COMMENTARY AND CASES
ON THE LAW OF
TRUSTS AND EQUITABLE REMEDIES

AUSTRALIA
LBC Information Services
Sydney

CANADA and USA
Carswell
Toronto – Ontario

NEW ZEALAND
Brooker's
Auckland

SINGAPORE and MALAYSIA
Thomson Information (S.E. Asia)
Singapore

HAYTON AND MARSHALL

COMMENTARY AND CASES
ON THE LAW OF
TRUSTS AND EQUITABLE REMEDIES

ELEVENTH EDITION

by

DAVID J. HAYTON, LL.D.
of the Inner Temple and Lincoln's Inn, Barrister;
Professor of Law, King's College, London University;
Acting Justice of the Bahamas' Supreme Court,
formerly Recorder, S.E. Circuit, 1984–2000

LONDON
SWEET & MAXWELL
2001

First edition 1939 by J. A. Nathan
Second edition 1951 by O. R. Marshall
Third edition 1955 by O. R. Marshall
Fourth edition 1961 by O. R. Marshall
Second impression 1966 by O. R. Marshall
Fifth edition 1967 by O. R. Marshall
Second impression 1971 by O. R. Marshall
Sixth edition 1975 by D. J. Hayton
Seventh edition 1980 by D. J. Hayton
Eighth edition 1986 by D. J. Hayton
Second impression 1988 by D. J. Hayton
Third impression 1989 by D. J. Hayton
Ninth edition 1991 by D. J. Hayton
Second impression 1994 by D. J. Hayton
Tenth edition 1996 by D. J. Hayton
Second impression 1997 by D. J. Hayton
Third impression 1999 by D. J. Hayton
Fourth impression 2000 by D. J. Hayton
Eleventh edition 2001 by D. J. Hayton
Reprinted 2001, 2003

Published by
Sweet & Maxwell Ltd of
100 Avenue Road,
Swiss Cottage, London NW3 3PF
(*http://www.sweetandmaxwell.co.uk*)

Phototypeset by LBJ Typesetting Ltd of Kingsclere
Printed and bound in Great Britain by The Bath Press, Bath

No natural forests were destroyed to make this product;
only farmed timber was used and replanted.

ISBN 0 421 717807

**A CIP catalogue record for this book is available
from the British Library**

PREFACE

If you really want to understand the principles of trust law and the scope of equitable remedies this is the book for you. It is a combined textbook and case-book, designed for those who intend to get to grips with the fundamentals of the subject so that they can appear in the top half of successful examinees in university or professional examinations. To help achieve this, questions and problems are posed at the end of relevant sections for, as someone once said, "To read without reflecting is like eating without digesting".

With the assistance of excerpts from cases, statutes, articles, Government White Papers, Charity Commissioners' Reports and Decisions and Attorney-General's Guidelines, the book aims to expand the law clearly and succinctly and to provide insights into the operation of trust law and equitable remedies and likely future developments therein; it encourages readers to develop their analytical faculties and to think for themselves. To this end reference is occasionally made to illuminating Commonwealth cases and statutes.

There is detailed investigation of those "grey" areas favoured by examiners. The syllabus for Equity and Trusts, as prescribed by the Law Society and the Bar Council and covered in University courses and the Common Professional Examination is fully catered for, while practitioners should find this book most useful for keeping in touch with modern developments.

Much has happened in the five years since the tenth edition, not least the Trustee Delegation Act 1999, the Trustee Act 2000 and the Child Support, Pension and Social Security Act 2000. Space has had to be found for excerpts from the following significant cases: *Neville v. Wilson, Associated Alloys Pty Ltd v. ACN, Yaxley v. Gotts, Re The Church of Scientology, Re Rabaiotti's Settlement, Glazier v. Australian Men's Health* (No. 2), *Co-operative Insurance Society Ltd v. Argyll Stores (Holdings) Ltd, Armitage v. Nurse* and *Foskett v. McKeown*.

So as not to lengthen the book—and to prune cases not now so significant as once they were—excerpts from the following cases have been deleted: *Oughtred v. IRC, Pascoe v. Turner, Stokes v. Anderson, Re Hetherington, Chichester Diocesan Fund v. Simpson, Re Duke of Norfolk's S.T., Re Harari's S.T., Re Vickery, Re Fawcett, Boe v. Alexander, Midland Bank Trustee (Jersey) Ltd v. Federated Pension Services, Stott v. Milne* and *Giles v. Morris*.

While much has been re-written in the light of developments over the last five years, there is particularly significant new material in the following areas as one progresses through the book : the modern utility, versatility and vitality of the trust; whether trusts are testamentary or not; the ambit of proprietary estoppel; the unilateral conduct of the settlor as the foundation of the trust; certainty of subject-matter;

distinguishing fiduciary and personal powers, *e.g.* of protectors; should the "beneficiary principle" be the "enforcer principle"; the nature of resulting and of constructive trusts; the need to distinguish breach of proscriptive fiduciary duty from breach of prescriptive equitable duties; recovery of property obtained by a voidable transaction; trustees' powers and obligations under the Trustee Act 2000; the duty to notify, and account to, beneficiaries; the significance of letters of wishes; exculpatory clauses; the measure of liability to account and equitable compensation; foreign forced heirship claims against trustees.

As with the tenth edition, I have my colleague, Raymond Davern MA Barrister, to thank for Chapter 11 sections 5 and 6 on Injunctions and Specific Performance. I am very grateful to him for such invaluable work.

The book is based upon sources available in February 2001, but at the proof stage some up-dating has been possible. It is hoped that the law is accurately stated as at June 11, 2001.

For further material and new material, the following websites are very useful: *www.bailii.org*, *www.austlii.edu.au*, *www.parliament.uk*, *www.charity-commission.gov.uk*, *www.open.gov.uk/lawcom/*, and for the work of Sir John Vinelott's Trust Law Committee (of which I am Deputy Chairman), *www.kcl.ac.uk/depsta/law/tlc.*

King's College London   David Hayton
June 11, 2001

ACKNOWLEDGMENTS

The Publishers and Author wish to thank the following for permission to reprint material from publications in which they have copyright:

Reproduced by permission of the Butterworths Division of Reed Elsevier (UK) Limited
  The All England Law Reports
  Chesterman *Charities, Trusts and Social Welfare*

Blackwell publishers
  Green: "Grey, Oughtred and Vandervell—A Contextual Reappraisal" (1984) 47 M.L.R. 385

Crown Copyright ©
  Various Acts

Her Majesty's Stationery Office:
  The Charity Commissions Annual Reports
  Charities: A Framework for the Future, White Paper Cm. 694 (1989)

Incorporated Council of Law Reporting for England & Wales:
  Appeal Cases
  Chancery Division Cases
  Weekly Law Reports

Jordan Publishing Limited
  Huntingford v. Hobbs [1993] 1 F.L.R. 736

Whilst every care has been taken to establish and acknowledge copyright and contact the copyright owners, the publishers tender their apologies for any accidental infringement. They would be pleased to come to a suitable arrangement with the rightful owner in each case.

CONTENTS

TABLE OF CASES

TABLE OF STATUTES

TABLE OF STATUTORY INSTRUMENTS

CIVIL PROCEDURE RULES

TABLE OF EUROPEAN AND FOREIGN LEGISLATION

EUROPEAN AND INTERNATIONAL CONVENTIONS & TREATIES

Chapter 1

Introduction

Section 1. What is a Trust?

A trust arises where ownership of property is transferred by a person to **1–01** trustees to be managed or dealt with for the benefit of beneficiaries or a charitable purpose: such property is not part of the trustee's patrimony but is a separate fiduciary patrimony not available for the trustee's private creditors, spouse or heirs. Usually, the transfer is by way of gift but it may be pursuant to a contract. The law of trusts is concerned with the utilisation and preservation of wealth, whether in the form of pension funds, unit trusts, charitable funds, union funds, club funds, family funds or rights (whether secured or unsecured) against a borrower intended as a commercial security device to be held by trustees for the benefit of a collection of lenders. It is also about settling property on trustees so as to minimise liability to the various taxes. Much of trust law has so far developed in regard to the preservation of family wealth, tying up property so that it can be enjoyed by successive generations, protecting the family from the depredations of creditors and of particular relatives with extravagant reckless dispositions, providing secretly for mentally defective relatives, for mistresses, for illegitimate children or for causes with which an open association is not desired. Case law used to be much concerned with lifetime or testamentary express family trusts or trusts for employees of family companies where the funds are a small fraction of the total value of all funds held on trust. Recently, problems have arisen in respect of pension funds leading to the Pensions Act 1995, in respect of alleged constructive trusts of family homes and of assets allegedly the traceable product of property subject to a trust or other fiduciary relationship, in respect of the ambit of personal liability to account as a constructive trustee for recipients of such property (who no longer have it) or for persons dishonestly involved in assisting in a breach of trust or other fiduciary relationship, and in respect of whether upon the liquidation of a company certain of its funds are trust funds not available for its general creditors.

The trust concept is extremely flexible and in English law can be used **1–02** to achieve almost any lawful end except that problems arise where it is sought to use it to provide directly for the furtherance of abstract non-charitable purposes.[1] Some rules of trust law make it difficult to give property to unincorporated associations on trust, though the courts now

---

[1] See *infra*, paras 3–208 *et seq.*

1

avoid this difficulty where possible by construing such gifts as out-and-out accretions to the association's funds subject to the contractual rights thereto of the members of the association under its constitution.[2] The trust concept has proved particularly useful in conveyancing so that whenever land is owned by two or more persons that land must be held on trust.[3] Maitland has quite rightly characterised the trust concept as "the greatest and most distinctive achievement performed by Englishmen in the field of jurisprudence."[4] No lawyer can claim to provide a proper service for his private or corporate clients without a thorough grasp of trust law and its potentialities.

1–03   Trusts are used not only for pension schemes, collective investment schemes (unit trusts), trade union funds, charitable purposes and for minimising the impact of tax on family wealth. Ownership of a family business can be transferred to trustees so as to prevent ownership becoming fragmented by inheritance and then, perhaps, passing to outsiders. Assets can be held by trustees to protect minors, persons of unsound mind, spendthrifts or young adults who might fall under the influence of an unscrupulous lover or religious guru. Persons can have transactions conducted anonymously, *e.g.* in a politically sensitive country by having trustees use their assets. The trust instrument revealing the names of beneficiaries does not have to be filed in any public register and is a private document which normally remains confidential between the trustees and the beneficiaries. Indeed, the names of beneficiaries do not always appear on the face of the trust instrument because the trustees, with the consent of the settlor or, after his death, of another person known as the protector, may have power to make anyone in the world a member of the class of beneficiaries.

1–04   A settlor can use a trust as a substitute for a will by transferring all his significant assets to trustees (of whom he may be one). On his death the assets remain in the surviving trustee(s) subject to the terms of the trust: no public grant of probate is required before those assets can be dealt with. If resident in a politically unstable country a person can transfer assets to trustees in some stable country so that the assets are beyond the reach of some new regime in his country of residence.

As part of some commercial venture the voting rights attached to shares or other securities can be vested in trustees to be managed as a block. As an independent security device there is the trust for debenture holders where a company mortgages property to trustees and confers rights on them to be held on trust for large numbers of debenture holders who actually lend money to the company in return for debenture

---

[2] See *infra*, paras 3–219 *et seq.*
[3] ss.34–36 of the Law of Property Act 1925, imposing a trust for sale with power to postpone sale which, under the Trusts of Land and Appointment of Trustees Act 1996 was replaced by a trust to hold land with power to sell or otherwise dispose of it as an absolute owner could. Trustees hold property as joint tenants so that on the death of one trustee the property automatically passes to the surviving trustees by virtue of the *ius accrescendi*. On the death of the last surviving trustee his personal representatives take over his function until they appoint new trustees: Trustee Act 1925, ss.18, 36.
[4] *Selected Essays*, p. 129.

stock. In the company sphere there are also tax-efficient employee share ownership plans under which the company transfers moneys to trustees to purchase shares in the company itself for the ultimate benefit of company employees.

A good lawyer can tailor a trust for any particular purpose not in **1–05** contravention of[5] the perpetuity and accumulation rules[6] or otherwise contrary to public policy or illegal.

What then is a trust? It is impossible to define such a flexible concept. However, four quasi-definitions are now set out to provide a rough and ready introduction to trust law.

Scott, Trusts, 4th ed., para. 2.3

"Even if it were possible to frame an exact definition of a legal concept, the **1–06** definition would not be of great practical value. A definition cannot properly be used as though it were a major premise so that rules governing conduct can be deduced from it. Our law, at least, has not grown in that way. When the rules have been arrived at from other sources, it may be possible to attempt to frame a definition. But the definition results from the rules, and not the rules from the definition.

All that one can properly attempt to do is to give such a description of a legal **1–07** concept that others will know in a general way what one is talking about. It is possible to state the principal distinguishing characteristics of the concept so that others will have a general idea of what the writer means. With this in mind, those responsible for the Restatement of Trusts proposed the following definition or description of an express trust. It is 'a fiduciary relationship with respect to property, subjecting the person by whom the title to property is held to equitable duties to deal with the property for the benefit of another person, which arises as a result of a manifestation of an intention to create it.' In this definition or description the following characteristics are to be noticed: (1) a trust is a relationship; (2) it is a relationship of a fiduciary character; (3) it is a relationship with respect to property, not one involving merely personal duties; (4) it involves the existence of equitable duties imposed upon the holder of the title to the property to deal with it for the benefit of another; and (5) it arises as a result of a manifestation of an intention to create the relationship."

Keeton's & Sheridan's Law of Trusts, 12th ed., p. 2

"A trust . . . is the relationship which arises wherever a person called the trustee **1–08** is compelled in equity to hold property, whether real or personal, and whether by legal or equitable title, for the benefit of some persons (of whom he may be one and who are termed beneficiaries) or for some object permitted by law, in such a way that the real benefit of the property accrues, not to the trustee, but to the beneficiaries or other objects of the trust."

---

[5] See *infra*, Chap. 3, section 5.
[6] See *infra*, Chap. 3, section 4.

Hague Convention on the Law Applicable to Trusts and on their Recognition

ARTICLE 2

1–09 "For the purposes of this Convention, the term 'trust' refers to the legal relationships created—*inter vivos* or on death—by a person, the settlor, when assets have been placed under the control of a trustee for the benefit of a beneficiary or for a specified purpose.

A trust has the following characteristics—

> *a* the assets constitute a separate fund and are not a part of the trustee's own estate;
> *b* title to the trust assets stands in the name of the trustee or in the name of another person on behalf of the trustee;
> *c* the trustee has the power and the duty, in respect of which he is accountable, to manage, employ or dispose of the assets in accordance with the terms of the trust and the special duties imposed upon him by law.

The reservation by the settlor of certain rights and powers, and the fact that the trustee may himself have rights as a beneficiary, are not necessarily inconsistent with the existence of a trust."

Principles of European Trust Law[7]

ARTICLE I

1–10 "(1) In a trust, a person called the "trustee" owns assets segregated from his private patrimony and must deal with those assets (the "trust fund") for the benefit of another person called the "beneficiary" or for the furtherance of a purpose.

(2) There can be more than one trustee and more than one beneficiary; a trustee may himself be one of the beneficiaries.

(3) The separate existence of the trust fund entails its immunity from claims by the trustee's spouse, heirs and personal creditors.

(4) In respect of the separate trust fund a beneficiary has personal rights and may also have ["and also has" for common law countries] proprietary rights against the trustee and against third parties to whom any part of the trust fund has been wrongfully transferred."

ARTICLE II

"The general rule is that in order to create a trust a person called the "settlor" in his lifetime or on death must, with the intention of creating a segregated trust fund, transfer assets to the trustee. However, it may also be ["it is also" for common law countries] possible to create a trust by making it clear that he is to be trustee of particular assets of his."

---

[7] Published 1999 by Kluwer Law International, edited by D. Hayton, S. Kortmann & R. Verhagen.

ARTICLE III

"(1) The trust fund consists not only of the original assets and those subsequently **1–11** added, but also of those assets from time to time representing the original or added assets."

It will be seen that the last two definitions or descriptions do not refer to beneficiaries having *equitable* property interests (as opposed to the legal property interests of the trustees) since this distinction originated in English law (where a Court of Equity developed separately from the Courts of Law) and was perpetuated in its colonies (e.g. America, Australia, Bermuda, Bahamas, Barbados, Cayman Islands) but does not appear in the trust laws of Scotland, India, Japan, Liechtenstein or South Africa.[8]

The Principles of European Trust Law were prepared by an international working group so as to assist countries interested in implementing The Hague Trusts Convention. Such Principles were concerned to counter the misleading superficial impression given by Article 2 of the Trusts Convention that the term "trust" could extend to agency or mandate relationships where O, the owner, placed some of his assets under the control of another (who, perhaps, had possession of them as bailee if they were not intangible assets where ownership and possession are coterminous in common law countries but not in civil law countries).

This possible agency construction arose from trying to deal from a **1–12** layman's viewpoint with the situation where a trustee, T, does not directly own 10,000 shares (that he thought he had bought) in XYZ plc because Custodian plc owns one million XZY plc shares, 10,000 of which are recorded by computer entry as held for T so that, technically, T owns a one hundredth fraction of Custodian's shareholding as equitable tenant in common. On a purposive construction, taking account of the fact that the Trusts Convention has a recital referring to the trust as a unique legal institution and has no provision as to its relationship with the earlier Hague Agency Convention and interpreting Article 2 in the light of Articles 11 and 13, the Article 2 "trust" should not extend to agency or mandate or bailment. As James L.J. stated in *Smith* v *Anderson*,[9] "A trustee is a man who is the owner of the property and deals with it as principal as owner and as master, subject only to an equitable obligation to account to some persons to whom he stands in the relation of trustee", while in *CCSD v. ISPT Pty*[10] Ltd Mason P emphasised, "It is of the essence of a trust that property is vested in the trustee."

The trustees' position

It will thus be seen that the ownership of trust property is vested in the **1–13** trustees (or their nominees, though the trustees can be regarded as then

---

[8] See J. Glasson (ed.) International Trust Laws (Jordans) and D. Hayton "The Development of the Trust Concept in Civil Law Jurisdictions" [2000] 8 Jo. Int. Trust & Corp P1 159.
[9] (1880) 15 Ch. D. 247 at 275.
[10] (1999) 2 ITELR 1 at 15.

owning an interest in the property owned by the nominees) to be managed and dealt with wholly for the benefit of the beneficiaries. Because the opportunities for trustees to take advantage of their position are so great Equity has imposed very strict rigorous duties or disabilities upon trustees.[11] Indeed, so onerous have these duties become that properly drawn trust instruments greatly relax the standards that Equity would otherwise demand: were it not for such relaxation few individuals or companies would be prepared to act as trustees. It should be noted that as long as illegality or public policy or uncertainty does not intervene then draftsmen of trust instruments have a free hand to vary or negative trust principles so long as the irreducible core content of the trust concept remains. In so far as the draftsman has not made the consent of someone other than the trustees (*e.g.* an individual or a committee or a company, usually designated as a "protector") requisite before certain things are done the trustees have an independent, unfettered discretion in their decisions though, of course, the income and capital managed by the trustees must be held according to the terms of the trust for the relevant beneficiaries.

1–14   The interests of the beneficiaries are paramount and the trustees must do their best to hold the balance fairly between those beneficiaries (with life interests) interested in income and those beneficiaries (with absolute interests in remainder) interested in capital.[12] Indeed, the trustees have a paternalistic function of protecting each beneficiary against himself. Even if all the beneficiaries interested in a particular trust are each *sui juris* and wish the trustees to do a certain thing the trustees can refuse if they consider that some of the beneficiaries are not objectively acting in their own best interests[13]: however, if all the beneficiaries are between them absolutely entitled to the trust property and are each *sui juris* then under the *Saunders v. Vautier*[14] principle, the beneficiaries have a fundamental proprietary power to call for the trust property to be vested in them (or their nominees) by the trustees, so terminating the trust.

1–15   Since the beneficiaries' interests are paramount the trustees cannot (in the absence of authorisation in the trust instrument) invest trust moneys as they might invest their own: they have to play "safe" and invest only in investments authorised under the Trustee Act 2000, replacing the Trustee Investments Act 1961.[15] Even if they have a broad express power of investment they cannot speculate because (in the absence of a contrary provision in the trust instrument) they have to exercise as much care as a prudent man of business would exercise if investing for other persons for whom he felt morally obliged to provide.[16] On the other hand, whilst trustees when selling their own houses might feel bound to

---

[11] See *infra*, Chap. 9.
[12] See *infra*, Chap. 9.
[13] *Re Brockbank* [1949] Ch. 206, subject to Trusts of Land & Appointment of Trustees Act 1996 s.19.
[14] *Saunders v. Vautier* (1841) 4 Beav. 115, see *infra*, at para. 9–152; *Re Smith* [1928] Ch. 915, see *infra*, at para. 4–98.
[15] See *infra*, Chap. 9.
[16] See *infra*, para 9–75..

honour the commercial morality code and reject out of hand a higher offer when they had orally agreed, subject to contract, to sell to a purchaser who had just submitted his part of the contract to them, trustees, when selling trust property in such circumstances, must not reject the higher offer without probing it with a view to acceptance.[17] Any authority given by the trust instrument to the trustees is deemed to exclude ordinary trust law as little as possible and will be presumed not to allow the trustees to act in a way detrimental to the beneficiaries.

A trust, unlike a company,[18] has no legal personality; thus, it cannot **1–16** own property or enter into contracts, sue or be sued. It is the trustees who own the trust property, enter into contracts, sue or are sued. A trustee as such has no distinct legal personality in his representative capacity separate from himself in his personal capacity.[19] Thus, he is personally liable to the extent of his whole personal fortune for debts contracted in managing the trust fund,[20] whether contracting in his own name or as trustee,[21] unless he makes it clear that he is to be liable only to the extent that the trust fund is available to him to satisfy the liability.[22] To discharge liabilities properly incurred by him as trustee he has a right of indemnity against the trust fund[23] (subject to any countervailing equities of the beneficiaries for breach of trust[24]) and creditors may be subrogated to this right.[25]

Generally, one can say that the external aspects of a trust are governed **1–17** by common law rules whilst the internal aspects are governed by rules of equity.[26] Thus, before turning the spotlight from the trustees to the beneficiaries one needs to consider the development of equity and the trust so that one can then examine the nature of the interest of a beneficiary under a trust.

---

[17] *Buttle v. Saunders* [1950] W.N. 255.

[18] A company needs to be created formally and registered under the Companies Act 1985. A trust can be created informally: see *infra*, Chap. 2.

[19] However, for some taxation purposes trustees are considered a single continuing body of persons distinct from the actual individuals who are from time to time trustees: Taxation of Chargeable Gains Act 1992, s.69; *Bond v. Pickford* [1983] STC 517.

[20] *Fraser v. Murdoch* (1881) 6 App. Cas. 855 at 874; *Staniar v. Evans* (1886) 34 Ch.D. 470 at 477.

[21] *Watling v. Lewis* [1911] 1 Ch. 414 at 423–424; *Burt, Boulton & Hayward v. Bull* [1895] 1 Q.B. 276 at 285.

[22] *Lumsden v. Buchanan* (1865) 4 Macq. 950 at 955; 13 L.T. 174; *Muir v. City of Glasgow Bank* (1879) 4 App. Cas. 337 at 355 and 388.

[23] *Re Blundell* (1888) 40 Ch.D. 370 at 377; *Re Exhall Coal Co. Ltd.* (1886) 35 Beav. 449 at 453.

[24] *Jacubs v. Rylance* (1874) L.R. 17 Eq. 341; *Doering v. Doering* (1889) 42 Ch.D. 203.

[25] *Re Johnson* (1880) 15 Ch.D. 548; *Re Firth* [1902] 1 Ch. 342; *Re Raybould* [1900] 1 Ch. 199; *Re Suco Gold Pty. Ltd.* (1983) 7 Australian C.L.R. 873.

[26] At common law no *ultra vires* doctrine (like that applicable to companies) applied to trustees who had the full powers of individuals, but the internal equitable interest of beneficiaries came in equity to bind all donees and all purchasers with notice. The trustee having legal ownership could enforce his legal rights against third parties in the common law courts. The beneficiary having only equitable rights could enforce these against the trustee in the Court of Chancery. If the trustee wrongfully refused to exercise his legal rights the beneficiary could be authorised to take legal proceedings in the trustee's name as plaintiff. Since 1875 in such a case the beneficiary will be plaintiff and will merely join the trustee as a co-defendant to ensure that all necessary parties will be bound by the decision in the case: *Parker-Tweedale v. Dunbar Bank plc* [1990] 2 All E.R. 577, 583.

Section 2. The Development of Equity and the Trust

1–18 A trust is the creature of Equity and not of the common law so what is "Equity?" In this context Equity can only be described as the body of rules which evolved from those rules applied and administered by the Court of Chancery before the Judicature Act 1873. Since that Act came into force on November 1, 1875 the rules of Equity and the rules of common law have been concurrently applied and administered in all Courts.[27]

The Court of Chancery grew out of the residuum of justice left in the King where his common law courts for some special reason brought about an unjust result, *e.g.* because they provided no remedy owing to the rigidity of the writ system or only an inadequate remedy or because a party could not succeed due to the power or wealth of the other party.[28] An aggrieved person would petition the King who would refer it to his Chancellor as his right-hand man. The Chancellor, who was an ecclesiastic, with some knowledge of Roman law and canon law, first advised the King and his Council, but towards the end of the fifteenth century began making decrees on his own authority. He was concerned with affording relief in hard cases and acted *in personam* against defendants who were imprisoned for contempt if they did not observe his decrees. At first, Equity varied according to the Chancellor's conscience—or the size of the Chancellor's foot as Selden remarked.[29] The work of hearing petitions led to increasing judicial activity of the Chancellor in what came to be known as the Court of Chancery. Lawyers, like Lord Nottingham at the end of the seventeenth century, instead of ecclesiastics, became Chancellors and began systematically developing a body of rules of equity. The Chancellor, Lord Eldon, observed in 1818,[30] "Nothing would inflict on me greater pain than the recollection that I had done anything to justify the reproach that the Equity of this Court varies like the Chancellor's foot." However, as Jessel M.R. commented in 1880[31]:

> "The rules of Courts of Equity are not supposed to have been established from time immemorial. It is perfectly well-known that they have been established from time to time—altered, improved and refined from time to time. The doctrines are progressive, refined and improved."

1–19 Subsequently,[32] Harman L.J. complained, that equitable principles are:

---

[27] Supreme Court of Judicature Act 1873, ss.24, 25, now Supreme Court Act 1981, s.49.
[28] For fuller accounts see Holdsworth's *History of English Law*, Vol. 1, at 395 *et seq.*; Potter's *Historical Introduction to English Law* (4th ed.), at 152 *et seq.*; Milsom's *Historical Foundations of the Common Law* (2nd ed.), at 82 *et seq.*; J. H. Baker's *Introduction to English Legal History* (3rd ed.), Chap. 6.
[29] *Table Talk of John Selden* (Pollock ed., 1927), at 43.
[30] *Gee v. Pritchard* (1818) 2 Swans. 402 at 414.
[31] *Re Hallett's Estate* (1880) 13 Ch.D. 696 at 710.
[32] *Campbell Discount Co Ltd. v. Bridge* [1961] 1 Q.B. 445 at 459, (similarly see *per* Lord Radcliffe in *Bridge v. Campbell Discount Co Ltd.* [1962] A.C. 600 at 626).

"rather too often bandied about in common law courts as though the Chancellor still had only the length of his own foot to measure when coming to a conclusion,"

though as Bagnall J. remarked in 1972[33]:

"In the field of equity the length of the Chancellor's foot has been measured or is capable of measurement. This does not mean that equity is past child-bearing; simply that its progeny must be legitimate—by precedent out of principle."

Nowadays, Megarry V.-C. has pointed out[34] there is a:

"tendency in equity to put less emphasis on detailed rules that have emerged from the cases and more weight on the underlying principles that engendered those rules, treating the rules less as rules requiring complete compliance and more as guidelines to assist the court in applying the principles."

It is crucial to appreciate that Equity is not a self-sufficient system[35]: it **1–20** is only a gloss on, or supplement to, the common law that is a self-sufficient system whose rigour needed mitigating in the interests of justice and of social and economic change. Thus, Equity's trust concept was used to enable landowners in their lifetimes in effect to devise land (viz. pass land on by will) or married women in effect to have separate property or merchant venturers to do business under deeds of settlement almost as if they were limited companies, when at common law such was not possible due respectively to the lack of testamentary power, to married men having control of their wives' property and to the absence of limited companies. Equity developed a modern law of mortgages (including tacking, marshalling, consolidation and the crucial doctrine of the equity of redemption) and of restrictive covenants when the common law had closed the category of negative easements, while Equity also gave effect to interests in land created for value without satisfying formal common law requirements. It developed its remedies of injunction and specific performance and its auxiliary jurisdiction to assist proceedings at law by interrogatories, discovery, set-off and the taking of accounts, while being ready to relieve against the rigidity of the law where there was proof of fraud, mistake, undue influence or misrepresentation.

The relationship between equity and the common law

There are three aspects to the relationship between Equity and the **1–21** common law as emphasised by the draftsman of the Judicature Acts 1873–75, Sir Arthur Wilson.[36] First, equity recognises and enforces rights

---

[33] *Cowcher v. Cowcher* [1972] 1 All E.R. 943 at 948.
[34] *Re Montagu's S.T.* [1987] Ch. 264 at 278, [1992] 4 All E.R. 308 at 324.
[35] F.W. Maitland, *Equity* (2nd ed.) pp. 18–19; Meagher, Gummow & Lehane (3rd ed.) Chap. 1.
[36] See (1875) 19 Sol. Jo. at pp. 633–634.

and duties known to the common law but then goes further in recognising and enforcing other rights and duties. The classic example is the trust, *e.g.* where property is vested in trustees for A for life, remainder to B absolutely. The common law protects the trustees' title to the property and facilitates their dealing with third parties but if A or B wishes to enforce his rights then it is equity that governs the position. Hence the trustees' rights are legal rights and the beneficiaries' rights are equitable rights.

1–22   The trust derives from the mediaeval practice of a "feoffor" conveying a legal estate in land to a "feoffee to uses" to hold it to the use of a "*cestui que use.*" This was done to enable a knight to go off to the Crusades, leaving someone to safeguard his land for himself and his family,[37] or to enable some body to benefit as a "*cestui que use*" which could not directly benefit as a feoffee owing to the Mortmain Statutes[38] or vows of poverty.[39] Indeed, lifetime "uses" could be exploited to enable land to be devised in effect and as a tax avoidance device to avoid burdensome feudal incidents. The number of trustees could be kept up so that there was never a death of a sole individual to provoke the levy of feudal dues on death of the estate owner. Accordingly, the Statute of Uses 1535, "executed" the use so that the legal estate vested automatically in the *cestui que use* and not the feoffee to uses.[40] What happened if a legal estate was purportedly conveyed to A to the use of B to the use of C? At first, B held the legal estate as his own property, the first use being executed and the second use being void as repugnant to the first use. However, by the middle of the seventeenth century the second use came to be enforced as a matter of course (not just to prevent fraud or remedy a mistake) and it came to be known as a trust to distinguish it from the first use. The drafting formula became "Unto and to the use of B and his heirs in trust for C and his heirs" and C came to be known as the *cestui que trust.* After the repeal of the Statute of Uses in 1925 land was conveyed "to B in fee simple on trust for C in fee simple."

Over the years C's equitable interest came to be enforced in the Court of Chancery not just against the trustee or a donee of the legal estate from the trustee but against anyone having the legal estate, other than a bona fide purchaser for value of it without notice ("equity's darling"). Notice comprised actual knowledge and knowledge which a person should have had if he had made reasonable inquiries and inspections ("constructive notice"); such actual or constructive notice of a purchaser's agent will be imputed to the purchaser ("imputed notice") unless the agent was acting in fraud of his principal and the matter of which he had notice was relevant to the fraud.

---

[37] To protect the land a "real" action to recover the land (the "*rem*") had to be brought by an adult male "seised" of the land by virtue of feoffment with livery of seisin and present in court.

[38] The Mortmain Statutes prevented land being conveyed without a royal licence into the "dead hand" of a corporation (not liable to the feudal dues payable on marriage, death or the heir being under age).

[39] *e.g.* the Order of Franciscan Friars.

[40] This soon led to a rebellion as it prevented land being indirectly devised: hence the Statute of Wills 1540 was enacted to enable land to be directly devised.

The second aspect is that common law and equity may provide **1–23** different remedies but each leave the plaintiff free to enjoy whatever remedy was allowed by the other. After all, the common law affords the "bad man" the fundamental freedom to break his contract or misappropriate another person's property and pay damages, while where circumstances justify the intervention of Equity, Equity insists that the man be a "good man" and does not allow him to maintain that he is a "bad man": Equity looks on as done that which ought to be done and declares that the bad man holds particular property on trust for the good man (who can then require legal ownership of the property to be transferred to him) or decrees specific performance or grants an injunction against a legal title owner.[41] Where the common law only allows damages for breach of contract or for nuisance Equity may decree specific performance or grant an injunction. A contract relating to land, before becoming void at law for lack of writing required by the Law of Property (Miscellaneous Provisions) Act 1989[42] was not enforceable in court if written evidence was lacking, though the deposit could be forfeited or recovered for failure of consideration, but in Equity specific performance could be ordered if there was an act of part performance. A voluntary, (*i.e.* gratuitous) covenant under seal enables the covenantee to obtain common law damages for breach thereof[43] but Equity will not decree specific performance since "Equity will not assist a volunteer," *i.e.* an intended donee. At common law a plaintiff can generally only obtain damages for his losses but if there is a breach of a trust or other fiduciary relationship a plaintiff always make the defendant account for any profit he has made.[44]

Beneficiaries do not sue trustees for damages but seek to make **1–24** trustees liable to account in equity so as to discover the proper amount due after finalising accounts. Thus, if a trustee breaks her personal obligations to the beneficiaries they can "falsify" or "surcharge" the trustee's accounts. If T wrongfully sells 1,000 ABC Ltd shares to purchase 2,000 XYZ Ltd shares which depreciate in value, the sale is "falsified", so that T's accounts should still reveal ownership of 1,000 ABC Ltd shares and T must sell the XYZ shares and purchase 1,000 ABC shares even if they have doubled in value. If T's negligence causes £10,000 loss to the trust fund then the accounts are "surcharged" by the addition of £10,000 to the trust fund, so requiring T to make up this loss. Moreover, if T wrongfully sells trust assets to purchase a house privately for herself, Equity looks on as done that which the beneficiaries claim ought to have been done and requires the house to be treated as trust

---

[41] *Att.-Gen. for Hong Kong v. Reid* [1994] 1 A.C. 324; *Bromage v. Genning* (1616) 1 Roll. Rep. 368; O.W. Holmes, *The Common Law* and (1897) 10 Harv. L.R. 457; Millett L.J. in [1993] Restitution L.R. 7 and 19–21.

[42] See *infra*, at para. 2–07.

[43] *Cannon v. Hartley* [1949] Ch. 213, *infra*, at para. 4–53.

[44] *Surrey C.C. v. Bredero Homes* [1993] 1 W.L.R. 1361 (plaintiff received only nominal damages, not being entitled to profit that defendant made from his breach). Exceptionally, the amount of profits may have to be paid over at common law: *Att-General v. Blake* [2000] 4 All E.R. 385

property, unless it is worth less than the replacement cost of sold trust assets; in this eventuality, T is personally liable for the amount of the replacement cost but the beneficiaries have an equitable charge over the house enabling them to be treated as secured creditors up to the value of the house.

1–25   The Chancellors also established that the beneficiaries have more than a personal right to seek the proper amount due to them from the trustee on a taking of accounts. The beneficiaries have an equitable proprietary interest in the trust fund in T's ownership. This has the effect of affording them priority over T's creditors, heirs or divorcing spouse. Moreover, because the beneficiaries have a property interest they can recover the property from X to whom T has wrongfully transferred the property, unless X is a bona fide purchaser of a legal interest in the property for value without notice of the trust (or a successor thereto). Indeed, if X is such a purchaser, then the beneficiaries can trace the proceeds of sale so as to recover any asset purchased by T with such proceeds considered to be the beneficiaries' moneys in the eyes of Equity. The input value of the beneficiaries can be traced from asset to asset (*e.g.*, to stocks and shares, to the proceeds of sale thereof, to a painting purchased therewith, to the proceeds of sale thereof and to a flat purchased therewith) until such value is wholly dissipated, *e.g.*, by being used to pay off unsecured debts.

1–26   The third aspect of the relationship between Equity and the common law is that there are some very rare cases where the rules of Equity and of common law actually conflict. In 1616[45] it was held that Equity prevailed because the Court of Chancery could effectively issue common injunctions restraining parties successful in common law courts from enforcing their judgments or restraining parties from continuing with a common law action. Now the Supreme Court Act 1981, s.49 (replacing the Judicature Act 1873, s.25(11) and the Judicature Act 1925, s.44) states, "Every Court exercising jurisdiction in England or Wales in any civil cause or matter shall continue to administer law and equity on the basis that, wherever there is any conflict or variance between the rules of equity and the rules of common law with reference to the same matter, the rules of equity shall prevail."

1–27   Examples of conflict are cases where in an action on a deed at law it was no defence for a defendant to plead a written variation for value not in a deed but such a defendant could obtain a common injunction in equity.[46] Similarly, if a legal estate owner purportedly granted a lease exceeding three years in writing, instead of by deed, and the document contained a term enabling the landlord to claim a year's rent in advance then at law the landlord (only being entitled to rent in arrear at law) could not sue for such rent or levy distress for such rent, so he could be liable to the tenant for illegal distress. Since Equity would be prepared to

---

[45] *Earl of Oxford's Case* (1615) 1 Rep. Ch. 1.
[46] *Berry v. Berry* [1929] 2 K.B. 316.

decree specific performance so as to have a legal lease by deed executed and before then look on as done that which ought to be done, the landlord could obtain a common injunction in respect of the tenant's action for legal distress.[47] An example of variance arises where a plaintiff seeks contribution from sureties where one of them is insolvent. At law if A, B and C are sureties for £30,000 and A becomes insolvent then B and C are only liable for £10,000 each. In equity B and C are liable for £15,000 each.[48] The plaintiff receives less at law than in equity so no question arose before 1875 of a defendant seeking a common injunction as happened in cases of conflict.

The fusion fallacy

The Judicature Act 1873 enabled the one Court concurrently to adminis- **1–28** ter the rules of common law and the rules of equity. It did not provide for the fusion of these two systems of principle; it only provided for the fusion of the Courts administering the two systems. As Sir George Jessel M.R. stated in *Salt v. Cooper*,[49] having himself as Solicitor General piloted the Act through the Commons, the main object of the Act

> "has been sometimes inaccurately called 'the fusion of Law and Equity'; but it is not any fusion, or anything of the kind; it was the vesting in one tribunal the administration of Law and Equity in every cause, action or dispute which should come before that tribunal."

After all, section 25(11) of the 1873 Act and its statutory replacements assume the continued existence of two separate systems for otherwise there would be no need to provide for the resolution of conflicts between them. In Ashburner's vivid metaphor,[50] "the two streams of jurisdiction though they run in the same channel run side by side and do not mingle their waters."

Surprisingly, Lord Diplock in *obiter dicta* has stated[51]:

> "My Lords, by 1977 this metaphor has in my view become both mischievous and deceptive. The innate conservatism of English lawyers may have made them slow to recognise that by the

---

[47] *Walsh v. Lonsdale* (1882) 21 Ch.D. 9, on which see *Chan v. Cresdon Pty. Ltd.* (1989) 168 C.L.R. 242.
[48] *Lowe & Sons v. Dixon & Sons* (1885) 16 Q.B.D. 455.
[49] (1880) 16 Ch.D. 544 at 549. In an extempore interlocutory judgment (where the right to specific performance was conceded) in *Walsh v. Lonsdale* (1882) 21 Ch.D. 9 at 14, Jessel M.R. got carried away and erroneously said: "There are not two estates as there were formerly, one estate at common law by reason of the payment of rent from year to year and an estate in equity under the agreement. There is only one court and the equity rules prevail in it." Legal leases and equitable leases co-exist without conflict: Megarry & Wade's *Law of Real Property* (6th ed.), paras 14–039 *et seq*; Meagher Gummow & Lehane, Equity (3rd ed.), paras. 220–245; *Tinsley v. Milligan* [1994] 1 A.C. 340.
[50] *Principles of Equity* (2nd ed., 1933), at 18.
[51] *United Scientific Holdings Ltd. v. Burnley Borough Council* [1978] A.C. 904 at 924–925. His common law colleagues all spoke in the same vein. See also Lord Denning in *Nelson v. Larholt* [1948] 1 K.B. 339 at 343 and *Errington v. Errington* [1952] 1 K.B. 290 at 298. *Cf.* Lord Brandon in *Bank of Boston v. European Grain* [1989] 1 All E.R. 545 at 557.

Judicature Act 1873 the two systems of substantive and adjectival law formerly administered by Courts of Law and Courts of Chancery were fused. As at the confluence of the Rhone and Saone, it may be possible for a short distance to discern the source from which each part of the combined stream came, but there comes a point at which this ceases to be possible. If Professor Ashburner's fluvial metaphor is to be retained at all, the waters of the confluent streams of law and equity have surely mingled now."

But how can law and equity be fused? In the law of trusts there is legal and equitable ownership and a beneficiary, having only an equitable title, cannot sue a third party at law for negligently damaging trust property[52]; in property law there are legal and equitable rights with different effects, especially as regards third parties who find that equitable rights are normally much less obvious than legal rights, common law claims in respect of breach of contract extend to losses caused to the plaintiff but not normally to profits made by the defendant[53]; equitable rights can only be enforced by equitable remedies and not by common law damages,[54] equitable defences like hardship and not affording assistance to volunteers or to those who come without "clean hands" cannot be defences to common law actions, *e.g.* for debt. It is a fallacy[55] to assume that law and equity have been fused into a new body of principles.

The modern trust concept

1–29 (1) The trustees own and manage segregated assets as a trust fund for the benefit of beneficiaries, who are not ordinary creditors of the trustees but have an interest in the fund that survives the insolvency, dissolution, death or divorce of the trustees.

(2) The beneficiaries, indeed, have an equitable proprietary interest binding not only the trustee's creditors, heirs or spouse but extending to property, whether the original trust property or property traceable[56] as representing the original trust property, either owned by the trustees or a third party transferee who is not a bona fide purchaser of a legal interest without notice of the trust nor protected by statutory provisions (*e.g.*, conferring a good

---

[52] *Leigh & Sillavan v. Aliakmon Shipping* [1986] 2 All E.R. 145 at 151; *Parker-Tweedale v. Dunbar Bank plc* [1990] 2 All E.R. 577.

[53] *Surrey C.C. v. Bredero Homes* [1993] 1 W.L.R. 1361; *In data v. ACL* [1997] *The Times,* August 14; for exceptional circumstances see *Attorney-General v. Blake* [2000] 4 All E.R. 385.

[54] *Downsview Nominees v. First City Corp* [1993] A.C. 295 at 315; *China & South Seas Bank Ltd v. Tan* [1990] 1 AC 536 at 543. By the Supreme Court Act 1981, s.50 (replacing provisions originally in Chancery Amendment Act 1858) damages may be awarded in lieu of or in addition to specific performance or an injunction, which is how the unexplained award of damages in *Seager v. Copydex* (1967) 2 All E.R. 414 is explained by Slade J. in *English v. Dedham Vale Properties Ltd.* [1978] 1 All E.R. 382 at 399.

[55] As emphasised by Holdsworth (1935) 51 L.Q.R. 142; Lord Evershed (1954) 70 L.Q.R. 326; P. V. Baker (1977) 93 L.Q.R. 529; Meagher Gummow & Lehane, Equity (3rd ed.) paras. 220–245; J.E. Martin [1994] Conv. 13; D. Capper (1994) 14 *Legal Studies* 315.

[56] See *infra* at paras 11–06 *et seq.*

title on a purchaser of land if paying the purchase moneys to two trustees or a trust corporation, irrespective of notice of the trust).

(3) In the absence of express provisions in the trust instrument there is implied a regime not just of trustees' powers but also of trusteeship obligations to ensure the trustees' impartiality, loyalty and prudence and so protect the beneficiaries[57]; but there are certain irreducible core obligations that cannot be ousted[58] *e.g.* to produce accounts to beneficiaries for falsification or surcharge.

(4) The trust instrument can create whatever flexible or inflexible structure the settlor desires, whether concerning the creation of a variety of rights for beneficiaries or concerning matters of internal management.

(5) It is the trustees who sue or are sued, the trust not being a legal person, so there is the possibility of "look-through" or "conduit" taxation of beneficiaries, avoiding entity-level taxation unless statute intervenes.

(6) The court, in addition to its usual punitive, regulatory role, has a paternalistic supporting role to advise trustees and resolve doubts or enlarge trustees' powers in the unforeseeable circumstances that can arise in the lengthy life of a trust.

(7) A trust is not a contract like a contract for the benefit of a third party or parties[59] or a contract of agency.

   (a) Once the settlor (gratuitously or pursuant to a contract) has made his unilateral transfer of his assets to the trustee to own as a segregated patrimony, he drops out of the picture and cannot tell the trustee what to do[60]: the trustee's obligations are independent obligations owed exclusively to the beneficiaries who alone have correlative rights against the trustee.[61]

   (b) The fact that the settlor later dies or becomes mentally incapacitated or discovers a breach of trust has been committed is totally immaterial.

   (c) The death or incapacity of the trustee does not affect the continuing existence of the trust: it only means that someone else will need to take over the office of trustee. Indeed, a trust can arise without the knowledge and agreement of the trustee (e.g. in the case of a testamentary trust or the case of property, like land or shares, that can be transferred into the name of another without the need to tell such person) but if the trustee refuses to act and disclaims, the settlor or his executor takes the property as trustee.[62]

---

[57] See *infra* at paras 9–08 *et seq.*
[58] See *infra* at paras 9–208, 9–308
[59] First permitted by Contracts (Rights of Third Parties) Act 1999
[60] *Re Astor's ST* [1952] Ch 534 at 542, *Bradshaw v. University College of Wales* [1987] 3 All E.R. 200 at 203
[61] Powers of appointment or of revocation or to direct or veto certain action may, however, be reserved to others, *e.g.* the settlor, his widow, a designated protector.
[62] Equity will not allow a trust to fail for want of a trustee: *infra* at para 8–39.

(d) A breach of trust confers no right to treat the trust as terminated: it merely enables the beneficiaries to falsify or surcharge the trustee's accounts and to apply to the court to replace the trustee.

The past utility, versatility and vitality of the trust

1–30 The trust has been to the fore in reflecting economic and social changes and leading to statutory reform of the law.

(a) It enabled land indirectly to be left on death to someone other than the owner's legal heir until Parliament made this possible directly in 1540.

(b) It enabled members of an unincorporated association to trade via trustees with the apparent benefit of limited liability until the courts after 80 years or so held the members to be personally liable, thereby compelling Parliament to enact legislation permitting limited liability corporations in the mid 19th Century.

(c) When married women would otherwise have no property rights, the father of a married woman could transfer property to trustees to hold to her "separate use", so that she had some financial independence before legislation conferred independence on wives.

(d) With the increase in cohabitation over the last 30 years, problems have arisen where W has moved into a house or flat owned by M and then acted in detrimental reliance on a belief encouraged by M that F is to acquire some share in the property. Here the courts have been prepared to impose a constructive or resulting trust upon M so that the property is regarded in equity as co-owned in shares decreed by the court. The Law Commission is now considering the preparation of draft legislation in this area.

1–31 Where the King or Parliament has considered that there has been an abuse of the trust then legislation has blocked such abuse.

(a) Thus, transfers to trustees with intent to avoid creditors were first blocked in 1376, while transfers to trustees to the use of a corporation (to whom transfers could not be made directly due to the Statute of Mortmain) were blocked in 1391.

(b) Transfers to trustees to avoid wardship rights of feudal lords were blocked in 1490, while the general device of using "uses" to avoid feudal incidents was blocked in 1535.

(c) More recently, transfers made within 6 years of death to trustees (or others) with intent to defeat claims of the transferor's dependants under the Inheritance (Provision for Family & Dependants) Act 1975 can be set aside as far as necessary, as can dispositions to trustees (or others) with intent to defeat the Matrimonial Causes Act 1973 claims of the transferor's spouse or children.

On the tax front, legislation ensures that settlors cannot make transfers to trustees so as to obtain unfair tax advantages *e.g.* settlors are taxed on trust income if creating a trust for their infant children or a trust under which the settlor or his spouse can receive any benefit, while taxes on death are not avoided by a settlor who is not entirely excluded from benefiting under his lifetime trust.

The modern utility, versatility and vitality of the trust

A. The family context

Trusts are particularly common to provide for the management of the **1–32** affairs of beneficiaries who are mentally or physically handicapped or who are spendthrift or who are young or who are old. They are also used to prevent the law of succession operating to vest the deceased's property absolutely in his adult children who could then dissipate the property. Thus a settlor's trust can preserve and generate family assets for three or four generations, successive family members benefiting from avoiding division of the assets into smaller and smaller shares each generation and from economies of scale in the management of the large pool of family assets.

Examples of family trusts are:

(a) a grandparent's fixed trust for such of the grandchildren who attain 25 years in equal shares;

(b) a testator's fixed trust for the surviving spouse for life, remainder to their children equally, but with power for the spouse by will or by deed to appoint the capital unequally between such of the children and the children's children as may be seen fit in the spouse's absolute discretion;

(c) a testator's fixed trust for the surviving spouse for life, remainder equally to each of their children for the life of each respective child, with the capital of such child's share to pass equally to such child's children, subject to an overriding power for the surviving spouse to appoint as in (b) and after the death of such spouse for the trustees to have such power of appointment;

(d) a discretionary trust for such of the descendants of the settlor/ testator as the trustees shall see fit in their absolute discretion from time to time to pay income or capital to, before expiry of an eighty year perpetuity period.

The settlor can provide a morally binding letter of wishes to guide the **1–33** trustees in the exercise of their discretions, while family members can be trustees and employ professional discretionary portfolio managers to manage investments and other professionals for other tasks. Often a professional trust corporation is trustee, while family input can be preserved via the trust instrument providing for a "protector" with arrangements for the appointment of successor protectors. The protector may be the settlor or his surviving spouse or a specified child or a committee or board or, even, a company whose shares are owned by family members. The protector may have powers of vetoing trustees' proposed distributions of capital or proposed sales of particular assets and power to replace the trustees, even with foreign trustees to be subjected to a new foreign trust law replacing English law as the law governing the trust. The protector will generally be subject to similar fiduciary duties as trustees in exercising his powers unless the trust instrument or special circumstances indicate otherwise.

Lifetime trusts are more useful than testamentary trusts because the probate process on death is a public one revealing the terms of the will and the taxable size of the deceased's estate. Moreover, if a settlor has assets in many jurisdictions he does not want those assets to pass on death subject to different succession laws and a variety of forced heirship regimes forcing different fractions of his estate to pass to his children and treating gifts made within differing periods before death as part of such estate.

To avoid such complex situations, well-advised wealthy persons with valuable assets in a variety of countries put most of their assets into a lifetime trust so as to escape the application of laws governing succession to a deceased's estate.

If a person dies intestate then his administrators hold his estate on a statutory trust with a power of sale. A similar trust arises whenever land is co-owned if an express trust is not created in the co-ownership documentation.

B. The commercial context

1–34   As seen, trusts developed in the context of preserving and developing family wealth and of furthering charitable purposes. Private client lawyers specialise in these areas, thereby helping their clients in generating family wealth and using any surplus to advance philanthropic purposes.

In the twentieth century, the story of the trust has been the story of corporate finance lawyers utilising the trust structure, so that it is estimated that only about 10 per cent of trust assets are comprised in family and charitable trusts. Thus, the most important dimension of the trust concept is as an instrument of commerce, particularly for money-raising, with the key attributes of protection against insolvency, the protective regime of fiduciary trust law and the flexibility of provisions that can be inserted in trust instruments. In this context the trust results from a contract rather than a gift.

The key attributes of trusts can be employed in whatever ways the ingenious mind of man can devise. Common uses of the trusts are as follows.

1. Pensions for employees

1–35   To ensure funding of pensions for retired employees, money is paid (pursuant to the contract of employment) to trustees to manage as a segregated fund. The retired employee then receives thereout either a percentage of his final salary or a lump sum that must be used to purchase an annuity.

2. Collective investment schemes

A trust is used as an open ended collective investment vehicle (with no **1–36** fixed or irreducible capital base) in which the value of units in the unit trust held for a particular unit-holder-investor is directly related to the value of the assets held by the custodian trustee to the order of the managing trustee. Investors can sell their units back to the manager whenever they wish, whereupon a charge to capital gains tax will arise (but no such charge arises against the trustees or the unit holders on the disposal and reinvestment of underlying trust assets).

"Unit trusts" (known as "mutual funds" in North America) differ from "investment trusts" (as featured in share price pages of newspapers) because the latter actually are companies so that the investor owns shares in the company, the value of which will depend not just on the value of the assets owned by the company but also upon the dividend policy of the company, so that the share price will stand at a discount to the net asset value. Open-ended investment companies (OEICs)—as open-ended as unit trusts—can now be created with share prices directly reflecting the value of underlying assets.

Unit trusts can quote one price for acquisition of units and another for redemption of units, while OEICs have a single pricing system. A unit trust can only issue "income" or "accumulation" units while an OEIC can issue different classes of share intended for different types of investment or investor.

3. Collective security trusts for holders of bonds or debenture stock

The trustee has the benefit of the borrower's promise to repay the loan **1–37** collectively provided by a group of lenders and often also has assets of the borrower as security for repayment.

The trustee is an independent professional person (not the agent of either the lenders or the borrower) who can be relied upon confidentially to monitor matters and to decide the proper response to any default or even to modify the terms of the loan without the expense and trouble of a meeting with the lenders except in defined special circumstances.

The rights of the trustee and any fruits of such rights (*e.g.*, proceeds of sale of a security) are held as a separate fund for the lenders (of whom there are too many to be co-owners of the security interest, four being the maximum for co-ownership of interests in land), so protecting them against the insolvency of the trustee whose office as trustee will then be filled by another trustee.

4. Syndicated loan trusts

Where slices of capital will be provided at differing times and may be **1–38** from lenders different from the original lenders, trustees of collective security trusts can have overriding powers to afford subsequent lenders the same priority as earlier lenders or even a higher priority but, perhaps, only if a specified proportion of the earlier lenders agree.

Indeed, to deal with the case where all the lenders are repaid but further loans are needed (*e.g.* in financing the Channel Tunnel) matters can be arranged so that the trustee continues to hold the security but for the new lenders without the need for anything further to be done (like registration of a new charge if the old charge were considered to have ceased when all the old lenders had been paid).

5. Subordination trusts

1–39   Subordination of a creditor occurs where one creditor, the "subordinated" or "junior" creditor, agrees not to be paid by a debtor until another creditor, the "senior" creditor, of the common debtor has been paid.

To avoid the insolvency rule that requires rateable distributions to creditors from an insolvent debtor, a trust deed is executed under which the junior debt is payable by the debtor to a trustee, who is to hold any payment made in respect of the junior debt on trust first for the benefit of the senior creditor to the amount of the senior debt, and then, if any money remains, for the junior creditor. The senior creditor is thus protected against the insolvency of both the junior creditor and the debtor. Prospective lenders will often not lend unless they obtain this priority over existing debts.

6. Securitisation trusts of special purpose vehicles (SPV)

1–40   For the purposes of enabling a complex portfolio of assets (*e.g.*, secured or unsecured debts, credit card receivables) to be available as security to investors, a company, known as an SPV, purchases the portfolio, borrowing the money via a collective security bond issue (as in 3 above). The shares in the SPV and the portfolio are held on trust to repay the bondholders with any (small) surplus held on trust for the bondholders or for charitable purposes (or for non-charitable purposes where expressly permitted by foreign laws *e.g.* of Bermuda, Cayman Islands, Isle of Man, Jersey).[63]

This avoids the original owner of the portfolio beneficially owning shares in the SPV, and so avoids the SPV's debt appearing on such owner's consolidated balance sheet. Where there is a shortage in the financial markets of AAA rated bonds or of high yielding bonds it is possible to use this securitisation trust device to put together a "ring-fenced" package of corporate bonds to help satisfy the shortage.

---

[63] Further on commercial and financial uses of trusts see S. Moerman, "Non-charitable purposes trusts" (1999–2000) 6 Trusts & Trustees at 7–13; C. Duffet, "Using Trusts in International Financial and Commercial Transactions" (1992) 1 Jo Int Planning at 23–30; J.H. Langbein "The Secret Life of the Trust: The Trust as an Instrument of Commerce (1997) 107 Yale L.J. pp. 165–189: and D.J. Hayton, Report on Trust Law, for the Association of Corporate Trustees (2001), dealing with analogous European arrangements as well as English trusts.

7. Project financing and future income streams

If L contracts to lend £50 million to B and actually pays over the money **1–41**
to B on the basis that B will hold on trust for L all money B expects to
acquire from a particular source once B acquires it, then as soon as B
does acquire it B holds it on trust for L[64]. Such acquired money is not
available for B's creditors: after all, by paying over the £50 million to B,
L made such available to B's creditors, who should not therefore benefit
further by also having available to them the asset purchased by L as the
price of the loan.

This enables B to acquire money now in respect of a future income
stream expected from a particular project *e.g.* a tunnel, a mine, an oil
well. Such income will be used to service the debt interest and to repay
capital.

*8. Temporary purpose trusts of money until debtor-creditor relationship
arises (Quistclose[65] trusts)*

C can transfer money to T or to D on trust for C until the money is used **1–42**
for a specified purpose benefiting D, whereupon D is merely to be a
debtor of C.

This protects C against the insolvency of D if the money is not so used
(unless C paid the money on trust to D, and D wrongfully dissipated it so
it became untraceable).

9. Client accounts e.g. of solicitors

If X, involved in a profession or business, has an office (or private)
account with a bank and a separate client account for clients' money,
then the client account money is held on trust for the clients, who are
thus safe if X becomes insolvent. It is a fundamental feature of the trust
concept that anyone can open in his own name an account designated as
a trust account for the benefit of others, who are then protected against
the insolvency of the account holder. In such event they are entitled to
the balance in the account and to assets wrongfully purchased by the
account holder in his own name with money drawn from the account or
wrongfully given away to a third party.

*10. Trusts affecting personal accounts of agents or purchasers so as to
protect interests of principals or vendors*

P Co may sell its fleet of cars or its airline tickets through the agency of **1–43**
A Co which will merely be in a debtor-creditor relationship with P Co,
having to pay it an amount corresponding to the proceeds of sale less A
Co's commission. Purchasers from A Co will not make out one cheque
in favour of A Co for its commission and a second cheque in favour of P

---

[64] *Re Lind* [1915] 2 Ch 345, *Palette Shoes Pty Ltd v. Krohn* (1937) 58 CLR 1 at 26–27
[65] *Barclays Bank v. Quistclose Investment Ltd* [1970] A.C. 567

Co for the balance, but just a cheque for the whole amount in favour of A Co, which will pay such cheque into its personal account. P Co then runs the risk of A Co's insolvency.

To avoid such risk,[66] P Co can negotiate an arrangement whereby A Co contractually agrees that it will hold a specified (fractional or percentage) part of the proceeds of sale that represents the whole proceeds less its commission on trust for P Co, it will pay an amount of money corresponding to such part to P Co within a specified period of, say, 5 working days (such payment to discharge the relevant indebtedness of A Co to P Co) and will not let the balance in the account within such period fall below the amount due to P Co.[67]

V Co may sell raw materials to P Co which P Co uses to produce manufactured products belonging wholly to P Co and which P Co then sells. To avoid the insolvency risk arising from P Co only being a debtor of V Co, V Co can negotiate in its contract of sale with P Co, that P Co will be trustee of such a (fractional or percentage) part of the proceeds of sale of the newly manufactured products as is equivalent to the amount owing to V Co by P Co at the time P Co received such proceeds,[68] P Co will pay to V Co such amount within a specified period of, say, 5 working days and will not let the balance in its account within such period fall below such amount due to V Co.

In both these instances of principal-agent and vendor-purchaser the principal or vendor will be able to invoke equitable tracing processes so as to have an equitable lien or charge for the amount of its money[69] over the personal bank account of the agent or purchaser and an equitable proprietary interest in any traceable product purchased with its money. Under the general law, the principal or vendor will not have such rights if the alleged trust was a sham, both parties from the outset agreeing on irregular payments under a debtor-creditor relationship to help the cash-flow of the agent or purchaser, or will lose such rights if expressly or impliedly agreeing to ouster of the trust relationship by a debtor-creditor relationship.

11. Building contracts: retention trusts

1–44 Standard form building construction contracts have a clause for the employer of the management contractor, which employs various works contractors, to set up a retention trust fund of a percentage (*e.g.,* three

---

[66] *Re Fleet Disposal Services Ltd* [1995] 1 B.C.L.C. 345; *Re Lewis of Leicester Ltd* [1995] 1 B.C.L.C. 428; *Re ILG Travel* [1995] 2 B.C.L.C. 128; *Air Canada v. M & L Travel Ltd* (1994) 108 DLR (4th) 592; background position to *Royal Brunei Airlines v. Tan* [1995] 2 A.C. 378

[67] One cannot trace beyond the lowest intermediate balance (*Roscoe v. Winder* [1915] 1 Ch. 62): this clause is not vital but serves to emphasise the trust relationship.

[68] *Associated Alloys Pty Ltd v. ACN 001 452 106 Pty Ltd* (in Liquidation) 2000 74 ALJR 862 where at 869 Gaudron, McHugh, Gummow & Hayne JJ. state "There being value [provided by V Co], and equity regarding as done that which ought to be done, a completely constituted trust would arise in respect of those proceeds as they were received by the Buyer [P Co]".

[69] Such charge arises by operation of law from the creation of the trust, and a trust affecting a company's property does not require registration under s.395 Companies Act 1985 unlike an expressly created charge. If the contract between V Co and P Co related not to a trust of a specific ascertainable part (say half) of the proceeds (say £100,000) received by P Co, but to a trust of an amount corresponding to the amount of the debt (say £50,000) a problem arises as to certainty of subject matter of a trust, there being no £50,000 fund segregated from the remaining £50,000, so that only a contractual charge would arise, falling within s.395.

or five percent) of each amount certified by the architect as due to the management contractor for itself and the works contractors. Half of this fund is payable when the architect issues the certificate of practical completion and the final half upon issue of the certificate of completion of making good defects.

Thus, the employer has a measure of security to ensure the building is properly completed and the management contractor and works contractors have some protection against the insolvency of the employer.

12. Sinking fund trusts

Where major expenditure will be needed after a number of years, money **1–45** can be paid regularly to a trustee so that an adequate amount will certainly be available to carry out a particular purpose, for example major repairs or renewals for blocks of flats, for old heritage property, or for good environmental land reclamation after working out of a mine.

13. Employee share ownership trusts

A company can arrange for some of its shares to be held on trust for allocation to particular employees in due course (who then receive favoured tax treatment if they do not sell their shares for three years). Thus its employees are encouraged to work hard (so helping it and the English economy to develop) The trust also provides a market for shares in the employer company. "All employee" trusts of shares are particularly encouraged by provisions in the Finance Act 2000, the Inland Revenue even publishing model trust deeds.

14. Trusts of shares to separate control from ownership of the company

It may be useful to have voting rights vested in independent trustees **1–46** rather than in those owning the economic value, for example where A and B who are 60:40 shareholders in a joint venture company transfer their shares to T who must vote 75 per cent as B directs, which provides B with greater protection than if A merely contracted with B to vote 35 of his 60 as B directs, in which case A could break his contract and harm B's interests.

Independent trustees may be controlling directors of a company so that those owning the economic value do not have control which would contravene public interest laws *e.g.* for the conduct of banking business or for regulating fair competition (where the regulatory authority may require the shares to be sold but afford the trustees a reasonable time for this, so avoiding a forced sale at a depressed price that would have had to occur if the beneficiary controlled the company).

15. Custodian trusts in the financial or securities markets

To facilitate speedy inexpensive dealings in stocks and shares, many of **1–47** such securities are held by a corporate custodian, often for a sub-custodian, which holds for a broker who holds for a client. Because there can be no bailment or custody of intangibles, intangibles must be owned by the custodian as trustee, with sub-custodians, brokers and their clients having only a proportionate equitable co-ownership interest in the fungible pool of securities legally owned by the custodian as trustee.

This trust of a pool of assets for persons entitled to proportionate shares therein as equitable co-owners provides purchasers of securities with a proprietary interest and avoids technical certainty problems concerning which specific securities belong to whom. Thus, if Nominee plc is registered shareholder of ten million shares in Bigg plc and Subcustodian plc is interested in two million shares out of which it sold 100,000 to P, P does not actually own a specific 100,000 shareholding. P owns a one twentieth share of Subcustodian's one fifth share of Nominee's shareholding.

16. Pledges of bills of lading

1–48 Pledging the bill of lading with the other shipping documents requires delivery to the lender, but the buyer-borrower needs these documents to obtain the goods from the shipping company. If the lender parts with the documents unconditionally the pledge will be extinguished.

Thus, the buyer provides the lender with a trust letter or receipt in which, in return for the release of the documents, the buyer undertakes he will hold the documents and then the goods and any proceeds of sale on trust for the lender, who is thereby deemed to continue in constructive possession of the documents, so that the pledge remains valid.

The nature of a beneficiary's interest

1–49 There has been much controversy over the nature of a beneficiary's interest under a trust based upon the differences between *in personam* rights against trustees and *in rem* rights against property.[70] However, much depends on the meaning in context of *in personam* and *in rem* and whether one is dealing with a *bare* trust (A holds on trust for X absolutely) or a *fixed* trust (A holds on trust for X for life, remainder to Y for life, remainder to Z absolutely) or a *discretionary* trust (A holds on trust to distribute the income and capital between such of X Y or Z or their spouses and issue as he sees fit).

1–50 In all cases X has an equitable chose in action, a right *in personam* against the trustee to verify or falsify the trusteeship accounts and to compel due administration of the trust: the *situs* of that chose is in the jurisdiction where the trustees reside and administer the trust. As beneficiary under a bare trust he may demand transfer of the legal title from the trustee and so obtain the trust property *in rem* for himself as legal and beneficial owner[71]; he may, instead, assign or declare a sub-

---

[70] Hart (1899) 15 L.Q.R. 294; Scott (1917) 17 Col.L.R. 269; Stone (1917) 17 Col.L.R. 467; Hanbury (1929) 45 L.Q.R. 198; Latham (1954) 32 Can.B.R. 520; Waters (1967) 45 Can.B.R. 219; *Baker v. Archer-Shee* [1927] A.C. 844.

[71] *Saunders v. Vautier* (1841) 4 Beav. 115; see *infra*, at 9–152.

trust of his equitable interest in the trust property; he may trace the trust property into the hands of third-party recipients from the trustee unless the third party is a bona fide purchaser of the legal title for value without notice of his equitable interest[72] or a purchaser who complies with the overreaching requirements of the Law of Property Act or the Settled Land Act[73] or a person who validly acquired title under a foreign *lex situs*.[74] Thus he has proprietary *in rem* rights in the relevant assets. However, in this last eventuality if the trustee has dissipated the proceeds of sale then X has lost his equitable proprietary interest and is left merely with his equitable chose in action against the trustee personally, which will be worthless if the trustee is bankrupt or disappears with all his assets. For tax purposes X is properly regarded as *in rem* owner of the relevant assets. However, X is properly regarded as enforcing an *in personam* right against A where A holds a French immovable on express or resulting task for X,[75] but refuses to transfer title to X, so that X's English proceedings against A resident in England are not "proceedings which have as their object rights *in rem* in, or tenancies of, immovable property" when the court of the *lex situs* has exclusive jurisdiction.[76] As the European Court stated[77]:

> "The aim of the proceedings before the national court is to obtain a declaration that the son holds the flat for the exclusive benefit of the father and that he is under a duty to execute the documents necessary to convey ownership of the flat to the father. The father . . . seeks only to assert rights as against the son. Consequently his action is an action *in personam* . . . the immovable nature of the property held in trust and its location are irrelevant to the issues which have to be determined in the main proceedings, which would have been the same if the dispute had concerned a flat situated in the U.K. or a yacht."

If X be a beneficiary with a limited interest under a fixed trust, he has a **1–51** disposable equitable proprietary interest but he cannot claim the trust capital unless the other beneficiaries, Y and Z, are each of full capacity and join in demanding it from the trustees so that they can then divide it between themselves as they agree. He has a right to the income produced by the trust assets and is regarded as having part of the equitable ownership of the assets themselves[78] so that if they are situate in New York State he is treated for tax purposes as interested in foreign

---

[72] *Re Diplock* [1948] Ch. 465.
[73] L.P.A. 1925, s.27; S.L.A. 1925, s.18.
[74] Article 11, para, 2(d) of The Hague Trust Convention, implemented by Recognition of Trusts Act 1987.
[75] *Webb v. Webb* [1994] QB 696 (Ct. of Justice of E.U.). See also *Ashurst v. Polland* [2000] 2 All E.R. 772, affirmed [2001] 2 All E.R. 75.
[76] Article 16(1) of Convention on Jurisdiction and the Enforcement of Judgments in Civil and Commercial Matters implemented by Civil Jurisdiction and Judgments Act 1982.
[77] [1994] 3 All E.R. 911 at 930–931.
[78] *New Zealand Insurance Co. Ltd. v. C.P.D. (Victoria)* [1973] V.R. 659.

assets, namely New York assets[79]; it being immaterial that the trustees
reside in and administer the trust in England so that his equitable chose
in action is English.

1–52   If he be a beneficiary under a discretionary trust, X cannot compel the
trustees to pay him anything (so that the source of any entitlement is the
exercise of the trustees' discretion) and cannot substitute another person
for himself as a potential recipient of discretionary sums but he can
release his rights[80] and he has *in rem* standing to trace for the benefit of
all those interested under the trust.[81] However, it seems that just as
personal representatives of an unadministered estate[82] and a company
subject to a winding-up order[83] have ownership subject to onerous duties
in circumstances where the devisees, legatees or creditors have no
equitable proprietary interest but only choses in action, so trustees of a
discretionary trust with a large fluctuating class of beneficiaries have
ownership subject to onerous fiduciary duties in circumstances where the
beneficiaries under the discretionary trust only have an equitable chose
in action.[84] Indeed, Viscount Radcliffe[85] has rejected the view that "for
all purposes and at every moment of time the law requires the separate
existence of two different kinds of estate or interest in property, the legal
and the equitable . . . Equity in fact calls into existence and protects
equitable rights and interests in property only where their recognition
has been found to be required in order to give effect to its doctrines."[86]

1–53   To conclude, in order to understand the working operation of a trust it
is better to regard the interest of a beneficiary as an *in personam* right to
compel the trustees to perform the trust, *i.e.* as an equitable chose in
action situated where the trustees reside and administer the trust.
However, where things have gone wrong and trust property finds its way
wrongly into the hands of a third party (other than equity's darling) then
it is appropriate to regard the interest of a beneficiary, as a result of his
equitable tracing rights, as an equitable *in rem* right.[87] One thus
distinguishes internal aspects of the trust from external aspects.[88]

Where the state is seeking to recover tax which hinges upon the *situs*
of the taxable asset the better approach (in the absence of express

---

[79] *Baker v. Archer-Shee* [1927] A.C. 844; *Hamilton-Russell's Executors v. I.R.C.* (1943) 25 TC 200 at 207–
208; *I.R.C. v. Berrill* [1982] 1 All E.R. 867 at 880. Where the trust is not an English trust but a New
York trust then, by the New York proper law, a life tenant only has an equitable chose in action and
not a proprietary interest in the trust assets: *Archer-Shee v. Garland* [1931] A.C. 212. Further see
Memec v. IRC [1996] STC 1336 at 1351 and, on appeal, [1998] STC 754 at 764.

[80] *Re Gulbenkian's Settlement (No. 2)* [1970] Ch. 408.

[81] After all, a residuary beneficiary under an unadministered estate can assert "the estate's right of
property": *Commissioner for Stamp Duties v. Livingston* [1965] A.C. 694 at 714.

[82] *Commissioner for Stamp Duties v. Livingston* [1965] A.C. 694.

[83] *Ayerst v. C. & K. Constructions Ltd.* [1976] A.C. 168.

[84] If the class is a fixed class of, say, seven persons of full capacity then the seven have *Saunders v. Vautier*
(1841) 4 Beav 115 proprietary interests.

[85] Trustees of a charitable purpose trust would seem to be in a similar position, having ownership subject
to onerous duties enforceable by the Attorney-General: see *Att.-Gen. v. Cocke* [1988] Ch. 414 and *Von
Ernst & Cie SA v. IRC* [1980] 1 All E.R. 677.

[86] [1965] A.C. 694 at 712.

[87] Unless the *lex situs* governing transfer of the relevant property was a foreign one having no concept of
equitable proprietary right in its code of property principles.

[88] As did the European Court in *Webb v. Webb* [1994] 3 All E.R. 911 at 923, 930.

statutory guidance) is to say that if X is a bare beneficiary or a life tenant he should in substance be regarded as having an *in rem* interest in the trust assets wherever they may be situated. But if X is a discretionary beneficiary then in substance he should be regarded as having an *in personam* equitable chose in action[89] situate where the trustees reside and administer the trust.

From a tax point of view a beneficiary's interest (leaving aside bare **1–54** trusts) will be one of two basic types. He will either have a current fixed entitlement to such net income as remains after a proper exercise of the trustees' administrative powers (an interest in possession,[90] *e.g.* a life interest) or he will have no fixed entitlement to anything, merely hoping that the trustees will from time to time give him some of the trust income (*i.e.* he will merely be beneficiary of a discretionary trust)[91] or will not use their dispositive powers to divert to others the income he would otherwise have received (*e.g.* to A for life subject to the trustees' power within six months of income arising to pay such income instead to B or C). Trust instruments thus begin by setting out the sorts of interests that the beneficiaries are to have and laying down any contingencies that beneficiaries may have to satisfy; then, they set out any special powers of the settlor or the trustees to affect the beneficial interests under the trusts; finally, a host of administrative powers are conferred upon the trustees in such a way as to relax or abrogate the rigorous duties and standards that trust law would otherwise impose.

Section 3. A Discretionary Trust Precedent (Modern and Traditional)

As seeing something for yourself is so much better than any description **1–55** there now follows a discretionary trust precedent. Read it now, read it after reading Chapter 3, section 1, and read it at later stages when the significance of its administrative clauses will be more apparent. The trust in question where no interest in possession exists usefully reveals the flexibility of a trust and common administrative clauses. It is worthwhile considering how you would explain to a lay person the effect of clauses 3 and 4 and how accountable (or free from accountability) are the trustees. Trust instruments are normally drafted so as drastically to lighten the otherwise onerous duties of trustees.

TRADITIONAL TRUST PRECEDENT

THIS SETTLEMENT is made the _____day of _____19 _____ **1–56**
BETWEEN _____of _____(hereinafter called "the Settlor") of the one part and _____ of _____and _____of _____ (hereinafter called "the Original Trustees")[92] of the other part

---

[89] *cf. Sainsbury v. I.R.C.* [1970] 1 Ch. 712.
[90] *Pearson v. I.R.C.* [1981] A.C. 753. The distinction between trusts with an interest in possession and trusts where no such interest exists, is crucial for inheritance tax purposes: Inheritance Tax Act 1984, ss.49–57, 58–85.
[91] See Chap. 4, section 2 and *infra*, at para. 3–64.
[92] As to the identity of the Trustees see clause 8(a).

WHEREAS:

(A) The Settlor is desirous of making irrevocable provision for the Specified Class as herein defined [and for charity[93]] in manner hereinafter appearing

(B) With the intention of making such provision the Settlor has prior to the execution hereof transferred to the Original Trustees the assets specified in the Second Schedule hereto and is desirous of declaring such trusts thereof as hereinafter appear

(C) The Settlor may hereafter pay or transfer further assets to or into the control of the Trustees hereof to be held by them on the trusts of this Settlement

NOW THIS DEED WITNESSETH as follows:

1.—(1) THE perpetuity period applicable to this Settlement under the rule against perpetuities shall be the period of eighty years from the execution of this deed

(2) IN this Settlement and the Schedules hereto the following expressions shall have the following meanings that is to say:

(a) "the Trustees" means the Original Trustees or other the trustees or trustee for the time being of this Settlement and "Trustee" has a corresponding meaning;

(b) subject to any and every exercise of the powers conferred by Clause 5 hereof "the Specified Class" has the meaning attributed to it in the First Schedule hereto;

(c) "the Appointed Day" means the day on which shall expire the period of eighty years less three days from the execution of this Deed;

(d) "The Trust Fund" means and includes:
 (i) the said assets specified in the Second Schedule hereto;
 (ii) all assets paid or transferred to or into the control of and accepted by the Trustees as additions to the Trust Fund; and
 (iii) the assets from time to time representing the said assets specified in the Second Schedule hereto and the said additions to the Trust Fund or any part or parts thereof respectively

(e) "Spouse" means a party to a marriage which is for the time being subsisting and does not include a party to a former marriage which has terminated by death or divorce or otherwise

[(f)[94] "charity" means any institution whether corporate or not (including a trust) which is established for exclusively charitable purposes and "charities" bears a corresponding meaning]

(g) "the Nominating Beneficiaries" means such of the persons referred to in the First Schedule hereto as are for the time being members of the Specified Class and *sui juris*

1–57   **2.** THE Trustees shall stand possessed of the Trust Fund UPON TRUST at their discretion to retain the same (so far as not consisting of cash) in its existing form of investment or to sell the same or any part or parts thereof and to invest or

---

[93] Delete reference to charity if settlor does not wish to benefit charity.
[94] Delete sub-clause (f) if charities are not intended to benefit.

apply the net proceeds of any sale and any other capital moneys in or upon any kind of investment or for any of the purposes hereinafter authorised with power at any time and from time to time to vary such investments or applications for others of any nature hereby authorised.

3.—(1)[95] THE Trustees shall stand possessed of the Trust Fund and the **1–58** income thereof UPON TRUST for all or such one or more exclusively of the others or other of the members of the Specified Class if more than one in such shares and either absolutely or at such age or time or respective ages or times upon and with such limitations conditions and restrictions and such trusts and powers (including discretionary trusts and powers over income and capital exercisable by any person or persons other than the Settlor or any Spouse of the Settlor whether similar to the discretionary trusts and powers herein contained or otherwise) and with such provisions (including provisions for maintenance and advancement and the accumulation of income for any period or periods authorised by law and provisions for investment and management of any nature whatsoever and provisions for the appointment of separate trustees of any appointed fund) and generally in such manner as the Trustees (being not less than two in number or being a corporate trustee) shall in their absolute discretion from time to time by any deed or deeds revocable or irrevocable appoint PROVIDED THAT:

(i) no such appointment shall invalidate any payment or application of capital or income previously made under the trusts or powers herein elsewhere contained; and

(ii) every appointment shall be made and every interest limited thereunder shall vest in interest (if at all) not later than the Appointed Day and no appointment shall be revoked later than the Appointed Day

[(2)[96] Subject to any appointment previously made by the Trustees under the powers hereinbefore contained the Trustees may in their absolute discretion and without prejudice to the generality of the said powers at any time and from time to time before the Appointed Day:

(a) pay or transfer the whole or any part or parts of the income or capital of the Trust Fund to any charity or charities or apply the same for any exclusively charitable purpose or purposes;

(b) revocably or irrevocably in writing appoint that the whole or any part or share of the income of the Trust Fund or any annual or other periodic sum out of the same income shall during any period or periods ending before the Appointed Day be paid to any charity or charities;

(c) enter into any covenant or other arrangement with any charity or charities to enable or facilitate the recovery of any tax by such charity or charities in respect of any such payment transfer or appointment (as aforesaid)

PROVIDED ALWAYS that the receipt of the person purporting or appearing to be the treasurer or other proper officer of any charity or (in the case of a charitable trust) of the persons purporting or appearing to be the trustees thereof shall be a

---

[95] Delete numeral (1) if sub-clause (2) deleted.
[96] Delete sub-clause (2) if charities are not intended to benefit.

good discharge to the Trustees for any capital or income paid or transferred to such charity without the necessity for the Trustees to see further to the application thereof]

1–59   **4.**—(1) IN default of and subject to and until any or every exercise of the powers conferred on the Trustees by the preceding clause hereof the Trustees shall until the Appointed Day hold the income of the Trust Fund upon the trusts and with and subject to the powers and provisions following namely:

(a) During the period of twenty-one years from the execution of this Deed the Trustees shall have power to pay or apply the whole or any part or parts of such income as it arises to or for the maintenance and support or otherwise for the benefit of all or such one or more exclusively of the others or other of the persons who shall for the time being be living and members of the Specified Class if more than one in such shares and in such manner as the Trustees shall in their absolute discretion without being liable to account for the exercise of such discretion think fit.

(b) Subject to any and every exercise of the last-mentioned power the Trustees shall during the said period of twenty-one years accumulate the whole or the balance (as the case may be) of the said income by investing the same in any manner hereby authorised and shall hold the accumulations so made as an accretion to the capital of the Trust Fund for all purposes.

(c) After the expiration of the same period of twenty-one years the Trustees shall until the Appointed Day pay or apply the whole of the annual income of the Trust Fund as it arises to or for the maintenance and support or otherwise for the benefit of all or such one or more exclusively of the others or other of the persons who shall for the time being be living and members of the Specified Class if more than one in such shares and in such manner as the Trustees shall in their absolute discretion without being liable to account for the exercise of such discretion think fit

(2) In default of and subject to any or every exercise of the said powers conferred on the Trustees by the preceding clause hereof the Trustees shall stand possessed of the Trust Fund on the Appointed Day UPON TRUST for such persons as shall be then living and members of the Specified Class if more than one in equal shares per capita absolutely

(3) Any income or capital of the Trust Fund which but for this present sub-clause would be undisposed of by this Deed shall be held by the Trustees Upon Trust for [[97] _____ and his/her executors administrators and assigns absolutely][98] [_____and _____ and their respective executors administrators and assigns in equal shares absolutely][99] _____ (as a registered charity) absolutely and in the event of the failure of this present trust then for charitable purposes generally][1]

1–60   **5.** THE Trustees (being not less than two in number or being a corporate trustee) may from time to time and at any time before the Appointed Day by any deed or deeds:

---

[97] The beneficiaries under this ultimate trust should not be the settlor or his spouse or anyone whom he might marry or detrimental tax consequences follow.
[98] These are alternatives, so delete as appropriate.
[99] *ibid.*
[1] *ibid.*

(a) declare that any person or class or description of person shall cease to be a member or members of the Specified Class and thereupon such person or class or description of person shall cease to be a member or members of the Specified Class in the same manner as if he she or they had originally been expressly excluded therefrom but without prejudice to any previous payment of capital or income to such person or any member of such class or description of person or application thereof for his her or their benefit PROVIDED that the removal of any such person or class or description of person as aforesaid shall not prejudice modify or affect any appointment of capital or income then already made [AND PROVIDED ALSO[2] that the removal of any such person or class or description of person as aforesaid shall not prejudice modify or affect the trust in favour of [_____ and his/her executors administrators and assigns][3] [_____ and _____ and their executors administrators and assigns][4] contained in sub-clause (3) of the last preceding clause hereof]

(b) declare that any person or persons (not being the Settlor or a Spouse of the Settlor or one of the Trustees) previously nominated in writing in that behalf by any one or more of the Nominating Beneficiaries shall thenceforth be included in the Specified Class and thereupon such person or persons shall become a member or members of the Specified Class for all the purposes hereof PROVIDED that (subject to obtaining any necessary Exchange Control consents) the Trustees shall have an absolute discretion whether or not to make any such declaration in relation to any person or persons nominated as aforesaid and PROVIDED FURTHER that any addition of any such person or persons to the Specified Class shall not prejudice modify or affect any appointment of capital or income then already made

(c) wholly or partially release or restrict all or any of the powers and discretions conferred upon them (including this present power) whether in relation to the whole Trust Fund or any part or parts thereof or the income thereof respectively

6. WHENEVER the Trustees shall determine to apply any income for the benefit of an infant the Trustees may either themselves so apply that income or for that purpose may pay the same to any parent guardian or other person for the time being having the care or custody of such infant (other than the Settlor or any Spouse of the Settlor) without being responsible for seeing to the further application thereof

7.—(1) MONEYS to be invested under this Settlement may be invested or otherwise applied on the security of or in the purchase or acquisition of real or personal property (including the purchase or acquisition of chattels and the effecting or maintaining of policies of insurance or assurance) rights or interests of whatsoever kind and wheresoever situate including any stocks funds shares securities or other investments of whatsoever nature and wheresoever (but including derivatives for the purpose only of controlling or limiting risk) whether producing income or not and whether involving liability or not or on personal loan with or without interest and with or without security to any person (other

---

[2] This proviso is not required if the ultimate trust in clause 4(3) is in favour of charity.
[3] Delete as appropriate, for these are alternatives.
[4] *ibid.*

than the Settlor or any Spouse of the Settlor) anywhere in the world including loans to any member of the Specified Class and the Trustees may grant indulgence to or release any debtor (other than as aforesaid) with or without consideration and may enter into profit sharing agreements and give and take options with or without consideration and accept substitution of any security for other security or of one debtor for another debtor to the intent that the Trustees (subject as herein provided) shall have the same unrestricted powers of investing and using moneys and transposing investments and altering the user of moneys arising under these presents as if they were absolutely entitled thereto beneficially

1–61   (2) IT IS HEREBY EXPRESSLY DECLARED that without prejudice to the generality of the foregoing sub-clause and without prejudice to any powers conferred by law the Trustees shall (subject to the terms of any appointment made under the powers hereinbefore contained) have the following additional powers-exercisable until the Appointed Day namely:

    (a) The Trustees may:
        (i) at any time or times lay out any part or parts of the Trust Fund in the purchase or acquisition of and paying the expenses of purchasing or acquiring and making improvements in or repairs to or on any land and buildings of freehold leasehold or of any other tenure or interest of whatsoever description situate in any part of the world whether or not in the occupation of or intended for occupation by any member or members of the Specified Class;
       (ii) at any time or times lay out any part or parts of the Trust Fund in the purchase of household furniture plate linen china cutlery and articles of household use ornament or equipment or any other chattels whatsoever for the use or enjoyment of any member or members of the Specified Class whether occupying a building purchased as aforesaid or otherwise

    (b)   (i) any land purchased by the Trustees shall if situate in England or Wales be assured to the Trustees upon trust for sale with power to postpone sale and if situate elsewhere be assured to the Trustees either with or without any trust for sale as the Trustees shall think fit but nevertheless with power to sell the same;
       (ii) in relation to any land situate outside England and Wales the powers and indemnities given to the Trustees in relation to land in England by English law shall apply as if expressed in this Deed and the net rents and profits thereof shall be applicable in like manner as if they arose from land in England;
      (iii) the Trustees shall stand possessed of any land so purchased and the net proceeds of sale thereof and other capital moneys arising under this Settlement upon the trusts and with and subject to the powers and provisions (including power to purchase land) upon with and subject to which the money laid out in the purchase of such land would have been held if the same had not been so laid out;
      (iv) until the sale of any land purchased as aforesaid the Trustees may permit any member or members of the Specified Class to occupy the same upon such terms (if any) as to payment or non-payment of rent rates taxes and other expenses and outgoings and as to repair and decoration and for such period or periods before the Appointed Day as the Trustees may think fit;

  (v) the Trustees shall be indemnified out of the Trust Fund against all costs rents covenants obligations and outgoings relating to any land purchased as aforesaid or for which the Trustees may be liable in respect of the said premises or the said purchase

(c) Any household furniture or other chattels purchased by the Trustees as **1–62** aforesaid may be handed over to any member or members of the Specified Class for his or her or their use or enjoyment for any period before the Appointed Day upon and subject to such terms and conditions (if any) as to maintaining such inventory or inventories (if any) and as to insurance and preservation as the Trustees shall think fit

(d) (i) The Trustees shall be at liberty to borrow money (otherwise than from the Settlor or any Spouse of the Settlor) for any of the purposes of this Settlement (including the provision of money to give effect to any appointment authorised hereunder or for the purpose of effecting or maintaining any policies or purchasing or subscribing for any shares or stocks securities properties options rights or interests or other property of whatsoever description) and they may pledge or mortgage the whole or any part of the Trust Fund or the future income thereof by way of security for any such loan and no lender shall be obliged to inquire as to the purpose for which any loan is required or whether the money borrowed exceeds any such requirement

  (ii) The Trustees may pledge or mortgage the whole or any part of the Trust Fund by way of principal collateral or other security or by way of guarantee to secure any bank overdraft or other moneys borrowed by any member or members of the Specified Class *Provided* that neither the Settlor nor any Spouse of the Settlor is the lender or one of the lenders in respect of or has any interest in such overdraft or other moneys and *Provided* further that no person other than a member or members of the Specified Class is liable for the repayment thereof

(e) The Trustees may at any time or times enter into any compromise or arrangement with respect to or may release all or any of their rights as shareholders stockholders or debenture stockholders or creditors of any company and whether in connection with a scheme of reconstruction or amalgamation or otherwise and may accept in or towards satisfaction of all or any of such rights such consideration as they shall in their discretion think fit whether in the form of shares stock debenture stock cash obligations or securities of the same or of any other company or companies or in any other form whatsoever

(f) (i) The Trustees may effect purchase or acquire any policy or policies **1–63** assuring payment to the Trustees in the event of the death of any person of such sum as the Trustees in their absolute discretion (having regard to any prospective liability for tax that may arise in respect of the Trust Fund or any part thereof on the death of such person) may think fit or any endowment or sinking fund policy or policies of whatsoever nature and may pay any premium or premiums thereon out of income or capital

  (ii) Without prejudice to the last-mentioned powers or to any powers vested in them under the general law the Trustees may from time to time apply any part or parts of the income or capital of the Trust Fund in or towards payment of the premium or premiums on any policy or policies in which any one or more of the members of the Specified Class shall (whether under this Settlement or any other deed or otherwise) have any beneficial interest whether vested or contingent and whether indefeasible or defeasible PROVIDED ALWAYS that no person except one or more of the members of the Specified Class shall have any beneficial interest whatsoever in the said policy or policies and so that (subject to the said proviso) the Trustees shall have power if they think fit to effect any such policy or policies on any life or lives in which any one or more of the members of the Specified Class shall have an insurable interest

(iii) PROVIDED ALWAYS that no income shall be paid or applied under the foregoing powers after the expiration of twenty-one years from the execution hereof if such payment or application would involve an accumulation of the said income

(iv) In relation to any policy held by them hereunder the Trustees shall have all the powers of a beneficial owner including (without prejudice to the generality of such powers) power to surrender any such policy or to convert the same into a paid up policy or into any other form of assurance or otherwise or to exercise any option thereunder or to sell mortgage charge or otherwise realise or dispose of the same

1–64 (g) The Trustees may exercise all voting rights appertaining to any investments comprised in the Trust Fund in as full free and absolute a manner as if they were absolute owners of such investments and in particular but without prejudice to the generality of the foregoing provisions shall be at liberty to exercise such voting rights either by voting or by abstaining from voting so as to ensure or further the appointment or reappointment of any one or more of their number to be directors secretaries or employees of any company in which any part of the Trust Fund may for the time being be invested or of any subsidiary of any such company and any Trustee receiving from any such company or subsidiary any fees salary bonuses or commissions for services rendered to such company or subsidiary shall be entitled to retain the same for his own benefit and shall not be required to account therefor to any person interested hereunder

(h) The Trustees shall not be bound or required to interfere in the management or conduct of the affairs or business of any company in which the Trust Fund may be invested (whether or not the Trustees have the control of such company) and so long as no Trustee has actual knowledge of any fraud dishonesty recklessness or negligence on the part of the directors having the management of such company they may leave the same (including the payment or non-payment of dividends) wholly to such directors without being liable for any loss thereby arising

1–65 (i) The Trustees shall have the powers of appropriation and other incidental powers conferred on a personal representative by Section 41 of the Administration of Estates Act 1925 but without the necessity of obtaining the consent of any person to the exercise thereof

(j) The Trustees may apportion as they think fit any funds subject to different trusts which may have become blended and (without prejudice to the jurisdiction of the Court) may determine as they shall consider just whether any money is to be considered as capital or income and whether any expense ought to be paid out of capital or income and all other questions and matters of doubt of whatsoever description arising in the execution of the trusts of these presents and none of the Trustees and no person having formerly been one of the Trustees and no estate of any deceased Trustee shall be liable for or for the consequences of any act done or omitted to be done or for any payment made or omitted to be made in pursuance of any such determination notwithstanding that such determination shall subsequently be held to have been wrongly made

(k) The Trustees may in addition and without prejudice to any powers to employ agents or attorneys conferred by law employ and remunerate on such terms and conditions as they shall think fit any Solicitors Brokers or other agents or advisers (being in each case a person firm or corporation other than and excluding the Settlor and any Spouse of the Settlor) for the purpose of transacting all or any business of whatever nature or doing any act or giving any advice requiring to be transacted done or given in relation to the trusts hereof including any business act or advice which a trustee not being in any profession or business could have transacted done or given personally and any such Solicitor Broker or other agent or adviser shall be entitled to retain any such remuneration or his share thereof notwithstanding that he or any partner of his is a trustee or the sole trustee hereof or is a member officer or employee of or is otherwise interested in any body corporate which is a trustee or the sole trustee hereof and notwithstanding that such agent or adviser is a body corporate of which one or more of the trustees is a member officer or employee or in which one or more of the Trustees is otherwise interested. And the Trustees shall not be responsible for the default of any such Solicitor Broker or other agent or adviser or for any loss occasioned by the employment thereof in good faith

(l) The Trustees may employ and remunerate as they see fit an investment **1–66** manager (who may be one of themselves or any person associated with any of themselves) so as to delegate to him full discretion to manage the Trust Fund or any part thereof within the limits and for the period stipulated by the Trustees providing his investment activities are subject to review by the Trustees no less than every six months and providing he is reasonably believed by the Trustees to be someone qualified and authorised to engage in the business of managing investments for others and the Trustees shall have authority to enter into an agreement with such investment manager on the same terms (including, for example, terms as to self-dealing and sub-delegation) as a prudent man of business can agree for the management of his own funds and the Trustees shall not be liable for any loss resulting from the exercise of the powers herein conferred so long as they act in good faith nor for any profit made by the investment manager if a Trustee or associated with a Trustee so long as management fees and commissions do not exceed those paid by an unassociated client with a portfolio of investments of similar value to that of the Trust Fund

(m) The Trustees may deposit any moneys deed securities or investments **1–67** (including shares and securities to bearer) held by them as trustees with any banker or any person firm or corporation (other than and excluding the Settlor and any Spouse of the Settlor) whether in the United Kingdom or abroad for safe custody or receipt of dividends and may pay out of the income or capital of such part of the Trust Fund as they shall think proper any sum payable for such deposit and custody

(n) Assets of the Trust may be held in the names of any two or more of the Trustees and the Trustees may vest such assets in a stakeholder or in a nominee or nominees anywhere in the world (other than the Settlor or any Spouse of the Settlor) on behalf of the Trustees and entrust or concur in entrusting the realisation and reinvestment of such assets to such stakeholder nominee or nominees upon such terms as the Trustees may deem reasonable

(o) The Trustees may (at the expense of the Trust Fund) incorporate or register or procure the incorporation or registration of any company (with limited or unlimited liability) in any part of the world for any purpose including the acquisition of the Trust Fund or any part thereof and so that (if thought fit) the consideration on the sale of the Trust Fund to any such company may consist wholly or partly of fully paid shares debentures debenture stock or other securities of the company credited as fully paid which shall be allotted to or otherwise vested in the Trustees and be capital moneys in the Trustees' hands

1–68 (p) The trustees may embark upon or carry on whether alone or in partnership or as a joint venture with any other person or persons (except the Settlor or any Spouse of the Settlor) or corporation or corporations at the expense of the Trust Fund and the income thereof any trade or business whatsoever including (without prejudice to the generality of the foregoing) any forestry timber farming development insurance banking or other agricultural commercial industrial financial or professional trade or business whatsoever and may assist or finance to any extent the commencement or carrying on of any trade or business by any other or others (except as aforesaid)

(q) The trustees may effect any transaction relating to the management administration or disposition of property within the Trust Fund which falls within the jurisdiction of a court to authorise under section 57 of the Trustee Act 1925 without the necessity of obtaining an order of the court authorising such transactions

8. The following provisions shall apply to the trusts and trusteeship hereof:

(a) The statutory powers of appointing trustees shall apply hereto and shall be exercisable by [the Settlor][5] during [his/her][6] life PROVIDED that neither the Settlor nor any Spouse of the Settlor shall be appointed a trustee of these presents

1–69 (b) Any person whether an individual or a body corporate may be appointed as a trustee of this settlement whether or not he or it shall be resident domiciled or incorporated in the United Kingdom and the appointment as sole trustee of a body corporate ranking as a trust corporation under the law governing its incorporation shall validly discharge the trustees from all the trusts of this settlement except those if any relating to English or Welsh land then comprised in this settlement

(c) The Trustees shall have power to carry on the administration of the trusts of this settlement in any part of the world whether inside or outside the United Kingdom and power to that end to appoint and pay

---

[5] Amend as appropriate.
[6] *ibid.*

agents and investment managers with general discretion as to investment and disinvestment of the whole or a specified part of the trust fund upon such terms (including, for example, terms as to self-dealing and sub-delegation) as a prudent man of business can agree for the management of his own funds

(d) No Trustee shall be capable of being removed or replaced on the grounds that he has remained out of the United Kingdom for more than 12 months

(e) Subject to subclause (b) hereof the law according to which the trusts powers and provisions of this settlement shall for the time being be governed and administered shall be the law of England and Wales

(f) The Trustees shall have power exercisable at any time or time by deed or **1–70** deeds executed before the Perpetuity Day in their absolute discretion (but during the lifetime of the Settlor not without his prior consent in writing) to declare that the law governing the validity of this settlement or the law governing the administration of this settlement shall from the date of such deed or from some later date specified therein and subject to any further exercise of this power be the law of some other State specified therein provided that such State has its own internal law of trusts and recognises the effectiveness of the exercise of this power and providing always that this power shall not be exercisable so as to render this settlement revocable or unenforceable in whole or in part or otherwise to affect the beneficial trusts and powers thereof other than the powers incorporated by Trustee Act 1925 sections 31 and 32 and analogous powers in other States and "administration" matters shall include all matters other than those governing the validity of the beneficial interests created or capable of being created under this settlement

(g) Any Trustee engaged in any profession or business shall be entitled to charge and be paid all professional or other charges made by him or his firm for business done by him or his firm in relation to the execution of the trusts hereof whether or not in the ordinary course of his profession or business and whether or not of a nature requiring the employment of a professional or business person

(h) Any corporation appointed to be a trustee hereof shall have the powers rights and benefits as to remuneration or otherwise as at or prior to its appointment may be agreed in writing between such corporation and the person or persons (or corporation or corporations) making such appointment

9. THE following provisions shall apply to the powers and discretions of the **1–71** Trustees hereunder:

(1) Any Trustee may concur in exercising any such power or discretion notwithstanding that he may have a direct or other personal interest in the mode or result of exercising the same Provided that at least one of the Trustees has no such direct or other personal interest

(2) The Trustees shall not be concerned to see to the insurance preservation repair or renewal of any freehold leasehold or other property household furniture or other chattels occupied used or enjoyed by any member of the Specified Class and in the professed execution of the trusts and powers hereof no Trustee shall be liable for any loss to the trust premises

arising by reason of any improper investment or application of the Trust Fund or any part thereof made in good faith

(3) Every discretion hereby conferred upon the Trustees shall be an absolute and unfettered discretion and the Trustees shall not be required to furnish to any beneficiary hereunder any reason or justification for the manner in which any such discretion may be exercised

(4) No power or discretion hereunder to which the rule against perpetuities applies shall be exercisable after the Appointed Day

1–72   **10.** NOTWITHSTANDING anything hereinbefore or in the schedules hereto contained:

(a) the Trust Fund and the income thereof shall be possessed and enjoyed to the entire exclusion of the Settlor and of any benefit to the Settlor by contract or otherwise;

(b) no part of the Trust Fund or the income thereof shall be paid lent or applied for the benefit of the Settlor or any Spouse of the Settlor nor shall any power or discretion hereunder be exercised so as to confer any benefit on the Settlor or any Spouse of the Settlor in any circumstances whatsoever

1–73   **11.** THIS Settlement and the dispositions hereby made are intended to be and are irrevocable

IN WITNESS whereof the parties hereto have hereunto set their respective hands or seals the day and year first before written

THE FIRST SCHEDULE[7] hereinbefore referred to

The Specified Class consists (subject to any exercise of the powers contained in Clause 5 of the foregoing Deed) of the following persons namely:

[(1) the children and remoter issue of the Settlor whether living at the date hereof or born hereafter;

(2) any person (other than a Trustee) who shall (whether before or after the date hereof) have married any of such children or remoter issue of the Settlor as aforesaid (whether or not such marriage shall for the time being be subsisting);

(3) A.B. (the brother of the Settlor);

(4) the children and remoter issue of the said A.B. whether living at the date hereof or born hereafter;

(5) any person (other than a Trustee) who shall (whether before or after the date hereof) have married any of such children or remoter issue of the said A.B. as aforesaid (whether or not such marriage shall for the time being be subsisting);

(6) any adopted child of the Settlor or of any of such children or remoter issue of the Settlor as aforesaid and the children and remoter issue of any such adopted child;

(7) any person (other than a Trustee) who shall (whether before or after the date hereof) have married any such adopted child or any child or remoter issue of any such adopted child as aforesaid (whether or not such marriage shall for the time being be subsisting)

---

[7] This schedule has been completed by way of example.

Provided that for the purposes of this present definition a person shall be deemed to be the adopted child of another person only if he or she shall be recognised as the adopted child of such other person by the Law of England for the time being in force.]

THE SECOND SCHEDULE hereinbefore referred to

MODERN TRUST SETTLEMENT

(From J. Kessler, *Drafting Trusts and Will Trusts*, 5th ed, (2000)

This settlement is made [date] between: **1–74**

1 [Name of settlor] of [address] ("the Settlor") of the one part and
2   2.1 [Name of first trustee] of [address] and
      2.2 [Name of second trustee] of [address]
("the Original Trustees") of the other part.

Whereas:

1 The Settlor has [two] children:
    1.1 [Adam Smith] ("[Adam]") who was born on [date] and
    1.2 [Mary Smith] ("[Mary]") who was born on [date].
2 This Settlement shall be known as the [Name-of-settlor Settlement 2000].

Now this deed witnesses as follows:

1. Definitions

In this settlement: **1–75**

1.1 **"The Trustees"** means the Original Trustees or the trustees of the settlement for the time being.
1.2 **"The Trust Fund"** means:
    1.2.1 property transferred to the Trustees to hold on the terms of this Settlement; and
    1.2.2 all property from time to time representing the above.
1.3 **"Trust Property"** means any property comprised in the Trust Fund.
1.4 **"The Trust Period"** means the period of 80 years beginning with the date of this Settlement. That is the perpetuity period applicable to this Settlement under the rule against perpetuities.
1.5 **"The Accumulation Period"** means the period of 21 years beginning with the date of this Settlement.
1.6 **"The Beneficiaries"** means:
    1.6.1 The children and descendants of the Settlor.
    1.6.2 The spouses, widows and widowers (whether or not remarried) of paragraph .1 of this sub-clause:
    1.6.3 The [widow] (whether or not remarried) of the Settlor.
    1.6.4 Any Person or class of Persons nominated to the Trustees by:
        1.6.4.1 the Settlor or
        1.6.4.2 two Beneficiaries (after the death of the Settlor)

and whose nomination is accepted in writing by the Trustees.

1.6.5 At any time during which there are no Beneficiaries within paragraph .1 of this sub-clause.

1.6.5.1 [specify "fall back" beneficiaries if desired, *e.g.* nieces and nephews and their families].

1.6.5.2 [any company, body or trust established for charitable purposes only].

1.7 **"Person"** includes a person anywhere in the world and includes a Trustee.

2. Trust Income

1–76 Subject to the Overriding Powers below:

2.1 The Trustees may accumulate the whole or part of the income of the Trust Fund during the Accumulation Period. That income shall be added to the Trust Fund.

2.2 The Trustees shall pay or apply the remainder of the income to or for the benefit of any Beneficiaries, as the Trustees think fit, during the Trust Period.

3. Overriding Powers

1–77 The Trustees shall have the following powers ("Overriding Powers"):

3.1 Power of appointment

3.1.1 The Trustees may appoint that they shall hold the Trust Fund for the benefit of any Beneficiaries, on such terms as the Trustees think fit.

3.1.2 An appointment may create any provisions and in particular:

3.1.2.1 discretionary trusts;

3.1.2.2 dispositive or administrative powers;

exercisable by any Person.

3.1.3 An appointment shall be made by deed and may be revocable or irrevocable.

3.2 *Transfer of Trust Property to new settlement*

The Trustees may by deed declare that they hold any Trust Property on trust to transfer it to trustees of a Qualifying Settlement, to hold on the terms of that Qualifying Settlement, freed and released from the terms of this Settlement.

"A Qualifying Settlement" here means any settlement, wherever established, under which every Person who may benefit is (or would if living be) a Beneficiary of this Settlement.

3.3 *Power of advancement*

The Trustees may pay or apply any Trust Property for the advancement or benefit of any Beneficiary.

3.4 The Overriding Powers shall be exercisable only:

3.4.1 during the Trust Period; and

3.4.2 at a time when there are at least two Trustees, or the Trustee is a company carrying on a business which consists of or includes the management of trusts.

4. Default Clause

1–78 Subject to that, the Trust Fund shall be held on trust for [Adam and Mary in equal shares—or specify default trusts as appropriate] absolutely.

5. Appointment of Trustees

The power of appointing trustees is exercisable by the Settlor during [his] life and by will.

6. Further Provisions

The provisions set out in the schedule below shall have effect [For a shorter form, say instead of the above:

> "The standard provisions of the Society of Trust and Estate Practitioners (1st Edition) shall apply with the deletion of paragraph 5. Section 11 Trusts of Land & Appointment of Trustees Act 1996 (consultation with beneficiaries) shall not apply."

And omit the schedule.]

7. Exclusion of Settlor and Spouse

Notwithstanding anything else in this Settlement, no power conferred by this **1–79** settlement shall be exercisable, and no provision shall operate so as to allow Trust Property or its income to become payable to or applicable for the benefit of the Settlor or the spouse of the Settlor in any circumstances whatsoever.
In witness, [etc.]

THE SCHEDULE: FURTHER PROVISIONS

1. Additional powers

The Trustees have the following additional powers: **1–80**

1.1 Investment

> 1.1.1 The Trustees may make any kind of investment that they could make if they were absolutely entitled to the Trust Fund. In particular the Trustees may invest in land in any part of the world and unsecured loans.
> 1.1.2 The Trustees are under no obligation to diversify the Trust Fund.
> 1.1.3 The Trustees may invest in speculative or hazardous investments but this power may only be exercised at the time when there are at least two Trustees, or the Trustee is a company carrying on a business which consists of or includes the management of trusts.

1.2 Joint property

The Trustees may acquire property jointly with any Person and may blend Trust Property with other property.

1.3 General power of management and disposition

The Trustees may effect any transaction relating to the management or disposition of Trust Property as if they were absolutely entitled to it.

1.4 Improvement

The Trustees may develop or improve Trust Property in any way. Capital expenses need not be repaid out of income under section 84(2) of the Settled Land Act 1925, if the Trustees think fit.

1.5 Income and capital

    1.5.1 The Trustees may acquire:
        1.5.1.1 wasting assets and
        1.5.1.1 assets which yield little or no income
        for investment or any other purpose.

    1.5.2 The Trustees are under no duty to procure distributions from a company in which they are interested.

    1.5.3 The Trustees may pay taxes and other expenses out of income although they would otherwise be paid out of capital

    1.5.4 Generally, the Trustees are under no duty to hold a balance between conflicting interests of Beneficiaries.

    1.5.5 The Trustees may (subject to the jurisdiction of the Court) determine whether receipts and liabilities are to be considered as capital or income, and whether expenses ought to be paid out of capital or income. The Trustees shall not be liable for any act done in pursuance of such determination (in the absence of fraud or negligence) even though it shall subsequently be held to have been wrongly made.

    1.5.6 Income may be set aside and invested to answer any liabilities which in the opinion of the Trustees ought to be borne out of income or to meet depreciation of the capital value of any Trust Property. In particular, income may be applied for a leasehold sinking fund policy.

1.6 Application of trust capital as income

1–81 The Trustees may apply Trust Property as if it were income arising in the current year. In particular, the Trustees may pay such income to a Beneficiary as his income, for the purpose of augmenting his income.

1.7 Use of trust property

    1.7.1 The Trustees may acquire any interest in property anywhere in the world for occupation or use by a Beneficiary.

    1.7.2 The Trustees may permit a Beneficiary to occupy or enjoy the use of Trust Property on such terms as they think fit.

    1.7.3 The Trustees may lend trust money to a Beneficiary. The loan may be interest free and unsecured, or on such terms as the Trustees think fit. The Trustees may charge Trust Property as security for any debts or obligations of a Beneficiary.

1.8 Trade

1–82 The Trustees may carry on a trade, in any part of the world, alone or in partnership.

1.9 Borrowing

    The Trustees may borrow money for investment or any other purpose. Money borrowed shall be treated as Trust Property.

1.10 Delegation

    A Trustee or the Trustees jointly (or other Person in a fiduciary position) may authorise any person to exercise all or any functions on such terms as to remuneration and other matters as they think fit. A Trustee shall not be responsible for the default of that Person (even if the delegation was not strictly necessary or convenient) provided he took reasonable care in his selection and supervision.

1.11 Nominees and custodians

1.11.1 The Trustees may appoint a person to act as their nominee in relation to such of the assets of the trust as they may determine. They may take such steps as are necessary to secure that those assets are vested in the nominee.

1.11.2 The Trustees may appoint a person to act as custodian in relation to such of the assets of the trust as they may determine. The Trustees may give the custodian custody of the assets and any documents or records concerning the assets. The Trustees are not obliged to appoint a custodian of securities payable to bearer.

1.11.3 The Trustees may appoint a person to act as nominee or custodian on such terms as to remuneration and other matters as they may think fit.

1.12 Offshore administration

The Trustees may carry on the administration of this Settlement anywhere they think fit.

1.13 Indemnities

The Trustees may indemnify any Person for any liability relating to the **1–83** Settlement.

1.14 Security

The Trustees may mortgage or charge Trust Property as security for any liability incurred by them as Trustees (and may grant a floating charge so far as the law allows).

1.15 Supervision of company

The Trustees are under no duty to enquire into the conduct of a company in which they are interested, unless they have knowledge of circumstances which call for inquiry.

1.16 Appropriation

The Trustees may appropriate Trust Property to any Person or class of Persons in or towards the satisfaction of their interest in the Trust Fund.

1.17 Receipt by charities

Where Trust Property is to be paid or transferred to a charity, the receipt of the treasurer or appropriate officer of the charity shall be a complete discharge to the Trustees.

1.18 Release of powers

The Trustees (or other persons in a fiduciary position) may by deed release **1–84** wholly or in part any of their rights or functions and (if applicable) so as to bind their successors.

1.19 Ancillary powers

The Trustees may do anything which is incidental or conducive to the exercise of their functions.

1.20 Insurance policies

The trustees may pay premiums of any insurance policy out of income.

2. Minors

1–85   2.1 Where the Trustees may apply income for the benefit of a minor, they may do so by paying the income to the minor's parent or guardian on behalf of the minor, or to the minor if he has attained the age of 16. The Trustees are under no duty to inquire into the use of the income unless they have knowledge of circumstances which call for inquiry.

2.2 Where the Trustees may apply income for the benefit of a minor, they may do so by resolving that they hold that income on trust for the minor absolutely and:

2.2.1 The Trustees may apply that income for the benefit of the minor during his minority.

2.2.2 The Trustees shall transfer the residue of that income to the minor on attaining the age of 18.

2.2.3 For investment and other administrative purposes that income shall be treated as Trust Property.

3. Mentally handicapped beneficiary

1–86   Where income or capital is payable to a Beneficiary who does not have the mental capacity to appoint an attorney with an enduring general power, the Trustees may (subject to the directions of the Court or his Receiver) apply that income or capital for his benefit.

4. Disclaimer

A Person may disclaim his interest in this Settlement wholly or in part.

5. Apportionment

Income and expenditure shall be treated as arising when payable, and not from day to day, so that no apportionment shall take place.

6. Conflicts of interest

1–87   6.1 In this paragraph:

6.1.1 **"A Fiduciary"** means a Person subject to fiduciary duties under the Settlement.

6.1.2 **"An Independent Trustee"**, in relation to a Person, means a Trustee who is not:

6.1.2.1 a brother, sister, ancestor, descendant or dependent of the Person;

6.1.2.2 a spouse of paragraph .1.2.1 above, or a spouse of the Person;

6.1.2.3 a company controlled by one or more of any of the above.

6.1.3 Subject to the next sub-clause a Fiduciary may:

    6.1.3.1 enter into a transaction with the Trustees, or

    6.1.3.2 be interested in an arrangement in which the Trustees are or might have been interested, or

    6.1.3.3 act (or not act) in any other circumstances;

    even though his fiduciary duty under the Settlement conflicts with other duties or with his personal interest;

6.1.4 The above sub-clause only has effect if:

    6.1.4.1 the Fiduciary first discloses to the Trustees the nature and extent of any material interest conflicting with his fiduciary duties, and

    6.1.4.2 there is an Independent Trustee in respect of whom there is no conflict of interest, and he considers that the transaction arrangement or action is not contrary to the general interest of the Settlement.

6.1.5 The powers of the Trustees may be used to benefit a Trustee (to the same extent as if he were not a Trustee) provided that there is an Independent Trustee in respect of whom there is no conflict of interest.

7. Absolute discretion clause

7.1 The Powers of the Trustees may be exercised: **1–88**

    7.1.1 at their absolute discretion; and

    7.1.2 from time to time as occasion requires.

7.2 The Trustees are not under any duty to consult with any Beneficiaries or to give effect to the wishes of any Beneficiaries.

8. Trustee remuneration

8.1 A Trustee acting in a professional capacity is entitled to receive reasonable remuneration out of the Trust Fund for any services that he provides on behalf of the Trust

8.2 For this purpose, a trustee acts in a professional capacity if he acts in the course of a profession or business which consists of or includes the provision of services in connection with:

    8.2.1 the management or administration of trusts generally or a particular kind of trust, or

    8.2.2 any particular aspect of the management or administration of trusts generally or a particular kind of trust.

8.3 The Trustees may make arrangements to remunerate themselves for work done for a company connected with the Trust Fund.

9. Commissions and bank charges

9.1 A Person may retain any reasonable commission or profit in respect of any **1–89** transaction relating to this Settlement even though that commission or profit was procured by an exercise of fiduciary powers (by that Person or some other Person) provided that:

    9.1.1 The Person would in the normal course of business receive and retain the commission or profit on such transaction.

    9.1.2 The receipt of the commission or profit shall be disclosed to the Trustees.

9.2 A bank may make loans to the Trustees and generally provide banking services upon its usual terms and shall not be liable to account for any profit so made even though the receipt of such profit was procured by an exercise of fiduciary powers (by the bank or some other Person).

10. Liability of trustees

1–90 10.1 The duty of reasonable care (set out in s. 1, Trustee Act 2000) applies to all the functions of the Trustees.

10.2 A Trustee shall not be liable for a loss to the Trust Fund unless that loss was caused by his own fraud or negligence.

10.3 A Trustee shall not be liable for acting in accordance with the advice of Counsel, of at least five years' standing, with respect to the settlement. A Trustee may recover from the Trust Fund any expenses where he has acted in accordance with such advice. The Trustees may in particular conduct legal proceedings in accordance with such advice without obtaining a court order.

10.4 The above paragraph does not apply if:

    10.4.1 the Trustee knows or has reasonable cause to suspect that the advice was given in ignorance of material facts; or

    10.4.2 proceedings are pending to obtain the decision of the court on the matter.

10.5 The Trustees may distribute Trust Property or income in accordance with this Settlement but without having ascertained that there is no Person who is or may be entitled to any interest therein by virtue of any illegitimate relationship. The Trustees shall not be liable to such a Person unless they have notice of his claim at the time of the distribution.

10.6 This paragraph does not prejudice any right of any Person to follow property or income into the hands of any Person, other than a purchaser, who may have received it.

11. Appointment and retirement of trustees

1–91 11.1 A Person may be appointed Trustee of the Settlement even though he has no connection with the United Kingdom.

11.2 A Trustee who has reached the age of 65 shall retire if:

    11.2.1 he is requested to do so by his co-trustees, or by a Person interested in Trust Property; and

    11.2.2 he is effectually indemnified against liabilities properly incurred as Trustee.

On that retirement a new Trustee shall be appointed if necessary to ensure that there will be at least two Trustees. This sub-paragraph does not apply to a Trustee who is the Settlor or the spouse or widow of the Settlor.

11.3 A Trustee may be discharged even though there is neither a trust corporation nor two Persons to act as trustees provided that there remains at least one trustee.

Section 4. Taxation Aspects of Trusts

1–92 Just as a swimmer's environment is water so a trust's environment is a fiscal system. Necessarily, space allows of only a superficial treatment here, especially as regards those anti-avoidance provisions designed to prevent the versatile flexibility of the trust from being manipulated to obtain tax advantages. After all, in trust law a settlor may himself be a trustee and a beneficiary, may have power to add or subtract beneficiaries, may have powers of appointing income and capital amongst the beneficiaries or on new trusts, and may have power to revoke his trust, whilst the trustees may have power to accumulate income within the trust and to invest in non-income-producing assets. A trust is like a sponge capable of soaking up liquid funds and retaining them without undue leakage, yet capable of being squeezed lightly or harshly or of being totally squashed so as to yield its contents into the required hands; it can even be split up into smaller pieces having the same qualities as the whole.

Income tax

(1) *The settlor's position.* An individual's taxable income is taxed **1–93** progressively at rates laid down annually in the Finance Act. There is a Starting Rate of 10 per cent (up to £1,880), then a 22 per cent Basic Rate (up to £29,400) and a 40 per cent Higher Rate (over £29,400), though, previously, progressively higher slices of taxable income were taxed at progressively higher rates (up to a top rate as high as 83 per cent). For dividend income the rate is 10 per cent for those below the Higher Rate limit, and 32.5 per cent for those above it. For other savings income there is a starting rate of 10 per cent, a lower rate of 20 per cent and then the higher rate of 40 per cent. The progressive nature of the tax is such that, in circumstances not covered by anti-avoidance provisions, a tax saving can be achieved by a wealthy person hiving off some of his income to trustees or an individual or a charity not taxable at the higher rates or at all. He can do this either by covenanting to pay income to them or by transferring the income-producing capital itself. If capital taxes have lower rates than income tax (as was the case until 1988) or have the advantage that the first £7,500 of gains each year are exempt from capital gains tax, further tax savings can be achieved by using trustees' powers of accumulation of income to convert income into capital and eventually pass it over to beneficiaries as capital, especially when the maximum rate of tax on accumulated trust income is 34 per cent.[8] Tax-efficient benefits in kind (*e.g.* free loans of cash, chattels, houses) may also be conferred on beneficiaries.

Anti-avoidance provisions, however, reduce the opportunities for settlements to be used to avoid income tax. In considering whether such provisions apply one must ask three questions:

(i) Do the settlor and his spouse retain any possibility of benefiting **1–94** from the settled property other than in very limited contingencies.[9] If so then the trust income is treated as wholly his.[10] If a settlor receives a

---

[8] Income and Corporation Taxes Act 1988 (I.C.T.A.), ss.686, 687.
[9] I.C.T.A., s.660A, substituted by Finance Act 1995, Sched. 17.
[10] *ibid.* and s.660E and F, enabling tax paid by the settlor to be recovered from the recipient of the income. Further see J. Tiley, *Revenue Law*, 4th ed., chaps 29, 31, 40, 70–73.

capital sum by way of loan from the trust or repayment of his loan to the trust, he is treated as receiving taxed net income (to the extent of available undistributed income for that year and the next 10 years) equal to such sum.[11]

(ii) If the settlor is not caught by (i) but income is actually paid by the trustees to or for the benefit of the settlor's minor unmarried children (or allocated on a bare trust to pay the income therefrom to such children[12]) such income ranks as the settlor's.[13] If income is accumulated, then any capital payment to or for the benefit of the unmarried minor is deemed to be a payment of income, ranking as the settlor's income, to the extent that there is accumulated income available to cover the payment.[14]

(iii) Was a covenanted payment of income either a maintenance payment for an ex-spouse or a separated spouse or an annual payment made for bona fide commercial reasons in connection with his trade profession or vocation or a covenant for charity capable of lasting for more than three years so that it is then deductible from the settlor's income.[15]

1–95   (2) *The trustees' position*. The trustees are liable to basic rate tax, or lower rate tax on savings (except for dividends taxed at 10 per cent) under the appropriate income tax schedules on all the income produced by the trust fund. Such income is quite separate from their own personal income. Trust income can have no deduction against it for personal allowances or for expenses incurred in administering the trust.[16] It cannot be liable to higher rate tax. Much income will be received by the trustees after deduction of tax (*e.g.* dividends or building society interest) but in other cases (*e.g.* profits of carrying on a trade[17]) the trustees will need to pay the basic rate tax.

In an exceptional case where trust income without passing through the hands of a trustee is paid directly to an interest in possession beneficiary who has no liability to income tax because of non-residence or charitable status the trustees will not be assessed to tax.[18]

1–96   Where no one such as a life tenant has an interest in possession[19] in the trust entitling him as of right to the income then the trustees have to pay tax at the section 686 rate applicable to trusts which is 34 per cent except for dividend income taxed at the 25 per cent schedule F trust rate.[20] This is because in such cases there would otherwise be too much

---

[11] I.C.T.A., s.677.
[12] Finance Act 1999 s.64.
[13] I.C.T.A., s.660B, substituted by F.A. 1995 Sched. 17.
[14] I.C.T.A., s.660B(2), (3).
[15] I.C.T.A., s.347A and s.660A as added by Finance Act 1995, Sched, 17.
[16] *Aikin v. Macdonald's Trustees* (1894) 3 TC 306.
[17] Of course, expenses incurred in earning the profits may be deducted and loss relief may be claimed.
[18] *Williams v. Singer* [1921] A.C. 65.
[19] For the meaning of interest in possession *see Pearson v. IRC* [1981] A.C. 753 and *infra*, at para. 1–104.
[20] F.A. 1973, ss. 16, 17 replaced by I.C.T.A., ss. 686, 687; *I.R.C. v. Berrill* [1982] 1 W.L.R. 1449. These provisions do not apply if the income is treated as the settlor's under the anti-avoidance provisions above.

scope for minimising liability to tax by exercising powers of accumulation or by delaying exercising discretionary powers over income until a tax-efficient beneficiary materialised. However, in the case of these accumulation trusts and discretionary trusts the expenses incurred in administering the trust which are properly chargeable to income (under the general law if ignoring express authority in the trust instrument) can be deducted from the income liable to the additional rate charge.[21]

(3) *The beneficiary's position.* A beneficiary who is currently entitled to **1–97** trust income as it arises (*i.e.* who has an interest in possession like a life tenant) is liable to income tax for the year of assessment in which that income arises, even if none of the income was actually paid to him that year[22] One should note that the effect of Trustee Act 1925, s.31[23] (which may be excluded by the trust instrument) is to convert a minor's apparent entitlement to income under a trust for him for life into a contingent interest, since it imposes a duty upon the trustees to accumulate income (so far as not needed for his maintenance, education or benefit) until his majority, and if he dies before attaining his majority the accumulated income passes with the capital, to which it has accrued, to the person entitled to capital after his death.[24] The beneficiary will be entitled to the balance after the trustees have paid basic rate tax or lower rate or the 10 per cent dividend tax and their administration expenses. This net sum (*e.g.* £7,000 where gross income of £10,000 has borne £2,200 basic rate tax and £800 expenses) is then grossed up by the relevant rate of tax.

$$(£7,000 \times \frac{100}{100 - 22} = £8,974)$$

to find the taxable sum to rank as part of the beneficiary's total taxable income. He is given a tax credit for the difference (£8,974 − £7,000 = £1,974) (except for the 10 per cent dividend tax) so if his total income is such that he bears basic rate tax only then this credit satisfies his liability.[25] If he is not liable to tax then he can reclaim the amount of the tax credit from the Revenue (£1,974, and not the £2200 actually paid by the trustees); if he is liable to higher rate tax then he only has to pay the difference between the amount of such liability and the amount of the tax credit.

---

[21] I.C.T.A., s.686(2)(d); *Carver v. Duncan* [1985] A.C. 1082.

[22] *Baker v. Archer-Shee* [1927] A.C. 844; *Hamilton-Russell's Executors v. I.R.C.* (1943) 25 TC 200; [1943] 1 All E.R. 474.

[23] *Infra*, at para. 9–224. One should also note that a person with a contingent right, *e.g.* upon attaining 30 years of age obtains a vested right to income on attaining majority: Trustee Act 1925, s.31(1)(ii), *infra*, at para. 9–224.

[24] *Stanley v. I.R.C.* [1944] 1 All E.R. 230.

[25] Where the trustees deduct their administration expenses the beneficiary is only entitled to gross up his net receipt *after* tax and these expenses, so his grossed-up income will be less than the trustees' gross income: *Macfarlane v. I.R.C.*, 1929 S.C. 453; 14 TC 532. If the trustees had paid him the gross £10,000 less £2,200 tax then if he were below the tax threshold he would reclaim the £2,200 and then pay the trustees their £800 expenses, so leaving him with £9,200 instead of £8,974 where the trustees first paid their expenses before paying him.

1–98   A beneficiary not entitled to trust income as it arises (*i.e.* who does not have an interest in possession but depends upon the discretion of the trustees) is charged[26] on what he receives. He will receive the income net of the section 686 trust rate tax of 34 per cent deducted by the trustees[27]: he obtains a tax credit for this deduction and will be able to reclaim some of this sum if his total income is such that he is assessable at some lower rate than 34 per cent. The imposition of tax at 34 per cent on the trustees is thus not a worrying factor where the trustees distribute the income to beneficiaries liable to basic rate tax or no tax at all. However, if the income is accumulated it will suffer tax at 34 per cent except in one case. If trust capital is so applied that it becomes *income* in the beneficiary's hands, then to the extent that the amount of capital distributed is less than the net amount of accumulated income after tax, the beneficiary will be treated as having received such gross amount of income as after deduction of tax at 34 per cent[28] leaves the amount of the capital distributed and he will be able to claim repayment of tax if liable to tax at a lower rate than 34 per cent.

Schedule F dividend income taxed at 25 per cent raises major problems for trustees who invest in shares. If the trustees receive a gross dividend of £1000 they actually receive a net £900 and need to pay a further £150 tax (£250 tax at 25 per cent, less £100 credit) so they can actually distribute £750 to a discretionary beneficiary. Such distribution must be grossed up to £1136 so that £750 is received after payment of 34 per cent tax on £1136. Other trust income must be found to pay the £236 on top of the £150.

1–99   Once income has been accumulated it loses its character as income and accrues to the capital fund becoming part thereof (*i.e.* it becomes capitalised), so payments of accumulated income will be payments of capital and will normally be receipts of capital in the beneficiary's hands and so not liable to income tax. However, if a beneficiary is given £x p.a. and the trustees have a duty or a power to make up that sum out of capital if trust income is less than £x, such "topping up" payments of capital will be taxed as income in the beneficiary's hands.[29] Moreover, regular payments out of capital may be characterised as income receipts of the beneficiary if paid to enable him to keep up his standard of living.[30] However, a disposition of capital in exercise of a power over capital will normally not rank as income in the beneficiary's hands even if used for what might be termed as an income purpose.[31]

Capital payments may involve liabilities to inheritance tax and capital gains tax.

---

[26] Under Sched. D, Case III.
[27] I.C.T.A., ss.686, 687.
[28] I.C.T.A., s.687. This tax will actually have been paid earlier when the income was accumulated.
[29] *Brodies's Will Trustees v. I.R.C.* (1933) 17 TC 432; *Lindus & Horton v. I.R.C.* (1933) 17 TC 442.
[30] *Cunard's Trustees v. I.R.C.* [1962] 1 All E.R. 159.
[31] *Stevenson v. Wishart* [1987] 1 W.L.R. 1204.

Inheritance tax

(1) *The settlor's position.* When a settlor transfers assets to trustees or **1–100** declares himself trustee of specific assets this amounts to a transfer of value (*i.e.* a disposition diminishing the value of the disposer's estate[32]).

A transfer of value may be chargeable, exempt or potentially exempt,[33] and on death the deceased is treated as making a transfer of value of the whole of his estate immediately before his death.[34] If a donor makes a gift on trusts (or outright) but reserves any benefit[35] then the gifted property is treated as still belonging to him so as to be taxable on his death with the rest of his estate at 40 per cent, *e.g.* if he is one of the beneficiaries of his discretionary trust or a remunerated trustee or, not being a beneficiary, retains the *de facto* use of the gifted property, so creating a major problem for parents who give away their house to their children but continue to live there.

Transferring property into a discretionary trust (other than a favoured **1–101** accumulation and maintenance trust) is a chargeable transfer[36] whilst transferring property into an interest in possession trust or accumulation and maintenance trust is a potentially exempt transfer[37] (so no I.H.T. is payable) ripening into an exempt transfer if the settlor survives for seven years. Inheritance tax ("I.H.T.") is charged at 40 per cent for death transfers and those within three years of death and half that for lifetime transfers unless the transferor dies within seven years, a sliding scale operating between three and seven years of the transfer.[38] No tax is payable if the transfer falls within the nil rate band, currently £242,000, taking account of the transferor's cumulative total in the seven years immediately preceding the relevant transfer. Thus, everyone who is wealthy enough can give away £242,000 every seven years without any I.H.T. liability.

If the settlor pays the I.H.T. *inter vivos* in respect of his discretionary **1–102** settlement, so diminishing his estate further, he is treated as having made a transfer of value of such amount as after payment of I.H.T. thereon leaves the value of the settled property, *i.e.* his gift is grossed up.[39] This does not happen if the trustees pay the I.H.T. out of the trust fund.[40]

(2) *Interest in possession trusts.* The person beneficially entitled to the **1–103** interest in possession (*e.g.* a life interest) is deemed to own the whole settled capital so when he disposes of his interest (*e.g.* gives it away or

---

[32] Inheritance Tax Act 1984 (I.H.T.A.), s.3(1). A transfer will be exempt from being a chargeable transfer if within the exemption for small annual amounts (£3,000), or for normal expenditure out of income or for a transfer between spouses, or gifts in consideration of marriage, or to charities, or to political parties or for certain national purposes: I.H.T.A., ss.18–29.
[33] I.H.T.A., s.3A.
[34] I.H.T.A., s.4.
[35] Finance Act 1986, s.102.
[36] I.H.T.A., s.2.
[37] I.H.T.A., s.3A(2).
[38] I.H.T.A., s.7.
[39] I.H.T.A., ss.3(1), 162(3), 164.
[40] *ibid.* and s.199(1)(c).

sells it) or his interest comes to an end[41] (other than upon his becoming absolutely entitled to the capital[42]) there is deemed to be a transfer of value equal to that of the whole settled capital. Where he sells his interest the amount of the transfer of value is reduced by the proceeds of sale.[43] His lifetime transfer of value will be potentially exempt but if he dies within seven years or died owning the interest the amount of I.H.T. payable will depend upon his cumulative total in the preceding seven years.[44] It is, however, the trustees who are primarily liable to pay the I.H.T. out of the trust property.[45]

According to an Inland Revenue Press Notice[46]:

1–104   "An interest in possession in settled property exists where the person having the interest has the immediate entitlement (subject to any prior claim by the trustees for expenses or other outgoings properly payable out of income) to any income produced by that property as the income arises; but that a discretion or power, in whatever form, which can be exercised after income arises so as to withhold it from that person negatives the existence of an interest in possession. For this purpose a power to accumulate income is regarded as a power to withhold it, unless any accumulations must be held solely for the person having the interest or his personal representatives.

On the other hand the existence of a mere power of revocation or appointment, the exercise of which would determine the interest wholly or in part (but which so long as it remains unexercised, does not affect the beneficiary's immediate entitlement to income) does not in the Board's view prevent the interest from being an interest in possession."

1–105   This Notice was needed since the legislation does not define the crucial concept "interest in possession." Since then this approach has been supported by the House of Lords in *Pearson v. IRC*,[47] which 3:2 rejected the traditional Chancery view that the mere existence of a power to accumulate or otherwise divert *income* from life tenant, L, did not prevent L having an interest in possession, L being entitled to income unless the trustees positively diverted it. Thus, a beneficiary does not have an interest in possession if the trustees have power to divert the income away from him (*e.g.* by accumulating it, so that it accrues to capital to which he has no certainty of succeeding, or by paying it or

---

[41] I.H.T.A., s.52(1). If the interest terminates on his death then the settled capital is aggregated with his estate: ss.4(1), 49(1).
[42] I.H.T.A., s.53(2) or if the capital reverts to the settlor or passes to the beneficiary's spouse: s.53(3), (4).
[43] I.H.T.A., s.52(2).
[44] I.H.T.A., ss.51(1), 52(2), 7.
[45] I.H.T.A., ss.201(1)(a), 212(1). A new beneficiary with an interest in possession may also be liable though he has power to recoup the tax: ss.20(1)(b), 212(1), (2).
[46] [1976] B.T.R. 418.
[47] [1981] A.C. 753; [1980] 2 All E.R. 479, developed in *Re Trafford* [1985] Ch. 32.

applying it for the benefit of another beneficiary). A power to terminate an interest in possession (*e.g.* a power to appoint or advance some or all the *capital* to X) does not prevent the interest being an interest in possession so long as the power is not exercised.

There is a distinction between *dispositive* powers, by which income can **1–106** be diverted away from a beneficiary, and *administrative* powers by which income can also be so diverted. Dispositive powers enabling net income after expenses to be diverted to another beneficiary prevent an interest in possession arising. Administrative powers enabling gross income to be used for payment of expenses and other outgoings properly payable out of income[48] do not prevent an interest in possession arising in the net income. Indeed, Viscount Dilhorne in *Pearson*[49] said *obiter* that a power [perhaps ancillary and not independent] to use income to pay taxes otherwise payable out of capital was an administrative power.[50]

Interests in remainder or reversion after an interest in possession are normally excluded property so that a transfer of them occasions no charge to I.H.T.[51]: after all, the beneficiary with the interest in possession is already treated as owning the whole settled capital.[52]

(3) *Trusts with no interest in possession.* Unless these are privileged **1–107** trusts (*infra*) they are liable to a periodic charge to I.H.T. every tenth anniversary[53] and it is up to the trustees to pay this out of the trust fund.[54] If during a 10-year period capital ceases to be subject to such trusts (*e.g.* because distributed to a beneficiary or because resettled or subsettled on interest in possession trusts or privileged trusts) there is an exit charge in respect of such capital.[55] Basically, the exit charge represents a proportion of the periodic charge payable on the next 10-year anniversary of the trust and depends on the time elapsed since the last such anniversary. Calculation of the tax actually payable is complex involving a hypothetical transfer of value by a hypothetical transferor with a cumulative total including that of the settlor in the seven years before creating the trust.[56] The rate of I.H.T. is calculated at 30 per cent of the lifetime rates applicable to the hypothetical transfer,[57] so the maximum rate is 6 per cent (30 per cent of 20 per cent). Thus

---

[48] For such expenses see *Carver v. Duncan* [1985] A.C. 1082.

[49] [1981] A.C. 753 at 775; [1980] 2 All E.R. 479, 486, followed in *Miller v. I.R.C.* [1987] STC 108.

[50] Powers to allow a beneficiary to have rent-free use of a house or interest-free use of cash raise thorny problems: the Revenue treat the exercise of such powers as creating interests in possession and so occasioning an I.H.T. charge if previously no interest in possession subsisted or if causing the partial termination of an existing interest in possession. While the house remains trust property for the user to have an interest in possession in trust property, loaned cash becomes the property of the borrower absolutely and his debt is the trust property. The trust property is thus transposed from cash into a debt due to the trust and it can hardly be said that the borrower has an interest in possession in that debt that is trust property.

[51] I.H.T.A., ss.47, 48. Certain exceptions exist to prevent use of such interests to avoid I.H.T.

[52] I.H.T.A., s.49(1).

[53] I.H.T.A., ss.61, 64.

[54] I.H.T.A., ss.201(1)(a), 212

[55] I.H.T.A., s.65.

[56] I.H.T.A., ss.66, 68, 69. The exit charge rate necessarily has to be calculated as a proportion of the effective rate of the last periodic charge.

[57] I.H.T.A., s.66(1).

discretionary trusts can still be useful propositions, especially if they are kept just below the £242,000 threshold and are made by settlors with small cumulative totals of chargeable transfers. Additions of property by the original settlor to his trust should be avoided since they will often cause more I.H.T. to be charged (at the next 10-year anniversary) than would be the case if he created a new separate settlement.[58]

If the trustees pay I.H.T. in respect of the exit charge out of property remaining in the discretionary settlement then the chargeable amount has to be grossed up[59]: This does not happen if the recipient of the capital ceasing to be subject to the discretionary trust pays the I.H.T.[60]

1–108   (4) *Privileged trusts.* For policy reasons some trusts which would otherwise fall to be taxed as trusts with no interest in possession receive privileged treatment. Accumulation and maintenance trusts for minors are the most significant privileged trusts for private tax planning. Such trusts are privileged so as not to discriminate between gifts to minors or to adults contingent upon attaining 25 years of age (which must take effect behind trusts) and outright gifts to adults of 25 years or more. No periodic or exit charges are payable and no charge arises when a beneficiary becomes entitled to the settled property.[61]

1–109   Such privileged treatment is accorded to settled property if[62]:

(1) One or more persons ("beneficiaries") *will*,[63] on or before attaining a specified age not exceeding 25,[64] become beneficially entitled to it or to an interest in possession in it; and

(2) No interest in possession subsists in it, and the income from it is to be accumulated so far as not applied for the maintenance education or benefit of a beneficiary; and

(3) Either (a) all the persons who are or have been beneficiaries are or were either (i) grandchildren of a common grandparent, or (ii) children, widows or widowers of such grandchildren who were themselves beneficiaries but died before the time when, had they survived, they would have become entitled as in (1) above, or (b) not more than 25 years have elapsed since the commencement of the settlement or, if it was later, since the time when the conditions in (1) and (2) became satisfied with respect to the property.

There are other privileged trusts which receive special treatment, *e.g.* charitable trusts and protective trusts.[65]

---

[58] I.H.T.A., s.67.

[59] I.H.T.A., s.65(2)(b).

[60] I.H.T.A., s.65(2)(a).

[61] I.H.T.A., ss.58(1)(b), 71(4).

[62] I.H.T.A., s.71(1), (2).

[63] "Will" means "must under the terms of the settlement become entitled" ignoring possibilities of the beneficiary dying, becoming bankrupt, assigning his interest or losing his interest under the Variation of Trusts Act 1958: *Inglewood v. I.R.C* [1983] 1 W.L.R. 366.

[64] No age need be specified in the settlement or an age greater than 25 can be specified for entitlement to *capital* so long as Trustee Act 1925, s.31(1)(ii) applies to confer a vested right to *income* on a beneficiary attaining majority.

[65] I.H.T.A., ss.72–77, 86–89.

Capital gains tax

(1) *The settlor's position.* On settling capital assets (other than cash or **1–110** his principal private residence[66]) *inter vivos* a settlor will be chargeable to C.G.T. on this disposal even if he (or his spouse) is a trustee or sole trustee or life tenant or if the settlement is revocable.[67] The chargeable gain will be the excess of the property's then market value over its March 31, 1982 value or its subsequent original acquisition (or "base") cost to the settlor.[68] However, on a transfer into a discretionary trust (a chargeable I.H.T. transfer taxable only if the nil band is exceeded) the settlor can elect that the gain be held over, the trustees taking the property over at the settlor's original base value.[69] The settlor should not settle assets on which he has made a loss since such loss can only be set off against gains on subsequent disposals to the trustees.[70] The rate of C.G.T. payable by the settlor will be the same as his income tax basic or higher rate, *i.e.* 22 per cent or 40 per cent.[71] An indexation allowance (to deal with inflation) calculated to 5 April 1998 is available to reduce the chargeable gain. Thereafter tapering relief[72] is available to reduce the gain by 5 per cent (for non-business assets) for each whole year of ownership of the disposed of asset up to a maximum of 10 years, but the reductions do not start till the third year of ownership, so the maximum reduction is 40 per cent for non-business assets thereby reducing the tax rate to the equivalent of 24 per cent. For business assets the maximum reduction is 75 per cent after four years (reducing the tax rate to 10 per cent) with reductions respectively of 12.5 per cent, 25 per cent, and 50 per cent after one, two and three years.

(2) *Actual disposals by trustees.* Normal principles apply to calculating **1–111** the gain or loss on sales of chargeable assets by trustees. However, they are chargeable merely at the trusts' rate of 34 per cent on their gains but only have an annual exemption of half that of individuals.[73] Losses must be set off against gains of the same year or of future years.[74] Any unrelieved losses when the trust ends and a beneficiary becomes absolutely entitled to the settled property will enure for the benefit of the beneficiary.[75] Incidentally, settled property is trust property other than nominee property where the trustees are bare trustees or nominees

---

[66] Taxation of Chargeable Gains Act 1992 (T.C.G.A.), s.21(1)(b) and ss.222–226.
[67] T.C.G.A., s.70: no charge to C.G.T. arises where a testator's will creates a trust since his estate is already liable to I.H.T.: the trustees (and then the legatees) take over the value of the property at the testator's death as their base value: T.C.G.A., s.62. However, if the settlor or his spouse retains any interest in the settled property subsequent capital gains of the trustees are charged to the settlor: *Billingham v. Cooper* [2000] S.T.C. 122.
[68] T.C.G.A., s.17: the first £7,500 of gains are exempt and there is an indexation allowance to cope with inflation until 5 April 1998, and tapering relief thereafter.
[69] T.C.G.A., s.260, *Melville v. IRC* [2000] S.T.C. 628.
[70] T.C.G.A., s.18.
[71] T.C.G.A., s.4.
[72] Finance Act 1998 s.122.
[73] Finance Act 1998 s.118 T.C.G.A., Sched. 1: the fraction dwindles to one-tenth if the settlor creates 10 or more settlements.
[74] T.C.G.A., s.2.
[75] T.C.G.A., s.71.

for a beneficiary (or beneficiaries between them) absolutely entitled to the trust property, subject to the trustees' lien for costs and expenses.[76] Bare trusts are ignored, the acts of the bare trustees being treated as the acts of the beneficiaries.[77]

1–112   (3) *Actual disposals of beneficiaries' equitable interests.* To prevent double taxation there is no C.G.T. charge when a beneficiary disposes of his underlying equitable interest in settled property so long as that interest had not at any time been acquired for money or money's worth (other than another interest under the settlement).[78]

(4) *Life interest in possession trusts.* On the death of a life tenant in possession where the settlement continues the trustees are deemed to dispose of and re-acquire the settled property at its then market value, but C.G.T. will not be charged.[79] After all, I.H.T. will be charged on the settled property.[80] Thus the property's base value gets a C.G.T.-free uplift. However, any held-over gain on the creation of the settlement will be chargeable, and payable by the trustees.[81]

1–113   If the life interest terminates other than on the life tenant's death but the settlement continues (*e.g.* to A for life or until remarriage, then B for life, then C absolutely and A remarries or releases her interest) there is no charge to C.G.T.[82] The original base value of the property in the trustees' hands remains unaltered.

If the life tenant dies and the settlement ends because a person becomes absolutely entitled to the settled property, the trustees are deemed to dispose of and re-acquire the settled property at its then market value, but C.G.T. will not be charged.[83] After all, I.H.T. will be charged on the property that has now become nominee property.[84] The absolutely entitled beneficiary will take over the property with its base value as at the life tenant's death. However, any held-over gain on the creation of the settlement will be chargeable at the beneficiary's expense.

If the life interest terminates other than on the life tenant's death and the settlement ends in respect of particular property because a person becomes absolutely entitled to the settled property, such property is deemed to have been disposed of by the trustees and C.G.T. is chargeable at the trusts' rate of 34 per cent.[85] The position is as set out in the next paragraph, except that no hold-over relief is available because the disposition will be a potentially exempt transfer for I.H.T. purposes.[86]

---

[76] T.C.G.A., ss.68, 60.
[77] T.C.G.A., s.60.
[78] T.C.G.A., s.76. If the trust is non-resident there will be a charge: T.C.G.A., s.855.
[79] T.C.G.A., s.72.
[80] I.H.T.A., ss.4, 49(1).
[81] T.C.G.A., ss.74, 65: hold-over relief was available for transfers to trustees of interest in possession trusts until March 14, 1989: Finance Act 1989, s.124.
[82] The event falls outside the charging provisions, T.C.G.A., ss.71, 72. However, I.H.T. will be payable: I.H.T.A., ss.51, 52.
[83] T.C.G.A., ss.71, 73.
[84] I.H.T.A., ss.4, 49(1).
[85] T.C.G.A., s.71, Finance Act 1998 s.118.
[86] Except where discretionary trustees become absolutely entitled against interest in possession trustees (not a potentially exempt transfer) when hold-over relief will be available; T.C.G.A., s.260.

If the trustees do not pay the tax within six months then the absolutely entitled person becomes liable.[87]

(5) *Trusts with no life interest in possession.* When a person becomes **1–114** absolutely entitled to any settled property as against the trustees, the assets comprised in the part to which he has become entitled are deemed to have been disposed of by the trustees for market value and C.G.T. is chargeable.[88] The rate of C.G.T. is the trusts' rate of 34 per cent.[89] However, because the absolute entitlement occasions an exit charge to IHT an election can be made to hold over the gain and this can extend to any held-over gain on the creation of the settlement.[90]

The charge to C.G.T. arises whether the person becoming absolutely **1–115** entitled does so in his personal capacity as beneficiary or in a fiduciary capacity as trustee of another trust.[91] If trust assets wholly cease to be subject to the trusts, powers and provisions of one settlement and become subject to the trusts, powers and provisions of another settlement, there is a deemed disposal of the assets even if the trustees of the two settlements happen to be the same persons.[92] The trustees of a settlement are treated as a single continuing body of persons distinct from the actual persons who may from time to time be the trustees[93] (so that a change of trustees occasions no charge to C.G.T. or I.H.T.).

Difficult questions arise where trustees of a settlement containing a **1–116** power of appointment or of allocation or of appropriation or of advancement exercise such power so that part of the settled property falls to be held by them on trusts other than those to which it was subject immediately beforehand. Does the exercise of the power create a new trust, whose trustees are absolutely entitled against the old trustees, so that there has been a deemed disposal, or does it merely create a sub-trust under the umbrella of the old original trust so that there has been no deemed disposal? If the power is in a wide form authorising an application of the trust fund freed and released from the original trusts of the settlement, so that the original trusts are replaced by other exhaustive trusts, then such an application of the trust fund will be a deemed disposal.[94] If the power is in a narrow form, *e.g.* a special power to appoint the trust fund on trusts for a class of beneficiaries, their spouses and children (but with no unusual provision allowing the trustees to delegate their duties to other persons or otherwise contemplating the creation of an entirely new trust) then any appointed

---

[87] T.C.G.A. s.69(4).
[88] T.C.G.A., s.7.
[89] Finance Act 1998 s.118.
[90] T.C.G.A., s.260. However, if the gain on an asset is held over then on a subsequent sale taper relief is only available for the seller's period of ownership.
[91] *Hoare Trustees v. Gardner* [1979] Ch. 10 at 13–14.
[92] *Hart v. Briscoe* [1979] Ch. 1. at 5; *Bond v. Pickford* [1983] STC517; *cf. Swires v. Renton* [1991] STC 490.
[93] *Roome v. Edwards* [1982] A.C. 279 (English trustees liable for gain on non-resident trustee's part of the trust property: see [1981] C.L.J. 240; *Bond v. Pickford, supra*; T.C.G.A., s.69(1).
[94] Hold-over relief will be available in respect of business or agricultural assets or if an I.H.T. charge arises because interest in possession trusts are the new trusts.

property will be regarded as a sub-trust within the original trust, even if the sub-trusts are exhaustive, so there will be no deemed disposal.[95]

Section 5. Significance of Matters of Construction

1–117 Before a court can apply a legal rule to validate or invalidate a provision in a document or something purportedly done thereunder it is vital to construe the provision to determine exactly what it means in the context of the document as a whole and in the light of such extrinsic evidence as is admissible, *e.g.* allowing the judge to put himself in the testator's armchair and take advantage of section 21 of the Administration of Justice Act 1982.[96]

1–118 Every provision requires minute scrutiny to see how many meanings it may have—nothing must be taken for granted. Words like "relatives" or "customers" may seem straightforward enough. But does "relatives of X" mean just those persons who would be his statutory next-of-kin taking under the intestacy rules if X were dead or does it cover the huge number who are descended like X from some common ancestor thousands of years ago?[97] Does "customer of the Y Co.," cover a purchaser who has not ordered any goods from the Y Co. for six months, one year, six years or more?[98] Can "small" have a meaning where a testator leaves his residuary estate on trust for "those who have only received small legacies?"[99] Can "gay guys" extend to lesbians and bi-sexuals?

1–119 It is often crucial whether words have any obligatory sense ("must") or merely a permissive sense ("may"), though complex clauses can make the distinction difficult to discern.[1] If a trustee is protected when lending on mortgage if acting upon a report as to the value of property "made by a person whom he reasonably believed to be an able practical surveyor or valuer instructed and employed independently of any owner of the property," must the valuer *in fact* be independently instructed or is the trustee's reasonable belief sufficient?[2] Does "charitable or benevolent" mean that a purpose can be charitable or instead it can be benevolent, so that the trust is void, or can it be treated as meaning that the purpose must be both charitable and benevolent so that the trust is valid?[3] If

---

[95] See *Bond v. Pickford, supra.* Trusts are exhaustive if the beneficial interest is fully disposed of so that there is no need to refer elsewhere to discover what happens after someone dies or fails to obtain a vested interest. See also *Swires v. Renton* [1991] STC 490 and *Revenue* SP 7/84. The taxation of non-resident trusts is ignored as a very complex topic containing many tax avoidance provisions; see R. Venables QC, *Non-Resident Trusts*, 8th ed, 2000 (Key Haven plc).

[96] See *infra*, at para. 3–70; *Re Williams* [1985] 1 W.L.R. 905; *Re Benham's W.T.* [1995] STC 210.

[97] *Re Baden's Deed Trusts (No. 2)* [1972] Ch. 607, *infra*, at para. 3–144.

[98] *Sparfax (1965) Ltd. v. Dommett, The Times,* July 14, 1972.

[99] *Re Steel* [1978] 2 All E.R. 1026; *cf. O'Rourke v. Binks* [1992] STC 703.

[1] See Chap. 3, sections 1 and 3 and *McPhail v. Doulton* [1971] A.C. 424.

[2] Contrast *Re Walker* (1890) 62 L.T. 449 at 452 and *Re Somerset* [1894] 1 Ch. 231 at 253 with *Re Stuart* [1897] 2 Ch. 583 at 592, *Shaw v. Cates* [1909] 1 Ch. 389 at 403 and *Re Solomon* [1912] 1 Ch. 261 at 281.

[3] *Chichester Diocesan Fund v. Simpson* [1944] A.C. 341, *infra*, at para. 7–231; *cf.* a trust for purposes connected with the education and welfare of children: *Att.-Gen. of Bahamas v. Royal Trust Co.* [1986] 1 W.L.R. 1001.

property is left to D "on condition she provides a home for her infirm sister, I," does this mean that if D takes the property she will be subject to this condition or can the apparent condition really be treated as only expressing the testator's motive.[4] Indeed, what does the condition mean? Is it certain enough to be enforceable and valid? If not, can the clause be treated as expressing motive only so that D can inherit the property?

If a testator leaves his residuary estate "for the Hull Judeans **1–120** Association in memory of my late wife to be used solely in the work of constructing the new buildings for the Association and/or improvements to the said buildings" can this be construed not as a purpose trust to endow the Association, (and so void) but as an out-and-out gift accruing to the Association's funds, subject to the contractual rights thereto of the Association members under its constitution?[5]

From the outset one has to be alert to the possibilities of construction. **1–121** Judges are only human and once they have seen the merits of a case they may be prepared to construe a document—or even interpret circumstances[6]—in a way that one would not normally construe it—or interpret them—coming "cold" to the situation. Some judges, however, do prefer to adopt a strict approach. The rest of this book contains plenty of examples of both sorts, though the modern judicial trend is to be facilitative and uphold trustlike arrangements so far as possible.

Section 6. Aspects of Wills and Intestacy Law

In a study of trust law there are many occasions when points relating to **1–122** wills or intestacies crop up. A general outline knowledge of the laws applicable thereto is thus useful before embarking on a detailed study of trust law.[7]

First, one needs to distinguish the position of personal representatives (P.R.s) winding up a deceased person's estate from the position of trustees holding the trust property. The P.R.s' function is to collect in the deceased's assets, pay off all debts, taxes and expenses and, then, to distribute the assets to those entitled under the will or intestacy. Their duty is owed to the estate as a whole so that they are under no duty to consider the effect of the exercise of their administrative powers so as to keep an even hand between those interested in income and those interested in capital.[8] Until they assent to the assets passing to the legatees or devisees the legal and beneficial title to the assets is vested in the P.R.s.[9] The legatees or devisees have no equitable interest in such

---

[4] *Re Brace* [1954] 1 W.L.R. 955; *cf. Re Frame* [1939] Ch. 700.

[5] *Re Lipinski's W.T.* [1976] Ch. 235, *infra*, at para. 3–252.

[6] *Re Vandervell's Trusts (No. 2)* [1974] Ch. 269, *infra*, para. 2–68; *Hammond v. Mitchell* [1991] 1 W.L.R. 1127; *Wayling v. Jones* (1993) 69 P. & C.R. 170.

[7] For further reference see *Theobald on Wills*; Parry & Clark's *Law of Succession*.

[8] *Re Hayes's W.T.* [1971] 1 W.L.R. 758, Trustees have such a duty.

[9] "Whatever property comes to the executor *virtute officii* comes to him in full ownership without distinction between legal and equitable interests: the whole property in his": *Commissioner for Stamp Duties v. Livingston* [1965] A.C. 694, 701. Thus "no legatee, devisee or next of kin has any beneficial interest in the assets being administered"; *Re Hayes's W.T.* [1971] 1 W.L.R. 758 at 764. See also *Kavenagh v. Best* [1971] N.I. 89 at 93–94; *Marshall v. Kerr* [1994] 3 All E.R. 106.

assets: they merely have a right to compel due administration of the estate though this chose in action (unlike the right of a beneficiary under a discretionary trust) can be assigned or bequeathed.[10] To assist them in their functions P.R.s have a statutory power to appropriate assets to legatees or devisees[11] and if only a sole P.R. has been appointed then, acting as such, he can give a valid receipt for capital moneys arising on a trust for sale of land.[12] P.R.s can only be appointed by will or by the court.[13] Finally, one of two or more P.R.s has full power to deal with the deceased's pure personalty[14] However, in respect of freehold or lease-hold land the concurrence of all the P.R.s is required to enter into any contract and then to convey the land.[15]

1–123   When P.R.s have completed administration of the deceased's estate they become trustees of the residuary estate[16] and their conduct will be sufficient to imply an assent of personalty to themselves as trustees.[17] As trustees they can exercise the statutory power that trustees have to appoint new or additional trustees.[18] Such appointment makes the new or additional trustees trustees of the trusts of the residuary estate but it does not obtain the benefit of Trustee Act 1925, s.40 (*infra* at para. 823): thus, to the extent that the residuary estate consists of land, the legal estate therein remains outstanding in the P.R.s until a written assent is executed by them (or their successors in title) in favour of such trustees,[19] no earlier implied assent from conduct being possible for legal[20] estates in land. Thus, personal representatives need to execute a written assent in favour of themselves or trustees so that subsequent appointments by them are effective under s.40.

1–124   If a testator leaves his residuary estate on trust for A absolutely or for A for life, remainder to B absolutely, it has already been seen that no trust arises until the P.R.s have completed winding up the estate and ascertained the residue. Before then where the P.R.s dispose of assets

---

[10] *Re Leigh's W.T.* [1970] Ch. 277; *P.V. Baker* (1970) 86 Q.L.R. 20; *Crowden v. Aldridge* [1993] 1 W.L.R. 433; *Marshall v. Kerr* [1994] 3 All E.R. 106 at 112, 119; *Wu v Wu* [1996] 3 WLR 778.

[11] Administration of Estates Act 1925, s.41. Trustees only have such power if expressly conferred upon them.

[12] Law of Property Act 1925, s.27(2). *cf.* Settled Land Act 1925, s.30(3).

[13] Trustees can be appointed under Trustee Act 1925, s.36, *infra*, at para. 8–01.

[14] *Attenborough v. Solomon* [1913] A.C. 76 where a P.R., three years after he had become a trustee of the deceased's silver, pledged it and this was invalid since trustees must act jointly.

[15] Law of Property (Miscellaneous Provisions) Act 1994 s.16.

[16] *Eaton v. Daines* [1894] W.N. 32; *Re Ponder* [1921] 2 Ch. 59; *Re Cockburn's W.T.* [1957] 1 Ch. 438.

[17] *Attenborough v. Solomon* [1913] A.C. 76; C. Stebbings [1984] Conv. 423.

[18] *Re Cockburn's W.T.* [1957] 1 Ch. 438.

[19] *Re King's W.T.* [1964] Ch. 542, criticised by Professor E. C. Ryder [1976] *Current Legal Problems* 60. The Limitation Act 1980 may remedy defects in title. Take E and F who completely administer T's estate and are to hold the residue (including Blackacre) upon trust for sale for A for life, remainder to B absolutely. Five years later E dies. Then F as surviving trustee purports to appoint G and H additional trustees with himself. Four years later F dies. G and H as trustees then sell and convey Blackacre to P. Later P contracts to sell to Q who objects to P's title. The objection is valid (unless P can prove 12 years' adverse possession). The legal estate is in F's personal representatives and not P since E and F never executed a written assent of Blackacre in favour of themselves in their new capacity as trustees. Thus they could not take advantage of Trustee Act 1925, s.40, *infra*, para. 8–23.

[20] An implied informal assent is possible for equitable interests if the P.R. is also beneficially entitled: *Re Edwards's W.T.* [1982] Ch. 30.

other than to legatees C.G.T. will be payable by the P.R.s.[21] However, for I.H.T. purposes a legatee with an interest in possession in a deceased's residuary estate is treated as having such interest from the deceased's death.[22] For income tax purposes sums paid to the legatees to the extent that residuary estate income is available are taxed on the grossed up equivalent of such sums:[23]

Basically, a will (unless made by a privileged military testator) must be **1–125** in writing signed at the end by the testator (or by some other person in his presence and by his direction).[24] The testator's signature has to be made or acknowledged by him in the presence of two witnesses both with the testator at the same time. The witnesses must then sign their names in the testator's presence. The document must be intended to take effect only on the testator's death.[25] Thus, if S by deed settles £50,000 upon trust for himself for life and then for R absolutely, the formalities for a will are not applicable since S's settlement takes effect immediately, giving R a present vested interest in remainder and entitling S only to the income from the £50,000 for the rest of his life. If S had made a will bequeathing £50,000 to R absolutely, S could use in his lifetime not only the income from the £50,000 but also the whole £50,000: he could also revoke his will and bequeath the £50,000 to X instead. Incidentally, personal property is said to be bequeathed to legatees and real property to be devised to devisees by will.

Gifts by will may fail to take effect by reason *inter alia* of ademption, **1–126** abatement, lapse, the beneficiary being an attesting witness or the spouse thereof[26] or the beneficiary disclaiming the gift or the beneficiary's marriage to the testator having been disolved or annulled unless a contrary intention appears in the will.[27] Ademption occurs if T specifically leaves some property such as "my Ming dynasty vase" or "my house Blackacre" but no longer has the property when he dies: the legacy or devise is adeemed and the legatee or devisee receives nothing. Abatement is a little less drastic: if T's debts are such that the Ming vase and Blackacre forming part of T's estate at T's death have to be sold but that a surplus remains after using the proceeds to pay off the debts then a rateable proportion will pass to the legatee and devisee. General legacies such as "I bequeath £5,000 to A, £3,000 to B and £1,000 to C" must first abate to their entire extent before resort can be had to specific gifts.[28]

---

[21] *Cochrane v. I.R.C.* [1974] STC 335; *Prest v. Bettinson* [1980] STC 607; T.C.G.A., s.62. P.R.s have the annual exemption (£7,500) for the year in which the deceased died and for the next two years of assessment. Where P.R.s' gains do not exceed their losses any surplus losses cannot be passed on to the legatees unlike the position for trustees and beneficiaries under T.C.G.A., s.71(2). Assets received by legatees are taken over at their base value at the deceased's death: T.C.G.A., s.62(4).

[22] I.H.T.A., s.91.

[23] I.C.T.A. 1988, ss.695 and 696 as amended by Finance Act 1995 Sched. 18.

[24] Wills Act 1837, s.9 *infra*, at para. 2–101.

[25] *Att.-Gen. v. Jones* (1817) 3 Price 368, *Governors of Foundling Hospital v. Crane* [1911] 2 KB 367.

[26] Wills Act 1837, s.15 as restricted by Wills Act 1968 for which see *infra*, at para. 2–128.

[27] Law Reform (Succession) Act 1995, s.3, substituting Wills Act 1837, s.18A.

[28] The order in which property has to be resorted to to pay debts, etc., is laid down in Part II, 1st Sched. to the Administration of Estates Act 1925.

1–127   Lapse occurs if a legatee or devisee predeceases the testator unless the legatee or devisee was a child (or other issue) of the testator and left issue alive at the testator's death: in such an exceptional case the gift is effective in favour of the surviving issue *per stirpes*.[29] Where lapse occurs the gift fails and will fall into any residuary gift of the testator (*e.g.* "I leave all the residue of my property not otherwise hereinbefore disposed of to R"). Necessarily, if it is the residuary legatee, R, who has predeceased the testator and occasioned the lapse, then the gifted property must be undisposed of and so pass to the next-of-kin under the intestacy rules applicable on the partial intestacy of the testator. Similarly, if a trust in a will fails, the property purportedly subject to the trust will pass under the residuary gift unless the trust was of the residuary property when the property will pass to the next-of-kin under the intestacy rules.

1–128   If it is uncertain whether or not a beneficiary predeceased the testator (*e.g.* where they are both killed by a bomb or in a car or plane crash) the younger is presumed to have survived the elder under the *commorientes* rule in section 184 of the Law of Property Act 1925.

1–129   A beneficiary under a will or intestacy may disclaim the gift to him.[30] The gift then falls back into the deceased's estate and passes to whomsoever would have been entitled if the disclaiming beneficiary had predeceased the deceased.[31] Once a beneficiary has accepted the gift he cannot disclaim it[32] but he can assign it on to whomsoever he wants. This will occasion another charge to C.G.T. or I.H.T. unless this occurs within two years of the deceased's death and takes the form of a written instrument varying the will or the intestacy rules and executed by the bountiful beneficiary, who then elects for such variation to take effect as if made by the deceased in his will.[33] Unfortunately, for income tax purposes the variation is not so treated so that the bountiful beneficiary will be treated[34] as a settlor of the benefit conferred by him.[35]

1–130   This leaves us with the intestacy rules but first it should be noted that, whilst a testator in his will can appoint "executors" to administer the testator's estate and who will obtain "probate" of the will, where a person dies intestate his closest relatives normally have to take out "letters of administration" and act as "administrators": the phrase "personal representatives" covers both executors and administrators. A testator's will, if professionally drafted, will, after specific gifts, usually

---

[29] Wills Act 1837, s.33, as substituted by Administration of Justice Act 1982, s.19. Illegitimate issue count: Family Law Reform Act 1969, s.16. *Per stirpes* means through their stocks of descent so that children of a deceased child take the share their parent would have taken had he survived.

[30] *Townson v. Tickell* (1819) 3 B. & Ald. 31; *Re Scott* [1975] 1 W.L.R. 1260. A gift of a single whole (*e.g.* residue) must be wholly accepted or wholly disclaimed, partial acceptance amounting to whole acceptance: *Re Joel* [1943] Ch. 311; *Guthrie v. Walrond* (1882) 22 Ch.D. 573.

[31] *Re Backhouse* [1931] W.N. 168.

[32] *Re Hodge* [1940] Ch. 260.

[33] I.H.T.A. 1984, s.142; T.C.G.A. 1992, s.62(6).

[34] See *Schnieder v. Mills* [1993] STC 430 at 435.

[35] If a variation is made by a beneficiary in favour of his minor unmarried child then the income arising (unless accumulated in a capital settlement) will be assessed as that of the beneficiary: I.C.T.A. 1988, s.660B, *supra*, at para. 1–94.

give everything to the executors on a trust for sale, and, on an intestacy, statute[36] directs the administrators to hold the intestate's property on a trust with a power of sale.

Where an intestate is survived by a spouse and issue[37] the spouse takes the intestate's personal chattels absolutely and the net sum of £125,000 free of death duties and costs[38]: the residue is held on "the statutory trusts" for the issue subject to the spouse having a life interest[39] in half the residue. If the intestate is survived by a spouse and one or more of the following, that is to say, a parent, a brother or sister of the whole blood, or issue of such a brother or sister, but leaves no issue, then, the spouse takes the personal chattels absolutely and the net sum of £200,000 free of death duties and costs: half of any residue is held for the surviving spouse absolutely and the other half is held for the surviving parents or parent or, if there is no surviving parent, it is held on "the statutory trusts" for the brothers and sisters of the whole blood. If the intestate leaves a spouse and no issue and no parent or brother or sister of the whole blood and no issue of such brother or sister then the surviving spouse takes everything.

If the intestate leaves issue, but no surviving spouse, everything is held **1–131** on "the statutory trusts" for the issue. If the intestate leaves no spouse and no issue any surviving parent or parents of the intestate take the assets absolutely. If, in such circumstances, there is no such surviving parent the intestate's relatives are entitled in the following order so that if any member of one class takes a vested interest he excludes all members of subsequent classes:

(i) the brothers and sisters of the whole blood on "the statutory trusts,"

(ii) brothers and sisters of the half blood on "the statutory trusts,"

(iii) grandparents,

(iv) uncles and aunts of the whole blood on "the statutory trusts,"

(v) uncles and aunts of the half blood on "the statutory trusts." In default the Crown (or the Duchy of Lancaster or of Cornwall) takes everything as *bona vacantia*.

---

[36] Administration of Estates Act 1925, s.33 as amended by Trusts of Land and Appointment of Trustees Act 1996 Sched. 2.

[37] "Issue" includes illegitimate issue: Family Law Reform Act 1987, s.1. Indeed, unless s.1 of that Act is excluded any disposition (by will or deed) referring to various relatives (*e.g.* child, nephew) covers both legitimate and illegitimate relatives.

[38] The rules are in A.E.A. 1925, s.46 and the current amount of the statutory legacies in Family Provision (Intestate Succession) Order 1993 (S.I. 1993 No. 2906). Interest of 6% is payable on unpaid statutory legacies: S.I. 1983 No. 1374. The spouse must survive the intestate by 28 days to take the legacy: Law Reform (Succession) Act 1995, s.1.

[39] The surviving spouse has a right to have the personal representatives purchase or redeem the life interest by paying over its capital value: Administration of Estates Act 1925, s.47A. For calculation see Intestate Succession (Interest and Capitalisation) Order 1977 (No. 1491). She also has a right to compel the personal representatives to appropriate the matrimonial home at a proper valuation towards satisfaction of her interest under the intestacy: Intestates' Estate Act 1952, s.5; *Re Phelps* [1980] Ch. 275.

1–132   If property is held on the statutory trusts, *e.g.* for issue, this means that the property is held upon trust equally for all the intestate's children living at his death who have attained or subsequently attain 18 years of age or who marry under that age: if a child predeceased the intestate, but left issue living or conceived at the death of the intestate, then such issue stand in the parent's shoes and take his share if they go on to attain 18 years of age or marry thereunder.[40] Thus, if an intestate widower dies leaving a 40-year-old son (with two daughters of his own) and two grandchildren aged 20 and 15, being the children of a deceased son of the intestate, then the 40-year-old son takes one-half of the intestate's property, and the two grandchildren acquire interests in the other half. The elder grandchild takes one-quarter of the property absolutely whilst the other quarter is held for the younger grandchild contingent upon his attaining 18 or marrying thereunder: if he should die before then his elder brother would then obtain the whole half share that would have passed to his father had he not predeceased the intestate.

1–133   Finally, mention may be made of the fact that if a testator's will or the intestacy rules fail to make reasonable financial provision for the testator's or intestate's dependants then an application under the Inheritance (Provision for Family and Dependants) Act 1975 can be made to the court for the court to order reasonable provision to be made. Sections 10 and 11 have special provisions to deal with dispositions within six years of death intended to defeat applications for financial provision and with contracts to leave property by will.

Section 7. Classification of Trusts

1–134   Traditionally trusts have been classified as express, implied, resulting or constructive. Classification is significant in the following respects. No formalities are required for implied, resulting or constructive trusts.[41] A person who is incapable of being an express trustee may become a resulting or constructive trustee.[42] A constructive trust imposed on A, the owner of Blackacre, in favour of B as to a half interest therein may be void against A's trustee in bankruptcy under section 339 of the Insolvency Act 1986 as not being a settlement upon B for valuable consideration.[43] A resulting trust imposed on A, the owner of Blackacre, in favour of B due to B contributing half the purchase moneys will not be void against A's trustees in bankruptcy under s.339.

There is no authoritative classification of trusts but for our purposes the following classification is adopted.

1–135   *Express trust*: a trust where the settlor has positively expressed his intention to create a trust of specific property whether using the word "trust" or other informal words expressing the same idea.

---

[40] Administration of Estates Act 1925, s.47(1).
[41] L.P.A. 1925, s.53(2), *infra*, at para. 2–06 and Law of Property (Miscellaneous Provisions) Act 1989 s.2(5).
[42] *Re Vinogradoff* [1935] W.N. 68.
[43] *Re Densham* [1975] 3 All E.R. 726.

Implied trust: a resulting or constructive trust.[44]

Resulting trust[45]: a *presumed* resulting trust, where A transfers property or causes property to be transferred without intending to dispose of his beneficial interest, so that if he transfers property to B gratuitously, then B is rebuttably presumed to hold such property on trust for A, or if A and B equally put up the purchase price but have Blackacre put into B's name alone, then B will hold on resulting trust for A and B equally; or an *automatic* resulting trust, where A transfers property to B on trusts which, for some reason, leave some or all of the beneficial interest undisposed of so B automatically holds such property on a resulting trust for A to the extent of the undisposed of beneficial interest.

Constructive trust[46]: a trust of specific property declared by Equity on proof of special circumstances (which require the owner's conscience to be affected by knowledge of the special circumstances) where Equity considers it unconscionable for the owner of specific property to hold it for his own benefit to the exclusion of the claimant. Thus, a proprietary interest subsists in that specific property which makes it necessary to prove facts which fit the accepted special circumstances directly or by analogy, because the court cannot impose a constructive trust whenever justice and good conscience require it and thereby indulge idiosyncratic notions of fairness and justice.[47]

Exceptionally, a person, though not constructive trustee of specific **1–136** property (so that this exception may more accurately be thought of as constructive *trusteeship*) may, through his dishonest involvement with a breach of trust or other fiduciary duty, be treated constructively as if he were a trustee so that he may be made personally liable to account like an express trustee, *i.e.* be personally liable to make good the loss of trust property.[48] Historically, the terminology of personal liability to account in equity as a constructive trustee has been utilised: logically, this equitable remedy of *personal* liability to account should be kept distinct from *proprietary* constructive trusts of property, so it is excluded from Chapter 6 and discussed in Chapter 11.

It is important to realise that just as Equity is a supplement to the **1–137** common law so are constructive trusts of property a supplement to express and resulting trusts of property. It is because the trustees have become express or resulting trustees of property they own that the court compels them to give effect to the plaintiff beneficiaries' rights therein. It is because the defendant is found by the court, as a result of some principle of Equity, to hold property or its traceable product knowingly subject to an express or resulting trust or other fiduciary obligations, that the defendant is a constructive trustee thereof: it is not because the defendant is a constructive trustee that he is compelled to hold such

---

[44] *Cowcher v. Cowcher* [1972] 1 All E.R. 943 at 949, though Trustee Act 1925, s.68(17) in speaking of "implied and constructive trusts" means "resulting and constructive trusts."
[45] See Chap. 5.
[46] See Chap. 6.
[47] See *infra*, at paras 6–96 to 6–139.
[48] See Chap. 11, section 4.

property in equity for the plaintiffs.[49] A constructive trust therefore arises in support of pre-existing rights in respect of property: it is a substantive proprietary right that is a natural incident of the trust institution. As such, it arises automatically on the occurrence of certain factual situations involving property subject to a trust or other fiduciary obligation, so that any court decree will be retrospective.

1–138 Different from the English constructive trust (sometimes referred to as an "institutional" or "substantive" constructive trust) is the remedial constructive trust found in the USA, Canada and Australia[50] which does not arise automatically in accordance with settled principles but which is imposed by the court as a remedy in its discretion when it discovers it just, the court's decree being prospective except to the rare extent it considers it should be retrospective against a specified person.[51] Once the defendant property owner is insolvent it is clear that no remedial constructive trust could be imposed by the courts because this would undermine the statutory regime covering assets of insolvent persons.[52] However, there is scope[53] for the courts to develop a doctrine enabling them to impose a remedial constructive trust against the property of a solvent defendant. Indeed, equitable proprietary estoppel claims may be recognised as equivalent to remedial constructive trust claims,[54] while it is possible that common intention constructive trusts could come to be regarded not as institutional constructive trusts but as proprietary estoppel or remedial constructive trust claims.[55]

1–139 It should be noted that in some judgments "constructive trust" is sometimes used to cover automatic resulting trusts which may be said to arise as a matter of construction. "Implied trust" is sometimes used to mean informally created express trusts not using the word "trust", sometimes to mean resulting trusts, sometimes to mean only presumed resulting trusts,[56] and sometimes to mean presumed resulting trusts and constructive trusts arising out of informally expressed common intentions.[57] This has created problems for parliamentary counsel.[58] Ideally, since the concept of "implied trust" has no useful function it should cease to be used, but the compendious expression "implied resulting or constructive trusts" has its attractions to judges and parliamentary counsel who act with abundant caution.

---

[49] Scott on Trusts (4th ed.) para. 462; *Muschinski v. Dodds* (1985) 62 A.L.R. 429 at 451–453.

[50] *Giumelli v. Giumelli* [1999] 73 A.L.J.R. 547 (Australia), *Peter v. Beblow* (1993) 101 D.L.R. (4th) 621 (Canada).

[51] *Westdeutsche Landesbank v. Islington B.C.* [1996] A.C. 669, 714.

[52] *Re Polly Peck (No. 2)* [1998] 3 All E.R. 812, 824, 830.

[53] *Westdeutsche Landesbank v. Islington B.C.* [1996] A.C. 669, 716, *Re Goldcorp* [1994] 2 All E.R. 806, 826–827.

[54] Cp. *Giumelli v. Giumelli* (1999) 73 A.L.J.R. 547.

[55] *infra* at para. 6–121.

[56] See, *e.g. Soar v. Ashwell* [1893] 2 Q.B. 390; *Cook v. Fountain* (1676) 3 Swan. 585; *Re Llanover Estates* [1926] Ch. 626; *Lloyd v. Spillil* (1740) Barn. Ch. 384 at 388; *Allen v. Snyder* [1977] 2 New South Wales L.R. 685.

[57] Sir Christopher Slade, *The Informal Creation of Interests in Land* (The Childe & Co. Oxford Lecture, 1984), at 4.

[58] *e.g.* L.P.A. 1925, s.53(2); Trustee Act 1925, s.68(17).

Chapter 2

FORMAL REQUIREMENTS

Section 1. Lifetime and testamentary dispositions distinguished

A testamentary disposition is one that requires to be made in the form of a will **2–01** complying with the Wills Act 1837, as amended. A will has been defined[1] as "an instrument by which a person makes a disposition of his property to take effect after his decease and which is in its own nature ambulatory and revocable during his life": such person is a testator or testatrix. As Lord Oliver remarked,[2] "It is, of course, axiomatic that an essential characteristic of a will is that, during the lifetime of the testator, it is a mere declaration of his present intention and may be freely revoked or altered. It does not follow that every document intended to operate on death and containing a power of revocation is necessarily testamentary in character."

He also stated[3] "the most obvious example of such a revocable but non-testamentary instrument is the exercise of a revocable power of appointment under a settlement *inter vivos*." A testator has to make a disposition of his own property. Thus if trustees hold property for T for life, and then to distribute the capital between such of T's descendants as the trustees shall select in their absolute discretion, but subject to T's power, revocably or irrevocably, to appoint shares of capital to such of his descendants as he may see fit, T is not disposing of his own property if he revocably appoints all the capital to pass on his death to his son, S.

What if T has disposed of his property in his lifetime to trustees on trusts for **2–02** himself for life, remainder to B and C equally, where he has expressly reserved to himself the power to revoke the trust wholly or partly at any time during his life or to appoint capital to such of XYZ as he might choose? In default of any exercise of the power, capital will pass equally to B and C on the death of the life tenant, T, but as a result of T's earlier *lifetime disposition* to the trustees which took effect immediately, conferring an equitable interest in capital on B and C, although subsequently defeasible if the power of revocation or appointment were exercised. Thus, a settlor's revocable trusts taking effect in his lifetime are not testamentary dispositions.[4]

What if T went further and disposed of his property in his lifetime to trustees **2–03** to hold the income *and the capital* on trust for himself or such other persons as he might direct and, then, on his death to distribute whatever remained to B and C equally? Here T has the full equitable interest in all the trust property to do whatever he wants with it: B and C have no interest whatsoever in the trust

---

[1] Lord Oliver in *Baird v. Baird* [1990] 2 AC 548 at 556 adopting Jarman on Wills (8th ed) 1951 p. 26
[2] *Baird v. Baird* [1990] 2 AC 548 at 557
[3] *ibid* at 556
[4] *Kauter v. Hilton* (1953) 90 CLR 86 at 98–99 and 100–101, *Young v. Sealey* [1949] Ch 279 at 284 and 294, *Anderson v. Patton* [1948] 2 DLR 202. The creation of a joint bank account is not a testamentary disposition: see para. 5–79 *infra*.

property, only a hope that something will remain at T's death and that it will then pass to them. At the outset T made a lifetime disposition of his legal (but not his beneficial) interest in the trust property: he retained the whole beneficial interest as his to do with as he wished in the rest of his lifetime. Thus, T's intentions to benefit B and C are testamentary intentions concerned with disposing of his beneficial interest in the trust property, so that such intentions will be ineffective unless complying with the Wills Act 1837 requiring two witnesses.[5] All the trust property is held from the outset to T's order in his lifetime until he orders how the remaining capital is to be dealt with on his death, such orders being testamentary in nature.

2–04   One needs to distinguish the situation where trustees hold to the order of the settlor from the outset and the situation where the trustees hold on trusts for various persons subject to the settlor's power (via a power of revocation or a power of appointment in his own favour) to defeat the existing equitable interests of the beneficiaries by directing the trustees for the future to hold to his order. In the former situation from the outset the full equitable interest is owned by the settlor, while in the latter situation such equitable interest from the outset is held by all the beneficiaries and it is only at some subsequent date that the settlor can acquire an equitable interest by exercising his reserved overriding powers. In the former case there is no lifetime disposition of the settlor's equitable interest, while in the latter case there is, the settlor only acquiring an equitable interest (that will need to be passed on upon his death by a testamentary disposition) if he exercises his overriding powers.

Section 2. Lifetime or Inter Vivos Trusts

THE STATUTORY PROVISIONS

Law of Property Act 1925

2–05 *Section* 52(1): "All conveyances of land or of any interest therein are void for the purpose of conveying or creating a legal estate unless made by deed."

Section 53(1): "Subject to the provisions hereinafter contained with respect to the creation of interests in land by parol:

(a) No interest in land can be created or disposed of except by writing signed by the person creating or conveying the same, or by his agent thereunto lawfully authorised in writing, or by will, or by operation of law;

(b) A declaration of trust respecting any land or any interest therein must be manifested and proved by some writing signed by some person who is able to declare such trust or by his will;

(c) A disposition of an equitable interest or trust subsisting at the time of the disposition, must be in writing signed by the person disposing of the same, or by his agent thereunto lawfully authorised in writing or by will.

---

[5] *Anderson v. Patton* (supra) and *Kauter v. Hilton* (supra) at 100 endorsing Dixon and Evatt JJ in *Russell v. Scott* (1936) 55 CLR 440 at 454 "What can be accomplished only by will is the voluntary transmission on death of an interest which up to the moment of death belongs absolutely and indefeasibly to the deceased." See also *Governors of Foundling Hospital v. Crane* [1911] 2KB 367 at 379–380. An agreement between T and L, intended to be a legatee under T's formally valid will, that L will hold the legacy on secret trust for B amounts to a testamentary disposition, but will be effective under a constructive trust: see section 3 below.

(2) This section does not affect the creation or operation of resulting, implied **2–06** or constructive trusts."

Section 54(1): "All interests in land created by parol and not put in writing and signed by the persons so creating the same, or by their agents thereunto lawfully authorised in writing, have, notwithstanding any consideration having been given for the same, the force and effect of interests at will only.

(2) Nothing in the foregoing provisions . . . shall affect the creation by parol of leases taking effect in possession for a term not exceeding three years at the best rent which can reasonably be obtained without taking a fine."

Section 55: "Nothing in the last two foregoing sections shall—

(*a*) Invalidate dispositions by will . . .

(*d*) Affect the operation of the law relating to part performance."

Section 205(1): "In this Act unless the context otherwise requires, the following expressions have the meanings hereby assigned to them— . . .

(ii) "Conveyance" includes a mortgage, charge, lease, assent, vesting declaration, vesting instrument, disclaimer, release and every other assurance of property or of an interest therein by any instrument, except a will; "convey" has a corresponding meaning; and "disposition" includes a conveyance and also a devise, bequest, or an appointment of property contained in a will; and "dispose of" has a corresponding meaning . . .

(ix) "Land" includes land of any tenure, and mines and minerals, whether or not held apart from the surface, buildings or parts of buildings . . . and other corporeal hereditaments; also a manor, an advowson, and a rent and other incorporeal hereditaments, and an easement, right, privilege, or benefit in, over, or derived from land; but not an undivided share in land . . .

(x) "Legal estates" mean the estates, interests and charges, in or over land (subsisting or created at law) which are by this Act authorised to subsist or be created as legal estates; "equitable interests" mean all the other interests and charges in or over land or in the proceeds of sale thereof."

LAW OF PROPERTY (MISCELLANEOUS PROVISIONS) ACT 1989

Section **2.**—(1) A contract for the sale or other disposition of an interest in **2–07** land can only be made in writing and only by incorporating all the terms which the parties have expressly agreed in one document or, where contracts are exchanged, in each.

(2) The terms may be incorporated in a document either by being set out in it or by reference to some other document.

(3) The document incorporating the terms or, where contracts are exchanged, one of the documents incorporating them (but not necessarily the same one) must be signed by or on behalf of each party to the contract.

(4) Where a contract for the sale or other disposition of an interest in land satisfies the conditions of this section by reason only of the rectification of one or

more documents in pursuance of an order of a court, the contract shall come into being, or be deemed to have come into being, at such time as may be specified in the order.

(5) This section does not apply in relation to—

2–08   (a) a contract to grant such a lease as is mentioned in section 54(2) of the Law of Property Act 1925 (short leases);
(b) a contract made in the course of a public auction; or
(c) a contract regulated under the Financial Services Act 1986;

and nothing in this section affects the creation or operation of resulting, implied or constructive trusts.

(6) In this section—
"disposition" has the same meaning as in the Law of Property Act 1925; "interest in land" means any estate, interest or charge in or over land or in or over the proceeds of sale of land.

(7) Nothing in this section shall apply in relation to contracts made before this section comes into force.

(8) Section 40 of the Law of Property Act 1925 (which is superseded by this section) shall cease to have effect.

CONTRACTS TO CREATE TRUSTS OR DISPOSE OF EQUITABLE INTERESTS

2–09   Section 2 of the 1989 Act applies to a contract to create a trust of any interest in land and to a contract to dispose of an equitable interest in land, *e.g.* a life interest or a co-owner's equitable interest under a trust of land. Unlike the position under Law of Property Act 1925 section 40,[6] which it has replaced as from September 27, 1989, the contract is void if all the terms are not in one document signed[7] by both parties or in exchanged documents signed by each exchanger (or on his behalf), though it is possible to incorporate terms set out in another document by referring to that document. Under section 40 the contract had not been required to be created by signed writing, but only to be evidenced by writing signed by or on behalf of the defendant by the time a court action was brought, and the contract was unenforceable by action,[8] but

---

[6] "(1) No action may be brought upon any contract for the sale or other disposition of land or any interest in land, unless the agreement upon which such action is brought, or some memorandum or note thereof, is in writing, and signed by the party to be charged or by some other person thereunto by him lawfully authorised.
(2) This section does not affect the law relating to part performance."
[7] Old, liberal authorities on what constituted a sufficient signature for Statute of Frauds 1677 and Law of Property Act 1925 are no longer relevant: the 1989 Act has a different philosophy, so a signature must be a handwritten signature: *Firstpost Homes Ltd v. Johnson* [1995] 4 All E.R. 355. The 1989 Act does not apply to the exercise of an option to purchase an interest in land (*Spiro v. Glencrown Properties Ltd* [1991] Ch. 537) nor to a lock-out agreement not to consider any further offers if the purchaser exchanges contracts within two weeks (*Pitt v. PHH Asset Management Ltd* [1994] 1 W.L.R. 327) nor to a collateral contract (*Record v. Bell* [1991] 1 W.L.R. 853) nor to an agreement supplemental to a completed contract (*Tootal Clothing Ltd v. Guinea Properties Management Ltd* (1992) 64 P. & C.R. 452): it applies to variations: *McCausland v. Duncan Lawrie* [1996] 4 All E.R. 995. If an agreed term is omitted then rectification can be obtained so that the rectified document complies with the 1989 Act: *Wright v. Robert Leonard (Developments) Ltd* [1994] E.G.C.S. 69.
[8] A deposit could be forfeited or recovered: *Monnickendam v. Leanse* (1923) 39 T.L.R. 445; *Pulbrook v. Lawes* (1876) 1 Q.B.D. 284.

not void, until the requisite signed written evidence materialised or part performance of the contract occurred.

For a claimant to rely on the equitable doctrine of part performance **2–10** to obtain specific performance or damages in lieu (under the equitable jurisdiction originally enshrined in Lord Cairns' Act 1858) he needed to show that he had acted to his detriment in reliance upon the inadequately evidenced contract and that his acts were such as to indicate, on a balance of probabilities, that they had been performed in reliance upon a contract with the defendant concerning land and consistent with the contract alleged.[9] The doctrine of part performance is not available in support of a void obligation but a claimant may, instead, rely on the imposition of a constructive trust[10] to prevent a defendant unconscionably relying upon lack of the necessary signed writing. Thus, if a defendant contracted to sell a building plot to the claimant for £30,000, so that the claimant then spent £200,000 on erecting a house on the plot, the defendant would not be able to take unconscionable advantage of the omission of some minor term from the terms of the written agreement. He would be compelled to hold the plot on constructive trust for the claimant, subject to payment of the £30,000 (if not already paid), so that the claimant would be entitled to a conveyance of the plot.[11]

A contract to create a trust of pure personalty need satisfy no special **2–11** formalities as also seems to be the case for a contract to dispose of an equitable interest in pure personalty.[12]

THE CREATION OF TRUSTS AND SECTION 53(1)(b)[13]

Transactions within section 53(1)(b), unlike those within section 53(1)(a) **2–12** or within section 53(1)(c), need only be evidenced at some time by signed writing and do not actually have to be carried out by signed writing if they are to be effective. It would seem that section 53(1)(a) needs to be construed as covering the creation of equitable interests in land (*e.g.* restrictive covenants) other than equitable interests under a trust, leaving section 53(1)(b) to cover creation of equitable interests in land under a trust.[14] This protects a landowner and his heirs from the perils of oral evidence and enables purchasers to know whether or not to pay the purchase money to at least two trustees.

A settlor may create a trust of Blackacre either by declaring that he **2–13** himself is henceforth to hold Blackacre on specified trusts or by conveying Blackacre to trustees and declaring specified trusts on which

---

[9] *Steadman v. Steadman* [1976] A.C. 536 as narrowly interpreted in *Re Gonin* [1979] Ch. 16.

[10] *Yaxley v. Gotts* [2000] 1 All E.R. 74. See s.2(5) of the 1989 Act and para. 2–29 (equitable proprietary estoppel interests) and Chap. 6, s.3.

[11] If D holds on trust for P who is *sui juris* then P can demand that D transfer the property to P. See *Saunders v. Vautier* principle, *infra*, para. 9–152. As a short-cut the court would here direct the defendant to execute a conveyance in the plaintiff's favour: *cf. Pascoe v. Turner* [1979] 1 W.L.R. 431.

[12] See *Chinn v. Collins* [1981] A.C. 533 at 548 and the discussion of *Oughtred v. I.R.C.* [1960] A.C. 206, *infra*, paras 2–48 to 2–50.

[13] Replacing Statute of Frauds 1677, s.7 with fresh wording: see *Grey v. I.R.C.* [1960] A.C. 1.

[14] In view of L.P.A. 1925, s.52(1), s.53(1)(a) cannot be restricted to legal interests and so that s.53(1)(a) does not make s.53(1)(b) otiose para. (b) should be construed applying the maxim *"generalia specialibus non derogant."*

the trustees are to hold Blackacre. In both cases the declaration of the trusts must be in writing specifying the beneficiaries, the trust property and the nature of the trusts.[15] As was the case with Law of Property Act 1925, section 40 the writing may be comprised in linked documents[16] and also the trust is unenforceable, but not void, until the requisite written evidence is present,[17] or part performance of the trusts occurs.[18]

The signing must be "by some person who is able to declare such trust," *e.g.* by A where A conveys Blackacre to B and contemporaneously declares signed written trusts for C or by T1 and T2 where they hold property on trust for A for life, remainder to B but with power for the trustees to declare new trusts in favour of C or his issue. It has been assumed that the absence from section 53(1)(b), unlike section 53(1)(a) or (c), of an express reference to an agent precludes the settlor's agent authorised in writing from being "some person who is able to declare" a trust on the settlor's behalf, but such assumption may yet prove to be unfounded because the duly authorised agent may be regarded as "some person who is able to declare such trust." The signatory should be the person who, at the time of the signature, would seem to be the beneficial owner (or, perhaps, the agent thereof) if the declaration of trust were ignored.[19] Such person will be A where A declares himself trustee of Blackacre for B, and such person will be B if, subsequently, B declares that he holds his equitable interest on trust for C for life, remainder to D.[20] However, if A conveys Blackacre to B and contemporaneously declares *oral* trusts for C, then subsequent written evidence of the trust signed by B satisfies section 53(1)(b)[21] though it may well be that until B signs such writing (or an act of part performance occurs) A retains the equitable interest[22] which he can dispose of as he wishes (unless C has earlier acted to his detriment, *e.g.* by building on Blackacre, such performance giving rise to an equitable estoppel).

2–14   If A had conveyed land or transferred other property to B to hold to A's order and on some subsequent date told B to hold on trust for C, this would amount to A disposing of his subsisting equitable interest in C's favour: such disposition would be void under section 53(1)(c) unless in writing signed by A or his agent.[23]

---

[15] *Smith v. Matthews* (1861) 3 De G.F. & J. 139; *Morton v. Tewart* (1842) 2 Y. & C.Ch. Case 67.

[16] *Forster v. Hale* (1798) 3 Ves. 696.

[17] *Rochefoucauld v. Boustead* [1897] 1 Ch. 1962, 206; *Gardner v. Rowe* (1828) 5 Russ. 258. (A granted a lease to B on oral trusts for C, and after B became bankrupt B executed a deed stating the trusts. *Held* valid declaration of trust prior to B's bankruptcy so his creditors had no claim to the lease. Note under the *Rochefoucauld* doctrine, *infra*, at para. 2–20, B was bound from the time he took the lease so if, instead, A orally declared *himself* trustee of land for C and provided written evidence only after his own bankruptcy he would not be bound by the trust until the written evidence, so his creditors would have a claim to the land, assuming C had not earlier acted to his detriment, *e.g.* by building a house on the land, in reliance on A's declaration of trust.)

[18] LPA s.55(d).

[19] See T. G. Youdan [1984] C.L.J. 306 at 316–320.

[20] *Tierney v. Wood* (1854) 19 Beav. 330; *Kronheim v. Johnson* (1877) 7 Ch.D. 60.

[21] *Gardner v. Rowe, supra; Smith v. Matthews, supra; Mountain v. Styak* [1922] N.Z.L.R. 131. If the oral trusts had been for A himself then he would have an equitable interest under a constructive trust which he could then sub-settle; *Tierney v. Wood, supra*.

[22] See *infra*, at para. 2–22.

[23] *Grey v. I.R.C.* [1960] A.C. 1

Declarations of trust of property other than land or interests in land can be made orally[24] since no special evidential or other requirements exist, but care must be taken where A purports to declare himself trustee of an equitable interest in any property for X absolutely where X is of full capacity. In substance it seems that the apparent sub-trust is a disposition of A's subsisting equitable interest within section 53(1)(c) because the head trustee, whom X can directly sue, is now holding on trust for X and not for A, who has no active duties to perform and so drops out of the picture.[25]

DISPOSITIONS OF EQUITABLE INTERESTS AND SECTION 53(1)(c)

In context the meaning of "equitable interest" must comprise interests in **2–15** land or in personality and "disposition" must comprise a disposition in writing or otherwise.[26]

The signed writing is essential to the validity of the disposition: failure to satisfy section 53(1)(c) makes the disposition void. Subsequent written evidence will be of no avail unless it can be construed as a "belt and braces" device capable of making a disposition as of its date insofar as necessary if the earlier disposition were void.[27] The signed writing may comprise linked documents.[28] Where the assignee is to hold the assigned equitable interest as trustee the writing need not contain the particulars of the trust which may thus be communicated orally,[29] though if the interest is in land some subsequent written evidence will be necessary to satisfy section 53(1)(b). If no communication of the particulars of the trust is made to the assignee, T, taking as trustee, then the assigned interest will be held on resulting trust for the assignor, A, and any subsequent disposition in favour of B by the assignor will fall within section 53(1)(c). It is vital to appreciate that A's direction to T to hold the property for B, instead of A, amounts to A disposing of his subsisting equitable interest to B within section 53(1)(c): *Grey v. I.R.C., infra* paras 2–51 *et seq.*

There is no disposition of a subsisting equitable interest when a legal **2–16** owner with full beneficial ownership makes a declaration of trust. He is not regarded as having two estates one legal and the other equitable,[30] the equitable or beneficial interest is merged or subsumed in the legal estate and will pass automatically when the legal estate is transferred.[31] If

---

[24] *Rowe v. Prance* [2000] WTLR 249 (boat), *Paul v. Constance* [1977] 1 W.L.R. 527 (a bank account, a chose in action)

[25] See *infra*, at para. 2–43.

[26] Assumed in *Grey v. I.R.C., supra*; *Oughtred v. I.R.C.* [1960] A.C. 206, *Vandervell v. I.R.C.* [1967] 2 A.C. 291, and treated as well established in *Re Tyler's Fund Trusts* [1967] 3 All E.R. 389 at 392. The context must oust L.P.A. 1925, s.205(1)(ii), (x).

[27] See *Grey v. I.R.C.* [1958] Ch. 690 at 706–707 and B. Green (1984) 47 M.L.R. 385 at 391–92.

[28] *Re Danish Bacon Co. Ltd Staff Pension Fund* [1971] 1 W.L.R. 248.

[29] *Re Tyler's Fund Trusts* [1967] 2 All E.R. 389.

[30] *Westdeutsche Landesbank v. Islington BC* [1996] AC 669 at 706; *D.K.L.R. Holding Co. v. C.S.D.(N.S.W.)* (1982) 40 Austr.L.R. 1; a person cannot hold on trust for himself: *Re Cook* [1948] Ch. 212.

[31] *Vandervell v. IRC* [1967] 2 A.C. 291.

he declares a trust this creates a new equitable interest so no evidential
or other writing will be necessary except in the case of land within
section 53(1)(b). Where trustees hold property on trust for B absolutely
and, pursuant to B's direction they transfer the property to X absolutely
then B's interest is extinguished and X obtains full legal and beneficial
ownership so there is no separate disposition by B of his equitable
interest that requires compliance with section 53(1)(c): *Vandervell v.
I.R.C., infra* pp. 00, 00. If this last example were extended one step
further because X had previously agreed to hold the property on trust
for Y one might think that this should make no difference. Nevertheless,
in substance B is responsible for disposing of his subsisting equitable
interest now in the hands of Y so that section 53(1)(c) should be
applicable,[32] there being a need for a paper trail where the equitable
interest has been separated from the legal interest so that Y can prove
his interest against X's executors after X's death. However, the need for
a paper trail could justify a need for writing where a legal beneficial
owner, A, declares he holds specific personalty on trust for Y, or a
trustee, T, who holds on trust for X, exercises an overriding power of
appointment to declare that T now holds for Y instead of X, but in
neither case is writing required.[33] The key in each case is that neither A
nor T owns a separate subsisting equitable interest which he disposes of
to Y.

2–17   It would seem that there is a disposition where there is a release or a
surrender of a subsisting equitable interest[34] but not where there is a
disclaimer.[35] Variations of trusts under the Variation of Trusts Act 1958
escape section 53(1)(c) either by implication under the 1958 Act or by
virtue of a constructive trust within section 53(2).[36] Also escaping section
53(1)(c) (and the Wills Act 1837) is the exercise of an employee's
contractual right to nominate revocably a person to receive moneys
payable under a pension trust fund in the event of the employee's death
in service: there is no subsisting interest in property to dispose of[37]
Similarly, if L takes out a policy on his life where rights to a money
payment only crystallise on his death, there is no disposition of a
subsisting equitable interest if he orally nominates X to receive the
money and hold it on trust for Y and Z.[38]

It also seems that section 53(1)(c) will not apply where V sells 10,000
shares to P, who replaces V in a computer recording that P now owns
those shares, where V actually owned on equitable interest as tenant in

---

[32] *cf. Grey v. I.R.C.* [1960] A.C. 1 where trustees held shares on trust for Mr. Hunter and he told them to
hold the shares not (so to speak) in their left hands for him but in their right hands as trustees of
existing trusts for his grandchildren: this ranks as a CGT disposal by one trustee to another even if the
same individual is concerned: *Hoare Trustees v. Gardner* [1978] 1 All E.R. 791.

[33] See note 24 supra and *Re Vandervell's Trusts (No 2)* [1974] Ch. 269

[34] L.P.A. 1925, s.205(1)(ii), G. Battersby [1979] Conv. 17 at 20–21.

[35] *Re Paradise Motor Co. Ltd* [1968] 1 W.L.R. 1125; disclaimer "operates by way of avoidance and not by
way of disposition." See also *Allied Dunbar Assurance plc v. Fowler* [1994] 25 Est. Gaz. 149 and L.P.A.
1925, s.52(2)(b).

[36] *Re Holt's S.T.* [1969] 1 Ch. 100, *infra*, at paras 2–49, 9–170.

[37] *Re Danish Bacon Co. Ltd Staff Pension Fund* [1971] 1 W.L.R. 248; *Baird v. Baird* [1990] 2 A.C. 548.

[38] *Gold v. Hill* (1998–99) 1 ITELR 27.

common in a pool of shares owned by the company with the computer records, so that V seemed to dispose of a subsisting equitable interest: see para. 3–92 *infra*.

STATUTE MAY NOT BE USED AS AN INSTRUMENT OF FRAUD,
CONSTRUCTIVE TRUSTS AND RESULTING TRUSTS

If A transfers land to B or buys land in B's name on an oral **2–18** understanding with B that B is to hold the land on trust for A, case law[39] assumes that A cannot prove the express trust owing to section 53(1)(b), so that it will be necessary for signed writing of B to satisfy section 53(1)(b).[40]

It would, however, be monstrous if B could plead the statute (passed to prevent fraud) so as fraudulently to keep the land for himself. Accordingly, A can have his claim to the land recognised on one of three grounds.

He can accept that section 53(1)(b) prevents proof of the express trust, **2–19** but then he can rely on section 53(2) on the basis of either a resulting trust[41] (arising from the gratuitous circumstances in which there was no intention to transfer any beneficial interest) or a constructive trust[42] (imposed upon B because it would be fraudulent and unconscionable for him to keep the land for himself and so unjustly enrich himself).

Alternatively, since there is a valid trust, though unenforceable by virtue of section 53(1)(b), A can rely on equity estopping B from raising the issue of unenforceability under section 53(1)(b)[43] since otherwise B would be using statute as an instrument of fraud, so that the court thus enforces the express trust.

As Lindley L.J. stated in *Rochefoucauld v. Boustead*.[44] **2–20**

> "It is a fraud on the part of a person to whom land is conveyed as a trustee and who knows it is so conveyed to deny the trust and to claim the land for himself. Consequently, notwithstanding the statute, it is competent for a person claiming land conveyed to another to prove by parol evidence that it was so conveyed upon trust for the claimant, and that the grantee, knowing the facts, is denying the trust and relying upon the form of conveyance and the statute in order to keep the land himself. . . . The trust which the plaintiff has established is clearly an express trust . . . one which

---

[39] *Hutchins v. Lee* (1737) 1 Atk 447; *Young v. Peachy* (1741) 2 Atk 255; *Re Duke of Marlborough* [1894] 2 Ch. 133.

[40] *Ambrose v. Ambrose* (1716) 1 P. Wms. 321; *Smith v. Matthews* (1861) 3 De G.F. & J. 139; *Gardner v. Rowe* (1828) 5 Russ. 258; *Mountain v. Styak* [1922] N.Z.L.R. 131.

[41] See *infra*, paras 5–75, 6–77; *Hodgson v. Marks* [1971] Ch. 892; *Davies v.Otty (No. 2)* (1865) 35 Beav. 208; *Haigh v. Kaye* (1872) L.R. 7 Ch. 469. The circumstances should oust the impact of L.P.A. 1925 s.60(3); see *infra*, para. 5–77.

[42] *Scheuerman v. Scheuerman* (1916) 28 D.L.R. 223; *Bannister v. Bannister* [1948] 2 All E.R. 133; *Binions v. Evans* [1972] Ch. 359; *British Railways Board v. Pickin* [1974] A.C. 765, 795–796.

[43] *cf.* the need for a defendant specifically to plead L.P.A. 1925, s.40.

[44] [1897] 1 Ch. 196 at 206, 208.

the plaintiff and the defendant intended to create. The case is not one in which an equitable obligation [*i.e.* a constructive trust] arises although there may have been no intention to create a trust."[45]

2–21　　This equitable maxim "Equity will not allow a statute to be used as an instrument of fraud" is not confined to cases in which the conveyance was itself fraudulently obtained. "The fraud which brings the principle into play arises as soon as the absolute character of the conveyance is set up for the purpose of defeating the beneficial interest."[46] So if A sells her two adjoining cottages to B for below market value, B orally agreeing to let her live in one cottage for the rest of her days, B will be compelled to hold that cottage on trust for A for life if he subsequently changes his mind and tries to defeat her interest by relying on section 53(1)(b).[47]

2–22　　Where A's oral understanding with B is that B will hold the land on trust for C, B clearly cannot keep the land for himself. Can A claim beneficial entitlement if he has repented of his intention to benefit C? After all, he can argue that his failure to satisfy section 53(1)(b) means that there is no completely constituted trust for C and equity will not perfect imperfect gifts, assuming C can make no special proprietary estoppel claim by virtue of detrimental reliance.[48] Thus B holds the land on resulting trust for A since A has failed effectively to dispose of his beneficial interest,[49] if indeed, he does not hold on constructive trust for A to prevent B's fraudulent conduct from unjustly enriching B.[50] Whilst B would be estopped from pleading section 53(1)(b) against A or C, A can argue that nothing should stop A from pleading section 53(1)(b) against C. It is true that A intended to make a gift of the beneficial interest to C but A had failed to comply with the requisite formalities, and intended donees cannot complain if the donor's original purported gift was ineffective and the donor then repents of his intentions and so refuses to perfect the gift.[51]

2–23　　C can invoke the analogous case where X by will devises land to Y on the oral understanding with Y that Y is to hold the land on trust for Z. After all, the wills formalities provisions and section 53 of the Law of Property Act were originally all contained in the Statute of Frauds. It is clear that X's secret trust in favour of Z will be enforced against Y.[52] However, Y is clearly intercepting property definitively intended by X for Z, X dying happy with the secret trust, while A is alive and the last thing he wants is for C to benefit.

---

[45] The trust was held to be an express trust for the purpose of the Statute of Limitations and such category was then broad so as to include some persons who would nowadays be classed as constructive trustees: see *Soar v. Ashwell* [1893] 2 Q.B. 390 at 396–397. For classification of trusts see *supra*, para. 1–34.

[46] *Bannister v. Bannister* [1948] 2 All E.R. 133 at 136; *Ungurian v. Lesnoff* [1990] Ch. 206.

[47] *ibid.*

[48] See *infra*, paras 2–29 *et seq.*

[49] *Hodgson v. Marks* [1971] Ch. 892. The circumstances should oust L.P.A. 1925, s.60(3), *infra*, para. 5–77.

[50] *Bannister v. Bannister, supra*; *Last v. Rosenfeld* [1972] 2 N.S.W.L.R. 923 at 937.

[51] See *Re Brooks' S.T., infra*, paras 4–32 and 4–67.

[52] *Ottaway v. Norman* [1972] Ch. 698, *infra*, para. 2–102.

C might then emphasise that the oral trust of land is valid, though **2–24** unenforceable due to section 53(1)(b),[53] so that if B wished B could carry out the trust and sign the necessary writing himself.[54] A will reply that B's authority to sign the required writing can be revoked by A's notification to him or by A's death.[55] Once A has so notified B then it would fly in the face of the statute to allow C to adduce oral evidence to establish his interest. Thus, C cannot prove any unjust deprivation to justify the imposition of a constructive trust.

After all, if A had orally declared himself trustee of Blackacre for C, C could adduce no oral evidence to establish the interest (unless taking advantage of detrimental reliance to establish an equitable proprietary claim).[56] It should make no difference that A transferred the land to B and declared oral trusts for C: if it did there would hardly be any scope for the application of section 53(1)(b) with its cautionary and evidentiary functions.[57]

It may be argued[58] that there should be no difference between (1) A **2–25** simply conveying Blackacre to B with intent manifested by oral evidence to make an outright gift to B (effective in B's favour) and (2) A conveying Blackacre to B with intent manifested by oral evidence for B to hold on trust for C as intended donee of an equitable gift. However, section 53(1)(b) deliberately creates a difference in expressly requiring written evidence of trusts of land where legal title is in one person (B) and equitable title is in another (C) so that A's claim should prevail over C's claim. This provides a paper trail to enable C to enforce his interest against B's executors after B's death, as is the case (though, instead, due to section 53(1)(c)) where X holds on trust for A and, in accordance with A's instructions, transfers the property to Y who has already orally agreed to hold on trust for C.

So far, we have been concerned with a gratuitous conveyance by A to B for C. However, if A sells and conveys land to B (so losing all interest therein) on the express understanding that B will hold the land on trust to give effect to an equitable interest of C or to a licence conferred by A on C, then C has enforceable rights against B.[59] B is not allowed to claim that C's rights are unenforceable against him as a purchaser because this would be fraudulent.

AMBIT AND NATURE OF EQUITABLE MAXIM

The equitable maxim is available not just against the transferee-trustee **2–26** but to volunteers claiming under him[60] and to purchasers with notice.

---

[53] *Gardner v. Rowe* (1828) 5 Russ. 258; *Rochefoucauld v. Boustead* [1897] 1 Ch. 196 at 206.
[54] *Ambrose v. Ambrose* (1716) 1 P. Wms. 321; *Smith v. Matthews* (1861) 3 De G.F. & J. 139; *Mountain v. Styak* [1922] N.Z.L.R. 131.
[55] *Rudkin v. Dolman* (1876) 35 L.T. 791; *Scheurman v. Scheurman* (1916) 52 S.C.R. 625 at 636.
[56] *Wratten v. Hunter* [1978] 2 N.S.W.L.R. 367; *Midland Bank v. Dobson* [1986] 1 F.L.R. 171; *Gissing v. Gissing* [1971] A.C. 886 at 905.
[57] J. D. Feltham [1987] Conv. 246.
[58] T. G. Youdan [1988] Conv. 267.
[59] *Ashburn Anstalt v. Arnold* [1989] Ch. 1; *Lyus v. Prowsa Developments Ltd* [1982] 1 W.L.R. 1044.
[60] *Lincoln v. Wright* (1859) 4 De G. & J. 16; *Re Duke of Marlborough* [1894] 2 Ch. 133.

Indeed, Ungoed-Thomas J. has held[61] that it is available against a bona fide purchaser for value without notice of the trusts affecting his vendor's title, taking the view that such a purchaser is acting fraudulently if he seeks to rely on section 53(1)(b) once he discovers the trusts. It is difficult to see why such purchaser is acting fraudulently. Even if the trusts had originally satisfied section 53(1)(b) a purchaser without notice would take free from the trusts, so that even if the trusts flouting section 53(1)(b) are allowed to be proved under *Rochefoucauld* a purchaser without notice should still take free from the trusts.

2–27   In cases[62] where A has transferred an interest in land to B but orally for the benefit of A, the effect of the equitable maxim is to create a resulting trust,[63] even though in *Bannister v. Bannister* Scott L.J.[64] described the doctrine as "the equitable principle on which a constructive trust is raised against a person who insists on the absolute character of a conveyance to himself for the purpose of defeating a beneficial interest." Subsequent purchasers are bound by resulting or constructive trusts if they have notice,[65] so it matters not whether the trusts be resulting or constructive trusts, each being within section 53(2) of the Law of Property Act. However, in cases where A has transferred an interest in land to B but orally for the benefit of C, and the court does not hold there to be a resulting trust in A's favour but, exceptionally, compels B to hold the land for C's benefit there is a constructive trust. These exceptional cases arise in testamentary situations where A leaves property by will to B on fully or half-secret trusts[66] or in *inter vivos* situations where the detrimental reliance of C creates an estoppel interest.[67] The key to the enforcement of C's interest against B is not just the intention of A (which is the key to express trusts[68]) but B's agreement to hold property for C, whether leading A to die happy in the belief that C's interests were secure so that he need not take other steps to secure C's interests (*viz.* secret trusts) or leading C to carry out detrimental acts of reliance in relation to the property (*viz.* proprietary estoppel interest).

2–28   As a final point on the equitable doctrine it is important to realise that where certain interests are required to be registered or protected under the Land Charges Act 1972[69] or the Land Registration Act 1925[70] or the Companies Act 1985[71] on pain of a purchaser taking free from such

---

[61] *Hodgson v. Marks* [1971] Ch. 892 at 909; see inconsistency with *Dodds v. Hill* (1865) 2 H. & M. 424 endorsed in *Macmillan v. Bishopsgate (No. 3)* [1995] 3 All E.R. 747 at 773.

[62] *Rochefoucauld v. Boustead* [1897] 1 Ch. 196; *Bannister v. Banister* [1948] 2 All E.R. 133.

[63] *Hodgson v. Marks* [1971] 1 Ch. 892.

[64] [1948] 2 All E.R. 133 at 136.

[65] In the case of unregistered land or if the beneficiary is in actual occupation with an overriding interest in registered land.

[66] See *infra*, paras 2–96 *et seq.*

[67] See *infra*, paras 2–29 *et seq.*

[68] See Ford & Lee, *Principles of Law of Trusts* (2nd ed.) p. 239.

[69] *Hollington Bros Ltd v. Rhodes* [1951] 2 T.L.R. 691; *Miles v. Bull (No. 2)* [1969] 3 All E.R. 1585; *Midland Bank Trust Co. v. Green* [1981] A.C. 513; *Lloyds Bank plc v. Carrick* [1996] 4 All E.R. 630.

[70] *De Lusignan v. Johnson* (1973) 230 Est.Gaz. 499; *Freer v. Unwins Ltd* [1976] Ch. 288; *Williams & Glyn's Bank v. Boland* [1981] A.C. 487.

[71] *Re Monolithic Building Co.* [1915] 2 Ch. 643.

interests, it is not fraud for the purchaser merely to take advantage of his strict statutory rights by relying on the absence of the registration or protection stipulated for in the statute. It is fraud, however, if he positively misleads the interest owner to leave the interest unprotected.

EQUITABLE PROPRIETARY ESTOPPEL
(BY ACQUIESCENCE OR ENCOURAGEMENT)

If O encourages or acquiesces in X acting to his detriment in reliance on **2–29** the belief that O's property is X's property or that O has given or will give X the property or an interest therein, then, to prevent unconscionable behaviour, equity will estop O from asserting his full legal and beneficial ownership and from claiming that non-compliance with statutory requirements bars X's claim. Such estoppel gives rise to an equity in X's favour which may entitle him to an injunction against O[72] or an equitable lien[73] on O's property for X's expenditure[74] or for the value of X's improvements,[75] or to compensation for his loss,[76] or to a decree perfecting O's imperfect gift and ordering O to convey[77] or lease[78] land to X unconditionally or on payment of some money by X,[79] or grant X an easement[80] or a licence as long as X uses the premises as his private residence[81] or as long as X's loan is not repaid by O.[82]

Court of Appeal cases[83] indicate a cautious approach to ensure that X **2–30** should receive the minimum equity to do justice to him, having regard to the way in which he changed his position for the worse[84] by reason of the acquiescence and encouragement of O. As Walker LJ stated in *Gillett* v. *Holt*,[85]

---

[72] *Jackson* v. *Cator* (1800) 5 Ves. 688 or damages in lieu of an injunction: *Shaw* v. *Applegate* [1978] 1 All E.R. 123.

[73] Instead of a lien the Court may make the order for possession in favour of O conditional upon repayment to X of X's expenditure: *Dodsworth* v. *Dodsworth* (1973) 228 Est. Gaz. 1115.

[74] *Unity Joint Stock Mutual Banking Assoc.* v. *King* (1858) 25 Beav. 72; *Hussey* v. *Palmer* [1972] 1 W.L.R. 1286; *Morris* v. *Morris* [1982] 1 N.S.W.L.R. 61; *Lee-Parker* v. *Izzet (No. 2.)* [1972] 2 All E.R. 800 at 804–805.

[75] *Raffaele* v. *Raffaele* [1962] W.R. 238; (1963) 79 L.Q.R. 228 (D. E. Allan).

[76] *Baker* v. *Baker* (1993) 25 H.L.R. 408; *Burrows* v. *Sharp* (1989) 23 H.L.R. 82; *Gillett* v. *Holt* [2000] 3 W.L.R. 815.

[77] *Pascoe* v. *Turner* [1979] 1 W.L.R. 431; *Gillett* v. *Holt* [2000] 3 W.L.R. 815. X may even obtain O's residuary estate: *Re Basham* [1986] 1 W.L.R. 1498. If the land has been sold X will be entitled to its proceeds of sale: *Wayling* v. *Jones* (1993) 69 P. & C.R. 170.

[78] *Siew Soon Wah* v. *Yong Tong Hong* [1973] A.C. 836; *Griffiths* v. *Williams* (1977) 248 E.G. 947; *Taylor Fashions Ltd* v. *Liverpool Victoria Trustees Co.* [1982] Q.B. 133; *Yaxley* v. *Goffs* [2000] 1 All E.R. 11.

[79] *Lim Teng Huan* v. *Ang Swee Chin* [1992] 1 W.L.R. 113 (O ordered to convey his half share to X upon X paying him its value as bare land, X having built upon it.).

[80] *Ward* v. *Kirkland* [1967] Ch. 194; *Ives Investments Ltd* v. *High* [1967] 2 Q.B. 379; *Crabb* v. *Arun D.C.* [1976] Ch. 179.

[81] *Inwards* v. *Baker* [1965] 2 Q.B. 29; *Greasley* v. *Cooke* [1980] 1 W.L.R. 1306.

[82] *Re Sharpe* [1980] 1 W.L.R. 219.

[83] *Crabb* v. *Arun D.C.* [1976] Ch. 179; *Pascoe* v. *Turner* [1979] 1 W.L.R. 431; *Stedmore* v. *Dalby* 1996 72 P & CR 1961; *Baker* v. *Baker* (1993) 25 H.L.R. 408; *Gillett* v. *Holt* [2000] 3 W.L.R. 815.

[84] *Pascoe* v. *Turner* [1979] 2 All ER 945 at 950. "The person claiming must have incurred expenditure or otherwise have prejudiced himself or acted to his detriment," *per* Dunn L.J. in *Greasley* v. *Cooke* [1980] 1 W.L.R. 1306 at 1313–14.

[85] [2000] 2 All E.R. 289 at 308, on which see R. Wells [2000] Conv. 13. The Court of Appeal rejected the judge's view that a promise to leave property by will had to be irrevocable and required some mutual understanding as to the quid pro quo for the promise, and also criticised *Taylor* v. *Dickens* [1998] 1 FLR 806 for misplaced emphasis on irrevocability of such a promise.

"Detriment is required. But the authorities show that it is not a narrow or technical concept. The detriment need not consist of the expenditure of money or other quantifiable financial detriment, so long as it is something substantial. The requirement must be approached as part of a broad inquiry as to whether repudiation of an assurance is or is not unconscionable in all the circumstances . . . There must be sufficient causal link between the assurance relied on and the detriment asserted. The issue of detriment must be judged at the moment when the person who has given the assurance seeks to go back on it. Whether the detriment is sufficiently substantial is to be tested by whether it would be unjust or inequitable to allow the assurance to be disregarded—that is, again, the essential test of unconscionability. The detriment alleged must be pleaded and proved."

2–31   Once it is proved that the assurance was made and that there has been conduct by the claimant of such a nature that inducement may be inferred, then the burden of proof switches to the defendant to establish that the claimant did not rely on the assurance[86]

2–32   Originally, the courts regarded matters from O's viewpoint so that it was considered that O had to be at fault in some way before X could claim an equity. So, if O did not know the true position and so did not know of his right to object when he either acquiesced in or encouraged X's belief then O was not estopped from subsequently asserting his rights against X.[87] This may still be the position in cases of acquiescence where O has stood by without protest while his rights were being infringed at a time when he did not realise he had such rights.[88]

2–33   In cases of encouragement the courts now regard matters from X's viewpoint. Fault on O's part is no longer crucial: attention is focused on X's position and how unconscionable it would be if he were to suffer from O enforcing his strict legal rights once O had discovered his rights.[89] Indeed, a broad approach is suggested "directed at ascertaining whether, in particular circumstances it would be unconscionable for a party to be permitted to deny that which, knowingly or unknowingly, he has allowed or encouraged another to assume to his detriment."[90] Lord Browne-Wilkinson thus stated.[91]

"In order to found a proprietary estoppel it is not essential that the representor should have been guilty of unconscionable conduct in

---

[86] *Wayling v. Jones* (1999) 69 P & CR 170 at 173 endorsed in *Gillett v. Holt* [2000] 2 All E.R. 289 at 303.
[87] *Wilmot v. Barber* (1880) 15 Ch. D. 96; *Falcke v. Scottish Imperial Insurance Co.* (1886) 34 Ch.D. 234 at 243, 253; *Re Vandervell's Trusts (No. 2)* [1974] Ch. 269 at 300–301.
[88] *Taylor Fashions Ltd v. Liverpool Victoria Trustees Co.* [1982] Q.B. 133 at 147; *Amalgamated Investment & Property Co. v. Texas Commerce International Bank* [1982] Q.B. 84 at 104.
[89] *Ibid.* See also *McMahon v. Kerry C.C.* [1981] ILRM 419.
[90] *Taylor Fashions Ltd v. Liverpool Victoria Trustees Co.* [1982] Q.B. 133 at 151; approved in *Habib Bank Ltd v. Habib Bank A.G. Zurich* [1981] 2 All E.R. 650 at 666. Compare the approach to consents to breach of trust, *infra*, para. 10–79.
[91] *Lim Teng Huan v. Ang Swee Chin* [1992] 1 W.L.R. 113 at 117 overlooked in *Matharu v. Matharu* (1994) 68 P. & C.R. 93.

permitting the representee to assume that he could act as he did: it is enough if, in all the circumstances, it is unconscionable for the representor to go back on the assumption that he permitted the representee to make."

O's ignorance of the true position and of his strict rights is merely one of **2–34** the relevant factors in the overall inquiry. The court considers whether it would be unconscionable for O to insist on his strict legal rights, and if it would, then the court, taking into account *all circumstances to the date of the trial*,[92] qualifies, suspends or extinguishes those rights (perhaps on monetary terms) so far as necessary for X to receive the minimum equity to do justice to him.

In family property cases the courts are very ready to find that once X **2–35** acted detrimentally this was in reliance upon O's representation: once detriment is shown the burden falls on O to prove that X did not act in reliance on the representation.[93] In *Wayling v. Jones*[94] O and X lived together as homosexuals for 16 years before O died, X being a chef who, for less than full wages, helped O run his hotel business. After 10 years O promised to leave X the hotel in his will, and did so. Unfortunately that hotel was sold and a new one purchased but without O changing his will: hence the gift of the old hotel was adeemed when O died. The new hotel was sold and X claimed the proceeds of sale successfully, despite having answered "Yes" in cross-examination to the question, "If he had not made the promise to you, would you still have stayed?" thereby indicating that he stayed with O for low wages because he loved him and had not relied on any promise that the hotel would be his on O's death.

The Court of Appeal held that since O did make the promise and **2–36** since X in his evidence in chief had said that if O had then reneged on his promise he, X, would have left, this was sufficient to prevent O's executors from showing that X had not relied upon the promise. Thus, the court acted not on evidence of what the promisee actually did in reliance on the promise but on speculation as to what the promisee might have done, which is capable of rendering many a bare promise enforceable.[95] Hence, in a subsequent commercial case,[96] the Court of appeal held:

"The court can only decide a question of promissory estoppel on the evidence put before it of what the promisee did in reliance on

---

[92] *Willis v. Willis* (1986) 277 EG 1133; *Williams v. Staite* [1979] Ch. 291; For a proportionality approach over a lengthy period see *Stedmore v. Dalby* (1996) 72 P & CR 196.

[93] *Greasley v. Cooke* [1980] 1 W.L.R. 1306; *Coombes v. Smith* [1986] 1 W.L.R. 808; *Grant v. Edwards* [1986] Ch. 638; *Maharaj v. Chand* [1986] A.C. 898.

[94] (1993) 69 P. & C.R. 170 discussed by E. Cooke (1995) 111 L.Q.R. 389.

[95] Thus the woman in *Coombes v. Smith* [1986] 1 W.L.R. 808 should have established detrimental reliance because if her lover had told her he was reneging on his promise to her she would surely have left him because that would have wholly undermined their relationship. Further see the conjecture of Walter LJ in *Gillett v. Holt* [2000] 2 All ER 289 at 310 as to what the Gilletts would have done if Mr Holt told them he was not bound by his stated intentions, so they should not count their chickens before they hatched.

[96] *Meghraj Bank Ltd v. Arsiwalla*, February 10, 1994; discussed by E. Cooke, (1995) 111 L.Q.R. 389.

the promise rather than on speculation as to what the promisee might have done."

2–37   In its discretionary prevention of unconscionable conduct the court tailors the remedy to fit the wrong and so is not upholding crystallised rights of a proprietary nature.[97]

"The court's aim is, having identified the maximum [extent of the equity], to form a view as to what is the minimum required to satisfy it and do justice between the parties."[98] The minimum, from a narrow view of reversing or preventing detriment, is to compensate the claimant for his financial loss flowing from his reliance, while on a broad view the claimant should obtain what he expected so that no detriment results from the denial of the correctness of the assumption upon which he relied. The tendency for English[99] courts is to take the broader view[1] (the expectation basis and not the reliance basis) unless practical difficulties prevent fulfilment of expectations.[2]

2–38   The equity which arises by estoppel entitles the claimant to seek equitable relief from the court. If the court orders that a property interest be granted to him this takes effect from the date of the court's order,[3] so that if the claimant seeks to have his interest bind a third party (such as a mortgagee who knew of the claimant's claims when taking a mortgage from the defendant) he should join that party in the action. If the court considers that the conscience of such party was bound by the claimant's interest, the court order can also bind such party.[4] Since such party is bound in *personam* by such order it is then unnecessary to determine whether the claimant's inchoate interest amounted to a proprietary right capable of *in rem* effect against such party.

2–39   The right to rescind or rectify a conveyance for fraud or mistake amounts to a "mere equity" binding on a purchaser with notice of it or on a donee irrespective of notice.[5] The inchoate right to proprietary interest (a), failing which proprietary interest (b), failing which a compensation claim (preferably secured by a charge on the property) is, however, more flexible and less certain or stable than a right to rescind or rectify a conveyance. Once a writ is issued and a pending land action

---

[97] Meagher Gummow & Lehane, (3rd ed.) para 1724. Also see N. Hopkins, *The Informal Acquisition of Rights in Land*, Sweet & Maxwell (2000) at pp. 156–158

[98] *Gillett v. Holt* [2000] 2 All E.R. 289 at 312

[99] For Australian courts see *Waltons Stores Interstate Ltd v. Maher* (1987) 164 CLR 387; *Commonwealth v. Verwayen* 1990 170 CLR 394; *Giumelli v. Giumelli* (1999) 61 ALR 473.

[1] *Pascoe v. Turner* [1979] 1 W.L.R. 431; *Re Basham* [1986] 1 W.L.R. 1498; *Greasley v. Cooke* [1980] 1 W.L.R. 1306; *Wayling v. Jones* (1993) 69 P& CR 170. In *Gillet v. Holt* [2000] 2 All E.R. 289 at 308 Walker LJ endorsed the view of Dixon J in *Grundt v. Great Boulder Pty Ltd* (1937) 59 CLR 641, 674: "the basal purpose of the doctrine . . . is to avoid or prevent a detriment to the party asserting the estoppel by compelling the opposite party to adhere to the assumption upon which the former acted or abstained from acting. This means that the real detriment or harm from which the law seeks to give protection is that which would flow from the change of position if the assumption were deserted that led to it."

[2] *Dodsworth v. Dodsworth* (1973) 228 E.G. 1115; *Baker v. Baker* 1993 2 FLR 247.

[3] *Griffiths v. Williams* [1978] 1 EGLR 121 at 123; *Williams v. Staite* 1979 Ch 291 at 300, 301

[4] *Ashburn Anstalt v. Arnold* [1989] Ch 1

[5] See Megarry & Wade, *Real Property*, (6th ed. by C. Harpum) paras 5–012, 13–031.

arises it requires registration under the Land Charges Act 1972 (in the case of unregistered land) or it will not bind a purchaser unless he had express notice of it,[6] so that proprietary consequences affect such a purchaser. Perhaps, the implication is that there are no proprietary consequences for estoppel claims until formulated in a writ occasioning a greater measure of certainty than oral claims or convoluted claims in correspondence. For registered land, proprietary rights of actual occupiers are protected as overriding interests,[7] but the problem is whether inchoate estoppel claims (not formulated in legal proceedings instituted by writ) are such rights.

Obiter dicta leave the position unclear, although revealing a trend to **2–40** assume estoppel claims to interests in land are of a proprietary nature.[8] It is suggested the better view is that a purchaser, P, of a legal interest in the land (*e.g.* a mortgage) before X registered a pending action in respect of the land should take free of X's uncertain discretionary claim, unless X has some independent *in personan* claim against P by virtue of some representation or agreement involving X and P which makes it unconscionable for P personally to deny X's claim or by virtue of some blameworthy behaviour of P which prevented X from being able to take steps to protect herself, as discussed *infra*, paras 6–116, 117, 123.

IMPORTANCE OF FORMAL REQUIREMENTS

The validity and consequences of a transaction may depend on com- **2–41** pliance with a particular form. Through not having used the requisite formalities a man, like Mr. Vandervell, may find that he has not divested himself of all interest in property settled by him so as to be liable to a large amount of tax he had intended to avoid.[10] If a disposition can be effected orally then no stamp duty will be payable: stamp duty is payable on *instruments* (physically capable of being impressed with a stamp) transferring property or interests in property and so will be escaped if the transfer is effected orally and a subsequent written instrument merely records this for the benefit of the trustees. Section 82 of the Finance Act 1985 now makes conveyances or transfers by way of gift no longer subject to ad valorem duty if made after March 25, 1985.

If stamp duty were reintroduced on such conveyances or transfers **2–42** account would need to be taken of a recently developed far-reaching principle against tax avoidance. As Lord Oliver stated in *Craven v. White*:[11]

---

[6] s.5(7) LCA 1972

[7] s.70(1) (g) Land Registration Act 1925

[8] See *Lloyds Bank v. Carrick* [1996] 4 All ER 630 at 642, *Inwards v. Baker* [1965] 2QB 29 at 37, *Ives Investment Ltd v. High* [1967] 2 QB 379 at 400,405, *Voyce v. Voyce* (1991) 62 P & CR 290 at 244, 246; but cp *United Bank of Kuwait plc v. Sahib* [1997] Ch 107 at 142 and *Habermann v. Koehler* (1996) 73 P & CR 515. Further, see N. Hopkins, *The Informal Acquisition of Rights in Land*, Sweet & Maxwell (2000), at 150–155.

[10] *Vandervell v. I.R.C.* [1967] 2 A.C. 291.

[11] [1989] A.C. 398, 514. Further see *Fitzwilliam v. IRC* [1993] 1 W.L.R. 1189 and *IRC v. McGuckian* [1997] 3 All E.R. 817.

"The essentials emerging from *Furniss v. Dawson* [1984] A.C. 474 appear to me to be four in number (1) that the series of transactions was, at the time when the intermediate transaction was entered into, pre-ordained in order to produce a given result; (2) that that transaction had no other purpose than tax mitigation; (3) that there was at that time no practical likelihood that the preplanned events would not take place in the order ordained, so that the intermediate transaction was not even contemplated practically as having an independent life, and (4) that the pre-ordained events did in fact take place. In these circumstances the court can be justified in linking the beginning with the end so as to make a single composite whole to which the fiscal results of the single composite whole are to be applied."

EXAMPLES OF APPLICATION OF FORMALITIES

2–43 T1 and T2 hold property on trust for A absolutely in the following five examples:

(1) *A declares that he is to hold his equitable interest on trust either for B for life, remainder to C or for such of L to Z as he or T1 and T2 may appoint.* Here A remains in the picture with active trust duties so this is a declaration of trust where the declaration may be oral if the property is pure personalty but must be evidenced in writing within section 53(1)(b) if the property is land.[12]

(2) *A declares himself trustee of his interest for D absolutely.* Whilst superficially a declaration of trust requiring only compliance with section 53(1)(b) if the property is land, this probably amounts to a disposition of A's entire equitable interest which must itself be in writing within section 53(1)(c) whether the property is land or pure personality.[13] After all, A is a simple bare trustee with no active duties to perform, (having, essentially, made himself an agent for D), so that he should drop out of the picture, T1 and T2 now holding for D instead of A: by A's action A's equitable interest has passed to D who can directly enforce his rights against T1 and T2 merely joining A as a co-defendant to the action.[14]

2–44 (3) *A directs T1 and T2 to transfer the property to E absolutely for E's own benefit.* Here, the transfer of the legal title to E automatically carries with it the equitable interest so that there is no separate disposition by A of his equitable interest that requires compliance with section 53(1)(c):

---

[12] *Onslow v. Wallis* (1849) 1 Mac. & G. 506 approved in *Re Lashmar* [1891] 1 Ch. 253.

[13] *Grainge v. Wilberforce* (1889) 5 TLR 436, 437; *Re Lashmar* [1891] 1 Ch 253; *Grey v. I.R.C.* [1958] Ch. 375 at 382, *per* Upjohn J. [1958] Ch. 690 at 715, *per* Evershed M.R. *cf.* a tenant's purported sub-lease for the residue of his lease taking effect as an assignment: Megarry & Wade, *Law of Real Property* (6th ed.), para 14–110. Where A's equitable interest is in a pool of shares held by a financial intermediary and he declares himself trustee thereof for D (or sells his interest to D) see at para. 3–91 *infra*.

[14] Brian Green in (1984) 47 M.L.R. 385 at 396–399 prefers the declaration to be treated as a sub-trust carving out a subsidiary equitable entitlement in B's favour out of A's original equitable interest but he goes on to submit that it should fall within s.53(1)(c) as a part disposal of A's equitable interest, a disposal of the beneficial part of A's bundle of hitherto subsisting equitable rights.

Vandervell v. I.R.C. set out *infra*, at para 2–64. This is commercially convenient, *e.g.* where a stockbroker or bank as nominee holds shares for A and A directs the shares to be transferred to E it would be most inconvenient for signed writing to be required of A in addition to that of the legal transferor. However, the reasoning is not very satisfactory because in the case of a transfer by the legal and beneficial[15] owner the beneficial interest is merged or subsumed in the legal interest, whereas when T holds the legal title on trust for A the legal and equitable interests are obviously separated and the issue is whether they can be joined without a separate assignment or surrender by A, so that the beneficial interest is then at home with the legal interest in T and so capable of transfer by T to E.

The position may be better justified on the basis that where T does **2–45** transfer the legal title to E at the instigation of or with the concurrence of A, then A cannot claim there has been a breach of trust and assert his equitable interest against the new legal owner, E, so that by operation of law outside section 53(1)(c) A's equitable interest is extinguished, just as much as it would have been extinguished if A in signed writing had expressly surrendered his equitable interest to T so that T might then pass the legal, and thus therewith the beneficial, interest to E.[15a]

On either basis it is the transfer to E that is crucial so it would seem **2–46** that if before then A revoked his direction to T, then A would remain entitled to the equitable interest and E could not in law complain about the promised gift not materialising. In the case of shares (or registered land) the legal title is not actually transferred till the transferee becomes registered as owner (or the relevant documents are delivered to the appropriate District Land Registry) but equity treats the transfer as complete when the transferor has done everything necessary to be done by him,[16] *e.g.* delivery of the share or land certificate and the transfer form to the transferee. Pragmatically, it is likely that once A asks T to do such acts A will not be allowed to revoke his gift and claim that E on becoming registered owner holds the property on trust for A.[17]

(4) *A directs T1 and T2 to hold the property on trust for F absolutely.* This is a disposition of A's equitable interest and so must be in writing within section 53(1)(*c*): *Grey v. I.R.C.* set out *infra* para. 2–51. After all, as a result of A's direction T1 and T2 hold on trust for F instead of A, so A has been responsible for his equitable interest passing from himself to F.[18]

---

[15] No separate equitable interest subsists where A is sole legal beneficial owner: *Westdeutsche landesbank v. Islington BC* [1996] AC 669, 706.

[15a] See S. M. Spencer (1967) 31 Conv. 175; G. Battersby [1979] Conv. 17. If A had directed the trustees to transfer the property to E to hold on trust for X then this is likely to be a disposition of A's subsisting equitable interest to X: see *supra* n. 32, para. 2–16.

[16] *Re Rose* [1952] Ch. 499, *infra* para. 4–06.

[17] B. Green (1984) 47 M.L.R. 385 at 410, and see *infra*, n. 37, para. 2–67.

[18] An exception from the *Grey v. I.R.C.* principle is implicit in *Re Bowden* [1936] Ch. 31 and *Re Adlard* [1954] Ch. 29 on which see para. 4–34. No writing seems required where S has executed a voluntary "S" settlement and therein covenanted to transfer to his trustee (*e.g.* Lloyds Bank) after-acquired

2–47   If T1 and T2 held the property on trust for A until A *or the trustees* appointed the property amongst such of C to Z as might be seen fit, then such appointment by the trustees in favour of F absolutely would not be "a disposition of an equitable interest subsisting at the time of the disposition" within section 53(1)(*c*), but the creation of a new interest automatically extinguishing A's formerly subsisting equitable interest.[19] If, however, A, and not the trustees, appointed in favour of F absolutely this would seem a disposition of A's subsisting equitable interest since by virtue of A's act it passes from him to F. As Viscount Simonds stated in *Grey v. I.R.C.*,[20] "If the word 'disposition' is given its natural meaning it cannot be denied that a direction given by Mr. Hunter [the settlor-beneficiary] whereby the beneficial interest theretofore vested to him became vested in another is a disposition." However, in *obiter dicta* Lord Denning[21] seems to suggest that if T1 and T2 held property on a resulting trust for A until A or the trustees appointed new trusts then an appointment *by A* or the trustees should be treated as the creation of a new interest, A's equitable interest (under the resulting trust arising to plug the gap in the beneficial ownership) automatically ceasing "as soon as the gap is filled by the creation or declaration of a valid trust."[22] These dicta seem unsound where the appointment is by A: in *Re Vandervell's Trusts (No. 2)* it was surely only because *the trustees* made the appointment that there was created a valid trust to displace the resulting trust as emphasised by Stephenson L.J.

2–48   (5) *A contracts with G to transfer his equitable interest to G.* If A's equitable interest is in land, whether or not held on trust for sale, then all the terms of the contract must be in writing as required by section 2 of Law of Property (Miscellaneous Provisions) Act 1989. Otherwise, it seems writing is not required. Certainly, a contract to make a disposition of an equitable interest does not seem itself to be a disposition. However, it can be said that the constructive trusteeship imposed upon A when he enters into a specifically enforceable contract[23] to sell his equitable interest to G means that T1 and T2 hold on trust for A who

---

property appointed to him under the "T" trust or bequeathed to him under T's will and Lloyds Bank becomes trustee of the "T" trust or of T's will when property is appointed or bequeathed to S (giving S an equitable interest) and S authorises Lloyds Bank *qua* trustee of the "T" trust or of T's will to hold the property *qua* trustee of the "S" trust. Where CREST enables title to securities to be evidenced and transferred electronically without a written instrument (pursuant to Companies Act 1989, s.207) Regulation 32(5) of the Uncertificated Securities Regulations provides "sections 53(1)(c) and 136 of the Law of the Property Act 1925 shall not apply (if they otherwise would do so) to (a) any transfer of title to uncertificated units of a security through a relevant system and (b) any disposition or assignment of an interest in uncertificated units of a security, title to which is held by a relevant nominee."

[19] *Re Vandervell's Trusts (No. 2)* [1974] Ch. 269, see *infra*, at para. 2–68, criticised on its estoppel grounds by Brian Green, *infra*, at para. 2–88.
[20] [1960] A.C. 1 at 12.
[21] *Re Vandervell's Trusts (No. 2)* [1974] Ch. 269 at 320.
[22] One cannot restrict Lord Denning's views to equitable interests under *resulting* trusts, falling outside s.53(1)(*c*): equitable interests under *express* trusts are similarly displaced by the creation of new valid trusts. In *Re Tyler's Fund Trusts* [1967] 3 All E.R. 389, 391–392, Pennycuick J. applied s.53(1)(*c*) to an equitable interest under a resulting trust. In *Oughtred v. I.R.C.* [1960] A.C. 206 at 253, Lord Denning considered s.53(1)(*c*) to apply to an equitable interest under a constructive trust which falls under s.53(2) like a resulting trust.
[23] See *infra*, at para. 6–204.

holds on constructive trust for G so that if A is or becomes (after receipt of the purchase price) a simple bare trustee with no active duties to perform he disappears from the picture leaving T1 and T2 holding on trust for G. Thus A has disposed of his equitable interest and this requires writing within section 53(1)(c).[24]

Against such a conclusion is section 53(2) which states that section **2–49** 53(1) is not to affect the creation or operation of constructive trusts so that without the need for any section 53(1)(c) writing G becomes owner of the equitable interest due to the constructive trust in his favour: this view has been taken by Upjohn J.,[25] Lord Radcliffe,[26] Megarry J.[27] and by Goff and Shaw L.JJ,[28] and has been held correct by the Court of Appeal in *Neville v. Wilson*,[29] infra at para. 2–54. In any event as Lord Cohen has indicated[30] once G had paid the purchase price to A, A would not be able to put forward successfully any claim to the equitable interest. Furthermore, A's self-interested trusteeship in ensuring the contract is observed and the purchase price paid to him means that when the contract is first made he is not a simple bare trustee with no active duties so that the constructive trust in G's favour is a true sub-trust outside section 53(1)(c). The position is analogous to the case where A declares a sub-trust of his equitable interest for S for one month, remainder to T absolutely (outside section 53(1)(c)) and after a month S's interest automatically ceases and by operation of law T becomes full beneficial owner (outside section 53(1)(c)).

In *Chinn v. Collins* the House of Lords regarded the availability of **2–50** specific performance and the creation of a constructive trust immaterial in a case concerned with non-specifically enforceable contractual dealings relating to an equitable interest in shares (in an English public company held by an English private company as nominee for a Guernsey trustee). Lord Wilberforce asserted,[31] "Dealings related to the equitable interest in these [shares] required no formality. As soon as there was an agreement for their sale accompanied or followed by payment of the price, the equitable title passed at once to the purchaser and all that was needed to perfect his title was notice to the trustee or the nominee."[32]

GREY, V. INLAND REVENUE COMMISSIONERS

House of Lords [1960] A.C. 1; [1959] 3 W.L.R. 759; 103 S.J 896; [1959] 3 All **2–51** E.R. 603; [1959] T.R. 311 (Viscount Simonds, Lords Radcliffe, Cohen, Keith of Avonholm and Reid)

---

[24] See Lord Denning in *Oughtred v. I.R.C.* [1960] A.C. 206 at 233. Stamp duty may then be payable under Stamp Act 1891, s.59(1).
[25] *Oughtred v. I.R.C.* [1958] Ch. 383.
[26] *Oughtred v. I.R.C.* [1960] A.C. 206 at 227–228.
[27] *Re Holt's Settlement* [1969] 1 Ch. 100.
[28] *DHN Food Distributors Ltd v. Tower Hamlets London Borough Council* [1976] 1 W.L.R. 852 at 865,867.
[29] [1997] Ch. 144
[30] *Oughtred v. I.R.C.* [1960] A.C. 206 at 230.
[31] [1981] A.C. 533 at 548 without giving reasons, though the emphasis on payment of the price indicates support for Lord Cohen's view in *Oughtred, supra*. The other Law Lords agreed with him.
[32] Under the rule in *Dearle v. Hall* (1828) 3 Russ. 1 the first assignee to give notice of the dealing with the equitable interest to the trustee takes priority over other assignees.

On February 1, Mr. Hunter, as settlor, transferred 18,000 shares of £1 each to the appellants as nominees for himself. The appellants were the trustees of six settlements, which Mr. Hunter had previously created. On February 18, 1955, Mr. Hunter orally directed the trustees to divide the 18,000 shares into six parcels of 3,000 shares each and to appropriate the parcels to the trusts of the six settlements, one parcel to each settlement.

On March 25, 1955, the trustees executed six deeds of declaration of trust (which Mr. Hunter also executed in order to testify to the oral direction previously given by him) declaring that since February 18, 1955, they held each of the parcels of 3,000 shares on the trusts of the relevant settlement. The Commissioners of Inland Revenue assessed the deeds of declaration of trust to *ad valorem* stamp duty on the basis that the oral declaration did not effectively create trusts of the shares so that it was the subsequent deeds that created trusts of the shares and were stampable as instruments transferring an interest in property: they were not exempt as merely confirming an earlier effective transfer. The trustees appealed against this view upheld by a majority in the Court of Appeal.

2–52   LORD RADCLIFFE: "My Lords, if there is nothing more in this appeal than the short question whether the oral direction that Mr. Hunter gave to his trustees on February 18, 1955, amounted in any ordinary sense of the words to a 'disposition of an equitable interest or trust subsisting at the time of the disposition,' I do not feel any doubt as to my answer. I think that it did. Whether we describe what happened in technical or in more general terms, the full equitable interest in the eighteen thousand shares concerned, which at that time was his, was (subject to any statutory invalidity) diverted by his direction from his ownership into the beneficial ownership of the various equitable owners, present and future, entitled under his six existing settlements . . .

2–53   "In my opinion, it is a very nice question whether a parol declaration of trust of this kind was or was not within the mischief of section 9 of the Statute of Frauds. The point has never, I believe, been decided and perhaps it never will be. Certainly it was long established as law that while a declaration of trust respecting land or any interest therein required writing to be effective a declaration of trust respecting personalty did not. Moreover, there is warrant for saying that a direction to his trustee by the equitable owner of trust property prescribing new trusts of that property was a declaration of trust. But it does not necessarily follow from that that such a direction, if the effect of it was to determine completely or *pro tanto* the subsisting equitable interest of the maker of the direction, was not also a grant or assignment for the purposes of section 9 and therefore required writing for its validity. Something had to happen to that equitable interest in order to displace it in favour of the new interests created by the direction: and it would be at any rate logical to treat the direction as being an assignment of the subsisting interest to the new beneficiary or beneficiaries or, in other cases, a release or surrender of it to the trustee.

"I do not think, however, that that question has to be answered for the purposes of this appeal. It can only be relevant if section 53(1) of the Law of Property Act 1925 is treated as a true consolidation of the three sections of the Statute of Frauds concerned and as governed, therefore, by the general principle, with which I am entirely in agreement, that a consolidating Act is not to be read as effecting changes in the existing law unless the words it employs are too clear in their effect to admit of any other construction. But, in my opinion, it is impossible to regard section 53 of the Law of Property Act 1925 as a consolidating enactment in this sense."[33] *Appeal dismissed.*

NEVILLE V WILSON

Court of Appeal [1997] Ch. 144, [1996] 3 W.L.R. 460, [1996] 3 All ER 171 **2–54**
(Nourse, Rose and Aldous L.JJ)

NOURSE L.J.: "We are therefore of the opinion that in about April 1969 the shareholders of JEN entered into an agreement with one another for the informal liquidation of JEN as contended for by Mr Jacob and thus, as part of it, for the division of JEN's equitable interest in the 120 ordinary shares in UEC registered in the names of the widow and Mr Wilson amongst themselves, as Mr Hyde put it, 'on a shareholding basis'; in other words, in proportions correspond-ing to their existing shareholdings. . . . In consequence, JEN's equitable interest in the shares would, as the plaintiffs now claim, be divided amongst the shareholders in the proportions: 104 for the trustees of the will of the testator, and 4 each for the widow, Mr Neville, Mrs Hill and Mrs Wilson.

The effect of the agreement, more closely analysed, was that each shareholder **2–55** agreed to assign his interest in the other shares of JEN's equitable interest in exchange for the assignment by the other shareholders of their interests in his own aliquot share. Each individual agreement having been a disposition of a subsisting equitable interest not made in writing, there then arises the question whether it was rendered ineffectual by s 53 of the Law of Property Act 1925 . . .

The simple view of the present case is that the effect of each individual **2–56** agreement was to constitute the shareholder an implied or constructive trustee for the other shareholders, so that the requirement for writing contained in sub-s (1)(c) of s 53 was dispensed with by sub-s (2). That was the view taken by Upjohn J at first instance and by Lord Radcliffe in the House of Lords in *Oughtred v IRC*. In order to see whether it is open to us to adopt it in this court, we must give careful consideration to those views and to the other speeches in the House of Lords.

In *Oughtred v IRC* [1960] AC 206 a mother and son were the tenant for life **2–57** and absolute reversioner respectively under a settlement of shares in a private company. By an oral agreement made on 18 June 1956 they agreed that on 26 June the son would exchange his reversionary interest under the settlement for shares in the same company owned by the mother absolutely, to the intent that her life interest in the settled shares should be enlarged into an absolute interest. On 26 June the mother and the son released the trustees by a deed which recited, amongst other things, that the settled shares were "accordingly now held in trust for [the mother] absolutely", and that it was intended to transfer them to her. On the same day the trustees transferred the settled shares to the mother by deed, the consideration being expressed to be ten shillings. It was held by Lord Keith of Avonholm, Lord Denning and Lord Jenkins, (Lord Radcliffe and Lord Cohen dissenting), that the transfer was assessable to ad valorem stamp duty.

---

[33] Would *ad valorem* stamp duty have been avoided if (1) H had orally declared himself trustee of the shares on trust for his grandchildren; (2) H had retired as trustee in favour of the trustees of the six settlements, legal title to the shares being transferred to such trustees by instrument bearing fixed 50p duty; (3) the trustees later signed an instrument recording they hold the shares on specified trusts declared earlier by H?

The basis of decision adopted by the majority was that, even if the oral agreement was effective to pass the equitable interest in the settled shares to the mother, the transfer, as the instrument by which the transaction was completed, was none the less a conveyance on sale within s 54 of the Stamp Act 1891.

2–58   Upjohn J, having said that s 53(2) of the 1925 Act was a complete answer to the argument that s 53(1)(c) applied, continued ([1958] Ch 383 at 390):

> "This was an oral agreement for value, and, accordingly, on the making thereof Peter the vendor became a constructive trustee of his equitable reversionary interest in the trust funds for the appellant. No writing to achieve that result was necessary, for an agreement of sale and purchase of an equitable interest in personalty (other than chattels real) may be made orally, and s 53 has no application to a trust arising by construction of law."

Lord Radcliffe, having expressed the view that the judgment of Upjohn J was correct and agreeing with his reasons, said ([1959] 3 All ER 623 at 625, [1960] AC 206 at 227):

> "The reasoning of the whole matter, as I see it, is as follows: On June 18, 1956, the son owned an equitable reversionary interest in the settled shares; by his oral agreement of that date he created in his mother an equitable interest in his reversion, since the subject-matter of the agreement was property of which specific performance would normally be decreed by the court. He thus became a trustee for her of that interest sub modo; having regard to sub-s. (2) of s 53 of the Law of Property Act, 1925, sub-s. (1) of that section did not operate to prevent that trusteeship arising by operation of law."

2–59   Lord Cohen, the other member of the minority, said ([1960] AC 206 at 230):

> "Before your Lordships, counsel for the Crown was prepared to agree that, on the making of the oral agreement, Peter became a constructive trustee of his equitable reversionary interest in the settled funds for the appellant, but he submitted that, none the less, s. 53(1)(c) applied and, accordingly, Peter could not assign that equitable interest to the appellant except by a disposition in writing. My Lords, with that I agree, but it does not follow that the transfer was a conveyance of that equitable interest on which ad valorem stamp duty was payable under the Stamp Act, 1891."

Having held that the transfer was not such a conveyance, he dissented on that ground.

2–60   Lord Denning said [1960] AC 206 at 233):

> "I do not think it necessary to embark on a disquisition on constructive trusts; because I take the view that, even if the oral agreement of June 18, 1956, was effective to transfer Peter's reversionary interest to his mother, nevertheless, when that oral agreement was subsequently implemented by the transfer, then the transfer became liable to stamp duty. But I may say that I do not think the oral agreement was effective to transfer Peter's reversionary interest to his mother. I should have thought that the wording

of s. 53(1)(c) of the Law of Property Act, 1925, clearly made a writing necessary to effect a transfer, and s. 53(2) does not do away with that necessity."

The views of their Lordships as to the effect of s 53 can be summarised as **2–61** follows. Lord Radcliffe, agreeing with Upjohn J, thought that sub-s (2) applied. He gave reasons for that view. Lord Cohen and Lord Denning thought that it did not. Although neither of them gave reasons, they may be taken to have accepted the submissions of Mr Wilberforce QC (see [1960] AC 206 at 220–222). Lord Keith and Lord Jenkins expressed no view either way. We should add that when the case was in this court, Lord Evershed MR, in delivering the judgment of himself, Morris and Ormerod LJJ, said [1958] Ch 678 at 687):

> "In this court the case for the Crown has, we think, been somewhat differently presented, and in the end of all, the question under s. 53 of the Law of Property Act [1925] does not, in our judgment, strictly call for a decision. We are not, however, with all respect to the learned judge, prepared to accept, as we understand it, his conclusion on the effect of s. 53 of the Law of Property Act."

The basis of this court's decision was the same as that adopted by the majority of the House of Lords.

We do not think that there is anything in the speeches in the House of Lords **2–62** which prevents us from holding that the effect of each individual agreement was to constitute the shareholder an implied or constructive trustee for the other shareholders. In this respect we are of the opinion that the analysis of Lord Radcliffe, based on the proposition that a specifically enforceable agreement to assign an interest in property creates an equitable interest in the assignee, was unquestionably correct (cf *London and South Western Rly Co v Gomm* (1882) 20 Ch D 562 at 581 per Jessel MR). A greater difficulty is caused by Lord Denning's outright rejection of the application of s 53(2), with which Lord Cohen appears to have agreed.

So far as it is material to the present case, what sub-s (2) says is that sub-s (1)(c) does not affect the creation or operation of implied or constructive trusts. Just as in *Oughtred v IRC* the son's oral agreement created a constructive trust in favour of the mother, so here each shareholder's oral or implied agreement created an implied or constructive trust in favour of the other shareholders. Why then should sub-s (2) not apply? No convincing reason was suggested in argument and none has occurred to us since. Moreover, to deny its application in this case would be to restrict the effect of general words when no restriction is called for, and to lay the ground for fine distinctions in the future. With all the respect which is due to those who have thought to the contrary, we hold that sub-s (2) applies to an agreement such as we have in this case.

For these reasons, we have come to the conclusion that the agreement entered **2–63** into by the shareholders of JEN in about April 1969 was not rendered ineffectual by s 53 of the 1925 Act."

VANDERVELL V. INLAND REVENUE COMMISSIONERS

House of Lords [1967] 2 A.C. 291 [1967] 2 W.L.R. 97 [1967] 1 All ER 1 (Lords **2–64** Pearce, Upjohn and Wilberforce; Lords Reid and Donovan dissenting)

The detailed facts appear in the judgment of Lord Denning M.R. in *Re Vandervell's Trusts (No. 2)* set out *infra* para. 2–68.

The following extracts from the speeches in the House of Lords concern the point whether the transfer by the bare trustee of the legal title to shares carried with it the equitable interest of the taxpayer beneficiary without any separate written disposition by him.

LORD UPJOHN: ". . . the object of the section, as was the object of the old Statute of Frauds, is to prevent hidden oral transactions in equitable interests in fraud of those truly entitled, and making it difficult, if not impossible, for the trustees to ascertain who are in truth the beneficiaries. When the beneficial owner, however, owns the whole beneficial estate and is in a position to give directions to his bare trustee with regard to the legal as well as the equitable estate there can be no possible ground for invoking the section where the beneficial owner wants to deal with the legal estate as well as the equitable estate.

2–65   "I cannot agree with Diplock L.J. that prima facie a transfer of the legal estate carries with it the absolute beneficial interest in the property transferred; this plainly is not so, *e.g.* the transfer may be on a change of trustee; it is a matter of intention in each case. If, however, the intention of the beneficial owner in directing the trustee to transfer the legal estate to X is that X should be the beneficial owner, I can see no reason for any further document or further words in the document assigning the legal estate also expressly transferring the beneficial interest; the greater includes the less. X may be wise to secure some evidence that the beneficial owner intended him to take the beneficial interest in case his beneficial title is challenged at a later date but it certainly cannot, in my opinion, be a statutory requirement that to effect its passing there must be some writing under section 53(1)(c).

2–66   "Counsel for the Crown admitted that where the legal and beneficial estate was vested in the legal owner and he desired to transfer the whole legal and beneficial estate to another he did not have to do more than transfer the legal estate and he did not have to comply with section 53(1)(c); and I can see no difference between that case and this.

"As I have said, that section is, in my opinion, directed to cases where dealings with the equitable estate are divorced from the legal estate and I do not think any of their Lordships in *Grey v. I.R.C.*[34] and *Oughtred v. I.R.C.*[35] had in mind the case before your Lordships. To hold the contrary would make assignments unnecessarily complicated; if there had to be assignments in express terms of both legal and equitable interests that would make the section more productive of injustice than the supposed evils it was intended to prevent . . ."

2–67   LORD WILBERFORCE: ". . . On November 14, 1958, the taxpayer's solicitor received from the bank a blank transfer of the shares, executed by the bank, and the share certificate. So at this stage the taxpayer was the absolute master of the shares and only needed to insert his name as transferee in the transfer and to register it to become the full legal owner. He was also the owner in equity. On November 19, 1958, the solicitor . . . on behalf of the taxpayer, who intended to make a gift, handed the transfer to the College, which in due course, sealed it

---

[34] [1960] A.C. 1.
[35] [1960] A.C. 206.

and obtained registration of the shares in the College's name. The case should then be regarded as one in which the taxpayer himself has, with the intention to make a gift, put the College in a position to become the legal owner of the shares, which the College in fact became. If the taxpayer had died before the College had obtained registration, it is clear on the principle of *Re Rose*[36] that the gift would have been complete, on the basis that he had done everything in his power to transfer the legal interest, with an intention to give, to the College. No separate transfer, therefore, of the equitable interest ever came to or needed to be made and there is no room for the operation of the subsection. What the position would have been had there simply been an oral direction to the legal owner (*viz.* the bank) to transfer the shares to the College, followed by such a transfer, but without any document in writing signed by the taxpayer as equitable owner, is not a matter which calls for consideration here . . ."[37]

RE VANDERVELL'S TRUSTS (NO. 2)

Court of Appeal [1974] Ch. 269; [1974] 3 All E.R. 205 [1973] 3 W.L.R. 744 (Lord Denning M.R., Stephenson and Lawton L.JJ.)

LORD DENNING M.R.: "During his lifetime Mr. Vandervell was a very **2–68** successful engineer. He had his own private company—Vandervell Products Ltd—'the products company,' as I will call it—in which he owned virtually all the shares. It was in his power to declare dividends as and when he pleased. In 1949 he set up a trust for his children. He did it by forming Vandervell Trustees Ltd— 'the trustee company,' as I will call it. He put three of his friends and advisers in control of it. They were the sole shareholders and directors of the trustee company. Two were chartered accountants. The other was his solicitor. He transferred money and shares to the trustee company to be held in trust for the children. Such was the position at the opening of the first period.

The first period: 1958–61

"The first period covers the three years from October 1958 to October 1961. **2–69** Mr. Vandervell decided to found a chair of pharmacology at the Royal College of Surgeons. He was to endow it by providing £150,000. But he did not do it by a direct gift. In November 1958 he transferred to the Royal College of Surgeons 100,000 'A' shares in his products company. His intention was that his products company should declare dividends in favour of the Royal College of Surgeons which would amount in all to £150,000 or more. But, when that sum had been provided, he wanted to be able to regain the shares—so as to use the dividends for other good purposes. So, about the time of the transfer, on December 1, 1958, he got the Royal College of Surgeons to grant an option to the trustee company. By this option the Royal College of Surgeons agreed to transfer the 100,000 'A' shares to the trustee company for the sum of £5,000 at any time on

---

[36] [1949] Ch. 78; *post*, para. 4–06. However, in *Re Rose* the taxpayer was entitled legally and equitably to the shares and did all he could to transfer them by executing a share transfer and delivering the transfer and the share certificate to the donee. Vandervell was only equitably entitled and to say that he had done all he could to vest the shares in the College is to beg the s.53(1)(c) question of what was required of an owner of a subsisting equitable interest to achieve a disposition of that interest in the first place.

[37] See N. Strauss (1967) 30 M.L.R. 461; Gareth Jones [1966] C.L.J. 19–25; S. M. Spencer (1967) 31 Conv.(N.S.) 175–181; B. Green (1984) 47 M.L.R. 385, 410.

request within the next five years. (This £5,000 was far less than the real value of the shares.) At the time when the option was granted, Mr. Vandervell did not state definitely the trusts on which the trustee company was to hold the option. He meant the trustee company to hold the option on trust—not beneficially for itself—but on trust for someone or other. He did not specify the trusts with any kind of precision. But at a meeting with the chairman of the trustee company it was proposed—and Mr. Vandervell approved—that the option should be held *either* on trust for his children (as an addition to the children's settlement) *or* alternatively on trust for the employees of his products company. He had not made up his mind which of those should benefit. But one thing he was clear about. He thought that he himself had parted with all interest in the shares and in the option. Afterwards, during the years from 1958 to 1961, he saw to it that his products company declared dividends on these 100,000 shares which were paid to the Royal College of Surgeons. They amounted to £266,000 gross (before tax), or £157,000 net (after tax). So the Royal College of Surgeons received ample funds to found the Chair of Pharmacology.

2–70   "But there were other advantages hoped for. The Royal College of Surgeons thought that, being a charity, they could claim back the tax from the Revenue. And Mr. Vandervell thought that, having parted with all interest in the shares, he was not subject to pay surtax on these dividends. The Revenue authorities, however, did not take that view. They claimed that Mr. Vandervell had not divested himself of all interest in the shares. They argued that he was the beneficial owner of the option and liable for surtax on the dividends. Faced with this demand, in October 1961, the trustee company, on the advice of counsel, and with the full approval of Mr. Vandervell, decided to exercise the option. It did it so as to avoid any question of surtax thereafter being payable by Mr. Vandervell. This ended the first period (when the option was in being) and started the second period (after the option was exercised).

The second period: 1961–65

2–71   "In October 1961 the trustee company exercised the option. It did it by using the money of the children's settlement. It paid £5,000 of the children's money to the Royal College of Surgeons. In return the Royal College of Surgeons, on October 27, 1961 transferred the 100,000 'A' shares to the trustee company. The intention of Mr. Vandervell and of the trustee company was that the trustee company should hold the shares (which had replaced the option) on trust for the children as an addition to the children's settlement. The trustee company made this clear to the Revenue authorities in an important letter written by its solicitors on November 2, 1961, which I will read:

> *"G.A. Vandervell, Esq.—Surtax*
>
> 'Further to our letter of the 7th September last, we write to inform you that in accordance with the advice tendered by Counsel to Vandervell Trustees Ltd, the latter have exercised the option granted to them by the Royal College of Surgeons of the 1st December 1958, and procured a transfer to them of the shares referred to in the option, with funds held by them upon the trusts of the Settlement created by Mr. G. A. Vandervell and dated the 3rd December 1959, and consequently such shares will henceforth be held by them upon the trusts of that Settlement.'

2–72   "Mr. Vandervell believed that thenceforward the trustee company held the 100,000 'A' shares on trust for the children. He acted on that footing. He got his products company to declare dividends on them for the years 1962 to 1964 amounting to the large sum of £1,256,458 gross (before tax) and £769,580 10s. 9d. (after tax). These dividends were received by the trustee company and added to the funds of the children's settlement. They were invested by the trustee company for the benefit of the children exclusively. But even now Mr. Vandervell had not shaken off the demands of the Revenue authorities. They claimed that, even after the exercise of the option, Mr. Vandervell had not divested himself of his interest in the 100,000 'A' shares and that he was liable for surtax on the dividends paid to the children's settlement. Faced with this demand Mr. Vandervell, on the advice of counsel, took the final step. He executed a deed transferring everything to the trustee company on trust for the children. This ended the second period, and started the third.

The third period: 1965–67

"On January 19, 1965, Mr. Vandervell executed a deed by which he trans- **2–73** ferred to the trustee company all right, title or interest which he had on the option or the shares or in the dividends—expressly declaring that the trustee company was to hold them on the trusts of the children's settlement. At last the Revenue authorities accepted the position. They recognised that from January 19, 1965, Mr. Vandervell had no interest whatever in the shares or the dividends. They made no demands for surtax thenceforward.

On January 27, 1967, Mr. Vandervell made his will. It was in contemplation of **2–74** a new marriage. In it he made no provision for his children. He said expressly that this was because he had already provided for them by the children's settlement. Six weeks later, on March 10, 1967, he died.

Summary of the claims

"The root cause of all the litigation is the claim of the Revenue authorities.

"*The first period—1958–61.* The Revenue authorities claimed that Mr. Vandervell was the beneficial owner of the *option* and was liable for surtax on the dividends declared from 1958 to 1961. This came to £250,000. The claim of the Revenue was upheld by the House of Lords: see *Vandervell v. Inland Revenue Coms.*[38]

"*The second period—1961–65.* The Revenue authorities claimed that Mr. **2–75** Vandervell was the beneficial owner of the shares. They assessed him for surtax in respect of the dividends from October 11, 1961, to January 19, 1965, amounting to £628,229. The executors dispute the claim of the Revenue. They appealed against the assessments. But the appeal was, by agreement, stood over pending the case now before us. The executors have brought this action against the trustee company. They seek a declaration that, during the second period, the dividends belonged to Mr. Vandervell himself, and they ask for an account of them. The Revenue asked to be joined as parties to the action. This court did join them: see *Vandervell Trustees Ltd v. White;*[39] but the House of Lords reversed the decision.[40] So this action has continued—without the presence of the Revenue—whose claim to £628,229 has caused all the trouble.

"*The third period—1965–67.* The Revenue agreed that they have no claim against the estate for this period.

[38] [1967] 2 A.C. 291; [1967] 1 All E.R. 1.
[39] [1970] Ch. 44; [1969] 3 All E.R. 496.
[40] [1971] A.C. 912; [1970] 3 All E.R. 16.

The law for the first period

2–76   "The first period was considered by the House of Lords in *Vandervell v. Inland Revenue Comrs.*[41] They held, by a majority of three to two, that during this period the trustee company held the option as a trustee. The terms of the trust were stated in two ways. Lord Upjohn (with the agreement of Lord Pearce) said[42] that the proper inference was that—

> 'the trustee company should hold as trustee on such trusts as [Mr. Vandervell] or the trustee company should from time to time declare.'

Lord Wilberforce said[43] that 'the option was held [by the trustee company] on trusts not at the time determined, but to be decided on a later date.'

"The trouble about the trust so stated was that it was too uncertain. The trusts were not declared or defined with sufficient precision for the trustees to ascertain who the beneficiaries were. It is clear law that a trust (other than a charitable trust) must be for ascertainable beneficiaries: see *Re Gulbenkian's Settlement Trusts*[44] per Lord Upjohn. Seeing that there were no ascertainable beneficiaries, there was a resulting trust for Mr. Vandervell. But if and when Mr. Vandervell should declare any defined trusts, the resulting trust would come to an end. As Lord Upjohn said[44] 'until these trusts should be declared there was a resulting trust for [Mr. Vandervell].'

2–77   "During the first period, however, Mr. Vandervell did not declare any defined trusts. The option was, therefore, held on a resulting trust for him. He had not divested himself absolutely of the shares. He was, therefore, liable to pay surtax on the dividends.

The law for the second period

2–78   "In October and November 1961 the trustee company exercised the option. It paid £5,000 out of the children's settlement. The Royal College of Surgeons transferred the legal estate in the 100,000 'A' shares to the trustee company. Thereupon the trustee company became the legal owner of the shares. This was a different kind of property altogether. Whereas previously the trustee company had only a chose in action of one kind—an option—it now had a chose in action of a different kind—the actual shares. This trust property was not held by the trustee company beneficially. It was held by the company on trust. On this occasion a valid trust was created at the time of the transfer. It was manifested in clear and unmistakable fashion. It was precisely defined. The shares were to be held on the trusts of the children's settlement. The evidence of intention is indisputable: (i) the trustee company used the children's money—£5,000—with which to acquire the shares; this would be a breach of trust unless they intended the shares to be an addition to the children's settlement; (ii) the trustee company wrote to the Revenue authorities the letter of November 2, 1961, declaring expressly that the shares 'will henceforth be held by them upon the trusts of the children's settlement'; (iii) thenceforward all the dividends received by the trustee company were paid by it to the children's settlement and treated as part of the funds of the settlement. This was all done with the full assent of Mr.

---

[41] [1967] A.C. 291; [1967] 1 All E.R. 1.
[42] [1967] 2 A.C. 315 at 317; [1967] 1 All E.R. 10 at 11.
[43] [1967] 2 A.C. 325 at 328; [1967] 1 All E.R. 16 at 17.
[44] [1970] A.C. 508 at 523, 524; [1968] 3 All E.R. 785 at 792, 793.

Vandervell. Such being the intention, clear and manifest, at the time when the shares were conveyed to the trustee company, it is sufficient to create a trust.

"Counsel for the executors admitted that the intention of Mr. Vandervell and **2–79** the trustee company was that the shares should be held on trust for the children's settlement. But he said that this intention was of no avail. He said that during the first period Mr. Vandervell had an equitable interest in the property, namely, a resulting trust; that he never disposed of this equitable interest (because he never knew he had it); and that in any case it was the disposition of an equitable interest which, under section 53 of the Law of Property Act 1925, had to be in writing, signed by him or his agent, lawfully authorised by him in writing (and there was no such writing produced). He cited *Grey v. Inland Revenue Comrs.*[45] & *Oughtred v. Inland Revenue Comrs.*[46]

"There is a complete fallacy in that argument. A resulting trust for the settlor is born and dies without any writing at all. It comes into existence wherever there is a gap in the beneficial ownership. It ceases to exist whenever that gap is filled by someone becoming beneficially entitled. As soon as the gap is filled by the creation or declaration of a valid trust, the resulting trust comes to an end. In this case, before the option was exercised, there was a gap in the beneficial ownership. So there was a resulting trust for Mr. Vandervell. But, as the option was exercised and the shares registered in the trustees' name there was created a valid trust of the shares in favour of the children's settlement. Not being a trust of land, it could be created without any writing. A trust of personalty can be created without writing. Both Mr. Vandervell and the trustee company had done everything which needed to be done to make the settlement of these shares binding on them. So there was a valid trust: see *Milroy v. Lord*[47] *per* Turner L.J.

The law as to third period

"The executors admit that from January 19, 1965, Mr. Vandervell had no **2–80** interest whatsoever in the shares. The deed of that date operated so as to transfer all his interest thenceforward to the trustee company to be held by them on trust for the children. I asked counsel for the executors: what is the difference between the events of October and November 1961 and the event of January 19, 1965? He said that it lay in the writing. In 1965 Mr. Vandervell disposed of his equitable interest in writing, whereas in 1961 there was no writing. There was only conduct or word of mouth. That was insufficient. And, therefore, his executors were not bound by it.

"The answer to this argument is what I have said. Mr. Vandervell did not **2–81** dispose in 1961 of any equitable interest. All that happened was that his resulting trust came to an end—because there was created a new valid trust of the shares for the children's settlement.

Estoppel

"Even if counsel for the executors were right in saying that Mr. Vandervell **2–82** retained an equitable interest in the shares, after the exercise of the option, the question arises whether Mr. Vandervell can in the circumstances be heard to assert the claim against his children. Just see what happened. He himself

---

[45] [1967] 2 A.C. at 317; [1967] 1 All E.R. at 11.
[46] [1960] A.C. 206; [1959] 3 All E.R. 623.
[47] (1862) 4 De G.F. & J. 264 at 274; [1861–73] All E.R. Rep. 783 at 789.

arranged for the option to be exercised. He himself agreed to the shares being transferred to the trustee company. He himself procured his products company to declare dividends on the shares and to pay them to the trustee company for the benefit of the children. Thenceforward the trustee company invested the money and treated it as part of the children's settlement. If he himself had lived, and not died, he could not have claimed it back. He could not be heard to say that he did not intend the children's trust to have it. Even a court of equity would not allow him to do anything so inequitable and unjust. Now that he has died, his executors are in no better position. If authority were needed, it is to be found in *Milroy v. Lord*[48] In that case Thomas Medley assigned to Samuel Lord 50 shares in the Bank of Louisiana on trust for his niece; but the shares were not formally transferred into the name of Samuel Lord. The bank, however, paid the dividends to Samuel Lord.[49] He paid them to the niece, and then, at Thomas Medley's suggestion, the niece used those dividends to buy shares in a fire insurance company—taking them in the name of Thomas Medley. After Thomas Medley's death, his executors claimed that the bank shares belonged to them as representing him, and also the fire insurance shares. Knight-Bruce and Turner L.JJ. held that the executors were entitled to the bank shares, because 'there is no equity in this Court to perfect an imperfect gift.' But the executors were not entitled to the fire insurance shares. Turner L.J. said:[50]

> '. . . the settlor made a perfect gift to [the niece] of the dividends upon these shares, so far as they were handed over or treated by him as belonging to her, and these insurance shares were purchased with dividends which were so handed over or treated.'

2–83 "So here Mr. Vandervell made a perfect gift to the trustee company of the dividends on the shares, so far as they were handed over or treated by him as belonging to the trustee company for the benefit of the children. Alternatively, there was an equitable estoppel. His conduct was such that it would be quite inequitable for him to be allowed to enforce his strict rights (under a resulting trust) having regard to the dealings which had taken place between the parties: see *Hughes v. Metropolitan Railway Co.*[51]

"I would allow the appeal and dismiss the claim of the executors."

2–84 STEPHENSON L.J.: "I have had more doubt than my brethren whether we can overturn the judgment of Megarry J.[52] in what I have not found an easy case.

"To expound my doubts would serve no useful purpose; to state them shortly may do no harm. The cause of all the trouble is what the judge called 'the illfated option' and its incorporation in a deed which was 'too short and simple' to rid Mr. Vandervell of the beneficial interest in the disputed shares, as a bare majority of the House of Lords held, not without fluctuation of mind on the part of one of them (Lord Upjohn), in *Vandervell v. Inland Revenue Comrs.*[53] The operation of law or equity kept for Mr. Vandervell or gave him back an equitable interest which he did not want and would have thought he had disposed of if he

---

[48] 4 De G.F. & J. 264; [1861–73] All E.R. Rep. 783, *infra*, para. 4–03.
[49] Since he had a power of attorney from Medley authorising him to the dividends.
[50] 4 De G.F. & J. at 277; [1861–73] All E.R.Rep. at 790.
[51] (1877) 2 App.Cas. 439 at 448.
[52] [1973] 3 W.L.R. 744; [1974] 1 All E.R. 47.
[53] [1967] 2 A.C. 291; [1967] 1 All E.R. 1.

had ever known it existed. It is therefore difficult to infer that he intended to dispose or ever did dispose of something he did not know he had until the judgment of Plowman J. in *Vandervell v. Inland Revenue Comrs.*, which led to the deed of 1965, enlightened him, or to find a disposition of it in the exercise by the trustee company in 1961 of its option to purchase the shares. And even if he had disposed of his interest, he did not dispose of it by any writing sufficient to comply with section 53(1)(c) of the Law of Property Act 1925 . . .

"*But Lord Denning M.R. and Lawton L.J. are able to hold that no disposition is* **2–85** *needed because (1) the option was held on such trusts as might thereafter be declared by the trustee company or Mr. Vandervell himself, and (2) the trustee company has declared that it holds the shares in the children's settlement,*[54] I doubt the first, because it was apparently the view of the majority of the House of Lords in *Vandervell v. Inland Revenue Comrs.* I should be more confident of the second if it had been pleaded or argued either here or below and we had had the benefit of the learned judge's views on it. I see, as perhaps did counsel, difficulties in the way of a limited company declaring a trust by parol or conduct and without a resolution of the board of directors, and difficulties also in the way of finding any declaration of trust by Mr. Vandervell himself in October or November 1961, or any conduct then or later which would in law or equity estop him from denying that he made one.

"However, Lord Denning M.R. and Lawton L.J. are of the opinion that these **2–86** difficulties, if not imaginary, are not insuperable and that these shares went into the children's settlement in 1961 in accordance with the intention of Mr. Vandervell and the trustee company—a result with which I am happy to agree as it seems to me to be in accordance with the justice and the reality of the case."

Lawton L.J. began with the point that it was the late Mr. Vandervell's **2–87** intention that the trustee company should hold the option on such trusts as might thereafter be declared by the trustee company or Mr. Vandervell himself and held that the trustee company declared trusts for the children in 1961. He also held that Mr. Vandervell was estopped from denying the existence of a beneficial interest for his children.

He went on to create a most unlawyerlike distinction between the **2–87** option held on a resulting trust and the shares acquired upon exercising the option: he took the view that after the option had been exercised it had been extinguished, so no old equitable interest existed to be capable of assignment, so that only new equitable interests could be created! However, the option is not distinct from the shares but merely a limited right created out of the larger bundle of rights inherent in the ownership of the shares. For this very reason the House of Lords in *Vandervell v. I.R.C.* had held that Vandervell, the original beneficial owner of the shares, who had remained beneficial owner under a resulting trust of the option relating to the shares, had failed to divest himself absolutely of the shares which the option governed. If the right to the shares under the option was held by the trustee company under a resulting trust for Vandervell then any shares actually acquired by exercising the right should surely be similarly held under a resulting trust.

---

[54] Editor's italics.

B. GREEN (1984) 47 M.L.R. 418 (COMMENTING ON *RE VANDERVELL'S TRUST* (NO. 2)

2-88 "Lord Denning isolated estoppel as a basis for his decision quite separate to the declaration of new trusts ground upon which he primarily founded himself: but then complicated the picture by (i) intertwining his 'estoppel' reasoning with the 'perfect gift' approach of Turner L.J. in relation to the Louisiana Bank shares' dividends in *Milroy v. Lord*[55] and (ii) citing as his 'estoppel' authority *Hughes v. Metropolitan Railway*[56] Lawton L.J., on the other hand, concertinaed the declaration of new trusts and estoppel arguments; and it is not clear whether in his judgment it was V's procurement of the payment of the second phase dividends or his wilful agreement to V.T.'s exercise of the option using children's settlement monies, or both factors, which achieved the estoppel result. Both judgments ignored the question of whether V (and hence his executors) were merely estopped in respect of recovery of the second phase dividends or whether estoppel extended to recovery of the shares on which the dividends had been declared as well, no doubt since that question had become otiose since V's execution of his stage (10) assignment and release upon which the second phase had terminated.

2-89 "The estoppel raised by the majority was, despite the misleading citation of *Hughes*, 'estoppel by encouragement':[57] a genus of what is today increasingly referred to, along with the related doctrine of 'estoppel by acquiescence,' by the blanket term 'proprietary estoppel.' The difficulty here is not so much seeing how an 'estoppel by encouragement' might be made out on the facts of *Vandervell (No. 2)*, but rather as to how it could be said that the 'minimum equity' necessary to satisfy the objects of the children's settlement involved the retention of the £770,000 dividends appropriated on their behalf by V.T. It is clear that proprietary estoppels can be raised in respect of personalty just as in respect of realty.[58] Furthermore, even though it may not have been generally perceived in 1974,[59] it has now been convincingly established[60] that (whatever may be the position in regard to 'acquiescence'[61]) neither principle nor previous authority requires the person estopped in an 'encouragement' case to have known of his legal right inconsistent to that on the faith of which the person seeking to raise

---

[55] (1862) 2 De G.F. & J. 264. The shares could only be transferred by complying with all due forms, but there was no such obstacle to a gift of the money dividends arising on the shares where the donor was *not* merely entitled to those dividends in equity. Had Thomas Medley only been entitled to the dividends in equity, s.9 of the Statute of Frauds 1677 would have been just as great a problem to him as was s.53(1)(*c*) to V. Lord Denning's use of *Milroy v. Lord* in the present connection begs precisely the same question as does Lord Wilberforce in *Vandervell v. I.R.C.* where he adopts the view of Jenkins J. in *Re Rose*: see *supra*, at para. 2-67, n. 37.

[56] (1877) 2 App.Cas. 439. The root authority on the waiver of contractual rights doctrine of promissory estoppel: generally seen as unconnected with the present subject-matter. (Although see the widest treatment of this area by Robert Goff J. in *Amalgamated Investment & Property Co. Ltd v. Texas Commerce International Bank Ltd* [1981] 1 All E.R. 923, which was too much even for Lord Denning's wholesale adoption when that case reached the Court of Appeal: [1981] 3 All E.R. 577).

[57] The majority cast V in an active role: he is not alleged to have simply acquiesced but positively to have encouraged: see [1974] Ch. 269 at 321A–B and 325G; *per* Denning and Lawton L.JJ. respectively.

[58] See, *e.g. Falcke v. Scottish Imperial Insurance Co.* (1886) 34 Ch.D. 234.

[59] See Megarry J. in *Vandervell (No. 2)* at first instance [1974] Ch. 269, 301B espousing the conventional assumption in this regard.

[60] By Oliver J. in *Taylor Fashions Ltd. v. Liverpool Victoria Trustees Co. Ltd.* [1981] 1 All E.R. 897 pointing up the divergences between Cranworth L.C. and Lord Westbury in *Ramsden v. Dyson* (1866) L.R. 1 H.L. 129: a distinction obscured by the accessible "five probanda" of Fry J. in *Wilmot v. Barber* (1880) 15 Ch.D. 96 at 105–106, too easily cited as a substitute for analysis for too long.

[61] Where arguably *Wilmot v. Barber* (1880) 15 Ch.D. 96 stands. Had V merely "acquiesced," probandum number 4 would have prevented an estoppel being raised against him as one mistaken as to his legal rights. A mistake of secondary fact, not law: *cf. Cooper v. Phibbs* (1867) L.R. 2 H.L. 149.

an equity against him acted to his detriment. And the children's settlement had incurred a certain detriment in reliance on V's encouragement, since on such facts as were emergent V.T. had considered itself honour bound to follow V's wishes and it was V's wish (on the advice of his legal advisers) that the children's settlement should exercise the option with its own monies. But even if V's encouragement of V.T.'s actions for and on behalf of the children's settlement was theoretically capable of grounding an estoppel despite V's lack of knowledge of his true rights at all material times, it is impossible to see how the comparatively trivial estoppel thereby entailed could conceivably justify the children's settlement's retention of over £3/4 million. Under normal conditions it would require deeply unconscientious behaviour by a representor, which had induced an extremely substantial (if not wholly proportionate) irreversible act of detriment on the part of a representee to raise an equity of that extent.

"Yet when one searches for the villain in V, one finds an innocent. As for **2–90** substantial detriment, there was no evidence whatsoever that the children's settlement had changed its position at all in the face of V's encouragement, beyond expending £5,000 in exercise of the option in the first place. The £770,000 dividends had simply been credited to the children's settlement's account, none of it had been distributed, let alone dissipated, on an assumption that V.T. was entitled to deal with it as part of the children's fund[62] Nor does it even appear that the mechanism of estoppel was, on the facts, necessary to do justice to the objects of the children's settlement at all. The £5,000 could easily have been ordered to be repaid (with interest) by V's executors as a condition of the payment over of the dividends (with interest) to them.[63]

"The only party to the second phase transactions who had actually acted to his **2–91** detriment in reliance on the property and future legal defensibility of V.T. holding the £770,000 as an accretion to the children's settlement trust fund, was V himself. He had assumed that he had adequately provided for his children *inter vivos*, and hence cut them out of his will: an act of detrimental reliance rendered irreversible by his death. One is left with the impression that it was V's reliance on his own mistaken belief that he had successfully vested beneficial entitlement to the dividends in the children's settlement which was the real and substantial basis for raising an equity against his executors: which makes V the only person in English law ever to have stood in the shoes of both 'estopped' and 'estopper' at one and the same time."

QUESTIONS

1. T1 and T2 hold property on trust for X. What formalities are required if: **2–92**

   (i) X assigns his equitable interest to Y or to A and B on trust for Y;

  (ii) X directs T1 and T2 to hold the property on trust for Y;

 (iii) X contracts with Y to transfer his equitable interest to him;

 (iv) X declares himself a trustee of his interest for Y;

  (v) X declares himself trustee of his interest for himself for life, remainder for Y absolutely;

---

[62] *per* Megarry J. in *Vandervell (No. 2)* at first instance: [1974] Ch. 269 at 301F–G.
[63] Which is to cast *Vandervell (No. 2)* as the "trust unravelling" case it essentially should have been; with the children's settlement obtaining restitution of its £5,000 as money paid under a mistake of fact as to what it would be getting for it: *cf. Cooper v. Phibbs* (1867) L.R. 2 H.L. 149.

(vi) X directs T1 and T2 to transfer the property to P and Q on trust for Y; what should T1 and T2 do if X died or revoked his direction before T1 and T2 had transferred the legal title?

(vii) X directs T1 and T2 that they henceforth have power to appoint the property to such of Y, his spouse and issue as they may see fit, and a month later T1 and T2 declare they therefore hold the property on trust for Y for life, remainder to his children equally.

Does it matter if the property is land or personalty? Does it matter if the property were held on resulting trust for X?

2–93   2. All Heels' College, Durham, to which Archibald Alumnus who has just died has left all his property by will, seeks your advice on the property to which it is entitled.

On February 1, last year, Archibald did three things:

(i) he transferred £25,000 from his bank account into the bank account of Roger Randall as his nominee;

(ii) he executed a share transfer of his 15,000 shares in Up and Down Ltd in favour of Simon Sharp (not intending him to become beneficial owner) and Simon in due course became registered owner of the shares;

(iii) for no consideration he conveyed his holiday cottage, Tree-Tops, to Theodore Thin for an estate in fee simple in possession.

2–94   On March 1, Archibald orally stated, "I declare that I hold my interest in the £25,000, which I recently transferred into Roger Randall's name, upon trust for my two adult children in equal shares."

On April 1, by unsigned writing Archibald directed Simon to hold half the Up and Down Ltd shares upon trust for Gay Gibson and to transfer the other half into the name of Maud Molesworth legally and beneficially, which Simon duly did.

As far as Tree-Tops is concerned there is cogent evidence that prior to the execution of the conveyance Theodore had orally agreed with Archibald to hold it upon trust for Wendy Williams.

2–95   3. Two years ago Brian transferred his cottage to Tom, orally telling Tom to hold it for Brian for life and then for Clarissa absolutely. He also transferred 10,000 ICI plc shares, 8,000 Hanson plc shares and 6,000 British Gas shares to his sister, Susan, orally telling her to hold them for himself or for such of their relatives as she might select. He soon told her to hold the ICI shares for Clarissa absolutely. Susan complied but said that she was now going to hold the Hanson shares for her cousin, Joy. Brian then told her to transfer the British Gas shares to Tom, who had already orally agreed to hold them on the same trusts as he held the cottage. Susan did so transfer the shares.

A year ago Brian had a row with Clarissa and so told Tom, "Hold the cottage and the shares for me absolutely until I decide what to do about them." Last month he wrote a letter to Tom, "When I die I want you to transfer the cottage and the shares to Joy."

A fortnight ago Brian died, having, by will, left everything to Eric.

Advise Eric.

Section 3. Post Mortem Trusts: Secret Trusts

I. GENERAL

The doctrine of secret trusts is a product of equity not allowing statutes **2–96** to be used as an instrument of fraud.[64] It will already have been seen that statutes prescribe certain formalities for declarations of trust respecting land and for dispositions of equitable interests.[65] In addition, section 9 of the Wills Act 1837 set out *infra* at para. 2–101, prescribes special formalities for the validity of testamentary dispositions whilst the Administration of Estates Act 1925 lays down rules of intestate succession. All too often a person might be induced to die intestate leaving X as his intestate successor[66] or to leave property by will to X on the secret oral understanding that X was to hold the property he received on trust for B. If X were allowed to retain the property beneficially, instead of taking merely as trustee, then this would be allowing statutes to be used as an instrument of fraud by X. Accordingly, equity treats X as a trustee despite the absence of the requisite formalities.

Secret trusts most commonly concern trusts engrafted on wills and in **2–97** this context it is most important to distinguish between (1) fully secret trusts, (2) half-secret trusts, and (3) cases where the probate doctrine of incorporation by reference arises. Respective examples (where X has agreed to hold on trust for B) are (1) I devise Blackacre to X absolutely (2) I devise Blackacre to X upon trusts which I have communicated to him and (3) I devise Blackacre to X upon trusts which I have communicated to him by letter dated November 11, 1995. In this last example since the will refers to a written instrument, already existing at the date of the will, in such terms that the written instrument can be ascertained, the requirements of the doctrine of incorporation are satisfied[67] so that the incorporated document is admitted to public probate as part of the testator's will, the will's compliance with the requirements of section 9 of the Wills Act being sufficient to cover the unattested written instrument referred to in the will. It will be seen that the application of the doctrine of incorporation renders the imposition of a secret trust unnecessary as the requisite formalities for an express trust are present, preventing any possibility of fraud upon X's part.

Testators, today, who do not want their testamentary wishes to **2–98** become public by admission to probate as part of their will can take advantage of the doctrine of secret trusts to make provision for mistresses, illegitimate children, relatives whom they do not wish to appear to be helping or organisations which they do not wish to appear

---

[64] *McCormick v. Grogan* (1869) L.R. 4 H.L. 82 at 88–89; *Blackwell v. Blackwell* [1929] A.C. 318, *infra*, p. 94; *Jones v. Badley* (1868) 3 Ch. App. 362 at 364.

[65] Law of Property Act 1925, s.53, *supra*, at para. 2–05.

[66] *Sellack v. Harris* (1708) 2 Eq.Ca.Ab. 46.

[67] *In the goods of Smart* [1902] P. 238; *Re Jones* [1942] Ch. 328, restricted by *Re Edwards W.T.* [1948] Ch. 440.

to be helping. Indecisive, aged testators can also leave everything by will absolutely to their solicitors, from time to time calling upon or phoning their solicitors with their latest wishes.

2–99   Proving secret trusts can be a problem, though the standard of proof is the ordinary civil standard on a balance of probabilities unless fraud is involved when a higher standard is required.[68] A good practical precaution is for the testator to have a document signed by the intended trustee put into the possession of the secret beneficiaries.

II. FULLY SECRET TRUSTS

2–100   A fully secret trust is one where neither the existence of the trust nor its terms are disclosed by the will.[69]

If a testator makes a valid will bequeathing or devising property to X, apparently beneficially, and communicates to X his intention that X is to hold the property on certain trusts or subject to certain conditions or charges, which X accepts either expressly by promise or impliedly by silence, oral evidence is admissible to prove both the existence and the terms of the trust or conditions or charges which, if clearly proved, X will be compelled to carry out: *Ottaway v. Norman, infra*. Nothing short of an express or implied acceptance by X will raise a trust (or condition or charge): *Wallgrave v. Tebbs, infra*. Communication and acceptance must be of a definite legally binding obligation of X, not of a mere hope or confidence expressed by the testator.[70] Communication and acceptance[71] may be effected at any time during the life of the testator, whether before or after the execution of the will and communication may be made through an agent.[72] It may also be made by handing to X a sealed envelope containing the terms of the trust, and requiring X not to open it until after the testator's death: *Re Keen, infra*. If X is told in the testator's lifetime that he is to hold the property on trust, but is not informed of the terms of the trust, he holds the property on a resulting trust for the testator's residuary legatee or devisee, or if there is no such person, or the property is residuary property, then for the testator's

---

[68] *Re Snowden* [1979] 2 All E.R. 172 at 179 (disagreeing with *Ottaway v. Norman* [1971] 3 All E.R. 1325 at 1333), but if P has proved intent to create a trust on a balance of probabilities is it not illogical to require a higher standard of proof if the legatee is alleged to be fraudulent—see [1979] C.L.J. 260 (C. Rickett).

[69] It can also arise in cases of intestacy: *Sellack v. Harris* (1708) 2 Eq.Ca.Ab. 46.

[70] See *Kasperbauer v. Griffith* [2000] WTLR 333 at 343 *Att.-Gen. v. Chamberlain* (1904) 90 L.T. 581; *Re Snowden* [1979] Ch. 528 at 534. Whether the obligation is technically a trust or a condition or a charge (see *infra*, para. 3–24) it seems that equity will intervene.

[71] The full extent of the property to be covered by the obligation must be communicated and accepted so that where a secret trust for a £5,000 legacy has been communicated to and accepted by the trustee and the legacy is increased by £5,000 in a further codicill but nothing said to the trustee the further £5,000 is not caught by the secret trust: *Re Colin Cooper* [1939] Ch. 580 at 811. The further £5,000 is taken beneficially by the fully secret "trustee."

[72] *Moss v. Cooper* (1861) 1 J. & H. 352. If the agent were unauthorised but the legatee did not approach the testator to clarify the matter would this amount to acquiescence?

intestate successors:[73] *Re Boyes*.[74] If X is not so told he takes the property beneficially as is also the case if X is told that he is to take the property subject to a condition or charge but is not informed of the terms of the condition or charge.

Wills Act 1837

Section 9.[75] "No will shall be valid unless—

2–101

(*a*) it is in writing, and signed by the testator, or by some other person in his presence and by his direction; and

(*b*) it appears that the testator intended by his signature to give effect to the will; and

(*c*) the signature is made or acknowledged by the testator in the presence of two or more witnesses present at the same time; and

(*d*) each witness either—

    (i) attests and signs the will; or

    (ii) acknowledges his signature, in the presence of the testator (but not necessarily in the presence of any other witness), but no form of attestation shall be necessary."

OTTAWAY V. NORMAN

Chancery Division [1972] Ch. 698; [1972] 2 W.L.R. 50; [1971] 3 All E.R. 1325

A testator, Harry Ottaway, by will devised his bungalow (with fixtures, fittings **2–102** and furniture) to his housekeeper Miss Hodges in fee simple and gave her a legacy of £1,500 and half the residue of his estate. It was alleged that Miss Hodges had orally agreed with the testator to leave the bungalow, etc., by her will to the plaintiffs, who were the testator's son and daughter-in-law, Mr. and Mrs. William Ottaway, and that she had also orally agreed to leave to them whatever money was left at her death. By her will Miss Hodges left all her property away from the plaintiffs, who thus brought an action against Miss Hodges' executor, Mr. Norman, for a declaration that the appropriate parts of Miss Hodges' estate were held by him on trust for the plaintiffs.

Brightman J. upheld the plaintiffs' claim except in respect of the moneys.

BRIGHTMAN J.: ". . . It will be convenient to call the person on whom such a **2–103** trust is imposed the 'primary donee' and the beneficiary under that trust the 'secondary donee.' The essential elements which must be proved are: (i) the

---

[73] If X himself is the residuary beneficiary or next-of-kin it seems the court should not impose an arbitrary salutary rule removing all temptation to make self-serving statements by prohibiting X from taking *qua* residuary beneficiary or next-of-kin. Only if X appeared to be lying and it was impossible to ascertain the trust terms should public policy prevent X from obtaining any advantage from his own wrong and pass the property to the person who would have taken under the intestacy rules if X had not survived the testator; *cf. Re Sigsworth* [1935] Ch. 89.

[74] (1884) 26 Ch.D. 531.

[75] Superseding the Statute of Frauds 1677, s.5 and itself substituted by Administration of Justice Act 1982, s.17.

intention of the testator to subject the primary donee to an obligation in favour of the secondary donee; (ii) communication of that intention to the primary donee; and (iii) the acceptance of that obligation by the primary donee either expressly or by acquiescence. It is immaterial whether these elements precede or succeed the will of the donor. I am informed that there is no recent reported case where the obligation imposed on the primary donee is an obligation to make a will in favour of the secondary donee as distinct from some form of *inter vivos* transfer. But it does not seem to me that that can really be a distinction which can validly be drawn on behalf of the defendant in the present case. The basis of the doctrine of a secret trust is the obligation imposed on the conscience of the primary donee and it does not seem to me that there is any materiality in the machinery by which the donor intends that that obligation shall be carried out . . .

2–104   "I find as a fact that Harry Ottaway intended that Miss Hodges should be obliged to dispose of the bungalow in favour of the plaintiffs at her death, that he communicated that intention to Miss Hodges and that Miss Hodges accepted the obligation. I find the same facts in relation to the furniture, fixtures and fittings which passed to Miss Hodges under clause 4 of Harry Ottaway's will. I am not satisfied that any similar obligation was imposed and accepted as regards any contents of the bungalow which had not devolved on Miss Hodges under clause 4 of Harry Ottaway's will.

"I turn to the question of money. In cross-examination William Ottaway said the trust extended to the house, furniture and money:

> 'Everything my father left to Miss Hodges was to be in the trust. The trust comprised the lot. She could use the money as she liked. She had to leave my wife and me whatever money was left.'

2–105   In cross-examination Mrs. Ottaway said that her understanding was that Miss Hodges was bound to make a will giving her and her husband the bungalow, contents and any money she had left. "She could please herself about the money. She did not have to save it for us. She was free to spend it." It seems to me that two questions arise. First as a matter of fact what did the parties intend should be comprised in Miss Hodges's obligation? All money which Miss Hodges had at her death, including money which she had acquired before Harry's death and money she acquired after his death from all sources? Or, only money acquired under Harry's will? Secondly, if such an obligation existed would it as a matter of law create a valid trust? On the second question I am content to assume for present purposes but without so deciding that if property is given to the primary donee on the understanding that the primary donee will dispose by his will of such assets, if any, as he may have at his command at his death in favour of the secondary donee, a valid trust is created in favour of the secondary donee which is in suspense during the lifetime of the primary donee, but attaches to the estate of the primary donee at the moment of the latter's death. There would seem to be at least some support for this proposition in an Australian case to which I was referred: *Birmingham v. Renfrew*.[76] I do not, however, find sufficient evidence that it was Harry Ottaway's intention that Miss Hodges should be compelled to leave all her money, from whatever source derived, to the plaintiffs. This would seem to preclude her giving even a small pecuniary legacy to any friend or relative. I

---

[76] (1937) 57 C.L.R. 666, *infra*, para. 2–154.

do no think it is clear that Harry Ottaway intended to extract any such far-reaching undertaking from Miss Hodges or that she intended to accept such a wide obligation herself. Therefore the obligation, if any, is in my view to be confined to money derived under Harry Ottaway's will. If the obligation is confined to money derived under Harry Ottaway's will, the obligation is meaningless and unworkable unless it includes the requirement that she shall keep such money separate and distinct from her own money. I am certain that no such requirement was ever discussed or intended. If she had the right to mingle her own money with that derived from Harry, there would be no ascertainable property on which the trust could bite at her death.[77]

"There is another difficulty. Does money in this context include only cash or **2–106** cash and investments, or all moveable property of any description? The evidence is quite inconclusive. In my judgment the plaintiff's claim succeeds in relation to the bungalow and in relation to the furniture, fixtures and fittings which devolved under clause 4 of Harry Ottaway's will subject, of course, to normal wastage and fair wear and tear, but not to any other assets."

WALLGRAVE V. TEBBS

Vice-Chancellor (1855) 2 K. & J. 313; 25 L.J. Ch. 241; 26 L.T. (o.s.) 147; 20 J.P. 84; 4 W.R. 194; 2 Jur. 83

A testator bequeathed to the defendants, Mr. Tebbs and Mr. Martin, a legacy **2–107** of £12,000 as joint tenants, and also devised some freehold properties in Chelsea and a field at Earls Court "unto and to the use of Tebbs and Martin, their heirs and assigns, for ever, as joint tenants." There was oral and written evidence that the testator wanted such property used by them for purposes that contravened the Statute of Mortmain. However they knew nothing of this until after his death. They admitted that it would be proper for them to make use of the property in a manner consistent with the motives which had induced the testator to leave the property to them, but claimed to be entitled in law to hold it beneficially.

The plaintiffs (residuary beneficiaries) unsuccessfully claimed that a secret trust had been created which was rendered void by the Statute of Mortmain.

WOOD V.-C.: ". . . Where a person, knowing that a testator in making a **2–108** disposition in his favour intends it to be applied for purposes other than his own benefit, either *expressly promises*, or *by silence implies*, that he will carry the testator's intention into effect, and the property is left to him *upon the faith of that promise or undertaking*, it is in effect a case of trust; and, in such a case, the court will not allow the devisee to set up the Statute of Frauds—or rather the Statute of Wills, by which the Statute of Frauds is now, in this respect, superseded; and for this reason: the devisee by his conduct has induced the testator to leave him the property; and, as Turner L.J. says in *Russel v. Jackson*,[78] no one can doubt, that, if the devisee had stated that he would not carry into effect the intentions of the testator, the disposition in his favour would not have been found in the will. But in this the court does not violate the spirit of the

---

[77] On this principle see *Customs & Excise Commissioners v. Richmond Theatre Management Ltd* [1995] STC 257; *Re Goldcorp Exchange Ltd* [1995] A.C. 74; *Henry v. Hammond* (1913) 2 K.B. 515 at 521; endorsed in *R. v. Clowes* [1994] 2 All E.R. 316 at 325.
[78] (1852) 10 Hare 204 at 211.

statute: but for the same end, namely, prevention of fraud, it engrafts the trust on the devise, by admitting evidence which the statute would in terms exclude, in order to prevent a party from applying property to a purpose foreign to that for which he undertook to hold it.

2–109 "But the question here is totally different. Here there has been no such promise or undertaking on the part of the devisees. Here the devisees knew nothing of the testator's intention until after his death. That the testator desired, and was most anxious to have, his intentions carried out is clear. But, it is equally clear, that he has suppressed everything illegal. He has abstained from creating, either by his will or otherwise, any trust upon which this court can possibly fix. Upon the face of the will, the parties take indisputably for their own benefit. Can I possibly hold that the gift is void? If I knew perfectly well that a testator in making me a bequest, absolute on the face of the will, intended it to be applied for the benefit of a natural child, of whom he was not known to be the father, provided that intention *had not been communicated to me during the testator's life*, the validity of the bequests as an absolute bequest to me could not be questioned.

2–110 "Upon the face of this will the devisees are entitled to the property in question for their own absolute benefit. The statute prevents the court from looking at the paper-writing in which the testator's intentions are expressed; and the parties seeking to avoid the devise have failed to show that during the testator's lifetime, there was any bargain or understanding between the testator and the devisees, or any communication which could be construed into a trust, that they would apply the property in such a manner as to carry the testator's intentions into effect. The devise, therefore, is a valid devise, and the bill must be dismissed."

III. Half-Secret Trusts

2–111 A half-secret trust is one where the existence of the trust is disclosed by the will but the terms are not.

If a testator makes a valid will bequeathing or devising property to X on trust, without specifying in the will the objects of the trust, but communicates the objects to X *before or at the time of* the execution of the will, which states that the objects have been so communicated, and X accepts the trust then X will be compelled to carry out the trust for the specified objects:[79] *Blackwell v. Blackwell, infra.* If, however, the testator communicates the objects to X *after* the execution of the will, X will hold the property on trust, because the will has created a trust; but since the objects have not been effectively specified, the beneficial interest will belong to the testator's residuary legatee or devisee, or if there is no such

---

[79] The full extent of the property to be covered by the obligation must be communicated so that if £5,000 is bequeathed on a half-secret trust accepted by the trustee and then a codicil increases that sum to £15,000 but the trustee is not informed of this increase, the surplus £10,000 will not be held on the half-secret trust but on trust for the residuary legatee or next-of-kin: *cf. Re Colin, Cooper* [1939] Ch. 580 and 811. If the trustee had undertaken to hold the original legacy and anything extra that the testator might subsequently bequeath, then the trustee would be bound to hold everything bequeathed on the half-secret trust.

person, or if the property is residuary property, to the testator's intestate successors:[80] *Re Keen, infra.*

The supposed justification of this is that a testator cannot, through the **2–112** medium of a valid will which imposes a trust but does not create the beneficial interests of that trust, reserve to himself a power to create the beneficial interests in an informal non-testamentary manner, so giving the go-by to the requirements of the Wills Act 1837. After all, as we have seen, in the case of the probate doctrine of incorporation of documents by reference the documents must exist prior to or contemporaneously with the execution of the will, for to allow otherwise would be to give the go-by to the Wills Act. However, the doctrine of incorporation by reference operates within the ambit of the statutory formalities, whilst the whole justification for secret trusts is to impose them just where the statutory formalities have not been satisfied: they operate outside the will and independently of the Wills Act.[81] Fully secret trusts, allowing communication of the trusts between execution of the will and the testator's death, allow the go-by to be given to the Wills Act, and since a will is ambulatory, being of no effect till death, there is logically no difference between declarations of trusts before and after the will. After all, in the case of both fully and half-secret trusts communicated after the will it is fraudulent for X to deprive B of his beneficial interest which but for the testator relying on X's promise would have been secured to B by the testator altering his will, so choosing a compliant legatee as trustee. Logically, half-secret trusts in this respect should be assimilated to fully secret trusts, as in Ireland[82] and most American jurisdictions,[83] rather than have a different rule based upon a misplaced analogy with the doctrine of incorporation by reference. At present, there are the following differences between half-secret trusts and the probate doctrine of incorporation;

(i) In half-secret trusts the will need not specify the type of communi- **2–113** cation with any precision; in incorporation by reference the will must refer to the document to be incorporated with sufficient precision to enable it to be identified.[84]

---

[80] If a testator, having created a valid half-secret trust, subsequently tells the trustee not to hold for the old beneficiaries but to hold for new beneficiaries the trust for the new beneficiaries will fail by *Re Keen*, and it is possible that the revocation of the old trusts will fall on the basis that it was conditional on the creation of valid new trusts: it will succeed if construed as unconditional (*cf.* conditional revocation of wills, *e.g. Re Finnemore* [1992] 1 All E.R. 800) so the property will pass to the residuary legatee (or the statutory next-of-kin).

[81] *Re Young* [1951] Ch. 344; *Re Gardner (No. 2)* [1923] 2 Ch. 230; *Cullen v. Att.-Gen. for N. Ireland* (1866) L.R. 1 H.L. 190 at 198 (in the tax context); *Blackwell v. Blackwell* [1929] A.C. 318 at 340, 342; *Re Snowden* [1979] 2 All E.R. 172 at 177. However, as P. Critchley in (1999) 115 LQR 631 at 641 correctly states, "the mistake is to confuse 'outside the will' with 'outside the Wills Act' ": a disposition by way of secret trust is a testamentary disposition, being revocable and ambulatory, as made clear in section 1 of this Chapter, so as to fall within the Wills Act. It is the harmful effect of the secret trustee's wrongful conduct that justifies Equity's intervention.

[82] *Re Browne* [1944] Ir. R. 90; 67 L.Q.R. 413 (L. A. Sheridan; *Re Prendiville* (unreported) noted [1992] Conv. 202 by J. Mee). If a testator expressly specifies that Irish law shall govern the validity of any half-secret trust he creates should English law nullify such choice on public policy grounds? See *infra:* Articles 6 and 18 Hague Trusts Convention at paras 12–30, 12–35 *infra.*

[83] *Restatement of Trusts*, para. 55(c)(h). As *Scott on Trusts* (4th ed.) Vol. 1A states at p. 88, "It seems strange that the more the intention to create a trust appears on the will, the less ready the courts are to effectuate it."

[84] *Re Edwards' W.T.* [1948] Ch. 440.

(ii) In half-secret trusts the communication may be oral; in incorporation by reference the document to be incorporated must be in writing.

(iii) In half-secret trusts the testator must take the intended trustee into his confidence; in incorporation by reference the intended trustee need not be told of the document to be incorporated. Indeed, incorporation by reference may be effected in cases of absolute gift as well as in cases of trust.

2–114   (iv) In half-secret trusts the names of the beneficiaries are not made public; in incorporation by reference the incorporated document is admitted to probate and so made public.

(v) A beneficiary under a half-secret trust who witnesses the will does not forfeit his beneficial interest, whereas a beneficiary named in an incorporated document who witnesses the will does.[85]

(vi) The interest of a beneficiary under a half-secret trust who predeceases the testator does not lapse (*sed quaere infra*, para. 2–135): in like circumstances that of a beneficiary named in an incorporated document does.[86]

2–115   One special requirement for half-secret trusts which is inapposite for fully secret trusts and is probably derived from the false analogy with the probate doctrine of incorporation, is that the communication of the trusts and the terms of the trust must not conflict with the wording of the will, for to allow otherwise would be to allow oral evidence to contradict the express words of the will: *Re Keen, infra*. Thus, leaving property to four persons "to be dealt with in accordance with my wishes which I have made known *to them*" is ineffective to create a half-secret trust unless the wishes were communicated to all four:[87] communication to less than four would only be effective if the words "or any one or more of them" had been added.[88] Furthermore, if property is left by will to X as trustee, evidence is not admissible to show that X was meant to have some part of that property beneficially.[89]

2–116   By way of contrast if the wording of the will gives property "to X absolutely" or "to X relying on him, but not by way of trust, to carry out my wishes . . ." then oral evidence is admissible to prove a fully-secret trust, contradicting the express words of the will, for to allow otherwise would be to allow the possibility of the perpetration of fraud: *Re Spencer's Will*.[90]

---

[85] *Re Young* [1951] Ch. 344, *infra*, p. 104.

[86] *Re Gardner (No. 2)* [1923] 2 Ch. 230; *Bizzey v. Flight* (1876) 3 Ch.D. 269.

[87] *Re Spence* [1949] W.N. 237 following *Re Keen*, see *infra*.

[88] "to them or either of them" was used in *Re Keen*, see *infra*.

[89] *Re Rees* [1950] Ch. 204; *Re Tyler* [1967] 1 W.L.R. 1269; *Re Pugh's W.T.* [1967] 1 W.L.R. 1262; *Re Baillie* (1886) 2 T.L.R. 660; *Re Marsten* [1953] N.Z.L.R. 456. *Aliter* if property given under a fully secret trust when the possibilities of trust, conditional gift and equitable charge have to be examined: *Irvine v. Sullivan* (1869) L.R. 8 Eq. 673; *Re Foord* [1922] 2 Ch. 519.

[90] (1887) 57 L.T. 519; *Re Williams* [1933] 1 Ch. 244; *Irvine v. Sullivan, supra; cf. Re Falkiner* [1924] 1 Ch. 88; *Re Stirling* [1954] 1 W.L.R. 763.

Should there really be such distinctions between fully- and half-secret trusts if their basis[91] is that whilst the will must first operate to vest the property in the secret trustee, thereafter the secret trusts themselves arise outside the will for equity "makes him do what the will in itself has nothing to do with; it lets him take what the will gives him and then makes him apply it as the court of conscience directs, and it does so in order to give effect to the wishes of the testator which would not otherwise be effectual"? Is it not illogical in the case of half-secret trusts for the court to concern itself so strictly with the wording of the will and to require communication of the trust in accordance therewith before or at the time of the will?

BLACKWELL v. BLACKWELL

House of Lords [1929] A.C. 318; 98 L.J. Ch. 251; 140 L.T. 444 (Lord Hailsham **2–117** L.C., Viscount Sumner, Lords Buckmaster, Carson and Warrington)

A testator by a codicil bequeathed a legacy of £12,000 to five persons upon trust to invest according to their discretion and "to apply the income . . . for the purposes indicated by me to them." Before the execution of the codicil the objects of the trust were communicated in outline to four of the legatees and in detail to the fifth, and the trust was accepted by all of them. The legatee to whom the communication had been made in detail also made a memorandum, on the same day as (though a few hours after) the execution of the codicil, of the testator's instructions. The plaintiffs (the residuary legatees) now claimed a declaration that no valid trust in favour of the objects so communicated had been created, on the ground principally that parol evidence was inadmissible to establish the purposes indicated by the testator.

Eve J. and the Court of Appeal held that the evidence was admissible, and **2–118** here proved a valid secret trust for the persons named by the testator in his instructions to the legatees. The appellants appealed unsuccessfully.

VISCOUNT SUMNER: ". . . In itself the doctrine of equity, by which parol evidence is admissible to prove what is called 'fraud' in connection with secret trusts, and effect is given to such trusts when established, would not seem to conflict with any of the Acts under which from time to time the legislature has regulated the right of testamentary disposition. A court of conscience finds a man in the position of an absolute legal owner of a sum of money, which has been bequeathed to him under a valid will, and it declares that, on proof of certain facts relating to the motives and actions of the testator, it will not allow the legal owner to exercise his legal right to do what he will with his own. This seems to be a perfectly normal exercise of general equitable jurisdiction. The facts commonly, but not necessarily, involve some immoral and selfish conduct on the part of the legal owner. The necessary elements, on which the question turns, are intention, communication and acquiescence. The testator intends his absolute gift to be employed as he and not as the donee desires; he tells the proposed donee of this intention and, either by express promise or by the tacit

---

[91] *Blackwell v. Blackwell* [1929] A.C. 318 at 335; *Re Young* [1951] Ch. 344; *Re Snowden* [1979] 2 All E.R. 172 at 177.

promise, which is satisfied by acquiescence, the proposed donee encourages him to bequeath the money in the faith that his intentions will be carried out. For the prevention of fraud equity fastens on the conscience of the legatee a trust, a trust, that is, which otherwise would be inoperative; in other words it makes him do what the will in itself has nothing to do with; it lets him take what the will gives him and then makes him apply it as the court of conscience directs, and it does so in order to give effect to wishes of the testator which would not otherwise be effectual.

2–119   "To this, two circumstances must be added to bring the present case to the test of the general doctrine, first, that the will states on its face that the legacy is given on trust but does not state what the trusts are, and further contains a residuary bequest, and, second, that the legatees are acting with perfect honesty, seek no advantage to themselves, and only desire, if the court will permit them, to do what in other circumstances the court would have fastened it on their conscience to perform.

2–120   "Since the current of decisions down to *Re Fleetwood*[92] and *Re Huxtable*[93] has established that the principles of equity apply equally when these circumstances are present as in cases where they are not, the material question is whether and how the Wills Act affects this case. It seems to me that, apart from legislation, the application of the principle of equity which was made in *Fleetwood's* case and *Huxtable's* case was logical, and was justified by the same considerations as in the cases of fraud and absolute gifts. Why should equity forbid an honest trustee to give effect to his promise, made to a deceased testator, and compel him to pay another legatee, about whom it is quite certain that the testator did not mean to make him the object of his bounty? In both cases the testator's wishes are incompletely expressed in his will. Why should equity, over a mere matter of words, give effect to them in one case and frustrate them in the other? No doubt the words 'in trust' prevent the legatee from taking beneficially, whether they have simply been declared in conversation or written in the will, but the fraud, when the trustee, so called in the will, is also the residuary legatee, is the same as when he is only declared a trustee by word of mouth accepted by him. I recoil from interfering with decisions of long standing, which reject this anomaly, unless constrained by statute . . .

2–121   "The limits, beyond which the rules as to unspecified trusts must not be carried, have often been discussed. A testator cannot reserve to himself a power of making future unwitnessed dispositions by merely naming a trustee and leaving the purposes of the trust to be supplied afterwards, nor can a legatee give testamentary validity to an unexecuted codicil by accepting an indefinite trust, never communicated to him in the testator's lifetime: *Johnson v. Ball,*[94] *Re Boyes*[95] *Riordan v. Banon,*[96] *Re Hetley*[97] To hold otherwise would indeed be to enable the testator to 'give the go-by' to the requirements of the Wills Act, because he did not choose to comply with them. It is communication of the purpose to the

---

[92] (1880) 15 Ch.D. 594, where a testatrix by a codicil bequeathed to X all her personalty "to be applied as I have requested him to do." Before the execution of the codicil she had stated to X the trusts on which she intended the property to be held, and X made a memorandum of the details in her presence. Hall V.-C. held that external evidence was admissible to prove the terms of the understanding between X and the testatrix.

[93] [1902] 2 Ch. 793.

[94] (1851) 5 De G. & Son 85.

[95] (1884) 26 Ch.D. 531.

[96] (1876) 10 I.R.Eq. 469.

[97] [1902] 2 Ch. 866.

legatee, coupled with acquiescence or promise on his part, that removes the matter from the provision of the Wills Act and brings it within the law of trusts, as applied in this instance to trustees, who happen also to be legatees. . . ." *Appeal dismissed.*

RE KEEN, EVERSHED V. GRIFFITHS

Court of Appeal [1937] Ch. 236; 106 L.J. Ch. 177; 156 L.T. 207; 53 T.L.R. 320; 81 S.J. 97; [1937] 1 All E.R. 452 (Wright M.R., Greene and Romer L.JJ.)

The testator by clause 5 of his will, dated August 11, 1932, gave to his **2–122** executors and trustees, Captain Hazelhurst and Mr. Evershed, the sum of £10,000 free of duty "to be held upon trust and disposed of by them among such person, persons or charities as may be notified by me to them or either of them during my lifetime, and in default of such notification and so far as such notification shall not extend I declare that the said sum of £10,000 or such part thereof as shall not be disposed of in manner aforesaid shall fall into and form part of my residuary estate." Earlier, on March 31, 1932, the testator had made a will containing an identical gift. He had on that date handed to Mr. Evershed a sealed envelope containing the name of the intended beneficiary, but he had not disclosed its contents to Mr. Evershed, having directed that it was not to be opened until after his death. Mr. Evershed regarded himself as having undertaken to hold the £10,000 in accordance with the directions contained in the sealed envelope. A new will was executed on August 11, 1932, but no fresh directions were given. Mr. Evershed still regarded himself as being bound by the previous communication. On the testator's death the question arose whether the £10,000 was held by Captain Hazelhurst and Mr. Evershed on trust for the intended beneficiary or whether it fell into residue. It was held by Farwell J. and the Court of Appeal that it fell into residue.

LORD WRIGHT M.R.: "Farwell J. . . . decided adversely to the claims of the lady **2–123** [the intended beneficiary] on the short ground that she could not prove that she was a person notified to the trustees by the testator during his lifetime within the words of clause 5 [of the will]. His opinion seems to be that the clause required the name and identity of the lady to be expressly disclosed to the trustees during the testator's lifetime, so that it was not sufficient to place these particulars in the physical possession of the trustees, or one of them, in the form of a memorandum which they were not to read till the testator's death.

"I am unable to accept this conclusion, which appears to me to put too narrow a construction on the word 'notified' as used in clause 5 in all the circumstances of the case. To take a parallel, a ship which sails under sealed orders is sailing under orders though the exact terms are not ascertained by the captain till later. I note that the case of a trust, put into writing, which is placed in the trustees' hands in a sealed envelope, was hypothetically treated by Kay J. as possibly constituting a communication in a case of this nature[98] This, so far as it goes seems to support my conclusion. The trustees had the means of knowledge available whenever it became necessary and proper to open the envelope. I think Mr. Evershed was right in understanding that the giving of the sealed envelope was a notification within clause 5.

---

[98] *Re Boyes* (1884) 26 Ch.D. 531 at 536.

2–124   "This makes it necessary to examine the matter on a wider basis . . .

". . . The principles of law or equity relevant in a question of this nature have now been authoritatively settled or discussed by the House of Lords in *Blackwell v. Blackwell*[99] [in the case of half-secret trusts and *McCormick v. Grogan*[1] in the case of fully secret trusts. The Master of the Rolls then analysed the facts and decisions in those cases, and continued:] As, in my judgment, clause 5 should be considered as contemplating future dispositions, and as reserving to the testator the power of making such dispositions without a duly attested codicil, simply by notifying them during his lifetime, the principles laid down by Lord Sumner [in *Blackwell v. Blackwell*] must be fatal to the appellant's claim. Indeed, they would be equally fatal even on the construction for which Mr. Roxburgh contended, that the clause covered both anterior or contemporaneous notifications and future notifications. The clause would be equally invalid, but as already explained I cannot accept that construction. In *Blackwell v. Blackwell*[2] *Re Fleetwood*[3] and *Re Huxtable*[4] the trusts had been specifically declared to some or all of the trustees, at or before the execution of the will, and the language of the will was consistent with that fact. There was, in these cases, no reservation of a future power to change the trusts, in whole or in part. Such a power would involve a power to change a testamentary disposition by an unexecuted codicil, and would violate section 9 of the Wills Act. This was so held in *Re Hetley*.[5] *Johnson v. Ball*[6] is, again, a somewhat different example of the rule against dispositions made subsequently to the date of the will in cases where the will in terms leaves the property on trust, and shows that the position may be different from the position where the will in terms leaves the gift absolutely. The trusts referred to, but undefined in the will, must be described in the will as established prior to, or at least contemporaneously with, its execution.

2–125   "But there is a still further objection which, in the present case, renders the appellant's claim unenforceable: the trusts which it is sought to establish by parol evidence would be inconsistent with the express terms of the will. That such an objection is fatal appears from the cases already cited, such as *Re Huxtable*. In that case, an undefined trust of money for charitable purposes was declared in the will, as in respect of the whole corpus and, accordingly, evidence was held inadmissible that the charitable trust was limited to the legatee's life, so that he was free to dispose of the corpus after his death. Similarly in *Johnson v. Ball* the testator by the will left the property to trustees, upon the uses contained in a letter signed 'by them and myself': it was held that that evidence was not admissible to show that, though no such letter was in existence at the date of the will, the testator had made a subsequent declaration of trust; the court held that these trusts could not be enforced. Lord Buckmaster in *Blackwell's* case[7] described *Johnson v. Ball* as an authority pointing 'to a case where the actual trusts were left over after the date of the will to be subsequently determined by the testator.' That, in his opinion, would be a contravention of the Wills Act. I know of no authority which would justify such a contravention. Lord Buckmaster also quotes[8] the grounds on which Parker V.-C. based his decision as being both

---

[99] [1929] A.C. 318; see *supra*, para. 2–117.
[1] (1869) L.R. 4 H.L. 82.
[2] [1929] A.C. 318.
[3] (1880) 15 Ch.D. 594.
[4] [1902] 2 Ch. 793.
[5] [1902] 2 Ch. 866.
[6] (1851) 5 De G. & Sm. 85.
[7] [1929] A.C. 318, 331.
[8] *Ibid.* at 330.

'that the letter referred to in the will had no existence at the time when the will was made and that, supposing it referred to a letter afterwards signed, it is impossible to give effect to it as a declaration of the trusts since it would admit the document as part of the will and it was unattested.'

"In the present case, while clause 5 refers solely to a future definition, or to **2–126** future definitions, of the trust, subsequent to the date of the will, the sealed letter relied on as notifying the trust was communicated (as I find the facts) before the date of the will. That it was communicated to one trustee only, and not to both, would not, I think, be an objection (see Lord Warrington's observation in the *Blackwell* case).[9] But the objection remains that the notification sought to be put in evidence was anterior to the will, and hence not within the language of clause 5, and inadmissible simply on that ground, as being inconsistent with what the will prescribes. . . ." *Appeal dismissed*[10]

IV. THE BASIS OF SECRET TRUSTS

Before dealing with the basis of secret trusts it is as well to examine **2–127** certain unusual secret trust situations since they will shed light thereon.

(i) *Attestation of will by secret beneficiary*

Section 15 of the Wills Act 1837: "If any person shall attest the execution of any will to whom or to whose wife or husband any beneficial devise, legacy, estate, interest, gift, or appointment, of or affecting any real or personal estate (other than and except charges and directions for the payment of any debt or debts), shall be thereby given or made, such devise, legacy, estate, interest, gift, or appointment shall, so far only as concerns such person attesting the execution of such will, or the wife or husband of such person, or any person claiming under such person or wife or husband, be utterly null and void, and such person so attesting shall be admitted as a witness to prove the execution of such will, or to prove the validity or invalidity thereof, notwithstanding such devise, legacy, estate, interest, gift, or appointment mentioned in such will."

Section 1 of the Wills Act 1968: "For the purposes of section 15 of the **2–128** Wills Act 1837 the attestation of a will by a person to whom or to whose spouse there is given or made any such disposition as is described in that section shall be disregarded if the will is duly executed without his attestation and without that of any other such person."

Re Young [1951] Ch. 344 (Danckwerts J.): bequest by a testator to his wife with a direction that on her death she should leave the property for

---

[9] *Ibid.* at 341.
[10] In *Re Bateman's W.T.* [1970] 1 W.L.R. 1463; [1970] 3 All E.R. 817, *Re Keen* was followed without argument where a testator had directed his trustees to set aside £24,000 and pay the income thereof "to such persons and in such proportions *as shall* be stated by me in a sealed letter to my trustees": "[The direction] clearly imports that the testator may, in the future after the date of the will, give a sealed letter to his trustees. It is impossible to confine the words to a sealed letter already so given. If that be the true construction of the wording it is not in dispute that the direction is invalid": *per* Pennycuick V.-C. at 1468 and 820, respectively.

the purposes which he had communicated to her. Before execution of will, direction given and accepted by wife that she would leave a legacy of £2,000 to testator's chauffeur. The chauffeur had witnessed the testator's will. *Held* that the chauffeur had not forfeited his legacy under section 15 of the Wills Act 1837 for "the whole theory of the formulation of a secret trust is that the Wills Act has nothing to do with the matter because the forms required by the Wills Act are entirely disregarded, since the persons do not take by virtue of the gift in the will, but by virtue of the secret trusts imposed upon the beneficiary who does in fact take under the will."

2–129   But why is it that the secret beneficiary does not obtain an interest in the testator's property (or rights against the secret trustee) at the date of the testator's death by virtue of a testamentary disposition within the Wills Act when till the testator dies the relevant property is his absolutely to deal with as he pleases? Why should the attesting secret beneficiary be allowed to benefit if the function of section 15 is to ensure there is an impartial witness with nothing to gain or lose by his testimony? He may know he is a beneficiary at the time of attestation. He could be lying if he said he did not know: for this reason a beneficiary taking on the face of a will is subject to section 15 even if, in fact, he just witnessed the signature at the end of the will and so did not know of its contents.

2–130   It seems likely that persons taking under a fully secret trust would receive nothing if the trustee taking absolutely beneficially on the face of the will had witnessed the will so he should receive nothing on which the trusts could bite,[11] though some might argue[12] that the admission of oral evidence to establish the trusteeship should carry the day: half-secret trustees taking as trustees on the face of the will clearly cannot infringe section 15 of the Wills Act 1837.

(ii) *Trustee predeceasing testator*

2–131   Generally, a gift by will to X is said to lapse if X predeceases the testator and the gift fails.[13] If, however, the gift is to X on trust for B and B survives the testator then despite X's predecease the gift will not lapse for equity will not allow a trust to fail for want of a trustee: the testator's personal representative will take over as trustee.[14]

According to dicta of Cozens-Hardy L.J. in *Re Maddock*,[15] a case concerning a fully secret trust, "if the legatee renounces and disclaims, or dies in the lifetime of the testator, the persons claiming under the

---

[11] Compare "trustee predeceasing testator" in following paragraph.

[12] See *Inchiquin v. French* (1745) 1 Cox Eq. Cas. 1.

[13] Exceptionally, if issue predecease a testator leaving issue of their own surviving the testator, the gift takes effect in favour of the surviving issue: Wills Act 1837, s.33. The persons benefiting from this exception will not be able to disregard the deceased legatee-trustee's undertaking: *cf. Huguenin v. Baseley* (1807) 14 Ves. 273.

[14] *Sonley v. Clock Makers' Company* (1780) 1 Bro.C.C. 81; *Mallott' v. Wilson* [1903] 2 Ch. 494; *Re Smirthwaite's Trusts* (1871) L.R. 11 Eq. 251; *Re Armitage* [1972] Ch. 438. See *infra*, para. 8–39.

[15] [1902] 2 Ch. 220 at 231.

memorandum [*i.e.* the secret trusts] can take nothing." This is based upon the view that the secret trusts only arise when the property intended to be the subject-matter of the trust vests in someone under the terms of the will.[16] It follows that if by reason of the fully secret trustee's death the property does not so vest then no trust can arise.

(iii) *Trustee disclaiming after testator's death*

A beneficiary under a will after the testator's death can always **2–132** disclaim a legacy or devise before acceptance and a person can always disclaim the office of trustee before acceptance.[17] If a person named as a half-secret trustee disclaimed the office then it would seem that the testator's personal representative would hold on the trusts for the secret beneficiaries. Where disclaimer by fully secret trustees is concerned although Cozens-Hardy L.J. opined in *Re Maddock, supra* that no trusts would arise in such a case there are contrary dicta of Lord Buckmaster and Lord Warrington in *Blackwell v. Blackwell*:[18] "In the case where no trusts are mentioned the legatee might defeat the whole purpose by renouncing the legacy and the breach of trust would not in that case inure to his own benefit, but I entertain no doubt that the court having once admitted the evidence of the trust, would interfere to prevent its defeat." Lord Buckmaster's dicta presuppose the existence of a trust whereof the legatee is in breach and apply the maxim that equity will not allow a trust to fail for want of a trustee. Whether the trusts arose on the testator's death or at an earlier time is not stated by Lord Buckmaster. By analogy with mutual wills the testator's death should be the appropriate time, it being immaterial whether or not gifts are disclaimed.[19] Disclaimer might, however, be material if the testator's orally communicated intentions to the legatee were construed not as imposing trusts but as conferring a gift subject to a personal condition.[20]

(iv) *Trustee revoking acceptance before the testator's death*

Compare the three following examples: **2–133**

(a) Testator, T, bequeaths £10,000 to X absolutely, having told X that he wants X to hold the money on trust for Y and Z. A year later

---

[16] "The obligation can be enforced if the donee becomes entitled": *per* Romer J. in *Re Gardner* [1923] 2 Ch. 230, 232. "The doctrine must, in principle, rest on the assumption that the will has first operated according to its terms": *per* Viscount Sumner [1929] A.C. 318, 334. "The whole basis of secret trusts is that they operate outside the will, changing nothing that is written in it and allowing it to operate according to its tenor, but then fastening a trust on to the property in the hands of the recipient": *per* Megarry V.-C. *Re Snowden* [1979] 2 All E.R. 172 at 177.

[17] *Smith v. Smith,* [2001] *The Times,* June 18; *Re Sharman's W.T.* [1942] Ch. 311.

[18] [1929] A.C. 318 at 328, 341.

[19] *Re Dale* [1993] 4 All E.R. 129; see also *Blackwell v. Blackwell* [1929] A.C. 318 at 341, *per* Lord Warrington: "It has long been settled that if a gift be made to a person in terms absolutely but in fact upon a trust communicated to the legatee and accepted by him, the legatee, would be bound to give effect to the trust, on the principle that the gift may be presumed to have been made on the faith of his acceptance of the trust, and a refusal after the death of the testator to give effect to it would be a fraud on the part of the legatee." See also (1972) 36 Conv. (N.S.) 113 (R. Burgess).

[20] See *infra*, at para. 3–25.

X tells T that he is no longer prepared to hold the money on trust for anyone. Five years later T dies without having changed his will;

(b) The bequest as before but X tells T that he is no longer prepared to hold the money on trust for anyone only three days before T dies of a week-long illness;

(c) The bequest as before but T is incurably insane when informed by X as before and T remains so till his death five years later.

2–134 Does X take the £10,000 beneficially only in case (a)? Is X under any obligations before T's death? What if the trust had been half secret?

(v) Secret beneficiary predeceasing testator

2–135 If T by will left property to X on trust expressly for B and B predeceased T the gift to B would lapse just as an *inter vivos* trust for B fails if B is not alive when the trust is created.[21] One would have imagined that the result would be the same if T, having asked X to hold on trust for B, left property "to X absolutely" or "to X upon trusts that I have communicated to him." However, in *Re Gardner (No. 2)*[22] Romer J. held that B's interest did not lapse as B obtained an interest as soon as T communicated the terms of the trust to X and X accepted the trust. B's interest derived not from T's will (to which the rules regarding lapse would have applied) but under the agreement between T and X. "The rights of the parties appear to me to be exactly the same as though the husband (X), after the memorandum had been communicated to him by the testatrix (T) in the year 1909 had executed a declaration of trust binding himself to hold any property that should come to him upon his wife's (T's) partial intestacy upon trust as specified in the memorandum."[23] Such a declaration, however, does not create a properly constituted trust since the subject-matter is future property.[24] It may be that Romer J. considered that the vesting of the property in X on T's death in 1919 completely constituted the trust[25] but on the terms of the memorandum. However, the interests of those taking under the memorandum only became vested proprietorial interests after T's death: until then the so-called interests only amounted to mere *spes* that T would not change her mind and make a different testamentary disposition or die insolvent and that X would not revoke his acceptance, so that ultimately

[21] *Re Corbishley's Trusts* (1880) 14 Ch.D. 846; *Re Tilt* (1896) 74 L.T. 163, both concerned with personalty where a gift to B gave B an absolute interest: for realty a gift by will after 1837 to B gave an absolute interest whilst till 1925 a gift by deed to B gave B only a life interest in the absence of proper words of limitation.

[22] [1923] 2 Ch. 230.

[23] *ibid.* at 233. Here Romer J. may have been thinking that if B had an absolute vested interest in a 1909 settlement then funds accruing under a will taking effect in 1919 would be treated as an accretion to the 1909 settlement rather than as comprised in a separate 1919 referential settlement: see *Re Playfair* [1951] Ch. 4.

[24] *Re Ellenborough* [1903] 1 Ch. 697; *Re Northcliffe* [1925] Ch. 651; *Williams v. C.I.R.* [1965] N.Z.L.R. 395, see *infra*, at para. 4–79; *Brennan v. Morphett* (1908) 6 C.L.R. 22.

[25] *cf. Re Ralli's W.T.* [1964] Ch. 288; *Re Adlard* [1954] Ch. 29.

X would receive property to hold on trust for them. Just as an *inter vivos* trust constituted by X in 1919 declaring himself trustee of certain property for the benefit of A, B and C equally would give B no interest, if at that date B were dead and so no longer an existing legal entity, so the trust arising in *Re Gardner* after T's death in 1919 could give B no interest, B being dead by that date. It makes no difference that whilst B was alive he might have had some sort of *spes* that if he lived long enough a trust might come into existence for his benefit at a later date. The authority of *Re Gardener* is thus very doubtful indeed.

(vi) *Bequest to two on a promise by one*

The orthodox position is laid down in *Re Stead*[26] by Farwell J.: **2–136**

> "If A induced B either to make, or to leave unrevoked, a will leaving property to A and C as tenants in common, by expressly promising or tacitly consenting, that he and C will carry out the testator's wishes and C knows nothing of the matter until after the testator's death, A is bound, but C is not bound: *Tee v. Ferris*;[27] the reason stated being, that to hold otherwise would be to enable one beneficiary to deprive the rest of their benefits by setting up a secret trust. If, however, the gift were to A and C as joint tenants, the authorities have established a distinction between those cases in which the will is made on the faith of an antecedent promise by A and those in which the will is left unrevoked on the faith of a subsequent promise. In the former case the trust binds both A and C: *Russell v. Jackson*;[28] *Jones v. Bradley*,[29] the reason stated being that no person can claim an interest under a fraud committed by another; in the latter case A and not C is bound: *Burney v. Macdonald*[30] and *Moss v. Cooper*,[31] the reason stated being that the gift is not tainted with any fraud in procuring the execution of the will. Personally, I am unable to see any difference between a gift made on the faith of an antecedent promise and a gift left unrevoked on the faith of a subsequent promise to carry out the testator's wishes; but apparently a distinction has been made by the various judges who have had to consider the question. I am bound, therefore, to decide in accordance with these authorities . . ."

However, Bryn Perrins in (1972) 88 L.Q.R. 225 examines these **2–137** authorities to different effect, persuasively concluding that the only question to be asked is: was the gift to C induced by A's promise? If yes, C is bound; if no, he is not:

---

[26] [1900] 1 Ch. 231, 247, The principles here discussed apply only to fully secret trusts. In the case of half-secret trusts, if the will permits communication to be made to one only of several trustees, a communication made before or at the time of the execution of the will to one only of the trustees binds all of them, the trust being a joint office: *Blackwell v. Blackwell* [1929] A.C. 318; *Re Spence* [1949] W.N. 237; *Ward v. Duncombe* [1893] A.C. 369; *Re Gardom* [1914] 1 Ch. 662 at 673.
[27] (1856) 2 K. & J. 357.
[28] (1852) 10 Hare 204.
[29] (1868) L.R. 3 Ch. 362.
[30] (1845) 15 Sim. 6.
[31] (1861) 1 J. & H. 352.

BRYN PERRINS (1972) 88 L.Q.R. 225

2–138 "The reasons stated by Farwell J. in *Re Stead* are at first sight contradictory. One consideration is that a person must not be allowed, by falsely setting up a secret trust, to deprive another of his benefits under the will. Apparently this is decisive if the parties are tenants in common but not if they are joint tenants. On the other hand one person must not profit by the fraud of another. Apparently this is decisive only if the parties are joint tenants and not if they are tenants in common. Yet again it is apparently only fraud in procuring the execution of a will that is relevant, and not fraud in inducing a testator not to revoke a will already made. All very confusing, but add *Huguenin v. Baseley*[32] and the whole picture springs into focus and the confusion disappears. Returning to A and C, whether they are tenants in common or joint tenants, C is not bound *if his gift was not induced by the promise of A* because to hold otherwise would be to enable A to deprive C of his benefit by setting up a secret trust; but C is bound *if his gift was induced by the promise of A* because he cannot profit by the fraud of another; and if the trust was communicated to A after the will was made, then C takes free *if this gift was not* induced by the promise of A because if there is no inducement there is no fraud affecting C.

2–139 This, it is submitted, is what was decided by the cases cited in Farwell J.'s judgment."

CONCLUSIONS

In the light of the foregoing discussion of unusual secret trust situations it will be seen that the title of a beneficiary under a fully secret and a half-secret trust arises outside the will and is regarded by many judges[33] as arising outside the wills Act and so not by virtue of a testamentary disposition. Even then, it seems that, except in the case of disclaimer by a fully secret trustee after the testator's death, such a trust is conditional and dependent upon the gift by will taking effect according to its terms. Section 9 of the Wills Act 1837 should however, be relevant because the intended secret trust property belongs absolutely and indefeasibly to the testator who is free to deal with it howsoever he pleases before he dies,[34] so that the disposition thereof by the conduct outside his will[35] is a testamentary disposition.[36] How then does there arise an equitable obligation binding the trustee's conscience.

2–140 The equitable principle that equity will not allow a statute to be used as an instrument of fraud was the basis for not allowing the Statute of Frauds 1677 to be invoked by persons intended to be secret trustees of

---

[32] (1807) 14 Ves. 273. This is authority for the principle, "No man may profit by the fraud of another." A widow was persuaded by Rev. Baseley, who managed her property, to settle some of it on him and his family. Later, she married Mr. Huguenin and sought to set aside the conveyance for undue influence. She succeeded, for Lord Eldon held that the Rev. Baseley's wife and children, though innocent, were not purchasers but volunteers who could not profit from Baseley's fraud and retain their vested interests.

[33] *Re Snowden* [1979] 2 All E.R. 172 at 177, *Re Young* [1951] Ch 344, *Re Gardner* (No 2) [1923] 2 Ch 230, *Blackwell v. Blackwell* [1929] 2 AC 318 at 340, 342.

[34] *Kasperbauer v Griffith* [2000] WTLR 333 at 343.

[35] Since secret trusts operate outside the will it is illogical in the case of a half-secret trust not to allow communication after the date of the will but before the testator's death and claim that otherwise the Wills Act would be avoided: see *supra*, para. 2–112.

[36] See P. Critchley (1999) 115 LQR 631 at 639–641.

testamentary gifts or to be trustees of inter vivos trusts of land.[37] The provisions of the 1677 Statute are now to be found in the Wills Act 1837 and the Law of Property Act 1925. The equitable principle should apply since there would be fraud if the secret trustee attempted to rely on the statute to defeat a beneficial interest which he had led the testator to believe would belong to another. There would be not just a fraud on the testator in betraying the testator's confidence[38] but there would be harmful fraud on the secret beneficiary who would be deprived of the benefit which, but for the trustee agreeing to carry out the testator's wishes, would have been secured for him by other means.[39] Thus, in a fully secret trust and in a half-secret trust the trustee holds the testator's property not on resulting or constructive trust for the testator's residuary legatee (or next of kin as the case may be) but on the express trust for the beneficiary: it would be unconscionable for the trustee to hold the property otherwise by invoking the Wills Act for that would enable statute to be used as an instrument of fraud. Thus, C can enforce his interest where A devises land by will to B on an oral trust for C.[40]

The same result can better be achieved in accordance with statute if **2–141** one treats such trusts as constructive trusts—exempted from L.P.A., s. 53(1) by s.53(2)—on the ground that such trusts, unlike ordinary express trusts which can be created unilaterally, depend crucially upon the trustee's express or tacit promise to honour the trust in favour of the secret beneficiary.[41] As Robert Walker LJ states,[42] "There must be an agreement between A and B conferring a benefit on C because it is the agreement which would make it unconscionable for B to resile from his agreement." This was his view of secret trusts as well as mutual wills: "both doctrines show equity intervening to prevent unconscionable conduct".[43]

Section 4. Post Mortem Trusts: Mutual Wills[44]

The term "mutual wills" is used to describe documents of a testamentary **2–142** character made as the result of a contract between husband and wife, or other persons, to create irrevocable interests in favour of ascertainable

---

[37] *McCormick v. Grogan* (1868) L.R. 4 H.L. 82 at 88–89; *Jones v. Badley* (1868) 3 Ch. App. 362 at 364; *Wattgrave v. Tebbs* (1855) 2 K. & J. 313 at 321–322; *Rochefoucauld v. Boustead* [1897] 1 Ch. 196; R. Blumenstein (1978) 36 U. Toronto F.L.R. 108.

[38] As stated in *Re Dale* [1993] 4 All E.R. 129 at 142 in relation to mutual wills made by two testators; T1 and T2, where T1 dies and T2 makes a will departing from what was agreed, "I am unable to see why it should be any the less a fraud on T1 if the agreement was that each testator should leave his or her property to particular beneficiaries, *e.g.* their children, rather than to each other."

[39] D.R. Hodge [1980] Conv. 341. This point seems overlooked by B. Perrins in [1985], Conv. 248.

[40] *Ottaway v. Norman* [1972] Ch. 698 and see *supra*, para. 2–23. In *Re Baillie* (1886) 2 T.L.R. 660, 661 a half-secret trust of land failing for one reason also failed for not complying with written formalities: this seems erroneous.

[41] In *Re Cleaver* [1981] 2 All E.R. 1018 at 1024 Nourse J. categorised secret trusts as constructive trusts and Peter Gibson LJ endorsed this in *Kasperbauer v. Griffith* [2000] WTLR 333 at 342.

[42] *Gillett v. Holt* [2000] 2 All E.R. 289 at 305

[43] *Ibid* at 304

[44] See Oakley's *Constructive Trusts* (3rd ed) Chap. 5; Univ. Toronto L.J. 390 (T. G. Youdan); (1989) 105 L.Q.R. 534 (C. E. F. Rickett).

beneficiaries. The revocable nature of the wills under which the interests are created is fully recognised by the court of probate,[45] but, in certain circumstances, the court of equity will protect and enforce the interests created by the agreement despite the revocation of the will by one party after the death of the other without having revoked his will.

2–143   A typical case of mutual wills arises in the following circumstances: H(usband) and W(ife) agree to execute mutual wills (or a joint will) leaving their respective properties to the survivor of them for life, with remainder to the same ultimate beneficiary (B). H dies, W makes a fresh will leaving her property away from B to her second husband (S).

2–144   In these circumstances, H's will (or the joint will) is admitted to probate on his death and, under it, W gets a life interest and B an interest in remainder. On W's death, her second will is admitted to probate. Under it her property vests in her personal representatives upon trust, not for S, but to give effect to the terms of the agreement upon which the mutual wills were made, *i.e.* upon trust for B.

B's interest in W's property arises as soon as H dies. It prevails over the interest of S therein by virtue of the maxim that "where the equities are equal the first in time prevails." Indeed, if B survives H but predeceases W his interest in W's property does not lapse but is payable to his personal representatives, and forms part of his estate.[46] B's interest arises irrespective of whether W disclaims her benefit under H's will[47] and even if H and W left no property to each other, leaving everything to B.[48] It is the death[49] of H, no longer having the opportunity to revoke his own will, which concludes performance of the contract and renders the will of W irrevocable in equity, though, it is always revocable at law.

2–145   The courts will not infer a trust merely because mutual wills are made in almost identical terms. There must be evidence of an agreement to create interests under the mutual wills which are intended to be irrevocable after the death of the first to die. As Legatt LJ stated a *Re Goodchild*.[50] "A key feature of mutual wills is the irrevocability of the mutual intentions. Not only must they be [contractually] binding when made, but the testators must have undertaken, and so must be bound, not to change their intentions after the death of the first testator." Where there is no such evidence the fact that the survivor takes an absolute interest is a factor against the implication of an agreement.[51] Where, however, the evidence is clear, as, for example, where it is contained in recitals in the wills themselves, the fact that each testator gave the other an absolute interest with a substitutional gift in the event of the other's prior death does not prevent a trust from arising.[52]

---

[45] *Re Heys* [1914] P. 192.
[46] *Re Hagger* [1930] 2 Ch. 190.
[47] *Dufour v. Pereira* (1769) 1 Dick. 419 at 421; *Stone v. Hoskins* [1905] P. 194 at 197; *Re Hagger* 1930 2 Ch. 190; J. D. B. Mitchell (1951) 14 M.L.R. 136 at 138.
[48] *Re Dale* [1994] Ch. 31.
[49] *Quaere*: would incurable insanity on the part of H have the same effect? Consider Mental Health Act 1983, ss. 95, 96.
[50] [1997] 3 All E.R. 63 at 71.
[51] *Re Oldham* [1925] Ch. 75.
[52] *Re Green* [1951] Ch. 148.

The requirement for mutual wills sometimes expressed as the need for **2–146** "an agreement not to revoke" the wills is more aptly expressed as the need for "acceptance of an obligation imposed by the other party" as the obligation may well allow the will of the survivor to be revoked so long as a new will is made giving effect to the agreed arrangements.[53] The acceptance of an obligation may be difficult to prove in husband and wife situations where there is less likely to be an intention to impose legal relationships, neither party making the gifts by will on the faith of a promise by the other to accept legal obligations, but instead, making the gifts without any strings attached, confidently assuming the other party will do as asked.[54]

The principle is that the survivor becomes a trustee for the perfor- **2–147** mance of the mutual agreement after the death of the first to die. Accordingly, if the agreement is too vague to be enforced, there will be no trust. Subject to this, however, the agreement can define the property, which is to be subject to the trust, in any way it pleases. The trust may give the survivor nothing[55] or just give the survivor a life interest in all or a specific part of the deceased's property or it may also provide for him to have a life interest in all or a specific part of his own property at the date of death of the deceased.[56] The life interest may even extend to capital acquired after the deceased's death though practical problems arise if there is no power of appointment of capital.[57] Sometimes, it may appear that the survivor is to be absolute owner of the deceased's property passing to him under the will and of his own existing and subsequently acquired property, but that he is supposed to be under some binding obligation to bequeath whatever he has left at his death to the agreed beneficiaries.[58]

A purported trust of such uncertain property would normally be **2–148** void,[59] but it seems that the express contract between the parties that led the party first dying to leave his property in the agreed manner may give the ultimate beneficiaries a remedy by way of a "floating" trust, suspended during the survivor's lifetime and crystallising into a proper trust on his death: *Re Cleaver, infra*. The survivor will be under a fiduciary duty not to make *inter vivos* gifts deliberately intended to defeat the contract and, presumably, the proceeds of sale of any property within the fiduciary obligation and any property purchased with such proceeds

---

[53] *cf. Re Oldham* [1925] Ch. 75 where Mrs. O after Mr. O's death had revoked her mutual will but made another in similar terms, when it was not suggested that there had been a breach of her agreement with Mr. O, the breach only allegedly occurring when she made yet another will but in different terms.

[54] *Gray v. Perpetual Trustee Ltd* [1928] A.C. 391; *Re Oldham* [1925] Ch 75, *Re Goodchild* [1997] All E.R. 63

[55] *Re Dale* [1994] Ch. 31.

[56] *Re Hagger* [1930] 2 Ch. 190.

[57] J. D. B. Mitchell (1953) 14 M.L.R. 136; R. Burgess (1972) 36 Conv. 113.

[58] Such beneficiaries may well not have vested interests liable to be divested: the parties probably intend them to benefit only if alive on the survivor's death so that if they all predecease the survivor his fiduciary obligation will cease.

[59] *Re Jones* [1898] 1 Ch. 438 *Re Goodchild* [1997] 3 All E.R. 63 at 76 and see *infra*, at para. 3–85.

will be subject to such obligation.[60] Perhaps the "floating" trust may develop doctrinally by analogy with the floating charge over company assets and crystallise not only on the death of the survivor but also when the survivor attempts to make a mala fide gift or sale at an undervalue designed to defeat his contract,[61] especially if such intent is expressed in the contract.

2–149   Before the death of the first to die the agreement is a contractual one made in consideration of the mutual promises of H and W for the benefit of B, who neither is a party to the contract nor supplies consideration.[62] Whether H would be in breach of the contract if he told W that he no longer intended to give effect to their arrangement, or if his will was automatically revoked by remarriage to someone else after divorcing W, or if he revoked his will without informing W but predeceased W, depends on the construction of the contract. Prime facie it seems that the contract will be presumed revocable upon notice to the other party or upon the will automatically being revoked by marriage so as not to be broken if such circumstances occur.[63] However, if H makes a new will containing new arrangements without informing W, but predeceases W, it seems that W can sue H's executors for damages for losses flowing from the breach of contract (though W will be released from her obligations under contract) or for specific performance if willing to fulfil her obligations.[64]

2–150   If H died first, by his will carrying into effect the mutual arrangement, then, in order to protect B and to prevent W repudiating her obligations, a constructive trust is imposed since B is unable to bring an action for specific performance[65] of the express terms of the contract or was unable until advantage could be taken of the contract (Rights of Third Parties) Act 1999. If the contract relates not just to whatever assets might be owned at death but to interests in land then equity will not allow L.P.A. 1925, s.40 or now Law of Property (Miscellaneous Provisions) Act 1989, s.2 to be pleaded since this would be to use the statute as an instrument of fraud.[66]

2–151   It would seem that the principles underlying mutual wills could extend to an agreement subsequent to the making of the wills[67] and to an agreement between joint tenants not to sever their interest on terms that the survivor will dispose of the asset in an agreed manner.[68]

---

[60] The fiduciary relationship should give rise to a right to trace. The survivor might be compared to an executor who has full title to the testator's estate in which the beneficiaries have no proprietary interest (see *Commissioner for Stamp Duties v. Livingston* [1965] A.C. 694 at 701; *Re Diplock* [1948] Ch. 465). Because the obligation is rather nebulous a well-advised testator should leave the property to S for life, remainder to B but give S and the trustees a joint power to appoint capital to S.

[61] *cf. Re Manuwera Transport* [1971] N.Z.L.R. 909.

[62] *Dufour v. Pereira* (1769) 1 Dick. 419 at 421; *Lord Walpole v. Lord Oxford* (1797) 3 Ves. 402; *Gray v. Perpetual Trustee Co.* [1928] A.C. 391; *Birmingham v. Renfrew* (1937) 57 C.L.R. 666.

[63] *Dufour v. Pereira, supra* at 420; *Stone v. Hoskins* [1905] P. 194 at 197; *Re Marsland* [1939] Ch. 820.

[64] See C. E. F. Rickett (1991) 54 M.L.R. 581 and M. Cope, *Constructive Trusts*, pp. 534–537.

[65] *Birmingham v. Renfrew* (1937) 57 C.L.R. 666; *Re Dale* [1994] Ch. 31.

[66] *Birmingham v. Renfrew* (1937) 57 C.L.R. 666 at 690.

[67] *Re Fox* [1951] Ontario R. 378.

[68] *Re Newey* [1994] 2 N.Z.L.R. 590, *Manitoba University v. Sandeman* (1998) 155 DLR (4th) 40.

RE CLEAVER (DECEASED)

Chancery Division [1981] 1 W.L.R. 939; [1981] 2 All E.R. 1018

The testator and testatrix married in their seventies and in 1974 made wills on the same date and in similar terms, leaving their property to each other absolutely and in default of survival to the plaintiffs. The testator died in 1975. The testatrix made a new will in 1977 and cut out the plaintiffs and died in 1978. The plaintiffs successfully claimed her executors held her estate on the terms of the 1974 will.

NOURSE J.: "I have derived great assistance from the decision of the High **2–152** Court of Australia in *Birmingham v. Renfrew* (1936) 57 C.L.R. 666. That was a case where the available extrinsic evidence was held to be sufficient to establish the necessary agreement between two spouses. It is chiefly of interest because both Latham C.J. and more especially Dixon J. examined with some care the whole nature of the legal theory on which these and other similar cases proceed. I would like to read three passages from the judgment of Dixon J., which state, with all the clarity and learning for which the judgments of that most eminent judge are renowned, what I believe to be a correct analysis of the principles on which a case of enforceable mutual wills depends. First (at 682–683):

'I think the legal result was a contract between husband and wife. The **2–153** contract bound him, I think, during her lifetime not to revoke his will without notice to her. If she died without altering her will, then he was bound after her death not to revoke his will at all. She on her part afforded the consideration for his promise by making her will. His obligation not to revoke his will during her life without notice to her is to be implied. For I think the express promise should be understood as meaning that if she died leaving her will unrevoked then he would not revoke his. But the agreement really assumes that neither party will alter his or her will without the knowledge of the other. It has long been established that a contract between persons to make corresponding wills gives rise to equitable obligations when one acts on the faith of such an agreement and dies leaving his will unrevoked so that the other takes property under its dispositions. It operates to impose upon the survivor an obligation regarded as specifically enforceable. It is true that he cannot be compelled to make and leave unrevoked a testamentary document and if he dies leaving a last will containing provisions inconsistent with his agreement it is nevertheless valid as a testamentary act. But the doctrines of equity attach the obligation to the property. The effect is, I think, that the survivor becomes a constructive trustee and the terms of the trust are those of the will which he undertook would be his last will.'

"Next (at 689):

'There is a third element which appears to me to be inherent in the nature **2–154** of such a contract or agreement, although I do not think it has been expressly considered. The purpose of an arrangement for corresponding wills must often be, as in this case, to enable the survivor during his life to deal as absolute owner with the property passing under the will of the party first dying. That is to say, the object of the transaction is to put the survivor in a position to enjoy for his own benefit the full ownership so that, for instance, he may convert it and expend the proceeds if he choose. But when he dies he is to bequeath what is left in the manner agreed upon. It is only by the special doctrines of equity that such a floating obligation, suspended, so to speak, during the life-time of the survivor can descend upon the assets at his death and crystallise into a trust. No doubt gifts and settlements, *inter vivos*, if calculated to defeat the intention of the compact, could not be made by the survivor and his right of disposition, *inter vivos*, is, therefore, not unqualified. But, substantially, the purpose of the arrangement will often be to allow full enjoyment for the survivor's own benefit and advantage upon condition that at his death the residue shall pass as arranged.'

"Finally (at 690):

2–155   'In *Re Oldham* Astbury J. pointed out, in dealing with the question whether an agreement should be inferred, that in *Dufour v. Pereira* the compact was that the survivor should take a life estate only in the combined property. It was, therefore, easy to fix the corpus with a trust as from the death of the survivor. But I do not see any difficulty in modern equity in attaching to the assets a constructive trust which allowed the survivor to enjoy the property subject to a fiduciary duty which, so to speak, crystallised on his death and disabled him only from voluntary disposition *inter vivos*.'

"I interject to say that Dixon J. was there clearly referring only to voluntary dispositions *inter vivos* which are calculated to defeat the intention of the compact. No objection could normally be taken to ordinary gifts of small value. He went on:

2–156   'On the contrary, as I have said, it seems rather to provide a reason for the intervention of equity. The objection that the intended beneficiaries could not enforce a contract is met by the fact that a constructive trust arises from the contract and the fact that testamentary dispositions made upon the faith of it have taken effect. It is the constructive trust and not the contract that they are entitled to enforce.'

"It is also clear from *Birmingham v. Renfrew* that these cases of mutual wills are only one example of a wider category of cases, for example secret trusts, in which a court of equity will intervene to impose a constructive trust. A helpful and interesting summary of that wider category of cases will be found in the argument of counsel for the plaintiffs in *Ottaway v. Norman* [1972] Ch. 698 at 701–702. The principle of all these cases is that a court of equity will not permit a person to whom property is transferred by way of gift, but on the faith of an agreement or clear understanding that it is to be dealt with in a particular way for the benefit of a third person, to deal with that property inconsistently with that agreement or understanding. If he attempts to do so after having received the benefit of the gift equity will intervene by imposing a constructive trust on the property which is the subject-matter of the agreement or understanding. I take that statement of principle, and much else which is of assistance in this case, from the judgment of Slade J. in *Re Pearson Fund Trusts* (October 21, 1977, unreported).

"I would emphasise that the agreement or understanding must be such as to **2–157** impose on the donee a legally binding obligation to deal with the property in the particular way and that the other two certainties, namely those as to the subject-matter of the trust and the persons intended to benefit under it, are as essential to this species of trust as they are to any other. In spite of an argument by counsel for Mr. and Mrs. Noble to the contrary, I find it hard to see how there could be any difficulty about the second or third certainties in a case of mutual wills unless it was in the terms of the wills themselves. There, as in this case, the principal difficulty is always whether there was a legally binding obligation or merely an honourable engagement.

"Before turning in detail to the evidence which relates to the question whether there was a legally binding obligation on the testatrix in the present case or not I must return once more to *Birmingham v. Renfrew*. It is clear from that case, if from nowhere else, that an enforceable agreement to dispose of property in pursuance of mutual wills can be established only by clear and satisfactory evidence. That seems to me to be no more than a particular application of the general rule that all claims relating to the property of deceased persons must be scrutinised with very great care. However, that does not mean that there has to be a departure from the ordinary standard of proof required in civil proceedings. I have to be satisfied on the balance of probabilities that the alleged agreement was made, but before I can be satisfied of that I must find clear and satisfactory evidence to that effect."

QUESTIONS

1. Is a sound approach to gifts by will where secret trusts or mutual wills may **2–158** be involved as follows:

(1) Is there appearance of (a) incorporation by reference (b) half-secret trust (c) fully secret trust (d) mutual wills?

(2) If (a) does the will refer to an ascertainable already existing document or does it attempt to incorporate a future document or an assortment of present and future documents?

(3) If (b) so that on the face of the will there really was an intent to create a binding obligation were the terms of the obligation (i) communicated before or after the will and, if before, were they (ii) communicated in accordance with the will (iii) to a person who accepted them and (iv) who does not take beneficially under the trust if the obligation was a trust and not a gift upon condition?

(4) If (c) so that there was an intention outside of the will to create a binding obligation were the terms of the obligation (i) communicated in the testator's lifetime (ii) to a person who accepted the obligation?

(5) If (d) so that the arrangements were agreed by each testator, resulting in the alike wills, was there an acceptance that the survivor would be legally obliged to carry out the arrangements?

2. In 1991 Alan made his will as follows: "Whatever I die possessed of I give to **2–159** my wife Brenda." The will was witnessed by two of Alan's daughters, Diana and Edwina. Shortly afterwards, Alan asked Brenda if she would hold half the property she received under his will for their three daughters, Diana, Edwina and Freda equally. Brenda assented to this. In 1994 Freda ran away with a merchant

seaman, Wayne. As a result Alan told Brenda to keep Freda's share for herself. A year ago Diana died, childless, and a week later Alan died after a long illness. How should his £150,000 estate be distributed? Would it make any difference if Brenda disclaimed all benefits due to pass to her under the will and relied, instead, upon her rights under the intestacy rules?

2–160   3. H and W make wills in identical terms *mutatis mutandis* in pursuance of an agreement that they were each to leave their estates upon trust for sale for the survivor absolutely, the survivor being obliged to leave half of the property he owned at his death to their nephews. A and B equally. Each agreed not to withdraw from the arrangement without giving notice to the other. W died childless having left all her estate upon trust for sale for H absolutely.

H later married S and made a second will leaving half his property to A and B equally, one quarter to S absolutely and one quarter to S "upon trusts which have been communicated to her." In a sealed envelope given to S shortly before H made his second will there were directions that S was to hold the quarter share given to her as trustee on trust for X for life remainder to Y absolutely, whilst one month before his death H asked S to hold her absolute quarter share upon trust for Z and she agreed. H and S were involved in a bad car crash resulting in S predeceasing H by one day.

2–161   How should H's estate be distributed if the property received by H under W's will was worth £150,000 whilst the property passing under H's will was worth £100,000? Would it make any difference if two years after W's death and seven years before his own death H had created a settlement of £40,000 on trust for X for life, remainder to Y absolutely? Would the position be any different if W's estate had been worth £500,000 and she had died intestate owing to her will failing to comply with the formalities required by the Wills Act 1837?

4. A month before he died Tim conveyed his freehold estate, Longways, to Brian Bluff, having obtained Brian's oral agreement to hold it on trust for Lucy Lovejoy. Lucy first learned of this after Tim's death, she and Tim having had a major row two weeks before Tim's death so Tim then told Brian to hold Longways for Tim.

In 1996 Tim made his will in which he appointed Roger Robinson to be his executor, he gave Braeside to Bluff "to deal with as I have directed him" and he gave his residuary estate to his widow.

2–162   Tim's signature to his will was properly witnessed by Robinson and by Bluff. Tim contemporaneously handed Bluff a diskette from an Amstrad word processor saying, "This tells you what to do with Braeside after my death but you will not find the code word to its special contents until after my death, when the code word will be in my deed box at my Bank in Buty High Street." Bluff took the diskette saying, "That's fine by me."

Tim died last week in a car crash. Bluff discovered that in the deed box there were two undated slips of paper headed "Codeword," one containing the word "Scylla," the other containing the word "Charybdis." The former makes the diskette state: "Memo to B. Bluff. Please sell Braeside, invest the proceeds and pay the income to Sue Grabbitt till her death when you can have the capital." The latter makes the diskette state: "Memo to B. Bluff. Please transfer Braeside to Sue Grabbitt." Obviously, Tim had put both messages on the diskette before making his will but the codeword device left him still able to decide which message should be the binding one.

Bluff seeks your advice about entitlement to Braeside and to Longways.

5. If trustees hold property upon trust to pay or transfer the income and or **2–163** capital to the settlor or his nominee in accordance with such written directions as may from time to time be received by the trustees from the settlor in his lifetime, and on his death to transfer the property remaining to X Y and Z equally (or unequally if the settlor so directs in writing in his lifetime) then is this not a bare *Saunders v Vautier* (*infra* at para. 9–152) trusteeship or agency until the settlor's death (especially, if the trustees have to invest as the settlor directs or can only invest or disinvest with the settlor's consent) so that the property remains part of the settlor's disposable estate and the settlement actually amounts to a testamentary disposition requiring compliance with the Will Act 1837? Is this also the case where trustees hold a £10 million fund on trust to accumulate the income in the settlor's lifetime, remainder to X Y and Z equally (or unequally if the settlor so directs in his lifetime in writing), where the settlor retains a power to revoke the trust wholly or partly and a power to appoint income or capital to anyone (including himself) at any time?

Is there a distinction between (1) trustees holding to the order of the settlor and (2) trustees holding to the settlor's order if he orders it?

Chapter 3

THE ESSENTIALS OF A TRUST

3–01 To create a trust any requisite formalities for vesting property in the trustees (known as completely constituting the trust) must be complied with and the "three certainties" must be present: certainty of intention to create a trust, certainty of subject matter of the trust and certainty of beneficiaries, thereby making the trust administratively workable and capable of being "policed" by the court. To underpin the binding obligation inherent in the trust concept the trust must be directly or indirectly for the benefit of persons (individual or corporate) so that some person has *locus standi* to apply to the court to enforce the trust and make the trustees liable to account,[1] unless the trust is either for a limited anomalous number of testamentary non-charitable purposes relating to the maintenance of animals, tombs, etc.,[2] or for charitable purposes when the Attorney-General enforces the charitable purposes. Charitable trusts, where there is a general charitable intention, are also favoured in that they do not have to satisfy the requirement of certainty of objects (so long as the objects are sufficiently certain to be classified as exclusively charitable) and they can endure for ever whilst private trusts are limited by the perpetuity rules to a perpetuity period. As charitable trusts are a special category they are dealt with in Chapter 6.

3–02 In the vast majority of cases the trustees know that they are trustees, having agreed with the settlor to be trustees, and the beneficiaries know that they are beneficiaries, but a trust can be created unilaterally by a settlor in circumstances where the trustees do not know that they are trustees[3] and the beneficiaries do not know that they are beneficiaries.[4]

Take the case of a trust created by will where the testator before he dies does not tell the trustees or the beneficiaries about his testamentary trust, which arises as soon as he dies. Equity does not allow a trust to fail for want of a trustee,[5] so if the trustees refuse to act and disclaim the intended trust property, such property falls to be held on trust by the person in whom the deceased's estate is vested, the executor or the administrator with the will annexed to the grant of letters of administration. Such person holds the trust property (to the extent not properly

---

[1] See section 5, at paras 3–208 *et seq.*
[2] See *infra*, at paras 3–126 *et seq.*
[3] *Fletcher v. Fletcher* (1844) 4 Hare 67; *Childers v. Childers* (1857) 1 De G&J 482.
[4] *Fletcher v. Fletcher* (supra); *Re Lewis* [1904] 2 Ch 656, *Rose v. Rose* (1986) 7 NSWLR 679, 686, *Re Kayford* [1975] 1 W.L.R. 279. Indeed, there may be no beneficiaries for a period while income is being accumulated and the ultimate contingent beneficiary may not be born or otherwise ascertained for some time, especially for jurisdictions other than England where the accumulation period can be as long as the perpetuity period.
[5] *Mallott v. Wilson* [1903] 2 Ch 494, *Harris v. Sharp*, unreported, Court of Appeal March 21, 1989.

used for the payment of the deceased's debts and expenses) on trust for the beneficiaries until such person exercises his power[6] to appoint new trustees.

Similarly, a settlor in his lifetime might transfer legal title to his **3–03** registered land or his shares in a company[7] by making the transferee(s) registered proprietor(s) of the land or shares without telling them, and by signing a document showing he intends them to become trustees thereof for specified beneficiaries. If the trustees disclaim on learning the true situation, then, after rectification of the register, the legal title remains with the settlor to hold it as trustee on trust for the beneficiaries.

Thus, the key event that gives rise to a trust is the unilateral act of the settlor. The intended trustee's decision to accept the trust property and act as trustee then makes that trustee the trustee of the trust, but if he decided against it, the trust still subsists, albeit with the settlor or the settlor's personal representative as trustee until new trustees are appointed. The trustee is then entitled to remuneration under the trust instrument or statute[8] as an incident of the office of trustee and not by virtue of any agreement or contract with the settlor.[9] The trustee cannot sue the settlor for trusteeship fees, while the settlor cannot sue the trustee if the trustee in breach of trust carries out the trusteeship negligently or improperly. The trustee reimburses itself out of the trust fund for properly incurred expenses and pays its fees thereout, while it is the beneficiaries (and not the settlor) who can sue the trustee if it acts negligently or improperly so that the trustee tops up the trust fund to its proper level. A breach of contract can lead to termination of the contract, but a breach of trust does not terminate the trust, although enabling termination of the wrongdoing trustee's term of office and replacement by a new person as trustee.

A person cannot be burdened with the duties of trusteeship until that **3–04** person's conscience is affected by the trust,[10] *e.g.* by actual knowledge of the trust or by turning a "Nelsonian" blind eye to the trust or by being suspicious that a trust affects property but then deliberately or recklessly failing to make the further inquiries that an honest reasonable person would take.[11] However, property in the hands of a person whose conscience is not affected by any equitable interest is subject from the time of receipt by such person to equitable interests then burdening the property under the priority rules governing proprietary interests,[12]

---

[6] Trustee Act 1925 s. 36.

[7] S could also covenant on behalf of himself and his personal representatives with T that one year after his death his personal representatives will pay £100,000 to T to the intent that T will hold the benefit of this covenant on trust for S's illegitimate children who attain 25 years. There is an immediate trust of this chose in action (even if T subsequently disclaims on learning of the covenant): *Fletcher v. Fletcher* (1844) 4 Hare 67. There is a danger that if the intended trustee is kept in the dark, then the trust could be a sham, with the property remaining beneficially owned by the settlor, *e.g. Midland Bank plc v. Wyatt* [1995] 1 FLR 696.

[8] Trustee Act 2000 s.29 *infra* para. 9–68.

[9] *Re Duke of Norfolk's S.T* [1982] Ch 61.

[10] *Westdeutsche Landesbank v. Islington BC* [1996] AC 669, 705, 707.

[11] Further on such actual, "Nelsonian" or "naughty" knowledge see at para. 11–111 *infra*.

[12] *Westdeutsche Landesbank v. Islington BC* [1996] AC 669, 707.

whether such equitable interests are interests under trusts or charges (or equitable easements or restrictive covenants).

Section 1. Certainty of Intention to Create a Trust

RELATIONSHIPS OTHER THAN TRUSTS

3–05 A person may deal with his property in a variety of ways, His expressed wishes have to be examined in the context of the surrounding circumstances for indications as to the consequences he expects to flow from his actions, so that these indicia may then be seen as appropriate to the creation of a trust relationship or some other relationship. A person can create a trust without knowing it[13]; while, no matter how clear the intention to create a trust, if the essence of the obligation created is that of a charge[14] or of a debt[15] then a charge or a debt will arise and not a trust.

Bailment

3–06 If an owner delivers possession (as opposed to ownership) of her goods to another on condition that they will be redelivered to the owner or according to the owner's directions when the purpose of delivering the goods (*e.g.* for cleaning or for use for a year or for safe custody or as security for a loan) has been carried out, this will be a bailment.[16] This is a common law relationship where the bailee receives a special property in the goods, the general property in which remains in the bailor.

3–07 Bailment and trust can co-exist. Thus in *Lloyd's Bank v. Bank of America National Trust and Savings Associated*[17] the plaintiffs lent money on the security of bills of lading (shipping documents relating to particular merchandise) pledged to them. They released the bills of lading to the corporate pledgor "in order to enable the company to sell the merchandise as trustees for the plaintiffs" so the proceeds of sale would reimburse the plaintiffs. The pledgor, instead, fraudulently transferred the bills of lading to the defendant as security for a loan. The Court of Appeal held that the defendant was a bona fide purchaser for value without notice of the plaintiffs' equitable interest, the pledgor having general legal title to pass to the defendant, which took free from the plaintiffs' special legal title as bailee owing to the pledgor being a mercantile agent, so that the exception to *nemo dat quod non habet* in Factors Act 1889 section 2(1) applied.

---

[13] *e.g. Paul v. Constance* [1977] 1 W.L.R. 54; *Re Vandervell's Trusts (No. 2)* [1974] Ch: 269; *Re Chelsea Cloisters Ltd* (1980) 41 P. & C.R. 98.
[14] *Clough v. Martin* [1985] 1 W.L.R. 111; *Re Bond Worth Ltd* [1980] Ch. 228.
[15] *Commissioners of Customs & Excise v. Richmond Theatre Management Ltd* [1995] STC 257.
[16] See N. E. Palmer, *Bailment* (2nd ed.) and A. P. Bell, *Modern Law of Personal Property*, Chap. 5. There can be sufficient fiduciary relationship between bailor and bailee to give the bailor the equitable right to trace the bailed goods and their product: *Aluminium Industries Vaasen v. Romalpa* [1976] 1 W.L.R. 676 but this has been much restricted as a special case: *Clough Mill Ltd v. Martin* [1985] 1 WLR 111
[17] [1938] 2 K.B. 147.

Bailment of intangibles cannot exist because intangibles (*e.g.* copyrights, shares in companies, debts) cannot be possessed without being owned.

Agency

If an owner transfers ownership or possession of property to another to **3–08** enable him to do things on his behalf an agency relationship will arise. The principal can direct the agent and can terminate the agency (except in certain limited circumstances[18]). The agent (unlike a trustee *vis-à-vis* the settlor or beneficiaries) has power to subject his principal to liability in contract and in tort. The agency normally arises as a result of a contract between principal and agent. Thus, an agency normally creates a debtor-creditor relationship. However, if a principal sells his cars via an agent obliged to pay the proceeds of each sale into a designated account and to remit to the principal by separate cheques the proceeds of such sales less commission and costs within five days (but not to account for any interest earned in that period) then a trust arises.[19] This is crucial where the agent goes into liquidation.

Equitable charges and reservation of title

To protect his financial interests as much as possible against creditors' **3–09** insolvencies, S, a supplier of materials to a manufacturer, M Ltd, may seek to obtain[20] an equitable interest in (a) the materials; (b) any products produced using his materials and (c) any proceeds of sale of the materials or the products either until the price of the particular materials is paid or even until the price of all materials from time to time supplied by S to M Ltd is paid. If M Ltd did hold (a), (b) and (c) on trust for S then S would be entitled to such on the insolvency of M Ltd in priority to M Ltd's creditors. However, if S only had a charge then such would be void against M Ltd's liquidator unless registered under the Companies Act when (impractically) no dealings with the assets would take place without S's consent.

In *Re Bond Worth Ltd*[21] it was held that if S transfers legal title in fibre **3–10** to M Ltd, purporting to reserve equitable ownership of the fibre until resale and to become equitable owner of the proceeds of sale and of any products produced using the fibre and of the proceeds of sale thereof

---

[18] Neither the settlor nor beneficiaries of a trust (unless between them absolutely entitled and *sui juris* when they can terminate the trust) have such rights. A person can be a trustee but not an agent for unborn or unascertained persons: *Swain v. Law Society* [1981] 3 All E.R. 797 at 822. Further see Markesinis & Munday's *Outline of Agency*, Chap. 6.

[19] *Re Fleet Disposal Services Ltd* [1995] 1 B.C.L.C. 345 *supra* at para. 1–43 and for sales of airline tickets: *Royal Brunei Airlines v. Tan* [1995] 3 All E.R. 97; *Re Air Canada and M & L Travel Ltd* (1994) 108 D.L.R. (4th) 592.

[20] S is legal and beneficial owner: he cannot obtain a separate equitable interest until full ownership is vested in another: *Westdentsche Landesbank v. Islington BC* [1996] A.C. 669, 706, 714; *DKLR Holding Co (No 2) Pty Ltd v. Commissioner of Stamp Duties* (1982) 149 CLR 431

[21] [1980] Ch. 228. See also *Specialist Plant Ltd v. Braithwaite* [1987] BCLC, where the Court of Appeal held that the suppliers' attempt to become part owner of the products made with his suppliers till payment actually created an equitable charge.

until full payment be made for the relevant fibre, this amounts to the creation of an equitable charge by M Ltd by way of security. Such a charge needed to be registered under the Companies Act (now section 395 of the 1985 Act) and was not, and so was void against creditors and the liquidator.

3–11   The alternative effective approach for S to adopt is to retain full legal beneficial ownership in the materials supplied until full payment to S of money due from M Ltd[22] when there can be no question of M Ltd granting a registrable charge because M Ltd owns nothing out of which a grant can be made.[23] Thus S can recover such raw materials in the event of the insolvency of M Ltd. However, if S goes further and claims to obtain legal ownership of products produced using his materials with others supplied by M Ltd or a third party until paid the money due from M Ltd, this will normally be construed as giving rise to a charge on the products in S's favour.[24] Similarly, any clause purporting to make S owner of the proceeds of sale of such products until paid the money due from M Ltd will be construed as creating a charge.[25]

3–12   The substance of the matter is that M Ltd is intended to be entitled to the new products or the proceeds of sale thereof once it has paid the debt due to S, so that, really, S has a charge over property subject to M Ltd's equity of redemption. What, however, if M Ltd expressly contracted that it will be trustee of re-sale proceeds received by it, holding one fifth for S and four fifths for itself (so as to cover S's input and profit), or, better still, holding on trust for S such fractional part of such proceeds then received as is equivalent to the amount then owing by M Ltd to S and the rest on trust for itself? No charge within section 395 arises here.[26] On receipt of the proceeds "Equity looks on that as done which ought to be done", and because of this, "even if the proceeds were paid into a general bank account there could be a tracing remedy where the recipient was obliged to hold a particular portion of the proceeds on trust."[27] To reinforce S's position, M Ltd should be expressly placed under an obligation to transfer the relevant amount of money into M Ltd's account within a short period (between five to 10 working days) and under an obligation in that period not to permit the amount credited in the general account to fall below the relevant amount held on trust for S.

---

[22] *Armour v. Thyssen Edelstahlwerke A.G.* [1991] 2 A.C. 339.
[23] *Clough Mill Ltd v. Martin* [1985] 1 W.L.R. 111, *infra*, para. 3–26; *Re Highway Foods International Ltd* [1995] 1 BCLC 209.
[24] *Clough v. Martin* [1985] 1 W.L.R. 111; *Modelboard Ltd v. Outer Box Ltd* [1992] BCC 945; [1993] BCLC 623.
[25] *Pfeiffer v. Arbuthnot Factors* [1988] 1 W.L.R. 150; *Company Computer Ltd v. Abercorn Group* [1993] BCLC 603; *Re Highway Foods International Ltd* [1995] 1 BCLC 209.
[26] *Associated Alloys Pty Ltd v. ACN 001 452 106 Pty Ltd* (2000) 74 A.L.J.R 862. If the contract related not to a trust of a specific fraction or percentage but only to a trust of an amount of money then owed by M Ltd to S a problem arises as to certainty of subject matter because such amount is not segregated from the remaining amount of M Ltd's money, so that no more than a contractual charge can arise, requiring registration under s.395 Companies Act 1985.
[27] *ibid* at 870.

Where M Ltd is simply selling goods supplied by S then the contract **3-13** can contain a provision that M Ltd is to hold proceeds of sale of the goods forthwith as trustee thereof for S to the extent of the fraction thereof representing the amounts then due to S by M Ltd in respect of such goods, providing that moneys subject to such trust may be paid into M Ltds' general bank account subject to being transferred into S's own account within ten working days (but without liability to pay interest thereon for such ten days) and providing that the money to the credit of M Ltd in its general bank account shall never fall below the amount held on trust for S. S should then have equitable entitlement to such money[28] supported by equitable tracing rights,[29] though they will be valueless if such money is used to pay off creditors without notice of S's rights.

Loans

If A transfers to B £50,000 not by way of gift but as part of the **3-14** purchase price of Blackacre for £150,000 in B's name, then A will have one-third of the equitable interest in Blackacre (under a resulting trust) which will obviously appreciate or depreciate with the value of Black-acre. If A had merely lent B the £50,000 for B to have the whole beneficial interest in Blackacare then A would merely have a personal claim against B for the debt. If the £50,000 loan had been secured by a charge on Blackacre then A would have the right to sell Blackacre to repay himself the debt out of the proceeds of sale. It is also possible that A could also forgive the debt in consideration for purchasing a specified share of Blackacre.

The one arrangement cannot be both a loan and a trust since the **3-15** concepts are mutually exclusive.[30] However, a loan arrangement may commence as a primary temporary trust to carry out a purpose, resulting if the purpose is performed in a pure loan relationship excluding any trust relationship, but with a secondary final trust arising in the event of non-performance of the purpose.[31] Thus where Quistclose loaned Rolls Razor Ltd £209,000 only for the purpose of paying a dividend on July 24, and Rolls Razor went into liquidation on July 17, so preventing any dividend being paid, the House of Lords held the money was then held on trust for Quistclose. This approach was applied in *Re EVTR, infra*, at para. 3-51.

---

[28] *Associated Alloys Pty Ltd v. ACN 001 452 106 Pty Ltd* (2000) A.L.J.R 862. *Re Fleet Disposal Services Ltd* [1995] 1 BCLC 345; *Re Lewis's of Leicester Ltd* [1995] 1 BCLC 428, *Royal Trust Bank v. National Westminster Bank* [1996] 2 B.C.L.C. 128

[29] For the extensiveness of tracing via an equitable charge see *El Ajou v. Dollar Land Holdings* [1993] 3 All E.R. 717, 736–737, reversed on another point [1994] 2 All E.R. 685 and *infra* para. 11–34.

[30] *Re Sharpe* [1980] 1 W.L.R. 219; *Spence v. Browne* (1988) 18 Fam. Law 291. In an exceptional case, a female not seeking repayment of her loan to a male houseowner, with whom she cohabits, nor any interest on the loan may thereby act to her detriment on the basis of a common intention that she should acquire a share of the house so that she acquires such a share: *Risch v. McFee* [1991] 1 F.L.R. 105.

[31] *Barclays Bank Ltd v. Quistclose Investments Ltd* [1970] A.C. 567; *Carreras Rothmans v. Freeman Mathews Treasure Ltd* [1985] 1 All E.R. 155; *Re EVTR Ltd* [1987] B.C.L.C. 646; *Twinsectra Ltd v. Yardley* [2000] WTLR 527, 556–567 (CA). Further on purpose trusts and the beneficiary principle see *infra*, at paras 3–208 *et seq.*

Prepayments

3–16   When a company goes into liquidation (or an individual becomes bankrupt) it will be crucial whether a claimant has merely a personal claim, whether contractual or quasi-contractual, or has a proprietary claim under a trust or a charge. If a customer sent money to a company for goods and the company went into liquidation before supplying the goods the customer with his personal claim will be a mere unsecured creditor. If the customer in his letter had stipulated that his money was to be held in trust for him till he received title to the goods, then he will have an equitable interest giving him priority over the company's creditors in so far as it is possible to trace such money. If the company, fearful of liquidation, had expressly opened a trust bank account in which it had deposited customers' payments then, again, such a customer will have an equitable interest.[32]

3–17   One could take the view[33] that the company's unilateral declaration of trust is a voidable preference of the customers as creditors. The customer would expect to be a mere creditor, having done nothing to prevent his payment going into the ordinary bank account of the company to be available to creditors generally. The company's voluntary act preferred the customers' interests above those of ordinary creditors, and this is a voidable preference resulting in the customers being relegated to the position of ordinary creditors. However, the courts[34] have taken the view that the company's unilateral declaration of trust prevents the customers from becoming creditors by making them beneficiaries under a trust, just as if the customers themselves had created the trust, or does not result from the requisite subjective desire to prefer the customers. Indeed, even where there is no clear declaration of trust by the company the courts have become quite ready to infer the requisite intent to create a trust where a separate bank account has been opened when the company was in a parlous financial situation.[35]

3–18   The most extreme case is *Neste Oy v. Lloyd's Bank plc*[36] where the plaintiff shipowners made a series of payments to PSL, their agents, to discharge present and future liabilities relating to their vessels. Such were paid into PSL's general account with the Bank, without being subjected to any trusts.

> "[The last] payment was credited to PSL at a time when Peckston Group Ltd had already resolved that it and its group companies

---

[32] *Re Kayford Ltd* [1975] 1 W.L.R. 279. Also *see Re Chelsea Cloisters Ltd* (1980) 41 P.&C.R. 98 (tenants' damage deposit account moneys held on trust by company landlord in liquidation).

[33] Goodhart & Jones (1980) 43 M.L.R. 489 at 496–498 querying whether Kayford's unilateral voluntary declaration of trust contravened the Companies Act 1948, ss. 302, 320, now Insolvency Act 1986, ss.238, 239, but because Kayford could have declined the order and returned the prepayment could it not also accept the order only on the basis the prepayment was trust money as indicated by RM Goode, *Payment Obligations in Commercial & Financial Transactions* (2nd ed. 1989) at 18 n.64?

[34] *Re Kayford Ltd* [1975] 1 WLR 279; *Re Chelsea Cloisters Ltd* (1980) 41 P. & C.R. 989; *Re Lewis's of Leicester Ltd* [1995] 1 BCLC 428 applying *Re M.C. Bacon* [1991] 1 Ch. 127.

[35] *Re Chelsea Cloisters Ltd, supra; Re Lewis's of Leicester Ltd, supra;* M. Bridge (1992) 12 O.J.L.S. 333, 335–357.

[36] [1983] 2 Lloyds Rep. 658.

should cease trading immediately (one of the directors supporting the resolution being a director of PSL) at a time when PSL had not paid for the services for which the funds had been remitted and at a time when, in all the circumstances, there was no chance that PSL could pay for the services".[37]

The directors of PSL would at least have been liable for wrongful trading if PSL had continued in business. Bingham J. held,[38]

"Given the situation of PSL when the last payment was received, any honest and reasonable directors (or the actual directors had they known of it) would, I feel sure, have arranged for the repayment of that sum to the plaintiffs without hesitation or delay . . . and, accordingly, a constructive trust is to be inferred."

He thus refused to allow the Bank to set off the payment against money **3–19** due to it when he held that the Bank had constructive notice of the trust. Subsequently in *Re Japan Leasing (Europe) Plc*[39] the judge applied the views of Bingham J. to the case where a purchaser paid the instalment of the purchase price of an aeroplane to company A, the head vendor, to divide the instalment between itself and three companies B, C and D, A's co-vendors. The intended beneficial payment to A discharged the purchaser of its liability to A B C and D under contractual arrangements which also expressly excluded any trust relationship arising between A on the one hand and B, C and D on the other hand in respect of instalments received by A: A was only to be under a personal contractual obligation as agent to account to B, C and D in respect thereof. However, the judge held that when A received the instalment after its financial problems had led to it going into administration the exclusion clause did not extend to the constructive trust that the judge held to arise by operation of law against A because[40] "it would be unconscionable for the Company [A], as agent, to receive money as agent knowing that it could not account for it to its principal [B, C, and D]".

Thus, a contractual arrangement became a trust arrangement by **3–20** operation of law. It is equally possible, of course, for a contractual relationship to become a trust relationship upon events specified in the contract. Thus, it may be expressly stipulated that unit holders under a unit trust only have personal rights to a sum of money calculated by reference to the number of units owned and the underlying value of the assets subject to the unit trust (rather than a proprietary interest in the underlying assets) until the unit trust comes to the end of its life whereupon the then unit holders are to have a proprietary interest in the assets then owned by the trustees.[41] Similarly, a life policy may consist of

---

[37] *Ibid* at 666.
[38] *Ibid* at 665.
[39] [2000] WTLR 301.
[40] *ibid* at 316.
[41] See KF Sin, *The Legal Nature of the Unit Trust*, Oxford, 1997, Chap. 5.

an investment element linked with a unit trust, premiums being applied in the acquisition of units. However, unit-linked policies normally provide that the policy-holder has no proprietary interest in the units allocated to the policy which are merely to be units of account establishing the extent of the insurance company's personal liability.[42]

Privity of contract

3–21   The well-established common law rule is that only a party to a contract can sue on it, so that if A contracts with B for the benefit of C, C cannot enforce the contract or prevent A and B from varying its terms.[43] B alone can enforce the contract: normally he can only claim nominal damages for his own loss,[44] though sometimes the equitable remedy of specific performance may be available.[45] Statutory rules in the Contracts (Rights of Third Parties) Act 1999 now permit A and B if they wish, to enable C to enforce A's contract with B.

In contrast, if A transfers property to B on trust for C, then Equity has always held that only C can enforce the trust and compel restitution to the trust fund of any losses or profits because A drops out of the picture as a donor who has made an irrevocable gift.[46]

3–22   Exceptionally, where A contracted with B if it is positively provided[47] that they both[48] intended B to be the trustee of the benefit of A's promise (a chose in action capable of being the subject matter of a trust) for C, then C will be able to enforce the trust, subject to joining B as a necessary party to be bound by any judgment in the action.[49] In such circumstances A and B will not be able to vary their contract without C's consent, unless such a power was expressly or by necessary implication reserved at the creation of the contract in circumstances where the power is a personal one for the benefit of A or B and not a fiduciary power for the benefit of C.

3–23   In the absence of clear trust language it is difficult to forecast exactly what are the circumstances when a court will find that a trust has been affirmatively established.[50] The courts are reluctant[51] to find an intent to create a trust, suspecting that such a claim is normally a transparent device to avoid the privity of contract doctrine.

Where there is a contract between A and B for the benefit of C, B cannot unilaterally[52] improve's C's position (and worsen A's position) by

---

[42] *Foskett v. McKeown* [2000] 3 All E. R. 97, 135.
[43] *Dunlop v. Selfridge* [1915] A.C. 847; *Scruttons v. Midland Silicones* [1962] A.C. 440.
[44] *Panatown Ltd v. Alfred McAlpine Construction Ltd* [2000] 4 All ER 97 (HL).
[45] *Beswick v. Beswick* [1968] A.C. 58, *infra*, para. 11–310.
[46] *Paul v. Paul* (1882) 20 Ch. D. 742; *Re Astor's S.T.* [1952] Ch 534, 542; *Bradshaw v. University College of Wales* [1987] 3 All ER 200, 203; *Goulding v. James* [1997] 2 All E.R. 239, 247.
[47] *West v. Houghton* 1879 L.R. 4 C.P.D. 197 at 203.
[48] *Re Schebsman* [1994] Ch. 83 at 89, 104: B cannot unilaterally increase the measure of A's liability.
[49] *Vandepitte v. Preferred Accident Insurance Co* [1933] A.C. 70 at 79; *Parker-Tweedale v. Dunbar Bank plc* [1991] Ch. 26.
[50] See *Trident General Insurance Co. v. McNeice Bros* (1988) 165 C.L.R. 107, pointing out how *Re Foster* [1938] 4 All E.R. 357 and *Re Sinclair's Life Policy* [1938] Ch. 799 cannot logically be distinguished from *Royal Exchange Assurance v. Hope* [1928] Ch. 179 and *Re Webb* [1941] Ch. 225.
[51] *Re Schebsman* [1944] Ch. 538; *Green v. Russell* [1959] 2 Q.B. 220; *Beswick v. Beswick* [1966] Ch. 538; *Swain v. Law Society* [1983] 1 A.C. 598.
[52] *Re Schebsman, supra*, n.48; *Darlington B.C. v. Wiltshier Northern Ltd* [1995] 1 W.L.R. 68.

declaring himself trustee for C or assigning his rights to C where B's rights are inherently for nominal damages only. However, if both A and B contracted on the footing that B would be able to enforce contractual rights for the benefit of those who suffered from defective performance but who could not acquire any rights to hold A liable for breach, then B may assign such rights[53] and be regarded as trustee of such rights.[54] Such an exception to the general rule that refuses to recognise a *ius quaesitum tertio* may be regarded as "a judicial subterfuge"[55] providing "a remedy where no other would be available to a person sustaining loss which under a national legal system ought to be compensated by the person who has caused it."[56] "The legal position in cases such as these is now fundamentally affected by the Contracts (Rights of Third Parties) Act 1999"[57] which enables rights to be expressly enforceable by a third party like C if the contracting parties so wish.

Possibilities of construction for testamentary gifts

If a testator by will leaves property to B and requires B to make some **3–24** payment to C or perform some obligation in favour of C, there are five possible constructions open to a court. The testator's words may be treated as:

(i) Merely indicating his motive, so that B takes an absolute beneficial interest, *e.g.* "to my wife, B, so that she may support herself and the children according to their needs" or "to my daughter B, on condition she provides a home for my handicapped daughter, C."[58]

(ii) Creating a charge on the property given to B, so that B takes the property beneficially subject to the charge for securing payment of money to C,[59] *e.g.* "my office block, Demeter House, to my son, B, subject to paying thereout £10,000 p.a. to my widow, C."

(iii) Creating a trust in favour of C,[60] *e.g.* "my office block, Demeter **3–25** House, to B absolutely but so that he must pay an amount equal to the income therefrom to my widow C for the rest of her life."

(iv) Creating a personal obligation binding B to C so that if B accepts the property he must perform the obligation in C's favour[61] (even if it costs him more than the value of the property[62]) *e.g.* "my

---

[53] *Dunlop v. Lambert* (1839) 6 Cl. & F. 600; *The Albazero* [1977] A.C. 774; *St Martin's Property Corporation Ltd v. Sir Robert McAlpine Ltd* [1994] 1 A.C. 85; *Darlington B.C. v. Wiltshier Northern Ltd, Supra.*

[54] *Darlington B.C. v. Wiltshier Northern Ltd, supra*; *Panatown Ltd v. Alfred McAlpine Construction Ltd* [2000] 4 All ER 97, 151, 157–158.

[55] *Swain v. Law Society* [1983] 1 A.C. 598 at 611.

[56] *St Martin's Property Corporation Ltd v. Sir Robert McAlpine Ltd* [1994] A.C. 85 at 115.

[57] *Panatown Ltd v. Alfred McAlpine Construction Ltd* [2000] 4 All ER 97, 149.

[58] *Re Brace* [1954] 1 W.L.R. 955; *cf. Re Frame* [1939] Ch. 700 and *Re Lipinski* [1976] Ch. 235. Further see Administration of Justice Act 1982 s.22, *infra*, at para. 3–71.

[59] *Re Oliver* (1890) 62 L.T. 533. B is under no personal obligation to make up any deficiency caused by insufficiency of the property charged.

[60] *e.g. Irvine v. Sullivan* (1869) L.R. 8 Eq. 673.

[61] *Re Lester* [1942] Ch. 324.

[62] *Re Hodge* [1940] Ch. 260.

leasehold cottage currently subleased to X I hereby devise to B absolutely on condition that he agrees to pay my widow C £3,500 p.a. for the rest of her life."

(v) Creating a condition subsequent that affects the property in B's hands making B liable to forfeit the property if the condition is broken;[63] *e.g.* "my 500,000 £1 shares in Fantabulous Co. Ltd to B Charity Co. on condition that it pays my widow, C, an annuity of £10,000 for her life and properly maintains my family burial vault, and upon any failure to observe this condition then the R.S.P.C.A. shall become entitled to the shares."

CLOUGH MILL LTD v. MARTIN

Court of Appeal [1984] 3 All E.R. 982; [1985] 1 W.L.R. 111.

3–26 ROBERT GOFF L.J.: "This appeal is concerned with what is sometimes called 'a retention of title clause', but more frequently nowadays a 'Romalpa clause.' The appellants, Clough Mills Ltd, carry on business as spinners of yarn. Under four contracts entered into between December 1979 and March 1980 they contracted to supply yarn to a company called Heatherdale Fabrics Ltd (which I shall refer to as 'the buyers'), which carried on business as manufacturers of fabric. When the appellants entered into these contracts, they knew that the yarn to be supplied under them was to be used by the buyers for such manufacture. Each of the contracts incorporated the appellants' standard conditions. These included a condition (condition 12) entitled 'Passing of title'; this is the Romalpa clause, with the construction and effect of which this case is concerned . . . It reads as follows:

3–27 'However the ownership of the material shall remain with the Seller, which reserves the right to dispose of the material until payment in full for all the material has been received by it in accordance with the terms of this contract or until such time as the Buyer sells the material to its customers by way of bona-fide sale at full market value.

If such payment is overdue in whole or in part the Seller may (without prejudice to any of its other rights) recover or re-sell the material or any of it and may enter upon the Buyer's premises by its servants or agents for that purpose.

Such payments shall become due immediately upon the commencement of any act or proceeding in which the Buyer's solvency is involved.

If any of the material is incorporated in or used as material for other goods before such payment the property in the whole of such goods shall be and remain with the Seller until such payment has been made, or the other goods have been sold as aforesaid, and all the Seller's rights hereunder in the material shall extend to those other goods.'

3–28 On March 11, 1980 the respondent, Geoffrey Martin, was appointed receiver of the buyers. On that date the buyers still retained at their premises 375 kg of unused yarn supplied under contracts and still unpaid for. So on March 11, 1980

---

[63] *Att.-Gen. v. Cordwainers' Company* (1833) 3 My. & K.; 40 E.R. 203; *Re Oliver* (1890) 62 L.T. 533; *Re Tyler* [1891] 3 Ch. 252.

the appellants wrote to the receiver expressing their intention to repossess the unused yarn . . . the solicitors acting for the receiver replied that the appellants' retention of title clause was invalid for, *inter alia*, non-registration under section 95 of the Companies Act 1948 and that the receiver would therefore continue to allow the yarn to be used and would refuse the appellants admission to collect it. The appellants therefore commenced proceedings, claiming damages from the receiver for conversion of the yarn. His Honour Judge O'Donoghue, sitting as a judge of the High Court, dismissed the claim, holding that, on its true construction, condition 12 created a charge on the yarn and that such charge was void for non-registration under section 95. It is against that decision that the appellants now appeal to this court . . .

"The submission of counsel for the appellants as to the nature of the **3–29** appellants' retention of title under the first sentence of the condition was extremely simple. Under the Sale of Goods Act 1979 a seller of goods is fully entitled, after delivery of the goods to the buyer, to retain title in the goods until he has been paid: see section 19(1) of that Act. That is precisely what the appellants have done by condition 12. The appellants' title did not derive from the contract; on the contrary, it was simply retained by them, though under the contract power was conferred on the buyers both to sell the goods and to use them in manufacturing other goods. As the buyers never acquired any title to the unused yarn in question, they could not charge the yarn to the appellants. So the appellants were, quite simply, the owners of the yarn; and there was no question of there being any charge on the yarn in their favour, which was void if unregistered.

"This attractively simple approach was challenged by counsel for the receiver. **3–30** He submitted, first of all, that, if the first sentence of condition 12 is read literally, as counsel for the appellants suggested it should be read, the buyers can only have had possession of the yarn in a fiduciary capacity, whether as bailees or as fiduciary agents. But, he said, the power conferred on the buyers under the contract, not merely to sell the material but also to mix it with other materials in the manufacture of goods, was inconsistent with the existence of any fiduciary capacity in the buyers, or indeed with the appellants' unqualified ownership of the yarn.

"Now this is a submission which I am unable to accept. In every case, we have **3–31** to look at the relevant documents and other communications which have passed between the parties, and to consider them in the light of the relevant surrounding circumstances, in order to ascertain the rights and duties of the parties *inter se*, always paying particular regard to the practical effect of any conclusion concerning the nature of those rights and duties. In performing this task, concepts such as bailment and fiduciary duty must not be allowed to be our masters, but must rather be regarded as the tools of our trade. I for my part can see nothing objectionable in an agreement between parties under which A, the owner of goods, gives possession of those goods to B, at the same time conferring on B a power of sale and a power to consume the goods in manufacture, though A will remain the owner of the goods until they are either sold or consumed. I do not see why the relationship between A and B, pending sale or consumption, should not be the relationship of bailor and bailee, even though A has no right to trace the property in his goods into the proceeds of sale. If that is what the parties have agreed should happen, I can see no reason why the law should not give effect to that intention. I am happy to find that both Staughton and Peter Gibson J.J. have adopted a similar approach in *Hendy Lennox (Industrial Engines) Ltd v. Grahame Puttick Ltd* [1984] 1 W.L.R. 485 and *Re Andrabell Ltd* [1984] 3 All E.R. 407.

3–32   "Even so, it is necessary to examine counsel for the appellants' construction in a little more detail. If, under this condition, retention of title applied only to goods not yet paid for, I can see that his construction could be given effect to without any problem. But the difficulty with the present condition is that the retention of title applies to material, delivered and retained by the buyer, until payment in full for *all* the material delivered under the contract has been received by the seller. The effect is therefore that the seller may retain his title in material still held by the buyer, even if part of that material has been paid for. Furthermore, if in such circumstances the seller decides to exercise his rights and resell the material, questions can arise concerning (1) whether account must be taken of the part payment already received in deciding how much the seller should be entitled to sell and (2) whether, if he does resell, he is accountable to the buyer either in respect of the part payment already received, or in respect of any profit made on the resale by reason of a rise in the market value of the material . . .

3–33   "To me, the answer to these questions lies in giving effect to the condition in accordance with its terms, and on that approach I can discern no intention to create a trust. The condition provides that the seller retains his ownership in the material. He therefore remains owner; but, during the subsistence of the contract, he can only exercise his powers as owner consistently with the terms, express and implied, of the contract. On that basis, in my judgment, he can during the subsistence of the contract only resell such amount of the material as is needed to discharge the balance of the outstanding purchase price; and, if he sells more, he is accountable to the buyer for the surplus. However, once the contract has been determined, as it will be if the buyer repudiates the contract and the seller accepts the repudiation, the seller will have his rights as owner (including, of course, his right to sell the goods) uninhibited by any contractual restrictions; though any part of the purchase price received by him and attributable to the material so resold will be recoverable by the buyer on the ground of failure of consideration, subject to any set-off arising from a crossclaim by the seller for damages for the buyer's repudiation.

3–34   ". . . If this approach is right, I can see no reason why the retention of title in the first sentence of condition 12 should be construed as giving rise to a charge on the unused material in favour of the seller. In the course of his argument counsel for the receiver prayed in aid another proposition culled from the judgment of Slade J. in *Re Bond Worth Ltd* [1980] Ch. 228 at 248; [1979] 3 All E.R. 919 at 939 when he said:

> 'In my judgment, any contract which, by way of security for payment of a debt, confers an interest in property defeasible or destructible on payment of such debt, or appropriates such property for the discharge of the debt, must necessarily be regarded as creating a mortgage or charge, as the case may be. The existence of the equity of redemption is quite inconsistent with the existence of a bare trustee-beneficiary relationship.'

3–35   "However, so far as the retention of title in unused materials is concerned, I see no difficulty in distinguishing the present case from that envisaged by Slade J. Under the first sentence of the condition, the buyer does not, by way of security, *confer* on the seller an interest in property defeasible on the payment of the debt so secured. On the contrary, the seller *retains* the legal property in the material.
"There is however one further point which I must consider. Counsel for the receiver relied, in support of his argument, on the fourth sentence of the condition. It will be remembered that this reads as follows:

'If any of the material is incorporated in or used as material for other goods before such payment the property in the whole of such goods shall be and remain with the Seller until such payment has been made, or the other goods have been sold as aforesaid, and all the Seller's rights hereunder in the material shall extend to those other goods.'

"The submission of counsel for the receiver was that the effect of this **3–36** provision is to confer on the seller an interest in the buyer's property and so must have been to create a charge; and he further submitted that, having regard to the evident intention that the seller's rights in goods in which the material provided by him has been incorporated shall be the same as his rights in unused material, the seller's rights in unused material should likewise be construed as creating a charge.

"Now it is no doubt true that, where A's material is lawfully used by B to **3–37** create new goods, whether or not B incorporates other material of his own, the property in the new goods will generally vest in B, at least where the goods are not reducible to the original materials (see Bl. Com. (14th ed. pp. 404–405). But it is difficult to see why, if the parties agree that the property in the goods shall vest in A, that agreement should not be given effect to. On this analysis, under the fourth sentence of the condition as under the first, the buyer does not *confer* on the seller an interest in property defeasible on the payment of the debt; on the contrary, when the new goods come into existence the property in them *ipso facto* vests in the seller, and he thereafter retains his ownership in them, in the same way and on the same terms as he retains his ownership in the unused material. However, in considering the fourth sentence, we have to take into account not only the possibility that the buyer may have paid part of the price for the material, but also that he will have borne the cost of manufacture of the new goods, and may also have provided other materials for incorporation into those goods; and the condition is silent, not only about repaying such part of the price for the material as has already been paid by the buyer, but also about any allowance to be made by the seller to the buyer for the cost of manufacture of the new goods, or for any other material incorporated by the buyer into the new goods. Now, no injustice need arise from the exercise of the seller's power to resell such goods provided that, having applied the price received from the resale in satisfaction of the outstanding balance of the price owed to him by the buyer, he is bound to account for the remainder to the buyer. But the difficulty of construing the fourth sentence as simply giving rise to a retention by the seller of title to the new goods is that it would lead to the result that, on the determination of the contract under which the original material was sold to the buyer, the ownership of the seller in the new goods would be retained by the seller uninhibited by any terms of the contract, which had then ceased to apply; and I find it impossible to believe that it was the intention of the parties that the seller would thereby gain the windfall of the full value of the new product, deriving as it may well do not merely from the labour of the buyer but also from materials that were his, without any duty to account to him for any surplus of the proceeds of sale above the outstanding balance of the price due by him to the seller. It follows that the fourth sentence must be read as creating either a trust or a charge. In my judgment, however, it cannot have been intended to create a trust. Those who insert Romalpa clauses in their contracts of sale must be aware that other suppliers might do the same; and the prospect of two lots of material, supplied by different sellers, each subject to a Romalpa clause which vests in the seller the legal title in a product manufactured from both lots of material, is not at all sensible. Accordingly, consistent with the approach to a similar provision in *Re Peachdart Ltd* [1984] Ch. 131, I have come to the conclusion that, although it does indeed do violence to the language of the fourth sentence of the condition, that sentence must be read as giving rise to a charge on the new goods in favour of the seller.

3–38 "Even so, I do not see why the presence of the last sentence in the condition should prevent us from giving effect to the first sentence in accordance with its terms . . .

3–39 "I recognise that, on the view which I have formed of the retention of title in the first sentence of condition 12 in this case, its effect is very similar to that of a charge on goods created by the buyer in favour of the seller. But the simple fact is that under the first sentence of the condition the buyer does not in fact confer a charge on his goods in favour of the seller: on the contrary, the seller retains his title in his goods, for the purpose of providing himself with security. I can see no reason in law why a seller of goods should not adopt this course, and, if the relevant contractual term is effective to achieve that result, I can see no reason why the law should not give effect to it in accordance with its terms."

ASSOCIATED ALLOYS PTY LIMITED v. ACN 001 452 106 PTY LIMITED (IN LIQUIDATION)

High Court of Australia (2000) HCA 25, 74 ALJR 862

Gaudron, McHugh, Gummow & Hayne JJ

3–40 "The appellant, Associated Alloys Pty Ltd ('the Seller'), sold steel to the first respondent, ACN 001 452 106 Pty Limited (In Liquidation) (formerly Metro-politan Engineering and Fabrications Pty Ltd) ('the Buyer'), between 1981 and 1996. In about 1987 or 1988, the Seller began to issue invoices to the Buyer with the registration of title clause, the subject-matter of this appeal, printed on the reverse side.

"Invoices were issued by the Seller to the Buyer on August 31, September 26 and October 26, 1995. Each individually numbered invoice recorded the details of the supply and shipment of steel by the Seller, in accordance with an individually numbered order of the Buyer. Each invoice also recorded a particular United States dollar sum owed by the Buyer to the Seller in respect of the particular shipment of steel supplied thereunder. On the front of the Invoices was recorded, under the heading 'PAYMENT TERMS', 'PAYMENT DUE APPROX MID/END NOVEMBER '95'. The bottom of the front of the Invoices was marked 'Romalpa Clause set forth on the reverse side hereof applies' . . .

"The clause provided:

"Reservation of Title

3–41 '[1] It is expressly agreed and declared that the title of the subject goods/ product shall not pass to the [Buyer] until payment in full of the purchase price. The [Buyer] shall in the meantime take custody of the goods/product and retain them as the fiduciary agent and bailee of the [Seller].

[2] The [Buyer] may resell but only as a fiduciary agent of the [Seller]. Any right to bind the [Seller] to any liability to any third party by contract or otherwise is however expressly negatived. Any such resale is to be at arms length and on market terms and pending resale or utilisation in any

manufacturing or construction process, is to be kept separate from its own, properly stored, protected and insured.

[3] The [Buyer] will receive all proceeds whether tangible or intangible, direct or indirect of any dealing with such goods/product in trust for the [Seller] and will keep such proceeds in a separate account until the liability to the [Seller] shall have been discharged.

[4] The [Seller] is to have power to appropriate payments to such goods and accounts as it thinks fit notwithstanding any appropriation by the [Buyer] to the contrary.

[5] *In the event that the [Buyer] uses the goods/product in some manufac-* **3–42** *turing or construction process of its own or some third party, then the [Buyer] shall hold such part of the proceeds of such manufacturing or construction process as relates to the goods/product in trust for the [Seller]. Such part shall be deemed to equal in dollar terms the amount owing by the [Buyer] to the [Seller] at the time of the receipt of such proceeds'.*" (paragraph numbers and emphasis added)

It is the operation of the fifth paragraph of the clause ("the Proceeds Subclause") which is of prime importance for this appeal . . .

The Proceeds Subclause operates, conditionally, "[i]n the event that the **3–43** [Buyer] uses the goods/product in some manufacturing or construction process of its own or some third party". This event occurred on each occasion the Buyer used the steel supplied by the Seller to manufacture the Steel Products. No question arises as to the Seller retaining any proprietary interest in the steel it supplied under the Invoices to the Buyer. This is because the steel supplied by the Seller was no longer capable of being ascertained in the Steel Products manufactured by the Buyer. This loss of ascertainability may be contrasted with the circumstances in which the first paragraph of the reservation of title clause applies. This paragraph has an operation where the steel supplied by the Seller remains intact in the hands of the Buyer or is otherwise dealt with by the Buyer in such a way that the steel supplied does not lose its ascertainability. In such a case, the goods would remain the property of the Seller and an action in trover or detinue would lie against the Buyer[64] and, in support of such an action, injunctive relief might be available in an appropriate case.[65]

The remainder of the Proceeds Subclause is divisible into two parts. The first **3–44** part describes a subject-matter of commercial value. The second part operates to confer an interest in equity in that subject-matter . . .

The proper construction of the phrase "the proceeds" is revealed by a consideration of the Proceeds Subclause as a whole. The phrase has the meaning employed by Sir George Jessel MR in his ex tempore judgment in *In re Hallett's Estate*,[66] where the Master of the Rolls eloquently states the principles of tracing in equity. The phrase "the proceeds" is to be construed as referring to moneys received by the Buyer and not debts which may be set out in the Buyer's books (or computer records) from time to time.[67] The concluding sentence of the

---

[64] *Penfolds Wines Pty Ltd v. Elliott* (1946) 74 CLR 204 at 229; *Gollan v Nugent* (1988) 166 CLR 18 at 25.
[65] As was sought in *Penfolds Wines Pty Ltd v Elliott* (1946) 74 CLR 204, and see *Puma Australia Pty Ltd v. Sportsman's Australia Limited (No 2)* [1994] 2 Qd R 159 at 166–169, 171–173.
[66] (1880) 13 Ch D 696 at 708–709.
[67] Questions as to the application of moneys received, which it is unnecessary now to answer, may arise where a running account exists between a supplier (*e.g.* the Seller) and purchaser (*e.g.* the Buyer).

Proceeds Subclause would be strained if the phrase "the proceeds" were to include book debts. In the event that a debt were subject to conditions, it may prove to be difficult to determine when the Buyer is in "receipt" of that intangible obligation. Moreover, to attempt to equate a chose in action, "in dollar terms", to a sum of money, namely "the amount owing by the [Buyer] to the [Seller] at the time of the receipt of such proceeds", is, at the very least, conceptually problematic. In contrast, limiting the phrase "the proceeds" to refer to payments made to the Buyer results in this equation operating with certainty.

3–45   It is necessary to determine the equitable rights, liabilities and remedies which arise from the purported operation of the Proceeds Subclause. A pendent question also arises as to the manner in which the Buyer's contractual rights and obligations are affected by equitable considerations . . .

The contracts, in respect of each of the Invoices, spoke for the future and provided the attachment of a trust for "the proceeds" received from time to time. There being value, and equity regarding as done that which ought to be done, a completely constituted trust would arise in respect of those "proceeds" (giving that word the meaning considered above) as they were received by the Buyer.[68]

In their joint judgment in *Kauter v. Hilton*, Dixon CJ, Williams and Fullagar JJ identified[69]:

> "the established rule that in order to constitute a trust the intention to do so must be clear and that it must also be clear what property is subject to the trust and reasonably certain who are the beneficiaries".

3–46   In the present case, it is no objection to the effective creation of a trust that the property to be subjected to it is identified to be a proportion of the proceeds received by the Buyer; a proportion referable to moneys from time to time due and owing but unpaid by the Buyer to the Seller.

3–47   In respect of those proceeds from time to time bound by the trust, there is nothing in the terms of the trust to negative the ordinary consequence that the trustee (the Buyer) is bound to apply that sum by accounting to or at the direction of a beneficiary (the Seller). It is convenient to identify the condition which limits the beneficiary's entitlement to call upon the trust property later in this judgment. As Professor Hayton points out,[70] with reference to authority,[71] because equity treats as done that which ought to be done, even if the proceeds were paid into a general bank account of the Buyer there could be a tracing

---

[68] *Palette Shoes Pty Ltd v Krohn* (1937) 58 CLR 1 at 26–27; *Federal Commissioner of Taxation v Everett* (1980) 143 CLR 440 at 450. See also the United States authorities considered under the heading "Debtor Declaring Himself Trustee for Creditor" in Bogert, *The Law of Trusts and Trustees*, 2nd ed rev (1984), §19.

[69] (1953) 90 CLR 86 at 97.

[70] Underhill and Hayton, *Law Relating to Trusts and Trustees*, 15th ed (1995) at 12(n); cf Hayton, "The Uses of Trusts in the Commercial Context", in Hayton (ed), *Modern International Developments in Trust Law*, (1999) 145 at 168.

[71] Including that of the Supreme Court of Canada in *Air Canada v. M & L Travel Ltd* [1993] 3 SCR 787 at 804–805 in which reliance was placed upon the judgment of Hope JA in *Stephens Travel Service International Pty Ltd (Receivers and Managers Appointed) v. Qantas Airways Ltd* (1988) 13 NSWLR 331 at 348–349, with which Kirby P and Priestley JA agreed.

remedy where the recipient was obliged to hold a particular portion of the proceeds on trust.

In the situation just considered, where the trust is performed and discharged by appropriation of the proceeds by the Seller, the relevant trust relationship between the Buyer and the Seller is brought to an end. A question may then arise whether, despite the Seller having been funded in this way, it might retain a good claim for that amount by an action in debt against the Buyer. The answer to that will be found not in trust law but in the terms, express or implied, of the contract between the Buyer and the Seller. In the formulation of those terms, particularly any implied terms, there is, to adapt the words of Lord Wilberforce, "surely no difficulty in recognising the co-existence in one transaction of legal and equitable rights and remedies"[72] and the giving of effect to "practical arrangements" by "the flexible interplay of law and equity" . . .[73]

The contractual agreements of the Buyer and Seller, in respect of each of the **3–48** Invoices, included the amount to be paid by the Buyer for the steel supplied under each Invoice and stated "PAYMENT DUE APPROX MID/END NOVEMBER '95". This latter term operated as a period of credit, commercially benefiting the Buyer. The question that arises is whether this term is inconsistent with the intention to constitute a trust in the manner described above. That is, whether the purported liberty of the Buyer not to pay the Seller is consistent with the obligation to create a trust of "proceeds" which might be received by the Buyer during the period of credit. This question is resolved by reference to the contract as a whole, including the implied terms that arise.

The rules governing the implication of an implied term as a matter of fact **3–49** were stated by the Privy Council in *BP Refinery (Westernport) Pty Ltd v. Shire of Hastings* . . .[74]

The implication of an implied term operates to align, or give congruence to, the rights and obligations of the Buyer and Seller in contract and the intention of these parties to create a trust in the manner described above. An implied contractual term arises, as a matter of business efficacy, that upon the receipt by the Buyer of the relevant "proceeds" (and thus the constitution of a trust of part of those proceeds), the obligation in debt is discharged. The express term in the agreement (referred to above) which provides for a period of credit within which the debt need not be paid by the Buyer is, in turn, incorporated as an express term of the trust. This term thereby prescribes the period within which the Seller, as beneficiary, cannot call upon the trust property (if the trust is constituted during the credit period). The implied term thus provides one means of discharging the debt by performance. No relevant inconsistency arises between this implied term and the express term in the agreement providing for a period of credit for the Buyer . . .

Further, no inconsistency arises between the contractual agreement and the **3–50** creation of a trust of property "equal in dollar terms [to] the amount owing by the [Buyer] to the [Seller] at the time of the receipt" of the proceeds.[75] Manifestly, this term did not operate to constitute a trust in respect of the whole of the proceeds received by the Buyer except, perhaps, coincidentally.

The Proceeds Subclause is an agreement to constitute a trust of future-acquired property. It is therefore not a "charge" within the meaning of s. 9 of the

---

[72] *Quistclose Investments Ltd v. Rolls Razor Ltd* [1970] AC 567 at 581.
[73] *Quistclose Investments Ltd v. Rolls Razor Ltd* [1970] AC 567 at 582.
[74] (1977) 180 CLR 266 at 283.
[75] See Underhill and Hayton, *Law Relating to Trusts and Trustees*, 15th ed (1995) at 11–12.

Law and the detailed provisions of the Law governing charges thus do not apply to it. The Proceeds Subclause is not a "registrable charge" within s. 262 and the Seller had no obligation to lodge a notice under s. 263 within the prescribed period (s 266(1)(c)). In turn, the Proceeds Subclause is not void as against the administrators or liquidator of the Buyer (see s. 266(1))."

RE EVTR

Court of Appeal [1987] BCLC 646

3–51   The appellant, who had won £240,000 on premium bonds, wanted to help the penurious company, which had employed him, to purchase new equipment. He deposited £60,000 with the company's solicitors to be released to the company "for the sole purpose of buying new equipment." The money was paid into the company's general funds and paid out in pursuit of the purpose. Receivers were appointed and the company ceased trading before delivery of the equipment, so that £48,536 of the £60,000 was returned to the company. The trial judge rejected the appellants claim to the money but the Court of Appeal upheld it.

3–52   DILLON L.J.: "In the forefront of the appellant's case counsel for the appellant (Mr Jackson) refers to the decision of the House of Lords in *Barclays Bank Ltd v. Quistclose Investments Ltd* [1970] A.C. 567. There, Quistclose had lent money to a company (Rolls Razor Ltd) on an agreed condition that the money be used only for the purpose of paying a particular dividend which the company had declared. In the event the company went into liquidation, after receiving Quistclose's money, but without having paid the dividend. It was held that Quistclose could claim the whole of the money back, as on a resulting trust, the specific purpose having failed, and Quistclose was not limited to proving as an unsecured creditor in the liquidation of the company.

3–53   In the present case the £60,000 was released by Knapp-Fishers to the company on the appellant's instructions for a specific purpose only, namely the sole purpose of buying new equipment. Accordingly, I have no doubt, in the light of *Quistclose*, that, if the company had gone into liquidation, or the receivers had been appointed, and the scheme had become abortive before the £60,000 had been disbursed by the company, the appellant would have been entitled to recover his full £60,000, as between himself and the company, on the footing that it was impliedly held by the company as a resulting trust for him as the particular purpose of the loan had failed.

"At the other end of the spectrum, if after the £60,000 had been expended by the company as it was, the Encore System had been duly delivered to, and accepted by, the company, there could be no doubt that the appellant's only right would have been as an unsecured creditor of the company for the £60,000. There would have been no question of the Encore System, or any interest in it, being held on any sort of trust for the appellant, and if, after it had been delivered and installed, the company had sold the system, the appellant could have had no claim whatsoever to the proceeds of sale as trust moneys held in trust for him.

"The present case lies on its facts between those two extremes of the spectrum . . .

3–54   "On *Quistclose* principles, a resulting trust in favour of the provider of the money arises when money is provided for a particular purpose only, and that purpose fails. In the present case, the purpose for which the £60,000 was provided by the appellant to the company was, as appears from the authority to

Knapp-Fishers, the purpose of (the company) buying new equipment. But in any realistic sense of the words that purpose has failed in that the company has never acquired any new equipment, whether the Encore System which was then in mind or anything else. True it is that the £60,000 was paid out by the company with a view to the acquisition of new equipment, but that was only at half-time, and I do not see why the final whistle should be blown at half-time. The proposed acquisition proved abortive and a large part of the £60,000 has therefore been repaid by the payees. The repayments were made because of, or on account of, the payments which made up the £60,000 and those were payments of trust moneys. It is a long-established principle of Equity that, if a person who is a trustee receives money or property because of, or in respect of, trust property, he will hold what he receives as a constructive trustee on the trusts of the original trust property. It follows, in my judgment, that the repayments made to the receivers are subject to the same trusts as the original £60,000 in the hands of the company. There is now, of course, no question of the £48,536 [*i.e.* the repayments] being applied in the purchase of new equipment for the company, and accordingly, in my judgment, it is now held on a resulting trust for the appellant."

RE KAYFORD LTD

Chancery Division [1975] 1 W.L.R. 279; [1975] 1 All E.R. 604

The company conducted a mail order business. Customers either paid the full **3–55** price for goods in advance, or paid a deposit. Its suppliers got into difficulties and Kayford could not meet orders. Its accountants advised the company to open a separate "customers' trust deposit account" and pay into it all money received from customers for goods not yet delivered, withdrawing money only upon delivery of goods. The object was to allow the company fully to refund payments to customers should the company go into liquidation. The company accepted this advice except that the money was paid into a dormant account in the company's name, the title of the account being changed later. When the company went into liquidation, the liquidators sought a declaration as to the ownership of the sums of money paid into the account.

MEGARRY J.: "I may say at the outset that on the facts of the case counsel for **3–56** the joint liquidators was unable to contend that any question of a fraudulent preference arose. If one leaves on one side any case in which an insolvent company seeks to declare a trust in favour of creditors, one is concerned here with the question not of preferring creditors but of preventing those who pay money from becoming creditors, by making them beneficiaries under a trust.

". . . I feel no doubt that the intention was that there should be a trust. There are no formal difficulties. The property concerned is pure personalty, and so writing, though desirable, is not an essential. There is no doubt about the so-called 'three certainties' of a trust. The subject-matter to be held on trust is clear, and so are the beneficial interests therein, as well as the beneficiaries. As for the requisite certainty of words, it is well settled that a trust can be created without using the words 'trust' or 'confidence' or the like: the question is whether, in substance, a sufficient intention to create a trust has been manifested.

"In *Re Nanwa Gold Mines Ltd* [1955] 1 W.L.R. 1080; [1955] 1 All E.R. 219, the **3–57** money was sent on the faith of a promise to keep it in a separate account, but there is nothing in that case or in any other authority that I know of to suggest that this is essential. I feel no doubt that here a trust was created. From the outset the advice (which was accepted) was to establish a trust account at the bank. The whole purpose of what was done was to ensure that the moneys remained in the beneficial ownership of those who sent them, and a trust is the obvious means of achieving this. No doubt the general rule is that if you send money to a company for goods which are not delivered, you are merely a creditor of the company unless a trust has been created. The sender may create a trust by using appropriate words when he sends the money (though I wonder how many do this, even if they are equity lawyers), or the company may do it by taking suitable steps on or before receiving the money. If either is done, the obligations in respect of the money are transformed from contract to property, from debt to trust. Payment into a separate bank account is a useful (though by no means conclusive) indication of an intention to create a trust, but of course there is nothing to prevent the company from binding itself by a trust even if there are no effective banking arrangements.

3–58   ". . . In cases concerning the public, it seems to me that where money in advance is being paid to a company in return for the future supply of goods or services, it is an entirely proper and honourable thing for a company to do what this company did, on skilled advice, namely, to start to pay the money into a trust account as soon as there begin to be doubts as to the company's ability to fulfil its obligations to deliver the goods or provide the services."

TRUSTS AND POWERS

3–59   Special attention has to be given to the distinction between trusts and powers which is complicated by the fact that the trustees will in many cases not just have trusts which they *must* carry out (*e.g.* "on trust to distribute the income between such of my descendants as they see fit from time to time") but also distributive (as opposed to administrative) powers concerning distributing income or capital (*e.g.* "but so that my trustees may instead distribute the income between such charities as they may see fit from time to time") which they *may or may not* exercise. Furthermore, in construing a clause in a trust deed there may be a fine (and perhaps artificial) distinction between (a) a power of distribution of income coupled with a trust to dispose of the undistributed surplus and (b) a trust for distribution coupled with a power to withhold a portion and accumulate it or otherwise dispose of it, (*e.g.* (a) on trust to pay or apply the income to or for the benefit of such of my family company's employees, ex-employees and their relatives and dependants as my trustees may see fit but so that my trustees shall pay or apply any income not so paid or applied within three months of receipt by my trustees to or for the benefit of such of my issue as my trustees shall see fit and (b) on trust to pay or apply the income to or for the benefit of such of my family company's employees, ex-employees and their relatives and dependants as my trustees shall see fit but so that my trustees may pay or apply any income within three months of receiving it to or for the benefit of such of my issue as my trustees may see fit).

A trustee *must*[76] act in accordance with the terms of the trust and whilst such **3–60** terms may leave him no discretion (*e.g.* if holding on trust for A for life, remainder to B, when he must pay the income to A and then, on A's death, pay the capital to B) sometimes such terms may afford him some discretion, as in the case of a discretionary trust (*e.g.* on trust to distribute the income and capital as he sees fit between such of A, B, C, D and E and their spouses and issue as he may choose). Lack of someone to enforce a trust is fatal to its validity.[77]

A power, which is the authority to deal with property which one does **3–61** not own, may be legal where it is a statutory power of attorney[78] or a mortgagee's statutory power of sale,[79] but it is usually a power to choose who are to be the beneficial recipients of property and such power of appointment is equitable[80] and will arise under a trust. Such a power will be a special power unless the donee can on his own appoint to himself when it will be a general power.[81] Where a special power is exercisable in favour of everyone but a small excepted class (*e.g.* the settlor and his spouse and past and present trustees) it is often referred to as a hybrid or intermediate power.[82] The validity of a trust depends upon the existence of a person with *locus standi* positively to enforce it but this does not appear necessary for the validity of a power.[83]

The donee of a special power will usually be a trustee but, as far as the **3–62** power is concerned, the donee *may or may not* exercise it as he chooses, *e.g.* where he holds on trust with power to distribute income amongst such of V, W, X, Y, Z as he sees fit but in default of appointment upon trust for A for life, remainder to B absolutely. Here, he can choose whether or not to pay income to V, W, X, Y, Z but, if he does not so choose or does not exercise his discretion in respect of particular income within a reasonable time so that his discretion is extinguished,[84] then the income in question must be paid to A. A trustee with a special power must ask two interrelated questions: (1) "Shall I exercise the power?" (2) "If so, how shall I exercise it?" A trustee of a discretionary trust just asks "How shall I exercise my duty to distribute income amongst the beneficiaries?"

Powers are fiduciary or personal

Whilst the donee of a power of appointment need not exercise it he will, **3–63** if a trustee, be under an obligation bona fide to consider exercising the power and to this end to take reasonable steps to discover the identities and needs of objects of the power, before considering the appropriateness of individual appointments.[85] Someone who is donee of a special

---

[76] If he does not then the court will intervene to ensure that the trusts are carried out: *McPhail v. Doulton* [1971] A.C. 424 at 457, see *infra*, at para. 3–142.

[77] Except in limited anomalous cases where the "trusts" are in substance "powers," see *infra*, at para. 3–216.

[78] Powers of Attorney Act 1971; Trustee Delegation Act 1999.

[79] Law of Property Act 1925, ss. 88, 101, 104.

[80] *ibid.* s. 1(7).

[81] *Re Penrose* [1933] Ch. 793, Perpetuities Act 1964, s. 7.

[82] *Re Hay's Settlement* [1982] 1 W.L.R. 202.

[83] *Re Douglas* (1887) 35 Ch.D. 472, Morris Leach, *Rule Against Perpetuities* (2nd ed.) p. 320.

[84] *Re Allen-Meyrick's W.T.* [1966] 1 W.L.R. 499; *Re Gulbenkian's S.T. (No. 2)* [1970] Ch. 408.

[85] *McPhail v. Doulton* [1971] A.C. 424; *Re Manisty* [1974] Ch. 17; *Re Hay's S.T.* [1982] 1 W.L.R. 202, see *infra*, para. 3–157.

power in a personal, as opposed to a fiduciary, capacity is not under the obligation to consider exercising the power (*e.g.* where a testator's will trusts have E and F as trustees but the widow life tenant is given power to appoint capital between grandchildren). The personal donee of a special power can release it unlike a fiduciary donee who can only do so if authorised by the trust instrument.[86] Powers vested in trustees as such are fiduciary (*i.e.* the power is conferred upon a trustee the better to enable him to fulfil his trusteeship role and not for his personal use unconstrained by any obligations relating to its use[87]) unless there is express contrary intent in the trust instrument.

Position of beneficiaries

3–64   Beneficiaries under a discretionary trust and objects of a special power held by trustees have some common rights.[88] Both have a right to retain any sums properly paid by the trustees in exercise of their discretion; both have a right to be considered by the trustees with a view to a distribution in their favour, though the trustees' duty of inquiry of possible recipients is higher where they have to carry out discretionary trusts than where they merely have to consider whether or not to exercise a power.[89] However, where under discretionary trusts income has to be distributed year by year (an exhaustive discretionary trust)[90] amongst a discretionary class then if all members of such class are ascertained and of full capacity they can, if unanimous, call for the income and so have a collectively enforceable right: they can have a similar right if also similarly interested in capital.[91] The collective objects of a special power can have no such right. Furthermore, discretionary trusts over income remain exercisable despite the passing of time, though only in favour of such persons as would have been possible beneficiaries if the discretion had been exercised within a reasonable time, whilst if powers over income are not exercised within a reasonable time the discretion is extinguished and the default beneficiaries are entitled.[92] Finally, trustees are under a core duty, so far as practicable, to inform beneficiaries of full capacity that they are beneficiaries, so as to give substance to the beneficiaries' core right to make the trustees account for their steward ship of the trust fund[93]: Indeed, the settlor can

---

[86] *Re Wills's Trust Deeds* [1964] Ch. 219. See further, *infra*, para. 3–110.
[87] *Re Bacon* [1907] 1 Ch. 475 at 487; *Re Wills' Trust Deed* [1964] Ch. 219 at 231; *Re Gulbenkian's Settlements* [1970] A.C. 508 at 518.
[88] *Vestey v. I.R.C.* [1979] 2 All E.R. 225 at 235–236.
[89] *McPhail v. Doulton* [1971] A.C. 424.
[90] A discretionary trust is "exhaustive" where the trustees must distribute the income amongst class "A" and "non-exhaustive" where the trustees must distribute the income amongst class "A" *only* if they fail to exercise a power to withhold the income for some purpose such as accumulating it or using it for class "B." There is a fine line between the latter situation and a trust for accumulation or for benefiting discretionary class "B" with a power to benefit discretionary class "A." See *Sainsbury v. I.R.C.* [1970] 1 Ch. 712; *McPhail v. Doulton* [1971] A.C. 424 at 448.
[91] *Re Smith* [1928] Ch. 915; *Saunders v. Vautier* (1841) Cr. & Ph. 240. Rights to capital are often contingent upon being alive at the "closing date" of the trust, so preventing a *Saunders v. Vautier* right arising.
[92] *Re Locker's S.T.* [1977] 1 W.L.R. 1323; *Re Allen-Meyrick's W.T.* [1966] 1 W.L.R. 499.
[93] There is no trust for beneficiaries unless they have rights to enforce the trust: *Armitage v. Nurse* [1998] Ch 241, 253.

be forced to tell the beneficiaries the name and address of the trustees.[94] However, it is open to a settlor expressly to exclude any rights of objects of powers other than the two rights mentioned at the beginning of the paragraph.[95]

Problems can arise in ascertaining the intentions of a testator. He may **3–65** intend to leave property to his executors and trustees on trust for W for life with:

(1) a mere power for her to appoint the capital amongst such of their children as she may see fit, so that if the power is not exercised the capital is held on a resulting trust for the testator's estate[96];

(2) a mere power for her to appoint the capital amongst such of their children as she may see fit, but in default of appointment remainder for their children equally[97] (a fixed trust);

(3) a mere power for her to appoint the capital amongst such of their children as she may see fit, but in default of appointment for such of their children and in such shares as his executors and trustees shall select in their absolute discretion[98] (a discretionary trust);

(4) a "trust" power whereby she *must* exercise her power to appoint the capital (vested in the executors and trustees) amongst such of their children as she sees fit.[99] If this discretionary trust is unexercised at her death then the court will order equal division on the basis that equality is equity[1] unless some other basis for

---

[94] *Re Murphy's Settlements* [1999] 1 W.L.R. 282.

[95] See *Re Manisty's S.T.* [1974] Ch. 17 at, 25, 27–28, *infra*, para. 3–106 and *Rosewood Trust Ltd v. Schmidt* (unreported February 2001 decision of Manx appellate court), *infra*, para. 9–209.

[96] *Re Weekes's Settlement* [1897] 1 Ch. 289, see *infra*, at para. 3–68; *Re Combe* [1925] 1 Ch. 210 (after life interest, "in trust for such persons as my said son shall by will appoint but such appointment must be confined to relations of mine of the whole blood": held resulting trust when no appointment made); *Re Poulton's W.T.* (1987) 1 All E.R. 1068.

[97] *Wilson v. Duguid* (1883) 24 Ch.D. 244 (trust for A for life, remainder to such of his children as he should by any writing appoint: held children had vested interests, liable to be divested by exercise of power, since there was an *implied* gift to the children equally in default of appointment). If A's power had only been exercisable by will then the implied gift in default of appointment would have been only to those children alive at A's death, since any appointment could only have been in favour of those children: *Walsh v. Wallinger* (1830) 2 Russ. & M. 78 at 81. One should note that "to W for life, remainder to our children equally, but so that W may instead appoint the capital between our children in such shares as she may see fit" is equivalent to "to W for life, with power for her to appoint the capital amongst our children as she sees fit, but in default of appointment for our children equally": the children in both cases have immediate vested interests liable to be divested. See *Re Llewellyn's Settlement* [1921] 2 Ch. 281; *Re Arnold* [1947] Ch. 131.

[98] This gift on discretionary trust in default of appointment will need to be express, whereas a gift to beneficiaries equally in default of appointment may well be implied. If the trustees do not select beneficiaries then new trustees can be appointed or the court may order equal distribution in the absence of a more appropriate basis for distribution: *McPhail v. Doulton* [1971] A.C. 424 at 457.

[99] *Brown v. Higgs* (1803) 8 Ves. 561; M. C. Cullity (1976) 54 Can.B.R. 229.

[1] In *Wilson v. Duguid* (1883) 24 Ch.D. 244 at 249 Chitty J. adverts to the distinction between a trust power and a trust in default of appointment under a mere power. Where the class is small like "children," then the class members take equally on either view (*e.g. Burrough v. Philcox* (1840) 5 My. & Cr. 72) so why create the paradoxical concept of a trust power as inquired by M. G. Unwin (1962) 26 Conv. 92? See also [1984] Conv. 227 (Bartlett and Stebbings). However, unequal division is possible in the case of a trust power and this may be appropriate where the class is larger, *e.g.* my children and my nephews and nieces and their issue. Moreover, even where the class is as small as children it may be that the class includes children who predeceased W and the court may prefer to divide the capital only between those alive at W's death. If the class is children or grandchildren it is likely the gift to grandchildren will be treated as a substitutionary gift in the event of predeceasing children, so the children will take *per stirpes* like the statutory trusts on intestacy: *supra*, para. 1–132.

distribution appears more appropriate[2] (which may well be the case if the class of objects is broader, *e.g.*, my children and my nephews and nieces and the children of such persons).

3–66   Where the class of objects is so large that they cannot all be listed then, obviously, there can be no question of equal division under an implied gift in default of appointment. Thus, in welfare trusts for employees, ex-employees and their relations and dependants where the trustees are empowered to make grants to such persons, the question that arises is whether the relevant clause in the trust deed is a mere power or a "trust" power.[3] Where the person with the "trust" power has the trust property vested in him it has become the modern usage simply to say that he holds the property on discretionary trust.[4]

The similarities between discretionary trusts and powers have led to the certainty test being the same for both: both are valid if it can be said with certainty of any given beneficiary or object that he is or is not a member of the class of beneficiaries or objects.[5] For a fixed trust for equal division, however, since it is necessary to know the exact number of beneficiaries to arrange for equal arithmetical division, the trust will only be valid if a comprehensive list of all the beneficiaries can be drawn up.

3–67   In reading cases and textbooks it is necessary to be aware of the fact that discretionary trusts are sometimes referred to as trust powers or powers in the nature of a trust, and that the situation where, after a power, there is implied a trust in default for persons equally, is sometimes referred to as a trust power or a power in the nature of a trust or a power coupled with a trust.

In ascertaining whether or not only a mere power and no more is intended the following propositions[6] can be stated:

(1) If there is a gift over in default of appointment, the power is a mere power,[7] even where the gift over is void for some reason.[8]

(2) A residuary gift in favour of the donee of the power is not a gift over for this purpose.[9]

(3) To cause a power to be treated as a mere power only, the gift over must be in default of appointment, and not for any other event. Thus in the absence of a gift in default of appointment, a gift over on the failure of the appointees or any of them to reach

---

[2] *McPhail v. Doulton* [1971] A.C. 424, *infra*, at para. 3–131.

[3] *ibid.*

[4] *e.g. Re Baden's Deed Trusts (No. 2)* [1973] Ch. 9, *infra*, para. 3–144; *Re Hay's S.T.* [1982] 1 W.L.R. 202, *infra*, at para. 3–150.

[5] *McPhail v. Doulton* [1971] A.C. 424, *infra*, at para. 3–131.

[6] It should be noted that general powers of appointment are never considered to be in the nature of trusts, since there is no class of persons in whose favour the trust could operate. The question, therefore, arises only in connection with special powers of appointment.

[7] *e.g. Re Mills* [1930] 1 Ch. 654.

[8] *Re Sprague* (1880) 43 L.T. 236; *Re Sayer* [1957] Ch. 423.

[9] *Re Brierley* [1894] 43 W.R. 36.

a specified age will not necessarily prevent the power from being treated as a discretionary trust or prevent the implication of a trust for the objects equalty in default of appointment.[10]

(4) Where there is no gift over in default of appointment, the power may be only a mere power, or a power coupled with an implied trust in default of appointment, or a trust power or discretionary trust, according to the true intention of the settlor.[11]

RE WEEKES' SETTLEMENT

Chancery Division [1897] 1 Ch. 289; 66 L.J.Ch. 179; 76 L.T. 112.

A testatrix gave a life interest in property to her husband with a "power to **3–68** dispose of all such property by will amongst our children in accordance with the power granted to him as regards the other property which I have under my marriage settlements."[12] There was in her will no gift over in default of appointment, and the husband died intestate without having exercised the power. The surviving children of the marriage claimed the property in equal shares, on the ground that there was an implied gift to them in default of appointment.

ROMER J.: ". . . The husband did not exercise the power of appointment, and the question is whether the children take in default of appointment.

"Now, apart from the authorities, I should gather from the terms of the will that it was a mere power that was conferred on the husband, and not one coupled with a trust that he was bound to exercise. I see no words in the will to justify me in holding that the testatrix intended that the children should take if her husband did not execute the power.

"This is not a case of a gift to the children with power to the husband to select, **3–69** or to such of the children as the husband should select by exercising the power.

"If in this case the testatrix really intended to give a life interest to her husband and a mere power to appoint if he chose, and intended if he did not think fit to appoint that the property should go as in default of appointment according to the settlement, why should she be bound to say more than she has said in this will?

"I come to the conclusion on the words of this will that the testatrix only intended to give a life interest and a power to her husband—certainly she has not said more than that.

"Am I then bound by the authorities to hold otherwise? I think I am not. The authorities do not show, in my opinion, that there is a hard-and-fast rule that a gift to A for life with a power to A to appoint among a class and nothing more must, if there is no gift over in the will, be held a gift by implication to the class in default of the power being exercised. In my opinion the cases show (though there may be found here and there certain remarks of a few learned judges which, if not interpreted by the facts of the particular case before them, might seem to have a more extended operation) that you must find in the will an

---

[10] *Re Llewellyn's Settlement* [1921] 2 Ch. 281.

[11] *Burrough v. Philcax* (1840) 5 My. & Cr. 72; *Re Weekes's Settlement, infra; Re Combe* [1925] Ch. 210; *Re Perowne* [1951] Ch. 785; *Re Scarisbrick* [1951] Ch. 622; *Re Arnold's Trusts* [1947] Ch. 131; *McPhail v. Doulton* [1971] A.C. 424.

[12] There were gifts over in default of appointment in those settlements.

indication that the testatrix did intend the class or some of the class to take—intended in fact that the power should be regarded in the nature of a trust, only a power of selection being given, as, for example, a gift to A for life with a gift over to such of a class as A shall appoint . . ."

Held, the power was a mere power only so the children were therefore not entitled in default of appointment.

THE NECESSARY LANGUAGE TO REVEAL INTENT TO CREATE A TRUST

3–70   No technical expressions are necessary to create a trust so long as some imperative formula is used to indicate that the person with the property in question is to be subject to a legally binding obligation to hold and manage the property for others (or himself and others). Wills often create problems where a testator expresses his confidence, wish, hope or request that a particular legatee should use the legacy in a certain way. Originally, the courts[13] were only too ready to treat such precatory words as creating a trust and as James L.J. said in *Lamb v. Eames*[14] "the officious kindness of the Court of Chancery in interposing trusts where in many cases the father of the family never meant to create trusts, must have been a very cruel kindness indeed." Since the 1870s the courts have not allowed precatory words to create a trust unless on the consideration of the will as a whole it was clearly the intention of the testator to create a trust.[15] By Administration of Justice Act 1982, section 21 extrinsic evidence, including evidence of the testator's intention, may be admitted to assist in its interpretation (a) in so far as any part of the will is meaningless (b) in so far as the language used in any part of it is ambiguous on the face of it and (c) in so far as evidence, *other than evidence of the testator's intention*, shows that the language used in any part of it is ambiguous in the light of the surrounding circumstances.

3–71   The following clauses have been held, in context, not to create a trust: "feeling confident that she will act justly to our children in dividing the same when no longer required by her,"[16] "it is my desire that she allows A.G. an annuity of £25 during her life,"[17] "I wish them to bequeath the same equally between the families of O and P,"[18] "in the fullest trust and confidence that she will carry out my wishes in the following particulars,"[19] "I request that C on her death leave her property to my four sisters."[20] Nowadays, Administration of Justice Act 1982, section 22

---

[13] *Eade v. Eade* (1820) 5 Madd. 118 at 121; *Palmer v. Simmonds* (1854) 2 Drew 221; *Gutty v. Cregoe* (1857) 24 Beav. 185.
[14] (1871) 6 Ch.App. 597.
[15] *Lamb v. Eames* (1871) 6 Ch.App. 597; *Re Adams and Kensington Vestry* (1884) 27 Ch.D. 394. In *Re Steele's W.T.* [1948] Ch. 603 an unusual precatory formula for disposing of jewellery which Page-Wood V.-C. in *Shelley v. Shelley* (1868) L.R. 6 Eq. 540, had held created a trust was also apt to create a trust since it was likely the professional draftsman had the earlier formula in mind: (1968) 32 Conv. 361 (P. St. J. Langan).
[16] *Mussoorie Bank Ltd v. Raynor* (1882) 7 App.Cas. 221.
[17] *Re Diggles* (1888) 39 Ch.D. 253.
[18] *Re Hamilton* (1895) 2 Ch. 370.
[19] *Re Williams* [1897] 2 Ch. 12.
[20] *Re Johnson* [1939] 2 All E.R. 458.

states, "Except where a contrary intent is shown, it shall be presumed that if a testator devises or bequeaths property to his spouse in terms which in themselves would give an absolute interest to the spouse but by the same instrument purports to give his issue an interest in the same property, the gift to the spouse is absolute notwithstanding the purported gift to the issue", *e.g.* "all my property to my wife and after her death to our children."

In *Comiskey v. Bowring-Hanbury*[21] a testator left to his wife "the whole **3–72** of my real and personal estate in full confidence that she will make such use of it as I should have made myself and that at her death she will devise *it* to such one or more of my nieces as she may think fit and in default of any disposition by her thereof by her will I hereby *direct* that all my estate and property acquired by her under this my will *shall* at her death be equally divided among the surviving said nieces." The House of Lords (Lord Lindley dissenting) held a trust had been created: the widow could have the use of the property (*e.g.* income, occupation of the house) and could manage it (she was Settled Land Act tenant for life) but the capital had to pass on her death to the nieces equally if not passed to them in other shares by her will.

Recently the Court of Appeal[22] has not been as strict as formerly in **3–73** requiring clear evidence of an intent to create a trust, but it does recognise that a settlor does not actually need to know that it is technically a trust that he is creating: he is taken to intend the legal consequences that would be apparent to a lawyer[23]:

An intention to create a trust of property normally requires indications that the alleged trustee is to be obliged to keep the specific trust property separate from his own.[24] After all if a recipient of money:

> "is not bound to keep the money separate, but is entitled to mix it with his own money and deal with it as he pleases, and when called upon to hand over an equivalent sum of money, then he is not a trustee of the money but merely a debtor."[25]

However, mingling of funds will not be fatal to the funding of a trust **3–74** where T receives funds from A, B and C for such funds or investments purchased therewith to be held separately from T's own assets, on a trust

---

[21] [1905] A.C. 84.

[22] *Paul v. Constance, infra; Re Vandervell's Trusts (No. 2)* [1974] Ch. 269, *supra*, at para. 2–68; *Re Chelsea Cloisters Ltd* (1980) 41 P. & C.R. 98.

[23] See also Buckley L.J. on the creation of an equitable charge in *Swiss Bank Corporation v. Lloyds Bank* [1980] 2 All E.R. 419, 426: "notwithstanding that the matter depends on the intention of the parties, if on the true construction of the relevant documents in the light of any admissible evidence as to surrounding circumstances the parties have entered into a transaction the legal effect of which is to give rise to an equitable charge, the fact that they may not have realised this consequence will not mean that there is no charge. They must be presumed to intend the consequences of their acts." Also *Clough Mill Ltd v. Martin, supra*, paras 3–26 *et seq.*

[24] *Paragon Finance plc v. Thakerar & Co* [1999] 1 All ER 400, 416; *Re Goldcorp Exchange Ltd* [1995] 1 A.C. 74; *Re English & American Insurance Co. Ltd* [1994] 1 BCLC 345.

[25] *Henry v. Hammond* [1913] 2 K.B. 515 at 521; *R. v. Clowes (No. 2)* [1994] 2 All E.R. 316 at 325; *Commissioners of Customs & Excise v. Richmond Theatre Management Ltd* [1995] STC 257.

for A, B and C in their proportionate shares[26] or where T adds funds of A, B and C to funds of his in a separate account so that such funds or investments purchased therewith are held separately from T's own assets on trust for A, B and C and T in proportionate shares.[27] T can also contract with X that if he receives proceeds of sale materialising from some specified future property, he will hold all or a specified part on trust for X, such trust then affecting the certain whole or part of the ascertained proceeds when received by T. Thus, even if they are mingled with T's funds in T's general bank account X has a right to trace such amount until properly placed in a separate account for X.[28]

Shams

3–75   Even if language is used that would clearly suffice to create a trust for beneficiaries subsequent language in the trust instrument may indicate that there is no true trust for those beneficiaries, only a sham trust, the true trust being to hold the trust fund (as to capital and income) for the settlor absolutely, albeit with power to benefit beneficiaries, so the settlor remains full beneficial owner of the trust fund. An example would be where a later clause stipulates that during the life of the settlor no beneficiary is to be informed of the trust and any beneficiary who discovers the trust cannot sue the trustees in respect of anything occurring or not occurring in the lifetime of the settlor, so beneficiaries have no rights in the settlor's lifetime.[29]

3–76   Instead of a trust being a sham on the face of the trust instrument, a trust can be a sham in substance[30] because the common understanding at the outset between the settlor and the trustee is that the trustee is to do whatever the settlor wants with the trust property. Technically, it is only the intention of the settlor that is the key to the express creation of a trust, but a settlor intending a sham trust would hardly be so foolish as to transfer his property out of his power to a trustee without getting the trustee to understand that the trustee is to deal with it as the settlor orders (regardless of what would otherwise be the obligations of the trustee under trust law).

3–77   If for some reason (*e.g.* a settlor's poor understanding of English) a trust company put a simple discretionary trust for the settlor's descendants in front of the settlor and unknowingly allowed the settlor to believe the trust fund was held to his order like a bank account, although the trust company intended to run a proper trust for the settlor's

---

[26] *R. v. Clowes (No. 2), supra; Re Goldcorp Exchange Ltd, supra.*

[27] *Re Lewis's of Leicester Ltd* [1995] 1 BCLC 428.

[28] *Re Fleet Disposal Services Ltd* [1995] 1 BCLC 345: *Associated Alloys Pty Ltd ACN 001 452 106 Pty Ltd (in liquidation)* (2000) 74 A.L.J.R 862, *supra*, at para. 3–40; *cf. Re ILG Travel* [1995] 2 BCLC 128; *Pullan v. Koe* [1913] 1 Ch. 9; *Palette Shoes Pty Ltd. v. Krohn* (1937) 58 C.L.R. 1 at 27 and *infra*, para. 6–91.

[29] The disposition in their favour is a testamentary disposition requiring compliance with the formalities for wills. "If the beneficiaries have no rights enforceable against the trustees there are no trusts" for the beneficiaries: *Armitage v. Nurse* [1998] Ch. 241, 253 per Millett L.J.

[30] *R v. Dimsey, R v. Allen* [1999] S.T.C. 846, 870–871, *Rahman v. Chase Bank (C.I) Trust Co Ltd* [1991] Jersey L.R.

descendants, the settlor could recover the property as his own if the trust company refused his request to pay him monies after two years or so of giving effect to his requests because they were in favour of his children and the trust company itself considered it sensible to benefit the children as requested. Strictly, the trust property from the outset has been held to his order in accordance with his intention so he can order the return of the property, although if regarded as creating a true trust by mistake he could anyhow set it aside for mistake.[31]

PAUL v. CONSTANCE

Court of Appeal [1977] 1 W.L.R. 527; [1977] 1 All E.R. 195 (Scarman, Bridge and Cairns L.JJ.)

SCARMAN L.J.: "Mr. Dennis Albert Constance was a wage earner living in **3–78** Cheltenham until he died on March 9, 1974. He was married to Bridget Frances Constance, the defendant in this action. But they parted in June 1965. In 1967 Mr. Constance met Mrs. Doreen Grace Paul, who is the plaintiff in this action. The two of them set up house together in December of that year, and they lived to all appearances as man and wife up to the date of Mr. Constance's death. The house in which they lived was the property of the plaintiff.

"In August 1969 Mr. Constance was injured at his work. He claimed damages **3–79** against his employers . . . his claim was disposed of by the payment to him of a sum of £950. This money he received by cheque early in 1973. He discussed with the plaintiff what to do with the money, and the evidence is clear that they decided it was to go into a bank account. The two of them went to see the manager of the St. George's Square branch of Lloyds Bank in Cheltenham, and there they had a discussion about opening a bank account. According to the notes of evidence which the trial judge made, the two of them had a discussion with the bank manager. He explained to them the different sorts of accounts which they could open, and the decision was taken to open a deposit account. At that stage Mr. Constance revealed that they were not married. It is perhaps of some significance in understanding this interview if one recalls the evidence that was given by a Mr. Thomas, a fellow employee of Mr. Constance's, who said that he knew that they were not married but most people did not. After Mr. Constance had told the manager that they were not married the manager said: 'Well, it will be in your name only then?' Mr. Constance said; 'Yes.' Then Mr. Constance asked the manager what was to happen if the plaintiff wanted to draw on the account, or if he wanted the plaintiff to draw on it, and the manager said that that could be done if she used a note with Mr. Constance's signature on it authorising her to draw on the account.

"The account that was opened on that day in February 1973 is at the very **3–80** heart of this case. The account was maintained in Mr. Constance's name from that date until the date of his death. Over the period between 1973 and his death, some 13 months later in 1974, further sums were paid into the account including, in particular, some sums which represented 'bingo' winnings. It is clear from the evidence that Mr. Constance and the plaintiff did play 'bingo,' and they played it really as a joint venture. They did have winnings from time to time, and

---

[31] *Gibbon v. Mitchell* [1990] 3 All ER 338, *Dent v. Dent* [1996] 1 W.L.R. 683

at any rate three of such winnings—none of them very great—were paid into the account. It is clear from the plaintiff's evidence that they thought of those winnings as 'their winnings': neither hers nor his alone, but theirs. Nevertheless, when the account was closed on the death of Mr. Constance the ultimate balance, after the addition of interest, consisted largely of the initial sum of £950 representing Mr. Constance's damages as a result of his injury at work. There was one withdrawal during this period, a sum of £150, and the evidence was that that money was divided between the two of them after part of it had been used for buying Christmas presents and some food.

"The plaintiff began her action after the death of Mr. Constance against his lawful wife, the defendant, who took out letters of administration for his estate since he died intestate. The plaintiff claims that the bank account in his name, to which I have referred, was held by him on trust for the benefit of himself and the plaintiff jointly. She claims that it was an express trust declared orally by him on numerous occasions. The defendant maintains that the whole fund contained in the account was the beneficial property of the deceased at the time of his death, and, as such, became part of his estate after death.

"The matter came on for trial and on August 12 the Judge found in favour of the plaintiff. He found the existence of an express trust, a trust for the benefit of the plaintiff and the deceased jointly, and he ordered that the sum of £499.21 be paid to the plaintiff as representing one half share of the fund to which she was beneficially entitled.

3–81 "The only point taken by the defendant on her appeal to this court goes to the question whether or not there was, in the circumstances of this case, an express declaration of trust.

"Counsel for the defendant drew the attention of the court to the so- called three certainties that have to be established before the court can infer the creation of a trust. We are concerned only with one of the three certainties, and it is this (Snell's Equity 27th ed at 111):

> 'The words [that is the words of the declaration relied on] must be so used that on the whole they ought to be construed as imperative. [A little later on the learned author says:] No particular form of expression is necessary for the creation of a trust, if on the whole it can be gathered that a trust was intended. A trust may well be created, although there may be an absence of any expression in terms imposing confidence. A trust may thus be created without using the word "trust," for what the court regards is the substance and effect of the words used.'

3–82 "Counsel for the defendant has taken the court through the detailed evidence and submits that one cannot find anywhere in the history of events a declaration of trust in the sense of finding the deceased man, Mr. Constance, saying: 'I am now disposing of my interest in this fund so that you, Mrs. Paul, now have a beneficial interest in it.' Of course, the words which I have just used are stilted lawyers' language, and counsel for the plaintiff was right to remind the court that we are dealing with simple people, unaware of the subtleties of equity, but understanding very well indeed their own domestic situation. It is right that one should consider the various things that were said and done by the plaintiff and Mr. Constance during their time together against their own background and in their own circumstances.

"Counsel for the defendant drew our attention to two cases [*Jones v. Lock*[32] and *Richards v. Delbridge*],[33] and he relies on them as showing that, though a man may say in clear and unmistakable terms that he intends to make a gift to some other person, for instance his child or some other member of his family, yet that does not necessarily disclose a declaration of trust; and, indeed, in the two cases to which we have been referred the court held that, though there was a plain intention to make a gift, it was not right to infer any intention to create a trust . . .

"There is no suggestion of a gift by transfer in this case. The facts of those **3–83** cases do not, therefore, very much help the submission of counsel for the defendant, but he was able to extract from them this principle: that there must be a clear declaration of trust, and that means there must be clear evidence from what is said or done of an intention to create a trust, or as counsel for the defendant put it, 'an intention to dispose of a property or a fund so that somebody else to the exclusion of the disponent acquires the beneficial interest in it.' He submitted that there was no such evidence.

"When one looks to the detailed evidence to see whether it goes as far as that—and I think that the evidence does have to go as far as that—one finds that from the time that Mr. Constance received his damages right up to his death he was saying, on occasions, that the money was as much the plaintiff's as his. When they discussed the damages, how to invest them or what to do with them, when they discussed the bank account, he would say to her: 'The money is as much yours as mine.' The judge, rightly treating the basic problem in the case as a question of fact, reached this conclusion. He said:

> 'I have read through my notes, and I am quite satisfied that it was the intention of [the plaintiff] and Mr. Constance to create a trust in which both of them were interested.'

"In this court the issue becomes: was there sufficient evidence to justify the **3–84** judge reaching that conclusion of fact? In submitting that there was, counsel for the plaintiff draws attention first and foremost to the words used. When one bears in mind the unsophisticated character of Mr. Constance and his relationship with the plaintiff during the last few years of his life, counsel for the plaintiff submits that the words that he did use on more than one occasion namely: 'This money is as much yours as mine,' convey clearly a present declaration that the existing fund was as much the plaintiff's as his own. The judge accepted that conclusion. I think he was well justified in doing so and, indeed, I think he was right to do so. There are, as counsel for the plaintiff reminded us, other features in the history of the relationship between the plaintiff and Mr. Constance which support the interpretation of those words as an express declaration of trust. I have already described the interview with the bank manager when the account was opened. I have mentioned also the putting of the 'bingo' winnings into the account, and the one withdrawal for the benefit of both of them.

The question, therefore, is whether in all the circumstances the use of those words on numerous occasions as between Mr. Constance and the plaintiff constituted an express declaration of trust. The judge found that they did. For myself, I think he was right so to find. I therefore would dismiss the appeal."[34]

---

[32] (1865) 1 Ch.App. 25.
[33] (1874) L.R. 18 Eq. 11.
[34] Why was Mrs. Paul not entitled to the whole £998.42 as surviving joint tenant? *cf. Re Osoba* [1979] 2 All E.R. 393. Ought it not to be possible to identify a declaration of trust at a particular time, *e.g.* to know when Mrs. Paul's right commenced for limitation purposes, or for entitlement to interest?

Section 2. Certainty of Subject-matter

3–85   Certainty of subject-matter requires that the property to be held on trust must be certain for otherwise there will be nothing specific to which the trust can attach.[35] It is also necessary that the beneficial interests to be taken by the beneficiaries must be certain,[36] However, where a court is imposing a constructive trust to prevent fraudulent or unconscionable behaviour of a defendant trying to take advantage of uncertainty it will circumvent problems of uncertainty.[37] This justifies the imposition of the common intention constructive trust of a fair share in a family home and even the "floating trust" discussed in *Birmingham v. Renfrew*[38] (and accepted in *Re Ottaway v. Norman*[39] and *Re Cleaver*[40]) against a defendant who agreed (under a mutual will or a secret trust) with a deceased testator to accept such a trust.

3–86   Where property is transferred to a trustee to hold separately from the rest of his assets such property is necessarily identified by virtue of the transfer. Identifiability problems, however, arise if T purports to declare himself trustee of some of his property. "It makes no difference what the parties intended, if what they intend is impossible: as is the case with an immediate transfer of [legal or equitable] title to goods whose identity is not yet known"[41] Thus, if T gratuitously purports to declare himself trustee for B of 20 cases of Chateau Latour 1983 when he has 80 cases thereof, or 20 of his 80 gold bars, B acquires no equitable interest until 20 cases or 20 bars have been segregated and appropriated for B.[42] It similarly follows from the very nature of things (*viz.* that it is impossible to have title to specific assets when nobody knows to what assets the title relates) that if T declares himself trustee of 50 of his Wonder Ltd shares when he has 950 of them or £50 in his building society account (then containing £950) on trust for B, B acquires no equitable interest until such shares or moneys have been segregated from T's so as to be separately held for B.[43]

---

[35] *Palmer v. Simmonds* (1854) 2 Drew. 221, 227 ("the bulk of my residuary estate" cannot satisfy the certainty requirement though "my residuary estate" can where the person alleged to be trustee to use the residuary estate in various ways before distributing the bulk had predeceased the testator: if E were to hold T's residuary estate on trust to distribute the bulk thereof to X and the rest to Y, then it seems that X and Y could together demand all the residuary estate to divide it between themselves as they agreed); *Re London Wine Co. (Shippers) Ltd* [1986] *Palmer's Company Cases* 121 (settlor cannot declare itself trustee of unascertained 20 out of 80 bottles of Lafite 1970 in its cellar though it could declare it held its holding of 80 bottles on trust as for three-quarters for itself and one-quarter for X).

[36] *Boyce v. Boyce* (1849) 16 Sim. 476 where T devised four houses on trust to convey whichever one she chose to Maria and to convey the others to Charlotte; and upon Maria predeceasing T so that she could not choose any house it was held the trust in favour of Charlotte was void for uncertainty. However in *Re Golay's W.T.* [1965] 1 W.L.R. a trust for B to receive an objectively reasonable income was upheld.

[37] *Pallant v. Morgan* [1953] Ch. 43; *Banner Homes Group plc v. Luff Developments Ltd* [2000] 2 All E.R. 117; *Gissing v. Gissing* [1971] A.C. 886 at 909 ("fair" share of family home); *Eves v. Eves* [1975] 3 All E.R. 768 at 772; *Passee v. Passee* [1988] 1 F.L.R. 263 at 271.

[38] (1936) 57 C.L.R. 666 at 689, *supra* at para. 2–152.

[39] [1972] Ch. 698.

[40] [1981] 1 W.L.R. 939.

[41] *Re Goldcorp Exchange* [1994] 2 All E.R. 806 at 814 *per* Lord Mustill.

[42] *Ibid. Re London Wine Co. Shippers Ltd* [1986] P.C.C. 121; *Re Stapylton Fletcher Ltd* [1995] 1 All E.R. 192. These problems in the sale of goods context have now been remedied by Sale of Goods Amendment Act 1995.

[43] *cf. Re Innes* [1910] 1 Ch. 188 at 193; *MacJordan Construction Ltd v. Brookmount Erostin* [1992] BCLC 350.

Most surprisingly, in *Hunter v. Moss*[44] the Court of Appeal upheld a **3–87** gratuitous trust of 50 of T's shares in MEL when T had 950 of them on the basis that:[45]

> "just as a person can give by will a specified number of his shares in a certain company, so equally he can declare himself a trustee of 50 of his shares in MEL and that is effective to give a beneficial proprietary interest to the beneficiary under the trust".

This overlooks a crucial difference between inter vivos and testamentary dispositions. By his death a testator does everything necessary to divest himself of all his legal and beneficial title in all his assets in favour of his executor,[46] who is then obliged to implement his wishes subject to payment of debts, expenses and taxes. In his lifetime a donor-settlor only divests himself of his beneficial entitlement to his assets when he has done everything necessary to identify those assets to which he has relinquished entitlement, *i.e.* when he has separated 50 shares from the remaining 900 shares which he retains. Until then, how can one tell whether 100 shares sold by him are all his or only half his? Having made an imperfect gift, he is entitled to sell all as his own shares.

The problem facing B can be overcome easily enough[47] by T declaring **3–88** himself trustee of specified assets in proportionate undivided shares for himself and B. Thus, T himself could have declared that he held the chose in action representing his 950 shares on trust as to eighteen nineteenths for himself and one nineteenth for B: it is then clear that T and B have eighteen nineteenths and one nineteenth undivided shares in the *chose* thereby enabling B to take advantage of the tracing rules in respect of such one nineteenth, which cannot be done for an imperfect gift of 50 unsegregated shares because one cannot tell which 50 of the 950 shares were supposed to be beneficially B's.

An intention to create a trust of one nineteenth of a shareholding is a **3–89** different intention from an intention to create a trust of 50 shares, which is a feasible intention where T is registered shareholder of 950 shares. To give effect to such intention he can send the share certificate for 950 shares to the company registrar with a signed transfer form requesting a share certificate for 900 shares and one for 50 shares. He can then declare a trust of the 50 shares covered by the latter certificate, and tracing principles are available if such shares are sold or given away.

---

[44] [1994] 1 W.L.R. 452 criticised (1994) 110 L.Q.R. 335; it seems inconsistent with the later *Re Goldcorp Exchange* [1994] 2 All E.R. 806 at 814.

[45] *ibid.* at 459.

[46] See *supra*, at para. 1–122. If T in his lifetime declared himself trustee of 50 shares for A and 900 for B so as to have divested himself in equity of all interest in the 950 shares he owned, then A and B, between them absolutely entitled to the 950 shares, could demand transfer of legal title to themselves and treat themselves as entitled to one nineteenth and eighteen nineteenths of T's chose in action.

[47] Hence the approach in Sale of Goods Amendment Act 1995, s.1(3) deeming a vendor of a number of assets in a larger whole owned by him to be tenant in common as to the proportionate share reflecting the proportion that the number of goods contracted to be sold bears to the total owned by him. Thus, if he received the purchase price for 10 out of 40 cases of Ch. Lafite 1983 still in his cellar (without the 10 having been allocated by markings or otherwise to the purchaser) he is treated as holding a quarter of such stock of wine on trust for the purchaser, which is crucial if he has become insolvent.

3–90   However, what of the much more common situation where T owns shares in a public company, all of whose 5 million shares are registered in the name of Custodian plc, whose computer records it as holding 1 million shares for Cazenove & Co, whose computer records it as holding 20,000 shares for T? Here, T does not actually own 20,000 shares and so cannot declare a trust of 20,000 shares nor of 5,000 shares, for that matter. Actually, T owns a fiftieth equitable interest in Cazenove's one fifth equitable interest in the pool of 5 million shares legally owned by Custodian plc. Thus, the court has to construe T's declaration of trust of his notional 20,000 shares for B not as impossible and nonsensical but as reflecting an intention to make a declaration of trust of his one fiftieth interest in Cazenove's interest in the shares owned by Custodian plc. It seems to follow that if T happened to declare himself trustee of a notional 5,000 of his 20,000 shares, then, because he does not own any shares, he should be treated as intending to declare himself trustee of a quarter of the one fiftieth interest he does own in Cazenove's interest in the shares owned by Custodian plc. Thus certainty of subject matter of the trust is present.

3–91   One problem that remains concerns the application of section 53(1) (c) of the Law of Property Act 1925 which requires a disposition of a subsisting equitable interest to be in signed writing or be void. Prima facie, where T declares himself trustee of his equitable interest for B (where B is of full capacity) this is a disposition of his subsisting equitable interest to B because B replaces T as owner of the equitable interest,[48] just as where T sells his equitable interest to B.

Financial markets cannot accept the risks inherent in T's sale of his (equitable) interest in shares having to be carried out in signed writing. Thus, subsidiary legislation ousts the application of s.53 (1) (c) for dealings in shares held in the CREST system for paperless dealings in shares in United Kingdom public companies.[49]

3–92   However, without the need for any such legislation, it is likely that the replacement of T by a purchaser, P, on the computer list of a financial intermediary (like Cazenove & Co) is in itself effective to transfer T's interest (*e.g.* in shares in a foreign company) to P. After all, such a change in the membership list of a deed of settlement company (with trustees holding property on trusts for members of the company) or of an unincorporated society (with trustees holding property on trusts for members) has been accepted as valid without the need for any writing signed by the transferor.[50] The financial intermediary can be treated as running a membership list with existing members contractually bound by entries on such list (whether enlarging or diminishing existing members'

---

[48] See at para. 2–43 *supra*.

[49] Regulation 32(5) of the Uncertified Securities Regulations 1995 (SI 1999/3272); for gilts dealings settled through the Central Gilts Office see s.1(2) Stock Transfer Act 1982.

[50] *Ashby v. Blackwell & Milton Bank* (1765) Amb 503; KF Sin, *The Legal Nature of the Unit Trust*, Oxford 1997, at 17. It has thus been taken for granted that resigning members (or executors of deceased members) of a club do not need to provide signed writing to part with their equitable interests and new members do not need to show any signed assignments to them.

interests or creating new members by virtue of interests newly acquired by them or striking out old members who had fully parted with their interests). Alternatively, equitable title will have passed to the purchaser, P on payment of the purchase price and giving notice to the financial intermediary,[51] and replacement of T's name by P's name on the intermediary's list simply reflects this.

This is fine where there is a sale when it may not be vital that T's **3–93** name is replaced by P's name to the extent of T's interest in the relevant number of notional shares in the relevant company; but what of the situation where T merely gratuitously declares he holds his interest on trust for B, thereby disposing of his interest to B (assuming B is of full capacity). It appears that s.53 (1) (c) precludes B a volunteer, from having any interest unless and until the financial intermediary replaces T with B on its computer list of interest holders.

Section 3. Certainty of Beneficiaries and Administrative Workability

The comprehensive list test

Prior to the radical decision in *McPhail v. Doulton, infra*, a distinction **3–94** had to be drawn between trusts and powers for certainty purposes. Since trusts, even if discretionary, *have* to be carried out by trustees it must be possible in default for the courts to enforce and control the trust: for this reason there must be no linguistic or semantic uncertainty, otherwise known as conceptual uncertainty, in the description of the beneficiaries nor can the class of beneficiaries be so described that the trust is administratively unworkable. It used to be considered that if trustees failed to carry out a discretionary trust then, since it would be individious and injudicial for the courts to distinguish between the possible discretionary beneficiaries, the court would have to intervene positively by acting on the maxim "Equality is equity" and so distribute the trust assets equally. It followed that for an equal division it must be possible to draw up a comprehensive list of the beneficiaries. Accordingly, discretionary trusts used to fail for uncertainty if such a list could not be drawn up.[52] This must still be the position for "fixed" trusts which require equal division amongst the beneficiaries. Thus a trust for "my relations in equal shares," has to be construed as for "my statutory next-of-kin in equal shares" to save it from being void for uncertainty.[53]

The conceptually clear "is or is not" test

On the other hand, where powers of appointment for objects are **3–95** concerned, the court does not positively intervene to compel exercise of the power. So long as the trustees consider whether or not to exercise

---

[51] *Chinn v. Collins* [1981] AC 533, 548, and at para. 2–50 *supra*

[52] *I.R.C. v. Broadway Cottages Trust* [1955] Ch. 20.

[53] *Re Gansloser's W.T.* [1952] Ch. 30; *Re Poulton's W.T.* [1987] 1 All E.R. 1068 since it is impossible to establish all persons related by blood, however remotely.

the powers and do not go beyond the scope of the powers the courts cannot intervene in negative fashion unless the trustees can be shown to have acted mala fide or capriciously, *i.e.* for reasons which are irrational, perverse or irrelevant to any sensible expectation of the settlor. It is purely up to the trustees whether or not they exercise the powers, so all that is required is that they are in a proper position to consider the exercise of the powers, *i.e.* if they can say with certainty of any given person that he is or is not within the scope of the power: see *Re Gulbenkian's S.T., infra*, rejecting the view expressed in the Court of Appeal that it suffices if the trustees can say of any *one or a few* persons with certainty that he or they are within the scope of the power though uncertainty may exist in respect of many other persons. Accordingly, a power fails for uncertainty only if the court cannot with certainty determine whether any given individual is or is not within the scope of the power.

3–96   In *McPhail v. Doulton, infra*, the House of Lords were faced with a quasi-charitable trust that was a type of private pension trust where it would have been regarded as unsatisfactory on social policy grounds for such a discretionary trust to be void when it would have been valid if a discretionary power. They thus held by a 3:2 majority that the *Gulbenkian* test for powers is also the appropriate test for discretionary trusts as it was possible for the court to carry out a discretionary trust by distributing the trust assets not equally amongst all possible beneficiaries (surely the last thing the settlor ever intended) but in such proportions as appropriate in the circumstances "so as to give effect to the settlor's or testator's intentions. It may do so by appointing new trustees or authorising or directing representative persons of the classes of benefici- aries to prepare a scheme of distribution, or even, should the proper basis for distribution appear, by itself directing the trustees so to distribute."[54] The case was then remitted to the High Court for determination whether on the new test the trust was valid or void for uncertainty.

Application of the "is or is not" test

3–97   In *Re Baden's Deed Trusts (No. 2), infra*, on appeal from the High Court the Court of Appeal unanimously held the trust valid. Stamp L.J. considered the court must be able to say of any given postulant that he definitely is a member of the beneficiary class or he definitely is *not* such a member, *i.e.* the name of a postulant must be capable of being put either in a "Yes" box or a "No" box. Thus a discretionary trust would be void if some postulants' names had to go into a "Don't know" box: if "relatives" meant descendants of a common ancestor there would be a very large number of persons, neither known to be relatives nor to be non-relatives, needing to be placed within the "Don't know" box, so

---

[54] [1971] A.C. 424 at 457.

invalidating a discretionary trust for relatives. However, Stamp L.J. was prepared to treat relatives as meaning "next-of-kin" in which case any postulant would fall within the "Yes" box or the "No" box, so validating the trust.

Sachs and Megaw L.JJ., however, held the trust valid with "relatives" **3–98** bearing its broadest meaning as descendants of a common ancestor. Sachs L.J. took the robust practical view that if a postulant could not prove that his name should go into the "Yes" box then it went into the "No" box. Megaw L.J. treated Stamp L.J.'s view that a discretionary trust will fail if it cannot be shown of any individual that he definitely is or *definitely is not* a member of the class is to contend "in substance and reality that it does fail simply because it is impossible to ascertain every member of the class"[55] and draw up a comprehensive list thereof, a contention rejected by *McPhail v. Doulton*. However, in ascertaining whether *any* (as opposed to every) individual is or is not a class member it is surely not necessary to ascertain *every* class member and draw up a comprehensive list. Be that as it may, Megaw L.J. considered the "is or is not" test satisfied if "as regards a substantial number of objects it can be said with certainty that they fall within the trust, even though as regards a substantial number of other persons the answer would have to be not 'they are outside the trust' but 'it is not proven whether they are in or out.' What is a substantial number may well be a question of common sense and of some degree in relation to the particular trust."[56]

However, is it so wrong for Stamp L.J. to emphasise the need to **3–99** ascertain those who are *not* class members when a person alleging a breach of trust will need to prove that the trustees distributed to an individual who was *not* a class member? There is also obvious uncertainty in the word "substantial". What, indeed, if to a class like that in *McPhail v. Doulton* there was added a conceptually uncertain clause such as "or any of my company's customers or any of my old friends."[57] Moreover, the "substantial" view is only a question of degree removed from the view rejected by the Lords in *Re Gulbenkian* in relation to powers, and so in relation to trusts by *McPhail v. Doulton*, namely the view[58] that a power or discretionary trust is valid if it can be said with certainty of any one or a few persons[59] that he or they are within the scope of the power or discretionary trust though uncertainty exists as to whether other persons are within or without the power or discretionary trust.

---

[55] [1973] Ch. 9 at 23.

[56] *Ibid.* at 24.

[57] Is there scope for the court to develop a power to strike out an offending concept and sever it from the valid concepts within the class or classes of beneficiaries?: *Re Leek* [1969] 1 Ch. 563, 586; *Re Gulbenkian's Settlement* [1968] Ch. 126 at 138. It seems not: see *Re Gulbenkian's Settlement* [1970] A.C. 508 at 524; *McPhail v. Doulton* [1971] A.C. 424 at 456; *Tatham v. Huxtable* (1950) 81 CLR 639, 652.

[58] *Re Gulbenkian's Settlement* [1968] Ch. 126, C.A.

[59] Megaw L.J. in *Re Baden (No. 2)* [1973] Ch. 9 at 24, treats the rejected view as concerning one person but Lord Upjohn in *Re Gulbenkian's Settlement* [1970] A.C. 508 at 524, in his example of two or three individuals being clearly "old friends" treats the rejected view as concerning one or a few persons.

3–100 The crux of the matter is how the court will deal with B's allegation that the trustees committed a breach of trust by paying income to X, who is alleged to be not a relative of A. There is no evidence capable of proving that X is or is not such a relative. Does this mean that, since B has not discharged the burden of proving that X is not a relative of A, B's action fails? If so, then the trustees are free to pay income to X and, indeed, to any Tom, Dick or Harriet and so do whatever they like without the risk of any sanctions for breach of any obligation, if it is in practice impossible to prove that anyone is not a relative of A, for anyone might well be if we could go back far enough, *e.g.* to 4,000 B.C. However, if, although the *legal* burden of proving such a breach of trust lies on B, the *evidential* burden of proving payment to a beneficiary lies on the trustees once B has provided prima facie evidence that the payee is not a beneficiary, then B's action will succeed. If so, then the trustees will be under an enforceable duty to pay only those who can produce the relevant birth and marriage certificates or other sufficient evidence to prove relationship. Sachs[60] and Megaw L.JJ. expressly agreed with the judge of first instance, Brightman J., for the reasons he gave and these justify the pragmatic majority view in the Court of Appeal. He said[61]:

3–101 "In practice, the use of the expression 'relatives' cannot cause the slightest difficulty. A supposed relative to whom a grant is contemplated would, in strictness, be bound to produce the relevant birth and marriage certificates or other sufficient evidence to prove his or her relationship. If the relationship is sufficiently proved the trustees will be entitled to make the grant. If no sufficient evidence can be produced the trustees would have no option but to decline to make a grant."

Thus the trustees are liable if they do not discharge the evidential burden of proving payment to a relative. Nowadays, DNA testing makes this straightforward but creates administrative unworkability problems if the class size does not make the trust charitable.

Conceptual certainty, evidential certainty, ascertainability and administrative workability

3–102 As Carl Emery has emphasised,[62] questions concerning "certainty" of beneficiaries of trusts or objects of powers may relate to one or more of the following:

"(a) 'Conceptual uncertainty': this refers to the precision of language used by the settlor to define the classes of persons whom he intends to benefit.

---

[60] Sachs L.J. considered that if a postulant is not proved to be within the beneficial class then he is outside it, so placing the evidential burden on the trustees to prove the payee is a relative. See *Cross on Evidence*, Chap. 4 on legal and evidential burdens of proof.
[61] [1971] 3 All E.R. 985 at 995.
[62] (1982) 98 L.Q.R. 551 at 552.

(b) 'Evidential uncertainty': this refers to the extent to which the evidence available in a particular case enables specific persons to be identified as members of those classes—and so as beneficiaries or potential beneficiaries.

(c) 'Ascertainability': this refers to the extent to which 'the whereabouts or continued existence' of persons identified as beneficiaries or potential beneficiaries can be ascertained.

(d) 'Administrative workability': this refers to the extent to which it is practicable for trustees to discharge the duties laid upon them by the settlor towards beneficiaries or potential beneficiaries."

Evidential uncertainty does not invalidate a discretionary trust or a **3–103** power since if a person is not proved to be within the beneficial class then he is outside it.[63] Ascertainability problems (*e.g.* over the whereabouts or continued existence of a relative, A, or an ex-employee, B) do not invalidate a discretionary trust or a power because such problems are valid reasons for trustees deciding not to exercise their discretions or powers, and because, in the case of a trust, the court may give leave to distribute the trust fund on the basis that X is dead[64] or may direct a scheme for distribution amongst ascertained beneficiaries.[65]

If a discretionary trust is not conceptually certain or not admin- **3–104** istratively workable then the express trust fails and the property will be held on resulting trust for the settlor. If a trust is not conceptually certain then it cannot be administratively workable, *e.g.* a discretionary trust "for such persons as have moral claims upon me."[66] "for my old friends[67] and business associates," "for worthy causes,"[68] "for those of my friends and relations who are good citizens," "for my customers"[69] because uncertain when they become ex-customers), "for my fans" (unless restricted to members of a particular fan club), "for Cambridge students" (unless restricted to students from time to time studying as junior members of the University of Cambridge). As Lord Hailsham emphasised in *I.R.C. v. McMullen*,[70] "Where it is claimed that there is an ambiguity, a benignant construction should be given if possible. This was the maxim of the civil law: *semper in dubiis benigniora praeferenda sunt*. There is a similar maxim in English law: *ut res magis valeat quam pereat*. It applied where a gift is capable of two constructions one of which would make it void and the other effectual."

---

[63] *Re Baden's Deed Trust (No. 2)* [1973] Ch. 9 at 20, *per* Sachs L.J. [1972] Ch. 607, *per* Brightman J. The minority view of Stamp L.J. was to the effect that the evidential uncertainty (which he considered could not be resolved so simplistically) converted the apparent black and white certainty of concept into an uncertain grey concept.

[64] *Re Benjamin* [1902] 1 Ch. 723.

[65] *McPhail v. Doulton* [1971] A.C. 424 at 457; *Re Hain* [1961] 1 W.L.R. 440 and *Muir v. I.R.C.* [1966] 3 All E.R. 38 at 44 show that a trust will not be invalidated because some of the class of beneficiaries may have disappeared or become impossible to find or it has been forgotten who they were.

[66] *Re Leek* [1969] 1 Ch. 563.

[67] *Brown v. Gould* [1972] 53 at 57; *Re Barlow's W.T.* [1979] 1 All E.R. 296.

[68] *Re Atkinson* [1978] 1 All E.R. 1275.

[69] *Sparfax (1965) Ltd v. Dommett* [1972] *The Times,* July 14.

[70] [1981] A.C. 1 at 11, [1980] 1 All E.R. 884 at 890, *infra,* at para. 7–219.

3–105   In a very rare case a discretionary trust may be conceptually certain but, nonetheless, may be administratively unworkable, *e.g.* "for everyone in the world except the settlor, his spouse and past and present trustees"[71] or even "for the benefit of any or all or some of the inhabitants of the County of West Yorkshire."[72] Such a "trust" would not be capable of being effectively "policed" by the court when a default beneficiary complains of the trustee's exercise of a power in favour of an object. A court must act judicially according to some criteria, expressly or impliedly provided by the trust instrument or by extrinsic admissible evidence, so that it may control or execute the trusts: it cannot resort to pure guesswork for such is a non-justiciable function. If you were trustee of a discretionary trust for everyone in the world but five persons, how on earth would you begin to try to decide what to do?

3–106   However, trustees' *powers* to add anyone in the world (excepting the settlor, his spouse, past and present trustees) to the class of discretionary trust beneficiaries[73] and trustees' powers to appoint capital or income to anyone in the world (excepting the above small class) have been upheld by judges of first instance as not capable of being invalidated by the test of administrative workability which has been restricted to trusts.[74] The basis for this distinction is that in the case of a discretionary trust a trustee is under more extensive obligations which the beneficiaries can positively enforce because they may lead to the court seeing to the carrying out of the trusts. In the case of powers a trustee only need consider periodically whether or not he should exercise the power, taking into account the range of objects of the power and the appropriateness of possible individual appointments; the only control exercisable by the court in the words of Templeman J.[75] "is the removal of the trustees and the only 'due adminstration' which can be 'directed' is an order requiring the trustees to consider the exercise of the power, and, in particular a request from a person within the ambit of the power." He contemplated[76] it being possible for objects to have no right to be informed they were objects and no right to go through the trust accounts. However, he accepted[77] that the court must be able to intervene if a wide power is exercised capriciously, *i.e.* for reasons which are irrational, perverse or irrelevant to any sensible expectation of the settlor.

---

[71] *Re Hay's S.T.* [1982] 1 W.L.R. 202, *infra*, para. 3–150 *Yeap Cheo Neo v. Ong Chen Neo* (1875) L.R. 6 P.C. 381; *Blausten v. I.R.C.* [1972] Ch. 256 at 266, 271, 272. The question of conceptual certainty and of administrative workability must be determined at the date of creation of the trust: *Re Baden's Deed Trust (No. 2)* [1972] Ch. 607.

[72] *R. v. District Auditor, ex p. West Yorkshire County Council* (1985) 26 R.V.R. 24: there were about 2,500,000 potential beneficiaries. "Relatives" of X may be 5 million.

[73] *Re Manisty's Settlement* [1974] Ch. 17. In this case, as held by Templeman J, it is more easy to discern the intention of the settlor than is the case of a power to appoint to anyone but four specified persons—unless a settlor's letter of wishes is available.

[74] *Re Hay's S.T.* [1982] 1 W.L.R. 202, *infra*, para. 3–150, *Re Beatty's W.T.* [1990] 3 All E.R. 844. In *Re Denley's Trust Deed* [1969] 1 Ch. 373 Goff J. with little discussion upheld the power of trustees to allow any persons other than the trust beneficiaries to use the sports ground primarily intended for the beneficiaries' use.

[75] [1974] Ch. 17 at 27–28. Also see *Re Gulbenkian's S.T.* [1970] A.C. 508 at 525.

[76] *ibid* at 24–25. Also *Rosewood Trust Ltd v. Schmidt*, (unreported Manx CA, February 2001).

[77] *ibid* at 26.

But if this is the case, then for the trustees' power to be justiciable the **3–107** settlor's expectations must somehow be discerned.[78] If they cannot be discerned so that the power is not justiciable then it cannot be a fiduciary power, yet a power exercisable *virtute officii* can only be a fiduciary power unless expressly stated not to be fiduciary but only personal.[79] The object of a fiduciary power has, like a beneficiary in default of exercise of the power, a right to seek the court's removal of the trustees for exercising the power for reasons which are irrational, perverse or irrelevant to any sensible expectation of the settlor. If such expectation cannot be discerned then the court cannot adjudicate on the matter and cannot determine rights and duties. Thus, Buckley L.J. considered *obiter*[80] that a power to add anyone in the world to a class of trust beneficiaries (and, presumably, by parity of reasoning a power to appoint to anyone in the world) would be void. Templeman J.[81] and Megarry V.-C.[82] have rejected this, considering[83] that "dispositions ought, if possible, to be upheld and the court ought not to be astute to find grounds on which a power can be invalidated."

The need for justiciability underlies the requirement of administrative **3–108** workability yet the High Court has created a distinction between trusts where there is positive and negative justiciability and fiduciary powers where there is only negative justiciability. The distinction may well be disputed in an appellate court. After all, in *McPhail v. Doulton*[84] the House of Lords regarded discretionary trusts ("trust powers" in the terminology of Lord Wilberforce) and powers as so similar in substance that the same certainty test should apply to both, so why only have the test of administrative workability apply to discretionary trusts?

Furthermore, despite the views of Templeman J. in *Re Manisty*, the court may positively intervene in an extreme case where there is an improper refusal to consider exercising a power: so as to direct the exercise of the power in an obviously proper way (albeit a power to benefit a beneficiary as opposed to an object of a power of appointment).[85] This has recently taken on particular significance in the context of pension fund trusts in favour of beneficiaries who have earned their interest and have legitimate expectations that powers of augmenting pensions will be exercised in their favour.[86] Warner J.[87] indeed, regarded

---

[78] In *Re Manisty's Settlement* [1974] Ch. 17 at 24–25 Templeman J. significantly stated, "In the present case if the settlement is read as a whole the expectations of the settlor are not difficult to discern."

[79] *Re Gulbenkian's S.T.* [1970] A.C. 508 at 518, *per* Lord Reid, unless the trust instrument expressly states that the powers are to be regarded as personal and not fiduciary.

[80] *Blausten v. I.R.C.* [1972] Ch. 256 at 273 and Orr and Salmon L.J.J. agreed with him at 274 and 175. The moral is to couch the power as a power for the trustees to add to the class of beneficiaries anyone from a list submitted to them by any existing beneficiary: see trust precedent at para 1–60, *supra*.

[81] *Re Manisty's S.T.* [1974] Ch. 17.

[82] *Re Hay's S.T.* [1982] 1 W.L.R. 202, applied in *I.R.C. v. Schroder* [1983] STC. 480.

[83] *Ibid* at 212. So long as conceptual certainty is present it does not matter that in substance the testator is effectively delegating his function of choosing legatees to another: *Re Abraham's W.T.* [1969] 1 Ch. 463; *Re Park* [1932] 1 Ch. 580; *Re Nicholls* (1987) 34 D.L.R. (4th) 321; *Re Beatty's WT* [1990] 3 All E.R. 844.

[84] [1971] A.C. 424.

[85] *Klug v. Klug* [1918] 2 Ch. 67, *White v. Grane* (1854) 18 Beav 571, *Re Lofthause* (1885) 29 Ch.D. 921.

[86] *Mettoy Pension Trustees Ltd v. Evans* [1991] 2 All E.R. 513, *Thrells Ltd v. Lomas* [1993] 1 W.L.R. 456.

[87] *Mettoy, supra* at 549, *infra*, at para. 3–165.

Lord Wilberforce's remarks on how the court can positively see to the carrying out of discretionary trusts as equally applicable to fiduciary powers though in the context of a power to benefit beneficiaries (not objects of a power) who had earned their pension rights and expectations.

3–109   On the safety-first principle a power of appointment should be restricted to a workable ascertainable class of persons and a power to add persons to a beneficial class should be restricted, for example, to persons nominated in writing by existing members of the class who shall give written reasons why such an addition would have been likely to have met with the settlor's approval. Otherwise, a memorandum of wishes expressed to be of no binding legal effect, but merely indicative of the settlor's purposes in creating the trust, will assist in settling workable parameters for the exercise of the trustee's discretion. The power should clearly be upheld if the trust instrument expressly states that it is to be a personal power such that its exercise is to be unchallengeable unless providing the trustee with a tangible benefit.

Fiduciary powers and personal powers

3–110   There is a personal power where the holder of the power (known as the "donee" of the power) does not have to consider from time to time whether or not to exercise the power and can even release the power so it can never be exercised.[88] If he does decide to exercise the power, then he "is entitled to prefer one object to another from any motive he pleases, and however capriciously he exercises the power the Court will uphold it",[89] so long as he commits no fraud on the power by exercising it to benefit someone (like himself) outside the scope of the power[90] *e.g.* appoints to an object on the basis that the object will give him half the money appointed as a gift or to repay a debt due to him.

One type of a personal power can be regarded as a "beneficial" power where the holder of the power can exercise it for his own benefit[91] *e.g.* appoint money to himself or to another to satisfy a legal or moral obligation or refuse to consent to the trustee selling shares in a company of which he is a director or selling a house he occupies.

3–111   There is a fiduciary power where the settlor intends the donee to exercise a discretion to benefit beneficiaries or objects of a power of appointment in a responsible manner for the purposes for which the discretion was conferred on the donee by the settlor.[92] This requires the donee to consider periodically—or when consent is sought by the trustees—whether or not to exercise the discretion, and the discretion

---

[88] *Re Gulbenkian's S.T.* [1982] 1 W.L.R. 202, *Re Wills' Trust Deeds* [1964] Ch. 219.
[89] *Re Wright* [1920] 1 Ch. 108, 118. The court cannot take a personal power away from its holder: *Re Park* [1932] 1 Ch. 580.
[90] *Re Somes* [1896] 1 Ch. 250, 255, *Palmer v. Locke* (1880) 15 Ch. D. 294, 302–303.
[91] *Re Wills' Trust Deeds* [1964] Ch. 214, 228, *Steele v. Paz Ltd.* [1993–95] Manx LR 102 especially on appeal at 426, *Re Z Trust* [1997] Cayman ILR 248, *Rawson Trust v. Perlman* 1 Butts O.C.M 135 (Bahamas 1984).
[92] *Re Hay's S.T.* [1981] 3 All E.R. 788, 792, *Re Beatty's W.T.* [1990] 3 All E.R. 844, 846.

cannot be released or fettered in any way unless expressly authorised in the trust instrument.[93] The exercise or non-exercise of the discretionary power must take account of the range of possibilities within the power and must be in good faith and not be irrational, perverse or irrelevant to any sensible expectation of the settlor.[94] The donee cannot benefit from the discretionary power unless authorised expressly or by necessary implication.[95]

Powers vested in an office-holder like a trustee or a protector are presumed to be fiduciary powers,[96] while powers relating to distribution of capital or income to beneficiaries or objects and which are vested in individuals *qua* individuals like the settlor or a testator's widow or eldest child are presumed to be personal.[97] Powers vested in such individuals which relate to the appointment and replacement of trustees or the investment role thereof are, however, presumed fiduciary[98] because the trustees' investment role is at the core of the trust, protecting and furthering the interests of the beneficiaries as a whole.

One has to construe the terms of the trust instrument in the light of **3–112** the surrounding background circumstances to determine the obligations affecting the donee of a power,[99] so that express assistance from the draftsman is advisable. Indeed, expressly or by necessary implication a power could be semi-fiduciary.

For example, an individual donee of a power could be under no duty to consider periodically whether or not to exercise the power, and could even refuse to bother ever thinking about it, but if she did exercise the power then it would have to be exercised subject to the obligations affecting full fiduciary powers.[1] Alternatively, a trustee could be under an obligation to consider periodically whether or not to exercise a power (*e.g.* a power to appoint to anyone except the settlor, the settlor's spouse and the trustee) but if he did exercise the power then he would be treated as the donee of a personal power, so that the exercise of the power could not be challenged except under the fraud on a power doctrine (*e.g.* if property were appointed to X on condition X gave half of it to the settlor, the settlor's spouse or the trustee). This latter construction by way of an allegedly necessary implication could be used by the courts to justify the validity of trustees' powers to appoint to anyone in the world except X,Y and Z, courts being reluctant to overturn old cases on the basis of which property has changed hands over many years.

---

[93] *Re Hay's S.T. (supra).*
[94] *ibid* and *Re Manisty's Settlement* [1974] Ch. 17.
[95] *Re Z Trust* [1997] Cayman I.L.R. 248.
[96] *Re Wills' Trust Deeds* [1964] Ch. 219, *Re Gulbenkian's S.T.* [1970] A.C. 508, 518.
[97] *Re Somes* [1896] 1 Ch. 250, *Palmer v. Locke* (1880) 15 Ch. D. 294.
[98] *IRC v. Schroder* [1983] S.T.C. 480, *Commissioner of Stamp Duties v. Way* [1942] 1 All E.R. 191, *Vestey's Executors v. IRC* [1949] 1 All E.R. 1108.
[99] *Botnar v. IRC* [1999] S.T.C. 711 (CA), applying Lord Hoffmann's approach in *Investors Compensation Scheme v. West Bromwich B.S.* [1998] 1 W.L.R. 896.
[1] *Re Osiris Trustees Ltd* [2000] WTLR 933.

3–113   Normally, all the powers of a trustee are fidiciary,[2] while in the case of protectors their powers will be fiduciary if for the benefit of the beneficiaries as a whole, but it is possible for some powers to be conferred on the protector to safeguard the interests of the protector (*e.g.* if the protector be the settlor or a beneficiary[3]) or even of the settlor (*e.g.* if the protector be the settlor's lawyer and confidant[4]). While protectors can be indemnified as to expenses properly incurred in fulfilling the duties of their office, the draftsperson needs not only to consider spelling out the nature of their powers—and the implications for the trustees' relationship with them—but to provide for protectors to charge for their services and, perhaps, have the benefit of a clause exempting them from liability for negligent breach of their fiduciary duties. The court, having inherent jurisdiction to appoint a protector (*e.g.* if no name appears in the schedule to the trust where the protector's name was accidentally never inserted[5]) must also have similar jurisdiction to replace a protector in breach of his fiduciary duties.

3–114   There seems no reason why a personal power which does not have to be administratively workable[6] should have to satisfy the test for conceptual certainty of fiduciary powers. Instead of the concept being certain enough to enable the court to say of any given postulant that he definitely is or is not an object of the power, it should suffice that the court can say of one or more persons that they are within the "core" meaning of the concept (*e.g.* "friends"[7]) even if the penumbra may be so uncertain that the court cannot say of many persons whether they qualify or not.[8] Thus, a widow's personal power should be valid where her husband leaves his residuary estate to trustees upon particular discretionary trusts, but gives his widow power to appoint thereout up to 10 separate sums of £2,000 to up to 10 friends of the testator not otherwise benefited by his will, or power to appoint up to £20,000 thereout between business associates of the testator not otherwise benefited by his will as she might see fit. After all, this is not so different from a testator leaving his residuary estate to trustees upon discretionary trusts "for my old friends, A, B, C, and D, and for my good business associates, V, W, X and Y, with power for my widow to add as beneficiaries anyone else (apart from herself or past and present trustees) but particularly any person she considers to be other friends or business associates of mine as she may see fit." This last power would enable her to benefit the testator's "friends" and "business associates" by making them eligible to benefit from the exercise of the trustees' discretion.

---

[2] *Re Gulbenkian's S.T.* [1970] AC 508, 518.

[3] *Rawson Trust v. Perlman* 1 Butts O.C.M. 135, *Re Z Trust* [1997] Cayman ILR 248. Further see DJ Hayton (1999) 32 Vanderbilt Jo. of Transnational Law 559, 579–589.

[4] *Re Star, Knierem v. Bermuda Trust Co.* 1 Butts O.C.M. 116.

[5] *Steele v. Paz Ltd.* [1993–95] Manx LR 102 and, on appeal, 426.

[6] *Re Hay's Settlement* [1982] 1 W.L.R 202 *infra*.

[7] See Browne-Wilkinson J on "friends" in *Re Barlow's W.T.* [1979] 1 WLR 278 *infra* at para. 3–168.

[8] See C. T. Emery (1982) 98 L.Q.R. 551, 582 where he uses the expression "bare power" to distinguish a personal power from a fiduciary power. Exercise of the personal power would be effective so long as confined to those within the "core" meaning of the concept. Query whether it should be ineffective only when in favour of some person clearly outside the penumbra of meaning, *e.g.* where the alleged old friend had never met or corresponded with the testator: see *infra*, at para. 3–126.

Conditions subsequent and conditions precedent

Trusts may contain conditions subsequent or conditions precedent. If **3–115** property is held subject to a condition subsequent so that the beneficiary's vested interest will be liable to forfeiture on the subsequent happening of the proscribed event, the condition must be such that the court can see from the outset precisely and distinctly upon the happening of what event the interest is to be forfeited.[9] The circumstances involving forfeiture must be clearly known in advance so that the beneficiary knows precisely where he stands.

Where property is held on trust for persons subject to the fulfilment of **3–116** a condition so that it is up to them positively to show that they satisfy such condition precedent then a less strict standard of certainty is usually required, except where the trust is a fixed trust for equal division amongst all those who can satisfy a particular condition when the condition must be certain enough to enable a complete list to be drawn up of those who satisfy the condition.[10] However, if instead of a fixed trust for a class there is a discretionary trust or a fiduciary power for a class of people who can satisfy a particular condition, then the condition must contain conceptually clear criteria so that it can be said of any given postulant that he is or is not a member of the class.[11]

Where property is held on trust not for distribution between qualifying **3–117** members of a class but to enable qualifying individuals to benefit to a specified extent (*i.e.* not "£100,000 to be distributed between such of my relatives as marry persons of the Jewish faith and of Jewish parentage as my trustees may see fit" but "£5,000 to each of my relatives as marry persons of the Jewish faith and of Jewish parentage" or "£25,000 to my daughter Naomi if she marries a person of the Jewish faith and of Jewish parentage") Browne-Wilkinson J. has held[12] that the qualifying condition is valid if it is possible to say of one or more persons that he or they undoubtedly qualify, even though it may be impossible to say of others whether or not they qualify.

In *Re Barlow infra* Browne-Wilkinson J. was faced with a testatrix who **3–118** directed her executor "to allow any member of my family and any friends of mine who may wish to do so to purchase" particular paintings in the testatrix's estate at a low 1970 valuation. He held that the disposition was properly to be regarded as a series of individual gifts to persons answering the description friends or blood relations of the testatrix, since the effect of the disposition was to confer on such persons

---

[9] *Clavering v. Ellison* (1859) 7 H.L.Cas. 707; *Blathwayt v. Lord Cawley* [1976] A.C. 397 at 429.

[10] *e.g.* the case of a trust for my relatives in equal shares as envisaged in *Re Barlow's W.T.* [1979] 1 W.L.R. 278.

[11] *McPhail v. Doulton* [1971] A.C. 424.

[12] *Re Barlow's W.T.* [1979] 1 W.L.R. 278, *infra*, at para. 3–168. This was the test suggested by Lord Denning in *Re Gulbenkian's S.T.* [1968] Ch. 126 at 134 for judging certainty of powers and rejected by the House of Lords on appeal. "Jewish faith and parentage" was held void for uncertainty in *Clayton v. Ramsden* [1943] A.C. 320 but in *Re Tepper's W.T.* [1987] Ch. 358 Scott J. was reluctant to find "Jewish faith" uncertain and so adjourned the case to see if evidence of the Jewish faith as practised by the testator would clarify the matter. Both cases involved conditions subsequent.

a series of options to purchase. It was not necessary to discover who all the friends or relations were: all that was required was for the executors to be able to say of any individual coming forward that he had proved that he was a friend or relation on which qualifications he provided guidance.[13] He justified this on the basis of *Re Allen*[14] where the Court of Appeal had upheld a devise "to the eldest of the sons of A who shall be a member of the Church of England and an adherent to the doctrine of that Church," so allowing the eldest son to seek to establish that he qualified, even if the conditions were conceptually uncertain so that it would be impossible to say of others whether or not they qualified. He considered *Re Allen* still to be good law after *McPhail v. Doulton* since the Court of Appeal in *Re Tuck's S.T.*[15] had mentioned it approvingly (but only in the context of revealing a distinction between conditions precedent and conditions subsequent, which he overlooked).

3–119   He was much impressed by Lord Evershed's dictum[16] that a gift to A if he is a tall man will be valid, enabling A if he is 6ft. 6ins. to claim the gift. Where there is one ascertained individual, who is the only possible beneficiary, then one can accept his entitlement if he can prove he comes within the "core" meaning of the qualifying condition, even if the penumbra is so conceptually uncertain that it may often be impossible to judge whether the condition is satisfied.[17] This exception will cover several ascertained beneficiaries where each is the only possible beneficiary, *e.g.* "£15,000 to each of my sons A, B, C and D if he is tall."

3–120   However, one ought not to extend the exception beyond individuals whose identity is ascertained from the outset to individuals whose identity can only be ascertained after deciding whether or not others have satisfied a particular condition which is conceptually uncertain, *e.g.* £20,000 to my first daughter to marry (or to the eldest of my daughters who shall marry) a tall adherent to the doctrine of the Church of England. If the eldest daughter, A, marries someone within the penumbra of the conceptually uncertain condition so that it is impossible to say whether she qualifies or not then it cannot help B, the second eldest, if she is within the "core" of the condition by marrying a 6ft. 6ins. Church of England vicar. Whether B satisfies the condition depends on the *ex hypothesi* insoluble question whether or not A has satisfied the condition.[18] The condition would fail more clearly if the gift had been to "my first female friend to marry a tall adherent to Church of England doctrine" since "friend" is a highly imprecise concept.

---

[13] *Re Baden's Deed Trusts (No. 2)* [1973] Ch. 9 enables relations to be ascertained on the basis that he who does not prove he is a relation is not a relation, the concept of descendant of a common ancestor being clear. The concept of friendship is not clear. If one picture was particularly good and available at a particularly low price, so that everyone wanted this best bargain, would the purchaser have to be found by putting all possible names into a hat and drawing out one name? But would not this be impossible since the uncertain penumbra of meaning of friendship would make it impossible for the executor or the court to decide whether many persons were friends or not?

[14] [1953] Ch. 810.

[15] [1978] Ch. 49.

[16] [1953] Ch. 810 at 817.

[17] L. McKay [1980] Conv. 263 at 277; C. T. Emery (1982) 98 L.Q.R. 551 at 564.

[18] C. T. Emery (1982) 98 L.Q.R. 551 at 564–565. The Court of Appeal in *Re Allen* [1953] Ch. 810 did not face up to this when dealing with a claim by the eldest son (or rather, his executor).

Browne-Wilkinson J. considered that "a gift of £10 to each of my **3–121** friends" was valid, whilst accepting that a discretionary trust or power for "my friends" would be void[19] Such a less strict approach seems anomalous and illogical. After all, a trustee or executor directed to make payments to qualifying beneficiaries has a duty to make such payments which may be enforced by each qualifying beneficiary, unlike the weaker position of beneficiaries or objects under discretionary trusts or powers. Furthermore, the person entitled to the fund after payment thereout of the sums to the "friends" must have a clear right to sue the trustee or executor for paying sums out to persons not ranking as "friends", so that it needs to be possible to draw up a comprehensive fixed list of friends. To protect themselves the trustees or executors (caught between the claims of the alleged friend and the residuary beneficiary) must have a right to obtain the court's directions as to the comprehensive list of persons to whom to make the payments. "Friends" gives rise not just to evidential uncertainty but to conceptual uncertainty having an uncertain penumbra making it impossible in many instances for the court to say whether a person is or is not a friend. If, pragmatically, one is to have Browne-Wilkinson J.'s exception for persons within the "core" meaning of friend why not allow discretionary trusts and powers to be validly exercised in favour of persons within the "core" meaning of friend, though House of Lords authority[20] is against this?

Resolution of uncertainty

Questions of evidential uncertainty can be resolved by the court in the **3–122** last resort, though it is possible for the trust instrument to contain a clause empowering someone like the trustees[21] or the testator's widow, or the testator's business partner to resolve any evidential uncertainty.

Apparent conceptual uncertainty may not be such if the court restrictively construes the concept, *e.g.* restricts "Cambridge students" to students from time to time studying as junior members of the University of Cambridge or restrict "fans of Elvis Presley" to members of Elvis Presley fan clubs or restricts a residuary bequest to "those beneficiaries who have only received small amounts" to those who had received legacies of £25, £50 and £100 where other legatees had received legacies of £200 and £250.[22] A proviso that in cases of doubt the decision of the Registrary of the University of Cambridge or of the secretaries of official Elvis Presley fan clubs shall be conclusive may assist the court restrict the concept so that it is actually certain.

---

[19] *Re Barlow's W.T.* [1979] 1 W.L.R. 278 at 281, *infra*, para. 3–168
[20] *Re Gulbenkian's S.T.* [1970] A.C. 508, *infra*, para. 3–128; *McPhail v. Doulton* [1971] A.C. 424, *infra*, para. 3–131.
[21] *Dundee General Hospital Board v. Walker* [1952] 1 All E.R. 896.
[22] *Re Steel* [1978] 2 All E.R. 1026 at 1032; also see *O'Rourke v. Bicks* [1992] STC 703.

3–123 However, actual conceptual uncertainty cannot be resolved by such provisos,[23] except, it seems, where a person acting as an expert (as opposed to acting as an arbitrator) is given power to resolve the matter *e.g.* the Chief Rabbi is to determine whether or not beneficiaries are of the Jewish faith.[24] If the concept is "my tall relations" or "my old friends" or "my good business associates," and the testator's trustees are given power to resolve any doubts as to whether any persons qualify or not then since *ex hypothesi* the court cannot resolve the uncertainty caused by the conceptual uncertainty it is difficult to see how the trustees can. There are no clear conceptual criteria to guide them or, indeed, the court if their exercise of the power is challenged. An inherently irresolvable issue is just that; it cannot be resolved, whether by a judge or anyone else.

3–124 If the concept is "persons whom my trustees consider to be my tall relatives or my old friends or my good business associates" the concept still seems uncertain. As Jenkins J. said in *Re Coxen*[25]:

> "If the testator had insufficiently defined the state of affairs on which the trustees were to form their opinion he would not have saved the condition from invalidity on the ground of uncertainty merely by making their opinion the criterion, although the declaration by the trustees of this or that opinion would be an event about which in itself there could be no uncertainty."

3–125 This view was followed in *Re Jones*[26] and then in *Re Wright's W.T.*[27] where a gift of property to trustees "to use the same at their absolute discretion for such people and institutions as they think have helped me or my late husband" failed for conceptual uncertainty. How can the trustees consider someone to have helped a testatrix or to be a tall relative or old friend or good business associate without knowing what exactly they are supposed to consider as criteria justifying their conclusion? If their conclusion is challenged how can the court adjudicate upon the matter?[28]

3–126 If a power to resolve conceptual uncertainty is given not as a fiduciary power but as a personal power, for example, to the testator's widow, might this validate a prima facie uncertain trust? What if a testator left

---

[23] *Re Coxen* [1948] Ch. 747 at 761–762; *Re Jones* [1953] Ch. 125; *Re Wright's W.T.* [1981] L.S. Gaz. 841. Lord Denning's dicta to the contrary in *Re Tuck's S.T.* [1978] Ch. 49 at 60, 62 are out of line and seem based on a misinterpretation of *Dundee General Hospital Board, supra* as Eveleigh L.J. indicates [1978] Ch. 49 at 66. See also P. Matthews (1983) 133 New L.J. 915.

[24] Lord Denning's approach in *Re Tuck's ST* [1978] Ch 49, 60, 62 can nowadays be so justified e.g. *The Glacier Bay* [1996] 1 4 Rep 370, *Brown v. G10 Insurance Ltd* [1998] Lloyds Rep I.R. 201 [1998] *The Times* February 18.

[25] [1948] Ch. 747 at 761–762.

[26] [1953] Ch. 125: "if at any time B shall in the uncontrolled opinion of the trustee have social or other relationship with C."

[27] [1981] L.S. Gaz. 841. Also see *Tatham v. Huxtable* (1950) 81 CLR 639, 653.

[28] The jurisdiction of the court cannot be ousted: *Re Raven* [1915] 1 Ch. 673: *Re Wynn's W.T.* [1952] Ch. 271. One should note that a court should construe a discretionary trust "for my old friends but so that my trustees shall have power to resolve any doubts as to whether anyone is or is not an old friend of mine" as being a discretionary trust for "persons whom my trustees consider to be my old friends" so that the position should be the same on either construction.

his residuary estate to his executors and trustees on discretionary trust for his old friends but stated that if any doubts or disputes arose as to membership of such class then his widow's decision was to be final unless it was unreasonable, as rejecting a person clearly within the "core" meaning of "old friends" or admitting a person clearly outside the "penumbra" of meaning of "old friend," like someone whom the testator had never met or corresponded with?[29] It would seem unreasonable for a court not to accept the validity of such a personal power with the above express or implied limitation that it may not be exercised unreasonably. But if one concedes the validity of such power of the widow why should one not concede the validity of such power if vested in trustees in such terms indicating it is to be regarded not as a fiduciary power.[30] If such power was *expressly* limited as above the court might well accept it as conferring dispositive leeway on the trustees, just as much as on the widow, but the court would be reluctant to find such validating *implied* limitation on the power vested in the trustees as such.

Absence of certainties

If there is no intention to create a trust the alleged settlor or his estate **3–127** retains the beneficial interest in relevant property. If there is uncertainty of subject-matter then the alleged trust is ineffective since there is nothing for the alleged trust to "bite" on. If certainty of intention and of subject-matter are present but there is uncertainty of beneficiaries then the trustee holds the property on a resulting trust for the settlor or the testator's estate as the case may be.

If property is given by will or other instrument to someone absolutely and subsequently in that instrument trusts are imposed on that absolute interest then if these trusts fail for uncertainty or otherwise the donee takes the property for himself absolutely.[31]

RE GULBENKIAN'S SETTLEMENT TRUSTS

House of Lords [1970] A.C. 508; [1968] 3 W.L.R. 1127; [1968] 3 All E.R. 785.   **3–128**

Settlements were made including a special power for trustees to appoint in favour of Nubar Gulbenkian "and any wife and his children or remoter issue . . . and any person . . . in whose house or apartment or in whose company or under whose care or control or by or with whom [he] may from time to time be employed or residing," and with trusts in default of appointment.

---

[29] This is narrower than taking advantage of *Re Hay's S.T.* [1982] 1 W.L.R. 202, *infra*, para. 3–150 to give the widow power to add to the class of beneficiaries anyone else (apart from herself or past or present trustees) but particularly anyone she considers to be an old friend of the testator. Also see *Re Coates* [1955] Ch. 495 for the court's liberal approach before establishment of the "is or is not" test.

[30] Perhaps this may have been at the back of Harman L.J.'s mind in *Re Leek* [1969] 1 Ch. 563 at 579 when, whilst accepting that a discretionary trust for such persons as have moral claims on the settlor would be void for conceptual uncertainty, he uttered unorthodox dicta to the effect that if the trustees were arbiters of the class of beneficiaries, being such persons as the trustees considered to have a moral claim on the settlor, the trust would be valid.

[31] *Hancock v. Watson* [1902] A.C. 14: *Re Burton's S.T.* [1955] Ch. 348.

The House of Lords unanimously upheld the power and (Lord Donovan reserving his opinion though "inclined to share" Lord Upjohn's views) rejected *obiter* the broad view that a power was valid if any one person clearly fell within the scope of the power. The House construed the clause as meaning "and any person or persons by whom Nubar may from time to time be employed and any person or persons with whom N from time to time is residing whether in the house or apartments of such person or persons or whether in the company or under the care and control of such person or persons" and held that it could be said with certainty whether any given individual was or was not a member of that class so that the power was valid.

LORD UPJOHN (with whom Lords Guest and Hodson concurred): "My lords, that is sufficient to dispose of the appeal, but the reasons of two members of the Court of Appeal went further and so must be examined.

3–129 "Lord Denning M.R.,[32] propounded a test in the case of powers collateral, namely, that if you can say of one particular person meaning thereby, apparently, any one person only that he is clearly within the category the whole power is good though it may be difficult to say in other cases whether a person is or is not within the category, and he supported that view by reference to authority. Winn L.J. said[33] that where there was not a complete failure by reason of ambiguity and uncertainty the court would give effect to the power as valid rather than hold it defeated since it will not have wholly failed, which put—though more broadly—the view expressed by Lord Denning M.R. Counsel for the respondents in his second line of argument relied on these observations as a matter of principle but he candidly admitted that he could not rely on any authority. Moreover, Lord Denning M.R. expressed the view[34] that the different doctrine with regard to trust powers should be brought into line with the rule with regard to conditions precedent and powers collateral . . .

[After pointing out that a fixed trust for equal division among my old friends would be void even if two or three individuals plainly were old friends, he continued]

"Suppose the donor does not direct an equal division but gives a power of selection to his trustees among the class: exactly the same principles apply. The trustees have a duty to select the donees of the donor's bounty from among the class designated by the donor; he has not entrusted them with any power to select the donees merely from among known claimants within the class, for that is constituting a narrower class and the donor has given them no power to do this . . .

3–130 "But with respect to mere powers,[35] while the court cannot compel the trustees to exercise their powers, yet those entitled to the fund in default must clearly be entitled to restrain the trustees from exercising it save among those within the power. So the trustees, or the court, must be able to say with certainty who is within and who is without the power. It is for this reason that I find myself

---

[32] [1968] Ch. 126 at 133, 134.
[33] [1968] Ch. 126 at 138.
[34] *ibid.*
[35] He had just pointed out that in the case of trust powers (*viz.* discretionary trusts) "the trustees *must* exercise their power of selection and in default the court will", so he could not "see how it is possible to apply to the execution of a trust power the principles applicable to the permissible exercise by the donees, even if trustees, of mere powers."

unable to accept the broader position advanced by Lord Denning M.R. and Winn L.J., mentioned earlier.

"My lords, I would dismiss these appeals." *Appeals dismissed.*

MCPHAIL v. DOULTON

House of Lords [1971] A.C. 424; [1970] 2 W.L.R. 1110; [1970] 2 All E.R. 228.   **3–131**

The facts and the issues appear clearly in the following speech of Lord Wilberforce with which Lord Reid and Viscount Dilhorne concurred, though dissenting speeches were delivered by Lords Hodson and Guest.

LORD WILBERFORCE: "My Lords, this appeal is concerned with the validity of a trust deed dated July 17, 1941, by which Mr. Bertram Baden established a fund for the benefit, broadly, of the staff of the respondent company Matthew Hall & Co. Ltd

The critical clauses are as follows:

'9. (a) The Trustees shall apply the net income of the Fund in making at their absolute discretion grants to or for benefit of any of the officers and employees or ex-officers or ex-employees of the Company or any relatives or dependants of any such persons in such amounts at such times and on such conditions (if any) as they think fit and any such grant may at their discretion be made by payment to the beneficiary or to any institution or person to be applied for his or her benefit and in the latter case the Trustees shall be under no obligation to see to the application of the money.

'(b) The Trustees shall not be bound to exhaust the income of any year or other period in making such grants as aforesaid and any income not so applied shall be dealt with as provided by clause 6(a) hereof enabling moneys to be placed with any Bank or to be invested.

'(c) The Trustees may realise any investments representing accumulations of income and apply the proceeds as though the same were income of the Fund and may also (but only with the consent of all the Trustees) at any time prior to the liquidation of the Fund realise any other part of the capital of the Fund which in the opinion of the Trustees it is desirable to realise in order to provide benefits for which the current income of the Fund is insufficient.

'10. All benefits being at the absolute discretion of the Trustees, no person shall have any right title or interest in the Fund otherwise than pursuant to the exercise of such discretion, and nothing herein contained shall prejudice the right of the Company to determine the employment of any officer or employee.'

"Clause 11 defines a perpetuity period within which the trusts are, in any event, **3–132** to come to an end and clause 12 provides for the termination of the fund. On this event the trustees are directed to apply the fund in their discretion in one or more of certain specified ways of which one is in making grants as if they were grants under clause 9(a) . . .

"In this House, the appellants contended that the provisions of clause 9(a) constitute a trust and not a power. If that is held to be the correct result both sides agree that the case must return to the Chancery Division for consideration, on this footing, whether this trust is valid. But here comes a complication. In the present state of authority, the decision as to validity would turn on the question whether a complete list (or on another view a list complete for practical purposes) can be drawn up of all possible beneficiaries. This follows from the Court of Appeal's decision in *Inland Revenue Comrs. v. Broadway Cottages Trust*[36] as applied in later cases by which, unless this House decides otherwise, the Court of Chancery would be bound. The respondents invite your Lordships to review this decision and challenge its correctness. So the second issue which arises, if clause 9(a) amounts to a trust, is whether the existing test for its validity is right in law and if not, what the test ought to be.

3–133   "Before dealing with these two questions some general observations, or reflections, may be permissible. It is striking how narrow and in a sense artificial is the distinction, in cases such as the present, between trusts or as the particular type of trust is called, trust powers, and powers. It is only necessary to read the learned judgments in the Court of Appeal[37] to see that what to one mind may appear as a power of distribution coupled with a trust to dispose of the undistributed surplus, by accumulation or otherwise, may to another appear as a trust for distribution coupled with a power to withhold a portion and accumulate or otherwise dispose of it. A layman and, I suspect, also a logician, would find it hard to understand what difference there is.

3–134   "It does not seem satisfactory that the entire validity of a disposition should depend on such delicate shading. And if one considers how in practice reasonable and competent trustees would act, and ought to act, in the two cases, surely a matter very relevant to the question of validity, the distinction appears even less significant. To say that there is no obligation to exercise a mere power and that no court will intervene to compel it, whereas a trust is mandatory and its execution must be compelled, may be legally correct enough, but the proposition does not contain an exhaustive comparison of the duties of persons who are trustees in the two cases. A trustee of an employees' benefit fund, whether given a power or a trust power, is still a trustee and he would surely consider in either case that he has a fiduciary duty; he is most likely to have been selected as a suitable person to administer it from his knowledge and experience, and would consider he has a responsibility to do so according to its purpose. It would be a complete misdescription of his position to say that, if what he has is a power unaccompanied by an imperative trust to distribute, he cannot be controlled by the court if he exercised it capriciously, or outside the field permitted by the trust (*cf. Farwell on Powers*[38]). Any trustee would surely make it his duty to know what is the permissible area of selection and then consider responsibly, in individual cases, whether a contemplated beneficiary was within the power and whether, in relation to other possible claimants, a particular grant was appropriate.

3–135   "Correspondingly a trustee with a duty to distribute, particularly among a potentially very large class, would surely never require the preparation of a complete list of names, which anyhow would tell him little that he needs to know. He would examine the field, by class and category; might indeed make diligent and careful enquiries, depending on how much money he had to give away and the means at his disposal, as to the composition and needs of particular

---

[36] [1955] Ch. 20.
[37] [1969] 2 Ch. 388.
[38] (3rd ed., 1916), at 524.

categories and of individuals within them; decide on certain priorities or
proportions, and then select individuals according to their needs or qualifications. If he acts in this manner, can it really be said that he is not carrying out the
trust?

"Differences there certainly are between trusts (trust powers) and powers, but **3–136**
as regards validity should they be so great as that in one case complete, or
practically complete ascertainment is needed, but not in the other? Such
distinction as there is would seem to lie in the extent of the survey which the
trustee is required to carry out; if he has to distribute the whole of a fund's
income, he must necessarily make a wider and more systematic survey than if his
duty is expressed in terms of a power to make grants. But just as, in the case of a
power, it is possible to underestimate the fiduciary obligation of the trustee to
whom it is given, so, in the case of a trust (trust power), the danger lies in
overstating what the trustee requires to know or to enquire into before he can
properly execute his trust. The difference may be one of degree rather than of
principle; in the well-known words of Sir George Farwell (*Farwell on Powers*[39])
trusts and powers are often blended, and the mixture may vary in its ingredients.

"I now consider whether the provisions of clause 9(a) constitute a trust or a
power. Naturally read, the intention of the deed seems to me clear: clause 9(a),
whose language is mandatory ('shall'), creates, together with a power of
selection, a trust for distribution of the income, the strictness of which is
qualified by clause 9(b) which allows the income of any one year to be held up
and (under clause 6(a)) either placed, for the time, with a bank, or, if thought fit,
invested. Whether there is, in any technical sense an accumulation, seems to me
in the present context a jejune enquiry; what is relevant is that clause 9(c) marks
the difference between 'accumulations' of income and the capital of the fund: the
former can be distributed by a majority of the trustees, the latter cannot. As to
clause 10, I do not find in it any decisive indication. If anything it seems to point
in favour of a trust, but both this and other points of detail are insignificant in
the face of the clearly expressed scheme of clause 9. I therefore declare that the
provisions of clause 9(a) constitute a trust and remit the case to the Chancery
Division for determination whether on this basis clause 9 is (subject to the effects
of section 164 of the Law of Property Act 1925) valid or void for uncertainty.

"This makes it necessary to consider whether, in so doing, the court should **3–137**
proceed on the basis that the relevant test is that laid down in the *Broadway
Cottages* case[40] or some other test. That decision gave the authority of the Court
of Appeal to the distinction between cases where trustees are given a *power* of
selection and those where they are bound by a *trust* for selection. In the former
case the position, as decided by this House, is that the power is valid if it can be
said with certainty whether any given individual is or is not a member of the class
and does not fail simply because it is impossible to ascertain every member of the
class. (The *Gulbenkian* case.[41]) But in the latter case it is said to be necessary, for
the trust to be valid, that the whole range of objects (I use the language of the
Court of Appeal) should be ascertained or capable of ascertainment.

"The respondents invited your Lordships to assimilate the validity test for **3–138**
trusts to that which applies to powers. Alternatively, they contended that in any
event the test laid down in the *Broadway Cottages* case was too rigid, and that a

---

[39] *ibid.* at 10.
[40] [1955] Ch. 20.
[41] [1970] A.C. 508.

trust should be upheld if there is sufficient practical certainty in its definition for it to be carried out, if necessary with the administrative assistance of the court, according to the expressed intention of the settlor. I would agree with this, but this does not dispense from examination of the wider argument. The basis for the *Broadway Cottages* case principle is stated to be that a trust cannot be valid unless, if need be, it can be executed by the court, and that the court can only execute it by ordering an equal distribution in which every beneficiary shares. So it is necessary to examine the authority and reason for this supposed rule as to the execution of trusts by the court.

3–139   "Assuming, as I am prepared to do for present purposes, that the test of validity is whether the trust can be executed by the court, it does not follow that execution is impossible unless there can be equal division. As a matter of reason, to hold that a principle of equal division applies to trusts such as the present is certainly paradoxical. Equal division is surely the last thing the settlor ever intended; equal division among all may, probably would, produce a result beneficial to none. Why suppose that the court would lend itself to a whimsical execution? And as regards authority, I do not find that the nature of the trust, and of the court's powers over trusts, calls for any such rigid rule. Equal division may be sensible and has been decreed, in cases of family trusts for a limited class, here there is life in the maxim 'equality is equity,' but the cases provide numerous examples where this has not been so, and a different type of execution has been ordered, appropriate to the circumstances.

[He then dealt with the following examples of unequal division; *Moseley v. Moseley*[42]; *Clarke v. Turner*[43]; *Warburton v. Warburton*[44]; *Richardson v. Chapman*.[45]]

3–140   "So I come to *Inland Revenue Comrs. v. Broadway Cottage Trusts*.[46] This was certainly a case of trust, and it proceeded on the basis of an admission, in the words of the judgment, 'that the class of "beneficiaries" is incapable of ascertainment.' In addition to the discretionary trust of income, there was a trust of capital for all the beneficiaries living or existing at the terminal date. This necessarily involved equal division and it seems to have been accepted that it was void for uncertainty since there cannot be equal division among a class unless all the members of the class are known. The Court of Appeal[47] applied this proposition to the discretionary trust of income, on the basis that execution by the court was only possible on the same basis of equal division. They rejected the argument that the trust could be executed by changing the trusteeship, and found the relations cases of no assistance as being in a class by themselves. The court could not create an arbitrarily restricted trust to take effect in default of distribution by the trustees. Finally they rejected the submission that the trust could take effect as a power, a valid power could not be spelt out of an invalid trust.

3–141   "So I think we are free to review the *Broadway Cottages* case. The conclusion which I would reach, implicit in the previous discussion, is that the wide distinction between the validity test for powers and that for trust powers, is unfortunate and wrong, that the rule recently fastened on the courts by the

---

[42] (1673) Rep.temp. Finch 53.
[43] (1694) Freem.Ch. 198.
[44] (1702) 4 Bro.Parl.Cas. 1.
[45] (1760) 7 Bro.Parl.Cas. 318.
[46] [1955] Ch. 20.
[47] [1968] Ch. 126.

Broadway Cottages case ought to be discarded, and that the test for the validity of trust powers ought to be similar to that accepted by this House in *Re Gulbenkian's Settlement Trusts* for powers, namely that the trust is valid if it can be said with certainty that any given individual is or is not a member of the class.

"Assimilation of the validity test does not involve the complete assimilation of **3–142** trust powers with powers. As to powers, I agree with my noble and learned friend Lord Upjohn in *Re Gulbenkian's Settlement* that although the trustees may, and normally will, be under a fiduciary duty to consider whether or in what way they should exercise their power, the court will not normally compel its exercise. It will intervene if the trustees exceed their powers, and possibly if they are proved to have exercised it capriciously. But in the case of a trust power, if the trustees do not exercise it, the court will; I respectfully adopt as to this the statement in Lord Upjohn's opinion.[48] I would venture to amplify this by saying that the court, if called on to execute the trust power, will do so in the manner best calculated to give effect to the settlor's or testator's intentions. It may do so by appointing new trustees, or authorising or directing representative persons of the classes of beneficiaries to prepare a scheme of distribution, or even, should the proper basis for distribution appear, by itself directing the trustees so to distribute. The books give many instances where this has been done and I see no reason in principle why they should not do so in the modern field of discretionary trusts (see *Brunsden v. Woolredge*,[49] *Supple v. Lowson*,[50] *Liley v. Hey*[51] and Lewin on Trusts[52]). Then, as to the trustees' duty of enquiry or ascertainment, in each case the trustees ought to make such a survey of the range of objects or possible beneficiaries as will enable them to carry out their fiduciary duty (*cf. Liley v. Hey*). A wider and more comprehensive range of enquiry is called for in the case of trust powers than in the case of powers.

"Two final points: first, as to the question of certainty, I desire to emphasise **3–143** the distinction clearly made and explained by Lord Upjohn,[53] between linguistic or semantic uncertainty which, if unresolved by the court, renders the gift void, and the difficulty of ascertaining the existence or whereabouts of members of the class, a matter with which the court can appropriately deal on an application for directions. There may be a third case where the meaning of the words used is clear but the definition of beneficiaries is so hopelessly wide as not to form 'anything like a class' so that the trust is administratively unworkable or in Lord Eldon L.C.'s words one that cannot be executed (*Morice v. Bishop of Durham*[54]). I hesitate to give examples for they may prejudice future cases, but perhaps 'all the residents of Greater London' will serve. I do not think that a discretionary trust for 'relatives' even of a living person falls within this category . . ."

Appeal allowed. Declaration that the provisions of clause 9(a) constituted a trust. Case remitted for determination whether on this basis clause 9 was (subject to the effects of section 164 of the Law of Property Act 1925) valid or void for uncertainty.

---

[48] [1970] A.C. 508 at 525.
[49] (1765) Amb. 507.
[50] (1773) Amb. 729.
[51] (1842) 1 Hare 580.
[52] (16th ed., 1964), p. 630.
[53] [1970] A.C. 508 at 524.
[54] (1805) 10 Ves. at 527.

RE BADEN'S DEED TRUSTS (NO. 2)

Court of Appeal [1973] Ch. 9; [1972] 3 W.L.R. 250; [1972] 2 All E.R. 1304.

3–144   Upon remittance Brightman J.[55] and the Court of Appeal held the trust valid but there was a difference of approach in applying the test for certainty, Stamp L.J. not being prepared to hold the trust valid if relatives meant descendants of a common ancestor and not merely statutory next-of-kin.

SACHS L.J.: ". . . Once the class of persons to be benefited is conceptually certain it then becomes a question of fact to be determined on evidence whether any postulant has on enquiry been proved to be within it; if he is not so proved then he is not in it. That position remains the same whether the class to be benefited happens to be small (such as 'first cousins') or large (such as 'members of the X Trade Union' or 'those who have served in the Royal Navy'). The suggestion that such trusts could be invalid because it might be impossible to prove of a given individual that he was *not* in the relevant class is wholly fallacious."

MEGAW L.J.: ". . . The *Gulbenkian* test, as expressed by Lord Wilberforce[56] is this:

". . . the power is valid if it can be said with certainty whether any given individual is or is not a member of the class and does not fail simply because it is impossible to ascertain every member of the class."

3–145   "The executors' argument concentrates on the words 'or is not' in the first of the two limbs of the sentence quoted above; 'if it can be said with certainty whether any given individual is *or is not* a member of the class.' It is said that those words have been used deliberately, and have only one possible meaning; and that, however startling or drastic or unsatisfactory the result may be—and counsel for the defendant executors does not shrink from saying that the consequence is drastic—this court is bound to give effect to the words used in the House of Lords' definition of the test. It would be quite impracticable for the trustees to ascertain in many cases whether a particular person was *not* a relative of an employee. The most that could be said is: 'There is no proof that he is a relative.' But there would still be no 'certainty' that such a person was not a relative. Hence, so it is said, the test laid down by the House of Lords is satisfied, and the trust is void. For it cannot be said with certainty, in relation to any individual, that he is not a relative.

3–146   "I do not think it was contemplated that the words 'or is not' would produce that result. It would, as I see it, involve an inconsistency with the latter part of the same sentence: 'does not fail simply because it is impossible to ascertain every member of the class.' The executors' contention, in substance and reality, is that it *does* fail 'simply because it is impossible to ascertain every member of the class.'

3–147   "The same verbal difficulty, as I see it, emerges also when one considers the words of the suggested test which the House of Lords expressly rejected. That is set out by Lord Wilberforce in a passage[57] immediately following the sentence which I have already quoted. The rejected test was in these terms: '. . . it is said to be necessary . . . that the whole range of objects . . . shall be ascertained or

---

[55] [1972] Ch. 607.
[56] [1971] A.C. 424 at 450.
[57] [1971] A.C. 424 at 450. See *supra*, at para. 3–137.

capable of ascertainment.' Since that test was rejected, the resulting affirmative proposition, which by implication must have been accepted by their Lordships, is this: a trust for selection will not fail simply because the whole range of objects cannot be ascertained. In the present case, the trustees could ascertain, by investigation and evidence, many of the objects; as to many other theoretically possible claimants, they could not be certain. Is it to be said that the trust fails because it cannot be said with certainty that such persons are not members of the class? If so, is that not the application of the rejected test; the trust failing because 'the whole range of objects cannot be ascertained?'

"In my judgment, much too great emphasis is placed in the executors' **3–148** argument on the words 'or is not.' To my mind, the test is satisfied if, as regards at least a substantial number of objects, it can be said with certainty that they fall within the trust; even though, as regards a substantial number of other persons, if they ever for some fanciful reason fell to be considered, the answer would have to be, not 'they are outside the trusts,' but 'it is not proven whether they are in or out.' What is a 'substantial number' may well be a question of common sense and of degree in relation to the particular trust: particularly where, as here, it would be fantasy, to use a mild word, to suggest that any practical difficulty would arise in the fair, proper and sensible administration of this trust in respect of relatives and dependants.

"I do not think that this involves, as counsel for the defendant executors **3–149** suggested, a return by this court to its former view which was rejected by the House of Lords in the *Gulbenkian* case.[58] If I did so think, I should, however reluctantly, accept his argument and its consequences. But as I read it, the criticism in the House of Lords of the decision of this court in that case related to this court's acceptance of the view that it would be sufficient if it could be shown that *one single person* fell within the scope of the power or trust. The essence of the decision of the House of Lords in the *Gulbenkian* case, as I see it, is *not* that it must be possible to show with certainty that any given person is *or is not* within the trust; but that it is not, or may not be, sufficient to be able to show that one individual person is within it. If it does not mean that, I do not know where the line is supposed to be drawn, having regard to the clarity and emphasis with which the House of Lords has laid down that the trust does not fail because the whole range of objects cannot be ascertained. I would dismiss the appeal."

RE HAY'S SETTLEMENT TRUSTS

Chancery Division [1982] 1 W.L.R. 202; [1981] 3 All E.R. 786

By clause 4 of Lady Hay's settlement made in 1958, trustees held the trust **3–150** fund "on trust for such persons or purposes for such interests and with such gifts over and (if for persons) with such provisions for their respective maintenance or advancement at the discretion of the Trustees or of any other persons as the Trustees shall by any deed or deeds revocable or irrevocable (but if revocable not after the expiration of 21 years from the date hereof) executed within 21 years from the date hereof appoint . . . and in default of such appointment in trust for the nieces and nephews of the Settlor now living in equal shares." A proviso precluded any appointment being made to the settlor, any husband of her, and any trustee or past trustee. For the first five years income was to be accumulated

---

[58] [1970] AC 508.

and then the income was to be held on discretionary trusts for the nieces and nephews or charities until the clause 4 power of appointment was exercised or ceased to be exercisable (by expiry of the 21 years).

3–151   In 1969 a deed of appointment was executed, clause 1 conferring a power of appointment on the trustees (exercisable till expiry of the 21-year period in the 1958 settlement) to hold "the trust fund and the income thereof on trust for such persons and such persons as shall be appointed." Clause 2 directed that the undisposed-of income (until full exercise of the clause 1 power) be held on discretionary trusts for the benefit of any persons whatsoever (the settlor, any husband of her, any existing or former trustee excepted) or for any charity.

Was the vast power of appointment in the 1958 settlement valid or not? If valid was its exercise void in creating a vast discretionary trust that could be said to infringe the rule "*delegatus non potest delegare*" or the rule that a trust must be administratively workable?

3–152   MEGARRY V.-C.: ". . . The starting point must be to consider whether the power created by the first limb of clause 4 of the settlement is valid . . . The essential point is whether a power for trustees to appoint to anyone in the world except a handful of specified persons is valid. Such a power will be perfectly valid if given to a person who is not in a fiduciary position: the difficulty arises when it is given to trustees, for they are under certain fiduciary duties in relation to the power, and to a limited degree they are subject to the control of the courts. At the centre of the dispute there are *Re Manisty's Settlement Trusts*; [1974] Ch. 17; [1973] 2 All E.R. 1203 (in which Templeman J. differed from part of what was said in the Court of Appeal in *Blausten v. Inland Revenue Comrs.*; [1972] Ch. 256; [1972] 1 All E.R. 41; *McPhail v. Doulton*; [1971] A.C. 424; [1970] 2 All E.R. 228 (which I shall call *Re Baden (No. 1)*); and *Re Baden's Deed Trusts (No. 2)*; [1973] Ch. 9; [1972] 2 All E.R. 1304, which I shall call *Re Baden (No. 2)*. Counsel for the defendants, I may say, strongly contended that *Re Manisty's Settlement* was wrongly decided.

3–153   "In *Re Manisty's Settlement* a settlement gave trustees a discretionary power to apply the trust fund for the benefit of a small class of the settlor's near relations, save that any member of a smaller 'excepted class' was to be excluded from the class of beneficiaries. The trustees were also given power at their absolute discretion to declare that any person, corporation or charity (except a member of the excepted class or a trustee) should be included in the class of beneficiaries. Templeman J. held that this power to extend the class of beneficiaries was valid. In *Blausten v. Inland Revenue Comrs.* which had been decided some eighteen months earlier, the settlement created a discretionary trust of income for members of a 'specified class' and a power to pay or apply capital to or for the benefit of members of that class, or to appoint capital to be held on trust for them. The settlement also gave the trustees power 'with the previous consent in writing of the settlor' to appoint any other person or persons (except the settlor) to be included in the 'specified class.' The Court of Appeal decided the case on a point of construction; but Buckley L.J.; ([1972] Ch. 256 at 271; [1972] 1 All E.R. 41 at 49) also considered a contention that the trustees' power to add to the 'specified class' was so wide that it was bad for uncertainty, since the power would enable anyone in the world save the settlor to be included. He rejected this contention on the ground that the settlor's prior written consent was requisite to any addition to the 'specified class'; but for this, it seems plain that he would have held the power void for uncertainty. Orr L.J. simply concurred, but Salmon L.J. expressly confined himself to the point of construction, and said nothing about the power to add to the 'specified class.' In *Re Manisty's Settlement*; [1974] Ch. 17 at 29; [1973] 2 All E.R. 1203 at 1213, Templeman J. rejected the view of Buckley L.J. on this point on the ground that *Re Gestetner (deceased)*; [1953] Ch. 672; [1953] 1 All E.R. 1150, *Re Gulbenkian's Settlement Trusts*; [1970] A.C. 508 [1968] 3 All E.R. 785 and the two *Baden* cases did not appear to have been fully explored in the *Blausten* case, and the case did not involve any final pronouncement on the point. In general, I respectfully agree with Templeman J.

"I propose to approach the matter by stages. First, it is plain that if a power of **3–154** appointment is given to a person who is not in a fiduciary position, there is nothing in the width of the power which invalidates it per se. The power may be a special power with a large class of persons as objects; the power may be what is called a 'hybrid' power, or an 'intermediate' power, authorising appointment to anyone save a specified number or class of persons; or the power may be a general power. Whichever it is, there is nothing in the number of persons to whom an appointment may be made which will invalidate it. The difficulty comes when the power is given to trustees as such, in that the number of objects may interact with the fiduciary duties of the trustees and their control by the court. The argument of counsel for the defendants carried him to the extent of asserting that no valid intermediate or general power could be vested in trustees.

"That brings me to the second point, namely, the extent of the fiduciary obligations of trustees who have a mere power vested in them, and how far the court exercises control over them in relation to that power. In the case of a trust, of course, the trustee is bound to execute it, and if he does not, the court will see to its execution. A mere power is very different. Normally the trustee is not bound to exercise it, and the court will not compel him to do so. That, however, does not mean that he can simply fold his hands and ignore it, for normally he must from time to time consider whether or not to exercise the power, and the court may direct him to do this.

"When he does exercise the power, he must, of course (as in the case of all **3–155** trusts and powers) confine himself to what is authorised, and not go beyond it. But that is not the only restriction. Whereas a person who is not in a fiduciary position is free to exercise the power in any way that he wishes, unhampered by any fiduciary duties, a trustee to whom, as such, a power is given is bound by the duties of his office in exercising that power to do so in a responsible manner according to its purpose. It is not enough for him to refrain from acting capriciously; he must do more. He must 'make such a survey of the range of objects or possible beneficiaries' as will enable him to carry out his fiduciary duty. He must find out 'the permissible area of selection and then consider responsibly, in individual cases, whether a contemplated beneficiary was within the power and whether, in relation to the possible claimants, a particular grant was appropriate': per Lord Wilberforce in *Re Baden (No. 1)*; [1971] A.C. 424 at 449, 457; [1970] 2 All E.R. 228 at 240, 247 . . .

"That brings me to the third point. How is the duty of making a responsible **3–156** survey and selection to be carried out in the absence of any complete list of objects? This question was considered by the Court of Appeal in *Re Baden (No. 2)*. That case was concerned with what, after some divergences of judicial opinion, was held to be a discretionary trust and not a mere power; but plainly the requirements for a mere power cannot be more stringent than those for a discretionary trust. The duty, I think, may be expressed along the following lines. The trustee must not simply proceed to exercise the power in favour of such of the objects as happen to be at hand or claim his attention. He must first consider what persons or classes of persons are objects of the power within the definition in the settlement or will. In doing this, there is no need to compile a complete list of the objects, or even to make an accurate assessment of the number of them: what is needed is an appreciation of the width of the field, and thus whether a selection is to be made merely from a dozen or, instead, from thousands or millions . . . Only when the trustee has applied his mind to 'the size of the problem' should he then consider in individual cases whether, in relation to other possible claimants, a particular grant is appropriate. In doing this, no doubt he should not prefer the undeserving to the deserving; but he is not required to make an exact calculation whether, as between deserving claimants, A is more deserving than B: see *Re Gestetner (deceased)*; [1953] Ch. 672 at 688; [1953] 1 All E.R. 1150 at 1155, approved in *Re Baden (No. 1)* [1971] A.C. 424 at 453; [1970] 2 All E.R. 228 at 243–244.

3–157   "If I am right in these views, the duties of a trustee which are specific to a mere power seem to be threefold. Apart from the obvious duty of obeying the trust instrument, and in particular of making no appointment that is not authorised by it, the trustee must, first, consider periodically whether or not he should exercise the power; second, consider the range of objects of the power; and third, consider the appropriateness of individual appointments. I do not assert that this list is exhaustive; but as the authorities stand it seems to me to include the essentials, so far as relevant to the case before me.

          "On this footing, the question is thus whether there is something in the nature of an intermediate power which conflicts with these duties in such a way as to invalidate the power if it is vested in a trustee. The case that there is rests in the main on *Blausten v. Inland Revenue Comrs.* which I have already summarised. The power there was plainly a mere power; and it authorised the trustees, with the settlor's previous consent in writing, to add any other person or persons (except the settlor) to the specified class.

3–158   "After referring to *Re Park* [1932] 1 Ch. 581 at 583; [1931] All E.R. Rep. 633 at 634, Buckley L.J. went on; ([1972] Ch. 256 at 273 [1972] 1 All E.R. 41 at 50):

> ". . . this is not a power which suffers from the sort of uncertainty which results from the trustees being given a power of so wide an extent that it would be impossible for the court to say whether or not they were properly exercising it and so wide that it would be impossible for the trustees to consider in any sensible manner how they should exercise it, if at all, from time to time. The trustees would no doubt take into consideration the possible claims of anyone having any claim in the beneficence of the [settlor]. That is not a class of persons so wide or so indefinite that the trustees would not be able rationally to exercise their duty to consider from time to time whether or not they should exercise the power."

          "It seems quite plain that Buckley L.J. considered that the power was saved from invalidity only by the requirement for the consent of the settlor. The reason for saying that in the absence of such a requirement the power would have been invalid seems to be twofold. First, the class of persons to whose possible claims the trustees would be duty-bound to give consideration was so wide as not to form a true class, and this would make it impossible for the trustees to perform their duty of considering from time to time whether to exercise the power.

3–159   "I feel considerable difficulty in accepting this view. First, I do not see how mere numbers can inhibit the trustees from considering whether or not to exercise the power, as distinct from deciding in whose favour to exercise it.

Second, I cannot see how the requirement of the settlor's consent will result in any 'class' being narrowed from one that is too wide to one that is small enough. Such a requirement makes no difference whatever to the number of persons potentially included: the only exclusion is still the settlor. Third, in any case I cannot see how the requirement of the settlor's consent could make it possible to treat 'anyone in the world save X' as constituting any real sort of a 'class,' as that term is usually understood.

"The second ground of invalidity if there is no requirement for the settlor's **3–160** consent seems to be that the power is so wide that it would be impossible for the trustees to consider in any sensible manner how to exercise it, and also impossible for the court to say whether or not they were properly exercising it. With respect, I do not see how that follows. If I have correctly stated the extent of the duties of trustees in whom a mere power is vested, I do not see what there is to prevent the trustees from performing these duties. It must be remembered that Buckley L.J., though speaking after *Re Gulbenkian's Settlement* and *Re Baden (No. 1)* had been decided, lacked the advantage of considering *Re Baden (No. 2)*, which was not decided until some five months later. He thus did not have before him the explanation in that case of how the trustees should make a survey and consider individual appointments in cases where no complete list of objects could be compiled. I also have in mind that the settlor in the present case is still alive, though I do not rest my decision on that.

"From what I have said it will be seen that I cannot see any ground on which **3–161** the power in question can be said to be void. Certainly it is not void for linguistic or semantic uncertainty; there is no room for doubt in the definition of those who are or are not objects of the power. Nor can I see that the power is administratively unworkable. The words of Lord Wilberforce in *Re Baden (No. 1)* [1971] A.C. 424 at 457; [1970] 2 All E.R. 228 at 247 are directed to discretionary trusts, not powers. Nor do I think that the power is void as being capricious. In *Re Manisty's Settlement* [1974] Ch. 17 at 27; [1973] 2 All E.R. 1203 at 1211 Templeman J. appears to be suggesting that a power to benefit 'residents in Greater London' is void as being capricious 'because the terms of the power negative any sensible intention on the part of the settlor.' In saying that, I do not think that the judge had in mind a case in which the settlor was, for instance, a former chairman of the Greater London Council, as subsequent words of his on that page indicate. In any case, as he pointed out earlier, this consideration does not apply to intermediate powers, where no class which could be regarded as capricious has been laid down. Nor do I see how the power in the present case could be invalidated as being too vague, a possible ground of invalidity considered in *Re Manisty's Settlement* [1974] Ch. 17 at 24; [1973] 2 All E.R. 1203 at 1208. Of course, if there is some real vice in a power, and there are real problems of administration or execution, the court may have to hold the power invalid: but I think that the court should be slow to do this. Dispositions ought if possible to be upheld, and the court ought not to be astute to find grounds on which a power can be invalidated. Naturally, if it is shown that a power offends against some rule of law or equity, then it will be held to be void: but a power should not be held void on a peradventure. In my judgment, the power conferred by clause 4 of the settlement is valid.

"With that, I turn to the discretionary trust of income under clause 2 of the **3–162** deed of appointment. Apart from questions of the validity of the trust per se, there is the prior question whether the settlement enabled the trustees to create such a trust, or, for that matter, the power set out in clause 1 of the deed of appointment. The power conferred by clause 4 of the settlement provides that the trustees are to hold the trust fund on trust 'for such persons or purposes for such interests and with such gifts over and (if for persons) with such provision for their respective maintenance or advancement at the discretion of the Trustees or any other persons as the trustees shall appoint. Clause 2 of the deed of appointment provides that the trustees are to hold the trust fund on trust to pay the income 'to or for the benefit of any person or persons whatsoever . . . or to any charity' in such manner and shares and proportions as the trustees think fit. I need say nothing about purposes or charities as no question on them has arisen. The basic question is whether the appointment has designated the 'persons' to whom the appointment is made.

3–163   "Looked at as a matter of principle, my answer would be 'No.' There is no such person to be found in clause 2 of the deed of appointment. That seems to me to be a plain case of delegation.

"Counsel for the defendants relied on *Re Hunter's Will Trusts* [1963] Ch. 372; [1962] 3 All E.R. 1050 [and *Re Morris' S.T.* [1951] 2 All E.R. 528] as supporting his contention that clause 2 of the deed of appointment was void.

"Now it is clear that in these authorities the rule delegatus non potest delegare was in issue. Does this rule apply to intermediate powers? This was not explored in argument, but I think that it is clear from *Re Triffitt's Settlement* [1958] Ch. 852; [1958] 2 All E.R. 299 that the rule does not apply to an intermediate power vested in a person beneficially. Here, of course, the power is an intermediate power, but it is vested in trustees as such, and not in any person beneficially; and the rule is that 'trustees cannot delegate unless they have authority to do so': *per* Viscount Radcliffe in *Re Pilkington's Will Trusts* [1964] A.C. 612 at 639; [1962] 3 All E.R. 622 at 630. Accordingly, I do not think that the fact that the power is an intermediate power excludes it from the rule against delegation. On the contrary, the fact that the power is vested in trustees subjects it to that rule unless there is something in the settlement to exclude it. I can see nothing in the settlement which purports to authorise any such appointment or to exclude the normal rule against delegation. In my judgment, both on principle and on authority clause 2 of the deed of appointment is void as being an excessive execution of the power.

3–164   "That, I think, suffices to dispose of the case. I have not dealt with the submission which counsel for the defendants put in the forefront of his argument. This was that even if the power had been wide enough to authorise the creation of the discretionary trust, that trust was nevertheless as bad as being a trust in favour of 'so hopelessly wide' a definition of beneficiaries 'as not to form anything like a class so that the trust is administratively unworkable': see *per* Lord Wilberforce in *Re Baden (No. 1)*; [1971] A.C. 424 at 457; [1970] 2 All E.R. 228 at 247. I do not propose to go into the authorities on this point. I consider that the duties of trustees under a discretionary trust are more stringent than those of trustees under a power of appointment (see *Re Baden (No. 1)*; [1971] A.C. 424 at 457; [1970] 2 All E.R. 228 at 247), and as at present advised I think that I would, if necessary, hold that an intermediate trust such as that in the present case is void as being administratively unworkable. In my view there is a difference between a power and a trust in this respect. The essence of that difference, I think, is that beneficiaries under a trust have rights of enforcement which mere objects of a power lack."

[He then held that the nieces and nephews living at the date of the settlement had become entitled to the trust fund on the expiration of 21 years from the date of the settlement by virtue of the gift over in default of any valid appointment within the 21 years.]

METTOY PENSION TRUSTEES LTD v. EVANS

Chancery Division [1990] 1 W.L.R. 1587; [1991] 2 All E.R. 515.

On the liquidation of a company, which was sole trustee of its company **3–165** pension fund, it became impossible for it to exercise its fiduciary power as trustee to apply surplus trust funds to benefit the beneficiaries; nor could the liquidator exercise the power because of his conflicting duties to the creditors of the company otherwise entitled to the surplus and to the beneficiary. Could the court exercise the power in the same way that the court can give effect to discretionary trusts? Yes.

WARNER J.: "The question then arises, if the discretion is a fiduciary power **3–166** which cannot be exercised either by the receivers or by the liquidator, who is to exercise it? I heard submissions on that point. The discretion cannot be exercised by the directors of the company, because on the appointment of the liquidator all the powers of the directors ceased. I was referred to a number of authorities on the circumstances in which the court may interfere with or give directions as to the exercise of discretions vested in trustees, namely *Gisborne v. Gisborne* (1877) 2 App.Cas. 300; *Re Hodges, Dovey v. Ward* (1878) 7 Ch. D. 754; *Tabor v. Brooks* (1878) 10 Ch. D 273; *Klug v. Klug* [1918] 2 Ch. 67; *Re Allen-Meyrick's Will Trusts; Mangnall v. Allen-Meyrick* [1966] 1 All E.R. 740; [1966] 1 W.L.R. 499; *McPhail v. Doulton* [1970] 2 All E.R. 228; [1971] A.C. 424; *Re Manisty's Settlement* [1973] 2 All E.R. 1203 at 1209–1211; [1974] Ch. 17 at 25–26 and *Re Locker's Settlement Trusts; Meachem v. Sachs* [1978] 1 All E.R. 216; [1977] 1 W.L.R. 1323. None of those cases deals directly with a situation in which a fiduciary power is left with no one to exercise it. They point however to the conclusion that in that situation the court must step in. Mr Inglis-Jones and Mr Walker urge me to say that in this case the court should step in by giving directions to the trustees as to the distribution of the surplus in the pension fund. They relied in particular on this passage in the speech of Lord Wilberforce in *McPhail v. Doulton* [1970] 2 All E.R. 228 at 247; [1971] A.C. 424 at 456–457:

"As to powers, I agree with my noble and learned friend Lord Upjohn in *Re Gulbenkian's Settlement* [1968] 3 All E.R. 785; [1970] A.C. 508 that although the trustees may, and formally will, be under a fiduciary duty to consider whether or in what way they should exercise their power, the court will not normally compel its exercise. It will intervene if the trustees exceed their powers, and possibly if they are proved to have exercised it capriciously. But in the case of a trust power, if the trustees do not exercise it, the court will; I respectfully adopt as to this the statement in Lord Upjohn's opinion (see [1968] 3 All E.R. 785 at 793; [1970] A.C. 508 at 525). I would venture to amplify this by saying that the court, if called upon to execute the trust power, will do so in the manner best calculated to give effect to the settlor's or testator's intentions. It may do so by appointing new trustees, or by authorising or directing representative persons of the classes of beneficiaries to prepare a scheme of distribution, or even, should the proper basis for distribution appear, by itself directing the trustees so to distribute. The books give many instances where this has been done and I see no reason in principle why they should not do so in the modern field of discretionary trusts . . ."

3–167 "Clearly, in the first two sentences of that passage Lord Wilberforce was referring to a discretion in category 2[59] and in the following part of it to a discretion in category 4. In that latter part he was indicating how the court might give effect to a discretionary trust when called upon to execute it. It seems to me however that the methods he indicated could be equally appropriate in a case where the court was called upon to intervene in the exercise of a discretion in category 2. In saying that I do not overlook that in *Re Manisty's Settlement* [1973] 2 All E.R. 1203 at 1210; [1974] Ch. 17 at 25 Templeman J. expressed the view that the only right and the only remedy of an object of the power who was aggrieved by the trustees' conduct would be to apply to the court to remove the trustees and appoint others in their place. However, the earlier authorities to which I was referred, such as *Re Hodges* and *Klug v. Klug*, had not been cited to Templeman J. I conclude that, in a situation such as this, it is open to the court to adopt whichever of the methods indicated by Lord Wilberforce appears most appropriate in the circumstances."

RE BARLOW'S WILL TRUSTS

Chancery Division [1979] 1 W.L.R. 278; [1979] 1 All E.R. 296.

3–168 A testatrix directed her executor "to allow any members of my family and any friends of mine who may wish to do so to purchase any of such pictures at the prices shown in Mr. Fry's catalogue or at the values placed upon them by valuation for Probate purposes at the date of my death, whichever shall be the lower". The question arose whether "family" and "friends" were conceptually uncertain so that the gift failed.

BROWNE-WILKINSON J.: "The right to purchase conferred by clause 5(a) on the testatrix's family and friends is a beneficial right of some value.

"The main questions which arise for my decision are (a) whether the direction to allow members of the family and friends to purchase the pictures is void for uncertainty since the meaning of the word 'friends' is too vague to be given legal effect and (b) what persons are to be treated as being members of the testatrix's family.

3–169 "Those arguing against the validity of the gift in favour of the friends contend that, in the absence of any guidance from the testatrix, the question 'who were her friends?' is incapable of being answered. The word is said to be 'conceptually uncertain' since there are so many different degrees of friendship and it is impossible to say which degree the testatrix had in mind. In support of this argument they rely on Lord Upjohn's remarks in *Re Gulbenkian's Settlement Trusts*[60] and the decision of the House of Lords in *McPhail v. Doulton*[61] to the effect that it must be possible to say who is within and who without the class of

---

[59] Note that in Warner *J.'s* classification, category 1 comprises any power given to a person to determine the destination of trust properly without that person being under any obligation to exercise the power or to preserve it (a personal power); category 2 comprises any power conferred on the trustees of the property or on any other person as a trustee of the power itself (a fiduciary power); category 3 comprises any discretion which is really a duty to form a judgment as to the existence or otherwise of particular circumstances giving rise to particular consequences; and category 4 comprises discretionary trusts where someone, usually the trustees, is under a duty to select from among a class of beneficiaries those who are to receive amounts of income or capital of the trust fund.

[60] [1970] A.C. 508 at 523–524.

[61] [1971] A.C. 424.

friends. They say that since the testatrix intended all her friends to have the opportunity to acquire a picture it is necessary to be able to ascertain with certainty all the members of that class.

"Counsel for the fourth defendant, who argued in favour of the validity of the **3–170** gift, contended that the tests laid down in the *Gulbenkian case* and *McPhail v. Doulton* were not applicable in this case. The test, he says, is that laid down by the Court of Appeal in *Re Allen*[62] as appropriate in cases where the validity of a condition precedent or description is in issue, namely that the gift is valid if it is possible to say of one or more persons that he or they undoubtedly quality even though it may be difficult to say of others whether or not they qualify.

"The distinction between the *Gulbenkian* test and the *Re Allen* test is, in my judgment, well exemplified by the word 'friends.' The word has a great range of meanings; indeed, its exact meaning probably varies slightly from person to person. Some would include only those with whom they had been on intimate terms over a long period; others would include acquaintances whom they liked. Some would include people with whom their relationship was primarily business; others would not. Indeed, many people, it asked to draw up a complete list of their friends, would probably have some difficulty in deciding whether certain of the people they knew were really 'friends' as opposed to 'acquaintances.' Therefore, *if the nature of the gift was such that it was legally necessary to draw up a complete list of 'friends' of the testatrix, or to be able to say of any person that 'he is not a friend,' the whole gift would probably fail*[63] even as to those who, by any conceivable test, were friends. But in the case of a gift of a kind which does not require one to establish all the members of the class (*e.g.* 'a gift of £10 to each of my friends'), it may be possible to say of some people that, on any test, they qualify. Thus in *Re Allen*[64] Evershed M.R. took the example of a gift to X 'if he is a tall man'; a man 6 feet 6 inches tall could be said on any reasonable basis to satisfy the test, although it might be impossible to say whether a man, say 5 feet 10 inches high satisfied the requirement.

"So in this case, in my judgment, there are acquaintances of a kind so close **3–171** that, on any reasonable basis, anyone would treat them as being 'friends.' Therefore, by allowing the disposition to take effect in their favour, one would certainly be giving effect to part of the testatrix's intention even though as to others it is impossible to say whether or not they satisfy the test . . .

"such reasoning [in *Re Gulbenkian* and *McPhail v. Doulton*] has no application to a case where there is a condition or description attached to one or more individual gifts; in such cases, uncertainty as to some other persons who may have been intended to take does not in any way affect the quantum of the gift to persons who undoubtedly possess the qualfication. Hence, in my judgment, the different test laid down in *Re Allen*. The recent decision of the Court of Appeal in *Re Tuck's Settlement Trust*[65] establishes that the test in *Re Allen* is still the appropriate test in considering such gifts, notwithstanding the *Gulbenkian* and *McPhail v. Doulton* decisions: see *per* Lord Russell of Killowen.[66]

"The effect of clause 5(a) is to confer on friends of the testatrix a series of **3–172** options to purchase. Therefore, each person coming forward to exercise the option has to prove that he is a friend; it is not legally necessary, in my judgment,

---

[62] [1953] Ch. 810.
[63] Editor's Italics
[64] Ch. 810 at 817.
[65] [1978] Ch. 49.
[66] [1978] Ch. 49 at 65.

to discover who all the friends are. In order to decide whether an individual is entitled to purchase, all that is required is that the executors should be able to say of that individual whether he has proved that he is a friend. The word 'friend,' therefore, is a description or qualification of the option holder.

"It was suggested that by allowing undoubted friends to take I would be altering the testatrix's intentions. It is said that she intended all her friends to have a chance to buy any given picture, and since some people she might have regarded as friends will not be able to apply, the number of competitors for that picture will be reduced. This may be so, but I cannot regard this factor as making it legally necessary to establish the whole class of friends. The testatrix's intention was that a friend should acquire a picture. My decision gives effect to that intention.

3–173   "I therefore hold, that the disposition does not fail for uncertainty, but that anyone who can prove that by any reasonable test he or she must have been a friend of the testatrix is entitled to exercise the option. Without seeking to lay down any exhaustive definition of such test, it may be helpful if I indicate certain minimum requirements: (a) the relationship must have been a long-standing one; (b) the relationship must have been a social relationship as opposed to a business or professional relationship; (c) although there may have been long periods when circumstances prevented the testatrix and the applicant from meeting, when circumstances did permit they must have met frequently. If in any case the executors entertain any real doubt whether an applicant qualifies, they can apply to the court to decide the issue.

"I turn now to the question, who are to be treated as 'members of my family?' It is not suggested that this class is too uncertain. The contest is between those who say that only the next-of-kin of the testatrix are entitled and those who say that everyone related by blood to the testatrix is included." [He held that everyone related by blood to the unmarried testatrix was included.]

R. v. DISTRICT AUDITOR, ex p. WEST YORKSHIRE METROPOLITAN COUNTY COUNCIL

Divisional Court (1985) 26 R.V.R. 24.

3–174   To spend money under Local Government Act 1972, section 137 just before its abolition the Metropolitan Council resolved to create a trust (to which £400,000 would be transferred), in which the capital and income had to be spent within 11 months, "for the benefit of any or all or some of the inhabitants of the County of West Yorkshire" in any one of four specified ways: (i) to assist economic development in the county in order to relieve unemployment and poverty, (ii) to assist bodies concerned with youth and community problems, (iii) to assist and encourage ethnic and other minority groups, (iv) to inform all interested and influential persons of the consequences of the proposed abolition of the Council (and other metropolitan councils). Was the trust administratively workable?

3–175   LLOYD L.J. (with whom Taylor J. concurred): "Counsel for the county council did not seek to argue that the trust is valid as a charitable trust, though he did not concede the point in case he should have second thoughts in a higher court. His case was that the trust could take effect as an express private trust. For the creation of an express private trust three things are required. First, there must be a clear intention to create the trust. Secondly there must be certainty as to the subject matter of the trust; and thirdly there must be certainty as to the persons intended to benefit. Two of the three certainties, as they are familiarly called, were present here. Was the third? He argued that the beneficiaries of the trust were all or some of the inhabitants of the county of West Yorkshire. The class might be on the large side, containing as it does some two and a half million potential beneficiaries. But the definition, it was said, is straightforward and clear cut. There is no uncertainty as to the concept. If anyone were to come forward and claim to be a beneficiary, it could be said of him at once whether he was within the class or not.

"I cannot accept counsel for the county council's argument. I am prepared to **3–176** assume in favour of the council, without deciding, that the class is defined with sufficient clarity. I do not decide the point because it might, as it seems to me, be open to argument what is meant by 'an inhabitant' of the county of West Yorkshire. But I put that difficulty on one side. For there is to my mind a more fundamental difficulty. A trust with as many as two and a half million potential beneficiaries is, in my judgment, quite simply unworkable. The class is far too large. In *Re Gulbenkian's Settlements* [1970] A.C. 508 Lord Reid said at 518:

> 'It may be that there is a class of case where, although the description of a **3–177** class of beneficiaries is clear enough, any attempt to apply it to the facts would lead to such administrative difficulties that it would for that reason be held to be invalid.'

[His Lordship quoted Lord WILBERFORCE's final paragraph in *McPhail v. Doulton* [1971] A.C. 424 at 457, *supra*, para. 3–143, and continued]:

"It seems to me that the present trust comes within the third case to which Lord Wilberforce refers . . .

"There can be no doubt that the declaration of trust in the present case created a trust and not a power. Following Lord Wilberforce's dictum, I would hold that the definition of the beneficiaries of the trust is 'so hopelessly wide' as to be incapable of forming 'anything like a class.' I would therefore reject counsel for the county council's argument that the declaration of trust can take effect as an express private trust.

"Since, as I have already said, it was not argued that the trust can take effect as a valid charitable trust, it follows that the declaration of trust is ineffective. What we have here, in a nutshell, is a non-charitable purpose trust. It is clear law that, subject to certain exceptions, such trusts are void: see *Lewin on Trusts* (16th ed.), at 17–19. The present case does not come within any of the established exceptions. Nor can it be brought within the scope of such recent decisions as *Re Denley's Trust Deed* [1969] 1 Ch. 373, *infra*, at para. 3–242, and *Re Lipinski's Will Trusts* [1976] Ch. 235, *infra*, at para. 3–252, since there are, for the reasons I have given, no ascertained or ascertainable beneficiaries."

Section 4. Compliance with the Rules against Perpetuity

Reference is often made to a trust offending the perpetuity rule without **3–178** it being made clear whether the trust infringes the rule against remoteness of vesting, directed at persons' interests vesting at too remote a time, or infringes the rule against inalienability, directed at immediately effective interests which can go on for too long, so tying up the use of the income of trust property for too long. The two rules are mutually exclusive, the former applying to "people" trusts and the latter to "purpose" trusts. Thus, the 1964 Perpetuities and Accumulations Act, which helps to validate people trusts, leaves the rule against inalienability well alone because it cannot invalidate people trusts.

THE RULE AGAINST REMOTENESS[67]

The common law rule

3–179 Where capital is set on one side to be kept intact ("endowment" capital) with only the income thereof being used, this cannot last indefinitely. A settlor cannot be allowed to rule the living from his grave for thousands of years nor to compel capital to be used for ever as "safe" trust capital instead of absolutely owned capital available for risky entrepreneurial ventures. Thus, where a settlor created successive interests a future interest (contingent on birth or whatever) was, under the common law rule, void unless *at the creation of the trust* it was *absolutely certain* that the contingency would be satisfied—and so the interest would become "vested in interest"—within the perpetuity period.

3–180   The perpetuity period cannot exceed 21 years from the death of some expressly or impliedly relevant life in being at the creation of the trust. A settlor can expressly stipulate that his beneficiaries are only those described by him who take a vested interest before the expiry of 21 years from the death of the last survivor of all the descendants of King George VI living at the date of the settlement (a "royal lives" clause). If T died, leaving his estate on trust for his widow, W, for life, remainder to S, his only child, for life, remainder to such of his grandchildren who attained 21 years of age, all the trusts are valid. W has a life interest "vested in possession" (a present right of present enjoyment), S has a life interest "vested in interest" (a present right to future enjoyment), while grand-children under 21 have contingent interests (a contingent right to future enjoyment), which must become vested in interest within 21 years of the deaths of S and his spouse, even though in the case of class gifts a member's interest does not vest in interest (for perpetuity purposes) until the size of the share is fixed when the last class member is ascertained.[68] The grandchildren's parents' lives are impliedly causally relevant in restricting the period within which the contingent interests inevitably must, if at all, become vested interests.

The 1964 Act "wait and see" rule

3–181   If, by any stretch of the imagination, a contingent interest might possibly not become vested in interest within the perpetuity period, it was void. To mitigate this harshness the Perpetuities and Accumulations

---

[67] See Morris & Leach, *The Rule against Perpetuities* (2nd ed.), Megarry & Wade *Real Property*, Chap. 7 but in the light of J. Dukeminier (1986) 102 L.Q.R. 250 on relevant lives in being.

[68] The class gift to grandchildren would therefore have been void if the age to be attained exceeded 21 years; hence s. 163, Law of Property Act 1925 and s. 4 of the Perpetuities and Accumulations Act 1964.

Act 1964 radically reformed the rule against remoteness. Where a contingent future interest would have been void at common law one now "waits and sees" what actually happens in a statutory perpetuity period.[69] The interest is valid until it becomes clear that it must vest in interest (if at all) outside the period prescribed by statute, which replaces causally relevant common law lives by a list of statutory lives in being[70] and, as an alternative, expressly allows a specified period of years not exceeding 80 to be chosen as the perpetuity period.[71] Modern practice is to use the 80-year period because one then knows in advance exactly when the trust will terminate.

The 1964 Act only affects settlements created after July 16, 1964 but **3–182** in the case of settlements made by the exercise of a special power of appointment only applies where the head-settlement containing the special power was created after July 16, 1964.[72] The reason for this exception is that the perpetuity period for special powers runs not from the date the power is exercised but from the date of the head-settlement creating the power.[73]

Discretionary trusts

The rule against remoteness originated in dealing with contingent, life **3–183** or absolute, interests in remainder. How did it deal with the validity of discretionary trusts? It dealt with them by regarding them as trust *powers* and so, like special powers of appointment, they were void unless they were absolutely bound to be completely exercised within the perpetuity period so that all the trust property became absolutely owned by some of the discretionary beneficiaries within the period.[74] Under the 1964 Act discretionary trusts and special powers of appointment that would have been void at common law are valid to the extent that the trustees actually exercise their fiduciary powers within the statutory perpetuity period.[75] Thereafter, there will be a resulting trust of the property in favour of the settlor[76] (unless, exceptionally, there is a gift over to a person with a vested interest[77]).

Class gifts

The 1964 Act deals specifically with class gifts,[78] particularly where **3–184** beneficiaries have to attain an age greater than 21 years. Thus, if a testator, T, left property to his only child, C, for life, remainder to such

---

[69] Perpetuities and Accumulations Act 1964, s.3(1), (2), (3), *infra*, at para. 3–200.
[70] *ibid*. s.3(5), *infra*, at para. 3–202.
[71] *ibid*. s.1.
[72] *ibid*. s.15(5).
[73] *Pilkington v. I.R.C.* [1964] A.C. 612.
[74] *Re Coleman* [1936] Ch. 528.
[75] 1964 Act, ss.3(3), 15(2).
[76] 1964 Act, s.4(4), like the rest of s.4, only seems applicable to fixed trusts in favour of a class and not discretionary trusts, "class" gifts traditionally being restricted to cases where the property is divisible into shares varying according to the number of persons in the class and the "class-closing" rule in *Andrews v. Partington* (1791) 3 Bro. C.C. 401 applying when the first member of the class becomes entitled to claim his share.
[77] 1964 Act, s.6.
[78] See *supra*, n. 76, 1964 Act, s.4.

of his grandchildren as attained 25 years of age this remainder would have been wholly void at common law because a grandchild might theoretically attain 25 years of age more than 21 years after the death of impliedly relevant lives in being.[79] The 1964 Act reduces the age from 25 years to 24 years if the youngest grandchild is only three years old at the death of the last statutory life in being, so that in the next 21 years, if at all, the grandchild will obtain a vested interest, so the remainder is valid.

3–185   Where the problem relates not to attaining a specified age outside the perpetuity period but to persons by birth, or marriage or otherwise, becoming members of a class outside the period the Act provides a statutory guillotine. At the end of the period such persons will be excluded from the class of beneficiaries so the property will then be held absolutely for the then existing beneficiaries.[80] Thus, if a testator leaves £1 million to be distributed equally amongst any nephews and nieces whenever born and at the end of the period of statutory lives plus 21 years there are 12 nephews and nieces, then the class will close to the exclusion of future-born nephews and nieces. It also seems likely that if a testator leaves £50,000 and his cricket ground and pavilion thereon to the persons who are at his death the Chairman and Treasurer of the Slogworthy Cricket Club to hold the same on trust solely for present and future members of the club one waits and sees if the club is dissolved within the period of statutory lives plus 21 years, because the then members would divide the property (or, rather, its proceeds of sale) equally between themselves. Otherwise, because at the end of the period persons can still become members and so obtain an interest in the property, the 1964 Act may well apply[81] to exclude such future persons from the class of beneficiaries. Those happening to be members at the end of the period will become absolutely entitled to the property. Hopefully, they will agree (after buying out the relevant shares of any dissentients) that the property should then be vested in four club members on a bare trust to be administered for current members according to the rules of the club.

Re Denley-type locus standi purpose trusts

3–186   As will be seen in the next section, *Re Denley*[82] upheld a trust of land to be maintained and used as a recreation or sports ground for the benefit of employees from time to time of a particular company, while in *Wicks v. Firth*[83] the House of Lords assumed that there can be a valid

---

[79] A class gift could not be partly valid and partly void: the size of the benefit of each member of the class had to be certain before expiry of the perpetuity period so the possibility of the number of members increasing outside the period made the gift to the class wholly void.

[80] 1964 Act, s. 4(4).

[81] With members having fixed rights to property on dissolution under the Club rules the case seems more appropriately treated within s.4(4) (like a fixed trust for a class) rather than within s.3(3) as a discretionary trust followed by a resulting trust upon expiry of the perpetuity period or earlier dissolution of the club.

[82] [1969] 1 Ch. 373.

[83] [1983] A.C. 214.

trust to award scholarships to assist in the education of children of employees of a company from time to time. Both trusts were limited expressly to a valid perpetuity period but what would have happened if such trusts were left open-ended to last indefinitely?

It seems likely that for perpetuity purposes such a trust would be **3–187** regarded as analogous to a discretionary trust before the 1964 Act.[84] Thus, because the powers of the trustees to benefit the beneficiaries were not bound to have been exhaustively exercised within the common law perpetuity period the trusts would have been void. However, under the Act the trusts are valid to the extent that the trustees exercise their fiduciary powers within the statutory perpetuity period.[85] At the end of such period the property will be held on resulting trust for the settlor.[86] This would seem to be the position today if, for example, a testator left £50,000 and his cricket ground and pavilion thereon to his executors and trustees on trust to enable the villagers of Slogworthy to play cricket there forever.[87]

An alternative approach is to say that *Re Denley*-type purpose trusts **3–188** should be treated like other permitted non-charitable purpose trusts[88] and so be subject not to the rule against remoteness but to the rule against inalienability.[89] This will make them void unless at the outset it is certain that by the end of the perpetuity period the trust fund will be wholly alienable by some absolute owners.[90] Because of the modern, praiseworthy, judicial tendency to facilitate, rather than frustrate, the intentions of settlors and testators it seems likely that the courts will not invoke the harsh application of the rule against inalienability that applies to purpose trusts but will regard *Re Denley*-type purpose trusts as trusts for those persons with locus standi to sue.[91]

After all, under the rule in *Saunders v. Vautier*[92] if S creates a trust to **3–189** spend £10,000 in planting trees on land held for A for life, remainder to B, A and B can together claim the £10,000 since they are intended to benefit absolutely between them and so can choose how to take such benefit.[93] Similarly, if a testator leaves £10,000 to provide for publishing his manuscript books so that there will be sufficient money to provide for his grandson's university education, the grandson can claim the £10,000 if publication is not a paying proposition, because the request was solely for his benefit.[94]

---

[84] See *Re Grant's W.T.* [1979] 3 All E.R. 359 at 368.
[85] 1964 Act, s. 3(3).
[86] See *supra*, n.81.
[87] Contrast an endowment trust for the purpose of benefiting a class of members of a club as in the Slogworthy C.C. example in the ante-penultimate paragraph.
[88] See *infra*, at para. 3–194.
[89] *Re Northern Developments (Holdings) Ltd* (October 6, 1978, unreported) at (1991) 107 L.Q.R. 608 at 611.
[90] See next sub-heading.
[91] See Vinelott J. in *Re Grant's W.T.* [1979] 3 All E.R. 359 at 368; P.J. Millett Q.C. (now Lord Millett) (1985) 101 L.Q.R. 268 at 281–282.
[92] See *infra*, at para. 9–154.
[93] *Re Bowes* [1896] 1 Ch. 507.
[94] *Re Skinner's Trusts* (1860) 1 John & H 102.

3–190　　It should make no difference if the class of beneficiaries benefiting from a trust's purposes is a fluctuating class so that *Saunders v. Vautier* rights cannot be invoked,[95] e.g. present and future members of a club or present and future members of a class under a discretionary trust. The key question of construction[96] is whether the trust is primarily for the benefit of individuals, with the specified way in which they are to enjoy the benefits being secondary, or whether the specified purpose in which they will be involved to some extent is of the essence of the trust, with the indirect benefit to individuals being secondary.

3–191　　The former category will include trusts to provide a maintenance fund for historic buildings and gardens held by trustees for the benefit of individuals[97] or to provide a sinking fund for repairs to a block of flats for the benefit of lessees from time to time[98] or to provide for the education of employees' children.[99] The latter category will include trusts for furthering the overriding purposes of a political party[1] or a non-charitable religious order[2] or of an unincorporated society,[3] such trusts being void for infringing the rule against inalienability (if not restricted to the perpetuity period) and the beneficiary principle.

3–192　　The former category will have the benefit of the 1964 Act. Prima facie, there will be a discretionary trust for the benefit of the class until expiry of the statutory period of statutory lives plus 21 years, when a resulting trust in favour of the settlor's estate will arise.[4] Exceptionally, in the case of a class of club members with fixed rights under the club rules it may be that those members will be allowed to divide the property between themselves on dissolution of the club within the statutory perpetuity period or, if later, upon expiry of such period by virtue of section 4(4) of the Act.[5]

THE RULE AGAINST INALIENABILITY (OR PERPETUAL PURPOSE TRUSTS)

3–193　　The common law rule against remoteness ensured that endowment trusts for persons were void unless one could be absolutely sure from the outset that by the end of the perpetuity period the beneficiaries would have obtained vested interests enabling them to deal with the trust fund as they wished. Under the rule in *Saunders v. Vautier*[6] if trustees hold property on trust for A absolutely or for B for life, remainder to C absolutely then (assuming each is *sui juris*) A or B and C, as the case may be, can direct the trustees how to deal with the property, *e.g.* vest it

---

[95] *Re Levy* [1960] Ch. 346 at 363; *Re Westphal* [1972] N.Z.L.R. 792 at 794–795.
[96] See P.J. Millett Q.C. (now Lord Millett) (1985) 101 L.Q.R. 269, 282.
[97] *Re Aberconway's S.T.* [1953] Ch. 647; *Raikes v. Lygon* [1988] 1 W.L.R. 281.
[98] Landlord and Tenant Act 1987, s.42.
[99] *Wicks v. Firth* [1983] A.C. 214; see also *Re Sanderson's Trusts* (1857) 3 K & J; *Re Abbott Fund Trust* [1900] 2 Ch. 326; *Re Gillingham Bus Disaster Fund* [1958] Ch. 300.
[1] *Re Grant's W.T.* [1979] 3 All E.R. 359; *Bacon v. Pianta* (1966) 114 C.L.R. 634.
[2] *Leahy v. Att-Gen. for New South Wales* [1959] A.C. 457.
[3] *Came v. Long* (1860) 2 De. G.F. & J. 75; *Re Macauley's Estate* [1943] Ch. 435n.
[4] 1964 Act, s.3(3).
[5] See *supra*, at para. 3–185.
[6] (1841) 4 Beav. 115, *infra*, at para. 9–154.

in A absolutely or divide it absolutely between B and C in the shares agreed by B and C. Persons like B must obtain vested interests before the end of the perpetuity period but there is no requirement that their interests must terminate within the perpetuity period so that someone must become absolutely entitled to the relevant property in such period.[7] Thus, if at the end of the period B has a life interest the trust continues till C acquires the property on B's death.

The rule against inalienability makes the few permitted[8] non- **3–194** charitable endowment purpose trusts void unless from the outset it is certain that persons will become absolutely entitled beneficiaries by the end of the perpetuity period,[9] 21 years from the death of the last survivor of any causally relevant lives in being.[10] Such a rule was necessary because purposes unlike individuals can last forever and because a rule against remoteness of vesting is inappropriate when interests cannot vest in purposes as opposed to persons. Thus, testamentary trusts to erect and then maintain a sepulchral monument, to say private masses for the testator and to maintain the testator's horse or cat are void unless restricted to a specified perpetuity period, which will be 21 years unless, say, a royal lives clause is used.

Section 15(4) of the Perpetuities and Accumulation Act 1964 prevents the Act having any effect in relation to the rule against inalienability.[11]

Alienability of trust assets but inalienability of trust fund

Whatever happen from time to time to be the particular trust *assets* **3–195** comprised in the trust *fund* will be alienable under the Trustee Act 2000, the Settled Land Act 1925 or the Law of Property Act 1925. However, if trust income has to be used for a particular purpose then the trust fund producing that income must be kept intact for as long as the income is required for that purpose. The inalienability of the trust income inevitably leads to the inalienability of the trust fund. The rule against inalienability is concerned to ensure that the length of time for which trustees must retain the trust fund (in whatever assets it is from time to time invested) does not exceed the perpetuity period.

Only endowment trusts are subject to rule

If the trustees do not have to keep the capital intact and use only the **3–196** income thereof but can spend trust money on the trust purposes without the need to consider whether or not the money represents capital or

---

[7] *Re Chardon* [1928] Ch. 464; *Re Gage* [1898] 1 Ch. 506; *Wainwright v. Miller* [1897] 2 Ch. 255.

[8] See *infra*, para. 3–126.

[9] *Leahy v. Att.-Gen. for New South Wales* [1959] A.C. 457; *Cocks v. Manners* (1871) L.R. 12 Eq. 574.

[10] *Re Astor's S.T.* [1952] Ch. 534; *Re Khoo Cheng Teow* [1932] Straits Settlement Reports 226. The statutory period of 80 years is available only for the rule against remoteness: see *infra*, n. 11.

[11] See *infra*, para. 3–207. It is oddly worded. In context "the rule of law rendering void for remoteness" is the rule against inalienability (which the draftsman considers to make purpose trusts void if they can continue till too remote a time). The draftsman in s. 1 uses "the rule against perpetuities" when referring to the rule against remoteness of vesting and allowing the 80-year period expressly to be specified. One should add implicitly to the end of s. 15(4) "applicable to the relevant disposition under such rule of law."

income and whether the purpose is a "capital" or "income" type of purpose, then the rule against inalienability has no application.[12] Usually, the settlor will make it clear if the trustees are to hold his property on trust only to use the income within a specified perpetuity period for particular purposes and at the end of the period to distribute the capital to beneficiaries. Exceptionally, he may make it clear that his property is to be used without distinction between capital and income until fully consumed.

THE RULE AGAINST EXCESSIVE ACCUMULATIONS

3–197   Fearful of the implications for the English economy if megawealthy men like Thellusson could by will[13] have the income of their estate accumulated for the full perpetuity period of royal lives plus 21 years— and more fearful for the finances of themselves and their children— English MPs passed the Accumulations Act 1800 (the "Thellusson Act") to restrict the period for which income could be accumulated. The modern position is as follows.

If a trust is concerned with a trust or power to accumulate, it is crucial to restrict the accumulation to one of the six periods allowed by section 164 of the Law of Property Act 1925 and section 13 of the 1964 Act unless section 31 of the Trustee Act 1925 allows accumulations during a beneficiary's minority:

    (a) the life of the grantor or settlor;

    (b) twenty-one years from the death of the grantor, settlor or testator;

    (c) the duration of the minority or respective minorities of any person(s) living or *en venture sa mère* at the death of the grantor, settlor or testator;

    (d) the duration of the minority or respective minorities only of any persons(s) who under the limitations of the instrument directing the accumulations would, for the time being, if of full age, be entitled to the income directed to be accumulated;

    (e) twenty-one years from the date of the making of the disposition;

    (f) the duration of the minority or respective minorities of any person(s) in being at that date.

3–198   If an excessive accumulation infringes the perpetuity period it is void *in toto*.[14] If within the perpetuity period it is cut down to the nearest appropriate period of the six permitted, and only the excess is void.[15]

---

[12] *Re Lipinski's W.T.* [1976] Ch. 235 at 245, see *infra*, para. 3–252; *Re Drummond* [1914] 2 Ch. 90 at 98; *Re Prevost* [1930] 2 Ch. 383 at 388; *Re Price* [1943] Ch. 422 at 428, 430; *Re Macaulay's Estate* [1943] Ch. 435 at 436 (H.L); R. H. Maudsley, *The Modern Law of Perpetuities* 173. In *Leahy v. Att.-Gen. for New South Wales* [1959] A.C. 457 at 483, see *infra*, para. 3–233. Viscount Simonds doubted whether a society's liberty to spend the capital and income of a gift as it saw fit saved a gift on trust to the society unless its members are treated as the immediate beneficiaries capable of disposing of the gifted property. This is too restrictive a view of the beneficiary principle: there can be *Re Denley-type* purpose trusts benefiting individuals within a fluctuating class who have no right to make the trust property their own but do have a right to ensure that the property is used for their benefit.

[13] *Thellusson v. Woodford* (1799) 4 Ves 227.

[14] *Curtis v. Lukin* (1842) 5 Beav. 147.

[15] *Re Watt's W.T.* [1936] 2 All E.R. 1555 at 1562; *Re Ransome* [1957] Ch. 348 at 361.

Indirectly, "excessive" accumulation may be provided for by empowering trustees to transfer trust assets to a company formed by them in return for shares in the company: the company can then retain profits and not declare dividends. Indeed, the company can settle assets on accumulation trusts without being bound by the statute which only applies to natural persons.[16] It seems likely that a settlor can expressly choose a foreign law to govern accumulations without offending English public policy.[17] The English Accumulations Act 1800 never extended to colonies or dependencies under whose laws accumulations can continue for as long as the perpetuity period. The Law Commission has strongly recommended that the accumulation period should be the same as the perpetuity period which should be extended to 125 years.[18]

Power to specify perpetuity period

1.—(1)   Subject to section 9(2) of this Act and subsection (2) below,where the **3–199** instrument by which any disposition is made so provides, the perpetuity period applicable to the disposition under the rule against perpetuities, instead of being of any other duration, shall be of a duration equal to such number of years not exceeding eighty as is specified in that behalf in the instrument.

(2)   Subsection (2) above shall not have effect where the disposition is made in exercise of a special power of appointment, but where a period is specified under that subsection in the instrument creating such a power the period shall apply in relation to any disposition under the power as it applies in relation to the power itself.

Uncertainty as to remoteness

3.—(1)   Where, apart from the provisions of this section and sections 4 and 5 **3–200** of this Act, a disposition would be void on the ground that the interest disposed of might not become vested until too remote a time, the disposition shall be treated, until such time (if any) as it becomes established that the vesting must occur, if at all, after the end of the perpetuity period, as if the disposition were not subject to the rule against perpetuities; and its becoming so established shall not affect the validity of anything previously done in relation to the interest disposed of by way of advancement, application of intermediate income or otherwise.

(2)   Where, apart from the said provisions, a disposition consisting of the conferring of a general power of appointment would be void on the ground that the power might not become exercisable until too remote a time, the disposition shall be treated, until such time (if any) as it becomes established that the power will not be exercisable within the perpetuity period, as if the disposition were not subject to the rule against perpetuities.

(3)   Where, apart from the said provisions, a disposition consisting of the conferring of any power, option or other right would be void on the ground that the right might be exercised at too remote a time, the disposition shall be treated as regards any exercise of the right within the perpetuity period as if it were not

---

[16] *Re Dodwell & Co's Trust Deed* [1979] Ch. 301.
[17] Consider Articles 6 and 18 of Hague Convention on Trust and problem, *infra*, at para. 12–30.
[18] Law Commission Report No 251 (1998), accepted by the Government in March 2001.

subject to the rule against perpetuities and, subject to the said provisions, shall be treated as void for remoteness only if, and so far as, the right is not fully exercised within that period.

3–201   (4) Where this section applies to a disposition and the duration of the perpetuity period is not determined by virtue of section 1 or 9(2) of this Act, it shall be determined as follows:—

(a) where any persons falling within subsection (5) below are individuals in being and ascertainable at the commencement of the perpetuity period the duration of the period shall be determined by reference to their lives and no others, but so that the lives of any description of persons falling within paragraph (b) or (c) of that subsection shall be disregarded if the number of persons of that description is such as to render it impracticable to ascertain the date of death of the survivor;

(b) where there are no lives under paragraph (a) above the period shall be twenty-one years.

3–202   (5) The said persons are as follows:—

(a) the person by whom the disposition was made;

(b) a person to whom or in whose favour the disposition was made, that is to say—

(i) in the case of a disposition to a class of persons, any member or potential member of the class;

(ii) in the case of an individual disposition to a person taking only on certain conditions being satisfied, any person as to whom some of the conditions are satisfied and the remainder may in time be satisfied;

(iii) in the case of a special power of appointment exercisable in favour of members of a class, any member or potential member of the class;

(iv) in the case of a special power of appointment exercisable in favour of one person only, that person or, where the object of the power is ascertainable only on certain conditions being satisfied, any person as to whom some of the conditions are satisfied and the remainder may in time be satisfied;

(v) in the case of any power, option or other right, the person on whom the right is conferred;

(c) a person having a child or grandchild within sub-paragraphs (i) to (iv) of paragraph (b) above, or any of whose children or grandchildren, if subsequently born, would by virtue of his or her descent fall within those sub-paragraphs;

(d) any person on the failure or determination of whose prior interest the disposition is limited to take effect.

Reduction of age and exclusion of class members to avoid remoteness

3–203   **4.**—(1) Where a disposition is limited by reference to the attainment by any person or persons of a specified age exceeding 21 years, and it is apparent at the time the disposition is made or becomes apparent at a subsequent time—

(a) that the disposition would, apart from this section, be void for remoteness, but

(b) that it would not be so void if the specified age had been twenty-one years,

the disposition shall be treated for all purposes as if, instead of being limited by reference to the age in fact specified, it had been limited by reference to the age nearest to that age which would, if specified instead, have prevented the disposition from being so void.

(2) Where in the case of any disposition different ages exceeding 21 years are specified in relation to different persons—

(a) the reference in paragraph (b) of subsection (1) above to the specified age shall be construed as a reference to all the specified ages, and
(b) that subsection shall operate to reduce each such age so far as is necessary to save the disposition from being void for remoteness.

(3) Where the inclusion of any persons, being potential members of a class or **3–204** unborn persons who at birth would become members or potential members of the class, prevents the foregoing provisions of this section from operating to save a disposition from being void for remoteness, those persons shall thenceforth be deemed for all the purposes of the disposition to be excluded from the class, and the said provisions shall thereupon have effect accordingly.

(4) Where, in the case of a disposition to which subsection (3) above does not apply, it is apparent at the time the disposition is made or becomes apparent at a subsequent time that, apart from this subsection, the inclusion of any persons, being potential members of a class or unborn persons who at birth would become members or potential members of the class, would cause the disposition to be treated as void for remoteness, those persons shall, unless their exclusion would exhaust the class, thenceforth be deemed for all the purposes of the disposition to be excluded from the class.

(5) Where this section has effect in relation to a disposition to which section 3 above applies, the operation of this section shall not affect the validity of anything previously done in relation to the interest disposed of by way of advancement, application of intermediate income or otherwise.

Saving and acceleration of expectant interests

6. A disposition shall not be treated as void for remoteness by reason only that **3–205** the interest disposed of is ulterior to and dependent upon an interest under a disposition which is so void, and the vesting of an interest shall not be prevented from being accelerated on the failure of a prior interest by reason only that the failure arises because of remoteness.

Powers of appointment

7. For the purposes of the rule against perpetuities, a power of appointment shall be treated as a special power unless—

(a) in the instrument creating the power it is expressed to be exercisable by one person only, and
(b) it could, at all times during its currency when that person is of full age and capacity, be exercised by him so as immediately to transfer to himself the whole of the interest governed by the power without the consent of

any other person or compliance with any other condition, not being a formal condition relating only to the mode of exercise of the power:

Provided that for the purpose of determining whether a disposition made under a power of appointment exercisable by will only is void for remoteness, the power shall be treated as a general power where it would have fallen to be so treated as if exercisable by deed.

Administrative powers of trustees

3–206   8.—(1) The rule against perpetuities shall not operate to invalidate a power conferred on trustees or other persons to sell, lease, exchange or otherwise dispose of any property for full consideration, or to do any other act in the administration (as opposed to the distribution) of any other property, and shall not prevent the payment to trustees or other persons of reasonable remuneration for their services.

(2) Subsection (1) above shall apply for the purpose of enabling a power to be exercised at any time after the commencement of this Act notwithstanding that the power is conferred by an instrument which took effect before that commencement.

Short title, interpretation and extent

3–207   15.—(1) This Act may be cited as the Perpetuities and Accumulations Act 1964.

(2) In this Act—

"disposition" includes the conferring of a power of appointment and any other disposition of an interest in or right over property, and references to the interest disposed of shall be construed accordingly;
"in being" means living or en ventre sa mere;
"power of appointment" includes any discretionary power to transfer a beneficial interest in property without the furnishing of valuable consideration;
"will" includes a codicil;

and for the purposes of this Act a disposition contained in a will shall be deemed to be made at the death of the testator.

(3)   For the purposes of this Act a person shall be treated as a member of a class if in his case all the conditions identifying a member of the class are satisfied, and shall be treated as a potential member if in his case some only of those conditions are satisfied but there is a possibility that the remainder will in time be satisfied.

(4) Nothing in this Act shall affect the operation of the rule of law rendering void for remoteness certain dispositions under which property is limited to be applied for purposes other than the benefit of any person or class of persons in cases where the property may be so applied after the end of the perpetuity period.

(5) The foregoing sections of this Act shall apply (except as provided in section 8(2) above) only in relation to instruments taking effect after the commencement of this Act, and in the case of an instrument made in the exercise of a special power of appointment shall apply only where the instrument creating the power takes effect after that commencement:

Provided that section 7 above shall apply in all cases for construing the foregoing reference to a special power of appointment.

(6) This Act shall apply in relation to a disposition made otherwise than by an instrument as if the disposition had been contained in an instrument taking effect when the disposition was made.

Section 5. The Beneficiary (or Enforcer) Principle

Because enforceable obligations of the trustee are at the heart of the **3–208** trust it is a hallowed principle that Courts of Equity will not uphold any alleged trust that cannot be effectively supervised and sanctioned by the Courts at the behest of somebody in whose favour the Courts can decree performance.[19] Leaving aside charitable purpose trusts enforceable by the Crown in the public interest via the Attorney-General and the Charity Commissioners, a trust "to be effective must have ascertained or ascertainable beneficiaries", as Lord Evershed MR emphasised in *Re Endacott*.[20] Indeed, Viscount Simonds[21] explained "a trust may be created for the benefit of persons as *cestuis que trust* but not for a purpose or object unless the purpose or object be charitable, for a purpose or object cannot sue, but if it be charitable the Attorney General can sue to enforce it". In the case of a trust for persons it is those persons who sue to enforce their rights as beneficiaries against the trustees, the settlor dropping out of the picture like a donor who has made an outright gift.[22] It is thus taken for granted that "A trust for non-charitable purposes, as distinct from a trust for individuals, is clearly void because there is no beneficiary."[23]

Thus, a trust to further the abstract impersonal purposes of a **3–209** contemplative (non-charitable) Catholic Order of nuns[24] or of the Labour Party is void.[25] This sort of overriding purpose trust is in the words of Goff J in *Re Denley's Trust Deed*[26] (infra)

> "A purpose trust, the carrying out of which would benefit an individual or individuals but where that benefit is so indirect or intangible or which is otherwise so framed as not to give those persons any *locus standi* to apply to the court to enforce the trust, in which case the beneficiary principle would apply to invalidate

---

[19] *Morice v. Bishop of Durham* (1804) 9 Ves 399, 405, (1805) 10 Ves 521, 539. "A court of equity does not recognise as valid a trust which it cannot both enforce and control "per Roxburgh J in *Re Astor's S.T.* [1952] Ch. 534, 549.

[20] *Re Endacott* [1960] Ch. 232, 246. It suffices that a beneficiary is ascertained by the end of a relevant perpetuity or accumulation period so as then to be able retrospectively to call the trustees to account for their stewardship of the trust property: *Rosewood Trust Ltd v. Schmidt* (unreported Manx CA February 2001).

[21] *Leahy v. Att-Gen for New South Wales* [1959] A.C. 457, 479.

[22] *Re Astor's S.T.* [1952] Ch. 534, 542, *Bradshaw v. University College of Wales* [1987] 3 All E.R. 200, 203.

[23] *Re Recher's W.T.* [1972] Ch. 526, 538. A power to carry out abstract impersonal purposes can be valid: *Re Douglas* [1887] 35 in.D.472, *Goff v. Nairne* (1876) 3 Ch. D. 278, *Re Shaw* [1957] 1 W.L.R. 729

[24] *Leahy v. Att-Gen for New South Wales* [1959] A.C. 457

[25] *Re Grant's WT* [1979] 3 All E.R. 359. See also *Re Astor's S.T.* [1952] Ch. 534, *Re Shaw* [1957] 1 W.L.R. 729, *Re Endacott* [1960] Ch. 232.

[26] [1969] 1 Ch. 373, 382–383.

> the trust, quite apart from any question of uncertainty or perpetuity"

3–210   He then upheld a trust of a corporate settlor's land "to be maintained and used as and for the purposes of a recreation or sports ground primarily for the benefit of the employees of the company and secondarily for the benefit of such other persons (if any) as the trustees may allow to use the same." The attainment of these trust purposes was sufficiently for the benefit of individuals taken to be intended to have *locus standi* to enforce the trust positively in their favour.[27] After all, the trust was primarily for the benefit of people, with the specified way in which they were to be benefited being secondary: the specified purpose was not of the essence of the trust with an indirect secondary benefit to people.[28] As trusts for the benefit of people, such trusts should have the benefit of the liberal Perpetuities and Accumulations Act 1964 and not be subject to the strict rule against inalienability already discussed in the last section.

3–211   The orthodox view that non-charitable purpose trusts are void and that settlors (unless beneficiaries) have no rights to enforce their trusts enforceable only by beneficiaries has led to offshore jurisdictions filling a gap in the trusts "market" by enacting legislation validating non-charitable purpose trusts so long as the trust instrument appoints an enforcer (who could initially be the settlor) with provision for further enforcers after his death or retirement.

What then would happen under English conflict of law (or private international law) principles if the English court were faced with a non-charitable purpose trust of English assets governed by a foreign law (such as that of Jersey or the Isle of Man or Bermuda or the British Virgin Islands or the Cayman Islands) treating such a trust as valid where the terms of the trust appoint an enforcer and provide for the appointment of a successor to any enforcer? The English court could only hold the trust to be void for infringing the beneficiary principle (so that a resulting trust arises for the settlor, whose creditors, heirs or divorcing spouse can then enforce their claims against the trust assets) if such a foreign trust concept were either repugnant to the English trust concept or contrary to English public policy.[29]

3–212   Is the true English trust concept that just as a car needs an engine so a trust needs a beneficiary, or that just as a car needs an engine so a trust needs an enforcer, whether a beneficiary or the Attorney-General or Charity Commissioners for charitable purpose trusts or some person

---

[27] Also see *Wicks v. Firth* [1983] A.C. 214 and *Re Saxone Shoe Co's Trust Deed* [1962] 1 W.L.R. 934 (which would now be valid under the *McPhail v. Doulton* [1971] A.C. 424 test). Persons named in a trust deed and benefiting directly or indirectly but not intended to have a right to enforce the trust have no *locus standi* to apply to the court: *Shaw v. Lawless* (1838) 5 Cl. & Fin. 129, 153; *Gandy v. Gandy* (1885) 30 Ch. D. 57, 69–70; L. McKay (1973) 37 Conv. 420, 426–427.

[28] P.J. Millett Q.C. (now Lord Millett) (1985) 101 L.Q.R. 269, 282 and para. 3–190 *supra*.

[29] See approach to wide exemption clauses in *Armitage v. Nurse* [1998] Ch. 241, 253, and the right under the Recognition of Trusts Act 1987 to choose any foreign trust law to govern a trust so long as not "manifestly incompatible with public policy" (at para. 12–35 below).

expressly appointed by the trust instrument to be enforcer with *locus standi*[30] positively[31] to enforce the trust?

Take the case of an English trust (limited to a valid perpetuity period) to further the interests of the U.K. Conservative Party expressed to be enforceable by the Leader from time to time of such Party, or a trust to further the purposes of a specified contemplative Order of Nuns expressed to be enforceable by the Head from time to time of such order, or a trust to further "The professional interests of barristers entitled to practice in the English Courts expressed to be enforceable by the Chair from time to time of the Bar Council or a trust to further the business and reputation of a named Set of barristers' Chambers expressed to be enforceable only by the Head of Chambers from time to time. The trusts clearly supply a mechanism for the positive enforcement of the trusts so that the trustees are under an obligation to account to someone in whose favour the court can positively decree performance, unlike the cases of void non-charitable purpose trusts so far considered by the English courts[32] where there was no-one who had been given *locus standi* positively to sue to enforce the trust.

It is submitted it then becomes clear that the "beneficiary principle"   **3–213** should be regarded as the "enforcer principle."[33] However, where a settlor has created a trust for beneficiaries those beneficiaries must be enforcers because as Millett L.J. stated in *Armitage v. Nurse*[34] "If the beneficiaries have no rights enforceable against the trustees there are no trusts." Thus, an English "trust" for A for life remainder for such of the descendants of his children, B, C, and D as the trustees shall select in their absolute discretion (for a valid perpetuity period) would not be a trust for A and his descendants if the trust instrument[35] expressly stipulated that another person, E, alone was enforcer and that A and his descendants had no right to see the trust accounts or to enforce any rights against the trustees or E. Instead, there would be a resulting trust for the settlor with the trustees having power (until revoked by the settlor) to benefit A and his descendants, who would be characterised not as beneficiaries of a trust but as mere objects of a power of appointment entitling them to retain whatever was appointed to them.[36]

---

[30] See the emphasis on *locus standi* to enforce in *Re Denley's Trust Deed* [1969] 1 Ch. 373, 382–383, *Re Astor's S.T.* [1952] Ch. 534, 542, *Re Shaw* [1957] 1 W.L.R. 729, 745.

[31] The fact that the residuary legatees or the next-of-kin will take property in default of specific purposes being carried out does not indicate that the settlor-testator intended such "negatively" interested persons to be enforcers, so the presence of such persons will not save a trust for non-charitable purposes: *Re Shaw* [1957] 1 W.L.R. 729, 745; *Re Davidson* [1909] I Ch. 567, 571.

[32] *E.g. Re Nottage* [1895] 2 Ch. 649, *Re Wightwick's W.T.* [1950] Ch. 260, *Leahy v. Att-Gen for New South Wales* [1959] AC 457 (all void for perpetuity in any event, except for a saving statute in the New South Wales Case). But cp. *Re Price* [1945] Ch. 422, paras 3–256 and 3–258.

[33] D.J. Hayton, "Developing the Obligation Characteristic of the Trust" (2001) 117 L.Q.R. 96.

[34] [1998] Ch, 241, 253; D.J. Hayton, "The Irreducible Core Content of Trusteeship", Chapter 3 in A.J. Oakley (ed) *Trends in Contemporary Trust Law*, Oxford, 1996.

[35] Section 7 of the Cayman Special Trusts (Alternative Regime) Law 1997 surprisingly takes away all rights from the "beneficiaries" who then only have hopes that the enforcer and the trustees will act so as to benefit them.

[36] This could lead to a Cayman STAR trust being valid in Cayman but not in England (a "limping" trust) unless some beneficiaries had been appointed as enforcers.

However, there is no reason why *in addition to* the beneficiaries someone else should not have *locus standi* as enforcer to enforce the trust (*e.g.* the settlor while the beneficiaries are infants or unborn or otherwise unascertained) so as to strengthen the trustees' obligations.[37]

QUISTCLOSE MONEY PURPOSE TRUSTS

3–214 Where P (the payer) and R (the recipient) have agreed that P is to pay money to R for a specific purpose only *and* that R is not to have the full beneficial interest in the fund,[38] then P has a right to restrain misuse of the money by R (or by R's bank with notice of the agreement between P and R[39]) and the money is not available on R's insolvency for R's general creditors, as seen in *Re EVTR* supra at para. 3–51, applying *Quistclose Investments Ltd v. Barclays Bank*.[40] The primary purpose trust comes to an end when the express purpose is performed, in which event no question of a secondary trust arises (except for any balance remaining in R's hands), the money then becoming a debt due from R to P or being treated as a completed gift from P to R. If the purpose is not performed then a secondary trust of the money arises in favour of P, whether as an express or a resulting trust.[41]

As Potter LJ stated in *Twinsectra Ltd v. Yardley*[42]:

> "Whilst the *Quistclose*-type cases have generally concerned loans for the payment of specific debts, there seems to me no inherent reason why the imposition of a wider special purpose should not impose a trust so long as the terms of the restraint on the borrower's use of the money are sufficiently certain to be enforceable by the lender. Again, because the *Quistclose*-type trust is, in truth, a 'quasi-trust' (the trust arises from the restriction of the borrower's right to use the money rather than the existence of a conventional express trust), it does not seem to me essential that the nature of the special purpose need be such as to meet the usually strict requirements for a valid trust so far as 'certainty of object' is concerned: See *Re Rogers* (1891) 3 Morr 243 (to pay 'Pressing creditors'); also *Re EVTR* [1987] BCLC 646 (purchase of new video equipment). Thus, in principle, the degree of certainty need be no more than is necessary to enable the restriction on the recipient's use of the money to be identified and enforced. However, the position remains that, in a commercial setting, there must be some element or circumstance present additional to a simple declaration of purpose to give rise to a fiduciary obligation

---

[37] Further see D. J. Hayton op. cit. in n. 33 above.
[38] *Twinsectra Ltd v. Yardley* [2000] W.T.L.R. 527, 559 (CA).
[39] *Barclays Bank v. Quistclose Investments Ltd* [1970] A.C. 567 (H.L.)
[40] *ibid.* Also see *Re McKeown* [1974] N.I. 226.
[41] *Twinsectra Ltd v. Yardley* [2000] W.T.L.R. 527, 558, (C.A.).
[42] *ibid.* at 560. Also see R. Chambers, *Resulting Trusts* (Oxford 1997) at 68, 85–89.

on the recipient of a loan, such element or circumstance usually being found to exist in the form of a requirement by the lender that the loan moneys be held in a special account separate from the recipient's general funds."[43]

It was difficult, although not impossible,[44] to try to explain *Quistclose*- **3–215** type trusts as compatible with the beneficiary principle, but one no longer needs to make such efforts once the beneficiary principle is seen to be part of the wider enforcer principle discussed earlier in this Section.

ANOMALOUS VALID TESTAMENTARY PURPOSE TRUSTS

The Court of Appeal[45] has accepted that there are some anomalous **3–216** cases, not to be extended, where testamentary trusts infringing the beneficiary (or enforcer) principle have been held valid as concessions to human sentiment. These anomalous cases are:

(1) trusts for the maintenance of particular animals[46];
(2) trusts for the erection or maintenance of graves and sepulchral monuments[47];
(3) trusts for the saying of masses in private[48];
(4) trusts for the promotion and furtherance of fox-hunting.[49]

These trusts are sometimes referred to as trusts of imperfect obligation[50] since the trustees are not obliged to carry out the trusts in the

---

[43] See Federal Court of Australia in *Peter Cox Investments Pty, Ltd. v. International Air Transport Association* [1999] FCA 27 (www.austlii.edu.au).

[44] See P.J. Millett Q.C. in (1985) 101 L.Q.R. 269. Potter L.J. in *Twinsectra Ltd v. Yardley* [2000] W.T.L.R. 525, 559 took the view, "Although the lender's right to enforce the restriction is treated as arising on the basis of 'trust', the use of that word does not enlarge the lender's interest in the fund. The borrower is entitled to the beneficial use of the money, subject to the lender's right to prevent its misuse; the lender's limited interest in the fund is sufficient to prevent its use for other than the special purpose for which it was advanced".

[45] *Re Endacott* [1960] Ch. 232 (residuary gift to a parish council "for the purpose of providing some useful memorial to" the testator held void for uncertainty and for infringing the beneficiary principle).

[46] *Pettingall v. Pettingall* (1842) 11 L.J. Ch. 176; *Re Dean* (1889) 41 Ch.D. 552. Many trusts for animals generally are charitable: *Re Wedgwood* [1915] 1 Ch. 113.

[47] *Re Hooper* [1932] Ch. 38; *Mussett v. Bingle* [1876] W.N. 170; *Pirbright v. Salwey* [1896] W.N. 86; *Trimmer v. Danby* (1856) 25 L.J. Ch. 424. The maintenance of private graves may be possible for 99 years under the Parish Council and Burial Authorities (Miscellaneous Provisions) Act 1970, s.1. If the construction is part of the fabric of a church the trust is charitable and valid: *Hoare v. Osborne* (1866) L.R. 1 Eq. 585.

[48] *Bourne v. Keane* [1919] A.C. 815 at 874–875. Gifts for the saying of masses in public are charitable because of the public benefit in assisting in the endowment of priests but not for the saying of masses in private: *Re Hetherington* [1989] 2 All E.R. 129 (but the endowment ground seems applicable in both cases). In Malaysia and Singapore trusts for ancestor worship (Sin Chew or Chin Shong ceremonies) have been held valid anomalous non-charitable purpose gifts if restricted to the perpetuity period: *Tan v. Tan* (1946) 12 M.L.J. 159,; *Hong Kong Bank Trustee Co. v. Farrer Tan* [1988] 1 M.L.J. 485.

[49] *Re Thompson* [1934] Ch. 342, but the default beneficiary, a charity, only objected *pro forma*. If any of these anomalous cases is to be overruled this seems the prime candidate: it certainly should not be extended to other forms of sport like angling Romer J erroneously based his judgment on negative enforceability by the default beneficiary: positive enforceability is, however, necessary (*Re Davidson* [1909] 1 Ch. 567, 571; *Re Shaw* [1957] 1 W.L.R. 729, 745). Snell's *Equity*, Part II, Chap. 1, sect. 3.3.

[50] Snell's *Equity,* Part II, Chap. 1, sect. 3.3.

absence of anyone able to apply to the court to enforce the trust. The trusts are subject to the rule against inalienability and so must be restricted directly or indirectly[51] to the common law perpetuity period. If the trustees do not take advantage of what, in substance, amounts to a power to carry out a purpose, then the person otherwise entitled to the trust property will be able to claim it.

PURPOSES CONSTRUED AS TRUSTS FOR BENEFICIARIES

3–217   *Re Denley*-type purpose trusts typically involve a large fluctuating class of beneficiaries never intended to have, and never capable[52] of having, absolute ownership of the trust property, and only having a positive right to the performance of the trustee's duties in the form prescribed by the settlor. What of the cases, however, where there is a small class of identified beneficiaries who could be intended to have absolute ownership of the trust property, though the settlor purportedly qualifies this by requiring the property to be used for a specified purpose?

Take the case of a trust fund set up for the education of the seven children of a deceased clergyman. Once their formal education was over, Kekewich J.[53] held this to be an absolute gift with the reference to education expressing merely the motive of the gift. He applied the well-established, and difficult to rebut,[54] presumption of construction,[55] "If a gross sum be given, or if the whole income of property be given, and a special purpose be assigned for this gift this court regards the gift as absolute and the purpose merely as the motive of the gift, and therefore holds that the gift takes effect as to the whole sum or the whole income as the case may be."

3–218   This was applied by the Court of Appeal in *Re Osoba*[56] where a bequest to the testator's widow upon trust "for her maintenance and for the training of my daughter, Abiola, up to university grade and for the maintenance of my aged mother" was held to be a trust for the three females absolutely as joint tenants. In *Re Bowes*[57] a trust to spend £5,000

---

[51] *Pedulla v. Nasti* (1990) 20 N.S.W.L.R. 720. If a will restricts a bequest expressly "so far as the law allows" this is construed as restricting the period to 21 years so satisfying the rule against inalienability: *Re Hooper* [1932] Ch. 38. The court will not imply such a term: *Re Compton* [1946] 1 All E.R. 117. If the legacy does not have to be kept intact as endowment capital but can be spent as soon as practicable on the purpose then the rule against inalienability has no application: *Trimmer v. Danby* (1856) 25 L.J.Ch. 424; *Mussett v. Bingle* [1876] W.N. 170.

[52] A fluctuating class can never exercise *Saunders v. Vautier* rights to make the trust, property their own: *Re Levy* [1960] Ch. 346 at 363; *Re Westphal* [1972] N.Z.L.R. 792 at 764–765. Exceptionally, where the beneficial class consists of members from time to time of a club who, on dissolution of the club, are entitled to divide the assets between them, the beneficiariaries will be able to acquire absolute ownership if the gift is not construed only as a discretionary trust for club members while the club exists: see *supra*, at para. 3–185.

[53] *Re Andrew's Trust* [1905] 2 Ch. 48.

[54] *Re Abbott Fund Trust* [1900] 2 Ch. 326: fund subscribed for maintenance of two deaf and dumb ladies (so not of normal capacity) held after their deaths to pass to subscribers under resulting trust and not to survivor's estate. For other cases where the beneficiary was only entitled to claim what was necessary for the specified purpose see *Re Sanderson's Trusts* (1857) 3 K.&J. 497; *Re Gillingham Bus Disaster Fund* [1958] Ch. 300.

[55] *Re Sanderson's Trusts* (1857) 3 K. & J. 497 and see *Re Skinner* (1860) 1 J. & H. 102 at 105.

[56] [1979] 2 All E.R. 393.

[57] [1896] 1 Ch. 507.

on planting trees for shelter on the Wemmergill Estate was held to be a trust for the estate owners absolutely with the motive of having trees planted, so the owners could have the £5,000 to spend as they wished.

Thus, if S creates a trust for the maintenance of B for B's life and, subject thereto, for C absolutely, B will be absolutely entitled to the whole income for whatever purpose he wants,[58] being entitled by the *Saunders v. Vautier* principle[59] to obtain for himself any interest in property (whether capital or income) to which he is absolutely indefeasibly entitled *sui juris*. On the other hand, if S creates a trust for the trustees to apply so much of the income as is necessary for the maintenance of B for B's life, and subject thereto, for C absolutely B will only have *Saunders v. Vautier* rights to so much of the income as is necessary for the specified purpose.[60]

GIFTS FOR PURPOSES OF UNINCORPORATED BODIES

Unincorporated bodies, whether called associations, clubs or societies, **3–219** raise special problems since an unincorporated body, unlike a corporate body, is not a legal person capable of owning property or entering into contracts or floating charges or of being the subject of legal rights and duties.[61] For this reason clubs, like rugby clubs, often incorporated themselves by registration as an Industrial and Provident Society under the 1965 Act of that title, which is considerably cheaper than converting the club into a limited company under the Companies Act 1985 and which enables the structure of the club for the most practical purposes to remain fundamentally the same, so that the club is run by a committee elected by the member-shareholders. Tax legislation tackles an unincorporated body formed for business purposes as a partnership with tax liability attributed to the individual partners, but if not formed for business purposes then the unincorporated body is regarded as a beneficiary under a bare trust, so making the trustees liable for corporation tax or, until its abolition, development land tax.[62]

The body's property will be vested in trustees under a bare trust for **3–220** the members of the body (except to the extent that statute may prevent members of certain bodies from winding up the body and dividing its property between themselves.[63]) The trustees or other organ under the

---

[58] Unless the circumstances such as B's mental and physical incapacity indicate otherwise: *Re Sanderson's Trusts* (1859) 3 K.&J. 497.

[59] (1841) 4 Beav. 115, *infra*, at para. 9–154.

[60] See *Re Sanderson's Trusts, supra*. If the trustees had a discretion to decide how much income they considered to be necessary for B's maintenance then B would be bound to accept such subjectively determined amount (unless B could prove bad faith or invoke *Re Hastings-Bass* principles discussed below at para. 9–298).

[61] Trade unions are unincorporated associations (if not incorporated as a special register body) but by the Trade Union and Labour Relations Act 1974, s.2 they can make contracts in their own names, may sue or be sued in their own names, judgments can be enforced against them as if they were bodies corporate, and property may be vested in trustees on trust "for the union".

[62] *Conservative Central Office v. Burrell* [1982] 1 W.L.R. 522; *Frampton v. I.R.C.* [1985] STC 186, Income and Corporation Tax Act 1988, s.111; Development Land Tax Act 1976, s. 47, Interpretation Act 1978, s.5 and Sched. 1 defining person to include a body corporate or incorporate.

[63] *e.g.* Literary and Scientific Institutions Act 1854, s.30; *Re Bristol Athenaeum* (1899) 43 Ch.D. 236.

body's constitution may enter into contracts, thereby putting the body's property at risk *vis-à-vis* the claims of creditors, and may even be authorised to declare trusts binding the body's property.[64] To the extent such valid trusts have not been declared the body's property belongs to the members, subject to their contract made between themselves under the body's constitution and subject to any claims that third parties may have resulting from contracts made by the trustees.[65]

3–221   A member or his spouse (or anyone) may give property in their lifetime by will to the officers of the body as trustees upon certain trusts that are germane to the purpose of the body. Such trusts may be to use the property as soon as convenient in payment of everyday expenses so that the property is treated as part of the body's general assets. However, such trust property may not be intended to become the body's property to be spent as part of its general assets. The trust property may be intended to be held under a separate endowment account (so that income but not capital is spent) and managed separately from the body's general assets: neither the body's constitution nor the agreement of its members can then change the trustees' obligations as trustees of the trust property.

Associations with no unifying contract

3–222   An unincorporated body has the following features:

    (1) it is composed of two or more persons bound together for a common purpose;

    (2) these persons have mutual rights and duties arising from a contract between them;

    (3) the body has rules to determine (a) who controls the body and its funds and (b) the terms on which such control is exercisable;

    (4) the body can be joined or left at will.

For lack of the second and third features the Conservative Party was held not to be an unincorporated association liable to corporation tax.[66] The Revenue had argued that the party was an unincorporated association since members' contributions surely took effect as an accretion to the funds which were the subject-matter of a contract which such members had made between themselves. How else could there be a legal relationship between a contributor and the recipient of the contribution so as to safeguard the contributor's interest?

---

[64] Anything they do may be ratified by the membership since unincorporated associations have no capacity to be limited and so unlike companies cannot act *ultra vires*, though most of the *ultra vires* doctrine for companies has been abolished where outsiders dealing with the company are concerned: Companies Act 1989, s.108.

[65] *Re Bucks Constabulary Fund Friendly Society (No. 2)* [1979] 1 All E.R. 623, *infra*, at para. 5–50.

[66] *Conservative Central Office v. Burrell* [1982] 1 W.L.R. 522. The fourth feature was not in issue but it seems too restrictive since an association may well have restrictions on new membership or rules curtailing the freedom of members to leave at will.

Vinelott J.[67] suggested that the answer is that the contributor enters **3–223** into a contract with the treasurer whereby in consideration of payment of the subscription the treasurer undertakes to apply the subscription towards the association's purposes: breach of this undertaking can be enjoined on normal contractual principles at the suit of the contributor. On appeal,[68] Brightman L.J. opined that the contributor, by way of mandate or agency, gives his contribution to the treasurer to add it to the general funds of the association. Once that has been done the mandate becomes irrevocable but the contributor will have a remedy to restrain or have made good a misapplication of the mixed fund, unless it appeared on ordinary accounting principles that his own contribution had already been properly expended.

A gift for purposes (whether of an unincorporated body or otherwise[69]) may thus take effect by way of contract or of mandate (which may be gratuitous) if the donor is to retain some measure of control. Effect cannot be given to a testator's bequests in such fashion since one cannot imply a contract or mandate between a deceased person and another,[70] though a deceased may authorise or direct his personal representatives to enter into a contract or mandate. A deceased may also in his lifetime contract to leave property by will to someone for a purpose, and if he does die, leaving such a will, then his rights and duties under the contract will vest in his personal representatives who will be able to enforce the contractual undertakings given to him.

There is no need for any of the above artificial reasoning in the case of **3–224** gifts for unincorporated associations as Brightman L.J. has emphasised,[71] since lifetime or testamentary gifts can validly take effect "as an accretion to the funds which are the subject-matter of the contract which the members [of the unincorporated association] have made *inter se*."[72]

Different constructions of gifts to unincorporated bodies

Before the 1964 Perpetuities and Accumulations Act there were particular legal obstacles confronting gifts to unincorporated bodies. The gift could not be an absolute gift to such a body because such a body has no legal personality. It could not be a valid gift if construed as a gift to the present and future members of the body because the intent to ensure benefiting future members required the capital to be kept intact and held on trust for only the income to be used, so that the capital would remain available for the benefit of future members.[73] This rendered the gift void

---

[67] *Conservative Central Office v. Burrell* [1980] 3 All E.R. 42. He appears to suggest as an alternative that the treasurer by accepting the subscription comes under a special equitable obligation similar to an executor.
[68] [1982] 1 W.L.R. 522, and see [1983] Conv. 150 (P. Creighton) and (1983) 133 New L.J. 87 (C. T. Emery). Brightman L.J. made no comment on Vinelott J.'s views.
[69] *e.g.* a disaster appeal committee in a situation like that in *Re Gillingham Bus Disaster Fund* [1958] Ch. 300.
[70] As accepted by Vinelott J. and Brightman L.J. in the *Conservative Central Office* case, also *Re Wilson* [1908] 1 Ch. 839.
[71] *Conservative Central Office v. Burrell* [1982] 2 All E.R. 1 at 7.
[72] *ibid.*
[73] *Leahy v. Att.-Gen. for New South Wales* [1959] A.C. 457.

for infringing the rule against remoteness, though since the 1964 Act such a gift would be valid for the statutory perpetuity period.[74] If the gift were construed as a gift to the body on trust for carrying out purposes, with the gift being an endowment fund to be used for those purposes only, and not to be used without distinction between capital and income nor to be capable (on dissolution of the body) for sharing out between the then members, then such a purpose trust was void for infringing the rule against inalienability, unless it was a charitable purpose trust. The 1964 Act has not affected this.[75]

3-225   The gift would be valid if construed as an absolute gift to the persons happening to be current members of the body, so that any such person could claim his proportionate share. This might not be quite what the deceased donor wished but, at least, his gift was not void. There thus developed a sophisticated construction, more likely to give effect to a testator's intention to benefit future members, but without imposing a trust to benefit future members with the attendant void for remoteness problem before the 1964 Act.

The sophisticated construction construes the gift as an absolute gift to the current members beneficially, but as an accretion to the body's property held subject to the terms of the contract which the members are subjected to by virtue of their membership of the body. This contract determines how the body's assets are to be enjoyed and what are the rights of the members in respect of such assets, while the treasurer or other worthy members will hold the assets on a bare trust for current members to be dealt with according to the contract (the constitution of the body).

Possible constructions to consider

3-226   1. The gift is a valid absolute gift (and not a trust except to the extent a testator's executors may be under a fiduciary duty to give effect to the intended absolute gift after paying debts, etc.) to the persons currently members of the unincorporated body, so that any such person can claim his proportionate share.[76] The donor-testator is not providing endowment capital, but giving his property so that each donee can deal with his share as he wishes. Exceptionally, if the contract between the donees as members of the body requires gifts to members in their capacity, or under their description, as members to be treated as an accretion to the body's fund to be dealt with according to the body's rules[77] then the donor's property will have to be so treated.[78]

---

[74] See *supra*, at para. 3-181.

[75] See s.15(4) of 1964 Act, *supra*, para. 3-207.

[76] *Cocks v. Manners* (1871) L.R. 12 Eq. 574; *Re Smith* [1916] 1 Ch. 937; *Re Ogden* [1933] Ch. 678; *Re Clarke* [1901] 2 Ch. 110 (revealing that an expression of the purpose of the gift may merely be regarded as motive).

[77] Like property caught by a donee's covenant to settle after-acquired property: *Pullan v. Koe* [1913] 1 Ch. 9 and *infra*, at para. 4-42.

[78] P. Matthews [1995] Conv. 302; as Viscount Simonds stated in *Leahy v. Att.-Gen. for New South Wales* [1959] A.C. 457 at 478, "If it is a gift to individuals, each of them is entitled to his distributive share (unless he has previously bound himself by the rules of the society that it should be devoted to some other purpose)".

2. The gift is a valid absolute gift (and not a trust except to the extent a testator's executors may be under a fiduciary duty to give effect to the intended absolute gift) to the current members, taking effect as an accretion to the body's funds which are to be dealt with (under a bare trust) according to the rules of the body by which the members are all contractually bound.[79] The donor/testator is not providing endowment capital but giving his property to be freely spent[80] on day-to-day expenses or something of a more lasting nature, or to be divided up and pocketed by the members if the contractual rules allow this on dissolution or otherwise. It ought not to matter that because of some statute or subordination to some outside legal entity the members are unable to wind up the body and pocket its assets.[81] The gift in augmentation of the body's general assets is fairly alienable: it can be totally consumed in supporting the body's purposes directly or indirectly benefiting the members who all have *locus standi* to sue. The gift does not have to be kept intact as endowment capital, so no trust rules concerning remoteness or inalienability can be applicable. However, if the testator knew that it was impossible or very difficult in practice for members to wind up the body and pocket its assets, so that the body was designed to carry on indefinitely, his bequest could well be construed as intending to set up endowment capital so that the income would benefit members from time to time indefinitely as under construction 3.[82]

3. The gift is intended to ensure that present and future members **3–227** are either directly benefited or indirectly benefited (sufficiently to have *locus standi* to sue under *Re Denley's Trust Deed*) by the carrying out of the purposes of the body to which they belong. Thus, the gift is of endowment capital to be held upon trust (separate from the body's general assets available to be spent like current income) so that the income will always be available for the members from time to time or for purposes benefiting such members.

One can have an obvious example like £100,000 left on trust "to **3–228** The Club Treasurer to apply the income for the benefit qua members of those from time to time members of the Club" or a

---

[79] *Re Recher's W.T.* [1972] Ch. 526, *infra*, p. 209; *Re Lipinski's W.T.* [1976] Ch. 235, *infra*, at 211; *Universe Tankships Inc. of Monrovia v. International Transport Workers Federation* [1983] A.C. 366; *News Group Ltd v. Sogat* [1986] I.C.R. 716; *Re Bucks Constabulary Fund (No. 2)* [1979] 1 All E.R. 623, *infra*, at para. 5–50.

[80] *Re Macaulay's Estate* [1943] Ch. 435; *Re Price* [1943] Ch. 422; *Re Lipinski* [1976] Ch. 235; *Re Drummond* [1914] 2 Ch. 90 at 97–98; *Re Prevost* [1930] 2 Ch. 383.

[81] The suggestion of Vinelott J. in *Re Grant's W.T.* [1979] 3 All E.R. 359 that a "necessary characteristic" of any gift within this second construction is the members' power to alter the rules and divide the assets between them seems unsound. It surely suffices that the gifted property is not endowment capital but can be freely spent on purposes benefiting the members. The members' contractual rights to enforce spending the property for their benefit suffices even if they cannot personally "pocket" the property: their position is *a fanion* that of beneficiaries with *locus standi* to enforce purpose trusts directly benefiting them even if they have no *Saunders v. Vautier* right to "pocket" the trust property.

[82] *Carne v. Long* (1860) 2 De G.F. & J. 75; *Bacon v. Pianta* (1966) 114 C.L.R. 634 (to the Communist Party of Australia "for its sole use and benefit"); *Re Grant's W.T.* [1979] 3 All E.R. 359.

less obvious example like "to The Club Treasurer to apply the income for the general purposes of the Club" or for a particular purpose within its various purposes. Another example would be if a testator left £1 million to The Club Treasurer for the benefit of members from time to time of the Club or to ensure that the Club's purposes continue indefinitely. Here, by necessary implication the capital needs to be set aside as an endowment so that the income can be used indefinitely for the benefit of the members directly or indirectly. Such endownment gifts before the 1964 Perpetuities and Accumulation Act would have been void for infringing the rule against remoteness. Nowadays, the trend[83] is to stretch matters to hold that there is no endowment capital, so that there is an absolute gift accruing to the body's assets under the second construction above.

3–229   If the court cannot so hold then, where the members can wind up the body and make its capital assets their own, the court will wait and see if the members do so within the statutory perpetuity period of statutory lives in being plus 21 years. The court then has to determine whether the trust should be construed as a discretionary trust for members until dissolution of the body or the later expiry of the perpetuity period, because in such an eventuality there would arise a resulting trust in favour of the settlor's estate by virtue of section 3(3) of the 1964 Act, which could lead to practical problems in finding the person(s) to enjoy such a benefit that may be regarded as a windfall. Where the settlor has not contemplated providing for either of the above eventualities it seems likely that the court will be inclined to find that on dissolution the then members should be entitled to divide the trust capital between themselves according to the body's rules, or upon prior expiry of the statutory perpetuity period; then section 4(4) of the 1964 Act should close the class of members so as to exclude persons becoming members outside the perpetuity period. The current members at the end of that period should between them be absolutely entitled to the gifted capital. No doubt, in practice, they will be happy to transfer it to trustees as an accretion to the club's funds but a member could claim his proportionate share (at the risk of not having his membership renewed) unless the club rules expressly provided that any assets passing to a member by virtue of the membership must accrue to the club's funds.[84]

3–230   Where the members cannot make the club assets their own because statute prohibits this[85] or because on dissolution the assets must pass to another body[86] then the trust will be construed as a purpose trust under constructions 4 and 5, *infra*.

---

[83] See *supra*, n.79.
[84] See *supra*, n.76 and 78.
[85] *e.g.* Literacy and Scientific Institutions Act 1854, s.30. *Re Bristol Athenaeum* (1889) 43 Ch.D. 236.
[86] *e.g. Re Grant's W.T.* [1979] 3 All E.R. 359.

4. The gift is intended to be of endowment capital to be held on trust for the income to be applied to a charitable purpose. This is a valid charitable trust (exempt from the beneficiary principle and the rule against inalienability) whose funds will need to be kept separate from the non-charitable funds of the body and will remain subject to the charitable purpose, even after dissolution of the body.[87]

5. The gift is intended to be of endowment capital to be held on trust for the income to be applied for the club's abstract non-charitable purposes where any benefit for persons is so indirect or intangible that no person has *locus standi* to apply for enforcement of the trust. The trust will be void for infringing the beneficiary principle[88] unless it is one of the anomalous permitted testamentary purpose trusts,[89] but even these must be restricted to the common law perpetuity period if they are not to infringe the rule against inalienability.[90]

In *Re Grant's W.T.*[91] a testator left his estate "to the Labour **3–231** Party Property Committee for the benefit of the Chertsey Head-quarters of the Chertsey and Walton Constituency Labour Party" ("C.L.P.") providing that if the headquarters ceased to be in the Chertsey UDC area (1972) his estate should pass to the National Labour Party ("N.L.P.") absolutely. The C.L.P. constitution sub-ordinated it to the N.L.P., who could direct changes in the constitution and prevent the C.L.P. changing its constitution without N.L.P. approval. Vinelott J. held that the estate was meant to be kept intact as endowment capital on trust for Labour Party purposes and so was void for infringing the beneficiary principle and the rule against inalienability.

6. The gift is intended to be of endowment capital to be held on **3–232** trust for the income to be applied for the club's abstract non-charitable purposes, the chairman from time to time of the club to be sole enforcer of the trust. This ought to satisfy the wider form of the beneficiary principle that may be known as the enforcer principle,[92] but it would need to be restricted from the outset to a common law perpetuity period so as not to infringe the rule against inalienability, and the purposes would need to be

---

[87] *Brooks v. Richardson* [1986] 1 All E.R. 952; *Re Finger's W.T.* [1972] Ch. 300 revealing the predisposition of the court to treat a gift to an unincorporated charitable body as a trust for purposes, so as to prevent the gift lapsing if the body had been earlier dissolved and the second construction had been applied.

[88] *Leahy v. Att.-Gen. for New South Wales* [1959] A.C. 457.

[89] See *supra*, at para. 3–216.

[90] *ibid.*

[91] [1979] 3 All E.R. 359. *Obiter dicta* overlook the impact of the 1964. Perpetuities and Accumulations Act and the significance of *Re Lipinski's W.T.* [1976] Ch. 235. See further (1980) 39 Camb. L.J. 88 (C. E. F. Rickett) and (1980) 44 M.L.R. 459 (B. Green). In *News Group Newspapers Ltd v. Society of Graphical & Allied Trades* [1986] I.C.R. 716 Lloyd L.J. seems to accept that the NLP's power to obtain CLP assets for its own needs justified the conclusions of Vinelott J.

[92] See para. 3–211 *supra*

certain enough to enable the restrictions on the use of the income to be identified and enforced.[93]

LEAHY v. ATTORNEY-GENERAL FOR NEW SOUTH WALES

3–233   Privy Council [1959] A.C. 457; [1959] 2 All E.R. 300 (Viscount Simonds, Lords Morton of Henryton, Cohen, Somervell of Harrow and Denning)

By his will the testator provided as follows: "As to my property known as 'Elmslea' situated at Bungendore aforesaid and the whole of the land comprising the same and the whole of the furniture contained in the homestead thereon upon trust for such order of nuns of the Catholic Church or the Christian Brothers as my executors and trustees shall select."

Counsel for the trustees argued that the disposition made thereby was good as it stood. Once the trustees selected the recipient of the gift, whether an order of nuns or the Christian Brothers, the selected body became absolutely entitled to the gift. No question of uncertainty or perpetuity was therefore involved and the gift was valid. It should be observed that this argument, if successful, would enable the trustees to select as the recipient an order of nuns which was not charitable in the legal sense of that term. The phrase "order of nuns" included "contemplative" as well as "active" orders, the former of which were not charitable[94] Counsel, accordingly, argued, in the alternative, that, if the disposition made by clause 3 was not valid as it stood, it was nevertheless saved from invalidity by section 37D of the Conveyancing Act 1919–54, which would, at least, enable active (though not contemplative) orders to be selected.

3–234   VISCOUNT SIMONDS: "The disposition made by clause 3 must now be considered. As has already been pointed out, it will in any case be saved by the section so far as orders other than contemplative orders are concerned, but the trustees are anxious to preserve their right to select such orders. They can only do so if the gift is what is called an absolute gift to the selected order, an expression which may require examination.

3–235   "The the difficulty arises out of the artificial and anomalous conception of an unincorporated society which, though it is not a separate entity in law, is yet for many purposes regarded as a continuing entity and, however inaccurately, as something other than an aggregate of its members. In law a gift to such a society simpliciter (*i.e.*, where, to use the words of Lord Parker in *Bowman v. Secular Society Ltd*,[95] neither the circumstances of the gift nor the directions given nor the objects expressed impose on the donee the character of a trustee) is nothing else than a gift to its members at the date of the gift as joint tenants or tenants in common. It is for this reason that the prudent conveyancer provides that a receipt by the treasurer or other proper officer of the recipient society for a legacy to the society shall be a sufficient discharge to executors. If it were not so, the executors could only get a valid discharge by obtaining a receipt from every member. This must be qualified by saying that by their rules the members might have authorised one of themselves to receive a gift on behalf of them all.

---

[93] See *Twinsectra Ltd v. Yardley* [2000] W.T.L.R. 527, 560 on certainty of analogous *Quistclose*-type trust restrictions: where the purposes are spelled out in certain workable fashion one could have all the club members as enforcers.
[94] See *Gilmour v. Coats* [1949] A.C. 426; *infra*, at para. 7–149.
[95] [1917] A.C. 406 at 437.

"It is in the light of this fundamental proposition that the statements, to which **3–236** reference has been made, must be examined. What is meant when it is said that a gift is made to the individuals comprising the community and the words are added 'it is given to them for the benefit of the community?' If it is a gift to individuals, each of them is entitled to his distributive share (unless he has previously bound himself by the rules of the society that it shall be devoted to some other purpose). It is difficult to see what is added by the words 'for the benefit of the community.' If they are intended to import a trust, who are the beneficiaries? If the present members are the beneficiaries, the words add nothing and are meaningless. If some other persons or purposes are intended, the conclusion cannot be avoided that the gift is void. For it is uncertain and beyond doubt tends to a perpetuity.

"The question then appears to be whether, even if the gift to a selected order of nuns is prima facie a gift to the individual members of that order, there are other considerations arising out of the terms of the will, or the nature of the society, its organisation and rules, or the subject-matter of the gift, which should lead the court to conclude that though prima facie the gift is an absolute one (absolute both in quality of estate and in freedom from restriction) to individual nuns, yet it is invalid because it is in the nature of an endowment and tends to a perpetuity or for any other reason.

"The prima facie validity of such a gift (by which term their Lordships intend a **3–237** bequest or devise) is a convenient starting-point for the examination of the relevant law. For, as Lord Tomlin (sitting at first instance in the Chancery Division) said in *Re Ogden*,[96] a gift to a voluntary association of persons for the general purposes of the association is an absolute gift and prima facie a good gift. He was echoing the words of Lord Parker in *Bowman's* case[97] that a gift to an unincorporated association for the attainment of its purposes 'may . . . be upheld as an absolute gift to its members.' These words must receive careful consideration, for it is to be noted that it is because the gift can be upheld as a gift to the individual members that it is valid, even though it is given for the general purpose of the association. If the words 'for the general purposes of the association' were held to import a trust, the question would have to be asked, what is the trust and who are the beneficiaries? A gift can be made to persons (including a corporation) but it cannot be made to a purpose or to an object: so, also, a trust may be created for the benefit of persons as *cestuis que trust* but not for a purpose or object unless the purpose or object be charitable. For a purpose or object cannot sue, but, if it be charitable, the Attorney-General can sue to enforce it . . ." [He then considered *Cocks v. Manners* (1871) L.R. 12 Eq. 574; *Re Smith* [1914] 1 Ch. 937; *Re Clarke* [1901] 2 Ch. 110; *Re Drummond* [1914] 2 Ch. 90; *Re Taylor* [1940] Ch. 481; *Re Price* [1943] Ch. 422; *Re Prevost* [1930] 2 Ch. 383 and *Re Ray's W.T.* [1936] Ch. 520.]

"The cases that have been referred to are all cases in which gifts have been **3–238** upheld as valid either on the ground that, where a society has been named as legatee, its members could demand that the gift should be dealt with as they should together think fit; or on the ground that a trust has been established (as in *Re Drummond*) which did not create a perpetuity . . .

---

[96] [1933] Ch. 678 at 681.
[97] [1917] A.C. 406 at 442.

3-239   "Their Lordships must now turn to the recent case of *Re Macaulay's Estate*,[98] which appears to be reported only in a footnote to *Re Price*.[99] There the gift was to the Folkestone Lodge of the Theosophical Society absolutely for the maintenance and improvement of the Theosophical Lodge at Folkestone. It was assumed that the donee 'the Lodge' was a body of persons. The decision of the House of Lords in July 1933, to which both Lord Buckner and Lord Tomlin were parties, were that the gift was invalid. A portion of Lord Buckmaster's speech may well be quoted. He had previously referred to *Re Drummond* and *Carne v. Long*. 'A group of people,' he said, 'defined and bound together by rules and called by a distinctive name can be the subject of gift as well as any individual or incorporated body. The real question is what is the actual purpose for which the gift is made. There is no perpetuity if the gift is for the individual members for their own benefit, but that, I think, is clearly not the meaning of this gift. Nor again is there a perpetuity if the society is at liberty in accordance with the terms of the gift to spend both capital and income as they think fit . . . If the gift is to be for the endowment of the society to be held as an endowment and the society is according to its form perpetual, the gift is bad: but, if the gift is an immediate beneficial legacy, it is good.' In the result he held the gift for the maintenance and improvement of the Theosophical Lodge at Folkestone to be invalid. Their Lordships respectfully doubt whether the passage in Lord Buckmaster's speech in which he suggests the alternative ground of validity, viz, that the society is at liberty in accordance with the terms of the gift to spend both capital and income as they think fit, presents a true alternative. It is only because the society, *i.e.*, the individuals constituting it, are the beneficiaries that they can dispose of the gift. Lord Tomlin came to the same conclusion. He found in the words of the will 'for the maintenance and improvement' a sufficient indication that it was the permanence of the Lodge at Folkestone that the testatrix was seeking to secure and this, he thought, necessarily involved endowment. Therefore a perpetuity was created. A passage from the judgment of Lord Hanworth M.R. (which has been obtained from the records) may usefully be cited. He said: 'The problem may be stated in this way. If the gift is in truth to the present members of the society described by their society name so that they have the beneficial use of the property and can, if they please, alienate and put the proceeds in their own pocket, then there is a present gift to individuals which is good: but if the gift is intended for the good not only of the present but of future members so that the present members are in the position of trustees and have no right to appropriate the property or its proceeds for their personal benefit, then the gift is invalid. It may be invalid by reason of there being a trust created, or it may be by reason of the terms that the period allowed by the rule against perpetuities would be exceeded.'

3-240   "It is not very clear what is intended by the dichotomy suggested in the last sentence of the citation, but the penultimate sentence goes to the root of the matter. At the risk of repetition their Lordships would point out that if a gift is made to individuals, whether under their own names or in the name of their society, and the conclusion is reached that they are not intended to take beneficially, then they take as trustees. If so, it must be ascertained who are the beneficiaries. If, at the death of the testator, the class of beneficiaries is fixed and ascertained or ascertainable within the limit of the rule against perpetuities, all is well. If it is not so fixed and not so ascertainable, the trust must fail.

---

[98] [1943] Ch. 435n.
[99] [1943] Ch. 422.

"It must now be asked, then, whether in the present case there are sufficient indications to displace the prima facie conclusion that the gift made by clause 3 of the will is to the individual members of the selected order of nuns at the date of the testator's death so that they can together dispose of it as they think fit. It appears to their Lordships that such indications are ample.

"In the first place, it is not altogether irrelevant that the gift is in terms upon **3–241** trust for a selected order. It is true that this can in law be regarded as a trust in favour of each and every member of the order. But at least the form of the gift is not to the members, and it may be questioned whether the testator understood the niceties of the law. In the second place, the members of the selected order may be numerous, very numerous perhaps, and they may be spread over the world. If the gift is to the individuals it is to all the members who were living at the death of the testator, but only to them. It is not easy to believe that the testator intended an 'immediate beneficial legacy' (to use the words of Lord Buckmaster) to such a body of beneficiaries. In the third place, the subject-matter of the gift cannot be ignored. It appears from the evidence filed in the suit that Elmslea is a grazing property of about 730 acres, with a furnished homestead containing twenty rooms and a number of outbuildings. With the greatest respect to those judges who have taken a different view, their Lordships do not find it possible to regard all the individual members of an order as intended to become the beneficial owners of such a property. Little or no evidence has been given about the organisation and rules of the several orders, but it is at least permissible to doubt whether it is a common feature of them that all their members regard themselves or are to be regarded as having the capacity of (say) the Corps of Commissionaires (see *Re Clarke*) to put an end to their association and distribute its assets. On the contrary it seems reasonably clear that, however little the testator understood the effect in law of a gift to an unincorporated body of persons by their society name, his intention was to create a trust not merely for the benefit of the existing members of the selected order but for its benefit as a continuing society and for the furtherance of its work.

". . . Their Lordships, therefore, humbly advise Her Majesty that the appeal should be dismissed, but that the gift made by clause 3 of the will is valid by reason only of the provisions of section 37D of the Conveyancing Act 1919–54, and that the power of selection thereby given to the trustees does not extend to contemplative orders of nuns." *Appeal dismissed*.

RE DENLEY'S TRUST DEED

Chancery Division [1969] 1 Ch. 373; [1968] 3 W.L.R. 457; [1968] 3 All E.R. 65.

In 1936 land was conveyed by a company to trustees so that until the **3–242** expiration of 21 years from the death of the last survivor of certain specified persons the land should under clause 2(c) of a trust deed "be maintained and used as and for the purpose of a recreation or sports ground primarily for the benefit of the employees of the company and secondarily for the benefit of such other person or persons (if any) as the trustees may allow to use the same." The main question was dealt with as follows in a reserved judgment:

GOFF J.: "It was decided in *Re Astor's Settlement Trusts*,[1] that a trust for a number of non-charitable purposes was not merely unenforceable but void on

---

[1] [1952] Ch. 534.

two grounds; first that they were not trusts for the benefit of individuals, which I refer to as 'the beneficiary principle,' and, secondly, for uncertainty.

"Counsel for the first defendant has argued that the trust in clause 2(c) in the present case is either a trust for the benefit of individuals, in which case he argues that they are an unascertainable class and therefore the trust is void for uncertainty, or it is a purpose trust, that is a trust for providing recreation, which he submits is void on the beneficiary principle, or alternatively it is something of a hybrid having the vices of both kinds.

3–243 *"I think that there may be a purpose or object trust, the carrying out of which would benefit an individual or individuals, where that benefit is so indirect or intangible or which is otherwise so framed as not to give those persons any locus standi to apply to the court to enforce the trust, in which case the beneficiary principle would, as it seems to me, apply to invalidate the trust, quite apart from any question of uncertainty or perpetuity. Such cases can be considered if and when they arise. The present is not, in my judgment, of that character, and it will be seen that clause 2(d) of the trust deed expressly states that, subject to any rules and regulations made by the trustees, the employees of the company shall be entitled to the use and enjoyment of the land.*

"Apart from this possible exception, in my judgment the beneficiary principle of *Re Astor*,[2] which was approved in *Re Endacott (decd.)*,[3] see particularly by Harman L.J.,[4] *is confined to purpose or object trusts which are abstract or impersonal. The objection is not that the trust is for a purpose or object per se, but that there is no beneficiary or cestui que trust.* The rule is so expressed in *Lewin on Trusts* (16th ed.), p. 17, and, in my judgment, with the possible exception which I have mentioned, rightly so. In *Re Wood*[5] Harman J. said:

> 'There has been an interesting argument on the question of perpetuity, but it seems to me, with all respect to that argument, that there is an earlier obstacle which is fatal to the validity of this bequest, namely, that a gift on trust must have a cestui que trust, and there being here no cestui que trust the gift must fail.'

3–244 "Again, in *Leahy v. Att.-Gen. of New South Wales*[6] Viscount Simonds, delivering the judgment of the Privy Council, said:

> 'A gift can be made to persons (including a corporation) but it cannot be made to a purpose or to an object: so, also [and these are the important words] a trust may be created for the benefit of persons as cestuis que trust but not for a purpose or object unless the purpose or object be charitable. For a purpose or object cannot sue, but, if it be charitable, the Attorney-General can sue to enforce it.'

"Where, then, the trust, though expressed as a purpose, is directly or indirectly for the benefit of an individual or individuals, it seems to me that it is in general outside the mischief of the beneficiary principle.

"I am fortified in this conclusion by the dicta of Lord Evershed M.R. and Harman L.J. in *Re Harpur's Will Trusts, Haller v. Att.-Gen.*[7]

---

[2] [1952] Ch. 534. Editor's italics for cross-referencing purposes.
[3] [1960] Ch. 232.
[4] [1960] Ch. 232 at 250.
[5] [1949] Ch. 498 at 501.
[6] [1959] A.C. 457 at 478.
[7] [1962] Ch. 78 at 91, 96.

"Some further support for my conclusion is, I think, to be found in *Re Aberconway's Settlement Trusts*[8] where it was assumed that a trust for the upkeep and development of certain gardens which were part of a settled estate was valid.

"I also derive assistance from what was said by North J. in *Re Bowes*.[9] That was **3–245** a bequest of a sum of money on trust to expend the same in planting trees for shelter on certain settled estates. It happened that there was a father and a son of full age, tenant for life in possession and tenant in tail in remainder respectively; so that, subject to the son disentailing, they were together absolutely entitled, and the actual decision was that they could claim the money, but North J. said[10]:

> 'If it were necessary to uphold it, the trees can be planted upon the whole of it until the fund is exhausted. Therefore, there is nothing illegal in the gift itself . . .';

and[11]: 'I think there clearly is a valid trust to lay out money for the benefit of the persons entitled to the estate.'

"The trust in the present case is limited in point of time so as to avoid any infringement of the rule against perpetuities and, for the reasons which I have given, it does not offend against the beneficiary principle; and unless, therefore, it be void for uncertainty, it is a valid trust.

"There is, however, one other aspect of uncertainty which has caused me some **3–246** concern; that is, whether this is in its nature a trust which the court can control, for, as Lord Eldon L.C. said in *Morice v. Bishop of Durham*[12]:

> 'As it is a maxim that the execution of a trust shall be under the control of the court, it must be of such a nature that it can be under that control; so that the administration of it can be reviewed by the court; or, if the trustee dies, the court itself can execute the trust: a trust, therefore, which, in case of maladministration could be reformed; and a due administration directed; and then, unless the subject and the objects can be ascertained upon principles familiar in other cases, it must be decided that the court can neither reform maladministration nor direct a due administration.'

"In my judgment, however, it would not be right to hold the trust void on this ground. The court can, as it seems to me, execute the trust both negatively by restraining any improper disposition or use of the land, and positively by ordering the trustees to allow the employees and such other persons (if any) as they may admit to use the land for the purpose of a recreation or sports ground. Any difficulty there might be in practice in the beneficial enjoyment of the land by those entitled to use it is, I think, really beside the point. The same kind of problem is equally capable of arising in the case of a trust to permit a number of persons—for example, all the unmarried children of a testator or settlor—to use or occupy a house or to have the use of certain chattels; yet no one would suggest, I fancy, that such a trust would be void.

"In my judgment, therefore, the provisions of clause 2(c) are valid."

---

[8] [1953] Ch. 647.
[9] [1896] 1 Ch. 507.
[10] [1896] 1 Ch. 507 at 510.
[11] [1896] 1 Ch. 507 at 511.
[12] (1805) 10 Ves. 522 at 539.

RE RECHER'S WILL TRUSTS

3–247   Chancery Division [1972] Ch. 526; [1971] 3 W.L.R. 321; [1971] 3 All E.R. 401.

By will dated May 23, 1957, T gave a share of her residue to what the judge interpreted as "The London and Provincial Anti-Vivisection Society" which had ceased to exist on January 1, 1957. T died in 1962. In a reserved judgment consideration was first given to the question whether the gift would have been valid if the unincorporated society had existed at T's death:

BRIGHTMAN J.: "Having reached the conclusion that the gift in question is not a gift to the members of the London and Provincial Society at the date of death, as joint tenants or tenants in common so as to entitle a member as of right to a distributive share, nor an attempted gift to present and future members beneficially, and is not a gift in trust for the purpose of the society, I must now consider how otherwise, if at all, it is capable of taking effect.

3–248   "As I have already mentioned, the rules of the London and Provincial Society do not purport to create any trusts except insofar as the honorary trustees are not beneficial owners of the assets of the society, but are trustees on trust to deal with such assets according to the directions of the committee.

3–249   "A trust for non-charitable purposes, as distinct from a trust for individuals, is clearly void because there is no beneficiary. It does not, however, follow that persons cannot band themselves together as an association or society, pay subscriptions and validly devote their funds in pursuit of some lawful non-charitable purpose. An obvious example is a members' social club. But it is not essential that the members should only intend to secure direct personal advantages to themselves. The association may be one in which personal advantages to the members are combined with the pursuit of some outside purpose. Or the association may be one which offers no personal benefit at all to the members, the funds of the association being applied exclusively to the pursuit of some outside purpose. Such an association of persons is bound, I would think, to have some sort of constitution; *i.e.* the rights and liabilities of the members of the association will inevitably depend on some form of contract *inter se*, usually evidenced by a set of rules. In the present case it appears to me clear that the life members, the ordinary members and the associate members of the London Provincial Society were bound together by a contract *inter se*. Any such member was entitled to the rights and subject to the liabilities defined by the rules. If the committee acted contrary to the rules, an individual member would be entitled to take proceedings in the courts to compel observance of the rules or to recover damages for any loss he had suffered as a result of the breach of contract. As and when a member paid his subscription to the association, he would be subjecting his money to the disposition and expenditure thereof laid down by the rules. That is to say, the member would be bound to permit, and entitled to require, the honorary trustees and other members of the society to deal with that subscription in accordance with the lawful directions of the committee. Those directions would include the expenditure of that subscription, as part of the general funds of the association, in furthering the objects of the association. The resultant situation, on analysis, is that the London and Provincial Society represented an organisation of individuals bound together by a contract under which their subscriptions became, as it were, mandated towards a certain type of expenditure as adumbrated in rule 1. Just as the two parties to a bipartite bargain can vary or terminate their contract by mutual assent, so it must follow that the life members, ordinary members and associate members of the London and Provincial Society could, at any moment of time, by unanimous agreement (or by majority vote if the rules so prescribe), vary or terminate their multipartite contract. There would be no limit to the type of variation or termination to which all might agree. There is no private trust or trust for charitable purposes or other trust to hinder the process. It follows that if all members agreed, they could decide to wind up the London and Provincial Society and divide the net assets among themselves beneficially. No one would have any locus standi to stop them so doing. The contract is the same as any other contract and concerns only those who are parties to it, that is to say, the members of the society.

"The funds of such an association may, of course, be derived not only from the **3–250** subscriptions of the contracting parties but also from donations from non-contracting parties and legacies from persons who have died. In the case of a donation which is not accompanied by any words which purport to impose a trust, it seems to me that the gift takes effect in favour of the existing members of the association as an accretion to the funds which are the subject-matter of the contract which such members have made *inter se*, and falls to be dealt with in precisely the same way as the funds which the members themselves have subscribed. So, in the case of a legacy. In the absence of words which purport to impose a trust, the legacy is a gift to the members beneficially, not as joint tenants or as tenants in common so as to entitle each member to an immediate distributive share, but as an accretion to the funds which are the subject-matter of the contract which the members have made *inter se*.

"In my judgment the legacy in the present case to the London and Provincial **3–251** Society ought to be construed as a legacy of that type, that is to say, a legacy to the members beneficially as an accretion to the funds subject to the contract which they had made *inter se*. Of course, the testatrix did not intend the members of the society to divide their bounty between themselves, and doubtless she was ignorant of that remote but theoretical possibility. Her knowledge or absence of knowledge of the true legal analysis of the gift is irrelevant. The legacy is accordingly in my view valid, subject only to the effect of the events of January 1, 1957."

RE LIPINSKI'S WILL TRUSTS

Chancery Division [1976] Ch. 235; [1977] 1 All E.R. 33; [1976] 3 W.L.R. 522.

The testator bequeathed his residuary estate to trustees on trust "as to one **3–252** half thereof for the Hull Judeans (Maccabi) Association in memory of my late wife to be used solely in the work of constructing the new buildings for the association and/or improvements to the said buildings." Was this valid?

OLIVER J.: "I approach question 1 of the summons, therefore, on the footing that this is a gift to an unincorporated non-charitable association. Such a gift, if it is an absolute and beneficial one, is of course perfectly good: see, for instance, the gift to the Corps of Commissionaires in *Re Clarke*.[13] What I have to consider, however, is the effect of the specification by the testator of the purposes for which the legacy was to be applied. The principles applicable to this type of case were stated by Cross J. in *Neville Estates Ltd v. Madden*[14] and they are conveniently summarised in *Tudor on Charities*, where it is said[15]:

---

[13] [1901] 2 Ch. 110.
[14] [1962] Ch. 832.
[15] (6th ed., 1967), at 150.

3–253   "In *Neville Estates Ltd v. Madden* Cross J. expressed the opinion (which is respectfully accepted as correct) that every such gift might, according to the actual words used, be construed in one of three quite different ways: (*a*) As a gift to the members of the association at the date of the gift as joint tenants so that any member could sever his share and claim it whether or not he continues to be a member. (*b*) As a gift to the members of the association at the date of the gift not as joint tenants, but subject to their contractual rights and liabilities towards one another as members of the association. In such a case a member cannot sever his share. It will accrue to the other members on his death or resignation, even though such members include persons who become members after the gift took effect. If this is the effect of the gift, it will not be open to objection on the score of perpetuity or uncertainty unless there is something in its terms or circumstances or in the rules of the association which precludes the members at any given time from dividing the subject of the gift between them on the footing that they are solely entitled to it in equity. (*c*) The terms or circumstances of the gift or the rules of the association may show that the property in question—*i.e.* the subject of the gift—is not to be at the disposal of the members for the time being but is to be held in trust for or applied for the purposes of the association as a quasi-corporate entity. In this case the gift will fail unless the association is a charitable body."

3–254   "That summary may require, I think, a certain amount of qualification in the light of subsequent authority, but for the present purposes I can adopt it as a working guide. Counsel for the next-of-kin argues that the gift in the present case clearly does not fall within the first category, and that the addition of the specific direction as to its employment by the association prevents it from falling into the second category. This is, therefore, he says, a purpose trust and fails both for that reason and because the purpose is perpetuitous . . .

"Counsel for the next-of-kin points out, first, that the gift is in memory of the testator's late wife (which, he says, suggests an intention to create a permanent memorial or endowment); secondly, that the gift is *solely* for a particular purpose (which would militate strongly against any suggestion that the donees could wind up and pocket the money themselves, even though their constitution may enable them to do so); and, thirdly, that the gift contemplates expenditure on 'improvements,' which connotes a degree of continuity or permanence. All this, he says, shows that what the testator had in mind was a permanent endowment in memory of his late wife.

3–255   "For my part, I think that very little turns on the testator's having expressed the gift as being in memory of his late wife. I see nothing in this expression which suggests any intention to create a permanent endowment. It indicates merely, I think, a tribute which the testator wished to pay, and it is not without significance that this self-same tribute appeared in the earlier will in which he made an absolute and outright gift to the association. The evidential value of this in the context of a construction summons may be open to doubt, and I place no reliance on it. It does, however, seem to me that nothing is to be derived from these words beyond the fact that the testator wished the association to know that his bounty was a tribute to his late wife.

"I accept, however, the submission of counsel for the next-of-kin that the designation of the sole purpose of the gift makes it impossible to construe the gift as one falling into the first of Cross J.'s categories, even if that were otherwise possible. But I am not impressed by the argument that the gift shows an intention of continuity. Counsel prays in aid *Re Macaulay*[16] where the gift was for the 'maintenance and improvement of the Theosophical Lodge at Folkestone.' The House of Lords held that it failed for perpetuity, the donee being a non-charitable body. But it is clear from the speeches of both Lord Buckmaster and Lord Tomlin that their Lordships derived the intention of continuity from the reference to 'maintenance.' Here it is quite evident that the association was to be free to spend the capital of the legacy.

"*Re Price*[17] itself is authority for the proposition that a gift to an unincorpo- **3–256** rated non-charitable association for objects on which the association is at liberty to spend both capital and income will not fail for perpetuity, although the actual conclusion in that case has been criticised, the point that the trust there (the carrying on of the teachings of Rudolf Steiner) was a 'purpose trust' and thus unenforceable on that ground was not argued. It does not seem to me, therefore, that in the present case there is a valid ground for saying that the gift fails for perpetuity.

"But that is not the end of the matter. If the gift were to the association *simpliciter*, it would, I think, clearly fall within the second category of Cross J.'s categories. At first sight, however, there appears to be a difficulty in arguing that the gift is to members of the association subject to their contractual rights *inter se* when there is a specific direction or limitation sought to be imposed on those contractual rights as to the manner in which the subject-matter of the gift is to be dealt with. This, says counsel for the next-of-kin, is a pure 'purpose trust' and is invalid on that ground, quite apart from any question of perpetuity. I am not sure, however, that it is sufficient merely to demonstrate that a trust is a 'purpose' trust . . .

"There would seem to me to be, as a matter of common sense, a clear **3–257** distinction between the case where a purpose is described which is clearly intended for the benefit of ascertained or ascertainable beneficiaries, particularly where those beneficiaries have the power to make the capital their own, and the case where no beneficiary at all is intended (for instance, a memorial to a favourite pet) or where the beneficiaries are unascertainable (as for instance in *Re Price*[18]). If a valid gift may be made to an unincorporated body as a simple accretion to the funds which are the subject-matter of the contract which the members have made *inter se*, and *Neville Estates v. Madden*[19] and *Re Recher's Will Trusts*[20] show that it may, I do not really see why such a gift, which specifies a purpose which is within the powers of the unincorporated body and of which the members of that body are the beneficiaries, should fail. Why are not the beneficiaries able to enforce the trust or, indeed, in the exercise of their contractual rights, to terminate the trust for their own benefit? Where the donee body is itself the beneficiary of the prescribed purpose, there seems to me to be the strongest argument in common sense for saying that the gift should be construed as an absolute one within the second category, the more so where, if the purpose is carried out, the members can by appropriate action vest the resulting property in themselves, for here the trustees and the beneficiaries are the same persons.

---

[16] [1943] Ch. 435.
[17] [1943] Ch. 422.
[18] [1943] Ch. 422.
[19] [1962] Ch. 832.
[20] [1972] Ch. 526.

3–258 "Is such a distinction as I have suggested borne out by the authorities? The answer is, I think, 'Not in terms,' until recently. But the cases appear to me to be at least consistent with this. For instance, *Re Clarke*[21] (the case of the Corps of Commissionaires), *Re Drummond*[22] (the case of the Old Bradfordians) and *Re Taylor*[23] (the case of the Midland Bank Staff Association), in all of which the testator had prescribed purposes for which the gifts were to be used, and in all of which the gifts were upheld, were all cases where there were ascertainable beneficiaries; whereas in *Re Wood*[24] and *Leahy v. Attorney-General for New South Wales*[25] (where the gifts failed) there were none. *Re Price* is perhaps out of line, because there was no ascertained beneficiary and yet Cohen J. was prepared to uphold the gift even on the supposition that (contrary to his own conclusion) the purpose was non-charitable. But as I have mentioned, the point about the trust being a purpose trust was not argued before him.

3–259 "A striking case which seems to be not far from the present is *Re Turkington*,[26] where the gift was to a masonic lodge 'as a fund to build a suitable temple in Stafford." The members of the lodge being both the trustees and the beneficiaries of the temple, Luxmoore J. construed the gift as an absolute one to the members of the lodge for the time being. Directly in point is the more recent decision of Goff J. in *Re Denley's Trust Deed*,[27] where the question arose as to the validity of a deed under which land was held by trustees as a sports ground:

> ". . . primarily for the benefit of the employees of [a particular] company and secondarily for the benefit of such other person or persons . . . as the trustees may allow to use the same"

the latter provision was construed by Goff J. as a power and not a trust. The same deed conferred on the employees a right to use and enjoy the land subject to regulations made by the trustees. Goff J. held that the rule against enforceability of non-charitable "purpose or object" trusts was confined to those which were abstract or impersonal in nature where there was no beneficiary or *cestui que trust*. A trust which, though expressed as a purpose, was directly or indirectly for the benefit of an individual or individuals was valid provided that those individuals were ascertainable at any one time and the trust was not otherwise void for uncertainty.

"I respectfully adopt [the view of Goff J, italicised, *supra*, at para. 3–243], as it seems to me to accord both with authority and with common sense.

3–260 "If this is the right principle, then on each side of the line does the present case fall? Counsel for the Attorney-General has submitted in the course of his argument in favour of charity that the testator's express purpose 'solely in the work of constructing the new buildings for the association' referred and could only refer to the youth centre project, which was the only project for the erection of buildings which was under consideration at the material time. If this is right, then the trust must, I think, fail, for it is quite clear that that project is ultimately conceived embraced not only the members of the association, but the whole Jewish community in Hull, and it would be difficult to argue that there was any

---

[21] [1901] 2 Ch. 110.
[22] [1914] 2 Ch. 90.
[23] [1940] Ch. 481.
[24] [1949] Ch. 498.
[25] [1959] A.C. 457.
[26] [1937] 4 All E.R. 501.
[27] [1969] 1 Ch. 373 at 375.

ascertainable beneficiary. I do not, however, so construe the testator's intention. The evidence is that the testator knew the association's position and that he took a keen interest in it. I infer that he was kept informed of its current plans. The one thing that is quite clear from the minutes is that from 1965 right up to the testator's death there was great uncertainty about what was going to be done. There was a specific project for the purchase of a house in 1965. By early 1966 the youth centre was back in favour. By October 1966 it was being suggested that the association should stay where it was in its rented premises. The meeting of March 21, is, I think, very significant because it shows that it was again thinking in terms of its own exclusive building and that the patrons (of whom the testator was one) would donate the money when it was needed. At the date of the will, the association had rejected the youth centre plans and was contemplating again the purchase of premises of its own; and thereafter interest shifted to the community centre. I am unable to conclude that the testator had any specific building in mind; and, in my judgment, the reference to '*the* . . . buildings for the association' means no more than whatever buildings the association may have or may choose to erect or acquire. The reference to improvements reflects, I think, the testator's contemplation that the association might purchase or might, at his death, already have purchased an existing structure which might require improvement or conversion or even that it might, as had at one time been suggested, expend money in improving the premises which it rented from the Jewish Institute. The association was to have the legacy to spend in this way for the benefit of its members.

"I have already said that, in my judgment, no question of perpetuity arises **3–261** here, and accordingly the case appears to me to be one of the specification of a particular purpose for the benefit of ascertained beneficiaries, the members of the association for the time being. There is an additional factor. This is a case in which, under the constitution of the association, the members could, by the appropriate majority, alter their constitution so as to provide, if they wished, for the division of the association's assets among themselves. This has, I think, a significance. I have considered whether anything turns in this case on the testator's direction that the legacy shall be used 'solely' for one or other of the specified purposes. Counsel for the association has referred me to a number of cases where legacies have been bequeathed for particular purposes and in which the beneficiaries have been held entitled to override the purpose, even though expressed in mandatory terms.

"Perhaps the most striking in the present context is the case of *Re Bowes*,[28] **3–262** where money was directed to be laid out in the planting of trees on a settled estate. That was a 'purpose' trust, but there were ascertainable beneficiaries, the owners for the time being of the estate; and North J. held that the persons entitled to the settled estate were entitled to have the money whether or not it was laid out as directed by the testator. He said:[29]

"The owners of the estate now say 'It is a very disadvantageous way of spending this money; the money is to be spent for our benefit, and that of no one else; it was not intended for any purpose other than our benefit and that of the estate. That is no reason why it should be thrown away by doing what is not for our benefit, instead of being given to us, who want to have

---

[28] [1896] 1 Ch. 507.
[29] [1896] 1 Ch. 507 at 511.

the enjoyment of it.' I think their contention is right. I think the fund is devoted to improving the estate, and improving the estate for the benefit of the persons who are absolutely entitled to it."

3–263   "I can see no reason why the same reasoning should not apply in the present case simply because the beneficiary is an unincorporated non-charitable association. I do not think the fact that the testator has directed the application 'solely' for the specified purpose adds any legal force to the direction. The beneficiaries, as members of the association for the time being, are the persons who could enforce the purpose and they must, as it seems to me, be entitled not to enforce it or, indeed, to vary it.

"Thus, it seems to me that whether one treats the gift as a 'purpose' trust or as an absolute gift with a superadded direction or, on the analogy of *Re Turk-ington*,[30] as a gift where the trustees and the beneficiaries are the same persons, all roads lead to the same conclusion.

"In my judgment, the gift is a valid gift."

REFORM?

Section 16 of the Ontario Perpetuities Act 1966

3–264   (1) A trust for a specific non-charitable purpose that creates no enforceable equitable interest in a specific person shall be construed as a power[31] to appoint the income or the capital, as the case may be, and, unless the trust is created for an illegal purpose or a purpose contrary to public policy, the trust is valid so long as, and to the extent that it is exercised either by the original trustee or his successor, within a period of twenty-one years, notwithstanding that the limitation creating the trust manifested any intention, either expressly or by implication, that the trust should or might continue for a period in excess of that period, but, in the case of such a trust that is expressed to be of perpetual duration, the court may declare the limitation to be void if the court is of opinion that by so doing the result would more closely approximate to the intention of the creator of the trust than the period of validity provided by this section.

3–265   (2) To the extent that the income or capital of a trust for a specific non-charitable purpose is not fully expended within a period of twenty-one years, or within any annual or other recurring period within which the limitation creating the trust provided for the expenditure of all or a specified portion of the income or the capital, the person or persons, or his or their successors, who would have been entitled to the property comprised in the trust if the trust had been invalid from the time of its creation, are entitled to such unexpended income or capital.

Bermuda Trusts (Special Provisions) Amendment Act 1998

Purpose trusts

3–266   2. For Part II of the Trusts (Special Provisions) Act 1989 (trusts for a purpose) there shall be substituted—

---

[30] [1937] 4 All E.R. 501.
[31] The courts are not prepared to do this artificially of their own volition: cp. *IRC v. Broadway Cottages Trust* [1955] Ch 20, 36.

"PART II PURPOSE TRUSTS

Purpose trusts

12A—(1) A trust may be created for a non-charitable purpose or purposes provided that the conditions set out in subsection (2) are satisfied; and in this Part such a trust is referred to as a "purpose trust".

(2) The conditions are that the purpose or purposes are—

(a) sufficiently certain to allow the trust to be carried out,
(b) lawful, and
(c) not contrary to public policy.

(3) A purpose trust may only be created in writing.

(4) The rule of law (known as the rule against excessive duration or the rule against perpetual trusts) which limits the time during which the capital of a trust may remain unexpendable to the perpetuity period under the rule against perpetuities shall not apply to a purpose trust.

(5) The rule against perpetuities (also known as the rule against remoteness of vesting) as modified by the Perpetuities and Accumulations Act 1989 shall apply to a purpose trust.

Enforcement and variation of purpose trust by the court

12B—(1) The Supreme Court may make such order as it considers expedient **3–267** for the enforcement of a purpose trust on the application of any of the following persons—

(a) any person appointed by or under the trust for the purposes of this subsection;
(b) the settlor, unless the trust instrument provides otherwise;
(c) a trustee of the trust;
(d) any other person whom the court considers has sufficient interest in the enforcement of the trust;

and where the Attorney-General satisfies the court that there is no such person who is able and willing to make an application under this subsection, the Attorney-General may make an application for enforcement of the trust.

(2) On an application in relation to a purpose trust by any of the following persons—

(a) any person appointed by or under the trust for the purposes of this subsection;
(b) the settlor, unless the trust instrument provides otherwise;
(c) a trustee of the trust,

the court may if it thinks fit approve a scheme to vary any of the purposes of the trust, or to enlarge or otherwise vary any of the powers of the trustees of the trust.

(3) Where any costs are incurred in connection with any application under this section, the Supreme Court may make such order as it considers just as to payment of those costs (including payment out of the property of the trust).

QUESTIONS

3–268 **1.** A testator who died a month ago by his will made the following bequests:

(i) £10,000 to Alan and at his death the remaining part of what is left that he does not want for his own use to be divided equally between Xerxes and Yorick;

(ii) £50,000 to my trustees Tom and Tim to distribute amongst such of the inhabitants of Cambridge as they shall in their unfettered discretion think fit;

(iii) £100,000 to my said trustees to distribute amongst Brian, Charles, David, Ellen, Oswald, Peter, Quentin and Roger and such of my other business associates and old friends as they shall see fit;

(iv) £100,000 to my said trustees to use the income for 80 years from my death as the applicable perpetuity period or such other period as the law allows if less for providing holidays for employees and ex-employees their spouses and relatives of I.C.I. plc and of companies on whose boards of directors, directors of I.C.I. plc sit, and thereafter to use the income for the education of my relatives;

(v) residue to my son Simon trusting that he will see to it that my old friends shall have the contents of my wine cellar; and in case of any doubts he shall have power to designate who are my business associates and old friends.

Consider the validity of these bequests, the testator having lived in Cambridge all his life.

3–269 **2.** "If the practical distinctions between discretionary trusts and fiduciary powers are so slight as to justify the decision in *McPhail v. Doulton* it cannot be right to have one but not the other subject to the test of administrative workability; nor, in light of *McPhail v. Doulton*, can *Re Barlow's W.T.* be justified." Discuss.

3. Simon Small, who was only 4 feet 11 inches tall, has just died. In his home-made will, he directed his executors:

"(a) to pay £2,000 to each of my small relatives;

(b) to distribute £8,000 as they see fit amongst such persons as they consider to be friends of mine;

(c) to hold my residuary estate on trust to pay the income therefrom to my four daughters equally in their respective lifetimes but if a daughter marries a supporter of Watford Football Club the share of such daughter shall accrue to the other daughters, as shall also be the case on the death of a daughter, but on the death of my last surviving daughter they shall distribute the capital within one year amongst such persons connected with me who have been benefited by me in my lifetime as they shall see fit."

Advise on the validity of the above bequests.

4. By his will Tony left:

(a) "£1,000,000 to my executor and trustee Eric to use the income to further the purposes of the UK Socialist Party so far as the law allows, such trust to be enforceable by the Leader from time to time of such Party";

(b) "£50,000 to the Treasurer of the Cambridge University Law Society to deal with it as the Society wishes";

(c) "£50,000 to the Treasurer of the Manchester Literary and Philosophical Society on trust to apply the income for the benefit of its members";

(d) "£150,000 to be used at the discretion of the chairman and executive council of the Anthroposophical Society of Great Britain to further the teachings of Rudolph Steiner";

(e) "the proceeds of sale of my residuary estate to the Treasurer of the Manchester Real Tennis Club to apply half the income for the purposes of the Club and half the income for providing educational assistance to the children of Club members."

Statute prevents the members of the "Lit. and Phil." Society from winding up the Society and dividing its assets between themselves, while this is possible in the case of the Real Tennis Club only if membership falls below five, though the rules can be changed by a 90 per cent majority vote.

Advise on the validity of the above bequests.

5. How satisfactory are the reforms enacted in sections 12A and 12B of the **3–270** Bermudan Trusts (Special Provisions) Act 1989 (as substituted by the Trusts Special Provisions Amendment Act 1998). What happens if there is no protector? How is the Att.-Gen. to discover there is no protector or an unwilling or incapable protector? Where is the beneficial equitable ownership if a settlor transfers £500,000 and all the shares in Wonder Co. Ltd to trustees to the intent that he be forthwith divested of all interest in the assets which are to be used exclusively for the purpose of developing Wonder Co. Ltd? How does the position differ if the trustees are under a duty to accumulate the income for the full 100 year period allowed by Bermudan law and on the expiry thereof in their discretion to distribute the trust property between such of the settlor's relatives then alive as they see fit, but with the power at any earlier time to appoint capital or income to the settlor or any of his relatives as they may see fit or to any other person nominated in writing to them by the settlor?

Chapter 4

EXPRESS PRIVATE TRUSTS

Section 1. Completely and Incompletely Constituted Trusts[1]

4–01 There are two ways of completely constituting an *inter vivos* trust: (1) by the settlor transferring the property intended to be the subject-matter of the trust to persons as trustees upon certain trusts declared by him or (2) by the settlor declaring that he himself will hold certain of his property as trustee upon certain trusts.

There is no room for such a distinction in the case of testamentary trusts nor in such case is there any scope for the rule in *Milroy v. Lord*[2] that applies to incomplete gifts. By virtue of the death there is a perfect gift of the legal beneficial ownership to the executor(s)[3] or administrator(s)[4] who are under equitable obligations,[5] once debts, expenses and taxes have been paid, to transfer the relevant property to legatees or devisees entitled in their own right or as trustees for others. So long as the three certainties are present[6] and debts expenses and taxes do not exhaust the relevant property a testamentary trust will be constituted though the named trustee disclaims or is unable to take the property through incapacity or predeceasing the testator.[7] Whoever succeeds to the legal title takes subject to the trust, for equity will not allow a trust to fail for want of a trustee.[8]

I. Creation of Express Trusts by an Effectual Transfer upon Trust

4–02 A purported voluntary transfer of legal title is ineffectual both at law and in equity where something remains to be done by the transferor in order to render the transfer effectual: *Milroy v. Lord, infra*. When, however, the transferor has done everything which it is obligatory for him to do to render the transfer of legal title effectual, but something remains to be done by a third party, the transfer, though invalid at law, is nevertheless valid in equity: *Re Rose, infra*.

---

[1] For the formalities required for the creation of trusts, see Chap. 2.
[2] (1862) 4 De G.F. & J. 264 *infra*, para. 4–03.
[3] Administration of Estates Act 1925, ss.1, 25, 32.
[4] *ibid.* and s.9 as substituted by Law of Property Miscellaneous Provisions Act 1994, s. 14.
[5] *Commissioner of Stamp Duties v. Livingston* [1965] A.C. 694; *Marshall v. Kerr* [1995] 1 A.C. 148.
[6] See Chap. 3.
[7] *Sonley v. Clock Makers' Company* (1780) 1 Bro.L.L. 81; *Re Smirthwaite's Trusts* (1871) L.R. 11 Eq. 251.
[8] *Re Armitage* [1972] Ch. 438, 445 (where it is pointed out that very exceptionally the trust will fail if the personality of the named trustee is vital to the carrying out of the trust).

MILROY V. LORD

Court of Appeal in Chancery (1862) 4 De G.F. & J. 264; 31 L.J. Ch. 798; 7 L.T. 178; 8 Jur. 806 (Turner and Knight-Bruce L.JJ.)

Thomas Medley executed what was treated as a voluntary deed[9] purporting to assign 50 shares in the Louisiana Bank to Samuel Lord upon trust for the benefit of the plaintiffs. The shares were transferable only by entry in the books of the bank; *but no such transfer was ever made.* Samuel Lord held at the time a general power of attorney authorising him to transfer Thomas Medley's shares, and Thomas Medley, after the execution of the settlement, gave him a further power of attorney authorising him to receive the dividends on the bank shares. Thomas Medley lived three years after the execution of the deed, during which period the dividends were received by Samuel Lord and remitted by him to the plaintiffs, sometimes directly and sometimes through Thomas Medley. *There was thus a perfect gift of the dividends.*

Shortly after the execution of the deed, the settlor had delivered to Samuel Lord the certificates for the shares; and on the death of the settlor, Samuel Lord gave up the certificates to the settlor's executor. The shares stood in the settlor's name before and at the time of his death.

Stuart V.-C. held that a trust had been created for the plaintiffs but was reversed upon an appeal by the executor.

Turner L.J.: "Under the circumstances of this case, it would be difficult not to 4–03 feel a strong disposition to give effect to this settlement to the fullest extent, and certainly I have spared no pains to find the means of doing so, consistently with what I apprehend to be the law of the court; but, after full and anxious consideration, I find myself unable to do so. *I take the law of this court to be well settled, that, in order to render a voluntary settlement valid and effectual, the settlor must have done everything which, according to the nature of the property comprised in the settlement, was necessary to be done in order to transfer the property and render the settlement binding upon him. He may, of course, do this by actually transferring the property to the persons for whom he intends to provide, and the provision will then be effectual, and it will be equally effectual if he transfers the property to a trustee for the purposes of the settlement, or declares that he himself holds it in trust for those purposes;*[10] *and if the property be personal, the trust may, as I apprehend, be declared either in writing or by parol; but, in order to render the settlement binding, one or other of these modes must, as I understand the law of this court, be resorted to, for there is no equity in this court to perfect an imperfect gift. The cases, I think, go further to this extent: that if the settlement is intended to be effectuated by one of the modes to which I have referred, the court will not give effect to it by applying another of those modes. If it is intended to take effect by transfer, the court will not hold the intended transfer to operate as a declaration of trust,*[11] *for*

---

[9] The deed (apparently executed in Louisiana) was expressed to be made in consideration of one dollar. In *Mountford v. Scott* [1975] Ch. 258, the Court of Appeal treated £1 as valuable consideration enabling specific performance to be ordered. If a transfer or grant of a legal title for consideration fails (*e.g.* a purported legal lease is not granted by deed) equity will treat this as a contract to transfer or grant the legal title properly, and if the contract is specifically enforceable (complying with the requisite formalities in Law of Property Miscellaneous Provisions Act 1989, s.2) equity will treat it as having been carried out, so that the transfer or grant is effective to create an equitable interest: *Walsh v. Lonsdale* (1882) 21 Ch.D.9.

[10] See *infra*, section 1(II). The italicised passage has been much quoted and applied.

[11] See *infra*, section 1(III).

then every imperfect instrument would be made effectual by being converted into a perfect trust. These are the principles by which, as I conceive, this case must be tried.

4–04   "Applying, then, these principles to the case, there is not here any transfer either of the one class of shares or of the other[12] to the objects of the settlement, and the question therefore must be whether a valid and effectual trust in favour of those objects was created in the defendant Samuel Lord or in the settlor himself as to all or any of these shares. Now it is plain that it was not the purpose of this settlement, or the intention of the settlor, to constitute himself a trustee of the bank shares. The intention was that the trust should be vested in the defendant Samuel Lord, and I think therefore that we should not be justified in holding that by the settlement, or by any parol declaration made by the settlor, he himself became a trustee of these shares for the purposes of the settlement. By doing so we should be converting the settlement or the parol declaration to a purpose wholly different from that which was intended to be effected by it and, as I have said, creating a perfect trust out of an imperfect transaction. . . .

4–05   "The more difficult question is whether the defendant Samuel Lord did not become a trustee of these shares. Upon this question I have felt considerable doubt; but in the result, I have come to the conclusion that no perfect trust was ever created in him. The shares, it is clear, were never legally vested in him; and the only ground on which he can be held to have become a trustee of them is that he held a power of attorney under which he might have transferred them into his own name; but he held that power of attorney as the agent of the settlor; and if he had been sued by the plaintiffs as trustee of the settlement for an account under the trust, and to compel him to transfer the shares into his own name as trustee, I think he might well have said: 'These shares are not vested in me; I have no power over them except as the agent of the settlor, and without his express directions I cannot be justified in making the proposed transfer, in converting an intended into an actual settlement.' A court of equity could not, I think, decree the agent of the settlor to make the transfer, unless it could decree the settlor himself to do so, and it is plain that no such decree could have been made against the settlor. In my opinion, therefore, this decree cannot be maintained as to the fifty Louisiana Bank shares . . ."

RE ROSE, ROSE V. INLAND REVENUE COMMISSIONERS[13]

Court of Appeal [1952] Ch. 499; [1952] 1 T.L.R. 1577; [1952] 1 All E.R. 1217; [1952] T.R. 175; (Evershed M.R., Jenkins and Morris L.JJ.).

4–06   The transferor, Mr. Rose, was the registered owner of a number of shares in Leweston Estates Co. On March 30, 1943, he executed two transfers[14] of two blocks of these shares, one in favour of his wife, and the other in favour of his wife and another person to be held by them upon certain trusts. The transfers were registered by Leweston Estates Co. on June 30, 1943. The transferor died more than five years after executing the instruments of transfer but less than five years after the transfers were registered. The question was whether in these

---

[12] A similar question arose in the case with reference to a second set of shares.
[13] See criticism of L. McKay (1976) 40 Conv. 139, but *Re Rose* was rightly applied in *Mascall v. Mascall* (1984) 50 P. & C.R. 119.
[14] One was a gratuitous transfer, and the other was expressed to be for a nominal consideration.

circumstances the two blocks of shares should be taken into account for the purpose of assessing estate duty. If the shares were taken under a voluntary disposition made by a person more than five years before his death and purporting to operate as an immediate gift, no duty would be leviable.

Roxburgh J.[15] decided the case adversely to the Inland Revenue Commissioners, who appealed unsuccessfully to the Court of Appeal.

EVERSHED M.R. "The burden of the case presented by the Crown may be **4–07** briefly put as it was formulated by counsel. This document, he said, on the face of it, was intended to operate and operated, if it operated at all, as a transfer. If for any reason it was at its date incapable of so operating it is not legitimate, either by reference to the expressed intention in the document or on well-established principles of law, to extract from it a wholly different transaction, *i.e.* to make it take effect, not as a transfer, but as a declaration of trust. Now I agree that on the face of the document it was obviously intended (if you take the words used) to operate, and operate immediately, as a transfer . . . of rights. To some extent at least, it is said, it could not possibly do so. To revert to the illustration which has throughout been taken, if the company had declared a dividend during his interregnum, it is not open to question that the company must have paid that dividend to the donor. So that *vis-à-vis* the company this document did not and could not operate to transfer to Mrs. Rose the right against the company to claim and receive that dividend. Shares, it is said by counsel for the Crown, are property of a peculiar character consisting, as it is sometimes put, of a bundle of rights, *i.e.* rights against or in the company. It has followed from counsel's argument that, if such a dividend had been paid, Mr. Rose could, consistently with the document to which he has set his hand and seal, have retained that dividend, and if he had handed it over to his wife it would have been an independent gift. I think myself that such a conclusion is startling. Indeed, I venture to doubt whether to anybody but a lawyer such a conclusion would even be comprehensible, at least without a considerable amount of explanation. That again is not conclusive, but I confess that I approach a matter of this kind with a preconceived notion that a conclusion that offends common sense so much as this would prima facie do ought not to be the right conclusion.

[His Lordship then examined *Milroy v. Lord*[16] and after quoting the passage **4–08** from that case italicised *supra*, at para. 4–03 continued:] Those last few sentences form the gist of the Crown's argument, and on it is founded the broad, general proposition that if a document is expressed as, and on the face of it intended to operate as, a transfer, it cannot in any respect take effect by way of trust. In my judgment, that statement is too broad and involves too great a simplification of the problem, and is not warranted by authority. I agree that if a man purporting to transfer property executes documents which are not apt to effect that purpose, the court cannot then extract from those documents some quite different transaction and say that they were intended merely to operate as a declaration of trust which *ex facie* they were not; but if a document is apt and proper to transfer the property—is, in truth, the appropriate way in which the property must be transferred—then it does not seem to me to follow from the statement of Turner L.J. that, as a result, either during some limited period or otherwise, a trust may not arise, for the purpose of giving effect to the transfer. The simplest case will, perhaps, provide an illustration. If a man executes a document transferring all his

---

[15] [1951] 2 All E.R. 959.
[16] (1862) 4 De G.F. & J. 264.

equitable interest, say, in shares, that document, operating and intended to operate as a transfer, will give rise to and take effect as a trust, for the assignor will then be a trustee of the legal estate in the shares for the person in whose favour he has made an assignment of his beneficial interest. And for my part I do not think that *Milroy v. Lord* is an authority which compels this court to hold that in this case, where, in the terms of Turner L.J.'s judgment, the settlor did everything which, according to the nature of the property comprised in the settlement, was necessary to be done by him in order to transfer the property, the result necessarily negatives the conclusion that, pending registration, the settlor was a trustee of the legal interest for the transferee.

4–09   "The view of the limitations of *Milroy v. Lord* which I have tried to express was much better expressed by Jenkins J. in the recent case which also bears the name of *Re Rose*[17] (though that is a coincidence). The testator in that case, Rose, by his will had given a number of shares to one Hook, but the gift was subject to this qualification: 'If such . . . shares have not been transferred to him previously to my death.' The question was: Had the shares been transferred to him in these circumstances? He had executed (as had this Mr. Rose) a transfer in appropriate form, and handed the transfer and the certificate to Hook, but, at the time of his death, the transfer had not been registered. Jenkins J. considered *Milroy v. Lord* and in regard to it he used this language:[18] 'I was referred on that to the well-known case of *Milroy v. Lord* and also to the recent case of *Re Fry*.[19] Those cases, as I understand them, turn on the fact that the deceased donor had not done all in his power, according to the nature of the property given, to vest the legal interest in the property in the donee. In such circumstances it is, of course, well settled that there is no equity to complete the imperfect gift. If any act remains to be done by the donor to complete the gift at the date of the donor's death, the court will not compel his personal representatives to do that act and the gift remains incomplete and fails. In *Milroy v. Lord* the imperfection was due to the fact that the wrong form of transfer was used for the purpose of transferring certain bank shares. The document was not the appropriate document to pass any interest in the property at all.' Then he refers to *Re Fry*, which is another illustration, and continued: 'In this case, as I understand it, the testator had done everything in his power to divest himself of the shares in question to Mr. Hook. He had executed a transfer. It is not suggested that the transfer was not in accordance with the company's regulations. He had handed that transfer together with the certificate to Mr. Hook. There was nothing else the testator could do.'

4–10   "I venture respectfully to adopt the whole of the passage I have read which, in my judgment, is a correct statement of the law. If that be so, then it seems to me that it cannot be asserted on the authority of *Milroy v. Lord*, and I venture to think it also cannot be asserted as a matter of logic and good sense or principle, that because, by the regulations of the company, there had to be a gap before Mrs. Rose could, as between herself and the company, claim the rights which the shares gave her *vis-à-vis* the company, Mr. Rose was not in the meantime a trustee for her of all his rights and benefits under the shares. That he intended to pass all those rights, as I have said, seems to me too plain for argument. I think the matter might be put, perhaps, in a somewhat different fashion though it

---

[17] [1949] Ch. 78.
[18] *ibid*. at 89.
[19] [1946] Ch. 312. For inessential irregularities see *Re Paradise Motor Co.* [1968] 1 W.L.R. 1125.

reaches the same end. Whatever might be the position during the period between the execution of this document and the registration of the shares, the transfers were on June 30, 1943, registered. After registration, the title of Mrs. Rose was beyond doubt complete in every respect, and if Mr. Rose had received a dividend between execution and registration and Mrs. Rose had claimed to have that dividend handed to her, what would Mr. Rose's answer have been? It could no longer be that the purported gift was imperfect; it had been made perfect. I am not suggesting that the perfection was retroactive. But what else could he say? How could he, in the face of his own statement under seal, deny the proposition that he had, on March 30, 1943, transferred the shares to his wife? By the phrase 'transfer the shares' surely must be meant transfer to her 'the shares and all my right, title and interest thereunder.' Nothing else could sensibly have been meant."

Held, therefore, that the transfer was valid and effectual in equity from March 30, 1943, and accordingly the shares were not assessable for estate duty.

Note

A gift of shares is, therefore, valid in equity if (1) the transferor has **4–11** executed the form of transfer required by the company's articles[20] and (2) has done everything else, *e.g.* delivered the share certificate which it is obligatory for *him* to do to make the transfer effective and binding upon him.[21] The gift is effective at law when registration of the transfer is made, and until this is done a transferor who complies with (1) and (2) above is a constructive trustee for the transferee.

The identical principle applies to a gift of a debt or other legal chose in action. If, therefore, the donor makes an absolute written assignment of the debt,[22] the gift is good in equity, though it will not be valid at law until written notice is received by the debtor whether from the assignor or the assignee.[23] A voluntary oral assignment on the other hand would be ineffective both at law and in equity.[24]

---

[20] In *Milroy v. Lord, supra* the form used was a deed poll; in *Antrobus v. Smith* (1805) 12 Ves. 39, unsealed writing, both of which were inappropriate forms according to the company's articles. Under Companies Act 1989, s. 207 the Secretary of State for Trade and Industry has promulgated the Uncertificated Securities Regulations 1995 which have enabled securities to be evidenced and transferred without a written instrument. There is now a paperless computerised system (CREST) under which many companies are no longer obliged to issue share certificates (except where shareholders still wish to receive them) but are permitted to allow their securities to be transferred through an electronic share settlement system. Shareholders who are not system members with direct access to the system may hold share certificates and when selling will need to send a stock transfer form plus the share certificate to the system-member who will then dematerialise the shares into the paperless system; a buyer can require the shares to be materialised so that he has a share certificate. Regulation 32(5) of the above Regulations disapplies Law of Property Act 1925 s. 53(1)(c) for transfers of equitable interests in shares, the legal title to which is in another under the CREST system.

[21] *Corin v. Patton* (1990) 169 C.L.R. 540. In *Re Fry* [1946] Ch. 312 although the American donor had sent the necessary forms to obtain Treasury exchange control consent no consent had been obtained before his death. If the gift was imperfect because such consent had not been obtained why was the gift in *Re Rose* not imperfect because the directors' consent to register the shares had not been obtained at the relevant time? Is it because the directors' consent is the ultimate consent and is a negative requirement in that transfers must automatically be registered within two months unless the directors' discretion to refuse is exercised within the two months: Companies Act 1985, s. 183(5), *Re Swaledale Cleaners Ltd* [1968] 1 W.L.R. 1710?

[22] As required by s. 136 of the Law of Property Act 1925.

[23] *Holt v. Heatherfield Trust* [1942] 2 K.B. 1; *Norman v. F.C.T.* (1963) 109 C.L.R. 28.

[24] *Olsson v. Dyson* (1969) 120 C.L.R. 365; *cf. Tibbits v. George* (1836) 5 A. & E. 107.

4–12   In the case of a gift of an equitable interest statute[25] requires action only by the donor so that there is no scope for *Milroy v. Lord*. If the donor has made a written assignment, whether of the whole or a part of the equitable interest, the gift is good. This was so in *Kekewich v. Manning*,[26] where the donor made a voluntary assignment by deed of his equitable interest in a trust fund. A voluntary *promise* to assign an equitable interest is unenforceable even if in signed writing since it is not an assignment and the absence of consideration means the promisee is a volunteer whom equity will not assist.[27]

Legal estates in freehold or leasehold property must be transferred by deed or in the case of registered land by a transfer form which is subsequently registered. Delivery by the registered proprietor to the transferee of the executed transfer form and the land certificate will satisfy the *Re Rose* principle.[28]

Personal chattels must be transferred by delivery or by deed of gift. It is noteworthy that money is not effectively given by the donor giving his cheque for the money[29] for a cheque is merely a revocable authority or mandate. A bill of exchange must be transferred by endorsement[30] and copyright by writing.[31]

4–13   As will be seen (*infra*, at para. 4–24), existing rights to have property now or in the future and whether or not such rights are conditional (*e.g.* on marrying or attaining 25 years) or defeasible (*e.g.* by exercise of a power of appointment) are capable of being gratuitously assigned: a *spes* or expectancy (*e.g.* a hope of receiving property if a power of appointment is exercised or a hope of inheriting property under T's will) is not property and so cannot be assigned,[32] although a person can enter into a contract for sale of a *spes*.

II. Creation of an Express Trust by an Effectual Declaration of Trust

4–14   In each case where a declaration of trust of the settlor as trustee is relied on the court must be satisfied that the subject matter of the trust has been clearly identified or segregated from the settlor's other assets[33] and that a *present binding* declaration of trust has been made complying with

---

[25] s. 53(1)(c) of the Law of Property Act 1925.
[26] (1851) 1 De G.M. & G. 176; such an assignment may take the form of a written direction to the trustees to hold on trust for the third party; *Grey v. I.R.C., supra*, at para. 2–51.
[27] *Re McArdle* [1951] Ch. 669.
[28] *Re Ward* [1968] W.A.R. 33; *Scoones v. Galvin* [1934] N.Z.L.R. 1004; *Brunker v. Perpetual Trustee Co.* (1937) 57 C.L.R. 555; *Mascall v. Mascall* (1984) 49 P. & C.R. 119.
[29] *Re Swinburne* [1926] Ch. 38; *Re Owen* [1949] W.N. 201; [1949] 1 All E.R. 901.
[30] Bills of Exchange Act 1882, s. 31; Cheques Act 1957, ss. 1, 2.
[31] Copyright Designs and Patents Act 1988, s. 90(3).
[32] *Williams v. Commissioners of Inland Revenue* [1965] N.Z.L.R. 395, *infra* at para. 4–79.
[33] See *supra*, paras 3–86 *et seq*. A declaration of trust of £100 (of the larger sum of money) in my bank account should be ineffective, though a trust of all (or half) the money currently in my bank account should be an effective trust of a chose in action.

the requisite formalities,[34] though the trust interest may be defeasible upon exercise of a power of appointment or a power of revocation.[35]

A declaration of trust, to be effectual, need not be literal. It is not necessary for an intending declarant to say: "I declare myself a trustee." What is necessary is some form of expression which in the circumstances shows that he intended to constitute himself trustee and another a beneficiary even if he did not know that the obligation he was creating amounted to a trust, see *Paul v. Constance, supra*, para. 3–78. An illustration of this is *Choithram International S.A. v. Pagarani*.[36] A month before he died of cancer, TCP organised an elaborate ceremony at his London bedside to establish a philanthropic Foundation in the form of a Jersey trust of which he was Settlor and one of the Trustees. He executed the trust deed in the presence of three (of the other six) trustees, his accountant and the First Secretary of the Indian High Commission. They recollected him as orally making an immediate absolute gift to the Foundation of all his wealth in his shareholdings and credit balances with four British Virgin Island Companies. Indeed, the minutes of those companies' meetings later that day recorded that the directors (including TCP, who signed the minutes) acknowledged TCP's gift of such wealth to the Foundation and that the Trustees (who included TCP) of the Foundation were henceforth the holders of the shares and assets in the relevant companies. Before TCP died the gifted property was not vested in the other Trustees, so it was alleged the gift was an imperfect gift.

Lord Browne-Wilkinson for the Privy Council held in context that "the words 'I give to the Foundation' can only mean 'I give to the Trustees of the Foundation trust deed to be held by them on the trusts of the Foundation trust deed'. Although the words are apparently words of outright gift they are essentially words of gift on trust."

What of the fact that he had not actually transferred the gifted assets **4–15** to all seven Trustees, including himself as one of the Trustees? As Lord Browne-Wilkinson stated, "what then is the position where the trust property is vested in one of the body of Trustees *viz* TCP? TCP has, in the most solemn circumstances, declared that he is giving (and later that he has given) property to a trust which he himself has established and of which he has appointed himself to be a Trustee. All this occurs in one composite transaction taking place on February 17. There can in principle be no distinction between the case where the donor declares himself to be sole Trustee for a donee or a purpose and the case where he declares himself to be one of the Trustees. In both cases his conscience is affected and it would be unconscionable and contrary to

---

[34] Neville J. in *Re Cozens* [1913] 2 Ch. 478 at 486; Romilly M.R. in *Grant v. Grant* (1865) 34 Beav. 623 at 626.

[35] *Copp v. Wood* [1962] 2 D.L.R. 224; *Beecher v. Major* (1865) 2 Drew & Son 431 at 437; *Young v. Sealey* [1949] Ch. 278 at 284, 294; *Choithram International S.A. v. Pagarani* [2001] 2 All E.R. 492, 500. A transfer or declaration of trust of property is presumed irrevocable. *Newton v. Askew* [1848] 11 Beav. 145, *Miller v. Harrison* (1871) L.R. 5 Eq. 324.

[36] [2001] 2 All E.R. 492, 501–502.

the principles of equity to allow such a donor to resile from his gift . . . in the absence of special factors,[37] where one out of a larger body of trustees has the trust property vested in him he is bound by the trust and must give effect to it by transferring the trust property into the name of all the Trustees".

As it happened, the four companies had altered their share registers after TCP's death so that legal title to the shares actually vested in the remaining six Trustees. The Privy Council held that the administrators of TCP's intestate estate could not claim the shares or the deposit balances with the companies.

Neville J., in *Re Cozens*,[38] referred to a "present irrevocable declaration of trust." The distinction is apparently between these declarations: "I declare a trust for X to be entitled on my death" and "I declare that on my death I will declare a trust for X." The latter is a mere promise to create a testamentary trust in the future, an example being *Bayley v. Boulcott*.[39] The former could operate as a declaration of trust in favour of the declarant for life, remainder to X, an example being *Kelly v. Walsh*.[40]

An interesting example of a declaration of trust occurred in *Re Ralli's Will Trusts*.[41] H, the owner of a reversionary interest (after her mother's life interest) under the will of her deceased father, covenanted with the trustees of her marriage settlement to settle, as soon as circumstances would admit, all her existing and after-acquired property (thinking particularly of the future actual assets she would become entitled to on her mother's death) upon certain trusts (which failed) and ultimately upon trusts for the benefit of the children of H's sister who were volunteers. A declaration of trust clause in the marriage settlement declared that all property comprised within the terms of the covenant should be subject in equity to the trusts of the settlement pending transfer to the trustees. H never assigned the reversionary interest to the trustees before she died. Buckley J. held that the reversionary interest being existing property of H at the time of her declaration of trust there was a valid trust of the interest so that the actual assets materialising on the death of H's mother years after H's death passed (not under H's will or intestacy but) under her settlement to her sister's children. It would appear that if her reversionary interest had only been acquired by her subsequently to her settlement so as to be after-acquired property then no trust of the interest would have arisen in favour of the volunteer nieces and nephews as declarations of trust in respect of after-acquired property are ineffective at law and in equity where volunteers are concerned.[42]

---

[37] *e.g.* if the settlor intended no trust to arise until he had vested the intended trust property in the names of all the intended trustees.
[38] [1913] 2 Ch. 478 at 486.
[39] (1828) 4 Russ. 345.
[40] (1878) 1 L.R.Ir. 275; see also *Re Smith* (1890) 64 L.T. 13.
[41] [1964] Ch. 288 at 298, *infra* at para. 4–72.
[42] *Williams v. C.I.R.* [1965] N.Z.L.R. 395, *infra*, at para. 4–79.

III. Ineffectual Transfers not Saved by Being Regarded as Effectual Declarations

No matter how clearly there may have been an intention to create a **4–16** voluntary trust by transfer, if the intending transferor has used an ineffectual method of transfer, this will not be construed into a declaration of trust. *Milroy v. Lord*, *supra*, at para. 4–03 and *Paul v. Constance*, *supra*, at para. 3–78, show that the attempted out-and-out *transfer* to other persons as trustees is the clearest evidence that the donor did not intend to *retain* the property and himself be trustee thereof.

Exceptionally, in the case of shares within the *Re Rose* principle it seems that if the directors refuse to register the share transfer then the transferor remains indefinitely as constructive trustee of the shares for the transferee.[43] It would further seem that if the transferee lost the transfer form or it was destroyed in a fire then the equitable interest he had acquired should justify the court requiring the transferor to execute a fresh transfer.[44]

Where the transferee disclaims the intended trust as soon as he hears of it it has been held that the transfer is not void *ab initio* but is valid until disclaimer when the legal interest, now subject to the trust, revests in the settlor.[45]

IV. The Importance of the Distinction Between Completely and Incompletely Constituted Trusts

Position of volunteers

If a will creates trusts it is immaterial that the beneficiary is a **4–17** volunteer just as it is immaterial that a direct legatee is a volunteer: subject to payment of debts, expenses and liabilities the personal representatives must vest the subject-matter of the gift in the trustees or in the direct legatee.[46]

If an *inter vivos* trust is completely constituted, whether by a transfer to trustees upon trusts declared by the settlor or by the settlor himself declaring trusts of certain of his property, then the beneficiaries under the trust can enforce it despite being volunteers.[47] "Once a trust relationship is established between trustee and beneficiary, the fact that a beneficiary has given no value is irrelevant."[48] If the trust has not been

---

[43] *Re Rose* [1952] Ch. 499 at 510; *Tett v. Phoenix Property Investment Co.* [1984] BCLC 599 at 619, noted (1985) 48 M.L.R. 220; A.J. Oakley, *Constructive Trusts*, (3rd ed.), Chap. 8.

[44] Zines, (1965) 38 Australian L.J. 344; Seddon (1974) 48 A.L.J. 13; Trustee Act 1925, s. 51; *Mascall v. Mascall* (1984) 49 P. & C.R. 119.

[45] *Jones v. Jones* (1874) 31 L.T. 535; *Mallott v. Wilson* [1903] 2 Ch. 494, criticised by P. Matthews [1981] Conv. 141 but it is unlikely that this pragmatic exception will be overruled. Also see *Fletcher v. Fletcher* (1844) 4 Hare 67, *infra*, at para. 4–46.

[46] Until the personal representatives appropriate the assets, having decided recourse to them will not be necessary for payment of debts, etc., or having paid off all debts, etc., the legatees only have a chose in action and not a full equitable interest: see *supra*, at para. 1–122.

[47] *Paul v. Paul* (1882) 20 Ch.D. 742. If the trustees refuse to sue they will be joined as co-defendants: *Harmer v. Armstrong* [1934] 1 Ch. 65; *Parker-Tweedale v. Dunbar Bank plc* [1991] Ch. 26.

[48] Per Lord Browne-Wilkinson is *Choithram International S.A. v. Pagarini* [2001] 2 All E.R. 492, 501.

completely constituted then the "settlor" can only be treated as having promised to make a gift on trust and so if the "beneficiary" is only a volunteer, no consideration having been supplied for the promise, he cannot enforce the promise:[49] "equity will not assist a volunteer." However, if a beneficiary who is not a volunteer seeks to enforce the promise the court will enforce the promise so that the trust becomes completely constituted and then a volunteer beneficiary will be in a position to enforce the now completely constituted trust.[50]

4–18   A person is not a volunteer if he provided value or can bring himself within a marriage consideration: *Pullan v. Koe, infra*, para. 4–42. A promise to create a trust made before and in consideration of marriage is regarded as having been made for value. If the trust is created after marriage and contains a true recital that it was made in pursuance of an ante-nuptial promise to create the trust it will be treated as having been made for value.[51] Within the scope of marriage consideration are the parties to the marriage, their children and remoter issue.[52] Old cases allowing children of a former marriage or a possible later remarriage or illegitimate children to be within the scope of marriage consideration and to enforce trust deed covenants to settle after-acquired property, can now only be supported on the basis that such children's interests were so closely interwoven with the interests of the children of the marriage that the latter could only benefit on terms allowing the former to benefit.[53]

4–19   Once a trust is completely constituted a settlor cannot "undo" it or revoke it on the basis that the beneficiaries are only volunteers[54]—unless he reserved a power to revoke at the time he created the trust. After all, if A makes a birthday or Christmas gift to B, A cannot recover the property if she subsequently falls out with B.

Covenants to settle or transfer property

If A covenants (*i.e.* promises in a deed) to pay £11,000 or transfer 1,000 I.C.I. ordinary shares or transfer his unique fifth dynasty Ming vase to B, a volunteer, then B has a chose in action enforceable at law against A, the deed's formalities supplying the consideration.[55] However, equity does not regard the deed's formalities as consideration and so treats B as a volunteer and "equity will not assist a volunteer." Thus B cannot obtain specific performance of the Ming vase covenant but will have to be satisfied with common law damages, as for the £11,000 covenant or the 1,000 I.C.I. shares covenant, specific performance never being available in such cases where money compensation is itself adequate.[56]

---

[49] *Re Plumptre's Marriage Settlement* [1910] 1 Ch. 609; *Re D'Angibau* (1880) 15 Ch.D. 228.
[50] *Davenport v. Bishopp* (1843) 2 Y. & C.C.C. 451, affd. (1846) 1 Ph. 698.
[51] *Re Holland* [1902] 2 Ch. 360.
[52] *Att.-Gen. v. Jacobs-Smith* [1895] 2 Q.B. 341; *Re Cook's S.T.* [1965] Ch. 902.
[53] *Mackie v. Herbertson* (1884) 9 App.Cas. 303 at 337; *De Mestre v. West* [1891] A.C. 264 at 270; *Rennell v. I.R.C.* [1962] Ch. 329, 341; *Re Cook's S.T.* [1965] Ch. 902 at 914.
[54] *Re Bowden* [1936] Ch. 71; *Re Adlard* [1954] Ch. 29.
[55] *Cannon v. Hartley* [1949] Ch. 213, below, seals being required for deeds until August 1990.
[56] *Harnett v. Yielding* (1805) 2 Sch. & Lef. 549 at 552; *Beswick v. Beswick* [1968] A.C. 58.

Equity, however, will not frustrate a volunteer suing at law[57] and so B may recover as damages £11,000, or the money equivalent of the shares or the Ming vase.

Since B has a chose in action this is property that he himself as **4–20** beneficial owner can settle on trusts, whether declaring himself trustee of it or assigning it to trustees on trusts for C for life, remainder to D.

If A covenants with B to transfer £60,000 to B as trustee with express or implied intent that B shall hold the benefit of the covenant upon trust for C and D if they attain 21 years of age, then A has created a completely constituted trust of the benefit of the covenant held by B as trustee, so this may be enforced by C and D, though volunteers, just as trusts are ordinarily enforceable by volunteers: *Fletcher v. Fletcher,*[58] *infra*, para. 4–46.

If A merely covenants with B to pay money or transfer property[59] to B **4–21** on trust for C and D if they attain 21 the question arises whether A intended to create a trust *of the covenant* for C and D (an immediate equitable gift of the covenant) or intended only to create a trust *of the subject-matter of the covenant* if or when transferred to B (a future equitable gift of such subject-matter). Though volunteers, C and D will be able to enforce their claims if there is a completely constituted trust of the benefit of the covenant,[60] but they will fail if A is treated as merely promising to make a gift to B of the property to which the covenant relates, for a trust will only arise when the property is effectively given to B.[61]

Originally, the courts were quite sympathetic to the claims of the likes **4–22** of C and D, just as originally they were quite ready to find an intention to create a trust in precatory words like "wish," "request," "in full confidence that," etc.[62] In the twentieth century the courts have become

---

[57] *Cannon v. Hartley* [1949] Ch. 213, unless fraud, undue influence or oppressive unconscionable behaviour were involved: *Hart v. O'Connor* [1985] 2 All E.R. 880 at 891–892, *per* Lord Brightman. To succeed at law the volunteer, if not a covenantee under a deed poll, will have to be a party to the *inter partes* deed as well as a covenantee, L.P.A. 1925, s. 56, covering only land: *Beswick v. Beswick* (3:2 majority view) [1968] A.C. 58 at 76, 81, 87, 94, 105.

[58] (1844) 4 Hare 67 where the intention was not express but implied in rather special circumstances at a time when courts were more ready to find an intent to create a trust than they now are. Other examples are *Williamson v. Codrington* (1750) 1 Ves.Sen. 511; *Cox v. Barnard* (1850) 8 Hare 310; *Watson v. Parker* (1843) 6 Beav. 283; *Dowling v. Dowling* [1917] Victoria L.R. 208.

[59] M. W. Friend [1982] Conv. 280 distinguishes between covenants to settle (i) money; (ii) specific and presently existing property other than money and (iii) future or after-acquired property. For (i) a trust of the benefit of the covenant should be inferred simply because A has constituted himself the debtor of B in his capacity as trustee for C. For (ii) no debt is automatically created and B can only obtain nominal damages unless A intended to create a trust of the covenant. A covenant of type (iii) is incapable of being the subject-matter of a trust. His view on type (i) covenants is attractive but for other covenants full damages should always be available, and the covenant and damages relating thereto should be held on trust if A clearly intended such: see Feltham (1982) 98 L.Q.R. 17 and at paras 4–22 to 4–26, *infra*.

[60] *Fletcher v. Fletcher* (1844) 4 Hare 67; *Cox v. Barnard* (1850) 8 Hare 310 at 312, 313; *Milroy v. Lord* (1862) 4 De G.F. & J. 264, 278, and *Re Cavendish-Browne* [1916] W.N. 341, indicate that a covenant for further assurance may assist the court to find an intent to create a trust of a covenant to transfer property or of the covenant for further assurance itself. After all, the benefit of the covenant for further assurance can hardly be held on a resulting trust for the settlor without making the covenant futile and meaningless: see further nn.64 and 90 and text thereto.

[61] *Re Plumptre's Marriage Settlement* [1910] 1 Ch. 609.

[62] See *supra*, at para. 3–70.

reluctant to find an intention to create a completely constituted trust of the benefit of a covenant. This seems quite justifiable. Where in the context of a lengthy trust deed, typically a marriage settlement (wholly enforceable by the issue within the marriage consideration but not by the next-of-kin beneficiaries in default of issue so far as not completely constituted) there is a covenant by the settlor to transfer after-acquired property to the trustees, surely the settlor is only promising to make a gift of such property to the trustees, so that a completely constituted trust enforceable by next-of-kin volunteers will only arise upon the property being gifted to the trustees.[63] It would be most unusual for the settlor to intend to create a trust of the covenant forthwith enforceable by next-of-kin volunteers, so a clear express intention should be required, *e.g.* "to the intent that the benefit of this covenant shall be held by my trustees upon trust for." If a deed merely contains one covenant, *e.g.* "A covenants with B to transfer £10,000 to him on C's twenty-fifth birthday to hold on trust for C if C attains twenty-five" then since A has constituted himself debtor of B in his capacity as trustee for C and the deed would otherwise be futile[64] it seems it should be treated as creating a trust of the covenant as if it read "A covenants with B to transfer £10,000 to him on C's twenty-fifth birthday to the intent that B shall hold the benefit of this covenant on trust for C if he attains twenty-five."

4–23   It has been suggested[65] that since four[66] of the cases where there was held to be no trust of the benefit of the covenant concerned covenants to settle after-acquired property or analogous covenants, such covenants are never capable of being the subject-matter of a trust just as a *spes* or future property cannot be the subject of a trust or of an assignment. While one can *contract* to transfer not-yet-existing property one cannot *give* or transfer or declare a trust of not-yet-existing property. This calls for a digression which will show that future property is non-existent property so there is nothing for a trust to "bite" on, whilst a covenant relating to future property is an existing chose in action[67] which a trust can "bite" on. "A chose in action is no less a chose in action because it is not immediately recoverable by action" as Lord Oliver has made clear.[68]

4–24   Future property must be distinguished from existing vested or contingent rights to obtain property at some future time.[69] While a contingent equitable interest in remainder under a trust (*e.g.* to A for

---

[63] *Re Plumptre's M.S.* [1910] 1 Ch. 609; *Re Pryce* [1917] 1 Ch. 234. Really the settlor intends the covenant to be for the enforceable benefit of his spouse and issue and not the next-of-kin, while any actual transfer is to be for the benefit of all the beneficiaries. On this basis the position should not be affected by the Contracts Rights of Third Parties Act 1999: see s. 1(2) thereof and consider that the contract disappears on completion by execution of the settlement intended to replace the contract, so such covenants (that create specialty debts) seem outside the Act.

[64] *cf. Fletcher v. Fletcher* (1844) 6 Hare 67, *infra*, at para. 4–46. *Ex hypothesi* if B does not hold the benefit of the covenant on trust for C, he must hold it on resulting trust for A, and so cannot sue A for damages for breach of covenant.

[65] W. A. Lee (1969) 85 L.Q.R. 313.

[66] *Re Plumptre's M.S.* [1910] 1 Ch. 609; *Re Pryce* [1917] 1 Ch. 234; *Re Kay's Settlement* [1939] Ch. 329; *Re Cook's S.T.* [1965] Ch. 902, *infra*, at para. 4–64.

[67] L.P.A. 1925, s. 205(1)(xx) defines property as including any thing in action.

[68] *Kwok Chi Leung Karl v. Commissioner of Estate Duty* [1988] 1 W.L.R. 1035, 1040, applied in *Re Landau*, [1997] 3 All E.R. 322, 328.

[69] See *Re Earl of Midleton's W.T.* [1969] 1 Ch. 600 at 607.

life, remainder to B if he attains 30 and is alive on A's death, where B has an assignable, saleable interest) is existing property, examples of future property are the hope of inheriting upon the death of some live person or of receiving property under the exercise of a power of appointment or of acquiring book-debts arising in a business or of acquiring royalties arising on a book. At law an assignment of future property is void as an assignment of nothing,[70] though, if the assignee gave valuable consideration equity will treat the assignment as a contract to assign the property when received if received,[71] the assignment being wholly inoperative if no value was given.[72] Just as an assignment of future property to trustees is void at law and inoperative in equity unless for value, a declaration of trust by S that he holds future property on trust is inoperative unless for value: *Williams v. C.I.R.*, para. 4–79, *infra*. If S covenants to assign future property, when received if received, then equity will not enforce this in favour of volunteers but only in favour of someone who provided value or is within a marriage consideration.[73] However, at common law a covenantee can obtain full damages under a deed poll or, if also a party, where the deed is *inter partes*. Thus, if S in a deed with B covenants to assign to B, a volunteer, any property S may acquire under S's father's will or intestacy B may obtain full damages at common law if S breaks the covenant: *Cannon v. Hartley, infra*, para. 4–53.

In this case since B has the beneficial ownership of a presently existing **4–25** covenant it seems B may declare himself trustee of the covenant for C. It follows that S when entering into the after-acquired property covenant with B should be able intentionally to create a trust of the covenant for C, *e.g.* "I, S, hereby covenant to assign to B any property that I may inherit under my father's will or intestacy to the intent that B shall immediately hold the benefit of this covenant as trustee on trust for C." Since there is a completely constituted trust of the covenant it is then enforceable by C though a volunteer. In *Davenport v. Bishopp*[74] Knight-Bruce V.-C. indicated there could be a completely constituted trust of a covenant to settle after-acquired property *viz.* relating to an indefinite amount at an indefinite future time. Further, in *Lloyd's v. Harper*[75] the Court of Appeal held there was a trust of the benefit of a contractual promise to pay an uncertain amount on an uncertain future date, which is similar to a promise to assign an expectancy, and in *Royal Exchange Assurance v. Hope*[76] Tomlin J. upheld a trust of a contractual promise to pay a sum arising only on a person's death before a certain date which might or might not occur. Thus, a covenant to settle after-acquired

---

[70] *Holroyd v. Marshall* (1862) 10 H.L.Cas. 191 at 220; *Re Tilt* (1896) 74 L.T. 163.
[71] *Ibid.*
[72] *Re Ellenborough* [1903] 1 Ch. 697.
[73] *Ibid.*; *Re Lind* [1915] 2 Ch. 345; *Palette Shoes Pty. Ltd v. Krohn* (1937) CLR 1 at 27; *Re Brooks's S.T.* [1939] Ch. 993, *infra*, at para. 4–67.
[74] (1843) 2 Y. & C.C.C. 451, 460.
[75] (1880) 16 Ch.D. 290.
[76] [1928] Ch. 179.

property or an analogous covenant can itself be the subject-matter of a completely constituted trust,[77] though where the covenant relates to future property there should be a rebuttable presumption that the settlor intended not to create a trust of the covenant (an immediate equitable gift) but only a trust of the property when acquired and transferred to trustees (a future equitable gift of future property).[78]

4–26   The elliptical judgment of Buckley J. in *Re Cook's S.T., infra*, at para. 4–64 is best interpreted as based on the fact that there was no intention to create a trust of the covenant so as to be forthwith enforceable by the children volunteers, but only an intention to create a trust of the subject-matter of the covenant if or when it materialised and was transferred to the trustees for the children; so only then would the children have enforceable equitable rights, though, meanwhile, Sir Herbert would be able to enforce the covenant, having provided consideration therefor. It is considered that *if* the settlor had ended his covenant with the clause, "to the intent that the benefit of this covenant shall forthwith be held by my trustees upon the trusts hereof" Buckley J. surely would have upheld a trust of the covenant even though it related to a sum of money that might never arise. A good draftsman should, of course, expressly state the intention of the settlor.[79] Sir Herbert or, it seems,[80] his executors could have enforced his contractual rights and the proceeds of sale thereby placed in the trustees' hands would then be held on trust for the children volunteers. The trustees could not compel Sir Herbert or his executors to take such action nor could they join him or his executors as co-defendants in an attempt to take advantage of his contractual rights.[81]

Can the covenantee sue?

4–27   If A enters into a deed with B and gratuitously covenants with B to transfer existing or after-acquired property to B, but breaks the covenant, then equity will not assist B as a volunteer but it will not frustrate B from obtaining damages at common law: *Cannon v. Hartley, infra*, at para. 4–53. Similarly, if A covenants with X that he will transfer £20,000 to B on trust for C then A is liable at law only to X if he fails to transfer the money.[82]

4–28   If A covenants with B to transfer property to B on trust for C to the intent that B as trustee will hold the benefit of the covenant on trust for C then there is a completely constituted trust of the benefit of the

---

[77] Further, see (1976) 92 L.Q.R. 427 (Meagher and Lehane) (though not dealing with the resulting trust difficulty where the covenantee sues the settlor); (1975) 91 L.Q.R. 236 (J. L. Barton); D. Wright (1996) 70 Austr. L.J. 911 also dealing with Australian cases where the judges have become readier to infer a trust from an intent to benefit X in circumstances where a trust is the appropriate vehicle to deliver that benefit: *Trident General Insurance Co. Ltd. v. McNiece Bros. Pty. Ltd.* (1988) 165 C.L.R. 107, 121, 147, *Re Australian Elizabethan Theatre Trust* (1991) FCR 491, 503.

[78] See *Re Plumptre's M.S.* [1910] 1 Ch. 609.

[79] Just as where the settlor intends to create a trust of the benefit of a contract: see *supra*, at para. 4–25.

[80] *Beswick v. Beswick* [1968] A.C. 58.

[81] Since Sir Herbert and his executors are under no obligation to the trustees or the children to exercise Sir Herbert's contractual rights, they cannot be forced against their will to become parties to an action concerning such rights.

[82] *Colyear v. Lady Mulgrave* (1836) 2 Keen 81.

covenant.[83] As with all trusts B as trustee is under a duty to get in the trust property and so enforce the covenant so as to benefit C. If B breaks his duty then C can sue A and join B as co-defendant.[84]

If A covenants with B to transfer property to B on trust for C in circumstances where there is no intention to create a trust of the covenant then A is treated as voluntarily promising to make a gift of the property referred to in the covenant, so that C will only have enforceable rights as a volunteer if A actually carries out his promise and transfers the property to B.[85]

However, cannot B sue A for damages for breach of the covenant with **4–29** B[86] and recover full damages[87] to be held on trust for C? The difficulty is that *ex hypothesi* B does not hold the covenant on trust for C so that he must either hold the covenant for his own benefit or by way of resulting trust for A and it is clear that he is not intended to hold the covenant beneficially. If, therefore, the covenant and the right to damages for breach of covenant are held on resulting trust for the settlor, A, then surely so must any damages for breach of covenant.[88] Since A is, under the resulting trust, a *sui juris* absolutely entitled beneficiary he must under the *Saunders v. Vautier* principle[89] be able to terminate such trust and prevent the trustees from launching upon such a pointless exercise as a suit against himself for damages.[90] A further difficulty is that if B could choose to sue and so constitute a trust of the damages this would contravene the principle in *Re Brook's S.T.*, at para. 4–67, *infra* that only a settlor (or his authorised agent) can completely constitute his trust, whilst for the matter to be at the whim of B whether he sues or not, not only puts B in an invidious position, it contravenes the principle that the acts, neglects or defaults of the trustees cannot be allowed to affect the rights of their beneficiaries.[91]

---

[83] *Fletcher v. Fletcher, infra*, at para. 4–46.

[84] *Vandepitte v. Preferred Accident Insurance Co.* [1933] A.C. 70 at 79; *Wills v. Cooke* (1979) 76 Law Soc. Gaz. 706; *Parker-Tweedale v. Dunbar Bank plc (No. 1)* [1991] Ch. 26.

[85] *Re Plumptre's M.S.* [1910] 1 Ch. 609; *Re Pryce* [1917] 1 Ch. 234.

[86] Old cases tend to assume that B could be left to pursue his common law remedy without considering for whom such damages should be held: *Davenport v. Bishopp* (1843) 2 Y. & C.C.C. 451 at 460; *Milroy v. Lord* (1862) 4 De G.F. & J. 264 at 278; *Re Flavell* (1883) 25 Ch.D. 89 at 99; *Re Plumptre's M.S.* [1910] 1 Ch. 609 (damages claim statute-barred).

[87] *Robertson v. Wait* (1853) 8 Exch. 299; *Lamb v. Vice* (1840) 6 M. & W. 862 (J. L. Barton) (1975) 91 L.Q.R. 236, 238–239 though M. W. Friend has pointed out that *Lamb v. Vice* concerned a bond and the bond created a debt: [1982] Conv. 280, 283; surely, at law if a covenantor did not transfer property worth £X to the covenantee then the loss was £X, the position in equity of the beneficiaries being immaterial before the Judicature Act and the position has not changed since then: see D. Goddard [1988] Conv. 19 and *Re Cavendish-Browne's S.T.* [1916] W.N. 341, though this inadequately reported case may be an example of a completely constituted trust of a covenant for further assurance.

[88] *cf.* resulting trust of £500 in *Re Tilt* (1896) 74 L.T. 163.

[89] See at para. 9–152.

[90] See *I.R.C. v. Ingram* [1997] 4 All E.R. 395, 424 where Millett L.J. endorses *Hirachand Punamchand v. Temple* [1911] 2 K.B. 330, where plaintiff money-lenders accepted a lesser sum from the defendant's father in satisfaction of a debt and then sued the defendant for the balance. Vaughan Williams L.J. (at 337) and Fletcher-Moulton L.J. (at 342) held any moneys recovered would be held on trust for the father: "a court of equity would have regarded the plaintiffs as disentitled to sue except as trustees for the father and would have restrained them from suing" (at 342). Also see *Hunt v. Severs* [1994] A.C. 250 where the Lords held that a plaintiff claiming damages for personal injury can recover damages in respect of the care voluntarily provided by X and will hold them as trust for X except where X is also the defendant tortfeasor because it would be pointless and circular if the plaintiff were to recover £y from X which was then to be held in trust for X.

[91] *Fletcher v. Fletcher* (1844) 4 Hare 67 at 78; *Re Richerson* [1892] 1 Ch. 379.

4-30   In practice, if a trustee like B were considering suing A to benefit C he would seek to obtain the leave of the court for, otherwise, he would be at personal risk as to costs if he sued and could not prove his costs were properly incurred.[92] It is plain that the court will direct B that he must not sue for common law damages for breach of covenant where A did not create a completely constituted trust of the benefit of the covenant.[93] Equity thus goes beyond passively not assisting volunteers by positively intervening (which can only be justified on the grounds set out in the penultimate paragraph rather than the basis mouthed by the courts that "equity will not assist a volunteer"). This negative direction is so well-established that there is no need for trustees like B to bother the court: there is a complete defence if any beneficiary like C brings a breach of trust action against B for failing to sue the covenantor for damages.[94]

4-31   If a bold trustee like B did sue (*e.g.* because married to the beneficiary or fully indemnified as to costs by the beneficiary) it is submitted such action would fail on the basis that since the settlor had not created a trust of the voluntary covenant he must *ex hypothesi* have reserved to himself the right, if he chooses, at a later date to constitute a trust of the property referred to in his covenant, having lined up the trustee as his agent to receive the property, but who meanwhile is to hold the covenant on a resulting trust for the settlor, making any action against the settlor groundless.

Only the settlor (or his authorised agent) can constitute a trust

4-32   The settlor must be responsible for the trust property becoming duly vested in the trustees whether he or his duly authorised agent is directly responsible.[95] This is obvious where S has created the "S" settlement and a trustee, Y, whose daughter is life tenant, steals from S a painting (that S has talked about transferring to the trust but as to which S is still undecided) so that it will grace his daughter's lounge very nicely. Equity respects the common law rule that only a donor or his agent can make an effective gift so there is no trust of the painting. The position would be the same if S mistakenly left the painting behind at Y's house, having taken it there merely to show it to Y and his daughter.

4-33   If S in his 1998 voluntary settlement has covenanted to transfer to the trustees of his settlement after-acquired property appointed to S under a special power in the 1976 "T" trust or devolving upon S under T's will or intestacy, and property is appointed to S in 2001 or bequeathed to S on

---

[92] *Re Beddoe* [1893] 1 Ch. 547; *Re Yorke* [1911] 1 Ch. 370. Wherever trustees have reasonable doubts they may at the cost of the trust obtain directions from the court: R.S.C., Ord. 85, para. 2(5).

[93] *Re Pryce* [1917] 1 Ch. 234 (though Eve J.'s reasoning is fallacious in that the Judicature Act fusion did not make defences available to a defendant in Chancery also available to a defendant at law: *Cannon v. Hartley* [1949] Ch. 213; (1960) 76 L.Q.R. 100 at 109, 111 (D. W. Elliot); Meagher Gummow & Lehane's *Equity: Doctrines & Remedies*, para. 234); *Re Kay's Settlement* [1939] Ch. 329, discussed by Romer J., *infra*, at para. 4–54; *Re Cook's S.T.* [1965] Ch. 902.

[94] *Re Ralti's W.T.* [1964] Ch. 288 at 301–302.

[95] *Re Brooks's S.T.* [1939] 1 Ch. 993 (there could hardly be a clearer case for allowing a trustee to constitute the trust if the law were to allow this); *Re Adlard* [1954] Ch. 29; *Milroy v. Lord, supra*, at para. 4–05, last paragraph of quoted judgment of Turner L.J.

T's death in 2001, what happens if, fortuitously, the "S" trustees happen to be trustees of the "T" trust or of T's will, not so unlikely if the "S" trustees are a trust corporation like Barclays Bank Trust Co? Can the trustees of the "T" trust or of T's will claim to hold the appointed or bequeathed property as trustees of the "S" settlement, so completely constituting a trust of such property in the "S" settlement, even though S is himself demanding the appointed or bequeathed property? No, S is entitled to the property free from any trusts since his voluntary obligation is unenforceable and he is in no way responsible for vesting title to the property in the "S" trustees: *Re Brooks' S.T., infra*, para. 4–67.

However, if S in 2001 had authorised the trustees of the "T" trust or **4–34** of T's will to hold the appointed or bequeathed property *qua* trustees of the "S" settlement, the "S" settlement of such property would be completely constituted and so S would not be able to claim the property for himself.[96] Similarly, if S in his 1998 settlement had inserted a clause authorising the "S" trustees to receive property appointed or bequeathed to him and the "S" trustees had received such property from the trustees of the "T" trust or of T's will then the "S" settlement of such property would be completely constituted,[97] so long as the authority had not been revoked before such receipt, such authority being voluntary[98] and therefore unenforceable and revocable.[99]

In *Re Ralli's W.T.*, at para. 4–72, *infra* Buckley J. *obiter* took a view **4–35** inconsistent[1] with the *Re Brooks's S.T.* principle, that case not being cited to him. S voluntarily covenanted in her 1924 settlement to assign her interest in remainder under the "T" trust of 1899 to the "S" trustees as soon as circumstances might admit, but did not do so before she died in 1956. Her interest in remainder fell into possession in 1961 by which time it so happened that X, the sole surviving trustee of S's 1924 settlement (and one of the original trustees thereof) had been appointed by a third party to be a trustee of the 1899 "T" trust and was, in fact, sole surviving trustee of the "T" trust. Buckley J. considered that since X

---

[96] *Re Adlard* [1954] Ch. 29. If S had been deliberately misled by the trustees telling him he was bound to authorise them he might have a claim if he acted promptly after finding out.

[97] *Re Bowden* [1936] Ch. 71, discussed in *Re Ralli's W.T., infra*, at para. 4–72. By L.P.A. s. 53(1)(c) writing is required for the assignment of S's interest under the "T" trust or T's will to the trustees of S's settlement: see *Grey v. I.R.C.* [1960] A.C. 1, as discussed at para. 2–15. Where the same persons are trustees of both trusts it seems implicit in *Re Bowden* and *Re Adlard* [1954] Ch. 29, that there is an exception from the *Grey v. I.R.C.* [1960] A.C. 1 principle discussed at para. 2–15 where the S settlement with S's consent receives S's T property pursuant to an after-acquired property clause (whether general or specifically relating to property appointed under a special power or bequeathed under a will): it is then inequitable for S to claim the interest and so the Revenue will not be able to tax S as if the interest were still his.

[98] Or not otherwise binding as an irrevocable power of attorney or to give effect to a condition contained in a will: *Re Burton's Settlements* [1955] Ch. 82.

[99] *Re Bowden* [1936] Ch. 71, though *cf.* dicta in *Re Burton's Settlements* [1955] Ch. 82 at 104.

[1] Perhaps one can reconcile the cases on the basis that *Re Brooks' S.T.* concerned a live settlor who had changed his mind while in *Re Ralli's W.T.* the settlor had died happy without having changed her mind, having a continuing intention like that in *Re James* [1995] Ch. 449 if such extension of the *Strong v. Bird* principle is justifiable despite the countering view in *Re Gonin* [1979] Ch. 16, *infra*, at para. 4–38 and in *Re Pagarini* [1998/99] 2 O.F.L.R. 1 (B.V.I. Court of Appeal).

had the title to the covenanted property as sole[2] trustee of the 1899 "T"
trust and was also trustee of S's 1924 settlement containing the covenant,
this completely constituted S's voluntary settlement of the assets in
question. However, S was in no way responsible for the assets becoming
vested in X so that according to *Re Brooks's S.T., infra,* at para. 4–67, no
trust of the assets within the 1924 settlement should have arisen. The
position might have been different if S *herself* had appointed X to be
trustee of the "T" trust or if she had appointed X to be her executor, for
she would then have been responsible for X as trustee of her settlement
acquiring title to the covenanted property so impliedly authorising the
position. To appreciate this it is necessary to consider the rule in *Strong
v. Bird.*

The rule in Strong v. Bird

4–36   *Strong v. Bird*[3] decides that in certain circumstances equity should
allow the common law position to prevail where a deceased creditor had
appointed his debtor as his executor. The *common law* treated the
appointment[4] as extinguishing or releasing the debt on the basis[5] "that a
debt was no more than the right to sue for the money owing to the
creditor and that a personal action was discharged when it was suspended by the voluntary act of the person entitled to bring it . . . [the
true basis of the common law rule] lay in the significance attributed to
the voluntary act [of appointing the executor] on the part of the testator.
Once this is recognised the true character of the rule is perceived. It
reflected the presumed intention of the party having the right to bring
the action and was not absolute in its operation." Since administrators
are not chosen by the testator the common law did not treat the court
appointment of the administrator as the release of any debt due to the
deceased from the administrator.[6] In *equity* the debtor (whether the
deceased creditor's executor or administrator) had to account for the
debt to the estate so that such moneys were available to pay off creditors
of the estate or to be distributed amongst the estate beneficiaries.[7]

---

[2] If there had been another trustee, Y, then Y would need to seek the directions of the court. Trustees
hold property jointly and must act unanimously. Since Y is not a trustee-covenantee under the 1924
settlement does not Y hold the assets on trust for S's estate so that he will be liable for breach of trust
if he co-operates with X to transfer the assets to X to be held on the trusts of the 1924 settlement? If
this is so then X will need to co-operate with Y to transfer the assets to S's estate and X will not be
liable to the 1924 settlement beneficiaries since he was never able himself to obtain the assets for the
1924 settlement.

[3] (1874) L.R. 18 Eq. 315, Waters's *Law of Trusts in Canada,* pp. 166–174; Meagher Gummow &
Lehane's *Equity: Doctrines & Remedies,* paras. 2901–2908.

[4] Taking out the grant of probate or becoming an executor *de son tort* by intermeddling sufficed and, it
seems, the appointment itself, though the executor died before taking out probate or intermeddling;
Wankford v. Wankford (1704) 1 Salk. 299; *Re Bourne* [1906] 1 Ch. 697; *Jenkins v. Jenkins* [1928] 2 K.B.
501; *Bone v. Stamp Duties Commissioner* (1974) 132 C.L.R. 38; *Re Applebee* [1891] 3 Ch. 422; *Williams
on Wills* (15th ed.), p. 717.

[5] *Per* Mason J. in *Bone v. Stamp Duties Commissioner* (1974) 132 C.L.R. 38 at 53.

[6] *Wankford v. Wankford* (1704) 1 Salk. 299; *Seagram v. Knight* (1867) 2 Ch. App. 628; *Re Gonin* [1977] 2
All E.R. 720 at 734. Now see Administration of Estates Act 1925, s. 21A added by Limitation
Amendment Act 1980, s. 10.

[7] *Berry v. Usher* (1805) 11 Ves. 87; *Jenkins v. Jenkins* [1928] 2 K.B. 501.

In *Strong v. Bird* the court of equity decided that the common law should prevail, and thus the executor did not have to account for the debt, if the testator had manifested an intent to forgive the debt in his lifetime and this intent had continued till death.

Where a donor intends to make an immediate gift of specific property **4–37** but fails to satisfy the legal formalities for vesting legal title in the intended donee and goes on to appoint the donee his executor and then dies, the appointment itself is no perfect gift at law of the specific property although it is in the case of a release of a debt due from an imperfectly released debtor. However, Neville J. in *Re Stewart*[8] extended *Strong v. Bird*, which *negatively* left the situation as it was at law, since he *positively* treated a gift as effective though the law did not, so perfecting an imperfect gift made by the testator in his lifetime to his wife who was one of his appointed executors. He said:[9]

> "Where a testator has expressed the intention of making a gift of personal estate to one who upon his death becomes his executor, the intention continuing unchanged, the executor is entitled to hold the property for his own benefit. The reasoning is first that the vesting of the property in the executor at the testator's death completes the imperfect gift made in the lifetime and secondly that the intention of the testator to give the beneficial interest to the executor is sufficient to countervail the equity of beneficiaries under the will, the testator having vested the legal estate in the executor."

Re Stewart has been followed many times at first instance[10] and treated **4–38** as good law by the Court of Appeal.[11] In *Re James*[12] Farwell J. extended *Re Stewart* to perfect an imperfect gift of real property made by a donor to his housekeeper who, on the donor's intestacy, had herself appointed by the court one of two administratrices of the deceased donor's estate, thereby obtaining legal title to the house. This extension has been doubted by Walton J. in *Re Gonin*[13] and rejected by the British Virgin Islands' Court of Appeal in *Re Pagarini*:[14] after all, it is the voluntary act of the testator in appointing his debtor as his executor that extinguishes the debt at law, so that the fortuitous appointment by the court of an administrator who was a debtor of the intestate did not extinguish the debt, and so *Strong v. Bird* would have been differently decided if the defendant had been an administrator and not an executor. However, the reasoning in the above-cited dicta of Neville J. suggests that, what,

---

[8] [1908] 2 Ch. 251.
[9] *ibid.* at 254.
[10] *Re Comberback* (1929) 73 Sol. J. 403; *Re James* [1935] Ch. 449; *Re Nelson* (1967) 91 Sol. J. 533: see also *Re Ralli's W.T.* [1964] Ch. 288; *Re Gonin* [1979] Ch. 16.
[11] *Re Freeland* [1952] Ch. 110, counsel unreservedly accepting *Re Stewart*.
[12] [1935] Ch. 449.
[13] [1979] Ch. 16. The extension is acceptable to P. V. Baker (1977) 93 L.Q.R. 485 and G. Kodilinye [1982] Conv. 14.
[14] [1998/99] 2 O.F.L.R. 1.

perhaps, should more aptly be known as the rule in *Re Stewart* is only concerned with the acquisition of legal title like the *tabula in naufragio* doctrine.[15]

4-39 What is traditionally known as the rule in *Strong v. Bird* has now developed into the principle that an imperfect *immediate*[16] gift of specific[17] existing[18] real or personal property[19] will be perfected if the intended donee is appointed the testator's executor or administrator alone or with others so long as the intention to make the gift continues unchanged till the testator's death.[20] The gift is perfected *vis-à-vis* those beneficially entitled to the deceased's estate but probably not *vis-à-vis* creditors since a common law extinguishment of a debt by appointment of the debtor as executor did not avail against creditors.[21]

Where the imperfect gift is to trustees and one (or more) of them is appointed the donor's executor this should perfect the trust, the equity of the beneficiaries under the intended trust of the property being sufficient to countervail the equity of the testamentary residuary beneficiaries.[22]

4-40 With voluntary covenants, where there is no completely constituted trust of such covenants, difficulties arise in applying the rule in *Strong v. Bird* where one of the trustee-covenantees is appointed executor of the deceased settlor. First, the rule requires separate specific identifiable property[23] so as to be incapable of applying where S has voluntarily covenanted to pay £20,000 or transfer shares to the value of £20,000. Secondly, *ex hypothesi* S has neither transferred the property nor completely constituted a trust of the covenant itself and so does not have "a present intention to make an immediate gift"[24] of the subject-matter, if indeed the covenant does not expressly refer to transferring the subject-matter at a future date. The covenant is thus "an announcement of what a man intends to do in the future and is not intended by him as a gift in the present"[25] so as not to comply with the requirement of a present intention to make an immediate gift. Query whether this requirement is logically justifiable since once the pass has been sold by

---

[15] This doctrine confers priority upon later equitable interests whose owners somehow manage to obtain the legal estate: it was particularly significant before 1926 and still can have some effect: Megarry & Wade, *Law of Real Property* (6th ed.) 19–244 *McCarthy & Stone Ltd v. Hodge* [1971] 1 W.L.R. 1547. *MacMillan v. Bishopsgate Investment Management (No. 3)* [1995] 3 All E.R. 747 at 770–773.

[16] *Re Innes* [1910] 1 Ch. 188; *Re Freeland* [1952] Ch. 110; *Re Gonin* [1979] Ch. 16; *Re Pink* [1912] 2 Ch. 528 at 536–539; *Simpson v. Simpson* [1992] 1 F.L.R. 423. *Re Goff* (1914) 111 L.T. 34 is out of line since the donor only intended to forgive the debt if the donor predeceased the donee.

[17] *Re Innes* [1910] 1 Ch. 188 at 193.

[18] *Morton v. Brighouse* [1927] 1 D.L.R. 1009.

[19] *Re James* [1935] Ch. 449.

[20] It seems contrary expressions before death may be ignored if the intent to make the imperfect gift is confirmed in the will: *Re Stoneham* [1919] 1 Ch. 149 at 158. For cases on contrary intention see *Re Freeland* [1952] Ch. 110; *Re Eiser's W.T.* [1937] 1 All E.R. 244; *Re Wale* [1956] 1 W.L.R. 1346; *Morton v. Brighouse* [1927] 1 D.L.R. 1009 (property imperfectly given to X subsequently specifically bequeathed to Y).

[21] *Bone v. Stamp Duties Comr.* (1974) 132 C.L.R. 38.

[22] *Re Ralli's W.T.* [1964] Ch. 288.

[23] *Re Innes* [1910] 1 Ch. 188.

[24] *Re Freeland* [1952] Ch. 110 at 118, the Court of Appeal assuming this to be good law since counsel did not argue that *Re Innes* was wrong on this point.

[25] *Re Innes* [1910] 1 Ch. 188 at 193.

equity assisting a volunteer and perfecting an imperfect immediate gift it seems inconsistent for equity to refrain from assisting a volunteer under an imperfect gift of specific property to be made at a future time (other than the donor's death when testamentary formalities must be complied with[26]) once that time has arrived.[27] Thirdly, it may be difficult to show that the settlor's intention continued unchanged till death.

If S makes an imperfect gift to trustees of his settlement and dies, his **4–41** intention to make the gift continuing unchanged till his death, and his executor, mistakenly believing himself legally bound to perfect the gift, does so, Astbury J. opined[28] this would be effective against the beneficiaries entitled under S's will. Can this really be so when an executor does not have as much freedom as the deceased to release debts and perfect gifts since the executor holds the estate under fiduciary obligations owed to the will beneficiaries and not as absolute owner like the deceased?[29] Would *Strong v. Bird* not have been decided differently (and the debtor remain accountable in equity if the executor could not personally satisfy all creditors' claims) if the debtor had not been appointed executor but whoever was the executor had released the debt?

PULLAN V. KOE

Chancery Division [1913] 1 Ch. 9; 82 L.J. Ch. 37.

A marriage settlement of 1859 contained a covenant by the husband and wife **4–42** to settle the wife's after-acquired property of the value of £100 or upwards.

In 1879 the wife received £285 and paid it into her husband's banking account, on which she had power to draw. Part of it was shortly after invested in two bearer bonds which remained at the bank till the husband's death in 1909 and were now in his executors' possession:

Held, that the moment the wife received the £285 it was specifically bound by the covenant[30] and was consequently subject in equity to a trust enforceable in favour of all persons within the marriage consideration, and therefore, the trustees were entitled to follow and claim the bonds as trust property, though their legal remedy on the covenant was statute-barred.

SWINFEN EADY J. (in a reserved judgment): "The defence of laches and acquiescence was given up by the defendants, but they insisted that, although

---

[26] *Re Pink* [1912] 2 Ch. 528 at 536, 538–539.
[27] In *Re Ralli's W.T.* [1964] Ch. 288, Buckley J. assumed a covenant to transfer property as soon as circumstances would admit could come within the rule in *Strong v. Bird*. See also *Re Goff* (1914) 111 L.T. 34.
[28] *Carter v. Hungerford* [1917] 1 Ch. 260 at 273–274.
[29] *Stamp Duties Comr. v. Livingstone* [1965] A.C. 694; *Re Diplock* [1948] Ch. 465.
[30] Where consideration has been provided (so that equitable remedies are not precluded by the maxim "Equity will not assist a volunteer") and specific ascertained sums of money come into the hands of X, who is bound to hold them on particular trusts, "Equity looks on as done that which ought to be done", so treating the money as forthwith subject to the relevant trusts: *Pullan v. Koe* [1913] 1 Ch. 9; *Re Lind* [1915] 2 Ch. 345; *Re Gillott's Settlements* [1934] Ch. 97; *Palette Shoes Pty. Ltd v. Krohn* (1937) C.L.R. 1 at 27, However, if X covenants for value or contracts that X will hold, or transfer to trustees, £10,000 of his money on trust for certain beneficiaries the lack of an ascertained segregated £10,000 ousts any equitable remedy if common law damages are inadequate: *Stone v. Stone* (1869) 5 Ch.App. 74; *MacJordan Construction Ltd v. Brookmount Erostin Ltd* [1992] BCLC 350.

they still retained the bonds, they were under no liability to the plaintiffs. They put their case in this way—that the plaintiff trustees could not follow the bonds into their hands, that the only liability of the husband was upon his covenant, and the claim of the trustees was for damages only, and that as this claim accrued in 1879 it was long since barred by the Statutes of Limitation. . . .

4–43   "[The husband] received the bonds, purchased with his wife's money, with full notice of the trusts of the settlement, and knowing that the £285 and the bonds purchased with part of it were bound by the covenant. The trustees having traced the property into his hands are entitled to claim it from his executors.

"It was contended that the bonds never in fact became trust property, as both the wife and husband were only liable in damages for breach of covenant, and that the case was different from cases where property which has once admittedly become subject to the trusts of an instrument has been improperly dealt with, and is sought to be recovered. In my opinion as soon as the £285 was paid to the wife it became in equity bound by and subject to the trusts of the settlement. The trustees could have claimed that particular sum, could have obtained at once the appointment of a receiver of it, if they could have shown a case of jeopardy, and, if it had been invested and the investment could be traced, could have followed the money and claimed the investment.

4–44   "This point was dealt with by Jessel M.R. in *Smith v. Lucas*,[31] where he said: 'What is the effect of such a covenant in equity? It has been said that the effect in equity of the covenant of the wife, as far as she is concerned, is that it does not affect her personally, but that it binds the property: that is to say, it binds the property under the doctrine of equity that that is to be considered as done which ought to be done. That is in the nature of specific performance of the contract no doubt. If therefore, this is a covenant to settle the future-acquired property of the wife, and nothing more is done by her, the covenant will bind the property.'

"Again in *Collyer v. Isaacs*[32] Jessel M.R. said: 'A man can contract to assign property which is to come into existence in the future, and when it has come into existence, equity, treating as done that which ought to be done, fastens upon that property, and the contract to assign thus becomes a complete assignment. If a person contract for value, *e.g.* in this marriage settlement, to settle all such real estate as his father shall leave him by will, or purports actually to convey by the deed all such real estate, the effect is the same. It is a contract for value which will bind the property if the father leaves any property to his son.'

4–45   "Again the trustees are entitled to come into a Court of Equity to enforce a contract to create a trust, contained in a marriage settlement, for the benefit of the wife and the issue of the marriage, all of whom are within the marriage consideration. The husband covenanted that he and his heirs, executors, and administrators should, as soon as circumstances would admit, convey, assign, and surrender to the trustees the real or personal property to which his wife should become beneficially entitled. The trustees are entitled to have that covenant specifically enforced by a Court of Equity. In *Re D'Angibau*[33] and in *Re Plumptre's Marriage Settlement*[34] it was held that the Court would not interfere in favour of volunteers, not within the marriage consideration, but here the plaintiffs are the contracting parties and the object of the proceeding is to benefit the wife and issue of the marriage."

---

[31] 18 Ch.D. 531 at 543.
[32] 19 Ch.D. 342 at 351.
[33] (1880) 15 Ch.D. 228 at 242.
[34] [1910] 1 Ch. 609 at 616.

FLETCHER V. FLETCHER

Vice-Chancellor (1844) 4 Hare 67; 14 L.J.Ch. 66; 8 Jur.(O.S.) 1040.

The bill was filed by Jacob, a natural son of the testator, Ellis Fletcher, **4–46** demanding payment by the defendants, who were the testator's executors of the sum of £60,000 from the assets (and interest calculated from a date 12 months after the death of the testator). The claim was founded upon a voluntary deed executed by the testator some years before his death and discovered for the first time some years after his death. The deed had been retained by the testator in his own possession and, so far as appeared, he had not communicated its contents either to the trustees or to the beneficiaries.

The indenture in question was made on September 1, 1829, between Ellis Fletcher and five trustees therein named; it recited that Ellis Fletcher, being desirous of making provision for his two natural sons, John and Jacob, thereby covenanted for himself, his heirs, executors and administrators, with the said trustees, their heirs, executors, administrators and assigns, that if either or both of the sons should survive the testator, the latter's heirs, etc., would pay to the trustee, their heirs, etc., the sum of £60,000 within twelve months of the death of the testator to be held upon the following trusts: if both sons were alive at the testator's death and attained the age of twenty-one the trustees were to hold the money on trust for them both in equal shares as tenants in common; if only one son fulfilled these conditions the money was to be held on trust for him alone. In the event of either or both of the sons surviving the testator but neither attaining the age of twenty-one, the money was to fall back into residue.

Both sons survived the testator but John died without attaining twenty-one. **4–47** Jacob accordingly claimed that he had become solely entitled to the £60,000 and interest under the indenture of covenant.

The executors admitted assets. The surviving trustees said that they had not accepted or acted in the trusts of the indenture; and they declined to accept or act in such trusts.

At the close of the argument, Wigram V.-C. said: "It is not denied that, if the plaintiff in this case had brought an action in the name of the trustees, he might have recovered the money; and it is not suggested that, if the trustees had simply allowed their name to be used in the action, their conduct could have been impeached. There are two classes of cases, one of which is in favour of, and the other, if applicable, against, the plaintiff's claim. The question is to which of the two classes it belongs.

"In trying the equitable question I shall assume the validity of the instrument **4–48** at law. If there was any doubt of that it would be reasonable to allow the plaintiff to try the right by suing in the name of the surviving trustee. The first proposition relied upon against the claim in equity was that equity will not interfere in favour of a volunteer. That proposition, though true in many cases, has been too largely stated. A court of equity, for example, will not, in favour of a volunteer, enforce the performance of a contract *in specie*. That it will, however, sometimes act in favour of a volunteer is proved by the common case of a volunteer on a bond who may prove his bond against the assets. Again, where the relation of trustee and *cestui que trust* is constituted, as where property is transferred from the author of the trust into the name of a trustee, so that he has lost all power of disposition over it, and the transaction is complete as regards him, the trustee, having accepted the trust, cannot say he holds it, except for the purposes of the trust; and the court will enforce the trust at the suit of a volunteer. According to the authorities I cannot, I admit, do anything to perfect the liability of the author of the trust if it is not already perfect. The covenant, however, is already perfect. The covenantor is liable at law, and the court is not called upon to do any act to perfect it. One question made in argument has been whether there can be a trust of a covenant the benefit of which shall belong to a third party; but I cannot think there is any difficulty in that. Suppose, in the case of a personal covenant to pay a certain annual sum for the benefit of a third person, the trustee were to bring an action against the covenantor; would he be afterwards allowed to say he was not a trustee? If he cannot do so after once acknowledging the trust, then there is a case in which there is a trust of a covenant for another. In the case of *Clough v. Lambert*[35] the question arose; the point does not appear to have been taken during the argument, but the Vice-Chancellor was of opinion that the covenant bound the party; that the *cestui que trust* was entitled to the benefit of it; and that the mere intervention of a trustee made no difference. The proposition, therefore, that in no case can there be a trust of a covenant is clearly too large, and the real question is whether the relation of trustee and *cestui que trust* is established in the present case.

4–49   WIGRAM V.-C.: "The objections made to the relief sought by the plaintiff under the covenant in the trust deed of September 1829 were three: first, that the covenant was voluntary; secondly, that it was executory; and, thirdly, that it was testamentary, and had not been proved as a will. For the purpose of considering these objections I shall first assume that the surviving trustee of the deed of September 1829 might recover upon the covenant at law; and upon that assumption the only questions will be, first, whether I shall assist the plaintiff in this suit so far as to allow him the use of the name of the surviving trustee, upon the latter being indemnified, a course which the trustee does not object to if the court shall direct it; and, secondly, whether I shall further facilitate the plaintiff's proceeding at law by ordering the production of the deed of covenant for the purposes of the trial.

4–50   "Now, with regard to the first objection, for the reasons which I mentioned at the close of the argument, I think the proposition insisted upon, that because the covenant was voluntary therefore the plaintiff could not recover in equity, was too broadly stated. I referred to the case of a volunteer by specialty claiming payment out of assets, and to the case of one claiming under a voluntary trust, where a fund has been transferred. The rule against relief to volunteers cannot, I conceive, in a case like that before me, be stated higher than this, that a court of equity will not, in favour of a volunteer, give to a deed any effect beyond what the law will give to it. But if the author of the deed has subjected himself to a liability at law, and the legal liability comes regularly to be enforced in equity, as in the cases before referred to, the observation that the claimant is a volunteer is of no value in favour of those who represent the author of the deed. If, therefore, the plaintiff himself were the covenantee,[36] so that he could bring the action in his own name, if follows, from what I have said, that in my opinion he might enforce payment out of the assets of the covenantor in this case. Then, does the interposition of the trustee of this covenant make any difference? I think it does not. Upon this part of the case I have asked myself the question, proposed by Vice-Chancellor Knight-Bruce in *Davenport v. Bishopp*,[37] whether, if the surviving

---

[35] (1839) 10 Sim. 174.
[36] A case of this type is *Cannon v. Hartley* [1949] Ch. 213.
[37] (1843) 2 Y. & C.C.C. 451.

trustee chose to sue, there would be any equity on the part of the estate to restrain him from doing so,[38] or, which is the same question, in principle, whether in a case in which the author of the deed has conferred no discretion on the trustees (upon which supposition the estate is liable at law) the right of the plaintiff is to depend upon the caprice of the trustee, and to be kept in suspense until the Statute of Limitations might become a bar to an action by the trustee.

Or, in the case of new trustees being appointed (perhaps by the plaintiff **4–51** himself, there being a power to appoint new trustees), supposing his own nominees to be willing to sue, the other trustees might refuse to sue. I think the answer to these and like questions must be in the negative. The testator has bound himself absolutely. There is a debt created and existing. I give no assistance against the testator. I only deal with him as he has dealt by himself, and, if in such a case the trustee will not sue without the sanction of the court, I think it is right to allow the *cestui que trust* to sue for himself, in the name of the trustee, either at law, or in this court, as the case may require. The rights of the parties cannot depend upon mere accident and caprice. Having come to this conclusion upon abstract reasoning, it was satisfactory to me to find that this view of the case is not only consistent with, but is supported by, the cases of *Clough v. Lambert*[39] and *Williamson v. Codrington*.[40] If the case, therefore, depended simply upon the covenant being voluntary my opinion is that the plaintiff would be entitled to use the name of the trustee at law, or to recover the money in this court, if it were unnecessary to have the right decided at law, and, where the legal right is clear, to have the use of the deed, if that use is material.

"The second question is whether, taking the covenant to be executory, the title **4–52** of the plaintiff to relief is affected by that circumstance. The question is answered by what I have already said. Its being executory makes no difference, whether the party seeks to recover at law in the name of the trustee, or against the assets in this court.

"The third question is whether the plaintiff is precluded from relief in this court, on the ground suggested that this is a testamentary paper . . . There is, therefore, no ground for the argument that the interest is testamentary.

"The only other question arises from the circumstances of the instrument having been kept in the possession of the party—does that affect its legal validity? In the case of *Dillon v. Coppin*[41] I had occasion to consider that subject, and I took pains to collect the cases upon it. The case of *Doe v. Knight*[42] shows that, if an instrument is sealed and delivered, the retainer of it by the party in his possession does not prevent it from taking effect. No doubt the intention of the parties is often disappointed by holding them to be bound by deeds which they have kept back, but such unquestionably is the law . . .

"Declare that the deed of September 1, 1829, constitutes a debt at law, and decree payment of the principal and interest on the same to the plaintiff."

CANNON V. HARTLEY

Chancery Division [1949] Ch. 213.

By a deed of separation made on January 23, 1941, between the defendant of **4–53** the first part, his wife of the second part and the plaintiff, their daughter, of the third part, the defendant covenanted, *inter alia*, "If and whenever during the

---

[38] See (1960) 76 L.Q.R. 100 (Elliott).
[39] (1839) 10 Sim. 174.
[40] (1750) 1 Ves.Sen. 511.
[41] (1839) 4 Myl. & Cr. 647 at 660.
[42] (1826) 5 B. & C. 671.

lifetime of the wife or the daughter the husband shall become entitled . . . under
the will or codicil . . . of either of his parents . . . to any money or property
exceeding in net amount or value £1,000, he will forthwith at his own expense . . .
settle one-half of such money or property upon trust for himself for life and for
the wife for life after his death and subject thereto in trust for the daughter
absolutely . . ." In 1944 the defendant became entitled, subject to a prior life
interest therein of his mother, to a quarter share of a fund of approximately
£50,000. The defendant's wife died in 1946. The defendant refused to execute a
settlement in accordance with the said covenant. On a claim by the plaintiff for
damages for breach of the covenant:

Held, that the plaintiff was entitled to damages.

4–54   ROMER J.: "It has been argued on behalf of the defendant that the plaintiff,
not having given any consideration for this covenant by her father, is not only
unable to apply to a court of equity for the enforcement of the covenant by way
of specific performance, but that she is also disqualified from suing at common
law for damages for breach of the covenant.

"It is, of course, well established that in such a case as this a volunteer cannot
come to a court of equity and ask for relief which is peculiar to the jurisdiction of
equity, *viz*. Specific performance; but for my part I thought it was reasonably
clear that, the document being under seal, the covenantee's claim for damages
would be entertained, and that is still my belief . . .

"But the defendant relies upon some observations made by Eve J. in *Re
Pryce*,[43] and on the subsequent decision of Simonds J. in *Re Kay's Settlement*.[44] I
think the point of the observations of Eve J. in *Re Pryce* appear sufficiently in *Re
Kay's Settlement*. The headnote of that case is: 'A voluntary settlement executed
by a spinster contained a covenant in the usual form to settle any after-acquired
property, with certain exceptions. The settlor afterwards married and had three
children. Having become entitled under a will to a legacy and a share of residue
which fell within the covenant, and a share in an appointed fund, she was asked
by the trustees of the settlement to settle this property, but refused to do so:
Held, on an application by the trustees for directions, that the children, being
volunteers, had no right to enforce the covenant, and therefore the trustees
ought to be directed not to take any proceedings to enforce the covenant, by
action for damages for breach or otherwise.'

4–55   "Simonds J., after referring to the facts of the case, said at 338:

'It is in these circumstances that the trustees have issued this summons,
making as parties to it, first, the settlor herself and, secondly, her infant
children, who are beneficiaries under the settlement. But, be it observed,
though beneficiaries, her children are, for the purpose of this settlement,
to be regarded as volunteers, there being no marriage consideration, which
would have entitled them to sue, though they are parties to this application. The trustees asked whether, in the event which has happened of
the settlor having become entitled to certain property, they should take
proceedings against her to compel performance of the covenant or to
recover damages on her failure to implement it.

4–56   'I am bound to say that that does not seem to me to be a very happy
form of proceeding, though perhaps it is difficult to see how else the
trustees should act. It is to be observed that one of the persons made a

---

43 [1917] 1 Ch. 234.
44 [1939] Ch. 329 at 338.

party is the very person as to whom the trustees ask the question whether she should be sued. She, the settlor, has appeared by Mr. Evershed and has contended, as she was entitled to contend, that the only question before the court was whether the trustees ought to be directed to take such proceedings; that is to say, she contended that the only question before the court was precisely that question which Eve J. had to deal with in *Re Pryce*. She has said that the question before me is not primarily whether, if she were sued, such an action would succeed (as to which she might have a defence, I know not what), but whether, in the circumstances as they are stated to the court, the trustees ought to be directed to take proceedings against her.

'As to that, the argument before me has been, on behalf of the children **4–57** of the marriage, beneficiaries under the settlement, that, although it is conceded that the trustees could not successfully take proceedings for specific performance of the agreements contained in the settlement, yet they could successfully, and ought to be directed to, take proceedings at law to recover damages for the non-observance of the agreements contained in the settlement, first, the covenant for further assurance of the appointed share of the first-mentioned £20,000 and, secondly, the covenant with regard to the after-acquired property. In the circumstances I must say that I felt considerable sympathy for the argument which was put before me by Mr. Winterbotham on behalf of the children, that there was, at any rate, on the evidence before the court today, no reason why the trustees should not be directed to take proceedings to recover what damages might be recoverable at law for breach of the agreements entered into by the settlor in her settlement. But on a consideration of *Re Pryce* it seemed to me that so far as this court was concerned the matter was concluded and that I ought not to give any directions to the trustees to take the suggested proceedings.

'In *Re Pryce* the circumstances appear to me to have been in no wise **4–58** different from those which obtain in the case which I have to consider. In that case there was a marriage settlement made in 1887. It contained a covenant to settle the wife's after-acquired property. In 1904 there was a deed of gift under which certain interests in reversion belonging to the husband were assured by him absolutely to his wife. The husband was also entitled to a one-third share in certain sums appointed to him by the will of his father in exercise of a special power of appointment contained in a deed of family arrangements. The share of the £9,000 fell into possession in 1891 on the death of his father, and was paid to him, unknown to the trustees of his marriage settlement, and spent. The interests given by the husband to the wife and his share of the £4,700 came into possession in 1916 on the death of the husband's mother, and were outstanding in the trustees of his parents' settlement and of the deed of family arrangement respectively. The husband died in 1907, and there was no issue of the marriage. Subject to his widow's life interest in both funds, the ultimate residue of the wife's fund was held in trust for her statutory next-of-kin, and the husband's fund was held in trust for him absolutely. The widow was also tenant for life under her husband's will. The trustees of the marriage settlement in that case took out a summons 'to have it determined whether these interests and funds were caught by the provisions of the settlement, and, if so, whether they should take proceedings to enforce them.' In those proceedings, apparently, the plaintiffs were the trustees of the **4–59** marriage settlement, and the only defendant appears to have been the widow of the settlor; that is to say, there were no other parties to the proceedings to whose beneficial interest it was to argue in favour of the enforceability and enforcement of the covenant, but the trustees no doubt argued in favour of their interests, as it was their duty to do. Eve J., in a considered judgment, held that although the interests to which I have referred were caught by the covenant of the wife and the agreement by the husband respectively, yet the trustees ought not to take any steps to recover any of them. In the case of the wife's fund he said that her next of kin were volunteers, who could neither maintain an action to enforce the covenant nor for damages for breach of it, and that the court would not give them by indirect means what they could not obtain by direct procedure; therefore he declined to direct the trustees to take proceedings either to have the covenant specifically enforced or to recover damages at law. Many of the cases which have been cited to me, though not

4–60   all of them apparently, were cited to him, and after deciding that no steps should be taken to enforce specific performance of the covenant he used these words: "The position of the wife's fund is somewhat different, in that her next of kin would be entitled to it on her death; but they are volunteers, and although the court would probably compel fulfilment of the contract to settle at the instance of any persons within the marriage consideration—see, *per* Cotton L.J. in *Re D'Angibau*[45] and in their favour will treat the outstanding property as subjected to an enforceable trust— *Pullan v. Koe*[46] "volunteers have no right whatever to obtain specific performance of a mere covenant which has remained as a covenant and has never been performed": see, *per* James L.J. in *Re D'Angibau*. Nor could damages be awarded either in this court, or, I apprehend, at law,[47] where, since the Judicature Act, 1873, the same defences would be available to the defendant as would be raised in an action brought in this court for specific performance or damages."

4–61   "That is the exact point which has been urged on me with great insistence by Mr. Winterbotham. Whatever sympathy I might feel for his argument, I am not justified in departing in any way from this decision, which is now twenty-one years old. The learned judge went on: "In these circumstances, seeing that the next-of-kin could neither maintain an action to enforce the covenant nor for damages for breach of it, and that the settlement is not a declaration of trust constituting the relationship of trustee and cestui que trust between the defendant and the next of kin, in which case effect could be given to the trusts even in favour of volunteers, but is a mere voluntary contract to create a trust, ought the court now for the sole benefit of these volunteers to direct the trustees to take proceedings to enforce the defendant's covenant? I think it ought not; to do so would be to give the next of kin by indirect means relief they cannot obtain by any direct procedure, and would in effect be enforcing the settlement as against the defendant's legal right to payment and transfer from the trustees of the parents' marriage settlement." It is true that in those last words the learned judge does not specifically refer to an action for damages, but it is clear that he has in his mind directions both with regard

---

[45] (1880) 5 Ch.D. 228 at 242, 246.
[46] [1913] 1 Ch. 9.
[47] But see *supra* at para. 4–30, n. 93.

to an action for specific performance and an action to recover damages at law—or, now, in this court. In those circumstances it appears to me that I must follow the learned judge's decision and I must direct the trustees not to take any steps either to compel performance of the covenant or to recover damages through her failure to implement it."

"Now it appears to me [this is Romer J. after the lengthy citation of Simonds **4–62** J.] that neither in *Re Pryce*[48] nor in *Re Kay's Settlement*[49] is any authority for the proposition which has been submitted to me on behalf of the defendant. In neither case were the claimants parties to the settlement in question, nor were they within the consideration of the deed. When volunteers were referred to in *Re Pryce* it seems to me that what Eve J. intended to say was that they were not within the class of non-parties, if I may use that expression, to whom Cotton L.J. recognised in *Re D'Angibau*[50] that the court would afford assistance. In the present case the plaintiff, although a volunteer, is not only a party to the deed of separation but is also a direct covenantee under the very covenant upon which she is suing. She does not require the assistance of the court to enforce the covenant for she has a legal right herself to enforce it. She is not asking for equitable relief but for damages at common law for breach of covenant.

"For my part, I am quite unable to regard in *Re Pryce*, which was a different **4–63** case dealing with totally different circumstances, or anything which Eve J. said therein, as amounting to an authority negativing the plaintiff's right to sue in the present case. I think that what Eve J. was pointing out in *Re Pryce* was that the next of kin who were seeking to get an indirect benefit had no right to come to a court of equity because they were not parties to the deed and were not within the consideration of the deed and, similarly, they would have no right to proceed at common law by an action for damages, as the court of common law would not entertain a suit at the instance of volunteers who were not parties to the deed which was sought to be enforced, any more than the court of equity would entertain such a suit.

"I shall accordingly direct an inquiry as to the damages sustained by the plaintiff for breach by the defendant of the covenant with the plaintiff contained in clause 7 of the deed of separation and the plaintiff will have her costs of the action."

RE COOK'S S.T.

Chancery Division [1965] Ch. 902; [1965] 2 W.L.R. 179; [1964] 3 All E.R. 898.

Sir Herbert as life tenant and his son, Sir Francis, as remainderman agreed **4–64** that certain settled property (including a Rembrandt) should become Sir Francis's absolutely subject to Sir Francis resettling some of the property (not the Rembrandt) and covenanting with the trustees of the resettlement that in case any of certain pictures (including the Rembrandt) should be sold during Sir Francis's lifetime the net proceeds of sale should be paid over to the trustees to be held by them on the resettlement trusts in favour of Sir Francis's children. A settlement was executed pursuant to this contract.

---

[48] [1917] 1 Ch. 234.
[49] [1939] Ch. 329.
[50] (1880) 15 Ch. D. 228.

Sir Francis gave the Rembrandt to his wife who desired to sell it. The trustees, therefore, took out a summons as to whether or not upon any sale of the Rembrandt the trustees would be obliged to take steps to enforce the covenant.

Held, (1) Since Sir Francis's children were volunteers they could not enforce the covenant so that the trustees would be directed not to enforce the covenant on the principles in *Re Pryce*[51] and *Re Kay*[52] but (2) that in any case the covenant operated only upon a sale by Sir Francis and not by his wife.

As to (1):

4–65   BUCKLEY J.: ". . . Counsel appearing for Sir Francis submitted that as a matter of law the covenant . . . is not enforceable against him by the trustees of the settlement . . . [He] submits that the covenant was a voluntary and executory contract to make a settlement in a future event and was not a settlement of a covenant to pay a sum of money to the trustees. He further submits that, as regards the covenant, all the beneficiaries under the settlement are volunteers with the consequence that not only should the court not direct the trustees to take proceedings on the covenant but also that it should positively direct them not to take proceedings. He relies on *Re Pryce* and *Re Kay's Settlement*.

4–66   "Counsel for the second and third defendants have contended that, on the true view of the facts, there was an immediate settlement of the obligation created by the covenant, and not merely a covenant to settle something in the future. It was said, as counsel for the second defendant put it, that, by the agreement, Sir Herbert bought the rights arising under the covenant for the benefit of the cestuis que trust under the settlement and that, the covenant being made in favour of the trustees, these rights became assets of the trust. He relied on *Fletcher v. Fletcher*;[53] *Williamson v. Codrington*[54] and *Re Cavendish Browne's Settlement Trusts*.[55] I am not able to accept this argument. The covenant with which I am concerned did not, in my opinion, create a debt enforceable at law, that is to say, a property right, which, although to bear fruit only in the future and on a contingency, was capable of being made the subject of an immediate trust, as was held to be the case in *Fletcher v. Fletcher*. Nor is this covenant associated with property which was the subject of an immediate trust, as in *Williamson v. Codrington*. Nor did the covenant relate to property which then belonged to the covenantor, as in *Re Cavendish Browne's Settlement Trusts*. In contrast to all these cases, this covenant on its true construction is, in my opinion, an executory contract to settle a particular fund or particular funds of money which at the date of the covenant did not exist and which might never come into existence. It is analogous to a covenant to settle an expectation or to settle after-acquired property. The case, in my judgment, involves the law of contract, not the law of trusts . . .

"Accordingly, the second and third defendants are not in my judgment entitled to require the trustees to take proceedings to enforce the covenant, even if it is capable of being construed in a manner favourable to them."

RE BROOKS' SETTLEMENT TRUSTS

Chancery Division [1939] 1 Ch. 993.

---

[51] [1917] 1 Ch. 234.
[52] [1939] Ch. 329.
[53] (1844) 4 Hare 67.
[54] (1750) 1 Ves.Sen. 511.
[55] (1916) 61 S.J. 27.

By the terms of a marriage settlement the income of the settled fund was **4–67** directed to be paid to the wife during her life and the fund was to be held in trust for such of her issue as she might by deed or will appoint; in default of any appointment the fund was to be held in trust for all her children who being sons should attain the age of twenty-one years or being daughters should attain that age or marry in equal shares. In 1929 one of her children. A.T., executed a voluntary settlement whereby he assigned to Lloyds Bank as trustees "all the part or share, parts or shares and other interest whether vested or contingent to which the settlor is now or may hereafter become entitled whether in default of appointment, or under any appointment hereafter to be made or on failure of any such appointment of and in the trust property" subject to the marriage settlement. By an appointment in pursuance of the power executed in 1939, his mother appointed him a sum of £3,517 and released her life interest. Thereupon Lloyds Bank Ltd, who had by then become trustees of the marriage settlement as well as the voluntary settlement took out a summons asking whether they should pay A.T. the £3,517.

Held, that A.T. was entitled to require payment of the sum appointed, and **4–68** could not be compelled to permit the bank to retain the £3,517.

FARWELL J.: "When one looks at the voluntary settlement, at first sight the answer would seem to be quite clearly that the trustees' duty was to retain the sum of £3,517 as part of the funds which the son had voluntarily settled, and the language of the voluntary settlement would seem to leave no doubt on that score, because the settlor assigned to the bank 'all the part or share parts or shares and other interest whether vested or contingent to which the settlor is now or may hereafter become entitled whether in default of appointment or under any appointment hereafter to be made or on failure of any such appointment of and in the trust property which is now or may at any time hereafter become subject to the trusts of the wife's settlement.' One would say, looking at the language of the settlement, that it would be difficult to find words more apt to embrace in the voluntary settlement all the interests which the son had then or might thereafter have under the marriage settlement and that accordingly the answer should be that it is the duty of the trustees to retain this as part of the voluntary settlement fund. But, when one considers the legal position in this matter, a different aspect seems to appear. If the matter could be tested simply as one of construction, the answer would appear to be in favour of the trustees of the voluntary settlement; but the question is not one of construction only, and I have to consider whether the attempt to assign that which the son has now become entitled to by virtue of the exercise of the power is enforceable against him.

"The legal position in the case of a special power of appointment is not in any **4–69** doubt at all. Referring to *Farwell on Powers*, (3rd ed.), p. 310, I find this statement of principle, which will be found in exactly the same language in earlier editions of the book, and therefore is not in any way the creation of the editor: 'The exercise of a power of appointment divests (either wholly or partially according to the terms of the appointment) the estates limited in default of appointment and creates a new estate, and that, too, whether the property be real or personal.' The effect of this is that in the case of a special power the property is vested in the persons who take in default of appointment, subject, of course, to any prior life interest, but liable to be divested at any time by a valid exercise of the power, and the effect of such an exercise of the power is to defeat wholly or *pro tanto* the interests which up to then were vested in the persons entitled in default of appointment and to create new estates in those persons in whose favour the appointment had been made. That being so, it is, in my judgment, impossible to say that until an appointment has been made in favour of this son the son had any interest under his mother's settlement other than an interest as one of the people entitled in default of appointment; he had an interest in that; but that interest was liable to be divested, and, if an appointment was made in favour of the son, then to that extent the persons entitled in default were defeated and he was given an interest in the funds which he had never had before and which came into being for the first time when the power was exercised. No doubt it is quite true to say that the appointment has to be read in to the marriage settlement, but, in my judgment, that is not sufficient ground for saying that at the time when this voluntary settlement was made the son had any interest at all in the fund other than his vested interest in default of appointment; for the rest, he had nothing more than a mere expectancy, the hope that at some date his mother might think fit to exercise the power of appointment in his favour, but, until she did so choose, he had nothing other than his interest in default of appointment to which he could point and say: 'That is a fund to which I shall become entitled in future or to which I am contingently entitled.' Apart from this he was not contingently entitled at all; he had no interest whatever in the fund until the appointment had been executed.

4–70   "If that be the true view, as I believe it to be, the result must be that, whatever the language of the settlement may be, the settlor under the voluntary settlement was purporting to assign to the trustees something to which he might in certain circumstances become entitled in the future, but to which he was not then entitled in any sense at all, and if that be so, then it is plain on the authorities that the son cannot be compelled to hand over or to permit the trustees to retain this sum and that he is himself entitled to call upon them to pay it over to him.

     "There are two cases to which I have been referred. One of them is a decision of Buckley J. (as he then was) in a case of *In re Ellenborough*.[56] What Buckley J. said was this: 'The question is whether a volunteer can enforce a contract made by deed to dispose of an expectancy. It cannot be and is not disputed that if the deed had been for value the trustees could have enforced it. If value be given, it is immaterial what is the form of assurance by which the disposition is made, or whether the subject of the disposition is capable of being thereby disposed of or not. An assignment for value binds the conscience of the assignor. A Court of Equity as against him will compel him to do that which ex hypothesi he has not yet effectually done. Future property, possibilities, and expectancies are all assignable in equity for value: *Tailby v. Official Receiver*.[57] But when the assurance is not for value, a Court of Equity will not assist a volunteer, the reason for that being, that, since it is merely a voluntary act and not an act for consideration at all, the conscience of the assignor is not affected so as in equity to prevent him from saying: "I am not going to hand over this property to which now for the first time I have become entitled." ' If that be the true view, it must follow that this particular interest, which for the first time came into being when the appointment was made, is not caught by the settlement.

4–71   "Notwithstanding the fact that the language of this voluntary settlement as a matter of construction is wide enough to comprise this interest, the principle of law which I have stated makes it impossible to enforce the settlement to that extent and prevents the settlor from being compelled by this Court to transfer or permit the trustees to retain this money as part of the funds subject thereto.

---

[56] [1903] 1 Ch. 697 at 700.
[57] (1888) 13 App.Cas. 523.

"I regret to have to come to this conclusion, because I think it is quite plainly contrary to what was intended at the date when the voluntary settlement was executed, but none the less I feel compelled by the principles to which I have referred to hold that the answer to the summons must be that the trustees ought to pay to the defendant the sum in question on the footing that that settlement does not operate as a valid assignment or declaration of trust in respect thereof. I make that declaration accordingly."[58]

RE RALLI'S WILL TRUSTS

Chancery Division [1964] Ch. 288; [1963] 3 All E.R. 940.

From 1899 Helen was entitled to one-half of her father's residuary estate **4–72** subject to her mother's life interest. The mother died in 1961 so Helen's reversionary interest then fell into possession. In 1924 Helen in her marriage settlement had covenanted to assign to the trustees thereof as soon as circumstances would admit all her existing and after-acquired property upon certain trusts for her children which failed (Helen dying a childless widow) and ultimately upon trusts for the benefit of the children of Helen's sister, Irene, who were volunteers. A subsequent clause in the marriage settlement was held on its proper construction to declare that all property comprised within the terms of the covenant should be subject in equity to the trusts of the settlement pending assignment to the trustees. Helen never assigned the reversionary interest before dying in 1956.

The plaintiff was one of the three original trustees of the 1924 marriage settlement and was sole surviving trustee thereof. It so happened that in 1946 he had also become a trustee of Helen's father's will and was indeed sole surviving trustee. He claimed that Helen's reversion in half the residue was held on the trusts of the marriage settlement whilst the defendants, Helen's personal representatives, claimed her estate was entitled.

BUCKLEY J. held that the vested reversionary interest, being existing property **4–73** of Helen at the time she made what he construed as an independent declaration of trust pending assignment to the trustees of her marriage settlement, was held on the trusts of the marriage settlement. He then continued:

"If this view is right, this disposes of the case, but I think I should go on to state what would be my view, if I were mistaken in the view I have expressed. The investments representing the share of residue in question stand in the name of the plaintiff. This is because he is now the sole surviving trustee of the testator's will. Therefore, say the defendants, he holds these investments primarily on the trusts of the will, that is to say, in trust for them as part of Helen's estate. The plaintiff is, however, also the sole surviving covenantee under clause 7 of the settlement, as well as the sole surviving trustee of that settlement. This, however, affords him no answer, say the defendants, to their claim under the will unless the plaintiff, having transferred the property to them in pursuance of the trusts of the will, could compel them to return it in pursuance of their obligation under the covenant, and this, they say, he could not do. In support of this last contention they rely on *Re Plumptre's Marriage Settlement*,[59] *Re Pryce*,[60] and *Re Kay's Settlement*.[61]

---

[58] Also see last cited paragraph of Turner L.J. in *Milroy v. Lord* (1862) 4 De G.F. & J. 265, *supra* at para. 4–03.
[59] [1910] 1 Ch. 609.
[60] [1917] 1 Ch. 234.
[61] [1939] Ch. 329.

4–74   "The plaintiff, on the other hand, contends that, as he already holds the investments, no question of his having to enforce the covenant arises. The fund having come without impropriety into his hands is now, he says, impressed in his hands with the trusts on which he ought to hold it under the settlement; and because of the covenant it does not lie in the mouth of the defendants to say that he should hold it in trust for Helen's estate. He relies on *Re Bowden*[62] in which case a lady by a voluntary settlement purported to assign to trustees *inter alia* such property as she should become entitled to under the will of her father, who was still alive, and authorised the trustees to receive the property and give receipts for it. In due course her father died and the property to which the lady became entitled under his will was transferred to the trustees of the settlement. Many years later the lady claimed that the property belonged to her absolutely. Bennett, J. [held] that she was not entitled to the property.

4–75   "Counsel for the defendants says that *Re Bowden*[63] and *Re Adlard's Settlement Trust* are distinguishable from the present case because in each of those cases the fund had reached the hands of the trustees of the relevant settlement and was held by them in that capacity, whereas in the present case the fund is, as he maintains, in the hands of the plaintiff in the capacity of trustee of the will and not in the capacity of trustee of the settlement. He says that *Re Burton's Settlements*,[64] the complicated facts of which I forbear to set out here, should be distinguished on the ground that, when the settlement there in question was made, the trustee of that settlement and the trustee of the settlement under which the settlor had expectations was the same, so that the settlor by her settlement gave directions to the trustee of the settlement under which she had expectations, who then already held the relevant fund.

4–76   "Counsel for the plaintiff says that the capacity in which the trustee has become possessed of the fund is irrelevant. Thus in *Strong v. Bird*,[65] an imperfect gift was held to be completed by the donee obtaining probate of the donor's will of which he was executor, notwithstanding that the donor died intestate as to her residue and that the donee was not a person entitled as on her intestacy. Similarly in *Re James*,[66] a grant of administration to two administrators was held to perfect an imperfect gift by the intestate to one of them, who had no beneficial interest in the intestate's estate.

4–77   "In my judgment the circumstance that the plaintiff holds the fund because he was appointed a trustee of the will is irrelevant. He is at law the owner of the fund and the means by which he became so have no effect on the quality of his legal ownership. The question is: for whom, if any one, does he hold the fund in equity? In other words, who can successfully assert an equity against him disentitling him to stand on his legal right? It seems to me to be indisputable that Helen, if she were alive, could not do so,[67] for she has solemnly covenanted under seal to assign the fund to the plaintiff and the defendants can stand in no better position. It is, of course, true that the object of the covenant was not that the plaintiff should retain the property for his own benefit, but that he should hold it on the trusts of the settlement. It is also true that, if it were necessary to enforce performance of the covenant, equity would not assist the beneficiaries

---

[62] [1936] Ch. 71.
[63] [1954] Ch. 29.
[64] [1955] Ch. 82.
[65] (1874) L.R. 18 Eq. 315.
[66] [1935] Ch. 449.
[67] Is this right in view of *Re Brooks's S.T.* [1939] 1 Ch. 993, *supra*, at para. 4–67

under the settlement, because they are mere volunteers; and that for the same reason the plaintiff, as trustee of the settlement, would not be bound to enforce the covenant and would not be constrained by the court to do so, and indeed, it seems, might be constrained by the court not to do so. As matters stand, however, there is no occasion to invoke the assistance of equity to enforce the performance of the covenant. It is for the defendants to invoke the assistance of equity to make good their claim to the fund. To do so successfully they must show that the plaintiff cannot conscientiously withhold it from them. When they seek to do this, he can point to the covenant which, in my judgment, relieves him from any fiduciary obligation that he would otherwise owe to the defendants as Helen's representatives. In so doing the plaintiff is not seeking to enforce an equitable remedy against the defendants on behalf of persons who could not enforce such a remedy themselves: he is relying on the combined effect of his legal ownership of the fund and his legal right to enforce the covenant. That an action on the covenant might be statute-barred is irrelevant, for there is no occasion for such an action.

"Had someone other than the plaintiff been the trustee of the will and held **4–78** the fund, the result of this part of the case would, in my judgment, have been different; and it may seem strange that the rights of the parties should depend on the appointment of the plaintiff as a trustee of the will in 1946, which for present purposes may have been a quite fortuitous event. The result, however, in my judgment, flows—and flows, I think, quite rationally—from the consideration that the rules of equity derive from the tenderness of a court of equity for the consciences of the parties. *There would have been nothing unconscientious in Helen or her personal representatives asserting her equitable interests under trusts of the will against a trustee who was not a covenantee under clause 7 of the settlement,*[68] and it would have been unconscientious for such a trustee to disregard those interests. Having obtained a transfer of the fund, it would not have been unconscientious in Helen to refuse to honour her covenant, because the beneficiaries under her settlement were mere volunteers: nor seemingly would the court have regarded it as unconscientious in the plaintiff to have abstained from enforcing the covenant either specifically or in damages, for the reason, apparently, that he would have been under no obligation to obtain for the volunteers indirectly what they could not obtain directly. In such circumstances Helen or her personal representatives could have got and retained the fund. In the circumstances of the present case, on the other hand, it is not unconscientious in the plaintiff to withhold from Helen's estate the fund which Helen covenanted that he should receive: on the contrary, it would have been unconscientious in Helen to seek to deprive the plaintiff of that fund, and her personal representatives can be in no better position. The inadequacy of the volunteers' equity against Helen and her estate consequently is irrelevant, for that equity does not come into play; but they have a good equity as against the plaintiff, because it would be unconscientious in him to retain as against them any property which he holds in consequence of the provisions of the settlement.

"For these reasons I am of opinion that in the events which have happened the plaintiff now holds the fund in question on the trusts of the marriage settlement, and I will so declare."

---

[68] Author's italics.

WILLIAMS V. COMMISSIONERS OF INLAND REVENUE

New Zealand Court of Appeal [1965] N.Z.L.R. 395.

4–79   Williams, who had a life interest under a trust, executed a voluntary deed, in which "the assignor by way of gift hereby assigns to the assignee for the religious purposes of the Parish of the Holy Trinity Gisborne for the four years commencing on June 30, 1960 the first £500 of the net income which shall accrue to the assignor personally while he lives in each of the said four years from the Trust. . . . And the assignor hereby declares that he is trustee for the sole use and benefit of the assignee for the purpose aforesaid of so much (if any) of the said income as may not be capable of assignment (or may come to his hands)."

The question arose whether Williams had effectively divested himself of his interest in the £500 so as not to be liable for income tax on it. The New Zealand Court of Appeal held that he had not.

TURNER J. (delivering the judgment of North P. and himself) said: "Mr. Thorp, for the appellant, submitted that what was assigned by this document was a defined share in the existing life estate of the assignor in the trust property, and hence that the deed of assignment took effect, as at its date, to divest the assignor of the annual sums of £500 so that he did not thereafter derive them for taxation purposes in the years under consideration. For the respondent Commissioner it was contended that the deed was ineffective to divest the assignor of the sums, and that its effect was no more than that of an order upon the trustees still revocable by the assignor until payment.

4–80   "The life interest of the appellant in the trust was at the date of the execution of the deed an existing equitable interest. Being an existing interest, it was capable in equity of immediate effective assignment. Such an assignment could be made without consideration, if it immediately passed the equitable estate: *Kekewich v. Manning.*[69] There is no doubt that if the deed before us had purported to assign, not 'the first £500,' but the whole of the appellant's life interest under the trust, such an assignment would have been good in equity.

"But while equity will recognise a voluntary assignment of an existing equitable interest, it will refuse to recognise in favour of a volunteer an assignment of an interest, either legal or equitable, not existing at the date of the assignment, but to arise in the future. Not yet existing, such property cannot be owned, and what may not be owned may not be effectively assigned: *Holroyd v. Marshall.*[70] If, not effectively assigned, it is made the subject of an agreement to assign it, such an agreement may be good in equity, and become effective upon the property coming into existence but if, and only if, the agreement is made for consideration (as in *Spratt v. Commissioner of Inland Revenue*[71]), for equity will not assist a volunteer: In *Re Ellenborough.*[72]

4–81   "The deed on which this appeal is founded was not made for consideration. The simple question is therefore—was that which it purported to assign (*viz.* 'the first five hundred pounds of the net income which shall accrue') an existing property right, or was it a mere expectancy, a future right not yet in existence? If the former, counsel agree that the deed was effective as an immediate assignment: if the latter, it is conceded by Mr. Thorp that it could not in the circumstances of this case have effect.

---

[69] (1851) 1 De G.M. & G. 176; 42 E.R. 519.
[70] (1862) 10 H.L.C. 191, 210; 11 E.R. 999 at 1006, *per* Lord Westbury L.C.
[71] [1964] N.Z.L.R. 272.
[72] [1903] 1 Ch. 697.

"What then was it that the assignor purported to assign? What he had was the life interest of a *cestui que trust* in a property or partnership adventure vested in or carried on by trustees for his benefit. Such a life interest exists in equity as soon as the deed of trust creating it is executed and delivered. Existing, it is capable of immediate assignment. We do not doubt that where it is possible to assign a right completely it is possible to assign an undivided interest in it. The learned Solicitor-General was therefore right, in our opinion, in conceding that if here, instead of purporting to assign 'the first £500 of the income,' the assignor had purported to assign (say) an undivided one-fourth share in his life estate, then he would have assigned an existing right, and in the circumstances effectively.

"But in our view, as soon as he quantified the sum in the way here attempted, **4–82** the assignment became one not of a share or a part of his right, but of moneys which should arise from it. Whether the sums mentioned were ever to come into existence in whole or in part could not at the date of assignment be certain. In any or all of the years designated the net income might conceivably be less than five hundred pounds; in some or all of them the operations of the trust might indeed result in a loss. The first £500 of the net income, then, might or might not (judging the matter on the date of execution of the deed) in fact have any existence.

"We accordingly reject Mr. Thorp's argument that what was here assigned was a part or share of the existing equitable right of the assignor. He did not assign part of his right to income; he assigned a right to a part of the income, a different thing. The £500 which was the subject of the purported assignment was five hundred pounds *out of the net income*. There could be no such income for any year until the operations of that year were complete, and it became apparent what debits were to be set off against the gross receipts. For these reasons we are of opinion that what was assigned here was money; and that was something which was not presently owned by the assignor. He had no more than an expectation of it, to arise, it is true, from an existing equitable interest—but that interest he did not purport to assign. . . .

"It was argued in the alternative by Mr. Thorp, but somewhat faintly that if the **4–83** document were not effective as an assignment it was effective as a declaration of trust, and that this result was sufficient to divest the appellant of the enjoyment of the annual sums so that he did not derive them as income. It will be recalled in this regard that the text of the deed includes an express declaration of trust. Mr. Thorp's submission was that this express declaration is effective even if the assignment fails. We agree that there may be circumstances in which a purported assignment, ineffective for insufficiency of form or perhaps through lack of notice, may yet perhaps be given effect by equity by reason of the assignor having declared himself to be a trustee; but it is useless to seek to use this device in the circumstances of the present case. Property which is not presently owned cannot presently be impressed with a trust any more than it can be effectively assigned; property which is not yet in existence may be the subject of a present agreement to impress it with a trust when it comes into the hands of the donor; but equity will not enforce such an agreement at the instance of the *cestui que trust* in the absence of consideration: *Ellison v. Ellison*.[73] For the same reasons therefore as apply in this case to the argument on assignment Mr. Thorp's second alternative submission must also fail."

---

[73] (1802) 6 Ves.Jun. 656 at 662, *per* Lord Eldon.

V. Exceptions to the Rule That Equity Will not Assist a Volunteer

4–84 There seem to be four exceptions.

1. *Equitable exceptions*

(a) The rule in *Strong v. Bird*.[74] This has already been considered, *supra*, at paras 4–36 to 4–40.

(b) *Donationes mortis causa*.[75] Cases of *donationes mortis causa* sometimes provide an exception to the rule that equity will not perfect an imperfect gift. A *donatio mortis causa* must comply with the following essential requirements:

(i) The donor must have made the gift in contemplation though not necessarily in expectation of death.

(ii) He must have delivered the subject-matter of the gift to the donee or transferred to him the means or part of the means of getting at that subject-matter, *e.g.* delivering a key, like car keys[76] or a key to a box containing essential indicia of title,[77] intending to part with dominion over the property to which the key relates.

4–85 (iii) The circumstances must have been such as to establish that the gift was to be absolute and complete only on the donor's death so as to be revocable before then. A condition to this effect need not be expressed and will normally be implied from the fact that the gift was made when the donor was ill.[78]

Since, in the case of a chose in action, physical delivery is impossible, it follows that the title of the donee will not be completely vested at the death of the donor. The question is, therefore, whether the donee can, as a volunteer, compel the personal representatives of the donor to complete the gift. Equity will not grant its assistance to the donee in every such case; it will do so only in those cases in which the donor has delivered to the donee a document which is necessary to prove title to the chose in action, *i.e.* a document the possession or production of which is necessary in order to entitle the possessor or producer to payment of the money as property purported to be given.[79] It is not necessary that the document should contain all the terms on which the subject-matter of the chose in action is held.[80] In the case of a bank deposit book, delivery of the book is sufficient to pass the money in the

---

[74] (1874) L.R. 18 Eq. 315.
[75] See Pettit, pp. 112–117.
[76] *Woodard v. Woodard* (1991) 21 Fam. Law 470 (not necessary to hand over log book).
[77] *Re Lillingston* [1952] 2 All E.R. 184, *Sen v. Headley* [1991] Ch. 425.
[78] *See Re Eillingston* [1952] 2 All E.R. 184; *Re Mustapha* (1891) 8 T.L.R. 160.
[79] *Moore v. Darton* (1851) 4 De G. & Sm. 517; *Re Dillon* (1890) 44 Ch.D. 76; *Birch v. Treasury Solicitor* [1951] Ch. 298.
[80] *Birch v. Treasury Solicitor* [1951] Ch. 298; disapproving dicta in *Re Weston* [1902] 1 Ch. 680 and *Delgoffe v. Fader* [1939] Ch. 922.

deposit account if the bank insists on production of the book before paying out. Delivery of title deeds to land or of share certificates is capable of amounting to a *d.m.c.* of the land[81] or of the shares.[82] Delivery of a donor's own cheque cannot amount to a *d.m.c.* of the sum represented by the cheque,[83] although delivery of a cheque payable to the donor can amount to a *d.m.c*[84]

(c) *Equitable proprietary estoppel*. As already seen *supra* at paras 2–29   **4–86** to 2–39, In some circumstances equity will prevent an owner of land, who has made an imperfect gift of some estate or interest in it, from asserting his title against the donee. The equity of the donee exists where he has expended money on the land in the mistaken belief that he has or will acquire an interest in it and the owner, knowing of the mistake, stood by and allowed the expenditure to be incurred. This type of equity has a wider sphere of operation than an estoppel of the ordinary kind, and in some cases nothing short of a conveyance of the owner's estate or interest to the donee will be sufficient to satisfy the quity.

2. *Statutory exception*

The Trusts of land and Appointment of Trustees Act 1996 provides a   **4–87** further exception to the rule.

Conveyance to an infant. Although after 1925 an infant cannot hold a legal estate in land, an attempt to transfer a legal estate to him is not wholly ineffective. It operates as a declaration of trust by the grantor in favour of the minor.[85]

QUESTIONS

1. Sam is freehold owner of some unregistered land in Wales, registered shareholder of 10,000 OK Ltd shares, a depositor of £12,000 with Bigg Bank and of £14,000 with Great Bank, and is entitled to XYZ Ltd shares held for him by Eric, executor of his father's will.

Sam gives the title deed to the Welsh land to Dawn, signing a hand-written endorsement on the conveyance to himself, "Dawn, this is now yours." He orally tells Frances he is holding 4,000 of his OK shares on trust for her, tells George he is holding his Bigg account on trust for him, has Great Bank write a letter to Harriet informing her that at Sam's telephoned request it is now holding his £14,000 on trust for her, tells Ian he is holding one half of his remaining 6,000 OK shares on trust for him, and tells Eric to transfer the XYZ shares to Jennifer. Eric signs a duly completed share transfer form and encloses it with the relevant

---

[81] *Sen v. Headley* [1991] 2 All E.R. 636 (appeal to H.L. settled).
[82] *Dufficy v. Mollica* [1968] 3 NSWLR 751 at 759. This clearly should be the position if a share transfer form is properly executed and handed over; *Staniland v. Willott* (1850) 3 Mac. & G. 664; *Re Craven's Estate* [1937] Ch. 423; or if land is actually conveyed; *Cooper v. Seversen* (1955) 1 D.L.R. (2d) 161.
[83] *Re Beaumont* [1902] 1 Ch. 889; *Re Leaper* [1916] 1 Ch. 579.
[84] *Re Mead* (1880) 15 Ch.D. 651.
[85] Trusts of Land and Appointment of Trustees Act 1996 Sched. 1.

share certificate in an envelope which he gives to Jennifer, who accidentally throws it out with some old newspapers and empty envelopes.

One month later a financial disaster strikes Sam, who seeks to recover the above property if at all possible. Advise him. Would your answer be different in respect of the OK shares if he had made a further declaration of trust of 3,000 OK shares in favour of Keith?

4–88   2. Under A's father's will trusts property is settled on trust for W for life, remainder to his sons A and B equally, but W has express power to appoint the capital between A and B as she sees fit. If A assigns *inter alia* "All my interest under my father's will trusts to Bigg Bank on trust for" X for life, remainder to Y, advise the bank if W dies either (i) without having made an appointment so that A receives £450,000, or (ii) having appointed £500,000 to A a month before her death, so that A's half share on her death brings him assets worth £200,000.

Would your advice differ if, instead, A had assigned to the Bank *inter alia* "all such assets whatsoever as shall come into my possession on my mother's death under the terms of my father's will trusts"? Would it matter if these words were followed by "but pending transfer of such assets I shall hold all my interest under my father's will trusts on the trusts applicable to such assets"?

Would any of your advice to the bank differ if unknown to A the bank happened to be trustee of his father's will trusts?

4–89   3. Five years ago, 26-year-old Sheila executed a voluntary settlement of certain property and further assigned to Barclays Bank as her trustee all property to which she might become entitled under anybody's will or intestacy and she covenanted with the bank[86] to transfer to it upon the trusts of the settlement the sum of £30,000 to which she would become entitled under another trust if she attained 30.

Last year Sheila's mother died, by her will appointing Barclays Bank her executor and leaving £20,000 to Sheila. After receiving the £30,000 on attaining 30 Sheila, who then banked with Lloyds Bank, sent off her cheque for that sum in favour of Barclays Bank but stopped the cheque before it was met and sent off a cheque for £12,000 in its place. This cheque was cashed.

Sheila now claims to be entitled to recover this £12,000 and to be under no obligation to pay the £18,000 balance. She further demands that Barclays Bank pay her the £20,000 due to her under her mother's will. Advise the bank.

Would it make any difference if Sheila had died last month having appointed Barclays Bank executor of her will and having left everything to her husband, Barry, whom she had married last year and who persisted with her claims and demands?

4–90   4. "When it comes to Chancery judges directing trustees not to sue on covenants, that are not themselves the subject-matter of a trust, the judges cannot justify their directions simply on the negative basis that 'Equity will not assist a volunteer' because Equity is positively intervening to prevent trustees exercising their common law rights." Discuss.

5. On Albert's hundredth birthday he asked his three children Maud, George and Emma, to visit him.

---

[86] Would it have been better for the bank (and the beneficiaries under Sheila's voluntary settlement) if Sheila had, instead, expressly assigned to the bank her contingent equitable interest in £30,000 or had, additionally, declared herself trustee of such interest on the trusts of her voluntary settlement?

To Maud he said, "Here is a large envelope for you but don't open it till you've left me." To George he said, "Here is my share certificate for 4,000 ordinary shares in P.Q. Ltd, together with a transfer in your favour which I've signed. You can also have my car." To Emma he said, "I feel awful. If I die I want you to have everything else including this house and all my furniture. All the necessary papers are in this deed box underneath my bed. Here is the only key."

Albert died in his sleep that very night. His will appointed George his executor and left everything equally amongst his children.

In Maud's envelope were a cheque for £2,000 and the deeds of some freehold land and on the last conveyance to Albert he had written and signed, "I hold this for Maud." In the deed box Emma found several share certificates, Albert's Trustee Savings Bank passbook showing a balance of £1,000, and a receipt acknowledging that the bank had the safe custody of the title deeds to the house. George was unable to get himself registered in respect of the 4,000 shares as the directors refused to register him and were entitled to do so under the company's articles.

Advise Albert's executor on the distribution of Albert's estate.

6. Is the following approach to completely and incompletely constituted trusts **4–91** a sound one?

(1) Has a trust been completely constituted by a declaration of trust by S himself or by property having been effectively given by him to trustees, bearing in mind that the strict rules as to gifts have been attenuated by *Strong v. Bird* principles and *donatio mortis causa* principles and that if the intent is clear there may be a completely constituted trust of a covenant?

(2) If a trust is incompletely constituted is the beneficiary seeking to enforce the trust
   (a) a convenanting party,
   (b) someone who gave consideration for the settlor's covenant,
   (c) someone within the marriage consideration if the settlement was made in consideration of marriage?

(3) If a beneficiary cannot enforce the trust can the trustees as convenantees sue at common law and hold the damages on trust—but for whom?[87]

Section 2. Discretionary and Protective Trusts[88]

Discretionary Trusts

If a settlor wishes to provide for B by creating a trust for the benefit of B **4–92** (*e.g.* conferring a life interest upon B) he ought to consider whether his intention will best be carried out by conferring a distinct fixed interest upon B. After all, if B becomes bankrupt his life interest like his other property will pass to his trustee in bankruptcy for the benefit of his

---

[87] If the trustee-covenantee assigned the benefit of the covenant to the person beneficially claiming the subject-matter of the covenant should the covenant not still be held on resulting trust for the settlor? Similarly, if the trustee resigned on appointing the alleged beneficiary to be trustee.

[88] See generally Sheridan, "Discretionary Trusts" (1957) 21 Conv. (N.S.) 55; "Protective Trusts," *Ibid.* 110; A. J. Hawkins (1967) 31 Conv. (N.S.) 117.

creditors. Moreover, B himself could sell his life interest and lose the proceeds on a gambling holiday so as then to be unprovided for.

4–93   If, however, B were merely a beneficiary of a discretionary trust[89] B would have no right to any of the trust income: he would merely have a hope that the trustees' discretion would be exercised in his favour. The essence of a discretionary trust is, of course, the complete discretion of the trustees as to the amount of income, if any, to be paid to the various beneficiaries of the trust. If the trustees have no power to retain income for accumulation the whole income[90] has to be distributed though only amongst such of the beneficiaries and in such proportions as the trustees see fit.[91] Only if all the beneficiaries of the discretionary trust are each of full capacity and between themselves absolutely entitled to either the income or the income and capital of the trust and call for the trustees to transfer the income or the trust property (as the case may be) to them (or to their nominee) do the trustees' discretions determine: *Re Smith, infra.* Till then neither individually nor collectively do the beneficiaries have an interest in possession.[92]

4–94   If B is beneficiary of a discretionary trust and then sells his interest or becomes bankrupt his assignee or trustee in bankruptcy has no more right than he to demand payment from the trustees. If the trustees do exercise their discretion in favour of B by paying money to him or delivering goods to him then B's assignee or trustee in bankruptcy is entitled to the money or goods.[93] Indeed, where the trustees have had notice of the assignment or bankruptcy but have still paid money to B they have been held liable to his assignee or trustee in bankruptcy for the money so paid.[94] It seems, however, that if the trustees spend trust money on the maintenance of B by paying third parties for food, clothes or accommodation for B then the assignee or trustee in bankruptcy will have no claim.[95]

Discretionary trusts thus have the advantage of protecting beneficiaries from themselves besides the obvious advantages of flexibility. However, there is the corresponding disadvantage that such trusts create uncertainty for a beneficiary since he has no fixed entitlement as he would have, say, if he had a life interest.

---

[89] For the nature of an interest under a discretionary trust see *Gartside v. I.R.C.* [1968] A.C. 553; *Re Weir's Settlement* [1969] 1 Ch. 657 (reversed [1971] Ch. 145 on grounds not affecting these principles); *McPhail v. Doulton* [1971] A.C. 424. For an example of a draft discretionary settlement see *supra*, at para. 1–56.

[90] An "exhaustive" discretionary trust: *Sainsbury v. I.R.C.* [1970] 1 Ch. 712.

[91] *Re Gourju's W.T.* [1943] Ch. 24; *Re Gulbenkian's Settlements (No. 2)* [1970] Ch. 408; *Re Allen Meyrick's W.T.* [1966] 1 W.L.R. 499.

[92] *Re Trafford* [1984] 1 All E.R. 1108; *Vestey v. I.R.C. (No. 2)* [1979] 2 All E.R. 225 at 235–236.

[93] *Re Coleman* (1888) 39 Ch.D. 443. The assignment must be for value if the assignment of what B hopes to receive from an exercise of the trustees' discretion is to be enforceable once B has actually received property from the trustees; see *infra*, at para. 6–91.

[94] *Re Neil* (1890) 62 L.T. 649; *Re Bullock* (1891) 60 L.J. Ch. 341 though *Re Ashby* [1892] 1 Q.B. 872 has created some uncertainty by indicating that an assignee or a trustee in bankruptcy can only claim to the extent to which sums paid are in excess of the amount necessary for B's maintenance: see Hardingham & Baxt's *Discretionary Trusts*, p. 144.

[95] *Re Coleman* (1888) 39 Ch.D. 443 at 451; *Re Allan-Meyrick's W.T.* [1966] 1 W.L.R. 499.

Protective Trusts

To tackle this disadvantage there arose the protective trust[96] confer- **4–95** ring upon B a life (or lesser) interest determinable upon the bankruptcy of B or upon any other event which would deprive B of the right to receive all the income of the trust, whereupon a discretionary trust springs up in favour of B and her spouse and issue. It has long been established that, whilst a condition or proviso for forfeiture of an interest on bankruptcy or attempted alienation of the interest is void, a determinable limitation of an interest to last until bankruptcy or attempted alienation is valid,[97] except that where a settlor purports to create such a protective trust for himself the determining event will be void against his trustee in bankruptcy for reasons of public policy.[98] The justification for such a distinction is that a limitation merely sets a natural limit to an interest whilst a condition or proviso cuts down an interest before it reaches its natural limit: if such a condition or proviso is void for being contrary to a course of devolution prescribed by law, in cutting down the natural length of an interest to prevent creditors obtaining the benefit of the interest, or for being repugnant to the nature of the alienable interest granted, then the whole natural interest is available for creditors and for alienation. A limitation, however, creates a determinable interest lasting until the limiting event happens and such interest itself is the whole natural interest. The conceptual difference between conditional and determinable interests may be stated as the difference between giving someone a 12-inch ruler subject to being cut down to a six-inch ruler in certain conditions and giving someone a six-inch ruler in the first place.

Protective trusts are now normally created by use of the shorthand **4–96** phrase "protective trusts" which invokes the detailed trusts set out in section 33 of the Trustee Act 1925, *infra*. It is also quite common in the cause of fiscal flexibility to insert some express provision enabling the protected life tenant during the currency of his determinable life interest, if he obtains the written approval of the trustees, to enter into arrangements with the other beneficiaries under the settlement for dividing up the trust funds or otherwise rearranging the beneficial interests as if he had an absolute life interest. Indeed, the protected life tenant may be given a general power of appointment exercisable only with the written consent of the trustees (for this purpose being a trust corporation or not less than two persons other than or in addition to the protected life tenant) so as to be able to vary the beneficial or administrative provisions of the settlement or even completely to revoke

---

[96] See the statutory form invoked by use of the phrase "protective trusts" set out in the Trustee Act 1925, s.33, *infra*, at para. 4–101. They have favoured treatment for inheritance tax purposes: Inheritance Tax Act 1984, s.88; *Cholmondeley v. IRC* [1986] STC 384.

[97] *Brandon v. Robinson* (1811) 18 Ves. 429; *Rochford v. Hackman* (1852) 9 Hare 475, *Re Leach* [1912] 2 Ch. 422.

[98] *Re Burroughs-Fowler* [1916] 2 Ch. 251, *infra*, at para. 4–123, *Official Assignee v. NZI Life Assurance* [1995] 1 N.Z.L.R. 684.

the settlement.[99] For the reasons set out in an extract *infra* para. 4–103 from a case note by R.E. Megarry (later Vice-Chancellor) it became not uncommon to create a series of protective trusts, *e.g.* one set until a beneficiary is 30, another from 30 to 40, a third from 40 to 50 and another for the rest of his life. Nowadays, particularly to deal with eventualities where it may or may not be clear whether forfeiture has occurred and where forfeiture may or may not be a "good" thing, a settlor seeking to provide for a profligate beneficiary may as well give the beneficiary a fixed interest but revocable at the trustees' discretion. The beneficiary then has a transferable but unsaleable interest, and whenever it would help the beneficiary to avoid claims the trustees can revoke his interest in favour of his having an interest under a discretionary trust or no interest at all for a few years till things have blown over.

4–97   As will be seen upon examining section 33 of the Trustee Act 1925 a protective trust contains three parts: (1) a life or lesser interest determinable on certain events; (2) a forfeiture clause specifying the determining events; (3) a discretionary trust which arises after forfeiture.

RE SMITH, PUBLIC TRUSTEE v. ASPINALL

Chancery Division [1928] Ch. 915; 97 L.J. Ch. 441; 140 L.T. 369.

4–98   The testator by his will directed his trustees to stand possessed of one-fourth of his residuary estate upon trust during the life of the defendant Mrs. Aspinall at their absolute discretion and in such manner as they should think fit "to pay or apply the whole or any part of the annual income of such one-fourth and the investments thereof or if they shall think fit from time to time any part of the capital thereof unto or for the maintenance and personal support or benefit of the said Lilian Aspinall or as to the income thereof but not as to the capital for the maintenance education support or benefit of all or any one or more of the children of the said Lilian Aspinall and either themselves so to apply the same or to pay the same for that purpose to any other person or persons without seeing to the application thereof. And during the period of twenty-one years from my death if the said Lilian Aspinall shall live so long to accumulate the surplus if any of such income at compound interest by investing the same and the resulting income thereof in any of the investments aforesaid by way of addition to the capital of such fund as aforesaid and so as to be subject to the same trusts as are hereby declared concerning the same. And after the death of the said Lilian Aspinall as regards both capital and income both original and accumulated in trust for the child or children of the said Lilian Aspinall who either before or after her decease shall being a son or sons attain the age of twenty-one years or being a daughter or daughters attain that age or marry and if more than one in equal shares." Mrs. Aspinall had three children, all of whom attained the age of twenty-one years, and one of whom died before the proceedings in this summons. Mrs. Aspinall was of an age when it was quite impossible that she

---

[99] Such a general power falls to be treated as a special power for perpetuity purposes so that the perpetuity period runs not from the date of the exercise of the power of appointment but from the date of the settlement creating the power: *Re Earl of Coventry's Indentures* [1974] Ch. 77; Perpetuities and Accumulations Act 1964, s. 7.

should have any further issue. In those circumstances Mrs. Aspinall, the two surviving children and the legal personal representatives of the deceased child all joined in executing a mortgage to the defendants the Legal and General Assurance Company, which took the form of an assignment to the assurance company of all the interests that Mrs. Aspinall and the three children took under the will in any event.

ROMER J.: "The question I have to determine is whether the Legal and **4–99** General Assurance Company are now entitled to call upon the trustees to pay the whole of the income to them. It will be observed from what I have said that the whole of this share is now held by the trustees upon trusts under which they are bound to apply the whole income and eventually pay over or apply the whole capital to Mrs. Aspinall and the three children or some or one of them. So far as the income is concerned they are obliged to pay it or apply it for her benefit or to pay it or apply it for the benefit of the children. So far as regards the capital, they have a discretion to pay it, and to apply it for her benefit and subject to that, they must hold it upon trust for the children. Mrs. Aspinall, the two surviving children and the representatives of the deceased child are between them entitled to the whole fund. In those circumstances it appears to me, notwithstanding the discretion which is reposed in the trustees, under which discretion they could select one or more of the people I have mentioned as recipients of the income, and might apply part of the capital for the benefit of Mrs. Aspinall and so take it away from the children, that the four of them, if they were all living, could come to the court and say to the trustees: 'Hand over the fund to us.' It appears to me that that is in accordance with the decision of the Court of Appeal in a case of *Re Nelson*,[1] of which a transcript of the judgments has been handed to me, and is in accordance with principle. What is the principle? As I understand it it is this. Where there is a trust under which trustees have a discretion as to applying the whole or part of a fund to or for the benefit of a particular person, that particular person cannot come to the trustees, and demand the fund; for the whole fund has not been given to him but only so much as the trustees think fit to let him have. But when the trustees have no discretion as to the amount of the fund to be applied, the fact that the trustees have a discretion as to the method in which the whole of the fund shall be applied for the benefit of the particular person does not prevent that particular person from coming and saying: 'Hand over the fund to me.' That appears to be the result of the two cases which were cited to me: *Green v. Spicer*[2] and *Younghusband v. Gisborne*.[3]

"Now this third case arises. What is to happen where the trustees have a **4–100** discretion whether they will apply the whole or only a portion of the fund for the benefit of one person, but are obliged to apply the rest of the fund, so far as not applied for the benefit of the first-named person, to or for the benefit of a second-named person? There, two people together are the sole objects of the discretionary trust and, between them, are entitled to have the whole fund applied to them or for their benefit. It has been laid down by the Court of Appeal in the case to which I have referred that, in such a case as that, you treat all the people put together just as though they formed one person, for whose benefit the trustees were directed to apply the whole of a particular fund. The case before the Court of Appeal was this: A testator had directed his trustees to

---

[1] [1928] Ch. 920n.
[2] (1830) 1 Russ. & My. 395.
[3] (1844) 1 Coll.C.C. 400.

stand possessed of one-third of his residuary estate upon trust during the lifetime of the testator's son Arthur Hector Nelson: 'to apply the income thereof for the benefit of himself and his wife and child or children or of any of such persons to the exclusion of the others or other of them as my trustees shall think fit.' What happened was something very similar to what happened in the case before me. Hector Nelson, his wife and the only existing child of the marriage joined together in asking the trustees to hand over the income to them, and it was held by the Court of Appeal that the trustees were obliged to comply with the request, in other words, to treat all those persons who were the only members of the class for whose benefit the income could be applied as forming together an individual for whose benefit a fund has to be applied by the trustee without any discretion as to the amount so to be applied.

"There will, consequently, be a declaration that, in the events which have happened, the plaintiff is bound to pay the whole of the income of the one-fourth to the defendant society during the lifetime of Mrs. Aspinall, or until the mortgage is discharged."

The Trustee Act 1925

4–101　　Section 33.—(1)　Where any income, including an annuity or other periodical income payment, is directed to be held on protective trusts for the benefit of any person[4] (in this section called "the principal beneficiary") for the period of his life or for any less period, then, during that period (in this section called the "trust period") the said income shall, without prejudice to any prior interest, be held on the following trusts, namely:

(i)　Upon trust for the principal beneficiary during the trust period or until he, whether before or after the termination of any prior interest, does or attempts to do or suffers any act or thing, or until any event happens, other than an advance under any statutory or express power,[5] whereby, if the said income were payable during the trust period to the principal beneficiary absolutely during that period, he would be deprived of the right to receive the same or any part thereof, in any of which cases, as well as on the termination of the trust period, whichever first happens, this trust of the said income shall fail or determine.

(ii)　If the trust aforesaid fails or determines during the subsistence of the trust period, then, during the residue of that period, the said income shall be held upon trust for the application thereof[6] for the maintenance or support, or otherwise for the benefit, of all or any one or more exclusively of the other or others of the following persons (that is to say)—

(a)　the principal beneficiary and his or her wife or husband, if any, and his or her children or more remote issue, if any; or

(b)　if there is no wife or husband or issue of the principal beneficiary in existence, the principal beneficiary and the persons who would, if he

---

[4] Person means a human being and not a company: *IRC v. Brandenburg* [1982] S.T.C. 555 at 565, 569.

[5] See *Re Hodgson* [1913] 1 Ch. 34; *Re Shaw's Settlement* [1951] Ch. 833; *Re Rees* [1954] Ch. 202; *cf. Re Stimpson's Trusts* [1931] 2 Ch. 77, which should now be confined to its own facts, that is where an express advancement clause is lacking and where no use is made of s. 33 of the Trustee Act. Even so, it must be regarded as of doubtful authority: see *Re Rees* [1954] Ch. 202 at 209.

[6] The income must be distributed: *Re Gourju's W.T.* [1934] Ch. 24.

were actually dead, *be entitled to the trust property or the income thereof* or to the annuity fund, if any, or arrears of the annuity, as the case may be; as the trustees in their absolute discretion, without being liable to account for the exercise of such discretion, think fit.

(2) This section does not apply to trusts coming into operation before the **4–102** commencement of this Act, and has effect subject to any variation[7] of the implied trusts aforesaid contained in the instrument creating the trust.

(3) Nothing in this section operates to validate any trust which would, if contained in the instrument creating the trust, be liable to be set aside.[8]

R. E. MEGARRY (1958) 74 L.Q.R. 184

"This sequence of events [in *Re Richardson's W.T.* [1958] Ch. 504] points a moral **4–103** for draftsmen. Hitherto the normal course of drafting has been to give a life interest simply 'on protective trusts,' with or without variations. The result is that a single mistaken act by the beneficiary may deprive him of his determinable life interest and reduce him for the rest of his life to the status of merely one of the beneficiaries of a discretionary trust. *Re Richardson* suggests that there may be advantages in setting up a series of protective trusts, *e.g.* one set until the beneficiary is twenty-five, another from twenty-five to thirty-five, a third from thirty-five to forty-five, and another for the rest of his life. The result would be that a youthful indiscretion at, say, twenty-two, would not irretrievably condemn the beneficiary to the mere hopes of a beneficiary under a discretionary trust, dependent upon the exercise of the trustees' discretion, but would give him a fresh start when he was twenty-five. Again, a bankruptcy at the age of thirty would not *per se* mean that when he was twice that age he would still have not an income as of right, but a mere hope of a well-exercised discretion. Indeed, instead of relating the stages to the age of the beneficiary, they might be related to a period of time (*e.g.* five years) after the occurrence of any event which had made the initial trust pass from Stage 1 to Stage 2. England lacks the device of the spendthrift trust in the American sense, but it is far from clear that the fullest possible use is being made of the existing machinery of protective and discretionary trusts." [The American spendthrift trust is a result of most American jurisdictions allowing inalienable beneficial interests to be created, though legislation sometimes intervenes to allow creditors to reach income in excess of a specified amount.]

Forfeiting Events

Whether the interest of the beneficiary is determined in the events which **4–104** have happened is a question of construction of the forfeiture clause in each particular case. It is sometimes said that forfeiture clauses should

---

[7] See, *e.g. Re Wittke* [1944] Ch. 166: bequest of residue upon protective trusts for testatrix's sister, no period being specified, but trustees being given a power to pay capital to the sister from time to time. *Held* by Vaisey J. that a protected life interest had been created, for, had an absolute interest been given, it would have been open to the sister to call for an immediate transfer of the capital, which would have been inconsistent with the power given to the trustees.

[8] This preserves *inter alia* the rule that although a settlor may validly create in favour of another person a life interest determinable by bankruptcy, such a limitation in favour of himself is void against his trustee in bankruptcy. See *Re Burroughs-Fowler* [1916] 2 Ch. 251; *Re Detmold* (1889) 40 Ch.D. 585 (where a determining event, other than bankruptcy, occurred, and it was held that the life interest determined). See *infra*, Sect. 3.

be construed in favour of the principal beneficiary, but it must be remembered that he is not the sole object of the testator's bounty, and that there are other persons upon whom the testator intended to confer a benefit.[9] It is only if, after construing the clause, a doubt remains that this should be resolved in favour of the principal beneficiary, for "the burden is upon those who allege a forfeiture to satisfy the court that a forfeiture has occurred."[10]

4–105   The forfeiture clause contained in section 33 of the Trustee Act 1925 is very wide, for it includes not only the acts and omissions of the principal beneficiary, but also the happening of any event which deprives him of his right to receive the income or any part thereof. Such an event was the Trading with the Enemy Act 1939 and orders made thereunder, whereby the property of those resident in enemy territory vested in the Custodian of Enemy Property.[11] It was otherwise with express forfeiture clauses which were drafted in narrower terms. Thus in *Re Hall*[12] forfeiture was to occur "if the annuitant should alienate or charge her annuity or become bankrupt or do or suffer any act or thing whereby the said annuity or any part thereof would or might become vested in or payable to any other person." It was held by Uthwatt J. that the clause was directed to the forfeiture of the annuity in the event of the annuitant doing *personally* certain classes of things whereby she would be deprived of her annuity. Accordingly, the Trading with the Enemy Act 1939 did not bring about a forfeiture.

4–106   Apart from these special cases, involving the application of the Trading with the Enemy Act to protective trusts, the following events have been held to cause a forfeiture:

Re Balfour's Settlement[13]: the impounding by the trustees of part of the income of the principal beneficiary to repair a breach of trust committed by them in paying part of the trust fund to him at his own instigation.

Re Walker[14]: the bankruptcy of the principal beneficiary, even if this had occurred before the trust first came into operation.

Re Baring's Settlement Trusts[15]: an order of sequestration of the income for contempt of court, even though the contempt is subsequently purged.

Re Dennis's Settlement Trusts[16]: the execution by the principal beneficiary of a deed of variation relinquishing his right to part of the income in certain events.

---

[9] *Re Sartoris's Estate* [1892] 1 Ch. 11 at 16.
[10] *Re Baring's Settlement Trusts* [1940] Ch. 737 (Morton J.).
[11] *e.g.* Trading with the Enemy (Custodian) Order 1939 (S.R. & O. 1939 No. 1198). Later orders contained a proviso that vesting in the custodian should not take place if it would cause a forfeiture (*e.g.* S.R. & O. 1945 No. 887).
[12] [1944] Ch. 46; so too *Re Furness, Wilson v. Kenmare (No. 1)* [1944] 1 All E.R. 575; *Re Harris* [1945] Ch. 316; *Re Pozot's Settlement Trusts* [1952] Ch. 427.
[13] [1938] Ch. 928.
[14] [1939] Ch. 974.
[15] [1940] Ch. 737.
[16] [1942] Ch. 283; see (1942) 58 L.Q.R. 312. It may be possible to set aside a deed for mistake as in *Gibbon v. Michell* [1990] 1 W.L.R. 1304.

Re Richardson's W.T.[17]: an order of the Divorce court attempting to **4–107** impose a charge (to secure maintenance of £50 p.a.) which though ineffectual for that purpose was sufficient to bring about a forfeiture thereby conveniently benefiting the principal beneficiaries, who had been adjudicated bankrupt a year after such order and who would still benefit under the discretionary trusts of income (whereas the trustee in bankruptcy would have acquired all the income but for the forfeiture).

On the other hand no forfeiture occurred in the following cases:

Re Tancred's Settlement[18]: the appointment by the principal beneficiary of an attorney to receive the income, even though the attorney's expenses are to be deducted from the income, and the balance paid over to the principal beneficiary.

Re Mair[19]: the making by the court of an order under section 57 of the Trustee Act 1925 authorising capital moneys to be raised to enable the principal beneficiary to pay certain pressing liabilities: section 57 is an overriding section whose provisions are read into every settlement. Contrast *Re Salting*,[20] where the scheme sanctioned by the court under section 57 involved the doing of certain acts by the principal beneficiary—and *his* omission to do them caused a forfeiture. The scheme provided for the life tenant to pay premiums on insurance policies with a proviso that the trustees were to pay the premiums out of his income if the premiums were not duly paid: his failure to pay was held to create a forfeiture.

Re Westby's Settlement[21]: the charge of a lunacy percentage upon the **4–108** estate of a lunatic under section 148(3) of the Lunacy Act 1890 (now Mental Health Act 1983, s.106(6)), since the fees payable were to be regarded as management expenses, and, even if a charge was created by the section, it was not such an incumbrance as was contemplated by the forfeiture clause.[22]

Re Longman[23]: a testatrix left the income of her residuary estate on **4–109** certain trusts for her son under which he would forfeit his interest if he should "commit permit or suffer any act default or process whereby the said income or any part thereof would or might but for this present proviso become vested in or payable to any other person." The son authorised the trustee to pay his creditors specified sums out of a particular future dividend due on shares forming part of the residuary

---

[17] See also *Edmonds v. Edmonds* [1965] 1 W.L.R. 58 (attachment of earnings order to secure former wife's maintenance held to cause forfeiture of husband's protected interest in pension fund). Further see [1993] So.Jo. 919, indicating that no attachment can be made to sums paid to the pensioner under the discretionary trusts arising upon forfeiture of the pensioner's fixed entitlements.

[18] [1903] 1 Ch. 715.

[19] [1935] Ch. 562.

[20] [1932] 2 Ch. 57.

[21] [1950] Ch. 296; overruling *Re Custance's Settlements* [1946] Ch. 42; see also *Re Oppenheim's Will Trusts* [1950] Ch. 633 (appointment of receiver of person of unsound mind did not effect a forfeiture).

[22] The same result was then achieved, independently of the cases, by the Law Reform (Miscellaneous Provisions) Act 1949, s. 8.

[23] [1955] 1 W.L.R. 197.

estate. The son later withdrew this authority, and the company afterwards did not declare a dividend. It was held by Danckwerts J. that the
withdrawal of authority would not by itself prevent forfeiture;[24] but the
failure to declare a dividend did, since the income of the residuary estate
never included anything to which the authority could possibly have
attached.

4–110   *General Accident Fire and Life Assurance Corporation Ltd v. I.R.C.*[25]:
order of the Divorce court diverting income from husband to wife and
taking effect in priority to the protective trusts was held by the Court of
Appeal not to create a forfeiture, so the husband retained a life interest
liable to estate duty on death. Although the case turned on a narrow
ground of construction of section 33 it is possible to treat it on the same
basis as *Re Mair, supra* (order under section 57 of the Trustee Act): all
protective trusts must be read as subject to the court's jurisdiction to
make orders under section 57 of the Trustee Act and sections 24 and 31
of the Matrimonial Causes Act 1973. If this be the case then *Re
Richardson's W.T.*[26] *Supra* (not cited to the Court of Appeal) is out of
line like *Re Carew*[27] which the Court of Appeal overruled.

4–111   An order of the court may sometimes do more than cause a forfeiture:
it may destroy the protected life interest and discretionary trusts
altogether. This happened in *Re Allsopp's Marriage Settlement Trusts,*[28]
where an express protective trust was created by a marriage settlement in
1916 with discretionary trusts after forfeiture. In 1928 on the dissolution
of the marriage the court made an order varying the marriage settlement
by *extinguishing* the rights of the husband as if he were already dead.
Vaisey J. held that the husband's protected life interest was extinguished
for all purposes and the discretionary trusts were so closely connected
with the life interest that they also were destroyed.

4–112   The effect of the forfeiture is to determine the principal beneficiary's
life interest and to bring the discretionary trusts into operation. Thus in
Re Gourju's Will Trusts,[29] the Trading with the Enemy Act 1939 and
orders made thereunder having brought about a forfeiture of the
principal beneficiary's interests, and the discretionary trusts having
arisen, it was held by Simonds J. that income which had accrued due
before the forfeiture was payable to the Custodian of Enemy Property,
but income which accrued due after that event was to be held on the
discretionary trusts for the benefit of the beneficiaries, and that since the
Act contemplated a continuous benefit to those beneficiaries, the
trustees were not to retain the income, but were to apply it for the
beneficiaries as and when it came in, subject to such reasonable
exceptions as the exigencies of the case demanded.[30] Thus the trustees

---

[24] See *Re Baker* [1904] 1 Ch. 157.
[25] [1963] 1 W.L.R. 1207; (1963) 27 Conv.(N.S.) 517 (F. R. Crane).
[26] [1958] Ch. 504 Further see Parker & Mellows, *The Modern Law of Trusts* 7th ed. A.J. Vakley, at 236.
[27] (1910) 103 L.T. 658.
[28] [1959] Ch. 81.
[29] [1943] Ch. 24.
[30] If the trustees fail to exercise their discretion, the discretionary trusts over income remain exercisable
    despite the passing of time though only in favour of such persons as would have been objects of the
    discretion had it been exercised within a reasonable time: *Re Locker's S.T.* [1978] 1 All E.R. 216.

could not accumulate the income so as to pay it at the end of the war to the principal beneficiary (a woman marooned in German-occupied Nice).

Section 3. Attempts by a Settlor to Deprive his Creditors

Although a settlor may validly create in favour of another person a life **4–113** interest determinable upon bankruptcy such a limitation in favour of himself is void as a matter of public policy[31] against his trustee in bankruptcy though effective between himself and the other beneficiaries under the settlement; *Re Burroughs-Fowler, infra*. Where there are several determinable events including bankruptcy then the occurrence before bankruptcy of some other determinable event is, however, valid against the trustee in bankruptcy.[32] A settlement upon discretionary trusts where the settlor is one of the discretionary beneficiaries is prima facie valid but may be impeached under section 423 of the Insolvency Act 1986 (replacing section 172 of the Law of Property Act 1925) or sections 339 and 341 of the Insolvency Act 1986 (replacing section 42 of the Bankruptcy Act 1914).

INSOLVENCY ACT 1986, SECTIONS 423–425, 339–342

These sections are broad enough to catch many dispositions by a settlor **4–114** in favour of third parties. Section 423, at para. 4–126, *infra* operates *independently of any bankruptcy* of the settlor and covers all voluntary settlements and settlements in consideration of marriage (whenever made) if the settlor made the settlement *"for the purpose* (a) of putting assets beyond the reach of a person who is making, or may at some time make, a claim against him, or (b) of otherwise prejudicing the interests of such a person in relation to the claim which he is making or may make."

Sections 339 and 341, *infra*, paras 4–130 to 4–133, only apply *if the* **4–115** *settlor is adjudged bankrupt* (and apply only in favour of the trustee in bankruptcy) and only if the settlement[33] was not created more than five years before the bankruptcy, but no purposive intent to defraud creditors is required: merely entering into a transaction at an undervalue suffices. This includes a man trying to prevent his major creditor obtaining his farm by granting a protected agricultural tenancy to his wife at full

---

[31] Some offshore trust juridictions (*e.g.* Belize and the Cook Islands) have abolished the rule that a settlor may not create a protective trust determinable on his bankruptcy so as to prevent his interest passing on bankruptcy to his trustee in bankruptcy. If property subject to such a Belize trust is found in England it is almost certain that it will be made available to the trustee in bankruptcy, taking advantage of Article 18 of The Hague Trusts Convention implemented by Recognition of Trusts Act 1987.

[32] *Re Detmold* (1889) 40 Ch.D. 585.

[33] Exercise of a special power of appointment under a settlement created more than 5 years before the settlor's bankruptcy is outside s.339 even if occurring well within the 5 years: *Clarkson v. Clarkson* (unreported C.A. April 26, 1994, Underhill & Hayton, *Law of Trusts*, 15th ed. at 262–263).

market rent, but depreciating the value of the man's interest, where the wife thereby would safeguard the family home and the farming business and obtain a "ransom" surrender-value against the creditor.[34]

The basic period is within two years of presentation of the bankruptcy petition but is extended to five years if the settlor-transferor was insolvent, as defined in section 341(3), at the time of the transfer or became so as a result of the transfer. It is rebuttably presumed that such insolvency existed if the transfer benefited "associates", including relatives of the bankrupt or spouse, as defined in section 435.

4–116   Section 423, replacing Law of Property Act 1925 section 172 (itself replacing a statute of 1571) probably encapsulates in modern language the effect of the old case law. The section clearly extends to "present" creditors (with existing enforceable claims) and "subsequent" creditors (identifiable persons who have claims that may reasonably be anticipated to mature into existing enforceable claims, *e.g.* holders of guarantees executed by the donor, or persons who had issued writs or informed the donor that they would be issuing a writ or would have so informed the donor if they had his knowledge, such as his knowledge of his negligence in relation to them).

In some circumstances the section is capable of extending to "potential future" creditors, *viz.* presently unidentifiable persons, who may or may not surface in the future to bring presently unascertainable claims of indeterminate amounts against the donor.

In *Re Butterworth*[35] Butterworth, who had been a successful baker for many years, decided to expand and buy a grocery business, a trade in which he had no experience. He therefore settled most of his property on his family just before buying the grocery business. It was not a success but Butterworth was able to sell it six months later for the same price he had paid. He continued with his bakery until it failed three years later. The Court of Appeal held that the settlement was made "with intent to defraud" under the 1571 Statute of Elizabeth and so could be upset by the creditors of the bakery.

4–117   Jessel M.R. said,[36] "The principle of *Mackay v. Douglas* is this, that a man is not entitled to go into a hazardous business, and immediately before doing so settle all his property voluntarily, the object being this: 'If I succeed in business, I make a fortune for myself. If I fail, I leave my creditors unpaid. They will bear the loss.' That is the very thing which the Statute of Elizabeth was meant to prevent. The object of the settlor was to put his property out of the reach of his future creditors. He contemplated engaging in this new trade and he wanted to preserve his property from his future creditors. That cannot be done by a voluntary settlement. That is, to my mind, a clear and satisfactory principle."

4–118   In these days when lawyers, accountants and doctors may find that they can only insure themselves against negligence up to a ceiling of £x, but that they may possibly become liable for £2x, what can they do? They

---

[34] *Agricultural Mortgage Corporation v. Woodward* [1995] 1 BCLC 1, [1996] 1 F.L.R. 226.
[35] (1882) 19 Ch.D. 588.
[36] *Ibid.* at 598, also see Lindley L.J. at 60 and *Cadogan v. Cadogan* [1977] 1 W.L.R. 1041.

can, of course, settle their property on their families, but can one distinguish their activities as professions and not hazardous trades so as to fall outside Jessel M.R.'s statement of principle? Should it matter whether a business is a trade or a profession in these days when there should be no room for class distinction? Can section 423(3) be treated as changing the law through speaking of "putting assets beyond the reach of *a* person who may at some time make a claim" rather than "*any* person," so that it could be said to contemplate only an identifiable person rather than any future potential creditors?[37]

This point was not raised in *Midland Bank plc v. Wyatt*[38] where section **4–119** 423, following *Re Butterworth* was held to cover the voluntary disposition of assets to trustees to avoid future but unknown creditors, whether or not the transferor was about to go into a "hazardous business", and whether or not the transferor was about to undertake the business as a sole trade or a partnership or via a limited liability company he controlled. Section 423 applies if the predominant[39] or substantial[40] purpose is avoiding existing, potential or future creditors but not if such purpose is estate planning. Once there is a strong prima facie case that the purpose of a transaction was to prejudice the interests of creditors no legal privilege attaches to documents relating to such transactions.[41]

To avoid problems one may seek to take advantage of favourable asset **4–120** protection trust legislation in some off-shore trust jurisdictions (*e.g.* The Bahamas, Belize, Cook Islands) which protects a settlor against potential future creditors and also introduces a short limitation period where present and subsequent creditors are concerned, but assets could be at risk if they can be traced to England or the USA where the courts could find such legislation contrary to public policy. By sections 352 and 357 of the Insolvency Act 1986 a bankrupt is guilty of an offence if in the 5 years before his bankruptcy commenced he made or caused to be made any gift or transfer of or charge on his property unless he proves that at the time he had no intent to defraud creditors under section 423 or to conceal the state of his affairs. Assisting such a person to commit such a crime is an offence.

The burden of proving the settlor's purpose is on the applicant while **4–121** the burden of proving exemption under section 425(2) is on the transferee who seeks exemption.[42] Proving the settlor's purpose is a question of fact and the surrounding circumstances may be capable of establishing a rebuttable presumption that the requisite purpose was present, *e.g.* where the settlor settles virtually all his assets, or settles so

---

[37] A question posed by Moffat & Chesterman, *Trusts Law: Text & Materials*, (3rd ed.) p. 231. After all, a prospective hazardous trader can form a company with limited liability to engage in the trade (though creditors may well insist on him personally guaranteeing company debts).

[38] [1995] 1 F.L.R. 696.

[39] *ibid. Re M. C. Bacon Ltd* [1991] Ch. 127.

[40] *Royscott Spa Leasing Ltd v. Lovett* [1994] NPC146, the retired Slade L.J. favouring "substantial": see G. Miller [1998] Conv. 362, 368–372.

[41] *Barclays Bank plc v. Eustice* [1995] 1 W.L.R. 1238.

[42] *Lloyds Bank Ltd v. Marcan* [1974] 1 W.L.R. 370 on L.P.A. 1925, s. 172 but similar principles seem applicable to s. 423.

much of his assets that his liabilities then exceed what he has left, or makes the settlement secretly and hastily.[43]

Dispositions to defeat spouses

Under section 37 of the Matrimonial Causes Act 1973 the Family Division has jurisdiction to set aside dispositions made with the intention of defeating a spouse's claim to financial relief,[44] such an intention being presumed for a disposition made within three years of the application to the court if it actually has the effect of defeating such claim: section 37(5).

Dispositions to defeat heirs

4-122   Under the Inheritance (Provision for Family and Dependants) Act 1975 the court has power to make various orders in relation to dispositions effected by a deceased, other than for full valuable consideration, and made with the intention of defeating applications for financial provision.[45] Section 10 applies to dispositions made less than six years before the deceased's death but not including appointments made in exercise of a special power of appointment. Section 13 provides protection for trustee-disponees against liability beyond trust property at hand.

RE BURROUGHS-FOWLER

Chancery Division [1916] 2 Ch. 251.

4-123   By an ante-nuptial settlement dated March 24, 1905, freeholds and leaseholds belonging to W. J. Fowler, the intended husband, were conveyed to the trustees upon trust to sell subject to certain consents and "to pay the rents profits and income thereof to the said W. J. Fowler or to permit him to receive the same during his life or until he shall be outlawed or be declared bankrupt or become an insolvent debtor within the meaning of some Act of Parliament for the relief of insolvent debtors or shall do or suffer something whereby the said rents profits and income or some part thereof respectively might if absolutely belonging to him become vested in or payable to some other person or persons. And from and immediately after the death of the said W. J. Fowler or other the determination of the trust for his benefit in his lifetime to pay the said rents profits and income unto the" wife if she should survive him during her life for her separate use without power of anticipation, and after the death of the survivor upon the usual trusts for the children of the marriage.

---

[43] *Re Wise* (1886) 17 Q.B.D. 290; *Freeman v. Pope* (1870) 5 Ch.App. 538; *Re Sinclair* (1884) 26 Ch.D. 319; *Lloyds Bank Ltd v. Marcan* [1974] 1 W.L.R. 370; *Agricultural Mortgage Corporation v. Woodward* [1995] 1 BCLC 1.

[44] e.g. *Kemmis v. Kemmis* [1988] 1 W.L.R. 1307; *Sherry v. Sherry* [1991] 1 F.L.R. 307; but a notice to quit given to a landlord by a joint tenant of a periodic tenancy is not a disposition of any property, such notice merely signifying the tenant was not willing to consent to the continuation of the tenancy beyond the date when if would otherwise expire: *Newlon Housing Trust v. Alsulaimen* [1998] 4 All E.R. 1 (H.L.).

[45] e.g. *Re Dawkins* [1986] 2 F.L.R. 360.

After the marriage the husband took the name of Burroughs-Fowler. He was **4–124** adjudicated bankrupt in 1915. The trustee in bankruptcy offered for sale the husband's life interest under the settlement, but the intending purchaser objected that the debtor's life interest remained defeasible if the debtor should do or suffer any of the other specified acts of forfeiture.

PETERSON J.: "Now the limitation until the settlor is declared bankrupt is void **4–125** against the trustee in bankruptcy, and therefore, so far as the trustee in bankruptcy is concerned, the words relating to the bankruptcy and insolvency of the settlor must be treated as if they were omitted altogether from the clause. But on the other hand the provision as to bankruptcy and insolvency is not void as between the husband and the wife; for it was decided in *Re Johnson*[46] that, while the provision for the cessation of the life interest on bankruptcy was void as against the trustee in bankruptcy, it was effective for the purpose of producing a forfeiture as between the person who had the protected life interest and the persons interested in remainder. What, then, is the result? It is said that the result may be that the trustee in bankruptcy will be in a position to dispose of more than was vested in the bankrupt himself. That would be so in any case, because, so far as the trustee is concerned, the provisions for terminating the protected life interest upon bankruptcy are void. It seems to me that the true view is that, so far as the trustee in bankruptcy is concerned, the provisions as to bankruptcy and insolvency must be treated as excluded from the settlement, and the trustee is therefore in a position to deal with the interest of the husband under the settlement, whatever it may be, as if those provisions were excluded. So far, however, as the wife is concerned the forfeiture by reason of the bankruptcy has already taken place, and, therefore, it is no longer possible for the husband hereafter to do or suffer something which would determine his interest. The result is that the trustee in bankruptcy is in possession of the life interest of the bankrupt, which is now incapable of being affected by any subsequent forfeiture."

Insolvency Act 1986

423. Transactions defrauding creditors.—(1) This section relates to trans- **4–126** actions entered into at an undervalue; and a person[47] enters into such a transaction with another person if—

 (a) he makes a gift to the other person or he otherwise enters into a transaction with the other on terms that provide for him to receive no consideration;

 (b) he enters into a transaction with the other in consideration of marriage; or

 (c) he enters into a transaction with the other for a consideration the value of which, in money or money's worth, is significantly less than the value, in money or money's worth, of the consideration provided by himself.

(2) Where a person has entered into such a transaction, the court may, if **4–127** satisfied under the next subsection, make such order as it thinks fit[48] for—

---

[46] [1904] 1 K.B. 134.
[47] The section has extra-territorial effect: *Re Paramount Airways* [1993] Ch. 223.
[48] s. 425(1) sets out specific orders "without prejudice to the generality of s. 423."

    (a) restoring the position to what it would have been if the transaction had
        not been entered into, and

    (b) protecting the interests of persons who are victims of the transaction.

(3) In the case of a person entering into such a transaction, an order shall only
be made if the court is satisfied that it was entered into by him for the purpose—

    (a) of putting assets beyond the reach of a person who is making, or may at
        some time make, a claim against him, or

    (b) of otherwise prejudicing the interests of such a person in relation to the
        claim which he is making or may make. . . .

(5) In relation to a transaction at an undervalue, references here and below to
a victim of the transaction are to a person who is, or is capable of being,
prejudiced by it; and in the following two sections the person entering into the
transaction is referred to as "the debtor."

4–128   **424. Those who may apply for an order under s.423.**—(1) An application for
an order under section 423 shall not be made in relation to a transaction
except—

    (a) in a case where the debtor has been adjudged bankrupt or is a body
        corporate which is being wound up or in relation to which an administra-
        tion order is in force, by the official receiver, by the trustee of the
        bankrupt's estate or the liquidator or administrator of the body corporate
        or (with the leave of the court) by a victim of the transaction. . . .
        (c) in any other case, by a victim of the transaction.

(2) An application made under any of the paragraphs of subsection (1) is to
be treated as made on behalf of every victim of the transaction.

4–129   **425. Provision which may be made by order under s.423.**—(2) An order under
section 423 may affect the property of, or impose any obligation on, any person
whether or not he is the person with whom the debtor entered into the
transaction; but such an order—

    (a) shall not prejudice any interest in property which was acquired from a
        person other than the debtor and was acquired in good faith, for value
        and without notice[49] of the relevant circumstances, or prejudice any
        interest deriving from such an interest, and

    (b) shall not require a person who received a benefit from the transaction in
        good faith, for value and without notice of the relevant circumstances to
        pay any sum unless he was a party to the transaction.

(3) For the purposes of this section the relevant circumstances in relation to a
transaction are the circumstances by virtue of which an order under section 423
may be made in respect of the transaction.

4–130   **339. Transactions at an undervalue.**—(1) Subject as follows in this section and
sections 341 and 342, where an individual is adjudged bankrupt and he has at a
relevant time (defined in section 341) entered into a transaction with any person

---

[49] Notice will include constructive notice: *Lloyds Bank Ltd v. Marcan* [1973] 1 W.L.R. 339 at 345.

at an undervalue, the trustee of the bankrupt's estate may apply to the court for an order under this section.

(2) The court shall, on such an application, make such order as it thinks fit for restoring the position to what it would have been if that individual had not entered into that transaction.

(3) For the purposes of this section and sections 341 and 342, an individual enters into a transaction with a person at an undervalue if—

(a) he makes a gift to that person or he otherwise enters into a transaction with that person on terms that provide for him to receive no consideration,

(b) he enters into a transaction with that person in consideration of marriage, or

(c) he enters into a transaction with that person for a consideration the value of which, in money or money's worth, is significantly less than the value, in money or money's worth, of the consideration provided by the individual.

341. "Relevant time" under ss.339, 340.—(1) Subject as follows, the time at **4–131** which an individual enters into a transaction at an undervalue . . . is a relevant time if the transaction is entered into or the preference given—

(a) in the case of a transaction at an undervalue at a time in the period of 5 years ending with the day of the presentation of the bankruptcy petition on which the individual is adjudged bankrupt . . .

(2) Where an individual enters into a transaction at an undervalue . . . at a time mentioned in paragraph (a) . . . of subsection (1) (not being, in the case of a transaction at an undervalue, a time less than 2 years before the end of the period mentioned in paragraph (a)), that time is not a relevant time for the purposes of section 339 . . . unless the individual—

(a) is insolvent at that time, or

(b) becomes insolvent in consequence of the transaction . . . but the requirements of this subsection are presumed to be satisfied, unless the contrary is shown, in relation to any transaction at an undervalue which is entered into by an individual with a person who is an associate of his (otherwise than by reason only of being his employee).

(3) For the purposes of subsection (2), an individual is insolvent if—

(a) he is unable to pay his debts as they fall due, or

(b) the value of his assets is less than the amount of his liabilities, taking into account his contingent and prospective liabilities.

342. Orders under ss.339, 340.—(2) An order under section 339 or 340 may **4–132** affect the property of, or impose any obligation on, any person whether or not he is the person with whom the individual in question entered into the transaction . . . but such an order—

(a) shall not prejudice any interest in property which was acquired from a person other than that individual and was acquired in good faith and for value or prejudice any interest deriving from such an interest, and

(b) shall not require a person who received a benefit from the transaction . . . in good faith and for value to pay a sum to the trustee of the bankrupt's estate, except where he was a party to the transaction . . .

4–133   (2A)[50]   Where a person has acquired an interest in property from a person other than the individual in question, or has received a benefit from the transaction . . ., and at the time of that acquisition or receipt—

(a) he had notice of the relevant surrounding circumstances and of the relevant proceedings, or

(b) he was an associate of, or was connected with, either the individual in question or the person with whom that individual entered into that transaction . . .

then, unless the contrary is shown, it shall be presumed for the purposes of para. (a) or para. (b) of subsection (2) that the interest was acquired or the benefit was received otherwise than in good faith.

(4) For the purposes of subsection (2A)(a), the relevant surrounding circumstances are

(a) the fact that the individual in question entered into the transaction at an undervalue; or

(b) . . .

(5) For the purposes of subsection (2A)(a), a person has notice of the relevant proceedings if he has notice—

(a) of the fact that the petition on which the individual in question is adjudicated bankrupt has been presented; or

(b) of the fact that the individual in question has been adjudged bankrupt.

QUESTIONS

4–134   1. Sharp transferred various assets to trustees to be held on trust for Sharp himself for life or until he should become bankrupt or his property should otherwise become available to his creditors. On any such event occurring the trustees were directed to pay the income to Sharp's wife for her life. Subject to those trusts the trustees were to hold on trust for Sharp's children absolutely in equal shares.

Four years after making the settlement Sharp was adjudicated bankrupt when he had a wife and two adult children.

Advise Sharp's trustee in bankruptcy as to the position if he wishes (1) to sell or (2) to retain Sharp's interest under the settlement.

4–135   2. Valiant has just been asked to become a partner in the ten partner firm of solicitors, "Chance & Hope." He knows that the firm has not been able to obtain sufficient insurance cover in respect of negligence claims, so the partners would

---

[50] These provisions came into force on July 26, 1994 by virtue of Insolvency (No., 2) Act 1994, s.6 to remove the previous difficulties for purchasers of property that had been given away in the previous 5 years and who could be adversely affected merely because they had notice of such a transaction at an undervalue. A purchaser will now be protected if his conveyancing searches do not reveal any bankruptcy proceedings being brought against the donor.

then be personally liable for any excess claims which might amount to £20 million. He owns a £½ million house and has just inherited £1,680,000. His wife is likely to be elected a local councillor in the next election. Her party is likely to win and impose financial policies contravening the law, so that she could be surcharged by the District Auditor and be bankrupted if unable to pay. They have twin sons, aged two years.

He seeks your advice on what they can do to safeguard their assets, and mentions the possibility that his wife's involvement with politics might lead them to divorce, ultimately.

Chapter 5

RESULTING TRUSTS OF PROPERTY

5–01 Megarry J. has classified resulting trusts from the way in which they arise as being either "automatic resulting trusts" or "presumed resulting trusts": *Re Vandervell's Trusts, infra.* The former arise automatically wherever some or all of the beneficial interest has not been effectively exhausted by the express trusts. The latter are presumed to arise where property is bought by X in Y's name or gratuitously transferred by X to Y in which case Y will rebuttably be presumed to hold the property on trust for X. It seems a convenient classification for expository purposes because it divides resulting trusts into two easily remembered types, rebuttable "presumed" resulting trusts and apparently irrebuttable "automatic" resulting trusts. However, is it not the case that "automatic" resulting trusts are imposed because it is presumed that a settlor expects property to result to him so far as not fully disposed of? As Lord Browne-Wilkinson stated in a published lecture:[1]

5–02 "A resulting trust arises in order to give effect to the intention of the parties. Where there is an express declaration of trust which does not exhaust the whole beneficial interest in the property Equity presumes an intention that the trust property is to revert to the original settlor, *i.e.* is held on a resulting trust. A second instance of a resulting trust is where property is purchased with money provided by two or more people: Equity presumes that they intended the property to belong to those who provided the purchase money. Accordingly, in the absence of any contrary evidence, the property is held on a resulting trust for them in shares proportionate to their contributions. A resulting trust depends on presumed intention . . . Under a resulting trust, the existence of the trust is established once and for all at the date on which the property is acquired [by the trustee(s)]".[2]

---

[1] Birmingham University Holdsworth Lecture 1991, "Constructive Trusts and Unjust Enrichment", pp. 4, and 6 reprinted in (1996) 10 Trust L.I. 98, 99–100, 100.

[2] As Hoffmann L.J. stated in *Pietrantoniou v. Fazzari* (unreported 1993 C.A. set out in Lim & Green, *Cases & Materials in Land Law* (2nd ed.) at 270) "the beneficial interest has to be taken as crystallising at the time of acquisition" unless, as Slade L.J. pointed out in *Huntingford v. Hobbs* [1993] 1 F.L.R. 736 at 745 and *Springette v. Defoe* (1992) 65 P. & C.R. 9, the parties *at such time* had agreed that their respective shares should not crystallise but should be assessed only when the property came to be sold, taking account of the parties' then direct or indirect contributions to discharging the purchase price and mortgage, or unless, *subsequent to the time of acquisition*, the parties agree on different shares or one represents to the other that the other is to have more than before, so that in either situation a party is led to act to his or her detriment or significantly alter his or her position in reliance thereon, thereby giving rise to a common intention constructive trust or an equitable proprietary estoppel:

Subsequently in *Westdeutsche v. Islington B.C.*[3] he pointed out that **5–03** "automatic" resulting trusts were not necessarily irrebuttable: "If the settlor has expressly, or by necessary implication, abandoned any beneficial interest in the trust property, there is in my view no resulting trust: the undisposed-of equitable interest vests in the Crown as *bona vacantia*." However, the law is very reluctant to find that abandonment was intended.[4]

Thus, in *Air Jamaica Ltd. v. Charlton*[5] the Privy Council held that clause 4 of a pension trust deed stating "No moneys which at any time have been contributed by the Company under the terms hereof shall in any circumstances be repayable to the Company" did not prevent a resulting trust arising in favour of the Company in respect of surplus funds arising from the trust being found unexpectedly to be void for perpetuity. Lord Millett stated,[6] "Like a constructive trust, a resulting trust arises by operation of law, though unlike a constructive trust it gives effect to intention. But it arises whether or not the transferor intended to retain a beneficial interest—he almost certainly does not—since it responds to the absence of any intention on his part to pass a beneficial interest to the recipient. It may even arise where the transferor positively wished to part with the beneficial interest as in *Vandervell v. IRC*" (where, as seen,[8] the option reserved by Vandervell for the re-purchase of his shares at a great undervalue was held on a resulting trust due to Vandervell's lack of intention as to what was ultimately going to be done with such option).

Essentially, it is the lack of evidence of X's actual intention to make a **5–04** gift or loan of his property to Y so as to benefit Y[9] that makes Equity presume that Y is intended by X to hold the property for X's benefit on a resulting trust for X. Resulting trusts are thus a response to the presumed intention of the transferor-settlor and provide a default mechanism as part of the law of property to locate beneficial ownership of property.[10]

Lloyd's Bank v. Rosset [1991] 1 A.C. 107; *Ivin v. Blake* (1994) 67 P. & C.R. 263; but *cf. Midland Bank plc v. Cooke* [1995] 4 All E.R. 465, discussed *infra*, at paras 6–105, 6–181. If property is acquired by a series of payments (unlike the normal house purchase when the vendor receives the whole purchase price at completion) a resulting trust in respect of the due proportion may arise from the payments of one or more in the series *e.g.* hire purchase or instalment payments: *Foskett v. McKeown* [1997] 3 All ER 392, 423, and, on appeal, [2000] 3 All ER 97, *infra* at para. 11–81.

[3] [1996] A.C. 669, 708

[4] *Jones v. Williams* unreported March 15, 1998, Knox J, cited by C. Rickett & R. Grantham (2000) 116 L.Q.R. 15, 20.

[5] [1999] 1 W.L.R. 1399.

[6] ibid, 1412.

[8] *Supra* at para. 2–68.

[9] *Air Jamaica Ltd. v. Charlton* [1999] 1 W.L.R. 1399, 1412 (Lord Millett); *Twinsectra Ltd. v. Yardley* [2000] WTLR 527, 562 (Potter L.J.); R. Chambers, *Resulting Trusts*, Clarendon Press Oxford, 1997 *passim*.

[10] C.E.F. Rickett & R. Grantham (2000) 116 L.Q.R. 15, 19. It matters not that at the time of the transfer Y might not have known anything of X's intentions, except that in *Quistclose* trust cases Y must have known of the restrictions imposed by X on the use of the transferred money, while in the case of joint purchases of land by X and Y the intentions of each are relevant: R. Chambers, *Resulting Trusts*, Clarendon Press Oxford, 1997, pp 35–38, Lord Millett (1998) 114 L.Q.R. 399, 401.

An alternative unorthodox approach[11] is to regard resulting trusts as arising by operation of law to reverse or prevent the unjust enrichment of Y, the recipient of the property. Taking this to the logical limit would mean that if X's actual intention to transfer the beneficial interest to Y was vitiated by any mistake or misrepresentation making the transfer voidable or was conditional on the happening of a certain event which failed to materialise, then Y holds the property on resulting trust for X. However, if X's real or mistaken intention was for Y to treat the transferred assets as a freely available part of Y's general assets, this is surely inconsistent with any proprietary trust relationship,[12] just as in the case of money paid over under a contract of loan that was void for being beyond the powers of the borrower in *Westdeutsche Landesbank v. Islington B.C. infra.* Where X has a right to rescind, then this and the working out of this equitable remedy ought to have nothing to do with resulting or constructive trusts.[13]

5–05   It is also suggested[14] that just as a resulting trust for X arises where X, as the legal beneficial owner, transfers particular property to Y without intending to benefit Y (by way of a gift or bailment or loan), so a resulting trust for X should arise where it is T, as trustee of property for X, who wrongfully without X's consent transfers the property to Y, if X did not intend to benefit Y even if T as apparent true owner did intend to benefit Y. The orthodox view[15] is that T as apparent legal beneficial owner has power[16] intentionally to transfer full legal beneficial title to Y who will, as a matter of property law, take free of X's equitable interest if a bona fide purchaser of the property without notice of X's interest. If not such a purchaser, Y will take the legal title subject to X's equitable interest. X can then compel Y to transfer the legal title to X or X's nominee, Y being constructive trustee of the property for X from the time Y was aware of X's interest and so personally accountable in equity to X for Y's stewardship of X's property. A better semantic viewpoint[17] to explain the situation is to regard Y as resulting or constructive trustee of the property for X as soon as Y received the property (a trust being regarded as arising once it is proved that "the legal title was in the plaintiff and the equitable title in the defendant"[18]), although Y does not

---

[11] P.B.H. Birks, "Restitution and Resulting Trusts" in S. Goldstein, *Equity and Contemporary Legal Developments* (Jerusalem, 1992) 361; Lord Millett, "Restitution and Constructive Trusts" in (1998) 114 L.Q.R. 399, 401 but accepting at p. 402 that "Evidence that he transferred the property by mistake or for a consideration which wholly failed will rebut any presumption of resulting trust," as brought out in "A new role for resulting trusts?" by W. Swadling (1996) 16 Legal Studies 110, endorsed by Lord Browne-Wilkinson in *Westdeutsche Landesbank v. Islington B.C.* [1996] A.C. 669, 703.

[12] Lord Millett (1998) 114 L.Q.R. 399, 406–407.

[13] Lord Millett (1998) 114 L.Q.R. 399, 416 and in "The Law of Restitution: Taking Stock", *Amicus Curiae*, February 1999, Issue 14, pages 7–8.

[14] Lord Millett (1998) 114 L.Q.R. 399, 401, and as Millett J. in *El Ajou v. Dollar Land Holdings Plc.* [1993] 3 All E.R. 717, 734; but cp. Millett LJ in *Boscawan v. Bajwa* [1996] 1 W.L.R. 318, 334–336.

[15] *Westdeutsche Landesbank v. Islington B.C.* [1996] A.C. 669, 705–706, 707, 709.

[16] without any need for signed writing of X to dispose of X's equitable interest: *Vandervell v. I.R.C.* [1967] 2 A.C. 291. Presumptions of advancement in favour of children and wives to rebut presumed resulting trusts are irrelevant, it being unnecessary to determine whether it should be Y's relationship to T or to X that is crucial.

[17] Lord Millett (1998) 114 L.Q.R. 399, 404–406.

[18] *Hardoon v. Belilios* [1901] A.C. 118, 123 endorsed by Lord Millett (1998) 114 L.Q.R. 399, 404. After all, the equitable title affects the defendant from the time the property was transferred to him (*Tinsley v. Milligan* [1993] 3 All E.R. 65, 89, *Westdeutsche* [1996] A.C. 669, 705–706)

become personally accountable in equity to X for Y's stewardship of the property until Y becomes aware of X's interest in the property.[19]

Because X's interest under a trust binds Y from the moment Y **5–06** received title to the property affected by X's interest (assuming Y was not a bona fide purchaser without notice), there is much to be said for regarding Y as trustee of the property from the outset,[20] although no fiduciary obligations affect Y till he becomes aware of X's interest.[21] However, he must produce accounts for the period of his ownership of the property so that X may vindicate his proprietary rights and trace profits made from use of the property, subject to a possible defence of change of position by Y for the period when Y was unaware of X's interest.

Resulting trusts, like constructive trusts, are exempt from the formal requirements of the Law of Property Act 1925, s.53 and, in particular, take on significance where spouses or cohabitees or relatives contribute towards property without any writing being used to set out the respective size of each contributor's interest in the property.

RE VANDERVELL'S TRUST (NO. 2)

Chancery Division [1974] Ch. 269; [1974] 1 All E.R. 47 **5–07**

See paras 2–68 *et seq.* for the facts of the case revealing that whilst the Court of Appeal disagreed with Megarry J.'s view of the facts no adverse comment was made on his propositions on resulting trusts.

MEGARRY J. (in a reserved judgment): "It seems to me that the relevant points on resulting trusts may be put in a series of propositions as follows.

"(1) If a transaction fails to make any effective disposition of any interest it does nothing. This is so at law and in equity, and has nothing to do with resulting trusts.

"(2) Normally the mere existence of some unexpressed intention in the breast of the owner of the property does nothing: there must at least be some expression of that intention before it can effect any result. To yearn is not to transfer.

"(3) Before any doctrine of resulting trust can come into play, there must at least be some effective transaction which transfers or creates some interest in property.

"(4) Where A effectually transfers to B (or creates in his favour) any interest **5–08** in any property, whether legal or equitable, a resulting trust for A may arise in two distinct classes of case. For simplicity, I shall confine my statement to cases in which the transfer or creation is made without B providing any valuable consideration, and where no presumption of advancement can arise; and I shall state the position for transfers without specific mention of the creation of new interests.

---

[19] For this personal liability to account in equity ("as constructive trustee") from the date one's conscience is affected by actual, "Nelsonian" or "naughty" knowledge of the circumstances see para. 11–111.
[20] Lord Millett's view in (1998) 114 L.Q.R. 399, 404–406; and see para. 6–04 *infra*.
[21] Lord Browne-Wilkinson's view in *Westdeutsche Landesbank v. Islington B.C.* [1996] A.C. 669, 705–706, 707, 709.

"(a) The first class of case is where the transfer to B is not made on any trust. If, of course, it appears from the transfer that B is intended to hold on certain trusts, that will be decisive, and the case is not within this category; and similarly if it appears that B is intended to take beneficially. But in other cases there is a rebuttable presumption that B holds on a resulting trust for A. The question is not one of the automatic consequences of a dispositive failure by A, but one of presumption: the property has been carried to B, and from the absence of consideration and any presumption of advancement B is presumed not only to hold the entire interest on trust, but also to hold the beneficial interest for A absolutely. The presumption thus establishes both that B is to take on trust and also what that trust is. Such resulting trusts may be called 'presumed resulting trusts.'

5–09 "(b) The second class of case is where the transfer to B is made on trusts which leave some or all of the beneficial interest undisposed of. Here B automatically holds on a resulting trust for A to the extent that the beneficial interest has not been carried to him or others. The resulting trust here does not depend on any intentions or presumptions but is the automatic consequence of A's failure to dispose of what is vested in him. Since *ex hypothesi* the transfer is on trust, the resulting trust does not establish the trust but merely carries back to A the beneficial interest that has not been disposed of. Such resulting trusts may be called 'automatic resulting trusts.'

"(5) Where trustees hold property in trust for A, and it is they who, at A's direction, make the transfer to B, similar principles apply, even though on the face of the transaction the transferor appears to be the trustees and not A. If the transfer to B is on trust, B will hold any beneficial interest that has not been effectually disposed of on an automatic resulting trust for the true transferor, A. If the transfer to B is not on trust, there will be a rebuttable presumption that B holds on a resulting trust for A."

5–10 Significantly, Megarry J. does not go on to treat under a new heading (6) a resulting trust as arising where trustees hold property in trust for A and, without A's consent or knowledge, transfer the property in breach of trust to B. Under heading (5) A is the real transferor so that from his lack of intention to make a gift a resulting trust arises in his favour, the beneficial interest remaining in the transferor. In the situation under the notional heading (6) the trustees are the real transferors intending to pass legal and beneficial ownership (and so ousting any resulting trust) to the transferee, B, who under the property law rules of priorities will hold the property, if a donee or a purchaser with notice, subject to A's equitable interest, so that once he has knowledge of this he comes to owe fiduciary obligations to A as constructive trustee of the property, as discussed at the beginning of this Chapter.

WESTDEUTSCHE LANDESBANK GIROZENTRALE V. ISLINGTON B.C.

House of Lords, [1996] AC 669; [1996] [1996] 2 W.L.R. 802; 2 All E.R. 961 (Lords Goff, Browne-Wilkinson, Slynn, Woolf and Lloyd)

5–11 The Bank sued the Council to recover £1,145,525 paid under a void interest swap transaction that was beyond the powers of the Council. The House of Lords unanimously held the money was recoverable at law as money had and received but not in equity as money subject to a resulting trust; by 3:2 it followed that, unfortunately, only simple interest was payable (though Lords Goff and Woolf considered that compound interest should be awarded by way of an equitable remedy in aid of the common law, so that full justice be given to the prevention of unjust enrichment).

LORD BROWNE-WILKINSON: *"The relevant principles of trust law*

  (i) Equity operates on the conscience of the owner of the legal interest. In the case of a trust, the conscience of the legal owner requires him to carry out the purposes for which the property was vested in him (express or implied trust) or which the law imposes on him by reason of his unconscionable conduct (constructive trust).

 (ii) Since the equitable jurisdiction to enforce trusts depends upon the conscience of the holder of the legal interest being affected, he cannot be a trustee of the property if and so long as he is ignorant of the facts alleged to affect his conscience, *i.e.* until he is aware that he is intended to hold the property for the benefit of others in the case of an express or implied trust, or, in the case of a constructive trust, of the factors which are alleged to affect his conscience.

(iii) In order to establish a trust there must be identifiable trust property. The only apparent exception to this rule is a constructive trust[21a] imposed on a person who dishonestly assists in a breach of trust who may come under fiduciary duties even if he does not receive identifiable trust property.

(iv) Once a trust is established, as from the date of its establishment the beneficiary has, in equity, a proprietary interest in the trust property, which proprietary interest will be enforceable in equity against any subsequent holder of the property (whether the original property or substituted property into which it can be traced) other than a purchaser for value of the legal interest without notice.

"These propositions are fundamental to the law of trusts and I would have **5–12** thought uncontroversial. However, proposition (ii) may call for some expansion. There are cases where property has been put into the name of X without X's knowledge but in circumstances where no gift to X was intended. It has been held that such property is recoverable under a resulting trust: *Birch v. Blagrave* (1755) Amb. 264; *Childers v. Childers* (1875) 1 De G. & J. 482; *Re Vinogradoff* [1935] W.N. 68; *Re Muller* [1953] N.Z.L.R. 879. These cases are explicable on the ground that, by the time action was brought, X or his successors in title have become aware of the facts which gave rise to a resulting trust: his conscience was affected as from the time of such discovery and *thereafter* he held on a resulting trust under which the property was recovered from him. There is, so far as I am aware, no authority which decides that X was a trustee, and therefore accountable for his deeds, at any time before he was aware of the circumstances which gave rise to a resulting trust.

"Those basic principles are inconsistent with the case being advanced by the **5–13** Bank. The latest time at which there was any possibility of identifying the 'trust property' was the date on which the monies in the mixed bank account of the

---

[21a] Editor's note: this *personal* liability to account in equity "as a constructive trustee" arises to make someone who is not a trustee personally liable as if he had been a trustee, and needs to be distinguished from a constructive trust *of property* that gives rise to *proprietary* remedies: *Paragon Finance plc v. D.B. Thakerar & Co* [1999] 1 All E.R. 400, 409 (Millett L.J.), and *infra* at para. 6–09.

local authority ceased to be traceable when the local authority's account went into overdraft in June 1987. At that date, the local authority had no knowledge of the invalidity of the contract but regarded the monies as its own to spend as it thought fit. There was therefore never a time at which both (a) there was defined trust property and (b) the conscience of the local authority in relation to such defined trust property was affected. The basic requirements of a trust were never satisfied.

"I turn then to consider the Bank's arguments in detail . . .

The retention of title point

5–14   "It is said that, since the Bank only intended to part with its beneficial ownership of the monies in performance of a *valid* contract, neither the legal nor the equitable title passed to the local authority at the date of payment. The legal title vested in the local authority by operation of law when the monies became mixed in the bank account but, it is said, the Bank 'retained' its equitable title.

"I think this argument is fallacious. A person solely entitled to the full beneficial ownership of money or property, both at law and in equity, does not enjoy an equitable interest in that property. The legal title carries with it all rights. Unless and until there is a separation of the legal and equitable estates, there is no separate equitable title. Therefore to talk about the Bank 'retaining' its equitable interest is meaningless. The only question is whether the circumstances under which the money was paid were such as, in equity, to impose a trust on the local authority. If so, an equitable interest arose for the first time under that trust.

"This proposition is supported by *Re Cook* [1948] Ch. 212; *Vandervell v. I.R.C.* [1967] 2 A.C. 291 at 311g, *per* Lord Upjohn, and 317f, *per* Lord Donovan; *Commissioner of Stamp Duties (Queensland) v. Livingston* [1965] A.C. 694 at 712b–e; Underhill and Hayton, *Law of Trusts and Trustees* (15th ed, 1995), p. 866.

The separation of title point

5–15   "The Bank's submission, at its widest, is that if the legal title is in A but the equitable interest in B. A holds as trustee for B.

"Again I think this argument is fallacious. There are many cases where B enjoys rights which, in equity, are enforceable against the legal owner, A, without A being a trustee, *e.g.* an equitable right to redeem a mortgage, equitable easements, restrictive covenants, the right to rectification, an insurer's right by subrogation to receive damages subsequently recovered by the assured: *Lord Napier and Ettrick v. Hunter* [1993] A.C. 713. Even in cases where the whole beneficial interest is vested in B and the bare legal interest is in A, A is not necessarily a trustee, *e.g.* where title to land is acquired by estoppel as against the legal owner: a mortgagor who has fully discharged his indebtedness enforces his right to recover the mortgaged property in a redemption action, not an action for breach of trust.

5–16   "The Bank contended that where, *under a pre-existing trust*, B is entitled to an equitable interest in trust property, if the trust property comes into the hands of a third party, X (not being a purchaser for value of the legal interest without notice), B is entitled to enforce his equitable interest against the property in the hands of X because X is a trustee for B. In my view the third party, X, is not necessarily a trustee for B: B's equitable right is enforceable against the property in just the same way as any other specifically enforceable equitable right can be enforced against a third party. Even if the third party, X, is not aware that what he has received is trust property B is entitled to assert his title in that property. If X has the necessary degree of knowledge, X may himself become a constructive trustee for B on the basis of knowing receipt. But unless he has the requisite degree of knowledge he is not personally liable to account as trustee: *Re Diplock* [1948] Ch. 465 at 478; *Re Montagu's Settlement* [1987] Ch. 264. Therefore, innocent receipt of property by X subject to an existing equitable interest does not by itself make X a trustee despite the severance of the legal and equitable titles. Underhill and Hayton, *Law of Trusts and Trustee*, (15th ed.), pages 369–370, whilst accepting that X is under no personal liability to account unless and until he becomes aware of B's rights, does describe X as being a constructive trustee. This may only be a question of semantics: on either footing, in the present case the local authority could not have become accountable for profits until it knew that the contract was void.

Resulting Trust

"This is not a case where the Bank had any equitable interest which predated **5–17** receipt by the local authority of the upfront payment. Therefore, in order to show that the local authority became a trustee, the Bank must demonstrate circumstances which raised a trust for the first time either at the date on which the local authority received the money or at the date on which payment into the mixed account was made. Counsel for the Bank specifically disavowed any claim based on a constructive trust. This was plainly right because the local authority had no relevant knowledge sufficient to raise a constructive trust at any time before the monies, upon the bank account going into overdraft, became untraceable. Once there ceased to be an identifiable trust fund, the local authority could not become a trustee: *Re Goldcorp Exchange Ltd* [1995] 1 A.C. 74. Therefore, as the argument for the Bank recognised, the only possible trust which could be established was a resulting trust arising from the circumstances in which the local authority received the upfront payment.

"Under existing law a resulting trust arises in two sets of circumstances: **5–18**

(A) Where A makes a voluntary payment to B or pays (wholly or in part) for the purchase of property which is vested either in B alone or in the joint names of A and B, there is a presumption that A did not intend to make a gift to B: the money or property is held on trust for A (if he is the sole provider of the money) or in the case of a joint purchase by A and B in shares proportionate to their contributions. It is important to stress that this is only a *presumption*, which presumption is easily rebutted either by the counter-presumption of advancement or by direct evidence of A's intention to make an outright transfer: see *Underhill and Hayton, supra*, p. 317 *et seq.*; *Vandervell v. I.R.C.* [1967] 2 A.C. 291 at 312 *et seq.*; *Re Vandervell (No. 2)* [1974] Ch. 269 at 288 *et seq.*

(B) Where A transfers property to B *on express trusts*, but the trusts declared do not exhaust the whole beneficial interest: *ibid.* and *Barclays Bank v. Quistclose Investments Ltd* [1970] A.C. 567.

Both types of resulting trust are traditionally regarded as examples of trusts giving effect to the common intention of the parties. A resulting trust is not imposed by law against the intentions of the trustee (as a constructive trust) but gives effect to his presumed intention. Megarry J. in *Re Vandervell (No. 2)* suggests that a resulting trust of type (B) does not depend on intention but operates automatically. I am not convinced that this is right. If the settlor has expressly, or by necessary implication, abandoned any beneficial interest in the trust property, there is in my view no resulting trust: the undisposed-of equitable interest vests in the Crown as *bona vacantia*: see *Re West Sussex Constabulary's Widows, Children and Benevolent (1930) Fund Trusts* [1971] Ch. 1.

5–19   "Applying these conventional principles of resulting trust to the present case, the Bank's claim must fail. There was no transfer of money to the local authority on express trusts: therefore a resulting trust of type (B) above could not arise. As to type (A) above, any presumption of resulting trust is rebutted since it is demonstrated that the Bank paid, and the local authority received, the upfront payment with the intention that the monies so paid should become the absolute property of the local authority. It is true that the parties were under a misapprehension that the payment was made in pursuance of a valid contract. But that does not alter the actual intentions of the parties at the date the payment was made or the monies were mixed in the bank account. As the article by William Swadling (16 Legal Studies 110) demonstrates the presumption of resulting trust is rebutted by evidence of any intention inconsistent with such a trust, not only by evidence of an intention to make a gift.

5–20   "Professor Birks (in Goldstein (ed.), *Equity: Contemporary Legal Developments* (1992)), whilst accepting that the principles I have stated represent 'a very conservative form' of definition of a resulting trust (page 360), argues from restitutionary principles that the definition should be extended so as to cover a perceived gap in the law of 'subtractive unjust enrichment' (page 368) so as to give a plaintiff a proprietary remedy when he has transferred value under a mistake or under a contract the consideration for which wholly fails. He suggests that a resulting trust should arise wherever the money is paid under a mistake (because such mistake vitiates the actual intention) or when money is paid on a condition which is not subsequently satisfied.

5–21   "As one would expect, the argument is tightly reasoned but I am not persuaded. The search for a perceived need to strengthen the remedies of a plaintiff claiming in restitution involves, to my mind, a distortion of trust principles. First, the argument elides rights in property (which is the only proper subject matter of a trust) into rights in 'the value transferred': see page 361. A trust can only arise where there is defined trust property: it is therefore not consistent with trust principles to say that a person is a trustee of property which cannot be defined. Second, Professor Birks' approach appears to assume (for example in the case of a transfer of value made under a contract the consideration for which subsequently fails) that the recipient will be deemed to have been a trustee from the date of his original receipt of money, *i.e.* the trust arises at a time when the 'trustee' does not, and cannot, know that there is going to be a total failure of consideration. This result is incompatible with the basic premise on which all trust law is built, *viz*, that the conscience of the trustee is affected. Unless and until the trustee is aware of the factors which give rise to the supposed trust, there is nothing which can affect his conscience. Thus neither in the case of a subsequent failure of consideration nor in the case of payment under a contract subsequently found to be void for mistake or failure of condition will there be circumstances, at the date of receipt, which can impinge on the conscience of the recipient, thereby making him a trustee. Thirdly, Professor Birks has to impose on his wider view an arbitrary and admittedly unprincipled modification so as to ensure that a resulting trust does not arise when there has only been a failure to perform a contract, as opposed to total failure of consideration: see pages 356–359 and 362. Such arbitrary exclusion is designed to preserve the rights of creditors in the insolvency of the recipient. The fact that it is necessary to exclude artificially one type of case which would logically fall within the wider concept casts doubt on the validity of the concept.

"If adopted, Professor Birks' wider concepts would give rise to all the practical **5–22** consequences and injustices to which I have referred. I do not think it right to make an unprincipled alteration to the law of property (*i.e.* the law of trusts) so as to produce in the law of unjust enrichment the injustices to third parties which I have mentioned and the consequential commercial uncertainty which any extension of proprietary interests in personal property is bound to produce.

The authorities

"Three cases were principally relied upon in direct support of the proposition that a resulting trust arises where a payment is made under a void contract.

(A) Sinclair v. Brougham [1914] A.C. 398

"The case concerned the distribution of the assets of the Birkbeck Building **5–23** Society, an unincorporated body which was insolvent. The Society had for many years been carrying on business as a bank which, it was held, was *ultra vires* its objects. The bank had accepted deposits in the course of its *ultra vires* banking business and it was held that the debts owed to such depositors were themselves void as being *ultra vires*. In addition to the banking depositors, there were ordinary trade creditors. The Society had two classes of members, the A shareholders who were entitled to repayment of their investment on maturity and the B shareholders whose shares were permanent. By agreement, the claims of the ordinary trade creditors and of the A shareholders had been settled. Therefore the only claimants to the assets of the Society before the Court were the *ultra vires* depositors and the B shareholders, the latter of which could take no greater interest than the Society itself.

"The issues for decision arose on a summons taken out by the liquidator for directions as to how he should distribute the assets in the liquidation. In the judgments, it is not always clear whether this House was laying down general propositions of law or merely giving directions as to the proper mode in which the assets in that liquidation should be distributed. The depositors claimed, first, in quasi contract for money had and received. They claimed secondly, as the result of an argument suggested for the first time in the course of argument in the House of Lords (at 404), to trace their deposits into the assets of the Society.

Money had and received

"The House of Lords was unanimous in rejecting the claim by the *ultra vires* **5–24** depositors to recover in quasi-contract on the basis of monies had and received. In their view, the claim in quasi-conract was based on an implied contract. To imply a contract to repay would be to imply a contract to exactly the same effect as the express *ultra vires* contract of loan. Any such implied contract would itself be void as being *ultra vires*.

"Subsequent developments in the law of restitution demonstrate that this reasoning is no longer sound. The common law restitutionary claim is based not on implied contract but on unjust enrichment: in the circumstances the law imposes an obligation to repay rather than implying an entirely fictitious agreement to repay: *Fibrosa v. Fairbairn* [1943] A.C. 32 at 63–64 *per* Lord Wright; *Pavey & Matthews Pty. Ltd v. Paul* [1987] 69 A.L.R. 579 at 583, 603;

Lipkin Gorman v. Karpnale Ltd [1991] 2 A.C. 548 at 578c; *Woolwich Equitable Building Society v. I.R.C.* [1993] A.C. 70. In my judgment, Your Lordships should now unequivocally and finally reject the concept that the claim for monies had and received is based on an implied contract. I would overrule *Sinclair v. Brougham* on this point.

5–25   "It follows that in *Sinclair v. Brougham* the depositors should have had a personal claim to recover the monies at law based on a total failure of consideration. The failure of consideration was *not* partial: the depositors had paid over their money in consideration of a promise to repay. That promise was *ultra vires* and void: therefore the consideration for the payment of the money wholly failed. So in the present swaps case (though the point is not one under appeal) I think the Court of Appeal were right to hold that the swap monies were paid on a consideration that wholly failed. The essence of the swap agreement is that, over the whole term of the agreement, each party thinks he will come out best; the consideration for one party making a payment is an obligation on the other party to make counter-payments over the whole term of the agreement.

"If in *Sinclair v. Brougham* the depositors had been held entitled to recover at law, their personal claim would have ranked *pari passu* with other ordinary unsecured creditors, in priority to the members of the society who could take nothing in the liquidation until all creditors had been paid.

The claim in rem

5–26   "The House of Lords held that, the ordinary trade creditors having been paid in full by agreement, the assets remaining were to be divided between the *ultra vires* depositors and the members of the Society *pro rata* according to their respective payments to the Society . . .

"As has been pointed out frequently over the 80 years since it was decided, *Sinclair v. Brougham* is a bewildering authority: no single ratio decidendi can be detected; all the reasoning is open to serious objection; it was only intended to deal with cases where there were no trade creditors in competition and the reasoning is incapable of application where there are such creditors. In my view the decision as to rights *in rem* in *Sinclair v. Brougham* should also be overruled. Although the case is one where property rights are involved, such overruling should not in practice disturb long-settled titles. However, Your Lordships should not be taken to be casting any doubt on the principles of tracing as established in *Re Diplock*.

"If *Sinclair v. Brougham*, in both its aspects, is overruled the law can be established in accordance with principle and commercial common sense: a claimant for restitution of monies paid under an *ultra vires*, and therefore void, contract has a personal action at law to recover the monies paid as on a total failure of consideration; he will not have an equitable proprietary claim which gives him either rights against third parties or priority in an insolvency; nor will he have a personal claim in equity, since the recipient is not a trustee.

(B) Chase Manhattan Bank N.A. v. Israel-British Bank (London) Ltd [1981] Ch. 105

5–27   "In that case Chase Manhattan, a New York bank, had by mistake paid the same sum twice to the credit of the defendant, a London bank. Shortly thereafter, the defendant bank went into insolvent liquidation. The question was whether Chase Manhattan had a claim *in rem* against the assets of the defendant bank to recover the second payment.

"Goulding J. was asked to assume that the monies paid under a mistake were capable of being traced in the assets of the recipient bank: he was only concerned with the question whether there was a proprietary base on which the tracing remedy could be founded: at 116b. He held that, where money was paid under a mistake, the receipt of such money *without more* constituted the recipient a trustee: he said that the payer 'retains an equitable property in it and the conscience of [the recipient] is subject to a fiduciary duty to respect his proprietary right'; at 119d–e.

"It will be apparent from what I have already said that I cannot agree with this **5–28** reasoning. First, it is based on a concept of retaining an equitable property in money where, prior to the payment of the recipient bank, there was no existing equitable interest. Further, I cannot understand how the recipient's 'conscience' can be affected at a time when he is not aware of any mistake. Finally, the Judge found that the law of England and that of New York were in substance the same. I find this a surprising conclusion since the New York law of constructive trusts has for a long time been influenced by the concept of a *remedial* constructive trust, whereas hitherto English law has for the most part only recognised an institutional constructive trust: see *Metall & Rohstoff v. Donaldson Inc.* [1990] 1 Q.B. 391 at 478–480. In the present context, that distinction is of fundamental importance. Under an institutional constructive trust, the trust arises by operation of law as from the date of the circumstances which give rise to it: the function of the court is merely to declare that such trust has arisen in the past. The consequences that flow from such trust having arisen (including the possibily unfair consequences to third parties who in the interim have received the trust property) are also determined by rules of law, not under a discretion. A remedial constructive trust, as I understand it, is different. It is a judicial remedy giving rise to an enforceable equitable obligation: the extent to which it operates retrospectively to the prejudice of third parties lies in the discretion of the court. Thus for the law of New York to hold that there is a remedial constructive trust where a payment has been made under a void contract gives rise to different consequences from holding that an institutional constructive trust arises in English law.

"However, although I do not accept the reasoning of Goulding J., *Chase* **5–29** *Manhattan* may well have been rightly decided. The defendant bank knew of the mistake made by the paying bank within two days of the receipt of the monies: see at 115a. The judge treated this fact as irrelevant (at 114f) but in my judgment it may well provide a proper foundation for the decision. Although the mere receipt of the monies, in ignorance of the mistake, gives rise to no trust, the retention of the monies after the recipient bank learned of the mistake may well have given rise to a constructive trust: see *Snell's Equity*, p. 193; *Pettit Equity and the Law of Trusts* (7th ed.) p. 168; *Metall and Rohstoff v. Donaldson Inc.* [1990] 1 Q.B. 391 at pages 473–474.

(C) Re Ames' Settlement [1946] 1 Ch. 217

. . . In either event, the decision has no bearing on the present case. On either view, the fund was vested in trustees on trusts which had failed. Therefore the monies were held on a resulting trust of type (b) above. The decision casts no light on the question whether, there being no express trust, monies paid on a consideration which wholly fails are held on a resulting trust.

The stolen bag of coins

"The argument for a resulting trust was said to be supported by the case of a **5–30** thief who steals a bag of coins. At law those coins remain traceable only so long as they are kept separate: as soon as they are mixed with other coins or paid into a mixed account they cease to be traceable at law. Can it really be the case, it is asked, that in such circumstances the thief cannot be required to disgorge the property which, in equity, represents the stolen coins? Monies can only be traced in equity if there has been at some stage a breach of fiduciary duty, *i.e.* if either before the theft there was an equitable proprietary interest (*e.g.* the coins were stolen trust monies) or such interest arises under a resulting trust at the time of the theft or the mixing of the monies. Therefore, it is said, a resulting trust must arise either at the time or the theft or when the monies are subsequently mixed. Unless this is the law, there will be no right to recover the assets representing the stolen monies once the monies have become mixed.

"I agree that the stolen monies are traceable in equity. But the proprietary interest which equity is enforcing in such circumstances arises under a constructive, not a resulting, trust. Although it is difficult to find clear authority for the proposition, when property is obtained by fraud equity imposes a constructive trust on the fraudulent recipient: the property is recoverable and traceable in equity. Thus, an infant who has obtained property by fraud is bound in equity to restore it: *Stocks v. Wilson* [1913] 2 K.B. 235 at 244; *R. Leslie Ltd v. Shiell* [1914] 3 K.B. 607. Monies stolen from a bank account can be traced in equity: *Bankers Trust Co. v. Shapira* [1980] 1 W.L.R. 1274 at 1282 c–e. See also *McCormick v. Grogan* L.R. 4 H.L. 82 at 97.

Restitution and equitable rights

5–31   "Those concerned with developing the law of restitution are anxious to ensure that, in certain circumstances, the plaintiff should have the right to recover property which he has unjustly lost. For that purpose they have sought to develop the law of resulting trusts so as to give the plaintiff a proprietary interest. For the reasons that I have given in my view such development is not based on sound principle and in the name of unjust enrichment is capable of producing most unjust results. The law of resulting trusts would confer on the plaintiff a right to recover property from, or at the expense of, those who have not been unjustly enriched at his expense at all, *e.g.* the lender whose debt is secured by a floating charge and all other third parties who have purchased an equitable interest only, albeit in all innocence and for value.

"Although the resulting trust is an unsuitable basis for developing proprietary restitutionary remedies, the remedial constructive trust, if introduced into English law, may provide a more satisfactory road forward. The court by way of remedy might impose a constructive trust on a defendant who knowingly retains property of which the plaintiff has been unjustly deprived. Since the remedy can be tailored to the circumstances of the particular case, innocent third parties would not be prejudiced and restitutionary defences, such as change of position, are capable of being given effect. However, whether English law should follow the United States and Canada by adopting the remedial constructive trust will have to be decided in some future case where the point is directly in issue."

Section 1. Automatic Resulting Trusts (for Failing Trusts)

Where they arise

5–32   These trusts arise in favour of the settlor where he has settled his property on express trusts which fail whether for failure of marriage consideration, uncertainty, lapse, disclaimer, perpetuity, illegality, non-compliance with requisite statutory formalities, or for any other reason.[22] They also arise if settlors fail to dispose exhaustively of the whole beneficial interest under their express trusts[23] or create a *Quistclose*[24] money trust for a purpose (agreed with the recipient) which fails.[25] Fiscal considerations these days often make a resulting trust in favour of the settlor in a particular eventuality the very last thing intended by the settlor, though, logically and arithmetically, the settlor must expect that what he has not effectively divested himself of must remain in him.[26]

Where express trusts of funds subscribed by many settlors do not exhaust the funds there is a resulting trust in favour of the settlors rateably in proportion to the amounts subscribed by them.[27] In the case of charitable trusts that fail the funds will usually be applied *cy-près* as will be seen in Chapter 7.

Whether or not the settlor has failed to dispose effectively of the **5–33** entire beneficial interest is often a difficult matter. In *Re Abbott*[28] a fund had been subscribed for the maintenance and support of two deaf and dumb ladies and Stirling J. held, not as a matter of construction of the documents by which the subscriptions had been sought, but as an inference from all the facts, that the surplus left after both ladies died was held on a resulting trust for the subscribers. In *Re Andrew's Trust*[29] a fund was subscribed solely for the education of the children of a deceased clergyman and not for exclusive use of one child or for equal division among them but as necessary, and after the formal education of the children had been completed Kekewich J. held that the children were entitled to the balance equally. He construed "education" in the broadest sense as not being exhausted upon formal education ending and treated the reference to education as expressing merely the motive of the gift.[30] "If a gross sum be given, or if the whole income of property be given, and a special purpose be assigned for the gift this court [rebuttably] regards the gift as absolute and the purpose merely as the motive of the gift, and therefore holds that the gift takes effect as to the whole sum or the whole income as the case may be."

This was applied by the Court of Appeal in *Re Osoba*[31] holding that a **5–34** bequest to the testator's widow upon trust "for her maintenance and for the training of my daughter Abiola up to university grade and for the

---

[22] *Hodgson v. Marks* [1971] Ch. 892 at 933, *per* Russell L.J.; *Re Ames's Settlement* [1946] Ch. 217 though see now sections 16 and 24 of the Matrimonial Causes Act 1973. If the settlor were a testator then the property results to the testator's estate: if the property were specifically devised or bequeathed it falls into residue, whilst if the property were comprised in the residuary gift the property passes to the next-of-kin under the intestacy rules set out in the Administration of Estates Act 1925 as amended. On the impact of illegality see *infra* paras 5–100 to 5–133.

[23] *Re Gillingham Bus Disaster Fund*, [1958] Ch. 300; *Re West* [1900] 1 Ch. 84.

[24] *Barclays Bank Ltd v. Quistclose Investments Ltd.* [1970] A.C. 567.

[25] *Re EVTR* [1987] B.C.L.C. 646, *supra* at para. 3–51.

[26] *Re Vandervell's Trusts (No. 2)* [1974] Ch. 269 *supra*, para. 2–68.

[27] *Air Jamaica Ltd v. Charlton* [1999] 1 W.L.R. 1399 (P.C.); *Re British Red Cross Balkan Fund* [1914] 2 Ch. 419 (where in the absence of the Att.-Gen. a resulting trust was erroneously admitted: *Re Welsh Hospital Fund* [1921] 1 Ch. 655 at 662); *Re Hobourn Aero Components Ltd's Air Raid Disaster Fund* [1946] Ch. 194.

[28] [1900] 2 Ch. 326. See *supra*, at para. 3–217.

[29] [1905] 2 Ch. 48.

[30] *ibid.* at 52–53 citing Page-Wood V.-C. in *Re Sanderson's Trust* (1857) 3 K. & J. 497; 503.

[31] [1979] 2 All E.R. 393. See *supra*, at para. 3–218.

maintenance of my aged mother" was a trust for the three females absolutely as joint tenants so that nothing resulted to the testator's estate after Abiola finished her university education, the widow and the mother having died by then, so that Abiola was absolutely entitled.

Where there can be no resulting trust

5–35   There is no resulting trust in favour of the donor or his estate if the donee is intended to take the property beneficially subject only to a charge for some purpose. Thus, in *Re Foord*[32] where a testator left his estate to his sister "absolutely . . . on trust" to pay his widow an annuity and the estate income exceeded the annuity the sister was held beneficially entitled to the balance.

There is no resulting trust if the rule in *Hancock v. Watson*[33] applies. This is the rule "that if you find an absolute gift to a legatee in the first instance, and trusts are engrafted or imposed on that absolute interest which fail, either from lapse or invalidity or any other reason, then the absolute gift takes effect so far as the trusts have failed to the exclusion of the residuary legatee or next-of-kin as the case may be."[34] The rule is equally applicable to *inter vivos* settlements.[35]

5–36   There is no resulting trust if the doctrine of acceleration applies to prevent there being a temporary failure to exhaust the beneficial interest under a trust.[36] Thus, if T by will leaves property to A for life and after A's death to B absolutely and A disclaims his interest, B's interest is accelerated so as to take effect immediately, thereby ousting any possible resulting trust of the income till A's death. For the doctrine to apply the remainderman must have a vested interest and there must be no contrary intention manifested in the trust document.[37]

5–37   There can normally be no resulting trust where a donor has parted with his property in pursuance of some contract (except for the very rare case of money paid over for a purpose benefiting persons which, if implemented, gives rise to a debtor-creditor relationship but, if unimplemented, gives rise to a resulting trust as exemplified by *Barclays Bank Ltd v. Quistclose Investments Ltd*[38] and *Re EVTR*[39] *ante*): see para. 3–15. Thus, in the case of a society, formed to raise funds by subscriptions from its members for the purpose of providing for their widows, which had surplus funds after the death of the last widow, there could be no resulting trust for the deceased members' estates: each member had parted absolutely with his money in return for contractual benefits for his

---

[32] [1922] 2 Ch. 519. Contrast the resulting trust in *Re West* [1900] 1 Ch. 84.
[33] [1902] A.C. 14.
[34] *ibid.* at 22, *per* Lord Davey.
[35] *Att.-Gen. v. Lloyds Bank* [1935] A.C. 382; *Re Burton's S.T.* [1955] Ch. 348; *Watson v. Holland* [1985] 1 All E.R. 290.
[36] *Re Flower's S. T.* [1957] 1 W.L.R. 401; *Re Davies* [1957] 1 W.L.R. 922; *Re Harker* [1969] 1 W.L.R. 1124 (rightly not following *Re Davies* on the impact of acceleration upon the class closing rules); *Re Hodge* [1963] Ch. 300; A. M. Prichard [1973] Camb.L.J. 246.
[37] *Re Scott* [1975] 2 All E.R. 1033.
[38] [1970] A.C. 567.
[39] [1987] B.C.L.C. 646.

widow.[40] Similarly, no resulting trust can arise where donors part absolutely with their money for tickets contractually entitling them to participate in raffles, sweepstakes, beetle drives, whist drives, discotheques, or to watch live entertainment, and the purposes for which such money has been raised fail to exhaust the profits arising after deducting expenses.[41]

Exceptionally, as revealed by *Davis v. Richard & Wallington Ltd*[42] **5–38** where, pursuant to a contract, money was transferred to trustees of a trust like a pension fund (rather than paid absolutely to a treasurer of an unincorporated society) and the trust deed was silent as to the destination of surplus, and there was no possibility of amending the deed to deal with such surplus[43] the law supplies a resulting trust in favour of the provider of the funds in question unless such be clearly expressly or impliedly excluded. Thus, Scott J. opined that the surplus derived primarily from the overfunding arising from the contributions of the employer (which was obliged to make up any deficiencies if the employees' contributions proved inadequate) would be held on resulting trust for the employer. However, as regards the surplus derived from employees' contributions he opined that it would pass to the Crown as *bona vacantia* because the circumstances of the case pointed "firmly and clearly to the conclusion that a resulting trust in favour of the employees is excluded." Why? Because equity should not impute to the employees an intention that would lead to an unworkable result,[44] the value of benefits being different for each employee, or lead to employees receiving more than the legislature intended in its legislative limits on maximum benefits under exempt approved schemes.

Lord Millett in *Air Jamaica Ltd. v. Charlton*[45] did not find these **5–39** reasons convincing when tax law considerations should not distort legal principle and the resulting trust concept is a response to a lack of intention. Air Jamaica had set up a pension trust in 1969 with clause 4 of the Trust Deed stating, "No moneys which at any time have been contributed by the Company under the terms hereof shall in any circumstances be repayable to the Company." Section 13 of the Pension Plan enabled the Company to discontinue the Plan at any time, in which event, after providing defined benefits to Members, additional benefits were to be provided for Members, surviving spouses or designated beneficiaries. There was a large 400 million dollar surplus at the time the Plan was held to have been discontinued, but the discontinuance provisions for additional benefits were held void for perpetuity.

---

[40] *Cunnack v. Edwards* [1896] 2 Ch. 679.
[41] *Re West Sussex Constabulary's Benevolent Fund Trusts* [1971] Ch. 1, *infra*, at para. 5–44.
[42] [1990] 1 W.L.R. 1511 discussed by J. Martin [1991] Conv. 366; S. Gardner [1992] Conv. 41.
[43] Now see Pensions Act 1995, ss.68, 69.
[44] But if proportionate return under a resulting trust were unworkable why not have a per capita distribution to cut the Gordian Knot? According to Goff J. in *Re West Sussex Constabulary's Fund Trusts* [1970] 1 All E.R. 544 at 548, "The Court will not find itself baffled but will cut the Gordian knot." Note also that Scott J. treated the *bona vacantia* approach of *Re West Sussex Constabulary's Fund Trusts* [1971] Ch. 1 as valid, overlooking the negative impact thereon of *Re Bucks Constabulary Fund* [1979] 1 W.L.R. 936, discussed *infra*, at para. 5–43.
[45] [1999] 1 W.L.R. 1399

Lord Millett held[46] that "the surplus is held on a resulting trust for those who provided it . . . Contributions were payable by the Members with matching contributions by the Company . . . the surplus must be treated as provided as to one half by the Company and as to one half by the Members." Clause 4 did not oust a resulting trust for the Company because it was not intended to cover what had happened outside, rather than within, the terms of the contributory pension scheme.

5–40 The Jamaican Government's submission that it was entitled to the Members' half share of the surplus as *bona vacantia* (ownerless property) because the Members' had received their contractual entitlement was rejected "because they have not received what they bargained for"[47] when the provisions of section 13 were held void. Therefore, the Members' share of surplus should not be treated as abandoned assets but should be divided proportionately among the Members and the estates of deceased Members in proportion to contributions made by each Member, without regard to the benefits received by each of them and irrespective of the dates on which contributions were made.

It can thus be seen that there can be no resulting trust where a transferor has transferred property by way of out-and-out abandonment of all interest in it, though it can be difficult, where money is raised for certain purposes, to show that donors had a general intention to part with their money out-and-out beyond all recall rather than merely part with their money *submodo* to the intent that the certain purposes be carried out. However, where street collections are concerned, with thousands of anonymous donors, the courts are becoming increasingly ready to find a general intention to part utterly with contributed money so as to exclude any resulting trust in favour of the donors with the result that unused moneys pass as *bona vacantia* to the Crown,[48] unless accruing to the funds of an unincorporated association[49] for whom the collections were made.

Dissolution of unincorporated associations

5–41 When an unincorporated association is dissolved it is necessary to ascertain whether its property falls to be distributed on a resulting trust basis to persons providing such property or on a contractual basis to the association members or as *bona vacantia* to the Crown.

5–42 The old view[50] that rights to such property are founded in resulting trust has been totally discredited. It is now well established that the interests and rights of persons who are members of any type of

---

[46] *ibid* at 1411

[47] *ibid* at 1413. This concern with failure of consideration could be regarded as justifying the imposition of a resulting trust to prevent unjust enrichment rather than as a response to lack of intention of Members to benefit others (as earlier emphasised at 1412) but in context it was natural for Lord Millett to counter the Government's argument in its own terms.

[48] *Re West Sussex Constabulary's Fund Trusts* [1971] Ch. 1 infra para. 5–44; contrast *Re Gillingham Bus Disaster Fund* [1958] Ch. 300.

[49] *Re Bucks Constabulary Fund Friendly Society (No. 2)* [1979] 1 W.L.R. 936, *infra*, para. 5–50.

[50] *Re Printers and Transferrers Amalgamated Trades Protection Society* [1899] 2 Ch. 184; *Re Lead Co.'s Workmen's Fund Society* [1904] 2 Ch. 196.

unincorporated association are governed exclusively by contract.[51] Whilst the assets of the association are usually vested in trustees on trust for the members this is a quite separate and distinct trust bearing no relation to the claims of the members *inter se* to the surplus assets. Thus, as between a number of people contractually interested in a fund, if the terms of the contract do not provide some other method of distribution then distribution is on the basis of equality, subject only to third-party rights against the fund. Such rights will arise either by the duly authorised procedure in the association's constitution for creating contracts or express trusts or by declarations of trust imposed by a donor upon giving property to the association. However, where such a donor is concerned, since such a trust would be likely to fail for offending the rule against remoteness before the 1964 Perpetuities and Accumulations Act or the rule against inalienability or the beneficiary principle, the tendency of the courts is to validate such a gift as not imposing a trust, unless there are clear words to such effect, but as an out-and-out beneficial gift to members of the association as an accretion to the funds which are the subject-matter of the contract which the members have made between themselves, so that it falls to be dealt with in precisely the same way as the funds which the members themselves have subscribed as a matter of contract.[52]

Only if the association has become moribund, as where all the members or all but one have died, will the assets be treated as *bona vacantia* and pass to the Crown.[53]

The present position is clearly apparent from the decision of Walton J. **5–43** in *Re Bucks Constabulary Fund Friendly Society (No. 2), infra*. Whilst, as he pointed out, one can distinguish the decision of Goff J. in *Re West Sussex Constabulary's Benevolent Fund, infra*, on the footing that it concerned a simple unincorporated association whilst *Re Bucks* concerned a friendly society affected by the Friendly Societies Act 1896, s.49(1), it seems clear that the reasoning underlying *Re West Sussex* and distinguishing a club for members from a club of members for third parties or purposes is erroneous[54] and that Walton J. would have decided it differently in favour of the members rather than the Crown as to members' subscriptions and contributions and the proceeds of entertainment, raffles, collecting boxes, etc. Indeed, in view of the dicta in *Re Recher's W.T.*[55] cited by Walton J it is likely that donations and legacies would also, if he had decided the case, have passed to the members rather than be held on resulting trust for the donors or testators.

---

[51] *Tierney v. Tough* [1914] 1 I.R. 142; *Re St. Andrew's Allotment Association* [1969] 1 W.L.R. 229; *Re William Denby Ltd's Sick Fund* [1971] 1 W.L.R. 973; *Re West Sussex Constabulary's Benevolent Fund* [1971] Ch. 1; *Re Sick & Funeral Society of St. John's Sunday School* [1973] Ch. 51 (per capita basis but child members only to have a half share); *Re GKN Bolts and Nuts Ltd Sports and Social Club* [1982] 1 W.L.R. 774; *Re Bucks Constabulary Fund Friendly Society (No. 2)* [1979] 1 All E.R. 623.

[52] *Re Recher's W.T.* [1972] Ch. 526; *Re Lipinski's W.T.* [1976] Ch. 235, discussed *supra*, para. 3–225 *et seq.*

[53] *Re Bucks Constabulary Fund Friendly Society (No. 2)* [1979] 1 All E.R. 623; *Cunnack v. Edwards* [1896] 2 Ch. 679; *Re West Sussex Constabulary's Benevolent Fund* [1971] Ch. 1 is probably erroneous. If under the association's rules the last member can claim the property without having to call a meeting, *e.g.* in the case of a tontine society then he or his estate will be entitled to the property.

[54] See *Re Grant's W.T.* [1979] 3 All E.R. 359 at 365.

[55] [1972] Ch. 526, 538–539, *supra*, at paras 3–249, 3–250.

RE WEST SUSSEX CONSTABULARY'S BENEVOLENT FUND TRUSTS

Chancery Division [1971] Ch. 1; [1970] 2 W.L.R. 848: [1970] 1 All E.R. 544

5–44   In 1930 a fund was set up to provide for widows and orphans of deceased members. The W. Sussex Constabulary amalgamated with other forces in 1968 so that it was doubtful as to how its funds were to be dealt with. The funds came from (1) contributions of past and present members; (2) entertainments, raffles, sweepstakes; (3) collecting boxes; (4) donations and legacies.

In a reserved judgment Goff J. held that (4) were held on resulting trusts for the donors whilst (1), (2) and (3) were *bona vacantia* though these holdings are now of doubtful authority in view of the next case, *Re Bucks Constabulary Fund Friendly Society (No. 2)*. However, the following dicta are good law.

GOFF J.: ". . . I must now turn to the moneys raised from outside sources. Counsel for the Attorney-General made an overriding general submission that there could not be a resulting trust of any of the outside moneys because in the circumstances it is impossible to identify the trust property. No doubt something could be achieved by complicated accounting, but this, he submitted, would not be identification but notional reconstruction. I cannot accept that argument. In my judgment in a case like the present, equity will cut the gordian knot by simply dividing the ultimate surplus in proportion to the sources from which it has arisen . . .

5–45   "There may be cases of tolerable simplicity where the court will be more refined, but in general where a fund has been raised from mixed sources interest has been earned over the years and income and possibly capital expenditure has been made indiscriminately out of the fund as an entirety, and when the venture comes to an end, prematurely or otherwise, the court will not find itself baffled but will cut the gordian knot as I have said.

5–46   "Then counsel divided the outside moneys into three categories: first, the proceeds of entertainments, raffles and sweepstakes; secondly, the proceeds of collecting boxes; and thirdly, donations including legacies, if any, and he took particular objections to each. I agree that there cannot be any resulting trust with respect to the first category. I am not certain whether Harman J. meant to decide otherwise in the *Gillingham Bus Disaster* case.[56] The statement of facts[57] refers to 'street collections and so forth.' There is mention of whist drives and concerts in the argument,[58] but the judge himself did not speak of anything other than gifts. If he did, however, I must respectfully decline to follow his judgment in that regard, for whatever may be the true position with regard to collecting boxes, it appears to me to be impossible to apply the doctrine of resulting trust to the proceeds of entertainments and sweepstakes and such-like money raising operations for two reasons. First, the relationship is one of contract and not of trust. The purchaser of a ticket may have the motive of aiding the cause or he may not. He may purchase a ticket merely because he wishes to attend the particular entertainment or to try for the prize, but whichever it be he pays his money as the price of what is offered and what he receives. Secondly, there is in such cases no direct contribution to the fund at all. It is only the profit, if any, which is

---

[56] [1958] Ch. 300.
[57] [1958] Ch. 300 at 304.
[58] [1958] Ch. 300 at 309.

ultimately received, and there may even be none. In any event the first category cannot be any more susceptible to the doctrine than the second to which I now turn.

"Here one starts with the well-known dictum of P.O. Lawrence J. in *Re Welsh* **5–47** *Hospital (Netley) Fund, Thomas v. Att.-Gen.*[59]

> 'So far as regards the contributors to entertainments, street collections, etc., I have no hesitation in holding that they must be taken to have parted with their money out and out. It is inconceivable that any person paying for a concert ticket or placing a coin in a collecting box presented to him in the street should have intended that any part of the money so contributed should be returned to him when the immediate object for which the concert was given or the collection made had come to an end. To draw such an inference would be absurd on the face of it.'

This was adopted by Upjohn J. in *Re Hillier, Hillier v. Att.-Gen.*,[60] where the point was actually decided.

"In *Re Ulverston & District New Hospital Building Fund*,[61] Jenkins L.J. threw **5–48** out a suggestion that there might be a distinction in the case of a person who could prove that he put a specified sum in a collecting box, and in the *Gillingham* case[62] Harman J. after noting this, decided that there was a resulting trust with respect to the proceeds of collections. He said[63]:

> 'In my judgment the Crown has failed to show that this case should not follow the ordinary rule merely because there was a number of donors who, I will assume, are unascertainable. I see no reason myself to suppose that the small giver who is anonymous has any wider intention than the large giver who can be named. They all give for the one object. If they can be found by inquiry the resulting trust can be executed in their favour. If they cannot I do not see how the money could then, with all respect to Jenkins L.J., change its destination and become *bona vacantia*. It will be merely money held on a trust for which no beneficiary can be found. Such cases are common, and where it is known that there are beneficiaries, the fact that they cannot be ascertained does not entitle the Treasury Solicitor to come in and claim. The trustees must pay the money into court like any other trustee who cannot find his beneficiary. I conclude, therefore, that there must be an inquiry for the subscribers to this fund.'

For my part I cannot reconcile the decision of Upjohn J. in *Re Hillier* with that of **5–49** Harman J. in the *Gillingham* case. I agree that all who put their money into collecting boxes should be taken to have the same intention, but why should they not all be regarded as intending to part with their money out and out, absolutely, in all circumstances? I observe that P.O. Lawrence J. used very strong words. He said any other view was inconceivable and absurd on the face of it. That commends itself to my humble judgment, and I, therefore, prefer and follow the judgment of Upjohn J. in *Re Hillier*."

---

[59] [1921] 1 Ch. 655 at 660, 661.
[60] [1954] 1 W.L.R. 9.
[61] [1956] Ch. 622 at 633.
[62] [1958] Ch. 300.
[63] [1958] Ch. 300 at 314.

RE BUCKS CONSTABULARY FUND FRIENDLY SOCIETY (NO. 2)

Chancery Division [1979] 1 W.L.R. 936; [1979] 1 All E.R. 623

5–50   The Bucks Constabulary Fund Friendly Society was established to provide for the relief of widows and orphans of deceased members of the Bucks Constabulary. It was an unincorporated association registered under the Friendly Societies Act 1896 but it had no rules providing for the distribution of its assets in the event of it being wound up.

On being wound up the question arose whether the surplus assets were *bona vacantia* passing to the Crown or whether they should be distributed amongst members at the date of dissolution, in which case should distribution be equally *per capita* or on some other basis?

WALTON J. read the following judgment: "There are basically two claimants to the fund, the Solicitor for the Affairs of Her Majesty's Treasury, who claims the assets as ownerless property, *bona vacantia*, and the members of the friendly society at the date of its dissolution on October 14, 1969.

5–51   "Before considering the relevant legislation, it is I think desirable to view the question of the property of unincorporated associations in the round. If a number of persons associate together, for whatever purpose, if that purpose is one which involves the acquisition of cash or property of any magnitude, then, for practical purposes, some one or more persons have to act in the capacity of treasurers or holders of the property. In any sophisticated association there will accordingly be one or more trustees in whom the property which is acquired by the association will be vested. These trustees will of course not hold such property on their own behalf. Usually there will be a committee of some description which will run the affairs of the association; though of course in a small association the committee may well comprise all the members; and the normal course of events will be that the trustee, if there is a formal trustee, will declare that he holds the property of the association in his hands on trust to deal with it as directed by the committee. If the trust deed is a shade more sophisticated it may add that the trustee holds the assets on trust for the members in accordance with the rules of the association. Now in all such cases it appears to me quite clear that, unless under the rules governing the association the property thereof has been wholly devoted to charity, or unless and to the extent to which the other trusts have validly been declared of such property, the persons, and the only persons, interested therein are the members. Save by way of a valid declaration of trust in their favour, there is no scope for any other person acquiring any rights in the property of the association, although of course it may well be that third parties may obtain contractual or proprietary rights, such as a mortgage, over those assets as the result of a valid contract with the trustees or members of the committee as representing the association.

5–52   "I can see no reason for thinking that this analysis is any different whether the purpose for which the members of the association associate are a social club, a sporting club, to establish a widows' and orphans' fund, to obtain a separate Parliament for Cornwall, or to further the advance of alchemy. It matters not. All the assets of the association are held in trust for its members (of course subject to the contractual claims of anybody having a valid contract with the association) save and except to the extent to which valid trusts have otherwise been declared of its property. I would adopt the analysis made by Brightman J. in *Re Recher's Will Trusts*[64] (set out, *supra*, paras 3–249 to 3–250) . . .

---

[64] [1972] Ch. 526 at 538–539.

"All this doubtless seems quite elementary, but it appears to me to have been lost sight of to some extent in some of the decisions which I shall hereafter have to consider in detail in relation to the destination on dissolution of the funds of unincorporated associations.

"Now in the present case I am dealing with a society which was registered **5–53** under the Friendly Societies Act 1896. This does not have any effect at all on the unincorporated nature of the society, or (as I have in substance already indicated) on the way in which its property is held. But the latter point is in fact made very explicit by the provisions of section 49(1) of the 1896 Act which reads as follows:

'All property belonging to a registered society, whether acquired before or after the society is registered, shall vest in the trustees for the time being of the society, for the use and benefit of the society and the members thereof, and of all persons claiming through the members according to the rules of the society.'

"There can be no doubt, therefore, that in the present case the whole of the **5–54** property of the society is vested in the trustees for the use and benefit of the society and the members thereof and of all persons claiming through the members according to the rules of the society. I do not think I need go through the rules in detail. They are precisely what one would expect in the case of an association whose main purpose in life was to enable members to make provision for widows and orphans. Members paid a contribution in exchange for which in the event of their deaths their widows and children would receive various benefits. There is a minimal benefit for which provision is made in the case of a member suffering very severe illness indeed, but, as counsel for the Treasury Solicitor was able to demonstrate from an analysis of the accounts, virtually the entire expenditure of the association was, as indeed one would expect, on the provision of widows' and orphans' benefits. But, of course, there is no trust whatsoever declared in their favour. I am not called on, I think, to decide whether they are, within the meaning of section 49(1), persons claiming through the members according to the rules of the society, or whether they are simply the beneficiaries of stipulations by the members for the benefit of third parties. All parties are agreed that accrued rights of such persons must be given full effect. There is indeed no rule which says what is to happen to surplus assets of the society on a dissolution. But in view of section 49(1) there is no need. The assets must continue to be held, the society having been dissolved, and the widows and orphans being out of the way, simply for the use and benefit of the members of the society, albeit they will all now be former members.

"In a work of great authority on all matters connected with friendly societies, **5–55** Baden Fuller,[65] the learned author says this:

'If the rules provide for the termination of the society they usually also provide for the distribution of the funds in that event, but if on the termination of a society no provision has been made by the rules for the distribution of its funds, such funds are divisible among the existing members at the time of the termination or dissolution in proportion to the amount contributed by each member for entrance fees and subscriptions,

---

[65] *The Law of Friendly Societies* (4th ed., 1926), p. 186.

and irrespective of fines or payments made to members in accordance with the rules.'

5-56   "In my judgment this accurately represents the law, at any rate so far as the beneficiaries of the trust on dissolution are concerned, although not necessarily so far as the *quantum* of their respective interests is concerned; a matter which still remains to be argued. The effective point is that the claims of the Treasury Solicitor to the funds as *bona vacantia* are unsuitable in the present case. I say 'in the present case' because there are undoubtedly cases where the assets of an unincorporated association do become *bona vacantia*. To quote Baden Fuller again[66]:

> 'A society may sometimes become defunct or moribund by its members either all dying or becoming so reduced in numbers that it is impossible either to continue the society or to dissolve it by instrument; in such cases the surplus funds, after all existing claims (if any) under the rules have been satisfied or provided for, are not divisible among the surviving members . . . or the last survivor . . . or the representative of the last survivor . . . nor is there any resulting trust in favour of the personal representatives of the members of the society . . . not even in favour of honorary members in respect of donations by them . . . In these circumstances two cases seem to occur: if the purposes of the society are charitable, the surplus will be applicable *cy-près* . . . but if the society is not a charity, the surplus belongs to the Crown as *bona vacantia*.'

5-57   "Before I turn to a consideration of the authorities, it is I think pertinent to observe that all unincorporated societies rest in contract to this extent, that there is an implied contract between all of the members *inter se* governed by the rules of the society. In default of any rule to the contrary, and it will seldom if ever be that there is such a rule, when a member ceases to be a member of the association he *ipso facto* ceases to have any interest in its funds. Once again, so far as friendly societies are concerned, this is made very clear by section 49(1), that it is the members, the present members, who, alone, have any right in the assets. As membership always ceases on death, past members or the estates of deceased members therefore have no interest in the assets. Further, unless expressly so provided by the rules, unincorporated societies are not really tontine societies, intended to provide benefits for the longest liver of the members. Therefore, although it is difficult to say in any given case precisely when a society becomes moribund, it is quite clear that if a society is reduced to a single member neither he, still less his personal representatives on his behalf, can say he is or was the society and therefore entitled solely to its fund. It may be that it will be sufficient for the society's continued existence if there are two members, but if there is only one the society as such must cease to exist. There is no association, since one can hardly associate with oneself or enjoy one's own society. And so indeed the assets have become ownerless.

5-58   "I now turn to the authorities. The first case is that of *Cunnack v. Edwards*.[67] The association there in question was established in 1810 to raise a fund by the subscriptions, fines and forfeitures of its members, to provide annuities for the

---

[66] *ibid.* at 186–187.
[67] [1895] 1 Ch. 489; *on appeal* [1896] 2 Ch. 679.

widows of its deceased members. It was later registered under the Friendly Societies Act 1829. This Act was repealed later, but its material provisions remained in force with regard to societies registered thereunder. There was no provision in that Act corresponding to section 49(1) of the 1896 Act. Sections 3, 8 and 26 are material[68] . . .

"The scheme of the 1829 Act thus was that the rules must specify all the **5–59** circumstances under which any member of the society might become entitled to any part of its assets, and that on a dissolution the distribution of the assets had to conform to the general intents and purposes of the society. It is at once apparent why in that case an alteration of the rules was essential before any member could take any part of the assets, as, on their face, the rules were exclusively concerned with the provision of the relief of the widows of deceased members. There was no provision whatsoever relating to any members. In the course of time the society was reduced to two members, one an honorary member who was in fact the ultimate survivor, but who had disclaimed any interest in the society's assets, the other an ordinary member who died and whose personal representative claimed the surplus of the assets of the society after provision had been made for the payment of the last annuity to the last widow . . . In the Court of Appeal[69] the only point argued apart from the question of charity was the third, the resulting trust point, and Lord Halsbury L.C. did indeed decide against this point on the contractual basis.

"A careful examination of that case reveals that the really crucial fact was that **5–60** the rules were required to state all the uses applicable to the assets of the society and they stated none in favour of members. On dissolution section 26 governed, and following on the absence of any provision in favour of members in the rules the members were not entitled to any interest in the assets. Hence the inescapable conclusion that the surplus assets had no owner and must go to the Crown. At the risk of repetition, the combined effect of the rules and the 1829 Act made it quite impossible for any argument to the effect that on dissolution the assets vested in the then members in some shares and proportions, which is the normal argument to be put forward in such a case. The case therefore did not decide that this was not the usual position in the case of an unincorporated association not then registered under the Friendly Societies Act. [The judge then referred to *Re Printers and Transferrers Amalgamated Trades Protection Society*[70]; *Braithwaite v. Attorney-General*[71]; *Tierney v. Tough*[72] and *Re St. Andrews Allotment Association's Trusts*[73] and *Re William Denby & Sons Ltd Sick and Benevolent Fund.*[74]]

"Finally, there comes a case which gives me great concern, *Re West Sussex* **5–61** *Constabulary's Widows, Children and Benevolent (1930) Fund Trusts.*[75] The case is indeed easily distinguishable from the present case in that what was there under consideration was a simple unincorporated association and not a friendly society, so that the provisions of section 49(1) of the 1896 Act do not apply. Otherwise the facts in that case present remarkable parallels to the facts in the present case. Goff J. decided that the surplus funds had become *bona vacantia*. [See *supra*, at para. 5–44.]

---

[68] See *per* Rigby L.J. in [1896] 2 Ch. 679 at 687–689.
[69] [1896] 2 Ch. 679.
[70] [1899] 2 Ch. 184.
[71] [1909] Ch. 510.
[72] [1914] I.R. 142.
[73] [1969] 1 W.L.R. 229.
[74] [1971] 1 W.L.R. 973 at 978; [1971] 2 All E.R. 1196 at 1201.
[75] [1971] Ch. 1; [1970] 1 All E.R. 544.

5–62   The material parts of that judgment read as follows[76]:

5–63   'First it was submitted that it belongs exclusively and in equal shares to all
those persons now living who were members on December 31, 1967 and
the personal representatives of all the then members since deceased, to all
of whom I will refer collectively as 'the surviving members.' The argument
is based on the analogy of the members' club cases. I cannot accept that as
applicable, for these reasons. First, it simply does not look like it. This was
nothing but a pensions or dependent relatives fund not at all akin to a
club. Secondly, in all the cases where the surviving members have taken,
with the sole exception of *Tierney's* case,[77] the club, society or organisation
existed for the benefit of the members for the time being exclusively,
whereas in the present case as in *Cunnack v. Edwards*,[78] only third parties
could benefit. Moreover, in *Tierney's* case the exception was minimal and
discretionary and can, I think, fairly be disregarded. Finally, this very
argument was advanced and rejected by Chitty J. in the *Cunnack* case[79] at
first instance, and was abandoned on the hearing of the appeal. That
judgment also disposes of the further argument that the surviving members
had power to amend the rules under rule 14 and could, therefore, have
reduced the fund into possession and so ought to be treated as the owners
of it or the persons for whose benefit it existed at the crucial moment.
They had the power but they did not exercise it, and it is now too late.

5–64   Then it was argued that there is a resulting trust, with several possible
consequences. If this be the right view there must be a primary division
into three parts, one representing contributions from former members,
another contributions from the surviving members, and the third moneys
raised from outside sources. The surviving members then take the second,
and possibly by virtue of rule 10 the first also. Rule 10 is as follows: "Any
member who voluntarily terminates his membership shall forfeit all claim
against the Fund except in the case of a member transferring to a similar
Fund of another force in which instance the contributions paid by the
member to the West Sussex Constabulary's Widows, Children and Benevolent (1930) Fund may be paid into the Fund of the force to which the
member transfers." Alternatively, the first may belong to the past members
on the footing that rule 10 is operative so long only as the fund is a going
concern, or may be *bona vacantia*. The third is distributable in whole or in
part between those who provide the money, or again is *bona vacantia*. In
my judgment the doctrine of resulting trust is clearly inapplicable to the
contributions of both classes. Those persons who remained members until
their deaths are in any event excluded because they have had all they
contracted for, either because their widows and dependants have received
or are in receipt of the prescribed benefits, or because they did not have a
widow or dependants. In my view that is inherent in all the speeches in the
Court of Appeal in *Cunnack v. Edwards*.[80] Further, whatever the effect of
rule 10 may be on the contribution of those members who left prematurely, they and the surviving members alike are also unable to claim

---

[76] [1971] Ch. 1 at 8–10.
[77] [1914] I.R. 142.
[78] [1896] 2 Ch. 679.
[79] [1895] 1 Ch. 489.
[80] [1896] 2 Ch. 679.

under a resulting trust, because they put up their money on a contractual basis and not one of trust: see *Re Gillingham Bus Disaster Fund*.[81] Accordingly, in my judgment all the contributions of both classes are *bona* **5–65** *vacantia*, but I must make a reservation with respect to possible contractual rights. In *Cunnack v. Edwards* and *Braithwaite v. Att.-Gen.*,[82] all the members had received or provision had been made for all the contractual benefits. Here the matter has been cut short. Those persons who died whilst still in membership cannot, I conceive, have any rights, because in their case the contract has been fully worked out, and on a contractual basis I would think that members who retired would be precluded from making any claim by rule 10, although that is perhaps more arguable. The surviving members, on the other hand, may well have a right in contract on the ground of frustration or total failure of consideration, and that right may embrace contributions made by past members, though I do not see how it could apply to moneys raised from outside sources. I have not, however, heard any argument based on contract and therefore the declarations I propose to make will be subject to the reservation which I will later formulate. This will not prevent those parts of the fund which are *bona vacantia* from being paid over to the Crown as it has offered to give a full indemnity to the trustees;"

and the judge then turned to consider the destination of moneys from outside sources, with which of course I am not here concerned.

"It will be observed that the first reason given by the judge for his decision is **5–66** that he could not accept the principle of the members' clubs as applicable. This is a very interesting reason, because it is flatly contrary to the successful argument of Mr. Ingle Joyce who appeared for the Attorney-General in the case Goff J. purported to follow, *Cunnack v. Edwards*. His argument was as follows[83]:

'This society was nothing more than a club, in which the members had no transmissible interest: *Re St. James' Club*.[84] Whatever the members, or even the surviving member, might have done while alive, when they died their interest in the assets of the club died with them';

and in the Court of Appeal[85] he used the arguments he had used below. If all **5–67** that Goff J. meant was that the purposes of the fund before him were totally different from those of a members' club then of course one must agree, but if he meant to imply that there was some totally different principle of law applicable one must ask why that should be. His second reason is that in all the cases where the surviving members had taken, the organisation existed for the benefit of the members for the time being exclusively. This may be so, so far as actual decisions go, but what is the principle? Why are the members not in control, complete control, save as to any existing contractual rights, of the assets belonging to their organisation? One could understand the position being different if valid trusts had been declared of the assets in favour of third parties, for example charities, but that this was emphatically not the case was demonstrated by the fact that

---

[81] [1958] Ch. 300 at 314.
[82] [1909] 1 Ch. 510.
[83] [1895] 1 Ch. 489 at 494.
[84] [1852] 2 De G.M. & G. 383 at 387.
[85] [1896] 2 Ch. 679.

Goff J. recognised that the members could have altered the rules prior to dissolution and put the assets into their own pockets. If there was no obstacle to their doing this, it shows in my judgment quite clearly that the money was theirs all the time. Finally he purports to follow *Cunnack v. Edwards*[86] and it will be seen from the analysis which I have already made of that case that it was extremely special in its facts, resting on a curious provision of the 1829 Act which is no longer applicable. As I have already indicated, in the light of section 49(1) of the 1896 Act the case before Goff J.[87] is readily distinguishable, but I regret that, quite apart from that, I am wholly unable to square it with the relevant principles of law applicable.

5–68   "The conclusion therefore is that as on dissolution there were members of the society here in question in existence, its assets are held on trust for such members to the total exclusion of any claim on behalf of the Crown. The remaining question under this head which falls now to be argued is, of course, whether they are simply held *per capita*, or, as suggested in some of the cases, in proportion to the contributions made by each . . .

"I think that there is no doubt that, as a result of modern cases springing basically from the decision of O'Connor M.R. in *Tierney v. Tough*,[88] judicial opinion has been hardening and is now firmly set along the lines that the interests and rights of persons who are members of any type of unincorporated association are governed exclusively by contract, that is to say the rights between themselves and their rights to any surplus assets. I say that to make it perfectly clear that I have not overlooked the fact that the assets of the society are usually vested in trustees on trust for the members. But that is quite a separate and distinct trust bearing no relation to the claims of the members *inter se* on the surplus funds so held on trust for their benefit.

5–69   "That being the case, prima facie there can be no doubt at all but that the distribution is on the basis of equality, because, as between a number of people contractually interested in a fund, there is no other method of distribution if no other method is provided by the terms of the contract, and it is not for one moment suggested here that there is any other method of distribution provided by the contract. We are, of course, dealing here with a friendly society, but that really makes no difference to the principle. The Friendly Societies Acts do not incorporate the friendly society in any way and the only effect that it has is, as I pointed out in my previous judgment in this case, that there is a section which makes it crystal clear in the Friendly Societies Act 1896 that the assets are indeed held on trust for the members.

5–70   "Now the fact that the prima facie rule is a matter of equality has been recently laid down, not of course for the first time, in two cases to which I need do no more than refer, *Re St. Andrew's Allotment Association's Trusts*,[89] a decision of the late Ungoed-Thomas J., and *Re Sick and Funeral Society of St. John's Sunday School, Golcar*, a decision of Megarry J.[90] Neither of those cases was, however, the case of a friendly society, and there are a number of previous decisions in connection with friendly societies, and, indeed, *Tierney v. Tough*[91]

---

[86] [1896] 2 Ch. 679.
[87] [1971] Ch. 1.
[88] [1914] I.R. 142.
[89] [1969] 1 W.L.R. 229.
[90] [1973] Ch. 51. (where the society's rules indicated a per capita basis of one share for each full member and one half-share for each child member).
[91] [1914] I.R. 142.

itself is such a case, where the basis of distribution according to the subscriptions paid by the persons among whom the fund is to be distributed has been applied, and it has been suggested that perhaps those decisions are to be explained along the lines that a friendly society, or similar society, is thinking more of benefits to members, and that, thinking naturally of benefits to members, you think, on the other side of the coin, of subscriptions paid by members. But in my judgment that is not a satisfactory distinction of any description, because one is now dealing with what happens at the end of the life of the association; there are surplus funds, funds which have not been required to carry out the purposes of the association, and it does not seem to me it is a suitable method of distribution to say that one then looks to see what the purposes of the society were while the society was a going concern.

"An ingenious argument has been put by counsel for the third and fifth **5–71** defendants: the members of the society are entitled in equity to the surplus funds which are distributable among them, therefore they are to be distributed among them according to equitable principles and those principles should, like all equitable principles, be moulded to fit the circumstances of the case, and in one case it would therefore be equitable to distribute in equal shares, in another case it might be equitable to distribute in proportion to the subscription that they have paid, and I suppose that in another case it might be equitable to distribute according to the length of their respective feet, following a very well known equitable precedent. Well, I completely deny the basic premise. The members are not entitled in equity to the fund; they are entitled at law. It is a matter, so far as the members are concerned, of pure contract, and, being a matter of pure contract, it is, in my judgment, as far as distribution is concerned, completely divorced from all questions of equitable doctrines. It is a matter of simple entitlement, and that entitlement must be, and can only be, in equal shares."

Section 2. Presumed Resulting Trusts (for Apparent Gifts)

I. PRESUMPTION OF A RESULTING TRUST

These trusts arise in X's favour where X purchases property but in Y's name **5–72** or in the name of X and Y or where X and Y purchase property in Y's name. They may also arise in cases where X gratuitously transfers his interest in property to others. The presumption is "no more than a long-stop to provide the answer when the relevant facts and circumstances fail to yield a solution."[92] "Presumptions may be looked on as the bats of the law flitting in the twilight but disappearing in the sunrise of the actual facts."[93] The presumption arises from X's lack of intention to benefit Y,[94] and can be countered by the presumption of advancement (*infra* paras 5–96 *et seq.*) if X is the father or husband of Y or stands in *loco parentis* to Y.

---

[92] *Vandervell v. I.R.C.* [1967] 2 A.C. 291 at 313, *per* Lord Upjohn.
[93] *Mackowick v. Kansas City* (1906) 945 W. 256 at 264, *per* Lamm J. The presumptions are a "last resort" and where X purchases property or gratuitously transfers it to a company or trust controlled by X the proper natural inference is that beneficial ownership is intended to pass to the company or trustees: *Nightingale Mayfair Ltd v. Mehta* [2000] W.T.L.R. 901, 925–926.
[94] R. Chambers, *Resulting Trusts*, Clarendon Oxford 1997, 26, *Air Jamaica Ltd v. Charlton* [1999] 1 W.L.R. 1399, 1412 (P.C.), *Twinsectra Ltd v. Yardley* [2000] W.T.L.R. 527 562 (C.A.); *Brown v. Brown* [1993] 31 N.S.W.L.R. 582 (C.A.)

5–73   Where property is purchased with the aid of X's moneys it is vital whether X paid over the moneys as purchaser or lender. If X provided £25,000 of a £100,000 purchase price of a house put in Y's name then if X lent the £25,000 he is only entitled as a personal creditor to the £25,000 and any agreed interest, whereas if he provided the £25,000 as purchaser he is entitled to a quarter share in the house. Loan and purchase by way of resulting trust are thus mutually exclusive,[95] though in an exceptional case a loan arrangement may commence as a primary temporary trust to carry out a purpose which, if carried out, results in a pure loan relationship but which, if not carried out, gives rise to a secondary final express or resulting trust as in *Barclays Bank Ltd v. Quistclose Investments Ltd* (discussed *supra*, para. 3–214). If Y alleges that X provided moneys by way of gift and not by way of loan or purchase then the onus is on Y to prove this.[96]

5–74   If X and Y purchase a yearly tenancy for £3,000 each in Y's name then Y holds it on resulting trust. However, if no capital sum is paid and Y alone takes on the tenancy, having arranged for X to share the rent and gas and electricity bills, and X does so, X cannot claim a half share under a resulting trust in the tenancy or in the freehold purchased by Y on favourable terms (subject to reimbursing Y half the price of the freehold).[97] Payments of a capital, as opposed to an income, nature are required to establish a resulting trust. Thus, if X and Y buy a home in Y's name for £100,000 X having paid £50,000 directly, but Y providing £50,000 by way of mortgage, Y cannot claim a greater share than half if repayments of capital with interest amount to £100,000. It makes no difference whether Y has such a repayment mortgage or instead, an endowment mortgage where the £50,000 remains due for the duration of an endowment assurance policy (*e.g.* 20 or 25 years) so that interest on the full £50,000 is paid during such period until the policy matures to provide at least £50,000 to pay off the mortgage debt.

The Types of Transactions

(a) Purchase in the name of another

5–75   X purchases property (real or personal) in the name of Y. Ordinarily, if X wishes to make a gift to Y, he will purchase the property in his own name and then convey it to Y. Here he has paid the purchase-money, but has required his vendor to convey to Y. Y is then presumed in equity to hold the property on a resulting trust for X.[98]

(b) Purchase by one in joint names of himself and another

X purchases property (real or personal) in the *joint* names of himself *and* Y. As in (a) above, X has paid the purchase-money, but instead of

---

[95] *Aveling v. Knipe* (1815) 19 Ves. 441; *Re Sharpe* [1980] 1 All E.R. 198 at 201; at para. 3–15, *supra; Winkworth v. Edward Baron Development Co.* [1987] 1 All E.R. 114 at 118, *per* Lord Templeman.
[96] *Seldon v. Davidson* [1968] 1 W.L.R. 1083; *Dewar v. Dewar* [1975] 1 W.L.R. 1532.
[97] *Savage v. Dunningham* [1974] Ch. 181.
[98] *Dyer v. Dyer* (1788) 2 Cox 92; *Vandervell v. I.R.C.* [1967] 2 A.C. 291.

requiring his vendor to convey to Y alone, he takes a conveyance to himself and Y jointly. Here again equity presumes that X and Y hold the property on a resulting trust for X.[99]

(c) Joint purchase in name of one

X *and* Y jointly purchase property (real or personal) in the name of Y **5–76** alone. Both X and Y have contributed towards the purchase-money, but the conveyance is taken in the name of Y alone. There will be a presumption that Y holds the property on resulting trust for X and Y in shares proportionate to their contributions.[1]

(d) Transfer from one to another

X gratuitously *transfers* property into the name of Y. In (a), (b) and (c) above the transaction was a *purchase*; here it is a *transfer*. Property already stands in the name of X, who gratuitously transfers it into the name of Y. It is presumed that Y holds the property on resulting trust for X although, as in (a) (b) and (c) above, if X is the father of Y or stands *in loco parentis* (*patris*) to Y or is husband of Y, there will be a rebuttable[2] presumption of advancement in favour of Y.[3]

Exceptionally, no resulting trust arises if the property is land,[4] by **5–77** virtue of section 60(3) of the Law of Property Act 1925, which provides: "In a voluntary conveyance a resulting trust for the grantor shall not be implied merely by reason that the property is not expressed to be conveyed for the use or benefit of the grantee." By section 205(1)(ii) of the Act the expression "conveyance" includes a "mortgage, charge, lease . . . and every other assurance of property or of an interest therein by any instrument, except a will," unless the context otherwise requires; and by section 205(1)(xx) the expression "property" includes any interest in property real *or* personal, unless the context otherwise requires. The context of section 60 appears, however, to restrict the meaning of "property" in subsection (3) to land. For other property, *e.g.* stocks and shares, the stranger, Y, will hold the property rebuttably upon a resulting trust for X.[5] Slight circumstances should enable the presumption to be rebutted in the case of chattels and cash where it will not be considered so likely that the donor intends to retain the beneficial interest.

(e) Transfer into joint names of transferor and another

X gratuitously transfers property into the *joint* names of himself and **5–78** Y. As in (d) above, property already stands in the name of X, but instead of transferring it into the *sole* name of Y, he gratuitously transfers it into

---

[99] *Benger v. Drew* (1721) 1 P.Wms. 781; *Rider v. Kidder* (1805) 10 Ves. 360.
[1] *The Venture* [1908] P. 218; *Bull v. Bull* [1955] 1 Q.B. 234.
[2] *Re Gooch* (1890) 62 L.T. 384 (shares); *Shephard v. Cartwright* [1955] A.C. 431.
[3] *Currant v. Jago* (1844) 1 Coll. 261 (cash); *May v. May* (1863) 33 Beav. 81 (land).
[4] *Lohia v. Lohia* [2001] W.T.L.R. 101. Oral evidence revealing that the transferor intended to retain the equitable interest will oust any presumption of resulting trust: *Hodgson v. Marks* [1971] Ch. 892.
[5] *Vandervell v. I.R.C.* [1967] 2 A.C. 291 at 312; *Re Vandervell's Trusts (No. 2)* [1974] Ch. 269; *Fowkes v. Pascoe* (1875) 10 Ch.App. 343 at 348; *Hepworth v. Hepworth* (1870) L.R. 11 Eq. 10.

the *joint* names of himself and Y. There will be a presumption of a resulting trust in favour of X[6] for property other than land as discussed in (d) above. An example is *Young v. Sealey*,[7] in which X opened a joint banking account with Y, but during her life X retained complete control of the account, and Y neither paid anything into nor drew anything out of it. On X's death Y took the legal title by survivorship. Did he, however, hold it on trust for X's estate? Romer J. held that the presumption of a trust in favour of X's estate arose, but that this was rebutted by the evidence of Y as to X's intentions. If X is Y's husband then the presumption of advancement applies unless the joint account was opened merely for conveniently managing X's affairs (*e.g.* if X is ill).[8] If it was opened with the intention of making provision for the wife, as is quite likely if X alone opened the account, then the wife will be entitled to the balance on X's death.[9]

5–79   The further question arises whether X's provision for whatever is left in the joint account with Y to pass to Y amounts to a testamentary disposition where X controls the account, Y having no sole drawing rights till X's death. Following the Australian High Court's lead,[10] English courts of first instance[11] have held that no testamentary disposition is involved, there being[12] "an immediate gift [at the time of opening the joint account] of a fluctuating asset consisting of the chose in action for the time being constituting the balance in the bank account." The Irish Supreme Court in *Lynch v. Burke*[13] overruled an earlier decision of its own to hold that no testamentary disposition is involved either because there is a gift subject to the contingency of surviving the donor or because the donee has been given contractual rights under documents signed by the donee and enforceable against the bank and the donor's executor, assuming the donor's intentions exclude the possibility of a resulting trust.

(f) Joint purchase and joint mortgage

5–80   Where X and Y, though providing the money in unequal shares, purchase property in their joint names or jointly advance money on mortgage in their joint names, and X dies, Y takes the legal title to the whole by survivorship but will be treated as a tenant in common in equity and holds the share of the purchase or mortgage money advanced by X on trust for X's estate.[14]

---

[6] *Re Vinogradoff* [1935] W.N. 68.
[7] [1949] Ch. 278; *Re Reid* (1921) 50 Ont.L.R. 595; *Russell v. Scott* (1936) 55 C.L.R. 440.
[8] *Marshal v. Crutwell* (1875) L.R. 20 Eq. 328.
[9] *Re Figgis* [1969] 1 Ch. 123; see (1969) 85 L.Q.R. 530 (M. C. Cullity).
[10] *Russell v. Scott* (1936) 56 C.L.R. 440.
[11] *Young v. Sealey* [1943] Ch. 278; *Re Figgis* [1969] 1 Ch. 123.
[12] *Re Figgis* [1969] 1 Ch. 123, 149 per Megarry J.
[13] [1995] 2 I.R. 159 discussed by P. Capper (1996) 47 N.I.L.Q. 281
[14] *Re Jackson* (1887) 34 Ch.D. 732; *Cobb v. Cobb* [1955] 2 All E.R. 696 (C.A.); Law of Property Act 1925, s.111 enabling the survivor to give a good receipt.

Joint purchases of homes

As Lord Browne-Wilkinson has stated,[15] "Under a resulting trust, the existence of the trust is established once and for all at the date on which the property is acquired." It is based upon presumed intention flowing from the absence of an intention to benefit another person. When X and Y purchase a house but, foolishly, do not make an express written declaration of trust as to their shares, they are presumed to intend at the time of purchase that they then acquired the equitable shares therein that they paid for, being proportionate to their share of the purchase price.[16]

Thus in the case of a house costing £100,000 if X pays £40,000 and Y **5-81** pays £60,000 X will be equitably entitled to 40 per cent and Y to 60 per cent. The position is the same if X does not actually pay £40,000 but, as sitting tenant of the house, obtained a £40,000 discount off the market price of the house.[17]

Nowadays, of course, most houses are purchased with the assistance of a mortgage, the vendor receiving the whole purchase price upon completion of the contract of sale, but the purchaser(s) being under an obligation to repay to the mortgagee that part of the purchase price provided by the mortgagee. So what happens if X provides £40,000 but the £60,000 balance is provided by way of mortgage?

Clearly, the legal mortgage will have to be granted by the new legal **5-82** owner(s) of the house who will thereby be directly liable to the mortgagee for the mortgage money. Where the legal title is taken in the names of X and Y this means that X and Y will be jointly and severally liable to the mortgagee, with a right of indemnity against each other for half the money unless they have agreed otherwise. Thus, if X and Y undertake liability for a £60,000 mortgage on their £100,000 house they will prima facie be regarded as thereby providing £30,000 of the purchase price each.[18] If, however, X had already provided £40,000 and so had agreed with Y that Y should be solely responsible for the £60,000 mortgage then Y will be regarded as providing £60,000 of the purchase price,[19] just as if title had been taken in the name only of Y who then alone would have the burden of the legal mortgage.

---

[15] Birmingham University Holdsworth Lecture (1991) "Constructive Trusts and Unjust Enrichment", p. 6; (1996) 10 Trust L.I. 98, 100; *Scott on Trusts* (4th ed.) Vol. V pp. 278–279; J. Hayes [1993] So.Jo. 606; P. Matthews (1994) 8 Trust L.I. 43; *Sekhon v. Alissa* [1989] 2 F.L.R. 94, 100; *Huntingford v. Hobbs* [1993] 1 F.L.R. 736, *infra*, para. 5–86. In *Foskett v. McKeown* [1997] 3. All E.R. 392, 423 Morritt L.J. states "In most cases in which there has been found to be a resulting trust the property was acquired once and for all by simultaneous payments or assumptions of liability. But if property is acquired by a series of payments a resulting trust is respect of the due proportion may arise from the payment of one or more in the series: hire purchase or instalment payment transactions would be examples.

[16] *Pettit v. Pettit* [1970] A.C. 777 at 814. Acquisition costs, *e.g.* legal fees, stamp duty are part of the price: *Huntingford v. Hobbs, supra*. An express written declaration of trust signed by the parties is conclusive in the absence of fraud or mistake: *Goodman v. Gallant* [1986] Fam. 106.

[17] *Springette v. Defoe* (1992) 65 P. & C.R. 1; *Abbey National B.S. v. Cann* (1989) 59 P. & C.R. 381.

[18] *Harwood v. Harwood* [1991] 2 F.L.R. 274, 292; *Springette v. Defoe* (1992) 65 P. & C.R. 1, *Ammala v. Savimaa* (1993) 17 Fam.L.R. 529 (Federal Ct. Australia)

[19] *Huntingford v. Hobbs, supra; Ivin v. Blake* (1994) 67 P. & C.R. 265.

5–83   The shares of X and Y under a resulting trust crystallise at the date of acquisition just as if there had been an express written declaration of trust of such shares.[20] If any subsequent improvements to the house paid for by one party or any subsequent mortgage payments paid for by one party are alleged to give her a larger share than subsisting under the resulting, or express formal, trust this can only be if she can establish some agreement with or representation by the other party generating a common intention constructive trust or a proprietary estoppel interest.[21] If the parties split up and one makes all the mortgage payments and spends money on the property while enjoying rent-free occupation then, on sale of the property, equitable accounting principles can require deductions to be made against a party's share of the proceeds of sale.[22]

5–84   An example of the above principles is *Huntingford v. Hobbs, infra*. Before reading the judgment of the retired Lord Justice, Sir Christopher Slade, to appreciate a preliminary point he makes, one needs to know that in an exceptional case the court may find that the parties did not intend their shares to crystallise upon acquisition of the house, but intended themselves to have fair shares fixed when the house is sold, based on their direct and indirect financial contributions to the acquisition of, and any subsequent improvements to, the house.[23] This gives rise to what is known as a common intention constructive trust which may, perhaps, be regarded as a proprietary estoppel interest (see *infra*, paras 6–118 *et seq*).

5–85   It is worth noting at this stage that an inferred common intention constructive trust can arise from X and Y equally providing the deposit on a house purchased in the name of one or both of them (see *infra*, para. 6–105).

HUNTINGFORD V. HOBBS

Court of Appeal [1993] 1 F.L.R. 736; (1992) 24 H.L.R. 652.

5–86   Early in 1986 Mr. Huntingford and Mrs. Hobbs bought a house in joint names for £63,860 (£63,250 plus £610 fees). She provided £38,860 from the proceeds of her house while the £25,000 balance was provided by a joint mortgage supported by an endowment policy to produce £25,000 on maturity. She had no income and they agreed he would see to the mortgage interest and endowment premiums. He left her in August 1988. He sought a sale under LPA 1925 s.30 and a share of the proceeds when the house was valued at £95,000 but still subject to the £25,000 mortgage, so the equity was worth £70,000. The judge ordered sale

---

[20] See n. 18 above.

[21] *Pettit v. Pettit* [1970] A.C. 777 at 818; *Davis v. Vale* [1971] 1 W.L.R. 1022 at 1025; *Thomas v. Fuller-Brown* [1988] 1 F.L.R. 237; *Harwood v. Harwood* [1991] 2 F.L.R. 274 at 294; *Austin v. Keele* (1987) 61 ALJR 605, P.C. Exceptionally, in the case of married or engaged couples the court can treat improvements as giving rise to a proportionate fair share under section 37 Matrimonial Property and Proceedings Act 1970.

[22] *e.g. Huntingford v. Hobbs, supra; Bernard v. Josephs* [1982] Ch. 391; *Re Gorman* [1990] 1 W.L.R. 616; *Re Pavlou* [1993] 1 W.L.R. 1046. Further see E. Cooke [1995] Conv. 391.

[23] *e.g. Stokes v. Anderson* [1991] 1 F.L.R. 39; *Passee v. Passee* [1988] 1 F.L.R. 240.

subject to paying £3,500 of the proceeds to Mr. Huntingford who appealed successfully.

SIR CHRISTOPHER SLADE: "There is no dispute that when the property was **5–87** placed in joint names, the two parties intended that they should each have a beneficial interest in it. The difficulty lies in establishing the extent of those beneficial interests in the absence of any declaration of trust.

In the absence of any declaration of trust, the parties' respective beneficial interests in the property fall to be determined not by reference to any broad concepts of justice, but by reference to the principles governing the creation or operation of resulting, implied or constructive trusts which by s.53(2) of the Law of Property Act 1925 are exempted from the general requirements of writing imposed by s.53(1).

In *Walker v. Hall* [1984] F.L.R. 126 at 133, Dillon L.J. made the following statement of well-known general principle:

"... the law of trusts has concentrated on how the purchase money has been provided and it has been consistently held that where the purchase money for property acquired by two or more persons in their joint names has been provided by those persons in unequal amounts, they will be beneficially entitled as between themselves in the proportions in which they provided the purchase money. This is the basic doctrine of the resulting trust and it is conveniently and cogently expounded by Lord Upjohn in *Pettit v. Pettit* [1970] A.C. 777 at 814."

The application of this principle ordinarily gives rise to no difficulty where the **5–88** whole of the initial purchase price has been contributed by the two or more interested parties in the form of cash derived out of their respective resources without the benefit of a loan. Greater problems arise in cases such as the present, where part of the money required has been borrowed on mortgage. On the particular facts of some such cases the court, for the purpose of ascertaining the parties' proportionate interests in the property, has thought it right to impute to them the intention that their contributions to the purchase should be ascertained as at the date when the property eventually came to be sold. In *Gissing v. Gissing* [1971] A.C. 886, Lord Diplock, in the context of a case where the conveyance had been taken in the name of one spouse only, said (at 909):

"And there is nothing inherently improbable in their acting on the understanding that the wife should be entitled to a share which was not to be quantified immediately upon the acquisition of the home but should be left to be determined when the mortgage was repaid or the property disposed of, on the basis of what would be fair having regard to the total contributions, direct or indirect, which each spouse had made by that date. Where this was the most likely inference from their conduct it would be for the court to give effect to that common intention of the parties by determining what in all the circumstances was a fair share."

Inferences of this nature as to the common intentions of the parties were **5–89** drawn by this court on the particular facts of *Young v. Young* [1984] F.L.R. 375 and *Passee v. Passee* [1988] 1 F.L.R. 263.

However, in a case where a purchase in the joint names of two parties has been financed partly in the form of cash provided by one or both of them, and partly by way of a loan on mortgage, another approach open to the court is to assess the parties' contributions to the purchase, and thus their proportionate interests in the property, by reference to the time of the initial purchase, having regard to what sums each of them actually paid and what obligations each of them actually assumed in relation to the mortgage. This, for example, was the approach adopted by this court in *Crisp v. Mullings* [1976] 239 E.G. 119 and by Bush J. in *Marsh v. von Sternberg* [1986] 1 F.L.R. 526.

5–90   In my opinion, the judge in the present case was mistaken in his view that the decision in *Young v. Young* precluded him from holding that Mr. Huntingford was entitled to a share in the property ascertained by reference to the liability which he had originally assumed under the mortgage, as opposed to his actual payments towards the purchase. In the present case, in contrast, while both parties as joint proprietors had to join in the mortgage and assume joint and several liability to the mortgagee building society, there was a clear agreement or understanding that, as between the two of them, Mr. Huntingford would pay all the interest due under the mortgage and all the endowment policy premiums which would in due course, if the policy were duly kept up, discharge the capital debt owed to the lender. As at the date of the purchase, while Mrs. Hobbs no less than Mr. Huntingford was assuming a liability to the lender, it was not contemplated that, as between the two of them, she would have to pay anything towards discharge of this liability.

> "It is of course always possible to look at the subsequent conduct of the parties to see if it throws any light on what they originally agreed, but in the absence of a new or varied agreement, subsequent conduct cannot affect what was originally agreed." (*Marsh v. von Sternberg* (above) at 533 *per* Bush J.)

5–91   Drawing the most likely inference from the conduct of the parties in the present case, in my judgment the proper common intention to impute to them is a common intention as at the date of purchase that Mrs. Hobbs should be treated as having contributed her cash contribution, Mr. Huntingford should be treated as having contributed the whole of the sum borrowed on mortgage, and that the property should be owned by the two of them in shares proportionate to such contributions. This approach to the problem is consistent with that of Bagnall J. in *Cowcher v. Cowcher* [1972] 1 W.L.R. 425 at 431E and of Vinelott J. in *Re Gorman* [1990] 2 F.L.R. 284, where he said (at 291):

> "In circumstances of this kind, the court is concerned to ascertain, so far as is possible, from the evidence, what was the intention of the parties when the property was purchased, or what intention is to be imputed to them. Prima facie, if the purchase is financed in whole or in part on mortgage, the person who assumed liability for the mortgage payments, as between the joint owners, is to be treated as having contributed the mortgage monies."

5–92   I can see no sufficient grounds for not following this prima facie approach in the present case. Both parties intended that the property should be purchased as a joint venture, and while Mr. Huntingford could not and would not have purchased it on his own without Mrs. Hobbs' cash contribution, the reasonable inference is that she could not and would not have purchased it on her own without the support of the commitments which he was undertaking in relation to the mortgage, both to the building society and to her personally.

On the basis of the parties' respective contributions and as at the date of original completion of the purchase:

(a) Mrs. Hobbs was beneficially entitled to:

$\dfrac{38,860}{63,860}$ (say 61%) of the property or its proceeds of sale.

(b) Mr. Huntingford was beneficially entitled to:

$\dfrac{25,000}{63,860}$ (say 39%) of the property or its proceeds of sale.

These, I think, are the basic proportions which should govern the calculation of the sums which the parties are to receive out of the proceeds of sale of the property or the price which Mrs. Hobbs is to pay on the purchase of Mr. Huntingford's interest.

In any such calculation Mr. Huntingford will, in my opinion, be entitled to be **5–93** credited for the £2,000 (approximately) paid by him for the erection of the conservatory. On either of the two alternative possible explanations of the sum of £3,500 arrived at by the judge in his judgment, it would appear that the judge at least implicitly found that this sum represented expenditure in respect of which the parties intended that Mr. Huntingford would be entitled to claim reimbursement on a subsequent sale.

Mr. Huntingford will not, in my judgment, be entitled to be credited with any **5–94** of the sums which he has paid either by way of interest under the mortgage or premiums due under the policy. His original 39 per cent share came into being on the footing that he would be paying all such sums.

Correspondingly, in my judgment, in the course of the accounting between the parties, Mr. Huntingford should be debited with the whole of the capital debt of £25,000 still outstanding under the mortgage for the discharge of which he was to be responsible and which has not been discharged.

If Mrs. Hobbs had not continued to occupy the property after his departure, I would have considered that he should be debited with any sums by way of mortgage interest or policy premiums which he had thereafter failed to pay and she herself had paid. However, since that date she has had the benefit of continued occupation of the property and I think that broad justice will be done if she is treated as having made these payments in place of paying an occupation rent. In short, I would propose that the calculations provided for by the order of this court should not, on the one hand, refer either to the mortgage interest and policy premiums paid since Mr. Huntingford left the property or, on the other hand, provide for any occupation rent payable by Mrs. Hobbs."

STEYN L.J.: "In my judgment it is impossible to infer any actual common **5–95** intention as a basis for this conclusion [*viz* 61 per cent to the woman and 39 per cent to the man]. Reluctantly I concur in the result."

DILLON L.J.: "If the interests of the parties are to be calculated by reference to their contributions, the interests must be calculated as percentages when the arrangements were set up and the expenditure was incurred.

Since the mortgage of £25,000 was only available because of the plaintiff's income, and the defendant, without the assistance of the plaintiff's acceptance of liability under the mortgage, could not have purchased the property, the plaintiff is, in my judgment, entitled to say that either a half or the whole of the liability under the mortgage is to be treated as his contribution to the purchase of the property. On the evidence at the trial however the defendant had no income out of which to make any payments in respect of the mortgage or the endowment policy. Moreover both the plaintiff and the defendant agreed in their evidence that as between themselves, he was to pay the mortgage.

Basically, therefore, the plaintiff ought to have been credited with a contribution of £25,000 in respect of the mortgage loan."

II. PRESUMPTION OF ADVANCEMENT

5–96   Where a special relationship exists between X and Y there is no presumption of resulting trust but a presumption of advancement. The principle is stated by Lord Eldon in *Murless v. Franklin*[24] as follows: "The general rule that on a purchase by one man in the name of another, the nominee is a trustee for the purchaser, is subject to exception where the purchaser is under a species of natural obligation to provide for the nominee."

The presumption of advancement always arises where X is the father of Y or stands *in loco parentis* to Y,[25] or is the husband or engaged fiancé of Y.[26] It does not arise where X is merely cohabiting with Y,[27] nor, according to old case law, where X is the wife of Y.[28] The strength of the presumption between husband and wife is nowadays very weak[29] but the existence of the presumption can be crucial where property was transferred for an illegal purpose which has been partly or wholly performed.[30]

5–97   It was apparently held in *Sayre v. Hughes*[31] and *Re Grimes*[32] that a presumption of advancement arises also where X is the *mother* of Y, at any rate if she is a *widowed* mother. This is supported by a dictum in *Garrett v. Wilkinson*[33]; but *Re De Visme*[34] and *Bennet v. Bennet*[35] are to the opposite effect. The ground of the decision in these two cases was that whether the father is alive or not, the mother is under no equitable

---

[24] (1818) 1 Swans. 13, 17. Where T holds property on trust for X, and T transfers it to Y, then as a matter of property law Y takes subject to X's equitable interest, unless Y is a bona fide purchaser without notice, and so Y is regarded as constructive trustee of the property for X although owing no duties to X until aware of X's interest: there is no scope for the presumption of advancement and no need to consider the relationship between Y and T or X.

[25] *Shephard v. Cartwright* [1955] A.C. 431; *Hepworth v. Hepworth* (1870) L.R. 11 Eq. 10; *Re Cameron* [1999] Times April 2.

[26] *Tinker v. Tinker* [1970] P. 136; *Silver v. Silver* [1958] 1 W.L.R. 259; *Moate v. Moate* [1948] 2 All E.R. 486 (intended husband: marriage afterwards solemnised); Law Reform (Miscellaneous Provisions) Act 1970, s.2(1); *Mossop v. Mossop* [1988] 2 All E.R. 202.

[27] *Rider v. Kidder* (1805) 10 Ves. 360; *Napier v. Public Trustee* (1980) 32 A.L.R. 153, 158; *Calverley v. Green* (1984) 56 A.L.R. 483.

[28] *Re Curtis* (1885) 52 L.T. 244; *Mercier v. Mercier* [1903] 2 Ch. 98; *Abrahams v. Trustee of Property of Abrahams [2000] W.T.L.R.* 593.

[29] *Pettitt v. Pettitt* [1970] A.C. 777; *McGrath v. Wallis* [1995] 2 F.L.R. 114 (C.A.). Usually, there will be at least circumstantial evidence to clarify the position.

[30] *Tinsley v. Milligan* [1994] 1 A.C. 340, *infra*, para. 5–106.

[31] (1868) L.R. 5 Eq. 376.

[32] [1937] Ir.R. 470.

[33] (1848) 2 De G. & Sm. 244 at 246.

[34] (1863) 2 De G.J. & S. 17.

[35] (1879) 10 Ch.D. 474.

obligation which will raise the presumption of advancement. In *Gross v. French*[36] the Court of Appeal held that even if the presumption of advancement operates against a mother in favour of her child, there was sufficient evidence to rebut any such presumption: usually there will be some evidence to affirm or negative the presumption as in *Sekhon v. Alisse*,[37] where Hoffmann J. took the traditional view that a presumption of resulting trust (and not of advancement) applied where a mother provided most of the purchase price of a house bought in her daughter's name.

Modern ideas of equality indicate that the presumption of advance- **5–98** ment should extend to mothers *vis-à-vis* their children[38] and wives *vis-à-vis* their husbands. In practice, it is easier for courts to pay lip-service to the old case law whilst being satisfied on flimsy evidence that the old-fashioned presumption has been rebutted.[39]

III. REBUTTING THE PRESUMPTIONS

Both the presumption of a resulting trust and the presumption of **5–99** advancement can be rebutted by evidence within the limits laid down by the House of Lords in *Shepherd v. Cartwright*.[40] That case reaffirms the rule that evidence of subsequent acts, though not admissible in favour of the party doing the acts, is admissible against him.[41] Before the First World War it was held that acquiescence by a child, in whose name a purchase had been made, in the receipt by his father during his life of the rents or the income of the property does not rebut the presumption of advancement,[42] at any rate where the child has not already been fully advanced to set him up in life[43]; for if the child is an infant it is natural that the father should receive the profits, while if the child is an adult, it is an act of good manners on his part not to dispute their reception by his father. In the 2000s one can hardly expect a court to allow good manners to explain the child's conduct. The retention of the title deeds by the father with a contemporaneous declaration by him that the transaction was not a gift is sufficient to rebut the presumption of advancement,[44] though retention of the title deeds without such a declaration may be insufficient.[45] Nowadays, it seems that the presumptions are readily rebutted by comparatively slight evidence.[46] Rebuttal

---

[36] (1976) 238 E.G. 39.

[37] [1989] 2 F.L.R. 94.

[38] *Nelson v. Nelson* (1995) 184 C.L.R. 538; *Re Brownlee* [1990] 3 N.Z.L.R. 243; *Brown v. Brown* (1993) 31 N.S.W.L.R. 582 at 591; *Re Dreger Estate* (1994) 97 Manitoba R. (2d) 39.

[39] *e.g.* the approach in *McGrath v. Wallis* [1995] 2 F.L.R. 114.

[40] [1955] A.C. 431.

[41] E.g. *Midland Bank plc v. Wyatt* [1995] 1 F.L.R. 696.

[42] *Commissioner of Stamp Duties v. Byrnes* [1911] A.C. 386; *cf.* Wickens V.-C. in *Stock v. McAvoy* (1872) L.R. 15 Eq. 55 at 59; *Northern Canadian Trust Co. v. Smith* [1947] 3 D.L.R. 135; *Re Gooch* (1890) 62 L.T. 384 (presumption of advancement rebutted where father bought shares in son's name to qualify the son to be a director, the son passed the dividends to his father and later handed over the share certificates to his father).

[43] *Grey v. Grey* (1677) 2 Swans. 594; and see *Hepworth v. Hepworth* (1870) L.R. 11 Eq. 10.

[44] *Warren v. Gurney* [1944] 2 All E.R. 472.

[45] *Scawin v. Scawin* (1841) 1 Y. & C.C.C. 65.

[46] *Pettitt v. Pettitt* [1970] A.C. 777 at 813, 824; *Falconer v. Falconer* [1970] 1 W.L.R. 1333; *McGrath v. Wallis* [1995] 2 F.L.R. 114.

may be partial enabling the transferee to have a life interest or to have the beneficial interest only on the transferor's death.[47]

IV. ILLEGALITY

5–100 In considering evidence offered to rebut the presumptions one must consider the maxims "he who comes to equity must come with clean hands," *"ex turpi causa actio non oritur"* ("no legal action arises in favour of vile conduct"), *"in pari delicto potior est conditio defendentis* (or *possidentis)"* "when both parties are in the wrong the defendant (or possessor of property) is in the stronger position". After all, a person may transfer property to another to defraud the Revenue, to defeat his creditors or to defeat his wife's claims on divorce.[48]

Where the presumption of advancement applies (*e.g.* where H transfers property to his wife, W, or son, S) the onus is on the transferor, H, to produce evidence rebutting the presumption. If he honestly transferred the property to defeat his creditors then this could not lawfully be achieved without the beneficial ownership passing with the legal title, so the presumption of advancement is strengthened that this was intended, as held in *Tinker v. Tinker*.[49] If he dishonestly transferred the legal title to W or S to cloak the truth so that he went on to deceive or prejudice his creditors then he cannot rely on his illegal purpose to rebut the presumption of advancement.[50] However, *Tribe v. Tribe infra* at para. 5–120 establishes that he can so rely if no deception was actually practised on the creditor in question (*e.g.* because matters were resolved without her being made aware of the relevant transfer of property): he can recover his property so long as the illegal purpose has not "been wholly or partly carried into effect".[51] Thus, a plaintiff can recover his property where his illegal plan has become unnecessary, so he may as well try out such plan, rather than being deferred. Is this satisfactory?

5–101 Where the presumption of resulting trust applies (*e.g.* where A transfers property to his brother, B or buys property in B's name) A may plead that B holds on resulting trust for him without disclosing any illegality, merely by pleading the gratuitous transfer or a transfer apparently for a consideration but which has never been paid, so that A is entitled to recover his property according to the majority view in *Tinsley v. Milligan*,[52] *infra* para. 5–106. Indeed on this basis once the coast

---

[47] *Napier v. Public Trustee* (1980) 32 A.L.R. 153; *Young v. Sealey* [1949] Ch. 278.

[48] But note Insolvency Act 1986, ss.339–342, 423–425; Matrimonial Causes Act 1973, s.37; Inheritance (Provision for Family and Dependants) Act 1975, s.10, *supra*, at para. 4–113 *et seq.*

[49] [1970] P. 136; but note Insolvency Act 1986 ss.339–342, 423–425, *supra.* at para. 4–133 *et seq.*

[50] *Gascoigne v. Gascoigne* [1918] 1 K.B. 223, (where there were existing creditors and where tax was paid on the basis the bungalow belonged to the wife); *Re Emery's Investment Trusts* [1959] Ch. 410 (where, it seems, American withholding tax was evaded).

[51] *Tribe v. Tribe* [1995] 4 All E.R. 236, 259 per Millett L.J.; *Symes v. Hughes* (1875) L.R. 9 Eq. 475; *Sekhon v. Alissa* [1989] 2 F.L.R. 94; *Chettiar v. Chettiar* [1962] A.C. 294, 302; *Petherpermal Chetty v. Muniandi Servai* (1908) 24 T.L.R. 462; *Perpetual Executors Association of Australia Ltd v. Wright* (1917) 23 C.L.R. 185; *Martin v. Martin* (1959) 110 C.L.R. 297.

[52] [1994] 1 A.C. 340; applied in *Silverwood v. Silverwood* (1997) 74 P. & C.R. 453 (C.A.) and *Lowson v. Coombes* [1999] 2 W.L.R. 720. As Council states in (1993) 143 N.L.J. 1577 the effect of *Tinsley* can be summarised as "He who comes to equity should keep unclean hands in his pockets."

is clear and the creditors have been defrauded A can recover his property as has been held in Canada.[53] To prevent such iniquitous result, Millett L.J. has suggested[54] that if X transfers property to his nephew Y to conceal it from creditors and then settles with his creditors on the basis he owns no interest in such property, he should not be able to recover the property as held on a resulting trust for him: "The transferor's own conduct would be inconsistent with the retention of any beneficial interest in the property."[55] Y should be able to give evidence of X's dealings with his creditors to rebut the presumption of a resulting trust and show that a gift to Y must have been intended. After all, "the only way in which a man can protect his property from his creditors is by divesting himself of all beneficial interest in it."[56]

Thus, to prevent arbitary unjust results flowing from the narrow **5–102** *Tinsley v. Milligan* approach, the court has fact-finding leeway to conclude that X did not have any illegal purpose in the first place, X not intending to give the appearance of transferring property to Y (when actually wanting Y to be merely a nominee or bare trusteee for X) but actually intending Y to be full legal beneficial owner, so that X's creditors could then have no claim against such property except under the Insolvency Act 1986 sections 339–342 and 423–425. However, if the court does find that X had the illegal purpose of creating only the appearance that he had transferred the property to Y (when the actual arrangement was for Y to be merely a nominee or bare trustee for X) then it is surely inconsistent with the *Tinsley v. Milligan* approach to try and prevent X from relying on the presumption of resulting trust.[57]

To make X's recovery of property simply turn upon the adventitious **5–103** application of the presumption of resulting trust or the presumption of advancement is unfair and unsatisfactory, especially when there is uncertainty as to which presumption applies to transfers from mother to child or wife to husband and when land is treated differently from other property. Thus, the minority (Lords Goff and Keith) in *Tinsley v. Milligan* favoured the harsh but certain approach that[58] "a court of equity will not assist a claimant who does not come to equity with clean hands" so that the transferred property is left in the hands of the defendant.[59] All their Lordships rejected the flexible rule relied upon by the Court of Appeal[60] which depended upon the extent to which the public conscience would be affronted by recognising rights resulting from illegal transactions. Lord Goff (with whom Lord Keth concurred) commented,[61]

---

[53] *Gorog v. Kiss* (1977) 78 D.L.R. (3d) 690 endorsed by *Tinsley v. Milligan* [1994] 1 A.C. 340 at 376; also see *Tribe v. Tribe* [1995] 4 All E.R. 236 at 238 where Nourse L.J. points out that it was inherent in that decision that it made no difference whether or not the illegal purpose had been carried into effect.
[54] *Tribe v. Tribe* [1996] Ch. 107, 129.
[55] *ibid* 129; but Milligan's conduct in defrauding the DHSS on the basis she had no beneficial interest was inconsistent with her having any beneficial interest, yet the Lords' majority did not suggest Tinsley could exploit this against Milligan.
[56] *ibid* 134; *Tinker v. Tinker* [1970] P. 136.
[57] *Lowson v. Coombes* [1999] 2 W.L.R. 720
[58] [1994] 1 A.C. 340
[59] "Let the estate lie where it falls": *Muckleston v. Brown* (1801) 6 Ves. 52, 69
[60] [1992] Ch. 310
[61] [1994] 1 A.C. 340,

"Everything points to the conclusion that, if there is to be a reform aimed at substituting a system of discretionary relief for the present rules, the reform is one which should only be instituted by the legislature after a full inquiry into the matter by the law Commission."

5–104   In 1998 the Law Commission produced a Consultation Paper No 154[62] assisted by the Australian High Court's critical view of *Tinsley v. Milligan* in *Nelson v. Nelson*.[63] There the High Court applied the presumption of advancement to a mother's purchase of property in the name of her children, but allowed her to rebut such presumption by evidence that that this was only for the illegal purpose of enabling her to declare that she owned no house, so as to obtain a housing subsidy on the purchase of another house in her name that would not otherwise have been available: "she who comes to equity has to do equity", so she was obliged to pay back the housing subsidy as a condition of the relief sought.

5–105   The Commission's provisional view[64] is that there should be a structured statutory discretion to decide the effects of illegality. Factors to be taken into account should be "(a) the seriousness of the illegality; (b) the knowledge and intent of the illegal trust beneficiary; (c) whether invalidity would tend to deter the illegality; (d) whether invalidity would further the purpose of the rule which renders the trust 'illegal'; and (e) whether invalidity would be a proportionate response to the claimant's participation in the illegality." Such statutory discretion would oust[65] the equitable maxim "he who comes to equity must come with clean hands," but views were sought[66] on a discretion to make relief conditional on a payment or transfer of property that could come within the maxim "he who comes to equity must do equity."

Finally, it should be noted that if the transferor cannot recover then his personal representative is in no better position.[67] Query whether public policy should allow his trustee in bankruptcy to be in a better position.[68]

TINSLEY V. MILLIGAN

House of Lords [1994] 1 A.C. 340; [1993] 3 W.L.R. 126; [1993] 3 All E.R. 65.

5–106   Stella Tinsley and Kathleen Milligan jointly purchased a house which they registered only in Tinsley's name to enable Milligan (with the knowledge and assent of Tinsley) to make false social security benefit claims for the benefit of both of them cohabiting as lovers. Their relationship ended after 4 years so

---

[62] "Illegal Transactions; The Effect of Illegality on Contracts and Trusts" on which see N. Enonchong, "Illegal Transactions: The Future", [2000] R.L.R. 82, 99–104.
[63] (1995) 184 C.L.R. 538.
[64] Para. 8. 63.
[65] Para. 8. 91
[66] Para. 8. 88
[67] *Ayerst v. Jenkins* (1873) L.R. 16 Eq. 275 at 281, *per* Lord Selborne L.C.. The contrary view of Lord Eldon in *Muckleston v. Brown* (1801) 6 Ves. 52 at 68 seems unsound.
[68] *cf. Trautwein v. Richardson* [1946] Argus L.R. 129, 134, *per* Dixon J.; *Ayerst v. Jenkins* (1873) 16 Eq. 275 at 283.

Tinsley moved out and claimed possession of the house as owner, while Milligan counterclaimed for an order for sale and a declaration that the house was held by Tinsley on trust for the two of them equally. Milligan confessed her fraud to the Dept. of Social Security, made her peace with it and then obtained benefit on a lawful basis, while Tinsley was prosecuted, convicted and fined and had to make some repayment, to the Dept.

LORD BROWNE-WILKINSON: "My Lords, I agree that the consequences of being a party to an illegal transaction cannot depend, as the majority in the Court of Appeal held, on such an imponderable factor as the extent to which the public conscience would be affronted by recognising rights created by illegal transactions.

"Neither at law nor in equity will the court enforce an illegal contract which **5–107** has been partially, but not fully, performed. However, it does not follow that all acts done under a partially performed contract are of no effect. In particular it is now clearly established that at law (as opposed to in equity), property in goods or land can pass under, or pursuant to, such a contract. If so, the rights of the owner of the legal title thereby acquired will be enforced, provided that the plaintiff can establish such title without pleading or leading evidence of the illegality. It is said that the property lies where it falls, even though legal title to the property was acquired as a result of the property passing under the illegal contract itself. I will first consider the modern authorities laying down the circumstances under which an illegal transaction will be enforced by the courts. I will then consider whether the courts adopt a different attitude to equitable proprietary interests so acquired . . .

"From these authorities the following propositions emerge: (1) property in chattels and land can pass under a contract which is illegal and therefore would have been unenforceable as a contract; (2) a plaintiff can at law enforce property rights so acquired provided that he does not need to rely on the illegal contract for any purpose other than providing the basis of his claim to a property right; (3) it is irrelevant that the illegality of the underlying agreement was either pleaded or emerged in evidence; if the plaintiff has acquired legal title under the illegal contract that is enough.

"I have stressed the common law rules as to the impact of illegality on the **5–108** acquisition and enforcement of property rights because it is the appellant's contention that different principles apply in equity. In particular it is said that equity will not aid Miss Milligan to assert, establish or enforce an equitable, as opposed to a legal, proprietary interest since she was a party to the fraud on the D.S.S. The house was put in the name of Miss Tinsley alone (instead of joint names) to facilitate the fraud. Therefore, it is said, Miss Milligan does not come to equity with clean hands: consequently, equity will not aid her.

"Most authorities to which we were referred deal with enforcing proprietary **5–109** rights under a trust: I will deal with them in due course. But before turning to them, I must point out that if Miss Tinsley's argument is correct, the results would be far reaching and, I suggest, very surprising. There are many proprietary rights, apart from trusts, which are only enforceable in equity. For example, an agreement for a lease under which the tenant has entered is normally said to be as good as a lease, since under such an agreement equity treats the lease as having been granted and the "lessee" as having a proprietary interest enforceable against the whole world except the bona fide purchaser for value without notice. Would the result in *Ferrel v. Hill*, 15 C.B. 207 have been different if there had only been an agreement for a lease? Say that in *Taylor v. Chester*, L.R. 4 Q.B. 309

the plaintiff had deposited by way of security share certificates instead of half a bank note (thereby producing only an equitable security): would the outcome have been different? Similarly, if the plaintiff were relying on an assignment of a chose in action would be succeed if the assignment was a legal assignment but fail if it were equitable?

5–110   "In my judgment to draw such distinctions between property rights enforceable at law and those which require the intervention of equity would be surprising. More than 100 years has elapsed since law and equity became fused. The reality of the matter is that, in 1993, English law has one single law of property made up of legal and equitable interests. Although for historical reasons legal estates and equitable estates have differing incidents, the person owning either type of estate has a right of property, a right in rem not merely a right in personam. If the law is that a party is entitled to enforce a property right acquired under an illegal transaction, in my judgment the same rule ought to apply to any property right so acquired, whether such right is legal or equitable.

"In the present case, Miss Milligan claims under a resulting or implied trust. The court below have found, and it is not now disputed, that apart from the question of illegality Miss Milligan would have been entitled in equity to a half share in the house in accordance with the principles exemplified in *Gissing v. Gissing* [1971] 1 A.C. 886; *Grant v. Edwards* [1986] Ch. 638 and *Lloyds Bank Plc v. Rosset* [1991] A.C. 107. The creation of such an equitable interest does not depend upon a contractual obligation but on a common intention acted upon by the parties to their detriment. It is a development of the old law of resulting trust under which, where two parties have provided the purchase money to buy a property which is conveyed into the name of one of them alone, the latter is presumed to hold the property on a resulting trust for both parties in shares proportionate to their contributions to the purchase price. In arguments, no distinction was drawn between strict resulting trusts and a *Gissing v. Gissing* type of trust.

5–111   "A presumption of resulting trust also arises in equity when A transfers personalty or money to B: see *Snell's Equity*, 29th ed. (1990), at 183–184; *Standing v. Bowring* (1885) 31 Ch.D. 282, 287, *per* Cotton L.J.; *Dewar v. Dewar* [1975] 1 W.L.R. 1532, 1537. Before 1925, there was also a presumption of resulting trust when land was voluntarily transferred by A to B: it is arguable, however, that the position has been altered by the 1925 property legislation: see *Snell's Equity*, at 182. The presumption of a resulting trust is, in my view, crucial in considering the authorities. On that presumption (and on the contrary presumption of advancement) hinges the answer to the crucial question "does a plaintiff claiming under a resulting trust have to rely on the underlying illegality?" Where the presumption of resulting trust applies, the plaintiff does not have to rely on the illegality. If he proves that the property is vested in the

5–112   defendant alone but that the plaintiff provided part of the purchase money, or voluntarily transferred the property to the defendant, the plaintiff establishes his claim under a resulting trust unless either the contrary presumption of advancement displaces the presumption of resulting trust or the defendant leads evidence to rebut the presumption of resulting trust. Therefore, in cases where the presumption of advancement does not apply, a plaintiff can establish his equitable interest in the property without relying in any way on the underlying illegal transaction. In this case Miss Milligan as defendant simply pleaded the common intention that the property should belong to both of them and that she contributed to the purchase price: she claimed that in consequence the property belonged to them equally. To the same effect was her evidence in chief.

Therefore Miss Milligan was not forced to rely on the illegality to prove her equitable interest. Only in the reply and the course of Miss Milligan's cross-examination did such illegality emerge: it was Miss Tinsley who had to rely on that illegality.

"Although the presumption of advancement does not directly arise for **5–113** consideration in this case, it is important when considering the decided cases to understand its operation. On a transfer from a man to his wife, children or others to whom he stand in loco parentis, equity presumes an intention to make a gift. Therefore in such a case, unlike the case where the presumption of resulting trust applies, in order to establish any claim the plaintiff has himself to lead evidence sufficient to rebut the presumption of gift and in so doing will normally have to plead, and give evidence of, the underlying illegal purpose.

"Against this background, I turn to consider the authorities dealing with the position in equity where A transferred property to B for an illegal purpose. The earlier authorities, primarily Lord Eldon, support the appellant's proposition that equity will not aid a plaintiff who has transferred property to another for an illegal purpose. [He then considered *Collington v. Fletcher*, 2 Atk. 155, *Muckleston v. Brown*, 6 Ves. 52, *Curtis v. Perry*, 6 Ves. 739, *Ex parte Yallop*, 15 Ves. 60 and *Groves v. Groves*, 3 Y. & J. 163.]

However, in my view, the law was not so firmly established as at first sight it appears to have been . . .

The law was developing in another direction during the 19th century. There **5–114** was originally a difference of view as to whether a transaction entered into for an illegal purpose would be enforced at law or in equity if the party had repented of his illegal purpose before it had been put into question, *i.e.* the doctrine of locus poenitentiae. It was eventually recognised both at law and in equity that if the plaintiff had repented before the illegal purpose was carried through, he could recover his property: see *Taylor v. Bowers*, 1 Q.B.D. 291; *Symes v. Hughes*, L.R. 9 Eq. 475. The principle of locus poenitentiae is in my judgment irreconcilable with any rule that where property is transferred for an illegal purpose no equitable proprietary right exists. The equitable right, if any, must arise at the time at which the property was voluntarily transferred to the third party or purchased in the name of the third party. The existence of the equitable interest cannot depend upon events occurring after that date. Therefore if, under the principle of locus poenitentiae, the courts recognise that an equitable interest did arise out of the underlying transaction, the same must be true where the illegal purpose was carried through. The carrying out of the illegal purpose cannot, by itself, destroy the pre-existing equitable interest. The doctrine of locus poenitentiae therefore demonstrates that the effect of illegality is not to prevent a proprietary interest in equity from arising or to produce a forfeiture of such right: the effect is to render the equitable interest unenforceable in certain circumstances. The effect of illegality is not substantive but procedural. The question therefore is, "In what circumstances will equity refuse to enforce equitable rights which undoubtedly exist."

"It is against this background that one has to assess the more recent law. **5–115** Although in the cases decided during the last 100 years there are frequent references to Lord Eldon's wide principle, with one exception (*Cantor v. Cox*, 239 E.G. 121) none of the English decisions are decided by simply applying that principle. They are all cases where the unsuccessful party was held to be precluded from leading evidence of an illegal situation in order to rebut the presumption of advancement. Lord Eldon's rule would have provided a complete answer whether the transfer was made to a wife or child (where the presumption

of advancement would apply) or to a stranger. Yet with one exception none of
the cases in this century has been decided on that simple basis.

5–116   The majority of cases have been those in which the presumption of advancement applied: in those authorities the rule has been stated as being that a
plaintiff cannot rely on evidence of his own illegality to rebut the presumption
applicable in such cases that the plaintiff intended to make a gift of the property
to the transferee. Thus in *Gascoigne v. Gascoinge* [1918] 1 K.B. 223; *McEvoy v.
Belfast Banking Co. Ltd* [1934] N.I. 67; *Re Emery's Investments Trusts* [1959] Ch.
410; *Palaniappa Chettiar v. Arunasalum Chettiar* [1962] A.C. 294 and *Tinker v.
Tinker* [1970] P. 136, 142c, 143 the crucial point was said to be the inability of the
plaintiff to lead evidence rebutting the presumption of advancement. In each case
the plaintiff was claiming to recover property voluntarily transferred to, or
purchased in the name of, a wife or child, for an illegal purpose. Although
reference was made to Lord Eldon's principle, none of those cases was decided
on the simple ground (if it were good law) that equity would not in any
circumstances enforce a resulting trust in such circumstances. On the contrary in
each case the rule was stated to be that the plaintiff could not recover because he
had to rely on the illegality to rebut the presumption of advancement.

5–117   "In my judgment, the explanation for this departure from Lord Eldon's
absolute rule is that the fusion of law and equity has led the courts to adopt a
single rule (application both at law and in equity) as to the circumstances in
which the court will enforce property interests acquired in pursuance of an illegal
transaction, viz., the *Bowmakers* rule [1945] K.B. 65. A party to an illegality can
recover by virtue of a legal or equitable property interest if, but only if, he can
establish his title without relying on his own illegality. In cases where the
presumption of advancement applies, the plaintiff is faced with the presumption
of gift and therefore cannot claim under a resulting trust unless and until he has
rebutted that presumption of gift: for those purposes the plaintiff does have to
rely on the underlying illegality and therefore fails.

5–118   "The position is well illustrated by two decisions in the Privy Council. [*Singh v.
Ali* [1960] A.C. 167 and *Chettiar v. Chettiar* [1962] A.C. 294 were then
considered].

"In my judgment these two cases show that the Privy Council was applying
exactly the same principle in both cases although in one case the plaintiff's claim
rested on a legal title and in the other on an equitable title. The claim based on
the equitable title did not fail simply because the plaintiff was a party to the
illegal transaction; it only failed because the plaintiff was bound to disclose and
rely upon his own illegal purpose in order to rebut the presumption of
advancement. The Privy Council was plainly treating the principle applicable
both at law and in equity as being that a man can recover property provided that
he is not forced to rely on his own illegality.

5–119   "I therefore reach the conclusion that, although there is no case overruling the
wide principle stated by Lord Eldon, as the law has developed the equitable
principle has become elided into the common law rule. In my judgment the time
has come to decide clearly that the rule is the same whether a plaintiff founds
himself on a legal or equitable title: he is entitled to recover if he is not forced to
plead or rely on the illegality, even if it emerges that the title on which he relied
was acquired in the course of carrying through an illegal transaction.

"As applied in the present case, that principle would operate as follows. Miss
Milligan established a resulting trust by showing that she had contributed to the
purchase price of the house and that there was common understanding between
her and Miss Tinsley that they owned the house equally. She had no need to

allege or prove why the house was conveyed into the name of Miss Tinsley alone, since that fact was irrelevant to her claim: it was enough to show that the house was in fact vested in Miss Tinsley alone. The illegality only emerged at all because Miss Tinsley sought to raise it. Having proved these facts, Miss Milligan had raised a presumption of resulting trust. There was no evidence to rebut that presumption. Therefore Miss Milligan should succeed. This is exactly the process of reasoning adopted by the Ontario Court of Appeal in *Gorog v. Kiss* (1977) 78 D.L.R. (3d) 690 which in my judgment was rightly decided."

TRIBE V. TRIBE

Court of Appeal (Nourse, Millett, Otton L.JJ.) [1995] 4 All E.R. 237.

Fearful of dilapidations claims against him as tenant of two properties, the **5–120** plaintiff transferred 459 out of 500 shares in the family company that operated from such properties to one of his four children purportedly for £78,030 never paid or intended to be paid. The presumption of advancement was allowed to be rebutted by the plaintiff's evidence that the purpose of the transfer was to deceive his creditors by creating an appearance that he no longer owned the shares because such illegal purpose had not been carried into effect because, without disclosing the transfer, the plaintiff for value surrendered one lease and purchased the reversion on the other lease.

(1) The presumption of advancement

MILLETT L.J.: "Prior to *Tinsley v. Milligan* no transferor had ever succeeded in recovering his property by enforcing a resulting trust where he had transferred the property for an illegal purpose and that purpose had been carried out. In *Re Great Berlin Steamboat Co.* the transferor failed to recover for this very reason; in other cases where the transferor has succeeded he did so only because the illegal purpose had not been carried out.

"In *Tinsley v. Milligan* the parties, who both contributed to the purchase of a **5–121** house, arranged for the conveyance to be taken in the name of the appellant alone but on the understanding that it was to belong to them jointly. The purpose of this arrangement was to enable the respondent to perpetrate frauds on the Departments of Social Security, and over a number of years the respondent, with the connivance of the appellant, made false claims for benefit. Despite this the respondent was allowed to recover.

"In his dissenting speech Lord Goff refused to draw any distinction between **5–122** cases where the presumption of advancement applied and cases in which the plaintiff could rely on a resulting trust. From the authorities he derived a single principle; that if one party puts property in the name of another for a fraudulent or illegal purpose neither law nor equity will allow him to recover the property. Even if he can establish a resulting trust in his favour he cannot enforce it. Given Lord Goff's opinion that there was but one principle in play, it was natural for him to describe the doctrine of the *locus poenitentiae* as an exception to that principle. Since the respondent could not bring himself within the exception, he would have allowed the appeal.

"This was not, however, the view of the majority. Lord Browne-Wilkinson **5–123** expressly held that the rule was the same whether the plaintiff founded himself on a legal or an equitable title: he was entitled to succeed if he was not forced to rely on his own illegality, even if it emerged that the title on which he relied was acquired in the course of carrying through an illegal transaction. The respondent had established a resulting trust by showing that she had contributed to the purchase price and that there was a common understanding between her and the appellant that they should own the house equally. She had no need to allege or prove why she had allowed the house to be conveyed into the sole name of the appellant, since that fact was irrelevant to her claim.

5–124   "The necessary consequence of this is that where he can rely on a resulting trust the transferor will normally be able to recover his property if the illegal purpose has not been carried out. In *Tinsley v. Milligan* she recovered even though the illegal purpose had been carried out. It does not, however, follow that the transferor will invariably succeed in such circumstances, so that the presence or absence of a locus poenitentiae is irrelevant where the transfer gives rise to a resulting trust. A resulting trust, like the presumption of advancement, rests on a presumption which is rebuttable by evidence (see *Standing v. Bowring* (1885) 31 Ch.D. 282 at 287. The transferor does not need to allege or prove the purpose for which property was transferred into the name of the transferee; in equity he can rely on the presumption that no gift was intended. But the transferee cannot be prevented from rebutting the presumption by leading evidence of the transferor's subsequent conduct to show that it was inconsistent with any intention to retain a beneficial interest. Suppose, for example, that a man transfers property to his nephew in order to conceal it from his creditors, and suppose that he afterwards settles with his creditors on the footing that he has no interest in the property. Is it seriously suggested that he can recover the property? I think not. The transferor's own conduct would be inconsistent with the retention of any beneficial interest in the property. I can see no reason why the nephew should not give evidence of the transferor's dealings with his creditors to rebut the presumption of a resulting trust and show that a gift was intended. He would not be relying on any illegal arrangement but implicitly denying it. The transferor would have to give positive evidence of his intention to retain a beneficial interest and dishonestly conceal it from his creditors, evidence which he would not be allowed to give once the illegal purpose had been carried out.

5–125   "This analysis is not, in my view, inconsistent with a passage in Lord Browne-Wilkinson's speech where he said ([1994] 1 A.C. 340 at 374):

> 'The equitable right, if any, must arise at the time at which the property was voluntarily transferred to the third party or purchased in the name of the third party. The existence of the equitable interest cannot depend upon events occurring after that date. Therefore if, under the principle of locus poenitentiae, the courts recognise that an equitable interest did arise out of the underlying transaction, the same must be true where the illegal purpose was carried through. The carrying out of the illegal purpose cannot, by itself, destroy the pre-existing equitable interest.'

5–126   But it does not follow that subsequent conduct is necessarily irrelevant. Where the existence of an equitable interest depends upon a rebuttable presumption or inference of the transferor's intention, evidence may be given of his subsequent conduct in order to rebut the presumption or inference which would otherwise be drawn.

"*Tinsley v. Milligan* is, in my opinion, not authority for the proposition that a party who transfers property for an illegal purpose in circumstances which give rise to a resulting trust can invariably enforce the trust and recover the property even though the illegal purpose has been carried into effect. I do not accept the suggestion that cases such as *Re Great Berlin Steamboat Co.* have been impliedly overruled or that the dicta in the many cases, including *Taylor v. Bowers* and *Sajan Singh v. Sandara Ali*, indicating that the result would have been otherwise if the illegal purpose had or had not been carried out, must be taken to have been overruled.

The question in the present case is the converse: whether the transferor can **5–127** rebut the presumption of advancement by giving evidence of his illegal purpose so long as the illegal purpose has not been carried into effect.

"There is no modern case in which restitution has been denied in circumstances comparable to those of the present case where the illegal purpose has not been carried out. In *Tinsley v. Milligan* Lord Browne-Wilkinson expressly recognised the availability of the doctrine of the locus poenitentiae in a restitutionary context, and cited *Taylor v. Bowers* as well as *Symes v. Hughes* without disapproval. In my opinion the weight of the authorities supports the view that a person who seeks to recover property transferred by him for an illegal purpose can lead evidence of his dishonest intention whenever it is necessary for him to do so provided that he has withdrawn from the transaction before the illegal purpose has been carried out. It is not necessary if he can rely on an express or resulting trust in his favour; but it is necessary (i) if he brings an action at law and (ii) if he brings proceedings in equity and needs to rebut the presumption of advancement. The availability of the locus poenitentiae is well documented in the former case. I would not willingly adopt a rule which differentiated between the rule of the common law and that of equity in a restitutionary context . . .

"At heart the question for decision in the present case is one of legal policy. **5–128** The primary rule which precludes the court from lending its assistance to a man who founds his cause of action on an illegal or immoral act often leads to a denial of justice. The justification for this is that the rule is not a principle of justice but a principle of policy (see the much-quoted statement of Lord Mansfield C.J. in *Holman v. Johnson* (1775) 1 Cowp 341 at 343, [1775–1802] All E.R. Rep 98 at 99). The doctrine of the locus poenitentiae is an exception which operates to mitigate the harshness of the primary rule. It enables the court to do justice between the parties even though, in order to do so, it must allow a plaintiff to give evidence of his own dishonest intent. But he must have withdrawn from the transaction while his dishonesty still lay in intention only. The law draws the line once the intention has been wholly or partly carried into effect.

"Seen in this light the doctrine of the locus poenitentiae, although an **5–129** exception to the primary rule, is not inconsistent with the policy which underlies it. It is, of course, artificial to think that anyone would be dissuaded by the primary rule from entering into a proposed fraud, if only because such a person would be unlikely to be a studious reader of the law reports or to seek advice from a lawyer whom he has taken fully into his confidence. But if the policy which underlies the primary rule is to discourage fraud, the policy which underlies the exception must be taken to be to encourage withdrawal from a proposed fraud before it is implemented, an end which is no less desirable. And if the former objective is of such overriding importance that the primary rule must be given effect even where it leads to a denial of justice, then in my opinion the later objective justifies the adoption of the exception where this enables justice to be done.

5–130   "To my mind these considerations are even more compelling since the decision in *Tinsley v. Milligan*. One might hesitate before allowing a novel exception to a rule of legal policy, particularly a rule based on moral principles. But the primary rule, as it has emerged from that decision, does not conform to any discernible moral principle. It is procedural in nature and depends on the adventitious location of the burden of proof in any given case. Had Mr. Tribe transferred the shares to a stranger or distant relative whom he trusted, albeit for the same dishonest purpose, it cannot be doubted that he would have succeeded in his claim. He would also have succeeded if he had given them to his son and procured him to sign a declaration of trust in his favour. But he chose to transfer them to a son whom he trusted to the extent of dispensing with the precaution of obtaining a declaration of trust. If that is fatal to his claim, then the greater the betrayal, the less the power of equity to give a remedy.

"In my opinion the following propositions represent the present state of the law.

5–131   "(1) Title to property passes both at law and in equity even if the transfer is made for an illegal purpose. The fact that title has passed to the transferee does not preclude the transferor from bringing an action for restitution.

"(2) The transferor's action will fail if it would be illegal for him to retain any interest in the property.

"(3) Subject to (2) the transferor can recover the property if he can do so without relying on the illegal purpose. This will normally be the case where the property was transferred without consideration in circumstances where the transferor can rely on an express declaration of trust or a resulting trust in his favour.

"(4) It will almost invariably be so where the illegal purpose has not been carried out. It may be otherwise where the illegal purpose has been carried out and the transferee can rely on the transferor's conduct as inconsistent with his retention of a beneficial interest.

"(5) The transferor can lead evidence of the illegal purpose whenever it is necessary for him to do so provided that he has withdrawn from the transaction before the illegal purpose has been wholly or partly carried into effect. It will be necessary for him to do so (i) if he brings an action at law or (ii) if he brings proceedings in equity and needs to rebut the resumption of advancement.

"(6) The only way in which a man can protect his property from his creditors is by divesting himself of all beneficial interest in it. Evidence that he transferred the property in order to protect it from his creditors, therefore, does nothing by itself to rebut the presumption of advancement; it reinforces it. To rebut the presumption it is necessary to show that he intended to retain a beneficial interest and conceal it from his creditors.

5–132   "(7) The court should not conclude that this was his intention without compelling circumstantial evidence to this effect. The identity of the transferee and the circumstances in which the transfer was made would be highly relevant. It is unlikely that the court would reach such a conclusion where the transfer was made in the absence of an imminent and perceived threat from known creditors.

(2) The doctrine of the locus poenitentiae

5–133   "It is impossible to reconcile all the authorities on the circumstances in which a party to an illegal contract is permitted to withdraw from it. At one time he was allowed to withdraw so long as the contract had not been completely performed but later it was held that recovery was barred once it had been partly performed (see *Kearley v. Thompson* (1890) 24 Q.B.D. 742. It is clear that he must withdraw voluntarily, and that it is not sufficient that he is forced to do so because his plan has been discovered. In *Bigos v. Bousted* [1951] 1 All E.R. 92 this was (perhaps dubiously) extended to prevent withdrawal where the scheme has been frustrated by the refusal of the other party to carry out his part.

"I would hold that genuine repentance is not required. Justice is not a reward for merit; restitution should not be confined to the penitent. I would also hold that voluntary withdrawal from an illegal transaction when it has ceased to be needed is sufficient. It is true that this is not necessary to encourage withdrawal, but a rule to the opposite effect could lead to bizarre results. Suppose, for example, that in *Bigos v. Bousted* exchange control had been abolished before the foreign currency was made available: it is absurd to suppose that the plaintiff should have been denied restitution. I do not agree that it was correct in *Groves v. Groves* (1829) 3 Y. & J. 163, 148 E.R. 1136 and similar cases for the court to withhold its assistance from the plaintiff because 'if the crime has not been completed, the merit was not his'."

QUESTIONS

1. "A resulting trust is a default mechanism for the location of beneficial **5–134** ownership of property and not a mechanism to prevent unjust enrichment." Discuss.

2. The Ravers Anonymous Club which is not a charitable organisation has just dissolved itself one week after having received £10,000 donated by Sir Launcelot Hellfire for the purposes of the Club and one month after having received £1,000 from certain raffles and sweepstakes and £150 from collections taken at a public meeting called to publicise the Club. In accordance with the rules the Club had given its members 10 days written notice of the meeting called to dissolve the Club. What should be done with the above sums?

3. The Black Sheep Club was formed in 1928 to encourage the breeding and improvement of Black Sheep and also to provide sick benefits for the widows of members. The members paid an annual subscription of £5 unless aged less than 35 years when they paid half that. Funds were also raised from annual covenants from well-wishers, from collections made at the annual show and from the profits of an annual dance and monthly beetle drives. The Club has been inactive since 1990. There are four surviving members (aged 34, 40, 50 and 60 years) and one widow of a deceased member. Its assets amount to £50,000. Advise as to the distribution of the Club's assets.

4. Six years before her death Miss Spry opened a current account with Barclays **5–135** Bank in the joint names of herself and her nephew, Neal Smug. Both of them called on the manager when they came to open the joint account. Miss Spry told the manager that as she was getting frail her nephew would look after her banking matters for her. She also said that if she died before her nephew he could keep any credit balance in the account at her death. It was arranged that cheques drawn by either Miss Spry or Neal would be honoured. Although Miss Spry kept the cheque book in her desk Neal signed all the cheques.

As had been envisaged only Miss Spry contributed moneys to the joint account and at her death a credit balance of £2,000 remained. Who is entitled to this if Miss Spry by will had left everything to the RSPCA?

5. Ms. F and Mr. M are registered proprietors of Cosyacre, which they bought **5–136** from the Council which had been Ms. F's landlord. The purchase price was £100,000 less a £30,000 discount for Ms. F as sitting tenant, so that Ms. F and

Mr. M took out a joint mortgage for the £70,000 balance, though they agreed that Mr. M would see to mortgage repayments.

Three years later Mr. M went to live with Mrs. X, leaving Ms. F to pay the mortgage instalments, she having just won £10,000 on a premium bond. Before he left Mr. M had paid mortgage instalments amounting to £10,000 (£3,000 representing repayment of capital and £7,000 interest).

Advise Ms. F on equitable entitlement to the house.

Would your answer differ if they had a joint bank account and agreed that the mortgage payments would be paid by a standing order on that account, Mr. M closing that account when he left Ms. F for Mrs. X?

Would your answer differ if they had executed a written declaration of trust of Cosyacre on trust for themselves as joint tenants?

5–137 6. Fearing that his wife might divorce him at some time and that a new business venture might prove financially damaging, Harold transferred "Cosy Cottage" and 10,000 ICI plc shares to Simon, who agreed that when matters had resolved themselves so that it was safe to do so he would reconvey the cottage to Harold. The conveyance purported to be for £80,000 but, in fact, as agreed Simon actually paid nothing.

Advise Harold who seeks to recover the cottage. Does it matter (a) if Simon is Harold's brother or his son, or (b) if only six months have elapsed and Harold's wife is still living with him and he can pay his debts as they fall due?

7. "The presumptions of presumed resulting trusts and of advancement are today false and outmoded, so that only lip-service is paid to them in establishing where the onus of proof lies; instead, the courts should presume that the legal title reflects the intentions of the parties unless there are circumstances (not the outdated, false presumptions) which displace it in equity." Discuss.

8. "The attempt of Millett L.J. in *Tribe v. Tribe* to rely on the fact-finding discretion of the trial judge to undermine the arbitrariness of the approach in *Tinsley v. Milligan* is inappropriate: far better for the court openly to have the flexible statutory discretion provisionally proposed by the Law Commission." Discuss.

Chapter 6

CONSTRUCTIVE TRUSTS OF PROPERTY[1]

INTRODUCTION

Proprietary rights under constructive trusts

Beneficiaries have equitable proprietary rights under express or result- **6–01** ing or constructive trusts of property as a response to particular events. A beneficiary's proprietary right under an express trust arises from the settlor's intention to create a trust of identified property retained by the settlor or transferred to a trustee even if the trustee does not learn of the transfer until some months later, *e.g.* where the trust was created on death by a will or by a settlor in her lifetime registering shares in the trustee-transferee's name. If the trustee disclaims[2] or the private company refuses to register the transfer,[3] then the settlor or her personal representative becomes trustee for the beneficiary still entitled to the trust property (and its fruits and any traceable product thereof) from the earlier date.

The equitable proprietary right of a settlor under a resulting trust **6–02** arises from her transfer of property to—or purchase of property in the name of—another person without intent that such person should have her beneficial interest therein, whether or not such person knows of the transfer or of the lack of beneficial intent. As Lord Browne-Wilkinson stated in *Tinsley v. Milligan*,[4] "The equitable right must arise at the time at which the property was voluntarily transferred to the third party or purchased in the name of the third party." Indeed, in *Westdeutsche Landesbanke v. Islington B.C.*[5] he stated, "once a trust is established, as from the date of its establishment the beneficiary has, in equity, a proprietary interest in the trust property which will be enforceable in equity against any subsequent holder of the property (whether the original or substituted property into which it can be traced) other than a bona fide purchaser for value of the legal estate without notice."

As an equitable mechanism to vindicate the equitable interests of **6–03** beneficiaries under express or resulting trusts, "It is a long-established principle of Equity that, if a person who is a trustee receives money or

---

[1] See A. W. Scott, "Constructive Trusts" (1955) 71 L.Q.R. 39; Ford & Lee, *Principles of the Law of Trusts* (3rd ed) Chap. 22; Goff and Jones' *Law of Restitution*, Chap. 2; A.J. Oakley's *Constructive Trusts*; G. Ellias, *Explaining Constructive Trusts*; A.J. Oakley (ed) Parker & Mellows, *Modern Law of Trusts* (7th ed) Chap. 10; C.E.F. Rickett. "The Classification of Trusts", (1999) 18 N.Z.L.R. 305.
[2] *Mallott v. Wilson* [1903] 2 Ch. 49, *Harris v. Sharp* unreported Court of Appeal March 21, 1989. However, in virtually all trusts the settlor sensibly obtains the agreement of the trustee to act as trustee.
[3] *Re Rose* [1952] Ch. 459.
[4] [1993] 3 All E.R. 65, 89.
[5] [1996] 2 All E.R. 961, 988.

property because of, or in respect of, trust property, he will hold what he receives as a constructive trustee on the trusts of the original trust property."[6] Similarly, a third party (other than a bona fide purchaser for value of the legal interest without notice) who, through a breach of trust, receives property subject to an express or resulting or constructive trust will hold it (and its traceable product) as constructive trustee on the trusts affecting such property.[7] Finally, a person not within such two categories, but who has obtained or enhanced his interest in property, by virtue of well-established types of behaviour to another person in respect of such property, will be constructive trustee of the whole or part thereof for such person where it would be unconscionable for him to act inconsistently with such behaviour[8] or otherwise exploit his behaviour.[9]

Because the defendant's conscience has been affected by his behaviour he will become subject to *personal* fiduciary or equitable obligations to the claimant at the same time as he becomes subject to the claimant's equitable *proprietary* interest. In the case of the former two categories and, indeed, generally in the case of express or resulting trusts, it is possible for a defendant unknowingly to be subject to the claimant's proprietary interest, and yet not be subject to any personal obligations because they cannot bind him until his conscience is affected by awareness of the claimant's interest.[10]

6–04 It is important to realise that while a beneficiary always has an equitable proprietary right from the date of establishment of an express or resulting or constructive trust,[11] at which date the property owner should be regarded as an express or resulting or constructive trustee of the property,[12] no fiduciary obligations or equitable duties can be imposed upon him until the time his conscience becomes aware of the relevant trust.[13] To vindicate the claimant's proprietary rights the defendant is then retrospectively forced to account for what has happened to the property and its fruits and the traceable product thereof and after such time the accounts may be surcharged or falsified in respect of any subsequent breaches of the extensive duties then attaching to the express trust, if he be an express trustee, or the limited duties[14] attaching to a resulting or constructive trust for B if he be a resulting or a constructive trustee for B *e.g.* requiring him to transfer the relevant property to B or B's nominee as soon as practical.

---

[6] Per Dillon L.J. in *Re EVTR* [1987] B.C.L.C. 646, 651, *supra*, para. 3–54.

[7] *Boscawen v. Bajwa* [1996] 1 W.L.R. 328, 334–335 per Millett L.J.

[8] *e.g.* trusts of land unenforceable under s. 53(1)(b) L.P.A. 1925 but enforceable as so-called "common intention" constructive trusts, or a defendant seeking on other technical grounds to retain wholly for himself property agreed to be held in uncertain fashion for a co-purchaser.

[9] *e.g.* murdering X so as to benefit from X's will or intestacy or a joint tenancy with X.

[10] *Westdeutsche Landesbanke v. Islington B.C.* [1996] A.C. 669, 705–706, 707, 709.

[11] *ibid.* at 705.

[12] Lord Millett (1998) 114 L.Q.R. 399, 403–406.

[13] *Westdeutsche Landesbanke v. Islington B.C.* [1996] A.C. 669, 705–706, 707, 709.

[14] Lord Millett (1998) 114 L.Q.R. 399, 403–406, and in *Lonhro plc v. Fayed (No 2)* [1992] 1 W.L.R. 1, 12.

The institutional constructive trust of property

As seen, the equitable interest under a constructive trust arises by **6–05** operation of law from the date of the event giving rise to it and any subsequent court decision simply confirms and clarifies the pre-existing position.[15] Like the express trust and the resulting trust, the constructive trust arises and exists independently of any order of the court.

In America,[16] Canada[17] and, it seems, Australia[18] the courts have developed a flexible remedy that enables the court in its discretion to alter proprietary rights by imposing a "remedial constructive trust" in respect of particular property. The English Court of Appeal[19] has rejected the possible imposition of a remedial constructive trust on particular property of an insolvent defendant because it is not open to the judiciary thereby to oust the effect of the statutory insolvency rules. However, Lord Browne-Wilkinson[20] contemplates that it could be used against a solvent defendant. "The court by way of remedy might impose a constructive trust on a defendant who knowingly retains property of which the plaintiff has been unjustly deprived. Since the remedy can be tailored to the circumstances of the particular case, innocent third parties would not be prejudiced and restitutionary defences, such as change of position, are capable of being given effect." However, whether English law should adopt the remedial constructive trust "will have to be decided in some future case where the point is directly in issue."[21]

Earlier he illuminated the current gulf between the institutional and **6–06** the remedial constructive trust as follows[22]:

"Under an institutional constructive trust, the trust arises by operation of law as from the date of the circumstances which give rise to it: the function of the court is merely to declare that such trust has arisen in the past. The consequences that flow from such trust having arisen (including the possibly unfair consequences to third parties who in the interim have received the trust property) are also determined by rules of law, not under a discretion. A remedial constructive trust is different. It is a judicial remedy giving rise to an enforceable equitable obligation: the extent to which it operates retrospectively to the prejudice of third parties lies in the discretion of the court."

---

[15] *Westdeutsche Landesbank v. Islington B.C.* [1996] A.C. 669, 711; *Fortex Group Ltd v. Macintosh* [1998] 3 N.Z.L.R. 171, 172–173.
[16] Scott on Trusts 4th ed paras 461, 462.
[17] *Sorochan v. Sorochan* (1986) 29 D.L.R. (4th) 1, *Lac Minerals v. International Corona Resources* (1989) 61 D.L.R. (4th) 14, *Korkontzilas v. Saulos* (1997) 146 D.L.R. (4th) 214.
[18] *Muschinski v. Dodds* (1985) 160 C.L.R. 583 (prospective order), *Bathurst C. C. v. PWC Properties* (1998) 157 A.L.R. 414, *Giumelli v. Giumelli* (1999) 73 A.L.J.R. 547.
[19] *Re Polly Peck International plc (No 2)* [1998] 3 All E.R. 812.
[20] *Westdeutsche Landesbanke v. Islington B.C.* [1996] A.C. 669, 716; (also see *Metall und Rohstoff AG v. Donaldson Lufkin & Jenrette* [1990] 1 Q. B. 391, 473–474).
[21] *ibid.*, 716. Further see D. Wright, *The Remedial Constructive Trust*, Butterworths Australia (1998) and review thereof by P.B.H. Birks (1999) 115 L.Q.R. 681.
[22] *ibid.* 714.

6–07   In English law there is, of course, already the flexible discretionary doctrine of equitable proprietary estoppel[23] which enables the court to tailor the remedy (*e.g.* a constructive trust of a home for life or as co-equal beneficial owner or an equitable charge over the home) to fit the circumstances of a particular case. Indeed, extra-judicially,[24] Lord Browne-Wilkinson has considered that judges have been exploiting and distorting the law of resulting and constructive trusts in family home cases in order to prevent the legal owner getting away with unconscionable conduct when it would have been more appropriate to rely on equitable estoppel principles. The court's judgment will have prospective effect and so not affect a third party earlier acquiring any interest (*e.g.* under a mortgage) unless it would be unconscionable in all the circumstances for such party to take free from the interest awarded by the court to the successful claimant.[25]

6–08   Prospective remedial constructive trusts are fine but if retrospective effect is sought for a remedial constructive trust this is unlikely to find favour with English courts[26] whose approach is to regard rights of property as fixed and ascertainable in advance and immutable except with the consent of the owner[27] or of the court under the Variation of Trusts Act 1958 for persons incapable of consenting on their own behalf.[28]

Personal liability of strangers to account ("as constructive trustee")

To provide beneficiaries with a personal (as opposed to a proprietary) remedy against a stranger who was not a trustee, but who had dishonestly assisted a trustee's breach of trust or who had received trust property and then dishonestly dealt with it inconsistently with the trusts affecting it, Equity constructively treats such stranger as if he were a trustee and therefore, like a proper trustee, personally accountable for losses or profits.[29] No proprietary claim can be made, of course, where the stranger never had the trust property which he dishonestly helped the trustee dispose of in breach of trust or where the stranger who received the property no longer has it or its traceable product.

6–09   In establishing the personal liability of a stranger, Courts of Equity as a fictitious formula for equitable relief[30] used the catch-phrase[31] "personally liable to account as a constructive trustee" and called the stranger "a constructive trustee" even though he was not constructive trustee of any

---

[23] See paras 2–29 *et seq*, *supra* and close relationship of constructive trusts and proprietary estoppels in *Yaxley v. Gotts* [2000] 1 All E.R. 711 (CA) and *Re Basham* [1986] 1 W.L.R. 1488.

[24] "Constructive trusts and unjust enrichment", Holdsworth Lecture, 1991, in (1996) 10 Trust L. J. 98.

[25] See para. 6–117 *infra*.

[26] *Re Goldcorp Exchange Ltd* [1995] 1 A. C. 74, *Re Polly Peck International plc (No 2)* [1998] 3 All E.R. 812.

[27] Lord Millett (1998) 114 L.Q.R. 399 and in *Foskett v. McKeown* [2000] 3 All E.R. 97, 119–120.

[28] See paras 9–164 *et seq.*

[29] See paras 11–110 *et seq*, *infra*.

[30] *English v. Dedham Vale Properties Ltd* [1978] 1 All E.R. 382, 398, *Selangor United Rubber Estates v. Cradock (No 3)* [1968] 1 W.L.R. 1555, 1582.

[31] *Paragon Finance Ltd v. Thakerar* [1999] 1 All E.R. 400, 414.

property, so that if he was insolvent the personal claim abated with those of his other general creditors. Lord Browne-Wilkinson still used this terminology in *Westdeutsche Landesbanke v. Islington B.C.*[32] but Lord Millett[33] and modern commentators[34] rightly point out that "as constructive trustee" should not be taken literally and, indeed, should surely be discarded: a person should only be designated a constructive trustee if he holds property as a constructive trustee.

The personal remedy of the beneficiary has no place in a chapter dealing with the institutional constructive trust of property: it is dealt with later in Chapter 11.

Personal and proprietary liability of trustees of property

Where A is trustee of an *express* or *resulting* or *constructive* trust of **6–10** property for B, then B has an equitable proprietary right to claim such property or its traceable product and the fruits thereof. This proprietary right will prevail over A's trustee in bankruptcy and any other person deriving title from A who is not a bona fide purchaser of a legal interest for value without notice. B also has a personal claim to make A account for his trusteeship and any losses or profits resulting from breach of any duties as trustee. If A is wealthy enough it does not matter whether B relies on A's proprietary liability or on A's personal liability or on both. If the property has doubled in value B can claim that specific property or a sum of money amounting to the value of such property, though A can then insist on handing over the specific property if he prefers. Until trial B can preserve the position by obtaining (virtually[35] as of right) an interlocutory injunction restraining dealings with "his" trust property.

If A is insolvent then B's personal claim to make A liable to account **6–11** for losses or profits will abate with the claims of all unsecured creditors. Thus B, instead, will exercise his proprietary claim and, if need be, obtain an interlocutory injunction to preserve his property.

Categories of constructive trusts of property

At the highest level of generality it is clear that a constructive trust arises whenever the circumstances are such that it is unconscionable for the owner of property to assert his own beneficial interest therein to the exclusion of the beneficial interest of another.[36] This generalisation can cover the cases where the imposition of the constructive trust is merely an equitable mechanism for vindicating the subsisting equitable interests of beneficiaries under trusts (or other fiduciary relationships) whether against the trustees (or other fiduciaries) or against third parties not

---

[32] [1996] A. C. 669, 705.
[33] (1998) 114 L.Q.R. 399, 400 and in *Paragon Finance Ltd v. Thakerar* [1999] 1 All E.R. 400, 414.
[34] D. J. Hayton (1985) 27 Malaya L.R. 313, 314; P.B.H. Birks in E. McKendrick (ed) *Commercial Aspects of Trusts and Fiduciary Obligations* (1992 Oxford) Chap 8; A. J. Oakley (ed) Parker & Mellows, *Modern Law of Trusts* (7th ed) at 268.
[35] *Polly Peck International plc v. Nadir (No. 2)* [1992] 4 All E.R. 769 at 784 (claim too speculative).
[36] *e.g.* Lord Millett in (1998) 114 L.Q.R. 399, 400.

protected as bona fide purchasers or by protective legislation. The owner of an equitable proprietary interest can (with the assistance of the tracing process, if need be) directly assert his equitable ownership over assets in the hands of the trustee (or fiduciary) or the third parties, so that the imposition of the constructive trust over such assets is a direct response to the interference with pre-existing equitable proprietary rights.

6–12   Thus, the vindication or enforcement of equitable property rights could be dealt with separately as such,[37] rather that conventionally subsumed within the heading of "Constructive Trusts of Property" but convention will be followed in this Chapter in sections 1 and 2 below. The third section then deals with established, but open-textured, categories of circumstances where a Court of Equity regards it as unconscionable to allow an owner of property to assert his own beneficial interest therein to the exclusion of the beneficial interest of the claimant.

Section 1. The Trustee or other Fiduciary as constructive Trustee of Profits
Who is fiduciary?

6–13   A well-established category of constructive trust arises to flesh out the obligations of a trustee or other fiduciary. The relationship of trustee and beneficiary is the original fiduciary relationship and provides the guidelines for determining when other persons are in a fiduciary relationship to each other by virtue of the position and power of one in respect of the other and the latter's reasonably induced expectation that the former will act exclusively in the interests of the latter or of their joint interest.[37a] Trustees are persons who are under a duty to act exclusively in the interests of the trust beneficiaries, who are vulnerable, if the trustees seek to abuse their position, because the trustees have rights and powers that are capable of being exercised so as detrimentally to affect the beneficiaries. Thus, if such aspects are present in other relationships these are treated as fiduciary relationships as a matter of law, *e.g.* personal representatives and beneficiaries of deceased's estate,[38] solicitor and client,[38a] principal and agent,[39] partner and partner,[40]

---

[37] C.E.F. Rickett (1999) 18 N. Z. L. R. 305, 320–321. Indeed, Lord Browne-Wilkinson in *Westdeutsche Landesbanke v. Islington B.C.* [1996] A.C. 669, 707 regards the treatment of the defendant as a constructive trustee inappropriate where equitable property rights affect his title and the equitable owner seeks to vindicate her property rights, while Lord Millett in *Foskett v. McKeown* [2000] 3 All E.R. 97, 121 considered the claimant beneficiaries "seek to vindicate their property rights, not to reverse unjust enrichment" via the tracing process, as did the Court of Appeal in *Re Diplock* [1948] Ch. 465 at 525, concerned with the "beneficent powers of equity to protect and enforce what it recognises as equitable rights of property which subsist until they are destroyed by the operation of a purchase for value without notice."

[37a] Generally see P. D. Finn, "The Fiduciary Principle" in Equity, Trusts and Fiduciary Relationships (T. G. Youdan, ed.) pp. 1–56; Meagher, Gummow & Lehane, *Equity: Doctrines and Remedies*, Chap. 5; Goff & Jones, *Law of Restitution* (5th ed.), Chap 33; P. D. Finn, "Fiduciary law and the Modern Commercial World" in E. McKendrick (ed.), *Commercial Aspects of Trusts and Fiduciary Obligations*; P.B.H. Birks (ed) *Privacy and Loyalty*, Clarendon Oxford 1997 Chapters 8, 10 and 11.

[38] *Re Diplock* [1948] Ch. 465.

[38a] *Clark Boyce v. Mouat* [1994] 1 A.C. 428, *Nocton v. Lord Ashburton* [1914] A.C. 932.

[39] *Boston Deep Sea Fishing Co. v. Ansell* (1888) 39 Ch. D. 389; *Att.-Gen. of Hong Kong v. Reid* [1994] 1 A.C. 324 on how *Lister v. Stubbs* (1890) 45 Ch. D. 1 should have been decided.

[40] *Thompson's Trustee v. Heaton* [1974] 1 All E.R. 1239.

promoter and company,[41] director and company,[42] employee and employer while the employment relationship subsists,[43] although any fiduciary obligation of confidence arising in such employment will continue until the information ceases to be confidential.[44]

As a matter of public policy, to maintain the integrity, credibility and **6–14** utility of such relationships, it is vital that the fiduciary loyally serves the interests of his beneficiaries. Except with the fully-informed, freely-given consent of his beneficiaries, he cannot misuse his position of trust to his own or a third party's possible advantage and he cannot place himself in a position where there is a conflict between his duty and self-interest or between his duty to his beneficiaries and his duty to others.[45] It is thus not prescriptive but proscriptive duties that Equity imposes on a fiduciary.[46]

Separate from fiduciary relationships arising as a matter of law from status[47] are fact-based fiduciaries who become subject to fiduciary duties because of a particular factual situation where the imposition of such duties is considered appropriate in the interests of justice because of the claimant's particular vulnerability to being taken advantage of by the defendant upon whose loyalty he is reasonably relying, *e.g.* in the case of a financier using confidential information imparted by A (when seeking a loan) to help B conclude a deal to the exclusion of A and to the profit of B and the financier,[48] or of the parties to a joint venture where they were entitled to expect that the other would act in their joint interest to the exclusion of his own several interest.[49]

The distinction between fact-based fiduciaries and status-based fiduci- **6–15** aries is illuminated by contrasting the position of financial advisers and of discretionary portfolio managers. It seems that the latter should be regarded automatically as fiduciaries with their unilateral powers to invest and disinvest as they see fit.[50] In the case of the former it is a question of fact whether or not the parties' relationship was such as to give rise to a fiduciary duty on the part of the adviser: the circumstances can cover the whole spectrum from total reliance upon the adviser to total independence of the adviser.[51]

---

[41] *Gluckstein v. Barnes* [1990] A.C. 240.

[42] *Regal Hastings Ltd v. Gulliver* [1942] 1 All E.R. 378.

[43] *Att.-Gen. v. Blake* [1998] Ch. 439 (C.A.).

[44] *ibid.* since the information had ceased to be confidential, on appeal, the House of Lords held (4:1) that, very exceptionally, the Russian spy, Blake, should be subject to an account of profits as a new remedy for breach of contract: *Att.-Gen. v. Blake* [2000] 4 All E.R. 385.

[45] *Boardman v. Phipps* [1967] 2 A.C. 46; *Warman International Ltd v. Dwyer* (1995) 64 ALJR 362, 367; *Chan v. Zachariah* (1984) 154 C.L.R. 178.

[46] *Breen v. Williams* (1996) 70 ALJR 772, 793, 794; *Bristol & West B.S. v. Mothew* [1996] 4 All E.R. 698, 710, 712.

[47] *Hodgkinson v. Simms* (1994) 117 D.L.R. (4th) 161 at 176, 215; P. D. Finn, in T. G. Youdan (ed.) *Equity, Trusts and Fiduciary Relationships*, pp. 33–44; Law Commission No. 124 "Fiduciary duties & Regulatory Rules" para. 2.4.3.

[48] *United Pan Europe Ltd v. Deutsche Bank* [2000] 2 B.C.L.C. 461 (C.A.).

[49] *Lac Minerals Ltd v. International Corona Resources Ltd* (1989) 61 D.L.R. (4th) 14; *Hospital Products Ltd v. U.S. Surgical Corp.* (1984) 156 C.L.R. 41; *Noranda Australia Ltd v. Lachlan Resources* (1988) 14 NWSLR 1.

[50] *Glennie v. McDougall* [1935] S.C.R. 357 at 276; *Hewson v. Stock Exchange* [1968] 2 NSWLR 245.

[51] *Hodgkinson v. Simms* (1994) 117 D.L.R. (4th) 161.

Scope of fiduciary duties

6–16   The scope of a defendant's fiduciary obligations depends upon the
nature and scope of his relationship with the claimant.[52] He is not to be
made liable in respect of profits derived by him outside the scope of the
plaintiff's business nor to be obliged to prefer the claimant's interests to
his own outside such scope. "A person may be in a fiduciary position
quoad a part of his activities and not quoad other parts."[53] Thus, a
partner is not accountable to his partners for profits made from a
business outside the scope of the partnership business.[54] A director is a
fiduciary in relation to his company[55] but not to any shareholder[56] (unless
exceptionally the shareholder had turned to the director so as to place
special reliance on the director[57]), while the director's obligations,
particularly in respect of business opportunities, depend upon the actual
and prospective line(s) of business of the company.[58]

6–17   While a solicitor is a status-based fiduciary, his negligence in carrying
out his duties does not amount to a breach of fiduciary duty.[59] Such a
breach requires breach of the fiduciary's obligation of loyalty, *e.g.* acting
for a client in a matter that the solicitor has a personal interest without
fully disclosing this or acting for both sides in a transaction without
disclosing this to one of them.[60] While an agent is a status-based
fiduciary, if the principal allows the agent to mix moneys paid in respect
of sums due to the principal with the agent's own money and account
monthly to the principal for the moneys owed to the principal, the agent
is only personally liable in debt to the principal.[61] However, if the agent
had agreed to hold all money received on the principal's behalf from the
principal's debtors separate from his own money for the principal's
exclusive benefit, the principal would have an equitable proprietary
interest in the money held by the agent as fiduciary.[62]

6–18   In the case of fact-based fiduciary obligations imposed because of the
claimant's particular vulnerability to the power of the defendant, upon
whom the claimant is manifestly relying, these obligations will be

---

[52] "To say that a man is a fiduciary only begins analysis: it gives direction to further enquiry. To whom is
he a fiduciary? What obligations does he owe as a fiduciary? In what respect has he failed to discharge
these obligations? And what are the consequences of his deviation from duty?" *per* Frankfurter J. in
SEC v. Chenery Corp (1943) 318 U.S. 80 at 85–86 endorsed by Lord Mustill in *Re Goldcorp Exchange
Ltd* [1994] 2 All E.R. 806 at 821.

[53] *New Zealand Netherlands Society Oranje Inc v. Kuys* [1973] 2 All E.R. 1222 at 1225.

[54] *Aas v. Benham* [1891] 2 Ch. 244.

[55] *Regal Hastings Ltd v. Gulliver* [1967] 2 A.C. 134n; *Industrial Development Consultants v. Cooley* [1972]
1 W.L.R. 443.

[56] *Percival v. Wright* [1902] 2 Ch. 421; *North-west Transportation v. Beatty* (1887) 12 App. Cas. 589.

[57] *Coleman v. Myers* [1977] 2 N.Z.L.R. 225.

[58] See *infra*, para. 9–29; *Queensland Mines Ltd v. Hudson* (1978) 52 ALJR 394; *Canadian Aero Services
Ltd v. O'Malley* (1973) 40 D.L.R. (3rd) 371.

[59] *Bristol & West B. S. v. Mothew* [1998] Ch. 1 (C.A.). As Lord Mustill said in *Re Goldcorp Exchange Ltd*
[1994] 2 All E.R. 806 at 821, "The essence of a fiduciary relationship is that it creates obligations of a
different character from those deriving under the contract itself".

[60] *Clark Boyce v. Mouat* [1994] 1 A.C. 428; *Farrington v. Row McBride & Partners* [1985] 1 N.Z.L.R. 83;
Witten-Hannah v. Davis [1995] 2 N.Z.L.R. 141.

[61] *Henry v. Hammond* [1953] 2 K.B. 515; *Commissioners of Customs & Excise v. Richmond Theatre* [1995]
STC 257; *R. v. Clowes (No. 2)* [1994] 2 All E.R. 316.

[62] *Napier and Ettrick (Lord) v. Hunter* [1993] A.C. 713 at 744 *per* Lord Goff; *Re Fleet Disposal Services
Ltd* [1995] 1 BCLC 345.

restricted to the defendant's activities which result from his power and play upon the vulnerability of the claimant.[63]

Where the fiduciary relationship arises from a contract or a partnership or trust deed or other instrument then the terms of the instrument are relevant for qualifying the scope of the fiduciary's obligations.[64] However, a fiduciary relationship can arise in the course of negotiating the terms of a contract or trust,[65] in which case abuse of such relationship or the exercise of undue influence can prevent the fiduciary relying on a clause exempting him from negligence or breach of fiduciary duties.[66]

Nature of fiduciary remedies: temptation to extend fiduciary situations

The establishment of a fiduciary situation affords scope for an extensive **6–19** range of equitable remedies for breach of fiduciary duty. The transaction with the fiduciary can be avoided[67] or equitable compensation for loss caused by the defendant's breach of fiduciary duty will be available,[68] while in respect of profits[69] the courts can impose a personal liability to account[70] or a proprietary constructive trust of the profits and their traceable product.[71] Moreover, advantages flow from suing in equity rather than common law due to the strict deterrent liability for profits imposed by equity[72] and equity's assessment of losses (once proved to be caused by the breach of fiduciary duty[73]) with the full benefit of hindsight[74] and ignoring any contributory negligence.[75]

The utility, and the extent, of fiduciary obligations and the remedies **6–20** for breach thereof are such that claimants and courts are tempted to stretch the concept of fiduciary relationship as if it were an "accordion term"[76] However, the courts have rejected claims that treat any breach of a fiduciary's obligations as a breach of fiduciary duty. As Millett L.J. stated in *Bristol & West B.S. v. Mothew*[77]:

---

[63] See "Fiduciary duties & Regulatory Rules": Law Com Consultation Paper No. 124, para. 2.4.8.
[64] *Kelly v. Cooper* [1993] A.C. 205, *New Zealand Netherlands Society Oranje Inc v. Kuys* [1973] 2 All E.R. 1222.
[65] *Swain v. Law Society* [1981] 3 All E.R. 797 at 817.
[66] *Tate v. Williamson* (1866) 2 Ch. App. 55 at 61; *Baskerville v. Thurgood* (1992) 100 Sask L.R. 214.
[67] *Wright v. Morgan* [1926] A.C. 788.
[68] Gummow J. "Compensation for breach of Fiduciary Duty" in *Equity, Trusts and Fiduciary Relationships* (T. G. Youdan, ed.) at 57–92; *Nocton v. Lord Ashburton* [1914] A.C. 932; *O'Sullivan v. Management Agency Ltd* [1985] Q.B. 428; *Mahoney v. Purnell* [1996] 3 All E.R. 61 89–91; *Swindle v. Harrison* [1997] 4 All E.R. 705 (C.A.).
[69] In the case of a claim for profits whether the claimant suffered any loss is altogether irrelevant because the object is to ensure that the defaulting fiduciary does not retain any profit: *Att.-Gen. v. Blake* [2000] 4 All E.R. 385, 393; *United Pan Europe Ltd v. Deutsche Bank* [2000] 2 B.C.L.C. 461.
[70] *Reading v. Att.-Gen.* [1951] A.C. 507; *Regal Hastings Ltd v. Gulliver* [1967] 2 A.C. 134n; *English v. Dedham Vale Properties Ltd* [1978] 1 All E.R. 382.
[71] *Att.-Gen. of Hong Kong v. Reid* [1994] 1 A.C. 324; *Boardman v. Phipps* [1967] 2 A.C. 46, *Re EVTR* [1987] B.C.L.C. 646.
[72] See paras 9–21 *et seq.*
[73] *Swindle v. Harrison* [1997] 4 All E.R. 705 (C.A.).
[74] *Target Holdings v. Redferns* [1996] A.C. 421.
[75] See Handley J. A. in Finn (ed.) *Essays on Damages* (1992) pp. 126–127; Gummow J. in *Equity, Trusts and Fiduciary Relationships* (T. G. Youdan ed.) pp. 83–87.
[76] See P. D. Finn in *Equity, Trusts and Fiduciary Relationships* (T. G. Youdan ed.) p. 10.
[77] [1998] Ch. 1, 16

"The expression 'fiduciary duty' is properly confined to those duties which are peculiar to fiduciaries and the breach of which attracts legal consequences differing from those consequent upon breach of other duties . . . not every breach of a duty by a fiduciary is a breach of fiduciary duty . . . It is inappropriate to apply the expression to the obligation of a trustee or other fiduciary to use proper skill and care in he discharge of his duties . . . The distinguishing obligation of a fiduciary is the obligation of loyalty . . . A fiduciary must act in good faith; he must not make a profit out of his position; he must not place himself in a position where his duty and his interest may conflict; he may not act for his own benefit or the benefit of a third person without the informed consent of his principal . . . where the fiduciary deals with his principal . . . he must prove affirmatively that the transaction is fair and that he made full disclosure of all the facts material to the transactions . . . Breach of fiduciary obligation connotes disloyaly or infidelity. Mere incompetence is not enough"

6–21   Until recently, the courts were too inclined to stretch the circumstances giving rise to a fiduciary obligation, so converting the defendant into a fiduciary,[78] in order to enable them to make the defendant account for profits or to utilise the tracing process so as to impose an equitable lien or constructive trust against the defendant's property. Nowadays, such accounting remedy has been made available in an exceptional type of a breach of contract,[79] while the tracing rules for identifying substituted assets are now available in support of legal claims as well as equitable claims.[80] Thus there is less need to stretch the circumstances giving rise to a fiduciary obligation.

The constructive trust of property

6–22   As Dillon L.J. stated in *Re EVTR*[81] "It is a long established principle of equity that if a person who is a trustee receives money or property because of, or in respect of, trust property, he will hold what he receives as a constructive trustee on the trusts of the original trust property" until such money or property is duly vested in the trustees on the trusts of the trust fund. The trustees are express trustees of the fund comprising whatever happens from time to time to be duly vested in them as representing the original trust property.[82] However, the trustee will be regarded as constructive trustee of a rights issue of shares relating to a trust shareholding where he purchased them purportedly for himself with his own money, or of a lease renewed in favour of himself and not

---

[78] A Fiduciary "is not subject to fiduciary obligations because he is a fiduciary; it is because he is subject to them that he is a fiduciary": *Bristol & West B.S. v. Mothew* [1998] Ch. 1, 18
[79] *Att.-Gen. v. Blake* [2000] 4 All E.R. 385.
[80] *Foskett v. McKeown* [2000] 3 All E.R. 97, 106, 121.
[81] [1987] B.C.L.C. 646, 651, *Supra* para. 3–54.
[82] *Re Earl of Strafford* [1979] 1 All E.R. 513 at 521.

the trust,[83] or of the freehold reversion to a trust's lease,[84] or of shares in his own company formed specially to develop trust land sold by him to the company at an undervalue,[85] or of property bought in his own name with a cheque drawn on his private account containing trust money wrongfully mixed with his own money.[86] Similarly, an agent engaged to buy property for his principal will hold it on constructive trust for his principal if he buys it for himself[87] and a director diverting to himself a profitable contract which he should have taken up on behalf of the company will hold it on constructive trust for the company.[88] If a bribe is taken by a trustee or director or agent or senior employee then the bribe will forthwith be held upon a constructive trust as will property purchased therewith: *Att.-Gen. of Hong Kong v. Reid*,[89] *infra*, para. 6–71. "That which is the fruit of trust property or of the trusteeship is itself trust property"[90] so that profits made from exploiting the fiduciary property or the position of fiduciary[91] are held on constructive trust.

Strict liability and its justification

A proprietary constructive trust (with a personal liability to account) **6–23** arises as a sanction for the fundamental, strict rule that a fiduciary must not place himself where his fiduciary duty does, or may sensibly, conflict with his private interest[92]—unless duly authorised by his principal or the court. It is immaterial that the fiduciary, T, acted honestly and in his principal's best interest, that the principal suffered no loss but even made a profit which he could not otherwise have obtained and that the profit was obtained through use of T's own assets and by virtue of T's skills,—though T will have a lien for his expenditure and, in exceptional circumstances, may obtain an allowance for his skills.[93] The rule is very strict in order to maintain confidence in the trust or other fiduciary relationship by deterring any slipping from the high standards required of trustees and other fiduciaries: just as a dishonest loss-causing defendant in the same situation would be liable for losses, so an honest profit-making defendant should be liable for profits. Equity has a strict **6–24** prophylactic approach to prevent a wrong which may enrich the defendant or harm the claimant. To relax standards for situations where the defendant allegedly acted "properly" cannot be allowed because most of the relevant evidence will be peculiarly within the defendant's knowledge

---

[83] *Keech v. Sandford* (1726) 2 Eq.Cas.Abr. 741, *infra*, at 341.
[84] *Protheroe v. Protheroe* [1968] 1 W.L.R. 519.
[85] *cf. Aberdeen Railway Co. v. Blaikie Bros.* (1854) 1 Macq. 461.
[86] *cf. Re Tilley's W.T.* [1967] Ch. 1179.
[87] *Longfield Parish Council v. Robson* (1913) 29 T.L.R. 357; *Lees v. Nuttall* (1834) 2 My. & K. 819; *Lonrho v. Fayed (No. 2)* [1991] 4 All E.R. 901 at 969–970.
[88] *Cook v. Deeks* [1916] 1 A.C. 554, *Industrial Developments Consultants Ltd v. Cooley* [1972] 1 W.L.R. 443.
[89] [1994] 1 A.C. 324.
[90] *Swain v. Law Society* [1981] 3 All E.R. 797, 813 per Oliver L.J.
[91] *Att.-Gen. of Hong Kong v. Reid* [1994] 1 A.C. 324; *Phipps v. Boardman* [1967] 2 A.C. 46.
[92] *Phipps v. Boardman* [1967] 2 A.C. 46, 123, *N.Z. Netherlands Society Inc. v. Kuys* [1973] 1 W.L.R. 1126, 1129. See *infra*, paras 9–21 *et seq.*
[93] *Phipps v. Boardman* [1967] 2 A.C. 46; *O'Sullivan v. Management Agency & Music Ltd* [1985] Q.B. 428.

and control, so making it very difficult for the disadvantaged plaintiff beneficiaries to know whether or not they have a case for saying the defendant acted "improperly." Thus, it is *per se* (in itself) improper for a defendant fiduciary to enter into transactions where there is a conflict or sensible possibility of a conflict between his fiduciary duty and his self-interest. It is up to the defendant to avoid any problems by obtaining the informed consent of his principal(s) or of the court.

6–25 He "must account . . . for any benefit or gain which has been obtained or received in circumstances where a conflict or significant possibility of conflict existed between his fiduciary duty and his personal interest in the pursuit or possible receipt of such a benefit or gain."[94] He also "must account . . . for any benefit or gain which was obtained or received by use or by reason of his fiduciary position or of opportunity or knowledge resulting from it" where he is "actually misusing his position for his personal advantage" rather than for the advantage of his principal(s). However, if information is acquired by a fiduciary in the course of his duties and it is not classified as confidential information he is free to use the information for the benefit of himself or of another trust of which he is trustee if there is no reasonably foreseeable possibility of his needing to use that information for his original principal(s).[95] Where information acquired by a fiduciary or his "tippee" (to whom he passes the information) is confidential so that its disclosure could be prevented by a court injunction then, although such information has insufficient "property" nature for the law of theft, it may have sufficient "property" nature for profits made by use of such information to be held on constructive trust,[96] though since then abuse of position (in addition to exploitation of fiduciary property) has been held sufficient to justify the imposition of a constructive trust on property obtained as a result of such abuse.[97]

Proprietary and/or personal liability

6–26 If there is a proprietary liability because T (a trustee or other fiduciary) holds specific property as constructive trustee then there is a co-extensive personal liability to account and if T is wealthy enough the plaintiffs will usually be happy enough to rely on T's personal liability and take the cash profits from him (rather than take the property upon paying T sufficient for his lien on the property for its cost to him). Thus, a House of Lords case like *Regal Hastings Ltd v. Gulliver*[98] was pleaded only as a personal claim to account and in *Phipps v. Boardman*[99] counsel and judges concentrated upon making the wealthy Boardman personally liable to account. In *Phipps v. Boardman, infra*, at para. 6–46 the plaintiff

---

[94] *Chan v. Zachariah* (1984) 154 C.L.R. 178, 199 where all the citations in this para. are to be found. Also see *Warman International Ltd v. Dwyer* (1995) 69 ALJR 362 at 367.
[95] *Phipps v. Boardman* [1967] 2 A.C. 46, 130; see *infra*, para. 6–46.
[96] *Nanus Asia Co. Inc. v. Standard Chartered Bank* [1990] Hong Kong L.R. 396.
[97] *Att.-Gen. for Hong Kong v. Reid* [1994] 1 A.C. 324.
[98] [1967] 2 A.C. 134 *infra*, at paras 6–46 *et seq*.
[99] [1967] 2 A.C. 46.

with a five-eighteenths interest under a trust claimed (i) a declaration that the defendants held five-eighteenths of the shareholding obtained by them through using information acquired by them when representing the trust as constructive trustees for him, (ii) an account of the profits made by the defendants, and (iii) an order that they should transfer to him the shares held by them as constructive trustees and should pay him five-eighteenths of profits found to be due upon taking the account. Wilberforce J. gave the plaintiff the relief requested under (i) and (ii) but adjourned (iii) having ordered an inquiry as to a liberal allowance for the defendant's work. Presumably, this was to allow the taking of accounts of profits made on sale of some of the shares and the inquiry as to the proper payment to be allowed to the defendants for their skilful efforts, whereupon the balance would be due to the plaintiff, who could then consider whether to call for the remaining shares subject to reimbursing the defendants for their costs in purchasing the shares. No doubt, at the end of the day the plaintiff preferred to receive all cash rather than cash plus shares, and the defendants agreed to this.

The Court of Appeal and the House of Lords, due to counsels' **6–27** concentration on personal accountability, held that the defendants were constructive trustees who were liable to account for their profits but they confirmed Wilberforce J.'s order which included a proprietary declaration of constructive trust.[1]

Where the gain emanates from property entrusted to the fiduciary it is **6–28** clear that the gain should be held on a proprietary constructive trust, but three[2] of the five Law Lords held that the defendants' information obtained *qua fiduciaries* was not trust property so that the shares purchased as a result of using such information did not thereby constructively become trust property. Two Law Lords[3] thought that there was no sensible possibility of conflict of duty and interest. However, the majority[4] thought that there was: the defendant as solicitor to the trustees was not in a position to give disinterested impartial advice at the stage when he was almost about to make large profits for himself and yet when he ought, if consulted, to have been advising the trustees to obtain wider investment powers from the court so as to enable the trust (and not himself) to make large profits. Thus, the defendants had to account for their profits on the shares because they had acquired the knowledge and the opportunity to purchase the shares while purporting to represent the trust.

The Lords did not openly consider the question of a proprietary **6–29** constructive trust but the court order accepts the existence of such a trust, so that the use of position as opposed to the use of trust property seemed capable of generating a proprietary constructive trust of the profit made in breach of the duty to avoid conflicts of interest, despite an

---

[1] See [1964] 2 All E.R. 187 at 208; [1965] Ch. 992, 1006, 1021; (1967) 2 A.C. 46 at 99, 112.
[2] Lords Cohen and Upjohn and Viscount Dilhorne.
[3] Viscount Dilhorne and Lord Upjohn.
[4] Lords Hodson, Guest and Cohen; see *infra*, at paras 6–50 *et seq.*

earlier contrary Court of Appeal decision, *Lister v. Stubbs*,[5a] rejecting any constructive trust of a bribe obtained by a fiduciary abusing his position, so that the dishonest fiduciary was only personally accountable for the bribe and his employer could not trace the bribe into assets purchased therewith. Lord Templeman, delivering the advice of the Privy Council in *Att.-Gen. for Hong Kong v. Reid*,[5b] rejected that decision and explained that *Boardman v. Phipps* "demonstrates the strictness with which equity regards the conduct of a fiduciary and the extent to which equity is willing to impose a constructive trust on property obtained by a fiduciary by virtue of his office . . . the solicitor was held to be a constructive trustee . . . because the solicitor obtained the information . . . and the opportunity of acquiring the shares as a result of acting for certain purposes on behalf of the trustees. If a fiduciary acting honestly in good faith and making a profit which his principal could not make for himself becomes a constructive trustee of that profit, then a fiduciary acting dishonestly who accepts a bribe must also be a constructive trustee." Thus, the Attorney General could enter a *caveat* against three New Zealand properties purchased with bribes received by Reid as public prosecutor to drop prosecutions, such properties being held on constructive trust for the Crown.

6–30   It seems easier to support a proprietary constructive trust in *Lister* and *Reid* than in *Boardman*. In a bribe case is there not an incontrovertible assumption that the victim has lost property of a value at least equal to the bribe, so that the bribe may justifiably be regarded as representing the victim's property? As between the victim and the fiduciary surely the victim has a better claim not only to the bribe but to the fruits thereof: the fiduciary would certainly be unjustly enriched if allowed to retain the bribe and its fruits. If he himself should not benefit from his dishonest wrongdoing why should his creditors be better off and receive a windfall if he is insolvent?

6–31   In *Boardman* the case for a proprietary constructive trust for profits gained by use of position seems weaker. The profit, literally speaking, was not made at the expense of the beneficiaries, though it was made at the expense of the fiduciary not being able to give disinterested advice to the beneficiaries (if asked) and so at the risk of harming the beneficiaries' interests. Should the latter honest but wrongful breach of his duty to avoid a conflict make the fiduciary subject to a proprietary constructive trust of his profit as opposed to a mere personal liability to account?[6]

English law has an "all or nothing" approach. Boardman was unlucky that the majority did not take the view that the remote possibility of him being asked to advise the trustees at the time of the third phase (see para. 6–49 *infra*) was immaterial, particularly when, if the possibility

---

[5a] (1890) 45 Ch.D.
[5b] [1994] 1 A.C. 324, see *infra*, at para. 6–71.
[6] Further see G. Elias, *Explaining Constructive Trusts* (O.U.P. 1990), at 77; P. Birks, *Introduction to the Law of Restitution* (O.U.P. 1985), at 341, 388; G. H. Jones (1968) 84 L.O.R. 472.

materialised, he could have openly declared his interest or have declined to advise them, other than to seek the advice of another solicitor.

KEECH v. SANDFORD[7]

Lord Chancellor (1726) 2 Eq.Cas.Abr. 741; Sel.Cas.Ch. 61

A person being possessed of a lease of the profits of a market devised his **6–32** estate to a trustee in trust for his infant. Before the expiration of the term the trustee applied to the lessor for a renewal, for the benefit of the infant, which he refused, since the lease being only of the profits of a market, there could be no distress, and its enforcement must rest in covenant, by which the infant could not be bound.

The infant sought to have the lease assigned to him, and for an account of the profits, on the principle that wherever a lease is renewed by a trustee or executor it shall be for the benefit of the *cestui que use*, which principle was agreed on the other side, though endeavoured to be differenced on account of the express proof of refusal to renew to the infant.

LORD KING L.C.: "I must consider this as a trust for the infant, for I very well **6–33** see, if a trustee, on the refusal to renew, might have a lease to himself, few trust estates would be renewed to *cestui que use*. Though I do not say there is fraud in this case, yet he should rather have let it run out than to have had the lease to himself. This may seem hard, that the trustee is the only person of all mankind who might not have the lease; but it is very proper that the rule should be strictly pursued, and not in the least relaxed; for it is very obvious what would be the consequences of letting trustees have the lease on refusal to renew to *cestui que use*."

So decreed, that the lease should be assigned to the infant, and that the trustee should be indemnified from any covenants comprised in the lease, and an account of the profits made since the renewal.[8]

Note

The rule applies whether the trustee obtains a renewal by virtue of a **6–34** provision in the lease to that effect or whether he obtains it by virtue of the advantage which his position as sitting tenant gives him.[9] The principle applies not only to trustees and tenants for life,[10] but also to mortgagees,[11] directors[12] and partners.[13] But unlike trustees and tenants

---

[7] The rule in *Keech v. Sandford* is derived from the principle that a trustee must not put himself in a position where his interest conflicts with his duty: in case of conflict, duty prevails over interest. Several instances of this principle occur in the administration of express trusts: *infra*, at paras 9–08 to 9–66. See also Hart, "The Development of the Rule in *Keech v. Sandford*" (1905) 21 L.Q.R. 258; Cretney (1969) 33 Conv.(N.S.) 161.

[8] Also, see *Re Jarvis* [1958] 1 W.L.R. 815.

[9] *Re Knowles' Will Trusts* [1948] 1 All E.R. 866.

[10] *James v. Dean* (1808) 15 Ves. 236; *Lloyd-Jones v. Clark-Lloyd* [1919] 1 Ch. 424; ss.16, 107 of the Settled Land Act 1925.

[11] *Rushworth's Case* (1676) Freem.Ch. 13; *Leigh v. Burnett* (1885) 29 Ch.D. 231.

[12] *G. E. Smith Ltd v. Smith* [1952] N.Z.L.R. 470; *Crittenden & Cowler Co. v. Cowler*, 72 New York State 701 (1901).

[13] *Featherstonhaugh v. Fenwick* (1810) 17 Ves. 298; *cf. Piddock v. Burt* [1894] 1 Ch. 343.

for life the latter group of persons are not irrebuttably precluded from taking the renewal of a lease. In *Re Biss*,[14] a lease formed part of the personalty of an intestate, and after the lessor had refused to renew to the administratrix, one of her sons (helping her run the deceased's business at the premises) obtained a renewal for himself. It was held, however, to be unimpeachable, since he could show affirmatively that he acted bona fide and did not take advantage of the other persons interested. Romer L.J. said,[15] "where the person renewing the lease does not clearly occupy a fiduciary position" he "is only held to be a constructive trustee of the renewed lease if, in respect of the old lease, he occupied some special position and owed, by virtue of that position, a duty towards the other persons interested."

6–35   In *Protheroe v. Protheroe*[16] the Court of Appeal in a one-page extempore judgment of Lord Denning held that under the *Keech v. Sandford* principle there was "a long-established rule of equity" that a trustee purchasing the reversion upon a lease held by him *automatically* held the reversion upon the same trusts as the lease. This is unsound as till then such constructive trusts of the reversion were only imposed where the lease was renewable by custom or contract (the purchase thus cutting off the right of renewal) or where the trustee obtained the reversion by virtue of his position *qua* leaseholder (*e.g.* a landlord offering enfranchisement to all his leaseholders).[17] The reason for the distinction is that "whereas in the case of a renewal the trustee is in effect buying a part of the trust property, in the case of a reversion this is not so; it is a separate item altogether."[18] However, *Protheroe* can be justified because purchasers of a reversion fall foul of the strict principles illustrated by *Boardman v. Phipps, infra*, para. 6–46 especially since the trustee would personally be the landlord of the trust tenancy.

CHAN v. ZACHARIA

High Court of Australia (1984) 154 C.L.R. 178 (1984) 53 A.L.R. 417

6–36   DEANE J.: "There is a wide variety of formulations of the general principle of equity requiring a person in a fiduciary relationship to account for personal benefit or gain. The doctrine is often expressed in the form that a person 'is not

---

[14] [1903] 2 Ch. 40.

[15] *ibid.* at 61. See *Chan v. Zacharia infra*, at para. 6–36.

[16] [1968] 1 W.L.R. 519; followed in *Thompson's Trustee v. Heaton* [1974] 1 W.L.R. 605. See (1968) 84 L.Q.R. 309; (1974) 38 Conv.(N.S.) 288; *Metlej v. Cavanagh* [1981] 2 N.S.W.L.R. 339 at 348; *Brenner v. Rose* [1973] 1 W.L.R. 443 seems erroneous.

[17] *Bevan v. Webb* [1905] 1 Ch. 620; *Longton v. Wilsby* (1887) 76 L.T. 770; *Randall v. Russell* (1817) 3 Mer. 190; *Phillips v. Phillips* (1884) 29 Ch.D. 673; *Phipps v. Boardman* [1964] 1 W.L.R. 993, 1009; *Brenner v. Rose* [1973] 1 W.L.R. 443, 448, but *cf. Thompson's Trustee v. Heaton* [1974] 1 W.L.R. 605; *Popat v. Shonchhatra* [1995] 4 All E.R. 646.

[18] *Phipps v. Boardman (ibid.)*; *cf.* different treatment of renewals and reversions for purposes of rule against remoteness: *Woodall v. Clifton* [1905] 2 Ch. 257.

allowed to put himself in a position where his interest and duty conflict' (*Bray v. Ford*[19]) or 'may conflict' (*Phipps v. Boardman*[20]) or that a person is 'not to allow a conflict to arise between duty and interest': *New Zealand Netherlands Society 'Oranje' Inc. v. Kuys*.[21] As Sir Frederick Jordan pointed out, however (see *Chapters on Equity*, (6th ed., Stephen) (1947), p. 115, reproduced in Jordan, *Select Legal Papers* (1983), p. 115), this, read literally, represents 'rather a counsel of prudence than a rule of equity': indeed, even as an unqualified counsel of prudence, it may, in some circumstances, be inappropriate: see *e.g. Hordem v. Hordem*[22]; *Smith v. Cock*.[23] The equitable principle governing the liability to account is concerned not so much with the mere existence of a conflict between personal interest and fiduciary duty as with the pursuit of personal interest by, for example, actually entering into a transaction or engagement 'in which he has, or can have, a personal interest conflicting . . . with the interests of those whom he is bound to protect' (*per* Lord Cranworth L.C., *Aberdeen Railway Co. v. Blaikie Brothers*[24]) or the actual receipt of personal benefit or gain in circumstances where such conflict exists or has existed.

"The variations between more precise formulations of the principle governing **6–37** the liability to account are largely the result of the fact that what is conveniently regarded as the one 'fundamental rule' embodies two themes. The first is that which appropriates for the benefit of the person to whom the fiduciary duty is owed any benefit or gain obtained or received by the fiduciary in circumstances where there existed a conflict of personal interest and fiduciary duty or a significant possibility of such conflict: the objective is to preclude the fiduciary from being swayed by considerations of personal interest. The second is that which requires the fiduciary to account for any benefit or gain obtained or received by reason of or by use of his fiduciary position or of opportunity or knowledge resulting from it: the objective is to preclude the fiduciary from actually misusing his position for his personal advantage. Notwithstanding authoritative statements to the effect that the 'use of fiduciary position' doctrine is but an illustration or part of a wider 'conflict of interest and duty' doctrine (see, *e.g. Phipps v. Boardman*;[25] *N.Z. Netherlands Society 'Oranje' Inc. v. Kuys*,[26] the two themes, while overlapping, are distinct. Neither theme fully comprehends the other and a formulation of the principle by reference to one only of them will be incomplete. Stated comprehensively in terms of the liability to account, the **6–38** principle of equity is that a person who is under a fiduciary obligation must account to the person to whom the obligation is owed for any benefit or gain (i) which has been obtained or received in circumstances where a conflict-or significant possibility of conflict existed between his fiduciary duty and his personal interest in the pursuit or possible receipt of such a benefit or gain, or (ii) which was obtained or received by use or by reason of his fiduciary position

---

[19] [1896] A.C. 44 at 51.
[20] [1967] 2 A.C. 46 at 123.
[21] [1973] 1 W.L.R. 1126 at 1129.
[22] [1910] A.C. 465 at 475.
[23] (1911) 12 C.L.R. 30 at 36, 37.
[24] (1854) 1 Macq. 461.
[25] [1967] 2 A.C. 46 at 123.
[26] [1973] 1 W.L.R. 1126 at 1129.

or of opportunity or knowledge resulting from it. Any such benefit or gain is held by the fiduciary as constructive trustee: see *Keith Henry & Co. Pty. Ltd v. Stuart Walker & Co. Pty. Ltd*[27] That constructive trust arises from the fact that a personal benefit or gain has been so obtained or received and it is immaterial that there was no absence of good faith or damage to the person to whom the fiduciary obligation was owed. In some, perhaps most, cases, the constructive trust will be consequent upon an actual breach of fiduciary duty: *e.g.* an active pursuit of personal interest in disregard of fiduciary duty or a misuse of fiduciary power for personal gain. In other cases, however, there may be no breach of fiduciary duty unless and until there is an actual failure by the fiduciary to account for the relevant benefit or gain: *e.g.* the receipt of an unsolicited personal payment from a third party as a consequence of what was an honest and conscientious performance of a fiduciary duty. The principle governing the liability to account for a benefit or gain as a constructive trustee is applicable to fiduciaries generally including partners and former partners in relation to their dealings with partnership property and the benefits and opportunities associated therewith or arising therefrom: see *Birtchnell v. Equity Trustees*[28]; *Consul Development Pty. Ltd v. D.P.C. Estates Pty. Ltd*[29]

6–39   "In *Keech v. Sandford*[30] Lord King L.C. held that it was a 'rule' that 'should be strictly pursued, and not in the least relaxed,' that a trustee of a tenancy who obtains a renewal of the lease for himself holds the interest in the renewed lease as part of the trust estate. Lord King's admonition that the rule should be not in the least relaxed has been largely obeyed in that, in its application to the case of the ordinary trustee, the 'rule' has been accepted as being applicable regardless of whether the original lease was renewable by right or custom or whether the lessor was willing to grant a new lease for the benefit of the trust or whether there would, in the circumstances, be nothing inequitable in the trustee obtaining a renewal of the lease for his own benefit. The rule has been extended, either in its strict or in a modified form, to persons under obligations arising from certain other fiduciary relationships (*e.g.* executor or agent) and to certain other relationships which are not fiduciary but are said to be special (*e.g.* tenants for life and remaindermen: mortgagee and mortgagor). In particular, it has been applied to a member of a partnership in respect of the renewal of a lease which was held on behalf of the partnership: see *Featherstonhaugh v. Fenwick*[31]; *Clegg v. Edmondson*.[32] It has, in my view correctly, been accepted as being so applicable notwithstanding that the partnership has been dissolved: see *Thompson's Trustee v. Heaton*.[33]

6–40   "One can point to impressive support both for the view that the rule in *Keech v. Sandford* is an independent doctrine of equity with no more than an 'illusory' link with the general equitable principle governing the liability of a fiduciary to account for personal benefit or gain (see the discussion of both the rule and the general equitable principle in Finn, *Fiduciary Obligations* (1977), Chs. 21 and 23) and for the contrary view that that rule is no more than a manifestation of that general principle: see, *e.g., per* Dixon C.J., McTiernan and Fullagar JJ., *Keith*

---

[27] (1958) 100 C.L.R. 342 at 350.
[28] (1929) 42 C.L.R. 384 at 395–397, 408–409.
[29] (1975) 132 C.L.R. 373 at 394.
[30] (1726) Sel.Cas.t.King 61 at 62.
[31] (1810) 17 Ves.Jr. 298.
[32] (1857) 8 De G.M. & G. 787 at 807.
[33] [1974] 1 W.L.R. 605.

Henry & Co. Pty. Ltd v. Stuart Walker & Co. Pty. Ltd[34] and *per* Lord Russell of Killowen, *Regal (Hastings) Ltd v. Gulliver*.[35] It would plainly be futile to attempt to reconcile all that has been said in the cases as to the nature and scope of the rule in *Keech v. Sandford*. It is preferable to acknowledge the existence of unresolved difficulties and differences about both the precise nature of the rule and its application to persons who are not trustees. Those difficulties and differences are, however, such as to encourage rather than preclude the search in this Court for unity of principle. With all respect to those who have expressed a contrary view, I consider that the rule should not be seen as either a completely independent principle of equity or as a mere manifestation of the general principle governing the liability of a beneficiary to account for personal benefit or gain. The case itself is an illustration of that general principle: indeed, it is one of the cases which established it. The 'rule' in *Keech v. Sandford* is, however, a rule concerned with the operation of presumptions in the application of that general principle to particular types of property. 'In the case both of leases renewable by right or custom and of leases not so renewable the renewal is prima facie considered to have been obtained by virtue of the interest' under the prior lease: *per* Parker J., *Griffith v. Owen*.[36]

"In its primary application to the renewal of a lease by a trustee, the rule in **6–41** *Keech v. Sandford*[37]—'depends partly on the nature of leasehold property and partly on' the position of special opportunity which a trustee occupies: see *per* Parker J., *Griffith v. Owen*,[38] and *per* Collins M.R., *Re Biss*.[39] The effect of the rule in such a case is that there is an irrebuttable presumption (a presumption of law: *per* Collins M.R., *Re Biss*[40]) that the lease was obtained by use of the position of advantage which the trustee enjoyed as the tenant at law, that is to say, by the use by the trustee of his fiduciary position, with the result that he holds the new lease as constructive trustee under the general principle governing the liability of a fiduciary to account for a personal benefit or gain. The presumption which the rule creates in its application to a fiduciary other than a trustee is irrebuttable or rebuttable according to the nature of the powers and obligations of the fiduciary with respect to the leasehold property and the extent to which the interposition of the fiduciary represents, as it were, a barrier between the person to whom the fiduciary duty is owed and the lessor: *cf. per* Collins M.R., *Re Biss*. In the extension, by analogy, of the rule in *Keech v. Sandford* to certain 'special' non-fiduciary relationships under which a person is under an obligation to advance or preserve the interests of another, the presumption would appear, at least ordinarily, to be a rebuttable one: see, *per* Romer L.J., *Re Biss*,[41] *cf.* Collins M.R.[42]

Notwithstanding the difficulties and differences in and between the judgments **6–42** of Collins M.R. and Romer L.J. in *Re Biss*, there are clear statements in both judgments (with each of which Cozens Hardy L.J. agreed) which support the conclusion that the presumption that a partner holds a renewed lease as constructive trustee—or, as I would enunciate the primary rule in *Keech v.*

---

[34] (1958) 100 C.L.R. 342 at 350.
[35] [1967] 2 A.C. 134(n), 149–150.
[36] [1907] 1 Ch. 195 at 204.
[37] (1726) Sel.Cas.t.King 61.
[38] [1907] 1 Ch. 195 at 203.
[39] [1903] 2 Ch. 40 at 57.
[40] [1903] 2 Ch. 40, 55.
[41] [1903] 2 Ch. 40 at 61–67.
[42] [1903] 2 Ch. 40 at 56–57.

Sandford the presumption that the renewed lease was obtained by use of the partner's fiduciary position—is a rebuttable one. Those statements are consistent with overall authority and should be accepted as correct and applicable both to the case where the renewed lease is obtained by a partner in a subsisting partnership and the case where the renewed lease is obtained by a member of a partnership which has been dissolved but whose assets are in the course of realization: see *Clegg v. Fishwick*.[43]

6–43   "Prima facie, the rule in *Keech v. Sandford* has a dual operation in the present case: there is an irrebuttable presumption that any rights in respect of a new lease of the Mansfield Park premises were obtained by Dr. Chan by use of his position as a trustee of the previous tenancy and there is a rebuttable presumption of fact that any such rights were obtained by use of his position as a partner in the dissolved partnership whose assets were under receivership and in the course of realization. It follows that Dr. Chan holds and will hold any rights to or under a new lease of the premises as a constructive trustee unless there be some reason for excluding the ordinary application of the general principle.

6–44   "Many of the statements of the general principle requiring a fiduciary to account for a personal benefit or gain are framed in absolute terms—'inflexible,' 'inexorably,' 'however honest and well-intentioned,' 'universal application'— which sound somewhat strangely in the ears of the student of equity and which are to be explained by judicial acceptance of the inability of the courts, 'in much the greater number of cases,' to ascertain the precise effect which the existence of a conflict with personal interest has had upon the performance of fiduciary duty: see, *per* Lord Eldon, *Ex parte James*;[44] *per* Rich, Dixon and Evatt JJ., *Furs Ltd v. Tomkies*.[45] The principle is not however completely unqualified. The liability to account as a constructive trustee will not arise where the person under the fiduciary duty has been duly authorized, either by the instrument or agreement creating the fiduciary duty or by the circumstances of his appointment or by the informed and effective assent of the person to whom the obligation is owed, to act in the manner in which he has acted. The right to require an account from the fiduciary may be lost by reason of the operation of other doctrines of equity such as laches and equitable estoppel: see, *e.g. Clegg v.*

6–45   *Edmondson*.[46] It may still be arguable in this Court that, notwithstanding general statements and perhaps even decisions to the contrary in cases such as *Regal (Hastings) Ltd v. Gulliver*[47] and *Phipps v. Boardman*,[48] the liability to account for a personal benefit or gain obtained or received by use or by reason of fiduciary position, opportunity or knowledge will not arise in circumstances where it would be unconscientious to assert it or in which, for example, there is no possible conflict between personal interest and fiduciary duty and it is plainly in the interests of the person to whom the fiduciary duty is owed that the fiduciary obtain for himself rights or benefits which he is absolutely precluded from seeking or obtaining for the person to whom the fiduciary duty is owed: *cf. Peso Silver Mines Ltd (N.P.L.) v. Cropper*.[49] In that regard, one cannot but be conscious of the danger that the over-enthusiastic and unnecessary statement of

---

[43] (1849) 1 Mac. & G. 294 at 298–299.
[44] (1803) 8 Ves.Jr. 337 at 345.
[45] (1936) 54 C.L.R. 583.
[46] (1857) 8 De G.M. & G. at 807–810 [44 E.R. at 602].
[47] [1967] 2 A.C. 134.
[48] [1967] 2 A.C. 46.
[49] (1966) 58 D.L.R. (2d) 1 at 8.

broad general principles of equity in terms of inflexibility may destroy the vigour which it is intended to promote in that it will exclude the ordinary interplay of the doctrines of equity and the adjustment of general principles to particular facts and changing circumstances and convert equity into an instrument of hardship and injustice in individual cases: see *Canadian Aero Service Ltd v. O'Malley*[50]; Cretney, *loc. cit.*, pp. 168 *et seq.*; Oakley, *Constructive Trusts* (1978), pp. 57 *et seq.* There is 'no better mode of undermining the sound doctrines of equity than to make unreasonable and inequitable applications of them': *per* Lord Selborne L.C., *Barnes v. Addy.*"[51]

BOARDMAN AND ANOTHER v. PHIPPS

House of Lords [1967] 2 A.C. 46; [1966] 3 All E.R. 721 (Lords Cohen, Hodson **6–46** and Guest; Viscount Dilhorne and Lord Upjohn dissenting)

The respondent, Mr. J. A. Phipps, was one of the residuary legatees under the will of his father, Mr. C. W. Phipps, who died in 1944. The residuary estate included 8,000 out of 30,000 issued shares in a private company, Lester & Harris Ltd. By his will the testator left an annuity to his widow and subject thereto five-eighteenths of his residuary estate to each of his three sons and three-eighteenths to his only daughter. At the end of 1955 the trustees of the will were the testator's widow (who was senile and took no part in the affairs of the trust), his only daughter, Mrs. Noble, and an accountant, Mr. W. Fox. The first appellant, Mr. T. G. Boardman, was at all material times solicitor to the trustees and also to the children of the testator (other than the respondent). The second appellant, Mr. T. E. Phipps, was the younger brother of the respondent and in the transactions which gave rise to this action he was associated with and represented by the first appellant, Mr. Boardman.

In 1956 Mr. Boardman and Mr. Fox decided that the recent accounts of Lester **6–47** & Harris Ltd were unsatisfactory and with a view to improving the position the appellants attended the annual general meeting of the company in December 1956 with proxies obtained from two of the trustees, Mrs. Noble and Mr. Fox. They were not satisfied with the answers given at the meeting regarding the state of the company's affairs.

Shortly after this meeting the appellants decided with the knowledge of Mrs. Noble and Mr. Fox to try to obtain control of Lester & Harris Ltd by themselves making an offer for all the outstanding shares in that company other than the 8,000 held by the trustees. The trustees had no power to invest in the shares of the company without the sanction of the court and Mr. Fox said in evidence that he would not have considered seeking such sanction. The appellants originally offered £2 5s. per share, which they later increased to £3, but by April 1957 they had received acceptances only in respect of 2,925 shares and it was clear that as things then stood they would not go through with their offer. This ended the first phase in the negotiations which ultimately led to the acquisition by the appellants of virtually all the outstanding shares in Lester & Harris Ltd During this phase the appellants attended the annual general meeting as proxies of the two trustees and obtained information from the company as to the prices at which shares had recently changed hands; but they made the offer to purchase on their own behalf.

---

[50] (1973) 40 D.L.R. (3d) 371.
[51] (1874) L.R. 9 Ch.App. 244 at 251.

6–48   The second phase lasted from April 1957 to August 1958. Throughout this period Mr. Boardman carried on negotiations with the chairman of Lester & Harris Ltd with a view to reaching agreement on the division of the assets of that company between the Harris family and the directors on the one hand and the Phipps family on the other. During this phase Mr. Boardman obtained valuable information as to the value of the company's assets and throughout he purported to act on behalf of the trustees. These negotiations proved abortive.

6–49   The third phase began in August 1958 with the suggestion by Mr. Boardman that he and Mr. T. E. Phipps should acquire for themselves the outstanding shares in the company. The widow died in November 1958 and a conditional agreement for the sale of the shares was made on March 10, 1959. On May 26, 1959, the appellants gave notices making the agreements unconditional to buy 14,567 shares held by the chairman of the company and his associates at £4 10s. per share. This, in addition to the earlier agreements to purchase 2,925 shares at £3 each and the purchase of a further 4,494 shares at £4 10s. each, made the appellants holders of 21,986 shares.

Thereafter the business of the company was reorganised, part of its assets was sold off at considerable profit, and substantial sums of capital, amounting in the aggregate to £5 17s. 6d. per share, were returned to the shareholders, whose shares were still worth at least £2 each after the return of capital. The appellants acted honestly throughout.

6–50   The respondent, like the other members of the Phipps family, was asked by Mr. Boardman whether he objected to the acquisition of control of the company by the appellants for themselves; but Mr. Boardman did not give sufficient information as to the material facts to succeed in the defence of consent on the part of the respondent. At first the respondent expressed his satisfaction but later he became antagonistic and issued a writ claiming (i) that the appellants held five-eighteenths of the above-mentioned 21,986 shares as constructive trustees for him[52] and (ii) an account of the profits made by the appellants out of the said shares. Wilberforce J. granted this relief[53] and his decision was affirmed by the Court of Appeal.[54] The appellants appealed to the House of Lords.

LORD COHEN: ". . . As Wilberforce J. said,[55] the mere use of any knowledge or opportunity which comes to the trustee or agent in the course of his trusteeship or agency does not necessarily make him liable to account. In the present case had the company been a public company and had the appellants bought the shares on the market, they would not, I think have been accountable. The company, however, is a private company and not only the information but also the opportunity to purchase these shares came to them through the introduction which Mr. Fox gave them to the board of the company and, in the second phase, when the discussions related to the proposed split up of the company's undertaking, it was solely on behalf of the trustees that Mr. Boardman was purporting to negotiate with the board of the company. The question is this: when in the third phase the negotiations turned to the purchase of the shares at £4 10s. a share, were the appellant debarred by their fiduciary position from purchasing on their own behalf the 21,986 shares in the company without the informed consent of the trustees and the beneficiaries?

---

[52] The appellants would, of course, have a lien for their outlay on the purchase of the shares.
[53] [1964] 1 W.L.R. 993.
[54] [1965] Ch. 992 (Lord Denning M.R., Pearson and Russell L.JJ.).
[55] [1964] 1 W.L.R. 993 at 1011.

"Wilberforce J.[56] and, in the Court of Appeal,[57] both Lord Denning M.R. and **6–51** Pearson L.J. based their decision in favour of the respondent on the decision of your Lordships' House in *Regal (Hastings) Ltd v. Gulliver*[58] I turn, therefore, to consider that case. Counsel for the respondent relied on a number of passages in the judgments of the learned Lords who heard the appeal, in particular on (i) a passage in the speech of Lord Russell of Killowen where he said.[59] 'The rule of equity which insists on those, who by use of a fiduciary position make a profit, being liable to account for that profit, in no way depends on fraud, or absence of bona fides; or upon such questions or considerations as whether the profit would or should otherwise have gone to the plaintiff, or whether the profiteer was under a duty to obtain the source of the profit for the plaintiff, or whether he **6–52** took a risk or acted as he did for the benefit of the plaintiff, or whether the plaintiff has in fact been damaged or benefited by his action. The liability arises from the mere fact of a profit having, in the stated circumstances, been made'; (ii) a passage in the speech of Lord Wright where he says[60]: 'That question can be briefly stated to be whether an agent, a director, a trustee or other person in an analogous fiduciary position, when a demand is made upon him by the person to whom he stands in the fiduciary relationship to account for profits acquired by him by reason of his fiduciary position, and by reason of the opportunity and the knowledge, or either, resulting from it, is entitled to defeat the claim upon any ground save that he made profits with the knowledge and assent of the other person. The most usual and typical case of this nature is that of principal and agent. The rule in such cases is compendiously expressed to be that an agent must account for net profits secretly (that is, without the knowledge of his principal) acquired by him in the course of his agency. The authorities show how manifold and various are the applications of the rule. It does not depend on fraud or corruption.' These paragraphs undoubtedly help the respondent but they must be considered in relation to the facts of that case. In that case the profit arose through the application by four of the directors of Regal for shares in a subsidiary company which it had been the original intention of the board **6–53** should be subscribed for by Regal. Regal had not the requisite money available but there was no question of it being *ultra vires* Regal to subscribe for the shares. In the circumstances Lord Russell of Killowen said[61]: 'I have no hesitation in coming to the conclusion, upon the facts of this case, that these shares, when acquired by the directors, were acquired by reason, and only by reason, of the fact that they were directors of Regal, and in the course of their execution of that office.' He went on to consider whether the four directors were in a fiduciary relationship to Regal and concluded that they were. Accordingly, they were held accountable. Counsel for the appellants argued that the present case is distinguishable. He puts his argument thus. The question one asks is whether the information could have been used by the principal for the purpose for which it was used by his agents. If the answer to that question is no, the information was not used in the course of their duty as agents. In the present case the information could never have been used by the trustees for the purpose of purchasing shares in the company; therefore purchase of shares was outside the scope of the appellants' agency and they are not accountable.

---

[56] *ibid.*
[57] [1965] Ch. 992.
[58] [1942] 1 All E.R. 378.
[59] *ibid.* at 386.
[60] *ibid.* at 392.
[61] *ibid.* at 387.

6–54   "This is an attractive argument, but it does not seem to me to give due weight to the fact that the appellants obtained both the information which satisfied them that the purchase of the shares would be a good investment and the opportunity of acquiring them as a result of acting for certain purposes on behalf of the trustees. Information is, of course, not property in the strict sense of that word and, as I have already stated, it does not necessarily follow that, because an agent acquired information and opportunity while acting in a fiduciary capacity, he is accountable to his principals for any profit that comes his way as the result of the use he makes of that information and opportunity. His liability to account must depend on the facts of the case. In the present case much of the information came the appellants' way when Mr. Boardman was acting on behalf of the trustees on the instructions of Mr. Fox, and the opportunity of bidding for the shares came because he purported for all purposes except for making the bid to be acting on behalf of the owners of the 8,000 shares in the company. In these circumstances it seems to me that the principle of the *Regal* case applies and that the courts below came to the right conclusion.

6–55   "That is enough to dispose of the case but I would add that an agent is, in my opinion, liable to account for profits which he makes out of the trust property if there is a possibility of conflict between his interest and his duty to his principal. Mr. Boardman and Mr. Tom Phipps were not general agents of the trustees, but they were their agents for certain limited purposes. The information which they had obtained and the opportunity to purchase the 21,986 shares afforded them by their relations with the directors of the company—an opportunity they got as the result of their introduction to the directors by Mr. Fox—were not property in the strict sense but that information and that opportunity they owed to their representing themselves as agents for the holders of the 8,000 shares held by the trustees. In these circumstances they could not, I think, use that information and that opportunity to purchase the shares for themselves if there was any possibility that the trustees might wish to acquire them for the trust. Mr. Boardman was the solicitor whom the trustees were in the habit of consulting if they wanted legal advice. Granted that he would not be bound to advise on any point unless he were consulted, he would still be the person they would consult if they wanted advice. He would clearly have advised them that they had no power to invest in shares of the company without the sanction of the court. In the first phase he would also have had to advise on the evidence then available that the court would be unlikely to give such sanction: but the appellants learnt much more during the second phase. It may well be that even in third phase the answer of the court would have been the same but, in my opinion, Mr. Boardman would not have been able to give unprejudiced advice if he had been consulted by the trustees and was at the same time negotiating for the purchase of the shares on behalf of himself and Mr. Tom Phipps. In other words, there was, in my opinion, at the crucial date (March 1959) a possibility of a conflict between his interest and his duty.

6–56   "In making these observations I have referred to the fact that Mr. Boardman was the solicitor to the trust. Mr. Tom Phipps was only a beneficiary and was not as such debarred from bidding for the shares, but no attempt was made in the courts below to differentiate between them. Had such an attempt been made it would very likely have failed, as Mr. Tom Phipps left the negotiations largely to Mr. Boardman, and it might well be held that, if Mr. Boardman was disqualified from bidding, Mr. Tom Phipps could not be in a better position. Be that as it may, counsel for the appellants rightly did not seek at this stage to distinguish between the two. He did, it is true, say that Mr. Tom Phipps as a beneficiary would be entitled to any information that the trustees obtained. This may be so, but nonetheless I find myself unable to distinguish between the two appellants. They were, I think, in March 1959, in a fiduciary position *vis-à-vis* the trust. That fiduciary position was of such a nature that (as the trust fund was distributable) the appellants could not purchase the shares on their own behalf without the informed consent of the beneficiaries: it is now admitted that they did not obtain that consent. They are therefore, in my opinion, accountable to the respondent for his share of the net profits which they derived from the transaction.

"I desire to repeat that the integrity of the appellants is not in doubt. They **6–57** acted with complete honesty throughout, and the respondent is a fortunate man in that the rigour of equity enables him to participate in the profits which have accrued as the result of the action taken by the appellants in March 1959 in purchasing the shares at their own risk. As the last paragraph of his judgment clearly shows, the trial judge evidently shared this view. He directed an inquiry as to what sum was proper to be allowed to the appellants or either of them in respect of their or his work and skill in obtaining the said shares and the profits in respect thereof. The trial judge concluded by expressing the opinion that payment should be on a liberal scale. With that observation I respectfully agree . . ."

LORD HODSON: ". . . The proposition of law involved in this case is that no person standing in a fiduciary position, when a demand is made on him by the person to whom he stands in the fiduciary relationship to account for profits acquired by him by reason of his fiduciary position and by reason of the opportunity and the knowledge, or either, resulting from it, is entitled to defeat the claim on any ground save that he made profits with the knowledge and assent of the other person . . .

". . . it is said on behalf of the appellants that information as such is not **6–58** necessarily property and it is only trust property which is relevant. I agree, but it is nothing to the point to say that in these times corporate trustees, *e.g.* the Public Trustee and others, necessarily acquire a mass of information in their capacity of trustees for a particular trust and cannot be held liable to account if knowledge so acquired enables them to operate to their own advantage, or to that of other trusts. Each case must depend on its own facts, and I dissent from the view that information is of its nature something which is not properly to be described as property. We are aware that what is called 'know-how' in the commercial sense is property which may be very valuable as an asset. I agree with the learned judge[62] and with the Court of Appeal[63] that the confidential information acquired in this case, which was capable of being and was turned to account, can be properly regarded as the property of the trust. It was obtained by Mr. Boardman by reason of the opportunity which he was given as solicitor acting for the trustees in the negotiations with the chairman of the company, as the correspondence demonstrates. The end result was that, out of the special position in which they were standing in the course of the negotiations, the appellants got the opportunity to make a profit and the knowledge that it was there to be made . . .

"*Regal (Hastings) Ltd v. Gulliver* differs from this case mainly in that the **6–59** directors took up shares and made a profit thereby, it having been originally intended that the company should buy these shares. Here there was no such

---

[62] [1964] 1 W.L.R. 993 at 1008–1011.
[63] [1965] Ch. 992.

intention on the part of the trustees. There is no indication that they either had the money or would have been ready to apply to the court for sanction enabling them to do so. On the contrary, Mr. Fox, the active trustee and an accountant who concerned himself with the details of the trust property, was not prepared to agree to the trustees buying the shares and encouraged the appellants to make the purchase. This does not affect the position. As *Keech v. Sandford* shows, the inability of the trust to purchase makes no difference to the liability of the appellants, if liability otherwise exists. The distinction on the facts as to intention to purchase shares between this case and *Regal (Hastings) Ltd v. Gulliver* is not relevant. The company (Regal) had not the money to apply for the shares on which the profit was made. The directors took the opportunity which they had presented to them to buy the shares with their own money and were held accountable. Mr Fox's refusal as one of the trustees to take any part in the matter on behalf of the trust, so far as he was concerned, can make no difference. Nothing short of fully informed consent, which the learned judge found not to have been obtained, could enable the appellants in the position which they occupied, having taken the opportunity provided by that position, to make a profit for themselves . . .

6–60   "The confidential information which the appellants obtained at a time when Mr. Boardman was admittedly holding himself out as solicitor for the trustees was obtained by him as representing the trustees, the holders of 8,000 shares of Lester & Harris Ltd As Russell L.J. put it:[64] 'The substantial trust shareholding was an asset of which one aspect was its potential use as a means of acquiring knowledge of the company's affairs, or of negotiating allocations of the company's assets, or of inducing other shareholders to part with their shares.' That aspect was part of the trust assets. Whether this aspect is properly to be regarded as part of the trust assets is, in my judgment, immaterial. The appellants obtained knowledge by reason of their fiduciary position, and they cannot escape liability by saying that they were acting for themselves and not as agents of the trustees. Whether or not the trust, or the beneficiaries in their stead, could have taken advantage of the information is immaterial, as the authorities clearly show. No doubt it was but a remote possibility that Mr. Boardman would ever be asked by the trustees to advise on the desirability of an application to the court in order that the trustees might avail themselves of the information obtained. Nevertheless, whenever the possibility of conflict is present between personal interest and the fiduciary position the rule of equity must be applied . . ."

6–61   LORD GUEST: ". . . I take the view that from first to last Mr. Boardman was acting in a fiduciary capacity to the trustees. This fiduciary capacity arose in phase 1 and continued into phase 2, which glided into phase 3. In saying this I do not for one moment suggest that there was anything dishonest or underhand in what Mr. Boardman did. He has obtained a clean certificate below and I do not wish to sully it; but the law has a strict regard for principle in ensuring that a person in a fiduciary capacity is not allowed to benefit from any transactions into which he has entered with trust property. If Mr. Boardman was acting on behalf of the trust, then all the information that he obtained in phase 2 became trust property. The weapon which he used to obtain this information was the trust holding; and I see no reason why information and knowledge cannot be trust property . . ."

---

[64] [1965] Ch. 992 at 1031.

LORD UPJOHN (dissenting): "On the evidence there was never any suggestion at **6–62** any subsequent stage [after 1956] that Mr Fox or any other trustee would ever have contemplated any purchase of further shares . . . In *Aberdeen Railway Co. v. Blaikie Bros*[65] Lord Cranworth L.C. said, 'and it is a rule of universal application that no-one having such duties to discharge shall be allowed to enter into engagements in which he has or can have a personal interest conflicting or which possibly may conflict with the interests of those whom he is bound to protect.' The phrase "possibly may conflict" requires consideration. In my view it means that the reasonable man would think that there was a real sensible possibility of conflict; not that you could imagine some situation arising which might, in some conceivable possibility in events not contemplated as real sensible possibilities by any reasonable person, result in a conflict . . . [*Regal (Hastings) Ltd v. Gulliver* and *Keech v. Sandford* bear no relation to this case.]

"This case, if I may emphasise it again, is one concerned not with trust property or with property of which the persons to whom the fiduciary duty was owed were contemplating a purchase but, in contrast to the facts in *Regal*, with property which was not trust property or property which was ever contemplated as the subject-matter of a possible purchase by the trust . . .

"This question whether the appellants were accountable requires a closer **6–63** analysis than it has received in the lower courts.

"This analysis requires detailed consideration:

1. The facts and circumstances must be carefully examined to see whether in fact a purported agent and even a confidential agent is in a fiduciary relationship to his principal. It does not necessarily follow that he is in such a position.
2. Once it is established that there is such a relationship, that relationship must be examined to see what duties are thereby imposed on the agent, to see what is the scope and ambit of the duties charged on him.
3. Having defined the scope of those duties one must see whether he has committed some breach thereof by placing himself within the scope and ambit of those duties in a position where his duty and interest may possibly conflict. It is only at this stage that any question of accountability arises.
4. Finally, having established accountability it only goes so far as to render the agent accountable for profits made within the scope and ambit of his duty.

"Before applying these principles to the facts, however, I shall refer to the **6–64** judgment of Russell L.J. which proceeded on a rather different basis. He said:

"The substantial trust shareholding was an asset of which one aspect was its potential use as a means of acquiring knowledge of the company's affairs, or of negotiating allocations of the company's assets, or of inducing other shareholders to part with their shares. That aspect was part of the trust assets."

My Lords, I regard that proposition as untenable.

"In general, information is not property at all. It is normally open to all who have eyes to read and ears to hear. The true test is to determine in what circumstances the information has been acquired. If it has been acquired in such circumstances that it would be a breach of confidence to disclose it to another, then courts of equity will restrain the recipient from communicating it to another. In such cases such confidential information is often and for many years has been described as the property of the donor, the books of authority are full of such references; knowledge of secret processes, 'know-how,' confidential information as to the prospects of a company or of someone's intention or the expected results of some horse race based on stable or other confidential information. But in the end the real truth is that it is not property in any normal sense, but equity will restrain its transmission to another if in breach of some confidential relationship.

6–65 "With all respect to the views of Russell L.J., I protest at the idea that information acquired by trustees in the course of their duties as such is necessarily part of the assets of trust property which cannot be used by the trustees except for the benefit of the trust. Russell L.J. referred to the fact that two out of three of the trustees could have no authority to turn over this aspect of trust property to the appellants except for the benefit of the trust; this I do not understand, for if such information is trust property not all the trustees acting together could do it for they cannot give away trust property.

6–66 "We heard much argument on the impact of the fact that the testator's widow was at all material times incapable of acting in the trust owing to disability. Of course trustees must act all of them and unanimously in matters affecting trust affairs, but they never performed any relevant act on behalf of the trust at all; I quoted Mr. Fox's answer earlier for this reason. At no time after going to the meeting in December 1956, did Mr. Boardman or Tom rely on any express or implied authority or consent of the trustees in relation to trust property. They understood rightly that there was no question of the trustees acquiring any further trust property by purchasing further shares in the company, and it was only in the purchase of other shares that they were interested.

"There is, in my view, and I know of no authority to the contrary, no general rule that information learnt by a trustee during the course of his duties is property of the trust and cannot be used by him. If that were to be the rule it would put the Public Trustee and other corporate trustees out of business and make it difficult for private trustees to be trustees of more than one trust. This would be the greatest possible pity for corporate trustees and others may have much information which they may initially acquire in connection with some particular trust but without prejudice to that trust can make it readily available to other trusts to the great advantage of those other trusts.

6–67 "The real rule is, in my view, that knowledge learnt by a trustee in the course of his duties as such is not in the least property of the trust and in general may be used by him for his own benefit or for the benefit of other trusts unless it is confidential information which is given to him (i) in circumstances which, regardless of his position as a trustee, would make it a breach of confidence for him to communicate to anyone, for it has been given to him expressly or impliedly as confidential; or (ii) in a fiduciary capacity, and its use would place him in a position where his duty and his interest might possibly conflict. Let me give one or two simple examples. A, as trustee of two settlements X and Y holding shares in the same small company, learns facts as trustee of X about the company which are encouraging. In the absence of special circumstances (such, for example, that X wants to buy more shares) I can see nothing whatever which would make it improper for him to tell his co-trustees of Y who feel inclined to sell that he has information that this would be a bad thing to do. Another example: A as trustee of X learns facts that make him and his co-trustees want to sell. Clearly he could not communicate this knowledge to his co-trustees of Y until at all events the holdings of X have been sold for there would be a plain conflict, reflected in the prices that might or might possibly be obtained.

"My Lords, I do not think for one moment that Lord Brougham in *Hamilton v.* **6–68** *Wright*,[66] quoted in the speech of my noble and learned friend, Lord Guest, was saying anything to the contrary; one has to look and see whether the knowledge acquired was capable of being used for his own benefit *to injure* the trust (my italics). That test can have no application to the present. There was no possibility of the information being used to injure the trust. The knowledge obtained was used not in connection with trust property but to enhance the value of the trust property by the purchase of other property in which the trustees were not interested . . .

"As a result of the information the appellants acquired, admittedly by reason of the trust holding, they found it worthwhile to offer a good deal more for the shares than in phase 1 of chapter 2. I cannot see that in offering to purchase non-trust shares at a higher price they were in breach of any fiduciary relationship in using the information which they had acquired for this purpose. I cannot see that they have, from start to finish, in the circumstances of this case, placed themselves in a position where there was any possibility of a conflict between their duty and interest.

"I have dealt with the problems that arise in this case at considerable length **6–69** but it could, in my opinion, be dealt with quite shortly. In *Barnes v. Addy*,[67] Lord Selborne L.C., said:

> "It is equally important to maintain the doctrine of trusts which is established in this court, and not to strain it by unreasonable construction beyond its due and proper limits. There would be no better mode of undermining the sound doctrines of equity than to make unreasonable and inequitable applications of them."

That, in my judgment, is applicable to this case.[68]

"The trustees were not willing to buy more shares in the company. The active **6–70** trustees were very willing that the appellants should do so themselves for the benefit of their large minority holding. The trustees, so to speak, lent their name to the appellants in the course of prolonged and difficult negotiations and, of course, the appellants thereby learnt much which would have otherwise been denied to them. The negotiations were in the end brilliantly successful. How successful Tom was in his reorganisation of the company is apparent to all. They ought to be very grateful.

"In the long run the appellants have bought for themselves with their own money shares which the trustees never contemplated buying and they did so in circumstances fully known and approved of by the trustees. To extend the doctrines of equity to make the appellants accountable in such circumstances is, in my judgment, to make unreasonable and inequitable applications of such doctrines."

---

[66] (1842) 9 Cl. & Fin. 111.
[67] (1874) 9 Ch.App. 244 at 251.
[68] Now see *Queensland Mines v. Hudson, infra*, at para. 9–29.

ATT.-GEN. FOR HONG KONG v. REID

[1994] 1 A.C. 324 [1993] 3 W.L.R. 1143 [1994] 1 All E.R. 1 Privy Council (Lords
Templeman, Goff, Lowry, Lloyd and Sir Thomas Eichelbaum)

6–71   LORD TEMPLEMAN: "Bribery is an evil practice which threatens the foundations
of any civilised society. In particular, bribery of policemen and prosecutors brings
the administration of justice into disrepute. Where bribes are accepted by a
trustee, servant, agent or other fiduciary, loss and damage are caused to the
beneficiaries, master or principal whose interests have been betrayed. The
amount of loss or damage resulting from the acceptance of a bribe may or may
not be quantifiable. In the present case the amount of harm caused to the
administration of justice in Hong Kong by Mr. Reid in return for bribes cannot
be quantified.

6–72   "When a bribe is offered and accepted in money or in kind, the money or
property constituting the bribe belongs in law to the recipient. Money paid to the
false fiduciary belongs to him. The legal estate in freehold property conveyed to
the false fiduciary by way of bribe vests in him. Equity however which acts in
personam insists that it is unconscionable for a fiduciary to obtain and retain a
benefit in breach of duty. The provider of a bribe cannot recover it because he
committed a criminal offence when he paid the bribe. The false fiduciary who
received the bribe in breach of duty must pay and account for the bribe to the
person to whom that duty was owed. In the present case, as soon as Mr. Reid
received a bribe in breach of the duties he owed to the Government of Hong
Kong, he became a debtor in equity to the Crown for the amount of that bribe.
So much is admitted. But, if the bribe consists of property which increases in
value or if a cash bribe is invested advantageously, the false fiduciary will receive
a benefit from his breach of duty unless he is accountable not only for the
original amount or value of the bribe but also for the increased value of the
property representing the bribe. As soon as the bribe was received it should have
been paid or transferred instanter to the person who suffered from the breach of
duty. Equity considered as done that which ought to have been done. As soon as
the bribe was received, whether in cash or in kind, the false fiduciary held the
bribe on a constructive trust for the person injured. Two objections have been
raised to this analysis. First it is said that, if the fiduciary is in equity a debtor to
the person injured, he cannot also be a trustee of the bribe. But there is no
reason why equity should not provide two remedies, so long as they do not result
in double recovery. If the property representing the bribe exceeds the original
bribe in value, the fiduciary cannot retain the benefit of the increase in value
6–73   which he obtained solely as a result of his breach of duty. Secondly, it is said that
if the false fiduciary holds property representing the bribe in trust for the person
injured, and if the false fiduciary is or becomes insolvent, the unsecured creditors
of the false fiduciary will be deprived of their right to share in the proceeds of
that property. But the unsecured creditors cannot be in a better position than
their debtor. The authorities show that property acquired by a trustee innocently
but in breach of trust and the property from time to time representing the same
belong in equity to the cestui que trust and not to the trustee personally whether
he is solvent or insolvent. Property acquired by a trustee as a result of a criminal
breach of trust and the property from time to time representing the same must
also belong in equity to his cestui que trust and not to the trustee whether he is
solvent or insolvent.

    "When a bribe is accepted by a fiduciary in breach of his duty then he holds
that bribe in trust for the person to whom the duty was owed. If the property

representing the bribe decreases in value the fiduciary must pay the difference between that value and the initial amount of the bribe because he should not have accepted the bribe or incurred the risk of loss. If the property increases in value, the fiduciary is not entitled to any surplus in excess of the initial value of the bribe because he is not allowed by any means to make a profit out of a breach of duty . . ."

QUESTION

Tom and Trevor, holding *inter alia* a lease with two years unexpired on **6–74** trust for Brian for life, remainder for Brian's children equally, were trying to sell the lease as they were likely to receive a heavy dilapidations schedule for remedying at the expiry of the lease. They had tried to purchase the freehold reversion for the trust but the landlord had refused. Tom's friend Joe, hearing of their predicament, had relieved the trust of the lease at the proper, but low, market price. Joe happened to play golf regularly with the landlord and after persisting for four months was able to contract to purchase the freehold.

Joe, only having half the purchase price, went to see Tom and **6–75** suggested that Tom put up the other half for he had been a good friend and without him Joe would never have heard of the property and obtained the opportunity to buy the freehold. Tom was only too happy to put up half the purchase price, delighted that Joe was letting him in on the deal rather than merely borrow the money from Tom or a bank. Shortly afterwards Joe and Tom sold the property with vacant possession making £25,000 profit each.

Brian seeks your advice.

Section 2. The Stranger as Constructive Trustee of Property

Positive assumption of trusteeship: trustee de son tort

As A. L. Smith L.J. stated in *Mara v. Browne*,[69] "If one, not being a **6–76** trustee and not having authority from a trustee, takes upon himself to intermeddle with trust matters or to do acts characteristic of the office of trustee he may thereby make himself a trustee of his own wrong, *i.e.* a trustee *de son tort*, or as it is also termed, a constructive trustee."

A trustee *de son tort* does not purport to act in his own behalf but for **6–77** the beneficiaries and his assumption to act is not of itself a ground of liability (save in the sense of thereafter being liable to account and liable for any failure in the duty assumed) so that his status as trustee precedes the occurrence which may be the subject of a claim against him.[70] From

---

[69] [1896] 1 Ch. 199 at 209, endorsed by Danckwerts L.J. in *Carl Zeiss Stiftung v. Herbert Smith (No. 2)* [1969] 2 Ch. 276 at 289. In some circumstances an executor *de son tort* can become regarded as a trustee *de son tort* or a constructive trustee: *James v. Williams* [1999] 3 All E.R. 309, but it overlooked *Paragon Finance Ltd v. Thakerar* [1999] 1 All E.R. 450.

[70] *Selangor United Rubber Ltd v. Cradock (No. 3)* [1968] 1 W.L.R. 1555 at 1579. One could, perhaps, regard the defendant in *English v. Dedham Vale Properties Ltd*: [1978] 1 W.L.R. 93 as a fiduciary *de son tort*.

the outset he will be constructive trustee of the property acquired by him as a result of intervening and assuming the duties of trustee,[71] and thereafter he may be liable for any breach of these duties of administration. It matters not that the intermeddler was honest and well-intentioned.[72] However, to be a trustee *de son tort* he must have the trust property vested in him or so far under his control that he could require it to be vested in him.[73]

The proprietary constructive trust of property or its product unauthorisedly in the hands of a stranger

6–78   If trust property (or other property subject to a fiduciary relationship) has been improperly disposed of and it, or its traceable equivalent,[74] is in the hands of a stranger, then such property can be claimed for the beneficiaries unless the stranger (or a person through whom he claims) was a purchaser of the legal interest therein for value without notice[75] (actual, constructive or imputed), or was protected by the overreaching provisions of the 1925 property legislation or the exceptions to the *nemo dat quod non habet* principle in the Factors Acts, the Sale of Goods Acts and the Hire Purchase Acts. This position is the result of the property law of priorities and the application of the tracing process which enable the beneficiaries to vindicate their equitable proprietory rights.

6–79   To give effect to these rights, one can regard the constructive trust as arising as soon as the defendant receives the property affected by the claimant's interest, although it is only when the defendant becomes aware of the claimant's interest that he becomes personally liable to account for the property and to give effect to the claimant's rights.[76] Imputed notice is actual or constructive notice of an agent[77] of the

---

[71] *Lyell v. Kennedy* (1889) 14 App.Cas. 437 (agent of deceased landlord collected rents which held on constructive trust for the heir when identified); *Blyth v. Fladgate* [1891] 1 Ch. 337. If an agent is employed by trustees who have not been validly appointed one can argue like North J. in *Mara v. Browne* [1895] 2 Ch. 69, that the agent should be treated as a principal and regarded as an intermeddler so as to be liable as trustee *de son tort*, irrespective of the agent's knowledge. However, if the agent has no actual or Nelsonian knowledge (turning a blind eye) of the lack of title of the "trustees" or did not wilfully and recklessly fail to make such inquiries as an honest and reasonable man would make, should he not be in the same position as an agent of validly appointed trustees since it is surely too much to expect him to carry out a detailed inquiry into the title or authority of his trustee-principal: see *Mara v. Browne* [1896] 1 Ch. 199 at 207, *per* Lord Herschell.

[72] *Lyell v. Kennedy* (1889) 14 App.Cas. 437 at 459; *Life Association of Scotland v. Siddall* (1861) 3 De G.F. & J. 58.

[73] *Re Barney* [1892] 2 Ch. 265, 273 (two businessmen who looked over trustee-widow's business accounts and checked expenditure, so that bank would not honour widow's cheques unless bearing their initials, not liable as trustees *de son tort* when unauthorised business failed since they had no control of the trust property). One can e.g. regard ICI plc shares held by a custodian for X as trust property controlled by X rather than X's chose in action against the custodian as trust property.

[74] See *infra*, at paras 11–04 *et seq.*

[75] e.g. *Boursot v. Savage* (1866) L.R. 2 Eq. 134.

[76] *Supra* at paras 6–02 to 6–04.

[77] Where the matter of which the agent has notice arises from the agent's own fraud (which he could not be expected to disclose to his principal) notice of such matter will not be imputed to the principal. Similarly, if a solicitor acts for A and B (borrower and lender) and he obtains knowledge from A of a fact which it is his duty not to disclose to B without A's consent and which it is his duty to B to communicate it to B; the solicitor's knowledge of the fact is not to be imputed to B: *Halifax Mortgage Services Ltd v. Stepsky* [1995] 4 All E.R. 656, appeal dismissed by C.A. [1996] 2 All E.R. 277 on basis that L.P.A. 1925, s.199 only imputed to the principal notice received by agent when acting for principal and not notice obtained earlier by agent before instructed by principal; *Clark Boyce v. Mouat* [1993] 4 All E.R. 268.

stranger in the relevant transaction. A person has actual notice of matters within his own knowledge and constructive notice of matters that would have come to his knowledge if such inquiries and inspections had been made as a reasonably prudent person ought to have made. What *ought* to have been done in all the circumstances and thus the nature and extent of the *duty* to make reasonable inquiries will vary according to the circumstances.[78] The duty is at its greatest where purchases of land are concerned. In other commercial transactions the courts are most reluctant to import a duty to make inquiries, which would restrict the flow of commerce, unless the defendant knows of some suspicious circumstances and a donee is under no duty of inquiry unless he knows of suspicious circumstances.[79]

Where an agent, such as a solicitor or an accountant, is worried that **6–80** he might be holding fiduciary property on constructive trust for a third party, such as the claimant in an action against his principal, and is worried that the claimant may seek to recover fees paid by the principal to the agent allegedly out of the claimant's money, no assistance can be obtained by an application to the High Court for administration directions under Order 85 of the Rules of the Supreme Court. The court is not in a position to ascertain the state of the agent's conscience in respect of the claimant's alleged money and so cannot declare that fees received by the agent will be immune from any claim by the claimant[80] until trial of any action against the agent. This may lead the agent to withdraw his assistance to his principal as defendant to the proprietary claim unless his fees clearly come from an untainted source.

Section 3: The Prevention of Fraudulent or Other Unconscionable Conduct

The prevention of fraudulent or other unconscionable conduct underlies **6–81** a miscellaneous category of cases where equity imposes a constructive trust over the defendant's property to prevent him or her from owning the property to the exclusion of any beneficial interest of the claimant.

Cases considered by various commentators to be instances of constructive trusts will now be considered.

MUTUAL WILLS AND SECRET TRUSTS

As we have seen,[81] under the doctrine of mutual wills the survivor of two **6–82** testators is forced to observe the contract between them by the

---

[78] *Re Diplock* [1948] Ch. 465, 478–479; *Carl Zeiss Stiftung v. Herbert Smith (No. 2)* [1969] 2 Ch. 276 at 297.
[79] *Joseph v. Lyons* (1884) 15 Q.B.D. 280; *Manchester Trust v. Furness* [1895] 2 Q.B. 539; *Feuer Leather Co. v. Frank Johnstone & Sons* [1981] Com.L.R. 251; *Macmillan v. Bishopsgate Investment Trust* [1995] 3 All E.R. 747; *Polly Peck International v. Nadir (No. 2)* [1992] 4 All E.R. 769.
[80] *United Mizrahi Bank v. Doherty* [1998] 2 All E.R. 230.
[81] See *supra*, paras 2–14 *et seq.*

imposition of a constructive trust designed to give effect to the contract in favour of a third party. The constructive trust affecting the survivor arises on the death of the predeceasing testator leaving a will in accordance with the contract, so complying with her side of the bargain.

In the case of secret trusts it has been seen[82] that a deceased's informally expressed wishes are effectuated where he has made his will or died intestate on the faith of an undertaking by a legatee or the next-of-kin that his wishes would be carried out. It is possible to regard a beneficiary under a secret trust as vindicating her right under an express trust which is enforced because "Equity will not allow a statute to be used as an instrument of fraud," but it seems better[83] to regard her as having a right under a constructive trust since it is the acceptance of the secret trustee—and not just the intention of the testator—that is crucial to the trust arising at the testator's death.

EFFECTING INCOMPLETE TRANSFERS UNDER RE ROSE

6–83 A constructive trust is imposed to give effect to a donor's intentions where he has not yet assigned the legal title but he has done all that is necessary for him to do to achieve that end, so that Equity will regard the donee as beneficial owner (*e.g.* in the case of shares or land requiring registration of the new owner to transfer legal title to him).[84] Once Equity so regards the donee it becomes fraudulent or otherwise unconscionable for the donor to retain benefits, like dividends or rents, arising from the property.

NO KILLER OR OTHER CRIMINAL[85] MAY BENEFIT FROM HIS CRIME

6–84 When Crippen murdered his wife her property did not on her intestacy pass to him and via his will to Miss Le Neve, but passed to his wife's blood relatives; and where R murdered both his parents (Mr and Mrs S) who died intestate, R could not inherit their property and nor could his son, T, (a child only inheriting the property otherwise passing to the child's parent if that parent predeceased the intestate), so that Mr S's sister inherited his estate and Mrs. S's sister's children inherited her estate.[86] If the property is not intercepted before passing to the killer it seems he will hold it on constructive trust for those really entitled to it.[87] Their claims will have priority if he becomes bankrupt still owning such

---

[82] See *supra*, paras 2–96 *et seq.*

[83] *e.g.* Nourse J. in *Re Cleaver* [1981] 1 W.L.R. 939; see *supra*, para. 2–152.

[84] *Re Rose* [1952] Ch. 499, *supra*, para. 4–06; *Mascall v. Mascall* (1984) 49 P. & C.R. 119.

[85] *e.g.* the inciter of murder (*Evans v. Evans* [1989] 1 F.L.R. 351) or the aider and abetter of suicide (*Dunbar v. Plant* [1997] 4 All E.R. 289).

[86] *Re Crippen* [1911] P. 108 (also see *Re Sigsworth* [1935] Ch. 89) and *Re DWS (deceased)* [2001] 1 All E.R. 98 (C.A.).

[87] *Schobelt v. Barber* (1966) 60 D.L.R. (2nd) 519; *Re Pechar* [1969] N.Z.L.R. 574; *Rasmanis v. Jurewitsch* [1970] N.S.W.L.R. 650; *Beresford v. Royal Insurance* [1938] A.C. 586 at 600. See (1973) 89 L.Q.R. 235 (T. G. Youdan); (1974) 37 M.L.R. 481 (Earnshaw & Pace); Goff & Jones, Chap. 38.

property, and they will have the right to trace the property or its product into the hands of anyone other than a bona fide purchaser of the legal interest for value without notice.

If one joint tenant murders another he should hold the property on **6–85** constructive trust for himself and his victim in equal shares.[88] If a remainderman murders the life-tenant the victim should be deemed to live his actuarial life-span (except for a death-bed mercy killing), so that for the notional life-span the victim's interest should be held on constructive trust for his estate: thereafter, devolution should occur normally.[89]

Murder and manslaughter including manslaughter by reason of dimin- **6–86** ished responsibility invoke the principle, but not a finding of not guilty by reason of insanity.[90] The inflexibility of the forfeiture rule applying to all types of manslaughter would, as Phillips L.J. pointed out,[91] have led to judges modifying the rule where the facts involved a low degree of culpability or a high degree of mitigation so that forfeiture was a disproportionate sanction. He continued,[92] "I can see no reason now for the court to attempt to modify the forfeiture rule. The appropriate course where the application of the rule appears to conflict with the ends of justice is to exercise the powers given by the Forfeiture Act."

Except for murder cases, the Forfeiture Act 1982 now enables the court to modify the effect of the forfeiture rule where the justice of the case requires it, if the killer brings proceedings within three months of his conviction. In *Re K*[93] full relief against forfeiture was ordered in favour of a wife convicted of manslaughter of her husband. He had been violently attacking her for years. During one attack she picked up a loaded shotgun to frighten him and deter him from following her out of the room: the gun went off and killed him. The moral judgment for the judiciary to make was not too difficult here, but in other cases[94] the task could be an unenviable one, calling for the judgment of Solomon. Thus in *Dunbar v. Plant*[95] the Court of Appeal was divided on what the justice of the case required after taking account of all material circumstances involving the survivor of a suicide pact.

---

[88] *Rasmanis v. Jurewitsch* [1970] N.S.W.L.R. 650; *Re K* [1985] 1 All E.R. 403 (if A's murder of B severs their joint tenancy A holds legal title on constructive trust for A and B's estate equally). If X, Y and Z are joint tenants and X kills Y then X should become tenant in common of one-third and Z of two-thirds. For destination of surplus endowment assurance moneys payable on death of murderer's co-owner see *Davitt v. Titcomb* [1990] 1 Ch. 110.

[89] (1973) 89 L.Q.R. 231, 250–251 (T. G. Youdan).

[90] *Re Giles* [1972] Ch. 544; *Re Pitts* [1931] 1 Ch. 546.

[91] *Dunbar v. Plant* [1997] 4 All E.R. 279, 310.

[92] *ibid.*, 311, rejecting *Re S (deceased)* [1996] 1 W.L.R. 235.

[93] [1986] Ch. 180 and see *Re H* [1990] 1 F.L.R. 441 and S. Cretney (1990) 3 Ox. J.L.S. 289.

[94] See *Jones v. Roberts* [1995] 2 F.L.R. 422 discussed by R. A. Buckley (1995) 111 L.Q.R. 196.

[95] [1997] 4 All E.R. 279; material circumstances include the gravity of the offence, the conduct of the offender and the deceased, their relationship to each other, the source and value of the relevant property, and the wishes of those taking the property if the forfeiture rule fully applied.

PROPERTY OBTAINED BY A VOIDABLE TRANSACTION

6-87   Under a voidable transaction the claimant, O, deliberately transfers legal and beneficial[96] ownership in particular assets to the recipient, R, but O's intention is vitiated by factors such as fraud, undue influence, unconscionable bargain, misrepresentation or mistake so that O has an equitable right to rescind the transaction and a claim that the court should exercise its discretion to restore to him the assets of which he had been deprived.[97] Once O elects to rescind it seems that the court in its discretion can treat equitable title as retrospectively vesting in her for the purpose of enabling her to trace what happened to her assets in R's hands,[98] although if the contract had been a contract of loan O cannot be placed in any better position than if the contract had been valid.[99] Thus, if R fraudulently obtained a £1 million mortgage enabling him to buy a house that has doubled in value O can only recover the £1 million with interest at the contractual rate. However, if R fraudulently obtained a £1 million gift from O, then O should be able to claim equitable entitlement to a house purchased by R with such £1 million.[1]

6-88   Since R, his trustee in bankruptcy and his personal representatives are bound[2] on demand from O, electing to rescind the transaction, to transfer the original assets or their traceable product to O, one can regard R as constructive trustee of assets for O always from the time of such demand[3] and, in many cases, probably from the time R received the original assets on the basis that from that time his conscience was affected by an obligation to re-transfer the assets to O[4] because he was aware that if O was fully in the picture O would demand such re-transfer. However, if R was an innocent recipient and not a wrongdoer, his conscience would not be affected till the time of O's demand and the tracing process could result only in a lien being imposed in support of R's personal liability to O.[5]

A difficult case in this area is *Chase Manhattan Bank N.A. v. Israel-British Bank (London) Ltd*[6] where by a clerical mistake on 3 July 1974

---

[96] Lord Millett (1998) 114 L.Q.R. 399, 416; a case of undue inluence "assumes a transfer of the beneficial interest but in circumstances which entitle the transferor to recall it" *Hodgson v. Marks* [1971] Ch. 892, 929 per Russell L.J. and so assumed in *Cheese v. Thomas* [1994] 1 All E.R. 35.

[97] *Lonhro plc v. Fayed (No 2)* [1992] 1 W. L. R. 1, 9; *Re Goldcorp Exchange Ltd* [1995] 1 A.C. 74, 103; *Cheese v. Thomas* [1994] 1 All E.R. 35, 42.

[98] *El Ajou v Dollar Land Holdings plc* [1993] 3 All E. R. 717, 734; *Bristol & West B.S. v. Mothew* [1996] 4 All E.R. 698, 716; *O'Sullivan v. Management Agency & Music Ltd* [1985] Q. B. 428, 457.

[99] *Halifax B. S. v. Thomas* [1996] Ch 217; *Daly v. Sydney Stock Exchange* (1986) 60 A.L.J.R. 311; *Chief Constable of Leicestershire v. M* [1988] 3 All E. R. 1055.

[1] See S. Worthington, *Proprietary Interests in Commercial Transactions* (Clarendon Oxford, 1996) p.166 although her view that vitiated gifts give rise to a resulting trusts seems outdated and unsound in view of *Westdeutsche Landesbank v. Islington B.C.* [1996] A.C. 669 and cf. Lord Millett (1998) 114 L.Q.R. 399, 401–402, 416–417. The working out of equitable rescission will normally reach the same outcome as the application of resulting trust principles e.g. *Cheese v. Thomas* [1994] 1 All E.R. 35, 41.

[2] S. Worthington (supra) p.167, *Tilley v. Bowman* [1910] 1 K.B. 745, 750.

[3] Lord Millett (1998) 114 L.Q.R. 399, 416, although also pointing out that any right to a reconveyance on rescission should be regarded better as a working out of the rescission remedy rather than as a response to a constructive trust.

[4] *Westdeutsche Landesbank v. Islington B.C.* [1996] A.C. 669, 705–706, 707, 709,

[5] S. Worthington (supra) p.179 and para. 11–42 et seq.

[6] [1981] Ch. 105.

the plaintiff paid the defendant a second 2 million dollars. Two days later the defendant discovered the mistake but made no attempt to correct it. Four weeks later the insolvent defendant petitioned for itself to be compulsorily wound up. Goulding J held a fiduciary relationship subsisted between the parties to enable the plaintiff to invoke a proprietary remedy via the tracing process: "A person who pays money to another under a factual mistake retains an equitable property in it and the conscience of that other is subjected to a fiduciary duty to respect his proprietary right".[7] Whether or not there was a proprietary remedy was left open.

Lord Browne-Wilkinson[8] and Lord Millett[9] have rejected the reason- **6–89** ing of Goulding J. on the basis that the payee became the full legal beneficial owner to the exclusion of any equitable interest in the payer. Lord Browne-Wilkinson went on to indicate[10] that "the retention of the money after the recipient bank learnt of the mistake may well have given rise to a constructive trust" in his sense[11] of a personal liability to account as a constructive trustee.[12] However, such personal liability does not provide the proprietary base necessary for establishing a proprietary remedy via the tracing process. To provide a proprietary base one needs to rely on the court treating equitable title as retrospectively vesting in the payer when the payer elected to rescind, although major obstacles remained in the way of the tracing process.[13] Alternatively one can apply the principles developing from *Nest Oy v. Lloyds Bank plc*[14] and *Re Japan Leasing (Europe) plc*[15]: in the light of the defendant's parlous financial position when the two million dollars were mistakenly paid to it, any honest and reasonable person in the defendant's shoes would have forthwith regarded himself as holding the money to the plaintiff's order and arranged for it to be repaid so that a constructive trust is imposed on the money to prevent the defendant unconscionably benefiting from the payment.

O's interest is capable of being devised[16] or assigned,[17] and one would **6–90** have thought that for priority purposes against subsequent interests it should rank as an equitable interest,[18] so prevailing over any subsequent equitable interest unless prevented, essentially on estoppel grounds.

---

[7] *ibid*. 119

[8] *Westdeutsche Landesbank v. Islington B.C.* [1996] A.C. 669, 706, 715.

[9] Lord Millett (1998) 114 L.Q.R. 399, 412–413,

[10] [1996] A. C. 669, 715

[11] *ibid*, 705. See para. 6–09 *supra*.

[12] He relied on authorities involving personal liability to account as a constructive trustee, and if he were to be regarded as finding the plaintiff's proprietary interest not to be a continuing one but arising for the first time 2 days after receipt of the relevant property this would be inconsistent with his view that the remedial constructive trust of property has not yet been introduced into English law: Further see D. J. Hayton in P. B. H. Birks (ed) *Privacy and Loyalty* (Clarendon Oxford) 1997, at 301–302.

[13] *e.g.* not being able to trace below the lowest intermediate credit balance: *Roscoe v. Winder* [1915] 1 Ch. 62.

[14] [1983] 2 Lloyd's Rep. 658.

[15] [2000] W.T.L.R. 301. See paras 3–18 to 3–19 *supra*.

[16] *Stump v. Gaby* (1852) 2 De G.M. & G. 623.

[17] *Dickinson v. Burrell* (1866) E.R. 1 Eq. 337; *Bruty v. Edmundson* (1915) 85 L.J. Ch. 568.

[18] *Eyre v. Burmester* (1862) 10 H.L.C. 90.

Current authority,[19] however, indicates that policy considerations justify treating O's interest as a mere equity. Thus, it will not bind a third party who is a volunteer or a purchaser with notice: it will not bind a bona fide purchaser of any interest legal *or equitable* without notice.[20] There will be an equitable right to trace the property, but it seems that this right will only have the characteristics of a mere equity because the interest protected by such right is a mere equity.

ASSIGNMENTS FOR VALUE OF FUTURE PROPERTY

As Swinten-Eady L.J. stated in *Re Lind*[21]:

6–91   "An assignment for value of future property actually binds the property itself directly it is acquired—automatically on the happening of the event, and without any future act on the part of the assignor—and does not merely rest in, and amount to, a right in contract, giving rise to an action. The assignor, having received the consideration, becomes in equity on the happening of the event, trustee for the assignee of the property devolving upon or acquired by him, and which he had previously sold and been paid for."

6–92   Here a constructive trust arises as a result[22] of the maxim, "Equity regards as done that which ought to be done." Thus, if A in his settlement in consideration of marriage covenanted to pay to trustees any money inherited from X, such money is automatically subject to the settlement once received by A.[23] Similarly, if F, for a consideration received from G, contracted to hold on trust for G any future receipts arising in respect of payments for specified future sales or services, then such payments are subject to such trust immediately F receives them.[24] It is crucial that G has actually paid over the consideration to F because "Equity will not assist a volunteer", and F, having received the benefit of such consideration, cannot complain of the burden arising therefrom.

PURCHASERS' UNDERTAKINGS

6–93   Although a contractual licence to occupy a house or a flat is not an interest in land[25] and so only binds the contracting parties a purchaser, P, may undertake to the vendor, V, that he will take the property positively

---

[19] *Phillips v. Phillips* (1861) 4 De. G. F. & J. 208 at 218, 221–223 endorsed by Lord Millett (1998) 114 L.Q.R. 399, 416, *Latec Investments v. Terrigal Pty Ltd* (1965) 113 C.L.R. 265; *Blacklocks v. J. B. Developments Ltd* [1981] 3 All E.R. 392 at 400.

[20] *Lancashire Loans Ltd v. Black* [1934] 1 K.B. 380; *Phillips v. Phillips* (1861) 4 De G.F. & J. 208; *Latec Investments v. Terrigal Pty. Ltd* (1965) 113 C.L.R. 265.

[21] [1915] 2 Ch. 354 at 300.

[22] *Palette Shoes Pty Ltd v. Krohn* (1937) 58 C.L.R. at 16; *Associated Alloys Pty Ltd v. ACN 001 452 106 Pty Ltd* (in liquidation), at para. 3–40 *supra*.

[23] *Pullman v. Koe* [1913] 1 Ch. 9; *Re Gillott's Settlement* [1934] Ch. 97 at 158–159.

[24] *Barclays Bank plc v. Willowbank International Ltd* [1987] B.C.L.C. 717; *Associated Alloys Pty Ltd* (*supra*).

[25] *Ashburn Anstalt v. Arnold* [1989] Ch. 1.

subject to the rights of C, a contractual licensee. After completion of the purchase, if C cannot take advantage of a term in the contract between V and P for C's benefit that is enforceable by C under the Contracts (Rights of Third Parties) Act 1999, it then becomes unconscionable for P to evict C[26] by claiming that C only has contractual *in personam* rights binding V. Equity gives C an *in personam* right against P, compelling P to recognise C's rights under the contractual licence: *Ashburn Anstalt v. Arnold, infra,* para. 6–138. However, as this case also reveals, if V conveys or contracts to convey Blackacre defensively subject to whatever rights C may happen to have, so as to satisfy V's obligation to disclose all possible incumbrances and to protect him against any possible claim by P, then P is not bound by C's rights which are merely personal and not proprietary.

Where title to land is registered and C has a property interest which **6–94** he has not protected by entry on the register, so that it would ordinarily be void against P, P will personally be bound by it if he has so undertaken with V or C.[27] As Brennan J. has stated[28]:

> "A registered proprietor who has undertaken that his transfer should be subject to an unregistered interest and who repudiates the unregistered interest when his transfer is registered is, in equity's eye, acting fraudulently and he may be compelled to honour the unregistered interest. A means by which equity prevents the fraud is by imposing a constructive trust on the purchaser when he repudiates the unregistered interest . . . The fraud which attracts the intervention of equity consists in the unconscionable attempt by the registered proprietor to deny the unregistered interest to which he has undertaken to subject his registered title."

In these circumstances of giving effect to a contractual licence or an **6–95** estate contract, the court finds that the defendant's conscience is personally affected by an obligation to give effect to the claimant's interest and, as a formula to achieve such effect, treats the defendant constructively as a trustee to the extent of such personal obligation. The imposition of constructive trusteeship upon the defendant as a formula for equitable relief[29] however, does not confer on the claimant an equitable interest in the land to which the claim relates for, otherwise, the claimant's contractual licence would be a valid equitable interest binding the land, as would an unregistered void estate contract.

---

[26] Indeed, from *Snelling v. Snelling* [1973] 1 Q.B. 87, it would seem that V could intervene in proceedings between P and C so as to have P's action stayed indefinitely and so dismissed.

[27] *Lyus v. Prowsa Developments* [1982] 2 All E.R. 953; *IDC Group v. Clark* [1992] 1 E.G.L.R. 187, 190.

[28] *Bahr v. Nicolay (No. 2)* (1988) 62 A.L.J.R. 268 at 288–289.

[29] See similar imposition to make strangers to a trust personally accountable to beneficiaries: at para. 6–09 *supra.*

COMMON INTENTION CONSTRUCTIVE TRUSTS AND EQUITABLE PROPRIETARY ESTOPPEL

Problems where legal title in name of one party

6–96   Over the last 40 years the courts have increasingly had to deal with the problems that a female[30] cohabitee, F, can face when title to the family home is in the sole name of the man, M, and the relationship has broken down. F then wants a share in the property or some compensation from M. Because they are not married she cannot claim against M under liberal divorce legislation which takes into account a wife's non-financial contributions to the welfare of her family.[31]

6–97   F will have to rely on alleging an equitable right under a resulting trust or a common intention constructive trust or an equitable estoppel claim.[32] If at the outset F directly contributed or undertook with M to contribute a proportion of the purchase price paid at the outset for the home (*e.g.* using money lent on mortgage) M will hold the legal title on resulting trust for M and F in proportion to their respective contributions or undertakings.[33] Thus, F obtains only the share she paid for or undertook to pay for at the outset, though if she does not fulfil any undertaking she will have to make an equitable accounting[34] to M in due course, even if this be due to her lower earnings and demands of childbirth and childcare. Because of these limitations and because she may not have paid for (or undertaken to have paid for) any part of the initial purchase price, though subsequently, directly or indirectly, making financial contributions to discharging the mortgage or making improvements to the home it has become preferable for F to claim instead, on common intention constructive trust principles to enable her to obtain the share expressly or implied agreed between M and F, normally a half share or, perhaps a "fair"[35] share. One thus commences by establishing the resulting trust position and then seeing if any such trust has been ousted by an agreement or representation leading to a constructive trust or a proprietary estoppel.[36]

---

[30] The same principles will apply whether the cohabitee without the legal title is male or female and even if the cohabitees are of the same sex. If the dispute is not between a husband and wife but with a third party, like a mortgagee, a spouse without the legal title may take advantage of these principles.

[31] For disputes between spouses Matrimonial Causes Act 1973, s.24 affords the courts plenty of discretion to take into account the wife's home-making and child-rearing functions. Substantial contributions to the improvements of M's property can enable M's spouse or fiancée to obtain a beneficial interest under Matrimonial Property and Proceedings Act 1970, s.37.

[32] After September 27, 1989 all the terms of a contract disposing of an interest in land must actually be in writing signed by both parties or the contract will be void, and the equitable doctrine of part-performance of valid but unenforceable contracts will not be available: Law of Property (Miscellaneous Provisions) Act 1989, s.2 which does not affect interests arising under resulting or constructive trusts. Even before the 1989 Act it was difficult to establish a contract, *e.g.* because of uncertainty of terms or lack of intention to create legal relations.

[33] Thus, if M paid £10,000 of the £70,000 purchase price and took on a mortgage on the house in his name for £60,000 which F agreed with him to pay equally, there will be a resulting trust in the proportion 4:3 (40,000:30,000); *Cowcher v. Cowcher* [1972] 1 All E.R. 943 at 949–950. Further see *supra*, at paras 5–81 to 5–82.

[34] See *supra*, at para. 5–83.

[35] On a "fair" share, see *Gissing v. Gissing* [1971] A.C. 887 at 909; *Eves v. Eves* [1975] 3 All E.R. 768 at 772; *Passee v. Passee* [1988] 1 F.L.R. 263 at 271; *Stokes v. Anderson* [1991] 1 F.L.R. 391.

[36] See *e.g.* Dillon L.J. in *Springette v. Defoe* [1992] 2 F.L.R. 388 referring to the presumption of a resulting trust not being displaced.

Recently, problems over finding an implied agreement have led to the **6–98** invocation of equitable proprietary estoppel principles to avoid difficulties flowing from the requirements for a common intention constructive trust.[37] Indeed, in the light of the views of the Australian High Court,[38] English courts may ultimately come to decide that the distinction between common intention constructive trusts and equitable estoppel interests which both prevent unconscionable conduct is illusory, and that, therefore, the courts have a flexible range of remedies, whether prospective or retrospective, enabling justice to be done between M and F (perhaps even taking domestic as well as financial contributions into account), and between them and third parties who had earlier acquired interests, like mortgages, in the family home.[39]

Common intention constructive trusts

(a) Originally a *quid pro quo* was required. Conventionally, the **6–99** common intention constructive trust requires a bilateral understanding or agreement that if F acts in a particular way[40] then she will obtain the agreed share in the family home, usually a half share (leaving the court no discretion) or a "fair" share[41] (leaving the court plenty of discretion). It can be said that Equity acts *in personam* to prevent M pleading the lack of formalities, so F gets what was agreed.[42] Her interest should date from the time she commences to act to her detriment in the contemplated manner so that it is then inequitable for M to deny her an interest. Her interest will be capable thereafter of binding a mortgagee or a purchaser if she is occupying the property.[43]

A distinction must be made[44] between cases based on evidence capable of establishing an *express agreement* and cases based on conduct allegedly enabling the court to *infer an agreement*.

Where there is direct evidence of express discussions between the **6–100** parties, however imperfectly remembered and however imprecise their terms may have been, the court may find as a fact that there was an express common intention that if F acted in a particular way she would obtain an agreed interest in the property. Whatever the agreed *quid pro quo* was (whether relating to financial contributions, labouring work on improving the property, staying at home looking after M's children by a previous marriage and any children M and F may have) it will suffice if F furnishes it.[45]

---

[37] *Grant v. Edwards* [1986] Ch. 638 at 657 (approved by C.A. in *Lloyds Bank v. Rossett* [1989] Ch. 350) and *Mollo v. Mollo* [2000] W.T.L.R. 227.
[38] *Baumgartner v. Baumgartner* (1988) 62 A.L.J.R. 29; *Waltons Stores Interstate Ltd v. Maher* (1988) 62 A.L.J.R. 110.
[39] See *infra*, at para. 6–117.
[40] See Lord Diplock in *Gissing v. Gissing* [1971] A.C. 887 at 905 and Lord Oliver in *Austin v. Keele* (1987) 61 A.L.J.R. 605 at 610.
[41] See cases cited in *supra*, n. 35.
[42] Until then, there is a merely voluntary declaration of trust unenforceable for want of writing: under LPA 1925 section 53(1)(b), *supra* para. 2–05.
[43] Assumed in *Midland Bank v. Dobson* [1986] 1 F.L.R. 171 and *Lloyds Bank v. Rosset* [1989] Ch. 350.
[44] Emphasised by H.L. in *Lloyds Bank v. Rosset* [1991] 1 A.C. 107.
[45] *Grant v. Edwards* [1986] Ch. 638.

A claimant most provide in her statement of claim as much particularity as possible of express discussions, although this "means that the tenderest exchanges of courtship may assume an unforeseen significance many years later when they are brought under equity's microscope and subjected to an analysis under which many thousands of pounds of value may be liable to turn on fine questions as to whether the words were spoken in earnest or in dalliance and with or without representational effect."[46] It does not suffice that each party happened separately to form the same intention because an express common intention means one that is communicated between the parties.[47] It is the external manifestation of intention by one party to the other that is crucial, regardless of uncommunicated private intentions.[48]

6–101   As Lord Bridge states,[49] "In sharp contrast with this situation is the very different one where there is no evidence to support a finding of an agreement or arrangement to share, however reasonable it might have been for the parties to reach such an arrangement if they had applied their minds to the question, and where the court must rely entirely on the conduct of the parties both as the basis from which to infer a common intention to share the property beneficially and as the conduct relied on to give rise to a constructive trust. In this situation direct contributions to the purchase price by the partner who is not the legal owner, whether initially or by payment of mortgage instalments, will readily justify the inference necessary to the creation of a constructive trust. But, as I read the authorities, it is at least extremely doubtful whether anything less will do."

6–102   In *Lloyds Bank Ltd v. Rosset*, in delivering the only speech in the House of Lords, Lord Bridge held that the facts fell within the second situation and emphasised the distinction between the shared use of assets and shared ownership, stating,[50] "Neither a common intention by spouses that a house is to be renovated as a 'joint venture' nor a common intention that the house is to be shared by parents and children as the family home throws any light on their intentions with respect to the beneficial ownership of the property."

6–103   With such common intention H and W had decided to buy a semi-derelict farmhouse for £57,000, using money provided by trustees of a family trust who insisted the property be bought in H's name alone. Without W's knowledge, H mortgaged the property to Lloyds Bank to secure a £15,000 loan with interest. W spent some time supervising the builders doing renovatory works, did some preparatory cleaning work and did some skilful painting and decorating herself. The House of Lords held that such conduct was insufficient to justify any inference that there was a common intention for her to acquire a beneficial interest in

---

[46] *Hammond v. Mitchell* [1991] 1 W.L.R. 1127 at 1139.
[47] *Springette v. Defoe* (1992) 24 H.L.R. 552.
[48] *Mollo v. Mollo* [2000] W.T.L.R. 227, 242–243.
[49] *Lloyds Bank v. Rosset* [1991] A.C. 107 at 132–133 *infra*, at para. 6–166.
[50] *ibid.* at 130.

the farmhouse capable of binding a mortgagee. The value of her work in relation to a farmhouse costing about £72,000 was trifling. More significantly,[51] "It would seem the most natural thing in the world for any wife, in the absence of her husband abroad, to spend all the time she could spare and to employ any skills she might have, such as the ability to decorate a room, in doing all she could to accelerate progress of the work, quite irrespective of any expectation she might have of enjoying a beneficial interest in the property. The judge's view that some of this work was work 'on which she could not reasonably have been expected to embark unless she was to have an interest in the house' seems to me quite untenable." Thus, the bank as mortgagee could evict her as well as H in order to be able to sell the property with vacant possession.

It is clear[52] that domestic stay-at-home contributions to the welfare of the household cannot justify the inference that the parties agreed that F would obtain an agreed share in the house if she made such contributions. It is the most natural thing in the world for F to bear and rear children, to cook and clean and to sew and darn out of love for M and a desire to live in a pleasant, happy environment.[53] It is most unnatural, and therefore requires an express agreement, for F to do such things in the belief that she is thereby acquiring a beneficial interest in the home. **6–104**

Lord Bridge in his *obiter dicta*[54] indicates that to justify an inferred agreement between M and F it is necessary to find *direct* contributions by F to the purchase price, whether initially or by payment of mortgage instalments, such financial contributions clearly representing conduct upon which F could not reasonably have been expected to embark unless she was thereby to obtain an interest in the home. Payment by F towards the deposit will clearly give rise to an interest under a resulting trust, the size of which will depend on how F and M have agreed to bear the burden of the mortgage taken out to pay the balance of the purchase price, such burden being borne according to the legal effect of the mortgage in the absence of a contrary agreement at the outset between F and M. Thus, if F pays £5,000 of a £10,000 deposit on a home costing £100,000 vested in M's name, so that M alone is legal mortgagor responsible for paying the £90,000 balance paid to the vendor, then M prima facie holds on trust for M and F in the proportion 95:5. However, the courts are ready to oust such resulting trust by finding they can infer a common intention from the payment of the deposit by M and F that F was to obtain an equal share or a fair share taking account of the whole course of dealing between them relevant to their ownership and occupation of the home and their sharing of its burdens and advantages, **6–105**

---

[51] *ibid.* at 131.

[52] *Gissing v. Gissing* [1971] A.C. 887; *Burns v. Burns* [1984] Ch. 317; *Lloyds Bank v. Rosset* [1991] 1 A.C. 107, *infra*, at para. 6–166.

[53] *e.g. Coombes v. Smith* [1986] 1 W.L.R. 808.

[54] See *supra*, n. 49. However, as pointed out in *Mollo v. Mollo* [2000] W.T.L.R. 227, 236, "It is difficult in the extreme to conceive of both parties contributing to the purchase price without some form of express discussion sufficient to create an [express] agreement or understanding."

e.g. contributions to mortgage instalments from pooled funds or indirect contributions.[55]

6–106   What, then, is the position where F indirectly pays M's mortgage, *i.e.* she goes out to work and uses her earnings to pay a substantial part of the household expenses, so enabling M to pay all the mortgage instalments which he would not have been able to do and keep up their standard of living without F seeing to the other expenses? If there is no evidence of an express agreement and no contribution to the deposit *dicta* of Fox and May L.JJ. in *Burns v. Burns*[56] indicate that the courts will infer from F's substantial financial contributions to household expenses, which are necessary to enable M alone to keep up the mortgage payments without affecting their standard of living, that there was a common intention for F to have an interest in the home; but, presumably, only for her to have that share which corresponds to that proportion of the home represented by that part of the mortgage paid off by her. In reality one would expect a court to be sympathetic enough to F's claim to be able to find some evidence of an express agreement behind F's conduct.

6–107   Lord Bridge did not refer to *Burns v. Burns* but he did say[57] that F's conduct in *Grant v. Edwards*[58] in making substantial financial contributions to household expenses so as to enable M alone to pay the mortgage "fell far short of such conduct as would by itself have supported the claim in the absence of an express representation by the male partner that she was to have such an interest." These cited words also applied to F's conduct in *Eves v. Eves*[59] where M led F to believe she was to have a fair share in the dilapidated house, taking account of her renovatory work. She cleaned the house and did extensive decorative work and painted the brickwork on the front of the house. She wielded a 14lb sledge-hammer to demolish the concrete surface of the front garden and disposed of the rubble in a skip and prepared the front garden for turfing. She worked in the back garden and, with M, demolished an old shed and erected a new shed. The Court of Appeal held she was entitled to a quarter share in the house under a constructive trust.

6–108   In the absence of any common intention or unilateral representation Lord Bridge clearly considers that Janet Eves's conduct would have been referable to her love for Stuart Eves and a desire to live in pleasant surroundings, so that she would have obtained no interest in the home. To enable an inference to be drawn that she was to have an interest in the home, it would seem that a major capital contribution to the value of the home would be needed, such as using a £25,000 legacy to pay a building contractor's bill for an extension of a garage with a bedroom

---

[55] Resulting trust not displaced in *Springette v. Defoe* (1992) 65 P. & C.R. 1 but it was in *McHardy v. Warren* [1994] 2 F.L.R. 338 (applied in *Halifax B.S. v. Brown* (1995) 27 H.L.R. 511 at 518), *Mollo v. Mollo* [2000] W.T.L.R. 227 and *Midland Bank plc v. Cooke* [1994] 4 All E.R. 562, *infra*, at para. 6–181.
[56] [1984] Ch. 317 at 329, 344–345. Also see *Gissing v. Gissing* [1971] A.C. 887 at 903, 909.
[57] [1990] 1 All E.R. 1111 at 1119.
[58] [1986] Ch. 638, *infra*, at para. 6–146.
[59] [1975] 1 W.L.R. 1338.

above it or herself building such extension over a six-month period.[60] In practice, in such a case it would seem most unlikely for there not to have been some express discussion about F thereby acquiring an interest in the home, but in the absence of such discussion such conduct clearly seems conduct on which F "could not reasonably have been expected to embark unless she was to have an interest in the home."[61]

(b) Common intention without *quid pro quo*.

As Nicholls L.J. stated in *Lloyds Bank v. Rosset*[62]: **6–109**

> "I can see no reason in principle why, if the parties' common intention is that the wife should have a beneficial interest in the property, and if thereafter to the knowledge of the husband she acts to her detriment in reliance on that common intention, the wife should not be able to assert an equitable interest against the husband just as much as she could in a case where the common intention was that, by acting in a certain way, she would acquire a beneficial interest. In each case the question is whether, having regard to what has occurred, it would be inequitable to permit the party in whom the legal estate is vested to deny the existence of the beneficial interest which they both intended should exist."

On appeal, Lord Bridge implicitly accepted this. He stated that once there is a finding that there was an express common intention for the property to be shared beneficially,[63] "It will only be necessary for the partner asserting a claim to a beneficial interest against the partner entitled to the legal estate to show that he or she has acted to his or her detriment or significantly altered his or her position in reliance on the agreement in order to give rise to a constructive trust or proprietary estoppel."

This reference to proprietary estoppel is particularly significant **6–110** because a proprietary estoppel claim requires only unilateral conduct by M which leads F to believe that she has an interest in the home, so that in this belief she acts to her detriment, so that it then becomes unconscionable for M to insist on his formal 100 per cent. ownership of the home.[64] Indeed, in *Grant v. Edwards*[65] Browne-Wilkinson V.-C. had earlier suggested that useful guidance for constructive trust cases could be obtained from the principles underlying the law of proprietary estoppel. After all, Lord Oliver had pointed out[66] "In essence, the common intention doctrine is an application of proprietary estoppel."

(c) Size of F's interest.

---

[60] The "real and substantial equivalent" of a financial contribution: *Burns v. Burns* [1984] Ch. 317 at 344.

[61] *Grant v. Edwards* [1986] Ch. 638 at 648.

[62] [1989] Ch. 350, 381.

[63] [1990] 1 All E.R. 1111 at 1118–1119. However, be expressed "considerable doubt whether Mrs Rosset's contribution to the renovation was sufficient to support a claim to a constructive trust" even if there had been an express common intention.

[64] See *infra*, at para. 6–115.

[65] [1986] Ch. 638, 656 *infra*, at para. 6–146.

[66] *Austin v. Keele* (1987) 61 ALJR 605 at 609; see also *Maharaj v. Chand* [1986] A.C. 898 at 907.

6–111   Where the common intention is for F to have a half share it has been assumed that she will obtain the half share if she fully provides the *quid pro quo*,[67] *e.g.* contributes what she can to help with mortgage payments and household expenses, taking account of the exigencies of their family life. No court has considered what would happen if she only provided half the *quid pro quo*, *e.g.* if she held back (for her private nest-egg) half of what she could have contributed. Would she only obtain half of the half share? Indeed, what would happen if due to much unemployment F only made small financial contributions towards household expenses and holidays for two years before leaving M and running off with Roger?

The problem becomes greater where no *quid pro quo* is required, M merely carrying F over the threshold and saying, "This house is as much yours as mine" and F then acts to her detriment in reliance on the belief that she has a half share in the house. Detrimental acts may be placed on a scale of one to 99: does a tiny scale one detriment entitle F to the half share just as a colossal scale 99 detriment must so entitle F?[68]

6–112   The way forward must be that diffidently suggested by Browne-Wilkinson V.- C., namely, following guidance in the law of proprietary estoppel, for the court to act only to the extent necessary to prevent M unconscionably asserting his formal 100 per cent. ownership: "Equity is displayed at its most flexible."[69] Thus, in certain circumstances, instead of the promised half share, F might only obtain a quarter share, or a charge on the property to secure the sum of £2,000 representing F's contributions, or a licence to live in the property until paid the sum of £2,000.[70]

6–113   Where the court finds an intention to have a fair or unspecified share (which may arise from the springboard of the common intention behind a purchase money resulting trust) then it has plenty of leeway to determine the proper share in surveying the whole course of dealing between the parties relevant to their ownership and occupation of the property and their sharing of its burdens and advantages and taking account of all conduct throwing light on the question.[71]

(d) Impact upon third parties.

6–114   Where equity confers upon F the interest she would originally have had if M's express trust had been declared in signed writing, so that the imposition of a constructive trust arguably vindicates the express oral trust,[72] the court's decree is assumed to be retrospective.[73] However, the

---

[67] *Gissing v. Gissing* [1971] A.C. 887 at 905, 908; *Midland Bank Ltd v. Dobson* [1986] 1 F.L.R. 171; *Allen v. Snyder* [1977] 2 N.S.W.L.R. 685; *Grant v. Edwards* [1986] Ch. 638 at 657; *Savill v. Goodall* [1993] 1 F.L.R. 755.

[68] In *Lloyds Bank v. Rosset* [1990] 1 All E.R. 1111 at 1118 Lord Bridge opined that Mrs. Rosset's acts would have been insufficient even if she had proved an oral declaration of trust in her favour. See also *Bothe v. Amos* [1976] Fam. 46 at 55–56.

[69] *Grant v. Edwards* [1986] Ch. 638 at 657.

[70] *Re Sharpe* [1980] 1 All E.R. 198 at 202; *Maharaj v. Chand* [1986] A.C. 898; *Lim Teng Huan v. Ang Jwee Chuan* [1992] 1 W.L.R. 113; *Burrows v. Sharp* [1989] 23 H.L.R. 82; *cf. Tanner v. Tanner* [1975] 1 W.L.R. 1346.

[71] *Stokes v. Anderson* [1991] 1 F.L.R. 391, *Midland Bank plc v. Cooke* [1995] 4 All E.R. 562, *infra*, at para. 6–181, *Drake v. Whipp* [1996] 1 F.L.R. 826; (1996), 112 LQR 381.

[72] See *Allen v. Snyder* [1977] 2 N.S.W.L.R. 685, *per* Glass J.A.; C. Harpum (1982) 2 O.J.L.S. 277 at 279.

[73] *Midland Bank v. Dobson* [1986] 1 F.L.R. 171; *Lloyds Bank v. Rosset* [1989] Ch. 350.

date of the oral declaration cannot be the relevant date because the trust is then unenforceable.[74] If there is no detrimental reliance by F before M mortgages the home to X it seems that just as M is not subject to an enforceable trust so neither is X, who derives title from M. The priority of X over F crystallises at this stage[75] so as not to be affected if F subsequently acts to her detriment or subsequently persuades M to sign a memorandum evidencing the trust within the Law of Property Act 1925, section 53(1)(b).[76]

What of the case where X acquires a mortgage after F has allegedly acted detrimentally and some years later F alleges that she has an interest that binds X? Courts assume without argument[77] that any interest established in due course by F will bind X. It will be submitted that it is correct that F's interest binds X whether on the basis that the court decree retrospectively recognises F's pre-existing proprietary interest or preferably on the same basis that would confer priority on F against X if F's interest arose only on proprietary estoppel principles.

Equitable proprietary estoppels

(a) Unilateral conduct followed by detrimental reliance. A successful **6–115** equitable estoppel claim requires only unilateral conduct by M leading F to believe that she has an interest in the family home, so that she acts to her detriment in reliance thereon and it then becomes unconscionable for M to insist on his strict legal rights.[78]

(b) Size of F's interest and its impact upon third parties. The **6–116** "minimum equity to do justice"[79] to F and prevent M's unconscionable assertion of his strict legal rights depends upon the conduct and relationship of the parties from the date of M's original conduct till the court makes its decree—the likely outcome of F's claim may fluctuate in this period.[80] The court is apparently tailoring the remedy to fit the wrong and is not upholding already-existing rights of a proprietary nature[81] F cannot insist on having the expected interest: she is a supplicant for the court's discretionary assistance. However, the court tends to award her the promised interest but it may, instead, award her a lesser interest or even merely a sum of money,[82] to reverse her

---

[74] *Gissing v. Gissing* [1971] A.C. 887; *Midland Bank v. Dobson* [1986] 1 F.L.R. 171.
[75] cf. *London & Cheshire Insurance Co. Ltd v. Laplagrene* [1971] Ch. 499.
[76] See T. G. Youdan [1984] Camb. L.J. 306 at 321–322.
[77] See *supra*, n. 73 and *Midland Bank plc v. Cooke* [1995] 4 All E.R. 562, *infra*, at para. 6–181.
[78] See *supra*, at paras 2–29 *et seq.*
[79] *Crabb v. Arun D.C.* [1976] Ch. 179 at 198, *per.* Scarman L.J. endorsed in *Pascoe v. Turner* [1979] 1 W.L.R. 431; *Baker v. Baker* (1993) 25 H.L.R. 408; *Waltons Stores (Intestate) Ltd v. Maher* (1988) 164 C.L.R. 387; *Commonwealth of Australia v. Verwayen* (1990) 170 C.L.R. 394.
[80] *Crabb v. Arun D.C.* [1976] Ch. 179; *Williams v. Staite* [1979] Ch. 291; *Dodsworth v. Dodsworth* (1973) 228 E.G. 1115; *Griffiths v. Williams* (1977) 248 E.G. 947; *Sledmore v. Dalby* (1996) 72, P. & C.R. 196.
[81] See *supra* paras 2–38 *et seq.*
[82] See As Oliver L.J. stated in *Savva v. Costa* [1980] C.A. Transcript 723, Maudsley & Burn, *Land Law Cases & Materials* (5th ed.), at 556, "The expenditure gives rise to an equity to which the court will give effect in such way as may be appropriate in the circumstances giving rise to the estoppel claim. It may be by injunction, it may be by declaring a trust of the beneficial interest or it may be by a declaration of lien for monies expended."

detrimental reliance, though it may be supported by granting F a licence to occupy the premises till the sum is paid or a charge on the property.

When the court puts an end to the great uncertainty[83] and the effect of its decree is that M holds the house on constructive trust[84] for F as to an equitable half share or quarter share or an equitable life interest, it seems that this should[85] only have prospective effect normally so that it is a "remedial constructive trust" that arises.[86] Thus, at first sight, if M had sold or mortgaged the house to X after some detrimental reliance of F, X should not be bound by F's rights unless he had agreed with M or F positively to take subject to F's rights so that it would be unconscionable for him to deny her rights on *Ashburn Anstalt v. Arnold* principles.[87] However, if F had been in actual occupation and X had inquired, as he obviously ought to do,[88] whether F had any interest under a resulting trust or a constructive trust or protected by her co-occupation under section 70(1)(g) of the Land Registration Act 1925, this would have alerted F to what M and X were up to. If she is happy with this, but tells X she has a proprietary estoppel or a constructive or resulting trust claim or interest, then X must obtain her written consent to protect himself and, if the loan is for M's benefit (and not the joint benefit of M and F), take steps to check that her consent is not vitiated by undue influence or fraudulent misrepresentation.[89] If F is unhappy with M's plans to grant X (or other persons in the future) a mortgage with priority over her, she should take steps to have M expressly grant her a prior interest, involving the issue of a writ[90] against M if he refuses: such a writ can seek an injunction restraining him from mortgaging the property and demand that she be appointed co-trustee of the property. Thus she can fully safeguard her interests.

6–117　　If X deliberately or recklessly failed to take the elementary conveyancing precaution of asking the occupier, F, whether she claims any interest in the property so that F failed to learn of M's plan and so was divested of her opportunity to take the above precautions to safeguard herself, is it not clearly unconscionable for X to try to take advantage of his own lapse to claim priority over whatever interest the court decides F to have on proprietary estoppel principles? Surely, X will have to accord priority

---

[83] The claim is more uncertain than a mere equity to set aside a deed or rectify a deed where the ultimate court decision is predestined if the case to set aside or rectify is made out.

[84] *Yaxley v. Gotts* [2000] Ch. 162 (C.A.), *infra*, para. 6–173.

[85] Lord Browne-Wilkinson in 1991 Holdsworth Lecture "Constructive Trusts and Unjust Enrichment," reprinted in (1996) 10 Trust L.I. 98, though some *obiter dicta, e.g. Voyce v. Voyce* (1991) 62 P. & C.R. 290, 294 assume that donees or purchasers with notice will be bound by inchoate estoppel interests, though this can be justified not only if the court decree is always retrospective but if retrospective only on grounds of conscience.

[86] *Metall und Rohstoff A.G. v. Donaldson Lufkin & Jenrette Inc.* [1990] 1 Q.B. 391 at 479; *Westdeutsche Landesbank v. Islington B.C.* [1996] AC 669, 716.

[87] See *infra*, p. 037.

[88] *Kingsworth Finance Ltd v. Tizard* [1986] 1 W.L.R. 119, *Williams & Glyn's Bank v. Boland* [1981] A.C. 487.

[89] *Barclays Bank plc v. O'Brien* [1994] 1 A.C. 180; Dixon & Harpum [1994] Conv. 421, S. Cretney [1994] R.L.R. 3.

[90] As a *lis pendens* this can be protected on the register.

to F because X's conscience is affected[91] like that of a purchaser taking subject to a contractual licence on *Ashburn Anstalt v. Arnold*[92] principles.

The illusory distinction between common intention constructive trusts and equitable estoppels

Consider the following three scenarios.

(1) M says to F, "This house is as much yours as mine, so long as you **6–118** contribute what you can to household expenses and mortgage payments in the exigencies of our life together." F replies, "Lovely. I agree."

(2) M says to F, "This house is as much yours as mine" when asked by her whether she has a share in the house. "I'm glad you agree," she replies.

(3) Proudly carrying F over the threshold of his house, M states, "My darling, this house is as much yours as mine from this day forth." "Oh, thank you. How wonderful!" exclaims F.

It will be seen that (1) is a common intention constructive trust with a **6–119** *quid pro quo*, (2) such a trust without a *quid pro quo*, while (3) is a unilateral representation upon which an estoppel claim may be based. However, all three claims hinge upon F's detrimental reliance which makes it unconscionable for M to assert his 100 per cent. formal ownership. One can see that there is not very much difference between the scenarios and that to obtain the best scenario for F there will be a heavy premium upon skilled professional assistance in the preparation of relevant evidence and in encouraging F to say that she acted not out of love and affection but out of an express or tacit understanding or expectation that she had a half share so long as she contributed what cash she could in the exigencies of their life together or so long as she was a good housekeeper.

In scenarios (2) and (3), M is making a unilateral gift of half his **6–120** ownership, so that it is his intention as donor that is the foundation for an estoppel claim, which then requires F to know of that intention, so that in reliance thereon she can act to her detriment and make it unconscionable for M to assert his strict legal rights. It follows that scenario (2) should be treated as an equitable estoppel claim.[93]

Even in the case of scenario (1), M is making a unilateral gift, albeit conditionally, so that F knows of the condition and thus of M's intention,

---

[91] Query whether nowadays (*e.g.* in light of Cooke P. in *Phillips v. Phillips* [1993] 3 N.Z.L.R. 159, 167 and of S. Gardner in (1993) 109 L.Q.R. 263, 288) it could be successfully argued that M owed a particular fiduciary duty to F in respect of the house, having placed her in a vulnerable position where he had led her to expect that he would at least act in their joint interests (in respect of the legal estate) to the exclusion of his own separate interest. In breach of M's fiduciary duty X received an interest with notice, if not "Nelsonian" or "naughty" knowledge, of such breach so that it would be inequitable or unconscionable if he did not take his interest subject to F's rights as subsequently crystallised by the court.

[92] [1989] Ch. 1, see *infra*, at para. 6–138.

[93] *e.g.* facts of *Lloyds Bank plc v. Rosset* [1991] 1 A.C. 107.

so that she can act detrimentally in reliance thereon. Thus in *Yaxley v. Gotts*[94] and *Mollo v. Mollo*[95] the courts held that express common intention *quid pro quo* constructive trusts co-existed with a proprietary estoppel interest. The key factor is what M leads F reasonably to believe so that she then acts detrimentally in reliance thereon.[96] It is the external manifestation of intention that is crucial, so that M's real intention is irrelevant where he provides an excuse for not putting the home into joint names, so leading F reasonably to believe that she is really to have some interest, though on the face of things this is not to be recorded.[97]

6–121   Lord Oliver in *Austin v. Keele*[98] states of the common intention constructive trust doctrine, "in essence, the doctrine is an application of proprietary estoppel" and Browne-Wilkinson V.-C.[99] and Nicholls[1] and Nourse L.JJ.[2] have accepted that this is so, while Lord Bridge[3] treats "constructive trust or proprietary estoppels" as if they are interchangeable terms. This has led Robert Walker L.J. to state,[4] "in the area of a joint enterprise for the acquisition of land the two concepts coincide." The proprietary estoppel approach affords extra flexibility with a broad approach to behaviour that can amount to detriment.[5] As investigated,[6] it also seems that it can afford proper protection against third parties, while producing a sensible result between the squabbling parties themselves. It is thus submitted that the way ahead is for proprietary estoppel principles (whether or not re-characterised as remedial constructive trusts) to be used to create interests with prospective effect except where it would be unconscionable for a third party to exploit such position. It is time to abandon the distorting use of the institutional constructive trust to do justice in family home situations.

Discretionary prevention of unconscionable conduct

6–122   Is it not time that the courts and counsel moved beyond pigeon-holing circumstances into common intention constructive trusts and equitable estoppels and concentrated upon the basic principle of unconscionability

---

[94] [2000] Ch. 162.

[95] [2000] W.T.L.R. 227.

[96] *Gissing v. Gissing* [1971] A.C. 886 at 906 and *Mollo v. Mollo* [2000] W.T.L.R. 227, 242–243 where the claimant's contributions in money and labour were from the legal houseonwer's viewpoint intended to benefit the claimant, who actually intended to benefit their children.

[97] *e.g. Eves v. Eves* [1975] 1 W.L.R. 1338, *Grant v. Edwards* [1986] Ch. 638.

[98] (1987) ALJR 605 at 609.

[99] *Grant v. Edwards* [1986] Ch. 638 and 1991 Holdsworth Lecture, "Constructive Trusts and Unjust Enrichment" reprinted in (1996) 10 Trust L.I. 198.

[1] *Lloyds Bank v. Rosset* [1989] Ch. 350.

[2] *Stokes v. Anderson* [1991] 1 F.L.R. 391; and 1991 Hong Kong Law Lectures for Practitioners "Unconscionability and the unmarried Couple" discussed by Cooke P. in *Phillips v. Phillips* [1993] 1 N.Z.L.R. 159 at 168.

[3] *Lloyds Bank v. Rosset* [1991] A.C. 107.

[4] *Yaxley v. Gotts* [2000] Ch 162, 176, (endorsed in *Banner Homes v. Luff Developments Ltd* [2000] 2 All E.R. 126 by C.A.) and in *Birmingham Midshires v. Sabherwal* (1999) 80 P. & C.R. 256, 263.

[5] "The detriment need not consist of the expenditure of money or other quantifiable financial detriment, so long as it is something substantial. The requirement must be approached as part of a broad inquiry as to whether repudiation of an assurance is or is not unconscionable in all the circumstances": *Gillett v. Holt* [2000] 2 All E.R. 289, 308.

[6] *Supra*, paras 6–116 to 6–117.

underlying both doctrines? As Browne-Wilkinson V.-C. has pointed out,[7] in a passage endorsed by Robert Walker L.J.,[8] "In both the claimant must to the knowledge of the legal owner have acted in the belief that the claimant has or will have an interest in the property. In both the claimant must have acted to his or her detriment in reliance on such belief. In both equity acts on the conscience of the legal owner to prevent him from acting in an unconscionable manner." As Megarry V.-C. has indicated[9]: "There is today a tendency in equity to put less emphasis on detailed rules and more weight on the underlying principles that engendered those rules, treating the rules less as rules requiring complete compliance and more as guidelines to assist the court in applying the principles." Thus, the High Court of Australia in *Baumgartner v. Baumgartner* in dealing with a dispute between M and F where there was insufficient evidence to establish a common intention constructive trust held[10] "the appellant's assertion, after the relationship had failed, that the Leumeah property is his property beneficially to the exclusion of any interest at all on the part of the respondent, amounts to unconscionable conduct which attracts the intervention of equity and the imposition of a constructive trust at the suit of the respondent . . . We consider that the constructive trust to be imposed [prospectively] should declare the beneficial interest of the parties in the proportion 55 per cent to the appellant and 45 per cent to the respondent."

Shortly afterwards, the Australian High Court accepted that the **6–123** discretionary prevention of unconscionable conduct underlies not just constructive trust claims but also estoppel claims.[11]

Whether or not M is unconscionably asserting his 100 per cent formal ownership and so is unconscionably retaining a benefit at F's expense may be said to turn on an apparently vague standard. For this reason unconscionability factors should not affect third parties as a matter of property law but only if their consciences are affected. As has been seen, the court's decree should not recognise any pre-existing proprietary rights but should prospectively remedy the "wrong" of unconscionable conduct. The broad flexible range of remedies should just affect M and F and to the extent that any remedy confers a proprietary right on F it should not retrospectively affect X, a third party, unless in all the circumstances it would be unconscionable for X to claim priority over F.[12] Thus, the courts should not be inhibited by worries about third parties in developing a flexible range of remedies as between cohabitees.

As between M and F, who have full inside knowledge of all uncons- **6–124** cionability factors, it should matter little that there is a grey penumbra of uncertainty for which they have only themselves to blame. There should

---

[7] *Grant v. Edwards* [1986] Ch. 638 at 656.
[8] *Yaxley v. Gotts* [2000] Ch. 162, 177 and by Chadwick L.J. in *Banner Homes v. Luff Developments Ltd* [2000] 2 All E.R. 117, 126.
[9] *Re Montagu's Settlement* [1987] Ch. 264 at 278. Also see *Ashburn Anstali v. Arnold* [1989] Ch. 1 at 22 and 25.
[10] (1987) 164 C.L.R. 137 at 149. Subsequently, State courts have confined *Baumgartner* to unconscionability arising from financial contributions: see (1997) 113 L.Q.R. 227.
[11] *Waltons Stores (Interstate) Ltd v. Maher* (1988) 164 C.L.R. 387.
[12] See *supra*, paras 6–116 to 6–117.

be an interpretative community of judges and lawyers who can come to a significant consensus on what is unconscionable in particular circumstances in the light of current decided cases on constructive trusts and equitable estoppels and future cases decided on unconscionability principles. Judges and lawyers already cope with whether or not a term in a mortgage[13] or a bargain with a poorly-educated member of the lower income group[14] is "unconscionable", whether it is "unconscionable" to allow a plaintiff amenable to the English jurisdiction to bring a claim against the defendant in a foreign court,[15] and whether or not a landlord is "unreasonably" withholding his consent to an assignment or sublease.[16] Indeed, they also cope with taking a spouse's domestic contributions to family life into account in arranging financial provision on divorce.[17]

6–125   A cohabitee's domestic contributions to the welfare of the family can be taken into account in the rare case where they are the *quid pro quo* of a common intention constructive trust. More commonly, M will state that the home is as much F's as his or, otherwise, lead F to believe that she is to have a fair share in the home, and F may then spend the next 15 years of her life staying at home looking after the home and M and the children they have. The key question after M and F separate is whether F would have done the acts relied upon as a detriment even if she thought she had no interest in the home: if so, she cannot successfully plead that she did the acts in reliance on her belief that she had an interest in the home and so it is not unconscionable to deny her any interest in the home.

As Browne-Wilkinson V.-C. states[18]:

6–126   "Setting up house together, having a baby, making payments to general housekeeping expenses (not strictly necessary to enable the mortgage to be paid) may all be referable to the mutual love and affection of the parties and not specifically referable to the claimant's belief that she has an interest in the house. As at present advised, once it has been shown that there is a common intention that the claimant should have an interest in the house [or unilateral conduct of the houseowner reasonably leading the claimant to believe she should have an interest in the house],[19] any act done by her to her detriment relating to the joint lives of the parties is, in my judgment, sufficient detriment to qualify. The acts do not have to be

---

[13] *Multiservice Bookbinding Ltd v. Marden* [1979] Ch. 84.
[14] *Cresswell v. Potter* [1978] 1 W.L.R. 255; *Portman B.S. v. Dusangh* [2000] 2 Comm 221 (C.A.).
[15] *British Airways Board v. Laker Airways Ltd* [1985] A.C. 58. An equity also arises where its would be "unconscionable or inequitable" to allow one party to treat as its own property that had been acquired by it in furtherance of a pre-acquisition non-contractual arrangement with the other party: the acquiring party thereby gaining an advantage cannot act inconsistently with the arrangement, and will hold the property on constructive trust for the other party in accordance with the arrangement: *Banner Homes v. Luff Developments Ltd* [2000] 2 All E.R. 117 (C.A.).
[16] *Birkel v. Duke of Westminster* [1977] Q.B. 517; *International Drilling Fluids Ltd v. Louisville Investments (Uxbridge) Ltd* [1986] 1 All E.R. 321.
[17] Matrimonial Causes Act 1973, ss. 23, 24, 25.
[18] *Grant v. Edwards* [1986] Ch. 638 at 657. Further see *Wayling v. Jones* (1993) 69 P. & C.R. 170 discussed *supra*, para. 2–35.
[19] In view of the assimilation of the two concepts: see paras 6–118 *et seq supra*.

inherently referable to the house . . . The holding out to the claimant that she had a beneficial interest in the house is an act of such a nature as to be part of the inducement to her to do the acts relied on. Accordingly, in the absence of evidence to the contrary, the right inference is that the claimant acted in reliance on such holding out and the burden lies on the legal owner to show that she did not do so: see *Greasley v. Cooke*."[20]

The Privy Council and the Court of Appeal[21] have subsequently **6–127** endorsed this approach derived from proprietary estoppel and misrepresentation principles. The implication to be derived from the House of Lords in *Lloyds Bank v. Rosset*[22] is that once there is a finding of an express common intention or unilateral intention made known to F by M, then F only needs to show that she acted to her detriment or significantly altered her position in reliance on the intention to establish a constructive trust or a proprietary estoppel.[23] This appears to leave unaffected the presumption that F did so act unless M can prove to the contrary.

If M does not so prove then the court has jurisdiction to grant F **6–128** whatever remedy is necessary to undo M's unconscionable behaviour such remedy usually giving effect to F's expectations rather than simply reversing F's detrimental reliance,[24] *e.g.* give F a half share, a lesser fair share, a licence to reside in the home till the children reach adulthood or until M pays her £X compensation.

Where there is no finding of an express or inferred common intention **6–129** or unilateral intention made known to F by M, then it is not unconscionable for M to assert his 100 per cent. formal ownership of the property. F's domestic conduct was clearly not induced by any beliefs encouraged by M: her domestic services were provided by way of gift out of love and of liking to live in a pleasant family environment.[25] The courts have no jurisdiction to benefit F unless it is conferred by legislation along the lines of the New South Wales De Facto Relationship Act 1984.[26]

By this Act a court can "make such order adjusting the interests of the parties in the property as to it seems just and equitable having regard to:

(a) the financial and non-financial contributions made directly or indirectly by or on behalf of the de facto partners[27] to the

---

[20] [1980] 1 W.L.R. 1306.
[21] *Maharaj v. Chand* [1986] A.C. 898; *Lloyds Bank v. Rosset* [1989] Ch. 350; *Wayling v. Jones* (1993) P. &. C.R. 170, 173; *Gillett v. Holt* [2000] 2 All E.R. 289, 303.
[22] [1991] 1 A.C 107, 132.
[23] In *Gillett v. Holt* [2000] 2 All E.R. 289, 308 Robert Walter L.J. states, "The detriment need not consist of the expenditure of money or other quantifiable financial detriment, so long as it is something substantial. The requirement must be approached as part of a broad enquiry as to whether repudiation of an assurance is or is not unconscionable in all the circumstances . . . whether the detriment is sufficiently substantial is to be tested by whether it would be unjust or in equitable to be disregarded—the essential test of unconscionability."
[24] See at para. 2–37 *supra*.
[25] *e.g. Coombes v. Smith* [1986] 1 W.L.R. 808; *Gillies v. Keogh* [1991] 2 N.Z.L.R. 327.
[26] For background see (1985) 48 M.L.R. 61.
[27] These are heterosexual partners. The Australian Capital Territory's Domestic Relationships Act 1991 extends to homosexual partners.

acquisition, conservation or improvement of any of the property
of the partners of either or them; and

(b) the contributions, including any contributions made in the capacity of homemaker or parent, made by either of the de facto
partners to the welfare of the other de facto partner or to the
welfare of the family constituted by the partners and one of more
of the family, namely (i) a child of the partners; (ii) a child
accepted by the partners or either of them into the household of
the partners."

6–130 However, in the absence of such an Act, it may well be that social
attitudes in England may change so as readily to lead to expectations by
those within apparently stable and enduring *de facto* relationships that
assets used by the family, particularly the family home, are ordinarily
shared and not the exclusive property of M or of F unless it is otherwise
agreed or made plain.[28] There will thus be a presumption of a common
intention to share ownership of the family home and F's conduct will be
presumed to have been in reliance upon such intention. Time will tell
unless the courts are forestalled by legislation dealing with the matter; a
Consultation Paper is expected from the Law Commission shortly.

UNJUST ENRICHMENT

6–131 The concept of unjust enrichment in England is "a broad organisational
tool or 'umbrella' beneath which a series of sometimes quite different
actions for unjust gain can defensibly be collected"[29] although Lord
Steyn[30] would like it to rank "next to contract and tort as part of the law
of obligations as an independent source of rights and obligations." The
preventing or reversing of unjust enrichment underlies the action for
money had and received,[31] subrogation claims (outside of contract),[32]
and claims to restore profits, so covering unjust enrichment by subtrac-
tion and unjust enrichment by wrong doing,[33] but not the vindication of
proprietary rights via the tracing process[34] or the location of proprietary
rights under resulting trusts.[35]

Extra-judicially, Lord Browne-Wilkinson has rejected[36] the use of
unjust enrichment to deal with family home cases the way the Canadian

---

[28] As in New Zealand: *Gillies v. Keogh* [1989] 2 N.Z.L.R. 327; *Lankon v. Rose* [1995] 1 N.Z.L.R. 277. In
Canada, too, F is not presumed to be making a gift of her services: *Herman v. Smith* (1984) 34 Alta
L.R. (2nd) 90; *Everson v. Rich* (1988) 53 D.L.R. (4th) 470; *Peter v. Beblow* (1991) 101 D.L.R. (4th) 621
at 633–634.

[29] See K. Barker & L. Smith, "Unjust Enrichment" in D. J. Hayton (ed) *Law's Future(s)* Hart
Publishing, 2000, at 412. Also see Goff & Jones, *Law of Restitution* (5th ed) Chapter 1 and A. Burrows
The Law of Restitution, (2nd ed) Chap. 1.

[30] *Banque Financière de la Cité. Parc (Battersea) Ltd* [1998] 2 W.L.R. 475, 479

[31] Hence a mistake of law no longer precludes recovery: *Kleinwort Benson Ltd v. Lincoln C. C.* [1999] 2
A. C. 349

[32] *ibid.*, 483 per Lord Hoffmann.

[33] This terminology was invented by P.B.H. Birks in *Introduction to the Law of Restitution*, Oxford, 1985
and adopted by Lord Steyn in *Banque Financière supra*.

[34] *Foskett v. McKeown* [2000] 3 All E.R. 97

[35] *Westdeutsche Landesbank v. Islington B.C.* [1996] A.C. 669, and see para. 5–04 *supra*.

[36] 1991 Holdsworth Lecture, "Constructive trusts and unjust enrichment," reprinted (1996) 10 Trust L.I.
198.

courts deal with them. He favours the pragmatic flexibility of equitable estoppel, a doctrine the English courts are familiar with, though as we have just seen such doctrine has as its basis the prevention of unconscionable conduct. The difference between unconscionable conduct and unjust enrichment is that[37]:

> "The former looks to the conduct of the person who takes **6–132** unconscientious advantage of the person in the position of disadvantage and requires an assessment of that conduct, whereas the latter looks to the expectations of the parties and inquires whether there was an enrichment and a corresponding deprivation, and the absence of any juristic reason for the enrichment. But that is not to say that the expectations of the parties are irrelevant to the concept of unconscionable conduct."

In Canada,[38] though not quite yet in Australia,[39] the principle of unjust **6–133** enrichment is now recognised as a general basis of liability, though its limits remain to be fully probed. As Goff J. pointed out in an English case[40]: "The principle of unjust enrichment presupposes three things:

(i) receipt by the defendant of a benefit,
(ii) at the plaintiff's expense,
(iii) in such circumstances that it would be unjust to allow the defendant to retain the benefit."

The first two requirements raise few difficulties, though a benefit may **6–134** include a negative benefit, such as the savings made in not needing to employ a housekeeper because of services provided to M by F,[41] and something may be done at the plaintiff's expense where he suffers no loss but he could have been at risk of suffering a loss due to the defendant's wrongdoing.[42] The third requirement is obviously the one requiring refined development to make it clear that there is no scope for the unjust enrichment principle where the benefit was conferred by virtue of a gift or a contract or other legal obligation owed to the defendant or where the defendant did not freely accept the benefit. On these matters readers are referred to Goff and Jones, *The Law of Restitution* (5th ed.). A defence of change of position or of bona fide purchaser will also be relevant.

Prima facie, unjust enrichment leads to personal liability but it may **6–135** lead to proprietary liability *e.g.* by way of subrogation or lien or a constructive trust. In assessing whether a proprietary "constructive trust

---

[37] Sir Anthony Mason, Chief Justice of Australia, (1994) 110 L.Q.R. 238 at 251.
[38] *Sorochan v. Sorochan* (1988) 29 D.L.R. (4th) 12; *Petkus v. Becker* (1980) 117 D.L.R. (3rd) 259.
[39] *Baumgartner v. Baumgartner* (1987) 164 C.L.R. 137; *Pavey v. Paul* (1987) 62 C.L.R. 221 at 227, 256–257; Mason C.J. (1994) 110 L.Q.R. 238 at 251.
[40] *B.P. Exploration Co. (Libya) Ltd v. Hunt* [1979] 1 W.L.R. 783 at 839. Also see Lord Millett in (1998) 114 L.Q.R. 399, 408.
[41] See *Sorochan v. Sorochan* (1986) 29 D.L.R. (4th) 1 approving *Hermann v. Smith* (1984) 34 Alta L.R. (2nd) 90 in this respect; *Peter v. Beblow* (1993) 101 D.L.R. (4th) 621, 645.
[42] See Birks, *op. cit.*, at 132–139, 338–342.

404 Constructive Trusts of Property

remedy is appropriate we must direct our minds to the specific question of whether the claimant reasonably expected to receive an actual interest in the property and whether the respondent was or ought reasonably to have been cognisant of that expectation."[43] So long as M, with legal title to the family home, reasonably believes that F is making a gift of her housewifely services, F obtains no interest in the home. The position thus turns upon what M led F to believe about ownership of the home and what current social attitudes should have led M and F to believe so as to place the onus of proof on the cohabitee going against such social attitudes. In England it seems that social attitudes presume a gift[44] unlike the position in Canada[45] or New Zealand.[46]

Clearer position where legal title in both parties

6–136   Where legal title is taken in the name of M and F the position will usually be concluded by an express written declaration of trust[47] that the lawyers involved should advise M and F to provide. The fact that title has been put in both names reveals a common intention that the beneficial interest is to be shared in some fashion,[48] with the joint liability of the parties under any mortgage leading them to be regarded for resulting trust purposes as each contributing to the price half the mortgage money, unless at the outset the parties agreed between themselves that one was to be responsible for more than half the repayments to the mortgagee.[49] Thus, prima facie the parties' respective shares will be determined on resulting trust principles.

6–137   However, there will normally be plenty of scope arising from the parties' discussions that led the home to be purchased in joint names to find evidence of an express common intention that the parties are to have equal shares or fair shares "to be determined when the mortgage was repaid or the property disposed of, on the basis of what would be fair having regard to the total contributions, direct or indirect, which each had made by that date".[50] Even in the absence of evidence of an express common intention the courts are ready to infer from the legal title having been put in joint names that the parties are to have fair shares or even half shares if the deposit was provided equally.[51]

---

[43] *Sorochan v. Sorochan* (1986) 29 D.L.R. (4th) 1 at 12, *per* Dickson C.J.; *Peter v. Beblow* (1993) 101 D.L.R. (4th) 621.
[44] *Windeler v. Whitehall* [1990] 2 F.L.R. 505; *Coombes v. Smith* [1986] 1 W.L.R. 808; *Burns v. Burns* [1984] Ch. 317; *Lloyds Bank v. Rosset* [1990] 1 All E.R. 1111 at 1118.
[45] *Everson v. Rich* (1988) 53 D.L.R. (4th) 470; *Peter v. Beblow* (1993) 101 D.L.R. (4th) 621.
[46] *Gillies v. Keogh* [1989] 2 N.Z.L.R. 727; *Lankow v. Rose* [1995], 1 N.Z.L.R. 277.
[47] *Goodman v. Gallant* [1986] Fam. 106.
[48] *Bernard v. Josephs* [1982] Ch. 391; *Burns v. Burns* [1984] Ch. 317; *Springette v. Defoe* [1992] 2 F.L.R. 388.
[49] *Springette v. Defoe, ibid*; *Huntingford v. Hobbs* [1993] 1 F.L.R. 736; *Cowcher v. Cowcher* [1972] 1 W.L.R. 425 at 431.
[50] *Gissing v. Gissing* [1971] A.C. 886 at 909; *Burns v. Burns* [1984] Ch. 317 at 344 where May L.J. emphasises that "the court is only to look at their financial contributions or their real or substantial equivalent." Further see *Stokes v. Anderson* [1991] F.L.R. 391 at 400.
[51] *cf. Midland Bank plc v. Cooke* [1995] 4 All E.R. 562, *infra*, at para. 6–181

ASHBURN ANSTALT v. ARNOLD

Court of Appeal [1989] Ch. 1; [1988] 2 All E.R. 147; [1988] 2 W.L.R. 706 (Fox, Neill and Bingham L.JJ.)

Fox L.J. delivering the reserved judgment of the court: "The constructive trust **6–138** principle, to which we now turn, has been long established and has proved to be highly flexible in practice. It covers a wide variety of cases from that of a trustee who makes a profit out of his trust or a stranger who knowingly deals with trust properties, to the many cases where the courts have held that a person who directly or indirectly contributes to the acquisition of a dwelling house purchased in the name of and conveyed to another has some beneficial interest in the property. The test, for the present purposes, is whether the owner of the property has so conducted himself that it would be inequitable to allow him to deny the claimant an interest in the property: see *Gissing v. Gissing* [1971] A.C. 886, 905, *per* Lord Diplock.

"In *Bannister v. Bannister* [1948] 2 All E.R. 133, on the plaintiff's oral **6–139** undertaking that the defendant continue to live in a cottage rent free for as long as she wished, the defendant agreed to sell to him that and an adjacent cottage. The conveyance contained no reference to the undertaking. The plaintiff thereafter occupied the whole cottage save for one room which was occupied by the defendant. The plaintiff after a time sought to expel the defendant. The Court of Appeal held that he was not entitled to. Scott L.J., giving the judgment of the court, said, at p. 136:

> 'It is, we think, clearly a mistake to suppose that the equitable principle on which a constructive trust is raised against a person who insists on the absolute character of a conveyance to himself for the purpose of defeating a beneficial interest, which, according to the true bargain, was to belong to another, is confined to cases in which the conveyance itself was fraudulently obtained. The fraud which brings the principle into play arises as soon as the absolute character of the conveyance is set up for the purpose of defeating the beneficial interest . . . Nor is it, in our opinion, necessary that the bargain on which the absolute conveyance is made should include any express stipulation that the grantee is in so many words to hold as trustee. It is enough that the bargain should have included a stipulation under which some sufficiently defined beneficial interest in the property was to be taken by another.'

"We come then to cases in which the application of the principle to particular **6–140** facts has been considered.

"In *Binions v. Evans* [1972] Ch. 359, the defendant's husband was employed by an estate and lived rent free in a cottage owned by the estate. The husband died when the defendant was 73. The trustees of the estate then entered into an agreement with the defendant that she could continue to live in the cottage during her lifetime as tenant at will rent free; she undertook to keep the cottage in good condition and repair. Subsequently the estate sold the cottage to the plaintiffs. The contract provided that the property was sold subject to the tenancy. In consequence of that provision the plaintiffs paid a reduced price for the cottage. The plaintiffs sought to eject the defendant, claiming that she was tenant at will. That claim failed. In the Court of Appeal Megaw and Stephenson

L.JJ. decided the case on the ground that the defendant was a tenant for life under the Settled Land Act 1925. Lord Denning M.R. did not agree with that. He held that the plaintiffs took the property subject to a constructive trust for the defendant's benefit. In our view that is a legitimate application of the doctrine of constructive trusts. The estate would certainly have allowed the defendant to live in the house during her life in accordance with their agreement with her. They provided the plaintiffs with a copy of the agreement they made. The agreement for sale was subject to the agreement, and they accepted a lower purchase price in consequence. In the circumstances it was a proper inference that on the sale to the plaintiffs, the intention of the estate and the plaintiffs was that the plaintiffs should give effect to the tenancy agreement. If they had failed to do so, the estate would have been liable in damages to the defendant.

6–141 "In *D.H.N. Food Distributors Ltd v. Tower Hamlets Borough Council* [1976] 1 W.L.R. 852, premises were owned by Bronze Investments Ltd but occupied by an associated company (D.H.N.) under an informal agreement between them—they were part of a group. The premises were subsequently purchased by the council and the issue was compensation for disturbance. It was said that Bronze was not disturbed and that D.H.N. had no interest in the property. The Court of Appeal held that D.H.N. had an irrevocable licence to occupy the land. Lord Denning M.R. said, at p. 859:

> 'It was equivalent to a contract between the two companies whereby Bronze granted an irrevocable licence to D.H.N. to carry on their business on the premises. In this situation Mr. Dobry cited to us *Binions v. Evans* [1972] Ch. 359 to which I would add *Bannister v. Bannister* [1948] 2 All E.R. 133 and *Siew Soon Wah v. Young Tong Hong* [1973] A.C. 836. Those cases show that a contractual licence (under which a person has a right to occupy premises indefinitely) gives rise to a constructive trust, under which the legal owner is not allowed to turn out the licensee. So, here. This irrevocable licence gave to D.H.N. a sufficient interest in the land to qualify them for compensation for disturbance.'

Goff L.J. made this a ground for his decision also.

6–142 "In *Lyus v. Prowsa Developments Ltd* [1982] 1 W.L.R. 1044, the plaintiffs contracted to buy a plot of registered land which was part of an estate being developed by the vendor company. A house was to be built which would then be occupied by the plaintiffs. The plaintiffs paid a deposit to the company, which afterwards became insolvent before the house was built. The company's bank held a legal charge, granted before the plaintiffs' contract, over the whole estate. The bank was under no liability to complete the plaintiffs' contract. The bank, as mortgagee, sold the land to the first defendant. By the contract of sale it was provided that the land was sold subject to and with the benefit of the plaintiffs' contract. Subsequently, the first defendant contracted to sell the plot to the second defendant. The contract provided that the land was sold subject to the plaintiffs' contract so far, if at all, as it might be enforceable against the first defendant. The contract was duly completed. In the action the plaintiffs sought a declaration that their contract was binding on the defendants and an order for specific performance. The action succeeded. This again seems to us to be a case where a constructive trust could justifiably be imposed. The bank were selling as mortgagees under a charge prior in date to the contract. They were therefore not bound by the contract and on any view could give a title which was free from it. There was, therefore, no point in making the conveyance subject to the contract unless the parties intended the purchaser to give effect to the contract. Further, on the sale by the bank a letter had been written to the bank's agents, Messrs. Strutt & Parker, by the first defendant's solicitors, giving an assurance that their client would take reasonable steps to make sure the interests of contractual purchasers were dealt with quickly and to their satisfaction. How far any constructive trust so arising was on the facts of that case enforceable by the plaintiffs against owners for the time being of the land we do not need to consider.

"We come to the present case. It is said that when a person sells land and **6–143** stipulates that the sale should be 'subject to' a contractual licence, the court will impose a constructive trust upon the purchaser to give effect to the licence: see *Binions v. Evans* [1972] Ch. 359, 368, *per* Lord Denning M.R. We do not feel able to accept that as a general proposition. We agree with the observations of Dillon J. in *Lyus v. Prowsa Developments Ltd* [1982] 1 W.L.R. 1044, 1051:

> 'By contrast, there are many cases in which land is expressly conveyed subject to possible incumbrances when there is no thought at all of conferring any fresh rights on third parties who may be entitled to the benefit of the incumbrances. The land is expressed to be sold subject to incumbrances to satisfy the vendor's duty to disclose all possible incumbrances known to him, and to protect the vendor against any possible claim by the purchaser. ... So, for instance, land may be contracted to be sold and may be expressed to be conveyed subject to the restrictive covenants contained in a conveyance some 60 or 90 years old. No one would suggest that by accepting such a form of contract or conveyance a purchaser is assuming a new liability in favour of third parties to observe the covenants if there was for any reason before the contract or conveyance no one who could make out a title as against the purchaser to the benefit of the covenants.'

The court will not impose a constructive trust unless it is satisfied that the **6–144** conscience of the estate owner is affected. The mere fact that that land is expressed to be conveyed "subject to" a contract does not necessarily imply that the grantee is to be under an obligation, not otherwise existing, to give effect to the provisions of the contract. The fact that the conveyance is expressed to be subject to the contract may often, for the reasons indicated by Dillon J., be at least as consistent with an intention merely to protect the grantor against claims by the grantee as an intention to impose an obligation on the grantee. The words "subject to" will, of course, impose notice. But notice is not enough to impose on somebody an obligation to give effect to a contract into which he did not enter. Thus, mere notice of a restrictive covenant is not enough to impose upon the estate owner an obligation or equity to give effect to it: *London County Council v. Allen* [1914] 3 K.B. 642.

"In matters relating to the title to land, certainty is of prime importance. We do not think it desirable that constructive trusts of land should be imposed in reliance on inferences from slender materials. In our opinion the available evidence in the present case is insufficient. The deputy judge, while he did not have to decide the matter, was not disposed to infer a constructive trust, and we agree with him.

"In general, we should emphasise that it is important not to lose sight of the **6–145** question: 'Whose conscience are we considering?' It is the plaintiff's, and the issue is whether the plaintiff has acted in such a way that, as a matter of justice, a trust must be imposed on it. For the reasons which we have indicated, we are not satisfied that it should be." [They indicated that a "subject to" clause in a 1973 contract was a defensive protective provision only].

GRANT v. EDWARDS

Court of Appeal [1986] Ch. 638; [1986] 3 W.L.R. 114; [1986] 2 All E.R. 426 (Sir Nicholas Browne-Wilkinson V.-C., Mustill and Nourse L.JJ.)

NOURSE L.J.: "In order to decide whether the plaintiff has a beneficial interest in 96, Hewitt Road we must climb again the familiar ground which slopes down from the twin peaks of *Pettitt v. Pettitt* [1970] A.C. 777 and *Gissing v. Gissing* [1971] A.C. 886. In a case such as the present, where there has been no written declaration or agreement, nor any direct provision by the plaintiff of part of the purchase price so as to give rise to a resulting trust in her favour, she must establish a common intention between her and the defendant, acted upon by her, that she should have a beneficial interest in the property. If she can do that, equity will not allow the defendant to deny that interest and will construct a trust to give effect to it.

6–146   "I must summarise the crucial facts as found, expressly or impliedly, by the judge. They are the following. (1) The defendant told the plaintiff that her name was not going onto the title because it would cause some prejudice in the matrimonial proceedings between her and her husband. The defendant never had any real intention of replacing his brother with the plaintiff when those proceedings were at an end. Just as in *Eves v. Eves* [1975] 1 W.L.R. 1338, these facts appear to me to raise a clear inference that there was an understanding between the plaintiff and the defendant, or a common intention, that the plaintiff was to have some sort of proprietary interest in the house; otherwise no excuse for not putting her name onto the title would have been needed. (2) Except for any instalments under the second mortgage which may have been paid by the plaintiff as part of the general expenses of the household, all the instalments under both mortgages were paid by the defendant. Between February 1970 and October 1974 the total amount paid in respect of the second mortgage was £812 at a rate of about £162 each year. Between 1972 and 1980 the defendant paid off £4,745 under the first mortgage at an average rate of £527 per year. (3) The £6 per week which the defendant admitted that the plaintiff paid to him, at least for a time after they moved into the house, was not paid as rent and must therefore have been paid as a contribution to general expenses. (4) From August 1972 onwards the plaintiff was getting the same sort of wage as the defendant, *i.e.* an annual wage of about £1,200 in 1973, out of which she made a very substantial contribution to the housekeeping and to the feeding and bringing up of the children. From June 1973 onwards she also received £5 a week from her former husband which went towards the maintenance of her two elder sons.

6–147   "As stated under (1) above, it is clear that there was a common intention that the plaintiff was to have some sort of proprietary interest in 96, Hewitt Road. The more difficult question is whether there was conduct on her part which amounted to an acting upon that intention or, to put it more precisely, conduct on which she could not reasonably have been expected to embark unless she was to have an interest in the house.

"From the above facts and figures it is in my view an inevitable inference that the very substantial contribution which the plaintiff made out of her earnings after August 1972 to the housekeeping and to the feeding and to the bringing up of the children enabled the defendant to keep down the instalments payable under both mortgages out of his own income and, moreover, that he could not have done that if he had had to bear the whole of the other expenses as well. For example, in 1973, when he and the plaintiff were earning about £1,200 each, the defendant had to find a total of about £643 between the two mortgages. I do not see how he would have been able to do that had it not been for the plaintiff's very substantial contribution to the other expenses. There is certainly no evidence that there was any money to spare on either side and the natural inference is to the contrary.

"In the circumstances, it seems that it may properly be inferred that the **6–148** plaintiff did make substantial indirect contributions to the instalments payable under both mortgages.

"Was the conduct of the plaintiff in making substantial indirect contributions to the instalments payable under both mortgages conduct upon which she could not reasonably have been expected to embark unless she was to have an interest in the house? I answer that question in the affirmative. I cannot see upon what other basis she could reasonably have been expected to give the defendant such substantial assistance in paying off mortgages on his house. I therefore conclude that the plaintiff did act to her detriment on the faith of the common intention between her and the defendant that she was to have some sort of proprietary interest in the house.

"Finally, it is necessary to determine the extent of the plaintiff's beneficial **6–149** interest in 96, Hewitt Road. There is a particular feature of the present case to which we can turn for guidance. That is the crediting of the £1,037 balance of the fire insurance moneys to what the judge found was intended as a joint account. I think that this act of the defendant, when viewed against the background of the initial common intention and the substantial indirect contributions made by the plaintiff to the mortgage repayments from August 1972 onwards, is the best evidence of how the parties intended that the property should be shared. I would therefore hold that the plaintiff is entitled to a half interest in the house.

MUSTILL L.J.: "I agree. For my part, I do not think that the time has yet arrived when it is possible to state the law in a way which will deal with all the practical problems which may arise in this difficult field, consistently with everything said in the cases. For present purposes it is unnecessary to attempt this. I believe that the following propositions, material to this appeal, can be extracted from the authorities. (For convenience it is assumed that the 'proprietor'—*viz.* the person who has the legal title—is male, and the 'claimant' who asserts a beneficial interest is female).

"(1) The law does not recognise a concept of family property, whereby people **6–150** who live together in a settled relationship ipso facto share the rights of ownership in the assets acquired and used for the purposes of their life together. Nor does the law acknowledge that by the mere fact of doing work on the asset of one party to the relationship the other party will acquire a beneficial interest in that asset.

"(2) The question whether one party to the relationship acquires rights to property the legal title to which is vested in the other party must be answered in terms of the existing law of trusts. There are no special doctrines of equity, applicable in this field alone.

"(3) In a case such as the present the inquiry must proceed in two stages. First, by considering whether something happened between the parties in the nature of bargain, promise or tacit common intention, at the time of the acquisition. Second, if the answer is 'Yes,' by asking whether the claimant subsequently conducted herself in a manner which was (a) detrimental to herself, and (b) referable to whatever happened on acquisition. (I use the expression 'on acquisition' for simplicity. In fact, the event happening between the parties which, if followed by the relevant type of conduct on the part of the claimant, can lead to the creation of an interest in the claimant, may itself occur after acquisition. The beneficial interests may change in the course of the relationship).

6–151   "(4) For present purposes, the event happening on acquisition may take one of the following shapes. (a) An express bargain whereby the proprietor promises the claimant an interest in the property, in return for an explicit undertaking by the claimant to act in a certain way. (b) An express but incomplete bargain whereby the proprietor promises the claimant an interest in the property, on the basis that the claimant will do something in return. The parties do not themselves make explicit what the claimant is to do. The court therefore has to complete the bargain for them by means of implication, when it comes to decide whether the proprietor's promise has been matched by conduct falling within whatever undertaking the claimant must be taken to have given sub silentio. (c) An explicit promise by the proprietor that the claimant will have an interest in the property, unaccompanied by any express or tacit agreement as to a quid pro quo. (d) A common intention, not made explicit, to the effect that the claimant will have an interest in the property, if she subsequently acts in a particular way.

"(5) In order to decide whether the subsequent conduct of the claimant serves to complete the beneficial interest which has been explicitly or tacitly promised to her the court must decide whether the conduct is referable to the bargain, promise or intention. Whether the conduct satisfies this test will depend upon the nature of the conduct, and of the bargain, promise or intention.

6–152   "(6) Thus, if the situation falls into category (a) above, the only question is whether the claimant's conduct is of the type explicitly promised. It is immaterial whether it takes the shape of a contribution to the cost of acquiring the property, or is of a quite different character.

"(7) The position is the same in relation to situations (b) and (d). No doubt it will often be easier in practice to infer that the quid pro quo was intended to take the shape of a financial or other contribution to the cost of acquisition or of improvement, but this need not always be so. Whatever the court decides the quid pro quo to have been, it will suffice if the claimant has furnished it.

"(8) In considering whether there was a bargain or common intention, so as to bring the case within categories (b) and (d) and, if there was one, what were its terms, the court must look at the true state of affairs on acquisition. It must not impute to the parties a bargain which they never made, or a common intention which they never possessed.

6–153   "(9) The conduct of the parties, and in particular of the claimant, after the acquisition may provide material from which the court can infer the existence of an explicit bargain, or a common intention, and also the terms of such a bargain or intention. Examining the subsequent conduct of the parties to see whether an inference can be made as to a bargain or intention is quite different from examining the conduct of the claimant to see whether it amounts to compliance with a bargain or intention which has been proved in some other way. (If this distinction is not observed, there is a risk of circularity. If the claimant's conduct is too readily assumed to be explicable only by the existence of a bargain, she will always be able to say that her side of the bargain has been performed.) . . .

"Whatever the defendant's actual intention, the nature of the excuse which he **6–154** gave must have led the plaintiff to believe that she would in the future have her name on the title, and this in turn would justify her in concluding that she had from the outset some kind of right to the house. The case does not fall precisely within either of categories (b), (c) or (d) above, but the defendant's conduct must now preclude him from denying that it is sufficiently analogous to these categories to make the relevant principles apply.

"Assuming therefore that the case must be approached as if the defendant had **6–155** promised the plaintiff some kind of right to the house, or as if they had a common intention to this effect—and I do not think it matters which formula is chosen—what kind of right was this to be? In particular was it to be a right which was to arise only if the plaintiff gave something in exchange; and if so, what was that something to be? These are not easy questions to answer, especially since the judge never approached, or was asked to approach, the matter in this way. Nevertheless I consider it legitimate to hold that there must have been an assumption that the transfer of rights to the plaintiff would not be unilateral, and that the plaintiff would play her own part. Moreover, the situation of the couple was such that the plaintiff's part must have included a direct or indirect contribution to the cost of acquisition: for the defendant could not from his own resources have afforded both to buy their new home and to keep the joint household in existence.

"Finally, there remains the question whether the conduct of the plaintiff can **6–156** be regarded as referable to the bargain or intention thus construed. On the facts as analysed by Nourse L.J. I consider that it can. For the reasons given by Nourse L.J. I agree that the interest should be quantified at 50 per cent."

Sir Nicholas Browne-Wilkinson V.-C.: "I agree. In my judgment, there has been a tendency over the years to distort the principles as laid down in the speech of Lord Diplock in *Gissing v. Gissing* [1971] A.C. 886 by concentrating on only part of his reasoning. For present purposes, his speech can be treated as falling into three sections: the first deals with the nature of the substantive right; the second with the proof of the existence of that right; the third with the quantification of that right.

1. The nature of the substantive right: [1971] A.C. 886, 905B–G
"If the legal estate in the joint home is vested in only one of the parties ('the legal owner') the other party ('the claimant'), in order to establish a beneficial interest, has to establish a constructive trust by showing that it would be inequitable for the legal owner to claim sole beneficial ownership. This requires two matters to be demonstrated: (a) that there was a common intention that both should have a beneficial interest; (b) that the claimant has acted to his or her detriment on the basis of that common intention.

2. The proof of the common intention
"(a) Direct evidence (p. 905H). It is clear that mere agreement between the **6–157** parties that both are to have beneficial interests is sufficient to prove the necessary common intention. Other passages in the speech point to the admissibility and relevance of other possible forms of direct evidence of such intention: see pp. 907c and 908c.

"(b) Inferred common intention (pp. 906A–908D). Lord Diplock points out that, even where parties have not used express words to communicate their intention (and therefore there is no direct evidence), the court can infer from their actions an intention that they shall both have an interest in the house. This part of his speech concentrates on the types of evidence from which the courts are most often asked to infer such intention, *viz.* contributions (direct and indirect) to the deposit, the mortgage instalments or general housekeeping expenses. In this section of the speech, he analyses what types of expenditure are capable of constituting evidence of such common intention: he does not say that if the intention is proved in some other way such contributions are essential to establish the trust.

3. The quantification of the right (pp. 908D–909)

6–158   "Once it has been established that the parties had a common intention that both should have a beneficial interest *and* that the claimant has acted to his detriment, the question may still remain 'what is the extent of the claimant's beneficial interest?' This last section of Lord Diplock's speech shows that here again the direct and indirect contributions made by the parties to the cost of acquisition may be crucially important.

"If this analysis is correct, contributions made by the claimant may be relevant for four different purposes, *viz.*: (1) in the absence of direct evidence of intention, as evidence from which the parties' intentions can be inferred; (2) as corroboration of direct evidence of intention; (3) to show that the claimant has acted to his or her detriment in reliance on the common intention: Lord Diplock's speech does not deal directly with the nature of the detriment to be shown; (4) to quantify the extent of the beneficial interest.

6–159   "I have sought to analyse Lord Diplock's speech for two reasons. First, it is clear that the necessary common intention can be proved otherwise than by reference to contributions by the claimant to the cost of acquisition. Secondly, the remarks of Lord Diplock as to the contributions made by the claimant must be read in their context.

"In cases of this kind the first question must always be whether there is sufficient direct evidence of a common intention that both parties are to have a beneficial interest. Such direct evidence need have nothing to do with the contributions made to the cost of acquisition. Thus in *Eves v. Eves* [1975] 1 W.L.R. 1338 the common intention was proved by the fact that the claimant was told that her name would have been on the title deeds but for her being under age. Again, in *Midland Bank Plc. v. Dobson* [1986] 1 F.L.R. 171 this court held that the trial judge was entitled to find the necessary common intention from evidence which he accepted that the parties treated the house as 'our house' and had a 'principle of sharing everything.' It is only necessary to have recourse to inferences from other circumstances (such as the way in which the parties contributed, directly or indirectly, to the cost of acquisition) in cases such as *Gissing v. Gissing* [1971] A.C. 886 and *Burns v. Burns* [1984] Ch. 317 where there is no direct evidence of intention.

6–160   "Applying those principles to the present case, the representation made by the defendant to the plaintiff that the house would have been in the joint names but for the plaintiff's matrimonial disputes is clear direct evidence of a common intention that she was to have an interest in the house: *Eves v. Eves* [1975] 1 W.L.R. 1338. Such evidence was in my judgment sufficient by itself to establish the common intention: but in any event it is wholly consistent with the contributions made by the plaintiff to the joint household expenses and the fact that the surplus fire insurance moneys were put into a joint account.

"But as Lord Diplock's speech in *Gissing v. Gissing* [1971] A.C. 886, 905D and the decision in *Midland Bank Plc. v. Dobson* make clear, mere common intention by itself is not enough: the claimant has also to prove that she has acted to her detriment in the reasonable belief by so acting she was acquiring a beneficial interest.

"There is little guidance in the authorities on constructive trusts as to what is necessary to prove that the claimant so acted to her detriment. What 'link' has to be shown between the common intention and the actions relied on? Does there have to be positive evidence that the claimant did the acts in conscious reliance on the common intention? Does the court have to be satisfied that she would not have done the acts relied on but for the common intention, *e.g.* would not the claimant have contributed to household expenses out of affection for the legal owner and as part of their joint life together even if she had no interest in the house? Do the acts relied on as a detriment have to be inherently referable to the house, *e.g.* contribution to the purchase or physical labour on the house?

"I do not think it is necessary to express any concluded view on these **6–161** questions in order to decide this case. *Eves v. Eves* [1975] 1 W.L.R. 1338 indicates that there has to be some 'link' between the common intention and the acts relied on as a detriment. In that case the acts relied on did inherently relate to the house (that is the work the claimant did to the house) and from this the Court of Appeal felt able to infer that the acts were done in reliance on the common intention. So, in this case, as the analysis of Nourse L.J. makes clear, the plaintiff's contributions to the household expenses were essentially linked to the payment of the mortgage instalments by the defendant: without the plaintiff's contributions, the defendant's means were insufficient to keep up the mortgage payments. In my judgment where the claimant has made payments which, whether directly or indirectly, have been used to discharge the mortgage instalments, this is a sufficient link between the detriment suffered by the claimant and the common intention. The court can infer that she would not have made such payments were it not for her belief that she had an interest in the house. On this ground therefore I find that the plaintiff has acted to her detriment in reliance on the common intention that she had a beneficial interest in the house and accordingly that she has established such beneficial interest.

"I suggest that in other cases of this kind, useful guidance may in the future be **6–162** obtained from the principles underlying the law of proprietary estoppel which in my judgment are closely akin to those laid down in *Gissing v. Gissing* [1971] A.C. 886. In both, the claimant must to the knowledge of the legal owner have acted in the belief that the claimant has or will obtain an interest in the property. In both, the claimant must have acted to his or her detriment in reliance on such belief. In both, equity acts on the conscience of the legal owner to prevent him from acting in an unconscionable manner by defeating the common intention. The two principles have been developed separately without cross-fertilisation between them: but they rest on the same foundation and have on all other matters reached the same conclusions.

"In many cases of the present sort, it is impossible to say whether or not the **6–163** claimant would have done the acts relied on as a detriment even if she thought she had no interest in the house. Setting up house together, having a baby, making payments to general housekeeping expenses (not strictly necessary to enable the mortgage to be paid) may all be referable to the mutual love and affection of the parties and not specifically referable to the claimant's belief that she has an interest in the house. As at present advised, once it has been shown that there was a common intention that the claimant should have an interest in the house, any act done by her to her detriment relating to the joint lives of the parties is, in my judgment, sufficient detriment to qualify. The acts do not have to be inherently referable to the house: see *Jones (A.E.) v. Jones (F.W.)* [1977] 1

W.L.R. 438 and *Pascoe v. Turner* [1979] 1 W.L.R. 431. The holding out to the claimant that she had a beneficial interest in the house is an act of such a nature as to be part of the inducement to her to do the acts relied on. Accordingly, in the absence of evidence to the contrary, the right inference is that the claimant acted in reliance on such holding out and the burden lies on the legal owner to show that she did not do so: see *Greasley v. Cooke* [1980] 1 W.L.R. 1306.

"The possible analogy with proprietary estoppel was raised in argument. However, the point was not fully argued and since the case can be decided without relying on such analogy, it is unsafe for me to rest my judgment on that point. I decide the case on the narrow ground already mentioned.

6–164   "What then is the extent of the plaintiff's interest? It is clear from *Gissing v. Gissing* [1971] A.C. 886 that, once the common intention and the actions to the claimant's detriment have been proved from direct or other evidence, in fixing the quantum of the claimant's beneficial interest the court can take into account indirect contributions by the plaintiff such as the plaintiff's contributions to joint household expenses: see *Gissing v. Gissing* [1971] A.C. 886 at 909A and D–E. In my judgment, the passage in Lord Diplock's speech at pp. 909G–910A is dealing with a case where there is no evidence of the common intention other than contributions to joint expenditure: in such a case there is insufficient evidence to prove any beneficial interest and the question of the extent of that interest cannot arise.

6–165   "Where, as in this case, the existence of some beneficial interest in the claimant has been shown, prima facie the interest of the claimant will be that which the parties intended: *Gissing v. Gissing* [1971] A.C. 886 at 908G. In *Eves v. Eves* [1975] 1 W.L.R. 1338 at 1345G Brightman L.J. plainly felt that a common intention that there should be a joint interest pointed to the beneficial interests being equal. However, he felt able to find a lesser beneficial interest in that case without explaining the legal basis on which he did so. With diffidence, I suggest that the law of proprietary estoppel may again provide useful guidance. If proprietary estoppel is established, the court gives effect to it by giving effect to the common intention so far as may fairly be done between the parties. For that purpose, equity is displayed at its most flexible: see *Crabb v. Arun D.C.* [1976] Ch. 179. Identifiable contributions to the purchase of the house will, of course be an important factor in many cases. But in other cases, contributions by way of labour or other unquantifiable actions of the claimant will also be relevant.

"Taking into account the fact that the house was intended to be the joint property, the contributions to the common expenditure and the payment of the fire insurance moneys into the joint account, I agree that the plaintiff is entitled to a half interest in the house." *Appeal allowed with costs.*

LLOYDS BANK PLC v. ROSSET

House of Lords [1991] 1 A.C. 107; [1990] 2 W.L.R. 867; [1990] 1 All E.R. 1111
(Lords Bridge, Griffiths, Ackner, Oliver and Jauncey)

6–166   LORD BRIDGE (with whose speech the others all simply concurred) after citing the judge's findings on Mrs. Rosset's cleaning, painting and decorating: "It is clear from these passages in the judgment that the judge based his inference of a common intention that Mrs. Rossett should have a beneficial interest in the property under a constructive trust essentially on what Mrs. Rosset did in and about assisting in the renovation of the property between the beginning of

November 1982 and the date of completion on 17 December 1982. Yet by itself this activity, it seems to me, could not possibly justify any such inference. It was common ground that Mrs. Rosset was extremely anxious that the new matrimonial home should be ready for occupation before Christmas if possible. In these circumstances, it would seem the most natural thing in the world for any wife, in the absence of her husband abroad, to spend all the time she could spare and to employ any skills she might have, such as the ability to decorate a room, in doing all she could to accelerate progress of the work quite irrespective of any expectation she might have of enjoying a beneficial interest in the property. The judge's view that some of this work was work 'on which she could not reasonably have been expected to embark unless she was to have an interest in the house' seems to me, with respect, quite untenable.

"On any view the monetary value of Mrs. Rosset's work expressed as a **6–167** contribution to a property acquired at a cost exceeding £70,000 must have been so trifling as to be almost de minimis. I should myself have had considerable doubt whether Mrs. Rosset's contribution to the work of renovation was sufficient to support a claim to a constructive trust in the absence of writing to satisfy the requirements of s.53 of the Law of Property Act 1925 even if her husband's intention to make a gift to her of half or any other share in the equity of the property had been clearly established or if he had clearly represented to her that that was what he intended. But here the conversations with her husband on which Mrs. Rosset relied, all of which took place before November 1982, were incapable of lending support to the conclusion of a constructive trust in the light of the judge's finding that by that date there had been no decision that she was to have any interest in the property. The finding that the discussions 'did not exclude the possibility' that she should have an interest does not seem to me to add anything of significance.

"These considerations lead me to the conclusion that the judge's finding that **6–168** Mr. Rosset held the property as constructive trustee for himself and his wife cannot be supported and it is on this short ground that I would allow the appeal. In the course of the argument your Lordships had the benefit of elaborate submissions as to the test to be applied to determine the circumstances in which the sole legal proprietor of a dwelling house can properly be held to have become a constructive trustee of a share in the beneficial interest in the house for the benefit of the partner with whom he or she has cohabited in the house as their shared home. Having in this case reached a conclusion on the facts which, although at variance with the views of the courts below, does not seem to depend on any nice legal distinction and with which, I understand, all your Lordships agree, I cannot help doubting whether it would contribute anything to the illumination of the law if I were to attempt an elaborate and exhaustive analysis of the relevant law to add to the many already to be found in the authorities to which our attention was directed in the course of the argument. I do, however, draw attention to one critical distinction which any judge required to resolve a dispute between former partners as to the beneficial interest in the home they formerly shared should always have in the forefront of his mind.

"The first and fundamental question which must always be resolved is whether, **6–169** independently of any inference to be drawn from the conduct of the parties in the course of sharing the house as their home and managing their joint affairs, there has at any time prior to acquisition, or exceptionally at some later date, been any agreement, arrangement or understanding reached between them that the property is to be shared beneficially. The finding of an agreement or arrangement to share in this sense can only, I think, be based on evidence of express discussions between the partners, however imperfectly remembered and however imprecise their terms may have been. Once a finding to this effect is made it will only be necessary for the partner asserting a claim to a beneficial interest against the partner entitled to the legal estate to show that he or she has acted to his or her detriment or significantly altered his or her position in reliance on the agreement in order to give rise to a constructive trust or proprietary estoppel.

6–170   "In sharp contrast with this situation is the very different one where there is no evidence to support a finding of an agreement or arrangement to share, however reasonable it might have been for the parties to reach such an arrangement if they had applied their minds to the question, and where the court must rely entirely on the conduct of the parties both as the basis from which to infer a common intention to share the property beneficially and as the conduct relied on to give rise to a constructive trust. In this situation direct contributions to the purchase price by the partner who is not the legal owner, whether initially or by payment of mortgage instalments, will readily justify the inference necessary to the creation of a constructive trust. But, as I read the authorities, it is at least extremely doubtful whether anything less will do.

6–171   "The leading cases in your Lordships' House are *Pettitt v. Pettitt* [1970] A.C. 777 and *Gissing v. Gissing* [1971] A.C. 886. Both demonstrate situations in the second category to which I have referred and their Lordships discuss at great length the difficulties to which these situations give rise. The effect of these two decisions is very helpfully analysed in the judgment of Lord MacDermott L.C.J. in *McFarlane v. McFarlane* [1972] N.I. 59.

"Outstanding examples on the other hand of cases giving rise to situations in the first category are *Eves v. Eves* [1975] 1 W.L.R. 1338 and *Grant v. Edwards* [1986] Ch. 638. In both these cases, where the parties who had cohabited were unmarried, the female partner had been clearly led by the male partner to believe, when they set up home together, that the property would belong to them jointly. In *Eves v. Eves* the male partner had told the female partner that the only reason why the property was to be acquired in his name alone was because she was under 21 and that, but for her age, he would have had the house put into their joint names. He admitted in evidence that this was simply an 'excuse.' Similarly, in *Grant v. Edwards* the female partner was told by the male partner that the only reason for not acquiring the property in joint names was because she was involved in divorce proceedings and that, if the property were acquired jointly, this might operate to her prejudice in those proceedings. As Nourse L.J. put it ([1986] Ch. 638 at 649):

'Just as in *Eves v. Eves*, these facts appear to me to raise a clear inference that there was an understanding between the plaintiff and the defendant, or a common intention, that the plaintiff was to have some sort of proprietary interest in the house; otherwise no excuse for not putting her name onto the title would have been needed.'

6–172   The subsequent conduct of the female partner in each of these cases, which the court rightly held sufficient to give rise to a constructive trust or proprietary estoppel supporting her claim to an interest in the property, fell far short of such conduct as would by itself have supported the claim in the absence of an express representation by the male partner that she was to have such an interest. It is significant to note that the share to which the female partners in *Eves v. Eves* and

Grant v. Edwards were held entitled were one-quarter and one-half respectively. In no sense could these shares have been regarded as proportionate to what the judge in the instant case described as a "qualifying contribution" in terms of the indirect contributions to the acquisition or enhancement of the value of the houses made by the female partners.

"I cannot help thinking that the judge in the instant case would not have fallen into error if he had kept clearly in mind the distinction between the effect of evidence on the one hand which was capable of establishing an express agreement or an express representation that Mrs. Rosset was to have an interest in the property and evidence on the other hand of conduct alone as a basis for an inference of the necessary common intention." *Appeal allowed.*

YAXLEY v. GOTTS

Court of Appeal [2000] Ch. 162, [2000] 1 All E.R. 711

ROBERT WALKER L.J.

Proprietary estoppel and constructive trusts

At a high level of generality, there is much common ground between the **6–173** doctrines of proprietary estoppel and the constructive trust, just as there is between proprietary estoppel and part performance. All are concerned with equity's intervention to provide relief against unconscionable conduct, whether as between neighbouring landowners, or vendor and purchaser, or relatives who make informal arrangements for sharing a home, or a fiduciary and the beneficiary or client to whom he owes a fiduciary obligation. The overlap between estoppel and part performance has been thoroughly examined in the defendants' written submissions, with a survey of authorities from *Gregory v Mighell* (1811) 18 Ves 328 to *Take Harvest Ltd v Liu* [1993] AC 552.

The overlap between estoppel and the constructive trust was less fully covered in counsel's submissions but seems to me to be of central importance to the determination of this appeal. Plainly there are large areas where the two concepts do not overlap: when a landowner stands by while his neighbour mistakenly builds on the former's land the situation is far removed (except for the element of unconscionable conduct) from that of a fiduciary who derives an improper advantage from his client. But in the area of a joint enterprise for the acquisition of land (which may be, but is not necessarily, the matrimonial home) the two concepts coincide. Lord Diplock's very well-known statement in *Gissing v Gissing* [1971] AC 886 at 905 brings this out:

> "A resulting, implied or constructive trust—and it is unnecessary for **6–174** present purposes to distinguish between these three classes of trust—is created by a transaction between the trustee and the cestui que trust in connection with the acquisition by the trustee of a legal estate in land, whenever the trustee has so conducted himself that it would be inequitable to allow him to deny to the cestui que trust a beneficial interest in the land acquired. And he will be held so to have conducted himself if by his words or conduct he has induced the cestui que trust to act to his own detriment in the reasonable belief that by so acting he was acquiring a beneficial interest in the land."

Similarly Lord Bridge said in *Lloyds Bank plc v Rosset* [1991] 1 AC 107 at 132:

6–175   "The first and fundamental question which must always be resolved is whether, independently of any inference to be drawn from the conduct of the parties in the course of sharing the house as their home and managing their joint affairs, there has at any time prior to acquisition, or exceptionally at some later date, been any agreement, arrangement or understanding reached between them that the property is to be shared beneficially. The finding of an agreement or arrangement to share in this sense can only, I think, be based on evidence of express discussions between the partners, however imperfectly remembered and however imprecise their terms may have been. Once a finding to this effect is made it will only be necessary for the partner asserting a claim to a beneficial interest against the partner entitled to the legal estate to show that he or she has acted to his or her detriment or significantly altered his or her position in reliance on the agreement in order to give rise to a constructive trust or proprietary estoppel."

6–176   It is unnecessary to trace the vicissitudes in the development of the constructive trust between these two landmark authorities, except to note the important observations made by Browne-Wilkinson V-C in *Grant v Edwards* [1986] Ch 638 at 656, where he said:

"I suggest that, in other cases of this kind, useful guidance may in the future be obtained from the principles underlying the law of proprietary estoppel which in my judgment are closely akin to those laid down in *Gissing v Gissing*. In both, the claimant must to the knowledge of the legal owner have acted in the belief that the claimant has or will obtain an interest in the property. In both, the claimant must have acted to his or her detriment in reliance on such belief. In both, equity acts on the conscience of the legal owner to prevent him from acting in an unconscionable manner by defeating the common intention. The two principles have been developed separately without cross-fertilisation between them; but they rest on the same foundation and have on all other matters reached the same conclusions."

6–177   In this case the judge did not make any finding as to the existence of a constructive trust. He was not asked to do so, because it was not then seen as an issue in the case. But on the findings of fact which the judge did make it was not disputed that a proprietary estoppel arose, and that the appropriate remedy was the grant to Mr Yaxley, in satisfaction of his equitable entitlement, of a long leasehold interest, rent free, of the ground floor of the property. Those findings do in my judgment equally provide the basis for the conclusion that Mr Yaxley was entitled to such an interest under a constructive trust. The oral bargain which the judge found to have been made between Mr Yaxley and Mr Brownie Gotts, and to have been adopted by Mr Alan Gotts, was definite enough to meet the test stated by Lord Bridge in *Lloyds Bank plc v Rosset* [1991] 1 AC 107 at 132.

6–178   To recapitulate briefly: the species of constructive trust based on "common intention" is established by what Lord Bridge in *Lloyds Bank plc v Rosset* [1991] 1 AC 107 at 132 called an "agreement, arrangement or understanding" actually reached between the parties, and relied on and acted on by the claimant. A constructive trust of that sort is closely akin to, if not indistinguishable from, proprietary estoppel. Equity enforces it because it would be unconscionable for

the other party to disregard the claimant's rights. Section 2(5) expressly saves the creation and operation of a constructive trust.
Clarke LJ. . . .

(2) Constructive trust

I entirely agree with Robert Walker LJ's analysis under this head. I also agree **6–179** that it follows from the findings of fact made by the judge that the plaintiff was entitled to a long leasehold interest under a constructive trust. I also agree with his construction of s 2(5) of the Law Reform (Miscellaneous Provisions) Act 1989. Since s 2(5) expressly provides that nothing in s 2 affects the creation or operation of a constructive trust, it follows that nothing in s 2(1) prevents the plaintiff from relying upon the constructive trust created by the facts which have been summarised by both Beldam and Robert Walker LJJ. I agree that the appeal should be dismissed on this basis.
Beldam LJ. . . .

For my part I cannot see that there is any reason to qualify the plain words of s **6–180** 2(5). They were included to preserve the equitable remedies to which the Commission had referred. I do not think it inherent in a social policy of simplifying conveyancing by requiring the certainty of a written document that unconscionable conduct or equitable fraud should be allowed to prevail.

In my view the provision that nothing in s 2 of the 1989 Act is to affect the creation or operation of resulting, implied or constructive trusts effectively excludes from the operation of the section cases in which an interest in land might equally well be claimed by relying on constructive trust or proprietary estoppel.

That, to my mind, is the case here. There was on the judge's findings, as I interpret them, a clear promise made by Brownie Gotts to the plaintiff that he would have a beneficial interest in the ground floor of the premises. That promise was known to Alan Gotts when he acquired the property and he permitted the plaintiff to carry out the whole of the work needed to the property and to convert the ground floor in the belief that he had such an interest. It would be unconscionable to allow either Alan or Brownie Gotts to resile from the representations made by Brownie Gotts and adopted by Alan Gotts. For my part I would hold that the plaintiff established facts on which a court of equity would find that Alan Gotts held the property subject to a constructive trust in favour of the plaintiff for an interest in the ground floor and that that interest should be satisfied by the grant of a 99-year lease. I consider the judge was entitled to reach the same conclusion by finding a proprietary estoppel in favour of the plaintiff. I, too, would dismiss the appeal."

Appeal dismissed. Permission to appeal to the House of Lords refused.

MIDLAND BANK PLC v. COOKE

Court of Appeal [1995] 4 All E.R. 565.

WAITE L.J. (with whom SCHIEMANN and STUART-SMITH L.JJ. simply agreed): **6–181** "Mr Bergin, for the bank, contends as follows.

"(1) The evidence did not establish that the contribution made by Mr. Cooke's parents to the original purchase price of the property included any element of gift to Mrs. Cooke: it was a present to their son alone (this is the basis for the cross-appeal).

"(2) If that be wrong, and the parents' contribution is to be regarded as a gift to the spouses jointly, it is conceded that Mrs. Cooke would fall on that footing to be treated as a party who has contributed directly to the purchase price; but her beneficial interest is restricted, on basic principles of the law of resulting trusts, to the proportion borne by her cash contribution (£550) to the price of the property (£8,500). All her subsequent conduct, in the admitted absence of any further direct contribution to the purchase price on her part, is irrelevant, and can have no retrospective effect upon the quantification of her share.

"(3) If (contrary to (2)) subsequent conduct is prima facie capable of being taken into account as evidence from which the court could infer an implied agreement between the spouses that the proportions in which they share beneficial ownership should be different from the strict proportions resulting from direct contribution to the purchase price, no such agreed intention can be inferred in the present case because both spouses have stated on oath that they neither made nor intended any agreement—and the court cannot impute an agreement to parties who have expressly stated that there never was one.

"I will deal separately with those submissions.

(A) Was there a gift by Mr. Cooke's parents to both spouses?

6–182　　"The judge was in my view fully entitled, on the evidence which I have quoted, to hold that there was. In a case where the bride's parents were paying for the wedding and reception and the bridegroom's parents were providing a contribution to the purchase price of the matrimonial home, it would not only be sensible to draw the inference that the bridegroom's parents intended to make a present to them both of the moneys which were to be applied in the purchase, but highly artificial to draw any other inference.

(B) Is the proportion of Mrs. Cooke's beneficial interest to be fixed solely by reference to the percentage of the purchase price which she contributed directly, so as to make all other conduct irrelevant?

"In contending that it is, Mr. Bergin submits as follows.

6–183　　"(a) It is now well settled that in determining (in the absence of evidence of express agreement) whether a party unnamed in the deeds has any beneficial interest in the property at all the test is the stringent one stated by Lord Bridge of Harwich in *Lloyds Bank plc v. Rosset* [1991] 1 A.C. 107 at 133:

'In this situation direct contributions to the purchase price by the partner who is not the legal owner, whether initially or by payment of mortgage instalments, will readily justify the inference necessary to the creation of a constructive trust. But, as I read the authorities, it is at least extremely doubtful whether anything less will do.'

(b) By parity of reasoning, in cases where a direct contribution has been duly proved by the partner who is not the legal owner (thus establishing a resulting trust in his or her favour of *some* part of the beneficial interest) the proportion of that share will be fixed at the proportion it bears to the overall price of the property. Although the proportion may be enlarged by subsequent contribution to the purchase price, such contributions must be direct—*i.e.* further cash payments or contribution to the capital element in instalment repayments of any mortgage under which the unpaid proportion of the purchase remains secured. Nothing less will do.

"Mr. Bergin derives support for that submission from *Springette v. Defoe* [1992] **6–184**
2 F.L.R. 388. That was a case where cohabitees of mature years bought in their
joint names (so there was no dispute that they both had some beneficial interest)
a council house of which one of them had been the sitting tenant. After crediting
the former tenant with the discount in the purchase price attributable to her
rights as a sitting tenant and taking account of the contributions to that price
which each partner had made in cash, the proportions of their initial contributions stood at 75 per cent to 25 per cent. Part of the purchase price was provided
by a mortgage, and by express agreement the parties contributed to the mortgage
instalments equally. The judge held that the beneficial interests were equal. He
was overruled on appeal, where it was held that the parties were beneficially
entitled in the proportions of 75 per cent to 25 per cent. Dillon L.J. said in
regard to the common intention to be imputed to the parties, in the absence of
express agreement, as to what their precise shares should be (at 393):

> 'The common intention must be founded on evidence such as would **6–185**
> support a finding that there is an implied or constructive trust for the
> parties in proportions to the purchase price. The court does not as yet sit,
> as under a palm tree, to exercise a general discretion to do what the man
> in the street, on a general overview of the case, might regard as fair . . .
> Since, therefore, it is clear in the present case that there never was any
> discussion between the parties about what their respective beneficial
> interests were to be, they cannot, in my judgment, have had in any relevant
> sense any common intention as to the beneficial ownership of the property
> . . . The presumption of a resulting trust is not displaced.'

"The decision has to be compared with *McHardy v. Warren* [1994] 2 F.L.R. **6–186**
338, a case in which (as here) it became necessary to quantify the interests of
husband and wife on a strict equitable basis because of third party claims against
the property. The purchase of the first matrimonial home was (again, as in this
case) partly financed by a contribution from the husband's parents, but with the
difference that in that instance the husband's parents paid the whole of the
deposit (using that term in the sense of the net purchase price not covered by a
mortgage) for the property, which was registered in the husband's sole name.
The two subsequent homes successively purchased by the parties out of the net
proceeds of sale of the former home were similarly taken in his name alone. The
husband then executed a charge on the current home to secure his indebtedness
to the plaintiffs, who were trade creditors. In proceedings by the plaintiffs against
both husband and wife to enforce their charge, the plaintiffs asserted that the
wife either had no beneficial interest or at most an interest equivalent to 8.97 per
cent, representing the proportion that half the initial deposit of £650 bore to the
total purchase price of the first home. The judge rejected that claim, holding that
the parties were beneficially entitled in equal shares. He was upheld on appeal. It
does not appear from the law report that *Springette v. Defoe* was cited, but the
presiding Lord Justice was again Dillon L.J. who said (at 340):

> 'To my mind it is the irresistible conclusion that where a parent pays the **6–187**
> deposit, either directly or to the solicitors or to the bride and groom, it
> matters not which, on the purchase of their first matrimonial home, it is
> the intention of all three of them that the bride and groom should have
> equal interests in the matrimonial home, not interests measured by the
> reference to the percentage half the deposit [bears] to the full price . . .'

"I confess that I find the differences of approach in those two cases mystifying. In the one a strict resulting trust geared to mathematical calculation of the proportion of the purchase price provided by cash contribution is treated as virtually immutable in the absence of express agreement: in the other a displacement of the cash-related trust by inferred agreement is not only permitted but treated as obligatory. Guidance out of this difficulty is to be found, fortunately, in the passage in the speech of Lord Diplock in *Gissing v. Gissing* [1971] A.C. 886 at 908–909, where he is dealing with the approach to be adopted by the court when evaluating the proportionate shares of the parties, once it had been duly established through the direct contributions of the party without legal title, that *some* beneficial interest was intended for both. He said:

6–188   'Where in any of the circumstances described above contributions, direct or indirect, have been made to the mortgage instalments by the spouse into whose name the matrimonial home has not been conveyed, and the court can infer from their conduct a common intention that the contributing spouse should be entitled to *some* beneficial interest in the matrimonial home, what effect is to be given to that intention if there is no evidence that they in fact reached any express agreement as to what the respective share of each spouse should be? I take it to be clear that if the court is

6–189   satisfied that it was the common intention of both spouses that the contributing wife should have a share in the beneficial interest and that her contributions were made on this understanding, the court in the exercise of its equitable jurisdiction would not permit the husband in whom the legal estate was vested and who had accepted the benefit of the contributions to take the whole beneficial interest merely because at the time the wife made her contributions there had been no express agreement as to how her share in it was to be quantified. In such a case the court must first do its best to discover from the conduct of spouses whether any inference can reasonably be drawn as to the probable common understanding about the amount of the share of the contributing spouse on which each must have acted in doing what each did, even though that understanding was never expressly stated by one spouse to the other or even consciously formulated in words by either of them independently. It is only if no such inference can be drawn that the court is driven to apply as a rule of law, and not as an inference of fact, the maxim "equality is equity", and to hold that the beneficial interest belongs to the spouses in equal shares. The same result however may often be reached as an inference of fact. The instalments of a mortgage to a building society are generally repayable over a period of many years. During that period, as both must be aware, the ability of each spouse to contribute to the instalments out of their separate earnings is likely to alter, particular in the case of the wife if any children are born of

6–190   the marriage. If the contribution of the wife in the early part of the period of repayment is substantial but is not an identifiable and uniform proportion of each instalment, it may well be a reasonable inference that their common intention at the time of acquisition of the matrimonial home was that the beneficial interest should be held by them in equal shares and that each should contribute to the cost of its acquisition whatever amounts each could afford in the varying exigencies of family life to be expected during the period of repayment. In the social conditions of today this would be a natural enough common intention of a young couple who were both earning when the house was acquired but who contemplated having children whose birth and rearing in their infancy would necessarily affect the future earning capacity of the wife. The relative size of their respective contributions to the instalments in the early part of the period of repayment, or later if a subsequent reduction in the wife's contribution is not to be accounted for by a reduction in her earnings due to motherhood or some other cause from which the husband benefits as well, may make it a more probable inference that the wife's share in the beneficial interest was intended to be in some proportion other than one-half. And there is nothing inherently improbable in their acting on the understanding that the wife should be entitled to a share which was not to be quantified immediately on the acquisition of the home but should be left to be determined when the mortgage was repaid or the property disposed of, on the basis of what would be fair having regard to the total contributions, direct or indirect, which each spouse had made by that date. Where this was the most likely inference from their conduct it would be for the court to give effect to that common intention of the parties by determining what in all the circumstances was a fair share. Difficult as they **6–191** are to solve, however, these problems as to the amount of the share of a spouse in the beneficial interest in a matrimonial home where the legal estate is vested solely in the other spouse, only arise in cases where the court is satisfied by the words or conduct of the parties that it was their common intention that the beneficial interest was not to belong solely to the spouse in whom the legal estate was vested but was to be shared between them in some proportion or other.'

"The decision of this court in *Grant v. Edwards* [1986] Ch. 638 also affords **6–192** helpful guidance. The context was different, in that the court was there dealing with a legal owner who has made representations to the occupier on which the latter has relied to her detriment so as to introduce equities in the nature of estoppel. Once a beneficial interest had been established by that route, however, the court then proceeded—to fix the proportions of all the beneficial interests on general grounds which were regarded as applying in all cases. That appears from the judgments of Nourse L.J. ([1986] Ch. 638 at 650) and of Browne-Wilkinson V.-C., where (after citing the passage I have quoted from Lord Diplock in *Gissing v. Gissing*) he says:

'Where, as in this case, the existence of some beneficial interest in the **6–193** claimant has been shown, prima facie the interest of the claimant will be that which the parties intended: see *Gissing v. Gissing* [1971] A.C. 886 at 908. In *Eves v. Eves* [1975] 1 W.L.R. 1338 at 1345 Brightman L.J. plainly felt that a common intention that there should be a joint interest pointed to the beneficial interests being equal. However, he felt able to find a lesser beneficial interest in that case without explaining the legal basis on which he did so. With diffidence, I suggest that the law of proprietary estoppel may again provide useful guidance. If proprietary estoppel is established, the court gives effect to it by giving effect to the common intention so far as may fairly be done between the parties. For that purpose, equity is displayed at its most flexible: see *Crabb v. Arun D.C.* [1976] Ch. 179. Identifiable contributions to the purchase of the house will of course be an important factor in many cases. But in other cases, contributions by way of the labour or other unquantifiable actions of the claimant will also be relevant. Taking into account the fact that the house was intended to be the joint property, the contributions to the common expenditure and the payment of the fire insurance moneys into the joint account, I agree that the plaintiff is entitled to a half interest in the house.' (See [1986] Ch. 638 at 657–658.)

6–194   "The general principle to be derived from *Gissing v. Gissing* and *Grant v. Edwards* can in my judgment be summarised in this way. When the court is proceeding, in cases like the present where the partner without legal title has successfully asserted an equitable interest through direct contribution, to determine (in the absence of express evidence of intention) what proportions the parties must be assumed to have intended for their beneficial ownership, the duty of the judge is to undertake a survey of the whole course of dealing between the parties relevant to their ownership and occupation of the property and their sharing of its burdens and advantages. That scrutiny will not confine itself to the limited range of acts of direct contribution of the sort that are needed to found a beneficial interest in the first place. It will take into consideration all conduct which throws light on the question what shares were intended. Only if that search proves inconclusive does the court fall back on the maxim that 'equality is equity'.

6–195   "My answer to question B would therefore be No. The court is not bound to deal with the matter on the strict basis of the trust resulting from the cash contribution to the purchase price, and is free to attribute to the parties an intention to share the beneficial interest in some different proportions.

"Mr. Bergin submits, however, that in the particular circumstances of this case, that is an approach which the court is precluded from following by the evidence of actual intention given by the spouses themselves.

(C) Can an agreement be attributed by inference of law to parties who have expressly stated that they reached no agreement?

6–196   "Mr. Bergin begins by pointing out (rightly) that this is an area of the law in which there is no scope for discretion. The entire jurisdiction rests upon the very limited exception provided by Parliament to the general requirement in s.53 of the Law of Property Act 1925 that trusts must be evidenced in writing. It is an exception in favour of trusts that are 'resulting, implied or constructive'. Mr. Bergin then submits that the resulting trust is that which results from a contribution to the purchase price, and prima facie that fixes the proportion of the beneficial interest. Any implied or constructive trust relied on to alter or enlarge that prima facie entitlement must rest upon an imputed agreement inferred from conduct by equity. If the parties themselves testify on oath that they made no agreement, there is no scope for equity to make one for them.

6–197   "That is a submission which, if it fell to be considered without assistance from authority, I would reject instinctively on the ground that it runs counter to the very system of law—equity—on which it seeks to rely. Equity has traditionally been a system which matches established principle to the demands of social change. The mass diffusion of home ownership has been one of the most striking social changes of our own time. The present case is typical of hundreds, perhaps even thousands, of others. When people, especially young people, agree to share their lives in joint homes they do so on a basis of mutual trust and in the expectation that their relationship will endure. Despite the efforts that have been made by many responsible bodies to counsel prospective cohabitants as to the risks of taking shared interests in property without legal advice, it is unrealistic to expect that adice to be followed on a universal scale. For a couple embarking on a serious relationship, discussion of the terms to apply at parting is almost a contradition of the shared hopes that have brought them together. There will inevitably be numerous couples, married or unmarried, who have no discussions about ownership and who, perhaps advisedly, make no agreement about it. It would be anomalous, against that background, to create a range of home-buyers who were beyond the pale of equity's assistance in formulating a fair presumed basis for the sharing of beneficial title, simply because they had been honest enough to admit that they never gave ownership a thought or reached any agreement about it.

"Mr. Bergin submits, however, that his proposition is supported by authority. **6–198** He relies upon the passage already quoted from the judgment of Dillon L.J. in *Springette v. Defoe* [1992] 2 F.L.R. 388 at 393. He also relies on the judgment in ther same case of Steyn L.J. . . . commented as follows (at 395):

> 'The assistant recorder had already found as a matter of fact that no such common intention was communicated between the parties. The simple answer to the man's case is that there was no communicated common intention. Given that no actual intention to share the property in equal beneficial shares was established, one is driven back to the equitable principle that the shares are presumed to be in proportion to the contributions.'

"These observations of Dillon and Steyn L.JJ. (with which Sir Christopher Slade agreed) are of course entitled to the highest respect, and if they formed part of the ratio of the decision would be binding on us. But they are observations which need to be read in the context of a decision relating to the part-pooling of resources by a middle-aged couple already established in life whose house-purchasing arrangements were clearly regarded by the court as having the same formality as if they had been the subject of a joint venture or commercial partnership. I cannot for my part believe that it was intended in that case to lay down a principle, applicable to all instances, that absence of express agreement precluded inference of presumed agreement. This impression is confirmed by the subsequent participation of Dillon L.J. in the decision in the *McHardy* case.

"I would therefore hold that positive evidence that the parties neither **6–199** discussed nor intended any agrement as to the proportions of their beneficial interest does not preclude the court, on general equitable principles, from inferring one.

Conclusion

"It follows from the answers I have given to the last two questions that the judge was in my view in error when he proceeded to treat the cash contribution to the purchase price as wholly determinative of the issue of the current proportions of beneficial entitlement, without regard to the other factors emerging from the whole course of dealing between the husband and wife.

"When the proper approach (that is to say the approach I have summarised in **6–200** dealing with question B) is applied to the present case, I have little doubt as to what the answer should be. Mrs. Cooke is a wife who in addition to bringing up three children (one of whom is still only 11) was working full or part-time as a teacher and paying out her earnings in relief of household bills. When a second charge was taken out on the property within a few months after the marriage, she undertook joint and several liability to repay it. When her husband wanted her to sign the consent form in respect of the mortgage to the bank for the benefit of his business, she did so, despite the anxiety and distress which provided part of the grounds for the judge's ruling that it had been obtained by undue influence. Thereafter she again undertook liability under a second charge on the property for the benefit of his business. One could hardly have a clearer example of a couple who had agreed to share everything equally: the profits of his business while it prospered, and the risk of indebtedness suffered through its failure; the upbringing of their children; the rewards of her own career as a teacher; and, most relevantly, a home into which he had put his savings and to which she was to give over the years the benefit of the maintenance and improvement contribution. When to all that there is added the fact (still an important one) that this was a couple who had chosen to introduce into their relationship the additional commitment which marriage involves, the conclusion becomes inescapable that their presumed intention was to share the beneficial interest in the property in equal shares. I reach this result without the need to rely on any equitable maxim as to equality.

6–201   "For all these reasons I would allow the appeal and substitute for the declaration granted by the judge a declaration that Mrs. Cooke has a beneficial one-half interest in the property."

QUESTIONS

6–202   1.   "If legal title is taken in the names of both M and F, F is bound to obtain a fair share at the very least. Indeed, even where the legal title is taken only in M's name, if F pays part of the deposit it seems very likely that she will obtain a fair share that will be larger than an interest under a resulting trust corresponding to the proportion between the amount she paid towards the deposit and the total purchase price. It is only if she paid nothing towards the deposit and there was no agreement between M and her that she was to take responsibility to him for part of the mortgage taken on by him as sole legal owner, that the courts have difficulty preventing M from insisting on 100 per cent beneficial ownership." Discuss.

6–203   2.   Fifteen years ago, Martin purchased a freehold house in Shrewsbury (which was not then a compulsory registration of title area) for £100,000 of which £75,000 was borrowed by way of a legal mortgage in favour of the Greenwich BS which retained the title deeds to the house. Four years ago, he and Fiona decided to cohabit but first had a long weekend in Dublin before he carried her over the threshold of the house, saying, "This house is now as much yours as mine." "How wonderful," she replied, feeling reassured because a week earlier she had given notice to quit her protected tenancy of a flat.

She continued working as a hair tinter but used her money to buy clothes for herself and to buy holidays and restaurant dinners for herself and Martin because he refused to let her use her money to help pay the mortgage or other household outgoings. However, two years ago Martin was dismissed from his job, although within a week he obtained new employment at half his former salary.

Fiona then offered to pay half the monthly mortgage instalments but Martin refused this, telling her instead that it was simpler if he just used his money to pay the mortgage while she used her money for the other expenses of their cohabitation. Six months ago Fiona left Martin, who had been drinking and gambling too much, and moved in with Roderick. In this 18 months period Martin paid out £15,000 to cover the mortgage while Fiona paid £15,000 for other household outgoings. Of the mortgage payments £10,000 represented interest and £5,000 repayment of capital.

Martin is now bankrupt. His house is worth £300,000 but Fiona has just discovered that not only is there the original mortgage (though now only to secure £40,000) but there is a three-year-old legal mortgage for £150,000 in favour of Fairdeal Finance Co. and a one-year-old legal mortgage for £100,000 in favour of Martin's brother, Julian, who works in New York and made no inspection of the house. Fairdeal's surveyor inspected the house when Fiona was away on a residential course but commented to Martin on some feminine bits and pieces on a dressing table. Martin replied that he kept them as a memento of his recently-deceased wife.

Advise Fiona on her rights.

Would your answer differ if on carrying her over the threshold Martin had said, "This house is as much yours as mine so long as you'll help out as best you can with mortgage payments and household bills whenever I need it," and Fiona had replied, "Of course my darling, I'll help as much as I can"?

3.   Kevin, a chef, lived with Sharon, a hairdresser, in a rented flat but they **6–204** had separate bank accounts. Upon hearing that Sharon was pregnant, Kevin's parents gave him £1,000 to enable him to put down a deposit on a £10,000 flat of which he became registered proprietor twenty years ago subject to a registered charge for £9,000 in favour of Bigg Building Society. When the baby was born Sharon gave up her job and her separate bank account. She subsequently had two more children by Kevin.

Eight years ago Sharon returned to work, receiving a weekly pay packet. She used the money for housekeeping and holidays. This afforded Kevin the opportunity to take on and service a further loan from Bigg Building Society of £40,000 secured on the flat so that he and his mistress, Lucy, a keen gambler and cocaine user, could have a good time. She dropped him when the money was spent. Kevin took solace in alcohol and was then sacked from his job four years ago and has not worked since.

Fortunately, at this time Sharon became manageress of the hair salon where she worked. At her suggestion, "Because I love you, you silly sausage, and we have to keep the building society happy," his bank account was made into a joint account into which she had her salary paid and out of which the mortgage instalments continued to be paid. He alone monitored the monthly bank statements.

To finance his gambling habits, Kevin mortgaged the flat two years ago to Great Finance plc to secure a loan of £50,000, having forged financial references. Sharon has now discovered that all the £40,000 remaining due to Bigg Building Society represents the further loan of £40,000 of which she knew nothing, Kevin having told Bigg Building Society that he was living on his own as a bachelor and its surveyor visiting the flat when Sharon was at work. This was also the case for Great Finance plc (now owed £60,000 including interest) whose mortgage Sharon has also just discovered. The value of the flat is only £100,000.

Sharon and Kevin never discussed ownership of the flat though in conversation with friends they habitually referred to it as "our flat" or "our home".

Sharon seeks your advice as to whether she may have any interest in the flat and what considerations will determine whether any interest will bind Bigg Building Society and Great Finance plc.

To what extent would your answer differ if it was upon the marriage of Kevin and Sharon that Kevin's parents provided Kevin with the £1,000 deposit?

Section 4. The Vendor as Constructive Trustee[52]

6–205   Once a vendor has received the purchase price for his land[53] it is clear that he holds it on constructive trust for the purchaser until he has transferred title to the purchaser. As an exceptional *sui generis* matter even when a vendor enters into a specifically enforceable contract for the sale of property he becomes a modified constructive trustee thereof for the purchaser until the contract is completed by a conveyance of the property.[54] "Equity regards as done that which ought to be done" but the doctrine of conversion does not operate until the vendor has made title in accordance with the contract or the purchaser has agreed to accept a title not in accordance with the contract. Once conversion has so occurred its operation is retrospective from the date of the contract.[55]

6–206   The vendor has to "use reasonable care to preserve the property in a reasonable state of preservation, and, so far as may be, as it was when the contract was made" or "to take reasonable care that the property is not deteriorated in the interval before completion."[56] This may be exploited by a purchaser upon whom a vendor has served a notice to complete[57] making time of the essence of the contract: the purchaser can claim that the notice was invalid because the vendor was not ready, able and willing to complete the contract owing to breach of his equitable duty of preservation.[58] However, if the contract goes off the vendor cannot be liable to the purchaser for failing to preserve the property.[59]

6–207   Till completion the vendor is a quasi-trustee with a highly interested trusteeship: he has a paramount right to protect his own interest.[60] He is entitled to keep the rents and profits till the date fixed for completion[61] and to retain possession of the property until the contract is completed by payment of the price.[62] If he parts with possession to the purchaser before actual completion or even conveys the land he may fall back on his equitable lien to ensure that he is paid.[63] If the vendor in breach of

---

[52] Barnsley's *Conveyancing Law and Practice* (3rd ed.) at 226–238; Oakley's *Constructive Trusts*, Chap. 6; M. Cope, *Constructive Trusts* (Law Book Co. of Australia 1992) Chap. 25.

[53] Or other property of such a special character that a contract for such property will be specifically enforceable: *Oughtred v. IRC* [1960] A.C. 206.

[54] *Wall v. Bright* (1820) 1 Jac. & W. 494 at 503; *Royal British P.B.S. v. Bomash* (1887) 35 Ch.D. 390 at 397; *Rayner v. Preston* (1881) 18 Ch.D. 1 at 6. For conflicting views of Stamp and Goff L.JJ. on a sub-purchaser's position see *Berkeley v. Poulett* (1977) 241 Est. Gaz. 911; 242 Est. Gaz. 39.

[55] *Lysaght v. Edwards* (1876) 2 Ch.D. 499 at 506–507. The Trusts of Land and Appointment of Trustees Act 1996 negatives the doctrine of conversion for trusts for sale.

[56] *Clarke v. Ramuz* [1891] 2 Q.B. 456 at 460, 468; *Davron Estates Ltd v. Turnshire* (1983) 133 New L.J. 937; risk, however, passes to the purchaser after exchange of contracts in so far as concerns anything not caused by a breach of the vendor's duties: *Rayner v. Preston* (1881) 18 Ch.D. 1 (affected by Law of Property Act 1925, s.47, now) unless under the contract the vendor retains the risk as under the Standard Conditions of Sale, Condition 5.1. (subject to contrary agreement).

[57] Standard Conditions of Sale, Condition 6.6.

[58] Purchasers have taken this point where squatters have managed to break into the property the subject of the contract: so far the cases appear to have been settled without the need to spend days in court arguing whether or not the vendor's precautions were reasonable.

[59] *Plews v. Samuel* [1904] 1 Ch. 464; *Ridoul v. Fowler* [1904] 1 Ch. 658; [1904] 2 Ch. 93.

[60] *Shaw v. Foster* (1872) L.R. 5 H.L. 321 at 338; *Re Watford Corporation's Contract* [1943] Ch. 82 at 85.

[61] *Cuddon v. Tite* (1858) 1 Giff. 395.

[62] *Gedge v. Montrose* (1858) 26 Beav. 45; *Phillips v. Silvester* (1872) L.R. 8 Ch. 173.

[63] *Nives v. Nives* (1880) 15 Ch.D. 649; *Re Birmingham* [1959] Ch. 523; *London & Cheshire Insurance Co. Ltd v. Laplagrene* [1971] Ch. 499.

the constructive trust sells the property to X, the purchaser may trace the property into the proceeds of sale received by the vendor subject to accounting to the vendor for the price agreed between them. This will be useful if the contractual claim against the vendor for damages is not worthwhile, *e.g.* if he is bankrupt or more financial benefit can be obtained from the tracing claim than the damages claim.[64]

A vendor of shares in an unquoted company can use his votes to protect his lien for the price but, because he is a fiduciary, he cannot use them for any purpose that might damage the purchaser.[65]

---

[64] *Lake v. Bayliss* [1974] 1 W.L.R. 1073.
[65] *Michaels v. Harley House (Marylebone) Ltd* [2000] Ch. 104.

Chapter 7

CHARITABLE (OR PUBLIC) TRUSTS[1]

Section 1. The Advantages of Charity

Tax advantages

7–01   United Kingdom[2] charities do not pay income tax on their investment income which is applicable to charitable purposes only and is in fact applied solely for those purposes.[3] They can recover basic rate or corporation tax paid by donors in respect of four year covenants drawn up in their favour[4] or in respect of any gifts under the gift aid scheme.[5] Where trading income is concerned, however, they are only exempt from tax if either the trade is exercised in the course of the actual carrying out of a primary purpose of the charity or the work in connection with the trade is mainly carried out by beneficiaries of the charity.[6]

7–02   Charities do not pay capital gains tax in respect of gains made upon disposals by them[7] and individuals are encouraged to make *inter vivos* gifts to charities since no charge to capital gains tax arises upon such gifts.[8] Where inheritance tax is concerned transfers to charities are exempt.[9] Charities can obtain 80 per cent relief as of right in respect of non-domestic rates for premises wholly or mainly used for charitable purposes and some discretionary relief in respect of the rest.[10] Charities are also exempt in respect of stamp duty[11] but only have a very few

---

[1] *Tudor on Charities* and Picarda's *The Law and Practice to Charities* are the authoritative legal works. The recent P. Luxton, *Law of Charities* (2001) is also very useful. Goodman Committee: *Charity Law and Voluntary Organisations* (1976); Wolfenden Committee: *The Future of Voluntary Organisations*; Chesterman; *Charities, Trusts and Social Welfare*; F. Gladstone, *Charity Law and Social Justice*; 16th Report of Committee of Public Accounts 1987–88; Charities: *A Framework for the future* (1989) Cm. 694 (Government White Paper) Deakin Report, *Meeting the Challenge of Change* (1996).

[2] *Camille and Henry Dreyfus Foundation Inc. v. I.R.C.* [1956] A.C. 39.

[3] Income and Corporation Taxes Act 1988, ss.505, 506. See *I.R.C. v. Educational Grants Association Ltd* [1967] Ch. 123, *infra*, para. 7–122.

[4] I.C.T.A. 1988, ss.660, 683, Finance Act 1989, ss.56, 59. Money can also be given (with tax relief) by employees under a payroll deduction scheme: I.C.T.A. 1988, s.202, Finance Act 2000 s. 41.

[5] Finance Act 1990 ss.25, 26 as amended by Finance Act 2000 s.39.

[6] I.C.T.A. 1988, s.505; G. N. Glover [1972] B.T.R. 346. If substantial trading is being carried on which is not within the exemption the charity may form a company to run the trade and have the company covenant to pay its net profits to the charity for a period capable of exceeding 3 years; the company then deducts the payment as a charge on income for the purposes of corporation tax: I.C.T.A. 1988, s.338(5)(6)(8). By concession the Revenue do not charge tax in respect of profits from occasional fund-raising bazaars, jumble sales, etc. Further see Trading by Charities; Guidelines on the Tax Treatment of Trades carried out by Charities (CS2) produced by Inland Revenue; and CC 35—Charities and Trading produced by Charity Commission.

[7] I.C.T.A. 1970, s.345(2); Taxation of Chargeable Gains Act 1992, s.256.

[8] T.C.G.A. 1992, s.257. The value of gifted shares is also deductible against taxable income.

[9] Inheritance Tax Act 1988, s.23.

[10] Local Government Finance Act 1988, ss.43, 47, 64.

[11] F.A. 1982, s.129.

reliefs from value added tax[12] in prescribed circumstances e.g. relating to medical supplies.

The fiscal advantages of charities are such that in 1997 terms over **7–03** £1,700 million tax is lost to the Exchequer each year and probably over £500 million rates is lost to the rating authorities each year.[13] By making up the loss the taxpayer and the ratepayer are subsidising all sorts of charities and so have a direct personal interest in the integrity and efficiency of charities: as one-man's philanthropy is another man's tax burden it is only right that legal safeguards should exist to ensure that there is proper philanthropy properly carried out. The Charity Commission's Annual Report 1999–2000 estimated the total gross income of registered charities in that year to be £24 thousand million. There are over 185,000 registered charities and about 110,000 excepted or exempt from registration. Positive Government funding (directly or indirectly) of charities amounts to over £2,000 million a year, quite apart from the tax subsidy.

Trust law advantages

Charitable trusts have further advantages in that they are not subject **7–04** to the rule against inalienability[14] that applies exclusively to pure purpose trusts and, to the extent that a charity might be a company or regarded as a trust for purposes benefiting individuals with locus standi to sue, it enjoys one limited exemption from the rule against remoteness. At common law a gift over from one person to another that might possibly take effect outside the perpetuity period was void.[15] However, a gift over from one charity to another charity was valid, the property being treated as belonging to charity throughout so as not to be caught by the rule against remoteness,[16] if that rule be applicable as opposed to the rule against inalienability from which charities are in any event exempt.[17] If the gift were a gift over from a charity to a non-charity[18] or from a non-charity to a charity[19] then the rule against remoteness applied. Since the Perpetuities and Accumulations Act 1964 came into force it is now possible in these two latter instances to wait and see[20] when the gift over takes effect: if it takes effect within the perpetuity period then it is good, if not it is bad and the first gift becomes absolute, no longer subject to defeasance or determination.[21] Of course, the validity of gifts over from one charity to another charity is unaffected by the 1964 Act.

---

[12] Value Added Tax Act 1994, Sched. 8, Group 15 and Sched. 9 Groups 7, 8, 10, 12.
[13] Treasury Press Statement, July 2, 1997. See White Paper: Charities: A Framework for the Future (1989) Cm. 694, para. 1 for the 1988 position.
[14] *e.g. Re Banfield* [1968] 1 W.L.R. 846 compared with *Re Warre's W.T.* [1953] 1 W.L.R. 725 or *Re Gwyon* [1930] 1 Ch. 255; see *infra*. n.17.
[15] *Re Frost* (1889) 43 Ch.D. 246.
[16] *Christ's Hospital v. Grainger* (1849) 1 Mac. & G. 460; *Re Tyler* [1891] 3 Ch. 252.
[17] The two rules are mutually exclusive, hence the 1964 Perpetuities & Accumulations Act did not need to deal also with the rule against inalienability to save trusts for persons: see *supra*, at para. 3–193.
[18] *Re Bowen* [1893] 2 Ch. 491.
[19] *Re Dalziel* [1943] Ch. 277; *Re Peel's Release* [1921] 2 Ch. 218.
[20] Perpetuities and Accumulations Act 1964, s.3.
[21] P.A.A. 1964, s.12 treats determinable interests in the same way as conditional interests.

7–05   Furthermore, a charitable trust is valid though a pure purpose trust because the Attorney-General can enforce it, and the trust requirement of certainty of objects is satisfied so long as the settlor manifested a general charitable intention to enable a *cy-près* scheme to be formulated for giving effect to his intention as nearly as possible.[22] Thus a trust "for world-wide charitable purposes" or "for poor persons" or "for the following charitable religious societies" without specifying any is valid, whilst a discretionary trust for everyone in the United Kingdom is void. The *cyprès* doctrine is peculiar to charitable trusts and will be dealt with at the end of this chapter. Finally, charitable trustees can act by a majority instead of unanimously which is the position for private trusts unless the trust deed authorises majority decisions.[23]

CHARITABLE COMPANIES

7–06   At this stage it might usefully be noted that a charity will often take the form of a charitable trust with individual or corporate trustees[24] but it may take the form of a company[25] incorporated under the Companies Act 1985, but limited by guarantee (rather than by shares geared to distributing profits to shareholders), with the charitable provisions in its memorandum of association. Such provisions will not be trusts in the strict equitable sense but will be "trusts" for the purposes of the Charities Act 1993 (concerned with the proper administration of charities) by virtue of section 97(1) thereof. Section 96 defines a charity as "any institution, corporate or not, which is established for charitable purposes and is subject to the control of the High Court in the exercise of the court's jurisdiction with respect to charities." A gift to a company which is incorporated under the Companies Acts, so that its general property is held for charitable purposes (without distinguishing between capital and income) without the intervention of trusts, is usually treated as intended to be held as an addition to the company's general property

---

[22] The court has inherent jurisdiction to resolve any problems of administrative unworkability so long as the settlor has manifested a general charitable intention. If the trust is one the administration of which the court could not undertake and control and no exclusively charitable intent appears so as to found a *cy-près* scheme then the trust fails: *Re Hummultenberg* [1923] 1 Ch. 237 (legacy to the treasurer of the London Spiritualistic Alliance for the purpose of establishing a college for the training of suitable persons as mediums); *Re Koeppler's W.T.* [1984] 2 All E.R. 111 (legacy to trustees for the formation of an informed international public opinion and the promotion of greater co-operation in Europe and the West, though held charitable in the Court of Appeal [1985] 2 All E.R. 869); *Att-Gen of Cayman Islands v. Wahr-Hansen* [2000] 3 All E.R. 642 (trust for organisations operating for the public good held void by Privy Council).

[23] *Re Whiteley* [1910] 1 Ch. 600 at 608. Yet another distinction is that the six year limitation period in Limitation Act 1980, s.21(3) applies to an action by a beneficiary under a trust but not an action by the Att.-Gen.: *Att.-Gen. v. Cocke* [1988] 2 All E.R. 391.

[24] Under sections 50 to 52 of the Charities Act 1993 the Individual-trustees may collectively become a body corporate (*e.g.* to make title holding easier by avoiding the need to transfer title to individuals becoming new trustees) but the trustees remain liable personally as if no incorporation had been effected: s.54 of 1993 Act. Further see CC 43 "Incorporation of Charity Trustees", produced by Charity Commission.

[25] See "The trust versus the company under the Charities Acts by Judith Hill in (1993–1994) Vol. 2 Charity Law & Practice Review reproduced in NLJ Xmas Appeals Supplement, December 16, 1994, pp. 22–32.

and not upon trusts unless the donor uses express words importing a trust.[26] Although a company can always change its objects clause in its memorandum under section 4 of the Companies Act 1985 it cannot do so without the prior written consent of the Charity Commissioners.[27] Of course, where property was gifted upon express (endowment or non-endowment) trusts then the company must always give effect to those trusts unless and until a *cy-près* scheme is finalised. A charitable company's own general property is also subject to the court's *cy-près* jurisdiction, *e.g.* on its winding up.[28] In the rare case where the Commissioners may allow a company to change its objects so as to cease to be a charity this cannot affect the application of any property acquired other than for full consideration or any property representing property so acquired or the income from any such property.[29]

Section 2. The Scope of Charity

1. INTRODUCTORY

The spirit and intendment of the 1601 preamble

Before the Statute of Charitable Uses 1601, the Court of Chancery **7–07** exercised jurisdiction in matters relating to charity (although in administering deceaseds' estates of personalty the ecclesiastical courts exercised a significant jurisdiction sanctioned by fines and excommunication), but notions of what was a charity were imprecise. The preamble to that statute contained a list of charitable objects which the courts used as "an index or chart" for the decision of particular cases, with the result that, in addition to the objects enumerated in the preamble, other objects analogous to them or within the spirit and intendment of the preamble came to be regarded as charitable: *see Scottish Burial Reform and Cremation Society v. Glasgow Corporation, infra*, at para. 7–23 holding the provision of crematoria charitable by analogy with the provision of burial grounds by analogy with the upkeep of churchyards by analogy with the repair of churches. This enables the courts to avoid direct assessment of the social worth of putative charitable trusts and to avoid overt value judgments.

The 1601 statute was enacted as part of a comprehensive poor law **7–08** code and provided for commissioners to be appointed to investigate misappropriations of charity property. Its preamble commenced: "Whereas lands, chattels, money have been given by sundry well disposed persons: some for the relief of aged, impotent and poor people; the maintenance of sick and maimed soldiers and mariners, schools of

---

[26] *Re Finger's W.T.* [1972] 1 Ch. 286 and see Charity Commissioners' Report for 1971, paras. 22–30.
[27] Charities Act 1993 s.64(2); also see s.66.
[28] *Liverpool and District Hospital v. Att.-Gen.* [1981] Ch. 193.
[29] Charities Act 1993 s.64(1).

learning, free schools, and scholars in universities; the repair of bridges, ports, havens, causeways, churches, sea banks and highways; the education and preferment of orphans; the relief, stock, or maintenance for houses of correction; the marriage of poor maids; the supportation aid and help of young tradesmen, handicraftsmen and persons decayed; the relief or redemption of prisoners or captives; the aid or ease of any poor inhabitants concerning payment of fifteens, setting out of soldiers and other taxes; which lands, chattels and money have not been employed according to the charitable intent of the givers by reason of frauds, breaches of trust and negligence."

7–09   The Statute of Charitable Uses 1601 was repealed by the Mortmain and Charitable Uses Act 1888, but section 13(2) of the latter Act expressly preserved the preamble to the former statute, and on the basis of its continued existence Lord Macnaghten in *Commissioners of Income Tax v. Pemsel* enunciated his famous fourfold classification of charity: "Charity in its legal sense comprises four principal divisions: trusts for the relief of poverty; trusts for the advancement of education; trusts for the advancement of religion; and trusts for other purposes beneficial to the community, not falling under any of the preceding heads."

The Mortmain and Charitable Uses Act 1888, and with it the preamble to the Statute of Charitable Uses 1601, were repealed by the Charities Act 1960, section 38(4) of which provides: "Any reference in any enactment or document to a charity within the meaning, purview and interpretation of the Charitable Uses Act 1601, or of the preamble to it, shall be construed as a reference to a charity within the meaning which the word bears as a legal term according to the law of England and Wales."

7–10   This provision is not free from obscurity,[30] but the courts treat the somewhat ossificatory classification to which the preamble gave rise as still surviving in the decided cases.[31]

Historical overview

It seems that the 1601 Act was intended to be almost wholly confined to purposes which would operate for the benefit of the public as a whole, rich and poor, by reducing the burden of parish poor relief and other parochial obligations.[32] If gifts for the specified purposes were properly employed they should relieve poverty and so reduce the burden of poor rates.

7–11   Worries about testators disinheriting their families in favour of charity by wills or gifts made within 12 months of death (so as to curry favour with their Maker) led to the Mortmain and Charitable Uses Act 1736 (now repealed) which made void most of such charitable trusts of land.

---

[30] See O.R. Marshall (1961) 24 M.L.R. 444.
[31] *e.g. Incorporated Council of Law Reporting v. Att.-Gen.*, [1972] Ch. 73; *I.R.C. v. McMullen* [1991] A.C. 1.
[32] See Francis Moore's (1607) Reading on the 1601 Statute, G. H. Jones, *History of Charity Law* 1532–1827, p. 27.

These same sentiments led to the legal requirement that if a gift of personalty to charity was initially impossible or impracticable to take effect then the property reverted to the testator's estate (for his family's benefit) unless there was a clear general charitable intention evinced, when the property would be applied *cy-près* for closely allied purposes.[33]

To favour families and make charitable trusts of land void under the 1736 Act the courts divorced the enumerated objects from the preamble and the 1601 legislative and historical context.[34] The argument that charity involved something in the nature of a relief was rejected.[35] It sufficed that public benefit existed and this could exist where any section of the community benefited even if not poor. Thus, while the words in the preamble were originally thought to cover free schools only,[36] they became used to uphold a bequest to establish a school for educating the sons of gentlemen.[37] Providing schools, hospitals[38] and sheltered accommodation for the elderly[39] albeit at a cost came to be charitable objects so long as the profits are ploughed back into the enterprise and not distributed. However, it became established[40] that purposes will not qualify for charitable status if they are substantially political in the broad sense of seeking to change or preserve the law or government policy.

Concern over the negligent or fraudulent mismanagement of charita- **7–12** ble funds led to the establishment of the Charity Commission under the Charitable Trusts Acts 1853, 1855 and 1860 to supervise the administration of charities. Similar concerns in the 1980s led to reports[41] resulting in the Government White Paper[42] "Charities: A Framework for the Future" (May 1989). Extensive new powers have been given to the Commission by the Charities Act 1993. In particular the Commission now has powers, corresponding to and concurrent with those possessed by the Attorney-General, to go directly to the courts for the enforcement of obligations against defaulting trustees and others. The Commission has the leading role in enforcement litigation but is required to obtain the Attorney-General's consent before commencing proceedings.[43] As well as investigating possible misconduct and abuse of charitable assets with a view to taking remedial action, the Commission maintains a public register of charities, gives advice to charity trustees to make the administration of their charity more effective, and makes schemes and orders to modernise the purposes and administrative machinery of charities and to give trustees useful additional powers. It provides much

---

[33] See *infra*, at paras 7–320 and 7–324.
[34] *e.g. Townley v. Bedwell* (1801) 6 Ves. 194, *Thornton v. Howe* (1862) 31 Beav. 14.
[35] *Trustees of the British Museum v. White* (1826) 2 Sim. & Stu. 594 at 596.
[36] *Att.-Gen. v. Hewer* (1700) 2 Vern. 387.
[37] *Att.-Gen. v. Lord Lonsdale* (1827) 1 Sim. 105.
[38] *Re Resch's W.T.* [1969] 1 A.C. 514.
[39] *Rowntree Memorial Trust Housing Association v. Att.-Gen.* [1983] Ch. 159.
[40] *Bowman v. Secular Society Ltd* [1917] A.C. 406 at 442; *National Anti-Vivisection Society v. I.R.C.* [1948] A.C. 31; *McGovern v. Att.-Gen.* [1982] Ch. 321.
[41] 16th Report of Committee of Public Accounts 1987–88; Sir Philip Woodfield Efficiency Scrutiny of the Supervision of Charities (1987).
[42] Cm. 694.
[43] Charities Act 1993, s.32(5).

useful guidance in publications that can easily be accessed on its website www.charity-commission.gov.uk.

Public benefit

7–13 A valid charitable trust must also promote some public benefit for a section of the public, as opposed to a private class, unless it is within Lord Macnaghten's first category of trusts for the relief of poverty.[44] This exception is anomalous but well established in the House of Lords: *Dingle v. Turner, infra*, para. 7–64.

The public benefit test requires the trust to confer a tangible benefit[45] directly or indirectly upon the public but does not require a benefit available to all the public: it suffices that the possibility of benefiting is conferred upon some section of the public such that the trust is a public one as opposed to a private one. The House of Lords in *Oppenheim* v. *Tobacco Securities Trust Co. Ltd, infra*, para. 7–105, used the personal nexus test put forward in *Re Compton*[46] to distinguish between public trusts and private trusts: they held that except in "poverty" trusts no class of beneficiaries can constitute a section of the public if the distinguishing quality which links them together is relationship to a particular person either through a common ancestor or a common employer. Thus a trust for the education of children of employees or former employees of British American Tobacco Co. Ltd or any of its subsidiary or allied companies was not a valid charitable trust though there were over 110,000 current employees. If the trust had been for the education of children of those employed or formerly employed in the tobacco industry it would have been valid as it would if confined to children of those engaged in the tobacco industry in a particular county or town.[47]

7–14 The weaknesses of the personal nexus test are revealed in the dissenting speech of Lord MacDermott in *Oppenheim, infra*, at para. 7–110 and with whose broad approach the House of Lords were in agreement obiter in *Dingle v. Turner, infra*, at para. 7–64 where Lord Cross indicated that whether or not the potential beneficiaries can fairly be said to constitute a section of the public is a question of degree in all the circumstances of the case and that much must depend upon the purpose of the trusts.[48] If charity of purpose and benefit to the public are not separate, but interrelated issues, then there can be no universal test of public benefit. Indeed, the cases reveal that minute public benefit is required for religious trusts,[49] a substantial amount of public benefit is

---

[44] *Oppenheim v. Tobacco Securities Trust Co. Ltd, infra*, at para. 7–105; *Gilmour v. Coats, infra*, at para. 7–149; *I.R.C. v. Baddeley* [1955] A.C. 572.
[45] *Gilmour v. Coats*, [1949] A.C. 426; *Re Pinion* [1965] Ch. 85.
[46] [1945] Ch. 123.
[47] [1951] A.C. 297 at 318; *Re Morgan* [1955] 1 W.L.R. 738. Similarly, on this basis a trust for the education of children of inhabitants of Bournville will be valid but not a trust for the education of children of employees of Cadbury-Schweppes Ltd: *I.R.C. v. Educational Grants Association* [1967] Ch. 993 at 1009.
[48] D. J. Hayton (1972) 36 Conv. (N.S.) 209; Gareth Jones (1974) C.L.J. 63. For comments of Lord Cross see *Carter v. Race Relations Board* [1973] A.C. 868 at 907.
[49] *Re Watson* [1973] 1 W.L.R. 1472; *Thornton v. Howe* (1862) 31 Beav. 14; *Dingle v. Turner, infra*, paras 7–64 *et seq*, *Neville Estates Ltd v. Madden* [1962] Ch. 832 (members for the time being of the Catford Synagogue).

required for educational trusts[50] and slightly more public benefit still is required for trusts for other purposes beneficial to the community.[51] This is dealt with when examining these categories of trusts.

Owing to the conflicting views expressed in the Lords in *Oppenheim* **7–15** and in *Dingle v. Turner* lower courts will face an unenviable dilemma when the case arises that compels a choice between the two views. In its favour the broad approach at least concerns itself with the substance of the matter and is not unduly preoccupied with form as is the narrow personal nexus approach. The narrow formal approach, though conducive to certainty, also leads to artificial manipulation of the legal forms so as to obtain fiscal advantages, *e.g.* in the case of a trust for the education of children of inhabitants of Bournville which might well be invalidated under the broad approach as in substance a trust benefiting employees of Cadbury-Schweppes Ltd[52]

Indeed, the law of charitable trusts is bedevilled by the fact that such **7–16** trusts enjoy not just immunity from the rules against uncertainty and inalienability but also automatically fiscal privileges. The two questions of the validity of the trust and of exemption from rates and taxes are joined together in an unholy and unnatural union. It is most noticeable that in "Chancery" cases, where the validity of a trust is attacked by the residuary legatee or next of kin, there are many doubtful first instance cases in favour of charity, whereas in "Revenue" cases, where exemption from taxes is the real bone of contention, there are many appellate cases restricting the scope of charity.[53] Is it too much to ask that fresh consideration should be given to the recommendations of the Radcliffe Commission on Taxation[54] that the question whether a trust should be regarded as a charitable trust for the purpose of general validity as a trust should be separated from the question whether it should enjoy any fiscal privileges?[55] It is noteworthy that in *Dingle v. Turner* the Lords disagreed over the influence of fiscal considerations in an application of a broad public benefit test. It would seem that Lords Simon and Cross thought that fiscal considerations would require a case like *Oppenheim* to be decided the same way today on the basis that it was not sufficiently altruistic to merit tax exemptions, merely providing a perquisite to attract and retain employees.

Most charities have to be registered with the Charity Commissioners **7–17** under the Charities Act 1960 now replaced by the 1993 Act[56] so that in the vast majority of instances it is the Charity Commissioners who alone

---

[50] *Oppenheim v. Tobacco Securities Trust., infra,* para. 7–105; *I.R.C. v. Educational Grants Association Ltd, infra.,* para. 7–120.

[51] *I.R.C. v. Baddeley* [1955] A.C. 572; *Williams' Trustees v. I.R.C., infra,* para. 7–179.

[52] In tax matters the courts nowadays take a broad approach: see *Furniss v. Dawson* [1984] A.C. 474, *Craven v. White* [1989] A.C. 398; but there are some limits: *Fitzwilliam v. I.R.C.* [1993] 1 W.L.R. 1189.

[53] See Cross (1956) 72 L.Q.R. 187 though *I.R.C. v. McMullen* [1981] A.C. 1 is an exception to this trend.

[54] (1955) Cmd. 9474.

[55] See [1989] Conv. 28 (S. Bright).

[56] Charities Act 1993, s.3, appeal to the courts is possible under s.4(3) though the cost of appeal is a deterrent: between 1960 and 1971 only one appeal resulted from 1,380 refusals of charitable status (*New Law Journal Annual Charities Review* 1974, at 34).

determine the issue of charity or not though they do consult the Inland Revenue. They produce Annual Reports and have produced volumes of "Decisions of Charity Commissioners" showing what their practice is in interpreting the case law. As to be expected they feel it their duty to err on the side of a conservative restrictive interpretation, while it is to be expected that their recommendations on draft trusts are accepted rather than fought in the courts (although there is an informal procedure of internal appeal within the Commission for an aggrieved applicant for registration as a charity). This has brought them some criticism especially from recently established philanthropic bodies which to a greater or lesser extent pursue political activities. However, some of the criticism would be better directed at the anomalous state of the law for as the Commissioners write in their defence, "The Law is, of course, what it is and we cannot change it."[57]

Trusts with political purposes

7–18   Trusts for political purposes are non-charitable trusts on the basis that the courts have no means of judging whether a proposed change in the law would or would not be for the public benefit,[58] and the law could not stultify itself by holding that it was for the public benefit that the law itself should be changed.[59] Political purposes comprise not only attempts to change the law by legislation or to oppose proposed changes but also attempts to influence local or national government home or foreign policy. Thus a university student union cannot indulge in a campaign against the Government ending free milk for school children or against the Government's support of a foreign war like that in the Gulf between Iraq and Kuwait.[60] The following bodies are not registered as charities: the National Anti-Vivisection Society, National Council for Civil Liberties, Campaign against Racial Discrimination, Martin Luther King Fund, Human Rights Society, United Nations Association, Amnesty International, Animal Abuse, Injustice and Defence Society (on which see Decision of Charity Commissioners Vol. 2, p. 1.) and the Disablement

7–19   Income Group. However, if a body, particularly a long established one, which exists for much wider charitable purposes,[61] incidentally indulges

---

[57] 1971 Report, para. 10.

[58] *Bowman v. Secular Society* [1917] A.C. 406 at 442, *per* Lord Parker.

[59] *National Anti-Vivisection Society v. I.R.C.*, [1948] A.C. 31 at 49, 62, infra, para. 7–188. See also *Bonar Law Memorial Trust v. I.R.C.* (1933) 49 T.L.R. 220 (Conservative); *Re Ogden* [1933] Ch. 678 (Liberal); *Re Hopkinson* [1949] W.N. 29 (Socialist); *Re Strakosch* [1949] Ch. 529 (appeasing racial feeling); *Re Bushnell* [1975] 1 All E.R. 721; (1975) 38 M.L.R. 471 (furthering socialised medicine in a socialist state); C.J. Forder [1984] Conv. 263.

[60] See *Baldry v. Feintuck* [1972] 2 All E.R. 81; *Webb v. O'Doherty* (1991) 3 Admin. L.R. 731, and also *Re Koeppler's W.T.* [1984] Ch. 243. In *Southwood v. Att.-Gen.* [2000] W.T.L.R. 1199 the Court of Appeal held that a trust to educate the public to accept that peace is best secured by demilitarisation and disarmament is political and non-charitable.

[61] These purposes do not in practice have to be much wider in the case of respectable long established charities like the Anti-Slavery Society, the Lords Day Observance Society and the Howard League for Penal Reform. By way of contrast the Humanist Trust, the National Secular Society and the Sexual Law Reform Society are not charities. The Upper Teesdale Defence Fund was registered as a charity, though its *raison d'être* seemed to be oppose a private Bill in Parliament, since the Commissioners take the view that virtually all private Bills are free from the taint of political activity: see 1969 Annual report, para. 15.

in political activity so as to put pressure on the public and politicians this does not affect the charitable status of the body, *e.g.* the RSPCA fighting vivisection, the British Legion fighting for better pensions for ex-servicemen, Guide Dogs for the Blind resisting VAT on dog food, the National Association for Mental Health in their MIND campaign organising and presenting a petition to Parliament. Certain registered charities such as the Child Poverty Action Group and Shelter have been walking the tightrope so precariously as to lead the Charity Commissioners to publish some guidance in their 1969 Annual Report paras. 10–16, their 1981 Annual Report, and their CCA publication (July 1995), revised as CC9 in September 1999, "Political Activities and Campaigning by Charities," *infra*, at para. 7–37.

Since Parliament in the Race Relations Act 1976 has decided that **7–20** promoting good race relations, endeavouring to eliminate discrimination on racial grounds and encouraging equality of opportunity between persons of different racial groups are for the public benefit, the Charity Commissioners in their 1983 Annual Report now consider such purposes as charitable. Previously they had not been so considered on the authority of *Re Strakosch*[62] where the appeasement of racial feelings (between the Dutch and English speaking South Africans) had been held to be a political and, therefore, non-charitable purpose.

Since the essence of any living law and of any healthy democracy is **7–21** change, it is difficult to see why trusts for political purposes should not be capable of being valid trusts, though not charitable trusts with fiscal advantages. It has already been submitted (para. 3–212 *supra*) that such trusts should be valid if an enforcer has been appointed in the trust instrument and the trust is administratively workable and restricted to the perpetuity period.

For the present, bodies that are sufficiently hard-pressed to need relief on rates and taxes are not prepared to risk the costs of fighting the decisions of the Charity Commissioners in the Law Courts, especially when it is possible to hive off part of their funds for such activities as are certainly charitable, *e.g.* Amnesty with its Prisoners of Conscience Fund for relieving the poverty of such prisoners and their families, the National Council for Civil Liberties with its Cobden Trust for educational activities, the Martin Luther King Fund with its Martin Luther King Foundation for educational activities; UNA and the Anti-Apartheid Movement also have their own separate educational trusts.

Profit-making trusts

A trust can make a profit by charging fees (*e.g.* for educational, **7–22** medical or housing purposes) and still be a charitable trust so long as the profits are not distributed to benefit individuals but used for the purposes of the trust.[63]

---

[62] [1949] Ch. 529.
[63] *Re Resch's W.T.* [1969] 1 A.C. 514; *Re Rowntree Memorial Trust Housing Association* [1983] Ch. 159; *Customs & Excise Commissioners v. Bell Concord Education Trust Ltd* [1989] 2 All E.R. 217.

SCOTTISH BURIAL REFORM AND CREMATION SOCIETY LTD v. GLASGOW CORPORATION

House of Lords [1968] A.C. 138; [1967] 3 W.L.R. 1132; [1968] 3 All E.R. 215.

7–23   The appellants were a non-profit-making limited company with a main object of promoting inexpensive and sanitary methods of disposal of the dead, in particular promoting cremation. For rating purposes they claimed a declaration that they were a charity, it being common ground that English law determined the issue. The Society charged fees but was non-profit-making.[64]

On appeal from the Court of Session the House of Lords held that the appellants were a charity within Lord Macnaghten's fourth category of charitable purposes and indicated the approach adopted by the courts as follows:

7–24   LORD REID: ". . . The appellants must also show, however, that the public benefit is of a kind within the spirit and intendment of the statute of Elizabeth. The preamble specifies a number of objects which were then recognised as charitable. But in more recent times a wide variety of other objects have come to be recognised as also being charitable. The courts appear to have proceeded first by seeking some analogy between an object mentioned in the preamble and the object with regard to which they had to reach a decision. Then they appear to have gone farther, and to have been satisfied if they could find an analogy between an object already held to be charitable and the new object claimed to be charitable. This gradual extension has proceeded so far that there are few modern reported cases where a bequest or donation was made or an institution was being carried on for a clearly specified object which was for the benefit of the public at large and not of individuals, and yet the object was held not to be within the spirit and intendment of the statute of Elizabeth. Counsel in the present case were invited to search for any case having even the remotest resemblance to this case in which an object was held to be for the public benefit but not yet to be within that spirit and intendment; but no such case could be found.

7–25   "There is, however, another line of cases where the bequest did not clearly specify the precise object to which it was to be applied, but left a discretion to trustees or others to choose objects within a certain field. There the courts have been much more strict, so that if it is possible that those entrusted with the discretion could, without infringing the testator's direction, apply the bequest in any way which would not be charitable (for example, because it did not benefit a sufficiently large section of the public) then the claim that the bequest is charitable fails. That line of cases, however, can have no application to the present case, and it is easy to fall into error if one tries to apply to a case like the present judicial observations made in a case where there was a discretion which could go beyond objects strictly charitable. In the present case the appellants make a charge for the services which they provide. It has never been held, however, that objects, otherwise charitable, cease to be charitable if beneficiaries are required to make payments for what they receive. It may even be that public demand for the kind of service which the charity provides becomes so large that there is room for a commercial undertaking to come in and supply similar

---

[64] Organisations out to make a profit for their members are obviously not charitable: *Re Smith's W.T.* [1962] 2 All E.R. 563; *Re Girls Public Day School Trust* [1951] Ch. 400.

services on a commercial basis; but no authority and no reason has been put forward for holding that when that state is reached the objects and activities of the non-profit earning charitable organisation cease to be charitable.

"If, then, all that is necessary to bring the objects and activities of the appellants within the spirit and intendment of preamble to the statute of Elizabeth is to find analogous decided cases, I think that there is amply sufficient analogy with the series of cases dealing with burial.[65] I would therefore allow this appeal."

Charity Commissioners' Annual Report 1966

36. Some of our non-legal correspondents have questioned the justification for **7–26** the importance which the law attaches to the words used rather than to the institution's activities. It is felt by such correspondents that it should be enough to examine the activities of the institution to decide whether it is a charity and that two organisations both doing the same things should be equally qualified for registration. But this fails to take account of the fact that the law must be concerned principally with the obligation imposed on the institution to pursue certain objects. It is this obligation which established it as a charity; and so long as an institution is free to pursue any activities it wishes it cannot be treated as an established charity however much its current activities may resemble those of other recognised charities.

37. The problem of interpreting words presents a somewhat different aspect **7–27** when we are asked to consider draft documents intended to set up proposed charities. It is not unusual to find an attempt to dress up the purposes of the proposed institution in words which it is hoped will be accepted as charitable even though the purposes, so phrased, are quite remote from the true intentions of the promoters. We are convinced that this is a highly unsatisfactory course and that the governing instrument of every institution should show unequivocally what the institution really sets out to achieve. Three particular devices call for comment.

38. The first is the over-working of the word "education." Ingenious draftsmen **7–28** have found it possible to embrace within this word a vast variety of activities, mainly propagandist, which do not come within the meaning of the "advancement of education" as it is used in charity law. A purpose which is not charitable cannot be made charitable merely by representing it to be a form of education.

39. The second device is the use of very wide general terms. It is of course true that there are some founders of charities, particularly those who are settling part of their own personal fortune, who genuinely expect to apply the settled property for all manner of charitable purposes; in such a case the general words are not intended to conceal a more limited true purpose. But, nonetheless, they may be difficult to interpret and it is undesirable that they should be used in any case where the proposed charity has a more limited purpose, particularly if the charity is intending to appeal to the public and not be merely the vehicle for the founder's own benevolence.

40. The third device is that of enumerating a number of objects, some perhaps **7–29** charitable and others less obviously so, and then declaring that the institution is to be confined to carrying out such of the listed objects as are charitable. We have already commented on this device in paragraph 25 of our report for 1964.

---

[65] See also *Incorporated Council of Law Reporting v. Att.-Gen.* [1972] Ch. 73 at 88, *per* Russell L.J.

This approach begs the question, prevents the real purpose of the institution from being readily recognised and quite unnecessarily introduces difficulty in construing and acting upon the documents in which it is used. If a proposed charity shows us a draft instrument incorporating such a phrase we consider ourselves entitled to enquire what are intended to be its activities, with a view to seeing whether those activities can be authorised in terms of clearly defined charitable purposes.

CC40 Disaster Appeals—Attorney-General's Guidelines

The Making of the Appeal

7-30   Those who use these guidelines must remember that no two appeals can ever be quite the same, and should do all they can to ensure that their own appeal is appropriate to the particular circumstance of their case, and runs into no unforeseen difficulties, whether personal, administrative, or fiscal. Amongst the most important and urgent decisions which must be made will be whether or not a charitable appeal is called for, and it may well be desirable to take advice on such question before the appeal is issued. Generally speaking, the terms of the appeal will be all-important in deciding the status and ultimate application of the fund. Once the terms are agreed, it will generally be desirable to publish the appeal as soon as possible, and as widely as appropriate in the circumstances.

Sometimes gifts may be sent before publication of the appeal. If there are more than can be acknowledged individually, the published appeal should indicate that gifts already made will be added to the appeal fund unless the donors notify the organisers (say within ten days) that this is not their wish.

Pros and Cons of the Types of Appeal

7-31   *Charitable funds* attract generous tax reliefs; donations to them may do so, especially through the Gift Aid scheme details of which are obtainable from your local tax office. In particular, donations will also for the most part be exempt from inheritance tax. But charitable funds, being essentially public in their nature, cannot be used to give individuals benefits over and above those appropriate to their needs; and the operation of a charitable trust will be subject to the scrutiny of the Charity Commissioners.

Non-charitable funds attract no particular tax reliefs; donations to them are subject to no special tax treatment (and will have to be taken into account for inheritance tax purposes unless, as is likely to be the case for the bulk of donations, they are within the normal reliefs). But under a non-charitable trust there is no limit on the amount which can be paid to individual beneficiaries if none has been imposed by the appeal, and only the court acting on behalf of the beneficiaries will have control over the trust, which will not be subject to scrutiny by us.

7-32   The terms of the non-charitable appeal must be prepared with particular care to ensure that there is no doubt who is to benefit, whether or not their benefit is to be at the discretion of the trustees, and whether or not the entire benefit is to go to the beneficiaries, and if not, for example because specific purposes are laid down and the funds may be more than is required for those purposes, or because the beneficiaries are only to take as much as the trustees think appropriate, what is to happen to any surplus. If specific purposes are laid down, and after they have been fulfilled a surplus remains for which no use has been specified, the surplus will belong to the donors, which may lead to expensive and wasteful problems of administration.

Forms of Appeal

If a *charitable* fund is intended then the appeal could take the following form: **7–33** "This appeal is to set up a charitable fund to relieve distress caused by the accident/disaster at .... on .... The purpose is to use the funds to relieve those who may be in need of help (whether now or in the future) as a result of this tragedy in accordance with charity law. Any surplus after their needs have been met will be used for charitable purposes in one or more of the following ways. (i) To help those who suffer in similar tragedies. (ii) To benefit charities with related purposes. (iii) To help the locality affected by the accident/ disaster."

If a *non-charitable* fund is intended and those affected are to take the entirety of the fund in such shares as the trustees think fit the appeal could take the following form:
"This appeal is to set up a fund, the entire benefit of which will be used for those injured or bereaved in the accident/disaster at .... and their families and dependants as the trustees think fit. This fund will not be a charity."

A non-charitable fund in which the trustees would have a discretion to give as much as they think fit to those who have suffered with any surplus going to charity could be set up on the basis of the following form:
"This appeal is to set up a fund for those injured or bereaved in the accident/ disaster at .... and their families and dependants. The trustees will have a discretion how and to what extent to benefit individual claimants: the fund will not itself be a charity but any surplus will be applied for such charitable purposes as the trustees think most appropriate to commemorate those who died."

Appeals for Individuals

It sometimes happens that publicity given to individual suffering moves people **7–34** to give. In such a case it is particularly desirable for those who make appeals to indicate whether or not the appeal is for a charitable fund. It is also desirable for those who give to say whether their gift is meant for the benefit of the individual, or for charitable purposes including helping the individual so far as that is charitable; if no such intention is stated, then the donation should be acknowledged with an indication how it will be used if the donor does not dissent. Those who make appeals should bear in mind the possibility that a generous response may produce more than is appropriate for the needs of the individual and should be sure to ask themselves what should be done with any surplus.

Thus, if a child suffers from a disease, there are two alternatives: to appeal for **7–35** the benefit of the child, or to appeal for charitable purposes relating to the suffering of the child, such as may help him and others in the same misfortune, for example by helping find a cure. It may be that the child will not live long, and so may not be able to enjoy generosity to him as an individual; alternatively, he may be intended to receive as much as possible because he faces a lifetime's suffering. Once again, the pros and cons of setting up a charitable fund or a non-charitable fund should be considered before the appeal is made and the appeal should indicate which alternative is intended; once again, even if a non-charitable appeal is made, it may be thought right to make it on terms that any surplus can be used for charity.

Generally

The suggestions made in this memorandum are only examples of forms which **7–36** can be used; and before making an appeal it is always wise to seek advice on what form to use. We will always be ready as a matter of urgency to advise on the terms of any intended charitable appeal, or to consider whether a proposed appeal is likely to be charitable and if so to advise on the likely consequences.

In conclusion, the Attorney-General would like to emphasise that those organising an appeal should do all they can to make sure that the purpose of the appeal is clear and that donors know how their gifts will be used. This will do much to reduce the risk of confusion and distress. It is considered undesirable to make a general appeal postponing until the size of the fund is known decisions on whether the fund ought to be charitable and whether those affected should take the entire benefit; this can all too easily lead both donors and beneficiaries to form the view that the ultimate result is not what was intended, as well as giving rise to legal problems. [On Penlee Lifeboat Disaster, see (1982) 132 New L.J. 223; on Aberfan Disaster Fund and the Charity Commission see (1999) 19 Legal Studies 380 (McLean & Johnes), and generally, see Celia Wells, *Negotiating Tragedy: Law and Disasters*.]

CC9 Political Activities and Campaigning by Charities (September 1999)

Section 3: Extent to which charities may engage in political activities

9. Although an organisation established for political purposes can never be a charity, the trustees of a charity may do some things of a political nature as a means of achieving the purposes of the charity.

7–37 10. This principle, although easy to state, is not always easy to apply in practice. In applying it charity trustees must take particular care, since the dividing line between proper debate in the public arena and improper political activity is a difficult one to judge. The guidance given in this publication, which is drawn from the principles established by the Courts, is designed to help trustees to determine that line in relation to a range of activities. Any political activity undertaken by trustees must be in furtherance of, and ancillary to, the charity's stated objects and within its powers.

11. To be ancillary, activities must serve and be subordinate to the charity's purposes. They cannot therefore, be undertaken as an end in themselves and must not be allowed to dominate the activities which the charity undertakes to carry out its charitable purposes directly. The trustees must be able to show that there is a reasonable expectation that the activities will further the purposes of the charity, and so benefit its beneficiaries, to an extent justified by the resources devoted to those activities.

7–38 12. Where these requirements are met, trustees of charities may properly enter into dialogue with government on matters relating to their purposes or the way in which the trustees carry out their work. They may publish the advice or views they express to Ministers. They may also seek to inform and educate the public on particular issues which are relevant to the charity and its purposes, including information about their experience of the needs met in their field of activities and the solutions they advocate. But they must do so on the basis of a reasoned case and their views must be expressed with a proper sense of proportion.

13. Trustees must not advocate policies, nor seek to inform and educate, on subjects and issues which do not bear on the purposes of their charity. Moreover, the manner and content of any advocacy of, or opposition to, legislative or policy change must be consistent with these guidelines.

7–39 14. In summary, therefore, a charity can engage in political activity if:

- there is a reasonable expectation that the activity concerned will further the stated purposes of the charity, and so benefit its beneficiaries, to an extent justified by the resources devoted to the activity;

- the activity is within the powers which the trustees have to achieve those purposes;
- the activity is consistent with these guidelines;
- the views expressed are based on a well-founded and reasoned case and are expressed in a responsible way.

Section 5 of this publication gives more detailed guidance on the acceptability of particular kinds of political activity.

15. Because of the need to meet these requirements it is important that any charity undertaking political activities has adequate arrangements in place for the commissioning, control and evaluation of such activities by its trustees (who are, of course, ultimately responsible for ensuring that they are properly conducted).

Section 4: Campaigning

16. Campaigning by charities to mobilise public opinion to influence govern- **7–40** ment policy can arouse strong feelings. On the one hand, many people think that charities should be allowed, and indeed have a duty, to campaign freely to change public policy on any issue if it is relevant to their work and if they have direct experience to offer. On the other hand, some argue that such campaigning is a misuse of charity funds, a misdirection of effort by charities and a misuse of the fiscal concessions from which charities benefit. This is particularly so if the charity appears to favour a particular political party or a policy of a political party.

17. By the very nature of their knowledge and social concern, however, some charities are well placed to play a part in public debate on important issues of the day and to make an important contribution to the development of public policy. Others will invariably be drawn into such debate. It would be wrong to think that this cannot and should not happen: it is open to charities to engage in campaigning activities, provided the requirements set out in section 3 of this publication are satisfied.

18. Whether a charity can properly engage in campaigning will therefore **7–41** depend upon the nature of its purposes, its powers and the way in which it contributes to public debate. Where charities wish to raise issues in a way which will inform public debate and influence decisions of public bodies, great care must be taken to ensure that the issues concerned are relevant to their purposes and that the means by which they raise them are within their powers and consistent with these guidelines.

19. A charity should not seek to organise public opinion to support or oppose a political party which advocates a particular policy favoured or opposed by the charity. It is inevitable that sometimes a policy put forward by a charity coincides with that of a particular political party, or a political party decides to adopt such a policy. It does not follow that the charity is prevented from promoting its policy on the issue. However, it may influence how it does so. In such cases the charity should take particular care—especially to ensure that the independence of its view is explained and understood.

20. Where a charity can properly campaign, the information provided to the **7–42** public in support of the campaign as a whole must be accurate and sufficiently full to support its position. In arguing its case a charity is not restricted to using print media alone. If it uses a communications medium the nature of which makes it impracticable to set out the full basis of the charity's position, the

charity can simply state its position, without the need to set out the full factual basis and argument lying behind that position. It must be able to set out its full position, however, if called upon to do so.

21. Provided all other requirements are met, material produced in support of a campaign may have emotional content. Indeed, the Commission accepts that in the areas in which many charities work it is difficult to avoid engaging the emotions of the public. But it would be unacceptable (except where the nature of the medium makes it impracticable to set out the basis of the charity's position) for a charity to seek to persuade government or the public on the basis of material which was *merely* emotive.

Section 5: What political activities are allowed?

22. A charity may undertake only those activities which further its purposes and which are authorised by its governing document. If the activity involves campaigning, then in all cases the manner in which it is conducted must be in accordance with the principles set out in section 4 of this publication.

23. Where this is the case, a charity may engage in activities of the kinds shown below. Examples of activities in which a charity must *not* engage are shown in *italics*.

Influencing government or public opinion

7–43   24. A charity may seek to influence government or public opinion through well-founded, reasoned argument based on research or direct experience on issues either relating directly to the achievement of the charity's own stated purposes or relevant to the wellbeing of the charitable sector.

25. A charity may provided information to its supporters or the public on how individual Members of parliament or parties have voted on an issue, provided they do so in a way which will enable its supporters or the public to seek to persuade those Members or parties to change their position through well-founded, reasoned argument rather than *merely* through public pressure.

26. A charity may provide its supporters, or members of the public, with material to send to Members of Parliament or the government, provided that the material amounts to well-founded, reasoned argument.

27. A charity may organise and present a petition to either House of Parliament or to national or local government, provided that the purpose of the petition is stated on each page:

7–44   28. *A charity must not base any attempt to influence public opinion or to put pressure on the government, whether directly or indirectly through supporters or members of the public, to legislate or adopt a particular policy on data which it knows (or ought to know) is inaccurate or on a distorted selection of data in support of a preconceived position.*

29. *A charity must not participate in party political demonstrations.*

30. *A charity must not claim evidence of public support for its position on a political issue without adequate justification.*

31. *Except where the nature of the medium being employed makes it impracticable to set out the basis of the charity's position, a charity must not seek to influence government or public opinion on the basis of material which is merely emotive.*

32. *A charity must not invite its supporters, or the public, to take action in support of its position without providing them with sufficient information to enable them to decide whether to give their support and to take the action requested. In particular, a charity must not invite its supporters or the public to write to their Members of*

Parliament or the government without providing them with sufficient information to enable them to advance a reasoned argument in favour of the charity's position.

33. *A charity whose stated purposes include the advancement of education must not overstep the boundary between education and propaganda in promoting that purpose. The distinction is between providing balanced information designed to enable people to make up their own mind and providing one-sided information designed to promote a particular point of view.*

Responding to proposed legislation

34. A charity may provide, and publish comments on possible or proposed **7–45** changes in the law or government policy, whether contained in a Green or White Paper or otherwise.

35. A charity may, in response to a Parliamentary Bill, supply to Members of either House for use in debate such relevant information and reasoned arguments as can reasonably be expected to assist the achievement of its charitable purposes.

Advocating and opposing changes in the law and public policy

36. A charity may advocate a change in the law or public policy which can **7–46** reasonably be expected to help it to achieve its charitable purposes and may oppose a change in the law or public policy which can reasonably be expected to hinder its ability to do so. In either case the charity can present government with a reasoned memorandum in support of its position. It may publish its views and may seek to influence public opinion in favour of its position by well-founded reasoned argument.

Supporting, opposing and promoting legislation

37. A charity may support the passage of a Bill which can reasonably be expected to help it to achieve its charitable purposes and may oppose the passage of a Bill which can reasonably be expected to hinder its ability to do so.

38. A charity may spend its funds on the promotion of public general legislation provided it has the power to do so and the legislation can reasonably be expected to further its charitable purposes.

Commenting on public issues

39. A charity may comment publicly on social, economic and political issues if **7–47** these relate to its purpose or the way in which the charity is able to carry out its work.

Supporting political parties

40. A charity may advocate a particular solution if it can reasonably be expected to further the purposes of the charity, even though that solution is advocated by a political party. If it does so it must make plain that its views are independent of the political party.

41. *A charity must not support a political party.*

Acting with other bodies

42. A charity may affiliate to a campaigning alliance, even if the alliance **7–48** includes non-charitable organisations, provided certain conditions are met. First, the charity must carefully consider the alliance's activities, and the implications

of the charity's being associated with them, and should only affiliate if affiliation can reasonably be expected to further the charity's own charitable purposes. Second, since a charity may not undertake through an alliance activities which it would be improper for it to undertake directly, if the alliance engages in such activities the charity must dissociate itself from them and take reasonable steps to ensure that its name, and any funds it has contributed, are not used to support them.

Providing information

7–49   43. A charity may provide factual information to its members and those interested in its work in seeking to inform their Members of Parliament and others on matters related to the purposes of the charity.

44. A charity may employ Parliamentary staff to inform Members of Parliament on matters relevant to its purposes.

45. *A charity must not provide information which it knows, or ought to know, to be inaccurate, or which has been distorted by selection to support a preconceived position.*

46. *A charity must not provide supporters or members of the public with material specifically designed to underpin a party political campaign or for or against a government or particular MPs.*

47. *A charity must not issue material which supports or opposes a particular political party or the government.*

Forthcoming elections

7–50   48. A charity may respond to forthcoming elections, whether local, national or to the European Parliament, by analysing and commenting on the proposals of political parties which relate to its purposes or the way in which it is able to carry out its work, provided that it comments in a way which is consistent with these guidelines and complies with all the relevant provisions of electoral law.

49. A charity may also bring to the attention of prospective candidates issues relating to its purposes or the way in which it is able to carry out its work, and raise public awareness about them generally, provided that the promotional material is educational, informative, reasoned and well-founded.

50. *A charity must not seek to persuade members of the public to vote for or against a candidate or for or against a political party.*

Conducting and publishing research

7–51   51. A charity which conducts research must ensure that it is properly conducted using a methodology appropriate to the subject. If the research is undertaken to test a hypothesis arising from a charity's own experience or earlier research, it must be undertaken objectively to test that hypothesis rather than merely to support a preconceived position or objective. The aim in publishing the results of the research must be to inform and educate the public.

52. *A charity must not distort research, or the results of research, to support a preconceived position or objective.*

53. *A charity must not promote the results of research conducted by itself or others which it knows, or ought to know, to be flawed.*

54. *A charity must not undertake research for another body where it is clear that body intends to use the research for party political or propagandist purposes.*

55. The Commission will be producing a further leaflet on charities and research, which will give further guidance in this area.

Seeking support for government grants

56. A charity may seek the support of Members of the Parliament where a question arises as to whether a government grant to the charity is to be made or continued.

Section 6: Charities involvement in demonstrations and direct action

57. Charities may wish, as part of a campaign, to organise, promote or participate in some kind of demonstration or direct action. If this involves nothing more than the provision of reasoned argument or information (such as the handing out of leaflets in a public place) the principles stated earlier in the publication will apply to it and no particular difficulties should normally arise, whether from the point of view of organising the event or of deciding whether it is one in which the charity can properly be involved. **7-52**

58. Different considerations apply if an event moves beyond the mere provision of reasoned argument or information (as may be the case, for example, with marches, rallies, or peaceful picketing). This will be so even if elements of the event, such as the speeches made before a march, involve the provision of reasoned argument or information.

59. As in the case of other types of political activity, a charity can only organise, promote or take part in activity of this kind if it forms part of a well-founded and properly argued campaign which, seen as a whole, satisfies the requirements set out in *Section 3*. We will respond to any failure to meet this basic requirement in the same way as any other breach of these guidelines (*see Section 7*).

60. There are other matters which must also be considered by charities proposing to engage in demonstrations or direct action.

61. Whilst events of this nature may be thought to offer significant opportunities in terms of publicising a charity's position or showing the extent of public support for it on the matter in question, they can also involve significant risks. **7-53**

62. Precisely because they go beyond the merely educative or informative, some people will regard any involvement by a charity in activities of this kind as inappropriate. As a result, the participation of a charity in a demonstration or direct action may damage public support for it, or even for charities generally. The further the activity moves away from reasoned argument and debate, and the more it affects the rights of others, the more likely it is that this will happen.

63. Additionally, events such as demonstrations and rallies can of course present real problems of control. Since the law relating to public order is complex and in parts unclear, there is considerable potential for the commission of an offence by the charity, its officers or those taking part.

64. The risks of incurring civil or criminal liability, and of adverse publicity, are of course increased significantly if an event is badly organised or if other groups who do not share the aims of the organisers become involved.

65. In our view, therefore, any charity considering taking part in demonstrations or direct action must consider the implications of doing so very carefully, from the point of view of both the possible impact on public support and potential civil or criminal liability. **7-54**

66. A charity should assess whether or not it needs to seek its own legal advice on the lawfulness of what it has in mind, with a view to satisfying itself that there is no significant risk of any civil or criminal proceedings being brought against it, its trustees or members or those taking part. The greater the risk of interference with the rights of others, the more important it is that such advice should be **7-55**

taken, and the less likely that the activity can be justified in terms of the charity trustees' duties not to expose the property of the charity to risk.

7–56   67. If the charity decides to proceed, the duty imposed on all charity trustees to act prudently will require its charity trustees to take reasonable steps to ensure that the event in question:

- receives thorough and appropriate advance preparation (including, where necessary, liaison with the police and other authorities);
- is at all times fully under the control of the charity (or of the organisers of the event, where the charity is not solely responsible for organising it);
- is peaceful;
- does not take such a form, and is not conducted in such a way, as to give rise to a significant risk of civil or criminal proceedings being brought against the charity, its trustees or members or those participating in the event; and
- does not take such a form, and is not conducted in such a way, as to bring the charity, or charities generally, into disrepute (as a result, for example, of being intimidatory, provocative or excessively disruptive of the life of the community).

7–57   68. If the charity trustees fail to take such reasonable steps, and their charity incur financial loss as a result (*e.g.* by incurring a liability to a third party following a demonstration which gets out of control) the trustees may be exposed to a claim for want of prudence in their administration of the charity, which could result in financial claims against them personally.

69. We recommend that a charity consider carefully before requiring its staff to take part in a demonstration or other form of direct action. One important consideration is that it is an implied term of employment contracts than the employer must not require the employee to do an unlawful act. While no charity will deliberately require its staff to do something that the charity knows is unlawful, equally it must take care that any instructions it gives to its staff are capable of being fully carried out in a way which will not involve, or be likely to involve, the staff in any unlawful act.

7–58   70. Finally, there can generally be no objection to members or officers of a charity participating in an individual capacity in demonstrations or direct action organised by others. Charities need to take reasonable steps, however, to ensure that if members or officers do take part **in an individual capacity**, there is no misunderstanding as to the basis of their participation. In particular, a charity should not do anything (such as supplying placards or badges for the purpose) which might suggest that participants are taking part as official representatives of the charity.

Section 7: What penalties are there for carrying out unacceptable political activities?

7–59   71. The pursuit of improper political activities by charities is a misuse of charity funds and can lead to the loss of tax relief on funds applied for that purpose. It may also be regarded as amounting to the use of a charity as a vehicle for the personal views of its trustees. It can therefore bring about a loss of support for the charity and damage the good name of charities generally.

72. The Commission therefore expects trustees to comply with these guidelines. Where it appears that they have failed to do so the Commission will take the matter up with them to seek an explanation.

73. In the absence of a satisfactory explanation a range of possibilities arise, including simply giving advice to the trustees, taking proceedings against them for repayment of the funds applied on the activities in question (including any additional tax liability incurred as a result) and restricting future political activity.

74. The action taken by the Commission will depend upon all the circumstances of the case, including the scale and nature of the activity in question, whether the charity has enaged in improper political activities before and the attitude of the charity trustees.

75. Political activity by the trustees of a charity would not normally affect its **7–60** charitable status and be a reason for removing it from the Register of Charities, as the issue would concern the propriety of the trustees' management of the charity rather than the nature of the charity's purposes. If, however, the trustees could argue successfully that the express purposes of the institution were wide enough to cover impermissible political activities, then the question of whether the organisation was established for exclusively charitable purposes would arise, and could lead to its removal from the Register of Charities.

Section 8: Conclusion

76. The extent to which charities are allowed to promote, support or take part **7–61** in political activities has to be considered in each case in the light of all the relevant circumstances. It is not sufficient for the trustees simply to *believe* that their activities will effectively further the purposes of the charity; there must be a *reasonable expectation* that this is so. Trustees should not hesitate to consult their legal advisers, or to seek advice from us, before undertaking any activity which might be beyond the proper scope of the charity.

II. TRUSTS FOR THE RELIEF OF POVERTY

This group of charitable trusts has its origins in that part of the preamble **7–62** to the Statute of Charitable Uses 1601 which speaks of "the relief of aged, impotent and poor people." It has been held that these words must be read disjunctively so that a trust is charitable if the beneficiaries are either elderly or ill or poor.[66] The word "relief" implies that the persons in question have a need attributable to their condition as aged, ill or poor persons which requires alleviating and which those persons could not alleviate or would find difficulty in alleviating themselves from their own resources. The word "relief" is not synonymous with "benefit."[67-69] A trust for aged millionaires of Mayfair would thus not be charitable.

"Poverty" is a relative term and the expression "poor people" is not **7–63** necessarily confined to the destitute poor: it includes persons who have to "go short" in the ordinary acceptation of that term, due regard being had to their station in life and so forth.[70] Thus, a trust fund for "poor and needy" relatives could be used to assist those who may need a

---

[66] Age; *Re Robinson* [1951] Ch. 198; *Re Glyn's W.T.* [1950] 2 All E.R. 1150n.; *Re Bradbury* [1950] 2 All E.R. 1150n.; *Rowntree Memorial Trust Housing Association v. Att.-Gen.* [1983] Ch. 159; impotence: *Re Elliott* (1910) 102 L.T. 528; *Re Hillier* [1944] 1 All E.R. 480; *Re Lewis* [1955] Ch. 104.
[67-69] *Rowntree Memorial Trust* [1983] Ch. 159 at 171, *per* Peter Gibson J.
[70] *Re Segelman* [1996] Ch. 171; *Re Coulthurst* [1951] Ch. 661 at 666; *Re Young* [1953] 3 All E.R. 689.

helping hand from time to time in order to overcome an unforeseen crisis: the failure of a business venture, urgent repairs to a dwelling house or expenses brought on by reason of failing health while the "working classes" do not *ipso facto* constitute a section of the poor.[71] In *Re Niyazi's* W.T.[72] a gift of residue worth about £15,000 for "the construction of or as a contribution towards the construction of a working men's hostel" in Famagusta was held charitable. The size of the gift, the grave housing shortage in Famagusta, and the term "working men's hostel" provided a sufficient connotation of poverty to make the gift charitable.

7–64   If a trust may be brought under any of the other three heads, then it is no objection that it may incidentally benefit the rich as well as the poor; but if it cannot be brought under any head save that of the relief of poverty, then the benefits contemplated by the trust must be directed exclusively to that end: *Re Gwyon*,[73] where clothing for boys would benefit rich and poor boys.

7–65   Trusts for the relief of poverty (but not for the relief of elderly[74] or ill persons[75]) form an exception to the principle that every charitable trust must be for the public benefit so that the beneficiaries must not be a private class defined by reference to a personal nexus with a particular person. The exception covers both the poor relations of a named individual[76] and the poor employees of a particular employer and their families: *Dingle v. Turner, infra.* However, there must be a primary intent to relieve poverty, though amongst a particular class of person. If the primary intent is to benefit particular persons (*e.g.* A, B, C and their children for their relief in needy circumstances) the trust is a private one and not charitable.[77]

DINGLE v. TURNER

House of Lords [1972] A.C. 601; [1972] 2 W.L.R. 523; [1972] 1 All E.R. 878.

The facts sufficiently appear in Lord Cross' speech, *infra*.

7–66   VISCOUNT DILHORNE: "My Lords, I agree with Lord Cross that this appeal should be dismissed and with the reasons he gives for the conclusion.

"With Lord MacDermott, I too do not wish to extend my concurrence to what my noble and learned friend Lord Cross has said with regard to the fiscal privileges of a legal charity. Those privileges may be altered from time to time by

---

[71] *Re Sanders' W.T.* [1954] Ch. 265, ("dwellings for the working classes and their families resident in the area of Pembroke Dock or within a radius of 5 miles therefrom" held not charitable).
[72] [1978] 3 All E.R. 785. Also see *Cresswell v. Potter* [1978] 1 W.L.R. 255 at 257 treating "poor" as a member of the lower income group," covering post office telephonists.
[73] [1930] 1 Ch. 255.
[74] *Re Dunlop* [1984] N.I. 408 (trust to found a home for old Presbyterian persons held to be for sufficient section of public to be charitable under fourth head of charity).
[75] *Re Resch's W.T.* [1969] 1 A.C. 514.
[76] *Re Scarisbrick* [1951] Ch. 662.
[77] *Re Scarisbrick* [1951] Ch. 662; *Re Cohen* [1973] 1 W.L.R. 415; *Re Segelman* [1995] 3 All E.R. 676 at 687–692 (26 persons in class which would increase with birth of further members).

Parliament and I doubt whether their existence should be a determining factor in deciding whether a gift or trust is charitable."

LORD MACDERMOTT: "My Lords, the conclusion I have reached on the facts of **7–67** this case is that the gift in question constitutes a public trust for the relief of poverty which is charitable in law. I would therefore dismiss the appeal.

"I do not find it necessary to state my reasons for this conclusion in detail. In the first place, the views which I have expressed at some length in relation to an educational trust in *Oppenheim v. Tobacco Securities Trust Co. Ltd.*[78] seem to me to apply to this appeal and to mean that it fails. And, secondly, I have had the advantage of reading the opinion prepared by my noble and learned friend, Lord Cross of Chelsea, and find myself in agreement with his conclusion for the reasons he has given. But I would prefer not to extend my concurrence to what my noble and learned friend goes on to say respecting the fiscal privileges of a legal charity. This subject may be material on the question whether what is alleged to be a charity is sufficiently altruistic in nature to qualify as such, but beyond that, and without wishing to express any final view on the matter, I doubt if these consequential privileges have much relevance to the primary question whether a given trust or purpose should be held charitable in law."

LORD HODSON: "My Lords, I agree with my noble and learned friend, Lord **7–68** Cross of Chelsea, that this appeal should be dismissed and with his reasons for that conclusion. With this reservation: that I share the doubts expressed by my noble and learned friends, Lord MacDermott and Viscount Dilhorne, as to the relevance of fiscal considerations in deciding whether a gift or trust is charitable."

LORD SIMON OF GLAISDALE: "My Lords, I have had the advantage of reading the opinion of my noble and learned friend, Lord Cross of Chelsea, with which I agree."

LORD CROSS OF CHELSEA: "My Lords, . . . Clause 8(*e*) was in the following **7–69** terms:

'(*e*) To invest the sum of ten thousand pounds in any of the investments for the time being authorised by law for the investment of trust funds in the names of three persons (hereinafter referred to as "the Pension Fund Trustees") to be nominated for the purpose by the persons who at the time at which my Executors assent to this bequest are directors of E. Dingle & Company Limited and the Pension Fund Trustees shall hold the said sum and the investments for the time being representing the same (hereinafter referred to as "the Pensions Fund") UPON TRUST to apply the income thereof in paying pensions to poor employees of E. Dingle & Company Limited or of any other company to which upon any reconstruction or amalgamation the goodwill and the assets of E. Dingle & Company Limited may be transferred who are of the age of Sixty years at least or who being of the age of Forty five years at least are incapacitated from earning their living by reason of some physical or mental infirmity PROVIDED ALWAYS that if at any time the Pension Fund Trustees shall for any reason be unable to apply the income of the Pension Fund in paying such pensions to such employees as aforesaid the Pension Fund Trustees

---

[78] [1951] A.C. 297. See *infra*, at para. 7–105.

shall hold the Pensions Fund and the income thereof UPON TRUST for the aged poor in the Parish of St. Andrew, Plymouth.'

Finally by clause 8(*g*) the testator directed his trustees to hold the ultimate residue of his estate on the trusts set out in clause 8(*e*).

7–70   "The testator died on January 10, 1950. His widow died on October 8, 1966, having previously released her testamentary power of appointment over her husband's shares in E. Dingle & Co. Ltd, which accordingly fell into the residuary estate. When these proceedings started in July 1970, the value of the fund held on the trusts declared by clause 8(*e*) was about £320,000 producing a gross income of about £17,800 per annum.

7–71   "E. Dingle and Co. Ltd was incorporated as a private company on January 20, 1935. Its capital was owned by the testator and one John Russell Baker and it carried on the business of a departmental store. At the time of the testator's death the company employed over 600 persons and there was a substantial number of ex-employees. On October 23, 1950, the company became a public company. Since the testator's death its business has expanded and when these proceedings started it had 705 full-time and 189 part-time employees and was paying pensions to 89 ex-employees.

"The trustees took out an originating summons asking the court to determine whether the trust declared by clause 8(*e*) were valid and if so to determine various subsidiary questions of construction—as, for example, whether part-time employees or employees of subsidiary companies were eligible to receive benefits under the trust. To this summons they made defendants (1) representatives of the various classes of employees or ex-employees, (2) those who would be interested on an intestacy if the trusts failed, and (3) Her Majesty's Attorney-General. It has been common ground throughout that the trust at the end of clause 8(*e*) for the aged poor in the Parish of St. Andrew Plymouth is dependent on the preceding trust for poor employees of the company so that although it will catch any surplus income which the trustees do not apply for the benefit of poor employees it can have no application if the preceding trust is itself void.

7–72   "The contentions of the appellant and the respondents may be stated broadly as follows. The appellant says that in the *Oppenheim* case this House decided that in principle a trust ought not to be regarded as charitable if the benefits under it are confined either to the descendants of a named individual or individuals or the employees of a given individual or company and that although the 'poor relations' cases may have to be left standing as an anomalous exception to the general rule because their validity has been recognised for so long, the exception ought not to be extended to 'poor employees' trusts which had not been recognised for long before their status as charitable trusts began to be called in question. The respondents, on the other hand, say, first, that the rule laid down in the *Oppenheim* case with regard to educational trusts ought not to be regarded as a rule applicable in principle to all kinds of charitable trust and, secondly, that in any case it is impossible to draw any logical distinction between 'poor relations' trusts and 'poor employees' trusts, and, that as the former cannot be held invalid today after having been recognised as valid for so long, the latter must be regarded as valid also.

7–73   "By a curious coincidence within a few months of the decision of this House in the *Oppenheim* case the cases on gifts to 'poor relations' had to be considered by the Court of Appeal in *Re Scarisbrick*.[79] Most of the cases on this subject were

---

[79] [1951] Ch. 622.

decided in the eighteenth or early nineteenth centuries and are very inadequately reported but two things at least were clear. First, that it never occurred to the judges who decided them that in the field of 'poverty' a trust could not be a charitable trust if the class of beneficiaries was defined by reference to descent from a common ancestor. Secondly, that the courts did not treat a gift or trust as necessarily charitable because the objects of it had to be poor in order to qualify, for in some of the cases the trust was treated as a private trust and not a charity. The problem in *Re Scarisbrick* was to determine on what basis the distinction was drawn. The Court of Appeal held that in this field the distinction between a public or charitable trust and a private trust depended on whether as a matter of construction the gift was for the relief of poverty amongst a particular description of poor people or was merely a gift to particular poor persons. The fact that the gift took the form of a perpetual trust would no doubt indicate that the intention of the donor could not have been to confer private benefits on particular people whose possible necessities he had in mind; but the fact that the capital of the gift was to be distributed at once did not necessarily show that the gift was a private trust.

[His Lordship then reviewed the earlier cases leading up to *Gibson v. S.* **7–74** *American Stores.*]

"The facts in *Gibson v. South American Stores (Gath & Chaves) Ltd*[80]—the case followed by Megarry J. in this case—were that a company had vested in trustees a fund derived solely from its profits to be applied at the discretion of the directors in granting gratuities, pensions or allowances to persons—

> 'who . . . are or shall be necessitous and deserving and who for the time being are or have been in the company's employ . . . and the wives widows husbands widowers children parents and other dependants of any person who for the time being is or would if living have been himself or herself a member of the class of beneficiaries.'

The Court of Appeal held that this trust was a valid charitable trust but it did so **7–75** without expressing a view of its own on the question of principle involved, because the case of *Re Laidlaw*[81] which was unearthed in the course of the hearing showed that the Court of Appeal had already accepted the decision in *Re Gosling*[82] as correct.

"In *Oppenheim v. Tobacco Securities Trust Co. Ltd*[83] this House had to consider the principle laid down by the Court of Appeal in *Re Compton*.[84] There the trustees of a fund worth over £125,000 were directed to apply its income and also if they thought fit all or any part of the capital—

> "in providing for or assisting in providing for the education of children of employees or former employees of British-American Tobacco Co., Ltd . . . or any of its subsidiary or allied companies . . .'

"There were over 110,000 such employees. The majority of your Lordships— **7–76** namely Lord Simonds (in whose judgment Lord Oaksey concurred), Lord Normand and Lord Morton of Henryton—in holding that the trust was not a

---

[80] [1950] Ch. 177.
[81] (January 11, 1935) unreported, the decision (and not the reasoning) only being available.
[82] (1900) 48 W.R. 300.
[83] [1951] A.C. 297.
[84] [1945] Ch. 123.

valid charitable trust gave unqualified approval to the *Compton* principle. They held, that is to say, that although the 'poverty' cases might afford an anomalous exception to the rule, it was otherwise a general rule applicable to all charitable trusts that no class of beneficiaries can constitute a 'section of the public' for the purpose of the law of charity if the distinguishing quality which links them together is relationship to a particular individual either through common descent or common employment. My noble and learned friend, Lord MacDermott, on the other hand, in his dissenting speech, while not challenging the correctness of the decisions in *Re Compton* or in the *Hobourn Aero* case[85] said that he could not regard the principle stated by Lord Greene M.R. as a criterion of general applicability and conclusiveness. He said:[86]

7-77   '. . . I see much difficulty in dividing the qualities or attributes which may
                serve to bind human beings into classes into two mutually exclusive groups,
                the one involving individual status and purely personal, the other dis-
                regarding such status and quite impersonal. As a task this seems to me no
                less baffling and elusive than the problem to which it is directed, namely,
                the determination of what is and what is not a section of the public for the
                purposes of this branch of the law.'

He thought that the question whether any given trust was a public or a private trust was a question of degree to be decided in the light of the facts of the particular case and that viewed in that light the trust in the *Oppenheim* case was a valid charitable trust . . .

7-78   "The *Oppenheim* case was a case of an educational trust and although the majority evidently agreed with the view expressed by the Court of Appeal in the *Hobourn Aero* case,[87] that the *Compton* rule was of universal application outside the field of poverty, it would no doubt be open to this House without overruling *Oppenheim* to hold that the scope of the rule was more limited. If ever I should be called on to pronounce on this question—which does not arise in this appeal—I would as at present advised be inclined to draw a distinction between the practical merits of the *Compton* rule and the reasoning by which Lord Greene M.R. sought to justify it. That reasoning—based on the distinction between personal and impersonal relationships—has never seemed to me very satisfactory and I have always—if I may say so—felt the force of the criticism to which my noble and learned friend Lord MacDermott subjected it in his dissenting speech in the *Oppenheim* case.[88] For my part I would prefer to approach the problem on far broader lines. The phrase 'a section of the public' is in truth a phrase which may mean different things to different people. In the law of charity judges have sought to elucidate its meaning by contrasting it with another phrase 'a fluctuating body of private individuals.' But I get little help from the supposed contrast for as I see it one and the same aggregate of persons may well be describable both as a section of the public and as a fluctuating body of private individuals. The ratepayers in the Royal Borough of Kensington and Chelsea, for example, certainly constitute a section of the public; but would it be a misuse of language to describe them as a 'fluctuating body of private

---

[85] [1946] Ch. 194.
[86] [1951] A.C. 297 at 317.
[87] [1946] Ch. 194.
[88] [1951] A.C. 297. (See also G. Cross, as Lord Cross then was, (1956) 72 L.Q.R. 187.)

individuals'? After all, every part of the public is composed of individuals and being susceptible of increase or decrease is fluctuating. So at the end of the day one is left where one started with the bare contrast between 'public' and 'private.' No doubt some classes are more naturally describable as sections of the public **7-79** than as private classes while other classes are more naturally describable as private classes than as sections of the public. The blind, for example, can naturally be described as a section of the public; but what they have in common—their blindness—does not join them together in such a way that they **7-80** could be called a private class. On the other hand, the descendants of Mr. Gladstone might more reasonably be described as a 'private class' than as a section of the public, and in the field of common employment the same might well be said of the employees in some fairly small firm. But if one turns to large companies employing many thousands of men and women most of whom are quite unknown to one another and to the directors the answer is by no means so clear. One might say that in such a case the distinction between a section of the public and a private class is not applicable at all or even that the employees in such concerns as ICI or GEC are just as much 'sections of the public' as the residents in some geographical area. In truth the question whether or not the potential beneficiaries of a trust can fairly be said to constitute a section of the public is a question of degree and cannot be by itself decisive of the question whether the trust is a charity. Much must depend on the purpose of the trust. It may well be that, on the one hand, a trust to promote some purpose, prima facie charitable, will constitute a charity even though the class of potential beneficiaries might fairly be called a private class and that, on the other hand, a trust to promote another purpose, also prima facie charitable, will not constitute a charity even though the class of potential beneficiaries might seem to some people fairly describable as a section of the public.

"In answering the question whether any given trust is a charitable trust the **7-81** courts—as I see it—cannot avoid having regard to the fiscal privileges accorded to charities. As counsel for the Attorney-General remarked in the course of the argument the law of charity is bedevilled by the fact that charitable trusts enjoy two quite different sorts of privilege. On the one hand, they enjoy immunity from the rules against perpetuity and uncertainty and although individual potential beneficiaries cannot sue to enforce them the public interest arising under them is protected by the Attorney-General. If this was all there would be no reason for the courts not to look favourably on the claim of any 'purpose' trust to be considered as a charity if it seemed calculated to confer some real benefit on those intended to benefit by it whoever they might be and if it would fail if not held to be a charity. But that is not all. Charities automatically enjoy fiscal privileges which with the increased burden of taxation have become more and more important and in deciding that such and such a trust is a charitable trust the court is endowing it with a substantial annual subsidy at the expense of the taxpayer. Indeed, claims of trusts to rank as charities are just as often challenged by the Revenue as by those who would take the fund if the trust was invalid. It is, of course, unfortunate that the recognition of any trust as a valid charitable trust should automatically attract fiscal privileges, for the question whether a trust to further some purpose is so little likely to benefit the public that it ought to be declared invalid and the question whether it is likely to confer such great benefits on the public that it should enjoy fiscal immunity are really two quite different questions. The logical solution would be to separate them and to say—as the Radcliffe Commission proposed—that only some charities should enjoy fiscal **7-82** privileges. But as things, are, validity and fiscal immunity march hand in hand

7–83 and the decisions in the *Compton*[89] and *Oppenheim*[90] cases were pretty obviously influenced by the consideration that if such trusts as were there in question were held valid they would enjoy an undeserved fiscal immunity. To establish a trust for the education of the children of employees in a company in which you are interested is no doubt a meritorious act; but however numerous the employees may be the purpose which you are seeking to achieve is not a public purpose.[91] It is a company purpose and there is no reason why your fellow taxpayers should contribute to a scheme which by providing 'fringe benefits' for your employees will benefit the company by making their conditions of employment more attractive. The temptation to enlist the assistance of the law of charity in private endeavours of this sort is considerable—witness the recent case of the Metal Box scholarships—*Inland Revenue Comrs. v. Educational Grants Association Ltd.*[92]— and the courts must do what they can to discourage such attempts. In the field of poverty the danger is not so great as in the field of education—for while people are keenly alive to the need to give their children a good education and to the expense of doing so, they are generally optimistic enough not to entertain serious fears of falling on evil days much before they fall on them. Consequently the existence of company 'benevolent funds,' the income of which is free of tax does not constitute a very attractive 'fringe benefit.' This is a practical justification— although not, of course, the historical explanation—for the special treatment accorded to poverty trusts in charity law. For the same sort of reason a trust to promote some religion among the employees of a company might perhaps safely be held to be charitable provided that it was clear that the benefits were to be purely spiritual. On the other hand, many 'purpose' trusts falling under Lord Macnaghten's fourth head if confined to a class of employees would clearly be open to the same sort of objection as educational trusts. As I see it, it is on these broad lines rather than for the reasons actually given by Lord Greene M.R. that the *Compton* rule can best be justified.

"My Lords, I would dismiss this appeal." *Appeal dismissed.*

III. TRUSTS FOR THE ADVANCEMENT OF EDUCATION

Educational purposes

7–84 This group of charitable trusts has its origins in those parts of the preamble to the Statute of Charitable Uses 1601 which speak of "the maintenance of schools of learning, free schools and scholars in universities" and "the education and preferment of orphans." It is now clear that trusts endowing fee-paying schools are charitable if the school is non-profit-making or if, though profit-making, its profits are used for school purposes only.[93] Similarly, the Incorporated Council of Law Reporting is a charity because its charges are retained for its purposes and do not enure for the benefit of its members: it provides essential material for the study of law so as to be for the advancement of

---

[89] [1945] Ch. 123.
[90] [1951] A.C. 297.
[91] For a critical view of this approach see T. G. Watkin [1978] Conv. 277.
[92] [1967] Ch. 993, *infra*, p. 447.
[93] *Abbey Malvern Wells Ltd v. Ministry of Local Government* [1951] Ch. 728; *Customs & Excise Commissioners v. Bell Concord Education Trust* [1989] 2 All E.R. 217.

education, it being immaterial that thereby lawyers are able to make money because one must not confuse the results flowing from the achievement of the purpose with the purpose itself.[94]

Education is not confined to matters formally taught in schools and **7–85** universities. It includes the promotion or encouragement of the arts and graces of life: see *Re Shaw's Will Trusts*[95] ("the teaching, promotion and encouragement in Ireland of self-control, elocution, oratory, deportment, the arts of personal contact, of social intercourse, and the other arts of public, private, professional and business life"); *Royal Choral Society v. I.R.C.*[96] (choral singing in London); *Re Levien*[97] (organ music); *Re Delius*[98] (the music of the composer Delius); *Re Dupree's Deed Trusts*[99] (encouragement of chess-playing among young people in Portsmouth); and *Re South Place Ethical Society*[1] (the study and dissemination of ethical principles and the cultivation of a rational religious sentiment). Indeed, the Charity Commissioners have upheld as charitable[2] a Cult **7–86** Information Centre (researching into and making people aware of movements concerned with the exploration of spiritual life) and Public Concern at Work (concerned with promoting business ethics and advising and protecting employees faced with ethical dilemmas at work).

The decision of Harman J. in *Re Shaw*[3] (denying charitable status **7–87** where George Bernard Shaw had bequeathed funds for pursuing inquiries into a new 40 letter alphabet) appeared to render doubtful the validity of trusts for the advancement of research, at any rate where no element of teaching was involved; but the decision of Wilberforce J. in *Re Hopkins' Will Trusts, infra*[4] removes most of the doubts. Wilberforce J. held "that the word 'education', as used by Harman J, must be used in a wide sense, certainly extending beyond teaching, and that the requirement is that, in order to be charitable, research must either be of educational value to the researcher or must be so directed as to lead to something which will pass into the store of educational material or so as to improve the sum of communicable knowledge in an area which education may cover . . . research of a private character, for the benefit only of the members of a society, would not normally be educational or otherwise charitable but I do not think that the research in the present case [into the works of Francis Bacon and whether he might have been the author of plays ascribed to Shakespeare] can be said to be of private character, for it is inherently inevitable and manifestly intended that the result of any discovery should be published to the world."

---

[94] *Incorporated Council of Law Reporting v. An.-Gen.* [1972] Ch. 73 where two L.JJ. held the Council to fall within the educational head of charity and all three L.JJ. held it within the fourth head.
[95] [1952] Ch. 163.
[96] [1943] 2 All E.R. 101; contrast *Associated Artists Ltd v. I.R.C.* [1956] 1 W.L.R. 752 (production of artistic dramatic works).
[97] [1955] 1 W.L.R. 964.
[98] [1957] Ch. 299; contrast *Re Pinion* [1965] Ch. 85 (bequest of worthless works of art to found a museum); *Sutherland's Trustees v. Verschoyle*, 1968 S.L.T. 43.
[99] [1945] Ch. 16.
[1] [1980] 1 W.L.R. 1565.
[2] See respectively Decisions Vol. 1, p. 1 and Vol. 2, p. 5.
[3] [1965] Ch. 699; [1957] 1 W.L.R. 729.
[4] See (1965) 29 Conv. (N.S.) 368 (Newark and Samuels).

7–88   In *McGovern v. Att.-Gen.*[5] Slade J. summarised the principles as follows:

> "(1) A trust for research will ordinarily qualify as a charitable trust if, but only if (a) the subject matter of the proposed research is a useful subject of study; and (b) it is contemplated that knowledge acquired as a result of the research will be disseminated to others; and (c) the trust is for the benefit of the public, or a sufficiently important section of the public. (2) In the absence of a contrary context, however, the court will be readily inclined to construe a trust for research as importing subsequent dissemination of the results thereof. (3) Furthermore, if a trust for research is to constitute a valid trust for the advancement of education, it is not necessary either (a) that a teacher/pupil relationship should be in contemplation, or (b) that the persons to benefit from the knowledge to be acquired should be persons who are already in the course of receiving 'education' in the conventional sense."

7–89   The promotion of sport as such is not a charitable object: see *Re Nottage*[6] (yacht-racing); *Re Clifford*[7] (angling); *Re Patten*[8] (cricket); *Re King*[9] (general sport); *Re Birchfield Harriers*[10] (competitive athletics for both sexes from 10 years old); *I.R.C. v. Baddeley*[11] (moral, social and physical training and recreation). In certain circumstances trusts for similar objects may now be charitable by virtue of being a recreational trust for the public within the fourth head of charitable trusts,[12] or of the Recreational Charities Act 1958, *infra*.[13] On the other hand, where the promotion of sport is ancillary to a charitable object, it will itself be charitable: *Re Mariette*[14] (sport in a school—educational), *Re Gray*[15] (sport in a regiment—general public benefit in promoting the efficiency of the Army), *London Hospital Medical College v. I.R.C.*[16] (athletic, social and cultural activities of Students Union charitable as furthering educational purposes of College), *I.R.C. v. McMullen, infra*, para. 7–93 (soccer and other sports in the physical education and development of pupils at schools and universities).

---

5 [1982] Ch. 321 at 352.
6 [1885] 2 Ch. 649.
7 (1911) 106 L.T. 14.
8 [1929] 2 Ch. 276.
9 [1931] W.N. 232.
10 [1989] Report of Charity Commissioners, paras. 48–55.
11 [1955] A.C. 572.
12 See *infra*, pp. 460–463, *Re Morgan* [1955] 2 All E.R. 632, *Re Oxford Ice Skating Rink* [1984] Report of Charity Commissioners, paras. 19–25.
13 See *infra*, at paras 7–123 *et seq.*
14 [1915] 2 Ch. 284; *Re Geere's W.T.* [1954] C.L.Y. 388 (swimming bath at Marlborough College).
15 [1925] Ch. 362; but this has been doubted in *I.R.C. v. City of Glasgow Police Athletic Association* [1953] A.C. 380 at 391, 401.
16 [1976] 2 All E.R. 113; *Att.-Gen. v. Ross* [1985] 3 All E.R. 334 (N. London Polytechnic Students' Union charitable).

Public benefit

The promotion of a particular type of political education[17] is not **7–90** charitable; and some other forms of education may also not be for the public benefit: *Re Hummeltenberg*[18] (training of spiritualistic mediums). In *Southwood v. Attorney–General*[19] the Court of Appeal held that a trust to educate the public that peace is best secured by disarmament and pacifism was not charitable because "the court cannot determine whether or not it promotes the public benefit for the public to be" so educated: "there are differing views as to how best to secure peace and avoid war . . . on the one hand it can be argued that war is best avoided by bargaining through strength; on the other hand it can be argued that peace is best secured through disarmament—if necessary, by unilateral disarmament." The court and not the settlor determines whether public benefit is present so that a testator cannot set up a charitable museum of his artistic collection if it has no artistic merit.[20] The fact that it is by means of an educational process that non-charitable purposes are to be achieved does not render such purposes charitable.[21]

A trust for the education of beneficiaries who are ascertained by **7–91** reference to some personal tie (*e.g.* of blood or contract), such as the relations of a particular individual, the members of a particular family, the employees of a particular firm, or the members of a particular trade union, lacks the element of public benefit and is not charitable: *Oppenheim v. Tobacco Securities Trust Co. Ltd, infra*, para. 7–105, though this may require reconsideration in the light of *Dingle v. Turner*[22] where large-scale trusts are concerned. A trust to educate residents of a town[23] or children of members of a particular profession[24] or to provide "closed" scholarships from a specified school to a specified Oxbridge College will be valid.[25]

Merely creating a clearly valid charitable trust, *e.g.* "for the advancement of the education of children in the United Kingdom" will not confer tax advantages if the trustees run the trust as a private trust for certain associated persons: *I.R.C. v. Educational Grants Association, infra*, para. 7–120. Indeed, the trustees will be acting beyond their powers and so be liable for breach of trust.

If a trust for a broad charitable class of beneficiaries gives the trustees **7–92** a power, without being under any duty, to prefer a certain private class within the broader public class this does not vitiate the validity of the

---

[17] *Bonar Law Memorial Trust v. I.R.C.* (1933) 49 T.L.R. 220; *Re Hopkinson* [1949] 1 All E.R. 346; *cf. Re Scowcroft* [1898] 2 Ch. 638 which nowadays should be regarded as of doubtful authority; and *see Re McDougall* [1957] 1 W.L.R. 81 (study of methods of government is a charitable object).

[18] [1923] 1 Ch. 237. *Cf. Funnel v. Stewart* [1996] 1 All E.R. 715.

[19] [2000] W.T.L.R. 1199, 1217.

[20] *Re Pinion* [1965] Ch. 85.

[21] *Re Koeppler's W.T.* [1984] 2 All E.R. 111 though reversed by the Court of Appeal [1985] 2 All E.R. 869 since the purpose was held charitable.

[22] [1972] A.C. 601, set out *supra.* at para. 7–64. However the majority there seemed to favour the result in *Oppenheim*, tax advantages preventing the trust being sufficiently altruistic.

[23] *Re Tree* [1945] Ch. 325: a restriction to Methodists or members of the Church of England would seem valid.

[24] *Hall v. Derby Sanitary Authority* (1885) 16 Q.B.D. 163 approved in *Oppenheim v. Tobacco Securities Trust Co.* [1951] A.C. 297, *infra*, p. 442.

[25] Picarda *Law & Practice Relating to Charities* (2nd ed.), p. 49.

trust as a charitable trust.[26] However, payments to members of the private class will have unfortunate tax consequences if regarded as of such significance that they ought fairly to be considered as misuse of public funds for a private purpose. Rather than put the tax inspector on his mettle some settlors may omit the preference from the trust deed and rely on the sensible selection of beneficiaries by trustees.

7–93 If the trust for the broad charitable class imposes a duty upon the trustees to use the whole, if possible, or an uncertain part of the funds for a specified private class then the trust cannot be a valid charitable trust.[27] If only a maximum specified part of the fund is directed to be used for the private class then whilst such part should not be charitable the remainder, presumably, should be severed as charitable since it can **7–94** be used for exclusively charitable purposes. However, in *Re Koettgen*[28] (doubted in *I.R.C. v. Educational Grants Association*[29] *infra*, at para. 7–120). Upjohn J. in a brief extempore judgment held that if there was a broad primary class that was charitable the trust remained charitable despite an imperative direction imposing a duty to prefer a private class for up to a maximum of 75 per cent. of the trust income. This is difficult to justify logically, but pragmatically it validates the trust, whilst leaving it open to the Revenue to charge tax if the trust is operated as a private trust and enabling charitable purposes to be carried out to the extent it is impossible or impracticable to benefit the preferred class. The Charity Commissioners have accepted *Re Koettgen* as good law.[30]

INLAND REVENUE COMMISSIONERS v. MCMULLEN

House of Lords [1981] A.C. 1; [1980] 1 All E.R. 884.

7–95 LORD HAILSHAM: "Four questions arose for decision below. In the first place neither the parties nor the judgments below were in agreement as to the proper construction of the trust deed itself. Clearly this is a preliminary debate which must be settled before the remaining questions are even capable of decision. In the second place the trustees contend and the Crown disputes that, on the correct construction of the deed, the trust is charitable as being for the advancement of education. Thirdly, the trustees contend and the Crown disputes that if they are wrong on the second question the trust is charitable at least because it falls within the fourth class of Lord Macnaghten's categories as enumerated in *Income Tax Special Purposes Comrs. v. Pemsel*[31] as a trust beneficial to the community within the spirit and intendment of the preamble to

---

[26] *Re Koettgen* [1954] Ch. 252; *Caffoor v. Comr. of Income Tax, Colombo* [1961] A.C. 584; *I.R.C. v. Educational Grants Association* [1967] Ch. 123, dealing with above cases *infra*, para. 7–120.

[27] *Re Martin* (1977) 121 Sol. J. 828, *The Times*, November 17, 1977. An anomalous exception exists for the ancient English institution of educational provision for Founder's Kin in certain schools and colleges "though there seems to be virtually no direct authority as to the principle on which they rested and they should probably be regarded more as belonging to history than to doctrine": *Caffoor v. Comr. of Income Tax* [1961] A.C. 584, at 602.

[28] [1954] Ch. 252.

[29] [1967] Ch. 123.

[30] [1978] Annual Report, paras. 86, 89.

[31] [1891] A.C. 531 at 583: [1891–94] All E.R. Rep. 28 at 55.

the statute 43 Eliz. I, c. 4.[32] Fourthly, the trustees contend and the Crown disputes that, even if not otherwise charitable, the trust is a valid charitable trust as falling within section I of the Recreational Charities Act 1958, that is as a trust to provide or to assist in the provision of facilities for recreation or other leisure time occupation provided in the interests of social welfare.

"Since we have reached the view that the trust is a valid educational charity **7–96** their Lordships have not sought to hear argument nor, therefore, to reach a conclusion on any but the first two disputed questions in the dispute. Speaking for myself, however, I do not wish my absence of decision on the third or fourth points to be interpreted as an indorsement of the majority judgments in the Court of Appeal nor as necessarily dissenting from the contrary views contained in the minority judgment of Bridge L.J. For me at least the answers to the third and fourth questions are still left entirely undecided.

"I now turn to the question of construction, for which it is necessary that I reproduce the material portions of the deed . . .

"The objects of the Trusts are:—

'(a) to organise or provide or assist in the organisation and provision of **7–97** facilities which will enable and encourage pupils of Schools and Universities in any part of the United Kingdom to play Association Football or other games or sports and thereby to assist in ensuring that due attention is given to the physical education and development of such pupils as well as to the development and occupation of their minds and with a view to furthering this object (i) to provide or assist in the provision of Association Football or games or sports equipment of every kind for the use of such pupils as aforesaid (ii) to provide or assist in the provision of courses lectures demonstrations and coaching for pupils of Schools and Universities in any part of the United Kingdom and for teachers who organise or supervise playing and coaching of Association Football or other games or sports at such Schools and Universities as aforesaid (iii) to promote provide or assist in the promotion and provision of training colleges for the purpose of training teachers in the coaching of Association Football or other games or sports at such Schools and Universities as aforesaid (iv) to lay out manage equip and maintain or assist in the laying out management equipment and maintenance of playing fields or appropriate indoor facilities or accommodation (whether vested in the Trustees or not) to be used for the teaching and playing of Association Football or other sports or games by such pupils as aforesaid

'(b) to organise or provide or assist in the organisation or provision of **7–98** facilities for physical recreation in the interests of social welfare in any part of the United Kingdom (with the object of improving the conditions of life for the boys and girls for whom the same are provided) for boys and girls who are under the age of twenty-one years and who by reason of their youth or social and economic circumstances have need of such facilities.'

"I pause here only to say that no question arises as to clause 3(b) above which clearly corresponds to the language of the Recreational Charities Act 1958. Controversy therefore revolves solely around clause 3(a), since it is obvious that, if this cannot be shown to be solely for charitable purposes, the whole trust ceases to be a charitable trust . . .

---

[32] Charitable Uses Act 1601.

"I agree with [the judgment of Bridge L.J.] . . . that what the deed means is that the purpose of the settlor is to promote the physical education and development of pupils at schools and universities as an addition to such part of their education as relates to their mental education by providing the facilities and assistance to games and sports in the manner set out at greater length and in greater detail in the enumerated sub-clauses of clause 3(a) of the deed . . .

7–99　　"On a proper analysis, therefore, I do not find clause 3(a) ambiguous. But, before I part with the question of construction, I would wish to express agreement with a contention made on behalf of the trustees and of the Attorney-General, but not agreed to on behalf of the Crown, that in construing trust deeds the intention of which is to set up a charitable trust, and in others too, where it can be claimed that there is an ambiguity, a benignant construction should be given if possible. This was the maxim of the civil law: semper in dubiis benigniora praeferenda sunt. There is a similar maxim in English law: ut res magis valeat quam pereat. It certainly applies to charities when the question is one of uncertainty (*Weir v. Crum-Brown*[33]) and, I think, also where a gift is capable of two constructions one of which would make it void and the other effectual (*cf. Bruce v. Deer Presbytery,*[34] *Houston v. Burns*[35] and *Bain, Public Trustee v. Ross*[36]). In the present case I do not find it necessary to resort to benignancy in order to construe the clause, but, had I been in doubt, I would certainly have been prepared to do so . . .

7–100　　"I must now turn to the deed, construed in the manner in which I have found it necessary to construe it, to consider whether it sets up a valid charitable trust for the advancement of education.

"It is admitted, of course, that the words 'charity' and 'charitable' bear, for the purposes of English law and equity, meanings totally different from the senses in which they are used in ordinary educated speech, or for instance, in the Authorised Version of the Bible But I do not share the view, implied by Stamp and Orr L.JJ. in the instant case,[37] that the words 'education' and 'educational' bear, or can bear, for the purposes of the law of charity, meanings different from those current in present day educated English speech. I do not believe that there is such a difference. What has to be remembered, however, is that, as Lord Wilberforce pointed out in *Re Hopkins' Will Trusts*[38] and in *Scottish Burial Reform and Cremation Society Ltd v. Glasgow City Corpn,*[39] both the legal conception of charity, and within it the educated man's ideas about education are not static, but moving and changing. Both change with changes in ideas about social values. Both have evolved with the years. In particular in applying the law to contemporary circumstances it is extremely dangerous to forget that thoughts concerning the scope and width of education differed in the past greatly from those which are now generally accepted.

7–101　　"In saying this I do not in the least wish to cast doubt on *Re Nottage*,[40] which was referred to in both courts below and largely relied on by the Crown here. Strictly speaking *Re Nottage* was not a case about education at all. The issue there was whether the bequest came into the fourth class of charity categorised

---

[33] [1908] A.C. 162 at 167.
[34] (1867) L.R. 1 Sc. & Div. 96 at 97.
[35] [1918] A.C. 337 at 341–342.
[36] [1930] 1 Ch. 224 at 230.
[37] [1979] 1 W.L.R. 130 at 135, 139.
[38] [1965] Ch. 669 at 678.
[39] [1968] A.C. 138 at 154.
[40] [1895] 2 Ch. 649.

in Lord Macnaghten's classification of 1891.[41] The mere playing of games or enjoyment of amusement or competition is not per se charitable, nor necessarily educational, though they may (or may not) have an educational or beneficial effect if diligently practised. Neither am I deciding in the present case even that a gift for physical education per se and not associated with persons of school age or just above would necessarily be a good charitable gift. That is a question which the courts may have to face at some time in the future. But in deciding what is or is not an educational purpose for the young in 1980 it is not irrelevant to point out what Parliament considered to be educational for the young in 1944 when, by the Education Act of that year in sections 7 and 53 (which are still on the statute book), Parliament attempted to lay down what was then intended to be the statutory system of education organised by the state, and the duties of the local education authorities and the Minister in establishing and maintaining the system. Those sections are so germane to the present issue that I cannot forbear to quote them both. Section 7 provides (in each of the sections the emphasis being mine):

> 'The statutory system of public education shall be organised in three **7–102** progressive stages to be known as primary education, secondary education, and further education; and it shall be the duty of the local education authority for every area, so far as their powers extend, to contribute towards *the spiritual, moral, mental, and physical development of the community by securing that efficient education throughout those stages shall be available to meet the needs of the population of their area'*

and in section 53 of the same Act it is said:

> '(1) It shall be the duty of every local education authority to secure that the facilities for primary, secondary and further education provided for their area include adequate facilities for recreation d social and physical training, and for that purpose a local education authority, with the approval of the Secretary of State, may establish maintain and manage, or assist the establishment, maintenance, and management of *camps, holiday classes, playing fields, play centres and other places (including playgrounds, gymnasiums, and swimming baths not appropriated to any school or college), at which facilities for recreation and for such training as aforesaid are available for persons receiving primary, secondary or further education, and may organise games, expeditions and other activities for such persons, and may defray or contribute towards the expenses thereof.*

"I find the first instance case of *Mariette*,[42] a decision of Eve J., both **7–103** stimulating and instructive. Counsel for the Crown properly reminded us that this concerned a bequest effectively tied to a particular institution. Nevertheless, I cannot forbear to quote a phrase from the judgment, always bearing in mind the danger of quoting out of context. Eve J. said[43]:

> "No one of sense could be found to suggest that between those ages [10 to 19] any boy can be properly educated unless at least as much attention is

---

[41] See *Income Tax Special Purposes Comrs. v. Pemsel* [1891] A.C. 531 at 583.
[42] [1915] 2 Ch. 284.
[43] [1915] 2 Ch. 284 at 288.

given to the development of his body as is given to the development of his mind."

7–104   "Apart from the limitation to the particular institution I would think that these words apply as well to the settlor's intention in the instant appeal as to the testator's in *Re Mariette*, and I regard the limitation to the pupils of schools and universities in the instant case as a sufficient association with the provision of formal education to prevent any danger of vagueness in the object of the trust or irresponsibility or capriciousness in application by the trustees. I am far from suggesting either that the concept of education or of physical education even for the young is capable of indefinite extension. On the contrary, I do not think that the courts have as yet explored the extent to which elements of organisation, instruction or the disciplined inculcation of information, instruction or skill may limit the whole concept of education. I believe that in some ways it will prove more extensive, in others more restrictive than has been thought hitherto. But it is clear at least to me that the decision in *Re Mariette*[44] is not to be read in a sense which confines its application for ever to gifts to a particular institution. It has been extended already in *Re Mellody*[45] to gifts for annual treats for schoolchildren in a particular locality (another decision of Eve J), to playgrounds for children (*Re Chester*,[46] possibly *not* educational, but referred to in *Inland Revenue Comrs. v. Baddeley*[47]); to a children's outing (*Re Ward's Estate*[48]), to a prize for chess to boys and young men resident in the City of Portsmouth (*Re Dupree's Deed Trusts*,[49] a decision of Vaisey J.) and for the furthering of the Boy Scouts' movement by helping to purchase sites for camping, outfits, etc. (*Re Webber*,[50] another decision of Vaisey J.).

7–105   "It is important to remember that in the instant appeal we are dealing with the concept of physical education and development of the young deliberately associated by the settlor with the status of pupillage in schools or universities (of which, according to the evidence, about 95 per cent are within the age-group 17 to 22). We are not dealing with adult education, physical or otherwise, as to which some considerations may be different.

"I am at pains to disclaim the view that the conception of this evolving, and therefore not static, view of education is capable of infinite abuse or, even worse, proving void for uncertainty. Quite apart from the doctrine of the benignant approach to which I have already referred, and which undoubtedly comes to the assistance of settlors in danger of attack for uncertainty, I am content to adopt the approach of my predecessor Lord Loreburn L.C. in *Weir v. Crum-Brown*,[51] to which attention was drawn by counsel for the Attorney-General, that if the bequest to a class of persons, is as here capable of application by the trustees, or, failing them, the court, the gift is not void for uncertainty. Lord Macnaghten also said[52]:

> "The testator has taken pains to provide competent judges. It is for the trustees to consider and determine the value of the service on which a candidate may rest his claim to participate in the testator's bounty."

---

[44] [1915] 2 Ch. 284.
[45] [1918] 1 Ch. 228.
[46] (July 25, 1934) unreported.
[47] [1955] A.C. 572 at 596.
[48] [1937] 81 SJ. 397.
[49] [1945] Ch. 16.
[50] [1954] 1 W.L.R. 1500.
[51] [1908] A.C. 162 at 167.
[52] [1908] A.C. 162 at 169.

"*Mutatis mutandis*, I think this kind of reasoning should apply here. Granted **7–106** that the question of application may present difficulties for the trustees, or, failing them, for the court, nevertheless it is capable of being applied, for the concept in the mind of the settlor is an object sufficiently clear, is exclusively for the advancement of education, and, in the hands of competent judges, is capable of application.

"My Lords, for these reasons I reach the conclusion that the trust is a valid charitable gift for the advancement of education, which, after all, is what it claims to be. The conclusion follows that the appeal should be allowed."

Lords Diplock and Salmon merely concurred while Lords Russell and Keith, concurred and gave brief speeches.

OPPENHEIM v. TOBACCO SECURITIES TRUST CO. LTD

House of Lords [1951] A.C. 297; [1951] 1 T.L.R. 118; [1951] 1 All E.R. 31 (Lord **7–107** Simonds, Normand, Oaksey and Morton; Lord MacDermott dissenting)[53]

Investments were held by the respondents, Tobacco Securities Trust Co. Ltd, on trust to apply the income in providing for the education of children of employees or former employees of British-American Tobacco Co. Ltd . . . or any of its subsidiary or allied companies without any limit of time being specified. The High Court and Court of Appeal held the trust void for perpetuity because it was not charitable on the ground that it lacked public benefit.

LORD SIMONDS: "In the case of trusts for educational purposes the condition of **7–108** the public benefit must be satisfied. The difficulty lies in determining what is sufficient to satisfy the test, and there is little to help your Lordships to solve it.

"If I may begin at the bottom of the scale, a trust established by a father for the education of his son is not a charity. The public element, as I will call it, is not supplied by the fact that from that son's education all may benefit. At the other end of the scale the establishment of a college or university is beyond doubt a charity. 'Schools of learning and free schools, and scholars of universities' are the very words of the preamble to the [Charitable Uses Act 1601 (43 Eliz. I, c. 4)]. So also the endowment of a college, university or school by the creation of scholarships or bursaries is a charity, and nonetheless because competition may be limited to a particular class of persons. It is on this ground, as Lord Greene M.R. pointed out in *Re Compton*,[54] that the so-called 'founder's kin' cases can be rested. The difficulty arises where the trust is not for the benefit of any institution either then existing or by the terms of the trust to be brought into existence, but for the benefit of a class of persons at large. Then the question is whether that class of persons can be regarded as such a 'section of the community' as to satisfy the test of public benefit. These words 'section of the community' have no special sanctity, but they conveniently indicate (1) that the possible (I emphasise the word 'possible') beneficiaries must not be numerically negligible, and (2) that the quality which distinguishes them from other members of the community, so that they form by themselves a section of it, must be a quality which does not depend on their relationship to a particular individual. It

---

[53] See also *Davies v. Perpetual Trustee Co.* [1959] A.C. 439; 75 L.Q.R. 292. These broad employee benefit discretionary trusts were usually void as private trusts before *McPhail v. Doulton* [1971] A.C. 424 liberalised the test for certainty of beneficiaries.
[54] [1945] Ch. 123.

is for this reason that a trust for the education of members of a family or, as in *Re Compton*, of a number of families cannot be regarded as charitable. A group of persons may be numerous, but, if the nexus between them is their personal relationship to a single *propositus* or to several *propositi*, they are neither the community nor a section of the community for charitable purposes.

7–109   "I come, then, to the present case where the class of beneficiaries is numerous, but the difficulty arises in regard to their common and distinguishing quality. That quality is being children of employees of one or other of a group of companies. I can make no distinction between children of employees and the employees themselves. In both cases the common quality is found in employment by particular employers. The latter of the two cases, by which the Court of Appeal held itself to be bound, the *Hobourn* case, is a direct authority for saying that such a common quality does not constitute its possessors a section of the public for charitable purposes. In the former case, *Re Compton*, Lord Greene M.R. had by way of illustration placed members of a family and employees of a particular employer on the same footing, finding neither in common kinship nor

7–110   in common employment the sort of nexus which is sufficient. My Lords, I am so fully in agreement with what was said by Lord Greene in both cases, and by my noble and learned friend, then Morton L.J., in the *Hobourn* case, that I am in danger of repeating without improving upon their words. It appears to me that it would be an extension [of the legal definition of charity], for which there is no justification in principle or authority, to regard common employment as a quality which constitutes those employed a section of the community. It must not, I think, be forgotten that charitable institutions enjoy rare and increasing privileges, and that the claim to come within that privileged class should be clearly established. With the single exception of *Re Rayner*,[55] which I must regard as of doubtful authority, no case has been brought to the notice of the House in which such a claim as this has been made, where there is no element of poverty in the beneficiaries, but just this and no more, that they are the children of those in a common employment.

7–111   "Learned counsel for the appellant sought to fortify his case by pointing to the anomalies that would ensue from the rejection of his argument. For, he said, admittedly those who follow a profession or calling—clergymen, lawyers, colliers, tobacco-workers and so on—are a section of the public; how strange then it would be if, as in the case of railwaymen, those who follow a particular calling are all employed by one employer. Would a trust for the education of railwaymen be charitable,[56] but a trust for the education of men employed on the railways by the Transport Board not be charitable? And what of service of the Crown, whether in the civil service or the armed forces? Is there a difference between soldiers and soldiers of the King? My Lords, I am not impressed by this sort of argument and will consider on its merits if the occasion should arise, the case where the description of the occupation and the employment is in effect the same, where in a word, if you know what a man does, you know who employs him to do it. It is to me a far more cogent argument, as it was to my noble and learned friend in the *Hobourn* case, that, if a section of the public is constituted by the personal relation of employment, it is impossible to say that it is not constituted by a thousand as by 100,000 employees, and if by a thousand, then by a hundred, and, if by a hundred, then by ten. I do not mean merely that there is a

---

[55] (1920) 89 L.J.Ch. 369.
[56] As to this see *Hall v. Derby Sanitary Authority* (1885) 16 Q.B.D. 163.

difficulty in drawing the line, though that, too, is significant. I have it also in mind that, though the actual number of employees at any one moment might be small, it might increase to any extent, just as, being large, it might decrease to any extent. If the number of employees is the test of validity, must the court take into account potential increase or decrease, and, if so, as at what date?

LORD MACDERMOTT (dissenting)[57]: ". . . The question is whether it is of a **7–112** public nature, whether, in the words of Lord Wrenbury in *Verge v. Somerville*,[58] 'it is for the benefit of the community or of an appreciably important class of the community.' The relevant class here is that from which those to be educated are to be selected. The appellant contends that this class is public in character; the respondent bank (as personal representative of the last surviving settlor) denies this and says that the class is no more than a group of private individuals.

"Until comparatively recently the usual way of approaching an issue of this sort, at any rate where educational trusts were concerned, was, I believe, to regard the facts of each case and to treat the matter very much as one of degree. No definition of what constituted a sufficient section of the public for the purpose was applied, for none existed; and the process seems to have been one of reaching a conclusion on a general survey of the circumstances and considerations regarded as relevant rather than of making a single, conclusive test. The investigation left the course of the dividing line between what was and what was not a section of the community unexplored, and was concluded when it had gone far enough to establish to the satisfaction of the court whether or not the trust was public; and the decision as to that was, I think, very often reached by determining whether or not the trust was private.

"If it is still permissible to conduct the present inquiry on these broad if **7–113** imprecise lines, I would hold with the appellant. The numerical strength of the class is considerable on any showing. The employees concerned number over 110,000, and it may reasonably be assumed that the children, who constitute the class in question, are no fewer. The large size of the class is not, of course, decisive but in my view it cannot be left out of account when the problem is approached in this way. Then it must be observed that the *propositi* are not limited to those presently employed. They include former employees (not reckoned in the figure I have given) and are, therefore, a more stable category than would otherwise be the case. And, further, the employees concerned are not limited to those in the service of the 'British American Tobacco Co. Ltd or any of its subsidiary or allied companies'—itself a description of great width—but include the employees, in the event of the British American Tobacco Co. Ltd being reconstructed or merged on amalgamation, of the reconstructed or amalgamated company or any of its subsidiary companies. No doubt the settlors here had a special interest in the welfare of the class they described, but, apart from the fact that this may serve to explain the particular form of their bounty, I do not think it material to the question in hand. What is material, as I regard the matter, is that they have chosen to benefit a class which is, in fact, substantial in point of size and importance and have done so in a manner which, to my mind, manifests an intention to advance the interests of the class described as a class rather than as a collection or succession of particular individuals . . .

---

[57] See (1951) 67 L.Q.R. 162 (R.E.M.); *ibid.* 164 (A. L. G.) and the support in *Dingle v. Turner* [1972] A.C. 601 set out *supra*, at para. 7–75.
[58] [1924] A.C. 496 at 499.

7–114 "The respondent bank, however, contends that the inquiry should be of quite a different character to that which I have been discussing. It advances as the sole criterion a narrower test derived from the decisions of the Court of Appeal in *Compton*,[59] and in *Hobourn*.[60] The basis and nature of this test appear from the passage in the judgment of the court in *Compton*,[61] where Lord Greene M.R., says: 'In the case of many charitable gifts it is possible to identify the individuals who are to benefit, or who at any given moment constitute the class from which the beneficiaries are to be selected. This circumstance does not, however, deprive the gift of its public character. Thus, if there is a gift to relieve the poor inhabitants of a parish the class to benefit is readily ascertainable. But they do not enjoy the benefit, when they receive it, by virtue of their character as

7–115 individuals but by virtue of their membership of the specified class. In such a case the common quality which unites the potential beneficiaries into a class is essentially an impersonal one. It is definable by reference to what each has in common with the others, and that is something into which their status as individuals does not enter. Persons claiming to belong to the class do so not because they are A.B., C.D. and E.F., but because they are poor inhabitants of the parish. If, in asserting their claim, it were necessary for them to establish the fact that they were the individuals A.B., C.D. and E.F., I cannot help thinking that on principle the gift ought not to be held to be a charitable gift, since the introduction into their qualification of a purely personal element would deprive the gift of its necessary public character. It seems to me that the same principle ought to apply when the claimants, in order to establish their status, have to assert and prove, not that they themselves are A.B., C.D., and E.F., but that they stand in some specified relationship to the individuals A.B., C.D., and E.F., such as that of children or employees. In that case, too, a purely personal element enters into and is an essential part of the qualification, which is defined by reference to something, *i.e.*, personal relationship to individuals or an individual which is in its essence non-public.'

7–116 "The test thus propounded focuses upon the common quality which unites those within the class concerned and asks whether that quality is essentially impersonal or essentially personal. If the former, the class will rank as a section of the public and the trust will have the element common to and necessary for all legal charities; but, if the latter, the trust will be private and not charitable. It is suggested in the passage just quoted, and made clear beyond doubt in *Hobourn*,[62] that in the opinion of the Court of Appeal employment by a designated employer must be regarded for this purpose as a personal and not as an impersonal bond of union. In this connection and as illustrating the discriminating character of what I may call 'the *Compton*[63] test' reference should be made to that part of the judgment of the learned Master of the Rolls in *Hobourn*,[64] in which he speaks of the decision in *Hall v. Derby Borough Urban Sanitary Authority*.[65] The passage runs thus:

> "That related to a trust for railway servants. It is said that if a trust for railway servants can be a good charity, so too a trust for railway servants in

---

[59] [1945] Ch. 123.
[60] [1946] Ch. 194.
[61] [1945] Ch. 123 at 129–30.
[62] [1946] Ch. 194.
[63] [1945] Ch. 123.
[64] [1946] Ch. 194 at 206.
[65] (1885) 16 Q.B.D. 163

the employment of a particular railway company is a good charity. That is not so. The reason, I think, is that in the one case the trust is for railway servants in general and in the other case it is for employees of a particular company, a fact which limits the potential beneficiaries to a class ascertained on a purely personal basis."

"My Lords, I do not quarrel with the result arrived at in the *Compton* and **7–117** *Hobourn* cases, and I do not doubt that the *Compton* test may often prove of value and lead to a correct determination. But, with the great respect due to those who have formulated this test, I find myself unable to regard it as a criterion of general applicability and conclusiveness. In the first place I see much difficulty in dividing the qualities or attributes, which may serve to bind human beings into classes, into two mutually exclusive groups, the one involving individual status and purely personal, the other disregarding such status and quite impersonal. As a task this seems to me no less baffling and elusive than the **7–118** problem to which it is directed, namely, the determination of what is and what is not a section of the public for the purposes of this branch of the law. After all, what is more personal than poverty or blindness or ignorance? Yet none would deny that a gift for the education of the children of the poor or blind was charitable; and I doubt if there is any less certainty about the charitable nature of a gift for, say, the education of children who satisfy a specified examining body that they need and would benefit by a course of special instruction designed to remedy their educational defects.

"But can any really fundamental distinction, as respects the personal or **7–119** impersonal nature of the common link, be drawn between those employed, for example, by a particular university and those whom the same university has put in a certain category as the result of individual examination and assessment? Again, if the bond between these employed by a particular railway is purely personal, why should the bond between those who are employed as railway men be so essentially different? Is a distinction to be drawn in this respect between those who are employed in a particular industry before it is nationalized and those who are employed therein after that process has been completed and one employer has taken the place of many? Are miners in the service of the National Coal Board now in one category and miners at a particular pit or of a particular district in another? Is the relationship between those in the service of the Crown to be distinguished from that obtaining between those in the service of some other employer? Or, if not, are the children of, say, soldiers or civil servants to be regarded as not constituting a sufficient section of the public to make a trust for their education charitable?

"It was conceded in the course of the argument that, had the present trust **7–120** been framed so as to provide for the education of the children of those engaged in the tobacco industry in a named county or town, it would have been a good charitable disposition, and that even though the class to be benefited would have been appreciably smaller and no more important than is the class here. That concession follows from what the Court of Appeal has said. But if it is sound and a personal or impersonal relationship remains the universal criterion I think it shows, no less than the queries I have just raised in indicating some of the difficulties of the problem, that the *Compton* test is a very arbitrary and artificial rule. This leads me to the second difficulty that I have regarding it. If I understand it aright it necessarily makes the quantum of public benefit a consideration of little moment; the size of the class becomes immaterial and the need of its members and the public advantage of having that need met appear alike to be irrelevant. To my mind these are considerations of some account in the sphere of educational trusts for, as already indicated, I think the educational value and scope of the work actually to be done must have a bearing on the question of public benefit.

"Finally, it seems to me that, far from settling the state of the law on this particular subject, the *Compton* test is more likely to create confusion and doubt in the case of many trusts and institutions of a character whose legal standing as charities has never been in question. Take, for instance, a trust for the provision of university education for boys coming from a particular school. The common quality binding the members of that class seems to reside in the fact that their parents or guardians all contracted for their schooling with the same establishment or body. That the school in such a case may itself be a charitable foundation seems altogether beside the point and quite insufficient to hold the *Compton* test at bay if it is well founded in law.

7–121   I therefore return to what I think was the process followed before the decision in *Compton's* case, and, for the reasons already given, I would hold the present trust charitable and allow the appeal. I have only to add that I recognize the imperfections and uncertainties of that process. They are as evident as the difficulties of finding something better. But I venture to doubt if it is in the power of the courts to resolve those difficulties satisfactorily as matters stand. It is a long cry to the age of Elizabeth and I think what is needed is a fresh start from a new statute." *Appeal dismissed.*

I.R.C. v. EDUCATIONAL GRANTS ASSOCIATION LTD

Chancery Division [1967] Ch. 123; [1966] 3 W.L.R. 724; [1966] 3 All E.R. 708

7–122   The Revenue appealed from a decision of the Special Commissioners of Income Tax that the respondents were a charity entitled to exemption from income tax under section 447(1)(*b*) of the Income Tax Act 1952 (now section 505 of the Income and Corporation Taxes Act 1988).

The respondents were a company limited by guarantee formed for the advancement of education. However, the promoters of the company and its management were very much connected with Metal Box Ltd. Virtually all the income came from a seven-year deed of covenant executed by Metal Box Ltd. Care was taken that details of the company's objects did not leak out except to the higher ranks of Metal Box employees and their associates. Between 75 and 85 per cent. of payments were for the benefit of children of Metal Box employees.

The Revenue conceded that the respondents were established for charitable purposes only and so the case turned upon whether or not the payments had been applied to charitable purposes only.

Pennycuick J. allowed the appeal holding that the absence of public benefit had the consequence that the payments had not been applied to charitable purposes only. The Court of Appeal[66] in short extempore judgments affirmed his decision but without pursuing his doubts over *Re Koettgen*. The reserved judgment of Pennycuick J. appears below as illuminating the issues more clearly than the Court of Appeal decision.

7–123   PENNYCUICK J.: "I will next read the relevant part of section 447 of the Income Tax Act 1952.[67]

---

[66] [1967] Ch. 993.
[67] See now Income and Corporation Taxes Act 1988, s.505, replacing I.C.T.A. 1970, s.360.

'(1) Exemption shall be granted . . . (*b*) . . . from tax chargeable under Sch. D in respect of any yearly interest or other annual payment, forming part of the income of any body of persons or trust established for charitable purposes only, or which, according to the rules or regulations established by Act of Parliament, charter, decree, deed of trust or will, are applicable to charitable purposes only, and so far as the same are applied to charitable purposes only.'

"It will be observed that the subsection imposes two distinct requirements: (i) **7–124** the income must form part of the income of a body of persons or trust established for charitable purposes only, or must, according to the rules established by the relevant instrument, be applicable to charitable purposes only; and (ii) the exemption is available only so far as the income is applied to charitable purposes only. The first requirement depends on the construction of the relevant instrument; the second requirement depends on what is in fact done with the income as it arises from time to time. I will, for convenience, consider these requirements in their application to a corporate body, since that is the case now before me. They apply equally, mutatis mutandis, in the case of a trust created by a will or settlement.

"The objects of the corporation, in order that they may be exclusively **7–125** charitable, must be confined to objects for the public benefit. Equally, the application of the income, if it is to be within those objects, must be for the public benefit. Conversely, the application of income otherwise than for the public benefit must be outside the objects and *ultra vires*. For example, under an object for the advancement of education, once that is accepted as an exclusively charitable object, the income must be applied for the advancement of education by way of public benefit. An application of income for the advancement of education by way of private benefit would be *ultra vires*, and nonetheless so by reason that, in the nature of things, the members of a private class are included in the public as a whole. This may perhaps explain the repetition of the words 'for charitable purposes only' in the second requirement of the subsection.

"Counsel for the taxpayers advanced a simple and formidable argument: *viz.* **7–126** (i) the taxpayers are established for specified educational purposes; (ii) those purposes are admittedly charitable purposes, so the first requirement is satisfied; (iii) the income has been applied for the specified educational purposes; and (iv) therefore the income has been applied for charitable purposes, and the second requirement is satisfied. It seems to me that this argument leaves out of account the element of public benefit. It is true that it is claimed by the taxpayers and admitted by the Crown that the educational purposes specified in the taxpayers' memorandum are charitable purposes, but this by definition implies that the purposes are for the public benefit. In order that the second requirement may be satisfied, it must equally be shown that their income has been applied not merely for educational purposes as expressed in the memorandum but for those educational purposes by way of public benefit. An application of income by way of private benefit would be *ultra vires*. It is not open to the taxpayers first to set up a claim which can only be sustained on the basis that the purposes expressed in the memorandum are for the public benefit, and then, when it comes to the application of the income, to look only to the purposes expressed in the memorandum, leaving the element of public benefit out of account. This point may be illustrated by considering the familiar example of a case in which a fund is settled on trust for the advancement of education in general terms and the income is applied for the education of the settlor's children. Counsel for the taxpayer does not shrink from the conclusion that such an application comes within the terms of the trust and satisfies the second requirement of the subsection. I think that it does neither.

7–127 "Counsel for the Crown based his argument on construction broadly on the lines which I have indicated above as being correct. He devoted much of his argument to repelling the application of the *Koettgen* case to the present one. In the *Koettgen*[68] case a testatrix bequeathed her residuary estate on trust 'for the promotion and furtherance of commercial education . . .' The will provided that

> "The persons eligible as beneficiaries under the fund shall be persons of either sex who are British born subjects and who are desirous of educating themselves or obtaining tuition for a higher commercial career but whose means are insufficient or will not allow of their obtaining such education or tuition at their own expense . . ."

The testatrix further directed that in selecting the beneficiaries

7–128
> "It is my wish that the . . . trustees shall give a preference to any employees of J.B. & Co. (London), Ltd, or any members of the families of such employees; failing a sufficient number of beneficiaries under such description then the persons eligible shall be any persons of British birth as the . . . trustees may select provided that the total income to be available for benefiting the preferred beneficiaries shall not in any one year be more than seventy-five per cent. of the total available income for that year."

In the event of the failure of those trusts there was a gift over to a named charity. It was admitted that the trust was for the advancement of education, but it was contended for the charity that having regard to the direction to prefer a limited class of persons the trusts were not of a sufficiently public nature to constitute valid charitable trusts. It was held that the gift to the primary class from whom the trustees could select beneficiaries contained the necessary element of benefit to the public, and that it was when that class was ascertained that the validity of the trust had to be determined; so that the subsequent direction to prefer, as to 75 per cent. of the income, a limited class did not affect the validity of the trust, which was accordingly a valid and effective charitable trust. *Oppenheim v. Tobacco Securities Trust Co. Ltd.*,[69] was distinguished.

7–129 "The other case considered by the Special Commissioners was *Caffoor (Trustees of the Abdul Gaffoor Trust) v. Comr. of Income Tax, Colombo*[70] in the Privy Council. In that case by the terms of a trust deed executed in Ceylon in 1942 the trust income after the death of the grantor was to be applied by the board of trustees, the appellants, in their absolute discretion for all or any of a number of purposes, which included '(2)(b) the education instruction or training in England or elsewhere abroad of deserving youths of the Islamic Faith' in any department of human activity. The recipients of the benefits were to be selected by the board 'from the following classes of persons and in the following order: (i) male descendants along either the male or female line of the grantor or of any of his brothers or sisters' failing whom youths of the Islamic Faith born of Muslim parents of the Ceylon Moorish community permanently resident in Colombo or

---

[68] [1954] Ch. 252.
[69] [1951] A.C. 297.
[70] [1961] A.C. 584.

elsewhere in Ceylon. It was held that in view of what was in effect the absolute priority to the benefit of the trust income which was conferred on the grantor's own family by clause 2(b)(i) of the trust deed this was a family trust and not a trust of a public character solely for charitable purposes, and the income thereof was accordingly not entitled to the exemption claimed. In his speech, Lord Radcliffe, giving the decision of the Privy Council, made the following comments[71] on the *Koettgen* case:

> "It was argued with plausibility for the appellants that what this trust **7–130** amounted to was a trust whose general purpose was the education of deserving young people of the Islamic Faith, and that its required public character was not destroyed by the circumstances that a preference in the selection of deserving recipients was directed to be given to members of the grantor's own family. Their Lordships go with the argument so far as to say that they do not think that a trust which provides for the education of a section of the public necessarily loses its charitable status or its public character merely because members of the founder's family are mentioned explicitly as qualified to share in the educational benefits or even, possibly, are given some kind of preference in the selection. They part with the argument, however, because they do not consider that the trust which is now before them comes within the range of any such qualified exception."

Lord Radcliffe went on to say that, there, the grantor's own family had, in effect, **7–131** absolute priority. Then he said of the *Koettgen* case[72]:

> "It is not necessary for their Lordships to say whether they would have put the same construction on the will there in question as the learned judge did, or whether they regard the distinction which he made as ultimately maintainable. The decision edges very near to being inconsistent with *Oppenheim's* case, but it is sufficient to say that the construction of the gift which was there adopted does not tally with the construction which their Lordships are bound to place on the trust which is now before them. Here, the effect of the wording of para. 2(b)(i) is to create a primary disposition of the trust income in favour of the family of the grantor."

I am not concerned with the construction placed by Upjohn J. on the particular **7–132** will before him in the *Koettgen* case. I will assume that the effect of the will was as he construed it, *i.e.*, that it constituted a primary public class and then directed that the trustees should give preference to employees of a named company and their families, those employees being necessarily members of the whole public class. Upjohn J., held the trust to be charitable. In the *Caffoor* case, Lord Radcliffe gave a very guarded and qualified assent to that principle. The decision in *Koettgen's* case is concerned with the character of a trust on the construction of the relevant instrument, and not with the application of income. Its relevance in the latter connection is presumably that, if in the instrument creating a trust for a public class a private class whose members are included in the public class can be mentioned specifically and accorded a preference, then a preferential application of income for the benefit of a private class whose members are

[71] [1961] A.C. 297 at 603.
[72] [1961] A.C. 297 at 604.

comprised in a public class is a proper execution of a trust for the public class. This is a long step, and I do not feel obliged to take it.

7–133   "For myself I find considerable difficulty in the *Koettgen* decision. I should have thought that a trust for the public with preference for a private class comprised in the public might be regarded as a trust for the application of income at the discretion of the trustees between charitable and non-charitable objects. However, I am not concerned here to dispute the validity of the *Koettgen* decision. I only mention the difficulty which I feel as affording some additional reason for not applying the *Koettgen* decision by analogy in connection with the second requirement of the subsection.

"I return now to the present case. The taxpayers have claimed that the purposes of the taxpayers are exclusively charitable, which imports that the purposes must be for the public benefit. The Crown have admitted that claim. I have then to consider whether the taxpayers have applied their income within their expressed objects and by way of public benefit. There is no doubt that the application has been within their expressed objects, but has it been by way of the public benefit? In order to answer this question, I must, I think, look at the individuals and institutions for whose benefit the income has been applied, and seek to discern whether these individuals and institutions possess any, and if so, what, relevant characteristics by virtue of which the income has been applied for their benefit. One may for this purpose look at the minutes of the council, circular letters and so forth. Counsel for the Crown at one time appeared to suggest that one might look at the actual intention of the members of the council. I do not think that is so.

7–134   "When one makes this enquiry, one finds that between 75 per cent and 85 per cent of the income of the taxpayers has been expended on the education of children connected with Metal Box Co. Ltd The taxpayers are intimately connected with Metal Box Co. Ltd, in the many respects found in the Case Stated. They derive most of their income from Metal Box Co. Ltd The council of management, as the Special Commissioners found, has followed a policy of seeking applications for grants from employees and ex-employees of Metal Box Co. Ltd, though these applications are not, of course, always successful. The inference is inescapable that this part of the taxpayer's income—*i.e.* 75 per cent to 85 per cent—has been expended for the benefit of these children by virtue of a private characteristic: *i.e.*, their connection with Metal Box Co. Ltd Such an application is not by way of public benefit. It is on all fours with an application of 75 per cent to 85 per cent. of the income of a trust fund on the education of a settlor's children. It follows, in my judgment, that, as regards the income which has been applied for the education of children of Metal Box Co. Ltd's employees, the taxpayers have failed to satisfy the second requirement in the subsection, and that the claim for relief fails. No reason has been suggested why the taxpayers should not obtain relief in respect of income applied for the benefit of institutions and outside individuals; see the words 'so far as' in the section.

7–135   "I recognise that this conclusion involves a finding that the council of management has acted *ultra vires* in applying the income of the taxpayers as it has done, albeit within the expressed objects of the taxpayers' memorandum. This conclusion follows from the basis on which the taxpayers have framed their objects and based their claim. It is of course open to a comparable body to frame its objects so as to make clear that its income may be applied for private as well as public purposes, but in that case it may not obtain tax relief. It does not seem to me that such a body can have it both ways. I propose, therefore, to allow this appeal." *Appeal allowed.*

IV. TRUSTS FOR THE ADVANCEMENT OF RELIGION

Religious purposes

This category of charitable trusts has its origin in the preamble to the **7–136** 1601 Statute which speaks of "the repair of churches" but the courts soon held that the equity of the Statute extended to trusts advancing orthodox religion. With increasing religious toleration "the present position is that any religious body is entitled to charitable status so long as its tenets are not morally subversive and so long as its purposes are directed to the benefit of the public."[73] In rejecting the claim of an ethical society to be a charity for the advancement of religion Dillon J. said[74]:

> "Religion is concerned with man's relations with God, and ethics **7–137** are concerned with man's relations with man. The two are not the same, all are not made the same by sincere inquiry into the question: what is God? If reason leads people not to accept Christianity or any known religion, but they do believe in the excellence of qualities, such as truth, beauty and love, or believe in the platonic concept of the ideal, their beliefs may seem to them to be the equivalent of a religion, but viewed objectively they are not religion . . . It seems to me that two of the essential attributes of religion are faith and worship: faith in a god and worship of that god. The Oxford English Dictionary gives as one of the definitions of religion: 'A particular system of faith and worship.' Then: 'Recognition on the part of man of some higher unseen power as having control of his destiny, and as being entitled to obedience, reverence and worship.' "

No distinction is drawn between monotheistic and polytheistic reli- **7–138** gions. Charitable trusts have been registered for the advancement of the Church of England, Catholic,[75] Baptist,[76] Quaker,[77] Exclusive Brethren,[78] Jewish,[79] Sikh, Islamic, Buddhist and Hindu[80] religions. The Unification Church (the "Moonies") has registered charitable status[81] but not the Church of Scientology. The Charity Commission[82] rejected its application for registration because although it believed in a supreme being

---

[73] Charities: A Framework for the Future (1989) Cm. 694, para. 2.20.

[74] *Re South Place Ethical Society* [1980] 1 W.L.R. 1565 at 1571. The society was charitable under the second and fourth heads of charity.

[75] *Bradshaw v. Tasker* (1834) 2 Myl. & K. 221.

[76] *Re Strickland's W.T.* [1936] 3 All E.R. 1027.

[77] *Re Manser* [1905] 1 Ch. 68.

[78] *Holmes v. Att.-Gen., The Times*, February 12, 1981.

[79] *Neville Estates Ltd v. Madden* [1962] Ch. 832 but not a trust for the settlement of Jews in Palestine: *Keren Kayemeth Le Jisroel v. I.R.C.* [1932] A.C. 650.

[80] See (1989) Cm. 694, para. 2.19; [1962] S.I. 1962 No. 1421; [1963] S.I. 1963 No. 2074; *Varsani v. Jesani* [1998] 3 All E.R. 273.

[81] [1982] Charity Commissioners Annual Report paras. 36–38. The Att.-Gen. dropped his action to deprive them of charitable status: Hansard February 3, 1988, p. 977.

[82] Decision of November 17, 1999 taking account of *R.v. Registrar General ex p. Segerdal* [1970] 2 Q.B. 697. Its creed was more of a philosophy of the existence of man rather than a religion; such creed was described as "dangerous material" (*per* Lord Denning in *Hubbard v. Vosper* [1972] 2 Q.B. 84 at 96) and as "pernicious nonsense" (*per* Goff J. in *Church of Scientology v. Kaufman* [1973] R.P.C. 635 at 658).

such belief did not find expression in conduct indicative of reverence or veneration for the supreme being: study and therapy or counselling did not amount to such worship. However, in Australia[83] Scientology (as exemplified by the Church of New Faith) has been accepted as a charitable religion.

Mason A.C.J. and Brennan J. in the Australian High Court said[84]:

7–139

> "We would hold that the criteria of religion are twofold: first, belief in a supernatural Being, Thing or Principle; and, second, the acceptance of canons of conduct in order to give effect to that belief, though canons of conduct which offend against the ordinary law are outside the area of any immunity, privilege or right conferred on the grounds of religion. Those criteria may vary in their comparative importance, and there may be a different intensity of belief or of acceptance of canons of conduct among religions or among the adherents to a religion . . . Variations in emphasis may distinguish one religion from other religions, but they are irrelevant to the determination of an individual's or a group's freedom to profess and exercise the religion of his or their choice."

Wilson and Deane JJ. stated[85]:

7–140

> "One of the more important indicia of 'religion' is that the particular collection of ideas and/or practices involves belief in the supernatural, that is to say, belief that reality extends beyond that which is capable of perception by the senses. If that be absent it is unlikely that one has a 'religion.' Another is that the ideas relate to a man's nature and place in the universe and his relation to things supernatural. A third is that the ideas are accepted by adherents as requiring or encouraging them to observe particular standards or codes of conduct or to participate in specific practices having supernatural significance. A fourth is that, however loosely knit and varying in beliefs and practices adherents may be, they constitute an identifiable group or groups. A fifth, and perhaps more controversial, indicium is that the adherents themselves see the collection of ideas and/or practices as constituting a religion. . . . No one of the above indicia is necessarily determinative of the question whether a particular collection of ideas of and/or practices should be objectively characterised as a 'religion.' They are no more than aids in determining that question. . . . All of those indicia are, however, satisfied by most or all leading religions."

[83] *Church of the New Faith v. Commissioner of Pay-roll Tax* [1982–1983] 154 C.L.R. 120. The broad Australian view has been applied in New Zealand: *Centrepoint Community Growth Trust v. I.R.C.* [1985] 1 N.Z.L.R. 673.
[84] [1982–1983] 154 C.L.R. 120 at 136.
[85] *ibid.* at 174.

Public anxiety has been expressed about some religious movements **7–141** that may cause dissension in, and a break-up of, family life but the question is usually not whether their *objects* are contrary to morality or the public interest but whether *conduct* of the movement causes harm. Here the Government has emphasised that the Charity Commissioners have powers of inquiry available to them under section 6 of the 1960 Charities Act (now section 8 of the 1993 Act) and stated[86]:

> "Where conduct is in breach of trust or is marginal to the pursuit **7–142** of an organisation's objects, action can generally be taken to restrain the trustees or their agents. Action of this kind does not affect an organisation's charitable status. But in exceptional circumstances where from a careful examination of all the circumstances the activities complained of appeared to them to be directly and essentially expressive of the objects and tenets of a particular movement, the Commissioners might conclude that the pursuit of those objects was not beneficial, and hence not therefore being directed to charitable purposes. Should they reach this conclusion the Commissioner could remove the organisation from the register of charities under section 4(3) of the 1960 Act (now s.3(4) of 1993 Act). Under section 5(3) (now s.4(3) of 1993 Act) the Att.- Gen. can appeal against any decision of the Commissioners to remove or not to remove an organisation from the register."

The Freemasons[87] and the Oxford Group[88] (as originally formed) are **7–143** not religious charities, though a trust for the publication of the writings of Joanna Southcott (who claimed to be with child by the Holy Ghost and so about to give birth to a new Messiah) was held to be charitable[89] (and so void under the 1736 Mortmain and Charitable Uses Act). Indeed, a trust "for the continuance of the work of God as it has been maintained by H and myself since 1942" was held charitable[90] where the work consisted mainly in the free distribution of fundamentalist Christian tracts written by H, though the tracts were of no intrinsic merit except in confirming the beliefs of H's circle.

Trusts for adding to or repairing the fabric of a church[91] or for the **7–144** upkeep of a churchyard[92] are charitable but not for the erection or upkeep of a particular tomb in a churchyard.[93] If a gift is made to an ecclesiastic in his official name and by virtue of his office then if no purposes are expressed in the gift the gift is for charitable religious

---

[86] (1989) Cm. 694, para. 2.32.

[87] *United Grand Lodge of Freemasons v. Holborn B.C.* [1957] 1 W.L.R. 1080.

[88] *Re Thackrach* [1939] 2 All E.R. 4, *Oxford Group v. I.R.C.* [1949] 2 All E.R. 537.

[89] *Thornton v. Howe* (1862) 31 Beav. 14.

[90] *Re Watson* [1973] 1 W.L.R. 1472.

[91] *Re Raine* [1956] Ch. 417; *Hoare v. Osborne* (1866) L.R. 1 Eq. 585.

[92] *Re Douglas* [1905] 1 Ch. 279; *Re Vaughan* (1866) 33 Ch.D. 187 at 192.

[93] *Lloyd v. Lloyd* (1852) 2 Sim. (N.S.) 225; *Re Hooper* [1932] 1 Ch. 38; see Parish Councils and Burial Authorities Miscellaneous Provisions Act 1970, s.1 (a burial or local authority may contract to maintain a grave or memorial for not exceeding 99 years).

purposes inherent in the office.[94] However, if the purposes are expressed in terms not confining them to exclusively charitable purposes then the charitable character of the trustee will not make the gift charitable.[95] A trust for religious purposes will be treated as for charitable religious purposes[96] but a trust for religious institutions will not be a charitable trust because some religious institutions (like a purely contemplative order of nuns) lack the necessary public benefit for a charitable trust.[97]

Public benefit

7–145   A trust for the advancement of religion (in the sense previously discussed) is presumed to be for the public benefit unless there is evidence to the contrary.[98] This presumption reflects the reluctance of the courts to enter into questions of the comparative worth of different religions. However, in *Gilmour v. Coats infra*, at para. 7–149 the House of Lords held that a trust for a contemplative order of nuns who did not leave their cloisters nor allow the public into them was not charitable. The benefits of their edifying example and their intercessory prayers were too vague and incapable of being proved to be of tangible benefit for the public. The court does not have to accept as proved whatever a particular religion believes. Nonetheless, in *Neville Estates Ltd v. Madden*[99] Cross J. upheld as charitable a trust for the members from time to time of the Catford Jewish Synagogue because[1] "the court is entitled to assume that some benefit accrues to the public from the attendance at places of worship of persons who live in this world and mix with their fellow citizens." Moreover, the Charity Commissioners[2] registered as charitable The Society of the Precious Blood. This was an enclosed contemplative society of Anglican Nuns but their activities included within their walls public religious services, religious and secular education of the public and the relief of suffering, sickness, poverty and distress through their counselling service.

7–146   A further issue is whether or not the saying of Catholic Masses for the repose of particular souls is for the public benefit. The benefit of intercessory prayer is incapable of legal proof, but if Masses are said in public this has an edifying and improving effect on members of the

---

[94] *Re Rumball* [1956] Ch. 105.
[95] *Re Simson* [1946] Ch. 299 (gift to vicar "for his work in the parish" charitable); *Farley v. Westminster Bank* [1939] A.C. 430 (gift to vicar "for parish work" not charitable) applying *Dunn v. Byrne* [1912] A.C. 407.
[96] *MacLaughlin v. Campbell* [1906] I.R. 588 to trustees "for such Roman Catholic purposes in the parish of Coleraine or elsewhere as they deem fit" void because possibility of Catholic political economic or social purposes, while there and in *Re White* [1893] 2 Ch. 41 it was accepted that a gift for "religious purposes" means impliedly "charitable religious purposes."
[97] *Gilmour v. Coats* [1949] A.C. 426.
[98] 1989 Cm. 694, para. 2.26, [1973] 1 W.L.R. 1472 at 1482.
[99] *Neville Estates Ltd v. Madden* [1962] Ch. 832. Clearly, the benefited class was small, and in *Dingle v. Turner* [1972] A.C. 601 at 625 Lord Cross said, "A trust to promote some religion among the employees of a company might perhaps be held to be charitable, provided it was clear that the benefits were to be purely spiritual."
[1] *Ibid.* 853; *Re Warre's W.T.* [1953] 1 W.L.R. 725 (retreat house not charitable) is of dubious authority.
[2] [1989] Annual Report paras. 56–62, *Decisions*, Vol. 3, p. 11.

public who happen to be in attendance, Masses held in private only edifying a private and not a public class of people. In both cases, however, one can argue that the money paid to the priest for saying Masses relieves the Catholic Church to that extent of its liability to provide stipends for priests and so benefits the Catholic Church and its members. In *Re Hetherington*[3] it was held that this in itself is not enough, so that the trust for Masses for the repose of particular souls was held to be charitable only by implicitly restricting it to Masses that had to be held in public.

On this basis, the Charity Commissioners, in rejecting the application **7–147** for registration as a charity of the Church of Scientology (*infra* para. 7–157), held that it is the public nature of the religious practice which is essential to the trust being charitable. The Commissioners also considered that it was clearly possible that the European Convention on Human Rights, as applied in the United Kingdom by the Human Rights Act 1999, could apply to their decisions so that they needed to interpret the case law consistently with the Convention.

In particular under Article 9 (1) "everyone has the right to freedom of **7–148** thought, conscience and religion; this right includes freedom to change his religion or belief and freedom either alone or in community with others and in public or private to manifest his religion or belief in worship, teaching, practice and observance", while by Article 9(2) "Freedom to manifest one's religion or beliefs shall be subject only to such limitations as are prescribed by law and are necessary in a democratic society in the interests of public safety, for the protection of public order, health or morals, or for the protection of the rights or freedoms of others".

Article 14 may be used in conjunction with Article 9: "The enjoyment **7–149** of the rights and freedoms set forth in this Convention shall be secured without discrimination on any ground such as sex, race, colour, language, religion, political or other opinion, national or social origin, association with a national minority, property, birth or other status."

A reasonable case can be made that to decline registration of a body **7–150** as a charity, with the fiscal privileges attaching thereto, would impair protected freedoms as it limits the body's ability to manifest its beliefs through teaching and evangelical activities designed to encourage persons to change their religious affiliations.[4] Nevertheless, the Commissioners held that the Church of Scientology failed the public benefit test as prescribed by English cases that satisfied the requirements of the Convention.

GILMOUR v. COATS

House of Lords [1949] A.C. 426; [1949] 1 All E.R. 848 (Lords Simonds, du **7–151**
 Parcq, Normand, Morton and Reid)

---

[3] [1990] Ch.1 criticised by C. Rickett [1990] Conv.34; further see *Nolan v. Downes* (1917) 23 C.L.R. 546 and *Carrigan v. Redwood* (1910) 30 N.Z.L.R. 244.
[4] *Kokkinakis v. Greece* (1997) 24 EHRR (C.D.) 52. In other respects the recognition or non-recognition as a charity does not appear to interfere with the manifestation of a person's belief, so that the State's declining to confer a privilege would not breach Article 9.

The income of a trust fund was to be applied to the purposes of a Carmelite convent, if those purposes were charitable. The convent was comprised of an association of strictly cloistered and purely contemplative nuns who were concerned with prayers and meditation, and who did not engage in any activities for the benefit of people outside the convent. In the view of the Roman Catholic Church, however, their prayers and meditation caused the intervention of God for the benefit of members of the public, and their life inside the convent provided an example of self-denial and concentration on religious matters which was beneficial to the public. All courts held that the trust was not a charitable one.

7–152   LORD SIMONDS: ". . . I need not go back beyond the case of *Cocks v. Manners*,[5] which was decided nearly eighty years ago by Wickens V.-C. In that case the testatrix left her residuary estate between a number of religious institutions, one of them being the Dominican convent at Carisbrooke, a community not differing in any material respect from the community of nuns now under consideration. The learned judge used these words,[6] which I venture to repeat, though they have already been cited in the courts below: 'On the Act [the statute of Elizabeth] unaffected by authority I should certainly hold that the gift to the Dominican convent is neither within the letter nor the spirit of it; and no decision has been referred to which compels me to adopt a different conclusion. A voluntary association of women for the purpose of working out their own salvation by religious exercises and self-denial seems to me to have none of the requisites of a charitable institution, whether the word 'charitable' is used in its popular sense or in its legal sense. It is said, in some of the cases, that religious purposes are charitable, but that can only be true as to religious services tending directly or indirectly towards the instruction or the edification of the public; an annuity to an individual, so long as he spent his time in retirement and constant devotion, would not be charitable, nor would a gift to ten persons, so long as they lived together in retirement and performed acts of devotion, be charitable. Therefore the gift to the Dominican convent is not, in my opinion, a gift on a charitable trust.'

7–153   "Apart from what I have called the final argument, which I will deal with later, the contention of the appellant rests, not on any change in the lives of the members of such a community as this, nor, from a wider aspect, on the emergence of any new conception of the public good, but solely on the fact that for the first time certain evidence of the value of such lives to a wider public together with new arguments based on that evidence has been presented to the court. Never before, it was urged, has the benefit to be derived from intercessory prayer and from edification been brought to the attention of the court; if it had been, the decision in *Cocks v. Manners* would, at least should, have been otherwise.

7–154   "My Lords, I would speak with all respect and reverence of those who spend their lives in cloistered piety, and in this House of Lords spiritual and temporal, which daily commences its proceedings with intercessory prayers, how can I deny that the Divine Being may in His Wisdom think fit to answer them? But, my Lords, whether I affirm or deny, whether I believe or disbelieve, what has that to do with the proof which the court demands that a particular purpose satisfies the

---

[5] (1871) L.R. 12 Eq. 574.
[6] *ibid.* at 585.

test of benefit to the community? Here is something which is manifestly not susceptible of proof. But, then it is said, this is a matter not of proof but of belief, for the value of intercessory prayer is a tenet of the Catholic faith, therefore, and in such a prayer there is benefit to the community. But it is just at this 'therefore' that I must pause. It is, no doubt, true that the advancement of religion is, generally speaking, one of the heads of charity, but it does not follow from this that the court must accept as proved whatever a particular church believes. The faithful must embrace their faith believing where they cannot prove: the court can act only on proof. A gift to two or ten or a hundred cloistered nuns in the belief that their prayers will benefit the world at large does not from that belief alone derive validity any more than does the belief of any other donor for any other purpose. The importance of this case leads me to state my opinion in my own words but, having read again the judgment of the learned Master of the Rolls, I will add that I am in full agreement with what he says on this part of the case.

"I turn to the second of the alleged elements of public benefit, edification by **7–155** example, and I think that this argument can be dealt with very shortly. It is, in my opinion, sufficient to say that this is something too vague and intangible to satisfy the prescribed test. The test of public benefit has, I think, been developed in the last two centuries. Today it is beyond doubt that that element must be present. No court would be rash enough to attempt to define precisely or exhaustively what its content must be. But it would assume a burden which it could not discharge if now for the first time it admitted into the category of public benefit something so indirect, remote, imponderable and, I would add, controversial as the benefit which may be derived by others from the example of pious lives.

"I must now refer to certain cases on which the appellant relied. They consist **7–156** of a number of cases in the Irish courts and *Re Caus*,[7] a decision of Luxmoore J. A consideration of the Irish cases shows that it has there been decided that a bequest for the saying of masses, whether in public or in private, is a good charitable bequest: see, *e.g., Att.-Gen. v. Hall*[8] and *O'Hanlon v. Logue*.[9] And in *Re Caus* Luxmoore J. came to the same conclusion. I would expressly reserve my opinion on the question whether these decisions should be sustained in this House. So important a matter should not be decided except on a direct consideration of it. It is possible that, particularly in regard to the celebration of masses in public, good reason may be found for supporting a gift for such an object as both a legal and a charitable purpose. But it follows from what I have said in the earlier part of this opinion that I am unable to accept the view, which at least in the Irish cases is clearly expressed, that in intercessory prayer and edification that public benefit which is the condition of legal charity is to be found. Of the decision of Luxmoore J. in *Re Caus*, I would only say that his *ratio decidendi* is expressly stated to be,[10] 'first, that it (*i.e.*, a gift for the saying of masses) enables a ritual act to be performed which is recognised by a large proportion of Christian people to be the central act of their religion, and, secondly, that it assists in the endowment of priests whose duty it is to perform the ritual act.' The decision, therefore, does not assist the appellant's argument in the present case and I make no further comments on it.[11]

---

[7] [1934] Ch. 162.
[8] [1897] 2 I.R. 426.
[9] [1906] 1 I.R. 247.
[10] [1934] Ch. 162 at 170.
[11] See *Re Hetherington* [1990] Ch 1 on *Re Caus*.

7–157 "It remains, finally, to deal with the argument that the element of public benefit is supplied by the fact that qualification for admission to membership of the community is not limited to any group of persons but is open to any woman in the wide world who has the necessary vocation. Thus, it is said, just as the endowment of a scholarship open to public competition is a charity, so also a gift to enable any woman (or, presumably, any man) to enter a fuller religious life is a charity. To this argument, which, it must be admitted, has a speciously logical appearance, the first answer is that which I have indicated earlier in this opinion. There is no novelty in the idea that a community of nuns must, if it is to continue, from time to time obtain fresh recruits from the outside world. That is why a perpetuity is involved in a gift for the benefit of such a community, and it is not to be supposed that, to mention only three masters of this branch of the law, Wickens V.-C., Lord Lindley or Lord Macnaghten failed to appreciate the point. Yet, by direct decision or by way of emphatic example, a community such as this is by them regarded as the very type of religious institution which is not

7–158 charitable. I know of no consideration applicable to this case which would justify this House in unsettling a rule of law which has been established so long and by such high authority. But that is not the only, nor, indeed, the most cogent reason why I cannot accede to the appellant's argument. It is a trite saying that the law is life, not logic. But it is, I think, conspicuously true of the law of charity that it has been built up, not logically, but empirically. It would not, therefore, be surprising to find that, while in every category of legal charity some element of public benefit must be present, the court had not adopted the same measure in regard to different categories, but had accepted one standard in regard to those gifts which are alleged to be for the advancement of religion, and it may be yet another in regard to the relief of poverty. To argue by a method of syllogism or analogy from the category of education to that of religion ignores the historical process of the law. Nor would there be lack of justification for the divergence of treatment which is here assumed. For there is a legislative and political background peculiar to so-called religious trusts, which has, I think, influenced the development of the law in this matter."[12] *Appeal dismissed*.

CHARITY COMMISSIONERS' DECISION ON APPLICATION FOR REGISTRATION OF
THE CHURCH OF SCIENTOLOGY

The legal test of public benefit under the third head of charity

7–159 The **Commissioners** noted that it is clear (from the dicta of Lord Greene M.R. in *Coats v. Gilmour*) that the burden is upon the religious organisation in question to demonstrate both its impact upon the community and that the impact is beneficial, if public benefit is to be demonstrated.

Some clear principles emerge from the decided cases:

- a gift for the advancement of religion must be beneficial to the public (or a sufficient section of the public)[13] and not simply for the benefit of the adherents of the particular religion themselves.[14]

---

[12] The Nathan Committee on Charitable Trusts rejected the suggestion of the representatives of the Roman Catholic Church that trusts for the advancement of religion should be defined to include "the advancement of religion by those means which that religion believes and teaches are means by which it does advance it": (1952) Cmnd. 8710, paras. 129–130.

[13] *National Anti-Vivisection Society v. IRC* [1948] A.C. 31.

[14] *Holmes v. Attorney General The Times,* February 12, 1981.

- It is settled law that the question whether a particular gift satisfies the requirement of public benefit must be determined by the court and the opinion of the donor or testator is irrelevant.[15]
- The court must decide whether or not there is a benefit to the community in the light of evidence of a kind cognisable by the court[16]

The presence or absence of the necessary element of public benefit has also been considered in a number of cases. The essential distinguishing feature seems to be whether or not the practice of the religion is essentially public. The case **In re Hetherington decd. [1990] Ch. 1** focused on the question of public benefit in relation to religion. In that case the Judge summarised the principles established by the legal authorities. In concluding that a gift for the celebration of masses (assumed to be in public) was charitable he drew upon cases concerning a variety of religious practices and concluded as follows:

1. A trust for the advancement of education, the relief of poverty or the **7–160** advancement of religion is charitable and assumed to be for the public benefit. The assumption can be rebutted by showing that in fact the particular trust in question cannot operate so as to confer a legally recognised benefit on the public—as in *Gilmour v. Coats*;
2. The celebration of a religious rite in public does confer sufficient public benefit because of the edifying and improving effect of such celebration on the members of the public who attend; and
3. The celebration of a religious rite in private does not contain the necessary element of public benefit since any benefit of prayer or example is incapable of proof in the legal sense and any element of edification is limited to a private not public class of those present at the celebration. Following *Gilmour v. Coats*,[17] *Yeap Cheah Neo v. Ong Cheng Neo*[18] and *Hoare v. Hoare*[19]; and
4. Where there is a gift for a religious purpose which could be carried out in a way which is beneficial to the public, (*i.e.* by public masses) but could also be carried out in a way which would not have a sufficient element of public element (ie by private masses) the gift is to be construed as a gift to be carried out by methods that are charitable, all non charitable methods being excluded.

It is clear from **In re Hetherington decd.**[20] and the cases cited there that it is the **7–161** public nature of the religious practice which is essential to the gift being charitable.

The **Commissioners** concluded that the decided cases indicated that where the practice of the religion is essentially private or is limited to a private class of

---

[15] *Re Hummeltenberg* [1923] 1 Ch 237 and *National Anti-Vivisection Society v. IRC* (*supra*).
[16] *Gilmour v. Coats* [1949] A.C. 426.
[17] [1949] A.C. 426.
[18] [1875] LR 6PC 381.
[19] [1886] 56 LT 147.
[20] [1990] Ch. 1.

individuals not extending to the public generally, the element of public benefit will not be established.[21]

The legal test of public benefit under the fourth head

The **Commissioners** turned next to the legal test of public benefit under the fourth head of charity and considered the test to be that set out by Lord Wright in *National Anti-Vivisection Society v. IRC*.[22] Lord Wright said that:

7–162   "I think the whole tendency of the concept of charity in a legal sense under the fourth head is towards tangible and objective benefits, and at least, that approval by the common understanding of enlightened opinion for the time being, is necessary before an intangible benefit can be taken to constitute a sufficient benefit to the community to justify admission of the object into the fourth class."

It seemed to the **Commissioners** that the benefit that arises from the moral or spiritual welfare or improvement of the community is likely to be an intangible rather than a tangible one. The **Commissioners** considered the test in respect of an intangible benefit to mean a common consensus of opinion amongst people who were fair minded and free from prejudice or bias.

The **Commissioners** considered in particular whether the representations which it had received about Scientology generally and **CoS** in particular, both favourable and unfavourable amounted to such "common understanding" and concluded that they did not. The representations were not easily substantiated and in effect represented opposing ends of the spectrum of opinion about **CoS** or Scientology generally.

7–163   The **Commissioners** further indicated that a key factor in assessing whether the test in that case was met (ie whether there was a common understanding of enlightened opinion that public benefit flowed from the advancement of Scientology by **CoS**), was the extent to which the core practices of Scientology were readily accessible by the public generally.

Accordingly, the **Commissioners** would need to consider whether there was approval by the common understanding of enlightened opinion that pursuit of Scientology doctrines and practices is beneficial to the community such that **CoS** may be regarded as charitable under the fourth head.

Consideration of CoS's arguments as to public benefit under the fourth head of charity

The **Commissioners** noted **CoS**'s arguments in this respect. One interpretation of **CoS**'s legal arguments was to the effect that public benefit under the fourth head of charity does not have to be *proved*, but that it is only necessary to *show* that the organisation's activities *may* have that result.

7–164   The **Commissioners** considered CoS's argument apparently based upon *Berry v. St Marylebone Corporation* [1959] Ch 406 concerning the Theosophical Society in England seeking relief from paying rates under section 8 of the Ratings and Valuation (Miscellaneous Provisions) Act 1955. The **Commissioners** noted that **CoS** appeared to rely on dicta of Romer L.J. in that case as support for the proposition that public benefit under the fourth head of charity need not be proven but should only be shown.

The **Commissioners** did not accept this argument, as it was not clear to them that the case cited—*Berry v. St Marylebone Corporation*—was authority for this

---

[21] *In re Hetherington decd.*, *(supra)* *Coats v. Gilmour* [1948] Ch 340, 347 *per* Lord Evershed.
[22] [1948] A.C. 31, 49.

proposition, rather it seemed to the **Commissioners** that it was authority for the proposition that it was necessary to show that the purpose (in that case the advancement of religion) may be likely to be advanced. This they had considered above. In any event the case related specifically to the requirements of section 8 of the Ratings and Valuation (Miscellaneous Provisions) Act 1955 and was not a discussion about charitable status such that the judge's comments were not directly applicable to charity law.

In relation to the question of public benefit it seemed clear to the Commis- **7–165** sioners from the dicta of Lord Wright in *National Anti-vivisection Society v. IRC* that public benefit must positively be shown under the fourth head of charity. Lord Wright's comments in that case that the whole tendency of the concept of charity under the fourth head is towards tangible and objective benefits, seemed to the **Commissioners** to indicate quite clearly that the benefits must be identifiable and demonstrable, and that a common consensus of approval is necessary before an intangible benefit can be regarded as sufficient to satisfy the requirement of public benefit.

Whether CoS is established for the public benefit, whether under the third or fourth heads of charity

The **Commissioners** next sought to address the question of whether **CoS** had **7–166** shown itself to be established for the public benefit. The **Commissioners** considered the considerable volume of evidence supplied by **CoS** in support of its arguments that **CoS** was established for the public benefit whether under the third or fourth heads of charity because

- Individual churches of Scientology conduct numerous religious services freely accessible by members of the public.
- **CoS** sufficiently benefits the public through extensive charitable and public benefit programmes including anti drug campaigns, eradicating illiteracy, disaster relief and raising public morality.
- The Company (**CoS**) is limited by guarantee and its members make no profit.
- It is of the essence of Scientology "like most other religions" to seek to make itself available to all.
- Many of Mr Hubbard's teachings are already recognised as charitable and applied by existing registered charities.
- The Scientology movement engages in other activities which could potentially give rise to public benefit eg volunteer and relief programmes; rituals and practices such as "assists" (described as a form of healing); work in the field of criminal rehabilitation; observance of a moral code by individual Scientologists and promulgation of that moral code through the "Way to Happiness Foundation".

The **Commissioners** *considered* that the evidence and arguments supplied by **CoS** **7–167** may indicate ways in which Scientology organisations, and individual Scientologists, seek to benefit the wider community. They noted that in terms of English charity law some of that work may potentially be charitable in its own right, albeit not as promoting the moral or spiritual welfare or improvement of the community nor as advancing religion.[23] However, the **Commissioners** noted that

---

[23] Much Scientology activity appeared to the Commissioners to be in the fields of education and what might broadly be termed "relief in need"

the evidence and argument put to them by **CoS** did not address the central question of whether the advancement of Scientology (whether as a religion or as a non-religious belief system) confers recognisable benefit upon the public in English charity law. **CoS** states that its principal activities are auditing and training and that it is through these core activities that Scientology is advanced. In the **Commissioners** view it therefore had to be demonstrated that the advancement of Scientology through auditing and training is beneficial to the public. The **Commissioners** considered that it is to the central activities of auditing and training that the question of public benefit should be addressed.

7–168   The **Commissioners** went on to consider whether it was demonstrated that public benefit flowed from the core practices of Scientology. The **Commissioners** again noted that the test of public benefit was slightly different in relation to the third and fourth heads of charity. In relation to the third head the decided cases indicated that the public or private nature of the "religious practice" of the organisation in question was central to determining the presence or absence of public benefit. In relation to the purpose of promoting the moral or spiritual welfare or improvement of the community under the fourth head of charity the legal test was that set out by Lord Wright in the *National Vivisection Society v. IRC* case.

In relation to the test of public benefit for the advancement of religion the **Commissioners** *concluded that*

7–169

(1) The central "religious" practices of Scientology are conducted in private and not in public.

The "religious practices" of Scientology are auditing and training. Scientologists regard these as worship. Auditing is conducted in private on a one to one basis. It appears akin to a form of counselling and is described by Scientologists as such.[24] Training is essentially a private activity requiring the study of specialist material and access to specialist trainers. Whilst members of the public may sign up for a course of auditing and training, generally upon payment of the appropriate requested donation, these activities are not carried out "in public". Further, progression beyond introductory or initial levels of auditing and training necessitated membership of the Church.

Attendance at a session of auditing or training by members of the public generally does not appear to be a possibility. The **Commissioners** found it difficult therefore to see how any edifying and improving effects upon the public generally might flow from the "religious" practices of Scientology.

7–170   In relation to the fourth proposition in In *re Hetherington* decd., there was no suggestion that auditing and training could be carried out in a way that was public rather than private. It did not seem possible to construe auditing and training as religious rites which could be conducted in public rather than in private such as to render them charitable.

(2) Auditing and training are in their nature private rather than public activities

7–171   The **Commissioners** considered that even if a member of the public could attend an auditing and/or training session other than as a participant but rather

---

[24] Video presentation "The Church of Scientology at Saint Hill—A Special presentation to the Charity Commission of England and Wales".

as an observer, these Scientology services are by their very nature directed to the particular individual receiving them. Auditing appears akin to a form of counselling and is described by Scientologists who receive it as "counselling". It is directed to the private needs of the individual receiving it. The **Commissioners** found it difficult to see how the public could be edified or otherwise benefited by attending and observing at such a session.

Both the above factors—that Scientology services are conducted in private, and are in their nature private being directed to the needs of the private individual in receipt of them seemed to the **Commissioners** to indicate that these actual activities are of a private rather than a public kind. In any event it seemed to the **Commissioners** that any benefit to the public that may flow from auditing and training is incapable of proof, any edification or improving effect being limited to the private individual engaging in the auditing or training. Accordingly, the **Commissioners** concluded that these activities conferred no legally recognised benefit on the public.

In addition the **Commissioners** noted that the apparent dependence of participa- **7–172** tion in those activities upon payment of the requested donation referred to by **CoS** strengthened their perception that these activities were of a private rather than a public kind. Whilst **CoS** states that there are ways in which adherents can and do participate in auditing and training without making any form of monetary contribution, so that a lack of financial means is no bar to a member's progress in Scientology, access to auditing and training through requested donations is the norm. The **Commissioners** noted that the fact that a practice existed of requesting and making these payments strengthened the **Commissioners** in their perception that the activities were of a private rather than a public kind.

The **Commissioners** further noted that in its published and promotional literature, including the book "What is Scientology?", Scientology on balance presented its benefits in private rather than public terms.

In addition the **Commissioners** noted that a not insignificant number of **7–173** individual Scientologists described the benefits of Scientology in private and personal terms this being borne out both by a number of the statements printed in Scientology's published literature and by a significant proportion of the letters of support for **CoS** received from individual Scientologists.

The fact that Scientology describes its benefits in private rather than public terms in its published and promotional literature, and that individual Scientologists described the benefits of Scientology to them in private and personal terms confirmed the **Commissioners** conclusion that **CoS** is not established for the public benefit.

In relation to the test of public benefit under the fourth head of charity law for the moral or spiritual welfare or improvement of the community the Commissioners concluded that:

The question of accessibility by the public was key to the existence of public **7–174** benefit. As indicated above, the **Commissioners** had already concluded that the central practices of Scientology (auditing and training) were conducted in private rather than in public, and were in their nature private rather than public activities. In addition there was the practice of requesting donations in advance of receipt of those services. This led the **Commissioners** to conclude that the restricted access to those practices meant that any benefit flowing from Scientology as advanced by **CoS** is of a private rather than a public kind. In addition the description of the benefits of Scientology, both in Scientology published and promotional literature and by individual Scientologists, as already acknowledged by the **Commissioners**, confirmed them in this conclusion.

The **Commissioners** concluded that it could not be said that **CoS** had demonstrated that it was established for the public benefit so as to satisfy the legal test of public benefit of a charitable purpose for the advancement of religion or for the moral or spiritual welfare or improvement of the community."

V. TRUSTS FOR OTHER PURPOSES BENEFICIAL TO THE COMMUNITY

Other beneficial purposes which are charitable

7–175   This group of charitable trusts has its origin in the remaining charitable purposes enumerated in the preamble to the Statute of Charitable Uses 1601, and like the other groups it includes purposes within the spirit and intendment of those enumerated.

This category is limited to purposes not falling within the previous three categories but which are beneficial to the community in a way recognised by the law to be charitable. In 1972 the Court of Appeal[25] indicated that the proper approach after a finding that a purpose is beneficial to the community is to hold it charitable unless there are grounds for holding it outside the equity of the 1601 Statute. While one can strongly sympathise with such approach Dillon J. has taken the justifiable view[26] (adopted by the Charity Commissioners[27] and the Australian High Court[28]) that this ignores House of Lords decisions,[29] so that the proper approach remains that of analogy from the statutory preamble or from decided cases, though the Commissioners and the courts are ready to be liberal in looking for an analogy nowadays. Indeed, the Privy Council recently in *Att.-Gen. of Cayman Islands v. Wahr-Hansen*[30] opined that "Russell L.J.'s approach has much to commend it" before holding that "it has no application at all to the quite different problem which is raised in the present case *viz.* are general words [for institutions or organisations operating for the public good] to be artificially restricted to purposes which are within the spirit and intendment of the statute and thereby rendered charitable." A negative answer was given. It is, of course, the opinion of the court and not of the settlor that determines whether or not a trust is beneficial to the community: *National Anti-Vivisection Society v. I.R.C. infra*, at para. 7–190.

---

[25] *Incorporated Council of Law Reporting v. I.R.C.* [1972] Ch. 73 at 88 *infra*, at para. 7–204. Further see E. B. Bromley, "Contemporary Philanthropy—Is the Legal Concept of Charity Any Longer Adequate" in D. W. M. Waters (ed.), *Equity Fiduciaries & Trusts*, 1993 Carswell, Canada.

[26] *Re South Place Ethical Society* [1980] 1 W.L.R. 1565 *infra*, para. 7–210, and see *Brisbane City Council v. Att.-Gen. for Queensland* [1978] 3 All E.R. 30 at 33 (Lord Wilberforce), *I.R.C. v. McMullen* [1979] 1 All E.R. 588 at 592 (Stamp L.J.).

[27] [1985] Annual Report paras. 5, 26 and Decisions of Charity Commissioners, Vol 2 (1994) p.9.

[28] *Royal National Agricultural Association v. Chester* (1974) 48 A.L.J.R. 304.

[29] *e.g. Williams Trustees v. I.R.C.* [1947] A.C. 447, see *infra*, p. 469.

[30] [2000] 3 All E.R. 642, 647.

The following types of activities are charitable: the relief of the aged[31] **7–176** or sick[32] or disabled[33]; providing public works and public amenities[34]; protecting human life, the environment and property[35]; providing for social rehabilitation and welfare[36]; protecting or benefiting animals so long as this benefits, or promotes the moral improvement of, the community;[37] promoting patriotic purposes.[38] Notions of charity change with the times so that early cases may become unreliable as authorities.[39] There was some authority that trusts within this fourth category are not charitable if carried out overseas unless there is some benefit, albeit indirectly, for the United Kingdom community, *e.g.* cancer research abroad.[40] However, the Charity Commissioners, following the lead of the Ontario Court of Appeal,[41] now presume[42] that a body operating abroad is charitable if it would be regarded as charitable if its operations were confined to the U.K., unless recognition of such overseas operations would be contrary to public policy.[43]

---

[31] *Re Dunlop* [1984] N.I. 408 (Home for elderly Presbyterians), *Rowntree Memorial Trust Housing Association v. Att.-Gen.* [1983] Ch. 159 (sheltered accommodation for elderly for payment).

[32] *Re Resch's W.T.* [1969] 1 A.C. 514 (private hospital for fee-paying patients).

[33] *Re Lewis* [1955] Ch. 104 (the blind). "Relief" is not synonymous with "benefit": a trust for aged or blind millionaires will not relieve a need of theirs as aged or blind persons: *Rowntree* [1983] Ch. 159 at 171.

[34] *Att.-Gen. v. Shrewsbury Corp.* (1843) 6 Beav. 220 (repair, improvement of town's bridges, towers and walls); *Scottish Burial Reform and Cremation Society v. Glasgow Corp.* [1968] A.C. 138 (crematorium); *Re Hadden* [1932] 1 Ch. 133 and *Re Morgan* [1955] 1 W.L.R. 738 (public recreation ground); *Re Oxford Ice Skating Association Ltd* [1984] Annual Report of Charity Commissioners paras. 19–25 (public ice-skating rink); *Goodman v. Saltash Corporation* (1882) 7 App.Cas. 633 (for benefit of inhabitants of particular locality) but anomalous and not to be extended: *Williams Trustees v. I.R.C.* [1947] A.C. 447 at 459–460, see next section on Recreational Charities Act 1958.

[35] *Re Wokingham Fire Brigade Trusts* [1951] Ch. 373; *Johnston v. Swann* (1818) 3 Madd. 457 (lifeboat service); *Re Upper Teesdale Defence Fund* [1969] Annual Report of Ch. Comms. paras. 23–24 (preservation of flora and fauna of Upper Teesdale), The National Trust.

[36] *e.g.* rehabilitation of drug addicts and criminals, crime victim support schemes, family conciliation services, provision for "latch-key" children, but a trust for the welfare of children and young persons is too wide to be charitable: *Att.-Gen. of Bahamas v. Royal Trust Co.* [1986] 1 W.L.R. 1001, P.C. as is the provision of advice and aid on life's problems and medical, legal, matrimonial and social values (*D'Aguiar v. Guyana I.R.C.* [1970] T.R. 31).

[37] *Re Wedgwood* [1915] 1 Ch. 113 at 122: "A gift for the benefit and protection of animals tends to promote and encourage kindness towards them, to discourage cruelty, and thus to stimulate humane and generous sentiments in man towards the lower animals, and by these means promote feelings of humanity and morality generally, repress brutality and thus elevate the human race." But in *Re Grove-Grady* [1929] 1 Ch. 557, C.A. held a trust to set up an animal refuge safe from human interference not charitable. Animal sanctuaries involving the public can be charitable and, with the increasing recognition nowadays of the need to preserve wild life, a non-public animal sanctuary might now be held charitable, certainly if some element of education from films taken by the warden were incorporated: *cf. Att.-Gen. (N.S.W.) v. Sawtell* [1978] 2 N.S.W. L.R. 200.

[38] A gift "for patriotic purposes" is not necessarily charitable, and so is void: *Att.-Gen. v. Nat Provincial Bank* [1924] A.C. 262 but some particular patriotic purposes are charitable: trusts for helping defence of the realm *Re Stratheden* [1895] 3 Ch. 265; *Re Corbyn* [1941] Ch. 400; *Re Gray* [1925] Ch. 362; gifts to the National Revenue *Nightingale v. Goulburn* (1848) 2 Ph. 594 or to erect a statue of Earl Mountbatten [1981] Annual Report of Ch. Comms. paras. 68–70.

[39] *e.g. Re Strakosch* [1949] Ch. 529 appeasement of racial feelings between Dutch- and English-speaking South Africans too political to be charitable but Charity Commissioners' Annual Report 1983 paras. 18–20 reveals that "promoting good race relations, endeavouring to eliminate discrimination on grounds of race and encouraging equality of opportunity" are charitable purposes in light of Race Relations Act 1976.

[40] [1963] Annual Report of Ch. Comms. paras. 72–73, *Camille & Henry Dreyfuss Foundation Inc. v. I.R.C.* [1954] Ch. 672 at 684; *McGovern v. Att.-Gen.* [1981] 3 All E.R. 493 at 507; *cf. Re Jacobs* (1970) 114 So.Jo. 515 (upholding trust to plant trees in Israel but unclear whether overseas point argued).

[41] *Re Levy Estate* (1989) 58 D.L.R. (4th) 375: Ontario C.A. upheld bequest to State of Israel for charitable purposes only (which were likely to be restricted to Israel).

[42] Decisions of Charity Commissioners Vol. 1, p. 17.

[43] *e.g. Att.-Gen. v. Guise* (1692) 2 Vern 266; *Harbershon v. Varnon* (1851) 4 De. G. & Sm. 467.

7-177   In considering proposed new charitable trusts the Commissioners and the court will be particularly concerned to see that the purposes are not tainted by politics in the broad sense,[44] that any profits from charging fees are reapplied to charitable purposes and not distributed privately,[45] and that the purposes do not benefit too narrow a class to be a sufficient section of the public.[46]

Public benefit

7-178   The trust must provide some tangible benefit for a sufficient section of the community which must not be defined by reference to a personal nexus with a named propositus,[47] *e.g.* an individual or a corporate employer. This creates problems for dependants of particular victims of a disaster, so disaster relief funds, if charitable, are restricted to relieving needs within the poverty category of charitable trust.[48]

7-179   The degree of benefit required for this residual category is very much greater than that required for religion and greater than that required for education. In *I.R.C. v. Baddeley infra*, para. 7–181, Lords Simonds and Somervell opined[49] that a residual category trust involving recreational facilities for Methodists resident in West Ham and Leyton was not for a sufficient section of the public. They constituted "a class within a class" because they were "a class of persons not only confined to a particular area but selected from within it by reference to a particular creed." However, a trust to establish a school for the children of Methodists resident in West Ham and Leyton would be a charitable educational trust.[50]

7-180   The Law Lords pointed out that a trust to build a bridge only for the use of Methodists would not be charitable. Here, one can understand that there must be a sensible relationship between the benefit conferred and the group chosen to receive it. To restrict use of a recreation ground to Methodists seems eccentric and not for the benefit of the public. However, a trust to establish a home for old Presbyterian persons is sensibly restricted to a sufficient section of the public to be charitable,[51] while The Community Security Trust to provide protection for the Jewish Community has been registered as a charity by the Commissioners.[52]

---

[44] *National Anti-Vivisection Society v. I.R.C.* [1948] A.C. 31; Animal Abuse, Injustice and Defence Society: Decisions of Charity Commissioners Vol. 2, p. 1.

[45] *Re Resch's W.T.* [1969] 1 A.C. 514.

[46] *I.R.C. v. Baddeley* [1955] A.C. 572; *Re Birchfield Harriers*, [1989] Annual Report, paras. 48–55.

[47] *Re Hobourn Aero Components Ltd's Air Raid Disaster Fund* [1946] Ch. 194 (fund limited to employees so not charitable); *Re Mead* [1981] 1 W.L.R. 1244 (limited to trade union members so convalescent home non-charitable).

[48] Following suggestions of Charity Commissioners: Annual Reports, 1965, paras. 54–58, 1966, paras. 9–12.

[49] [1955] A.C. 572 at 592.

[50] *cf. Commissioner of Income Tax v. Pemsel* [1991] A.C. 531; *Re Tree* [1945] Ch. 325 and valid charitable trusts for specific C. of E. or Methodist schools. A fourth category trust for the Freemen of Huntingdon and their widows was initially a valid charitable trust but a cy-près scheme made all inhabitants of the borough objects of the trust when the number of Freemen had dwindled to 15 and the income had increased to £550,000 p.a.: *Peggs v. Lamb* [1994] Ch. 172.

[51] *Re Dunlop* [1984] N.I. 408; [1987] Conv. 114 (N. Dawson).

[52] 1994 Annual Report, at 21.

The *ratio* of *I.R.C. v. Baddeley* was that the social element in the recreational purposes prevented the purposes from being charitable in nature. This led to the Recreational Charities Act 1958 discussed in the next section.

INLAND REVENUE COMMISSIONERS v. BADDELEY

House of Lords [1955] A.C. 572; [1955] 1 All E.R. 525

Land was conveyed to trustees on trust to be used by certain Methodist leaders **7–181** "for the promotion of the religious social and physical well-being of persons resident in . . . West Ham and Leyton . . . *by the provision of facilities for religious services and instruction and for the social and physical training and recreation of such aforementioned persons* who for the time being are in the opinion of such leaders members or likely to become members of the Methodist Church and of insufficient means otherwise to enjoy the advantages provided by these presents and by the provision of facilities for religious social and physical training and education and by promoting and encouraging all forms of such activities as are calculated to contribute to the health and well-being of such persons." A second conveyance was in the same terms but with the omission of the italicized words. The conveyances were held not to be charitable and so not exempt from stamp duty.

VISCOUNT SIMONDS: "This brings me to another aspect of the case, which was **7–182** argued at great length and to me at least presents the most difficult problems in this branch of the law. Suppose that, contrary to the view that I have expressed that the social element prevented the trust being charitable, the trust would be a valid charitable trust, if the beneficiaries were the community at large or a section of the community defined by some geographical limits, is it the less a valid trust if it is confined to members or potential members of a particular church within a limited geographical area?

"The starting point of the argument must be, that this charity (if it be a **7–183** charity) falls within the fourth class in Lord Macnaghten's classification. It must therefore be a trust which is, to use the words of Sir Samuel Romilly in *Morice v. Bishop of Durham* (1805) 10 Ves. 522 at 532, of 'general public utility,' and the question is what these words mean. It is, indeed, an essential feature of all 'charity' in the legal sense that there must be in it some element of public benefit, whether the purpose is educational, religious or eleemosynary . . . and, as I have said elsewhere, it is possible, particularly in view of the so-called 'poor relations' cases,' the scope of which may one day have to be considered, that a different degree of public benefit is requisite according to the class in which the charity is said to fall. But it is said that if a charity falls within the fourth class, it must be for the benefit of the whole community or at least of all the inhabitants of a sufficient area. And it has been urged with much force that, if, as Lord Greene said in *Re Strakosch* [1949] Ch. 529, this fourth class is represented in the preamble to the Statute of Elizabeth by the repair of bridges, etc., and possibly by the maintenance of Houses of Correction, the class of beneficiaries or potential beneficiaries cannot be further narrowed down. Some confusion has arisen from the fact that a trust of general public utility, however general and however public, cannot be of equal utility to all and may be of immediate utility to few. A sea wall, the prototype of this class in the preamble, is of remote, if any, utility to those who live in the heart of the Midlands. But there is no doubt **7–184** that a trust for the maintenance of sea walls generally or along a particular stretch of coast is a good charitable trust. Nor, as it appears to me, is the validity of a trust affected by the fact that by its very nature only a limited number of people are likely to avail themselves, or are perhaps even capable of availing themselves, of its benefits. It is easy, for instance, to imagine a charity which has for its object some form of child welfare, of which the immediate beneficiaries could only be persons of tender age. Yet this would satisfy any test of general public utility. It may be said that it would satisfy the test because the indirect benefit of such a charity would extend far beyond its direct beneficiaries, and that aspect of the matter has probably not been out of sight. Indirect benefit is certainly an aspect which must have influenced the decision of the 'cruelty to animal' cases. But, I doubt whether this sort of rationalization helps to explain a branch of the law which has developed empirically and by analogy upon analogy.

7–185   "It is, however, in my opinion, particularly important in cases falling within the fourth category to keep firmly in mind the necessity of the element of general public utility, and I would not relax this rule. For here is a slippery slope. In the case under appeal the intended beneficiaries are a class within a class; they are those of the inhabitants of a particular area who are members of a particular church: the area is comparatively large and populous and the members may be numerous. But, if this trust is charitable for them, does it cease to be charitable as the area narrows down and the numbers diminish? Suppose the area is confined to a single street and the beneficiaries to those whose creed commands few adherents: or suppose the class is one that is determined not by religious belief but by membership of a particular profession or by pursuit of a particular trade. These were considerations which influenced the House in the recent case of *Oppenheim*. That was a case of an educational trust, but I think that they have even greater weight in the case of trusts which by their normal classification depend for their validity upon general public utility.

7–186   "It is pertinent, then, to ask how far your Lordships might regard yourselves bound by authority to hold the trusts now under review valid charitable trusts, if the only question in issue was the sufficiency of the public element . . .

7–187   "In [*Verge v. Somerville* [1924] A.C. 496 at 499] in which the issue was as to the validity of a gift 'to the trustees of the Repatriation Fund or other similar fund for the benefit of New South Wales returned soldiers,' Lord Wrenbury, delivering the judgment of the Judicial Committee, said that, to be a charity, a trust must be 'for the benefit of the community or of an appreciably important class of the community. The inhabitants,' he said, 'of a parish or town or any particular class of such inhabitants, may, for instance, be the objects of such a gift, but private individuals, or a fluctuating body of private individuals, cannot.' Here, my Lords, are two expressions: 'an appreciably important class of the community' and 'any particular class of such inhabitants,' to which in any case it is not easy to give a precise quantitative or qualitative meaning. But I think that in consideration of them the difficulty has sometimes been increased by failing to observe the distinction, at which I hinted earlier in this opinion, between a form of relief accorded to the whole community yet by its very nature advantageous only to the few and a form of relief accorded to a selected few out of a larger number equally willing and able to take advantage of it. Of the former type repatriated New South Wales soldiers would serve as a clear example. To me it would not seem arguable that they did not form an adequate class of the community for the purpose of the particular charity that was being established. It was with this type of case that Lord Wrenbury was dealing, and his words are apt to deal with it. Somewhat different considerations arise if the form, which the purporting charity takes, is something of general utility which is nevertheless made available not to the whole public but only to a selected body of the public—an important class of the public it may be. For example, a bridge which is available for all the public may undoubtedly be a charity and it is indifferent how many people use it. But confine its use to a selected number of persons, however numerous and important: it is then clearly not a charity. It is not of general public utility: for it does not serve the public purpose which its nature qualifies it to serve.

"Bearing this distinction in mind, though I am well aware that in its application it may often be very difficult to draw the line between public and private purposes, I should in the present case conclude that a trust cannot qualify as a charity within the fourth class . . . if the beneficiaries are a class of persons not only confined to a particular area but selected from within it by reference to a particular creed. The Master of the Rolls in his judgment cites a rhetorical question asked by Mr. Stamp in argument [1953] Ch. 504 at 519: 'Who has ever heard of a bridge to be crossed only by impecunious Methodists?' The *reductio ad absurdum* is sometimes a cogent form of argument, and this illustration serves to show the danger of conceding the quality of charity to a purpose which is not a public purpose. What is true of a bridge for Methodists is equally true of any other public purpose falling within the fourth class and of the adherents of any other creed."

LORD REID [dissenting, and disagreeing with Viscount Simonds on the "public" **7–188** point] "But your Lordships are bound by a previous decision in this House, and it appears to me to be unquestionable that in *Goodman v. Mayor of Saltash* (1882) 7 App. Cas. 633 this House decided that there was a valid charitable trust where there was no question of poverty or disability or of education or religion, and where the beneficiaries were not by any means all the inhabitants of any particular area . . . [If] the members of a religious denomination do not constitute a section of the public (or the community) then a trust solely for the advancement of religion or of education would not be a charitable trust if limited to members of a particular church. Of course, the appellants do not contend that that is right: they could not but admit that the members of a church are a section of the community for the purpose of such trusts. But they maintain that they cease to be a section of the community when it comes to trusts within the fourth class . . . Poverty may be in a special position but otherwise I can see no justification in principle or authority for holding that when dealing with one deed for one charitable purpose the members of the Methodist or any other church are a section of the community, but when dealing with another deed for a different charitable purpose they are only a fluctuating body of private individuals. I therefore reject this argument and on the whole matter I am of opinion that this appeal ought to be dismissed."

LORD SOMERVELL OF HARROW: "I agree with the Court of Appeal in rejecting **7–189** the argument that as a matter of law a trust to qualify under Lord Macnaghten's fourth class must be analgous to the repair of 'bridges portes havens causwaies seabankes and highewaies,' being the examples given in the preamble outside the three main categories of poverty, religion and education . . . I think, however, that a trust to be valid under this head would normally be for the public or all members of the public who needed the help or facilities which the trust was to provide. The present trust is not for the public.

"I cannot accept the principle submitted by the respondents that a section of the public sufficient to support a valid trust in one category must as a matter of law be sufficient to support a trust in any other category. I think that difficulties are apt to arise if one seeks to consider the class apart from the particular nature of the charitable purpose. They are, in my opinion, interdependent. There might well be a valid trust for the promotion of religion benefiting a very small class. It would not at all follow that a recreation ground for the exclusive use of the same class would be a valid charity, though it is clear from the Mortmain and Charitable Uses Act 1888, that a recreation ground for the public is a charitable purpose."

[LORDS PORTER AND TUCKER expressed no opinion on the "public" point.]

NATIONAL ANTI-VIVISECTION SOCIETY v. INLAND REVENUE COMMISSIONERS

House of Lords [1948] A.C. 31; 177 L.T. 226; [1947] 2 All E.R. 217 (Lords Simon, Wright, Simonds and Normand; Lord Porter dissenting)

7–190   The question was whether the appellant society was a body established for charitable purposes only within the meaning of section 37 of the Income Tax Act 1918 and accordingly entitled to exemption from income tax upon the income of its investments. The Special Commissioners for the purposes of the Income Tax Acts held that they were so entitled, but this decision was reversed by Macnaghten J.,[53] whose judgment was upheld by the Court of Appeal[54] (Mackinnon and Tucker L.JJ., Greene M.R. dissenting). The society appealed unsuccessfully.

7–191   LORD SIMONDS: ". . . The first point is whether a main purpose of the society is of such a political character that the court cannot regard it as charitable. The second point is whether the court, for the purpose of determining whether the object of the society is charitable, may disregard the finding of fact that any assumed public benefit in the direction of the advancement of morals and education was far outweighed by the detriment to medical science and research and, consequently, to the public health, which would result if the society succeeded in achieving its objects, and that, on balance, the object of the society, so far from being for the public benefit, was gravely injurious thereto.

"My Lords, on the first point the learned Master of the Rolls cites in his judgment[55] a passage from the speech of Lord Parker in *Bowman v. Secular Society Ltd*[56]: '. . . a trust for the attainment of political objects has always been held invalid, not because it is illegal . . . but because the court has no means of judging whether a proposed change in the law will or will not be for the public benefit . . .' Lord Parker is here considering the possibility of a valid charitable trust, and nothing else, and when he says 'has always been held invalid' he means 'has always been held not to be a valid charitable trust.' The learned Master of the Rolls found this authoritative statement upon a branch of the law, with which no one was more familiar than Lord Parker, to be inapplicable to the present case for two reasons, first, because he felt difficulty in applying the words to 'a change in the law which is in common parlance a "non-political" question' and, secondly, because he thought they could not in any case apply when the desired legislation is 'merely ancillary to the attainment of what is *ex hypothesi* a good charitable object.'

---

[53] [1945] 2 All E.R. 529.
[54] [1946] K.B. 185.
[55] [1946] K.B. 185 at 207.
[56] [1917] A.C. 406 at 442.

"My Lords, if I may deal with this second reason first, I cannot agree that in **7–192** this case an alteration in the law is merely ancillary to the attainment of a good charitable object. In a sense, no doubt, since legislation is not an end in itself, every law may be regarded as ancillary to the object which its provisions are intended to achieve. But that is not the sense in which it is said that a society has a political object. Here the finding of the commissioners is itself conclusive. 'We are satisfied,' they say, 'that the main object of the society is the total abolition of vivisection . . . and (for that purpose) the repeal of the Cruelty to Animals Act 1876, and the substitution of a new enactment prohibiting vivisection altogether.' This is a finding that the main purpose of the society is the compulsory abolition of vivisection by Act of Parliament. What else can it mean? And how else can it be supposed that vivisection is to be abolished?

"Abolition and suppression are words that connote some form of compulsion. It can only be by Act of Parliament that that element can be supplied. . . . Coming to the conclusion that it is a main object, if not the main object, of the society to obtain an alteration of the law, I ask whether that can be a charitable object, even if its purposes might otherwise be regarded as charitable.

"My Lords, I see no reason for supposing that Lord Parker, in the cited **7–193** passage, used the expression 'political objects' in any narrow sense or was confining it to objects of acute political controversy. On the contrary, he was, I think, propounding familiar doctrine, nowhere better stated than in a textbook which has long been regarded as of high authority, but appears not to have been cited for this purpose to the courts below (as it certainly was not to your Lordships), *Tyssen on Charitable Bequests.* The passage[57] is worth repeating at length: 'It is a common practice for a number of individuals amongst us to form an association for promoting some change in the law, and it is worth our while to consider the effect of a gift to such an association. It is clear that such an association is not of a charitable nature. However desirable the change may really be, the law could not stultify itself by holding that it was for the public benefit that the law itself should be changed. Each court in deciding on the validity of a gift must decide on the principle that the law is right as it stands. On the other hand, such a gift could not be held void for illegality.'

"Lord Parker uses slightly different language, but means the same thing, when **7–194** he says that the court has no means of judging whether a proposed change in the law will or will not be for the public benefit. It is not for the court to judge and the court has no means of judging. The same question may be looked at from a slightly different angle. One of the tests, and a crucial test, whether a trust is charitable lies in the competence of the court to control and reform it. I would remind your Lordships that it is the King as *parens patriae* who is the guardian of charity, and that it is the right and duty of his Attorney-General to intervene and inform the court if the trustees of a charitable trust fall short of their duty. So too it is his duty to assist the court, if need be, in the formulation of a scheme for the execution of a charitable trust. But, my Lords, is it for a moment to be supposed that it is the function of the Attorney-General, on behalf of the Crown, to intervene and demand that a trust shall be established and administered by the court, the object of which is to alter the law in a manner highly prejudicial, as he and His Majesty's Government may think, to the welfare of the state? This very case would serve as an example if upon the footing that it was a charitable trust it became the duty of the Attorney-General on account of its maladministration to

---

[57] (1st ed., 1898), at 176.

intervene. There is, undoubtedly, a paucity of judicial authority on this point. But in truth the reason of the thing appears to me so clear that I neither expect nor require much authority. I conclude upon this part of the case that a main object of the society is political and for that reason the society is not established for charitable purposes only. I would only add that I would reserve my opinion upon the hypothetical example of a private enabling Act, which was suggested in the course of the argument.

7–195 "The second question raised in this appeal . . . is of wider importance, and I must say at once that I cannot reconcile it with my conception of a court of equity, that it should take under its care and administer a trust, however well intentioned its creator, of which the consequence would be calamitous to the community. [His Lordship made a brief review of the origin of the equitable jurisdiction in matters of charity, and continued:]

7–196 "My Lords, this then being the position, that the court determined 'one by one' whether particular named purposes were charitable, applying always the overriding test whether the purpose was for public benefit, and that the King as *parens patriae* intervened *pro bono publico* for the protection of charities, what room is there for the doctrine, which has found favour with the learned Master of the Rolls, and has been so vigorously supported at the Bar of the House, that the court may disregard the evils that will ensue from the achievement by the society of its ends? It is to me a strange and bewildering idea that the court must look so far and no farther, must see a charitable purpose in the intention of the society to benefit animals, and thus elevate the moral character of men, but must **7–197** shut its eyes to the injurious results to the whole human and animal creation. I will readily concede that, if the purpose is within one of the heads of charity forming the first three classes in the classification which Lord Macnaghten borrowed from Sir Samuel Romilly's argument in *Morice v. Bishop of Durham*,[58] the court will easily conclude that it is a charitable purpose. But even here to give the purpose the name of 'religious' or 'educational' is not to conclude the matter. It may yet not be charitable if the religious purpose is illegal or the educational purpose is contrary to public policy. Still there remains the overriding question: Is it *pro bono publico*? It would be another strange misreading of Lord Macnaghten's speech in *Pemsel's* case[59] to suggest that he intended anything to the contrary. I would rather say that, when a purpose appears broadly to fall within one of the familiar categories of charity, the court will assume it to be for the benefit of the community and therefore charitable unless the contrary is shown, and further that the court will not be astute in such a case to defeat upon doubtful evidence the avowed benevolent intention of a donor. But, my Lords, the next step is one that I cannot take. Where upon the evidence before it the court concludes that, however well intentioned the donor, the achievement of his object will be greatly to the public disadvantage, there can be no justification for saying that it is a charitable object. If and so far as there is any judicial decision to the contrary, it must, in my opinion, be regarded as inconsistent with principle and be overruled." *Appeal dismissed.*

WILLIAMS' TRUSTEES v. INLAND REVENUE COMMISSIONERS

House of Lords [1947] A.C. 447; 176 L.T. 462; 63 T.L.R. 352; [1947] 1 All E.R. 513 (Lords Simon, Wright, Porter, Simonds and Normand)

---

[58] (1805) 10 Ves. 522.
[59] [1891] A.C. 531.

A trust was established for the purpose of maintaining an institute "for the **7–198** benefit of Welsh people resident in or near or visiting London with a view to creating a centre in London for promoting the moral, social, spiritual and educational welfare of Welsh people, and fostering the study of the Welsh language and of Welsh history, literature, music and art."[60] The trust property, consisted of two blocks of property, one of which was let out to tenants, and the other occupied by the London Welsh Association Ltd. This association had been incorporated for substantially the same purposes as those contained in the deed of trust which are set out above. The trustees applied the rents of the first block and made certain gifts to the association intending that they should be directed to the following purposes: public lectures and debates, a music club, literary and educational classes, the maintenance of the headquarters' premises, badminton and table-tennis clubs, dances, whist- and bridge-drives, an annual dinner and garden-party, a weekly social and dance, and the provision of a central information bureau. The trustees admitted that the purposes of the association were not exclusively charitable, but contended that they themselves were trustees of a trust established for charitable purposes only, and that in applying the rents of the first block of trust property to the purposes of the association they had applied them to charitable purposes only and that accordingly they were entitled to exemption from income tax in respect of the rents of that property.

The Court of Appeal held[61] that on the true construction of the trust deed the **7–199** property was not vested in the trustees for charitable purposes only, and on the facts the rents applied to the purpose of the association were not applied for charitable purposes only. The trustees appealed unsuccessfully.

LORD SIMONDS: "Lord Cave said 'Lord Macnaghten did not mean that all trusts for purposes beneficial to the community are charitable, but that there were certain beneficial trusts which fell within that category: . . . it is not enough to say that the trust in question is for public purposes beneficial to the community; you must also show it to be a charitable trust.' See *Att.-Gen. v. National Provincial Bank*.[62] But . . . it is just because the purpose of the trust deed in this case is said to be beneficial to the community or a section of the community, and for no other reason, that its charitable character is asserted. It is not alleged that the trust is (1) for the benefit of the community and (2) beneficial in a way which the law regards as charitable. Therefore, as it seems to me, in its mere statement the claim is imperfect and must fail.

"My Lords, the cases in which the question of charity has come before the **7–200** courts are legion, and no one who is versed in them will pretend that all the decisions, even of the highest authority, are easy to reconcile, but I will venture to refer to one or two of them . . . In *Houston v. Burns*[63] the question was as to the validity of a gift 'for such public benevolent or charitable purposes in connection with the parish of Lesmahagow or the neighbourhood' as might be thought proper. This was a Scottish case, but upon the point now under

---

[60] These purposes might today be regarded as charitable by the Recreational Charities Act 1958, *infra*, para. 7–213. It would still be necessary to prove the existence of the other criterion, namely, an element of public benefit. *Williams' Trustees v. I.R.C.* remains an important authority on the latter requirement. The Charitable Trusts (Validation) Act 1954 (*infra*, para. 7–235) has been applied to validate the *Williams* trusts: see Charity Commissioners Annual Report 1977, paras. 71–80, considering the beneficial class to be a sufficient section of the public.

[61] [1945] 2 All E.R. 236.

[62] [1924] A.C. 262, 265.

[63] [1918] A.C. 337.

consideration there is no difference between English and Scottish law. It was argued that the limitation of the purpose to a particular locality was sufficient to validate the gift, that is to say, though purposes beneficial to the community might fail, yet purposes beneficial to a localised section of the community were charitable. That argument was rejected by this House. If the purposes are not charitable *per se*, the localisation of them will not make them charitable. It is noticeable that Lord Finlay L.C. expressly overrules a decision or dictum of Lord Romilly to the contrary effect in *Dolan v. MacDermot*[64] . . .

7–201   "My Lords, I must mention another aspect of this case. It is not expressly stated in the preamble to the statute, but it was established in the Court of Chancery that a trust to be charitable must be of a public character. It must not be merely for the benefit of particular private individuals. If it is it will not be in law a charity, though the benefit taken by those individuals is of the very character stated in the preamble. The rule is thus stated by Lord Wrenbury in *Verge v. Somerville*.[65] 'To ascertain whether a gift constitutes a valid charitable trust so as to escape being void on the ground of perpetuity, a first inquiry must be whether it is public—whether it is for the benefit of the community or of an appreciably important class of the community. The inhabitants of a parish or town, or any particular class of such inhabitants, may for instance be the objects of such a gift, but private individuals, or a fluctuating body of private individuals,

7–202 cannot.' It is, I think, obvious that this rule, necessary as it is, must often be difficult of application, and so the courts have found. Fortunately, perhaps, though Lord Wrenbury put it first, the question does not arise at all if the purpose of the gift, whether for the benefit of a class of inhabitants or of a fluctuating body of private individuals, is not itself charitable. I may, however, refer to a recent case in this House which in some aspects resembles the present case. In *Keren v. Inland Revenue Commissioners*[66] a company had been formed which had as its main object (to put it shortly) the purchase of land in Palestine, Syria or other parts of Turkey in Asia and the peninsula of Sinai for the purpose of settling Jews on such lands. In its memorandum it took numerous other powers which were to be exercised only in such a way as should, in the opinion of the company, be conducive to the attainment of the primary object. No part of the income of the company was distributable among its members. It was urged that the company was established for charitable purposes for numerous reasons, with only one of which I will trouble your Lordships, namely, that it was

7–203 established for the benefit of the community or of a section of the community, whether the association was for the benefit of Jews all over the world, or of the Jews repatriated in the Promised Land. Lord Tomlin,[67] dealing with the argument that I have just mentioned on the footing that if benefit to a 'community' could be established the purpose might be charitable, proceeded to examine the problem in that aspect and sought to identify the community. He failed to do so, finding it neither in the community of all Jews throughout the world nor in that of the Jews in the region presented for settlement. It is perhaps unnecessary to pursue the matter. Each case must be judged on its own facts and the dividing-line is not easily drawn, but the difficulty of finding the community in the present case, when the definition of 'Welsh people' in the first deed is remembered, would not, I think, be less than that of finding the community of Jews in *Keren's* case."

---

[64] (1867) L.R. 5 Eq. 60 at 62.
[65] [1924] A.C. 496 at 499.
[66] [1932] A.C. 650.
[67] *ibid.* at 659.

INCORPORATED COUNCIL OF LAW REPORTING FOR ENGLAND AND WALES v. ATTORNEY-GENERAL

Court of Appeal [1972] Ch. 73; [1971] 3 W.L.R. 853; [1971] 3 All E.R. 1029

This decision turned primarily upon Lord Macnaghten's second category but **7–204** the following extract from the judgment of Russell L.J. reveals a new approach to Lord Macnaghten's fourth category which Sachs L.J. agreed with.

RUSSELL L.J.: ". . . I come now to the question whether, if the main purpose of **7–205** the Association is (as I think it is) to further the sound development and administration of the law in this country, and if (as I think it is) that is a purpose beneficial to the community or of general public utility, that purpose is charitable according to the law of England and Wales. On this point the law is rooted in the Statute of Elizabeth, a statute whose object was the oversight and reform of abuses in the administration of property devoted by donors to purposes which were regarded as worthy of such protection as being charitable. The preamble to the statute listed certain examples of purposes worthy of such protection. These **7–206** were from an early stage regarded merely as examples, and have through the centuries been regarded as examples or guide-posts for the courts in the differing circumstances of a developing civilisation and economy. Sometimes recourse has been had by the courts to the instances given in the preamble in order to see whether in a given case sufficient analogy may be found with something specifically stated in the preamble, or sufficient analogy has been found. Of this approach perhaps the most obvious example is the provision of crematoria by analogy with the provision of burial grounds by analogy with the upkeep of churchyards by analogy with the repair of churches. On other occasions a decision in favour or against a purpose being charitable has been based in terms on a more general question whether the purpose is or is not within 'the spirit and intendment' of the Elizabethan statute and in particular its preamble. Again (and at an early stage in development) whether the purpose is within 'the equity' or within 'the mischief' of the statute. Again whether the purpose is charitable 'in the same sense' as purposes within the purview of the statute. I have much sympathy with those who say that these phrases do little of themselves to elucidate any particular problem. 'Tell me' they say, 'what you define when you speak of spirit, intendment, equity, mischief, the same sense, and I will tell you whether a purpose is charitable according to law. But you never define. All you do is sometimes to say that a purpose is none of these things. I can understand it when you say that the preservation of sea walls is for the safety of lives and property, and therefore by analogy the voluntary provision of lifeboats and fire brigades are charitable. I can even follow you as far as crematoria. But these other generalities teach me nothing.' I say I have much sympathy for such an approach; but it seems to me to be unduly and improperly restrictive. The Statute of Elizabeth was a statute to reform abuses; in such circumstances and in that age the courts of this country were not inclined to be restricted in their implementation of Parliament's desire for reform to particular examples given by the statute, and they deliberately kept open their ability to intervene when they thought necessary in cases not specifically mentioned, by applying as the test whether any particular case of abuse of funds or property was within the 'mischief' or the 'equity' of the statute.

"For myself I believe that this rather vague and undefined approach is the **7–207** correct one, with analogy its handmaid, and that when considering Lord Macnaghten's fourth category in *Pemsel's* case[68] of 'other purposes beneficial to

---

[68] [1891] A.C. 531 at 583.

the community' (or as phrased by Sir Samuel Romilly[69] 'objects of general public utility') the courts, in consistently saying that not all such are necessarily charitable in law, are in substance accepting that if a purpose is shown to be so beneficial or of such utility it is prima facie charitable in law, but have left open a line of retreat based on the equity of the statute in case they are faced with a purpose (*e.g.* a political purpose) which could not have been within the contemplation of the statute even if the then legislators had been endowed with the gift of foresight into the circumstances of later centuries.

7–208 "In a case such as the present, in which in my view the object cannot be thought otherwise than beneficial to the community and of general public utility, I believe the proper question to ask is whether there are any grounds for holding it to be outside the equity of the statute; and I think the answer to that is here in the negative. I have already touched on its essential importance to our rule of law. If I look at the somewhat random examples in the preamble to the statute I find in the repair of bridges, havens, causeways, sea banks and highways examples of matters which if not looked after by private enterprise must be a proper function and responsibility of government, which would afford strong ground for a statutory expression by Parliament of anxiety to prevent misappropriation of funds voluntarily dedicated to such matters. It cannot I think be doubted that if there were not a competent and reliable set of reports of judicial decisions, it would be a proper function and responsibility of government to secure their provision for the due administration of the law. It was argued that the specific topics in the preamble that I have mentioned are all concerned with concrete matters, and that so also is the judicially accepted opinion that the provision of a court house is a charitable purpose. But whether the search be for analogy or for the equity of the statute this seems to me to be too narrow or refined an approach. I cannot accept that the provision, in order to facilitate the proper administration of the law, of the walls and other physical facilities of a court house is a charitable purpose, but that the dissemination by accurate and selective reporting of knowledge of a most important part of the law to be there administered is not.

7–209 "In my judgment accordingly the purpose for which the Association is established is exclusively charitable in the sense of Lord Macnaghten's fourth category."

RE SOUTH PLACE ETHICAL SOCIETY

Chancery Division [1980] 1 W.L.R. 1565; [1980] 3 All E.R. 918

DILLON J.: . . . "The fourth category developed from the matters specified in the preamble to the . . . Charitable Uses Act 1601 but it has long been recognised that it is not limited to those matters actually listed in the preamble which do not fall within Lord Macnaghten's other three categories of the relief of poverty, the advancement of education and the advancement of religion. It is also clear, as stated in *Tudor on Charities* (6th Ed., 1967, at 85, 120) that the fourth category can include trusts for certain purposes tending to promote the mental or moral improvement of the community. It is on the basis of mental or moral improvement of the community that animal welfare trusts have been

---

[69] In *Morice v. Bishop of Durham* (1805) 10 Ves. 522 at 531.

supported. But it is plain that not all objects which tend to promote the moral improvement of the community are charitable.

"Again, as Wilberforce J. pointed out in *Re Hopkins' Will Trusts* [1965] Ch. 669 **7–210** at 680–681, beneficial in the fourth category is not limited to the production of material benefit, but includes at least benefit in the intellectual or artistic fields.

"In *Incorporated Council of Law Reporting for England and Wales v. Attorney General* [1972] Ch. 73 at 88–89, Russell L.J. seems to have taken the view that the court can hold that there are some purposes 'so beneficial or of such utility' to the community that they ought prima facie to be accepted as charitable. With deference, I find it difficult to adopt that approach in view of the comments of Lord Simonds in *Williams' Trustees v. Inland Revenue Commissioners* [1947] A.C. 447 at 455 where, in holding that the promotion of the moral, social, spiritual and educational welfare of the Welsh people was not charitable, he pointed out that it was really turning the question upside down to start with considering whether something was for the benefit of the community. He said:

> "My Lords, there are, I think, two propositions which must ever be borne **7–211** in mind in any case in which the question is whether a trust is charitable. The first is that it is still the general law that a trust is not charitable and entitled to the privileges which charity confers unless it is within the spirit and intendment of the preamble to 43 Eliz., c. 4, which is expressly preserved by section 13(2) of the Mortmain and Charitable Uses Act 1888. The second is that the classification of charity in its legal sense into four principal divisions by LORD MACNAGHTEN in *Pemsel's* case ([1891] A.C. 583) must always be read subject to the qualification appearing in the judgment of LINDLEY L.J. in *Re Macduff* ([1896] 2 Ch. 446): 'Now SIR SAMUEL ROMILLY did not mean, and I am certain that LORD MACNAGHTEN did not mean to say, that every object of public general utility must necessarily be a charity. Some may be and some may not be.' This observation has been expanded by VISCOUNT CAVE L.C. in this House in *A.G. v. National Provincial Bank* [1924] A.C. 265 in these words: 'LORD MACNAGHTEN did not mean that all trusts beneficial to the community are charitable, but that there were certain beneficial trusts which fall within that category: and accordingly to argue that because a trust is for a purpose beneficial to the community it is therefore a charitable trust is to turn round his sentence and to give it a different meaning. So here it is not enough to say that the trust in question is for public purposes beneficial to the community or is for the public welfare; you must also show it to be a charitable trust.' "

"Therefore it seems to me that the approach to be adopted in considering **7–212** whether something is within the fourth category is the approach of analogy from what is stated in the preamble to the Statute of Elizabeth or from what has already been held to be charitable within the fourth category.

"The question is whether the trust is within the spirit and intendment of the preamble, and the route that the courts have traditionally adopted is the route of precedent and analogy as stated by Lord Wilberforce in *Brisbane City Council v. Att. Gen.* [1979] A.C. 411 at 422." [But see para. 7–175 *supra*.]

VI. THE PROVISION OF FACILITIES FOR RECREATION IN THE INTERESTS OF SOCIAL WELFARE

The Recreational Charities Act 1958[70]

Section 1.—(1) Subject to the provisions of this Act, it shall be and be deemed always to have been charitable to provide, or assist in the provision of, facilities for recreation or other leisure-time occupation, if the facilities are provided in the interests of social welfare:

7–213 Provided that nothing in this section shall be taken to derogate from the principle that a trust or institution to be charitable must be for the public benefit.

(2) The requirement of the foregoing subsection that the facilities are provided in the interests of social welfare shall not be treated as satisfied unless—

   (a) the facilities are provided with the object of improving the conditions of life for the persons for whom the facilities are primarily intended; and
   (b) either—
      (I) Those persons have need of such facilities as aforesaid by reason of their youth, age, infirmity or disablement, poverty or social and economic circumstances; or
      (ii) The facilities are to be available to the members or female members of the public at large.

7–214 (3) Subject to the said requirement, subsection (1) of this section applies in particular to the provision of facilities at village halls, community centres and women's institutes, and to the provision and maintenance of grounds and buildings to be used for purposes of recreation or leisure-time occupation, and extends to the provision of facilities for those purposes by the organising of any activity.

[Section 2 makes special provision for trusts for miners' welfare; section 3 makes it clear that the Act does not restrict the purposes which are charitable independently of the Act.]

Note

7–215 The Act was passed to remedy a defect in the law revealed by the House of Lords in *I.R.C. v. Baddeley*.[71] The objects of the trusts were "the moral, social and physical well-being of persons resident in West Ham and Leyton who for the time being were or were likely to become members of the Methodist Church and who were of insufficient means otherwise to enjoy the advantages provided." The method by which the objects were to be attained was "by the provision of facilities for moral, social and physical training and recreation and by promoting and encouraging all forms of such activities." The House of Lords by a

---

[70] See S. G. Maurice, "Recreational Charities" (1959) 23 Conv.(N.S.) 15; (1958) 21 M.L.R. 534 (L. Price). There is a Northern Ireland Recreational Charities Act 1958 in similar terms.

[71] [1955] A.C. 572 at para. 7–181 *supra*. The provision of a recreation ground for the inhabitants of a particular area is, however, charitable: *Re Morgan* [1955] 1 W.L.R. 738. See also *Brisbane City Council v. Att.-Gen. for Queensland* [1978] 3 All E.R. 30.

majority (Lord Reid dissenting) held that the objects were not exclusively charitable. The word "social" included worthy objects of benevolence which were not charitable in the legal sense and the trust accordingly failed.[72] Lord Simonds also held[73] that "a trust cannot qualify as a charity within the fourth class in *Pemsel's* case (*i.e.* as being of general public utility) if the beneficiaries are a class of persons not only confined to a particular area but selected from within it by reference to a particular creed." Lord Somervell appeared to agree with this. Lords Porter and Tucker expressed no opinion on the point and Lord Reid dissented.[74] In *Universe Tankships Inc v. International Transport Workers Federation*[75] the Court of Appeal accepted that it had been rightly conceded that a trust to provide welfare social and recreational facilities in ports around the world for seafarers of all nations was not charitable, primarily it seems because of the trustees' wide discretion under ITWF rules as to what amounted to "welfare."

The Act established two criteria for the validity of a recreational **7–216** charity: first, the trust must be for the public benefit; and, secondly, the facilities must be provided in the interests of social welfare. The second criterion itself has two elements: the first is constant, namely, that the object of providing the facilities must be to improve the conditions of life of the beneficiaries; but the second may be satisfied in alternative ways— by showing *either* that the beneficiaries have need of the facilities by reason of the factors enumerated in the Act, *or* that the facilities are available to the members or female [but not male] members of the public at large.

The Act is not free from difficulties of interpretation. For example, **7–217** what is the test of "public benefit" to be applied? If it is Lord Simonds' test for trusts of general public utility, a trust like that in *I.R.C. v. Baddeley* would still not be charitable. Moreover, the "social welfare" criterion would not be satisfied in that the beneficiaries did not have need of the facilities by reason of the factors comprised in the Act. Similarly, *Williams v. I.R.C.*[76] may be unaffected on the footing that the London Welsh factor is not a sufficient qualifying factor. There would even be some difficulty forcing *I.R.C. v. Glasgow Police Athletic Association*[77] (encouragement and promotion of "all forms of athletic sports and general pastimes" for Glasgow Police held not charitable) within the Act as police are not normally considered as persons needing recreational facilities by reason of age or social and economic circumstances. Furthermore, a sports club open for membership for a fee to the public at large or for persons by reason of their youth desirous of physical

---

[72] See *Williams' Trustees v. I.R.C.* [1947] A.C. 447, *supra*, at para. 7–198.

[73] [1955] A.C. 572, 592. See discussion *supra*, at para. 7–178 *et seq.*

[74] Citing *Verge v. Somerville* [1924] A.C. 496; and *Goodman v. Mayor of Saltash* (1882) 7 App.Cas. 633.

[75] [1980] 2 L.I.R. 523 at 538.

[76] [1947] A.C. 447, see *supra*, para. 7–198. However, the Charity Commissioners have treated the Charitable Trusts (Validation) Act 1954, as applying to such trusts as benefiting a sufficient section of the public: [1977] Annual Report, paras. 71–80.

[77] [1953] A.C. 380 regarded as really a trust for the private advantage of members. Trusts for promoting the efficiency of the police or the armed forces are valid: [1953] A.C. 380 at 409.

development, will not be registered as charitable on the application of members seeking to improve the conditions of life of themselves rather than others.[78]

7–218   In *Wynn and Others v. Skegness U.D.C.*[79] a convalescent home and holiday centre for North Derbyshire mineworkers was conceded to be within the terms of the Act but Ungoed-Thomas J. discussed some of the difficulties inherent in the Act. More recently in *I.R.C. v. McMullen*, the Court of Appeal[80] highlighted the difficulty over whether the persons for whom the facilities are primarily intended must be to some extent and in some way deprived persons to satisfy section 1(2) or whether it suffices that objectively the facilities are of a type capable of improving the conditions of life for such persons. The Charity Commissioners and then the House of Lords in *Guild v. I.R.C. infra*, have come down in favour of the latter broad approach.

GUILD v. I.R.C.

House of Lords [1992] 2 A.C. 310.

7–219   LORD KEITH OF KINKEL.[81] "My Lords, the late James Young Russell (the testator), who resided in North Berwick, died on September 11, 1982 leaving a will dated April 7, 1971 in which, after bequeathing a number of pecuniary legacies, he provided as follows:

> 'And I leave the whole, rest, residue and remainder of my said means and estate to the Town Council of North Berwick for the use in connection with the Sports Centre in North Berwick or some similar purpose in connection with sport and the receipt of the Treasurer for the time being of the Burgh of North Berwick shall be a sufficient receipt and discharge for my Executor.'

7–220   "In the course of his argument in relation to the first branch of the bequest counsel for the Crown accepted that it assisted in the provision of facilities for recreation or other leisure-time occupation within the meaning of sub-s (1) of s.1 of the 1958 Act, and also that the requirement of public benefit in the proviso to the subsection was satisfied. It was further accepted that the facilities of the sports centre were available to the public at large so that the condition of sub-s (2)(b)(ii) was satisfied. It was maintained, however, that these facilities were not provided 'in the interests of social welfare' as required by sub-s (1), because they did not meet the condition laid down in sub-s (2)(a), namely that they should be 'provided with the object of improving the conditions of life for the persons for whom the facilities are primarily intened'. The reason why it was said that this condition was not met was that on a proper construction it involved that the facilities should be provided with the object of meeting a need for such facilities in people who suffered from a position of relative social disadvantage. Reliance

---

[78] See Decisions of Charity Commissioners Vol 5 (1997) at 11 dealing with North Tawton R.U.F.C.
[79] [1967] 1 W.L.R. 52. The 1984 Annual Report of the Charity Commissioners, para. 25 shows they treated the provision by a benefactor of a public ice-skating rink in Oxford as within the 1958 Act.
[80] [1979] 1 All E.R. 588.
[81] Lords Roskill, Griffiths, Jauncey and Lowry simply concurred with Lord Keith.

was placed on a passage from the judgment of Walton J. in *I.R.C. v. McMullen* [1978] 1 W.L.R. 664 at 675. He said in relation to the words 'social welfare' in sub-s(1):

> 'In my view, however, these words in themselves indicate that there is some sort of deprivation, not, of course, by any means necessarily of money, which falls to be alleviated; and I think that this is made even clearer by the terms of s.1(2)(a) of the 1958 Act. The facilities must be provided with the object of improving the conditions of life for persons for whom the facilities are primarily intended. In other words, they must be to some extent and in some way deprived persons.'

"When the case went to the Court of Appeal (see [1979] 1 W.L.R. 130) the **7–221** majority (Stamp and Orr L.JJ.) affirmed the judgment of Walton J. on both points, but Bridge L.J. dissented. As regards the 1958 Act point he said [1979] 1 W.L.R. 130 at 142–143):

> 'I turn therefore to consider whether the object defined by cl. 3(a) is **7–222** charitable under the express terms of s.1 of the Recreational Charities Act 1958. Are the facilities for recreation contemplated in this clause to be "provided in the interests of social welfare" under s.1(1)? If this phrase stood without further statutory elaboration, I should not hesitate to decide that sporting facilities for persons undergoing any formal process of education are provided in the interests of social welfare. Save in the sense that the interests of social welfare can only be served by the meeting of some social need, I cannot accept the judge's view that the interests of social welfare can only be served in relation to some "deprived" class. The judge found this view reinforced by the requirement of s.1(2)(a) that the facilities must be provided "with the object of improving the conditions of life for the persons for whom the facilities are primarily intended". Here again I can see no reason to conclude that only the deprived can have their conditions of life improved. Hyde Park improves the conditions of life for residents in Mayfair and Belgravia as much as for those in Pimlico or the Portobello Road, and the village hall may improve the conditions of life for the squire and his family as well as for the cottagers. The persons for whom the facilities here are primarily intended are pupils of schools and universities, as defined in the trust deed, and these facilities are in my judgment unquestionably to be provided with the object of improving their conditions of life. Accordingly the ultimate question on which the appli- **7–223** cation of the statute to this trust depends, is whether the requirements of s.1(2)(b)(i) are satisfied on the ground that such pupils as a class have need of facilities for games or sports which will promote their physical education and development by reason either of their youth or of their social and economic circumstances, or both. The overwhelming majority of pupils within the definition are your persons and the tiny majority of mature students can be ignored as *de minimis*. There cannot surely be any doubt that young persons as part of their education do need facilities for organised games and sports both by reason of their youth and by reason of their social and economic circumstances. They cannot provide such facilities for themselves but are dependent on what is provided for them.'

"In the House of Lords the case was decided against the Crown upon the ground that the trust was one for the advancement of education, opinion being reserved on the point under the 1958 Act. Lord Hailsham of St Marylebone L.C. said [1981] A.C. 1 at 11):

> '. . . I do not wish my absence of decision on the third or fourth points to be interpreted as an indorsement of the majority judgments in the Court of Appeal nor as necessarily dissenting from the contrary views contained in the minority judgment of Bridge L.J.'

7–224   "Counsel for the executor, for his part, relied on part of the judgment of Lord MacDermott L.C.J. in *Valuation Comr. for Northern Ireland v. Lurgan B.C.* [1968] N.I. 104. A local authority which was the owner and occupier of an indoor swimming pool claimed exemption from rates in respect of it under s.2 of the Valuation (Ireland) Act 1854 on the ground, inter alia, that it was used exclusively for the purposes of a recreational charity under the Recreational Charities Act (Northern Ireland) 1958. A majority of the Court of Appeal held that this ground of exemption was established.

7–225   "Lord MacDermott L.C.J. makes the point that s.1(2) of the 1958 Act does not exactly contain a definition but that it does state the essential elements which must be present if the requirements that the facilities should be provided in the interests of social welfare is to be met. It is difficult to envisage a case where, although these essential elements are present, yet the facilities are not provided in the interests of social welfare. Nor do I consider that the reference to social welfare in sub-s (1) can properly be held to colour sub-s (2)(a) to the effect that the persons for whom the facilities are primarily intended must be confined to those persons who suffer from some form of social deprivation. That this is not so seems to me to follow from the alternative conditions expressed in sub-s (2)(b). If it suffices that the facilities are to be available to the members of the public at large, as sub-para (ii) provides, it must necessarily be inferred that the persons for whom the facilities are primarily intended are not to be confined to those who have need of them by reason of one of the forms of social deprivation mentioned in sub-para. (1).

7–226   "The fact is that persons in all walks of life and all kinds of social circumstances may have their conditions of life improved by the provision of recreational facilities of suitable character. The proviso requiring public benefit excludes facilities of an undesirable nature. In my opinion the view expressed by Bridge L.J. in *I.R.C. v. McMullen* is clearly correct and that of Walton J. in the same case is incorrect. Lord MacDermott L.C.J. in the *Lurgan B.C.* case plainly did not consider that the category of persons for whom the facilities were primarily intended was subject to any restriction. I would therefore reject the argument that the facilities are not provided in the interests of social welfare unless they are provided with the object of improving the conditions of life for persons who suffer from some form of social disadvantage. It suffices if they are provided with the object of improving the conditions of life for members of the community generally. The Lord President, whose opinion contains a description of the facilities available at the sports centre which it is unnecessary to repeat, took the view that they were so provided (see [1991] STC 281 at 288–289). I respectfully agree, and indeed the contrary was not seriously maintained.

7–227   "It remains to consider the point upon which the executor was unsuccessful before the First Division, namely whether or not the second branch of the bequest of residue, referring to 'some similar purpose in connection with sport', is so widely expressed as to admit of the funds being applied in some manner which falls outside the requirements of s.1 of the 1958 Act. Counsel for the executor invited your Lordships, in construing this part of the bequest, to adopt the benignant approach which has regularly been favoured in the interpretation of trust deeds capable of being regarded as evincing a charitable intention. That approach is appropriate where the language used is susceptible of two constructions one of which would make it void and the other effectual (see *I.R.C. v. McMullen* [1980] 1 All E.R. 884 at 890; [1981] A.C. 1 at 14 per Lord Hailsham of St Marylebone L.C. and *Weir v. Crum-Brown* [1908] A.C. 162 at 167 per Lord Loreburn L.C.). It was argued for the Crown that the benignant approach was not apt in the present case, since the question was not whether the trust was valid or invalid, but whether it qualified for exemption from tax by virtue of the 1958 Act. But the importation into Scots law, for tax purposes, of the technical English law of charities involves that a Scottish judge should approach any question of construction arising out of the language used in the relevant instrument in the same manner as would an English judge who had to consider its validity as a charitable gift. The English judge would adopt the benignant approach in setting about that task, and so the Scottish judge dealing with the tax consequences should do likewise.

"The matter for decision turns upon the ascertainment of the intention of the **7–228** testator in using the words he did. The adjective 'similar' connotes that there are points of resemblance between one thing and another. The points of resemblance here with the sports centre cannot be related only to location in North Berwick or to connection with sport. The first of these is plainly to be implied from the fact of the gift being to the town council of North Berwick and the second is expressly stated in the words under construction. So the resemblance to the sports centre which the testator had in mind must be ascertained by reference to some other characteristics possessed by it. The leading characteristics of the sports centre lie in the nature of the facilities which are provided there and the fact that those facilities are available to the public at large. These are the characteristics which enable it to satisfy s.1 of the 1958 Act. Adopting so far as necessary a benignant construction, I infer that the intention of the testator was that any other purpose to which the town council might apply the bequest or any part of it should also display those characteristics. In the result I am of opinion, the first part of the bequest having been found to be charitable within the meaning of s.1 of the 1958 Act, that the same is true of the second part, so that the funds in question qualify for exemption from capital transfer tax.

"My Lords, for these reasons I would allow the appeal and set aside the determination of the commissioners."

VII. No Unlawful Discrimination

Race Relations Act 1976

It is not against public policy or unlawful in a private trust to **7–229** discriminate on grounds of race, religion, nationality or colour.[82] However, the Race Relations Act 1976 prohibits discrimination *against* persons on the ground of colour, race, nationality, or ethnic or national

---

[82] *Re Lysaght* [1986] Ch. 191; *Re Dominion Students' Hall Trusts* [1947] Ch. 183; *Blathwayt v. Lord Cawley* [1976] A.C. 397. The Human Rights Act 1999 may affect religious conditions.

origins in the case of charitable trusts, though it allows discrimination in *favour* of persons of a class defined by reference to race, nationality or ethnic or national origins,[83] though not by reference to colour. The colour qualification is disregarded even where favourable discrimination is concerned.[84] Thus, a trust to educate "black youngsters of West Indian origin in Brixton" would have the word "black" deleted. In exceptional circumstances the removal of any discriminatory provision unacceptable to the original trustees is possible under the *cy-près* jurisdiction.[85]

Sex Discrimination Act 1975

7–230 Sexually discriminating provisions in private trusts are valid. Where a charitable trust contains a provision for benefiting persons of one sex only it is valid,[86] *e.g.* Boy Scouts, Girl Guides, retired schoolmasters, research fellowships available for men only.[87] In the case of an educational charity, however, the trustees can apply to the Secretary of State for Education to make the trust's benefits open to both sexes. He will make the order if satisfied that to do so would conduce to the advancement of education without sex discrimination and 25 years have elapsed since creation of the trust, unless the donor (or his personal representatives) or the personal representatives of the testator have consented in writing.[88]

Disability Discrimination Act 1995

Discrimination against the disabled is prescribed except that charities can treat some categories of disabled more favourably than others[89] *e.g.* so the Royal National Institute for the Blind can prefer employing visually impaired persons. Discrimination in favour of the disabled against the able is authorised.[90]

VIII. THE PURPOSE OF THE TRUST MUST BE EXCLUSIVELY CHARITABLE

7–231 If, consistently with its terms, a trust may be applied exclusively for purposes which are not charitable, it is a non-charitable trust notwithstanding that, consistently with its terms, it may be applied exclusively for purposes which are charitable. Thus a trust to apply income to "registered charities or to such bodies as in the opinion of the trustees have charitable objects" is not charitable since the final clause does not state "*exclusively* charitable objects" and, even if it did, bodies *in the opinion of the trustees* having exclusively charitable objects might not be

---

[83] s.34(2)(3).
[84] s.34(1).
[85] See Lysaght [1966] Ch. 191; *Re Woodhams* [1981] 1 W.L.R. 493; see *infra* at para. 7–317, n. 41.
[86] Sex Discrimination Act 1975, s.43.
[87] *Hugh-Jones v. St. John's College Cambridge* (1979) 123 So.Jo. 603.
[88] 1975 Act, s. 78.
[89] Disability Discrimination Act 1995 s.10.
[90] *ibid., s. 19(5)(K).*

regarded by the courts as having exclusively charitable objects.[91] More obviously, the following trusts are not exclusively charitable and so are void: "for worthy causes," "for benevolent purposes," for "charitable or benevolent purposes,[92] for purposes[93] "connected with the education and welfare of children" or "for the public good".[94] However, a benignant construction may save a charitable trust as in *Guild v. I.R.C.*[95] where the trust deed required funds to be used for a Sports Centre in North Berwick qualifying as a valid recreational charity under the 1958 Recreational Charities Act "or some similar purpose in connection with sport", where the House of Lords held such "similar purpose" must likewise be a charitable purpose.

Exceptions

There are some exceptions to the rule that a trust cannot be charitable unless its purposes are exclusively charitable.

(i) Incidental Purposes

If the main purpose of a corporation or trust is charitable and the only **7–232** elements in its constitution and operations, which are non-charitable, are merely incidental to the effective promotion of that main purpose, the corporation and trust are established for charitable purposes only.[96] If the non-charitable object is itself a main object, neither the corporation nor the trust is established for charitable purposes only; but there is this difference between them: the corporation remains validly constituted, but the trust is void.[97] As Slade J. states,[98] "The distinction is between (a) those non-charitable activities authorised by the trust instrument which are merely incidental or subsidiary to a charitable purpose and (b) those non-charitable activities so authorised which themselves form part of the trust purpose. In the latter but not the former case the reference to non-charitable activities will deprive the trust of its charitable status."

(ii) Apportionment

Where a trustee is directed to apportion between charitable and non- **7–233** charitable objects the trust is always good as to the charitable objects. The trust will be valid *in toto* if the non-charitable objects are certain and

---

[91] *Re Wootton's W.T.* [1968] 2 All E.R. 618. In poverty cases the courts seem ready to restrict the opinion of trustees as to persons in needy circumstances or special need to such persons that the law recognises as within the poverty head of charity: *Re Scarisbrick* [1951] Ch. 622; *Re Cohen* [1973] 1 All E.R. 889.

[92] *Chichester Diocesan Fund v. Simpson* [1944] A.C. 341.

[93] *Att.-Gen. of the Bahamas v. Royal Trust Co.* [1986] 1 W.L.R. 1001 (welfare purposes not restricted to educational welfare purposes so as to qualify as charitable).

[94] *Att.-Gen. of Cayman Islands v. Wahr-Hansen* [2000] 3 All E.R. 642.

[95] [1992] 2 A.C. 310, *supra*, para. 7–219.

[96] *Royal College of Surgeons of England v. National Provincial Bank Ltd* [1952] A.C. 631; *Re Coxen* [1948] Ch. 747; *London Hospital Medical College v. I.R.C.* [1976] 1 W.L.R. 613; N. Gravells [1978] Conv. 92.

[97] *Oxford Group v. I.R.C.* [1949] W.N. 343; *Chichester Diocesan Fund and Board of Finance (Incorporated) v. Simpson* [1944] A.C. 341; *Associated Artists Ltd v. I.R.C.* [1956] 1 W.L.R. 752.

[98] *McGovern v. Att.-Gen.* [1981] 3 All E.R. 493 at 510.

valid,[99] and, in the absence of apportionment by the trustee, the court will divide the fund equally between both classes of objects in accordance with the maxim that "equality is equity."[1] If the non-charitable objects are uncertain, the trust will be good as to the charitable objects only[2] so long as defined sufficiently enough to reveal a general charitable intention.[3]

7–234   If there is no direction to apportion, and if the trust is partly for a non-charitable purpose, and then to apply the remainder to a charitable purpose, some cases decide that where the court is satisfied that an inquiry is practicable as to the portion required for the non-charitable purpose, it will direct such an inquiry and uphold the charitable part of the gift.[4] If, on the other hand, such an inquiry is impracticable, it will divide the fund into equal shares, the share applicable to non-charitable purposes falling into residue.[5] Other cases, however, have held that the whole of the gift goes to charity, independently of the question whether the portion which would otherwise have been required for the non-charitable purpose is ascertainable.[6] Yet another case decides that if the non-charitable part of the gift cannot be carried out without also performing the charitable part the whole gift will be valid.[7]

7–235   In *Re Coxen*,[8] Jenkins J. (as he then was) emphasised that, where the amount applicable to the non-charitable purpose cannot be quantified, the whole gift fails for uncertainty. He pointed out, however, that there were two exceptions to this general rule: first, an exception of a general character to the effect that, where, as a matter of construction, the gift to charity was a gift of the entire fund subject to the payments thereout required for the non-charitable purpose, the amount set free by the failure of the non-charitable gift was caught by, and passed under, the charitable gift;[9] and, secondly, an exception of a more limited character, applicable in the "tomb" cases, to the effect that where there is a primary trust (imposing a merely honorary obligation[10]) to apply the income in perpetuity to the repair of a tomb not in a church, followed by a charitable trust in terms extending only to the balance of the income, the established rule is to ignore the invalid trust for the repair of the tomb and treat the whole income as given to charity.

---

[99] *Re Douglas* (1887) 35 Ch.D. 472.

[1] *Salusbury v. Denton* (1857) 3 K. & J. 529.

[2] *Re Clarke* [1923] 2 Ch. 407.

[3] The *cy-près* doctrine is available if required.

[4] *Re Rigley* (1867) 36 L.J.Ch. 147; *Re Vaughan* (1886) 33 Ch.D. 187. The distinction between the invalid "charitable or benevolent purposes" cases and the apportionment cases is made by Page-Wood V.-C. in *Salusbury v. Denton* (1857) 3 K. & J. 529 at 539. "It is one thing to direct a trustee to give a *part* of a fund to one set of objects and the *remainder* to another, and it is a distinct thing to direct him to give either to one set of objects or to another."

[5] *Adnam v. Cole* (1843) 6 Beav. 353; *Hoare v. Osborne* (1866) L.R. 1 Eq.585; *cf. Fowler v. Fowler* (1864) 33 Beav. 616, where the whole gift failed.

[6] *Fisk v. Att.-Gen.* (1867) L.R. 4 Eq. 521; *Hunter v. Bullock* (1872) L.R. 14 Eq. 45; *Dawson v. Small* (1874) L.R. 18 Eq. 114; *Re Williams* (1877) 5 Ch.D. 735; *Re Birkett* (1878) 9 Ch.D. 576; *Re Rogerson* [1901] 1 Ch. 715; *cf. Re Porter* [1925] Ch. 746.

[7] *Re Eighmie* [1935] Ch. 524.

[8] [1948] Ch. 747 at 752.

[9] *cf. Hancock v. Watson* [1902] A.C. 14; *supra*, para. 5–35.

[10] *Re Morton's W.T.* [1948] 2 All E.R. 842; *Re Dalziel* [1943] Ch. 277 at 278; *supra*, para. 3–216; *Picarda on Charities*, (3rd ed.), p. 218.

(iii) The Charitable Trusts (Validation) Act 1954

This Act only applies to the terms of a trust which took effect before December 16, 1952[11] and so nowadays will apply to few trusts. Consideration of this complex Act is therefore omitted in this edition.

IX. A NEW DEFINITION OF CHARITY?

Whither Charity Law?

M. R. Chesterman: Charities, Trusts and Social Welfare, pp. 397–409

"SHOULD FISCAL AND TRUSTS LAW PRIVILEGES BE SEPARATED?"

It has been contended[12] on a number of recent occasions that the linking of fiscal **7–236** and trusts law privileges to the same definition of "charitable" produces unsatisfactory results: in other words, that the decision in *Pemsel's* case should be reversed. To break this link by confining the fiscal privileges to a narrower range of purposes than those which attract the trusts law privileges would, it is alleged, be advantageous in two respects. First, fiscal privileges would cease to be available to a range of organizations (such as animal charities, or obscure religious sects) which are on the periphery of "charity" and do not really deserve them. Secondly, purpose trusts of a public nature which presently fall foul of the rules as to certainty of objects because fiscal pressures have excluded them from the definition of "charitable" would no longer be thus deprived of the right to exist. According to one version of this argument,[13] there would accordingly be "charitable trusts," privileged under both tax and trusts law, and "public purpose trusts," privileged only under trusts law provided that they could show at least a modicum of "public benefit."

"Reform along these lines would eliminate an unsatisfactory tension within **7–237** charity law and would accord with recent relaxations of the rules regarding certainty of objects for discretionary trusts. There would, however, be problems to resolve with regard to 'public purpose' trusts. Would they have the privilege of perpetual existence as well as freedom from certainty requirements?[14] If so, would there be some procedure for *cy-près* modification of their purposes? If, as would seem unavoidable, the Attorney-General or some other public body such as the government department most closely concerned with their activities should be retained as a representative plaintiff to enforce them (and perhaps to instigate *cy-près* alterations of their purpose), what level of 'public benefit' would justify the necessary expenditure of public funds? Would grant-making trusts be allowed

---

[11] The date on which the Report of the Nathan Committee on Charitable Trusts was presented to Parliament. The Act gives effect to certain recommendations of that Committee (Cmnd. 8710 Chap. 12).

[12] *Dingle v. Turner* [1972] A.C. 601 at 624–625; (1956) 72 L.Q.R. 187 at 206 (G. Cross); N. P. Gravells (1977) 40 M.L.R. 397; Culyer, Wiseman & Posnett in *Social and Economic Administration*, Vol. 10 (1976), at 32.

[13] Gravells, *op. cit.*

[14] If, as has been recommended, charitable trusts were to lose their privilege on the ground that it causes charity resources to become tied to out-of-date purposes (see *infra*) this particular issue is more easily resolved.

to retain the fiscal privileges attached to genuine "charities" if they made grants to 'public purpose trusts'? These and other side-issues would have to be worked out.

7–238 "Pursuing this general line of argument, one may ask next whether the category of genuinely charitable organizations should all continue to enjoy the same 'package' of fiscal privileges? At present, some charities derive considerably more benefit than others from the operation of these privileges: for example, the covenant system discriminates in favour of longer-term charities which are supported by corporate donors and by donors who are prepared to commit money in advance. Furthermore, the policies underlying particular taxes are arguably not served by allowing all charities to claim automatic exemption from them. The provisions for relief from local rates take account of this problem to some degree, though the fifty per cent relief enjoyed by large national or international charities still imposes a significant burden on the local authority which has to grant this exemption.[15] But the other tax reliefs are not flexible in this way, so that (for example) there is little scope to withdraw even partially the exemption from tax on investment income when a charity is both wealthy and prone to accumulate income, or to deny the exemption from capital transfer tax to a gift or bequest to such a charity on the ground that a major objective of this tax is to break down concentrations of wealth.

7–239 "The spirit of some of these recommendations is discernible in the tax policies of the United States, where actual expenditure of funds on a charity's beneficiaries is made a condition of tax relief,[16] and in Sweden, where tax relief is granted on a sliding scale according to the charity's degree of 'social merit.'[17] In these two systems, the fiscal policy underlying privileged treatment for charities is implemented with more sophistication than is to be found in the United Kingdom package of automatic reliefs. But where a system (like the Swedish system) creates 'class one charities'; 'class two charities,' etc., or where it grants different measures of relief from different groups of taxes to different groups of charities, it significantly 'fragments' the concept of charity. Within tax law, no single, comprehensive form of treatment is meted out to organisations of a legally charitable nature.

7–240 "A more far-reaching recommendation along the same lines is that automatic fiscal relief for charities should be wholly abolished and replaced by a system of discriminatory cash subsidies.[18] According to one version of this recommendation,[19] charitable status might be retained as a precondition for obtaining such a subsidy, but would not confer any entitlement to it. We have, however, seen that under present law voluntary organizations may usually obtain discretionary grants-in-aid from public funds without having to prove that their purposes are charitable. Government agencies dispensing funds in this way may decide for themselves whether the organization merits financial assistance without being technically bound to refuse assistance merely because it is not a charity. It would seem to follow that *either* charitable status should be made a considerably more reliable indicator of the genuine worth of an organization's welfare activities in

---

[15] It has accordingly been suggested that the cost of mandatory rating relief should be borne by central government, *i.e.* through increases in the "rate support grant": Goodman Report, para. 132; Layfield Committee into Local Government Finance (Cmnd. 6453, 1976), at 167–168.

[16] B. Whitaker, *The Foundations* (1974), at 131, 234–235.

[17] B. Nightingale, *Charities*, at 66–67.

[18] Culyer, Wiseman & Posnett, *op. cit.*, at 44–46; S. Surrey, *Pathways to Tax Reform* (1973), at 223–232; *contra* the Expenditure Committee Report, paras. 90–92.

[19] Culyer, Wiseman & Posnett, *op. cit.* at 46.

current social conditions, *or* such status should not be a necessary condition of obtaining a subsidy under the proposed scheme. The latter recommendation, once again, threatens to deprive charitable status of legal significance; the former, as we shall see, also tends in this direction.

"A further major issue arising out of the recommendations just discussed is the **7–241** reformulation of the legal definition of 'charitable' so as to comply explicitly with the demands of fiscal policy and with the consideration that charitable status facilitates access to funds from grant-making trusts, the state and the public."

THE "DEATH OF CHARITY"?

"In the eyes of many, charity would straightway be smothered to death by **7–242** bureaucracy if reform proposals along the lines considered in this chapter were ever implemented. The free exercise of a philanthropist's power to dedicate his property to the benevolent purposes of his choice and to frame these purposes within a trust; the autonomy of charity trustees to manage the funds committed to their care, free from heavy-handed state intervention; the enthusiasm of voluntary or underpaid workers giving their time and energy to a worthy cause— all these would be discouraged out of existence if an overpowering and overbearing Charity Commission were allowed to peer and pry into every corner of charitable activity.

"In a more legalistic sense, 'charity' may 'die' simply because it ceases to describe a meaningful category within any branch of the law. In the course of this chapter, it has been envisaged that charitable trusts, 'public purpose' trusts and private discretionary trusts might all become similarly regulated under trusts law, that different charities might enjoy different privileges under tax laws, that tax privileges might be replaced by a subsidy system not confined to charities, that the criteria for determining charitable status might be highly flexible and that the supervision of different classes of charity might be divided amongst different governmental bodies. Also relevant here are (a) the equivalence (more or less) of charitable and non-charitable voluntary organisations with regard to access to public subsidies and (b) the blurring of fiscal lines between these two groups of organisations. Collectively, these existing and projected trends amount to a fragmentation or dissolution of the concept of charity, in the sense that one could no longer speak of a common legal regime for 'charities.'

"If this is correct, social democratic reform of the law of charity may, in this **7–243** specific sense, be ultimately destructive. By attempting to bring this branch of the law in line with the policy demands of the welfare state, reformers may simply destroy its identity. In fact, one recent proposal explicitly seeks this result. This is the recommendation of the Charity Law Reform Committee that the tax privileges associated with charity should be granted to all genuinely non-profit-distributing organisations (NPDOs). The committee put forward this idea in a leaflet entitled 'Charity Law—Only a New Start Will Do'[20]; a better title might have been 'Charity Law Should Be Abolished.' In contending that the anomalies and inconsistences in the present legal definition of charity were so serious and so intractable that 'charity' should have no fiscal significance whatsoever, they were attempting to pluck the heart out of charity law.

---

[20] A long extract is printed as their principal "Evidence to the Expenditure Committee." See also the "Evidence of A. Steen, M.P." (Qs. 1526–1544).

7–244   "Both the fiscal wisdom of extending charity's motley array of tax privileges to all NPDOs and the likelihood in practice that distribution of profit by tax-exempt NPDOs could ever be effectively prohibited are matters of some doubt.[21] But the radical implications of the suggestion are far-reaching, particularly in the sense that English law without 'charity' would be shorn of a number of ideological notions. These suggest not only that the freedoms associated with the workings of the 'voluntary spirit' are valuable and worth preserving, but also that a number of non-egalitarian enterprises within society have a traditionally charitable nature which helps to justify their continuance with state support and that, due to the absence of any 'political' taint from 'true' charity, charitable provision of social welfare cannot have political implications least of all conservative ones. Within notions such as these, there are moral values which should not be jettisoned, at least while the principal mode of distribution of material resources within society pays homage to entitlements to wealth and property rather than to meeting the needs of society's members. Yet these notions also contribute to the perpetuation of social inequalities by helping to mask their true causes and to erect misleading justifications for them.

7–245   "The radical response to these equivocal aspects of legal 'charity' is itself equivocal. Most of the progressive recommendations discussed in this chapter are concerned to bring the law's concept of charity in line with the popular concept of charity or philanthropy by insisting, in particular, that only genuinely altruistic, redistributive and socially useful projects be labelled as charitable. But a more profoundly radical approach, based ultimately on a Marxist view of social relations, is that when charity, even thus 'purified,' exists as a systematic instrument of social welfare in society, it retards progress towards true socialism because it presupposes the inequalities which it purports to try to eliminate. When a rich individual directly or indirectly distributes welfare benefits amongst the working classes, he is simply restoring property which was stolen from them in the first place by way of the process of commodity production. He calls it a 'charitable gift' in order to conceal the element of theft. It accordingly matters not whether legal 'charity' appears genuinely altruistic: indeed, the more self-seeking it is allowed to be, the more obvious the element of pretence the whole process becomes.

"According to this argument, systematised charity would thus have no place in a truly socialist society. Yet in the meantime it continues to exhibit moral values which no society can ignore. We are back where this book began: there is a great deal of ambiguity in charity."

CHARITIES: A FRAMEWORK FOR THE FUTURE

Government White Paper Cm. 694 (May 1989) Development of the Law

7–246   2.7   The loose framework, which was set by the 1601 preamble and clarified by Lord Macnaghten, has enabled the courts over the years to develop the law in a way which has been sensitive to changing needs whilst maintaining the fundamental principles on which the concept of charity rests. It has been argued that on the whole, given the increasing complexity of society, this development has been remarkably coherent and consistent. The scope of education, for

---

[21] See, *e.g.* the objections in the "Expenditure Committee Report," paras. 25–34 and in the "Evidence of the Inland Revenue" (Qs. 552–557).

example, has been gradually extended to cover not just free schooling but a whole range of objects of a broadly educational nature, such as research and information services, which are considered to be of public benefit.

2.8 The scope of charity, as it applies to organisations concerned with the **7–247** advancement of religion, has been similarly widened in response to increasing religious toleration and to cultural diversity. Under the fourth head, in particular, the courts have admitted, under the umbrella of charity, a remarkable range of bodies which have been established by benefactors who have discerned new public needs and who have responded to them.

2.9 If the main lines of the law's development are clear, it is fair to say that its results in detail are not always tidy and can sometimes be confusing, even to experts. It is perhaps not surprising that, as the threads reaching back to 1601 get longer and as the analogies which the courts employ become more extended, so the rationale for decisions on charitable status should not always be immediately apparent. This has undoubtedly led to a degree of uncertainty about the interpretation of the law which can inhibit innovative bodies from seeking charitable status. Some critics, however, go further. The law, they say, is now so complex and tangled that it is bound to lead to some decisions which can only be described as illogical or capricious.

2.10 Against this background, it has been proposed from time to time, that a **7–248** definition of charity should be formulated and given statutory effect. This might be achieved in one of the following ways:

(i) by listing the purposes which are deemed to be charitable;
(ii) by enacting a definition of charity based on Lord Macnaghten's classification; or
(iii) by defining "charitable purposes" as "purposes beneficial to the community."[22]

2.11 The Government consider that an attempt to define charity by any of these means would be fraught with difficulty, and might put at risk the flexibility of the present law which is both its greatest strength and its most valuable feature. In particular, they consider that there would be great dangers in attempting to specify in statute those objects which are to be regarded as charitable.

2.12 Even if it was possible to draw up a list which could command a reasonable measure of agreement it might well lead to the exclusion of trusts which have long been treated as charitable, depriving them of any means of enforcement. A list might be inflexible and quickly outdated by changing public opinion. Listing the details in statute would not evade for long the problems which are inherent in any system of case law. Disputes would undoubtedly quickly arise on which the courts would be asked to adjudicate. There is no reason to believe that a new body of case law would be any less complex than the old.

2.13 In the Government's view, it would be scarcely less difficult to try to **7–249** enact the whole of Lord Macnaghten's classification. As a classification, the formulation has proved of enduring use. As a definition, its advantages are much less compelling.

---

[22] Subsequently para 3.2.6 of the Deakin Report, *Meeting the Challenge* (1996) recommended this: "It would embody the essential altruism implicit in an organisation being established for the benefit of the community rather than for any private or sectional interest. The 'community' in this context would be a sufficiently important section of the public and would include any identifiable black and minority groups."

2.14 Unless it were proposed to preserve the present case law, the incorporation of Lord Macnaghten's classification into statute would throw the law into confusion and uncertainty by depriving the courts of recourse to previous decisions when they were asked to interpret the new statutory provisions. On the other hand, if some form of words were to be found which would successfully preserve the present valuable case law, it is hard to see what the new definition would achieve.

2.15 Defining "charitable purposes" as "purposes beneficial to the community" would have the merit of simplicity but this would also be open to major objections. Such a definition would allow the courts to admit to charitable status virtually any organisation which was not obviously for private benefit or profit. A definition on these simple lines, which was intended to supersede existing case law, would greatly expand the ambit of charity in ways which might be far from desirable. It would be notably subjective and would be likely to give rise to a great deal of litigation.

7–250   **2.16** An attempt might be made to make clearer exactly what is meant by "public benefit" by reference to existing case law and by incorporating the other heads of charity into the general formula. The more that detail becomes added in this way, however, the fewer appear the advantages of a new definition. Instead of being simplified the law would be ossified.

2.17 There would appear, therefore, to be few advantages in attempting a wholesale redefinition of charitable status—and many real dangers in doing so.[23]

Section 3. Administration of Charities

7–251   Overall supervision of charities is carried on by the Charity Commissioners under the powers now conferred on them by the Charities Act 1993. Their aim is to ensure that charities are able to operate for their proper purposes within an effective legal, accounting and governance framework, to improve the governance, accountability, efficiency and effectiveness of charities and to identify and deal with abuse and poor practices, as made clear in their 1999–2000 Annual Report. Their Annual Reports contain much useful information, while they also produce "Decisions of Charity Commissioners" and many useful leaflets or booklets, available at the website "www. charity-commission. gov. uk" *e.g.* "Responsibilities of Charity Trustees," "Political Activities and Campaigning by Charities," "Payment of Charity Trustees," "Investment of Charitable Funds," "Fundraising and Charities," "Registering as a Charity." They are always ready to provide free advice to trustees under section 29 of the Charities Act 1993 and cannot be liable for damages if such advice negligently causes loss.[24]

7–252   In exceptional cases the Attorney-General may authorise trustees to make *ex gratia* payments out of charitable funds to persons outside the class of charitable beneficiaries and to whom it would be morally wrong

---

[23] However in the 1998 Charity Commission Consultation paper, "Review of organisations on the Register" it was proposed that "social value" of organisations might be the key to determine charitable status, such being "a way of expressing what is the underlying value or uniqueness of charity as a contribution to the well-being of society." For an impressive overview of the issues see C. Mitchell (1999) Trust L.I. 21.

[24] *Mills v. Winchester Diocesan Board of Finance* [1989] 2 All E.R. 317.

to refuse such payments.[25] Trustees must be most careful to restrict their payments to the specific purposes of their charity.[26] Charitable trustees may act by majority, and not unanimous decision: *Re Whiteley*.[27] In the absence of a scheme, the only person competent to consent to matters affecting the beneficial interests under charitable trusts seems to be the Attorney-General.[28] From time to time he issues guidelines to assist trustees as do the Charity Commissioners.

Control of fund-raising for charitable institutions is strictly governed by Part II of the Charities Act 1992 (Part I thereof being replaced to a great extent by Charities Act 1993) but this is outside the scope of this chapter.

Attorney-General's Guidelines on Expenditure by Student Unions

". . . It has been held in the courts that a Student Union has charitable objects if **7–253** it exists to represent and foster the interests of the students at an educational establishment in such a way as to further the educational purposes of the establishment itself. The Attorney-General believes that that will be the case with the great majority of Student Unions, including those provided for in the constitutions of their parent establishments (unless those establishments do not themselves have charitable objects). If a Student Union has charitable objects it follows as a matter of law that, whatever may be stated in its constitution, those objects cannot be changed, even by unanimous vote of its members, so as to include non-charitable objects; and Union funds may be spent only on those charitable objects or for properly incidental purposes.

"The Attorney-General recognises the difficult position in which officers of **7–254** Student Unions with charitable objects may find themselves. They may have no experience of charity law, and their members may believe that Union funds can be spent on anything that they think to be of general interest. However, the officers are trustees of the funds, and they have a duty to see that the funds are used only for purposes permitted by charity law. The complaints which have been made in recent years contain allegations of considerable expenditure of an improper nature. Such investigation as has been undertaken confirms that there are grounds for concern. Although perhaps the items taken individually appear not to be very great, they represent in total a major abuse of charitable funds.

"In the circumstances the Attorney-General considers it right that he should issue guidelines to assist Union officers in the discharge of their responsibility for Union funds. In the event of wrongful application of funds, such officers would potentially be at personal risk to a claim that they have been party to a breach of trust, and might well find themselves bound to make good any loss to the funds of their Union at their own expense. It is therefore important that they should be aware of their responsibilities.

---

[25] *Re Snowden* [1970] Ch. 700 (very substantial gift of shares by will was adeemed and its value fell into residue giving charitable residuary legatees ten times the value of their intended legacies: it was held they could make *ex gratia* payments to the adeemed legatees). Further see *Annual Report* for 1969, paras. 26–31.

[26] *e.g. Baldry v. Feintuck* [1972] 1 W.L.R. 552; [1972] Annual Report paras. 19–22; "Political Activities by Charities" paras 56–60, *supra*, paras 7–37 *et seq*; *I.R.C. v. Educational Grants Association Ltd* [1967] Ch. 123 and 993.

[27] [1910] 1 Ch. 600.

[28] *Re Freeston's Charity* [1978] 1 All E.R. 481 at 490; affd; [1979] 1 All E.R. 51; but this point was left open since there had been no full consent on the part of the school governors even if their consent could be sufficient.

7–255   "The Attorney-General considers that expenditure of a Student Union's charitable funds is proper if it can be said to be appropriate for the purpose of representing and furthering the interests of the students at the relevant college (and 'college' here includes 'university') in such a way as to assist in the educational aims of the college—for example, by providing channels for the representation of student views within the college, or by improving the conditions of life of the students and in particular providing facilities for their social and physical well-being.

"It is clear, for example, that if a college is to function properly, there is a need for the normal range of clubs and societies so as to enable each student to further the development of his abilities, mental and physical. Equally, it is likely that the college will gain from the fact that the students hold meetings to debate matters of common concern, and publish some form of campus newspaper. Reasonable expenditure on such purposes is, in the view of the Attorney-General, plainly permissible for a Student Union.

7–256   "On the other hand, for the students to offer financial support to a political cause in a foreign country—as opposed to merely debating the merits of that cause—is, in the Attorney-General's view, irrelevant to the educational purpose of the college. Such expenditure must accordingly be rejected as improper.

"Between these extremes there is a wide range of cases for which the Attorney-General believes the best touchstone to be the question: does the matter in issue affect the interests of either the students *as such* or the affairs of the college *as such*? If the answer is 'no,' then the case is likely to be one on which the students may hold debates and express views but not charge expenditure to the charitable funds of the Union.

"A major area of difficulty appears to be that of political issues. While the Attorney-General recognises that it is entirely natural that students will wish to express their views on political matters, the law sets strict limits to the expenditure of charitable funds for political purposes. Such expenditure is permissible only if the political purposes are merely *incidental* to the necessarily non-political objects of the charity. Thus, for a Union to expend its charitable funds in supporting a political campaign or demonstration is extremely unlikely to be justifiable[29] unless the issue directly affects students as students. It may be helpful to mention that in this context politics is not to be limited to party politics, but extends essentially to all aspects of the making and changing of laws. Thus it would be no less improper, in the view of the Attorney-General, for charitable funds of a Union to be devoted to a campaign for or against the legalisation of drugs, even though this is not a matter of party political debate, than it would be for such funds to be used either in support of or opposition to a campaign concerning, say, nuclear weapons or some controversial parliamentary debate not concerned with the interests of students as such.

7–257   "Another area of difficulty appears to be that of industrial disputes. The Attorney-General accepts that students may often wish to express a view on a current dispute, particularly if it be centred upon the neighbourhood of the college of which they are students. There is, however, in his view no justification for applying charitable funds in support of either side to the dispute. It would be as wrong for charitable funds to be spent on the hire of coaches, say, for the purpose of taking demonstrators to the scene of the dispute as it would be to hire coaches to take students to a demonstration in respect of the political issues referred to in the last paragraph.

---

[29] *e.g. Webb v. O'Doherty* (1991) 3 Admin. L.R. 731.

"There is, of course, no objection whatsoever to students joining together to collect their own monies for a particular purpose for which union funds cannot be used. The Attorney-General wishes to stress that the objection is not to student participation in activities outside the educational sphere, but to the use of charitable funds for purposes for which they cannot properly be applied according to the law.

"In issuing these guidelines the Attorney-General is anxious solely to assist **7–258** those who may find themselves called to account for their actions as trustees of charitable monies. Officers should, of course, bear in mind that it will be amongst their most important duties to identify and keep proper accounts of all Union funds (including, for example, not merely subscriptions to the Union, but income from Union investments, and profits from Union activities, such as the running of a bar or dance at the expense of the Union and with the assistance of its employees). They have a further duty to ensure that expenditure not only is within the proper bounds within which the funds of their Union can be used, but also has been approved and recorded as the Constitution of the Union requires.

"They should also bear in mind that a trustee is at all times entitled to seek advice, if necessary at the expense of the trust fund, on any aspect of his trust which causes him doubt or concern; in particular, under section 29 of the Charities Act 1993 the Charity Commissioners are empowered on the written application of a charity trustee to give him their opinion or advice on any matter affecting the performance of his duties as such.

"The Attorney-General would add that he hopes that the senior members of **7–259** the college concerned will always be willing to assist Student Union officers in considering doubtful items of expenditure. It must be borne in mind that where the parent body is itself a charitable body and thus has a duty to ensure that its funds are properly applied for purposes within, or incidental to, its own charitable educational purposes, it might well be that upon becoming aware of major items of improper expenditure by the Union it ought properly to cease to fund the Union until the position had been rectified."

CHARITIES ACT 1993

For present purposes significant sections are as follows.   **7–260**

Registration of charities

3.—(1) The Commissioners shall continue to keep a register of charities, which shall be kept by them in such manner as they think fit.

(2) There shall be entered in the register every charity not excepted by subsection (5) below; and a charity so excepted (other than one excepted by paragraph (a) of that subsection) may be entered in the register at the request of the charity, but (whether or not it was excepted at the time of registration) may at any time, and shall at the request of the charity, be removed from the register.

(3) The register shall contain—

(a) the name of every registered charity; and
(b) such other particulars of, and such other information relating to, every such charity as the Commissioners think fit.

(4) Any institution which no longer appears to the Commissioners to be a charity shall be removed from the register, with effect, where the removal is due

to any change in its purposes or trusts, from the date of that change; and there shall also be removed from the register any charity which ceases to exist or does not operate.

(5) The following charities are not required to be registered[30]—

7–261   (a) any charity comprised in Schedule 2 to this Act (in this Act referred to as an "exempt charity");

(b) any charity which is excepted by order or regulations;

(c) any charity which has neither—
    (i) any permanent endowment, nor
    (ii) the use or occupation of any land,
and whose income from all sources does not in aggregate amount to more than £1,000 a year

and no charity is required to be registered in respect of any registered place of worship.

(6) With any application for a charity to be registered there shall be supplied to the Commissioners copies of its trusts (or, if they are not set out in any extant document, particulars of them), and such other documents or information as may be prescribed by regulations made by the Secretary of State or as the Commissioners may require for the purpose of the application.

(7) It shall be the duty—

7–262   (a) of the charity trustees of any charity which is not registered nor excepted from registration to apply for it to be registered, and to supply the documents and information required by subsection (6) above; and

(b) of the charity trustees (or last charity trustees) of any institution which is for the time being registered to notify the Commissioners if it ceases to exist, or if there is any change in its trusts or in the particulars of it entered in the register, and to supply to the Commissioners particulars of any such change and copies of any new trusts or alterations of the trusts.

(8) The register (including the entries cancelled when institutions are removed from the register) shall be open to public inspection at all reasonable times; and copies (or particulars) of the trusts of any registered charity as supplied to the Commissioners under this section shall, so long as it remains on the register, be kept by them and be open to public inspection at all reasonable times, except in so far as regulations made by the Secretary of State otherwise provide.

7–263   (9) Where any information contained in the register is not in documentary form, subsection (8) above shall be construed as requiring the information to be available for public inspection in legible form at all reasonable times.

(10) If the Commissioners so determine, subsection (8) above shall not apply to any particular information contained in the register and specified in their determination . . .

(13) The reference in subsection (5)(b) above a charity which is excepted by order or regulations is to a charity which—

---

[30] These include universities, grant maintained schools, British Museum, Church Commissioners and institutions administered by them, societies registered under Industrial and Provident Societies Acts or Friendly Societies Acts. These fall outside the Charity Commissioner's supervisory or inquisitorial jurisdiction.

(a) is for the time being permanently or temporarily excepted by order of the Commissioners; or

(b) is of a description permanently or temporarily excepted by regulations made by the Secretary of State,

and which complies with any conditions of the exception . . .

4.—(1) An institution shall for all purposes other than rectification of the **7–264** register be conclusively presumed to be or to have been a charity at any time when it is or was on the register of charities.

(2) Any person who is or may be affected by the registration of an institution as a charity may, on the ground that is not a charity, object to its being entered by the Commissioners in the register, or apply to them for it to be removed from the register; and provision may be made by regulations made by the Secretary of State as to the manner in which any such objection or application is to be made, prosecuted or dealt with.

(3) An appeal against any decision of the Commissioners to enter or not to enter an institution in the register of charities, or to remove or not to remove an institution from the register, may be brought in the High Court by the Attorney General, or by the persons who are to claim to be the charity trustees of the institution, or by any person whose objection or application under subsection (2) above is disallowed by the decision.

(4) If there is an appeal to the High Court against any decision of the **7–265** Commissioner to enter an institution in the register, or not to remove an institution from the register, then until the Commissioners are satisfied whether the decision of the Commissioners is or is not to stand, the entry in the register shall be maintained, but shall be in suspense and marked to indicate that it is in suspense; and for the purposes of subsection (1) above an institution shall be deemed not to be on the register during any period when the entry relating to it is in suspense under this subsection.

(5) Any question affecting the registration or removal from the register of an institution may, notwithstanding that it has been determined by a decision on appeal under subsection (3) above, be considered afresh by the Commissioners and shall not be concluded by that decision, if it appears to the Commissioners that there has been a change of circumstances or that the decision is inconsistent with a later judicial decision, whether given on such an appeal or not . . .

Commissioners' Information Powers

8.—(1) The Commissioners may from time to time institute inquiries with **7–266** regard to charities or a particular charity or class of charities, either generally or for particular purposes, but no such inquiry shall extend to any exempt charity.

(2) The Commissioners may either conduct such an inquiry themselves or appoint a person to conduct it and make a report to them.[31]

(3) For the purposes of any such inquiry the Commissioners, or a person appointed by them to conduct it, may direct any person (subject to the provisions of this section)—

---

[31] See *Jones v. Att.-Gen.* [1974] Ch. 148; [1989] Annual Report, paras. 63–71; the Commissioners can now debar a person from trusteeship (ss. 18, 20, 72 of 1993 Act). Inquiry Reports are on the website www. charity—commission.gov.uk.

   (a) to furnish accounts and statements in writing with respect to any matter in question at the inquiry, being a matter on which he has or can reasonably obtain information, or to return answers in writing to any questions or inquiries addressed to him on any such matter, and to verify any such accounts, statements or answers by statutory declaration;

   (b) to furnish copies of document in his custody or under his control which relate to any matter in question at the inquiry, and to verify any such copies by statutory declaration;

   (c) to attend at a specified time and place and give evidence or produce any such documents.

7–267   (4) For the purposes of any such inquiry evidence may be taken on oath, and the person conducting the inquiry may for that purpose administer oaths, or may instead of administering an oath require the person examined to make and subscribe a declaration of the truth of the matters about which he is examined.

   (5) The Commissioners may pay to any person the necessary expenses of his attendance to give evidence or produce documents for the purpose of an inquiry under this section, and a person shall not be required in obedience to a direction under paragraph (c) of subsection (3) above to go more than ten miles from his place of residence unless those expenses are paid or tendered to him.

   (6) Where an inquiry has been held under this section, the Commissioners may either—

   (a) cause the report of the person conducting the inquiry, or such other statement of the results of the inquiry as they think fit, to be printed and published, or

   (b) publish any such report or statement in some other way which is calculated in their opinion to bring it to the attention of persons who may wish to make representations to them about the action to be taken.

7–268   (7) The council of a county or district, the Common Council of the City of London and the council of a London borough may contribute to the expenses of the Commissioners in connection with inquiries under this section into local charities in the council's area.

   9.—(1) The Commissioners may by order—

   (a) require any person to furnish them with any information in his possession which relates to any charity and is relevant to the discharge of their functions or of the functions of the official custodian;

   (b) require any person who has in his custody or under his control any document which relates to any charity and is relevant to the discharge of their functions or of the functions of the official custodian—

     (i) To furnish them with a copy of or extract from the document, or

     (ii) (unless the document forms part of the records or other documents of a court or of a public or local authority) to transmit the document itself to them for their inspection.

7–269   (2) Any officer of the Commissioners, if so authorised by them, shall be entitled without payment to inspect and take copies of or extracts from the records or other documents of any court, or of any public registry or office of records, for any purpose connected with the discharge of the functions of the Commissioners or of the official custodian.

(3) The Commissioners shall be entitled without payment to keep any copy or extract furnished to them under subsection (1) above; and where a document transmitted to them under that subsection for their inspection relates only to one or more charities and is not held by any person entitled as trustee or otherwise to the custody of it, the Commissioners may keep it or may deliver it to the charity trustees or to any other person who may be so entitled.

(4) No person properly having the custody of documents relating only to an exempt charity shall be required under subsection (1) above to transmit to the Commissioners any of those documents, or to furnish any copy of or extract from any of them.

(5) The rights conferred by subsection (2) above shall, in relation to informa- **7–270** tion recorded otherwise than in legible form, include the right to require the information to be made available in legible form for inspection or for a copy or extract to be made of or from it . . .

Powers of Commissioners to make schemes and act for protection of charities etc.

16.—(1) Subject to the provisions of this Act, the Commissioners may by order exercise the same jurisdiction and powers as are exercisable by the High Court in charity proceedings for the following purposes—

(a) establishing a scheme for the administration of a charity;
(b) appointing, discharging or removing a charity trustee or trustee for a charity, or removing an officer or employee;
(c) vesting or transferring property, or requiring or entitling any person to call for or make any transfer of property or any payment.

(2) Where the court directs a scheme for the administration of a charity to be established, the court may by order refer the matter to the Commissioners for them to prepare or settle a scheme in accordance with such directions (if any) as the court sees fit to give, and any such order may provide for the scheme to be put into effect by order of the Commissioners as if prepared under subsection (1) above and without any further order of the court.

(3) The Commissioners shall not have jurisdiction under this section to try or **7–271** determine the title at law or in equity to any property as between a charity or trustee for a charity and a person holding or claiming the property or an interest in it adversely to the charity, or to try or determine any question as to the existence or extent of any charge or trust.

(4) Subject to the following subsections, the Commissioners shall not exercise their jurisdiction under this section as respects any charity, except—

(a) on the application of the charity; or
(b) on an order of the court under subsection (2) above; or
(c) in the case of a charity other than an exempt charity, on the application of the Attorney General.

(5) In the case of a charity which is not an exempt charity and whose income from all sources does not in aggregate exceed £500 a year, the Commissioners may exercise their jurisdiction under this section on the application—

(a) of any one or more of the charity trustees; or
(b) of any person interested in the charity; or

(c) of any two or more inhabitants of the area of the charity if it is a local charity.

7–272   (6) Where in the case of a charity, other than an exempt charity, the Commissioners are satisfied that the charity trustees ought in the interests of the charity to apply for a scheme, but have unreasonably refused or neglected to do so and the Commissioners have given the charity trustees an opportunity to make representations to them, the Commissioners may proceed as if an application for a scheme had been made by the charity but the Commissioners shall not have power in a case where they act by virtue of this subsection to alter the purposes of a charity, unless forty years have elapsed from the date of its foundation.

(7) Where—

(a) a charity cannot apply to the Commissioners for a scheme by reason of any vacancy among the charity trustees or the absence or incapacity of any of them, but

(b) such an application is made by such number of the charity trustees as the Commissioners consider appropriate in the circumstances of the case,

the Commissioners may nevertheless proceed as if the application were an application made by the charity.

7–273   (8) The Commissioners may on the application of any charity trustee or trustee for a charity exercise their jurisdiction under this section for the purpose of discharging him from his trusteeship.

(9) Before exercising any jurisdiction under this section otherwise than on an order of the court, the Commissioners shall give notice of their intention to do so to each of the charity trustees, except any that cannot be found or has no known address in the United Kingdom or who is party or privy to an application for the exercise of the jurisdiction; and any such notice may be given by post, and, if given by post, may be addressed to the recipient's last known address in the United Kingdom.

(10) The Commissioners shall not exercise their jurisdiction under this section in any case (not referred to them by order of the court) which, by reason of its contentious character, or of any special question of law or of fact which it may involve, or for other reasons, the Commissioners may consider more fit to be adjudicated on by the court.

7–274   (11) An appeal against any order of the Commissioners under this section may be brought in the High Court by the Attorney General.

(12) An appeal against any order of the Commissioners under this section may also, at any time within the three months beginning with the day following that on which the order is published, be brought in the High Court by the charity or any of the charity trustees, or by any person removed from any office or employment by the order (unless he is removed with the concurrence of the charity trustees or with the approval of the special visitor, if any, of the charity).

(13) No appeal shall be brought under subsection (12) above except with a certificate of the Commissioners that it is a proper case for an appeal or with the leave of one of the judges of the High Court attached to the Chancery Division.

(14) Where an order of the Commissioners under this section establishes a scheme for the administration of a charity, any person interested in the charity shall have the like right of appeal under subsection (12) above as a charity

trustee, and so also, in the case of a charity which is a local charity in any area, shall any two or more inhabitants of the area and the council of any parish or (in Wales) any community comprising the area or any part of it.

18.—(1) Where, at any time after they have instituted an inquiry under section **7–275** 8 above with respect to any charity, the Commissioners are satisfied—

(a) that there is or has been any misconduct or mismanagement in the administration of the charity, or

(b) that it is necessary or desirable to act for the purpose of protecting the property of the charity or securing proper application for the purposes of the charity of that property or of property coming to the charity,

the Commissioners may of their own motion do one or more of the following things—

(i) by order suspend any trustee, charity trustee, officer, agent or employee of the charity from the exercise of his office or employment pending consideration being given to his removal (whether under this section or otherwise);

(ii) by order appoint such number of additional charity trustees as they consider necessary for the proper administration of the charity;

(iii) by order vest any property held by or in trust for the charity in the official **7–276** custodian, or require the persons in whom any such property is vested to transfer it to him, or appoint any person to transfer any such property to him;

(iv) order any person who holds any property on behalf of the charity, or of any trustee for it, not to part with the property without the approval of the Commissioners;

(v) order any debtor of the charity not to make any payment in or towards the discharge of his liability to the charity without the approval of the Commissioners;

(vi) by order restrict (notwithstanding anything in the trusts of the charity) the transactions which may be entered into, or the nature or amount of the payments which may be made, in the administration of the charity without the approval of the Commissioners;

(vii) by order appoint (in accordance with section 19 below) a receiver and manager in respect of the property and affairs of the charity.

(2) Where, at any time after they have instituted an inquiry under section 8 **7–277** above with respect to any charity, the Commissioners are satisfied—

(a) that there is or has been any misconduct or mismanagement in the administration of the charity; and

(b) that it is necessary or desirable to act for the purpose of protecting the property of the charity or securing a proper application for the purposes of the charity of that property or of property coming to the charity,

the Commissioners may of their own motion do either or both of the following things—

(i) by order remove any trustee, charity trustee, officer, agent or employee of the charity who has been responsible for or privy to the misconduct or mismanagement or has by his conduct contributed to it or facilitated it;

(ii) by order establish a scheme for the administration of the charity.

(3) The references in subsection (1) or (2) above to misconduct or mismanagement shall (notwithstanding anything in the trusts of the charity) extend to the employment for the remuneration or reward of persons acting in the affairs of the charity, or for other administrative purposes, of sums which are excessive in relation to the property which is or is likely to be applied or applicable for the purposes of the charity.

7–278   (4) The Commissioners may also remove a charity trustee by order made of their own motion—

    (a) where, within the last five years, the trustee—
        (i) having previously been adjudged bankrupt or had his estate sequestrated, has been discharged, or—
        (ii) having previously made a composition or arrangement with, or granted a trust deed for, his creditors, has been discharged in respect of it;
    (b) Where the trustee is a corporation in liquidation;
    (c) where the trustee is incapable of acting by reason of mental disorder within the meaning of the Mental Health Act 1983;
    (d) where the trustee has not acted, and will not declare his willingness or unwillingness to act;
    (e) where the trustee is outside England and Wales or cannot be found or does not act, and his absence or failure to act impedes the proper administration of the charity.

7–279   (5) The Commissioners may by order made of their own motion appoint a person to be a charity trustee—

    (a) in place of a charity trustee removed by them under this section or otherwise;
    (b) where there are no charity trustees, or where by reason of vacancies in their number or the absence or incapacity of any of their number the charity cannot apply for the appointment;
    (c) where there is a single charity trustee, not being a corporation aggregate, and the Commissioners are of opinion that it is necessary to increase the number for the proper administration of the charity;
    (d) where the Commissioners are of opinion that it is necessary for the proper administration of the charity to have an additional charity trustee because one of the existing charity trustees who ought nevertheless to remain a charity trustee either cannot be found or does not act or is outside England and Wales.

7–280   (6) The powers of the Commissioners under this section to remove or appoint charity trustees of their own motion shall include power to make any such order with respect to the vesting in or transfer to the charity trustees of any property as the Commissioners could make on the removal or appointment of a charity trustee by them under section 16 above.

(7) Any order under this section for the removal or appointment of a charity trustee or trustee for a charity, or for the vesting or transfer of any property, shall be of the like effect as an order made under section 16 above.

(8) Subject to subsection (9) below, subsections (11) to (13) of section 16 above shall apply to orders under this section as they apply to orders under that section.

(9) The requirement to obtain any such certificate or leave as is mentioned in section 16(13) above shall not apply to

(a) an appeal by a charity or any of the charity trustees of a charity against an order under subsection (1)(vii) above appointing a receiver and manager in respect of the charity's property and affairs, or

(b) an appeal by a person against an order under subsection (2)(i) or (4)(a) above removing him from his office or employment.

(10) Subsection (14) of section 16 above shall apply to an order under this **7–281** section which establishes a scheme for the administration of a charity as it applies to such an order under that section.

(11) The power of the Commissioners to make an order under subsection (1)(i) above shall not be exercisable so as to suspend any person from the exercise of his office or employment for a period of more than twelve months; but (without prejudice to the generality of section 89(1) below), any such order made in the case of any person may make provision as respects the period of his suspension for matters arising out of it, and in particular for enabling any person to execute any instrument in his name or otherwise act for him and, in the case of a charity trustee, for adjusting any rules governing the proceedings of the charity trustees to take account of the reduction in the number capable of acting.

(12) Before exercising any jurisdiction under this section otherwise than by **7–282** virtue of subsection (1) above, the Commissioners shall give notice of their intention to do so to each of the charity trustees, except any that cannot be found or has no known address in the United Kingdom; and any such notice may be given by post and, if given by post, may be addressed to the recipient's last known address in the United Kingdom.

(13) The Commissioners shall, at such intervals as they think fit, review any order made by them under paragraph (i), or any of paragraphs (iii) to (vii), of subsection (1) above; and, if on any such review it appears to them that it would be appropriate to discharge the order in whole or in part, they shall so discharge it (whether subject to any savings or other transitional provisions or not).

(14) If any person contravenes an order under subsection (1)(iv), (v) or (vi) above, he shall be guilty of an offence and liable on summary conviction to a fine not exceeding level 5 on the standard scale.

(15) Subsection (14) above shall not be taken to preclude the bringing of **7–283** proceedings for breach of trust against any charity trustee or trustee for a charity in respect of a contravention of an order under subsection (1)(iv) or (vi) above (whether proceedings in respect of the contravention are brought against him under subsection (14) above or not).

(16) This section shall not apply to an exempt charity.

20.—(1) The Commissioners shall not make any order under this Act to establish a scheme for the administration of a charity, or submit such a scheme to the court or the Secretary of State for an order giving it effect, unless not less than one month previously there has been given public notice of their proposals, inviting representations to be made to them within a time specified in the notice, being not less than one month from the date of such notice, and, in the case of a scheme relating to a local charity, other than on ecclesiastical charity, in a parish or (in Wales) a community, a draft of the scheme has been communicated to the parish or community council or, in the case of a parish not having a council, to the chairman of the parish meeting.

Additional powers of Commissioners

7–284   **26.**—(1) Subject to the provisions of this section, where it appears to the Commissioners that any action proposed or contemplated in the administration of a charity is expedient in the interests of the charity, they may by order sanction that action, whether or not it would otherwise be within the powers exercisable by the charity trustees in the administration of the charity; and anything done under the authority of such an order shall be deemed to be properly done in the exercise of those powers.

(2) An order under this section may be made so as to authorise a particular transaction, compromise or the like, or a particular application of property, or so as to give a more general authority, and (without prejudice to the generality of subsection (1) above) may authorise a charity to use common premises, or employ a common staff, or otherwise combine for any purpose of administration, with any other charity.

(3) An order under this section may give directions as to the manner in which any expenditure is to be borne and as to other matters connected with or arising out of the action thereby authorised; and where anything is done in pursuance of an authority given by any such order, any directions given in connection therewith shall be binding on the charity trustees for the time being as if contained in the trusts of the charity; but any such directions may on the application of the charity be modified or superseded by a further order.

7–285   (4) Without prejudice to the generality of subsection (3) above, the directions which may be given by an order under this section shall in particular include directions for meeting any expenditure out of a specified fund, for charging any expenditure to capital or to income, for requiring expenditure charged to capital to be recouped out of income within a specified period, for restricting the costs to be incurred at the expense of the charity, or for the investment of moneys arising from any transaction . . .

27.—(1) Subject to subsection (3) below, the Commissioners may be order exercise the same power as is exercisable by the Attorney General to authorise the charity trustees of a charity—

(a) to make any application of property of the charity, or
(b) to waive to any extent, on behalf of the charity, its entitlement to receive any property,

in a case where the charity trustees—

(i) (apart from this section) have no power to do so, but
(ii) in all the circumstances regard themselves as being under a moral obligation to do so.

7–286   (2) The power conferred on the Commissioners by subsection (1) above shall be exercisable by them under the supervision of, and in accordance with such directions as may be given by, the Attorney General; and any such directions may in particular require the Commissioners, in such circumstances as are specified in the directions—

(a) to refrain from exercising that power; or

(b) to consult the Attorney General before exercising it.

(3) Where—

(a) an application is made to the Commissioners for them to exercise that power in a case where they are not precluded from doing so by any such directions, but

(b) they consider that it would nevertheless be desirable for the application to be entertained by the Attorney General rather than by them,

they shall refer the application to the Attorney General.

(4) It is hereby declared that where, in the case of any application made to **7–287** them as mentioned in subsection (3)(a) above, the Commissioners determine the application by refusing to authorise charity trustees to take any action falling within subsection (1)(a) or (b) above, that refusal shall not preclude the Attorney General, on an application subsequently made to him by the trustees, from authorising the trustees to take that action . . .

29.—(1) The Commissioner may on the written application of any charity trustee give him their opinion or advice on any matter affecting the performance of his duties as such.

(2) A charity trustee or trustee for a charity acting in accordance with the opinion or advice of the Commissioners given under this section with respect to the charity shall be deemed, as regards his responsibility for so acting, to have acted in accordance with his trust, unless, when he does so, either

(a) he knows or has reasonable cause to suspect that the opinion or advice was given in ignorance of material facts; or

(b) the decision of the court has been obtained on the matter or proceedings are pending to obtain one.

Legal proceedings relating to charities

32.—(1) Subject to subsection (2) below, the Commissioners may exercise the **7–288** same powers with respect to—

(a) the taking of legal proceedings with reference to charities or the property or affairs of charities, or

(b) the compromise of claims with a view to avoiding or ending such proceedings,

as are exercisable by the Attorney General acting ex officio.

(2) Subsection (1) above does not apply to the power of the Attorney General under section 63(1) below to present a petition for the winding up of a charity.

(3) The practice and procedure to be followed in relation to any proceedings taken by the Commissioners under subsection (1) above shall be the same in all respects (and in particular as regards costs) as if they were proceedings taken by the Attorney General acting ex officio.

(4) No rule of law or practice shall be taken to require the Attorney General to be a party to any such proceedings.

(5) The powers exercisable by the Commissioners by virtue of this section shall be exercisable by them of their own motion, but shall be exercisable only with the agreement of the Attorney General on each occasion.

7–289   **33.**—(1) Charity proceedings[32] may be taken with reference to a charity either by the charity, or by any of the charity trustees, or by any person interested[33] in the charity, or by any two or more inhabitants of the area of the charity if it is a local charity, but not by any other person.

(2) Subject to the following provisions of this section, no charity proceedings relating to a charity (other than an exempt charity) shall be entertained or proceeded with in any court unless the taking of the proceedings is authorised by order of the Commissioners.

(3) The Commissioners shall not, without special reasons, authorise the taking of charity proceedings where in their opinion the case can be dealt with by them under the powers of this Act other than those conferred by section 32 above.

(4) This section shall not require any order for the taking of proceedings in a pending cause or matter or for the bringing of any appeal.

(5) Where the foregoing provisions of this section require the taking of charity proceedings to be authorised by an order of the Commissioners, the proceedings may nevertheless be entertained or proceeded with if, after the order had been applied for and refused, leave to take the proceedings was obtained from one of the judges of the High Court attached to the Chancery Division.

(6) Nothing in the foregoing subsections shall apply to the taking of proceedings by the Attorney General, with or without a relator, or to the taking of proceedings by the Commissioners in accordance with section 32 above.

7–290   (7) Where it appears to the Commissioners, on an application for an order under this section or otherwise, that it is desirable for legal proceedings to be taken with reference to any charity (other than an exempt charity) or its property or affairs, and for the proceedings to be taken by the Attorney-General, the Commissioners shall so inform the Attorney-General, and send him such statements and particulars as they think necessary to explain the matter.

(8) In this section "charity proceedings" means proceedings in any court in England or Wales brought under the court's jurisdiction with respect to charities, or brought under the court's jurisdiction with respect to trusts in relation to the administration of a trust for charitable purposes.

Charity accounts reports and returns

7–291   **41.**—(1) The charity trustees of a charity shall ensure that accounting records are kept in respect of the charity which are sufficient to show and explain all the charity's transactions, and which are such as to—

---

[32] "Charity proceedings" as defined in s.28(8) do not cover proceedings by way of construction of a will or of a conveyance to determine whether or not the will or conveyance is effective to create a charitable trust: *Re Belling* [1967] Ch. 425; *Hauxwell v. Burton-upon-Humber U.D.C.* [1974] Ch. 432.

[33] In *Richmond London B.C. v. Rogers* [1988] 2 All E.R. 761, C.A. rejected an interested person needing either (a) to be capable of benefiting from the charity or taking some interest under the trusts or (b) to be entitled to participate in the management of the charity because this could be too wide or too narrow in some respects. If a person has an interest in securing the due administration of the trust materially greater than, or different from, that possessed by the ordinary public that interest may well qualify him as a "person interested," *e.g.* Richmond B.C. due to the close relationship between the council's welfare services and the activities of the charity and its power to appoint 3 of 11 trustees. Further see *Scott v. National Trust* [1998] 2 All E.R. 705, 712–715 and *Muman v. Nagasena* [1999] 4 All E.R. 178, but proceedings in respect of a charity established under a foreign law and not registered as a charity in England cannot be charity proceedings": *Gaudiya v. Brahmachary* [1997] 4 All E.R. 957.

(a) disclose at any time, with reasonable accuracy, the financial position of the charity at that time, and

(b) enable the trustees to ensure that, where any statements of accounts are prepared by them under section 42(1) below, those statements of accounts comply with the requirements of regulations under that provision.

(2) The accounting records shall in particular contain—

(a) entries showing from day to day all sums of money received and expended by the charity, and the matters in respect of which the receipt and expenditure takes place; and

(b) a record of the assets and liabilities of the charity.

(3) The charity trustees of a charity shall preserve any accounting records **7–292** made for the purposes of this section in respect of the charity for at least six years from the end of the financial year of the charity in which they are made.

(4) Where a charity ceases to exist within the period of six years mentioned in subsection (3) above as it applies to any accounting records, the obligation to preserve those records in accordance with that subsection shall continue to be discharged by the last charity trustees of the charity, unless the Commissioners consent in writing to the records being destroyed or otherwise disposed of.

(5) Nothing in this section applies to a charity which is a company.

42.—(1) The charity trustees of a charity shall (subject to subsection (3) below) prepare in respect of each financial year of the charity a statement of accounts complying with such requirements as to its form and contents as may be prescribed by regulations made by the Secretary of State.

(2) Without prejudice to the generality of subsection (1) above, regulations under that subsection may make provision—

(a) for any such statement to be prepared in accordance with such methods and principles as are specified or referred to in the regulations;

(b) as to any information to be provided by way of notes to the accounts;

and regulations under that subsection may also make provision for determining the financial years of a charity for the purposes of this Act and any regulations made under it.

(3) Where a charity's gross income in any financial year does not exceed **7–293** £25,000, the charity trustees may, in respect of that year, elect to prepare the following, namely—

(a) a receipts and payments account, and

(b) a statement of assets and liabilities,

instead of a statement of accounts under subsection (1) above.

(4) The charity trustees of a charity shall preserve—

(a) any statement of accounts prepared by them under subsection (1) above, or

(b) any account and statement prepared by them under subsection (3) above,

for at least six years from the end of the financial year to which any such statement relates or (as the case may be) to which any such account and statement relate.

7–294 (5) Subsection (4) of section 41 above shall apply in relation to the preservation of any such statement or account and statement as it applies in relation to the preservation of any accounting records (the reference to subsection (3) of that section being read as references to subsection (4) above).

(6) The Secretary of State may by order amend subsection (3) above by substituting a different sum for the sum for the time being specified there.

(7) Nothing in this section applies to a charity which is a company.

43.—(1) Subsection (2) below applies to a financial year of a charity ("the relevant year") if the charity's gross income or total expenditure in any of the following, namely—

    (a) the relevant year,
    (b) the financial year of the charity immediately preceding the relevant year (if any), and
    (c) the financial year of the charity immediately preceding the year specified in paragraph (b) above (if any),

exceeds £100,000.

7–295 (2) If this subsection applies to a financial year of a charity, the accounts of the charity for that year shall be audited by a person who—

    (a) is, in accordance with section 25 of the Companies Act 1989 (eligibility for appointment), eligible for appointment as a company auditor, or
    (b) is a member of a body for the time being specified in regulations under section 44 below and is under the rules of that body eligible for appointment as auditor of the charity.

(3) If subsection (2) above does not apply to a financial year of a charity, then (subject to subsection (4) below) the accounts of the charity for that year shall, at the election of the charity trustees, either—

    (a) be examined by an independent examiner, that is to say an independent person who is reasonably believed by the trustees to have the requisite ability and practical experience to carry out a competent examination of the accounts, or
    (b) be audited by such a person as is mentioned in subsection (2) above.

(4) Where it appears to the Commissioners—

7–296   (a) that subsection (2), or (as the case may be) subsection (3) above, has not been complied with in relation to a financial year of a charity within ten months from the end of that year, or
    (b) that, although subsection (2) above does not apply to a financial year of a charity, it would nevertheless be desirable for the accounts of the charity for that year to be audited by such a person as is mentioned in that subsection,

the Commissioners may by order require the accounts of the charity for that year to be audited by such a person as is mentioned in that subsection.

(5) If the Commissioners make an order under subsection (4) above with respect to a charity, then unless—

(a) the order is made by virtue of paragraph (b) of that subsection, and
(b) the charity trustees themselves appoint an auditor in accordance with the order,

the auditor shall be a person appointed by the Commissioners.

(6) The expenses of any audit carried out by an auditor appointed by the **7–297** Commissioners under subsection (5) above, including the auditor's remuneration, shall be recoverable by the Commissioners—

(a) from the charity trustees of the charity concerned, who shall be personally liable, jointly and severally, for those expenses; or
(b) to the extent that it appears to the Commissioners not to be practical to seek recovery of those expenses in accordance with paragraph (a) above, from the funds of the charity.

(7) The Commissioners may—

(a) give guidance to charity trustees in connection with the selection of a person for appointment as an independent examiner;
(b) give such directions as they think appropriate with respect to the carrying out of an examination in pursuance of subsection (3)(a) above;

and any such guidance or directions may either be of general application or apply to a particular charity only.

(8) The Secretary of State may by order amend subsection (1) above by substituting a different sum for the time being specified there.

(9) Nothing in this section applies to a charity which is a company . . .

45.—(1) The charity trustees of a charity shall prepare in respect of each **7–298** financial year of the charity an annual report containing—

(a) such a report by the trustees on the activities of the charity during that year, and
(b) such other information relating to the charity or to its trustees or officers,

as may be prescribed by regulations made by the Secretary of State.

(2) Without prejudice to the generality of subsection (1) above, regulations under that subsection may make provision—

(a) for any such report as is mentioned in paragraph (a) of that subsection to be prepared in accordance with such principles as are specified or referred to in the regulations;
(b) enabling the Commissioners to dispense with any requirement prescribed by virtue of subsection (1)(b) above in the case of a particular charity or a particular class of charities, or in the case of a particular financial year of a charity or of any class of charities.

(3) The annual report required to be prepared under this section in respect of **7–299** any financial year of a charity shall be transmitted to the Commissioners by the charity trustees—

(a) within ten months from the end of that year, or
(b) within such longer period as the Commissioners may for any special reason allow in the case of that report.

(4) Subject to subsection (5) below, any such annual report shall have attached to it the statement of accounts prepared for the financial year in question under section 42(1) above or (as the case may be) the account and statement so prepared under section 42(3) above, together with—

(a) where the accounts of the charity for that year have been audited under section 43 above, a copy of the report made by the auditor on that statement of accounts or (as the case may be) on that account and statement;
(b) where the accounts of the charity for that year have been examined under section 43 above, a copy of the report made by the independent examiner in respect of the examination carried out by him under that section.

7–300   (5) Subsection (4) above does not apply to a charity which is a company, and any annual report transmitted by the charity trustees of such a charity under subsection (3) above shall instead have attached to it a copy of the charity's annual accounts prepared for the financial year in question under Part VII of the Companies Act 1985, together with a copy of the auditors' report on those accounts.

(6) Any annual report transmitted to the Commissioners under subsection (3) above, together with the documents attached to it, shall be kept by the Commissioners for such period as they think fit.

7–301   **46.**—(1) Nothing in section 41 to 45 above applies to any exempt charity; but the charity trustees of an exempt charity shall keep proper books of account with respect to the affairs of the charity, and if not required by or under the authority of any other Act to prepare periodical statements of account shall prepare consecutive statements of account consisting on each occasion of an income and expenditure account relating to a period of not more than fifteen months and a balance sheet relating to the end of that period.

(2) The books of accounts and statements of account relating to an exempt charity shall be preserved for a period of six years at least unless the charity ceases to exist and the Commissioners consent in writing to their being destroyed or otherwise disposed of.

(3) Nothing in section 43 to 45 above applies to any charity which—

(a) falls within section 3(5)(c) above, and
(b) is not registered.

(4) Except in accordance with subsection (7) below, nothing in section 45 above applies to any charity (other than an exempt charity or a charity which falls within section 3(5)(c) above) which—

(a) is excepted by section 3(5) above, and
(b) is not registered.

7–302   (5) If requested to do so by the Commissioners, the charity trustees of any such charity as is mentioned in subsection (4) above shall prepare an annual report in respect of such financial year of the charity as is specified in the Commissioners' request.

(6) Any report prepared under subsection (5) above shall contain—

(a) such a report by the charity trustees on the activities of the charity during the year in question, and
(b) such other information relating to the charity or to its trustees or officers,

as may be prescribed by regulations made under section 45(1) above in relation to annual reports prepared under that provision.

(7) Subsections (3) to (6) of section 45 above shall apply to any report **7–303** required to be prepared under subsection (5) above as if it were an annual report required to be prepared under subsection (1) of that section.

(8) Any reference in this section to a charity which falls within section 3(5)(c) above includes a reference to a charity which falls within that provision but is also excepted from registration by section 3(5)(b) above.

47.—(1) Any annual report or other document kept by the Commissioners in pursuance of section 45(6) above shall be open to public inspection at all reasonable times—

(a) during the period for which it is so kept; or
(b) if the Commissioners so determine, during such lesser period as they may specify.

(2) Where any person—

(a) requests the charity trustees of a charity in writing to provide him with a copy of the charity's most recent accounts, and
(b) pays them such reasonable fee (if any) as they may require in respect of the costs of complying with the request,

those trustees shall comply with the request within the period of two months beginning with the date on which it is made . . .

(d) in the case of an exempt charity, a reference to the accounts of the charity most recently audited in pursuance of any statutory or other requirement or, if its accounts are not required to be audited, the accounts most recently prepared in respect of the charity.

48.—(1) Every registered charity shall prepare in respect of each of its **7–304** financial years an annual return in such form, and containing such information, as may be prescribed by regulations made by the Commissioners.

(2) Any such return shall be transmitted to the Commissioners by the date by which the charity trustees are, by virtue of section 45(3) above, required to transmit to them the annual report required to be prepared in respect of the financial year in question.

(3) The Commissioners may dispense with the requirements of subsection (1) above in the case of a particular charity or a particular class of charities, or in the case of a particular financial year of a charity or of any class of charities.

49.—(1) Any person who, without reasonable excuse, is persistently in default **7–305** in relation to any requirement imposed—

(a) by section 45(3) above (taken with section 45(4) or (5), as the case may require), or

(b) by section 47(2) or 48(2) above,

shall be guilty of an offence and liable on summary conviction to a fine not exceeding level 4 on the standard scale.

Disqualification for acting as charity trustee

7–306　　72.—(1) Subject to the following provisions of this section, a person shall be disqualified for being a charity trustee or trustee for a charity if—

(a) he has been convicted of any offence involving dishonesty or deception;

(b) he has been adjudged bankrupt or sequestration of his estate has been awarded and (in either case) he has not been discharged;

(c) he has made a composition or arrangement with, or granted a trust deed for, his creditors and has not been discharged in respect of it;

(d) he has been removed from the office of charity trustee or trustee for a charity by an order made—

　(i) By the Commissioners under section 18(2)(i) above, or

　(ii) By the Commissioners under section 20(1A)(i) of the Charities Act 1960 (power to act for protection of charities) or under section 20(1)(i) of that Act (as in force before the commencement of section 8 of the Charities Act 1992), or

　(iii) By the High Court,
　　on the grounds of any misconduct or mismanagement in the administration of the charity for which he was responsible or to which he was privy, or which he by his conduct contributed to or facilitated;

7–307　　(e) he has been removed, under section 7 of the Law Reform (Miscellaneous Provisions) (Scotland) Act 1990 (powers of Court of Session to deal with management of charities), from being concerned in the management or control of any body;

(f) he is subject to a disqualification order under the Company Directors Disqualification Act 1986 or to an order made under section 429(2)(b) of the Insolvency Act 1986 (failure to pay under county court administration order).

(2) In subsection (1) above—

(a) paragraph (a) applies whether the conviction occurred before or after the commencement of that subsection, but does not apply in relation to any conviction which is a spent conviction for the purposes of the Rehabilitation of Offenders Act 1974;

(b) paragraph (b) applies whether the adjudication of bankruptcy or the sequestration occurred before or after the commencement of that subsection;

(c) paragraph (c) applies whether the composition or arrangement was made, or the trust deed was granted, before or after the commencement of that subsection; and

(d) paragraphs (d) to (f) apply in relation to orders made and removals effected before or after the commencement of that subsection.

(3) Where (apart from this subsection) a person is disqualified under subsec- **7–308** tion (1)(b) above for being a charity trustee or trustee for any charity which is a company, he shall not be so disqualified if leave has been granted under section 11 of the Company Directors Disqualification Act 1986 (undischarged bankrupts) for him to act as director of the charity; and similarly a person shall not be disqualified under subsection (1)(f) above for being a charity trustee or trustee for such a charity if—

(a) in the case of a person subject to a disqualification order, leave under the order has been granted for him to act as director of the charity, or
(b) in the case of a person subject to an order under section 429(2)(b) of the Insolvency Act 1986, leave has been granted by the court which made the order for him to so act.

(4) The Commissioners may, on the application of any person disqualified **7–309** under subsection (1) above, waive his disqualification either generally or in relation to a particular charity or a particular class of charities; but no such waiver may be granted in relation to any charity which is a company if—

(a) the person concerned is for the time being prohibited, by virtue of—

    (i) a disqualification order under the Company Directors Disqualification Act 1986, or
    (ii) section 11(1) or 12(2) of that Act (undischarged bankrupts; failure to pay under county court administration order),

from acting as director of the charity; and
(b) leave has not been granted for him to act as director of any other company.

(5) Any waiver under subsection (4) above shall be notified in writing to the **7–310** person concerned.

(6) For the purposes of this section the Commissioners shall keep, in such manner as they think fit, a register of all persons who have been removed from office as mentioned in subsection (1)(d) above either—

(a) by an order of the Commissioners made before or after the commencement of subsection (1) above, or
(b) by an order of the High Court made after the commencement of section 45(1) of the Charities Act 1992;

and, where any person is so removed from office by an order of the High Court, the court shall notify the Commissioners of his removal.

(7) The entries in the register kept under subsection (6) above shall be available for public inspection in legible form at all reasonable times.

73.—(1) Subject to subsection (2) below, any person who acts as a charity **7–311** trustee or trustee for a charity while he is disqualified for being such a trustee by virtue of section 72 above shall be guilty of an offence and liable—

(a) on summary conviction, to imprisonment for a term not exceeding six months or to a fine not exceeding the statutory maximum, or both;

(b) on conviction on indictment, to imprisonment for a term not exceeding two years or to a fine, or both.

(2) Subsection (1) above shall not apply where—

(a) the charity concerned is a company; and

(b) the disqualified person is disqualified by virtue only of paragraph (b) or (f) of section 72(1) above.

(3) Any acts done as charity trustee or trustee for a charity by a person disqualified for being such a trustee by virtue of section 72 above shall not be invalid by reason only of that disqualification . . .

Manner of executing instruments

7–312   82.—(1) Charity trustees[34] may, subject to the trusts of the charity, confer on any of their body (not being less than two in number) a general authority, or an authority limited in such manner as the trustees think fit, to execute in the names and on behalf of the trustees assurances or other deeds or instruments for giving effect to transactions to which the trustees are a party; and any deed or instrument executed in pursuance of an authority so given shall be of the same effect as if executed by the whole body.

(2) An authority under subsection (1) above—

(a) shall suffice for any deed or instrument if it is given in writing or by resolution of a meeting of the trustees, notwithstanding the want of any formality that would be required in giving an authority apart from that subsection;

(b) may be given so as to make the powers conferred exercisable by any of the trustees, or may be restricted to named persons or in any other way;

(c) subject to any such restriction, and until it is revoked, shall, notwithstanding any change in the charity trustees, have effect as a continuing authority given by the charity trustees from time to time of the charity and exercisable by such trustees.

7–313   (3) In any authority under this section to execute a deed or instrument in the names and on behalf of charity trustees there shall, unless the contrary intention appears, be implied authority also to execute it for them in the name and on behalf of the official custodian or of any other person, in any case in which the charity trustees could do so.

(4) Where a deed or instrument purports to be executed in pursuance of this section, then in favour of a person who (then or afterwards) in good faith acquires for money or money's worth an interest in or charge on property or the benefit of any covenant or agreement expressed to be entered into by the charity trustees, it shall be conclusively presumed to have been duly executed by virtue of this section.

---

[34] Charities are not limited to four trustees (Trustees Act 1925 s.34) and charitable trustees may act by majority: *Re Whiteley* [1915] 1 Ch. 600.

(5) The powers conferred by this section shall be in addition to and not in derogation of any other powers.

83.—(1) Where, under the trusts of a charity, trustees of property held for the **7–314** purposes of the charity may be appointed or discharged by resolution of a meeting of the charity trustees, members or other persons, a memorandum declaring a trustee to have been so appointed or discharged shall be sufficient evidence of that fact if the memorandum is signed either at the meeting by the person presiding or in some other manner directed by the meeting and is attested by two persons present at the meeting.

(2) A memorandum evidencing the appointment or discharge of a trustee under subsection (1) above, if executed as a deed, shall have the like operation under section 40 of the Trustee Act 1925 (which relates to 1925 (which relates to vesting declarations as respects trust property in deeds appointing or discharging trustees) as if the appointment or discharge were effected by the deed.

(3) For the purposes of this section, where a document purports to have been signed and attested as mentioned in subsection (1) above, then on proof (whether by evidence or as a matter of presumption) of the signature the document shall be presumed to have been so signed and attested, unless the contrary is shown.

(4) This section shall apply to a memorandum made at any time, except that subsection (2) shall apply only to those made after the commencement of the Charities Act 1960.

Section 4. The Cy-près Doctrine[35]

As already seen in Chapter 5 where a private trust is initially ineffective **7–315** or subsequently fails there arises a resulting trust for the settlor or his estate if he is dead. If a charitable trust is *initially* impracticable or impossible it is presumed that there is a resulting trust in favour of the settlor or, if he is dead, his estate (thereby normally benefiting his family[36]) unless the settlor had a general charitable intention.[37] If he had such an intention, then the trust property will be applied *cy-près* under a scheme formulated by the Charity Commissioners or the court, *i.e.* it will be applied to some other charitable purposes as nearly as possible resembling the original purposes. If an effective charitable trust *subsequently* becomes impracticable or impossible then the trust property will be applied *cy-près* irrespective of the question of general charitable intention[38]: the settlor or, if he is dead, his residuary legatee or next of kin are forever excluded once the property has been effectually dedicated to charity absolutely.

---

[35] See *Tudor on Charities*, Chap. 5; *Picarda on Charities*, Chap. 25; 1989 Annual Report of the Ch. Commrs., paras. 73–80.

[36] This presumption in favour of a testator's family seems less strong than it used to be, particularly when disinherited family members can make a claim that the charitable bequest be reduced in their favour under the Inheritance (Provision for Family and Dependants) Act 1975 replacing the 1938 Family Provisions Act.

[37] *Re Rymer* [1895] 1 Ch. 19; *Re Stemson* [1970] Ch. 16. Gifts to particular Churches or to augment particular vicars' stipends may be saved under special legislation, *e.g.* Methodist Church Act 1976, s.15 or Endowments and Glebe Measures 1976 of the Church of England.

[38] Assuming the gift is an absolute one or made absolute by Perpetuities and Accumulations Act 1964, s.12.

It is the duty of trustees to secure the effective use for charity of trust property by a *cy-près* application where appropriate,[39] although the Commissioners may make a scheme of their own volition if satisfied that the trustees "ought in the interests of the charity to apply for a scheme but have unreasonably refused or neglected to do so" after being approached by the Commissioners.[40]

7–316   Section 14 of the Charities Act 1993, *infra*, may be relied upon if need be in special circumstances to establish general charitable intention and section 13, *infra*, has relaxed the requirements of impracticability or impossibility. Such provisions have been in force since the 1960 Charities Act.

One must appreciate that the case law reveals how much leeway a court has in determining whether there has been an initial failure of charitable purposes and, if so, whether there was a general charitable intention manifested by the testator or donor.

Whether or not there is Initial Lapse or Failure

There are three basic ways in which a testator might bequeath property: (1) for the relief of the blind in Batley (2) for Batley Blind Home, High Street, Batley, the receipt of the treasurer for the time being to be sufficient discharge to the executors (3) for Batley Blind Home Ltd [a company limited by guarantee under the Companies Act 1985], High Street, Batley.

7–317   No problem arises in the *first case* since the purpose is not initially impracticable or impossible and purposes live for ever, though particular institutions carrying out purposes may die. If the purpose had been more specific such as building a blind home at a particular site, where there was no reasonable chance of such a blind home being erected whether because of planning permission problems or lack of cash so the purpose failed *ab initio* then the legacy would lapse unless a general charitable intention was present[41] to enable a *cy-près* application to be made. However, if the site for the testator's project is merely incidental to his charitable intention and the preservation or use of that site is not an

---

[39] Section 13(5) Charities Act 1993.
[40] Section 16(6).
[41] *Re Wilson* [1913] 1 Ch. 314 (to endow a school at a particular place where there was no reasonable chance of such a school being established); *Re Good's W.T.* [1950] 2 All E.R. 653 (funds insufficient for erection and upkeep of rest-homes); *Re Ulverston and District New Hospital Building Trusts* [1956] Ch. 622 (funds always insufficient for required purpose); *Re Mackenzie* [1962] 2 All E.R. 890 (trust to provide bursaries for education at secondary schools rendered impossible by provision of free education by state); *Re Lysaght* [1966] Ch. 191 (gift to Royal College of Surgeons on trust to provide studentships for persons not of Jewish or Catholic faith failed as the college was not prepared to act as trustees of such a trust and Buckley J., rather remarkably, held that this was the rare type of case where the identity of the trustees was vital to the trust. He further held that a paramount charitable intent was present so that a *cy-près* scheme could be directed omitting the offending religious conditions. This reveals the flexibility of *cy-près* applications which can even provide remedies in special circumstances); *Re Woodhams* [1981] 1 W.L.R. 493 (music scholarship for British boys restricted to orphans from two institutions but the trustee, the London College of Music, would not accept the trust as so restricted so Vinelott J. removed the restrictions by *cy-près* scheme).

original purpose of the charitable gift then an alternative site may be used without the need for a *cy-près* scheme.[42] The time for determining whether failure has occurred is the date of the *inter vivos* gift or, in the case of a testamentary gift, the date of the testator's death,[43] *i.e.* when the gift vests in interest not when it vests in possession, *e.g.* after a life interest. If need be, an inquiry will be directed "whether at the date of the death of the testator it was practicable to carry his intentions into effect or whether at the said date there was any reasonable prospect that it would be practicable to do so at some future time."[44] Where a future gift is defeasible an inquiry as to its practicability should be undertaken on the basis that the gift will not be defeated but will take effect at some future time as an interest in possession.[45] The onus of proving impracticability is on the person who is asserting it.[46]

Problems arise in the *second case*, where an unincorporated charitable **7–318** association runs the home, if the home has ceased to exist by the testator's death. Since the association is unincorporated and charitable (not being a private members' club) the gift must necessarily be construed as a gift on trust for purposes: *Re Vernon's W.T., infra*, para. 7–332. The purposes may be (a) the relief of the blind from time to time in the Batley Blind Home and nothing more (b) the relief of the Blind in Batley (c) the augmentation[47] of the endowed trust funds of the Batley Blind Home for whatever purposes such endowed trust funds might become held, *e.g.* if amalgamated with the Bury Blind Home and the Dewsbury Deaf Home.

In (a) where the gift is construed as a gift to a particular charitable **7–319** institution just for its particular purposes then the gift lapses if the institution ceases to exist before the testator's death[48] unless, which is most unlikely,[49] a general charitable intention can be found to justify a *cy-près* application.[50]

In (b) where the gift is construed as a gift for a charitable purpose in circumstances where the existence of the particular institution carrying out the purpose is not material to the gift's validity, the gift does not lapse so long as the purpose can be carried out by other means which are to be determined by the court in cases of doubt.[51]

---

[42] *Oldham B.C. v. Att.-Gen.* [1993] Ch. 210. The council was trustee of The Clayton Playing Fields "for the benefit and enjoyment of the inhabitants of Oldham, Chatterton and Rayton" and was allowed to sell the land for supermarket development and purchase an alternative site for playing fields to benefit such inhabitants. Nothing could have been done if the purpose of the original gift was that the particular land conveyed should be used for ever as playing fields, none of the section 13 criteria for a *cy-près* application being applicable.

[43] *Re Wright* [1954] Ch. 347, *Harris v. Sharp* (unreported, C.A. March 21, 1989).

[44] *Re Wright* [1954] Ch. 347; *Re White* [1955] Ch. 188; *Re Martin* (1977) 121 Sol.J. 828.

[45] *Re Tacon* [1958] Ch. 447.

[46] *Ibid. Harris v. Sharp* (unreported, C.A. March 21, 1989).

[47] *cf.* accretion to funds of unincorporated members' club: *Re Recher's W.T.* [1972] Ch. 526, *supra*, para. 3–247.

[48] *Re Rymer* [1895] 1 Ch. 19, *Re Slatter's W.T.* [1964] Ch. 512. *Re Spence's W.T.* [1979] Ch. 483. On the possible constructions see J.B.E. Hutton (1969) 32 M.L.R. 283; R.M.B. Cotterell (1972) 36 Conv. 198; J. Martin (1974) 38 Conv. 187.

[49] *Re Harwood* [1936] Ch. 285; *Re Stemson* [1970] Ch. 16, 21.

[50] As happened in *Re Finger's W.T.* [1972] 1 Ch. 286 on which Megarry V.-C. had some reservations in *Re Spence's W.T.* [1978] 3 All E.R. 92, see *infra*, para. 7–334.

[51] *Re Watt* [1932] 2 Ch. 243; *Re Roberts* [1963] 1 W.L.R. 406; *Re Finger's W.T.* [1972] 1 Ch. 286.

7–320   Construction (c) ensures that so long as there are endowment funds held in trust for the named charity's purposes the gift augments such funds despite any alteration in its name or constitution or any amalgamation with other charities.[52] Thus the bequest in (c) unlike (b) could be used for the Bury Blind Home and the Dewsbury Deaf Home. However, if the constitution of the named charity does not provide for there to be a fund in existence for ever devoted to charity so that the charity is liable to dissolution under its own constitution and chooses to dissolve itself, whereupon its surplus funds on its winding up are transferred to some other charity, the gift will lapse on the basis that the charity has ceased to exist.[53]

7–321   In the *third case* where the bequest is to the Batley Blind Home Ltd, High Street, Batley the bequest is presumed to be an out and out gift to the corporate institution beneficially as part of its general funds, unless there is something positive in the will to justify the bequest being treated as on trust for the purposes of the company's charitable objects. In the former case the gift will lapse if the company is would up before the testator dies unless, which is most unlikely, a general charitable intention can be found to justify a *cy-près* application.[54] In the latter case the trust purposes will be (a) the relief of the blind from time to time in the Batley Blind Home, High Street, Bately, as run by the Bately Blind Home Ltd, or (b) the relief of the blind from time to time in premises run by the Batley Blind Home Ltd, or (c) the relief of the blind in Bately, In (a) lapse will occur if such home ceases to exist before the testator's death, in (b) lapse will occur if the company is wound up before the testator's death whilst in (c) lapse will not occur.[55]

Where there is Initial Lapse or Failure

7–322 If matters of construction cannot save the gift then the gift lapses unless the court can find a general charitable intention present. There have been many judicial statements on the meaning of the phrase: *e.g.* Kay J. in *Re Taylor*[56] "If upon the whole scope and intent of the will you discover the paramount object of the testator was to benefit not a particular institution but to effect a particular form of charity independently of any special institution or mode, then, although he may have indicated the mode in which he desires that to be carried out, you are to regard the primary paramount intention chiefly, and if the particular mode for any reason fails, to use the phrase familiar to us, execute that *cy-près*, that is, carry out the general paramount intention indicated without which his intention itself cannot be effected." Also Buckley J. in

---

[52] *Re Lucas* [1948] Ch. 424 (on which see *Re Spence's W.T.* [1978] 3 All E.R. 92); *Re Faraker* [1912] 2 Ch. 488; *Re Bagshaw* [1954] 1 W.L.R. 238.
[53] *Re Stemson's W.T.* [1970] Ch. 16.
[54] *Ibid.*
[55] *Re Meyers* [1951] Ch. 534.
[56] (1888) 58 L.T. 538 at 543.

Re Lysaght[57]: "A general charitable intention . . . may be said to be a paramount intention on the part of a donor to effect some charitable purpose which the court can find a method of putting into operation, notwithstanding that it is impracticable to give effect to some direction by the donor which is not an essential part of his true intention—not, that is to say, of his paramount intention.

"In contrast, a particular charitable intention exists when the donor **7–323** means his charitable disposition to take effect if, but only if, it can be carried into effect in a particular specified way, for example, in connection with a particular school to be established at a particular place,[58] or by establishing a home in a particular house . . ."[59]

Where the gift is to an institution described by a particular name and the institution has never existed, a general charitable intent is presumed if the name imports a charitable object[60]; but the presumption may be easily rebutted if the will also includes a residuary gift in favour of charity.[61] On the other hand, the court is assisted in discovering a general charitable intention if the gift to the non-existent institution is of a share of residue and the other residuary legatees are charities.[62]

Subsequent Failure

If at the testator's death the designated charity existed or it was not then **7–324** impossible or impracticable to carry out the designated charitable purposes then the gifted property has become charitable property to the perpetual exclusion of the testator's residuary legatee or next of kin.[63] Accordingly, the *cy-près* doctrine is available upon any subsequent failure[64]: there is no need to prove any general charitable intent.[65]

---

[57] [1966] Ch. 191 at 202, approved in *Re Woodhams* [1981] 1 All E.R. 202 at 209.

[58] *Re Wilson* [1913] 1 Ch. 314.

[59] *Re Packe* [1918] 1 Ch. 437.

[60] *Re Davis* [1902] 1 Ch. 876; *Re Harwood* [1936] Ch. 285 (though Peace Societies are probably not charitable: *Re Koeppler's W.T.* [1984] 2 All E.R. 111 at 122, 124); but *cf. Att.-Gen. for N.S.W. v. Public Trustee* (1987) 8 NSWLR 550.

[61] *Re Goldschmidt* [1957] 1 W.L.R. 524; 73 L.Q.R. 166 (V.T.H. Delany).

[62] *Re Knox* [1937] Ch. 109. See also *Re Satterthwaite's W.T.* [1966] 1 W.L.R. 277, where a misanthropic testatrix left her residuary estate in nine shares to nine named institutions, seven of which were animal charities, an anti-vivisection society (once thought charitable but now in law non charitable) and the London Animal Hospital (not ascertainable): a general charitable intent was found to infect the latter two shares of residue. In *Re Jenkin's W.T.* [1966] Ch. 249 residue was divided into sevenths, six for charitable institutions and one for "the British Union for the Abolition of Vivisection to do all in its power to urge and get an Act passed prohibiting atrocious unnecessary cruelty to animals": no general charitable intent was found since there was such a clearly expressed non-charitable purpose.

[63] Assuming the gift is an absolute one or made absolute by Perpetuities and Accumulations Act 1964, s.12.

[64] Assuming the gift is an absolute one or made absolute by Perpetuities and Accumulations Act 1964, s.12.

[65] *Re Slevin* [1891] 2 Ch. 236; *Re Moon's W.T.* [1948] 1 All E.R. 300; *Re Wright* [1954] Ch. 347; *Re King* [1923] 1 Ch. 243; *Re Raine* [1956] Ch. 417; *Re Tacon* [1958] Ch. 447. Peter Luxton [1983] Conv. 107 accepts the position for simple legacies to bodies corporate or unincorporate, but submits it is open to the House of Lords to deal differently with legacies on trust for purposes which should be regarded as only disposing of the testator's equitable interest to the extent that the stated purposes are achieved. Thus, failure of the purposes after as well as before, the testator's death, should be capable of giving rise to a resulting trust unless ousted by a general charitable intention.

7–325   The position is the same for *inter vivos* gifts effectively dedicated to charity, whether the surplus funds are general assets of a charitable company that has been wound up[66] or assets held on charitable trusts by trustees for an unincorporated association that has been dissolved or for purposes that have been carried out.[67] As Jenkins L.J. remarked,[68] "Once the charity for which the fund was raised had been effectively brought into action the fund was to be regarded as permanently devoted to charity to the exclusion of any resulting trust" for the subscribers. He endorsed[69] the decision of Danckwerts J.[70] that no general charitable intention need be proved in such cases, though there are some illogical cases[71] where the courts have gone to the lengths of excluding any resulting trust by holding that the subscribers intended to give their money out and out under a general charitable intention.

Cy-près under Charities Act 1960, s.14

7–326 In the case of initial failure of charitable purposes section 14 (replacing section 14 of the 1960 Act) permits a *cy-près* application as if a general charitable intention had been present. It is necessary to show that the donors cannot be traced or have executed written disclaimers. The idea is to prevent resulting trusts arising in favour of anonymous donors contributing in the course of street collections, etc., to specific charitable appeals. However, the section seems to be superfluous as pointed out by David Wilson.[72]

The problem is that the section only applies where[73] "any difficulty in applying property to those purposes makes that property or the part not applicable *cy-près* available to be returned to the donors." Thus, it applies only where under the general law the property is held on a resulting trust for donors. It does not apply where the property passes to the Crown as *bona vacantia*, as an out and out gift without any general charitable intention, nor where the property is in any event applicable *cy-près* as an out and out gift under a general charitable intention. Since 1970 it has been clear that cash put into collection boxes is by way of out and out gift[74] so there is no scope for section 14 to apply to such cash collections.

---

[66] *Liverpool & District Hospital v. Att.-Gen.* [1981] Ch. 193.
[67] *Re Wokingham Fire Brigade Trusts* [1951] Ch. 373.
[68] *Re Ulverston & District New Hospital Building Trusts* [1956] Ch. 622 at 636. To similar effect see Upjohn J. in *Re Coopers Conveyance* [1956] 1 W.L.R. 1096.
[69] *ibid.* at 637.
[70] *Re Wokingham Fire Brigade Trusts* [1951] Ch. 373.
[71] *Re Welsh Hospital (Netley) Fund* [1921] 1 Ch. 655; *Re North Devon & West Somerset Relief Fund Trusts* [1953] 1 W.L.R. 1260; *Re British School of Egyptian Archaeology* [1954] 1 W.L.R. 546; *Picarda on Charities*, (2nd ed.) at 299–301.
[72] [1983] Conv. 40, but *cf. Beggs v. Kirkpatrick* [1961] V.R. 764.
[73] Charities Act 1993, s.14(7).
[74] *Re West Sussex Constabulary's Benevolent Fund Trusts* [1971] Ch. 1, *supra* at. 295; *Re Hillier* [1954] 1 W.L.R. 700 (out-and-out gift and general charitable intention imputed); *Re Ulverston & District New Hospital Building Fund* [1956] 1 Ch. 622 (out-and-out gift but *bona vacantia* since no general charitable intention imputed). In *bona vacantia* cases the Att.-Gen. normally waives the Crown's rights and has the property applied *cy-près* as emerges from *Re Ulverston* [1956] 1 Ch. 622 at 634.

At face value, the section purports to cover the proceeds of lotteries, **7–327** competitions, entertainments or sales, but in most cases the so-called donors will have provided contractual consideration for their tickets, so there is no question of returning their money to them by way of a resulting trust,[75] so the section is inapplicable to such proceeds. If the money paid is *ex gratia* and not contractual then this will be by way of out and out gift[76] so that the section will be inapplicable.

In the case of supervening failure of charitable purposes where the property has been given out and out to charity then such property is regarded as permanently devoted to charity to the exclusion of any resulting trust[77] so that section 14 can have no scope.

Extension of Cy-près under Charities Act 1993, s.13

Before section 13 of the 1960 Act (replaced by the 1993 Act) was **7–328** enacted failure justifying *cy-près* occurred when the purposes of a trust became impossible or impracticable or there was a surplus after the purposes had been carried out. "Impracticable" came to be liberally interpreted over the years so as to include "highly undesirable,"[78] but failure did not occur just because performance in another way would be more suitable or more beneficial.[79] Section 13 now extends the occasions when *cy-près* may be available but in cases of initial failure it is still necessary to show general charitable intention.[80] The section deals with difficulties over the original purposes of the trust (*e.g.* where £3 p.a. for clergyman and rest to poor when total income was £5 in 1716 and the income then rose to £800 p.a.)[81] and not over provisions as to administration of the trust (*e.g.* a provision for distribution of all capital for charitable purposes within 10 years of the settlor's death).[82] However, matters relating to administration of the trust may be dealt with under the court's inherent jurisdiction.[83]

Section 13 has no application of course, if there would have been no **7–329** need for a scheme before section 13 of the 1960 was enacted, as appears from *Oldham B.C. v. Att.-Gen.*[84] where the Council held land "upon trust to preserve and manage the same at all times hereafter as playing fields

---

[75] *Re West Sussex Constabulary's Benevolent Fund Trust* [1971] Ch. 1, *supra* at para. 5–44. Previously, the courts had overlooked this and so too, naturally, did the 1960 Act.

[76] See *supra*, para. 5–40.

[77] *Re Wright* [1954] Ch. 347; *Re Ulverston* [1956] 1 Ch. 622 at 636; *Re Wokingham Fire Brigade Trusts* [1951] Ch. 373.

[78] *Re Dominion Students' Hall Trust* [1947] Ch. 183 (scheme removing provision restricting Hall for Dominion students to students of European origin, *i.e.* white students).

[79] *Re Weir Hospital* [1910] 2 Ch. 124.

[80] Charities Acts 1960 and 1993, s.13(2). In *Re J.W. Laing Trust* [1984] 1 All E.R. 50 at 53 counsel surprisingly (and erroneously) conceded that general charitable intent was necessary for property effectively dedicated to charity in 1922.

[81] *Re Lepton's Charity* [1972] Ch. 276.

[82] *Re J. W. Laing Trust* [1984] 1 All E.R. 50.

[83] *Ibid. Att.-Gen. v. Dedham School* (1857) 23 Beav. 350.

[84] [1993] Ch. 210. Before sections 36–38 of the Charities Act 1993 the Commissioners' consent was still needed to dispose of charity land.

for the benefit and enjoyment of" local inhabitants. The Council wanted to sell the land to developers and use the proceeds to buy other land with better facilities. The Court of Appeal held that this did not involve an alteration of the "original purposes" of the charitable gift so that the sale could proceed without the need for a *cy-près* scheme.

7–330   For section 13 to apply the circumstances must be fitted into one or other of the "pigeonholes" in paragraphs (a) to (e), the largest pigeonhole being (e)(iii) "where the original purposes, in whole or in part, have, since they were laid down ceased to provide a suitable and effective method of using the property available by virtue of the gift, regard being had to the spirit of the gift". This requires the court to make a value judgment taking account of "the basic intention underlying the gift or the substance of the gift"[85]: "to look beyond the original purposes as defined by the objects specified in the declaration of trust and to seek to identify the spirit in which the donors gave property upon trust for those purposes . . . with the assistance of the document as a whole and any relevant evidence as to the circumstances in which the gift was made."[86]

7–331   In *Varsani v. Jesani*[87] a group of Hendon Hindus in 1967 set up a trust to promote the faith of Swaminarayan as practised in accordance with the teaching and tenets of Muktajivandasji, to provide facilities for a small united community of his followers in the Hendon area of London. After his death problems arose over his successor as divine leader of the sect so that the community divided into two factions, each claiming that it adhered to the true faith while the other did not. The Court of Appeal held that to appropriate the property to one faction to the exclusion of the other would be contrary to the spirit in which the gift to the charitable trust was made, and that the impasse between the two factions with the majority faction excluding the minority faction meant that a *cy-près* scheme could be made under paragraph (e) (iii) to divide the trust property between the two factions.

RE VERNON'S WILL TRUSTS

7–332   [1972] Ch. 300n., 303

BUCKLEY J.: "Every [charitable] bequest to an unincorporated charity by name without more must take effect as a gift for a charitable purpose. No individual or aggregate of individuals could claim to take such a bequest beneficially. If the gift is to be permitted to take effect at all, it must be as a bequest for a purpose, *i.e.*, that charitable purpose which the named charity exists to serve. A bequest which is in terms made for a charitable purpose will not fail for lack of a trustee but will be carried into effect either under the sign manual or by means of a scheme. A bequest to a named unincorporated charity, however, may on its true interpretation show that the testator's intention to make the gift at all was dependent on

---

[85] *Varsani v. Jesani* [1998] 3 All E.R. 273, 283.
[86] *ibid*, 288.
[87] [1998] 3 All E.R. 273.

the named charitable organisation being available at the time when the gift takes effect to serve as the instrument for applying the subject-matter of the gift to the charitable purpose for which it is by inference given. If so and the named charity ceases to exist in the lifetime of the testator, the gift fails (*Re Ovey*[88]). A bequest to a corporate body, on the other hand, takes effect simply as a gift to that body beneficially, unless there are circumstances which show that the recipient is to take the gift as a trustee. There is no need in such a case to infer a trust for any particular purpose. The objects to which the corporate body can properly apply its funds may be restricted by its constitution, but this does not necessitate inferring as a matter of construction of the testator's will a direction that the bequest is to be held in trust to be applied for those purposes: the natural construction is that the bequest is made to the corporate body as part of its general funds, that is to say, beneficially and without the imposition of any trust. That the testator's motive in making the bequest may have undoubtedly been to assist the work of the incorporated body would be insufficient to create a trust."

Note

This dictum was applied by Goff J. in *Re Finger's W.T.*[89] so as to hold a **7–333** gift to a dissolved unincorporated charity, the National Radium Commission, to be a purpose trust for the sort of work carried on by the Commission so as not to lapse, whilst a gift to a dissolved corporate charity, the National Council for Maternity and Child Welfare, he held to be for such charity absolutely beneficially, so as to lapse unless a general charitable intention could be found to justify a *cy-près* application: he found such an intention enabling the gift to pass to the National Association for Maternity and Child Welfare. Earlier he had said,[90] "If the matter were *res integra* I would have thought there would be much to be said for the view that the status of the donee, whether corporate or unincorporate, can make no difference to the question whether as a matter of construction a gift is absolute or on trust for purposes. Certainly drawing such a distinction produces anomalous results."

Nevertheless, the dictum of Buckley J was applied in *Re ARMS (Multiple Sclerosis Research) Ltd*[91] where the recipient company went into compulsory insolvent liquidation after the testator's will was made but before the testator's death, by which date the company had not been formally dissolved. Neuberger J held that the company took the money as part of its general assets available for its creditors.

RE SPENCE'S WILL TRUSTS

[1979] Ch. 483; [1978] 3 All E.R. 92; [1978] 3 W.L.R. 483

---

[88] (1885) 29 Ch.D. 560.
[89] [1972] Ch. 286; and also see *Re Koeppler's W.T.* [1986] Ch. 423 at 434, taking the *Re Vernon's W.T.* [1972] Ch. 300 approach.
[90] [1972] Ch. 286, 294. See also *Montefiore Jewish Home v. Howell* [1984] 2 N.S.W.L.R. 407, for treating corporate and unincorporate charities similarly.
[91] [1997] 1 W.L.R. 877.

7–334 MEGARRY V.-C. read the following judgment: "The testatrix, Mrs. Spence, . . . made her will on December 4, 1968, and died on May 30, 1972 . . . She gave her residuary estate to her trustees on trust to sell it and to pay her funeral and testamentary expenses and debts, and then:

> 'to pay and divide the residue thereof equally between The Blind Home, Scott Street, Keighley and the Old Folks Home at Hillworth Lodge, Keighley for the benefit of the patients.'

The will next provided that the receipt of the treasurer for the time being of 'each of the above-mentioned institutions' should be a sufficient discharge to her trustees. Subject to the expenses of administration and to the costs of these proceedings, the net residue is now worth some £17,000 . . .

7–335 "I shall first consider the gift to 'The Blind Home, Scott Street, Keighley . . . for the benefit of the patients.' I think it is clear that these last six words apply to the gift to the Blind Home as they apply to the gift to the Old Folks Home; and nobody contended to the contrary. The question is whether this gift carries a moiety of residue to the Keighley and District Association for the Blind and, if so, on what terms. That charity was founded in 1907 and, over the years, it has changed its name thrice. It has borne its present name for nearly 20 years and is at present governed by a trust deed dated October 25, 1963. For over 25 years it has been running a blind home at 31 Scott Street, Keighley, which provides permanent accommodation for the blind in Keighley and district. Since 1907 there have been no other premises or associations connected with the blind in Keighley. The premises in Scott Street are often called 'The Blind Home'; and a memorandum of the appointment of new trustees made on June 9, 1970, refers to the meeting for that purpose held at 'The Blind Home, Scott Street, Keighley.' Other names are used. A board on the building calls it 'The Keighley and District Home for the Blind,' and a brochure in evidence calls it 'Keighley Home for the Blind.' It seems clear beyond a peradventure that the language of the will fits the home run by the charity at these premises.

7–336 "In those circumstances, counsel for the plaintiff felt unable to advance any argument that the gift of this moiety failed and passed as on intestacy; and in this I think he was right. That, however, does not dispose of the matter, since the charity also carries on a home for the blind at Bingley, and may of course expend some or all of its funds on this or other purposes within its objects. There is therefore the question whether the moiety should go to the charity as an accretion to its endowment, and so be capable of being employed on any of its activities, or whether it is to be confined to the particular part of the charity's activities that are carried on at The Blind Home in Scott Street, Keighley. I confess that but for the decision of the Court of Appeal in *Re Lucas*[92] I should have had little hesitation in resolving this question in the latter and narrower sense, confining the moiety to the particular Blind Home in Scott Street, Keighley.

"In *Re Lucas* the testatrix made her will on October 12, 1942, and died on December 18, 1943. The will made gifts to 'the Crippled Children's Home, Lindley Moor, Huddersfield'; and it provided that the receipt of the treasurer or other officer for the time being should be a sufficient discharge. From 1916 there had been an establishment called 'The Huddersfield Home for Crippled Children' at Lindley Moor, governed by the charitable trusts established by a deed

---

[92] [1948] Ch. 424.

dated March 29, 1915; but according to the statement of facts in the report[93] 'On October 17, 1941, this home was closed and a scheme for the future administration of its assets was made by the charity commissioners.' Under that scheme the charity thereby created was to be known as 'The Huddersfield Charity for Crippled Children,' and the income was to be applied in sending poor crippled children to holiday or convalescent homes.

In the All England Law Reports,[94] passages in the judgments which are **7–337** omitted from the Law Reports explicitly state that the scheme of the Charity Commissioners was sealed on October 17, 1941. They also show that the home had been closed not on that day but some two-and-a-half years before, on April 6, 1939, when the lease had run out. The statement of facts in the Law Reports is thus wrong in this respect. When the testatrix came to make her will on October 12, 1942, the home had been closed for some three-and-a-half years, and the charity had for almost a year had a name which, in accord with its new objects, had had the word 'Home' in it replaced by 'Charity.' The All England Law Reports also show that the original name, 'The Huddersfield Home for Crippled Children,' had been given to the charity by the trust deed. The question for resolution in *Re Lucas* was thus whether the gifts to 'the Crippled Children's Home, Lindley Moor, Huddersfield' took effect as gifts to 'The Huddersfield Charity for Crippled Children,' or whether they were gifts for the upkeep of a particular home for crippled children which had ceased to exist before the will had been made, so that they failed.

"At first instance, Roxburgh J. held that the latter was the correct view: *Re* **7–338** *Lucas*.[95] On appeal, Lord Greene M.R. delivered the reserved judgment of himself, Somervell L.J. and Jenkins J. This reversed the decision below, and held that the gifts were gifts which contributed to the endowment of the charity, and so did not fail. I have found the judgment puzzling in places. Lord Greene M.R. discussed the misdescription in the will as follows.[96]

> 'As to the misdescription (*i.e.* "The Crippled Children's Home" for "the Huddersfield Home for Crippled Children") the description given by the testatrix was no more an accurate description of the particular home than it was of the charity.'

Later the judgment considers the position if the testatrix 'did know the correct name of the charity (*i.e.* "The Huddersfield Home for Crippled Children").'

"I find this puzzling. My difficulty is this. Nearly a year before the will was **7–339** made, the correct name of the charity had ceased to be what the judgment says it was. The 'description given by the testatrix' was 'the Crippled Children's Home, Lindley Moor, Huddersfield.' This, said the judgment, was 'no more an accurate description of the particular home [that is, the Huddersfield Home for Crippled Children which was at Lindley Moor] than it was of the charity.' Yet when the will was made the name of the charity had for nearly a year been 'The Huddersfield Charity for Crippled Children,' a name which did not include the word 'Home.' I find it difficult to see why a gift to a 'Home' does not fit an entity with 'Home' in its title better than it fits an entity without the word 'Home' in its title, but the word 'Charity,' instead. If in referring to the 'correct name' of the

---

[93] [1948] Ch. 424 at 425.
[94] [1947] 2 All E.R. 773 at 774; [1948] 2 All E.R. 22 at 24.
[95] [1948] Ch. 175.
[96] [1948] Ch. 424 at 428.

charity the judgment intends to refer to what had once been the correct name of the charity, I cannot see what it was that made the court reject the state of affairs when the will was made in favour of the past, particularly when there appears to have been no evidence about what the testatrix knew about the charity. I say what I say with all due humility, and a ready recognition that the fault may be an inability on my part to see what is plain to others; but, though humble, I remain puzzled.

7–340   "The main factors in the decision of the Court of Appeal seem to have been that the words used in the will fitted the home that had been closed down no better than the charity which continued in existence, and that the will had omitted to make any specific reference to the upkeep or maintenance of the home which would indicate that the gifts were to be confined to the upkeep of the home. The gifts were accordingly gifts to the charity, and so did not fail. The question for me is whether on the case before me there ought to be a similar result, so that the moiety of residue would go to the Keighley, and District Association for the Blind as an addition to its endowment generally, and would not be confined to the Blind Home in Scott Street, Keighley, carried on by the association.

7–341   "Counsel for the first defendant submitted that there were two substantial points of distinction between the present case and *Re Lucas*.[97] First, the words of the will fitted the Blind Home far better than they fitted the association. Indeed, although the Blind Home was from time to time described by different names, all the names used included both 'Blind' and 'Home': and, as I have mentioned, the appointment of new trustees in June 1970 uses the name 'The Blind Home, Scott Street, Keighley,' which is the precise expression used in the will. The title of the charity, 'The Keighley and District Association for the Blind,' is very different. True, it has the word 'Blind' in common with the title used in the will. There is also the word 'Keighley,' though this is used adjectively and not as part of the address. But otherwise there is nothing in common. In particular, there is not the use of the word 'Home' in both titles which the Court of Appeal in *Re Lucas* said was present in that case; and I think the words 'Home' and 'Association' are different in a real and significant sense.

7–342   "Secondly, in the case before me, there are the words 'for the benefit of the patients' which follow and govern the expression 'The Blind Home, Scott Street, Keighley.' In *Re Lucas* there was no counterpart to this. Indeed, the absence of any reference to the upkeep or maintenance of the home in that case was, as I have indicated, one of the grounds on which the decision was based. Here, there is no reference to upkeep or maintenance as such: but I think 'patients' must mean 'patients of the Blind Home,' and the upkeep and maintenance of the home is an obvious means of providing a benefit for the patients in it.

"In my judgment both these distinctions are valid and substantial. It therefore seems to me that the case before me is distinguishable from *Re Lucas*, so far as I have correctly understood that case. The testatrix was making provision for the benefit of the patients for the time being at a particular home, namely, the home usually known as The Blind Home at Scott Street, Keighley. She was giving the money not to augment generally the endowment of the charity which runs that home, with the consequences that the money might be used for purposes other than the benefit of the patients at that home, but was giving the money so that it would be used exclusively for the benefit of those patients. The only way in which

---

[97] [1948] Ch. 424.

this can conveniently be done is to give the money to the charity but to confine its use to use for the benefit of the patients for the time being at the home. That, I think, requires a scheme; but I see no need to direct that a scheme should be settled in chambers. Instead, I think that I can follow the convenient course taken by Goff J. in *Re Finger's Will Trusts*.[98] I shall therefore order by way of scheme (the Attorney-General not objecting) that the moiety be paid to the proper officer of the charity to be held on trust to apply it for the benefit of the patients for the time being of the home known as The Blind Home, Scott Street, Keighley.

"I now turn to the other moiety of residue, given by the will to 'the Old Folks **7–343** Home at Hillworth Lodge, Keighley for the benefit of the patients.' Hillworth Lodge was built as a workhouse in 1858. Shortly before the outbreak of war in 1939 the West Riding Country Council, in whom it had become vested, closed it down: but during the war it was used to house what were generally but inelegantly called 'evacuees.' In 1948 it became an aged persons' home under the National Assistance Act 1948, and it continued as such until January 28, 1971, when it was finally closed down. There had been between 120 and 140 residents in it as late as 1969, but the numbers were then progressively run down, until in January 1971, just before it closed, only ten residents were left; and these were transferred to another establishment in Pudsey. The aged of the area had over the years been increasingly accommodated in purpose-designed old people's homes which provided better accommodation for the aged than could the old workhouse, despite many improvements to it. Since the building ceased to house old people it has been used as Divisional Social Services Offices.

"When the testatrix made her will in 1968 the building was accordingly still in **7–344** use as an old people's home run by the local authority in accordance with their duty under the National Assistance Act 1948. As an old people's home it had no assets of its own, and residents contributed towards their maintenance in accordance with the Ministry of Social Security Act 1966, Part III. When the testatrix died on May 30, 1972, the building was no longer used as an old people's home, and was being used, or was soon to be used, as offices. The home had been run neither as nor by a charity. It formerly provided homes for those living in a large area of the West Riding, and not merely Keighley; and it has not been replaced by any one home. Instead, there are many old people's homes serving the area.

"Now without looking at the authorities I would have said that this was a fairly **7–345** plain case of a will which made a gift for a particular purpose in fairly specific terms. The gift was for the benefit of the patients at a particular home, namely the Old Folks Home at Hillworth Lodge, Keighley. At the date of the will there were patients at that home. When the testatrix died, there was no longer any home there, but offices instead; and so there were no longer any patients there, or any possibility of them. The gift was a gift for a charitable purpose which at the date of the will was capable of accomplishment and at the date of death was not. Prima facie, therefore, the gift fails unless a general charitable intention has been manifested so that the property can be applied *cy-près*. Buttressed by authority, counsel for the plaintiff contended that the court would be slow to find a general charitable intention where the object of the gift is defined with some particularity, as it was here.

"Against that, counsel for the Attorney-General advanced two main conten- **7–346** tions. First, he said that as a matter of construction it was wrong to construe the gift as being merely for the benefit of patients who were actually at the Old Folks

---

[98] [1972] 1 Ch. 286 at 300.

Home at Hillworth Lodge; admittedly, of course, there are none of these. Instead, those who were intended to benefit included all those who would have been sent to that home if it had still existed, irrespective of the type of home in which in fact they are being or will be accommodated. He emphasised that the gift was essentially a gift for old people in Keighley, and the home was merely a means of providing a benefit for them.

"I do not think that this argument can be right. When the testatrix made her will there were patients at the Old Folks Home at Hillworth Lodge. The gift to that home 'for the benefit of the patients' is, on this construction, to be treated as being a gift for the benefit not only of the patients who successively were for the time being at the home, but of others who never go near the home but who might or would have been sent to it in certain circumstances. The words of the will were perfectly capable of being satisfied by confining their meaning to their natural sense, namely, as relating to those who are or will in the future be patients at the home. Why is there to be forced on to those words a notional extension of uncertain effect? If at the time they were being written those words could not have their natural effect, one might indeed look round for a secondary meaning; but that is not the case.

7–347　　"There are further difficulties. If the notional extension is made, who are within it? As I have said, the defunct home provided for a large area of the West Riding, and not merely Keighley. How is it to be determined who can hope to benefit under the gift? Which of the occupants of the other old people's homes in such an area (the extent of which is undefined) can claim to be objects of the testatrix's bounty? Who is to decide whether any particular individual could (or would) have been sent to the defunct home had it still existed, and so would fall within the scope of the gift? I do not see how such an extension of meaning can fairly be placed on the words of the will. No doubt a scheme could cure much, but my difficulty is in seeing what on this footing, was the intention of the testatrix. For the reasons that I have given, I reject this contention.

"Counsel's other contention for the Attorney-General was that the will displayed a sufficient general charitable intention for the moiety to be applied *cy-près*. In doing this he had to contend with *Re Harwood*.[99] This, and cases which apply to it, such as *Re Stemson's Will Trusts*[1] establish that it is very difficult to find a general charitable intention where the testator has selected a particular charity, taking some care to identify it, and the charity then ceases to exist before the testator's death. This contrasts with cases where the charity described in the will has never existed, when it is much easier to find a general charitable intention.

7–348　　"These cases have been concerned with gifts to institutions, rather than gifts for purposes. The case before me, on the other hand, is a gift for a purpose, namely, the benefit of the patients at a particular old folks home. It therefore seems to me that I ought to consider the question, of which little or nothing was said in argument, whether the principle in *Re Harwood*, or a parallel principle, has any application to such a case. In other words, is a similar distinction to be made between, on the one hand, a case in which the testator has selected a particular charitable purpose, taking some care to identify it, and before the testator dies that purpose has become impracticable or impossible of accomplishment, and on the other hand a case where the charitable purpose has never been possible or practicable?

---

[99] [1936] Ch. 285.
[1] [1970] Ch. 16.

"As at present advised I would answer yes to that question. I do not think that **7–349** the reasoning of the *Re Harwood* line of cases is directed to any feature of institutions as distinct from purposes. Instead, I think the essence of the distinction is in the difference between particularity and generality. If a particular institution or purpose is specified, then it is that institution or purpose, and no other, that is to be the object of the benefaction. It is difficult to envisage a testator as being suffused with a general glow of broad charity when he is labouring, and labouring successfully, to identify some particular specified institution or purpose as the object of his bounty. The specific displaces the general. It is otherwise where the testator has been unable to specify any particular charitable institution or practicable purpose, and so, although his intention of charity can be seen, he has failed to provide any way of giving effect to it. There, the absence of the specific leaves the general undisturbed. It follows that in my view in the case before me, where the testatrix has clearly specified a particular charitable purpose which before her death became impossible to carry out, counsel for the Attorney-General has to face that level of great difficulty in demonstrating the existence of a general charitable intention which was indicated by *Re Harwood*.

"One way in which counsel sought to meet that difficulty was by citing *Re* **7–350** *Finger's Will Trusts*.[2] There, Goff J. distinguished *Re Harwood* and held that the will before him displayed a general charitable intention. He did this on the footing that the circumstances of the case were 'very special.' The gift that failed was a gift to an incorporated charity which had ceased to exist before the testatrix died. The 'very special' circumstances were, first, that apart from a life interest and two small legacies, the whole estate was devoted to charity, and that this was emphasised by the direction to hold the residue in trust for division 'between the following charitable institutions and funds.' Secondly, the charitable donee that had ceased was mainly, if not exclusively, a co-ordinating body, and the judge could not believe that the testatrix meant to benefit that body alone. Thirdly, there was evidence that the testatrix regarded herself as having no relatives.

"In the case before me neither of these last two circumstances applies, nor **7–351** have any substitute special circumstances been suggested. As for the first, the will before me gives 17 pecuniary legacies to relations and friends, amounting in all to well over one-third of the net estate. Further, in *Re Rymer*,[3] which does not appear to have been cited, the will had prefaced the disputed gift by the words 'I give the following charitable legacies to the following institutions and persons respectively.' These words correspond to the direction which in *Re Finger's Will Trusts* was regarded as providing emphasis, and yet they did not suffice to avoid the conclusion of Chitty J. and the Court of Appeal that a gift to an institution which had ceased to exist before the testator's death lapsed and could not be applied *cy-près*. I am not sure that I have been able to appreciate to the full the cogency of the special circumstances that appealed to Goff J.; but however that may be I can see neither those nor any other special circumstances in the present case which would suffice to distinguish *Re Harwood*.

"The other way in which counsel for the Attorney-General sought to meet his **7–352** difficulty was by relying on *Re Satterthwaite's Will Trusts*[4] and on *Re Knox*.[5] The doctrine may for brevity be described as charity by association. If the will gives

---

[2] [1972] 1 Ch. 286.
[3] [1895] 1 Ch. 19.
[4] [1966] 1 W.L.R. 277.
[5] [1937] Ch. 109.

the residue among a number of charities with kindred objects, but one of the apparent charities does not in fact exist, the court will be ready to find a general charitable intention and so apply the share of the non-existent charity *cy-près*. I have not been referred to any explicit statement of the underlying principle, but it seems to me that in such cases the court treats the testator as having shown the general intention of giving his residue to promote charities with that type of kindred objects, and then, when he comes to dividing the residue, as casting round for particular charities with that type of objects to name as donees. If one or more of these are non-existent, then the general intention will suffice for a *cy-près* application. It will be observed that, as stated, the doctrine depends, at least to some extent, on the detection of 'kindred objects' (a phrase which comes from the judgment of Luxmoore J. in *Re Knox*[6]) in the charities to which the shares of residue are given; in this respect the charities must in some degree be *ejusdem generis*.

7–353 "In *Re Satterthwaite's Will Trusts*[7] the residuary gift was to nine charitable bodies which were all concerned with kindness to animals; but the gifts to two of them failed as no bodies could be found which sufficiently answered the descriptions in the will. Harman L.J. said[8] that he 'felt the gravest doubts' whether a general charitable intent had been shown. However, at first instance the judge had held that in respect of one of the bodies a sufficient general charitable intention had been displayed, and as there had been no appeal as to that share, he (Harman L.J.) would reach the same conclusion in respect of the other share, which was the subject of the appeal. On the other hand, Russell L.J. had no doubt that a general charitable intention had been shown.[9] Diplock L.J. delivered a single-sentence judgment agreeing with both the other judgments. The support which this case provides for counsel for the Attorney-General accordingly seems to me to be a trifle muted.

7–354 "In *Re Knox* Luxmoore J. distilled a general charitable intention out of a residuary gift in quarters to two named infirmaries, a named nursing home and Dr. Barnardo's Homes. No institution existed which correctly answered the description of the nursing home, and it was held that the quarter share that had been given to it should be applied *cy-près*. I am not entirely sure what genus the judge had in mind as embracing the infirmaries and Dr. Barnardo's Homes when he said that 'the object of each of the other charities is a kindred object to that which is to be inferred from the name' of the nursing home: perhaps it was the provision of residential accommodation for those in need. "It will be observed that these are all cases of gifts to bodies which did not exist. In such cases, the court is ready to find a general charitable intention: see *Re Davis*.[10] The court is far less ready to find such an intention where the gift is to a body which existed at the date of the will but ceased to exist before the testator died, or, as I have already held, where the gift is for a purpose which, though possible and practicable at the date of the will, has ceased to be so before the testator's death.

7–355 The case before me is, of course, a case in this latter category, so that counsel for the Attorney-General has to overcome this greater difficulty in finding a general charitable intention. Not only does counsel have this greater difficulty: he also has, I think, less material with which to meet it. He has to extract the general

---

[6] [1937] Ch. 109 at 113.
[7] [1966] 1 W.L.R. 277.
[8] [1966] 1 W.L.R. 277 at 284.
[9] [1966] 1 W.L.R. 277 at 286.
[10] [1902] 1 Ch. 876 at 884.

charitable intention for the gift which fails from only one other gift: the residue, of course, was simply divided into two. In *Re Knox* and *Re Hartley (deceased)*[11] the gifts which failed were each among three other gifts, and in *Re Satterthwaite's Will Trusts* there were seven or eight other gifts. I do not say that a general charitable intention or a genus cannot be extracted from a gift of residue equally between two: but I do say that larger numbers are likely to assist in conveying to the court a sufficient conviction both of the genus and of the generality of the charitable intention.

"A further point occurred to me which I think that I should mention. There **7–356** are, of course, cases where there is merely a single gift, but the court is nevertheless able to see a clear general charitable intention underlying the particular mode of carrying it out that the testator has laid down. Thus in the well known case of *Biscoe v. Jackson*,[12] which I read in the light of *Re Wilson*,[13] the gift was to provide a soup kitchen and cottage hospital 'for the parish of Shoreditch.' Despite a considerable degree of particularity about the soup kitchen and the cottage hospital that were to be provided, the court found a general charitable intention to provide a benefit for the sick and poor of the parish. In that case, of course, there would have been no real difficulty in ascertaining those who were intended to benefit. Whatever the practical difficulties, at least the concept of those who were to be included is clear enough. The only real difficulty or impossibility lay in the particular method of carrying out that intention which the testator had specified. In the present case, on the other hand, the difficulty lies not only in the particular method but also in the very nature of the general charitable intention that is said to underlie that method. For the reasons that I have already given, I find it far from clear which 'patients' are intended to benefit once the touchstone of the Old Folks Home at Hillworth Lodge is removed. There is no geographical or other limitation to provide a guide. Where the difficulty or impossibility not only afflicts the method but also invades the concept of the alleged general charitable intention, then I think that the difficulty of establishing that the will displays any general charitable intention becomes almost insuperable.

"From what I have said it follows that I have been quite unable to extract from **7–357** the will, construed in its context, any expression of a general charitable intention which would suffice for the moiety to be applied *cy-près*. Instead, in my judgment, the moiety was given for a specific charitable purpose which, though possible when the will was made, became impossible before the testatrix died. The gift of the moiety accordingly fails, and it passes as on intestacy."

Charities Act 1993

Occasions for applying property cy-près

13.—(1) Subject to subsection (2) below, the circumstances in which the **7–358** original purposes of a charitable gift can be altered to allow the property given or part of it to be applied *cy-près* shall be as follows.[14]

(a) where the original purposes, in whole or in part,—

---

[11] March 15, 1978 (unreported decision of Megarry J.).
[12] (1887) 35 Ch.D. 460.
[13] [1913] 1 Ch. 314.
[14] The section is available for initial and subsequent failure, subs. (2) preserving the requirement of general charitable intention for cases of initial failure.

    (i) Have been as far as may be fulfilled; or

    (ii) Cannot be carried out, or not according to the directions given and to the spirit of the gift; or

(b) Where the original purposes provide a use for part only of the property available by virtue of the gift; or

(c) where the property available by virtue of the gift and other property applicable for similar purposes can be more effectively used in conjunction, and to that end can suitably, regard being had to the spirit of the gift, be made applicable to common purposes; or

(d) where the original purposes were laid down by reference to an area which then was but has since ceased to be a unit for some other purpose, or by reference to a class of persons or to an area which has for any reason since ceased to be suitable, regard being had to the spirit of the gift, or to be practical in administering the gift; or

(e) where the original purposes,[15] in whole or in part, have, since they were laid down,—

    (i) been adequately provided for by other means; or

    (ii) ceased,[16] as being useless or harmful to the community or for other reasons, to be in law charitable; or

    (iii) Ceased in any other way to provide a suitable and effective method of using the property available by virtue of the gift, regard being had to the spirit of the gift.[17]

7–359   (2) Subsection (1) above shall not affect the conditions which must be satisfied in order that property given for charitable purposes may be applied *cy-près*, except in so far as those conditions require a failure of the original purposes.

    (3) References in the foregoing subsections to the original purposes of a gift shall be construed, where the application of the property given has been altered or regulated by a scheme or otherwise, as referring to the purposes for which the property is for the time being applicable.

    (5) It is hereby declared that a trust for charitable purposes places a trustee under a duty, where the case permits and requires the property or some part of it to be applied *cy-près*, to secure its effective use for charity by taking steps to enable it to be so applied.

Application cy-près of gifts of donors unknown or disclaiming

7–360   **14.**—(1) Property given for specific charitable purposes which fail shall be applicable *cy-près* as if given for charitable purposes generally, where it belongs—

(a) to a donor who, after—

    (i) the prescribed advertisements and inquiries have been published and made, and

---

[15] "The original purposes" are apt to apply to the trusts as a whole where the trust is for payment of a fixed annual sum out of the income of a fund to charity A and payment of the residue of the income to charity B: the phrase is not read severally in relation to the trust for payment of the fixed annual sum and the trust for payment of residuary income: *Re Lepton's Charity* [1972] 1 Ch. 276.

[16] See Lord Simonds in *National Anti-Vivisection Society v. I.R.C.* [1948] A.C. 31 at 64, 65.

[17] This broad head is very useful indeed. The phrase "spirit of the gift" was recommended by the Nathan Committee (Cmd. 8710, para. 365) who borrowed it from s.116 of the Education (Scotland) Act 1946 where it appears as "the spirit of the intention of the founders as embodied either (i) in the original deed constituting the endowment where it is still the governing instrument, or (ii) in any scheme affecting the endowment." See also *Re Lepton's Charity* [1972] 1 Ch. 276 and *Varsani v. Jesani* [1998] 3 All E.R. 373 (C.A.).

(ii) the prescribed period beginning with the publication of those
advertisements has expired,

cannot be identified or cannot be found; or

(b) to a donor who has executed a disclaimer in the prescribed form of his
right to have the property returned.

(2) Where the prescribed advertisements and inquiries have been published and
made by or on behalf of trustees with respect to any such property, the trustees
shall not be liable to any person in respect of the property if no claim by him to
be interested in it is received by them before the expiry of the period mentioned
in subsection (1)(a)(ii) above.

(3) For the purpose of this section property shall be conclusively presumed **7–361**
(without any advertisement or inquiry) to belong to donors who cannot be
identified, in so far as it consists—

(a) of the proceeds of cash collections made by means of collecting boxes or
by other means not adapted for distinguishing one gift from another; or

(b) of the proceeds of any lottery, competition, entertainment, sale or similar
money-raising activity, after allowing for property given to provide prizes
or articles for sale or otherwise to enable the activity to be undertaken.

(4) The court may be order direct that property not falling within subsection
(3) above shall for the purposes of this section be treated (without any
advertisement or inquiry) as belonging to donors who cannot be identified where
it appears to the court either—

(a) that it would be unreasonable, having regard to the amounts likely to be
returned to the donors, to incur expense with a view to returning the
property; or

(b) that it would be unreasonable, having regard to the nature, circumstances
and amounts of the gifts, and to the lapse of time since the gifts were
made, for the donors to expect the property to be returned.

(5) Where property is applied *cy-près* by virtue of this section, the donor shall **7–362**
be deemed to have parted with all his interest at the time when the gift was
made; but where property is so applied as belonging to donors who cannot be
identified or cannot be found, and is not so applied by virtue of subsection (3) or
(4) above—

(a) the scheme shall specify the total amount of that property; and

(b) the donor of any part of that amount shall be entitled, if he makes a
claim not later than six months after the date on which the scheme is
made, to recover from the charity for which the property is applied a sum
equal to that part, less any expenses properly incurred by the charity
trustees after that date in connection with claims relating to his gift; and

(c) the scheme may include directions as to the provisions to be made for
meeting any such claim.

(6) Where—

(a) any sum is, in accordance with any such directions, set aside for meeting **7–363**
any such claims, but

(b) the aggregate amount of any such claims actually made exceeds the relevant amount,

then, if the Commissioners so direct, each of the donors in question shall be entitled only to such proportion of the relevant amount as the amount of his claim bears to the aggregate amount referred to in paragraph (b) above; and for this purpose "the relevant amount" means the amount of the sum so set aside after deduction of any expenses properly incurred by the charity trustees in connection with claims relating to the donor's gifts.

(7) For the purposes of this section, charitable purposes shall be deemed to "fail" where any difficulty in applying property to those purposes makes that property or the part not applicable cy-près available to be returned to the donors.

7–364   (8) In this section "prescribed" means prescribed by regulations made by the Commissioners; and such regulations may, as respects the advertisements which are to be published for the purposes of subsection (1)(a) above, make provision as to the form and content of such advertisements as well as the manner in which they are to be published.

(9) Any regulations made by the Commissioners under this section shall be published by the Commissioners in such manners as they think fit.

(10) In this section, except in so far as the context otherwise requires, references to a donor include persons claiming through or under the original donor, and references to property given include the property for the time being representing the property originally given or property derived from it.

(11) This section shall apply to property given for charitable purposes, notwithstanding that it was so given before the commencement of this Act.

QUESTIONS

7–365   1.   Are the following trusts charitable, and, if not, are they otherwise valid?

    (i) To apply the income from £500,000 amongst such persons having the surnames Smith or Hayton, with preference so far as practicable for 50 per cent of the income to be used for the relatives of David Hayton, as my trustees may consider to merit educational assistance.

    (ii) £400,000 to my trustees to invest and apply the income therefrom in educating the children of needy employees or ex-employees of London Transport for 21 years whereupon the income shall be used to provide an English Public School education for such children of European origin living in Oxford as my trustees shall determine provided that in either case no person of the Roman Catholic faith shall be so assisted.

    (iii) A £10 million trust set up by I.C.I. plc and Barclays Bank plc for the income to be used at the trustees' discretion in assisting towards the education of the children or grandchildren of any persons employed or formerly employed by I.C.I. or Barclays Bank or any of their subsidiary or associated companies.

2. In 2000 a public appeal for funds to establish a recreation and **7–366** sports centre for the City of London Police was launched. £200,000 was donated by Hank Badman, £80,000 was obtained from street collections, £110,000 profit was made out of a pop festival in aid of the appeal and £20,000 was donated anonymously. It has now proved completely impossible in view of the size of the fund to obtain any suitable site. What should be done with the moneys?

3. By his will dated April 1, 1999, Oscar O'Flaherty (who died three months ago) bequeathed £60,000 to his executors to use part thereof for benevolent purposes and the remainder for charitable purposes and £50,000 to the "Torquay Home for Distressed Gentlefolk for the benefit of the needy who happen to be there." The Home, an unincorporated body, closed down six months before Oscar's death, its funds and many of its inhabitants going to the Bournemouth Home for the Handicapped. Advise Oscar's executors. Would your answer differ at all if the gift had been to the Torquay Home for Distressed Gentlefolk Ltd which had gone into compulsory insolvent liquidation six months before Oscar's death although it had not been formally dissolved by his death?

4. By his will Alan left his residuary estate to Tim and Tom "upon **7–367** trust to apply the income therefrom for such of the adult residents of Greater London as my Trustees in their absolute discretion shall think fit having due regard to the need to combat the stress, squalor and expense of residing in Greater London provided that my Trustees shall have power to add as further possible beneficiaries adult residents of any other city in the United Kingdom where the stress, squalor and expense are in my Trustees' absolute discretion comparable to that of Greater London provided further that one day before the expiration of the period of eighty years from my death (which period I hereby specify as the perpetuity period applicable hereto) the aforesaid Trust shall determine and the capital shall be distributed equally between United Reform Churches in West Ham and Leyton to use the income therefrom to assist in the burial or cremation of members of their congregations."

Alan has just died and Tim and Tom seek advice on the validity of the Trust.

5. During a motor race in Birmingham a car spun out of control killing the driver, a marshall and four mechanics. The Lord Mayor wants to appeal for funds for the families of the deceased and for the distressed surviving drivers, marshalls, mechanics and spectators. Advise him.

6. "In assessing the merits of putative charitable trusts the judges and **7–368** the Charity Commissioners make the best of a bad job: the alternative is to go back to first principles and have a special tribunal concerned with cost-benefit analyses and value-judgments on social merits and whose decisions could not be overturned unless no reasonable person could have made such a decision." Discuss.

Chapter 8

APPOINTMENT, RETIREMENT AND REMOVAL OF TRUSTEES

Section 1. Appointment of Trustees

I. APPOINTMENT UNDER THE STATUTORY POWER

The Trustee Act 1925

8–01   Section 36.[1]—(1)   Where a trustee,[2] either original or substituted, and whether appointed by a court or otherwise, is dead, or remains out of the United Kingdom for more than twelve months,[3] or desires to be discharged from all or any of the trusts or powers reposed in or conferred on him, or refuses or is unfit to act therein, or is incapable of acting therein, or is an infant, then, subject to the restrictions imposed by this Act on the number of trustees[4]—

(a) the person or persons nominated for the purpose of appointing new trustees by the instrument, if any, creating the trust;[5] or

(b) if there is no such person, or no such person able and willing to act, then the surviving or continuing[6] trustees or trustee for the time being, or the personal representatives of the last surviving or continuing trustee; [7]

---

[1] This section reproduces, with amendments and additions, the Trustee Act 1893, s.10(1), (3) and (4). Wolstenholme & Cherry's *Conveyancing Statutes* (13th ed.), by J. T. Farrand, Vol. 4, provides a most useful commentary on all sections of the Trustee Act.

[2] "Trustee" is used as to exclude personal representatives. Accordingly, no power is conferred to appoint executors. By the Administration of Estates Act 1925, s.7, an executor of a sole or last surviving executor of a testator is the executor by representation of that testator.

[3] It does not follow that there is an absolute bar to the appointment of non-resident trustees: *Re Whitehead's W.T.* [1971] 1 W.L.R. 833. Further see *Richard v. Mackay* (1997) 11 Trust L-I(1),22 discussed by R. Bramwell O.C. in (1990) 1 OTPR 1: para. 8–08.

[4] Maximum of four trustees except for charities: Trustee Act 1925, s.34 and see s.36(5).

[5] See *Re Wheeler* [1896] 1 Ch. 315: a decision on s.10(1) of the Trustee Act of 1893, which is re-enacted by s.36(1) of the Act of 1925. In that case the settlor, instead of nominating X the person to appoint new trustees generally—as in *Re Walker and Hughes* (1883) 24 Ch.D. 698—nominated X to appoint new trustees in certain specified events. One of the trustees became bankrupt and absconded, whereupon he became "unfit" to act, but not "incapable" of acting. The events specified by the settlor included the event of a trustee becoming "incapable," but not that of a trustee becoming "unfit." The question was whether the proper person to nominate a new trustee was X, as being "the person or persons nominated for the purpose of appointing new trustees by the instrument, if any, creating the trust"—s.36(1)(a)—or whether the proper person was the surviving or continuing trustees or trustee under s.36(1)(b). Kekewich J. held that if a power of appointment contained in the instrument of trust is a limited one, and the event which has actually happened is not one of the events contemplated by that power, then the nominee is not "the person or persons nominated for the purpose of appointing new trustees by the instrument, if any, creating the trust." Hence the proper person to appoint a new trustee in *Re Wheeler* was to be found in s.36(1)(b). *Re Wheeler* was followed, with reluctance, by Neville J. in *Re Sichel* [1916] 1 Ch. 358. The Act of 1925 does not seem to alter the position.

[6] A continuing trustee is one who is to continue to act after completion of the intended appointment: *Re Coates to Parsons* (1886) 34 Ch.D. 370.

[7] Persons appointed executors and trustees of wills of land must formally assent in favour of themselves *qua* trustees so as to take advantage of s.40: *Re King's W.T.* [1964] Ch. 542 discussed *supra*, at para. 1–123. An executor who has not proved his testator's will can exercise the power but the trustee appointed in such circumstances can only prove his title by reference to a proper grant of representation so that such a grant is, in practice, vital: *Re Crowhurst Park* [1974] 1 W.L.R. 583. If a will creates trusts but the trustees predecease the testator then s.36 is inapplicable: *Nicholson v. Field* [1893] 2 Ch. 511.

may, by writing,[8] appoint one or more other persons[9] (whether or not being the persons exercising the power) to be a trustee or trustees in the place of the trustee so deceased, remaining out of the United Kingdom, desiring to be discharged, refusing, or being unfit or being incapable, or being an infant, as aforesaid.

(2)   Where a trustee has been removed under a power contained in the **8–02** instrument creating the trust, a new trustee or new trustees may be appointed in the place of the trustee who is removed, as if he were dead, or, in the case of a corporation, as if the corporation desired to be discharged from the trust, and the provisions of this section shall apply accordingly, but subject to the restrictions imposed by this Act on the number of trustees.

(3)   Where a corporation being a trustee is or has been dissolved, either before or or after the commencement of this Act, then, for the purposes of this section and of any enactment replaced thereby, the corporation shall be deemed to be and to have been from the date of the dissolution incapable of acting in the trusts or powers reposed in or conferred on the corporation.

(4)   The power of appointment given by subsection (1) of this section or any similar previous enactment to the personal representatives of a last surviving or continuing trustee shall be and shall be deemed always to have been exercisable by the executors for the time being (whether original or by representation) of such surviving or continuing trustee who have proved the will of their testator or by the administrators for the time being of such trustee without the concurrence of any executor who has renounced or has not proved.

(5)   But a sole or last surviving executor intending to renounce, or all the **8–03** executors where they all intend to renounce, shall have and shall be deemed always to have had power, at any time before renouncing probate, to exercise the power of appointment given by this section, or by any similar previous enactment, if willing to act for the purpose and without thereby accepting the office of executor.

(6)   Where, in the case of any trust, there are not more than three trustees[10]

> (a)   the person or persons nominated for the purpose of appointing new trustees by the instrument, if any creating the trust; or
>
> (b)   if there is no such person, or no such person able and willing to act, then the trustee or trustees for the time being;

may, by writing, appoint another person or other persons[11] to be an additional trustee or additional trustees, but it shall not be obligatory to appoint any additional trustee, unless the instrument, if any, creating the trust, or any statutory enactment provides to the contrary, nor shall the number of trustees be increased beyond four by virtue of any such appointment.

(7)   Every new trustee appointed under this section as well before as after all **8–04** the trust property becomes by law, or by assurance, or otherwise, vested in him, shall have the same powers, authorities, and discretions, and may in all respects

---

[8] For the desirability of making the appointment by deed, see s.40 of the Trustee Act 1925, *infra*, para. 8–23.

[9] Not being infants: Law of Property Act 1925, s.20. Corporations may be appointed.

[10] This broad provision was inserted by the Trusts of Land and Appointment of Trustees Act 1996 Schedule 3 para. 3(11).

[11] This 1996 amendment ensures that the appointors should be able to appoint themselves as additional trustees, so reversing the previous position; *Re Power's S.T.* [1951] Ch.1074.

act as if he had been originally appointed a trustee by the instrument, if any, creating the trust.

(8) The provisions of this section relating to a trustee who is dead include the case of a person nominated trustee in a will but dying before the testator, and those relative to a continuing trustee include a refusing or retiring trustee, if willing to act in the execution of the provisions of this section.[12]

(9) Where a trustee is incapable, by reason of mental disorder within the meaning of the Mental Health Act, 1983, of exercising his functions as trustee and is also entitled in possession to some beneficial interest in the trust property, no appointment of a new trustee in his place shall be made by virtue of paragraph (b) of subsection (1) of this section unless leave to make the appointment has been given by the authority having jurisdiction under Part VII of the Mental Health Act 1983.[13]

8–05   Section 37.—(1)   On the appointment of a trustee for the whole or any part of trust property—

(a) the number of trustees may, subject to the restrictions imposed by this Act on the number of trustees, be increased; and

(b) a separate set of trustees, not exceeding four, may be appointed for any part of the trust property held on trusts distinct from those relating to any other part or parts of the trust property, notwithstanding that no new trustees or trustee are or is to be appointed for other parts of the trust property, and any existing trustee may be appointed or remain one of such separate set of trustees, or, if only one trustee was originally appointed, then, save as hereinafter provided, one separate trustee may be so appointed; and

(c) it shall not be obligatory, save as hereinafter provided, to appoint more than one new trustee where only one trustee was originally appointed, or to fill up the original number of trustees where more than two trustees were originally appointed, but, except where only one trustee was originally appointed, and a sole trustee when appointed will be able to give valid receipts for all capital money, a trustee shall not be discharged from his trust unless there will be either a trust corporation[14] or at least two persons[15] to act as trustees to perform the trust; and

(d) any assurance or thing requisite for vesting the trust property, or any part thereof, in a sole trustee, or jointly in the persons who are the trustees, shall be executed or done.

8–06   (2)   Nothing in this Act shall authorise the appointment of a sole trustee, not being a trust corporation where the trustee, when appointed, would not be able to give valid receipts for all capital money arising under the trust.

---

[12] In *Re Stoneham's Settlement Trusts* [1953]Ch. 59, X and Y were the trustees of a settlement. Y remained out of the United Kingdom for a period longer than 12 months. X executed a deed retiring from the trust and appointing C and D to be trustees in place of himself and Y. Y challenged the validity of the new appointments on the ground that he was entitled to participate in making them. Danckwerts J. rejected his contention, first because he had been validly removed from the trust owing to his continuous absence from the United Kingdom for more than 12 months, even though the removal might have been against his will, and secondly because he was not a "continuing trustee" within the meaning of s.36(8) of the Act of 1925. He was not a "refusing or retiring" trustee but a trustee who had been compulsorily removed from the trust and so his concurrence in the new appointments could be dispensed with: *Re Coates to Parsons* (1886) 34 Ch.D. 370 explained.

[13] As amended by the Mental Health Act 1983, s.148 and Sched. 4, para. 4.

[14] See limited meaning of "trust corporation" para. 8–36 *infra*.

[15] "Persons" replaced "individuals" under Trusts of Land and Appointment of Trustees Act 1996 Schedule 3 para. 3 (12).

It should be noted that the power of appointment of trustees is a fiduciary power[16] exercisable by the current trustees having due regard to the interests of the trust and of the conflicting interests of the beneficiaries. Indeed, the trustees' function is a paternalistic one requiring them to protect the beneficiaries from themselves.[17] Thus, before 1996 if the beneficiaries were all of full capacity and between them absolutely entitled they could not compel the trustees under section 36 to appoint their nominee: the trustees were entitled to exercise their independent judgment.[18] All that the beneficiaries could do was put an end to the existing settlement under the rule in *Saunders v. Vautier*[19] and then create a new settlement of which, as settlors, they were be able to appoint new trustees—but this had fiscal disadvantages.

However, after section 19 of the Trusts of Land and Appointment of Trustees Act 1996 if all the beneficiaries are ascertained and of full age and capacity they have a right to require the trustees to retire and to direct the trustees to appoint specified persons to be new trustees, such right not existing where a person nominated in the trust instrument (and not the current trustees) has the power to appoint new trustees.[20]

Appointment of foreign trustees

The provision in Trustee Act 1925, s.36(1) which enables a trustee **8–07** who remains out of the United Kingdom for more than 12 months to be replaced does not make persons resident abroad ineligible to be appointed as trustees, as held by Pennycuick V.-C. in *Re Whitehead's W.T.*[21] However, while accepting that the appointment of non-resident trustees had been a proper valid one in the case before him, he went on to say that in the absence of special circumstances (e.g. the beneficiaries having taken up permanent residence in a foreign country where the newly-appointed trustees reside) the appointment of non-residents was improper (though neither void nor illegal) so that the court would be likely to interfere at the instance of the beneficiaries.[22]

This approach is now out of date where the trustees are exercising **8–08** their discretion to appoint foreign trustees and are merely seeking the declaratory authorisation of the court for their own protection. In *Richard v. Mackay*[23] Millett J. stated:

> "The appropriateness is for the trustees to decide, and different minds may have different views on what is appropriate in particular circumstances. Certainly, in the conditions of today when one can have an

---

[16] Indeed, even if the power of appointing new trustees is reserved to the settlor while alive it will be presumed to be a fiduciary power: *IRC v. Schroder* [1983] STC 480; *Re Osiris Trustees Ltd* [2000] W.T.L.R. 933.

[17] *Head v. Gould* [1898] 2 Ch. 250.

[18] *Re Brockbank* [1948] Ch. 206.

[19] See *infra*, para. 9–154.

[20] Section 19(1)(a). Section 19 is inapplicable to a pre-Act trust if the settlor subsequently executes a deed stating it is to be inapplicable: s. 21(6).

[21] [1971] 1 W.L.R. 833.

[22] It thus seems that the appointment is voidable by the beneficiaries: the Revenue will have no *locus standi* to object unless the appointment was void as part of a criminal conspiracy to defraud the Revenue.

[23] (1997) ll Trust L. I. (1) 22 noted by R. Bramwell Q.C. in (1990) 1 O.T.P.R. 1 and followed in *Re Beatty's W.T. (No 2)* (1997) 11 Trust L.I(3) 77.

international family with international interests and where they are as likely to make their home in one country as in another and as likely to choose one jurisdiction as another for the investment of their capital, I doubt that the language of Sir John Pennycuick is really in tune with the times. In my judgment, where the trustees retain their discretion, as they do in the present case, the court should need to be satisfied only that the proposed transaction is not so inappropriate that no reasonable trustee could entertain it."

8–09   Thus, the trustees (in case United Kingdom exchange control was reintroduced) could properly transfer part of the trust fund to the trustees of a trust to be established in Bermuda with Bermudan resident trustees, Bermuda having a stable English system of law and very experienced corporate trustees, even though the beneficiaries had no connection with Bermuda. Although the proposal was not to appoint new trustees of an existing trust nothing turns on the distinction, as recognised in *Re Whitehead's W.T.*[24]

However, Millett J. contrasted cases where the court is asked to exercise a discretion of its own (*e.g.* under the Variation of Trusts Act 1958[25] or s.41[26] of the Trustee Act 1925) with cases where the trustees are exercising their own discretion. In the former situation the applicants have to make out a positive case for the court's exercise of its discretion "and the court is unlikely to assist them where the scheme is nothing more than a device to avoid tax and has no other advantages of any kind."

8–10   Tax-saving is, of course, a proper consideration for trustees[27] and where it is clear that the proposed transaction is not so inappropriate that no reasonable trustee could entertain it the appointment of foreign trustees can now proceed without seeking any confirmation from the court.

The foreign trust corporation trap

Under Trustee Act 1925, s.37(1)(c) "a trustee shall not be discharged from his trust unless there will be either a trust corporation or at least two persons to act as trustees to perform the trust." It is important to notice that the broader expression "persons" (including companies) has replaced "individuals" and that "trust corporation" cannot cover a company that is not incorporated in a Member State of the European Community.[28] If a sole corporate trustee is appointed then the purportedly replaced trustees remain as trustees if such trustee does not rank as a "trust corporation."[29]

---

[24] [1971] 1 W.L.R. 833 at 838.
[25] See *infra*, para. 9–164, *Re Weston's Settlements* [1969] 1 Ch. 223, though in *Re Chamberlain* (1976) 126 New L.J. 1034 the Court approved Guernsey trustees where the primary beneficiaries were domiciled in France and the remaindermen in Indonesia.
[26] See *infra*, at para. 8–13.
[27] [1971] 1 W.L.R. 833 at 839.
[28] See Trustee Act 1925, s.68(18) and at para. 8–36.
[29] *Eg. Adams & Company International Trustees Ltd. v. Theodore Goddard* (2000) 2 I.T.E.L.R. 634, [2000] W.T.L.R. 349.

However, it seems that section 37(1)(c) is subject to express contrary **8–11**
intention so that the trust instrument can expressly authorise the
discharge of trustees from the trusts by replacing them with the
appointment as sole trustee of a corporation ranking as a trust corporation by the law of the State of its incorporation, except for trust property
consisting of land in England and Wales.[30] After all, a valid receipt for
the proceeds of sale of such land can only be given by a trust corporation
or two persons acting as trustees.[31]

II. APPOINTMENT BY THE COURT

The court has power to appoint new trustees under section 41[32] of the **8–12**
Trustee Act 1925, *infra*, but application should not be made to the court
where the power of appointing new trustees contained in section 36(1) of
the Act, *supra*, can be exercised: *Re Gibbon's Trusts*.[33] The principles
which guide the court in making an appointment are set out in *Re
Tempest*, *infra*. If non-resident trustees are to be appointed the beneficiaries must usually[34] have a real and substantial connection with the
country where the proposed trustees are resident.

The Trustee Act 1925

Section 41—(1)   The court, may, whenever it is expedient to appoint a new
trustee or new trustees, and it is found inexpedient, difficult or impracticable so
to do without the assistance of the court, make an order appointing a new trustee
or trustees either in substitution for or in addition to any existing trustee or
trustees, or although there is no existing trustee.

In particular and without prejudice to the generality of the foregoing **8–13**
provision, the court may make an order appointing a new trustee in substitution
for a trustee who is incapable, by reason of mental disorder within the meaning
of the Mental Health Act 1983, of exercising his functions as trustee, or is a
bankrupt, or is a corporation which is in liquidation or has been dissolved.

RE TEMPEST

Court of Appeal in Chancery (1866) L.R. 1 Ch. 485; 35 L.J.Ch. 632; 14
L.T. 688; 12 Jur.(N.S.) 539; 14 W.R. 850 (Turner and Knight-Bruce L.JJ.)
TURNER L.J.: " In making such appointments the court acts upon and exercises **8–14**
its discretion; and this, no doubt, is generally true; but the discretion which the
court has and exercises in making such appointments is not, as I conceive, a mere

---

[30] Trustee Act 1925, ss.69(2), 71(3); *London Regional Transport Pension Fund Trust Co. v. Hatt* [1993]
O.P. L.R. 227, 260.

[31] *ibid.* s.14(2), (3); Law of Property Act 1925, s.27(2).

[32] Under the section a trustee may be displaced against his will: *Re Henderson* [1940] Ch. 764. The
section authorises removal of trustees by replacement but not otherwise: *Re Harrison's S.T.* [1965] 3
All E.R. 795 at 799.

[33] (1882) 30 W.R. 287; 45 L.T. 756. Otherwise, if it is uncertain whether the power under s.36(1) of the
Act is exercisable: *Re May's Will Trusts* [1941] Ch. 109.

[34] In *Re Chamberlain* [1976] 126 New Law Jo. 1034 (reported in article by J. B. Morcom) the court
approved Guernsey trustees where the beneficiaries were domiciled and resident some in France some
in Indonesia. See *supra.* paras 8–07 to 8–09.

arbitrary discretion, but a discretion in the exercise of which the court is, and ought to be, guided by some general rules and principles, and, in my opinion, the difficulty which the court has to encounter in these cases lies not so much in ascertaining the rules and principles by which it ought to be guided, as in applying those rules and principles to the varying circumstances of each particular case. The following rules and principles may, I think, safely be laid down as applying to all cases of appointments by the court of new trustees.

"First, the court will have regard to the wishes of the persons by whom the trust has been created, if expressed in the instrument creating the trust, or clearly to be collected from it.[35] I think this rule may be safely laid down, because if the author of the trust has in terms declared that a particular person, or a person filling a particular character, should not be a trustee of the instrument, there cannot, as I apprehend, be the least doubt that the court would not appoint to the office a person whose appointment was so prohibited, and I do not think that upon a question of this description any distribution can be drawn between express declarations and demonstrated intention. The analogy of the course which the court pursued in the appointment of guardians affords, I think, some support to this rule. The court in those cases attends to the wishes of the parents, however informally they may be expressed.

8–15   "Another rule which may, I think, safely be laid down is this—that the court will not appoint a person to be trustee with a view to the interest of some of the persons interested under the trust, in opposition either to the wishes of the testator or to the interests of others of the *cestuis que trust*. I think so for this reason, that it is of the essence of the duty of every trustee to hold an even hand between the parties interested under the trust. Every trustee is in duty bound to look to the interests of all, and not of any particular member or class of members of his *cestuis que trust*.

"A third rule which, I think, may safely be laid down is that the court in appointing a trustee will have regard to the question whether his appointment will promote or impede the execution of the trust, for the very purpose of the appointment is that the trust may be better carried into execution . . .[36]

8–16   "There cannot, I think, be any doubt that the court ought not to appoint a trustee whose appointment will impede the due execution of the trust; but, on the other hand, if the continuing or surviving trustee refuses to act with a trustee who may be proposed to be appointed . . . I think it would be going too far to say that the court ought, on that ground alone, to refuse to appoint the proposed trustee; for this would, as suggested in the argument, be to give the continuing or surviving trustee a veto upon the appointment of the new trustee. In such a case, I think it must be the duty of the court to inquire and ascertain whether the objection of the surviving or continuing trustee is well founded or not, and to act or refuse to act upon it accordingly. . . ."[37]

---

[35] See also *Re Badger* [1915] W.N. 166; 84 L.J.Ch. 567: the court will not appoint an additional trustee against the wishes of a sole trustee appointed by the settlor, in the absence of allegations against his honesty, even at the unanimous request of the beneficiaries of full capacity (not between them absolutely entitled to the whole beneficial interest so as to be able to invoke s. 19 of the 1996 Trusts of Land and Appointment of Trustees Act), except where land is trust property since a valid receipt cannot be given by less than two trustees or a trust corporation: Law of Property Act 1925, s.27(2).

[36] A person will thus not be appointed if so to do would place him in a position in which his interest and duty would be likely to conflict: *Re Parsons* [1940] Ch. 973.

[37] The court may postpone an order for appointment of new trustees in order to protect the interests of the existing trustees, *e.g. Re Pauling S.T. (No. 2)* [1963] Ch. 576.

III. Appointment indirectly by Beneficiaries

Trusts of Land and Appointment of Trustees Act 1996

19.—(1) This section applies in the case of a trust where—

(a) there is no person nominated for the purpose of appointing new trustees **8–17**
by the instrument, if any, creating the trust, and

(b) the beneficiaries under the trust are of full age and capacity and (taken
together) are absolutely entitled to the property subject to the trust.

(2) The beneficiaries may give a direction or directions of either or both of
the following descriptions—

(a) a written direction to a trustee or trustees to retire from the trust, and

(b) a written direction to the trustees or trustee for the time being (or, if
there are none, to the personal representative of the last person who was
a trustee) to appoint by writing to be a trustee or trustees the person or
persons specified in the direction.

(3) Where—

(a) a trustee has been given a direction under subsection (2)(a),   **8–18**

(b) reasonable arrangements have been made for the protection of any rights
of his in connection with the trust,

(c) after he has retired there will be either a trust corporation or at least two
persons to act as trustees to perform the trust, and

(d) either another person is to be appointed to be a new trustee on his
retirement (whether in compliance with a direction under subsection
(2)(b) or otherwise) or the continuing trustees by deed consent to his
retirement,

he shall make a deed declaring his retirement and shall be deemed to have
retired and be discharged from the trust.

(4) Where a trustee retires under subsection (3) he and the continuing
trustees (together with any new trustee) shall (subject to any arrangements for
the protection of his rights) do anything necessary to vest the trust property in
the continuing trustees (or the continuing and new trustees).

(5) This section has effect subject to the restrictions imposed by the Trustee **8–19**
Act 1925 on the number of trustees.

20.—(1) This section applies where—

(a) a trustee is incapable by reason of mental disorder of exercising his
functions as trustee,

(b) there is no person who is both entitled and willing and able to appoint a
trustee in place of him under section 36(1) of the Trustee Act 1925, and

(c) the beneficiaries under the trust are of full age and capacity and (taken
together) are absolutely entitled to the property subject to the trust.

(2) The beneficiaries may give to—

(a) a receiver of the trustee,

(b) an attorney acting for him under the authority of a power of attorney created by an instrument which is registered under section 6 of the Enduring Powers of Attorney Act 1985, or

(c) a person authorised for the purpose by the authority having jurisdiction under Part VII of the Mental Health Act 1983.

a written direction to appoint by writing the person or persons specified in the direction to be a trustee or trustees in place of the incapable trustee.

8–20   21.—(1) For the purposes of section 19 or 20 a direction is given by beneficiaries if—

(a) a single direction is jointly given by all of them, or

(b) (subject to subsection (2)) a direction is given by each of them (whether solely or jointly with one or more, but not all, of the others),

and none of them by writing withdraws the direction given by him before it has been complied with.

(2)   Where more than one direction is given each must specify for appointment or retirement the same person or persons.

(3)   Subsection (7) of section 36 of the Trustee Act 1925 (powers of trustees appointed under that section) applies to a trustee appointed under section 19 or 20 as if he were appointed under that section.

(4)   A direction under section 19 or 20 must not specify a person or persons for appointment if the appointment of that person or those persons would be in contravention of section 35(1) of the Trustee Act 1925 or section 24(1) of the Law of Property Act 1925 (requirements as to identity of trustees).

(5)   Sections 19 or 20 do not apply in relation to a trust created by a disposition in so far as provision that they do not apply is made by the disposition.

8–21   (6)   Sections 19 and 20 do not apply in relation to a trust created before the commencement of this Act by a disposition in so far as provision to the effect that they do not apply is made by a deed executed—

(a) in a case in which the trust was created by one person and he is of full capacity, by that person, or

(b) in a case in which the trust was created by more than one person, by such of the persons who created the trust as are alive and of full capacity.

(7)   A deed executed for the purpose of subsection (6) is irrevocable.

(8)   Where a deed is executed for the purposes of subsection (6)—

(a) it does not affect anything done before its execution to comply with a direction under section 19 or 20, but

(b) a direction under section 19 or 20 which has been given but not complied with before its execution shall cease to have effect.

IV. Protection of a Purchaser of Land of which New Trustees Have Been Appointed

The Trustee Act 1925

8–22   Section 38.—(1) A statement, contained in any instrument coming into operation after the commencement of this Act by which a new trustee is appointed for any purpose connected with land, to the effect that a trustee has remained out of the United Kingdom for more than twelve months or refuses or is unfit to act, or is incapable of acting, or that he is not entitled to a beneficial interest in the trust property in possession, shall, in favour of a purchaser of a legal estate, be conclusive evidence of the matter stated.

(2) In favour of such purchaser any appointment of a new trustee depending on that statement, and any vesting declaration, express or implied, consequent on the appointment, shall be valid.

Where an appointment is invalid the general rule is that the old trustee remains trustee with the powers and liabilities of a trustee[38] though the invalidly appointed new trustee will become liable as trustee *de son tort* if he intermeddles with the property.[39]

V. VESTING OF TRUST PROPERTY IN NEW OR CONTINUING TRUSTEES

The Trustee Act 1925

Section 40.—(1) Where by a deed a new trustee is appointed to perform any **8–23** trust, then—

(a) if the deed contains a declaration by the appointor to the effect that any estate or interest in any land subject to the trust, or in any chattel so subject, or the right to recover or receive any debt or other thing in action so subject, shall vest in the persons who by virtue of the deed become or are the trustees for performing the trust, the deed shall operate,[40] without any conveyance or assignment, to vest in those persons as joint tenants and for the purposes of the trust the estate interest or right to which the declaration relates; and

(b) if the deed is made after the commencement of this Act and does not contain such a declaration, the deed shall, subject to any express provision to the contrary therein contained, operate as if it had contained such a declaration by the appointor extending to all the estates interests and rights with respect to which a declaration could have been made.

(2) Where by a deed a retiring trustee is discharged under the statutory **8–24** power without a new trustee being appointed, then—

(a) if the deed contains such a declaration as aforesaid by the retiring and continuing trustees, and by the other person, if any, empowered to appoint trustees, the deed shall, without any conveyance or assignment, operate to vest in the continuing trustees alone, as joint tenants, and for

---

[38] *Adams & Company International Trustees Ltd v. Theodore Goddard* (2000) 2 I.T.E.L.R. 634, [2000] W.T.L.R. 389.

[39] *Pearce v. Pearce* (1856) 22 Beav. 248.

[40] Even when the estate, interest or right is not vested in the person making the appointment. *cf.* s.9 of the Law of Property Act 1925; but not as in *Re King's W.T.* [1964] Ch. 542, *supra*, at para. 1–123, where the legal estate is held by the appointor in his capacity as personal representative, not having executed an assent in his favour as trustee. Entry on the register is needed for registered land. The practice is for the current registered proprietor(s) to execute a transfer to the new trustees as new registered proprietors: this saves the Registrar from having to check on the validity of the deed of appointment and then altering the register under the Land Registration Act 1925, s.47.

the purposes of the trust, the estate, interest, or right to which the declaration relates; and

(b) if the deed is made after the commencement of this Act and does not contain such a declaration, the deed shall, subject to any express provision to the contrary therein contained, operate as if it had contained such a declaration by such persons as aforesaid extending to all the estates, interests and rights with respect to which a declaration could have been made.

8–25   (3) An express vesting declaration, whether made before or after the commencement of this Act, shall, notwithstanding that the estate, interest or right to be vested is not expressly referred to, and provided that the other statutory requirements were or are complied with, operate and be deemed always to have operated (but without prejudice to any express provision to the contrary contained in the deed of appointment on discharge) to vest in the persons respectively referred to in subsections (1) and (2) of this section, as the case may require, such estates, interests and rights as are capable of being and ought to be vested in those persons.

(4) This section does not extend—

(a) to land conveyed by way of mortgage for securing money subject to the trust, except land conveyed on trust for securing debentures or debenture stock;

(b) to land held under a lease which contains any covenant, condition or agreement against assignment or disposing of the land without licence or consent, unless, prior to the execution of the deed containing expressly or impliedly the vesting declaration, the requisite licence or consent has been obtained, or unless, by virtue of any statute or rule of law, the vesting declaration, express or implied, would not operate as a breach of covenant or give rise to a forfeiture;

(c) to any share, stock, annuity or property which is only transferable in books kept by a company or other body, or in manner directed by or under an Act of Parliament.

8–26   In this subsection "lease" includes an underlease and an agreement for a lease or underlease.

(5) For purposes of registration of the deed in any registry, the person or persons making the declaration expressly or impliedly, shall be deemed the conveying party or parties, and the conveyance shall be deemed to be made by him or them under a power conferred by this Act.

(6) This section applies to deeds of appointment or discharge executed on or after the first day of January, eighteen hundred and eighty-two.

Section 2. Retirement of Trustees

8–27   Where a trustee retires and a new trustee is appointed[41] to fill the vacancy, the retirement and new appointment are effected under section 36(1) of the Trustee Act 1925, *supra*. Where all the beneficiaries require

---

[41] If no one else can be found the Public Trustee will usually be willing to act.

retirement under section 19 of the 1996 Act, the retiring trustee must execute a deed discharging himself or herself under section 19(3). Where a new trustee is not appointed to fill the vacancy, the retirement is effected under section 39, *infra*.

The Trustee Act 1925

Section 39.[42]—(1) Where a trustee is desirous of being discharged from the trust, and after his discharge there will be either a trust corporation or at least two individuals to act as trustees to perform the trust, then, if such trustee as aforesaid by deed declares that he is desirous of being discharged from the trust, and if his co-trustees and such other person, if any, as is empowered to appoint trustees, by deed consent to the discharge of the trustee, and to the vesting in the co-trustees alone of the trust property, the trustee desirous of being discharged shall be deemed to have retired from the trust, and shall, by the deed, be discharged therefrom under this Act, without any new trustee being appointed in his place.

(2) Any assurance or thing requisite for vesting the trust property in the continuing trustees alone shall be executed or done.

Section 3. Disclaimer by Trustees

A person appointed trustee may naturally *disclaim*, for "a man cannot **8–28** have an estate put into him in spite of his teeth." The disclaimer of a trust by a person appointed trustee—

  (i) ought to be in writing (or by deed); but it may be

    (a) oral[43];

    (b) by conduct[44];

    (c) by mere inactivity (it seems)[45];

    (d) signified on behalf of the person appointed trustee by counsel at the Bar[46];

  (ii) must be a disclaimer of the whole trust; it cannot be partial.[47]

If a person is appointed both executor and trustee and he proves the will, he thereby accepts the trust. But if he renounces probate, he does not thereby necessarily disclaim the trust.[48]

---

[42] Independently of statute a trustee may retire (i) under a power of retirement contained in the trust instrument: *Camoys v. Best* (1854) 19 Beav. 414; (ii) by the consent of all the beneficiaries, the latter being of full capacity: *Wilkinson v. Parry* (1828) 4 Russ. 472 at 476; (iii) by authority of the court, to which the trustee has a right to apply to be discharged from the trust; but costs will depend on whether he has reasonable grounds for desiring to be discharged: *Gardiner v. Downes* (1856) 22 Beav. 395; *Barker v. Peile* (1865) 2 Dr. & Sm. 340; *Re Chetwynd* [1902] 1 Ch. 692. Section 39 like s.37(1)(c) is subject to contrary intention *e.g.* if the trust instrument authorises retirement if a non European Union trust corporation remains a trustee: *Adams & Company International Trustee Ltd v. Theodore Goddard* (2000) 2 I.T.E.L.R. 634, [2000] W.T.L.R. 349.

[43] *Bingham v. Clanmorris* (1828) 2 Moll. 253; doubted by Wood V.-C. in *Re Ellison* (1856) 2 Jur. 62.

[44] *Stacey v. Elph* (1883) 1 My. & K. 195; *Re Birchall* (1889) 40 Ch.D. 436.

[45] *Re Clout and Frewer* [1924] 2 Ch. 230.

[46] *Landbroke v. Bleaden* (1852) 16 Jur.(o.s.) 630; *Foster v. Dawber* (1860) 8 W.R. 646.

[47] *Re Lord and Fullerton* [1896] 1 Ch. 228.

[48] *Mucklow v. Fuller* (1821) Jac. 198; *Ward v. Butler* (1824) 2 Moll. 533; Romilly M.R. in *Dix v. Burford* (1854) 19 Beav. 409 at 412.

Section 4. Removal of Trustees

8–29 The trust instrument may confer a power of removal,[49] though if it is conferred on a majority of the trustees and they are not unanimous then a meeting will need to be held.[50] It needs to be borne in mind that the benefit of property passing from the old trustees to the new trustees under section 40 only applies if a new trustee is appointed in place of the old trustee and not if the old trustee is simply removed.

The court has a jurisdiction, independent of statute, to remove trustees (*Letterstedt v. Broers, infra*) and under section 41 on appointing a new trustee it may remove a trustee.[51] On appointment of a new trustee under section 36 the appointors may remove a trustee. If hostility between trustees prevents them from acting unanimously (as they must do unless the trust instrument authorises otherwise) then one or all should be removed and replaced.[52]

In an emergency trustees may be removed on an *ex parte* interlocutory application and a receiver appointed of the trust assets until appointment of new trustees at an *inter partes* hearing.[53]

The Occupational Pensions Regulatory Authority has power under sections 4 to 9 of the Pensions Act 1995 to suspend or remove trustees and appoint new trustees in the case of pension trust schemes, while the Charity Commissioners have similar powers under section 18 of the Charities Act 1993.

LETTERSTEDT v. BROERS

8–30 Privy Council (1884) 9 App.Cas. 371; 51 L.T. 169 (Lord Blackburn, Sir Robert P. Collier, Sir Richard Couch and Sir Arthur Hobhouse)

The Board of Executors of Cape Town were the sole surviving executors and trustees of a will under which the appellant was a beneficiary. The appellant alleged misconduct in the administration of the trust, and claimed that the Board were unfit to be entrusted with the management of the estate and should be removed in favour of a new appointment. The Supreme Court of the Cape of Good Hope had refused the application to remove the Board. The beneficiary appealed successfully.

8–31 LORD BLACKBURN: ". . . The whole of the matters which have been complained of, and the whole that, if this judgment stands, may yet have to be done by the Board, are matters which they had to do, as having accepted the burden of

---

[49] A power of removal, *e.g.* vested in a protector, will be presumed a fiduciary power not to be exercised for the personal benefit of the power-holder but for the beneficiaries as a whole or perhaps even for the benefit of the settlor (although the trust instrument should spell this out): *Von Knierem v. Bermuda Trust Co.* (1994) Butts, O.C.M. Vol. 1 at 116.

[50] *Att.-Gen. v. Scott* (1750) 1 Ves. Sen. 413.

[51] If there is a dispute as to fact then instead of taking out a summons under section 41 a writ should be issued for administration or execution of the trusts invoking the inherent jurisdiction to remove trustees: *Re Henderson* [1940] Ch. 764.

[52] *Re Consigli's Trusts (No. 1)* (1973) 36 D.L.R. (3d) 658. On exercise of court's jurisdiction see *Monty v. Delmo* [1996] 1 VR65 and *Titterton v. Oates* [2001] W.T.L.R. 319.

[53] *Clarke v. Heathfield* (1985) 82 Law Soc.Gaz. 599; [1985] I.C.R. 203.

carrying out the trusts which on the true construction of the will were imposed upon them, and so become trustees. What they had to do as executors merely, such as paying debts, collecting assets, etc., have long ago been over, and by the terms of the compromise the plaintiff cannot now say they have not been done properly. There may be some peculiarity in the Dutch colonial law, which made it proper to make the prayer in the way in which it was done to remove them from the office of executor; if so, it has not been brought to their Lordships' notice; the whole case has been argued here, and, as far as their Lordships can perceive, in the court below, as depending on the principles which should guide an English court of equity when called upon to remove old trustees and substitute new ones. It is not disputed that there is a jurisdiction 'in cases requiring such a remedy,' as is said in Story's *Equity Jurisprudence*, s.1287, but there is very little to be found to guide us in saying what are the cases requiring such a remedy; so little that their Lordships are compelled to have recourse to general principles.

"Story says, section 1289: 'But in cases of positive misconduct, courts of equity **8–32** have no difficulty in interposing to remove trustees who have abused their trust; it is not indeed every mistake or neglect of duty, or inaccuracy of conduct of trustees, which will induce courts of equity to adopt such a course. But the acts or omissions must be such as to endanger the trust property or to show a want of honesty, or a want of proper capacity to execute the duties, or a want of reasonable fidelity.'

"It seems to their Lordships that the jurisdiction which a court of equity has no difficulty in exercising under the circumstances indicated by Story is merely ancillary to its principal duty, to see that the trusts are properly executed. This duty is constantly being performed by the substitution of new trustees in the place of original trustees for a variety of reasons in non-contentious cases. And therefore, though it should appear that the charges of misconduct were either not made out, or were greatly exaggerated, so that the trustee was justified in resisting them, and the court might consider that in awarding costs, yet if satisfied that the continuance of the trustee would prevent the trusts being properly executed, the trustee might be removed. It must always be borne in mind that trustees exist for the benefit of those to whom the creator of the trust has given the trust estate.

"The reason why there is so little to be found in the books on this subject is **8–33** probably that suggested by Mr. Davey in his argument. As soon as all questions of character are as far settled as the nature of the case admits, if it appears clear that the continuance of the trustee would be detrimental to the execution of the trusts, even if for no other reason than that human infirmity would prevent those beneficially interested, or those who act for them, from working in harmony with the trustee, and if there is no reason to the contrary from the intentions of the framer of the trust to give this trustee a benefit or otherwise, the trustee is always advised by his own counsel to resign, and does so. If, without any reasonable ground, he refused to do so, it seems to their Lordships that the court might think it proper to remove him; but cases involving the necessity of deciding this, if they ever arise, do so without getting reported. It is to be lamented that the case was not considered in this light by the parties in the court below, for, as far as their Lordships can see, the Board would have little or no profit from continuing to be trustees, and as such coming into continual conflict with the appellant and her legal advisers, and would probably have been glad to resign, and get out of an onerous and disagreeable position. But the case was not so treated.

8-34   "In exercising so delicate a jurisdiction as that of removing trustees, their Lords do not venture to lay down any general rule beyond the very broad principle above enunciated, that their main guide must be the welfare of the beneficiaries. Probably it is not possible to lay down any more definite rule in a matter so essentially dependent on details often of great nicety.[54] . . .

"It is quite true that friction or hostility between trustees and the immediate possessor of the trust estate is not of itself a reason for the removal of the trustees. But where the hostility is grounded on the mode in which the trust has been administered, where it has been caused wholly or partially by substantial overcharges against the trust estate, it is certainly not to be disregarded.

"Looking, therefore, at the whole circumstances of this very peculiar case, the complete change of position, the unfortunate hostility that has arisen, and the difficult and delicate duties that may yet have to be performed, their Lordships can come to no other conclusion than that it is necessary, for the welfare of the beneficiaries, that the Board should no longer be trustees.

"Probably if it had been put in this way below they would have consented. But for the benefit of the trust they should cease to be trustees, whether they consent or not . . ."

The charge of misconduct was not proved: no costs were awarded.

Section 5. Special Types of Trustee

Custodian trustees[55]

8-35   These are distinct from the usual managing trustees. They hold the trust property and the trust documents of title (*e.g.* title deeds, share certificates) and all sums payable to or out of the income or capital of the trust property are paid to or by them except that dividends and other income derived from the trust property may be paid to such other persons as they direct, *e.g.* the managing trustees or a beneficiary.[56] The day-to-day running of the trust is left to the managing trustees whose instructions must be obeyed by the custodian trustee unless aware that they involve a breach of trust.[57] The following may be appointed custodian trustees: the Public Trustee, the Official Custodian for Charities and trust corporations.[58] A trustee cannot be custodian trustee and managing trustee of the same trust.[59]

---

[54] "You must find," said Warrington J. in *Re Wrightson* [1908] 1 Ch. 789 at 803, "something which induces the court to think either that the trust property will not be safe, or that the trust will not properly be executed in the interests of the beneficiaries."

[55] Generally see S. G. Maurice (1960) 24 Conv.(N.S.) 196; P. Pearce (1972) 36 Conv.(N.S.) 260–261; Keeton's *Modern Developments in the Law of Trusts*, Chap. 3.

[56] Public Trustee Act, s.4(2).

[57] *ibid.* Exceptionally, in the case of an authorised unit trust, the trustee, which must be a corporate E.U. trustee independent of the manager of the unit trust, has to take reasonable care to ensure that the manager acts within its powers, keeps adquate records and manages the scheme in accordance with the Financial Service Authority's Regulations for Collective Investment Schemes.

[58] Public Trustee Rules 1912 r. 30, as substituted by the Public Trustee (Custodian Trustees) Rules 1975, S.I. 1975 No. 1189 and amended by S.I. 1976 No. 836, S.I. 1981 No. 358, S.I. 1984 No. 109, S.I. 1985. No. 132; S.I. 1987 No. 1891.

[59] *Forster v. Williams Deacon's Bank Ltd* [1935] Ch. 359; *Arning v. James* [1936] Ch. 58.

Trust corporations

A trust corporation can act alone where otherwise two trustees would be **8–36** required, *e.g.* receipt of capital moneys on a sale of land. The following are trust corporations[60]: the Public Trustee, the Treasury Solicitor, the Official Solicitor, certain charitable corporations and corporations either appointed by the court in any particular case or entitled to act as custodian trustees under the Public Trustee Act 1906. Corporations so entitled include those constituted under United Kingdom law or the law of an EU state and having a place of business in the United Kingdom and empowered to undertake trust business, which are either incorporated by special Act or Royal Charter or else registered United Kingdom or other European Union state companies with an issued capital of at least £250,000 (or its foreign equivalent) of which at least £100,000 (or its equivalent) has been paid up in cash.

The Public Trustee[61] in the Official Solicitor's Office

The Public Trustee was established in 1906 as a corporation sole available to deal with the difficulty persons might have in finding someone willing to act as trustee especially of low value trusts. However, it cannot accept charitable trusts, insolvent estates or, normally, trusts involving the carrying on of a business. It can act as personal representative, ordinary managing trustee, custodian trustee or judicial trustee. Since April 1, 2001 the Official Solicitor is also the Public Trustee.

Judicial trustee

The Judicial Trustees Act 1896 established judicial trustees in order **8–37** "to provide a middle course in cases where the administration of the estate by the ordinary trustees had broken down and it was not desired to put the estate to the expense of a full administration" by the court.[62] Judicial trustees can only be appointed by the court upon a claim in existing proceedings or an original part 8 claim. Trouble-shooting accountants are often appointed to sort out the muddled situation. The judicial trustee is an officer of the court so that he can at any time obtain the court's directions as to the way in which he should act without the necessity of a formal application by summons though he has as much authority as ordinary trustees to act on his own initiative, and, for example, compromise claims.[63]

---

[60] See *supra.* n.58 and Law of Property Act 1925 s.205(1)(xxviii); Trustee Act 1925, s.68(18); Law of Property (Amendment) Act 1925, s.3 (including trustees in bankruptcy).

[61] The Hutton Committee of Enquiry into the Public Trustee Office (1972) Cmnd. 4913 recommended that it be wound up and merged with the Official Solicitor's Department but the government did not take any action on the Committee's recommendations. By Public Trustee and Administration of Funds Act 1986 the Public Trustee was given the powers of a judge of the Court of Protection concerned with mental patients' property and affairs, but its financial management of trusts and mental patients' estates came in for much criticism by the National Audit office so that since April 1, 2001 the mental health functions were taken from the Public Trustee by the Public Guardian's Office.

[62] *per* Jenkins J. in *Re Ridsdell* [1947] Ch. 597, 605.

[63] *Re Ridsdell* [1947] Ch. 597.

Can there be a controlling trustee?

The basic position is that all trustees are equal and must act unanimously, trusteeship being a joint office *par excellence*, so one trustee cannot be "controlling" or "managing" trustee whom the other trustees can safely[64] leave on his or her own to deal with all trust matters. However, as where two trustees are needed to give a good receipt for capital moneys derived from land, the trust instrument can effectively provide for T2 always to do whatever T1 decides without being liable in any way for any breach of trust unless T2 was aware that he was assisting T1 to commit a breach of trust.[65] Similarly, there is no reason why a trust instrument might not effectively provide for T1 to have a casting vote if T1 and T2 cannot agree on a trust matter.[66]

Section 6. Trusts do not Fail for want of Trustees

8–39   If the testator failed to appoint trustees or if the trustees appointed refuse or are unable to act or have ceased to exist the trust does not fail[67] (unless its operation was conditional upon a specific trustee undertaking the trust[68]) nor does if fail if the intended trustees disclaim ownership of shares or land secretly transferred into their names by a settlor. The property or the beneficial interest therein remains in the settlor or the personal representatives of the testator to be held upon the trusts of the settlement or the will as the case may be.[69]

On the death of a sole or sole surviving trustee the trust property vests in his personal representatives subject to the trusts and by the Trustee Act 1925, s.18(2), they are capable of exercising or performing any power or trust which the deceased trustee could have exercised or performed. They are not bound to accept the position and duties of trustees and may exercise their power of appointing new trustees under s.36 with a right to payment of the costs thereof from the trust moneys.[70] If need be the court may appoint new trustees under section 41[71] or itself execute the trust.[72]

8–40   Where a deceased trustee's powers have devolved upon his personal representative who then dies (without having appointed new trustees) it seems that if he accepted the trustee role under s.18(2) then he should

---

[64] It is a breach of trust to leave matters to a co-trustee: all co-trustees must positively involve themselves with all trust matters; see at para. 10–12 *infra*.

[65] *Re Arnott* [1899] I.R. 201.

[66] After all, the settlor can provide for trustees, to act by majority decisions, but if only an even number of trustees subsists then the chairman of the trustees is to have a casting vote where the trustees are equally divided.

[67] *Re Willis* [1921] 1 Ch. 44; *Re Armitage* [1972] Ch. 438; *Re Morrison* (1967) 111 S.J. 758.

[68] *Re Lysaght* [1966] 1 Ch. 191.

[69] *Mallot v. Wilson* [1903] 2 Ch. 494, accepted as good law by the Court of Appeal in *Harris v. Sharp* (unreported March 21, 1989). P. Matthews [1981] *Conv.* 141 contends that disclaimer of an *inter vivos* transfer to a trustee should make the transfer void and the trust fail; but one may treat the transferor as constructive trustee by *Re Rose* [1952] Ch. 499 principles and *Tett v. Phoenix* [1984] B.C.L.C. 599: *supra*, para. 4–06. See also *Standing v. Bowring* (1885) 31 Ch.D. 282 at 288. On the unilateral and bilateral nature of gifts see J. Hill (2001) 117 LQR 127.

[70] *Re Benett* [1906] 1 Ch. 216.

[71] *Jones v. Jones* (1874) 31 L.T. 538.

[72] *McPhail v. Doulton* [1971] A.C. 424 at 457, *supra*, at para. 3–131; (A. J. Hawkins) (1967) 31 (Conv. (N.S.) 117).

himself be treated as a trustee for his powers to devolve under s.18(2) to his own personal representative.[73] If he was executor of the deceased trustee and himself appointed an executor then his executor would be executor by representation of the trustee[74] and so have the s.18(2) powers in any event.

---

[73] P. W. Smith (1977) 41 Conv. 423; *Williams on Title* (4th ed.), p. 490.
[74] Administration of Estates Act 1925, s.7.

Chapter 9

THE OBLIGATIONS OF TRUSTEESHIP

Section 1. General Introduction

9–01 THE office of trustee is onerous. Equity, supplemented by the Trustee
Act 2000, imposes many duties upon a trustee. A trustee has two roles to
fulfil: a distributive role, concerned with distributing income and capital
to appropriate beneficiaries, and an administrative or managerial role,
concerned with safeguarding and developing the value of the trust fund.

In exercising these roles, a trustee is subject to the proscriptive
obligation of exhibiting undivided loyalty to the beneficiaries and to
prescriptive equitable duties of skill and care. A trustee is under
fiduciary obligations not to act in bad faith and not (without authorisation) to profit from the trust nor place himself in a position where his or
her duty as trustee may conflict with his or her personal interest nor to
act for his or her own benefit or benefit of a third party.[1] As Millett L.J.
states[2]:

> "The various obligations of a fiduciary merely reflect different
> aspects of his core duties of loyalty and fidelity. Breach of fiduciary
> obligation, therefore, connotes disloyalty or infidelity. Mere incom-
> petence is not enough."

Incompetence is a breach of the equitable duty of skill and care in the
administration or management of the trust property.

9–02 In carrying out the distributive role the trustee does not have to afford
individual beneficiaries or objects of powers the opportunity to make
their case[3] but must ensure that trust money or other property is not
distributed to a person who is not entitled to benefit under the trust
instrument[4] and must exercise any discretionary power in responsible
fashion only for the purposes intended by the settlor (not capriciously or
perverse to any sensible expectation of the settlor),[5] while taking account
of all relevant factors and ignoring all irrelevant factors, so that any
decision cannot be vitiated on the basis that the trustee would have

---

[1] *Bristol & West B.S. v. Mothew* [1998] Ch. 1, 18.
[2] *ibid.*
[3] *R v. Charity Commissioners, ex parte Baldwin* [2001] W.T.L.R. 137; *Re B* [1987] 2 All E.R. 475, 478.
[4] Equity does not allow the trustee's accounts to show that he transferred property to X not entitled to
receive such property; the property is treated as still trust property in the accounts, so the trustee must
replace the property wrongfully transferred to X: see para. 10–04 *infra.*
[5] *Re Hay's S.T.* [1981] 3 All E.R. 786, 792; *Re Beatty's W.T.* [1990] 3 All E.R. 844, 846; *McPhail v.
Doulton* [1971] A.C. 424, 449, *Re Manisty's Settlement* [1994] Ch. 17, 26.

decided otherwise if he had taken account of all relevant factors and ignored all irrelevant factors.[6] There is a modern trend[7] to introduce issues of public law *Wednesbury*[8] unreasonableness into the private law of trusts where application of the traditional principles just described seems to cover the same ground and so ought to make it unnecessary to ask the question "is this decision so unreasonable that no properly informed body of trustees could have reached such decision?" in which event the decision can be set aside for the body to reconsider when it is properly informed.

In administering and managing the trust property Lord Watson said,[9] **9–03** "As a general rule, the law requires of a trustee no higher degree of diligence than a man of ordinary prudence would exercise in the management of his own private affairs". However, in the investment sphere Lindley L.J. stated[10] in a much-endorsed[11] passage, "The duty of a trustee is not to take such care only as a prudent man would take if he had only himself to consider; the duty rather is to take such care as an ordinary prudent man would take if he were minded to make an investment for the benefit of other people for whom he felt morally bound to provide". With the advent of professional paid trustees and trust companies it became established that a higher degree of care was expected of them so that they were to be judged on the standards they professed and which had led to their appointment.[12] This equitable duty of care has now been replaced by a statutory duty of care covering most, but not all, activities of trustees from February 1, 2001.

Section 1 of the Trustee Act 2000 lays down "the duty of care" applicable to the activities mentioned in schedule 1 relating to investments, using agents, nominees and custodians, compounding liabilities, insuring, valuing and auditing—but the duty does not apply so far as it appears from the trust instrument that it is not meant to apply.[13] Thus, as concerns such activities, a trustee:

> "must exercise such care and skill as is reasonable in the circum- **9–04** stances, having regard in particular—
>
> (a) to any special knowledge or experience that he has or holds himself out as having, and
> (b) if he acts as a trustee in the course of a business or profession, to any special knowledge or experience that it is reasonable to expect of a person acting in the course of that kind of business or profession".

---

[6] *Re Hastings-Bass* [1975] Ch. 25, 41; *Mettoy Pensions Trustees Ltd v. Evans* [1991] 2 All E.R. 513, 553.
[7] *Edge v. Pensions Ombudsman* [1998] Ch. 512, 534, on appeal [1999] 4 All E.R. 546, 569–570, *Scott v. National Trust* [1998] 2 All E.R. 705, 718.
[8] *Associated Provincial Picture House v. Wednesbury Corporation* [1948] 1 K.B. 223.
[9] *Learoyd v. Whiteley* (1887) 12 A.C. 727, 733.
[10] *Re Whiteley* (1886) 33 Ch.D. 347, 355.
[11] *e.g. Cowan v. Scargill* [1985] Ch. 270, 289, *Nestle v. National Westminster Bank* [1994] 1 All E.R. 118, 126, 140.
[12] *Bartlett v. Barclays Bank Trust Co* [1980] 1 All E.R. 139, 152, Lord Nicholls (1995) 9 Trust L.I. 71, 73.
[13] Trustee Act 2000 Schedule 1, para. 7.

It will be noted that (a) involves a subjective element relating to the trustee personally, while (b) objectively relates to persons engaged in the trustee's business or profession generally. In (b) there is a distinction between a trustee who carries on trust business in the course of practising generally as a solicitor or accountant or financial adviser and a trustee who specialises in trust work in the course of the specific business of being a trustee: the latter will normally be governed by a higher standard.

If the appropriate standard of care is honestly taken but loss occurs the trustee will not be liable (*e.g.* for the dramatic depreciation of a trust holding in apparently safe companies like Rolls-Royce or Polly Peck) nor will he be liable for profits that the trust would have made if he had been more dynamic and skilful (*e.g.* in more actively selling and buying shares or in manipulating a significant minority shareholding in a private company so as either to sell at a very high price or to take over the company and strip it of its assets). In making decisions (*e.g.* on selling or buying particular investments) that are alleged to be negligent breaches of trust the position of a trustee is equated[14] with that of other professionals facing a claim for professional negligence who can only be "liable for damage caused by their advice, acts or omissions in the course of their professional work which no member of the profession who was reasonably well-informed and competent would have given or done or omitted to do."[15]

9–05   If any doubts arise then the trustee should apply to the Chancery Division for directions. As a last resort the trustee may under section 61 of the Trustee Act be excused liability wholly or partly for breach of trust if he acted "honestly and reasonably, and ought fairly to be excused for the breach of trust *and* for omitting to obtain the directions of the court in the matter in which he committed such breach." A paid trustee will be much less likely to be excused than an unpaid trustee.[16]

9–06   Where there is more than one trustee, as is usually the case, each trustee is personally responsible for the acts performed in the administration of the trust and so should personally consider each act requiring to be done: it is no defence that one was a "sleeping trustee" blindly relying on one's co-trustees.[17] It is not possible to delegate a trustee's duties except where authorised under the trust instrument or by statute

---

[14] *Wight v. Olswang (No 2)* (2000) 2 I.T.E.L.R 689, [2000] W.T.L.R. 783, and on appeal [2001] W.L.T.R. 291, applying *dicta* in *Bristol & West B.S. v. Mothew* [1998] Ch. 1, 17–18.

[15] Per Lord Diplock in *Saif Ali v. Sydney Mitchell & Co* [1980] A.C. 198, 218, applied in *Wight v. Olswang (No 2) supra.*

[16] *Re Rosenthal* [1972] 1 W.L.R. 1273; *Re Pauling's S.T.* [1964] Ch. 303 at 338 and 339; *National Trustee Co. of Australasia v. General Finance Co.* [1905] A.C. 373. See *infra*, para. 10–78.

[17] *Bahin v. Hughes* (1886) 31 Ch.D. 390; *Munch v. Cockerell* (1840) 5 Myl. & Cr. 178; *Re Turner* [1897] 1 Ch. 536; *Head v. Gould* [1898] 2 Ch. 250. There is no automatic vicarious liability for co-trustees' breaches, *e.g. Re Lucking's W.T.* [1968] 1 W.L.R. 866.

which from February 1, 2001,[18] confers broad powers of delegation of managerial, but not distributive, functions. The trustees must act unanimously except where the settlement or the court otherwise directs or, in the case of charitable trusts or pension trusts, where the trustees may act by a majority.[19] It follows that if there is a trust to sell with power to postpone sale then the power is only effective so long as all trustees wish to postpone sale: once one wishes a sale the trust to sell must be carried out, all the trustees being under a duty to sell so long as the power to postpone sale is not effectively exercised unanimously.[20] *Mutatis mutandis* the position is the same where the trust is to hold land with power to sell it.[21]

Upon accepting[22] trusteeship in order to safeguard himself against claims for breach of trust the new trustee should ascertain the terms of the trust and check that he has been properly appointed. He should inspect all trust documents and ensure that all trust property is properly invested and is in the joint names of himself and his co-trustees[23] or in the name of a duly authorised nominee or custodian.[24] It is often best to have title deeds or share certificates deposited at a bank in the joint names but in the absence of special circumstances the court will not order one trustee who has possession of the documents so to deposit them.[25] If appointed new trustee of an existing trust then it is necessary to investigate any suspicious circumstances which indicate a prior breach of trust so that action may be taken to recoup the trust fund if necessary.[26]

Equity is seen at its strictest in the duty it imposes upon a trustee not **9–07** to allow himself to be put in a position where there may be a conflict between his position as trustee and his personal interest—as the next section shows. This overriding duty of loyalty to the trust must always be borne in mind by trustees.

---

[18] Trustee Art 2000 Part IV. Further see paras 9–130 *et seq.*

[19] *Luke v. South Kensington Hotel Ltd* (1879) 11 Ch.D. 121; *Re Whiteley* [1910] 1 Ch. 600, 608 (Charities); Pensions Act 1995, s.32; *Re Butlin's S.T.* [1976] Ch. 251 (rectification to allow majority decisions). If decision by majority is allowed it is not enough that a majority sign a paper recording the decision: the trustees must meet (*Att.-Gen. v. Scott* (1750) 1 Ves. Sen. 413).

[20] *Re Mayo* [1943] Ch. 302. However, the letter of the trust will not be enforced if so to do would defeat the spirit of the trust: *Jones v. Challenger* [1961] 1 Q.B. 176.

[21] As normal for co-ownership under Trusts of Land and Appointment of Trustees Act 1996.

[22] Of course, no one is bound to accept office as trustee and office should be refused if one wishes to buy property owned by the trust, or run a business likely to compete with a business owned by the trust, or if one is likely to be in a position where it might be said that profits had been made through advantage being taken of the office.

[23] *Hallows v. Lloyd* (1888) 39 Ch.D. 686 at 691; *Harvey v. Olliver* (1887) 57 L.T. 239; *Tiger v. Barclays Bank* [1952] W.N. 38; *Lewis v. Nobbs* (1878) 8 Ch.D. 591. For those classes of property not vesting in the new trustee under Trustee Act 1925, s.40, the ordinary modes of transferring the property will have to be utilised.

[24] Trustee Act 2000, ss.16–23.

[25] *Re Sisson's Settlements* [1903] 1 Ch. 262. Bearer securities have to be deposited with a custodian unless otherwise authorised by the trust instrument: Trustee Act 2000, s.18.

[26] *Re Strahan* (1856) 8 De G.M. & G. 291; *Re Forest of Dean Coal Co.* (1878) 10 Ch.D. 250.

Section 2. Conflict of Interest and Duty[27]

1. PURCHASE OF TRUST PROPERTY BY TRUSTEES

9–08 Of course, at law and in equity T cannot sell, lease or contract to sell or lease property to himself or herself,[28] but often there is more than one trustee. The rule is that a purchase of trust property by a trustee is voidable *ex debito justitiae*, however fair the price, at the instance of any beneficiary, unless authorised by the trust instrument expressly or by necessary implication,[29] or by the court, or by section 68 of the Settled Land Act 1925 (purchases by tenant for life), or made pursuant to a contract or option[30] arising before the trusteeship arose, or acquiesced in by the beneficiary or very special circumstances exist that would make the application of the strict rule unfair as in *Holder v. Holder*. Here it was held by the Court of Appeal, boldly examining the mischief underlying the supposed arbitrary rule, that a renouncing executor who remained executor owing to technical acts of intermeddling and who acquired no special knowledge as executor and who took no part in preparing for a sale by public auction took a valid title as the highest bidder. He had never acted as executor in a way which could be taken to amount to acceptance of a duty to act in the interests of the beneficiaries under the will.

HOLDER v. HOLDER

Court of Appeal [1968] Ch. 353; [1968] 2 W.L.R. 237; [1968] 1 All E.R. 665

The plaintiff beneficiary sought to rescind the sale of trust property to the third defendant in circumstances sufficiently appearing below.

9–09 HARMAN L.J.: "The cross-appeal raises far more difficult questions, and they are broadly three. First, whether the actions of the third defendant before probate made his renunciation ineffective. Second, whether on that footing he was disentitled from bidding at the sale. Third, whether the plaintiff is disentitled from taking this point because of his acquiescence.

"It was admitted at the Bar in the court below that the acts of the third defendant were enough to constitute intermeddling with the estate and that his renunciation was ineffective. On this footing he remained a personal representative even after probate had been granted to his co-executors and could have been obliged by a creditor or a beneficiary to re-assume the duties of an executor. The judge decided in favour of the plaintiff on this point because the third defendant at the time of the sale was himself still in a fiduciary position and, like any other

---

[27] See A. W. Scott, "The Trustee's Duty of Loyalty" (1936) 49 H.L.R. 521; Marshall, "Conflict of Interest and Duty" (1955) 8 C.L.P. 91; Gareth Jones, "Unjust Enrichment and the Fiduciary's Duty of Loyalty" (1968) 84 L.Q.R. 472.

[28] *Rye v. Rye* [1962] A.C. 496, *Ingram v. I.R.C.* [2000] 1 A.C. 293 as affected by s.72 Law of Property Act 1925. Further see McPherson J in Chapter 6, *Trends in Contemporary Trust Law* (ed. A. J. Oakley) Oxford 1996.

[29] *Sargeant v. National Westminster Bank* (1990) 61 P & C.R. 518; *Edge v. Pensions Ombudsman* [1998] Ch 512, affirmed [2000] Ch. 602.

[30] *Re Mulholland's W.T.* [1949] 1 All E.R. 460.

trustee, could not purchase the trust property. I feel the force of this argument, but doubt its validity in the very special circumstances of this case. The reason for the rule is that a man may not be both vendor and purchaser; but the third defendant was never in that position here. He took no part in instructing the valuer who fixed the reserves or in the preparations for the auction. Everyone in the family knew that he was not a seller but a buyer. In this case the third defendant never assumed the duties of an executor. It is true that he concurred in signing a few cheques for trivial sums and endorsing a few insurance policies, but he never so far as appears interfered in any way with the administration of the estate. It is true he managed the farms, but he did that as tenant and not as executor. He acquired no special knowledge as executor. What he knew he knew as tenant of the farms.

"Another reason lying behind the rule is that there must never be a conflict of **9–10** duty and interest, but in fact there was none here in the case of the third defendant, who made no secret throughout that he intended to buy. There is of course ample authority that a trustee cannot purchase. The leading cases are decisions of Lord Eldon L.C.—*ex p. Lacey*[31] and *ex p. James*.[32] In the former case Lord Eldon L.C. expressed himself thus[33]:

> 'The rule I take to be this: not, that a trustee cannot buy from his *cestui que trust*, but, that he shall not buy from himself. . . ., A trustee, who is entrusted to sell and manage for others, undertakes in the same moment, in which he becomes a trustee, not to manage for the benefit and advantage of himself.'

"In *ex p. James* Lord Eldon L.C. said this[34]:

> 'This doctrine as to purchases by trustees, assignees, and persons having a confidential character, stands much more upon general principle than upon the circumstances of any individual case. It rests upon this, that the purchase is not permitted in any case, however honest the circumstances, the general interests of justice requiring it to be destroyed in every instance.'

These are no doubt strong words, but it is to be observed that Lord Eldon was **9–11** dealing with cases where the purchaser was at the time of sale acting for the vendors. In this case the third defendant was not so acting: his interference with the administration of the estate was of a minimal character, and the last cheque that he signed was in August before he executed the deed of renunciation. He took no part in the instructions for probate, nor in the valuations or fixing of the reserves. Everyone concerned knew of the renunciation and of the reason for it, namely that he wished to be a purchaser. Equally, everyone including the three firms of solicitors engaged assumed that the renunciation was effective and entitled the third defendant to bid. I feel great doubt whether the admission made at the Bar was correct, as did the judge, but assuming that it was right, the acts were only technically acts of intermeddling and I find no case where the circumstances are parallel. Of course, I feel the force of the judge's reasoning

---

[31] (1802) 6 Ves. 625.
[32] (1803) 8 Ves. 337.
[33] (1802) 6 Ves. 625 at 626.
[34] (1803) 8 Ves. 337 at 344.

that if the third defendant remained an executor he is within the rule, but in a case where the reasons behind the rule do not exist I do not feel bound to apply it. My reasons are that the beneficiaries never looked to the third defendant to protect their interests. They all knew he was in the market as purchaser; that the price paid was a good one and probably higher than anyone not a sitting tenant would give. Further, the first two defendants alone acted as executors and sellers: they alone could convey: they were not influenced by the third defendant in connection with the sales.

9–12　　　"I hold, therefore, that the rule does not apply in order to disentitle the third defendant to bid at the auction, as he did."

DANCKWERTS L.J.: "There is no allegation of fraud in the present case. The third defendant acted in complete innocence and did not know that he was regarded as debarred from purchasing the farms. He bought them at a public auction, in respect of which he took no part in regard to the arrangements for the auction, and the judge found[35] that the prices that he paid were good prices. They were well above the reserve prices. The third defendant and the two proving executors were at arm's length. There was no question of knowledge which the third defendant might have acquired as an executor. He had a great amount of knowledge of the farms acquired by him, while he was a tenant or when he helped his father in the carrying on of the farms, and he was the obvious person to purchase these farms and likely to offer the best price. I agree with Harman L.J. that there was no reason why he should not bid at the auction and purchase the farms."

The Width of the "Self-dealing" Rule

9–13　　　In *Movitex Ltd v. Bulfield*[36] Vinelott J. stated, "The self-dealing rule is founded on and exemplifies the wider principle that 'no one who has a duty to perform shall place himself in a situation to have his interests conflicting with that duty.'[37] To that should be added for completeness 'nor to have his duty to one conflicting with his duty to another.'[38] So, the fiduciary owes a duty to the person whose interest he is bound to protect not to place himself in a position in which duty and interest or duty and duty are in conflict."[39]

9–14　　　The prohibition against purchase by the trustee applies whether or not he himself fixes the price. Thus in *Wright v. Morgan*,[40] a testator left land on trust for sale with power to postpone sale for seven years and provided that it should be offered at a price to be fixed by valuers to one of his sons, X, who was one of the trustees. X assigned his right (which was treated as an option and not a right of pre-emption) to his brother, Y, who was also one of the trustees but who was not authorised to purchase by the terms of the will. Y arranged for the sale to himself, retired from the trust and purchased at a price fixed by the valuers, and

---

[35] [1966] 3 W.L.R. 229 at 237.
[36] [1988] BCLC 104 at 117.
[37] *Broughton v. Broughton* (1855) 5 De G.M. & G. 160 at 164.
[38] *Re Haslam & Hier-Evans* [1902] 1 Ch. 765.
[39] See also *Chan v. Zachariah* (1984) 154 C.L.R. 178, see *supra*, at para. 6–36.
[40] [1926] A.C. 788.

it was held that the sale could be set aside. After all, Y as a trustee was one of those responsible for determining when the land was first to be offered for sale (and prices could fluctuate over the years) and for determining the terms of payment, *e.g.* cash or instalments with interest payable. If X had assigned to a stranger, Z, then assuming the right was assignable and not personal to X, Z could quite properly have purchased the land. Of course, if X had exercised his right and had the land conveyed to him, then a subsequent conveyance to Y would have been proper.

The prohibition against purchase by the trustee is applicable where the **9–15** sale is conducted at an auction held by the trustee himself,[41] since the trustee is in a position to discourage bidders. Further, where the sale is conducted, not by the trustee, but a third party, as, for example, where a trustee holds trust property subject to a mortgage and the mortgagee sells under his power of sale, the trustee is nevertheless not allowed to buy the property, since to hold otherwise might be to permit him to prefer his own interest to his duty,[42] and this is so whether or not he could have prevented the sale.[43] The rule is a strong one and is not circumvented by the device of the trustee selling to a third party to hold on trust for him.[44] But if there is no prior agreement and the sale is in all respects bona fide there is no objection to the trustee subsequently buying the trust property from the person to whom he sold it,[45] though if the trustee contracts to sell the property to X, a stranger, and before the conveyance is made he purchases the benefit of the contract from X, the contract can be set aside.[46] Further, if the trustee has retired from the trust with a view to purchasing the property the sale can be avoided,[47] but it is otherwise if at the date of his retirement he had no idea of making the purchase, unless the circumstances show that when he made the purchase he used information acquired by him while a trustee.[48] But a trustee who has disclaimed is not caught by the rule.[49]

Moreover, the rule is sufficiently strong and elastic to prevent a trustee **9–16** from selling the trust property to a company of which he is the principal shareholder,[50] managing director or other principal officer,[51] or to a

---

[41] *Whelpdale v. Cookson* (1747) 1 Ves.Sen. 9; *Campbell v. Walker* (1800) 5 Ves. 678 at 682.
[42] A. W. Scott, "The Trustee's Duty of Loyalty" (1936) 49 H.L.R. 521 at 529–530.
[43] *Griffith v. Owen* [1907] 1 Ch. 195, where it was held that the tenant for life of an equity of redemption could not purchase the property for himself from the mortgagee selling under his power of sale.
[44] *Michoud v. Girod* (1846) 4 How. 503 (U.S.).
[45] *Re Postlethwaite* (1888) 37 W.R. 200.
[46] *Williams v. Scott* [1900] A.C. 499.
[47] *Wright v. Morgan* [1926] A.C. 788.
[48] *Re Boles and British Land Co.'s Contract* [1902] 1 Ch. 244.
[49] *Stacey v. Elph* (1833) 1 Myl. & K. 195; *cf. Clark v. Clark* (1884) 9 App.Cas. 733 at 737, P.C.
[50] *Silkstone & Haigh Moor Coal Co. v. Edey* [1900] 1 Ch. 167; *Farrars v. Farrars Ltd* (1888) 40 Ch.D. 395. Sale to a trustee's wife is risky (see *Ferraby v. Hobson* (1847) 2 Ph. 255 at 261) but perhaps not absolutely prohibited (see *Burrell v. Burrell's Trustees*, 1915 S.C. 33; (1949) 13 Conv.(N.S.) 248; *Re King's W.T.* (1959) 173 Est.Gaz. 627; *Tito v. Waddell (No. 2)* [1977] 3 All E.R. 129 at 241) though see *Re McNally* [1967] N.Z.L.R. 521. A mortgagee can exercise his power of sale in favour of a company in which he is interested only if he shows he acted in good faith and took all reasonable steps to obtain the best price reasonably obtainable: *Tse Kwong Lam v. Wong Chit Sen* [1983] 3 All. E.R. 54.
[51] *Eberhardt v. Christiana Window Glass Co.* (1911) 9 Del.Ch. 284 (U.S.).

partnership of which he is a member.[52] Of course, the rule applies to corporate trustees, so that a trust corporation cannot in the absence of authorisation by the trust instrument or consent of the beneficiaries or approval of the court sell the trust property either to itself or to its subsidiaries.[53]

9–17　　Where a sale takes place in breach of the rules outlined above, the beneficiaries have a number of remedies open to them. Thus they may claim any profit made by the trustee on a resale of the property. If the property has not been resold they can insist on a reconveyance or alternatively they can demand that it be offered for sale again. If on this occasion a higher price is bid than which the trustee paid, it will be sold at that price. If not, the trustee may at the option of the beneficiaries be allowed to retain the property, and in the nature of things the beneficiaries will confer this doubtful favour upon him where the property has fallen in value since he purchased it.[54] The right which the beneficiaries have to avoid the sale is an equitable one, and as such is liable to be lost through laches, but for laches to apply the beneficiaries must have full knowledge of the facts and must acquiesce in the situation for an unreasonably long period.[55] Further, the right to have the sale set aside may be lost if the court in the exercise of its inherent jurisdiction sets the seal of its approval on the transaction, and it seems that not only may the court authorise a sale which is about to take place, but in a suitable case it may ratify one which has already occurred.[56]

9–18　　The above presupposes that the sale has taken place without the consent of the beneficiaries. Where, however, the beneficiaries are of full capacity they may authorise the sale, which will then stand, provided that the trustee made a full disclosure, and did not induce the sale by taking advantage of his relation to the beneficiaries or by other improper conduct, and the transaction was in all respects fair and reasonable.[57] The onus of proof is on the trustee to show affirmatively that these conditions existed, but there is no objection to the consent of the beneficiaries being obtained after the sale to the trustees.[58]

The "fair dealing" rule

9–20　　Of course, a trustee may purchase his beneficiary's equitable interest under the trust (subject to making full disclosure and negativing undue influence) so as to acquire the trust property itself when he has acquired

---

[52] *Colgate's Executor v. Colgate* (1873) 23 N.J.Eq. 372 (U.S.). The self-dealing rule extends to cases where a trustee concurs in a transaction which cannot be effected without his consent and where he also has an interest in, or holds a fiduciary duty to another in relation to, the same transaction: *Re Thompson* [1985] 2 All E.R. 720.

[53] *Purchase v. Atlantic Safe Deposit and Trust Co.* (1913) 81 N.J.Eq. 334 (U.S.).

[54] For further details, see *Holder v. Holder* [1966] 2 All E.R. 116 at 130, *per* Cross J.

[55] *Infra*, para. 10–96; *Holder v. Holder* [1968] Ch. 353.

[56] *Farmer v. Dean* (1863) 32 Beav. 327; *Campbell v. Walker* (1800) 5 Ves. 678.

[57] *Coles v. Trecothick* (1804) 9 Ves. 234; *Morse v. Royal* (1806) 12 Ves. 355; *Gibson v. Jeyes* (1801) 6 Ves. 266; *cf. Fox v. Mackreth* (1788) 2 Bro.C.C. 400. These factors can make it difficult for the trustee to find a purchaser when he himself wishes to sell, as a purchaser will be bound by a beneficiary's equity to set aside the transaction if he has actual or constructive notice.

[58] T. B. Ruoff, "Purchases in Breach of Trust: A Suggested Cure" (1954) 18 Conv.(N.S.) 528.

all the equitable interests. In *Tito v. Waddell (No. 2)*[59] Megarry V.-C. categorised this as subject to the "fair-dealing" rule that "if a trustee purchases the beneficial interest of any of his beneficiaries, the transaction is not voidable *ex debito justitiae*, however fair the transaction, [as under the 'self-dealing' rule] but can be set aside by the beneficiary unless the trustee can show that he has taken no advantage of his position and has made full disclosure to the beneficiary, and that the transaction is fair and honest."

II. PROFITS INCIDENTAL TO TRUSTEESHIP

In order to maintain confidence in the trust institution by maintaining **9–21** high standards of conduct in the trustee role equity has developed the rule that a trustee may not place himself in a position where his trusteeship duties and his personal interest may possibly conflict[60] and the allied rule that, unless authorised,[61] he is strictly liable to account for any profit made by using trust property or his position as trustee. Indeed, the court, if need be, will be prepared to find that the property acquired by such use is held on constructive trust for the trust beneficiaries, the purpose being to ensure that the defaulting fiduciary does not retain such property for herself and not to compensate the beneficiaries for any losses.[62] Of course, an injunction may also lie against any trustee who is in breach of or is about to break his duties to the trust.

The rules applicable to trustees have been extended to all persons in a **9–22** fiduciary relationship.[63] The categories of fiduciary relationships are not closed. The following relationships have been held to be fiduciary: director,[64] senior management employee,[65] promoter[66] and the company; solicitor and client[67]; agent (including a self-appointed agent[68]) and principal[69]; partner and co-partner[70]; mortgagee and mortgagor.[71] Once a

---

[59] [1977] 3 All E.R. 129 at 241. A mortgagee may purchase the mortgagor's equity of redemption by a subsequent transaction independent of and separate from the mortgage: *Alec Lobb Garages Ltd v. Total Oil* [1983] 1 All E.R. 944 at 965.

[60] See *supra*, para. 6–23; *Bray v. Ford* [1896] A.C. 44 at 51; *Parker v. McKenna* (1874) L.R. 10 Ch.App. 96 at 124–125; *Boardman v. Phipps* [1967] 2 A.C. 46. Generally see Goff & Jones, Chap. 33; Oakley, Chap. 3. In *Swain v. Law Society* [1981] 3 All E.R. 797 at 813 Oliver L.J. preferred to consider the rule "as an application of the principle that that which is the fruit of trust property or of the trusteeship is itself trust property." In *Movitex Ltd v. Bulfield* [1988] BCLC 104 at 117, Vinelott J. pointed out that "the fiduciary owes a duty to the person whose interest he is bound to protect not to place himself in a position in which duty and interest *or duty and duty* are in conflict."

[61] See *infra*, at para. 9–30.

[62] See Chap. 6, s.1, *supra*, at para. 6–23 and *United Pan-Europe Communications NV v. Deutsche Bank AG* [2000] 2 B.C.L.C. 461 (C.A.).

[63] Generally see P. D. Finn, *Fiduciary Obligations* and *supra*, at para. 6–13.

[64] *Regal (Hastings) Ltd v. Gulliver* [1967] 2 A.C. 134; L. S. Sealy [1967] C.L.J. 83.

[65] *Canadian Aero Services Ltd v. O'Malley* (1973) 40 D.L.R. (3d) 371 at 381.

[66] *Lydney Iron Ore Co. v. Bird* (1886) 33 Ch.D. 85 at 94.

[67] *McMaster v. Byrne* [1952] 1 All E.R. 1362.

[68] *English v. Dedham Vale Properties Ltd* [1978] 1 All E.R. 382.

[69] *Lowther v. Lowther* (1806) 13 Ves. 95 at 103; *Parker v. McKenna* (1874) 10 Ch.App. 96 at 124–125. To the extent the agent-principal relationship is a debtor-creditor relationship no constructive trusteeship or tracing can be allowed: *Halifax B.S. v. Thomas* [1995] 4 All E.R. 673.

[70] *Bentley v. Craven* (1853) 18 Beav. 75.

[71] *Farrars v. Farrars Ltd* (1888) 40 Ch.D. 395.

fiduciary relationship has been established it is necessary to ascertain the scope and ambit of the fiduciary's duties. Then one can examine whether or not the fiduciary has placed himself in a position where his personal interest may possibly conflict with those duties. If so, then he is accountable for all profits made from acting within the scope and ambit of those duties[72] whether the profit arises before or after his resignation, retirement or dismissal from his fiduciary post, *e.g.* where information concerning certain economic opportunities has been gained *qua* fiduciary which leads to the fiduciary resigning his post so that *he* can profit from the opportunity rather than his principal.[73]

9-23   The English courts have retained a strict deterrent approach to fiduciaries. *Boardman v. Phipps* (*supra*, at para. 6–46) establishes that the fiduciary must disgorge any benefit obtained by him "even though he acted honestly and in his principal's best interest, even though his principal benefited as well as he from his conduct, even though his principal could not otherwise have obtained the benefit and even though the benefit was obtained through the use of the fiduciary's own assets and in consequence of his personal skill and judgment."[74]

9-24   As will be seen from reading *Boardman v. Phipps* the majority thought there was a feasible possibility of conflict: since the trustees might possibly have changed their minds and have sought Boardman's advice on an application to the court to acquire power to purchase the outstanding shares in the company, when there would be required not just legal advice but practical advice as to the likelihood of the assured success of the proposed takeover and reorganisation of the company. Boardman would hardly have been able to give unprejudiced advice if, when his plans were well advanced, he had been consulted by the trustees as to whether they should then try to take advantage of what he had done so as to obtain profits otherwise passing to him. However, the minority considered that a reasonable man would not think there was a real sensible possibility of conflict when there seemed virtually no chance the trustees would have changed their minds and so consult Boardman: indeed, in that exceptionally unlikely event, Boardman could have declined to advise and have referred them to another solicitor.

9-25   *Regal (Hastings) Ltd v. Gulliver*[75] discussed, *infra*, para. 9–45, is another important case, though dealing with the director-company relationship. Similarly, in *Cook v. Deeks*[76] where directors diverted to themselves contracts which they should have taken up on behalf of the

---

[72] *Boardman v. Phipps* [1967] 2 A.C. 46 at 128–129, *per* Lord Upjohn; *Patel v. Patel* [1982]1 All E.R. 68 (no breach of trust and so no accountability where trustees live in a house held on trust for young children adopted by trustees on death of their parents). Further see *Warman International Ltd v. Dwyer* (1995) 69 ALJR 362.

[73] *Industrial Development Consultants Ltd v. Cooley* [1972] 1 W.L.R. 443; *Canadian Aero Services Ltd v. O'Malley* (1973) 40 D.L.R. (3d) 371; *Abbey Glen Pty. Co. v. Stumborg* (1978) 85 D.L.R. (3d) 35. Contrast *Queensland Mines v. Hudson* (1978) 18 A.L.R. 1.

[74] (1968) 84 L.Q.R. 472 at 474, Prof. G. H. Jones. The prophyllactic approach is reflected in *Guinness plc v. Saunders* [1990] 2 A.C. 663.

[75] [1967] 2 A.C. 134.

[76] [1916] 1 A.C. 554.

company, the Privy Council found the directors held the benefit of the contracts on constructive trust for the company. In *Industrial Development Consultants v. Cooley*[77] the managing director of the plaintiff company was held constructive trustee of the benefit of a contract with the Eastern Gas Board and made liable to account for the profits thereof. The Gas Board had privately told him he would not obtain a contract from them for the benefit of his company but that he would have a good chance of privately obtaining the contract for himself if he left the company. Pretending poor health and concealing his true reason, he secured his release from his employment with the company. He then personally obtained the contract with the Gas Board which he had tried unsuccessfully to obtain for the company. He was held liable to account for all the profit, though the chance of his persuading the Gas Board to contract with the company was estimated by the judge as no greater than 10 per cent.

In *English v. Dedham Vale Properties*[78] self-appointed agents were held **9–26** liable to account for profits. The plaintiff sold her property to the defendant for £7,750. However, seven days before contracts were exchanged the defendant had applied for planning permission, making the application in the plaintiff's name and signed by the defendant as agent for the plaintiff. Under the Planning Acts the plaintiff did not then need to be notified of the application or informed of its outcome. Planning permission was granted after exchange of contracts but before completion. When, after completion, the plaintiff discovered the position she successfully claimed an account of profits since Slade J. was prepared to treat the defendant as a fiduciary who should have disclosed the planning application to the plaintiff before the contract and the price had been concluded.

In *Swain v. Law Society*[79] a solicitor sought to make the Law Society **9–27** accountable for commission received by it from an insurance company in respect of premiums paid by solicitors under the Solicitors' Indemnity Insurance Scheme which the Law Society had negotiated with the company. Oliver L.J. stated[80]:

> "What one has to do is to ascertain first of all whether there was a fiduciary relationship and, if there was, from what it arose and what, if there was any, was the trust property; and then to inquire whether that of which an account is claimed either arose, directly or indirectly, from the trust property itself or was acquired not only in the course of, but by reason of, the fiduciary relationship."

---

[77] [1972] 1 W.L.R. 443. For Canadian cases where directors were liable see *Canadian Aero Services Ltd v. O'Malley* (1973) 40 D.L.R. (3d) 371 noted (1974) 37 M.L.R. 464; *Abbey Glen Pty. Co. v. Stumborg* (1978) 85 D.L.R. (3d) 35 noted (1979) 42 M.L.R. 215; (1975) 51 Can.B.R. 771 (Beck).
[78] [1978] 1 All E.R. 382.
[79] [1982] 1 W.L.R. 17; reversed [1982] 2 All E.R. 827; [1983] 1 A.C. 598.
[80] [1982] 1 W.L.R. 17 at 37.

9–28   On appeal, Lord Brightman (with whom the other Law Lords agreed) endorsed[81] this approach but held that no fiduciary relationship existed since the Law Society was performing a public duty under section 37 of the Solicitors Act 1974.

9–29   In *Queensland Mines Ltd v. Hudson*[82] the Privy Council took a liberal view on a case of unusual merits to produce a decision that is out of line with earlier strict cases. Queensland was formed to exploit the anticipated award of mining licences: its managing director was Hudson. At the last minute Queensland's financial backing collapsed so Hudson took the licences in his own name in 1961 and resigned as managing director, though remaining a director for a further 10 years. At a 1962 board meeting Hudson admitted he held the licences for Queensland and candidly warned of the risks attendant on exploiting the licences. So the board resolved Queensland would not pursue the matter further, so Hudson was free to go it alone. It was held that Hudson was not liable for his profits for either of two reasons since the board had (1) given their fully informed consent, and (2) placed the licences venture outside the scope of the fiduciary relationship of director and company. As to (1) the consent of the board is not enough: one needs the consent of the majority vote of shareholders at a general meeting at the very least,[83] if not the consent of all the shareholders.[84] As to (2) to allow fiduciary managers to define the scope of their own fiduciary obligations, and so immunise themselves from liability, is startling when there will be such a conflict of interest involved if the directors can then acquire for themselves what they have rejected on behalf of the company. The decision seems rather weak when contrasted with the House of Lords decisions in *Regal (Hastings)*[85] and in *Boardman*.[86] The Privy Council were over-influenced by the fact that Hudson seemed a good chap who had worked hard and risked all, while Queensland had risked nothing, and watched him becoming very successful and then had tried to take away everything he had worked for.

Defences

9–30   It will be a defence to show that the conduct generating the profit was authorised by the trust instrument expressly or by necessary implication,[87] or by the contract of agency,[88] or the deed of partnership, or the articles of a company,[89] or by the court.[90] A further defence is to show

---

[81] [1982] 2 All E.R. 827 at 838; [1983] A.C. 598 at 619.
[82] (1978) 18 A.L.R. 1, well criticised by G. R. Sullivan (1979) 42 M.L.R. 711.
[83] *Imperial Credit Association v. Coleman* (1871) 6 Ch.App. 556 at 557; *Regal (Hastings) Ltd v. Gulliver* [1967] 2 A.C. 134 at 150, 154; *Prudential Assurance Co. v. Newman Industries (No. 2)* [1980] 2 All E.R. 841 at 862.
[84] *Cook v. Deeks* [1916] 1 A.C. 554; *Daniels v. Daniels* [1978] 2 All E.R. 89 at 95.
[85] [1967] 2 A.C. 134.
[86] [1967] 2 A.C. 46.
[87] *Re Llewellin* [1949] Ch. 225. *Sargeant v. National Westminister Bank*, (1990) 61 P. & C.R. 518, *Edge v. Pensions Ombudsman* [1998] Ch. 512.
[88] *Kelly v. Cooper* [1993] A.C. 205.
[89] *Movitex Ltd v. Bulfield* [1988] B.C.L.C. 104; *Guiness plc v. Saunders* [1990] 2 A.C. 663.
[90] *e.g.* Trustee Act, s.42; R.S.C., Ord. 85, r. 2.

the informed consent of all the beneficiaries being each of full capacity and between them absolutely entitled to the trust property.[91] A partner will need the consent of the other partners; a director the consent of all the members of the company for it will be a fraud on the minority to expropriate property held on a constructive trust for the company.[92] It would seem that someone employed by trustees in a fiduciary position (*e.g.* a solicitor or accountant) or a beneficiary acquiring special information while purportedly representing the trust so as to be treated as a fiduciary, may have a defence if obtaining the informed consent of independent trustees.[93]

Where a fiduciary in his professional capacity may have clients with **9–31** differing interests he has to cope with his need not to have his fiduciary duty to one conflicting with his duty to another. He can take advantage of the principle that the scope of the fiduciary duties owed by him to his clients is to be defined by the express or implied terms of his contract with each of them.[94] Indeed, "it is the contractual foundation which is all-important . . . The fiduciary relationship, if it is to exist at all, must accommodate itself to the terms of the contract so that it is consistent with, and conforms to, them."[95]

The fact that a fiduciary could have avoided problems by an apt contractual term or by obtaining an informed consent or court approval before entering into the profit-making situation and the practical problems in the way of the principal finding out for himself what exactly the fiduciary was involved in, combine to indicate that the strict deterrent approach is likely to be maintained.

In an exceptional case, like *Boardman v. Phipps*, the court can grant **9–32** the defendant an allowance for his valuable services and, perhaps, even an element of the profit, though the court should be very cautious in this: it does not want to encourage trustees or other fiduciaries to put themselves in a position where their interests conflict with their duties.[96]

---

[91] *Boardman v. Phipps* [1967] 2 A.C. 46.

[92] *Cook v. Deeks* [1916] 1 A.C. 554; *Borland's Trustees v. Steel Bros. Ltd* [1901] Ch. 279. In contrast a majority by resolution in general meeting may waive a director's personal liability to account if they consider he acted in the company's best interests: *Regal (Hastings) Ltd v. Gulliver* [1967] 2 A.C. 134.

[93] *Regal (Hastings) Ltd v. Gulliver* [1967] 2 A.C. 134 (solicitor not liable though closely involved with the directors as emerges from *Luxor (Eastbourne) Ltd v. Cooper* [1941] A.C. 108, especially [1939] 4 All E.R. 411 at 414–417); *Boardman v. Phipps* [1967] 2 A.C. 46 at 93, 117 and implicit in Lord Upjohn's speech 130–133; *Anson v. Potter* (1879) 13 Ch.D. 141. The trustees should be independent just like company directors must be if disclosure to them is to protect a promoter: *Gluckstein v. Barnes* [1900] A.C. 240. If to the fiduciary's knowledge a fund is distributable under a bare trust because the beneficiaries are each of full capacity and between them absolutely entitled to call for the capital then according to Lord Cohen in *Boardman v. Phipps* [1967] 2 A.C. 46 at 104, the informed consent of the beneficiaries is required. Presumably, trustees can employ an agent to exploit information on terms he receives as fee a percentage of the profit.

[94] *Kelly v. Cooper* [1993] A.C. 205, *Clark Boyce v. Mouat* [1994] 1 A.C. 428.

[95] *Hospital Products Ltd v. United States Surgical Corporation* (1984) 156 C.L.R. 41 at 97 endorsed in *Kelly v. Cooper, supra.*

[96] See Lord Goff in *Guinness plc v. Saunders* [1990]2 A.C. 663 at 701, though the Court of Appeal were flexible in *O'Sullivan v. Management Agency and Music Ltd* [1985] Q.B. 428 at 468. Indeed, in *Re Badfinger* [2001] W.T.L.R. 1 the High Court held that not only a flat fee but a fee based on a percentage of profits could and would be allowed to the sound-engineer hired by the fiduciary: it was open to allow a percentage fee to the fiduciary himself but in the circumstances only a flat fee would be allowed.

The equitable obligation of confidence

9–33   This equitable right of confidentiality is still in course of development. It is usually protected by the grant of an injunction to prevent disclosure of the confidence or by damages in lieu of an injunction under Lord Cairns's Act or by making the confidant liable to account to the confider for profits made from exploiting the confidence or, perhaps, by making a *quantum meruit* award. The right "depends on the broad principle of equity that he who has received information in confidence shall not take unfair advantage of it. He must not make use of it to the prejudice of him who gave it without obtaining his consent": *Seager v. Copydex*,[97] *infra*. Thus the information must have the necessary quality of confidentiality, must have been imparted in circumstances importing an obligation of confidence, and there must have been unauthorised use of the information.[98] If the circumstances are such that any reasonable man, standing in the shoes of the recipient of the information, would have realised upon reasonable grounds that the information was being given to him in confidence, then this should suffice to impose upon him the equitable obligation of confidence.[99] Indeed, Lord Goff[1] has stated that:

> "a duty of confidence arises when confidential information comes to the knowledge of a person (the confidant) in circumstances where he has notice, or is held to have agreed, that the information is confidential, with the effect that it would be just in all the circumstances that he should be precluded from disclosing the information to others."

It will be a defence to show that disclosure was in the public interest[2] or that the obligation of confidentiality was at an end at the relevant time because the information was in the public domain available to all on reasonable inquiry.[3]

9–34   If the confidant consciously breaks the plaintiff's confidence the court will grant an injunction and direct an account of profits, treating the confidant as constructive trustee of the profits or any patent or copyright which is the product of the confidential information.[4] Indeed in *LAC*

---

[97] [1967] 1 W.L.R. 923 at 931; See *Malone v. Commissioner of Police (No. 2)* [1979] 2 All E.R. 620 at 633; Goff & Jones, Chap. 36; Law Commission *Breach of Confidence*, Law. Com. No. 110; Meagher, Gummow & Lehane, Chap. 41, and especially, F. Gurry's *Breach of Confidence* (Clarendon, 1984).

[98] See *Coco v. Clark (Engineers) Ltd* [1969] R.P.C. 41 at 47 endorsed by C.A. in *Murray v. Yorkshire Fund Managers* [1998] 2 All E.R. 1015, 1020; *Att.-Gen. v. Jonathan Cape* [1975] 3 All E.R. 484 at 494; *Dunford & Elliott Ltd v. Johnson* [1977] 1 Lloyd's Rep. 505; *Fraser v. Thames Television* [1983] 2 All E.R. 101 at 116. See also Braithwaite (1979) 42 M.L.R. 94.

[99] *Coco v. Clark (Engineers) Ltd* [1969] R.P.C. 41 at 48; *Att.-Gen. v. Guardian Newspapers (No. 2)* [1988] 3 All E.R. 545.

[1] *Att.-Gen. v. Guardian Newspapers Ltd (No. 2)* [1990] 1 A.C. 109 at 281.

[2] *Initial Services Ltd v. Putterill* [1968] 1 Q.B. 396 at 405; *Lion Laboratories Ltd v. Evans* [1984] 2 All E.R. 417; *Francome v. Mirror Group Newspapers* [1984] 2 All E.R. 408.

[3] *Satnam Investments Ltd v. Dunlop Heywood & Co Ltd* [1999] 3 All E.R. 652, 672; *Bunn v. BBC* [1998] 3 All E.R. 552.

[4] *Peter Pan Manufacturing Co. v. Corsets Silhouette Ltd* [1964] 1 W.L.R. 96; *British Syphon Co. v. Homewood* [1956] 1 W.L.R. 1190; *Att.-Gen. v. Guardian Newspapers (No. 2)* [1988] 3 All E.R. 545; *Nanus Asia Co. Inc. v. Standard Chartered Bank* [1990] Hong Kong L.R. 396 holding that even a tippee may be constructive trustee of his profits.

Minerals Ltd v. International Corona Resources Ltd[5] the Supreme Court
of Canada held that LAC was constructive trustee of land it had bought
because told in confidence by a potential joint-venturer that it could well
contain gold deposits. If the confidant acted honestly but foolishly in
believing that he was not breaching confidence then damages[6] under
Lord Cairns's Act[7] or a *quantum meruit*[8] will be awarded, at least if the **9–35**
information had only partially contributed to the product marketed to
produce the profits. If the information were the *sine qua non* and the
confidant was foolish in thinking he was not breaching the plaintiff's
confidence the confidant should be liable to account for his unjust
enrichment.[9] If a person uses information without having reason to think
that it had been imparted to him in breach of another's confidence, and
later discovers the truth of the matter, he should not be liable for use of
the information in the prior period.[10] Thereafter he should be liable
whether he be a volunteer or a purchaser,[11] so that if he continues with a
project with the informant he should be liable to be restrained as
participating in a dishonest design in breach of confidence.[12] The general
defence of change of position will be available in appropriate
circumstances.[13]

Recently, the Court of Appeal[14] in developing English law consistently
with the European Convention on Human Rights, implemented by the
Human Rights Act 1999, has recognised a right of privacy grounded in
the equitable doctrine of breach of confidence, without any longer
needing to construct an artificial relationship of confidentiality between
intruder and victim.

---

[5] (1989) 61 D.L.R. (4th) 14.

[6] For principles of assessment see *Seager v. Copydex (No. 2)* [1969] 1 W.L.R. 809 and *Dowson & Mason Ltd v. Potter* [1986] 2 All E.R. 418. If the plaintiff is a manufacturer loss of manufacturing profits is an appropriate basis but not if the plaintiff instead intended to exploit the information by licensing it to others when the value to the plaintiff of the information is an appropriate basis.

[7] The damages were treated as in lieu of an injunction under Lord Cairns's Act 1858 by Slade J. in *English v. Dedham Vale Properties Ltd* [1978] 1 All E.R. 382 at 399, and Megarry V.-C. in *Malone v. Commissioner of Police (No. 2)* [1979] 2 All E.R. 620 at 633; and Lord Goff in *Att.-Gen. v. Guardian Newspapers Ltd (No. 2)* [1990] 1 A.C. 109 at 286. It is probable that Lord Cairns's Act is concerned purely with damages in aid of legal rights and that where the plaintiff has suffered a loss and seeks relief within the exclusive jurisdiction of equity he is entitled to equitable compensation (see *infra*, paras 10–04 *et seq.*) so that the court should award this restitutionary remedy and not damages: Meagher, Gummow & Lehane, *Equity* (3rd ed.) pp. 888–889.

[8] See Goff & Jones, p. 758.

[9] Prof. G. H. Jones (1970) 86 L.Q.R. 463 at 476.

[10] "It may be a reason for limiting the account of profits to the period subsequent to the date at which he becomes aware of the true facts": *Att.-Gen. v. Spalding* (1915) 32 R.P.C. 273 at 283.

[11] The defence of bona fide purchaser for value without notice does not apply since the equitable obligation is not a property right, *e.g. Oxford v. Moss* (1978) 68 Cr.App.R. 183; [1979] Crim. L.R. 119. Even if the property analogy were adopted the equitable nature of the right would mean that the confider's claim would prevail as being the equitable right first in time.

[12] *cf.* the constructive trusteeship imposed on strangers to a trust to make them accountable: *supra*, Chap. 11, section 2; *Wheatley v. Bell* [1982] 2 N.S.W.L.R. 544; [1984] F.S.R. 16; J. D. Davies (1984) 4 Ox.J.L.S. 142; *Malone v. Commissioner of Police* [1979] 2 All E.R. 620 at 634.

[13] See *infra*, paras. 11–46 *et seq.*

[14] *Douglas v. Hello Ltd* [2001] 2 All E.R. 289 applied in *Venables v. News Group Newspapers* [2001] *The Times*, January 16.

Use of information acquired qua fiduciary

9–36   Information acquired by a trustee in the course of his duties as such may
be used by him for his own benefit or for the benefit of other trusts
unless its use would place him in a position where his duty and his
interest might possibly conflict or it was imparted to him in circumstances placing an obligation of confidence upon him.[15] Thus if A is
trustee of S1 and of S2 and as trustee of S1 learns facts that make him
and his co-trustees wish to sell X Co. shares he cannot use this
knowledge for S2 until S1's X Co. shares have been sold, for a prior sale
of S2's shares could well drive down the price of X Co. shares. If A as
trustee of S1 learnt encouraging facts about Y Co. shares and his S2 co-
trustees were thinking of selling Y Co. shares then A could tell them this
would be unsatisfactory unless S1 was thinking of purchasing more Y Co.
shares. If A obtains as trustee of S2 information subject to the equitable
obligation of confidence then he cannot use it for the benefit of S1 and,
it seems, even if he became trustee of S1 before he became trustee of S2,
he cannot be sued by the S1 beneficiaries for breach of trust for failing to
take advantage of the confidential information obtained *qua* S2 trustee.[16]

9–37   A partner may make a profit from information obtained in the course
of the partnership business where he does so in another firm with
business outside the scope of the partnership business.[17] As Lord
Hodson stated in *Boardman v. Phipps*,[18] "Partnership is special in that a
partner is the principal as well as the agent of the other partners and
works in a defined area of business so that it can normally be determined
whether the particular transaction is within or without the scope of the
partnership. It is otherwise in the case of a general trusteeship or
fiduciary position such as was occupied by Mr. Boardman the limits of
which are not readily defined."

The scope of a trustee's duties to the trust is unclear where he
acquired useful information privately but not in circumstances placing
him under the equitable obligation of confidence. Obviously, he can first
make as much use of the information for himself as he likes. If he uses
the information to make a profit for himself should he not also go on to
use it for the benefit of the trust if a trustee with his special knowledge
should be expected so to act?[19] If use of the information could enable
the shares to be sold quickly before the share price drops dramatically
should he not use such information to save the trust suffering a loss?

---

[15] *Boardman v. Phipps* [1967] 2 A.C. 46 at 128–129, *per* Lord Upjohn who also provides the next two
examples. Further see *Kelly v. Cooper* [1993] A.C. 205; *Mortgage Express Ltd v. Bowerman* [1996] 2 All
E.R. 836, C.A.

[16] *cf. North & South Trust Co. v. Berkeley* [1971] 1 W.L.R. 470 and see B. A. K. Rider [1978] Conv. 114.

[17] *Aas v. Benham* [1891] 2 Ch. 244.

[18] [1967] 2 A.C. 46 at 108. For companies see *Queensland Mines, supra*, para. 9–29. On the position of an
agent acting for two principals (*e.g.* a solicitor acting for a purchaser and the purchaser's prospective
mortgagee) see *Bristol & West B.S. v. Mothew* [1998] Ch. 1 (C.A.).

[19] See what approximates to a trustee's duty to gazump in *Buttle v. Saunders* [1950] 2 All E.R. 193. Is
there a distinction between a profit-making situation when there are so many different ways of
investing money for profit and a loss-making situation when there is only one way of avoiding the loss,
viz. selling the shares as soon as possible?

RE GEE, WOOD AND OTHERS v. STAPLES AND OTHERS

Chancery Division [1948] Ch. 284; [1948] 1 All E.R. 498

The capital of a private company, Gee & Co. (Publishers) Ltd, was £5,000 in **9–38** £1 shares. Alfred Lionel Gee ("the testator") was the registered owner of 4,996 shares, of which he held 1,996 in his own right and 3,000 as sole surviving executor of his father's will upon the trusts relating thereto. The remaining four shares were held, one each, by the testator's sister, Miss Gee; his second wife, who remarried after his death and at the time of this action had become Mrs. Haynes; his daughter, Mrs. Hunter; and Mr. Staples.

The testator appointed Mrs. Haynes, Mrs. Hunter and Mr. Staples to be the executors and trustees of his will. After the death of the testator Mr. Staples was appointed managing director of the company by unanimous agreement of the executors and Miss Gee, who together constituted all the registered share-holders. The appointment and remuneration of Mr. Staples were subsequently confirmed by an annual general meeting.

The testator's will was proved on March 24, 1939, by all three executors, and **9–39** the 3,000 shares, previously vested in the testator as executor of his father's will, were registered in the names of the beneficiaries entitled under that will. The testator was himself so entitled to 334 shares.

Mr. Staples received £15,721 as remuneration between the date of the testator's death and March 31, 1947. Some of the beneficiaries under the testator's will claimed that Mr. Staples was liable to account.

HARMAN J.: ". . . [The claim] raises in a complicated form the vexed question of the liability of trustees who become salaried officers of companies in which their testator's estate is largely interested . . .

"The allegation made against Mr. Staples is that he made use of his position of **9–40** trust under the testator's will to obtain his remuneration, and it is this which needs examination. The cases on the subject are not numerous, nor do I find them very helpful. None of them deals with a position where more than one trust estate is involved. The principle that a trustee, in the absence of a special contract, cannot make a profit out of his trust, nor be paid for his time and trouble, is an old one, and is spoken of as established in *Robinson v. Pett.*[20] It is most clearly stated by Lord Herschell in *Bray v. Ford*[21] in these words: 'It is an inflexible rule of a court of equity that a person in a fiduciary position . . . is not, unless otherwise expressly provided, entitled to make a profit; he is not allowed to put himself in a position where his interest and duty conflict.' The difficulty of applying this principle arises where the payment is made not directly out of the trust estate, but by a third party or body, and, in particular, by a limited company. The modern cases begin with *Re Francis*,[22] from which it appears that Kekewich J. declined to allow trustees to retain for their own use remuneration received by them from a company in which the testator held substantially all the shares. The remuneration was voted at a general meeting, and appears to have been procured by the trustees by the exercise of the voting powers attached to the trust shares which had become registered in their names. This case was not cited in *Re Dover Extension Ltd*,[23] which has been sometimes thought to be incon-sistent with it.[24] This, however, in my judgment is not so. The trustees there had

---

[20] (1734) 3 P.Wms. 250 at 261.
[21] [1896] A.C. 44 at 51.
[22] (1905) 74 L.J.Ch. 198.
[23] [1908] 1 Ch. 65.
[24] See, *e.g. Underhill on Trusts,* (9th ed.) p. 353.

9–41

become directors before they held any trust shares. The trust shares were, by their own procurement, registered in their names in order to qualify them to continue as directors, but it was not by virtue of the use of these shares that they either became entitled or continued to earn their fees. Warrington J., however, in this case does suggest,[25] that remuneration paid for acting as director of a company can never be a profit for which a trustee needs to account, and it is this expression of opinion which is reflected in the headnote and has given rise to a good deal of misconception about the case. This view was not necessary to the decision and may be regarded as mere *obiter dictum*. It is, in my judgment, too wide, if applied to a case where either the use of the trust shares brings about the appointment, or there is no independent board of the employing company to strike a proper bargain with the employed trustee. Moreover, it leaves out of account the second leg of the principle stated by Lord Herschell in *Bray v. Ford*.[26] The beneficiaries are entitled to the advantage of the unfettered use by the trustee of his judgment as to the government of the company in which they are interested. This they do not get if his judgment is clouded by the prospect of the pecuniary advantage he may acquire if he makes use of the trust shares to obtain for himself a directorship carrying remuneration. *Re Lewis*[27] is again an instance where the trustee did not receive the remuneration by virtue of the use of his position as a trustee, but by an independent bargain with the firm employing him.

9–42

"There follow two cases on the other side of the line, first, *Williams v. Barton*[28] where one of the trustees, a half-commission agent in the Stock Exchange, had persuaded his co-trustees to employ his firm to value the trust securities, thus increasing his commission from his firm and making a profit directly by the use of his position as a trustee. Russell J. held him accountable. Last, there is the decision of Cohen J. in *Re Macadam*,[29] where the cases are reviewed. There certain trustees had a power as such, and by virtue of the articles of the company, to appoint two directors of it. By the exercise of this power they appointed themselves and were held liable to account for the remuneration they received because they had acquired it by the direct use of their trust powers. Cohen J. felt (and I respectfully concur) that he ought to do nothing to weaken the principle, and he expressed the view that[30] 'the root of the matter . . . is: Did the trustee acquire the position in respect of which he drew the remuneration by virtue of his position as trustee?' The judge also held[31] that the liability to account for a profit could not 'be confined to cases where the profit is derived directly from the trust estate.'

9–43

"I conclude from this review that a trustee who either uses a power vested in him as such to obtain a benefit, as in *Re Macadam*, or who (as in *Barton's* case) procures his co-trustees, to give him, or those associated with him, remunerative employment, must account for the benefit obtained. Further, it appears to me that a trustee, who has the power, by the use of trust votes, to control his own appointment to a remunerative position, and refrains from using them, with the result that he is elected to the position of profit, would also be accountable. On the other hand, it appears not to be the law that every man who becomes a

---

[25] [1907] 2 Ch. 76 at 83.
[26] [1896] A.C. 44 at 51.
[27] [1910] 103 L.T. 495.
[28] [1927] 2 Ch. 9.
[29] [1946] Ch. 73.
[30] *Ibid.* at 82.
[31] *Ibid.*

trustee, holding, as such, shares in a limited company, is made *ipso facto* accountable for remuneration received from that company independently of any use by him of the trust holding, whether by voting or refraining from doing so. For instance, A, who holds the majority of the shares in a limited company, becomes the trustee of the estate of B, a holder of a minority interest. This cannot, I think, disentitle A to use his own shares to procure his appointment as an officer of the company, nor compel him to disgorge the remuneration he so receives, for he cannot be disentitled to the use of his own voting powers, nor could the use of the trust votes in a contrary sense prevent the majority prevailing. Many other instances could be given of a similar kind of these, *Re Dover Coalfield Extension Ltd* is really one. There the trustees did not earn their fees by virtue of the trust shares, though, no doubt, the holding of those shares was a qualification necessary for the continued earning of the fees. In so far as Warrington J. goes further than this, as he seems to do by suggesting that remuneration paid by a company could not be a 'profit,' it being a mere wage equivalent in value to the work done for it, I feel he goes too far. Certainly this view was not taken in *Re Macadam*. It would gravely encroach on the principle which Cohen J. [in that case] and Russell J. in *Williams v. Barton* felt to be so important.

"I turn now to an examination of the facts in this case to see what (if any) use **9–44** was made of the trust shares in the appointment of Mr. Staples. In my judgment, when the facts are examined, no such use was made. After the death of the testator, only four persons remained on the register of this company, and they alone could attend meetings of it. As I have said before, the meeting [at which Mr. Staples was appointed managing director] was attended by all the corporators. Each of them held one share, and, as the resolutions were passed unanimously, they must be supposed to have voted in favour by the use of that share. If the corporators, as I think, held their shares beneficially, they were entitled to vote as they chose. If, on the other hand, they were nominees of the testator, there were still three of them whose votes outweighed the vote of Mr. Staples if it was his duty to vote against his own interest. In neither event did the trust shares come into the picture at all. If this be too narrow a view to take, and it is right for this purpose to look behind the register at the beneficial interests in the shares of the company, then it will be seen that the majority interest belonged to the estate of [the testator's father] and that the persons entitled to have his shares registered in their names . . . were in favour of the appointment and the payment of the stipulated remuneration. If then the shares in which the testator's estate was interested had all been used against the resolutions, they would still have been carried, and, therefore, the appointment was not procured by the use of the trust interest vested in the defendant executors, or any of them, by the will of the testator, in which alone the plaintiffs are interested. On the evidence tendered to me, I think it is clear that the persons present at this meeting had no notion that they were using trust votes, or that trust votes controlled the company. They merely met as the four corporators to decide the company's future and were entitled to come to the conclusion at which they arrived . . ."[33]

---

[33] See also *Re Liewellin* [1949] Ch. 225 (testator authorised trustees to use trust shares to secure appointment as directors. *Held* he must be deemed to have authorised them to retain directors' fees).

GARETH JONES (1968) 84 L.Q.R. 474

9–45 *"Regal (Hastings) Ltd v. Gulliver*[34] is a good illustration of the approach of the English courts. The appellant company owned a cinema in Hastings and wanted to acquire two more cinemas, with a view to selling the property of the company as a going concern. For the purpose of acquiring the cinemas a subsidiary company was formed. The landlord was prepared to offer a lease of these properties but required the directors to guarantee the rent unless the paid-up capital of the subsidiary was £5,000. The appellant company, which was to hold all the shares of the subsidiary company, could only afford to subscribe for 2,000 shares; and the directors did not want to give personal guarantees for the rest. Accordingly the directors (on their own behalf and on behalf of certain third parties) and the company solicitor arranged to finance the transaction by personally taking up the other 3,000 shares. This arrangement was formalised by a resolution at a board meeting at which the solicitor was present, and the shares were duly paid up and allotted. The trial judge found that the directors and the solicitor had acted in perfect good faith and in the best interests of the appellant company. Shortly afterwards the proposed sale and purchase of the three cinemas as going concerns fell through. But it was replaced by another proposal which involved a sale of the shares in the appellant company and its subsidiary. This proposal was accepted. From the sale of their shares in the subsidiary, the directors and the solicitor made a profit of £2 16s. 1d. per share. In this action the appellant company, now controlled by the purchasers, sought to recover this profit from the former directors and the solicitor.

9–46 "The House of Lords held that the directors, but not the solicitor, must disgorge their profits to the company, for the opportunity and special knowledge to acquire the shares had come to them *qua* fiduciaries. As Lord Russell of Killowen said[35]:

> "The rule of equity which insists on those who by use of a fiduciary position make a profit, being liable to account for that profit, in no way depends on fraud, or absence of bona fides: or upon such questions or considerations as whether the profit would or should otherwise have gone to the plaintiff, or whether the profiteer was under a duty to obtain the source of the profit for the plaintiff, or whether he took a risk or acted as he did for the benefit of the plaintiff, or whether the plaintiff has in fact been damaged or benefited by his action. The liability arises from the mere fact of a profit having, in the stated circumstances, been made. The profiteer, however honest and well intentioned, cannot escape the risk of being called upon to account . . .

9–47 > "I am of the opinion that the directors' standing in a fiduciary relationship to Regal [the appellant company] in regard to the exercise of their powers as directors, and having obtained these shares by reason and only by reason of the fact that they were directors of Regal and in the course of the execution of that office, are accountable for the profits which they have made out of them. The equitable rule laid down in *Keech v. Sandford* . . . and similar authorities applies to them in full force. It was contended that these cases were distinguishable by reason of the fact that

---

[34] [1967] 2 A.C. 134n.
[35] [1967] 2 A.C. 134 at 145, 149.

it was impossible for Regal to get the shares owing to lack of funds, and that the directors in taking the shares were really acting as members of the public. I cannot accept this argument. It was impossible for the *cestui que trust* in *Keech v. Sandford* to obtain the lease, nevertheless the trustee was accountable. The suggestion that the directors were applying simply as members of the public is a travesty of the facts.'

"The solicitor, however, was not in a fiduciary position.[36] Because he had taken **9–48** the shares at the directors' request, he was not compelled to account for his profits. The chairman of the company who had bought his shares only as a nominee of the third parties was also not liable to account to the appellant company. "Neither the shares nor the profit ever belonged to [him]."[37]

"The company's claim lacked all merit.[38] As a result of the House of Lords' **9–49** decision, the purchasers of the shares 'receive[d] in one hand part of the sum which ha[d] been paid by the other.' For the shares in Amalgamated [the subsidiary] they paid £3 16s. 1d. per share, yet part of that sum may be returned to the group, though not necessarily to the individual shareholders by reason of the enhancement in the value of the shares in Regal—an enhancement brought about as a result of the receipt by the company of the profit made by some of its former directors on the sale of Amalgamated shares."[39] Only Lord Porter, from whose speech this quotation is taken, chose to mention this point. He recognised that Regal, and hence its purchasers, had received an "unexpected windfall." But, he concluded,[40]

> "whether it be so or not, the principle that a person occupying a fiduciary relationship shall not make a profit by reason thereof is of such vital importance that the possible consequence in the present case is in fact as it is in law an immaterial consideration."

"But did the House too easily assume that principle to be of 'vital import- **9–50** ance'? The critical issue was whether directors, acting in good faith, should be allowed to retain profits made from the sale of shares in circumstances where the company wanted to acquire them but was financially unable to do so. It may well be necessary in such a case to impose a prophylactic rule. As Judge Swan of the Court of Appeals, Second Circuit, pointed out in *Irving Trust Co. v. Deutsch*,[41] if directors could justify their conduct on the theory that their corporation was financially unable to undertake their venture,

> "there will be a temptation to refrain from exerting their strongest efforts on behalf of the corporation since, if it does not meet the obligations, an opportunity of profit will be open to them [the directors] personally . . .
> "If the directors are uncertain whether the corporation can make the necessary outlays, they need not embark it upon the venture; if they do, they may not substitute themselves for the corporation any place along the line and divert possible benefits into their own pockets."

---

[36] He was rather lucky to escape liability: see *Luxor (Eastbourne) Ltd v. Cooper* [1939] 4 All E.R. 414–417 for his close involvement with the directors.
[37] At 151, *per* Lord Russell of Killowen.
[38] L. C. B. Gower, *Modern Company Law* (2nd ed., London 1957), p. 487.
[39] [1967] 2 A.C. 134 at 152, *per* Lord Porter.
[40] At 152.
[41] 73 F. 2d 121, 124 (1934). But *cf. Zeckendorf v. Steinfeld*, 12 Ariz. 245, 100 P. 784 (1909); *Beaumont v. Folsom*, 136 Neb. 235, 285 N.W. 547 (1939).

9–51   "But directors are business men. In the Court of Appeal in *Regal (Hastings) Ltd v. Gulliver*,[42] Lord Greene sympathised with the dilemma of the Regal directors:

> "[A]s a matter of business . . . there was only one way left of raising the money, and that was putting it up themselves. . . . That being so, the only way in which [they] could secure that benefit for the company was by putting up the money themselves. Once that decision is held to be a bona fide one and fraud drops out of the case, it seems to me that there is only one conclusion, namely, that the [company's] appeal must be dismissed with costs."

9–52   "The House of Lords rejected Lord Green's reasoning and followed *Keech v. Sandford*.[43] Yet it is not easy to see why because Lord King decided in 1726 that a trustee could not renew a trust lease for his own benefit, it *must* follow that the Regal directors, acting honestly and in the best interests of the company should disgorge the profit from the sale of the shares. The relevant policy considerations were delicately balanced. But the House of Lords' unquestioning adherence to the inexorable rule of equity meant that they were never properly weighed against each other."

SEAGER v. COPYDEX

9–53   Court of Appeal [1967] 1 W.L.R. 923; [1967] 2 All E.R. 415 (Lord Denning M.R., Salmon and Winn L.JJ.)

LORD DENNING M.R. (in a reserved judgment): "Summarised, the facts are these—

"(i) The plaintiff invented the 'Klent' carpet, grip and took out a patent for it. He manufactured this grip and sold it. He was looking for a selling organisation to market it.

"(ii) The plaintiff negotiated with the defendant company with a view to their marketing the 'Klent' grip. These negotiations were with Mr. Preston, the assistant manager, and Mr. Boon, the sales manager. These negotiations lasted more than a year, but came to nothing.

"(iii) In the course of those negotiations, the plaintiff disclosed to Mr. Preston and Mr. Boon all the features of the 'Klent' grip. He also told them of an idea of his for an alternative carpet grip with a 'V' tang and strong point. But they rejected it, saying that they were only interested in the 'Klent' grip.

"(iv) Both Mr. Preston and Mr. Boon realised that the information was given to them in confidence. Neither of them had any engineering skills, nor had invented anything.

"(v) As soon as the negotiations looked like coming to nothing, the defendant company decided to make a carpet grip of their own, which was to be basically similar to the 'Klent' grip, but with spikes which would not infringe the plaintiff's patent.

9–54   "(vi) The defendant company did in fact make a carpet grip which did not infringe the plaintiff's patent for a 'Klent' grip. But it embodied the very idea of an alternative grip (of a 'V-tang' with strong point) which the plaintiff mentioned

---

[42] The decision of the Court of Appeal is not reported. This quotation from Lord Greene's judgment was cited by Viscount Sankey in his speech in the House of Lords (at p. 381). It was adopted and followed in *Peso Silver Mines Ltd (N.P.L.) v. Cropper* (1966) 58 D.L.R. (2d) 1.

[43] (1726) Cas.temp. King 61.

to them in the course of the negotiations. They made an application to patent it, and gave the name of Mr. Preston as the true and first inventor.

"(vii) The defendant company gave this carpet grip the name 'Invisigrip' which was the very name which the plaintiff says that he mentioned to Mr. Preston and Mr. Boon in the course of the negotiations.

"(viii) The defendant company say that their alternative grip was the result of their own ideas and was not derived in any way from any information given to them by the plaintiff. They say also that the name of 'Invisigrip' was their own spontaneous idea.

"(ix) I have no doubt that the defendant company honestly believed the **9–55** alternative grip was their own idea; but I think that they must unconsciously have made use of the information which the plaintiff gave them. The coincidences are too strong to permit of any other explanation.

"*The Law*. I start with one sentence in the judgment of Lord Greene M.R. in *Saltman Engineering Co. Ltd v. Campbell Engineering Co. Ltd*[44]:

> 'If a defendant is proved to have used confidential information, directly or indirectly obtained from the plaintiff, without the consent, express or implied, of the plaintiff, he will be guilty of an infringement of the plaintiff's rights.'

To this I add a sentence from the judgment of Roxburgh J. in *Terrapin Ltd v. Builders' Supply Co. (Hayes) Ltd*,[45] which was quoted and adopted as correct by Roskill J. in *Cranleigh Precision Engineering Co. Ltd v. Bryant*[46]:

> 'As I understand it, the essence of this branch of the law, whatever the **9–56** origin of it may be, is that a person who has obtained information in confidence is not allowed to use it as a springboard for activities detrimental to the person who made the confidential communication, and springboard it remains even when all the features have been published or can be ascertained by actual inspection by any member of the public.'

The law on this subject does not depend on any implied contract. It depends on **9–57** the broad principle of equity that he who has received information in confidence shall not take unfair advantage of it. He must not make use of it to the prejudice of him who gave it without obtaining his consent. The principle is clear enough when the whole of the information is private. The difficulty arises when the information is in part public and in part private. As for instance in this case. A good deal of the information which the plaintiff gave to the defendant company was available to the public, such as the patent specification in the Patent Office, or the 'Klent' grip, which he sold to anyone who asked. But there was a good deal of other information which was private, such as, the difficulties which had to be overcome in making a satisfactory grip; the necessity for a strong, sharp tooth; the alternative forms of tooth; and the like. When the information is mixed, being partly public and partly private, then the recipient must take special care to use only the material which is in the public domain. He should go to the public source and get it: or, at any rate, not be in a better position than if he had gone to the public source. He should not get a start over others by using the

---

[44] [1963] 3 All E.R. 413 at 414.
[45] [1960] R.P.C. 130.
[46] [1965] 1 W.L.R. 1293.

information which he received in confidence. At any rate, he should not get a start without paying for it. It may not be a case for injunction but only for damages, depending on the worth of the confidential information to him in saving him time and trouble.

"*Conclusion.* Applying these principles, I think that the plaintiff should succeed. On the facts which I have stated, he told the defendant company a lot about the making of a satisfactory carpet grip which was not in the public domain. They would not have got going so quickly except for what they had learned in their discussions with him. They got to know in particular that it was possible to make an alternative grip in the form of a 'V-tang,' provided the tooth was sharp enough and strong enough, and they were told about the special shape required. The judge thought that the information was not significant. But I think it was. It was the springboard which enabled them to go on to devise the 'Invisigrip' and to apply for a patent for it. They were quite innocent of any intention to take advantage of him. They thought that, as long as they did not infringe his patent, they were exempt. In this they were in error. They were not aware of the law as to confidential information.

9–58　　"I would allow the appeal and give judgment to the plaintiff for damages to be assessed . . .

"The court grants neither an account of profits, nor an injunction, but only damages to be assessed by the Master. Damages should be assessed on the basis of reasonable compensation for the use of the confidential information which was given to the defendant company."[47]

III. Competition with the Trust

9–59　　The general rule is that a trustee may not, after accepting a trust which comprises a business, set up a private business which competes or may compete with the business of the trust since, if he did so, his interest would conflict with his duty. Thus in *Re Thomson*,[48] the testator's estate included a yachtbroker's business which he bequeathed to his executors on trust to continue it. One of the executors claimed the right to set up a similar business in competition with the trust, but the court granted an injunction to restrain him.[49] On the other hand, in the Irish case of *Moore v. M'Glynn*,[50] the court refused to restrain a trustee from setting up a competing business, but considered that it would be a good ground for removing him from his trusteeship. Chatterton V.-C. observed[51]: "I

---

[47] In *Seager v. Copydex (No. 2)* [1969] 1 W.L.R. 809 the measure of damages was held to be a consultant's fee, if the information could have been acquired by employing a consultant, or the sale price between a willing seller and buyer if the information was of a special inventive nature using damages for conversion as an analogy. In *Satnam Investments Ltd v. Dunlop Heywood & Co Ltd* [1999] 3 All E.R. 652 confidential information obtained at an early stage before it became public was not regarded as a springboard.

[48] [1930] 1 Ch. 203. Where at 215 Clauson J. said, "An executor and trustee having duties to discharge of a fiduciary nature towards the beneficiaries under the will shall not be allowed to enter into any engagement in which he has or can have a personal interest conflicting or which possibly may conflict with the interests of those whom he is bound to protect."

[49] For the grant of an injunction against a business competitor allegedly taking advantage of confidential financial information see *United Pau-Europe Communications NV. v. Deutsche Bank A.G.* [2000] 2 B.C.L.C. 461 (C.A.).

[50] [1894] 1 I.R. 74.

[51] *ibid.* at 89.

have not been referred to, nor am I aware of, any case deciding that an executor or trustee of a will carrying on the business of his testator is disabled from setting up a similar business in the same locality on his own account. . . . I am not prepared to hold that a trustee is guilty of a breach of trust in setting up for himself in a similar line of business in the neighbourhood, provided that he does not resort to deception or solicitation of custom from persons dealing at the old shop." A distinction between this case and *Re Thomson* is that in the latter the business was highly specialised and the locality was very small so that the competition was inevitable whether or not there was solicitation of custom.

Any profits made in breach of duty should be held on trust for the **9–60** beneficiaries as the profits are their profits which have been lost by the trustee's competition.[52] Whilst partners are under a statutory obligation[53] not to engage in a competing business it seems that non-service directors are not so obliged (unless their contract so provides) but they must be very careful as to the information they disclose to rival companies[54] since confidential information must not be disclosed.

IV. GRATUITOUS ADMINSTRATION OF TRUST UNLESS OTHERWISE AUTHORISED

Trustees must, in the absence of some special dispensation, administer **9–61** the trust gratuitously for otherwise "the trust estate might be loaded and made of little value."[55] There is an obvious conflict between their self-interest and their fiduciary duty, but the position has been much liberalised and modernised by the Trustee Act 2000.

The cases in which the trustee is entitled to payment for his services are as follows.

First, in a suitable case the court has an inherent jurisdiction to be excercised sparingly to authorise a trustee to receive remuneration prospectively or retrospectively and it may increase the remuneration authorised by the trust instrument. In order to do so the court must be satisfied that the services of the particular trustee will be or have been of exceptional benefit to the estate.[56] The court, when appointing a *corporation* (other than the Public Trustee or Guardian) to act, also has

---

[52] Goff and Jones, p. 728 citing *Somerville v. Mackay* (1810) 16 Ves. 382; *Dean v. MacDowell* (1877) 8 Ch.D. 345 at 353; *Trimble v. Goldberg* [1906] A.C. 494; Restatement of Restitution, para. 199.
[53] Partnership Act 1890, s.30.
[54] *London & Mashonaland Exploration Co. v. New Mashonaland Exploration Co.* [1891] W.N. 165 approved by Lord Blanesburgh in *Bell v. Lever Bros.* [1932] A.C. 161, 195; *Aubanei & Atabaster Ltd v. Aubanel* (1949) 66 R.P.C. 343.
[55] *Robinson v. Pett* (1734) 3 P. Wms, 249 at 251.
[56] *Re Duke of Norfolk's S.T.* [1982] Ch. 61; *Marshall v. Holloway* (1820) 2 Swans. 432; *Docker v. Somes* (1834) 2 My. & K. 655; *Re Freeman* (1887) 37 Ch.D. 148; *Re Masters* [1953] 1 W.L.R. 81; *Re Macadam* [1946] Ch. 73; *Boardman v. Phipps* [1967] 2 A.C. 46; *Re Barbour's Settlement* [1974] 1 All E.R. 1188, 1192; *Re Keeler's S.T.* [1981] 1 All E.R. 888 (though it overlooks *Re Llewellin's W.T.* [1949] Ch. 225); *Foster v. Spencer* [1996] 2 All E.R. 672. Even a wrongdoer may benefit: *O'Sullivan v. Management Agency & Music Ltd* [1985] 3 All E.R. 351; *John v. James* [1986] S.T.C. 352 at 358; *Re Badfinger* [2001] W.T.L.R. 1.

a statutory jurisdiction[57] under section 42 of the Trustee Act 1925 to authorise it to charge for its services.

9–62   Second, if the settlement authorises the trustee to charge for his services he is entitled to be paid, but charging clauses are construed strictly in the sense that the onus is on the trustee to show that the charge which he proposes to make is covered by the terms of the settlement. Thus, where a solicitor-trustee was authorised to make "professional charges," and even where the words "for his time and trouble" were added, he was not be allowed to charge for time and trouble expended other than in his position as solicitor.[58] But where a will authorised the solicitor-trustee to make "the usual professional or *other proper and reasonable* charges for all business done and time expended in relation to the trusts of the will, *whether such business is usually within the business of a solicitor or not,*" the solicitor was permitted to charge for business not strictly of a professional nature transacted by him in relation to the trust,[59] though, apparently, not for work altogether outside his professional vocation that a layman could do.[60] However, in radical fashion section 28(2) of the Trustee Act 2000

9–63   treats a trustee entitled under the trust instrument to charge for services provided by him as entitled to receive payment "in respect of services even if they are services which are capable of being provided by a lay trustee", so long as the trustee is "a trust corporation or is acting in a professional capacity"—and the services were provided after January 2001.[61] A trustee acts in a professional capacity[62] "if he acts in the course of a profession or business which consists of or includes the provision of services in connection with (a) the management or administration of trusts generally or a particular kind of trust, or (b) any particular aspect of the management or administration of trusts generally or a particular kind of trust." A person acts as a "lay trustee" if he does not act in a professional capacity and is not a trust corporation.[63] For deaths after January 2001 payments of remuneration to a personal representative who (or whose spouse) witnesses the will will not be treated as legacies that fail due to such witnessing and will not abate with other legacies if the estate is unable to pay all legacies in full but will be paid in priority thereto.[64]

9–64   Third, by section 29 of the Trustee Act 2000 (unless provision as to entitlement to remuneration has been made by the trust instrument or by primary or subordinate legislation[65]—and unless the trust is a

---

[57] The Public Trustee or Guardian has a statutory right to charge under the Public Trustee Act 1906, s.9, as have custodian trustees acting as custodian trustees *only* under the Public Trustee Act 1906, s.4: *Forster v. Williams Deacon's Bank* [1935] Ch. 359. Judicial trustees may charge under Judicial Trustees Act 1896, s.1.

[58] *Re Chapple* (1884) 27 Ch.D. 584; *Re Orwell* [1982] 3 All E.R. 177.

[59] *Re Ames* (1883) 25 Ch.D. 72.

[60] *Clarkson v. Robinson* [1900] 2 Ch. 722.

[61] Section 33(1) Trustee Act 2000.

[62] s.28(5) *ibid.*

[63] s.28(6) *ibid.*

[64] s.33(2) *ibid.*

[65] s.29(5) *ibid.*

charitable trust[66]) a trustee which is a trust corporation is entitled to "reasonable remuneration",[67] while a trustee who acts in a "professional capacity" (as defined in the last paragraph) and is not a sole trustee, is also entitled to reasonable remuneration if each other trustee has agreed in writing that he may be remunerated for the services he provides to the trust,[68] including services capable of being provided by a lay trustee.[69] The power for a trustee to agree that another trustee be remunerated for her services is a power to be exercised in the interests of the beneficiaries as a whole and not for the personal benefit of the trustee to be remunerated or of the power-exerciser,[70] hoping perhaps for a reciprocal agreement for him to be remunerated. However, because it is the legislation that has placed a trustee in an individious position where there is a sensible possibility of a conflict between self-interest and fiduciary duty, the exercise of the power to agree remuneration of a trustee is not impeachable by reason only that a conflict situation has arisen.[71] Where T_1 and T_2 are to be trustees it is better not to rely on section 29 but on an express remuneration clause: in the absence of the latter, T_1 and T_2 agreeing to each other being remunerated would be vulnerable to attack by disaffected beneficiaries so that to protect themselves T_1 and T_2 would want to obtain the prior consent of adult beneficiaries[72] or the authorisation of the court.[73]

Fourth, if the beneficiaries are all of full capacity and between them **9–65** absolutely entitled to the trust estate, they may authorise the trustee to be paid. If the beneficiaries then sue the trustee for breach of trust in paying trust moneys to himself the trustee has their authorisation as a defence unless undue influence was exercised by him.

Fifth, the general rule of gratuitous service was particularly severe in the case of solicitor-trustees. Thus in *Christophers v. White*,[74] it was held that a solicitor-trustee's firm was not entitled to charge for professional services rendered to the trust by a partner in the firm even though the partner was not one of the trustees.[75] But where a solicitor-trustee employed his partner, as distinct from his firm, under an *express* agreement that the partner should be individually entitled to charges, these were allowed on the ground that where such an agreement is carried out there is no infringement of the rule that a trustee may not make his office a source of remuneration.[76] Moreover, the severity of the

---

[66] s.29(1)(b), (2)(b) *ibid.* By s.30 the Secretary of State can make regulations for remuneration of trustees of charitable trusts who are trust corporations or act in a professional capacity.
[67] As defined in s.29(3).
[68] s.29(2).
[69] s.29(4).
[70] See Report on Trustees' Powers and Duties, Law Com No. 260 (1999) para. 7.10 and Explanatory Note to Trustee Bill 2000, para. 103.
[71] Cp *Edge v. Pensions Ombudsman* [1998] Ch. 512.
[72] A trustee can invoke s.62 of the Trustee Act 1925 to claim an indemnity from a beneficiary who consented to a breach of trust, so inhibiting action by a descendant of such a beneficiary.
[73] See *Lewin on Trusts* (17th ed.), para. 20–149D.
[74] (1847) 10 Beav. 523.
[75] See also *Re Gates* [1933] Ch. 913 and *Re Hill* [1934] Ch. 623.
[76] *Clack v. Carlon* (1861) 30 L.J.Ch. 639.

rule was relaxed by the case of *Cradock v. Piper*,[77] in which a solicitor-trustee acted as solicitor for himself and his co-trustees in legal proceedings relating to the trust, and was held to be entitled to his usual charges. The rule is that unlike a sole trustee acting as solicitor to the trust, a solicitor-trustee acting in legal proceedings[78] for a body of trustees, of whom he himself is one, is entitled to his usual charges if the fact of his appearing for himself and his co-trustees jointly has not increased the costs which would have been incurred if he had appeared for those co-trustees only.

9–66　　Sixth, where the trust property is situate abroad and the law of the foreign country permits payment, the trustee is entitled to keep any remuneration which he has received. Thus in *Re Northcote*,[79] a testator who left assets both in this country and in the United States died domiciled in England, and the principal forum of administration was therefore English. The executors took out an English grant, and on doing so they were put on terms by the Revenue, the English effects being insufficient to pay the English duty, to undertake themselves personally to obtain a grant in New York in respect of the American assets. In due course they obtained such a grant, and got in the assets. Under the law of New York they were entitled to commission for so doing, and Harman J. held that they were under no duty to account for it to the beneficiaries.

PART V

REMUNERATION

9–67　　**28.**—(1) Except to the extent (if any) to which the trust instrument makes inconsistent provision, subsections (2) to (4) apply to a trustee if—

  (a) there is a provision in the trust instrument entitling him to receive payment out of trust funds in respect of services provided by him to or on behalf of the trust, and
  (b) the trustee is a trust corporation or is acting in a professional capacity.

  (2) The trustee is to be treated as entitled under the trust instrument to receive payment in respect of services even if they are services which are capable of being provided by a lay trustee.
  (3) Subsection (2) applies to a trustee of a charitable trust who is not a trust corporation only—

  (a) if he is not a sole trustee, and

---

[77] (1850) 1 Mac. & G. 664.
[78] Legal proceedings need not necessarily be hostile litigation but may be friendly proceedings in chambers: *Re Corsellis* (1887) 34 Ch.D. 675. It must be work in connection with a writ or an originating summons rather than general advisory work not relating to legal proceedings.
[79] [1949] 1 All E.R. 442; see also *Chambers v. Goldwin* (1802) 9 Ves. 271.

(b) to the extent that a majority of the other trustees have agreed that it should apply to him.

(4) Any payments to which the trustee is entitled in respect of services are to be treated as remuneration for services (and not as a gift) for the purposes of—

(a) section 15 of the Wills Act 1837 (gifts to an attesting witness to be void), and
(b) section 34(3) of the Administration of Estates Act 1925 (order in which estate to be paid out).

(5) For the purposes of this Part, a trustee acts in a professional capacity if he acts in the course of a profession or business which consists of or includes the provision of services in connection with—

(a) the management or administration of trusts generally or a particular kind of trust, or
(b) any particular aspect of the management or administration of trusts generally or a particular kind of trust,

and the services he provides to or on behalf of the trust fall within that description.

(6) For the purposes of this Part, a person acts as a lay trustee if he—

(a) is not a trust corporation, and
(b) does not act in a professional capacity.

29.—(1) Subject to subsection (5), a trustee who—   **9–68**

(a) is a trust corporation, but
(b) is not a trustee of a charitable trust,

is entitled to receive reasonable remuneration out of the trust funds for any services that the trust corporation provides to or on behalf of the trust.

(2) Subject to subsection (5), a trustee who—

(a) acts in a professional capacity, but
(b) is not a trust corporation, a trustee of a charitable trust or a sole trustee,

is entitled to receive reasonable remuneration out of the trust funds for any services that he provides to or on behalf of the trust if each other trustee has agreed in writing that he may be remunerated for the services.

(3) "Reasonable remuneration" means, in relation to the provision of services by a trustee, such remuneration as is reasonable in the circumstances for the provision of those services to or on behalf of that trust by that trustee and for the purposes of subsection (1) includes, in relation to the provision of services by a trustee who is an authorised institution under the Banking Act 1987 and provides the services in that capacity, the institution's reasonable charges for the provision of such services.

(4) A trustee is entitled to remuneration under this section even if the services in question are capable of being provided by a lay trustee.

(5) A trustee is not entitled to remuneration under this section if any provision about his entitlement to remuneration has been made—

(a) by the trust instrument, or
(b) by any enactment or any provision of subordinate legislation.

(6) This section applies to a trustee who has been authorised under a power conferred by Part IV or the trust instrument—

(a) to exercise functions as an agent of the trustees, or
(b) to act as a nominee or custodian,

as it applies to any other trustee.

9–69   **30.**—(1) The Secretary of State may by regulations make provision for the remuneration of trustees of charitable trusts who are trust corporations or act in a professional capacity.

(2) The power under subsection (1) includes power to make provision for the remuneration of a trustee who has been authorised under a power conferred by Part IV or any other enactment or any provision of subordinate legislation, or by the trust instrument—

(a) to exercise functions as an agent of the trustees, or
(b) to act as a nominee or custodian.

(3) Regulations under this section may—

(a) make different provision for different cases;
(b) contain such supplemental, incidental, consequential and transitional provision as the Secretary of State considers appropriate.

(4) The power to make regulations under this section is exercisable by statutory instrument, but no such instrument shall be made unless a draft of it has been laid before Parliament and approved by a resolution of each House of Parliament.

9–70   **31.**—(1) A trustee—

(a) is entitled to be reimbursed from the trust funds, or
(b) may pay out of the trust funds,

expenses properly incurred by him when acting on behalf of the trust.

(2) This section applies to a trustee who has been authorised under a power conferred by Part IV or any other enactment or any provision of subordinate legislation, or by the trust instrument—

(a) to exercise functions as an agent of the trustees, or
(b) to act as a nominee or custodian,

as it applies to any other trustee.

32.—(1) This section applies if, under a power conferred by Part IV or any **9–71** other enactment or any provision of subordinate legislation, or by the trust instrument, a person other than a trustee has been—

(a) authorised to exercise functions as an agent of the trustees, or
(b) appointed to act as a nominee or custodian.

(2) The trustees may remunerate the agent, nominee or custodian out of the trust funds for services if—

(a) he is engaged on terms entitling him to be remunerated for those services, and
(b) the amount does not exceed such remuneration as is reasonable in the circumstances for the provision of those services by him to or on behalf of that trust.

(3) The trustees may reimburse the agent, nominee or custodian out of the trust funds for any expenses properly incurred by him in exercising functions as an agent, nominee or custodian.

33.—(1) Subject to subsection (2), sections 28, 29, 31 and 32 apply in relation **9–72** to services provided to or on behalf of, or (as the case may be) expenses incurred on or after their commencement on behalf of, trusts whenever created.
(2) Nothing in section 28 or 29 is to be treated as affecting the operation of—

(a) section 15 of the Wills Act 1837, or
(b) section 34(3) of the Administration of Estates Act 1925,

in relation to any death occurring before the commencement of section 28 or (as the case may be) section 29.

Section 3. Investment of Trust Funds

A fundamental function of the trustees is to invest and manage the trust **9–73** fund so that there is adequate income and capital available for the beneficiaries when the trustees come to exercise their other fundamental function, their distributive function. First, the trustees must familiarise themselves with their powers of investment so that they know which investments are within or outside their powers. Second, in deciding whether to sell or purchase investments within the authorised range of investments, the trustees must comply with further duties.

I. THE RANGE OF INVESTMENTS

Trustees are under a fundamental duty to invest the trust funds in **9–74** investments authorised expressly or impliedly by the trust instrument or by the court[80] or in default by the Trustee Act 2000 which as of February

---

[80] The court's powers are in Trustee Act 1925, s.57 and the Variation of Trusts Act 1958.

1, 2001 replaced the Trustee Investments Act 1961. A properly drafted trust instrument will contain very extensive powers of investment so that there is no need to apply to the court for wider powers or otherwise rely upon the Trustee Act 2000 which applies to pre-existing trusts as well as new trusts. If a testator by specific gift leaves certain investments (*e.g.* my apartments in Tenerife) to trustees for A for life, then B absolutely, this impliedly authorises the trustees to retain such investments but not to purchase any more.[81] If personal representatives appropriate property to trustees under section 41 of the Administration of Estates Act 1925, then such property is by such section thereafter treated as an authorised investment for purposes of retention but not for purchasing more of the same.

If an express investment power is void for uncertainty[82] (*e.g.* to invest in blue chip shares and such other investments as my trustees know I would approve of) then the trustees are relegated to the powers under the 2000 Act unless they obtain wider powers from the court.

II. Duties when Investing

To exhibit the statutory duty of care like a prudent person conducting another's affairs

9–75   To exhibit the statutory duty of care[83] like a prudent person, investing not for himself but for others, is required of trustees when exercising their powers of investment, reviewing investments in the light of the standard investment criteria and obtaining and considering proper advice.[84] It is considered that "such care and skill as is reasonable in the circumstances" must take account of the fact, as old case law did,[85] that prudent business persons may reasonably select some speculative investments for themselves, which they would avoid if investing for the future of someone who was depending on the trust fund as a safe and sound basis for securing her future. Thus, the Trustee Act 2000 has not affected the following statement of Lord Nicholls.[86] "It is not enough that a trustee should act honestly. Promotion of the trust purpose requires a trustee to be prudent and exercise the degree of care he would in conducting his own affairs but mindful, when making investment decisions, that he is dealing with another's property. The classic formulation of this standard of conduct was enunciated by Lindley L.J. in *Re Whiteley*[87] The duty of a trustee is not to take such care only as a prudent man would take if he had only himself to consider; the duty is rather to

---

[81] *Re Pugh* [1887] W.N. 143; *Re Whitfield* (1920) 125 L.T. 61.

[82] *Re Kolb's W.T.* [1962] Ch. 531.

[83] Set out at para. 9–04 *supra*; it may be excluded or modified by the trust instrument: Trustee Act 2000 Sched. 1, para. 7.

[84] Trustee Act 2000, Sched. 1 paras 1 and 2.

[85] *Re Whiteley* (1886) 33 Ch.D. 347, 355 endorsed thereafter in every case involving trustees' alleged breaches of their investment duties.

[86] (1995) 9 Trust L.I. 71, 73.

[87] (1886) 33 Ch.D. 347 at 355.

take such care as an ordinary prudent man would take if he were minded to make an investment for the benefit of other people for whom he felt morally bound to provide. . . . This 'ordinary prudent person conducting another's affairs' is the equitable counterpart of the reasonable man who is so ubiquitous in the common law . . . A comment is needed here on the ordinary prudent person. His standards are the minimum standards expected of trustees. If the trustee is a person professing particular expertise in the management of trusts, and he has been appointed for that reason, his conduct will be judged by the standards he professes. A professional person, a trust corporation, held out as an expert, will be expected to display the degree of skill and care and diligence such an expert would have."

He went on to endorse the view of Hoffmann J. (as he then was) who **9–76** had stated[88] "Modern trustees acting within their investment powers are entitled to be judged by the standards of current portfolio theory, which emphasises the risk level of the entire portfolio rather than the risk attaching to each investment taken in isolation." After all, as Dillon L.J. has emphasised,[89] "What the prudent man should do at any time depends on the economic and financial conditions of that time not on what judges of the past, however eminent, have held to be the prudent course in the conditions of 50 or 100 years before . . . when investment conditions were very different."

As Lord Nicholls states,[90] "Investment policy is aimed at producing a **9–77** portfolio of investments which is balanced overall and suited to the needs of the particular trust. Different investments are accompanied by different degrees of risk, which are reflected in the expected rate of return. A large fund with a widely diversified portfolio of securities might justifiably include modest holdings of high risk securities which would be imprudent and out of place in a smaller fund. In such a case it would be inappropriate to isolate one particular investment out of a vast portfolio and enquire whether that can be justified as a trust investment. Such a "line by line" approach is misplaced. The inquiry, rather, should be to look at a particular investment and enquire whether that is justified as a holding in the context of the overall portfolio. Traditional warnings against the need for trustees to avoid speculative or hazardous investments are not to be read as inhibiting trustees from maintaining portfolios of investments which contain a prudent and sensible mixture of low risk and higher risk securities. They are not to be so read, because they were not directed at a portfolio which is a balanced exercise in risk management."

---

[88] *Nestlé v. National Westminster Bank plc* June 29, 1988, [2000] W.T.L.R. 795.
[89] *Nestlé v. National Westminster Bank plc* [1994] 1 All E.R. 118 at 126.
[90] Article cited in n.86 above. On modern portfolio theory see J. Langbein (1996) 81 Iowa L.R. 641 and I.N. Legair (2000) 14 Trust L.I. 75.

9–78   The ordinary prudent person conducting another's affairs will of course review the portfolio of investments regularly[91] and if lacking investment knowledge will of course seek professional advice and consider such advice before acting upon it.[92]

9–79   Sections 4 and 5 of the Trustee Act 2000 now expressly impose such duties upon trustees as follows:

Section 4:

"(1)   In exercising any power of investment, whether arising under this Part or otherwise, a trustee must have regard to the standard investment criteria.

(2)   A trustee must from time to time review the investments of the trust and consider whether, having regard to the standard investment criteria, they should be varied.

(3)   The standard investment criteria, in relation to a trust, are—
　　(a)   the suitability to the trust of investments of the same kind as any particular investment proposed to be made or retained and of that particular investment as an investment of that kind, and
　　(b)   the need for diversification of investments of the trust, in so far as is appropriate to the circumstances of the trust."

Section 5:

9–80   "(1)   Before exercising any power of investment, whether arising under this Part or otherwise, a trustee must (unless the exception applies) obtain and consider proper advice about the way in which, having regard to the standard investment criteria, the power should be exercised.

(2)   When reviewing the investments of the trust, a trustee must (unless the exception applies) obtain and consider proper advice about whether, having regard to the standard investment criteria, the investments should be varied.

(3)   The exception is that a trustee need not obtain such advice if he reasonably concludes that in all the circumstances it is unnecessary or inappropriate to do so.

(4)   Proper advice is the advice of a person who is reasonably believed by the trustee to be qualified to give it by his ability in and practical experience of financial and other matters relating to the proposed investment."

9–81   It will be seen that proper advice is not needed if the trustee reasonably concludes (an objective test) that in all the circumstances it is unnecessary or inappropriate (*e.g.* the investment seems a safe one and a small

---

[91] *Nestlé v. National Westminster Bank plc* [1994] 1 All E.R. 118.
[92] *Cowan v. Scargill* [1985] Ch. 270; *Jones v. AMP Perpetual Trustee Co. N.Z. Ltd* [1994] 1 N.Z.L.R. 690.

one or the trustee is an experienced knowledgeable investor), while it would seem proper advice could be that of a co-trustee or employee reasonably believed by the trustee to be qualified to give it.[93] It will be advisable to have the advice in writing and to record in writing when advice is considered unnecessary or inappropriate.

Often trustees will delegate their asset management functions[94] to a land agent or a discretionary portfolio manager and have investments held by a nominee or custodian.[95] There must be a written agreement as to the terms of asset management delegation coupled with a policy statement, while there is a duty to keep the delegation arrangements and the policy statement under regular review—as is considered *infra* para. 9–138.

To act fairly

A "trustee must act fairly in making investment decisions which may **9–82** have different consequences for differing classes of beneficiaries,"[96] *e.g.* life tenant and remainderman.

> "The trustees have a wide discretion. They are, for example, entitled to take into account the income needs of the tenant for life or the fact that the tenant for life was a person known to the settlor and a primary object of the trust whereas the remainderman is a remoter relative or stranger. Of course, these cannot be allowed to become the overriding considerations but the concept of fairness between classes of beneficiaries does not require them to be excluded. It would be an inhuman rule which required trustees to adhere to some mechanical rule for preserving the real value of the capital when the tenant for life was the testator's widow who had fallen upon hard times and the remainderman was young and well-off."[97]

On appeal Staughton L.J. stated[98]:

> "A life tenant may be anxious to receive the highest possible **9–83** income while the remainderman will wish the real value of the fund to be preserved. If the life tenant is living in penury and the remainderman already has ample wealth common sense suggests that a trustee should be able to take that into account, not necessarily by seeking the highest possible income at the expense of capital but by inclining in that direction. However, before adopting that course a trustee should require some verification of

---

[93] See subsections (3) and (4) between which there may be an overlap.
[94] Trustee Act 2000, ss.11,12,13,14,15.
[95] *ibid.*, ss.16,17,19,20. Pension trustees are governed by Pensions Act 1995, s.36, *infra* at para. 9–403.
[96] *Nestlé v. National Westminster Bank*, June 29, 1988, [2000] W.T.L.R. 795.
[97] *ibid.*
[98] *Nestlé v. National Westminster Bank plc* [1994] 1 All E.R. 118 at 137.

the facts . . . Similarly, I would not regard it as a breach of trust for
the trustees to pay some regard to the relationship between Mr.
George Nestlé and Miss Nestlé. He was merely her uncle and she
would have received nothing from his share of the fund if he had
fathered a child who survived him. The trustees would be entitled
to incline towards income during his life tenancy . . . I do not think
it would be a breach of the duty to act fairly or impartially."

9–84   Where there is a life tenant the distinction between income and
capital is crucial because the life tenant is entitled to income but, if as
will almost always be the case for a well-drafted trust, there is a power to
appoint capital to the life tenant, the trustees will have the flexibility to
invest a greater part than otherwise would be possible in assets yielding
little or no income but where much capital growth is expected, so that
they can then sell some of such assets and appoint the proceeds (capital)
to the life tenant to make up for the income lost by investing in fewer
assets yielding a good income.

9–85   After all, economists and investors are concerned with the concept of
total return, *i.e.* income yield plus capital growth. The legal concept of
capital based on land settled on persons in succession regards capital as
the tree and income as the fruit of the tree,[99] though the economist's
view of income is exemplified by the well-known definition of Hicks:[1]
"Income is the maximum amount the individual can consume in a week
and still expect to be as well-off at the end of the week as he was at the
beginning." Thus, if £1 million of trust assets appreciate to be worth
£1,100,000 at the end of the year and yield income of £40,000 then the
total return of £140,000 less an amount for inflation can be spent without
the trust fund being any worse off than it was at the outset. To make
allowance for annual ups and downs of the stock market it may be
advisable to have a policy, if the terms of the trust allow it, to pay out the
equivalent of 5 per cent of the value of the fund at the end of the year
including the income produced that year. This can be done not just for
many charitable[2] and pension trusts but also for well-drafted discretionary trusts or even well-drafted fixed interest trusts where the trustees
have power to appoint capital to any beneficiary.

9–86   Judges nowadays emphasise the total return. Megarry V.-C. stated[3]
that the power of investment "must be exercised so as to yield the best
return for the beneficiaries, judged in relation to the risks of the
investments in question; and the prospects of the yield of income and of
capital appreciation both have to be considered in judging the return
from the investment" while Nicholls V.-C. stated[4] that charity trustees
should seek:

---

[99] L. H. Seltzer, *The Nature and Tax Treatment of Capital Gains and Losses* 1951, Chap. 2.
[1] J. R. Hicks, *Value and Capital*, (1938) p. 172. Further see J. Flower, A Note on Capital and Income in
the Law of Trusts in Edey & Yamey (eds.) *Debits, Credits, Finance and Profits* (1974) pp. 85–87.
[2] But not in respect of endowment capital providing the permanent base for the charity's activities.
[3] *Cowan v. Scargill* [1985] Ch. 270 at 287.
[4] *Harries v. Church Commissioners* [1992] 1 W.L.R. 1241 at 1246.

"the maximum return, whether by income or capital growth, which is consistent with commercial prudence . . . having due regard to the need to diversify, the need to balance income against capital growth and the need to balance risk against return."

To do the best they can financially for the beneficiaries as a whole

The last two quotations of Megarry V.-C. and Nicholls V.-C. make plain **9–87** the fundamental duty of trustees to do the best they can financially for the beneficiaries. Indeed, if trustees have agreed to sell Blackacre so as to be morally bound but not yet legally bound by a contract, they are under a duty to gazump (*i.e.* negotiate with someone putting in a serious higher offer) so as to obtain a higher price for the beneficiaries, even if as honourable men they would prefer to implement the bargain to which they felt in honour bound: *Buttle v. Saunders.*[5] If they have strong opinions against alcohol or investment in "Genocidia" then if such investments would be likely to be more beneficial financially than other proposed investments they must purchase those investments despite finding them disagreeable.[6] However, if trustees obtain professional advice that particular investments other than in alcohol or in Genocidia are equally satisfactory for the portfolio from the financial point of view then, of course, they can proceed to purchase those other investments. Thus, "all things being equal," trustees can refuse to invest in companies whose products or policies they find disagreeable.[7] Indeed Lord Nicholls has concluded,[8]

"In practice in these cases where trustees or [beneficiaries] have **9–88** strong views about particular investments on non-financial grounds it should be possible for trustees to exercise their investment powers in a manner avoiding embarrassment to all concerned without upsetting the balance of the portfolio . . . The range of investment is so extensive that there is scope for trustees to give effect to moral considerations without thereby prejudicing beneficiaries' financial interests."

A settlor, of course, can always restrict the trustees' powers of **9–89** investment by excluding certain types of investments and can always reduce the duties owed by the trustees, *e.g.* by permitting or directing the trustees to invest only in companies whose products or policies are ecologically more beneficial than those of other competing companies in the opinion of the trustees and by exempting[9] the trustees from liability so long as they acted in good faith.

---

[5] [1950] 2 All E.R. 193.
[6] *Cowan v. Scargill* [1985] Ch. 270.
[7] See R. E. Megarry in *Equity, Fiduciaries and Trusts* (T. G. Youdan ed.), pp. 149–159.
[8] In "Trustees and Their Broader Community: Where Duty, Morality and Ethics Converge" (1995) 9 Trust L.I. 71 at 75.
[9] On exemption clauses see *infra* at paras 9–308 *et seq.*

9–90   In the case of charitable trusts, the trustees must consider whether a particular investment is consistent with its charitable purposes so that, for example, it would not be proper for a trust concerned to rehabilitate alcoholics and prevent alcoholism to invest in companies manufacturing and distributing alcoholic drinks or for a trust for the Society of Friends to invest in shares in companies engaged in the armaments industry.[10]

American guidance on investment considerations

The American Uniform Prudent Investor Act seems to reflect the English position when it states in section 2(c) "Among circumstances that a trustee shall consider in investing and managing trust assets are such of the following as are relevant to the trust or its beneficiaries:

(1) general economic conditions;
(2) the possible impact of inflation or deflation;
(3) the expected tax consequences[11] of investment decisions or strategies;
(4) the role that each investment or course of action plays within the overall trust portfolio;
(5) the expected total return from income and the appreciation of capital;
(6) other resources of the beneficiaries;
(7) needs for liquidity, regularity of income, and preservation or appreciation of capital; and
(8) an assets special relationship or special value, if any, to the purposes of the trust or to one or more of the beneficiaries."

This is buttressed by section 2(d), "A trustee shall make a reasonable effort[12] to verify facts relevant to the investment and management of the trust assets." In England, statute[13] only provides detailed guidance for pensions trustees, as discussed *infra*, para. 9–383

Extent of liability

9–91 Liability will normally be to account for a loss caused by purchasing an unauthorised investment or by purchasing a wholly inappropriate authorised investment.[14] Exceptionally, it may be possible to make out a case that the trustee should be liable to account for a profit that ought to have been made, *e.g.* fair compensation taking account of the proper percentage that should have been invested in shares and not just

---

[10] *Martin v. Edinburgh D.C.* [1989] I Pensions L.R. 9; *Harries v. Church Commissioners* [1992] 1 W.L.R. 1241. Trustees should shun holdings of investments which might hamper a charity's work by making potential receipients of aid unwilling to be helped or by alienating some of those who support the charity financially or by voluntary work.
[11] See *Nestlé v. National Westminster Bank plc* [1993] 1 W.L.R. 1260.
[12] *ibid.*
[13] Pensions Act 1995, ss.35, 36.
[14] See paras 10–04 *et seq. infra.*

interest-yielding gilts or bonds, and of the average performance of shares in the period.[15] However, as Hoffmann J. said,[16] "In reviewing the conduct of trustees over a period of more than 60 years, one must be careful not to endow the prudent trustee with prophetic vision or expect him to have ignored the received wisdom of his time," *e.g.* as to the balance between gilt-edged securities and company shares. Where trustees invest in authorised investments it is difficult to make them liable for negligent breach of their equitable and statutory duties of care. It has to be proved that the trustees' course of conduct was a course which no properly informed[17] prudent trustee could have followed, so affording trustees plenty of leeway.[18]

COWAN v. SCARGILL

Chancery Division [1985] Ch. 270; [1984] 2 All E.R. 750; [1984] 3 W.L.R. 501

MEGARRY V.-C.: "I turn to the law. The starting point is the duty of trustees to **9-92** exercise their powers in the best interests of the present and future beneficiaries of the trust, holding the scales impartially between different classes of beneficiaries. This duty of the trustees towards their beneficiaries is paramount. They must, of course, obey the law; but subject to that, they must put the interests of their beneficiaries first. When the purpose of the trust is to provide financial benefits for the beneficiaries, as is usually the case, the best interests of the beneficiaries are normally their best financial interests. In the case of a power of investment, as in the present case, the power must be exercised so as to yield the best return for the beneficiaries, judged in relation to the risks of the investments in question; and the prospects for the yield of income and capital appreciation both have to be considered in judging the return from the investment.

"The legal memorandum that the union obtained from their solicitors is **9-93** generally in accord with these views. In considering the possibility of investment for 'socially beneficial reasons which may result in lower returns to the fund,' the memorandum states that 'the trustees' only concern is to ensure that the return is the maximum possible consistent with security'; and then it refers to the need for diversification. However, it continues by saying that:

> 'Trustees cannot be criticised for failing to make a particular investment for social or political reasons, such as in South African stock for example, but may be held liable for investing in assets which yield a poor return or for disinvesting in stock at inappropriate times for non-financial criteria.'

This last sentence must be considered in the light of subsequent passages in the **9-94** memorandum which indicate that the sale of South African securities by trustees might be justified on the ground of doubts about political stability in South

---

[15] *Nestlé v. National Westminster Bank plc* [1993] 1 W.L.R. 1260, 1268 and 1280 applied in *Re Mulligan* [1998] 1 N.Z.L.R. 481.

[16] *Nestlé v. National Westminster Bank*, June 29, 1988, [2000] W.T.L.R. 795.

[17] Taking account of relevant considerations like those set out in the American Uniform Prudent Investor Act and ignoring irrelevant considerations: *Re Hastings—Bass* [1975] Ch. 25, *Stannard v. Fisons Pensions Trust Ltd* [1992] I.R.L.R. 27.

[18] *Wight v. Olswang* (No. 2) (2000) 2 I.T.E.L.R. 689, [2000] W.T.L.R. 783 reversed on appeal [2001] W.T.L.R. 291, *Nestlé v. National Westminster Bank* [1993] 1 W.L.R. 1260, 1281 *per* Staughton L.J. "I cannot accept that failure to diversify in that decade was a course which no prudent trustee would have followed."

Africa and the long-term financial soundness of its economy, whereas trustees could not properly support motions at a company meeting dealing with pay levels in South Africa, work accidents, pollution control, employment conditions for minorities, military contracting and consumer protection. The assertion that trustees could not be criticised for failing to make a particular investment for social or political reasons is one that I would not accept in its full width. If the investment in fact made is equally beneficial to the beneficiaries, then criticism would be difficult to sustain in practice, whatever the position in theory. But if the investment in fact made is less beneficial, then both in theory and in practice the trustees would normally be open to criticism.

9–95 "This leads me to the second point, which is a corollary of the first. In considering what investments to make trustees must put on one side their own personal interests and views. Trustees may have strongly held social or political views. They may be firmly opposed to any investment in South Africa or other countries, or they may object to any form of investment in companies concerned with alcohol, tobacco, armaments or many other things. In the conduct of their own affairs, of course, they are free to abstain from making any such investments. Yet under a trust, if investments of this type would be more beneficial to the beneficiaries than other investments, the trustees must not refrain from making the investments by reasons of the views that they hold.

"Trustees may even have to act dishonourably (though not illegally) if the interests of their beneficiaries require it. Thus where trustees for sale had struck a bargain for the sale of trust property but had not bound themselves by a legally enforceable contract, they were held to be under a duty to consider and explore a better offer that they received, and not to carry through the bargain to which they felt in honour bound: see *Buttle v. Saunders* [1950] 2 All E.R. 193. In other words, the duty of trustees to their beneficiaries may include a duty to 'gazump,' however honourable the trustees. As Wynn-Parry J. said (at 195), trustees 'have an overriding duty to obtain the best price which they can for their beneficiaries.' In applying this to an Official Receiver, Templeman J. said in *Re Wyvern Developments Ltd* [1974] 1 W.L.R. 1097 at 1106 that he—

'. . . must do his best by his creditors and contributories. He is in a fiduciary capacity and cannot make moral gestures, nor can the court authorise him to do so.'

9–96 In the words of Wigram V.-C. in *Balls v. Strutt* (1841) 1 Hare 146 at 149:

'It is a principle in this court that a trustee shall not be permitted to use the powers which the trust may confer upon him at law, except for the legitimate purposes of his trust.'

Powers must be exercised fairly and honestly for the purposes for which they are given and not so as to accomplish any ulterior purpose, whether for the benefit of the trustees or otherwise: see *Duke of Portland v. Topham* (1864) 11 H.L. Cas. 32 a case on a power of appointment that must apply a fortiori to a power given to trustees as such.

9–97 "Third, by way of a caveat I should say that I am not asserting that the benefit of the beneficiaries which a trustee must make his paramount concern inevitably and solely means their financial benefit, even if the only object of the trust is to provide financial benefits. Thus if the only actual or potential beneficiaries of a trust are all adults with very strict views on moral and social matters, condemning all forms of alcohol, tobacco and popular entertainment, as well as armaments, I can well understand that it might not be for the "benefit" of such beneficiaries to know that they are obtaining rather larger financial returns under the trust by reason of investments in those activities than they would have received if the trustees had invested the trust funds in other investments. The beneficiaries might well consider that it was far better to receive less than to receive more money from what they consider to be evil and tainted sources. 'Benefit' is a word with a very wide meaning, and there are circumstances in which arrangements which work to the financial disadvantage of a beneficiary may yet be for his benefit: see, for example, *Re Towler's Settlement Trusts* [1964]Ch. 158; *Re C L* [1969] 1 Ch. 587. But I would emphasise that such cases are likely to be very rare, and in any case I think that under a trust for the provision of financial benefits the burden would rest, and rest heavy, on him who asserts that it is for the benefit of the beneficiaries as a whole to receive less by reason of the exclusion of some of the possibly more profitable forms of investment. Plainly the present case is not one of this rare type of case. Subject to such matters, under a trust for the provision of financial benefits, the paramount duty of the trustees is to provide the greatest financial benefits for the present and future beneficiaries.

"Fourth, the standard required of a trustee in exercising his powers of **9–98** investment is that he must—

'. . . take such care as an ordinary prudent man would take if he were minded to make an investment for the benefit of other people for whom he felt morally bound to provide.'

See *Re Whiteley* (1886) 33 Ch.D. 347 at 355 *per* Lindley L.J. and see also at 350, 358; *Learoyd v. Whiteley* (1887) 12 App. Cas. 727. That duty includes the duty to seek advice on matters which the trustee does not understand, such as the making of investments, and on receiving that advice to act with the same degree of prudence. This requirement is not discharged merely by showing that the trustee has acted in good faith and with sincerity. Honesty and sincerity are not the same as prudence and reasonableness. Some of the most sincere people are the most unreasonable; and Mr. Scargill told me that he had met quite a few of them. Accordingly, although a trustee who takes advice on investments is not bound to accept and act on that advice, he is not entitled to reject it merely because he sincerely disagrees with it, unless in addition to being sincere he is acting as an ordinary prudent man would act.

"Fifth, trustees have a duty to consider the need for diversification of **9–99** investments. By section 6(1) of the Trustee Investments Act 1961[19]:

'In the exercise of his powers of investment a trustee shall have regard— (a) to the need for diversification of investments of the trust, in so far as is appropriate to the circumstances of the trust; (b) to the suitability to the trust of investments of the description of investment proposed and of the investment proposed as an investment of that description."

The reference to the 'circumstances of the trust' plainly includes matters such as the size of the trust funds: the degree of diversification that is practicable and

---

[19] Replaced by Trustee Act 2000, s.4(3), at para. 9–79 *supra*.

desirable for a large fund may plainly be impracticable or undesirable (or both) in the case of a small fund.

9–100   "In the case before me, it is not in issue that there ought to be diversification of the investments held by the fund. The contention of the defendants, put very shortly, is that there can be a sufficient degree of diversification without any investment overseas or in oil, and that in any case there is no need to increase the level of overseas investments beyond the existing level. Other pension funds got on well enough without overseas investments, it was said, and in particular the NUM's own scheme had, in 1982, produced better results than the scheme here in question. This was not so, said Mr. Jenkins, if you compared like with like, and excluded investments in property, which figure substantially in the mineworkers' scheme but not at all in the NUM scheme: and in any case the latter scheme was much smaller, being of the order of £7m.

"I shall not pursue this matter. Even if other funds in one particular year, or in many years, had done better than the scheme which is before me, that does not begin to show that it is beneficial to this scheme to be shorn of the the the ability to invest overseas. . . .

9–101   "Sixth, there is the question whether the principles that I have been stating apply, with or without modification, to trusts of pension funds. Counsel for the plaintiffs asserted that they applied without modification, and that it made no difference that some of the funds came from the members of the pension scheme, or that the funds were often of a very substantial size. Mr. Scargill did not in terms assert the contrary. He merely said that this was one of the questions to be decided, and that pension funds may be subject to different rules. I was somewhat unsuccessful in my attempts to find out from him why this was so, and what the differences were. What it came down to, I think, was that the rules for trusts had been laid down for private and family trusts and wills a long time ago; that pension funds were very large and affected large numbers of people; that in the present case the well-being of all within the coal industry was affected; and that there was no authority on the point except *Evans v. London Co-op Society Ltd The Times*, July 6, 1976 and certain overseas cases . . .

9–102   "I can see no reason for holding that different principles apply to pension fund trusts[20] from those which apply to other trusts. Of course, there are many provisions in pension schemes which are not to be found in private trusts, and to these the general law of trusts will be subordinated. But subject to that, I think that the trusts of pension funds are subject to the same rules as other trusts. The large size of pension funds emphasises the need for diversification, rather than lessening it, and the fact that much of the fund has been contributed by members of the scheme seems to me to make it even more important that the trustees should exercise their powers in the best interests of the beneficiaries. In a private trust, most, if not all, of the beneficiaries are the recipients of the bounty of the settlor, whereas under the trusts of a pension fund many (though not all) of the beneficiaries are those who, as members, contributed to the funds so that in due time they would receive pensions. It is thus all the more important that the interests of the beneficiaries should be paramount, so that they may receive the benefits which in part they have paid for. I can see no justification for holding that the benefits to them should run the risk of being lessened because the trustees were pursuing an investment policy intended to assist the industry that the pensioners have left, or their union . . .

---

[20] For detailed investment criteria now see Pension Act 1995, s.35 *infra* para. 9–402.

"On principle and on the two American cases,[21] I reach the unhesitating **9–103** conclusion that the trusts of pension funds are in general governed by the ordinary law of trusts, subject to any contrary provision in the rules or other provisions which govern the trust. In particular, the trustees of a pension fund are subject to the overriding duty to do the best that they can for the beneficiaries, the duty that in the United States is known as 'the duty of undivided loyalty to the beneficiaries' (see *Blankenship v. Boyle* 329 F.Supp. 1089 at 1095).

"In considering that duty, it must be remembered that very many of the beneficiaries will not in any way be directly affected by the prosperity of the mining industry or the union. Miners who have retired, and the widows and children of deceased miners, will continue to receive their benefits from the fund even if the mining industry shrinks: for the scheme is fully funded, and the fund does not depend on further contributions to it being made. I cannot regard any policy designed to ensure the general prosperity of coal mining as being a policy which is directed to obtaining the best possible results for the beneficiaries, most of whom are no longer engaged in the industry, and some of whom never were. The connection is far too remote and insubstantial. Further, the assets of even so large a pension fund as this are nowhere near the size at which there could be expected to be any perceptible impact from the adoption of the policies for which Mr. Scargill contends . . ."

NESTLÉ v. NATIONAL WESTMINSTER BANK PLC

Court of Appeal (Dillon, Staughton and Leggatt L.JJ.) [1995] 1 W.L.R. 1260; [1994] 1 All E.R. 118.

STAUGHTON L.J.: "When Mr. William Nestlé died in 1922, the value of his trust **9–104** fund (after payment of debts, legacies and estate duty) was about £50,000. In November 1986, when the plaintiff, his granddaughter Miss Georgina Nestlé, became absolutely entitled after the death of the last life tenant, it was worth £269,203. That, it might be thought, was a substantial improvement. But during the same period the cost of living had multiplied by a factor of 20, so that it would have required £1m. to provide equivalent wealth: see the B.Z.W. equity-gilt study of 1988. The same source shows that an equity price index rose by 5203 per cent. in that period. An equivalent appreciation in the value of the trust fund would have left it worth £2.6m. in 1986. It is true that a small portion of the fund was advanced to life tenants, that some capital was used to supplement income for an annuity, and that there were no doubt transaction costs; against that, a sum of about £5,000 was added to the fund in 1959 when Mr. Nestlé's house and contents were sold. Nevertheless, it is apparent that the investments retained or made by the trustees fell woefully short of maintaining the real value of the fund, let alone matching the average increase in price of ordinary shares.

"Of course it is not a breach of trust to invest the trust fund in such a manner **9–105** that its real value is not maintained. At times that will be impossible, and at others it will require extraordinary skill or luck. The highest that even the plaintiff puts her claim is that, if the equity portion in the fund as it stood in 1922 (74 per cent) had been invested so as to achieve no more than the index, the fund as a whole would have been worth over £1.8m. in 1986 . . .

[21] *Bankenship v. Boyle* 329 F. Supp. 1089 (1971); *Withers v. Teachers' Retirement System of New York* 447 F. Supp. 1248 (1978).

"In the experts' reports and during the course of the trial it appeared that there were four main strands to the plaintiff's case. (1) The trustees misunderstood the investment clause in the will. (2) The trustees failed to conduct a regular and periodic review of the investments. (3) Throughout the trust period, but in particular in the later stages when there were life tenants domiciled abroad, they retained or bought too high a proportion of fixed interest securities and too few ordinary shares. (4) To the extent that the trustees did invest in ordinary shares, they concentrated too heavily on shares in banking and insurance companies, to the exclusion of other sectors.

Misunderstanding, and failure to review

9–106   "In my judgment the first two charges were proved. It was admitted that at times the trustees misunderstood the investment clause; but the evidence showed that they continually misunderstood it, and there is nothing to show that they ever understood it correctly. To a novice in these matters it seems that they might deserve to be forgiven, since only among much other detail are to be found the words 'stocks shares bonds debentures or securities of any railway or other company.' But there is authority which shows plainly that the word 'company' in such a clause is not limited by its context. Trustees are not allowed to make mistakes in law; they should take legal advice, and if they are still left in doubt they can apply to the court for a ruling. Either course would have revealed their mistake in this case.

9–107   "I also consider that, for a substantial period, the trustees failed to conduct regular periodic reviews of the investments. From 1922 to 1959 there was only one change of an investment, other than changes which were forced on the trustees by rights issues or because a security reached its redemption date . . .

"However, the misunderstanding of the investment clause and the failure to conduct periodic reviews do not by themselves, whether separately or together, afford the plaintiff a remedy. They were symptoms of incompetence or idleness—not on the part of National Westminster Bank but of their predecessors; they were not, without more, breaches of trust. The plaintiff must show that, through one or other or both of those causes, the trustees made decisions which they should not have made or failed to make decisions which they should have made. If that were proved, and if at first sight loss resulted, it would be appropriate to order an inquiry as to the loss suffered by the trust fund.

"It may be difficult to discharge that burden, and particularly to show that decisions were not taken when they should have been. But that does not absolve a plaintiff from discharging it, and I cannot find that it was discharged in this case . . .

The balance of the fund between equities and gilts

9–108   "That brings me to what I regard as the substance of the case, the failure to invest a higher proportion of the trust fund in ordinary shares. Here one must take care to avoid two errors. First, the trustees' performance must not be judged with hindsight: after the event even a fool is wise, as a poet said nearly 3,000 years ago. Secondly (unless this is the same point), one must bear in mind that investment philosophy was very different in the early years of this trust from what it became later. Inflation was non-existent, overall, from 1921 to 1938. It occurred in modest degree during the war years, and became a more persistent phenomenon from 1947 onwards. Equities were regarded as risky during the 1920s and 1930s, and yielded a higher return then gilt-edged securities. It was only in 1959 that the so-called reverse yield gap occurred.

"During the period from 1922 until the death of Mrs. Barbara Nestlé in 1960, **9–109** the proportion of ordinary shares in the trust fund as a whole varied between 46 and 82 per cent. Until 1951 it never rose above 57 per cent.; there was then quite a sharp rise until 1960, not caused by any change in investment policy but presumably by a general rise in the value of ordinary shares (183 per cent., according to the index, between 1950 and 1960).

"In my judgment the trustees are not shown to have failed in their duties at any time up to 1959 in this respect. I cannot say that, in the light of investment conditions then prevailing, they were in breach of trust by not holding a higher proportion of ordinary shares. In addition, they were charged with the duty of providing an annuity of £1,500 after tax for the widow of Mr. William Nestlé, and of setting aside a fund for that purpose. The plaintiff's expert witnesses were themselves disinclined to criticise the balance of the fund, as between fixed interest and ordinary shares, in that period.

"After 1959 the situation had changed. Mrs. Barbara Nestlé died in October 1960, and the trustees were relieved of the task of providing for her annuity. The cult of the equity had begun by then, if not some years before. From that date I would accept the evidence of the plaintiff's experts that, all other things being equal, there should be at least 50 per cent. of the fund in ordinary shares.

"The trustees' experts countered that on two grounds. First, they pointed to **9–110** evidence that pension funds and life assurance companies continued to invest less than half their funds in equities, and a substantial proportion in gilt-edged securities. Counsel for the plaintiff provided us with a calculation which was said to disprove this in the case of pension funds. But it had not been made in the court below or put to witnesses, and was incomplete for this purpose . . .

"There is in my opinion a better answer to this comparison. Life assurance companies and pension funds have as their primary duty an obligation to pay at some future date a sum that is fixed in monetary terms. No doubt they offer profits, or an increase on the promised pension; and it may be that even in 1959 there was competition between companies by reference to their past records of success. But I am convinced that they could be expected to follow a policy of considerable caution in order to ensure that, come what may, their minimum obligations in monetary terms were fulfilled. I do not regard them as a reliable guide to what would have been done by private investors, or should have been done by trustees of a private family trust.

"The second point is this, Professor Briston, who gave evidence for the plaintiff, made a calculation on the basis that the part of the trust fund which was invested in ordinary shares initially remained in ordinary shares throughout. His calculation shows that, if one takes the 74 per cent proportion of equities when Mr. William Nestlé died, the fund as a whole would have grown to £1.8m. in 1986. Alternatively, the portfolio had a proportion of 54 per cent in equities after the setting up of the annuity fund and some restructuring between 1922 and 1924; if that part of the fund had remained in ordinary shares, the value of the fund as a whole would in 1986 have been £1.36m.

"I have already expressed the view that, in the light of investment conditions **9–111** then prevailing, the trustees are not to be criticised over the balance of the fund between fixed interest and equities in the period from 1922 to 1959. It follows that I do not accept the evidence of Professor Briston that they ought to have acted differently in that period. Neither did he persist in it when cross-examined . . .

"In my judgment they should, in the investment climate prevailing from 1960 onwards, have followed Professor Briston's policy, subject only to one important consideration—the overseas domicile of life tenants. If all the beneficiaries had been subject to United Kingdom tax, they should have regarded the 76.8 per cent. of the fund that was in ordinary shares in 1959 (or even the 82.6 per cent. in 1960) as devoted to equity investment, and only the balance as available for fixed interest securities. No doubt there were times during the period from 1960 to 1986 when it would not have been a breach of trust, and may even have been wise, to depart temporarily from that policy. But in the main I am convinced that it is the policy which they should have followed. With hindsight, one can see that the B.Z.W. Equity Index rose from 789.9 to 6353.2 in that period; the gilt index fell from 74.6 to 48.4. But my conclusion is based on the evidence of Professor Briston and Mr. Harris, not on hindsight.

9–112   "That, however, assumes that all the beneficiaries were subject to United Kingdom tax, which they were not. George Nestlé lived in Tanganyika from 1933 to 1963, when he moved to Malta and lived there until he died in 1972. Elsie, his widow, continued to live there until 1980, when she returned to England. She died in 1982. John Nestlé went to live in Cyprus in 1969, and died there in 1986. The fiscal effects of residence/ordinary residence/domicile overseas were, as I understand it, twofold: first, the life tenant would not be liable for United Kingdom income tax on investments outside the United Kingdom, or (more significantly) on the income from gilt-edged securities which were tax exempt; secondly, neither estate duty nor capital transfer tax would be payable on the death of a life tenant in respect of such securities.

"The obligation of a trustee is to administer the trust fund impartially, or fairly (I can see no significant difference), having regard to the different interests of beneficiaries. Wilberforce J. said in *Re Pauling's Settlement Trusts (No. 2)* [1963] Ch. 576, 586:

> 'The new trustees would be under the normal duty of preserving an equitable balance, and if at any time it was shown they were inclining one way or the other, it would not be a difficult matter to bring them to account.'

9–113   "At times it will not be easy to decide what is an equitable balance. A life tenant may be anxious to receive the highest possible income, whilst the remainderman will wish the real value of the trust fund to be preserved. If the life tenant is living in penury and the remainderman already has ample wealth, common sense suggests that a trustee should be able to take that into account, not necessarily by seeking the highest possible income at the expense of capital but by inclining in that direction. However, before adopting that course a trustee should, I think, require some verification of the facts. In this case the trustees did not, so far as I am aware, have any reliable information as to the relative wealth of the life tenants and the plaintiff. They did send an official to interview Mr. John Nestlé in Cyprus on one occasion; but the information which they obtained was conflicting and (as it turned out) incomplete.

"Similarly I would not regard it as a breach of trust for the trustees to pay some regard to the relationship between Mr. George Nestlé and the plaintiff. He was merely her uncle, and she would have received nothing from his share of the fund if he had fathered a child who survived him. The trustees would be entitled, in my view, to incline towards income during his life tenancy and that of his widow, on that ground. Again common sense suggests to me that such a course might be appropriate, and I do not think that it would be a breach of the duty to act fairly, or impartially.

"The dominant consideration for the trustees, however, was that George's **9–114** fund from 1960, and John's from 1969, would not be subject to United Kingdom income tax in so far as it was invested in exempt gilts. That was a factor which the trustees were entitled—and I would say bound—to take into account. A beneficiary who has been left a life interest in a trust fund has an arguable case for saying that he should not be compelled to bear tax on the income if he is not lawfully obliged to do so.

"It was no more than a factor for the trustees to bear in mind, and would rarely justify more than a modest degree of preference for income paid gross over capital growth.

"A trustee should also bear in mind, as these trustees did, that estate duty or capital transfer tax is likely to be reduced in such a case if part of the fund is invested in tax-exempt gilts. That may provide a compensating benefit for the remainderman. Of course it is by no means certain that the benefit will materialise; the life tenant may return to this country, as happened in the case of Mrs. Elsie Nestlé. It has been said that nothing in this world is certain except death and taxes. But even the tax benefit was imponderable, since it could not be forecast what rate of tax would be applicable on the death of a life tenant.

"It is said that the trustees should have anticipated that Elsie would return to **9–115** the United Kingdom, or at least have made inquiries as to her intentions. I can see some force in the second part of that argument. It would have been prudent to ask her to let them know if she planned to come back to this country. But this was never put to the bank's witnesses. And I cannot find that any loss to the trust fund resulted from failure to request information from Elsie. From time to time during her life tenancy there were indications that she might return, but it was only at a late stage that this attained any degree of probability; and I doubt whether even then it would have been right for the trustees to switch investments, thus reducing her income and foregoing any prospect of a saving in capital transfer tax.

"I do not consider it necessary to examine separately the balance of the two different funds from 1961 to 1986. From the point of view of the plaintiff, what mattered was the balance of the fund as a whole. The proportion in ordinary shares varied between 59.55 per cent. and 35.9 per cent. On occasion the lower figure may be attributable not to a change in investments but to a fall in the value of equities, for example in 1974 when there was a catastrophic fall. But there can be no doubt that there were other occasions when money was switched from ordinary shares to gilt-edged securities.

"The policy of the trustees during this period was to achieve a 50/50 split **9–116** between equities and fixed-interest. This was not to be an initial division of the kind favoured by Professor Briston, which would have resulted in a much higher proportion of equities by 1986; it was to be a division that was rebalanced from time to time, as envisaged by Professor Brealey. Whilst I much prefer Professor Briston's method in general for trust funds during this period, I consider that the circumstances of this trust and in particular the overseas life tenants, justified the policy which the trustees adopted. They did not fail to act fairly or impartially by adopting it.

"But it is said that the trustees failed to implement their own policy: the **9–117** proportion of ordinary shares fell on one occasion to 35.9 per cent, and in six years it was below 40 per cent. In my judgment the trustees were not obliged to rebalance the fund annually, still less at more frequent intervals. It would have been questionable to switch immediately into equities when they fell through the floor in 1974, merely because the ordinary shares then held were only 36.37 per cent of the fund. There was evidence that it is not a wise policy for trustees to be changing investments continually; and whilst I would not regard that as a justification for sheer inertia, I accept that an ordinary fund manager who has no special expertise should not busy himself with constant changes. The equity content started as 59.55 per cent in 1961 and ended as 51.31 per cent in 1986. Over those 26 years the average; according to my arithmetic, was 44.56 per cent. I would not regard that as revealing a serious departure from the trustees' policy, or a failure to act fairly and impartially. But I should add that, if I had found a breach of trust in this respect I would have been reluctant to accept that compensation should be measured by the difference between the actual performance of the fund and the very least that a prudent trustee might have achieved. There is said to be 19th century authority to that effect; but I would be inclined to prefer a comparison with what a prudent trustee was likely to have achieved— in other words, the average performance of ordinary shares during the period.

Diversification

9–118   "The complaint here is that there was undue emphasis on the shares of banks and insurance companies during the period from 1922 to 1960. Indeed the equities in the annuity fund when it was set up in 1922 were entirely of that description.

"However, there was evidence from the experts on both sides that bank and insurance shares were regarded as safest in the earlier period of this trust, 'a low risk portfolio.' I am inclined to agree with Professor Briston that there should have been diversification in the 1950s, rather than from 1960 onwards. But I cannot accept that failure to diversify in that decade was a course which no prudent trustee would have followed . . .

"I would dismiss the appeal. . . . It is not shown that there was loss arising from a breach of trust for which the trustees ought to compensate the trust fund . . .

LEGGATT L.J.: "There is no dispute about the nature of the bank's duty. It was, as Lindley L.J. has expressed it, a duty 'to take such care as an ordinary prudent man would take if he were minded to make an investment for the benefit of other people for whom he felt morally bound to provide:' *Re. Whiteley; Whiteley v. Learoyd* (1886) 33 Ch.D. 347 at 355. The power of investment

> 'must be exercised so as to yield the best return for the beneficiaries, judged in relation to the risks of the investments in question; and the prospects of the yield of income and capital appreciation both have to be considered in judging the return from the investment:' *Cowan v. Scargill* [1985] Ch. 270, 287.

9–119   "It is common ground that a trustee with a power of investment must undertake periodic reviews of the investments held by the trust. In relation to this trust, that would have meant a review carried out at least annually, and whenever else a reappraisal of the trust portfolio was requested or was otherwise requisite. It must also be borne in mind that, as expressed by the Report of the Scarman Committee on the Powers and Duties of Trustees (1982) ((Law Reform Committee: 23rd Report) Cmnd. 8733), at para. 2.15, 'Professional trustees, such as banks, are under a special duty to display expertise in every aspect of their administration of the trust.'

9–120   "The plaintiff alleges that the bank is in breach of trust because over the years since her grandfather set up the trust the bank has supposed that its power of investment was more limited than it was; has failed to carry out periodic reviews of the portfolio, and to maintain a proper balance between equities and gilts, and to diversify the equity investments; and has unduly favoured the interests of her father and her uncle as life-tenants at the expense of her own interest as remainderman. She says that in consequence the trust fund was worth less in 1986 than it should have been.

"The essence of the bank's duty was to take such steps as a prudent businessman would have taken to maintain and increase the value of the trust fund. Unless it failed to do so, it was not in breach of trust. A breach of duty will not be actionable, and therefore will be immaterial, if it does not cause loss. In this context I would endorse the concession of Mr. Nugee for the bank that 'loss' will be incurred by a trust fund when it makes a gain less than would have been made by a prudent businessman. A claimant will therefore fail who cannot prove a loss in this sense caused by breach of duty. So here in order to make a case for an inquiry, the plaintiff must show that loss was caused by breach of duty on the part of the bank . . .

"The plaintiff therefore had to prove that a prudent trustee, knowing of the **9–121** scope of the bank's investment power and conducting regular reviews, would so have invested the trust funds as to make it worth more than it was worth when the plaintiff inherited it. That was a matter for expert evidence. In the result there was evidence which the judge was entitled to accept and did accept that the bank did no less than expected of it up to the death of the testator's widow in 1960 . . .

"After 1960 investment of the trust funds preponderantly in tax-exempt gilts for the benefit of life-tenants resident abroad is not shown to have produced a less satisfactory result for the remainderman than an investment in equities after taking into account savings in estate duty and capital transfer tax, because this policy had the effect of preserving the capital. By the time that John Nestlé died the equities to replace the tax-exempt gilts would have had to be worth more than twice as much as the gilts in order to achieve the same benefit net of tax . . .

"No testator, in the light of this example, would choose this bank for the **9–122** effective management of his investment. But the bank's engagement was as a trustee; and as such, it is to be judged not so much by success as by absence of proven default. The importance of preservation of a trust fund will always outweigh success in its advancement. Inevitably, a trustee in the bank's position wears a complacent air, because the virtue of safety will in practice put a premium on inactivity. Until the 1950s active management of the portfolio might have been seen as speculative, and even in these days such dealing would have to be notably successful before the expense would be justified. The very process of attempting to achieve a balance, or (if that be old-fashioned) fairness, as between the interests of life-tenants and those of a remainderman inevitably means that each can complain of being less well served than he or she ought to have been. But by the undemanding standard of prudence the bank is not shown to have committed any breach of trust resulting in loss.

"I am therefore constrained to agree that the appeal must be dismissed."

III. The Trustee Act 2000 range of investments

In the absence of wider express powers in the trust instrument and **9–123** subject to any restriction or exclusion in such instrument or in primary or subordinate legislation,[22] the Trustee Act 2000 (after repealing most of

---

[22] Pension fund investment is dealt with in the Pensions Act 1995, *infra* at. para. 9–383.

the Trustee Investments Act 1961) confers on trustees of old or new trusts[23] first, a "general power of investment", extending to loans secured on land (whether by way of legal or equitable mortgage or charge) but not to acquiring land, and second, a power to acquire legal estates in freehold or leasehold land in the U.K. as an investment or for occupation by a beneficiary or for any other reason.

By section 3(1) "a trustee may make any kind of investment that he could make if he[24] were absolutely entitled to the assets of the trust", but by subsection (3) "the general power of investment does not permit a trustee to make investments in land other than in loans secured on land." Investments can thus properly be made in assets anywhere in the world, including loans secured on foreign land, so long, of course, as the various equitable and statutory duties of care are observed. An "investment" was originally considered to be an asset acquired for the sake of the income it was expected to yield[25] but, nowadays, with the emphasis on "total return",[26] taking account of income yield and capital appreciation in accordance with modern portfolio theory, an investment is considered to cover an asset acquired for the sake of either or both an income yield or a capital profit.[27] It follows, for example, that the purchase of depreciating chattels for a villa owned by the trustees or of a depreciating vehicle for use by a beneficiary would fall outside the general power of investment, so that the beneficiary will need to have trust income or capital properly distributed to him or her and then use it to purchase the chattels or vehicle for himself or herself.

9—124   By section 8(1) "a trustee may acquire freehold or leasehold land in the United Kingdom (a) as an investment, (b) for occupation by a beneficiary, or (c) for any other reason." In England and Wales "freehold or leasehold land"[28] means a legal estate in land and, particularly in purchasing leases, the trustees will need to ensure that they observe their equitable and statutory duties of care. Then, by section 8 (3), "for the purpose of exercising his functions as a trustee, a trustee who acquires land under this section has all the powers of an absolute owner in relation to the land." For trustees who have acquired land other than under section 8(3) e.g. because the settlor settled land[29] on the trustees, section 6(3) of the Trusts of Land and Appointment of Trustees Act 1996 (as amended by the Trustee Act 2000) provides, "The trustees of land have power to acquire land under the power conferred

---

[23] Trustee Act 2000 ss.7(1), 10(2).

[24] If the trustee were a corporation with powers less than those of an absolute beneficial owner this would limit the range of investments to that permitted to that corporation.

[25] *Re Wragg* [1919] 2 Ch. 58, 64, 65, *Re Power's W.T.* [1947] Ch. 576, *Tootal Broadhurst Lee Co. Ltd. v. I.R.C.* [1949] 1 Al E.R. 261, 265.

[26] See para. 9–86 *supra.*

[27] In *Cook v. Medway Housing Society* [1997] S.T.C. 90, 98 "investment" was said to amount to the "laying out of moneys in anticipation of a profitable capital or income return". See also Explanatory Notes to Trustee Act 2000 paras 22 and 23 and Law Com No. 260 p. 22 n.56.

[28] Trustee Act 2000, s.8(2). Interests in foreign land may be acquired via acquiring shares in a company that owns foreign land.

[29] But land that is within the Settled Land Act 1925 is governed exclusively by such Act: Trustee Act 2000, s.10(1).

by section 8 of the Trustee Act 2000." Under section 8(3) it seems that the use of the present tense enables trustees to acquire the land with the assistance of a mortgage and, to that extent, "gear up" the value of the trust fund, even though this could not be accomplished by relying on an express power of purchasing land.[30]

IV. EXPRESS INVESTMENT CLAUSES

Express investment clauses are found in virtually all trusts (other than **9–125** those arising on a person's death intestate or those arising without the assistance of legal advice), although clauses in trust instruments more than 40 or 50 years old will usually be much more limited than modern clauses drafted in the light of the variety of financial products now on offer. Powers in default of express powers of investment were conferred by the Trustee Act 1925 and then the Trustee Investments Act 1961, but such powers soon became increasingly out-dated and ineffective in safeguarding and developing the value of the trust fund.

Draftspersons have developed their own sophisticated investment clauses and will continue to use them (rather than rely on the default powers in the Trustee Act 2000) so as to confer the broadest possible powers on the trustees who, however broad their powers, have their opportunities much narrowed by the equitable and statutory duties of care imposed upon them (except to the extent expressly modified or excluded by the trust instrument). To confer the broadest possible powers, draftspersons will often employ clauses like "to apply or invest in the purchase or acquisition of assets or investments of whatsoever nature and wherever situated, and whether or not yielding income or being appreciating or depreciating assets, and including the acquisition of derivatives but only for the purpose of limiting risks and not for the purpose of speculation." However, if most exceptionally, speculation is desired, the draftsperson can insert "or speculate" after "or invest" and omit the limitation on the acquisition of derivatives, while providing that in exercising such flexible powers the trustees "are under a duty to speculate with the trust fund as would an absolute beneficial owner who could afford to lose an amount equivalent to the value of the trust fund without it affecting his standard of living in any way whatever" and "are not to be liable for any conduct unless acting dishonestly."[31] The draftsperson can also confer express power to "gear up" the trust fund by borrowing on the security of trust property in order to acquire further property for the trust[32] and express power to lend merely on the security of a personal promise of the borrower to repay,[33] when a high interest rate will of course be payable because a personal promise provides no security at all in the event of non-payment.

---

[30] *Re Suenson-Taylor's S.T.* [1974] 1 W.L.R. 1280.
[31] Such exemption clauses are valid if known of and approved by the settlor: *Armitage v. Nurse* [1998] Ch. 241, *Bogg v. Roper* (1998) 1 I.T.E.L.R. 267.
[32] Otherwise not permitted: *Re Suenson–Taylor's S.T.* [1974] 1 W.L.R. 1280.
[33] Otherwise not permitted: *Khoo Tek Keong v. Ch'ng Joo Tuan Neoh* [1934] A.C. 529.

9–126   At one stage the courts took a narrow restrictive approach to the interpretation of investment clauses as extending the default powers as little as possible, but for the last fifty years the courts[34] have been interpreting investment clauses[35] according to the natural and proper meaning of the words used in their context so as to empower investment in a fairly-construed wide range of investments. However, the courts have been strict in refusing to treat conferment of a power for the trustee to invest in his absolute discretion in all respects as if he were the absolute beneficial owner of the trust fund as exempting such trustee from the need to exhibit the appropriate duties of care.[36]

Section 4. Delegation by a Trustee

I. INTRODUCTION

9–127   The general rule of equity is *delegatus non potest delegare* ("a delegate is not able to delegate") "I must observe," said Langdale M.R. in *Turner v. Corney*[37] "that trustees who take on themselves the management of property for the benefit of others have no right to shift their duty on other persons; and if they employ an agent, they remain subject to the responsibility towards their *cestuis que trust*, for whom they have undertaken the duty". If, in breach of trust, trustees employed an agent then they were automatically liable for all losses that flowed from the unauthorised agent's activities in respect of the trust.[38] The trustees were, however, justified in delegating if authorised in the trust instrument or if, in the circumstances, delegation was either reasonably necessary or in the ordinary course of affairs.[39] Such delegation was normally permissible only in respect of the trustees employing agents to do things decided upon by the trustees,[40] but in the case of property situated abroad in the far-flung British Empire trustees could confer discretionary management powers (*e.g.* to sell, lease or buy property and to employ agents).[41]

9–128   However, where the employment of an agent to do specific acts was justified, the trustee had to be prudent in his selection and supervision of

---

[34] *Re Harari's S.T.* [1949] 1 All E.R. 430, *Re Peczenik's settlement* [1964] 1 W.L.R. 720, *Re Douglas' W.T.* [1959] 1 W.L.R. 744.

[35] In *R v. Clowes (No. 2)* [1994] 2 All E.R. 316, 327–330 the Court of Appeal held that a clause "to place any uninvested funds with any body on such terms and conditions as you see fit" was not an investment clause to be treated liberally: it merely allowed money to be placed temporarily pending investment.

[36] *Barlett v. Barclays Bank Trust Co* [1980] Ch. 515, 536; also see *Re Maberly* (1886) 33 Ch.D. 455, 458.

[37] (1841) 5 Beav. 515 at 517.

[38] *Att.-Gen. v. Scott* (1749) 1 Ves. Sen 413,417; *Rowland v. Witherden* (1851) 3 Mac & Cr 568; *Clough v. Bond* (1838) 3 My & Cr 440, 496–497; *Re Dewar* (1885) 54, L.J.Ch. 830, 832.

[39] *Exp. Belchier (1754) Amb. 218,* applied in *Speight v. Gaunt* (1883) 22 Ch.D. 727; 9 App.Cas. 1.

[40] Trustees' discretions could not be delegated (unless authorised by the trust deed); *Robson v. Flight* (1865) 4 De G.J. & S. 608, 613, *Re Airey* [1897] 1 Ch. 164, 170.

[41] In those days post took a long time to arrive by boat; there were no telephones or fax machines or e-mails. See *Stuart v. Norton* (1860) 14 M 00, P.C. In *Re Muffet* (1887) 56 L.J.Ch. 600 the Court of Appeal even assumed that trustees with 80 English rented properties to manage could delegate collecting rents and seeing to repairs and to re-letting of vacated premises, presumably in such a case such delegation in the 1880s, could be reasonably necessary.

his agent. He had to exercise the care of a prudent man of business in his choice of the agent and he could not employ an agent to do an act outside the scope of the agent's business.[42] If these conditions were satisfied the trustee would not be responsible for a loss arising through the default of the agent, provided he exercised a proper supervision over the agent.[43] In this respect an express or statutory provision[44] authorising a wide use of agents in ministerial matters and exempting a trustee from liability for loss caused by the acts or defaults of an agent unless the loss occurred through the trustee's 'wilful default' did not relieve the trustee of his duty to show the care of the prudent man of business both in the selection and in the supervision of agents.[45] A trustee was thus only liable for his *own* acts or defaults, *e.g.* negligent selection, or negligent supervision. There was no automatic liability for the agent's acts or defaults in those cases where delegation to agents was permissible.

The Trustee Act 1925 radically enlarged trustees' collective powers to **9–129** delegate implementation of their decisions to an agent because section 23(1) enabled them to delegate whether or not there was any reasonable need for this, and lazy trustees could even so delegate matters they could have seen to personally. However, they could not delegate the exercise of their own discretion to decide what should be done except as before in the case of managing overseas property, although under section 23(2) they could now do this whether or not there was any reasonable necessity for it.

While it was clear that, as before, trustees were not to be automatically liable for the acts of agents employable under the general law or under the section 23 extension thereof after 1925, it was uncertain whether trustees still owed a duty to select and supervise such agents with the care of the prudent business person. Traditionalists considered such duty continued after 1925, so that trustees would still be liable if personally guilty of wilful default in the traditional equitable sense which covered deliberate, reckless and negligent conduct.[46] Modernists believed in a literal, rather than a history-based, interpretation of section 23(1) so that in cases where use of agents was permissible trustees should not only never be automatically responsible but should not be personally "responsible for the default of any such agent if employed in good faith", although there could be personal liability for trustees guilty of wilful default in the common law sense of deliberate or reckless conduct.[47] In *Armitage v. Nurse* in *obiter dicta*[48] the Court of Appeal, without full

---

[42] *Fry v. Tapson* (1884) 28 Ch.D. 268; *Rowland v. Witherden* (1851) 3 Mac & Cr 508.

[43] *Matthews v. Brise* (1845) 10 Jur.(o.s.) 105.

[44] *Underwood v. Stevens* (1816) 1 Mer. 712; s.30(1) of the Trustee Act 1925, replacing s.24 of the Trustee Act 1893, replacing s.31 of the Law of Property Amendment Act 1859. Section 23 of the Trustee Act 2000 now governs the position.

[45] *Re Brier* (1884) 26 Ch.D. 238 at 243 (*per* Lord Selborne L.C.). Also *Re Chapman* [1896] 2 Ch. 763 at 776, *per* Lindley L.J., "Wilful default which includes want of ordinary prudence on the part of the trustees must be proved"; and in *Speight v. Gaunt* (1883) 9 App.Cas. 1 at 13–15, 22–23 the Lords treated wilful default as including want of ordinary prudence.

[46] G.H. Jones (1959) 22 M.L.R 381, J.E. Stannard [1979] Conv. 345.

[47] *Re Vickery* [1931] 1 Ch. 572.

[48] [1998] Ch. 241.

consideration of the arguments favouring the traditional approach, accepted the modernists' interpretation. It has to be said, however, that in modern times it does seem unsatisfactory that the default rule, in the absence of a higher duty imposed in the trust instrument, protects trustees unless not acting in good faith by being guilty of deliberate or reckless conduct. Hence the Trustee Act 2000 imposes the statutory duty of care in the employment and supervision of agents, nominees and custodians.[49]

II. Collective Delegation under Trustee Act 2000

9–130   In addition to powers conferred on trustees other than by the Trustee Act 2000, but subject to any restriction or exclusion imposed by the trust instrument or by any primary or subordinate legislation,[50] Part IV (sections 11 to 27) of the Trustee Act 2000 from 1st February 2001 confers the following powers on trustees collectively subject to the following duties.

1. Agents

(a) Power to employ agents

By section 11 of the Trustee Act 2000:

"(1) Subject to the provisions of this Part, the trustees of a trust may authorise any person to exercise any or all of their delegable functions as their agent.

(2) In the case of a trust other than a charitable trust, the trustees' delegable functions consist of any function other than—

(a) any function relating to whether or in what way any assets of the trust should be distributed,

(b) any power to decide whether any fees or other payment due to be made out of the trust funds should be made out of income or capital,

(c) any power to appoint a person to be a trustee of the trust, or

(d) any power conferred by any other enactment or the trust instrument which permits the trustees to delegate any of their functions or to appoint a person to act as a nominee or custodian.

9–131   (3) In the case of a charitable trust, the trustees' delegable functions are—

(a) any function consisting of carrying out a decision that the trustees have taken;

(b) any function relating to the investment of assets subject to the trust (including, in the case of land held as an investment, managing the land and creating or disposing of an interest in the land);

(c) any function relating to the raising of funds for the trust otherwise than by means of profits of a trade which is an integral part of carrying out the trust's charitable purpose;

---

[49] Generally see Law Com. No. 260 (1999) "Trustees' Powers and Duties" upon which the Trustee Act 2000 is based.

[50] Trustee Act 2000, s.26.

(d) any other function prescribed by an order made by the Secretary of State.

(4) For the purposes of subsection (3)(c) a trade is an integral part of carrying **9–132** out a trust's charitable purpose if, whether carried on in the United Kingdom or elsewhere, the profits are applied solely to the purposes of the trust and either—

(a) the trade is exercised in the course of the actual carrying out of a primary purpose of the trust, or
(b) the work in connection with the trade is mainly carried out by benefici- aries of the trust."

It will be seen that the section is concerned with trustees' management or administrative functions, not their discretionary distributive functions. It extends to a sole trustee[51] but not to trustees of authorised unit trusts[52] nor to enable pension trustees to delegate investment functions which are dealt with by sections 34 to 36 of the Pensions Act 1995.

(b) Persons eligible to be agents

By section 12 of the Trustee Act 2000:

"(1) Subject to subsection (2), the persons whom the trustees may under section 11 authorise to exercise functions as their agent include one or more of their number.
(2) The trustees may not authorise two (or more) persons to exercise the same function unless they are to exercise the function jointly.
(3) The trustees may not under section 11 authorise a beneficiary to exercise any function as their agent (even if the beneficiary is also a trustee)
(4) The trustees may under section 11 authorise a beneficiary to exercise any function as their agent even though he is also appointed to act as their nominee or custodian (whether under section 16, 17 or 18 or any other power)."

It is important that the trustees can employ one of themselves for **9–133** particular tasks so long as such trustee is not a beneficiary, there then being conflict of interest possibilities with a beneficiary-agent being vulnerable to the charge of preferring his or her own interests to those of other beneficiaries. Exceptionally under section 9(1) of the Trusts of Land and Appointment of Trustees Act 1996, "The trustees of land may, by power of attorney, delegate to any beneficiary or beneficiaries of full age and beneficially entitled to an interest in possession in land subject to the trust any of their functions as trustees which relate to the land." This power of attorney may be for any period or indefinite,[53] must be given by all the trustees jointly, may be revoked by any one or more of them and will be revoked by the appointment of a new trustee.[54] Such power can be exercised to enable a life tenant to decide upon sale or lease of the land but cannot enable the life tenant to receive or given

---

[51] *ibid*, s.25.
[52] *ibid*, s.37.
[53] Trusts of Land Appointment of Trustees Act 1996, s.9(5).
[54] *ibid*, s.9(3).

receipts for capital money,[55] two trustees being required for this purpose[56] (considering the practical danger of permitting an income beneficiary to receive capital moneys). Beneficiaries exercising delegated functions are in the same position as trustees (with the same duties and liabilities) but are not regarded "as trustees for any other purposes (including the purposes of any enactment permitting the delegation of functions by trustees or imposing requirements relating to the payment of capital money)."[57]

(c) Agent subject to duties and restrictions linked to function delegated

9–134 As to be expected if an agent is employed under section 11 to carry out a function (like investment) he is subject to the duties and restrictions attached to such function (like having regard to the standard investment criteria) if the trustees themselves were exercising such function.[58]

(d) Asset management restrictions

By section 15 of the Trustee Act 2000:

"(1) The trustees may not authorise a person to exercise any of their asset management functions as their agent except by an agreement which is in or evidenced in writing.

(2) The trustees may not authorise a person to exercise any of their asset management functions as their agent unless—

- (a) they have prepared a statement that gives guidance as to how the functions should be exercised ("a policy statement"), and
- (b) the agreement under which the agent is to act includes a term to the effect that he will secure compliance with—
    - (i) the policy statement, or
    - (ii) if the policy statement is revised or replaced under section 22, the revised or replacement policy statement.

(3) The trustees must formulate any guidance given in the policy statement with a view to ensuring that the functions will be exercised in the best interests of the trust.

(4) The policy statement must be in or evidenced in writing.

(5) The asset management functions of trustees are their functions relating to—

- (a) the investment of assets subject to the trust,
- (b) the acquisition of property which is to be subject to the trust, and
- (c) managing property which is subject to the trust and disposing of, or creating or disposing of an interest in, such property."

---

[55] *ibid*, s.9(7).
[56] Law of Property Act 1925, s.27, Trustee Act 1925, s.14.
[57] T.L.A.T.A. 1996, s.9(7).
[58] T.A. 2000, s.13.

Clearly, this authorises the common useful, if not necessary, practice of employing a discretionary portfolio manager, but it extends to employing an estate agent to sell a trust property at the best price. It is noteworthy that the section applies to all asset management delegations, whether under the Act or otherwise (*e.g.* under the terms of the trust instrument).

(e) Terms of engagement

By section 14 of the Trustee Act 2000:   **9–135**

"(1) Subject to subsection (2) and sections 15(2) and 29 to 32, the trustees may authorise a person to exercise functions as their agent on such terms as to remuneration and other matters as they may determine.

(2) The Trustees may not authorise a person to exercise functions as their agent on any of the terms mentioned in subsection (3) unless it is reasonably necessary for them to do so.

(3) The terms are—

   (a) a term permitting the agent to appoint a substitute;
   (b) a term restricting the liability of the agent or his substitute to the trustees or any beneficiary;
   (c) a term permitting the agent to act in circumstances capable of giving rise to a conflict of interest."

It will be seen that an objective test of what is "reasonably necessary" **9–136** in all the circumstances applies to use of section 14 to authorise the potentially detrimental terms specified in section 14(3). An express power may liberally permit trustees to authorise any terms if the trustees subjectively bona fide believe such terms to be reasonably necessary in the best interests of the beneficiaries. It is doubtful whether a term ousting the liability of an agent (*e.g.* by excluding some otherwise applicable duty) is covered as "a term restricting the liability of" an agent[59] although, in any event, it may be difficult to justify any such ouster as "reasonably necessary".

In engaging a discretionary portfolio manager[60] it may well be reasonably necessary to permit it to appoint a substitute for a foreign portfolio of shares, to permit it to exclude liability for negligence, to permit it as a market-maker in shares in a particular company to sell such shares to the trustees and to permit it to place business with a subsidiary or associated company entitled to charge for its services. At the time of the engagement it will be good practice for the trustees to record the factors making them consider that particular terms were reasonably necessary.

(f) Remuneration

Where a person other than a trustee has been appointed an agent (or **9–137** a nominee or custodian) section 32 of the Trustee Act 2000 provides:

---

[59] Ouster of one particular duty, however, may be said to reduce or restrict the overall possible liability of the agent.
[60] See D.J. Hayton (1990) 106 L.Q.R. 89–93.

"(1) This section applies if, under a power conferred by Part IV or any other enactment or any provision of subordinate legislation, or by the trust instrument, a person other than a trustee has been—

(a) authorised to exercise functions as an agent of the trustees, or
(b) appointed to act as a nominee or custodian.

(2) The trustees may remunerate the agent, nominee or custodian out of trust funds for services if—

(a) he is engaged on terms entitling him to be remunerated for those services, and
(b) the amount does not exceed such remuneration as is reasonable in the circumstances for the provision of those services by him to or on behalf of that trust.

(3) The trustees may reimburse the agent, nominee or custodian out of the trust funds for any expenses properly incurred by him in exercising functions as an agent, nominee or custodian."

If a trustee has been appointed agent, nominee or custodian, then he can claim properly incurred expenses out of the trust fund, but entitlement to remuneration for his services will be based on a clause in the trust instrument or, otherwise, section 29 of the Trustee Act 2000.

(g) Duty of care in appointing and supervising agents

9–138   Trustees are under the statutory duty of care[61] when selecting the person who is to act, when determining any terms on which that person is to act, and, if such person is to exercise asset management functions, when preparing a policy statement under section 15, such duty applying whether the appointment is made under the Trustee Act 2000 or otherwise[62] (*e.g.* under the terms of the trust instrument except, of course, to the extent the statutory duty is modified or excluded in the trust instrument[63]).

Under section 22 of the Trustee Act 2000, while the agent continues to act for the trustees (a) they must keep under review the arrangements under which the agent acts and how those arrangements are being put into effect, (b) if circumstances make it appropriate to do so, they must consider whether there is a need to exercise any power of intervention that they have (*e.g.* a power to revoke the appointment or to give directions to the agent) and (c) if they consider that there is a need to exercise such a power, they must do so. The position is the same[64] where trustees of land delegate their functions under section 9 of the Trusts of Land and Appointment of Trustees Act 1996. In the case of an agent authorised to exercise asset management functions, the trustees' duties

---

[61] See para. 9–04 *supra*.
[62] T.A. 2000, Sched. 1, para. 3 and s.21(3).
[63] *ibid*, para. 7.
[64] T.L.A.T.A. 1996, s.9A(2) to (5) inserted by TA 2000, Sched. 2, para. 47.

include a duty to consider whether there is any need to revise or replace the section 15 policy statement, a duty to revise or replace it if they consider that there is such a need, and a duty to assess whether the current policy statement is being complied with.[65] The revision or replacement must be in, or evidenced in, writing and must be formulated with a view to ensuring that the delegated functions will be exercised in the best interests of the trust beneficiaries s a whole.[66] The statutory duty of care applies to the exercise of these supervisory duties under section 22 of the Trustee Act 2000[67] and section 9A (3) of the Trusts of Land and Appointment of Trustees Act 1966,[68] but delegations made under section 9 before February 2001 remain subject to the old law, including the prospectively repealed section 9(8).[69] Breach of the duty of care will, of course, lead to liability for losses directly flowing from such breach.

(h) No duty of care in deciding whether or not to delegate (except for delegations under s.9 Trusts of Land and Appointment of Trustees Act 1996)

In deciding whether or not to exercise their powers of delegation **9–139** under the Trustee Act 2000 the trustees can suit themselves and do not need to prove it was reasonably necessary to exercise the power or that exercise of the power was in the best interests of the trust beneficiaries, although they cannot, of course, commit a fraud on the power[70] by exercising it for some ulterior purpose. However, the statutory duty of care applies to trustees of land in deciding whether or not to delegate any of their extensive functions under section 9 of the Trusts of Land and Appointment of Trustees Act 1996 to a beneficiary with an interest in possession[71]—because the extensive powers conferred upon such a beneficiary can be exercised with little constraint and much impact.

(i) Trustees exceeding their powers

If trustees fail to act within the limits of their powers under the **9–140** Trustee Act 2000 in authorising a person to act as their agent this does not invalidate the authorisation.[72] The Trustees, of course, will still be liable for losses flowing from the improper authorisation, while the agent may perhaps be liable as a trustee *de son tort*.

2. Nominees and Custodians

The need for speedy settlement of share dealings within 5 days and, now, within 3 days, the introduction of dematerialised holding and

---

[65] T.A. 2000, s.22(2).
[66] *ibid*, s.15.
[67] *ibid*, Sched. 1, para. 3(1)(e).
[68] T.L.A.T.A. 1996, s.9A(5).
[69] T.L.A.T.A. 1996, s.9A(7).
[70] For fraud on a power see para. 9–303 *infra*.
[71] T.L.A.T.A. 1996, s.9A(1).
[72] T.A. 2000, s.4(a).

transfer of shares via the London Stock Exchange CREST system, and the use of computerised clearing systems in other financial markets make it vital that there are broad powers to use nominees and custodians.

(a) Power to employ nominees and custodians

The position is governed as follows by sections 16, 17 and 18 of the Trustee Act 2000:

"16 (1) Subject to the provisions of this Part, the trustees of a trust may—

(a) appoint a person to act as their nominee in relation to such of the assets of the trust as they determine (other than settled land), and

(b) take such steps as are necessary to secure that those assets are vested in a person so appointed.

(2) An appointment under this section must be in or evidenced in writing.

(3) This section does not apply to any trust having a custodian trustee or in relation to any assets vested in the official custodian for charities.

9–141   17 (1) Subject to the provisions of the Part, the trustees of a trust may appoint a person to act as a custodian in relation to such assets of the trust as they may determine.

(2) For the purposes of this Act a person is a custodian in relation to assets if he undertakes the safe custody of the assets or of any documents or records concerning the assets.

(3) An appointment under this section must be in or evidenced in writing.

(4) This section does not apply to any trust having a custodian trustee or in relation to any assets vested in the official custodian for charities.

18 (1) If trustees retain or invest in securities payable to bearer, they must appoint a person to act as a custodian of the securities.

9–142   (2) Subsection (1) does not apply if the trust instrument or any enactment or provision of subordinate legislation contains provision which (however expressed) permits the trustees to retain or invest in securities payable to bearer without appointing a person to act as a custodian.

(3) An appointment under this section must be in or evidenced in writing.

(4) This section does not apply to any trust having a custodian trustee or in relation to any securities vested in the official custodian for charities."

(b) Persons eligible to be nominees or custodians

By section 19 of the Trustee Act 2000:

"(1) A person may not be appointed under section 16, 17 or 18 as a nominee or custodian unless one of the relevant conditions is satisfied.

9–143   (2) The relevant conditions are that—

(a) the person carries on a business which consists of or includes acting as a nominee or custodian;

(b) the person is a body corporate which is controlled by the trustees;

(c) the person is a body corporate recognised under section 9 of the Administration of Justice Act 1985.

(3) The question whether a body corporate is controlled by trustees is to be determined in accordance with section 840 of the Income and Corporation Taxes Act 1988.

(4) The trustees of a charitable trust which is not an exempt charity must act in accordance with any guidance given by the Charity Commissioners concerning the selection of a person for appointment as a nominee or custodian under section 16, 17 or 18.

(5) Subject to subsections (1) and (4), the persons whom the trustees may **9–144** under section 16, 17 or 18 appoint as a nominee or custodian include—

    (a) one of their number, if that one is a trust corporation, or
    (b) two (or more) of their number, if they are to act as joint nominees or joint custodians.

(6) The trustees may under section 16 appoint a person to act as their nominee even though he is also—

    (a) appointed to act as their custodian (whether under section 17 or 18 or any other power), or
    (b) authorised to exercise functions as their agent (whether under section 11 or any other power).

(7) Likewise, the trustees may under section 17 or 18 appoint a person to act **9–145** as their custodian even though he is also—

    (a) appointed to act as their nominee (whether under section 16 or any other power), or
    (b) authorised to exercise functions as their agent (whether under section 11 or any other power)."

(c) Terms of engagement

By section 20 of the Trustee Act 2000:

    (1) Subject to subsection (2) and sections 29 to 32, the trustees may under section 16, 17 and 18 appoint a person to act as a nominee or custodian on such terms as to remuneration and other matters as they may determine.
    (2) The trustees may not under section 16,17 or 18 appoint a person to act as a nominee or custodian on any of the terms mentioned in subsection (3) unless it is reasonably necessary for them to do so.
    (3) The terms are—

        (a) a term permitting the nominee or custodian to appoint a substitute;
        (b) a term restricting the liability of the nominee or custodian or his substitute to the trustees or to any beneficiary;
        (c) a term permitting the nominee or custodian to act in circumstances capable of giving rise to a conflict of interest."

(d) Remuneration

The position is set out in section 32 of the Trustee Act 2000 as discussed **9–146** earlier[73] in relation to agents.

---

[73] See para. 9–137 *supra*.

(e) Duty of care in appointing and supervising nominees and custodian

Trustees are under the statutory duty of care when selecting the nominee or custodian and determining the terms of engagement thereof, whether under the Trustee Act 2000 or otherwise[74] (*e.g.* under the trust instrument, except to the extent there is a contrary intention therein). They also need to keep under review the arrangements under which the nominee or custodian acts and how those arrangements are being put into effect, considering whether any power of intervention needs to be exercised and then exercising it if called for.[75] The statutory duty of care applies to this reviewing duty[76] but not to deciding whether or not to exercise the powers to utilise the services of custodians or nominees.

(f) Trustees exceeding their powers

If trustees exceed their powers under the Trustee Act 2000 in appointing a person to act as nominee or custodian this does not invalidate the appointment.[77]

III DELEGATION BY INDIVIDUAL TRUSTEES

9–147   Section 25 of the Trustee Act 1925 for the first time allowed an individual trustee to delegate all or any of his discretionary functions, whether distributive functions or administrative functions, if he would be absent from the UK for more than a month. The Powers of Attorney Act 1971 then amended section 25 of the 1925 Act so that the facility was generally available to a trustee (whether or not absent abroad for a period) but the period for delegation was confined to 12 months, although another power of attorney could then forthwith be created for another 12 months and so on, if appropriate. The Trustee Delegation Act 1999 slightly further amended section 25 and repealed section 3 (3) of the Enduring Powers of Attorney Act 1985. This subsection had been a last-minute amendment to the 1985 Act, to reverse a particular recent case involving co-owners of land[78] but it accidentally had the vastly greater effect of enabling a trustee by an enduring power of attorney to delegate all her trusteeships to another person for an unlimited period. The 1999 Act further made special provision[79] for co-owners of land so that a trustee who also has a beneficial interest in trust land (or the proceeds thereof) can simply grant an ordinary power of attorney under the Powers of Attorney Act 1971 to his co-owner, enabling such co-owner to make a valid overreaching sale of the land.

---

[74] T.A. 2000, s.21(3) and Sched. 1, para. 3.
[75] *ibid*, s.22.
[76] *ibid.*, Sched. 1, para. 3.
[77] T.A. 2000, s.24(b).
[78] *Walia v. Michael Naughton Ltd* [1985] 1 W.L.R. 1115; Hansard (H.L.) Vol. 465, June 24, 1985 cols. 548–549.
[79] Sections 1, 2, 3 Trustee Delegation Act 1999.

The amended section 25 of the Trustee Act 1925 reads as follows.

"(1) Notwithstanding any rule of law or equity to the contrary, a trustee may, **9–148** by power of attorney, delegate the execution or exercise of all or any of the trusts, powers and discretions vested in him as trustee either alone or jointly with any other person or persons.

(2) A delegation under this section—

(a) commences as provided by the instrument creating the power or, if the instrument makes no provision as to the commencement of the delegation, with the date of the execution of the instrument by the donor; and

(b) continues for a period of twelve months or any shorter period provided by the instrument creating the power.

(3) The persons who may be donees of a power of attorney under this section include a trust corporation.

(4) Before or within seven days after giving a power of attorney under this **9–149** section the donor shall give written notice of it (specifying the date on which the power comes into operation and its duration, the donee of the power, the reason why the power is given and, where some only are delegated, the trusts, powers and discretions delegated) to—

(a) each person (other than himself), if any, who under any instrument creating the trust has power (whether alone or jointly) to appoint a new trustee; and

(b) each of the other trustees, if any; but failure to comply with this subsection shall not, in favour of a person dealing with the donee of the power, invalidate any act done or instrument executed by the donee.

(5) A power of attorney given under this section by a single donor—

(a) in the form set out in subsection (6) of this section; or

(b) in a form to the like effect but expressed to be made under this subsection, shall operate to delegate to the person identified in the form as the single donee of the power the execution and exercise of all the trusts, powers and discretions vested in the donor as trustee (either alone or jointly with any other person or persons) under the single trust so identified.

(6) The form referred to in subsection (5) of this section is as follows—"THIS **9–150** GENERAL TRUSTEE POWER OF ATTORNEY is made on [date] by [name of one donor] of [address of donor] as trustee of [name or details of one trust]. I appoint [name of one donee] of [address of donee] to be my attorney [if desired, the date on which the delegation commences or the period for which it continues (or both)] in accordance with section 25 (5) of the Trustee Act 1925. [To be executed as a deed]".

(7) The donor of a power of attorney given under this section shall be liable for the acts or defaults of the donee in the same manner as if they were the acts or defaults of the donor.

(8) For the purpose of executing or exercising the trusts or powers delegated to him, the donee may exercise any of the powers conferred on the donor as trustee by statute or by the instrument creating the trust, including power, for the purpose of the transfer of any inscribed stock, himself to delegate to an attorney power to transfer, but not including the power of delegation conferred by this section."

9–151   This amended section 25 applies to powers of attorney created from March 1 2000 onwards.[80] The duration of the delegation cannot exceed 12 months reckoned from the specified date or, in default, from the date of execution of the power.[81] It is now possible to delegate to a sole co-trustee[82] but, unless this be a trust corporation, such sole attorney-co-trustee can give no valid overreaching receipt for capital moneys arising from a disposition of land.[83] Sub-delegation by the attorney is still prohibited.[84] A statutory short form of power of attorney is available for use but, if used, a separate one has to be used for each trust fund to which the delegation is to apply.[85] However, there is nothing to stop a partner in a firm of solicitors who is trustee of ten trusts from executing one power of attorney delegating to a fellow partner the trusteeship powers of all ten trusts while enjoying six months sabbatical leave.

9–152   Delegation under section 25 is intended as a temporary measure, the donor of the power being automatically liable for the acts and defaults of the donee as if the donor's[86] and also having to give written notification to the person, if any, having power to appoint new trustees *and* to the donor's co-trustees,[87] who have the same power in default of any such person.[88] They might then consider it more appropriate to replace the donor as trustee. If not, the delegation lasts till the expiry of the 12 months (or lesser specified period) unless the donor earlier dies or becomes mentally incompetent, except that if the power was executed as an enduring power of attorney then mental incapacity will not vitiate the delegation.[89]

Section 5. Deviations from the Terms of a Trust

In case it is overlooked it is, of course, possible to change the structure of fixed or discretionary interests under a settlement or the terms of a trust if there is an overriding power of appointment in this behalf conferred by the settlement[90] (*e.g.* upon the trustees, or the life-tenant or settlor) or an overriding power of amendment of the trust vested in the trustees or the settlor (*e.g.* of a pension trust or of an insurance premiums trust deed), but the latter power is confined to such amendments as can reasonably be considered to have been within the contemplation of the parties and trustees are constrained to observe their undivided duty of loyalty.[91]

---

[80] Trustee Delegation Act 1999 Commencement Order 2000, S. I. 2000 No. 216.
[81] Trustee Act 1925 s.25(2) (as substituted by Trustee Delegation Act 1999 s.5).
[82] *ibid.*, s.25(3), contrast previous s.25(2).
[83] Trustee Delegation Act 1999, s.7.
[84] Trustee Act 1925 s.25(8).
[85] *ibid*, s.25(5)(6).
[86] *ibid*, s.25(7).
[87] *ibid*, s.25(4).
[88] Trustee Act 1925, s.36.
[89] Trustee Delegation Act 1999, ss.6 and 9.
[90] For capital gains tax purposes it is vital whether the power is exerciseable and exercised to create a re-settlement (as a separate settlement occasioning a charge to tax) or merely a sub-settlement (no charge): *Roome v. Edwards* [1982] A.C. 279; *Swires v. Renton* [1991] S.T.C. 490.
[91] *Napier and Ettrick v. Kershaw Ltd* (No. 2) [1999] 1 W.L.R. 756; *Hillsdown Holdings plc v. Pensions Ombudsman* [1997] 1 All E.R. 862.

I. WHERE THE BENEFICIARIES ARE OF FULL CAPACITY

If property is given not contingently but absolutely to a person of full age *any* restriction on his enjoyment of it is inconsistent with his absolute interest.[92] Hence a beneficiary of full capacity and entitled *absolutely* can call for a transfer: *Saunders v. Vautier, infra*; and he may do so even if the settlor purports to remove this right.[93] As a matter of property law the absolute owner(s) of property can do whatever be desired, irrespective of any material purpose that the donor might have had in mind. So also *several* beneficiaries who are all of full capacity and between them entitled absolutely may call for a transfer, if they act together.[94] Even beneficiaries who are entitled *in succession* can combine to call for a transfer, provided they are of full capacity and are collectively entitled absolutely.[95] Thus a fluctuating body of beneficiaries from time to time within a class cannot exercise *Saunders v. Vautier* rights.[96] However the rule in *Saunders v. Vautier, infra*, operates also in favour of a charity.[97] But it does not apply where other persons have an interest in the accumulations of income which the beneficiaries are seeking to stop.[98] Nor does it give beneficiaries the right to control the trustee in the exercise of any discretion conferred upon him by statute or the trust instrument.[99]

In the case of income accruing to a closed class of discretionary trust **9–153** beneficiaries the sole member of the class for the time being can claim an entitlement to that income. If such class were open such sole member cannot claim such entitlement so long as it is possible for another member of the class to come into existence before a reasonable time for the distribution of the accrued income has elapsed.[1]

Where trusts arise out of contractual relationships it is possible for the parties who are beneficiaries to contract out of their *Saunders v. Vautier* rights *e.g.* so that unit-holders in a unit trust cannot terminate the trust and claim the trust property while the trust is operating as a going concern and before it is wound up as agreed pursuant to the trust deed.

---

[92] *Weatherall v. Thornburgh* (1978) 8 Ch.D. 261 at 270 (Cotton L.J.).
[93] *Stokes v. Cheek* (1860) 28 Beav. 620.
[94] *Re Sandeman* [1937] I All E.R. 368; *Magrath v. Morehead* (1871) L.R. 12 Eq. 491; *Re Smith* [1928] Ch. 915, *supra*, para. 4–98.
[95] *Haynes v. Haynes* (1866) 35 L.J. Ch. 303; *Re Millner* (1872) L.R. 14 Eq. 245; *Anson v. Potter* (1879) 13 Ch.D. 141; *Re White* [1901] 1 Ch. 570; *Re Bowes* [1896] 1 Ch. 507; *Re Bellville's S.T.* [1964] Ch. 163.
[96] *Re Westphal* [1972] N.Z.L.R. 792 at 794–795, *Re Levy* [1960] Ch. 346 at 363.
[97] *Wharton v. Masterman* [1895] A.C. 186; but see *Re Levy* [1960] Ch. 346. Whilst an indefinite gift of income to an individual carries the right to the capital, this is not necessarily so in the case of a similar gift to charity, for such a gift can be enjoyed by the charity in perpetuity.
[98] *Berry v. Geen* [1938] A.C. 575.
[99] *Re Brockbank* [1948] Ch. 206; *Holding and Management Ltd v. Property Holdings plc* [1990] 1 All E.R. 938 at 948; *Re George Whichelow Ltd* [1954] 1 W.L.R. 5; *cf. Butt v. Kelson* [1952] Ch. 197 at 207. Exceptionally, where property is held on trust for beneficiaries all of whom are ascertained and of full age and capacity all such beneficiaries may force the trustees to retire in favour of new trustees nominated unanimously by the beneficiaries: Trust of Land and Appointment of Trustees Act 1996, ss.19, 20.
[1] *Re Trafford's Settlement* [1984] 1 All E.R. 1108; *Re Weir's Settlement* [1971] Ch. 145.

One must distinguish between the rights of the beneficial interest holders collectively and the rights of one of the co-owners: the latter are much more restricted as is made clear in *Stephenson v. Barclays Bank, infra*.

SAUNDERS v. VAUTIER

Master of the Rolls (1841) 4 Beav. 115; Cr. & Ph. 240; 10 L.J.Ch. 354

9–154   A testator bequeathed his stock on trust to accumulate the dividends until V. should attain the age of twenty-five, and then to transfer the principal, together with the accumulated dividends, to V. V., having attained twenty-one, claimed to have the fund transferred to him. It was contended for him that he had "a vested interest, and that as the accumulation and postponement of payment was for his benefit alone, he might waive it and call for an immediate transfer of the fund."

LORD LANGDALE M.R.: "I think that principle has been repeatedly acted upon; and where a legacy is directed to accumulate for a certain period, or where the payment is postponed the legatee, if he has an absolute indefeasible interest in the legacy, is not bound to wait until the expiration of that period, but may require payment the moment he is competent to give a valid discharge."

On a question raised, with reference to a previous order for maintenance, as to whether there was a vested interest in V. before he attained twenty-five, the petition stood over, with liberty to apply to the Lord Chancellor.

Held, by the Lord Chancellor, the fund was intended wholly for the benefit of V., although the enjoyment of it was postponed: it vested immediately, and he could now claim the transfer.[2]

STEPHENSON v. BARCLAYS BANK

Chancery Division [1975] 1 All E.R. 625; [1975] 1 W.L.R. 88

9–155   WALTON J.: "I think it may be desirable to state what I conceive to be certain elementary principles. (1) In a case where the persons who between them hold the entirety of the beneficial interests in any particular trust fund are all *sui juris* and acting together ('the beneficial interest holders'), they are entitled to direct the trustees how the trust fund may be dealt with. (2) This does not mean, however, that they can at one and the same time override the pre-existing trusts and keep them in existence. Thus, in *Re Brockbank*[3] itself the beneficial interest holders were entitled to override the pre-existing trusts by, for example, directing the trustees to transfer the trust fund to X and Y, whether X and Y were the trustees of some other trust or not, but they were not entitled to direct the existing trustees to appoint their own nominee as a new trustee of the existing trust. By so doing they would be pursuing inconsistent rights. (3) Nor, I think, are the beneficial interest holders entitled to direct the trustees as to the particular investment they should make of the trust fund. I think this follows for the same reasons as the above. Moreover, it appears to me that once the beneficial interest holders have determined to end the trust they are not entitled, unless by

---

[2] Joyce J., in *Re Couturier* [1907] 1 Ch. 470 at 473, points out the distinction between giving a person a *vested* interest and postponing the enjoyment to a certain age, and giving him an interest *contingent* on his attaining a certain age. Also see *Gosling v. Gosling* (1859) John 265.
[3] [1948] Ch. 206.

agreement, to the further services of the trustees. Those trustees can of course be compelled to hand over the entire trust assets to any person or persons selected by the beneficiaries against a proper discharge, but they cannot be compelled, unless they are in fact willing to comply with the directions, to do anything else with the trust fund which they are not in fact willing to do. (4) Of course, the rights of the beneficial interest holders are always subject to the right of the trustees to be fully protected against such matters as duty, taxes, costs or other outgoings; for example, the rent under a lease which the trustees have properly accepted as part of the trust property.

"So much for the rights of the beneficial interest holders collectively. When **9–156** the situation is that a single person who is *sui juris* has an absolutely vested beneficial interest in a share of the trust fund, his rights are not, I think, quite as extensive as those of the beneficial interest holders as a body. In general, he is entitled to have transferred to him (subject, of course, always to the same rights of the trustees as I have already mentioned above) an aliquot share of each and every asset of the trust fund which presents no difficulty so far as division is concerned. This will apply to such items as cash, money at the bank or an unsecured loan, stock exchange securities and the like. However, as regards land, certainly, in all cases, as regards shares in a private company in very special circumstances (see *Re Weiner's Will Trusts*[4]) and possibly (although the logic of the addition in facts escapes me[5]) mortgage debts (see *Re Marshall*[6] per Cozens-Hardy M.R.) the situation is not so simple, and even a person with a vested interest in possession in an aliquot share of the trust fund may have to wait until the land is sold, and so forth, before being able to call on the trustees as of right to account to him for his share of the assets."

II. WHERE THE BENEFICIARIES ARE NOT OF FULL CAPACITY

A. Introduction[7]

The decision of the House of Lords in *Chapman v. Chapman*[8] in 1954 **9–156** made it clear that the court did not possess plenary powers to alter a trust because alteration was thought to be advantageous to infant or unborn beneficiaries except in certain limited cases. Some of these exceptions related to acts done by the trustees in regard to the trust property in the administration of the trust, while others went beyond this and conferred a limited power to remould the beneficial interests when this was to the advantage of the beneficiaries.

---

[4] [1956] 1 W.L.R. 579. Now see *Lloyds Bank v. Duker* [1987] 1 W.L.R. 1324 where a beneficiary entitled to 46/80 of the testator's residuary estate claimed therefore to have 574 of 999 shares in a private company transferred to her. Such a majority shareholding was worth much more than 46/80 of the proceeds of sale of the whole 999 shares. It was held that the duty to maintain an even hand or fair balance between the beneficiaries prevailed so that the shares must be sold and the claimant beneficiary receive 46/80 of the proceeds.

[5] In *Crowe v. Appleby* [1975] 3 All E.R. 529 at 537, Goff J. endorsed Walton J.'s views and pointed out "the logic of the addition of mortgages is that they include not only the debt but the estate and powers of the mortgagee."

[6] [1914] 1 Ch. 192 at 199.

[7] See O. R. Marshall (1954) 17 M.L.R. 420; (1957) 21 Conv.(N.S.) 448.

[8] [1954] A.C. 429. The variation of the trust in that case was later effected under the Variation of Trusts Act 1958, *infra*, at para. 9–164; see *Re Chapman's Settlement Trusts (No. 2)* [1959] 1 W.L.R. 372.

(a) Exceptions relating to acts done in administration of trust

(i) *Salvage.* This group of cases involved the alienation of infants' property and established the proposition that the court could sanction a mortgage or sale of part of an infant's beneficial interest for the benefit of the part retained in cases of absolute necessity.[9]

9–157   (ii) *Emergency.* This exception can be regarded as an extension of the salvage cases. The salvage cases required proof of absolute necessity. The principle of the emergency cases was somewhat wider and enabled the court to sanction departure from the terms of a trust where an emergency had arisen which the settlor had not foreseen and which required to be dealt with by the conferment of extraordinary powers on the trustees.[10]

(iii) *Expediency*—Section 57 of the Trustee Act 1925. Section 57 of the Trustee Act 1925 rested the jurisdiction on expediency—a basis which, it is conceived, is wider than that of salvage or emergency. The section provides:

> "Where in the management or administration of any property vested in trustees, any sale, lease, mortgage, surrender, release or other disposition or any purchase, investment, acquisition, expenditure, or other transaction is in the opinion of the court expedient, but the same cannot be effected by reason of the absence of any power for that purpose vested in the trustees by the trust instrument, if any, or by law, the court may by order confer upon the trustees, either generally or in any particular instance, the necessary power for the purpose, in such terms, and subject to such provisions and conditions, if any, as the court may think fit and may direct in what manner any money authorised to be expended, and the costs of any transaction, are to be paid or borne as between capital and income."

9–158   The object of the section is to enable the court to authorise specific dealings with the trust property which it might not have been able to do on the basis of salvage or emergency, but it was no part of the legislative aim to disturb the rule that the court will not rewrite a trust.[11]

This is an overriding section, the provisions of which are read into every settlement.[12] The powers of the court are limited only by expediency, though the proposed transaction must be for the benefit not of one beneficiary but of the whole trust.[13] The power has been used to authorise the sale of chattels settled on trusts which prevent sale,[14] the sale of land where a consent requisite to sale has been refused,[15] the

---

[9] See *Re Jackson* (1882) 21 Ch.D. 786; *Conway v. Fenton* (1888) 40 Ch.D. 512; *cf. Re De Teissier* [1893] 1 Ch. 153; *Re Montagu* [1897] 2 Ch. 8.

[10] *Re New* [1901] 1 Ch. 534; *Re Tollemache* [1903] 1 Ch. 457. The jurisdiction has been used to resolve a retention trust fund problem in a construction contract: *Rafidain Bank v. Saipem* (unreported March 2, 1994, Underhill & Hayton, *Law of Trusts & Trustees* (15th ed.) at 495).

[11] *Re Downshire* [1953] Ch. 218.

[12] *Re Mair* [1935] Ch. 562.

[13] *Re Craven's Estate (No. 2)* [1937] Ch. 431.

[14] *Re Hope's Will Trust* [1929] 2 Ch. 136.

[15] *Re Beale's Settlement Trusts* [1932] 2 Ch. 15.

partitioning of land where there was no power to partition,[16] and the blending of two charitable funds into one.[17] In 1990, the powers of the court under section 57 were utilised to enable efficient investment management of a trust. In *Anker-Petersen v. Anker-Petersen*[18] the trustees were given power to invest in assets of any kind as if they were beneficial owners subject to obtaining advice from an "Investment Adviser" as defined, power to use an Investment Adviser as a discretionary portfolio manager, power to hold investments in the names of nominees and power to borrow money.

(b) Exceptions relating to the remoulding of the beneficial interests

(i) *Maintenance.*[19] Where a settlor made a provision for a family but **9–159** postponed the enjoyment, either for a particular purpose or generally for the increase of the estate, it was assumed that he did not intend that the children should be left unprovided for, or in a state of such moderate means that they could not be educated properly for the position which he intended them to have, and the court accordingly broke in upon the accumulation and provided maintenance for the children. The exercise of this jurisdiction resulted in an alteration of beneficial interests since income was applied in maintaining beneficiaries notwithstanding the fact that the settlor had directed that it should be accumulated or applied in reduction of incumbrances. The jurisdiction was not confined to cases of emergency or necessity.[20]

(ii) *Compromise.* It has long been clear that where the rights of the **9–160** beneficiaries under a trust are the subject of doubt or dispute, the court has jurisdiction on behalf of all interested parties, whether adult, infant or unborn, to sanction a compromise by substituting certainty for doubt.[21] The issue in *Re Downshire*, *Re Blackwell* and *Re Chapman* before the Court of Appeal,[22] and in the last-named case[23] before the House of Lords, was whether the court had jurisdiction to do the same with regard to rights which were admittedly not in dispute. Their Lordships emphatically rejected the view that the courts had so ample a jurisdiction; but Lord Cohen, alone, was prepared to give an extended meaning to the word "compromise." In his opinion, even where there was no dispute, the court could sanction arrangements between tenants for life on the one hand and remaindermen on the other; but it could not vary the rights of members of a class which the settlor had directed should be treated in a particular way.

---

[16] *Re Thomas* [1930] 1 Ch. 194.

[17] *Re Harvey* [1941] 3 All E.R. 284; for other cases on s.57, see *Municipal and General Securities Ltd v. Lloyds Bank Ltd* [1950] Ch. 212; *Re Pratt* [1943] 2 All E.R. 375.

[18] (1991) 88 Law Soc. Gaz. Part 16, p. 32, [2000] W.T.L.R. 581.

[19] *Havelock v. Havelock* (1880) 17 Ch.D. 807; *Re Collins* (1886) Ch.D. 229; *Re Walker* [1901] 1 Ch. 879; *Greenwell v. Greenwell* (1800) 5 Ves. 194; *Errat v. Barlow* (1807) 14 Ves. 202.

[20] See *Haley v. Bannister* (1820) 4 Madd. 275.

[21] *Brooke v. Mostyn* (1864) 2 De G.J. & S. 415; *Re Barbour's Settlement* [1974] 1 All E.R. 1188.

[22] [1953] Ch. 218.

[23] [1954] A.C. 429. In *Mason v. Farbrother* [1983] 2 All E.R. 1078 it was held that doubts over the scope of narrow investment powers should not be compromised in the court's discretion by insertion of a new wide investment clause.

9–161   (iii) *Section 64 of the Settled Land Act* 1925. Section 64(1) of the Settled Land Act 1925 provides that any transaction affecting or concerning the settled land, or any part thereof, or any other land (not being a transaction otherwise authorised by the Act, or by the settlement) which in the opinion of the court would be for the benefit of the settled land, or any part thereof, or the persons interested under the settlement, may, under an order of the court, be effected by a tenant for life, if it is one which could have been validly effected by an absolute owner. "Transaction" is defined by subsection (2) to include "any sale, extinguishment of manorial incidents, exchange, assurance, grant, lease, surrender, reconveyance, release, reservation or other disposition, any purchase or other acquisition, any covenant, contract, or option, and any application of capital money . . . and any compromise or other dealing or arrangement. . . ."

9–162   Roxburgh J. in *Re Downshire*[24] thought that the section did nothing more than authorise, with the sanction of the court, the carrying out of transactions in the nature of practical steps of an administrative character; it did not authorise the remoulding of beneficial interests. On appeal Lord Evershed M.R. and Romer L.J. expressed the view that the jurisdiction conferred by the section was more ample.[25] "Transaction" is a word of very wide import, and is defined by the section itself to include "compromise, and any other dealing or other arrangement." Practical steps of an administrative character are provided for by section 71 of the Settled Land Act. Therefore it was improbable that section 64 was meant to act merely as a supplement to section 71. Nor was the fact that the transaction has to be effected by the tenant for life an indication that a restricted meaning should be given to the word "transaction," since section 75(2) of the Act permitted the tenant for life to give directions to the trustees with regard to the application of capital moneys. The factors limiting the scope of the section were, first, that the transaction must be for the benefit either of the settled land or of the persons interested under the settlement, though not necessarily of both; secondly, it must affect or concern the settled land, or any other land whether settled or not, and whether within or without England; and, thirdly, when it concerns settled land, it must have an effect which is real and substantial by ordinary common-sense standards as distinct from one which is oblique or remote and merely incidental.[26] It has since been held that the powers conferred by section 64 are also available to trustees for sale.[27] Section 64 has been held wide enough to enable trustees to transfer part of their trust property to another settlement of which they were trustees even though benefiting some other persons,[28] and to enable the Eleventh Duke of Marlborough to convey the Blenheim estate to trustees of a new

---

[24] *Sub nom. Re D's Settled Estates* [1952] W.N. 428 at 432.
[25] [1953] Ch. 218.
[26] See also *Re Scarisbrick* [1944] Ch. 229; *Re Mount Edgcumbe* [1950] Ch. 615; *Re White-Popham* [1936] Ch. 725.
[27] *Re Simmon's Trusts* [1956] Ch. 125.
[28] *Raikes v. Lygon* [1988] 1 W.L.R. 28.

settlement giving his troublesome son a protected life interest instead of a fee tail.[29]

(iv) *Section 53 of the Trustee Act 1925.* Section 53 of the Trustee Act **9–163** provides that where an infant is beneficially entitled to *any* property the court may with a view to the *application* of the capital or income thereof for the maintenance, education or *benefit* of the infant make an order appointing a person to convey such property upon such terms as the court may think fit. The effect of this section may be summarised as follows:
Where:

(a) an infant is beneficially entitled to any interest in property, whether real or personal;

(b) the interest itself is not under the settlement applicable for his maintenance, education or benefit, nor is it producing any income which is so applicable;

(c) a proposal is made that the court should authorise a "conveyance"[30] of the infant's interest with a view to the application of the capital or income, arising out of such conveyance, for the maintenance, education or benefit of the infant;

then the court has jurisdiction to sanction the proposal upon such terms as it thinks fit. Thus the sale of an infant's contingent reversionary interest to the life-tenant in order to minimise liability to estate duty was made with a view to, and was, an application of the proceeds of sale for the infant's benefit, where they amounted to more than he would have been likely to receive if no sale had taken place, and they were to be settled upon[31] and not paid outright to him.[32]

B. The Variation of Trusts Act 1958

The decision in *Chapman v. Chapman*[33] was criticised by the Law **9–164** Reform Committee whose report[34] led to the passing of the Variation of Trusts Act 1958, *infra*.

Essentially, the Act enables the court on behalf of persons who cannot themselves give their approval (*e.g.* because unborn, unascertainable or minors) to approve arrangements varying or revoking beneficial and administrative provisions under trusts so long as such arrangements are

---

[29] *Hambro v. Duke of Marlborough* [1994] Ch. 158.
[30] Including a mortgage: *Re Gower's Settlement* [1934] Ch. 365; *Re Bristol's Settled Estates* [1965] 1 W.L.R. 469.
[31] *Re Meux's Will Trusts* [1957] 3 W.L.R. 377; *Re Lansdowne's W.T.* [1967] 1 All E.R. 888.
[32] *Re Heyworth's Contingent Reversionary Interest* [1956] Ch. 364. Other exceptions under this head which are outside the scope of this note are the *cy-près* jurisdiction of the court in relation to charitable trusts, the statutory jurisdiction of the court in regard to mental patients' settlements under the Mental Health Act 1983, s.96, and the statutory jurisdiction of the Family Division of the High Court to vary ante-nuptial and post-nuptial settlements. See Matrimonial Causes Act 1973, ss.24, 31.
[33] [1954] A.C. 429.
[34] (1957) Cmnd. 310; [1958] C.L.J. 1 (S. J. Bailey).

for the benefit of the individual persons in question. Exceptionally, in the case of persons with contingent discretionary interests under protective trusts, where the interest of the protected beneficiary has not failed or determined, the court can give an approval on behalf of (and against the will of) ascertained adults and no benefit to them is required.[35] Jurisdiction extends to foreign settlements where the property and the trustees are within the physical jurisdiction[36] and the foreign law governing validity of the trust allows variation of the trust.[37] It also extends to the approval of an arrangement substituting a foreign settlement for an English one[38] but the court in its discretion may require that the beneficiaries have a genuine foreign connection.[39] The Act has been useful for saving tax by exporting trusts and by a partition of the trust fund between the life tenant (who might have a protected interest) and the remaindermen (who might be minors, unborn or unascertained). Where new administrative provisions are needed it is simpler and cheaper to invoke section 57 of the Trustee Act which also obviates the need to obtain the consent of every adult beneficiary.

Variation cannot be resettlement

9–165 The Act does not extend beyond a variation to a completely new resettlement as pointed out by Megarry J. in *Re Holt's Settlement*.[40] Later, in *Re Ball's Settlement*[41] Megarry J. enunciated a substratum test for ascertaining upon which side of this jurisdictional line a proposed arrangement falls[42]: "If an arrangement changes the whole substratum of the trust, then it may well be that it cannot be regarded merely as varying that trust. But if, an arrangement, whilst leaving the substratum, effectuates the purpose of the trust by other means, it may still be possible to regard that arrangement as merely varying the original trusts, even though the means employed are wholly different and even though the form is completely changed." In the case a settlement conferred a life interest on the settlor (subject to a power of appointment in favour of his sons and grandchildren) and the capital was in default of appointment to be divided between the two sons of the settlor or their

---

[35] s.1(1)(d) and proviso thereto in Variation of Trusts Act 1958. Here the settlor's intentions have much significance: *Re Steed's W.T.* [1960] Ch. 407 *Goulding v. James* [1997] 2 All E.R. 239, 250.

[36] *Re Ker's S.T.* [1963] Ch. 553; *Re Paget's Settlement* [1965] 1 W.L.R. 1046 at 1050.

[37] Recognition of Trusts Act 1987 incorporating Article 8 of The Hague Convention on The Law Applicable to Trusts and on their Recognition, *infra*, para. 12–31. The safest course is to vary the trust in the jurisdiction of the governing law.

[38] *Re Seale's Settlement* [1961] Ch. 574; *Re Windeat's W.T.* [1969] 1 W.L.R. 692.

[39] *Re Weston's Settlement* [1969] 1 Ch. 224 where the Court of Appeal refused to make the settlement a Jersey settlement for the reason *inter alia* that it doubted whether the beneficiaries, having only moved to Jersey three months before making the application, would stay in Jersey very long after the approval of the arrangement, if approved, and the saving of the liability to capital gains tax of £163,000. Also see *Re Chamberlain* unreported but discussed in (1976) 126 N.L.J. 1034 (J. B. Morcom): see *supra*, para. 8–09. Nowadays the courts are likely to take a move relaxed attitude, given the free choice of law permitted by the Recognition of Trusts Act 1987: see *Richard v. Mackay* (1997) 11 Trust L.I. 123.

[40] [1969] 1 Ch. 100.

[41] [1968] 1 W.L.R. 899; (1968) 84 L.Q.R. 458.

[42] [1968] 1 W.L.R. 899 at 904.

issue *per stirpes* if either son predeceased the settlor. The approved arrangement revoked the beneficial and administrative provisions of the settlement and replaced them with new provisions whereby each half of the trust fund was held on trust for one of the sons for life and, subject thereto, for such of that son's children equally as were born before a certain date. This jurisdictional limit is thus unlikely in practice to cause much difficulty.

Benefit

"Benefit" may be financial, moral or social[43] or the facilitation of the **9–166** administration of the settlement.[44] Unfortunately, the reported cases all too often show, as one commentator puts it,[45] "that benefit and the measure of it is simply what the court says it is." An extreme case is *Re Remnant's W.T.*[46] where the children of two sisters, Dawn and Merrial, had contingent interests under a testamentary trust which contained a forfeiture provision in respect of any child who practised Roman Catholicism or was married to a Catholic at the time of vesting, with an accruer provision in favour of the children of the other sister. Dawn's children were Protestant whilst Merrial's children were Catholic. In the interests of family harmony an application was made *inter alia* for deletion of the forfeiture provision. Pennycuick J. acceded to the application in the interests of family harmony and freedom of marital choice, though defeating the testator's clear intentions and though financially disadvantageous to Dawn's children who otherwise had a good chance of gaining under the accruer clause. *Re Tinker's Settlement*[47] was not cited where Russell J. had refused approval to inserting a provision (omitted in error) which would have taken away a sister's children's chance of obtaining property under an accruer clause on the brother's death under 30. Further, Pennycuick J. did not consider whether the Protestant children, when adult, would in all probability be happy to forgo a larger share in the trust fund resulting from their cousins' Catholicism, this being the test taken by Cross J. in *Re C.L.*[48] to distinguish *Re Tinker* from *Re C.L.*, where he approved a mental patient giving up certain life interests in favour of her adopted daughters with interests in remainder. Perhaps one may artificially reconcile *Re Remnant's W.T.* with *Re Tinker's Settlement* on the basis that in the former both sides of the family could benefit in theory while in the latter only one side of the family could benefit.[49]

---

[43] *Re Towler's S.T.* [1964] Ch. 158; *Re Holt's Settlement* [1969] 1 Ch. 100; *Re Weston's Settlement* [1969] 1 Ch. 224; *Re Remnant's S.T.* [1970] 1 Ch. 560, but *cf. Re Tinker's Settlement* [1960] 1 W.L.R. 1011. See also G. R. Bretten (1968) 32 Conv. (N.S.) 194.
[44] *Re University of London Charitable Trusts* [1964] Ch. 282; *Re Seale's Marriage Settlement* [1961] Ch. 574.
[45] R. B. M. Cotterell (1971) 34 M.L.R. 98.
[46] [1970] 1 Ch. 560.
[47] [1960] 1 W.L.R. 1011.
[48] [1969] 1 Ch. 587.
[49] P. J. Clarke [1987] Conv. 69.

9–167   So long as the arrangement is for the benefit of the incapable or unborn beneficiaries it does not matter that it is contrary to the settlor's wishes,[50] the operation of the rule in *Saunders v. Vautier* entitling the beneficiaries collectively to deal with their property as they want and the court's approval operating as the collective consent of the unborn or incapable beneficiaries. Exceptionally, in the case of protective trust cases under section 1(1)(d) of the 1958 Act where it is immaterial that there is no benefit for the class of contingent beneficiaries the settlor's purpose to protect the protected life tenant from improvident dealings is a significant consideration.[51]

The court may sanction a proposed arrangement which involves an element of risk to infant or unborn beneficiaries if the risk is one which an adult might well be prepared to take.[52] It will not sanction an arrangement involving an appointment made under a special power considered to be a fraud on the power.[53]

Parties to the application

9–168   Application is by claim form (under Part 8 of the Civil Procedure Rules) supported by affidavits to which a draft scheme of arrangement will be exhibited. The proper claimants are the adult beneficiaries and not the trustees.[54] The trustees are supposed to be "watch-dogs" concerned with the interests of those who may possibly be adversely affected by the arrangement proposed. The defendant should be the trustees, the settlor, any beneficiary not a claimants, and any person who may become entitled to an interest under the trusts as being at a future date or on the happening of a future event a person of any specified description or a member of any specified class (*e.g.* next-of-kin of S, still alive) who would be of that description or of that class if the said date had fallen or the said event had happened (*e.g.* S's death) at the date of the application to the court, being the date of issue of the claim form.[55] No other persons who might eventually fulfil that description or be members of that class (*e.g.* distant relatives who might be next-of-kin if the nearer relatives conveniently died) need be made parties, nor need possible objects of a power of appointment which has not actually been exercised in their favour, or persons whose only interest is under discretionary trusts in a protective trust where the interest of the protected beneficiary has not failed or determined. A person who has an actual interest conferred

---

[50] *Goulding v. James* [1997] 2 All E.R. 239 (CA.). Four fifths of the costs of affidavits filed by the trustee relating to the testator's wishes of "little if any relevance or weight" were disallowed.

[51] *ibid*, pp 249–251, based on *Re Steed's W.T.* [1960] Ch. 407 (C.A.).

[52] *Re Cohen's W.T.* [1959] 1 W.L.R. 865; (1960) 76 L.Q.R. (R.E.M.); *Re Holt's Settlement* [1969] 1 Ch. 100; *Re Robinson's S.T.* [1976] 1 W.L.R. 806.

[53] *Re Brook's Settlement* [1968] 1 W.L.R. 1661, *infra*, para. 9–321; S. M. Cretney (1969) 32 M.L.R. 317.

[54] *Re Druce's S.T.* [1962] 1 W.L.R. 363; trustees should only act as claimants where they are satisfied that the proposed arrangement is beneficial and that no beneficiary is willing to make the application.

[55] *Knocker v. Youle* [1986] 1 W.L.R. 934, 938; Rules of Supreme Court, Order 93. For infants or unborn beneficiaries evidence in a witness statement verified by a statement of truth or in an affidavit must show that their litigation friends and the trustees support the arrangement as in their interests and exhibit counsel's opinion to this effect; Further, see *Lewin on Trusts* 17th ed. (2000) pp 1455–1462.

directly on him by a settlement, however remote or contingent, has been held not to be a person who *may* become entitled to an interest so the court cannot approve on his behalf: *Knocker v. Youle, infra*, para. 9–174.

The effect of approval by the court

The variation takes effect as soon as the order of the court is made **9–169** without any further instrument,[56] and the order may be liable to stamp duty.[57]

A fundamental question is whether it is the order of the court or the arrangement which that order approves which has the effect of varying the trusts. The former view was taken in *Re Hambleden's W.T.*[58] The latter view is supported by dicta of Lords Reid and Wilberforce in *Re Holmden's Settlement*.[59] In particular, Lord Reid said[60]:

> "Under the Variation of Trusts Act 1958 the court does not itself amend or vary the trusts of the original settlement. The beneficiaries are not bound by variations because a court has made the variation. Each beneficiary is bound because he has consented to the variation. If he was not of full age when the arrangement was made he is bound because the court was authorised by the Act of 1958 to approve of it on his behalf and did so by making an order. If he was of full age and did not in fact consent he is not affected by the order of the court and he is not bound. So the arrangement must be regarded as an arrangement made by the beneficiaries themselves. The court merely acted on behalf of or as representing those beneficiaries who were not in a position to give their own consent and approval."

In *Re Holt's Settlement*,[61] decided before *Re Holmden's Settlement*[62] was **9–170** reported, Megarry J. rejected the view taken in *Re Hambleden's W.T.*, canvassed the difficulties arising from such rejection and accepted counsel's submission that,[63] "when the adults by their counsel assented to the arrangement and the court on behalf of the infants by order approved the arrangement then there was an arrangement which varied the trusts." The variation is thus effected by the consent of all parties on *Saunders v. Vautier*[64] principles, the court supplying the consents of the unborn, the unascertained and infants, and new trusts replace the old so that since July 16, 1964, the Perpetuities and Accumulations Act 1964 has been available to provide new perpetuity and accumulation periods for trusts varied under the Variation of Trusts Act.[65]

---

[56] *Re Holmden's Settlement* [1968] A.C. 685; *Re Holt's Settlement* [1969] 1 Ch. 100.
[57] Practice Note [1966] 1 W.L.R. 345; *Re Holt's Settlement, supra; Thorn v. I.R.C.* [1976] 1 W.L.R. 915, though *ad valorem* duty on gifts abolished by Finance Act 1985, s.82.
[58] [1960] 1 W.L.R. 82.
[59] [1968] A.C. 685 at 701, 702, 710, 713.
[60] *ibid.* at 701–702.
[61] [1969] 1 Ch. 100.
[62] [1968] A.C. 685.
[63] [1969] 1 Ch. 100 at 115.
[64] *supra*, p. 631.
[65] So held in *Re Holt's Settlement* [1969] 1 Ch. 100. It is thought that as it is the court that orders variations under Matrimonial Causes Act 1973, s.24 such orders in the Family Division, like the exercise of special powers, are subject to the periods laid down in the original settlement.

This was endorsed in *Goulding v. James* by Mummery L.J.[66]: "The court is merely contributing on behalf of infants and unborn and unascertained persons the binding assents to the arrangements which they, unlike an adult beneficiary, cannot give. The 1958 Act has thus been viewed by the courts as a statutory extension of the consent principle embodied in the rule in *Saunders v. Vantier*. The principle recognises the rights of beneficiaries who are *sui juris* and together absolutely entitled to the trust property, to exercise their proprietary rights to overbear and defeat the intention of a testator or settlor."

9–171   Adult beneficiaries who give their own consents to the variation would seem to be *pro tanto* disposing of their subsisting equitable interests so that signed writing is required by section 53(1)(*c*) of the Law of Property Act 1925. However, in *Re Holt's Settlement*[67] Megarry J. held that the court's power under the 1958 Act was to approve arrangements that actually did vary the trusts effectively so the court's order approving the arrangement makes it effective irrespective of whether there is any signed writing provided by the consenting adults. The 1958 Act by implication ousted section 53(1)(*c*). Furthermore, where the arrange ment consisted of a specifically enforceable contract the beneficial interests would have passed under a constructive trust to the purchasers, such a trust being effective under section 53(2) without signed writing.

Variation of Trusts Act 1958

9–172   **Section 1.**—(1) Where property, whether real or personal, is held on trusts arising, whether before or after the passing of this Act, under any will, settlement or other disposition, the court may if it thinks fit by order approve on behalf of—

(a) any person having, directly or indirectly, an interest, whether vested or contingent, under the trusts who by reason of infancy or other incapacity is incapable of assenting,[68] or

(b) any person (whether ascertained or not) who may[69] become entitled, directly or indirectly, to an interest under the trusts as being at a future date or on the happening of a future event a person of any specified description[70] or a member of any specified class of persons, so however that this paragraph shall not include any person[71] who would be of that description, or a member of that class, as the case may be, if the said date had fallen or the said event had happened at the date of the application to the court,[72] or

(c) any person unborn, or

---

[66] [1997] 2 All E.R. 239, 247.
[67] [1969] 1 Ch. 100 at 115–116.
[68] Objects of a discretionary trust are treated as included: *Re Clitheroe's S.T.* [1959] 3 All E.R. 784.
[69] See *Knocker v. Youle* [1986] 2 All E.R. 914, *infra*, para. 9–174.
[70] Unascertained future spouses are included: *Re Steed's W.T.* [1960] Ch. 407.
[71] This is tacitly assumed to cover only "ascertained" persons so as not to cover all females who may possibly marry a bachelor beneficiary and so become a beneficiary.
[72] This refers *inter alia* to the potential next-of-kin of a living person, who must make up their own minds whether or not to give their consent: *Re Suffert's Settlement* [1961] Ch. 1. The relevant date is the date of issue of the claim form; *Knocker v. Youle* [1986] 1 W.L.R. 934, 938.

(d) any person[73] in respect of any discretionary interest of his under protective trusts where the interest of the principal beneficiary has not failed or determined,

any arrangement (by whomsoever proposed,[74] and whether or not there is any other person beneficially interested who is capable of assenting thereto) varying or revoking all or any of the trusts, or enlarging[75] the powers of the trustees of managing or administering any of the property subject to the trusts:

Providing that except[76] by virtue of paragraph (d) of this subsection the court **9–173** shall not approve an arrangement on behalf of any person unless the carrying out thereof would be for the benefit[77] of that person.

(2) In the foregoing subsection "protective trusts" means the trusts specified in paragraphs (i) and (ii) of subsection (1) of section thirty-three of the Trustee Act 1925 or any like trusts, "the principal beneficiary" has the same meaning as in the said subsection (1) and "discretionary interest" means an interest arising under the trust specified in paragraph (ii) of the said subsection (1) or any like trust.[78]

(3) The jurisdiction conferred by subsection (1) of this section shall be exercisable by the High Court, except that the question whether the carrying out of any arrangement would be for the benefit of a person falling within paragraph (a) of the said subsection (1) shall be determined by order of the authority having jurisdiction under Part VII of the Mental Health Act 1983 if that person is a patient within the meaning of the said Part VII.

(5) Nothing in the foregoing provisions of this section shall apply to trusts affecting property settled by Act of Parliament.

(6) Nothing in this section shall be taken to limit the powers conferred by section sixty-four of the Settled Land Act 1925, section fifty-seven of the Trustee Act 1925, or the powers of the authority having jurisdiction under Part VII of the Mental Health Act 1983.

---

[73] Including an unascertained or unborn person: *Re Turner's Will Trusts* [1960] Ch. 122; (1959) 75 L.Q.R. 541 (R.E.M.). This approval may be given without the need to show "benefit."

[74] The arrangement need not be in the nature of a contract between parties: *Re Steed's W.T.* [1959] Ch. 354; but must not amount to a completely new settlement: *Re T's S.T.* [1964] Ch. 158; *Re Ball's S.T.* [1968] 1 W.L.R. 899; and it must be practical and businesslike: *Re Van Jenisen's W.T.* [1964] 1 W.L.R. 449.

[75] *e.g.* conferring wider investment powers: see *Re Coates's Trusts* [1959] 1 W.L.R. 375; *Re Byng's Will Trusts* [1959] 1 W.L.R. 375; *Re Allen's Settlement Trusts* [1960] 1 W.L.R. 6; *Re Royal Naval and Royal Marine Children's Homes, Portsmouth* [1959] 1 W.L.R. 755. Where no alteration of beneficial interests is sought, only larger administrative powers, it is more convenient to use Trustee Act 1925, s.57: the advantages of s.57 are that the trustees are normally the applicants, the consent of each *sui juris* beneficiary is not required, the court considers the interest of the beneficiaries collectively not individually: *Anker-Petersen v. Anker-Petersen* [2000] W.T.L.R. 581.

[76] Even in the excepted case the court must exercise its discretion judicially: *Re Burney's Settlement* [1961] 1 W.L.R. 545; *Re Baker's S.T.* [1964] 1 W.L.R. 336.

[77] In *Re Cohen's W.T.* [1959] 1 W.L.R. 865 at 868 Danckwerts J. said that the court could take a risk on behalf of an infant if it was a risk an adult would be prepared to take. This was criticised at (1960) 76 L.Q.R. 22 (R. E. M.). In a case of the same name [1965] 1 W.L.R. 1229, Stamp J. stressed, however, that (i) the court had to be satisfied that there was a benefit in the case of each individual infant and not merely of the whole class to which the infant belonged; and (ii) while the court need not be satisfied that each individual infant is bound to be better off than he would otherwise have been, it must be sure that he is making a bargain which is a reasonable one which an adult would be prepared to make. The court may take a broad reasonable view but not a galloping gambling view: *Re Robinson's S.T.* [1976] 1 W.L.R. 806. The court will not approve an arrangement which is a fraud on a power (*Re Robertson's W.T.* [1960] 1 W.L.R. 1050) or is contrary to public policy (*Re Michelham's W.T.* [1964] Ch. 550). Nor will the court use the Act as a justification for rectifying a settlement on the basis of mistake (*Re Tinker's Settlement* [1960] 1 W.L.R. 1011) or for making an order which can be made without the aid of the Act (*Re Pettifor's W.T.* [1966] Ch. 257 where the female beneficiary was 70 years old and so well past child-bearing age.)

[78] For "like" trusts, see *Re Wallace's Settlement* [1968] 1 W.L.R. 711 at 716.

KNOCKER v. YOULE

Chancery Division [1986] 2 All E.R. 914; [1986]1 W.L.R. 934

9–174 WARNER J.: "I have before me three originating summonses under the Variation of Trusts Act 1958 which are interconnected. The first relates to the trusts of a settlement made by the late Charles McMahon Knocker, whom I will call 'the settlor,' on 25 November 1932, as varied by three subsequent deeds; the second relates to the trusts of a settlement made by the settlor on 22 December 1937; and the third relates to the trusts of the will and codicil of the settlor.

"The settlor had three children: a daughter Augusta, who was born in 1932 and who is now Mrs Youle, a daughter Ann, who was born in 1933 and died unmarried, without issue, in 1977, and a son Charles Cyprian Knocker, who was born in 1936 and whom I will call 'Mr Knocker.' Mrs Youle has three children, all now of age. Mr Knocker has two children, both still minors. The plaintiffs, in the case of each of the originating summonses, are Mr Knocker and Mrs Youle.

9–175 "A problem has arisen which particularly affects the second settlement, that dated 22 December 1937. The trusts of that settlement were unusual and are now effectively these. In the case of a share of the trust fund settled on Mrs Youle (referred to in the settlement as 'Augusta') cl. 3(2) provides:

> '*If* Augusta shall attain the age of twenty-one years [which of course she did long ago] the Trustees shall thereafter pay the income of the first share to Augusta during the reminder of her life and after her death shall hold such share and the future income thereof in trust for such person or persons for such purposes and in such manner as Augusta shall by Will or Codicil appoint.'

"In default of appointment there is an accruer clause to a share of the trust fund settled on Mr Knocker. The trusts of that share are, *mutatis mutandis*, the same. Then there is, in cl. 7, an ultimate trust in these terms:

> 'IN the event of the failure or determination of the trusts hereinbefore declared concerning the Trust Fund and subject to the trusts powers and provisions hereinbefore declared and contained concerning the same and to every or any exercise of such powers and to any statutory provisions which may be applicable the Trustees shall hold the Trust Fund upon trust to pay the income thereof to the Settlor's Wife Mildred Alice Knocker for her life or until she remarries and subject thereto shall hold the Trust Fund and the income thereof in trust for such of the Settlor's four sisters Emily Mills the said Ada Florence Potter Annie Maude Leveaux and Alice Augusta Baker as shall be living at the time of such failure or determination and the issue then living and attaining the age of twenty-one years of such of the said four sisters as shall then be dead in equal shares per stirpes.'

9–176 "The settlor's wife, Mildred Alice Knocker, and his four named sisters have all long since died. The problem is this. None of the issue of the four sisters, whom I will call, for convenience, 'the cousins,' has been made a party to any of these originating summonses. They are very numerous and some of them live in Australia. It is not practicable to get their approval of the proposed arrangement. There are 17 of them who, if the failure or determination of the prior trusts had occurred at the date of the issue of the originating summonses, would have been members of the class of issue entitled to take under the ultimate trust in cl. 7 of the settlement.

"What is said by counsel is that I have power under s.1(1)(b) of the Variation of Trusts Act 1958 to approve the arrangement on behalf of the cousins.

"There are two difficulties. First, it is not strictly accurate to describe the cousins as persons 'who may become entitled . . . to an interest under the trusts.' There is no doubt of course that they are members of a 'specified class.' Each of them is, however, entitled now to an interest under the trusts, albeit a contingent one (in the case of those who are under 21, a doubly contingent one) and albeit also that it is an interest that is defeasible on the exercise of the general testamentary powers of appointment vested in Mrs Youle and Mr Knocker. None the less, it is properly described in legal language as an interest, and it seems to me plain that in this Act the word 'interest' is used in its technical, legal sense. Otherwise, the words 'whether vested or contingent' in para. (a) of s.1(1) would be out of place.

"What counsel invited me to do was in effect to interpret the word 'interest' in **9–177** s.1(1) loosely, as a layman might, so as not to include an interest that was remote. I was referred to two authorities: *Re Moncrieff's Settlement Trusts* [1962] 1 W.L.R. 1344 and the earlier case of *Re Suffert's Settlement* [1961] Ch. 1. In both those cases, however, the class in question was a class of prospective next of kin, and, of course it is trite law that the prospective or presumptive next of kin of a living person do not have an interest. They have only a *spes successionis*, a hope of succeeding, and quite certainly they are the typical category of persons who fall within s.1(1)(b). Another familiar example of a person falling within that provision is a potential future spouse. It seems to me, however, that a person who has an actual interest directly conferred on him or her by a settlement, albeit a remote interest, cannot properly be described as one who 'may become' entitled to an interest.

"The second difficulty (if one could think of a way of overcoming the first) is that there are, as I indicated earlier, 17 cousins who, if the failure or determination of the earlier trusts declared by the settlement had occurred at the date of the application to the court, would have been members of the specified class, in that they were then living and over 21. Therefore, they are *prima facie* excluded from s.1(1)(b) by what has been conveniently called the proviso to it, that is to say the part beginning 'so however that this paragraph shall not include . . .' They are in the same boat, if I may express it in that way, as the first cousins in *Re Suffert's Settlement* and the adopted son in *Re Moncrieff's Settlement Trusts*. The court cannot approve the arrangement on their behalf; only they themselves can do so.

"Counsel for the plaintiffs suggested that I could distinguish *Re Suffert's* **9–178** *Settlement* and *Re Moncrieff's Settlement Trusts* in that respect for two reasons.

"First, he suggested that the proviso applied only if there was a single event on the happening of which one could ascertain the class. Here, he said, both Mr Knocker and Mrs Youle must die without exercising their general testamentary powers of appointment to the full before any of the cousins could take anything. But it seems to me that what the proviso is referring to is the event on which the class becomes ascertainable, and that that is a single event. It is, in this case, the death of the survivor of Mrs Youle and Mr Knocker, neither of them having exercised the power to the full; in the words of cl. 7 of the settlement, it is 'the failure or determination of the trusts hereinbefore declared concerning the trust fund.'

"The second reason suggested why I should distinguish the earlier authorities was that the event hypothesised in the proviso was the death of the survivor of Mr Knocker and Mrs Youle on the date when the originating summonses were issued, that is to say on 6 January 1984. There is evidence that on that day there were in existence wills of both of them exercising their testamentary powers to the full. The difficulty about that is that the proviso does not say '. . . so however that this paragraph shall not include any person who would have become entitled if the said event has happened at the date of the application to the court.' It says:

> '. . . so however that this paragraph shall not include any person who would be of that description, or a member of that class, as the case may be, if the said date had fallen or the said event had happened at the date of the application to the court.'

9–179   "So the proviso is designed to identify the presumptive members of the class at the date of the application to the court and does not advert to the question whether at that date they would or would not have become entitled.

"I was reminded by counsel of the principle that one must construe Acts of Parliament having regard to their purpose, and it was suggested that the purpose here was to exclude the need to join as parties to applications under the Variation of Trusts Act 1958 people whose interests were remote. In my view, however, that principle does not enable me to take the sort of liberty with the language of this statute that I was invited to take. It is noteworthy that remoteness does not seem to be the test if one thinks in terms of presumptive statutory next of kin. The healthy issue of an elderly widow who is on her deathbed, and who has not made a will, have an expectation of succeeding to her estate; that could hardly be described as remote. Yet they are a category of persons on whose behalf the court could, subject of course to the proviso, approve an arrangement under this Act. On the other hand, people in the position of the cousins in this case have an interest that is extremely remote. None the less, it is an interest, and the distinction between an expectation and an interest is one which I do not think that I am entitled to blur. So, with regret, having regard to the particular circumstances of this case, I have to say that I do not think that I have jurisdiction to approve these arrangements on behalf of the cousins."

Section 6. The Trustee's Duty of Impartiality

9–180   It is the trustees' duty to balance the conflicting interests of life-tenants interested in income and remaindermen interested in capital and certain rules have evolved to guide trustees and, in some cases, to provide what is to be done if the rules have been broken.[79] In an exceptional case it may even be necessary for them to balance fairly the interests of beneficiaries entitled to capital. Thus, they can reject the claim of a beneficiary entitled to 46/80 of a trust fund to have 574 of the 999 shares in a private company owned by the trust where such majority shareholding is worth much more than 46/80 of the proceeds of sale of the 999

---

[79] Generally, see Josling's *Apportionments for Executors and Trustees* (Oyez Publications); also the Trust Law Committee's Consultation Paper, "Capital and Income of Trusts" published by Butterworths Tolley, June 1999. The Law Commission is now busy with this topic.

shares.[80] To maintain an even hand or fair balance between the beneficiaries the shares should be sold and the proceeds divided in the relevant fractions between the beneficiaries. In making investments we have already seen[81] that the trustees must act fairly in making decisions which may have different consequences for different classes of beneficiaries.

I. THE RULE IN *ALLHUSEN V. WHITTELL*[82]

Take a case where a testator has left his residuary estate to A for life **9–181** remainder to B absolutely and in accordance with the general law debts, funeral and testamentary expenses and legacies have to be paid out of the residue. It would be unfair to apply all the income of the gross residue towards payment of debts, expenses and legacies, so favouring B. Similarly, it would be unfair to apply capital only towards such payments, so favouring A. The rule in *Allhusen v. Whittell* thus treats the payments as coming partly from income and partly from capital. It requires that sum to be ascertained which together with interest for the year succeeding death would amount to the total expended on payment of debts, expenses and legacies: the sum so ascertained will be borne by B and the excess of the total expenditure over that sum will be borne by A. The rate of interest to be taken depends on the ratio subsisting between the actual net income after tax[83] for the year succeeding death and the gross capital of the estate. The rule assumes payment at the end of the executor's year and should be modified if payment is significantly before or after that year.[84] Exact calculations are not required: rough and ready bona fide calculations will suffice.[85] In practice many wills exclude the rule (as any contrary intention displaces it).[86] Moreover, the rule is often ignored, especially as few beneficiaries know about the rule and most beneficiaries are so pleased to receive the testator's bounty that they do not "look a gift horse in the mouth."[87]

II. THE DUTY TO CONVERT

Once the net residue to which A and B are successively entitled has been **9–182** ascertained there are still further problems. The residue may comprise wasting, hazardous or other unauthorised investments producing a high

---

[80] *Lloyds Bank plc v. Duker* [1987] 1 W.L.R. 1324.

[81] See *supra*, para. 9–82.

[82] (1887) L.R. 4 Eq. 295. For a good general statement of the rule see *per* Romer L.J. in *Corbett v. I.R.C.* [1938] 1 K.B. 567, although the tax position is now different in Income and Corporation Taxes Act 1988 Part XVI.

[83] *Re Oldham* [1927] W.N. 113.

[84] *Re McEwen* [1913] 2 Ch. 704; *Re Wills* [1915] 1 Ch. 769.

[85] *Re Wills* [1915] 1 Ch. 769 at 779.

[86] *Re Ullswater* [1952] Ch. 105 holding that a common form clause for excluding the rule in *Howe v. Dartmouth* failed to exclude the rule in *Allhusen v. Whitell*.

[87] (1946) 10 Conv.(n.s.) 125 (George and George).

income for A and making B worry whether the capital will have depreciated considerably by the time he receives it. Alternatively, the residue may comprise some reversionary (or other non-income-producing asset maturing in the future) such that A receives no income whilst the capital value of the reversionary interest increases all the time as the life-tenant grows older and poorer.

Three questions then have to be borne in mind:

(1) is there a duty to convert property from its present state into an authorised investment;
(2) *if so*, is there a duty to apportion income pending conversion;
(3) *if so*, what is the method of apportionment?

9–183   A duty to convert arises: (a) if the trust instrument so directs whether by an express trust for sale or by other indications that the property must be sold or (b) if the rule in *Howe v. Dartmouth*[88] applies. This rule ensures that where a *will*[89] contains a *residuary*[90] bequest of *personal*[91] property to be enjoyed by persons in succession then unauthorised[92] investments (of which there are relatively few after the conferment of wide powers of investment in the Trustee Act 2000) are held upon an implied trust to sell them and invest the proceeds in authorised investments unless (since the rule is based upon presumed intention) the will reveals an intention that no such sale is to take place.

9–184   There is a clear contrary intention where the testator indicates that there is to be no trust or duty to sell at all as where the trustees are given the right to decide to sell only if they see fit since such right not to sell but to retain is inconsistent with any duty to sell.[93] A contrary intent is also present if there is an express duty to sell at some future date (*e.g.* the death of the life-tenant), where there is nothing else to oust the implication that there is no duty to sell till then but rather a duty to retain.[94] A mere provision that the residue is to be divided between certain persons after the life-tenant's death does not exclude *Howe v.*

---

[88] (1802) 7 Ves. 137; generally see L. A. Sheridan (1952) 16 Conv. 349. The "rule in *Howe v. Dartmouth*" is confusingly used sometimes not just for the duty to convert but compendiously for the apportionment rules where there is an express or a *Howe v. Dartmouth* trust for sale.

[89] Deeds necessarily deal with specific authorised property: *Re Van Straubenzee* [1901] 2 Ch. 779. On an intestacy a statutory trust for sale arises: Administration of Estates Act 1925, s.33.

[90] A specific bequest of assets makes them authorised for the purposes of retention but not for further purchases: *Harris v. Poyner* (1852) Drew 174.

[91] Realty is presumed meant to be enjoyed *in specie*: *Re Woodhouse* [1941] Ch. 332; *Lottman v. Stanford* (1980) 107 D.L.R. (3d) 28. Since L.P.A. 1925, s.28(2) income from land is in any event treated as income passing to the life-tenant even where the land is not settled land within S.L.A. 1925, and even where the land was leasehold and so personalty (*Re Gough* 1957 Ch. 323), such now being the position for all UK land as an authorised investment under Trustee Act 2000 s.8.

[92] No *Howe v. Dartmouth* implied trust for sale arises for authorised investments, even if wasting or hazardous: *Re Gough* [1957] Ch. 323, Lewin on Trusts (17th ed) para. 25–39, J. Kessler, *Drafting Trusts and Will Trusts* (5th ed) para. 18.33, although the cautious approach is still expressly to exclude *Howe v. Dartmouth* just in case it might still be held to apply to wasting or hazardous authorised investments: R. Mitchell [1999] Conv. 84.

[93] *Re Sewell* (1870) L.R. 11 Eq. 80; *Re Pitcairn* [1896] 2 Ch. 199; *Re Bates* [1907] 1 Ch. 22 pointing out that another way of regarding the matter is to view the right to retain shares, for example, as making them authorised investments.

[94] *Alcock v. Sloper* (1833) 2 My. & K. 699; *Rowe v. Rowe* (1861) 29 Beav. 276; *Re North* [1909] 1 Ch. 625.

Dartmouth since the division may be of the residue as converted under *Howe v. Dartmouth*.[95]

Where the trustees have a power to decide *when* to sell, rather than a right to decide *if* to sell, this presupposes a sale is intended to occur so this situation is really not an instance of an implied *Howe v. Dartmouth* trust for sale but an instance of the will itself expressly or impliedly imposing a duty to convert.

Where a contrary intention is present so that there is no duty to convert then obviously the life-tenant will be entitled to the income actually produced by the property—no more, no less.[96]

III. DUTY TO APPORTION

Even if there is a duty to convert it does not follow that pending **9–185** conversion the tenant for life will get an apportioned part of the income only. The duty to apportion may itself be excluded by an intention of specific enjoyment of income pending conversion. The rules are:

(i) If the property is land so that a duty to convert can only exist under an express trust for sale the tenant for life gets the actual income,[97] unless the will directs an apportionment, or there is an improper postponement of conversion: *Wentworth v. Wentworth*.[98]

(ii) If the property is personalty of the prescribed kind[99] and the will is treated as indicating expressly or impliedly that there is an express trust for conversion the tenant for life gets an apportionment only, unless the will expressly or impliedly gives him the actual income: *Re Chaytor*.[1] A mere trust for conversion with an ancillary power to postpone conversion does not of itself give the income of the property before conversion *in specie* to the life-tenant.[2] More is required in the way of showing an intention that the power was intended not for the more convenient realisation of the estate but for the special benefit of the life-tenant.[3] Even then until the trustees consciously exercise this power for the life-tenant's benefit the life-tenant is entitled to an apportioned income and not the actual income.[4]

---

[95] *Re Evans* [1921] 2 Ch. 309.

[96] *Re Pitcairn* [1896] 2 Ch. 199; *Rowlls v. Bebb* [1900] 2 Ch. 107.

[97] The Law of Property Act 1925, s.28(2) until its repeal by the Trusts of Land and Appointment of Trustees Act 1996. All UK land is now an authorised investment under Trustee Act 2000 s.8.

[98] [1900] A.C. 163: testator gave trustees power to postpone sale of realty for 21 years. Trustees improperly postponed for longer. *Held* by the Privy Council the tenant for life entitled to a reasonable percentage yield based upon the value of the property estimated as at the expiration of the period of 21 years.

[99] Residuary movable property comprising unauthorised investments.

[1] [1905] 1 Ch. 233.

[2] *Re Chaytor* [1905] 1 Ch. 233; *Re Slater* (1915) 113 L.T. 691 at 693; *Re Berry* [1962] Ch. 97 pointing out deficiencies in *Re Fisher* [1943] Ch. 377.

[3] *Re Inman* [1915] 1 Ch. 187.

[4] *Rowlls v. Bebb* [1900] 2 Ch. 107; *Re Fisher* [1943] Ch. 377 (intestacy trust for sale); *Re Hey's S.T.* [1945] Ch. 294; *Re Guinness's Settlement* [1966] 1 W.L.R. 1355.

   (iii) If the property is personalty of the prescribed kind and there
         is an implied trust for conversion under the rule in *Howe v.
         Dartmouth* there will be an apportionment.

   There is, of course, no duty to apportion income of property
invested in authorised investments: the life-tenant takes all such income.
This will normally be the case due to the extensive powers of investment
conferred by the Trustee Act 2000.

IV. THE METHOD OF APPORTIONMENT

9–186 If the tenant for life is entitled to an apportionment only it will be
calculated[5] as follows:
   (a) Where there is for the benefit of the estate as a whole[6] a power to
postpone conversion and the trustees postpone:

   (i) The subject-matter being unauthorised property, the tenant for
       life is entitled, as from the testator's death, to the current
       percentage[7] of the value of the property estimated *as at the death*,
       plus the income from investing the difference[8] (if any) between
       that percentage and the income actually produced: *Re Owen,*[9] *Re
       Parry.*[10] Valuation is at the date of death as no other date is
       appropriate in view of the power to postpone sale.
   (ii) The subject-matter being reversionary interests or other non-
        income-producing property maturing in the future (*e.g.* a 10-year
        interest-free loan to a charity), the mode of apportionment is that
        adopted in *Re Chesterfield's Trusts, infra.*

9–187   (b) Where there is no power to postpone sale but an immediate sale
would be disadvantageous to the estate:

---

[5] For calculations see J. F. Josling's *Apportionments for Executors and Trustees*; Rowland's *Trust Accounts*, Ranking Spicer & Pegler's *Executorship Law and Accounts*.
[6] If given exceptionally to benefit the life-tenant then he takes the income *in specie* so no question of apportionment arises: *Re Inman* [1915] 1 Ch. 187.
[7] It is surprising that no one has asked for directions from the court as to whether or not a higher rate than 4 per cent. (confirmed in *Re Berry* [1962] Ch. 97) is now proper since an intestate's statutory legacies now carry 6 per cent. In *Bartlett v. Barclays Bank Trust Co.* [1980] Ch. 515 at 547 the rate applied to compensation for breach of trust was that allowed on the court's short-term investment account under Administration of Justice Act 1965, s.6(1), *infra*, para. 10–72, though where this is a high rate such as 12 per cent. This reflects compensation for loss of capital value because of inflation so Brightman L.J. said, "It seems arguable that a proportion of the interest should be added to capital in order to help maintain the value of the corpus of the trust estate." Indeed, in *Jaffray v. Marshall* [1994] 1 All E.R. 143 at 154 actual interest at the court's special account rate on lost capital was divided equally between life tenant and remainderman. The current percentage is intended to represent a fair yield so why not take the mean between the "higher rate" and the "lower rate" prescribed by the Treasury under Inheritance Tax Act 1984, s.50(3) to prevent manipulation of artificial values for I.H.T.? The higher rate is that shown in the F.T. Actuaries Share Indices for British Government Stocks and the lower rate is the current gross dividend yield on the F.T. Actuaries All-Share Index.
[8] The difference is authorised capital to the income of which the life-tenant is entitled.
[9] [1912] 1 Ch. 519.
[10] [1947] Ch. 23.

(i) The subject-matter being unauthorised property, the tenant for life is entitled, as from the testator's death to the current percentage[11] of the value of the property estimated *as at the expiration of the executor's year, i.e.*[12] one year from the death, plus the income from investing the difference (if any) between that percentage and the income actually produced: *Re Fawcett*.[13]

(ii) The subject-matter being reversionary interests or other non-income-producing property maturing in the future, the mode of apportionment is as in *Re Chesterfield's Trusts, infra*, once the apportionable capital figure has materialised either on sale of the interest or on the property coming into hand, *e.g.* on the life-tenant's death.

(c) To illustrate the situation in (a)(i) and how adjustments are made **9–188** if the tenant for life received too much or too little actual income, assume that the testator died on January 1, 2000, and that it is now January 1, 2002. It is estimated that a sale of the unauthorised securities at the death of the testator would have produced £1,000. The tenant for life is entitled for two years to the current percentage—say, 4 per cent—of that sum, *i.e.* £80. The income in fact produced during the two years is £200. The difference of £120—being the difference between the percentage on the notional conversion and the income actually produced—forms part of the capital. The interest or income on that £120 when invested henceforth goes to income. If the tenant for life actually received the whole of the £200, he has received £120 more than he was entitled to, so that an adjustment will be made out of subsequent payments; and if the tenant for life dies before a complete adjustment, the balance may apparently be recouped out of his estate.[14]

The difference might also be the other way round. The percentage on the notional conversion is £80, but the income actually produced and actually received by the tenant for life might have been only £50, so that he has received £30 *less* than the sum he was entitled to. Here also an adjustment will be made. The deficiency in the income payable to the tenant for life is primarily payable out of any excess income produced by the unauthorised assets in a subsequent accounting period, and, failing that, out of the proceeds of sale of the unauthorised assets. Any excess income received in a previous year cannot be resorted to in order to make good the deficiency, as such excess income must be regarded as capital and invested accordingly.[15]

RE EARL OF CHESTERFIELD'S TRUSTS

Chancery Division (1883) 24 Ch.D. 643; 52 L.J.Ch. 958; 49 L.T. 261

---

[11] See *supra*, n. 7.
[12] If sale takes place before the end of the executor's year then the actual sale price is taken: *Re Fawcett* [1940] Ch. 402.
[13] [1940] Ch. 402.
[14] *cf. Hood v. Clapham* (1854) 19 Beav. 90.
[15] See *Re Fawcell* [1940] Ch. 402.

9–189   A testator who died on December 1, 1871, devised and bequeathed his residuary estate to trustees on trust for conversion, with a discretionary power to postpone conversion, for the benefit of one for life, with remainders over. This residue included outstanding personal estate consisting of (*inter alia*) a mortgage debt with arrears of interest. The trustees postponed the conversion of the outstanding estate, which eventually fell in (with interest) a number of years later.

    Held, following *Beavan v. Beavan*,[16] that the property was to be apportioned between capital and income "by ascertaining the respective sums which, put out at 4 per cent per annum on December 1, 1871 . . . and accumulating at compound interest calculated at that rate with yearly rests, and deducting income tax, would, with the accumulations of interest, have produced, at the respective dates of receipt, the amounts actually received; and that the aggregate of the sums so ascertained ought to be treated as principal and be applied accordingly, and the residue should be treated as income."[17]

Note

9–190   A testator who dies on December 1, bequeaths his residuary personalty on trust for conversion, with a power of postponement, for A for life, remainder to B. Part of this residue consists of a reversionary interest under a marriage settlement of which the tenant for life is the testator's wife, and the remainderman the testator. The testator's trustees postpone, and it is assumed, in order to eliminate the necessity of calculating with yearly rests (compound interest), that the wife dies exactly one year after the testator, whereupon the reversionary interest falls in and produces £1,030. Of this sum £1,000 goes to capital for B, and £30 goes to income for A; for the sum which, with interest at 4 per cent for one year, minus income tax at, say, 25p in the pound, would produce £1,030 is £1,000. Henceforth A receives the income of this £1,000 when invested. Calculation becomes involved if a lengthy period has elapsed between the testator's death and the apportionment, for after the first year of calculation there is interest upon interest. The position would be the same if the trustees had sold the reversionary interest at the end of the year for £1,030. As the £30 passing to A is part of the £1,030 capital it is not liable to income tax: the notional tax deducted in the calculation enures for B's benefit. As reversionary interests fetch relatively little owing to the imponderable factors involved, it is best if possible to wait till they fall into possession.[18]

    The same method of apportionment applies to a *contingent* reversionary interest.[19] But it does not apply where the interest is vested in possession, but the income therefrom is temporarily charged in favour of

---

[16] (1883) 24 Ch.D. 649n.

[17] So also *Re Morley* [1895] 2 Ch. 738; *Rowells v. Bebb* [1900] 2 Ch. 107; *Re Hollebone* [1919] 2 Ch. 93; *Re Hey's S.T.* [1945] Ch. 294; *Re Guinness's Settlement* [1966] 1 W.L.R. 1355; *cf. Re Hengler* [1893] 1 Ch. 586; *Re Chance* [1962] Ch. 593.

[18] As administrators are directed to do under an intestacy by the Administration of Estates Act 1925, s.33(1).

[19] *Re Hobson* (1885) 55 L.J.Ch. 422.

a third party,[20] and it does not apply to realty.[21] On the other hand, it can apply where the sum to be apportioned includes both principal and interest.[22]

V. OVERRIDING DUTY TO ACT FAIRLY AND PRUDENTLY

In case it might be thought that section 8 of the Trustee Act 2000 **9–191** scandalously enables trustees to purchase or retain a short lease of premises leased out so that the life-tenant can receive all rents during the last 10 or 12 years of the authorised lease, leaving nothing for the remainderman, it should be remembered that the trustees have an overriding duty to keep an even hand between the beneficiaries as well as a duty to invest prudently.[23] They would be in breach of this duty[24] if they retained the leases till they expired or for any longer period than reasonably necessary to sell the depreciating leases. While purchasing such a lease would not be prudent.[25] It would also seem that the remainderman could specifically invoke sections 14 and 15 of the Trusts of Land and Appointment of Trustees Act 1996 for the court to compel the trustees to sell or he could take advantage of his inherent right to call for conversion.[26]

Hoffmann J. has pointed out[27] that the duty to keep an even hand **9–192** between the beneficiaries in making or retaining investments is more appropriately the less mechanical duty to act fairly. His approach indicates that English courts would reach the same result as the Ontario Court of Appeal in *Re Smith*[28] circumstances. The trust property comprised only Imperial Oil Co. stock held on trust for S's mother for life, remainder to S. From the outset there was only an average dividend of 2 1/2 per cent when returns of 8 to 10 per cent were available in respect of good quality bonds and mortgages. S did not want the stock sold and the trustee was happy to agree with this and ignore the life tenant's requests to obtain a higher income for her. The Court of Appeal upheld the judge's finding that the trustee was in breach of trust and should be removed and replaced by a new trustee.

---

[20] *Re Holliday* [1947] Ch. 402.

[21] *Re Woodhouse* [1941] Ch. 332; *Lottman v. Stanford* (1980) 107 D.L.R. (3d) 28.

[22] *Re Chance's W.T.* [1962] Ch. 593 (the aggregate of principal sums payable out of the compensation fund established under the Town and Country Planning Act 1947, as subsequently amended, together with the interest thereon held to be apportionable in accordance with the rule).

[23] See *supra*, para. 9–82.

[24] *e.g. Beauclerk v. Ashburnham* (1845) 8 Beav. 322; 14 L.J.Ch. 241 where trustees were *authorised and required* by and with the consent and direction in writing of the life-tenant to invest in leaseholds. Obviously, the trustees could not object to investment in leaseholds as such, but they had a discretion whether or not to agree to a particular investment proposed "because it must be agreed at once that it would not be fit for them to lay out the trust moneys in a low, bad and deteriorating situation," *per* Lord Langdale M.R. at 8 Beav. 328.

[25] *e.g. Re Maberly* (1886) 33 Ch.D. 455 (should not invest as directed in Irish land but in statutorily authorised investments).

[26] *Thornton v. Ellis* (1852) 15 Beav. 193; *Wightwick v. Lord* (1857) 6 H.L.C. 217.

[27] *Nestlé v. National Westminster Bank* [2000] W.T.L.R. 795.

[28] (1971) 16 D.L.R. (3d) 130; 18 D.L.R. (3d) 405. Also see *Re Mulligan* [1998] 1 N.Z.L.R. 481 (where it was the life tenant who was unfairly benefited).

QUESTION

What is the purpose and effect of the following clause in a will?

9–193   "I give all my property of whatsoever kind and wheresoever situate of which I have any power of testamentary disposition and not otherwise disposed of by this my will or by any codicil hereto to my trustees upon the following trusts:

Upon trust to sell, call in and convert the same into money with power to postpone such sale, calling in and conversion for so long as they in the exercise of their absolute discretion shall think fit without being liable for loss and so that the income of my real, leasehold and personal estate howsoever constituted and invested (including the income of property required for the payment of debts and other payments in due course of administration in payment whereof the proceeds of such sale, calling in and conversion are hereinafter directed to be applied) shall as from my death be treated as income and that a reversionary or future interest shall not be sold prior to falling into possession unless my trustees shall see special reason for such earlier sale and that the net rents and profits of my real and leasehold estate for the time being remaining unsold after payment thereout of all outgoings which my trustees shall consider to be properly payable out of income shall go and be applied as if the same were income of authorised investments of such proceeds of an actual sale thereof and no property not actually producing income shall be treated as producing income."

VI. PROPOSALS OF LAW REFORM COMMITTEE 23RD REPORT 1982

9–194   3.31 Our experience, confirmed by the evidence we received, is that in practice the rules of apportionment are in well-drawn settlements almost always excluded. It is quite clear that in present-day investment conditions the rules both of conversion and apportionment pending conversion have little if any relevance. When they do apply they require, in effect, the sale of equities, other than those authorised by the Trustee Investments Act 1961, and re-investment in gilt-edged securities. At a time when investment in equities may be the only way in which the capital value of the fund can in fact be maintained the traditional theory that re-investment is necessary to protect those interested in the capital no longer holds good. Conversely, the yield on fixed interest investments is now such as to provide the tenant for life with an income which is as high and may be higher than the average yield on unauthorised equities. The second reason why the equitable rules are frequently excluded in practice is that the calculations they require are so complex that the costs and administrative difficulties involved are quite out of proportion to any advantage that they might, in very exceptional cases, confer. Nearly all our witnesses took particular exception to the rule in *Allhusen v. Whittell*, which was described as complex, fiddlesome and resulting in a disproportionate amount of work and expense. It was suggested that where not excluded it was often simply ignored . . .

9–195   3.36 After careful consideration, we agree that the best solution would be for the rules both as to conversion and apportionment in *Howe v. The Earl of Dartmouth, Re Chesterfield* and *Allhusen v. Whittell* to be subsumed in a new statutory duty to hold a fair balance between the beneficiaries, in particular those entitled to capital and those entitled to income. Coupled with such a general duty should be an express power for such purposes to convert income into capital and vice-versa. In compliance with such a general duty to act impartially and to protect the various interests in the trust, the trustees could, if they thought fit, continue to convert investments and to apportion pending conversion. But in deciding whether or not this was necessary, trustees would be able to have regard to the whole investment policy of the trust. Where they decided that apportionment was desirable or where it was required by virtue of an express duty to convert, the existing rules would not have to be rigidly applied although, where their application was the best way of achieving justice between the beneficiaries, they would continue to be used. To provide for conversion and apportionment in this way within the context of a statutory duty to hold an even hand would, we think, make it clear to trustees that they must consider whether or not apportionment is necessary whilst at the same time allowing them a sufficient degree of flexibility.

3.37 Clearly it should be open to the beneficiaries to ensure that this general **9–196** duty is fulfilled and we therefore recommend that any beneficiary should be entitled to apply to the court for an order directing the trustees either to make or to adjust an apportionment. The onus would, however, be upon the beneficiary seeking such an order to show that the trustees' exercise of their discretion had substantially prejudiced his interests. This would mean, for example, that trustees would not be bound to apportion in accordance with the existing equitable rules if satisfied that a fair result could be achieved in some other way. But on the application of a beneficiary, the court would be empowered to order the application of the existing rules if it were shown that this would make a substantial difference to the result. What is "substantial" would clearly depend upon the size of the trust. On such an application, the court would have to examine the overall administration of the trust fund and, bearing in mind the vast choice of investments available to trustees, in practice it would be exceptional for it to conclude that they had not held an even balance. The practical importance of the existing apportionment rules would be diminished although, in as much as they are an attempt by equity to do exact mathematical justice, they might continue to be applied in exceptional cases. Should the court order an adjustment of the division between the beneficiaries, trustees should not, we think, be open to an action for breach of trust, provided that they acted in good faith throughout.

VII. Other Apportionment Instances[29]

Losses on realisation of authorised securities, e.g. mortgages, debentures. **9–197** Where a trust security turns out to be insufficient, then the proceeds of the security are divisible between income and capital in shares bearing the same proportion to each other as the arrears of interest and capital: *Re Atkinson*.[30]

Losses on realisation of unauthorised investments made by the trustees. If the personal remedy against the trustees is worthless, then the life tenant cannot be compelled to refund income received by him over the current percentage to make up the capital.[31] Otherwise, the loss is borne rateably by dividing the sum realised (including both the proceeds of sale

---

[29] Generally see Josling's *Apportionments for Executors and Trustees*.
[30] [1904] 2 Ch. 160; *Re Morris's W.T.* [1960] 1 W.L.R. 1210. For the position where trustee mortgages foreclose, see Law of Property Act 1925, s.31; *Re Horn's Estate* [1924] 2 Ch. 222.
[31] *Re Bird* [1901] 1 Ch. 916. For the current percentage see para. 9–186; *supra*, n. 7.

and any income received before sale) in the proportion which the income which the life tenant ought to have received had the unauthorised investment not been made bears to the value of the sum wrongly invested, but the life tenant must bring into hotchpot[32] all the income actually received during the currency of the unauthorised investment: *Re Bird*. If no loss of capital has been sustained, then the remainderman is not entitled to have the capital increased by adding to it the difference between the income actually paid to the life tenant and the current percentage.[33]

9–198   *General apportionment rule.* By section 2 of the Apportionment Act 1870 "all rents, annuities, dividends and other periodical payments in the nature of income . . . shall . . . be considered as accruing from day to day and shall be apportionable in respect of time accordingly." The Law Reform Committee (Cmnd. 8733, para. 3.40) recommended in 1982 that subject to express contrary intention, the 1870 Act should not apply on any death where a settlement arises as a result of that death, and where it does apply to a trust it should be amended so that income is treated as belonging to the person entitled to the income of the trust on the date when that income falls due.

    Stocks or shares bought or sold cum dividend. By the rule in *Bulkeley v. Stephens*[34] there is no apportionment here unless a really glaring injustice would otherwise be caused.

9–199   *Capitalised profits of companies.* Where a company instead of distributing its profits by way of dividend capitalises those profits by issuing bonus shares, debentures or redeemable loan stock, the company's decision binds those interested under trusts so that those interested in capital benefit: *Bouch v. Sproule*.[35] Of course, if the issue of shares is a rights issue (entitling current shareholders to subscribe new capital in proportion to their existing share holdings) the new shares, being bought with capital moneys, form part of capital.

    As Lord Reid stated in *Rae v. Lazard Investments Co. Ltd*[36] "there is no doubt that every distribution of money or money's worth by an English company must be treated as income in the hands of the shareholders unless it is either a distribution in liquidation, a repayment in respect of reduction of capital (or a payment out of a special premium account) or an issue of bonus shares (or it may be bonus debentures)." To these exceptions must be added the proceeds of a purchase by a company of its own shares (by analogy with reductions of share capital)

---

[32] *Stroud v. Gwyer* (1860) 28 Beav. 130 at 141; *Re Appleby* [1903] 1 Ch. 565.
[33] *Slade v. Chaine* [1908] 1 Ch. 522; *Re Hoyles* [1912] 1 Ch. 67.
[34] [1896] 2 Ch. 241; *Re Henderson* [1940] Ch. 368.
[35] (1887) 12 App.Cas. 385; *Hill v. Permanent Trustee Co. of New South Wales Ltd* [1930] A.C. 720; *Re Maclaren's S.T.* [1951] 2 All E.R. 414; *Re Outen's W.T.* [1963] Ch. 291.
[36] [1963] 1 W.L.R. 555 at 565.

and shares distributed to shareholders by virtue of an indirect[37] (as opposed to direct[38]) demerger.

With conventional scrip dividends, where a company declares a **9–200** dividend but affords shareholders the option to take the dividend either as cash or as bonus shares, the receipt is income in nature, even if the shareholder opts for the shares, because the company's intention was to pay a dividend and not to capitalise its profits. In the case of enhanced scrip dividends the bonus shares are issued at a price below market value and the issuing company has lined up a third party ready to pay the market price for the shares so that most shareholders will be better off taking (and then selling) the bonus shares rather than taking the dividends. Prima facie, the company's intention seems to be to capitalise the profits. However, so long as the trustees are consistent, the Revenue[39] will accept the trustees' decision that the bonus shares and the proceeds of the sale of the bonus shares are capital or income or capital subject to a lien in favour of the life tenant to the amount of the cash dividend,[40] such lien being satisfied out of the proceeds of sale of the bonus shares.

Section 7. The Trust Property

I. REDUCTION OF TRUST PROPERTY INTO POSSESSION

The position upon accepting trusteeship has been considered at para. 9–06 *supra* but one needs also to be aware of the following statutory powers.

The Trustee Act 1925

Power to compound liabilities

Section 15. A personal representative or two or more trustees acting together, **9–201** subject to the restrictions[41] imposed in regard to receipts by a sole trustee not being a trust corporation, a sole acting trustee where by the instrument, if any, creating the trust, or by statute, a sole trustee is authorised to execute the trusts and powers reposed in him, may, if and as he or they think fit—

    (a) accept any property, real or personal, before the time at which it is made transferable or payable; or

    (b) sever and apportion any blended trust funds or property; or

    (c) pay or allow any debt or claim on any evidence that he or they think sufficient; or

---

[37] *Sinclair v. Lee* [1993] Ch. 497 where ICI hived off its bioscience activities in to Zeneca Group (having the capital value of ICI shares) and had the Zeneca shares given to ICI shareholders, *prima facie* ranking as an income distribution, which would have given life tenants a windfall of half the capital value of the ICI shares held on trust for them but for the bold sensible decision of Nicholls V–C.

[38] *Briggs v. I.R.C.* (1932) 17 T.C. 11.

[39] Statement of Practice 4/94.

[40] *Re Malam* [1894] 3 Ch. 578.

[41] See s.27 of the Law of Property Act 1925; s.14 of the Trustee Act 1925.

(d) accept any composition or any security, real or personal, for any debt or
for any property, real or personal, claimed; or

(e) allow any time of payment of any debt; or

(f) compromise, compound, abandon, submit to arbitration, or otherwise
settle any debt, account, claim or thing whatever relating to the testator's
or intestate's estate or to the trust[42];

and for any of those purposes may enter into, give, execute, and do such
agreements, instruments of composition or arrangement, releases, and other
things as to him or them seem expedient, without being responsible for any loss
occasioned by any act or thing so done by him or them if he has or they have
discharged the duty of care set out in section 1(1) of the Trustee Act 2000.[43]

9–202   [This section replaces, with amendments and additions, section 21 of the
Trustee Act 1893 which replaced section 37 of the Conveyancing Act 1881. In *Re
Brogden*[44] the Court of Appeal laid it down that trustees must demand payment
of funds due to the trust, and take legal proceedings, if necessary, to enforce
payment if the demand is not complied with within a reasonable time, unless
they reasonably believe that such action would be fruitless. In this case the
breach of trust occurred before the Conveyancing Act 1881 came into force. In
Re Owens[45] Jessel M.R. said *obiter*: "[Section 37 of the Conveyancing Act 1881]
may have a revolutionary effect on this branch of the law. It looks as if the only
question left would be whether the executors [or trustees] have acted in good
faith or not." But Eve J. in *Re Greenwood*[46] put a strict interpretation on the
section by holding that it involved the exercise of an *active discretion* on the part
of the trustee. The Trustee Act 2000 Schedule 2 paragraph 20 new requires full
compliance with the statutory duty of care.]

Reversionary interests, valuations and audit

9–203   **Section 22.**—(1) Where trust property includes any share or interest in
property not vested in the trustees, or the proceeds of the sale of any such
property, or any other thing in action, the trustees on the same falling into
possession, or becoming payable or transferable may—

(a) agree or ascertain the amount or value thereof or any part thereof in
such manner as they may think fit;

(b) accept in or towards satisfaction thereof, at the market or current value,
or upon any valuation or estimate of value which they may think fit, any
authorised investments;

(c) allow any deductions for duties, costs, charges and expenses which they
may think proper or reasonable;

(d) execute any release in respect of the premises so as effectually to
discharge all accountable parties from all liability in respect of any matter
coming within the scope of such release;

without being responsible in any such case for any loss occasioned by any act or
thing so done by them if they have discharged the duty of care set out in section
1(1) of the Trustee Act 2000.[47]

---

[42] See *Re Strafford (Earl of)* [1980] Ch. 28 for a useful examination of the scope of this.
[43] Before February 1, 2001 trustees only needed to have acted "in good faith".
[44] (1888) 38 Ch.D. 546.
[45] (1882) 47 L.T. 61 at 64.
[46] (1911) 105 L.T. 509.
[47] Before February 1, 2001 trustees only needed to have acted "in good faith".

(2) The trustees shall not be under any obligation and shall not be chargeable **9–204** with any breach of trust by reason of any omission—

(a) to place any distringas notice or apply for any stop or other like order upon any securities or other property out of or on which such share or interest or other thing in action as aforesaid is derived, payable or charged; or

(b) to take any proceedings on account of any act, default, or neglect on the part of the persons in whom such securities or other property or any of them or any part thereof are for the time being, or had at any time been, vested;

unless and until required in writing so to do by some person, or the guardian of some person, beneficially interested under the trust, and unless also due provision is made to their satisfaction for payment of the costs of any proceedings required to be taken:

Provided that nothing in this subsection shall relieve the trustees of the obligation to get in and obtain payment or transfer of such share or interest or other thing in action on the same falling into possession.

(3) Trustees may, for the purpose of giving effect to the trust, or any of the **9–205** provisions of the instrument, if any, creating the trust or of any statute, from time to time (by duly qualified agents) ascertain and fix the value of any trust property in such manner as they think proper, and any valuation so made shall be binding upon all persons interested under the trust if the trustees have discharged the duty of care set out in section 1(1) of the Trustee Act 2000.

(4) Trustees may, in their absolute discretion, from time to time, but not more than once in every three years unless the nature of the trust or any special dealings with the trust property make a more frequent exercise of the right reasonable, cause the accounts of the trust property to be examined or audited by an independent accountant, and shall, for that purpose, produce such vouchers and give such information to him as he may require; and the costs of such examination or audit, including the fee of the auditor, shall be paid out of the capital or income of the trust property, or partly in one way and partly in the other, as the trustees, in their absolute discretion, think fit, but, in default of any direction by the trustees to the contrary in any special case, costs attributable to capital shall be borne by capital and those attributable to income by income.

Public Trustee Act 1906

Investigation and audit of trust accounts

Section 13.—(1) Subject to rules under this Act and unless the court otherwise **9–206** orders, the condition and accounts of any trust shall, on an application being made and notice thereof given in the prescribed manner by any trustee or beneficiary, be investigated and audited by such solicitor or public accountant as may be agreed on by the applicant and the trustees or, in default of agreement, by the public trustee or some person appointed by him:

Provided that (except with the leave of the court) such an investigation or audit shall not be required within twelve months after any such previous investigation or audit, and that a trustee or beneficiary shall not be appointed under this section to make an investigation or audit.

(2) The person making the investigation or audit (hereinafter called the **9–207** auditor) shall have a right of access to the books, accounts, and vouchers of the trustees, and to any securities and documents of title held by them on account of

the trust, and may require from them such information and explanation as may be necessary for the performance of his duties and upon the completion of the investigation and audit shall forward to the applicant and to every trustee a copy of the accounts, together with a report thereon, and a certificate signed by him to the effect that the accounts exhibit a true view of the state of the affairs of the trust and that he has had the securities of the trust fund investments produced to and verified by him (or as the case may be) that such accounts are deficient in such respects as may be specified in such certificate.

(3) Every beneficiary under the trust shall, subject to rules under this Act, be entitled at all reasonable times to inspect and take copies of the accounts, report, and certificate, and, at his own expense, to be furnished with copies thereof or extracts therefrom.

[The Law Reform Committee (Cmnd. 8733, para. 4.48) recommend that Public Trustee Act 1906, s.13 be repealed: there are no powers to enforce the Public Trustee's findings and Trustee Act 1925, s.22(4) provides adequate protection.]

II. Duty to Notify Beneficiaries and Account to Them

9–208   As Millet L.J. (as he then was) stated in *Armitage v. Nurse*[48] "there is an irreducible core of obligations owed by the trustees to the beneficiaries and enforceable by them which is fundamental to the concept of a trust. If the beneficiaries have no rights enforceable against the trustees there are no trusts" [for beneficiaries, only a resulting trust for the settlor]. The rights of a beneficiary to obtain accounts from the trustee[49] so that they can then be falsified or surcharged[50] is at the heart of the trust concept. To give substance to this right, a beneficiary of full age has a right to be told by the trustee that she is a beneficiary[51] and, indeed, a right to be told by the settlor the name and address of the trustee to whom a request can then be made for a discretionary distribution.[52]

"Every beneficiary is entitled to see the trust accounts, whether his interest is in possession or not."[53] Thus, any beneficiary with a future

---

[48] [1998] Ch. 241, 253 and D.J. Hayton, "The Irreducible Core Content of Trusteeship", Chap. 3 of A.J. Oakley (ed) *Trends in Contemporary Trust Law*, (1996, Oxford). Also see *Raak v. Raak* 428 NW 2d 778, 780 (1988), Michigan C.A.

[49] Trustees are under a duty to keep proper accounts and be ready to provide them and supporting oral or documentary information: *White v. Lady Lincoln* (1803) 8 Ves Jr 363; *Pearse v. Green* (1819) 1 Jac & W. 135, 140, *Eglin v. Sanderson* (1862) 3 Giff 434, 440; but legacies to parents for maintaining and educating their infant children do not create trusts: *Re Rogers* [1944] Ch. 297. Defaulting trustees will have to pay for expenses and costs arising from such default: *Re Skinner* [1904] 1 Ch. 289, *Re Den Haag Trust* (1997/98) 1 O.F.L.R. 495.

[50] See paras 10–04 *et seq. infra.* In the case of charitable trusts or non charitable purpose trusts one needs the Attorney–General or an appointed enforcer to have the right to make the trustees account.

[51] The right to make trustees account is meaningless unless the beneficiaries know they are beneficiaries *Hawkesley v. May* [1956] 1 Q.B. 304, *Brittlebank v. Goodwin* (1868) L.R.5 Eq. 541, 550; cp. *Scally v. Southern Health & Social Services Board* [1992] 1 A.C. 294, 306–307. In the case of a testamentary trust or the statutory intestacy trust, the executor is under no duty to disclose the gift to the specified beneficiaries (*Re Lewis* [1904] Ch. 656) until the estate has been fully administered and the net trust fund ascertained in which the beneficiaries for the first time acquire an equitable proprietary interest (different from the equitable chose in action to have the estate duly administered): see para. 1–122 *supra*).

[52] *Re Murphy's Settlement* [1998] 3 All E.R. 1 where from p. 3 and the p. 9 reference to *Re Manisty's Settlement* [1974] Ch. 17 it appears the judge treated the claimant as the object of a power of appointment in a discretionary trust.

[53] *Armitage v. Nurse* [1998] Ch. 241, 261 per Millett L.J. Unless there is a possibility of income being accumulated and added to capital it seems that a capital beneficiary is, however, not entitled to see the income accounts disposing of income to income beneficiaries: *Nestlé v. National Westminster Bank* [2000] W.T.L.R. 795, 822.

interest,[54] normally including (so far as practicable) a person who is merely the object of a discretionary trust or power[55] which may never be exercised in his favour, has the means to discover a breach of trust, although time does not begin to run against him till he obtains a present interest in trust property because "he should not be compelled to litigate (at considerable personal expense) in respect of an injury to an interest which he may never live to enjoy".[56]

Normally, the settlor naturally wants objects of powers of appointment **9–209** to have the same rights to accounts and supporting information as the beneficiaries under his trust. This is particularly the case where for a lengthy period income and capital is subject to powers of appointment (and to no trusts other than to accumulate income), with trusts only arising for beneficiaries or charitable purposes at the end of such lengthy period. Until expiry of such period, one assumes that the objects of the power are the main objects of the settlor's bounty and so should be able to monitor the trustee's conduct in such period. However, it is considered that the fact that, ultimately, at the end of the trust period there will be ascertained one or more beneficiaries entitled retrospectively to falsify or surcharge the accounts for the whole trust period is sufficient foundation for the basic obligation underlying any trust.[57] Thus, a settlor, if so minded, could expressly exclude the rights of objects of powers of appointment to be told they are such and to see the trust accounts, the enforceable personal and proprietary interests of the beneficiaries entitled in default of appointment sufficing to provide the irreducible core content of the trust. The settlor's intention is the key.

A trust cannot exist without there ultimately being some beneficiary **9–210** (or other enforcer like the Attorney-General) with the right to make the trustee account, but can exist if objects of powers of appointment have no rights other than the right to retain whatever is appointed to them,[58] *e.g.* because the obligation burdening the donee of the power (even if otherwise a trustee) is not a full fiduciary obligation but the lowest fiduciary obligation only to act in good faith and altruistically or is even

---

[54] Including contingent interests: *Re Tillott* [1892] 1 Ch. 86; *Att-Gen of Ontario v. Stavro* (1995) 119 DLR (4th) 750. Note that descendants who are both objects of a power of appointment and contingent beneficiaries under a discretionary trust if alive on expiry of the trust period will have rights to see accounts *qua* contingent beneficiary, it being possible (as under possibilities taken account of by equity for the purposes of the rule against remoteness) they could still be alive (even aged 150 years) at the expiry of the trust period.

[55] *Chaine-Nickson v. Bank of Ireland* [1976] I.R. 393; *Spellson v. George* (1987) 11 N.S.W.L.R. 300, 315–316; *Hartigan Nominees Pty. Ltd. v. Rydge* (1992) 29 N.S.W.L.R. 405; *Lemos v. Coutts* [1992–93] C.I.L.R. 460; *Re Rabbaiotti's 1989 Settlement* [2000] W.T.L.R. 953. The trustee's duty to inform is only so far as this is reasonably practicable: *Re Hay's Settlement* [1981] 3 All E.R. 786, 793, while if objects of a power consist of more than one category of person, *e.g.* for issue, relatives and employees of the settlor the court is likely to consider that by necessary implication the settlor only intended the first category as the prime object of his bounty to be informed: *Re Manisty's Settlements* [1974] Ch. 17, 25.

[56] *Armitage v. Nurse* [1988] Ch. 241, 261.

[57] In *Rosewood Trust Ltd v. Schmidt* (unreported February 2001 Manx Appellate Court) it was held objects of a power had no right to see accounts and make trustees account.

[58] As Megarry V-C stated in *Re Hay's S.T.* [1982] 1 W.L.R. 202, 213–214, "Beneficiaries under a trust have rights of enforcement which mere objects of a power lack."

expressed to be merely personal.[59] However, if such power is fully fiduciary so the donee must periodically properly survey the range of objects and consider whether a particular grant is appropriate,[60] then an object who knows she is an object has a right to provide information for consideration for a grant, has a right to check that the donee is exercising the power in a responsible manner according to its purpose and a right to seek a court order for removal of the fiduciary-donee.[61] How then does an object get to know she is an object? In *Re Manisty's Settlement*,[62] where the objects were the settlor's issue, his relatives and the employees of his company, there was only a duty to inform the settlor's children that they were objects and to consider any information from them as to their needs, no breach of trust arising if the trustees did not inform the relatives or the employees and did not seek any information from them. Thus, to give substance to the fiduciary duties attached to the power it is only necessary to inform the primary objects that they are objects of the power. There certainly is no need to tell everyone in the world (other than existing beneficiaries and "excepted persons") that they are objects of a power to appoint to anyone in the world (except for "excepted persons" as defined) or a power to add anyone (except as aforesaid) to the class of beneficiaries or objects of a power.[63]

9–211   It is submitted that it is inherent in, and fundamental to, the status of beneficiary that a beneficiary is able to enforce his rights against the trustees (so that they are under the correlative obligation to account to their beneficiary which is at the core of the trust) and that, because a beneficiary cannot enforce her rights as beneficiary unless she knows she is a beneficiary, the trustees must be under a duty to notify a beneficiary of full capacity that he is a beneficiary. So long as there is an ascertained or ascertainable beneficiary, the objects of a power of appointment need not be given any rights other than the right to retain whatever is appointed to them.

What then if a settlor or testator creates a discretionary trust of income and capital for his four children, his grandchildren and great grandchildren, with a power of appointment in favour of persons who are spouses or cohabitees of beneficiaries or who are designated in writing by a beneficiary as being a friend of the designator or of an object of the power; and the trust instrument states that no-one is to be informed of the position except for the four children and the persons after their deaths who become the eldest of the next generation in that branch of the family, such four children and then the eldest members of

---

[59] See para. 3–110 *supra* for the distinction between personal and fiduciary powers, while the validity of trustee's powers to appoint to anyone in the world (but four "excepted persons") is explicable if such powers can be considered personal even though, otherwise, the trustees are subject to fiduciary obligations: see para. 3–112 *supra*.

[60] As explained in *Re Hay's S.T.* [1982] 1 W.L.R. 202.

[61] *Re Manisty's Settlement* [1974] Ch. 17, 25.

[62] [1974] Ch. 17.

[63] See *Re Murphy's Settlement* [1998] 3 All E.R. 1, 17; *Rosewood Trust Ltd v. Schmidt* (unreported February 2001 Manx C.A.).

the successor generation in each family branch alone to have the right to see trust accounts and to sue the trustees if any branches of trust have occurred. If child B dies, survived by three sons C, D and E born in that order, can D and E, having fortuitously learned of the trust, succeed in a claim to see trust accounts and to sue the trustees in respect of any breaches then discovered?

It is submitted that effect should be given to the settlor's intentions so **9–212** such claim should not succeed, whether (i) because C alone of C, D and E ranks as a beneficiary with the rights necessary for the status of beneficiary, so that D and E without such rights have to be recharacterised as merely being objects of a power of appointment or (ii) because D and E rank as "lesser" beneficiaries, while C is a "full" beneficiary. Basis (i) seems preferable to (ii) and to be in line with the views of Millett L.J. in *Armitage v. Nurse*. One can concede that peripheral powers of appointment in a trust deed can confer greater or lesser rights on the objects of such powers,[64] but does not the status of beneficiary need to be linked with an equitable proprietary interest in the trust property that can be protected or vindicated by the beneficiary's right to make the trustee account for stewardship of the trust property, and, if need be, to trace the fruits or exchange product of trust property into the hands of the trustee or of a third party who is not a bona fide purchaser without notice? A person without such a right is simply not a beneficiary with a beneficial interest, the English trust concept conferring personal and proprietary rights on a beneficiary.[65]

The right to inspect trust documents and take copies at own expense

A person who, as above, has the right to see trust accounts, so that he **9–213** or she can falsify or surcharge the accounts and have the trustee top up the trust fund by the amount due on finalising a proper account, has a right at all reasonable times to inspect documents concerning stewardship of the trust fund,[66] and at his or her own expense[67] to make copies thereof or to pay the trustee for copies provided by the trustee for an agreed sum representing the cost to the trustee.

---

[64] Must the trustee tell an object he is an object, then periodically consider whether or not to exercise the power, consider the range of objects, and the appropriateness of an individual appointment, or need the trustee only act honestly and altruistically when deciding to make an appointment? In the example, because a "beneficiary" cannot exercise his power to make a designation unless he knows of it, it seems every beneficiary must be entitled to be informed of this power, the purported exclusion of this right being disregarded as repugnant to, and inconsistent with, such right, although consistently with such right it is still possible to exclude the rights of some "beneficiaries", but not all, to see trust accounts and to sue for breach of trust if need be.

[65] A foreign statute like the Cayman (Special Trusts Alternative Regime) Law 1997 can define a "beneficiary" as having no interest whatsoever in any trust property and having no right to sue the trustee or the enforcer of the trust in any way whatsoever, so a "beneficiary" therefore has only a right to retain whatever the trustees distribute to the "beneficiary". However, if S creates a STAR trust of English assets for B C and D and their children and grandchildren enforceable only by the enforcer, X, the English court should hold there is a resulting trust for S with power to benefit the so-called "beneficiaries" characterised as merely being objects of a power, Millett L.J. having stated in *Armitage v. Nurse* [1998] Ch. 241, 253, "If the beneficiaries have no rights enforceable against the trustees there are no trusts."

[66] *Re Cowin* (1886) 33 Ch.D. 179; *Re Rabaiotti's 1989 Settlement* [2000] W.T.L.R. 953.

[67] *Re Watson* (1904) 49 S.J. 54; *Kemp v. Burn* (1863) 4 Giff. 348.

In *Re Londonderry's Settlement, infra,* para. 9–221, the Court of Appeal held that correspondence between the trustees themselves or between the trustees and beneficiaries and the agenda for trustees' meeting were not to be treated as trust documents that could be inspected by a beneficiary. However, minutes of trustees' meetings and other documents disclosing their deliberations on the exercise of their discretions or their reasons for any particular exercise of their discretions or "the material upon which such reasons were or might have been based," were exempt from the beneficiaries' right to inspect trust documents because, otherwise, the right of trustees not to be obliged to give reasons for the exercise of their discretionary distributive functions[68] would be undermined. This still enabled beneficiaries to see a factual aide-memoire on the state of the fund, past distributions and future possibilities, and legal advice as to the law relating to the manner in which trustees are entitled to exercise their discretions; but there is no right to see legal advice obtained by a trustee (which should be at his own expense) for his own protection when aware of likely proceedings against him[69] or to any evidence on a *Beddoe's* application by trustees for directions whether to take proceedings against a beneficiary.[70]

Trustees' discretion to withhold documents in interests of beneficiaries as a whole

9–214   Even where a beneficiary has a right to see trust documents, in an exceptional case[71] a trustee may decline to provide information to a particular beneficiary when the trustee has reasonable grounds for considering that providing the particular information to that particular beneficiary will not be in the interest of the beneficiaries as a whole and will be prejudicial to the ability of the trustee to discharge its obligations under the trust, especially a trust which involves the conduct or management of a business.[72] If the trustee does not seek the directions of the court as to the correctness of its refusal to disclose, then a dissatisfied beneficiary can seek the directions of the court for the court then to decide whether the strong presumption in favour of disclosure should be overridden in the best interests of the beneficiaries as a whole.

Beneficiaries' rights to disclosure in course of civil litigation

So far, one has been concerned with the rights of a party (like a beneficiary) to whom the trustee must account for the trusteeship to obtain disclosure of trust documents under the law of trusts. Quite

---

[68] *Re Beloved Wilkes' Charity* (1851) 3 Mac. 8 G. 440; *Wilson v. Law Debenture Trust Corp.* [1995] 2 All E.R. 337.
[69] *Talbot v. Marshfield* (1865) 2 Dr. & Sm. 549; *Bacon v. Bacon* (1876) 3 4 L.T. 349.
[70] *Re Eaton* [1964] 1 W.L.R. 1269; *Midland Bank Trust Co. Ltd v. Green* [1980] Ch. 590, 604–609.
[71] *e.g.* where one beneficiary's interest conflicts with the interests of the beneficiaries as a whole: *Rouse v. 100F Australia Trustees Ltd.* [2000] W.T.L.R. 111, 128–129.
[72] *Re Rabaiotti's 1989 Settlement* [2000] W.T.L.R. 953, 962; *Rouse v. 100F Australia Trustees Ltd.* [2000] W.T.L.R. 111, 128–129.

separately, under the Civil Procedure Rules governing civil litigation,[73] if a beneficiary can make out a properly particularised claim (so that it cannot be struck down as a mere "fishing expedition" to see if material can be found to support a claim) then this triggers standard disclosure of documents that can advance or hinder either party's case and subsequent applications can made in relation to specific disclosure of documents not disclosed pursuant to standard disclosure. Previously, a similar procedure was known as "discovery", and the order in *Re Londonderry's Settlement* was expressly "without prejudice to any right of the defendant to discovery in separate proceedings against the plaintiffs." As Robert Walker J. has pointed out.[74] "If a decision taken by trustees is directly attacked in legal proceedings, the trustees may be compelled either legally (through discovery or subpoena) or practically (in order to avoid adverse inferences being drawn) to disclose the substance of the reasons for their decision".

Letters of wishes

Finally, difficult issues arise in respect of a letter of wishes which a **9–215** settlor provides for the trustee to have some legal significance in guiding the trustee as to the purposes for which broad discretionary powers were conferred by the settlor on the trustee. Such a letter, brought into existence for the purposes of the operation of the trust, needs to be handed on from a retiring trustee to the new trustee, some regard needing to be had to it before a discretionary decision is taken on a matter referred to in the letter of wishes, even if the trustee exercising its independent discretion then decides to ignore a particular wish.[75] Thus, the letter is a trust document of some significance, although not so significant as the trust deed itself unless, exceptionally, the settlor intended the letter to be legally binding so as to override the trust deed to the extent necessary to give effect to what was laid down in the letter.

However, in *Re Rabaiotti's 1989 Settlement, infra,* para. 9–229, the Jersey Royal Court held a beneficiary had no right to see a letter of wishes because it was "material upon which reasons were or might have been based" within the terms of the Court order in *Re Londonderry's Settlement,*[76] and in any event, "to require disclosure of a letter of wishes would be likely in practice to undermine the immunity from the provision of reasons and to lead to just the sort of problems which the immunity was designed to avoid."[77] Furthermore, "as an additional ground", "the letter of wishes need not be disclosed on the ground of confidentiality": although the letter was not expressed to be confidential,

---

[73] Part 31 and Practice Direction thereon.
[74] *Scott v. National Trust* [1998] 2 All E.R. 705, 719, and to similar effect Buxton L.J. in *Taylor v. Midland Bank Trust Co.* (2000) 2 I.T.E.L.R. 439, 459–461.
[75] *Bank of Nova Scotia Trust Co (Bahamas) Ltd v. Ricart de Barletta* 1 Butterworths Offshore Cases & Materials 5 discussed by H. Thompson in (1994) 3 Jo. Int. Tr. & Corp. Pl 35. Further see D.J. Hayton (1999) 32 Vanderbilt Jo. of Transnat. Law 555, 573–576.
[76] [1965] Ch. 918, 938.
[77] *Re Rabbaiotti's 1989 Settlement* [2000] W.T.L.R. 953, 968.

"the fact that the settlor writes a separate letter addressed privately to trustees raises a strong implication that he intended the document to be confidential."[78]

9–216   As pointed out in *Lewin on Trusts*,[79] because the letter is given by the settlor to provide guidance to the trustees on the sound administration of the trust and the exercise of their discretions, the obligation of confidence to the settlor should permit the trustees to disclose the contents of the letter to the extent they consider it appropriate for the sound administration of the trust and the proper exercise of their discretions. Upon reaching this stage, one wonders why the beneficiaries should not have a right to see the letter of wishes where it concerns a matter of which the beneficiary complains involving the sound administration of the trust and the proper exercise of the trustees' discretions. After all, the trustees' discretions can only be exercised in a responsible manner for the purposes for which they were conferred upon the trustees[80] as indicated by the settlor in his legally significant letter of wishes. How can a beneficiary take advantage of the accountability to him of the trustees in exercising their discretions unless he knows the purposes for which such were conferred upon the trustees? Without knowing such purposes how can there be any meaningful substance to the fundamental right to make the trustees account for their trusteeship? In essence, in trying to establish a *prima facie* case the beneficiary is fighting the trustee in circumstances where the beneficiary is blind-folded and has one arm tied behind his back.

9–217   Consider the case of a discretionary trust for A, B, C, D, E and F where the trustees are directed not to inform D, E and F that they are beneficiaries, and so are not to show them the trust deed, and that the settlor's letter of wishes is expressly confidential to the trustees and A, B and C. Should the Court not hold that not only are D, E and F entitled to be told they are beneficiaries, and to see the trust deed but they are also entitled to see the letter of wishes. The first two restrictions, amounting to keeping the trust deed confidential, are repugnant to, or inconsistent with the trust concept which requires the beneficiaries having an irreducible core of rights against the trustees.[81] Is not a confidentiality restriction in a letter of wishes similarly repugnant to the trust concept because, if it prevents a beneficiary from knowing what is the purpose behind a particular discretionary power, how can he possibly allege the trustee is not responsibly exercising the power for the purpose for which it was conferred on the trustee by the settlor? Thus, the beneficiary has no meaningful right to make the trustee account for the trusteeship.

---

[78] This was also the majority view in *Hartigan Nominees Pty. Ltd v. Rydge* (1992) 29 N.S.W.L.R 405.
[79] 17th ed. (2000) at 632.
[80] *Re Hay's S.T.* [1981] 3 All E.R. 786, 792; *Re Beatty's W.T.* [1990] 3 All E.R. 844, 846; *McPhail v. Doulton* [1971] A.C. 424, 449.
[81] *Armitage v. Nurse* [1998] Ch. 241, 253; D. J. Hayton, "The Irreducible Core Content of Trusteeship", Chapter 3 of A. J. Oakley (ed.) *Trends in Contemporary Trust Law*.

However, A, B and C do have such a right so that the trustee is under **9–218** a meaningful trust obligation to each of them: the position of D, E and F can be recharacterised as that of an object of a power. But what if the letter of wishes was expressed to be confidential between the settlor and the trustee so as not to be disclosed to A, B, C, D, E or F? Is the position the equivalent of the trust deed being expressed to be similarly confidential, which would clearly be ignored as repugnant to the trust concept unless one accepted it as forming the basis of a claim that the trust was a sham?

Such argument has a logical attraction which may appeal to an appellate court. To avoid problems, the letter of wishes should provide for it to be disclosed to, say, two responsible members of the class of beneficiaries or if, as yet, there are no ascertained beneficiaries of full capacity to, say, two members of a class of objects of the power who have a right to make the trustees account; or, if there are none yet ascertained of full capacity, then to a protector until there is an ascertained person of full capacity with a right to make the trustees account.

Alternatively, a settlor could rely upon a morally binding letter of **9–219** wishes which is not treated as of any legal significance: "This letter is not to be regarded as indicating in a legally significant way the purposes for which the powers in my trust deed have been conferred on my trustees because I do not want my trustees to have any extra legal obligations placed upon them by this letter so as to have to go out of their way to justify the exercise of their powers. I believe the imposition of such extra legal obligations would cause more difficulties than benefits to accrue, creating greater cost burdens and proving likely to upset relationships between my beneficiaries. Thus, my trustees are only to be under a moral obligation to take into account the following wishes of mine and shall not be accountable before the courts in relation to taking into account or failing to take into account such wishes. I accept that if they wish my trustees may destroy this letter and not pass it on to any successor trustees." There is no case law on this but, in principle, there is no reason why facilitative effect should not be given by the courts to the settlor's genuine intention to create a merely morally binding letter of no legal significance even if it omitted the last sentence.

"Blind trusts"

Exceptionally, legally binding restrictions on a particular beneficiary **9–220** for a limited period may prevent such beneficiary from discovering how the trustees have performed their investment role. Thus, the Prime Minister or the Chancellor of the Exchequer or the Director of the Serious Fraud Office can place their investments in a "blind trust" so as to be free from allegations that they abused their inside information for their own ends while in office.

RE LONDONDERRY'S SETTLEMENT, PEAT AND OTHERS v. WALSH

Court of Appeal [1965] Ch. 918; [1965] 2 W.L.R. 229; [1964] 3 All E.R. 855
(Harman, Danckwerts and Salmon L.JJ.)

9–221   On December 5, 1934, the seventh Marquess of Londonderry settled a trust fund upon trusts as to the capital for members of a specified class in such shares and generally in such manner as the trustees with the consent of certain named persons, called "the appointors," might in writing from time to time appoint. There were provisions in default of that appointment.

The settlement then directed the trustees to hold the income until disposal of the capital upon trust for such member or members of the same class as the trustees might from time to time within twelve months after the receipt of such income with the written consent of the appointors determine and subject thereto upon trust to pay an annuity of £5,000 to the settlor's wife and subject thereto to pay the income to the settlor's eldest son and after his death to the settlor's other children.

The settlor's wife and eldest son having died, the settlor's daughter, Lady Helen Maglona Walsh, became entitled to share in the income of the trust fund under the above gift of income in default of appointment. There were other children of the marriage.

9–222   The trustees had from time to time appointed considerable sums to various beneficiaries and in December 1962 they unanimously decided with the consent of the appointors to make further substantial appointments of capital with a view to bringing the settlement to an end. The settlor's daughter was dissatisfied with the amounts proposed to be appointed to her and asked the trustees to supply her with copies of various documents relating to the settlement. The trustees supplied copies of the appointments and of the accounts up to date but refused to disclose any other documents. The settlor's daughter remained dissatisfied.

Accordingly on January 30, 1964, the trustees issued a summons, to which the settlor's daughter was defendant, asking which, if any, of the following documents the trustees were bound to disclose: (a) the minutes of the meetings of the trustees of the settlement; (b) agendas and other documents prepared for the purposes of the meetings or otherwise for the consideration of the trustees; (c) correspondence relating to the administration of the trust property or otherwise to the execution of the trusts and passing between (i) the trustees and the appointors; (ii) the trustees and the appointors on the one hand and the solicitors to the trustees on the other; and (iii) the trustees and the appointors on the one hand and the beneficiaries on the other.

Plowman J.[82] made a declaration that the trustees were bound to disclose all the documents in the categories set out above.

9–223   HARMAN L.J.: "I have found this a difficult case. It raises what in my judgment is a novel question on which there is no authority exactly in point although several cases have been cited to us somewhere near it. The court is really required here to resolve two principles that come into conflict, or at least apparent conflict. The first is that . . . trustees exercising a discretionary power are not bound to disclose to their beneficiaries the reasons actuating them in coming to a decision. This is a long-standing principle and rests largely, I think, on the view that nobody could be called upon to accept a trusteeship involving

---

[82] [1964] Ch. 594.

the exercise of a discretion unless, in the absence of bad faith, he were not liable to have his motives or his reasons called in question either by the beneficiaries or by the court. To this there is added a rider, namely, that if trustees do give reasons, their soundness can be considered by the court . . .

"It would seem on the face of it that there is no reason why this principle should be confined to decisions orally arrived at and should not extend to a case, like the present, where, owing to the complexity of the trust and the large sums involved, the trustees, who act subject to the consent of another body called the appointors, have brought into existence various written documents, including, in particular, agenda for and minutes of their meetings from time to time held in order to consider distributions made of the fund and its income. It is here that the conflicting principle is said to emerge. All these documents, it is argued, came into existence for the purposes of the trust and are in the possession of the trustees as such and are, therefore, trust documents, the property of the beneficiaries, and as such open to them to inspect . . .

"The judge, though he felt the strength of the trustees' submission that it was **9–224** undesirable to wash family linen in public which would be productive only of family strife and also odium for the trustees and embarrassment in the performance of their duties, felt constrained by a decision of Kindersley V.-C. in *Talbot v. Marshfield*.[83] It now appears, however, in the light of documents obtained from the Record Office and the other reports of the case that this case was not at all in point . . .

"Apart from this, the defendant relied on certain observations in *O'Rourke v. Darbishire*.[84] The decision was that the plaintiff was not entitled to the production of what were called the 'trust documents,' and I find Lord Parmoor making this observation[85]: 'A *cestui que trust*, in an action against his trustees, is generally entitled to the production for inspection of all documents relating to the affairs of the trust. It is not material for the present purpose whether this right is to be regarded as a paramount proprietary right in the *cestui que trust*, or as a right to be enforced under the law of discovery.' Lord Wrenbury says[86]: 'If the plaintiff is right in saying that he is a beneficiary, and if the documents are documents belonging to the executors as executors, he has a right to access to the documents which he desires to inspect upon what has been called in the judgments in this case a proprietary right. The beneficiary is entitled to see all the trust documents because they are trust documents and because he is a beneficiary. They are in a sense his own. Action or no action, he is entitled to access to them. This has nothing to do with discovery. The right to discovery is a right to see someone else's documents. A proprietary right is a right to access to documents which are your own. No question of professional privilege arises in such a case. Documents containing professional advice taken by the executors as trustees contain advice taken by trustees for their *cestuis que trust*, and the beneficiaries are entitled to see them because they are beneficiaries.'

"General observations of this sort give very little guidance, for first they beg **9–225** the question what are trust documents, and secondly their Lordships were not considering the point here that papers are asked for which bear on the question of the exercise of the trustees' discretion. In my judgment category (a) . . . *viz.*, the minutes of the meetings of the trustees . . .; and part of (b), *viz.*, agenda

---

[83] (1865) 2 Drew. & Sm. 549.
[84] [1920] A.C. 581.
[85] *ibid.* at 619.
[86] *ibid.* at 626.

prepared for trustees' meetings, are, in the absence of an action impugning the trustees' good faith, documents which a beneficiary cannot claim the right to inspect. If the defendant is allowed to examine these, she will know at once the very matters which the trustees are not bound to disclose to her, namely, their motives and reasons. Trustees who wish to preserve their rights in this respect must either commit nothing to paper or destroy everything from meeting to meeting. Indeed, if the defendant be right, I doubt that if the last course is open, for she must succeed, if at all, on the ground that the papers belong to her, and if so, the trustees have no right to destroy them.

9–226   "I would hold that even if documents of this type ought properly to be described as trust documents, they are protected for the special reason which protects the trustees' deliberations on a discretionary matter from disclosure. If necessary, I hold that this principle over-rides the ordinary rule. This is, in my judgment, no less in the true interest of the beneficiary than of the trustees. Again, if one of the trustees commits to paper his suggestions and circulates them among his co-trustees; or if inquiries are made in writing as to the circumstances of a member of the class; I decline to hold that such documents are trust documents the property of the beneficiaries. . . . On the other hand, if the solicitor advising the trustees commits to paper an *aide-mémoire* summarising the state of the fund or of the family and reminding the trustees of past distributions and future possibilities, I think that must be a document which any beneficiary must be at liberty to inspect. It seems to me, therefore, that category (b) [as set out *supra*, para. 9–222] embraces documents on both sides of the line.

"As to (c) I cannot think that communications passing between individual trustees and appointors are documents in which beneficiaries have a proprietary right. On the other hand, as to category (ii) in general the letters of the trustees' solicitors to the trustees do seem to me to be trust documents in which the beneficiaries have a property. As to category (iii) I do not think letters to or from an individual beneficiary ought to be open to inspection by another beneficiary . . ."[87]

R. E. MEGARRY (1965) 81 L.Q.R. 196

9–227   "It seems safe to say that the last of *Re Londonderry's Settlement* has not been heard. Perhaps the most obvious point which may arise is whether a beneficiary who is determined to discover all he can about the grounds upon which a discretion has been exercised may not achieve this by instituting litigation alleging that the trustees have exercised their discretion in some improper way, and then obtaining discovery of documents in those proceedings, as in *Talbot v. Marshfield* (1865) 2 Drew. & Sm. 549. Will the courts permit the bonds of secrecy to be invaded by the simple process of commencing hostile litigation against the trustees? It is not easy to see how the courts can prevent this. True, questions of relevance may obviously arise; but on discovery the test of relevance is wide. The classical statement is that of Brett L.J.: an applicant is entitled to discovery of any document 'which may fairly lead him to a train of inquiry'[88] that may 'either directly or indirectly enable the party requiring the affidavit either to advance his

---

[87] See also *Re Cowin* (1886) 33 Ch.D. 179; *Re Bosworth* (1889) 55 L.J.Ch. 432; *Re Dartnall* [1895] 1 Ch. 474; *Tiger v. Barclays Bank Ltd* [1952] W.N. 38; *Hawkesley v. May* [1956] 1 Q.B. 304; generally (1965) 81 L.Q.R. 192 (R.E.M.).

[88] Civil Procedure Rules Part 31 now confers less extensive rights of discovery—or "disclosure" as the modern process is called.

own case or to damage the case of his adversary' (*Compagnie Financière et Commerciale du Pacifique v. Peruvian Guano Co.* (1882) 11 Q.B.D. 55 at 63). Indeed, the formal order of the court, . . . seems to recognise this possibility.

"The other main point which plainly needs further exploration is the ambit of **9–228** the term 'trust documents.' The negative proposition is now plain: not all documents held by trustees as such are 'trust documents.' But even after a detailed examination of the judgments it is difficult to frame any positive proposition with any degree of confidence. Nor does the formal order of the court (see at [1965] Ch. 938) lessen the difficulty; indeed, it contributes its own quota of problems. The order states that without prejudice to any right of the defendant to discovery in any subsequent proceedings against the trustees, and subject to any order of the court in any particular circumstances, there are four categories of documents which the trustees are not bound to disclose to the defendant. The first of these categories is 'The agenda of the meetings of the trustees of the settlement'; the second and third categories consist of correspondence of the trustees *inter se* and with the beneficiaries; and the fourth category consists of minutes of the meetings of the trustees and other documents disclosing their deliberations as to the manner in which they should exercise their discretion or disclosing their reasons for any particular exercise of their discretion, or the materials therefor. It is thus only the minutes and the other documents in the fourth category which appear to be qualified by words relating to disclosure of the trustees' reasons for exercising their discretion in a particular way; the freedom from disclosure seems to apply to all agenda and correspondence, whether or not they would reveal any such reasons or the material on which they were based. Nor does the order make it plain how it applies to documents in the fourth category which not only disclose confidential matters but also deal with other points as well; the inclusion of any confidential matter seems to confer exemption upon the entire document, and not merely upon the confidential matter. The order did, however, declare that the trustees were bound to disclose to the defendant any written advice from their solicitors or counsel as to the manner in which the trustees were in law entitled to exercise their discretion.

"Putting all the material together, it seems at present to be difficult to say more than that all documents held by trustees *qua* trustees are prima facie trust documents, but that there is a class of exceptions from this rule which is ill-defined but includes confidential documents which the beneficiaries ought not to see. For greater precision than that we must await further decisions by the courts. The Court of Appeal has taken a firm step in the right direction; but that is all."

RE RABAIOTTI'S 1989 SETTLEMENT

Jersey Royal Court [2000] W.T.L.R. 953 (Deputy Bailiff Birt with Jurats Myles and Georgelin

The Deputy Bailiff "In our judgment, the Court does have a discretion to refuse **9–229** to order disclosure of trust documents that a beneficiary is normally entitled to see. Clearly, the general principle is that a beneficiary is entitled to see trust documents which show the financial position of the trust, what assets are in the trust, how the trustee has dealt with those assets, etc. This is an essential part of the mechanism whereby the trustee can be held accountable for his trusteeship to a beneficiary.

But the need for an individual beneficiary to obtain trust documents has to be weighed against the interests of the beneficiaries as a whole. The trustee has a duty to the beneficiaries as a class. If, as in some of the cases referred to above, the trustee forms the view in good faith that disclosure of documents to which a beneficiary would normally be entitled, would be prejudicial to the interests of the beneficiaries as a whole, it may refuse to make that disclosure and seek the directions of the Court. Should the trustee fail to seek the directions of the Court, it is open to any beneficiary to bring the matter before the Court for resolution. To that extent, the Court thinks the position is simpler than is suggested at the end of the first paragraph quoted from the judgment in *Rouse*. The remedy of a dissatisfied beneficiary is not to seek to have the trustee removed, but to seek the directions of the Court as to whether the particular trust document should or should not be disclosed. The Court will then have to balance the competing considerations and decide what is best for the beneficiaries as a whole. In short, the Court agrees with the way in which Doyle CJ puts the matter at 128F-H of the judgment in *Rouse v. 100F Australia Trustees Ltd* [2000] W.T.L.R. 111.

9–230   The Court does not wish to encourage trustees to refuse disclosure on weak grounds. One starts with a strong presumption that a beneficiary is entitled to see trust documents of the nature described. There would have to be good reason to refuse disclosure of such documents. But the Court is satisfied that, as a matter of general equitable principle, the Court has an overriding discretion to withhold documents where it is satisfied that this is in the best interests of the beneficiaries as a whole . . .

An additional issue raised in the Consultation Paper of the Jersey Law Commission, (see paragraphs 4.2.24–4.2.26) is whether the right of a beneficiary to inspect trust documents is a proprietary right. There is no doubt that *O'Rourke v. Darbishire* asserts a proprietary right on the part of a beneficiary (see the dictum of Lord Wrenbury at para. 9–224 above). This was followed in *Londonderry*. Conversely, a majority of judges in the Court of Appeal of New South Wales in *Hartigan Nominees Pty Ltd v. Rydge* (1992) 29 N.S.W.L.R. 405 appeared to be of the view that a better basis was the trustee's fiduciary duty to account to the beneficiary. In particular, at 422, Kirby P cited with approval an extract from Ford & Lee, *Principles of the Law of Trusts*, which was as follows:

> '. . . the legal title and rights to possession are in the trustees: all the beneficiary has are equitable rights against the trustees . . . The beneficiary's rights to inspect trust documents are founded therefore not upon any equitable proprietary right which he or she may have in respect of those documents but upon the trustee's fiduciary duty to keep the beneficiary informed and to render accounts. It is the extent of that duty that is in issue. The equation of the right to inspect trust documents with the beneficiary's equitable proprietary rights gives rise to unnecessary and undesirable consequences. It results in the drawing of virtually incomprehensible distinctions between documents which are trust documents and those which are not; it casts doubts upon the rights of beneficiaries who cannot claim to have an equitable proprietary interest in the trust assets, such as the beneficiaries of discretionary trusts; and it may give trustees too great a degree of protection in the case of documents, artificially classified as not being trust documents, and beneficiaries too great a right to inspect the activities of trustees in the case of documents which are, equally artificially, classified as trust documents.'

In *In re a Settlement* (*supra*) the Royal Court did not find it necessary to **9–231** determine whether the beneficiaries of a trust have a proprietary interest in trust documents. It is similarly not necessary for us to resolve the issue definitively for the purposes of this case, but, as at present advised, the Court is of the view that the opinions in *Hartigan* referred to above are persuasive and the Court would concur with the view of the Jersey Law Commission at 4.2.26 of the Consultation Paper when it said:

> 'In principle, whilst it can be seen that beneficiaries can assert proprietary rights to the trust property (thus being able to join together and demand an outright transfer to themselves if they are all absolutely entitled), it is less clear who such rights should extend over the trust documents, which are in the trustees' hands so that effective management can be carried out. In short, we would agree with Professor Hayton when he says:
>
>> "The beneficiaries' rights to inspect trust documents are now seen to be better based not on equitable proprietary rights but on the beneficiaries' rights to make the trustees account for their trusteeship."'

The letter of wishes

We turn now to consider whether a letter of wishes is a document which a **9–232** beneficiary is entitled to see. In referring to a letter of wishes, we mean a document addressed by a settlor to trustees which is not binding upon the trustees, but which indicates the settlor's thoughts and wishes as to how the trustees might exercise their discretionary powers.

In *Londonderry* the Court of Appeal endorsed earlier authority to the effect that trustees exercising a discretionary power are not bound to disclose the reasons for their decision. The Court then had to reconcile that principle with the rule that a beneficiary is entitled to see documents concerning the administration of the trust. The Court resolved this conflict by holding that the general entitlement to see trust documents did not apply to documents which would or might disclose the reasons for a discretionary decision. This included the agenda for a trustees' meeting, correspondence between trustees, correspondence between trustees and individual beneficiaries and, most importantly, minutes of meetings of the trustees and other documents disclosing the deliberations of the trustees as to the manner in which they should exercise the discretionary power, or disclosing the reason for any particular exercise of such power or the material upon which such reasons were or might have been based. However, the position of a letter of wishes did not arise for consideration in that case.

Londonderry was quoted with approval by this Court in *Re a Settlement* (*supra*), **9–233** when, at p148, it was said that the propositions contained in *Londonderry* offered general guidance as to the documents which need not be disclosed. The principles underlying the decision in *Londonderry* were also supported by the Court at p146 where it said:

> 'Those paragraphs make it clear that, subject to the terms of the trust and to any order of the Court, trustees are entitled to refuse to disclose matters touching upon the exercise of a power or discretion or the performance of a duty imposed on them. In the context of discretionary trusts, it seems to us eminently sensible and reasonable that trustees should be able to weigh

conflicting considerations as between different beneficiaries and to judge the merits and de-merits of particular courses of action without being exposed to minute examination as to their motives and processes of reasoning at the instance of disaffected beneficiaries. Trustees of such a trust have been entrusted with a confidential role and should, in general, be permitted to exercise their functions away from the glare of publicity. Of course, if they are not acting in good faith, that is an entirely different matter.'

9–234　　In *Bhander v. Barclays Private Bank and Trust Company Ltd*, (April 7, 1997, Jersey, unreported) a letter of wishes was disclosed voluntarily by the trustees and the court did not therefore address the issue. Counsel's researches have unearthed only one case where the position of a letter of wishes has been considered. That case is *Hartigan Nominees Pty Ltd v. Rydge (supra)*, a decision of the court of appeal of New South Wales, Australia. The court of appeal subjected *Londonderry* to detailed scrutiny. The court held by a majority that the letter of wishes in that case did not have to be disclosed to a beneficiary. However, the reasoning differed on a number of issues.

Kirby P. believed that *Londonderry* was based on old-fashioned principles which were no longer appropriate. A beneficiary should be entitled to know the reasons for the exercise of a discretionary power. The rule that documents disclosing reasons for the exercise of a discretionary power by trustees need not be disclosed was therefore wrong. Even if, contrary to his views, *Londonderry* was still good law, he held that, because trustees were likely to have regard to a letter of wishes when considering their powers under a trust deed, the letter of wishes should be regarded as a document which was ancillary to the trust deed and therefore a 'trust document', so that it was disclosable on *Londonderry* principles. Whilst reserving his position in a case where a settlor imposed an express provision of confidentiality in a letter of wishes, he declined to imply any duty of confidentiality in relation to letters of wishes generally and he would therefore have ordered that the letter be disclosed to the beneficiary.

9–235　　Mahoney J.A. approved *Londonderry*. He declined to order disclosure of the letter of wishes on three grounds. First, he held that a letter of wishes was not a trust document, in the sense that it was not part of the property of the trust. Secondly, he drew the inference that a letter of wishes was given by a settlor on a confidential basis to the trustees and it would be wrong to breach that confidentiality. Thirdly, he held that a letter of wishes was a document which related to the reasons for the exercise of a trustee's discretionary power, disclosure of which would be likely to lead to family difficulties, and was therefore a document which fell within the category of documents which *Londonderry* said need not be disclosed.

Sheller J.A. also supported the principle laid down by *Londonderry*. Documents which disclosed the reasons for the exercise of a trustee's discretion need not be disclosed to a beneficiary. However, he was of the view that *Londonderry* went too far in including in that category material upon which reasons were or might have been based, unless that material would reveal the reasons themselves or the reasoning process. Furthermore, he held that a letter of wishes was not a document which would disclose the reasons for a trustee's decision and therefore did not fall within the category of documents which *Londonderry* held need not be disclosed. However, he agreed with Mahoney J.A. that it was to be inferred that a letter of wishes written privately to trustees was intended to remain confidential and that, for that reason, it should not be disclosed to beneficiaries.

In short, a majority, (Mahoney and Sheller J.A.) held that a trustee was not **9–236** required to disclose a letter of wishes on the grounds of confidentiality. A different majority (Kirby P and Sheller J.A.) held that a letter of wishes was not a document which fell within the category of documents which *Londonderry* held need not be disclosed because they might disclose the reasons for the exercise of a discretionary power.

Mr Kelleher argued that the Court should follow the approach of Kirby P. to the effect that the reasoning in *Londonderry* is out of date. A beneficiary should be entitled to know the reasons for a trustee's decision. We do not agree. We think that the arguments for confidentiality in relation to the reasons for trustees' decisions given in *Londonderry* remain as valid today as they were then. Salmon L.J. summarised these at 240 as follows:

> 'The settlement gave the absolute discretion to appoint to the trustees and not to the courts. So long as the trustees exercise this power . . . *bona fide* with no improper motive, their exercise of the power cannot be challenged in the courts, and their reasons for acting as they did are, accordingly, immaterial. This is one of the grounds for the rule that trustees are not obliged to disclose to beneficiaries their reasons for exercising a discretionary power. Another ground for this rule is that it would not be for the good of the beneficiaries as a whole, and yet another that it might make the lives of trustees intolerable should such an obligation rest upon them . . . Nothing would be more likely to embitter family feelings and the relationship between the trustees and members of the family, were trustees obliged to state their reasons for the exercise of the powers entrusted to them. It might indeed well be difficult to persuade any persons to act as trustees were a duty to disclose their reasons, with all the embarrassment, arguments and quarrels that might ensue, added to their present not inconsiderable burdens.'

It seems to us important that discussion should be uninhibited by fear of **9–237** publication. In order to fulfil their duties properly, the trustees may need to consider weaknesses of character of a beneficiary, the relationship between different beneficiaries, and many other sensitive matters. One can readily understand that, should such personal information about beneficiaries be freely available to any individual beneficiary who asks for it, it may lead to difficulty. Furthermore, the fact that the views and reasoning of trustees on such sensitive matters could be made available to any disaffected beneficiary would, the Court believes, inhibit full and free discussion, and be likely to lead to ill feeling and to fruitless litigation. The Court cannot improve on the language of Bailhache, Bailiff, in *Re a Settlement* set out at para. 9–233 above and fully endorses it.

Mr Benest, on behalf of the trustees, argued that Mahoney J.A. was correct to hold that a letter of wishes is a document which falls within the category of documents which *Londonderry* held need not be disclosed, because it was a document which might disclose the deliberation of the trustees or the reasons for any particular exercise of the discretionary power or constitute material upon which such reasons were or might have been based.

Although the exact wording used in the order drawn up in *Londonderry* did **9–238** not have a letter of wishes in mind, we are satisfied that such a letter is covered by the principle which governed the decision in *Londonderry*. A letter of wishes will usually set out in some detail how the settlor would like the trustees to exercise their discretionary powers of distribution and, perhaps, of management of the trust fund. When trustees come to consider the exercise of a discretionary power, they will normally have the letter of wishes before them. The letter is of course not binding. If trustees slavishly follow a letter of wishes, their decision can be quashed, on the grounds that it is not, in truth, the decision of the trustees. The trustees must make up their own minds as to how they should exercise their discretion in the best interests of one or more of the beneficiaries. However, discussion is almost certain to involve references to the contents of the letter of wishes, such as whether the settlor's wishes remain appropriate; whether there are reasons to depart from his wishes; if so, what those reasons are and how they might impact on the wishes expressed by the settlor. Circumstances will, of course, vary and the weight given to the letter of wishes will vary from case to case. Nevertheless, in general terms, the contents of the letter of wishes will undoubtedly form an important part of the trustees' consideration of the exercise of their powers. We are quite satisfied that a letter of wishes is a document which is closely related to the decision-making process and to the reasons for a decision, even where the trustees decide to depart from the letter. However, we disagree with Kirby P. in *Hartigan* that it is therefore a document which is to be treated as being ancillary to the trust deed. It is an informal document which the trustees are free to ignore. It is merely an expression of the settlor's wishes.

9–239　　Nevertheless, it may, in many cases, be a document which discloses the reasons for a decision and is, in almost all cases, likely to be material upon which such reasons were or might have been based, even in cases where the trustee chooses to depart from it. We note the criticism of this last category of documents referred to in *Londonderry*, by Sheller J.A. in *Hartigan* and we can envisage a case in which material upon which reasons were or might have been based, should nevertheless be disclosed. However, in general, we think it reasonable that such material should be covered by the protection given to the reasons themselves as they will often be so closely inter-linked that the protection given to the reasons will not be achieved unless the material upon which those reasons were based is also protected.

　　We are conscious that the wording used to describe the relevant categories of documents in *Londonderry* should not be construed as a statute. The wording is simply taken from an order made in a particular case. Although we hold that the letter of wishes is covered by the wording in *Londonderry*, that is not necessary to our decision. We would rest our decision additionally upon the general principle that a trustee does not have to disclose the reasons for the exercise of a discretion and upon the justification for that principle as given in *Londonderry* and in *In re a Settlement*. We hold that to require disclosure of a letter of wishes would be likely in practice to undermine the immunity from the provision of reasons and to lead to just the sort of problems which the immunity was designed to avoid.

9–240　　We would also endorse, as an additional ground, the decision of the majority in *Hartigan*, that the letter of wishes need not be disclosed on the ground of confidentiality. We agree that the fact that the settlor writes a separate letter addressed privately to trustees raises a strong implication that he intended the document to be confidential. In some cases, he may have stated expressly that it is confidential. We agree with the majority in *Hartigan* that the Court should ordinarily respect that confidentiality. The settlor will often wish to communicate to the trustees thoughts about individual beneficiaries which would cause upset, distress, and possibly family strife if they became generally known. The settlor is always able to make these thoughts known to his family if he wishes. But should he prefer to keep them confidential, he should be entitled to do so. It will often be in the interests of the family as a whole that such thoughts should remain confidential. Where information is provided in confidence, the law will respect that confidence unless there are good grounds for it not do so. For the reasons which we have set out above, we believe that, far from there being good reason not to respect the confidentiality of the settlor's wishes in such cases, there are good grounds for saying that it should be respected and that it would be damaging to ignore it."

III. Distribution of Trust Property

A. Maintenance

The statutory power of maintenance in the Trustee Act 1925, section 31 is of fundamental importance in the administration of trusts for the assistance it may provide to minors, for the taxation repercussions flowing from the way in which it can convert what are vested interests under the terms of the trust into contingent interests and also flowing from a beneficiary's entitlement to income at eighteen years of age, and for the apportionment problems it creates where there is a class of beneficiaries.

The trustees must be aware of these points and they must consciously **9–241** exercise their discretion. In *Wilson v. Turner*[89] they automatically paid over the income to the minor's father without any request from him and without any attempt to ascertain whether any income was required for the minor's maintenance: the father was ordered to repay the income. Trustees should particularly review the situation a month or two before the minor attains eighteen years since the statutory power to apply income and its accumulations over the years expires on his eighteenth birthday.

Under the statutory power, so long as income is legally available,[90] there is a *duty* to accumulate the income, so far as not used under a *power* to apply it for the maintenance education or benefit of the beneficiary, for the period of the beneficiary's minority. During such period accumulations may be used as if they were current income despite having accrued to the capital.[91] Once the beneficiary attains eighteen the trustees *must* pay the income from the capital (including the accumulations which become part of the capital) to the beneficiary even if the beneficiary's interest is still contingent under the trust terms, *e.g.* to B if he attains 25 years.[92]

Section 31(2) may convert what appear to be indefeasible vested **9–242** interests into defeasible or contingent interests[93] since accumulations of income will not pass to a beneficiary with a vested interest in income

---

[89] (1883) 22 Ch.D. 521.

[90] A trust instrument may oust s.31 expressly or by necessary implication and s.31 only applies in the case of a contingent interest if the interest carries the intermediate income: see *infra*, para. 9–248.

[91] s.31(2).

[92] This gives the beneficiary an interest in possession which has much significance for inheritance tax purposes: Inheritance Tax Act 1984, ss.49–53 and *supra* para. 1–103. Also see *Swales v. I.R.C.* [1984] 3 All E.R. 16 at 24.

[93] Thus making 10 per cent additional income tax payable under Income and Corporation Taxes Act 1988 ss.686, 687, see *supra* para. 1–96.

under the terms of the trust unless he satisfies a contingency within section 31(2)(i) or unless he is entitled not just to income but also to the capital to which the accumulations automatically accrue, as where personalty is settled on a minor not for life but absolutely (s.31(2)(ii)). The contingencies within section 31(2)(i) are (a) attaining the age of eighteen or marrying thereunder when having a vested interest in income during his infancy and (b) attaining the age of eighteen or marrying thereunder when thereupon becoming entitled to the capital from which the income arose in fee simple absolute or determinable[94] (realty) or absolutely and indefeasibly[95] (personalty) or for an entailed interest (realty and personalty). Thus, if B is an unmarried minor and under a trust an apparently indefeasible vested interest is conferred on him (*e.g.* to B for life) in substance B's interest in income is defeasible or contingent[96] since he has no right to income as it arises (the trustees being under a duty to accumulate it in so far as not exercising their power to use it if they see fit for B's maintenance, education or benefit) and he has no right to accumulated income unless he attains eighteen or marries thereunder.[97]

9–243   The Apportionment Act 1870 requiring apportionment of income on a day to day basis has an odd effect when a beneficiary attains eighteen. Take dividends received after the eighteenth birthday in respect of a period before and after the birthday. The income apportioned to the pre-birthday period "cannot be applied for maintenance, etc., because the trustees cannot exercise their discretion in advance so as to affect the income when it is received and they cannot apply it in arrear because the infancy will have ceased."[98]

The 1870 Act also applies when a class member dies or is born. So much of a particular beneficiary's share of income that is not used for his maintenance but accumulated must be allocated to him and kept separate from the other beneficiaries' allocations. The particular share of income will vary with births or deaths of class members. If a minor dies before obtaining a vested interest the income provisionally accumulated and allocated to him is treated as an accretion to the capital of the whole fund, divisible among all beneficiaries ultimately becoming entitled to capital even if not alive during the period when such accumulation occurred.[99]

---

[94] *Re Sharp's S.T.* [1973] Ch. 331 treats this as a determinable fee in the strict sense distinct from a fee simple on condition though the Settled Land Act 1925, s.117(1)(iv) (not cited) treats "determinable fee" as meaning a fee determinable whether by limitation or condition. Consider Trustee Act 1925, s.68(1)(18).

[95] The interest will not be absolute if defeasible by an overriding power or a condition: *Re Sharp's S.T.*, *supra.*

[96] *Stanley v. I.R.C.* [1944] K.B. 255, *Re Delamere's S.T.* [1984] 1 All E.R. 584.

[97] The Income and Corporation Taxes Act 1988 s.686 applies to tax the income at 10 per cent above the standard rate.

[98] *Re Joel's W.T.* [1967] Ch. 14 at 29. The Law Reform Committee (Cmnd. 8733, para. 3.41) recommend replacing time apportionment by apportionment between the class of beneficiaries as constituted on the date the income is received by the trustees.

[99] *Re Joel's W.T.* [1967] Ch. 14. If trustees hold property on discretionary trusts and allocate income absolutely to a minor beneficiary such income does not fall within s.31 (though income arising from such income will): *Re Vestey's Settlement* [1951] Ch. 209.

Section 31 may be ousted wholly or partly by a contrary intention expressed directly or indirectly in the trust instrument. Its provisions will be inapplicable if on a fair reading of the instrument in question one can say that such application would be inconsistent with the purport of the instrument.[1]

The Trustee Act 1925

Power to apply income for maintenance[2] and to accumulate surplus income during a minority

Section 31.—(1) Where any property is held by trustees in trust for any person **9–244** for any interest whatsoever, whether vested or contingent, then, subject to any prior interests[3] or charges affecting that property—

> (i) during the infancy of any such person, if his interest so long continues, the trustees may, at their sole discretion, pay to his parent or guardian, if any, or otherwise apply for or towards his maintenance, education, or benefit, the whole or such part, if any, of the income of that property as may, in all the circumstances, be reasonable, whether or not there is—
>
> > (a) any other fund applicable to the same purpose; or
> > (b) Ny person bound by law to provide for his maintenance or education; and
>
> (ii) if such person on attaining the age of [eighteen][4] years has not a vested[5] interest in such income, the trustees shall[6] thenceforth pay the income of that property and of any accretion thereto under subsection (2) of this section to him, until he either attains a vested interest therein or dies, or until failure of his interest:

Provided that, in deciding whether the whole or any part of the income of the **9–245** property is during a minority to be paid or applied for the purposes aforesaid, the trustees shall have regard to the age of the infant and his requirements and generally to the circumstances of the case, and in particular to what other

---

[1] *I.R.C. v. Bernstein* [1961] Ch. 399 at 412; *Re Delamere's S.T.* [1984] 1 All E.R. 584 at 588.

[2] See B. S. Ker, "Trustees' Power of Maintenance" (1953) 17 Conv.(N.S.) 273 and Wolstenholme & Cherry's *Conveyancing Statutes* Vol. 4 (13th ed., by J. T. Farrand).

[3] If there is a prior direction to set apart and accumulate income, the trustees have no power to apply intermediate income for maintenance under this section: *Re Reade-Revell* [1930] 1 Ch. 52, but the court may do so under its inherent jurisdiction: *Re Walker* [1901] 1 Ch. 879; *supra*, para. 9–159

[4] Substituted by the Family Law Reform Act 1969, s.1(3), Sched. 1, Pt. 1. For interests under any instruments made before Jan. 1, 1970, 21 years remain the relevant age: Sched. III, para. 5(1). In such a case money may be paid direct to the beneficiary once he attains 18 instead of to his parent or guardian, Sched. III, para. 5(2). For appointments made after 1969 under a pre-1970 settlement the relevant age is 18: *Re Delamere's S.T.* [1984] 1 All E.R. 584 at 588 *Begg-McBrearty v. Stilwell* [1996] 4 All E.R. 205.

[5] The section does not apply if the person has a vested interest, even if it is liable to be divested: *Re McGeorge* [1963] Ch. 544.

[6] The word "shall" prima facie imports a "duty" as distinct from a "power." In this context, however, it imports a "power" which can be overriden by the expression of a contrary intention: see s.69(2) of the Trustee Act 1925; *Re Turner's Will Trusts* [1937] Ch. 15. Provisions made by the settlor or testator if inconsistent with the statutory power amount to contrary intention, *e.g.* a direction to accumulate; *Re Erskine's S.T.* [1971] 1 W.L.R. 162; *Re Henderson's Trusts* [1969] 1 W.L.R. 651 at 659. But if there is no contrary intention the trustees are under a duty to pay the income to the beneficiary on his attaining the age of 18; *Re Jones' Will Trusts* [1947] Ch. 48. Even though the beneficiary may not be entitled to the capital till attaining 30 years of age the fact that he is entitled to the income will give him an interest in possession for inheritance tax purposes.

income, if any, is applicable for the same purposes; and where trustees have notice that the income of more than one fund is applicable for those purposes, then, so far as practicable, unless the entire income of the funds is paid or applied as aforesaid or the court otherwise directs, a proportionate part only of the income of each fund shall be so paid or applied.

(2) During the infancy of any such person, if his interest so long continues, the trustees shall accumulate[7] all the residue of that income by investing it, and any profits from so investing it[8] from time to time in authorised investments, and shall hold those accumulations as follows:

(i) If any such person—
  (a) attains the age of [eighteen][9] years, or marries under that age, and his interest in such income during his infancy or until his marriage is a vested interest; or
  (b) on attaining the age of [eighteen][10] years or on marriage under that age becomes entitled to the property from which such income arose in fee simple, absolute or determinable,[11] or absolutely,[12] for an entailed interest;
  the trustees shall hold the accumulations in trust for such person absolutely, but without prejudice to any provision with respect thereto contained in any settlement by him made under any statutory powers during his infancy, and so that the receipt of such person after marriage, and though still an infant, shall be a good discharge; and
(ii) In any other case the trustees shall,[13] notwithstanding that such person had a vested interest in such income, hold the accumulations as an accretion to the capital of the property from which such accumulations arose,[14] and as one fund with such capital for all purposes, and so that, if such property is settled land, such accumulations shall be held upon the same trusts as if the same were capital money arising therefrom;

but the trustees may, at any time during the infancy of such person if his interest so long continues, apply those accumulations, or any part thereof, as if they were income arising in the then current year.

9–246   (3) This section applies in the case of a contingent interest only if the limitation or trust carries the intermediate income[15] of the property, but it applies to a future or contingent legacy by the parent of, or a person standing in *loco parentis* to, the legatee, if and for such period as, under the general law, the legacy carries interest for the maintenance of the legatee, and in any such case as last aforesaid the rate of interest shall (if the income available is sufficient, and

---

[7] See A. M. Prichard [1973] C.L.J. 246.

[8] These last 10 words substituted by Trustee Act 2000 Schedule 2 para. 25.

[9] See *supra*, n. 4.

[10] See *supra*, n. 4.

[11] See *supra*, n. 94.

[12] This applies exclusively to personalty and requires the interest in personalty to be indefeasible so that there is an odd distinction between realty and personalty: *Re Sharp's S.T.* [1973] Ch. 331.

[13] This may be excluded if its application would be inconsistent with the purport of the instrument in question, *e.g.* where an appointment of income to six minors "in equal shares *absolutely*" reveals in context an intention that each was to take an indefeasible share even if dying before attaining 18: *Re Delamere's S.T.* [1984] 1 All E.R. 584.

[14] Thus accumulation subject to an overriding power of appointment form an accretion to the respective shares of the beneficiaries subject to the overriding power. *Re Sharp's S.T.* [1973] Ch. 331 following *Re Joel's W.T.* [1967] Ch. 14.

[15] As to this, see s.175 of the Law of Property Act 1925, *infra* para. 9–247; (1963) 79 L.Q.R. 184 (P.V.B.).

subject to any rules of court to the contrary[16]) be five pounds per centum per annum.

(4) This section applies to a vested annuity in like manner as if the annuity were the income of property held by trustees in trust to pay the income thereof to the annuitant for the same period for which the annuity is payable, save that in any case accumulations made during the infancy of the annuitant shall be held in trust for the annuitant or his personal representatives absolutely.

(5) This section does not apply where the instrument, if any, under which the interest arises came into operation before the commencement of this Act.[17]

The Law of Property Act 1925

Contingent and future testamentary gifts carry intermediate income

Section 175.—(1) A contingent or future specific devise or bequest of **9–247** property, whether real or personal, and a contingent residuary devise of freehold land, and a specific or residuary devise of freehold land to trustees upon trust for persons whose interests are contingent or executory shall, subject to the statutory provisions relating to accumulations, carry the intermediate income of that property from the death of the testator, except so far as such income, or part thereof, may be otherwise expressly disposed of.

(2) This section applies only to wills coming into operation after the commencement of this Act.

Need for available income or interest

In the case of an infant with a vested interest section 31 of the Trustee Act 1925, *supra*, requires income to be accumulated except so far as it is applied for the maintenance of the infant unless the income is disposed of in favour of someone else or directed only to be accumulated.[18] But if the infant's interest is contingent, by section 31(3) income is not so required to be dealt with unless the limitation or trust carries the intermediate income. The rules in regard to this are as follows (subject to any contrary intention):

1. A contingent gift by will of residuary personalty carries with it all **9–248** the income which it produces after the testator's death: *Re Adams*.[19] If the income is accumulated until the contingency occurs, the rules in sections 164–166 of the Law of Property Act 1925, and section 13 of the Perpetuities and Accumulations Act 1964, which limit the period of accumulation, must be complied with: *Countess of Bective v. Hodgson*.[20] On the other hand, a residuary bequest, whether vested or contingent, which is expressly deferred to a future date does not carry intermediate income: *Re Oliver*[21]; *Re Gillett's Will Trusts*[22]; *Re Geering*.[23]

---

[16] 6 per cent is now prescribed by R.S.C., O. 44, r. 10.
[17] The section applies to an appointment made after 1925 under a power created before 1926: *Re Dickinson's Settlements* [1939] Ch. 27. S. 43 of the Conveyancing Act 1881, which was more limited in its scope than the present section, applies to instruments coming into operation before 1926.
[18] *Re Turner's W.T.* [1937] Ch. 15; *Re Ransome* [1957] Ch. 348; *Re Reade-Revell* [1930] 1 Ch. 52; *Re Stapleton* [1946] 1 All E.R. 323.
[19] [1893] 1 Ch. 329 at 334.
[20] (1864) 10 H.L.C. 656.
[21] [1947] 2 All E.R. 162 at 166.
[22] [1950] Ch. 102.
[23] [1964] Ch. 136.

2. A contingent residuary devise of freehold land and a residuary devise of freehold land to trustees upon trust for persons, whose interests are contingent, carry the intermediate income which they produce: s.175 of the Law of Property Act 1925, *supra*.

3. A contingent or future specific bequest of personalty carries the intermediate income: *ibid*.

4. So does a contingent or future specific devise of realty: *Re McGeorge*, *infra*, para. 9–252.

5. An *inter vivos* contingent interest will be of specific property and will carry the intermediate income (unless the income is disposed of in favour of someone else or directed to be accumulated).

6. Where a testator directs that a general or pecuniary contingent legacy (*e.g.* "a thousand ICI plc shares" or "£15,000") be set apart from the rest of his estate for the benefit of the minor contingent legatee this will carry the intermediate income produced by such separate fund.[24]

9–249   Section 31(3) further makes section 31 apply to a future or contingent legacy by a parent or person *in loco parentis* so far as under the general law the legacy *carries interest* for the maintenance of the legatee. Where a future or contingent legacy has not been directed to be set apart so as itself to produce intermediate income, it will be paid in due course at the appropriate time out of the residuary estate, and usually the legatee just receives the legacy without being allowed any interest for the period before the legacy became payable.[25] Exceptionally, a legacy carries 6 per cent interest[26] payable from the testator's death out of the residuary estate income if the testator was the parent or *in loco parentis* to the minor legatee, the legacy was direct to the minor and not to trustees for him,[27] no other fund was set aside for the maintenance of the minor,[28] and, if the legacy was contingent, the contingency related to the legatee's minority and so was not the attaining of an age greater than the age of majority.[29] In this exceptional case the provisions of section 31 apply.

9–250   There is a further exceptional case where a contingent legacy carries 6 per cent interest before it becomes payable: where the testator's will reveals an intention that the legacy should carry interest from the testator's death for the maintenance of the minor.[30] Here the testator need not be the parent of or *in loco parentis* to the minor and the contingency may be the attainment of an age exceeding majority.[31] It would seem that this was overlooked so that, strictly, section 31 is

---

[24] *Re Medlock* (1886) 55 L.J.Ch. 738; *Re Woodin* [1895] 2 Ch. 309; *Re Couturier* [1907] 1 Ch. 470. Income will be carried from the end of the executor's year unless intended to provide for the maintenance of a minor legatee as from the testator's death.

[25] *Re Raine* [1929] 1 Ch. 716.

[26] Trustee Act 1925, s.31(3); R.S.C., Ord. 44, r. 10.

[27] *Re Pollock* [1943] Ch. 338.

[28] *Re West* [1913] 2 Ch. 345.

[29] *Re Abrahams* [1911] 1 Ch. 108.

[30] *Re Churchill* [1909] 2 Ch. 431 (intention implied from a power to apply the whole or any part of the contingent legacy for the advancement or otherwise for the benefit of the legatee at any time before attaining 21 years of age, which clearly authorised payments for the minor's maintenance), *Re Selby Walker* [1949] 2 All E.R. 178.

[31] *Re Jones* [1932] 1 Ch. 108 (beware the incorrect headnote).

inapplicable, so that there must be used for the maintenance of the legatee interest at 6 per cent. rather than the higher actual income produced if, on winding up the testator's estate, the executors for convenience sake set aside the capital to which the legatee will be entitled on attaining, say, 25 years of age. It will be troublesome that the balance of income over the sum representing 6 per cent. interest will fall into residue. However, it would probably strain section 31(3) too much to construe "contingent interest" which "carries the intermediate income" to include contingent legacies to the extent they indirectly (via interest payable out of the residuary estate income) carry intermediate income so as to cover this further exceptional case,[32] especially when the latter half of the subsection deals with legacies which carry interest for maintenance.

Tax considerations should always be borne in mind. Income applied **9–251** for an infant unmarried child of the settlor is treated as the settlor's income.[33] Moreover, any sum paid out of trust funds to the settlor's child is treated as income and not capital to an amount equal to the total undistributed income of the trust to that date.[34]

RE MCGEORGE

Chancery Division [1963] Ch. 544; [1963] 2 W.L.R. 767; [1963] 1 All E.R. 519

A testator devised land to his daughter and declared that "the devise . . . shall **9–252** not take effect until after the death of my wife should she survive me." The testator also provided that if the daughter should die during the lifetime of the wife leaving issue, then the issue on attaining twenty-one were to "take by substitution the aforesaid devise in favour of" the daughter. The testator bequeathed his residuary estate on trust for his wife for life and after her death to be divided equally between his son and daughter.

Cross J. held that the declaration that the devise should not take effect until a **9–253** future time deferred its vesting in possession until that time but not its vesting in interest, read the terms of section 175 of the Law of Property Act 1925, *supra*, p. 672, and continued: "The devise is, it is said, a future specific devise within the meaning of the section; the testator has not made any express disposition of the income accruing from it between his death and the death of his widow, and so that income is carried by the gift. At first sight it is hard to see how Parliament could have enacted a section which produces such a result. If a testator gives property to A after the death of B, then whether or not he disposes of the income accruing during B's life he is at all events showing clearly that A is not to have it. Yet if the future gift to A is absolute and the intermediate income is carried with it by force of this section, A can claim to have the property **9–254** transferred to him at once, since no one else can be interested in it. The section, that is to say, will have converted a gift in remainder into a gift in possession in defiance of the testator's wishes. The explanation for the section taking the form

---

[32] But see B. S. Ker (1953) 17 Conv. 273 at 279, 283–284.
[33] The Income and Corporation Taxes Act 1988, ss.663, 664.
[34] *ibid.* s.664(2)(3), and see *supra*, para. 1–94.

which it does is, I think, probably as follows. It has long been established that a gift of residuary personalty to a legatee in being on a contingency or to an unborn person at birth carried the intermediate income so far as the law would allow it to be accumulated, but that rule had been held, for reasons depending on the old land law, not to apply to gifts of real property, and it was apparently never applied to specific dispositions of personalty. Section 175 of the Law of Property Act 1925 was plainly intended to extend the rule to residuary devises and to specific gifts whether of realty or of personalty. It is now established, at all events so far as courts of first instance are concerned, that the old rule does not apply to residuary bequests whether vested or contingent which are expressly deferred to a future date which must come sooner or later (see *Re Oliver*,[35] *Re Gillett's Will Trusts*[36] and *Re Geering*[37]). There is a good reason for this distinction. If a testator gives property to X contingently on his attaining the age of thirty it is reasonable to assume, in the absence of a direction to the contrary, that the testator would wish X, if he attains thirty, to have the income produced by the property between the testator's death and the happening of the contingency. If, on the other hand, he gives property to X for any sort of interest after the death of A, it is reasonable to assume that he does not wish X to have the income accruing during A's lifetime unless he directs that he is to have it. This distinction between an immediate gift on a contingency and a gift which is expressly deferred was not drawn until after the Law of Property Act 1925 was passed. There were statements in textbooks and even in judgments to the effect that the rule applied to deferred as well as to contingent gifts of residuary personalty.[38] The legislature, when it extended this rule to residuary devises and specific gifts, must, I think, have adopted this erroneous view of the law. I would have liked, if I could, to construe the reference to 'future specific devises' and 'executory interest' in section 175(1) of the Act of 1925 in such a way as to make it consistent with the recent cases on the scope of the old rule applicable to residuary bequests. To do that, however, would be to rectify the Act, not to construe it, and I see no escape from the conclusion that whereas before 1926 a specific gift or a residuary devise which was not vested in possession did not prima facie carry intermediate income at all, now such a gift may carry intermediate income in circumstances in which a residuary bequest would not carry it.

9–255   "It was argued in this case that the fact that the will contained a residuary gift constituted an express disposition of the income of the land in question which prevented the section from applying. I am afraid that I cannot accept this submission. I have little doubt that the testator expected the income of the land to form part of the income of residue during his widow's lifetime, but he has made no express disposition of it. I agree with what was said in this connection by Eve J. in *Re Raine*.[39] As the devise is not vested indefeasibly in the daughter but is subject to defeasance during the mother's lifetime the intermediate income which the gift carries by virtue of section 175 ought prima facie to be accumulated to see who eventually becomes entitled to it. It was, however, submitted by counsel for the daughter that she could claim payment of it under section 31(1) of the Trustee Act 1925. [His Lordship summarised the subsection,

---

[35] [1947] 2 All E.R. 162.
[36] [1950] Ch. 102.
[37] [1964] Ch. 136.
[38] See *Jarman on Wills* (7th ed.), p. 1006.
[39] [1929] 1 Ch. 716 at 719.

and continued:] There are, as I see it, two answers to the daughter's claim. The first—and narrower—answer is that her interest in the income of the devised land is a vested interest. It is a future interest liable to be divested but it is not contingent. Therefore section 31(1) does not apply to it. The second—and wider—answer is that the whole framework of section 31 shows that it is inapplicable to a future gift of this sort and that a will containing such a gift expresses a contrary intention within section 69(2) which prevents the subsection from applying. By deferring the enjoyment of the devise until after the widow's death the testator has expressed the intention that the daughter shall not have the immediate income. It is true that as he has not expressly disposed of it in any other way, section 175 of the Law of Property Act 1925 defeats that intention to the extent of making the future devise carry the income, so that the daughter will get it eventually, if she survives her mother or dies before her leaving no children to take by substitution. Even if, however, the words of section 31(1) of the Trustee Act 1925 fitted the case, there would be no warrant for defeating the testator's intention still further by reading section 31(1) into the will and thus giving the daughter an interest in possession in the income during her mother's lifetime. In the result, the income . . . must be accumulated, in my judgment, for twenty-one years if the widow so long lives."

B. Advancement[40]

Trustees must be particularly careful in exercising the statutory power of **9–256** advancement in order to "benefit" a beneficiary, for a mistake will mean that both capital and income disappear, probably for good. Danckwerts J. has said,[41] " 'benefit' is the widest possible word one could have and it must include payment direct to the beneficiary but that does not absolve the trustees from making up their minds whether the payment in the particular manner which they contemplate is for the benefit of the beneficiary." Viscount Radcliffe has said,[42] it "means any use of money which will improve the material situation of the beneficiary." In *Re Clore's S.T.*[43] making a donation to a charity at a wealthy beneficiary's request to discharge what he felt to be a moral obligation was held an advancement for his benefit. In *Re Hampden*[44] a transfer to trustees for the benefit of the beneficiary's children was held authorised by an express power to benefit the beneficiary.

Re Pauling's S.T.[45] provides a sorry, salutary story for compulsory **9–257** reading before trustees exercise their power of advancement. It is a fascinating but overlengthy case to set out in any detail. Essentially, the father of the beneficiaries was so charming and forceful that the trustees frittered away much of the capital in ways that enabled the wife's overdraft to be paid off, a house to be bought for the father and his wife

---

[40] See Wolstenholme & Cherry's *Conveyancing Statutes*, Vol. 4 (13th ed. by J. T. Farrand).
[41] *Re Moxon's W.T.* [1958] 1 W.L.R. 165. For "benefit" under an express clause see *Re Buckinghamshire's S.T., The Times*, March 29, 1977.
[42] *Pilkington v. I.R.C.* [1964] A.C. 612 at 635.
[43] [1966] 1 W.L.R. 955.
[44] [1977] T.R. 177, [2001] W.T.L.R. 195; *Re Esteem Settlement* [2001] W.T.L.R. 641.
[45] [1964] Ch. 303.

absolutely and an overly high standard of living to be maintained for the family. The lessons to be drawn are that requests for advancements from young adults unemancipated from the undue influence of their parents must be treated with caution and the moneys requested applied by the trustees themselves for a particular purpose if previous experience indicates that otherwise the purported purpose is unlikely to be effected.

9–258   An advancement may be by way of settlement that benefits someone other than the beneficiary so long as the beneficiary receives significant benefit,[46] *e.g.* receiving a life interest in the advanced moneys, remainder to his widow for life, remainder to his children equally. To deal with a dictum of Upjohn J.[47] and cases narrowly construing powers of appointment in outdated fashion the power of advancement has often been expressly extended to permit delegation of duties and discretions to make clear that a re-settlement may be by way of discretionary trusts or by way of protective trusts which may end up after forfeiture as discretionary trusts. However, the modern consensus,[48] supported by Viscount Radcliffe in *Pilkington v. I.R.C.*,[49] is that no question of delegation of the trustees' functions arises where they transfer property to be held on new trusts which may contain discretionary trusts and powers, because the new trustees are not exercising delegated functions but are exercising new original functions of their own as a result of the outright advancement. It is necessary to ensure that the rule against remoteness is not infringed, for the perpetuity period relevant to the exercise of the power of advancement runs from the date of the settlement and not from the date of the exercise of the power[50]: *Pilkington v. I.R.C., infra*, para. 9–264. If part of the exercise of the

9–259   power of advancement is void for remoteness *and* the resultant effect of the intended advancement is such that it could not reasonably be regarded as being beneficial to the beneficiary intended to be advanced, then the advancement fails for it cannot be authorised as within the powers of the trustees under section 32: otherwise the part of the advancement not void for remoteness will stand as within the trustees' powers,[51] *e.g.* C's life interest stands where the advancement is to trustees for C for life with remainders to his issue where the remainders are void for remoteness. The fact that in such a case no effective beneficial trusts of capital are created does not mean that there has been no payment or application of capital as required by section 32: the transfer of capital to the trustees of the settlement for C for life is an application of capital

---

[46] *Pilkington v. I.R.C.* [1964] A.C. 612, *Re Hampden* [1977] T.R. 177.

[47] *Re Wills' Trusts* [1959] Ch. 1, 13.

[48] See J. Kessler, *Drafting Trusts and Will Trusts* (5th ed.) paras 10.6 and 10.12; Parker & Mellows, *The Modern Law of Trusts* (7th ed. by A.J. Oakley) pp. 626–627; *Lewin on Trusts* (17th ed.) para. 32.18.

[49] [1964] A.C. 612, 639.

[50] The exercise of a power of advancement is treated as the exercise of a special power so that the Perpetuities and Accumulations Act 1964 is of no avail unless the original settlement was created after July 15, 1964: s.15(5) of the Perpetuities and Accumulations Act 1964.

[51] *Re Abraham's W.T.* [1969] 1 Ch. 463 as cut down by the interpretation of the Court of Appeal in *Re Hastings-Bass* [1975] Ch. 25 explored in *Mettoy Pension Trustees v. Evans* [1991] 2 All E.R. 513.

within section 32.[52] A capital gains tax charge arises not only on an advance to a beneficiary absolutely but also where the advancement is on new trusts even where T1 and T2 appropriate the property on new trusts and are themselves trustees of the appropriated property.[53] No capital gains tax charge will arise if the trustees instead of creating a new separate settlement merely sub-settle some trust assets. To help distinguish between a new settlement and a sub-settlement the Revenue issued a Statement of Practice as follows:

> "It is now clear that a deemed disposal under C.G.T.A. 1979, section 54(1) **9–260** (now T.C.G.A. 1992, s.71) cannot arise unless the power exercised by the trustees, or the instrument conferring the power, expressly or by necessary implication, confers on the trustees authority to remove assets from the original settlement by subjecting them to the trusts of a different settlement. Such powers (which may be powers of advancement or appointment) are referred to by the Court of Appeal as 'powers in the wider form.' However, the Board considers that a deemed disposal will not arise when such a power is exercised and trusts are declared in circumstances such that:
> (a) the appointment is revocable, or
> (b) the trusts declared of the advanced or appointed funds are not exhaustive so that there exists a possibility at the time when the advancement or appointment is made that the funds covered by it will on the occasion of some event cease to be held upon such trusts and once again come to be held upon the original trusts of the settlement.
> Further, when such a power is exercised the Board considers it unlikely **9–261** that a deemed disposal will arise when trusts are declared if duties in regard to the appointed assets still fall to the trustees of the original settlement in their capacity as trustees of that settlement, bearing in mind the provision in CGTA 1979 section 52(1) (now T.C.G.A. 1992, s.69(1)) that the trustees of a settlement form a single and continuing body (distinct from the persons who may from time to time be the trustees).
> Finally, the Board accept that a power of appointment or advancement can be exercised over only part of the settled property and that the above consequences would apply to that part."

When advances are brought into account they are accounted for at their value at the time of the advance and not at their value prevailing at the time of the final distribution.[54] This is unjust in these inflationary times so the Law Reform Committee (Cmnd. 8733, para. 4.47) recommended that advances should be accounted for at their value at the time

---

[52] *Re Hastings-Bass* [1975] Ch. 25. At 40 the court laid down the general proposition, "where by the terms of a trust (as under s.32) a trustee is given a discretion as to some matter under which he acts in good faith, the court should not interfere with his action notwithstanding that it does not have the full effect intended unless (1) what he has achieved is unauthorised by the power conferred on him or (2) it is clear that he would not have acted as he did (a) had he not taken into account considerations which he should not have taken into account or (b) had he not failed to take into account considerations which he ought to have taken into account."

[53] *Hart v. Briscoe* [1979] Ch. 110; *Roome v. Edwards* [1981] 1 All E.R. 736; *Bond v. Pickford* [1983] S.T.C. 517; Taxation of Chargeable Gains Act 1992, s.71.

[54] *Re Gollins' Declaration of Trust* [1969] 3 All E.R. 1591, but trustees may get a beneficiary to consent to his advancement being treated as of a fraction of the fund: *Re Leigh's S.T.* [1981] C.L.Y. 2453.

of the advance multiplied by any increase in the retail price index up to the time of the final distribution.

The Trustee Act 1925

9–262   **Section 32.**—(1) Trustees may[55] at any time or times pay or apply any capital money[56] subject to a trust, for the advancement or benefit, in such manner as they may, in their absolute discretion, think fit, of any person entitled to the capital[57] of the trust property or of any share thereof, whether absolutely or contingently on his attaining any specified age or on the occurrence of any other event, or subject to a gift over on his death under any specified age or on the occurrence of any other event, and whether in possession or in remainder or reversion, and such payment or application may be made notwithstanding that the interest of such person is liable to be defeated by the exercise of a power of appointment or revocation, or to be diminished by the increase of the class to which he belongs:

Provided that—

9–263   (a) the money so paid or applied for the advancement or benefit of any person shall not exceed altogether in amount *one-half*[58] of the presumptive or vested share or interest of that person in the trust property; and

(b) if that person is or becomes absolutely and indefeasibly entitled to a share in the trust property the money so paid or applied shall be brought into account as part of such share; and

(c) *no such payment or application shall be made so as to prejudice any person entitled to any prior life or other interest*,[59] whether vested or contingent, in the money paid or applied *unless* such person is in existence and of full age and *consents in writing* to such payment or application.

(2) This section applies only where the trust property consists of money or securities or of property held upon trust for sale calling in and conversion, and

---

[55] The section confers a power; it does not impose a duty: hence it cannot be utilised if the settlement contains a contrary intention: see *Inland Revenue Commissioners v. Bernstein* [1960] Ch. 444 (Danckwerts J.); [1961] Ch. 399, C.A.; *Re Henderson's Trusts* [1969] 1 W.L.R. 651; *Re Evans' Settlement* [1967] 1 W.L.R. 1294. Whilst a duty to accumulate is necessarily inconsistent with the power of maintenance it is not necessarily inconsistent with the power of advancement: *I.R.C. v. Bernstein* [1961] Ch. 399. S.32 is not excluded by the accumulation trust in s.31 nor by express accumulation and maintenance trusts in similar form to s.31.

[56] Assets can be transferred *in specie*: *Re Collard's W.T.* [1961] Ch. 293 noted (1961) 77 L.Q.R. 161. When brought into account on final distribution of the trust property they will be taken into account as of their cash value when originally received: *Re Gollins' Declaration of Trust* [1969] 3 All E.R. 1591.

[57] The section does not apply where the beneficiary is given only an interest in income: *Re Winch's Settlement* [1917] 1 Ch. 633.

[58] If A and B are the two beneficiaries contingently equally entitled to a trust fund of £200,000 and B receives the maximum advancement of £50,000 does this mean that the power can no longer be exercised in his favour or if the fund remaining appreciates to £250,000 can B maintain that the fund is now notionally worth £250,000 plus his advanced £50,000 so that an advancement of half of half of £300,000, *i.e.*, £75,000, may be made to him so that he may receive a further £25,000 on top of the £50,000 he has already received? Consider s.32(1) proviso (b) and *Re Marquess of Abergavenny's Estate Act Trusts* [1981] 2 All E.R. 643 (trustees had express power to advance to the life tenant "any part or parts not exceeding in all one half in value of the settled fund." Goulding J. held an advance of half the value of the settled fund exhausted the exercise of the power so that it ceased to be exercisable in the future even though the retained assets had later increased in value).

[59] A beneficiary under a discretionary trust is not entitled to such a prior interest as to render his consent requisite: *Re Beckett's Settlement* [1940] Ch. 279 but where income is held on the protective trusts in Trustee Act 1925, s.33, and there has been no forfeiture the "principal beneficiary" has a prior interest within para. (c) his consent not incurring a forfeiture: *Re Harris' Settlement* (1940) 162 L.T. 358; *Re Rees' W.T.* [1954] Ch. 202. Further see *I.R.C. v. Bernstein* [1960] Ch. 444; [1961] Ch. 399. Often the power to advance is extended to the whole, rather than half, of the prospective share but the life tenant's consent remains requisite: *Henley v. Wardell, The Times*, January 29, 1988.

such money or securities, or the proceeds of such sale calling in and conversion are not by statute or in equity considered as land, or applicable as capital money for the purposes of the Settled Land Act 1925.

(3) This section does not apply to trusts constituted or created before the commencement of this Act.[60]

PILKINGTON AND ANOTHER v. INLAND REVENUE COMMISSIONERS

House of Lords [1964] A.C. 612; [1962] 3 W.L.R. 1051; [1962] 3 All E.R. 622; 40 T.C. 416 (Viscount Radcliffe, Lords Reid, Jenkins, Hodson and Devlin)

By will the testator left his residuary estate to trustees on trust, for his nephew, **9–264** Richard Godfrey Pilkington ("Richard"), upon protective trusts during his life with a provision that any consent which he might give to the exercise of any applicable form of advancement should not cause a forfeiture of his life interest. After Richard's death the trustees were to hold the residuary estate upon trust for such of Richard's children or remoter issue at such age in such shares and with such trusts for their respective benefit and such provisions for their respective advancement and maintenance and education as Richard should by deed or will without transgressing the rule against perpetuities appoint. In default of appointment the trustees were to hold the residuary estate on trust for such of Richard's children as, being male, attained the age of twenty-one, or, being female, attained that age or married under it, and, if more than one, in equal shares.

The testator's will did not confer any express power of advancement upon the trustees, but, by implication, the power of advancement under section 32 of the Trustee Act 1925, *supra*, was applicable.

Richard had three children, of whom the defendant Penelope Margaret Pilkington ("Penelope") was one.

Richard's father, Guy Reginald Pilkington ("the settlor"), proposed to make a **9–265** settlement, to be executed by himself, Richard and the trustees of the testator's will, upon the following trusts: (i) Until Penelope attained the age of twenty-one the trustees of the settlement were to have power to apply income for her maintenance whether or not there was any other income available for that purpose and were to accumulate and capitalise surplus income; (ii) If Penelope attained the age of twenty-one the trustees were to be under a duty to pay the income to her until she reached the age of thirty or died under that age; (iii) If Penelope attained the age of thirty the trustees were to hold the capital of the trust fund upon trust for her absolutely; (iv) If Penelope died under the age of thirty, leaving a child or children who attained the age of twenty-one, the trustees were to hold the trust fund and the income thereof in trust for such child or children, and, if more than one, in equal shares.

Subject to these trusts, the trustees of the settlement were to hold the trust **9–266** fund in trust equally for all of Richard's children (other than Penelope) who, being male, attained the age of twenty-one, or, being female, attained that age or married under it. In the case of the failure of the trust, the fund was to be held

---

[60] If the trust is a testamentary one and the testator dies after 1925, the power contained in s.32 of the Act, *supra*, is available to the trustees: *Re Taylor's Will Trusts* (1950) 66 T.L.R.(Pt. 2) 507. *Aliter* if the trusts arose under a special power of appointment created before 1926 but exercised after 1925: *Re Batty* [1952] Ch. 280; criticised (1952) 68 L.Q.R. 319 (J. H. C. M., citing *Re Stimpson* [1931] 2 Ch. 77).

on the trusts of the testator's will which would take effect after Richard's death as if he had died without having been married.

The proposed settlement provided that the power of maintenance contained in section 31 of the Trustee Act 1925, subject to certain modifications, and the power of advancement contained in section 32 of the Act in an unmodified form, should be available to the trustees.

9–267 The trustees of the testator's will took out an originating summons to determine the question whether they could lawfully exercise the powers conferred on them in relation to the expectant interest of the defendant Penelope, in the testator's residuary estate by applying (with the consent of the defendant Richard, her father) some part not exceeding one-half of the capital of such interest in such manner as to make it subject to the trusts, powers and provisions of the settlement proposed to be executed by the plaintiff, the settlor. Danckwerts J.[61] held that the exercise of the power of advancement in this way would not be objectionable; but his decision was reversed by the Court of Appeal.[62] Richard and Penelope appealed.

9–268 VISCOUNT RADCLIFE: "The word 'advancement' itself meant in this context the establishment in life of the beneficiary who was the object of the power or at any rate some step that would contribute to the furtherance of his establishment. Advancement had, however, to some extent a limited range of meaning, since it was thought to convey the idea of some step in life of permanent significance, and accordingly, to prevent uncertainties about the permitted range of objects for which moneys could be raised and made available, such words as 'or otherwise for his or her benefit' were often added to the word 'advancement'. It was always recognised that these added words were 'large words' (see Jessel M.R. in *Re Breeds' Will*[63]) and indeed in another case (*Lowther v. Bentinck*[64]) the same judge spoke of preferment and advancement as being 'both large words' but of 'benefit' as being the 'largest of all.' Recent judges have spoken in the same terms—see Farwell J. in *Re Halsted's Will Trusts*[65] and Danckwerts J. in *Re Moxon's Will Trusts*.[66] This wide construction of the range of the power, which evidently did not stand upon niceties of distinction provided that the proposed application could fairly be regarded as for the benefit of the beneficiary who was the object of the power, must have been carried into the statutory power created by section 32, since it adopts without qualification the accustomed wording 'for the advancement or benefit in such manner as they may in their absolute discretion think fit.'

9–269 "So much for 'advancement,' which I now use for brevity to cover the combined phrase 'advancement or benefit.' It means any use of the money which will improve the material situation of the beneficiary. It is important, however, not to confuse the idea of 'advancement' with the idea of advancing the money out of the beneficiary's expectant interest. The two things have only a casual connection with each other. The one refers to the operation of finding money by way of anticipation of an interest not yet absolutely vested in possession or, if so vested, belonging to an infant: the other refers to the status of the beneficiary and the improvement of his situation. The power to carry out the operation of

[61] [1959] Ch. 699.
[62] [1961] Ch. 466.
[63] [1875] 1 Ch.D. 226 at 228.
[64] [1874] L.R. 19 Eq. 166 at 169.
[65] [1937] 2 All E.R. 570 at 571.
[66] [1958] 1 W.L.R. 165 at 168.

anticipating an interest is not conferred by the word 'advancement' but by those other words of the section which expressly authorise the payment or application of capital money for the benefit of a person entitled 'whether absolutely or contingently on his attaining any specified age or on the occurrence of any other event, or subject to a gift over on his death under any specified age or on the occurrence of any other event, and whether in possession or in remainder or reversion,' etc.

"I think, with all respect to the Commissioners, a good deal of their argument **9–270** is infected with some of this confusion. To say, for instance, that there cannot be a valid exercise of a power of advancement that results in a deferment of the vesting of the beneficiary's absolute title (Penelope, it will be remembered, is to take at thirty under the proposed settlement instead of at twenty-one under the will) is in my opinion to play upon words. The element of anticipation consists in the raising of money for her now before she has any right to receive anything under the existing trusts: the advancement consists in the application of that money to form a trust fund, the provisions of which are thought to be for her benefit.

"I have not been able to find in the words of section 32, to which I have now referred, anything which in terms or by implication restricts the width of the manner or purpose of advancement. It is true that, if this settlement is made, Penelope's children, who are not objects of the power, are given a possible interest in the event of her dying under thirty leaving surviving issue. But if the disposition itself, by which I mean the whole provision made, is for her benefit, it is no objection to the exercise of the power that other persons benefit incidentally as a result of the exercise. Thus a man's creditors may in certain cases get the most immediate advantage from an advancement made for the purpose of paying them off, as in *Lowther v. Bentinck*; and a power to raise money for the advancement of a wife may cover a payment made direct to her husband in order to set him up in business (*Re Kershaw's Trusts*[67]). The exercise will not be bad, therefore, on this ground.

"Nor in my opinion will it be bad merely because the moneys are to be tied up **9–271** in the proposed settlement. If it could be said that the payment or application permitted by section 32 cannot take the form of a settlement in any form but must somehow pass direct into or through the hands of the object of the power, I could appreciate the principle upon which the Commissioners' objection was founded. But can that principle be asserted? Anyone can see, I think, that there can be circumstances in which, while it is very desirable that some money should be raised at once for the benefit of an owner of an expectant or contingent interest, it would be very undesirable that the money should not be secured to him under some arrangement that will prevent him having the absolute disposition of it. I find it very difficult to think that there is something at the back of section 32 which makes such an advancement impossible. Certainly neither Danckwerts J. nor the members of the Court of Appeal in this case took the **9–272** view. Both Lord Evershed M.R. and Upjohn L.J.[68] explicitly accept the possibility of a settlement being made in exercise of a power of advancement. Farwell J. authorised one in *Re Halsted's Will Trusts*,[69] a case in which the trustees had left their discretion to the court. The trustees should raise the money and 'have' it 'settled,' he said. So, too, Harman J. in *Re Ropner's Settlement Trusts*[70] authorised

---

[67] (1868) L.R. 6 Eq. 322.
[68] [1961] Ch. 466 at 481, 486.
[69] [1937] 2 All E.R. 570 at 572.
[70] [1956] 1 W.L.R. 902 at 906.

the settlement of an advance provided for an infant, saying that the child could not 'consent or request the trustees to make the advance, but the transfer of a part of his contingent share to the trustees of a settlement for him must advance his interest and thus be for his benefit . . .' All this must be wrong in principle if a power of advancement cannot cover an application of the moneys by way of settlement.

9–273   "The truth is, I think, that the propriety of requiring a settlement of moneys found for advancement was recognised as long ago as 1871 in *Roper-Curzon v. Roper-Curzon* and, so far as I know, it has not been impugned since. If, then, it is a proper exercise of a power of advancement for trustees to stipulate that the money shall be settled, I cannot see any difference between having it settled that way and having it settled by themselves paying it to trustees of a settlement which is in the desired form.

"The Commissioners' objections seem to be concentrated upon such propositions as that the proposed transaction is 'nothing less than a resettlement' and that a power of advancement cannot be used so as to alter or vary the trusts created by the settlement from which it is derived. Such a transaction, they say, amounts to using the power of advancement as a way of appointing or declaring new trusts different from those of the settlement. The reason why I do not find that these propositions have any compulsive effect upon my mind is that they seem to me merely vivid ways of describing the substantial effect of that which is proposed to be done and they do not in themselves amount to convincing arguments against doing it. Of course, whenever money is raised for advancement on terms that it is to be settled on the beneficiary, the money only passes from one settlement to be caught up in the other. It is therefore the same thing as a resettlement. But, unless one is to say that such moneys can never be applied by way of settlement, an argument which, as I have shown, has few supporters and is contrary to authority, it merely describes the inevitable effect of such an advancement to say that it is nothing less than a resettlement. Similarly, if it is part of the trusts and powers created by one settlement that the trustees of it should have power to raise money and make it available for a beneficiary upon new trusts approved by them, then they are in substance given power to free the money from one trust and to subject it to another. So be it: but, unless they cannot require a settlement of it at all, the transaction they carry out is the same thing in effect as an appointment of new trusts.

"In the same way I am unconvinced by the argument that the trustees would be improperly delegating their trust by allowing the money raised to pass over to new trustees under a new settlement conferring new powers on the latter. In fact, I think that the whole issue of delegation is here beside the mark. The law is not that trustees cannot delegate: it is that trustees cannot delegate unless they have authority to do so. If the power of advancement which they possess is so read as to allow them to raise money for the purpose of having it settled, then they do have the necessary authority to let the money pass out of the old settlement into new trusts. No question of delegation of their powers or trusts arises."

9–274   "I ought to note for the record (1) that the transaction envisaged does not actually involve the raising of money, since the trustees propose to appropriate a block of shares in the family's private limited company as the trust investment, and (2) there will not be any actual transfer, since the trustees of the proposed settlement and the will trustees are the same persons. As I have already said, I do not attach any importance to these factors, nor, I think, do the Commissioners. To transfer or appropriate outright is only to do by short cut what could be done in a more roundabout way by selling the shares to a consenting party, paying the money over to the new settlement with appropriate instructions and arranging for it to be used in buying back the shares as the trust investment. It cannot make any difference to follow the course taken in *Re Collard's Will Trusts*[71] and deal with the property direct. On the other point, so long as there are separate trusts, the property effectually passes out of the old settlement into the new one, and it is of no relevance that, at any rate for the time being, the persons administering the new trusts are the same individuals.

"I have not yet referred to the ground which was taken by the Court of Appeal **9–275** as their reason for saying that the proposed settlement was not permissible. To put it shortly, they held that the statutory power of advancement could not be exercised unless the benefit to be conferred was 'personal to the person concerned, in the sense of being related to his or her own real or personal needs.'[72] Or, to use other words of the learned Master of the Rolls,[73] the exercise of the power 'must be an exercise done to meet the circumstances as they present themselves in regard to a person within the scope of the section, whose circumstances call for that to be done which the trustees think fit to do.' Upjohn L.J.[74] expressed himself in virtually the same terms.

"My Lords, I differ with reluctance from the views of judges so learned and **9–276** experienced in matters of this sort: but I do not find it possible to import such restrictions into the words of the statutory power which itself does not contain them. First, the suggested qualification, that the considerations or circumstances must be 'personal' to the beneficiary, seems to me uncontrollably vague as a guide to general administration. What distinguishes a personal need from any other need to which the trustees in their discretion think it right to attend in the beneficiary's interest? And, if the advantage of preserving the funds of a beneficiary from the incidence of death duty is not an advantage personal to that beneficiary, I do not see what is. Death duty is a present risk that attaches to the settled property in which Penelope has her expectant interest, and even accepting the validity of the supposed limitation, I would not have supposed that there was anything either impersonal or unduly remote in the advantage to be conferred upon her of some exemption from that risk. I do not think, therefore, that I can support the interpretation of the power of advancement that has commended itself to the Court of Appeal, and, with great respect, I think that the judgments really amount to little more than a decision that in the opinion of the members of that court this was not a case in which there was any occasion to exercise the power. That would be a proper answer from a court to which trustees had referred their discretion with a request for its directions; but it does not really solve any question where, as here, they retain their discretion and merely ask whether it is impossible for them to exercise it.

"To conclude, therefore, on this issue, I am of opinion that there is no **9–277** maintainable reason for introducing into the statutory power of advancement a qualification that would exclude the exercise in the case now before us. It would not be candid to omit to say that, though I think that that is what the law requires, I am uneasy at some of the possible applications of this liberty, when advancements are made for the purposes of settlement or on terms that there is to be a settlement. It is quite true, as the Commissioners have pointed out, that you might have really extravagant cases of resettlements being forced on

---

[71] [1961] Ch. 293.
[72] [1961] Ch. 466 at 484.
[73] [1961] Ch. 466 at 481.
[74] *ibid.*

beneficiaries in the name of advancement, even a few months before an absolute vesting in possession would have destroyed the power. I have tried to give due weight to such possibilities, but when all is said I do not think that they ought to compel us to introduce a limitation of which no one, with all respect, can produce a satisfactory definition. First, I do not believe that it is wise to try to cut down an admittedly wide and discretionary power, enacted for general use, through fear of its being abused in certain hypothetical instances. And moreover, as regards this fear, I think that it must be remembered that we are speaking of a power intended to be in the hands of trustees chosen by a settlor because of his confidence in their discretion and good sense and subject to the external check that no exercise can take place without the consent of a prior life-tenant; and that there does remain at all times a residual power in the court to restrain or correct any purported exercise that can be shown to be merely wanton or capricious and not to be attributable to a genuine discretion. I think, therefore, that, although extravagant possibilities exist, they may be more menacing in argument than in real life . . ."

9–278 [However, their Lordships also held that the power of advancement under section 32 was to be regarded in the same way as a special power of appointment so far as the application of the rule against perpetuities was concerned so that the proposed advancement would be void.]

C. Payment of Trust Funds to Beneficiaries

Trustees must pay trust moneys to the right beneficiaries, for otherwise it is a breach of trust. In *Eaves v. Hickson*,[75] trustees were induced by a forgery to pay trust funds to persons not entitled, and Romilly M.R. held that, as between trustee and beneficiary, the loss fell on the former.[76]

Section 61 of the Trustee Act 1925, *infra*, is now available as a defence to a trustee who honestly and reasonably makes a wrongful payment through circumstances similar to those in *Eaves v. Hickson*, or through an erroneous construction of the trust instrument.[77]

9–279 Before paying trust funds to an alleged *assignee* from a beneficiary a trustee must investigate the assignee's title. If he relies merely on the alleged assignee's statement, he is not acting reasonably. If the assignee happens also to be solicitor to the trust the trustee will still be liable[78] unless excused under section 61 of the Trustee Act.[79] But although the trustee must investigate the assignee's title, he cannot require actual delivery up to him of the assignee's document of title.[80]

If a trustee, through inadvertence or a mistake of construction or of fact, has overpaid one beneficiary at the expense of another, and the

---

[75] (1861) 30 Beav. 136. However, only if the forger or the wrong recipients could not compensate the beneficiary.

[76] See also *Ashby v. Blackwell* (1765) 2 Eden 299 at 302; *Sutton v. Wilders* (1871) L.R. 12 Eq. 373, *Boulton v. Beard* (1853) 3 De G.M. & G. 608; *Sporle v. Barnaby* (1864) 10 Jur. 1142.

[77] *Re Smith, Smith v. Thompson* (1902) 71 L.J.Ch. 411; *National Trustees Company of Australasia v. General Finance Co. of Australasia* [1905] A.C. 381; *Re Allsop* [1914] 1 Ch. 1.

[78] *Davis v. Hutchings* [1907] 1 Ch. 356.

[79] *Re Allsop* [1914] 1 Ch. 1. It is possible protection may be available under Trustee Act 2000 sections 11 and 23.

[80] *Re Palmer* [1907] 1 Ch. 486; see *Warter v. Anderson* (1853) 11 Hare 301.

court is administering the estate, it will adjust accounts out of future payments.[81] If the estate is not being administered by the court, an adjustment can be made with the court's assistance; and might presumably be made without any application to the court. If the underpaid beneficiary can identify the fund erroneously paid, he has, in addition, the remedy of tracing it into the hands of the overpaid beneficiary or an assignee (except a bona fide purchaser or a person with the defence of change of position),[82] and if beneficiary under a will he will also have a personal action against a recipient under *Ministry of Health v. Simpson* principles.[83]

But if a *trustee-beneficiary* underpays *himself*, then, according to *Re* **9–280** *Horne*,[84] he suffers by his mistake though it may be that, nowadays, he should be allowed to recoup himself out of trust property in his hands.[85]

The Law Reform Committee (Cmnd. 8733, para. 5.4) made the following recommendation: "where it appears that the cost of taking out a summons is out of all proportion to the amount at stake, trustees should be empowered to take the advice of counsel (in the case of trusts having adult beneficiaries only) or Chancery Queens Counsel or conveyancing counsel of the court (where there are infant beneficiaries) and to distribute on the basis of that advice if no adult beneficiary starts proceedings within three months of being sent a copy of the relevant opinion." As a half-way measure section 48 of the Administration of Justice Act 1985 gives the court power (without an oral hearing) to authorise action to be taken concerning the construction of a will or trust in reliance on a written opinion of a person with a ten year High Court qualification within section 71 of the Courts and Legal Services Act 1990.

IV. STATUTORY AND JUDICIAL PROTECTION OF TRUSTEES IN RESPECT OF THE DISTRIBUTION OF THE TRUST PROPERTY

The Trustee Act 1925

Protection against liability in respect of rents and covenants

Section 26.—(1) Where a personal representative or trustee liable as such[86] **9–281** for—

(a) any rent, covenant, or agreement reserved by or contained in any lease; or

---

[81] *Dibbs v. Goren* (1849) 11 Beav. 483; *Re Musgrave* [1916] 2 Ch. 417. Not until *Kleinwort Benson Ltd v. Lincoln C.C.* [1999] 2 A.C. 349 did the common law allow recovery for mistakes of law as well as fact.
[82] *Re Diplock* [1948] Ch. 465; *Lipkin Gorman v. Karpnale Ltd* [1991] 2 A.C. 548.
[83] [1951] A.C. 251, see *infra*, para. 11–103.
[84] [1905] 1 Ch. 76.
[85] See *Re Reading* [1916] W.N. 262, *Lewin on Trusts* (17th ed) para 42.08.
[86] The protection of the section avails a personal representative or trustee in respect of his representative liability *as such*. Personal liability, unprotected by the section, is incurred if the personal representative or trustee takes possession of the leaseholds and so becomes personally liable by privity of estate or enters into a lease in course of administration so becoming personally liable by privity of contract. It seems a trustee is liable "as such" only where liability on a contract is limited to the value of the trust fund, the trustee not being personally liable beyond that. *Re Owers (No. 2)* [1941] Ch. 389; *Re Bennett* [1943] 1 All E.R. 467; *Youngmin v. Health* [1974] 1 W.L.R. 135 at 138.

(b) any rent, covenant or agreement payable under or contained in any grant made in consideration of a rentcharge; or

(c) any indemnity given in respect of any rent, covenant or agreement referred to in either of the foregoing paragraphs:

satisfies all liabilities under the lease or grant which may have accrued, or been claimed, up to the date of the conveyance hereinafter mentioned, and where necessary, sets apart a sufficient fund to answer any future claim that may be made in respect of any fixed and ascertained sum which the lessee or grantee agreed to lay out on the property demised or granted, although the period for laying out the same may not have arrived, then and in any such case the personal representative or trustee may convey the property demised or granted to a purchaser, legatee, devisee or other person entitled to call for a conveyance thereof and thereafter—

9–282   (i) he may distribute the residuary real and personal estate of the deceased testator or intestate, or, as the case may be, the trust estate (other than the fund, if any, set apart as aforesaid) to or amongst the persons entitled thereto, without appropriating any part, or any further part, as the case may be, of the estate of the deceased or of the trust estate to meet any future liability under the said lease or grant;

(ii) notwithstanding such distribution, he shall not be personally liable in respect of any subsequent claim under the said lease or grant.

(1A) Where a personal representative or trustee has as such entered into, or may as such[87] be required to enter into, an authorised guarantee agreement[88] with respect to any lease comprised in the estate of a deceased testator or intestate or a trust estate (and, in a case where he has entered into such an agreement, he has satisfied all liabilities under it which may have accrued and been claimed up to the date of distribution)—

(a) he may distribute the residuary real and personal estate of the deceased testator or intestate, or the trust estate, to or amongst the persons entitled thereto—

(i) without appropriating any part of the estate of the deceased, or the trust estate, to meet any future liability (or, as the case may be, any liability) under any such agreement, and

(ii) notwithstanding any potential liability of his to enter into any such agreement; and

(b) notwithstanding such distribution, he shall not be personally liable in respect of any subsequent claim (or as the case may be, any claim) under any such agreement.

9–283   (2) This section operates without prejudice to the right of the lessor or grantor, or the persons deriving title under the lessor or grantor, to follow the assets of the deceased or the trust property into the hands of the persons amongst whom the same may have been respectively distributed, and applies notwithstanding anything to the contrary in the will or other instrument, if any, creating the trust.

---

[87] See n. 86 *supra*.
[88] Defined in the Landlord and Tenant (Covenants) Act 1995.

(3) In this section "lease" includes an underlease and an agreement for a lease or underlease and any instrument giving any such indemnity as aforesaid or varying the liabilities under the lease; "grant" applies to a grant whether the rent is created by limitation, grant, reservation, or otherwise, and includes an agreement for a grant and any instrument giving any such indemnity as aforesaid or varying the liabilities under the grant; "lessee" and "grantee" include persons respectively deriving title under them.

Protection by means of advertisements

Section 27.[89]—(1) With a view to the conveyance to or distribution among the **9–284** persons entitled to any real or personal property, the trustees of a settlement, trustees of land,[90] trustees for sale of personal property or personal representatives, may give notice by advertisement in the Gazette, and in a newspaper circulating in the district in which the land is situated, and such other like notices, including notices elsewhere than in England and Wales, as would, in any special case, have been directed by a court of competent jurisdiction in an action for administration, of their intention to make such conveyance or distribution as aforesaid, and requiring any person interested[91] to send to the trustees or personal representatives within the time, not being less than two months, fixed in the notice or, where more than one notice is given, in the last of the notices, particulars of his claim in respect of the property or any part thereof to which the notice relates.

(2) At the expiration of the time fixed by the notice the trustees or personal **9–285** representatives may convey or distribute the property or any part thereof to which the notice relates, to or among the persons entitled thereto, having regard only to the claims, whether formal or not, of which the trustees or personal representatives then had notice[92] and shall not, as respects the property so conveyed or distributed, be liable to any person of whose claim the trustees or personal representatives have not had notice[93] at the time of conveyance or distribution; but nothing in this section—

(a) prejudices the right of any person to follow the property, or any property representing the same, into the hands of any person, other than a purchaser, who may have received it; or

(b) frees the trustees or personal representatives from any obligation to make searches or obtain official certificates of search similar to those which an intending purchaser would be advised to make or obtain.

(3) This section applies notwithstanding anything to the contrary in the will or other instrument, if any, creating the trust.

---

[89] For the form which the advertisement should take, see *Re Aldhous* [1955] 1 W.L.R. 459.

[90] "Trustees of land" extends to a trust comprising partly land and partly personalty under the Trusts of Land and Appointment of Trustees Act 1996.

[91] Protection is afforded against belated claims of creditors, next of kin or beneficiaries under a will: *Re Aldhous* [1955] 1 W.L.R. 459 at 462.

[92] The Law Reform Committee (Cmnd. 873, para. 5.1) recommend that trustees should be empowered to write to any potential creditors, enclosing a copy of counsel's opinion, informing them they should make their claim within three months of receiving the opinion. If no claim is then made the trustees should be free to make the proposed distributions without liability, but without prejudice to the creditor's right to follow the trust assets.

[93] In view of s.27(2)(b) this may well cover constructive notice as well as actual notice. See also Law Com. No. 157 (Illegitimacy) 1986, para. 3.10, n. 22. If they have notice of a claim it cannot be ignored even if the claimant fails to respond to the advertisements: *Guardian Trust & Executor Co. of New Zealand v. Public Trustee* [1942] A.C. 115, 127.

Payment into court by trustees

9–286   **Section 63.**[94]—(1) Trustees, or the majority of trustees, having in their hands or under their control money or securities belonging to a trust, may pay the same into court; and the same shall, subject to rules of court, be dealt with according to the orders of the court.

(2) The receipt or certificate of the proper officer shall be a sufficient discharge to trustees for the money or securities so paid into court.

(3) Where money or securities are vested in any persons as trustees, and the majority are desirous of paying the same into court, but the concurrence of the other or others cannot be obtained, the court may order the payment into court to be made by the majority without the concurrence of the other or others.

(4) Where any such money or securities are deposited with any banker, broker, or other depositary, the court may order payment or delivery of the money or securities to the majority of the trustees for the purpose of payment into court.

(5) Every transfer payment and delivery made in pursuance of any such order shall be valid and take effect as if the same had been made on the authority by the act of all the persons entitled to the money and securities so transferred, paid, or delivered.

Miscellaneous statutory protection

9–287   Trustees and personal representatives have protection under the Adoption Act 1976, s.45 and the Legitimacy Act 1976, s.7, if they do not have notice of illegitimate or legitimated or adopted persons where the existence of such persons affects entitlement to the trust property. However, protection under section 27 of the Trustee Act may be sufficient.[95]

Judicial Protection Under Rules of Supreme Court, Order 85

Administration and Similar Actions

Interpretation (Ord. 85, r. 1).

1. In this Order "administration claim" means claim for the administration under the direction of the Court of the estate of a deceased person or for the execution under the direction of the Court of a trust.

Determination of questions, etc., without administration (Ord. 85, r. 2)

9–288   **2.**—(1) A claim may be issued for the determination of any question or for any remedy which could be determined or granted, as the case may be, in an administration claim and a claim need not be made in the action for the

---

[94] This section replaces s.42 of the Trustee Act 1893, which replaced s.1 and s.2 of the Trustees' Relief Act 1847. Unless trustees have reasonable cause, they may be made liable for the costs of paying funds into, and getting them out of, court. In case of doubt as to the claim, share or identity of a beneficiary the practice today is to submit the matter to the court for determination by way of Part 8 claim under Ord. 85, r.2 of the Rules of the Supreme Court. See A.J. Hawkins (1968) 84 L.Q.R. 65.
[95] See repeal of Family Law Reform Act 1969, s.17 by F.L.R.A. 1987, s.20 and comments of G. Miller [1988] Conv. 410 at 417–419.

administration or execution under the direction of the Court of the estate or trust in connection with which the question arises or the remedy is sought.

(2) Without prejudice to the generality of paragraph (1), an action may be brought for the determination of any of the following questions:

(a) any question arising in the administration of the estate of a deceased person or in the execution of a trust;

(b) any question as to the composition of any class of persons having a claim against the estate of a deceased person or a beneficial interest in the estate of such a person or in any property subject to a trust;

(c) any question as to the rights or interests of a person claiming to be a creditor of the estate of a deceased person or to be entitled under a will or on the intestacy of a deceased person or to be beneficially entitled under a trust.

(3) Without prejudice to the generality of paragraph (1), an action may be **9–289** brought for any of the following remedies:

(a) an order requiring an executor, administrator or trustee to furnish and, if necessary, verify accounts;

(b) an order requiring the payment into court of money held by a person in his capacity as executor, administrator or trustee;

(c) an order directing a person to do or abstain from doing a particular act in his capacity as executor, administrator or trustee;

(d) an order approving any sale, purchase, compromise or other transaction by a person in his capacity as executor, administrator or trustee;

(e) an order directing any act to be done in the administration of the estate of a deceased person or in the execution of a trust which the Court could order to be done if the estate or trust were being administered or executed, as the case may be, under the direction of the Court.

Parties

(3).—(1) All the executors or administrators of the estate or trustees of the **9–290** trust, as the case may be, to which an administration claim or such a claim as is referred to in rule 2 relates must be parties to the proceedings, and where the proceedings are made by executors, administrators or trustees, any of them who does not consent to being joined as a claimant must be made a defendant.

(2) Notwithstanding anything in CPR Rule 19.2 and without prejudice to the powers of the Court under that CPR Part, all the persons having a beneficial interest in or claim against the estate or having a beneficial interest under the trust, as the case may be, to which such a claim as is mentioned in paragraph (1) relates need not be parties to the proceedings; but the plaintiff may make such of those persons, whether all or any one or more of them, parties as, having regard to the nature of the remedy claimed in the proceedings, he thinks fit.

It is noteworthy that not only can order 85 be invoked to provide judicial guidance for the trustees as to the scope and obligations of a discretionary power,[96] but a particular discretion can be surrendered to the court for it to exercise if presented with adequate information[97] as appears from the case-note below of R.E. Megarry (later Megarry V-C).

R.E. MEGARRY (1966) 82 L.Q.R. 306

9–291   "The facts in *Re Allen-Meyrick's Will Trusts* ([1966] 1 W.L.R. 499; [1966] 1 All E.R. 740), were simple and elegant. A testratrix gave her residue to trustees in trust to apply the income thereof 'in their absolute discretion for the maintenance of my . . . husband,' and subject to the exercise of this discretion, she gave the residue in trust for her two godchildren equally. The trustees had made certain payments for the benefit of the husband, who was bankrupt, but had been unable to agree whether any further income should be so applied. In these circumstances the trustees sought to surrender their discretion to the court, and also sought to have it determined whether their discretion still existed in relation to past accumulations of income.

9–292   "It is well settled that trustees confronted by a particular problem may surrender their discretion to the court, and so be relieved both of the agony of decision and the responsibility for the result. But it is another matter where it is sought to surrender discretion which is not merely present and confined but prospective and indefinite. The Court of Chancery had a long history of administrative jurisdiction; but it exercised this jurisdiction not on its own investigations but on facts duly put before it in evidence by those concerned. It is not surprising, therefore, that Buckley, J. refused to accept the proffered general surrender of discretion. Whenever a specific problem arose upon specific facts, the aid of the court could be sought; but that was all. As regards past accumulations of income, the position was simple. The whole of the property, capital and income, belonged to the two godchildren except in so far as the trustees had effectually exercised their discretionary power to apply income to the husband. Trustees must, of course, be unanimous in exercising any powers vested in them, and so if within a reasonable time of receiving any income they had failed to exercise their discretion in favour of the husband, it ceased to be exercisable, and the godchildren became entitled to it. The principles are old, the facts new, and the result satisfactory."

It might be added that in cases where it is likely that there will be further disagreements necessitating expensive applications to the court it is best for the trustees to retire to allow the appointment of more compatible trustees.

Section 8. Judicial Control of Trustees

9–293   Wherever trustees have a discretion to exercise, the question arises as to the extent to which the court can control (including imposing sanctions in respect of) the exercise of the discretion at the behest of a complaining beneficiary. The discretion may be a distributive discretion (under a

---

[96] Including whether or not the proposed appointment of a reputable Foreign trustee would be a proper exercise of the trustees' powers: *Richard v. Mackay* (1997) 11 Trust L. I. 23; *Public Trustee v. Cooper* (Hart J, December 20, 1999) pointing out that this does not involve any surrender of discretionary powers.

[97] *Marley v. Mutual Security Merchant Bank & Trust Co* [1991] 3 All E.R. 198.

discretionary trust or a power of appointment or of maintenance or of advancement) or an administrative discretion (under a power of investment, for example). A purported appointment may be held void, compensation may need to be paid on surcharging or falsifying the accounts, trustees may be removed or declarations made as to the scope of trustees' duties.

Distributive discretions

Under a discretionary trust the trustees, of course, have a duty to exercise their discretion by distributing income (or, ultimately, capital) in some sort of amounts to some of the beneficiaries (unless, under a power to accumulate, they have decided to accumulate income). If the trustees neglect or refuse or are unable (till the outcome of a case), to discharge their duty, then the court will let them remedy this[98] or will positively have the settlor's intentions carried out "by appointing new trustees or by authorising or directing representative persons of the classes of beneficiaries to prepare a scheme for distribution, or even, should the proper basis for distribution appear, by itself directing the trustees so to distribute."[99]

In the case of distributive powers of appointment, advancement or **9–294** maintenance, the trustees have a duty to consider from time to time whether or not to exercise the power but they need not exercise the power.[1] Thus, if a power to distribute income to X instead of to trust beneficiaries is not exercised within a reasonable period (in default of an expressly specified period) the power lapses in respect of that income so that the income devolves on the trust beneficiaries entitled in default of a valid exercise of the power.[2]

If a trustee's attitude is that she is not going to bother about using any **9–295** powers to benefit a beneficiary, B, as B does not deserve any consideration, (*e.g.* because B married against her wishes) the court will intervene to remove the trustee or direct a payment that no trustee could refuse to make unless being spiteful or malicious: *Klug v. Klug*.[3] In that case legacy duty had to be paid by a beneficiary in four equal instalments but the beneficiary's income was insufficient to pay these instalments. Neville J. said,[4] "When the summons was previously before me, I decided that the trustees could in the exercise of their discretion under the powers of advancement, if they thought fit, advance out of capital a sum sufficient

---

[98] *Re Locker's S.T.* [1978] 1 All E.R. 216, *supra*, para. 3–64.
[99] *McPhail v. Doulton* [1971] A.C. 424, 451, A.J. Hawkins (1967) 31 Conv.(N.S.) 117.
[1] *Re Hay's S.T.* [1981] 3 All E.R. 786 at 792–793, *supra*, para. 3–150
[2] *Re Allen-Meyrick's W.T.* [1966] 1 W.L.R. 499.
[3] [1918] 2 Ch. 67. See *Re Lofthouse* (1885) 29 Ch.D. 921 (where trustees had refused to pay maintenance to a beneficiary under a discretionary power and Bacon V.-C. ordered £400 p.a. to be paid; on appeal his order was discharged without more ado since the trustees were agreeable to pay £250 p.a.) There was an interventionist attitude in some 19th century cases concerning powers to benefit a beneficiary, especially if the beneficiary was a ward of court: *Re Hodges* (1878) 7 Ch.D. 754, *Re Roper's Trusts* (1879) 11 Ch.D. 271.
[4] *ibid.* at 71.

to pay this legacy duty. The public trustee thinks that their discretion should be so exercised, but his co-trustee, the mother, declines to join him in so doing, not because she has considered whether or not it would be for her daughter's welfare, that the advance should be made, but because her daughter has married without her consent, and her letters show, in my opinion, that she has not exercised her discretion at all . . . In such circumstances, it is the duty of the court to interfere and to direct a sum to be raised out of capital sufficient to pay off . . . the legacy duty."

9–296   Exceptionally in the pensions fund context the courts[5] have also been prepared positively to exercise fiduciary powers in favour of beneficiaries where there is no one who can exercise the power, the employer-trustee being a company in liquidation and the liquidator being in the irreconcilable position of acting for the creditors interested in a non-exercise of the power to benefit the ordinary beneficiary-members of the pension scheme, while acting as trustee required to look after such members' interests. The court[6] acts in the manner in which a reasonable trustee could be expected to act in the light of all the material circumstances so as to do what is just and equitable.

9–297   One accepts this in the pensions context where the member-beneficiaries have earned their entitlements as deferred pay and have some justified expectations that powers to augment their entitlement out of surpluses will be seriously considered for exercising in certain circumstances. In the private family trust context however, where the trustees are in a position to exercise their powers in favour of persons who are not beneficiaries but only objects of a power of appointment but choose not to exercise them, having stated that they fairly considered exercising their powers but chose not to, then that should be the end of the matter, despite dicta of Warner J.[7] (not restricted expressly to the pensions context he was concerned with) that discretionary powers can be positively exercised by the court in any of the ways that discretionary trusts can be carried into effect by the court.

9–298   Once powers are consciously[8] exercised, then the court will not intervene[9] unless it can be shown that the particular purported exercise of the powers is unauthorised by the powers or that the trustees acted in bad faith, oppressively, corruptly or with improper motive or for reasons which can be said to be irrelevant to any sensible expectation of the

---

[5] *Mettoy Pension Trustees Ltd v. Evans* [1991] 2 All E.R. 513.
[6] *Thrells Ltd v. Lomas* [1993] 1 W.L.R. 456.
[7] *Mettoy Pension Trustees Ltd v. Evans* [1991] 2 All E.R. 513 at 549 citing Lord Wilberforce on discretionary trusts in *McPhail v. Doulton* [1971] A.C. 424 at 457 set out *supra* in para. 3–142.
[8] *Wilson v. Turner* (1883) 22 Ch.D. 521 (no conscious exercise of discretion so recipient liable to repay); *Turner v. Turner* [1983] 2 All E.R. 745 (deed of appointment void since trustees signed it at settlor's behest without understanding they had a discretion to exercise).
[9] *Re Beloved Wilkes' Charity* (1851) 3 Mac. & G. 440; *Re Charteris* [1917] 2 Ch. 379; *Re Steed's W.T.* [1960] Ch. 407; *Re Hastings-Bass* [1975] Ch. 25, at 41.

settlor[10] or if it can be shown under the *Hastings-Bass* principle[11] that they would not have acted as they did (a) had they not taken into account considerations which they should not have taken into account or (b) had they not failed to take into account considerations which they ought to have taken into account. For this principle to apply, however, it is not enough that it is shown that the trustees did not have a proper understanding of the effect of their act—it must also be clear that, had they had a proper understanding of it, they *would* not have acted as they did.[12] The sanction is to declare the purported exercise of the discretion void (or in a special case perhaps just to declare a particular provision in a deed of appointment void). Thus in *Stannard v. Fison Pension Trust Ltd*[13] the Court of Appeal invalidated the exercise of a discretion where due to an out-dated valuation of the trust assets the trustees had not been able to give fully informed consideration as to whether the amount of assets to be transferred from one pension fund to another should be calculated on the total service reserve method or the past service reserve method. **9–299**

Recently, judges[14] have introduced into private trust law the public law doctrine of *Wednesbury*[15] unreasonableness whereby a decision of a public body (that could otherwise not be impugned under private law principles) can be set aside if the court considers the decision to be one that no properly informed reasonable body could have reached, there being a legitimate expectation of persons capable of being affected by the decision that such a public body should not make a decision that no reasonable body could make. Thus, in *Edge v. Pensions Ombudsman*,[16] after holding that discretionary trustees of a pension trust were entitled honestly to favour some beneficiaries over others, Scott V-C stated, "The judge may disagree with the manner in which the trustees have exercised their discretion, but unless they can be seen to have taken into account irrelevant, improper or irrational factors, or unless their decision can be said to be one that no reasonable body of trustees properly directing themselves could have reached, the judge cannot interfere." **9–300**

---

[10] *Re Lofthouse* (1885) 29 Ch.D. 921 at 930; *Re Manisty's Settlement* [1973] 2 All E.R. 1203 at 1210; *Dwyer v. Ross* (1992) 34 F.L.R. 463. This is very difficult to prove especially if the trustees, as they are entitled to do, refuse to give any reasons for their acts: see *Re Londonderry's Settlement, supra,* p. 664 and comment of R.E.M. thereon (1965) 81 L.Q.R. 196. It would seem that trustees do not need to observe the rules of natural justice by allowing a beneficiary entitled in default of appointment to make representations to them before exercising their power of appointment: *Karger v. Paul* [1984] V.L.R. 161, 186; *Re B* [1987] 2 All E.R. 475 at 478.

[11] *Re Hastings-Bass* [1975] Ch. 25 at 41. Also see *Dundee General Hospital v. Walker* [1952] 1 All E.R. 896 at 905 and N. Parry [1989] Conv. 244.

[12] *Mettoy Pension Trustees Ltd v. Evans* [1991] 2 All E.R. 513 at 552–555; *Breadner v. Granville–Grossman* [2000] 4 All E.R. 705, 721, 732; *Green v. Cobham* [2000] W.T.L.R. 1101, 1109 (potentially disastrous capital gains tax consequences of deed of appointment of new trustees was overlooked, so deed ineffective). It ought not to suffice that the trustees *might* have acted differently, except, perhaps, in the pensions context, because this would make too many decisions of trustees susceptible to challenge: but see *AMP (U.K.) Ltd v. Baker* (2001) 3 I.T.E.L.R. 414.

[13] [1992] 1 I.R.L.R. 27.

[14] *Harris v. Lord Shuttleworth* [1995] O.P.L.R. 79, 86–87; *Wild v. Pensions Ombudsman* [1996] O.P.L.R. 129, 135; *Edge v. Pensions Ombudsman* [1998] Ch. 512, 534, 536 affd [2000] Ch.602, 628–630.

[15] *Associated Provincial Picture House v. Wednesbury Corp.* [1948] 1 K.B. 223.

[16] [1998] Ch 512, 534. The Court of Appeal rejected the appellant's criticisms of the approach of Scott V-C but considered it unnecessary to examine how far to press the analogy with *Wednesbury* public law principles; [2000] Ch. 602, 628–630.

9–301   In public law, judicial review principles require the public body to afford the claimants an opportunity to make their case so that both sides' arguments can be fully considered. In trust law, trustees are only under a duty to ensure they have adequate factual and/or legal background information to enable them to reach an informed decision[17]: they do not, for example, need to give a fair hearing to objects of a power of appointment and those beneficiaries entitled in default of exercise of the power.[18] Once in possession of such information they cannot exercise their discretions in a way that is capricious, irrational or perverse to any sensible expectation of the settlor.[19] In the light of such traditional terminology that creates rights under private trust law there is surely no need by analogy with public law to hold that trustees cannot exercise their discretions in a way that no reasonable body of trustees would have done. After all, is it not perverse to any sensible expectation of the settlor to permit trustees to make a decision that no adequately informed reasonable body of trustees could possibly have made?

9–302   Robert Walker J opined in *Scott v. National Trust*[20] that "legitimate expectation may have some part to play in trust law as well as in judicial review" when indicating that, if trustees had paid £1,000 a quarter to an elderly impoverished beneficiary for the last ten years, the latter has a legitimate expectation that no reasonable body of trustees would discontinue the payment without any warning and without giving her the opportunity of trying to persuade the trustees to continue the payment, at least temporarily. Under the traditional approach it would surely be perverse to any sensible expectation of the settlor for the trustees to dispense or withhold his bounty in such arbitrary fashion. Specialist trust-law judges surely have enough techniques at their disposal for controlling trustees without introducing some public law considerations which could mislead non-specialist judges into wrongfully introducing other public law notions, *e.g.* so that all 70 discretionary beneficiaries or objects of powers of appointment have to be sent a standardised grant application form to fill in.

9–303   One must also consider the doctrine of a fraud on a power[21] if the donee of a fidiciary or personal special power of appointment (*e.g.* A, where there is a trust for A for life then to such of his children as he shall appoint and in default of appointment for his children equally) exercises it other than bona fide for the purpose for which it was given him, *e.g.* if he exercises it for a corrupt or foreign purpose or pursuant to

---

[17] *R v. Charity Commissioners ex p. Baldwin* [2001] W.T.L.R. 137, 148–151. In the pensions context, however, of earned rights where the trustees have to form an opinion (*e.g.* as to whether the claimant is disabled or could be "able" but for an unreasonable refusal to submit to treatment) trustees may need to take more steps to be properly informed so that a proper decision can be made, and a breach of duty may be inferred if the decision is one which no reasonable trustee could make on the material before it: *Telstra Super Pty. Ltd. v. Flegeltaub* [2000] Victoria S.C.A. 180.

[18] *Re B* [1987] 2 All E.R. 475, 478; *Scott v. National Trust* [1998] 2 All E.R. 705, 718.

[19] *Re Manisty's settlement* [1974] Ch 17.

[20] [1998] 2 All E.R. 705, 718.

[21] G. Thomas, *Powers* (1999) pp. 453 *et seq.*; Hardingham & Baxt, *Discretionary Trusts* (2nd ed.), pp. 102–110, Maclean; *Trusts and Powers*, pp. 85–126.

a bargain to benefit non-objects of the power. The doctrine in modern times has become particularly relevant where for fiscal reasons the life tenant donee of the power has wished to appoint capital to certain adult (or infant) beneficiaries in order that the trust property can then be divided up between them. The strict view is laid down in *Re Brook's Settlement*[22]: "an appointment made partly for the purpose of enabling part of the capital of the appointed fund, however small, to be put in the pocket of the appointor is a fraud on the power." However, certain judges[23] have taken a more liberal line in answering the question of fact "was the appointment made for the ulterior purpose, or partly for the ulterior purpose, of enabling a division of the trust fund?" If a fraud on the power is involved then the appointment is void but the appointor can still make a fresh appointment.[24] Purchasers from appointees to whom "fraudulent" appointments have been made have a limited amount of protection under section 157 of the Law of Property Act 1925.

The doctrine of fraud on a power does not apply to releases of powers **9–304** as they simply benefit those entitled in default of appointment, who have all along had the property vested in them subject only to divestment upon an exercise of the power. Thus in *Re Somes*[25] where a father had a power of appointment in favour of a daughter or her issue, the daughter also being entitled in default of appointment, the father was able to release his power so that his daughter could mortgage the property to secure a sum of £10,000 to be paid to the father for his own purposes.[26]

It should be noted that whilst powers[27] given to individuals in their private capacity can be released (or exercised spitefully), powers given to trustees as fiduciaries cannot be released[28] (except under an express authority in the trust instrument or under the Variation of Trusts Act 1958) though the beneficiaries can validly release the trustees from their duties towards them, *e.g.* so as even to cease to be objects of a discretionary trust: *Re Gulbenkian's Trusts (No. 2)*.[29]

Management discretions

Questions concerning the exercise of trustees' managerial discretions **9–305** often arise in the investment sphere. Here it has been seen[30] that trustees are *inter alia* under a duty to act fairly as between beneficiaries interested

---

[22] [1968] 1 W.L.R. 1661, *infra*, para. 9–321; *Re Esteem Settlement* [2001] W.T.L.R. 641.
[23] *e.g.* Megarry J. in *Re Wallace's Settlements* [1968] 1 W.L.R. 711. See also S. M. Cretney (1969) 32 M.L.R. 317, J. G. Monroe [1968] B.T.R. 424.
[24] *Topham v. Duke of Portland* (1869) 5 Ch.App. 40; *Re Chadwick's Trusts* [1939] 1 All E.R. 850.
[25] [1896] 1 Ch. 250.
[26] Similarly the doctrine of fraud on a power does not apply to the revocation of a revocable appointment even though the revoking appointor thereby intends to obtain a benefit: *Re Greaves* [1954] Ch. 434.
[27] Also note a life tenant is under no duty to consent to an advancement to a remainderman.
[28] This is basically the position but the borderlines are difficult to draw though an attempt was made in *Re Wills' Trust Deeds* [1964] Ch. 219. See A. J. Hawkins (1968) 84 L.Q.R. 64.
[29] [1970] Ch. 408.
[30] See *supra*, paras 9–75 *et seq*. To protect himself a trustee may surrender his discretion to the court upon putting all relevant information before it: *Marley v. Mutual Security Merchant Bank* [1991] 3 All E.R. 198.

in income and beneficiaries interested in capital and to exhibit the statutory standard of care that a prudent man of business would take in conducting another's affairs.

In *Tempest v. Lord Camoys, infra*, para. 9–316, the trustees on selling real estate had to purchase real estate "in their absolute discretion." One trustee wanted to purchase particular real estate for £60,000 with £30,000 borrowed on mortgage pursuant to the trustees' power to raise money by mortgage "at their absolute discretion." The other trustee refused to concur in the purchase, considering it not to be a prudent exercise of the power. The Court of Appeal held that it could not interfere with the dissenting trustee's discretion. Jessel M.R. pointed out that all the court will do is prevent the trustees from exercising their power "improperly."

9–306 As Slade L.J. subsequently said,[31] "In other words the court was of opinion that even a power expressed in terms that it should be exercisable at the trustees' absolute discretion was subject to the implicit restriction that it should be exercised properly within the limits of the general law."

Because trustees must act unanimously[32] (unless charitable trustees or pension trustees or otherwise provided by the trust instrument) any trustee with some fairly slight basis for doubt about the proposed exercise of a discretion can prevent such an exercise. A beneficiary can obtain an injunction against a proposed exercise of an investment discretion only if such exercise is plainly improper or not in accordance with the trustees' duty of safe investment. If the beneficiary does not find out about an improper or unsafe investment until after the event, then his remedy will be to have the investment sold and to make the trustees liable to account for any losses[33] that arise.

9–307 Exceptionally, where the trustees are trustees of land then the court has a vast positive discretion under sections 14 and 15 of the Trusts of Land and Appointment of Trustees Act 1996 to make such order as it thinks fit, though, except in favour of creditors, it will not enforce a sale if so to do would defeat the spirit or purpose of the trust.[34]

Exemption clauses

It should first be noted that the jurisdiction of the court as to pure matters of law cannot be ousted by provisions in the trust instrument giving the trustees power to determine all questions arising in the execution of the trusts under the instrument.[35] However, the decision of trustees or of a third party can be binding and conclusive on matters of

---

[31] *Bishop v. Bonham* [1988] 1 W.L.R. 742 at 751–752; also see *Elder's Trustee and Executor Co. Ltd v. Higgins* (1965) 113 C.L.R. 426 at 448.

[32] *Luke v. South Kensington Hotel Ltd* (1879) 11 Ch.D. 121. *supra*, p. 568.

[33] For difficulties in establishing that (i) losses flowed from (ii) a breach of duty see *Nestlé v. National Westminster Bank* [1993] 1 W.L.R. 1290 and *Wight v. Olswang* (No. 2) [2001] W.T.L.R. 291.

[34] *The Law of Real Property*. This is generally treated as a land law topic so see Megarry & Wade (6th ed.), pp. 510–517. In bankruptcy cases see the Insolvency Act 1986, s.335A.

[35] *Re Wynn* [1952] Ch. 271.

fact, assuming that the specified factual circumstances are conceptually certain,[36] while the decision of someone with expert knowledge in the relevant factual area can even conclusively determine an incidental question of construction.[37]

If trustees prove that the settlor knew of, and approved, a clause in the trust instrument exempting the trustees from liability for the complained of breach of trust upon a restrictive construction of the clause,[38] then the trustees escape liability for such breach unless it was a dishonest or reckless breach of trust. This was held by the Court of Appeal in *Armitage v. Nurse*[39] in giving effect to a clause protecting the trustee from liability "unless such loss or damage shall be caused by his own actual fraud." "Fraud" was held simply to mean dishonesty which[40] "connotes at the minimum an intention on the part of the trustee to pursue a particular course of action, either knowing that it is contrary to the interests of the beneficiaries or being recklessly indifferent whether it is contrary to their interests or not."

Thus, it is permissible for an exemption clause to exempt a trustee **9–308** from liability for gross negligence as well as ordinary negligence. The Court of Appeal, unfortunately, did not have bailment cases[41] cited to it, so it erroneously assumed that in English law no distinction could be made between ordinary and gross negligence. It therefore erroneously assumed that exemption from all varieties of negligence either had to be accepted or outlawed, while in modern conditions one could not possibly hold that exemption from liability for ordinary negligence was contrary to public policy or repugnant to the trust concept. Scope therefore remains to challenge the view of the Court of Appeal and try to establish that exemption clauses (as in Scotland[42]) cannot extend to protect trustees from liability for gross negligence.

Further uncertainty exists where trustees consciously act beyond their **9–309** powers (*e.g.* making an investment which they know to be unauthorised, like buying a villa in Lanzarote) so deliberately committing a breach of trust, but do so in good faith and in the honest belief that they are acting in the best interests of the beneficiaries as a whole. Lord Nicholls[43] considered this to be fraudulent because the trustees are taking a risk to the prejudice of another's rights, which risk is known to be one which there is no right to take. Millett L.J.[44] (as he then was) considered this not to be fraudulent, perhaps assuming that if the trustees honestly think there is a risk which they ought to take, then they can justifiably believe

---

[36] *Re Coxen* [1948] Ch. 747; *Re Jones* [1953] Ch. 125; *Re Wright's W.T.* [1981] Law.S. Gaz 841.
[37] *The Glazier* (1996) 1 Ll. Rep. 370; *Re Tuck's S.T.* [1978] Ch.49; *Dundee General Hospitals Board v. Walker* [1952] 1 All E.R. 896.
[38] *Wight v. Olswang* (1998/99) 1 I.T.E.L.R. 783.
[39] [1998] Ch. 241.
[40] *ibid*, 251.
[41] *Gibbon v. McMullen* (1865) L.R. 2 P.C. 317; *Beal v. Smith Devon Rly. Co* (1864) 3 H 8 C 332: gratuitous bailees are liable for gross negligence only.
[42] *Lutea Trustees Ltd v. Orbis Trustees* [1997] S.C.L.R. 735, [1998] S.L.T. 471.
[43] *Royal Brunei Airlines v. Tan* [1995] 2 A.C. 378, 390.
[44] *Armitage v. Nurse* [1998] Ch. 241, 252.

they have a right to take it, although he accepted that[45] "a trustee who relied on the presence of an exemption clause to justify what he proposed to do would thereby lose its protection: he would be acting recklessly in the proper sense of the term."

The retired Slade L.J., faced with these two approaches, in *Walker v. Stones*[46] ducked the issue, holding that if the trustee, deliberately committing a breach of trust and taking a risk honestly believing it to be in the interests of the beneficiaries, is a solicitor, then he cannot rely on a clause exempting him from liability unless fraudulent if no reasonable solicitor-trustee could have held such belief.

9–310   Trustees will be well-advised to accept Lord Nicholl's view and not to commit a deliberate breach of trust in the belief it will be profitable or, if not, will be covered by a wide exemption clause. They should not proceed except with extended powers conferred by the court[47] or, perhaps, if they have sufficient beneficiaries of full capacity to provide them with an indemnity backed with some security.

A trustee who is a solicitor who inserts a clause into the settlor's trust instrument to exempt himself from liability for breaches of trust unless fraudulent, will also be well-advised if he tells the settlor to seek independent legal advice. After all, such solicitor-prospective trustee is in a fiduciary relationship with the settlor, so that one would expect that he would be disabled from relying on such a broad clause unless independent legal advice was suggested.[48] Somewhat surprisingly, however, the Court of Appeal[49] has held that the solicitor—prospective executor and trustee, who drafted the testamentary trusts, did not have to prove he had advised the testator to take independent legal advice, so long as it was proved the testator knew and approved the will—which must be the case where probate of the will had been granted.

Millett L.J. stated:

9–311   "The fundamental fallacy in the [plaintiffs'] argument is that clause 12 does not confer a benefit on the persons responsible for advising the testator on the contents of the will. In the first place, it does not discriminate between the persons who advised the testator in connection with his will and other persons who become executors or trustees and who have had no part in the preparation of his will. In the second place, it does not confer a benefit on the executors and trustees but defines the extent of the potential liabilities. Unlike a trustee charging clause, it does not enable the executors and trustees to profit from their position, but it protects them from loss thereby. The inclusion of the clause does not, therefore, conflict with the rule that, in the absence of clear words, a trustee may not profit form his trust."

With respect, is there not much to be said for the view that the solicitor-executor-trustee did profit from being unjustly enriched at the

---

[45] *ibid.*, 254.
[46] [2000] W.T.L.R. 975, [2000] 4 All E.R. 412.
[47] Under Trustee Act 1925, s.57.
[48] *Rutanen v. Ballard* 1997 424 Mass. 723, 733; *Baskerville v. Thurgood* [1992] Sask. LR. 214.
[49] *Bogg v. Raper* (1998)/99) 1 I.T.E.L.R. 267 at 285 for the cited passage in the text.

expense of the beneficiaries?[50] Did he not profit from saving the insurance premiums otherwise needed to protect against liability for losses? Did he not profit from being saved from liability to pay the beneficiaries the £8 million losses flowing from his alleged gross and ordinary negligence? Should he not have been under a fiduciary duty to advise the testator to obtain independent legal advice; and should breach of such duty not have prevented him from relying on the clause?

So far, it has been the basic type of exemption clause that has been **9–312** considered, namely a clause exempting from liability for a breach of duty. However, a clause may oust any duty in the first place so that there can then be no breach of duty.

In *Hayim v. Citibank*,[51] for example, Citibank was appointed executor of the testator's American will on terms that the executor "shall have no responsibility or duty with respect to" a Hong Kong house until the deaths of the testator's very elderly brother and sister who resided in the house. This house was given by a Hong Kong will to another executor on trust for Citibank as executor of the American will. Citibank declined to take steps to have the house sold for the benefit of the beneficiaries under the American will who wanted the house to be sold and the siblings to be evicted from it. Substantial losses flowed from the delayed sale of the house. The Privy Council held the clause was "understandable and explicable". To avoid death duties (payable if the siblings had interests in possession in the house) and to avoid placing them at the mercy of the beneficiaries, the clause enabled Citibank to permit the siblings to remain living in the house without Citibank owing any duties to the beneficiaries (other than to account to them if Citibank used the house for its own purposes).

It is also not uncommon to see clauses that oust the trustee's duty to **9–313** diversify investments, *e.g.* where 90 per cent of the value of the trust fund is in the controlling shareholding of a company transferred by the settlor to the trustees. The statutory duty of care when investing can also be excluded. Thus, a big lottery winner might settle £2 million on trustees to speculate with it as if they were the absolute beneficial owners of it and could afford to lose all of it without it affecting their standard of living in any way.

Of course, all the duties of trustees cannot be ousted or the trustees would either be nominee-resulting trustees for the settlor or themselves be absolute beneficial owners. The trustees must be left under a duty to perform the trust honestly and in good faith for the benefit of beneficiaries having a correlative right to make the trustees account for performance of their duty.[52]

While it seems the Unfair Contract Terms Act 1977 does not apply to trustees entitled to their remuneration as a beneficial incident of their

---

[50] The saving of expense is a benefit or profit: *Peel v. Canada* (1992)98 D.L.R. (4th) 140, *Peter v. Beblow* (1993) 101 D.L.R. 621, 645.
[51] [1987] A.C. 730.
[52] *Armitage v. Nurse* [1998] Ch. 241.

burdensome office,[53] some other statutes apply to particular types of trust to outlaw exemption clauses in the public interest.

9–314   Section 192 of the Companies Act 1985 specifically intervenes where there is a trust deed for securing an issue of debentures. In such a deed a borrower, which is a company, charges some of its property by way of fixed or floating charges in favour of the trustees as security for money lent. The trustees hold these secured rights on trust for the debenture holders who hold debenture stock in proportion to the amounts provided by them by way of loan. This device is very useful for raising a large sum of money from a large number of people. The deed states when the security will become enforceable and confers much discretion on the trustees subject to varying degrees of control by the debenture holders. Any provision in the deed is void under section 192 "in so far as it would have the effect of exempting a trustee of the deed from, or indemnifying him against, liability for breach of trust where he fails to show the degree of care and diligence required of him as trustee, having regard to the provisions of the trust deed conferring on him any powers, authorities or discretions." Section 192(2) makes it clear that subsection (1) does not

9–315   invalidate any release given to a trustee for things done or undone under a power for a three-quarters majority of debenture holders to give such a release.[54] For authorised unit trusts section 84 of the Financial Services Act 1986 makes any provision void so far as it would have the effect of exempting the manager or trustee from liability for failing to exercise due care and diligence. For pension trusts section 34 of the Pensions Act 1995 prohibits exclusion or restriction of liability for breach of an obligation under any rule of law to take care or exercise skill in the performance of any investment functions.

The Law Commission, building upon work of the Trust Law Committee Consultation Paper, "Trustee Exemption Clauses,[55] is now examining the general position of trustees. There seems little reason to allow professional trustees, whether corporate or individual, in selling their skilled services to exempt themselves from liability for grossly negligent breaches of trust or even ordinarily negligent breaches.

TEMPEST v. LORD CAMOYS[56]

Court of Appeal (1882) 21 Ch.D. 571; 51 L.J.Ch. 785; 48 L.T. 13; (Jessel M.R., Brett and Cotton L.JJ.)

9–316   The headnote summarises the facts as follows: "A testator gave his trustees a power to be exercised at their absolute discretion of selling real estates, with a declaration that the proceeds should be applied, at the like discretion, in the

---

[53] W. Goodhart (1996) 10 Trust L.I. 38, 43 (changing his mind from [1980] Conv. 333) based on *Re Duke of Norfolk's S.T.* [1982] Ch 61.

[54] For the relationship between s.192 and Table A article 85 see *Movitex Ltd v. Bulfield* [1988] B.C.L.C. 104.

[55] Trust Law Committee Report and Consultation Papers, June 1999, Butterworths Tolley, ISBN 0 75450 453–0.

[56] See also *Gisbome v. Gisbome* (1877) 2 App.Cas. 300; *Camden v. Murray* (1880) 16 Ch.D. 161 at 170; *Re Blake* (1885) 29 Ch.D. 913 at 917; *Re Courtier* (1886) 34 Ch.D. 136; *Re Horsnaill* [1909] 1 Ch. 631; *Re Kipping* [1914] 1 Ch. 62; *Re Charteris* [1917] 2 Ch. 379 at 391.

purchase of other real estates. He also gave them power at their absolute discretion to raise money by mortgage for the purchase of real estates. A suit having been instituted for the execution of the trusts of the will, and a sum of money, the proceeds of the sale of real estate, having been paid into court, one of the trustees proposed to purchase a large estate and to apply the fund in court in part-payment of the purchase-money, and to raise the remainder of the purchase-money by mortgage of the purchased estate. The other trustee refused to concur in the purchase."

Some of the beneficiaries being in favour of the proposal, a petition was presented for the purpose of having the purchase carried out. It was contended that it was desirable to purchase at a moderate price—£60,000, there being some £30,000 in court—an estate which had previously been in the family for a long while. The dissentient trustee, Mr. Fleming, objected that the transaction would not be a prudent exercise of the power. Chitty J. held, in accordance with *Gisborne v. Gisborne*,[57] that the court had no power to interfere with Mr. Fleming's bona fide exercise of his discretion. The petitioners appealed.

JESSEL M.R.: "It is very important that the law of the court on this subject **9–317** should be understood. It is settled law that when a testator has given a pure discretion to trustees as to the exercise of a power, the court does not enforce the exercise of a power against the wish of the trustees, but it does prevent them from exercising it improperly. The court says that the power, if exercised at all, is to be properly exercised. This may be illustrated by the case of persons having a power of appointing new trustees. Even after a decree in a suit for administering the trusts has been made they may still exercise the power, but the court will see that they do not appoint improper persons.

"But in all cases where there is a trust or duty coupled with the power the court will then compel the trustees to carry it out in a proper manner and within a reasonable time. In the present case there was a power which amounts to a trust to invest the fund in question in the purchase of land. The trustees would not be allowed by the court to disregard that trust, and if Mr. Fleming had refused to invest the money in land at all the court would have found no difficulty in interfering. But that is a very different thing from saying that the court ought to take from the trustees their uncontrolled discretion as to the particular time for the investment and the particular property which should be purchased. In this particular case it appears to me that the testator in his will has carefully distinguished between what is to be at the discretion of his trustees and what is obligatory on them.

"There is another difficulty in this case. The estate proposed to be purchased **9–318** will cost £60,000, and only £30,000 is available for the purchase, and the trustees will have to borrow the remaining £30,000. There is power to raise money by mortgage at the absolute discretion of the trustees, and assuming that such a transaction as this is within the power, and that the trustees can mortgage the estate before they have actually bought it, there is no trust to mortgage, it is purely discretionary. The court cannot force Mr. Fleming to take the view that it is proper to mortgage the estate in this way; he may well have a different opinion from the other trustee. Here again the court cannot interfere with his discretion. The appeal must therefore be dismissed." *Appeal dismissed.*

---

[57] (1877) 2 App.Cas. 300.

RE BELOVED WILKES'S CHARITY[58]

Lord Chancellor (1851) 3 Mac. & G. 440

9–319   Charitable trustees had to select a boy to be educated at Oxford for the Anglican ministry, preference to be given to boys from four named parishes if in the trustees' judgment a fit and proper candidate therefrom could be found. Without giving any reasons, but stating that they had acted impartially, the trustees selected Charles Joyce who did not come from the named parishes but who had a brother who was a minister who had put forward Charles's merits to the trustees. The court was asked to set aside the selection, and to select William Gale, whose father was a respectable farmer residing in one of the specified parishes.

Held. In the absence of evidence that the trustees had exercised their discretion unfairly or dishonestly, the court would not interfere.

9–320   LORD TRURO L.C.: "The question, therefore, is, whether it was the duty of the trustees to enter into particulars, or whether the law is not, that trustees who are appointed to execute a trust according to discretion, that discretion to be influenced by a variety of circumstances (as, in this instance, by those particular circumstances which should be connected with the fitness of a lad to be brought up as a minister of the Church of England), are not bound to go into a detail of the grounds upon which they come to their conclusion, their duty being satisfied by shewing that they have considered the circumstances of the case, and have come to their conclusion accordingly. Without occupying time by going into a lengthened examination of the decisions, the result of them appears to me so clear and reasonable, that it will be sufficient to state my conclusion in point of law to be, that in such cases as I have mentioned it is to the discretion of the trustees that the execution of the trust is confided, that discretion being exercised with an entire absence of indirect motive, with honesty of intention, and with a fair consideration of the subject. The duty of supervision on the part of this Court will thus be confined to the question of the honesty, integrity, and fairness with which the deliberation has been conducted, and will not be extended to the accuracy of the conclusion arrived at, except in particular cases. If, however, as stated by Lord Ellenborough in *The King v. The Archbishop of Canterbury* ((1812) 15 East 117), trustees think fit to state a reason, and the reason is one which does not justify their conclusion, then the Court may say that they have acted by mistake and in error, and that it will correct their decision; but if, without entering into details, they simply state, as in many cases it would be most prudent and judicious for them to do, that they have met and considered and come to a conclusion, the court has then no means of saying that they have failed in their duty, or to consider the accuracy of their conclusion.[59] It seems, therefore, to me, that having in the present case to look to the motives of the trustees as developed in the affidavits, no ground exists for imputing bad motives. The Petitioners, indeed, candidly state, on the face of their petition, that they do not impute such motives, they merely charge the trustees with a miscarriage as regards the duty which they had to perform. I cannot, therefore, deal with the case as if the petition had contained a statement of a different kind, and if I

---

[58] Applied in *Wilson v. Law Debenture Trust Corp.* [1995] 2 All E.R. 337 at 343.
[59] See *Re Londondeny's Settlement* [1965] Ch. 918, *supra*, para. 9–221.

could, still I should say, having read the affidavits, that I see nothing whatever which can lay the foundation for any judicial conclusion that the trustees intentionally and from bad motives failed in their duty, if they failed at all."

RE BROOK'S SETTLEMENT

Chancery Division [1968] 1 W.L.R. 1661; [1968] 3 All E.R. 416

STAMP J. read the following judgment: "By the originating summons which was **9–321** issued under the Variation of Trusts Act, 1958, on February 28, 1968, the plaintiff asks that the court may approve on behalf of the infant defendant, Ann Brook, and on behalf of all persons who may become interested under the discretionary trust to arise in the event of a forfeiture of the plaintiff's life interest, a variation of the trust of the settlement affecting the fund constituting the plaintiff's share. By the effect of the proposed variation a part of the fund would be held on trust for the plaintiff absolutely, the *quid pro quo* being in effect the release of the remainder of the fund from the protected life interest of the plaintiff and the consequent acceleration of the interests of those entitled in reversion expectant on the determination of that protected life interest.

"The proposed variation, however, and this is the point at which the difficulty **9–322** arises, proceeds on the footing that the two existing children are alone entitled to a share in the capital of the fund and the part of the fund which is to be freed from the protected life interest of the plaintiff is, under the proposed variation, to be held on trust, in effect, for them to the exclusion of after-born children. The court is not asked to approve the variation on behalf of after-born children. Plainly this would not do because even if the court could properly have approved the variation on the ground that it was for the benefit of Miss Ann Brook, the interest of after-born children would not be bound and the trustees could not have given effect to the variation. Nor could this court have bound the interest of after-born children because as the proposed variation stood, and still stands, they are to take nothing. When the plaintiff's counsel considered the matter a few days before the hearing he, of course, appreciated the difficulty; and in reliance, perhaps, on a recent decision of this court in *Re Wallace's Settlements*[60] an appointment was executed by the plaintiff of the whole of the plaintiff's share in favour of his two existing children. The question then arises was this appointment an effective appointment or was it a fraud on the power of appointment? This is a question which must be decided because, until it is decided, the trustees of the settlement will not know to whom the fund belongs; and counsel for the trustees in accordance with his duty on behalf of the trustees, was bound to argue, as he did, that the appointment was a fraud on the power.

"I observe first that the question whether an appointment is made for the **9–323** ulterior purpose, or partly for the ulterior purpose, of enabling a division of a trust fund or without any such ulterior purpose is one of fact; secondly, that the protestation that the appointor had no such ulterior purpose but that the appointment was a separate and independent transaction made irrespective of the scheme of division, is more easily acceptable if the apparent ulterior purpose—here a division of the trust fund under which the appointor takes part—could from the appointor's point of view have been better or equally well achieved had there been no appointment. In the present case counsel for the

---

[60] [1968] 1 W.L.R. 711.

infant defendant, found no difficulty in submitting that the division proposed is one which is for her benefit; but had there been no appointment it is at least less clear, because after-born children will not have the same advantage of accelera- tion, that the proposed division, under which the plaintiff is to have a half share of the fund, could have been supported as beneficial to any after-born child of the plaintiff. It appears, moreover, from what counsel told me, that in the course of the negotiations and discussions leading up to the formulation of the proposed variation it became apparent, as in my experience is very often the case, that the plaintiff wished to obtain as much as he could fairly do on the division and the fact that he might be able to receive less if there was no appointment was very present in the minds of his advisers.

9–324   "It was, however, submitted in reliance on *Re Wallace's Settlements*, that where you find that under the scheme for the division of the fund contemplated by the appointing tenant for life and the appointee, the tenant for life is to take no more than the equivalent of the market value of his life interest, there is no such benefit to the tenant for life as to render the appointment *ipso facto* a fraud on the power. It was for the purpose of considering the implications of this submission that I reserved my judgment.

9–325   "The facts in *Re Wallace's Settlements* were not quite the same as the facts of this case, but there is a clear finding in *Re Wallace's Settlements* that the appointments there in question were not fraudulent. The considerations which led Megarry J. to conclude that the extent to which the appointments there had become embrangled with the arrangements for the variation of the trusts had not tainted the appointments, were I think these: first, that as regards such advantages as there might be in the certainty and flexibility of capital as opposed to the limitations of an inalienable and defeasible life interest, the judge was satisfied that in relation to other material circumstances of life tenants there was no real advantage to either of them: secondly, that, on the facts of the cases there before him, the prospects of the life interests determining in the lifetime of either life tenant seemed to him to be negligible; and, thirdly, the excess of the actuarial value of the protected life interests, which was what each life tenant was to receive under the division, over the market value of the life interests, had those life interests not been protected, was negligible; so that the life tenants under the two settlements were receiving no more than the value to them of their life interests. In effect, therefore, Megarry J. took the view that the receipt by the life tenant of part of the capital of the appointed fund, if of no more value to him than the market value of his protected life interest if sold as an unprotected life interest, was not a benefit to the tenant for life, or at least not such a benefit as was referred to by Lord St. Leonards in *Duke of Portland v. Lady Topham*.[61] In so holding, the judge followed decisions of the Court of Session to which he referred and in which the Court of Session placed reliance on a late decision of Lord Romilly M.R., in *Re Huish's Charity*.[62]

9–326   "Consistently with *Portland v. Topham*[63] and *Vatcher v. Paull*,[64] *Re Wallace's Settlements* and the cases in the Court of Session which it followed, can in my judgment go no further than this: that if you find an appointment such as is here in question and, on the contemplated division of the fund, the appointor takes no more of the appointed fund than the value of his life interest, the appointment is

---

[61] (1864) 11 H.L.Cas. 32 at 55.
[62] (1870) L.R. 10 Eq. 5.
[63] (1864) 11 H.L.Cas. 32 at 55.
[64] [1915] A.C. 372.

not invalidated by the mere fact that it is made in contemplation of the division. It does not in my judgment, however follow that an appointment made by one entitled to a life interest not with an entire and single object of benefiting the appointee, but with a view also to having part of the capital of the appointed fund to spend, would be unobjectionable if the capital to be received was less than the market value of the life interest. The question must be one of fact. If my view of the earlier high authorities is correct and it is the purpose and the object of the appointment which is the test of its validity or invalidity, it must, I think, follow that, an appointment made partly for the purpose of enabling part of the capital of the appointed fund, however small, to be put in the pocket of the appointor is a fraud on the power: for if that be part of the motive for the appointment there is not the absence of an ulterior object necessary to support it. Nor do I find it easy to accept that, in an age when income tax and surtax rests so **9–327** heavily on the recipients of income, the advantage of having the capital equivalent of the value of a life interest is not a benefit, or may not prompt an appointment which would not otherwise be made thereby excluding other objects of the power and those entitled in default of appointment. If, however, one finds that just before the issue of the originating summons or, as in this case, just before its hearing, that an appointment has been made and that the court is being invited to approve on behalf of some person a variation of the trusts of a settlement under which part of the appointed fund is to be paid or transferred to the appointor, then in the absence of evidence that the appointment was a separate transaction or would have been made irrespective of the division, it may be—for I find nothing in *Re Wallace's Settlements* to suggest that this is not so— that the proper prima facie inference is that the appointment was not made "with the entire and single view' that the appointee should have the property. Suppose a fund be settled on A for life and after his death on trust for such of his three children in such shares as he shall appoint and in default of appointment on trust for those same named children in equal shares. Then suppose that the tenant for life partly in order to avoid estate duty, partly in order to put a capital sum into his own pocket and partly in order to benefit one of the three children, makes an appointment in favour of that child with a view to a division of the fund between himself and that child. I cannot doubt that in that case the appointment constitutes a fraudulent appointment as against the other two children who might have been willing to give him only a lesser price. Moreover in my view it would be none the less a fraudulent appointment if the amount received by the tenant for life was less than the amount which he could have obtained by selling his life interest on the market. I have come to the conclusion, however, in accordance with the recent authorities, that the mere fact that the tenant for life makes the appointment as part of a scheme for the division of the appointed fund does not *ipso facto* show that the appointment was made for an ulterior purpose not permitted by the instrument creating the power; at least in a case where the part of the appointed fund to be taken by the appointor is not more valuable than the life interest which the appointor gives up. If that were the position here I would, but subject to the caution at the end of this judgment, hold that the appointment which I have to consider was not a fraud on the power and make the order asked for.

"The facts of this case are, however, in my judgment clearly distinguishable **9–328** from the facts in *Re Wallace's Settlements* and the cases on which Megarry J. rested his judgment in that case: for here, first, the known effect of the appointment was to produce, by defeating the interests of future children, a state of affairs under which the court might be expected to approve a division more favourable to the tenant for life than would have been the case if the division had had to be shown to be for the benefit of the after-born children: and secondly, because of the fact that the tenant for life here was anxious to obtain all he could on the division. As counsel for the trustees pointed out, prima facie an appointment should be treated as made for the object which it achieved and I am constrained to hold that one of the objects of this appointment was to obtain a benefit for the appointor which he might not otherwise have had, and was a fraud on the power."

ARMITAGE v. NURSE

Court of Appeal [1998] Ch. 241 [1997] 3 W.L.R. 1048 [1997] 2 All E.R. 705
(Hirst, Millett and Hutchison L. JJ.)

9–329   Under clause 15 of the settlement, "No Trustee shall be liable for any loss or damage which may happen . . . from any cause whatsoever unless such loss or damage shall be caused by his own actual fraud." As a matter of construction, the court first held "clause 15 exempts the trustee from liability for loss or damage to the trust property no matter how indolent, imprudent, lacking in diligence, negligent or wilful he may have been, so long as he has not acted dishonestly."

MILLETT L.J. (with whom Hirst and Hutchison L.JJ. concurred)

"The permitted scope of trustee exemption clauses

9–330   It is submitted on behalf of Paula that a trustee exemption clause which purports to exclude all liability except for actual fraud is void, either for repugnancy or as contrary to public policy. There is some academic support for the submission (notably an article by Professor Matthews. "The Efficacy of Trustee Exemption Clauses in English Law" [1989] Conv 42 and *Hanbury and Martin's Modern Equity* (14th edn, 1993) pp 473–474) that liability for gross negligence cannot be excluded, but this is not the view taken in *Underhill and Hayton's Law of Trusts and Trustees* (15th edn, 1995) pp 560–561 (where it appears to be taken only because the editor confusingly uses the term "gross negligence" to mean reckless indifference to the interests of the beneficiaries). In its consultation paper *Fiduciary Duties and Regulatory Rules, A Summary* (Law Com No 124) (1992) para 3.3.41 the Law Commission states:

> "Beyond this, trustees and fiduciaries cannot exempt themselves from liability for fraud, bad faith and wilful default. It is not, however, clear whether the prohibition on exclusion of liability for "fraud" in this context only prohibits the exclusion of common law fraud or extends to the much broader doctrine of equitable fraud. It is also not altogether clear whether the prohibition on the exclusion of liability for "wilful default" also prohibits exclusion of liability for gross negligence although we incline to the view that it does."

9–331   This passage calls for two comments. First, the expression "wilful default" is used in the cases in two senses. A trustee is said to be accountable on the footing of wilful default when he is accountable not only for money which he has in fact received but also for money which he could with reasonable diligence have received. It is sufficient that the trustee has been guilty of a want of ordinary prudence (see *e.g. Re Chapman, Cocks v. Chapman* [1896] 2 Ch. 763). In the context of a trustee exclusion clause, however, such as s.30 of the Trustee Act 1925, it means a deliberate breach of trust (*Re Vickery, Vickery v. Stephens* [1931] 1 Ch 572, The decision has been criticised, but it is in line with earlier authority (see *Lewis v. Great Western Rly Co* (1877) 3 Q.B.D. 195, *Re Trusts of Leeds City Brewery Ltd's Debenture Stock Trust Deed, Leeds City Brewery Ltd v. Platts* [1925] Ch 532 and *Re City Equitable Fire Insurance Co Ltd* [1925] Ch. 407. Nothing less than conscious and wilful misconduct is sufficient. The trustee must be—

> "conscious that, in doing the act which is complained of or in omitting to do the act which it said he ought to have done, he is committing a breach of his duty, or is recklessly careless whether it is a breach of his duty or not." (See *Re Vickery* [1931] 1 Ch 572 at 583 per Maugham J.)

A trustee who is guilty of such conduct either consciously takes a risk that loss will result, or is recklessly indifferent whether it will or not. If the risk eventuates he is personally liable. But if he consciously takes the risk in good faith and with the best intentions, honestly believing that the risk is one which ought to be taken in the interests of the beneficaries, there is no reason why he should not be protected by an exemption clause which excludes liability for wilful default.

Secondly, the Law Commission was considering the position of fiduciaries as **9–332** well as trustees, and in such a context it is sensible to consider the exclusion of liability for so-called equitable fraud. But it makes no sense in the present context. The nature of equitable fraud may be collected from the speech of Viscount Haldane LC in *Nocton v. Lord Ashburton* [1914] AC 932 at 953 and *Snell's Equity* (29th edn, 1990) pp. 550–551. It covers breach of fiduciary duty, undue influence, abuse of confidence, unconscionable bargains and frauds on powers. With the sole exception of the last, which is a technical doctrine in which the word "fraud" merely connotes excess of vires, it involves some dealing by the fiduciary with his principal and the risk that the fiduciary may have exploited his position to his own advantage. In *Earl of Aylesford v. Morris* (1873) LR 8 Ch.App. 484 at 490–491. Lord Selborne LC said:

> "Fraud does not here mean deceit or circumvention; it means an unconscientious use of the power arising out of these circumstances and conditions . . ."

A trustee exemption clause such as cl 15 of the settlement does not purport to **9–333** exclude the liability of the fiduciary in such cases. Suppose, for example, that one of the respondents had purchased Paula's land at a proper price from his fellow trustees. The sale would be liable to be set aside. Clause 15 would not prevent this. This is not because the purchasing trustee would have been guilty of equitable fraud, but because by claiming to recover the trust property (or even equitable compensation) Paula would not be suing in respect of any "loss or damage" to the trust. Her right to recover the land would not depend on proof of loss or damage. Her claim would succeed even if the sale was at an overvalue; the purchasing trustee could never obtain more than a defeasible title from such a transaction. But cl 15 would be effective to exempt his fellow trustees from liability for making good any loss which the sale had occasioned to the trust estate so long as they had acted in good faith and in what they honestly believed was Paula's interests.

Accordingly, much of the argument before us which disputes the ability of a trustee exemption clause to exclude liability for equitable fraud or unconscionable behaviour is misplaced. But it is unnecessary to explore this further, for no such conduct is pleaded. What is pleaded is, at the very lowest, culpable and probably gross negligence. So the question reduces itself to this: can a trustee exemption clause validly exclude liability for gross negligence?

9–334 It is a bold submission that a clause taken from one standard precedent book and to the same effect as a clause found in another, included in a settlement drawn by Chancery counsel acting for an infant settlor and approved by the court on her behalf, should be so repugnant to the trusts or contrary to public policy that it is liable to be set aside at her suit. But the submission has been made and we must consider it. In my judgment it is without foundation.

There can be no question of the clause being repugnant to the trust. In *Wilkins v. Hogg* (1861) 31 L.J.Ch. 41 at 42 Lord Westbury LC challenged counsel to cite a case where an indemnity clause protecting the trustee from his ordinary duty had been held so repugnant as to be rejected. Counsel was unable to do so. No such case has occurred in England or Scotland since.

9–335 I accept the submission made on behalf of Paula that there is an irreducible core of obligations owed by the trustees to the beneficiaries and enforceable by them which is fundamental to the concept of a trust. If the beneficiaries have no rights enforceable against the trustees there are no trusts. But I do not accept the further submission that these core obligations include the duties of skill and care, prudence and diligence. The duty of the trustees to perform the trusts honestly and in good faith for the benefit of the beneficiaries is the minimum necessary to give substance to the trusts, but in my opinion it is sufficient. As Mr Hill pertinently pointed out in his able argument, a trustee who relied on the presence of a trustee exemption clause to justify what he proposed to do would thereby lose its protection: he would be acting recklessly in the proper sense of the term.

It is, of course, far too late to suggest that the exclusion in a contract of liability for ordinary negligence or want of care is contrary to public policy. What is true of a contract must be equally true of a settlement. It would be very surprising if our law drew the line between liability for ordinary negligence and liability for gross negligence. In this respect English law differs from civil law systems, for it has always drawn a sharp distinction between negligence, however gross, on the one hand and fraud, bad faith and wilful misconduct on the other. The doctrine of the common law is that: "Gross negligence may be evidence of mala fides, but is not the same thing." (See *Goodman v. Harvey* (1836) 4 A & E 870 at 876, 111 ER 1011 at 1013 per Lord Denman C.J.) But while we regard the difference between fraud on the one hand and mere negligence, however gross, on the other as a difference in kind, we regard the difference between negligence and gross negligence as merely one of degree. English lawyers have always had a healthy disrespect for the latter distinction. In *Hinton v. Dibbin* (1842) 2 Q.B. 646, 114 ER 253 Lord Denman C.J. doubted whether any intelligible distinction exists; while in *Grill v. General Iron Screw Collier Co* (1866) 35 LJCP 321 at 330 Willes J. famously observed that gross negligence is ordinary negligence with a vituperative epithet. But civilian systems draw the line in a different place. The doctrine is *culpa lata dolo aequiparetur*; and although the maxim itself is not Roman the principle is classical. There is no room for the maxim in the common law; it is not mentioned in Broom *Selection of Legal Maxims Classified and Illustrated* (10th edn, 1939).

9–336 The submission that it is contrary to public policy to exclude the liability of a trustee for gross negligence is not supported by any English or Scottish authority. The cases relied on are the English cases of *Wilkins v. Hogg* (1861) 31 L.J.Ch. 41 and *Pass v. Dundas* (1880) 43 LT 665; and the Scottish cases of *Knox v.*

Mackinnon (1888) 13 App.Cas. 753 and *Rae v. Meek* (1889) 14 App.Cas. 558, *Wyman or Ferguson (Pauper) v. Paterson* [1900] A.C. 271 and *Clarke v. Clarke's Trustees* 1925 SC 693. These cases, together with two other Scottish cases, *Seton v. Dawson* (1841) 4 D 310 and *Carruthers v. Carruthers* [1896] A.C. 659, and cases from the Commonwealth and America, were reviewed by the Jersey Court of Appeal in *Midland Bank Trustee (Jersey) Ltd v. Federated Pension Services Ltd* [1995] Jersey L.R. 352, [1996] PLR 179 in a masterly judgment delivered by Sir Godfray Le Quesne Q.C.

In *Wilkins v. Hogg* Lord Westbury L.C. accepted that no exemption clause **9–337** could absolve a trustee from liability for knowingly participating in a fraudulent breach of trust by his co-trustee. But subject thereto, he was clearly of opinion that a settlor could, by appropriate words, limit the scope of the trustee's liability in any way he chose. The decision was followed in *Pass v. Dundas*, where the relevant clause was held to absolve the trustee from liability. In the course of his judgment Bacon V.-C. stated the law in the terms in which counsel for the unsuccessful beneficiaries had stated it, *viz* that the clause protected the trustee from liability unless gross negligence was established; but this was plainly obiter.

Each of the Scottish cases contains dicta, especially in the speeches of the **9–338** Scottish members of the House of Lords, which have been taken by academic writers to indicate that no trustee exemption clause in a Scottish settlement could exonerate a trustee from his own culpa lata. But in fact all the cases were merely decisions on the true construction of the particular clauses under consideration, which were in common form at the time. In *Knox v. Mackinnon* (1888) 13 App Cas 753, for example, it was unnecessary to consider the exemption clause since the transaction in question was outside its scope. Lord Watson, nevertheless, speaking of "a clause conceived *in these or similar terms*", said that it was the settled law of Scotland that "*such a clause* is ineffectual to protect a trustee against the consequences of culpa lata, or gross negligence on his part," and added (quoting Lord Ivory, Lord Gillies and Lord Murray in *Seton v. Dawson* (1841) 4 D 310 at 318) that "*clauses of this kind* do not protect against positive breach of duty" (see 13 App.Cas. 753 at 765–766; my emphasis). In *Seton v. Dawson* the judges who were in the majority spoke to the same effect both of "the protecting clause which occurs in this particular deed" and of "the usual clauses framed for the same object". In *Rae v. Meek* (1889) 14 App Cas 558 at **9–339** 572–573 Lord Herschell pointed out that the clause in question was a common one found in many trust deeds and did not come before the court for construction for the first time. He said that its effect had been considered in *Seton v. Dawson* and adopted the passage in Lord Watson's speech in *Knox v. Mackinnon* to which I have already referred. In *Carruthers v. Carruthers* the House was concerned with a standard trustee exemption clause which was to be treated as inserted into the trust deed. Their Lordships held that the terms of such a clause would not exempt trustees from liability for culpa lata. *Wyman v. Paterson* was not a case of negligence at all, but of a plain failure to perform a positive obligation. It turned on the true construction of the particular clause under consideration. In *Clarke v. Clarke's Trustees* 1925 SC 693 the Lord President (Clyde) held that the clause in question did not protect the trustees from the consequence of their negligence. He added (at 707):

> "It is difficult to imagine that any clause of indemnity in a trust settlement could be capable of being construed to mean that the trustees might with impunity neglect to execute their duty as trustees, in other words, that they were licensed to perform their duty carelessly. There is at any rate no such clause in this settlement."

It is not easy to know what to make of this (save that it was obiter). Sir Godfray Le Quesne Q.C. read the passage as directed to the construction of the indemnity clauses common in Scottish settlements at the time. I do not so read it. I tend to think that the Lord President (Clyde) was saying that it was difficult to conceive of a settlor permitting the inclusion of a clause which would have the effect stated. But I agree with Sir Godfray that the Lord President (Clyde) was emphasising the need to exclude liability for negligence by clear and unambiguous words, and was not purporting to exclude the possibility of such a clause on the grounds of public policy.

9–340   I agree with the conclusion of the Jersey Court of Appeal that all these cases are concerned with the true construction of the particular clauses under consideration or of similar clauses in standard form in the nineteenth century. None of them deals with the much wider form of clause which has become common in the present century, and none of them is authority for the proposition that it is contrary to public policy to exclude liability for gross negligence by an appropriate clause clearly worded to have that effect.

At the same time, it must be acknowledged that the view is widely held that these clauses have gone too far, and that trustees who charge for their services and who, as professional men, would not dream of excluding liability for ordinary professional negligence, should not be able to rely on a trustee exemption clause excluding liability for gross negligence. Jersey introduced a law in 1989 which denies effect to a trustee exemption clause which purports to absolve a trustee from liability for his own "fraud, wilful misconduct or gross negligence". The subject is presently under consideration in this country by the Trust Law Committee under the chairmanship of Sir John Vinelott. If clauses such as cl 15 of the settlement are to be denied effect, then in my opinion this should be done by Parliament which will have the advantage of wide consultation with interested bodies and the advice of the Trust Law Committee."[65]

Section 9. The Control of Pension Funds

THE BACKGROUND[66]

9–341   British pension funds are worth over £660 billion, the top 10 funds alone being responsible for almost £120 billion. There are, in the U.K., nearly 11 million employees who are members of occupational pension schemes. About 3.6 million are members of unfunded, pay-as-you-go, central government or local authority schemes governed by special statutes, while the rest are members of private or public sector schemes, the majority of which are set up under irrevocable trusts. A further 7 million people in the U.K. are currently in receipt of occupational pensions. Millions also have personal pension plans because the State pension is at a low bare subsistence level except for State Earnings Re

---

[65] The matter has now been referred to the law commission so that legal and economic matters can be considered together.

[66] Generally see R. Nobles, *Pensions, Employment and the Law* (1993, Clarendon Press) on the background leading to the Pensions Act 1995 tilting the balance away from the employer to the employees. Otherwise, see R. Ellison, *Pensions Law & Practice* and Inglis-Jones & Hand, *The Law of Occupational Pension Schemes*.

lated Pension Schemes ("SERPS") which will be phased out in 2002 in favour of Stakeholder Pensions under the Welfare Reform and Pensions Act 1999.

An individual's pension rights are very significant private assets. The nature and extent of these rights under a funded scheme is determined usually by two documents, the Trust Deed and the Rules of the Scheme, by principles of trust law, by contractual principles of employment law, and by statutory intervention, *e.g.* Social Security Acts 1973 and 1990, Pensions Schemes Act 1993, Pensions Act 1995, Welfare Reform and Pensions Act 1999 and Child Support, Pensions and Social Security Act 2000.

Pensions are often provided by a final salary scheme (otherwise known **9–342** as a defined benefit plan) determining a pension by a formula related to an employee's earnings on retirement and the number of years worked, *e.g.* one-sixtieth or one eightieth of final pensionable salary for each year worked, not exceeding 40 years. In advance, the employee and the employer contribute money to trustees of the trust fund (a self-administered scheme of which there are about 17,000, covering about 6 million employees) so that assets will be available safe from the employer's creditors if the employer has financial problems. Benefits may be provided for the employee's dependants despite the absence of privity of contract between such persons and the employer.

In the 1980s a surplus developed in many of these trust funds, a **9–343** surplus being the amount by which the actuarially determined value of the assets of a pension scheme exceeds the actuarially determined value of the liabilities to the employees and other beneficiaries of the scheme. The surpluses arose because of greater than anticipated investment returns, many employees leaving before reaching retirement age, overly conservative assumptions made by actuaries in determining the amount of funding required, and employers for tax reasons (or out of ignorance) contributing more than was necessary. The question of ownership of the surplus became a crucial concern on the liquidation of the employer or on the taking over of the employer by a predator, the employer arguing that since it had the burden of making up any deficit in the pension fund it should have the benefit of any surplus.[67]

Such surpluses did not arise in the rarer case of pensions being **9–344** provided by a money purchase scheme (otherwise known as a defined contribution plan). Here, the level of an employee's contribution is fixed in the scheme and the benefit depends upon the interest and bonuses allocated to the employee each year depending upon how well the fund containing his contribution performs. It will also depend on the level of annuity rates after retirement when an annuity must under Revenue rules be purchased with the available capital amount before the age of 75 years is attained, but the Government is under much pressure to change

---

[67] *e.g. Davis v. Richards and Wallington Ltd* [1990] 1 W.L.R. 1511; *Re Courage Group's Pension Scheme* [1987] 1 W.L.R. 495; *Wrightson Ltd v. Fletcher Challenge Nominees Ltd* [2001] UKPC 23.

this. The employee is like a person having an endowment assurance policy in that the amount of contributions is certain but the ultimate benefit is speculative, as in the case of the new stakeholder pensions which are money purchase arrangements. Each employee has an individual account so that single people with no dependants are not cross-subsidising their married colleagues nor do early leavers from the scheme subsidise those who stay to retirement as in final salary schemes where it is the employer who underwrites the defined benefits. In the case of money purchase schemes the trustees will normally place the employer's and employees' contributions with a life assurance company.

Money purchase schemes are now much favoured by employers because they transfer the risks of investment returns from employers to employees and no surpluses arise over which to have morale-sapping rows. The costs of final salary schemes have also increased due to the statutory minimum funding requirement being too severe and due to removal of tax relief on share dividend income. Employers are striving to see if the pension trust deed can be construed widely enough to enable them to close down a final salary scheme and open up a money purchase section and use the surplus in the salary section for their contributions to the new scheme.[68]

Contributions to, pension funds attract exceptional tax advantages[69] if the pension scheme is approved by the Pension Schemes Office of the Inland Revenue. The P.S.O. will not approve schemes if they do not satisfy the requirements of the Occupational Pensions Regulatory Authority ("OPRA") set up under the Pensions Act 1995 (to replace the Occupational Pensions Board Board set up under the Social Security Act 1973).

9–345   The new regime introduced by the Pensions Act 1995 was a response to the perceived lack of security of pension trust funds when Robert Maxwell looted about £450 million of such funds of his group of companies and when other companies became insolvent after some of their pension trust funds had been used to try to keep the companies solvent. The House of Commons Select Committe on Social Security demanded action[70] believing "that trust law gives an inadequate legal underpinning to occupational pension schemes." The Government appointed the Pensions Law Review Committee[71] under Professor Goode to review the legal framework. It reported that:

---

[68] Contrast *Kemble v. Hicks* [1999] P.L.R. 287 with *Barclays Bank v. Holmes* [2000] Pens. L.R. 339 [2000] *The Times* Business Section, November 22, pp 27 & 29. Also see the case of the *British Airways Pension Fund* [2001] *The Daily Telegraph* Business Section, February 17, pp. 29 & 31 where the Final Salary scheme, closed in 1984, was worth £6 billion and effectively had a £1.2 billion surplus, although the actuarial accounting approach under the minimum funding requirement led to less than a 5 per cent notional surplus. Lloyd J. held the members had no right to require the surplus to be used for their benefit: it was open to the trustees to use it to enable BA to have a 30-year contributions holiday.

[69] For exempt approved schemes, under Income and Corporation Taxes Act 1988, s.592 the employee is not taxed on the employer's contributions, which are an allowable expense of the employer, while employee contributions up to a limit of 15 per cent of pay are free of tax and premiums paid for life assurance are free of any charge to tax. However, such schemes no longer have tax relief on dividend income, so raising the costs of final salary schemes.

[70] "The operation of Pension Funds", March 4, 1992, HC61–11, on which See D.J. Hayton "Trust Law and Occupational Pension Schemes" [1993] Conv. 283.

[71] "Pension Law Reform", 1993 Cm 2342.

"Trust law in itself is broadly satisfactory and should continue to provide the foundation for . . . pension schemes. But some of the principles of trust law require modification in their application to pensions"

because they afforded too much freedom to the employer on setting up **9–346** the terms of the trust. The Government accepted this in a White Paper (accepting most of the Committee's other recommendations) which was implemented in the Pensions Act 1995.[72] This Act introduced, inter alia, a new regulatory scheme under the Occupational Pensions Regulatory Authority ("OPRA") with an ultimate limited fall-back to compensation awarded by a Pensions Compensation Board, while extending the powers of the Pensions Ombudsman and providing a minimum funding requirement for funded pension trust schemes.

SPECIAL FEATURES OF PENSION TRUSTS

Leaving aside the special regulatory regime under the Pensions Act **9–347** 1995, a feature of pension trusts is their duration in benefiting employees, their surviving spouses, relatives and dependants, when the corporate employee or the industry (in an industry-wide scheme) may exist for hundreds of years. While the employer in setting up the pension trust with a nominal amount of money is a settlor, it is now clear that when an employer joins the scheme and make his or her first contribution he or she becomes settlor of his or her settlement.[73] Thus, benefits payable by way of lump sum and an annuity on the death or retirement of the employee are valid, the employee being a life in being for perpetuity purposes. However, trusts arising on discontinuance of the scheme possibly more than 21 years after the death of the employee raise perpetuity problems, as does any trust for a widow when she might not take any interest or exercise any power till more than 21 years after the employee's death and might not have been ascertainable[74] when the employee commenced employment and became a settlor. Therefore, approved pension schemes are exempted from the perpetuity rules.[75]

The size of a pension trust fund has long been regarded as a special **9–348** feature, while there is something of a public element in it, such private provision reducing claims on the public purse. Investment powers can justifiably be very wide-ranging indeed, entitling a court under the Variation of Trusts Act 1958 or section 57 of the Trustee Act 1925 to confer such wide powers if so requested[76] before the broad statutory

---

[72] On which see R. Nobles (1996) 59 M.L.R. 241.

[73] *Air Jamaica Ltd v. Charlton* [1999] 1 W.L.R. 1399, 1409, (P.C.). holding that the perpetuity period did not run from the date the employer set up the pension fund, in which event the trust would have been void from the outset at common law, so leading to the Superannuation and other Funds (Validation) Act 1927.

[74] The "unborn widow" trap dealt with by s.5 of the English Perpetuities and Accumulations Act 1964.

[75] Pension Schemes Act, s.163.

[76] *Mason v. Farbrother* [1983] 2 All E.R. 1078 at 1087. For problems caused by too narrow powers of investment see the Monaghan Report on the Superannuation Fund Investment Trust (Australian Government Publishing Service, Canberra, 1984).

power in section 34(1) of the Pensions Act 1995 took effect on April 6, 1997. However, some pension funds are small, being restricted to fewer than 12 members and being established wholly or partly for directors with shareholdings of at least 20 per cent. in their company. The trustees are directors who invest the funds with an eye to assisting the companies and themselves, though conflicts of interest can arise between the trustee-rôle and the director-rôle. As a result, in the case of these small self-administered schemes, known as pensioneer trusts, the P.S.O. will not normally approve such a scheme unless there is an independent external trustee approved by the P.S.O. and known as a Pensioneer Trustee.[77]

An independent trustee is also needed upon the insolvency of the employer-settlor of the pension trust scheme to ensure that the scheme is properly wound up with due regard to the interests of the scheme members and creditors of the company. The insolvency practitioner involved in the liquidation of the employer is responsible for seeing that there is an independent trustee appointed. The public interest in such a course of action to safeguard the interests of members of the scheme was first appreciated in 1990 when the Social Security Act 1990 was enacted. Its provisions were replaced and improved by the Pension Schemes Act 1993 and the Pensions Act 1995. Under section 25(2) thereof all the discretionary powers conferred on the trustees and all fiduciary powers conferred on the employer become exercisable only by the independent trustee. Further safeguards are provided by Child Support, Pensions and Social Security Act 2000, Section 47.

9–349   Indeed, the public interest in safeguarding pension benefits led to the Social Security Act 1990[78] introducing a regulation-making power to restrict the proportion of an occupational pension scheme's resources which may be invested in "employer-related investments." A regulation was made in 1992 to prohibit schemes (other than small self-administered schemes) from having more than five per cent invested in employer-related investments other than land after a transitional period. The position is now governed by Pension Act 1995 section 40 and the Occupational Pension Schemes (Investment) Regulations 1996 which, in addition, prohibit any employer-related loans.

Since pension rights are a form of deferred pay (employers' contributions matching or exceeding employees' contributions), the trustees' duty of disclosure is extended to documents covered by the Occupational Pension Schemes (Disclosure of Information) Regulation 1996 as amended (replacing 1986 Regulations) but pension trustees, like ordinary trustees, are under no obligation to allow beneficiaries to see

---

[77] Income and Corporation Taxes Act 1988, s.591(6).
[78] Sched. 4, para. 3 inserting s.57A of the Social Security Pensions Act 1975.

documents indicating the reasons for the exercise of trustees' discretions.[79]

A key feature of pension fund trusts is that since the employer is **9–350** responsible (albeit with consultation with representatives of the employees) for the drafting of the trust deed, such deeds normally contain broad flexible powers, if the employer consents, to increase or reduce the benefits or the range of beneficiaries or to alter the trust deed to cope with mergers or take-overs involving the employer. On the other hand, the scheme members are not in the position of volunteers under a discretionary trust absolutely at the mercy of the trustees. Their rights derive from a commercial contractual origin: they earn their pension rights as deferred remuneration[80] so in a special situation where there is no trustee capable of exercising a fiduciary power to benefit scheme members the court exceptionally may intervene to exercise such power in favour of the members.[81] Furthermore, even where the employer's powers (*e.g.* to consent or withhold consent or to amend) are personal and not fiduciary they are[82] "impliedly subject to the limnitation that the rights and powers of the company can only be exercised in accordance with the implied obligation of good faith" arising out of the contractual employment relationship. Employee members may well have expectations or hopes that if a surplus materialises then it should be used to reduce employees' contributions or provide a contributions "holiday" or to keep in line with inflation if possible the value of retired employees' pensions of half or two-thirds of final salary.

However, the employer may regard the surplus as belonging to it so **9–351** that it can have a contributions holiday or have the surplus paid over. A company taking over the employer might want to merge the surplus with its own less profitable pension fund and then even sell on the employer with a reduced pension fund of an amount lowly valued on the past service reserve basis.[83] The decision on using surplus will usually be that of the trustees or of a management committee (whose wishes the trustees, like custodian trustees, must follow) but normally such decision can only be taken if the employer consents.[84] The influence of the

---

[79] In *Wilson v. Law Debentures Trust Corp.* [1995] 2 All E.R. 337 Rattee J. rejected the claims of beneficiary-employees to see documents relating to how the trustees determined what proportion of the pension fund should pass to another scheme for employees being transferred to that scheme. Robert Walker J. (now L.J.) criticised this in A.J. Oakley (ed), *Trends in Contemporary Trust Law* (1996) pp. 130–131, believing trustees should be ready to justify their decisions to those whose interests they represent, subject only to protection for what is truly confidential.

[80] See *Kerr v. British Leyland (Staff) Trustees Ltd and Mihlenstedt v. Barclays Bank International Ltd* [1989] I.R.L.R. 522 cited in *Davis v. Richards & Wallington* [1990] 1 W.L.R. 1511 at 1538; *Swan v. Charlesworth* [1987] I.C.R. 288; *Mettoy Pension Trustees Ltd v. Evans* [1991] 2 All E.R. 513.

[81] *Mettoy Pension Trustees Ltd v. Evans* [1990] 1 W.L.R. 1587; *Thrells v. Lomas* [1993] 1 W.L.R. 456. In *Mettoy* the power would probably not have seen held to be a fiduciary power had the case been decided after the *Imperial Group Case* [1991] 1 W.L.R. 590; D.J. Hayton [1993] Conv. 292 and *National Grid Co plc v. Laws* [1997] P.L.R. 157 at para. 91.

[82] *Imperial Group Pension Trust Ltd v. Imperial Tobacco Ltd* [1991] 1 W.L.R. 590 at 597; applied in *British Coal Corp. v. British Coal Staff Superannuation Scheme Trustees Ltd* [1995] 1 All E.R. 912 at 926 where Vinelott J. emphasised the employer has to have regard to the legitimate expectations of the employees even in exercising personal powers due to the implied obligation of good faith: contrast *Schmidt v. Air Products of Canada Ltd* (1994) 115 D.L.R. (4th) 631.

[83] *cf. Re Courage Group's Pension Scheme* [1987] 1 W.L.R. 495.

[84] Assuming that the employer is not a trustee.

employer can be considerable if the trustees or the management committee are appointed and dismissed by the employer, especially if such persons as employees may be dismissed or not promoted if they do not comply with the employer's wishes. Many conflicts of interest and duty may arise! To help trustees and committee members to stand firm they may need the protection of seeking the guidance and instruction of the court, although after the Pensions Act 1995 member-nominated trustees[85] cannot be removed without the agreement of all the other trustees.

9–352   As fiduciaries they are under a duty to act honestly and in good faith, to act fairly[86] between the different classes of beneficiaries, to consider from to time whether or not to exercise a fiduciary power and to ascertain the relevant facts to enable such duty and any discretion to be properly exercised[87] and a duty to act in the interests of the beneficiaries by exercising the fiduciary power for its proper purposes and upon relevant (as opposed to irrational or perverse or irrelevant) considerations.[88] A fiduciary cannot exercise his power so as to benefit himself unless expressly allowed or unless there is a very necessary implication from the trust deed or unless the court authorises it under its ancient jurisdiction to secure the competent administration of the trust, especially where the trustees in question are also members of the pension scheme who will incidentally benefit (qua members) with the other members and who had not deliberately put themselves in the position of conflict of interest and duty except, technically, in succumbing to pressure to allow themselves to be appointed trustees.[89] To avoid the problem[90] for trustee-members section 39 of the Pensions Act 1995 now provides:

> "No rule of law that a trustee may not exercise the powers vested in him so as to give rise to a conflict between his personal interest and his duties to the beneficiaries shall apply to a trustee of a trust scheme, who is also a member of the scheme, exercising the powers vested in him in any manner, merely because their exercise in that manner benefits, or may benefit, him as a member of the scheme."

---

[85] One third of the trustees had to be nominated by the members unless they were happy with alternative arrangements so as to opt out, as occurred in the great majority of cases (see Nat. Assoc. Pension Funds Annual Survey 1997) so opting out under Pensions Act 1995, s.17. is no longer to be possible; Child Support, Pensions and Social Security Act 2000, s.43.

[86] *Edge v. Pensions Ombudsman* [1998] Ch. 512, [2000] Ch. 602 (C.A.).

[87] *Scott v. National Trust* [1998] 2 All E.R. 705; *R. v. Church Commissioners, ex p. Baldwin* [2001] W.T.L.R. 137.

[88] *Hillsdown Holdings plc v. Pensions Ombudsman* [1997] 1 All E.R. 862; *Re Hay's S.T.* [1981] 3 All E.R. 786 at 792–793; *Dundee General Hospital v. Walker* [1952] 1 All E.R. 896 at 905; *Mills v. Mills* (1938) 60 C.L.R. 150; *Nestlé v. National Westminster Bank* discussed *supra*, p. 604; *Vidovic v. Email Superannuation Pty. Ltd* (unreported but discussed in 1995 69 A.L.J. 412–413),

[89] *Re Drexel Burnham Lambert Holdings Ltd's Pension Plan* [1995] 1 W.L.R. 32.

[90] In *Edge v. Pensions Ombudsman* [1998] Ch. 512, Scott V.-C. considered that the problem did not exist, it being "ridiculous" to prevent a member receiving benefits authorised to be given to all members of his class merely because the member was one of the authorising trustees.

A person who is not a trustee but who has a power, *e.g.* to withhold **9–353** consent, will be treated prima facie as having a merely personal, as opposed to a fiduciary, power[91] so that he can act spitefully and for his personal benefit. However, it is necessarily implicit in the contract of employment that the employer will duly discharge its pensions scheme rights and powers in good faith: *Imperial Group Pension Trust Ltd v. Imperial Tobacco Ltd.*[92] It can have regard to its own financial interests in any surplus but only to the extent that in so doing it does not breach the obligation of good faith to its employees: this is the obligation not to conduct itself in a manner likely seriously to damage the relationship of confidence between employer and employee. In *National Grid Co plc v. Laws*[93] it was emphasised, "the *Imperial Tobacco* duty does not prevent the employer from looking after its own financial interests, even where they conflict with those of members and pensioners."

Further special features of pension trusts are that (by virtue of Pensions Act 1995 sections 91 and 92 Pension Schemes Act 1993 sections 159 and 159A, Welfare Reform and Pensions Act 1999 sections 11 and 12) interests thereunder cannot be forfeited on bankrupty nor can they be made available to creditors, while on divorce pension sharing orders may be made in favour of the member-beneficiaries' spouse as a result of reforms introduced by sections 19–46 of the Welfare Reform and Pensions Act 1999.

SURPLUSES

Introduction

In balance of costs schemes (as final salary schemes are also known) **9–354** where the employers make up the necessary money so far as the employees' fixed proportions of their salaries are insufficient, the problem was one of deficits until the 1980s produced major surpluses for the reasons already mentioned. Indeed, the Revenue became so concerned that pension funds were deliberately being used as a tax shelter that the Finance Act 1986[94] required reduction of surplus[95] of assets over liabilities to not more than 5 per cent. Surplus can be reduced by improving benefits, reducing or suspending contributions (a contributions "holiday") for up to five years by employers or employees, or by making a payment to the employer. If surplus is not maintained at less

---

[91] But see *Mettoy Pension Trustees Ltd v. Evans* [1990] 1 W.L.R. 1587, although the power would probably not have been held to be fiduciary had the case been heard after *Imperial Group Pension Trust Ltd v. Imperial Tobacco Ltd* [1991] 1 W.L.R. 590.

[92] [1991] 2 All E.R. 597. Also see *Mihlenstedt v. Barclays Bank International Ltd* [1989] I.R.L.R. 522 where Nourse L.J. states, "It is necessarily implicit in the contract of employment that the Bank agrees with the employee that it will duly discharge those functions [it has under the pension scheme] in good faith."

[93] [1997] P.L.R. 157, 177 implicitly confirmed by Court of Appeal [1999] P.L.R. 39, 46.

[94] Now see Income and Corporation Taxes Act 1988, ss.601–603, Sched. 22.

[95] In an on-going scheme "surplus" is very notional, so much depending on assumptions but the Finance Act 1986 introduced rules for ascertaining the notional surplus on a standard basis: Pension Scheme Surpluses (Valuation) Regs 1987 S.I. 412.

than 5 per cent tax exemptions on investment income are lost. Surplus returned to the employer is taxed at 40 per cent.

9–355 A major problem arose where the trust deed did not provide the trustees with the necessary power to pay surplus to the employer (especially if the other methods of reducing surplus were inadequate to reduce surplus only to 5 per cent), tax rules for years having required schemes to contain provisions prohibiting returns to the employer. The O.P.R.A. (previously O.P.B.) now has power[96] to make modification orders enabling schemes to reduce surplus by returning it to the employer if the proposal is approved by the P.S.O., if the trustees or managers are satisfied that it is in the interests of the beneficiaries, if annual pension increases (in accordance with the increase in the Retail Price Index up to a ceiling of 5 per cent per annum) are already provided for or are included in the package for reducing the surplus, and if the O.P.R.A. is satisfied that it is reasonable in all the circumstances to make the order.

9–356 The application to the O.P.R.A. must state whether the trustees have taken independent advice in reaching their decision and enclose a copy of the notice given to employees informing them of the O.P.R.A. application and their opportunity to make representations to the O.P.R.A. There will thus need to be co-operation between employer and employees: the *quid pro quo* for paying some surplus to the employer should be generous treatment for employees and pensioners, so helping to maintain good industrial relations with the workforce. The destination of surplus after satisfying employees' legitimate expectations is thus the employer but it is left to a bargaining process to determine exactly what expectations are legitimate.

Thus the interests of employees in the surplus, which is a notional one while the employer is a going concern and liable to make up any subsequent deficits are to be regarded as rights to have the trust fund administered properly with processes taking due account of their "expectations",[97] but as the Court of Appeal has made clear,[98] "the language used by Knox J. in the *LRT*[99] case must not be elevated into a general proposition that members of a contributory pension scheme have interests in the surplus equivalent to rights of property. They do not."

Surpluses on liquidation of employer where Pensions Act 1995 in applicable

9–357 Where the trust deed as amended deals fully with entitlement to the surplus there are no loose ends, and where the company employer is a going concern the powers of the O.P.R.A. should be available to amend the trust deed so as to obviate problems, especially that of the surplus

---

[96] Pensions Act 1995 ss.69–71; Occupational Pension Schemes (Payments to Employers) Regulations 1996 S.I. 2156.
[97] *London Regional Transport v. Hatt* [1993] P.L.R. 227 (at paras 157 *et seq.*).
[98] *National Grid plc v. Laws* [1999] P.L.R. 37 at para. 46.
[99] See note 97 *supra*. Also Privy Council in *Wrightson Ltd v. Fletcher Challenge Nominees Ltd* [2001] UKPC 23.

being regarded as *bona vacantia*. After all, subject to consideration of *Air Jamaica Ltd v. Charlton*,[1] if the employer has no entitlement to surplus due to a prohibition in the trust deed and if the employees are regarded as having contractual rights simply to two-thirds of final salary at the date of retirement then such contractual rights exclude the possibility of a resulting trust so that the surplus must pass to the Crown as *bona vacantia* on liquidation of the company employer.[2]

This seems harsh on the employees. They are settlors of the trust fund **9–358** as well as beneficiaries. Why should an employee just because he is a beneficiary be precluded from asserting his rights as a settlor to the return of his contributions? Alternatively, should the pension scheme for members not be regarded as analogous to a club for members, between whom the assets would be distributed on the dissolution of the club as indicated by Walton J. in *Re Bucks Constabulary Fund Friendly Society*?[3]

On liquidation of a company its pension fund trust deed may deal **9–359** comprehensively with the position, so ousting any question of *bona vacantia*. However, if the company is a trustee with power to pay surplus to the company (and therefore to its creditors) or to use it to augment employees' pensions there is an obvious conflict of interest, but this could be authorised by the trust deed expressly authorising the exercising of discretionary powers notwithstanding any personal interest of the exerciser.[4] Accordingly, sections 22–25 of the Pensions Act 1995 replacing the Social Security Act 1990[5] now require that if there is not at least one independent trustee then the insolvency practitioner liquidating the company must appoint an independent trustee, who alone can exercise fiduciary discretions. If the discretionary power to augment benefits is vested not in the trustees but in the employer as such, then Warner J. has held[6] that this is a fiduciary power so that it cannot be exercised on the company's behalf by a receiver or liquidator (whose duties are owed to the creditors alone) or, if it is a solvent voluntary winding-up, by the directors (when the only class of members whose interests can be considered are the employees[7]). The discretionary power thus had to be exercised by the court, although now it would be the independent trustee who would exercise the power by virtue of section 25(2) of the Pensions Act 1995.

How should such power be exercised by the court or by the indepen- **9–360** dent trustees? The starting point could be the view that the surplus belongs morally to the employer for the reasons given by Millett J., as follows[8]:

---

[1] [1999] 1 W.L.R. 1399 (P.C.), discussed *infra* para. 9–366.
[2] *Palmer v. Abney Park Cemetery Co. Ltd* (unreported) cited in *Davis v. Richards and Wallington Ltd* [1990] 1 W.L.R. 1511 at 1539.
[3] [1979] 1 W.L.R. 936, *supra*, para. 5–50.
[4] *cf. Icarus (Hertford) Ltd v. Driscoll* [1990] Pensions L.R. 1 and see necessarily implied authorisation in *Edge v. Pensions Ombudsman* [1998] Ch. 512.
[5] Sched. 4, para. 1 inserting ss.57C, 57D of the Social Security Pensions Act 1975.
[6] *Mettoy Pension Trustees Ltd v. Evans* [1991] 2 All E.R. 513.
[7] See *Parke v. Daily News Ltd* [1962] Ch. 927 as modified by Companies Act 1980, s.74.
[8] *Re Courage Group's Pension Scheme* [1987] 1 All E.R. 528 at 545.

"Employees are obliged to contribute a fixed proportion of their salaries or such lesser sum as the employer may from time to time determine. They cannot be required to pay more, even if the fund is in deficit; and they cannot demand a reduction or suspension of their own contributions if it is in surplus. The employer, by way of contrast, is obliged only to make such contributions if any as may be required to meet the liabilities of the scheme. If the fund is in deficit, the employer is bound to make it good; if it is in surplus, the employer has no obligation to pay anything. Employees have no right to complain if, while the fund is in surplus, the employer should require them to continue their contributions while itself contributing nothing. If the employer chooses to reduce or suspend their contributions, it does so ex gratia and in the interests of maintaining good industrial relations.

From this, two consequences follow. First, employees have no legal right to a "a contributions holiday." Second, any surplus arises from past overfunding not by the employer and the employees pro rata to their respective contributions but by the employer alone to the full extent of its past contributions and only subject thereto by the employees."

9–361   However, can the power to pay surplus to the employer or use it to augment pensions not be regarded as for the purpose of holding a fair balance between the employees and the employer, but then can it be unfair to return to the employer the surplus generated by the employer's over-funding? If an independent trustee ascertained the relevant facts concerning employees and the employer's liabilities and in good faith then decided to pay the surplus to the employer's liquidator why should the decision not to favour the employee-objects of the power be impeachable? The employees' hopes may not materialise but that is the common fate for the objects of discretionary powers.

However, Warner J. has stated[9]:

9–362   "One cannot in my opinion, in construing a provision in the rules of a 'balance of cost' pension scheme relating to surplus, start from the assumption that any surplus belongs morally to the employer . . . in deciding whether the employer owed a duty to the objects of the power, one must have regard to the fact that the beneficiaries under a pension scheme are not volunteers . . . their rights are derived from the contract of employment as well as from the trust instrument. Those rights have been earned by the service of the members under those contracts as well as by their contributions . . . In construing the trust instrument one must bear in mind as an important part of the background the origins of the beneficiaries' rights under it."

Thus, the discretionary power is a fiduciary one requiring regard to be had to the interests of the employee-members of the scheme; but this is a weak duty leaving it open to the power-exerciser to consider them but still pay the surplus to the employer's liquidator.[10] It is arguable that the

---

[9] *Mettoy Pension Trustees Ltd v. Evans* [1991] 2 All E.R. 513, 549.
[10] See R. Nobles (1990) 53 M.L.R. 377–380 discussing *Mettoy* and *Icarus (Hertford) Ltd v. Driscoll* [1990] Pensions L.R. 1.

courts should go further and require the power to be exercised according to the purpose of advancing the interests of the employee-beneficiaries as much as possible,[11] and treat failure to exercise the power (thereby benefiting third parties at the expense of the beneficiaries) as a breach of duty to the employee-beneficiaries. In *Mettoy* the surplus was ultimately divided between members and the employer in the ratio 2:1.

It will thus be seen that even if the rules of the scheme are not **9–363** comprehensive there should normally be no question of the surplus on liquidation of the company going to the Crown as *bona vacantia* unless the trust deed clearly excludes any right to surplus of the company or its employees. Scott J. considered the position in *Davis v. Richards and Wallington Industries Ltd*[12] where the employer went into liquidation before the execution of a definitive trust deed dealing with distribution of surplus funds. He held that a definitive deed executed after liquidation was effective in the circumstances but that even if it had been ineffective its inefficacy could have been remedied by treating an interim deed as constituting an executory trust which would be executed by a court order bringing into effect provisions corresponding to those in the definitive deed. Thus the trustees, using the discretion conferred on them by the definitive deed, could use the surplus for the purpose of augmenting members' benefits.

In *obiter dicta* he considered the situation where the scheme did not **9–364** prohibit the return of surplus money to the employer and opined that a resulting trust did arise in favour of the employer, the surplus being regarded as primarily arising from overfunding by the employer. However, so far as part of the surplus derived from employees' contributions he opined that it devolved as *bona vacantia*.

He considered that where a trust deed is silent as to destination of a surplus the law will supply a resulting trust in favour of the provider of the funds in question and that it is only where it is "absolutely clear,"[13] expressly or by necessary implication, that in no circumstances is a resulting trust to arise that such trust will be excluded. "Therefore, the fact that a payment to a fund has been made under a contract and that the payer has obtained all that he or she bargained for under the contract is not necessarily a decisive argument against a resulting trust."[14]

Surprisingly, Scott J. then discovered that the employee-contributors **9–365** intended that there should be no resulting trust in their favour. Why was this "absolutely clear"? First, because an intention to have a resulting trust would be "unworkable," the employees' entitlements (taking benefits received into account) being so various. Secondly, because an intention to have a resulting trust would give them more than the

---

[11] Millett J. in *Re Courage Group's Pension Scheme* [1987] 1 All E.R. 528, 541 stated, "A pension scheme is established, not for the benefit of a particular company, at *for the benefit of those employed* in a commercial undertaking."

[12] [1990] 1 W.L.R. 1511.

[13] [1990] 1 W.L.R. 1511 at 1541, endorsing *Re ABC T.V. Pension Scheme* (unreported May 22, 1973).

[14] *ibid.* at 1541–1542.

legislature intended in its legislative requirements for benefits under exempt approved schemes. These two reasons are not at all convincing: would these thoughts have crossed the employees' minds? Each employee would probably expect to be able to work out what he was entitled to[15] and why should the *legislature's* intention provide evidence of the *employees'* intention (though if the legislation clearly prevents a resulting trust arising in favour of the employees then *cadit quaestio*, regardless of the employees' intentions)? One may also note that Scott J. treated as gospel truth the *bona vacantia* findings of Goff J. in the *West Sussex Constabulary* case[16] whereas, as has been seen,[17] such findings are probably incorrect in view of Walton J.'s later reasoning in the *Bucks Constabulary* case[18] applied in subsequent members' club cases with which an analogy could be drawn for members' pension fund schemes.

9–366   Recently Lord Millett in delivering the advice of the Privy Council in *Air Jamaica Ltd. v. Charlton*[19] was critical of the views of Scott V.-C. observing[20] "in the ordinary case of an actuarial surplus, it is not obvious that when employees are promised certain benefits under a scheme to which they have contributed more than was necessary to fund them, they should not expect to obtain a return of their excess contributions". As to tax legislation placing limits he stated[21]: "Allowing the employees to enjoy any part of the surplus by way of a resulting trust would probably exceed those limits. This fact is not, however, in their Lordships view, a proper ground on which to reject the operation of a resulting trust in favour of the employees . . . There is no call to distort principle in order to meet [Revenue] requirements. The resulting trust arises by operation of the general law *dehors* the pension scheme and the scope of the relevant tax legislation".

9–367   The Air Jamaica defined benefit or salary scheme pension trust had been discontinued with a surplus of over 400 million dollars arising from the failure for perpetuity reasons of some of the trusts. This meant the employees did not receive all they bargained for because of the invalidity of the provisions for the trustees to pay them additional benefits upon discontinuance of the scheme. Thus, the Privy Council rejected the argument that the employees in receiving their due entitlement to a share of their salaries had received all they were entitled to, so as to exclude any resulting trust.

The Privy Council also rejected the argument that clause 4 of the trust Deed ousted the employer's claim under a resulting trust when it

---

[15] Distribution of the surplus could be proportionate to the amounts contributed by employees and pensioners.

[16] [1971] Ch. 1. Scott J. also held that if any part of the surplus was derived from funds transferred from the pension schemes of other companies such transfers were outright transfers, excluding any resulting trust possibility, so that any surplus therefrom was *bona vacantia*, but why could such surplus not accrue to the shares of the employees and the employer?

[17] See *supra*, para. 5–43.

[18] [1979] 1 W.L.R. 936.

[19] [1999] 1 W.L.R. 1399.

[20] *ibid.*, 1412.

[21] *ibid.*, 1413.

provided, "No moneys which at any time have been contributed by the Company under the terms hereof shall in any circumstances be repayable to the company". Their Lordships held,[22] "clauses of this kind in a pension scheme should generally be construed as forbidding the repayment of contributions under the scheme and not as a pre-emptive but misguided attempt to rebut a resulting trust *dehors* the scheme". Thus, 1994 amendments to the scheme to enable moneys to be repaid to the Company were prohibited by clause 4, but the clause did not prevent the company from retaining a beneficial interest by way of a resulting trust in so much of the surplus as was attributable to its contributions.

As to this,[23] "Contributions were payable by the Members with **9–368** matching contributions by the Company . . . the surplus must be treated as provided as to one half by the Company and as to one-half by the Members . . . The Members' share of the surplus should be divided *pro rata* among the Members and the estates of deceased Members in proportion to the contributions made by each Member without regard to the benefits each has received and irrespective of the dates on which the contributions were made". No contributions therefore fell to be treated as *bona vacantia*, as the Jamaican Government claimed.

Surpluses where ss. 76 and 77 Pensions Act 1995 applicable

Where an exempt approved scheme[24] is being wound up and there is a power conferred on the employer or the trustees to distribute assets to the employer, this power cannot be exercised until (1) any power to distribute assets to persons other than the employer has been exercised or a decision has been made not to exercise it, (ii) the annual rates of pensions have been increased by the appropriate percentage[25] and (iii) notice has been given to the members of the proposal to distribute assets to the employer.[26] Where an exempt approved scheme prohibits the distribution of assets to an employer, and a power to distribute assets to pensions other than the employer has been exercised or a decision has been made not to exercise it, than the annual rates of pensions must be increased by the appropriate percentage so far as possible, and, if a surplus then remains, the trustees must use the surplus for the purpose of providing additional benefits or increasing the value of any benefits subject to the prescribed Revenue limits, and "the trustees may then distribute [any remaining surplus] to the employer".[27]

Thus, the trustees can avoid any possibility of *bona vacantia* passing to **9–369** the Crown, while persons other than the employer receive the maximum permitted by the Revenue rules where there is a prohibition in the trust deed against benefiting the employer, although where there is a power to

---

[22] *ibid.*, 1412.
[23] *ibid.*, 1411, 1413.
[24] As defiend in s.592(1) of Income and Corporation Taxes Act 1988.
[25] See Pension Act 1995 s.54 *infra* para. 9–417.
[26] *ibid.*, s.76.
[27] *ibid.*, s.77. Provisions to speed up the winding up of occupational pension schemes are found in Child Support, Pensions ad Social Security Act 2000, ss.47 to 50.

benefit the employer a difficult balancing decision is still needed in considering the extent to benefit the employer or the member-beneficiaries taking account of the matters discussed in the proceeding part hereof and the fact that annual rates of pensions have to be increased to the appropriate percentage.

Sale of employer and related pension fund

Problems involving ownership of surplus pension moneys also arise where a controlling company sells a subsidiary company to a purchaser. Where the trust deed provides for a portion of the group pension fund to be transferred to the purchaser of the subsidiary company and for the amount of the portion to be determined by an appointed actuary then the court cannot intervene with the actuary's expert decision in the absence of bad faith.[28] Thus a valuation made by him on the past service reserve method (the amount required to meet pension benefits for service rendered to date) with allowance for future pay and pension increases was unimpeachable. Indeed, the judge regarded such approach more appropriate than the higher valued share of fund basis, the notional temporary surplus being capable of being dealt with by the employer, primarily responsible for the surplus, in various ways which could lead to disappearance of the surplus over a period without the surplus necessarily being used for the benefit of the relevant employees even if they stayed within the scheme. On transfers the past service reserve method is now regularly used.

9–370   The Hanson Group tried to take advantage of this when buying the Imperial Group and selling Imperial's Courage brewing division to Elders. The Courage division had its own pension fund surplus so Hanson tried to merge the Courage scheme (with its £80 million surplus) into the Imperial Group scheme, substituting Hanson for the Imperial Group as principal employer under a purported power in that behalf, so that the Courage brewing division could then be sold on to Elders with a pension fund of an amount based only on the past service reserve method, so that £70 million of the surplus would remain in the main Imperial Group Scheme controlled by Hanson.

9–371   Hanson took advantage of a provision allowing the trust deed to be varied, if it did not have the effect of altering the main purpose of the fund, to add a broad power to substitute the employer company by another company. Millett J. held[29] that the addition of such power was *ultra vires* but, even if it were not, the exercise of such power in the circumstances was for a purpose foreign to the purpose for which the power could be conferred and so was invalid. He explained that he did not base his decision on the ground that Hanson's proposals would deprive the employees of an accrued legal entitlement to surplus because in his views the surplus derived from past overfunding by the employer. He further said[30]:

---

[28] *Re Imperial Foods Ltd Pension Scheme* [1986] 1 W.L.R. 717.
[29] *Re Courage Group's Pension Scheme* [1987] 1 All E.R. 528.
[30] *ibid.* at 545.

"It will, however, only be in rare cases that the employer will have any legal right to repayment of any part of the surplus.[31] Regulations are expected to confer power on the Occupational Pensions Board to author-ise modifications to pension schemes in order to allow repayment to employers.[32] Repayment will, however, still normally require amendment to the scheme, and thus co-operation between the employer and the trustees or committee of management. Where the employer seeks repay-ment, the trustees or committee can be expected to press for generous treatment of employees and pensioners, and the employer to be influenced by a desire to maintain good industrial relations with its workforce.

It is, therefore, precisely in relation to a surplus that the relationship **9–372** between 'the company' as the employer and the members as its present or past employees can be seen to be an essential feature of a pension scheme. In the present case, the members of these schemes object to being compulsorily transferred to a new scheme of which they know nothing except that it has a relatively small surplus. While they have no legal right to participate in the surpluses in the existing schemes, they are entitled to have them dealt with by consultation and negotiation between their employers with a continuing responsibility towards them and the com-mittee of management with a discretion to exercise on their behalf, and not to be irrevocably parted from these surpluses by the unilateral decision of a take-over raider with only a transitory interest in the share capital of the companies which employ them."

The O.P.B. then provided trustees with guidance in its booklet, *Pension Trust* **9–373** *Principles*, where it states:

"You will need to be particularly clear about your duty to act in accordance with the trust deed and rules if the employer is engged in the sale and purchase of an undertaking which involves a bulk transfer of members and assets out of or into the scheme. The two employers involved will have entered into a sale agreement which will cover the pension terms of the transferring employees and the associated financial arrangements. You and your fellow trustees will not normally be parties to the agreement, and indeed the trustees of the two schemes may not have been consulted fully, if at all. You must ensure that you act strictly in accordance with the trust deed and rules. The employers will have to solve any difficulties that then arise."

Clearly, the trustees of the vendor company's scheme must not **9–374** transfer too great a proportion of their fund while the trustees of the purchasing company's scheme must not receive inadequate new funding. To look after the transferring employees' interest to a minimum extent, the actuary to the transferring scheme must (under the Preservation of Benefit Regulations allowing bulk transfers of members from one

---

[31] In *Hillsdown Holdings v. Pensions Ombudsman* [1997] 1 All E.R. 862 it was held a fraud on a power for trustees of pension fund "B" to exercise their power to transfer the fund to pension fund "C" for the trustees thereof to look after the interests of members of both funds where the reason for exercising the power was that under the rules of pension fund "C", unlike "B", surplus could be paid to the employer.

[32] This is now the case under Pensions Act 1995, ss.69–71 for O.P.R.A.

scheme to another without their consent) certify that the past service rights and expectations to be provided to the transferring members in the new scheme are equivalent on an overall basis to their past service rights and expectations in the original scheme. Such certificate, however, does not of itself absolve the trustees of the transferring scheme from their fiduciary duties to their member-beneficiaries.

THE SOCIAL SECURITY ACT 1990 AND THE PENSIONS OMBUDSMAN

9–375 The Act provided for a register of occupational and personal pension schemes[33] and, most significantly, created[34] the post of Pensions Ombudsman with retrospective powers involving matters arising before the 1990 Act came into force. The idea was to provide a cheap, speedy, efficient method for dealing with "maladministration" by trustees or managers of pension schemes. From the outset, the Pensions Ombudsman took a broad pro-active view of his powers[35] while the courts took a restrictive approach, cutting down his powers until Parliament responded by expressly conferring particular broad powers upon him. He can deal with the law and the facts relating to maladministration in the sense of "bias, neglect, inattention, delay, incompetence, ineptitude, perversity, turpitude, arbitrariness and so on".[36] His jurisdiction extends to complaints from actual or potential beneficiaries against the trustees or the managers or the employer, from trustees against each other or the employer, including complaints from the independent trustee (where there is an insolvency of the employer) about the other trustees or former trustees.

9–376 Section 54 of the Child Support, Pension and Social Security Act 2000 reverses the effect of *Edge v. Pension Ombudsman*[37] which was to prevent the Ombudsman from investigating a complaint if his ruling would affect the interests of third parties not directly involved in the dispute and for whom there was no procedure to enable them to be involved and to be bound by the ruling. Now[38] a representative can be appointed by the Ombudsman to represent a group with a common interest that may be affected by a ruling even if having no direct interest in the particular complaint or dispute. The Ombudsman may also order costs (or certain expenses up to given limit) to be met from the pension fund.

9–377 Everyone who has had the opportunity (whether individually or via a representative) to make representations will be bound by the Ombudsman's ruling but will be able to appeal to the High Court Chancery Division on a point of law. The Ombudsman is expected to accept the

---

[33] See s.13. O.P.R.A. keeps a register of disqualified trustees.
[34] s.12. Now see ss.145–152 of Pension Schemes Act 1993 as amended by Pensions Act 1995, ss.157–160 and Child Support, Pensions and Social Security Act 2000, ss.53 and 54.
[35] J.T. Farrand (the Ombudsman himself), "*Courts v. Pensions Ombudsman—Stepping on Toes?*" (2000) 14 Trust L.I. 146.
[36] *Hillsdown Holdings plc v. Pensions Ombudsman* [1997] 1 All E.R. 862, 884.
[37] [2000] Ch. 602.
[38] Child Support, Pension and Social Security Act 2000, s.54.

High Court decision and not appeal unless there are conflicting High Court decisions on a point of principle which make it difficult for him to perform his functions without appellate guidance.[39]

THE EUROPEAN COMMUNITY DIMENSION

In *Barber v. Guardian Royal Exchange Assurance Group*[40] the European **9–378** Court of Justice held that occupational pension schemes fall within Article 119 (now renumbered 141) of the EEC Treaty of Rome requiring the application of the principle that men and women should receive equal pay for equal work. "Pay" includes the wage or salary "and any other consideration which the worker receives, directly or indirectly, in respect of his employment from his employer" and so the Court held that pension rights of the employee or his dependants constitute "pay," albeit deferred pay. It has since been held that the *Barber* judgment only applies prospectively[41] to rights *earned* by virtue of pensionable service in pay periods after May 16, 1990.

In the *Coloroll*[42] case the ECJ also held "The direct effect of Article 119 may be relied upon by both employees and their dependants against the trustees of an occupational pension scheme who are bound in the exercise of their powers and performance of their obligations as laid down in the trust deed, to observe the principle of equal treatment. . . . In so far as national law prohibits employers and trustees from acting beyond the scope of their respective powers or in disregard of the provisions of the trust deed, they are bound to use all the means available under domestic law, such as recourse to the national courts, in order to eliminate all discrimination in the matter of pay."

Periods of pensionable service after May 16, 1990 but before a pension **9–379** scheme's rules are changed to eliminate sexual discrimination must give rise to equal benefits by granting to the disadvantaged sex the same advantages as those previously enjoyed by the advantaged sex. However, equal treatment for periods of pensionable service after the date the scheme rules are changed can be achieved by reducing the advantages which the advantaged sex used to enjoy.

Recently in *Preston v. Wolverhampton Health Care NHS Trust*[43] the House of Lords has applied the ruling of the European Court of Justice[44] in relation to part-time employees' access to pension provision, thousands of women retiring after long periods of part-time service with little or no pension while their male colleagues, who did not have to work part-time to look after their families, receive pensions based on all their

---

[39] *Edge v. Pensions Ombudsman* [2000] Ch. 602. The High Court seems to accept that compensation for distress can be awarded: *Wild v. Smith* [1996] O.P.L.R. 129 (and *Westminster C.C. v. Heywood* [1998] Ch. 377, 410–411).
[40] [1991] 1 Q.B. 344, discussed (1991) 54 M.L.R. 271.
[41] *cf. Defrenne v. Sabena* [1976] E.C.R. 455.
[42] [1995] 1 All E.R. (E.C.) 23 at 76.
[43] [2001] All E.R. (D) 99 (Feb).
[44] [2000] I.C.R. 961, (Case C–78/98).

service. The rule in the Equal Pay Act 1975 limiting any claim to a maximum of two years pensionable service contravenes Article 119 (or 141), so claims can be retrospective to service after April 8, 1976, the date when Article 119 was first held[45] to have direct effect on member States, subject to the employee paying any relevant contributions. However, for a claim to be valid it has to be brought within six months of the termination of employment, as under the Equal Pay Act, but where there were a series of separate contracts at regular intervals in respect of the same employment in a stable employment relationship, the six months runs from the end of the last contract forming part of that relationship. Obviously this has massive implications for employers and for part-time employees.

THE PENSIONS ACT 1995 AS REINFORCED BY CHILD SUPPORT, PENSIONS AND SOCIAL SECURITY ACT 2000

9–380 Equal treatment of the sexes is provided by section 62 which also places the onus of justifying a different treatment due to a material factor not related to gender upon the trustees. If the trustees do not have the power to make alterations to the trust deed or rules or if the procedure is likely to be unduly complex, protracted or involve consents which cannot be obtained or can only be obtained with great difficulty, section 65 empowers trustees to modify the trust deed and rules by simple resolution so that the scheme reflects the equal treatment rule set out in the Act.

Besides enacting the principle of equal treatment in accordance with European Union law, the Act in 181 sections and seven schedules introduces a new regulatory system under OPRA with a compensation scheme and limits to the generally unlimited scope of trust law; extends significantly the powers of the Pensions Ombudsman (so saving recourse to the courts); alters arrangements for the financial levy on schemes to pay for the new regime; introduces limited annual pension rises in line with retail price indexation up to a 5 per cent maximum; equalises state pension ages for men and women; allows greater flexibility for purchasing annuities; provides for the division of a pension following divorce; and, tidies up a number of pension related matters.

9–381 OPRA has extensive powers to direct that a scheme be wound up to protect the interests of the generality of members and to suspend, remove and appoint new trustees, particularly in the light of the duty imposed by section 48 upon auditors and actuaries to "blow the whistle" and inform OPRA in writing of failures to comply with the law that are likely to be of material significance in the exercise by OPRA of any of its functions. Taking account of safeguards in the Act, compensation is to be payable only in limited criminal circumstances by an independent

---

[45] *Defrenne v. Sabena* [1976] I.C.R. 547.

Pensions Compensation Board. The compensation will be provided by a post-event levy paid by other pension schemes.

The Act then modifies freedom of contract and of trust law to deal with problems arising from the employer's reservation of rights to determine who are the trustees, the nature of scheme amendments, the appointment of professional advisers, the basis of bulk transfer payments on transferring employee's rights with parts of the company's undertakings and the resolution of disputes. If these rights were not fiduciary rights exercisable only in the members' interests but were personal beneficial rights of the employer, then the employer need only exercise them in good faith so as not to jeopardise the relationship of confidence and trust that should subsist between employer and employee. This made the employer's pension promise to the employee depend too heavily on the continuing goodwill of the employer and allowed too much scope for oppressive conduct by the employer.

Sections 16 to 21 were designed to ensure that there are member- **9–382** nominated trustees or directors of the pension trust company (unless opting out arrangements are agreed with the members) so that one third of the trustees are member-nominated, with a minimum of two of the total number of trustees (or one if the scheme has fewer than 100 members). Section 43 of the Child Support, Pensions and Social Security Act 2000 now prevents opting out, although current opt-outs will be allowed to finish their natural term.

Sections 22 to 26 (as reinforced by section 47 of the Child Support, Pensions and Social Security Act 2000) require the appointment of an independent trustee when the employer becomes insolvent. An employer which is sole trustee before the appointment of an independent trustee ceases to be a trustee on that appointment, while any fiduciary power exercisable by an employer not a trustee becomes exercisable only by the independent trustee, and all trustee discretions are exercisable only by the independent trustee.

Sections 27 and 28 make a trustee (and any associate or connected person) ineligible to act as an auditor or actuary of the scheme, while sections 29 and 30 automatically disqualify certain categories of persons from being a trustee, *e.g.* undischarged bankrupts and those convicted of offences involving dishonesty or deception. Section 31 prohibits the trustees from being indemnified out of the trust assets for fines or civil penalties or being covered by insurance paid out of trust assets, though an employer can agree with a trustee to provide an indemnity.

Section 32 allows for decisions of the trustees to be by a majority. **9–383** Sections 33 to 36 confer upon trustees very broad powers of investment and of delegating investment discretions, though trustees cannot exempt themselves from liability for breach of their duties of care in relation to their investment functions. However, if they delegate to a discretionary portfolio manager authorised under the Financial Services Act 1986 they cannot be liable for its acts or defaults if they took all such steps as are reasonable to satisfy themselves that it had the appropriate knowledge and experience, that it was carrying out its work competently and complying with all the requirements of the Act relating to investment management. For investment business outside the 1986 Financial Services Act (*e.g.* cash or land or foreign assets) similar protection is available. The requirements of the Act as to a written statement of investment principles and the choosing of investments are set out in sections 35 and 36.

9–384 Section 37 regulates payment of any surplus to the employer while the scheme is on-going, while section 76 deals with excess assets on winding up the scheme, both sections ensuring that annual increases in pensions are properly provided for. Section 38 empowers trustees to defer winding up a scheme but then no new members are to be admitted to the scheme.

Section 39 enables member-trustees to benefit themselves when benefiting members. Section 40 imposes restrictions on employer-related investments and section 41 imposes disclosure duties in respect of trust documents.

Employee trustees have by sections 42 and 43 to be allowed paid time off for performance of their duties and for training and by section 46 have a right not to suffer detriment in employment or be unfairly dismissed by virtue of functions performed or proposed to be performed *qua* trustee.

Section 47 insists that the trustees and not the employer appoint the auditor, the actuary, the discretionary portfolio manager or other manager, or the legal or medical or other professional advisers. Under section 48 the auditor and actuary are under a duty to report to O.P.R.A. any reasonable belief that any statutory or other breach of duty has occurred which is likely to be of material significance to O.P.R.A. exercise of its functions.[46]

Section 49 ensures that proper receipts, records and separate bank accounts are kept, while section 50 ensures that there are proper procedures for resolution of disputes.

9–385 In support of the crucial minimum funding requirements sections 57 to 61 require trustees to obtain actuarial valuations and certificates, to provide schedules of contributions by the employer and active members and to give notice to OPRA and the scheme members if the employer or active members do not pay their contributions by the due dates. If the value of the scheme assets falls below 90 per cent of scheme liabilities the employer must make good the 90 per cent level within a year, while the function of contributions schedules (based on valuations every three years) is to ensure that the 100 per cent level is reached within five years if a valuation reveals a shortfall.

In the crucial area of powers to modify schemes, section 67 prevents such powers being exercised in any way which would or might affect any entitlement or accrued right of any scheme member unless certain

---

[46] Civil, rather than criminal, penalities are now imposed for non-fraudulent failure to pay contributions (and produce accounts): Occupational and Personal Pension Schemes (Penalties) Regulations, 2000.

requirements are satisfied, *e.g.* the approval of the trustees where the power is exercisable by the employer or the consent of the members. Section 68 further confers extensive powers upon trustees by resolution to modify their scheme to reflect the impact of the Act or with the employer's consent to extend the class who may receive benefits in respect of the death of a scheme member. Section 69 then further enables OPRA to modify schemes for achieving particular purposes.

The more important sections of the Act are now set out, as amended by the Child Support, Pensions and Social Security Act 2000.

Member-nominated trustees and directors

16.—(1) The trustees of a trust scheme must secure— **9–386**

(a) that such arrangements for the selection of persons nominated by members of the scheme to be trustees of the scheme as are required by this section are made, and
(b) that those arrangements are implemented.

(2) Persons who become trustees under the arrangements required by subsection (1) are referred to in this Part as "member-nominated trustees".
(3) The arrangements must provide—

(a) for any person who has been nominated and selected as a member-nominated trustee to become a trustee by virtue of his selection, and
(b) for the removal of such a person to require the agreement of all the other trustees.

(4) Where a vacancy for a member-nominated trustee is not filled because insufficient nominations are received, the arrangements must provide for the filling of the vacancy, or for the vacancy to remain, until the expiry of the next period in which persons may be nominated and selected in accordance with regulations.
(5) The arrangements must provide for the selection of a person as a member- **9–387**
nominated trustee to have effect for a period of not less than three nor more than six years but for a member-nominated trustee to be eligible for selection again at the end of any period of service as such a trustee.
(6) The arrangements must provide for the number of member-nominated trustees to be—

(a) at least two or (if the scheme comprises less than 100 members) at least one, and
(b) at least one-third of the total number of trustees;

but the arrangements must not provide for a greater number of member-nominated trustees than that required to satisfy that minimum unless the employer has given his approval to the greater number.
(6A) The arrangements must provide that, where the employer so requires, a person who is not a qualifying member of the scheme must have the employer's approval to qualify for selection as a member-nominated trustee.
(7) The arrangements must not provide for the functions of member-nominated trustees to differ from those of any other trustee but, for the purposes of this subsection—

(a) any provision made by an order under section 8(4), and

(b) section 25(2),

shall be disregarded.

9–388   (8) The arrangements (a) must provide that, if a member-nominated trustee who was a member of the scheme when he was appointed ceases to be a member of the scheme, he ceases to be a trustee by virtue of that fact; and (b) may provide for a member-nominated trustee who

(i) is a qualifying member of one of the following descriptions, an active, deferred or pensioner member, and

(ii) ceases (without ceasing to be a qualifying member) to be a qualifying member of that description, to cease, by virtue of that fact, to be a trustee.

(9) [Empowers regulations to be made in relation to the above arrangements] [Section 18 creates parallel provisions concerning member-nominated directors of a trustee company connected with the employer.]

[Sections 17, 19 and 20 that allowed opt-outs have been repealed].

Trustees: general

27.—(1) A trustee of a trust scheme, and any person who is connected with, or an associate of, such a trustee, is ineligible to act as an auditor or actuary of the scheme.

(2) Subsection (1) does not make a person who is a director, partner or employee of a firm of actuaries ineligible to act as an actuary of a trust scheme merely because another director, partner or employee of the firm is a trustee of the scheme.

(3) Subsection (1) does not make a person who falls within a prescribed class or description ineligible to act as an auditor or actuary of a trust scheme.

(4) A person must not act as an auditor or actuary of a trust scheme if he is ineligible under this section to do so.

(5) In this section and section 28 references to a trustee of a trust scheme do not include—

(a) a trustee, or

(b) a trustee of a scheme,

falling within a prescribed class or description.

3–389   **29.**—(1) Subject to subsection (5), a person is disqualified for being a trustee of any trust scheme if—

(a) he has been convicted of any offence involving dishonesty or deception,

(b) he has been adjudged bankrupt or sequestration of his estate has been awarded and (in either case) he has not been discharged,

(c) where the person is a company, if any director of the company is disqualified under this section,

(d) where the person is a Scottish partnership, if any partner is disqualified under this section,

(e) he has made a composition contract or an arrangement with, or granted a trust deed for the behoof of, his creditors and has not been discharged in respect of it, or

(f) he is subject to a disqualification order under the Company Directors Disqualification Act 1986 or to an order made under section 429(2)(b) of the Insolvency Act 1986 (failure to pay under county court administration order).

(2) In subsection (1)—

(a) paragraph (a) applies whether the conviction occurred before or after the **9–390** coming into force of that subsection, but does not apply in relation to any conviction which is a spent conviction for the purposes of the Rehabilitation of Offenders Act 1974,
(b) paragraph (b) applies whether the adjudication of bankruptcy or the sequestration occurred before or after the coming into force of that subsection,
(c) paragraph (e) applies whether the composition contract or arrangement was made, or the trust deed was granted, before or after the coming into force of that subsection, and
(d) paragraph (f) applies in relation to orders made before or after the coming into force of that subsection.

(3) Where a person—

(a) is prohibited from being a trustee of a trust scheme by an order under **9–391** section 3, or
(b) has been removed as a trustee of a trust scheme by an order made (whether before or after the coming into force of this subsection) by the High Court or the Court of Session on the grounds of misconduct or mismanagement in the administration of the scheme for which he was responsible or to which he was privy, or which he by his conduct contributed to or facilitated,

the Authority may, if in their opinion it is not desirable for him to be a trustee of any trust scheme, by order disqualify him for being a trustee of any trust scheme.

(4) The Authority may by order disqualify a person for being a trustee of any trust scheme where—

(a) in their opinion he is incapable of acting as such a trustee by reason of mental disorder (within the meaning of the Mental Health Act 1983 or, as respects Scotland, the Mental Health (Scotland) Act 1984), or
(b) the person is a company which has gone into liquidation (within the meaning of section 247(2) of the Insolvency Act 1986).

(5) The Authority may, on the application of any person disqualified under **9–392** this section—

(a) give notice in writing to him waiving his disqualification,
(b) in the case of a person disqualified under subsection (3) or (4), by order revoke the order disqualifying him,

either generally or in relation to a particular scheme or particular class of schemes.

(6) A notice given or revocation made at any time by virtue of subsection (5) cannot affect anything done before that time.

30.—(1) A trustee of a trust scheme who becomes disqualified under section 29 shall, while he is so disqualified, cease to be a trustee.

(2) Where—

(a) a trustee of a trust scheme becomes disqualified under section 29, or
(b) in the case of a trustee of a trust scheme who has become so disqualified, his disqualification is waived or the order disqualifying him is revoked or he otherwise ceases to be disqualified,

the Authority may exercise the same jurisdiction and powers as are exercisable by the High Court or, in relation to a trust scheme subject to the law of Scotland, the Court of Session for vesting any property in, or transferring any property to, the trustees.

9–393 (3) A person who purports to act as a trustee of a trust scheme while he is disqualified under section 29 is guilty of an offence and liable—

(a) on summary conviction to a fine not exceeding the statutory maximum, and
(b) on conviction on indictment, to a fine or imprisonment or both.

(4) An offence under subsection (3) may be charged by reference to any day or longer period of time: and a person may be convicted of a second or subsequent offence under that subsection by reference to any period of time following the preceding conviction of the offence.

(5) Things done by a person disqualified under section 29 while purporting to act as trustee of a trust scheme are not invalid merely because of that disqualification.

(6) Nothing in section 29 or this section affects the liability of any person for things done, or omitted to be done, by him while purporting to act as trustee of a trust scheme.

(7) The Authority must keep, in such manner as they think fit, a register of all persons who are disqualified under section 29(3) or (4); and the Authority must, if requested to do so, disclose whether the name of a person specified in the request is included in the register in respect of a scheme so specified.

9–394 **31.**—(1) No amount may be paid out of the assets of a trust scheme for the purpose of reimbursing, or providing for the reimbursement of, any trustee of the scheme in respect of—

(a) a fine imposed by way of penalty for an offence of which he is convicted, or
(b) a penalty which he is required to pay under section 10 or under section 168(4) of the Pension Schemes Act 1993.

(2) For the purposes of subsection (1), providing for the reimbursement of a trustee in respect of a fine or penalty includes (among other things) providing for the payment of premiums in respect of a policy of insurance where the risk is or includes the imposition of such a fine or the requirement to pay such a penalty.

(3) Where any amount is paid out of the assets of a trust scheme in contravention of this section, sections 3 and 10 apply to any trustee who fails to take all such steps as are reasonable to secure compliance.

(4) Where a trustee of a trust scheme—   **9–395**

(a) is reimbursed, out of the assets of the scheme or in consequence of
    provision for his reimbursement made out of those assets, in respect of
    any of the matters referred to in subsection (1)(a) or (b), and

(b) knows, or has reasonable grounds to believe, that he has been reim-
    bursed as mentioned in paragraph (a),

then, unless he has taken all such steps as are reasonable to secure that he is not
so reimbursed, he is guilty of an offence.

(5) A person guilty of an offence under subsection (4) is liable—

(a) on summary conviction, to a fine not exceeding the statutory maximum,
    and

(b) on conviction on indictment, to imprisonment, or a fine, or both.

Functions of trustees

32.—(1) Decisions of the trustees of a trust scheme may, unless the scheme **9–396**
provides otherwise, be taken by agreement of a majority of the trustees.

(2) Where decisions of the trustees of a trust scheme may be taken by
agreement of a majority of the trustees—

(a) the trustees may, unless the scheme provides otherwise, by a determina-
    tion under this subsection require not less than the number of trustees
    specified in the determination to be present when any decision is so
    taken, and

(b) notice of any occasions at which decisions may be so taken must, unless
    the occasion falls within a prescribed class or description, be given to
    each trustee to whom it is reasonably practicable to give such notice.

(3) Notice under subsection (2)(b) must be given in a prescribed manner and
not later than the beginning of a prescribed period.

(4) This section is subject to sections 8(4)(b), 16(3)(b) and 25(2).

(5) If subsection (2)(b) is not complied with, sections 3 and 10 apply to any
trustee who has failed to take all such steps as are reasonable to secure
compliance.

33.—(1) Liability for breach of an obligation under any rule of law to take **9–397**
care or exercise skill in the performance of any investment functions, where the
function is exercisable—

(a) by a trustee of a trust scheme, or

(b) by a person to whom the function has been delegated under section 34,

cannot be excluded or restricted by any instrument or agreement.

(2) In this section, references to excluding or restricting liability include—

(a) making the liability or its enforcement subject to restrictive or onerous
    conditions,

(b) excluding or restricting any right or remedy in respect of the liability, or
    subjecting a person to any prejudice in consequence of his pursuing any
    such right or remedy, or

(c) excluding or restricting rules of evidence or procedure.

(3) This section does not apply—

(a) to a scheme falling within any prescribed class or description, or
(b) to any prescribed description of exclusion or restriction.

9–398   **34.**—(1) The trustees of a trust scheme have, subject to any restriction imposed by the scheme, the same power to make an investment of any kind as if they were absolutely entitled to the assets of the scheme.

(2) Any discretion of the trustees of a trust scheme to make any decision about investments—

(a) may be delegated by or on behalf of the trustees to a fund manager to whom subsection (3) applies to be exercised in accordance with section 36, but
(b) may not otherwise be delegated except under section 25 of the Trustee Act 1925 (delegation of trusts during absence abroad) or subsection (5) below.

9–399   (3) This subsection applies to a fund manager who, in relation to the decisions in question, falls, or is treated as falling, within any of paragraphs (a) to (c) of section 191(2) of the Financial Services Act 1986 (occupational pension schemes: exemptions where decisions taken by authorised and other persons).

(4) The trustees are not responsible for the act or default of any fund manager in the exercise of any discretion delegated to him under subsection (2)(a) if they have taken all such steps as are reasonable to satisfy themselves or the person who made the delegation on their behalf has taken all such steps as are reasonable to satisfy himself—

(a) that the fund manager has the appropriate knowledge and experience for managing the investments of the scheme, and
(b) that he is carrying out his work competently and complying with section 36.

(5) Subject to any restriction imposed by a trust scheme—

9–400   (a) the trustees may authorise two or more of their number to exercise on their behalf any discretion to make any decision about investments, and
(b) any such discretion may, where giving effect to the decision would not constitute carrying on investment business in the United Kingdom (within the meaning of the Financial Services Act 1986), be delegated by or on behalf of the trustees to a fund manager to whom subsection (3) does not apply to be exercised in accordance with section 36;

but in either case the trustees are liable for any acts or defaults in the exercise of the discretion if they would be so liable if they were the acts or defaults of the trustees as a whole.

(6) Section 33 does not prevent the exclusion or restriction of any liability of the trustees of a trust scheme for the acts or defaults of a fund manager in the exercise of a discretion delegated to him under subsection (5)(b) where the

trustees have taken all such steps as are reasonable to satisfy themselves, or the person who made the delegation on their behalf has taken all such steps as are reasonable to satisfy himself—

(a) that the fund manager has the appropriate knowledge and experience for managing the investments of the scheme, and

(b) that he is carrying out his work competently and complying with section 36;

and subsection (2) of section 33 applies for the purposes of this subsection as it applies for the purposes of that section.

(7) The provisions of this section override any restriction inconsistent with the **9–401** provisions imposed by any rule of law or by or under any enactment, other than an enactment contained in, or made under, this Part or the Pension Schemes Act 1993.

35.—(1) The trustees of a trust scheme must secure that there is prepared, maintained and from time to time revised a written statement of the principles governing decisions about investments for the purposes of the scheme.

(2) The statement must cover, among other things—

(a) the trustees' policy for securing compliance with sections 36 and 56, and

(b) their policy about the following matters.

(3) Those matters are—

(a) the kinds of investments to be held,

(b) the balance between different kinds of investments,

(c) risk,

(d) the expected return on investments,

(e) the realisation of investments, and

(f) such other matters as may be prescribed.[47]

(4) Neither the trust scheme nor the statement may impose restrictions **9–402** (however expressed) on any power to make investments by reference to the consent of the employer.

(5) The trustees of a trust scheme must, before a statement under this section is prepared or revised—

(a) obtain and consider the written advice of a person who is reasonably believed by the trustees to be qualified by his ability in and practical experience of financial matters and to have the appropriate knowledge and experience of the management of the investments of such schemes, and

(b) consult the employer.

(6) If in the case of any trust scheme—

---

[47] S.I. 1999/1849 adding Reg. 11A to S.I. 1996/3127 prescribes the extent, if at all, to which social, environmental or ethical considerations are taken into account (all things being equal) and the trustees' policy, if any, in relation to the rights, including voting rights, attaching to investments.

(a) a statement under this section has not been prepared or is not being maintained, or

(b) the trustees have not obtained and considered advice in accordance with subsection (5),

sections 3 and 10 apply to any trustee who has failed to take all such steps as are reasonable to secure compliance.

(7) This section does not apply to any scheme which falls within a prescribed class or description.

9–403 **36.**—(1) The trustees of a trust scheme must exercise their powers of investment in accordance with subsections (2) to (4) and any fund manager to whom any discretion has been delegated under section 34 must exercise the discretion in accordance with subsection (2).

(2) The trustees or fund manager must have regard—

(a) to the need for diversification of investments, in so far as appropriate to the circumstances of the scheme, and

(b) to the suitability to the scheme of investments of the description of investment proposed and of the investment proposed as an investment of that description.

9–404 (3) Before investing in any manner (other than in a manner mentioned in Part I of Schedule 1 to the Trustee Investments Act 1961) the trustees must obtain and consider proper advice on the question whether the investment is satisfactory having regard to the matters mentioned in subsection (2) and the principles contained in the statement under section 35.

(4) Trustees retaining any investment must—

(a) determine at what intervals the circumstances, and in particular the nature of the investment, make it desirable to obtain such advice as is mentioned in subsection (3), and

(b) obtain and consider such advice accordingly.

(5) The trustees, or the fund manager to whom any discretion has been delegated under section 34, must exercise their powers of investment with a view to giving effect to the principles contained in the statement under section 35, so far as reasonably practicable.

(6) For the purposes of this section "proper advice" means—

9–405 (a) where giving the advice constitutes carrying on investment business in the United Kingdom (within the meaning of the Financial Services Act 1986), advice—

(i) given by a person authorised under Chapter III of Part I of that Act,

(ii) given by a person exempted under Chapter IV of that Part who, in giving the advice, is acting in the course of the business in respect of which he is exempt,

(iii) given by a person where, by virtue of paragraph 27 of Schedule 1 to that Act, paragraph 15 of that Schedule does not apply to giving the advice, or

(iv) given by a person who, by virtue of regulation 5 of the Banking Coordination (Second Council Directive) Regulations 1992, may give the advice though not authorised as mentioned in sub-paragraph (i) above.

(b) in any other case, the advice of a person who is reasonably believed by the trustees to be qualified by his ability in and practical experience of financial matters and to have the appropriate knowledge and experience of the management of the investments of trust schemes.

(7) Trustees shall not be treated as having complied with subsection (3) or (4) unless the advice was given or has subsequently been confirmed in writing.

(8) If the trustees of a trust scheme do not obtain and consider advice in accordance with this section, sections 3 and 10 apply to any trustee who has failed to take all such steps as are reasonable to secure compliance.

37.—(1) This section applies to a trust scheme if—

(a) apart from this section, power is conferred on any person (including the **9–406** employer) to make payments to the employer out of funds which are held for the purposes of the scheme,

(b) the scheme is one to which Schedule 22 to the Taxes Act 1988 (reduction of pension fund surpluses in certain exempt approved schemes) applies, and

(c) the scheme is not being wound up.

(2) Where the power referred to in subsection (1)(a) is conferred by the scheme on a person other than the trustees, it cannot be exercised by that person but may be exercised instead by the trustees; and any restriction imposed by the scheme on the exercise of the power shall, so far as capable of doing so, apply to its exercise by the trustees.

(3) The power referred to in subsection (1)(a) cannot be exercised unless the requirements of subsection (4) and (in prescribed circumstances) (5), and any prescribed requirements, are satisfied.

(4) The requirements of this subsection are that— **9–407**

(a) the power is exercised in pursuance of proposals approved under paragraph 6(1) of Schedule 22 to the Taxes Act 1988,

(b) the trustees are satisfied that it is in the interests of the members that the power be exercised in the manner so proposed,

(c) where the power is conferred by the scheme on the employer, the employer has asked for the power to be exercised, or consented to it being exercised, in the manner so proposed,

(d) the annual rates of the pensions under the scheme which commence or have commenced are increased by the appropriate percentage, and

(e) notice has been given in accordance with prescribed requirements to the members of the scheme of the proposal to exercise the power.

(5) The requirements of this subsection are that the Authority are of the opinion that—

(a) any requirements prescribed by virtue of subsection (3) are satisfied, and

(b) the requirements of subsection (4) are satisfied.

(6) In subsection (4)—

(a) "annual rate" and "appropriate percentage" have the same meaning as in section 54, and
(b) "pension" does not include—
    (i) any guaranteed minimum pension (as defined in section 8(2) of the Pension Schemes Act 1993) or any increase in such a pension under section 109 of that Act, or
    (ii) any money purchase benefit (as defined in section 181(1) of that Act).

9–408   (7) This section does not apply to any payment to which, by virtue of section 601(3) of the Taxes Act 1988, section 601(2) of that Act does not apply.

(8) If, where this section applies to any trust scheme, the trustees purport to exercise the power referred to in subsection (1)(a) by making a payment to which this section applies without complying with the requirements of this section, sections 3 and 10 apply to any trustee who has failed to take all such steps as are reasonable to secure compliance.

(9) If, where this section applies to any trust scheme, any person, other than the trustees, purports to exercise the power referred to in subsection (1)(a) by making a payment to which this section applies, section 10 applies to him.

(10) Regulations may provide that, in prescribed circumstances, this section does not apply to schemes falling within a prescribed class or description, or applies to them with prescribed modifications.

9–409   **38.**—(1) If, apart from this section, the rules of a trust scheme would require the scheme to be wound up, the trustees may determine that the scheme is not for the time being to be wound up but that no new members are to be admitted to the scheme.

(2) Where the trustees make a determination under subsection (1), they may also determine—

(a) that no further contributions are to be paid towards the scheme, or
(b) that no new benefits are to accrue to, or in respect of, members of the scheme;

but this subsection does not authorise the trustees to determine, where there are accrued rights to any benefit, that the benefit is not to be increased.

(3) This section does not apply to—

(a) a money purchase scheme, or
(b) a scheme falling within a prescribed class or description.

39.—(1) No rule of law that a trustee may not exercise the powers vested in him so as to give rise to a conflict between his personal interest and his duties to the beneficiaries shall apply to a trustee of a trust scheme, who is also a member of the scheme, exercising the powers vested in him in any manner, merely because their exercise in that manner benefits, or may benefit, him as a member of the scheme.

Functions of trustees or managers

40.—(1) The trustees or managers of an occupational pension scheme must **9–410** secure that the scheme complies with any prescribed restrictions with respect to the proportion of its resources that may at any time be invested in, or in any description of, employer-related investments.

(2) In this section—

"employer-related investments" means—

(a) shares or other securities issued by the employer or by any person who is connected with, or an associate of, the employer,

(b) land which is occupied or used by, or subject to a lease in favour of, the employer or any such person,

(c) property (other than land) which is used for the purposes of any business carried on by the employer or any such person,

(d) loans to the employer or any such person, and

(e) other prescribed investments,

"securities" means any asset, right or interest falling within paragraph 1, 2, 4 or 5 of Schedule 1 to the Financial Services Act 1986.

(3) To the extent (if any) that sums due and payable by a person to the trustees or managers of an occupational pension scheme remain unpaid—

(a) they shall be regarded for the purposes of this section as loans made to that person by the trustees or managers, and

(b) resources of the scheme shall be regarded as invested accordingly.

(4) If in the case of a trust scheme subsection (1) is not complied with, **9–411** sections 3 [removal by OPRA] and 10 [civil penalties] apply to any trustee who fails to take all such steps as are reasonable to secure compliance.

(5) If any resources of an occupational pension scheme are invested in contravention of subsection (1), any trustee or manager who agreed in the determination to make the investment is guilty of an offence and liable—

(a) on summary conviction, to a fine not exceeding the statutory maximum, and

(b) on conviction on indictment, to a fine or imprisonment, or both.

41.—(1) Regulations may require the trustees or managers of an occupational **9–412** pension scheme—

(a) to obtain at prescribed times the documents mentioned in subsection (2), and

(b) to make copies of them, and of the documents mentioned in subsection (3), available to the persons mentioned in subsection (4).

(2) The documents referred to in subsection (1)(a) are—

(a) the accounts audited by the auditor of the scheme,

(b) the auditor's statement about contributions under the scheme,

(c) a valuation by the actuary of the assets and liabilities of the scheme, and a statement by the actuary concerning such aspects of the valuation as may be prescribed.

(3) The documents referred to in subsection (1)(b) are—

9–413
    (a) any valuation, or certificate, prepared under section 57 or 58 by the actuary of the scheme,
    (b) any report prepared by the trustees or managers under section 59(3).

(4) The persons referred to in subsection (1)(b) are—

    (a) members and prospective members of the scheme,
    (b) spouses of members and of prospective members,
    (c) persons within the application of the scheme and qualifying or prospectively qualifying for its benefits,
    (d) independent trade unions recognised to any extent for the purposes of collective bargaining in relation to members and prospective members of the scheme.

9–414
(5) Regulations may in the case of occupational pension schemes to which section 47 does not apply—

    (a) prescribe the persons who may act as auditors or actuaries for the purposes of subsection (2), or
    (b) provide that the persons who may so act shall be—
        (i) persons with prescribed professional qualifications or experience, or
        (ii) persons approved by the Secretary of State.

(6) Regulations shall make provision for referring to an industrial tribunal any question whether an organisation is such a trade union as is mentioned in subsection (4)(d) and may make provision as to the form and content of any such document as is referred to in subsection (2).

Indexation

9–415
51.—(1) Subject to subsection (6) this section applies to a pension under an occupational pension scheme if—

    (a) the scheme—
        (i) is an approved scheme, within the meaning of Chapter I of Part XIV of the Taxes Act 1988 (retirement benefit schemes approved by the Commissioners of Inland Revenue) or is a scheme for which such approval has been applied for under that Chapter and not refused, and
        (ii) is not a public service pension scheme, and
    (b) apart from this section, the annual rate of the pension would not be increased each year by at least the appropriate percentage of that rate.

(2) Subject to sections 51A and 52, where a pension to which this section applies, or any part of it, is attributable to pensionable service on or after the appointed day or, in the case of money purchase benefits, to payments in respect of employment carried on on or after the appointed day—

    (a) the annual rate of the pension, or

    (b) if only part of the pension is attributable to pensionable service or, as the case may be, to payments in respect of employment carried on on or after the appointed day, so much of the annual rate as is attributable to that part,

must be increased annually by at least the appropriate percentage.

    (3) Subsection (2) does not apply to a pension under an occupational pension **9–416** scheme if the rules of the scheme require—

    (a) the annual rate of the pension, or
    (b) if only part of the pension is attributable to pensionable service or, as the case may be, to payments in respect of employment carried on on or after the appointed day, so much of the annual rate as is attributable to that part,

to be increased at intervals of not more than twelve months by at least the relevant percentage and the scheme complies with any prescribed requirements.

    (4) For the purposes of subsection (3) the relevant percentage is—

    (a) the percentage increase in the retail prices index for the reference period, being a period determined, in relation to each periodic increase, under the rules, or
    (b) the percentage for that period which corresponds to 5 per cent per annum,

whichever is the lesser.

    (5) Regulations may provide that the provisions of subsections (2) and (3) **9–417** apply in relation to a pension as if so much of it as would not otherwise be attributable to pensionable service or to payments in respect of employment were attributable to pensionable service or, as the case may be, payments in respect of employment—

    (a) before the appointed day,
    (b) on or after that day, or
    (c) partly before and partly on or after that day.

    (6) This section does not apply to any pension or part of a pension which, in the opinion of the trustees or managers, is derived from the payment by any member of the scheme of voluntary contributions.

    54.—(1) The first increase required by section 51 in the rate of a pension must take effect not later than the first anniversary of the date on which the pension is first paid; and subsequent increases must take effect at intervals of not more than twelve months.

    (2) Where the first such increase is to take effect on a date when the pension has been in payment for a period of less than twelve months, the increase must be of an amount at least equal to one twelfth of the amount of the increase so required (apart from this subsection) for each complete month in that period.

    (3) In sections 51 to 53 and this section—

"annual rate", in relation to a pension, means the annual rate of the pension, as previously increased under the rules of the scheme or under section 51, "the appointed day" means the day appointed under section 180 for the commencement of section 51,

"appropriate percentage", in relation to an increase in the whole or part of the annual rate of a pension, means the revaluation percentage for the latest revaluation period specified in the order under paragraph 2 of Schedule 3 to the Pensions Scheme Act 1993 (revalation of accrued pension benefits) which is in force at the time of the increase (expressions used in this definition having the same meaning as in that paragraph),

"pension", in relation to a scheme, means any pension in payment under the scheme and includes an annuity . . .

Minimum funding requirement

9–418   **56.**—(1) Every occupational pension scheme to which this section applies is subject to a requirement (referred to in this Part as "the minimum funding requirement") that the value of the assets of the scheme is not less than the amount of the liabilities of the scheme.

(2) This section applies to an occupational pension scheme other than—

(a) a money purchase scheme, or
(b) a scheme falling within a prescribed class or description.

(3) For the purposes of this section and sections 57 to 61, the liabilities and assets to be taken into account, and their amount or value, shall be determined, calculated and verified by a prescribed person and in the prescribed manner.

(4) In calculating the value of any liabilities for those purposes, a provision of the scheme which limits the amount of its liabilities by reference to the amount of its assets is to be disregarded.

9–419   (5) In sections 57 to 61, in relation to any occupational pension scheme to which this section applies—

(a) the amount of the liabilities referred to in subsection (1) is referred to as "the amount of the scheme liabilities",
(b) the value of the assets referred to in that subsection is referred to as "the value of the scheme assets",
(c) an "actuarial valuation" means a written valuation prepared and signed by the actuary of the scheme of the assets and liabilities referred to in subsection (1), and
(d) the "effective date" of an actuarial valuation is the date by reference to which the assets and liabilities are valued.

57.—(1) The trustees or managers of an occupational pension scheme to which section 56 applies must—

9–420   (a) obtain, within a prescribed period, an actuarial valuation and afterwards obtain such a valuation before the end of prescribed intervals, and
(b) on prescribed occasions or within prescribed periods, obtain a certificate prepared by the actuary of the scheme—
  (i) stating whether or not in his opinion the contributions payable towards the scheme are adequate for the purpose of securing that the minimum funding requirement will continue to be met throughout the prescribed period or, if it appears to him that it is not met, will be met by the end of that period, and

    (ii) indicating any relevant changes that have occurred since the last actuarial valuation was prepared.

(2) Subject to subsection (3), the trustees or managers must—

    (a) if the actuary states in such a certificate that in his opinion the contributions payable towards the scheme are not adequate for the purpose of securing that the minimum funding requirement will continue to be met throughout the prescribed period or, if it appears to him that it is not met, will be met by the end of that period, or

    (b) in prescribed circumstances,

obtain an actuarial valuation within the period required by subsection (4).

(3) In a case within subsection (2)(a), the trustees or managers are not **9–421** required to obtain an actuarial valuation if—

    (a) in the opinion of the actuary of the scheme, the value of the scheme assets is not less than 90 per cent. of the amount of the scheme liabilities, and

    (b) since the date on which the actuary signed the certificate referred to in that subsection, the schedule of contributions for the scheme has been revised under section 58(3)(b).

(4) If the trustees or managers obtain a valuation under subsection (2) they must do so—

    (a) in the case of a valuation required by paragraph (a), within the period of six months beginning with the date on which the certificate was signed, and

    (b) in any other case, within a prescribed period.

(5) A valuation or certificate obtained under subsection (1) or (2) must be **9–422** prepared in such manner, give such information and contain such statements as may be prescribed.

(6) The trustees or managers must secure that any valuation or certificate obtained under this section is made available to the employer within seven days of their receiving it.

(7) Where, in the case of an occupational pension scheme to which section 56 applies, subsection (1), (2) or (6) is not complied with—

    (a) section 3 applies to any trustee who has failed to take all such steps as are reasonable to secure compliance, and

    (b) section 10 applies to any trustee or manager who has failed to take all such steps.

58.—(1) The trustees or managers of an occupational pension scheme to **9–423** which section 56 applies must secure that there is prepared, maintained and from time to time revised a schedule (referred to in sections 57 to 59 as a "schedule of contributions") showing—

    (a) the rates of contributions payable towards the scheme by or on behalf of the employer and the active members of the scheme, and

(b) the dates on or before which such contributions are to be paid.

(2) The schedule of contributions for a scheme must satisfy prescribed requirements.

(3) The schedule of contributions for a scheme—

(a) must be prepared before the end of a prescribed period beginning with the signing of the first actuarial valuation for the scheme,
(b) may be revised from time to time where the revisions are previously agreed by the trustees or managers and the employer and any revision in the rates of contributions is certified by the actuary of the scheme, and
(c) must be revised before the end of a prescribed period beginning with the signing of each subsequent actuarial valuation.

9–424   (4) The matters shown in the schedule of contributions for a scheme—

(a) must be matters previously agreed by the trustees or managers and the employer, or
(b) if no such agreement has been made as to all the matters shown in the schedule, must be—
(i) rates of contributions determined by the trustees or managers, being such rates as in their opinion are adequate for the purpose of securing that the minimum funding requirement will continue to be met throughout the prescribed period or, if it appears to them that it is not met, will be met by the end of that period, and
(ii) other matters determined by the trustees or managers;

and the rates of contributions shown in the schedule must be certified by the actuary of the scheme.

9–425   (5) An agreement for the purposes of subsection (4)(a) is one which is made by the trustees or managers and the employer during the prescribed period beginning with the signing of the last preceding actuarial valuation for the scheme.

(6) The actuary may not certify the rates of contributions shown in the schedule of contributions—

(a) in a case where it appears to him that minimum funding requirement was met on the prescribed date; unless he is of the opinion that the rates are adequate for the purpose of securing that the requirement will be me throughout the prescribed period, and
(b) in any other case, unless he is of the opinion that the rates are adequate for the purpose of securing that the requirement will be met by the end of that period.

(7) The Authority may in prescribed circumstances extend (or further extend) the period referred to in subsection (6).

(8) Where, in the case of any occupational pension scheme to which section 56 applies, this section is not complied with—

(a) section 3 applies to any trustee who has failed to take all such steps as are reasonable to secure compliance, and

(b) section 10 applies to any trustee or manager who has failed to take all such steps.

59.—(1) Except in prescribed circumstances, the trustees or managers of an **9–426** occupational pension scheme to which section 56 applies must, where any amounts payable by or on behalf of the employer or the active members of the scheme in accordance with the schedule of contributions have not been paid on or before the due date, give notice of that fact, within the prescribed period, to the Authority and to the members of the scheme.

(2) Any such amounts which for the time being remain unpaid after that date (whether payable by the employer or not) shall, if not a debt due from the employer to the trustees or managers apart from this subsection, be treated as such a debt.

(3) If, in the case of an occupational pension scheme to which section 56 applies, it appears to the trustees or managers, at the end of any prescribed period that the minimum funding requirement is not met, they must within such further period as may be prescribed prepare a report giving the prescribed information about the failure to meet that requirement.

(4) If in the case of any such scheme, subsection (1) or (3) is not complied with—

(a) section 3 applies to any trustee who has failed to take all such steps as are reasonable to secure compliance, and
(b) section 10 applies to any trustee or manager who has failed to take all such steps.

60.—(1) Subsection (2) applies where, in the case of an occupational pension **9–427** scheme to which section 56 applies, an actuarial valuation shows that, on the effective date of the valuation, the value of the scheme assets is less than 90 per cent of the amount of the scheme liabilities (the difference shown in the valuation being referred to in this section as "the shortfall").

(2) The employer must—

(a) by making an appropriate payment to the trustees or managers, or
(b) by a prescribed method,

secure an increase in the value of the scheme assets which, taken with any contributions paid, is not less than the shortfall.

(3) The required increase in that value must be secured—

(a) before the end of a prescribed period beginning with the signing of the valuation, or
(b) if the actuarial valuation was obtained by reason of such a statement in a certificate as is referred to in section 57(2), before the end of a prescribed period beginning with the signing of the certificate.

(4) Except in prescribed circumstances, if the employer fails to secure the required increase in value before the end of the period applicable under subsection (3), the trustees or managers must, within the period of fourteen days (or such longer period as is prescribed) beginning with the end of that period, give written notice of that fact to the Authority and to the members of the scheme.

9–428　　(5) If the employer fails to secure the required increase in value before the end of the period applicable under subsection (3), then so much of the shortfall as, at any subsequent time, has not been met by an increase in value under subsection (2) made—

　　(a) by making an appropriate payment to the trustees or managers,
　　(b) by a prescribed method, or
　　(c) by contributions made before the end of that period,

shall, if not a debt due from the employer to the trustees or managers apart from this subsection, be treated at that time as such a debt.

　　(6) Where an increase in value is secured by a prescribed method, the increase is to be treated for the purposes of this section as being of an amount determined in accordance with regulations.

　　(7) The Authority may in prescribed circumstances extend (or further extend) the period applicable under subsection (3).

　　(8) If subsection (4) is not complied with—

　　(a) section 3 [enabling OPRA to remove him] applies to any trustee who has failed to take all such steps as are reasonable to secure compliance, and
　　(b) section 10 [prescribing civil penalties] applies to any trustee or manager who has failed to take all such steps.

Equal treatment

9–429　　**62.**—(1) An occupational pension scheme which does not contain an equal treatment rule shall be treated as including one.

　　(2) An equal treatment rule is a rule which relates to the terms on which—

　　(a) persons become members of the scheme, and
　　(b) members of the scheme are treated.

(3) Subject to subsection (6), an equal treatment rule has the effect that where—

　　(a) a woman is employed on like work with a man in the same employment,
　　(b) a woman is employed on work rated as equivalent with that of a man in the same employment, or
　　(c) a woman is employed on work which, not being work in relation to which paragraph (a) or (b) applies, is, in terms of the demands made on her (for instance under such headings as effort, skill and decision) of equal value to that of a man in the same employment,

but (apart from the rule) any of the terms referred to in subsection (2) is or becomes less favourable to the woman than it is to the man, the term shall be treated as so modified as not to be less favourable.

9–430　　(4) An equal treatment rule does not operate in relation to any difference as between a woman and a man in the operation of any of the terms referred to in subsection (2) if the trustees or managers of the scheme prove that the difference is genuinely due to a material factor which—

(a) is not the difference of sex, but

(b) is a material difference between the woman's case and the man's case.

(5) References in subsection (4) and sections 63 to 65 to the terms referred to in subsection (2), or the effect of any of those terms, include—

    (a) a term which confers on the trustees or managers of an occupational pension scheme, or any other person, a discretion which, in a case within any of paragraphs (a) to (c) of subsection (3)—

        (i) may be exercised so as to affect the way in which persons become members of the scheme, or members of the scheme are treated, and

        (ii) may (apart from the equal treatment rule) be so exercised in a way less favourable to the woman than to the man, and

    (b) the effect of any exercise of such a discretion;

and references to the terms on which members of the scheme are treated are to be read accordingly.

(6) In the case of a term within subsection (5)(a) the effect of an equal **9–431** treatment rule is that the term shall be treated as so modified as not to permit the discretion to be exercised in a way less favourable to the woman than to the man.

65.—(1) The trustees or managers of an occupational pension scheme may, if—

    (a) they do not (apart from this section) have power to make such alterations to the scheme as may be required to secure conformity with an equal treatment rule, or

    (b) they have such power but the procedure for doing so—

        (i) is liable to be unduly complex or protracted, or

        (ii) involves the obtaining of consents which cannot be obtained, or can only be obtained with undue delay or difficulty,

by resolution make such alterations to the scheme.

(2) The alterations may have effect in relation to a period before the alterations are made . . .

Modification of schemes

67.—(1) This section applies to any power conferred on any person by an **9–432** occupational pension scheme (other than a public service pension scheme) to modify the scheme.

(2) The power cannot be exercised on any occasion in a manner which would or might affect any entitlement, or accrued right, of any member of the scheme acquired before the power is exercised unless the requirements under subsection (3) are satisfied.

(3) Those requirements are that, in respect of the exercise of the power in that manner on that occasion—

    (a) the trustees have satisfied themselves that—

        (i) the certification requirements, or

        (ii) the requirements for consent,

are met in respect of that member, and

  (b) where the power is exercised by a person other than the trustees, the trustees have approved the exercise of the power in that manner on that occasion.

9–433   (4) In subsection (3)—

  (a) "the certification requirements" means prescribed requirements for the purpose of securing that no power to which this section applies is exercised in any manner which, in the opinion of an actuary, would adversely affect any member of the scheme (without his consent) in respect of his entitlement, or accrued rights, acquired before the power is exercised, and

  (b) "the consent requirements" means prescribed requirements for the purpose of obtaining the consent of members of a scheme to the exercise of a power to which this section applies.

(5) Subsection (2) does not apply to the exercise of a power in a prescribed manner.

(6) Where a power to which this section applies may not (apart from this section) be exercised without the consent of any person, regulations may make provision for treating such consent as given in prescribed circumstances.

9–434   **68.**—(1) The trustees of a trust scheme may by resolution modify the scheme with a view to achieving any of the purposes specified in subsection (2).

(2) The purposes referred to in subsection (1) are—

  (a) to extend the class of persons who may receive benefits under the scheme in respect of the death of a member of the scheme,

  (b) to enable the scheme to conform with such arrangements as are required by section 16(1) or 18A(1),

  (c) to enable the scheme to comply with such terms and conditions as may be imposed by the Compensation Board in relation to any payment made by them under section 83 or 84,

  (d) to enable the scheme to conform with section 37(2), 76(2), 91 or 92, and

  (e) prescribed purposes.

(3) No modification may be made by virtue of subsection (2)(a) without the consent of the employer.

(4) Modifications made by virtue of subsection (2)(b) may include in particular—

  (a) modification of any limit on the number of, or of any category of, trustees, or

  (b) provision for the transfer or vesting of property.

9–435   (5) Nothing done by virtue of subsection (2)(d), or any corresponding provisions in force in Northern Ireland, shall be treated as effecting an alteration to the scheme in question for the purposes of section 591B (cessation of approval) of the Taxes Act 1988.

(6) Regulations may provide that this section does not apply to trust schemes falling within a prescribed class or description.

69.—(1) The Authority may, on an application made to them by persons competent to do so, make an order in respect of an occupational pension scheme (other than a public service pension scheme)—

    (a) authorising the modification of the scheme with a view to achieving any of the purposes mentioned in subsection (3), or

    (b) modifying the scheme with a view to achieving any such purpose.

      (2) Regulations may make provision about the manner of dealing with applications under this section.

      (3) The purposes referred to in subsection (1) are—

    (a) in the case of a scheme to which Schedule 22 to the Taxes Act 1988 **9–436** (reduction of pension fund surpluses in certain exempt approved schemes) applies, to reduce or eliminate on any particular occasion any excess in accordance with any proposal submitted under paragraph 3(1) of that Schedule, where any requirements mentioned in section 37(4), and any other prescribed requirements, will be satisfied in relation to the reduction or elimination,

    (b) in the case of an exempt approved scheme (within the meaning given by section 592(1) of the Taxes Act 1988) which is being wound up, to enable assets remaining after the liabilities of the scheme have been fully discharged to be distributed to the employer, where prescribed requirements in relation to the distribution are satisfied, or

    (c) to enable the scheme to be so treated during a prescribed period that an employment to which the scheme applies may be contracted-out employment by reference to it.

(4) The persons competent to make an application under this section are— **9–437**

    (a) in the case of the purposes referred to in paragraph (a) or (b) of subsection (3), the trustees of the scheme, and

    (b) in the case of the purposes referred to in paragraph (c) of that subsection—

      (i) the trustees or managers of the scheme,

      (ii) the employer, or

      (iii) any person other than the trustees or managers who has power to alter the rules of the scheme.

(5) An order under subsection (1)(a) must be framed—

    (a) if made with a view to achieving either of the purposes referred to in subsection (3)(a) or (b), so as to confer the power of modification on the trustees, and

    (b) if made with a view to achieving the purposes referred to in subsection (3)(c), so as to confer the power of modification on such persons (who may include persons who were not parties to the application made to the Authority) as the Authority think appropriate.

(6) Regulations may provide that in prescribed circumstances this section does not apply to occupational pension schemes falling within a prescribed class or description or applies to them with prescribed modifications.

9–438   **70.**—(1) The Authority may not make an order under section 69 unless they are satisfied that the purposes for which the application for the order was made—

(a) cannot be achieved otherwise than by means of such an order, or
(b) can only be achieved in accordance with a procedure which—
    (i) is liable to be unduly complex or protracted, or
    (ii) involves the obtaining of consents which cannot be obtained, or can only be obtained with undue delay or difficulty.

(2) The extent of the Authority's powers to make such an order is not limited, in relation to any purposes for which they are exercisable, to the minimum necessary to achieve those purposes.

(3) The Authority may not make an order under section 69 with a view to achieving the purpose referred to in subsection (3)(c) of that section unless they are satisfied that it is reasonable in all the circumstances to make it.

9–439   **71.**—(1) An order under paragraph (a) of subsection (1) of section 69 may enable those exercising any power conferred by the order to exercise it retrospectively (whether or not the power could otherwise be so exercised) and an order under paragraph (b) of that subsection may modify a scheme retrospectively.

(2) Any modification of a scheme made in pursuance of an order of the Authority under section 69 is as effective in law as if it had been made under powers conferred by or under the scheme.

(3) An order under section 69 may be made and complied with in relation to a scheme—

(a) in spite of any enactment or rule of law, or any rule of the scheme, which would otherwise operate to prevent the modification being made, or
(b) without regard to any such enactment, rule of law or rule of the scheme as would otherwise require, or might otherwise be taken to require, the implementation of any procedure or the obtaining of any consent, with a view to the making of the modification.

(4) In this section, "retrospectively" means with effect from a date before that on which the power is exercised or, as the case may be, the order is made. [s 71A added by Child Support Pensions and Social Security, Act 2000 confers power upon O.P.R.A. to make an order modifying the scheme with a view to ensuring it is properly wound up.]

Section 10. Indemnity of Trustees[48]

I. Indemnity and Lien Against the Trust Property[49]

9–440   By section 31 (1) of the Trustee Act 2000 "A trustee (a) is entitled to be reimbursed from the trust funds, or (b) may pay out of the trust

---

[48] See generally A. W. Scott, "Liabilities Incurred in the Administration of Trusts" (1915) 28 H.L.R. 725; Stone. "A Theory of Liability of Trust Estates for the Contracts and Torts of the Trustee" (1922) 22 Col. L.R. 527; A. J. Hawkins, "The Personal Liability of Charity Trustees" (1979) 95 L.Q.R. 99; D. J. Hayton, "Trading Trusts", Chapter in J. Glasson (ed), *International Trust Laws*.
[49] For indemnity against the beneficiaries personally, see Part II of this section, *infra*, para. 9–445; for indemnity against the beneficiary's beneficial interest under s.62 of the Trustee Act 1925, see *infra*, para. 10–81; for a trustee's indemnity against his co-trustee, see *infra*, para. 10–105.

funds, expenses *properly* incurred by him when acting on behalf of the trust." What then, if he employs an agent or nominee or custodian and such appointee incurs expenses and charges remuneration? By section 32 (3) "The trustees may reimburse the agent, nominee or custodian out of the trust funds for any expenses *properly* incurred by him in exercising functions as an agent, nominee or custodian." However, by section 32 (2) the trustees can only "remunerate the agent, nominee or custodian out of the trust funds for services" if "the amount does not exceed such remuneration as is *reasonable* in the circumstances for the provision of those services by him to or on behalf of that trust."

These provisions reflect the established position that trustees only **9–441** have power to pay "proper costs incident to the execution of the trust."[50] As Lord Templeman stated in *Carver v. Duncan*,[51] "Trustees are entitled to be indemnified out of the capital and income of their trust fund against all obligations incurred by the trustees in the due performance of their duties and the due exercise of their powers. The trustees must then debit each item of expenditure either against income or against capital. The general rule is that income must bear all ordinary outgoings of a recurrent nature, such as rates and taxes and interest on charges and incumbrances. Capital must bear all costs, charges, and expenses incurred for the benefit of the whole estate."

In *Stott v. Milne*[52] the Earl of Selborne L.C. stated, "The right of trustees to indemnity against all costs and expenses properly incurred by them in the execution of the trust is a first charge on all the trust properly, both income and *corpus*. The trustees, therefore, had a right to retain the costs out of the income until provision could be made for raising them out of the *corpus*." Similarly if mortgage interest is paid out of capital because no income is available, capital must be reimbursed out of future income.[53]

Section 39 (1) of the Trustee Act 2000 defines "the trust funds" to **9–442** mean "income or capital funds of the trust", so that trustees can still initially pay expenses out of either income or capital before any adjustment is made for the burden of the expenses falling ultimately upon income or capital depending on the nature of the expenses. It appears that the Law Commission specifically intended trustees to have complete discretion to allocate the ultimate incidence of "the costs of employing a nominee or custodian between income and capital"[54] and believed this was achieved by the definition of "trust funds", which applies also to reimbursement of expenses in section 31 (1) and to remuneration of agents (as to which no general or specific recommendations were made by the Commission). It is not considered that the definition of "trust funds" is sufficient to alter the law so as dramatically

---

[50] *Holding and Management Ltd v. Property Holding and Investment Trust plc* [1998] 1 W.L.R. 1313, 1324 per Nicholls L.J.; *Re Grimthorpe* [1958] Ch. 615, 623.
[51] [1985] 2 All E.R. 645, 652.
[52] (1884) 25 Ch.D. 710, 715.
[53] *Honywood v. Honywood* [1902] 1 Ch. 347.
[54] "Trustees' Powers and Duties" Law Com No. 260 paras 5.13 and 8.33.

to afford trustees complete discretion on the ultimate incidence of expenses between income and capital.[55]

No indemnity can be claimed by a trustee in respect of a liability improperly[56] incurred to X, *e.g.* because of:

(i) lack of power under the trust instrument;
(ii) lack of due authorisation under internal requirements (*e.g.* for trustee unanimity, or consent of B, or for a meeting to be duly held before any decision is taken);
(iii) breach of equitable duties (*e.g.* to diversify investments, to supervise agents, to invest with the statutory duty of care, to take account of relevant considerations and ignore irrelevant considerations which would have led to a different decision).

Moreover, (iv), a trustee cannot reimburse itself if indebted to the trust by reason of some unconnected breach of trust.[57] After all, its right to reimbursement depends ultimately on the state of accounts between it and the beneficiaries and is limited to the balance, if any, in its favour.

9–443   Finally, (v) no right of indemnity exists to the extent that it has been excluded in the trust instrument, as may happen where the trustee has a liberal right to remuneration under a charging clause intended to cover expenses.[58]

The trustee can protect itself against the problems in (i) and (ii) above by taking the advice of lawyers or even the guidance of the court. It can also protect itself against allegations that in breach of its equitable duties it involved itself as claimant or defendant in an action involving the trust and a third party so that it should personally pay its own costs and the costs of the other (winning) side in the action. To do this, it seeks in private a Beddoe's Order[59] from the court which will entitle it to be reimbursed costs out of the trust fund no matter the result of the litigation, so long as full and frank disclosure was made to the court. However, where the claim seeks to undermine the trust wholly or partly (*e.g.* claims by the settlor's creditors or trustee in bankruptcy[60] or an adverse proprietary tracing claim) the trustee may be required to be neutral and only have a right of indemnity for the costs of acting neutrally,[61] unless no other person is appropriate to represent the interests of beneficiaries who are unborn or otherwise unascertained.[62]

---

[55] *Lewin on Trusts* (17th ed), para. 25–26B has the same view.
[56] Exceptionally, if the trustee acted in good faith and the transaction benefited the trust fund he should have a right of indemnity to the extent of the benefit to prevent unjust enrichment of the beneficiaries: *Vyse v. Foster* (1872) 8 Ch.App. 309, 336–337, *Conway v. Fenton* (1888) 11 Ch.D. 512, 518—or the trust deed might expressly permit indemnity even beyond the extent of the benefit to the whole expense.
[57] *Ex p. Edmonds* (1862) 4 De G.F. & J. 488, 498; *Re Johnson* (1880) 15 Ch.D. 548; *Re British Power Traction & Lighting Co Ltd* [1910] 2 Ch. 470.
[58] *Ex p. Chippendale, Re German Mining Co* (1854) 4 De G.M. & G 19, 52; *McLean v. Burns Philip Trustee Co Pty. Ltd* [1985] 2 N.S.W.L.R. 623 (the right to indemnity excluded in unit trusts so as not to affect the marketability of units).
[59] *Re Beddoe* [1893] 1 Ch.547: this is in a separate action and the judge who hears it will not hear the main action. For details see *Lewin on Trusts* (17th ed.) paras 21–106 to 21–119.
[60] See ss.339–342, 423–425 Insolvency Act 1986.
[61] *Alsop Wilkinson v. Neary* [1996] 1 W.L.R. 1220.
[62] *Re Hall* [1994–95] Cayman I.L.R. 456, *Lloyds Bank v Bylevan Corp. S.A.* [1994–95] C.I.L.R. 519.

The right of indemnity of a trustee is bolstered by an equitable **9–444**
proprietary right in the nature of a non-possessory lien,[63] which enables
the trustee to retain assets against actual, contingent or possible
liabilities[64] or to seek a sale of the assets[65] if in the ownership of a
sucessor trustee. The equitable lien will continue to bind successor
trustees[66] but will not bind beneficiaries to whom the assets are
distributed unless expressly preserved by the distributing trustee(s), the
recipient beneficiary receiving the assets (whether expressly or by
necessary implication) discharged from the interests of other beneficiaries and from the prior equitable interests of trustees.[67]

Trustees should reimburse themselves as soon as possible because they
are not entitled to interest on the money they paid out to meet
expenses.[68]

II. INDEMNITY AGAINST THE BENEFICIARY PERSONALLY

A trustee's right of indemnity in respect of expenses properly incurred— **9–445**
e.g. in respect of costs, a call on shares, solicitor's, stockbroker's or
auctioneer's charges—is a right of indemnity against the trust *estate*, not
against the beneficiary. Hence, the trustees of an ordinary club are
entitled to be indemnified out of the club property, not by the club
members,[69] unless, as is often the case, the club rules allow this. But in
the following circumstances a trustee's indemnity extends beyond the
estate to the *beneficiary* personally:

First, where the trustee accepted the trust at the request of the settlor
who is also a beneficiary so as to raise an implied contract of indemnity[70]
and secondly, where the beneficiary is a *sole* beneficiary *sui juris* and
entitled absolutely[71] or there are *several* beneficiaries who are *sui juris*
and between them collectively entitled absolutely.[72] This can prove very
useful where a trustee for such beneficiaries properly borrows money to

---

[63] *Jennings v. Mather* [1901] 1 K.B. 108, 113–114, [1902] 1 K.B. 1, 6, 9; *Stott v. Milne* (1884) 25 Ch.D. 710, 715; *Commissioner of Stamp Duties v. ISPT* (1999) 2 I.T.E.L.R. 1, 18; *Octavo Investments Pty Ltd v. Knight* (1979) 114 C.L. R 360; *Dimos v. Dikeatos Nominees Ltd* (1997) 149 A.L.R. 113, [1996] 68 F.C.R. 39.

[64] *X v. A* [2000] 1 All E.R. 490.

[65] *Re Pumfrey* (1882) 22 Ch.D. 255, 262.

[66] *Dimos v. Dikeatos Nominees Ltd* (1997) 149 Aust L.R. 113, (1996) 68 F.C.R. 39.

[67] Australian cases (like *Dimos, supra*, and *Chief Commissioner of Stamp Duties v. Buckle* (1998) 72 A.L.J.R. 242) treat the trustee's right not as an "encumbrance" but as a proprietary right equivalent to (but ranking ahead of) the equitable interests of beneficiaries. Further see *Lewin on Trusts* (17th ed.), paras 14–50 and 26–22 and Trust Law Committee Consultation Paper, December 1999, "The Proper Protection by Liens, Indemnities or otherwise of Those who Cease to be Trustees."

[68] *Foster v. Spencer* [1996] 2 All E.R. 672.

[69] *Wise v. Perpetual Trustee Co.* [1903] A.C. 139.

[70] *Ex p. Chippendale* (1854) 4 De G.M. & G. 19 at 54; *Jervis v. Wolferstan* (1874) L.R. 18 Eq. 18 as explained by Lord Blackburn in *Fraser v. Murdoch* (1881) 6 App.Cas. 855 at 872; *Matthews v. Ruggles-Brise* [1911] 1 Ch. 194. In that case it was also held that where a beneficiary is personally liable to indemnify his trustee, an assignment by him of his beneficial interest does not affect that liability as it stood at the date of the assignment.

[71] *Hardoon v. Belilios* [1901] A.C. 118.

[72] *Buchan v. Ayre* [1915] 2 Ch. 474 at 477; *Re Reid* (1971) 17 D.L.R. (3d) 199. *Balkin v. Peck* (1997) 43 N.S.W.L.R. 766, (1998) 1 I.T.E.L.R. 717. (English executor recovered from Australian beneficiaries overlooked the tax payable on proceeds remitted to Australia).

carry out authorised trading or investing and the borrowings exceed the assets when things go dreadfully wrong as occurred in *J. W. Broomhead (Vic.) Pty. Ltd (in liq.) v. J. W. Broomhead Pty. Ltd*[73] where McGarvie J. held "where there are several beneficiaries entitled to separate benefits, a beneficiary who gets a proportion of the benefit should bear that proportion of its burdens unless he can show why the trustee shold bear the proportion of them himself." He further held that where a beneficiary is insolvent the loss in respect of his proportion falls on the trustee and not the other beneficiaries. He also accepted that "a request from a beneficiary to the trustee to assume the office of trustee or to incur liabilities obviously justifies the imposition of a personal liability to indemnify on the beneficiary and this should be so even if the beneficiary has only a limited interest."

Section 11: Third Parties and Trustees

9–446 In carrying out the trusts or powers a trustee is personally liable to the extent of his whole fortune or patrimony for debts, contracts, torts or taxes arising in respect of his acts or omissions as trustee. After all, the trust property is not an entity that can be regarded as a person to be made liable. Having transferred his property, usually by way of gift, to the trustees the settlor has disappeared from the picture. The trustees are not agents for the beneficiaries nor are they in a partnership with them so there is no legal connection between the beneficiaries and any creditors. Thus, the trustees are personally liable and remain so even after retiring as trustees: hence the need for an indemnity from the new trustees or reliance upon their equitable lien.

As a matter of contract law a trustee and a third party may agree that the trustee may limit or exclude his personal liability and that the trustee shall pay the debt out of the trust property under his statutory right of indemnity.[74] The onus lies on the trustee to displace the strong presumption of personal liability so that contracting descriptively "as trustee" is not sufficient,[75] but contracting "as trustee and not otherwise" will suffice since the phrase would be meaningless if not excluding personal liability.[76]

9–447 Where a trustee does not pay a creditor out of her own moneys or out of trust moneys available under her statutory right of indemnity the creditor may have a claim by way of subrogation to the trustee's right of

---

[73] [1985] V.R. 891 at 936–939.

[74] *Muir v. City of Glasgow Bank* (1879) 4 App.Cas. 337 at 355. It is possible for the trustee, if authorised, to go further and charge the trust property with payment of the debt: such an intention to create a charge is not likely to be inferred merely from an agreement that the creditor is to look to the trust property and not to the trustee for payment: *cf. Swiss Bank Corporation v. Lloyds Bank* [1980] 2 All E.R. 419 at 426; affd. [1981] 2 All E.R. 449. See also Law Reform Committee's proposls *infra* at para. 9–455 concerning a floating, as opposed to a fixed, charge.

[75] *Watling v. Lewis* [1911] 1 Ch. 414 at 424, *Marston Thompson & Evershed plc. v. Benn* [1998] C.L.Y.N. 4875 The Trust Law Committee in paras 3.14 and 10.4 of "Creditors' Right", against Trustees and Trust Funds" (June 1999) recommends removal of this trap for unwary trustees or executors so that contracting "as trustee" (or "executor") should exclude personal liability for properly incurred contractual liabilities, if the trust fund (or estate) is inadequate.

[76] *Re Robinson's Settlement* [1912] 1 Ch. 717 at 729; *Muir v. City of Glasgow Bank* (1879) 4 App.Cas. 337 at 362.

indemnity.[77] The problem is that the creditor's right is derivative: he stands in the shoes of the trustee and has no better right than the trustee.[78] Thus, for the creditor to be paid out of the trust assets he will need to show that the right of indemnity was not excluded by the trust instrument,[79] that the debt was properly incurred in the authorised carrying-on of the trust, and that the state of accounts between the trustee and the beneficiaries (taking into account any losses caused by any breach of trust on the trustee's part) is such that there is some balance in the trustee's favour to which the right of indemnity may attach.[80] However, where there are two or more trustees and one of them does not have a clear account (*e.g.* because of an outstanding claim against him for a breach of trust) the creditor can rely on the right to indemnity enjoyed by the other trustee.[81]

In addition to his proprietary right of indemnity, a trustee in some **9–448** limited circumstances (already discussed *supra*, para. 9–445) may have a personal right of indemnity against a beneficiary personally. The right of subrogation in respect of the proprietary right of a trustee to an indemnity from the trust property arose out of the Court of Chancery's practice in administration of trust estates in an administration action. There was no similar practice for allowing a right of subrogation in respect of a trustee's right of indemnity against a beneficiary personally but, in principle, it seems there should be such a right of subrogation.[82]

A person contracting with a trustee is in a particularly invidious position due to her derivative right being worthless if the trustee happens to be or become indebted to the trust fund for some unconnected breach of trust or if the trustee happens to be in breach of some equitable duty of care in negotiating the contract. In the absence of a power to create a fixed charge over specific assets or to create an equitable interest in the fluctuating trust fund in the nature of a floating charge,[83] what can be done to protect the creditor's interests?

---

[77] *Re Johnson* (1880) 15 Ch.D. 548 at 552; *Re Blundell* (1889) 44 Ch.D. 1, 11; *Vaccum Oil Pty. Ltd v. Wiltshire* (1945) 72 C.L.R. 319 at 325, 336; *Re Raybould* [1900] 1 Ch. 199. He may bring an action under R.S.C. Ord. 85, r. 2, *supra*, para. 9–288) if a judgment against the trustee would be fruitless, *e.g.* if he seems insolvent.

[78] *ex p. Edmonds* (1862) 4 De G.F. & J. 488 at 498; *Re Johnson* (1880) 15 Ch.D. 548; *Re British Power Traction & Lighting Co. Ltd.* [1910] 2 Ch. 470.

[79] Unlike Trustee Act 1925, s.69(2) which expressly allowed s.30(2) to be subject to contrary intent, no provision in Trustee Act 2000 allows this in respect of s.31 (the successor to s.30(2) of the 1925 Act), but it is considered that no court would permit a trustee to exploit s.31 if its generous remuneration was premised upon no recovery of expenses. A court could hold s.31 inapplicable on the basis the trustee was acting not "on behalf of the trust" but on behalf of itself in order to earn its generous remuneration or could hold the benefit of the remmuneration was only available as burdened by the obligation not to claim expenses.

[80] See section 10, *supra*, para. 9–442.

[81] *Re Frith* [1902] 1 Ch. 342 at 346; "The indemnity is not to the trustees as a body but to each of the trustees. Each of them who has acted properly is entitled to be indemnified against the debts properly incurred by him in the performance of the trusts. The Court prevents a trustee from insisting upon that right unless he comes in with clear accounts; but if he comes in with clear accounts he is not the less entitled to be indemnified because he has a co-trustee who has run away with certain moneys. I am, of course, excluding the case where a trustee who has a clear account is responsible for a co-trustee who has not."

[82] Para 2.29 of Trust Law Commitee consultations paper on Rights of Creditors against Trustees and Trust Funds, April 1997.

[83] See *infra* para. 9–453 for proposal of Law Reform Committee.

9–449 To deal with the unconnected indebtedness problem it seems possible[84] to negotiate as part of the price of the contract a necessarily incidental, but express, term that the trustee is in no way personally liable upon the contract, but the creditor shall have a personal[85] non-proprietary direct independent right of recourse to the trust fund, so that it is immaterial whether or not the trustee's right of indemnity has been extinguished by indebtedness to the trust fund. It would be better, however, if statute were to provide (as recommended by the Trust Law Committee)[86] that the indebtedness of a trustee to the trust at the time a contractual creditor (or a victim of a tort) seeks an indemnity out of the trust fund should not be a reason for refusing such an indemnity to such creditor (or victim).

9–450 Dealing with a trustee who may be in breach of his equitable duty of care is fraught with danger. If the creditor believes he is getting too good a bargain perhaps he should disclose this to help ensure that the trustee satisfies the equitable duty—but this would seem to place intending contractors with trustees under a fiduciary obligation which seems inappropriate and impractical in the commercial context. Perhaps, the House of Lords or even the Court of Appeal might restrict "properly incurred" to mean incurred by virtue of authority in the trust instrument and complying with any internal procedures[87] so that it would be immaterial[88] that there had been a breach of equitable duties of care in investing or in supervising agents or that the trustees would not have entered into the contract but for ignoring relevant considerations or taking account of irrelevant considerations. It would be better if statute were to provide (as recommended by the Trust Law Committee)[89] that a trustee's breach of equitable duties should not prevent a creditor having a right of indemnity out of the trust fund unless dishonestly implicated in such breach. Furthermore, where a trustee's conduct made him a tortfeasor and such conduct amounted to a breach of his equitable duties (*e.g.* of care) this should not prevent the victim from having a right of indemnity out of the trust fund. In *Re Raybould infra* it was fortunate for the claimant that the subsidence damage was caused by the proper management of the colliery by the trustee.

9–451 Where a deceased's estate includes a business, special problems arise since it is necessary to consider not just the beneficiaries interested in the estate, but also the claims of creditors of the deceased and the claims of creditors of the business carried on by the deceased's executors. The applicable principles appear most clearly from a judgment of the High Court of Australia in *Vacuum Oil Company Pty. Ltd v. Wiltshire, infra.*

---

[84] Trust Law Committee Consultation Paper "Rights of Creditors against Trustees and Trust Funds" (April 1997) para. 2. 35; *Scott on Trusts* (4th ed.) Vol. IIIA pp 499–500; Stone (1922)22 Col.L.R.527; J.G. Merralls (1993) 10 Austr. Bar Rev. 248.

[85] So affording no priority over other creditors.

[86] Report on "Rights of Creditors against Trustees and Trust Funds" (June 1999) paras 3.4 and 10.2.

[87] See para. 9–442 *supra*.

[88] Assuming the problem of indebtedness to the trust fund for such breach of trust was overcome.

[89] Paras 3.11 and 10.3 of Report in not 85 *supra*.

In dealing with third parties, especially in borrowing money, it is **9–452** useful if the trustees have power to create a charge over the trust *fund* (as distinct from particular assets happening at the time to be comprised in the trust fund) so to provide security for third parties. The Law Reform Committee (Cmnd. 8733) discussed this issue as follows:

> "2.20 . . . our conclusion is that where the trust is of such a kind that the trustees are likely to wish to engage in commercial operations such as large scale borrowing, the right solution would be for the trust deed to confer upon the trustees a power to create a charge upon the trust fund in favour of a creditor. The effect of such a charge would be to make the third party, in whose favour it was created, a *cestiu que trust*. His rights as chargee would be analogous to those conferred by a floating charge, just as the rights of any other *cestui que trust* subsist in the assets from time to time comprised in the trust fund. The trustees would retain all their powers of dealing with the trust fund although they would, of course, have to exercise them with due regard for the interest of the chargee as of any other beneficiary.
>
> 2.21 We see no reason to doubt that a trust instrument could be **9–453** so worded under the present law as to confer on trustees just the sort of power that we have in mind. Trustees can be, and frequently are, given power to appoint beneficial interests without consideration and we think it would in fact be possible to empower them to create beneficial interests for valuable consideration, the consideration being part of the trust fund in which the beneficial interest will thereafter subsist. However, because there is some doubt whether this would be permissible under the present law, we think that legislation is needed to make it clear that a power to create a charge upon the trust fund as a continuing entity can be conferred upon trustees by the trust deed, thus enabling them to give the maximum possible security tothird parties. However, we do not think that the trustees of an existing trust should be able to make use of this new statutory provision: in our view it would not be right to allow the imposition of such a power on an existing trust where the settlor had not envisaged it would be needed. If the power is needed, it will always be possible for a trustee in this position to apply to the court under the Variation of Trusts Act 1958 . . .
>
> 2.24 Whilst the form of any legislation following our report is, of **9–454** course, a matter for Parliamentary Counsel to determine, we do not think that it should be necessary to define or in any way to limit the nature of the power that we envisage. The suggested new clause below, which is no doubt capable of a good deal of improvement, is intended simply to draw attention to the fact that trustees can, under existing law, be given the sort of powers we have in mind:

Charges for value on trust funds

    (1) Where under the terms of any trust instrument the trustees have power to charge the trust fund or any part thereof (as distinct from any assets for the time being comprised in the trust fund) to secure obligations created by them for valuable consideration, the persons in whose favour such obligations are created shall take equitable interests in the trust fund or part with such priority and subject to such conditions and provisions as the trustees have power under the trust instrument and are expressed by the instrument creating the charge to create.

9–455
    (2) Subject to subsection (4) of this section, a person in whose favour such a charge is created may require that

        (a) a memorandum of the charge be endorsed, written on or permanently annexed to the instrument creating the trust;

        (b) the instrument be produced to him by the person having the possession or custody thereof to prove that a sufficient memorandum has been placed thereon or annexed thereto.

Without prejudice to any other manner in which persons dealing with trustees may acquire notice of such a charge, such memorandum shall, as respects priorities, be deemed to constitute actual notice to all persons and for all purposes of the matters therein stated.

    (3) Subsections (5) and (6) of section 137 of the Law of Property Act 1925 shall apply in relation to any memorandum authorised by this section.

    (4) Section 138 of the Law of Property Act 1925 (power to nominate a trust corporation to receive notices) shall apply for the purposes of this section with the omission of subsection (7), and the obligation imposed on the trust corporation by subsection (9) shall extend to any person authorised by the trustees to inspect and take copies of the register and notices held by the trust corporation."

RE RAYBOULD

Chancery Division [1900] 1 Ch. 199, 69 L.J. Ch. 249.

9–456 The surviving trustee and executor of a deceased's estate properly worked one of the testator's collieries. Earthworks caused a subsidence damaging the buildings and machinery of the adjoining owners, Roberts & Cooper. They obtained a judgment against the trustee for damage and costs. In the present proceedings they sought an order that this amount and cost be paid out of the testator's estate.

9–457 BYRNE J.: "The first question I have to consider is whether the same principle ought to be applied to the case of a trustee claiming a right to indemnity for liability for damages for a tort, as is applied to the simpler case of claims made against a trustee by ordinary business creditors, where they have been allowed the benefit of his right to indemnity, by proving directly against the assets: the kind of case of which *Dowse v. Gorton* [1891] A.C. 190 is a recent illustration. It has been argued that there is no authority to justify me in holding that, where damages have been recovered against a trustee in respect of a tort, the person so recovering can avail himself of the trustee's right to indemnity, and so go direct against the trust estate; but the authority of *Bennett v. Wyndham* (1862) D.F. & J. 259 goes to show that if a trustee in the course of the ordinary management of his testator's estate, either by himself or his agent, does some act whereby some third person is injured, and that third person recovers damages against the trustee in an action for tort, the trustee, if he has acted with due diligence and reasonably, is entitled to be indemnified out of his testator's estate. When once a trustee is entitled to be this indemnified out of his trust estate, I cannot myself see why the person who has recovered judgment against the trustee should not have the benefit of this right to indemnify and go direct against the trust estate or the assets, as the case may be, just as an ordinary creditor of a business carried on by a trustee or executor has been allowed to do, instead of having to go through the double process of suing the trustee, recovering the damages from him and leaving the trustee to recoup himself out of the trust estate. I have the parties interested in defending the trust estate before me, and I have also the trustee, and he claims indemnity, and, assuming that a proper case for indemnifying him is made out by the evidence, I think his claim should be allowed.

"The next question I have to decide is whether this trustee has worked the colliery in such a way as to be entitled to be indemnified. Having considered all the evidence, I am not prepared to say that the injury done to the applicants' land was occasioned by reckless or improper working, or otherwise than by the ordinary and reasonable management of the colliery; and I therefore come to the conclusion that the trustee is entitled to be indemnified out of the assets against the damages and costs which he has been ordered to pay to Messrs. Roberts & Cooper. It follows, therefore, for the reasons already given, that Messrs. Roberts & Cooper are entitled to stand in the trustee's place for the purpose of obtaining this indemnity direct from this testator's estate. The result, therefore, is that this summons succeeds . . . ."

VACUUM OIL COMPANY PTY LTD v. WILTSHIRE

High Court of Australia (1945) 72 C.L.R. 319

Questions arose as to the priority of the claims of creditors of a testator (such **9–458** as Vacuum Oil) and creditors of the business carried on by the testator's executor, in the course of administration of the testator's bankrupt estate.

LATHAM C.J.: "In the first place I refer to the general principles of law which have been developed in relation to the rights and liabilities of the parties concerned when an executor carries on the business of his testator. These parties are the executor, the beneficiaries who claim under the will, the creditors of the testator (who may be called estate creditors) and the creditors to whom debts have been incurred in the course of trading by the executor (who may be called trading creditors).

"1. an executor is entitled (apart from any express authority given by the will) as against both beneficiaries and estate creditors to carry on the business of his testator for the purpose of realisation, but only for that purpose (*Collinson v. Lister* (1855) 20 Beav. 356). In respect of debts incurred by him in so carrying on the business he is personally liable to the trading creditors—the debts are his debts, and not the debts of his testator (*Labouchere v. Tupper* (1857) 11 Moo.P.C. 198; *Ex p. Garland* (1804) 10 Yes. Jun. 110). But as against beneficiaries and both classes of creditors he is entitled to indemnity in respect of those debts out of the assets of the estate (*Dowse v. Gorton* [1891] A.C. 190 at 199).

"2. If an executor is authorised by the will to carry on the business not merely **9–459** for the purpose of realisation, then it is still the case that debts incurred by him are his debts for which he is liable to the new creditors. The authority given by the testator is part of his disposition of his estate and binds beneficiaries under his will. Thus, as against the beneficiaries in such a case the executor is entitled to an indemnity against the new debts out of the assets of the estate which the testator authorised to be used for the purpose of carrying on the business and out of any assets acquired in the course of carrying on (*Ex p. Garland*).

"But the testator cannot by his will prejudice the rights of his own creditors (*Re Oxley* [1914] 1 Ch. 604 at 613). They may insist upon payment of the debts and upon realisation of the assets of the estate in due course in order to obtain payment, notwithstanding any provisions in the will with respect to the carrying on of the business. They can make the executor account upon the basis of the assets which came to his hands or which he has subsequently acquired as executor, leaving the new creditors to get such remedy as they can against the executor himself, but with the added right of subrogation to his indemnity against the estate—an indemnity which will be worth nothing if the old creditors exhaust the estate (*Dowse v. Gorton*).

9–460   "3. If an executor carries on a business otherwise than for the purpose of realisation and without authority given by the will of his testator, he acts at his own risk, the debts which he incurs are his debts, and he has no authority as against either beneficiaries or creditors to come upon the assets of the estate for the purpose of meeting them (*Labouchere v. Tupper*).

"4. But if a beneficiary actually authorises him to carry on the business, he is entitled as against that beneficiary to indemnity out of the estate in respect of the debts which, in the course of such carrying on, he incurs to the trading creditors. Similarly, if a creditor of the testator actually authorises him to carry on the business he is entitled as against that creditor to a similar indemnity, which in each case enures by subrogation for the benefit of the new creditors (*Dowse v. Gorton*).

9–461   "5. The position is the same if a creditor of the testator *actively* and positively *assents* to the executor carrying on the business, but it is not easy to determine, on the authorities, what kind of conduct should be held to amount to the necessary active and positive assent. The principle upon which the right of the executor in such a case to indemnity out of assets of the estate as against an estate creditor has been variously stated. In *Dowse v. Gorton* (at 208), Lord Macnaghten said: 'If the business is carried on by the executors at the instance of the creditors without regard to the terms of the will, the executors, I suppose, have the ordinary rights of agents against their principals.; In *Re Millard; Ex p. Yates* (1895) 72 L.T. 823, Smith L.J. referred to the words of Lord Macnaghten and applied the principle suggested by him. In the same case, however, Lord Esher M.R. pointed out that it could hardly be said that the executor in such a case was the agent of the creditors, because, if he were, the creditors would be undisclosed principals in the business and would be liable to new creditors for goods supplied to the business. The law, however, had held otherwise. Lord Esher took the view that the executor carrying on was in the position of a trustee for the creditors and that Lord Herschell in *Dowse v. Gorton* had based his judgment in that case upon the view that the executor was such a trustee. Upon either view the result followed that the executor was entitled to an indemnity as against the estate creditors—in one case the indemnity to which an agent is entitled against his principal and in the other case the indemnity which a *cestui que trust* is bound to give to his trustee against liabilities reasonably incurred in performing the trust—to use the words of Lord Esher M.R. in *Millard's* case.

9–462   "There are difficulties in adopting the theory of agency (as pointed out by Lord Esher) and there is no clear binding decision of any court (as distinct from *obiter dicta*) that the executor is a trustee in respect of creditors who have assented to the carrying on, but is not a trustee in the same sense with respect to creditors who have not assented to the carrying on.

"6. The principle which has been developed in the cases appears to be *sui generis*. It was decided in *Dowse v. Gorton* that knowledge by estate creditors that the business is being carried on otherwise than for purposes of realisation does not amount to such an assent as to entitle the executors to an indemnity out of assets of the estate as against those creditors. There must be something more than mere knowledge and inaction—more than 'standing by' with knowledge.

"7. But the principle which has been applied is not an example of the **9–463** application of the equitable doctrine of acquiescence. A person may lose his rights by acquiescence, that is, by quiescence in such circumstances that assent to an infringement of his rights which is taking place may reasonably be inferred. Acquiescence is an instance of estoppel by words or conduct. (*De Bussche v. Alt* (1878) 8 Ch.D. 286 at 314.) A person who so acquiesces is not allowed in equity to complain of the violation of his right because he has really induced the person infringing his right to pursue a course of action from which the latter person might otherwise have abstained. It is a condition, however, of the application of the doctrine of acquiescence that the person who acts in infringement of the right should be acting under a mistake as to his own rights. If he knows that he is infringing the right of another person he takes the risk of those rights being asserted against him (*Ramsden v. Dyson* (1866) L.R. 1 H.L. 129 at 141). Further, the person whose rights are infringed must know that other person is acting under a mistaken belief (*Ramsden v. Dyson; Russell v. Watts* (1883) 25 Ch.D. 559 at 576). A case of acquiescence by an estate creditor in this sense in the executor trading might be made out in some cases. But there is no evidence of such acquiescence in the present case—no evidence of any such mistake or inducement—and I therefore set the equitable doctrine of acquiescence on one side.

"8. There is one other matter to which reference may be made before **4–464** endeavouring to apply the law to the present case. In *Dowse v. Gorton*, Lord Macnaghten expressed the opinion that estate creditors could not claim the assets of the business which had been acquired after the death of the testator and then refuse the executors indemnity in respect of liabilities incurred in carrying on the business. If they so acted, it was said, they would be reprobating after approbating. The same view is expressed in *Re Oxley*, by Cozens-Hardy M.R. at 610 and by Buckley L.J. at 614. These observations were not necessary for the decision of either case, because Lord Macnaghten in *Dowse v. Gorton* and the majority in *Re Oxley* held that the creditors were not making any claim in respect of assets acquired subsequently to the death of the testator. I find much difficulty in reconciling these observations with the clearly established rule of law that assets acquired by an executor in carrying on the business of his testator are assets of the testator's estate in every respect in the same way as the testator's assets which came to the hands of the executor at the time of his testator's death. See the statement of the law by Herschell L.C. in *Dowse v. Gorton* (at 198) and the many cases cited in *Williams on Executors & Administrators* (11th ed., 1921), Vol. 2, 1271 *et seq.*, where the law is stated as it existed before the Administration of Estates Act 1925 (Imp.). When an estate creditor sues an executor for his debt or takes an administration order the assets upon which execution can be levied under a judgment *de bonis testatoris* or which can be administered in the suit are all the assets which the executor has obtained in his capacity as executor. A creditor so suing does not "claim against" any particular part of the assets. He is entitled as of course to the application to estate liabilities of all the estate assets, including assets acquired after the death. He may not have known that the business had been carried on. It would be a remarkable thing if the result of such a creditor taking the only possible steps to compel payments of his debt should be that he must be taken to have assented to the carrying on so as to be postponed to the trading creditors.

9–465   "9. In the present case the testator's estate is being administered in bankruptcy under the provisions of section 155 of the Bankruptcy Act. It is clear that all the assets in the hands of the executor as executor will be administered and that no distinction will be drawn between assets which belonged to the testator and assets which have been subsequently acquired by the executor in the course of carrying on the business. Thus all the estate creditors in the present case are, simply because they have lodged proofs of debt, claiming against all the assets. If the *obiter dicta* in *Dowse v. Gorton* and *Oxley's* case to which I have referred were to be taken as accurately stating the relevant law the result would be that all the estate creditors, independently of any assent by them in fact to the business being carried on, would be treated as having assented on the ground that they could not "approbate' the business being carried on by claiming the after-acquired assets, and 'reprobate' by refusing to allow the executor an indemnity out of those assets. If this were the law, then the result would be that all the estate creditors would be deemed to have assented because they have made claims to the satisfaction of which any assets in the executor's hands can be applied, even though some of them may have been completely unaware that the business had been carried on. The statements to which I have referred were not necessary for the decision of the cases mentioned and should not, I think be regarded as an authoritative statement of the law.

9–466   "10. Strictly it would appear, the trading creditors, whose debts are owed only by the executor personally, should not be admitted as creditors in the administration under the Bankruptcy Act section 155 of the estate of the testator. They are not creditors of the testator's estate. But, as the executor may have a right of indemnity out of the estate assets in respect of the trading debts against some beneficiaries or some estate creditors, the trading creditors will be entitled to the benefit of his indemnity, and so will be entitled, through him, though not directly, to the application of estate assets to the satisfaction of their debts in priority to the claims of such beneficiaries or creditors. It is only in this way that the claims of trading creditors can come into consideration in these proceedings."

QUESTIONS

9–467   1. David, Eric and Ferdinand are trustees of a fund whose portfolio of investments includes some 10,000 shares out of an issued 30,000 shares in a private company. The Fund is held upon protective trusts for Ferdinand during his life and after his death for George and Harry equally. Ian, who is the trustees' solicitor, discussed with them the possibility of them acquiring a sufficient number of shares in the company to give them a majority holding. The trustees refused for though they had power to retain their existing shares they had no power to invest in further shares in any private companies. Ian told them that they had a chance of applying successfully to the court for such a power but the trustees considered that it would not be worth it. In consideration of Ian agreeing not to charge legal fees for his unbilled work for the preceding year they told Ian that if he wished he could personally go ahead and try to obtain control for himself for as far as they could see this could only enhance the value of the trust's shareholding.

Ian then acquired all the remaining shares in the company, disposed **9–468** of some of its assets, reorganised the business and increased the value of the shares from £1 each to £4 each. In the meantime, Ferdinand had become bankrupt and David and Eric removed him from his trusteeship on the ground of his unfitness to act (without replacing him) and refused to apply any income for his benefit.

How far is Ian entitled to keep the profit on these transactions?

How far is the conduct of David and Eric legally justified?

Can Ferdinand call for the correspondence which passed between David and Eric, on the one hand, and Ian, on the other, relating to his removal from office and to the decision not to pay him any money?

2. David Rockechild is beneficially interested under a will trust of his **9–469** grandfather who died on April 1, 1990. Sir Malcolm Place and Sir Frank Haddock are the trustees of the settlement (with the broadest possible powers of investment) currently holding investments worth about £4 million upon trust for Alan Rockechild for life, with overriding power for the trustees to appoint that upon or before Alan Rockechild's death the capital be distributed to any one or more of Alan's children in such shares as the trustees in their absolute discretion may think fit, but with remainder in default of appointment to Alan's three children, Brian, Charles and David equally if they attain 30 years of age.

The trustees have recently refused to pay an already agreed advancement of money to David in the following circumstances. David is a qualified pharmacist and he was offered the opportunity to become co-owner of a good chemist's shop for £150,000. His father and the trustees recognised that this was a very worthwhile opportunity so arrangements were made for David to call upon the trustees to receive the moneys under an exercise of the statutory power of advancement and David gave three months' notice of leaving his present job.

When David arrived he was told that he would have to sign a **9–470** particular document before he could have the moneys. Upon examining the document he discovered it to be a deed already signed by his father and his brothers consenting to certain share transactions carried out in 1997 and authorising the trustees to retain any profits made by them in respect of those transactions.

Apparently, at tea at the 1997 Annual General Meeting of Quickgains Ltd attended by the trustees as representatives of the settlement, which had a not insubstantial shareholding, the trustees had obtained information about some prospective profitable contracts, that might lead to a take-over bid in a year or so, from one of the directors who was an old friend of theirs. The trustees discussed this information with Alan, Brian and Charles (for David, then aged 15 years and the youngest son by 5 years, was away at boarding school) and they all agreed that it would be worth risking investing a further £100,000 (but no more) of trust moneys in the company and that the trustees could spend as much of their moneys as they wished once the £100,000 trust moneys had been invested.

The trustees invested the £100,000 and then their own moneys and the shares had quadrupled in value between 1997 and 2001 when the trust shareholding was sold upon the written advice of the trust's stockbrokers.

9–471   When pressed by David the trustees refused to disclose how much of their own moneys had been invested in Quickgains Ltd, how much profit they had made or when or if they had sold their shares. The trustees merely pointed out that David should be very grateful for the profits which they had enabled the trust to make. However, David refused to sign the deed whereupon the trustees refused to advance any moneys to him. They also pointed out that if he did not be sensible like his father and his brothers and sign the deed, then it might well be that the power of appointment might be exercised in a way that might not be favourable to him. Two days later David received a letter from his father saying that as the father's personal circumstances had changed he was no longer prepared to consent to any advancement being made to David. Instructing solicitors imagine that the trustees put the father up to this.

Consider what courses of action may be available to David.

9–472   3. In September 2000 Tim died, bequeathing his coin collection and £800,000 to his executor and trustee, Eric, on trust for his widow for life, remainder to his children Alan, Brian and Charles equally. Their children were then aged 30, 25 and 15 years respectively. The will contained various administrative provisions including wide powers of investment, and also a clause exempting the trustee from liability for any breach of trust that is not dishonest.

Although Eric was himself an experienced investor, upon winding up Tim's estate in March 2001 he gave the £800,000 for investment to Whizz Kid & Co. which specialises in discretionary portfolio management for clients and for itself. Eric signed the Company's current customer agreement in 2001. Its terms enable the Company *inter alia* to sell its own shares to the trust at a price no higher than that generally available at the time and to purchase for itself the trust's shares at a price no lower than that generally available at the time and provide that the Company shall not be liable for any loss arising from its negligence. The Company reports back to Eric every six months and follows his written policy statement concerning income and capital growth.

9–473   The investments are now only worth £400,000. At the end of 2001 the Company sold £30,000 of its own ABC plc shares to the trust and these shares are now only worth £5,000. In 2001 the Company bought from the trust for £20,000 XYZ plc shares now worth £80,000. About £200,000 of the loss is due to the negligence of Jason, an employee of the Company, who is addicted to cocaine. Eric's son knew about Jason's addiction and had told Eric about it.

A year ago Eric gave the coin collection to Donald, an apparently reputable dealer in coins, to sell as soon as someone was found prepared to pay about £25,000 for the collection. At first Eric phoned Donald every new month to see if a purchaser had materialised. After four months Donald told Eric not to bother phoning because he would phone Eric if a sale occurred. Last week Eric tried to phone Donald and discovered that Donald had sold the collection for £22,500 six months ago, had used the proceeds in his business and then been made bankrupt a month ago.

Advise Tim's widow, who has heard that Whizz Kid & Co is having financial problems and would also like to have the trust property sold up and its proceeds divided between her and her children.

4. A domineering, secretive, prospective settlor seeks your advice on how much he can keep in the dark persons interested under a very flexible discretionary trust and whether he can sensibly insert a provision, "No breach of trust action may be brought where the trustees have received written permission from the settlor in the relevant matter unless the action is brought within one month of the grant of such permission."

Chapter 10

LIABILITY FOR BREACH OF TRUST

Section 1. Introduction

10–01 THIS chapter is concerned with the personal liability of a trustee for breach of trust. In some circumstances the beneficiaries may be able to take advantage of the equitable tracing process so as to have an equitable proprietary remedy against trust property and its product in the hands of all but a bona fide purchaser for value of the legal interest without notice of the trust or a person to whom the defence of change of position is available.[1] Then the beneficiaries can choose whether to sue the trustees or to exercise their proprietary right to trace against the person in possession of the property.[2]

In what follows it will, of course, be assumed that the trust instrument does not contain any clause qualifying the extent of the trustee's duties or otherwise exempting it from liability unless guilty of some dishonesty. Any such clause is strictly construed against any trustee attempting to rely upon it.[3] It needs also to be noted that even if a clause ousts the trustee's duty[4] as controlling shareholder of a company to seek information on the company's activities and to monitor such activities unless having actual knowledge of dishonesty in the running of the company, the trustee by virtue of its controlling shareholding has *power* to intervene and so could still be liable for negligent failure to exercise this power in circumstances considered by the court to require the power to be exercised.

10–02 Any act or neglect on the part of a trustee which is not authorised or excused by the terms of the trust instrument or by law or which fails to satisfy the duties imposed on a trustee conducting authorised activities is a breach of trust. Where a loss results the claimant beneficiary can obtain compensation requiring the trustee to restore to the trust fund (or to an absolutely entitled beneficiary) what is found due after proper accounts of the trusteeship have been drawn up. Where a trustee has made a private profit in breach of trust from misusing trust property or the office of trustee he must account for the profit. The claimant will need to elect between these two remedies where they are inconsistent

---

[1] See Chap. 11, section 1.
[2] Denning J. (as he then was) in (1949) 65 L.Q.R. at p. 44; *Hagan v. Waterhouse* (1994) 34 N.S.W.L.R. 308 at 369–370.
[3] *Brumridge v. Brumridge* (1858) 27 Beav. 5; *Re Brier* (1884) 26 Ch.D. 238; *Bartlett v. Barclays Bank Trust Co. Ltd* [1980] 1 All E.R. 139 at 154; *Wight v. Olswang* (1999) 1 I.T.E.L.R. 783 (CA.).
[4] *Bartlett v. Barclays Bank Trust Co Ltd* [1980] Ch. 515.

alternatives,[5] *e.g.* where she seeks an account of the actual rental profits from 16 houses and also compensation for the rent she would have obtained but for the trustee not transferring title to her so as to enable her to rent out the houses.

Where there has been a breach of fiduciary duty (as opposed to **10–03** equitable duties, *e.g.* of care) the remedy of rescission may be available as an alternative to a claim for compensation. Other reliefs include removal of the trustee(s) and replacement by a new trustee or trustees, interim injunctions to preserve the trust property, the appointment of a judicial trustee (or, exceptionally, the appointment of a receiver of the trust property[6]), and summary orders for accounts under Part 24 of the Civil Procedure Rules, while declarations may also be sought.

The trustee may have a defence open to it: the claim is time-barred under the Limitation Act 1980[7] or there was concurrence, acquiescence or release by the claimant beneficiary.[8] In exceptional circumstances the court has power to relieve a trustee from liability,[9] *e.g.* if misled by an excellent forged birth or marriage certificate to make a distribution of assets to someone not actually a beneficiary.

Section 2. Accountability and Equitable Compensation

The fundamental obligation of a trustee is to provide accounts of the **10–04** trusteeship of the trust property to the beneficiaries.[10] It is then up to the beneficiaries to falsify or to surcharge those accounts. A falsification is a showing of an entry which is false and needs to be corrected. A surcharge is the showing of an omission where there should be a credited item.

Falsification will occur, for example, where the trustee, T, has made an unauthorised distribution of £x to C, an unauthorised investment of £x in, say, a villa in South Africa, an unauthorised transfer of trust assets assets worth £x to an agent, nominee or custodian. Because T had no power under the trust so to deal with the £x, he is treated as having acted as a proper good trustee would have acted, and so is regarded as having spent his own £x and retained the £x or the assets worth £x in the trust fund[11]: "Equity looks on as done that which ought to have been done". It matters not that the assets worth £x were lost by the dishonesty or insolvency of the agent, nominee or custodian: T is liable to make good the loss to the trust estate because had it not been for the unauthorised transfer to such person the loss would not have occurred.[12]

---

[5] *Tang v. Capacious Investments Ltd* [1996] A.C. 514.
[6] *Att-Gen v. Schonfield* [1980] 1 W.L.R. 1182; *Clarke v. Heathfield* [1985] ICR 203; *Younghams v. Candoora No. 19 Pty Ltd* (2000) 3 I.T.E.L.R. 154.
[7] See *infra* para. 10–96.
[8] See *infra* para. 10–79.
[9] Trustee Act 1925 s. 61, *infra* para. 10–77.
[10] See *supra* para. 9–208.
[11] See Lord Millett in [1993] Restitution L.R. 7, 20; *Wallersteiner v. Moir (No 2)* [1975] Q.B. 373, 397; *Knott v. Cottee* (1852) 19 Beav. 77.
[12] *Clough v. Bond* (1838) 3 My & Cr 490, 496–497 endorsed in *Target Holdings v. Redferns* [1996] 1 A.C. 421, 434.

Indeed, if the assets worth £x that had been wrongfully transferred will cost £2x to replace or if an authorised investment that had been sold for £x to enable the purchase of the unauthorised investment will cost £2x to replace, then T will have to pay £2x to restore to the trust fund the assets lost by reason of the breach of trust.[13]

10–05   It will be appreciated that this stringent approach is designed to encourage T to observe to the full T's basic duty to do only what it is authorised to do in relation to the trust property. Questions of foreseeability and causation do not come into the equation.

A surcharge will occur, for example, where T fails to exhibit the requisite duty of care in negligently making an authorised investment or negligently supervising an authorised agent or negligently failing to sue a former trustee for breach of trust or a third party for breach of contract or for some tort in respect of the trust property. It is the failure to take care which is the crucial dimension, not the fundamental trustee-beneficiary fiduciary relationship which is only an incidental factor.[14] There is no special reason to treat breach of an equitable duty of care much differently from breach of a contractual or tortious duty of care,[15] although Lord Browne-Wilkinson has indicated[16] that compensation should restore to the trust fund or the beneficiaries "a loss in fact suffered by the beneficiaries and which, using hindsight and common-sense, can be said to have been caused by the breach."

10–06   Where a loss is alleged to have been caused by a trustee's failures, *e.g.* to diversify investments[17] or to sell particular investments[18] or to monitor the activities of a 99 per cent owned company,[19] it needs to be shown that but for T failing to do what no reasonable trustee (*viz.* a properly informed trustee exhibiting the due standard of care) could possibly have failed to do the loss would not have occurred. Where trustees do positively decide to take specific action *e.g.* to sell particular shares as soon as practicable, but then fail to implement their decision without any conscious reason, it would seem that they are failing to do what no reasonable trustee could possibly have failed to do, so that if such failure caused loss then the accounts should be surcharged with a credit item for the amount of the loss.[20] It would, however, be possible to draw an analogy with the case where the trust instrument required a particular original investment to be sold as soon as practicable. The trustees' decision to sell requires the sale to be made, so that the wrongful retention of the investment in the accounts should be falsified and

---

[13] *Target Holdings v. Redferns* [1996] 1 A.C. 421; *Re Massingberd* (1890) 63 L.T. 296. Further, see *Shepherd v. Mouls* (1845) 24 Hare 500, 504, *infra* para. 10–67.
[14] *Bank of New Zealand v. New Zealand Guardian Trust Co* [1999] 1 N.Z.L.R. 664, 687.
[15] *Bristol & West BS v. Mothew* [1998] Ch. 1, 17.
[16] *Target Holdings v. Redferns* [1996] 1 A.C. 421, 439.
[17] *Nestlé v. National Westminster Bank* [1993] 1 W.L.R. 1265, 1281.
[18] *Wight v. Olswang (No 2)* [2000] W.T.L.R. 783, reversed [2001] W.T.L.R. 291.
[19] *Bartlett v. Barclays Bank Trust Co Ltd* [1980] Ch. 515.
[20] *Wight v. Olswang (No 2)* [2001] W.T.L.R. 291.

replaced with the sum that would have been received if the investment had been sold as soon as practicable.[21]

The court can make an order for an account of *administration in* **10–07** *common form* which requires the defendant to account only for what has actually been received and what has been disbursed for expenses, *etc.* and what has been distributed to beneficiaries. It is then open to the claimant to falsify or surcharge those accounts to ascertain the sum ultimately owed by the defendant, but the making of the order need not imply any wrongdoing by the defendant,[22] just a need to clarify matters.

In contrast the court can make an order for an account of *administration on the basis of wilful default* which is entirely grounded on the defendant's misconduct[23] and which requires the defendant to account not only for what has actually been received but for what might have been received but for the defendant's wilful default which covers deliberate, reckless and negligent breaches of trust.[24] The court cannot make the order unless at least one instance of wilful default has been proved and the court considers that the past conduct of the trustees is such as to give rise to a reasonable prima facie inference that other breaches of trust not yet known to the claimant or the court have occurred.[25] A wilful default order then casts a substantial burden of proof on the defendant who has to justify the account (unless it is an already settled account).[26]

Where the claimant alleges that the defendant trustee should account **10–08** for profits arising from specific misuse of the trust property or the office of trustee, then a separate order for an account of profits can be made by the court.[27] The accounting relates to specific gains rather than the general administration of the trust property (although a wilful default order can be restricted to an account of part only of the administration[28]). As a sanction, underpinning and emphasising the fiduciary duty of undivided loyalty of a trustee or other fiduciary, when an account of profits is taken of assets, like shares, improperly received in breach of fiduciary duty, the defendant is liable to restore to the trust fund (or any absolutely entitled beneficiary) the value of those assets at the highest value between the date of breach and the date of judgment.[29]

---

[21] *Fry v. Fry* (1859) 27 Beav. 144; *Fales v. Canada Permament Trust Co* (1976) 70 D.L.R. (3d) 257, 274. Consider also where the trustees decide to make an appointment of capital to O by executing the requisite deed before 2 August 1989 when the power expires, but they do not get round to executing the deed till 2 August so the deed is void and the beneficiaries remain entitled to that capital: *Breadner v. Granville-Grossman* [2000] 4 All E.R. 705. O should receive equitable compensation for breach of a duty created in O's favour but incapable of binding the trust beneficiaries after 1 August.

[22] *Partington v. Reynolds* (1858) 4 Drew 253, 256.

[23] *ibid.*

[24] *Re Tebbs* [1976] 1 W.L.R. 924; *Bartlett v. Barclays Bank Trust Co Ltd* [1980] Ch. 515; *Coulthard v. Disco Mix Club Ltd* [1999] 2 All E.R. 457, 481; *Glazier v. Australian Men's Health (No 2)* [2001] N.S.W.S.C 6, *infra* para. 10–14.

[25] *Glazier, supra.*

[26] *Glazier, supra.*

[27] *Glazier, supra.*

[28] *Re Tebbs* [1976] 1 W.L.R. 924.

[29] *Nant-y-glo and Blaina Ironworks Co v. Grave* (1878) 12 Ch.D. 738 accepted in *Target Holdings v. Redferns* [1996] 1 A.C. 421, 440.

Where losses result from breach of the fiduciary duty of undivided loyalty, then equitable compensation is payable to restore to the trust fund (or any absolutely entitled beneficiary[30]) the value it would have had but for the losses caused by such breach; and it seems that the onus is on the defendant to prove that the losses would have occurred even if there had been no breach.[31] However, this escape route is not open to a fraudulent defendant so as to deter fraud.[32] Instead of claiming compensation it may be possible for the claimant to rescind the relevant transaction.[33]

10–09 Recently, it was too easy for pleaders to claim equitable compensation (or, broadly "damages") for breach of fiduciary duty of a wide range of fiduciaries going beyond the trustee as the paradigm fiduciary, but *Bristol & West BS v. Mothew*[34] has corrected this by emphasising the difference between prescriptive equitable duties and the proscriptive fiduciary duty of undivided loyalty, while *Target Holdings v. Redferns, infra* has made it clear that in equity it is "compensation" and not "damages" that should be claimed.

Important nineteenth century case law on falsification and surcharge of accounts on the basis of wilful default has also been overlooked despite its crucial significance for analysing the measure of compensation for which the defendant must ultimately account at the date of judgment. Some knowledge of this apparently old-fashioned law (as set out in *Glazier v. Australian Men's Health (No 2), infra*) is useful. Indeed, *Target Holdings v. Redferns, infra* can usefully be analysed in the following way, as indicated extra-judicially by Lord Millett.[35]

10–10 The defendant solicitor held the claimant-mortgagee's money on trust to pay it over to the mortgagor only in exchange for a duly executed charge over the premises to be bought with the assistance of the money, together with the supporting documents of title. When the solicitor paid the money over to the mortgagor's order without obtaining the charge and other documents this unauthorised disbursement could be falsified, the solicitor being treated as still retaining the money. However, the subsequent obtaining of the charge and other documents perfected the authorised task so that there could be no falsification. The possibility of surcharging the account then only arose if the claimant could prove that the loss caused by a mortgage fraud (the claimant lending one and a half million pounds on premises subsequently sold for half a million pounds) would not have happened but for the premature payment of the loaned moneys without contemporaneously obtaining the charge and other documents.

---

[30] *Target Holdings v. Redferns* [1996] 1 A.C. 421.
[31] *Bank of New Zealand v. New Zealand Guardian Trust Co* [1999] 1 N.Z.L.R. 664, 687 (CA); *Swindle v. Harrison* [1997] 4 All E.R. 705.
[32] *Swindle v. Harrison, supra*; the position is the same as for the tort of deceit.
[33] *Armstrong v. Jackson* [1917] 2 K.B. 822.
[34] [1998] Ch. 1, 16 endorsed by CA in *Companhia de Seguros Imperio v Heath Ltd* [2001] 1 W.L.R. 112.
[35] (1998) 114 L.Q.R. 214, 225–227.

An advantageous feature of the defaulting trustee's obligation to **10-11** restore to the trust fund (or an absolutely entitled beneficiary) that which has been lost to it is that no deduction is made for any tax that would have been payable but for the breach of trust.[36] Beneficiaries' tax liabilities do not enter into the picture because they arise not at the point of restitution to the trust fund but at the point of distribution of capital or income out of the fund.

Contributory negligence of a beneficiary cannot be relied on to assist a defendant trustee or other fiduciary, the beneficiary being entitled to sit back and expect the trustee to perform its duties properly.[37] However, if a beneficiary does become aware that her trustee or other fiduciary is not to be trusted, then losses resulting from clearly unreasonable behaviour on the beneficiary's part will be adjudged to flow from such behaviour and not from the breach.[38] Punitive damages or damages for distress and inconvenience have no place in equitable claims.[39]

Liability for co-trustees

While trustees are only liable for their *own* breaches of trust, it is a **10-12** trustee's own breach of trust to leave a matter to be dealt with as a co-trustee thinks fit[40] or to allow trust funds to be in the sole control of a co-trustee[41] or to stand by while having actual, Nelsonian or naughty knowledge[42] that a breach of trust ie being committed by a co-trustee,[43] or to take no steps to obtain redress on becoming aware that a co-trustee has committed a breach of trust,[44] or to retire from being a trustee with the object of facilitating the breach of trust which was then committed by the remaining or new trustees.[45] However, no liability arises from merely retiring in circumstances where there is an awareness that this will make it possible for the remaining or new trustees to commit a breach of trust.

Exceptionally, the settlor can provide for T2 always to do as directed by T1 and not to be liable unless dishonestly assisting T1 commit a breach of trust.[46]

Trustees liable for a breach of trust are "jointly and severally" liable: a **10-13** beneficiary can call upon any two of the trustees jointly or any one of them "severally", *viz.* separately, to discharge the liability. The trustee

---

[36] *Bartlett v. Barclays Bank Trust Co Ltd* [1980] Ch. 515, 543; *Re Bell's Indenture* [1980] 1 W.L.R. 1217; *John v. James* [1986] S.T.C. 352, 361.

[37] *Magnus v. Queensland National Park* (1888) 37 Ch. D 466.

[38] *Canson Enterprises Ltd v. Boughton & Co* (1991) 85 D.L.R. (4th) 129, 162–163 endorsed in *Corporaçion Naccional del Cobre de Chile v. Sogemin Metals Ltd* [1997] 1 W.L.R. 1396, 1403–1404; *Lipkin Gormale v. Karpnale* [1992] 4 All E.R. 331, 361; also see approach in *Swindle v. Harrison* [1997] 4 All E.R. 705.

[39] *West v. Lazard Brothers & Co Jersey Ltd* [1993] J.L.R. 165; *Miller v. Stapleton* [1996] 2 All E.R. 449.

[40] *Wynne v. Tempest* (1897) 13 T.L.R. 360; *Re Lucking's W.T.* [1968] 1 W.L.R. 866, assuming no proper delegation e.g. under Trustee Act 2000 ss 11, 12.

[41] *Lewis v. Nobbs* (1878) 8 Ch. D. 591 assuming the co-trustee is not an authorised nominee or custodian under Trustee Act 2000 s. 19.

[42] See para. 11–111 *infra* as to defendant's conscience being affected by such knowledge.

[43] *Booth v. Booth* (1838) 1 Beav. 125; *Gough v. Smith* [1872] W.N. 18.

[44] *Wilkins v. Hogg* (1861) 8 Jur. 25, 26.

[45] *Head v. Gould* [1898] 2 Ch 250; *Kingdom v. Castleman* (1877) 36 L.T. 141.

[46] *Re Arnott* [1899] I.R. 201.

who is made fully liable has a right of contribution from the other trustees unless he was a fraudulent trustee, although in exceptional circumstances a trustee can obtain a complete indemnity from the co-trustee, so as to throw the whole loss on the co-trustee.[47]

Partners of an express trustee are not vicariously liable for a breach of trust committed by him in his professional capacity.[48]

Set off of profit against losses

A trustee cannot set off profits made on breaches of trust against losses made on breaches of trust except where they may be regarded as flowing from the same breach of trust.[49] The need to apply modern portfolio investment principles should, therefore, oust any argument that a loss on one particular investment in a share portfolio should not be set off against a profit on another when investments were made in pursuance of such principles.

GLAZIER v. AUSTRALIAN MEN'S HEALTH (NO. 2) [2001] New South Wales Supreme Court 6

10–14 AUSTIN J. "Whether, having regard to my reasons for judgment of 3 April 2000 and the evidence admitted on the application, the plaintiff has established an entitlement to an order for the taking of accounts on the basis of wilful default, is the issue to which I now turn.

Accounting for administration in common form and for wilful default, and accounting for profit or replenishing loss

In equity an order for the taking of accounts may be made in a wide variety of circumstances. In the present context it is important to distinguish between two kinds of orders. One kind (which I shall call an order for an account of administration) is made where the overall administration of a business enterprise or fund or other property is to be established or accounted for. Another kind (which I shall call an order for an account of profits) is made to provide a remedy for specific equitable wrongdoing.

Order for an account of administration

10–15 An order for an account of administration is made for the taking of accounts of money received and disbursed by the person who is responsible for the administration of a business enterprise or fund or other property, and for payment of any amount found to be due by that person upon the taking of the accounts. For example, the Court routinely orders the taking of accounts of the administration of an estate

---

[47] See para. 10–105 *infra*.
[48] *Walker v. Stones* [2000] 4 All E.R. 412 (CA).
[49] *Dimes v. Scott* (1828) 4 Russ. 195; *Fletcher v. Green* (1864) 33 Beav. 426; *Bartlett v. Barclays Bank Trust Co Ltd* [1980] Ch. 515, *infra* para. 10–31 where a £271,000 profit on a speculative Guildford development was set off against a £580,000 capital loss on a speculative Old Bailey development.

by an executor, or upon the dissolution of a partnership, or of the administration of property by a mortgagee in possession, or of a trust fund such as a solicitor's trust account. In such a case the making of the order need not imply any wrongdoing by the defendant.

Order for an account of administration in common form

The usual form of order, referred to as an order in common form or for common accounts, requires the defendant to account only for what he or she has actually received, and his or her disbursement and distribution of it. The defendant prepares accounts and it is open to the other parties to surcharge or falsify items in those accounts. A surcharge is the showing of an omission for which credit ought to have been given, while a falsification is the showing of a charge which has been wrongly inserted, the falsifying party alleging that money shown in the account as paid was either not paid or improperly paid: Parker's Practice in Equity (New South Wales) (2nd ed by GP Stuckey and CD Irwin, 1949), p. 269. Part 48 Rule 6 of the Supreme Court Rules preserves these procedures for challenging the account, while abandoning the arcane terminology of the chancery practice.

Order for an account of administration on basis of wilful default

Sometimes the Court orders that accounts be taken on the basis of **10–16** wilful default (or in the earlier cases, wilful neglect or default). The order is "entirely grounded on misconduct", the defendant being required to account not only for what he or she has received, but also for what he or she might have received had it not been for the default: *Partington v. Reynolds* (1858) 4 Drew 253, 255–6; 62 ER 98, 98–9. To obtain an order for the taking of accounts in common form against an executor, for example, the plaintiff need only show that the defendant is the executor, and need not show anything about the defendant's dealings with the estate; whereas to obtain an order on the basis of wilful default the plaintiff must allege and prove "that there is some part of the deceased's personal estate which ought to have been and might have been received by the defendant, and which he has omitted to receive by his own wilful neglect or default": *Partington v. Reynolds*, at 256 (ER at 99).

It appears that in the present context, the concept of "wilful default" is confined to cases where there has been "a loss of assets received, or assets which might have been received": *Re Stevens* [1898] 1 Ch 162, 171. In that case the failure of executors to cause the proceeds of an insurance policy to be paid to the policy's mortgagee for nearly seven years, during which time interest accrued to the mortgagee, was held not to amount to wilful default for the purposes of an application for an accounting on that basis. However, the concept is evidently not confined to cases of conscious wrongdoing: *Bartlett v. Barclays Trust Co Ltd* [1980] 1 Ch 515, 546. Obviously the concept here is not necessarily the same as the concept of "wilful default" used in other parts of the law: see, for

example, *Wilkinson v. Feldworth Financial Services Pty Ltd* (1998) 29
A.C.S.R. 642, 696–700.

10–17   As will be seen, the court may make an order that general accounts be
taken on the footing of wilful default if at least one instance of wilful
default has been proved. However the court has a discretion whether to
make such an order. The test is this: "is the past conduct of the trustees
such as to give rise to a reasonable prima facie inference that other
breaches of trust not yet known to the plaintiff or the court have
occurred?" (*Re Tebbs* [1976] 1 All E.R. 858, 863; see also *Russell v.
Russell (1891) 17 VLR 729*).

An order for accounts based on wilful default has the effect of casting
a much more substantial burden of proof on the accounting party than
applies in the case of common accounts. On a falsification, the onus is on
the accounting party to justify the account, unless the account is a settled
account (not relevant in the present case): Parker, p 269; Daniell's
Practice of the High Court of Chancery (5th ed, 1871), p 1120ff, p 575ff;
Seton's Forms of Judgment and Orders (6th ed, 1901), Vol II, p 1356ff,
p 1382ff; and note the forms of falsification and surcharge in Miller and
Horsell's Equity Forms and Precedents (1934), p 195–196; and as to
settled accounts, see *Pit v. Cholmondeley* (1754) 2 Ves 565, 28 ER 360.
An accounting on the footing of wilful default leads to an order
requiring the defendant to replenish funds wrongfully depleted by him or
her and in that sense to make restitution for the benefit of the plaintiff.

Order for account of profits for specific equitable wrongdoing

10–18   An order for an account of profits is made where specific wrongdoing
such as breach of trust or fiduciary duty has been found or is suspected.
It is usually ancillary to the grant of an injunction: *Colbeam Palmer Ltd
v. Stock Affiliates Pty Ltd* (1968) 122 CLR 25, 34. An order for an
account of profits typically requires the wrongdoer to account to the
plaintiff for profits made in consequence of the wrongdoing, although
the court has a discretion to fashion the order to suit the circumstances
of the case, and (for example) will not order the defendant to account
for the entire profits of a business established in breach of fiduciary duty,
where it would be inequitable to do so: *Warman International Ltd v.
Dwyer* (1995) 182 CLR 544. The accounting relates to specified gains
rather than the general administration of a fund. Since the order is
premised upon a finding of specific wrongdoing, the distinction between
an order in common form and an order on the basis of wilful default is
irrelevant.

Comparison of order for account of profits with orders for account of
administration in common form and on basis of wilful default

10–19   The contrast between an order for an account of profits and an order
for an account of administration in common form is obvious. The former
provides a remedy for specific wrongdoing, while the latter "supposes no
misconduct" (*Partington v. Reynolds* at 256 (ER at 99)). The difference
between an order for an account of profits and an order for an account

of administration on the basis of wilful default is much less sharp. This is especially so when one bears in mind that an order on the footing of wilful default can be limited to an account of part only of the administration, and even to that part of the administration in respect of which wilful default has been proved (as in *Re Tebbs*). Confusion has arisen because in both cases, it is necessary to establish at least one instance of wrongdoing, and yet in one case the order is directed only to the specific wrongdoing that has been proved, while in the other case proof of an instance of wrongdoing leads to a process which "assumes the probability that other improper transactions may have occurred" (*Re Tebbs*, at 864) throughout the administration or some specified part of it.

There is an another source of confusion between cases where it is appropriate to order the taking of accounts on the basis of wilful default, and cases where relief is sought because of a specific breach of trust or duty. In an action for breach of trust or duty, an order for an account of profits is one of the many equitable remedies available if the plaintiff makes out an appropriate case. Another remedy is an order that the defendant replenish the fund that he or she has wrongfully depleted (in an administration action, this may take the form of an order charging the executor with the asset). Confusion can arise because an order of that kind is similar in effect to, though more specific than, an order for the taking of accounts on the basis of wilful default, since the latter order includes a provision requiring that the defendant replenish the fund by the amount certified to be due when accounts have been taken.

Active and passive misconduct

In a case where an account of administration on the basis of wilful **10-20** default is appropriate, emphasis is placed on whether the defendant has failed to discharge his or her duty, rather than whether the plaintiff has established active conduct in breach of duty. This could lead one to infer that the difference between accounting on the basis of wilful default and accounting for profit is that in the first case the wrongdoing is passive whereas in the second case there is active wrongdoing. In my view that would be an oversimplification.

[His Lordship then considered *Re Wrightson* [1908] 1 Ch 789, *Bartlett v. Barclays Trust Co* (No 2) [1980] Ch 539 and *Gava v. Grljusich* [1999] W.A.S.C. 13].

In my view, the distinction drawn in these cases is not the mere distinction between active and passive conduct. The circumstances that give rise to a breach of trust will commonly involve active and passive elements. For example, in *Re Tebbs* the wrongdoing was active conduct, involving the sale of land at an undervalue, but it was regarded as wilful default by Slade J. and his characterisation of it was accepted by Kennedy J. in *Gava v. Grljusich* (at paragraph 31). In *Bartlett v. Barclays Trust Co Ltd* the wrongdoing was found to be wilful default, although it involved the "active" conduct of allowing directors to occupy residential premises at an undervalue as well as the "passive" default of not intervening to prevent the unauthorised investment. In *Re Symons* (1882) 21 ChD 757, the plaintiffs' complaints related to conduct with active and passive elements but the case was treated as one of wilful default. Similarly, in the present case there is evidence that the trustee failed to keep proper accounting records. That involved omission to make accurate and complete entries recording the receipt and disbursement of trust money (passive breaches), and preparation and maintenance of accounting records that were not in proper form for a trust (active conduct). More importantly, it is hard to see why in principle there should be such a dramatic difference in consequences between cases where the breach is active and cases where it is passive. The true distinction identified by the quoted passages is the distinction between an order for administration, made in cases where the defendant is required to administer a fund for the benefit of others over time, and fails to do so properly (and is therefore guilty of "passive" breaches by not doing what he or she ought to have done), and an order for an account of profits or replenishment of a fund, made in cases where the complaint is about specific instances of wrongdoing ("active" breaches, although they may be as much non-feasance as misfeasance).

The present case

10–21　　Purporting to adopt the reasoning of Kennedy J. in *Gava v. Grljusich*, the respondents say that Glazier's claim for an account on the footing of wilful default is made under a misunderstanding as to the nature of an order of that kind. At the hearing of the proceedings before Young J, Glazier contended that there had been active breaches of trust by the first defendant, aided by the respondents. It sought, and obtained, an order for removal of the first defendant as trustee on the ground of breach of trust, as well as an order for the taking of accounts. The respondents submit that this is a case of alleged breaches of trust rather than wilful default, and that an order for the taking of accounts on the basis of wilful default is not appropriate where the case is simply one of breach of trust.

　　I disagree with this submission. In the first place, *Gava v. Grljusich* is distinguishable. There was a full hearing before Kennedy J, who heard the evidence and submissions of the parties with respect to the plaintiffs' complaints. He was able to say that the plaintiff did not rely upon the breaches of trust which he found to exist for the purpose of taking accounts, but only for the purpose of removing the trustees. That cannot be said in the present case, since the orders were made by consent without a full hearing. Secondly, the issue whether the plaintiffs' complaints related to wilful default was not fully argued, and the decision was based on the unfairness of allowing a very late amendment to the statement of claim which would have necessitated a reopening of the hearing. Kennedy J's remarks about the distinction between active breach and wilful default were therefore obiter.

10–22　　If, as I have said, the true distinction is between cases where the defendant is required to administer a fund over time and fails to do so properly, and cases where the defendant has engaged in specific acts of equitable wrongdoing (whether or not in the course of administering a fund), then the distinction must hold good even where numerous specific acts of wrongdoing are pleaded. However, if the specific acts of wrongdoing are so extensive and numerous that the plaintiff's case amounts to a challenge to the whole course of administration of the fund by the defendant, the case ought to be regarded as one in which an account of administration on the basis of wilful default is appropriate, provided that the case has been properly pleaded and one or more instances of wilful default have been proved. I have listed the complaints made about the trustees' conduct in *Gava v. Grljusich* to show that numerous specific complaints were made. Nevertheless, it was open to Kennedy J. to see the case as one about specific breaches, though numerous, rather than as a challenge to the whole course of administration of the trust.

The present case, in contrast, is one in which from the outset, the plaintiff has made numerous specific complaints which add up together to a challenge to the whole course of administration of the trust by the defendants. Mr Madden's report ranges over the whole course of administration of the trust and finds failures in the accounting area and substantial deficiencies of information, though not any specific breaches of trust except as regards the preparation of accounts and the maintenance of accounting records. The entire circumstances of the case signal that is a case about failure of the defendants properly to administer a fund over time, justifying an order for an account of administration rather than simply orders on the basis of specific breaches of trust, and warranting that the order be on the basis of wilful default if one or more such defaults have been properly pleaded and proved.

Must at least one act of wilful default be established, and if so, is that requirement satisfied here?

By the time of Lord Eldon, Chancery had developed the rule that in **10–23** order to obtain an inquiry, or the taking of accounts, on the basis of wilful neglect and default against an executor or trustee, it was necessary for the plaintiff to allege and prove at least one act of wilful neglect or default. It was for the plaintiff to fix upon any item he may choose, but having done so, it was then up to him to adduce proper evidence to show that but for the wilful neglect or default of the defendant, that item might have been received: *Sleight v. Lawson* (1857) 3 K & J 292, 298, 69 ER 1119, 1121–2. In *Coope v. Carter* (1852) 2 De G McN & G 297; 42 ER 884 the rule was relaxed to the extent that, if wilful neglect or default was alleged in the plaintiff's bill but the facts only raised a case of suspicion in the mind of the Court without proving any instance of such default, the Court could direct a preliminary inquiry to clarify the particular facts alleged. If that preliminary inquiry established one or more instances of wilful neglect or default, the Court might then order the remainder of the inquiry to proceed on the basis of wealth neglect or default.

In Lord Eldon's time the item of wilful default had to be proved at that the hearing, because an inquiry as to wilful default could not be added afterwards. By the time the Court of Appeal decided *Re Youngs* (1885) 30 Ch D 421, however, proof of an item of wilful default could be made after the hearing, in consequence of the prosecution of inquiries under an ordinary decree for the taking accounts (per Cotton L.J. at 431–2). But there was no weakening of the requirement that at least one item of wilful default had to be proved.

10–24   In my opinion the plaintiff has satisfied the requirement to prove at least one instance of wilful default in the present case. I do not agree with the plaintiff that the consent orders imply any such finding. However, the Madden report is in evidence. After hearing evidence about that report including the cross-examination of Mr Madden, I reviewed the report extensively in my reasons for judgment of 3 April 2000. I accept the findings in the Madden report, for the reasons given earlier in this judgment and more fully set out in my previous judgment. Mr Madden's general conclusions included his finding that AMH had failed to maintain adequate books and records which would enable true and fair accounts to be produced, and had failed to comply with the requirement of the unitholders' deed that monthly management accounts be prepared, and that financial records be maintained for that purpose. My acceptance of these conclusions now constitutes a finding of wilful default, for the purpose of making an order for the taking of accounts on that basis.

My view that the Madden report disclosed numerous occasions giving rise to real concern as to breach of trust is more than enough to satisfy the requirement that the past conduct of the trustees must be such as to give rise to a reasonable prima facie inference that other breaches of trust have occurred: *cf. Re Tebbs* at 863.

Must relief on the basis of wilful default be sought in the pleadings, and if so, is that requirement satisfied here?

10–25   As I have mentioned, the statement of claim alleges numerous specific breaches of trust, especially with respect to distributions, the keeping of accounts and related party transactions. The prayers for relief include an order for removal of the trustee, no doubt because of the breaches of trust previously pleaded. When the case was opened on behalf of the plaintiff, an outline of issues was handed up which specified alleged breaches of trust by reference to the affidavits and documentary evidence. But I have found that the order actually made should be treated as an order for an account of administration in common form. The question before me now is not whether it would have been open to Young J. on March 18, 1998 to make an order for an account of administration on the footing of wilful default, but whether it is open to me to do so now.

There have been significant developments since March 18, 1998. Most importantly, the administration of the trust by the defendants has been the subject of an extensive report by Mr Madden, vigorously challenged by the defendants in Mr Madden's interlocutory application to me for judicial advice, leading to my findings of April 3, 2000. Can the Court make a new order for the taking of accounts on the footing of wilful default in light of these developments? It appears to me that there are two potential obstacles to such an order. The first is that an order in that form was not specifically sought in the statement of claim. The second is that the order in fact made in consequence of the final hearing of the proceedings was for an account in common form (as I have held) and there has been no appeal against that order. I shall deal with these potential obstacles together.

In my opinion, under the modern law these potential obstacles are in **10–26** fact no barrier to the Court making a new order for an account of administration on the footing of wilful default. Nineteenth century Chancery practice was different. In order to obtain a decree for accounts on the basis of wilful default, it was necessary for the plaintiff to allege the misconduct in the bill and prove it at the hearing, and if the plaintiff only obtained the usual decree in common form, misconduct could not be noticed in the taking of accounts under the decree, nor on the hearing of the cause for further directions. If the plaintiff obtained the usual decree and in the course of the taking of accounts under the decree, or in a hearing for further directions, a ground for charging the defendant on the basis of wilful default emerged, the decree could not be varied to encompass wilful default but the plaintiff could file a supplemental bill which would operate as a bill of review: *Partington v. Reynolds*, at 258 (ER at 99). In that case it was held that the introduction, by legislation in 1852, of the new proceeding by summons in chambers did not alter these principles. The case recognised an exception to the general rule, however, where the question was whether an executor ought to be made liable for interest on funds improperly retained uninvested in his hands: see also *Knott v. Cottee* (1852) 16 Beav 77; 51 ER 705; *Re Barclay* [1899] 1 Ch 674.

The old chancery practice changed late in the nineteenth century. In **10–27** *Job v. Job* (1877) 6 Ch D 562 Jessel MR said (at 564):

> "a further rule is that though he is liable in equity in case of wilful default, he cannot be charged with it unless an account is ordered against him on that footing: you cannot charge him with wilful default without making out a case; and therefore, under the old practice, unless wilful default was charged in the bill, you could not so charge him in the accounts. I think, however, that under the new practice an order charging him with wilful default may be made at any time on a proper case being made . . ."

In *Re Symons* (1882) 21 Ch D 757 the residuary beneficiary took proceedings against the executors and trustees of an estate alleging that the defendants, in breach of trust, had failed to get in parts of the estate and had accepted interest on outstanding purchase money at a lower rate than they were entitled to charge. As Kennedy J. noted in *Gava v. Grljusich* (at paragraph 30) *Re Symons* was a case where the plaintiff pleaded in effect, though not in form, both wilful default and breach of trust. In addition to claims for the "ordinary accounts and inquiries" (at 757–8), the plaintiff claimed an order that the defendants make good to him the difference between the amount of interest actually received on the purchase money and the amount which should properly have been received. The plaintiff obtained judgment for administration upon admissions of fact contained in the statement of defence, and the court directed the ordinary accounts and inquiries to be taken and made. In terms of the distinction made above, the order was for the taking of accounts of administration, rather than for an account of profits for breach of trust, although the plaintiff had asserted various specific breaches of trust. No order was made on the footing of wilful default and the claims of breach of trust and breach of duty were not dismissed.

10–28   During the taking of accounts the plaintiff brought in a surcharge, seeking to charge the defendants with additional interest on the purchase money. The Chief Clerk decided that, the surcharge being in the nature of a charge of wilful default, the court's order did not permit him to proceed on that basis. When the matter came before Fry J. for further consideration, two years after the initial order for accounts and inquiries, evidence of wilful default was adduced. The defendant argued that, as there had already been a judgment for the taking of accounts in common form and the accounts had been taken and a certificate had been issued, thereafter it was too late to add a direction for an account on the footing of wilful default.

Fry J. disagreed, and directed accounts and inquiries on the footing of wilful default. He said (at 761) that "if wilful default is charged in the pleadings, and evidence of it is adduced, accounts and inquiries on that footing may be directed at any stage of the proceedings". He found that there was a charge of wilful default against the defendants in the statement of claim, because it alleged breaches of duty and breaches of trust in failing to get in the estate and to charge adequate interest on purchase money. Though the claim was not, in terms, for relief on the footing of wilful default, it was in his view a sufficient claim for relief on that footing (at 760). He noted the convenience of the Court being able to direct an account on the footing of wilful default after judgment, "because in many cases the evidence of wilful default comes out naturally in the course of taking the accounts" (at 761).

10–29   In *Gava v. Grljusich* (at paragraph 30) Kennedy J. observed that the reference by Fry J. to "any stage of the proceedings" was intended to mean any stage of the proceedings before judgment, as he expressly adopted the passage in the judgment of Jessel M.R. in *Mayer v. Murray*. I respectfully agree that the words "any stage of the proceedings" should be limited by reference to Jessel M.R.'s remarks, but in my opinion the limitation only applies if wilful default was not initially pleaded and must be introduced by amendment, and moreover, the correct limitation is that an order on the basis of wilful default cannot be made except at a stage of the action at which the pleadings may be amended to claim relief in that form. Amendments could only be made before judgment at the time when Jessel M.R. spoke, but today much depends on the nature of the judgment and the proceedings in question. I shall return to this point.

In my opinion, Fry J.'s judgment in *Re Symons* is a correct statement of the modern law with respect to the "pleading" requirement for an order for an account of administration. Even though Fry J. relies on cases (*Job v. Job, Mayer v. Murray* and *Barber v. Mackrell*) in which accounting for administration on the basis of wilful default did not strictly arise, his statements of principle were accepted by Stirling J. in *Re Barclay*, [1899] 1 Ch at 681 (although, as Kennedy J. pointed out in *Gava v. Grljusich* (at paragraph 34) that case did not concern a claim for wilful default). There is some support for Fry J.'s approach, in a different but analogous context, in *Wilkinson v. Feldworth* at 696–7.

In the present case, applying the reasoning of Fry J, I regard it as sufficient that the statement of claim alleges numerous specific breaches of trust, some of an inherently serious character, ranging over the whole administration of the trust by AMH and its directors, which would undoubtedly amount to wilful defaults if proved. This is true even though the statement of claim does not assert in respect of any of them that the breach amounts of "wilful default". The plaintiff's affidavits depose to numerous breaches of trust of the same character. It is not necessary for the prayers for relief to contain an explicit request for accounts on the footing of wilful default. In *Re Symons* there was no such request.

Fry J. took the view that accounts on the basis of wilful default could **10–30** be ordered at any stage in the pleadings, provided that wilful default was adequately charged in the pleadings and there was evidence of it. It would be just as unsatisfactory if the Court was precluded from responding to evidence of wilful default, vigorously contested, simply because the evidence has emerged from a process of receivership after the final hearing, as it would be if the Court were prevented from doing so because the evidence of wilful default arose during the taking of accounts after judgment.

Given these conclusions, it is strictly unnecessary for the plaintiff to seek to amend the statement of claim to seek an accounting on the basis of wilful default. However such an amendment may assist to clarify the position and so on balance, I am prepared to make the order sought by the plaintiff for leave to amend.

BARTLETT v. BARCLAYS BANK TRUST CO. LTD.

Chancery Division [1980] Ch. 515; [1980] 1 All E.R. 139

The plaintiff sued the trustees for failing to exercise proper supervision over the **10–31** management of a family company, "BTL," which they controlled through having a 99.8 per cent shareholding. Subsequently BTL became a wholly-owned subsidiary of "BTH" which the trustees controlled through a 99.8 per cent shareholding. The trustees' failure to supervise BTL and then BTH led to the company losing over £¹/₂ million in a disastrous property speculation.

BRIGHTMAN J.: "The situation may be summed up as follows. BTH made a large loss as a result of the involvement of itself and BTL in the Old Bailey project. This loss reduced the value of the BTH shares and thereby caused a loss to the trust fund of the 1920 settlement. The bank, had it acted in time, could by reason of its shareholding have stopped the board of BTL embarking on the Old Bailey project; and, had it acted in time, could have stopped the board of BTL and later the board of BTH (it is unnecessary to differentiate) from continuing with the project; and could, had it acted in time, have required BTH to sell its interest in Far [a company interested in the Old Bailey site] to Stock Conversion on the no-loss or small-loss terms which (as I find) were available for the asking. This would not have necessitated the draconian course of threatening to remove, or actually removing, the board in favour of compliant directors. The members of the board were reasonable persons, and would (as I find) have followed any reasonable policy desired by the bank had the bank's wishes been indicated to the board. The loss to the trust fund could have been avoided (as I find) without difficulty or disruption had the bank been prepared to lead, in a broad sense, rather than to follow.

10–32   "What, then was the duty of the bank and did the bank fail in its duty? It does not follow that because a trustee could have prevented a loss it is therefore liable for the loss. The questions which I must ask myself are: (1) what was the duty of the bank as the holder of 99.8 per cent of the shares of BTL and BTH? (2) was the bank in breach of duty in any and if so what respect? (3) if so, did that breach of duty cause the loss which was suffered by the trust estate? (4) if so, to what extent is the bank liable to make good that loss? In approaching these questions, I bear in mind that the attack on the bank is based, not on wrongful acts, but on wrongful omissions, that is to say, non-feasance not misfeasance.

"The cases establish that it is the duty of a trustee to conduct the business of the trust with the same care as an ordinary prudent man of business would extend towards his own affairs: see *Re Speight*[50] *per* Jessel M.R. and Bowen L.J. (affirmed on appeal[51] and see Lord Blackburn[52]). In applying this principle, Lindley L.J. added in *Re Whiteley*:[53]

10–33   '. . . care must be taken not to lose sight of the fact that the business of the trustee, and the business which the ordinary prudent man is supposed to be conducting himself, is the business of investing money for the benefit of persons who are to enjoy it at some future time, and not for the sole benefit of the person entitled to the present income. The duty of a trustee is not to take such care only as a prudent man would take if he had only himself to consider; the duty rather is to take such care as an ordinary prudent man would take if he were minded to make an investment for the benefit of other people for whom he felt morally bound to provide. That is the kind of business the ordinary prudent man is supposed to be engaged in; and unless this is borne in mind the standard of a trustee's duty will be

---

[50] (1883) 22 Ch.D. 727 at 739, 762.
[51] (1883) 9 App.Cas. 1.
[52] 9 App.Cas. 1 at 19.
[53] (1886) 33 Ch.D. 347 at 355.

fixed too low; lower than it has ever yet been fixed, and lower certainly than the House of Lords or this court endeavoured to fix it in *Speight v. Gaunt.*'[54]

"If the trust had existed without the incorporation of BTL, so that the bank **10–34** held the freehold and leasehold properties and other assets of BTL directly on the trusts of the settlement, it would in my opinion have been a clear breach of trust for the bank to have hazarded trust money in the Old Bailey development project in partnership with Stock Conversion. The Old Bailey project was a gamble, because it involved buying into the site at prices in excess of the investment values of the properties, with no certainty or probability, with no more than a chance, that planning permission could be obtained for a financially viable redevelopment, that the numerous proprietors would agree to sell out or join in the scheme, that finance would be available on acceptable terms, and that the development would be completed, or at least become a marketable asset, before the time came to start winding up the trust. However one looks at it, the project was a hazardous speculation on which no trustee could properly have ventured without explicit authority in the trust instrument. I therefore hold that the entire expenditure in the Old Bailey project would have been incurred in breach of trust, had the money been spent by the bank itself. The fact that it was a risk acceptable to the board of a wealthy company like Stock Conversion has little relevance.

"I turn to the question, what was the duty of the bank as the holder of shares **10–35** in BTL and BTH? I will first answer this question without regard to the position of the bank as a specialist trustee, to which I shall advert later. The bank, as trustee, was bound to act in relation to the shares and to the controlling position which they conferred, in the same manner as a prudent man of business. The prudent man of business will act in such manner as is necessary to safeguard his investment. He will do this in two ways. If facts come to his knowledge which tell him that the company's affairs are not being conducted as they should be, or which put him on enquiry, he will take appropriate action. Appropriate action will no doubt consist in the first instance of enquiry of and consultation with the directors, and in the last but most unlikely resort, the convening of a general meeting to replace one or more directors. What the prudent man of business will *not* do is to content himself with the receipt of such information on the affairs of the company as a shareholder ordinarily receives at annual general meetings. Since he has the power to do so, he will go further and see that he has sufficient information to enable him to make a responsible decision from time to time either to let matters proceed as they are proceeding, or to intervene if he is dissatisfied. This topic was considered by Cross J. in *Re Lucking's Will Trusts.*[55] In that case nearly 70 per cent of the shares in the company were held by two trustees, L and B, as part of the estate of the deceased; about 29 per cent belonged to L in his own right, and 1 per cent belonged to L's wife. The directors in 1954 were Mr. and Mrs. L and D, who was the manager of the business. In 1956 B was appointed trustee to act jointly with L. The company was engaged in the manufacture and sale of shoe accessories. It had a small factory employing about 20 people, and one or two travellers. It also had an agency in France. D wrongfully drew some £15,000 from the company's bank account[56] in excess of

---

[54] (1883) 22 Ch.D. 727; 9 App.Cas. 1.
[55] [1968] 1 W.L.R. 866.
[56] [1968] 1 W.L.R. 866 at 874–875.

his remuneration, and later became bankrupt. The money was lost. Cross J. said this:

10–36   'The conduct of the defendant trustees is, I think, to be judged by the standard applied in *Speight v. Gaunt*,[57] namely, that a trustee is only bound to conduct the business of the trust in such a way as an ordinary prudent man would conduct a business of his own. Now, what steps, if any, does a reasonably prudent man who finds himself a majority shareholder in a private company take with regard to the management of the company's affairs? He does not, I think, content himself with such information as to the management of the company's affairs as he is entitled to as share-holder, but ensures that he is represented on the board. He may be prepared to run the business himself as managing director or, at least, to become a non-executive director while having the business managed by someone else. Alternatively, he may find someone who will act as his nominee on the board and report to him from time to time as to the company's affairs. In the same way, as it seems to me, trustees holding a controlling interest ought to ensure so far as they can that they have such information as to the progress of the company's affairs as directors would have. If they sit back and allow the company to be run by the minority shareholder and receive no more information than shareholders are entitled to, they do so at their risk if things go wrong.'

10–37   "I do not understand Cross J. to have been saying that in every case where trustees have a controlling interest in a company it is their duty to ensure that one of their number is a director or that they have a nominee on the board who will report from time to time on the affairs of the company. He was merely outlining convenient methods by which a prudent man of business (as also a trustee) with a controlling interest in a private company, can place himself in a position to make an informed decision whether any action is appropriate to be taken for the protection of his asset. Other methods may be equally satisfactory and convenient, depending on the circumstances of the individual case. Alternatives which spring to mind are the receipt of the copies of the agenda and minutes of board meetings if regularly held, the receipt of monthly management accounts in the case of a trading concern, or quarterly reports. Every case will depend on its own facts. The possibilities are endless. It would be useless, indeed misleading, to seek to lay down a general rule. The purpose to be achieved is not that of monitoring every move of the directors, but of making it reasonably probable, so far as circumstances permit, that the trustee (or as in *Re Lucking's Will Trusts*[58]) one of them will receive an adequate flow of information in time to enable the trustees to make use of their controlling interest should this be necessary for the protection of their trust asset, namely the shareholding. The obtaining of information is not an end in itself, but merely a means of enabling the trustees to safeguard the interests of their beneficiaries.

10–38   "So far, I have applied the test of the ordinary prudent man of business. Although I am not aware that the point has previously been considered, except briefly in *Re Waterman's Will Trusts*,[59] I am of opinion that a higher duty of care is plainly due from someone like a trust corporation which carries on a

---

[57] (1883) 22 Ch.D. 727.
[58] [1968] 1 W.L.R. 866.
[59] [1952] 2 All E.R. 1054.

specialised business of trust management. A trust corporation holds itself out in its advertising literature as being above ordinary mortals. With a specialist staff of trained trust officers and managers, with ready access to financial information and professional advice, dealing with and solving trust problems day after day, the trust corporation holds itself out, and rightly, as capable of providing an expertise which it would be unrealistic to expect and unjust to demand from the ordinary prudent man or woman who accepts, probably unpaid and sometimes reluctantly from a sense of family duty, the burdens of trusteeship. Just as, under the law of contract, a professional person possessed of a particular skill is liable for breach of contract if he neglects to use the skill and experience which he professes, so I think that a professional corporate trustee is liable for breach of trust if loss is caused to the trust fund because it neglects to exercise the special care and skill which it professes to have. The advertising literature of the bank was not in evidence (other than the scale of fees) but counsel for the bank did not dispute that trust corporations, including the bank, hold themselves out as possessing a superior ability for the conduct of trust business, and in any event I would take judicial notice of that fact. Having expressed my view of the higher duty required from a trust corporation, I should add that the bank's counsel did not dispute the proposition.

"In my judgment the bank wrongfully and in breach of trust neglected to **10–39** ensure that it received an adequate flow of information concerning the intentions and activities of the boards of BTL and BTH. It was not proper for the bank to confine itself to the receipt of the annual balance sheet and profit and loss account, detailed annual financial statements and the chairman's report and statement, and to attendance at the annual general meetings and the luncheons that followed, which were the limits of the bank's regular sources of information. Had the bank been in receipt of more frequent information it would have been able to step in and stop, and ought to have stopped, Mr Roberts and the board embarking on the Old Bailey project. That project was imprudent and hazardous and wholly unsuitable for a trust whether undertaken by the bank direct or through the medium of its wholly owned company. Even without the regular flow of information which the bank ought to have had, it knew enough to put it on enquiry. There were enough obvious points at which the bank should have intervened and asked questions. Assuming, as I do, that the questions would have been answered truthfully, the bank would have discovered the gamble on which Mr Roberts and his board were about to embark in relation to the Old Bailey site, and it could have, and should have, stopped the initial move towards disaster, and later on arrested further progress towards disaster.

"I hold that the bank failed in its duty whether it is judged by the standard of **10–40** the prudent man of business or of the skilled trust corporation. The bank's breach of duty caused the loss which was suffered by the trust estate. If the bank had intervened as it could and should have, that loss would not have been incurred. By 'loss,' I mean the depreciation which took place in the market value of the BTL and BTH shares, by comparison with the value which the shares would have commanded if the loss of the Old Bailey project had not been incurred, and reduction of dividends through loss of income. The bank is liable for the loss so suffered by the trust estate, except to the extent that I shall hereafter indicate. . . .

"The bank also relies on clause 18 of the settlement. Clause 18 entitled the bank to—

'. . . act in relation to [BTL] or any other company and the shares securities and properties thereof in such way as it shall think best calculated to benefit the trust premises and as if it was the absolute owner of such shares securities and property.'

In my judgment this is a clause which confers on the bank power to engage in a transaction which might otherwise be outside the scope of its authority; it is not an indemnity protecting the bank against liability for a transaction which is a breach of trust because it is one that a prudent man of business would have eschewed . . .

10–41   "Section 61 of the Trustee Act 1925 is pleaded. There is no doubt that the bank acted honestly. I do not think it acted reasonably. Nor do I think it would be fair to excuse the bank at the expense of the beneficiaries.

"There remains this defence, which I take from paragraph 26 of the amended pleading:

> 'In about 1963 the Old Company purchased a site at Woodbridge Road, Guildford, pursuant to the policy pleaded in paragraph 19 hereof, for the sum of £79,000 and re-sold the same for £350,000 to MEPC Ltd in 1973. The net profit resulting from such sale was £271,000. If, which is denied, the Defendant is liable for breach of trust, whether as alleged in the amended Statement of Claim or otherwise, the Defendant claims credit for such sum of £271,000 or other sum found to be gained in taking any accounts or inquiries.'

"The general rule as stated in all the textbooks, with some reservations, is that where a trustee is liable in respect of distinct breaches of trust, one of which has resulted in a loss and the other in a gain, he is not entitled to set off the gain against the loss, unless they arise in the same transaction. The relevant cases are, however, not altogether easy to reconcile. All are centenarians and none is quite like the present. The Guildford development stemmed from exactly the same policy and (to a lesser degree because it proceeded less far) exemplified the same folly as the Old Bailey project. Part of the profit was in fact used to finance the Old Bailey disaster. By sheer luck the gamble paid off handsomely, on capital account. I think it would be unjust to deprive the bank of this element of salvage in the course of assessing the cost of the shipwreck. My order will therefore reflect the bank's right to an appropriate set-off. . . ."

RE DAWSON

[1966] 2 N.S.W.R. 211, 214–216 endorsed by Brightman L.J. in *Bartlett v. Barclays Bank Trust Co. Ltd (No. 2)* [1980] Ch. 515 at 543

10–42   STREET J.: "The obligation of a defaulting trustee is essentially one of effecting a restitution to the estate. The obligation is of a personal character and its extent is not to be limited by common law principles governing remoteness of damage. In *Caffrey v. Darby*,[60] trustees were charged with neglect in failing to recover possession of part of the trust assets. The assets were lost and it was argued by the trustees that the loss was not attributable to their neglect. The Master of the Rolls, in stating his reasons, asked 'will they be relieved from that by the circumstance that the loss has ultimately happened by something that is not a

---

[60] (1801) 6 Ves. 488.

direct and immediate consequence of their negligence?' His answer to this question was that, even supposing that 'they could not look to the possibility' of the actual event which occasioned the loss, 'yet, if they have already been guilty of negligence they must be responsible for any loss in any way to that property; for whatever may be the immediate cause the property would not have been in a situation to sustain that loss if it had not been for their negligence. If they had taken possession of the property it would not have been in his possession. If the loss had happened by fire, lightning, or any other accident, that would not be an excuse for them, if guilty of previous negligence. That was their fault.' *Caffrey v. Darby* is consistent with the proposition that if a breach has been committed then the trustee is liable to place the trust estate in the same position as it would have been in if no breach had been committed. Considerations of causation, fore-seeability and remoteness do not readily enter into the matter. To the same effect is the case of *Clough v. Bond*.[61] It was argued before Lord Cottenham L.C. that 'the principle of the court is to charge persons in the situation of trustees as parties to a breach of trust, wherever they have acted irregularly, and the irregularity, however well intended, has in the result enabled their co-trustees to commit a breach of trust, or has been, however remotely, the origin of the loss.' . . . The principles embodied in this approach do not appear to involve any inquiry as to whether the loss was caused by or flowed from the breach. Rather the inquiry in each instance would appear to be whether the loss would have happened if there had been no breach. . . . The cases to which I have referred demonstrate that the obligation to make restitution, which courts of equity have from very early times imposed on defaulting trustees and other fiduciaries, is of a more absolute nature than the common-law obligation to pay damages for tort or breach of contract. It is on this fundamental ground that I regard the principles in *Tomkinson's Case*[62] as distinguishable. Moreover the distinction between common law damages and relief against a defaulting trustee is strikingly demonstrated by reference to the actual form of relief granted in equity in respect of breaches of trust. The form of relief is couched in terms appropriate to require the defaulting trustee to restore to the estate the assets of which he deprived it. Increases in market values between the date of breach and the date of recoupment are for the trustee's account: the effect of such increases would, at common law, be excluded from the computation of damages but in equity a defaulting trustee must make good the loss by restoring to the estate the assets of which he deprived it notwithstanding that market values may have increased in the meantime. The obligation to restore to the estate the assets of which he deprived it necessarily connotes that, where a monetary compensation is to be paid in lieu of restoring assets, that compensation is to be assessed by reference to the value of the assets at the date of restoration and not at the date of deprivation. In this sense the obligation is a continuing one and ordinarily, if the assets are for some reason not restored *in specie*, it will fall for quantification at the date when recoupment is to be effected, and not before."

10–43

TARGET HOLDINGS LTD V. REDFERNS

House of Lords (Lords Keith, Ackner, Jauncey, Browne-Wilkinson, and Lloyd)
[1996] 1 A.C. 421 [1995] 3 W.L.R. 352 [1995] All E.R. 785.

---

[61] (1838) 3 My. & Cr. 490.
[62] [1961] A.C. 1007.

10–44   The plaintiff mortgagee alleged it was a victim of a mortgage fraud where the insolvent second defendant valued the mortgaged property at £2 million and where the first defendant, a firm of solicitors, acted not just for the plaintiff but for the mortgagor, Crowngate Ltd, and also for Kohli Ltd and Panther Ltd. The owner of the property, Mirage Ltd, had agreed to sell to Crowngate for £775,000 but Crowngate arranged matters so that Mirage would sell to Panther for £775,000 which would then sell to Kohli for £1,250,000, which would then sell to Crowngate for £2 million. The plaintiff knew nothing of these arrangements but paid £1,525,000 to the defendant solicitors to be held on a bare trust to pay to the order of Crowngate only when the property was transferred to Crowngate and charges over it were executed in the plaintiff's favour.

   In breach of trust the money was paid over a month before the charges were executed. Crowngate became insolvent and the plaintiff sold the property for only £500,000.

   The plaintiff sued Redferns for breach of its duty of care as a solicitor to the plaintiff in not alerting the plaintiff of the suspicious circumstances and for breach of trust in paying the money away without authority. Summary judgment under RSCO 14 for breach of trust was sought.

   Warner J. gave leave to defend conditional on payment into court of £1 million. The Court of Appeal 2:1 granted summary judgment.

10–45   LORD BROWNE-WILKINSON (with whom all the other law lords simply concurred): "Peter Gibson L.J. (with whom Hirst L.J. agreed) held that the basic liability of a trustee in breach of trust is not to pay damages but to restore to the trust fund that which has been lost to it or to pay compensation to the beneficiary for what he has lost. He held that, in assessing the compensation payable to the beneficiary, causation is not irrelevant but common law rules of causation, as such, do not apply: the beneficiary is to be put back in the position he would have been in but for the breach of trust. He held that in cases where the breach of trust does not involve paying away trust money to a stranger (e.g. making an unauthorised investment), the answer to the question whether any loss has been thereby caused and the quantification of such loss will depend upon events subsequent to the commission of the breach of trust. But he held that in cases, such as the present, where the trustee has paid away trust moneys to a stranger, there is an immediate loss to the trust fund and the causal connection between the breach and the loss is obvious: the trustee comes under an immediate duty to restore the moneys to the trust fund. He held that the remedies of Equity are sufficiently flexible to require Target (as it has always accepted) to give credit for the moneys received on the subsequent realisation of its security. But otherwise Redferns liability was to pay to Target the whole of the moneys wrongly paid away . . .

10–46   "Before considering the technical issues of law which arise, it is appropriate to look at the case more generally. Target allege, and it is probably the case, that they were defrauded by third parties (Mr. Kohli and Mr. Musafir and possibly their associates) to advance money on the security of the property. If there had been no breach by Redferns of their instructions *and the transaction had gone through*, Target would have suffered a loss . . .

   "[But] Such loss would have been wholly caused by the fraud of the third parties. The breach of trust committed by Redferns left Target in exactly the same position as it would have been if there had been no such breach: Target advanced the same amount of money, obtained the same security and received the same amount on the realisation of that security. In any ordinary use of words, the breach of trust by Redferns cannot be said to have caused the actual loss ultimately suffered by Target unless it can be shown that, but for the breach of trust, the transaction would not have gone through *e.g.* if Panther could not have obtained a conveyance from Mirage otherwise than by paying the purchase money to Mirage out of the moneys paid out, in breach of trust, by Redferns to Panther on June 29. If that fact can be demonstrated, it can be said that Redferns' breach of trust was a cause of Target's loss: if the transaction had not gone through, Target would not have advanced the money at all and therefore Target would not have suffered any loss. But the Court of Appeal decided (see Ralph Gibson L.J. 1100B-C: Peter Gibson L.J. 1104B) and it is common ground before your Lordships that there is a triable issue as to whether, had it not been for the breach of trust. the transaction would have gone through. Therefore the decision of the Court of Appeal in this case can only be maintained on the basis that, even if there is no causal link between the breach of trust and the actual loss eventually suffered by Target (*i.e.* the sum advanced less the sum recovered) the trustee in breach is liable to bear (at least in part) the loss suffered by Target . . .

"At common law there are two principles fundamental to the award of **10–47** damages. First, that the defendant's wrongful act must cause the damage complained of. Second, that the plaintiff is to be put "in the same position as he would have been in if he had not sustained the wrong for which he is now getting his compensation or reparation": *Livingston v. Rawyards Coal Company* (1880) 5 App. Cas. 25. 39. *per* Lord Blackburn. Although, as will appear. in many ways equity approaches liability for making good a breach of trust from a different starting point, in my judgment those two principles are applicable as much in equity as at common law. Under both systems liability is fault based: the defendant is only liable for the consequences of the legal wrong he has done to the plaintiff and to make good the damage caused by such wrong. He is not responsible for damage not caused by his wrong or to pay by way of compensation more than the loss suffered from such wrong. The detailed rules of equity as to causation and the quantification of loss differ, at least ostensibly, from those applicable at common law. But the principles underlying both systems are the same. On the assumptions that had to be made in the present case until the factual issues are resolved (i.e. that the transaction would have gone through even if there had been no breach of trust), the result reached by the Court of Appeal does not accord with those principles. Redferns as trustees have been held liable to compensate Target for a loss caused otherwise than by the breach of trust. I approach the consideration of the relevant rules of equity with a strong predisposition against such a conclusion.

"The considerations urged before your Lordships, although presented as a **10–48** single argument leading to the conclusion that the views of the majority in the Court of Appeal are correct, on analysis comprise two separate lines of reasoning, *viz.*

(A) an argument developed by Mr. Patten (but not reflected in the reasons of the Court of Appeal) that Target is *now* (*i.e.* at the date of judgment) entitled to have the "trust fund" restored by an order that Redferns reconstitute the trust fund by paying back into client account the moneys paid away in breach of trust. Once the trust fund is so reconstituted, Redferns as bare trustee for Target will have no answer to a claim by Target for the payment over of the moneys in the reconstituted "trust fund". Therefore, Mr. Patten says, it is proper now to order payment direct to Target of the whole sum improperly paid away, less the sum which Target has received on the sale of property;

(B) the argument accepted by the majority of the Court of Appeal that, because immediately after the moneys were paid away by Redferns in breach of trust there was an immediate right to have the "trust fund" reconstituted, there was *then* an immediate loss to the trust fund for which loss Redferns are now liable to compensate Target direct.

10–49 "The critical distinction between the two arguments is that argument (A) depends upon Target being entitled *now* to an order for restitution to the trust fund whereas argument (B) quantifies the compensation payable to Target as beneficiary by reference to a right to restitution to the trust fund at an earlier date and is not dependent upon Target having any right to have the client account reconstituted now.

"Before dealing with these two lines of argument, it is desirable to say something about the approach to the principles under discussion. The argument both before the Court of Appeal and your Lordships concentrated on the equitable rules establishing the extent and quantification of the compensation payable by a trustee who is in breach of trust. In my judgment this approach is liable to lead to the wrong conclusions in the present case because it ignores an earlier and crucial question, viz., is the trustee who has committed a breach under any liability at all to the beneficiary complaining of the breach? There can be cases where, although there is an undoubted breach of trust, the trustee is under no liability at all to a beneficiary. For example, if a trustee commits a breach of trust with the acquiescence of one beneficiary, that beneficiary has no right to complain and an action for breach of trust brought by him would fail completely. Again there may be cases where the breach gives rise to no right to compensation. Say, as often occurs, a trustee commits a judicious breach of trust by investing in an unauthorised investment which proves to be very profitable to the trust. A carping beneficiary could insist that the unauthorised investment be sold and the proceeds invested in authorised investments: but the trustee would be under no liability to pay compensation either to the trust fund or to the beneficiary because the breach has caused no loss to the trust fund. Therefore, in each case the first question is to ask what are the rights of the beneficiary: only if some relevant right has been infringed so as to give rise to a loss is it necessary to consider the extent of the trustee's liability to compensate for such loss.

10–50 "The basic right of a beneficiary is to have the trust duly administered in accordance with the provisions of the trust instrument, if any, and the general law. Thus, in relation to a traditional trust where the fund is held in trust for a number of beneficiaries having different, usually successive, equitable interests, (*e.g.* A for life with remainder to B), the right of each beneficiary is to have the whole fund vested in the trustees so as to be available to satisfy his equitable interest when, and if, it falls into possession. Accordingly, in the case of a breach of such a trust involving the wrongful paying away of trust assets, the liability of the trustee is to restore to the trust fund, often called "the trust estate", what ought to have been there.

"The equitable rules of compensation for breach of trust have been largely developed in relation to such traditional trusts, where the only way in which all the beneficiaries' rights can be protected is to restore to the trust fund what ought to be there. In such a case the basic rule is that a trustee in breach of trust must restore or pay to the trust estate either the assets which have been lost to the estate by reason of the breach or compensation for such loss. Courts of

Equity did not award damages but, acting in personam, ordered the defaulting trustee to restore the trust estate: see *Nocton v. Lord Ashburton* [1914] A.C. 932 at 952, 958, *per* Viscount Haldane L.C. If specific restitution of the trust property is not possible, then the liability of the trustee is to pay sufficient compensation to the trust estate to put it back to what it would have been had the breach not been committed: *Caffrey v. Darby* (1801) 6 Ves. 488; *Clough v. Bond* (1838) 3 My. and Cr. 490. Even if the immediate cause of the loss is the dishonesty or failure of a third party, the trustee is liable to make good that loss to the trust estate if, but for the breach, such loss would not have occurred: see *Underhill and Hayton, Law of Trusts and Trustees* (14th ed., (1987) pp. 734–736; *Re Dawson decd.; Union Fidelity Trustee Co. Ltd v. Perpetual Trustee Co. Ltd* [1966] 2 N.S.W.R. 211; *Bartlett v. Barclays Bank Trust Co. Ltd (Nos. 1 and 2)* [1980] Ch. 515. Thus the common law rules of remoteness of damage and causation do not apply. However there does have to be some causal connection between the breach of trust and the loss to the trust estate for which compensation is recoverable *viz.* the fact that the loss would not have occurred but for the breach: see also *Re Miller's Deed Trusts* (1978) 75 L.S.G. 454; *Nestlé v. National Westminster Bank Plc.* [1993] 1 W.L.R. 1260.

"Hitherto I have been considering the rights of beneficiaries under traditional **10–51** trusts where the trusts are still subsisting and therefore the right of each beneficiary, and his only right, is to have the trust fund reconstituted as it should be. But what if at the time of the action claiming compensation for breach of trust those trusts have come to an end. Take as an example again the trust for A for life with remainder to B. During A's lifetime B's only right is to have the trust duly administered and, in the event of a breach, to have the trust fund restored. After A's death, B becomes absolutely entitled. He of course has the right to have the trust assets retained by the trustees until they have fully accounted for them to him. But if the trustees commit a breach of trust, there is no reason for compensating the breach of trust by way of an order for restitution and compensation *to the trust fund* as opposed to the beneficiary himself. The beneficiary's right is no longer simply to have the trust duly administered: he is, in equity, the sole owner of the trust estate. Nor, for the same reason, is restitution to the trust fund necessary to protect other beneficiaries. Therefore, although I do not wholly rule out the possibility that even in those circumstances an order to reconstitute the fund may be appropriate, in the ordinary case where a beneficiary becomes absolutely entitled to the trust fund the court orders, not restitution to the trust estate, but the payment of compensation directly to the beneficiary. The measure of such compensation is the same i.e. the difference between what the beneficiary has in fact received and the amount he would have received but for the breach of trust . . .

Argument A

"As I have said, the critical step in this argument is that Target is *now* entitled to **10–52** an order for reconstitution of the trust fund by the repayment into client account of the moneys wrongly paid away, so that Target can now demand immediate repayment of the whole of such moneys without regard to the real loss it has suffered by reason of the breach.

"Even if the equitable rules developed in relation to traditional trusts were directly applicable to such a case as this, as I have sought to show a beneficiary becoming absolutely entitled to a trust fund has no automatic right to have the fund reconstituted in all circumstances. Thus, even applying the strict rules so developed in relation to tradition trusts, it seems to me very doubtful whether

Target is now entitled to have the trust fund reconstituted. But in my judgment it is in any event wrong to lift wholesale the detailed rules developed in the context of traditional trusts and then seek to apply them to trusts of quite a different kind. In the modern world the trust has become a valuable device in commercial and financial dealings. The fundamental principles of equity apply as much to such trusts as they do to the traditional trusts in relation to which those principles were originally formulated. But in my judgment it is important, if the trust is not to be rendered commercially useless, to distinguish between the basic principles of trust law and those specialist rules developed in relation to traditional trusts which are applicable only to such trusts and the rationale of which has no application to trusts of quite a different kind.

10–53　　"This case is concerned with a trust which has at all times been a bare trust. Bare trusts arise in a number of different contexts: e.g. by the ultimate vesting of the property under a traditional trust, nominee shareholdings and, as in the present case, as but one incident of a wider commercial transaction involving agency. In the case of moneys paid to a solicitor by a client as part of a conveyancing transaction, the purpose of that transaction is to achieve the commercial objective of the client, be it the acquisition of property or the lending of money on security. The depositing of money with the solicitor is but one aspect of the arrangements between the parties, such arrangements being for the most part contractual. Thus, the circumstances under which the solicitor can part with money from client account are regulated by the instructions given by the client: they are not part of the trusts on which the property is held. I do not intend to cast any doubt on the fact that moneys held by solicitors on client account are trust moneys or that the basic equitable principles apply to any breach of such trust by solicitors. But the basic equitable principle applicable to breach of trust is that the beneficiary is entitled to be compensated for any loss he would not have suffered but for the breach. I have no doubt that, until the underlying commercial transaction has been completed, the solicitor can be required to restore to client account moneys wrongly paid away. But to import into such trust an obligation to restore the trust fund once the transaction has been completed would be entirely artificial. The obligation to reconstitute the trust fund applicable in the case of traditional trusts reflects the fact that no one beneficiary is entitled to the trust property and the need to compensate all beneficiaries for the breach. That rationale has no application to a case such as the present. To impose such an obligation in order to enable the beneficiary solely entitled (i.e. the client) to recover from the solicitor more than the client has in fact lost flies in the face of common sense and is in direct conflict with the basic principles of equitable compensation. In my judgment, once a conveyancing transaction has been completed the client has no right to have the solicitor's client account reconstituted as a "trust fund"."

Argument B

10–54　　"The key point in the reasoning of the Court of Appeal is that where moneys are paid away to a stranger in breach of trust, an immediate loss is suffered by the trust estate: as a result, subsequent events reducing that loss are irrelevant. They drew a distinction between the case in which the breach of trust consisted of some failure in the administration of the trust and the case where a trustee has actually paid away trust moneys to a stranger. There is no doubt that in the former case, one waits to see what loss is in fact suffered by reason of the breach i.e. the restitution or compensation payable is assessed at the date of trial, not of breach. However, the Court of Appeal considered that where the breach consisted of paying away the trust moneys to a stranger it made no sense to wait: it seemed to Peter Gibson L.J. [1994] 1 W.L.R. 1089, 1103G-H obvious that in such a case "there is an immediate loss, placing the trustee under an immediate duty to restore the moneys to the trust fund". The majority of the Court of Appeal therefore considered that subsequent events which diminished the loss in fact suffered were irrelevant, save for imposing on the compensated beneficiary an obligation to give credit for any benefit he subsequently received. In effect, in the view of the Court of Appeal one "stops the clock" at the date the moneys are paid away: events which occur between the date of breach and the date of trial are irrelevant in assessing the loss suffered by reason of the breach.

"A trustee who wrongly pays away trust money, like a trustee who makes an **10–55** unauthorised investment commits a breach of trust and comes under an immediate duty to remedy such breach. If immediate proceedings are brought, the court will make an immediate order requiring restoration to the trust fund of the assets wrongly distributed or, in the case of an unauthorised investment, will order the sale of the unauthorised investment and the payment of compensation for any loss suffered. But the fact that there is an accrued cause of action as soon as the breach is committed does not in my judgment mean that the quantum of the compensation payable is ultimately fixed as at the date when the breach occurred. The quantum is fixed at the date of judgment at which date, according to the circumstances then pertaining, the compensation is assessed at the figure then necessary to put the trust estate or the beneficiary back into the position it would have been in had there been no breach. I can see no justification for "stopping the clock" immediately in some cases but not in others: to do so may, as in this case, lead to compensating the trust estate or the beneficiary for a loss which, on the facts known at trial, it has never suffered.

"Moreover, in my judgment the distinction is not consistent with the decision **10–56** in *Re Dawson decd.* [1966] 2 N.S.W.R. 211. In that case a testator had established separate executors for his New Zealand and his Australian estates. In 1939 the New Zealand estate was under the administration of attorneys for, amongst others, P.S.D. P.S.D. arranged that N.Z. £4,700 should be withdrawn from the New Zealand estate and paid away to a stranger. X, who in turn was supposed to lend the moneys to an Australian company in which P.S.D. was interested. X absconded with money. In that case, therefore, the trust money had been paid away to a stranger. Stret J. had to decide whether the liability of P.S.D. to compensate the estate was to be satisfied by paying sufficient Australian pounds to buy N.Z. £4,700 at the rate of exchange at the date of breach (when there was parity between the two currencies) or at the date of judgment (when the Australian pound had depreciated against the New Zealand pound). He held that the rate of exchange was to be taken as at the date of judgment. Although, contrary to the present case, this decision favoured the beneficiaries at the expense of the defaulting trustee, the principle is of general application whether operating to the benefit or the detriment of the beneficiaries. The equitable compensation for breach of trust has to be assessed as at the date of judgment and not at an earlier date."

"In *Canson Enterprises Ltd v. Boughton and Co.* (1991) 85 D.L.R. (4th) 129 the **10–57** plaintiffs had bought some property in a transaction in which they were advised by the defendant, a solicitor. To the knowledge of the solicitor, but not of the plaintiffs, there was an improper profit being made by the vendors. If the plaintiffs had known that fact, they would not have completed the purchase. The defendant's solicitor was in breach of his fiduciary duties to the plaintiffs. After completion the plaintiffs built a warehouse on the property, which due to the negligence of engineers and builders, was defective. The question was whether the defendant solicitor was liable to compensate the plaintiffs for the defective building, the plaintiffs contending that "but for" the defendant's breach of fiduciary duty they would not have bought the property and therefore would not have built the warehouse. Although the Supreme Court of Canada were unanimous in dismissing the claim, they reached their conclusions by two differing routes. The majority considered that damages for breach of fiduciary duty fell to be measured by analogy with common law rules of remoteness, whereas the minority considered that the equitable principles of compensation applied. Your Lordships are not required to choose between those two views. But the judgment of McLachlin J. (expressing the minority view) contains an illuminating exposition of the rules applicable to equitable compensation for breach of trust. Although the whole judgment deserves study, I extract the following statements (at pp. 160C, 162E and 163E):

10–58   'While foreseeability of loss does not enter into the calculation of compensation for breach of fiduciary duty, liability is not unlimited. Just as restitution in specie is limited to the property under the trustee's control, so equitable compensation must be limited to loss flowing from the trustee's acts in relation to the interest he undertook to protect. Thus, Davidson states "It is imperative to ascertain the loss *resulting from breach of the relevant equitable duty.*" ' (at p. 354, emphasis added) . . .

'A related question which must be addressed is the time of assessment of the loss. In this area tort and contract law are of little help . . . The basis of compensation at equity, by contrast, is the restoration of the actual value of the thing lost through the breach. The foreseeable value of the items is not in issue. As a result, the losses are to be assessed as at the time of trial, *using the full benefit of hindsight.* (emphasis added) . . .

'In summary, compensation is an equitable monetary remedy which is available when the equitable remedies of restitution and account are not appropriate. By analogy with restitution, it attempts to restore to the plaintiff what has been lost as a result of the breach, i.e., the plaintiff's loss of opportunity. The plaintiff's actual loss as a consequence of the breach is to be assessed with the full benefit of hindsight. Foreseeability is not a concern in assessing compensation but it is essential that the losses made good are only those which, *on a common sense view of causation*, were caused by the breach.' (emphasis added).

"In my view this is good law. Equitable compensation for breach of trust is designed to achieve exactly what the word compensation suggests: to make good a loss in fact suffered by the beneficiaries and which, using hindsight and common sense, can be seen to have been caused by the breach . . .

10–59   "Mr. Patten (for Target) relied on *Nant-y-Glo and Blaina Ironworks Company v. Grave* (1878) 12 Ch. D. 738 as showing that a trustee can be held liable to recoup to the trust fund the value of shares at the highest value between the date of breach and the date of judgment. In my view that case has no relevance. The claim there was not for breach of trust but for account of profits made by a fiduciary (a company director) from shares which he had improperly received in breach of his duty. The amount recoverable in an action claiming an account of profits is dependent upon the profit made by the fiduciary, not the loss suffered by the beneficiary.

"Mr. Patten also relied on *Jaffray v. Marshall* [1993] 1 W.L.R. 1285 where the principles applicable in an action for an account of profits were, to my mind wrongly, applied to a claim for compensation for breach of trust. In my judgment that case was wrongly decided not only because the wrong principle was applied but also because the judge awarded compensation by assessing the quantum on an assumption (viz. that the house in question would have been sold at a particular date) when he found as a fact that such sale would not have taken place even if there had been no breach of trust.

"For these reasons I reach the conclusion that, on the facts which must **10–60** currently be assumed, Target has not demonstrated that it is entitled to any compensation for breach of trust. Assuming that moneys would have been forthcoming from some other source to complete the purchase from Mirage if the moneys had not been wrongly provided by Redferns in breach of trust, Target obtained exactly what it would have obtained had no breach occurred *i.e.* a valid security for the sum advanced. Therefore, on the assumption made, Target has suffered no compensatable loss. Redferns are entitled to leave to defend the breach of trust claim.

"However, I find it very difficult to make that assumption of fact. There must be a high probability that, at trial, it will emerge that the use of Target's money to pay for the purchase from Mirage and the other intermediate transactions was a vital feature of the transaction. The circumstances of the present case are clouded by suspicion, which suspicion is not dissipated by Mr. Bundy's untruthful letter dated 30 June informing Target that the purchase of the property and the charges to Target had been completed. If the moneys made available by Redferns' breach of trust were essential to enable the transaction to go through, but for Redferns' breach of trust Target would not have advanced any money. In that case the loss suffered by Target by reason of the breach of trust will be the total sum advanced to Crowngate less the proceeds of the security. It is not surprising that Mr. Sumption was rather muted in his submission that Redferns should have had unconditional leave to defend and that the order for payment into court of £1m. should be set aside. In my judgment such an order was fully justified.

"I would therefore allow the appeal, set aside the order of the Court of Appeal and restore the order of Warner J."

I. MAKING UNAUTHORISED INVESTMENTS AND NEGLIGENTLY INVESTING

Where trustees make an unauthorised investment they are liable for all loss **10–61** incurred when it is realised as held in *Knott v. Cottee, infra,* para. 10–62. However, "what the prudent man should do at any time depends on the economic and financial conditions of that time—not on what judges of the past, however eminent, have held to be the prudent course in the conditions if 50 or 100 years before" as Dillon L.J. has indicated.[63] Thus, he and his brethren further indicated[64] that if a negligent investment policy (one that no prudent trustee could have pursued) causes loss, the trustee can be required to make good to the trust fair compensation for the capital growth there would have been if a proper investment policy had been followed *i.e.* compensation for loss of profit taking account, it seems, of the average performance of authorised investments during the period. It would seem to follow that if trustees invest in unauthorised

---

[63] *Nestlé v. National Westminster Bank plc* [1994] 1 All E.R. 118 at 126.
[64] *ibid.* at 126–127 (criticising *Robinson v. Robinson* (1851) 1 De. G.M. & G. 247), 138 at 141.

investments (as contrasted with negligent investment in authorised investments) they could be similarly accountable for the profit that would have been made if they had properly invested in authorised investments.

In *Re Mulligan*[65] in order to favour the life tenant the trustees did not diversity by investing in equities. It was held that they should have diversified in 1972 to the extent of 40 per cent of the capital and such 40 per cent holdings in equities would have appreciated at 75 per cent of an appropriate index of equities. The 25 per cent discount took account of dealing costs and the fact that the fund was not large enough for the trustees to be expected to rival the index. Nowadays investment can be in "tracker funds" which track and reflect the index, so obviating the need for such a discount.

KNOTT V. COTTEE

Master of the Rolls (1852) 16 Beav. 77; 16 Jur.(o.s.) 752

10–62   A testator who died in January 1844 directed his executor-trustees to invest in "the public or Government stocks or funds of Great Britain, or upon real security in England and Wales." In 1845 and 1846, the defendant executor-trustee invested part of the estate in Exchequer bills, which in 1846 were ordered into court, and in the same year sold at a loss. By a decree made in 1848, the court declared that the investment in Exchequer bills was improper. If, however, the investment had been retained, its realisation at the time of the decree of 1848 would have resulted in a profit.

Held, "that the executor ought to be charged with the *amount improperly invested*, and credited with the produce of the Exchequer bills in 1846." Thus he was liable for the loss incurred when the unauthorised investments were realised.

ROMILLY M.R.: "Here is an executor who had a direct and positive trust to perform, which was, to invest the money upon government stocks or funds, or upon real securities, and accumulate at compound interest all the balances after maintaining the children. He has made certain investments, which the court has declared to be improper. The case must either be treated as if these investments had not been made, or had been made for his own benefit out of his own moneys, and that he had at the same time retained moneys of the testator in his hands. I think, therefore, that there must be a reference back, to ascertain what balances the executor retained from time to time, it being clear that he has retained some balances . . .

10–63   "As to the mode of charging the executor in respect of the Exchequer bills, I treat the laying out in Exchequer bills in this way: The persons interested were entitled to earmark them, as being bought with the testator's assets, in the same manner as if the executor had bought a house with the trust funds; and though they do not recognise the investment, they had a right to make it available for what was due; and though part of the property of the executor, it was specifically applicable to the payment. When the Exchequer bills were sold and produced £3,955, the court must consider the produce as a sum of money refunded by the executor to the testator's estate on that day; and on taking the account, the master must give credit for this amount as on the day on which the Exchequer bills were sold . . ."

---

65 [1998] 1 N.Z.L.R. 481.

If a trustee makes an unauthorised investment, the beneficiaries may, **10–64** if they choose, and if they are all *sui juris*, adopt the investment as part of the trust.[66] The difficulty is as to the *extent* of their remedy. If they decide to adopt the investment, but it has caused a loss to the estate, can they also require the trustee to replace that loss? According to *Re Lake*,[67] they apparently can. But Wood V.-C. in *Thornton v. Stokill*[68] seems to have held that if they adopt the investment, it settles the matter. To play safe the beneficiaries should refuse to authorise or adopt the investment but accept the investment *in specie* as part satisfaction of the trustees' personal liability.

Where the unauthorised investment has not or cannot be adopted (*e.g.* where the beneficiaries are not each *sui juris*) the beneficiaries have a lien over it until the trust fund loss is made up, whether by the trustees using their own resources to replace the loss so that they can take over the investment themselves, or by the sale of the investment with the balance to make up the loss coming from the trustees' own resources. Of course, if the investment is of an *authorised* nature, the beneficiaries have no option of adopting or rejecting it, for it is necessarily part of the trust.[69]

II. Improper Retention of Unauthorised Investments[70]

Where trustees retain an unauthorised investment they are liable for the **10–65** difference between the price obtainable on sale at the proper time and the proceeds of sale of the unauthorised investment when eventually sold.

FRY V. FRY

Master of the Rolls (1859) 27 Beav. 144; 28 L.J.Ch. 591; 34 L.T.(o.s.) 51; 5 Jur. 1047

A testator who died in March 1834, after devising his residuary real estate to two trustees on trust to pay the rents (except those of the Langford Inn) to his wife during her widowhood, with remainder over, and bequeathing his residuary personal estate upon trust for conversion for his wife during her widowhood, with remainder over, directed the trustees: "And as for and concerning all that messuage or dwelling-house called Langford Inn . . . upon trust, as soon as convenient after my decease, to sell and dispose of the same, either by auction or private sale, and for the most money that could be reasonably obtained for the same." In April 1836 the trustees advertised the Langford Inn for sale for £1,000. They refused an offer of £900, made in 1837. One of the trustees died in 1842. A

---

[66] *Re Patten* (1883) 52 L.J. Ch. 787; *Re Jenkins* [1903] 2 Ch. 362; *Wright v. Morgan* [1926] A.C. 788 at 799.
[67] [1903] 1 K.B. 439; and see *ex p. Biddulph* (1849) 3 De. G. & Sm. 587.
[68] (1855) 1 Jur. 751. See also *Re Cape Breton* (1885) 29 Ch.D. 795.
[69] *Re Salmon* (1889) 42 Ch.D. 351.
[70] The assumption being that the investment has depreciated; otherwise any gain belongs of course to the trust. See Arden M.R. in *Piety v. Stace* (1799) 4 Ves. 620 at 622, 623.

railway opened in 1843 caused the property to depreciate in value through the diversion of traffic. The property was again advertised for sale in 1845, but no offer was received. The other trustee died in 1856. Langford Inn was still unsold and could not be sold except at a low price.

10–66   *Held*, by Romilly M.R., the trustees had committed a breach of trust by reason of their negligence in not selling the property for so many years, that the property must be sold, and that the estates of the trustees were "liable to make good the deficiency between the amount which should be produced by the sale of the inn and the sum of £900, in case the purchase-money thereof should not amount to that sum."[71]

It was held by the Court of Appeal in *Re Chapman*[72] and in *Rawsthorne v. Rowley*,[73] that a trustee is not liable for a loss arising through the retention of an *authorised* investment unless he was guilty of *wilful default*,[74] which requires proof of want of ordinary prudence on the part of the trustee.[75] The position is now governed by sections 1, 4 and 5 of the Trustee Act 2000. The trustees must from time to time obtain and consider proper advice on whether retention of the investment is satisfactory having regard to the need for diversification and the suitability of the investments. In deciding what to do the statutory duty of care needs to be observed (except to the extent excluded).

III. IMPROPER REALISATION OF PROPER INVESTMENTS

10–67   It is clearly a breach of trust if trustees sell an authorised investment for the purpose of investing in an unauthorised investment or for the purpose of paying the proceeds to the life-tenant in breach of trust. In such cases the trustees are liable to replace the authorised investment or the proceeds of sale of the authorised investment, whichever is the greater burden.[76] Replacement of the authorised investment will be at its value at the date it is actually replaced or at the date of the court judgment if not earlier replaced or, exceptionally, at the date the authorised investment would, in any event, have been sold.[77]

---

[71] See also *Grayburn v. Clarkson* (1868) 3 Ch.App. 605; *Dunning v. Gainsborough* (1885) 54 L.J.Ch. 891. Where the proper time during which the unauthorised investments, *e.g.* shares, should have been sold is a period during which fluctuations occur in the value of the shares one may take half the sum of the lowest and highest prices at which the shares might have been sold in the period commencing when the shares could first have been sold to advantage and ending at the date by which they should reasonably have been sold: *Fales v. Canada Permanent Trust Co.* (1976) 70 D.L.R. (3d) 257 at 274.

[72] [1896] 2 Ch. 763.

[73] [1909] 1 Ch. 409n.

[74] See also *Baud v. Fardell* (1855) 4 W.R. 40; *Henderson v. Hunter* (1843) 1 L.T.(o.s.) 359 at 385; *Robinson v. Murdoch* (1881) 45 L.T. 417; Joyce J. in *Re Oddy* (1910) 104 L.T. 128 at 131; *Re Godwin* (1918) 87 L.J.Ch. 645.

[75] *per* Lindley L.J. in *Re Chapman* [1896] 2 Ch. 763 at 776.

[76] Thus, if an authorised investment is sold for £10,000, then invested in an unauthorised investment sold for £8,000 when matters were discovered when the authorised investment could be repurchased for £7,000, the trustees must top up the £8,000 to £10,000, the true figure that should be in the accounts (after falsifying them) as retained for the beneficiaries: *Shepherd v. Mouls* (1845) 4 Hare 500, 504; *Watts v. Girdlestone* (1843) 6 Beav. 188.

[77] *Re Bell's Indenture* [1980] 3 All E.R. 425 at 437–439, pointing out that in *Re Massingberd* (1890) 63 L.T. 296 the reference to the date of the writ for ascertaining the value of the property sold in breach of trust was *per incuriam* and should be the date of the judgment.

Vice-Chancellor (1848) 6 Hare 26; affirmed (1850) 7 Hare 516; 2 H. & Tw. 459; **10–68**
    12 L.T.(o.s.) 445; 13 Jur.(o.s.) 318

The trustees of a sum of consols, who had power to convert and reinvest in the
public funds or upon real security, realised part of the stock and invested it in an
*un*authorised investment.

WIGRAM V.-C.: ". . . Then comes another material question—are the trustees
to replace the stock, or the money produced by the sale? Mr. Wood argued that
they were liable to make good the money only, distinguishing the sale, which he
said was lawful, from the investment, which I have decided to have been a breach
of trust. My opinion is, that the trustees must replace the stock. There was no
authority to sell, except with a view to the reinvestment; and here the sale was
made with a view to the investment I have condemned. It was all one transaction,
and the sale and investment must stand or fall together . . ."

Held, therefore, the trustees must replace the stock improperly realised.
Affirmed on appeal.[78]

IV. NON-INVESTMENT OF TRUST FUNDS

A trustee ought not to leave trust moneys uninvested for an unreason- **10–69**
able length of time. If he unnecessarily retains trust moneys which he
ought to have invested, he is chargeable with interest.[79]

While an investment is being sought, however, a trustee has statutory
powers to pay trust moneys into an interest-bearing account.[80]

If a trustee, having been *directed* to invest in a *specific* investment,
makes no investment at all, and the price of the specified investment
rises, he may be required to purchase so much of that investment as
would have been obtained by a purchase at the proper time.[81] This
applies equally where he is directed to invest in a specific investment and
he makes some investment other than the one specified.[82] But if he is
directed to invest in a specified *range* of investments, and he makes no
investment at all, it has been held that he is chargeable only with the
trust fund itself, and not with the amount of one or other of the
investments which might have been purchased.[83] The reason was stated
by Wigram V.-C in *Shepherd v. Mouls*[84] as follows: "The discretion given
to the trustees to select an investment among several securities makes it
impossible to ascertain the amount of the loss (if any) which has arisen
to the trust from the omission to invest, except, perhaps, in the possible
case (which has not occurred here) of a particular security having been

---

[78] Followed in *Re Massingberd* (1890) 63 L.T. 296.
[79] *Re Jones*, For lost capital appreciation see *Midland Bank Trustee Ltd v. Federated Pension Services*
[1995] Jersey L.R. 352 (1883) 49 L.T. 91.
[80] Trustee Act 2000 ss. 3, 16–24.
[81] *Byrchall v. Bradford* (1822) 6 Madd. 235.
[82] *Pride v. Fooks* (1840) 2 Beav. 430 at 432.
[83] *Shepherd v. Mouls* (1845) 4 Hare 500; *Robinson v. Robinson* (1851) 1 De G.M. & G. 247.
[84] *ibid.* at 504.

offered to the trustees, in conformity with the terms of the trust."
Nowadays, however, in view of *Nestlé v. National Westminster Bank*[85] as
discussed *supra*, para. 9–91 the trustees would be charged with the loss of
profit that would have been made taking account of the average
performance of the investments within the specified range.

V. TRUST FUNDS IN TRADE

10–70 If a trustee in breach of trust lends funds to a third party who knows they
are trust funds but not that the loan is a breach of trust and employs the
trust funds in trade, the beneficiaries cannot claim from the third party a
share of the profits. For example, a trustee in breach of trust lends
£1,000 of trust moneys to X, who employs the fund in his trade. The
agreement between the trustee and X provides that X is to pay interest
at the rate of 15 per cent. By employing this fund of £1,000 in his trade,
X makes a profit during the first year of £300. The beneficiaries cannot
claim from X a share of that profit; all that they can require is that he
replace, with interest, the fund which he borrowed. What is the position
if X knew, not merely that the funds were trust funds, but also *that the
loan was itself a breach of trust*? In this latter case, it would seem that X
is a constructive trustee, that he may not "traffic in his trust," and must
therefore account for his profit.[86] Of course, if the instrument of trust
authorises a loan of trust funds to a third party, and such a loan is made,
the beneficiaries have no right to claim profits.[87]

10–71 On the other hand, if it is the trustee himself who in breach of trust
employs trust funds in *his own* trade, the beneficiaries may, instead of
taking interest, require him to account for the profit. Thus, if in breach
of trust he employs £1,000 of trust moneys in his own trade and thereby
makes a profit during the first year of £200, the beneficiaries (on calling
upon him to replace the fund of £1,000), may, instead of taking interest
on that sum, claim the profit of £200.[88]

Even if the trust funds so employed by the trustee in his own trade
were mixed up with his private moneys, so that the fund used by him was
a mixed one, the beneficiaries may still claim a proportionate share of
the profits.[89] But it is either the one or the other, *either* interest *or* profit.
They cannot, even if they find it advantageous to do so, claim interest for
part of the time and profit for the other part.[90]

---

[85] [1994] 1 All E.R. 118.
[86] See *Stroud v. Gwyer* (1860) 25 Beav. 130; *Vyse v. Foster* (1872) 8 Ch.App. 309 at 334; *Belmont Finance Co. Ltd v. Williams Furniture Ltd* [1979] Ch. 250.
[87] *Parker v. Bloxam* (1855) 20 Beav. 295 at 302–304; *Evans v. London Co-operative Society Ltd, The Times*, July 6, 1976.
[88] *Jones v. Foxall* (1852) 15 Beav. 388; *Williams v. Powell* (1852) 15 Beav. 461; *Townsend v. Townsend* (1859) 1 Giff. 201; *Re Davis* [1902] 2 Ch. 314.
[89] *Docker v. Somes* (1834) 2 My. & K. 655; *Edinburgh T.C. v. Lord Advocate* (1879) 4 App.Cas. 823. Indeed, if the trust funds were the *sine qua non* of the purchase of a valuable asset later sold at a profit it is arguable that the trust should take the whole profit for to allow the trustee a proportion for himself would be to allow him to profit from his position.
[90] *Heathcote v. Hume* (1819) 1 Jac. & W. 122; *Vyse v. Foster* (1872) 8 Ch. App. 309 at 334; *Tang Man Sit v. Capacious Investments Ltd* [1996] 1 All E.R. 193.

VI. SUMMARY OF INCOME POSITION

(a) Rate of interest

If the life-tenant has lost income owing to the trustee's default he is **10–72** entitled to interest on the capital moneys at what one may term the "trustees' rate" or, exceptionally, at a higher rate. In the nineteenth century the trustees' rate was 4 per cent, with 5 per cent in cases of fraud or active misconduct in using money for trading purposes of the trustee.

The rate depends on the court's discretion but trustees' rate in the 1980s and 1990s became the rate of the court's special account[91] replacing the short-term investment account, reflecting the rate a trust fund would have earned if invested in authorised securities. *Lewin*[92] states "These rates ceased to be generally available and now the judgment rate is a possible substitute but, at eight per cent, is at present more than could be obtained on deposit." Clearly, in its discretion the court must award less than the higher rate and so award in the region of five or, perhaps, six per cent.

However, a higher rate will be charged: **10–73**

(i) where the trustee actually received a higher rate—when the life tenant takes the actual interest[93];

(ii) where the trustee ought to have received a higher rate (*e.g.* if he realised an authorised investment bearing 10 per cent and bought an unauthorised investment bearing five per cent[94]) when the life-tenant is entitled to interest at that higher rate;

(iii) where the trustee is presumed to have received a commercial rate as where he has made unauthorised use of trust moneys for his own purposes and the profits actually made by the trustee are unascertainable[95] or are less than the amount produced by applying the commercial rate—when the life-tenant is entitled to interest at the commercial rate instead of the actual interest or profit.[96] The commercial rate that is now presumed is one per cent above the London and Scottish clearing banks' base lending rate now that Bank of England minimum lending rate no longer exists.[97]

---

[91] *Bartlett v. Barclays Bank Trust Co. Ltd* [1980] Ch. 515 at 547; *Jaffray v. Marshall* [1994] 1 All E.R. 143. The Court Fund Rules 1987, rules 26, 27 deal with special account rates for funds invested with the court. The rates change much less frequently than commercial bank rates: usually they keep in line with National savings rates.

[92] 17th ed. (2000) para 39–32.

[93] *Re Emmet's Estate* (1881) 17 Ch.D. 142; *Matthew v. T. M. Sutton Ltd* [1994] 1 W.L.R. 1455. This should include the case where the trustee has used the money to reduce his overdraft and to save paying an actual interest rate: *Farnell v. Cox* (1898) 19 L.R.(N.S.W.)Eq. 142.

[94] *Jones v. Foxall* (1852) 15 Beav. 388; *Att.-Gen. v. Alford* (1855) 4 De G.M. & G. 843 explained in *Mayor of Berwick v. Murray* (1857) 7 De G.M. & G. 497.

[95] *Wallersteiner v. Moir (No. 2)* [1975] Q.B. 373.

[96] *Burdick v. Garrick* (1870) 5 Ch.App. 233; *Vyse v. Foster* (1872) 8 Ch.App. 309 at 329 (affd. L.R. 7 H.L. 318); *Gordon v. Gonda* [1955] 1 W.L.R. 885; *O'Sullivan v. Management Agency Ltd* [1985] Q.B. 428.

[97] *Belmont Finance Ltd v. Williams Furniture Ltd (No. 2)* [1980] 1 All E.R. 393; *O'Sullivan v. Management Agency Ltd* [1985] Q.B. 428; *John v. James* [1986] STC 352 at 363; *Shearson Lehman Inc. v. Maclaine Watson & Co. Ltd* [1990] 3 All E.R. 723 at 732–734; *Guardian Ocean Cargoes Ltd v. Banco da Brazil (No. 3)* [1992] 2 L.I.Rep. 193; *Westdeutsche Landesbank Girozentrale v. Islington B.C.* [1994] 4 All E.R. 890.

(b) Simple or compound interest

10–74 Nowadays there seems a presumption that in its discretion the court will award compound interest with yearly rests not just where there was a duty to accumulate income,[98] not just where the trustee or fiduciary was fraudulent or actually used the money in his own trade,[99] but where it is presumed against the wrongdoing fiduciary that he retained the misapplied money and used it for his own purposes most beneficially.[1] Compound interest is not to be awarded only as a punishment but as representing what the fiduciary should reasonably have obtained.

(c) Apportioning only real rate to life tenant

Where the trustee rate or the higher rate of the clearing banks reflects the continued erosion in the value of money by reason of significant inflation then a proportion of the income should be added to capital leaving the beneficiaries only with a real rate of interest. Thus in *Jaffray v. Marshall*[2] the interest at the special investment account rate was divided equally between capital and income, though the equitable life interest of the instigating life tenant benefiting from the breach was impounded under section 62 of the Trustee Act 1925.

Section 3. Impounding the Trustee's Beneficial Interest; Rule in *Re Dacre*[3]

10–75 If a beneficiary is also trustee, but is in default to the estate in his character of trustee, he is not entitled to receive any further part of his beneficial interest until his default is made good. His beneficial interest may also be applied in satisfaction of his liability. Take X who is a trustee, for himself for life, remainder to Y. X commits a breach of trust, and has not yet satisfied his liability. Until he does so, he cannot receive any further part of his beneficial interest, and that interest may be applied in satisfaction of his liability. The rule holds good where X's beneficial interest is *derivative* as well as where it is original. For example, X holds on trust for several beneficiaries, of which he is not himself one. He is in default to the estate in his character of trustee. One of the beneficiaries dies, and then X becomes entitled to that beneficiary's share as intestate successor or as legatee or devisee. X is now derivatively a beneficiary, and the rule applies as stated above.

---

[98] *Re Barclay* [1899] 1 Ch. 674; *Wallersteiner v. Moir (No. 2)* [1975] Q.B. 373.

[99] *Jones v. Foxall* (1852) 15 Beav. 388; *Re Barclay* [1899] 1 Ch. 674; *Burdick v. Garrick* (1870) 5 Ch.App. 233; *O'Sullivan v. Management Agency Ltd* [1985] Q.B. 428; *John v. James* [1986] S.T.C. 352 at 363–364.

[1] See *Wallersteiner v. Moir (No. 2)* [1975] Q.B. 373 at 388 where Lord Denning MR stated, "It should be presumed that the wrongdoer made the most beneficial use of it" while Buckley L.J. pointed out (p. 397) that a trustee who misapplied trust funds was forthwith liable to replace them with interest "on the notional ground that the money so applied was, in fact, the trustee's own money and that he has retained the misapplied trust money in his own hands and used it for his own purposes."

[2] [1993] 1 W.L.R. 128.

[3] [1916] 1 Ch. 344; *Jacubs v. Rylance* (1874) L.R. 17 Eq. 341; *Re Brown* (1886) 32 Ch.D. 597.

What is the position of an *assignee* from the trustee-beneficiary X? The assignee is in the same position as his assignor, *i.e.* he takes subject to the equity available against the trustee-beneficiary.[4] He takes subject to that equity even if the trustee-beneficiary's default to the estate was *subsequent* to the assignment.[5]

It can, in fact, be most unsafe to take an assignment of the beneficial **10–76** interest of a trustee-beneficiary, especially if that interest is reversionary. But it was held in *Re Towndrow*[6] that the rule does not apply to a case in which the trustee-beneficiary's liability relates to one trust (of a specific legacy) and his beneficial interest is derived from another trust (of the residuary estate), even though he is trustee of both trusts and both trusts are created by the same will. The rule in *Re Dacre* therefore applies only where the default relates to, and the beneficial interest is derived from, the same trust.

Section 4. Relief of Trustees

I. POWER OF THE COURT TO RELIEVE TRUSTEES FROM PERSONAL LIABILITY

Section 61[7] of the Trustee Act 1925 states, "If it appears to the court that **10–77** a trustee, whether appointed by the court or otherwise, is or may be[8] personally liable for any breach of trust, whether the transaction alleged to be a breach of trust occurred before or after the commencement of this Act, but has acted honestly and reasonably, and ought fairly to be excused for the breach of trust and for omitting to obtain the directions of the court in the matter in which he committed such a breach, then the court *may* relieve him either wholly or partly from personal liability for the same." This enables the court to excuse not just breaches of trust in the management of trust property but also payments to the wrong persons.[9] The question of fairness should be considered separately from whether the trustee acted honestly and reasonably: is it fair for the trustee to be excused when the inevitable result is to deny compensation to the beneficiaries? The burden is on the trustee[10] to satisfy the threefold obligation[11] of proving he acted honestly, reasonably and ought fairly to be excused. An appellate court will be reluctant to interfere with the lower court's exercise of discretion.[12]

---

[4] *Irby v. Irby (No. 3)* (1858) 25 Beav. 632.
[5] *Doering v. Doering* (1889) 42 Ch.D. 203; *Re Knapman* (1881) 18 Ch.D. 300 at 307.
[6] [1911] 1 Ch. 662.
[7] Re-enacting s.3 of the Judicial Trustees Act 1896. See Sheridan, "Excusable Breaches of Trust" (1955) 19 Conv.(N.S.) 420; Lord Maugham, "Excusable Breaches of Trust" (1898) 14 L.Q.R. 159. For similar protection of officers of a company, see s.727 of the Companies Act 1985.
[8] This does not authorise relief in respect of future anticipated breaches of trust: it relates to an existing situation where the trustee may or may not be liable for breach of trust: *Re Rosenthal* [1972] 1 W.L.R. 1273.
[9] *Re Alsop* [1914] 1 Ch. 1; *Ward-Smith v. Jebb* (1964) 108 So. Jo. 919; *Re Wightwick* [1950] 1 Ch. 260.
[10] *Re Stuart* [1897] 2 Ch. 583; *Re Turner* [1897] 1 Ch. 536.
[11] *Marsden v. Regan* [1954] 1 W.L.R. 423 at 434–435, *per* Evershed M.R.
[12] *Marsden v. Regan* [1954] 1 W.L.R. 423 (C.A.).

10–78   The court is rather reluctant to grant relief to a paid trustee but may do so in special circumstances.[13] The taking of legal advice will be a significant consideration if such advice is followed but a breach of trust occurs because the advice was erroneous: the standing of the legal adviser and the value of the property affected by the advice will be relevant considerations.[14] If the adviser were a negligent solicitor then the trustee should sue the solicitor to recover the loss for the trust and it seems hardly likely that the court would excuse the trustee if he failed to sue.[15] One must distinguish between trustees obtaining advice on behalf of the trust beneficiaries and trustees obtaining advice for their own personal protection and benefit. In the former case any cause of action arising from negligent advice will be a trust asset so that, if not barred by the limitation period, the beneficiaries could sue for themselves on joining the trustees as co-defendants with the adviser if the trustees refused to sue; in the latter case the beneficiaries have no rights against the adviser, being able only to sue the trustees for any breach of trust.[16]

II. An Instigating or Consenting Beneficiary Cannot Sue the Trustee and the Court has Power to Make Such Beneficiary Indemnify Trustee for Breach of Trust

10–79   A beneficiary[17] who is of full capacity[18] and knowingly[19] concurs in a breach of trust cannot afterwards complain of it against the trustees[20] unless they knew or ought to have known that the beneficiary's concurrence was the result of undue influence.[21] The position is summarised by Wilberforce J.[22] (as he then was) in a passage approved by the Court of Appeal[23]: "The court has to consider all the circumstances in which the concurrence of the *cestui que trust* was given with a view to seeing whether it is fair and equitable that, having given his concurrence, he should afterwards turn round and sue the trustees: that, subject to this, it is not necessary that he should know that what he is concurring in is a

---

[13] *National Trustees Co. of Australasia v. General Finance Co.* [1905] A.C. 373; *Re Windsor Steam Coal Co.* [1929] 1 Ch. 151; *Hawkesley v. May* [1956] 1 Q.B. 304; *Re Pauling's S.T.* [1964] Ch. 303 (partial relief); *Re Rosenthal* [1972] 1 W.L.R. 1273.

[14] *National Trustees Co. of Australasia, supra; Re Allsop* [1914] 1 Ch. 1 at 13; *Marsden v. Regan* [1954] 1 All E.R. 475 at 482.

[15] *National Trustees Co. of Australasia, supra.*

[16] *Wills v. Cooke* (1979) 76 L.S.G. 706 *per* Slade J.; *Parker-Tweedale v. Dunbar Bank plc* [1990] 2 All E.R. 577 at 583.

[17] In charitable trusts only the Attorney-General can consent or acquiesce in a breach of trust: *Re Freeston's Charity* [1978] 1 All E.R. 481 at 490, though the Court of Appeal found it unnecessary to say anything on this point: [1979] 1 All E.R. 51 at 63.

[18] *Wilkinson v. Parry* (1828) 4 Russ. 272 at 276; *Montford v. Cadogan* (1816) 19 Ves. 635. He may not fraudulently misrepresent his age to obtain money and then claim the money again on majority: *Overton v. Banister* (1844) Hare 503.

[19] *Phipps v. Boardman* [1964] 2 All E.R. 187 at 204–205, 207; the point was not appealed.

[20] *Fletcher v. Collis* [1905] 2 Ch. 24, *infra*, para. 10–82. If he instigates or requests the breach then *a fortiori* he cannot sue.

[21] *Re Pauling's S.T.* [1964] Ch. 303 at 338. Trustees must take special care in the case of young adults living with their parents.

[22] *Re Pauling's S.T.* [1962] 1 W.L.R. 86 at 108.

[23] *Holder v. Holder* [1968] Ch. 353; *Re Freeston's Charity* [1978] 1 W.L.R. 741.

breach of trust, provided that he fully understands what he is concurring in, and that it is not necessary that he should himself have directly benefited by the breach of trust." It would thus seem that if B consents to an act which the trustees know to be unauthorised but refrain from so telling B then B may still sue the trustees. The trustees must put the beneficiaries fully in the picture and must not withhold crucial information.[24] If, however, they themselves do not appreciate that what they propose is a breach of trust and B fully understands and agrees with the proposal then B should not be able to sue them if things turn out badly.

The above equitable principles apply whether the beneficiary's consent **10–80** or acquiescence[25] is before or after the breach of trust. They operate to prevent that particular beneficiary from suing for breach of trust, whether or not he benefited from consenting to such breach: *Fletcher v. Collis, infra*.

Where the beneficiary instigated, requested or consented to a breach of trust which the trustees then committed and another beneficiary called upon the trustee to make good the breach of trust, the court has always had jurisdiction to order the trustee to be indemnified out of the interest of the beneficiary who, being of full capacity, either instigated, requested or concurred in the breach. A motive of personal benefit on the part of the beneficiary was sufficient to invoke the jurisdiction in cases of instigation[26] or request[27]; but personal benefit actually derived by the beneficiary was necessary in cases of concurrence.[28] In order to succeed in claiming an indemnity, the trustee had to show that the beneficiary knew the facts which constituted the breach of trust although it was not necessary to show that the beneficiary knew that these facts amounted in law to a breach of trust: *Re Somerset, infra*.[29]

Section 62 of the Trustee Act 1925[30] enlarges the jurisdiction as **10–81** follows: "Where a trustee commits a breach of trust at the instigation or request or with the consent in writing[31] of a beneficiary, the court may if it thinks fit make such order as to the court seems just for impounding all or any part of the interest of the beneficiary in the trust estate by way

---

[24] *Phipps v. Boardman* [1964] 2 All E.R. 187 at 204–205.

[25] Mere delay (subject to Limitation Act 1980) is not enough; there must be conduct and circumstances making it inequitable to assert a claim *e.g.* having knowledge of entitlement to sue but doing nothing, so trustee does things that would otherwise not have been done: *De Busche v. Act* (1877) 8 Ch.D. 286, 314; *Nelson v. Rye* [1996] 1 W.L.R. 1378.

[26] *Trafford v. Boehm* (1746) 3 Atk. 440 at 442; *Raby v. Ridehalgh* (1855) 7 De G.M. & G. 104.

[27] *M'Gachen v. Dew* (1851) 15 Beav. 84; *Hanchett v. Briscoe* (1856) 22 Beav. 496.

[28] *Cocker v. Quayle* (1830) 1 Russ. & M. 535 at 538; *Booth v. Booth* (1838) 1 Beav. 125 at 130; *Blyth v. Fladgate* [1891] 1 Ch. 337 at 363. It makes no difference that the concurring beneficiary became a beneficiary after the date of his concurrence; *Evans v. Benyon* (1887) 37 Ch.D. 329 at 344. These factors of motive and actual benefit may still influence the exercise of discretion of the court determining whether all or any part of the beneficial interest should be impounded: *Bolton v. Curre* [1895] 1 Ch. 544 at 549; *Re Somerset* [1894] Ch. 231 at 275.

[29] See also *Rehden v. Wesley* (1861) 29 Beav. 213 at 215.

[30] Replacing Trustee Act 1893, s.45 replacing Trustee Act 1888, s.6.

[31] The requirement of writing only refers to consent and not instigation or request: *Re Somerset* [1894] 1 Ch. 231.

of indemnity to the trustee[32] or persons claiming through him."[33] However, the factors of motive and actual benefit are likely to continue to influence the court in exercising its discretion.

The section provides for impounding the interest of the "beneficiary in the trust estate." In *Ricketts v. Ricketts*[34] there was a marriage settlement for a mother for her life, remainder to her son. The son, on his marriage, assigned his reversionary interest under that settlement to the trustees of his own marriage settlement, under which latter settlement he was a beneficiary for life. Notice of the assignment was given to the trustees of the first settlement. By that assignment the son divested himself of his character of beneficiary under the first settlement, and substituted in his place the trustees of the second settlement. Afterwards the son instigated the trustees of the first settlement to commit a breach of trust in his favour by applying trust capital in discharging his debts, and when those trustees proceeded against him under the section for an indemnity, they discovered that he was not a beneficiary against whom they could proceed. Their beneficiary was now to be found in the trustees of the second settlement, who were trustees for the son who instigated the breach of trust to pay off his debts. He was not a "beneficiary in the trust estate."

FLETCHER V. COLLIS

Court of Appeal [1905] 2 Ch. 24; (Vaughan Williams, Romer and Stirling L.JJ)

10–82 Securities were settled on trust for the husband for life, remainder to the wife for life, remainder to children. At the request of the wife and with the (written) consent of the husband, the trustee in 1885 sold off the whole of the trust fund and handed the proceeds to the wife, who spent them. In June 1891 the husband was adjudicated bankrupt. In August 1891 the present action was commenced by the *remaindermen* against the trustee to make him replace the loss, but proceedings were stayed on an undertaking by the trustee, on the security of (*inter alia*) certain policies on his life, to make good the trust fund. By means of payments by the trustee and of the policies which fell in on his death in 1902, the whole of the trust fund was replaced, together with interest from August 1891.

The personal representative of the deceased trustee then took out a summons for a declaration that she was entitled, during the life of the husband, to the income of the trust fund replaced by the deceased trustee. It was argued for her that a beneficiary who concurs in a breach of trust cannot afterwards complain of it against his trustee. The capital had in fact been replaced by the trustee at the instance of the remaindermen, but since the husband himself had by virtue of his concurrence no claim against the trustee, the income of the capital so replaced should (during the life of the husband) go to her as personal representative of the trustee who replaced it.

---

[32] An order for indemnity can be made in favour of a former trustee: *Re Pauling's S.T. (No. 2)* [1963] Ch. 576. It would be absurd if the trustee who, ex hypothesi, is in breach of trust had to remain trustee in order to have an impounding order for an indemnity.

[33] Would the section be available if the sole trustee had fled the country leaving only trust assets behind and the remaindermen claimed to be subrogated to the trustee's right to impound the instigating life-tenant's income?

[34] (1891) 64 L.T. 263.

For the husband's trustee in bankruptcy, who resisted the claim of the personal representative, it was contended that the authorities showed that mere concurrence by a beneficiary does not preclude him from complaining against his trustee: it must be shown that the beneficiary also derived a personal benefit from the breach of trust, which was not the case here.

ROMER L.J.: "There was one proposition of law urged by the counsel on behalf **10–83** of the respondents before us to which I accede. It is this: If a beneficiary claiming under a trust does not *instigate* or *request* a breach of trust, is not the active moving party towards it, but merely *consents* to it, *and* he obtains no personal benefit from it, then his interest in the trust estate would not be impoundable in order to indemnify the trustee liable to make good loss occasioned by the breach. I think this is what was meant and referred to by Chitty J. in his judgment in *Sawyer v. Sawyer*,[35] where he says: 'It strikes me as a novelty in law, and a proposition not founded on principle, to say that the person who merely consents is bound to do more than what he says he consents to do. It does not mean that he makes himself personally liable, nor does he render any property liable to make it good.' But that proposition of law must be taken to be subject to the following right of the trustee as between himself and the beneficiaries. In the case I have before referred to in respect to the general proposition, the beneficiary who knowingly consented to the breach could not, if of full contracting age and capacity, and in the absence of special circumstances, afterwards be heard to say that the conduct of the trustee in committing the breach of trust was, as against him the particular beneficiary, improper, so as to make the trustee liable to the beneficiary for any damage suffered in respect of that beneficiary's interest in the trust estate by reason of the loss occasioned by the breach, and of course if satisfactorily proved the consent of the beneficiary to the breach need not be in writing.

"I will illustrate what I have said by a concrete case, not only to make my **10–84** meaning perfectly plain, but also because the illustration will have a bearing upon the case now before us. Take a simple case of a trust under a settlement, say, of £3,000, for a tenant for life, and after the death of the tenant for life for certain remaindermen. Suppose the trustee commits a breach of trust and sells out £1,000, and pays it over to some third person, so that the *cestui que trust* does not benefit by it himself, and suppose that the tenant for life, being of full age and *sui juris*, knows of that act of the trustee and consents to it. What would be the position of the trustee in reference to that breach of trust if he were made liable at the instance of the remaindermen for the loss accruing to the trust estate by the breach of trust, assuming the £1,000 to have been lost? The remaindermen would have the right of saying, so far as their interest in remainder is concerned, the capital must be made good by the trustee; but the tenant for life who consented could not himself have brought an action against the trustee to make him liable for the loss of income suffered by the tenant for life by reason of the breach of trust as to the £1,000. On the other hand, the trustee would not have had a right, as against the *cestui que trust*, the tenant for life, to have impounded the tenant for life's interest on the remaining £2,000 of the trust fund in order to indemnify himself. Now suppose the remaindermen having brought an action to make good the breach of trust against the trustee, and the tenant for life is a co-plaintiff, a defence is put in by the trustee raising

---

[35] (1885) 28 Ch.D. 595 at 598.

10–85   his right as against the tenant for life seeking relief in respect of the loss of income, but admitting the right of the remaindermen: what would the court in such a case do if the question between the tenant for life and the trustee had to be tried out, and the tenant for life was found to have consented knowingly to the breach of trust? To my mind the right thing for the court to do would have been clear. It might order the £1,000 to be paid into court by the trustee; but, pending the life of the tenant for life, it might also order the income to be paid to the trustee, because the income of the £1,000 would have been out of the pocket of the trustee just as much as the corpus from which it proceeded, and not to have given that relief to the trustee would have been to ignore his right, and to have acceded to the claim of the tenant for life in the action by him that I have indicated. Now suppose that the tenant for life is not a plaintiff, but co-defendant with the trustee, so that the question cannot be tried out at the trial as between the tenant for life and the trustee: what might the court do, if so advised, in that case? It might order the £1,000 to be paid into court by the trustee, and it might reserve the question of the right as between the tenant for life and the trustee to the income to be determined at some later period. It will be found that that illustration is pertinent to the case that is now before us. In such a case when the question as to income arose the trustee would be able to say: "The remaindermen are clearly not entitled to the income on the trust fund I have replaced, if the tenant for life is not entitled to it as against me. I replaced it; it is my money, and I am entitled to it"; and, therefore, when the question came to be tried out ultimately as between the tenant for life and the trustee, if that income was still under the control of the court, the court would again have the right to say to the trustee who replaced the corpus: "The income is yours in the absence of the right of the beneficiary, the tenant for life, to claim as against you to make you liable for that income."

10–86   "Now that right of a trustee which I have been dealing with, the right to resist the claim by the beneficiary to make good as against him the income, has clearly not been affected either by section 6 of the Trustee Act of 1888, or by section 45 of the Trustee Act of 1893. As I pointed out in *Bolton v. Curre*,[36] those sections were intended to and did *extend* the powers of the court for the benefit of the trustee. They clearly extended the powers of court so far as concerns the case of a married woman restrained from anticipation; but they also extended them in another respect by giving power to the court to impound any part of the interest in the trust property of any beneficiary who consented to a breach of trust, provided that consent was in writing. But clearly there was nothing in those sections which was intended to, and nothing in my opinion which operated so as to, deprive the trustee of the right I previously indicated, namely, the right of saying as against a beneficiary who has consented to a breach of trust that the beneficiary cannot make him, the trustee, personally liable to recoup, to the beneficiary who consented, the loss accruing to that beneficiary by the breach of trust committed with his consent. The beneficiary, if he consented to the breach of trust, could not be heard to make that a ground of complaint or a ground of action as against the trustee . . .

Is not this matter that we have to deal with on this appeal in substance one where a beneficiary who has consented to a breach of trust is now for his own benefit calling upon the trustee to make good the loss accruing to the beneficiary by reason of the breach? I think it is . . ."

---

[36] [1895] 1 Ch. 544 at 549.

Held, therefore, by the Court of Appeal that the personal representative of the deceased trustee was entitled, during the life of the husband tenant for life, to the income of the fund replaced by the trustee.

HOLDER V. HOLDER

Court of Appeal [1968] Ch. 353; [1968] 2 W.L.R. 237; [1968] 1 All E.R. 665

The plaintiff was seeking to set aside a sale made to the third defendant by the **10–87** first two defendant trustees when the third defendant was technically a trustee. The facts have already been set out at para. 9–09 and Harman L.J. with whom Danckwerts and Sachs L.JJ. expressly agreed on this point dealt as follows with the defence of the plaintiff's consent or acquiescence.

HARMAN L.J.: ". . . There arises a further defence, namely, that of acquiescence, and this requires some further recital of the facts.

"Completion of the sale was due for Michaelmas, 1961, but by that time the third defendant was not in a position to find the purchase money. The proving executors served a notice to complete in October, 1961, and, the validity of this notice being questioned, served a further notice in December. In February 1962 the plaintiff's solicitor pressed the defendants to forfeit the third defendant's deposit and this was a right given by the contract of sale and is an affirmation of it. Further, in May, 1962, the plaintiff issued a writ for a common decree of administration against the proving executors, seeking thus to press them to complete the contract and wind up the estate. The contract was in fact completed in June, 1962, and in the same month £2,000 on account was paid to and accepted by the plaintiff as his share and he thereupon took no further steps with his action. In order to complete, the third defendant borrowed £21,000 from the Agricultural Mortgage Corporation with interest at $7^{1}/_{2}$ per cent. He also borrowed £3,000 from his mother with interest at $6^{1}/_{2}$ per cent, and a like sum from his sister at a similar rate of interest. In November 1962 the third defendant demanded possession of Glebe Farm house from the plaintiff, who at that time changed his solicitors, and it was suggested by the new solicitors in February 1963 that the third defendant was disqualified from bidding at the auction. This was the first time any such suggestion had been made by anyone. The writ was not issued till a year later.

"I have found this question a difficult one. The plaintiff knew all the relevant **10–88** facts but he did not realise nor was he advised till 1963 that the legal result might be that he could object to his brother's purchase because he continued to be a personal representative. There is no doubt strong authority for the proposition that a man is not bound by acquiescences until he knows his legal rights. In *Cockerell v. Cholmeley*[37] Sir John Leach M.R. said this:

'It has been argued that the defendant, being aware of the facts of the case in the lifetime of Sir Henry Englefield has, by his silence, and by being a party to the application to Parliament, confirmed the title of the plaintiffs. In equity it is considered, as good sense requires it should be, that no man can be held by any act of his to confirm a title, unless he was fully aware at the time, not only of the fact upon which the effect of title depends, but of

---

[37] (1830) 1 Russ. & M. 418 at 425.

the consequence in point of law; and there is no proof that the defendant, at the time of the acts referred to, was aware of the law on the subject . . .'

10–89   There, however, the judge was asked to set aside a legal right. In *Wilmott v. Barber*[38] Fry J. said this:

'A man is not to be deprived of his legal rights unless he has acted in such a way as would make it fraudulent for him to set up those rights. What, then, are the elements or requisites necessary to constitute fraud of that description? In the first place the plaintiff must have made a mistake as to his legal rights. Secondly, the plaintiff must have expended some money or must have done some act (not necessarily upon the defendant's land) on the faith of his mistaken belief. Thirdly, the defendant, the possessor of the legal right, must know of the existence of his own right which is inconsistent with the right claimed by the plaintiff. If he does not know of it he is in the same position as the plaintiff, and the doctrine of acquiescence is founded upon conduct with a knowledge of your legal rights.'

On the other hand, in *Stafford v. Stafford*[39] Knight Bruce L.J. said this:

'Generally, when the facts are known from which a right arises, the right is presumed to be known . . .'

10–90   "Like the judge, I should desire to follow the conclusion of Wilberforce J. who reviewed the authorities in *Re Pauling's Settlement Trusts*[40]; and this passage was mentioned without dissent in the same case in the Court of Appeal[41]:

'The result of these authorities appears to me to be that the court has to consider all the circumstances in which the concurrence of the *cestui que trust* was given with a view to seeing whether it is fair and equitable that, having given his concurrence, he should afterwards turn round and sue the trustees: that, subject to this, it is not necessary that he should know that what he is concurring in is a breach of trust, provided that he fully understands what he is concurring in, and that it is not necessary that he should himself have directly benefited by the breach of trust.'

There is, therefore, no hard and fast rule that ignorance of a legal right is a bar, but the whole of the circumstances must be looked at to see whether it is just that the complaining beneficiary should succeed against the trustee.[42]

10–91   "On the whole I am of the opinion that in the circumstances of this case it would not be right to allow the plaintiff to assert his right (assuming he had one) because with full knowledge of the facts he affirmed the sale. He has had £2,000 as a result. He has caused the third defendant to embark on liabilities which he cannot recoup. There can in fact be no *restitutio in integrum* which is a necessary element in rescission.

---

[38] (1880) 15 Ch.D. 96 at 105.
[39] (1857) 1 De G. & J. 193 at 202.
[40] [1961] 3 All E.R. 713 at 730.
[41] [1964] Ch. 303.
[42] Endorsed in *Re Freeston's Charity* [1979] 1 All E.R. 51 at 62. The third proposition of Fry J. in *Wilmott v. Barber* (1880) 15 Ch.D. 96 at 105 has also been rejected in *Taylor Fashions Ltd v. Liverpool Victoria Trustees Co. Ltd* [1981] 1 All E.R. 897 at 915–918 and *Habib Bank Ltd v. Habib Bank A.G. Zurich* [1981] 2 All E.R. 650 at 666, 668. See *supra*, paras 2–32 to 2–33.

"The plaintiff is asserting an equitable and not a legal remedy. He has by his conduct disentitled himself to it. It is extremely doubtful whether the order if worked out would benefit anyone, I think we should not assent to it, on general equitable principles."

RE SOMERSET, SOMERSET V. EARL POULETT

Court of Appeal [1894] 1 Ch. 231; (Lindley, A. L. Smith and Davey L.JJ.)

Kekewich J. held that a £34,612 mortgage was a proper investment except in **10–92** so far as the trustees had advanced too much, so that they were liable for a breach of trust in respect only of the amount excessively advanced: Trustee Act 1888, s.5. He considered that the largest sum which in the circumstances the trustees could properly have advanced was £26,000. He further held that the trustees were entitled to have the plaintiff's life interest impounded by way of indemnity under the Trustee Act 1888, s.6; as to which the plaintiff appealed.

LINDLEY L.J.: ". . . The second question is whether, in order to indemnify the trustees, the court ought to impound the income of the trust funds during the life of the appellant. This question turns on the construction of section 6, and on the conduct of the parties. [Section 6 is now Trustee Act 1925, s.62.]

"Did the trustees commit the breach of trust for which they have been made **10–93** liable at the instigation or request, or with the consent in writing, of the appellant? The section is intended to protect trustees, and ought to be construed so as to carry out that intention. But the section ought not, in my opinion, to be construed as if the word 'investment' had been inserted instead of 'breach of trust.' An enactment to that effect would produce great injustice in many cases. In order to bring a case within this section the *cestui que trust* must instigate, or request or consent in writing to some act or omission which is itself a breach of trust and not to some act or omission which only becomes a breach of trust by reason of want of care on the part of the trustees. If a *cestui que trust* instigates, requests or consents in writing to an investment not in terms authorised by the power of investment, he clearly falls within the section; and in such a case his ignorance or forgetfulness of the terms of power would not, I think, protect him—at all events, not unless he could give some good reason why it should, *e.g.*, that it was caused by the trustee. But if all that a *cestui que trust* does is to instigate, request or consent in writing to an investment which is authorised by the terms of the power, the case is, I think, very different. He has a right to expect that the trustees will act with proper care in making the investment, and if they do not they cannot throw the consquences on him unless they can show that he instigated, requested or consented in writing to their non-performance of their duty in this respect. This is, in my opinion, the true construction of this section.

"As regards the necessity for a writing, I agree with the decision of Mr. Justice **10–94** Kekewich in *Griffith v. Hughes*,[43] that an instigation or request need not be in writing, and that the words 'in writing' apply only to the consent.

"I pass now to the facts. It is, in my opinion, perfectly clear that the appellant instigated, requested and consented in writing to the investment by the trustees of the trust money on a mortgage of Lord Hill's estate. This, indeed, was not

---

[43] [1892] 3 Ch. 105.

disputed. But the evidence does not, that I can see, go further than this. He certainly never instigated, requested or consented in writing to an investment on the property without inquiry; still less, if upon inquiry the rents payable in respect of the lands mortgaged were found to be less than the interest payable on the mortgage.

"Whether the appellant knew the rental is a very important question. Mr. Justice Kekewich has found that he did. But the evidence does not, in my opinion, warrant this inference . . .

10–95   "The solicitors obtained the valuation for and on behalf of the trustees; they obtained the second opinion of the valuers for the benefit of the borrower, and for the protection of the trustees. In obtaining the valuation and opinion the solicitors were not acting for or on behalf of the appellant; and considering that they never disclosed the valuation or opinion to the appellant, and never informed him of their effect, he cannot, in my opinion, be held to have known them. It is important to observe that the statute does not make a *cestui que trust* responsible for a breach of trust simply because he had actual or constructive notice of it; he must have instigated or requested it, or have consented to it in writing. Even if the knowledge of his solicitors could be imputed to him for some purposes, it is not true in fact that the appellant did by himself or his agent instigate, request or consent in writing to a breach of trust.[44] Even if the appellant had constructive notice through his solicitors of the valuation, the court, in exercising the power conferred on it by the statute, would, in my opinion, be acting unjustly, and not justly, if, under the circumstances of this case, it held the appellant liable to indemnify the trustees. The court would be treating the appellant as having done more than he did, and I can see no justification for such a course. It must be borne in mind that the plaintiff was not seeking to benefit himself at the expense of the remaindermen as in *Raby v. Ridehalgh*.[45] He was seeking a better security for the trust money for the benefit of everyone interested in it . . ."

Held, therefore, by the Court of Appeal that the defendants were not entitled to have the plaintiff's life interest impounded by way of indemnity.[46]

III. Statutes of Limitation

Equitable rules

10–96   The doctrine of "laches" is expressly preserved by the Limitation Act 1980, section 36 of which provides that "nothing in the Act shall affect any equitable jurisdiction to refuse relief on the ground of acquiescence or otherwise." The doctrine is available "where it would be practically

---

[44] On this point, A. L. Smith L.J. observed (at 270): "In my opinion, upon the true reading of this section, a trustee, in order to obtain the benefit conferred thereby, must establish that the beneficiary knew the facts which rendered what he was instigating, requesting or consenting to in writing a breach of trust." Davey L.J. observed (at 274): ". . . in order to bring the case within the section the beneficiary must have requested the trustee to depart from and go outside the terms of his trust. It is not, of course, necessary that the beneficiary should know the investment to be in law a breach of trust."

[45] (1855) 7 De G.M. & G. 104.

[46] In accordance with this case is *Mara v. Browne* [1892] 2 Ch. 69 at 92–93, where North J. held that the trustee was not entitled to impound the interest of the beneficiary because the beneficiary, though she had consented in writing, had not consented to those acts which constituted the breach of trust. On appeal [1896] 1 Ch. 199 the point did not arise. The life tenant's interest was impounded in *Jaffray v. Marshall* [1993] 1 W.L.R. 1285.

unjust to give a remedy, either because the party has, by his conduct, done that which might fairly be regarded as equivalent to a waiver of it, or where by his conduct and neglect he has, though perhaps not waiving that remedy, yet put the other party in a situation in which it would not be reasonable to place him if the remedy were afterwards asserted."[47] The doctrine really consists of a substantial lapse of time coupled with the existence of circumstances which make it inequitable to enforce the plaintiff's claim.

The field of operation of the doctrine has been narrowed by statute.[48] Nowadays, it is the statutory six-year period which operates against a beneficiary in respect of a claim against the trustee for a breach of trust[49] and not the equitable doctrine of "laches." But there are cases outside the Act (*e.g.* claims against trustees who have purchased trust property or beneficial interests therein[50] and cases under the Act[51] in which the liability of the trustee is subject to no *statutory* period of limitation at all (*e.g.* a claim against trustees for property or proceeds thereof retained by them). In such a case the right of the beneficiary will only be barred by an unreasonably long period of delay amounting to laches.[52]

The ability of equity to act by analogy to the statute is expressly **10–97** recognised and preserved, for section 36(1) of the 1980 Act provides that the six-year period which it lays down is not to apply to "any claim for specific performance of a contract or for an injunction or for *other equitable relief*" save in so far as a court of equity may apply it by analogy.[53] But the analogous application of section 36(1) is limited to claims for which no express provision is to be found elsewhere in the statute.[54]

Thus it was held in *Re Diplock*[55] that even if the claims in equity were analogous to the common law action for money had and received (which they were not), they were also "actions in respect of a claim to the personal estate of a deceased person" for which under section 20 of the 1939 Act (now s.22 of the 1980 Act) the relevant period of limitation was one of 12 years from the date when the right to receive the share or

---

[47] *per* Lord Selborne L.C. in *Lindsay Petroleum Co. v. Hurd* (1874) L.R. 5 P.C. 221 at 239–240. See also *Weld v. Petre* [1929] 1 Ch. 33 at 51–52; *Holder v. Holder* [1968] Ch. 353; *Nelson v. Rye* [1986] 2 All E.R. 186, 200–205, although incorrect on other points: *Paragon Finance plc v. Thakerar & Co.* [1999] 1 All E.R. 400, 415–416; *Companhia de Seguros Imperio v. Heath Ltd* [2001] 1 W.L.R. 112.
[48] Trustee Act 1888, s.8; Limitation Act 1939 replaced by Limitation Act 1980.
[49] See Limitation Act 1939, s.19(2) replaced by Limitation Act 1980, s.21(3), *infra*, para. 10–101; *Re Pauling's S.T.* [1964] Ch. 303. For reform see Law Com No. 270, *Limitation of Actions*.
[50] *Tito v. Waddell (No. 2)* [1977] Ch. 106 at 250.
[51] Limitation Act 1980, s.21(1), *infra*, para. 10–100.
[52] See *McDonnell v. White* (1865) 11 H.L.C. 271; *Sleeman v. Wilson* (1871) L.R. 13 Eq. 36; *Tito v. Waddell (No. 2)* [1977] Ch. 106 at 248–250.
[53] On this and actions for accounts, see *Tito v. Waddell (No. 2)* [1977] Ch. 106 at 250–252 discussing Limitation Act 1939, s.2(7) replaced by Limitation Act 1980, s.36(1).
[54] A case like *Re Robinson* [1911] 1 Ch. 502 would be decided today in accordance with the provisions of s.21(3) of the Limitation Act 1980 and not by the use of any analogy to the statute.
[55] [1948] Ch. 465 at 502–516; when the case reached the House of Lords, *sub nom. Ministry of Health v. Simpson* [1951] A.C. 251, their Lordships approved the views of the Court of Appeal on the applicability of s.20 of the Limitation Act 1939 (now s.22 of the 1980 Act) and it therefore became unnecessary to express an opinion on the applicability of s.26 thereof (now s.32 of the 1980 Act). It seems s.22 of the 1980 Act applies even after the personal representatives have become trustees.

interest accrued; accordingly, there was no scope for applying any other period by way of analogy or otherwise.

However, the six-year period applicable to an action for damages for fraud at common law has been held[56] to apply by analogy to equitable claims to make a person who is not a trustee personally liable for dishonest assistance in a breach of fiduciary duty or for knowingly dealing inconsistently with fiduciary obligations affecting property received even if not initially aware that it was trust property.

The equitable rule that time would not run against the plaintiff in cases of fraud and mistake is adopted by section 32(1) of the 1980 Act (replacing and amending s.26 of the 1939 Act) which provides:

10–98 "Where in the case of any action for which a period of limitation is prescribed by this Act, either:

    (a) the action is based upon the fraud of the defendant or his agent or of any person through whom he claims or his agent, or

    (b) any fact relevant to the plaintiff's right of action has been deliberately concealed from him by any such person as aforesaid, or

    (c) the action is for relief from the consequences of mistake,

the period of limitation shall not begin to run until the plaintiff has discovered the fraud concealment or mistake, as the case may be, or could with reasonable diligence have discovered it."[57] Subsection (3) goes on to protect purchasers taking under transactions without notice of the fraud having been committed or the concealment or mistake having been made, as the case may be. "Deliberate commission of a breach of duty in circumstances in which it is unlikely to be discovered for some time amounts to deliberate concealment of the facts involved in that breach of duty."[58] The House of Lords[59] has held that where after a cause of action has arisen there was a deliberate concealment of facts relevant to the plaintiff's cause of action time does not begin to run until the concealment was or should have been discovered. Surprisingly, it has been held it is only necessary to show that the breach was intentional, not that the trustee was also aware that his conduct was a breach of trust.[60]

10–99 It was decided in *Phillips-Higgins v. Harper*[61] that paragraph (c) does not apply to the case of a right of action concealed from the plaintiff by a mistake. Its scope is limited to actions where a mistake has been made

---

[56] *Coulthard v. Disco Mix Club Ltd* [1999] 2 All E.R. 457; *Companhia de Seguros Imperio v. Heath Ltd* [2001] 1 W.L.R. 112.

[57] See *Nocton v. Lord Ashburton* [1914] A.C. 932 at 936, 958; *Kitchen v. R.A.F. Association* [1958] 1 W.L.R. 563 at C.A. (solicitor's negligence); *Baker v. Medway Supplies* [1958] 1 W.L.R. 1216 (fraudulent conversion of money); *Bartlett v. Barclays Bank Trust Co.* [1980] 1 All E.R. 139 at 154; *Peco Arts Inc. v. Hazlitt Gallery Ltd* [1983] 3 All E.R. 193 (reasonable diligence in discovering drawing not an original).

[58] Limitation Act 1980 s.32(2); *King v. Victor Parsons & Co.* [1973] 1 W.L.R. 29 at 33, *per* Lord Denning M.R. This reflects the old case law on (b) when it was known as fraudulent concealment in Limitation Act 1939, s.26.

[59] *Sheldon v. R. H. Outhwaite (Underwriting Agencies) Ltd* [1996] A.C. 102.

[60] *Brockleby v. Armitage & Guest* [2000] 1 All E.R. 172; *Cave v. Robinson* [2001] EW CA Civ. 245.

[61] [1954] 1 Q.B. 411.

and has had certain consequences and the plaintiff is seeking to be relieved from those consequences, *e.g.* actions to recover money paid under a mistake; to rescind or rectify contracts on the ground of mistake; to reopen accounts settled in consequence of mistakes. It applies, in fact, only where mistake is an essential ingredient of the cause of action, and it does not help a plaintiff to ascertain the amount still due to him after the ordinary period of limitation has expired. The anomalous result is that a person who has by mistake paid too much can take advantage of the section, but the person who has by mistake received too little cannot avail himself of it.

Statutory rules affording little protection to trustees

Section 21 of the Act reads as follows:

> "(1) No period of limitation prescribed by this Act shall apply to an action **10–100** by a beneficiary under a trust, being an action:
> (a) in respect of any fraud or fraudulent breach of trust to which the trustee was a party or privy; or
> (b) to recover from the trustee trust property or the proceeds thereof in the possession of the trustee, or previously received by the trustee and converted to his use.
>
> (2)   Where a trustee who is also a beneficiary under the trust receives or retains trust property or its proceeds as his share on a distribution of trust property under the trust, his liability in any action brought by virtue of subsection (1)(b) above to recover that property or its proceeds after the expiration of the period of limitation prescribed by this Act for bringing an action to recover trust property shall be limited to the excess over his proper share.
> This subsection only applies if the trustee acted honestly and reasonably in making the distribution.
> (3) Subject to the preceding provisions of this section an action by a **10–101** beneficiary to recover trust property or in respect of any breach of trust, not being an action for which a period of limitation is prescribed by any other provision of this Act,[62] shall not be brought after the expiration of six years from the date on which the right of action accrued. For the purposes of this subsection the right of action shall not be treated as having accrued to any beneficiary entitled to a future interest in the trust property until the interest fell into possession.
> (4) No beneficiary as against whom there would be a good defence under this Act shall derive any greater or other benefit from a judgment or order obtained by any other beneficiary than he could have obtained if he had brought the action and this Act had been pleaded in defence."

The following observations may be made upon the effect of the section.

---

[62] Where personal representatives have become trustees upon completing administration of an estate the relationship between s.21(3) and s.22 is unclear. It would seem that the breadth of s.22 (formerly s.20 of the 1939 Act) makes the 12-year period applicable: *Re Diplock* [1948] Ch. 465 at 511–513; *Ministry of Health v. Simpson* [1951] A.C. 251 at 276–277.

10–102   The word "trustee" is defined by reference to section 68(17) of the
Trustee Act 1925. This definition excludes the duties incident to an
estate conveyed by way of mortgage,[63] but includes implied and constructive trusts and personal representatives. It has been held to include
the directors of a company,[64] but not trustees in bankruptcy[65] nor
apparently the liquidators of companies in voluntary liquidation.[66]

The Court of Appeal[67] recently distinguished two classes of "constructive trustees": (1) where the defendant acquired the property,
agreeable to it being held by him as a trustee or as a fiduciary before the
conduct complained of by the claimant; (2) where the wrongful conduct
of the defendant in asserting his selfish interest led to him being a
constructive trustee of property or personally liable to account as a
constructive trustee for dishonest assistance in a breach of trust or
fiduciary duty or for receiving trust or fiduciary property for his own
benefit when unaware it was such property but later dealing inconsistently with it after becoming aware it was such property. Instances
within (1) include trustees *de son tort* (assuming trusteeship functions in
the beneficiaries' interests) but not the type of executor *de son tort* who
acts in her own interest,[68] and include agents, like solicitors receiving
trust property knowing it to be such and agreeing to treat it as such but
who subsequently treat it as if not trust property but their own. Perpetual
liability under section 21(1) only applies to the first class of constructive
trustee.

The section is limited to actions by *beneficiaries* in respect of trust
property. It is thought, however, that a newly-appointed trustee would
have the same rights as the beneficiaries themselves against the surviving
trustees.[69] A claim by the Attorney-General against trustees of a
charitable trust (which has no beneficiary) is outside the section.[70]

Perpetual liability is confined under this section as under the 1888 Act
for express trustees to cases of (a) fraudulent[71] breaches of trust and (b)
of retention or conversion of the trust property. It appears from *Thorne
v. Heard*[72] that the negligence of a trustee, resulting in his solicitor
embezzling the trust funds, was insufficient to render the trustee "party
or privy" to the fraud. On the face of it it appears that there could be
perpetual liability for an innocent recipient of trust property from a

---

[63] But a prior mortgagee of land exercising his power of sale is a trustee of the surplus for subsequent
mortgagees after meeting his own claims. See *Thorne v. Heard* [1894] 1 Ch. 599; the Law of Property
Act 1925, s.105.
[64] *Re Lands Allotments Co.* [1894] 1 Ch. 616 at 631, 638, 643 and *Whitwam v. Watkin* (1898) 78 L.T. 188.
[65] *Re Cornish* [1896] 1 Q.B. 99.
[66] *Re Windsor Steam Coal Co. (1901) Ltd* [1928] Ch. 609; affd. on a different ground [1929] 1 Ch. 151.
[67] *Paragon Finance plc v. Thakerar & Co* [1999] 1 All E.R. 400, 408–409; *Companhia de Seguros Imperio
v. Health Ltd [2001] 1 W.L.R. 112*
[68] *Jones v. Williams* [2000] Ch. 1 was decided in ignorance of the above two-fold classification, with the
second class seemingly being the appropriate one.
[69] See *Re Bowden* (1890) 45 Ch.D. 444, a case decided under the 1888 Act which was not limited to
actions by beneficiaries. Also see *Lewin on Trusts* (17th ed) para. 44–21.
[70] *Att.-Gen. v. Cocke* [1988] Ch. 414.
[71] See *North American Land Co. v. Watkins* [1904] 1 Ch. 242; [1904] 2 Ch. 233; *Vane v. Vane* (1872) L.R.
8 Ch. 383; *Armitage v. Nurse* [1998] Ch. 241, 260.
[72] [1895] A.C. 495.

fraudulent trustee,[73] although it would be fairer for there only to be such liability if the recipient were privy to the fraud.

The section speaks of property "previously received by the trustee and **10–103** converted to his use." In *Re Howlett*[74] it was contended that this referred to an *actual* receipt of property, but Danckwerts J. held that it included a *notional* receipt, and so he was able to charge a trustee who had occupied trust property for some 20 years with an occupation rent. To fall foul of section 21(1)(b) a trustee's retention or conversion must be some wrongful application in his own favour.[75]

Exceptionally, he has some protection under section 21(2) so that if he had distributed one-third of the trust property to himself, honestly and reasonably believing that only three beneficiaries existed, he will be liable to a fourth beneficiary turning up after six years not for a quarter share but only for the one-twelfth difference between the one-third share he took and the one-quarter share which was truly his.

Section 21(3) of the Act prescribes a six-year period of limitation for breach of trust[76] cases not falling within section 21(1) or (2) or within any other provision of the Act. Thus, if a trustee can show that an innocent or negligent breach of trust led him to part with the trust property the six-year period is the appropriate one to limit his liability. The six-year period will also be appropriate if the trust funds were dissipated by a co-trustee.[77] It is also applicable for personal and proprietary claims against third parties who received trust property[78] for their own benefit unless, perhaps, from a fraudulent trustee.[79]

The last sentence of section 21(3) protects reversionary interests by **10–104** enacting that time shall not run against a beneficiary until his interest has fallen into possession.[80] Even before that date a remainderman can sue for breach of trust. In such a case if the prior beneficiary is himself barred the trustees must nevertheless replace the fund at the suit of the remainderman, but during the continuance of the prior beneficiary's interest they will be entitled to the income of the property: for a judgment recovered by one beneficiary is not to improve the position of one who is already barred.[81]

Where a beneficiary is merely interested under a discretionary trust until obtaining a life interest in possession on attaining 25 years, the Court of Appeal has held[82] that time does not run until the beneficiary

---

[73] *G. L. Baker Ltd v. Medway Building and Supplies Ltd.* [1958] 1 W.L.R. 1216, 1221–1222.
[74] [1949] Ch. 767.
[75] *Re Gurney* [1893] 1 Ch. 590; *Re Page* [1893] 1 Ch. 304; *Re Fountaine* [1909] 2 Ch. 382.
[76] Purchases by a trustee (or other fiduciary) of trust property or beneficial interests therein are not breaches of trust for this purpose but fall within a general disability of fiduciaries: *Tito v. Waddell (No. 2)* [1977] Ch. 106 at 248–250 revealing the doctrine of laches applies.
[77] *Re Tufnell* (1902) 18 T.L.R. 705; *Re Fountaine* [1909] 2 Ch. 382.
[78] But not the personal estate of a deceased where the 12-year limit under s.22 Limitation Act 1980 applies: *Ministry of Health v. Simpson* [1951] A.C. 251.
[79] See note 73 above.
[80] Consent by a life-tenant to an advance in favour of a remainderman does not amount to a release of the life interest so as to convert the remainderman's interest into an interest in possession: *Re Pauling's S.T.* [1964] Ch. 303.
[81] *Re Somerset* [1894] 1 Ch. 231; s.19(3) of the Limitation Act 1939 and s.21(4) of the 1980 Act; *Mara v. Browne* [1895] 2 Ch. 69 reversed on another point [1896] 1 Ch. 199.
[82] *Armitage v. Nurse* [1998] Ch. 241.

obtains the interest in possession on his 25th birthday. It matters not that at 18 a beneficiary, whether her interest is in possession or not, is entitled to see trust accounts, etc., so as to be able to discover a breach of trust. The rationale for section 23(1) "is not that a beneficiary with a future interest has not the means of discovery, but that the beneficiary should not be compelled to litigate (at considerable personal expense) in respect of an injury to an interest which he may never live to enjoy. Similar reasoning would apply to exclude a person who is merely the object of a discretionary trust or power which may never be exercised in his favour."[83] Thus, the liability of trustees of a discretionary trust is open-ended, except presumably for those objects who received a distribution (thereby acquiring an absolute interest in possesion before the relevant breach of trust and so have six years in which to act).

Section 5. Liability of Trustees *inter se*

10–105   Since trustees are jointly and severally liable one trustee may be compelled to replace the whole loss or more than his share of the loss.[84] In such a case he will have a right of contribution from the others unless he was a fraudulent trustee.[85] Exceptionally, a trustee can obtain a complete indemnity so as to throw the whole loss on his co-trustee if (a) his co-trustee has exclusively benefited from the breach of trust as by using trust money for his own purposes when he would be unjustly enriched if he could obtain contribution from his co-trustees or (b) his co-trustee is someone with special qualifications on whom he could reasonably be expected to rely, such as a solicitor[86] whose advice and control caused his passive participation in the breach of trust or (c) his co-trustee has a beneficial interest liable to impounding under general equitable principles or section 62 of the Trustee Act which is large enough to satisfy the loss: *Chillingworth v. Chambers*.[87] In respect of an unsatisfied loss in this last instance the trustee is left to his right of contribution against the co-trustee.

10–106   If, *e.g.* the trustees are a professional corporate trustee and a private person and the beneficiaries sue only the corporate trustee then it may bring in the private trustee as a party to the proceedings. If the beneficiaries recover the whole sum from the corporate trustee it may claim half from the private trustee except to the extent the court may relieve him under the Trustee Act 1925, s.61.[88]

---

[83] *ibid*, 261.
[84] A trustee may take proceedings against his co-trustee who derived all the benefit from the breach to make good the loss to the trust estate: *Baynard v. Woolley* (1855) 20 Beav. 583; *Elwes v. Barnard* (1865) 13 L.T. 426; 11 Jur.(N.S.) 1035.
[85] *Att.-Gen. v. Wilson* (1840) Cr. & Ph. 1, 28.
[86] As in *Re Partington* (1887) 57 L.T. 654. What about Chancery barristers, bank managers, professional trustees? See broad dicta of Cotton L.J. in *Bahin v. Hughes* (1886) 31 Ch.D. 390, *infra*, para. 10–108.
[87] [1896] 1 Ch. 685, *infra*, para. 10–112.
[88] *Wohleben v. Canada Permanent Trust Co. & Wohleben* (1976) 70 D.L.R. (3d) 257 totally relieving the private trustee, commented on by D. W. M. Waters (1977) 55 Can. Bar Rev. 342.

The Civil Liability (Contribution) Act 1978 (*infra*, paras 10–116 to 10–118) effective from January 1, 1979 for persons becoming trustees after 1978, has superseded the equitable right of contribution but not the right to an indemnity. It gives the court a vast discretion to fix the contribution anywhere between 1 and 99 per cent. However, in the case of trustees it is considered that the court's discretion will be exercised along the old equitable guidelines. It would need to be a very special case indeed for unequal treatment to be accorded to co-trustees (except in the exceptional indemnity cases) since the sanction of equal liability serves a useful salutary function for breach of what is a joint obligation *par excellence*. After all, to make the active trustee indemnify the passive co-trustee would discourage trustees from playing the active role required for the proper administration of the trust and the safeguarding of beneficiaries' interests.

BAHIN V. HUGHES

Court of Appeal (1886) 31 Ch.D. 390; 55 L.J.Ch. 472; 54 L.T. 188; 34 W.R. 311; 2 T.L.R. 276 (Cotton, Bowen and Fry L.JJ.)

A testator, Robert Hughes, bequeathed a legacy of £2,000 to his three **10–107** daughters—Eliza Hughes, Mrs. Burden and Mrs. Edwards—on trust to invest in specified securities and in real securities in England and Wales. Eliza Hughes, who was the active trustee, and Mr. Burden invested the fund on the (unauthorised) security of leasehold properties, an investment discovered by Mr. Burden. Mrs Edwards had been informed of the proposal, but her concurrence was not obtained. The security proving insufficient, the tenant for life and remaindermen brought this action against Eliza Hughes, Mr. Edwards (whose wife had died) and Mr. and Mrs. Burden, claiming that the defendants were liable to make good the trust fund.[89] Edwards served a third-party notice on Eliza Hughes claiming to be indemnified by her, on the ground that she had assumed the role of sole trustee, that the investment had been made at her instigation, and that she had represented to Mrs. Edwards that the mortgage was a proper and sufficient security.

Held, by Kay J., that the defendants were jointly and severally liable to replace the £2,000, and that the defendant Edwards had no right of indemnity against Eliza Hughes. Edwards appealed.

COTTON L.J.: ". . . On going into the authorities, there are very few cases in **10–108** which one trustee, who has been guilty with a co-trustee of breach of trust and held answerable, has successfully sought indemnity as against his co-trustee. In *Lockhart v. Reilly*[90] it appears from the report of the case in the *Law Journal* that the trustee by whom the loss was sustained had been not only trustee, but had been and was a solicitor, and acting as solicitor for his self and his co-trustee, and it was on his advice that Lockhart had relied in making the investment which gave rise to the action of the *cestui que trust*. The Lord Chancellor (Lord

---

[89] Prior to s.18 of the Married Women's Property Act of 1882 (which did not apply to the present case) a married woman could not act as trustee without the participation of her husband (Mr. Edwards); he was necessarily a trustee through her trusteeship, and was responsible for her breaches of trust.
[90] (1856) 25 L.J.Ch. 697 at 702.

Cranworth) refers to the fact that he was a solicitor, and makes the remark: 'The whole thing was trusted to him. He was the solicitor, and, independently of the consideration that one cannot help seeing it was done with a view of favouring his own family, yet if that had not been so, the co-trustee leaves it with the solicitor-trustee, by whose negligence (I use no harsher word) all this evil, in a great degree, has arisen.' Therefore the Lord Chancellor, in giving his decision, relies upon the fact of the trustee being a solicitor. In *Thompson v. Finch*[91] was conceded to prove against the estate of the deceased trustee for the full loss sustained; but it appears that in this case also he was a solicitor, and that he really took this money to himself, for he mixed it with his own money, and invested it on a mortgage; and therefore it was held that the trustee was entitled to indemnity from the estate of the co-trustee, who was a solicitor. This was affirmed in the Court of Appeal; and the Court of Appeal took so strong a view of the conduct of the solicitor that both of the judges concurred in thinking that he ought to be called on to show cause why he should not be struck off the rolls. Of course, where one trustee has got the money into his own hands, and made use of it, he will be liable to his co-trustee to give him an indemnity. Now I think it wrong to lay down any limitation of the circumstances under which one trustee would be held liable to the other for indemnity, both having been held liable to the *cestui que trust*; but so far as cases have gone at present, relief has only been granted against a trustee who has himself got the benefit of the breach of trust, or between whom and his co-trustees there has existed a relation which will justify the court in treating him solely liable for the breach of trust . . .

10–109   "Miss Hughes was the active trustee and Mr. Edwards did nothing, and in my opinion it would be laying down a wrong rule that where one trustee acts honestly, though erroneously, the other trustee is to be held entitled to indemnity who by doing nothing neglects his duty more than the acting trustee. That Miss Hughes made an improper investment is true, but she acted honestly, and intended to do the best she could, and believed that the property was sufficient security for the money, although she made no inquiries about their being leasehold houses. In my opinion the money was lost just as much by the default of Mr. Edwards as by the innocent though erroneous action of his co-trustee, Miss Hughes. All the trustees were in the wrong, and every one is equally liable to indemnify the beneficiaries." *Appeal dismissed.*

HEAD V. GOULD

Chancery Division [1898] 2 Ch. 250; 67 L.J.Ch. 480; 78 L.T. 739

10–110   Miss Head and Mr. Gould were appointed new trustees of certain marriage settlements (the beneficial interests being the same under both settlements), and thenceforth Gould acted as solicitor to the trusts. Miss Head was one of the remaindermen under these settlements, the tenant for life being her mother. The new trustees sold a house forming part of the trust, and in breach of trust handed the proceeds of sale to the tenant for life. Part of the trust property consisted also of certain policies on the life of Mrs. Head, policies which Mrs. Head had mortgaged to the trust by way of security for advances of trust capital which the former trustees had made to her at her urgent request for the purpose of assisting the family. These policies were (in breach of trust) surrendered by the new trustees with the concurrence of Mrs. Head.

---

[91] (1856) 25 L.J.Ch. 681.

Miss Head claimed to be indemnified by her co-trustee, Gould, under circumstances which appear from the judgment:

KEKEWICH J.: ". . . It will be convenient here at once to deal with the claim made by Miss Head against her co-trustee, Gould. By her third party notice she seeks to be indemnified by him against loss by reason of the breaches of trust, on the ground that the loss and misapplication (if any) of the trust funds, or any part thereof, were occasioned entirely by his acts or defaults, and that he assumed to act as solicitor to the trust estate and as the sole trustee thereof, and exercised control of the administration of the trust funds, and that whatever was done by herself in connection with the trust was at his instigation and in reliance upon his advice.

"This is a serious charge, and if it had been proved would have entitled her to **10–111** the relief claimed according to well-known and well-recognised principles. . . There is before me no evidence bringing the case within those principles, or showing that the charge which is correctly formulated on them is consistent with the facts. My conclusion from such evidence as there is before the court is distinctly adverse to the claim. I know that, before the appointment of herself and Gould as trustees, Miss Head was an active party to the importunities of her mother which induced the former trustees to commit a breach of trust for their benefit, and that she looked to the change of trustees as a means of, in some way or other, obtaining further advances. I know, further, that she was well acquainted with the position of the trust, and that it was all-important to maintain the policies and to appropriate the rents of the house to that purpose. She now affects to ignore all that has been done since her appointment, and professes not to remember having executed the several instruments which must have been executed by her for the sale of the house and the surrender of the policies, or the receipt of moneys arising therefrom. With regret, and under a painful sense of duty, I am bound to say that I do not credit her testimony. True it is that the defendant, Gould, is a solicitor, and that he was appointed a trustee for that very reason. True no doubt, also, that the legal business was managed by him, and I do not propose to absolve him from any responsibility attaching to him on that ground; but I do not myself think that Byrne J. or any other judge ever intended to hold that a man is bound to indemnify his co-trustee against loss *merely* because he was a solicitor, when that co-trustee was an active participator in the breach of trust complained of, and is not proved to have participated merely in consequence of the *advice and control* of the solicitor. . . ."

Held therefore, the trustee, Miss Head, had no claim of indemnity against her co-trustee.[92]

Chillingworth v. Chambers[93]

The decision of the Court of Appeal in the above case has been said to **10–112** lie on the border between contribution and indemnity. It is to the effect that a *trustee-beneficiary* who has participated in, and, as between himself and his co-trustee, benefited exclusively, by a breach of trust for which he and his co-trustee are equally to blame must indemnify his co-trustee to

---

[92] On indemnity between trustees, see also *Blyth v. Fladgate* [1891] 1 Ch. 337 at 364, 365; *Re Turner* [1897] 1 Ch. 536 at 544; *Re Linsley* [1904] 2 Ch. 785.
[93] [1896] 1 Ch. 685. See *Re Dacre* [1916] 1 Ch. 344, *supra*, para. 10–751.

the extent of his beneficial interest. X and Y were trustees. X was also a beneficiary, his share being (say) £500. X and Y, with the object of increasing the rate of dividend, invested trust funds in a mortgage which was held to be a breach of trust. As between X and Y, X benefited exclusively by this breach of trust; at any rate, he was so treated by the Court of Appeal. The mortgage was eventually realised at a loss of £400, the whole of which was in fact made good out of X's beneficial share (the trust fund now being in court). X's claim of contribution against Y, that Y should share the loss with him, failed; for X was held liable to indemnify his co-trustee Y to the extent of his beneficial interest. Since X's beneficial interest (£500) exceeded the actual loss (£400), the result was that Y managed to shift the whole of that loss on to X. Strictly speaking, Y did not shift the loss on to X; he shifted it on to X's beneficial interest.

10–113   Lindley L.J. summed up the position between X and Y as follows[94]: "To the extent to which the [trustee-beneficiary's] right as trustee is neutralised by his obligation as *cestui que trust* he will have no right to contribution." The trustee-beneficiary's right as trustee is a right of contribution from his co-trustee. His obligation as beneficiary is to indemnify that trustee out of his beneficial interest, for where a beneficiary is an active party in a breach of trust committed with a view towards his benefit he is liable to indemnify his trustee out of his beneficial interest.[95]

Lindley L.J. continued: "But except so far as it is thus neutralised his right of contribution will remain." If, therefore, X's beneficial interest had been £300, and not £500, that £300 would have been used up in indemnifying Y as to three-quarters of the loss of £400 for which they are jointly and severally liable, but the remaining £100 would have been shared between them.

In considering *Chillingworth v. Chambers* it is of advantage to approach the matter in three stages:

10–114   First, the set of circumstances which brings it into operation, *viz.*, a trustee-beneficiary and his co-trustee have between them committed a breach of trust from which the former benefited and the latter did not;

Secondly, the trustee-beneficiary's obligation to indemnify which arises from his character of beneficiary, the rule being that a beneficiary who participates in a breach of trust committed with a view towards his benefit must indemnify his trustees out of his beneficial interest; and

Thirdly, the trustee-beneficiary's right of contribution which arises from his character of trustee.

It would seem that, in order to bring the rule in *Chillingworth v. Chambers* into operation, it is not necessary that the trustee-beneficiary *actually benefit* from the breach of trust. The decisions on this particular

---

[94] *ibid.* at 698.
[95] See *supra*, para. 10–80.

point establish that it is quite sufficient if a beneficiary actively participates in a breach of trust with *a motive of personal benefit.*[96] Thus
simplified, the decision in *Chillingworth v. Chambers* decides only one
new point, *viz.*, that where a right of contribution *qua* trustee conflicts
with an obligation to indemnify *qua* beneficiary, the obligation to
indemnify must be discharged before the right of contribution may be
exercised.

Just as *Chillingworth v. Chambers* was based on liability *qua* benefici- **10–115**
ary to have a beneficial interest impounded under the old law so it would
appear that its principles have been extended by section 62 of the
Trustee Act 1925 which extends the law on impounding beneficial
interests.

In *Chillingworth v. Chambers* it was also held that it made no
difference that the trustee-beneficiary was not a beneficiary at the time
the breach of trust was committed, but became a beneficiary *after* that
date. This part of the decision was based on the analogy of *Evans v.
Benyon,*[97] where it was held that the rule that a beneficiary who concurs
in a breach of trust cannot complain of it against his trustee holds good
even if the beneficiary was not a beneficiary at the time of his
concurrence, but became a beneficiary after that date.

CIVIL LIABILITY (CONTRIBUTION) ACT 1978

1.—(1) Subject to the following provisions of this section, any person liable in **10–116**
respect of any damage suffered by another person may recover contribution from
any other person liable in respect of the same damage (whether jointly with him
or otherwise).[98]

(2) A person shall be entitled to recover contribution by virtue of subsection
(1) above notwithstanding that he has ceased to be liable in respect of the
damage in question since the time when the damage occurred, provided that he
was so liable immediately before he made or was ordered or agreed to make the
payment in respect of which the contribution is sought.

(3) A person shall be liable to make contribution by virtue of subsection (1)
above notwithstanding that he has ceased to be liable in respect of the damage in
question since the time when the damage occurred, unless he ceased to be liable
by virtue of an expiry of a period of limitation or prescription which extinguished
the right on which the claim against him in respect of the damage was based.

(4) A person who has made or agreed to make any payment in bona fide
settlement or compromise of any claim made against him in respect of any
damage (including a payment into court which has been accepted) shall be
entitled to recover contribution in accordance with this section without regard to
whether or not he himself is or ever was liable in respect of the damage,

---

[96] See *supra*, para. 10–80; and see s.62 of the Trustee Act 1925. In *Chillingworth v. Chambers* Lindley L.J.
at 700 considered personal benefit immaterial though Kay L.J. at 707 was not prepared so to commit
himself as the plaintiff in the circumstances had received a personal benefit. They were concerned only
with liability to impound on general equitable principles as the action was pending before section 6 of
the Trustee Act 1888 was enacted: see *per* Kay L.J. at 707.
[97] (1887) 37 Ch.D. 329 at 344; *supra*, para. 10–80, n. 28.
[98] For the width of this see *K. v. P.* [1993] Ch. 140; *Friends Provident Life Office v. Hillier Parker* [1995] 4
All E.R. 260; and *Birse Construction Ltd v. Haiste Ltd* [1996] 2 All E.R. 1.

provided, however, that he would have been liable assuming that the factual basis of the claim against him could be established.

10–117   (5) A judgment given in any action brought in any part of the United Kingdom by or on behalf of the person who suffered the damage in question against any person from whom contribution is sought under this section shall be conclusive in the proceedings for contribution as to any issue determined by that judgment in favour of the person from whom the contribution is sought.

2.—(1) Subject to subsection (3) below, in any proceedings for contribution under section 1 above the amount of the contribution recoverable from any person shall be such as may be found by the court to be just and equitable having regard to the extent of that person's responsibility for the damage in question.

(2) Subject to subsection (3) below, the court shall have power in any such proceedings to exempt any person from liability to make contribution, or to direct that the contribution to be recovered from any person shall amount to a complete indemnity.

(3) Where the amount of the damages which have or might have been awarded in respect of the damage in question in any action brought in England and Wales by or on behalf of the person who suffered it against the person from whom the contribution is sought was or would have been subject to—

(a) any limit imposed by or under any enactment or by any agreement made before the damage occurred;

(b) any reduction by virtue of section 1 of the Law Reform (Contributory Negligence) Act 1945 or section 5 of the Fatal Accidents Act 1976; or

(c) any corresponding limit or reduction under the law of a country outside England and Wales;

the person from whom the contribution is sought shall not by virtue of any contribution awarded under section 1 above be required to pay in respect of the damage a greater amount than the amount of those damages as so limited or reduced.

10–118   6.—(1) A person is liable in respect of any damage for the purposes of this Act if the person who suffered it (or anyone representing his estate or dependants) is entitled to recover compensation from him in respect of that damage (whatever is the legal basis of his liability, whether tort, breach of contract, breach of trust or otherwise).

7.—(1) Nothing in this Act shall affect any case where the debt in question became due or (as the case may be) the damage in question occurred before the date on which it comes into force [January 1, 1979].

(2) A person shall not be entitled to recover contribution or liable to make contribution in accordance with section 1 above by reference to any liability based on breach of any obligation assumed by him before the date on which this Act comes into force.[99]

(3) The right to recover contribution in accordance with section 1 above supersedes any right, other than an express contractual right, to recover contribution (as distinct from indemnity) otherwise than under this Act in corresponding circumstances; but nothing in this Act shall affect—

(a) any express or implied contractual or other right to indemnity; or

---

[99] Persons becoming trustees before 1979 thus are excluded from the Act: *Lampitt v. Poole B.C.* [1990] 2 All E.R. 887 at 892.

(b) any express contractual provision regulating or excluding contribution.

which would be enforceable apart from this Act (or render enforceable any agreement for indemnity or contribution which would not be enforceable apart from this Act).

QUESTIONS

1. What should the measure of liability be in the following alternative circum- **10–119** stances where, in breach of trust, Samantha Smith and Roger Robinson, trustees of a family trust:

   (a) transfer the £2 million portfolio of investments and cash to a discretionary portfolio manager and either (i) two months later before any of the investments have been replaced there is a stock-market collapse, so that the portfolio is worth only £1½ million or (ii) four years later, after the original investments have all been replaced, there is a stock-market collapse, so that the portfolio is worth only £1½ million, having been work £2¼ million earlier;

   (b) transfer investments worth £200,000 to their children Amanda Smith and Jack Robinson in consideration of their marriage and either (i) two months later before any of the investments have been sold there is a stock-market collapse, so that the investments are worth only £150,000 or (ii) four years later, after the investments have been sold and used to purchase a £200,000 house (now worth £280,000) there is a stock-market collapse, so that if the investments had been retained they would suddenly have depreciated from £250,000 to £175,000.

2. Ted and Tom are trustees of a £500,000 fund held on trust for Ted himself, **10–120** Arthur, Brian, Charles and David in equal shares contingent upon each attaining 30 years of age. To allay any suspicions of the other beneficiaries Ted takes little part in running the trust affairs, relying to a large extent on Tom, a 50-year old solicitor.

Tom and Arthur consider in 1998 that it would be desirable to buy shares in Exploration Syndicate Co. Ltd but realise that the trustees have no power to do so under the Trustees Investments Act 1961, the will creating the trust conferring no express powers of investment. Nevertheless, Tom writes to Ted telling him that his City connections lead him to consider it a very good idea to buy shares in Exploration Syndicate Co. Ltd For this purpose they can call in £30,000 deposited with the Countrywide Building Society bringing in a gross 8 per cent interest. Ted replies by letter, "If you wish us to invest that £30,000 in the Exploration Syndicate Co. Ltd that is all right by me."

Tom then wrote to Brian, Charles and David, "Ted and I as trustees are considering investing £30,000 of the trust funds in buying shares in the Exploration Syndicate Co. Ltd That is quite a lot of money but we would consider it well spent on such shares. However, before we go ahead we would like to have your consent. Arthur has already consented and we look forward to receiving replies from you and the other beneficiaries quite soon."

Brian and David replied briefly consenting. Charles replied, "I am quite happy **10–121** for the £30,000 to be invested in the shares proposed. Of course, I assume they are authorised investments." The beneficiaries, Ted, Arthur, Brian, Charles and

David were then respectively aged 29, 27, 25, 23 and 17 years. After the replies had been received the £30,000 was invested in buying the proposed shares.

Three years later the company collapsed and the whole £30,000 was lost, the shares only having produced a gross 3 per cent yield in the first year and nothing thereafter.

Advise the trustees of their position *vis-à-vis* (1) the beneficiaries and (2) themselves.

3. Frank Shoal is a grandchild-beneficiary under a discretionary trust of income and capital set up in 1980 by Simon Shoal for his three sons Alan, Brian, and Charles, their spouses and their children.

Simon Shoal, Frank's grandfather, settled his 75 per cent shareholding in Shoal Fishing Co. Ltd (of which he was founder and managing director) along with other investments. The settlement conferred upon the trustees power to appoint capital amongst the beneficiaries as the trustees saw fit from time to time (Clause 4), power to add/or subtract persons (other than the settlor or his spouse) to or from the class of beneficiaries (Clause 5), and power "to invest or otherwise use or apply moneys as if they were absolutely entitled thereto beneficially, so long as the settlor or his spouse do not benefit in any way thereby" (Clause 6). Clause 8 provided that "any Trustee may exercise any power or discretion notwithstanding that he may have a direct or other personal interest in the mode or result of exercising the same," and by Clause 9, "No Trustee shall be liable for any loss to the Trust unless the same happens through his own wilful default."

10–122   The original trustees were Simon Shoal, his solicitor, Sebastian Shallow and his accountant, Nigel Nexus. In 1984 Nexus died and Simon Shoal retired from the trust, being replaced by Alan and Brian Shoal. The third brother, Charles, held no interest in the family fishing company and had left in 1970 to seek his fortune in Australia. Simon Shoal died in 1986 and Shallow in 1990.

In 1993 the family company was in difficult straits. Alan and Brian, who had taken over from their father as joint managing directors, reckoned that they had either to contract the size of the business significantly or expand to obtain the economies afforded by larger-scale operations. They considered the latter alternative preferable and raised the money for expansion by a rights issue, which involved the settlement in paying up £150,000 to take up its entitlement to further shares in the family company. After this the settlement's shares in the family company were valued at £225,000, whilst its other investments were valued at £120,000.

Owing to industrial troubles and the international situation things unfortunately went from bad to worse. In January 1995 in a last-ditch attempt to save the family company, Alan and Brian on behalf of the settlement lent the company £50,000 at 4 per cent interest. Even this failed to save the company which went into liquidation in January 1996. The company shares are worthless and the settlement has lost its £50,000 loan.

10–123   Alan and Brian were adjudicated bankrupt in March 1996, having used their own assets in their attempt to save the company, but in January 1990 they had exercised their powers under Clause 4 of the settlement to appoint £60,000 of capital to each of their respective wives to provide *inter alia* new matrimonial homes secure from grasping creditors. In September 1996 Brian won £130,000 on the football pools and used £61,288 to pay off all his debts in full, and so have his bankruptcy adjudication annulled.

Charles died a widower in Australia in 1984 but his only son, Frank, aged 26, has just come to England and discovered the above facts. He seeks to have the settlement losses made good. However, the trustees, Alan and Brian, have told him he has nothing to gain in pursuing the matter since they did their best in difficult circumstances and are fully protected by the terms of the settlement under which he must bear in mind both Clause 5 and the fact that he is merely a discretionary beneficiary.

4. Julian, a Chancery barrister, and his housewife sister, Sarah, are trustees of **10–124** a 1984 testamentary trust for the testator's widow, Wendy, for life, remainder for her twin daughters (born in 1980) Horatia and Camilla equally. No express power of investment was conferred on the trustees, who have employed Cave & Co Ltd as investment advisers and to keep the accounts of wider-range and narrower-range investments under the 1961 Trustee Investments Act. An exemption clause expressly exempts the trustees from liability "unless guilty of dishonesty".

In 1996, with Wendy's written consent, the trustees in good faith decided it would be financially advantageous to invest £50,000 in shares of an American company and £50,000 in shares of a Japanese company that Cave & Co had recommended to Julian for his personal investments. Cave & Co carried out these purchases for them.

For sentimental reasons, Wendy had been happy for the trustees to retain her **10–125** husband's stamp collection but let her have custody of it. However, six months ago she came across a philatelist, Philip, on a train journey and invited him to see the collection. He enthused over it, told her it was worth around £40,000, and that he could probably find a buyer for it. She subsequently discussed matters with Julian and they decided to sell the collection, informing Sarah of this. Five months ago, Wendy handed the collection to Philip. At monthly intervals he phoned her on his mobile phone to say it was not going to be as easy as he hoped, but he should find a buyer within the next month. Two months ago, Julian obtained the number from Wendy but found it was no longer operational. Wendy and he then went to the address Philip had given them, only to discover the numbers of the houses in that road did not go as high as the number Philip had given. He seems to be untraceable.

The Japanese shares are now worthless, although the American shares are now worth £60,000.

Horatia and Camilla are suing Julian and Sarah and Cave and Co in respect of the loss of £50,000 flowing from the purchase of the Japanese shares, and Julian and Sarah in respect of the lost stamp collection.

Sarah, who tells you that Julian had told her that she could rely on falling in with whatever he wanted done as trustee, seeks your advice, as does Cave & Co.

Chapter 11

EQUITABLE REMEDIES

Section 1. Introduction

The key distinction between proprietary remedies and personal remedies

11–01 A proprietary remedy, *e.g.* an equitable lien (or charge) or an equitable interest under a constructive trust, is enforceable against a particular fund or a specific property held by the defendant and will be unaffected by the insolvency of the defendant, who has never owned the relevant asset free from the claimant's proprietary rights. If those assets have appreciated in value then this accrues to the advantage of the claimant when he recovers the assets as his assets. If the assets have depreciated in value or are mixed moneys that have passed into currency,[1] then the claimant has an equitable charge over them as security for the amount of his claim against the defendant. Pending the hearing of his claim the claimant is entitled almost[2] as of right to an interlocutory injunction preserving the claimed relevant assets intact until the outcome of the trial.

A personal claim is only enforceable against a defendant personally, so that a judgment making him personally liable is of little use if he is insolvent, the claimant ranking as an unsecured creditor. However, if the defendant is good for the money he is liable for the full value received by him rather than for any lesser value of the surviving enrichment in his hands, as in the case of proprietary liability.[3] Pending the hearing of a personal action it is possible only in exceptional circumstances to obtain an interlocutory freezing (formerly called a *Mareva*) injunction to freeze specified assets, though this does not confer upon the claimant any rights superior to the general body of unsecured creditors if the defendant becomes insolvent before the action is heard.[4]

---

[1] See F. A. Mann, *The Legal Aspect of Money* (5th ed.) at p. 7–13, S. Gleeson in P. B. H. Birks (ed.), *Laundering and Tracing* (1995) at 121.

[2] If part of his proprietary claim is weak the court has discretion to grant the requested injunction only over part of the claimed assets: *Polly Peck International plc v. Nadir (No. 2)* [1992] 4 All E.R. 769.

[3] If the value of the surviving enrichment is greater than the original value then there is co-extensive proprietary and personal liability for the surviving enrichment value. The useful phraseology of "value received" and "surviving enrichment" was coined by P. B. H. Birks in *Introduction to the Law of Restitution* (1985).

[4] See *infra*, para. 11–204.

The key role of "Equity regards as done that which ought to be done"

In certain circumstances Equity will not allow a defendant the option to **11–02** break his obligations by taking on a personal liability only to pay compensation, but will impose a proprietary liability upon him in respect of specific property of which he is the legal owner. Thus, a defendant who has contracted to sell an interest in land or a painting cannot be a "bad" man and avoid his obligation to vest title in the claimant merely by paying damages. On conclusion of the contract Equity regards equitable title to the property as passing to the claimant[5] subject to an obligation to pay the price (for which the defendant has an equitable lien over the property). Similarly, if a trustee or other fiduciary in breach of duty claims only to be personally liable to replace £x where he invested the money in an asset now worth £2x he will hold the asset on constructive trust for the beneficiaries regarded as having equitable title to the asset.[6]

Indeed, if a defendant for valuable consideration received by him **11–03** agrees that when he receives future property (*e.g.* whatever he inherits on his parents' deaths, or whatever payments he receives in respect of future sales or royalties) he will hold it on trusts for certain beneficiaries, then on actual receipt of such materialised property he will forthwith hold it on the relevant trusts without ever having for any *scintilla temporis* any beneficial equitable interest in what was received: thus such property will not be available for his creditors.[7]

Exceptionally, whether a plaintiff be a purchaser or donee, where the defendant has done everything required to be done by him to transfer to the claimant legal title to registered land or to shares, then Equity will regard equitable title to the land or shares as having passed to the claimant.[8]

Section 2. Proprietary Tracing Rights

Equitable lien or equitable ownership

Equity has developed sophisticate identification rules[9] to protect a **11–04** claimant's proprietary interest so that the value of the original property can be traced into new assets to ascertain the value surviving in the defendant's hands, no matter how many substitutions of one asset for another have occurred *e.g.* tracing a painting into its proceeds of sale

---

[5] See *supra*, para. 6–204.
[6] *Att.-Gen. for Hong Kong v. Reid* [1994] 1 A.C. 324.
[7] *Pullan v. Koe* [1913] 1 Ch. 9; *Re Lind* [1915] 2 Ch. 345; *Palette Shoes Pty Ltd v. Krohn* (1937) 58 C.L.R. 1 at 26–27; *Barclays Bank v. Willowbrook International Ltd* [1987] B.C.L.C. 717; see *supra*, para. 6–91.
[8] See *supra*, para. 6–83.
[9] See D. J. Hayton in P. B. H. Birks (ed.), *Laundering and Tracing* (1995), at. 1–21.

into a vintage car into its proceeds of sale into some stocks and shares into their proceeds of sale into a flat. The claimant needs to prove that his claim has a "proprietary base"[10] and that there are "transactional links"[11] between the original property and the new assets enabling the value of the original property to be matched with the new assets.[12]

Once the traceable assets have been identified the claimant will claim either an equitable lien (or charge) over the new assets or equitable ownership of the whole or a proportionate part of the new assets (held upon constructive trust for him). If the flat in the above example is worth £80,000 when the original painting was worth £100,000, then the claimant will only claim an equitable lien over the flat to secure part of his claim for £100,000 while looking to the personal liability of the defendant to make up the difference if the defendant is good for the money. Of course, if the defendant is wealthy enough then the claimant will not need to have recourse to his equitable lien to ensure recovery of the £100,000.[13]

11–05   If the flat, instead, happened to be worth £130,000 then the claimant will claim equitable ownership of the whole flat which will be held by the defendant upon constructive trust for him. If the flat happened to be worth £260,000 because purchased half with the defendant's own money then the claimant will claim equitable ownership of half the flat.

Exceptionally, an equitable lien (or charge) may indirectly arise by way of subrogation in favour of the claimant. Thus, if the claimant's money has been used to discharge a mortgage over the defendant's property the court will treat such property as subject to a charge by way of subrogation in favour of the claimant: the claimant stands in the shoes of the mortgagee whose charge is kept alive by Equity for the benefit of the claimant.[14]

Tracing as a preliminary process at law and in equity

11–06   The tracing process is concerned not with following a particular asset such as a painting passing through the hands of four people before ending up in an art gallery. It is concerned with tracing value passing through substitutions of assets in place of the original asset in which the claimant had a proprietary interest[15] *e.g.* the proceeds of sale of a painting held on trust for the plaintiff invested in stocks and shares then sold to purchase a flat. Special property law rules[16] govern cases where the claimant's asset is mixed with D's asset (*commixtio confusio*) or fixed to D's asset (*accessio*) or turned by D into something new (*specificatio*)

---

[10] See P. B. H. Birks in *Introduction to the Law of Restitution* (1985) at. 378 *et seq.*
[11] See D. A. Oesterle (1983) 68 Cornell L.R. 172.
[12] Such proprietary links justify affording the plaintiff priority over the defendant's unsecured creditors in the event of his bankruptcy.
[13] Or any higher replacement value: see *supra*, para. 10–04.
[14] *Boscawen v. Bajwa* [1995] 4 All E.R. 769.
[15] See P. B. H. Birks "Overview" in Birks (ed.), *Laundering and Tracing* (1995) pp. 292 and 299–300.
[16] See P. Matthews "Limits of Common Law Tracing" in Birks (ed.), *supra*, pp. 42–46. Also see *Foskett v. McKeown* [2000] 3 All E.R. 97, 113–114, 124–125 and L. Smith, *The Law of Tracing*, Chap. 2.

so that the claimant's asset loses its separate identity though not its physical continuity with the new asset.

Over the years the common law and equitable rules on the tracing process have become increasingly assimilated though an equitable tracing claim generates an equitable security interest (a non-possessory lien or charge) or a beneficial interest in the surviving enrichment, while a common law tracing claim generates only a personal claim not dependent upon any surviving enrichment in the defendant's hands[17] and not subject to the general equitable defence of bona fide purchaser of a legal interest for value without notice, though subject to the defence of change of position.

At common law[18] the ownership of and the right to possession of **11–07** chattels was protected by the tort actions of conversion and detinue, now known as wrongful interference with goods,[19] or in quasi-contract through the action for money had and received. A person who proved a tort had been committed could waive the tort[20] and bring an action for money had and received in respect of benefits received by the tortfeasor. Otherwise, the action for money had and received lay to recover money paid by the plaintiff to the defendant under a mistake or compulsion or for a consideration which had wholly failed; the plaintiff could also recover money which the defendant had received from a third party when the defendant was accountable to the plaintiff in respect of the money.

These common law actions are actions *in personam* following upon interference with proprietary rights. "Tracing" at common law is concerned with identifying property in a changed form and in whosoever hands in order to found a personal action to support the proprietary right discovered by the "tracing" process.[21] If A's original property is in B's hands and B disposes of such property in return for the new property in such circumstances that the new property belongs to A then, if B goes bankrupt, the title to the new property does not belong to B's trustee in bankruptcy. However, if he attempts to hold on to the property he can be personally sued for wrongful interference with goods so that he must either deliver the new property to A or pay damages to their value to A. Thus A obtains priority over B's creditors.

---

[17] In *Agip (Africa) Ltd v. Jackson* [1990] Ch. 265 Millett J. opined that the quantum for a money had and received action against an innocent third party donee should be limited to the surviving enrichment in the donee's hands. The better view is that there should be strict liability for the value received subject to the defence of change of position: Goff & Jones, *Law of Restitution* (5th ed.) pp. 94, 745–746; S. Gleeson in Birks (ed.), *supra*, p. 123.

[18] Even an equitable beneficiary in possession of a chattel can sue a third party (*Healey v. Healey* [1915] 1 K.B. 938; *The Aliakmon* [1986] A.C. 785 at 812) or his trustee in conversion where wrongfully deprived of it: *International Factors Ltd v. Rodriguez* [1979] Q.B. 351 at 357–358; *Stroud Architectural Systems Ltd v. John Laing Construction Ltd* [1994] 2 B.C.L.C. 276 at 283. Otherwise, a beneficiary has no sight to sue in tort: *MCC Proceeds Inc. v. Lehman Bros* [1998] 4 All E.R. 675.

[19] Torts (Interference with Goods) Act 1977.

[20] See Goff & Jones, Chap. 38. Waiver of tort is not based on any ratification or adoption of the wrongful acts: *United Australia Ltd v. Barclays Bank* [1941] A.C. 1, 18 at 28–29. For a modern view of the so-called waiver of tort doctrine see S. Hedley (1984) 100 L.Q.R. 653.

[21] See M. Scott (1966) 7 W.A.L.R. 463.

11–08　　　　The modern view,[22] owing to a mistaken belief that *Taylor v. Plumer*[23] and other cases concerned the common law position and not the position in equity, is that if A owns property which B without authority exchanges for cash or other property from C, then A can claim the "exchange product," either as owner or at least as having sufficient right to immediate possession to enable him to maintain a claim for conversion or, now, wrongful interference with goods, so as to bring a tort claim or waive the tort and sue in quasi-contract.

　　　　The better view[24] is that if C has not passed title to A directly via B's agency then title has passed to B so that unless B specifically appropriates the property to A, thereby passing title to A, then A has no title to the property nor sufficient right to immediate possession to enable him to bring a claim in tort. This is a significant limitation upon the common law position because it means that there are rarely common law tracing rights in respect of substitute assets.

11–09　　　　However, it seems that the courts[25] will accept that long-standing error makes law (*communis error facit ius*) especially where unification of tracing processes is achieved at common law and in equity. After all, the presumption that evidential difficulties must be resolved against the wrongdoer who created them is a principle common to both common law and equity[26] as is the "first in, first out" rule in *Clayton's Case*[27] and also, it seems, the *pari passu* principle of proportionate abatement of innocent contributors' claims to a fund.[28]

11–10　　　　Money raises particular problems since it soon ceases to be identifiable when mixed by passing into currency in the hands of a transferee for value.[29] The conventional view[30] has been that equity was far ahead of the common law in its flexible rules for tracing moneys, though mixed in bank accounts; whilst it may well have been that the common law was equally flexible.[31] However, the usefulness of equity in such situations has

---

[22] *Banque Belge v. Hambrouck* [1921] 1 K.B. 321; *Re J. Leslie Engineering Co. Ltd* [1976] 1 W.L.R. 292; *Agip (Africa) Ltd v. Jackson* [1991] Ch. 547; *Lipkin Gorman v. Karpnale* [1991] 2 A.C. 548, all misconceiving *Taylor v. Plumer* (1815) 3 M. & S. 562 which was concerned with equitable tracing, and where Lord Ellenborough's derogatory remarks about the limitations of tracing were directed at equitable tracing owing to his ignorance of equitable developments, as pointed out by Jessel M.R. in *Re Hallett's Estate* (1880) 13 Ch.D. 696; M. Scott, *op. cit.*; R. A. Pearce (1976) 40 Conv. 277; Khurshid & Matthews (1979) 95 L.Q.R. 78; P. Matthews, "Limits of Common Law Tracing" in Birks (ed.) *Laundering and Tracing* (1995), pp. 44–61 (pointing out the inconsistency of Lord Goff's *Lipkin Gorman* [1991] 2 A.C. 548 at 570, 573, 574 holding that the money obtained by the rogue was the plaintiff's for the purposes of money had and received but not for the purposes of conversion).
[23] (1815) 3 M. & S. 562; L. Smith, "Tracing in *Taylor v. Plumer*: Equity in the Court of King's Bench" [1995] L.M.C.L.Q. 240; *Trustee of F. C. Jones v. Jones* [1997] Ch. 159.
[24] R. M. Goode (1976) 92 L.Q.R. 360 at 367, n. 27; Khurshid & Matthews, *op. cit.*; Matthews in Birks (ed.) *Laundering and Tracing*, pp. 44–61 and Birks, *ibid.*, at 298.
[25] *Trustee of F.C. Jones v. Jones* [1997] Ch. 159.
[26] *Lupton v. White* (1808) 15 Ves. 432 at 434, 439–441; *Jones v. De Marchant* (1916) 28 DLR 561; *Frith v. Cartland* (1865) 2 Hem 814 417; *Re Oatway* [1903] 2 Ch. 356.
[27] *The Mecca* [1897] A.C. 286 at 290.
[28] *Spence v. Union Marine Insurance Co.* (1868) L.R. 2., C.P. 427; *Sinclair v. Brougham* [1914] A.C. 398.
[29] *King v. Milson* (1809) 2 Comp. 5; *Re Diplock* [1948] Ch. 465 at 539; F. A. Mann, *The Legal Aspect of Money* (5th ed.) pp. 7–13.
[30] *Sinclair v. Brougham* [1914] A.C. 419; *Re Diplock* [1948] Ch. 465; *Banque Belge v. Hambrouck* [1921] 1 K.B. 321.
[31] R. M. Goode (1976) 92 L.Q.R. 360 at 395–396; Khurshid & Matthews (1979) 95 L.Q.R. 78 at 81–82; *Jackson v. Anderson* (1811) 4 Taunt. 24. Point conceded in *Lipkin Gorman v. Karpnale* [1991] 2 A.C. 548.

been such that the common law position remains unclear, *Banque Belge v. Hambrouck*[32] being the rather unsatisfactory decision in point when there are two ways of explaining in a more satisfactory way[33] why A could recover £315 from C's bank account into which her lover, B, had arranged his bank to pay money fraudulently obtained by B from A. The case does establish that money paid into a bank account can certainly be identified at law if not mixed with other moneys and, perhaps, even if mixed with other moneys. Since then, the Court of Appeal[34] has upheld a common law claim to recover £50,000 from the defendant wife of a bankrupt innocently investing £11,700 (to which she had no legal or equitable title) in potato futures to profitable effect, but Mrs Jones had not mixed these moneys with others. It was also not necessary to trace the passage of money through the bank clearing system, Mrs Jones being considered to have simply the right to payment of the balance of her account. At common law clearing systems were regarded as insuperable obstacles to tracing.[35]

Equitable tracing can, however, trace money through a clearing system, the Court of Appeal having accepted backwards tracing to the extent of identifying a credit with a debit even where the credit entry was first in time[36] and Millett J. (as he then was) allowing tracing through back to back credit facilities.[37] Extra-judicially, he has stated,[38] "The question is whether there is a sufficient nexus between the debit to A's account and the credit to B's account that in contemplation of law the latter can be treated as representing the former. We must stop thinking in terms of identifying each item of property with its exchange product on a one to one basis. We must adopt a different test, and ask instead whether the debit and credit are both causally and transactionally linked."

In the light of *Foster v. McKeown*[39] *infra* it should now be recognised **11–11** as Lord Steyn says,[40] that "in truth, tracing is a process of identifying assets: it belongs to the realm of evidence. It tells us nothing about legal or equitable rights to the assets traced . . . there is a unified regime for tracing and it allows tracing to be cleanly separated from the business of asserting rights in assets successfully traced." As Lord Millett states,[41] "one set of tracing rules is enough. There is certainly no logical justification for allowing any distinction between them to produce capricious results in cases of mixed substitutions by insisting on the existence of a fiduciary relationship as a precondition for applying equity's tracing rules. The existence of such a relationship may be

---

[32] [1921] 1 K.B. 321.
[33] R. M. Goode (1976) 92 L.Q.R. 360 at 378–381; Khurshid & Matthews (1979) 95 L.Q.R. 78 at 91–94.
[34] *Trustee of F.C. Jones v. Jones* [1997] Ch. 159.
[35] *Agip (Africa) Ltd v. Jackson* [1990] Ch. 265, 290; [1991] Ch. 547, 566 (C.A.).
[36] *Agip (Africa) Ltd v. Jackson* [1991] Ch. 547.
[37] *El Ajou v. Dollar Land Holdings* [1993] 1 All E.R. 717 (not doubted on appeal).
[38] (1995) 6 K.C.L.J. 1 at 12, "Equity—The Road Ahead."
[39] [2000] 3 All E.R. 97.
[40] *ibid.*, 106.
[41] *ibid.*, 121.

relevant to the nature of the claim, whether personal or proprietary, but that is a different matter."

The right to the equitable proprietary remedy of a lien or a proportionate share

Thus tracing principles should enable equitable proprietary remedies to be available to legal (as well as equitable) owners if legal remedies are inadequate, although as a product of the exclusive jurisdiction of the Court of Chancery it has been held that for tracing to lead to a proprietary remedy it requires "a continuing right of property recognised in equity or its concomitant, a fiduciary or quasi-fiduciary relationship." Goulding J. stated[42] that this is the interpretation accorded to the House of Lords decision in *Sinclair v. Brougham*[43] by the Court of Appeal in *Re Diplock*.[44] This has also been the view of the Court of Appeal in *Agip (Africa) Ltd v. Jackson*[45] and in *Boscawen v. Bajwa*.[46]

11–12　　　As a result, to allow plaintiffs to use equitable tracing rules to acquire a proprietary remedy in circumstances where the court considers it to be just, the concept of fiduciary or quasi-fiduciary relationship has been stretched to the limit.[47] It has been held to cover bailor and bailee,[48] principal and agent where their relationship is not simply that of debtor and creditor,[49] directors of a company and persons making *ultra vires* deposits with the company,[50] and employer and employee,[51] as well as the obvious cases of solicitor and client[52] and trustee (express, resulting or constructive[53]) and beneficiary.

---

[42] *Chase Manhatten Bank v. Israel-British Bank* [1981] Ch. 105 at 119.
[43] [1914] A.C. 398.
[44] [1948] Ch. 465.
[45] [1992] 4 All E.R. 451 at 466.
[46] [1995] 4 All E.R. 769 at 777.
[47] This is unnecessary in view of *Foskett v. McKeown* [2000] 3 All E.R. 97, 106, 121; Goff & Jones, *Law of Restitution* (5th ed.) at 104–106.
[48] But the presumption of a fiduciary relationship between bailor and bailee may be rebutted: *Hendy Lennox Ltd v. Grahame Puttick Ltd* [1984] 2 All E.R. 152 at 162–163. Suppliers of goods to manufacturers, in order to give themselves security on the manufacturers' insolvency leaving the goods unpaid for, have tried by contract to make the manufacturer a fiduciary bailee or agent till payment, required to keep the goods and the proceeds of sale thereof separate from the manufacturers' property so that the supplier can trace the goods and the proceeds: *Aluminium Industrie Vaasen v. Romalpa* [1976] 1 W.L.R. 676. There are problems discussed, *supra*, para. 3–11, for the seller trying to trace into the manufactured product in which his goods are mixed and in Companies Act 1985, s.395 making equitable charges by companies void if unregistered: *Borden (U.K.) Ltd v. Scottish Timber Products Ltd* [1981] Ch. 25; *Re Bond Worth Limited* [1980] Ch. 228; *Re Andrabell Ltd* [1984] 3 All E.R. 407; *Re Peachdart Ltd* [1984] Ch. 131; *Clough Mill Ltd v. Martin* [1984] 3 All E.R. 982, *supra*, para. 3–26.
[49] *Re Goode* (1974) 4 Austr.L.R. 579. Clients, who dealt with a stockbroker one transaction at a time, had full rights to trace (if vendors) their shares into a pool of shares held by the broker or to recover (if purchasers) money entrusted to the broker for settlement; clients who operated on a running account with periodic balances and settlements were in a mere debtor-creditor relationship with no tracing remedy.
[50] *Sinclair v. Brougham* [1914] A.C. 398 but the House of Lords in *Westdeutsche Landesbank v. Islington B.C.*, [1996] A.C. 669 overruled this proprietary point because the depositors intended the company to become legal beneficial owner of the deposits and only be a debtor.
[51] *Banque Belge v. Hambrouck* [1921] 1 K.B. 321; *Black v. Freedman* (1910) 12 C.L.R. 105.
[52] *Re Hallett's Estate* (1880) 13 Ch.D. 696; *Hopper v. Conyers* (1866) L.R. 2 Eq. 549.
[53] *Lake v. Bayliss* [1974] 2 All E.R. 1114 (vendor under contract of sale of land to P1 held on constructive trust for P1 so that when V sold to P2, P1 could trace those proceeds of sale).

Indeed, there have been cases where the recipient of moneys under a mistaken[54] or void[55] or voidable transaction[56] had not been in a prior fiduciary relationship with the claimant, but the very payment of the moneys to the recipient was held to give rise to the payer's separate equitable proprietary right to recover his moneys, the recipient being under a fiduciary duty to respect such proprietary right. These cases require reconsideration when one considers the fundamental principle that a "proprietary base"[57] is at the core of proprietary tracing rights, so that if P pays money over to D for D to be absolute owner thereof (with the right to mix it with his own money and deal with it as he wishes) subject to an obligation to repay P a corresponding amount of money (with or without interest), P has no rights whatever in the money given to D[58] or in any property purchased with such money that has appreciated in value.[59]

There can be no right to trace between P and D where the **11–13** relationship is creditor and debtor so that D can do what he likes with *his* property. Similarly, if V enters into a non-specifically enforceable contract to sell goods to P but then, in breach of contract, sells the goods instead at a greater profit to Q, P cannot trace the proceeds of sale in V's hands because P had no proprietary interest in V's goods.[60] Again, if V contracts to sell gold bars to P, who pays over the price to V in circumstances where no gold bars are specifically appropriated and set aside for P, so that no title to any gold passes to P, P cannot trace his purchase money in V's hands upon discovering that V is insolvent.[61]

Thus, what should happen if P by mistake of fact or of law[62] (*e.g.* believing the contract under which the money is paid to be valid and not *ultra vires* the transferee and void) pays money to D for D to mix with his own money and use as his own, intending to create only a debtor-creditor relationship? On discovering the true position can P claim to have retained throughout an equitable proprietary interest in the money and its traceable product when his interest in the money was surely

---

[54] *Chase Manhattan Bank v. Israel-British Bank* [1981] Ch. 105 at 119 but now restrictively interpreted by Lord Browne-Wilkinson in *Westdeutsche Landesbank v. Islington B.C.*, [1996] A.C. 669 but he seems to confuse a constructive trust of property with personal liability as a constructive trustee.

[55] *Sinclair v. Brougham* [1914] A.C. 398 overruled on this by House of Lords in *Westdeutsche Landesbank v. Islington B.C.* [1996] A.C. 669.

[56] *El Ajou v. Dollar Land Holdings* [1993] 3 All E.R. 717. On which see comment of Lord Millett in *Bristol & West B.S. v. Motthew* [1996] 4 All E.R. 698, 716 desirous that the equitable tracing rules should be able to support a personal knowing receipt claim: see Cornish, Nolan, Sullivan & Virgo (eds.), *Restitution, Past Present and Future* (1998) p. 229.

[57] P. B. H. Birks, *Introduction to the Law of Restitution* (1985) pp. 378 *et seq.* and P. B. H. Birks (ed.), *Laundering and Tracing* (1995), pp. 311 *et seq.*; Millett J. in *Lonrho plc v. Fayed (No. 2)* [1991] 4 All E.R. 961 at 969.

[58] *Customs & Excise Commissioners v. Richmond Theatre Management Ltd* [1995] S.T.C. 257; *Daly v. Sidney Stock Exchange* (1986) 106 CLR 371; *Space Investments Ltd v. Canadian Imperial Bank of Commerce Trust Co.* [1986] 1 W.L.R. 1072. Note the emphasis on certainty of proprietary rights in *Westdeutsche Landesbank v. Islington B.C.*, see *supra*, para. 5–11.

[59] *Halifax B.S. v. Thomas* [1995] 4 All E.R. 673; *Chief Constable of Leicestershire v. M.* [1989] 1 W.L.R. 20.

[60] *ibid.*

[61] *Re Goldcorp Exchange Ltd* [1995] 1 A.C. 74.

[62] The traditional artificial distinction between mistakes of fact and mistakes of law has been abolished: *Kleinwort Benson Ltd v. Glasgow C.C.*, [1999] 1 A.C. 153 (H.L.).

extinguished when he paid it over and it was mixed with D's money, P not intending D to create a separate trust fund? In principle, P ought not to be able to claim any equitable proprietary remedy, and support for this can be found in the speech of Lord Browne-Wilkinson in *Westdeutsche Landesbank v. Islington B.C.*[64]

11–14   Indeed, Lord Browne-Wilkinson indicated that the equitable proprietary remedy over traced assets can be available not just in the case where the legal and equitable ownership of assets is split up but also where the equitable interest is subsumed within the legal title of a sole beneficial owner. Thus, if P's money is stolen from him (*e.g.* under a bogus criminal "scam" or by D accepting a payment of £1 million from P when D knew this was a mistake because P had already paid the £1 million due) P should be able to trace the money (or any other property stolen from him) if his legal remedies are inadequate *e.g.* because D is bankrupt. Mann L.J., taking his cue from Lord Templeman's apparent endorsement of *Black v. Freedman*,[65] has, indeed, taken the view[66] that "the thief becomes a constructive trustee of what he steals", his conscience presumably being under a fiduciary duty to return what he has stolen to its rightful owner. Lord Browne-Wilkinson in *Westdeutsche Landesbank v. Islington B.C.* has now stated,[67] "I agree that stolen monies are traceable in equity."

Thus, also taking account of the views of Lords Steyn and Millett (*supra* para. 11–11), equitable proprietary remedies imposed following the tracing process may be regarded as part of equity's auxiliary jurisdiction where common law damages are inadequate.

Interlocutory injunctions

11–15   If a plaintiff does have a sufficient proprietary base to trace assets as "his" he is entitled to obtain an interim injunction, to preserve such assets until the trial of the action,[68] though in a very special case the balace of convenience may lead the court to take lesser steps for the preservation of the claimant's interest.[69] To make his tracing rights effective a court will be very ready to make ancillary orders to enable him to discover traceable assets, *e.g.* ordering a bank or the defendant to make disclosure of all relevant documents, ordering a defendant to

---

[64] [1996] A.C. 669.
[65] (1910) 12 C.L.R. 105 at 110 endorsed in *Lipkin Gorman v. Karpnale Ltd* [1991] 2 A.C. 548 at 565–566.
[66] *Bishopsgate Investment Management Ltd v. Maxwell* [1993] Ch. 1 at 70. See also Millett J. in (1991) 107 L.Q.R. 71 at 76; Goff & Jones, *Law of Restitution* (5th ed.), p. 104.
[67] [1996] A.C. 669, 715–716. After all, if a thief sells 2 paintings stolen from X, where X is owner of one and tenant for life of the other, and uses the proceeds of £100,000 to purchase a flat for himself before being bankrupted why should there not be a proprietary remedy in respect of both paintings?
[68] See Lord Denning M.R. in *Bankers Trust v. Shapira* [1980] 3 All E.R. 353 at 357 citing Templeman L.J. in an unreported case.
[69] *Polly Peck International plc v. Nadir (No. 2)* [1992] 4 All E.R. 769 where a weak tracing claim against £8.9 million received by the Central Bank of Northern Cyprus led the court on the *American Cyanamid Co. v. Ethicon Ltd* [1975] A.C. 396 balance of convenience test just to require the Bank to earmark the £8.9 million in a separate account and not to deal with it otherwise than in the normal cause of business and unless and to the extent that no other funds in England were available to be used.

answer requests for further information before being allowed to leave the jurisdiction. Once the claimant proves his tracing claim he will be entitled to the frozen assets with priority over any creditors of the defendant.

Where the claimant merely has a personal claim (*e.g.* for damages at **11–16** common law for a tort or a breach of contract) then (as discussed below paras 11–204) *et seq.* in an exceptional case an interim freezing injunction may be obtained[70] to freeze assets not exceeding the amount of the plaintiff's claim and his costs. However, the injunction only operates *in personam* against the defendant. It affords the plaintiff no proprietary right in the frozen asset nor priority over other creditors.[71] Indeed, the injunction may be varied to enable the frozen assets to be partly unfrozen so that the defendant may make payments in good faith in the ordinary course of business or for legal or living expenses.[72] Exceptionally, a Chief Constable has sufficient interest to obtain an injunction freezing assets such as a confidence trickster's bank account, since he has a duty to seize and detain stolen or unlawfully obtained goods for restoring them to their true owner and, by analogy, a similar duty in respect of intangible assets such as a bank account.[73]

No need to sue trustee first

As *Foster v. McKeown* makes clear[74] "the transmission of a claimant's **11–17** property rights from one asset to its traceable proceeds is part of our laws of property": the claim is an[75] "assertion of" an "equitable proprietary interest in identified property" and "such proprietary interest is not dependent on any discretion vested in the court." Thus, as held in *Hagan v. Waterhouse*,[76] it is not considered that before a claimant can utilise the tracing process and enforce his equitable proprietary interest against third parties he must first sue the trustee or other fiduciary responsible for the assets passing into the hands of third parties. This is an important distinction between the proprietary tracing claim and the personal claim (discussed *infra*, para. 11–103) available to unpaid or underpaid creditors, legatees or next of kin against recipients of a deceased's estate only after they have first exhausted their remedies against the deceased's personal representatives.

In *Re Diplock* the Court of Appeal said[77]:

---

[70] *Mareva Cia Naviera Sa v. International Bulkeavviers SA* [1975] 2 Lloyd's Rep. 509. It will be without notice to the other party in the first instance but may be continued after a hearing with notice to the other party.
[71] *Iraqi Ministry of Defence v. Arcepey Shipping Co.* [1981] Q.B. 65.
[72] *PCW (Underwriting Agencies) Ltd v. Dixon* [1983] 2 All E.R. 158.
[73] *Chief Constable of Hampshire v. A* [1984] 2 All E.R. 385 as restricted by *Chief Constable of Leicestershire v. M* [1989] 1 W.L.R. 20.
[74] [2000] 3 All E.R. 97, 119.
[75] *ibid.*, 101. But see A. Burrows (2001) 117 L.Q.R. 412.
[76] (1994) 34 N.S.W.L.R. 308 at 369–370.
[77] [1948] Ch. 465 at 556.

"Prima facie and subject to discussion,[78] it appears to us that the sums so recovered [£15,000 recovered from the personal representatives] ought to be credited rateably to all the charities [the third parties who had innocently received the deceased's estate] for all purposes, *i.e.* for the purposes of the claims *in rem* [the proprietary tracing claim] as well as the claim *in personam*."

In context, since it so happened that £15,000 had already been received, it was only right and proper that the claims against the charities should be reduced *pro tanto*. The case is thus not authority for the view that claims against the fiduciary must first be exhausted before any tracing claim can be pursued against third party recipients.[79]

One may note that it is not only a beneficiary who can take advantage of the tracing remedy, *e.g.* into mixed bank accounts and claiming a charge over an amalgam of assets. A trustee may also trace where his remedies as legal owner are inadequate to safeguard his beneficiaries' interests, especially if the beneficiaries are as yet unborn or unascertained.[80]

The scope of the equitable proprietary remedy

11–18 Where the trust property or its product is intact, then the court will order the person having such property or product to restore it to the trustees (or to the beneficiaries if each is of full capacity and between them they are absolutely entitled to the trust fund).[81] Thus, if in breach of trust the trustee gives a trust painting to his brother, who sells it and uses the proceeds to buy a flat for his mistress as sole beneficial owner, she will be compelled to transfer the flat to the trustees (the original trustee no doubt having resigned or having been removed from his office). If the flat is worth more than the painting it is taken over as if it had been an authorised investment. If it is worth less there is a charge on the flat for the value of the painting so that the flat is taken over and its value credited against the personal liability for breach of trust. In other words, the beneficiaries can elect to treat the flat as trust property or as security for the recouping of trust assets.

11–19 Where trust funds are used by a trustee to purchase a house in the trustee's name, with the existence of a mortgage under which the trustee as legal owner personally covenants to repay the mortgage moneys, the courts do not treat the trustee as personally contributing the mortgage

---

[78] This seems to have been inserted in case it was necessary to marshall the £15,000 in different manner, *e.g.* if charity A had dissipated all it received should any of the £15,000 have been used in reduction of the barren tracing claim against it?

[79] Significantly, in *Re Leslie Engineers Co. Ltd* [1976] 2 All E.R. 85 at 91 Oliver J., having mentioned the restriction on the personal claim, did not mention it when referring to a possible tracing claim.

[80] *Price v. Blakemore* (1843) 6 Beav. 507 (where the trustees let the life tenant have £8,124 of proceeds of sale of trust land and the life tenant used the money towards purchasing a £17,400 house for himself in fee simple and the trustees' tracing claim succeeded); *Carson v. Sloane* (1884) 13 L.R. Ir. 139. The principle of non-derogation from grant may estop a trustee from pursuing a claim at law.

[81] *Re Hallett's Estate* (1880) 13 Ch.D. 709; *Re Diplock* [1948] Ch. 465.

money so as to be able to claim three quarters of the house where the trust contributed £25,000 and the mortgage £75,000. Instead, the trust beneficiaries can claim the whole house worth, say, £150,000 when the facts emerge[82]; but for the £25,000 of trust funds the trustee would not have had the proprietary interest to provide the necessary security for the mortgage loan. Where there has not been a clean substitution" because the trust property or its product has been mixed with other property the position is more complex.

If there is a mixture of heterogeneous goods in a manufacturing process so that the original trust property (*e.g.* resin) loses its character and what emerges is a wholly new product (*e.g.* chipboard), then in a case where the mixing had been authorised tracing has been held to be impossible because the manufacturing process is regarded as akin to the process of consumption.[83] However, if the mixing had been unauthorised it is difficult to see why the beneficiaries should not be entitled to claim every portion of the blended property that the wrongdoer cannot prove to be his own.[84] However, where it is known how much of the trust's property went into a fungible mixture then, it seems, the trust will be regarded as owning a share proportionate to the value of the contributed trust property.[85]

If the goods mixed are of a homogenous character as where trust corn **11–20** is mixed with a corn factor's own corn[86] or if trust shares are mixed with a trustee's private shares of the same type in the same company then the right to trace remains. Thus, if a trustee mixes 32,280 trust shares, held by him on trust for A absolutely, with 1,300 of his own shares of the same type in the same company, and then gives 17,000 to C so as to retain 16,580, he will be ordered to transfer his 16,580 to A's trustee in bankruptcy and C will be ordered so to transfer 15,700 of his 17,000 shares.[87] Similarly, if 50 tons of trust corn are mixed with 100 tons of a fiduciary bailee's own corn and the amalgam sold for £15,000 and the proceeds banked, the plaintiff may trace into the bank account moneys for £5,000. If the proceeds had been used to buy a car which was a vintage car that appreciated in value then the plaintiff could claim

---

[82] *Paul Davies Pty Ltd v. Davies* [1983] N.S.W.L.R. 440; *Re Marriage of Wagstaff* (1990) 99 F.L.R. 390.

[83] *Borden (U.K.) Ltd v. Scottish Timber Products Ltd* [1981] Ch. 25, though the point seems to have been conceded by counsel [1981] Ch. 25 at 31, 35, 44. Tracing would have been possible if there had been agreement that the supplier's interest in the resin should continue as part ownership of the product: *Coleman v. Harvey* [1989] 1 N.Z.L.R. 723. Perhaps *Borden* can be explained as regarding the resin owner as authorising his proprietary right to be replaced by a debtor-creditor relationship upon the resin being used to produce chipboard; otherwise, co-ownership according to the value of the mixed goods seems appropriate: *Silsbury v. McCoon* (1850) 8 N.Y. 379, 1 N.Y.C.A. 471.

[84] See *Jones v. De Marchant* (1916) 28 D.L.R. 561, endorsed in *Foskett v. McKeown* [2000] 3 All E.R. 97, 125; *Lupton v. White* (1808) 15 Ves. 432; *Westdeutsche Landesbank v. Islington B.C.* [1994] 4 All E.R. 890 at 938 and *Southern Cross Commodities v. Martin* 1991 S.L.T. 83. The conscious wrongdoer in an exceptional case could have an allowance for his personal skills and financial or other contributions: *O'Sullivan v. Management Agency and Music Ltd* [1985] Q.B. 428; *Badfinger Music v. Evans* [2001] W.T.L.R., 1 *cf. Guinness v. Saunders* [1990] 2 A.C. 663, 701.

[85] *cf. Indian Oil Corp. v. Greenstone Shipping SA* [1988] Q.B.; *Foskett v. McKeown [2000] 3 All E.R. 97; Glencore International AG v. Metro Trading Inc.* [2001] 1 Lloyd's Rep 283.

[86] An example given by Bridge L.J. in *Borden (U.K.) Ltd, Supra,* or if crude oil is mixed with crude oil: *Indian Oil Co. v. Greenstone Shipping S.A.* [1987] 3 All E.R. 893.

[87] *Brady v. Stapleton* (1952) 88 C.L.R. 322.

ownership of one third of the car, but if the car had depreciated then he would have a charge on the car for £5,000. Where the traced asset has depreciated this equitable charge or lien for the amount of the trust money is a most useful equitable device for securing the claimant beneficiaries' interests.

Usually, it is trust money that is mixed with other moneys, whether belonging to the trustee personally or as trustee of another trust or belonging to an innocent volunteer.

Mixing of trust money with trustee's own money

11-21 If T spends £20,000 of trust money and £40,000 of his own money on a flat worth £100,000 when the facts come to light, then the trust is entitled to a one-third interest in the flat[88] together with one-third of the actual rent produced by the flat, such being an incident of the rights established in the flat.[89] If T, instead, had bought a car worth only £18,000 when the facts came to light, then the trust would be entitled to a charge on the car for £18,000,[90] with a personal claim for the £2000 capital balance and lost interest on the £20,000. Thus, where the value of the purchased asset appreciates the beneficiaries will claim a proportionate share but where it depreciates they will claim an equitable charge.

(a) *The Re Hallett Presumption of Honesty.* If T has a bank account which is empty until paying in £5,000 of trust money and he then pays in £3,000 of his own and he then spends the £8,000 the applicable principles are set out in the preceding paragraph. But what if he spends only £2,500 which happens to be dissipated so as to be untraceable? Can he allege this was trust money, perhaps by invoking the rule in *Clayton's* case applicable to the running account between banker and customer whereby first payments in are treated as first payments out? No, because[91] "where a man does an act which may be rightfully performed . . . he is not allowed to say against the person entitled to the property or the right that he has done it wrongfully." Thus a trustee is not allowed to deny his beneficiaries' allegation that he was rightfully withdrawing his own funds. Therefore, the beneficiaries will allege that T rightfully dissipated his own £2,500 so that the trust moneys are still intact.

---

[88] *Scott v. Scott* (1962) 109 C.L.R. 649; *B.C. Teachers' Credit Union v. Betterley* (1975) 61 D.L.R. (3d) 755; *Re Tilley's W.T.* [1967] Ch. 1179. If the trustee could not have taken advantage of the opportunity to buy the property but for the trust money query whether he should obtain a proportionate share of the profit for taking advantage of his position, *e.g.* if a development syndicate requires a minimum £100,000 contribution and T, only having £10,000 of his own uses £90,000 trust moneys. If the investment doubles should T really get £20,000 or just a return of £10,000 plus interest? If the opportunity arises for T *qua* trustee (e.g. to purchase shares or a freehold reversion) then the shares or freehold will be held on constructive trust, with T only having a lien for his expenditure.
[89] *Banton v. CIBC Corporation* (1999) 182 D.L.R (4th) 486, 504–505; L. Smith, *The Law of Tracing* (1997) p. 24. It seems that compensation for loss of use of the stolen capital (*e.g.* interest on money) is a separate independent personal remedy so there is no justification for preferential treatment over ordinary unsecured creditors by securing such compensation by a charge over the traced property, but such securing of interest seems to have been conceded in *Foskett v. McKeown* [1998] Ch. 265, 277–278.
[90] *Re Hallett's Estate* (1880) 13 Ch.D. 606.
[91] *Re Hallett's Estate* (1880) 13 Ch. D. 686 at 727.

(b) *The Re Oatway election of rules by beneficiaries.* However, if T had **11–22** spent the £2,500 on purchasing Whizzo Ltd shares, now worth £10,000, and had then dissipated the £5,500 balance in the account, the beneficiaries will not allege that T first rightfully withdrew his own £2,500. Moreover, T, whose wrongful mixing of trust funds with his own made them indistinguishable, "cannot maintain that the investment which remains represents his money alone and what has been spent and can no longer be traced or recovered was money belonging to the trust."[92] Thus, in *Re Oatway*[93] where the beneficiaries' £3,000 had been added to T's bank account already containing £4,077, and £2,137 was spent on shares and the rest of the moneys subsequently frittered away, the beneficiaries were entitled to a charge on the shares, then worth £2,474, as security for their £3,000 claim for breach of trust against T. If the shares, for example, had appreciated to £5,000 then the beneficiaries instead of claiming a charge on the shares would have elected to adopt the unauthorised investment as purchased with their £2,137, so entitling them to the shares (and any dividends declared thereon if not dissipated) and leaving them with a personal claim for the £863 balance of trust moneys.

In *Re Oatway* it so happened that after purchase of the shares the **11–23** balance of the money in the account was dissipated. In principle, it should make no difference to the beneficiaries' rights whether, fortuitously, a balance remains in the account and whether this balance is large enough to represent all the moneys due to the beneficiaries. Where a trustee amalgamates trust property with his own he cannot also control the bookkeeping and allocate profitable investments to himself. The beneficiaries are entitled to elect either to have a charge on the amalgam (consisting of bank account moneys remaining and shares or other property purchased with account moneys) as security for their claim or to adopt the purchased property as trust property.[94] In the absence of specific authority it seems that basic principle should apply as follows.

Take the case where T already has £10,000 in his bank account when he adds £10,000 of trust money to it. He spends £15,000 on shares, so leaving £5,000 in the account. The shares double in value. Clearly at least £5,000 of trust moneys must have been used in the purchase. The beneficiaries can claim that £10,000 of trust moneys were used so that they can adopt two thirds of the shares as trust property now happily worth £20,000. The trustee by virtue of his wrongful act, in creating an amalgam where it is impossible to distinguish his property from the trust property, cannot disprove the beneficiaries' claim and the burden of proof is on him.[95]

---

[92] *Re Oatway* [1903] 2 Ch. 356 at 360.
[93] [1903] 2 Ch. 356.
[94] *Scott v. Scott* (1962) 109 C.L.R. 649; *Re Tilley's W.T.* [1967] Ch. 1179; *Foskett v. McKeown* [2000] 3 All E.R. 97, 123. If such property is not an authorised investment it will need to be sold (unless all the beneficiaries are of full capacity and agree otherwise).
[95] *Westdeutsche Landesbank v. Islington B.C.* [1994] 4 All E.R. 890 at 938. Persons deriving title under the wrongdoer are in no better position than the wrongdoer: "they certainty cannot do better than the claimant by confining him to a lien and keeping any profit for themselves": *Foskett v. McKeown*, [2000] 3 All E.R. 97, 124, *per* Lord Millett.

11–24   If, instead, T had spent £10,000 on shares in Wonder Limited and then either left the £10,000 balance in the account or spent it on shares in Tacky Limited, the beneficiaries should still be able to claim the Wonder Limited shares which double in value rather than be left, on the word of the wrongdoing T, with the £10,000 or the shares in Tacky Limited which have halved in value. T's speculation should be at his risk and not at his beneficiaries' risk.

Essentially, the wrongdoing trustee cannot be allowed to take advantage of his own wrongdoing to put himself in the position of "Heads I win, tails you lose" whereas the wronged beneficiaries can and the trustee cannot complain. His conduct prevented proper accounts from being kept so it is up to the beneficiaries and not him to resolve the bookkeeping as they wish: "everything is presumed against him."[96]

11–25   Take the case where T pays £10,000 trust money into his bank account containing £2,000 of his own money and then draws out £5,000 (leaving £7,000) which he uses with £15,000 of a legacy to him in his building society account to purchase for £20,000 shares now worth £40,000. The beneficiaries can elect either (1) for a charge for their £10,000 on the amalgam of the shares and the remaining money in the account, or (2) for one-quarter of the shares to be adopted as trust property, so satisfying their claim to the extent of £5,000 of their moneys, and for a charge for £5,000 to be imposed on the moneys remaining in the account.

(c) *Necessary action for trustee to right his wrong.* A trustee, of course, may reinstate the trust fund, and so right the wrong, and thenceforward, having distinguished his own private property from the trust property, he may invest his private property profitably or unprofitably as he wishes.[97] If T mixes £10,000 of trust money with his own £10,000 to purchase £20,000 of shares, which he later sells for £40,000, he does not reinstate the trust fund by paying £10,000 into his empty account redesignated as a trust account.[98] He would only do so if he paid £20,000 into the new trust account, when he would be free to deal as he wished with the other £20,000 put into his private building society account.

11–26   (d) *Restriction to lowest intermediate balance.* If beneficiaries do seek to trace moneys remaining in a trustee's personal bank account, originally containing a mixture of their moneys and the trustee's private moneys, they cannot claim as their money an amount exceeding the lowest balance in the account since the date of mixing the moneys. Withdrawals reducing the amount of the account to a level below that of the trust money originally mixed must be withdrawals of trust money. The trust money once so reduced remains reduced despite any subsequent payments in to the account by the trustee (unless such payments represent

---

[96] *Gray v. Haig* (1855) 20 Beav. 214 at 226, *per* Romilly M.R.; and *Foster v. McKeown* [2000] 3 All E.R. 97, 125. As Staughton J. stated in *Indian Oil Corp. v. Greenstone Shipping SA* [1987] 3 All E.R. 893 at 906, "the wrongdoer must suffer from the resulting uncertainty."
[97] *Re Oatway* [1903] 2 Ch. 356; *Scott v. Scott* (1962) 109 C.L.R. 649.
[98] *Scott v. Scott* (1962) 109 C.L.R. 649; also see *Re Hughes* [1970] I.R. 237.

the proceeds of sale of traceable assets), since payments by him into his personal account are not presumed to be repayments of trust moneys so as to remedy his misconduct.[99] Thus, if T adds £2,000 trust moneys to his private £1,000, then dissipates £2,800 and then pays in £1,200 so that his account stands at £1,400, the beneficiaries can only claim the £200 lowest intermediate balance. If T had paid £1,200 into a trust account set up for the beneficiaries then he would be treated as intending his money to become trust money, as also if the £1,200 was the proceeds of sale of property purchased earlier with trust moneys in the mixed account.

(e) *Tracing through trustee's bank account and "backwards tracing".* **11–27** The starting point is that the beneficiaries will have a first charge or lien for their money on the mixed fund in T's account and any property purchased thereout,[1] though the mixed fund amount can be reduced to the lowest intermediate balance, as just discussed above, unless subsequent payments in represent the proceeds of traceable assets. Thus, once the account becomes overdrawn there will normally be no proprietary right against the account, just as where payment of trust money was initially made into an overdrawn account, thereby discharging the trustee's debt to his bank, there is normally no right to trace, the moneys having been dissipated in favour of a bona fide purchaser without notice.[2]

Exceptionally, where the trustee acquires an asset with moneys **11–28** borrowed from an overdrawn or loan account but intended when he incurred the borrowing to repay it out of trust moneys or where he paid trust money into his overdrawn account so as to reduce the overdraft and to make finance available within his overdraft limit to purchase a particular asset it seems[3] such asset can be traced so as to be subject to a lien or the beneficiaries' partial or total ownership under a constructive trust. Indeed, if the trustee bought an asset on credit putting up 25 per cent of the purchase price out of his own money, and then used trust money to pay off the outstanding 75 per cent balance this payment of the debt should be regarded by backwards tracing as just the delayed payment of part of the purchase price, so that the beneficiaries should be entitled to 75 per cent of the asset or a charge thereon for their money used to purchase the asset.[4] However, the stricter view is to consider that T's creditworthiness made him 100 per cent legal beneficial owner so the beneficiaries' moneys were dissipated in paying off a debt of T.[5]

---

[99] *Roscoe v. Winder* [1915] 1 Ch. 62 at 69; endorsed by CA in *Bishopsgate Investment Management Ltd v. Homan* [1995] Ch. 211 and P.C. in *Re Goldcorp Exchange Ltd* [1996] 2 All E.R. 806, 827, 831. *Lofts v. Macdonald* (1974) 3 A.L.R. 404; *Re Norman Estate* [1952] 1 D.L.R. 174.
[1] *Re Hallett's Estate* (1880) 13 Ch.D. 696; *Re Oatway* [1903] 2 Ch. 356; *Re Diplock* [1948] Ch. 465 at 538; *El Ajou v. Dollar Land Holdings plc* [1993] 3 All E.R. 713 at 735; [1994] 2 All E.R. 685 at 659, 701.
[2] *Bishopsgate Investment Management Ltd v. Homan* [1994] 3 W.L.R. 1270 at 1274.
[3] Scott V.-C. favours this in *Foskett v. McKeown* [1998] Ch. 265, 283–284, as do Vinelott J. and Dillon L.J. but not Leggatt L.J. in *Bishopsgate*, see *supra*.
[4] See L. Smith [1985] Camb. L.J. 90, and in *The Law of Tracing* (1997) p. 146.
[5] The position would be different if T were to purchase an asset one quarter at a time with each of four instalments and T only provided the first instalment.

Equity[6] has no difficulty in tracing money through bank clearing systems: it can trace money through back to back credit facilities[7] and can trace backwards by identifying a credit with a debit even where the credit entry was first in time.[8]

11–29 (f) *The swollen assets theory.* The lowest intermediate balance rule in *Roscoe v. Winder*[9] means that the right to trace normally disappears once the balance in an account falls to nil. Thus if P's £2 million is paid by D in breach of trust to D's bank account P's right to trace is worthless once the balance falls to nil. It has therefore been suggested[10] that, to prevent the unjust enrichment of D at P's expense and because D's assets were swollen by the payment, the court should grant P an equitable charge over all D's unencumbered assets, even though none of those assets can be identified on traditional tracing principles.

11–30 The riposte is that where D has used P's money to pay off X's debt (so that the balance falls to nil) D's assets have not been swollen. How can one say that the satisfaction of X's debt by incurring another of equal amount either decreases D's liabilities or increases his assets?[11] Thus, the general body of D's creditors does not benefit from D's wrong at P's expense.

However, Professor Jones has pointed out[12] that it should make a difference that P has come upon the scene so that, instead of a contest only between D's general creditors, the contest is now between P and the remaining general creditors of D. While the other general creditors did intend to advance credit to D and take the risk of his insolvency P never did. Thus, P should have priority over the general creditors' claim whose only possible claim is that D's payment to X was a preferential payment which should be set aside under the Insolvency Act 1986.

11–31 Lord Templeman in the Privy Council[13] subsequently provided some *obiter dicta* to support an equitable charge in P's favour in the above circumstances, though the force of his *dicta* are weakened by the fact that he appears to have thought that he was uttering conventional rather than heterodox (or even heretical) views. In the case, the bank trustee had lawfully (pursuant to a power in the trust instrument) deposited money as a loan with a bank (itself) which went into liquidation. The beneficiaries' claims therefore ranked as unsecured debts.

Lord Templeman contrasted this situation with the one where a bank trustee unlawfully dissipated trust moneys for its own purposes in circumstances where[14] "it is impossible for the beneficiaries to trace their

---

[6] Conventionally the common law cannot trace where moneys are mixed; *Agip (Africa) Ltd v. Jackson* [1991] Ch. 547; *Bank Tejerat v. Hong Kong & Shanghai Banking Co. Ltd* [1995] LL. Rep. 239.
[7] *El Ajou v. Dollar Land Holdings plc* [1993] 3 All E.R. 713; [1994] 2 All E.R. 685.
[8] *Agip (Africa) Ltd v. Jackson* [1991] Ch. 547, Millett L.J. (1995) K.C.L.J. 1 at 12.
[9] [1915] 1 Ch. 62.
[10] Goff & Jones Law of Restitution (5th ed.), pp. 98, 132.
[11] *Slater v. Oriental Mills* (1893) 27 A 443 at 444.
[12] (1988) 37 King's Counsel 15, 19.
[13] *Space Investments Ltd v. Canadian Imperial Bank of Commerce Trust Co.* [1986] 3 All E.R. 75.
[14] *ibid.* at 76–77.

money to any particular asset belonging to the trustee bank. But equity allows the beneficiaries to trace the trust money to all the assets of the bank and to recover the trust money by the exercise of an equitable charge over all the assets of the bank. . . . This priority is conferred because the customers and other unsecured creditors voluntarily accept the risk that the trustee bank might become insolvent and unable to discharge its obligations in full. On the other hand, the settlor and the beneficiaries under the trust never accept any risks involved in the possible insolvency of the bank. On the contrary, the settlor could be certain that if the trusts were lawfully administered the trustee bank could never make use of trust money for its own purposes and would always be obliged to segregate trust money . . . free from any risks involved in the possible insolvency of the trustee bank. It is therefore equitable that where the trustee bank has unlawfully misappropriated trust money by treating the trust money as though it belonged to the bank beneficially . . . then the claims of the beneficiaries should be paid in full out of the assets of the bank in priority to the claims of the customers and other unsecured creditors of the bank: 'if a man mixes trust funds with his own, the whole will be treated as the trust property' (*per* Jessel M.R. in *Re Hallett's Estate*[15])."

In these *dicta* Lord Templeman seems to be assuming that all the **11–32** assets of the trustee bank constitute one colossal fund so that the totality of its assets is subject to an equitable charge once the bank treats any trust property as part of its own assets. Jessel M.R., however, was only concerned with the case where a trustee mixes £X of trust money with his own £Y in a particular account and did not regard the rest of the trustee's property as affected by any equitable proprietary claim.

Professor Goode thus concludes,[16] "When the route taken by the money or property is clearly visible and leads to its dissipation, the notion that the claimant's proprietary rights are then replaced by a new equitable charge over the defendant's free assets at the expense of his unsecured creditors surely cannot be countenanced either in principle or in policy, for their infusion of funds against a defeated expectation is as much a contribution to the swelling of the debtor's estate as the infusion of the tracing claimant."

Recently, the Privy Council[17] and the Court of Appeal[18] have rejected **11–33** the swollen assets theory and restrictively distinguished Lord Templeman's remarks as not concerned at all with the situation where trust assets have been dissipated (via overdrawn accounts or otherwise), reaffirming *Roscoe v. Winder*[19] and the statement of the Court of Appeal in *Re Diplock*[20]:

---

[15] (1880) 13 Ch.D. 696 at 719.
[16] (1987) 103 L.Q.R. 433 at 447.
[17] *Re Goldcorp Exchange* [1995] 1 A.C. 74.
[18] *Bishopsgate Investment Management Ltd v. Homan* [1995] Ch. 211; in *Re Hallett & Co.* [1894] 2 Q.B. 237 at 245 Davey L.J. rejected the swollen assets approach.
[19] [1915] 1 Ch. 62, *supra*, para. 11–29.
[20] [1948] Ch. 465 at 521.

"The equitable remedies presuppose the continued existence of the money either as a separate fund or as part of a mixed fund or as latent in property acquired by means of such a fund. If such continued existence is not established equity is as helpless as the common law itself."

11–34   Thus, if the beneficiaries' £100,000 has been dissipated by T there can be no general equitable charge or lien over the whole of T's assets to secure the beneficiaries' claim to £100,000. However, if T mixed the £100,000 with moneys in his No. 1 account and then transferred money from it into his No. 2 account and his No. 3 account, and then purchased a painting with some money from his No. 2 account and a flat with some money from his No. 3 account, then Equity[21] imposes a charge over the No. 1 account which affects derivatively the No. 2 and No. 3 accounts and the painting and the flat, but not other assets of T. The beneficiaries thus have a charge for their £100,000 against an amalgam consisting of the No. 1, No. 2 and No. 3 accounts (subject to the effect of the *Roscoe v. Winder* intermediate balance rule) and the painting and the flat. Only if they seek a proportionate share of the painting or flat because of an appreciation in value thereof will they need to rely on the presumption[22] T acted honestly in using his own money first or on the presumption[23] that he used trust money because he cannot allege or prove he used his own money till he has reinstated the trust fund in a separate trust account. "As against the wrongdoer and his successors in title, the beneficiary is entitled to locate his contribution in any part of the mixture and to subordinate their claims to share in the mixture till his own contribution has been satisfied."[24]

Mixing of two or more trust funds by the trustee

11–35   If a trustee purchases property using moneys from different trusts then the trusts will share the property in the proportions in which they contributed to the purchase, whether the property appreciates or depreciates.[25] To this equitable result there is an exception where the trust moneys had been mixed in the same unbroken running account since by *Clayton's* case[26] payments out of such an account are presumed

---

[21] *e.g. El Ajou v. Dollar Land Holdings plc* [1993] 3 All E.R. 713 at 735–736; [1994] 2 All E.R. 685 at 659, 701; *Boscawen v. Bajwa* [1995] 4 All E.R. 769.

[22] *Re Hallett's Estate* (1880) 13 Ch.D. 696 at 727–728.

[23] *Re Oatway* [1903] 2 Ch. 356.

[24] *Foskett v. McKeown* [2000] 3 All E.R. 97, 124, *per* Lord Millett.

[25] They will adopt the purchased property as trust property where it has appreciated. If it has depreciated they will claim a charge on the property as security towards their personal claim, *e.g.* if T used £10,000 cash from Trust A's account and £5,000 from Trust B's account to purchase a car now depreciated in value the car will be charged to Trust A and to Trust B in the proportion 2:1, so if sold for £9,000 Trust A will receive £6,000 and Trust B £3,000. *Lord Provost of Edinburgh v. Lord Advocate* (1879) 4 App.Cas. 823; *Re Diplock* [1948] Ch. 465 at 533, 534, 539; *Sinclair v. Brougham* [1914] A.C. 398.

[26] (1816) 1 Mer. 572. There must be an unbroken account between the parties, *e.g.* a current account, a solicitor's trust account, a moneylender's account: it does not apply where there are distinct and separate debts. See *The Mecca* [1897] A.C. 286; *Re Sherry* (1884) 25 Ch.D. 692 at 702. The rule does not apply to entries on the same day: it is the end-of-day balance that counts: *The Mecca* at 291.

to be made in the same order as payments in (*i.e.* first in first out) and the courts have been surprisingly ready to apply this rule between banker and customer to regulate the position between beneficiary and beneficiary.[27]

Take the following payments into T's empty bank account: (i) £1,000 from Trust A (ii) £2,000 from Trust B (iii) £3,000 from Trust C. Then T withdraws £2,000 which he dissipates on a holiday, and on his return he purchases shares for £4,000 which are now worth £6,000. The most equitable course would be to divide the shares between Trusts A, B and C in the proportions 1:2:3 so that each trust would recover its original moneys, £1,000, £2,000 and £3,000.[28] But if *Clayton's* case is applied, the withdrawn £2,000 exhausts the funds of Trust A and reduces Trust B's funds to £1,000. Thus the £4,000 invested in shares represents £1,000 of Trust B's funds and £3,000 of Trust C's funds. Therefore, one-quarter of the shares belongs to Trust B and three-quarters to Trust C, and poor Trust A has lost all its money. If T sold a quarter of the shares this would not be treated as sale of Trust B's shares but as a sale of a shareholding made up as to one-quarter with Trust B's shares and three-quarters with Trust C's shares.[29]

Clayton's case can easily lead to arbitrary and inconvenient results and **11–36** it is surprising to see Chancery courts happy to apply a common-law rule, as to the appropriation of payments between debtor and creditor in a running account, to the equitable proprietary rights of beneficiaries between themselves.[30] In a simple example, like that above where the proportions attributable to the possible claimants are easily ascertainable, it is difficult to see the justification for applying *Clayton's* case. At best, it ought to be restricted to fiduciaries (like solicitors or investment managers and custodians) who keep what are virtually banking accounts for their clients where there are so many transactions with so many clients spread over a considerable period that it would be controversial and impracticable to attempt to ascertain the amount of each client's contribution. It was for such a situation that the "first in, first out" rule was developed.

In England, the Court of Appeal[31] in 1992 reaffirmed the general **11–37** application of *Clayton's* case as a convenient rule, except where its application would be impracticable or would result in injustice between

---

[27] *Hancock v. Smith* (1889) 41 Ch.D. 456 at 461; *Re Stenning* [1895] 2 Ch. 433; *Re Diplock* (1948) Ch. 465 at 554; Fry J. in *Re Hallett's Estate* (1879) 13 Ch.D. 696 at 704.

[28] In *Re British Red Cross Balkan Fund* [1914] 2 Ch. 419, £28,682 was subscribed by 3,254 persons and at the end of the war £12,655 remained. If *Clayton's* case applied subscriptions before November 8, 1912 would be treated as having been withdrawn from the bank account, so that subscribers after that date would be entitled to the surplus. Astbury J. held that the surplus belonged to all 3,254 subscribers rateably, saying *Clayton's* case was "a mere rule of evidence and not an invariable rule of law." See also the rateable division of assets between depositors and shareholders in *Sinclair v. Brougham* [1914] A.C. 398 and between sets of beneficiaries in *Re Ontario Securities Commission* (1987) 30 D.L.R. (4th) 1, affirmed on appeal (1988) 52 D.L.R. (4th) 767, and between clients of an insolvent futures dealer who kept the clients' moneys in a separate account regarded as a trust account: *Re Eastern Capital Futures Ltd* [1989] B.C.L.C. 223.

[29] *Re Diplock* [1948] Ch. 465 at 554–555: each parcel of shares withdrawn from the whole shareholding is treated as made up of an aliquot proportion of the shareholding bought with the trust moneys.

[30] D. A. McConville (1963) 79 L.Q.R. 388.

[31] *Barlow Clowes International Ltd v. Vaughan* [1992] 4 All E.R. 22.

the claimants because a relatively small number would obtain most of the funds or it would be contrary to the express or implied intention of the claimants. The Court of Appeal found that the claimants expected their moneys to be pooled in what was effectively a collective investment scheme so that they should share rateably what was left in the pool. However, Woolf and Leggatt L.JJ.[32] indicated that the "rolling charge" solution might be fairer than a rateable sharing so that beneficiaries should share loss in proportion to their interest in the account immediately before each withdrawal[33] unless such a calculation should prove too difficult and expensive. Thus, a first instance judge seems to have leeway not to apply the "first in first out" rule but a rateable sharing or the "rolling charge" solution except where this would be too difficult and expensive in relation to the sums involved.

In New Zealand,[34] Canada[35] and New South Wales[36] the application of *Clayton's Case* has been rejected where an investment manager or solicitor has mixed hundreds of clients' moneys in a trust account. After the size of the net global fund of such clients has been ascertained, taking account of the lowest intermediate balance rule and traceable assets representing invested moneys, such net trust fund is divided rateably according to the amounts of clients' contributions to it. The court does not try to earmark each client's contribution and treat it as a separate trust subject to the lowest intermediate balance rule and so untraceable once the contribution has been dissipated in accordance with any "first in first out" rule.

11-38 Finally, if the mixed fund contains not just the money of two or more trusts but the trustee's own money as well, one must first apply the principles applicable to a trustee's own money and trust money of an amount corresponding to the aggregate value of all the mixed trust funds. Once the total entitlement of these trust funds has thereby been determined one applies the principles just discussed to apportioning this entitlement between the funds.

Mixing of trust money with an innocent volunteer's money

11-39 A volunteer (*i.e.* someone who has provided no consideration) must be distinguished from a purchaser, since the equitable tracing remedy fails where the property sought to be traced has reached the hands of a bona fide purchaser for value without notice of the claimant's equitable rights.[37] If, at the time of purchase or receipt, a purchaser or a volunteer has knowledge of the breach of trust, then they rank as constructive trustees[38] and so are treated as trustees if they knowingly mix their own assets with trust assets.

---

[32] *ibid.* at 35 and 44.
[33] *e.g.*, if in the above example of Trusts A, B and C with £1,000, £2,000 and £3,000 respectively, £3,000 were dissipated and then £3,000 were spent on an asset now worth £12,000, the £3,000 spent would be treated as owned by A, B and C in the ratio 1:2:3 so A would contribute £500, B £1,000 and C £1,500.
[34] *Re Registered Securities* [1991] 1 N.Z.L.R. 545.
[35] *Ontario Securities Commission v. Greymac Credit Corp.* (1998) 52 D.L.R. (4th) 767.
[36] *Keefe v. Law Society* (1998) 44 N.S.W.L.R. 45.
[37] *Taylor v. Blakelock* (1886) 32 Ch.D. 560; *Re Diplock* [1948] Ch. 465 at 539.
[38] See *infra*, paras 11–110 *et seq.*

If an innocent volunteer happens to mix trust moneys with his own moneys and purchase property therewith,[39] then he and the trust beneficiaries will share the property in the proportions in which they contributed to the purchase, whether the property appreciates or depreciates.[40] Their position *vis-à-vis* one another is the same as that between beneficiaries of separate trust funds whose moneys have been mixed together.[41] It follows that there is the same exceptional result where the innocent volunteer's moneys and the trust moneys have been mixed in the same current bank account. Prima facie the court will apply *Clayton's* case and presume that withdrawals from the account are made in the order in which moneys were first paid into the account.[42] This has already been considered and criticised and it will be seen (*infra* at para. 11–48) that the new defence of change of position should significantly help some innocent volunteers. If the innocent volunteer, who has paid trust moneys into his current account, pays into an interest-bearing account designated as the trust account as soon as he learns of the trust claim, then this will be regarded as effectively unmixing the fund so that the trust claim will relate only to the money in the designated trust account.[43]

Equitable lien or equitable ownership: whose election?

The remedy of an equitable lien or charge is an effective persistent **11–40** remedy because if trust moneys are mixed in the trustee's private account the equitable charge follows such mixed fund when part thereof is paid into other accounts of the trustee or of third parties who are not bona fide purchasers without notice or is used to purchase assets. There is a charge over the amalgam of those accounts and assets to secure the beneficiaries' claims.[44]

---

[39] If the moneys are dissipated the loss is borne rateably: *Re Diplock* [1948] Ch. 465; K. Hodkinson [1983] Conv. 135 at 138–139.

[40] *Re Diplock* [1948] Ch. 465 at 524, 539. Ideally, there should further be an allowance made to the volunteer in respect of any efforts or skills utilised in enhancing the value of the asset by analogy with *Boardman v. Phipps* [1967] 2 A.C. 46, *supra*, at para. 6–26. This should be enforceable as a personal claim against the trust beneficiaries: K. Hodkinson [1983] Conv. 135. Indeed, to prevent the claimant recovering "a windfall" benefit (*e.g.* where fortuitously £5 of trust moneys was used to help purchase £10 of lottery tickets, which the innocent volunteer would have bought with his own money if he knew the £5 was tainted and which produce £6 million winnings) the innocent volunteer ought not to have to share the winnings half and half but only have the winnings subject to a charge for £10, as discussed under the next heading.

[41] *ibid.* Placing the innocent volunteer on a par with the trust beneficiaries does not infringe the principle that equitable rights prevail except against a bona fide purchaser of a legal interest for value without notice. Here we are concerned with the earlier identification process ascertaining in what assets the beneficiaries' equitable rights subsist and ascertaining what assets are to be treated as the volunteer's own property.

[42] *Re Diplock* [1948] Ch. 465 at 554.

[43] *Re Diplock* [1948] Ch. 465 at 551–552 dealing with the claim against the National Institute for the Deaf, reversed on an amended statement of facts: *ibid.* at 559. Similarly, it would seem that if a trustee mixes two trust funds in one account and purports to withdraw a sum for a beneficiary of one trust but actually uses it for his own purposes the sum should be allocated to that particular trust: *Re Stillman and Wilson* (1950) 15 A.B.C. 68; *Re Registered Securities* [1991] 1 N.Z.L.R. 545.

[44] *e.g. Re Goldcorp Exchange* [1994] 2 All E.R. 806 at 831, "In the case of a bank which employs all borrowed money as a mixed fund for the purpose of lending out money or making investments any trust money unlawfully borrowed by a bank trustee may be said to be latent in the property acquired by the bank and the court may impose an equitable lien on that property for the recovery of the trust money." Also see *El Ajou v. Dollar Land Holdings plc* [1993] 3 All E.R. 717; [1994] 2 All E.R. 685 and *Foskett v. McKeown* [2000] 3 All E.R. 97.

If, due to an appreciation in value of particular assets that can be traced by transactional proprietary links, the beneficiaries seek equitable ownership under a constructive trust rather than a lien are they always entitled to do this? Does it depend upon whether or not the defendant is insolvent—or whether or not the defendant is a trustee or an innocent volunteer?

11–41   Indeed, what is the nature of the beneficiaries' claim? Do they have a vested equitable interest, so that if T uses trust money to purchase land and subsequently creates an equitable mortgage over it, the mortgagee will take subject to the beneficiaries' interests, even where he is a purchaser of his equitable interest without notice of the beneficiaries' interest? Conventionally so, according to *Cave v. Cave*,[45] though in Ireland[46] Porter M.R., fearing for equitable mortgagees unable to discover tracing rights, has preferred to regard the beneficiaries as having a mere equity or a mere power to recover the property, so that a purchaser of an equitable interest without notice will be safe. More recently,[47] there was support for the view that the beneficiaries' proprietary claim to a lien or proportionate share contingent on tracing principles is in the nature of a power floating above the relevant property until the power is exercised and crystallises into a full equitable interest affecting the relevant property. However, it is now apparent from *Foskett v. McKeown*[48] that the proprietary claim is a continuing equitable interest.

Anyhow, to return to the question of electing between the two possible remedies, let us consider the case where T, a trustee, in breach of trust pays £10,000 trust money into his account containing £40,000 and purchases a £50,000 flat, now worth £100,000, or wrongfully pays the £10,000 to D, an innocent donee, who uses it with his own £40,000 to purchase a £50,000 flat, now worth £100,000.

11–42   Let us assume in favour of D that he is wealthy and would, anyhow, have bought the flat wholly with his own money if he knew that he was not entitled to the £10,000: indeed, let us assume he had a £15,000 overdraft facility which would have been called upon pro tanto if he had not received the £10, 000. Should D not therefore be able to resist the beneficiaries' claim to 20 per cent of the flat rather than a charge for £10, 000? Should the law not be that they should need to go further than

---

[45] (1880) 15 Ch.D. 639.

[46] *Re French's Estate* (1887) 21 L.R. (Ir) 283 at 312: FitzGibbon and Barry L.J. rested their judgments on the conduct of the beneficiaries and the trustees but overlooked *Shrophsire Union Railways v. R.* (1875) L.R. 7 H.L. 496.

[47] *El Ajou v. Dollar Land Holdings plc* [1993] 3 All E.R. 717 at 737 ("notional" right to obtain an equitable charge sufficed while traceable assets passing through non-trust countries not recognising any equitable rights) and *Lipkin Gorman v. Karpnale Ltd* [1991] 2 A.C. 548 (firm's interest not sufficient to support an action for conversion) discussed by P. B. H. Birks (ed.) *Laundering and Tracing* (1995), pp. 307–311. In *Boscawen v. Bajwa* [1995] 4 All E.R. 769 at 783 Millett L.J. significantly left open the position of a purchaser of an equitable interest without notice of an equitable right of subrogation.

[48] [2000] 3 All E.R. 97, 120: "A beneficiary of a trust is entitled to a continuing beneficial interest not merely in the trust property but in its traceable proceeds also, and his interest binds everyone who takes the property or its traceable proceeds except a bona fide purchaser [of a legal interest] for value without notice."

simply proving transactional proprietary links and as a matter of causation prove that property in which they claim a proportionate share would not have been bought but for their money?[49] If they were joint purchasers there would, of course, be a purchase money presumed resulting trust in the proportions contributed. However, D did not intend to be a joint purchaser but sole purchaser. He was misled to change his position by fortuitously using the trust money rather than his own available resources, so why should the beneficiaries benefit to the detriment of D or D's trustee in bankruptcy? They surely cannot prove that D would be unjustly enriched at their expense if allowed to retain the flat subject only to a lien to satisfy the beneficiaries's claim.

Support for this view is provided by *Re Tilley's W.T.*[50] where the **11–43** plaintiffs could not prove as a matter of causation that the defendant would not have bought the land in question but for using the plaintiffs' money which represented a small percentage of the purchase price which could have come, anyway, from ample overdraft facilities available for the wealthy defendant. However, the judge would have imposed a lien[51] on the land purchased out of mixed funds in the defendant's account except that this was unnecessary when the defendant was clearly good for the money claimed, namely £2,237 trust moneys.

It so happened that the defendant was actually the sole trustee and life tenant of her husband's will trusts who had "innocently", but mis-guidedly, intermingled trust moneys with her own in very successful property speculations. It is most surprising that the judge developed the concept of an "innocent" trustee to allow such to escape liability unless the plaintiffs could establish as a matter of causation that the defendant was unjustly enriched at the plaintiffs' expense because but for the value input of the plaintiffs' property the defendant would not have acquired the land in which the plaintiffs claimed a proportionate share.

It is submitted that such "but for" causation should be necessary if a **11–44** constructive trust of a proportionate share is to be imposed on persons innocent of any knowledge that they are dealing will trust money, so as to capture the profit for the plaintiffs and make it unavailable to the defendants or their creditors on their insolvency. Where, however, it is the trustee who wrongfully uses trust money then, whether the trustee be wicked or innocent, it is submitted that actual causation is immaterial and that the trustee should not be allowed to dispute the beneficiaries' claims and try to wriggle off the hook upon which he has placed himself: the public interest in the integrity of trusteeship and conscientious performance of their duties requires a strict approach to liability.[52] The beneficiaries should be entitled to their pound of flesh if they want. It should make no difference whether the defendant trustee be solvent or

---

[49] See D.J. Hayton in P. B. H. Birks (ed.), *op. cit.* at 4–12 and 21.
[50] [1967] Ch. 1179. Significantly, in *Westdeutsche Landesbank v. Islington B.C.* [1994] 4 All E.R. 890 at 938, Hobhouse J. endorsed the *Re Tilley's W.T.* approach to the Plaintiff's burden of proof.
[51] *ibid.* at 1193. This accords with basic principle as expounded in cases in n. 44.
[52] *e.g. Boardman v. Phipps* [1967] 2 A.C. 46, *supra* para. 6–46; D. J. Hayton in P. B. H. Birks (ed.) *op. cit.* pp. 10–11; *Foskett v. McKeown* [2000] 3 All E.R. 97, 126.

insolvent, though on pragmatic policy grounds some commercial lawyers[53] would prefer to favour the creditors of an insolvent trustee by requiring the plaintiffs, if they seek not a charge but a proportionate share, to discharge the onus of proving that the asset in which they claim a beneficial interest would not have been purchased but for the use of their money or other value input.

Loss of right to trace

11-45 (1) If property has reached the hands of a bona fide purchaser of a legal interest for value without notice,[54] though any proceeds of sale of such property may be traceable.[55]

(2) If the plaintiff acquiesced in the wrongful mixing or distribution.[56]

(3) If property has been dissipated so that tracing is physically impossible, *e.g.* trust moneys were spent on a world cruise, a party, extinguishing a debt.[57] However, if a trustee pays off a mortgage over his private property by using trust moneys then the equitable doctrine of subrogation comes into play so that the beneficiaries are subrogated to the security of the mortgage[58]: the trustee cannot be heard to say that he had paid out the beneficiaries' money otherwise than for their benefit and so is treated as having an intention to keep the mortgage alive in equity.[59]

(4) If it would be inequitable to allow the plaintiff to trace against an innocent volunteer in the particular circumstances?[60] or if the new general defence of change of position is otherwise available.[61] Thus if an innocent volunteer spends money on altering or improving his land there can be no declaration of charge and consequently no tracing for the method of enforcing a charge is by sale which would force the volunteer to exchange his land and buildings for money: an inequitable possibility, particularly if it may be that the alterations had not enhanced the value of the property.

---

[53] *Westdeutsche Landesbank v. Islington B.C.* [1994] 4 All E.R. 890 at 938 *per* Hobhouse J; and Goff & Jones, *Low of Restitution* (5th ed.), pp. 81 and 118.

[54] *Re Diplock* [1948] Ch. 465 at 539; *Foskett v. McKeown*, [2000] 3 All E.R. 97, 120. Except where land is purchased the concept of constructive notice is rather restricted: see *infra*, para. 11–112. If the wrongdoing trustee acquired the property from such a purchaser without notice he would be susceptible to tracing: *Re Stapleford Colliery Co.* (1880) 14 Ch.D. 432 at 445.

[55] *Lake v. Bayliss* [1974] 2 All E.R. 1114 (vendor under contract of sale of land to P1 held on constructive trust for P1 so that when V sold to P2, P1 could trace those proceeds of sale).

[56] *Blake v. Gale* (1886) 32 Ch.D. 571.

[57] *Re Diplock* [1948] Ch. 465 at 521, 549.

[58] *Boscawen v. Bajwa* [1995] 4 All E.R. 769.

[59] *ibid.* at 781. However, the House of Lords in *Banque Financière de la Cite v. Parc (Battersea) Ltd* [1998] 1 All E.R. 737 has held that, unlike contractual subrogation cases, equitable subrogation does not entirely hinge on questions of intention but is based simply on the prevention of unjust enrichment.

[60] *Re Diplock* [1948] Ch. 465 at 546–550; *Boscawen v. Bajwa* [1995] 4 All E.R. 769, 783.

[61] *Boscawen v. Bajwa* [1995] 4 All E.R. 769, 776, "If all else fails he will raise the defence of innocent change of position" per Millett L.J.

The general defence of change of position

The USA Restatement of Restitution[62] defines the defence as follows: **11–46**

> "(1) The right of a person to restitution from another because of a benefit received is terminated or diminished if, after the receipt of the benefit, circumstances have so changed that it would be inequitable to require the other to make full restitution.
>
> (2) Change of circumstances may be a defense or a partial defense if the conduct of the recipient was not tortious and he was no more at fault for his receipt, retention or dealing with the subject matter than was the claimant."

The Lords in *Lipkin Gorman v. Karpnale*[63] have now recognised change of position as a defence to restitutionary actions, while leaving its scope to develop on a case by case basis. "Where an innocent defendant's position has so changed that he will suffer an injustice if called upon to repay in full, the injustice of requiring him so to repay outweighs the injustice of denying the plaintiff restitution. If the plaintiff pays money to the defendant under a mistake of fact, and the defendant then, in good faith, pays the money or part of it to charity, it is unjust to require him to make restitution to the extent that he has so changed his position. Likewise, if a thief steals my money and pays it to a third party who gives it away to charity, that third party should have a good defence to an action for money had and received." This should enable a more generous approach to be taken to the recognition of the right to restitution in the knowledge that the defence is available in appropriate cases.[64] Significantly, Lord Goff also stated,[65] "At present, I do not wish to state the principle any less broadly than this: that the defence is available to a person whose position has so changed that it would be inequitable in all the circumstances to require him to make restitution, or alternatively, to make restitution in full. I wish to stress, however, that the mere fact the defendant has spent the money, in whole or in part, does not of itself render it inequitable that he should be called upon to repay, because the expenditure might in any event have been incurred by him in the ordinary course of things."

A plaintiff has a right to restitution[66] where the defendant was (i) **11–47** enriched (ii) at the expense of the plaintiff (iii) in unjust circumstances where there was no legitimate ground for the defendant's enrichment and (iv) there has been no change of position by the defendant justifying refusal to make restitution in full or in part. Most restitutionary claims are personal claims for enrichment received (the first measure of

---

[62] Para. 142; see also para. 69.
[63] [1991] 2 A.C. 548 at 579.
[64] *ibid.*, 581.
[65] [1991] 2 A.C. 548, 580. Also *Derby v. Scottish Equitable plc* [2001] EWCA Civ 369.
[66] P. B. H. Birks, *Introduction to the Law of Restitution* (1985); Goff & Jones, *Law of Restitution* (5th ed.); A. S. Burrows, *The Law of Restitution* (2nd ed.).

restitutionary liability). Some restitutionary claims are claims for enrichment traceably surviving (the second measure) and these claims will usually be proprietary claims.

In *Foskett v. McKeown*[67] the House of Lords, however, rejected the view that a proprietary tracing claim is a restitutionary action to prevent unjust enrichment, the claimants seeking[68] "to vindicate their property rights, not to reverse unjust enrichment." Lord Millett pointedly stated,[69] "A claim in unjust enrichment is subject to a change of position defence, which usually operates by reducing or extinguishing the element of enrichment. An action like the present [a proprietary tracing claim] is subject to the bona fide purchaser for value defence, which operates to clear the defendant's title", but by implication not to the change of position defence, although in *Boscawen v. Bajwa*[70] he had accepted that there could be such a defence to a proprietary tracing claim, regarding such defence to be a logical development from the *Re Diplock*[71] discretion not to permit a proprietary claim if it would be inequitable (or "unfair" as Lord Browne–Wilkinson stated[72] in accepting such discretion). It is submitted that it is in accord with Lord Goff's broad view of the developing defence of change of position to follow Lord Millett's *dicta* in *Boscawen* rather than those in *Foskett*.

Where the defendant makes out the defence of change of position[73] any claims will be reduced to the extent that he can deny that his estate remains enriched, so that they will be reduced to the amount by which his wealth remains enhanced. Thus, if he innocently receives £10,000 of trust money which he uses to take up an opportunity to buy Good Ltd shares and, then, decides to spend £8,000 from his building society deposit account to have a special holiday which he would not have done but for receiving the £10,000 increase in his wealth, he should not be liable beyond £2,000 for which there can be a lien over the shares or, as a condition of the claimant obtaining the Good shares, he should remedy the defendant's £8,000 change of position.

11–48   Indeed, it seems likely that the developing defence of change of position will compel reconsideration of the traditional[74] pro rata or first in first out approaches where trust moneys are mixed with those of an innocent volunteer. Take the case where D is wrongly paid £1,200 from a trust fund of which P is a beneficiary and innocently pays this into his deposit account containing £600. Then, D takes a holiday costing £1,200 which he would not have taken but for receiving the £1,200. Traditional case law requires the £600 remaining in the account to be charged pro rata as to £400 for P and £200 for D, while if the account had been a

---

[67] [2000] 3 All E.R. 97.
[68] *ibid.*, 121.
[69] *ibid.*, 22.
[70] [1995] 4 All E.R. 769, 776, 783. Also at All Souls College Oxford Symposium, April 19, 2001.
[71] [1948] Ch. 465, 548.
[72] [2000] 3 All E.R. 97, 102.
[73] See P. Key (1995) 58 M.L.R. 505; R. C. Nolan and P. B. H. Birks in Birks (ed.) *Laundering and Tracing* Chaps. 6 and 11 respectively; Goff & Jones, Law of Restitution (5th ed.), p. 825.
[74] See *supra*, para. 11–39.

current account D would have been taken to spend his £600 first so that the £600 remaining would belong to P.[75] The impact of D's change of position ought to be that the remaining £600 should belong to D because he should have a complete defence to the claim for £1,200, excluding P's claim to have a restitutionary proprietary power to trace the trust money.

Voluntary expenditure made in detrimental reliance upon receipt of the plaintiff's property is the main basis for change of position and this will exclude expenditure that the defendant would have made anyway and the discharging of the defendant's pre-existing debts.[76] Loss of enrichment by theft or destruction should also suffice for change of position because the defendant is no longer enriched and would suffer detriment if he had to make restitution because he would then be in a worse position than the one he would have occupied if he had never received the enrichment.

Where detriment was incurred prior to receipt of the enrichment it **11–49** has been held at first instance[77] that the plea of change of position cannot be maintained. Clearly, this is right where the pre-receipt loss was not the result of detrimental reliance on the expectation of receiving an enrichment. However, where the causal connection is made out and the defendant has then actually received the anticipated enrichment which he is asked to return, he should be allowed to subtract the amount of his pre-receipt detrimental reliance from the amount claimed.[78] How arbitrary and capricious it would be if D had a defence when he or his bank paid out £x one hour after he received £x but not if the £x was paid out one hour before the expected £x was received (so that the risk of non-receipt of £x did not materialise and can be disregarded).

However, D cannot maintain change of position if he is a wrongdoer **11–50** or does not act in good faith.[79] Clearly, once D has actual Nelsonian or naughty knowledge[80] of the facts entitling P to restitution he cannot in all honesty take advantage of any subsequent change of position. Where D has constructive notice (because he ought to have known in all the circumstances[81]) so that he has failed to take reasonable precautions, so as to act unreasonably in assuming the enrichment is his, it seems likely that change of position should not be open to him.[82] However, if D has

---

[75] Correspondingly, if P's £1,200 had been paid in before D's £600 then the £600 remaining would belong to D.

[76] *Scottish Equitable plc v. Derby* [2000] 3 All E.R. 793; *Philip Collins Ltd v. Davis* [2000] 3 All E.R. 808, which cases also reveal that the all or nothing defence of estoppel (*Avon C.C. v. Howlett* [1983] 1 W.L.R. 605) is no longer apt for restitutionary claims where the more flexible change of position defence is available.

[77] *South Tyneside M.B.C. v. Svenska International* [1995] 1 All E.R. 545.

[78] P. Key (1995) 58 M.L.R. 505 at 513–514; R. C. Nolan and P. B. H. Birks in Birks (ed.) *Laundering and Tracing*, pp. 168 and 329; Goff & Jones, *Law of Restitution* (5th ed.), p. 823.

[79] *Lipkin Gorman v. Karpnale Ltd* [1991] 2 A.C. 548 at 580.

[80] See *infra*, para. 11–111.

[81] In the commercial context (outside the conveyancing mechanics on purchase of land), however, it seems a purchaser will only have constructive notice where he has actual, Nelsonian or naughty knowledge (*Polly Peck International plc v. Nadir (No. 2)* [1992] 4 All E.R. 769) while donees need make no inquiry unless they are aware of suspicious circumstances that would make an honest donee inquire further.

[82] R. C. Nolan and P. B. H. Birks in Birks (ed.) *Laundering and Tracing* pp. 155–156 and 325; but *cf.* Goff & Jones, *Law of Restitution* (5th ed.) p. 826 requiring "a want of probity."

no knowledge or constructive notice of the facts entitling P to restitution, so that he thinks he is free to deploy the resources apparently at his disposal, then the reasonableness of D's conduct ought not to be a relevant factor, *e.g.* if his negligence is responsible for loss or destruction of a relevant asset.[83]

Detailed rigorous guidelines ought to be developed by the courts as to the new defence of change of position so that they avoid intuitive value judgments in the loaded simple question, "Is it inequitable to require restitution or for the defendant's property to be subject to a charge in favour of the claimant or to be wholly or partly owned by the claimant?"

BOSCAWEN V. BAJWA

Chancery Division [1995] 4 All E.R. 769.

11–51   Dave & Co., solicitors for the prospective purchaser of Bajwa's house acted also for the Abbey National, which transferred £140,000 to Dave & Co. to be used only to complete the purchase and until then to be held for the Abbey National. In breach of trust Dave paid £137,405 to Bajwa's solicitors to hold to Dave's order till completion and then sent them Dave's cheque for £2,595 which "bounced" just after Bajwa's solicitors had precipitately paid £140,000 to Bajwa's mortgagee, the Halifax B.S. to discharge its mortgage on Bajwa's house.

The sale fell through. The plaintiff, a judgment creditor of Bajwa, obtained a charging order absolute over the house, which was sold and the £105,311 net proceeds of sale were paid into court.

It was held that the Abbey National was entitled to all these proceeds. It had priority over the plaintiff because its moneys could be traced into the payment to the Halifax B.S. and it was entitled to be subrogated to Halifax's legal charge. Bajwa's freehold was subject to a charge in equity by way of subrogation in favour of the Abbey National when the plaintiff obtained his interest under the charging order.

11–52   MILLETT J. *"Tracing and subrogation.:* The submission that the deputy judge illegitimately conflated two different causes of action, the equitable tracing claim and the claim to a right of subrogation, betrays a confusion of thought which arises from the admittedly misleading terminology which is traditionally used in the context of equitable claims for restitution. Equity lawyers habitually use the expressions "the tracing claim" and "the tracing remedy" to describe the proprietary claim and the proprietary remedy which equity makes available to the beneficial owner who seeks to recover his property in specie from those into whose hands it has come. Tracing properly so-called, however, is neither a claim nor a remedy but a process. Moreover, it is not confined to the case where the plaintiff seeks a proprietary remedy; it is equally necessary where he seeks a personal remedy against the knowing recipient or knowing assistant. It is the process by which the plaintiff traces what has happened to his property, identifies the persons who have handled or received it, and justifies his claim that the money which they handled or received. Unless he can prove this, he cannot (in the traditional language of equity) raise an equity against the defendant or (in

---

[83] R. C. Nolan, *op. cit.* at 158, P. Key (1995) 58 M.L.R. 505 at 515–516, 522.

the modern language of restitution) show that the defendant's unjust enrichment was at his expense.

"In such a case, the defendant will either challenge the plaintiff's claim that **11–53** the property in question represents his property (*i.e.* he will challenge the validity of the tracing exercise), or he will raise a priority dispute (*e.g.* by claiming to be a bona fide purchaser without notice). If all else fails, he will raise the defence of innocent change of position. This was not a defence which was recognised in England before 1991, but it was widely accepted throughout the common law world. In *Lipkin Gorman (a firm) v. Karpnale Ltd* [1991] 2 A.C. 548 the House of Lords acknowledged it to be part of English law also. The introduction of this defence not only provides the court with a means of doing justice in future, but allows a re-examination of many decisions of the past in which the absence of the defence may have led judges to distort basic principles in order to avoid injustice to the defendant.

"If the plaintiff succeeds in tracing his property, whether in its original or in **11–54** some changed form, into the hands of the defendant and overcomes any defences which are put forward on the defendant's behalf, he is entitled to a remedy. The remedy will be fashioned to the circumstances. The plaintiff will generally be entitled to a personal remedy; if he seeks a proprietary remedy he must usually prove that the property to which he lays claim is still in the ownership of the defendant. If he succeeds in doing this, the court will treat the defendant as holding the property on a constructive trust for the plaintiff and will order the defendant to transfer it in specie to the plaintiff. But this is only one of the proprietary remedies which is available to a court of equity. If the plaintiff's money has been applied by the defendant, for example, not in the acquisition of a landed property but in its improvement, then the court may treat the land as charged with the payment to the plaintiff of a sum representing the amount by which the value of the defendant's land has been enhanced by the use of the plaintiff's money. And if the plaintiff's money has been used to discharge a mortgage on the defendant's land, then the court may achieve a similar result by treating the land as subject to a charge by way of subrogation in favour of the plaintiff.

"Subrogation, therefore, is a remedy, not a cause of action (see Goff and **11–55** Jones *Law of Restitution* (4th ed., 1993) at 589 ff, *Orakpo v. Manson Investments Ltd* [1978] A.C. 95 at 104 *per* Lord Diplock and *Re TH Knitwear (Wholesale) Ltd* [1988] Ch. 275 at 284 *per* Slade L.J.). It is available in a wide variety of different factual situations in which it is required in order to reverse the defendant's unjust enrichment. Equity lawyers speak of a right of subrogation, or of an equity of subrogation, but this merely reflects the fact that it is not a remedy which the court has a general discretion to impose whenever it thinks it just to do so. The equity arises from the conduct of the parties on well-settled principles and in defined circumstances which make it unconscionable for the defendant to deny the proprietary interest claimed by the plaintiff. A constructive trust arises in the same way. Once the equity is established the court satisfies it by declaring that the property in question is subject to a charge by way of subrogation in the one case or a constructive trust in the other.

"Accordingly, there was nothing illegitimate in the deputy judge's invocation of the two doctrines of tracing and subrogation in the same case. They arose at different stages of the proceedings. Tracing was the process by which the Abbey National sought to establish that its money was applied in the discharge of the Halifax's charge; subrogation was the remedy which it sought in order to deprive Mr Bajwa (through whom the appellants claim) of the unjust enrichment which he would thereby otherwise obtain at the Abbey National's expense.

Tracing

11–56　　"It is still a prerequisite of the right to trace in equity that there must be a fiduciary relationship which calls the equitable jurisdiction into being (see *Agip (Africa) Ltd v. Jackson* [1991] Ch. 547 at 566 *per* Fox L.J.). That requirement is satisfied in the present case by the fact that from the first moment of its receipt by Dave in its general client account the £140,000 was trust money held in trust for the Abbey National. The appellants do not dispute that the Abbey National can successfully trace £137,405 of its money into Hill Lawson's client account. But they do dispute the judge's finding that it can trace the sum further into the payment to the Halifax.

"The £137,405 was paid into Hill Lawson's general client account at the bank because it was only intended to be kept for a short time. Funds which were held for clients for any length of time were held in separate designated accounts. Hill Lawson's ledger cards showed Mr Bajwa as the relevant client. According to Mr Duckney, Hill Lawson also held other funds for Mr Bajwa which were the result of an inheritance which he had received. These were the source from which Hill Lawson made good the shortfall of £2,595 which arose when Dave's cheque was dishonoured. The amount of these other funds is unknown, though it was certainly nothing like £140,000. The evidence does not show whether they were held in Hill Lawson's general client account or whether they were held in a separate designated account. If they were held in the general client account, the £137,405 received from Dave was (quite properly) mixed not only with moneys belonging to other clients but also with money belonging to Mr Bajwa. Hill Lawson can be presumed not to have committed a breach of trust by resorting to moneys belonging to other clients, but they were perfectly entitled to use Mr Bajwa's own money to discharge the Halifax's charge on his property. Whether they did so or not cannot be determined in the absence of any evidence of the amount involved. Accordingly, it is submitted, the Abbey National has failed to establish how much of its money was applied in the discharge of the Halifax's charge and how much of the money which was applied for this purpose was Mr Bajwa's own money.

11–57　　"The Abbey National answers this submission in two ways. First, it submits that Hill Lawson's ledger cards show that Hill Lawson appropriated the £137,405 which it had received from Dave towards the payment of the sum of £140,000 to the Halifax, and resorted to Mr Bajwa's other funds only when Dave's cheque for the balance was dishonoured. The ledger cards were, of course, made up after the event, though long before any litigation ensued, so they are not primary evidence of actual appropriation; but they are reliable evidence of the appropriation which Hill Lawson believed that they had made.

"I accept this submission. It is not necessary to apply artificial tracing rules where there has been an actual appropriation. A trustee will not be allowed to defeat the claim of his beneficiary by saying that he has resorted to trust money when he could have made use of own; but if the beneficiary asserts that the trustee has made use of the trust money there is no reason why he should not be allowed to prove it.

11–58　　"The second way in which the Abbey National answers the appellants' submission is by reliance on equity's ability to follow money through a bank account where it has been mixed with other moneys by treating the money in the account as charged with the repayment of his money. As against a wrongdoer the claimant is not obliged to appropriate debits to credits in order to ascertain where his money has gone. Equity's power to charge a mixed fund with the repayment of trust moneys enables the claimant to follow the money, not because it is his, but because it is derived from a fund which is treated as if it were subject to a charge in his favour (see *Re Hallett's Estate; Knatchbull v. Hallett* (1880) 13 Ch. D. 696; *Re Oatway, Hertslet v. Oatway* [1903] 2 Ch. 356 and *El Ajou v. Dollar Land Holdings plc* [1993] 3 All E.R. 717).

"The appellants accept this, but submit that for this purpose Mr Bajwa was not a wrongdoer. He was, as I have said, not guilty of any impropriety or want of probity. He relied on his solicitors, and they acted unwisely, perhaps negligently, and certainly precipitately, but not dishonestly. Mr Bajwa, it is submitted, was an innocent volunteer who mixed trust money with his own. As such, he was not bound to give priority to the Abbey National, but could claim parity with it. Accordingly, Mr Bajwa and the Abbey National must be treated as having contributed pari passu to the discharge of the Halifax's charge; and in the absence of the necessary evidence the amounts which were provided by Mr Bajwa and the Abbey National respectively cannot be ascertained. (In fact, on this footing the Abbey National would be entitled to succeed to the extent of one-half of its claim, but that is by the way.)

"For this proposition the appellants rely on a passage in *Re Diplock's Estate,* **11–59** *Diplock v. Wintle* [1948] Ch. 465 at 524 as follows:

> 'Where an innocent volunteer (as distinct from a purchaser for value without notice) mixes "money" of his own with "money" which in equity belongs to another person, or is found in possession of such a mixture, although that other person cannot claim a charge on the mass superior to the claim of the volunteer, he is entitled, nevertheless, to a charge ranking *pari passu* with the claim of the volunteer . . . But this burden on the conscience of the volunteer is not such as to compel him to treat the claim of the equitable owner as paramount. That would be to treat the volunteer as strictly as if he himself stood in a fiduciary relationship to the equitable owner which *ex hypothesi* he does not. The volunteer is under no greater duty of conscience to recognise the interest of the equitable owner than that which, lies on a person having an equitable interest in one of two trust funds of "money" which have become mixed towards the equitable owner of the other. Such a person is not in conscience bound to give precedence to the equitable owner of the other of the two funds.'

"This would be highly relevant if the distinction which the court was there **11–60** making was between the honest and the dishonest recipient. But it was not. The distinction was between the innocent recipient who had no reason to suspect that the money was not his own to dispose of as he pleased, and the recipient who knew or ought to have known that the money belonged to another. In *Re Diplock's Estate* the defendants were the recipients of grants made to them by the personal representatives of a deceased testator in accordance with the terms of the residuary gift in his will. The gift was afterwards held by the House of Lords to be ineffective, with the result that the testator's residue passed on intestacy. The next of kin then brought proceedings to recover the moneys paid away. The defendants found themselves in an unenviable position. Not only had they received the money honestly and in good faith, but they had had no reason to think that it was not theirs. There was no question of their having consciously mixed money which belonged to another with their own.

"But the present case is very different. Neither Mr Bajwa nor his solicitors **11–61** acted dishonestly, but nor were they innocent volunteers. Hill Lawson knew that the money was trust money held to Dave's order pending completion and that it would become available for use on behalf of their client only on completion. They were manifestly fiduciaries. Mr Bajwa, who was plainly intending to redeem the Halifax's mortgage out of the proceeds of sale of the property, must be taken to have known that any money which his solicitors might receive from the purchasers or their mortgagees would represent the balance of the proceeds of sale due on completion and that, since he had made no arrangement with the purchasers to be advanced any part of that amount before completion, it would be available to him only on completion. He cannot possibly have thought that he could keep both the property and the proceeds of sale. Had he thought about the matter at all, he would have realised that the money was not his to mix with his own and dispose of as he saw fit. The only reason that he and his solicitors can be acquitted of dishonesty is that he relied on his solicitors and they acted in the mistaken belief that, save for the tidying up of some loose ends, they were on the point of completing.

"It follows that Mr Bajwa cannot avail himself of the more favourable tracing rules which are available to the innocent volunteer who unconsciously mixes trust money with his own.

Subrogation

11–62 "The appellants submit that the mere fact that the claimant's money is used to discharge someone else's debt does not entitle him to be subrogated to the creditor whose debt is paid. There must be 'something more': *Paul v. Speirway Ltd (in liq)* [1976] Ch. 220 at 230 *per* Oliver J; and see *Orakpo v. Manson Investments Ltd* [1978] A.C. 95 at 105. From this the appellants derive the proposition that in order to be subrogated to the creditor's security the claimant must prove (i) that the claimant intended that his money should be used to discharge the security in question (that being the 'something more' required by Oliver J) and (ii) that he intended to obtain the benefit of the security by subrogation.

"I cannot accept that formulation as a rule of general application regardless of the circumstances in which the remedy of subrogation is sought. The cases relied on were all cases where the claimant intended to make an unsecured loan to a borrower who used the money to discharge a secured debt. In such a case the claimant is not entitled to be subrogated to the creditor's security since this would put him in a better position than he had bargained for.

11–63 "The mere fact that the payer of the money intended to make an unsecured loan will not preclude his claim to be subrogated to the personal rights of the creditor whose debt is discharged if the contractual liability of the original borrower proves to be unenforceable: see *e.g. Re Wrexham, Mold & Connah's Quay Rly Co* [1899] 1 Ch. 440 (where the borrowing was *ultra vires*) and *B Liggett (Liverpool) Ltd v. Barclays Bank Ltd* [1928] 1 K.B. 48 (where the borrowing was unauthorised) . . .

11–64 "In cases such as *Butler v. Rice* [1910] 2 Ch. 277 and *Ghana Commercial Bank v. Chandiram* [1960] A.C. 732, where the claimant paid the creditor direct and intended to discharge his security, the court took the claimant's intention to have been to keep the original security alive for his own benefit save in so far as it was replaced by an effective security in favour of himself. In the present case the Abbey National did not intend to discharge the Halifax's charge in the events which happened, that is to say in the event that completion did not proceed. But it did not intend its money to be used at all in that event. If *Butler v. Rice* and similar cases are relied upon to support the proposition that there can be no subrogation unless the claimant intended to keep the original security alive for its own benefit save in so far as it was replaced by a new and effective security, with the result that the remedy is not available where the claimant had no direct dealings with the creditor and did not intend his money to be used at all, then I respectfully dissent from that proposition. I prefer the view of Slade L.J. in *Re TH Knitwear (Wholesale) Ltd* [1988] Ch. 275 at 286 that in some situations the doctrine of subrogation is capable of applying even though it is impossible to infer a mutual intention to this effect on the part of the creditor and the person claiming to be subrogated to the creditor's security. In the present case the payment was made by Hill Lawson, and it is their intention which matters. As fiduciaries, they could not be heard to say that they had paid out their principal's money otherwise than for the benefit of their principal. Accordingly, their intention must be taken to have been to keep the Halifax's charge alive for the benefit of the Abbey National pending completion. In my judgment this is sufficient to bring the doctrine of subrogation into play.

"The application of the doctrine in the present case does not create the problem which confronted Oliver J in *Paul v. Speirway*. The Abbey National did not intend to be an unsecured creditor of anyone. It intended to retain the beneficial interest in its money unless and until that interest was replaced by a first legal mortgage on the property. The factual context in which the claim to subrogation arises is a novel one which does not appear to have arisen before, but the justice of its claim cannot be denied. The Abbey National's beneficial interest in the money can no longer be restored to it. If it is subrogated to the Halifax's charge its position will not be improved nor will Mr Bajwa's position be adversely affected. Both parties will be restored as nearly as may be to the positions which they were respectively intended to occupy."[84]

BISHOPSGATE INVESTMENT MANAGEMENT LTD V. HOMAN

Court of Appeal [1995] Ch. 211; [1994] 3 W.L.R. 1270; [1995] 1 All E.R. 347.

DILLON L.J.: This is an appeal, by Bishopsgate Investment Management Ltd. **11–65** ("B.I.M.") against an order of Vinelott J. made on December 21 1993. B.I.M., which is now in liquidation, is the trustee of certain of the assets of various pension schemes for employees of companies with which the late Robert Maxwell was associated.

"The respondents to the appeal, Mr. Homan and three colleagues who are partners in Price Waterhouse & Co., are the court-appointed administrators of Maxwell Communication Corporation Plc. ("M.C.C."). The judge's order was made on an application by the administrators under the Insolvency Act 1986 for directions. M.C.C., which was known at an earlier stage as the British Printing Corporation Ltd., was a publicly quoted company and the most prominent of a large number of companies, for which it was the holding company.

"On the unexpected death of Robert Maxwell on 5 November 1991 it was discovered that very large amounts of pension fund moneys of B.I.M. had been improperly paid, during his lifetime, directly or indirectly into various bank accounts of the private sector companies and of M.C.C. with National Westminster Bank. At the time of each wrongful payment of B.I.M.'s pension fund moneys

---

[84] The House of Lords in *Banque Financiere de la Cité v. Parc (Battersea) Ltd* [1998] 1 All E.R. 737 held that for equitable subrogation to be available as a restitutionary remedy the issues now are (1) whether the defendant would be enriched at the plaintiff's expense (2) whether such enrichment would be unjust and (3) whether there were nevertheless reasons of policy for denying such remedy.

into M.C.C.'s accounts those accounts were overdrawn, or later became overdrawn. It was also found that M.C.C. was hopelessly insolvent.

11–66 "The administrators, who have realised a substantial amount of M.C.C.'s assets although the administration is far from complete, wanted to make an interim distribution among the creditors of M.C.C. But the liquidators claimed that B.I.M. was entitled to an equitable charge, in priority to all other unsecured creditors of M.C.C., on all the assets of M.C.C. for the full amount of the pension moneys of B.I.M. wrongly paid to M.C.C. Accordingly the administrators applied to the Companies Court for directions.

"Vinelott J. approached the application on the basis that if the claims of B.I.M. were plainly not maintainable in law the court ought to make a declaration to that effect, in order that an interim distribution could be made without regard to unfounded claims. But, if it was possible that on a further investigation of the facts there might be a claim, valid in law, by B.I.M. to an equitable charge on a particular asset, the proceeds of that asset ought not to be distributed until the particular facts had been investigated.

"The judge declared by his order that the administrators were entitled to deal with specified notices of claim as if they do not give rise to any proprietary claims, and he declared also that B.I.M. was not entitled to any equitable charge over the assets of M.C.C. in respect of proprietary claims notified to the administrators to the extent that such assets were acquired before any moneys or assets misappropriated from B.I.M. were paid or transferred to or so as to be under the control of M.C.C. and were not acquired in anticipation of or otherwise in connection with the misappropriation of such assets or moneys. In essence the judge held that B.I.M. could only claim an equitable charge on any assets of M.C.C. in accordance with the recognised principles of equitable tracing and these principles do not permit tracing through an overdrawn bank account—whether an account which was already overdrawn at the time the relevant moneys were paid into it or an account which was then in credit, but subsequently became overdrawn by subsequent drawings.

11–67 "The judge reserved, however, the position if it were shown that there was a connection between a particular misappropriation of B.I.M.'s moneys and the acquisition by M.C.C. of a particular asset. The judge gave as an instance of such a case what he called "backward tracing"—where an asset was acquired by M.C.C. with moneys borrowed from an overdrawn or loan account and there was an inference that when the borrowing was incurred it was the intention that it should be repaid by misappropriations of B.I.M.'s moneys. Another possibility was that moneys misappropriated from B.I.M. were paid into an overdrawn account of M.C.C. in order to reduce the overdraft and so make finance available within the overdraft limits for M.C.C. to purchase some particular asset.

"By a respondent's notice by way of cross-appeal, the administrators ask us to overrule these reservations of the judge, and hold that even if the possible facts which the judge envisages were clearly proved that could not in law give B.I.M. any equitable charge on the particular asset acquired. For my part I would not interfere at all with this aspect of the judge's exercise of his discretion. In my judgment, if the connection he postulates between the particular misappropriation of B.I.M.'s money and the acquisition by M.C.C. of a particular asset is sufficiently clearly proved, it is at least arguable, depending on the facts, that there ought to be an equitable charge in favour of B.I.M. on the asset in question of M.C.C.

11–68 "But the main claims of B.I.M. are put much more widely as claims to an equitable charge on all the assets of M.C.C. These claims are not founded on proving any particular intention of Robert Maxwell or others in charge of M.C.C.

but on general principles which it is said that the court ought to apply. They are founded primarily on certain observations of Lord Templeman in giving the judgment of the Privy Council in *Space Investments Ltd. v. Canadian Imperial Bank of Commerce Trust Co. (Bahamas) Ltd.* [1986] 1 W.L.R. 1072. In particular, in that case Lord Templeman said, at 1074:

> 'In these circumstances it is impossible for the beneficiaries interested in trust money misappropriated from their trust to trace their money to any particular asset belonging to the trustee bank. But equity allows the beneficiaries, or a new trustee appointed in place of an insolvent bank trustee . . . to trace the trust money to all the assets of the bank and to recover the trust money by the exercise of an equitable charge over all the assets of the bank. . . . that equitable charge secures for the beneficiaries and the trust priority over the claims of the customers . . . and . . . all other unsecured creditors.'

"What Lord Templeman there said was strictly obiter, in that on the facts the **11–69** Privy Council held that the bank trustee was authorised by the trust instruments to deposit trust money with itself as banker and so there had been no misappropriation. The beneficiaries or their new trustee therefore could merely prove with the other general creditors of the insolvent bank trustee for a dividend in respect of the moneys so deposited.

"Vinelott J. rejected the submissions of B.I.M. founded on the *Space Investments* case. He considered that Lord Templeman could not have intended to effect such a fundamental change to the well-understood limitations to equitable tracing; Lord Templeman was only considering the position of an insolvent bank which had been taking deposits and lending money.

"In the notice of appeal to this court, B.I.M.'s first ground of appeal relies on the *Space Investments* case and it is said that the judge erred in his interpretation of what Lord Templeman had said. There is a second, and alternative, ground of appeal to which I will refer later . . .

"As I read the judgment of the Privy Council in *Re Goldcorp Exchange Ltd.* **11–70** delivered by Lord Mustill, it makes it clear that Lord Templeman's observations in the *Space Investments* case [1986] 1 W.L.R. 1072 were not concerned at all with the situation we have in the present case where trust moneys have been paid into an overdrawn bank account, or an account which has become overdrawn. Lord Mustill said in the clearest terms, [1994] 3 W.L.R. 199 at 222:

> 'Their Lordships should, however, say that they find it difficult to understand how the judgment of the Board in *Space Investments Ltd. v. Canadian Imperial Bank of Commerce Trust Co. (Bahamas) Ltd.* [1986] 1 W.L.R. 1072, on which the claimants leaned heavily in argument, would enable them to overcome the difficulty that the moneys said to be impressed with the trust were paid into an overdrawn account and thereupon ceased to exist: see, for example, *Re Diplock* [1948] Ch. 465. The observations of the Board in the *Space Investments* case were concerned with a mixed, not a non-existent, fund.'

"Thus the wide interpretation of those observations put forward by Cooke P., which is the basis of the first ground of appeal in the present case, is rejected. Instead the decision of the Court of Appeal in *Re Diplock* [1948] Ch. 465 is endorsed. There it was said, at p. 521:

'The equitable remedies presuppose the continued existence of the money either as a separate fund or as a part of a mixed fund or as latent in property acquired by means of such a fund. If, on the facts of any individual case, such continued existence is not established, equity is as helpless as the common law itself.'

11–71   "Also endorsed, in my judgment, in the decision of the Board delivered by Lord Mustill is the long-standing first instance decision in *James Roscoe (Bolton) Ltd. v. Winder* [1915] 1 Ch. 62, which Mr. Heslop for B.I.M., in his submissions in March, invited us to overrule. That was a decision that, in tracing trust moneys into the bank account of a trustee in accordance with *Re. Hallett's Estate* (1880) 13 Ch.D. 696, tracing was only possible to such an amount of the balance ultimately standing to the credit of the trustee as did not exceed the lowest balance of the account during the intervening period. Thus as is said in the headnote to the report [1915] 1 Ch. 62:

'Payments into a general account cannot, without proof of express intention, be appropriated to the replacement of trust money which has been improperly mixed with that account and drawn out.'

That reflects the statement by Sargant J. in the *James Roscoe* case, at p. 69:

'it is impossible to attribute to him'—*i.e.* the account holder—'that by the mere payment into the account of further moneys, which to a large extent he subsequently used for purposes of his own, he intended to clothe those moneys with a trust in favour of the plaintiffs.'

11–72   "Mr. Heslop, for B.I.M., referred, however, to later passages in the opinion of Lord Mustill. First Lord Mustill stated [1994] 3 W.L.R. 199, 227 that the law relating to the creation and tracing of equitable proprietary interests is still in a state of development. He referred to two recent decisions (*Attorney-General for Hong Kong v. Reid* [1994] A.C. 324 and *Lord Napier and Ettrick v. Hunter* [1993] A.C. 713) on facts not particularly relevant to the present case as instances where equitable proprietary interests have been recognised in circumstances which might previously have been regarded merely as circumstances for common law relief . . .

"Mr. Heslop submitted that the beneficiaries under the pension schemes of which B.I.M. is trustee are in a different position from the other creditors, who are mainly banks, of B.I.M. He did say that the beneficiaries under the pension schemes never undertook the risk that their pension funds would be misappropriated and paid into the overdrawn bank account of an insolvent company, whereas all the banks which lent money to M.C.C. took their chance, as a commercial risk, on M.C.C.'s solvency.

11–73   "Mr. Heslop therefore relied on the second ground in the notice of appeal, whereby B.I.M. claims (as it has been explained to us) to be entitled to an equitable charge as security for its claims against M.C.C. (i) over any moneys standing to the credit at the time of the appointment of the administrators of M.C.C. of any banking account maintained by M.C.C. into which any moneys of B.I.M. or the proceeds of any assets of B.I.M. misappropriated from it were paid and (ii) over any assets acquired out of any such bank account, whether or not in credit as at the date such assets were acquired.

"So far as (i) is concerned, the point is that the National Westminster Bank account into which the misappropriated B.I.M. trust moneys were paid happened to be in credit when the administrators were appointed. B.I.M. therefore claims a lien on that credit balance in the National Westminister Bank account for the amount of the misappropriated trust moneys. It is difficult to suppose, however, in the circumstances of Robert Maxwell's last days—and I know no evidence— that Robert Maxwell intended to make good the misappropriation of the B.I.M. pension moneys by the cryptic expedient of arranging to put M.C.C.'s account with National Westminster Bank into credit—but without repaying the credit balance this created to B.I.M. But in the absence of clear evidence of intention to make good the depredations on B.I.M. it is not possible to assume that the credit balance has been clothed with a trust in favour of B.I.M. and its beneficiaries: see *James Roscoe (Bolton) Ltd. v. Winder* [1915] 1 Ch. 62.

"As to (ii), this seems to be going back to the original wide interpretation of **11–74** what Lord Templeman said in the *Space Investments* case [1986] 1 W.L.R. 1072 and applying it to an overdrawn account because the misappropriated moneys that went into the account were trust moneys and thus different from other moneys that may have gone into that account. But the moneys in the *Space Investments* case were also trust moneys, and so, if argument (ii) is valid in the present case, it would also have been valid, as a matter of law, in the *Space Investments* case. But that was rejected in *Re Goldcorp Exchange Ltd.* [1994] 3 W.L.R. 199 because equitable tracing, though devised for the protection of trust moneys misapplied, cannot be pursued through an overdrawn and therefore non-existent fund. Acceptance of argument (ii) would, in my judgment, require the rejection of *Re Diplock* [1948] Ch. 465, which is binding on us, and of Lord Mustill's explanation of Lord Templeman's statement in the *Space Investments* case in *Re Goldcorp Exchange Ltd* [1994] 3 W.L.R. 199 at 222.

"It is not open to us to say that because the moneys were trust moneys the fact that they were paid into an overdrawn account or have otherwise been dissipated presents no difficulty to raising an equitable charge on assets of M.C.C. for their amount in favour of B.I.M. The difficulty Lord Mustill referred to is not displaced.

"Accordingly I would reject both grounds of appeal, and dismiss both the appeal and the cross-appeal.

"On consideration, I do not regard it as appropriate to give any further directions to the judge."

LEGGATT L.J.: "There can be no equitable remedy against an asset acquired **11–75** *before* misappropriation of money takes place, since ex hypothesi it cannot be followed into something which existed and so had been acquired before the money was received and therefore without its aid.

"The concept of a 'composite transaction' is in my judgment fallacious. What is envisaged is (a) the purchase of an asset by means of an overdraft, that is, a loan from a bank, and (b) the discharge of the loan by means of misappropriated trust money. The Judge thought that the money could be regarded as having been used to acquire the asset. His conclusion was that 'It is sufficient to say that proof that trust moneys were paid into an overdrawn account of the defaulting trustee may not always be sufficient to bar a claim to an equitable charge."

"I see the force of Mr. Kosmin's submission that, if an asset were used as security for an overdraft which was then discharged by means of misappropriated money, the beneficiary might obtain priority by subrogation. But there can ordinarily be no tracing into an asset which is already in the hands of the defaulting trustee when the misappropriation occurs.

"In *Liggett v. Kensington* [1993] 1 N.Z.L.R. 257 Cooke P. applied the principle **11–76** which he derived from the *Space Investments* case [1986] 1 W.L.R. 1072 that those who do not take a risk of insolvency are entitled to an equitable charge over all the assets of the trustee, giving them priority over those who are to be regarded as having taken such a risk. That decision is authority for no wider proposition than that, where a bank trustee wrongly deposits money with itself, the trustee can trace into all the bank's credit balances.

"Consistently with Mr. Kosmin's submissions on this appeal, Lord Mustill, delivering the judgment of the Board in *Re Goldcorp Exchange Ltd.* [1994] 3 W.L.R. 199, 222F, stated that their Lordships found it difficult to understand how it would enable the claimants in that case to "overcome the difficulty that the moneys said to be impressed with the trust were paid into an overdrawn account and thereupon ceased to exist." Lord Mustill emphasised that the observations of the Board were concerned with a mixed, not a non-existent, fund. He also cited with approval *James Roscoe (Bolton) Ltd. v. Winder* [1915] 1 Ch. 62 as conventionally exemplifying the principles of tracing.

"I therefore consider that the judge came to the right conclusion, though I do not accept that it is possible to trace through an overdrawn bank account or to trace misappropriated money into an asset bought before the money was received by the purchaser. I agree that the appeal should be dismissed."

HENRY L.J.: "I agree with both judgments." *Appeal dismissed with costs.*

LIPKIN GORMAN V. KARPNALE LTD

House of Lords [1991] 2 A.C., 548 [1991] 3 W.L.R. 10, [1992] 4 All E.R. 512.

11–77 LORD GOFF, whose views on change of position were endorsed by Lords Bridge, Griffith and Ackner, has stated: "Where an innocent defendant's position is so changed that he will suffer an injustice if called upon to repay or to repay in full, the injustice of requiring him so to repay outweighs the injustice of denying the plaintiff restitution. If the plaintiff pays money to the defendant under a mistake of fact, and the defendant then, acting in good faith, pays the money or part of it to charity, it is unjust to require the defendant to make restitution to the extent that he has changed his position. Likewise, on facts such as those in the present case, if a thief steals my money and pays it to a third party who gives it away to charity, the third party should have a good defence to an action for money had and received. In other words, bona fide change of position should of itself be a good defence in such cases as these.

11–78 ". . . I am most anxious that, in recognising this defence to actions of restitution, nothing should be said at this stage to inhibit the development of the defence on a case by case basis, in the usual way. It is of course, plain that the defence is not open to one who has changed his position in bad faith, as where the defendant has paid away the money with knowledge of facts entitling the plaintiff to restitution; and it is commonly accepted that the defence should not be open to a wrongdoer. These are matters which can, in due course, be considered in depth in cases where they arise for consideration. They do not arise in the present case. Here there is no doubt that the club have acted in good faith throughout, and the action is not founded upon any wrongdoing of the club. It is not, however, appropriate in the present case to attempt to identify all those actions in restitution to which change of position may be a defence. A prominent example will, no doubt, be found in those cases where the plaintiff is seeking repayment of money paid under a mistake of fact; but I can see no reason why the defence should not also be available in principle in a case such as the present, where the plaintiff's money has been paid by a thief to an innocent donee, and the plaintiff then seeks repayment from the donees in an action for money had and received. At present I do not wish to state the principle any less broadly than this: that the defence is available to a person whose position has so changed that it would be inequitable in all the circumstances to require him to make restitution, or alternatively to make restitution in full. I wish to stress, however, that the mere fact that the defendant has spent the money, in whole or in part, does not of itself render it inequitable that he should be called upon to repay, because the expenditure might in any event have been incurred by him in the ordinary course of things. I fear that the mistaken assumption that mere expenditure of money may be regarded as amounting to a change of position for present purposes has led in the past to opposition by some to recognition of a defence which in fact is likely to be available only on comparatively rare occasions. In this connection I have particularly in mind the speech of Lord Simonds in *Ministry of Health v. Simpson* [1950] 2 All E.R. 1137 at 1147, [1951] AC 251 at 276.

"I wish to add two further footnotes. The defence of change of position is akin **11–79** to the defence of bona fide purchase; but we cannot simply say that bona fide purchase is a species of change of position. This is because change of position will only avail a defendant to the extent that his position has been changed; whereas, where bona fide purchase is invoked, no inquiry is made (in most cases) into the adequacy of consideration. Even so the recognition of change of position as a defence should be doubly beneficial. It will enable a more generous approach to be taken to the recognition of the right to restitution, in the knowledge that the defence is, in appropriate cases, available; and, while recognising the different functions of property at law and in equity, there may also in due course develop a more consistent approach to tracing claims, in which common defences are recognised as available to such claims, whether in law or in equity."

LORD TEMPLEMAN earlier stated: "in a claim for money had and received by a **11–80** thief, the plaintiff victim must show that money belonging to him was paid by the thief to the defendant and that the defendant was unjustly enriched. An innocent recipient of stolen money may not be enriched at all. If Cass had paid £20,000 derived from the solicitors to a car dealer for a motor car priced at £20,000 the car dealer would not have been enriched. The car dealer would have received £20,000 for a car worth £20,000. But an innocent recipient of stolen money will be enriched if the recipient has not given full consideration. If Cass had given £20,000 of the solicitors' money to a friend as a gift, the friend would have been enriched and unjustly enriched because a donee of stolen money cannot in good conscience rely on the bounty of the thief to deny restitution to the victim of the theft. Complications arise if the donee innocently expends the stolen money in reliance upon the validity of the gift before the donee receives notice of the victim's claim for restitution. Thus, if the donee spent £20,000 in the purchase of a motor car which he would not have purchased but for the gift, it seems to me that the donee has altered his position on the faith of the gift and has only been unjustly enriched to the extent of the secondhand value of the motor car at the date when the victim of the theft seeks restitution. If the donee spends the £20,000 in a trip round the world, which he would not have undertaken without the gift, it seems to me that the donee has altered his position on the faith of the gift and that he is not unjustly enriched when the victim of the thief seeks restitution. In the present case Cass stole and the club received £229,908.48 of the solicitors' money. If the club was in the same position as a donee, the club nevertheless in good faith allowed Cass to gamble with the solicitors' money and paid his winnings from time to time so that, when the solicitors sought restitution, the club only retained £154,695 derived from the solicitors. The question is whether the club which was enriched by £154,695 at the date when the solicitors sought restitution was unjustly enriched."

He held, as did the other Law Lords, that the club had been unjustly enriched to the tune of £154,695 and so was liable therefor.

FOSKETT V. MCKEOWN

11–81 House of Lords [2000] 2 W.L.R. 1299, [2000] 3 All E.R. 97. Lords Browne-Wilkinson, Hoffmann and Millett, all Chancery judges, (with Lords Steyn and Hope from civil law backgrounds dissenting) held the claimant purchasers, whose purchase moneys were held on trust for Mr Murphy and were wrongfully used by him to pay at least two of the five annual premiums on a life policy held by him on trust for his children, were entitled on his death to the proportion of the £1 million policy proceeds representing their proportion of the premiums- and not just to a charge over the policy proceeds for the amount of their contributions to the premium payments.

11–82 LORD MILLETT. "My Lords, this is a textbook example of tracing through mixed substitutions. At the beginning of the story the purchasers were beneficially entitled under an express trust to a sum standing in the name of Mr Murphy in a bank account. From there the money moved into and out of various bank accounts where in breach of trust it was inextricably mixed by Mr Murphy with his own money. After each transaction was completed the purchasers' money formed an indistinguishable part of the balance standing to Mr Murphy's credit in his bank account. The amount of that balance represented a debt due from the bank to Mr Murphy, that is to say a chose in action. At the penultimate stage the purchasers' money was represented by an indistinguishable part of a different chose in action, *viz.* the debt prospectively and contingently due from an insurance company to its policyholders, being the trustees of a settlement made by Mr Murphy for the benefit of his children. At the present and final stage it forms an indistinguishable part of the balance standing to the credit of the respondent trustees in their bank account.

Tracing and following

11–83 The process of ascertaining what happened to the purchasers' money involves both tracing and following. These are both exercises in locating assets which are or may be taken to represent an asset belonging to the purchasers and to which they assert ownership. The processes of following and tracing are, however, distinct. Following is the process of following the same asset as it moves from hand to hand. Tracing is the process of identifying a new asset as the substitute for the old. Where one asset is exchanged for another, a claimant can elect whether to follow the original asset into the hands of the new owner or to trace its value into the new asset in the hands of the same owner. In practice his choice is often dictated by the circumstances. In the present case the purchasers do not seek to follow the money any further once it reached the bank or insurance company, since its identity was lost in the hands of the recipient (which in any case obtained an unassailable title as a bona fide purchaser for value without notice of the purchasers' beneficial interest). Instead the purchasers have chosen at each stage to trace the money into its proceeds, *viz.* the debt presently due from the bank to the account holder or the debt prospectively and contingently due from the insurance company to the policy holders.

Having completed this exercise, the purchasers claim a continuing beneficial **11–84** interest in the insurance money. Since this represents the product of Mr Murphy's own money as well as theirs, which Mr Murphy mingled indistinguishably in a single chose in action, they claim a beneficial interest in a proportionate part of the money only. The transmission of a claimant's property rights from one asset to its traceable proceeds is part of our law of property, not of the law of unjust enrichment. There is no "unjust factor" to justify restitution (unless "want of title" be one, which makes the point). The claimant succeeds if at all by virtue of his own title, not to reverse unjust enrichment. Property rights are determined by fixed rules and settled principles. They are not discretionary. They do not depend upon ideas of what is "fair, just and reasonable". Such concepts, which in reality mask decisions of legal policy, have no place in the law of property.

A beneficiary of a trust is entitled to a continuing beneficial interest not merely in the trust property but in its traceable proceeds also, and his interest binds every one who takes the property or its traceable proceeds except a bona fide purchaser for value without notice. In the present case the purchasers' beneficial interest plainly bound Mr Murphy, a trustee who wrongfully mixed the trust money with his own and whose every dealing with the money (including the payment of the premiums) was in breach of trust. It similarly binds his successors, the trustees of the children's settlement, who claim no beneficial interest of their own, and Mr Murphy's children, who are volunteers. They gave no value for what they received and derive their interest from Mr Murphy by way of gift.

Tracing

We speak of money at the bank, and of money passing into and out of a bank **11–85** account. But of course the account holder has no money at the bank. Money paid into a bank account belongs legally and beneficially to the bank and not to the account holder. The bank gives value for it, and it is accordingly not usually possible to make the money itself the subject of an adverse claim. Instead a claimant normally sues the account holder rather than the bank and lays claim to the proceeds of the money in his hands. These consist of the debt or part of the debt due to him from the bank. We speak of tracing money into and out of the account, but there is no money in the account. There is merely a single debt of an amount equal to the final balance standing to the credit of the account holder. No money passes from paying bank to receiving bank or through the clearing system (where the money flows may be in the opposite direction). There is simply a series of debits and credits which are causally and transactionally linked. We also speak of tracing one asset into another, but this too is inaccurate. The original asset still exists in the hands of the new owner, or it may have become untraceable. The claimant claims the new asset because it was acquired in whole or in part with the original asset. What he traces, therefore, is not the physical asset itself but the value inherent in it.

Tracing is thus neither a claim nor a remedy. It is merely the process by which **11–86** a claimant demonstrates what has happened to his property, identifies its proceeds and the persons who have handled or received them, and justifies his claim that the proceeds can properly be regarded as representing his property. Tracing is also distinct from claiming. It identifies the traceable proceeds of the claimant's property. It enables the claimant to substitute the traceable proceeds for the original asset as the subject matter of his claim. But it does not affect or establish his claim. That will depend on a number of factors including the nature of his interest in the original asset. He will normally be able to maintain the same claim to the substituted asset as he could have maintained to the original asset. If he held only a security interest in the original asset, he cannot claim more than a security interest in its proceeds. But his claim may also be exposed to potential defences as a result of intervening transactions. Even if the purchasers could demonstrate what the bank had done with their money, for example, and could thus identify its traceable proceeds in the hands of the bank, any claim by them to assert ownership of those proceeds would be defeated by the bona fide purchaser defence. The successful completion of a tracing exercise may be preliminary to a personal claim (as in *El Ajou v. Dollar Land Holdings plc* [1993] 3 All E.R. 717) or a proprietary one, to the enforcement of a legal right (as in *Trustees of the Property of FC Jones & Sons (a firm) v. Jones* [1997] Ch 159) or an equitable one.

11–87   Given its nature, there is nothing inherently legal or equitable about the tracing exercise. There is thus no sense in maintaining different rules for tracing at law and in equity. One set of tracing rules is enough. The existence of two has never formed part of the law in the United States: see Scott *The Law of Trusts* (4th edn, 1989) pp 605–609. There is certainly no logical justification for allowing any distinction between them to produce capricious results in cases of mixed substitutions by insisting on the existence of a fiduciary relationship as a precondition for applying equity's tracing rules. The existence of such a relationship may be relevant to the nature of the claim which the plaintiff can maintain, whether personal or proprietary, but that is a different matter. I agree with the passages which my noble and learned friend Lord Steyn has cited from Professor Birks' essay "The Necessity of a Unitary Law of Tracing" in *Making Commercial Law: essays in honour of Roy Goode* (1997), and with Dr Lionel Smith's exposition in his comprehensive monograph *The Law of Tracing* (1997) see particularly pp 120–130, 277–279 and 342–347.

11–88   This is not, however, the occasion to explore these matters further, for the present is a straightforward case of a trustee who wrongfully misappropriated trust money, mixed it with his own, and used it to pay for an asset for the benefit of his children. Even on the traditional approach, the equitable tracing rules are available to the purchasers. There are only two complicating factors. The first is that the wrongdoer used their money to pay premiums on an equity linked policy of life assurance on his own life. The nature of the policy should make no difference in principle, though it may complicate the accounting. The second is that he had previously settled the policy for the benefit of his children. This should also make no difference. The claimant's rights cannot depend on whether the wrongdoer gave the policy to his children during his lifetime or left the proceeds to them by his will; or if during his lifetime whether he did so before or after he had recourse to the claimant's money to pay the premiums. The order of events does not affect the fact that the children are not contributors but volunteers who have received the gift of an asset paid for in part with misappropriated trust moneys.

The cause of action

11–89   As I have already pointed out, the purchasers seek to vindicate their property rights, not to reverse unjust enrichment. The correct classification of the purchasers' cause of action may appear to be academic, but it has important consequences. The two causes of action have different requirements and may attract different defences.

A plaintiff who brings an action in unjust enrichment must show that the defendant has been enriched at the plaintiff's expense, for he cannot have been unjustly enriched if he has not been enriched at all. But the plaintiff is not concerned to show that the defendant is in receipt of property belonging beneficially to the plaintiff or its traceable proceeds. The fact that the beneficial ownership of the property has passed to the defendant provides no defence; indeed, it is usually the very fact which founds the claim. Conversely, a plaintiff who brings an action like the present must show that the defendant is in receipt of property which belongs beneficially to him or its traceable proceeds, but he need not show that the defendant has been enriched by its receipt. He may, for example, have paid full value for the property, but he is still required to disgorge it if he received it with notice of the plaintiff's interest.

Furthermore, a claim in unjust enrichment is subject to a change of position defence, which usually operates by reducing or extinguishing the element of enrichment. An action like the present is subject to the bona fide purchaser for value defence, which operates to clear the defendant's title.

The tracing rules

The insurance policy in the present case is a very sophisticated financial **11–90** instrument. Tracing into the rights conferred by such an instrument raises a number of important issues. It is therefore desirable to set out the basic principles before turning to deal with the particular problems to which policies of life assurance give rise.

The simplest case is where a trustee wrongfully misappropriates trust property and uses it exclusively to acquire other property for his own benefit. In such a case the beneficiary is entitled *at his option* either to assert his beneficial ownership of the proceeds or to bring a personal claim against the trustee for breach of trust and enforce an equitable lien or charge on the proceeds to secure restoration of the trust fund. He will normally exercise the option in the way most advantageous to himself. If the traceable proceeds have increased in value and are worth more than the original asset, he will assert his beneficial ownership and obtain the profit for himself. There is nothing unfair in this. The trustee cannot be permitted to keep any profit resulting from his misappropriation for himself, and his donees cannot obtain a better title than their donor. If the traceable proceeds are worth less than the original asset, it does not usually matter how the beneficiary exercises his option. He will take the whole of the proceeds on either basis. This is why it is not possible to identify the basis on which the claim succeeded in some of the cases.

Both remedies are proprietary and depend on successfully tracing the trust **11–91** property into its proceeds. A beneficiary's claim against a trustee for breach of trust is a personal claim. It does not entitle him to priority over the trustee's general creditors unless he can trace the trust property into its product and establish a proprietary interest in the proceeds. If the beneficiary is unable to trace the trust property into its proceeds, he still has a personal claim against the trustee, but his claim will be unsecured. The beneficiary's proprietary claims to the trust property or its traceable proceeds can be maintained against the wrongdoer and anyone who derives title from him except a bona fide purchaser for value without notice of the breach of trust. The same rules apply even where there have been numerous successive transactions, so long as the tracing exercise is successful and no bona fide purchaser for value without notice has intervened.

A more complicated case is where there is a mixed substitution. This occurs where the trust money represents only part of the cost of acquiring the new asset.

As James Barr Ames pointed out in "Following Misappropriated Property into its Product" (1906) 19 Harv LR 511, consistency requires that, if a trustee buys property partly with his own money and partly with trust money, the beneficiary should have the option of taking a proportionate part of the new property or a lien upon it, as may be most for his advantage. In principle it should not matter (and it has never previously been suggested that it does) whether the trustee mixes the trust money with his own and buys the new asset with the mixed fund or makes separate payments of the purchase price (whether simultaneously or sequentially) out of the different funds. In every case the value formerly inherent in the trust property has become located within the value inherent in the new asset.

11–92   The rule, and its rationale, were stated by Samuel Williston in "The Right to Follow Trust Property when Confused with Other Property" (1888) 2 Harv LR 28 at 29:

> "If the trust fund is traceable as having furnished in part the money with which a certain investment was made, and the proportion it formed of the whole money so invested is known or ascertainable, the *cestui que trust* should be allowed to regard the acts of the trustee as done for his benefit, in the same way that he would be allowed to if all the money so invested had been his; that is, he should be entitled in equity to an undivided share of the property which the trust money contributed to purchase—such a proportion of the whole as the trust money bore to the whole money invested. The reason in one case as in the other is that the trustee cannot be allowed to make a profit from the use of the trust money, and if the property which he wrongfully purchased were held subject only to a lien for the amount invested, any appreciation in value would go to the trustee."

If this correctly states the underlying basis of the rule (as I believe it does), then it is impossible to distinguish between the case where mixing precedes the investment and the case where it arises on and in consequence of the investment. It is also impossible to distinguish between the case where the investment is retained by the trustee and the case where it is given away to a gratuitous donee. The donee cannot obtain a better title than his donor, and a donor who is a trustee cannot be allowed to profit from his trust.

11–93   In *Re Hallett's Estate, Knatchbull v. Hallett* (1880) Ch D 696 at 709 Jessel MR acknowledged that where an asset was acquired exclusively with trust money, the beneficiary could either assert equitable ownership of the asset or enforce a lien or charge over it to recover the trust money. But he appeared to suggest that in the case of a mixed substitution the beneficiary is confined to a lien. Any authority that this dictum might otherwise have is weakened by the fact that Jessel MR gave no reason for the existence of any such rule, and none is readily apparent. The dictum was plainly obiter, for the fund was deficient and the plaintiff was only claiming a lien. It has usually been cited only to be explained away (see for example *Re Tilley's Will Trusts, Burgin v. Croad* [1967] Ch 1179 at 1186 per Ungoed-Thomas J, Burrows *The Law of Restitution* (1993) p 368). It was rejected by the High Court of Australia in *Scott v. Scott* (1963) 109 C.L.R. 649 (see the passage at 661–662 cited by Morritt L.J. below [1998] Ch 265 at 300–301)). It has not been adopted in the United States: see the American Law Institute, *Restatement of the Law, Trusts 2d* (1959) at § 202(h). In *Primeau v. Granfield* (1911) 184 F 480 at 482 Learned Hand J. expressed himself in forthright terms: "On principle there can be no excuse for such a rule."

In my view the time has come to state unequivocally that English law has no **11–94** such rule. It conflicts with the rule that a trustee must not benefit from his trust. I agree with Burrows that the beneficiary's right to elect to have a proportionate share of a mixed substitution necessarily follows once one accepts, as English law does, (i) that a claimant can trace in equity into a mixed fund and (ii) that he can trace unmixed money into its proceeds and assert ownership of the proceeds.

Accordingly, I would state the basic rule as follows. Where a trustee wrongfully uses trust money to provide part of the cost of acquiring an asset, the beneficiary is entitled *at his option* either to claim a proportionate share of the asset or to enforce a lien upon it to secure his personal claim against the trustee for the amount of the misapplied money. It does not matter whether the trustee mixed the trust money with his own in a single fund before using it to acquire the asset, or made separate payments (whether simultaneously or sequentially) out of the differently owned funds to acquire a single asset.

Two observations are necessary at this point. First, there is a mixed substitu- **11–95** tion (with the result already described) whenever the claimant's property has contributed in part only towards the acquisition of the new asset. It is not necessary for the claimant to show in addition that his property has contributed to any increase in the *value* of the new asset. This is because, as I have already pointed out, this branch of the law is concerned with vindicating rights of property and not with reversing unjust enrichment. Secondly, the beneficiary's right to claim a lien is available only against a wrongdoer and those deriving title under him otherwise than for value. It is not available against competing contributors who are innocent of any wrongdoing. The tracing rules are not the result of any presumption or principle peculiar to equity. They correspond to the common law rules for following into physical mixtures (though the consequences may not be identical). Common to both is the principle that the interests of the wrongdoer who was responsible for the mixing and those who derive title under him otherwise than for value are subordinated to those of innocent contributors. As against the wrongdoer and his successors, the beneficiary is entitled to locate his contribution in any part of the mixture and to subordinate their claims to share in the mixture until his own contribution has been satisfied. This has the effect of giving the beneficiary a lien for his contribution if the mixture is deficient.

Innocent contributors, however, must be treated equally *inter se*. Where the **11–96** beneficiary's claim is in competition with the claims of other innocent contributors, there is no basis upon which any of the claims can be subordinated to any of the others. Where the fund is deficient, the beneficiary is not entitled to enforce a lien for his contributions; all must share rateably in the fund.

The primary rule in regard to a mixed fund, therefore, is that gains and losses are borne by the contributors rateably. The beneficiary's right to elect instead to enforce a lien to obtain repayment is an exception to the primary rule, exercisable where the fund is deficient and the claim is made against the wrongdoer and those claiming through him. It is not necessary to consider whether there are any circumstances in which the beneficiary is confined to a lien in cases where the fund is more than sufficient to repay the contributions of all parties. It is sufficient to say that he is not so confined in a case like the present. It is not enough that those defending the claim are innocent of any wrongdoing if they are not themselves contributors but, like the trustees and Mr Murphy's children in the present case, are volunteers who derive title under the wrongdoer otherwise than for value. On ordinary principles such persons are in no better position than the wrongdoer, and are liable to suffer the same subordination of their interests to those of the claimant as the wrongdoer would have been. They certainly cannot do better than the claimant by confining him to a lien and keeping any profit for themselves.

11–97   Similar principles apply to following into physical mixtures: see *Lupton v. White, White v. Lupton* (1808) 15 Ves 432; and *Sandeman & Sons v. Tyzack and Branfoot Steamship Co Ltd* [1913] A.C. 680 at 695 where Lord Moulton said: "If the mixing has arisen from the fault of 'B.', 'A.' can claim the goods." There are relatively few cases which deal with the position of the innocent recipient from the wrongdoer, but *Jones v. DeMarchant* (1916) 28 D.L.R. 561 may be cited as an example. A husband wrongfully used 18 beaver skins belonging to his wife and used them, together with four skins of his own, to have a fur coat made up which he then gave to his mistress. Unsurprisingly the wife was held entitled to recover the coat. The mistress knew nothing of the true ownership of the skins, but her innocence was held to be immaterial. She was a gratuitous donee and could stand in no better position than the husband. The coat was a new asset manufactured from the skins and not merely the product of intermingling them. The problem could not be solved by a sale of the coat in order to reduce the disputed property to a divisible fund, since (as we shall see) the realisation of an asset does not affect its ownership. It would hardly have been appropriate to require the two ladies to share the coat between them. Accordingly it was an all or nothing case in which the ownership of the coat must be assigned to one or other of the parties. The determinative factor was that the mixing was the act of the wrongdoer through whom the mistress acquired the coat otherwise than for value.

11–98   The rule in equity is to the same effect, as Page Wood V.-C. observed in *Frith v. Cartland* (1865) 2 Hem & M 417 at 420:

> ". . . if a man mixes trust funds with his own, the whole will be treated as the trust property, except so far as he may be able to distinguish what is his own."

This does not, in my opinion, exclude a pro rata division where this is appropriate, as in the case of money and other fungibles like grain, oil or wine. But it is to be observed that a pro rata division is the best that the wrongdoer and his donees can hope for. If a pro rata division is excluded, the beneficiary takes the whole; there is no question of confining him to a lien. *Jones v. De Marchant* is a useful illustration of the principles shared by the common law and equity alike that an innocent recipient who receives misappropriated property by way of gift obtains no better title than his donor, and that if a proportionate sharing is inappropriate the wrongdoer and those who derive title under him take nothing.

Insurance policies

11–99   In the case of an ordinary whole-life policy the insurance company undertakes to pay a stated sum on the death of the assured in return for fixed annual premiums payable throughout his life. Such a policy is an entire contract, not a contract for a year with a right of renewal. It is not a series of single premium policies for one year term assurance. It is not like an indemnity policy where each premium buys cover for a year after which the policyholder must renew or the cover expires. The fact that the policy will lapse if the premiums are not paid makes no difference. The amounts of the annual premiums and of the sum assured are fixed in advance at the outset and assume the payment of annual premiums throughout the term of the policy. The relationship between them is based on the life expectancy of the assured and the rates of interest available on long term government securities at the inception of the policy.

In the present case the benefits specified in the policy are expressed to be payable "in consideration of the payment of the first Premium already made and of the further Premiums payable". The premiums are stated to be "£10220.00 payable at annual intervals from 06 Nov 1986 throughout the lifetime of the life assured". It is beyond argument that the death benefit of £1m paid on Mr Murphy's death was paid in consideration for *all* the premiums which had been paid before that date, including those paid with the purchasers' money, and not just some of them. Part of that sum, therefore, represented the traceable proceeds of the purchasers' money.

It is, however, of critical importance in the present case to appreciate that the **11–100** purchasers do not trace the premiums directly into the insurance money. They trace them first into the policy and thence into the proceeds of the policy. It is essential not to elide the two steps. In this context, of course, the word "policy" does not mean the contract of insurance. You do not trace the payment of a premium into the insurance contract any more than you trace a payment into a bank account into the banking contract. The word "policy" is here used to describe the bundle of rights to which the policyholder is entitled in return for the premiums. These rights, which may be very complex, together constitute a chose in action, *viz.* the right to payment of a debt payable on a future event and contingent upon the continued payment of further premiums until the happening of the event. That chose in action represents the traceable proceeds of the premiums; its current value fluctuates from time to time. When the policy matures, the insurance money represents the traceable proceeds of the policy and hence indirectly of the premiums.

It follows that, if a claimant can show that premiums were paid with his **11–101** money, he can claim a proportionate share of the policy. His interest arises by reason of and immediately upon the payment of the premiums, and the extent of his share is ascertainable at once. He does not have to wait until the policy matures in order to claim his property. His share in the policy and its proceeds may increase or decrease as further premiums are paid; but it is not affected by the realisation of the policy. His share remains the same whether the policy is sold or surrendered or held until maturity; these are merely different methods of realising the policy. They may affect the amount of the proceeds received on realisation but they cannot affect the extent of his share in the proceeds. In principle the purchasers are entitled to the insurance money which was paid on Mr Murphy's death in the same shares and proportions as they were entitled in the policy immediately before his death.

Since the manner in which an asset is realised does not affect its ownership, **11–102** and since it cannot matter whether the claimant discovers what has happened before or after it is realised, the question of ownership can be answered by ascertaining the shares in which it is owned immediately before it is realised. Where A misappropriates B's money and uses it to buy a winning ticket in the lottery, B is entitled to the winnings. Since A is a wrongdoer, it is irrelevant that he could have used his own money if in fact he used B's. This may seem to give B an undeserved windfall, but the result is not unjust. Had B discovered the fraud before the draw, he could have decided whether to keep the ticket or demand his money back. He alone has the right to decide whether to gamble with his own money. If A keeps him in ignorance until after the draw, he suffers the consequence. He cannot deprive B of his right to choose what to do with his own money; but he can give him an informed choice.

The application of these principles ought not to depend on the nature of the chose in action. They should apply to a policy of life assurance as they apply to a bank account or a lottery ticket." [Appeal allowed: policy proceeds to be divided between the purchaser-claimants and the children in proportions in which they contributed to premiums]

Section 3. Personal Claims against Recipients of Improperly Distributed Property

I. Improperly Distributed Estates of Deceased Persons

11–103   The House of Lords in *Ministry of Health v. Simpson*[85] (where the "reasoning and conclusions" of the Court of Appeal[86] on the personal claim were said to be "unimpeachable") held that where a deceased's estate has been wrongfully distributed to persons not entitled to it, then an unpaid or underpaid creditor, legatee or next of kin has an equitable personal claim against those persons, but *only* after he has first exhausted his claim against the personal representatives responsible for the blunder.[87] Naturally, he must give credit for the money he obtains from the personal representatives. He must bring his action within 12 years of the date when the right to receive the money from the personal representative accrued.[88] His claim lies only for the principal sum due from the estate and not for any interest thereon, assuming that the wrong recipient, R, had no knowledge[89] that his receipt was wrongful. R cannot be charged interest because he is under no obligation to the claimant to make productive use of the money or property which he innocently received.[90]

11–104   The personal claim is not restricted to cases where the personal representatives' mistake was one of fact and not of law. As Lord Simonds stated[91]:

> "It is difficult to see what relevance the distinction can have where a legatee [claimant] does not plead his own mistake or his own ignorance, but, having exhausted his remedy against the executor who has made the wrongful payment, seeks to recover money from him who has been

---

[85] [1951] A.C. 251.
[86] *Re Diplock* [1948] Ch. 468. The appeal to the Lords concerned the personal claim and not the proprietary tracing claim.
[87] It is a strict requirement that the blundering personal representatives must be sued before the innocent recipients of the property: *Re J. Leslie Engineers Ltd* [1976] 2 All E.R. 85 at 91, *Butler v. Broadhead* [1975] Ch. 97 at 107–108. They should take full advantage of Trustee Act 1925, s.27 and, if need be, act solely upon a court order.
[88] Limitation Act 1939, s.20 replaced by Limitation Act 1980, s.22.
[89] Including "Nelsonian" and "naughty knowledge": see discussion *infra*, para. 11–111.
[90] If he does make productive use of it, he should account for profits actually earned: neither the "tree" nor its "fruits" should logically be his (see Ford and Lee p. 751 and *Re Diplock* [1948] Ch. 468 at 517 deciding that charities which had invested moneys in interest-bearing securities should repay such investments and interest under the proprietary tracing claim).
[91] [1951] A.C. 251, 270. The bar to recovery for mistake of law has now been removed by *Kleinwort Benson v. Lincoln C.C.* [1998] 3 W.L.R. 1095 (H.L.).

wrongfully paid. To such a suit the executor was not a necessary party and there was no means by which the plaintiff could find out whether his mistake was of law or fact or, even, whether his wrongful act was deliberate or mistaken. He could guess and ask the court to guess, but he could prove nothing. I reject, therefore, the suggestion that the equitable remedy in such circumstances was thus restricted."

The executor's mistake of law was to accept the validity of a residuary bequest "for such charitable institution or institutions or other charitable or benevolent object or objects" as they should in their absolute discretion select. Such a non-charitable bequest was void for uncertainty[92] so that the next of kin were entitled to the undisposed of property. However, the executors distributed the estate between various charities whom the next of kin sued, after having first sued the executors and compromised the action with the court's approval.

The Court of Appeal held that[93]:

> "persons in the position of the respondents [the charities], themselves **11–105** unversed in the law, are entitled to assume that the executors are properly administering the estate, and if, as admitted in this case, they took the money bona fide believing themselves to be entitled to it, they should not have imposed on them the heavy obligations of trusteeship. We do not think it necessary or desirable to attempt an exhaustive formulation of the law applicable as regards notice in the case of payments to legatees, save to say that every case of this kind will depend on its own facts and that the principles are not the same as the principles in regard to notice of defects in title applicable to transfer of land where regular machinery has long since been established for inquiry and investigation."

In delivering the judgment of the House of Lords, Lord Simonds based **11–106** himself on the following statement of Lord Davey,[94] which he said[95] "explains the basis of the jurisdiction, the evil to be avoided and its remedy":

> "The Court of Chancery in order to do justice and to avoid the evil of allowing one man to retain what is really and legally applicable to the payment of another man devised a remedy by which where the estate had been distributed without regard to the rights of a creditor, it has allowed the creditor to recover back what has been paid to the beneficiaries or the next of kin who derive title from the deceased testator or intestate."

As Lord Simonds then remarked[96]:

> "It would be strange if a court of equity, whose self-sought duty it was to see that the assets of a deceased person were duly administered and came

---

[92] *Chichester Diocesan Fund v. Simpson* [1944] A.C. 341; see *supra*, p. 481.
[93] [1948] Ch. 465 at 478–479.
[94] *Harrison v. Kirk* [1904] A.C. 1 at 7.
[95] [1951] A.C. 251 at 266.
[96] *ibid.*

into the right hands and not into the wrong hands, devised a remedy for the protection of the unpaid creditor but left the unpaid legatee or next of kin unprotected."

11–107   However, he was careful to restrict himself to the improper administration of a deceased's estate where the Court of Chancery had inherited the strict approach of the ecclesiastical courts[97]:

> "It is important to remember that the particular branch of the jurisdiction of the Court of Chancery with which we are concerned relates to the administration of assets of a deceased person . . . I do not find in history or in logic any justification for an argument which denies the possibility of an equitable right in the administration of assets because, as it is alleged, no comparable right existed in the execution of trusts."

II. Improperly Distributed Trust Funds

Potential for new strict restitutionary approach

11–108   Despite the different historical basis[98] for the strict liability of recipients of improperly distributed estates of deceased persons a case can be made for extending this strict liability to recipients of improperly distributed trust funds now that the general defence of change of position is available to set reasonable limits to an expanded right to restitution. After all, recipients of a windfall benefit from a deceased's estate or from a trust fund are equally enriched at the expense of the rightful owner in circumstances where there is no lawful excuse for such enrichment. Thus, in each case they should be strictly liable to restore what they have received, unless they can prove that the defence of change of position is available or of bona fide purchaser of a legal interest for value without notice.[99]

11–109   The defence of change of position does not extend to someone who does not act in good faith or is a wrongdoer which, prevents the defence being made out if the defendant had actual, Nelsonian or naughty knowledge[1] of the circumstances affording the plaintiff a right to restitution. It should not, however, be a defence that the claimant has not first sued the blundering trustee.

Moreover, in the light of the House of Lords' broad approach to equitable subrogation in *Banque Financière v. Parc (Battersea) Ltd*,[2] if a trustee improperly distributes £5,000 to an innocent recipient R, who then uses it to discharge a £5,000 debt due to X then the beneficiaries

---

[97] See Birks *Introduction to the Law of Restitution* (1985), pp. 441–443.
[98] See S. J. Whittaker (1983) 4 Jo. Legal Hist. 3 and C. Harpum "Knowing Assistance and Knowing Receipt" in P. B. H. Birks (ed.) *Frontiers of Liability* (1994), Vol. 1.
[99] See C. Harpum, *op. cit.* and P. B. H. Birks therein pp. 31 *et seq.*; Sir Peter Millett (1991) 107 L.Q.R. 71; Lord Nicholls in Cornish, Nolan, O'Sullivan & Virgo (eds), *Restitution: Past, Present and Future* (1998) pp. 231–245.
[1] see *infra*, para. 11–111.
[2] [1998] 1 All E.R. 737. Also see *Wenlock v. River Dee Co* (1887) 19 Q.B.D. 155.

should be subrogated to X's right: otherwise, R would be unjustly enriched at the beneficiaries' expense in circumstances where there seems no policy reason for denying the beneficiaries a personal subrogation claim (or a proprietary subrogation claim if X were a secured creditor.[3]) However, liability to account for compound interest (as a constructive trustee) would not arise until R's conscience was affected by actual, Nelsonian or naughty knowledge of the trust as discussed below.

Traditional personal liability (as constructive trustee) if conscience affected

A person who has improperly received trust or other property subject to **11–110** a fiduciary relationship for his own benefit (and not as agent[4]) has traditionally been held personally liable to account as a constructive trustee (as a formula for equitable relief[5]) for so-called "knowing receipt" if the transfer to him was not protected by statutory overreaching provisions or exceptions to the rule nemo dat quod non habet and he received the property with knowledge[6] that it was fiduciary property transferred improperly or if he received it without such knowledge but subsequently discovered the facts. As a matter of the property rules as to priorities he is bound forthwith by the beneficiaries' equitable interests but he only becomes personally accountable as a constructive trustee liable to restore the trust property to its rightful owner from the time he had actual, Nelsonian or naughty knowledge of the equitable interests,[7] *e.g.* so as to become liable to account for compound interest on moneys received which he ought to have returned.

Notice and Knowledge

The classification of *notice* into actual or constructive or imputed notice **11–111** has developed to determine whether or not a purchaser (particularly of land) takes *property subject to an equitable interest*. Imputed notice is the

---

[3] *Boscawen v. Bajwa* [1995] 4 All E.R. 769, *supra* para. 11–51.
[4] Agents can be liable as accessories if they dishonestly assist in a breach of trust or other fiduciary duty: *Royal Brunei Airlines v. Tan* [1995] 2 A.C. 378 or as principals if they decide to ignore the trust and treat the assets as for their own benefit. A person receives for his own benefit where he is beneficially entitled as donee or purchaser: *Polly Peck International plc v. Nadir (No. 2)* [1992] 4 All E.R. 769 at 777; *Agip (Africa) Ltd v. Jackson* [1990] Ch. 265 at 291–293. In the case of a bank it becomes the owner of money paid to it but normally there is no meaningful receipt for the bank's own benefit except where the money reduces an overdraft: *Gray v. Johnson* (1868) L.R. 3 H.L. 1, 4; *Coleman v. Bucks, and Oxon Union Bank* [1897] 2 Ch. 243, 254; *Agip Africa Ltd v. Jackson* [1990] Ch. 265, 292; *Polly Peck International plc v. Nadir* [1992] 4 All E.R. 769, 777.
[5] *Selangor United Rubber Estates v. Cradock* [1968] 2 All E.R. 1073, at 1097.
[6] *El Ajou v. Dollar Land Holdings plc* [1994] 2 All E.R. 685 at 700, *per* Hoffmann L.J. endorsed by Nourse L.J. in *Bank of Credit and Commerce (overseas) Ltd v. Akindale* [2000] 4 All E.R. 221, 229; *Eagle Trust plc v. SBC Securities* [1992] 4 All E.R. 488; *Re Montagu's S.T.* [1987] Ch. 264. References to receipt with notice (*e.g. Agip (Africa) Ltd v. Jackson* [1990] Ch. 265 at 291 *per* Millett J.) should take account of constructive notice outside the conveyancing context being restricted to "naughty" knowledge; see *infra*, para. 11–112.
[7] *Re Montagu's S.T.* [1987] Ch. 264 endorsed in *Westdeutsche Landesbank Girozentrale v. Islington B.C.* [1996] 2 All E.R. 961, *supra*, para. 5–16.

actual or constructive notice of an agent[8] that is imputed to his principal, the purchaser. Constructive notice is notice of those matters that would have come to the knowledge of the agent or purchaser if such inquiries and inspections had been made as ought reasonably to have been made by him.[9]

It is then very easy to assume that because a third party receiving trust property with notice thereof is subject to a *proprietary* obligation to return it, and so is constructive trustee thereof till such return, he must also be *personally* accountable as a constructive trustee even if he parted with the property before having knowledge it was trust? However a person cannot become so personally accountable until his conscience is affected by knowledge that he had received property in breach of trust or other fiduciary duty.

The classification of *knowledge* into actual, "Nelsonian" and "naughty" knowledge has developed to determine whether a person's conscience is sufficiently affected for Equity to impose upon him the *personal burdens of accountability* as a constructive trustee. "Nelsonian" knowledge (named after Nelson putting his telescope to his blind eye to avoid seeing flag signals ordering him to withdraw) covers knowledge obtainable but for shutting one's eyes to what would otherwise be obvious.[10] A defendant has "naughty knowledge" where his suspicions were aroused that the transaction was probably improper but he deliberately or recklessly failed to make the inquiries an honest reasonable man would make in the circumstances.[11] If these circumstances were such as to arouse the suspicions of an honest reasonable man, then the court will be ready to infer that the defendant's suspicions were aroused despite his self-serving protestations to the contrary.[12] Normally, matters are reduced to a question of fact, a jury question,[13] as to whether or not the defendant was dishonest, exhibiting a lack of probity through his actual, Nelsonian or naughty knowledge. However, it is possible for a person with actual knowledge of circumstances amounting to a breach of fiduciary duty to believe himself honestly entitled to receive property affected by a fiduciary relationship because he did not believe there had been a breach of fiduciary duty; but it is not considered conscionable for him to rely on his drawing the wrong inference from the factual circumstances to try to escape liability for what[14] he knew to have happened.

---

[8] Acting as such in the particular transaction: *Halifax Mortgage Service Ltd v. Stepsky* [1996] 2 All E.R. 277.

[9] Law of Property Act 1925, s.199(1)(ii); *Barclays Bank plc v. O'Brien* [1994] 1 A.C. 180 at 195–196.

[10] *Baden v. Société Générale* [1992] 4 All E.R. 161 at 235.

[11] *Ibid. Re Montagu's S.T.* [1987] Ch. 264; *Jones v. Gordon* (1877) 2 App.Cas. 616 at 629; *Assets Co. U.K. v. Mere Roihi* [1905] A.C. 176 at 201, *Belmont Finance Corp v. Williams Furniture* [1979] Ch. 250.

[12] *Eagle Trust plc v. SBC Securities* [1992] 4 All E.R. 488 at 509; *El Ajou v. Dollar Land Holdings plc* [1993] 3 All E.R. 717 at 739.

[13] *Agip (Africa) Ltd v. Jackson* [1992] 4 All E.R. 385 at 405.

[14] *Belmont Finance Corp. v. Williams Furniture (No 2)* [1980] 1 All E.R. 393; *Hillsdown plc v. Pensions Ombudsman* [1997] 1 All E.R. 862; *Bank of Credit and Commerce International (Overseas) Ltd v. Akindele* [2000] 4 All E.R. 221, 235.

Since Megarry V.-C.[15] carefully distinguished "notice" and **11–112** "knowledge" in 1985 the borderline between the two has become blurred when the courts have examined what amounts to constructive notice outside the conveyancing context where a purchaser has to investigate title using well-established procedures. Outside such context, in commercial dealings it seems that a person will only have constructive notice of matters of which he has naughty knowledge.[16] Millett J. has stated,[17] "A recipient is not expected to be unduly suspicious and is not to be held [to have notice] unless he went ahead without further inquiry in circumstances in which an honest and reasonable man would have realised that the money was probably trust money and was being misapplied". As Millett L.J. has stated,[18] "In order to establish constructive notice it is necessary to prove that the facts known to the defendant made it imperative for him to seek an explanation, because in the absence of an explanation it was obvious that the transaction was probably improper".

In the case of donees, equitable interests bind them on property law principles irrespective of notice because they are not purchasers for value, but they should not have the burdens of personal accountability as a constructive trustee thrust upon them (eg to account for compound interest on moneys received) unless their consciences are bound by actual, Nelsonian or naughty knowledge.[19]

What must the claimant plead? Need want of probity be alleged?

Where the claimant pursues his equitable proprietary remedy he needs **11–113** to allege that the defendant improperly received the trust property and must return it or its traceable product, leaving it to the defendant to raise the defence that he has dissipated the property or has the defence of change of position or of bona fide purchaser of a legal interest without notice.[20] However, where the claimant alleges the defendant is personally accountable as a constructive trustee[21] he needs to allege that the defendant's conscience is bound because he had actual, Nelsonian or naughty knowledge of the facts giving rise to the claimant's claim. As

---

[15] *Re Montagu's S.T.* [1987] Ch. 264.
[16] *Polly Peck International plc v. Nadir (No. 2)* [1992] 4 All E.R. 769 at 777, 782.
[17] *El Ajou v. Dollar Land Holdings plc* [1993] 3 All E.R. 717 at 739.
[18] *Macmillan Inc. v. Bishopsgate Investment Trust plc* [1995] 1 W.L.R. 978 at 1014.
[19] *Westdeutsche Landesbank Girozentrale v. Islington B.C.* [1996] 2 All E.R. 961, 988c, 990b, 991; 997a, per Lord Browne-Wilkinson; *Hillsdown plc v. Pensions Ombudsman* [1997] 1 All E.R. 862, 902d.
[20] Surprisingly in *Polly Peck International plc v. Nadir (No. 2)* [1992] 4 All E.R. 769 the Court of Appeal rejected the view that the onus lay on the defendant to prove the bona fide purchaser defence: this reversal of the usual onus (*Barclays Bank v. Boulter* [1999] 4 All E.R. 513, 518) may be peculiar to banking or, perhaps the transfer of money; *Union Bank of Australia Ltd v. Murray Aynsley* [1898] A.C. 693.
[21] Historically, to make a non-trustee personally liable like an express trustee, he was constructively treated as a trustee if the state of his conscience justified this and so made personally liable as a constructive trustee. Nowadays "as a constructive trustee" is surplus to requirements and creates confusion with constructive trusts of property, so personal liability to account for equitable wrongdoing should become the recognised liability: Lord Nicholls in Cornish Nolan, O'Sullivan & Virgo (eds) *Restitution: Past, Present and Future* (1998) pp. 243–245; Lord Millett (1998) 114 L.R. 400.

Hoffmann L.J. has stated,[22] "the plaintiff must show, first, a disposal of his assets in breach of fiduciary duty; secondly, the beneficial receipt by the defendant of assets which are traceable as representing the assets of the plaintiff; and, thirdly, knowledge on the part of the defendant that the assets he received are traceable to a breach of fiduciary duty".

Once the defendant has such actual, Nelsonian or naughty knowledge, a denial of the claimant's personal claim will be unconscionable and will usually but not necessarily involve a want of probity.[23] Thus, want of probity—or dishonesty—need not be alleged. A solicitor receiving fees from trying to defend a defendant alleged to have obtained £x in breach of fiduciary duty and to have paid part of it as fees has cause to be anxious. A freezing order on the defendant's funds except for paying legal fees does not protect the solicitor from potential liability.[24]

The onus of proof lies on the claimant to prove that the conscience of the defendant is sufficiently affected to make him personally liable to account for the value received: it will be time to abandon the historical baggage of liability "as a constructive trustee" once that label has served the purpose of emphasising the need for the defendant's conscience to be affected to justify the intervention of Equity.

11–114	If the restitutionary strict approach were to prevail in the House of Lords, then the plaintiff would only need to plead the receipt by the defendant of the relevant property, whereupon the defendant would have to make full disclosure[25] and would have to discharge the onus of proving the defence of change of position which is, as yet, in an uncertain phase of its development, though it seems it will require him to prove that he acted in good faith without actual, Nelsonian or naughty knowledge of the circumstances. The distinction between the equitable approach and the restitutionary approach is not a distinction without a difference; the switching of the onus of proof if the latter approach is adopted is, in practice, a crucial distinction and, it is submitted, militates against the courts adopting such approach.

---

[22] *El Ajou v. Dollar Land Holdings plc* [1994] 2 All E.R. 685 at 700 endorsed by Nourse L.J. in *Bank of Credit and Commerce (Overseas) Ltd v. Akindele* [2000] 4 All E.R. 221, 229; *Eagle Trust plc v. SBC Securities Ltd* [1993] 1 W.L.R. 484; *Cowan de Groot Properties Ltd v. Eagle Trust plc* [1992] 4 All E.R. 700. Old cases stating that receipt with notice sufficed were confusing the proprietary tracing claim with the personal claim, though nowadays, they could be explained on the basis that, outside of the conveyancing context, constructive notice is restricted to naughty knowledge as indicated by *Polly Peck International plc v. Nadir (No. 2)* [1992] 4 All E.R. 769 at 777, 782; *El Ajou v. Dollar Land Holdings plc* [1993] 3 All E.R. 717 at 739; *Macmilan Inc v. Bishopsgate Investment Trust plc* [1995] 1 W.L.R. 978 at 1014. Further see S. Gardner (1996) 112 L.Q.R. 56.

[23] *Belmont Finance Corp. v. Williams Furniture (No 2)* [1980] 1 All E.R. 393, *Hillsdown plc v. Pensions Ombudsman* [1997] 1 All E.R. 862; *Bank of Credit and Commerce (Overseas) Ltd v. Akindele* [2000] 4 All E.R. 221 where Nourse L.J. at 235 lays down a single test of knowledge for knowing receipt: "The recipient's knowledge must be such as to make it unconscionable for him to retain the benefit of the receipt".

[24] *United Mizrahi Bank Ltd v. Doherty* [1998] 1 W.L.R. 435. Doherty, the bank's chief lending officer pleaded guilty at his subsequent trial and was jailed for 5 years. Some protection against liability for dishonest assistance in a breach of fiduciary duty may be obtained on applying to the court: *Finers v. Miro* [1991] 1 W.L.R. 35.

[25] He could not reject the claim (as he currently can) on the basis that it is a fishing expedition and should be struck out for not particularising knowledge on the part of the defendant, *e.g. Eagle Trust plc v. SBC Securities Ltd* [1993] 1 W.L.R. 484.

Section 4. Personal Claim for Dishonest Assistance in a Breach of Fiduciary Duty

The Privy Council in *Royal Brunei Airlines Sdn Bhd v. Tan*[26] *infra* para. **11–115** 11–152 has recently clarified an untidy area of the law concerned with the secondary liability of an accessory involved in a breach of trust or other fiduciary duty. Previously, persons who never received any trust property or only received it and dealt with it as agent were made personally liable to account (where they could not be liable at common law) by Equity treating them as constructive trustees where their conscience was affected, because they had knowingly assisted in a *dishonest* breach of fiduciary duty or had knowingly dealt with that property in an honest or dishonest manner[27] inconsistent with the fiduciary relationship.

Lord Nicholls has now made it clear that the secondary liability of an accessory requires dishonesty on the part of the accessory but it is not necessary that in addition the trustee or other fiduciary was acting dishonestly. He states,[28] "A liability in equity to make good resulting loss attaches to a person who dishonestly procures or assists in a breach of trust or fiduciary obligation".

He also indicates[29] that "knowingly" is better avoided as a defining **11–116** ingredient of liability and that the *Baden v. Société Generale*[30] scales of actual, Nelsonian, naughty and constructive[31] knowledge should best be forgotten. He thus concentrates on explaining dishonesty but as an objective standard. Essentially, his idea is that the test is whether the honest person would regard it as honest to behave as the defendant did, taking account of the external effects of the defendant's actions and the motives and attitudes with which he acted.

However, this indicates that the defendant's knowledge when he performed the relevant actions must be an issue. Does the defendant not need to have actual Nelsonian or naughty knowledge that there is a trust or other fiduciary obligation in respect of particular property and that his actions will prejudice those beneficially interested in such property?[32] As Simon Gardner writes,[33] "It is doubtful, then, that the new law of direct reference to a concept of dishonesty obviates any need for an exegesis upon cognisance".

---

[26] [1995] 2 A.C. 378.

[27] *Agip (Africa) Ltd v. Jackson* [1990] Ch. 265 at 292.

[28] [1995] 2 A.C. 378, 392. Query whether the fiduciary obligation can be free-standing or needs to involve particular property: *Brown v. Bennett* [1999] 1 B.C.L.C. 649, 658–659.

[29] *ibid.*

[30] [1992] 4 All E.R. 161.

[31] For the 2 types of constructive knowledge see the 5 types of knowledge set out in the judgment of *Re Montagu's Settlement*, *infra* para. 11–121.

[32] Dishonesty requires "the taking of a risk to the prejudice of another's right, which risk is known to be one which there is no right to take": *Baden* [1992] 4 All E.R. 161 at 234. The test is "whether the accused was acting dishonestly by the standards of ordinary and decent people and, if so, whether he himself must have realised that what he was doing was, by those standards, dishonest: *R. v. Ghosh* [1982] Q.B. 1053 applied in *R. v. Clowes (No. 2)* [1994] 2 All E.R. 316.

[33] (1996) 112 L.Q.R. 56 at 67.

11–117   Indeed, in *Brinks Ltd v. Abu Saleh (No. 3)*[34] Rimer J. pointed out that Lord Nicholls' speech proceeded on the basis that a dishonest assistance claim could only be brought against someone who knew of the existence of the trust or at least of the facts giving rise to the trust[35]: the speech was simply directed at what further needed to be shown to make the accessory liable.

If agents like solicitors or accountants (*e.g.* in the course of complying with the Money-Laundering Regulations[36] under the Criminal Justice Act 1988) become worried about possible liability as accessories then they should apply to the High Court under RSC O.85 for directions. The court's directions can even override the legal professional privilege of confidentiality of the client if the court believes he could well be involved in iniquity.[37]

RE MONTAGU'S SETTLEMENT

Chancery Division [1987] 1 Ch. 264; [1992] 4 All E.R. 308 [1987] 2 W.L.R. 1192.

11–118   SIR ROBERT MEGARRY V.-C.: ". . . What is in issue is the result of the receipt by the tenth Duke of a large number of settled chattels, and his disposal of them during his lifetime. On many matters the evidence is slender or obscure, since the tenth Duke (whom I shall call simply "the Duke") received the chattels in the late 1940s and disposed of many of them then; he died in 1977 and others concerned have also died. What has to be resolved was whether the Duke held the chattels as a constructive trustee so that his estate is accountable for them or their proceeds.

"The issue centred on clause 14(B) of the 1923 settlement. That settlement assigned a large number of chattels to the trustees of the settlement upon certain trusts. In the events which happened, the trustees had a fiduciary duty on the death of the ninth Duke to select and make an inventory of such of the chattels as they considered suitable for inclusion in the settlement, and to hold the residue of the chattels in trust for the Duke absolutely. In the event, the trustees made no selection or inventory but instead treated all the chattels as being the absolute property of the Duke. The Duke's solicitor, Mr. Lickfold, undoubtedly knew the terms of clause 14(B) and understood its effect, and the Duke had a copy of the settlement: but the time came when Mr. Lickfold, Col. Nicholl (a solicitor advising the trustees), the trustees themselves and Mr. Gilchrist, an American lawyer advising the Duke, all seemed to have treated clause 14(B) as allowing the trustees to assent to the Duke taking any of the chattels that he wished and either keeping them or else selling them and keeping the proceeds of

---

[34] [1995] *The Times*, October 23, 1995 (wife's presence in husband's car on six trips to Zurich to courier money there at request of husband's boss concerned, she believed, to evade tax on his business profits did not constitute relevant assistance in laundering £3 million stolen from Brinks Ltd with the help of a dishonest fiduciary).

[35] Thus, since the wife thought tax evasion (and not a breach of an employee's fiduciary duty) was involved she would not be liable. However, the view of Millett J. in *Agip (Africa) Ltd v. Jackson* [1990] Ch. 265, 295 should prevail: it is no defence to say that "only" tax evasion or foreign exchange control evasion was believed to be involved, because a person who consciously assists others by making arrangements which she knows to be calculated to conceal what is happening from a third party, takes the risk they are part of a fiduciary fraud against the third party.

[36] S.I. 1993 No. 1933.

[37] *Finers v. Miro* [1991] 1 W.L.R. 35. See also *Bank of Scotland v. A Ltd* [2001] 3 All E.R. 58.

sale. In 1949 there were two large sales of the chattels; and many chattels were shipped out to Kenya, where the Duke was living.

"There is no suggestion that anyone concerned in the matter was dishonest. **11–119** There was a muddle, but however careless it was, it was an honest muddle. Further, I do not think that the Duke was at any relevant time conscious of the fact that he was not entitled to receive the chattels and deal with them as beneficial owner. Of course, if clause 14(B) is singled out for attention and read carefully it could be seen by a reasonably intelligent layman not to empower the trustees simply to release chattels to the Duke, but to require them first to select chattels for inclusion in the settlement and to provide that only when they had done that would the chattels not selected become the Duke's property. But clause 14(B) was deeply embedded in a long and complex document, and in view of the advice and information that the Duke received from his solicitor I can see no reason why the Duke should be expected to attempt to construe the settlement himself. If expressed in terms of the doctrine of notice, I have held, ante, p. 268F-G, that the Duke had notice, both actual and imputed, of the terms of clause 14(B)." But I have also said, ante, pp. 271H–272A:

> "I do not think that the tenth Duke had any knowledge at any material time that the chattels that he was receiving or dealing with were chattels that were still subject to any trust. I think that he believed that they had been lawfully and properly released to him by the trustees."

"That brings me to the essential question for decision. The core of the **11–120** question is what suffices to constitute a recipient of trust property a constructive trustee of it. I can leave on one side the equitable doctrine of tracing: if the recipient of trust property still has the property or its traceable proceeds in his possession, he is liable to restore it unless he is a purchaser without notice. But liability as a constructive trustee is wider, and does not depend upon the recipient still having the property or its traceable proceeds. Does it suffice if the recipient had 'notice' that the property he was receiving was trust property, or must he have not merely notice of this, but knowledge, or 'cognizance,' as it has been put?

"In the books and the authorities the word 'notice' is often used in place of the word 'knowledge,' usually without any real explanation of its meaning. This seems to me to be a fertile source of confusion; for whatever meaning the layman may attach to those words, centuries of equity jurisprudence have attached a detailed and technical meaning to the term 'notice,' without doing the same for 'knowledge.' The classification of 'notice' into actual notice, constructive notice and imputed notice has been developed in relation to the doctrine that a bona fide purchaser for value of a legal estate takes free from any equitable interests of which he has no notice. I need not discuss this classification beyond saying that I use the term 'imputed notice' as meaning any actual or constructive notice that a solicitor or other agent for the purchaser acquires in the course of the transaction in question, such notice being imputed to the purchaser. Some of the cases describe any constructive notice that a purchaser himself obtains as being 'imputed' to him; but I confine 'imputed' to notice obtained by another which equity imputes to the purchaser.

"Now until recently I do not think there had been any classification of **11–121** 'knowledge' which corresponded with the classification of 'notice.' However, in the *Baden* case [1992] 4 All E.R. at p. 235, the judgment sets out five categories of knowledge, or of the circumstances in which the court may treat a person as having knowledge. Counsel in that case were substantially in agreement in treating all five types as being relevant for the purpose of a constructive trust; and the judge agreed with them: at 415. These categories are (i) actual knowledge; (ii) wilfully shutting one's eyes to the obvious; (iii) wilfully and recklessly failing to make such inquiries as an honest and reasonable man would make; (iv) knowledge of circumstances which would indicate the facts to an honest and reasonable man; and (v) knowledge of circumstances which would put an honest and reasonable man on inquiry. If I pause there, it can be said that these categories of knowledge correspond to two categories of notice: Type (i) corresponds to actual notice, and types (ii), (iii), (iv) and (v) correspond to constructive notice. Nothing, however, is said (at least in terms) about imputed knowledge. This is important, because in the case before me Mr. Taylor strongly contended that Mr. Lickfold's knowledge must be imputed to the Duke, and that this was of the essence of his case.

11–122   "It seems to me that one must be very careful about applying to constructive trusts either the accepted concepts of notice or any analogy to them. In determining whether a constructive trust has been created, the fundamental question is whether the conscience of the recipient is bound in such a way as to justify equity in imposing a trust on him. The rules concerning a purchaser without notice seem to me to provide little guidance on this and to be liable to be misleading. First, they are irrelevant unless there is a purchase. A volunteer is bound by an equitable interest even if he has no notice of it; but in many cases of alleged constructive trusts the disposition has been voluntary and not for value, and yet notice or knowledge is plainly relevant. Second, although a purchaser normally employs solicitors, and so questions of imputed notice may arise, it is unusual for a volunteer to employ solicitors when about to receive bounty. Even if he does, he is unlikely to employ them in order to investigate the right of the donor to make the gift or of the trustees or personal representatives to make the distribution; and until this case came before me I had never heard it suggested that a volunteer would be fixed with imputed notice of all that his solicitors would have discovered had he employed solicitors and had instructed them to investigate his right to receive the property.

11–123   "Third, there seems to me to be a fundamental difference between the questions that arise in respect of the doctrine of purchaser without notice and constructive trusts. As I said in my previous judgment, ante, pp. 272H–273B:

> 'The former is concerned with the question whether a person takes property subject to or free from some equity. The latter is concerned with whether or not a person is to have imposed upon him the personal burdens and obligations of trusteeship. I do not see why one of the touchstones for determining the burdens on property should be the same as that for deciding whether to impose a personal obligation on a man. The cold calculus of constructive and imputed notice does not seem to me to be an appropriate instrument for deciding whether a man's conscience is sufficiently affected for it to be right to bind him by the obligations of a constructive trustee.'

"I can see no reason to resile from that statement, save that to meet possible susceptibilities I would alter "man" to "person." I would only add that there is more to being made a trustee then merely taking property subject to an equity.

11–124   "There is a further consideration. There is today something of a tendency in equity to put less emphasis on detailed rules that have emerged from the cases and more weight on the underlying principles that engendered those rules, treating the rules less as rules requiring complete compliance, and more as guidelines to assist the court in applying the principles. A good illustration of this approach is to be found in the judgment of Oliver J. in *Taylors Fashions Ltd. v. Liverpool Victoria Trustees Co. Ltd. (Note)* [1981] Q.B. 133 at 145–155. This view was adopted by Robert Goff J. in *Amalgamated Investment & Property Co. Ltd. v. Texas Commerce International Bank Ltd.* [1982] Q.B. 84 at 104, 105, and it was, I think, accepted, though not cited, by the Court of Appeal in the latter case: see at pp. 116–132. Certainly it was approved in terms by the Court of Appeal in *Habib Bank Ltd. v. Habib Bank A.G. Zurich* [1981] 1 W.L.R. 1265 at 1285, 1287. The *Taylors Fashions case* [1981] Q.B. 133 concerned equitable estoppel and the five probanda to be found in the judgment of Fry J. in *Willmott v. Barber* (1880) 15 Ch. D. 96, 105; and on the facts of the case before him Oliver J. in the *Taylors Fashions* case concluded that the question was not whether each of those probanda had been satisfied but whether it would be unconscionable for the defendants to take advantage of the mistake there in question. Accordingly, although I readily approach the five categories of knowledge set out in the *Baden* case [1983] B.C.L.C. 325 as useful guides, I regard them primarily as aids in determining whether or not the Duke's conscience was affected in such a way as to require him to hold any or all of the chattels that he received on a constructive trust.

"There is one further general consideration that I should mention, and that is **11–125** that 'the court should not be astute to impute knowledge where no actual knowledge exists': see the *Baden* case at 415, *per* Peter Gibson J. This approach goes back at least as far as *Barnes v. Addy* (1874) 9 Ch. App. 244, 251, 252. The view of James L.J., at 256, was that the court had in some cases

> "gone to the very verge of justice in making good to cestuis que trust the consequences of the breaches of trust of their trustees at the expense of persons perfectly honest, but who have been, in some more or less degree, injudicious."

"Of the five categories of knowledge set out in the *Baden* case [1983] B.C.L.C. 325, Mr. Chadwick, as well as Mr. Taylor, accepted the first three. What was in issue was nos. (iv) and (v), namely, knowledge of circumstances which 'would indicate the facts to an honest and reasonable man' or 'would put an honest and reasonable man on inquiry.' On the view that I take of the present case I do not think that it really matters whether or not categories (iv) and (v) are included, but as the matter has been argued at length, and further questions on it may arise, I think I should say something about it.

"First, as I have already indicated, I think that one has to be careful to **11–126** distinguish the notice that is relevant in the doctrine of purchaser without notice from the knowledge that suffices for the imposition of a constructive trust. This is shown by a short passage in the long judgment of the Court of Appeal in In *Re Diplock* [1948] Ch. 465 at 478, 479. There, it was pointed out that on the facts of that case persons unversed in the law were entitled to assume that the executors were properly administering the estate, and that if those persons received money bona fide believing themselves to be entitled to it, 'they should not have imposed upon them the heavy obligations of trusteeship.' The judgment then pointed out:

> "the principles applicable to such cases are not the same as the principles in regard to notice of defects in title applicable to transfers of land where regular machinery has long since been established for inquiry and investigation."

11-127   "With that, I turn to the cases on constructive knowledge. Mr. Taylor relied strongly on *Selangor United Rubber Estates Ltd. v. Cradock (No. 3)* [1968] 1 W.L.R. 1555 and *Karak Rubber Co. Ltd. v. Burden (No. 2)* [1972] 1 W.L.R. 602. Each was a knowing assistance case. In the *Selangor* case at 1582, Ungoed-Thomas J., immediately after speaking of tracing property into the hands of a volunteer, said that equity

> "will hold a purchaser for value liable as constructive trustee if he had actual or constructive notice that the transfer to him was of trust property in breach of trust . . .";

and at 1583 he went on to refer to equitable rights and to say that in general "it is equitable that a person with actual notice or constructive notice of those rights should be fixed with knowledge of them." I find this view hard to reconcile with the passage in *Re Diplock* [1948] Ch. 465 (a case not cited to the judge) which I have just mentioned; and with all respect, it also seems to me to tend to confuse the absence of notice which shields a purchaser from liability under the doctrine of tracing, with the absence of knowledge of the trust which will prevent the imposition of a constructive trust. The judge went on to consider the meaning of "knowledge" in various judgments, and reached a conclusion that knowledge was not confined to actual knowledge; and with this, as such, Mr. Chadwick had no quarrel. But he strongly contended that the cases cited on the extended meaning of "knowledge" were cases within the "wilful and reckless" head in the classification in the *Baden* case [1983] B.C.L.C. 325 (*i.e.* type (iii)), and that there was nothing to justify the inclusion of types (iv) an (v). The essential difference, of course, is that types (ii) and (iii) are governed by the words "wilfully" or "wilfully and recklessly," whereas types (iv) and (v) have no such adverbs. Instead, they are cases of carelessness or negligence being tested by what an honest and reasonable man would have realised or would have inquired about, even if the person concerned was, for instance, not at all reasonable. Yet Ungoed-Thomas J. in his conclusion, at p. 1590, applied the standard of what would have been indicated to an honest and reasonable man, or would have put him on inquiry, and so, I think, included all five of the *Baden* types of knowledge, and not only the first three.

11-128   In the *Karak* case [1972] 1 W.L.R. 602, Brightman J. considered this conclusion. Again *Re Diplock* [1948] Ch. 465 was not cited, but *Williams v. Williams* (1881) 17 Ch.D. 437, another case not cited to Ungoed-Thomas J. in the *Selangor* case [1968] 1 W.L.R. 1555, was duly examined. Brightman J. distinguished that case by pointing out that it was a knowing receipt case, whereas the case before him was a knowing assistance case; and he said, at 638, that *Williams v. Williams* had "no relevance at all to the case before me." In *Williams v. Williams* Kay J. had held that the recipient of the trust property, a solicitor, was not liable as a constructive trustee, and, at 445, the judge said that the case would be "very different" if the recipient had "wilfully shut his eyes." He then referred to the "very great negligence" of the solicitor, qua solicitor, in ignoring the trust, though holding that he was not liable as a constructive trustee. I do not see how Kay J. could have reached that conclusion if he had thought that knowledge of *Baden* types (iv) and (v) had sufficed; and, of course, what is before me is a case of knowing receipt, like *Williams v. Williams* and unlike the *Karak* case.

11-129   "There is also In *Re Blundell* (1888) 40 Ch.D. 370, a case not cited in the *Selangor* case [1968] 1 W.L.R. 1555. It was cited but not mentioned in the judgment in the *Karak* case [1972] 1 W.L.R. 602, but like *Williams v. Williams, 17*

Ch.D. 437 and In *Re Diplock* [1948] Ch. 465 it does not appear in the *Baden* case [1983] B.C.L.C. 325: all three, I may say, were duly cited in the *Carl Zeiss* case [1969] 2 Ch. 276. In *Re Blundell*, Stirling J. refused to hold that a solicitor was a constructive trustee of costs that a trustee of property had allowed him to take out of the estate, even though he knew that the trustee was guilty of a breach of trust, 'unless there are facts brought home to him which show that to his knowledge the money is being applied in a manner which is inconsistent with the trust": see p. 381. Both *Williams v. Williams* and In *Re Blundell* figure prominently in the judgments of Sachs and Edmund Davies L.JJ. in the *Carl Zeiss* case, in support of their conclusion that negligence is not enough and that there must be dishonesty, a conscious impropriety or a lack of probity before liability as a constructive trustee is imposed . . .

"I shall attempt to summarise my conclusions.

(1) The equitable doctrine of tracing and the imposition of a constructive trust **11–130** by reason of the knowing receipt of trust property are governed by different rules and must be kept distinct. Tracing is primarily a means of determining the rights of property, whereas the imposition of a constructive trust creates personal obligations that go beyond mere property rights.

(2) In considering whether a constructive trust has arisen in a case of the knowing receipt of trust property, the basic question is whether the conscience of the recipient is sufficiently affected to justify the imposition of such a trust.

(3) Whether a constructive trust arises in such a case primarily depends on the knowledge of the recipient, and not on notice to him; and for clarity it is desirable to use the word "knowledge" and avoid the word "notice" in such cases.

(4) For this purpose, knowledge is not confined to actual knowledge, but includes at least knowledge of types (ii) and (iii) in the *Baden* case [1983] B.C.L.C. 325, 407, *i.e.* actual knowledge that would have been acquired but for shutting one's eyes to the obvious, or wilfully and recklessly failing to make such inquiries as a reasonable and honest man would make; for in such cases there is a want of probity which justifies imposing a constructive trust.

(5) Whether knowledge of the *Baden* types (iv) and (v) suffices for this purpose is at best doubtful; in my view, it does not, for I cannot see that the carelessness involved will normally amount to a want of probity.

(6) For these purposes, a person is not to be taken to have knowledge of a **11–131** fact that he once knew but has genuinely forgotten: the test (or a test) is whether the knowledge continues to operate on that person's mind at the time in question.

(7)(a) It is at least doubtful whether there is a general doctrine of "imputed knowledge" that corresponds to "imputed notice." (b) Even if there is such a doctrine, for the purposes of creating a constructive trust of the "knowing receipt" type the doctrine will not apply so as to fix a donee or beneficiary with all the knowledge that his solicitor has, at all events if the donee or beneficiary has not employed the solicitor to investigate his right to the bounty, and has done nothing else that can be treated as accepting that the solicitor's knowledge should be treated as his own. (c) Any such doctrine should be distinguished from the process whereby, under the name "imputed knowledge," a company is treated as having the knowledge that its directors and secretary have.

(8) Where an alleged constructive trust is based not on "knowing receipt" but on "knowing assistance," some at least of these considerations probably apply; but I need not decide anything on that; and I do not do so.

"From what I have said, it must be plain that in my judgment the Duke did not become a constructive trustee of any of the chattels. I can see nothing that affected his conscience sufficiently to impose a constructive trust on him."

Order accordingly.

EL AJOU V. DOLLAR LAND HOLDINGS PLC

Chancery Division [1993] 3 All E.R. 717; Court of Appeal [1994] 2 All E.R. 685.

MILLETT J: *"Tracing the money*

11–132   In *Agip (Africa) Ltd v. Jackson* [1991] Ch 547 at 566 Fox L.J. restated the principle, settled by *Re Diplock's Estate: Diplock v. Wintle* [1948] Ch 465, that it is a prerequisite of the right to trace in equity that there must be a fiduciary relationship which calls the equitable jurisdiction into being. This makes it necessary to consider separately the common law and equitable tracing rules. In the present case, it is manifestly impossible to follow the money at common law. The international transfers of money were made electronically; the plaintiff's money was mixed, not merely with the money of other victims or of the fraudsters themselves, but with the money of innocent third parties in the accounts of Valmet Geneva and Valmet Gibraltar, and passed on several occasions through the clearing systems of New York and London; while the back-to-back financing arrangements with Banque Scandinave and Scandinavian Bank would seem to present an insuperable obstacle to the common law, even if it had not lost the trail long before.

11–133   "As counsel for DLH properly concedes, however, none of these features creates a problem for equity. Nor has the plaintiff any difficulty in satisfying the precondition for equity's intervention. Mr Murad was the plaintiff's fiduciary, and he was bribed to purchase the shares. He committed a gross breach of his fiduciary obligations to the plaintiff, and that is sufficient to enable the plaintiff to invoke the assistance of equity. Other victims, however, were less fortunate. They employed no fiduciary. They were simply swindled. No breach of any fiduciary obligation was involved. It would, of course, be an intolerable reproach trace to our system of jurisprudence if the plaintiff were the only victim who could trace and recover his money. Neither party before me suggested that this is the case; and I agree with them. But if the other victims of the fraud can trace their money in equity it must be because, having been induced to purchase the shares by false and fraudulent misrepresentations, they are entitled to rescind the transaction and revest the equitable title to the purchase money in themselves, at least to the extent necessary to support an equitable tracing claim: see *Daly v. Sydney Stock Exchange Ltd* (1986) 160 C.L.R. 371 at 387–390 per Brennan J. There is thus no distinction between their case and the plaintiff's. They can rescind the purchases for fraud, and he for the bribery of his agent; and each can then invoke the assistance of equity to follow property of which he is the equitable owner . . .

11–134   "Subject to two points, counsel for DLH concedes that the plaintiff can successfully trace the money from Amsterdam to London. He submits (1) that plaintiff has not established that the money which reached the Keristal No 2 account on 12 and 16 May 1986 represented the money which was last seen leaving Gibraltar for Panama on 30 March and 1 April 1986, and (2) that the equitable remedy depends on the continuing subsistence of the plaintiff's equitable title, and cannot be invoked where the money is transferred to recipients in civil law jurisdictions like Switzerland and Panama which do not recognise the trust concept or the notion of equitable ownership.

"I reject both submissions.

Tracing through Panama

"It is, of course, beyond dispute that the money which was received in the **11–135** Keristal No 2 account was the Canadians' money. It is, however, true that the plaintiff is unable by direct evidence to identify that money with the money which Mr D'Albis had sent to Panama only a few weeks before. If the question arose in proceedings between the plaintiff and the Canadians, then, in the absence of evidence to the contrary, the court would draw the necessary inference against the latter, for they would be in a position to dispel it. But DLH is not; it is as much in the dark as the plaintiff.

"Nevertheless, in my judgment there is sufficient, though only just, to enable the inference to be drawn. One of the two sums received in the Keristal No 2 account was $1,541,432 received on May 12, 1986 from Bank of America. That corresponds closely with the sum of $1,600,000 transferred to Bank of America, Panama on April 1, 1986. In relation to the later transaction, Bank of America may, of course, merely have been acting as a correspondent bank in New York and not as the paying bank; and the closeness of the figures could be a coincidence. It is not much, but it is something, and there is nothing in the opposite scale. The source of the other money received in the Keristal No. 2 account is not known, but from the way in which the Canadians appear to have dealt with the affairs, if one sum came from Panama, then the other probably did so, too.

"The plaintiff points out that the deposit was paid out of funds held by the **11–136** second tier Panamanian companies immediately before they were sent to Panama, and submits that it is a reasonable inference that the rest of the money came from the same source. If the Canadians had substantial funds elsewhere to invest in the project, the plaintiff asks, why did they not use them to provide the deposit? There is force in this submission. Against it, DLH points out that, by the time the money was sent to Panama, Roth had already struck the deal with Mr Stern, and the Canadians knew that another £1,030,000 would be needed in London within a few weeks. Why send it to Panama? Far simpler to leave it in Geneva, especially when the Canadians had already decided to use it to support a back-to-back guarantee, as the terms of Mr Ferdman's telex demonstrate. There is force in this observation, too. But, in my judgment, any attempt to weigh the Canadians' motives is too speculative to form the basis of any inference. They may have decided to remove the funds at least temporarily from Geneva in order to conceal from Mr D'Albis that they were transferring their allegiance to a different Swiss fiduciary agent, or they may have decided to launder the money through Panama before making any long-term investment in Europe. Their request to be given five days' notice before coming up with the money is neutral; it may have had more to do with the time needed to arrange the back-to-back guarantee than any additional time needed to bring back funds from Panama.

"But the fact remains that there is no evidence that the Canadians had any **11–137** substantial funds available to them which did not represent proceeds of the fraud. This is acknowledged by counsel for DLH. For the source of the money he points to the $1.45m received by Zawi and the payments totalling $4,927,000 made by Herron and Wilmington which cannot be accounted for. But it has not been shown that any of these moneys were still at the disposal of the Canadians in May 1986. They had many expenses to meet out of moneys received by Herron and Wilmington (commission to salesmen, for instance, not already accounted for); and Singer and Goldhar would presumably need to be looked after.

11–138   "But, in my judgment, this is irrelevant. The money in the accounts of Herron and Wilmington represented proceeds of the fraud. It can be traced in equity from those accounts to the Keristal No 2 account as well as through Zawi or any other intermediate recipient as through the first and second tier Panamanian companies. The victims of a fraud can follow their money in equity through bank accounts where it has been mixed with other moneys because equity treats the money in such accounts as charged with the repayment of their money. If the money in an account subject to such a charge is afterwards paid out of the account and into a number of different accounts, the victims can claim a similar charge over each of the recipient accounts. They are not bound to choose between them. Whatever may be the position as between the victims *inter se*, as against the wrongdoer his victims are not required to appropriate debits to credits in order to identify the particular account into which their money has been paid. Equity's power to charge a mixed fund with the repayment of trust moneys (a power not shared by the common law) enables the claimants to follow the money, not because it is theirs, but because it is derived from a fund which is treated as if it were subject to a charge in their favour.

"In my judgment, there is some evidence to support an inference that the money which reached the Keristal No 2 account represented part of the moneys which had been transmitted to Panama by the second tier Panamanian companies some six weeks previously, and the suggestion that it was derived from any other source is pure speculation.

(2) Tracing through civil jurisdictions

11–139   "Counsel for DLH next submits that the plaintiff's claim, whether personal or proprietary, depends on the continuing subsistence of his equitable title to the money, and cannot be established where the money had passed through the hands of recipients in civil law jurisdictions which do not recognise the concept of equitable ownership. In my judgment, this argument is not open to DLH. Foreign law is a question of fact. It must be pleaded and proved by expert evidence. . . . In the absence of evidence, foreign law is presumed to be the same as English law. In the present case no question of foreign law has been pleaded, and no evidence of foreign law has been tendered . . .

"DLH is answerable to the court's equitable jurisdiction as regards assets situate abroad, even in a civil law country. A fortiori, it is amenable to the court's equitable jurisdiction as regards assets which were formerly in a civil law country but which it has received in England in circumstances which are alleged to render it unconscionable for it to retain them.

11–140   "DLH's argument is based on the premise that, for the plaintiff to succeed in tracing his money in equity through successive mixed accounts, he must have been in a position to obtain an equitable charge against each successive account. Even if the premise were correct, however, it would not matter where the accounts were maintained. It would be sufficient (and necessary) that the account holders were within the jurisdiction. But, in my judgment, it is not correct. It is not necessary that each successive recipient should have been within the jurisdiction; it is sufficient that the defendant is. This is because the plaintiff's ability to trace his money in equity is dependent on the power of equity to charge a mixed fund with the repayment of trust moneys, *not upon any actual exercise of that power.* The charge itself is entirely notional:

"An English court of equity will compel a defendant who is within the jurisdiction to treat assets in his hands as trust assets if, having regard to their history and his state of knowledge, it would be unconscionable for him to treat them as his own. Where they have passed through many different hands in many different countries, they may be difficult to trace; but in my judgment neither their temporary repose in a civil law country nor their receipt by intermediate recipients outside the jurisdiction should prevent the court from treating assets in the legal ownership of a defendant within the jurisdiction as trust assets. In the present case, any obligation on the part of DLH to restore to their rightful owner assets which it received in England is governed exclusively by English law, and the equitable tracing rules and the trust concept which underlies them are applicable as part of that law. There is no need to consider any other system of law.

Knowing receipt

"The plaintiff seeks a personal remedy based on 'knowing receipt'. As I have **11–141** previously pointed out, this is the counterpart in equity of the common law claim for money had and received. The latter, at least, is a receipt-based claim to restitution, and the cause of action is complete when the money is received: see *Lipkin Gorman (a firm) v. Karpnale Ltd* [1992] 4 All E.R. 512 at 527; [1991] 2 A.C. 548 at 572. So, in my judgment, is the former, unless arbitrary and anomalous distinctions between the common law and equitable claims are to be insisted upon. But it is necessary at the outset to identify the assets which DLH received, and the occasions upon which it received them.

"The plaintiff could if he wished have an account of what DLH did with the £4.65m it received from Regalian, or the balance remaining after payment of the £1.75m to Yulara, in an attempt to identify it as still in the possession of DLH with a view to asserting a proprietary claim against it to the extent of £2,325,000. The plaintiff has not sought to do so, seeing no advantage in the attempt. DLH is solvent and good for £2,325,000, and there is nothing to be gained by making a proprietary claim.

"All this, of course, is dependent on the plaintiff establishing that DLH **11–142** possessed the requisite degree of knowledge at the time of its purchase of Yulara's interest. DLH claims to be a bona fide purchaser for value without notice. Unfortunately, the nature of the knowledge required is highly controversial, at least where the recipient is a volunteer and the plaintiff brings a personal claim. In *Re Montagu's Settlement Trusts, Duke of Manchester v. National Westminster Bank Ltd* [1992] 4 All E.R. 308 at 330; [1987] Ch. 264 at 285 Megarry V.-C. expressed the view obiter that, in such a case, dishonesty or want of probity involving actual knowledge or wilful blindness is required . . .

"In *Eagle Trust plc v. SBC Securities Ltd* [1992] 4 All E.R. 488 at 509–510; [1993] 1 W.L.R. 484 at 506–507, Vinelott J based liability firmly on inferred knowledge and not on constructive notice. For my own part, I agree that even where the plaintiff's claim is a proprietary one, and the defendant raises the defence of bona fide purchaser for value without notice, there is no room for the doctrine of constructive notice in the strict conveyancing sense in a factual situation where it is not the custom and practice to make inquiry. But it does not follow that there is no room for an analogous doctrine in a situation in which any honest and reasonable man would have made inquiry. Vinelott J held that knowledge might be inferred if the circumstances were such that an honest and reasonable man would have inferred that the moneys were probably trust moneys and were being misapplied. He left open the question whether a recipient might escape liability if the court was satisfied that, although an honest and reasonable man would have realised this, through foolishness or inexperience he did not in fact suspect it.

11–143   "That question does not arise in the present case. In the absence of full argument I am content to assume, without deciding, that dishonesty or want of probity involving actual knowledge (whether proved or inferred) is not a precondition of liability; but that a recipient is not expected to be unduly suspicious and is not to be held liable unless he went ahead without further inquiry in circumstances in which an honest and reasonable man would have realised that the money was probably trust money and was being misapplied . . .

"I turn, therefore, to the allegation that by June 1988, if not before, DLH possessed the necessary degree of knowledge that Yulara's funds represented the proceeds of fraud. DLH is a body corporate, and establishing knowledge on the part of an artificial person involves identifying particular individuals and attributing their knowledge to it. For this purpose, the plaintiff has singled out Mr Ferdman and Mr Stern as persons alleged to have possessed the necessary knowledge at the relevant time. [Millett J. held that Stern did not have the necessary knowledge.]

Mr Ferdman's knowledge

11–144   "I could not bring myself to describe Mr Ferdman as an honest man. He was deeply implicated in the original fraud . . . He must have realised that his clients' scheme was dishonest. He probably suspected the nature of the fraud from the start. . . . The service which he gave his clients was to provide them with the means of concealment. He was prepared to lie to the authorities rather than risk divulging a client's identity. . . . He obviously realised that his clients' transactions might be questionable. He preferred not to know why his clients needed to keep their activities hidden from the light of day. As he admitted to me, he could not function at all if he had to inquire what his clients were up to. Wilful blindness was part of his job description. . . ."

[Millett J., however, refused to attribute Mr Ferdman's knowledge to DLH but the Court of Appeal reversed this.]

HOFFMANN L.J.: "This is a claim to enforce a constructive trust on the basis of knowing receipt. For this purpose the plaintiff must show, first, a disposal of his assets in breach of fiduciary duty; secondly, the beneficial receipt by the defendant of assets which are traceable as representing the assets of the plaintiff; and thirdly, knowledge on the part of the defendant that the assets he received are traceable to a breach of fiduciary duty.

"There is no dispute that the first requirement is satisfied. The Canadians bribed the plaintiff's fiduciary agent to give them over $10m of his money in return for worthless shares. The argument in this appeal has been over, first, which assets were received beneficially by Dollar Land Holdings plc ('DLH'); secondly, whether they are traceable as representing the plaintiff's money; and thirdly, whether the admitted knowledge of the frauds on the part of Mr Ferdman, chairman of DLH, can be imputed to the company.

Identifying the Assets Beneficially Received

11–145   "The judge has found as a fact that certain assets received by DLH, namely the benefit of the deposit paid under the contract for the purchase of the Nine Elms site and Yulara Realty Ltd's ('Yulara') interest in the development, were traceable in equity as proceeds of fraud. Both sides have challenged certain aspects of this finding.

(a) The deposit. The plaintiff says that the asset received by DLH was not the benefit of the deposit but the money used to pay it. This had been sent on 25 March 1986 to DLH's subsidiary Dollar Land (London) Ltd ('DLH London'), which entered into the contract to buy the site and afterwards assigned that contract (with the benefit of the deposit) to DLH. The plaintiff says that DLH London received the money as agent for DLH. The only evidence for this claim is that it was paid pursuant to an agreement between Roth and DLH. But that in my judgment is no reason why DLH London should not have received the money beneficially and this would be consistent with its having been the contracting party and subsequently assigning that contract for a substantial consideration to DLH.

(b) The main investment. The plaintiff says that the other asset received by DLH was not Yulara's interest in the project, which it acquired on 16 March 1988, but the £1,030,000 invested by Yulara on 29 May 1986. In my judgment the judge was right in holding that money was not received by DLH beneficially but on trust to invest on behalf of Yulara. DLH and Yulara were joint venturers. Yulara was making an equity investment by which it acquired a proprietary interest in half the share of profits due to DLH under its arrangements with Regalian Properties (Northern) Ltd (Regalian) and the benefit of a guarantee by DLH that its capital would be repaid. DLH received no part of this investment beneficially until it bought out Yulara's interest.

2. Tracing

"DLH challenges the judge's finding that the money can be traced to the **11–146** proceeds of fraud which the Canadians had remitted to Panama. In my view, this was a finding which the judge was entitled to make. Mr Tager says that it might have been the proceeds of frauds on other people or even the money realised by the Canadians when they sold the business. It might have been, but as against the plaintiff I do not think that the Canadians would have been entitled to say so. Nor is DLH. The mixed fund was impressed with an equitable charge in favour of the plaintiff which was enforceable against the Canadians and persons claiming under them.

3. Knowledge

"The judge correctly analysed the various capacities in which Mr Ferdman was **11–147** involved in the transaction between DLH and the Canadians. First, he acted as a broker, introducing the Canadians to DLH in return for a 5 per cent commission. In this capacity he was not acting as agent for DLH but as an independent contractor performing a service for a fee. Secondly, he was authorised agent of DLH to sign the agreement with Yulara. Thirdly, he was at all material times a director and chairman of the board of DLH.

"There are two ways in which Mr Ferdman's knowledge can be attributed to DLH. The first is that as agent of DLH his knowledge can be imputed to the company. The second is that for this purpose he *was* DLH and his knowledge was its knowledge. The judge rejected both.

(a) The agency theory. The circumstances in which the knowledge of an agent is imputed to the principal can vary a great deal and care is needed in analysing the cases. They fall into a number of categories which are not always sufficiently clearly distinguished. I shall mention three such categories because they each include cases on which Mr Beloff Q.C. placed undifferentiated reliance. In fact, however, they depend upon distinct principles which have no application in this case . . .

"It follows that in my judgment Millett J was right to hold that Mr Ferdman's position as agent or broker does not enable his knowledge to be imputed to DLH.

11–148   (b) *The 'directing mind and will' theory.* The phrase 'directing mind and will' comes from a well-known passage in the judgment of Viscount Haldane LC in *Lennards Carrying Co Ltd v. Asiatic Petroleum Co Ltd* [1915] AC 705, [1914–15] All E.R. Rep. 280 which distinguishes between someone who is "merely a servant or agent" and someone whose action (or knowledge) is that of the company itself. Despite their familiarity, it is worth quoting the terms in which Viscount Haldane L.C. said that the directing mind could be identified ([1915] A.C. 705 at 713, [1914–15] All E.R. Rep. 280 at 282):

> "That person may be under the direction of the shareholders in general meeting; that person may be the board of directors itself, or it may be, and in some companies it is so, that that person has an authority co-ordinate with the board of directors given to him under the articles of association, and is appointed by the general meeting of the company, and can only be removed by the general meeting of the company. My Lords, whatever is not known about Mr. Lennard's position, this is known for certain, Mr. Lennard took the active part in the management of this ship on behalf of the owners, and Mr. Lennard, as I have said, was registered as the person designated for this purpose in the ship's register."

11–149   "Viscount Haldane L.C. therefore regarded the identification of the directing mind as primarily a *constitutional* question, depending in the first instance upon the powers entrusted to a person by the articles of association. The last sentence about Mr. Lennard's position shows that the position as reflected in the articles may have to be supplemented by looking at the actual exercise of the company's powers. A person held out by the company as having plenary authority or in whose exercise of such authority the company acquiesces, may be treated as its directing mind . . .

"Millett J. did not accept that Mr Fredman was the directing mind and will of DLH because he exercised no independent judgment. As a fiduciary he acted entirely upon the directions of the American beneficial owners and their consultant Mr Stern. All that he did was to sign the necessary documents and ensure that the company's paper work was in order. This involved seeing that decisions which had really been taken by the Americans and Mr Stern were duly minuted as decisions of the board made in Switzerland.

"But neither the Americans nor Mr Stern held any position under the constitution of the company. Nor were they held out as doing so. They signed no documents on behalf of the company and carried on no business in its name. As a holding company, DLH had no independent business of its own. It entered into various transactions and on those occasions the persons who acted on its behalf were the board or one or more of the directors.

11–150   "It seems to me that if the criterion is whether the candidate for being the 'directing mind and will' was exercising independent judgment, as opposed to acting upon off-stage instructions, not even the board of directors acting collectively would in this case have qualified. It also did what it was told. But Mr Tager was inclined to concede that the board, acting as a board, could properly be regarded as the directing mind and will. It was certainly held out in certain quarters as such. DLH claimed non-resident status from the Inland Revenue on the ground that its "central management and control" was situated in Switzerland.

"The authorities show clearly that different persons may for different purposes satisfy the requirements of being the company's directing mind and will. Therefore the question in my judgment is whether in relation to the Yulara transaction, Mr Ferdman as an individual exercised powers on behalf of the company which so identified him. It seems to me that Mr Ferdman was clearly regarded as being in a different position from the other directors. They were associates of his who came and went. SAFI charged for their services at a substantially lower rate. It was Mr Ferdman who claimed in the published accounts of DLH to be its ultimate beneficial owner. In my view, however, the most significant fact is that Mr Ferdman signed the agreement with Yulara on behalf of DLH. There was no board resolution authorising him to do so. Of course we know that in fact he signed at the request of Mr Stern, whom he knew to be clothed with authority from the Americans. But so far as the constitution of DLH was concerned, he committed the company to the transaction as an autonomous act which the company adopted by performing the agreement. I would therefore hold, respectfully differing from the judge, that this was sufficient to justify Mr Ferdman being treated, in relation to the Yulara transaction, as the company's directing mind and will. Nor do I think it matters that by the time DLH acquired, Yulara's interest in the Nine Elms project on 16 March 1988, Mr Ferdman had ceased to be a director. Once his knowledge is treated as being the knowledge of the company in relation to a given transaction, I think that the company continues to be affected with that knowledge for any subsequent stages of the same transaction. And in my judgment the subsequent acquisition of Yulara's interest was sufficiently connected with the original investment to be affected by the same knowledge.

"I would therefore allow the appeal. I do not regard this as an unsatisfactory **11–151** outcome. If the persons beneficially interested in a company prefer for tax or other reasons to allow that company to be for all legal purposes run by off-shore fiduciaries, they must accept that it may incur liabilities by reason of the acts or knowledge of those fiduciaries." *Appeal allowed. Case remitted to judge to determine relief to which plaintiff was entitled*, on which, see *El Ajou v. Dollar Land Holdings (No. 2)* [1995] 2 All E.R. 213. Further on knowledge attributed to a Company see *Meridian Global Funds Management Asia Ltd v. Securities Commission* [1995] 3 All E.R. 918. *The Appeal Committee of the House of Lords refused leave to appeal.*

ROYAL BRUNEI AIRLINES V. TAN

Privy Council [1995] 2 A.C. 378 [1995] 3 W.L.R. 64 [1995] 3 All E.R. 97.

The judgment of their Lordships was delivered by LORD NICHOLLS OF **11–152** BIRKENHEAD: "The proper role of equity in commercial transactions is a topical question. Increasingly plaintiffs have recourse to equity for an effective remedy when the person in default, typically a company, is insolvent. Plaintiffs seek to obtain relief from others who were involved in the transaction, such as directors of the company, or its bankers, or its legal or other advisers. They seek to fasten fiduciary obligations directly onto the company's officers or agents or advisers, or to have them held personally liable for assisting the company in breaches of trust or fiduciary obligations.

"This is such a case. An insolvent travel agent company owed money to an airline. The airline seeks a remedy against the travel agent's principal director and shareholder. Its claim is based on the much-quoted dictum of Lord Selborne

L.C., sitting in the Court of Appeal in Chancery, in *Barnes v. Addy* (1874) L.R. 9
Ch.App. 244 at 251–252:

> '[The responsibility of a trustee] may no doubt be extended in equity to
> others who are not properly trustees, if they are found . . . actually
> participating in any fraudulent conduct of the trustee to the injury of the
> cestui que trust. But . . . strangers are not to be made constructive trustees
> merely because they act as the agents of trustees in transactions within
> their legal powers, transactions, perhaps of which a court of equity may
> disapprove, unless those agents receive and become chargeable with some
> part of the trust property, or unless they assist with knowledge in a
> dishonest and fraudulent design on the part of the trustees.'

11–153   "In the conventional shorthand, the first of these two circumstances in which
third parties (non-trustees) may become liable to account in equity is 'knowing
receipt,' as distinct from the second, where liability arises from 'knowing
assistance.' Stated even more shortly, the first limb of Lord Selborne L.C.'s
formulation is concerned with the liability of a person as a *recipient* of trust
property or its traceable proceeds. The second limb is concerned with what, for
want of a better compendious description, can be called the liability of an
accessory to a trustee's breach of trust. Liability as an accessory is not dependent
upon receipt of trust property. It arises even though no trust property has
reached the hands of the accessory. It is a form of secondary liability in the sense
that it only arises where there has been a breach of trust. In the present case the
plaintiff airline relies on the accessory limb. The particular point in issue arises
from the expression "a dishonest and fraudulent design on the part of the
trustees . . .

"In short, the issue on this appeal is whether the breach of trust which is a
prerequisite to accessory liability must itself be a dishonest and fraudulent breach
of trust by the trustee.

The honest trustee and the dishonest third party

11–154   "It must be noted at once that there is a difficulty with the approach adopted on
this point in the *Belmont* case [1979] Ch. 250. Take the simple example of an
honest trustee and a dishonest third party. Take a case where a dishonest
solicitor persuades a trustee to apply trust property in a way the trustee honestly
believes is permissible but which the solicitor knows full well is a clear breach of
trust. The solicitor deliberately conceals this from the trustee. In consequence,
the beneficiaries suffer a substantial loss. It cannot be right that in such a case
the accessory liability principle would be inapplicable because of the innocence
of the trustee. In ordinary parlance, the beneficiaries have been defrauded by the
solicitor. If there is to be an accessory liability principle at all, whereby in
appropriate circumstances beneficiaries may have direct recourse against a third
party, the principle must surely be applicable in such a case, just as much as in a
case where both the trustee and the third party have been dishonest. Indeed, if
anything, the case for liability of the dishonest third party seems stronger where
the trustee is innocent, because in such a case the third party alone was dishonest
and that was the cause of the subsequent misapplication of the trust property.

11–155   "The position would be the same if, instead of *procuring* the breach, the third
party dishonestly *assisted* in the breach. Change the facts slightly. A trustee is
proposing to make a payment out of the trust fund to a particular person. He
honestly believes he is authorised to do so by the terms of the trust deed. He asks

a solicitor to carry through the transaction. The solicitor well knows that the proposed payment would be a plain breach of trust. He also well knows that the trustee mistakenly believes otherwise. Dishonestly he leaves the trustee under his misapprehension and prepares the necessary documentation. Again, if the accessory principle is not to be artificially constricted, it ought to be applicable in such a case.

"These examples suggest that what matters is the state of mind of the third party sought to be made liable, not the state of mind of the trustee. The trustee will be liable in any event for the breach of trust, even if he acted innocently, unless excused by an exemption clause in the trust instrument or relieved by the court. But *his* state of mind is essentially irrelevant to the question whether the *third party* should be made liable to the beneficiaries for the breach of trust. If the liability of the third party is fault-based, what matters is the nature of his fault, not that of the trustee. In this regard dishonesty on the part of the third party would seem to be a sufficient basis for his liability, irrespective of the state of mind of the trustee who is in breach of trust. It is difficult to see why, if the third party dishonestly assisted in a breach, there should be a further prerequisite to his liability, namely that the trustee also must have been acting dishonestly. The alternative view would mean that a dishonest third party is liable if the trustee is dishonest, but if the trustee did not act dishonestly that of itself would excuse a dishonest third party from liability. That would make no sense.

Earlier authority

"The view that the accessory liability principle cannot be restricted to fraudulent **11–156** breaches of trust is not to be approached with suspicion as a latter-day novelty. Before the accessory principle donned its *Barnes v. Addy*, L.R. 9 Ch. App.244 strait-jacket, judges seem not to have regarded the principle as confined in this way. In *Fyler v. Fyler* (1841) 3 Beav. 550, 568, Lord Langdale M.R. expressed the view that, if trustees invested in an unauthorised investment, solicitors who knowingly procured that to be done for their own benefit 'ought to be considered as partakers in the breach of trust' even though the trustees intended in good faith that the investment would be beneficial to the life tenant and not prejudicial to the beneficiaries with interests in capital. The same judge. Lord Langdale M.R., in *Attorney-General v. Corporation of Leicester* (1844) 7 Beav. 176 at 179, stated:

> 'it cannot be disputed that, if the agent of a trustee, whether a corporate body or not, knowing that a breach of trust is being committed, interferes and assists in that breach of trust, he is personally answerable, although he may be employed as the agent of the person who directs him to commit that breach of trust.'

In *Eaves v. Hickson* (1861) 30 Beav. 136 trustees, acting in good faith, paid over the fund to William Knibb's adult children on the strength of a forged marriage certificate produced to them by William Knibb. Sir John Romilly M.R. held that William Knibb was liable to replace the fund, to the extent that it was not recovered from his children, and to do so in priority to the liability of the trustees. Far from this being a case of fraud by the trustees, Sir John Romilly M.R., at p. 141, described it as a very hard case on the trustees, who were deceived by a forgery which would have deceived anyone who was not looking out for forgery or fraud.

"This point did not arise in *Barnes v. Addy*, L.R. 9 Ch. App. 244. There the **11–157** new sole trustee was engaged in a dishonest and fraudulent design. He intended to misapply the trust fund as soon as it reached his hands. The two solicitors were held not liable because there was no evidence that either of them had any knowledge or suspicion of this.

"What has gone wrong? Their Lordships venture to think that the reason is that, ever since the *Selangor* case [1968] 1 W.L.R. 1555 highlighted the potential uses of equitable remedies in connection with misapplied company funds, there has been a tendency to cite and interpret and apply Lord Selborne L.C.'s formulation in *Barnes v. Addy*, L.R. 9 Ch. App. 244 at 251–252, as though it were a statute. This has particularly been so with the accessory limb of Lord Selborne L.C.'s apothegm. This approach has been inimical to analysis of the underlying concept. Working within this constraint, the courts have found themselves wrestling with the interpretation of the individual ingredients, especially 'knowingly' but also 'dishonest and fraudulent design on the part of the trustees,' without examining the underlying reason why a third party who has received no trust property is being made liable at all . . .

"To resolve this issue it is necessary to take an overall look at the accessory liability principle. A conclusion cannot be reached on the nature of the breach of trust which may trigger accessory liability without at the same time considering the other ingredients including, in particular, the state of mind of the third party. It is not necessary, however, to look even more widely and consider the essential ingredients of recipient liability. The issue on this appeal concerns only the accessory liability principle. Different considerations apply to the two heads of liability. Recipient liability is restitution-based; accessory liability is not . . .

Fault-based liability

11–158 "Given, then, that in some circumstances a third party may be liable directly to a beneficiary, but given also that the liability is not so strict that there would be liability even when the third party was wholly unaware of the existence of the trust, the next step is to seek to identify the touchstone of liability. By common accord dishonesty fulfils this role. Whether, in addition, negligence will suffice is an issue on which there has been a well-known difference of judicial opinion. The *Selangor* decision [1968] 1 W.L.R. 1555 in 1968 was the first modern decision on this point. Ungoed-Thomas J., at p. 1590, held that the touchstone was whether the third party had knowledge of circumstances which would indicate to 'an honest, reasonable man' that the breach in question was being committed or would put him on inquiry. Brightman J. reached the same conclusion in *Karak Rubber Co. Ltd. v. Burden (No. 2)* [1972] 1 W.L.R. 602. So did Peter Gibson J. in 1983 in *Baden v. Société Générale pour Favoriser le Développement du Commerce et de l'Industrie en France S.A. (Note)* [1993] 1 W.L.R. 509. In that case the judge accepted a five-point scale of knowledge which had been formulated by counsel.

11–159 "Meanwhile doubts had been expressed about this test by Buckley and Goff L.JJ. in the *Belmont* case [1979] Ch. 250 at 267, 275. Similar doubts were expressed in Australia by Jacobs P. in *D. P. C. Estates Pty, Ltd. v. Grey and Consul Development Pty. Ltd.* [1974] 1 N.S.W.L.R. 443 at 459. When that decision reached the High Court of Australia, the doubts were echoed by Barwick C.J., Gibbs and Stephen JJ.: see *Consul Development Pty. Ltd. v. D.P. Estates Pty. Ltd.* (1975) 132 C.L.R. 373 at 376, 398, 412.

"Since then the tide in England has flowed strongly in favour of the test being one of dishonesty: see, for instance, Sir Robert Megarry V.-C. in In *Re Montagu's Settlement Trusts* [1987] Ch. 264, 285, and Millett J. in *Agip (Africa) Ltd v. Jackson* [1990] Ch. 265 at 293. In *Eagle Trust Plc. v. S.B.C. Securities Ltd* [1993] 1 W.L.R. 484 at 495, Vinelott J. stated that it could be taken as settled law that want of probity was a prerequisite to liability. This received the imprimatur of the Court of Appeal in *Polly Peck International Plc. v. Nadir (No. 2)* [1992] 4 All E.R. 769 at 777, *per* Scott L.J. . . .

Dishonesty

"Before considering this issue further it will be helpful to define the terms being **11–160** used by looking more closely at what dishonesty means in this context. Whatever may be the position in some criminal or other contexts (see, for instance, *Reg. v. Ghosh* [1982] Q.B. 1053), in the context of the accessory liability principle acting dishonestly, or with a lack of probity, which is synonymous, means simply not acting as an honest person would in the circumstances. This is an objective standard. At first sight this may seem surprising. Honesty has a connotation of subjectivity as distinct from the objectivity of negligence. Honesty, indeed, does have a strong subjective element in that it is a description of a type of conduct assessed in the light of what a person actually knew at the time, as distinct a from what a reasonable person would have known or appreciated. Further, honesty and its counterpart dishonesty are mostly concerned with advertent conduct, not inadvertent conduct. Carelessness is not dishonesty. Thus for the most part dishonesty is to be equated with conscious impropriety. However, these subjective characteristics of honesty do not mean that individuals are free to set their own standards of honesty in particular circumstances. The standard of what constitutes honest conduct is not subjective. Honesty is not an optional scale, with higher or lower values according to the moral standards of each individual. If a person knowingly appropriates another's property, he will not escape a finding of dishonesty simply because he sees nothing wrong in such behaviour.

"In most situations there is little difficulty in identifying how an honest person **11–161** would behave. Honest people do not intentionally deceive others to their detriment. Honest people do not knowingly take others' property. Unless there is a very good and compelling reason, an honest person does not participate in a transaction if he knows it involves a misapplication of trust assets to the detriment of the beneficiaries. Nor does an honest person in such a case deliberately close his eyes and ears, or deliberately not ask questions, lest he learn something he would rather not know, and then proceed regardless. However, in the situations now under consideration the position is not always so straightforward. This can best be illustrated by considering one particular area: the taking of risks.

Taking risks

"All investment involves risk. Imprudence is not dishonesty, although imprudence may be carried recklessly to lengths which call into question the honesty of the person making the decision. This is especially so if the transaction serves another purpose in which that person has an interest of his own.

"This type of risk is to be sharply distinguished from the case where a trustee, with or without the benefit of advice, is aware that a particular investment or application of trust property is outside his powers, but nevertheless he decides to proceed in the belief or hope that this will be beneficial to the beneficiaries or, at least, not prejudicial to them. He takes a risk that a clearly unauthorised transaction will not cause loss. A risk of this nature is for the account of those who take it. If the risk materialises and causes loss, those who knowingly took the risk will be accountable accordingly. This is the type of risk being addressed by Peter Gibson J. in the *Baden* case [1993] 1 W.L.R. 509 at 574, when he accepted that fraud includes taking 'a risk to the prejudice of another's rights, which risk is known to be one which there is no right to take.'

11–162   "This situation, in turn, is to be distinguished from the case where there is genuine doubt about whether a transaction is authorised or not. This may be because the trust instrument is worded obscurely, or because there are competing claims, as in *Carl Zeiss Stiftung v. Herbert Smith & Co. (No. 2)* [1969] 2 Ch. 276, or for other reasons. The difficulty here is that frequently the situation is neither clearly white nor clearly black. The dividing edge between what is within the trustee's powers and what is not is often not clear-cut. Instead there is a gradually darkening spectrum which can be described with labels such as clearly authorised, probably authorised, possibly authorised, wholly unclear, probably unauthorised and, finally, clearly unauthorised.

"The difficulty here is that the differences are of degree rather than of kind. So far as the trustee himself is concerned the legal analysis is straightforward. Honesty or lack of honesty is not the test for his liability. He is obliged to comply with the terms of the trust. His liability is strict. If he departs from the trust terms he is liable unless excused by a provision in the trust instrument or relieved by the court. The analysis of the position of the accessory, such as the solicitor who carries through the transaction for him, does not lead to such a simple, clear-cut answer in every case. He is required to act honestly; but what is required of an honest person in these circumstances? An honest person knows there is doubt. What does honesty require him to do?

11–163   "The only answer to these questions lies in keeping in mind that honesty is an objective standard. The individual is expected to attain the standard which would be observed by an honest person placed in those circumstances. It is impossible to be more specific. Knox J. captured the flavour of this, in a case with a commercial setting, when he referred to a person who is 'guilty of commercially unacceptable conduct in the particular context involved:' see *Cowan de Groot Properties Ltd v. Eagle Trust Plc* [1992] 4 All E.R. 700 at 761. Acting in reckless disregard of others' rights or possible rights can be a tell-tale sign of dishonesty. An honest person would have regard to the circumstances known to him, including the nature and importance of the proposed transaction, the nature and importance of his role, the ordinary course of business, the degree of doubt, the practicability of the trustee or the third party proceeding otherwise and the seriousness of the adverse consequences to the beneficiaries. The circumstances will dictate which one or more of the possible courses should be taken by an honest person. He might, for instance, flatly decline to become involved. He might ask further questions. He might seek advice, or insist on further advice being obtained. He might advise the trustee of the risks but then proceed with his role in the transaction. He might do many things. Ultimately, in most cases, an honest person should have little difficulty in knowing whether a proposed transaction, or his participation in it, would offend the normally accepted standards of honest conduct.

11–164   "Likewise, when called upon to decide whether a person was acting honestly, a court will look at all the circumstances known to the third party at the time. The court will also have regard to personal attributes of the third party, such as his experience and intelligence, and the reason why he acted as he did.

"Before leaving cases where there is real doubt, one further point should be noted. To inquire, in such cases, whether a person dishonestly assisted in what is later held to be a breach of trust is to ask a meaningful question, which is capable of being given a meaningful answer. This is not always so if the question is posed in terms of 'knowingly' assisted. Framing the question in the latter form all too often leads one into tortuous convolutions about the 'sort' of knowledge required, when the truth is that 'knowingly' is inapt as a criterion when applied to the gradually darkening spectrum where the differences are of degree and not kind.

Negligence

"It is against this background that the question of negligence is to be addressed. **11–165** This question, it should be remembered, is directed at whether an honest third party who receives no trust property should be liable if he procures or assists in a breach of trust of which he would have become aware had he exercised reasonable diligence. Should he be liable to the beneficiaries for the loss they suffer from the breach of trust?

"The majority of persons falling into this category will be the hosts of people who act for trustees in various ways: as advisers, consultants, bankers and agents of many kinds. This category also includes officers and employees of companies in respect of the application of company funds. All these people will be accountable to the trustees for their conduct. For the most part they will owe to the trustees a duty to exercise reasonable skill and care. When that is so, the rights flowing from that duty form part of the trust property. As such they can be enforced by the beneficiaries in a suitable case if the trustees are unable or unwilling to do so. That being so, it is difficult to identify a compelling reason why, in addition to the duty of skill and care vis-à-vis the trustees which the third parties have accepted, or which the law has imposed upon them, third parties should also owe a duty of care directly to the beneficiaries. They have undertaken work for the trustees. They must carry out that work properly. If they fail to do so, they will be liable to make good the loss suffered by the trustees in consequence. This will include, where appropriate, the loss suffered by the trustees, being exposed to claims for breach of trust.

"Outside this category of persons who owe duties of skill and care to the **11–166** trustees, there are others who will deal with trustees. If they have not accepted, and the law has not imposed upon them, any such duties in favour of the trustees, it is difficult to discern a good reason why they should nevertheless owe such duties to the beneficiaries.

"There remains to be considered the position where third parties are acting for, or dealing with, dishonest trustees. In such cases the trustees would have no claims against the third party. The trustees would suffer no loss by reason of the third party's failure to discover what was going on. The question is whether in this type of situation the third party owes a duty of care to the beneficiaries to, in effect, check that a trustee is not misbehaving. The third party must act honestly. The question is whether that is enough.

"In agreement with the preponderant view, their Lordships consider that dishonesty is an essential ingredient here. There may be cases where, in the light of the particular facts, a third party will owe a duty of care to the beneficiaries. As a general proposition, however, beneficiaries cannot reasonably expect that all the world dealing with their trustees should owe them a duty to take care lest the trustees are behaving dishonestly . . .

The accessory liability principle

"Drawing the threads together, their Lordships' overall conclusion is that **11–167** dishonesty is a necessary ingredient of accessory liability. It is also a sufficient ingredient. A liability in equity to make good resulting loss attaches to a person who dishonestly procures or assists in a breach of trust or fiduciary obligation. It is not necessary that, in addition, the trustee or fiduciary was acting dishonestly, although this will usually be so where the third party who is assisting him is acting dishonestly. 'Knowingly' is better avoided as a defining ingredient of the principle and in the context of this principle the *Baden* [1993] 1 W.L.R. 509 scale of knowledge is best forgotten.

Conclusion

11–168   "From this statement of the principle it follows that this appeal succeeds. The money paid to B.L.T. on the sale of tickets for the airline was held by B.L.T. upon trust for the airline. This trust, on its face, conferred no power on B.L.T. to use the money in the conduct of its business. The trust gave no authority to B.L.T. to relieve its cash flow problems by utilising for this purpose the rolling 30-day credit afforded by the airline. Thus B.L.T. committed a breach of trust by using the money instead of simply deducting its commission and holding the money intact until it paid the airline. The defendant accepted that he knowingly assisted in that breach of trust. In other words, he caused or permitted his company to apply the money in a way he knew was not authorised by the trust of which the company was trustee. Set out in these bald terms, the defendant's conduct was dishonest. By the same token, and for good measure, B.L.T. also acted dishonestly. The defendant was the company, and his state of mind is to be imputed to the company.

"The Court of Appeal held that it was not established that B.L.T. was guilty of fraud or dishonesty in relation to the amounts it held for the airline. Their Lordships understand that by this the Court of Appeal meant that it was not established that the defendant intended to defraud the airline. The defendant hoped, maybe expected, to be able to pay the airline, but the money was lost in the ordinary course of a poorly-run business with heavy overhead expenses. These facts are beside the point. The defendant had no right to employ the money in the business at all. That was the breach of trust. The company's inability to pay the airline was the consequence of that breach of trust."

QUESTIONS

11–169   1. "Debtor-creditor relationships where the recipient is intended to be able to use the moneys as its own and so mix them with its own moneys subject to an obligation to repay a corresponding amount with interest cannot create equitable interests in favour of the payer." Discuss.

2. When is it appropriate to claim an equitable charge rather than whole or part ownership? When is there a role for proprietary subrogation despite *Re Diplock*?

3. "In *Re Tilley* the judge was torn between his head and his heart; hence he illogically rejected part ownership while accepting that he would have been prepared to impose a charge on the properties as security for the trust money if Ms Tilley's estate had not been good for the money." Discuss.

4. "The flexibility of the charge where money is traced from a bank account, *e.g.* into other mixed bank accounts and assets purchased with mixed moneys provides in the light of *El Ajou* strong remedies against the wrongdoer and third parties with notice." Discuss.

5. "A beneficiary can pick and choose his tracing rules under *Re Hallett* and *Re Oatway* when the trustee has mixed trust moneys in his private current

account at his bank though this is unnecessary if only a charge is sought." Discuss.

6. "The rule in *Clayton's* case is too arbitrary for a court of equity to apply it." **11–170** Discuss.

7. "The tracing rules are too harsh on innocent volunteers, though wicked volunteers deserve their strict treatment. An innocent volunteer, in the sense of one without actual Nelsonian or naughty knowledge, should not be liable to share his profits if he would have been able to make them without the assistance of the claimants' moneys." Discuss.

8. "Lord Templeman in *Space Investments* has odd ideas on tracing." Discuss in light of the views in *Re Goldcorp* and *Bishopsgate v. Homan*.

9. "It is not obvious why if T wrongfully mixes £50,000 of trust funds with £50,000 of his own money to buy a house now worth £200,000 the beneficiaries should have a lesser claim than if T had used the beneficiaries' £50,000 to buy a £100,000 house with the assistance of a £50,000 endowment mortgage thereon (under which interest alone is paid until maturity of the endowment policy)." Discuss.

10. "Equity's identification rules enable a plaintiff to have an equitable lien or **11–171** charge over, or a proportionate interest in, the defendant's property. On the basis of Hohfield's analysis of rights giving rise to correlative duties one can then argue that from the time of receiving the property subject to the plaintiff's rights the defendant is objectively a constructive trustee, not just from the date he becomes aware of the plaintiff's interest. However, Equity is based on a subjective approach acting in personam agaisnt a defendant only when his conscience is affected. Thus, the defendant should only become personally accountable to the plaintiff (and so liable as a fiduciary to pay compound interest on money received) when becoming aware of the plaintiff's claim: until then the defendant, as an innocent volunteer, simply holds the property subject to the plaintiff's rights under the law of property priorities making him liable upon demand to deliver up the property. The plaintiff is unfairly advantaged if the courts impose strict personal accountability upon the defendant unless the defendant proves he is a bona fide purchaser or protected by the defence of change of position. The courts of Equity when voyaging upon uncharted seas should not give up reliance upon the polar star of conscience to guide them in the hope that the defence of change of position will ultimately provide a safe harbour." Discuss.

11. A stockbroker is directed by the two trustees, H and W, to sell an **11–172** authorised investment and use the proceeds to buy an unauthorised investment. He knowingly does so because he bona fide believes this to be in the best financial interests of the beneficiaries. Most surprisingly the unauthorised investment halves in value within a year. Can the beneficiaries sue the stock-broker if H and W are now insolvent?

12. Trevor, who is trustee, deposits £6,000 of trust moneys in his personal current account which is £100 in credit though he has overdraft facilities limited to £1,400. On the following day he attends an auction of paintings and buys a painting which he has always wanted for £6,500. He pays for it by a cheque drawn on his personal account. A month later he opens a trustee account into which he pays £6,000. The painting is now worth £13,000. Advise the benefici-aries. Would your advice be different if a fire had destroyed the painting?

13. Darby and Joan were trustee of a family trust for Joan for life, remainder **11–173** to Darby for life, remainder to their two children equally. On Joan's death, Darby became trustee of her testamentary trust for Darby for life, remainder as to one half for their grandchildren and the other half for the R.S.P.C.A.

In May 2000, Darby had £5,000 in his current bank account. On June 1 Darby paid into it £30,000, the proceeds of sale of some family trust investments. On 8 June he withdrew £5,000 to purchase shares in Whizzo Ltd; on June 15 he withdrew £20,000 to purchase shares in Zomko Ltd; on June 22 he withdrew £10,000 to pay the last instalment due on a painting he had purchased on an instalment basis for himself a year earlier.

In July, Darby decided to advance out of the testamentary trust £50,000 each to his grandson, Simon, and to the R.S.P.C.A. However, by mistake he paid them out of family trust moneys. As it happened, the R.S.P.C.A. had an option conferred by a benefactor to purchase for £50,000 some land worth £500,000, so it simply endorsed the £50,000 cheque over to the benefactor.

Simon paid his £50,000 into his building society deposit account containing £10,000. He then paid £600 thereout into his current bank account already containing £600, before withdrawing £100 cash and giving £50 thereof to his wife, Tara, who used £6 thereof to buy lottery tickets. One ticket won £6 million.

Later Simon withdrew £29,400 to buy a racehorse, which shortly afterwards broke a leg, so it had to be destroyed, while the remaining £30,000 was used to discharge Simon's mortgage on his home. This is now up for sale because Simon and Tara are going to emigrate to The Bahamas.

Advise Simon's childless uncle Jasper, who has discovered the above facts on Darby's recent death and seeks to maximise his entitlement under the family trust, taking account of the fact that the Whizzo shares have quadrupled in value, the Zonko shares are worthless, and the painting has doubled in value.

11–174   **14.** Bill died in 1975, having left his residuary estate to Charles and David upon trust for his sister, Samantha, for life, remainder to such of her legitimate children as attained 21 years if more than one in equal shares, but in default thereof for University College, Durham, which now seeks your advice.

Having spent a year in Italy, Samantha had returned to England in October 1954 with Romeo Mondello, pretending they had married each other in Rome on September 3, 1969. In 1970 Samantha gave birth to Luigi. In 1975 Romeo died. In 1976 Samantha had an illness which left her incapable of having further children.

In 1993 at Samantha's request the trustees were happy to advance £28,000 so that Luigi could purchase a house.

In 1997 Samantha married a wealthy Greek. She then released her life interest in the trust fund. Before transferring the trust fund to Luigi the trustees asked Samantha as a mere formality to produce her marriage certificate. Through the services of Mario an Italian hairdresser to whom she had confided her problem, Samantha managed to obtain a forged Italian marriage certificate. After seeing it the trustees transferred the trust fund, consisting of £110,000 cash and £10,000 gilt-edged securities, to Luigi.

11–175   Luigi opened a deposit account for the cash and spent £101,000 on buying an Italian restaurant. He transferred the £9,000 balance into his current account then containing £1,000. He withdrew £5,000 therefrom to buy shares in Go-go Hi-Sci Ltd. Within a year payment of bills for his restaurant put his account into overdraft.

In March 2001 Samantha told Luigi to his astonishment that he was illegitimate but that he need not worry about his inheritance since his uncle had really intended him to benefit believing he was legitimate.

Luigi then sold the gilt-edged securities and, to comfort Samantha, spent £6,000 of the proceeds on a holiday for them both, whilst spending the balance on bills for his restaurant.

At present Luigi's current account contains £2,500, though he has heavy outstanding debts in respect of his restaurant. However, the Go-go shares and Luigi's house have quadrupled in value. Mario has just won £50,000 on the football pools.

15. Alan, managing director and controlling shareholder of Widgets Ltd, **11–176** erroneously believed he could borrow money for his private purposes interest-free from Widgets for as long as he wanted. Thus he contracted to buy a restaurant for £200,000 using £20,000 borrowed interest-free from Widgets to pay the 10 per cent deposit. He took possession of the restaurant for a monthly fee. Just before completion of the purchase was due, the vendor agreed, at Alan's request, to defer completion for three years on the purchase price rising to £250,000 and on payment by Alan of a further deposit of £30,000 on May 15.

This £30,000 was paid out of Alan's personal current bank account. This **11–177** account had already contained £10,000 of his own money when, on May 1, Alan added £30,000 borrowed by him out of funds held by him as sole trustee of a family trust. On May 3 Alan sold for £10,000 a painting owned by Widgets to a customer, Charles, who had admired it when seeing it hanging in Alan's office. Alan wrongly told Charles that the painting was Alan's, so Charles made out his cheque in favour of Alan, who paid it into his personal account. The cheque was cleared on May 8. On May 10 Alan paid a further £20,000 of his own money. On May 15 £30,000 was drawn out to pay the further deposit of £30,000. On May 24 the account was cleared when Alan paid off debts of £15,000 and purchased Gobiotech Ltd shares for £25,000. These shares are now worth £50,000.

Alan thought he was justified in taking the £30,000 out of the family trust as a personal loan—and signed a note stating that he agreed to pay interest thereon at two per cent above Barclay's Bank rate from time to time—since the trust instrument expressly authorised investing in any investments that an absolute owner might invest in on his own behalf.

Alan duly completed the purchase of the restaurant on expiry of the three years, taking out a mortgage for the necessary £200,000 balance and personally covenanting to repay the loan. A year later in May 2001 Alan sold the restaurant for £350,000, paying off the mortgage out of the proceeds of sale. He then gave £50,000 of the profit to his mistress, Mandy, who used £40,000 to discharge the mortgage on her flat and £10,000 to discharge the outstanding money due under a consumer credit agreement for the purchase of her Porsche car.

Advice Widgets Ltd and the family trust beneficiaries on their best course of action.

16. Four years ago under the terms of the Hazzard Settlement Trust the 13th **11–178** Duke of Hazzard forfeited his life interest by marrying a Roman Catholic after his first wife had died. The terms of the Settlement then required the trustees to retain in the Settlement such settled chattels as they saw fit and to allow the new life tenant, the 13th Duke's son, Timon, to choose for himself absolutely any of the remaining chattels. The trustees were a solicitor, Sharp, and Colonel Bluster, who was accustomed to relying on Sharp in matters involving the Settlement.

The 13th Duke secretly gave Sharp £50,000 to let Timon have first choice of the settled chattels, so that Timon innocently took for himself chattels to the value of £380,000 and left in the Settlement chattels worth only £20,000.

Timon forthwith sold the chattels for £380,000 and spent £80,000 on the wedding reception of his only child, Ophelia and a further £200,000 on buying her a London flat in consideration of her marriage. He placed the remaining

£100,000 temporarily in his current bank account into which he had paid £20,000 one day beforehand. He then spent £20,000 on Grokle plc shares now worth £80,000 and the following day he used the remaining £100,000 to pay off his mortgage on Stately Towers.

Meanwhile, Sharp had invested his £50,000 in Wizard plc shares now worth £150,000.

Six months ago Timon died and Yorick became life tenant under the Settlement. Advise him on what remedies may be available to him.

11–179   17. Is the following approach sensible for a claimant beneficiary?

    (a) Go for a *proprietary* tracing claim, if possible.
    (b) Go for *personal* liability:
        (i) of trustee or other fiduciary for breach of trust or other fiduciary obligation;
      (ii) of third party who dishonestly assists in a breach of trust or other fiduciary obligation and so becomes liable as constructive trustee if he has actual knowledge of the breach or exhibits a lack of probity through deliberately shutting his eyes to the obvious or deliberately or recklessly failing to make such inquiries as an honest reasonable man would make;
     (iii) of third party who received for his own benefit trust or fiduciary property but parts with it after having actual, Nelsonian, or naughty knowledge that he had improperly received the property; or who spends the money received on paying off a secured or unsecured debt so that a proprietary or personal subrogation claim lies against him if he cannot prove the defence of change of position or bona fide purchaser without notice.

Section 5. Injunctions

11–180   Injunctions, like specific performance and rescission and rectification (the subject matter of the next two sections) are equitable remedies.[38] Equitable remedies are those which, historically, were granted by the courts exercising an exclusive equitable jurisdiction. Their most important and distinctive characteristic is that, precisely because equitable remedies are discretionary, there is no "right" to them. In this respect they are unlike common law remedies (damages, principally) which may be claimed as of right on proof of a wrong known to the law (with or without proof of consequent loss, depending on the cause of action). Equitable remedies, of which injunction and specific performance are but two very important examples, aim to achieve a more perfect justice than the common law can through its monetary awards. What they have in common is their effect of forcing a defendant, through the threat of punishment or otherwise, to comply with his obligations under the

---

[38] Others include cancellation and delivery up of documents. Discovery (now called disclosure), being the process whereby a party to a suit is obliged to divulge the existence of all documentation relevant to the issues in the claim, started life as an equitable remedy. Declaration, nowadays granted pursuant to statutory power, likewise.

general law *in kind*.[39] A defendant who is made the subject of injunctive relief or a decree of specific performance is no longer at liberty to leave his primary (contractual, tortious or other) obligations unfulfilled. He can no longer elect to fulfil the "secondary" obligation to pay damages which arises on breach of a primary (contractual, tortious or other) obligation. He must, on pain of punishment, act or refrain from acting in the manner specified in the court order. Indeed, even if he chooses to take the punishment rather than act as he should, the court may simply by-pass him and in an appropriate case empower someone else to do the act instead.[40]

The following passage, which is taken from Spry's *Equitable* **11–181** *Remedies*,[41] illustrates how pervasive the discretionary nature of equitable remedies is:

"Equitable discretions are exercised by taking into account all relevant matters which tend towards the justice or injustice of granting the remedy which is sought, such as hardship, laches, unfairness, the lack of clean hands, and so on, and by weighing them against each other in order to decide whether the particular relief which is in question should be granted in an absolute or conditional form or else refused. Any particular discretionary matter is decisive only if there are no countervailing matters of equal or greater weight. Indeed, as to any particular set of circumstances which is such as would induce a court of equity to exercise its discretion in a particular way it is possible to postulate additional circumstances which would lead to the exercise of that discretion in a different way. It is therefore incorrect to say, for example, that an equitable remedy will be refused if to grant it would give rise to hardship to the defendant. A more correct statement would be, that an equitable remedy will be refused by the court if it appears that the hardship which would be caused to the defendant through granting it would be so great that, taking into account the degree of injury and inconvenience which would be caused to the plaintiff by its refusal and by his relegation to such remedies at law as damages, and all the other material circumstances before the court, the case is one of those in which courts of equity regard the grant of relief as unjust and in which they hence refuse to intervene.

Equitable remedies are, unlike the case in civilian systems, the exceptional legal response to wrong-doing. In those systems it is in theory the case, to take a simple example, that a buyer of goods which are readily available in the market is entitled to an order for specific performance of the contract of sale against the defaulting vendor.[42] In English law, as will be seen, that is not the case: the buyer can sue only for damages and,

---

[39] *In specie* in Latin, from which root *specific* is derived.
[40] For example, it is possible for the court to order that a conveyance or transfer of the defendant's land which he has promised to convey to the claimant be executed by someone other than the defendant if he will not execute it himself.
[41] (2nd ed.), p. 4.
[42] In practice, of course, most (common law and civilian) buyers will simply buy elsewhere what the vendor has promised but failed to deliver and seek monetary compensation for any loss. Sensible people tend to avoid unnecessary litigation.

even then, only if he can prove loss consequent upon the vendor's breach. Specific performance is both in theory and practice, the exception rather than the rule. The same is true of injunction with which it is convenient to start.

(1) Definition and classification

11–182 An injunction is an order of the court forbidding the initiation or the continuance of some act or state of affairs or commanding that an act be done.[43] An injunction may therefore be *prohibitory* or *mandatory* and the distinction, as in the case of positive and negative covenants in regard to land, is one of substance not form:[44] while an order of the court requiring the demolition of a house wrongfully erected could be framed as an order not to leave it standing, the order would nonetheless be mandatory. A tell-tale sign is that mandatory injunctions normally require some expenditure on the part of the defendant. In addition, whereas the execution of prohibitory injunctions generally needs no supervision (the defendant simply has to refrain from committing the prohibited act), the execution of a mandatory order may do so *e.g.* in the case of an order to demolish a house in a particular manner.

(2) Distinguished from specific performance

11–183 *Positive* contractual obligations of certain kinds are normally enforced, in equity, by orders for specific performance[45] rather than mandatory injunctions.[46] What is the point of insisting on this difference? Does it really matter to a claimant or defendant whether the claimant obtains a mandatory injunction or a decree of specific performance? In terms of enforcement, it could not seriously matter for both remedies are enforced in the same way: in the case of an individual defendant, by imprisonment, fine, or sequestration of assets (or any combination of these) and in the case of a corporation (whose officers may, additionally, be punished in their individual capacities), by fine or sequestration of assets[47] or both. Yet, it *does* matter which a claimant is required to apply for because, as will be seen, the number of grounds on which a decree for specific performance may be refused is considerably greater than the number of grounds on which a final injunction may be refused. And this appears to be for a justifiable reason: by contract an individual may either, by negative stipulation, put himself under disabilities that he does not have under the general law (apart from the contract) or, by positive stipulation, impose on himself obligations which he does not have under the general law (apart from the contract). In the former case, he is merely restricting his freedom to act which restriction can, within limits,

---

[43] An exception to this definition appears to be the order of prohibition in judicial review proceedings.
[44] *Truckell v. Stock* [1957] 1 W.L.R. 161.
[45] See section 6 below.
[46] *Evans v. B.B.C. and I.B.A., The Times*, February 26, 1974 provides an exception to this rule. Additionally, the injunction granted was interlocutory.
[47] Rules of the Supreme Court, Ord. 45.

be enforced by a prohibitory injunction without imposing burdens on him over and above those which the general law imposes. But in the latter case, when the defendant has (albeit freely and for valuable consideration) taken upon himself the burden of doing something which the general law does not require him to do, a court of equity will be astute to enquire into the justice of making him do *in kind* that which he has promised. In particular, it will want to be certain that, for example, the claimant is ready, willing and able to perform the obligations which *he* has undertaken pursuant to the contract; it will want to ensure, moreover, that there is "mutuality" between the parties[48] and so on. When a defendant is required, at the behest of a claimant, to do more than the law generally requires of him, a court of conscience will test the justice of the claimant's claim more keenly than otherwise.[49]

Moreover, it is often said that, unlike the case with mandatory **11–184** injunctions, no decree of specific performance will lie on an interim (formerly referred to as "interlocutory") basis (*i.e.* pending trial). If true, it would matter very much whether a claimant's claim were for a mandatory injunction or a decree of specific performance for, in the first case he might obtain interim relief but in the second could not. The case of *Sky Petroleum Ltd v. VIP Petroleum Ltd*,[50] however, tends to blur the distinction and, moreover suggests that it is not true that specific performance will not lie on an interim basis. There, the plaintiff applied for an interlocutory prohibitory injunction restraining the defendant from failing to supply it with petrol, which failure was allegedly in breach of contract. Goulding J. treated the motion as one for an interlocutory decree of specific performance, looking at the substance rather than the form, and granted it.

(3) Perpetual or interim

All injunctions may be classified, in addition, as either *interim*[51] or **11–185** *perpetual*.[52] Interim injunctions are those granted pending the final resolution of an issue between the parties or some earlier specified

---

[48] See below, para. 11–290.

[49] It might be objected that some negative contractual obligations (*e.g.* not to build on land) can only be enforced by mandatory injunctions (*e.g.* where the building has gone up and the only way of satisfactorily remedying the wrong is to require it to be pulled down) and, yet, here, the plaintiff will not be required to satisfy the requirements which he would have had to satisfy on an application for specific performance of a positive contractual stipulation. Is the distinction morally defensible? It is suggested that it is: in this case, the defendant has not taken upon himself any burden over and above that imposed by the law. The burden which will be imposed on him by requiring him to demolish the building is both self-inflicted *and* the consequence of his own wrong-doing. It would be odd to allow him to plead that wrong in his own defence. In contrary fashion, the burden which is imposed on a defendant who has promised to do something *positive* is, of course, self-inflicted but not the result of wrong-doing and if a claimant promisee claims a remedy which will achieve more perfect justice than an award of damages (*i.e.* a decree of specific performance), then his moral entitlement to more justice than the law normally affords can legitimately be tested.

[50] [1974] 1 W.L.R. 576.

[51] Formerly *interlocutory*.

[52] Also termed "permanent" and "final. Although 'perpetual' is the preferred terminology under the Civil Procedure Rules, it is potentially misleading in that the injunction might not, on its terms, be intended to have perpetual effect at all. Indeed, all that is meant is that the injunction granted is finally decisive of the issue between the parties. The actual order granted, for example, in the case of a one year restrictive covenant being enforced against a former employee, will endure only for one year.

event[53] and the courts have developed a special approach to the granting of them, quite different from those applicable to perpetual injunctions.[54] It will be convenient to consider the principles on which perpetual injunctions are granted first. Before doing so, however, three other general points may usefully be made about the jurisdiction to grant injunctions.

(4) The statutory basis of the modern jurisdiction

11–186 The equitable and therefore discretionary nature of the jurisdiction to grant injunctions does not absolve a claimant from the requirement to show some legal or equitable cause of action despite the wording of section 37(1) of the Supreme Court Act 1981 which provides:

> "The High Court[55] may by order (whether interlocutory or final) grant an injunction . . . in all cases in which it appears to the court to be just and convenient to do so."

The case of *Normid Housing Association Ltd v. Ralphs*[56] illustrates this point. There, an injunction was refused to the plaintiffs who were suing their architects, the defendants, for negligence. The defendants, as would be expected, had professional insurance. The insurers, however, were desirous of settling whatever claim the defendants might have against them. The sum which the insurers offered the defendants was less than the sum claimed by the plaintiffs from the defendants. When the plaintiffs discovered this, they sought an injunction preventing the defendants from accepting the insurers' offer. They failed because the defendants owed no legal duty to the plaintiffs to insure at all, let alone for any particular sum.

(5) The quia timet jurisdiction

11–187 Second, the foregoing principle has not prevented the issuing of injunctions *quia timet*.[57] Equity, achieving more perfect justice than the common law (which was limited to the award of damages to make good

---

[53] Such as the disposal of an appeal against the dismissal of a motion seeking interim relief pending trial. The grant of an injunction in such case is purely so that, should the appeal against the substantive refusal succeed, an order made on appeal will not be in vain.

[54] See below, para. 11–198.

[55] By the County Courts Act 1984, section 38, (as substituted by the Courts and Legal Services Act 1990, section 3) the County Court may make any order within its jurisdiction that could be made by the High Court except those of a "prescribed kind", *i.e.* specified under regulations made by the Lord Chancellor. To date, such regulations have been made in the County Court Remedies Regulations 1991 where, by regulation 2, *Anton Piller* (now called "search") orders and *Mareva* (now called "freezing") injunctions (see below, para. 11–198) are prescribed *except* in (i) family proceedings, (ii) for the purpose of preserving property forming the subject matter of proceedings or (iii) in aid of execution of county court orders or judgments for the purpose of preserving assets until execution.

[56] *The Times*, July 18, 1988. See also *Day v. Brownrigg* (1878) 10 Ch.D. 294. The principle appears to be subject to two exceptions: the jurisdiction of the High Court (1) to restrain the prosecution or defence of proceedings in a lower court or in another country and (2), when proceedings are on foot to resolve a dispute, to grant an order to protect or further the functioning of the tribunal. One academic has argued, against the judicial trend, for the concept of the entirely autonomous injunction: Tettenborn, "Injunctions without damages", (1987) 38 N.I. Legal Q. 118.

[57] Literally, "because (the claimant) fears".

injury which had already occurred), acted to restrain *future* wrongs. Indeed, all (perpetual) prohibitory injunctions achieve as much, in that, although normally sought only where there has been an actual wrong done, they ensure, so far as any court order can, that the wrong will not be repeated, thus rendering unnecessary a multiplicity of suits. It was only one step from that to hold that a threatened future wrong should be restrained before it had occurred. However, "mere vague apprehension is not sufficient to support an action for a *quia timet* injunction. There must be an immediate threat to do something".[58] Nor is it sufficient, in order to obtain an injunction *quia timet* against a defendant, to show that he would *technically* be a joint tortfeasor with another defendant if the latter were not restrained: one must go further in such cases and show an inclination to join in the threatened act. Thus an injunction was issued in anticipation of a threatened wrong (the erection of a car wash) against a lessee but not against his freeholder who, despite being a technical joint tortfeasor, showed no inclination to join in the act.[59]

(6) In personam or in rem

The fact that the jurisdiction is equitable means that, in theory, the order **11–188** of the court operates *in personam* rather than *in rem*. These Latin tags refer to a traditional distinction between rights against *particular* persons (such as arise under contracts) and rights against persons *generally* (such as arise in ownership). Historically, the Chancellor acted to perfect the injustices of the operation of the common law, administered in the King's courts, not by changing any substantive rule of law but, rather, by requiring a legal rightholder not to enforce his right. The Chancellor's method of securing compliance was to threaten imprisonment. The jurisdiction, therefore, was said to be solely *in personam*: directed against particular persons. However the modern trust, which is descended from the practice of the Chancellors who would regularly require a legal owner to hold property for the benefit and enjoyment of another, is a good example of how blurred the distinction between personal and property rights can become: no-one nowadays would seriously defend the thesis that a beneficiary's rights under a trust are merely personal rights.[60] Far from it, the reason that a beneficiary's rights prevail over the rights of a trustee's creditors where the trustee becomes insolvent is precisely that the beneficiary's rights in the trust property are rights of ownership. It is necessary to treat with caution, therefore, statements that the equitable jurisdiction is purely personal.

---

[58] *Per* Lord Buckmaster in *Graigola Merthyr Co. Ltd. v. Swansea Corporation* [1929] A.C. 344, 353.

[59] *Celsteel Ltd. v. Alton House Holdings Ltd.* [1986] 1 W.L.R. 512. Given that breach of an injunction could expose a defendant to severe penalties this sort of limitation on the availability of the remedy is not a merely technical requirement.

[60] Although personal accountability of the trustee to the beneficiary is the hallmark of the trust and part of the "irreducible core content" of *trusteeship: Armitage v. Nurse* [1998] Ch. 241 *per* Millett L.J. This does not preclude, however, the idea that as against the rest of the world, the beneficiary's rights are *in rem*.

11–189   In relation to the equitable jurisdiction to issue injunctions a similar blurring of the traditional distinction may also be seen. In practice, injunctions may operate against people to whom they are not immediately directed, for example, as in *Att.-Gen. v. Newspaper Publishing Plc*[61] where it was said that "if C's conduct, in knowingly doing acts which would, if done by **B**, be a breach of the injunction against [B], results in impedance to or intereference with the administration of justice by the court in the action between A and B, then, so far as the question of C's conduct being a contempt of court is concerned, it cannot make any difference whether such conduct takes the form of aiding and abetting B on the one hand or acting solely of his own volition on the other"[62] Thus anyone *with notice*[63] of an injunction directed at another may independently contemn the court and will do so, for example, where "the subject matter of the action[64] is such that, if it is destroyed in whole or in part before the trial of the action, the purpose of the action will be wholly or partly nullified".[65]

(7) General equitable principles governing the grant of final injunctions

(i) adequacy of common law remedies

11–190   Equity had no cause to supplement an existing legal remedy which was adequate and it came to be a requirement of the first order that before any equitable remedy would lie, the legal remedy be shown to be inadequate—a matter to be determined having regard to the nature of the injury (whether it is assessable in monetary terms), the prospect of its being repeated (when, otherwise, a multiplicity of suits would be necessary) and, to a lesser extent, the ability of a defendant to satisfy an award of damages. In *Beswick v. Beswick*,[66] a case on specific performance, D had promised P to pay a weekly sum of £5 to P's widow for the rest of her life. When D indicated that he would not do so, P's estate succeeded in an application for specific performance of the agreement. One of the reasons why it succeeded was the fact that damages for D's breach would be nominal (on the principle that neither P nor his estate suffered any loss: that fell on his impoverished widow). That, it was felt, would be an inadequate remedy in a situation which, morally, cried out for something more to be done. Another reason given in that case to justify the award of a decree was that as the obligation to pay the weekly sum was a continuing one of indefinite duration, P's estate would have to institute a multiplicity of suits—on a weekly basis!—in order to obtain justice. A decree would obviously constitute a more adequate remedy.

---

[61] [1988] Ch. 333 and *sub nom. Att.-Gen. v. Times Newspaper Ltd* [1992] 1 A.C. 191.

[62] [1992] 1 A.C. 103 *per* Lord Brandon.

[63] Knowledge is, of course, the touchstone of (personal) equitable liability: see Lord Browne-Wilkinson in *Wesdeutsche Landesbank Girozentrale v. Islington BC* [1996] 2 All E.R. 961.

[64] In that case, the confidential nature of certain information.

[65] [1992] 1 A.C. at 104.

[66] [1968] A.C. 58. See, further, the discussion of this case in section 6 at para. 11–304.

There is, moreover, something to be said for the view that the nominal **11–191** nature of damages is taken into account quite routinely outside contractual cases: in tort, the fact that even a relatively trivial threatened trespass, may be restrained by injunction[67] suggests that this is so. Were it otherwise the law would be seen to tolerate serious inroads into the notion of ownership (*i.e.* with quiet enjoyment) of real property. But, still, it might plausibly be said that the court's willingness to grant injunctive relief in such situations is dependent not so much on the cause of action (distinguishing between contract and tort, for example) as on the fact that in these cases the wrong is *threatened* (*i.e.* future rather than present or past) and this allows the *quia timet* jurisdiction to be invoked. It is a curious feature of this jurisdiction that the "inadequacy of damages" requirement seems to diminish to vanishing point: if a promisor is either honest or silly enough to announce, in advance of the time for performance of his obligations, that he does not intend to fulfil them then, on the promisee's application, a court of equity will have no hesitation in giving him an added reason (threat of contempt proceedings) to do as he promised. And this appears to be the case even if the promise is one which, if breached, would cause loss which could be easily assessed in damages.

(ii) equity will not act in vain

This principle (or "maxim" of equity), like the last, is common to specific **11–192** performance.[68] The idea is that if issuing an injunction would be futile, no injunction will be issued. In *Wookey v. Wookey*,[69] a family case, it was said that where there was evidence that an order would not be complied with and that nothing would be done about the non-compliance in judicial terms (because the subject of the order would, on account of youth, not be imprisoned and, on account of impecuniosity, not be fined) then the order should not be made. This is perhaps an extreme application of the principle but can be defended. More regular applications of the principle are to be found in cases where it would be *impossible* for the defendant to comply with the order (because, for example, in a case where a mandatory injunction was sought requiring him to tear down a building, he no longer owned the land and had no right to tear down any building upon it) or, as in the *Spycatcher* litigation,[70] where a final injunction was refused against a newspaper

---

[67] *Woollerton and Wilson Ltd. v. Richard Costain Ltd.* [1970] 1 W.L.R. 411. But note *Jaggard v. Sawyer* [1995] 1 W.L.R. 269, below at para. 11–209.
[68] See section 6, at para. 11–289.
[69] [1991] Fam. 121.
[70] See *Att.-Gen. v. Observer Ltd.* [1990] 1 A.C. 109.

preventing it from publishing certain information. Although that information was initially confidential it had already been published in a book that had become widely available in the United Kingdom.[71]

(iii) delay and acquiescence

11–193   The requirement that one who seeks equitable relief must do so without delay, even within the statutory limitation period (the doctrine of laches[72]) is often factually indistinguishable from the doctrine of acquiescence whereby knowing failure to object to a wrong may give rise to an inability to resurrect an objection to it at a later date. The cases on delay diverge on the question whether *mere* delay (*i.e.* unaccompanied by acquiescence) will bar the grant of relief.[73] As to acquiescence, the test is whether the plaintiff represented that he would no longer enforce his rights.[74] A very recent example of how acquiescence may operate to bar not just equitable but *any* relief is to be found in *Gafford v. Graham*.[75] There, the defendant was in breach of a restrictive covenant which prevented him from converting his bungalow or extending his barn without the plaintiff's consent. He breached the covenant in 1986 but, as the Court of Appeal said, "the plaintiff made no complaint until his solicitor wrote to the defendant about three years after the acts complained of", despite full knowledge of the breaches. At first instance, the judge had awarded the plaintiff damages in respect of the conversion and extension. The Court of Appeal, however, held that his acquiescence was a bar not just to equitable relief but *all* relief and discharged the order for damages. It held that, in all the circumstances, it would be unconscionable for the plaintiff to enforce the (legal) rights which he undoubtedly had in 1986. This, notwithstanding that the plaintiff's action was begun well within the limitation period. The case is an example (closely related to proprietary estoppel) of how equity can operate to *extinguish* accrued legal rights. Not all cases in which equitable relief is refused, however, are so draconian: normally, a claimant's delay will, if it has any effect, merely serve to deprive him of his (presumably more adequate) *equitable* remedy. His legal rights (and the remedies he has in respect of infringements thereof) remain, in the absence of something like an estoppel, intact.

But even a claimant who, knowing of a threatened or incipient wrong, begins proceedings for an injunction timeously must weigh carefully the

[71] A recent application of this principle made the headlines, if not the law reports, when the High Court discharged an injunction preventing the publication in England & Wales of the identity of a Cabinet Minister whose son (a minor) had allegedly broken the law. Because the Minister was lawfully identified in Scotland (before any injunctions had been obtained against the press there), and anyone in England, by means of a telephone call to someone in Scotland, could identify the Minister (in fact the Home Secretary, the Rt. Hon. Jack Straw), it would be in vain to continue the injunction in England & Wales. This, it turned out, was much to the relief of the Home Secretary, who until the injunction was discharged, could not comment (so as to defend himself and/or his son) for that would be to breach the injunction.
[72] Pronounced "lay-cheese".
[73] *Fullwood v. Fullwood* (1878) 9 Ch. D. 176, per Fry J., no; *H.P. Bulmer Ltd. & Showerings Ltd. v. J. Bollinger S.A.* [1977] 2 C.M.L.R. 625: only if "inordinate", per Goff L.J.
[74] *Allen v. Veranne Builders Ltd.* [1988] E.G.C.S. 2.
[75] *The Times*, May 1 1998.

decision whether or not at an early stage of the action to seek interim injunctive relief: *Jaggard v. Sawyer*[76] shows how the very possibility of obtaining perptual injunctive relief may turn on that decision (the court awarded damages in lieu).

(iv) clean hands

Further discussion of this requirement, also common to specific perfor- **11–194** mance, is to be found in section 6.[77] It is accepted that a claimant who has himself defaulted on a contract cannot obtain injunctive relief to enforce any of its terms.[78] That is an application, in the field of contract, of the clean hands maxim. It is, however, a different requirement from the similar doctrine that he who comes to equity must do equity, which looks not to whether the claimant's hands are already soiled by wrong-doing, but rather to the future question whether the claimant is prepared to fulfil his outstanding obligations.[79] In applications for specific perfor-mance, this translates into a requirement that the claimant demonstrate that he is "ready, willing and able" to perform his side of the bargain. Both requirements are morally defensible in that, by seeking an equita-ble remedy over and above the legal one to which he is entitled, a claimant must appeal to a court of conscience. He cannot do so if his is not clear.

(v) no undue hardship

Interim and mandatory injunctions in particular provide scope for an **11–195** argument that an injunction ought to be refused as a matter of discretion on the ground of hardship to the defendant. In the former case, this is so because, by definition, the claimant has not yet established his right to any relief (because there has not yet been a trial) and in the latter because often, as was suggested above, what is distinctive of a mandatory injunction is that compliance will involve the defendant in expenditure which may be out of all proportion to the benefit which the claimant will derive from the grant of an injunction.

Some cases which sought to circumvent hardship to the defendant by granting an injunction but suspending its operation for a period[80] are now suspect in light of the decision in *Jaggard v. Sawyer*[81] where that practice was specifically disapproved. The jurisdiction to award damages in lieu of an injunction, now contained in section 50 of the Supreme Court Act 1981 (which jurisdiction was analysed closely in that case), is a statutory recognition of the fact that sometimes the award of an

---

[76] [1995] 1 W.L.R. 269 and below, at para. 11–209. *Gafford v. Graham* follows this decision on the question of damages in lieu of other breaches of which the plaintiff claimed.
[77] at para. 11–295.
[78] *Measures Bros. Ltd. v. Measures* [1910] 2 Ch. 248.
[79] Although Lord Denning M.R. appears to have confused the doctrines in *Shell (U.K.) Ltd. v. Lostock Garage Ltd.* [1976] 1 W.L.R. 1187.
[80] *e.g. Woollerton and Wilson Ltd v. Richard Costain ltd* [1970] 1 W.L.R. 411. See also Lane L.J.'s proposed solution to the problem raised in *Miller v. Jackson* [1977] Q.B. 966.
[81] [1995] 1 W.L.R. 269, and below, at para. 11–209.

injunction (particularly a mandatory one requiring, for example, the demolition of a building) can be oppressive to a defendant. By giving courts of equity the power to award damages in lieu, Parliament made it easier to justify declining to grant injunctions in such cases. But the practice of doing so existed prior to the statutory provision where undue hardship would have resulted. A plaintiff would, in those circumstances, be confined to his legal remedy of damages. The innovation of the provision (first introduced by Lord Cairns in 1858) was that where the injunction had been sought to restrain *future* wrongs, for which common law damages could not be awarded, a plaintiff would not be put out of court without *any* remedy: he might be given damages instead.

(vi) the public interest

11–196   Although in specific performance cases the notion has long been accepted that public considerations might affect the availability of equitable remedies in contract[82] (in which branch of the law, more generally, it is well accepted that private individuals cannot create rights and duties for each other which contravene public policy), the matter is more controversial as regards those torts which create a perimeter of inviolability around the notion of private ownership of land. In *Miller v. Jackson*[83] Lord Denning M.R. opined *obiter* that if the defendants in that case had committed the tort of nuisance (he held to the contrary), then an injunction should be refused on the ground that the public interest in (i) protecting the environment achieved by the preservation of playing fields and (ii) enabling youth to enjoy the benefits of outdoor games prevailed over the private interest in securing the privacy of home and garden without the intrusion or interference caused by cricket balls hit out of the defendants' neighbouring cricket ground. That aspect of the decision was disavowed by a later Court of Appeal in *Kennaway v. Thompson*,[84] which held that the public interest in motor-boat racing could not prevail over the private right of quiet enjoyment of the home.

11–197   It is suggested that the distinction which is drawn in this regard between tort and contract (or, indeed, between tort and trust) is defensible: both contract and trust are, at the most general level, facilitative institutions which allow individuals to write "local law", creating for themselves powers, disabilities, rights and obligations that do not otherwise exist. The danger that individuals might achieve or attempt to achieve undesirable purposes through these institutions has always been guarded against judicially in the doctrines which invalidate contracts and trusts on grounds of illegality and public policy. The law of tort (which comprises all the non-voluntary, non-statutory private law rules regulating behaviour) is itself a statement of public policy: the availability of an effective remedy for the unwelcome intrusion of cricket

---

[82] See, below, at para. 11–289.
[83] [1977] Q.B. 966.
[84] [1981] Q.B. 88.

balls upon the quiet enjoyment of one's home is merely an acknowledgement of the importance that is attached, as a matter of public policy, to such enjoyment. If there is some doubt about how much importance should be given to quiet enjoyment of home and garden it seems misleading, bordering on the disingenuous, to dress that up as a clash between public and private right: it is either a clash between two desirable public goals or between two desirable private goals. Either way, in the face of long-established authority, a judicial re-setting of the balance seems constitutionally inappropriate. With contract and trust, on the other hand, there is truly a potential clash between private right or obligation and public policy.

(8) General principles governing the award of interim injunctions[85]

Unlike perpetual injunctions, where the lawyer finds himself considering **11–198** principles of equity, interim injunctions are granted or refused on grounds which have nothing to do, either historically or logically, with the maxims of equity. The principles on which the court acts, or has acted up to the introduction of the Civil Procedure Rules at least, are designed to achieve justice between the parties under circumstances of ignorance or uncertainty (*i.e.* when it is not known whether the claimant's claim is well founded). It must be cautioned at this stage, however, that the new Civil Procedure Rules might have an effect on the substance of these principles and it will be necessary to qualify what follows.[86] Therefore, in order to circumvent the necessity, at an early stage of an action, of deciding disputed questions of fact or determining points of law with insufficient argument, the House of Lords laid down guidelines in *American Cyanamid Co. v. Ethicon Ltd.*[87] for the exercise of judicial discretion whether to grant an interim injunction. Prior thereto, the House had held in *J.T. Stratford & Son Ltd. v. Lindley*[88] that a claimant had to show a prima facie case that he would succeed at trial in obtaining injunctive relief. The decision in *Cyanamid* is to the effect that

---

[85] These may be applied for without notice (formerly referred to as *ex parte*) *i.e.* in the absence of the party against whom the order is being sought in cases where the nature of the relief sought requires that the defendant be taken by surprise (as with *Mareva* or "freezing" injunctions and *Anton Piller* or "search" orders) or urgency where, for example, relief, if it is to granted at all, must be granted immediately. An order may then be made, normally effective only over a short period, which will be reviewed at a hearing with notice to the other side at the end of that period or at such earlier time as the defendant applies to have the order discharged. Note, however, The Trade Unions and Labour Relations (Consolidation) Act 1992, section 221(1) which provides that an *ex parte* injunction shall not be granted in a case where it is likely that the defendant would plead that he acted in contemplation or furtherance of a trade dispute unless all reasonable steps have been taken to give notice and an opportunity to be heard to the defendant. The onus of full and frank disclosure on applications without notice of all facts in the applicant's knowledge (or within his grasp after due inquiry) relevant to the exercise of the court's discretion—which extends to disclosing to the court possible defences that the defendant may have—is taken very seriously: breach of the duty will entitle (although not oblige) the court to discharge the injunction without more and leave the applicant to apply again. See, generally, *Lloyd's Bowmaker Ltd v. Britannia Arrow Holdings Plc* [1988] 1 W.L.R. 1337 per Glidewell L.J. at 1343–1344.

[86] See para. 11–262.

[87] [1975] A.C. 396 and below at para. 224.

[88] [1965] A.C. 269. *Cyanamid* has been said to be irreconcilable with this decision but as *Cyanamid* was the later case, that is the one the Court of Appeal should follow: *Hubbard v. Pitt* [1976] Q.B. 142.

a claimant need only show that he has a case that is not frivolous or vexatious and that there is a serious question to be tried. Once that is established, the question whether an injunction should be granted turns on the balance of convenience, a much used shorthand phrase to describe the balancing exercise in which the court engages in order to minimize the risk of doing injustice.

11–199   That balancing exercise is undertaken as follows: once a serious question for trial is raised, unless there is no arguable defence to the claimant's claim (in which case an injunction should be granted until trial[89]), the court considers whether damages would be an adequate remedy for loss caused to the claimant by *not* granting an injunction pending trial. If so, *and* the defendant can afford to pay, the balance favours no injunction. If the loss likely to be caused is not remediable in damages (either as a matter of legal principle or practice, *i.e.* the defendant could not pay them) then the court considers to what extent the claimant would be able to compensate the defendant for any loss caused to him by *granting* an injunction pending trial. (Thus making the claimant's relief conditional on the provision of what is called a cross-undertaking in damages.[90]) This has the result that if damages would not be an adequate remedy for the claimant (either as a matter of principle or practice) then *if* the defendant's potential loss is compensable, the balance favours an injunction. Where damages would be inadequate for both parties, however, (either as a matter of principle or practice) then injustice is best avoided by maintaining the *status quo*.[91] "Special factors" might properly be taken into account, but only as a last resort can the merits be examined and, even then, only if the strength of one case is disproportionate to the other.

11–200   Much judicial ink has been spilled over the relationship of these guidelines to instant cases and, in particular, on the question whether apparent exceptions to the *Cyanamid* approach are truly exceptions or

---

[89] Unless, with the defendant's consent, the hearing of the motion is treated as the trial of the action in which case a perpetual injunction will lie.

[90] This undertaking is extracted, if the injunction is granted, as a matter of course. Not, however, from the Crown when it is seeking to enforce the law (as opposed to its own proprietary or contractual rights): *Hoffman-La Roche (F.) & Co. v. Secretary of State for Trade and Industry* [1975] A.C. 295. The same is true of (i) relator actions where an undertaking will be required of the relator but not of the Attorney-General and (ii) local authorities enforcing the law: *Kirkless B.C. v. Wickes Building Supplies Ltd* [1992] 3 W.L.R 170. Where the Attorney-General is seeking to enforce a charitable trust as *parens patriae* the position is otherwise and public funds ought not to be risked (as proprietary rights are being asserted). Rather, if there were someone (such as a receiver of charitable property) to give an undertaking limited to the funds available to the charity: *Att.-Gen. v. Wright* [1988] 1 W.L.R. 164, Hoffmann J. The same judge, in *Oxy Electric Ltd. v. Zainuddin* [1991] 1 W.L.R. 115, doubted the decision of Sir Nicolas Browne-Wilkinson V.-C. in *Blue Town Investments Ltd. v. Higgs & Hill Plc.* [1990] 1 W.L.R. 696 to strike out a claim for final injunctive relief as vexatious unless the plaintiff was prepared to apply for interlocutory relief and offer the usual cross-undertaking. Requiring a plaintiff to put his money where his mouth is in this way underestimates what a plaintiff is risking in not applying for interlocutory relief (see *Jaggard v. Sawyer* [1995] 1 W.L.R. 269) and, of course, as Hoffmann J. pointed out (at 120) with a rhetorical question, "Is a poor plaintiff's claim struck out when a rich plaintiff's claim would survive?"

[91] Which, in effect, means letting any alleged wrong already initiated continue and, in the case of *quia timet* relief, prohibiting the occurrence of any alleged wrong. See Lord Diplock in *Garden Cottage Foods Ltd. v. Milk Marketing Board* [1984] A.C. 130, 140.

merely different ways of striking the balance of convenience in instant cases. An instance of judicial divergence on that (rather semantic) issue is to be found in *Cambridge Nutrition Ltd. v. B.B.C.*[92] There certainly appear to be categories of cases (whether *Cyanamid* "exceptions" or not) where the claimant has to show more than that his case is not frivolous or vexatious, raising merely a serious question to be tried. They are as follows.

(i) *trade disputes*: The Trade Union and Labour Relations (Consolidation) Act 1992, section 221(2) provides that, on an application for an interlocutory injunction, where the defendant claims that he acted in contemplation or furtherance of a trade dispute, the court is to have regard to the likelihood of the defendant's establishing at the trial any of the matters which, under the Act, confer immunity from tortious liability.

(ii) *trial of action unlikely or delayed*: In *Cambridge Nutrition Ltd. v. B.B.C.*[93] the plaintiffs sought an injunction preventing the defendants from broadcasting a programme (in the making of which they had participated) until after the imminent publication of a government report on the plaintiffs' low calorie diet, the subject matter also of the programme. The programme, however, would have had no impact if broadcast after the publication of the report and, if an injunction were granted to trial, it would effectively prevent the broadcast for good. Clearly, if the *Cyanamid* principles are designed to achieve a fair resolution pending trial, others must be used to achieve such resolution where there is likely to be no trial. The court therefore looked at the merits of the plaintiffs' claim and, finding the basis of it to be implausible (an oral agreement not to broadcast until after publication of the report—for which there was remarkably little evidence) declined to grant an injunction.

(iii) *no arguable defence*: This has already been mentioned in the **11–201** discussion above of *Cyanamid*.

(iv) *injunctions to restrain the presentation of winding-up petitions*: It has been held since *Cyanamid* that the guidelines do not apply to an interlocutory injunction to restrain the bringing of other proceedings on the ground that these latter would be an abuse of the court's process: the grant of such injunction finally determines the matter.[94] So a plaintiff would fail unless he demonstrated not merely a serious issue whether the defendant's proceedings would be an abuse but, over and above that, that the defendant was bound to fail in those proceedings. In *Ward v. Coulson Sanderson and Ward Ltd.*[95] the Court of Appeal followed that reasoning to

---

[92] [1990] 3 All E.R. 523.

[93] [1990] 3 All E.R. 523. See also *Cayne v. Global Natural Resources Plc.* [1984] 1 All E.R. 225.

[94] *Bryanston Finance v. De Vries (No. 2)* [1976] Ch. 63, per Stephenson L.J. and Sir John Pennycuick. Buckley L.J. concurred in refusing the injunction but purported to follow *Cyanamid*.

[95] [1986] P.C.C. 57.

hold that *Cyanamid* did not apply to injunctions to restrain the presentation of a winding-up petition by a creditor.

(v) *mandatory interlocutory injunctions*: For the grant of a mandatory injunction on an interlocutory basis there must be a "high degree of assurance" that it will appear at trial that the injunction was rightly granted.[96]

11–202   The effect of the new Civil Procedure Rules ("CPR"): by virtue of section 2 of the Civil Procedure Act 1997 and the Civil Procedure Rules 1998,[97] all civil claims brought after April 25, 1999 fall to be dealt with according to the CPR. Based on a review of Civil Justice by Lord Woolf, the then Master of the Rolls, they were intended to effect a fundamental change in the administration of civil justice in this country. For present purposes, it is pertinent to note that the principles according to which the courts have, since *Cyanamid*, awarded interim relief, must now be read subject to the "overriding objective" of allowing the court (through, amongst other things, active "case management") to deal with cases justly. This may include taking steps to ensure that the parties are on an equal footing, saving expense, and dealing with a case in ways which are appropriate to the amount involved, the importance of the case, the complexity of the case and the financial situation of the parties. Some or all of these might well militate in favour of the approach boldly (and, it is suggested, sensibly) advocated by Laddie J in *Series 5 Software v. Clark*[98] which cannot be interpreted as anything other than a first instance rejection of the *Cyanamid* approach.

(9) Two special cases of interim injunction[99]

11–203   Both *Mareva* (now "freezing") injunctions and *Anton Piller* (now "search") orders are interim orders. As Lord Donaldson M.R. made plain in *Polly Peck International v. Nadir (No. 2)*,[1] there is no question of *Cyanamid* applying to *Mareva* injunctions ". . . which proceed on principles quite different from those applicable to other interlocutory injunctions."[2] The same is true of *Anton Piller* or search orders. Together they have been described by the same judge as the law's "nuclear weapons".[3]

(i) Freezing injunctions

Section 37 of the Supreme Court Act 1981 provides:

---

[96] *Shepherd Homes Ltd. v. Sandham* [1971] Ch. 340, Megarry J.; *Locabail International Finance Ltd v. Agroexport* [1986] 1 W.L.R. 657, holding that Megarry J.'s approach was not affected by *Cyanamid* which it had preceded. Note, however, Hoffmann J. in *Films Rover International Ltd. v. Cannon Film Sales Ltd.* [1987] 1 W.L.R. 670 observing that in exceptional cases where the risk of injustice was greater in not granting an injunction, the *Shepherd Homes* test need not be met.
[97] SI 3132.
[98] [1996] All E.R. 853, below, at para. 11–236.
[99] See generally Gee's *Mareva Injunctions and Anton Piller Relief* (3rd ed.); Ough and Flenley's *The Mareva Injunction and Anton Piller Order* (2nd ed.) and Sheridan's *Injunctions In General* (1994) and *Chancery Procedure & Anton Piller Orders* (1994).
[1] [1992] 4 All E.R. 769.
[2] Although different views have been advanced suggesting that the test for *Marevas* is compatible with *Cyanamid*. See Gee, *op. cit.* at 143 and the authority there cited.
[3] *Bank Mellat v. Nikpour* [1985] F.S.R. 87, 91–92.

(1) The High Court may by order (whether interlocutory or final) grant an injunction or appoint a receiver in all cases in which it appears to the court to be just and convenient to do so . . .

(3) The power of the High Court under subsection (1) to grant an interlocutory injunction restraining a party to any proceedings from removing from the jurisdiction of the High Court, or otherwise dealing with, assets located within that jurisdiction shall be exercisable in cases where that party is, as well as in cases where he is not, domiciled, resident or present within that jurisdiction.

This provision is now the statutory basis for the injunction that was first **11–204** granted in *Nippon Yusen Kaisha v. Karageorgis*[4] but which took its name from the second case of its grant, *Mareva Compania Naveira S.A. v. International Bulkcarriers S.A.*[5] The criteria for obtaining a freezing injunction are: (1) a good arguable case,[6] (2) that there is a real risk that any judgment will go unsatisfied by reason of the disposal by the defendant of his assets, unless he is restrained by court order from disposing of them and (3) it would be just and convenient in all the circumstances of the case to grant the relief sought.

On (1), it has been said that this amounts to "one which is more than barely capable of serious argument, but not necessarily one which the judge considers would have a better than 50 per cent chance of success".[7] The requirement in (2) is not that of "nefarious intent" (*i.e.* that the defendant will dissipate assets *so that* a judgment will be unsatisfied) but, rather an objective risk that there will be dissipation making it likely that the result of his dissipation will be that the judgment goes unsatisfied.[8] The requirement in (3) is no mere formula: it may be regarded as justifying the approach taken in *Polly Peck International v. Nadir (No. 2)* with regard to banks whose business, depending on the confidence of their investors, might be destroyed at a stroke: the claimant's cross-undertaking in damages would be of little consolation or utility.

It is important for third parties who, it has been seen, can contemn the **11–205** court if they have notice of the terms of an injunction with which they act inconsistently, to know just what acts are prohibited by the order.

The injunction is available both before and after judgment and may restrict dealings with *all* assets of the defendant[9] or merely assets up to a

---

[4] [1975] 1 W.L.R. 1093.
[5] [1975] 2 Lloyd's Rep. 509.
[6] The court is bound therefore to consider the merits of the case.
[7] Per Mustill J. in *Ninemia Corporation v. Trave Schiffahrtsgesellschaft GmbH (The "Niedersachsen")* [1983] 2 Lloyd's Rep. 600, 605.
[8] In *Derby & Co. Ltd. v. Weldon* [1990] Ch 48, the Court of Appeal rejected the subjective interpretation of the requirement even in the case of the wide ("draconian", per May L.J.) relief granted in that case. *A fortiori*, then, in a standard case.
[9] Such an order is not appropriate in matrimonial cases: *Ghoth v. Ghoth* [1992] 2 All E.R. 920. On the question whether a freezing injunction is available against property which appears to be jointly owned by the defendant and another, the standard form recognises that, in the case of bank accounts, moneys held to the account of the defendant are subject to the order whether held in the defendant's own name or jointly with some other party. In practice, in order to obtain such order, a claimant must be

certain value (*i.e.* the value of the claimant's claim plus costs). However, it gives the claimant no right *in rem* or security or priority over the defendant's creditors (of which the claimant has not yet shown himself to be one).

Prior to the enactment of the Civil Jurisdiction and Judgments Act 1982, there was no power in the High Court to grant a freezing injunction against a defendant who had assets in the jurisdiction but against whom there was no substantive claim subject to the jurisdiction, the claimant asserting no proprietary interest in the assets.[10] The Act, which gives effect to the Convention on Jurisdiction and the Enforcement of Judgments in Civil and Commercial Matters,[11] has been interpreted by the Court of Appeal[12] to provide that such injunction can be obtained in England before trial or after judgment even though the claimant has no cause of action, in England, against the defendant: so long as a court in another contracting state has jurisdiction, it suffices.

(ii) Search orders[13]

11–206   In *Anton Piller K.G. v. Manufacturing Process*[14] the Court of Appeal approved the making of an order, in substance an interim mandatory injunction, requiring the defendants to allow the plaintiff's solicitors to enter the defendants' premises to inspect documents and remove them to the plaintiffs' solicitors' custody. Failure to comply with the order is a contempt by the defendant and so, even though the order does not *entitle* the claimant to enter as if he had a search warrant, the defendant has good reason to allow him so to do. The order is made so as to safeguard vital evidence which is needed to prove the claimant's claim although it may be granted simply to obtain information necessary to safeguard the claimant's rights, to locate assets against which a judgment might be enforced and to preserve property which might otherwise be dissipated or destroyed.

---

prepared to satisfy the court that the asset constituted by the chose in action would be available in execution of the claimant's judgment or for distribution in the defendant's bankruptcy. The claimant might show this by establishing a tracing claim to the "contents" of the account or by showing that the defendant is the sole beneficial owner of them. If he cannot, then the third party's share will be released to him. Where the joint property is land, the defendant's interest (under the statutory trust) may be the subject of an injunction and, after judgment, a charging order. If the court is satisfied that the property is owned in equity solely by the defendant it may grant relief against both the defendant and the co-owning third party: *S.S.F. v. Masri* [1985] 1 W.L.R. 876.

[10] *Siskina (Owners of Cargo Lately Laden on Board) v. Distos Compania Naveira S.A.* [1979] A.C. 210 although in *Mercedes-Benz A.G. v. Leiduck* [1995] 3 All E.R. 929, 946–950, Lord Nicholls considered the law should move on to allow "free-standing" freezing injunctions auxiliary to foreign proceedings and in 1999 the Privy Council gave leave for an appeal from the Bahamas to raise the point, but the appeal ultimately was not proceeded with.

[11] Set out in Sched. 1 to the Act. See para. 11–274

[12] *Babanaft International Co S.A. v. Bassatne* [1990] Ch. 13. See also *Republic of Haiti v. Duvalier* [1990] Q.B. 202.

[13] The standard order now made, as with freezing injunctions, is provided for by CPR and is printed below at para. 11–260. Close scrutiny of its provisions (it was designed to be comprehensible to the lay reader) reveals much of what is judicially thought desirable in future practice and, by implication, undesirable in past practice. The jurisdiction has now been placed on a statutory footing by section 7 of the Civil Procedure Act 1997.

[14] [1976] Ch. 55. The first reported case of such order was in *E.M.I. v. Pandit* [1975] 1 W.L.R. 302 (Templeman J.).

Because of the truly draconian effect of an order of this sort which, to a greater extent than the freezing injunction, involves serious inroads into basic civil liberties,[15] it is now accepted that they are to be granted sparingly.[16] The three essential requirements (per Ormrod L.J in *Anton Piller*[17]) are (1) an extremely strong prima facie case; (2) the potential or actual damage to the claimant (if an order is not made) must be very serious and (3) there must be clear evidence that the defendant has in his possession incriminating documents or things and that there is a real possibility that he may destroy such material before any application with notice can be made.[18] Even if all the conditions are met, the court still has to be satisfied that the need for the order outweighs the injustice of making an order against a defendant without his having been heard.[19] This has the effect that an order will not be made against persons of good standing who are likely to obey an order of the court to deliver up.[20] *Emmanuel v. Emmanuel*[21] makes it plain that in matrimonial proceedings an order will only be granted on strong evidence.

There is a common law principle enshrined in section 14(1) of the **11–207** Civil Evidence Act 1968 that no person may be obliged in civil proceedings to produce any document or thing which may incriminate him (or his spouse). There are two important exceptions to this, for present purposes, namely section 72 of the Supreme Court Act 1981[22] and section 31 of the Theft Act 1968.[23] *Emmanuel v. Emmanuel*[24] clarifies, however, that an order may be made if the risk of incrimination extends only to a charge of perjury in the proceedings in the context of which the order is sought.

---

[15] *i.e.* the right to be heard before the making of an order against one (a feature which, in virtue of its essential *ex parte* nature, it shares with the freezing injunction), the right to be free from arbitrary search and seizure, and the right to privacy in one's own home (orders were commonly made against defendants to be executed at their places of residence).

[16] The frequency with which orders came to be granted (see Oliver L.J.'s reference to them as "very, very commonly employed" and "almost commonplace" in *Dunlop Holdings Ltd. v. Staravia Ltd.* [1982] Com. L.R. 3) led to the expression of judicial concern in a number of cases about plaintiffs' failures to demonstrate, and judicial failure to insist on demonstration, of the necessity of making an order (see Hoffmann J. in *Lock International Plc. v. Beswick*, [1989] 1 W.L.R. 1268) and led to the establishment of a committee under Staughton L.J. which made recommendations (largely followed in the model orders which precede the current model orders printed in this edition) on future practice.

[17] [1976] Ch. 55, 62.

[18] Staughton added a fourth requirement (*cf.* Hoffmann J.'s view in *Lock International Plc. v. Beswick*, [1989] 1 W.L.R. 1268) that the harm likely to be caused by the execution of the order to the defendant and his business affairs must not be excessive or out of proportion to the legitimate object of the order.

[19] This is no mere formula and is a more important element in the judicial balancing exercise in search order cases than in freezing injunction or other cases of applications without notice. This is for the reason that although interlocutory, once executed the order cannot be "unexecuted". There is often no sense in a defendant's bothering to discharge a search order at a hearing with notice to the other side once it has been executed (but see Hoffmann J. in *Lock International Plc v. Beswick*, below, at para. 11–276).

[20] *e.g.* barristers and their clerks: *Randolph M Fields v. Watts* (1985) 129 S.J. 67.

[21] [1982] 1 W.L.R. 669.

[22] Intellectual property cases. See para. 11–271.

[23] Para. 11–270. Although, having regard to the decision in *Sociedade Nacionale de Combustiveis de Angola U.E.E. v. Lundqvist* [1991] 2 Q.B. 310, which held that the section did not apply to charges of conspiracy under section 1 of the Criminal Law Act 1977, nor at common law, the practical effect of section 31 in commercial (non-intellectual property) cases will therefore be reduced: no search order may be granted where there is a real possibility of a conspiracy charge.

[24] [1982] 1 W.L.R. 669.

11–208   On the question of the court's jurisdiction to make orders in support of actions other than those proceeding in an English court, the principle in *Siskina*[25] has been reversed to the extent that section 25 of the Civil Jurisdiction and Judgments Act 1982 applies to search orders. The limitation arises from the restriction of "interim relief" in subsection (7) (to which the section applies) to interim orders *other than* those making provision for "obtaining evidence". Clearly most search orders are intended to do just that. Those which seek merely to preserve assets in jeopardy, on the other hand, clearly are not and the *Siskina* principle will not apply to them.

JAGGARD V. SAWYER

Court of Appeal [1995] 1 W.L.R. 269; [1995] 2 All E.R. 189 (BINGHAM MR, KENNEDY and MILLETT L.JJ.)

11–209   In a cul-de-sac residential development consisting of ten plots, the plaintiff and defendants each owned one, together with part of the private road immediately fronting each. Each plot was bound by a restrictive covenant preventing the user of any part of any plot not built upon from being used other than as a private garden. The defendants purchased land adjacent to their plot but inaccessible from the private road other than through their plot. They obtained, in 1988, planning permission to build on the adjacent land and (wrongly believing the road to be a public one) to construct a driveway leading to it, over their garden, from the road. The plaintiff threatened injunctive proceedings on the ground of (i) breach of covenant and (ii) trespass over her portion of the road but did not act on the threat. On 14 June 1989 the defendants began building and on 10 August 1989, the building at an advanced stage, the plaintiff began proceedings for an injunction. No interlocutory relief was sought and the building was completed thereafter. At trial it was common ground that the road was private but was the only means of access to the plot. The judge held that although the defendants were in breach of covenant, had committed trespass and would by using the road in future, continue to commit trespass, it would, in the circumstances, have been oppressive to grant an injunction and that damages should be awarded in lieu under section 50 of the Supreme Court Act 1981. The award would be £694.44, one ninth share of £6,250, the sum which the nine plot-owners might reasonably have demanded from the defendants as the price of release from the covenant and for the grant of a right of way. The plaintiff appealed.

11–210   SIR THOMAS BINGHAM M.R.: The judge recognised that a plaintiff who can show that his legal right will be violated by the defendant's conduct is prima facie entitled to the grant of an injunction. He accepted that the court will only rarely and reluctantly permit such violation to occur or continue. But he held that this case fulfilled the four tests laid down by A. L. Smith L.J. in *Shelfer's* case to bring this case within the exception. The real question in this appeal is whether that judgment is sustainable.

---

[25] *Siskina v. Distos S.A.* [1979] A.C. 210. For section 25 see para. 11–274.

"(1) He regarded the injury to the plaintiff's right as small. This is in my view so. It is not suggested that the increase in traffic attributable to the existence of No. 5A will be other than minimal, or that the cost of keeping up the road will be significantly increased. The defendants have in any event offered throughout to contribute to the cost of upkeep and are willing, if a draft is tendered to them, to execute a deed binding themselves by the same covenants as other residents of the Avenue. It is not suggested that the driveway to No. 5A impairs the visual amenity of the plaintiff's house or affects its value. There is of course a violation of the plaintiff's strict legal right, but that will be so in any case of this kind.

"(2) The judge considered the value of the injury to the plaintiff's right as capable of being estimated in money. He based himself on the *Wrotham Park* approach. In my view he was justified. He valued the right at what a reasonable seller would sell it for. In situations of this kind a plaintiff should not be treated as eager to sell, which he very probably is not. But the court will not value the right at the ransom price which a very reluctant plaintiff might put on it. I see no error in the judge's approach to this aspect.

"(3) The judge held that the injury to the plaintiff's legal right was one which **11–211** could be adequately compensated by a small money payment. I agree, and I do not think this conclusion can be faulted.

"(4) The judge concluded that in all the circumstances it would be oppressive to the defendants to grant the injunctions sought. Most of the argument turned on this condition, and in particular on the significance which the judge attached to the plaintiff's failure to seek interlocutory relief.

"It is important to bear in mind that the test is one of oppression, and the court should not slide into application of a general balance of convenience test. But oppression must be judged as at the date the court is asked to grant an injunction, and (as Brightman J. recognised in the *Wrotham Park* case) the court cannot ignore the reality with which it is then confronted. It is relevant that the plaintiff could at an early stage have sought interlocutory relief, which she would seem very likely to have obtained; but it is also relevant that the defendants could have sought a declaration of right. These considerations are not decisive. It would weigh against a finding of oppression if the defendants had acted in blatant and calculated disregard of the plaintiff's rights, of which they were aware, but the judge held that this was not so, and the plaintiff's solicitors may be thought to have indicated that damages would be an acceptable remedy. . . . The judge was in my view entitled to hold on all the facts before the court at trial that the grant of an injunction would be oppressive to the defendants, and I share that view.

"I am of the clear opinion that the appeal must be dismissed."

KENNEDY L.J.: "I agree."

MILLETT L.J.: "This appeal raises yet again the question: what approach should **11–212** the court adopt when invited to exercise its statutory jurisdiction to award damages instead of granting an injunction to restrain a threatened or continuing trespass or breach of a restrictive covenant? And if the court accedes to the invitation on what basis should damages be assessed?

"Before considering these questions, it is desirable to state some general propositions which are established by the authorities and which are, or at least ought to be, uncontroversial.

"(1) The jurisdiction was originally conferred by section 2 of the Chancery Amendment Act 1858, commonly known as Lord Cairns's Act. It is now to be found in section 50 of the Supreme Court Act 1981. It is a jurisdiction to award damages "in addition to or in substitution for such injunction or specific performance."

"(2) The principal object of Lord Cairns's Act is well known. It was described by Turner L.J. in *Ferguson v. Wilson* (1866) L.R. 2 Ch. App. 77, 88. It was to enable the Court of Chancery, when declining to grant equitable relief and leaving the plaintiff to his remedy at law, to award the plaintiff damages itself instead of sending him to the common law courts to obtain them. From the very first, however, it was recognised that the Act did more than this. The jurisdiction of the Court of Chancery was wider than that of the common law courts, for it could give relief where there was no cause of action at law. As early as 1863, Turner L.J. himself had recognised the potential effect of Lord Cairns's Act. In *Eastwood v. Lever* (1863) 4 De G.J. & S. 114, 128, he pointed out that the Act had empowered the courts of equity to award damages in cases where the common law courts could not. The Act, he said, was not "confined to cases in which the plaintiffs could recover damages at law." Damages at common law are recoverable only in respect of causes of action which are complete at the date of the writ; damages for future or repeated wrongs must be made the subject of fresh proceedings. Damages in substitution for an injunction, however, relate to the future, not the past. They inevitably extend beyond the damages to which the plaintiff may be entitled at law. In *Leeds Industrial Co-operative Society Ltd v. Slack* [1924] A.C. 851 the House of Lords confirmed the jurisdiction of the courts to award damages under the Act in respect of an injury which was threatened but had not yet occurred. No such damages could have been awarded at common law.

11–213   "(3) The nature of the cause of action is immaterial; it may be in contract or tort. Lord Cairns's Act referred in terms to "a breach of any covenant, contract, or agreement, or against the commission or continuance of any wrongful act." The jurisdiction to award damages in substitution for an injunction has most commonly been exercised in cases where the defendant's building has infringed the plaintiff's right to light or where it has been erected in breach of a restrictive covenant. Despite dicta to the contrary in *Woollerton and Wilson Ltd v. Richard Costain Ltd* [1970] 1 W.L.R. 411 there is in my opinion no justification for excluding cases of threatened or continuing trespass on the ground that trespass is actionable at law without proof of actual damage. Equitable relief, whether by way of injunction or damages under Lord Cairns's Act, is available because the common law remedy is inadequate; but the common law remedy of damages in cases of continuing trespass is inadequate not because the damages are likely to be small or nominal but because they cover the past only and not the future.

"(4) The power to award damages under Lord Cairns's Act arises whenever the court "has jurisdiction to entertain an application" for an injunction or specific performance. This question must be determined as at the date of the writ. If the court would then have had jurisdiction to grant an injunction, it has jurisdiction to award damages instead. When the court comes to consider whether to grant an injunction or award damages instead, of course, it must do so by reference to the circumstances as they exist at the date of the hearing.

11–214   "(5) The former question is effectively one of jurisdiction. The question is whether, at the date of the writ, the court *could* have granted an injunction, not whether it *would* have done: *City of London Brewery Co. v. Tennant* (1873) L.R. 9 Ch.App. 212. Russell L.J. put it neatly in *Hooper v. Rogers* [1975] Ch. 43 at 48 when he said that the question was "whether . . . the judge could have (however unwisely . . .) made a mandatory order." There have been numerous cases where damages under Lord Cairns's Act were refused because at the date of the writ it was impossible to grant an injunction or specific performance: for one well known example, see *Lavery v. Pursell* (1888) 39 Ch.D. 508. The recent case of *Surrey County Council v. Bredero Homes Ltd* [1993] 1 W.L.R. 1361 appears to have been a case of this character.

"(6) It is not necessary for the plaintiff to include a claim for damages in his writ. As long ago as 1868 Lord Chelmsford L.C. held that damages may be awarded under Lord Cairns's Act

> "though not specifically prayed for by the bill, the statute having vested a discretion in the judge, which he may exercise when he thinks the case fitting without the prayer of the party:' see *Betts v. Neilson* (1868) L.R. 3 Ch.App. 429 at 411.

It would be absurd as well as misleading to insist on the plaintiff including a claim for damages in his writ when he is insisting on his right to an injunction and opposing the defendant's claim that he should be content to receive damages instead. By a parity of reasoning it is not in my opinion necessary for a plaintiff to include a claim for an injunction in order to found a claim for damages under the Act. It would be absurd to require him to include a claim for an injunction if he is sufficiently realistic to recognise that in the circumstances he is unlikely to obtain one and intends from the first to ask the court for damages instead. But he ought to make it clear whether he is claiming damages for past injury at common law or under the Act in substitution for an injunction.

"(7) In *Anchor Brewhouse Developments Ltd v. Berkley House (Docklands* **11–215** *Developments) Ltd* (1987) 38 B.L.R. 87 Scott J. granted an injunction to restrain a continuing trespass. In the course of his judgment, however, he cast doubt on the power of the court to award damages for future trespasses by means of what he described as a 'once and for all payment.' This was because, as he put it, the court could not by an award of damages put the defendant in the position of a person entitled to an easement; whether or not an injunction were granted, the defendant's conduct would still constitute a trespass; and a succession of further actions for damages could accordingly still be brought. This reasoning strikes at the very heart of the statutory jurisdiction; it is in marked contrast to the attitude of the many judges who from the very first have recognised that, while the Act does not enable the court to license future wrongs, this may be the practical result of withholding injunctive relief; and it is inconsistent with the existence of the jurisdiction, confirmed in *Leeds Industrial Co-operative Society Ltd v. Slack* [1924] A.C. 851, to award damages under the Act in a quia timet action. It is in my view fallacious because it is not the award of damages which has the practical effect of licensing the defendant to commit the wrong, but the refusal of injunctive relief. Thereafter the defendant may have no right to act in the manner complained of, but he cannot be prevented from doing so. The court can in my judgment properly award damages 'once and for all' in respect of future wrongs because it awards them in substitution for an injunction and to compensate for those future wrongs which an injunction would have prevented. The doctrine of res judicata operates to prevent the plaintiff and his successors in title from bringing proceedings thereafter to recover even nominal damages in respect of further wrongs for which the plaintiff has been fully compensated . . .

"When the plaintiff claims an injunction and the defendant asks the court to **11–216** award damages instead, the proper approach for the court to adopt cannot be in doubt. Clearly the plaintiff must first establish a case for equitable relief, not only by proving his legal right and an actual or threatened infringement by the defendant, but also by overcoming all equitable defences such as laches, acquiescence or estoppel. If he succeeds in doing this, he is prima facie entitled to an injunction. The court may nevertheless in its discretion withhold injunctive relief and award damages instead. How is this discretion to be exercised? In a well known passage in *Shelfer v. City of London Electric Lighting Co.* [1895] 1 Ch. 287 at 322–323, A. L. Smith L.J. set out what he described as "a good working rule" that

> "(1) If the injury to the plaintiff's legal right is small, (2) And is one which is capable of being estimated in money, (3) And is one which can be adequately compensated by a small money payment, (4) And the case is one in which it would be oppressive to the defendant to grant an injunction:—then damages in substitution for an injunction may be given."

Laid down just 100 years ago, A. L. Smith L.J.'s check-list has stood the test of time; but it needs to be remembered that it is only a working rule and does not purport to be an exhaustive statement of the circumstances in which damages may be awarded instead of an injunction.

11–217   "Reported cases are merely illustrations of circumstances in which particular judges have exercised their discretion, in some cases by granting an injunction, and in others by awarding damages instead. Since they are all cases on the exercise of a discretion, none of them is a binding authority on how the discretion should be exercised. The most that any of them can demonstrate is that in similar circumstances it would not be wrong to exercise the discretion in the same way. But it does not follow that it would be wrong to exercise it differently.

"The outcome of any particular case usually turns on the question: would it in all the circumstances be oppressive to the defendant to grant the injunction to which the plaintiff is prima facie entitled? Most of the cases in which the injunction has been refused are cases where the plaintiff has sought a mandatory injunction to pull down a building which infringes his right to light or which has been built in breach of a restrictive covenant. In such cases the court is faced with a fait accompli. The jurisdiction to grant a mandatory injunction in those circumstances cannot be doubted, but to grant it would subject the defendant to a loss out of all proportion to that which would be suffered by the plaintiff if it were refused, and would indeed deliver him to the plaintiff bound hand and foot to be subjected to any extortionate demands the plaintiff might make. In the present case, as in the closely similar case of *Bracewell v. Appleby* [1975] Ch. 408, the plaintiff sought a prohibitory injunction to restrain the use of a road giving access to the defendants' house. The result of granting the injunction would be much the same; the house would not have to be pulled down, but it would be rendered landlocked and incapable of beneficial enjoyment . . .

11–218   "In considering whether the grant of an injunction would be oppressive to the defendant, all the circumstances of the case have to be considered. At one extreme, the defendant may have acted openly and in good faith and in ignorance of the plaintiff's rights, and thereby inadvertently placed himself in a position where the grant of an injunction would either force him to yield to the plaintiff's extortionate demands or expose him to substantial loss. At the other extreme, the defendant may have acted with his eyes open and in full knowledge that he was invading the plaintiff's rights, and hurried on his work in the hope that by presenting the court with a fait accompli he could compel the plaintiff to accept monetary compensation. Most cases, like the present, fall somewhere in between.

"In the present case, the defendants acted openly and in good faith and in the not unreasonable belief that they were entitled to make use of Ashleigh Avenue for access to the house that they were building. At the same time, they had been warned by the plaintiff and her solicitors that Ashleigh Avenue was a private road, that they were not entitled to use it for access to the new house, and that it would be a breach of covenant for them to use the garden of No. 5 to gain access to No. 5A. They went ahead, not with their eyes open, but at their own risk. On the other hand, the plaintiff did not seek interlocutory relief at a time when she would almost certainly have obtained it. She should not be criticised for that, but it follows that she also took a risk, namely, that by the time her case came on for trial the court would be presented with a fait accompli. The case was a difficult one, but in an exemplary judgment the judge took into account all the relevant considerations, both those which told in favour of granting an injunction and those which told against, and in the exercise of his discretion he decided to refuse it. In my judgment his conclusion cannot be faulted.

"Having decided to refuse an injunction and to award the plaintiff damages **11–219** instead, the judge had to consider the measure of damages. He based them on her share of the amount which, in his opinion, the plaintiff and the other residents of Ashleigh Avenue could reasonably have demanded as the price of waiving their rights. In this he applied the measure of damages which had been adopted by Brightman J. in *Wrotham Park Estate Co. Ltd v. Parkside Homes Ltd* [1974] 1 W.L.R. 798, a case which has frequently been followed. It would not be necessary to consider this matter further but for the fact that in the recent case in this court of *Surrey County Council v. Bredero Homes Ltd* [1993] 1 W.L.R. 1361 doubts were expressed as to the basis on which this measure of damages could be justified and whether it was consistent with the reasoning of Lord Wilberforce in *Johnson v. Agnew* [1980] A.C. 367. It is, therefore, necessary to examine those cases further.

"In *Surrey County Council v. Bredero Homes Ltd* [1993] 1 W.L.R. 1361 the plaintiffs claimed damages from the original covenantor, a developer, for breach of a restrictive covenant against building more than 72 houses, and sought to measure the damages by reference to the additional profit which the defendant had made by building the extra houses. Their claim to substantial damages failed. The case is not authority on the proper measure of damages under Lords Cairns's Act, since (as Dillon L.J. made clear, at p. 1367c) the plaintiffs' claim was for damages at common law and not under the Act . . .

Examination of the facts stated in the headnote reveals that the defendant had disposed of all the houses on the estate before the plaintiffs commenced proceedings, and that the purchasers were not joined as parties. Any claim to damages under Lord Cairns's Act must have failed; at the date of the writ the court *could* not have ordered the defendant to pull down the houses, since this was no longer something which was within its power to do.

"Unfortunately, however, Dillon L.J. cast doubt on the correctness of the **11–220** measure of damages which had been adopted by Brightman J. in *Wrotham Park Estate Co. Ltd v. Parkside Homes Ltd* [1974] 1 W.L.R. 798 a case which was decided under Lord Cairns's Act. He said [1993] 1 W.L.R. 1361 at 1366:

"The difficulty about the decision in the *Wrotham Park* case is that in *Johnson v. Agnew* [1980] A.C. 367 at 400G, Lord Wilberforce, after citing certain decisions on the scope and basis of Lord Cairns's Act which were

not cited to Brightman J., stated in the clearest terms that on the balance
of those authorities and on principle he found in the Act no warrant for
the court awarding damages differently from common law damages."

"This statement must not be taken out of context. Earlier in his speech Lord
Wilberforce had clearly recognised that damages could be awarded under Lord
Cairns's Act where there was no cause of action at law, and he cannot have been
insensible to the fact that, when the court awards damages in substitution for an
injunction, it seeks to compensate the plaintiff for loss arising from future
wrongs, that is to say, loss for which the common law does not provide a remedy.
Neither *Wroth v. Tyler* nor *Johnson v. Agnew* [1980] A.C. 367 was a case of this
kind. In each of those cases the plaintiff claimed damages for loss occasioned by
a single, once and for all, past breach of contract on the part of the defendant. In
neither case was the breach a continuing one capable of generating further
losses. In my view Lord Wilberforce's statement that the measure of damages is
the same whether damages are recoverable at common law or under the Act
must be taken to be limited to the case where they are recoverable in respect of
the same cause of action. It cannot sensibly have any application where the claim
at common law is in respect of a past trespass or breach of covenant and that
under the Act is in respect of future trespasses or continuing breaches of
covenant.

11–221   "Accordingly I am of opinion that the judge was not precluded by the decision
of the House of Lords in *Johnson v. Agnew* from adopting the measure of
damages which he did. It is, however, necessary to notice the observations of
Steyn L.J. in *Surrey County Council v. Bredero Homes Ltd* [1993] 1 W.L.R. 1361
at 1369.

> "In my view *Wrotham Park Estate Co. Ltd v. Parkside Homes Ltd* [1974] 1
> W.L.R. 798 is only defensible on the basis of the third or restitutionary
> principle . . . The plaintiffs' argument that the *Wrotham Park* case can be
> justified on the basis of a loss of bargaining opportunity is a fiction."

I find these remarks puzzling. It is plain from his judgment in the *Wrotham Park*
case that Brightman J.'s approach was compensatory, not restitutionary. He
sought to measure the damages by reference to what the plaintiff had lost, not by
reference to what the defendant had gained. He did not award the plaintiff the
profit which the defendant had made by the breach, but the amount which he
judged the plaintiff might have obtained as the price of giving its consent. The
amount of the profit which the defendant expected to make was a relevant factor
in that assessment, but that was all.

11–222   "Both the *Wrotham Park* and *Bredero Homes* cases (unlike the present) were
concerned with a single past breach of covenant, so that the measure of damages
at common law and under the Act was the same. Prima facie the measure of
damages in either case for breach of a covenant not to build a house on
neighbouring land is the diminution in the value of the plaintiff's land occasioned
by the breach. One element in the value of the plaintiff's land immediately
before the breach is attributable to his ability to obtain an injunction to prevent
the building. Clearly a defendant who wished to build would pay for the release
of the covenant, but only so long as the court could still protect it by the grant of
an injunction. The proviso is important. It is the ability to claim an injunction
which gives the benefit of the covenant much of its value. If the plaintiff delays
proceedings until it is no longer possible for him to obtain an injunction, he

destroys his own bargaining position and devalues his right. The unavailability of the remedy of injunction at one and the same time deprives the court of jurisdiction to award damages under the Act and removes the basis for awarding substantial damages at common law. For this reason, I take the view that damages can be awarded at common law in accordance with the approach adopted in the *Wrotham Park* case, but in practice only in the circumstances in which they could also be awarded under the Act.

"This may be what Steyn L.J. had in mind when he said that the loss of **11–223** bargaining opportunity was a fiction. If he mean it generally or in relation to the facts which obtained in the *Wrotham Park* case, then I respectfully disagree. But it was true in the circumstances of the case before him, and not merely for the reason given by Rose L.J. (that the plaintiffs did not object to the extra houses and would have waived the breach for a nominal sum). The plaintiffs did not bring the proceedings until after the defendant had sold the houses and was no longer susceptible to an injunction. The plaintiffs had thereby deprived themselves of any bargaining position. Unable to obtain an injunction, they were equally unable to invoke the jurisdiction to award damages under Lord Cairns's Act. No longer exposed to the risk of an injunction, and having successfully disposed of the houses, the defendant had no reason to pay anything for the release of the covenant. Unless they were able to recover damages in accordance with restitutionary principles, neither at common law nor in equity could the plaintiffs recover more than nominal damages.

"In the present case the plaintiff brought proceedings at a time when her rights were still capable of being protected by injunction. She has accordingly been able to invoke the court's jurisdiction to award in substitution for an injunction damages which take account of the future as well as the past. In my view there is no reason why compensatory damages for future trespasses and continuing breaches of covenant should not reflect the value of the rights which she has lost, or why such damages should not be measured by the amount which she could reasonably have expected to receive for their release.

"In my judgment the judge's approach to the assessment of damages was correct on the facts and in accordance with principle. I would dismiss the appeal."

AMERICAN CYANAMID V. ETHICON LTD

House of Lords [1975] A.C. 396, [1975] 1 All E.R. 504.

LORD DIPLOCK: "In my view the grant of interlocutory injunctions in actions for **11–224** infringement of patents is governed by the same principles as in other actions. I turn to consider what those principles are.

"My Lords, when an application for an interlocutory injunction to restrain a defendant from doing acts alleged to be in violation of the plaintiff's legal right is made upon contested facts, the decision whether or not to grant an interlocutory injunction has to be taken at a time when ex hypothesi the existence of the right or the violation of it, or both, is uncertain and will remain uncertain until final judgment is given in the action. It was to mitigate the risk of injustice to the plaintiff during the period before that uncertainty could be resolved that the practice arose of granting him relief by way of interlocutory injunction; but since the middle of the 19th century this has been made subject to his undertaking to pay damages to the defendant for any loss sustained by reason of the injunction if it should be held at the trial that the plaintiff had not been entitled to restrain the defendant from doing what he was threatening to do. The object of the interlocutory injunction is to protect the plaintiff against injury by violation of his right for which he could not be adequately compensated in damages recoverable in the action if the uncertainty were resolved in his favour at the trial; but the plaintiff's need for such protection must be weighed against the corresponding need of the defendant to be protected against injury resulting from his having been prevented from exercising his own legal rights for which he could not be adequately compensated under the plaintiff's undertaking in damages if the uncertainty were resolved in the defendant's favour at the trial. The court must weigh one need against another and determine where 'the balance of convenience' lies.

11–225   "In those cases where the legal rights of the parties depend upon facts that are in dispute between them, the evidence available to the court at the hearing of the application for an interlocutory injunction is incomplete. It is given on affidavit and has not been tested by oral cross-examination. The purpose sought to be achieved by giving to the court discretion to grant such injunctions would be stultified if the discretion were clogged by a technical rule forbidding its exercise if upon that incomplete untested evidence the court evaluated the chances of the plaintiff's ultimate success in the action at 50 per cent or less, but permitting its exercise if the court evaluated his chances at more than 50 per cent.

"The notion that it is incumbent upon the court to undertake what is in effect a preliminary trial of the action upon evidential material different from that upon which the actual trial will be conducted, is, I think, of comparatively recent origin, though it can be supported by references in earlier cases to the need to show "a probability that the plaintiffs are entitled to relief" (*Preston v. Luck* (1884) 27 Ch.D. 497 at 506, *per* Cotton L.J.) or "a strong prima facie case that the right which he seeks to protect in fact exists" (*Smith v. Grigg Ltd* [1924] 1 K.B. 655 at 659, *per* Atkin L.J.). These are to be contrasted with expressions in other cases indicating a much less onerous criterion, such as the need to show that there is "certainly a case to be tried" (*Jones v. Pacaya Rubber and Produce Co. Ltd* [1911] 1 K.B. 455 at 457, *per* Buckley L.J.) which corresponds more closely with what judges generally treated as sufficient to justify their considering the balance of convenience upon applications for interlocutory injunctions, at any rate up to the time when I became a member of your Lordships' House . . .

"*Hubbard v. Vosper* [1972] 2 Q.B. 84 was treated by Graham J. and the Court of Appeal in the instant appeal as leaving intact the supposed rule that the court is not entitled to take any account of the balance of convenience unless it has first been satisfied that if the case went to trial upon no other evidence than is before the court at the hearing of the application the plaintiff would be entitled to judgment for a permanent injunction in the same terms as the interlocutory injunction sought.

11–226   "Your Lordships should in my view take this opportunity of declaring that there is no such rule. The use of such expressions as 'a probability,' 'a prima facie case,' or 'a strong prima facie case' in the context of the exercise of a discretionary power to grant an interlocutory injunction leads to confusion as to the object sought to be achieved by this form of temporary relief. The court no doubt must be satisfied that the claim is not frivolous or vexatious; in other words, that there is a serious question to be tried.

"It is no part of the court's function at this stage of the litigation to try to resolve conflicts of evidence on affidavit as to facts on which the claims of either party may ultimately depend nor to decide difficult questions of law which call for detailed argument and mature considerations. These are matters to be dealt with at the trial. One of the reasons for the introduction of the practice of requiring an undertaking as to damages upon the grant of an interlocutory injunction was that 'it aided the court in doing that which was its great object, viz. abstaining from expressing any opinion upon the merits of the case until the hearing': *Walkefield v. Duke of Buccleugh* (1865) 12 L.T. 628 629. So unless the material available to the court at the hearing of the application for an interlocutory injunction fails to disclose that the plaintiff has any real prospect of succeeding in his claim for a permanent injunction at the trial, the court should go on to consider whether the balance of convenience lies in favour of granting or refusing the interlocutory relief that is sought.

"As to that, the governing principle is that the court should first consider **11–227** whether, if the plaintiff were to succeed at the trial in establishing his right to a permanent injunction, he would be adequately compensated by an award of damages for the the loss he would have sustained as a result of the defendant's continuing to do what was sought to be enjoined between the time of the application and the time of the trial. If damages in the measure recoverable at common law would be adequate remedy and the defendant would be in a financial position to pay them, no interlocutory injunction should normally be granted, however strong the plaintiff's claim appeared to be at that stage. If, on the other hand, damages would not provide an adequate remedy for the plaintiff in the event of his succeeding at the trial, the court should then consider whether, on the contrary hypothesis that the defendant were to succeed at the trial in establishing his right to do that which was sought to be enjoined, he would be adequately compensated under the plaintiff's undertaking as to damages for the loss he would have sustained by being prevented from doing so between the time of the application and the time of the trial. If damages in the measure recoverable under such an undertaking would be an adequate remedy and the plaintiff would be in a financial position to pay them, there would be no reason upon this ground to refuse an interlocutory injunction.

"It is where there is doubt as to the adequacy of the respective remedies in damages available to either party or to both, that the question of balance of convenience arises. It would be unwise to attempt even to list all the various matters which may need to be taken into consideration in deciding where the balance lies, let alone to suggest the relative weight to be attached to them. These will vary from case to case.

"Where other factors appear to be evenly balanced it is a counsel of prudence **11–228** to take such measures as are calculated to preserve the status quo. If the defendant is enjoined temporarily from doing something that he has not done before, the only effect of the interlocutory injunction in the event of his succeeding at the trial is to postpone the date at which he is able to embark upon a course of action which he has not previously found it necessary to undertake; whereas to interrupt him in the conduct of an established enterprise would cause much greater inconvenience to him since he would have to start again to establish it in the event of his succeeding at the trial.

"Save in the simplest cases, the decision to grant or to refuse an interlocutory injunction will cause to whichever party is unsuccessful on the application some disadvantages which his ultimate success at the trial may show he ought to have been spared and the disadvantages may be such that the recovery of damages to which he would then be entitled either in the action or under the plaintiff's undertaking would not be sufficient to compensate him fully for all of them. The extent to which the disadvantages to each party would be incapable of being compensated in damages in the event of his succeeding at the trial is always a significant factor in assessing where the balance of convenience lies; and if the extent of the uncompensatable disadvantage to each party would not differ widely, it may not be improper to take into account in tipping the balance the relative strength of each party's case as revealed by the affidavit evidence adduced on the hearing of the application. This, however, should be done only where it is apparent upon the facts disclosed by evidence as to which there is no credible dispute that the strength of one party's case is disproportionate to that of the other party. The court is not justified in embarking upon anything resembling a trial of the action upon conflicting affidavits in order to evaluate the strength of either party's case.

"I would reiterate that, in addition to those to which I have referred, there may be many other special factors to be taken into consideration in the particular circumstances of individual cases. The instant appeal affords one example of this."

VISCOUNT DILHORNE, LORD CROSS of CHELSEA LORD SALMON and LORD EDMUND-DAVIES all simply agreed with Lord Diplock.

CAMBRIDGE NUTRITION LTD V. BRITISH BROADCASTING CORPORATION

11–229   Court of Appeal [1990] 3 All E.R. 523. Kerr and Ralph Gibson L.JJ. and Eastham J.)

The plaintiffs were manufacturers of a widely used low-calorie diet and agreed to participate in the making of a programme thereon by the defendants. The plaintiffs contended and the defendants denied that it was a contractual term of their agreement that the programme would not be broadcast until after the publication of a government report on the medical aspects of diets such as the plaintiffs'. Having become increasingly concerned about the tone of the proposed programme, the plaintiffs applied for injunctive relief preventing broadcast until after publication of the government report and sought an interlocutory injunction pending trial. The nature of the programme as proposed was such that it was only appropriate for transmission before publication of the government report. The judge granted an injunction and the defendants appealed.

KERR L.J.: "I would unhesitatingly refuse such an injunction in this case, and I summarise my reasons as briefly as I can.

11–230   "First, I do not consider that the question whether or not an injunction should be granted should in this case be tested simply by reference to the guidelines laid down in the *American Cyanamid* case. I accept that the judge was entitled to conclude that he should be guided by that case, but in my view it is not suitable for that purpose. Although *Cayne v. Global Natural Resources plc* [1984] 1 All E.R. 225 was clearly an exceptional case, I would reiterate without repeating what I then said (at 234–235) and I refer equally to the tenor of the judgments of Eveleigh and May L.J.J. in that case, which are much to the same effect. It is important to bear in mind that the *American Cyanamid* case contains no principle of universal application. The only such principle is the statutory power of the court to grant injunctions when it is just and convenient to do so. The *American Cyanamid* case is no more than a set of useful guidelines which apply in many cases. It must never be used as a rule of thumb, let alone as a strait-jacket. Admittedly, the present case is miles away on its facts from the *Global Natural Resources* case, and it is also much weaker than *NWL Ltd v. Woods*

[1979] 3 All E.R. 614, [1979] 1 W.L.R. 1294, where Lord Diplock himself recognised the limitations of the *Cyanamid* guidelines. But nevertheless, I do not consider that it is an appropriate case for the *Cyanamid* guidelines because the crucial issues between the parties do not depend on a trial, but solely or mainly on the grant or refusal of the interlocutory relief. The *American Cyanamid* case provides an authoritative and most helpful approach to cases where the function of the court in relation to the grant or refusal of interlocutory injunctions is to hold the balance as justly as possible in situations where the substantial issues between the parties can only be resolved by a trial. In my view, for reasons which require no further elaboration, the present case is not in that category. Neither side is interested in monetary compensation, and once the interlocutory decision has been given, little, if anything, will remain in practice.

"But for present purposes the point can be put more narrowly. It seems to me **11–231** that cases in which the subject matter concerns the right to publish an article, or to transmit a broadcast, whose importance may be transitory but whose impact depends on timing, news value and topicality, do not lend themselves easily to the application of the *Cyanamid* guidelines. Longer term publications, such as films or books, may not be in the same category. I think that it would be an inappropriate test for the grant or refusal of interlocutory injunctions in such cases if the transmission of a broadcast, or the publication of an article, whose value and impact depended on their timing, could be prevented merely by the plausible, or not implausible, allegation of a term alleged to have been agreed orally in an informal conversation. In such cases it *should* matter whether the chances of success in establishing some binding agreement are 90 per cent or 20 per cent. I use that phraseology because counsel for the plaintiffs referred us to the decision of this court in *Alfred Dunhill Ltd v. Sunoptic SA* [1979] FSR 337 at 373, where Megaw L.J. said that in the application of the *Cyanamid* test it did not matter whether the chances of success in establishing liability were 90 per cent or 20 per cent. The *Dunhill* case, like *Cyanamid* itself, was a typical case in which the *Cyanamid* guidelines are of great value, because everything depended on the trial and the long-term rights of the parties. The present type of case is not in the same category.

"Accordingly, since I would not follow the structured approach of the **11–232** *American Cyanamid* case in the present case, in carrying out the necessary balancing exercise I would have some regard to the relative weakness of the plaintiffs' case in establishing the contract on which they rely. Counsel for the plaintiffs conceded that clearly no contract of any kind had been made in the telephone conversations themselves. It is obvious that neither party was bound to anything at that stage. The conversations were no more than preliminary discussions. At most, as suggested by counsel for the plaintiffs, they resulted in a statement of terms which would apply if the BBC went ahead with the programme and the plaintiffs co-operated in making it. Even then, either side could no doubt have resiled from the project; for some time at least. The whole situation was by its nature undefined, and not easily definable in legal terms. Moreover, the alleged conditions were to be confirmed in writing, but never were. The second alleged condition, concerning the featuring of users of the diet 'before and after' was never pursued. And no reference to the existence of any condition was made for five months or so, despite all that intervened.

"In my view it would be highly undesirable if, on evidence of that nature, which the judge rightly characterised as being no more than 'plausible' in support of the alleged condition, the court were driven to grant an injunction because of the application of the *Cyanamid* guidelines. In situations of this kind, quite apart from the alleged express reference to a written confirmation in the original telephone calls, it is essential that there should indeed be written confirmation of any fetter on transmission or other publication. In the absence of clear evidence of a contract having been made, I consider that the court should be extremely slow to grant an interlocutory injunction in such situations. And if the application of the *Cyanamid* test were to lead to a different conclusion, then that would demonstrate that it is not appropriate in these situations.

11–233   "However, in the same way as the judge, I do not think that it makes any difference whether this case is decided in accordance with the *Cyanamid* test or not. On either basis the answer is the same. The judge and I agree about that, even though our answers are different. That in itself serves to demonstrate that one must be careful not to lose sight of the real demands of justice in any given case by attaching too much importance to the *Cyanamid* guidelines. The only real difference of substance in the court's approach concerns the extent to which it is permissible or otherwise to have some regard to the relative strength of the parties' contentions on the merits. But in that connection it should also be remembered that the speech of Lord Diplock in the *American Cyanamid* case [1975] 1 All E.R. 504 at 511, [1975] A.C. 396 at 409 itself contains a later passage where he appears himself to qualify to some extent the earlier passage on this aspect. I can summarise the position by saying that in a context such as the present a doubtful contract should never prevail over the right of free speech, all other things being even.

"In these circumstances it seems to me to be obviously contrary to the public interest that the plaintiffs should be entitled to an order which has the effect of suppressing similar discussion of this topic by the BBC in a programme made with the plaintiffs' full co-operation, merely on the basis of a shadowy claim of an oral agreement concerning the timing of this programme alleged to have been made on the telephone some eight months ago.

"I would allow this appeal and lift the injunction."

11–234   RALPH GIBSON L.J.: "It is necessary to go back to the *Cyanamid* principles as set out by Lord Diplock. The judge had reached the point that the plaintiffs had a good arguable case for the injunction sought, and that the plaintiffs would not be adequately compensated by an award of damages at trial. The finding that the BBC would be adequately compensated by an award of damages, which the plaintiffs could pay, could have been regarded by the judge as sufficient to establish that, in the absence of any other relevant factor, there could be no reason to refuse an interlocutory injunction: see the *American Cyanamid* case [1975] 1 All E.R. 504 at 510, [1975] A.C. 396 at 408 *per* Lord Diplock. The judge in fact went on to consider the balance of justice or convenience, as I have said, and it is important to note that in my view it was essential that that balance be considered, because on the evidence, contrary to the judge's view, the remedy in damages was not adequate to compensate for the loss which would be suffered by either party if the injunction was wrongly granted or wrongly withheld.

"Since neither party would be adequately compensated by an award of damages, the guidance offered in the following paragraph in Lord Diplock's speech was of crucial importance [1975] 1 All E.R. 504 at 511, [1975] A.C. 396 at 408–409):

'Save in the simplest cases, the decision to grant or to refuse an interlocutory injunction will cause to whichever party is unsuccessful on the application some disadvantages which his ultimate success at the trial may show he ought to have been spared and the disadvantages may be such that the recovery of damages to which he would then be entitled either in the action or under the plaintiff's undertaking would not be sufficient to compensate him fully for all of them. The extent to which the disadvantages to each party would be incapable of being compensated in damages in the event of his succeeding at the trial is always a significant factor in assessing where the balance of convenience lies; and if the extent of the uncompensatable disadvantage to each party would not differ widely, it may not be improper to take into account in tipping the balance the relative strength of each party's case as revealed by the affidavit evidence adduced on the hearing of the application. This, however, should be done only where it is apparent on the facts disclosed by evidence as to which there is no credible dispute that the strength of one party's case is disproportionate to that of the other party. The court is not justified in embarking on anything resembling a trial of the action on conflicting affidavits in order to evaluate the strength of either party's case.'

"It is clear that what is there said is the setting out of guidelines for the **11–235** assistance of the judges. I quote this passage again:

". . . if the extent of the uncompensatable disadvantage to each party would not differ widely, it may not be improper to take into account in tipping the balance the relative strength of each party's case . . ."

"For my part, I would hold that on the evidence before the judge this case was at best for the plaintiffs clearly within that principle. The uncompensatable disadvantage of each party in this case is difficult to assess separately for this purpose, and therefore even more difficult to compare with any confidence that one is more grave than the other.

This is a case, therefore, in which I think that the relative strength of the parties' cases should be taken into account, and this can be done by reference to the undisputed evidence on the affidavits and documents . . .

"There is one further matter to be taken into account on the balance of justice. Since I am following the judge through the principles stated in the *American Cyanamid* case, I should point out that it comes under the heading: '. . . many other special factors to be taken into consideration in the particular circumstances of individual cases' (see [1975] 1 All E.R. 504 at 511, [1975] A.C. 396 at 409). I refer to the public interest in the exercise by the BBC of their rights and duties in communication to the people of this country . . .

I would allow this appeal.

EASTHAM J: "I agree that this appeal should be allowed . . . [following the approach of Ralph Gibson L.J.].

SERIES 5 SOFTWARE v. CLARKE

Chancery Division [1996] 1 All E.R. 853.

LADDIE J.: "It is, of course, comparatively rare for applications for interlocu- **11–236** tory relief to reach the House of Lords. However, 1975 was an exception. In that year two cases, both of which involved an analysis of the courts' power to grant interlocutory injunctions, were heard more or less one after the other. The first was *F. Hoffmann-La Roche & Co. Att.-Gen. v. Secretary of State for Trade and Industry* [1973] A.C. 295. . . . In the course of that case their Lordships considered the circumstances in which interlocutory injunctions were granted and the conditions to which their grant could be subject. In particular Lord Diplock said ([1975] A.C. 295 at 360–361):

> 'An interim injunction is a temporary and exceptional remedy which is available before the rights of the parties have been finally determined and, in the case of an ex parte injunction, even before the court had been apprised of the nature of the defendant's case. *To justify the grant of such a remedy the plaintiff must satisfy the court first that there is a strong prima facie case that he will be entitled to a final order restraining the defendant from doing what he is threatening to do,* and secondly that he will suffer irreparable injury which cannot be compensated by a subsequent award of damages in the action if the defendant is not prevented from doing it between the date of the application for the interim injunction and the date of the final order made on trial of the action. Nevertheless, at the time of the application it is not possible for the court to be absolutely certain that the plaintiff will succeed at the trial in establishing his legal right to restrain the defendant from doing what he is threatening to do. If he should fail to do so the defendant may have suffered loss as a result of having been prevented from doing it while the interim injunction was in force; and any loss is likely to be damnum absque injuria for which he could not recover damages from the plaintiff at common law. So unless some other means is provided in this event for compensating the defendant for his loss there is a risk that injustice may be done.' (My emphasis.)

11–237 Then, having explained that the imposition of the cross-undertaking is designed to mitigate the risk to the defendant, Lord Diplock proceeded:

> 'Beside mitigating the risk of injustice to the defendant the practice of exacting an undertaking as to damages facilitates the conduct of the business of the courts. It relieves the court of the necessity to embark at an interlocutory stage upon an enquiry as to the likelihood of the defendant's being able to establish facts to destroy *the strong prima facie case which ex hypothesi will have been made out by the plaintiff.* The procedure on motion is unsuited to inquiries into disputed facts. This is best left to the trial of the action . . .' (My emphasis.)

"This was consistent with the approach which was followed in many, but not all, cases before *American Cyanamid*. The court had to pay regard to the strength or otherwise of the plaintiff's case as revealed by a consideration of all the affidavit evidence.

"Judgment in *Hoffmann-La Roche* was given just before the long vacation on July 3, 1974.

11–238 "That brings me to *American Cyanamid*, the hearing for which commenced after the long vacation on November 12, 1974. It can be assumed that the panel read the parties' briefs before that date. The panel consisted of Lord Diplock, Viscount Dilhorne, Lord Cross, Lord Salmon and Lord Edmund-Davies—that is, it included two members of the panel which decided *Hoffmann-La Roche*. If the House of Lords intended to say that it was inappropriate on an application for interlocutory relief, save in rare cases, to take into account the apparent strength of the plaintiff's case, it would mean that Lord Diplock performed a volte face on this issue in a matter of four months. In my view it is inconceivable that Lord

Diplock and Lord Cross could have forgotten what was said in the *Hoffmann-La Roche* judgment a few months earlier. Therefore, if they were saying the opposite of what was said in *Hoffmann-La Roche*, they must have been aware that they were doing so but chose not to mention that fact or explain it in *American Cyanamid*. That is a proposition I find difficult to accept. It seems to me that it is therefore appropriate to consider whether what Lord Diplock said in *Hoffmann-La Roche* is incompatible with what he said in *American Cyanamid* only a few months later. For this it is necessary to consider the *American Cyanamid* decision with some care.

"The *American Cyanamid* case was concerned with the alleged infringement of the main claim in the plaintiff's patent for absorbable surgical sutures. In response to the allegation of infringement, Ethicon presented a classic squeeze argument beloved of patent lawyers. It said that its sutures did not fall within the monopoly defined by the claim--that is it did not infringe, or, in the alternative, if the claim was construed widely enough to include its product, the patent was invalid on a number of grounds under the Patents Act 1949.

"In the House of Lords, as in the High Court and the Court of Appeal, both **11–239** parties had addressed the question of whether the plaintiff had demonstrated a strong prima facie case. In the course of his judgment, Lord Diplock said [1975] 1 All E.R. 504 at 510, [1975] A.C. 396 at 407:

> 'Your Lordships should in my view take this opportunity of declaring that there is no such rule. The use of such expressions as "a probability", "a prima facie case", or "a strong prima facie case" in the context of the exercise of a discretionary power to grant an interlocutory injunction leads to confusion as to the object sought to be achieved by this form of temporary relief. The court no doubt must be satisfied that the claim is not frivolous or vexatious; in other words, that there is a serious question to be tried.'

"The first question to be answered is precisely what was 'such rule' the existence of which the House of Lords disapproved. This can be found in the early part of Lord Diplock's judgment. In the High Court, Graham J. had held that the plaintiff had made out a strong prima facie case and went on to say that the balance of convenience favoured the grant of interlocutory relief. The way in which the Court of Appeal dealt with the application was set out in the following passage in Lord Diplock's judgment [1975] A.C. 396 at 404–405):

> 'As Russell L.J. put it in the concluding paragraph of his reasons for **11–240** judgment with which the other members of the court agreed—". . . if there be no prima facie case on the point essential to entitle the plaintiff to complain of the defendant's proposed activities, that is the end of the claim to interlocutory relief." "Prima facie case" may in some contexts be an elusive concept, but the sense in which it was being used by Russell L.J. is apparent from an earlier passage in his judgment. After a detailed analysis of the more conflicting expert testimony he said: "I am not satisfied on the present evidence that on the proper construction of this specification, addressed as it is to persons skilled in the relevant art or science, the claim extends to sterile surgical sutures produced not only from a homopolymer of glycolide but also from a copolymer of glycolide and up to 15 per cent of lactide. That is to say that I do not consider that a prima facie case of infringement is established." In effect what the Court

of Appeal was doing was trying the issue of infringement on the conflicting affidavit evidence as it stood, without the benefit of oral testimony or cross-examination. They were saying: "If we had to give judgment in the action now without any further evidence we should hold that Cyanamid had not satisfied the onus of proving that their patent would be infringed by Ethicon's selling sutures made of XLG." The Court of Appeal accordingly did not find it necessary to go into the questions raised by Ethicon as to the validity of the patent or to consider where the balance of convenience lay.'

As Lord Diplock put it ([1975] A.C. 396 at 405):

'[The Court of Appeal] considered that there was a *rule of practice so well established as to constitute a rule of law* that precluded them from granting any interim injunction unless on the evidence adduced by both the parties on the hearing of the application the applicant had satisfied the court that on the balance of probabilities the acts of the other party sought to be enjoined would, if committed, violate the applicant's legal rights.' (My emphasis.)

Lord Diplock then made it clear that it was in order to enable the existence of that rule of law to be considered that leave to appeal had been granted.

11–241 "The result of applying that rule of law was that in the Court of Appeal the motion lasted for two working weeks while the parties argued questions of polymer chemistry, infringement and validity. In the House of Lords the defendant tried to do the same thing. The note of argument there shows that sophisticated arguments of patent ambiguity, construction, inutility, false suggestion, insufficiency and unfair basis were advanced. In effect, the Court of Appeal had abandoned any attempt to evaluate the pros and cons of granting an interlocutory injunction and had said that there was a mandatory initial hurdle at which the plaintiff had fallen. The flexible and absence of strict rules which had been advocated by the Court of Appeal in *Hubbard v. Vosper* was ignored. If such a rule of law as envisaged by the Court of Appeal in *American Cyanamid* did exist, it would inevitably force the parties to engage in trying to prove at the interlocutory stage all those issues which were for determination at the trial. In a case as complicated as *American Cyanamid* it was likely to be impossible to show a strong prima facie case of infringement and validity and any attempt to do so would force the parties to expound at length on complicated technical and legal issues. But those were issues which at an interlocutory stage the court could not hope to resolve. It would have followed that if such a rule of law existed, interlocutory injunctions in patent cases, or in any other complicated case, would become a thing of the past no matter how severe was the damage to be suffered by the plaintiff in the interim.

11–242 "When Lord Diplock said that there was no such rule, he was referring to the so-called rule of law which the Court of Appeal had followed. In dismissing this approach, the House of Lords approved of the decision in *Hubbard v. Vosper* and in particular that part of the decision in which the Court of Appeal deprecated any attempt to fetter the discretion of the court by laying down any rules which would have the effect of limiting the flexibiity of the remedy (see [1975] A.C. 396 at 407).

"Once it had disposed of the inflexible rule as applied by the Court of Appeal in the instant case, the House of Lords went on to consider what principles a court should bear in mind when deciding whether to grant interlocutory relief. First, it said ([1975] A.C. 396 at 408):

'. . . [the court should] consider whether if the plaintiff were to succeed at the trial in establishing his right to a permanent injunction he would be adequately compensated by an award of damages for the loss he would have sustained as a result of the defendant's continuing to do what was sought to be enjoined between the time of the application and the time of the trial. If damages in the measure recoverable at common law would be adequate remedy and the defendant would be in a financial position to pay them, no interlocutory injunction should *normally* be granted, *however strong the plaintiff's claim appeared to be at that stage.*' (My emphasis.)

It should be noticed from the emphasised words in that passage that this approach was not said to be invariably the correct one and furthermore the words used suggest that where damages for the plaintiff was *not* an adequate remedy the apparent strength of the plaintiff's claim might well be a relevant consideration.

"Having considered the issue of adequacy of damages, Lord Diplock pro- **11–243** ceeded as follows ([1975] A.C. 396 at 408):

'It is where there is doubt as to the adequacy of the respective remedies in damages available to either party or to both, that the question of balance of convenience arises. It would be unwise to attempt even to list all the various matters which may need to be taken into consideration in deciding where the balance lies, let alone to suggest the relative weight to be attached to them. These will vary from case to case.'

"The reality is that the balance of convenience issue will need to be considered in most cases because evidence relating to the adequacy of damages normally will be contradictory and there will be no possibility of resolving the differences by cross-examination. In the result, normally there will be doubt as to the adequacy of damages. It follows that in most cases it will be the exercise of taking into account all the issues relevant to the balance of convenience which will be the major task of the court faced with an application for interlocutory relief. As Lord Diplock went on to point out ([1975] A.C. 396 at 408–409):

'Save in the simplest cases, the decision to grant or to refuse an interlocutory injunction will cause to whichever party is unsuccessful on the application some disadvantages which his ultimate success at the trial may show he ought to have been spared and the disadvantages may be such that the recovery of damages to which he would then be entitled either in the action or under the plaintiff's undertaking would not be sufficient to compensate him fully for all of them. The extent to which the disadvantages to each party would be incapable of being compensated in damages in the event of his succeeding at the trial is always a significant factor in assessing where the balance of convenience lies . . .'

"In many cases before *American Cyanamid* the prospect of success was one of **11–244** the important factors taken into account in assessing the balance of convenience. The courts would be less willing to subject the plaintiff to the risk of irrecoverable loss which would befall him if an interlocutory injunction was refused in those cases where it thought he was likely to win at the trial than in those cases where it thought he was likely to lose. The assessment of the prospects of success therefore was an important factor in deciding whether the court should exercise its discretion to grant interlocutory relief. It is this consideration which *American Cyanamid* is said to have prohibited in all but the most exceptional case. so it is necessary to consider with some care what was said in the House of Lords on this issue.

"Lord Diplock said ([1975] A.C. 396 at 409):

> '. . . if the extent of the uncompensatable disadvantage to each party would not differ widely, it may not be improper to take into account in tipping the balance the relative strength of each party's case as revealed by the affidavit evidence adduced on the hearing of the application. . . . The court is not justified in embarking on anything resembling a trial of the aciton on conflicting affidavits in order to evaluate the strength of either party's case.'

11–245   It appears to me that there is nothing in this which is inconsistent with the old practice. Although couched in terms "it may not be improper", this means that it is legitimate for the court to look at the relative strength of the parties' case as disclosed by the affidavits. The warning contained in the second of the quoted sentences is to avoid courts at the interlocutory stage engaging in mini-trials, which is what happened, at least in the Court of Appeal, in *American Cyanamid* itself. Interlocutory applications are meant to come on quickly and to be disposed of quickly.

"The supposed problem with *American Cyanamid* centres on the following statement by Lord Diplock ([1975] A.C. 396 at 409):

> '[Assessing the relative strength of the parties' case], however, should be done only where it is apparent upon the facts disclosed by evidence as to which there is no credible dispute that the strength of one party's case is disproportionate to that of the other party.'

If this means that the court *cannot* take into account its view of the strength of each party's case if there is any dispute on the evidence, as suggested by the use of the words "only" and "no credible dispute", then a new inflexible rule has been introduced to replace that applied by the Court of Appeal. For example, all a defendant would have to do is raise a non-demurrable dispute as to relevant facts in his affidavit evidence and then he could invite the court to ignore the apparent strength of the plaintiff's case. This would be inconsistent with the flexible approach suggested in *Hubbard v. Vosper* [1972] 2 Q.B. 84 which was cited with approval earlier in *American Cyanamid* [1975] A.C. 396 at 407. Furthermore, it would be somewhat strange, since *American Cyanamid* directs courts to assess the adequacy of damages and the balance of convenience, yet these too are topics which will almost always be the subject of unresolved conflicts in the affidavit evidence.

11–246   "In my view Lord Diplock did not intend by the last-quoted passage to exclude consideration of the strength of the cases in most applications for interlocutory relief. It appears to me that what is intended is that the court should not attempt to resolve difficult issues of fact or law on an application for interlocutory relief. If, on the other hand, the court is able to come to a view as to the strength of the parties' case on the credible evidence, then it can do so. In fact, as any lawyer who has experience of interlocutory proceedings will know, it is frequently the case that it is easy to determine who is most likely to win the trial on the basis of the affidavit evidence and any exhibited contemporaneous documents. If it is apparent from that material that one party's case is much stronger than the other's then that is a matter the court should not ignore. To suggest otherwise would be to exclude from consideration an important factor and such exclusion would fly in the face of the flexibility advocated earlier in *American Cyanamid*. As Lord Diplock pointed out in *Hoffmann-La Roche*, one of the purposes of the cross-undertaking in damages is to safeguard the defendant if this preliminary view of the strength of the plaintiff's case proves to be wrong.

"Accordingly, it appears to me that in deciding whether to grant interlocutory **11–247** relief, the court should bear the following matters in mind. (1) The grant of an interlocutory injunction is a matter of discretion and depends on all the facts of the case. (2) There are no fixed rules as to when an injunction should or should not be granted. The relief must be kept flexible. (3) Because of the practice adopted on the hearing of applications for interlocutory relief, the court should rarely attempt to resolve complex issues of disputed fact or law. (4) Major factors the court can bear in mind are (a) the extent to which damages are likely to be an adequate remedy for each party and the ability of the other party to pay, (b) the balance of convenience, (c) the maintenance of the status quo, and (d) any clear view the court may reach as to the relative strength of the parties' cases.

"In coming to this conclusion I am encouraged by the following **11–248** considerations.

(1) The House of Lords in *American Cyanamid* did not suggest that it was changing the basis upon which most courts had approached the exercise of discretion in this important area.

(2) The only issue which it was expressly addressing was the existence of the inflexible rule of law which had been applied as a mandatory condition by the Court of Appeal.

(3) It would mean that there was no significant inconsistency between the *Hoffmann-La Roche* and *American Cyanamid* decisions.

(4) It would be consistent with the approval given by the House of Lords to the decision in *Hubbard v. Vosper* and, implicitly, the decision to the same effect in *Evans Marshall & Co. Ltd v. Bertola SA* [1973] 1 W.L.R. 349 (a decision of Lord Edmund-Davies when in the Court of Appeal).

(5) It would preserve what is one of the great values of interlocutory proceedings, namely an early, though non-binding, view of the merits from a judge. Before *American Cyanamid* a decision at the interlocutory stage would be a major ingredient leading to the parties resolving their differences without the need for a trial. There is nothing inherently unsatisfactory in this. Most clients ask for and receive advice on prospects from their lawyers well before there has been cross-examination. In most cases the lawyers have little difficulty giving such advice. 'It should also be remembered that in many jurisdictions on the continent trials are conducted without discovery or cross-examination. There is nothing inherently unfair in a court here expressing at least a preliminary view based on written evidence. After all, it is what the courts managed to do for a century and a half.

(6) Allowing parties to come to an earlier view on prospects would assist in reducing the costs of litigation. This is an issue to which much attention is being given at the moment.

(7) It would mean that the approach of the courts in England and Wales to the grant of interlocutory relief would be the same as that followed in Scotland . . ."

PRACTICE DIRECTION FORMS

11–249 1A. DOMESTIC FREEZING INJUNCTION

Freezing Injunction	IN THE [HIGH COURT OF JUSTICE]
Order to restrain assets in	[CHANCERY DIVISION]
England and Wales	[Strand, London WC2A 2LL]
Before The Honourable Mr Justice	[ ]

Claim No.

Dated

Applicant

Seal

Respondent

Name, address and reference of Respondent

Penal Notice

IF YOU THE WITHIN NAMED [   ] DISOBEY THIS ORDER YOU MAY BE HELD IN CONTEMPT OF COURT AND LIABLE TO IMPRISONMENT OR FINED OR YOUR ASSETS SEIZED

IMPORTANT NOTICE TO THE RESPONDENT

You should read the terms of the Order and the Guidance Notes very carefully. You are advised to consult a Solicitor as soon as possible.

This Order prohibits you, the Respondent, from dealing with your assets up to the amount stated in the Order, but subject to any exceptions set out at the end of the Order. You have a right to ask the Court to vary or discharge this Order. If you disobey this Order you may be found guilty of Contempt of Court and may be sent to prison or fined. In the case of a Corporate Respondent, it may be fined, its Directors may be sent to prison or fined or its assets may be seized.

The Order

An application was made today (*date*) by [Counsel] [Solicitors] (*or as may be*) for the Applicant to Mr Justice .... who heard the application. The Judge read the affidavits listed in Schedule A and accepted the undertakings set out in Schedule B at the end of this Order. As a result of the application IT IS ORDERED that until .... ("the return date") [or further Order of the Court]:

11–250 1 The Respondent must not remove from England and Wales or in any way dispose of or deal with or diminish the value of any of his assets which are in England and Wales whether in his own name or not and whether solely or jointly owned up to the value of £ . . .

This prohibition includes the following assets in particular:—

(a) the property known as (*title/address*) or the net sale money after payment of any mortgages if it has been sold;

(b) the property and assets of the Respondent's business known as [or carried on at (*address*)] or the sale money if any of them have been sold; and

(c) any money in the account numbered (*a/c number*) at (*title/address*).

2 If the total unencumbered value of the Respondent's assets in England and Wales exceeds £ . . . the Respondent may remove any of those assets from England and Wales or may dispose of or deal with them so long as the total unencumbered value of his assets still in England and Wales remains above £ . . .

3 Exceptions to this Order.

(1) This Order does not prohibit the Respondent from spending £ ...... a week towards his ordinary living expenses [and £ ...... a week towards his ordinary and proper business expenses] and also £ ...... a week [or a reasonable sum] on legal advice and representation. But before spending any money the Respondent must tell the Applicant's legal representatives where the money is to come from.

[(2) This Order does not prohibit the Respondent from dealing with or disposing of any of his assets in the ordinary and proper course of business.]

(3) The Respondent may agree with the Applicant's legal representatives that the above spending limits should be increased or that this Order should be varied in any other respect, but any agreement must be in writing.

(4) The Respondent may cause this Order to cease to have effect if the Respondent provides security by paying the sum of £ into Court or makes provision for security in that sum by another method agreed with the Applicant's legal representatives.

4 The Respondent must:

(1) Inform the Applicant in writing at once of all his assets in England and Wales and whether in his own name or not and whether solely or jointly owned, giving the value, location and details of all such assets.
[The Respondent may be entitled to refuse to provide some or all of this information on the grounds that it may incriminate him. (*This sentence may be inserted in cases not covered by the Theft Act 1968 s.31.*)]

(2) Confirm the information in an affidavit which must be served on the Applicant's legal representatives within . . . days after this Order has been served on the Respondent.

[5 *Where an Order for service by an alternative means or service out of the jurisdiction has been made*

(1) The Applicant may issue and serve a Claim Form on the Respondent at (*address*) by (*method of service*).

(2) If the Respondent wishes to defend the Claim where the Claim Form states that Particulars of Claim are to follow he must complete and return the Acknowledgement of Service within . . . days of being served with the Claim Form. Where the Particulars of Claim are served with the Claim Form, and the Respondent wishes to defend part or all of the

Claim he must complete and return an Acknowledgement of Service within . . . days of being served with the Claim Form or a Defence within . . . days.]

Guidance Notes

Effect of This Order

11–251

(1) A respondent who is an individual who is ordered not to do something must not do it himself or in any other way. He must not do it through others acting on his behalf or on his instructions or with his encouragement.

(2) A respondent which is a corporation and which is ordered not to do something must not do it itself or by its directors, officers, employees or agents or in any other way.

Variation or Discharge of This Order

The Respondent (or anyone notified of this Order) may apply to the court at any time to vary or discharge this Order (or so much of it as affects that person), but anyone wishing to do so must first inform the Applicant's legal representatives.

Parties Other Than the Applicant and Respondent

(1) Effect of this Order:

It is a Contempt of Court for any person notified of this Order knowingly to assist in or permit a breach of this Order. Any person doing so may be sent to prison, fined or have his assets seized.

(2) Set off by banks:

This injunction does not prevent any bank from exercising any right of set off it may have in respect of any facility which it gave to the respondent before it was notified of this Order.

(3) Withdrawals by the Respondent:

No bank need enquire as to the application or proposed application of any money withdrawn by the Respondent if the withdrawal appears to be permitted by this Order.

Interpretation of This Order

(1) In this Order, where there is more than one Respondent, (unless otherwise stated), references to "the Respondent" means both or all of them.

(2) A requirement to serve on the Respondent' means on each of them. However, the Order is effective against any Respondent on whom it is served.

(3) An Order requiring "the Respondent" to do or not to do anything applies to all Respondents.

Communications With the Court

All communications to the Court about this Order should be sent, where the Order is made in the Chancery Division, to [Room TM 510], Royal Courts of

Justice, Strand, London WC2A 2LL quoting the case number The telephone number is 020 7936 [6827]; and where the order is made in the Queen's Bench Division, to Room W11(020 7936 6009). The offices are open between 10 am. and 4.30 p.m. Monday to Friday.

Schedule A

Affidavits

The Applicant relied on the following affidavits:

(*name*)	(*number of affidavit*)	(*date sworn*)	(*filed on behalf of*)
(1)			
(2)			

Schedule B

Undertakings given to the Court by the Applicant

(1) If the Court later finds that this Order has caused loss to the Respond- **11–252** ent, and decides that the Respondent should be compensated for that loss, the Applicant will comply with any Order the Court may make.

(2) The Applicant will on or before (*date*) cause a written guarantee in the sum of £ . . . to be issued from a bank having a place of business within England or Wales, such guarantee being in respect of any Order the Court may make pursuant to paragraph (1) above. The Applicant will further, forthwith upon issue of the guarantee, cause a copy of it to be served on the Respondent.

(3) As soon as practicable the Applicant will [issue and serve on the Respondent a Claim Form in the form of the draft produced to the Court] [serve on the Respondent the Claim Form] claiming the appropriate relief, together with this Order.

(4) The Applicant will cause an affidavit to be sworn and filed [substantially in the terms of the draft affidavit produced to the Court] [confirming the substance of what was said to the Court by the Applicant's Counsel/ Solicitors].

[(5) (*Where a return date has been given.*) As soon as practicable the Applicant will serve on the Respondent an Application for the return date together with a copy of the affidavits and exhibits containing the evidence relied on by the Applicant.]

(6) Anyone notified of this Order will be given a copy of it by the Applicant's legal representatives.

(7) The Applicant will pay the reasonable costs of anyone other than the Respondent which have been incurred as a result of this Order including the costs of ascertaining whether that person holds any of the Respondent's assets and if the Court later finds that this Order has caused such person loss, and decides that such person should be compensated for that loss, the Applicant will comply with any Order the Court may make.

(8) If for any reason this Order ceases to have effect (including in particular where the Respondent provides security as provided for above or the Applicant does not provide a bank guarantee as provided for above), the applicant will forthwith take all reasonable steps to inform, in writing, any person or company to whom he has given notice of this Order, or

who he has reasonable grounds for supposing may act upon this Order, that it has ceased to have effect.

Name and Address of Applicant's Legal Representatives

The Applicant's Legal Representatives are:

11–253 [Name, address, reference, fax and telephone numbers both in and out of office hours.]

1B. WORLDWIDE FREEZING INJUNCTION

Freezing Injunction	**IN THE [HIGH COURT OF JUSTICE]**
Order to restrain assets worldwide	[CHANCERY DIVISION]
	[Strand, London WC2A 2LL]
Before The Honourable Mr Justice	[ ]

Claim No.

Dated

Applicant

Seal

Respondent

Name, address and reference of Respondent

PENAL NOTICE
IF YOU THE WITHIN NAMED [   ] **DISOBEY THIS ORDER YOU MAY BE HELD TO BE IN CONTEMPT OF COURT AND LIABLE TO IMPRISONMENT OR FINED OR YOUR ASSETS SEIZED**

IMPORTANT NOTICE TO THE RESPONDENT

You should read the terms of the Order and the Guidance Notes very carefully. You are advised to consult a Solicitor as soon as possible.

This Order prohibits you, the Respondent, from dealing with your assets up to the amount stated in the Order, but subject to any exceptions set out at the end of the Order. You have a right to ask the Court to vary or discharge this Order.

If you disobey this Order you may be found guilty of contempt of Court and may be sent to prison or fined. In the case of a Corporate Respondent, it may be fined, its Directors may be sent to prison or fined or its assets may be seized.

The Order

11–254 An application was made today (*date*) by [Counsel] [Solicitors](or *as may be*) for the Applicant to Mr Justice .... who heard the application. The Judge read the affidavits listed in Schedule A and accepted the undertakings set out in Schedule

B at the end of this Order. As a result of the application IT IS ORDERED that until .... ("the return date")] [further Order of the Court]:

1 The Respondent must not:

(1) remove from England and Wales or in any way dispose of or deal with or diminish the value of any of his assets which are in England and Wales whether in his own name or not and whether solely or jointly owned up to the value of £ . . ., or

(2) in any way dispose of or deal with or diminish the value of any of his assets whether they are in or outside England or Wales whether in his own name or not and whether solely or jointly owned up to the same value. This prohibition includes the following assets in particular:

    (a) the property known as (*title/address*) or the net sale money after payment of any mortgages if it has been sold:

    (b) the property and assets of the Respondent's business known as [or carried on at (*address*)] or the sale money if any of them have been sold; and

    (c) any money in the account numbered (*a/c number*) at (*title/address*).

2

(1) If the total unencumbered value of the Respondent's assets in England and Wales exceeds £ . . . , the Respondent may remove any of those assets from England and Wales or may dispose of or deal with them so long as the total unencumbered value of his assets still in England and Wales remains above £ . . .

(2) If the total unencumbered value of the Respondent's assets in England and Wales does not exceed £ . . . , the Respondent must not remove any of those assets from England and Wales and must not dispose of or deal with any of them, but if he has other assets outside England and Wales the Respondent may dispose of or deal with those assets so long as the total unencumbered value of all his assets whether in or outside England and Wales remains above £ . . .

3 Exceptions to this Order: **11–255**

(1) This Order does not prohibit the Respondent from spending £ . . . a week towards his ordinary living expenses [and £ . . . a week towards his ordinary and proper business expenses] and also £ . . . a week [*or a reasonable sum*] on legal advice and representation. But before spending any money the Respondent must tell the Applicant's legal representatives where the money is to come from.

(2) This Order does not prohibit the Respondent from dealing with or disposing of any of his assets in the ordinary and proper course of business.

(3) The Respondent may agree with the Applicant's legal representatives that the above spending limits should be increased or that this Order should be varied in any other respect, but any agreement must be in writing.

(4) The Respondent may cause this Order to cease to have effect if the Respondent provides security by paying the sum of £ . . . into Court or makes provision for security in that sum by another method agreed with the Applicant's legal representatives.

4 The Respondent must:

(1) Inform the Applicant in writing at once of all his assets whether in or outside England and Wales and whether in his own name or not and whether solely or jointly owned, giving the value, location and details of all such assets.

[The Respondent may be entitled to refuse to provide some or all of this information on the grounds that it may incriminate him. *This sentence may be inserted in cases not covered by the Theft Act 1968 s.31.*]

(2) Confirm the information in an affidavit which must be served on the Applicant's legal representatives within . . . days after this Order has been served on the Respondent.

[5 Where an Order for service by an alternative means or service out of the jurisdiction has been made]

(1) The Applicant may issue and serve a Claim Form on the Respondent at (*address*) by (*method of service*)
(2) If the Respondent wishes to defend the Claim he must complete and return the Notice of Intention to Defend within . . . days of being served with the Claim Form.]

Guidance Notes

Effect of This Order

11–256

(1) A Respondent who is an individual who is ordered not to do something must not do it himself or in any other way. He must not do it through others acting on his behalf or on his instructions or with his encouragement.
(2) A Respondent which is a corporation and which is ordered not to do something must not do it itself or by its directors, officers, employees or agents or in any other way.

Variation or Discharge of This Order

The Respondent (or anyone notified of this Order) may apply to the Court at any time to vary or discharge this Order (or so much of it as affects that person), but anyone wishing to do so must first inform the Applicant's legal representatives.

Parties Other Than The Applicant and Respondent

(1) Effect of this Order:

It is a Contempt of Court for any person notified of this Order knowingly to assist in or permit a breach of this Order. Any person doing so may be sent to prison, fined or have his assets seized.

(2) Effect of this Order outside England and Wales: The terms of this Order do not affect or concern anyone outside the jurisdiction of this Court until it is declared enforceable by or is enforced by a Court in the relevant country and then they are to affect him only to the extent they have been declared enforceable or have been enforced UNLESS the person is:

(i) a person to whom this Order is addressed or an officer or an agent appointed by power of attorney of that person; or

(ii) a person who is subject to the jurisdiction of this Court and (a) has been given written notice of this Order at his residence or place of business within the jurisdiction of this Court and (b) is able to prevent acts or omissions outside the jurisdiction of this Court which constitute or assist in a breach of the terms of this Order.

(3) Set off by Banks:

This injunction does not prevent any bank from exercising any right of set off it may have in respect of any facility which it gave to the Respondent before it was notified of this Order.

(4) Withdrawals by the Respondent: No bank need enquire as to the application or proposed application of any money withdrawn by the Respondent if the withdrawal appears to be permitted by this Order.

Interpretation of This Order

(1) In this Order, where there is more than one Respondent, (unless **11–257** otherwise stated) references to "the Respondent" means both or all of them.

(2) A requirement to serve on "the Respondent" means on each of them. However, the Order is effective against any Respondent on whom it is served.

(3) An Order requiring "the Respondent" to do or not to do anything applies to all Respondents.

Communications With The Court

All communications to the Court about this Order should be sent, where the Order is made in the Chancery Division, to [Room TM 510], Royal Courts of Justice, Strand, London WC2A 2LL quoting the case number. The telephone number is 020 7936 [6827]; and where the order is made in the Queen's Bench Division, to Room W11 (020 7936 6009). The offices are open between 10 a.m. and 4.30 p.m. Monday to Friday.

Schedule A

Affidavits

The Applicant relied on the following affidavits:

(*name*)	(*number of affidavit*)	(*date sworn*)	(*filed on behalf of*)
(1)			
(2)			

Schedule B

Undertakings Given to the Court by the Applicant

11–258   (1) If the Court later finds that this Order has caused loss to the Respondent, and decides that the Respondent should be compensated for that loss, the Applicant will comply with any Order the Court may make.

    (2) The Applicant will on or before (*date*) cause a written guarantee in the sum of £ . . . to be issued from a bank having a place of business within England or Wales, such guarantee being in respect of any Order the Court may make pursuant to paragraph (1) above. The Applicant will further, forthwith upon issue of the guarantee, cause a copy of it to be served on the Respondent.

    (3) As soon as practicable the Applicant will [issue and serve on the Respondent a Claim Form in the form of the draft produced to the Court] [serve on the Respondent the Claim Form] claiming the appropriate relief, together with this Order.]

    (4) The Applicant will cause an affidavit to be sworn and filed [substantially in the terms of the draft affidavit produced to the Court] [confirming the substance of what was said to the Court by the Applicant's Counsel/Solicitors].

    [(5) *Where a return date has been given*—As soon as practicable the Applicant will serve on the Respondent an application for the return date together with a copy of the affidavits and exhibits containing the evidence relied on by the Applicant.]

    (6) Anyone notified of this Order will be given a copy of it by the Applicant's legal representatives.

    (7) The Applicant will pay the reasonable costs of anyone other than the Respondent which have been incurred as a result of this Order including the costs of ascertaining whether that person holds any of the Respondent's assets and if the Court later finds that this Order has caused such person loss, and decides that such person should be compensated for that loss, the Applicant will comply with any Order the Court may make.

11–259   (8) If for any reason this Order ceases to have effect (including in particular where the Respondent provides security as provided for above or the Applicant does not provide a bank guarantee as provided for above), the Applicant will forthwith take all reasonable steps to inform, in writing, any person or company to whom he has given notice of this Order, or who he has reasonable grounds for supposing may act upon this Order, that it has ceased to have effect.

    [(9) The Applicant will not without the leave of the Court begin proceedings against the Respondent in any other jurisdiction or use information obtained as a result of an Order of the Court in this jurisdiction for the purpose of civil or criminal proceedings in any other jurisdiction.]

    [(10) The Applicant will not without the leave of the Court seek to enforce this Order in any country outside England and Wales [or seek an Order of a similar nature including Orders conferring a change or other security against the Respondent or the Respondent's assets].]

Name and Address of Applicant's Legal Representatives

11–260   The Applicant's Legal Representatives are:

[Name, address, reference, fax and telephone numbers both in and out of office hours.]

2. SEARCH ORDER

Search Order	IN THE [HIGH COURT OF JUSTICE]
Order to preserve evidence and property	[CHANCERY DIVISION] [Strand, London WC2A 2LL]
Before The Honourable Mr Justice	[ ]

Claim No.

Dated

Applicant

Seal

Respondent

Name, address and reference of Respondent

Penal Notice

IF YOU THE WITHIN NAMED [......] DISOBEY THIS ORDER YOU MAY BE HELD TO BE IN CONTEMPT OF COURT AND LIABLE TO IMPRISONMENT OR FINED OR YOUR ASSETS SEIZED

IMPORTANT NOTICE TO THE RESPONDENT

You should read the terms of the Order and the Guidance Notes very carefully. You are advised to consult a Solicitor as soon as possible.

This Order orders you, the Respondent, to allow the persons mentioned in the Order to enter the premises described in the Order and to search for, examine and remove or copy the articles specified in the Order. The persons so named will have no right to enter the premises or, having entered, to remain at the premises, unless you give your consent to their doing so. If, however, you withhold your consent you will be in breach of this Order and may be held to be in Contempt of Court.

The Order also requires you to hand over any of such articles which are under your control and to provide information to the Applicant's Solicitors, and prohibits you from doing certain acts.

If you, the Respondent, disobey this Order you may be found guilty of contempt of Court and may be sent to prison or fined. In the case of a Corporate Respondent, it may be fined, its Directors may be sent to prison or fined or its assets may be seized.

The Order

AN APPLICATION was made today (*date*) by [Counsel] [Solicitors] for the Applicant to Mr Justice .... who heard the application. The Judge read the affidavits listed in Schedule F at the end of this Order and accepted the undertakings by the Applicant, the Applicant's Solicitors and the Supervising Solicitor set forth in the Schedules at the end of this Order. As a result of the application IT IS ORDERED that until .... ("the return date")] [or further Order of the Court]:

11–261   **1**

(1) The Respondent must allow Mr/Mrs/Miss ...... ("the Supervising Solicitor"), together with Mr ...... a Solicitor of the Supreme Court, and a partner in the firm of ...... the Applicant's Solicitors and up to ...... other persons being (*their capacity*) accompanying them, to enter the premises mentioned in Schedule A to this Order and any other premises of the Respondent disclosed under paragraph 4(1) below and any vehicles under the Respondent's control on or around the premises so that they can search for, inspect, photograph or photocopy, and deliver into the safekeeping of the Applicant's Solicitors all the documents and articles which are listed in Schedule B to this Order ("the listed items") or which Mr . . . believes to be listed items.

(2) The Respondent must allow those persons to remain on the premises until the search is complete, and to re-enter the premises on the same or the following day in order to complete the search.

2

(1) No item may be removed from the premises until a list of the items to be removed has been prepared, and a copy of the list has been supplied to the person served with the Order, and he has been given a reasonable opportunity to check the list.

(2) The premises must not be searched, and items must not be removed from them, except in the presence of the Respondent or a person appearing to be a responsible employee of the Respondent or in control of the premises.

(3) If the Supervising Solicitor is satisfied that full compliance with paragraph 2(1) or (2) above is impracticable, he may permit the search to proceed and items to be removed without compliance with the impracticable requirements.

3

(1) The Respondent must immediately hand over to the Applicant's Solicitors any of the listed items which are in his possession or under his control save for any computer or hard disk integral to any computer.

(2) If any of the listed items exists only in computer readable form, the Respondent must immediately give the Applicant's Solicitors effective access to the computers, with all necessary passwords, to enable them to be searched, and cause the listed items to be printed out. A print-out of the items must be given to the Applicant's Solicitors or displayed on the computer screen so that they can be read and copied. All reasonable steps shall be taken by the Applicant to ensure that no damage is done to any computer or data. The Applicant and his representatives may not themselves search the Respondent's computers unless they have sufficient expertise to do so without damaging the Respondent's system.

4

(1) The Respondent must immediately inform the Applicant's **11–262**
Solicitors:—

    (a) where all the listed items are; and

    (b) so far as he is aware—

        (i) the name and address of everyone who has supplied him, or
offered to supply him, with listed items,

        (ii) the name and address of everyone to whom he has supplied,
or offered to supply, listed items, and

        (iii) full details of the dates and quantities of every such supply
and offer.

(2) Within . . . days after being served with this Order the Respondent
must swear an affidavit setting out the above information.

5

(1) Except for the purpose of obtaining legal advice, the Respondent or
anyone else with knowledge of this Order must not directly or indirectly
inform anyone of these proceedings or of the contents of this Order, or
warn anyone that proceedings have been or may be brought against him
by the Applicant until . . . 19/20 . . . (the return date) [or further Order
of the Court].

(2) The Respondent must not destroy, tamper with, cancel or part with
possession, power, custody or control of the listed items otherwise than
in accordance with the terms of this Order.

(3) (*Insert any negative injunctions.*)

(**6** *Insert any further order.*)

Guidance Notes

Effect of This Order

(1) A Respondent who is an individual who is ordered not to do something **11–263**
must not do it himself or in any other way. He must not do it through
others acting on his behalf or on his instructions or with his
encouragement.

(2) A Respondent which is a corporation and which is ordered not to do
something must not do it itself or by the directors officers employees or
agents or in any other way.

(3) This Order must be complied with either by the Respondent himself or
by an employee of the Respondent or other person appearing to be in
control of the premises and having authority to permit the premises to be
entered and the search to proceed.

(4) This Order requires the Respondent or his employees or other person
appearing to be in control of the premises and having that authority to
permit entry to the premises immediately the Order is served upon him,
except as stated in paragraph 6 below.

Respondent's Entitlements

(1) Before you the Respondent or the person appearing to be in control of
the premises allow anybody onto the premises to carry out this Order you
are entitled to have the solicitor who serves you with this Order explain
to you what it means in everyday language.

(2) You are entitled to insist that there is nobody [or nobody except Mr . . .] present who could gain commercially from anything he might read or see on your premises.

(3) You are entitled to refuse to permit entry before 9:30 a.m. or after 5:30 p.m. or at all on Saturday and Sunday unless the Court has ordered otherwise.

(4) Except in certain cases, you may be entitled to refuse to permit disclosure of any documents which may incriminate you ("incriminating documents") or to answer any questions if to do so may incriminate you. It may be prudent to take advice, because if you so refuse, your refusal may be taken into account by the Court at a later stage.

(5) You are entitled to refuse to permit disclosure of any documents passing between you and your Solicitors or Patent or Trade Mark Agents for the purpose of obtaining advice ("privileged documents").

(6) You are entitled to seek legal advice, and to ask the Court to vary or discharge this Order, provided you do so at once, and provided you do not disturb or move anything in the interim and that meanwhile you permit the Supervising Solicitor (who is a Solicitor acting independently of the Applicant) to enter, but not start to search.

(7) Before permitting entry to the premises by any person other than the Supervising Solicitor, you (or any other person appearing to be in control of the premises) may gather together any documents you believe may be [incriminating or] privileged and hand them to the Supervising Solicitor for the Supervising Solicitor to assess whether they are [incriminating or] privileged as claimed. If the Supervising Solicitor concludes that any of the documents may be [incriminating or] privileged documents or if there is any doubt as to their status the Supervising Solicitor shall exclude them from the search and shall retain the documents of doubtful status in his possession pending further order of the Court. While this is being done, you may refuse entry to the premises by any other person, and may refuse to permit the search to begin, for a short time (not to exceed two hours, unless the Supervising Solicitor agrees to a longer period). If you wish to take legal advice and gather documents as permitted, you must first inform the Supervising Solicitor and keep him informed of the steps being taken.

Restrictions on Service

11–264 Paragraph 1 of the Order is subject to the following restrictions:—

(1) This Order may only be served between 9:30 a.m. and 5:30 p.m. on a weekday unless the Court has ordered otherwise.

(2) This Order may not be carried out at the same time as a police search warrant.

(3) This Order must be served by the Supervising Solicitor, and paragraph 1 of the Order must be carried out in his presence and under his supervision. Where the premises are likely to be occupied by an unaccompanied woman and the Supervising Solicitor is a man, at least one of the persons accompanying him as provided by paragraph 1 of the Order shall be a woman.

(4) This Order does not require the person served with the Order to allow anyone [or anyone except Mr . . .] to enter the premises who in the view

of the Supervising Solicitor could gain commercially from anything he might read or see on the premises if the person served with the Order objects.

Variation or Discharge of This Order

The Respondent (or anyone notified of this Order) may apply to the Court at any time to vary or discharge this Order (or so much of it as affects that person), but anyone wishing to do so must first inform the Applicant's Solicitors.

Interpretation of This Order

(1) In this Order, where there is more than one Respondent, references to "the Respondent" means both or all of them.

(2) A requirement to serve on the "Respondent" means on each of them. However, the Order is effective against any Respondent on whom it is served.

(3) An Order requiring "the Respondent" to do or not to do anything applies to all Respondents.

(4) Any other requirement that something shall be done to or in the presence of "the Respondent" means to or in the presence of any one of them or in the case of a firm or company a director or a person appearing to the Supervising Solicitor to be a responsible employee.

Communications With the Court

All communications to the Court about this Order should be sent, where the **11–265** Order is made in the Chancery Division, to [Room TM 510], Royal Courts of Justice, Strand, London, WC2A 2LL quoting the case number. The telephone number is 020 7936 [6827]; and where the order is made in the Queen's Bench Division, to Room W11(020 7936 6009). The offices are open between 10 a.m. and 4.30 p.m. Monday to Friday.

Schedule A

The premises

Schedule B

The listed items

Schedule C

Undertakings Given to the Court by the Applicant

(1) If the Court later finds that this Order or carrying it out has caused loss to the Respondent, and decides that the Respondent should be compensated for that loss, the Applicant will comply with any Order the Court may make. Further, if the carrying out of this Order has been in breach of the terms of this Order or otherwise in a manner inconsistent with the Applicant's Solicitors' duties as Officers of the Court the Applicant will comply with any order for damages the Court may make.

[(2) As soon as practicable to issue a Claim Form [in the form of the draft produced to the Court] [claiming appropriate relief.].]

[(3) To [swear and file an affidavit] [cause an affidavit to be sworn and filed] [substantially in the terms of the draft produced to the Court] [confirming the substance of what was said to the Court by the Applicant's Counsel/Solicitors].]

11–266   (4) To serve on the Respondent at the same time as this Order is served upon him:
  (i) the Claim Form, or if not issued, the draft produced to the Court,
  (ii) an Application for hearing on (*date*),
  (iii) copies of the affidavits [or draft affidavits] and exhibits capable of being copied containing the evidence relied on by the Applicant [Copies of the confidential exhibits need not be served, but they must be made available for inspection by or on behalf of the Respondent in the presence of the Applicant's Solicitor while the Order is carried out. Afterwards they must be provided to a Solicitor representing the Respondent who gives a written undertaking not to permit the Respondent to see them or copies of them except in his presence and not to permit the Respondent to make or take away any note or record of the exhibits.], and
  (iv) a note of any allegation of fact made orally to the Judge where such allegation is not contained in the affidavits or draft affidavits read by the Judge.

(5) To serve on the Respondent a copy of the Supervising Solicitor's report on the carrying out of this Order as soon as it is received.

(6) Not, without the leave of the Court, to use any information or documents obtained as a result of carrying out this Order not to inform anyone else of these proceedings (including adding further Respondents) or commencing civil proceedings in relation to the same or related subject matter to these proceedings until after the return date.

[(7) To maintain pending further order the sum of £ . . . in an account controlled by the Applicant's Solicitors.]

[(8) To insure the items removed from the premises.]

Schedule D

Undertakings Given by the Applicant's Solicitors

11–267   (1) To answer at once to the best of their ability any question whether a particular item is a listed item.

(2) To return the originals of all documents obtained as a result of this Order (except original documents which belong to the Applicant) as soon as possible and in any event within two working days of their removal.

(3) While ownership of any item obtained as a result of this Order is in dispute, to deliver the article into the keeping of Solicitors acting for the Respondent within two working days from receiving a written undertaking by them to retain the article in safe keeping and to produce it to the Court when required.

(4) To retain in their own sale keeping all other items obtained as a result of this Order until the Court directs otherwise.

Schedule E

Undertaking Given by the Supervising Solicitor

11–268   (1) To offer to explain to the person served with the Order its meaning and effect fairly and in everyday language, and to inform him of his right to seek legal advice (such advice to include an explanation that the

Respondent may be entitled to avail himself of [the privilege against self-incrimination or] [legal professional privilege]) and apply to vary or discharge the Order as mentioned in the Respondent's Entitlements above.

(2) To make and provide to the Applicant's Solicitors and to the Judge who made this Order (for the purposes of the Court file) a written report on the carrying out of the Order.

Schedule F

Affidavits

The Applicant relied on the following affidavits:

(*name*)   (*number of affidavit*)   (*date swom*)   [filled on behalf of]

Name and Address of Applicant's Solicitors

The Applicant's Solicitors are:

(Name, address, reference, fax and telephone numbers both in and out of office hours.)

CIVIL EVIDENCE ACT 1968

14 Priviledge against incrimination of self or spouse

(1) The right of a person in any legal proceedings other than criminal proceedings to refuse to answer any question or produce any document or thing if to do so would tend to expose that person to proceedings for an offence or for the recovery of a penalty—

(a) shall apply only as regards criminal offences under the law of any part of the United Kingdom and penalties provided for by such law; and

(b) shall include a like right to refuse to answer any question or produce any document or thing if to do so would tend to expose the husband or wife of that person to proceedings for any such criminal offence or for the recovery of any such penalty.

(2) In so far as any existing enactment conferring (in whatever words) **11–269** powers of inspection or investigation confers on a person (in whatever words) any right otherwise than in criminal proceedings to refuse to answer any question or give any evidence tending to incriminate that person, subsection (1) above shall apply to that right as it applies to the right described in that subsection; and every such existing enactment shall be construed accordingly.

(3) In so far as any existing enactment provides (in whatever words) that in any proceedings other than criminal proceedings a person shall not be excused from answering any question or giving any evidence on the ground that to do so may incriminate that person, that enactment

shall be construed as providing also that in such proceedings a person shall not be excused from answering any question or giving any evidence on the ground that to do so may incriminate the husband or wife of that person.

THEFT ACT 1968

31 Effect on civil proceedings and rights

11–270 (1) A person shall not be excused, by reason that to do so may incriminate that person or the wife or husband of that person of an offence under this Act—

(a) from answering any question put to that person in proceedings for the recovery or administration of any property, for the execution of any trust or for an account of any property or dealings with property; or
(b) from complying with any order made in any such proceedings;

but no statement or admission made by a person in answering a question put or complying with an order made as aforesaid shall, in proceedings for an offence under this Act, be admissible in evidence against that person or (unless they married after the making of the statement or admission) against the wife or husband of that person.

SUPREME COURT ACT 1981

72 Withdrawal of privilege against incrimination of self or spouse in certain proceedings

11–271 (1) In any proceedings to which this subsection applies a person shall not be excused, by reason that to do so would tend to expose that person, or his or her spouse, to proceedings for a related offence or for the recovery of a related penalty—

(a) from answering any question put to that person in the first-mentioned proceedings; or
(b) from complying with any order made in those proceedings.

(2) Subsection (1) applies to the following civil proceedings in the High Court, namely—

(a) proceedings for infringement of rights pertaining to any intellectual property or for passing off;
(b) proceedings brought to obtain disclosure of information relating to any infringement of such rights or to any passing off; and
(c) proceedings brought to prevent any apprehended infringement of such rights or any apprehended passing off.

(3) Subject to subsection (4), no statement or admission made by a **11–272** person—

(a) in answering a question put to him in any proceedings to which subsection (1) applies; or

(b) in complying with any order made in any such proceedings,

shall, in proceedings for any related offence or for the recovery of any related penalty, be admissible in evidence against that person or (unless they married after the making of the statement or admission) against the spouse of that person.

(4) Nothing in subsection (3) shall render any statement or admission made by a person as there mentioned inadmissible in evidence against that person in proceedings for perjury or contempt of court.

(5) In this section—

"intellectual property" means any patent, trade mark, copyright, **11–273** design right, registered design, technical or commercial information or other intellectual property;

"related offence", in relation to any proceedings to which subsection (1) applies, means—

(a) in the case of proceedings within subsection (2)(*a*) or (*b*)—

    (i) any offence committed by or in the course of the infringement or passing off to which those proceedings relate; or

    (ii) any offence not within sub-paragraph (i) committed in connection with that infringement or passing off, being an offence involving fraud or dishonesty;

(b) in the case of proceedings within subsection (2)(*c*), any offence revealed by the facts on which the plaintiff relies in those proceedings;

"related penalty", in relation to any proceedings to which subsection (1) applies means—

(a) in the case of proceedings within subsection (2)(a) or (b), any penalty incurred in respect of anything done or omitted in connection with the infringement or passing off to which those proceedings relate;

(b) in the case of proceedings within subsection (2)(c), any penalty incurred in respect of any act or omission revealed by the facts on which the plaintiff relies in those proceedings.

CIVIL JURISDICTION & JUDGMENTS ACT 1982

25 Interim relief in England and Wales and Northern Ireland in the absence of substantive proceedings

(1) The High Court in England and Wales or Northern Ireland shall **11–274** have power to grant interim relief where—

(a) proceedings have been or are to be commenced in a *Contracting State* other than the United Kingdom or in a part of the United Kingdom other than that in which the High Court in question exercises jurisdiction; and

(b) they are or will be proceedings whose subject-matter is within the scope of the 1968 Convention as determined by Article 1 (whether or not *the Convention* has effect in relation to the proceedings).

(2) On an application for any interim relief under subsection (1) the court may refuse to grant that relief if, in the opinion of the court, the fact that the court has no jurisdiction apart from this section in relation to the subject-matter of the proceedings in question makes it inexpedient for the court to grant it.

11–275 (3) Her Majesty may by Order in Council extend the power to grant interim relief conferred by subsection (1) so as to make it exercisable in relation to proceedings of any of the following descriptions, namely—

(a) proceedings commenced or to be commenced otherwise than in a *Contracting State*;

(b) proceedings whose subject-matter is not within the scope of the 1968 Convention as determined by Article 1;

(c) arbitration proceedings.

(4) An Order in Council under subsection (3)—

(a) may confer power to grant only specified descriptions of interim relief;

(b) may make different provision for different classes of proceedings, for proceedings pending in different countries or courts outside the United Kingdom or in different parts of the United Kingdom, and for other different circumstances; and

(c) may impose conditions or restrictions on the exercise of any power conferred by the Order . . .

(7) In this section "interim relief", in relation to the High Court in England and Wales or Northern Ireland, means interim relief of any kind which that court has power to grant in proceedings relating to matters within its jurisdiction, other than—

(a) a warrant for the arrest of property; or

(b) provision for obtaining evidence.

11–276 **LOCK PLC v. BESWICK**

Chancery Division [1989] 1 W.L.R. 1268

HOFFMANN J.: "*The Anton Piller jurisdiction*

The growth in the *Anton Piller* jurisdiction, from the original invention of such orders in 1974 as the ultimate weapon against fraudulent copyright pirates, to their widespread use today has been described by Scott J. in *Columbia Picture Industries Inc. v. Robinson* [1987] Ch. 38. As Scott J. pointed out, they potentially involve serious inroads on principles which bulk large in rhetoric of English liberty, such as the presumption of innocence, the right not to be condemned unheard, protection against arbitrary searches and seizures, the sanctity of the home. My common experience of the evident surprise of counsel when I have refused applications leads me to indorse Scott J.'s observation, at 76:

> "the practice of the court has allowed the balance to swing much too far in favour of plaintiffs and that *Anton Piller* orders have been too readily granted and with insufficient safeguards for respondents."

"In the original *Anton Piller* case, *Anton Piller KG v. Manufacturing Processes Ltd* [1976] Ch. 55, 61, Lord Denning M.R. said:

> "It seems to me that such an order can be made by a judge ex parte, but it should only be made where it is essential that the plaintiff should have inspection so that justice can be done between the parties: and when, if the defendant were forewarned, there is a grave danger that vital evidence will be destroyed, that papers will be burnt or lost or hidden, or taken beyond the jurisdiction, and so the ends of justice be defeated: and when the inspection would be no real harm to the defendant or his case. . . . We are prepared, therefore, to sanction its continuance, but only in an extreme case where there is grave danger of property being smuggled away or of vital evidence being destroyed."

Ormrod L.J. said, at 62:   **11–277**

> "There are three essential pre-conditions for the making of such an order, in my judgment. First, there must be an extremely strong prima facie case. Secondly, the damage, potential or actual, must be very serious for the applicant. Thirdly, there must be clear evidence that the defendants have in their possession incriminating documents or things, and that there is a real possibility that they may destroy such material before any application inter partes can be made."

"These strict requirements were indorsed by the Court of Appeal in *Booker McConnell Plc. v. Plascow* [1985] R.P.C. 425, where Dillon L.J. referred to the passages from Lord Denning M.R. and Ormrod L.J., which I have cited, and commented, at p. 441:

> 'The phrase 'a real possibility' [used by Ormrod L.J.] is to be contrasted with the extravagant fears which seem to afflict all plaintiffs who have complaints of breach of confidence, breach of copyright or passing off. Where the production and delivery up of documents is in question, the courts have always proceeded, justifiably, on the basis that the overwhelming majority of people in this country will comply with the court's order, and that defendants will therefore comply with orders to, for example, produce and deliver up documents without it being necessary to empower the plaintiff's solicitors to search the defendant's premises.'

"*Anton Piller* orders are frequently sought in actions against former employees **11–278** who have joined competitors or started competing businesses of their own. I have learned to approach such applications with a certain initial scepticism.

There is a strong incentive for employers to launch a pre-emptive strike to crush the unhatched competition in the egg by causing severe strains on the financial and management resources of the defendants or even a withdrawal of their financial support. Whether the plaintiff has a good case or not, the execution of the *Anton Piller* order may leave the defendants without the will or the money to pursue the action to trial in order to enforce the cross-undertaking in damages.

"Some employers seem to regard competition from former employees as presumptive evidence of dishonesty. Many have great difficulty in understanding the distinction between genuine trade secrets and skill and knowledge which the employee may take away with him. In cases in which the plaintiff alleges misuse of trade secrets or confidential information concerning a manufacturing process, a lack of particularity about the precise nature of the trade secrets is usually a symptom of an attempt to prevent the employee from making legitimate use of the knowledge and skills gained in the plaintiff's service. That symptom is particularly evident in this case. Judges dealing with ex parte applications are usually also at a disadvantage in dealing with alleged confidential knowledge of technical processes described in technical language, such as the electric circuitry in this case. It may look like magic but turn out merely to embody a principle discovered by Faraday or Ampère.

11–279   "Even in cases in which the plaintiff has strong evidence that an employee has taken what is undoubtedly specific confidential information, such as a list of customers, the court must employ a graduated response. To borrow a useful concept from the jurisprudence of the European Community, there must be *proportionality* between the perceived threat to the plaintiff's rights and the remedy granted. The fact that there is overwhelming evidence that the defendant has behaved wrongfully in his commercial relationships does not necessarily justify an *Anton Piller* order. People whose commercial morality allows them to take a list of the customers with whom they were in contact while employed will not necessarily disobey an order of the court requiring them to deliver it up. Not everyone who is misusing confidential information will destroy documents in the face of a court order requiring him to preserve them.

"In many cases it will therefore be sufficient to make an order for delivery up of the plaintiff's documents to his solicitor or, in cases in which the documents belong to the defendant but may provide evidence against him, an order that he preserve the documents pending further order, or allow the plaintiff's solicitor to make copies. The more intrusive orders allowing searches of premises or vehicles require a careful balancing of, on the one hand, the plaintiff's right to recover his property or to preserve important evidence against, on the other hand, violation of the privacy of a defendant who has had no opportunity to put his side of the case. It is not merely that the defendant may be innocent. The making of an intrusive order ex parte even against a guilty defendant is contrary to normal principles of justice and can only be done when there is a paramount need to prevent a denial of justice to the plaintiff. The absolute extremity of the court's powers is to permit a search of a defendant's dwelling house, with the humiliation and family distress which that frequently involves . . .

Should the order have been made?

11–280   "I am conscious of the fact that I have had the benefit of adversarial argument and a much longer time to read the evidence than the judge in chambers had when he made the order. But I am bound to say that it did not in my view justify any form of ex parte relief, let alone an *Anton Piller* order. The evidence came nowhere near disclosing an 'extremely strong prima facie case' or 'clear evidence that the defendants [had] in their possession incriminating documents or things' or that there was a 'grave danger' or 'real possibility' that the defendants might destroy evidence. The lack of specificity in the plaintiff's affidavit was such that I have some doubt whether it could be said to have raised a triable issue. Furthermore, these defendants were no fly-by-night video pirates. They were former long service employees with families and mortgages, who had openly said that they were entering into competition and whom the plaintiff knew to be financed by highly respectable institutions.

"As for the searches of the private homes of Messrs. Dearman, Ives and Lock, including the seizure of Mr. Dearman's private diary and other papers relating to his industrial tribunal proceedings against the plaintiff, none of which have been subsequently relied on, I can only sympathise with the sense of outrage which they must have felt.

"Nor do I understand why it was necessary to make an order ex parte which **11–281** had the effect of allowing the plaintiff's employees to have immediate access to all of Safeline's confidential documents and prototypes. In the *Anton Piller* case, one of the conditions mentioned by Lord Denning M.R. for the grant of an order was that "inspection would do no real harm to the defendant or his case." [1976] Ch. 55, 61. Even if it was thought that the defendants were the kind of dishonest people who would conceal or destroy incriminating documents, it would surely have been sufficient at the ex parte stage to allow the plaintiff's solicitors to remove the documents and make copies for their own retention pending an application by the plaintiff inter partes for leave to inspect them. The defendants would then have had the opportunity to object or to ask for a restricted form of inspection, such as by independent expert only. I do not regard the right to apply to discharge the order as a sufficient protection for the defendants. The trauma of the execution of the *Anton Piller* order means that in practice it is often difficult to exercise until after substantial damage has been done.

Evidence obtained under the order

"The plaintiff says that whether or not its case was strong enough on the original **11–282** application, the material recovered when the order was executed amply justifies the order he made. I agree that in deciding whether the defendants have suffered injustice as a result of the order, I should not ignore evidence which the order itself has brought to light: *WEA Records Ltd v. Visions Channel 4 Ltd.* [1983] 1 W.L.R. 721. In my judgment, however, the material seized by the plaintiff improves its case very little and comes nowhere near demonstrating that the defendants were indeed the kind of dishonest people who would, but for the order, have destroyed incriminating documents . . .

The discharge order

I shall order that the *Anton Piller* order be discharged, that the defendants have leave to proceed to an inquiry before the master on the cross-undertaking in damages and that all copies retained by the plaintiff or its advisers of the documents, computer records and prototypes seized under the order be returned to the defendants."

Section 6. Specific Performance

Definition and general principles

11–283   A decree of specific[26] performance is an order[27] of the court[28] compelling the defendant[29] personally to do what he has promised to do.[30] While the common law allows a defendant to choose to be a "bad man" and break his contractual obligations and pay damages for the privilege, where equity intervenes it will compel a defendant to be a "good man" and fulfil his equitable obligations.[31] Compulsion may take various forms, *eg* empowering a person other than the defendant to execute a conveyance which the latter has promised but refused to execute,[32] or, more generally, committing the defendant to prison on account of his contempt[33] (*i.e.* disobedience to the order of the court) until he complies with the court order and purges his contempt.

11–284   Not all positive contractual stipulations or promises will be specifically enforced[34] and the purpose of this section is to examine the principles upon which the court's discretion will be exercised. It is nowadays refused only according to reasonably settled principles the most important of which are[35]: (i) lack of consideration; (ii) adequacy of common law

---

[26] Referring to the performance in kind (in Latin, *in specie*) of a contractual (or primary) obligation rather than the performance of the secondary obligation to pay damages for loss caused by breach of a primary obligation. Meagher, Gummow and Lehane's *Equity, Doctrines and Remedies* (3rd ed.) observes the technical distinction between specific performance *proper* (which applies only to executory contracts requiring something to be done such as the execution of a deed or conveyance) and specific performance of executed agreements (whereby the performance of *any* contractual obligation may be decreed): the principles applying to both are the same, but the distinction makes it easier to understand decisions such as *C.H. Giles & Co Ltd v. Morris* [1972] 1 W.L.R. 307 and *Posner v. Scott-Lewis* [1987] Ch. 25.

[27] *i.e.* a final order. An interim decree is not possible but see *Sky Petroleum Ltd v. VIP Petroleum Ltd* [1974] 1 W.L.R. 576 and *Hill v. C.A. Parsons & Co Ltd* [1972] Ch. 305, cases where injunctions amounting in substance to the specific performance of obligations were granted on an interlocutory (now "interim") basis.

[28] Both the High Court and the County Court have jurisdiction to grant specific performance and, whereas the County Court jurisdiction is limited in the case of contracts to sell or lease land to cases where the purchase price (or, in the case of leases, the value of the property) does not exceed the County Court limit, the County Court must give effect to every defence or counterclaim to which effect would be given in the High Court: County Courts Act 1984, s. 38. Even where a case falls outside the County Court's jurisdiction to *decree* specific performance, that court might still *declare* that a party would be entitled to such decree: *Rushton v. Smith* [1976] Q.B. 480.

[29] Specific performance does not lie against the Crown: (Crown Proceedings Act 1947, section 21 (1)(a)) but a declaration may be made as to the Crown's position.

[30] It is only available to enforce positive obligations. Negative ones must be enforced by injunction.

[31] See Sir Peter Millett in 1993 Restitution L.R. 7 at 19–20, developing the celebrated view of O.W. Holmes in *The Common Law* (1881) and in *The Path of the Law* (1897) 10 Harv. L.R. 457. The availability of specific performance enables "Equity to treat as done that which ought to be done" *e.g. Attorney-General for Hong Kong v. Reid* [1994] 1 A.C. 324.

[32] Supreme Court Act 1981, s. 39.

[33] Sequestration of assets until compliance is also available against both individuals and corporations and is the only way of proceeding against corporations for contempt, although their directors may, of course, be imprisoned. Fines may also be imposed. See, generally, R.S.C. Ord. 45 and Miller's *Contempt of Court* (2nd ed.), Chap. 14.

[34] It is important to keep distinct the notion of a contract's enforceability in general terms, whether at law (where it might be unenforceable, *e.g.* for mistake, uncertainty, illegality *etc.*) or in equity (likewise, *e.g.*, for mistake, undue influence, misrepresentation *etc.*) from its ability to be enforced specifically. The latter notion implies that there is no legal or equitable ground for avoiding the contract and that the claimant will not be confined to a remedy in damages. A non-specifically enforceable contract may nonetheless, therefore, be said to be enforceable.

[35] See generally Jones and Goodhart *Specific Performance* (1996).; Fry on *Specific Performance* (6th ed.); Spry's *Equitable Remedies* (4th ed.) Ch. 3; Sharpe's *Injunctions and Specific Performance* (1983), Part II and Meagher, Gummow and Lehane's *Equity, doctrines and remedies* (3rd ed.), Chaps. 20 and 36.

remedies, (iii) equity will not act in vain, (iv) illegality or public policy, (v) lack of mutuality of a sort irremediable by imposition of terms, (vi) that the contract is incapable of being enforced in its entirety, (vii) that the order could not be enforced without the constant supervision of the court, (viii) delay, (ix) lack of clean hands, (x) undue hardship, (xi) performance would involve the defendant in a breach of contract (or trust), (xii) set-off, (xiii) mistake and misrepresentation and (xiv) mis-description of subject-matter. These will be looked at in turn.

(i) Lack of consideration

Lack of consideration in fact prevents there being a contract at law at all **11–285** and, if so, there is nothing to perform,[36] *in specie* or otherwise. But the consideration provided by a deed, although sufficient at law, is insufficient in equity.[37] Yet, there is no equitable test of adequacy of consideration (it follows the law in that respect) and the provision of money or money's worth, however small the sum, suffices.[38] Likewise, past consideration will not support a suit in equity.[39]

(ii) Inadequacy of damages

The best way of illustrating how this principle operates in relation to the enforcement of positive contractual stipulations is to examine different categories of contracts. First, some that have been held to be specifically enforceable and then some that have been held not to be.

(a) contracts for the disposition of an interest in land

Each piece of real estate is regarded as unique and, therefore, damages **11–286** will be an inadequate remedy for a purchaser in the sense that damages will not enable him to buy a replacement in the market.[40] Although damages will, clearly, be an adequate remedy for a vendor (who wants only money), a decree will lie against a purchaser on grounds of mutuality.[41]

(b) Chattels of especial value

The Court of Chancery had always claimed jurisdiction to order the return of a specific chattel wrongly retained by another[42] (a quasi-

---

[36] A similar consideration requires that, for example, contracts for the sale or disposition of interests in land must comply with section 2 of the Law of Property (Miscellaneous Provisions) Act 1989 before specific performance may be ordered. Likewise contracts void at law for other reasons, *e.g.* mistake, illegality, and uncertainty.

[37] *Re Pryce* [1917] 1 Ch. 234 at 241 per Eve J. Mere covenantees are therefore volunteers in equity and can only enforce the covenant at law: *Cannon v. Hartley* [1949] Ch. 213. Children of a marriage are, in marriage settlement cases, treated in equity, however, as having provided consideration: *Re Pryce, ante; Re Kay's Settlement* [1939] Ch. 329 and may obtain specific performance.

[38] *Mountford v. Scott* [1975] Ch. 258. But cp. *Milroy v. Lord* (1862) 4 De G.F. & J. 264 and *Peffer v. Rigg* [1977] 1 W.L.R. 285.

[39] *Robertson v. St John* (1786) 2 Bro. C.C. 140

[40] *Hall v. Warren* (1804) 9 Ves. 605; *Adderley v. Dixon* (1824) 1 Sim. & St. 607. In *Verrall v. Great Yarmouth Borough Council* [1981] 1 Q.B. 202, the Court of Appeal affirmed the grant of specific performance to enforce a contractual licence to occupy premises. As no other premises could be found damages would have been an inadequate remedy, (the promisee being unable to hire any premises with any damages awarded).

[41] So the vendor can "thrust the property down the purchaser's throat", per Lindley LJ in *Hope v. Walter* [1900] 1 Ch. 257 at 258. But, on mutuality, see below, para. 11–290.

[42] *Pusey v. Pusey* (1684) 1 Vern. 273 (an ancient horn, reputedly a gift of Canute).

contractual rather than properly contractual claim) but, as rationalised by Lord Eldon,[43] its justification for so doing was that such chattels possessed a *pretium affectionis*[44] which could not be estimated in damages.[45] Extending that reasoning by one step in *Sky Petroleum Ltd v. VIP Petroleum Ltd,*[46] Goulding J. held that the court had jurisdiction to order specific performance of a contract to sell non-specific chattels in a case where the remedy of damages would be inadequate.

(c) Shares in a private limited company

11–287   There being no readily available market in such shares, in light of the restriction on the transferability of shares in private companies and of the criminal prohibition in section 81 of the Companies Act 1985,[47] damages will normally be an inadequate remedy.

(d) contracts for sale of personal property not within (b) or (c) above

Such contracts are not specifically enforceable so that, for example, contracts for the sale of shares in which there is a ready market, *i.e.* those of a quoted public company,[48] and, indeed, any other contract[49] for the disposition of personal property, tangible or intangible, will not be specifically enforced unless it can be shown in the instant case that damages would not be an adequate remedy.[50] A contract to leave personal or real property by will is not enforceable directly (which would interfere with freedom of testamentary power) but a legatee who

---

[43] *Nutbrown v. Thornton* (1804) 10 Ves. 160 at 163.

[44] Roughly, a "sentimental value".

[45] *Falcke v. Gray* (1859) 4 Dr. 651; *Thorn v. Commissioners of Public Works* (1863) 32 Beav. 490 (stones from Old Westminster Bridge); *Phillips v. Lamdin* [1949] 2 KB. 33 (ornate Adam door). Damages would clearly be an inadequate remedy if an award would not enable the promisee to go into the market place and purchase a similar chattel. By definition it could not do so in cases of this sort. Note also that section 52 of the Sale of Goods Act 1979 enables the court, additionally, to decree specific performance of contracts for the sale of "specific or ascertained goods", *i.e.* identified and agreed upon when the contract is made. Neither under the statutory nor equitable jurisdictions (both being discretionary) will specific performance be decreed of contracts for the sale of "ordinary articles of commerce", even though specific or ascertained goods within the Act, as damages would be an adequate remedy: *Cohen v. Roche* [1927] 1 K.B. 169, (set of Hepplewhite chairs); *Whiteley Ltd v. Hilt* [1918] 2 K.B. 808, at 819. Inadequacy of damages seems, therefore, to be the touchstone.

[46] [1974] 1 W.L.R. 576 (enforcement of obligation to supply petrol during petrol shortage, no alternative source available), para. 11–308.

[47] Prohibiting a private company (other than a company limited by guarantee and not having a share capital) from offering its securities to the public directly or indirectly.

[48] It seems whether a life interest under a settlement of such shares would be sufficiently unique to merit specific performance of a contract for its disposition.

[49] Note, however, that in the case of contracts to assign choses in action there is no need (save for the purpose of perfecting legal title) to obtain specific performance at all as an assignment for value operates without more as an assignment in equity on the principle that equity considers that done which ought to be done: per Lord Macnaghten in *Tailby v. Official Receiver* (1888) App. Cas. 523 at 547–548. The operation of that principle does not depend on the specific enforceability of the contract to assign.

[50] Additionally, a contract for the transfer of the goodwill of a business is too uncertain to enforce *in specie: Darbey v. Whitaker* (1857) 4 Drew. 134 (unless premises or other business assets are contracted to be transferred with it). This appears to be an example of a contract sufficiently certain at law but not specifically enforceable for lack of certainty, an odd conclusion save that, for specific performance to lie, the court must be able to supervise the exact performance of the contract (per Lord Hardwicke L.C. in *Buxton v. Lister* (1746) 3 Atk. 383 at 386. As imprisonment may result from non-compliance, this requirement is understandable.

receives it in breach will be ordered to yield it up[51] and, before death of the testator, the promisee can obtain a declaration of right and an injunction restraining any inconsistent disposition.[52]

(e) contracts for personal services

Contracts of employment, by statute,[53] are non-specifically enforceable. **11–288** The equitable approach is illustrated in *De Francesco v. Barnum*[54]: "The courts are bound to be jealous lest they should turn contracts of service into contracts of slavery", per Fry L.J. This approach applies to contracts *of* service not covered by the statute and any contract *for* personal services but there seems to be no hard and fast *rule*.[55]

(f) contracts to pay money

In *South African Territories Ltd v. Wallington*,[56] a contract to make a loan was not specifically enforced because damages would be an adequate remedy. In *Beswick v Beswick*[57] the contract was to pay an annuity to a third party. It was enforced because damages would have been an inadequate remedy in the sense that either (i) damages awarded to the promisee would have been nominal or (ii) a multiplicity of suits might need to be brought if there were future breaches or (iii) the worth of an annuity, depending on the longevity of the annuitant, might be too conjectural to quantify.[58] It remains doubtful whether a promisee could obtain specific performance of a promise to pay a lump sum to a third party: if he could, it would require an English court to uphold (i) as a sufficient reason for enforcing a promise *in specie* and, moreover, one which the promisee could not have enforced for his own benefit.[59]

(iii) Equity never acts in vain

Equity never acts in vain and, therefore, it will not decree performance **11–289** of the impossible or the futile. Therefore, a vendor of land who has

---

[51] *Synge v. Synge* [1894] 1 Q.B. 466 (on the ground that he is a volunteer and takes subject to the equity).
[52] *Schaefer v. Schumann* [1972] A.C. 572 (Privy Council).
[53] Trade Union and Labour Relations (Consolidation) Act 1992, section 236; "no court shall . . . by way of an order of specific performance . . . compel an employee to do any work or to attend at any place for the doing of any work."
[54] (1890) 45 Ch.D. 430. The authorities cited in *Fry on Specific Performance*, at 50–51 suggest that other (earlier) justifications were that equity would not act in vain and even the absence of a property right in the plaintiff.
[55] In *Giles (C.H.) & Co Ltd v. Morris* [1972] 1 W.L.R. 307, Megarry J. denied that there was a rule preventing enforcement: it was, rather, a question of looking at the particular obligations in question. In *Hill v. C.A. Parsons& Co Ltd* [1972] Ch. 305 the Court of Appeal by a majority enforced a contract for personal services in what were described as exceptional circumstances. See also *Lumley v. Wagner* (1852) 1 De G.M. & G. 604, a case where a singer was prevented by injunction from breaching her promise to sing only at the plaintiff's theatre, effectively thereby being forced to sing for the plaintiff.
[56] [1898] A.C. 309.
[57] [1968] A.C. 58.
[58] But query: actuaries and judges in personal injury cases do it routinely.
[59] Because in *that* case, damages clearly would be adequate. (Note that it is not to be thought that the question whether such promise be specifically enforceable is an academic one. A defendant is at risk of imprisonment for failure to comply with a decree of specific performance but cannot nowadays (since abolition of debtors' prison) be gaoled for inability to pay a civil debt.

wrongfully conveyed away the property will not be ordered to convey to a purchaser what he no longer has unless the transferee is, for example, a company controlled by the vendor and used as a crude device or sham to avoid specific performance.[60] Likewise, an agreement for a lease which has already expired will not be enforced,[61] nor an agreement for a partnership not being of fixed duration.[62] But *Verrall v. Great Yarmouth Borough Council*[63] makes clear that authorities from the last century on transient interests[64] are now suspect: an agreement to occupy premises for two days is, other things being equal, specifically enforceable.

(iv) Illegality and public policy

A contract which is illegal is void and there is nothing to enforce, specifically or otherwise. A contract which is valid but which, if executed, might achieve some goal contrary to public policy might not be enforced specifically. *Wroth v. Tyler*[65] provides a good example of this. In that case, a husband contracted to sell his property. After conclusion of the contract, his wife registered a charge against the property under the Matrimonial Homes Act 1967 which gave her the right (but no more than the right) not to be evicted. The vendor sought either specific performance or damages in lieu. Specific performance was refused on, amongst others, the ground that if it were ordered, the vendor would have to take the property subject to the wife's occupation. But he would be able to evict the husband and other members of the family. The splitting up of a family in that way would be an end contrary to public policy and the vendor would be awarded damages in lieu.

(v) Mutuality

11–290 It used to be said that specific performance will not be granted to a promisee who could not himself be the subject of a decree,[66] *i.e.* all the obligations imposed by the contract upon the plaintiff promisee must themselves be specifically enforceable. This is the traditional statement of the requirement of mutuality. Fry's statement of it, which required mutuality at the time of entering into the contract (rather than it sufficing at the date of the hearing) was rejected in *Price v. Strange.*[67]

---

[60] *Jones v. Lipman* [1962] 1 W.L.R. 832.
[61] *Turner v. Clowes* (1869) 20 L.T. 214 It might be otherwise if the lessee would derive some benefit by being granted legal rights under the lease, *Walters v. Northern Coal Mining Board Co* (1855) 5 De G.M. & G. 629.
[62] *Henry v. Birch* (1804) 9 Ves. 357: either partner might dissolve it at will.
[63] [1981] Q.B. 202 at 220. Contrast, *e.g. Glasse v. Woolgar and Roberts (No 2)* (1897) 41 Sol. Jo. 573: "It was almost ludicrous to ask for specific performance of a lease for a single day", per Lindley L.J.
[64] *e.g. Lavery v. Pursell* (1888) 39 Ch. D. 508 where, at 519, one reason for refusing specific performance of a contract for a one year lease was that it was not often possible to get a decree made within a year and therefore a decree would be in vain.
[65] [1974] Ch. 30.
[66] *Flight v. Bolland* (1828) 4 Russ. 298 (minor failing to obtain decree because, *qua* minor, suit could not be maintained against him).
[67] [1978] 1 Ch. 337.

Goff L.J.[68] stated "want of mutuality raises a question of the court's discretion to be exercised according to everything that has happened up to the decree" so that "the court will grant specific performance if it can be done without injustice or unfairness to the defendant" which may involve some payment to the defendant as in *Price v. Strange*.[69] Where injustice can be avoided by the imposition of terms on the plaintiff or an award of damages to the defendant, a decree may be made subject thereto. Indeed, since the decision in that case, there has been a steady academic and judicial retreat from the doctrine of mutuality as a coherent explanation for the outcome of older, decided cases or, indeed, as a sound objection as a matter of moral principle.[70] This is to be welcomed for it appears at times to have been used as a principle to justify the specific enforcement of certain types of contract (such as those for the disposition of land, when, quite plainly, damages would be an adequate remedy for a vendor[71]) and, capriciously, to deny the specific **11–291** enforceability of others. In other words, it was serving a dual role in the case law. The judicial retreat from it must now be almost complete in light of the decision of the High Court in *Rainbow Estates v. Tokenhold Ltd*.[72] A word of background explanation about this decision is necessary. A landlord's repairing covenant is enforceable by statute notwithstanding any equitable rule restricting the tenant's remedy "whether based on mutuality or otherwise".[73] This provision was enacted precisely because it was thought that repairing covenants were not specifically enforceable either because, the tenant's covenants not being so enforceable, the landlord's covenants could not be so for want of mutuality or, alternatively, because of the need for constant supervision. The court in this case, however, decided that neither of these reasons had been the *ratio* of any decided case and, there being no reason in principle why a tenant's repairing covenant should not be specifically enforced (so long as oppression was avoided and the work required to be done was sufficiently defined[74]), the court in an appropriate case would order specific performance of a tenant's repairing covenant. The qualifications in parentheses would mean, however, that appropriate cases were rare.

In any event, it appears that, so far as mutuality is a decisive doctrine in English law today, a defendant may disentitle himself by waiver to rely on lack of mutuality as a reason for refusing specific performance.[75]

---

[68] *ibid.* at 354. At 368–369 Buckley LJ. stated: "The court will not compel a defendant to perform his obligations specifically if it cannot at the same time ensure that any unperformed obligations of the plaintiff will be specifically performed unless, perhaps, damages would be an adequate remedy to the defendant for any default on the plaintiff's part."

[69] *ibid.* p357.

[70] For a summary of the academic attack, see Jones & Goodhart, *op. cit.*, at 38 *et seq.*

[71] But, as may be seen from para. 11–286, he is said to be entitled to specific performance on the ground of mutuality.

[72] [1999] Ch 64 (Mr Lawrence Collins Q.C, sitting as a deputy judge of the Chancery Division), noted P. Luxton [1998] J.B.L. 564.

[73] Landlord and Tenant Act 1985, section 17.

[74] On this last requirement para. 11–294.

[75] *Price v. Strange, supra; Halkett v. Dudley* [1907] 1 Ch. 590.

(vi) Entire contracts only

11–292   That the contract sought to be enforced *in specie* should be capable of being enforced in its entirety[76] is an old rule[77] but one which may now be more flexible. In *CH Giles & Co Ltd v. Morris*,[78] a case where specific performance was sought of a contract for the sale of shares, one of the terms of which required the vendors to procure the appointment of a particular individual as managing director of the company, Megarry J. said "the court may refuse to let the disadvantages and difficulties of specifically enforcing the obligation to perform personal services outweigh the suitability of the rest of the contract for specific performance . . .".[79] Where the contract can properly be construed as two distinct contracts, specific performance may be obtained to enforce one of them.[80]

(vii) The need for constant supervision

11–293   There is authority to the effect that breach of a contract which would need constant supervision by the court if it were to be performed *in specie* will only sound in damages.[81] In *Posner v. Scott-Lewis*,[82] however, Mervyn Davies J. at a tenant's request and on facts difficult to distinguish from *Ryan v. Mutual Tontine Westminster Chambers Association*,[83] made an order against the landlord for the appointment of a resident porter whom the landlord had covenanted to employ for the purpose of carrying out certain duties at a block of flats: he found that there was a sufficient definition of what had to be done in order to comply with the order of the court. The more recent and important case of *Co-operative Insurance Society Ltd. v. Argyll Stores (Holdings) Ltd*[84] provided the House of Lords with the opportunity to review and reconcile the authorities clustered around this principle. In that case the tenant (owners of *Safeway* supermarkets) had given a covenant to keep the demised premises open for retail trade during normal business hours. The tenant was the anchor-tenant in a new shopping mall in Hillsborough but had made a decision, based on national performance, to close all of its loss-making stores of which the demised premises were

---

[76] Distinguish this requirement, which stresses the need for all of the *defendant's* obligations to be enforceable from the requirement of mutuality which focuses on the (alleged) need for all the *claimant's* obligations to be enforceable against him.

[77] *Ogden v. Fossick* (1862) 4 De G.F. & J. 426.

[78] [1972] 1 W.L.R. 307.

[79] *ibid.* at p. 317–318.

[80] *e.g., Lewin v. Guest* (1826) 1 Russ. 325 (Separate contracts to purchase two plots; purchaser obliged to take one plot even though vendor could not show title to other). It would be otherwise where, *e.g.*, a vendor knew that from purchaser's point of view the purchases were interdependent: *Poole v. Shergold* (1786) 1 Cox Eq. Cas. 273.

[81] *Ryan v. Mutual Tontine Westminster Chambers Association* [1893] 1 Ch. 116 (lessor's covenant to provide resident porter who would always be in attendance at block of flats). See also *Dowty Boulton Paul Ltd v. Wolverhampton Corporation* [1971] 2 All E.R. 277 (mandatory injunction refused to enforce covenant to maintain aerodrome for period of over 60 years: same principle applied)

[82] [1987] Ch. 25.

[83] *supra.* n. 81.

[84] [1998] A.C. 1, below, at para 11–335.

one. The tenant was content to pay damages for breach but resisted an order for specific performance. The Court of Appeal, by a majority, granted a decree[85] which the House of Lords discharged. Lord Hoffmann, giving the only speech with which all other members of the Committee agreed, approved a long line of authority to the effect that **11–294** the court will not order anyone to run a business. He examined the normal reason for this: the need for constant supervision. In *C.H. Giles & Co. v. Morris* Megarry J.[86] had suggested that difficulties of supervision were "a narrow consideration": performance would normally be secured by the defendant's realisation that he is liable to contempt for failure to obey the order and, therefore, there would in practice be little need for the court to "supervise". This kind of consideration had been relied on by the Court of Appeal to justify its order. The House, however, distinguished between orders to carry on an activity, such as running a business over time, and orders requiring a defendant merely to achieve a result. In the former case, the risk of repeated, expensive and cumbersome applications to the court for guidance is much higher than in the latter: even if the result which the court has ordained that the defendant shall bring about is a complex thing (such as erecting a building in accordance with complex plans) the court will still only have to rule once, after the fact, to say whether or not there has been compliance. If a defendant, on the other hand, were ordered to run a retail grocery business during ordinary business hours, there might be innumerable applications. It was with this distinction in mind, said Lord Hoffmann, that courts had in the past ordered the specific performance of repairing covenants and building contracts. What the courts had been prepared to do in those cases (of orders to achieve a result) was not to be confused with the approach to orders to carry on an activity. That was where the majority in the Court of Appeal had fallen into error.

(viii) delay or laches

There being no statutory limit on the time after which a claim for **11–295** specific performance may be brought[87] equitable considerations govern and may deprive a claimant of the right to performance *in specie* where there is delay either sufficient to be evidence of the plaintiff's abandonment of the contract[88] or coupled with circumstances which make it unjust to order specific performance.[89]

(ix) lack of clean hands

If the claimant is guilty of some impropriety connected to the contract[90] ("reprehensible", "unfair" or "tricky" conduct being required) he may

---

[85] [1996] 3 W.L.R. 27 (Millett L.J. forcefully dissenting).

[86] [1972] 1 W.L.R. 307.

[87] Limitation Act 1980, section 36. Nor do the Limitation Acts apply by analogy: *Talmash v. Mugleston* (1826) 4 LJOS Ch. 200.

[88] *Parkin v. Thorold* (1852) 16 Beav. 59 at 73. The plaintiff will still have his legal remedy.

[89] *Lindsay Petroleum Co v. Hurd* (1874) L.R. 5 P.C. 221. Where the plaintiff took possession and waited 10 years before seeking a decree to have the legal title vested in him, mere delay with no injustice to the defendant was no bar: *Williams v. Greatrex* [1957 1 W.L.R. 31.

[90] *van Gestel v. Cann, The Times*, August 7, 1987 (claim that plaintiff guilty of fraud unconnected with contract of no assistance to defendant).

be disentitled to an equitable remedy. The jurisdiction of the court to consider this matter cannot be ousted by agreement.[91] However, this last point was decided in a case where a clause in a sale agreement, which provided that the consideration was to be paid in cash "free from any equity cross-claim set-off or other deduction whatsoever", was held not to prevent the purchaser from raising an unclean hands defence. This was for the reason that the wording was not apt to exclude such a claim but alternatively for the reason that, even if it had been apt, "it could not have the effect of fettering the discretion of the court. Once the court is asked for the equitable remedy of specific performance, its discretion cannot be fettered".[92] Although defensible on its own, this decision does not sit easily with the long-established practice[93] of parties contracting that a particular obligation, if breached, shall "sound only in damages". This is just as much an attempt to oust the discretionary jurisdiction of the court to award a specific remedy. Perhaps all that can be said about it is that it is not, all other things being equal, an objectionable one.

(x) Undue hardship

11–296 Specific performance may be refused if hardship will be caused to either of the parties or a third party.[94] The decisions in individual cases tend to turn on the facts (see, for an example, *Wroth v. Tyler*).[95] Although there is commonwealth authority requiring the hardship to have existed at the date of contract,[96] in England it has been held that specific performance could be refused on the ground of hardship arising after contract.[97] and *Wroth v. Tyler, infra* para 11–315, is an example thereof.

(xi) Breach of contract

It is a well-established principle that the court will not grant a decree if compliance with it would involve the defendant in breach of a prior contract (or, indeed, trust).[98]

(xii) Set-off

In *BICC Plc. v. Burndy Corpn.*[99] the Court of Appeal accepted by a majority that a right of equitable set-off (where a defendant seeks to

---

[91] *Quadrant Visual Communications Ltd v. Hutchison Telephone (U.K. Ltd* [1993] B.C.L.C. 442. See, generally, Snell's *Equity* (29th ed.) at 30 *et seq.*; 611 *et seq.*

[92] [1993] B.C.L.C. 442 at 451.

[93] Endorsed by the Court of Appeal in *Co-operative Insurance Society Ltd. v. Argyll Stores (Holdings) Ltd, supra* and not criticised on this point by the House of Lords.

[94] *Thomas v. Dering* (1837) 1 Keen 729 at 747–748.

[95] [1974] Ch. 30, para. 11–289. Other situations, *e.g.* include: trustee vendors, contractually obliged to discharge personally incumbrances on property, relieved from so doing as purchase price insufficient to cover secured amounts (*Wedgwood v. Adams* (1843) 6 Beav. 600); purchaser not obliged to take property which had no right of access, so no possibility of enjoyment (*Denne v. Light* (1857) 8 De G.M. & G. 774

[96] *e.g. Nicholas v. Ingram* [1958] N.Z.L.R. 972.

[97] *Patel v. Ali* [1984] Ch 283 at 288 (husband and wife vendors; husband bankrupted, causing delay; wife seriously ill; young children; wife dependent on proximity of relatives so moving difficult).

[98] *Harvela Investments Ltd. v. Royal Trust Co. of Canada Ltd.* [1985] Ch. 103 at 122, per Peter Gibson J.

[99] [1985] Ch. 232.

defend a claim on the basis that the plaintiff is liable, under a related cross-claim, to him in a sum equal to or greater than the claim made by the plaintiff) could stand as a complete defence to a claim by a plaintiff not merely for a debt but also for specific performance.

(xiii) Mistake and misrepresentation

A contract which is not avoidable in equity for mistake or misrepresenta- **11–297** tion might sound only in damages if, owing to misrepresentation or (even unilateral) mistake, performance *in specie* would involve real hardship for the defendant amounting to injustice.[1]

(xiv) misdescription of subject-matter[2]

Although the authorities on this relate to sales of land the principles ought to apply to contracts for the disposition of personalty which are otherwise specifically enforceable. A misdescription *in the contract* will amount to a breach because the vendor cannot then convey what he has contracted to convey. Quite apart from the common law rules determining the rights of an innocent party equity developed the following rules[3] to deal specifically with this kind of breach when a question arose, assuming the contract was not discharged at law, whether it should be performed *in specie*.

If the misdesription is substantial (so that the purchaser does not get what he wanted (*i.e.* but for the misdescription it is reasonable to suppose he would never have contracted at all[4]), the vendor cannot enforce either at law or in equity even with abatement of price.

If insubstantial, the vendor can enforce though with abatement of **11–298** price by way of compensation.[5]

Whether substantial or not, the *purchaser* can enforce and take whatever the vendor has *and* secure an abatement.[6]

Effect of decree

If a decree is granted, the contract is not merged in the judgment of the court but still exists so that, if the decree is or cannot be complied with, the claimant may return to court,[7] seek dissolution of the decree and obtain an award of common law damages.[8]

---

[1] *Tamplin v. James* (1880) 15 Ch. D. 215 (land correctly described in plans, not consulted by purchaser; purchaser obliged to buy despite unilateral error in thinking adjacent land included. No injustice.) Contrast *Denny v. Hancock* (1870) 6 Ch. App. 1 (similar error was caused by vendor's unsatisfactory plans: no decree). See also *Riverlate Properties v. Paul* [1975] Ch. 133.

[2] See, for a summary, Farrand's *Contract & Conveyance* (4th ed.) at 52–55.

[3] Applicable to open contracts. In practice, parties to contracts for the sale of land use Standard Conditions which moderate the position. These, however, are subject to the Unfair Contract Terms Act 1977 and to a judicial reluctance to allow parties to escape their equitable duties, *qv Rignall Developments Ltd v. Halil* [1988] Ch. 190. See also, for a discussion of the applicability to contracts relating to dealings in land of European Community Directive 93/13, O.J. L95/29, 21.4. 1993, Bright & Bright, *Unfair Terms in Land Contracts: Copy Out or Cop Out?* (1995) 11 L.Q.R. 655.

[4] *Flight v. Booth* (1834) 1 Bing. N.C. 370.

[5] *Jacobs v. Revell* [1900] 2 Ch. 858.

[6] *Rutherford v. Acton-Adams* [1915] A.C. 866 at p. 870.

[7] In fact, he *must* return to court if he does not want to follow through with the decree: *GKN Distributors Ltd v. Tyne Tees Fabrication Ltd* (1985) 50 P.&CR. 403. (sale to another purchaser); *Singh v. Nazeer* [1979] Ch. 474.

[8] *Johnson v. Agnew* [1980] A.C. 367.

Damages in addition to or in lieu of injunction and specific performance

11–299   Section 50 of the Supreme Court Act 1981[9] provides:

> Where the Court of Appeal or the High Court has jurisdiction to entertain an application for an injunction or specific performance, it may award damages in addition to, or in substitution for, an injunction or specific performance.

This provision embodies and confers upon the named courts the jurisdiction that was conferred upon the Court of Chancery by section 2 of the Chancery Amendment Act 1858 (Lord Cairn's Act) which was later repealed.[10] The recent decision of the Court of Appeal in *Jaggard v. Sawyer*,[11] has provided the occasion for a comprehensive review of existing judicial authority on the jurisdiction so far as it relates to damages in lieu of injunctions. It has also provided some material on which to make some interesting observations about how the section might apply to awards of damages in substitution for specific performance. It is convenient, however, to take injunctions first.

11–300   Lord Cairn's Act enabled the Court of Chancery (i) to award damages (previously only awardable in common law courts) for *past* unlawful conduct "in addition to" awarding injunctions to restrain *future* unlawful conduct and (ii) to award damages "in substitution for" the grant of an injunction to restrain future unlawful conduct. Authoritative guidance on the exercise of the discretion in (ii) had been given by A.L. Smith L.J. in *Shelfer v. City of London Electric Lighting Co*[12] in the form of four conditions that required, as a working rule, to be met: the injury to the claimant's rights had to be small, capable of being estimated in money, and adequately compensable by a small sum; it must also be oppressive to the defendant to grant the injunction. Despite judicial zeal not to allow a wrong-doer merely to purchase the right to engage in wrongful activity, the net effect of an award of damages under (ii) is to allow a wrong-doer to engage lawfully in conduct that infringed a plaintiff's legal or other right. This is because, per Sir Thomas Bingham M.R., "a succession of future actions based on that conduct would, if brought, be dismissed or struck out, since a plaintiff could not complain of that for which he had already been compensated"[13] or, per Millett L.J., "the doctrine of res judicata operates to prevent the plaintiff and his successors from bringing proceedings thereafter to recover even nominal damages in respect of further wrongs for which the plaintiff has already been fully compensated."[14] In addition, damages are awardable under

---

[9] See generally Jolowicz, *Damages in Equity—A Study of Lord Cairn's Act*, [1975] C.L.J. 224.
[10] The wording of the section is set out in the judgment of Sir Thomas Bingham M.R in *Jaggard v. Sawyer*, [1995] 1 W.L.R. 269. See also, now, the decision of the Court of Appeal in *Gafford v. Graham, The Times* May 1, 1998, discussed in para. 11–193.
[11] [1995] 1 W. L. R. 269.
[12] [1895] 1 Ch. 287, 322–323.
[13] [1995] 1 W.L.R. 269, 280–281.
[14] *ibid.* at 286.

(ii) if injunctive relief is refused on the grounds of delay, acquiescence etc. A.L. Smith L.J.'s "working rule" was, after all, no more than a crystallisation of the perceived practice of the courts of equity which, in the last analysis, awarded remedies according to the justice of the case.

On the measure of damages to be awarded in lieu, despite the *dicta* of **11–301** Lord Wilberforce in *Johnson v. Agnew*[15] to the effect that there could be no difference between the bases of assessment at common law and in equity, *Jaggard v. Sawyer* makes clear that as regards injunctions, Lord Wilberforce cannot be taken to have intended to deny that some awards of damages under Lord Cairn's Act compensate for *future* wrongs— wrongs, therefore, not compensable at law. It is submitted, with respect, that the view of Millett L.J. to the effect that "Lord Wilberforce's statement . . . must be taken to be limited to the case where [the damages] are recoverable in respect of the same cause of action"[16] is clearly correct in principle. This view, moreover, may have consequences even for contractual cases where the duty breached, as in *Beswick v. Beswick*[17] is an on-going one so that, should specific performance be refused on some discretionary ground, an award of damages in lieu could properly be assessed, indeed, would *require* to be assessed, on a basis other than that adopted by courts of common law. This is a convenient moment at which to turn to damages in lieu of specific performance.

The extent of the jurisdiction, preserved by section 50 of the Supreme **11–302** Court Act 1981 is a matter of some doubt. It is clear that, in order for there to arise a power to award damages in lieu of specific performance, there must have been *jurisdiction* to order specific performance (even if, as a matter of discretion it was likely to be refused) as at the date of the writ.[18] But which of the grounds for refusing a decree go to jurisdiction and which to discretion? Ultimately the matter is one of statutory construction. It is here suggested that the first seven grounds covered in this section ought to be seen as going to jurisdiction but the remainder only to discretion. This suggestion is put forward without any appeal to authority but principle enough can be advanced to defend it: it is impossible to enforce a promise made without consideration, unnecess- ary to grant a remedy where the common law remedy is adequate, pointless or impossible to act in vain, obnoxious to act contrary to public policy (and so on). Matters such as delay, hardship, mistake (and so on) can fairly be characterised as grounds on which, if appropriate, to exercise some grace but nothing more.

There is authority for the view that no damages can be awarded unless specific performance is claimed[19] but that must be read subject to the *dicta* of Millett L.J. in *Jaggard v. Sawyer*[20] which, in relation to injunc- tions, dissent from that view: if a claimant omitted to claim an injunction

---

[15] [1980] A.C. 367, 400.
[16] [1995] 1 W.L.R. 269, 291.
[17] [1968] A.C. 58.
[18] *Jaggard v. Sawyer* [1995] 1 W.L.R. 269, at 284–285.
[19] *Horsler v. Zorro* [1975] Ch. 302.
[20] *supra*, at 289–290.

because, realistically, it would not be granted, the jurisdiction to award damages in lieu still existed. As a matter of principle, that ought to apply to specific performance.

11–303 Note that the jurisdiction also allows damages *in addition* to specific performance. The purpose of this provision in relation to injunctions has already been explained[21] but in the present context, they might be awarded where, exceptionally, only part of a contract is specifically enforced the claimant being awarded damages for the defendant's failure to perform the rest.[22]

As to measure of damages, Lord Wilberforce in *Johnson v. Agnew*[23] rejected the view that damages could be assessed on different bases under the Act and at common law. Megarry J., in *Wroth v. Tyler*[24] had said that the purpose of an award was to offer a true substitute for specific performance—which could only be refused at trial. That date, rather than the date of breach, might be the relevant one, therefore, in assessing compensation. This view is, with respect, clearly right, and is reconcilable with Lord Wilberforce's view. The common law rule did not invariably select the date of breach as the relevant one in determining loss: that was merely the *normal* rule in commercial contracts. But as it is always reasonable to seek specific performance of a contract for the sale of land[25] any increase in loss caused by denial of the relief at trial (so late in the day) ought, as a matter of justice, to be taken into account because "if to follow [the normal rule] would give rise to injustice, the court has power to fix such other date as may be appropriate in the circumstances."[26] Millett LJ's view in *Jaggard v. Sawyer*[27] arguing against, so far as injunctions are concerned, the abstraction of Lord Wilberforce's view from its context must, by its nature, apply across the board: it is impossible to see why, if Mrs Beswick had been refused a decree of specific performance merely on the ground of hardship to the defendant, she should not have been awarded substantial damages in lieu. It clearly would not be a true substitute for specific performance (an adequate remedy) to award her nominal damages which according to the reasoning in the case would be an inadequate remedy. It should be no objection that Peter Beswick's estate would thus get substantial damages

11–304 for loss in reality suffered by another if the estate was in principle held entitled to specific performance. On the question whether the estate would be obliged to hand the damages over to Mrs Beswick personally, one would have to resolve the conflict between the principles (a) that, as a matter of law, it would have no duty so to do and, in equity,[28] Mrs

---

[21] See para. 11–195 and *Jaggard v. Sawyer, supra*, at 284–286.

[22] *e.g. Soames v. Edge* (1860) John 669 (agreement to build house and lease to plaintiff: damages for failure to build, decree that lease of land be executed).

[23] [1980] A.C. 367.

[24] [1974] Ch. 30.

[25] Except, perhaps, if one knows or ought to know that one's own hands are unclean.

[26] per Lord Wilberforce at 401. Note also Millett L.J.'s explanation, in *Jaggard v. Sawyer, supra*, at 290–291, of Lord Wilberforce's view as it affects injunction cases concerned with the prevention of future wrongs.

[27] *supra*.

[28] paras 4–17, 4–84.

Beswick is a volunteer, and (b) the view of Lord Pearce[29] who saw "no objection in principle to the estate enforcing the judgment, receiving the fruits on behalf of the widow and paying them over to the widow, *just as a bailee does when he recovers damages which should properly belong to the true owner of the goods*" (emphasis supplied), which is tantamount to recognising (through, presumably, a constructive trust) a proprietary interest in a volunteer in rather special circumstances. It should be noted, of course, that by reason of the Contract (Rights of Third Parties) Act 1999, applying to all contracts entered into after May 11, 2000, a claim like Mrs Beswick's personal claim might well now succeed. However, section 5 makes an oblique reference to the situation contemplated here: it provides that where a promisee has recovered in respect of a third party's loss, then, in any proceedings by the third party, the court shall reduce the award to the third party accordingly. The draftsman (and thus Parliament) seems to have assumed in this case that the promisee, contrary to the argument advanced here, might be able to resist either a personal or proprietary claim by the third party to receive any damages awarded to the promisee in respect of the third party's loss. Still, what Parliament *assumes* to be law is not itself law: only the *enactments* of the Queen in Parliament are recognised as law and the argument advanced in this paragraph must stand or fall independently of any assumption thought to underlie the Act[30]

ADDERLEY V. DIXON

High Court of Chancery (1824) 1 Sim. & St. 607

The plaintiffs took assignments of certain debts which had been proven in the estates of two bankrupts. This entitled them to whatever dividend might be declared on the debts in the bankruptcy. The plaintiffs then contracted to sell their rights under the assignments for 2 shillings and sixpence in the pound to the defendant. The plaintiffs sought specific performance of the purchaser's obligation to pay the price.

11–305

SIR JOHN LEACH V.-C.: "Courts of Equity decree the specific performance of contracts not upon any distinction between realty and personalty, but because damages at law may not in the particular case, afford a complete remedy. Thus a Court of Equity decrees performance of a contract for land, not because of the real nature of the land, but because damages at law, which must be calculated upon the general money value of land, may not be a complete remedy to the purchaser, to whom the land may have a peculiar and special value. So a Court of Equity will not, generally, decree performance of a contract for the sale of stock or goods, not because of their personal nature, but because damages at law, calculated upon the market price of the stock or goods, are as complete a remedy to the purchaser as the delivery of the stock or goods contracted for; inasmuch as, with the damages, he may purchase the same quantity of the like stock or goods.

---

[29] *Beswick v. Beswick*, [1968] A.C. 58, 92; further see Lord Upjohn on enforcement rights *ibid.* at 100.
[30] There is further support for the argument that the damages would be held on constructive trust from *Hunt v. Severs* [1994] 2 A.C. 350 (tort claimant holding damages on trust for carer).

11–306 "In *Taylor v. Neville*, cited in *Buxton v. Lister* (1746) 3 Atk 383 at 384), specific performance was decreed of a contract for sale of 800 tons of iron, to be delivered and paid for in a certain number of years and by instalments; and the reason given by Lord Hardwicke is that such sort of contracts differ from those that are immediately to be executed and they do differ in this respect, that the profit upon the contract, being to depend upon future events, cannot be correctly estimated in damages where the calculation must proceed upon conjecture. In such a case, to compel a party to accept damages for the non-performance of his contract, is to compel him to sell the actual profit which may arise from it, at a conjectural price. In *Ball v. Coggs* (1710) 1 Bro. P.C. 140, specific performance was decreed in the House of Lords of a contract to pay the plaintiff a certain annual sum for his life, and also a certain other sum for every hundred weight of brass wire manufactured by the defendant during the life of the plaintiff. The same principle is to be applied to this case. Damages might be no complete remedy, being to be calculated merely by conjecture; and to compel the plaintiff in such a case to take damages would be to compel him to sell the annual provision during his life for which he had contracted at a conjectural price. In *Buxton v. Lister* Lord Hardwicke puts the case of a ship carpenter purchasing timber which was peculiarly convenient to him by reason of its vicinity; and also the case of an owner of land covered with timber contracting to sell his timber in order to clear his land; and assumes that as, in both those cases, damages would not, by reason of the special circumstances, be a complete remedy, equity would decree specific performance.

11–307 "The present case being a contract for the sale of the uncertain dividends which may become payable from the estates of the two bankrupts, it appears to me that, upon the principle established by the cases of *Ball v. Coggs* and *Taylor v. Neville*, a Court of Equity will decree specific performance, because damages at law cannot accurately represent the value of the future dividends; and to compel this purchaser to take such damages would be to compel him to sell these dividends at a conjectural price.

It is true that the present bill is not filed by the purchaser, but by the vendor, who seeks, not the uncertain dividends, but the certain sum to be paid for them. It has, however, been settled, by repeated decision, that the remedy in equity must be mutual; and that, where a bill will lie for the purchaser, it will also lie for the vendor."

SKY PETROLEUM LTD V. VIP PETROLEUM LTD

11–308 Chancery Division [1974] 1 W.L.R. 576;

The plaintiffs had contracted to purchase all their petrol, at fixed prices, from the defendants. During a petrol shortage the defendants purported to terminate the contract on the ground of breach of certain credit provisions therein by the plaintiffs. Pending trial of that issue, the plaintiffs sought an injunction to restrain the defendants from witholding supplies.

11–309 "Goulding J.: "What I have to decide is whether any injunction should be granted to protect the plaintiffs in the meantime. There is trade evidence that the plaintiffs have no great prospect of finding any alternative source of supply for the filling stations which constitute their business. The defendants have indicated their willingness to continue to supply the plaintiffs, but only at prices which, according to the plaintiffs' evidence, would not be serious prices from a commercial point of view. There is, in my judgment, so far as I can make out on the evidence before me, a serious danger that unless the court interferes at this stage the plaintiffs will be forced out of business. In those circumstances, unless there is some specific reason which debars me from doing so, I should be disposed to grant an injunction to restore the former position under the contract until the rights and wrongs of the parties can be fully tried out. The most serious hurdle in the way of the plaintiffs is the well known doctrine that the court refuses specific performance of a contract to sell and purchase chattels not specific or ascertained. That is a well-established and salutary rule, and I am entirely unconvinced by Mr. Christie, for the plaintiffs, when he tells me that an injunction in the form sought by him would not be specific enforcement at all. The matter is one of substance and not of form, and it is, in my judgment quite plain that I am, for the time being, specifically enforcing the contract if I grant an injunction. However, the ratio behind the rule is, as I believe, that under the ordinary contract for the sale of non-specific goods, damages are a sufficient remedy. That, to my mind, is lacking in the circumstances of the present case. The evidence suggests, and indeed it is common knowledge that the petroleum market is in an unusual state in which a would-be buyer cannot go out into the market and contract with another seller, possibly at some sacrifice as to price. Here, the defendants appear for practical purposes to be the plaintiffs' sole means of keeping their business going, and I am prepared so far to depart from the general rule as to try to preserve the position under the contract until a later date. I therefore propose to grant an injunction."

BESWICK V. BESWICK

House of Lords [1968] A.C. 58 [1967] 2 All E.R. 1197 (Lords Pearce, Upjohn, **11–310** Reid, Hodson and Guest).

Peter Beswick agreed with his nephew to transfer to him his business in consideration of the nephew's (a) employing Peter as a consultant for life and (b) paying thereafter to Peter's widow an annuity at the rate of £5 per week for life. Peter died and the nephew refused to make any payments to the widow but the first. She sued for specific performance in her capacity as administratix of Peter's estate and in her personal capacity. The House unanimously rejected her personal claim as a *ius quaesitum tertio* but allowed her representative claim.

LORD UPJOHN: "As it is necessary to keep clear and distinct the right of the widow as administratix of her husband and personally, I think it will be convenient to use letters: letter A represents the deceased and A1 the widow, as personal representative. B the widow in her personal capacity and C the appellant. And in other examples I shall give, these letters will serve the same purpose.

"Much is common ground between the parties: (1) B was not a party to the agreement: (2) A did not enter into the agreement as trustee for B in relation to the annuity to be paid to her; (3) A1 stands for all relevant purposes in the shoes of A and is entitled to sue C for breach of his admitted repudiation of the agreement (see paragraph 5 of the defence), but the parties differ fundamentally as to the remedy to which A1 is entitled in such an action . . .

"Leaving section 56 out of account, there was no real dispute between the **11–311** parties as to their respective rights (as distinct from remedies) under the agreement. (a) B has no rights thereunder. But it was clear from the whole tenor of the agreement that the annuity was to be paid to her for her own beneficial enjoyment, so if C paid it to her she could keep it and did not hold it as a constructive trustee for A1; (b) C would completely perform his obligation under the contract by continuing to pay the annuity to B during her life. Neither A nor A1 could compel C to pay it to A or A1, but (c) A or A1 and C could, if they pleased, agree to modify, compromise or even discharge further performance of the contract by C, and B would have no right to complain. If authority be wanted for these fundamental propositions, it is to be found in *Re Schebsman* and *Re Stapleton-Bretherton*.

"But when A dies and his rights pass to A1, it is said that the remedy of specific performance is no longer appropriate against C. The argument was first that the estate of A suffered no damage by reason of C's failure to pay B, so A1 is entitled to nominal damages but as she is not otherwise interested in the agreement as such it would be wrong to grant specific performance; for that remedy is available only where damages will be an inadequate remedy. Here nominal damages are adequate. Further, it was argued, to do so would really be to confer upon B a right which she does not have in law or equity to receive the annuity. Then, secondly, it was said that if the remedy of specific performance is granted it might prejudice creditors of A so that the parties ought to be left to their strict rights at law. Thirdly, it is said that there are procedural difficulties in the way of enforcing an order for specific performance in favour of a third party. I will deal with these points, though in reverse order.

11–312   "As to procedural difficulties, I fear I do not understand the argument. The point if valid applies to an action for specific performance by A just as much as by A1 yet in the authorities I have quoted no such point was ever taken; in *Drimmie v. Davies* indeed the action was by executors. Further, it seems to me that if C fails to obey a four-day order obtained by A1, B could enforce it under the clear and express provisions of R.S.C. Ord. 45. r. 9 (formerly Ord. 42. r. 26). Alternatively A1 could move for and obtain the appointment of a receiver of the business upon which the annuity is charged and the receiver would then be directed by the Court to pay the annuity to B out of the profits of the business. Finally, A1 could issue a writ of fi. fa. under Ord. 45, r. 1, but as A1 would then be enforcing the contract and not modifying or compromising it the court would obviously in executing its order compel her to carry out the contract in toto and hand the proceeds of execution to B. This point is entirely without substance.

"Then as to the second point. Let me assume (contrary to the fact) that A died with substantial assets but also many creditors. The legal position is that prima facie the duty of A1 is to carry out her intestate's contracts and compel C to pay B; but the creditors may be pressing and the agreement may be considered onerous; so it may be her duty to try and compromise the agreement with C and save something for the estate even at the expense of B. See *Ahmed Angullia v. Estate & Trust Agencies* (1927) *Ltd. per* Lord Romer. So be it, but how can C conceivably rely upon this circumstance as a defence by him to an action for specific performance by A1? Of course not; he, C, has no interest in the estate; he cannot plead a possible jus tertii which is no concern of his. It is his duty to fulfil his contract by paying C. A1 alone is concerned with the creditors, beneficiaries or next of kin of A and this point therefore can never be a defence by C if A1 in fact chooses to sue for specific performance rather than to attempt a compromise in the interest of the estate. This point seems to me misconceived. In any event, on the facts of this case there is no suggestion that there are any unpaid creditors and B is sole next of kin, so the point is academic.

11–313   "Then, as to the first point. On this question we were referred to the well-known dictum of Lush L.J. in *Lloyd's v. Harper*:

'I consider it to be an established rule of law that where a contract is made with A for the benefit of B, A can sue on the contract for the benefit of B and recover all that B could have recovered if the contract had been made with B himself.'

While in the circumstances it is not necessary to express any concluded opinion thereon, if the learned Lord Justice was expressing a view on the purely common law remedy of damages, I have some difficulty in going all the way with him. If A sues for damages for breach of contract by reason of the failure to pay B he must prove his loss; that may be great or nominal according to circumstances.

"I do not see how A can, in conformity with clearly settled principle in assessing damages for breach of contract, rely at common law on B's loss. I agree with the observations of Windeyer J, in the as yet unreported case of *Coulls v. Bagot's Executor and Trustee Co. Ltd* in the High Court of Australia. But I note, however, that in *Lloyd's v. Harper* James and Cotton L.JJ. treated A as trustee for B and I doubt whether Lush L.J. thought otherwise.

"However, I incline to the view that on the facts of this case damages are nominal for it appears that A died without any assets save and except the agreement which he hoped would keep him and then his widow for their lives. At all events let me assume that damages are nominal. So it is said nominal damages are adequate and the remedy of specific performance ought not to be granted. That is, with all respect, wholly to misunderstand that principle. Equity will grant specific performance when damages are inadequate to meet the justice of the case.

"But in any event quantum of damages seldom affects the right to specific **11–314** performance. If X contracts with Y to buy Blackacre or a rare chattel for a fancy price because the property or chattel has caught his fancy he is entitled to enforce his bargain and it matters not that he could not prove any damage.

"In this case the court ought to grant a specific performance order all the more because damages *are* nominal. C has received all the property: justice demands that he pay the price and this can only be done in the circumstances by equitable relief. It is a fallacy to suppose that B is thereby obtaining additional rights: A1 is entitled to compel C to carry out the terms of the agreement. The observations of Holmes L.J. already quoted are very much in point.

"My Lords, in my opinion the Court of Appeal were clearly right to grant a decree of specific performance."

Lords Pearce, Reid, Hodson and Guest delivered speeches concurring in the grant of such decree.

WROTH V. TYLER

Chancery Division [1974] Ch. 30. **11–315**

The defendant contracted to sell his property to the plaintiffs for £6,000. The next day, the defendant's wife registered a charge against the property under the Matrimonial Homes Act 1967 which gave her the right not to be evicted or excluded from the property. She refused to remove the charge and the defendant told the plaintiffs he could not complete. The plaintiffs sought specific performance or damages in lieu. The property was worth £7,500 at the date fixed for completion and £11,500 at the date of the hearing.

MEGARRY J.: "The issues before me may be summarised as follows. (1) Delay apart, are the plaintiffs entitled to specific performance of the contract with vacant possession? If they are, a form of order is sought that will require the defendant to make an application to the court for an order against his wife terminating her rights of occupation under the Matrimonial Homes Act 1967 in accordance with section 1 (2). (2) Delay apart, are the plaintiffs, as an alternative, entitled to specific performance of the contract subject to the rights of occupation of the defendant's wife, with damages or an abatement of the purchase price in respect thereof? If they are, they will be able to make the application to the court under the Act of 1967, by virtue of section 1 (2) and section 2 (3). (3) If, apart from delay, the plaintiffs would be entitled to an order for specific performance under either of these two heads, is their right to it barred by delay? (4) If the plaintiffs have no right to specific performance, then it is common ground that they are entitled to damages. There is, however, an acute conflict as to the measure of damages . . .

11–316 "The defendant says that the damages must be assessed as at the date of the breach, in accordance with the normal rule: the plaintiffs says that this is a case where damages must be assessed as at the date of assessment, that is, today, if I assess the damages. . . . Damages assessed as at the date of breach would be £1,500, but as at the date of the hearing would be £5,500. At which figure should damages for the loss of the bargain be assessed? The defendant says that the former figure applies, in accordance with the general rule, but the plaintiffs say that the latter figure applies, for unless it does, they will be unable to acquire an equivalent house at today's prices . . .

"I may summarise my conclusions as to the essentials of the right given by the Act to an occupying spouse as follows. The right is in essence a personal and non-assignable statutory right not to be evicted from the matrimonial home in question during marriage or until the court otherwise orders; and this right constitutes a charge on the estate or interest of the owning spouse which requires protection against third parties by registration. For various reasons, the right may be said to be one which readily fits into no category known to conveyancers before 1967; the phrase sui generis seems apt, but of little help.

"With that in mind, I turn to the first question before me. Delay apart, are the plaintiffs entitled to specific performance of the contract with vacant possession? If they are, the form of order sought will require the defendant to make an application to the court under section 1(2) to terminate his wife's rights of occupation which arose and became a charge on the defendant's estate on January 1, 1968, and were protected by registration on May 28, 1971 . . .

11–317 "It seems to me that where a third party has some rights over the property to be sold, there are at least three categories of cases. First, there are those cases where the vendor is entitled as of right to put an end to the rights of the third party, or compel his concurrence or co-operation in the sale. Second, and at the other extreme, there are cases where the vendor has no right to put an end to the third party's rights, or compel his concurrence or co-operation in the sale, and can do no more than to try to persuade him to release his rights or to concur in the sale.

"A vendor must do his best to obtain any necessary consent to the sale; if he has sold with vacant possession he must, if necessary, take proceedings to obtain possession from any person in possession who has no right to be there or whose right is determinable by the vendor, at all events if the vendor's right to possession is reasonably clear; but I do not think that the vendor will usually be required to embark upon difficult or uncertain litigation in order to secure any requisite consent or obtain vacant possession. Where the outcome of any litigation depends upon disputed facts, difficult questions of law, or the exercise of a discretionary jurisdiction, then I think the court would be slow to make a decree of specific performance against the vendor which would require him to undertake such litigation. In such a case, the vendor cannot know where the litigation will end. If he succeeds at first instance, the defendant may carry him to appeal; if he fails at first instance, the purchaser may say that there ought to be an appeal. No doubt the line between simple and difficult cases will sometimes **11–318** be hard to draw; and it may be that specific performance will be readily decreed only where it is plain that the requisite consent is obtainable without difficulty. The form of decree appropriate to such cases might specifically require the defendant to undertake such litigation; the court moulds the decree as need be. But it may be that the court will do no more than direct the defendant to procure the requisite consent: see *Long v. Bowring* (1864) 33 Beav. 585; *Seton's Judgments and Orders*, 7th ed. (1912), p. 2204.

"In the present case the defendant has endeavoured to persuade his wife to concur in the sale, but has failed. It is true that after the failure of his initial attempt on the Friday night he then instructed his solicitors to withdraw from both the sale and his Norfolk purchase; but he again tried to persuade his wife on the Sunday, and there is some evidence of later attempts. As the evidence stands, I think that the defendant has sufficiently attempted to obtain her consent, short of litigation. The mere fact that he sought to withdraw from the contract before he had made all his attempts does not seem to me to make much difference; if a later attempt had succeeded, he could still have completed at the date fixed for completion.

"Persuasion having failed, I think that the court should be slow to grant a **11–319** decree of specific performance that would require an unwilling husband to make an application to the court under section 1 (2) of the Act of 1967, particularly as the decision of the court depends upon the application of phrases such as 'just and reasonable' under section 1 (3). In any case, the court would be reluctant to make an order which requires a husband to take legal proceedings against his wife, especially while they are still living together. Accordingly, although this is a contract of a type which the court is normally ready to enforce by a decree of specific performance, in my judgment it would, in Lord Redesdale L.C.'s phrase, be 'highly unreasonable' to make such a decree if there is any other form of order that could do justice; and that I must consider in due course. Let me add that I would certainly not regard proceedings under the Act by the defendant against his wife as being without prospect of success. As the evidence stands (and of course I have not heard the defendant's wife) there is at least a real prospect of success for the defendant. He does not in any way seek to deprive his wife of a home; the difference between them is a difference as to where the matrimonial home is to be. In that, the conduct of the wife towards the plaintiffs and the defendant must play a substantial part.

"In turn to the second main question, that of Mr. Blackburne's alternative **11–320** claim to specific performance for which he contended if he failed in his main claim to specific performance, and if he also was limited to damages assessed as at the date of the breach. This alternative claim was for specific performance of the contract, but with the plaintiffs taking subject to the charge in favour of the defendant's wife, and receiving damages or an abatement of the purchase money. By virtue of section 2 (3) of the Act of 1967, section 1 (2) to (5) would apply to the plaintiffs as they apply to the defendant, in that the plaintiffs would be persons deriving title under the defendant, and affected by the charge. If the plaintiffs took subject to the charge in favour of the defendant's wife, the result would be remarkable, for reasons which I have already indicated. The defendant

Equitable Remedies

has no rights of occupation under the Act, for his right of occupation stems from his estate in the land, and so section 1 (1) of the Act gives him no statutory rights of occupation. The defendant's daughter has no rights of occupation under the Act, for the Act does not purport to confer such rights on anyone except a spouse. The defendant's wife alone has statutory rights of occupation, and on the facts of this case, these are expressed as being no more than 'a right not to be evicted or excluded from the dwelling house or any part thereof.' It has not been contended that this language is wide enough to empower the wife to authorise others to occupy the house with her, so that on that footing the plaintiffs, after completion, would be unable to evict the wife without an order of the court made under the Act, whereas the defendant and the daughter would have no defence to proceedings to evict them.

11–321   "There seems to be considerable force in the contention that this would be the result. Neither the defendant nor the daughter would have any rights of their own to remain in the house, and what the statute gives the wife is not a positive right of occupation, whether a licence or otherwise, but a mere negative right not to be evicted or excluded. A person who is given a positive right of occupation might be envisaged as having been given the right to permit others to occupy with him or her: but a mere negative right not to be evicted or excluded cannot so readily be construed in this sense . . .

"If one leaves the position of the children on one side as being debatable, there remains the position of the defendant vis-à-vis the plaintiffs. Even if the wife not only is protected against eviction or exclusion, but also has the right to permit others to occupy the dwelling with her, the defendant has contracted to give vacant possession to the plaintiffs. Could he, then, in breach of his contract, remain in occupation under cover of his wife's statutory right not to be evicted or excluded? Would a decree of specific performance of the contract subject only to his wife's statutory rights in effect be nugatory as to his contractual obligation not himself to remain in occupation but to give vacant possession? The Act seems to me to have created much doubt and uncertainty in this sphere, but there is at least a real possibility that a decree of specific performance subject to the wife's right not to be evicted or excluded would enable the plaintiffs, by taking suitable proceedings, to evict the defendant and perhaps the daughter, and thus split up the family. These circumstances seem to me to make the case one in which the court should be slow to decree specific performance if any reasonable alternative exists. I shall accordingly turn to the question of damages to see whether they would provide the plaintiffs with an adequate remedy . . ."

[He then held that the measure of damages perhaps at common law but certainly in lieu of specific performance was to be assessed at the date of judgments and so awarded £5,500 damages; *Johnson v. Agnew, infra*, now makes it clear that common law and equitable damages have the same measure.]

JOHNSON V. AGNEW

11–322   House of Lords [1980] A.C. 367 (Lords Wilberforce, Salmon, Fraser, Keith and Scarman).

The plaintiffs, in arrears of mortgage, contracted to sell their properties to the defendant at a price in excess of the amount owing on mortgage and sufficient to allow them to purchase another property. The defendant failed to complete and an order for specific performance was made. Before it was carried out the plaintiffs' mortgagees enforced their securities so that (a) the plaintiffs could no longer convey the properties and (b) there was insufficient even to pay off the mortgages, let alone purchase another property with the proceeds. The plaintiffs therefore sought an order that the defendant should pay the purchase price, less the moneys received on the mortgagees' sales, and an inquiry as to damages.

LORD WILBERFORCE: "My Lords, this appeal arises in a vendors' action for specific performance of a contract for the sale of land, the appellant being the purchaser and the vendors respondents. The factual situation is commonplace, indeed routine. An owner of land contracts to sell it to a purchaser; the purchaser fails to complete the contract; the vendor goes to the court and obtains an order that the contract be specifically performed; the purchaser still does not complete; the vendor goes back to the court and asks for the order for specific performance to be dissolved, for the contract to be terminated or 'rescinded,' and for an order for damages. One would think that the law as to so typical a set of facts would be both simple and clear. It is no credit to our law that it is neither, . . .

"By April 3, 1975, specific performance of the contract for sale had become **11–323** impossible. The vendors took no action upon the order for specific performance [entered on November 26 1974] until November 5, 1976, when they issued a notice of motion seeking (*a*) an order that the purchaser should pay the balance of the purchase price and an inquiry as to damages or (*b*) alternatively a declaration that they were entitled to treat the contract as repudiated by the purchaser and to forfeit the deposit and an inquiry as to damages.

"On February 25, 1977, Megarry V.-C. dismissed the motion. He rejected the first claim on the ground that, as specific performance was no longer possible, it would be unjust to order payment of the full purchase price. The second claim was not pressed, on the ground that it was precluded by authority: *Capital and Suburban Properties Ltd, v. Swycher* [1976] Ch. 319.

"The vendors appealed to the Court of Appeal who again rejected each alternative: they followed the previous decision in *Swycher's* case. However they held that the vendors could recover damages under the Chancery Amendment Act 1858 (Lord Cairns' Act), which enables the court to award damages in addition to or in substitution for specific performance. They accordingly made an order discharging the order for specific performance and an order for an inquiry as to damages. They fixed the date on which damages should be assessed as November 26, 1974, being the date of entry of the order for specific performance. The purchaser is now appealing against this order.

"In this situation it is possible to state at least some uncontroversial proposi- **11–324** tions of law.

"First, in a contract for the sale of land, after time has been made, or has become, of the essence of the contract, if the purchaser fails to complete, the vendor can *either* treat the purchaser as having repudiated the contract, accept the repudiation, and proceed to claim damages for breach of the contract, both parties being discharged from further performance of the contract; *or* he may seek from the court an order for specific performance with damages for any loss arising from delay in performance. (Similar remedies are of course available of purchasers against vendors.) This is simply the ordinary law of contract applied to contracts capable of specific performance.

"Secondly, the vendor may proceed by action for the above remedies (*viz*, specific performance or damages) in the alternative. At the trial he will however have to elect which remedy to pursue.

"Thirdly, if the vendor treats the purchaser as having repudiated the contract and accepts the repudiation, he cannot thereafter seek specific performance. This follows from the fact that, the purchaser having repudiated the contract and his repudiation having been accepted, both parties are discharged from further performance.

11–325   "At this point it is important to dissipate a fertile source of confusion and to make clear that although the vendor is sometimes referred to in the above situation as 'rescinding' the contract, this so-called 'rescission' is quite different from rescission ab initio, such as may arise for example in cases of mistake, fraud or lack of consent. In those cases, the contract is treated in law as never having come into existence. (Cases of a contractual right to rescind may fall under this principle but are not relevant to the present discussion.) In the case of an accepted repudiatory breach the contract has come into existence but has been put an end to or discharged. Whatever contrary indications may be disinterred from old authorities, it is now quite clear, under the general law of contract, that acceptance of a repudiatory breach does not bring about 'rescission ab initio.'

"Fourthly, if an order for specific performance is sought and is made, the contract remains in effect and is not merged in the judgment for specific performance. This is clear law, best illustrated by the judgment of Sir Wilfrid Greene M.R. in *Austins of East Ham Ltd v. Macey* [1941] Ch. 338, 341 in a passage which deals both with this point and with that next following. It repays quotation in full.

11–326   'The contract is still there. Until it is got rid of, it remains as a blot on the title, and the position of the vendor, where the purchaser has made default, is that he is entitled, not to annul the contract by the aid of the court, but to obtain the normal remedy of a party to a contract which the other party has repudiated. He cannot, in the circumstances, treat it as repudiated except by order of the court and the effect of obtaining such an order is that the contract, which until then existed, is brought to an end. The real position, in my judgment, is that, so far from proceeding to the enforcement of an order for specific performance, the vendor, in such circumstances is choosing a remedy which is alternative to the remedy of proceeding under the order for specific performance. He could attempt to enforce that order and could levy an execution which might prove completely fruitless. Instead of doing that, he elects to ask the court to put an end to the contract, and that is an alternative to an order for enforcing specific performance.'

11–327   "Fifthly, if the order for specific performance is not complied with by the purchaser, the vendor may *either* apply to the court for enforcement of the order, *or* may apply to the court to dissolve the order and ask the court to put an end to the contract. This proposition is as stated in *Austins of East Ham Ltd v. Macey* [1941] Ch. 338 (and see *Singh (Sudagar) v. Nazeer* [1979] Ch. 474 at 480, *per* Megarry V.-C.) and is in my opinion undoubted law, both on principle and authority. It follows, indeed, automatically from the facts that the contract remains in force after the order for specific performance and that the purchaser has committed a breach of it of a repudiatory character which he has not remedied, or as Megarry V.-C. puts it [1979] Ch. 474 at 480, 790, that he is refusing to complete.

"These propositions being, as I think they are, uncontrovertible, there only remains the question whether, if the vendor takes the latter course, *i.e.*, of applying to the court to put an end to the contract, he is entitled to recover damages for breach of the contract. On principle one may ask 'Why ever not?' If, as is clear, the vendor is entitled, after, and notwithstanding that an order for specific performance has been made, if the purchaser still does not complete the contract, to ask the court to permit him to accept the purchaser's repudiation and to declare the contract to be terminated, why, if the court accedes to this, should there not follow the ordinary consequences, undoubted under the general law of contract, that on such acceptance and termination the vendor may recover damages for breach of contract?

"I now consider the arguments which are said to support the negative answer. **11–328**

"The principal authority lies in the case of *Henty v. Schröder*, 12 Ch.D. 666, 667 in which Sir George Jessel M.R. is briefly reported as having laid down that a vendor 'could not at the same time obtain an order to have the agreement rescinded and claim damages against the defendant for breach of the agreement.'

At first instance, if has been followed usually uncritically . . . Finally, *Henty v. Schröder* was endorsed by the Court of Appeal in *Capital and Suburban Properties Ltd v. Swycher* ("*Swycher's* case") [1976] Ch. 319, but on a new basis which I shall shortly consider, and in the present case.

This is however the first time that this House has had to consider the right of an innocent party to a contract for the sale of land to damages on the contract being put an end to by accepted repudiation, and I think that we have the duty to take a fresh look. I should certainly be reluctant to invite your Lordships to endorse a line of authority so weak and unconvincing in principle. Fortunately there is support for a more attractive and logical approach from another bastion of the common law whose courts have adopted a more robust attitude . . .

[He then considered *McDonald v. Dennys Lascelles Ltd.* (1933) 43 C.L.R. 457; *Holland v. Wiltshire* (1954) 90 C.L.R. 409 and *Mckenna v. Richey* [1950] V.L.R. 360.]

"My Lords, I am happy to follow the latter case. In my opinion *Henty v. Schröder*, 12 Ch.D. 666, cannot stand against the powerful tide of logical objection and judicial reasoning. It should no longer be regarded as of authority: the cases following it should be overruled . . .

"The second basis for denying damages in such cases as the present is that **11–329** which underlines the judgment of the Court of Appeal in *Swycher's* case. This is really a rationalisation of *Henty v. Schröder*, 12 Ch.D. 666, the weakness of which case the court well perceived. The main argument there accepted was that by deciding to seek the remedy of specific performance the vendor (or purchaser) has made an election which either is irrevocable or which becomes so when the order for specific performance is made. A second limb of this argument (but in reality a different argument) is that the vendor (or purchaser) has adequate remedies under the order for specific performance so that there is no need, or equitable ground, for allowing him to change his ground and ask for damages.

"In my opinion, the argument based on irrevocable election, strongly pressed **11–330** by the appellant's counsel in the present appeal, is unsound. Election, though the subject of much learning and refinement, is in the end a doctrine based on simple considerations of common sense and equity. It is easy to see that a party who has chosen to put an end a contract by accepting the other party's repudiation cannot afterwards seek specific performance. This is simply because the contract has gone—what is dead is dead. But it is no more difficult to agree that a party, who has chosen to seek specific performance, may quite well thereafter, if specific performance fails to be realised, say, 'Very well, then, the contract should be regarded as terminated.' It is quite consistent with a decision provisionally to keep alive, to say, 'Well, this is no use—let us now end the contract's life.' A vendor who seeks (and gets) specific performance is merely electing for a course which may or may not lead to implementation of the contract—what he elects for is not eternal and unconditional affirmation, but a continuance of the contract under control of the court which control involves the power, in certain events, to terminate it. If he makes an election at all, he does so when he decides not to proceed under the order for specific performance, but to ask the court to terminate the contract: see the judgment of Sir Wilfrid Greene M.R. in *Austins of East Ham Ltd v. Macey* [1941] Ch. 338 quoted above. The fact is that the election argument proves too much. If it were correct it would deny the vendor not just the right to damages, but the right to 'rescind' the contract, but there is no doubt that this right exists: what is in question is only the right on 'rescission,' to claim damages.

11–331   "In my respectful opinion therefore *Swycher's* case [1976] Ch. 319, whether it should be regarded as resting upon *Henty v. Schröder*, 12 Ch.D. 666, or upon an independent argument based on election was wrongly decided in so far as it denied a right to contractual damages and should so far be overruled. The vendors should have been entitled, upon discharge of the contract, on grounds of normal and accepted principle, to damages appropriate for a breach of contract.

"There is one final point, on this part of the case, on which I should make a brief observation. Once the matter has been placed in the hands of a court of equity, or one exercising equity jurisdiction, the subsequent control of the matter will be exercised according to equitable principles. The court would not make an order dissolving the decree of specific performance and terminating the contract (with recovery of damages) if to do so would be unjust, in the circumstances then existing, to the other party, in this case to the purchaser. This is why there was, in the Court of Appeal, rightly, a relevant and substantial argument, repeated in this House, that the non-completion of the contract was due to the default of the vendors: if this had been made good, the court could properly have refused them the relief sought. But the Court of Appeal came to the conclusion that this non-completion, and the ultimate impossibility of completion, was the fault of the purchaser. I agree with their conclusion and their reasons on this point and shall not repeat or add to them.

"It is now necessary to deal with questions relating to the measure of damages. The Court of Appeal, while denying the vendors' right to damages at common law, granted damages under Lord Cairns' Act. Since, on the view which I take, damages can be recovered at common law, two relevant questions now arise. (1) Whether Lord Cairns' Act provides a different measure of damages from the common law; if so, the respondents would be in a position to claim the more favourable basis to them. (2) If the measure of damages is the same, on what basis they should be calculated.

11–332   "Since the decision? of this House, by majority, in *Leeds Industrial Co-operative Society Ltd v. Slack* [1924] A.C. 851 it is clear that the jurisdiction to award damages in accordance with section 2 of Lord Cairns' Act (accepted by the House as surviving the repeal of the Act) may arise in some cases in which damages could not be recovered at common law; examples of this would be damages in lieu of a quia timet injunction and damages for breach of a restrictive covenant to which the plaintiff was not a party. To this extent the Act created a power to award damages which did not exist before at common law. But apart from these, and similar cases where damages could not be claimed at all at common law there is sound authority for the proposition that the Act does not provide for the assessment of damages on any new basis. The wording of section 2 'may be assessed in such manner as the court shall direct' does not so suggest, but clearly refers only to procedure . . .

[He examined various cases]

"On the balance of these authorities and also on principle, I find in the Act no warrant for the court awarding damages differently from common law damages, but the question is left open on what date such damages, however awarded, ought to be assessed.

"The general principle for the assessment of damages is compensatory, *i.e.,* **11–333** that the innocent party is to be placed, so far as money can do so, in the same position as if the contract had been performed. Where the contract is one of sale, this principle normally leads to assessment of damages as at the date of the breach—a principle recognised and embodied in section 51 of the Sale of Goods Act 1893. But this is not an absolute rule: if to follow it would give rise to injustice, the court has power to fix such other date as may be appropriate in the circumstances.

"In cases where a breach of a contract for sale has occurred, and the innocent party reasonably continues to try to have the contract completed, it would to me appear more logical and just rather than tie him to the date of the original breach, to assess damages as at the date when (otherwise than by his default) the contract is lost. Support for this approach is to be found in the cases. In *Ogle v. Earl Vane* (1867) L.R. 2 Q.B. 275; L.R. 3 Q.B. 272 the date was fixed by reference to the time when the innocent party, acting reasonably, went into the market; in *Hickman v. Haynes* (1875) L.R. 10 C.P. 598 at a reasonable time after the last request of the defendants (buyers) to withhold delivery. In *Radford v. De Froberville* [1977] 1 W.L.R. 1262, where the defendant had convenanted to build a wall, damages were held measurable as at the date of the bearing rather than at the date of the defendant's breach, unless the plaintiff ought reasonably to have mitigated the breach at an earlier date.

"In the present case if it is accepted, as I would accept, that the vendors acted **11–334** reasonably in pursuing the remedy of specific performance, the date on which that remedy became aborted (not by the vendor's fault) should logically be fixed as the date on which damages should be assessed. Choice of this date would be in accordance both with common law principle, as indicated in the authorities I have mentioned, and with the wording of the Act 'in substitution for . . . specific performance.' The date which emerges from this is April 3, 1975—the first date on which mortgages contracted to sell a portion of the property. I would vary the order of the Court of Appeal by substituting this date for that fixed by them—viz. November 26, 1974. The same date (April 3, 1975) should be used for the purpose of limiting the respondents' right to interest on damages. Subject to these modifications I would dismiss the appeal." [Lords Salmon, Fraser, Keith of Kinkel and Scarman agreed.]

CO-OPERATIVE INSURANCE & ARGYLL STORES LTD

House of Lords [1998] A.C.I (Lords Hoffman, Browne–Wilkinson Slynn of **11–335** Hadley, Hope of Craighead & Clyde)

LORD HOFFMANN

"1. The issue

In 1955 Lord Goddard C.J. said:

"No authority has been quoted to show that an injunction will be granted enjoining a person to carry on a business, nor can I think that one ever would be, certainly not where the business is a losing concern:" *Attorney-General v. Colchester Corporation* [1955] 2 Q.B. 207, 217.

In this case his prediction has been falsified. The appellant defendants. Argyll Stores (Holdings) Ltd. ("Argyll"), decided in May 1995 to close their Safeway supermarket in the Hillsborough Shopping Centre in Sheffield because it was losing money. This was a breach of a covenant in their lease, which contained in clause 4(19) a positive obligation to keep the premises open for retail trade during the usual hours of business. Argyll admitted the breach and, in an action by the landlord. Co-operative Insurance Society Ltd. ("C.I.S.") consented to an order for damages to be assessed. But the Court of Appeal [1996] Ch. 286, reversing the trial judge. ordered that the covenant be specifically performed. It made a final injunction ordering Argyll to trade on the premises during the remainder of the term (which will expire on 3 August 2014) or until an earlier subletting or assignment. The Court of Appeal suspended its order for three months to allow time for Argyll to complete an assignment which by that time had been agreed. After a short agreed extension, the lease was assigned with the landlord's consent. In fact, therefore, the injunction never took effect. The appeal to your Lordships is substantially about costs. But the issue remains of great importance to landlords and tenants under other commercial leases . . .

11–336 The judge refused to order specific performance. He said that there was on the authorities a settled practice that orders which would require a defendant to run a business would not be made. He was not content, however, merely to follow authority. He gave reasons why he thought that specific performance would be inappropriate. Two such reasons were by way of justification for the general practice. An order to carry on a business, as opposed to an order to perform a "single and well-defined act," was difficult to enforce by the sanction of committal. And where a business was being run at a loss, specific relief would be "too far-reaching and beyond the scope of control which the court should seek to impose." The other two related to the particular case. A resumption of business would be expensive (refitting the shop was estimated to cost over £1m.) and although Argyll had knowingly acted in breach of covenant, it had done so "in the light of the settled practice of the court to award damages." Finally, while the assessment of damages might be difficult, it was the kind of exercise which the courts had done in the past.

4. The settled practice

11–337 There is no dispute about the existence of the settled practice to which the judge referred. It sufficient for this purpose to refer to *Braddon Towers Ltd. v. International Stores Ltd*. [1987] 1 E.G.L.R. 209, 213, where Slade J. said:

> "Whether or not this may be properly described as a rule of law. I do not doubt that for many years practitioners have advised their clients that it is the settled and invariable practice of this court never to grant mandatory injunctions requiring persons to carry on business.

But the practice has never, so far as I know, been examined by this House and it is open to C.I.S. to say that it rests upon inadequate grounds or that it has been too inflexibly applied.

Specific performance is traditionally regarded in English law as an exceptional remedy, as opposed to the common law damages to which a successful plaintiff is entitled as of right. There may have been some element of later rationalisation of an untidier history, but by the 19th century it was orthodox doctrine that the power to decree specific performance was part of the discretionary jurisdiction of the Court of Chancery to do justice in cases in which the remedies available at common law were inadequate. This is the basis of the general principle that specific performance will not be ordered when damages are an adequate remedy. By contrast, in countries with legal systems based on civil law, such as France, Germany and Scotland, the plaintiff is prima facie entitled to specific performance. The cases in which he is confined to a claim for damages are regarded as the exceptions. In practice, however, there is less difference between common law and civilian systems than these general statements might lead one to suppose. The principles upon which English judges exercise the discretion to grant specific performance are reasonably well settled and depend upon a number of considerations, mostly of a practical nature, which are of very general application. I have made no investigation of civilian systems, but a priori I would expect that judges take much the same matters into account in deciding whether specific performance would be inappropriate in a particular case.

The practice of not ordering a defendant to carry on a business is not entirely **11–338** dependent upon damages being an adequate remedy. In *Dowty Boulton Paul Ltd. v. Wolverhampton Corporation* [1971] 1 W.L.R. 204. Sir John Pennycuick V.-C. refused to order the corporation to maintain an airfield as a going concern because: "It is very well established that the court will not order specific performance of an obligation to carry on a business:" see p. 211. He added: "It is unnecessary in the circumstances to discuss whether damages would be an adequate remedy to the company:" see p. 212. Thus the reasons which underlie the established practice may justify a refusal of specific performance even when damages are not an adequate remedy.

The most frequent reason given in the cases for declining to order someone to carry on a business is that it would require constant supervision by the court. In *J.C. Williamson Ltd. v. Lukey and Mulholland* (1931) 45 C.L.R. 282, 297–298, Dixon J. said flatly: "Specific performance is inapplicable when the continued supervision of the court is necessary in order to ensure the fulfillment of the contract."

There has, I think, been some misunderstanding about what is meant by **11–339** continued superintendence. It may at first sight suggest that the judge (or some other officer of the court) would literally have to supervise the execution of the order. In *C.H. Giles & Co. Ltd. v. Morris* [1972] 1 W.L.R. 307, 318 Megarry J. said that "difficulties of constant superintendence" were a "narrow consideration" because:

> "there is normally no question of the court having to send its officers to supervise the performance of the order . . . Performance . . . is normally secured by the realisation of the person enjoined that he is liable to be punished for contempt if evidence of his disobedience to the order is put before the court; . . ."

This is, of course, true but does not really meet the point. The judges who have said that the need for constant supervision was an objection to such orders were no doubt well aware that supervision would in practice take the form of rulings by the court, on applications made by the parties, as to whether there had been a breach of the order. It is the possibility of the court having to give an indefinite series of such rulings in order to ensure the execution of the order which has been regarded as undesirable.

11–340   Why should this be so? A principal reason is that, as Megarry J. pointed out in the passage to which I have referred, the only means available to the court to enforce its order is the quasi-criminal procedure of punishment for contempt. This is powerful weapon: so powerful, in fact, as often to be unsuitable as an instrument for adjudicating upon the disputes which may arise over whether a business is being run in accordance with the terms of the court's order. The heavy-handed nature of the enforcement mechanism is a consideration which may go to the exercise of the court's discretion in other cases as well, but its use to compel the running of a business is perhaps the paradigm case of its disadvantages and it is in this context that I shall discuss them.

11–341   The prospect of committal or even a fine, with the damage to commercial reputation which will be caused by a finding of contempt of court, is likely to have at least two undesirable consequences. First, the defendant, who ex hypothesi did not think that it was in his economic interest to run the business at all, now has to make decisions under a sword of Damocles which may descend if the way the business is run does not conform to the terms of the order. This is, as one might say, no way to run a business. In this case the Court of Appeal made light of the point because it assumed that, once the defendant had been ordered to run the business, self-interest and compliance with the order would thereafter go hand in hand. But, as I shall explain, this is not necessarily true.

Secondly, the seriousness of a finding of contempt for the defendant means that any application to enforce the order is likely to be a heavy and expensive piece of litigation. The possibility of repeated applications over a period of time means that, in comparison with a once-and-for-all inquiry as to damages, the enforcement of the remedy is likely to be expensive in terms of cost to the parties and the resources of the judicial system.

11–342   This is a convenient point at which to distinguish between orders which require a defendant to carry on an activity, such as running a business over or more or less extended period of time, and orders which require him to achieve a result. The possibility of repeated applications for rulings on compliance with the order which arises in the former case does not exist to anything like the same extent in the latter. Even if the achievement of the result is a complicated matter which will take some time, the court, if called upon to rule, only has to examine the finished work and say whether it complies with the order. This point was made in the context of relief against forfeiture in *Shiloh Spinners Ltd v. Harding* [1973] A.C. 691. If it is a condition of relief that the tenant should have complied with a repairing covenant, difficulty of supervision need not be an objection. As Lord Wilberforce said, at p. 724:

> "what the court has to do is to satisfy itself, ex post facto, that the covenanted work has been done, and it has ample machinery, through certificates, or by inquiry, to do precisely this."

This distinction between orders to carry on activities and orders to achieve results explains why the courts have in appropriate circumstances ordered specific performance of building contracts and repairing covenants: see *Wolverhampton Corporation v. Emmons* [1901] 1 K.B. 515 (building contract) and *Jeune v. Queens Cross Properties Ltd.* [1974] Ch. 97 (repairing covenant). It by no means follows, however, that even obligations to achieve a result will always be enforced by specific performance. There may be other objections, to some of which I now turn.

11–343   One such objection, which applies to orders to achieve a result and a fortiori to orders to carry on an activity, is imprecision in the terms of the order. If the terms of the court's order, reflecting the terms of the obligation, cannot be precisely drawn, the possibility of wasteful litigation over compliance is increased. So is the oppression caused by the defendant having to do things under threat of proceedings for contempt. The less precise the order, the fewer the signposts to the forensic minefield which he has to traverse. The fact that the terms of a contractual obligation are sufficiently definite to escape being void for uncertainty, or to found a claim for damages, or to permit compliance to be made a condition of relief against forfeiture, does not necessarily mean that they will be sufficiently precise to be capable of being specifically enforced. So in *Wolverhampton Corporation v. Emmons.* Romer L.J. said, at p. 525, that the first condition for specific enforcement of a building contract was that

> "the particulars of the work are so far definitely ascertained that the court can sufficiently see what is the exact nature of the work of which it is asked to order the performance."

Similarly in *Morris v. Redland Bricks Ltd.* [1970] A.C. 652, 666, Lord Upjohn **11–344** stated the following general principle for the grant of mandatory injunctions to carry out building works:

> "the court must be careful to see that the defendant knows exactly in fact what he has to do and this means not as a matter of law but as a matter of fact, so that in carrying out an order he can give his contractors the proper instructions."

Precision is of course a question of degree and the courts have shown themselves willing to cope with a certain degree of imprecision in cases of orders requiring the achievement of a result in which the plaintiffs' merits appeared strong; like all the reasons which I have been discussing, it is, taken alone, merely a discretionary matter to be taken into account: see *Spry. Equitable Remedies*, 4th ed. (1990). p. 112. It is, however, a very important one.

I should at this point draw attention to what seems to me to have been a misreading of certain remarks of Lord Wilberforce in *Shiloh Spinners Ltd. v. Harding.* at p. 724. He pointed out, as I have said, that to grant relief against forfeiture subject to compliance with a repairing covenant involves the court in no more than the possibility of a retrospective assessment of whether the covenanted work has been done. For this reason, he said:

> "Where it is necessary, and, in my opinion, right, to move away from some 19th century authorities, is to reject as a reason against granting relief, the impossibility for the courts to supervise the doing of work."

This is plainly a remark about cases involving the achievement of a result such as **11–345** doing repairs, and, within that class, about making compliance a condition of relief against forfeiture. But in *Tito v. Waddell (No. 2)* [1977] Ch. 106, 322 Sir Robert Megarry V.-C. took it to be a generalisation about specific performance and, in particular, a rejection of difficulty of supervision as an objection, even in cases of orders to carry on an activity. Sir Robert Megarry V.-C. regarded it as an adoption of his own views (based, as I have said, on incomplete analysis of what was meant by difficulty of supervision) in *C.H. Giles & Co. Ltd. v. Morris* [1972] 1 W.L.R. 307, 318. In the present case [1996] Ch. 286, 292–293. Leggatt L.J. took this claim at face value. In fact, Lord Wilberforce went on to say that impossibility of supervision "is a reality, no doubt, and explains why specific performance cannot be granted of agreements to this effect . . ." Lord Wilberforce was in my view drawing attention to the fact that the collection of reasons which the courts have in mind when they speak of difficulty of supervision apply with much greater force to orders for specific performance, giving rise to the possibility of committal for contempt, than they do to conditions for relief against forfeiture. While the paradigm case to which such objections apply is the order to carry on an activity, they can also apply to an order requiring the achievement of a result.

11–346 There is a further objection to an order requiring the defendant to carry on a business, which was emphasised by Millett L.J. in the Court of Appeal. This is that it may cause injustice by allowing the plaintiff to enrich himself at the defendant's expense. The loss which the defendant may suffer through having to comply with the order (for example, by running a business at a loss for an indefinite period) may be far greater than the plaintiff would suffer from the contract being broken. As Professor R. J. Sharpe explains in "Specific Relief for Contract Breach," ch. 5 of *Studies in Contract Law* (1980), edited by Reiter and Swan. p. 129:

> "In such circumstances, a specific decree in favour of the plaintiff will put him in a bargaining position vis-à-vis the defendant whereby the measure of what he will receive will be the value to the defendant of being released from performance. If the plaintiff bargains effectively, the amount he will set will exceed the value to him of performance and will approach the cost to the defendant to complete."

11–347 This was the reason given by Lord Westbury L.C. in *Isenberg v. East India House Estate Co. Ltd.* (1863) 3 De G.J. & S. 263, 273 for refusing a mandatory injunction to compel the defendant to pull down part of a new building which interfered with the plaintiff's light and exercising instead the Court of Chancery's recently-acquired jurisdiction under Lord Cairns's Act 1858 (21 & 22 Vict. c. 27) to order payment of damages:

> ". . . I hold it . . . to be the duty of the court in such a case as the present not, by granting a mandatory injunction, to deliver over the defendants to the plaintiff bound hand and foot, in order to be made subject to any extortionate demand that he may by possibility make, but to substitute for such mandatory injunction an inquiry before itself, in order to ascertain the measure of damage that has been actually sustained."

It is true that the defendant has, by his own breach of contract, put himself in such an unfortunate position. But the purpose of the law of contract is not to punish wrongdoing but to satisfy the expectations of the party entitled to performance. A remedy which enables him to secure, in money terms, more than the performance due to him is unjust. From a wider perspective, it cannot be in the public interest for the courts to require someone to carry on business at a loss if there is any plausible alternative by which the other party can be given compensation. It is not only a waste of resources but yokes the parties together in a continuing hostile relationship. The order for specific performance prolongs the battle. If the defendant is ordered to run a business, its conduct becomes the subject of a flow of complaints, solicitors' letters and affidavits. This is wasteful for both parties and the legal system. An award of damages, on the other hand, brings the litigation to an end. The defendant pays damages, the forensic link between them is severed, they go their separate ways and the wounds of conflict can heal.

The cumulative effect of these various reasons, none of which would neces- **11–348** sarily be sufficient on its own, seems to me to show that the settled practice is based upon sound sense. Of course the grant or refusal of specific performance remains a matter for the judge's discretion. There are no binding rules, but this does not mean that there cannot be settled principles, founded upon practical considerations of the kind which I have discussed, which do not have to be re-examined in every case, but which the courts will apply in all but exceptional circumstances. As Slade J. said, in the passage which I have quoted from *Braddon Towers Ltd. v. International Stores Ltd* [1987] 1 E.G.L.R. 209, 213, lawyers have no doubt for many years advised their clients on this basis. In the present case. Leggatt L.J. [1996] Ch. 286, 294 remarked that there was no evidence that such advice had been given. In my view, if the law or practice on a point is settled, it should be assumed that persons entering into legal transactions will have been advised accordingly. I am sure that Leggatt L.J. would not wish to encourage litigants to adduce evidence of the particular advice which they received. Indeed, I doubt whether such evidence would be admissible.

The decision of the Court of Appeal

I must now examine the grounds upon which the majority of the Court of Appeal **11–349** [1996] Ch. 286 thought it right to reverse the judge. In the first place, they regarded the practice which he followed as outmoded and treated Lord Wilberforce's remarks about relief against forfeiture in *Shiloh Spinners Ltd. v. Harding* [1973] A.C. 691, 724 as justifying a rejection of the arguments based on the need for constant supervision. Even Millett L.J., who dissented on other grounds, said, at p. 303, that such objections had little force today. I do not agree. As I have already said, I think that Lord Wilberforce's remarks do not support this proposition in relation to specific performance of an obligation to carry on an activity and that the arguments based on difficulty of supervision remain powerful.

The Court of Appeal said that it was enough if the contract defined the tenant's obligation with sufficient precision to enable him to know what was necessary to comply with the order. Even assuming that this to be right. I do not think that the obligation in clause 4(19) can possibly be regarded as sufficiently precise to be capable of specific performance. It is to "keep the demised premises open for retail trade." It says nothing about the level of trade, the area of the premises within which trade is to be conducted, or even the kind of trade, although no doubt the tenant's choice would be restricted by the need to comply with the negative covenant in clause 4(12)(a) not to use the premises "other than as a retail store for the sale of food groceries provisions and goods normally sold from time to time by a retail grocer food supermarkets and food superstores . . ." This language seems to me to provide ample room for argument over whether the tenant is doing enough to comply with the covenant.

The Court of Appeal thought that once Argyll had been ordered to comply **11–350** with the covenant, it was, as Roch L.J. said, at p. 298, "inconceivable that they would not operate the business efficiently." Leggatt L.J. said, at p. 292, that the requirement

> "was quite intelligible to the defendants, while they were carrying on business there . . . If the premises are to be run as a business, it cannot be in the defendants' interest to run it half-heartedly or inefficiently . . ."

This treats the way the tenant previously conducted business as measuring the extent of his obligation to do so. In my view this is a non sequitur: the obligation depends upon the language of the covenant and not upon what the tenant has previously chosen to do. No doubt it is true that it would not be in the interests of the tenant to run the business inefficiently. But running the business efficiently does not necessarily mean running it in the way it was run before. Argyll had decided that, from its point of view, the most efficient thing to do was to close the business altogether and concentrate its resources on achieving better returns elsewhere. If ordered to keep the business open, it might well decide that the next best strategy was to reduce its costs as far as was consistent with compliance with its obligations, in the expectation that a lower level of return would be more than compensated by higher returns from additional expenditure on more profitable shops. It is in my view wrong for the courts to speculate about whether Argyll might voluntarily carry on business in a way which would relieve the court from having to construe its order. The question of certainty must be decided on the assumption that the court might have to enforce the order according to its terms.

11–351 C.I.S. argued that the court should not be concerned about future difficulties which might arise in connection with the enforcement of the order. It should simply make the order and see what happened. In practice Argyll would be likely to find a suitable assignee (as it in fact did) or conduct the business so as to keep well clear of any possible enforcement proceedings or otherwise come to terms with C.I.S. This may well be true, but the likelihood of Argyll having to perform beyond the requirements of its covenant or buy its way out of its obligation to incur losses seems to me to be in principle an objection to such an order rather than to recommend it. I think that it is normally undesirable for judges to make orders in terrorem, carrying a threat of imprisonment, which work only if no one inquires too closely into what they mean.

11–352 The likelihood that the order would be effective only for a short time until an assignment is an equivocal argument. It would be burdensome to make Argyll resume business only to stop again after a short while if a short stoppage would not cause any substantial damage to the business of the shopping centre. On the other hand, what would happen if a suitable assignee could not be found? Would Argyll then have to carry on business until 2014? Mr. Smith, who appeared for C.I.S., said that if the order became oppressive (for example, because Argyll were being driven into bankruptcy) or difficult to enforce, they could apply for it to be varied or discharged. But the order would be a final order and there is no case in this jurisdiction in which such an order has been varied or discharged, except when the injuncted activity has been legalised by statute. Even assuming that there was such a jurisdiction if circumstances were radically changed. I find it difficult to see how this could be made to apply. Difficulties of enforcement would not be a change of circumstances. They would have been entirely predictable when the order was made. And so would the fact that Argyll would suffer unquantifiable loss if it was obliged to continue trading. I do not think that such expedients are an answer to the difficulties on which the objections to such orders are based.

11–353 Finally, all three judges in the Court of Appeal took a very poor view of Argyll's conduct. Leggatt L.J. said [1996] Ch. 286, 295, that they had acted "with gross commercial cynicism;" Roch L.J. began his judgment by saying that they had "behaved very badly" and Millett L.J. said, at p. 301, that they had no merits. The principles of equity have always had a strong ethical content and nothing which I say is intended to diminish the influence of moral values in their application. I can envisage cases of gross breach of personal faith, or attempts to use the threat of non-performance as blackmail, in which the needs of justice will override all the considerations which support the settled practice. But although any breach of covenant is regrettable, the exercise of the discretion as to whether or not to grant specific performance starts from the fact that the covenant has been broken. Both landlord and tenant in this case are large sophisticated commercial organisations and I have no doubt that both were perfectly aware that the remedy for breach of the covenant was likely to be limited to an award of damages. The interests of both were purely financial: there was no element of personal breach of faith, as in the Victorian cases of railway companies which refused to honour obligations to build stations for landowners whose property they had taken: compare *Greene v. West Cheshire Railway Co.* (1871) L.R. 13 Eq. 44. No doubt there was an effect on the businesses of other traders in the Centre, but Argyll had made no promises to them and it is not suggested that C.I.S. warranted to other tenants that Argyll would remain. Their departure, with or without the consent of C.I.S., was a commercial risk which the tenants were able to deploy in negotiations for the next rent review. On the scale of broken promises, I can think of worse cases, but the language of the Court of Appeal left them with few adjectives to spare.

It was no doubt discourteous not to have answered Mr. Wightman's letter. But **11–354** to say, as Roch L.J. did, at p. 299, that they had acted "wantonly and quite unreasonably" by removing their fixtures seems to me an exaggeration. There was no question of stealing a march, or attempting to present C.I.S. with a fait accompli, because Argyll had no reason to believe that C.I.S. would have been able to obtain a mandatory injunction whether the fixtures had been removed or not. They had made it perfectly clear that they were closing the shop and given C.I.S. ample time to apply for such an injunction if so advised.

Conclusion

I think that no criticism can be made of the way in which Judge Maddocks exercised his discretion. All the reasons which he gave were proper matters for him to take into account. In my view the Court of Appeal should not have interfered and I would allow the appeal and restore the order which he made."

All of their Lordships agreed with Lord Hoffmann.

Section 7. Rescission and Rectification[31]

Rescission

The equitable right to rescind[32] is the right of a party to a transaction to **11–355** set it aside and so to be restored to his former position. It must be distinguished as a voidable transaction from a transaction that is void *ab initio* (*e.g.* a contract void for illegality or a very fundamental mistake). It must also be distinguished from the case where a contract with no inherent invalidity is said to be rescinded for the future when the innocent party accepts the wrongdoer's repudiatory breach of contract as

---

[31] These remedies are dealt with in outline only as more appropriate to textbooks on Contract (or Obligations I of the Foundation Subjects) or Restitution: see Goff & Jones, *Law of Restitution* (5th ed.), Chapter 9.

[32] See *Alati v. Kruger* (1955) 94 C.L.R. 216 at 223–224 endorsed by Dunn L.J. in *O'Sullivan v. Management Agency & Music Ltd* [1985] 3 All E.R. 352 at 364–365.

terminating the contract, but leaving the innocent party free to sue the wrongdoer for his past breaches of a valid contract.[33]

Equity can set aside a transaction in circumstances where the common law would not and is more flexible in its view of restitution in integrum, *e.g.* taking accounts and making an allowance for services rendered or for deterioration of property.[34] Moreover, equity by applying the maxim "he who comes to equity must do equity" can grant relief on terms, *e.g.* so that a contract is set aside so long as the vendor offers the property in question to the purchaser at a proper price.[35]

The grounds for rescission include cases:

11–356
    (i) where both parties to a contract acted under a common mistake of fact or law[36] without which no such contract would have been made[37];

   (ii) where a party was induced to enter into a contract by a fraudulent misrepresentation—or even an innocent misrepresentation, but the court now has a discretion to award damages in lieu of rescission if it would be equitable to do so[38];

  (iii) where a party entered into a transaction as a result of another's undue influence[39];

  (iv) where a poor ignorant person entered into a disadvantageous transaction (*e.g.* at an undervalue) without any independent legal advice[40];

   (v) where the other party to a contract uberrimae fidei (*e.g.* a contract of insurance) is in breach of his duty of full disclosure[41];

  (vi) where the other party to a transaction is in breach of his fiduciary duty of full disclosure[42];

 (vii) where a donor made a gift under a unilateral mistake as to the effect of the gift (*e.g.* causing a forfeiture of a protected life interest[43] or causing a[44] beneficiary to be benefited twice forgetful of an earlier gift to that beneficiary);

(viii) where a donor made a gift by reason of another's misrepresentation or undue influence.[45]

---

[33] *Johnson v. Agnew* [1980] A.C. 367 at 396–398, para. 11–325; *Photo Production Ltd v. Securicor Transport Ltd* [1980] A.C. 827 at 844.

[34] See cases in n.92 above.

[35] *Grist v. Bailey* [1967] Ch. 532, *Magee v. Pennine Insurance Co Ltd* [1969] 2 Q.B. 507. Further see Goff & Jones, Law of Restitution Chap. 9.

[36] *Kleinwort Benson Ltd v. Glasgow C.C.* [1999] 1 A.C. 153, *Cooper v. Phibbs* (1867) L.R. 2HL 149.

[37] *ibid. Associate Japanese Bank (International) Ltd v. Credit du Nord* [1988] 3 All E.R. 902 at 912.

[38] Misrepresentation Act 1967, s. 2(2). Indeed section 2(1) allows damages of a tortious measure to be awarded for a negligent misrepresentation: *Royscot Trust Ltd v. Rogerson* [1991] 2 Q.B. 297. See also *Witter Ltd v. TBP Industries* [1996] 2 All E.R. 573.

[39] *Barclays Bank plc v. O'Brien* [1994] 1 A.C. 180; *CIBC Mortgages plc v. Pitt* [1994] 1 A.C. 200.

[40] *Cresswell v. Potter* [1978] 1 W.L.R. 255 *Crédit Lyonnais Nederland NV v. Burch* [1997] 1 All E.R. 144; *Portman B.S. v. Dusangh* [2001] W.T.L.R 117.

[41] *Pan Atlantic Insurance Co Ltd v. Pine Top Insurance Co Ltd* [1994] 3 All E.R. 581.

[42] *Daly v. Sidney Stock Exchange* (1986) 160 C.L.R. 371.

[43] *Gibbon v. Mitchell* [1990] 1 W.L.R. 1304.

[44] *Hood (Lady) of Avalon v. Mackinnon* [1909] 1 Ch. 476.

[45] *Re Glubb* [1900] 1 Ch. 354.

The English Court of Appeal in *TSB Bank v. Camfield*[46] has taken the **11–357** strict view that if a plaintiff can set aside a transaction, like a mortgage, for misrepresentation (or undue influence) then it must be set aside entirely rather than partially, even where a wife would have agreed to a maximum liability of £15,000 (rather than of £30,000) irrespective of the misrepresentation (or under influence). The Australian High Court[47] has subsequently rejected that view and applied the maxim, "He who seeks equity must do equity" so as to do what is practically just. Thus, in the above type of case the mortgage should be entirely set aside but on the terms that the wife affords the mortgagee security for £15,000 because she was prepared to undertake that liability independently of any misrepresentation (or undue influence). In England a first instance judge has held[48] that where (unlike *Camfield*) the wife had actually benefited from the loan sought to be set aside she had to make restitution of such benefit to be granted rescission. It seems likely that the House of Lords in due course will overrule *Camfield* and follow the Australian approach.

The right to rescind is lost if

(i) the party entitled to rescind affirms the transaction[49];
(ii) *restitutio in integrun* is not substantially possible, taking account of services rendered or for property deterioration[50];
(iii) an innocent third party acquires rights for value before the plaintiff sets the transaction aside or does everything he can to set it aside by communicating his intention to the other party.[51]
(iv) not exercised within a reasonable time.[52]

Rectification

Rectification is a discretionary remedy to rectify a document so that it **11–358** accords correctly with what the parties agreed[53] or in the case of a settlement with what the settlor intended.[54] For this purpose there is an exception to the "parole evidence rule" so that oral evidence may be given to establish the error with the "convincing proof"[55] that is required. When rectification occurs it is retrospective.[56]

---

[46] [1995] 1 All E.R. 951.
[47] *Vadasz v. Pioneer Concrete SA* (1995) 69 A.L.J.R. 678. Similarly in *Maguire v. Makaronis* (1998) 188 C.L.R. 449 it allowed mortgagors to rescind a mortgage (for non-disclosure that their solicitors were the mortgagees) on condition they repaid the capital with interest at a commercial rate, but not the higher rate in the mortgage deed.
[48] *Dunbar Bank plc v. Nadeem* [1997] 2 All E.R. 253 (£210,000 of the loan to H and W was used to buy a lease in the names of H and W, so to obtain rescission W had to pay the bank £105,000 plus interest).
[49] *Peyman v. Lanjani* [1985] Ch. 457; *Leaf v. International Galleries* [1950] 2 K.B. 86; *Mitchell v. Homfray* (1881) 8 Q.B.D. 587.
[50] *Erlanger v. New Sombrero Phosphate Co* (1873) 3 App. Cas. 1218; *O'Sullivan v. Management Agency & Music Ltd* [1985] Q.B. 428.
[51] *Oakes v. Turquand* (1869) L.R. 2 H.L 325; *Car & Universal Finance Co Ltd v. Caldwell* [1965] 1 Q.B. 525.
[52] *Car and Universal Finance Co Ltd v. Caldwell* [1965] 1 Q.B. 525, 554, *Leaf v. International Galleries* [1950] 2 K.B. 86, 92.
[53] *Joscelyne v. Nissen* [1970] 2 Q.B. 86; *Racal Group Services Ltd v. Ashmore* [1994] STC 416.
[54] *Re Butlin's S.T.* [1976] Ch. 251; *Lake v. Lake* [1989] STC 865.
[55] *Joscelyne v. Nissen* [1970] 2 Q.B. 86.
[56] *Lake v. Lake* [1989] STC 865.

In bilateral transactions the mistake must normally be common to both parties so that the document fails to record what they agreed.[57] Exceptionally, rectification will be available where there was a unilateral mistake in circumstances where the party who was not mistaken is fraudulent or estopped from resisting rectification by virtue of his unconscionable conduct.[58]

11–359 Rectification of a voluntary deed, like a settlement, can be obtained if the donor's real intention was not accurately reflected in the deed.[59] Strong evidence of his precise real intention will be required so that the judge can be convinced that the document which was executed differed by reason of some mistake from that which the settlor intended *e.g.*[60] an accidental departure from his instructions to the draftsman. It is not enough that it would have been better if the settlor had executed a deed which was from the outset in the form to which she seeks it to be changed, nor is it enough that if the settlor's attention had been drawn to the actual terms of the deed and she had been asked if she would rather have them changed, she would have said that she would. Thus, where the deed excluded the trustees from benefiting under the trust and the original trustees were replaced as trustees by the settlor's daughters who were primary beneficiaries and who subsequently received significant benefits, the court[61] refused to rectify the deed so that beneficiaries who were trustees could still benefit. It is immaterial that the purpose of rectification is to obtain an intended fiscal advantage, but the court must be convinced that the clause to be rectified was intended to be in some precisely different form from that ultimately appearing in the deed.[62]

As alternatives to rectification, it is worth nothing that if the donor did not intend the transaction to have the effect which it did (*e.g.* a surrender to have the effect of forfeiting his life interest under a protective trust) it may be totally set aside,[63] while the exercise of a power may be declared void if it would not have been so exercised but for ignoring a key factor.[64]

Rectification will not be granted where a bona fide purchaser for value without notice has acquired a proprietary interest under the document.[65]

---

[57] If they both agreed "x" believing "x" to be "y" then rectification cannot be ordered; *Frederick Rose (London) Ltd v. William Pim Jr Co Ltd* [1953] 2 Q.B. 450 criticised by Goff & Jones, Law of Restitution (5th ed.) p. 300.

[58] *Thomas Bates & Son Ltd v. Wyndham's (Lingerie) Ltd* [1981] 1 All E.R. 1077 at 1086; *Commission for New Towns v. Cooper (GB) Ltd* [1995] 2 All E.R. 929.

[59] *Re Butlin's S.T.* [1976] Ch. 251.

[60] *Tankel v. Tankel* [1999] 1 F.L.R. 676, *Re Smouha Family Trust* [2000] W.T.L.R. 133.

[61] *Tankel v. Tankel* [1999] 1 F.L.R. 676.

[62] *Racal Group Services v. Ashmore* [1995] S.T.C. 1151: a covenant in favour of charitable trustees for a period exceeding 3 years was clearly intended, so as to attract tax relief, but mistakenly the period in the covenant could not exceed 3 years; Court of Appeal refused rectification because not clear on what particular dates over what particular period payments would be made, the company's controller only having a general idea. Some offshore jurisdictions have a more benevolent approach: *Briggs v. Integritas Trust Management (Cayman) Ltd* [1988] C.I.L.R. 456.

[63] *Gibbon v. Mitchell* [1990] 1 W.L.R. 1304.

[64] *Re Hastings–Bass* [1975] Ch. 25; *Green v. Cobham* [2000] W.T.L.R. 1101. In *Tankel* should they have sought a declaration that the appointment of the daughters as trustees was void?

[65] *Smith v. Jones* [1954] 1 W.L.R. 1089, or nowadays, presumably if an innocent volunteer has changed his position (see *supra*, para. 11–46).

Laches or acquiescence will also bar the claim.[66] In the case of a voluntary settlement the court may refuse to rectify if a trustee, who took office in ignorance of the mistake, has a reasonable objection to rectification.[67]

Section 20 of the Administration of Justice Act 1982 allows a will to be rectified if the court is satisfied that it fails to carry out the testator's intentions in consequence of a clerical error or a failure to understand his instructions.[68]

---

[66] *Beale v. Kyte* [1907] 1 Ch. 564.
[67] *Re Butlin's S.T.* [1976] Ch. 251.
[68] e.g. *Wordingham v. Royal Exchange Trust Co* [1992] Ch. 412.

Chapter 12

TRUSTS AND THE CONFLICT OF LAWS

12–01 The conflict of laws is that part of the private law of the English and Welsh system of law which deals with issues which concern elements connected with other legal systems, *e.g.* of Scotland, Northern Ireland, the Republic of Ireland, Jersey, the Isle of Man, each of the American and Australian states, each of the Canadian or Spanish provinces. A settlor of British nationality domiciled[1] in California may create a trust of assets, half of which are in Bermuda and half in Ontario, and appoint four trustees, one habitually resident in Bermuda, one habitually resident in Ontario and two habitually resident in England. One-third of the beneficiaries may be habitually resident in California, one-third in England and one-third in Jersey. The trust instrument may specify Californian law as governing the validity of the trust, and Bermudian law as governing administration of trust assets there and Ontario law as governing administration of the assets there. It may also confer express powers on the trustees to change the law governing the validity of the trust and to change the place of administration and the law governing administration. An alleged breach of trust may lead the beneficiaries to bring an action against the trustees before the Chancery Division of the English High Court.

12–02 The two questions that arise are (1) does the English court have jurisdiction to hear the case, and, if so, (2) what system of law shall apply to each point in issue? Sometimes, the case may be an exceptional one where, though the English court technically has jurisdiction, it will stay or strike out the proceedings on the ground of *forum non conveniens*, because the defendant shows there is another forum to whose jurisdiction he is amenable, in which justice can be done at substantially less inconvenience and expense, and where the plaintiff will not be deprived of a legitimate personal or juridical advantage which would be available to him under the English jurisdiction.[2] Sometimes, the question arises whether the English court will recognise or enforce a foreign judgment

---

[1] Domicile is a technical concept: it does not mean habitual residence. No one can be without a domicile since it is this that connects him with some legal system for many conflict of laws purposes. A person has a domicile of origin at birth (being his father's domicile or if illegitimate, his mother's domicile) a domicile of dependency when the infant's parents change domicile and may acquire a domicile of choice by the *factum* of permanent residence with the *animus* of residing there permanently or indefinitely. Upon giving up a domicile of choice the domicile of origin applies until acquisition of a new domicile of choice. However, for the purposes of the Civil Jurisdiction and Judgments Act 1982 by s.41 an individual's domicile simply requires residence in and a substantial connection with a territorial unit having its own system of law.

[2] *Spiliada Maritime Corp. v. Cansulex Ltd* [1987] A.C. 460, but in E.U. and EFTA countries jurisdiction under the Brussels and Lugano Conventions Articles 21 and 23 is on a first come (or "first seised") basis.

purporting to determine an issue that relates to the action before the court.

Detailed matters relating to questions of jurisdiction, of *forum non* **12–03** *conveniens*, and of recognition or enforcement of foreign judgments are best left to the major works on conflict of laws,[3] though the Brussels and Lugano EU and EFTA Conventions on Civil Jurisdiction and Enforcement of Judgments in force in the United Kingdom will be considered in outline at the end of the chapter. For the moment it is the choice of law issue—determining the law applicable to the matter in question—that will be examined. However, as will be seen, there are some situations where if the English court has jurisdiction it will apply English domestic law. One is used to this in family matters relating to divorce, separation and maintenance, and guardianship, custody and adoption of children, but in *Chellaram v. Chellaram, infra*, Scott J. held that the machinery for the enforcement of beneficiaries' rights determined under the proper law, particularly the removal of trustees and the appointment of new ones, is a matter to be governed by English law where the English court has jurisdiction to hear the case,[4] even though the proper law governing the validity of the trust may not be English but Indian and regardless of whether the law governing administration may be English or Indian.[5] He was strongly influenced by the maxim "Equity acts *in personam*" enabling the court to make orders effective against trustees within the jurisdiction of the court.

Background Matters and "Characterisation"

A distinction needs to be made between the testator's will or the settlor's **12–04** trust document, which may be considered as the "rocket-launcher" on the one hand, and the trust itself—the "rocket"—on the other hand.[6] The law that governs whether or not the property of the testator or settlor has been effectively vested under a valid will or other instrument in personal representatives or trustees, free or not from third-party rights (*e.g.* under forced heirship regimes,[7] matrimonial property regimes[8] or

---

[3] Dicey and Morris on *Conflict of Laws*, Cheshire & North on *Private International Law*. On conflict of laws there is a very useful chapter in Honoré's *Law of Trusts in South Africa* and Glasson (ed), *International Trust Laws*.

[4] The English Court (ignoring the E.U. and EFTA Brussels and Lugano Conventions) has jurisdiction against persons served with proceedings in England, those voluntarily submitting to the jurisdiction, and those served abroad with the court's leave if a necessary or proper party to a claim against a duly served person or if a trustee of a trust governed by English law or if the subject-matter is located within England: Civil Procedure Rule 6.20.

[5] Essentially, Scott J. seems to be regarding the enforcement of beneficiaries' rights as a matter of procedure and so governed by the *lex fori*. Also see *Stirling-Maxwell v. Cartwright* (1879) 11 Ch.D. 5 at 22; *Re Lord Cable* [1976] 3 All E.R. 417 at 431–432.

[6] *Re Lord Cable* [1976] 3 All E.R. 417 at 431. *Att.-Gen. v. Campbell* (1872) L.R. 5 H.L. 524, Article 4 of Hague Convention, see *infra*, para. 12–29.

[7] *e.g.* under French law a deceased's children have rights to part of his estate so that if he has three children he may only freely dispose of, say, one-quarter of his estate; *Re Annesley* [1926] Ch. 692; *Re Adams* [1967] I.R. 424. In ascertaining the size of his estate, gifts of capital in his lifetime are notionally added back to the value of his estate and if the actual estate at death is insufficient to satisfy the heirs' claims they have personal claims to make up the amount of their fixed or forced shares from donees, starting with the most recent donee.

[8] *e.g.* a husband cannot dispose of property within the matrimonial regime without his wife's participation: cp *Pullan v. Koe* position, para. 4–42 *supra*.

bankruptcy or defranding creditor[9] laws) may well be different from the law that governs the trust provisions once the intended trust property has wholly or partly survived the application of the law, or laws, relating to the preliminary issues.

Clearly, the formal requirements of the *lex situs* (the law of the jurisdiction of the location of the assets) need to be satisfied for transferring assets or declaring trusts thereof. If H wrongfully transfers to trustees property subject to a matrimonial property regime without W's written consent it may be that she will have a personal claim in tort or unjust enrichment against the trustees or a proprietary half share in the transferred assets and their traceable product. It is up to the *lex fori* (the law of the jurisdiction whose court is hearing the case) to characterise the issue which arises[10] and then give effect to a personal or a proprietary claim as the case may be.

12–05   This raises difficult problems where a forced heirship claim arises[11] because the deceased died domiciled in Civilopia which requires three quarters of his estate to pass to his three children absolutely, such estate being notionally increased for this purpose by earlier lifetime gifts of capital made by the deceased. Let us assume, the deceased, D, a widower, left an actual estate worth £6 million, but nine years before death transferred English assets worth £18 million to English trustees of a trust governed by English law. Thus, the three children sue the trustees for £12 million to make up their £18 million forced heirship claim.[12] Civilopia[13] characterises their claims as succession claims governed by the Civilopian *lex successionis* as the jurisdiction of D's last habitual residence, which as D's last domicile is also regarded by the English court as the *lex successionis*.

The heirs' claims would not, of course, have arisen but for D's death, but the central issue is how to treat the lifetime gift when, of course, no-one could know what would ultimately be D's *lex successionis* and whether he would die with sufficient actual estate to satisfy his heirs' claims or whether he would even be survived by any descendants. It would appear that the English *lex fori* would characterise the £18 million gift as a lifetime transfer valid by the English *lex situs*,[14] although potentially impeachable by the Insolvency Act 1986 or if he died domiciled in England within six years, having intended to defeat claims of his children to reasonable maintainance, by the Inheritance (Provision

---

[9] Insolvency Act 1986 ss.339–342, 423–425.

[10] Dicey and Morris, *Conflict of Laws* (13th ed.), para 2.034; *Macmillan Inc v. Bishopsgate Investment Trust (No. 3)* [1996] 1 All E.R. 585; *RZB v. Five Star LLC* [2001] 3 All E.R. 257.

[11] See D. J. Hayton (ed), *European Succession Laws*, (1998), for the mainland European forced heirship rules. The issue is not one of capacity (like infancy or lunacy) where it is because the lifetime gift was effective that the forced heirship claim arises.

[12] This could even occur if the trustees had transferred the assets on to trustees of a Cayman or Bermudan trust where legislation ousts forced heirship claims so no such claims could be brought there.

[13] Thus, assets found to be located in civil law jurisdictions can be frozen by the forced heirs in pursuing their claims.

[14] D. J. Hayton (ed), *European Succession Laws*, (1998), paras 1–65 to 1–68: *Lewin on Trusts* (17th ed) paras 11–59 to 11–60; P. Matthews (2001) 5 Chase Journal 15.

for Family and Dependants) Act 1975 when section 13 thereof protects trustees against being liable beyond the value of the property in their hands. No such potential having materialised, the lifetime transfer is unimpeachable and so falls outside D's estate[15] to which the Civilopian *lex successionis* applies. Such conclusion is reinforced when considering Article 15(1)(d) and (f) of The Hague Trust Convention (made English law by the Recognition of Trusts Act 1987) which require the application of the mandatory provisions of the *lex situs* designated by the English forum's choice of law rules concerning "the transfer of title to property" and "the protection, in other respects, of third parties acting in good faith", whether the trustees or the beneficiaries are regarded as "third parties".

Characterisation of a transaction as testamentary and so governed by **12–06** the *lex successionis*, or as a lifetime disposition (governed by the *lex situs*) is crucial from the perspective of formalities[16] and forced heirship claims where the deceased opened a joint account with X some years before death. The North American,[17] English[18] and Irish[19] approach is to treat property passing on death by virtue of being surviving joint tenant as being by virtue of a lifetime disposition and not a testamentary disposition.

Once the court of the forum has held that, under the applicable *lex situs*, assets have become owned by a person as trustee (including settlor-trustee), it seems it should be the applicable (or proper) law governing the trust that determines what interests have then arisen in favour of intended beneficiaries.[20]

In the case of immovables the *lex situs* has particular significance, especially for succession on the death of the owner thereof, while succession to movables is governed by the law of the deceased's last domicile in England and other common law countries—some civil law countries applying the law of the deceased's last habitual residence, some the law of the last nationality, and some applying such *lex successionis* to immovables as well as movables.[21]

---

[15] If the settlement were revocable or subject to the settlor's general power of appointment, there is a plausible case for permitting the trustees thereof to be subject (by analogy) to the forced heirship claims of heirs under the Civilopian mandatory family protection rules since the trust fund would automatically be regarded as part of the deceased's net estate subject to children's family provision claims under English family protection rules if the settlor had died domiciled in England: see Inheritance (Provision for Family and Dependants) Act 1975 s. 25(1) "net estate" definition. The section 10 position is very different: it only applies if D died within 6 years, had the requisite intent to defeat his children's claims and had not by virtue of lifetime and testamentary provisions (including trusts) made reasonable provision for them, in which circumstances the court may invade the trust to the extent necessary to make reasonable provision, but the trustees under s. 13 cannot be liable beyond the trust assets then in their hands. Any analogy between this specific narrow provision and general forced heirship rules would be false.

[16] See Chap. 2 *supra*.

[17] *Hutchinson v. Ross* 211 NE 2d 637 (1965); *Sanchez v. Sanchez* 547 So 2d 945 (1989); *Re Reid* (1921) 64 D.L.R. 598; *Edwards v. Bradley* [1956] O.R. 225.

[18] *Young v. Sealey* [1949] Ch. 278; *Re Figgis* [1969] 1 Ch 123, 149.

[19] *Lynch v. Burke* [1995] 1 IR 159.

[20] Further see J. Harris, Chapter C2 in J. Glasson (ed) *International Trust Laws* and Dicey and Morris, *Conflict of Laws* (13th ed), rules 115, 116, 117.

[21] Generally see D. J. Hayton (ed), *European Succession Laws*, (1998).

This distinction is not the same as that between real property and personal property. Leasehold interests in land, though personal property, are immovables.[22] Where Settled Land Act 1925 capital moneys have been invested in stocks and shares but by section 75(5) such capital moneys and investments therewith are regarded as "land" then the stocks and shares are immovables.[23]

General equitable principles of the Court of Chancery have a significant role, especially the maxim "Equity acts *in personam.*"[24] Other maxims that may be applicable are, for example, "equity will do nothing in vain" and "equity will not require persons to do acts illegal by the law of the place where the acts are to be performed," *e.g.* where foreign exchange laws prevent trustees from getting money out of the country for the beneficiaries.[25]

Choice of Applicable Law

12–07 As provided by Articles 6 and 7 of The Hague Convention, implemented by the Recognition of Trusts Act 1987, a trust is governed by the law expressly or impliedly chosen by the settlor, or in the absence of such choice, by the law with which the trust is most closely connected. It is easy to assume that there can be only one applicable law governing the trust except where the trust assets are physically situate in two or more countries where different applicable laws may be chosen to cover the assets situate in different countries. Upon a little reflection it can be seen that there may well be one law governing the validity of the trust provisions, often referred to as the "proper" law, and one law governing the administration of the trust. Upon further reflection, quite apart from preliminary issues concerning form or capacity with respect to the instrument creating the trust, there may be questions relating to formal validity of the trust itself[26] or capacity to act as trustee,[27] as well as questions relating to the substantive (or essential) validity of the trust provisions or questions affecting the interpretation (or construction) of such provisions. A settlor might thus state that his trust is to be governed by English law except that Queensland law is to govern matters of

---

[22] *Freke v. Carberry* (1873) L.R. 16 Eq. 461.

[23] *Re Cutcliffe's W.T.* [1940] Ch. 565.

[24] *e.g.* See also *Cook Industries Ltd v. Galliher* [1979] Ch. 439; *Derby & Co. Ltd v. Weldon (No. 2)* [1989] 1 All E.R. 1002, *Webb v. Webb* [1994] 3 All E.R. 911; [1992] 1 All E.R. 17.

[25] *Re Lord Cable* [1976] 3 All E.R. 417, for analogous contracts, see *Kahler v. Midland Bank Ltd* [1950] A.C. 24. See Articles 15 and 16, Hague Convention, *infra*, paras 12–34, 12–35.

[26] *e.g.* if the proper law applicable to the transfer of property allowed it to be done by conduct or by writing, whilst the proper law applicable to the creation of a trust of such property required use of a deed.

[27] *e.g.* if the proper law applicable to the transfer of property allowed transfer to any person of full capacity but the proper law applicable to the creation of a trust requires a trustee to be an official trust corporation or a male over 35 years of age.

interpretation[28] and Cayman Isles law is to govern matters of administration.

Where there is an express choice[29] the position is clear enough, except **12–08** for the finer points of the distinction between matters of validity and matters of administration and except for any rule of public policy that might invalidate such choice. Leaving these aside for the moment, it seems that a settlor may expressly go further and empower his trustees to change the law governing the validity of the trust (with the proviso that it does not invalidate the rights of the beneficiaries under the original law governing validity) and to change the law governing the administration of the trust, with or without changing the principal place of administration of the trust. It would seem that the law governing validity at the time of the disputed issue should determine whether that issue was a matter for the law governing validity or for the law governing administration and should, indeed, determine whether or not and by what formal methods the law governing administration may be replaced by another law.[30] This last point is particularly significant where there is no express power to change the law governing administration.

This leads one to implied choice of law for matters of validity or **12–09** matters of administration and to implied powers to change the law governing administration. If the addresses of the settlor and the trustees are English and the trust instrument refers to the English Trustee Act 1925 (*e.g.* in extending the powers in sections 31 and 32 thereof) then there will be an implied choice of English law as the applicable law governing the trust in all its aspects. At some stage implied subjective intent shades off into an imputed objective intent that the trust shall be governed by the law with which it is most closely connected at the time of its creation.[31] In ascertaining such objective law various factors are taken into account, with the weight to be attached to each factor varying according to the particular circumstances. In a testamentary trust the

---

[28] At first sight a Chancery lawyer might wonder how substantive validity and interpretation can be governed by different laws: validity almost inevitably depends on interpretation or construction. However, a trust provision may be valid whatever the interpretation, *e.g.* if "children" is legitimate children or children whether legitimate or illegitimate. Even if a trust provision would have been void under the old rule against remoteness if "issue" meant "descendants" and not just "children" the meaning of "issue" may be determined by the law expressly chosen by the testator even if different from the law governing validity. A testator may create his own dictionary of meanings whether by using specific foreign legal phrases or, generally incorporating a foreign law to govern interpretation: *Studd v. Cook* (1883) 8 App.Cas. 577.

[29] For split laws in a contractual context see *Forsikrings Vesta v. Butcher* [1986] 2 All E.R. 488 at 504–505; *Libyan Arab Bank v. Bankers Trust Co.* [1989] 3 All E.R. 252 at 267, and the Contracts (Applicable Law) Act 1990 implementing the 1980 Rome Convention, especially Articles 3 and 4.

[30] In England we consider the law governing validity as the "mother" law to which the law governing administration is attached by an umbilical cord: *cf. Marlborough v. Att.-Gen.* [1945] Ch. 78 at 85, *Iveagh v. I.R.C.* [1954] Ch. 364 at 370, *Fattorini v. Johannesburg Trust* (1948) 4 S.A.L.R. 806 at 812. So far, this seems the position in Australia and Canada. In the U.S.A. their greater experience of having different laws governing administration and of changing the place of and law of administration from time to time, has led them to consider the law governing validity as an "elder brother" and the law governing administration as a "younger brother": matters of administration are determined by the law governing administration but a change of the law governing administration cannot derogate from the beneficiaries' interests as established under the law governing validity. See Article 10, Hague Convention *infra*, para. 12–31.

[31] *Iveagh v. I.R.C.* [1954] Ch. 364.

domicile of the testator at his death has traditionally had much significance,[32] and still should have such significance under Article 7 as will obviously be the case where the home trust jurisdiction considers the matter as will normally be the case for matters concerning the internal trustee—beneficiary relationship. In the case of an *inter vivos* trust the domicile or habitual residence of the settlor at the time he created the trust has some significance as well as the place of execution of the trust instrument. Regard will also be had to the trustee's place of residence or business, though it must not be overlooked that trustees (other than professional corporate trustees) are often chosen for their personal qualities irrespective of where they live or work. Thus, if the testator or settlor expressly designates where the trust is to be administered this will be a more significant factor. Account will also be taken of the *situs* of the trust assets and the objects of the trust and the places where they are to be fulfilled.[33]

12–10   It seems there will be a presumption in favour of one implied or imputed applicable law governing all aspects of the trust,[34] the onus being upon he who alleges that one law governs validity and another law governs administration. If the original trustees appointed to administer the trust are foreign there will usually be other foreign elements and rarely will there be no express choice of the applicable law—in such rare case if there is a preponderant connection with one foreign system of law it is very likely that such law will govern both validity and administration and not just administration. If the trust instrument authorises the trustees to retire in favour of foreign trustees and to transfer the assets to such foreign trustees it seems likely that this power to change the place of administration impliedly carries with it the power to change the law governing administration to the law with which those foreign trustees are familiar, so far as this will be the law of a state that has its own internal law of trusts. For the law governing validity to be changed as well, it seems that the authority to transfer assets to foreign trustees will need to state that this is so so that such assets shall thereafter be exclusively governed by such foreign law, the "mother" law governing validity not being capable of change or exclusion except by clearly expressed intention. Indeed, where there is not a transfer of the whole trust find to trustees of a pilot settlement governed by a foreign law it may well be that declaring the trust to be governed henceforth by the law of Suntrustopia so far as not invalidating any beneficial interests under the original English trust will have Suntrustopian law operating under the continuing umbrella of English law like a sub-settlement[35] created in the exercise of a power of appointment or advancement.

---

[32] *Re Lord Cable* [1976] 3 All E.R. 417 at 431. Older cases tended to assume that the law of the testator's domicile because it governed the validity of the will must govern trust dispositions in that will: this may happen to be the case but such does not necessarily follow: *Chelleram v. Chelleram, infra.*

[33] *Fordyce v. Bridges* (1848) 2 Ph. 497; *Re Mitchner* [1922] St.R.Qd. 252. See Article 7, Hague Convention *infra*, para. 12–30.

[34] *Chelleram v. Chelleram* [1985] Ch. 409.

[35] See *Roome v. Edwards* [1982] A.C. 279; *Swires v. Renton* [1991] S.T.C. 490.

Matters of Validity Contrasted with Matters of Administration

Where there is an express power to change the law governing admin- **12–11** istration a wise settlor will specify what are matters of administration since there is precious little case law guidance on what amounts to matters of administration as opposed to matters of validity.

Some guidance may be found in *Pearson v. I.R.C.*,[36] which was concerned with "dispositive" powers of trustees that prevent a beneficiary having an interest in possession and "administrative" powers that do not. After all, dispositive powers affect the nature or *quantum* of a beneficiary's beneficial interest and so would appear not to be matters of administration. From *obiter dicta* in *Chellaram v. Chellaram, infra*, para. 12–38, it appears that the rights of the beneficiaries are matters of validity so that the corresponding duties of the trustees must also be matters of validity. This is obviously true where the beneficial interests are concerned but not as concerns the beneficiaries' rights and the trustees' duties relating to investments authorised only under the Trustee Act 2000. Matters of investment are clearly matters of administration. If the law governing administration changes from one jurisdiction to another which permits investment in "x" then beneficiaries have no right to object to investment in "x" if the trustees exhibit the requisite standard of care—even if this be of a lower standard than that required by the previous jurisdiction's law.[37]

Matters of administration, it seems, must include the powers of **12–12** trustees to administer and dispose and acquire trust assets, their powers of investment, their powers of delegation, their powers to pay debts and expenses and compromise claims, their rights to remuneration, their rights to contribution and indemnity between themselves, the appointment, retirement and removal of trustees and the devolution of trusteeship, the powers of the court to give advice and to confer powers upon trustees.

Powers of maintenance and advancement can affect the nature and extent of beneficiaries' interests, *e.g.* if the law of administration is changed to a foreign law which allows up to three-quarters of a beneficiary's contingent share to be advanced to him or gives no right to income at the age of 18 years to a beneficiary whose interest in capital is contingent on acquiring a greater age such as 30 years.[38] Thus sections 31 and 32 of the English Trustee Act should continue to apply even if the place and law of administration are changed to a different system of law, unless the clause that empowers such change can be broadly construed

---

[36] [1981] A.C. 753. A dispositive power prevents any beneficiary having an interest in possession because it enables net income to be diverted away from him after its has arisen: see *supra*, para. 1–106.

[37] It would be a fraud on the power if trustees exercised their power to change the law governing administration—or validity—for the purpose of benefiting themselves by reducing their duties of care.

[38] He will only be entitled to income on attaining the specified age in some jurisdictions. Some jurisdictions, indeed, exclude a beneficiary's rights under *Saunders v. Vautier* either altogether or only with the court's leave. The distinction between capital and income is probably a matter of validity because it affects beneficiaries' entitlements.

as authorising the foreign state's Trustee Act to apply to the exclusion of
the English Act.

12–13   Matters pertaining to the original validity of the trust provisions (*e.g.*
the rules against remoteness, accumulations and inalienability and
prohibiting purpose trusts unless charitable trusts) are for the law
governing validity. However, if an English testator in his will directs his
executors to transfer some Scottish property, whether movable or
immovable, that he himself had earlier inherited to two Scottish trustees
on public but non-charitable trusts (valid according to Scots law but not
English law) then although the law governing the testator's will and
other trust dispositions in it may be English it should be Scots law that
governs and upholds the validity of the public trusts.[39]

12–14   The Variation of Trusts Act position is special. Most jurisdictions have
such Acts. Since the legislation can drastically alter the nature and extent
of beneficiaries' interests one might have expected that the court's
jurisdiction should be restricted to those trusts whose validity is governed
by the *lex fori*. However, the English courts have arrogated to themselves
unlimited jurisdiction in the absence of restricting words in the Variation
of Trusts Act 1958.[40] "However, where there are substantial foreign
elements in the case, the court must consider carefully whether it is
proper to exercise the jurisdiction. If, for example, the court were asked
to vary a settlement which was plainly a Scottish settlement, it might well
hesitate to exercise its jurisdiction to vary the trusts simply because some
of, or even all, the trustees and beneficiaries were in this country. It may
well be that the judge would say that the Court of Session was the
appropriate tribunal to deal with the case."[41] In the light of Article
8(2)(h) of the Hague Convention it is very likely that an English court
will decline jurisdiction for trusts governed by a foreign law (unless
legislation thereof specifically authorised the English court). One must
remember that all the parties before the court will be anxious for the
jurisdiction to be exercised for family or for taxation reasons and that
the interests of infant or unborn beneficiaries will hardly ever[42] be
prejudiced by any variation. However, the taxation authorities in a
particular country may take the point that the variation is ineffective
except to the extent that adult beneficiaries are estopped from reverting
to the pre-variation position.

Court orders varying nuptial settlements[43] under Matrimonial Causes
Act 1973 section 24 (1)(c) and (d) can be made even in respect of
foreign trusts of foreign property held by foreign trustees[44] but will not

---

[39] *cf. Jewish National Fund v. Royal Trust Co.* (1965) 53 D.L.R. (2d) 577. The courts tend, where
possible, to choose as the applicable law one which will sustain the validity of the trust: *Augustus v.
Permanent Trustee Co. (Canberra) Ltd* (1971) 124 C.L.R. 245.
[40] *Re Ker's Settlement* [1963] Ch. 553; *Re Paget's Settlement* [1965] 1 W.L.R. 1046. The same has
happened in Alberta and in Western Australia: *Commercial Trust Co. v. Laing* unreported (Waters
Law of Trusts in Canada, at 1134); *Faye v. Faye* [1973] W.A.R. 66.
[41] *Re Paget's Settlement* [1965] 1 W.L.R. 1046 at 1050, *per* Cross J.
[42] See *Re Remnant's W.T.* [1970] 1 Ch. 560.
[43] *Brooks v. Brooks* [1995] 3 Au E.R. 257, 263.
[44] *E v. E* [1990] F.L.R. 233, 242; *T v. T* [1996] 2 F.L.R. 357, 363.

be made if they would be ineffective in the relevant foreign country.[45] One can invoke Articles 18 and 15(1)(b) to justify such English jurisdiction so that there can be a proper determination of all matters arising out of the divorce, application of the Act being an effect of the marriage. The Variation of Trusts Act jurisdiction is different in requiring the consent of all adult beneficiaries coupled with the court's consent, while the trustees have a non-partisan co-operative function.

Limitations upon Free Choice of Law

Obvious problems exist where immovables are concerned but under the **12–15** Trusts Convention the *lex situs* does not need to govern the validity of trusts of immovables. Take land in Spain (which does not have the trust concept within its code of law) or in Jersey (which allows trusts so long as they are not of land in Jersey). There are practical problems if recourse has to be had to Spanish or Jersey courts and so far as title to the land is concerned the trustees would appear as ordinary private beneficial owners. However, if the land comprised say one-twentieth of the aggregate of property subjected to trusts with an English proper law why should the English trustees not be under valid *in personam* trusteeship obligations to the English beneficiaries in respect of the land, *e.g.* to pay rents over to the beneficiaries and to keep the premises in reasonable repair?[46]

A settlor has total freedom of choice of law unless such choice is **12–16** manifestly incompatible with public policy.[47] Article 13 of the Hague Convention affords a discretion to refuse to recognise a trust if its significant elements, except for the choice of law, the place of administration and the habitual residence of the trustee, are more closely connected with a non-trust-State. The United Kingdom considered it unhelpful for its courts to have such a discretion and so the Recognition of Trusts Act 1987 deliberately omits the uncertainties of Article 13.

If, in what would otherwise be a trust governed by English law, an Englishman purports to create a trust of English land but expressly chooses a foreign law with the intent of enabling the land to be held for ever on valid public but non-charitable purpose trusts it is clear that the trust will be void. The English court will have to give effect to the English policy rules as to the administration of land within the jurisdiction. Indeed, the policy rules recognising the unenforceability of purpose trusts, where no one has *locus standi* to apply to the court to have the

---

[45] *Goff v. Goff* [1934] p. 107, 113.
[46] *cf. Re Fitzgerald* [1904] 1 Ch. 573; *Webb v. Webb* [1994] 3 All E.R. 911. Sufficient scope is afforded to the *lex situs* to govern preliminary or policy issues, *e.g. Re Ross* [1930] 1 Ch. 377 (*legitima portio*); *Re Hoyles* [1911] 1 Ch. 179, *Duncan v. Lawson* (1889) 41 Ch.D. 394 (Mortmain Acts); *Freke v. Carberry* (1873) L.R. 16 Eq. 461 (perpetuities and accumulations); *Re Pearse's Settlement* [1909] 1 Ch. 304 (Jersey land could not be conveyed by a married woman to someone except for adequate pecuniary compensation so that her after-acquired property convenant in an English settlement was construed as not intended to include after-acquired Jersey land within the scope of the convenant).
[47] See Articles 6 and 18 but note the safeguards in Articles 15 and 16 of The Hague Convention.

purposes positively carried out, would prevent the trust being effective even if the property was not land.

12–17   If, however, it was movable or immovable property in Scotland subjected to public non-charitable purpose trusts expressed to be subject to Scots law then there seems no policy reason for the English court to invalidate such trusts of an English testator in his English will. Indeed, if the trusts were private non-charitable purpose trusts of movables in the Isle of Man, Jersey, Bermuda or Cayman valid under special legislation with there being at least one person with standing to enforce the trust, the English court should not invalidate them, nor should it if such trusts purchase English assets as investments or even if such assets are directly transferred to the trustees to become original settled assets.[48] However, the purposes must not amount to a mere investment clause[49] or to a device purporting to put beneficial ownership in suspense protected from claims of creditors and tax inspectors.[50]

One should note that a choice of law (*e.g.* English law) to govern a trust makes that law govern the relationship between the trustees and the beneficiaries: that law governs the "internal" aspects of the trust. As far as the trustees' "external" relations with third parties are concerned, *e.g.* in contracting with them or transferring property to them one has to apply the conflict of laws rules applicable to contracts or to the transfer of property. Thus, a trustee of a trust governed by the law of Jersey may rely when contracting in Jersey on Article 32(1) of the Trusts Jersey Law 1983, "Where in any transaction or matter affecting a trust a trustee informs a third party that he is acting as trustee a claim by such third party in relation thereto shall extend only to the trust property." If the trustee contracts in England under English law (not expressly choosing Jersey law to govern the contract) he will be personally liable since any person contracting under English law is personally liable except to the extent he expressly restricts liability, for example to trust property to which he has a right of recourse for paying trust expenses.[51]

THE RECOGNITION OF TRUSTS ACT 1987

12–18   Since August 1, 1987, Articles 1 to 18 (except 13 and 16 para. 2) and 22 of The Hague Trusts Convention, *infra*, have been in force in the United Kingdom in respect of trusts whenever created, but this does not affect

---

[48] See D.J. Hayton, "Developing the Obligation Characteristic of the Trust" (2001) 117 L.Q.R. 96. Further on offshore developments see D.J. Hayton (ed) *Modern International Developments in Trust Law* (Kluwer 1999) Chapters 1 and 15; A.G.D. Duckworth, "The Role of Offshore Jurisdictions in the Development of the International Trust" (1999) 32 Vanderbilt Jo. Transnational Law 879; A.G.D. Dackworth "Trust Law in the New Millennium: Fundamentals" *Trusts & Trustees*, Feb 2001, at 9–15.

[49] *e.g.* a trust for the purpose of developing the income yield and capital growth of the trust fund, so in default of disposal of the beneficial interest there will be a resulting trust for the settlor.

[50] *e.g.* a trust to develop the business of X Co Ltd where X Co or its owner should be regarded as beneficiary. Under the Cayman Special Trusts Alternative Regime Law 1997 s.7 "beneficiaries" have no interests whatsoever in the trust property and have no rights to sue the trustees or the expressly appointed "enforcer", so unless a "beneficiary" has been appointed an enforcer the English court seems likely to treat "beneficiaries" as objects of a power, leaving a resulting trust for the settlor: *cf Armitage v. Nurse* [1998] Ch. 241, 253.

[51] See *supra*, para. 9–446

the law to be applied to anything done or omitted before August 1, 1987.[52] Section 1(2) extends the Convention's provisions to any other trusts of property arising (*e.g.* orally or by statute) under the law of any part of the United Kingdom or by virtue of a judicial decision in the United Kingdom or elsewhere. This is because Article 3 restricts the Convention to trusts created voluntarily and evidenced in writing.[53] Despite the superficial width of Article 2 the Convention does not extend beyond trusts to agency or mandate as earlier explained.[54]

LIMITED SCOPE OF TRUSTS CONVENTION

1. This (private international law) Convention does not introduce the **12–19** trust into the internal private law of States that do not have the concept of the trust; it simply makes foreign States recognise trusts of property as a matter of private international law, although, for recognition to mean something, the internal private law needs to recognise that the trust fund is separate from the owner's private patrimony, so as to be immune from claims of the owner's creditors heirs and spouse.[55]

2. This (private international law) Convention does not affect the internal private law of States that have the trust concept: the extent to which the applicable law can be expressly or impliedly changed and the distinction between matters of validity and matters of administration may vary according to the appropriate applicable law because State A's internal trust rules may differ from such rules of State B.

3. Non-trust states expect the home jurisdiction to resolve matters concerning the internal trustee—beneficiary relationship, so the Trusts Convention will help them where the external relationship of the trustees with third is concerned.

4. The Convention applies only to a trust ("the rocket") and not to the instrument launching the trust ("the rocket-launcher"). Antecedent preliminary issues that may affect the validity of wills, deeds or other acts by which property is allegedly subjected to a trust fall outside the Convention: Article 4. The Convention only applies if whatever is the applicable law governing capacity or formal or substantive validity of wills or *inter vivos* declarations of trust by the settlor or transfers of property to trustees has not operated to prevent the relevant property being available to be subjected to trusts.

5. While the Convention recognises the equitable proprietary right of **12–20** beneficiaries in trust property and its traceable product in States that have such equitable concept, it does not introduce such proprietary right

---

[52] S.I. 1987 No. 1177. The Convention is regarded as clarifying the common law position (on which see Wallace (1987) 36 I.C.L.Q. 454) but the non-retrospective provision was inserted in s.1(5) of the 1987 Act *ex abundante cautela*.

[53] The French text is "et dont la preuve est *apportée par écrit*" which appears to need dilution to reflect "evidenced" in writing and so to cover most trusts which are first established in respect of a nominal sum, with substantial assets being added subsequently and with written evidence subsequently arising, whether produced by the settlor or the trustees.

[54] See paras 1–11, 1–12. A settlor's declaration of himself as trustee of assets now controlled by him as trustee should be within Article 2.

[55] The Dutch implementing legislation provides for this: D.J. Hayton (1996) 5 J. Int. P. 127.

into States that have no concept of equitable proprietary interest in their fixed scheme of property interests. If trust property is transferred in such a State to X the *lex situs* will govern the effect of such transfer and deny the existence of any equitable proprietary interest except to the extent that any actual knowledge by X of a breach of trust may make it possible to take advantage of any *lex situs* rules on fraud: see the last sentence of Article 11 paragraph 3(d) and also Article 15(d)(f) and paragraph 113 of the Von Overbeck Official Report on the Trusts Convention.[56] However, in *El Ajou v. Dollar Landholdings plc*[57] the equitable tracing process was held not to be defeated if traceable assets passed through various civil law jurisdictions so as to end up in a common law jurisdiction.

12–21   6. Article 15 detracts hugely from Article 11. It ensures the application of the internal mandatory rules of a State whose law is applicable according to the conflicts rules of the forum, irrespective of the law applicable to the trust. A forum will have choice of law rules in areas such as succession, property, bankruptcy, matrimonial property regimes. Civil law states[58] know little of a distinction between a private patrimony and a fiduciary patrimony so that a separate fiduciary fund as a type of quasi-security for the personal claims of beneficiaries may only arise if the implementing legislation expressly ousts Article 15 paragraph (d) and (e) as in the Netherlands, unless one can boldly regard Article 11 as requiring recognition of a fiduciary patrimony separate from a private patrimony which alone is subject to Article 15. After all paragraph 108 of the Von Overbeck Report states that Article 11 paragraph 2 "determines that the assets of the trust are separate from those of the trustee. This is an essential element of the trust, without which its recognition would have no meaning." Mandatory succession rules (*réserve héréditaire, legitima portio, pflichtteil*) have special significance, especially if a settlor's trust assets are found in the civil law forum of a forced heir who seeks such assets: *Holzberg v. Sasson* 1986 Rev. crit. de dr. int. pr. 685. Choice of law rules may lead to the *lex successionis, lex situs* or *lex fori* being invoked so as wholly or partly to undo the effects of a trust. While an English court should characterise a Frenchman's transfer of assets in England to English trustees as a straightforward *inter vivos* transfer of property governed by the English *lex situs,* protected by Article 15(d) of the Convention, and then by the English applicable law of the trust, a French court will characterise such transfer as pertaining to the French *lex successionis* so far as it affects property subject to *réserve héréditaire.* So long as the trust property remains in England (or another common law country) it should remain intact but if the property is found in France (or a sympathetic civil law country) then the heirs may claim it in satisfaction of their *réserves héréditaires.*

---

[56] The Report is reproduced in Glasson (ed) *International Trust Laws* and will be taken account of by the court in construing the Convention as implemented by the 1987 Recognition of Trusts Act: *e.g. Three Rivers D. C. v. Bank of England* (No 2) [1996] 2 All E.R. 363.

[57] [1993] 3 All E.R. 717, 736–737, [1995] 2 All E.R. 213, 221 in respect of a personal claim but the position should be the same for a proprietary remedy despite the property vindication approach in *Foskett v. McKeown* [2000] 3 All E.R. 97: the life of the law has not always been logical.

[58] See Hayton, Kortmann & Verhagen (eds.) *Principles of European Trust Law* (Kluwer, 1999).

7. Under the first paragraph of Article 16 the *lex fori* court must of **12–22**
course apply its own international mandatory rules, *e.g.* if a beneficiary is
suing the trustee for failure to export to the beneficiary some thing or
animal whose export is prohibited by the *lex fori*.

Under the second paragraph the *lex fori* court has a discretion, to be
exercised only in the most exceptional case, to apply the international
mandatory rules of some other State with a sufficiently close connection
with the case, where the State's law is neither the *lex fori* nor the law
applicable to the trust as such.

Trust States find it difficult to appreciate the need for such a provision
since a Court of Equity will do nothing in vain (*i.e.* will not make orders
which cannot be carried out as where foreign immovables are concerned) and will not require a person to do an act that is illegal in the
place where it is to be done.[59] Thus, if the law of the trust is that of State
A, the law of the forum that of State B, and the law of State C makes it
illegal to take certain sorts of assets out of State C, any action by a
beneficiary against the trustees for not getting such assets out to the
beneficiary will fail, regardless of the second paragraph. The uncertain
ambit of the paragraph is also unsatisfactory for lawyers and for courts.
The United Kingdom government therefore made the reservation
allowed by the third paragraph.

8. By Article 13 a court in a trust or non-trust State has a **12–23**
discretionary power to refuse to recognise a trust if the significant
elements of the trust (*e.g.* situs of assets, settlor's and beneficiaries'
habitual residence) are more closely connected with non-trust than with
trust States, except for the choice of the applicable law, the place of
administration and the habitual residence of the trustee. It seems that it
is up to the court to decide in a particular case what are the significant
elements which connect the trust closely to a non-trust State. The
relevant time for these significant elements to be so connected seems to
be the time of the events occasioning the claim for recognition and not
the time of creation of the trust. The United Kingdom Recognition of
Trusts Act 1987 deliberately omitted Article 13 because it was considered unnecessary for such a discretion to be available.

9. The Convention is only concerned with trusts of property created
voluntarily and evidenced in writing[60] and not with the imposition of
constructive trusteeship upon a defendant so that he is personally liable
to account as a constructive trustee if he dishonestly assisted in a breach
of trust, whether or not any trust property was ever in his hands. Where
a defendant cannot be made personally liable in tort or contract but has
acted with want of probity equity constructively treats him as if he had
been a trustee as a formula for an equitable personal (as opposed to
proprietary) remedy, which will be of no assistance if the defendant is
deeply insolvent. A defendant in a State not having the trust and any

---

[59] *Re Lord Cable* [1976] 3 All E.R. 417, 435
[60] Seemingly of the settlor or the trustees in signing trust accounts e.g. in relation to property
subsequently added to trusts of nominal sums.

equitable jurisdiction can never be liable as a constructive trustee in that State.

CIVIL JURISDICTION & JUDGMENTS ACTS 1982 & 1991

12–24 These Acts make special provision for E.U. countries and for EFTA countries as required by the Brussels 1968 Convention on Civil Jurisdiction and Enforcement of Judgments and the parallel Lugano Convention of 1988. The basic principle is that jurisdiction is conferred on the courts of the "domicile" of the defendant,[61] but a person may be sued as settlor trustee or beneficiary in the courts of the contracting State in which the trust is "domiciled".[62] A trust is domiciled in the state having the system of law with which the trust has its closest and most real connection,[63] which seems to be the system that provides the applicable (or governing) law of the trust, so giving birth to the trust. The court first "seised" of the action hears it,[64] the *forum non conveniens* discretion being unavailable.

12–25 However, if a trust instrument confers jurisdiction on a particular system of law, the courts of that system will have exclusive jurisdiction in any proceedings brought against a settlor, trustee or beneficiary if relations betwen these persons or their rights or obligations under the trust are involved,[65] unless the proceedings have as their object rights *in rem* in immovable property or tenancies of immovable property, when the courts of the state in which such property is situated have exclusive jurisdiction.[66] If a father claims that French immovable property vested in his son is held on a resulting trust for the father this is regarded as a personal matter between them so that the French court does not have exclusive jursidiction: English Equity acts *in personam* and the English court has jurisdiction if the son is resident in England or the trust is an English trust.[67]

The Conventions and Acts do not apply to rights in property arising out of a matrimonial relationship, wills or succession or bankruptcy or insolvency,[68] thus excluding ante-nuptial marriage settlements. However, once under the relevant law governing wills and succession a testamentary trust has been permitted to arise, it seems that any subsequent dispute (*e.g.* arising 20 or 30 years later) should fall within the Conventions and the Act, just as in the case of a dispute arising under a trust set up in the settlor's lifetime.

---

[61] Requisting only residence in and a substantial connection with the relevant jurisdiction.
[62] Art. 5(6).
[63] s.45 of the 1982 Act.
[64] Articles 21 and 23 respectively of the Brussels and Lugano Conventions.
[65] Art. 17.
[66] Art. 16(1).
[67] *Webb v. Webb* [1994] Q.B. 696; [1994] 3 All E.R. 911 applied by CA in *Polland v. Ashurst* [2001] 2 All E.R. 75 upholding judge's order on behalf of husband's trustee in bankruptcy that husband and wife should sell their jointly owned Portugese villa to enable the trustee to obtain the husband's share of the proceeds.
[68] Art. 1(1).

Judgments given in a contracting State are to be recognised and **12–26** enforced in the other contracting States.[69] However, a judgment will not be recognised[70]:

(1) if such recognition is contrary to public policy;

(2) where it was given in default of appearance if the defendant was not duly served with the relevant proceedings in sufficient time to enable him to arrange for his defence;

(3) if the judgment is irreconcilable with a judgment in a dispute between the same parties in the State in which recognition is sought;

(4) if the court of the State of origin, in order to arrive at its judgment, has decided a preliminary question concerning the status or legal capacity of natural person, rights in property arising out of a matrimonial realtionship, wills or succession in a way that conflicts with a rule of the private international law of the State in which recognition is sought unless the same result would have been reached by the application of the rules of private international law of that State.[71]

CONVENTION ON THE LAW APPLICABLE TO TRUSTS AND ON THEIR RECOGNITION[72]

The States signatory to the present Convention,   **12–27**

Considering that the trust, as developed in courts of equity in common law jurisdictions and adopted with some modifications in other jurisdictions, is a unique legal institution,

Desiring to establish common provisions on the law applicable to trusts and to deal with the most important issues concerning the recognition of trusts,

Have resolved to conclude a Convention to this effect, and have agreed upon the following provisions—

CHAPTER I—SCOPE

Article 1

This Convention specifies the law applicable to trusts and governs their **12–28** recognition.

---

[69] Arts. 26, 31.

[70] Art. 27.

[71] Thus, if a Greek forced heir obtained a delict (or tort) judgment in Greece against trustee-owners of property refusing to transfer it to him, he could not enforce it in England if the English Court characterises the issue not as involving a tort but as involving rights "arising out of wills or succession."

[72] Generally see Explanatory Report by A.E. von Overbeck published by Permanent Bureau of The Hague Conference in Acts and Documents of the 15th Session of the Hague Conference pp. 370 *et seq.*, D. J. Hayton (1987) 36 I.C.L.Q. 260; Underhill & Hayton (15th ed.) Chapter 23; *Lewin on Trusts* (17th ed) Chapter 11; O'Sullivan [1993] 2 J.Int. P. 85; Albisini & Gambino [1993] 2 J.Int. P. 73; Schoenblum [1994] 1 J.Int. P. 5; Hayton [1994] J.Int. P. 23; Dicey & Morris, Chap. 29; Hayton in Borras (ed.) *Liber Amicorum Georges Droz* (1996). The Convention has been ratified (*i.e.* implemented) by Italy, Malta, Australia, Netherlands, Canada (for Alberta, New Brunswick, British Columbia, Newfoundland, Prince Edward Island, Manitoba, Saskatchewan) and the United Kingdom (including Isle of Man, Jersey, Guernsey, Gibraltar, Bermuda, Hong Kong, British Virgin Islands, Turks & Caicos, Montserrat, but not Cayman Islands). The USA, France and Luxembourg have signed the convention revealing an intention to ratify in due course. Indeed Luxembourg has introduced into its legislature a bill to implement the Convention while the Swiss Government is considering a report proposing ratification of the Convention.

Article 2

For the purposes of this Convention, the term "trust" refers to the legal relationships created—*inter vivos* or on death—by a person, the settlor, when assets have been placed under the control of a trustee for the benefit of a beneficiary or for a specified purpose.

A trust has the following characteristics—

(*a*) the assets constitute a separate fund and are not a part of the trustee's own estate;
(*b*) title to the trust assets stands in the name of the trustee or in the name of another person on behalf of the trustee;
(*c*) the trustee has the power and the duty, in respect of which he is accountable, to manage, employ or dispose of the assets in accordance with the terms of the trust and the special duties imposed upon him by law.

The reservation by the settlor of certain rights and powers and the fact that the trustee may himself have rights as a beneficiary, are not necessarily inconsistent with the existence of a trust.

Article 3

12–29 The Convention applies only to trusts created voluntarily and evidenced in writing.

Article 4

The Convention does not apply to preliminary issues relating to the validity of wills or of other acts by virtue of which assets are transferred to the trustee.

Article 5

The Convention does not apply to the extent that the law specified by Chapter II does not provide for trusts or the category of trusts involved.

CHAPTER II—APPLICABLE LAW

Article 6

12–30 A trust shall be governed by the law chosen by the settlor. The choice must be express or be implied in the terms of the instrument creating or the writing evidencing the trust, interpreted, if necessary, in the light of circumstances of the case.

Where the law chosen under the previous paragraph does not provide for trusts or the category of trust involved, the choice shall not be effective and the law specified in Article 7 shall apply.

Article 7

Where no applicable law has been chosen, a trust shall be governed by the law with which it is most closely connected.

In ascertaining the law with which a trust is most closely connected reference shall be made in particular to—

(*a*) the place of administration of the trust designated by the settlor;

(*b*) the situs of the assets of the trust;
(*c*) the place of residence or business of the trustee;
(*d*) the objects of the trust and the places where they are to be fulfilled.

Article 8

The law specified by Article 6 or 7 shall govern the validity of the trust, its **12–31** construction, its effects, and the administration of the trust. In particular that law shall govern—

(*a*) the appointment, resignation and removal of trustees, the capacity to act as a trustee, and the devolution of the office or trustee;
(*b*) the rights and duties of trustees among themselves;
(*c*) the right of trustees to delegate in whole or in part the discharge of their duties or the exercise of their powers;
(*d*) the power of trustees to administer or to dispose of trust assets, to create security interests in the trust assets, or to acquire new assets;
(*e*) the powers of investment of trustees;
(*f*) restrictions upon the duration of the trust, and upon the power to accumulate the income of the trust;
(*g*) the relationships between the trustees and the beneficiaries including the personal liability of the trustees to the beneficiaries;
(*h*) the variation or termination of the trust;
(*i*) the distribution of the trust assets;
(*j*) the duty of trustees to account for their administration.

Article 9

In applying this Chapter a severable aspect of the trust, particularly matters of administration, may be governed by a different law.

Article 10

The law applicable to the validity of the trust shall determine whether that law or the law governing the severable aspect of the trust may be replaced by another law.

CHAPTER III—RECOGNITION

Article 11

A trust created in accordance with the law specified by the preceding Chapter **12–32** shall be recognized as a trust. Such recognition shall imply, as a minimum, that the trust property constitutes a separate fund, that the trustee may sue and be sued in his capacity as trustee, and that he may appear or act in this capacity before a notary or any person acting in an official capacity.

In so far as the law applicable to a trust requires or provides, such recognition shall imply, in particular—

(*a*) that personal creditors of the trustee shall have no recourse against the trust assets;
(*b*) that the trust assets shall not form part of the trustee's estate upon his insolvency or bankruptcy;

(*c*) that the trust assets shall not form part of the matrimonial property of the trustee or his spouse nor part of the trustee's estate upon his death;

(*d*) that the trust assets may be recovered when the trustee, in breach of trust, has mingled trust assets with his own property or has alienated trust assets. However, the rights and obligations of any third party holder of the assets shall remain subject to the law determined by the choice of law rules of the forum.

Article 12

12–33 Where the trustee desires to register assets, movable or immovable, or documents of title to them, he shall be entitled, in so far as this is not prohibited by or inconsistent with the law of the State where registration is sought, to do so in his capacity as trustee or in such other way that the existence of the trust is disclosed.

Article 13

No State shall be bound to recognize a trust the significant elements of which, except for the choice of the applicable law, the place of administration and the habitual residence of the trustee, are more closely connected with States which do not have the institution of the trust or the category of trust involved.

Article 14

The Convention shall not prevent the application of rules of law more favourable to the recognition of trusts.

Chapter IV-General Clauses

Article 15

12–34 The Convention does not prevent the application of provisions of the law designated by the conflicts rules of the forum, in so far as those provisions cannot be derogated from by voluntary act, relating in particular to the following matters—

(*a*) the protection of minors and incapable parties;
(*b*) the personal and proprietary effects of marriage;
(*c*) succession rights, testate and intestate, especially the indefeasible shares of spouses and relatives;
(*d*) the transfer of title to property and security interests in property;
(*e*) the protection of creditors in matters of insolvency;
(*f*) the protection, in other respects, of third parties acting in good faith.

If recognition of a trust is prevented by application of the preceding paragraph, the court shall try to give effect to the objects of the trust by other means.

Article 16

12–35 The Convention does not prevent the application of those provisions of the law of the forum which must be applied even to international situations, irrespective of rules of conflict of laws.

If another State has a sufficiently close connection with a case then, in exceptional circumstances, effect may also be given to rules of that State which have the same character as mentioned in the preceding paragraph.

Any Contracting State may, by way of reservation, declare that it will not apply the second paragraph of this article.

Article 17

In the Convention the word "law" means the rules of law in force in a State other than its rules of conflict of laws.

Article 18

The provisions of the Convention may be disregarded when their application would be manifestly incompatible with public policy (*ordre public*).

Article 19

Nothing in the Convention shall prejudice the powers of States in fiscal matters.

Article 20

Any Contracting State may, at any time, declare that the provisions of the **12–36** Convention will be extended to trusts declared by judicial decisions.

This declaration shall be notified to the Ministry of Foreign Affairs of the Kingdom of the Netherlands and will come into effect on the day when this notification is received.

Article 31 is applicable to the withdrawal of this declaration in the same way as it applies to a denunciation of the Convention.

Article 21

Any Contracting State may reserve the right to apply the provisions of Chapter III only to trusts the validity of which is governed by the law of a Contracting State.

Article 22

The Convention applies to trusts regardless of the date on which they were **12–37** created.

However, a Contracting State may reserve the right not to apply the Convention to trusts created before the date on which, in relation to that State, the Convention enters into force.

Article 23

For the purpose of identifying the law applicable under the Convention, where a State comprises several territorial units each of which has its own rules of law in respect of trusts, any reference to the law of that State is to be construed as referring to the law in force in the territorial unit in question.

CHELLARAM V. CHELLARAM

Chancery Division [1985] 1 All E.R. 1043; [1985] Ch. 409

SCOTT J.: "The bedrock of counsel for the defendants' case is that these two **12–38** settlements are foreign settlements, the proper law of which is the law of India. Counsel for the plaintiffs contends, on the contrary, that the proper law is the law of England.

"It is important to be clear at the outset as to the relevance of this issue on the present application. The application seeks to prevent the plaintiffs from prosecuting in England a claim for the removal of the trustees and for the appointment of new trustees. Counsel for the defendants argues that the law by which the proposition that the trustees should be removed must be tested, and by which the question of who should be appointed in their places must be answered, is the proper law of the settlement. Counsel for the plaintiffs submits, however, that it is not the proper law of the settlement but the law of the place of administration that should govern such issues as removal of trustees and appointment of new ones. The place of administration, he submits, is London.

"The proper law of the settlement is, *per* Lord Greene M.R. in *Duke of Marlborough v. A.-G. (No. 1)* [1945] Ch. 78 at 83, the law which governs the settlement. He went on:

> "This law can only be the law by reference to which the settlement was made and which was intended by the parties to govern their rights and liabilities."

In Dicey and Morris on the *Conflict of Laws* (10th ed., 1980), p. 678, r. 120 states:

> "The validity, the interpretation and the effect of an *inter vivos* trust of movables are governed by its proper law, that is, in the absence of any express or implied selection of the proper law by the settlor, the system of law with which the trust has its closest and most real connection."

12–39   "When counsel for the defendants first opened the case to me, I was strongly inclined to regard the law of India as the obvious proper law of these two settlements, but as argument progressed I found myself progressively less certain. The beneficiaries are an Indian family. The trustees were all Indian in origin although one or other may have held a British passport. The settlements were drawn up in Bombay by Mr. Advani, an Indian practitioner, acting apparently in the course of his profession. The settlors were Indian in origin and Indian-domiciled at the date of the settlement. All these factors point, and I think point strongly, to the law of India being the proper law.

"Mr. Advani has sworn an affirmation in which he has stated in terms that he intended Indian law to apply to these settlements which he drafted. This evidence is inadmissible as evidence of the intentions of the parties to the settlements, but I may, I think, take it as indicating that the settlements are appropriate in form for the purposes of Indian law. Nevertheless, I am left with doubts. The trust property was Bermudian. The underlying assets, in the form of the operating companies, were all situated outside India. The purpose of the settlements was, it seems, in part to escape Indian taxation and, in part, to escape Indian exchange control regulations. But most important of all, it seems to me, is the identity of the three original trustees. Two, Mr. Rupchand and Mr. Bharwani, were permanently resident in England. The third, Ram Chellaram, was the member of the family who, in 1975, appeared to have the closest connection with England. The inference is inescapable that the parties to the settlements contemplated that administration thereof would take place in London. Indeed, counsel for the defendants accepted that this was an inference which was open to be drawn.

12–40   "The question why, if the parties intended the settlements to be governed by Indian law they should have arranged for an English administration, is a difficult one to answer. The parties' contemplation of an English administration seems to me to point strongly in favour of an English proper law. For the moment, however, I propose to leave the question open and to assume that counsel for the defendants is right that the law of India is the proper law of the settlement and to see where that leads. It leads, counsel for the defendants submitted, to the conclusion that the English courts should have nothing to do with the plaintiffs' claim for the removal of the trustees. You cannot have, he said, English courts removing foreign trustees of foreign settlements any more than you can have foreign courts removing English trustees of English settlements. Tied up in this *cri de coeur* are, in my view, three separate points. First, there is the question of jurisdiction. Does an English court have jurisdiction to entertain such a claim? Second, there is the question of power. If an English court does have jurisdiction, can it make an effective order removing foreign trustees of foreign settlements? Third, there is the *forum conveniens* point. Is this an action which an English court ought to be trying?

"I start with jurisdiction. In a sense, there is no doubt at all but that the court **12–41** has jurisdiction. Each of the defendants was either served personally or service was effected on Norton Rose Botterell & Roche who had authority to accept service. By reason of due service of the writ, the court has jurisdiction over each of the defendants in respect of each of the issues raised by the writ.

"As to subject matter, also there is in my judgment no doubt that the court has jurisdiction. In *Ewing v. Orr Ewing* (1883) 9 App.Cas. 34 it was held by the House of Lords that the English courts had jurisdiction to administer the trusts of the will of a testator who died domiciled in Scotland. The will was proved in Scotland by executors, some of whom resided in Scotland and some in England. The assets, the subject of the trusts, consisted mainly of hereditable and personal property in Scotland. An infant beneficiary resident in England brought an action in England for the administration of the trusts of the will by the English courts. It was clear that the proper law of the trusts was the law of Scotland. None the less, the House of Lords, affirming the Court of Appeal, upheld the jurisdiction of the English courts. The Earl of Selborne L.C. said (at 40–41):

> ". . . the jurisdiction of the English Court is established upon elementary **12–42** principles. The Courts of Equity in England are, and always have been, Courts of conscience, operating *in personam* and not *in rem*; and in exercise of this personal jurisdiction that have always been accustomed to compel the performance of contracts and trusts as to subjects which were not either locally or *ratione domicilii* within their jurisdiction. They have done so as to land, in Scotland, in Ireland, in the Colonies, in foreign countries. . . . A jurisdiction against trustees, which is not excluded *ratione legis rei sitae* as to land, cannot be excluded as to movables, because the author of the trust may have had a foreign domicil; and for this purpose it makes no difference whether the trust is constituted *inter vivos*, or by a will, or *mortis causâ* deed."

Lord Blackburn agreed (at 46):

> "The jurisdiction of the Court of Chancery is *in personam*. It acts upon the person whom it finds within its jurisdiction and compels him to perform the duty which he owes to the plaintiff."

Both the Earl of Selborne L.C. and Lord Blackburn went on to say that the jurisdiction of the court to administer the foreign trust was not truly discretionary and that the plaintiff was entitled to the order sought *ex debito justitae* (see 9 App.Cas. 34 at 41–42, 47–48).

12–43   "That view cannot, in my judgment, stand with more recent pronouncements in the House of Lords (see, *e.g.* Lord Diplock in *The Abidin Daver* [1984] A.C. 398 at 411–412). Current authority establishes that the court does have a discretion to decline jurisdiction on *forum non conveniens* grounds. But the principle that the English court has jurisdiction to administer the trusts of foreign settlements remains unshaken. The jurisdiction is *in personam*, is exercised against the trustees on whom the foreign trust obligations lie, and is exercised so as to enforce against the trustees the obligations which bind their conscience.

"The jurisdiction which I hold the court enjoys embraces, in my view, jurisdiction to remove trustees and appoint new ones. In *Letterstedt v. Broers* (1884) 9 App.Cas. 371 at 385–386, Lord Blackburn referred to a passage in Story's *Equity Jurisprudence* (12th ed., 1877), section 1289, which reads:

> '. . . Courts of equity have no difficulty in interposing to remove trustees who have abused their trust . . .'

Lord Blackburn then continued:

> 'It seems to their Lordships that the jurisdiction which a Court of Equity has no difficulty in exercising under the circumstances indicated by Story is merely ancillary to its principal duty, to see that the trusts are properly executed.'

Accordingly, in my judgment, the courts of this country, having jurisdiction to administer the trusts of the two settlements, have jurisdiction ancillary thereto to remove the trustees.

12–44   "The argument of counsel for the defendants that the court did not have jurisdiction to remove the trustees of a foreign settlement was based in part on the proposition that an order of removal would be ineffective to divest the present trustees of the fiduciary duties they owed under the proper law of the settlements. To some extent, this submission was based on the form of the relief sought in paragraph 4 of the writ. It seeks:

> 'An order removing the defendants as trustees of Mohan's Settlement and Harish's Settlement and appointing some fit and proper persons to be trustees in their place.'

An order in that form would not of itself, however, divest existing trustees and vest trust property in new trustees. Consequently, such an order would usually be accompanied by a vesting order under section 44 (in the case of land) section 51 (in the case of stocks and shares) of the Trustee Act 1925. It could not, in my opinion, sensibly be suggested (and counsel for the plaintiffs has not suggested) that a vesting order under section 51 could divest the defendants of the trust shares in the Bermudan holding companies or could vest those shares in new trustees. A vesting effect could be achieved by a vesting order only in respect of stocks and shares situated within the territorial jurisdiction of the court. Further, so long as the trust shares remain vested in the defendant trustees, their fiduciary obligations in respect thereof must remain. So, counsel for the defendants submitted, the court lacks the power to grant relief sought by paragraph 4 of the writ.

12–45   "This argument is, in my judgment, based on a point of form and not of substance. The jurisdiction of the court to administer trusts, to which the jurisdiction to remove trustees and appoint new ones is ancillary, is an *in* *personam* jurisdiction. In the exercise of it, the court will inquire what personal obligations are binding on the trustees and will enforce those obligations. If the obligations are owed in respect of trust assets abroad, the enforcement will be, and can only be, by *in personam* orders made against the trustees. The trustees can be ordered to pay, to sell, to buy, to invest, whatever may be necessary to give effect to the rights of the beneficiaries, which are binding on them. If the court is satisfied that, in order to give effect to or to protect the rights of the beneficiaries, the trustees ought to be replaced by others, I can see no reason in principle why the court should not make *in personam* orders against the trustees requiring them to resign and to vest the trust assets in the new trustees. The power of the court to remove trustees and to appoint new ones, owes its origin to an inherent jurisdiction and not to statute, and it must follow that the court has power to make such *in personam* orders as may be necessary to achieve the vesting of the trust assets in the new trustees. This is so, in my judgment, whether or not the trust assets are situated in England, and whether or not the proper law of the trusts in question is English law. It requires only that the individual trustee should be subject to the jurisdiction of the English courts. It does not matter, in my view, whether they have become subject to the jurisdiction by reason of service of process in England or because they have submitted to the jurisdiction, or because under R.S.C., Ord. 11 the court has assumed jurisdiction. In every case, orders *in personam* are made by the courts on the footing that those against whom they are made will obey them.

"Accordingly, and for these reasons, I do not accept counsel for the defen- **12–46** dants' submission that the English courts have no power to remove the defendants as trustees of these two settlements. Since, however, such removal would have to be effected by *in personam* orders, the plaintiffs have put before me an amended statement of claim which seeks such orders. In my judgment, the court would have power, if it thought it right to do so, to make those orders.

"There are two other associated points which I should now deal with. As an adjunct to his submission that the English courts lack the power to remove trustees of foreign settlements, counsel for the defendants submitted that if such an order in the *in personam* form were made the defendants could not safely obey the order without first obtaining confirmation from the Indian courts that it would be proper for them to do so. Further, he submitted, his clients ought not to be subjected to such an order unless it were clear that Indian law would regard them, if they did obey, as discharged from their fiduciary obligations under the settlement.

"It would be a matter entirely for the defendants and their advisers what steps **12–47** they take in the Indian courts, but for my part I am not impressed by the proposition that such confirmation would be necessary. The English courts have jurisdiction over these defendants. An objection to the exercise of jurisdiction on *forum conveniens* grounds has been taken and I must deal with it, but, if in the end the case continues in England, I would expect that the Indian courts, for reasons of comity would afford the same respect to orders of this court as in like circumstances and for the same reasons English courts would afford to theirs.

"Counsel for the defendants suggested to me that I would give short shrift to an order of a foreign court removing a trustee of an English trust; but if the English trustee had been subject to the jurisdiction of the foreign court exercised in like circumstances to those in which English courts claim and exercise jurisdiction, I can see no reason why I should recoil from an order *in personam* made by the foreign court against an English trustee. And if the order had been given effect to by, for example, the trustee transferring trust assets in England into the names of new trustees, I see no reason why an English court should question the efficacy of the transfer. All of this assumes, of course, that there were no vitiating features in the manner in which the foreign order was obtained.

12–48   "As to the point that the defendants might, notwithstanding that they had transferred the Bermudan shares to new trustees, still owe fiduciary duties under the settlements, there is, in my view, no substance to that point. Firstly, no party to the English action could so contend. Mohan and Lachmibai Chellaram are not parties to the action but could easily be joined, as also could any of the sisters who wished to be joined. This does not therefore seem to me to be a practical problem. Secondly, the point could be raised as a defence to the plaintiffs' claim for the removal of trustees, and, if the court were satisfied that the point was a sound one, I cannot imagine that the defendants would be ordered to transfer the shares. Thirdly, the status of trustee and the burden of the fiduciary obligations arising therefrom have, as it seems to me, no reality except in relation to assets which are vested in or under the control of the trustee. If a trustee is divested of the trust assets, I do not understand how it can be supposed that he can retain any fiduciary obligation thereafter in respect of those assets or in respect of the income derived from them.

12–49   "I do not, therefore, think, there is anything in counsel for the defendants' objections to the efficacy of the *in personam* orders, if such orders were made.

"I have dealt with counsel for the defendants' submission on jurisdiction and on the power of an English court to make the orders sought on the footing that Indian law is the proper law of the settlements. As an adjunct to his arguments on those matters, counsel for the defendants submitted that, if Indian law was the proper law of the settlements, then Indian law was the system of law which ought to be applied to the matter of removal of trustees of the settlements and to the appointment of new ones. He drew my attention to the relevant provisions of the Indian Trusts Act 1882, as amended up to 1969, and commented, rightly in my opinion, that the various provisions in that Act relevant to the removal and appointment of trustees by the Indian court could not be applied by an English court in the present case.

12–50   "Counsel for the defendants wielded this point as part of his argument on jurisdiction and also as relevant to his *forum conveniens* point. Counsel for the plaintiffs has contended that the proper law of the settlement is English law but he has submitted that, even if that is wrong, England is the place where the trusts were intended to be administered and the place where, in fact, the trusts have been administered, that the administration of a trust is governed not by the proper law of the trust but by the law of the place where administration takes place, and that the removal of trustees and the appointment of new ones is a matter of administration. It is a feature of the history of these settlements that there has been remarkably little administration. The reason for this is that the trust property has been represented simply by shares in Bermudan holding companies, and no trust income has been derived therefrom. Until recently, when in response to the plaintiffs' demand trust accounts were prepared, there were no such accounts. However, counsel for the plaintiffs is, in my view, right in pointing out that such administration as there has been has taken place in London. It was in London that the deeds of retirement and appointment of new trustees were prepared and executed; such legal advice as has been taken by the trustees seems to have been taken by Mr. Advani from Norton Rose Botterell & Roche in London, and there seems to me to be no room for any real doubt that the parties to the settlement contemplated that the administration would take place in London.

"Accordingly, in my judgment, the factual basis on which counsel for the **12-51** plaintiffs makes his submission is sound. As to law, counsel for the plaintiffs relies on the proposition stated in *Dicey and Morris*, p. 683, r. 121 that:

'The administration of a trust is governed (*semble*) by the law of its place of administration.'

Among the matters classified in the notes to rule 121 as matters of administration is "the question who can appoint a trustee and what persons may be so appointed." If this rule correctly states the law, it would seem to follow that the issue regarding removal of the trustees of these settlements should be governed by the law of the place of administration of the settlements. However, the tentative manner in which the rule is expressed is justified, in my view, by the lack of clear authority provided by the cases cited in the footnotes.

"There are two categories of case which must be distinguished from cases as the present case. Firstly, there are cases which establish that the administrative powers conferred on personal representatives by the Administration of Estates Act 1925 can be exercised by English personal representatives in relation to assets in England, whether or not the deceased died domiciled in England (see *Re Wilks*, [1935] Ch. 645). These cases exemplify the well-settled proposition that the administration of a deceased's assets is governed by the law of the country from which the administrator derives his authority.

"Secondly, there are cases which support the view that the provisions of **12-52** English trust legislation apply to trust property situated in England whether or not the trusts on which the trust property is held are the trusts of foreign settlements: see *Re Kehr (decd.), Martin v. Foges* [1952] Ch. 26, although Danckwerts J. doubted 'whether trustees constituted by the law of a foreign country would have the powers conferred on trustees regulated by English law' (see [1952] Ch. 26 at 30); see also *Re Ker's Settlement Trusts* [1963] Ch. 553. But neither of these lines of cases supports the proposition in *Dicey and Morris*, r. 121 when applied to a foreign settlement which is being administered in England but where the trust property is not in England.

"More cogent support is provided by *Re Pollak's Estate* [1937] T.P.D. 91. In that case the testator was domiciled in the Transvaal. He left movables in England and in South Africa as well as in other countries. By his will he appointed as his executor and trustee an English bank which had no branch in South Africa and left his residuary estate on trust for beneficiaries, the majority of whom were domiciled in England. A number of questions were raised for the decision of the Transvaal court, including a question as to the law which should determine the rights and duties of the bank as trustee in the execution of the testamentary trust. Since the testator was domiciled in the Transvaal, South African law governed the construction of the will, but the court concluded that the testator had intended the trust to be administered in England, and Davis J., with whose judgment Greenberg J. concurred, said (at 101):

'I have no doubt that in appointing an English bank . . . to administer a trust fund wherein the great majority of the persons interested were at the time domiciled in England, the testator . . . intended English law to govern.'

12–53 He cited with approval this passage in the American Law Institute's Restatement of the Law of Conflict of Laws (see [1937] T.P.D. 91 at 101–102):

> 'If the testator appoints as trustee a trust company of another state, presumptively his intention is that the trust should be administered in the latter state; the trust will therefore be administered according to the law of the latter state.'

Accordingly, the court held that the rights and duties of the bank as trustee were to be governed by English law, notwithstanding that the essential validity of the trust and the construction of the will were governed by the law of South Africa, the domicile of the testator. The reasoning which led the Transvaal court to this decision I respectfully accept. The court concluded that the testator in establishing a settlement to be administered in England must have intended English law to govern its administration. The court gave effect to that intention. But it does not follow from *Re Pollak's Estate* that the law of the place of the administration of a trust would govern the rights and duties of the trustee in a case where the circumstances did not enable the inference to be drawn that such was the testator's or settlor's intention. *Re Pollak's Estate* was a case of testamentary trust. It is well-established English law that the essential validity of a testamentary trust of movables is governed by the law of the testator's domicile. But there is no reason why a testator should not by will establish a trust to be governed by some law other than the law of his domicile. His ability to create the trust may be subject to the law of his domicile but subject thereto he is, in my view, as able by will to make a foreign settlement as he is able to do so *inter vivos*. *Re Pollak's Estate* supports the proposition that a testator can do so. It does not, in my view, support anything further and does not really support rule 121.

12–54 "As a matter of principle, I find myself unable to accept the distinction drawn by rules 120 and 121 in *Dicey and Morris* between 'validity, interpretation and effect' on the one hand and 'administration' on the other hand.[73] The rights and duties of trustees, for example, may be regarded as matters of administration but they also concern the effect of the settlement. The rights of the trustees are enjoyed as against the beneficiaries; the duties of the trustees are owed to the beneficiaries. If the rights of the beneficiaries are to be ascertained by applying the proper law of the settlement, I do not understand how the duties of the trustees can be ascertained by applying a different law, and vice versa. In my judgment, a conclusion that the law of the place of administration of a settlement governs such matters as the rights and duties of the trustees can only be right if that law is the proper law governing the settlement.

"But the right of beneficiaries to have trustees removed and new ones appointed is a right of a rather special nature. It is not, at least in the usual case, a right conferred by the settlement. If it were the case that a settlement conferred on particular beneficiaries or on a particular person such as the settlor the right to remove trustees and appoint new ones, that right (like any other rights conferred by the settlement on beneficiaries or trustees) would, in my view, require to be given effect in accordance with the proper law of the settlement. That would, in my view, be so, regardless of where the settlement was being administered. But no such right is conferred by the two settlements with which I am concerned.

---

[73] Dicey & Morris, *Conflict of Laws* (13th ed.), Rule 153 now reads, "The validity, construction, effects and administration of a trust are governed by the law chosen by the settlor, or, in the absence of any such choice, by the law with which the trust is most closely connected."

"The plaintiffs' claim for the removal of trustees and the appointment of new **12–55** ones is, in this case, as in most cases, not an attempt to enforce a corresponding right conferred by the settlements, but is an appeal to the inherent jurisdiction of the court to which Lord Blackburn referred in *Letterstedt v. Broers* (1884) 9 App.Cas. 371 at 385–386. The function of English courts in trust litigation is to enforce or protect the rights of the beneficiaries which bind the conscience of the trustee defendants. The identification and extent of those rights is a matter for the proper law of the settlement, but the manner of enforcement is, in my view, a matter of machinery which depends on the powers enjoyed by the English courts. Among the powers available to English courts is the power to order the removal of trustees and the appointment of new ones. This power is, in my view, machinery which, under English domestic law, can be exercised by English courts where necessary in order to enable the rights of beneficiaries to be enforced or protected. The exercise of the domestic power does not, in my view, depend on whether the rights of the beneficiaries are enjoyed under domestic settlements or foreign settlements, or on whether the trust property is situated in England or abroad. The locality of the trust property will, however, determine whether the removal can be achieved by an *in rem* order or whether an *in personam* order is appropriate. Accordingly, except where rights conferred by the settlement are under consideration, the removal of trustees and the appointment of new ones are not, in my judgment, a matter to be governed by the proper law of the settlement. Nor, in my opinion, is it a matter governed by the law of the place where the administration of the settlement has taken place. It is, in my judgment, a matter to be governed by the law of the country whose courts have assumed jurisdiction to administer the trusts of the settlement in question.

"In the view of the matter I take, therefore, I do not think that the **12–56** identification of the proper law of the settlement is a critical issue on this application. Any court before which the plaintiffs' case is litigated will have to consider the rights of the beneficiaries under these discretionary settlements in order to form an opinion whether the enforcement or protection of those rights requires the removal of the present trustees but no one has suggested that the nature of those rights is going to be different if tested under Indian law than if tested under English law. Any such difference is likely to be marginal only and to be immaterial for the purposes of the plaintiffs' claim for the removal of the trustees.

"It is, therefore, not necessary for me to decide on this application whether Indian law or English law is the proper law of the settlements. I am dealing with an interlocutory application. The relevant evidence has not been tested by cross-examination. In these circumstances, I would, I think, be unwise to express a conclusion on the proper law question and I do not do so.

"I have held, contrary to counsel for the defendants' submission, that the **12–57** English courts have both jurisdiction and power to deal with the plaintiffs' claim for the removal of trustees and for the appointment of new ones. In that event, counsel for the defendants submits that the court ought nevertheless to decline to exercise that jurisdiction on the ground, shortly stated, that there is another competent jurisdiction, India, in which justice can be done between the parties, and that by comparison with India, England is a *forum non conveniens* . . .

"In my judgment, the defendants have failed to cast England as a *forum non conveniens*. It is settled on authority that the onus lies on the defendants to satisfy me that I ought, in my discretion, to grant a stay. They have not done so, and I therefore refuse a stay and dismiss their application." *Application dismissed*.

QUESTIONS

12–58 1. S, an Italian national domiciled in Italy but resident in England, visits Dublin in 1975 and pays 100 Irish punts to A and B as Dublin resident trustees on specified trusts which confer on the trustees a power to accumulate income for 100 years or, if later, until the expiry of 20 years from the death of the last survivor of all the descendants of Queen Elizabeth II living at the date of his trust instrument which expressly makes Irish law govern the trust (so the accumulation power is valid).

On his return to his London residence S has £1 million transferred to A and B in Dublin who then use it to purchase shares in English companies for £500,000 and an English house for £500,000. A month later S transfers English company shares worth £1 million to A and B as well as two Italian restaurants in London worth £1 million.

A beneficiary claims that the trustees can no longer exercise their power of accumulation in respect of income from the above assets. Advise the trustees.

Would your advice differ if S had stayed in London and paid £100 to London resident trustees, though still creating such an extensive power of accumulation and expressly choosing Irish law to govern the trust and subsequently transferring the above assets to such English trustees? It is significant that the United Kingdom Government has let Turks & Caicos Islands (and Cayman for STAR trusts) abolish the rule against perpetuities and accumulations and did not extend *The Thellusson* Act 1800 to Ireland when part of the United Kingdom.

S died recently, and his widow and two children who are Italian nationals claim to have the trust set aside *pro tanto* to satisfy their reserved shares for three quarters of his estate, which under Italian law includes capital given away in the deceased's lifetime. Advise the trustees.

2. "In the light of *Pullan v. Koe* [1913] 1 Ch. 9 and *RZB v. Five Star LLC* [2001] 3 All E.R. 257, trustees need to check whether property about to be transferred to them is not subject to a foreign matrimonial community of property regime because the settlor's spouse (if not a party to such transfer) may well have a proprietary interest in such property." Discuss.

INDEX

EYEWITNESS TRAVEL GUIDES

CYPRUS

Grzegorz Micuła
Magdalena Micuła

LONDON, NEW YORK,
MELBOURNE, MUNICH AND DELHI
www.dk.com

Produced by Hachette Livre Polska sp. z o.o., Warsaw, Poland

SENIOR GRAPHIC DESIGNER
Paweł Pasternak

EDITORS
Agnieszka Majle,
Robert G. Pasieczny

MAIN CONTRIBUTORS
Elżbieta Makowiecka, Grzegorz Micuła, Magdalena Micuła

CARTOGRAPHERS
Magdalena Polak, Michał Zielkiewicz

PHOTOGRAPHERS
Dorota and Mariusz Jarymowicz, Krzysztof Kur

ILLUSTRATORS
Michał Burkiewicz, Paweł Marczak, Bohdan Wróblewski

TYPESETTING AND LAYOUT
Elżbieta Dudzińska, Paweł Kamiński, Grzegorz Wilk

Reproduced by Colourscan, Singapore.
Printed and bound in China by Toppan Printing Co., (Shenzhen
Ltd)

First published in Great Britain in 2006
by Dorling Kindersley Limited
80 Strand, London WC2R 0RL

ISBN-13: 978-1-40531-283-7
ISBN-10: 1-4053-1283 1
Front cover main image: Temple of Apollo, near Kourion

**The information in every
DK Eyewitness Travel Guide is checked regularly.**
Every effort has been made to ensure that this book is as
up-to-date as possible at the time of going to press. Some details,
however, such as telephone numbers, opening hours, prices,
gallery hanging arrangements and travel information are liable to
change. The publishers cannot accept responsibility for any
consequences arising from the use of this boook, nor for any
material on third party websites, and cannot guarantee
that any website address in this book will be a suitable
source of travel information.
We value the views and suggestions of our readers very highly.
Please write to: Publisher, DK Eyewitness Travel Guides, Dorling
Kindersley, 80 Strand, London WC2R 0RL, Great Britain.

◁ **Apollo Hylates temple at Kourion**

CONTENTS

**Cypriot saint, Agios Mamas, the
Byzantine Museum in Pafos**

INTRODUCING
CYPRUS

**Beach in the bustling resort of
Agia Napa in southeast Cyprus**

Ruins of the Apollo Hylates temple at Kourion

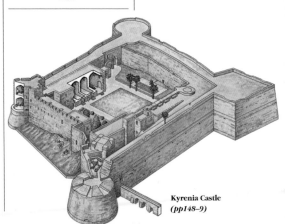

Kyrenia Castle
(pp148–9)

HOW TO USE THIS GUIDE

THIS GUIDE WILL HELP you to make the most out of your visit to Cyprus. The first section, *Introducing Cyprus*, locates the island geographically and gives an overview of its rich history, culture and natural environment. Individual sections describe the main historic sights and star attractions of each region of the island. Help with accommodation, restaurants, shopping, entertainment and many recreational activities can be found in the *Travellers' Needs* section, while the *Survival Guide* provides practical information and advice for visitors on everything from money and language to getting around and seeking medical attention.

CYPRUS REGION BY REGION

The guide divides Cyprus into six chapters: five regions plus South Nicosia – the capital of the Republic of Cyprus.

Getting There provides information on travel to and within each region.

1 Introduction
This provides a brief overview of each region, describing its history, geographical features and cultural characteristics as well as the main tourist attractions.

Pages devoted to individual regions are identified by colour-coded thumb tabs.

2 Regional Map
This shows the main roads and topography of the region. It also locates all the sights that are later described in detail.

Boxes contain information on events and people associated with the region.

3 Detailed Information
All the important sights in the region are described individually. The address, telephone number and other important practical information is given for each sight.

4 Major Towns
At least two pages are devoted to each major town, with a detailed description of the historic sights and local curiosities for which it is famous.

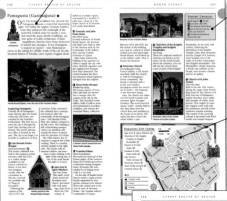

A Visitors' Checklist for each town and major sight provides tourist and transport information, including opening hours of tourist attractions, admission charges, and details of local festivals.

A Town Map shows the location of the main sights within the town centre, as well as tourist information offices, places of worship, car parks, and post offices.

5 Street-by-Street
This gives a bird's-eye view of a particularly interesting sightseeing area described in the region.

Photographs illustrate the most interesting areas and the most impressive sights within an attraction.

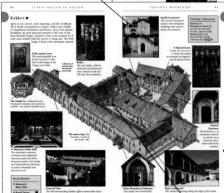

6 Star Sights
Two pages are dedicated to each major sight. Historic buildings are dissected to reveal their interiors, and parks are illustrated to show the main attractions.

Star Attractions point out the best sights or exhibits that no visitor should miss.

Cut-outs show the building with its surroundings and some parts of the interior.

INTRODUCING
CYPRUS

Putting Cyprus on the Map

Situated in the eastern Mediterranean Sea, Cyprus is its third largest island (after Sicily and Sardinia), covering an area of 9,250 sq km (3,571 sq miles) with a 720 km- (447-mile-) long coastline. Divided since 1974 into the Greek Cypriot-governed Republic of Cyprus in the south and the Turkish-sponsored Turkish Republic of North Cyprus in the north, both regions share Nicosia as a capital. The rocky Pentadaktylos mountain range runs along the north, while its central part is dominated by the mighty massif of the Troodos Mountains. The wildest and least accessible areas are the Akamas and Karpas peninsulas.

Satellite View of Cyprus
The entire island can be seen clearly, with the long, narrow Karpas peninsula to the right and the Troodos Mountains in the centre. Turkish Anatolia is visible to the north.

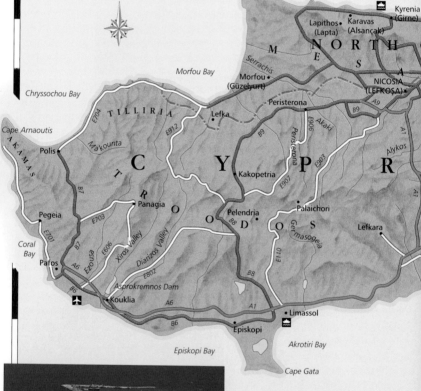

Cape Kormakiti

Kyrenia (Girne)

Lapithos (Lapta) · Karavas (Alsançak)

M E S A

NORTH

Serrachis

Morfou Bay

Morfou (Güzelyurt)

NICOSIA (LEFKOŞA)

Chryssochou Bay

Lefka

Peristerona

B9

Cape Arnaoutis

TILLIRIA

E704

E912

Makounta

Akaki

E906

Peristerona

A9

AKAMAS

Polis

B7

C

R

Y

Kakopetria

P

E907

E903

R

Alykos

A1

Panagia

E703

E606

Xiros Valley

Diarizos Valley

O

B8

Pelendria

D

Palaichori

Germasogeia

S

Lefkara

Pegeia

E701

Coral Bay

Pafos

B6

A6

Erousa

E802

Asprokremnos Dam

Kouklia

B6

A6

B8

E110

A1

Limassol

Episkopi

Akrotiri Bay

Episkopi Bay

Cape Gata

View from St Hilarion Castle
St Hilarion Castle in North Cyprus offers a magnificent, panoramic view of the coast. The view in this particular direction shows the town and harbour of Kyrenia.

◁ **Detail of the interior of Asinou Church in the Troodos Mountains**

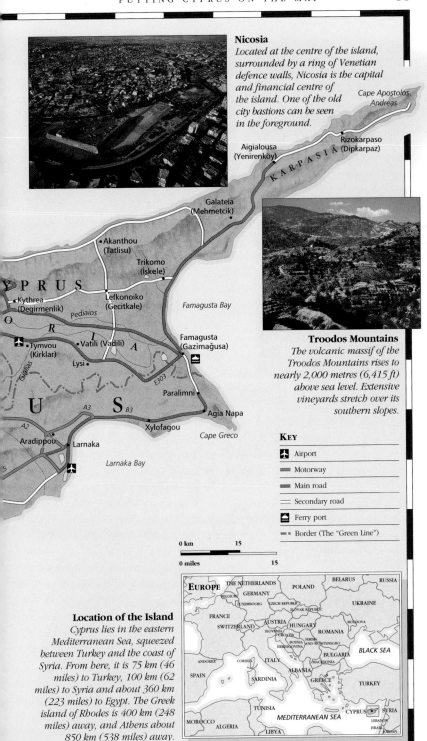

Nicosia
Located at the centre of the island, surrounded by a ring of Venetian defence walls, Nicosia is the capital and financial centre of the island. One of the old city bastions can be seen in the foreground.

Cape Apostolos Andreas

Aigialousa (Yenirenköy)

Rizokarpaso (Dipkarpaz)

K A R P A S I A

Galateia (Mehmetcik)

• Akanthou (Tatlisu)

Trikomo (İskele)

Y P R U S

• Kythrea (Degirmenlik)

Lefkonoiko (Gecitkale)

Pediaios

Famagusta Bay

O

R

• Tymvou (Kirklar)

I

• Vatili (Vadili)

A

Lysi •

Famagusta (Gazimağusa)

Gialias

U

S B3

E303

Paralimni •

A3

Agia Napa

A2

Xylofagou

Cape Greco

Aradippou •

Larnaka

Larnaka Bay

Troodos Mountains
The volcanic massif of the Troodos Mountains rises to nearly 2,000 metres (6,415 ft) above sea level. Extensive vineyards stretch over its southern slopes.

KEY

⤢ Airport

▬ Motorway

▬ Main road

— Secondary road

⚓ Ferry port

= = Border (The "Green Line")

0 km   15

0 miles   15

Location of the Island
Cyprus lies in the eastern Mediterranean Sea, squeezed between Turkey and the coast of Syria. From here, it is 75 km (46 miles) to Turkey, 100 km (62 miles) to Syria and about 360 km (223 miles) to Egypt. The Greek island of Rhodes is 400 km (248 miles) away, and Athens about 850 km (538 miles) away.

EUROPE
THE NETHERLANDS
BELGIUM
LUXEMBOURG
GERMANY
POLAND
BELARUS
RUSSIA
FRANCE
CZECH REPUBLIC
SLOVAK REPUBLIC
UKRAINE
AUSTRIA
HUNGARY
MOLDOVA
SWITZERLAND
SLOVENIA
CROATIA
BOSNIA AND HERZEGOVINA
SERBIA AND MONTENEGRO
ROMANIA
ANDORRA
CORSICA
ITALY
MACEDONIA
BULGARIA
BLACK SEA
SPAIN
SARDINIA
ALBANIA
GREECE
TURKEY
TUNISIA
MEDITERRANEAN SEA
CYPRUS
SYRIA
LEBANON
MOROCCO
ALGERIA
LIBYA
ISRAEL
JORDAN

A PORTRAIT OF CYPRUS

THE LEGENDARY BIRTHPLACE *of Aphrodite, Cyprus enjoys a hot, Mediterranean climate moderated by sea breezes. Visitors bask in the sun on its many beaches, but within an hour's drive can find themselves in the mountains, enjoying the shade of cool herb- and resin-scented cedar woods, villages set amid orchards and peaceful vineyards, as though time stands still here.*

Cyprus is an idyllic destination for romantics, with so many old castles, ancient ruins and secluded mountain monasteries to explore. The exploration of these historic sights is enhanced by plentiful sunshine – over 300 days of it per year. Cyprus also has a great number of scenic beaches, and the warm waters encourage bathing and relaxation.

Mosaic of Leda with the Swan, from Kouklia

Tucked away in the shady valleys are monasteries with ancient icons of the Virgin, at least one of which was supposedly painted by St Luke. The tiny churches, listed as UNESCO World Heritage Sites, hide unique frescoes – some of the most magnificent masterpieces of Byzantine art.

In the Pafos district, valleys overgrown with pine and cedar forests provide a home to the moufflon – a shy mountain sheep. Its image can be seen on Roman mosaics in Pafos.

Cypriot meadows are at their loveliest in springtime, when covered with motley carpets of colourful flowers: anemones, cyclamens, hyacinths, irises, peonies, poppies and tulips, among others. Orchid lovers will find over 50 species of these beautiful flowers growing in the sparsely populated regions of the island – in the Akamas Peninsula, in the Troodos Mountains and on the Pentadaktylos mountain range.

A symbol of Cyprus – an olive tree against the backdrop of a sapphire-blue sea

◁ A chapel next to a hotel complex near Polis

View over the northern part of Nicosia, with the Turkish Cypriot flag carved into the hillside

The island lies on a route for bird migration. Thousands of birds, including flamingos, cormorants and swans, can be seen wintering on the salt lakes at Larnaka and Akrotiri.

HISTORIC DIVISIONS

The winds of history have repeatedly ravaged this beautiful island. Cyprus has been ruled in turns by Egyptians, Phoenicians, Persians, Romans, Byzantines, Crusaders, Franks, Venetians, Turks and the British. Each of these cultures has left its mark on the architecture, style, cuisine, language and the mentality of the island's inhabitants.

Above all, the island has been shaped by the conflict between the Greeks and the Turks. The Greeks first arrived over 3,000 years ago. The Turks began to settle here following the conquest of the island by Sultan Selim II in 1571.

PEOPLE AND SOCIETY

Cypriot society has been composed of two completely separate cultures since the division of the island in 1974 into the Turkish-occupied North and the Greek-speaking Republic of Cyprus in the south. Greek Cypriot society has always been highly traditional, particularly among country people. This is partly due to the power of the Orthodox Church. Life proceeds at a slow pace in the villages, where it centres around cafés where men spend hours playing backgammon and discussing politics. Village women excel in sewing and embroidery. In recent years, there has been gradual change, with many villages becoming deserted as their residents move to towns, where life is easier and the

An Orthodox priest doing his shopping

standard of living higher, but this decline is gradually being reversed; old houses are frequently bought by artists, often foreigners, in search of tranquillity. In Fikardou, two abandoned houses have been turned into a museum of village life, and awarded the Europa Nostra medal for the preservation of architectural heritage. Overall, the Republic of Cyprus is highly urbanized. Women play a great role in the modern economy – running businesses, hotels and restaurants. Life in the cities of Larnaka, Nicosia and Limassol proceeds at a speedy pace.

The Cape Greco area – one of the most beautiful areas in Cyprus

In the Turkish North, life proceeds at a far gentler pace, partly due to the international boycott that has afflicted tourism and hampered development since 1974. The North is quite separate from southern Cyprus in both atmosphere and landscape, as well as politics. It is far less affluent and more sparsely populated, and Islam is the main religion.

A lace-maker at work

tens of thousands of its people, it seemed that the island would never recover, but the Republic of Cyprus has achieved an economic miracle. Over thirty years on, the southern part of the island is very prosperous. After the 1974 invasion, hundreds of thousands of refugees from the North found new homes and began their lives anew. Since then, national income has increased several fold. The economy is flourishing, based on tourism, maritime trade and financial services. The same cannot be said of the northern part of the island, where the standard of living is much lower, caused to a great extent by the international isolation of North Cyprus.

MODERN-DAY CYPRUS

The Republic of Cyprus lives off tourism. Its towns are bustling and – like the beaches – full of tourists. Tourist zones have been established in Limassol, Larnaka and Pafos, and around Agia Napa.

This small island provides everything for the holidaymaker, from beautiful scenery to delicious food, excellent hotels, gracious hosts and historic sights.

Following the Turkish invasion of Cyprus and the displacement of

Relaxing at an outdoor café on a summer afternoon

Landscape and Wildlife

THE CYPRIOT LANDSCAPE is surprisingly varied. Besides high mountains overgrown with pine and cedar forests, and the rugged crags of Kyrenia, the central part of the island is occupied by the fertile plain of Mesaoria. The crowded beaches of Limassol, Pafos and Agia Napa contrast with the less developed coastal regions of the Karpas and Akamas peninsulas. In the spring, the hills and meadows are covered with a carpet of colourful flowers. The forests are the habitat of the moufflon – mountain sheep – while the Karpas peninsula is home to wild donkeys.

A flock of goats grazing freely – a typical sight in the Cypriot landscape

THE COAST

Besides beautiful sandy and pebble beaches, the coastline features oddly shaped rocks jutting out of the sea and rugged cliffs, which descend steeply into the water. The northern part of Famagusta Bay and the Karpas and Akamas peninsulas feature virtually empty sandy beaches where female loggerheads and green turtles come to lay their eggs. The exposed Jurassic rocks near Coral Bay, northwest of Pafos, are being destroyed by erosion.

Lizards, *particularly the ubiquitous sand lizard, can be seen almost everywhere. The largest Cypriot lizard, Agama (Agama stelio cypriaca) can reach up to 30 cm (12 in) in length.*

Rocky coastlines *are created wherever mountain ranges reach the sea. The rocky coast near Petra tou Romiou (Rock of Aphrodite) is being worn away over time by erosion.*

Sandy coastlines *are found at Agia Napa, Famagusta Bay and the Karpas peninsula, but the loveliest beaches are on the Akamas peninsula.*

Salt lakes *– near Larnaca and on the Akrotiri peninsula – are a haven for pink flamingos, wild ducks and the Cyprus warbler (Sylvia melanthorax).*

ROCK FORMATIONS

The Troodos Mountains, in the central part of Cyprus, are formed of magma rock containing rich deposits of copper and asbestos. The Kyrenia Mountains (the Pentadaktylos range), running to the Karpas peninsula in the northeast part of the island, are made of hard, dense limestone. The lime soils in the southern part of the island, near Limassol, are ideally suited for the growing of vines.

Copper mine at Skouriotissa

MOUNTAINS

The island features two mountain ranges, separated by the fertile Mesaoria plain. The volcanic Troodos massif in central Cyprus, dominated by Mount Olympus at 1,951 m (6,258 ft) above sea level, is overgrown with pine and cedar forests. The constant mountain streams in the Troodos mountains even have waterfalls. Spring and autumn bring hikers to the cool forests and rugged valleys, while winter brings out skiers. The Kyrenia Mountains (the Pentadaktylos or "Five-Finger" range) in North Cyprus rise a short distance inland from the coast. The highest peak is Mount Kyparissovouno, at 1,024 m (3,360 ft).

The Troodos Mountains are largely forested but vines are grown on the southern slopes and apple and cherry orchards abound in the valleys.

Mountain streams flow year-round, bringing cooling water to lower ground.

In springtime wild flowers carpet the hillsides and meadows of the island with a colourful, fragrant display.

The Cypriot moufflon is a spry mountain sheep, living wild in the forests of Pafos, in the western part of the island.

OTHER REGIONS

The island's interior is occupied by the vast, fertile Mesaoria plain, given mainly to grain cultivation. The northern area around Morphou (Güzelyurt) is full of citrus groves, and to the south, in the region of Larnaka, runs a range of white semi-desert mountains stretching for kilometres. The sun-drenched region of Limassol, with its limestone soil, is a patchwork of vineyards, which yield grapes for the production of the sweet Commandaria wine.

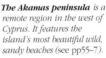

The Akamas peninsula is a remote region in the west of Cyprus. It features the island's most beautiful wild, sandy beaches (see pp55–7).

Donkeys can be seen in the Karpas peninsula. These ageing domesticated animals have been turned loose by their owners.

Pelicans with wingspans up to 2.5 m (8 ft) visit the island's salt lakes. Some stop for a few days, others remain longer. These huge birds can also be seen at the harbours of Pafos, Limassol and Agia Napa, where they are a tourist attraction.

The Karpas peninsula is a long, narrow strip of land jutting into the sea. Its main attractions are its wild environment and historical sights (see pp140–1).

Cypriot Architecture

T HE LONG AND RICH HISTORY of Cyprus is reflected in its architecture, and some true gems can be glimpsed amid the ocean of nondescript modern development. The island has a number of Neolithic settlements as well as Bronze Age burial chambers, ruins of ancient buildings (including vast Byzantine basilicas), medieval castles, churches and monasteries. From the Ottoman era, relics include mosques and caravanserais. The British left behind colonial buildings. In villages, particularly in the mountains, people today still live in old stone houses.

The Roman Hotel in Pafos, built to a design based on ancient Roman architecture

ANCIENT ARCHITECTURE

The Greeks, Phoenicians, Romans and Byzantines who once ruled over Cyprus left behind numerous ancient buildings. Archaeologists have uncovered the ruins of ancient Kourion, Amathous, Kition, Soloi, Salamis and Pafos with temples, theatres, basilicas, bathhouses and palaces. These ancient ruins include fragments of the old defence walls, sports stadiums, gymnasiums, and necropolises. Some Roman theatres are still in use today for shows and festivals.

The **palaestra** *in Salamis* (see pp134–5) *is surrounded by colonnades and statues. It was devoted to the training of athletes and to staging sporting competitions.*

Kourion, *a beautiful, prosperous city, was destroyed by an earthquake in the 4th century AD* (see pp66–7).

MEDIEVAL ARCHITECTURE

During the 300 years when Cyprus was ruled by the Crusaders and the Lusignans, many churches were built, including the opulent cathedrals in Famagusta and Nicosia. Added to these were charming village churches and chapels, Gothic monasteries and castles. The Venetians, who ruled the island for over 80 years, created the magnificent ring of defence walls around Nicosia and Famagusta, whose mighty fortifications held back the Ottoman army for almost a year.

Angeloktisi Church *in Kiti is one of a number of small stone churches on the island whose modest exteriors often hide magnificent Byzantine mosaics or splendid frescoes* (see p76).

This beautifully **carved capital** *crowns the surviving column of a medieval palace in South Nicosia.*

Bellapais, *with its ruins of a Gothic abbey, enchants visitors with its imposing architecture* (see p145). *Every spring international music festivals are held here* (see p22 and p25).

ISLAMIC ARCHITECTURE

Following the conquest of Cyprus by the army of Selim II, new stuctures appeared, including Turkish mosques (minarets were often added to Gothic cathedrals), bathhouses, caravanserais and covered bazaars. In many villages you can still see small mosques with distinctive pointed minarets.

Büyük Han in North Nicosia is a magnificent example of an Ottoman caravanserai, with a mescit (prayer hall) in the courtyard (see p128).

The Hala Sultan Tekke (see p76) is Cyprus's most sacred Muslim site. It comprises a mosque and a mausoleum with the tomb of Umm Haram, aunt of the Prophet Mohammed.

THE COLONIAL PERIOD

British rule on the island from the 18th to 19th centuries marked the beginning of colonial-style architecture, including churches, government offices, courts of law, army barracks, civil servants' villas, bridges and other public buildings. The British administration also admired the Greek Classical style, and commissioned, designed and built a great number of Neo-Classical buildings.

The Faneromeni School in South Nicosia (see p122) is an example of a Neo-Classical public building. When it was founded in 1852, it was seen as a connection to the students' Greek roots.

The Pierides Foundation Museum in Larnaca is a typical example of colonial architecture with shaded balconies resting on slender supports (see p78). Its flat roof and wooden shutters complement the image of a colonial residence.

MODERN ARCHITECTURE

Following independence in 1960, the architectural style of Cypriot buildings, particularly of public buildings such as town halls, offices, banks and hotels became more modern and functional. Most of these buildings were erected in Limassol, which has since become the international business capital of Cyprus. The majority of modern buildings lack architectural merit.

TRADITIONAL HOMES

For centuries Cypriot village houses, particularly in the mountains, were built of stone, offering the benefit of staying cool in summer and warm in winter. While some new homes imitate the traditional style, most are built of breeze-block and reinforced cement.

A modern stone building reminiscent of a traditional village home

Limassol's modern architecture is largely limited to functional office buildings constructed of glass, concrete and steel, located in the eastern business district of town.

Christianity and the Greek Orthodox Church

CHRISTIANITY GAINED AN EARLY FOOTHOLD in Cyprus, when saints Barnabas and Paul introduced the religion to the island in the first century AD. For 500 years the Church remained relatively unified. However, subsequent divisions led to the emergence of many parallel Christian creeds. The Great Schism of 1054 marked the split between East and West, resulting in the emergence of the Orthodox and Roman Catholic Churches. One of the groups of the Eastern Orthodox Church is the Greek Orthodox Church, and the majority of Greek Cypriots are devoutly Orthodox. Most of the churches in the south are still consecrated and can be visited; in the North, most have been converted into mosques or museums.

Byzantine frescoes, some of the most splendid in existence, decorate the walls of small churches in the Troodos Mountains. Nine of them feature on UNESCO's World Heritage List.

Father Kallinikos *from St Barbara's Monastery (Agia Varvara) is regarded as one of the greatest icon painters of recent times. His highly sought-after icons are sold at the monastery (see p76).*

Neo-Byzantine churches *are topped by a grooved cupola with a prominent cross. They have distinctive arched windows and portals.*

Saint Nicholas

Saints' days are celebrated by placing an icon of the saint on a small, ornamental table covered with a lace cloth.

SAINT BARNABAS AND SAINT PAUL

Two saints are associated with Cyprus – Barnabas (a citizen of Salamis, and patron saint of the island), and Paul. Together, they spread Christianity to Cyprus in 45 AD. Paul was captured and tied to a pillar to be flogged. It is said that the saint caused his torturer to go blind. Witnessing this miracle, the Roman governor of Cyprus, Sergius Paulus, was converted to Christianity. Barnabas was stoned to death in 57 AD.

St Paul's Pillar in Kato Pafos

Icons with images of Christ or the saints, depicted in traditional Byzantine style, play a major role in the Orthodox Church. They are painted on wood, according to strictly defined rules.

The Royal Doors *are found in the central part of an iconostasis. They symbolize the passage from the earthly to the spiritual world. The priest passes through them during the service.*

Royal Doors

The Iconostasis is a "wall of icons" that separates the faithful from the sanctuary.

MONASTICISM

Cypriot monasteries, some of then hundreds of years old, are scattered among the mountains. These religious communities of bearded monks live in accordance with a strict regime. Built on inaccessible crags or in shadowy green valleys, they were established in the mountains to be closer to God and further from the temptations of this world. The monasteries hide an extraordinary wealth of frescoes, intricate decorations and magnificent iconostases. The best known of the Cypriot monasteries is Kykkos – the Royal Monastery *(see pp90–91)* which is a place of pilgrimage for the island's inhabitants.

Two monks in the courtyard of Kykkos Monastery

DIVINE LITURGY

This is a liturgy celebrated in commemoration of the Last Supper. In the Greek Orthodox Church the service lasts longer than in the Catholic Church and there is no organ, only a choir. The service consists of two parts: the "catechumen liturgy", during which psalms and the Gospel are read; and the "liturgy of the faithful" – the main Eucharist when all worshippers (even children) receive holy communion in the form of bread and wine.

Icons on both sides of the Royal Doors depict Mary and Jesus. The second from the right usually depicts the patron saint of the church.

CYPRUS THROUGH THE YEAR

CYPRIOTS HOLD STRONGLY to their traditions, which are manifested in the celebration of numerous religious festivals. The Orthodox Church, to which most Greek Cypriots belong, has a great influence on their lives. Besides local village fairs and public holidays, the festivities include athletic events and beauty contests. Added to this, every village has its own *panagyri* – the patron saint's day

Girl in a folk costume

celebration – the equivalent of church fairs. The villagers celebrate them with copious food, drink, dancing and song. In North Cyprus, Muslim feasts are more common. The main ones include Şeker Bayrami, which ends the 40 days of Ramadan; Kurban Bayrami, which is held to commemorate Abraham's sacrifice (rams are slaughtered and roasted on a bonfire); and Mevlud, the birthday of Mohammed.

Olive trees flowering in the spring

SPRING

THIS IS the most beautiful season on the island. The slopes of the hills begin to turn green and the meadows are carpeted with colourful flowers, though it is still possible to ski. The main religious festival is Easter.

MARCH

International Skiing Competition *(mid-Mar)*, Troodos. Downhill races on the slopes of Mount Olympus *(see p92).*
Evangelismós, Feast of the Annunciation *(25 Mar).* Traditional folk fairs held in the villages of Kalavassos *(see p74)* and Klirou, as well as in Nicosia *(see pp112–23).*
Easter *(varies – Mar to May).* A week before Easter, the icon of St Lazarus is paraded through Larnaka. In all towns on Maundy Thursday, icons are covered

with veils, and on Good Friday the image of Christ adorned with flowers is carried through the streets. On Easter Saturday, icons are unveiled and in the evening an effigy of Judas is burned. Easter Day is celebrated with parties. Orthodox Easter is based on the Julian calendar,

Winners of the May Cyprus International Rally in Limassol

and may occur up to 5 weeks after Easter in the West.

APRIL

Wild Flower Festival *(Mar & Apr),* Every Saturday and Sunday in many towns throughout southern Cyprus.
International Spring Concerts *(Apr & May),* Bellapais. Performances by musical ensembles, singers and choirs are held in the Gothic abbey *(see p145).*
Classical Music Festival *(Apr),* Larnaka *(see pp78–81).* Organized by the municipality, this festival features recitals and concerts by internationally known musicians and ensembles.

MAY

Anthistiria Flower Festival *(mid-May),* Pafos, Limassol. The return of spring is celebrated by joyful processions and shows based on Greek myths.
Orange Festival *(mid-May),* Güzelyurt (Morfou) *(see p152).* Held since 1977, with parades and folk concerts.
Cyprus International Rally *(May),* 3-day car rally starting and ending in Limassol *(see pp68–71).*
Chamber Music Festival *(May–Jun),* Nicosia *(see pp112–23)* and Pafos *(pp48–51).* Top international orchestras and ensembles from abroad.

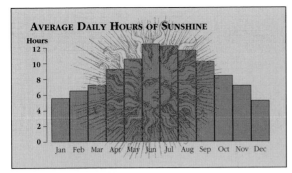

Average Hours of Sunshine

In June and July, the amount of sunshine reaches nearly 13 hours per day. These months mark the peak holiday season. December, January and February have the fewest hours of sunshine, but the winter sun is pleasant and warm.

Children at the Wild Flowers Festival in Larnaka

SUMMER

SUMMER IS rich in cultural events, especially art festivals, fairs and music concerts. Tourist resorts, hotels and attractions vie with one another to organize attractive cultural events for their guests. There are numerous folk fairs held in the mountain villages, particularly in August. This is also the hottest and sunniest time of the year.

The Limanaki Beach in Agia Napa

JUNE

Pancyprian Choirs Festival *(late Jun)*, Kato Pafos *(see pp52–3)*. During this festival, choirs perform in the ancient Odeon.
St Leontios' Day *(mid-Jun)*, Pervolia village. Traditional folk fair.
Pentecost-Kataklysmos Fair (Festival of the Flood) *(7 weeks after Easter)*. Coinciding with Pentecost, this is celebrated over 6 days with processions and sprinkling each other with water, to symbolize cleansing.
Shakespeare at Kourion *(late Jun)* *(see pp66–7)*. This charity performance of a Shakespeare play takes place at the ancient amphitheatre in Kourion.

JULY

International Music Festival *(Jun-Jul)*, Famagusta *(see pp136–9)*.
Moonlight Concerts *(Jul, during full moon)*, Pafos *(see pp48–51)*, Limassol *(pp68–71)*, Agia Napa *(p82)*. Concerts organized by the Cyprus Tourism Organisation.
Larnaka International Summer Festival *(Jul)*, Larnaka *(see pp78–81)*. Performances are staged by theatre, music and dance groups from Greece, the UK and Europe.

AUGUST

Ancient Greek Drama Festival *(Aug)*, Pafos ancient Odeon *(see pp52–3)*. Theatre festival with Greek dramas.
Assumption of the Virgin Mary *(15 Aug)*. Traditional fairs in Kykko *(see pp90–1)* and Chrysorrogiastissa monasteries and in the Chrysospiliotissa church *(see p106)* in Deftera village.
Commandaria Festival *(late Aug)*. Food, wine, music and theatre at Kalo Chorio village in the Limassol district to mark the beginning of the grape harvest.
Dionysia *(late Aug)*, Stroumbi near Pafos. Cypriot and Greek dances and music. An all-night party with local wine and food.

Pomegranate from the environs of Larnaka

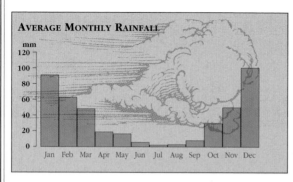

AVERAGE MONTHLY RAINFALL

mm

120 —
100 —
80 —
60 —
40 —
20 —
0 —

Jan Feb Mar Apr May Jun Jul Aug Sep Oct Nov Dec

Rainfall
The lowest rainfall occurs in July and August, the highest between November and February. Thunderstorms are rare in the summer. In the mountain regions, however, clouds may be thicker and rain more frequent than in the coastal areas.

AUTUMN

AFTER THE summer heat, autumn brings cooler weather. With the end of the peak holiday season many resorts slow down. The Cypriots celebrate successful harvests, with particular prominence given to the grape-gathering festivals. Many towns and villages hold local fairs. The Wine Festival in Limassol attracts hordes of visitors.

SEPTEMBER

Wine Festival *(early Sep)*, Limassol *(see pp68–71)*. Wine tasting and dancing in the Municipal Gardens.
Aphrodite Opera Festival *(Sep)*, Pafos *(see pp48–51)*. One of the main cultural festivals. Staged in front of the castle, the cast includes major international singers.
Agia Napa International Festival *(mid-Sep)*, Agia Napa *(see p82)*. This seaside resort

Autumn harvest of grapes in the wine-growing village of Vasa

Troodos Mountains in their autumn colours

becomes a gathering place for folk musicians and dancers, theatre groups, opera ensembles, traditional and modern singers, and magicians.
International North Cyprus Music Festival *(Sep–Oct)*, Bellapais *(see p145)*. Performances by musical virtuosos, symphony orchestras, piano recitals, vocal groups and soloists.
Elevation of the Holy Cross *(14 Sep)*. One of the oldest religious feasts in the Greek Orthodox Church calendar. In the past, men tucked basil leaves behind their ears on this day.

Participant in the Elevation of the Holy Cross

OCTOBER

Afamia Grape and Wine Festival *(early Oct)*, held in Koilani village *(see p94)* in the Limassol region.
Agios Ioannis Lampadistis *(early Oct)*, Kalopanagiotis *(see p89)*. Traditional folk festival combined with a fair.
International Dog Show *(mid-Oct)*, Pafos *(see pp48–51)* with the Kennel Club.

Agios Loukas *(mid-Oct)*. Traditional village fairs in Korakou, Koilani *(see p94)* and Aradippou.
Turkish National Day *(29 Oct)*.

NOVEMBER

Feast of Archangels Gabriel and Michael *(mid-Nov)*. Festival and fair in the St Michael monastery southwest of Nicosia *(see p106)*, in the village of Analiontas.
Cultural Winter *(Nov–Mar)*, Agia Napa *(see p82)*. A cycle of concerts, shows and exhibitions organized by the Agia Napa Municipality and Cyprus Tourism Organisation.
Cultural Festival *(Nov)*, Limassol *(see pp68–71)*. Music, dancing, films, theatre and opera performances held in the Rialto theatre.
TRNC Foundation Day *(15 Nov)*. Celebrating the foundation, in 1983, of the Turkish Republic of Northern Cyprus, which is recognized only by Turkey.

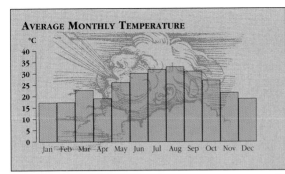

Average Monthly Temperature

Temperature
In the summer, temperatures may reach up to 40° C (104° F). Many people enjoy visiting the island out of the high season. Only the higher sections of the Troodos Mountains, which are covered with snow in winter, record temperatures below freezing.

WINTER

THE WINTERS in Cyprus are mild, and the days are usually sunny. At times winter brings rain, but snow is limited to the upper reaches of the Troodos Mountains. Many cultural events are organized by local authorities at this time. Christmas is traditionally celebrated within the family circle.

DECEMBER

Winter Solstice *(22 Dec)*. Observed at ancient Amathous *(see p74)*, the Sanctuary of Apollo and the Sanctuary of Aphrodite, Agios Tychonas in Limassol *(see pp68–71)*.
Christmas *(25 Dec)*. Family celebrations are held after attending church.
Carols Evening *(25 Dec)* occurs in the central square in Agia Napa *(see p82)*. Events include carol singing, rides in Santa's sleigh and tasting traditional Cypriot dishes.
Welcoming the New Year

(31 Dec), in all towns. In Agia Napa *(see p82)* delicacies are prepared in the main square, with free wine and fireworks displays.

JANUARY

New Year (Agios Vassilios) *(1 Jan)*, formally celebrated with the exchange of presents.
Fóta – the Epiphany *(6 Jan)*. Greek Orthodox churches hold processions and bless water. In coastal towns and villages, young men compete with each other to retrieve a crucifix hurled into the water.
St Neofytos' Day *(late Jan)*. A traditional fair held in the Agios Neofytos monastery *(see p47)* near Pafos.
Şeker Bayrami (Sugar Festival), *(varies)* North Cyprus. A religious feast and a family occasion marking the end of Ramadan, the annual Muslim fast.

FEBRUARY

Carnival, Limassol *(see pp68–71)*. Ten days of wild revelry preceding Lent end

Salt excavation from the salt lake near Larnaka

with Green Monday, which in Limassol features parades and fancy dress balls.
Presentation of Jesus to the Temple *(mid-Feb)*. Traditional fair in the Chrysorrogiatissa monastery *(see p58)*, in the Pafos district.
Kite-flying Competition *(late Feb)*, Deryneia *(see p83)*.

PUBLIC HOLIDAYS IN NORTH CYPRUS

New Year's Day (1 Jan)
Children's Day (23 Apr)
Labour Day (1 May)
Youth and Sports Day (19 May)
Peace and Freedom Day (20 Jul)
Communal Resistance Day (1 Aug)
Victory Day (30 Aug)
Turkish National Day (29 Oct)
Independence Day (15 Nov)
Şeker Bayrami (varies)
Kurban Bayram (varies)
Birth of the Prophet Mohammed (varies)

Winter sports on the slopes of the Troodos Mountains

THE HISTORY OF CYPRUS

L YING AT THE CROSSROADS *of the eastern Mediterranean, Cyprus has long been a prize coveted by surrounding lands: Egypt and Aegia, Persia and Greece, Rome and Byzantium, and finally Venice and Turkey. Its rich copper deposits ensured the island's continuing worth to the prehistoric world. Even the name Cyprus probably derives from the late Greek word for copper –* Kypros.

The location of Cyprus, at the point where the Eastern and Western civilizations met, determined its history to a large extent. Many rulers tried to conquer the island that occupied such a strategic position. Cyprus has been ruled in turn by the Egyptians, Mycenaeans, Phoenicians, Assyrians, Persians, Ptolemies, Romans, Byzantines, Crusaders, Franks, Venetians, Turks and British.

Ornate column capital from ancient Kourion

STONE AGE

Not much is known about the earliest inhabitants, who lived in coastal caves and did not leave much trace of their habitation. Recent evidence from archaeological discoveries at Aetokremmos (Eagle Cliff), however, indicates that Cyprus has been inhabited since at least 8,000 BC. The settlements of Petra tou Limnitis and Tenta existed here in the Neolithic era (late Stone Age), around 7,000-6,000 BC.

The first permanent settlements appeared in the 6th millennium BC. These early settlers are thought to have come from Asia Minor. They built round or oval huts of broken stone, covered with branches and clay. A settlement of this type was discovered in the area of Khirokitia. The inhabitants engaged in primitive farming, livestock rearing (one species of sheep was domesticated at that time) and fishing. The scarce flint stones and obsidian were used to make tools, and vessels were gouged out of limestone. Burial practices included weighing down the bodies with stones, in the belief that this would stop the dead disturbing the living.

From this period until around 4,500 BC there is a gap of information on the activities on the island. Archaeologists have discovered traces of settlements in the vicinity of Çatalköy (Agios Epikitotos), in the North, and Sotira in the South, where they found early "combed pottery" – the oldest ceramics in Cyprus. This pottery was produced by dragging a comb-like tool over the wet vessel to create straight or wavy lines.

After 4,000 BC the Chalcolithic era ushered in the first small-scale use of metal – copper, in addition to widespread use of stone.

TIMELINE

8000 BC	5000 BC	4000 BC	3500 BC	3000 BC
c.6000 BC Khirokitia is Cyprus' earliest known settlement	**5250 BC** Existence of monochromatic and linear-pattern painted ceramics	**after 4000 BC** Chalcolithic settlements emerging in the western part of the island		
c.8000 BC evidence of Neolithic era (Stone Age) human habitation			**3400–2300 BC** The earliest copper mines are established; copper vessels and steatite (soapstone) images of female idols are produced	

Howling Man *from Pierides Museum in Larnaka (5500–5000 BC)*

◁ **Richard the Lionheart, who conquered Cyprus in 1191**

Neolithic settlement of Tenta

THE COPPER AND BRONZE AGES

The transitional period between the Stone and Bronze ages was known as the Chalcolithic era (after the Greek words for copper and stone: *chalkos* and *lithos*); it saw the small-scale use of copper for tools and implements. Most Chalcolithic villages were discovered in the previously unsettled western part of Cyprus. Figurines of limestone fertility goddesses from Lempa and cruciform figurines in picrolite (blue-green stone) from Yala indicate the growing cult of fertility.

The Troodos Mountains contained large deposits of copper, and thanks to this the power of Cyprus began to increase in the third millennium BC. Cyprus became the largest producer and exporter of copper in the Mediterranean basin. The technology of bronze-smelting had by then spread throughout the entire Mediterranean basin. Copper, the main component of bronze, became the source of the island's wealth.

Trade with Egypt and the Middle East developed during this period. Along with vessels of fanciful, often zoomorphic shapes, human figurines and statuettes of bulls associated with the cult of fertility were produced. By the start of the second millennium BC, there were towns trading in copper. The most important of these was the eastern harbour town of Alasia (modern-day Enkomi). At that time, cultural influences brought by settling Egyptian and Phoenician merchants intensified.

Flourishing trade necessitated the development of writing. The oldest text found in Cyprus is a Minoan incised clay tablet from the ruins of Alasia (16th century BC), a form of writing which came about through links with the Minoan civilization of Crete.

During the 16th and 15th centuries BC, the most important towns were Kition (modern-day Larnaka) and Enkomi-Alasia. Mycenaean culture left a permanent imprint on the future development of Cypriot culture.

Khirokitia, one of the earliest settlements

Despite many diverse influences (from Egypt, Mesopotamia, Phoenicia and Persia), it was Greek culture that would dominate.

Around the 12th century BC, marauders known as the "sea peoples" invaded Cyprus, destroying Kition and Alasia. They settled in Maa (Paleo-kastro) in the west of the island, among other

Ruins of Phoenician-populated Kition

places. But with the mass arrival of Mycenaeans in the 11th century BC, balance was restored. The Greek language, customs and culture were widely adopted, and a flourishing cult of Aphrodite also developed. The Temple of Aphrodite in Palepafos rose in status and soon became the main shrine of the goddess in the ancient Greek world.

Around 1,050 BC, an earthquake devastated Cyprus, heralding the island's Dark Ages. Kition and Alasia were reduced to rubble, and their inhabitants relocated to Salamina.

Female figurine from the Temple of Aphrodite

IRON AGE

The first millennium BC ushered in the Iron Age throughout the entire Mediterranean area, although it in no way diminished the demand for copper from Cyprus. During this time, Cyprus was divided into kingdoms, ruled by local kings. The most important were Salamina, Marion, Lapithos, Soli, Pafos,

Tamassos and Kourion. By the 9th century BC the wealth of Cyprus lured Phoenicians from nearby Tyre, who established a colony at Kition. The joint influences from the Phoenicians, Mycenaeans and the Cypriots fuelled this era of outstanding cultural achievement, with the building of new towns and the development of metallurgy.

In about the 8th century BC Amathous (east of modern-day Limassol) began to develop, and Kition (modern-day Larnaka) became a major trading hub and the centre of the cult of the Phoenician goddess, Astarte.

ARCHAIC ERA

In about 700 BC, Cyprus fell into the hands of the Assyrian kings, who did not wish to rule but merely demanded payment of tributes. This period saw the creation of Ionian-influenced limestone statues, pottery decorated with images of people and animals, and votive terracotta figurines.

Amathous, one of the oldest Cypriot towns

		Gold jewellery 1650–1150 BC			
c.1400 BC Mycenaean merchants and craftsmen begin to settle on the island	**12th century BC** Invasion by the "sea peoples"	**1050–750 BC** Geometric era			
1600 BC	**1450 BC**	**1300 BC**	**1150 BC**	**1000 BC**	**850 BC**
				c.1000 BC Phoenicians arrive from Tyre and settle on the southern plains	
16th century BC The earliest Cypro-Minoan writing on a tablet found in the ruins of Alasia		**c.1050 BC** A violent earthquake destroys Cypriot towns, including Alasia and Kition			

Sarcophagus from Pierides Museum in Larnaka

CLASSICAL PERIOD

In the early 6th century BC, Cyprus was ruled by Egyptians, but their influence on local art was negligible. The most distinctive architectural features of the period are the subterranean burial chambers, resembling houses, unearthed in Tamassos. In 545 BC, Egypt was conquered by the Persians, under whose control Cyprus fell. The small Cypriot kingdoms were forced to pay tributes to the Persians and to supply battle-ships in the event of war.

Although the kingdoms were not at first involved in the Persian Wars (490–480 BC), strife akin to civil war erupted. Some kingdoms declared themselves on the side of the Greeks, while others sup-ported the Persians (especially the Phoenician inhabitants of Kition and Amathous, as well as Marion, Kourion and Salamis). In the decisive battle at Salamis, insurgents were defeated and the leader, Onesilos, was killed. The Persians went on to con-quer other kingdoms. The

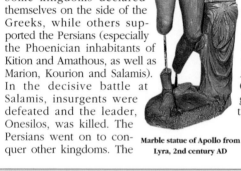
Marble statue of Apollo from Lyra, 2nd century AD

last to fall were Palepafos and Soloi (in 498 BC). Having quashed the revolt, the pro-Persian king of Marion built a palace to watch over Soloi.

By the start of the 5th century BC, Cyprus had ten kingdoms, the existing ones having been joined by Kyrenia, Idalion, Amathous and Kition, while Soloi submitted to the rule of the king of Marion. Cyprus became a battleground for the Greek-Persian Wars. The Athenian general, Kimon, who was sent to the island failed to conquer Cyprus, despite a few minor victories, and was killed during the siege of Kition.

Despite the difficult political situation, the influence of Greek culture on Cyprus grew considerably. This was especially noticeable in sculpture; hitherto the portrayal of gods and men had been stiff, endowed with an obligatory "archaic smile", and now it became more naturalistic.

HELLENISTIC ERA

When Alexander the Great attacked the Persian Empire in 325 BC, the Cypriot kingdoms welcomed him as a liber-ator, providing him with a fleet of battleships for his victorious siege of Tyre. The weakening of Phoenicia resulted in greater revenues from the copper trade for Cyprus. But the favourable situation did not last. After Alexander's death in 323 BC, Cyprus became a battle-ground for his successors – the victor was the Greek-Egyptian Ptolemy I Solter. Kition, Kyrenia, Lapithos and Marion were destroyed

TIMELINE

800 BC Phoenicians settle in Kition

570 BC Egyptians assume control of Cyprus

546 BC Start of Persian rule

Jug (5th century BC)

294 BC Island falls under the control of the Egyptian Ptolemys

| 700 BC | 600 BC | 500 BC | 400 BC | 300 BC |

8th century BC Assyrians leave control of the island to Cypriot kings, demanding only an annual tribute

c.500 BC Ionian cities revolt against the Persians

381 BC Evagoras, King of Salamis, leads revolt against the Persians

333 BC Alexander the Great occupies Cyprus

Lion from a tomb stele (5th century BC)

Ruins of Kambanopetra basilica in Salamis

by a governor, who resided in a magnificent palace in Nea Pafos. The largest town, port and main trading centre was still Salamis, which at that time numbered over 200,000 inhabitants. The imposing ruins of Salamis bear testimony to its prosperity, while the Roman floor mosaics in Pafos are among the most interesting in the Middle East. The flourishing city of Kourion was the site of the temple and oracle of Apollo – which continued to be of religious significance. Roman rule lasted in Cyprus until the end of the 4th century AD.

Mosaic from the house of Theseus in Kato Pafos

and Nicocreon, the King of Salamis who refused to surrender, committed suicide. Cyprus became part of the Kingdom of Egypt, and its viceroy resided in the new capital – Nea Pafos. Cultural life was influenced by Hellenism, with the Egyptian gods joining the pantheon of deities.

ROMAN RULE & CHRISTIANITY

In 58 BC, Cyprus was conquered by the legions of Rome. The island was given the status of a province ruled

Christianity came to Cyprus with the arrival from Palestine of the apostle Paul in AD 45. He was joined by Barnabas, who was to become the first Cypriot saint. In the same year they converted the Roman governor of Cyprus, Sergius Paulus. The new religion spread slowly, until it was adopted as the state religion by Emperor Constantine. His edict of 312 granted Christianity equal status with other religions of his Empire. St Helena, the mother of Constantine the Great, stopped in Cyprus on her way back from Jerusalem, where she found fragments of the True Cross. She founded Stavrovouni monastery, which is said to house a fragment of the cross.

Saranda Kolones in Kato Pafos

58 BC Rome annexes Cyprus

1st century BC Cyprus hit by violent earthquakes

Eros and Psyche (1st century AD)

| 200 BC | 100 BC | AD 1 | AD 100 | AD 200 | AD 300 |

AD 45 The apostles Paul and Barnabas arrive as missionaries to spread Christianity to Cyprus

313 Edict of Milan grants freedom of worship to Christians throughout the Roman Empire, including Cyprus

115–116 Jewish rebellion put down by Emperor Hadrian. Salamis destroyed

In 332 and 342, two cataclysmic earthquakes destroyed most of the Cypriot towns, including Salamis and Palepafos, marking the end of the era.

View from St Hilarion Castle

BYZANTINE PERIOD

The official division of the Roman realm into an Eastern and Western Empire in 395 naturally left Cyprus on the eastern side of the divide, under the Byzantine sphere of influence.

The 5th and 6th centuries were flourishing times. The centres of pagan culture linked to the cults of Aphrodite and Apollo (Pafos and Kourion) lost importance, while the role of Salamis increased. Renamed Constantia, it became the island's capital. New towns also arose, such as Famagusta and Nicosia, and vast basilicas were built.

Beginning around 647, the first of a series of pillaging raids by Arabs took place. In the course of the raids, which continued over three centuries, Constantia was sacked and many magnificent buildings were destroyed.

In 965, the fleet of the Byzantine emperor Nicephorus II Phocas rid the island of Arab pirates and Cyprus again became safe. But not for long. From the 11th century, the entire Middle East became the scene of new warfare. Anatolia,

Christ Pantocrator from the church of Panagiatou tou Araka

Syria and, above all, the Holy Land were captured by the Seljuk Turks. Byzantium was incapable of resisting the onslaught, and Crusades were organised in Europe to recover the Holy Land and other lost territories.

CRUSADES & LUSIGNAN PERIOD

Successive crusades took place throughout most of the 12th and 13th centuries to recover the Holy Land from the Muslims. After considerable effort, the first succeeded in capturing Jerusalem (1099). European knights set up the Kingdom of Jerusalem, but surrounded as it was by Turkish emirates, it was unable to survive. Further crusades were launched but mainly suffered defeats. The Sultan Saladin conquered nearly the entire Kingdom of Jerusalem in 1187. The next crusade was organised in 1190. One of its leaders was Richard I (the Lionheart),

TIMELINE

Pendant from the early Byzantine period

488 Following the discovery of the tomb of St Barnabas, Emperor Zenon confirms the independence of the Cypriot Church

688 Emperor Justinian II and Caliph Abd al-Malik sign a treaty dividing control of the island

300	450	600	750

395 Partition of the Roman Empire; Cyprus becomes part of the Eastern Roman Empire

7th century Arab raids

David in the Lion's Den, a 7th-century AD relief

King of England, whose ships were forced onto Cyprus by a storm. The local prince, Isaac Komnenos, who had proclaimed himself King of Cyprus, plundered the ships and tried to imprison the sister and the fiancée of Richard. In reprisal, Richard smashed the Komnenos artillery on the Mesaoria plain and chased his enemy, capturing him in Kantara Castle.

As spoils of war, Cyprus passed from hand to hand. Richard turned it over to the Knights Templar, and they in turn sold the island to the knight Guy de Lusignan, who started the Cyprian Lusignan Dynasty and introduced the feudal system to Cyprus. A period of prosperity for the nobility ensued, partly due to trade with Genoa and Venice, although local Cypriots experienced terrible poverty. Magnificent cathedrals and churches were built, and small churches in the Troodos mountains were decorated with splendid frescoes. The state was weakened by a devastating raid by the increasingly powerful Genoese in 1372, who captured Famagusta. Finally, the widow of James, the last Lusignan king, ceded Cyprus to the Venetians in 1489.

A costume from Venetian times

domains in the eastern Mediterranean from the Ottoman Empire. The most formidable fortifications around the ports and towns date from this period (including Kyrenia and Famagusta). Still, these were no match for the overwhelming power of the Ottoman Empire. When the Turkish army of Sultan Selim II landed on Cyprus in 1570, one town after another fell to the invaders. Nicosia was able to defend itself for just a few weeks; when it fell, the Turks slaughtered 20,000 people. The defence of Famagusta lasted longer – 10 months – and was one of the greatest battles of its time. The Venetian defenders did not survive to see the arrival of the relief army, and were forced to capitulate. The Turkish commander, Lala Mustafa Pasha, reneged on his promises of clemency and ordered the garrison to be slaughtered, and its leader Bragadino to be skinned alive.

VENETIAN RULE

Venetian rule over Cyprus lasted less than a century. The island was a frontier fortress, intended to defend the Venetian

A 16th-century map of Cyprus

THE OTTOMAN ERA

This was the start of 300 years of Turkish rule. The conquerors destroyed most of the monasteries and churches, turning others into mosques. They abolished the hated feudal system, and divided land among the peasants. The Orthodox clergy were allowed to adopt some Catholic churches and monasteries, and later the archbishop was recognized as the Greek community's representative.

The Turks brought their compatriots to settle on the island, and squashed the regular rebellions. In 1821, after the beginning of the Greek War of Independence, the Turkish governor ordered the execution of the popular Archbishop Kyprianos and many other members of the Orthodox clergy.

In the mid-19th century, Great Britain came to play an increasingly important role in the Middle East. In exchange for military aid in the war

Selima Mosque in North Nicosia

with Russia, Turkey handed over occupation and administrative rights of Cyprus to Britain in perpetuity in 1878, though the island would continue to be a Turkish possession.

BRITISH RULE

Cyprus's strategic location was vital in defending the sea routes to India and in safeguarding British interests in the Middle East. During their rule, the British introduced the English justice system, reduced crime, and built roads and waterworks. Following the outbreak of World War I, when Turkey declared itself on the side of Germany, Britain annexed Cyprus.

After World War II, Greek Cypriots pressed for *enosis* (unification with Greece), which was strongly opposed by the Turkish minority. Rising tensions led to the establishment of the organization EOKA (National

Hadjigeorgakis Kornesios mansion

Hoisting of the British flag in Cyprus

TIMELINE

1570 Cyprus invaded by Ottoman Turks	**1754** The sultan confirms the Orthodox archbishop as a spokesman for the Greek Cypriots	**1821** Bloody sup[of the Greek uprising by th
1600	**1650**	**1700** **1750** 18
1571–1878 Ottoman era	**1660** Ottoman authorities recognize the legitimacy of the Archbishop's office with the Greeks	**1779** Establishment of the dragoman (intercessor between the Turks and the Greeks)

Büyük Han in North Nicosia

Organization of Cypriot Fighters) in 1954 by Archbishop Makarios and Greek General George Grivas. Its aim was to free Cyprus from British control. EOKA embarked on a terrorist campaign, first aimed at property and later, at people. In 1958, Turkish Cypriots founded the Turkish Resistance Organisation (TNT), which provided a counterbalance to EOKA.

The terror and growing costs of maintaining order led the British to grant independence to Cyprus. A constitution was drafted that, among other things, excluded *enosis* and *taksim* (partition of Cyprus between Turkey and Greece favoured by Turkish Cypriots). Britain, Greece and Turkey signed a treaty that obliged them to ensure Cyprus's independence. Archbishop Makarios, who had been interned by the British, returned to Cyprus in triumph and was elected President of the Republic of Cyprus. Independence was officially declared on 16 August 1960.

Archbishop Makarios, first president of the Republic of Cyprus

Guard (led by Greek army officers), ousted Makarios. The conspirators killed several hundred Greeks and Turks, which provided the Turkish government in Ankara with a pretext to send troops to Cyprus. After a short battle, the invading army controlled the north, and the resettlement of the population began. The "Green Line" still divides the Turkish-occupied North from the South, and is patrolled by UN troops.

The Turks declared the Turkish Republic of Northern Cyprus (TRNC) in 1983, which was recognized only by Turkey. The subsequent repeated attempts at reunification have all failed. The greatest opportunity to reunify the island was provided by the 2004 referendum preceding Cyprus's entry into the European Union. The conditions laid down by the United Nations to unite both parts of the island were accepted only by the Turkish Cypriots – the Greek Cypriots rejected the proposal.

INDEPENDENT CYPRUS

In December 1963, animosity between Greek and Turkish Cypriots erupted into warfare. The Greek army intervened and the Turkish air force bombarded the environs of Polis. In 1964, United Nations troops arrived to restore peace between the warring parties within three months. The mission failed and troops remain to this day.

On 15 July 1974 a coup d'état, encouraged by Athens and staged by rebel units of the Cypriot National

Referendum on the reunification of Cyprus (2004)

The hanging of Archbishop Kyprianos

1925 Cyprus becomes a British colony

1950 Makarios is elected Archbishop

General George Grivas

1983 TRNC is declared

2004 (April) Referendum on reunification

1850	1900	1950	2000

1878 Great Britain takes over the administration of Cyprus

1914 Outbreak of World War I; Great Britain annexes Cyprus

1960 (16 August) Proclamation of independence. Archbishop Makarios III becomes President of the Republic of Cyprus

1974 Coup d'état against President Makarios. Turkish invasion of North Cyprus

1963–4 Fighting erupts between Greek and Turkish Cypriots; UN troops arrive

CYPRUS
REGION BY
REGION

Cyprus at a Glance

CYPRUS HAS A WIDE VARIETY of historic sites. Visitors can find everything from Neolithic settlements and ancient towns to medieval cathedrals and small mountain churches decorated with exquisite frescoes, castles built by the Crusaders and Venetian fortresses, and modern buildings and museums. The island abounds in picturesque towns and villages, beautiful coastal areas, and scenic mountains, with diverse wildlife and friendly people.

Nicosia *is the world's only divided capital city. A highlight of its southern part is the Byzantine-style Archbishop Makarios Cultural Centre, housing an impressive collection of icons (see pp118).*

Agios Nikolaos tis Stegis, a UNESCO World Heritage Site, is one of the many small churches hidden in the sheltered valleys of the Troodos Mountains that feature magnificent frescoes (see p198).

SOUTH NICOSI
Pages 112–

TROODOS MOUNTAINS
Pages 84–101

CENTRAL CYPRUS
Pages 102–111

WEST CYPRUS
Pages 40–59

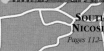

SOUTHERN CYPRUS
Pages 60–83

Pafos, divided into Kato Pafos (Lower Pafos) and Ktima, is full of history. With its picturesque harbour it is also one of the most beautiful towns in the Mediterranean (see pp48–53).

0 km   15

0 miles   15

◁ Herd of goats near Lara Bay in the Akamas peninsula

Buffavento Castle in the Kyrenia mountains was one of three castles, along with Kantara and St Hilarion, that defended Cyprus against attacks along the north coast (see p144).

NORTH CYPRUS
Pages 124–153

Salamis was the island's most important port and trading town for almost one thousand years, and also its capital. Now it is one of the largest archaeological sites (see pp134–5).

In Larnaka the remains of the 18th-century Kamares Aqueduct stand beside the Larnaka-Limassol highway. In ancient times the Kingdom of Kition, today Larnaka is a large port town with a thriving tourist zone (see pp78–81).

Famagusta, a city surrounded by Venetian defence walls, contains Gothic churches that have been transformed into mosques with minarets (see pp136–7).

WEST CYPRUS

UNTIL RECENTLY WEST CYPRUS, *which includes mountains and a stretch of a coastline with lovely beaches, was the most neglected part of the island, remote from the main cities and harbours. Now it is becoming a popular attraction due to its wild natural environment and small population. Lovers of antiquities are sure to be enchanted by the Roman mosaics in Pafos, while mythology buffs can see the place where the goddess Aphrodite emerged from the sea at Petra tou Romiou.*

Pafos's Hellenistic, Roman and Byzantine relics are among the most interesting in the island, especially the Roman mosaics.

The modern town is divided into a bustling tourist zone on the coast, with dozens of luxury hotels, taverns, pubs and restaurants, and Ktima – a typical small Cypriot town a short drive inland that seems a world away from the tourist zone.

This region has a slightly milder climate than the rest of the island, as witnessed by the banana plantations north of Pafos. And though there is practically no industry, it has the most extensive forest areas in Cyprus, including the famous Cedar Valley inhabited by wild moufflon. The Akamas Peninsula, with its rugged hills overgrown with forests, is home to many species of wild animals, and the beautiful beaches provide nesting grounds for sea turtles. This is a paradise for nature lovers and is one of the best places to hike in Cyprus. Movement around the peninsula is hindered by the lack of roads, but there are trails for use by walkers.

This is the land of Aphrodite, the goddess of love, born in the south of the island by the rocks jutting out of the sea, which are named after her. In the north, on the bay of Chryssochou, is the goddess's bath, which she used after her amorous frolics with Adonis.

Pafos harbour, the most picturesque in southern Cyprus

◁ *The bath of Achilles*, an ancient mosaic in Pafos

Exploring West Cyprus

THE BEST PLACE TO BEGIN exploring West Cyprus is Pafos, which has the largest concentration of hotels and the most developed tourist infrastructure. Here you will also find a wealth of historic relics that have made Kato Pafos a UNESCO World Heritage Site. They range from Bronze Age dwellings (Maa Paleokastro at Coral Bay), royal tombs dating from the Hellenic era and Roman floor mosaics to Byzantine castles and churches. Pafos forest is home to wild moufflon. Cape Lara, to the northwest of Pafos, has beautiful beaches, and further on is the Akamas peninsula.

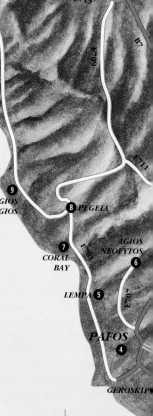

Lempa is a favourite place with water-sports enthusiasts

GETTING THERE

The easiest way to arrive is by air to the international airport east of Pafos. A few years ago a new motorway was finally completed, linking the town with Limassol, making it easier to reach the west coast. It is also possible to get here via a parallel road running along the coast and over the southern slopes of the Troodos Mountains. The mountain roads are not of the best quality, and driving around the Akamas peninsula is best done in a four-wheel-drive vehicle.

SIGHTS AT A GLANCE

Agios Georgios church at Cape Drepanon, which lies north of Coral Bay

SEE ALSO

• **Where to Stay** pp158–159

• **Where to Eat** pp170–171

15 **PANAGIA CHRYSORROGIATISSA**

16 **XIROS VALLEY**

17 **DIARIZOS VALLEY**

Troodos →

Asprokremmos Dam

2 **PALEPAFOS**

KOUKLIA

Limassol →

1 **PETRA TOU ROMIOU**

E704

Milkounta

E703

E702

E606

A6

B6

0 km   5

0 miles   5

KEY

Motorway

Major road

Scenic route

Other road

River

Viewpoint

Petra tou Romiou, the legendary birthplace of Aphrodite

Petra tou Romiou ❶

Road map B4. 25 km (16 miles) east of Pafos.

THE AREA between Pafos and Limassol includes what is probably the most beautiful stretch of the Cyprus coast, dominated by limestone crags rising from the blue sea. At Petra tou Romiou there are three huge, white limestone rocks known collectively as the **Rock of Aphrodite**. In Greek mythology it was here that Aphrodite, goddess of love, beauty and fertility, emerged from the sea foam. She sailed to the shore on a shell towed by dolphins and rested in nearby Palepafos, where a temple was built to her.

The location of these picturesque rocks is beautiful, with clear blue water beckoning swimmers. The large beach near the rocks is covered with fine pebbles and stones polished smooth by the action of the waves. A word of caution, however: the road between the car park and the beach is dangerous and you are advised to use the underground passage.

Nearby you can see trees on which infertile women tie handkerchiefs or scraps of fabric to appeal for help from Aphrodite. They are joined by others who are lonely and unlucky in love, beseeching the goddess of love to help them. A local legend says that swimming around the jutting rock at full moon will make you a year younger with each lap. Other legends lead us to believe that the amorous goddess, after a night spent in the arms of her lover, returned to this spot to regain her virginity by bathing in the sea.

On the slope of the hill rising above the Rock of Aphrodite, the Cyprus Tourism Organization has built a cafeteria where you can eat while taking in the beautiful view over Petra tou Romiou. Meaning "Rock of Romios", the name Petra tou Romiou also commemorates the legendary Greek hero Digenis Akritas, also known as Romios. He lived during the Byzantine era and, during an Arab raid by Saracen corsairs on Cyprus, hurled huge boulders into the sea to destroy the Arab ships. According to legend, the rocks here are the stones thrown by Romios.

ENVIRONS: A few kilometres east of Petra tou Romiou is the small resort community of **Pissouri**, surrounded by orchards. There are large purpose-built resorts here, and some smaller hotels, as well as a long, sandy beach. Nearby are two golf courses: Secret Valley and Aphrodite Hills.

Palepafos ❷

Road map A4. In the village of Kouklia, 14 km (9 miles) east of Pafos, by the Pafos–Limassol road. 📞 *264 32180.* 🕐 *9am–5pm (7pm in summer) Mon–Fri , 9am–4pm (5pm in summer) Sat–Sun.* 🖼

LYING JUST NORTH of the large village of Kouklia are the ruins of the famous Palepafos (Old Pafos), which was the oldest and most powerful city-state on the island in ancient times. According to tradition, it was founded by Agaperon – a hero of the Trojan Wars and the son of the King of Tegeia in Greek Arcadia. Palepafos was also the site of the **Temple of Aphrodite**, the most important shrine of the goddess in the ancient world, but now only of specialist interest.

APHRODITE

The cult of Aphrodite arrived in Cyprus from the East; she was already worshipped in Syria and Palestine as Ishtar and Astarte. She was also worshipped by the Romans as Venus. In Greek mythology Aphrodite was the goddess of love, beauty and fertility who rose from the sea foam off the shore of Cyprus. She was married to Hephaestus, but took many lovers, including Ares and Adonis. She was the mother of Eros, Hermaphrodite, Priap and Aeneas, among others. The main centres for her cult of worship were Pafos and Amathous. The myrtle plant is dedicated to her, as is the dove.

Marble statue of Aphrodite from Soloi

Archaeological evidence points to the existence of a much older town on this site, dating back to the Bronze Age. Legend says that Pygmalion, a local king and also a brilliant sculptor, carved many statues, including one of an extraordinarily beautiful woman with whom he fell madly in love. Aphrodite, moved by his love, turned the cold statue into a living woman. Their union produced a son, Pafos, who gave the town its name.

The most famous figure of Pafos was Kinyras, ruler of the city and great priest of Aphrodite, who introduced many religious mysteries and gave rise to the dynasty that ruled the city for centuries.

A large **centre of worship** devoted to Aphrodite was established here in the 12th century BC, at the end of the Bronze Age. All that is left now are its foundations and fragments of the walls. The sanctuary was destroyed during an earthquake and rebuilt in the 1st century, during Roman times. At this place of worship, the goddess was represented by a black stone shaped as a cone, symbolizing fertility. For centuries, crowds of pilgrims flocked to Pafos from all over the ancient world. Adorned with flowers, the pilgrims walked into the temple where they were met by the temple courtesans. Aphrodite was worshipped through ritual sexual intercourse between the pilgrims and Aphrodite's priestesses – young Cypriot women who

The small stone church of Agios Constantinos near Kouklion

were obliged to offer their virginity to the goddess by giving themselves to a pilgrim man within the temple area. These orgiastic rites were mainly held in the spring, and elements have survived in the form of the spring flower festival – the Anthistiria.

Palepafos was not always peaceful. It took part in the rebellion of the Ionian cities against the Persians. In 498 BC, the Persians laid siege to the city and, following a fierce battle, forced entry by scaling the ramparts, the remains of which can still be seen. In 325 BC, following a devastating earthquake that destroyed Palepafos, its last king, Nikikles, moved the city to Nea Pafos (present day Kato Pafos), but Aphrodite's sanctuary retained its importance until the end of the 4th century, when Emperor Theodosius banned pagan

Panagia Chrysopolitissa inscription

cults within the empire. The sanctuary is now a site of excavations, conducted by Swiss archaeologists.

Standing on the hill is a Gothic structure known as the **Lusignan Court**, built in the times of the Crusaders and subsequently remodelled by the Turks. It is built on a square floor plan, and leading onto a square yard is an old tower gate. The rooms in the east wing contain a museum that exhibits locally discovered ceramics, stone idols, bronze articles and the black stone worshipped by followers of Aphrodite. On the ground floor there is an impressive Gothic hall with cross vaulting.

In the nearby Roman villa, known as the **House of Leda**, archaeologists have uncovered a 2nd-century AD floor mosaic, which depicts the Spartan Queen Leda with Zeus in the guise of a swan.

Adjacent to the sanctuary is the small 12th-century church of **Panagia Chrysopolitissa**. It is dedicated to the early Christian Madonna, whose cult derives directly from Aphrodite – the pagan goddess of love. Until recently, women came here to light candles to the Virgin Mary – Giver of Mother's Milk. This church contains interesting 14th-century frescoes.

ENVIRONS: Standing in the nearby **Mandria** are 3 m- (10 ft-) tall pillars with square holes cut in them. It is not clear what purpose they served.

Ruins of the Sanctuary of Aphrodite

Folk Art Museum in Geroskipou

Geroskipou ❸

Road map A4. 3 km (1.8 miles) east of Pafos. 🏛 *25 & 26 Jun Agia Paraskevi.*

THE NAME Geroskipou *(hieros kipos)* means "sacred garden" in Greek. This testifies to the fact that this former village (now a suburban district bordering Pafos) was built on the site of a forest dedicated to Aphrodite. To this day, it is notable for its many flowers and fruit trees, especially citrus and pomegranate trees – symbols of the goddess.

The main street is lined with workshops producing the local delicacy – *loukoumia* (Turkish Delight). Made from water, sugar and citrus juice, thickened through evaporation, the resulting jelly is cut into cubes and coated with icing sugar. The workshops are open to visitors, who can view the production process and, while there, also buy other sweets including sugar-coated almonds and halva – made of nuts, honey and sesame seeds. The tree-shaded main square of the town is surrounded by colourful shops selling baskets, ceramics and the celebrated *loukoumia*; there are also numerous cafes.

Standing at the southern end of the market square is **Agia Paraskevi**, one of the most interesting Byzantine churches on the island. Built in the 9th century, this stone church features five domes arranged in the shape of a cross. The sixth one surmounts the reliquary located under the 19th-century belfry.

Originally, the church was a single-nave structure. Its interior is decorated with beautiful 15th-century murals depicting scenes from the New Testament, including the lives of Jesus and Mary, and the Crucifixion. The frescoes were restored in the 1970s.

The vault of the central dome is decorated with the painting of the Praying Madonna. The three images opposite the south entrance – – *The Last Supper, The Washing of the Feet* and *The Betrayal* – can be dated from the Lusignan period, due to the style of armour worn by the knights portrayed. Opposite are *The Birth and Presentation of the Virgin, The Entry into Jerusalem* and *The Raising of Lazarus.*

Another attraction, close to the market square, is the 19th-century historic house once home of the British Consul, Andreas Zamboulakis. Now the building houses the

The stone church of Agia Paraskevi in Geroskipou

Folk Art Museum, one of the most impressive on the island, including a collection of local folk costumes, textiles, embroidery and toys, as well as decorated gourds, furniture and domestic items.

🏛 **Folk Art Museum**
Leondiou. 🎫 *269 40216.*
🕐 *9am–2:30pm Mon–Fri (& 3-5pm Thu).* 🌑 *Sat & Sun, Jul–Aug.*
🔒 **Agia Paraskevi Church**
🎫 *269 61859,* 🕐 *8am–1pm & 2–5pm Mon–Sat, 10am–1pm Sun (until 4pm Oct–Apr).*

Pafos ❹

See pp48–51.

Reconstructed Chalcolithic houses in Lempa's Experimental Village

Lempa ❺

Road map A4. 4 km (2.5 miles) north of Pafos. 🚌 *3, 6 & 7 from Ktima Pafos.*

SET AMONG citrus groves between the villages of Chlorakas and Kissonerga just a short distance from the sea, Lempa is home to the **Cyprus College of Fine Arts**. The artists, craftsmen and students here have studios in restored village houses. The road to the college is lined with sculptures. The independent pottery workshops are worth visiting.

Lempa was home to the earliest islanders, who settled here more than 5,500 years ago. West of the village centre you can see the **Lempa Experimental Village** – a partially reconstructed settlement dating from the Chalcolithic (bronze) era (3500 BC). British archaeologists have rebuilt six complete houses from that era. The clay, cylindrical dwellings are covered with makeshift roofs.

Agios Neofytos monastery, founded in the 12th century

Cyprus College of Fine Arts

📞 269 70557.
🏛 **Lempa Experimental Village** ⭕ dawn–dusk daily.

ENVIRONS: Standing in a park in the centre of the nearby village of Empa, some 2 km (1.2 miles) southeast of Lempa, is the 12th-century monastery church of **Panagia Chryseleoussa**. Inside the church are the remains of frescoes that were initially destroyed by an earthquake in the mid-20th century, and subsequently damaged by a botched restoration job.

Agios Neofytos 6

Road map A4. 9 km north of Pafos, 2 km NW of Tala. ⭕ Apr–Sep: 9am–1pm & 2–6pm daily; Oct–Mar: 9am–4pm daily. 📷 🚫 24 Jan & 27 Sep.

THIS MONASTERY was founded in the 12th century by a monk named Neofytos, one of the main saints of the Cypriot church. He was a hermit and an ascetic, author of philosophical treatises and hymns, who spent dozens of years here. Some of his manuscripts survive, including the *Ritual Ordinance*, a handbook of monastic life, and a historic essay on the acquisition of Cyprus by the Crusaders.

The future saint dug three cells in the steep limestone rock with his bare hands. The murals covering its walls are reputed to have been painted by Neofytos himself. This, the oldest part of the monastery, is called the *encleistra* (hermitage). In two of the caves, murals depict the final days of the life of Christ – *The Last Supper, Judas's Betrayal* and the *Deposition from the Cross*, featuring Joseph of Arimathea whose face is thought to be a portrait of the saint. The dome, hewn from the soft rock, features the Ascension. The cell of the saint has bookshelves, benches and a desk at which St Neofytos used to work, all carved in the rock, as well as his sarcophagus presided over by an image of the Resurrection.

The main buildings, which are still inhabited by monks, include an inner courtyard, a small garden with an aviary, and a *katholikon* – the monastery church with a terrace dedicated to the Virgin Mary.

A woman potter

Coral Bay 7

Road map A4. 8 km (5 miles) north of Pafos. 🚌 10, 15.

THIS FINE SANDY beach between two promontories has a tropical air. All summer long it is covered by rows of sunbeds for hire, and there is a wide choice of water sports. There are a couple of bars, the giant 5-star Coral Beach Hotel with its own marina, and a campsite for more thrifty visitors. Live pop concerts are held here on summer evenings. This beach is popular with young Cypriots from Larnaka and Limassol, especially on summer weekends.

On the northern headland archaeologists discovered **Maa Paleokastro** – a fortified Achaian settlement dating from the Bronze Age. The site now houses the **Museum of the Mycenean Colonization of Cyprus**.

ENVIRONS: Opposite the village of Chlorakas on the road leading to Pafos is the **Church of St George**, which commemorates the landing of General George Grivas at this spot in 1954. The local museum has a boat that was used by EOKA guerrillas for weapons smuggling.

Several kilometres inland lies the Mavrokolympos reservoir. Above the car park are the **Adonis Baths**, whose main attraction is its 10m- (32 ft-) high waterfall. The road running along the Mavrokolympos river leads to more waterfalls.

The region also features numerous vineyards and banana plantations.

The picturesque crescent-shaped Coral Bay

Pafos ❹

P AFOS IS THE NAME given to the twin towns of Pano
Pafos (Upper Pafos, called Ktima by locals) and Nea
Pafos or Kato Pafos (Lower Pafos) *(see pp52–3)*. During
the Byzantine era, when coastal towns were threatened
by Arab raids, the town was moved inland to its
present hilltop location. This is now the modern
regional centre of trade, administration and culture,
while the lower town is the site of fine Roman ruins
and the majority of tourist facilities.

Exploring Pafos

Ktima is best explored on
foot. Most of its major historic
buildings and interesting
sites, except for the
Archaeological Museum, are
within walking distance. The
tourist area in the Old Town
has been restored. The main
shopping street is Makarios
Avenue, where you will find
a wide choice of jewellery,
clothing and footwear. After
strolling along the streets of
the Old Town it is worth
stopping for a rest in the
green district, to the south of
town, near the acropolis and
the Byzantine and
Ethnographic Museums. The
eastern part of town sports
wide avenues lined with
classical public buildings,
schools and libraries. The
western part is a maze of
narrow streets and traditional
architecture.

🅖 Grand Mosque
(Cami Kebir) Namik Kemil.
The Grand Mosque is a relic
of the past Turkish presence
in this area. Standing in the
former Mouttalos district, it
had been the Byzantine church
of Agia Sofia before being
turned into a mosque.

**The façade of Agios Kendas church,
which was built around 1930**

🏛 Agora
Agoras street
Rght in the centre, near to the
bus station, is an ornamental
covered market hall building,
dating from the early part of
the 20th century. Recently,
sweet and souvenir sellers
have replaced the fruit and
vegetables vendors.

🅛 Loutra (Turkish Baths)
Militiathou, next to the covered
bazaar (agora).
Among the trees south of the
Agora are the Turkish baths.
Originally this dome-covered
stone structure probably

served as a church. After
serving as the Turkish baths,
some of the rooms were used
to house the municipal
museum, but when the
museum moved to new
premises, the building stood
empty. A period of neglect
followed, but recently the
Loutra building has been
restored to its former glory.

🅐 Agios Kendas
Leoforos Archiepiskopou Makariou III
Built in 1930, the exterior is
not particularly exciting, but
the interior is well worth a
visit. Here you will find a
carved wooden iconostasis, a
bishop's throne and a number
of 19th-century icons.

🏛 Town Hall
Plateia 28 Octovriou.
The single-storey Neo-Classical
building standing on the edge
of the Municipal Garden,
redolent of ancient Greek
architecture, houses the Town
Hall and the Registry Office.
This is one of the most
popular wedding venues. On
the opposite side, behind the
slender Ionian column in the
middle of the square, is the
one-storey municipal library.

**The Neo-Classical Town Hall and
Registry Office of Pafos**

🅐 Agios Theodoros
(St Theodore's Cathedral)
Andrea Ioannou.
Built in 1896, Agios Theodoros
is the oldest church in Ktima
and is as important to the
Orthodox community as St
John's Cathedral (Agios
Ioannis) in Nicosia.
   Close to the square stands a
column commemorating the
victims of the Turkish
slaughter of 1821 that claimed
the lives of the Bishop of
Pafos, Chrysanthos, and
numerous other members of
the Greek clergy.

Agora fruit and vegetable market

Display in the Ethnographic Museum

🏛 Geological Exhibition

Ayios Theodoros 2. ⏰ *8am–1pm &*
4–7:30pm Mon-Sat.

One of a few places on the island where you can learn about the geology of Cyprus, this is a small private collection of rocks and minerals. On display are sedimentary rocks with fossils; volcanic rocks from the Troodos Mountains and the Akamas peninsula; and metallic minerals, particularly copper and asbestos that have been mined here for millennia.

🏛 Bishop's Palace and Byzantine Museum

Andrea Joannou. 📞 *269 1393.* ⏰
9am–5pm Mon–Fri, 10am–1pm Sat. 🖼

This beautiful Byzantine-style building is the residence of the Bishop of Pafos and the most important ecclesiastical

building after Agios Theodoros. It was built in 1910 by Iaskos, the Bishop of Pafos. Bishop Chrysostomos subsequently extended the palace, furnishing it with beautiful

The Dormition of the Virgin Mary,
the Byzantine Museum

arcades and allocating part of it to the Byzantine Museum. The museum houses a collection of icons, including the oldest on the island – the 9th-century *Agia Marina*, and the 12th-century *Panagia Eloussa* from the Agios Savras monastery. There are also religious books, including a 1472 Bible, a collection of documents produced by Turkish sultans, and other precious manuscripts.

🏛 Ethnographic Museum

Exo Vrysis 1. 📞 *269 3210.*
⏰ *Oct–Sep: 9am–1pm & 2–5pm*
Mon–Fri, 9am–1pm Sat; May–Sep:
9am–1pm & 3–7pm Mon–Fri,
10am–1pm Sun. 🖼

This musuem houses collections of coins, folk costumes, kitchen utensils and ceramics as well as axes, amphorae and carriages. In the garden is a wood-burning stove from an old bakery and a 3rd-century stone sarcophagus.

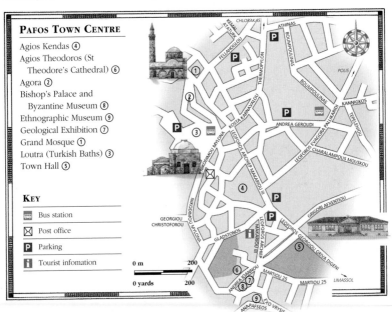

PAFOS TOWN CENTRE

Agios Kendas ④
Agios Theodoros (St
  Theodore's Cathedral) ⑥
Agora ②
Bishop's Palace and
  Byzantine Museum ⑧
Ethnographic Museum ⑨
Geological Exhibition ⑦
Grand Mosque ①
Loutra (Turkish Baths) ③
Town Hall ⑤

KEY

🚌	Bus station
⊠	Post office
P	Parking
ℹ	Tourist infomation

0 m   200
0 yards   200

⋔ Tombs of the Kings

Leoforos Tafon ton Vasileion.
☎ 263 06295. ◌ Jun–Jul: 8am–
7:30pm daily; Sep–May: 8am–5pm
daily. ▨ ▨ 15 from Kato Pafos.

The necropolis is a fascinating system of caves and rock
tombs dating from the Hellenic
and Roman eras (the 3rd century BC to 3rd century AD).
Situated north of Kato Pafos,
beyond the old city walls and
close to the sea, it consists of
imposing tombs carved in
soft sandstone.

Eight tomb complexes have
been opened for viewing; the
most interesting are numbers
3, 4 and 8. Stone steps lead to
underground vaults. Some
tombs are surrounded by
peristyles of Doric columns,
beyond which you can spot
burial niches. Others have
been decorated with murals.

The architectural style of
many tombs, particularly
those in the northern section,
reveals the Egyptian influence;
they were inspired by the
Ptolemy tombs in Alexandria.
One funerary custom that has
been documented is that on
the anniversary of the death,
relatives of the deceased
would gather around the
tomb for a ceremonial meal,
depositing the leftovers by
the actual sepulchre. Similar
customs prevail to this day in
some Greek Orthodox
communities.

Over the following centuries
the tombs were systematically

The 12th-century stone church of Agia Kyriaki

plundered. One of the more
notorious looters was the
American consul from Larnaka,
Luigi Palma de Cesnola, who
plundered many sites in
Cyprus, including Kourion
and the Tombs of the Kings
in Pafos. These sites were
built when there were no
longer kings on
Cyprus, and they
were probably
used to bury
prominent citizens
of Pafos, civil
servants and
army officers;
nevertheless, in
view of their opu-
lence they became known as
the Tombs of the Kings.

During times of persecution
they were used by Christians
as hiding places. Later the site
was used as a quarry. The
place has a unique atmos-
phere, best experienced in
the morning.

**Inscription on one of the
stones in Agia Kyriaki**

🔒 Agia Kyriaki

Odos Pafias Afroditis.
◌ daily.

The 12th-century
stone church of Agia
Kyriaki, with a later
small belfry and dome,
is also known as Pana-
gia Chrysopolitissa
(Our Lady of the
Golden City). It was
built on the ruins of
an earlier seven-aisled
Christian Byzantine
basilica, the largest in
Cyprus. A bishop's
palace also stood
nearby. Both buildings
were destroyed by the
Arabs, but the parts
that have survived
include 4th-century
religious floor mosaics.

The road to Agia Kyriaki leads
along a special platform built
over the archaeological digs,
from where you can see
several single columns. One
of them has been dubbed "St
Paul's Pillar". The apostle
came to Cyprus to preach
Christianity, but was captured
and led before the
Roman governor,
Sergius Paulus,
who sentenced
him to flogging.
St Paul blinded his
accuser, Elymas,
thus convincing
Sergius of his
innocence to such
an extent that the governor
converted to Christianity.

For more than a decade,
Agia Kyriaki has been used
jointly by the Catholic and
Anglican communities.

The beautiful church standing nearby, built on a rock
which forms part of the Kato
Pafos defence walls, is called
Panagia Theoskepasti –
"guarded by God". It is
apocryphally told that during
a scourging Arab attack a
miraculous cloud enveloped
it, hiding it from the enemy.

⋔ Catacombs of Agia
Solomoni and Fabrica Hill

Leoforos Apostolou Palou.
◌ dawn–dusk

Inside a former tomb, is a
subterranean church dedi-
cated to Solomoni, a Jewess,
whose seven children were
tortured in her presence, and
who is now regarded by the
Cypriots as a saint.

In Roman times the site was
probably occupied by a synagogue, and earlier on by a
pagan shrine. Steep steps
lead down to the sunken

The Tombs of the Kings necropolis

sanctuary. The adjacent cave contains a tank with what is believed to be miraculous water. Similar catacombs on the opposite side of the street are called Agios Lambrianos.

Beyond Agia Solomoni, to the right, is the limestone Fabrica Hill containing carved underground chambers. They were created during Hellenic and Roman times but their purpose is unknown.

On the southern slope of the hill, Australian archaeologists have unearthed a Hellenic amphitheatre hewn out of the living rock. Nearby are two small cave churches, Agios Agapitikos and Agios Misitikos. Tradition has it that when dust collected from the floor of Agios Agapitikos is placed in someone's house, it has the power to awaken their love (*agapi* means "love"), while dust collected from Agios Misitikos will awaken hate *(misos)*.

Fabric-festooned tree near the Catacombs of Agia Solomoni

A relief from the Hellenic era, Archaeological Museum

🏛 Archaeological Museum

Griva Digeni 43. 📞 *263 06215.*
🕐 *9am–5pm Mon–Fri, 10am–1pm Sat.* 🖼 🚻 🎫 ⛔ *1, 2.*

Housed in a small modern building outside the city centre, along the road leading to Geroskipou, this is one of the more interesting archaeological museums in Cyprus. The collection includes historic relics spanning thousands of years from the Neolithic era through the Bronze Age, Hellenic, Roman, Byzantine and medieval times, and up until the 18th century AD.

Particularly interesting are the Chalcolithic (copper age) figurines. There are steatite idols, a skeleton from Lempa, a 3rd-century AD mummy of a girl and an array of Hellenic ceramics, jewellery and glass. There are also ancient sarcophagi, sculptures, a coin collection, clay pots used for hot water and a set of Roman surgical instruments – evidence of the high standard of ancient medicine. There are also numerous exhibits from Kato Pafos, including a marble statue of an armed Aphrodite.

🐠 Aquarium

Odos Dionysou. 📞 *269 53920.*
🕐 *9am–8pm daily.* 🖼 🚻 🎫

Dedicated mainly to the Mediterranean Sea environment, the aquarium contains colourful sea and fresh-water fish from all over the world in large aquariums. The shark and piranha aquariums are especially popular with visitors.

🏖 Beaches

Pafos itself has only a few small beaches in front of hotels; these offer excellent conditions for water sports. A pleasant municipal beach is situated by Leoforos Poseidonos, at the centre of Kato Pafos, close to the Municipal Garden. Somewhat out of the way, to the north of the archaeological zone, lies the sandy-pebbly Faros Beach.

Good pebble beaches can be found north of Pafos. About 8 km (5 miles) along the coast is a small beach in the bay of Kissonerga fringed by banana plantations and relatively unused by tourists. The loveliest, most popular sandy beach is situated at Coral Bay, 10 km (6 miles) north of town *(see p47).* All the usual beach facilities are offered here, together with most water sports.

There are also several beaches to the east, including Alikes, Vrysoudia and Pahyammos. One of the most beautiful places to enjoy bathing is the beach near the Rock of Aphrodite, covered with smooth stones. The water here is crystal-clear and the environs truly enchanting. There are no facilities apart from toilets and a shower by the car park. It is worth coming to this beach either early in the morning or in the evening and staying to enjoy the beautiful sunset.

One of the alluring, popular beaches at Pafos

Kato Pafos

Column fragment

THE MOST ACCESSIBLE and inspiring archaeological park on the island, the ruins at Kato (Lower) Pafos were unearthed in 1962, shedding new light on Cyprus under the Roman Empire. In ancient times, this was the capital of Cyprus. Now a UNESCO World Heritage Site, the remains found here span over 2,000 years. The lavish mosaics found on the floors of four Roman villas indicate that this was a place of ostentatious wealth.

★ **House of Dionysos**
Some 2,000 sq m (21,500 sq ft) of magnificent mosaics can be viewed from wooden platforms.

House of Aion
This villa, with its interesting mosaics, was destroyed by an earthquake. It takes its name from the god Aion, whose image was once to the left of the entrance.

House of Theseus
The palace of the Roman governor contains a set of interesting mosaics portraying the myth of Theseus and Ariadne. The opulent villa discovered underneath dates from the Hellenic era.

Medieval Castle
The medieval Lusignan castle remodelled by the Turks now houses a museum; its flat roof affords a lovely view over the town and the harbour.

STAR SIGHTS

★ **House of Dionysos**

★ **Roman Odeon**

The East Tower
was a defence structure, guarding the town against attacks by Arab pirates in the early Middle Ages.

Lighthouse
The small, white lighthouse on top of the hill is not related to the Roman ruins below.

The Hellenic theatre is located near the agora.

★ **Roman Odeon**
This partly restored small music theatre, built of stone blocks, stands on a hillside overlooking the rest of the site. Summer concerts are held here.

Saranda Kolones
The castle, built by the Lusignans, was destroyed by an earthquake in 1222. It takes its name from the 40 columns found among its ruins.

Panagia Limeniotissa, the Byzantine basilica of Our Lady the Protectress of Harbours was destroyed in the 7th century by Arab raids.

PLAN OF KATO PAFOS

KEY

▨	Building
▬	Road
=	Footpath
--	Wall

PEGEIA   PAFOS
B20
Ancient Theatre
Agia Solomoni
Odeon   Agora   Cathedral Ruins
Asklepieion
House of Dionysos   Panagia Chrysopolitissa
Saranda Kolones
House of Orpheus   House of Aion   Panagia Limeniotissa   E705   GEROSKIPOU
House of Theseus
Castle   East Tower

0 m   300
0 yards   300

0 m   25
0 yards   25

Tree-lined avenue in the small town of Pegeia

Pegeia ❽

Road map A3. *19 km (12 miles) south of Pafos.* 2360.

THIS SMALL, PICTURESQUE hillside town, 5 km (3 miles) inland from Coral Bay, is the last sizeable settlement before entering the wilderness of Akamas. Pegeia, meaning "springs", was founded during the Byzantine era. It is famous for its abundant spring water – a great blessing in sun-parched Cyprus.

Pegeia has several good restaurants specializing in Greek cuisine, clustered around the cobbled central square with its fountains. Try the local Vasilikon wine.

ENVIRONS: On the hilltops north of Pegeia, at an altitude of some 600 m (1,970 ft), are the villages of the Laona region – **Inia**, **Drouseia**, **Arodes** and **Kathikas**, offering sweeping views of the surrounding area. In Inia you can visit the Basket Weaving Museum; in Drouseia the Textile Museum; the local school in Kathikas houses the Laona information centre.

Agios Georgios ❾

Road map A3.

DURING ROMAN times **Cape Drepanon**, north of Coral Bay, was the site of a late Roman and early Byzantine town and a harbour. The remains of a 6th-century early-Christian basilica have been unearthed here, revealing some well-preserved floor mosaics of sea creatures, a semi-circular bishop's throne and several columns.

The coastal cliffs contain caves that served as hiding places for the local population during enemy raids. Atop one craggy section is the picturesque **church of St George** (Agios Georgios Pegeias) built in the Byzantine style in 1928. St George, its patron saint, champions animals and those unlucky in love.

Close by there are several taverns and fishermen's cottages. The location affords a lovely view over the fishing harbour below, and the nearby island of Yeronissos with its remains of a Neolithic settlement. There are also remains of a small temple used during Greek and Roman times.

ENVIRONS: North of Agios Georgios is the **Avakas Gorge**. This deep ravine has steep craggy banks, a dozen or so metres high, and the river Avgas runs through the base of it. The Gorge is a

The picturesque church of St George

legally protected area; it can be visited only in organized groups led by a local guide.

Lara ❿

Road map A3.

THIS SANDY CRESCENT is home to two of the most attractive beaches in southwest Cyprus. To the south lies nearly 2 km (1 mile) of un-crowded sand, while to the north there is a shallow bay with a half-moon stretch of fine white sand frequented by sea turtles.

This is one of the few remaining Mediterranean nesting grounds for the rare green and loggerhead varieties. During breeding season (June to September) staff from the Lara Turtle Conservation Project close access to the beach. They arrange occasional night-time walks along the beach, when you can see the turtles struggling ashore.

Although marine animals, sea turtles lay their eggs on dry land, crawling out onto beaches during summer nights to do this. Females lay about 100 eggs at a time, which they bury up in the sand up to half a metre (one and a half feet) deep. After laying, the eggs are carefully removed to a protected area on the beach where they are safe from dogs, foxes and other predators.

After seven weeks the eggs hatch and the hatchlings head immediately for the water. Turtles reach maturity at about the age of 20, and the females return to lay eggs on the same beach where they were born.

The sandy beach at Lara Bay – a nesting ground for rare sea turtles

The Baths of Aphrodite ⓫

Road map A3. 8 km (5 miles) west of Polis, towards Akamas peninsula.

A PATH FROM the car park leads to the Baths of Aphrodite – a pool in a grotto shaded by overgrown fig trees, with water running down moss-covered stone. According to legend it was here that Aphrodite met her lover Adonis, who stopped by the spring to quench his thirst. It is said that bathing in this spot restores youth, but, sadly people are no longer allowed in the water.

Walking trails lead from the front of the Cyprus Tourism Organization (CTO) pavilion through the peninsula x The trails of Aphrodite, Adonis or Smigies will take you to the most interesting corners of the northwestern tip (*see pp56–7*). Detailed descriptions of the trails can be found in the *Nature Trails of the Akamas*, brochure published by the CTO .

Situated a few kilometres further west is another magnificent spring, the Fontana Amorosa (Fountain of Love). It was once believed that whoever took a sip of water from the spring would fall in love with the very first person they encountered afterwards.

ENVIRONS: On the way to the Baths of Aphrodite you will pass Latsi, a small town with

Akamas peninsula - the westernmost point of Cyprus

a fishing harbour. It was once a sponge-divers' harbour, and is now also the base for pleasure boats that offer tourist cruises along the Akamas peninsula. Latsi has numerous *pensions* and hotels; the harbour features several restaurants, including Yangos and Peter's, where you can get tasty and inexpensive fish and seafood dishes. The town has pebble and coarse sand beaches.

Akamas Peninsula ⓬

Road map A3. 18 km (11 miles) north of Agios Georgios.

S TRETCHING NORTH of Agios Georgios and Pegeia is the wilderness of the Akamas peninsula. The hillsides and headlands form the island's last undeveloped frontier, a region of spectacular, rugged scenery, sandy coves, clear water and hillsides covered with thick woodlands of pine and juniper. Its name comes from the legendary Akamas, son of Theseus, who arrived here on his triumphant return from the Trojan War and founded the town of Akamatis. Archaeologists are still searching for this site.

The peninsula's westward plain has rocks jutting out of the arid landscape, which is overgrown with tangles of trees and bushes. In

Spring flowers

the valleys and ravines the vegetation is lush due to more abundant water. The shoreline is characterized by steep cliffs dropping vertically into the sea, particularly around **Chryssochou Bay**.

Nowadays this area is practically deserted, inhabited only by wild animals and flocks of goat, but this was not always so. In ancient times, the region had Greek towns, and later Roman and Byzantine towns, that bustled with life. On **Cape Drepanon** you can see the ruins of a Roman harbour and a Byzantine basilica; in **Meleti Forest** you can visit the ruins of a Byzantine church, and tombs carved in rocks; and in the **Agios Konon region** archaeologists have discovered an ancient settlement. The Roman settlement, which once stood on the shores of the Tyoni Bay, is now submerged in water.

The only way to travel around the wild countryside of Akamas is by a four-wheel-drive vehicle or by a cruise along the coast from Latsi.

The westernmost point of the peninsula, and of the entire island, is **Cape Arnaoutis**, where you can see an unmanned lighthouse and the wreck of a ship that ran aground. The Cape is a magnet for divers, who will find vertical crags and caves where octopuses hide; fantastic arch-shaped rocks; or even come eye-to-eye with a barracuda.

The Baths of Aphrodite

Walking in the Akamas Peninsula

THIS IS THE WILDEST REGION of Cyprus, practically uninhabited and covered with forests. Its rich flora (over 530 species, including scores of orchid varieties) and fauna, the diverse geological features, the beautiful coastline and the legends and myths associated with this fascinating country make it a paradise for ramblers and nature lovers. The shortage of surfaced roads means that many places on the peninsula can be reached only on foot.

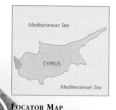

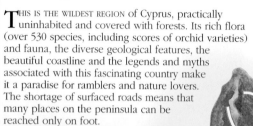

Bath
Aph

Bays
A section of the Aphrodite Trail hugs the peninsula's wild coastline. Here you'll find the most beautiful coves and deserted beaches.

Roads
Some sections of the trails run along dirt tracks; the best way to travel here is in a four-wheel-drive vehicle.

Caves
Water has carved many caves and rock niches in the lime rocks of the peninsula. These provide shelter for animals.

Rocks
Rocks, carved in fantastic shapes by wind and water, are a distinctive feature of the peninsula's landscape.

Neo Chorio

A stone church has survived here. There are plenty of places to stay in the village, as well as a few restaurants. To the south is the Petratis Gorge, famous for its bats' grotto.

TIPS FOR WALKERS

Length of trails: From 2 to 7.5 km (1.2 to 4.7 miles) long.

Where to stay: Accommodation can be found in Neo Chorio, Polis, Drouseia and at the Polis-Baths along the Aphrodite Trail.

Additional information: Bring adequate food and water when walking. The best starting point for trails 1–4 is the CTO office by the Baths of Aphrodite; for trail 5, start in the village of Kathikas.

Lizards

Lizards, particularly the wall lizard, are common on the island. You may be lucky enough to encounter the Agana, the largest Cypriot lizard (30 cm/12 in long).

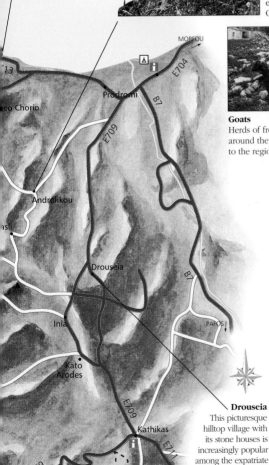

0 km 2

0 mile 1

MORFOU

E704

Prodromi

B7

eo Chorio

E709

Androlikou

asli

Drouseia

B7

PAFOS

Inia

Kato Arodes

E709

Kathikas

E711

E709

Pegeia

PAFOS

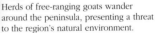

Goats

Herds of free-ranging goats wander around the peninsula, presenting a threat to the region's natural environment.

KEY

▬	Main road
=	Other road
•••	1. Aphrodite trail (7.5 km)
•••	2. Adonis trail (7.5 km)
•••	3. Smigies trail (7.5 km)
•••	4. Pissouromouttis trail (3 km)
•••	5. Kathikas trail (2 km)
≋	River
⚠	Campsite
ℹ	Tourist information
✸	Viewpoint

Drouseia

This picturesque hilltop village with its stone houses is increasingly popular among the expatriate community. There are restaurants, cafés and a hotel here.

The 16th-century church of Agios Andronikos in Polis

Polis ⑬

Road map A3. 35 km (22 miles) north of Pafos. 🏛 1890. 🛈 Vasileos Stasioikou 3, 263 22468. 🎭 Summer Cultural Festival (Jul, Aug)

T HIS SMALL TOWN, known until recently as Polis Chryssochous (Town of the Golden Land), stands on the site of the ancient city-state of Marion, surrounded by extensive orange groves. Polis provides an excellent base for exploring the Akamas peninsula and the wilderness of Tylliria. In the centre of Polis is the 16th-century **Agios Andronikos** church, featuring some fine frescoes. Under Turkish rule the church was turned into a mosque. The interior of the **Agios Rafael**, a new Byzantine-style church, is decorated with colourful frescoes.

Carved decoration above the entrance to Agios Andronikos in Polis

Polis is one of the most attractive, and fastest-growing seaside resorts of Cyprus. It is popular with backpackers; there are no luxury hotels here. Christos Georgiades, owner of the charming 3-star hotel Natura, offers organized nature trips.

ENVIRONS: Close to the town are some of the most beautiful beaches on the island, including a long sand-and-pebble beach stretching eastwards along Chryssochou Bay, a 15-minute walk from the centre of Polis. There are also picturesque villages and interesting churches, including the 16th-century Agia Aekaterini and the 15th-century Panagia Chorteni.

Marion ⑭

Road map A3.

F OUNDED in the 7th century BC by Greeks, the city-state of Marion was a major trading centre during the Classical and Hellenic eras. It owed its rapid development to the nearby copper mines. In 315 BC Marion was destroyed by the Egyptian king, Ptolemy I Soter. His son, Ptolemy II, rebuilt Marion under the name Arsinoe, but the town never regained its former power. Up to now archaeologists have managed to unearth only a small portion of the ancient town, with a burial ground dating from the Hellenic period. An interesting collection of artifacts from the site can be seen in the **Marion-Arsinoe Archaeological Museum**. Of special note are the amphorae decorated with images of people, animals and birds, as well as with geometric patterns. Growing near the museum is an olive tree, over 600 years old, which still bears fruit.

🏛 Marion-Arsinoe Archaeological Museum
Polis. Leoforos Makariou III. 🛈 263 22955. ◯ 8am–2pm Mon–Fri & 3–6pm Wed, 9am–5pm Sat. 🖼

Panagia Chrysorrogiatissa ⑮

Road map A3. 40 km (25 miles) northeast of Pafos, take a right turn before the village of Stroumpi. 1.5 km (1 mile) south of Pano Panagia. ◯ 9am–7pm daily. **Donations** welcome. 🎭 15 Aug.

I N A BEAUTIFUL setting 830 m (2723 ft) above the sea, the Chrysorrogiatissa monastery is dedicated to "Our Lady of the Golden Pomegranate". It features an unusual triangular cloister built of reddish stone.

The monastery was founded in 1152 by the hermit Ignatius, who came across an icon with the image of the Virgin Mary. The Virgin appeared to him and instructed him to build a monastery in which her name would be revered. The miraculous icon, wrapped in gauze, is kept in a special casket. It was supposedly painted by St Luke the Evangelist. Several other precious icons are stored in the monastery; the most famous of these is an 18th-century image of Mary

Entrance to Panagia Chrysorrogiatissa monastery

and Jesus covered with a cloak. Other objects include old Bibles, manuscripts, sculptures and crosses.

ENVIRONS: The **Agia Moni** church, located about 2 km (1.2 miles) from the monastery, is one of the oldest in the island. It was built in the 4th century on the site of an old pagan temple of the goddess Hera. This single-aisle church is dedicated to St Nicholas.

The nearby village of **Panagia** is the birthplace of Archbishop Makarios III, the statesman and politician, who was born the son of a shepherd here on 13 August 1913. In 1960 the Archbishop was elected president of the republic. He died on 3 August 1977 and was buried at Throni near Kykkos, overlooking his village.

🏛 **Makarios's Family Home**
Pano Panagia. ⭕ 10am–1pm & 2–6pm daily. **Donations** welcome.

Tomb of Archbishop Makarios at Throni above Panagia

Xiros Valley ⓰

Road map B4.

THE XIROS RIVER flows from the western slopes of the Troodos mountains through this scenic valley. The river initially flows through Pafos Forest and Cedar Valley, which is the main home of the Cypriot cedars of the local *cedrus brevifilia* species. The area, which has been declared a nature reserve, is also home to the mouflon.

A car is needed to explore the valley. Following the old road from Pafos, turn left in the village of Timi, opposite the airport, to reach **Asprokremmos** reservoir, a mecca for anglers, as it is fed by the

Xiros river. The valley of Xiros (which in Greek means "dry") was devastated by the tragic earthquake of 1953. Standing at the heart of the valley, away from the main roads, is the abandoned stone **Panagia tou Sinti** church. It can be reached via local roads from the village of Pentalia or Agia Marina. Further on, the road leads through hillside villages and vineyards.

Beyond the village of Vretsia the road steadily deteriorates, but after driving for a few more kilometres you can cross the Xiros river near the historic Venetian bridge of Roudia. The deserted village of **Peravasa** marks the start of the road leading south, towards the scenic Diarizos river valley.

Sheep in the Diarizos Valley

Diarizos Valley ⓱

Road map B3.

GREENER AND BETTER irrigated than the arid Xiros valley, the Diarizos valley is studded with medieval churches, farming villages and arched Venetian bridges. The clear-flowing river trickles southwest and, like the Xiros, feeds the Asprokremmos reservoir.

The village of **Nikokleia**, near Kouklia (*see p44*), is an ancient settlement named in honour of King Nikokles, who transferred his capital to what is now Kato Pafos. The village is scenically located on the

banks of the river. The old church contains fascinating icons. On the opposite side of the river, near the village of Souskiou, archaeologists unearthed a Chalcolithic settlement. In it they found pendants and figurines, as well as statues and ancient tombs. In the village of Agios Georgios are rock tombs.

Further northeast are the remains of a former monastery, **Agios Savvas tis Karonos**, built in the early 12th century and restored by the Venetians.

Above Kithasi the road climbs upwards and the views become increasingly beautiful. On the left side of the road is the restored church of **Agios Antonios**. The church in Praitori houses 16th-century icons. Above the village, the road climbs towards the resort of **Platres** and the peaks of the Troodos mountains.

The arid Xiros valley, a scenic, rugged nature reserve

SOUTHERN CYPRUS

T HE SOUTHERN REGION *of Cyprus features Neolithic settlements and ancient towns, medieval castles and monasteries, and the island's most beautiful beaches, around Agia Napa. Other attractions include charming hilltop villages and the ports of Limassol and Larnaka. The region is full of reminders of famous past visitors to Cyprus, including Zeno of Kition, Saint Helena, Richard the Lionheart and Leonardo da Vinci.*

The coast from Pissouri to Protaras is famous for its beautiful scenery and historic sites. It has the largest ports on the island and many crowded beaches, but just a short distance inland life flows at a gentle, lazy pace.

This region was the site of powerful city-states, including Kition (present-day Larnaka), Kourion – of which only magnificent ruins are left, and the more recently unearthed Amathous.

Among the oldest traces of man on Cyprus are the Neolithic settlements around Khirokitia and Kalavassos. There are reminders of subsequent settlers, too. There was a Phoenician presence at Kition; there are temples and stadia attesting to the Greek presence; and villas and theatres from the Romans.

The Byzantine legacy includes mosaics in vast basilicas, churches with beautiful murals, and monasteries – including the mountain-top Stavrovouni monastery and the cat-filled St Nicholas monastery on the Akrotiri peninsula.

The medieval castle in Limassol was used by the Crusaders; Richard the Lionheart married Berengaria of Navarre and crowned her Queen of England here; and from the Gothic castle in Kolossi knights oversaw the production of wine and sugar cane. A reminder of the Arab raids is the tomb of the Prophet's aunt at the Hala Sultan Tekke, on the shores of the salt lake near Larnaka, which attracts flamingoes, swans and pelicans.

Scenic village of Kato Lefkara

◁ Belfry of the Agia Napa monastery

Exploring Southern Cyprus

THE BEST-PRESERVED ancient town in Southern Cyprus is the Greco-Roman Kourion, with a beautifully located theatre, interesting mosaics, baths, a Byzantine stadium and the nearby Sanctuary of Apollo Hylates. The best beaches for swimming and sunbathing are in Agia Napa and Protaras, with their enchanting clear water and lovely sandy beaches. They also offer the greatest number of attractions for young people. When exploring this part of the island be sure to visit Lefkara, a charming Cypriot village where women produce beautiful lace by hand and men make silver jewellery. Nature lovers often head for the salt lakes around Limassol and Larnaka, and are rewarded with the sight of hundreds of birds.

Stavrovouni monastery, founded by St Helena, mother of Constantine the Great

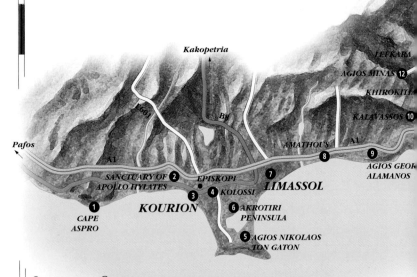

0 km   10

0 miles   1

Getting There

Most visitors to Cyprus arrive by air, and the biggest airport in the southern part of the island is outside Larnaka, serving a number of international flights. Motorways provide fast and safe travel links with Limassol and Agia Napa, as well as with Nicosia and Pafos. Alternatively, you can travel to Limassol by ferry from Piraeus (Greece), Egypt, Lebanon and Syria. Most of the historic sites of Limassol and Larnaka are best explored on foot. Public transport in the form of service taxis between major cities is good, but to reach smaller or more distant places a rental car is the best option for exploring Southern Cyprus.

See Also

• ***Where to Stay*** pp159–62

• ***Where to Eat*** pp171–3

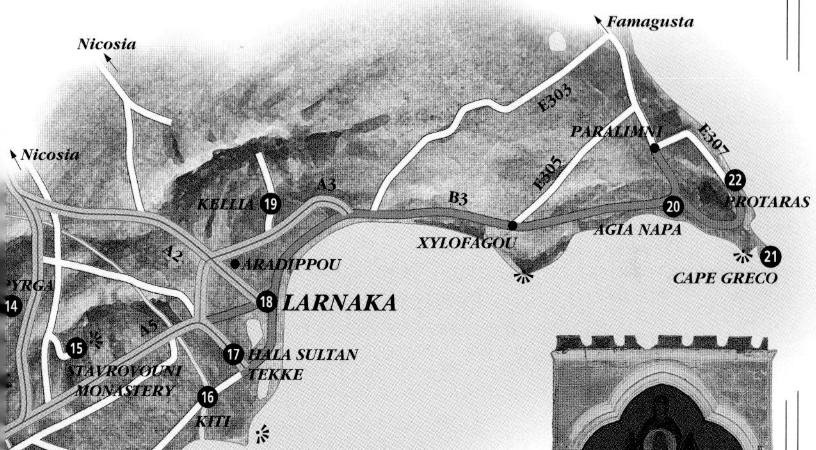

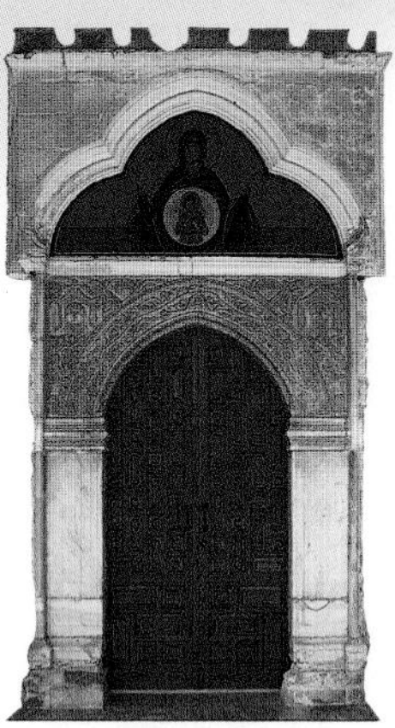

Doorway of Panagia Chrysopolitissa church in Larnaka

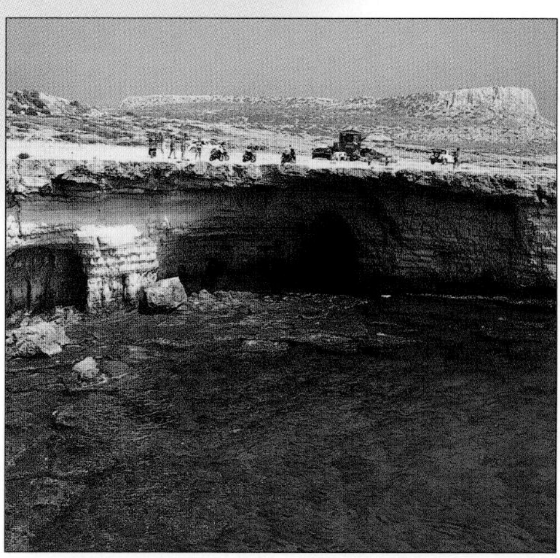

The craggy coastline of Cape Greco

Key

- Motorway
- Major road
- Scenic route
- Other road
- River
- Viewpoint

Cape Aspro ❶

Road map B4. 4 km (2.5 miles) south of Pissouri.

CAPE ASPRO is the highest point along the virtually deserted coast that stretches from Kourion to Pafos. Most of the coast along this, the southernmost point of the island (excluding the Akrotiri peninsula), is as flat as a pancake. Towering over the cape is the **Trachonas Hill**, which affords magnificent views over Episkopi Bay, the southern slopes of the Troodos mountains, the small town of Pissouri and the monastery church Moni Prophitis Ilias.

The area around **Pissouri** is famous for its orchards and vineyards; the fertile lime soil yields abundant crops of sweet grapes. The modern amphitheatre, which was built in 2000 with seating for a thousand people, affords a beautiful view over the sea and the southern coast. During the summer, plays and concerts are staged here.

The town of Pissouri has a pleasant little hotel – the Bunch of Grapes Inn – in a restored century-old home; there are also several rustic tavernas that offer typical local cuisine.

The rugged coastal cliffs rise to a height of 180 m (590 ft). They can be seen very clearly from the air, as planes usually approach Pafos airport from this direction. To the east of Cape Aspro is the pleasant and clean sandy-pebbly Pissouri beach with its clear, blue water.

Ruins of the Sanctuary of Apollo Hylates near Kourion

Sanctuary of Apollo Hylates ❷

Road map B4. 3 km (1.8 miles) west of Kourion. 259 97049. 9am–5pm daily (Jul & Aug until 7:30pm).

IN ANCIENT TIMES the Sanctuary of Apollo Hylates was an important shrine on the island. Stone fragments and toppled columns mark the site of this 7th-century BC shrine to the sun-god Apollo in his role as "Hylates", or god of the woods and forests. The present ruins date from early Roman times. It was in use until the 4th century AD, when Emperor Theodosius the Great declared a battle against pagans.

The sanctuary was surrounded by a holy garden, featuring laurel trees, myrtle and palms, and was home to deer.

When pilgrims arrived through the Curium and Pafian gates, they placed votive offerings by the residence of the Great Priests, which were then sent to the treasury. When the treasury became full, the priests stored the offerings *(tavissae)* in a nearby holy well. This hiding place was discovered centuries later by archaeologists, and the ancient offerings can be seen at the Kourion Archaeological Museum at Episkopi and in the Cyprus Museum in Nicosia.

Close by were baths and a *palaestra* (gymnasium), surrounded by a colonnaded portico and used as a venue for wrestling. Standing in one corner of the *palaestra* is a fragment of a large clay jug, which was used for storing water for the athletes. The remaining buildings of the complex include storehouses and pilgrims' dormitories.

The former pilgrims' inn marked the start of the holy procession route leading to the sanctuary. At the heart of the sanctuary there was a small temple with a pillared portico, devoted to Apollo. As reported by the ancient geographer Strabo, any unauthorized person who touched the altar was hurled from it to the sea, to placate Apollo. The front of the temple, with its two columns, a fragment of the wall and tympanum, has been partially reconstructed.

Earthquakes, the spread of Christianity and Arab raids all played a role in destroying the sanctuary, and now all that remains are the romantic ruins.

Some 500 m (1,640 ft) east of the sanctuary is a large, well-preserved Roman stadium, which could accommodate 6,000 spectators. Pentathlon events – consisting of running, long jump, wrestling, discus and javelin throwing – were staged here. The competitors appeared naked and only men were allowed to watch. In the 4th century the stadium was closed, regarded as a symbol of paganism.

Kourion ❸

See pp66–7.

The craggy coast of Cape Aspro

Kolossi ❹

Road map B4. 14 km (9 miles) west of Limassol. [259 34907. 9am–5pm daily (Jul–Aug: until 7:30pm).

THE BEST-PRESERVED medieval castle in Cyprus is situated south of the village of Kolossi. In 1210 the land passed to the hands of the Knights of St John of Jerusalem, who built a castle here to be used as the Grand Master's headquarters.

At the turn of the 14th and 15th centuries the castle was sacked several times by the Genoese and Muslims.

Kolossi castle in its present shape was built in 1454 by the Grand Master, Louis de Magnac. It is a three-storey structure, laid out on a square plan, 23 m (75 ft) high, with walls over 2.5 m (8 ft) thick. Entry is via a drawbridge, at the first floor level. The entrance is further guarded by an ornamental machicolation high above the gate, which permitted the pouring of boiling water, oil or melted tar over attackers.

The entrance led to the dining room, whose walls were once covered with paintings. You can still see a scene of the Crucifixion with Louis de Magnac's coat of arms underneath. The adjacent room used to be the castle kitchen; stores were kept on the lower floor, and above were the living quarters; you can see stone fireplaces and windows. From here a narrow staircase leads to the flat roof surrounded by battlements, affording extensive views of the surrounding area. From here it was possible to supervise the work on plantations and in vineyards, and to spot enemy ships in the distance.

The medieval Kolossi castle, used by the Knights of Jerusalem

Standing next to the castle is a large vaulted stone building, which was once a sugar refinery. To the north are the remains of a mill, formerly used for grinding the sugar, and beyond it lies the small 13th-century church of St Eustace which was used as the castle chapel by the Knights Templar and by the Knights of St John of Jerusalem.

Agios Nikolaos ton Gaton (St Nicholas of the Cats) ❺

Road map B4. 12 km (7.5 miles) from the centre of Limassol. daily, from dawn till dusk (closed noon–3pm).

THE MONASTERY of Agios Nikolaos ton Gaton stands on the Akrotiri Peninsula, between the salt lake and the military airport. According to tradition it was founded by St Helena, mother of Constantine the Great, who visited Cyprus while returning from a pilgrimage to the Holy Land. Appalled by the plague of snakes, she sent to the island a ship full of cats to deal with the reptiles.

Image of St Nicholas of the Cats

The monks fed the cats and rallied them to fight by the ringing of the bell. Another reference to the cats is the naming of the nearby Cape Gata – the Cape of Cats.

The monastery was founded in 325, but the buildings we see now are the result of remodelling that occurred during the 13th century. At the heart of the monastery is an old, small church with Gothic walls and Latin coats of arms above the entrance. Flickering candles inside the dark church illuminate the gilded iconostasis and the elongated faces on the icons, which appear to come to life.

A small section of the salt lake on the Akrotiri peninsula

Akrotiri Peninsula ❻

Road map B4.

AKROTIRI IS THE southernmost point of Cyprus. Most of the peninsula is occupied by a sovereign British base – Akrotiri-Episkopi, which includes an air force base and a radio communications station. This base, along with a second one at Dekelia, is a relic of the island's colonial past, when Cyprus was governed by the British.

The central part of the peninsula is occupied by a salt lake (one of the two on the island), a vantage point for watching flocks of water birds including swans, flamingoes and pelicans. Running along the east coast is the wide beach known as Lady's Mile, which was named after a mare used by an English army officer for his regular morning ride.

Kourion ❸

ANCIENT KOURION (or Curium) was a major centre of cultural, political and religious life. It was home to the centuries-old site of the Sanctuary of Apollo and later the seat of a Christian bishop. Perched on a bluff, the town was founded in the 12th century BC by Mycenaean Greeks, and was a large centre in the days of the Ptolemies and the Romans. Its trump card was its defensive location, and the control it wielded over the surrounding fertile land. Kourion was destroyed by two catastrophic earthquakes in the early 4th century.

Achilles' House
This takes its name from the 4th-century mosaic discovered inside the colonnade.

The House of the Gladiators was so named after the discovery of two mosaics depicting gladiator fights.

Public baths

Baptistry & Bishop's Palace
Adjacent to the basilica and close to the bishop's palace was a large baptistry. Its remains include floor mosaics and some columns.

Basilica
The impressive triple-aisle building, erected in the 5th century AD on the site of a pagan temple, was destroyed by Arabs.

Nymphaeum
This imposing complex of stone fountains was built close to the public baths, on the spot where the aqueduct brought water to the city of Kourion.

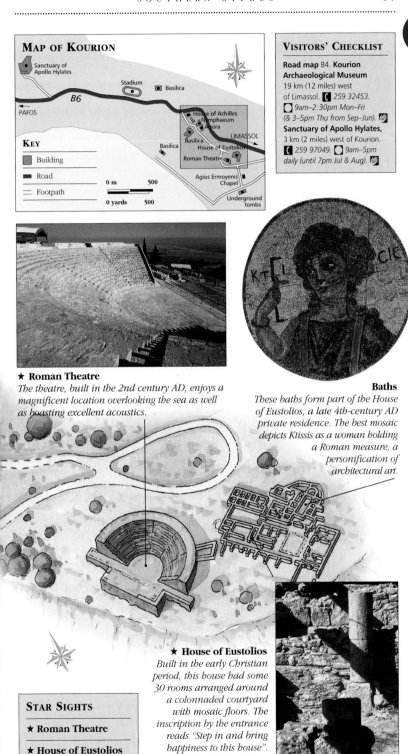

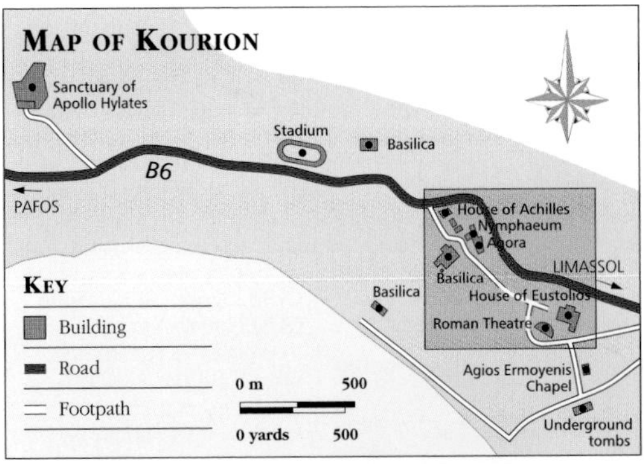
MAP OF KOURION
Sanctuary of Apollo Hylates
Stadium
Basilica
B6
PAFOS
House of Achilles
Nymphaeum
Agora
LIMASSOL
Basilica
Basilica
House of Eustolios
Roman Theatre
Agios Ermoyenis Chapel
Underground tombs
KEY
Building
Road
Footpath
0 m 500
0 yards 500

Visitors' Checklist

Road map B4. **Kourion Archaeological Museum** 19 km (12 miles) west of Limassol. *259 32453.* *9am–2:30pm Mon–Fri (& 3–5pm Thu from Sep–Jun).* **Sanctuary of Apollo Hylates,** 3 km (2 miles) west of Kourion. *259 97049.* *9am–5pm daily (until 7pm Jul & Aug).*

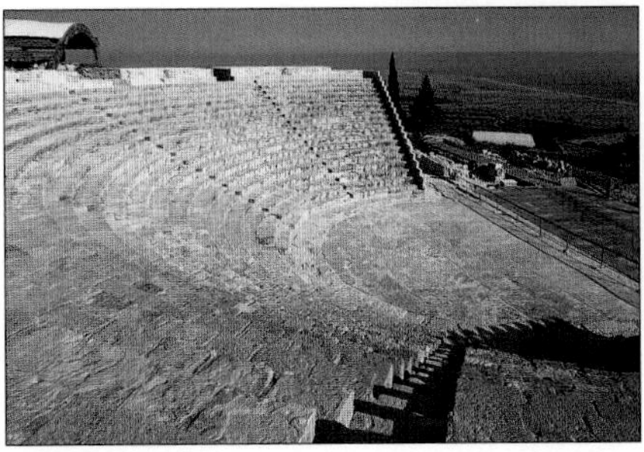

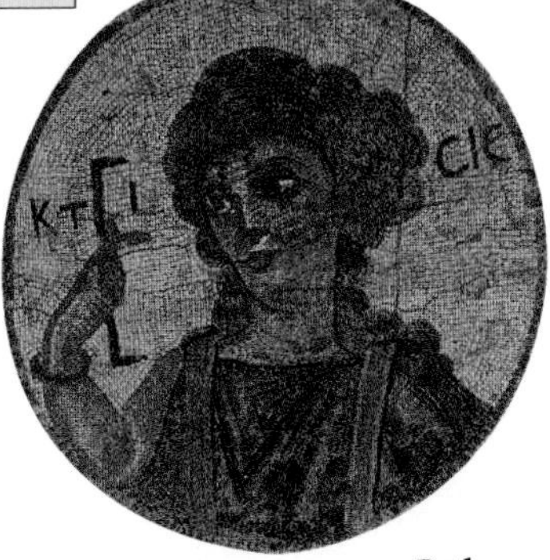
KT
CIE

★ Roman Theatre
The theatre, built in the 2nd century AD, enjoys a magnificent location overlooking the sea as well as boasting excellent acoustics.

Baths
These baths form part of the House of Eustolios, a late 4th-century AD private residence. The best mosaic depicts Ktissis as a woman holding a Roman measure, a personification of architectural art.

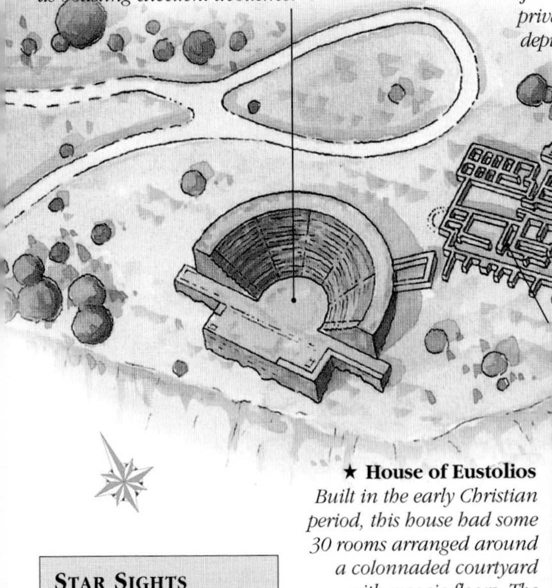

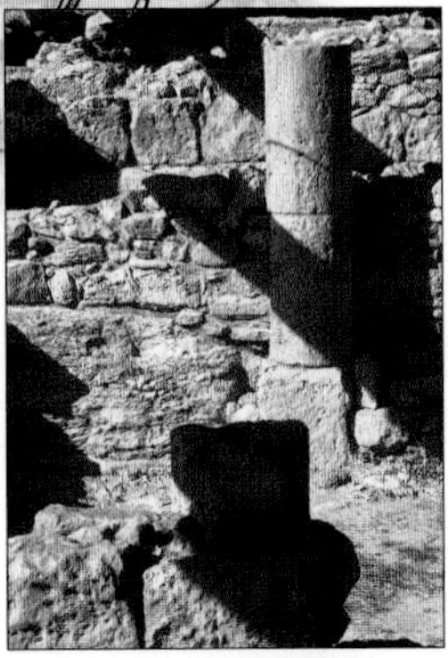

★ House of Eustolios
Built in the early Christian period, this house had some 30 rooms arranged around a colonnaded courtyard with mosaic floors. The inscription by the entrance reads "Step in and bring happiness to this house".

Star Sights

★ Roman Theatre

★ House of Eustolios

Limassol ❼

8th-century silver plate

LIMASSOL IS A MAJOR CENTRE of trade, business and tourism, and has the biggest harbour in southern Cyprus. It lies between the two ancient towns of Kourion and Amathous. Limassol is probably the most fun-filled city on Cyprus in terms of the numbers of fairs and festivals held here. The year starts with a riotous carnival; May marks the Flower Festival and September brings the famous Wine Festival. Hotels, restaurants and nightclubs are clustered mainly along the beach, within the resort area.

Strolling along the seaside promenade

Exploring Limassol

It is best to start from the medieval castle, the town's most interesting historic site. In the nearby restored Carob Mill is the Time Elevator – where you can watch a multimedia show on the history of the island – and nearby are a covered bazaar and a mosque.

The area has many restaurants with Cypriot and international cuisine, a wine bar and a brewery. From here it is not far to the old harbour, now used by fishing boats and pleasure craft. You can enjoy an extended walk along the seaside promenade, passing the Orthodox Agia Napia cathedral. More material distractions can be

Colourful stalls of fruit and vegetables at the Central Market

found just inland from here, along the main shopping street, Ayiou Andhreou, which runs parallel to the coast.

🏛 Central Market

Saripolou, in the old district near the town hall. ◯ 7am–2pm Mon–Sat.
The Central Market, housed in a graceful arcaded building dating from the British era in the early 20th century, is a great place to shop for handmade reed baskets, olive oil, *loukoumia* (Turkish delight) and other Cypriot delicacies, as well as fruit, vegetables, cheeses and meats. The stone market hall, its roof supported by metal pillars is of particular note, featuring two arched gates with Doric columns. It was recently refurbished to a design by Penelope Papadopoulou. The market is surrounded by old tavernas that make a welcome change from the modern eating-places and souvenir shops in the city's resort area. The stone-paved square in front of it is used as a venue for shows and fairs.

🏛 Cyprus Handicraft Centre

Themidos 25.◯ 7:30am–2:30pm daily (& 3–6pm Wed except Jul–Aug).
At this centre you can buy locally made gifts and souvenirs, including jewellery, lace, ceramics, mosaics and woodcarvings produced by Cypriot craftspeople using traditional methods.

All stock is government-vetted and the fixed prices offer a good gauge of how much visitors should be spending on products elsewhere.

🏛 Town Hall

Archiepiskopou Kyprianou.
Ⓦ www.limassolmunicipal.com.cy
The town hall is situated in the centre of Limassol, on a narrow street opposite the post office and near Agia Napa Cathedral. It was built to a design by the German architect Benjamin Gunzburg, based on the ancient Greek style of civic architecture. The columns by the entrance are redolent of the Tombs of the Kings in Pafos.

⛪ Agios Andronikos Church

Agiou Andreou. 🕒 Sat 6:30pm (in summer), 4:30pm (in winter); Sun 6:15–9:15am.
The church of Agios Andronikos and Athanosis (in Greek *athanosis* means immortality) was built in the 1870s in Neo-Byzantine style. For a while it served as the town's cathedral. The church is accessible only from the water-

Town Hall, dating from Colonial times

front. It is separated from the sea by the promenade, near the Agia Napa Cathedral and the Hotel Continental.

Seaside Promenade

Perfect for an evening stroll, this palm-fringed promenade stretches for nearly 3 km (1.8 miles) along the shoreline, starting at the old harbour and continuing eastward. It is lined with well-kept greenery and benches, from where you can watch ships awaiting entry to the harbour.

The Orthodox cathedral of Agia Napa

Agia Napa Cathedral

Genethliou Mitella. Sat 6:30pm (summer), 4:30pm (winter), Sun 6:15–9:15am.

On the fringe of Limassol's old quarter, this vast Byzantine-style structure was once built in the early 20th century on the ruins of a Byzantine church. It was consecrated in 1906. Today it serves as Limassol's Orthodox cathedral.

Greek architect Georgios Papadakis of Athens designed the cathedral, which represents Orthodox religious architecture at its florid best. This large stone church, sporting a twin-tower facade, is covered with a dome resting on a tambour over the intersection of the nave with the transept.

The cathedral was consecrated with the veil of St Veronica, with the imprinted image of Christ's face (the *veraikon*).

Grand Mosque

Genethliou Mitella
vary. **Donations** welcome.

The area around the harbour and castle was once inhabited mainly by Turks, and there are some remaining Turkish inscriptions and street names. The Grand Mosque – Cami Kebir – is still used by the handful of Turkish Cypriots resident in the city, and by Muslim visitors. The city's largest mosque with a graceful minaret is squeezed between old buildings behind the Turkish Bazaar.

The Grand Mosque with its distinctive pointed minaret

VISITORS' CHECKLIST

Road map C4. 161,200.
Spyrou Araouzou 115A, 253 62756. New harbour (ferries) 3 km (1.8 mile) east of the city.
Intercity to Larnaka and Nicosia (Old harbour), ALEPA to Nicosia and Pafos, Spyrou Araouzou, 996 25027. Carnival (Feb–Mar), Flower Festival (May), Wine Festival (early Sep).

Limassol Castle

See pp72–3.

Time Elevator

Vasilissis 1, by the castle. 257 62828. 9:30am–10pm daily.
In a cross between a roller coaster and a wide-screen cinema, this popular attraction offers a multimedia show of the island's history, from the earliest days (c.8500 BC) to 1974. The ride lasts half an hour. (For those prone to motion sickness, there are stationary seats from which to view the show.)

The most interesting segments are from the Middle Ages, including the conquest of Cyprus by Richard the Lionheart; his wedding to the Navarrese Princess Berengaria held in Limassol Castle; and the 16th-century Turkish conquest of the island.

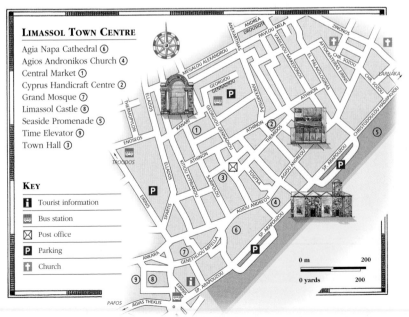

LIMASSOL TOWN CENTRE

Agia Napa Cathedral ⑥
Agios Andronikos Church ④
Central Market ①
Cyprus Handicraft Centre ②
Grand Mosque ⑦
Limassol Castle ⑧
Seaside Promenade ⑤
Time Elevator ⑨
Town Hall ③

KEY

i	Tourist information
🚌	Bus station
⊠	Post office
P	Parking
✝	Church

0 m   200
0 yards   200

Artifacts in the Archaeological Museum

Further Afield

Outside the city centre are a number of sights worth visiting, including St Catherine's Catholic Church, the Municipal Gardens and mini-zoo, the District Archaeological Museum and Folk Art Museum, as well as a theatre, municipal art gallery and among the best local attractions – the wineries. Stretching beyond the municipal beach to the east is the extensive tourist zone with dozens of hotels, tavernas, pubs, restaurants, souvenir shops and clubs.

♙ St Catherine's Catholic Church

28 Oktovriou 259. 📞 253 62946.
🕂 6:30pm Mon–Fri (English & Greek), 6:30pm Sat (English); Sundays: 8am (Greek), 9:30am (Greek), 11am (Latin) & 6:30pm (English).
This twin-tower church stands opposite the beach, near the end of Limassol's palm-lined promenade. Consecrated in 1879, it is one of several Catholic churches in this part of the island.

⋔ District Archaeological Museum

At the junction of Kanningos and Vyronos, next to the Municipal Gardens. 📞 253 05157.
🕐 Mon–Fri 9am–5pm, Sat 10am–1pm.
At the entrance to this museum is a mosaic depicting the bath of Eros and Aphrodite. The museum's collection includes artifacts found in excavations of the ancient city-states of Kourion and Amathous, as well as Neolithic tools and jewellery.

The highlights of the collection are the statue of the Egyptian god Bes – the god of harvest depicted in the guise of a dwarf; the statue of Hathor, Egyptian goddess of heaven, music and dance; the statue of Zeus discovered at Amathous; and the head of Zeus from Fasoula, carved from limestone. Other exhibits include a collection of glass and terracotta artifacts, votive statuettes, and Roman coins stamped with the images of emperors.

⚹ Municipal Gardens and Mini-Zoo

28 Oktovriou, on the seafront.
Gardens 🔲 all day. **Mini-Zoo**
9am–1pm & 2:30–6.30pm.
The charming Municipal Gardens feature ponds and fountains. Shaded by trees, they are full of exotic greenery and flowers. The gardens include an amphitheatre and a small zoo and aviary. Zebras, cheetahs and moufflon are among the animals here. In early September the Municipal Gardens become the venue for the famous Wine Festival. As well as grape trampling and folk dances, the crowds are treated to free wine from local producers.

⋔ Folk Art Museum

Agiou Andreou, 253. 📞 253 05419.
🕐 Jun–Sep: 8:30am–1pm & 3–5:30pm Mon–Tue & Thu–Fri, 8:30am–1pm Wed; Oct–May: 8:30am–1pm & 4–6pm Mon–Tue & Thu–Fri, 8:30am–1pm Wed.

Costume from the Folk Art Museum

The museum is housed in an attractive historic building dating from 1924. Arranged over six rooms is a good collection of 19th- and 20th-century Cypriot folk art. The exhibition includes tools and domestic utensils, traditional folk costumes, jewellery and handcrafted products such as net curtains, bedding and bedspreads, which were traditionally stored in *sentoukia* – decorative trunks used as a bride's dowry.

♜ Wineries

F. Roosevelt. 📞 253 62053.
🔲 year round. 🚍 19, 30.
Wine-growing is a long established tradition in the area surrounding Limassol. Along the avenue leading from the old town to the new harbour are the largest wineries in Cyprus, belonging to KEO, SODAP, ETKO and LOEL. These are open for tours, led by guides who explain the island's traditions of wine- and brandy-making. You can visit the vaults to see the huge barrels used to age and mellow the sweet dessert wine, Commandaria, that has been produced in Cyprus for over 800 years. At the end of the tour you will be offered a chance to taste and buy the

The leafy, pleasantly shaded Municipal Gardens

wines. Other distilleries produce *zivania*, a spirit distilled from grape seed left over from the production of wine and sherry. "Five Kings" brandy, commemorating a medieval banquet attended by five kings, including the King of Cyprus, is also produced here.

🏛 Pattichion Theatre
Agias Zonis. 📞 *253 43341.*

Musicals, drama and ballet productions are staged at the Pattichion, the oldest theatre in Limassol. The theatre was purchased by the Nicos and Despina Pattichi Foundation, then rebuilt and reopened in 1986. It is sponsored by the Limassol Municipality.

The theatre holds up to 760 people; backstage there are dressing rooms for 80 artists. In recent times the Pattichion theatre has hosted the Vienna Philharmonic Orchestra, the Athens Chamber Music Ensemble, the Vivaldi Orchestra from Moscow and Jazz Art Ballet from Paris.

🏛 Municipal Art Gallery
28 Oktovriou 103. 📞 *255 86212.*
🕐 *Jun–Sep: 8:30am–1pm & 4–6pm Mon–Fri; Oct–May: 8:30am–1pm & 3–5pm Mon–Fri.* 🖾

The gallery houses works by Cypriot painters, from early artists including Diamantis, Kashialos, Kanthos and Frangoudis, to contemporary painters. The gallery, designed by Benjamin Gunzburg (who also designed the Town Hall), was built in the 1930s.

Lady's Mile beach and the new harbour in Limassol

🎢 Wet'n Wild Waterpark
From A1 motorway take exit 23 in the direction of the sea. 📞 *253 18000.*
🕐 *Jun–Oct: 10am–6pm.* 🖾
🌐 www.wetnwild.com.cy

This popular waterpark has numerous water attractions including swimming pools, water slides and artificial waves. Great for families and kids of all ages.

🏛 New Port
4 km (2.5 miles) west of city centre.
📞 *255 71868.* 🚌 *6, 30.*

The new port in Limassol is the largest in Cyprus. It was enlarged after 1974, when Famagusta port fell under Turkish occupation. Besides the commercial port, it includes a terminal for passenger ferries as well as cruise ships.

The old harbour, situated near Limassol castle, is now used by fishing boats and pleasure craft. The modern yachting marina at the St Raphael resort, is situated around 12 km (7.5 miles) east of the city centre, in the tourist zone, near Amathous.

🏖 Beaches
Although long and wide, the municipal beach in Limassol is not among the island's most attractive beaches; it is covered with compressed soil and pebbles, and is located near a busy street.

Better beaches can be found further afield. Beyond the new harbour, in the eastern part of the Akrotiri peninsula, is Lady's Mile – a long and relatively quiet sandy beach (*see p65*). To the west, about 17 km (10.5 miles) from the city centre, Kourion beach enjoys a lovely location at the foot of the hill where ancient Kourion once stood. You can reach it by public transport from Limassol. Avdimou beach, a further 12 km (7.5 miles) along, has nice sand and a pleasant restaurant, although no shade.

The most pleasant sandy beach is found near Pissouri, some 44 km (27 miles) from Limassol. Here you can hire a deck chair and an umbrella, and nearby are several pleasant tavernas and restaurants.

The pre-war building of the Municipal Art Gallery

KING RICHARD THE LIONHEART

The English king, famed for his courage, was passing near Cyprus on his way to the Crusades when a storm blew one of his ships, carrying his sister and fiancée, to the shore. The ruler of Cyprus, the Byzantine Prince Isaac Komnenos, imprisoned both princesses and the crew. The outraged Richard the Lionheart landed with his army on the island, smashed the Komnenos army, imprisoned Komnenos and occupied Cyprus. In May 1191, in the chapel of Limassol castle, he married Princess Berengaria. Soon afterwards he sold the island to the Knights Templar.

English king Richard the Lionheart

Limassol Castle

Dionysos statue (4th–5th century)

THIS STRONGHOLD at the centre of the Old Town, near the harbour, was built by the Lusignan princes on foundations erected by the Byzantines. Later Venetian, Ottoman and British occupiers strengthened its defences. In 1191 the castle chapel was the venue for the wedding of Richard the Lionheart to Princess Berengaria of Navarre. The Turks later rebuilt the castle as a prison. During World War II it served as British Army headquarters. Nowadays it houses the Medieval Museum.

Castle Roof
The flat, stone roof of Limassol Castle was once used by its defenders. Today visitors admire the panoramic view of Limassol – the best view in town.

The Reliefs
The section devoted to Byzantine art houses not only numerous beautiful reliefs and mosaics from the oldest Christian basilicas, but also a number of religious icons.

Grape Press
This grape press is among the stone artifacts in the castle gardens.

★ **Knights' Hall**
The first-floor hall, in the south wing of Limassol Castle, houses two suits of armour and a collection of antique coins.

STAR SIGHTS

★ **Knights' Hall**

★ **Main Hall**

★ **Main Hall**
The Main Hall houses a large collection of Byzantine, Gothic and Renaissance sculptures, carvings and reliefs. Among them are carved images of the Lusignan kings from the portal of Agia Sofia Cathedral.

VISITORS' CHECKLIST

Irinis. Close to the old harbour.
🕐 9am–5pm Mon–Sat,
10am–1pm Sun. 🗙 There is
neither a café nor a shop in the
castle but close by are cafés,
restaurants and souvenir shops.

Main Lobby
Leading to the most opulent room, the lobby houses sculptures and coats of arms as well as photographs of Gothic and Renaissance architecture.

Fragment of a Portal
This fragment from Nicosia's Agia Sofia Cathedral forms part of the medieval stonemasonry exhibits in the museum collection.

Sarcophagi chamber
A chamber hidden in the shadowy recesses of the castle contains a collection of sarcophagi and tombstones.

Main Entrance
The castle is entered through a small bastion located on the east side of the castle.

Larnaka

Gargoyle

L ARNAKA STANDS ON THE SITE of ancient Kition. It takes its name from the Greek *larnax*, meaning "sarcophagus" (there were many ancient and medieval tombs in the district). The city has an international airport, a port, several interesting museums and a seaside promenade lined with numerous cafés and restaurants. The tourist zone has luxurious hotels, tavernas, nightclubs and souvenir shops.

Larnaka's seaside promenade lined with palm trees

Exploring Larnaka

The best place to begin is ancient Kition, followed by the Archaeological and Pierides Museums, with their priceless collections. From here continue with the church of St Lazarus (Agios Lazaros) and the Byzantine Museum, then proceed towards the sea, visiting the Turkish fort and mosque. The seaside promenade leads to the marina and beach.

⋔ Kition

0.5km (0.3 mile) NE of Archaeological Museum. ⬜ *Jul–Aug: 9am–2:30pm Mon–Fri; Sep–Jun: 9am–2:30pm Mon–Fri, & 3:30–5pm Thu.*

The ancient city of Kition (Kitium) lies in the northern part of Larnaka. According to tradition it was founded by Kittim, grandson of Noah. Archaeological excavations indicate, however, that the town was founded in the 13th century BC. Soon afterwards the Mycenaeans landed on the island; they reinforced the city walls and built a temple. The Phoenicians, who conquered the city in the 9th century BC,

turned the temple into a shrine to the goddess Astarte. Kition was a major trade centre for copper, which was excavated in mines near Tamassos.

⋔ Acropolis

Leontiou Kimonos.
Situated on top of Bamboula hill (immediately behind the Archaeological Museum) was the acropolis, which had its own defence walls. In the late 19th century the hill was plundered by British soldiers, who used the rubble to cover malaria-breeding swamps.
In the 1960s archaeologists stumbled upon ancient tombs filled with ceramics and jewellery, as well as fragments of stone and alabaster sculptures.

⋔ Mycenaean Site

Leoforos Archiepiskopu Kyprianou.
The main archaeological site (dubbed Area II) is near the cemetery for foreigners. There are wooden platforms from where you can view the dig. The defence walls dating from the late Bronze era were later strengthened by the Mycenaeans, who added fortifications built of stone and clay bricks.

A figurine from Pierides Museum

⋔ Archaeological Museum

Kalograion. ▐ *243 04169.*
⬜ *Jul–Aug: 9am–2:30pm Mon–Fri; Sep–Jun: 9am–2:30pm Mon–Fri, & 3–5pm Thu.* 🌐
The Archaeological Museum displays vases, sculptures and cult statues from Larnaka and the surrounding area. It has a collection of ceramics (mostly Mycenaean), votive terracotta figurines and glass objects from Roman times. There is also an interesting exhibition of Cypriot-Minoan inscriptions, as yet undeciphered.

Interior of Larnaka's Pierides Foundation Museum

⋔ Pierides Foundation Museum

Zinonos Kitieos 4. ▐ *248 17868.*
⬜ *Mon–Thu 9am–4pm, Fri–Sat 9am–1pm, Sun 11am–1pm.* 🌐
A part of this 1856 building houses the Pierides Museum, with the largest private collection in Cyprus. Comprising some 2,500 historical relics assembled by five generations of the Pierides family, the collection spans the period from the Neolithic era to medieval times. It was started in 1839 by Cypriot archaeologist Demetrios Pierides, who committed part of his fortune

Excavations of the ancient city of Kition

Natural History Museum in the municipal park

to the preservation of artifacts from the tombs pillaged by treasure hunters (in reality, grave robbers) such as the American consul in Larnaka, Luigi Palma di Cesnola.

The most precious objects include Neolithic-era stone idols and 3,000-year-old red polished ceramic vessels. There are also fascinating collections of terracotta figurines dating from the archaic era; miniature war chariots and cavalry soldiers; amphorae and goblets in geometric and archaic styles decorated with images of birds and fish; and Hellenic statues. Of particular note is the striking astronaut-like figure jumping on springs, painted on an archaic ceramic vessel. Other interesting exhibits include a collection of weaponry and a set of

historical maps of Cyprus and of the eastern Mediterranean.

In the rooms at the back of the building is a collection of handicrafts, including jewellery, embroidery, everyday items and richly carved furniture. There are also works by the primitive artist – Michael Kashialos, who was murdered by the Turks in his village studio, in 1974.

🏛 Natural History Museum

Leoforos Grigori Afxentiou.
📞 246 52569. ⏰ Jun–Aug:
10am–1pm & 4–6pm daily;
Sep–May: 10am–1pm &
3–5pm daily.
Located in Larnaka's municipal park, this small unassuming building houses a

Fountain in front of the town hall

diverse collection of exhibits illustrating the natural environment of Cyprus. Arranged across eight rooms are specimens of plants, insects and animals (from both land and sea), many of which are now rare in the wild.

There are also interesting geological exhibits. Besides the collection of copper minerals – the main source of the island's wealth since ancient times, you can see minerals belonging to the asbestos group. The large open mines from which these minerals came are located near Amiantos, on the southeastern slopes of the Troodos mountains. Other exhibits include fossils found in the island's limestone.

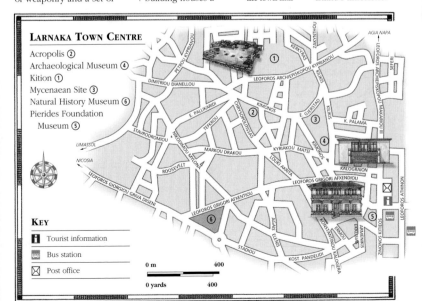

LARNAKA TOWN CENTRE

Acropolis ②
Archaeological Museum ④
Kition ①
Mycenaean Site ③
Natural History Museum ⑥
Pierides Foundation
    Museum ⑤

KEY

🛈 Tourist information

🚌 Bus station

⊠ Post office

0 m   400

0 yards   400

St Lazarus Church dating from AD 900

🔒 Agios Lazaros Church

Agiou Lazarou Square. 📞 246 52498.
⏰ Apr–Jul: 8am–12:30pm &
3:30–6:30pm; Sep–Mar:
8am–12:30pm & 2:30–5pm.

The Church of St Lazarus
(Agios Lazaros) stands in the
southern part of Old Larnaka.
It was built around AD 900
on the site of the
saint's grave.

Its architectural style
reveals the influence
of both eastern and
western trends.
Following its retrieval
from the hands of the
Turks in 1589, the
church was used by
Roman Catholic and
Orthodox communities
for 200 years, as
evidenced by Latin,
French and Greek
inscriptions on the
portico. The interior is built
around four vast pillars supporting a roof with three
small domes. Its main features are the Rococo pulpit,
around 300 years old, and a
small icon depicting Lazarus
emerging from his tomb, an
image reverently paraded
through the church at Easter.

**Icon from the
Byzantine Museum**

The magnificently
carved iconostasis
includes a number
of precious icons;
the best of these
dates from the 17th
century and por-
trays Lazarus rising.
On the right side
of the central nave
is a large gilded
reliquary contain-
ing the skull of the
saint. The crypt
houses several
stone sarcophagi.
One of them sup-
posedly housed
the relics of St Lazarus. The
tomb bore the Greek inscription: "Lazarus, friend of Jesus".

The graves in the courtyard
are mainly of British consuls,
civil servants and merchants.

Larnaka has other notable
places of worship, including
the metropolitan cathedral,
Agios Chrysotrios, built
in 1853; Agios Ioannis,
featuring a beautiful
iconostasis from the
beginning of the 17th
century and a marble
Venetian portal; and
the Roman Catholic
church Terra Santa.
Also of note is the
19th-century "Clown
Mosque" (Zahuri
Cami), with its
double dome and
truncated minaret.

🏛 Byzantine Museum

Agiou Lazarou Square. 📞 246 52498.
⏰ Apr–Jul: 8:30am–1pm & 4:30–6pm;
Sep–Mar: 8:30am–1pm & 3–5:30pm.
⚫ Wed & Sat afternoon. 🎫

Entry to this museum is from
the courtyard of Agios Lazaros
church. The collection consists
of icons and other objects
associated with the Orthodox

religion, including chasubles,
liturgical books and Bibles.

A previous, extensive
collection vanished during the
turbulent period between
1964 and 1974. It was kept in
the fort, which fell into the
hands of the Turks. When it
was finally regained by the
Greeks, most of the precious
items had simply vanished.

🔒 Agia Faneromeni

At the junction of Leoforos
Faneromeni and Artemidos.

This subterranean chapel is a
two-chambered cave hewn
into the rock. Its structure
suggests a pagan tomb,
probably dating from the
Phoenician era. The chapel
was famed for its magical
properties. The sick would
circle it twice, leaving behind
anything from a scrap of
clothing to a lock of hair in
the hope that they were also
leaving behind their illnesses.
Girls, whose boyfriends were
far away, would come here to
pray for their safe return.

🎭 Amphitheatre

Leoforos Artemidos.

The open-air amphitheatre,
used for staging events
during the July Festival, is
situated opposite the Zeno of
Kition Stadium, close to the
Agia Faneromeni chapel.

🔒 Büyük Cami

Standing beyond the fort, at
the border between the
Greek and Turkish districts, is
the Grand Mosque (Büyük
Cami). Originally the church
of the Holy Cross, this three-
aisled building now serves
Muslim visitors mostly from the
Middle East. Modest attire is
required, and before entering
you must remove your shoes.

SAINT LAZARUS

Lazarus, brother of Martha and Mary, was
resurrected by Jesus four days after his
death at Bethany. He moved to Cyprus,
becoming Bishop of Kition. After his
final death he was buried here; his tomb
was discovered in 890. Emperor Leo VI
helped to build St Lazarus church, in
exchange for which some of the saint's
relics were transferred to Constantinople,
from where they were stolen in 1204.
Today they are in Marseille Cathedral.

Painting showing the resurrection of Lazarus

For a small fee you can climb the narrow, steep stairs that lead to the top of the minaret. From here there is a lovely, panoramic view of Larnaka and the nearby Salt Lake. Stretching beyond the fort, right up to the fishing harbour is a large district that once belonged to the Turks. Its streets still bear Turkish names, but it is now inhabited by Greek Cypriot refugees from the area around Famagusta and the Karpas peninsula.

The imposing mid-18th-century aqueduct

A variety of yachts moored in Larnaka marina

🛥 Larnaka Harbours

The southern part of town has a small but picturesque fishing harbour. Larnaka marina is situated several hundred metres to the north of the coastal promenade, beyond a small beach. Only boat crews are allowed entry, but you can stroll along the breakwater. Beyond the marina there are cargo and passenger terminals; the passenger terminal is the second largest in Cyprus.

♜ Larnaka Fort and Medieval Museum

On the seashore, by the south end of the coastal promenade. 📞 *246 30576.* ◯ *9am–2:30pm Mon–Fri (& 3–5pm Thu in Jun–Aug).*

The fort in Larnaka was built by the Turks in c.1625 on the site of a medieval castle which had been destroyed by Mamelukes two centuries previously. When ships sailed into the harbour (which no longer exists), they were welcomed by a gun salute fired from the castle.

During the Byzantine period, the fort was used as a police headquarters, prison and execution site. In 1833, it was partially destroyed by a lightning strike. Today the fort houses a small Medieval Museum with arms and armour dating from Turkish times, and treasure troves unearthed in Kition and at the Hala Sultan Tekke. The crenellated wall, with menacing guns and cannons, is now a viewing platform. During summer the castle yard serves as a venue for concerts, occasional plays and other cultural events.

🏖 Beaches

The sandy municipal beach by the Finikoudes promenade, in the neighbourhood of the marina, owes its popularity mainly to a double row of shade-giving palm trees. Another municipal beach is situated to the south of the fishing harbour. Although small, it is popular with locals due to its water sports facilities and the numerous restaurants and cafés in the vicinity.

A cannon at Larnaka's Fort

The best sandy public beach in the area is located some 10 km (6 miles) east of the city and is run by the Cyprus Tourism Organization. About 10 km (6 miles) south of Larnaka, near Kiti, there is a rocky cove with patches of sand; this area is undeveloped and relatively free of people.

There are other beaches, some of them sandy, located a few kilometres north of Larnaka, within the tourist zone. However, your enjoyment of them may be hampered by the smell emanating from the nearby oil refinery.

🏛 Aqueduct (Kamares)

3 km (1.9 miles) from Larnaka.

On the outskirts of Larnaka, by the road leading to Limassol, are the remains of an aqueduct that formerly supplied the town with water taken from inlets on the River Thrimitus. The aqueduct was built in 1745 by the Turkish governor, Elhey Bekir Pasha, and functioned until 1930. Some 75 spans of this impressive structure still stand; they are illuminated at night.

Larnaka beach in high season

Octagonal fountain in the courtyard of Agia Napa monastery

Agia Napa ⑳

Road map E3. 🏛 *2500.*
ℹ *Leoforos Kryou Nerou 12, 237 21796.* 🎭 *Kataclysmos.*

UNTIL THE 1970s Agia Napa was a quiet fishing village with a scenic harbour. However, following the Turkish occupation of Varosha – the Greek Cypriot neighbourhood of Famagusta – Agia Napa assumed the role of Cyprus's prime bathing resort. Now a teeming holiday resort especially popular with British and Scandinavian young people, the town centre has scores of hotels, nightclubs and cafés that have given Agia Napa its reputation as the second most entertaining playground in the Mediterranean, after Ibiza.

An interesting historic relic of Agia Napa is the 16th-century Venetian **Monastery of Agia Napa**, enclosed by a high wall. According to legend, in the 16th century a hunter's dog led him to a spring in the woods where he found a sacred icon of the Virgin that had been lost 700 years earlier. (A church had been built here as early as the 8th century, hacked into the solid rock and named Agia Napa – Holy Virgin of the Forest). The spring was thus believed to have healing powers and the monastery of Agia Napa was built on the site. Soon after, Cyprus fell to the Turks and the Venetian monks fled, but villagers continued to use the beautiful **monastery church**.

The only church on the island with a freestanding belfry, it is built partly underground in a natural grotto. The route to its gloomy, mysterious interior leads through an entrance crowned with an arch and a rosette. Inside is a complex maze of grottoes, niches and shrines. From April until December, the church celebrates Anglican mass every Sunday at 11am and Roman Catholic mass at 5pm.

At the centre of the monastery's arcaded **courtyard** is an octagonal Renaissance fountain decorated with marble reliefs and topped with a dome resting on four columns. Nearby, water supplied by a Roman aqueduct flows from the carved marble head of a wild boar.

The monastery was restored in the 1970s and now houses the **World Council of Churches Ecumenical Conference Centre**.

The vaults of the town hall house the **Maritime Life Museum**. The majority of its exhibits come from the

Fountain detail, Agia Napa monastery

private collection of naturalist George Tomaritis. They include a range of preserved marine fauna as well as shells and maritime exhibits.

Another recently opened attraction is the **Thalassa Museum of the Sea** featuring a replica of the "Kyrenia Ship" dating from the times of Alexander the Great, which sank off the coast of Kyrenia some 2,300 years ago.

Beautiful sandy beaches can be found not only in Agia Napa, but also in the surrounding area. One of them is **Nissi Beach**, with its small island. Neighbouring **Makronissos Beach** is linked to the town centre by bicycle routes. Nearby, on a craggy peninsula, are 19 Hellenic tombs hacked into the rock. Two kilometres (1.2 miles) further west is a sandy beach, **Agia Thekla**, with a small chapel and a very old church in a rock cave.

🏛 **Maritime Life Museum**
Agia Mavri 25. ⏰ *May–Sep: 9am–2pm Mon–Sat .* 🎭

🏛 **Thalassa Museum of the Sea**
Leoforos Kryou Nerou.

Cape Greco ㉑

Road map E3.

THIS HEADLAND, lying at the south-eastern tip of Cyprus, rises in a steep crag above the sea. The neighbouring coves with their clear water are a paradise for scuba divers and snorkellers. The entire area, with its interesting variety of

Popular sandy beach in Agia Napa

The rugged coast of Cape Greco with its limestone cliffs

limestone rock formations, is a **protected nature reserve**.

Archaeologists have recently discovered the remains of two **temples**: the Hellenic temple of Aphrodite, and the Roman temple of Diana. The cape is surrounded by underwater **shipwrecks**, including a Genoese ship filled with looted treasure, which sank in the 15th century.

Walking along the shore towards Protaras you will come across a rock bridge over a small bay protruding inland, a Roman quarry, and a little further on, the **Agii Anargyri Church** above a grotto hidden in a craggy cliff underneath. The area in front of the church affords a truly magnificent view over Konnos Bay and the clifftop hotel.

Protaras ❷

Road map E3. ℹ️ *Leoforos Protaras Cape Greco 356, 238 32865.*

PROTARAS is a conglomeration of hotels, tavernas, cafés, water sports centres and an excellent to place to spend a holiday. In summer, its beautiful sandy beaches attract crowds of tourists ready to enjoy water sports, or to go for a cruise on one of the local pleasure boats.

The area is dominated by a rocky hill with the picturesque **chapel of Prophitis Elias** (the Prophet Elijah) affording a magnificent panoramic view of Protaras and nearby Varosha.

Further north are more beaches including Pernera, Minas and Agia Triada with a small church, situated in a coastal cove. Near the latter, close to the roundabout on

the road to Paralimni, is an **Aquarium**, where you can see crocodiles, penguins, fish and other marine creatures.

🐠 **Aquarium**
Paralimni. Protaras Ave. ◯ *daily;*
10am–dusk. 📞 *237 41111.*

ENVIRONS: The area encompassing Agia Napa, Paralimni and the tourist region of Protaras is known as **Kokkinohoria** (red villages) due to its red soil, rich in iron compounds. The scenery is dominated by windmills that drive pumps, which draw water from deep underground.

After 1974, the old village of **Paralimni** became the administrative centre of the district. Situated close to the occupied, northern part of Cyprus, it received a great many refugees after the invasion and now its population numbers about 11,000.

The village skyline is dominated by three churches. The oldest of these is Panagia (Virgin Mary) dating from the 18th century and lined with porcelain tiles typical of the period. It also houses a small Byzantine museum. Paralimni is famous for delicacies such as smoked pork *(pasta)* and pork sausages *(loukanika)*.

The neighbouring farming village of **Deryneia** perches atop a hill, right by the "Green Line". From here there

Statue of a diver in Protaras

are views of Varosha's abandoned houses, the former tourist district of Famagusta now resembling a ghost town, and the Gothic Cathedral of St Nicholas, which has been turned into a mosque.

Deryneia has three pretty churches – 15th-century Agia Marina, 17th-century Agios Georgios and the church of the Panagia.

The village of **Liopetri** is famous for the potatoes that are grown here, as well as the woven baskets used to collect them. You can still see local basket weavers at work.

The 15th-century village church of Agios Andronikos has a carved iconostasis with lovely icons and paintings in the apses.

The Akhyronas barn is Cyprus's national memorial. It was here that four EOKA fighters were killed in a battle with the British in 1958.

Potamos Liopetriou, to the south, is the most beautiful fishing village in Cyprus, situated on the shores of a long bay, next to the picturesque church of Agios Georgios and the crumbling walls of the Venetian watchtower. The seaside tavernas serve delicious fresh fish dishes.

The 18th-century church in Paralimni

TROODOS MOUNTAINS

Stretching some 120 km (75 miles) *over southwestern Cyprus, the Troodos mountain region is truly astonishing and completely different from the rest of the sun-baked island. In winter and early spring, the peaks are often capped with snow, and the forests fill the cool air with the scent of pine and cedar. The mountain villages and monasteries hidden in the forests seem a world away from the crowded coastal areas, even during the peak holiday season.*

The shady valleys and lofty peaks of the Troodos mountains have long been a refuge for people in search of calm and tranquillity, including the monks who came here looking for a place where they could be closer to God and farther from temptation.

Mount Olympus, the island's highest peak at 1,951 m (6,400 ft), rises above the other mountains in the mighty massif, crowned with the distinctive radar domes of the British army. In winter, its slopes swarm with skiers eager to enjoy a sport that is rare in this part of Europe.

The southern slopes are perfectly suited to growing the grapes used to produce the island's famous wine, the sweet Commandaria.

Almost half of the 140 species of plants unique to Cyprus grow in the Troodos region. The central section has been declared a nature reserve.

Travelling through the Troodos mountains brings visitors into contact with quiet, friendly villages, where the local people produce sweets of fruit and nuts soaked in grape juice *(soujouko)*, as well as excellent wine and flavourful goat cheese *(halloumi)*.

A trip to the region is not complete without seeing the Byzantine painted churches. The austere architecture of these Orthodox sanctuaries, hidden in remote valleys and glens, hides a wealth of amazingly rich murals (commonly referred to as frescoes) depicting scenes from the Bible.

A church hidden in the mountains – a distinctive feature of the region

◁ **The forested slopes of the Troodos Mountains**

Exploring the Troodos Mountains

AMONG THE HIGHLIGHTS of a visit to the Troodos
mountains are the many painted churches,
some dating from the Byzantine period. Ten of
these isolated churches have been listed as
UNESCO World Cultural Heritage Sites.
The tomb of Archbishop Makarios,
the first president of Cyprus,
lies near Kykkos
Monastery at Throni. The
Commandaria region's
villages have produced the
famous Cypriot dessert wine
since the 12th century. The
true treasures of the Troodos
mountains are their waterfalls
hidden among lush greenery –
unusual in the eastern Mediterranean.

Polis

Morf

① TYLLIRIA

KAMPO

② CEDAR VALLEY

③ KYKKO

Kon

**Theotokos Archangelos Church, one of the
many small churches in the region**

SIGHTS AT A GLANCE

0 km   5

0 miles   5

SEE ALSO

GETTING THERE

From Larnaka airport, follow the motorway signs toward the Troodos mountains, and then take the B8 road. The B9 road from Nicosia passes through Kakopetria. The best route from Pafos is along the scenic Diarizos valley. Leave the motorway at Mandria and turn towards Nikoklea. The mountain roads are of good quality, but winding and steep in places.

Winding roads and arid landscape typical of the region

Nicosia

Xeros

E908

Elaia

B9

22 PANAGIA
FORVIOTISSA
(ASINOU)

PANAGIA
TIS PODITHOU
21

PANAGIA TOU
MOUTOULLA
5

20 KAKOPETRIA

E907

STAVROS TOU
AGIASMATI
24

AGIOS IOANNIS
LAMPADISTIS
4

19

AGIOS NIKOLAOS
TIS STEGIS

6
PEDOULAS

23 PANAGIA TOU
ARAKA

MOUNT OLYMPUS 7
(CHIONISTRA)

8 TROODOS

ROODITISSA 9

PELENDRI

PLATRES
10

17 18

E801

TIMIOS
STAVROS

E802

OMODOS
11

14 KOILANI

POTAMIOU
12

13

LOFOU

VOUNI

15

MONAGRI
16

Limassol

KEY

▬	Major road
▬	Scenic route
═	Other road
═	River
✳	Viewpoint

10 km

Tylliria ❶

Road map B3.

Tylliria is a desolate region
east of Polis, on the northwestern slopes of the Troodos
mountains. Its forested hills
extend behind the former
monastery, Stavros tis Psokas,
in the direction of the Turkish
enclave of Kokkina, Kato
Pyrgos and the sea. This region
has never been inhabited,
although people came here to
work the long-since defunct
copper ore mines. It is ideal
for experienced hikers.

In ancient times, Cyprus was
overgrown with dense forests,
which were cut down to build
ships and fire the furnaces in
the copper-smelting plants.

Under British rule of the
island, action was taken to
restore the former character
of the Cypriot forests. The
extensive Pafos Forest was
created in the western region
of the Troodos Mountains.

**The wooded hills of the remote
Tylliria region – a hiker's paradise**

Cedar Valley ❷

Road map B3.

This valley, set in the midst
of the forest backwoods,
contains most of the island's
trees of the local *cedrus brevi-
folia* variety, different from
the better-known Lebanese
cedar. The valley is a nature
reserve, and with a bit of luck
visitors will see the moufflon –
a wild Cypriot sheep. In the
early 20th century, when the
British declared these animals
a protected species, only 15

of them remained in the wild;
now the forests of Cyprus are
home to over 1,200 of them.
The male displays powerful,
curled horns. The moufflon is
a symbol of Cyprus and
appears on its coins.

Environs: Standing in the
midst of the Pafos Forest is
the abandoned 19th-century
monastery of **Stavros tis
Psokas**, now used by the
Forestry Commission. It
contains a restaurant, several
guest rooms and a campsite.
The locals claim it to be the
coolest place on the island.
Close to the campsite is an
enclosure containing moufflon.

The Forestry Commission
building is the starting point
for hiking trails to the nearby
peaks of Tripylos and Zaharou.
Starting from the car park by
the spring and the junction
with the road leading towards
the sea, you can walk or drive
to Mount Tripylos – one of the
highest peaks in the district at
1,362 m (4,468 ft), which
affords a magnificent panorama
of the Pafos and Tylliria hills.

Kykkos ❸

See pp90–91.

Agios Ioannis Lampadistis ❹

Road map B3. Kalopanagiotis.
🏛 290. ⏰ 10am–noon & 3–6pm
daily. **Donations** *welcome.*

The monastery of St John of
Lampadou (ancient Lambas)
is one of the most interesting
in Cyprus. The old monastery
complex includes three
churches covered with one

**Kalopanagiotis village, scenically
located on a mountain slope**

vast roof. The oldest one,
dedicated to **St Irakleidios**,
dates from the 11th century
and is decorated with over 30
12th- and 15th-century frescoes
illustrating key events in the
life of Jesus. The painting on
the dome depicts Christ
Pantocrator. Others show the
Sacrifice of Abraham, the
Entry into Jerusalem and the
Ascension. The 15th-century
series of paintings seen on
the vaults, arches and walls
depicts various scenes from
the New Testament.

The second church, of
**Agios Ioannis (St John)
Lampadistis**, dating from the
11th century, is dedicated to
the saint who was born in
Lampadou. He renounced
marriage in favour of the
monastic life, went blind,
died at the age of 22, and was
canonised soon afterwards.
His tomb is inside the church
and the niche above contains
a silver reliquary with the
saint's skull. The church
interior is decorated with
12th-century paintings. The
richly gilded iconostasis dates

Monastery buildings of Agios Ioannis Lampadistis

from the 16th century. The narthex (portico) common to both churches, which was added in the 15th century, includes a cycle of paintings depicting the miracles of Christ.

The **Latin chapel**, added in the second half of the 15th century, is decorated with 24 magnificent Byzantine wall paintings with Greek texts written in about 1500.

Also in the grounds of the monastery is the **Icon Museum**.

🏛 Icon Museum
⬜ Mar–Sep: 9:30am–7pm Mon–Sat, 11am–7pm Sun; Oct–Feb: 9:30am–4:30pm Mon–Sat, 11am–4:30pm Sun.

ENVIRONS: The mountain village of **Kalopanagiotis** is scenically located and has existed since medieval times. It is now a small health resort with therapeutic sulphur springs (with beneficial properties for rheumatic conditions and gastric ailments). It is also known for its beautifully carved breadbaskets called *sanidha*. The village is believed to be descended from ancient Lambas, which produced the local saints, Ioannis and Irakleidios. Nearby is a medieval bridge.

Panagia tou Moutoulla ❺

Road map B3. 3 km (1.8 miles) from Pedoulas. Moutoullas. ⬜ varies. **Donations** welcome

THE VILLAGE of Moutoulla, situated in a valley below Pedoulas, is renowned for its mineral water spring and its tiny church of **Our Lady of Moutoulla** (Panagia tou Moutoulla) built in 1279–80.

This is the oldest of the Troodos mountain painted churches. Its most interesting features are the pitched roof and finely carved entrance door. Beyond these doors is another set of equally beautiful doors (wood carving has been a local speciality for centuries). Above them is the image of *Christ Enthroned*, flanked by *Adam and Eve*, and *Hell and Paradise*, with a procession of

Panoramic view of Pedoulas in the Marathassa valley

saints marching into Heaven. The cycle of paintings inside the church, illustrating key events in the life of Jesus and Mary, are similar to the wall paintings in the nearby Church of the Archangel Michael. The most distinctive of these faded paintings include *Mary with the Christ Child* in a cradle, and *St Christopher and St George Fighting the Dragon* with the head of a woman in a crown. There is also a portrait of the church founder, Ioannis Moutoullas, with his wife Irene.

Remains of a wall painting in Panagia tou Moutoulla

Pedoulas ❻

Road map B3. 🚶 190. 🚌 once a day from Nicosia. ⬜ varies. **Donations** welcome.

THIS SIZEABLE VILLAGE is located in the upper part of the Marathassa valley. The Setrakhos River that drains it flows down towards Morphou Bay. Pedoulas is famed for its surrounding orchards, gentle climate, bracing air and

bottled spring water, which you can buy in most shops in Cyprus. The most beautiful season here is spring, when the houses are completely enveloped by a sea of flowering cherry trees.

The most significant site in the village is the **Church of the Archangel Michael** (Archangelos Michail), dating from 1474. It is one of ten mountain churches listed as UNESCO World Cultural Heritage Sites, due to its magnificent interior wall paintings.

The paintings are unusually realistic. The north side of the tiny reading room is decorated with a painting of the Archangel Michael.

The recently renovated paintings are notable for their realistic images, including the *Sacrifice of Abraham*, the *Baptism in the Jordan River*, the *Kiss of Judas* and the *Betrayal of Christ in the Garden of Gethsemane*. The apse, usually decorated with an image of Christ Pantocrator, includes the Praying Mary *(Virgin Orans)* and the *Ascension*. Seen above the north entrance is the figure of the founder, Basil Chamados, handing a model of the church to the Archangel Michael.

ENVIRONS: The neighbouring village of Prodromos, which numbers only 150 inhabitants, is perched on top of a mountain range at an elevation of 1,400 m (4,593 ft). It is the highest village in Cyprus, and also, thanks to its decent accommodation facilities, a good base for starting to explore the Marathassa valley.

Kykkos ❸

THIS IS THE LARGEST, most imposing, and the wealthiest of all the monasteries in Cyprus. Built in the middle of magnificent mountains and forests, away from human habitation, its most precious treasure is the icon of the Most Merciful Virgin, claimed to have been painted by St Luke and credited with the power to bring rain. The holy image is kept in the monastery musem.

12th-century Icon
The most beautiful icon in the museum's collection is this image of the Virgin and Child.

Collection of manuscripts, documents and books

Belfry
The new belfry, with its distinctive architectural style, stands on top of a hill near the monastery.

The rotunda has a darkened room housing the museum's most precious exhibits – the ancient, beautiful icons.

The main wing of the monastery is home to the monks' cells.

★ Museum's Main Hall
The monastery museum contains some important treasures: gold and silver liturgical vessels, holy books, and embroidered vestments, as well as beautiful and precious icons.

STAR SIGHTS

★ Museum's
  Main Hall

★ Royal Doors
  (in the church)

General View
The hills surrounding Kykkos afford memorable views over the small monastery church and belfry, flanked by one-storey buildings with red roof tiles.

Small Courtyard
The church courtyard leads to the monastery buildings that used to house the museum.

VISITORS' CHECKLIST

Road map B3.
Monastery & church ☐
Apr–Sep: 8am–6pm daily;
Oct–Mar: 10am–5pm daily.
Museum ☐ *Apr–Sep:*
8am–6pm daily; Oct–Mar:
10am–5pm daily. 🖼 ☐ 🚫

★ Royal Doors
Inside the church is a richly decorated iconostasis incorporating the Royal Doors.

Church Entrance
The katholicon, *or monastery church, is entered via a doorway decorated with lovely mosaics.*

Main Monastery Entrance
This small, but wonderfully decorated entance is covered in beautiful mosaics.

Main Courtyard
The cloisters running along the edge of the main courtyard are decorated with mosaics depicting the history of Kykkos Monastery.

Timios Stavros ⑰

Road map B3. 8 km (5 miles) west of
Agros. ◯ *varies.* **Donations** *welcome.*

THE DESIGN of Timios Stavros
(Holy Cross) church is
different from that of other
Cypriot churches. Standing on
the lakeshore, at the southern
end of the village, this three-
aisled edifice was built on a
square plan and topped with a
slender dome on four columns.

Opposite the entrance are
the portraits of the church's
founders, as well as their
coats-of-arms, and the figure
of the apostle, Doubting
Thomas. The painting to the
right depicts the lineage of
Jesus. The series of 14
superbly preserved paintings
above the pulpit illustrates the
life of Mary, including the
Nativity and the *Presentation
of Jesus at the Temple*, with
figures dressed in Lusignan
period costumes.

The iconostasis includes a
silver reliquary containing
fragments of the True Cross,
for which the church is named.

Fragment of a painting in Timios Stavros Church

Lusignan, son of Hugo V (the
Franconian King of Cyprus).

At the centre of the village
is the **Panagia Katholiki
Church**, dating from the early
16th century, which has Italian-
Byzantine-style paintings.

It is worth spending some
time visiting the nearby
Pitsillia Winery, which
produces local wines using
traditional methods. The visit
must be arranged in advance
([**C**] 253 72928).

Agios Nikolaos
tis Stegis ⑲

Road map B3. 3 km (1.8 miles) NW
of Kakopetria. ◯ *9am–4pm Tue–Sat,
11am–4pm Sun.* **Donations** *welcome.*

THIS STONE CHURCH,
built in the form of
a cross, supports a
double roof, giving it
the name, St Nicholas
of the Roof. The oldest
section of the building
dates from the 11th
century; the dome and
narthex were added a
hundred years later,
and in the 15th century
the entire structure was
covered with a huge
ridge roof. This outer
roof was designed to
protect the building
from snow, which falls
here occasionally.

The church once
served as the chapel of
a monastery, no longer
in existence. Inside,
you can see some of

the oldest wall paintings
anywhere in the Troodos
mountain churches. Painted
over a period of about 500
years, between the 11th and
the 15th centuries, they
demonstrate the evolution of
Orthodox religious art,
making this church an
excellent place to study the
development of Byzantine
wall painting.

Along with paintings from
the early Byzantine period,
known as "hieratic" or
"monastic" styles influenced
by the art of Syria and
Cappadocia, you can also see
typical Komnenos and
Paleologos art styles. During
the Komnenos dynasty (1081-
1180), the Byzantine style,
which had been rigid and
highly formalized up to that
point, began to move towards
realism and emotional
expression in the figures and
in their settings.

The artists who created the
wall paintings during the
Paleologos dynasty continued
to display similar attention to
the emotional and aesthetic
qualities of their art.

Paintings inside the church
illustrate scenes from the New
Testament. Among the earliest
paintings here are the *Entry to
Jerusalem*, and the warrior
saints George and Theodore
brandishing their panoply of
arms. The ceiling of the main
vault depicts the **Transfiguration of the Lord** on
Mount Tabor and the **Raising
of Lazarus** from the dead,
conveying the startling

Pelendri ⑱

Road map B3. 8 km west of Agros,
32 km from Limassol.

IN THE MIDDLE AGES, the village
of Pelendri, on the southern
slopes of the Troodos mountains, was the seat of Jean de

Interior of Timios Stavros Church

◁ **Donkey riders in the Troodos mountains**

impression the events made on the disciples of Jesus and the relatives of Jesus.

The **Crucifixion** in the north transept shows the Sun and Moon personified weeping over the fate of the dying Jesus. Equally interesting is the painting of the **Resurrection**, in which the women coming to visit the grave are informed of the Lord's resurrection by an angel seated near the empty tomb. The painting dates from the Lusignan period.

The **Nativity** in the south transept vault shows the Virgin Mary breast-feeding the Christ Child. Painted around it is an idyllic scene with pipe-playing shepherds and gambolling animals. Adjacent is a shocking 12th-century painting of the 40 **Martyrs of Sebaste** – Roman soldiers who adopted Christianity and were killed for it – being pushed by soldiers into the freezing waters of an Anatolian lake. In the dome vault is an image of **Christ Pantocrator**.

A picturesque narrow street in old Kakopetria

Kakopetria ⑳

Road map B3. 80 km (50 miles) from Nicosia. ⌂ 1,200.

THIS OLD VILLAGE in the Solea region, in the valley of the Kargotis River, displays interesting stone architecture. At an elevation of 600 m (1,968 ft), its climate is mild enough to allow the cultivation of grapes. Besides wine, Kakopetria was once renowned for its production of silk. Now it is a weekend retreat for Nicosia residents.

Agios Nikolaos tis Stegis, featuring magnificent wall paintings

The village derives its name "Accursed Rocks" from the rocks which, during an earthquake, once killed a great number of people.

The surrounding district has several intriguing churches and chapels, including the **Archangelos Church** which dates from 1514, covered with a ridge roof. It is decorated with paintings depicting the life of Jesus. The paintings in the **Agios Georgios church** are influenced by folk tradition.

Panagia tis Podithou ㉑

Road map B3. **Panagia tis Podithou** Galata. ⌂ 10am–1pm & 2–5pm daily. ☎ 229 22245. **Donations** welcome.

DATING FROM 1502, this church is also known as Panagia Elousa (Our Lady of Mercy). Originally, it was a monastery church dedicated to St Eleanor. Later, it belonged to the Venetian family of Coro. The wall paintings that decorate the church date from the Venetian period. Created by Simeon Axenti, their style betrays both Byzantine and Italian influences. They are an example of the strong influence that Western art exerted at that time on Cypriot decorative art. The poignant **Crucifixion** is particularly interesting, painted within a triangle and revealing Italian

influences. Mary Magdalene can be seen at the foot of the Cross, her hair loose, alongside a Roman soldier and the two crucified thieves. The **Communion of the Apostles** in the apse is flanked by the figures of two Kings: Solomon and David. The painting in the narthex depicts **Our Lady the Queen of Heaven**; painted below it is the image of the church's founder – Dimitrios Coro – with his wife.

It is worth spending some time visiting the early 16th-century church, **Agios Sozomenos**, with its cycle of folk-style wall paintings created in 1513, also by Simeon Axenti. Take a closer look at the painting depicting St George fighting the dragon, whose tail is entwined around the hind legs of the knight's horse, as well as the image of St Mamas riding a lion while carrying a lamb in his arms. The nearby church of **Agia Paraskevi** features the remains of some 1514 wall paintings, probably created by a disciple of Axenti.

The charming church of Panagia tis Podithou

Fresco in Panagia Forviotissa church

Panagia Forviotissa (Panagia tis Asinou) ❷

Road map B3. 5 km (3 miles) SW of Nikitari village. ☐ *9am–3pm daily.* **Donations** *welcome.*

BEYOND THE VILLAGE of Nikitari, the road climbing towards the Troodos mountains leads through a dark forest and into a desolate valley overgrown with pine trees. Here, on a wooded hillside, stands the small 12th-century church of Panagia Forviotissa, also known as Panagia tis Asinou. With its red tiled roof, this church dedicated to Our Lady of the Meadows is listed as a UNESCO World Cultural Heritage Site.

The church was founded in 1206 by Nikiforos Maistros, a high-ranking Byzantine official, portrayed in the paintings inside. At first glance the building, with its rough stone walls and simple ridge roof, does not resemble a church. Nevertheless, this humble one-room structure hides a number of genuine treasures. There are frescoes dating from the 12th to the 16th centuries, which were restored in the 1960s and 1970s.

The wall and ceiling decorations are among the finest examples of Byzantine frescoes, starting with the *Christ Pantocrator* (Ruler of the World) on the vault of the narthex. There are also dignified figures of the apostles, saints, prophets and martyrs. The following frescoes date from 1105: the *Baptism in the Jordan River*, the *Raising of Lazarus*, the *Last Supper*, the *Crucifixion* and the *Resurrection*. They were painted by artists from Constantinople who represented the Komnenos style.

Altogether there are over 100 frescoes here, illustrating various religious themes. It is worth taking a closer look at the extraordinarily realistic painting covering the westernmost recess of the vault - the *Forty Martyrs of Sebaste*. Next to this are the *Pentecost* and the *Raising of Lazarus*.

The cycle of paintings in the nave illustrates the life of Jesus, from the Nativity to the Crucifixion and Resurrection. Seen in the apse is the *Communion of the Apostles*; Jesus offers the Eucharist to his disciples, with Judas standing aside.

The best paintings include the *Dormition of the Virgin*, above the west entrance, and the terrifying vision of the *Last Judgment*. Above the south entrance is a portrait of the founder, Nikiforos Maistros, presenting a model of the church to Christ.

The narthex offers further surprises. The moufflon and two hunting dogs on the arch of the door herald the arrival of the Renaissance; Byzantine iconography did not employ animals. Here, too, is another image of the church founders, praying to the Virgin and Child, with Christ Pantocrator surrounded by the Apostles.

Between 1965 and 1976, the frescoes underwent a process of meticulous cleaning and restoration, under supervision by experts on Byzantine art from Harvard University.

ENVIRONS: The village of **Vyzakia**, some 6 km (4 miles) down the valley from Panagia Forviotissa, is worth visiting to see the Byzantine **church of the Archangel Michael** with its frescoes depicting the life and the martyrdom of Jesus. Dating from the early 16th century, these wall paintings reveal a strong Venetian influence.

The little 12th-century church of Panagia Forviotissa

Panagia tou Araka ❸

Road map C3. Lagoudera. ☐ *10am–4pm daily.* **Donations** *welcome.* Feast of the Birth of the Virgin (6–7 Sep).

THE 12TH-CENTURY church Panagia tou Araka stands between the villages of Lagoudera and Saranti. Its interior is decorated with some of the island's most beautiful frescoes, painted in 1192 by Leon Authentou, who arrived from Constantinople and worked in the aristocratic

Panagia tou Araka Church, surrounded by mountains

Christ Pantocrator fresco in the Church of Panagia tou Araka

Komnenos style. This church contains some of the most interesting examples of pure Byzantine art in Cyprus.

The most magnificent of the paintings depicts Christ Pantocrator in a blue robe, surrounded by images of angels and prophets. In the apse are images of 12 early Christian saints, including St Barnabas, the patron saint of Cyprus. Above them is the Virgin Mary enthroned, with the Child Jesus on her knees, flanked by the Archangels Gabriel and Michael.

Another interesting fresco is the *Birth*, showing the Infant Jesus being bathed, watched by angels, shepherds, a flock of sheep and a white donkey.

The small, richly carved and gilded iconostasis contains only four icons. On the right is a larger-than-life painting of the Madonna of the Passion (*Panagia Arakiotissa*), to whom the church is dedicated.

Relief from Panagia tou Araka

ENVIRONS: The mountain hamlet of **Spilia** has a splendidly well preserved oil press housed in a stone building. In the central square are monuments commemorating the EOKA combatants who fought the British, blowing themselves up in a nearby hideout used to produce bombs. Some 2 km (1.3 miles) to the north of Spilia, in the village of **Kourdali**, is a three-aisle basilica, **Koimisis tis Panagias**, which once belonged to a former monastery. Inside, the Italian-Byzantine wall paintings depict figures dressed in Venetian clothes. The Virgin, fainting at the foot of the cross, wears a dress with exposed shoulders. Other interesting paintings here include: *Doubting Thomas*, the *Praying Virgin (Virgin Orans)* and the *Dormition of the Blessed Virgin*. The best times to visit are 14-15 August, which are local feast days.

Another site worth visiting is the diminutive **Church of Timiou Stavrou** in **Agia Eirini**, which contains more paintings depicting the life and death of Jesus. It also has a deisis – an image of the Mother of God and John the Baptist sitting on both sides of Christ, who holds in his hand the prophecy pronouncing him the Messiah and adjudicator on the Day of the Last Judgment. An attractive local walk leads along the Madhari ridge to the top of **Mount Adhelfi**, at 1,612 m (5,288 ft). From here there is a stunning panoramic view over the Troodos mountain region.

Stavros tou Agiasmati ㉔

Road map C3. 6 km (3.7 miles) north of Platanistassa. ⏱ *varies.*
Donations *welcome.* 🎟 *13 & 14 Sep.*

A ROUGH ROAD leads to the small church of Stavros tou Agiasmati in its isolated setting on the mountainside of Madhari. Originally built as the chapel for an older monastery, its very low main door was thus designed to prevent Arab and Turkish invaders from entering on horseback, a common way of desecrating churches.

Inside Stavros tou Agiasmati is the island's most complete cycle of paintings illustrating the Gospel. Some parts refer to the Old Testament. Another cycle of paintings illustrates the story of the Holy Cross. Together they form a fine assemblage of 15th-century frescoes.

The church's interior is divided into two horizontal zones of paintings: the lower zone displays life-size figures of the saints while the upper zone has 24 scenes from the New Testament.

Behind the iconostasis, the apse features a magnificent image of the Virgin uniting Heaven and Earth. Some of the paintings depict scenes not known anywhere else, like the fresco of the *Last Supper* in which only Christ is present; or the *Raising of Lazarus* in which a group of Jews is clearly offended by the smell of the resurrected Lazarus. The fresco of *Peter's Denial* includes a shockingly large image of a rooster. One of the niches in the north wall features a series of ten paintings that illustrate the discovery of the Holy Cross by St Helena, the mother of the Emperor Constantine. The frescoes are partly the work of Philip Goul, a Lebanese artist who is characterized by his spare yet profound style.

Standing in the north niche is a magnificently decorated cross, which gives Stavros tou Agiasmati (church of the Holy Cross) its name.

Stavros tou Agiasmati church, in its remote mountainside location

CENTRAL CYPRUS

WITH THE EXCEPTION *of the divided city of Nicosia, the heartland of Cyprus remains surprisingly unexplored by visitors. The plains are covered with colourful carpets of cultivated fields, crisscrossed by roads that link the small villages. They descend radially towards Nicosia* (see pp112–31), *whose suburbs sprawl across the Pentadaktylos range. The eastern part of the Troodos mountains – the Pitsillia area – is incorporated in this region.*

The vast plain on Mesaoria (meaning the land between mountains) is a gently undulating area dotted with small towns and old-fashioned villages. The watchtowers and fences occasionally seen from the road are reminders of the "Green Line" - the buffer zone border. The defunct airport to the west of Nicosia once provided international service.

Central Cyprus is the island's least developed region, from a tourist's point of view. It is almost devoid of hotels and restaurants, although here and there you can find a small agrotourism farm or a *kafeneion* - a local café. Tourists usually visit this region on their way to the beautiful Troodos mountains, or to the bustling seaside resorts in the south.

The most interesting historical sites of central Cyprus are the ruins of ancient Tamassos and Idalion. Tamassos, which was established around 4,000 BC, grew rich thanks to the copper ore deposits discovered nearby. Today, items made of this metal are among the most popular souvenirs from this region.

Also of interest are the Convent of Agios Irakleidios, the unusual subterranean Church of Panagia Chrysospiliotissa and Machairas Monastery on the northeastern slopes of the Troodos mountains, in the Pitsillia area. Nearby are the mountain villages of Fikardou, Lazanias and Gourri, and further south the town of Agros, which is famous for its roses.

Roadside vineyard in central Cyprus

◁ **The Byzantine Church of St Barnabas and St Hilarion at Peristerona, glowing in the light of the setting sun**

Exploring Central Cyprus

CENTRAL CYPRUS, stretching south of Nicosia and covering the Pitsillia area of the eastern Troodos mountains, has limited facilities for visitors. Nevertheless, when travelling to the Troodos mountains or Nicosia it is worth exploring this region, especially the ruins of ancient Tamassos, the centre of the copper-producing area since the Bronze Age. Peristerona, home to one of the most beautiful Byzantine churches in Cyprus, as well as a fine mosque, is well worth a visit. Life proceeds slowly in the picturesque villages, with their bougainvillea-clad houses.

The lively village of Dali, near ancient Idalion

GETTING THERE

Central Cyprus is easily accessible. From Larnaka airport the A2 motorway runs inland towards Nicosia. From the main port in Limassol, a motorway follows the coastline and branches off as the A1 road towards Nicosia. The route from Pafos airport leads through the mountains. The road is good and you can combine the journey with a tour of the Troodos mountains.

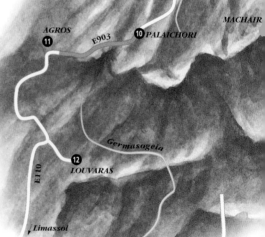

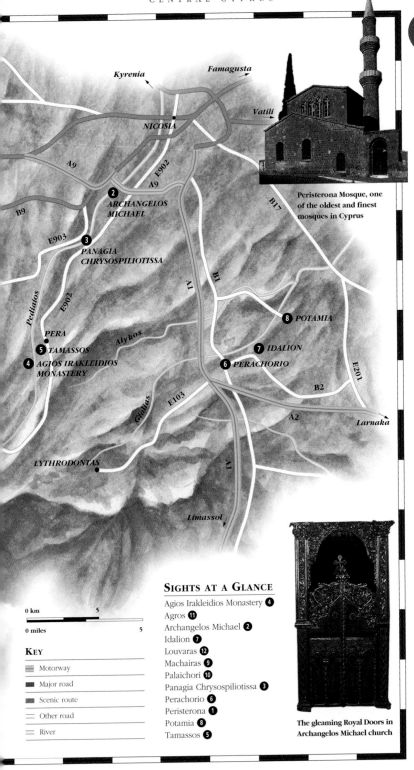

Kyrenia

Famagusta

Vatili

NICOSIA

A9

E902

A9

2
ARCHANGELOS
MICHAEL

B9

E903

B17

3
PANAGIA
CHRYSOSPILIOTISSA

A1

B1

Pediaios

E902

8 **POTAMIA**

PERA

Alykos

7 **IDALION**

5 **TAMASSOS**

4 **AGIOS IRAKLEIDIOS**
MONASTERY

6 **PERACHORIO**

E201

B2

Gialias

E103

A2

Larnaka

A1

LYTHRODONTAS

Limassol

Peristerona Mosque, one
of the oldest and finest
mosques in Cyprus

0 km   5

0 miles   5

KEY

▧	Motorway
▤	Major road
▨	Scenic route
═	Other road
═	River

SIGHTS AT A GLANCE

The gleaming Royal Doors in
Archangelos Michael church

Peristerona ●

Road map C3. 27 km (17 miles) west of Nicosia, along the road to Troodos.
🏛 *2,100.*

PERISTERONA is the centre of Cyprus's watermelon-growing district. The village straddles a usually dry river, and features the beautiful five-domed **Church of St Barnabas and St Hilarion**, whose tall slender belfry is topped with a cross. This is a prime example of early 10th-century Byzantine architecture. The domes, resting on tall tambours with conical tips, are arranged in the shape of a cross. (A similar five-domed structure, the Agia Paraskevi Church, can be seen near Pafos, in the village of Geroskipou.) The proprietor of the neighbouring café holds the key to the church; it is worth gaining entry.

The narthex, which houses a vast chest depicting the siege of a castle, provides a view of the nave, which is separated by arches from the side aisles. The remains of the 16th-century wall paintings illustrate the life of King David, and there is also a vast reading room. The gilded iconostasis, beautifully carved in wood, dates from 1549.

The nearby **mosque**, one of the oldest and most magnificent anywhere on the island, was built on a square floor plan. Its tall, arched tracery-laden windows indicate that this was once a Gothic church. Now the mosque stands empty, with pigeons nesting inside. The proximity of the church belfry and the mosque's minaret are reminders of a time when both

Fresco from the Archangelos Michael church

communities – Greeks and Turks – coexisted peacefully here in the village. Today, Peristerona is inhabited only by Greek Cypriots, while their Turkish Cypriot neighbours have moved north, beyond the demarcation line several kilometres away.

ENVIRONS: The Mesaoria plain lies between the Pentadak-tylos mountain range to the north and the Troodos massif to the south. The village of Orounda, a few kilometres south of Peristerona, is home to the **church of Agios Nikolaos**, part of the long deserted monastery here. Similar to other villages scattered on the north slopes of the Troodos mountains, such as Agia Marina, Xyliatos and Vyzakia, this area is home to small mountain churches, as well as numerous taverns and *kafenia* (cafés) where you can savour an original *meze* or relax over a cup of Cyprus coffee.

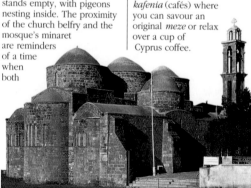

The five-domed church of St Barnabas and St Hilarion, in Peristerona

Archangelos Michael ●

Road map C3. On the outskirts of south Nicosia.
🎏 *Feast of the Archangels Michael and Gabriel (7–8 Nov.)*

THE Byzantine church of the Archangel Michael on the bank of the Pediaios River was built by Archbishop Nikiforos, whose tomb can be seen in the northern section of the building. It was rebuilt in 1636 and again in 1713, when it was bought by Kykkos Monastery. The austere edifice, constructed from a yellowish stone with small windows and a simple portico, is covered with a shallow white dome resting on a tall tambour.

The church interior has a lovely wooden iconostasis and frescoes depicting, among others, the Archangel Michael. The frescoes are more lively than some of their rivals. Their colours were brightened by restoration in 1980 and include a range of Gospel and Old Testament scenes.

ENVIRONS: To the north is a complex of playing fields and a market site; next to these is the church of Panagia Make-donitissa. Nearby is a military cemetery. On the opposite side of the river, at the end of Athalassa Avenue is Athalassa forest, the largest wooded area in the vicinity of Nicosia. It features pine, cedar and eucalyptus trees. There is also a reservoir where permit holders are allowed to fish. All this makes it a pleasant place during high summer.

Panagia Chrysospiliotissa ●

Road map C3. 12 km (8 miles) southwest of Nicosia.

THIS RARELY VISITED subter-ranean church, situated near the village of Kato Deftera, is dedicated to Our

Lady of the Golden Grotto. Originally a series of ancient catacombs, these were converted into a church in the early Christian era. The interior was once covered with beautiful frescoes, which are now severely damaged.

ENVIRONS: In the village of Agios Ioannis Malountas, a few kilometres away, is **Ostrich Wonderland**, Europe's largest ostrich ranch. A mini-train carries visitors around the park to admire these enormous flightless birds. Besides several dozen ostriches, there are donkeys, sheep, ponies and deer.

Ostrich Wonderland
🕐 *9am–8pm daily (summer) & 9am–6pm (winter).* 📞 *226 66178.* 📷

Inside the subterranean Panagia Chrysospiliotissa

Agios Irakleidios Monastery ❹

Road map C3. 20 km (12 miles) SW of Nicosia. 🕐 *9am–noon Mon, Wed & Thu (groups only).*

ST HERACLEIDIUS (Agios Irakleidios) Monastery stands close to the ruins of Tamassos. In the mid-1st century, in the course of their activities as missionaries on the island of Cyprus, the apostles Barnabas and Paul appointed a local man, Heracleidius, as the first Bishop of Tamassos. Bishop Heracleidius became famous for his many miracles; he was also a well-known exorcist. At the age of 60 he was killed by pagans and buried at this spot, where a small early Christian church and

Agios Irakleidios Monastery buildings

monastery were built. The monastery church, built in the 5th century, was repeatedly destroyed; the present building was erected in 1759.

Inside is a fresco depicting the baptism of Heracleidius administered by the apostles Paul and Barnabas, as well as beautiful geometric Byzantine mosaics and a monogram of Jesus. Relics of St Heracleidius – including his skull and forearm – are kept in a special silver reliquary.

From the side chapel to the south, a stairway descends to the catacombs, where Heracleidius spent his final years, and where he was buried.

The present buildings date from the late 18th century. The wall paintings of the period depict scenes from the life of St Heracleidius. At that time the monastery was famous for its icons, which were painted here. Now it is inhabited by nuns, who breed canaries and make delicious rose-petal jam and sugar-coated almonds.

Tamassos ❺

Road map C3. 18 km (11 miles) SW of Nicosia. **Excavation site** 🕐 *9am–3pm Tue–Fri, 10am–3pm Sat–Sun.* 📷

NEAR THE VILLAGE of Politico, along the route leading to Machairas Monastery, archaeologists have unearthed the remains of the ancient

town of Tamassos, founded by Trakofryges of Asia Minor in c.4,000 BC. In c.2,500 BC, rich copper deposits were discovered here, which led to the town's growth and prosperity. Temesa (an alternative name for Tamassos) is mentioned in Homer's *Odyssey*; an excerpt describes Athena's journey to Temesa in order to trade iron for copper.

Later, in about 800 BC, the town was taken over by the Phoenicians. Their King, Atmese of Tamassos, along with other Cypriot Kings, paid tribute to the Assyrian rulers.

Alexander the Great gave the local copper mines as a present to King Protagoras of Salamis, in gratitude for his help during the siege of Tyre. In 12 AD, the Judaean King Herod the Great leased the local copper mines; many Jews arrived on the island to supervise the excavation of this valuable commodity.

Archaeological works started in 1890 and continue to this day. The most important discoveries are the subterranean royal tombs dating from 650-600 BC, which have long since been looted. Two of them survive in perfect condition. Other discoveries include a citadel, the site of copper processing, the remains of houses and the Temple of Aphrodite (or Astarte). Many items discovered here are

Mosaic fragment from Tamassos

Perachorio ❻

Road map C3. 17 km (10.5 miles) south of Nicosia.

THE SMALL VILLAGE of Perachorio is the setting of the hilltop **church of the Holy Apostles** (Agioi Apostoloi). This domed, single-aisle building has several side chapels.

The church, in a scenic setting, conceals fragments of beautiful 12th-century frescoes, in a style similar to those in the Panagia tis Asinou Church (*see p100*). Experts regard these as the best examples of the Komnenos style anywhere on the island. The most interesting are the images of angels in the dome, below the damaged painting depicting Christ Pantocrator. Another interesting painting shows two shepherds conversing casually, their shoulder bags hanging from a tree, while the infant Jesus is bathed. The apse features a picture of the Virgin, flanked by St Peter and St Paul. Also depicted are saints, martyrs, emperors and demons.

Nearby is the 16th-century church of Agios Dimitrios.

Church in Perachorio with lovely 12th-century paintings

Idalion ❼

Road map D3. 20 km (12 miles) south of Nicosia. 🎨 *Adonis Festival (spring).*

THE ANCIENT IDALION, whose remains can be seen in the present-day village of Dali, was one of the oldest city-states on the island. According to legend, it was founded by King Chalcanor, a Trojan War hero.

The town is built on top of two hills; only a small portion of its ruins has so far been unearthed, including tombs along the road to Larnaka.

A stone church in the Potamia area

Idalion existed from the Bronze Age up to about 1,400 BC. The town had 14 temples, including those dedicated to Aphrodite, Apollo and Athena. Archaeological excavations are still under way. The best artifacts can be seen in the Cyprus Museum in Nicosia.

The remains of Idalion had already sparked interest in the 19th century. The American consul, Luigi Palma di Cesnola, plundered thousands of tombs in this area, robbing them of all their valuable items. Local farmers also found large numbers of votive figurines of Aphrodite while working in the fields, which indicates that this was a major site of the cult of Aphrodite, the most important Cypriot goddess.

Legend tells of Aphrodite's love for Adonis, son of Zeus and Hera. Ares, the jealous god of war, turned himself into a wild boar and killed Adonis in a nearby forest. Each spring, millions of red poppies and anemones cover the area, said to spring from his blood.

Ruins of the ancient city-state of Idalion, near present-day Dali

Potamia ❽

Road map D3.

SITUATED CLOSE to the Green Line, the little village of Potamia is one of the few places in the south with a small Turkish community. The excellent **Iy Myli** restaurant on the approach road specializes in well-prepared Cypriot cuisine.

Not far from the village are the ruins of the Lusignan Kings' summer palace, and several Gothic churches.

ENVIRONS: The surrounding area is not of great interest, due to the large number of factories and industrial estates built in the immediate vicinity of Nicosia. To the southwest of the derelict village of **Agios Sozomenos** are the ruins of **Agios Mamas church**, built in the Franco-Byzantine style. This is one of the best Gothic historic sites on the island. Construction began in the early 15th century, in the Gothic style which was prevalent on the island at that time. However, it was never completed. Today visitors can see the walls of the three-apsed aisles, separated by intricate arcades, and the monumental portico.

The village of Agios Sozomenos was abandoned early in 1964, when Greek Cypriot police attacked the village inhabited by Turkish Cypriots in retaliation for the killing of two Greeks. Both sides suffered severe losses. The stone wall surrounding the village stands as a remainder of these events.

Cypriot Church Frescoes

THE SHADY, FORESTED VALLEYS of the Troodos mountains hide small Byzantine churches; ten of these have been named UNESCO World Cultural Heritage Sites. Along with a few other churches and chapels throughout the island, they conceal frescoes representing some of the most magnificent masterpieces of Byzantine art. In keeping with Orthodox canons, the interior is divided according to theological

Asinou church paintings

order. The dome symbolizes Heaven, presided over by Christ Pantocrator, the Ruler of the World, usually surrounded by archangels and prophets. Below are the main scenes from the New Testament, including the saints and fathers of the Church. The apse behind the altar features an image of the Virgin with Child. The portico usually contains the Last Judgment, painted above the exit.

Christ Pantocrator
Often painted within the dome, the Omnipotent King of the World looks down from heaven. His right hand is raised in a gesture of benediction; his left hand holds a book as a symbol of the Law.

The Life of Jesus and Mary
The life of the Holy Family has been depicted in many frescoes, as illustrations of the New Testament.

Agios Mamas
Mamas is one of the most celebrated and popular of all Cypriot saints. His name has been given to many churches throughout the island.

The Praying Virgin (Virgin Orans)
Mary raises her hand towards heaven in a pleading gesture. Her eyes are turned towards the people, urging them to trust in Christ.

The 40 Martyrs of Sebaste
In the early days of Christianity, many followers suffered death for their faith. These men, despite being subjected to freezing temperatures and then fire, held to their faith and were martyred.

The Way of the Cross
The images of the way of the cross and the Lord's Passion are among the most dramatic subjects for fresco painters.

Machairas

Road map C3. 41 km (25 miles) SW of Nicosia. **Visitors** only pilgrim groups are permitted. 14–15 Aug and 20–21 Nov.

O N THE NORTHERN SLOPES of the Troodos Mountains, in the area known as Pitsillia, stands one of Cyprus's most famous monasteries – Machairas (Panagia tou Machaira). The monastery rises like a fortress from the mountainside of Kionia, almost 800 m (2,625 ft) above sea level. Its name originates from the word *mahera*, which means 'knife' and probably derives from the knife found next to an icon hidden in a cave. The locals believe that the icon, brought here by a monk from Constantinople, was painted by the Apostle Luke. Two hermits from Palestine found the icon in a cave, and then built a church dedicated to the Virgin Mary in 1148. In 1187, Emperor Manuel Komnenos provided the money to built a bigger church; he also exempted it from the jurisdiction of the local bishop.

The monastery buildings in their present form date from the early 20th century. The beautiful church, surrounded by cloisters, houses the icon attributed to St Luke, which depicts the Holy Virgin pierced with a sword. It also contains numerous other beautiful and well-preserved icons and cult objects. The Gospel, printed in Venice in 1588, is held in the treasury. The monks are extremely pious; their vows are as severe as those taken by the brothers from Mount Athos in Greece.

For Cypriots, this place is associated with EOKA commander, Grigorios Afxentiou, who hid here disguised as a monk. British soldiers ambushed him in a nearby bunker. His comrades surrendered, but Afxentiou chose to fight and resisted the attacks of 60 British soldiers for several hours. Only flame-throwers could put an end to this heroic battle. On the spot where Afxentiou fell now stands a larger-than-life statue, depicting the hero with an eagle by his side.

ENVIRONS: Beyond the village of Lythrodontas, where the paved road ends, is a small monastery dedicated to the Prophet Elijah (Prophitis Elias), hidden in the depth of Machairas Forest.

Palaichori

Road map C3.

T HE VILLAGE of Palaichori lies in a deep valley, near the source of the Peristerona River. The village and the surrounding area feature several churches and chapels, but the most interesting of

View of Palaichori village

these is the **Metamorfosis tou Sotiros chapel**. Erected in the early 16th century, this small church is decorated with frescoes. On the south wall is the scene that gives the chapel its name. It shows a luminous figure of Christ, with prophets and disciples, atop Tabor Mountain at the time of the Transfiguration.

Lions are the predominant motif of the remaining paintings: in the den with Daniel, preparing to bury the body of St Mary the Beatified of Egypt and finally, St Mamas riding a particularly elongated predator.

ENVIRONS: The three picturesque villages of **Fikardou**, **Gourri** and **Lazanias** at the eastern end of the Pitsillia area form a legally protected conservation zone, due to their unique traditional architecture. The largest number of typical folk buildings have survived in Fikardou, which now looks more like an open-air museum than a village. The village has been declared a monument of national culture, being the best example of rural architecture from the past few centuries. It has narrow alleys paved with stone, and neat little timber houses, two-storeys high, with wooden balconies.

The old houses of Katsinioros and Achilleas Dimitri,

Courtyard of the Machairas Monastery

which are some of the loveliest in the village, have been turned into a **Rural Museum** with a collection of tools and period furnishings. They include a loom, distillery equipment and an olive press.

🏛 **Rural Museum**

⬜ *summer: 9:30am–4pm Tue–Sat, 10:30am–2pm Sun; winter: 9:30am–3:30pm Tue–Sat, 10:30am–2pm Sun (winter).* 🈳

Agros ⓫

Road map C3. 🈁 *850.*

A RGOS IS A LARGE VILLAGE lying at an altitude about 1,000 m (3,280 ft) above sea level, in the picturesque Pitsillia area. The village is famous for its mouth-watering cold meats, particularly its sausages and hams, as well as its fruit preserves and products made of rose petals. The locally-cultivated Damask rose was brought here by the father of Chris Tsolakis, in 1948. Chris now owns a small factory of rose products, making rose water, liqueur, rose wine, rose-petal jam and rose-scented candles. Rose petals are harvested between late May and early June.

The charms of Agros and its environs are promoted enthusiastically by Lefkos Christodoulu who runs the largest local hotel – Rodon. His efforts have led to the creation of numerous walking trails. The neighbourhood has several Byzantine churches decorated with frescoes. Agros itself has no historic sites. The old monastery, which stood here until 1894, was pulled down by the villagers in a dispute with the local bishop. Agros boasts an excellent climate, reputedly good for a long lifespan.

Interior of the chapel of St Mamas, Louvaras, with frescoes of Jesus' life

Louvaras ⓬

Road map C4. 25 km (15.5 miles) north of Limassol.

L OUVARAS is a small village situated among the hills. The local attraction is the **Chapel of St Mamas**, decorated with exquisite late 15th-century frescoes depicting

Detail of a colourful fresco from St Mamas Chapel

scenes from the life of Jesus. They include the Teaching in the Temple, Meeting with the Samaritan Woman at the Well, and the Resurrection, in which the guards wear medieval suits of armour. The figures above the door, dressed in Lusignan clothes, are likely to represent the original donors.

St Mamas is one of the most popular Cypriot saints. He is portrayed on the north wall riding a lion while cradling a lamb in his arms. The scene is associated with an interesting legend. Mamas, a hermit, was ordered to pay taxes by the local governor. He refused to do so, claiming to live solely from alms. The governor lost patience and ordered Mamas to be thrown in jail. As the guards led Mamas away, a lion leapt from the bushes and attacked a lamb grazing peacefully nearby. The saint commanded the lion to stop, took the lamb into his arms and continued his journey on the back of the chastened lion. Seeing this miracle, the governor freed St Mamas, who became the patron saint of tax-evaders.

The village of Agros, scenically located among the hills

SOUTH NICOSIA

N EAR THE CENTRE *of the island, Nicosia (Lefkosia in Greek) is Europe's only divided capital city. The numerous historic sites and traditional atmosphere of South Nicosia have been carefully preserved. The Old Town lies within an imposing defence wall erected by the Venetians in the 16th century. In the evenings, the narrow streets fill with strolling crowds of Cypriots and tourists alike who come to dine and socialize in the pedestrianized Laiki Geitonia district.*

Nicosia is the business and financial centre of the Republic of Cyprus, as well as its seat of government, home to the president. It is composed of three districts: the Old Town, the modern city, and the sprawling suburbs where most families live, extending beyond the city far into the Mesaoria valley.

The charming, sleepy Old Town with its narrow, one-way streets, is surrounded by a Venetian wall stretching for 4.5 km (2.8 miles). The wall is punctuated by 11 bastions and 3 gates. The Porta Giuliana (Famagusta Gate) now houses a Cultural Centre. Visitors heading for the border foot-crossing to Turkish-controlled North Nicosia (near the Ledra Palace Hotel) are greeted by the grim Pafos Gate, near the demarcation line.

The Laiki Geitonia district, east of Eleftheria Square (Plateia Eleftherias), has narrow, winding alleys filled with restaurants, art galleries and boutiques set between traditional houses, typical of Cypriot urban architecture. Ledra Street – a prestigious pedestrian precinct with smart boutiques and garden restaurants – ends abruptly at the border wall with army checkpoints. At the heart of Nicosia stands the Archbishop's Palace and an 8-m (26-ft) tall statue of ex-President Makarios.

South Nicosia has a range of museums to visit, including the wonderful Cyprus Museum.

Shop-front in one of the bustling streets of Laiki Geitonia

◁ **The church of Panagia Faneromeni at sunset**

Exploring South Nicosia

THE MAJORITY of historical sites in Nicosia are found within the mighty town walls. The main attractions, not to be missed, are the Cyprus Museum, the Archbishop's Palace and St John's Cathedral. The latter contains pristine 18th-century frescoes on Biblical themes. The Cyprus Museum holds the island's largest collection of archaeological artifacts, gathered from many sites. The restored district of Laiki Geitonia makes a pleasant place to rest with its numerous cafés, as well as providing good shopping in the local stores. The Cyprus Tourism Organization also offers free tours of the capital *(see p121)*.

5th-century BC figurine from the Cyprus Museum

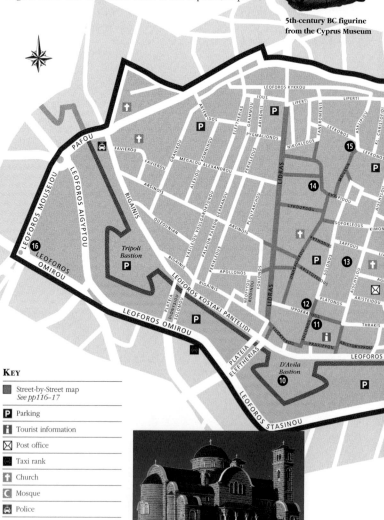

KEY

	Street-by-Street map *See pp116–17*
P	Parking
i	Tourist information
⊠	Post office
	Taxi rank
✝	Church
C	Mosque
	Police
—	City wall
▬	Pedestrianized street

Church along the border of South Nicosia

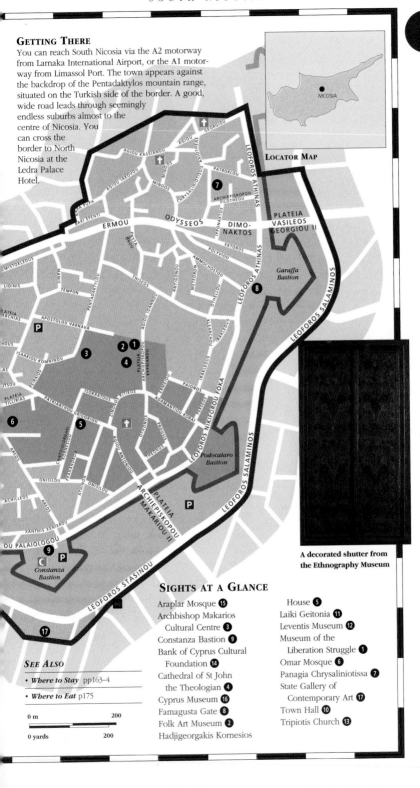

GETTING THERE
You can reach South Nicosia via the A2 motorway from Larnaka International Airport, or the A1 motorway from Limassol Port. The town appears against the backdrop of the Pentadaktylos mountain range, situated on the Turkish side of the border. A good, wide road leads through seemingly endless suburbs almost to the centre of Nicosia. You can cross the border to North Nicosia at the Ledra Palace Hotel.

LOCATOR MAP

A decorated shutter from the Ethnography Museum

SIGHTS AT A GLANCE

Araplar Mosque ⑮
Archbishop Makarios Cultural Centre ③
Constanza Bastion ⑨
Bank of Cyprus Cultural Foundation ⑭
Cathedral of St John the Theologian ④
Cyprus Museum ⑯
Famagusta Gate ⑧
Folk Art Museum ②
Hadjigeorgakis Kornesios House ⑤
Laiki Geitonia ⑪
Leventis Museum ⑫
Museum of the Liberation Struggle ①
Omar Mosque ⑥
Panagia Chrysaliniotissa ⑦
State Gallery of Contemporary Art ⑰
Town Hall ⑩
Tripiotis Church ⑬

SEE ALSO

• *Where to Stay* pp163–4

• *Where to Eat* p175

0 m — 200
0 yards — 200

Street-by-Street: South Nicosia

SOUTH NICOSIA is surrounded by Venetian defence walls and bastions, and has served as the capital since the 11th century. During the Lusignan era, this was a magnificent city, home of the Royal Palace and scores of churches. Today the area within the old walls is full of museums, sacred buildings and historical buildings, which help to recreate the atmosphere of bygone centuries. It is enjoyable to stroll along the streets of old Nicosia, stopping for coffee, or taking a shopping trip to the rebuilt district of Laiki Geitonia. The only drawback is the neglected zone of no man's land dividing the city.

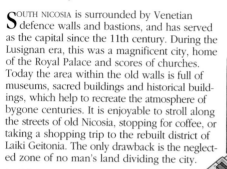

★ **Archbishop Makarios Cultural Centre**
The island's largest, most precious collection of magnificent icons and mosaics are housed here ❸

Richly decorated and well maintained 19th-century houses are the pride of the southern part of the Old Town.

← **Laiki Geitonia**

Omar Mosque
A former Augustinian church was converted into a mosque in 1571, following the capture of the city by Turks. It is the largest mosque in southern Cyprus ❻

The Archbishop's Palace was built in 1956–60 in Neo-Byzantine style.

Hadjigeorgakis Kornesios House
This historic 17th-century building, a former home of the Turkish dragoman, was awarded the Europa Nostra Prize following its restoration. Now it houses a small Ethnological Museum ❺

Folk Art Museum
The highlight here is the collection of 19th- and early 20th-century Cypriot folk art. The textiles, ceramics, wooden artifacts and folk costumes are housed in a former Bishop's Palace **2**

LOCATOR MAP
See pp114–15.

Museum of the Liberation Struggle
Here are documents, photographs and weapons associated with the Greek struggle for independence from 1855 to 1959 **1**

The statue of Archbishop Makarios is 8-m (26-ft) high.

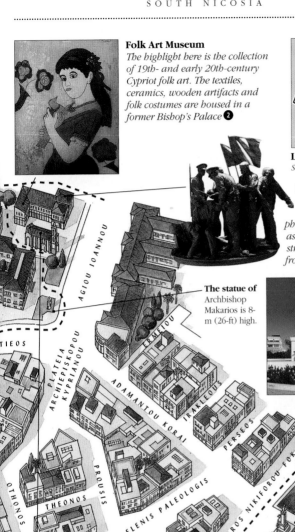

Liberty Monument on the Podocataro Bastion symbolizes the liberation of the Cypriot nation.

★ Cathedral of St John the Theologian
Erected by Archbishop Nikiforos, this small church contains beautiful 18th-century frescoes **4**

STAR SIGHTS

★ Archbishop Makarios Cultural Centre

★ Cathedral of St John the Theologian

KEY

- - - Suggested route

Museum of the Liberation Struggle ❶

Plateia Archiepiskopou Kyprianou.
📞 223 05878. ◷ 8am–2pm Mon–Fri & 3–5:30pm Thu. 📷

Housed in a new building just behind the old Archbishop's Palace is the Museum of the Liberation Struggle. Its collection of photographs, documents, weapons and other objects chronicles the bloody struggle of the EOKA organization against the colonial British army from 1955 to 1959. The exhibits illustrate the guerrilla warfare tactics carried out by EOKA against the British and those Cypriots who objected to the armed struggle.

The collection also includes materials documenting British reprisals, including arrests, interrogations and torture. The museum is primarily intended for Cypriots and school groups.

The Folk Art Museum, housed in the old Archbishop's Palace

Folk Art Museum ❷

Plateia Achiepiskopou Kyprianou. 📞 224 32578. ◷ 9am–2pm Mon–Fri. 📷

Behind the cathedral is the Old Archbishop's Palace, which now houses the Folk Art Museum. On display here is a diverse array of exhibits illustrating the culture of Cyprus. Outside, the main museum attractions are the wooden water wheel, olive presses and carriages. Inside are folk costumes dating from the 19th and 20th centuries, household furnishings and

Museum of the Liberation Struggle

other domestic implements, ceramics, textiles, embroidery, Lefkara laces and pieces of silver jewellery.

Archbishop Makarios Cultural Centre ❸

Plateia Achiepiskopou Kyprianou.
Byzantine Museum 📞 224 30008. ◷ 9am–4:30pm Mon–Fri, 9am–1pm Sat. 📷 **Municipal Arts Centre** Apostolou Varnava. 📞 224 32559. ◷ 10am–2pm & 5–11pm Tue–Sat, 10am–4pm Sun.

This centre, adjacent to the New Archbishop's Palace, houses several libraries, the School of Ecclesiastical Music and the Byzantine Museum, which was founded by Archbishop Makarios.

Also known as the Icon Museum, the Byzantine Museum contains the largest and most valuable collection of icons in Cyprus. Some 150 icons span the 8th to the 19th centuries. Through the exhibition you can follow the changing trends in the art of icon "writing", and see the idiosyncratic images of Jesus, the Virgin Mary, the saints and the apostles. The best exhibits include the 13th-century icon by the main door, portraying the Prophet Elijah being fed by a raven, and the image of the Virgin holding the dead body of Christ – the equivalent of the Roman Catholic *Pieta*.

The reconstructed apse was rescued from the church of

Crown exhibit from the Byzantine Museum

Agios Nikolaos tis Stegis in the Troodos mountains.

For several years the museum has displayed 6th-century Byzantine mosaics stolen during the 1970s from Panagia Kanakaria Church in Lythrangomi in the Turkish-occupied Karpas peninsula. Following a lengthy court battle, the Cypriot government recovered the mosaics. They include the Virgin Mary, the archangels Michael and Gabriel, and several apostles. The figure of Jesus, depicted in one of the mosaics clutching a scroll of parchment, has the appearance of a Hellenic god. All of the figures have unnaturally large eyes, a characteristic trait of early-Christian art.

In addition to mosaics and icons, the museum's collection includes ecclesiastical garments and books.

The New Archbishop's Palace was erected in 1956-60 in the Neo-Byzantine style to a design by Greek architect George Nomikos. Usually closed to visitors, it does open occasionally, when you can visit the bedroom of Archbishop Makarios, where his heart is kept. A giant statue of Makarios, the first president of the Republic of Cyprus, stands in front of the palace. It was produced by London-based Cypriot sculptor, Nicos Kotziamanis.

Near the Makarios Cultural Centre, located in a former power plant, is the Municipal Arts Centre, a venue for major art exhibitions.

Cathedral of St John the Theologian ❹

Plateia Achiepiskopou Kyprianou.
📞 224 32578. 🕐 8am–noon & 2–4pm Mon–Fri, 8am–noon Sat.

THE SMALL CATHEDRAL of St John (Agios Ioannis) dates from 1662. Built of yellow stone, and covered with a barrel vault, it stands on the ruins of a medieval Benedictine monastery. Its interior is decorated with magnificent paintings depicting Biblical scenes from the life of Jesus, from birth to crucifixion, including a striking Last Judgment above the entrance.

The four paintings on the right wall, next to the Archbishop's throne, show the discovery of the relics of the apostle Barnabas, founder of the Cypriot church. They also show the privileges granted by Byzantine Emperor Zeno to the Cypriot church, including *autokefalia* (independence from the Patriarch of Constantinople) and the right of the Archbishop to wear purple garments during ceremonies, to use the sceptre instead of the crosier, and to sign letters with red ink. The paintings tightly covering the walls and ceiling are by the 18th-century artist, Filaretos.

Among the furnishings are a fine carved and gilded iconostasis, and a pulpit with its double-headed eagle, a symbol of Byzantium.

To the right, by the door leading to the courtyard, stands a small marble bust of

A fragment of the decoration in the Hadjigeorgakis Kornesios House

Archbishop Kyprianos, who was hanged by the Turks in 1821 in retaliation for the outbreak of Greek national insurgence. Kyprianos founded the first secondary school in Cyprus. The Pancyprian Gymnasium, regarded as the most prestigious high school in the Greek part of the island, exists to this day. Its Neo-Greek building is on the opposite side of the street.

Hadjigeorgakis Kornesios House ❺

Ethnological Museum Odos Patriarchou Grigoriou 20. 📞 223 05316. 🕐 8:30am–3:30pm Mon–Fri. 📷

ONE OF THE town's most interesting buildings is the House of Hadjigeorgakis Kornesios, a well-preserved building from the late 18th century. Kornesios, a highly educated Greek Cypriot businessman and philanthropist, served from 1779 as a dragoman – a liaison between the Turkish government and the Greek Cypriot population. Despite serving

the Turks for a number of years, he was arrested and executed by them.

The opulent house is decorated with Anatolian-style columns and lattice-work. The bedroom and Turkish-style drawing room lined with carpets occupy the first floor. The ground floor contains servants' quarters and a *hammam* – Turkish bath. Part of the house holds a small ethnological exhibition.

Kornesios Patriarchou Grigoriou Street leads to the nearby Omar Mosque.

Omar Mosque (Ömeriye Cami) ❻

Trikoupi and Plateia Tyllirias. 🕐 Mon–Sat 10am–12.30pm & 1.30–3.30pm. **Donations** welcome.

THIS MOSQUE takes its name from Caliph Omar, who supposedly reached Nicosia in the course of the 7th-century Arab raids on Cyprus.

The site now occupied by this mosque was once home to a 14th-century church, which served the local Augustine monastery. The Church of St Mary drew pilgrims in great numbers from Cyprus and throughout Europe to visit the tomb of the Cypriot saint John de Montfort, a member of the Knights Templar.

Minaret of the Omar Mosque

The church was converted into a mosque after the town was captured by the Turks, led by Lala Mustapha Pasha, in the 16th century. On the floor of the mosque are Gothic tombstones, used by the Turks as building material.

The mosque is used by resident Muslims from Arab countries. It is open to visitors; please remove your shoes before entering. It is also possible to climb to the top of the minaret, from where are lovely views of Nicosia.

The small, yellow-stone Cathedral of St John the Theologian

Chrysaliniotissa Church, renowned for its collection of icons

Panagia Chrysaliniotissa ❼

Chrysaliniotissas.

THE CHRYSALINIOTISSA church, the capital's oldest house of worship, is dedicated to Our Lady of the Golden Flax. It stands at the centre of the district bearing the same name, right on the Green Line. It was built in c.1450 by Helen, the Greek-born wife of the Frankish King John II. The church takes its name from a miraculous icon found in a field of flax.

This L-shape building, with two domes and a slender belfry, is famous for its collection of rare Byzantine icons.

Located nearby at Dimonaktos 2 is the small **Chrysaliniotissa Crafts Centre**.

Chrysaliniotissa church detail

Here various types of Cypriot art and handicrafts can be seen and purchased. Eight workshops, a café and a souvenir shop surround the central courtyard, which is modelled on a traditional inn.

Prior to the division of Nicosia the opposite side of Ermou Street, called Tahtakale Cami after the mosque that stood here, was home to many Turkish Cypriots. In the last few years, based on the Nicosia Master Plan, the old houses are being renovated and new occupants are moving in. Thanks to the founding of the Municipal Cultural Centre in Famagusta Gate, the district is becoming more attractive.

Famagusta Gate ❽

Leoforos Athinon. **☎** 224 30877.
⏲ Jun–Aug: 10am–1pm & 5–8pm Mon–Fri; Sep–May: 10am–1pm & 4–7pm Mon–Fri.

ONE OF THREE city gates, Famagusta Gate is situated in the Caraffa bastion of the Venetian defence walls. Low-built and comprising a log tunnel ending at a wooden gate, it resembles the Venetian gate from Iraklion, on Crete. The side facing town is decorated with six Venetian coats-of-arms.

The structure was thoroughly renovated in the 1980s. Now it houses the **Municipal Cultural Centre**. The main room is used for exhibitions, concerts and theatrical performances. The smaller side room is devoted to art exhibitions. Thanks to the Cultural Centre, this part of town has been transformed into a pleasant artists' district.

ENVIRONS: The medieval Venetian defence walls are the most distinctive element of old Nicosia. They were erected during 1567–70 to a

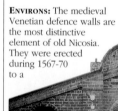

Famagusta Gate, housing Nicosia's Municipal Cultural Centre

design by Italian architect Giulio Savorgnano. The present-day Famagusta Gate was originally called the Porta Giuliana, in honour of the architect.

The 5-km (3-mile) long Venetian walls contain 11 artillery bastions and 3 gates – the other two are called the Pafos and Kyrenia Gates, after the towns they face.

The defence walls fit in well with Nicosia's overall appearance. The bastions and the areas between them have been converted into car parks and market squares. The d'Avila bastion, near the Plateia Elefteria (Eleftheria Square), is the site of the town hall and the municipal library. The Podocataro bastion features the Liberty Monument, which depicts the goddess of Liberty clad in ancient robes, while two EOKA soldiers at her feet open prison bars from which a group of Cypriots emerges.

Costanza Bastion ❾

Leoforos Konstantinou Palaiologou.
⬛ Wed. Bayraktar Mosque closed to visitors

ONE OF THE 11 bastions protruding from the Venetian walls encircling the old quarter of Nicosia, Costanza Bastion is the site of the Bayraktar mosque, which was erected to commemorate the Turkish soldier, who was killed as he scaled the defence wall during the siege of Nicosia.

Every Wednesday, the area in front of the mosque turns into a fruit and vegetable market.

Entrance to the town hall building, resting on Ionian columns

Town Hall ❿

Plateia Eleftheria (Eleftheria Square).

BUILT IN THE CLASSICAL Greek style, the single-storey town hall stands on the d'Avila bastion, next to the municipal library. An ornamental semicircular stairway leads to the portal, which rests on Ionian columns. **Plateia Eleftheria** (Eleftheria Square) opposite the town hall, is where Nicosians gather for public rallies.

Eleftheria Square is the starting point for the two main shopping streets of old Nicosia: **Onasagorou** and **Ledra**. Both are lined with dozens of shops selling shoes, clothes, textiles and souvenirs.

At the end of Ledra Street, whose name evokes the ancient town that once stood on the site of present-day Nicosia, is a barricade alongside the buffer zone, with a monument to those Greek Cypriots who disappeared during the Turkish invasion. There is also a small museum here.

Laiki Geitonia ⓫

THE PEDESTRIANIZED Laiki Geitonia (Popular Neighbourhood) is a restored section of Old Nicosia near the brooding Venetian defence walls, the town hall and Ledra – South Nicosia's main shopping street. Clustered within a small area of narrow, winding alleys in prettily restored houses are numerous restaurants, shady cafés, handicraft workshops and souvenir shops aimed primarily at tourists. Here you will also find tourist information offices, offering free maps and brochures.

The project to rebuild and restore the Laiki Geitonia district was honoured with the prestigious Golden Apple ("Pomme d'Or") Award, granted by the World Federation of Journalists and Travel Writers in 1988. The district has an inviting atmosphere, well suited to relaxing or a leisurely stroll.

Guided tours around South Nicosia start from outside the Cyprus Tourist Organization office located at 35 Odos Aristokyprou, in the Laiki Geitonia district. It is worth joining one of these tours, as they take visitors to many interesting sites that are normally closed to tourists.

Leventis Museum ⓬

Ippokratous 17, Laiki Geitonia.
📞 226 61475. ⏰ 10am–4:30pm Tue–Sun.

THE FASCINATING Leventis Museum houses a collection devoted to the history of Nicosia, from ancient times to the 1970s.

Its creators have succeeded in putting together an intriguing exhibition showing the everyday life of Nicosia's residents. Visitors are particularly drawn to the exhibits relating to the times of the Franks and the Venetians, including medieval manuscripts and the opulent clothes of the city's rulers. Also of note are the documents and photographs dating from the colonial era.

The restored building which houses the museum was built in 1885 by a rich merchant for his daughter.

An exhibit from the Leventis Museum

ENVIRONS: The pedestrianized Ledra street, which is full of shops, can be reached by walking along the Green Line. The military checkpoint here houses a small exhibition devoted to the island's northern territories, occupied by the Turks. Here, you can peer at the Turkish side through peep-holes in the concrete barricade, and also take photographs (photography at the other checkpoints is prohibited).

Inside a souvenir shop in Laiki Geitonia

Tripiotis Church  ⓭

Odos Solonos. ☐ *all day, except for lunch break.*

DEDICATED TO THE Archangel Gabriel, Tripiotis Church is the loveliest of the surviving Gothic churches in south Nicosia. This three-aisle, square edifice topped with a small dome was built in 1695 by Archbishop Germanos. Designed in the Franco-Byzantine style, it has an interesting interior with Gothic windows, while the exterior has a medieval stone relief depicting lions, mermaids and sea monsters. The pride of the church is its intricately carved iconostasis, which contains several old icons covered with silver revetments. The church takes its name from the district of Nicosia in which it stands, an area that was once inhabited by very wealthy families.

View of the three-aisled Tripiotis Church

Bank of Cyprus Cultural Foundation ⓮

Phaneromeni 86–90. **☎** 226 77134. ☐ *10am–7pm daily.*

ONE OF CYPRUS'S most prominent private art collections, the George and Nefeli Giabra Pierides collection, is housed here. The Cultural Foundation is an institution that sponsors scientific research and conducts educational and cultural activities. The magnificent exhibits representing works from the early Bronze Age (2,500 BC) to the end of the Middle Ages, are superbly displayed and illuminated in modern cabinets. The exhibits, numbering over 600 items, include ancient bronze and gold jewellery and Mycenaean amphorae and goblets decorated with images of bulls, dancers and octopuses. Also on display are terracotta figurines, anthropomorphic red-polished

Jug, Bank of Cyprus Cultural Foundation

vases and realistic limestone Hellenic statues depicting, among others, Apollo and Hercules. Glazed ceramics dating from the Middle Ages can also be seen.

Close to the Bank of Cyprus Cultural Foundation stands the **Agia Faneromeni church**, the largest church within the city walls, built in 1872 on the site of a former Greek Orthodox monastery. *Faneromeni* in Greek means "found through revelation". The church was built towards the end of Turkish rule on the island. Inside is a beautiful iconostas and a marble mausoleum containing the remains of the bishops and Greek priests who were murdered by the Turks in 1821.

Adjacent to the church is the imposing Neo-Classical building of the **Faneromeni High School**.

Araplar Mosque ⓯

Odos Lefkonos.

STANDING CLOSE to the Agia Faneromeni church, the Araplar Mosque was founded in the converted 16th-century Stavros tou Missirikou Church, which had been designed in the Gothic-Byzantine style.

Although the mosque is usually closed, it is sometimes possible to peek inside and see its imposing interior with the octagonal-drummed dome supported on columned arches.

Cyprus Museum ⓰

Leoforos Mouseiou 1. **☎** 228 65888. ☐ *9am–5pm Mon–Sat, 10am–1pm Sun.* 🖾

THE ISLAND'S LARGEST and best archaeological museum occupies a late 19th-century Neo-Classical building. The dozen or so rooms house a range of exhibits illustrating the history of Cyprus, from the Neolithic Era (7,000 BC) to the end of Roman rule (395 AD).

The museum is arranged in chronological order. **Room 1** displays the oldest traces of mankind's presence on the island. There are objects from the mid-5th century BC, as well as objects from Khirokitia, stone bowls, primitive human and animal figures carved in andesite, limestone idols, and jewellery made of shells and cornelian (which would have been imported to Cyprus). There are also early ceramics, both without decoration and with simple geometric patterns, Bronze Age amulets and cross-shaped figurines carved in soft, grey steatite.

Room 2 contains clay bowls and vessels of sometimes bizarre shapes, decorated with figurines of animals. Here you will find a miniature model of a temple and a collection of ceramic vessels and figurines. **Room 3**

houses a collection of ceramics up to Roman times, including lovely Mycenaean vases and craters dating from the 15th century BC. Later, the ceramics became gradually more Greek in style. There is also a collection of several thousand terracotta figurines depicting smiling gods.

Room 4 holds a collection of terracotta votive figurines found in the Agis Eirini sanctuary near the Kormakitis peninsula, in the north of the island. The most interesting exhibits in the sculpture gallery, in **Room 5**, include the statue of Zeus, the God of Thunder, hurling a lightning-bolt. Also here is a stone head of Aphrodite, the famous marble statue of Aphrodite of Soloi dating from the 1st century AD (by this time under Turkish occupation), and an exquisite Sleeping Eros.

Room 6 features a larger-than-life bronze statue of the Emperor Septimius Severus (c.193-211), a masterpiece of Roman sculpture. The adjoining rooms contain a bronze statue of a Horned God from Enkomi at the eastern end of the island, as well as interesting collections of coins, jewellery, seals and other small artifacts. There are also sarcophagi, inscriptions, alabaster vases and the mosaic of Leda with the Swan found in Palea Pafos **(Room 7a)**.

Further rooms contain reconstructed ancient tombs, as well as numerous items found during excavations in the Salamis area, including the marble statue of Apollo with a lyre. **Room 11** contains a reconstructed royal tomb from Salamis with the famous bronze cauldron decorated with griffon and heads of sphinxes that was found inside. **Room 12** houses items found in the Royal Tombs, including a throne decorated with ivory and a silver-encrusted sword. Other interesting exhibits include a collection of silver and gold Byzantine vessels – part of the Lambousa Treasure.

The **Municipal Garden**, on the opposite side of the street, is a green oasis set in the town centre, providing welcome shade on hot days. It is the site of the **municipal theatre** built in 1967. With an auditorium for 1,200, it is used as a venue for drama performances, concerts, recitals and other cultural events. A short distance away, in Leoforos Nehrou, stands the **Cyprus Parliament** building.

Adjacent to the nearby Pafos Gate, right by the demarcation line that divides the city, stands the Roman Catholic **Church of the Holy Cross** and the **Apostolic Nunciature**. A short distance away, by the hotel, is a UN-controlled border crossing, linking the two parts of the town. The **Ledra Palace Hotel** is the headquarters of the UN Peacekeeping Forces in Cyprus.

Neo-Classical facade of the Cyprus Museum

Bronze statue of Septimius Severus, the Cyprus Museum

State Gallery of Contemporary Art ⑰

Corner of Leoforos Stasinou and Kritis. ☎ 223 04947. ◷ 10am–5pm Mon–Fri, 10am–1pm Sat.

THIS GALLERY occupies a splendid building situated beyond the wall, level with the Constanza bastion. It displays a representative collection of the best works by Cypriot artists, dating from 1930-80.

When entering Nicosia from the south you will come across the **Cyprus Handicraft Centre**, situated in Athalassa Avenue, in a new building adjacent to St Barnabas Church. Here you can see the production of traditional Cypriot handicrafts, including embroidery, lace, woodcarvings, ceramics, metalwork, mosaics, the making of leather and textile goods and traditional costumes. The Centre was established in order to cultivate the tradition of artistic handicrafts in Cyprus, and give employment to refugees from the occupied territories. Visitors may watch artists at work and buy their products in the local shop.

ENVIRONS: In the suburban district of Strovolos, 2.5 km (1.5 miles) southwest of the Old Town, stands the **Presidential Palace**. It is located in an extensive park, with only its dome visible from the street. Built by the British, the palace was destroyed by fire during the riot of 1931. Rebuilt by the British Governor, Sir Ronald Storrs, it became his official residence. The first president of the independent Republic of Cyprus, Archbishop Makarios, had his office here and lived in the Archbishop's Palace in Old Nicosia.

NORTH CYPRUS

INHABITED AND GOVERNED BY THE TURKS, *and isolated from the southern Greek side of the island for over 30 years, North Cyprus is probably the most beautiful region of the entire island. The sandy beaches along Famagusta Bay and the wild Karpas peninsula attract thousands of tourists, although there are still far fewer here than in southern Cyprus. The heart of the region is North Nicosia, home to over one third of the population of North Cyprus.*

Most hotels and facilities can be found on the northern side of the Pentadaktylos mountains, whose rugged peaks contrast with the azure of the sea. Kyrenia (Girne) has a charming yacht harbour, one of the most attractive in the Mediterranean, with a vast, old castle recalling the time the island was under Byzantine rule. Nearby, on the northern slopes of the Pentadaktylos range (Beşparmak), lies the most beautiful village in Cyprus – Bellapais, with the romantic ruins of a Gothic abbey. Nearby St Hilarion Castle is one of three fortresses in North Cyprus, alongside the castles of Buffavento and Kantara.

The western plains, in the vicinity of Morphou (Güzelyurt), are planted with citrus orchards. Wedged between the mountains and the blue sea are the archaeological excavation sites of Soli and ruins of the Persian Palace, located on top of Vouni Hill.

Numerous fascinating relics from the Lusignan, Venetian and Ottoman eras are enclosed by the Venetian walls of north Nicosia. Old Famagusta, full of Gothic remains, is equally interesting, with its Othello's Tower and several fascinating historic relics close by – including ancient Salamis (the island's first capital), as well as Enkomi, and St Barnabas monastery.

Nature lovers will be enchanted by the Karpas peninsula, inhabited by tortoises and feral donkeys and boasting nearly 60 species of orchid.

A fruit and vegetable stall in Belediye Bazaar, in North Nicosia

◁ **A view through the Gothic Bellapais Abbey**

Exploring North Cyprus

U NTIL RECENTLY THIS REGION was fairly inaccessible,
but is now visited by increasing numbers of
tourists. The largest choice of hotels can be
found in the regions of Kyrenia and Famagusta.
North Nicosia (Lefkoşa) has only two hotels
recommended by the local Ministry of Tourism.
The area has good main roads, and is best
explored by car. Nicosia, the world's only
divided capital, is full of medieval churches,
caravansarais and museums. The same can be
said of Famagusta, whose old town, enclosed by
a ring of Venetian walls, has a unique atmosphere.
Nature lovers will be drawn to the wild Karpas
peninsula, while those interested in architecture
should travel to the Kyrenia mountains, with its
medieval castles and Bellapais Abbey.

**Window from the Church of St Mary
of Carmel Mountain, in Famagusta**

**CAPE KORMAKITIS
22 (KORUÇAM BURNU)**

**LAMBOUSA
(LAMBUSA) 18**

**KARAVAS
(ALSANCAK)** **KYRENIA
(GIRNE)**

**ANTIFONI
MONASTI**

21

**KORMAKITIS
(KORUÇAM)**

**LAPITHOS
(LAPTA) 19**

20

16

17

15 BELLAPAIS

**ST. HILARION
CASTLE**

**14 BUFFAVENTO
CASTLE**

**LARNAKA
TIS LAPITHOU
(KOZAN)**

**KYTHREA
(DEĞIRMEN**

**NORTH
NICOSIA
(LEFKOŞA) 1**

Serrachis

23

**VOUNI
26 (VUNI SARAYI)**

**MORPHOU
(GÜZELYURT)**

Kakopetria

**MOUSOULI
(KURUDER**

25 SOLOI (SOLI HARABELERI)

Kakopetria

**TYMVOU
(KIRKLAR)**

**V.
(VA**

24 LÉFKA (LEFKE)

Glafias

Apostolos Varnavas Monastery, built near the tomb of St Barnabas

KEY

▬▬	Major road
▬▬	Scenic route
=	Other road
=	River
✷	Viewpoint

GETTING THERE

There are no direct flights to Ercan (Tymbou) Airport from anywhere but Turkey, and ferries sail only from Turkish ports. These include a twice-daily service from Tasucu, a three-times-a-week sailing from Mersin and a catamaran ferry from Alanya (summer only). EU passport holders may cross from the south of the island to the north via the pedestrians-only Ledra Palace crossing point or via one of three vehicle crossing points (at Agios Dometios, Pergamos and Strovilia). North Cyprus is best explored by car but you will need to take out inexpensive special insurance if using a car rented in the South.

The picturesque harbour of Kyrenia

APOSTOLOS ANDREAS ⑫

RIZOKARPASO (DIPKARPAZ)

YIALOUSA (YENIERENKÖY) ⑪ **KARPAS PENINSULA**

0 km — 20
0 miles — 20

GALATEIA (MEHMETCIK) **KOMA TOU GIALOU (KUMYALI)**

KANTARA CASTLE ⑩

AKANTHOU (TATLISU)

BOGAZI (BOĞAZ) ⑨
TRIKOMO (İSKELE) ⑧

LEFKONOIKO (GECITKALE)

ST. BARNABUS MONASTERY

ROYAL TOMBS ④ ⑤ ⑥ **SALAMIS**
③ **ENKOMI-ALASIA**

⑦
FAMAGUSTA (GAZIMAĞUSA)

LYSI (AKDOĞAN)

Paralimni

The view from St Hilarion castle

SEE ALSO

SIGHTS AT A GLANCE

North Nicosia (Lefkoşa) ❶

Atatürk

FOLLOWING THE INVASION by Turkish troops in 1974, the northern part of Nicosia became the capital of the Turkish part of the island. It is home to over half the population of North Cyprus, as well as the seat of government. It is also the administrative, business, banking and commercial centre of North Cyprus. The majority of local historic relics are found within the old Venetian walls – Gothic churches turned into mosques, bazaars, Ottoman fountains, baths and caravansarais stand among the often ugly residential buildings.

Exploring North Nicosia

The Old Town is best explored on foot. At the bus station you can board a free bus that will take you to the centre of old Lefkoşa. Do not take photographs in the vicinity of the "Green Line" that divides the city, guarded by UN and Turkish troops.

The roof terrace of the Saray Hotel in Atatürk Square (Atatürk Meydani) provides a great view. The best place for coffee and rest is the former caravanserai, Büyük Han.

🕌 Büyük Han

Asma Alti Sokagi. 🎵 *Tue, Thu (evening).*

The Big Inn, a former caravanserai, is one of the most interesting Ottoman buildings on Cyprus. The Turks built it shortly after the capture of Nicosia in 1572, as an inn for visiting merchants. Its architectural style is redolent of other inns of that period, seen in Anatolia. Under British administration, it became Nicosia's main prison.

Following its restoration, the 68 former rooms spread around the inner court-

Colourful fruit and vegetable stalls in Belediy Ekpazari bazaar

yard now house souvenir shops, art galleries, cafés and a Cypriot wine-bar. The court-yard itself features an octagonal building of a small Muslim shrine and prayer hall *(mescit)* with an ablution fountain. Büyük Han is used as a venue for theatrical performances, concerts and exhibitions.

The nearby Ottoman "Gamblers' Inn" (Kumarcilar Han), in Asma Alti Square, was built in the late 17th century. Its entrance hall features two Gothic arches, since the inn was built on the ruins of a former monastery. Now it houses the North Cyprus centre for the conservation of historic sites.

🏛 Belediye Ekpazari

🕐 6am–3pm Mon–Fri, 6am–1pm Sat.

This covered bazaar, situated between the Bedesten and the "Green Line" that bisects old Nicosia, was the main shopping area in Ottoman times. It remains a market, where you can buy fresh meat and vegetables, as well as Turkish sweets and souvenirs. Hanging by the exit from the bazaar, on the wall of one of the houses, a plaque marks the centre of the Old Town.

🕌 Bedesten

By the Selima mosque. 🕐 *daily.*

This 12th-century Byzantine Church of St George was remodelled in the 14th century in the Gothic style by the Lusignan kings. Following the 16th-century occupation of Nicosia by the Turks, it was used as a warehouse, and subsequently as a market for selling jewellery and other precious metal objects. The word *bedesten* means "lockable bazaar". The north wall has an original Gothic portal, a variety of carved stonework elements and the escutcheons of the Venetian nobility.

Selima mosque, the former Gothic Cathedral Church of St Sophia

🇨 Selima Mosque (Selimiye Cami)

At the centre of the old town, in Arasta Sokagi. 🕐 *Mon–Fri.*

The former Cathedral Church of St Sophia (the Divine Wisdom), erected by the Lusignan kings from 1208 to 1326, is the oldest and finest example of Gothic architecture in Cyprus. It was once regarded as the most magnificent Christian sacred building in the Middle East. Its unique features include the entrance portal, stone-carved window and massive columns that support the criss-cross vaulting.

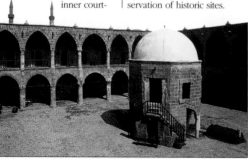

Büyük Han, a former caravanserai with a Muslim shrine in the courtyard

It was in this church that the Frankish rulers were crowned kings of Cyprus. This ceremony preceded a second, purely nominal, coronation as Kings of Jerusalem, performed in St Nicholas's Cathedral, in Famagusta.

The cathedral was destroyed, in turn, by the Genoese, the Mamelukes and several major earth-quakes. Following

Shield above entrance to Lapidary Museum

the capture of Nicosia by the Turks in 1570, the cathedral was transformed into Hagia Sophia mosque, which, in 1954, was renamed Selima Mosque (Cami Selimiye).

All images of people and animals have been removed, and the Gothic stone sculptures in the main portal have been chipped away. The interior has been stripped of all orna-mentation and painted white. Two 50-m (164-ft) tall minarets, entirely out of keeping with the rest of the building, have been added on the sides of the main facade.

Other adaptations made to the interior include the addition of three *mihrabs* indicating the direction of Mecca, and carpets.

🏛 Sultan Mahmut II Library

Kirilzade Sokagi. ⬭ *Mon–Sat.* 🔖
This small domed, stone build-ing is a classic example of Ottoman architecture. It was erected in 1829 by Turkish governor, Al Ruchi. It con-tains a collection of 1,700 books and oriental manu-scripts, richly orna-mented copies of the Koran and exquisite works of Turkish and Persian calligraphers.

🏛 Lapidary Museum

Kirilzade Sokagi. ⬭ *Mon–Fri.*
The 15th-century Venetian building at the rear of the Selima Mosque, near Sultam Mahmut II Library, houses a collection of stone sculptures removed from Gothic tombs, old houses and churches.

The garden includes a Lusignan royal sarcophagus, fragments of columns, stone rosettes and Venetian winged lions of St Mark.

🅲 Haydarpaşa Mosque

Haydarpasa Sokagi. ⬭ *9am–1pm & 2–5pm Mon–Fri, 9am–1pm Sat.*
This building was originally St Catherine's Church, erected by the Lusignans in the 14th century in flamboyant Gothic

VISITORS' CHECKLIST

Road map D3. 🏠 102,000.
ⓘ *Kyrenia Gate, 815 2145.* 🚌
Kemal Asik (adjacent to Atatürk Cad.) ✈ *Ercan, 20 km (12 miles) southeast of North Nicosia. The border crossing to South Nicosia is by the Ledra Palace Hotel.*

style. Their coats of arms can be seen on the south portal in magnificently carved stone.

Following the occupation of Nicosia, the Turks converted the beautiful church into Camii Haydarpaşa (Haydarpaşa Mosque), adding a dispropor-tionate minaret. Today it houses a modern art gallery.

Haydarpaşa Mosque, originally the Gothic church of St Catherine

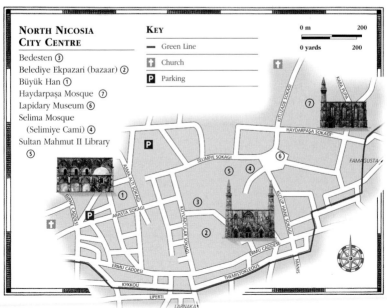

NORTH NICOSIA CITY CENTRE

Bedesten ③
Belediye Ekpazari (bazaar) ②
Büyük Han ①
Haydarpaşa Mosque ⑦
Lapidary Museum ⑥
Selima Mosque (Selimiye Cami) ④
Sultan Mahmut II Library ⑤

KEY

— Green Line
🔒 Church
🅿 Parking

0 m — 200
0 yards — 200

⚜ Venetian Walls

Construction of the Venetian defence walls that encircle the Old Town of Nicosia was completed in 1567, three years before the Turkish invasion. Of the 11 bastions in the walls, five are now in the northern, Turkish sector. The **Quirini** (Cephane) bastion is now the official residence of the president of the Republic of North Cyprus. The **Barbaro** (Musalla) bastion houses the National Struggle Museum set up by the army. The **Roccas** (Kaytazağa) bastion is now a park. The other two in the Turkish sector are **Mula** (Zahra) and **Loredano** (Cevizli). A sixth bastion – **Flatro** – is split across the "Green Line" between the Greek and Turkish Cypriots.

Also on the north side is the **Kyrenia Gate**, one of the three original gates leading to the Venetian fortress.

At this point, the "no man's land" close to the Pafos Gate is at its narrowest; a mere few metres separate the Greeks strolling along the street from the Turks on the bastion.

⚜ Kyrenia Gate

Girne Caddesi, by Inönu Meydani.
The Kyrenia Gate between the Quirini and Barbaro bastions was once the main entrance to north Nicosia. It was originally named Porta del Proveditore, in honour of the Venetian engineer who supervised the fortification works. The gate walls bear inscriptions dating from the Venetian and Ottoman eras. The Turks erected the square, domed building above the gate

The northernmost Kyrenia Gate

Figures of Whirling Dervishes in Mevlevi Tekke

in 1812. The street on either side of the gate was laid out in 1931 by the British, who took down part of the Venetian wall. Today, Kyrenia Gate houses a tourist information office.

Between the gate and the Atatürk monument are two huge iron cannons; several more have been placed along the walls. Although badly corroded, some of them still display British insignia. The cannons were cast in the late 18th century and used during the Napoleonic Wars.

🅒 Mevlevi Tekke

Girne Caddesi. ⭕ winter: 9am–1pm & 2–4:45pm; summer: 7:30am–2pm. 📷
Less than 100 m (328 ft) south of Kyrenia Gate is the entrance to this small museum. It is housed in the former Muslim monastery (*tekke*) of the Mevlevi order (the Whirling Dervishes) that existed here until the middle of the 20th century. A kind of monastic brotherhood, it was founded in 13th century in Konya by the poet Celaleddin Rumi, later known as Mevlana and revered as one of Islam's greatest mystics. Dervishes whirl to the music of a reed flute, a Levantine lute and a drum. To them, the dance represents the spiritual search

A tombstone from Mevlevi Tekke

for Divine Love, and provides a means of inducing ecstasy that frees human beings from all suffering and fear.

The museum includes figures of Whirling Dervishes accompanied by an instrumental trio sitting in the gallery. The display cabinets contain musical instruments, traditional costumes, small metal objects (such as knives), embroidery, photographs, illuminated copies of the Koran and other Turkish mementoes. The adjacent hall features a replica of a dervish's living quarters. Next to this is a mausoleum with sarcophagi covered with green cloth, containing the bodies of 15 religious leaders, including the last leader of the order, Selim Dede, who died in 1953. In the courtyard are several tombstones from a former cemetery that occupied this site.

🛁 Büyük Hamam

Irfanbey Sokagi 9. ⭕ 10am–10pm daily. 📷 for a bath.
This building, erected in the 14th century, was originally the Church of St George. After capturing the town, the Turks converted it into municipal baths. Steep stairs lead down through a Gothic portal to the large hall, and from there to the bathing rooms.

The baths are open to the public; you can also treat yourself to a Turkish massage. Visitors are charged higher prices than the locals.

🏛 Atatürk Square (Saray Square)

Atatürk Meydani, also known as Sarajönü, was the political centre of Cyprus for many centuries. On the north side of the square stood a palace inhabited, in turn, by the Frankish, Venetian and Turkish rulers, or their commissioners. In 1904, the British dismantled the 700-year-old palace complex, with its splendid throne room, opulent staterooms and cloistered courtyard.

Atatürk Square is the main square of Turkish Nicosia. The grey granite column at its centre was brought here from Salamis by the Venetians. In Venetian times, the column bore the Lion of St Mark, while its base was decorated with the coats-of-arms of the Venetian nobility. The Turks overturned the column; the British raised it again in 1915 and added a globe in place of the lion.

The northern end of the square features a stone platform with the British national emblem, erected here in 1953 to commemorate the coronation of Queen Elizabeth II.

Nearby are the courts of law, police headquarters, numerous banks and a post office, which was built by the British.

Atatürk Meydani, the main square in the Turkish zone of Nicosia

The Dervish Pasha Mansion

🏛 Dervish Pasha Mansion

Belig Paşa Sokagi. ◯ winter: 9am–1pm & 2–4:45pm; summer: 9am–7pm. 📷

This two-storey building, typical of early 19th-century Turkish architecture, was owned by Dervish Pasha, the publisher of Cyprus's first Turkish newspaper, *Zaman* (meaning "Time"). Archival copies of the paper, published since 1891, can be seen among the other exhibits here.

Following its restoration, the building has been turned into an ethnographic museum, where you can see a panelled and carpet-lined drawing room, dining room, bedroom, and even a bridal room. The exhibits include embroidery, jewellery, hookahs, lamps, ceramics and copperware.

The ground floor, intended as servants' quarters, is built of stone, while the upper floor, which was occupied by the owner, is built of brick.

🏛 Arabahmet District

Stretching southwest of Kyrenia Gate (Girne Caddesi), the Arabahmet district is full of imposing Ottoman houses, restored partly with funding from the European Union. At the junction of Zahra and Tanzimat, close to the Mula bastion, is an octagonal Ottoman fountain, somewhat neglected today.

Until 1963, this district was home to residents from a variety of countries, including Greece and Armenia. There was even an Armenian church dedicated to the Virgin Mary, which was originally a Benedictine monastery. Nowadays the church stands in the closed military zone.

The **Holy Cross Church**, straddling the border, has an entrance from the Greek side. Its tower, topped with a cross, dominates the entire Arabahmet district.

The **Roccas bastion** (Kaytazaga), which overlooks the "Green Line", was turned into a municipal garden in the 1990s. This is the only place in Nicosia where the buffer zone vanishes and the inhabitants of both sides of divided Nicosia can see each other. Photography, as is to be expected, is prohibited.

🕌 Arabahmet Mosque (Arabahmet Cami)

Salahi Sevket Sokagi.

Standing at the centre of the Arabahmet district is the Arabahmet Cami, covered with a vast dome. Built in the early 17th century on the site of a former Lusignan church, it was remodelled in 1845. The mosque was named after the Turkish military commander, Arab Ahmet Pasha.

The floor is paved with medieval tombstones taken from the church that formerly stood on this site. In the courtyard is a fountain and several tombs, including that of Kemal Pasha, Grand Vizier of the Ottoman Empire. The mosque holds a relic – a hair believed to come from the beard of the Prophet Mohammed – that is shown to the faithful once a year.

The Arabahmet district with its traditional Ottoman houses

Lysi (Akdoğan) ②

Road map D3. 12 km (7.5 miles)
southwest of Dörtyol (Prastio).

A SMALL FARMING VILLAGE in
the southeastern part of
the Mesaoria plain, Lysi lies
close to the "Green Line". Its
most interesting historic site is
the unfinished Byzantine-style
church decorated with Neo-
Gothic architectural elements.

ENVIRONS: Along the road to
Ercan airport are the remains
of Ottoman aqueducts.
   The surrounding area is
home to several neglected
Orthodox churches, including
Agios Themonianos, Agios
Synesios, Agios Andronikos,
Agios Fotios and Moni Agiou
Spyridona monastery in
Erdemli (Tremetousha). The
latter is guarded and visitors
should not approach it.

**The unfinished Neo-Byzantine
church in Lysi**

Enkomi-Alasia ③

Road map E3. ◯ winter: 9am–1pm
& 2–4:45pm; summer: 9am–7pm. ▨

R EMAINS OF A Bronze Age
town have been found
near the village of Enkomi-
Alasia. Archaeologists estimate
that Alasia was founded in
the 18th century BC. The
town grew rich on trading in
copper, which was excavated
on the island and exported to
Anatolia, Syria and Egypt.
   Alasia was the capital of
Cyprus and its main town –
its name synonymous with
the entire island. In the 12th
century BC, when the
Mycenaeans arrived here, the
town's population numbered

**Ruins near the village of Enkomi,
a few kilometres west of Salamis**

some 15,000 – a mind-boggling
number for that time.
Following an earthquake in
the 11th century BC, the town
was deserted and its inhabitants moved to Salamis.
   Excavation works conducted
since 1896 have unearthed
the ruins of a Late Bronze
Age settlement, with low
houses lining narrow streets.
   The Alasia ruins yielded a
tablet with Cypriot-Minoan
writing, not yet deciphered,
and the famous bronze statue
of the Horned God, dating
from the 12th century BC,
which is now kept in the
Cyprus Museum in Nicosia.
Strolling around the excavation
site you will come across the
Horned God's sanctuary and
the "House of Bronzes",
where many bronze objects
were discovered.

ENVIRONS: Along the road to
Famagusta is the village of
Enkomi (Tuzla). Next to the
shop is a white platform,
known as the **cenotaph of
Nikokreon**. It contains the
remains of Nikokreon – the
last King of Salamis. Refusing
to surrender to the Hellenic
king of Egypt, Ptolemy I,
Nikokreon committed suicide

by setting fire to the royal
palace. He perished, along
with his entire family, in the
flames that day.

Royal Tombs ④

Road map E3. ◯ winter: 9am–1pm
& 2–4:45pm; summer: 9am–7pm. ▨

T HE ROYAL necropolis by the
side of the road leading to
St Barnabas monastery contains
over 100 tombs from the 8th
and 7th centuries BC. Some
have been given names, and
others designated numbers.
Almost all of the tombs are
opened to the east. Each one
was approached by a slanting
corridor known as a *dromos*,
on which the most interesting
artifacts were found.
   Most of the tombs were
looted in antiquity, but some,
in particular numbers 47 and
49, contained a multitude of
objects that could be useful to
the royals in the next world.
The most famous finds
include the ivory inlaid royal
bed and throne, showing
clear Phoenician and Egyptian
influences. The Kings of
Salamis were buried with
their servants and horses.
   Tomb number 50, the so-
called "St Catherine's prison",
was built during Roman times
on top of older tombs.
According to legend, the
Alexandrian saint, a native of
Salamis, was imprisoned by
her father, the Roman governor, for refusing to marry the
man chosen by him. The
tomb's walls bear the remnants
of Christian decorations.
   The site also features a
small museum with plans and
photographs of the tombs,
and a reconstructed chariot
used to carry the kings of
Salamis on their final journey.

Royal Tombs from the 8th and 7th centuries BC, west of Salamis

St Barnabas Monastery, built near the tomb of the apostle Barnabas

St Barnabas Monastery ❺

Road map E3. ☐ winter: 9am–1pm & 2–4:45pm; summer: 9am–7pm. 🏛

THE MONASTERY OF St Barnabas was erected in 477 on the western end of the Constantia (Salamis) necropolis, near the spot where the apostle's grave was discovered. The construction of the church and monastery was financed by the Byzantine Emperor, Zeno, himself.

Two centuries later, it was demolished in one of the devastating Arab raids on Cyprus. All that remains of the original Byzantine edifice are the foundations. The present church and monastery were constructed in 1756 on the orders of Archbishop Philotheos, during Ottoman rule. The three-aisled church is covered with two flat domes resting on high drums. It now houses an **Icon Museum**.

Much more interesting, however, is the small **Archaeological Museum** occupying former monks' cells around the courtyard of the monastery. Displayed in a series of rooms are Neolithic tools and stone vessels, as well as a large number of ceramic items such as amphorae, jugs, vases and cups. Among the more curious items are a polished

A terracotta figurine, Archaeological Museum

bronze mirror, swords, hatchets and spearheads, made of the same metal. There are also terracotta figurines of people and animals, including an unusual horse with wheels instead of hooves, and clay baby rattles shaped like boars.

Other interesting exhibits are the black-glazed ceramics imported from Attica. These are decorated with intricate motifs of animal and human figures, including lions, wild boars and hares. There is also gold jewellery, a collection of Roman glass, and a stone figure of a woman holding a poppy – probably the goddess Demeter. The Classical period is further represented by sphinxes, showing the Egyptian influence, and carved lions.

A short distance east of the monastery stands a small **Byzantine-style church**. This rectangular, domed chapel was erected over the tomb of the apostle Barnabas. A stone staircase leads down to two chambers hewn into the rock where, according to legend, St Barnabas was buried. The saint was killed near Salamis for preaching Christianity, and his body was cast into the sea. His disciples fished the body out, and he was buried with St Matthew's gospel on his chest, under a lonely breadfruit tree to the west of Salamis.

From 1971 until the Turkish occupation of 1974, the St Barnabas Monastery was inhabited by the last three monks, the brothers Barnabas, Chariton and Stephen, who made a humble living by selling honey and painting icons.

SAINT BARNABAS

Born in Salamis, Barnabas accompanied St Paul on his missionary travels around Cyprus and Asia Minor. After parting from his master, Barnabas continued to promote Christianity on the island, for which he was killed in the year 57 AD. St Mark buried the body in secret.

St Barnabas acquired fame following a miracle that occurred after his death, when he revealed the site of his burial to Anthemios, the Bishop of Salamis. The discovery of the saint's relics, and the prestige they brought, helped preserve the autonomy of the Cypriot Church.

The tomb of St Barnabas

Salamis ❻

Gymnasium Statue

THE FORMER ROMAN SALAMIS, which later became Byzantine Constantia, was the island's main port and capital for a thousand years. Destroyed by the Arabs in 648, Salamis is still the largest and the most interesting archaeological excavation site on Cyprus. The unearthed relics date from the Roman and Byzantine periods. Allow a full day for a visit, including a relaxing break on the nearby beach.

★ Caldarium
The hot bath chamber, fitted with a central heating system, had walls decorated with abstract mosaics.

Sudatorium
The Greek-Roman baths complex included a steam bath, which was also decorated with mosaics. An underfloor heating system is in evidence.

Latrines
This semicircular colonnaded struc-ture contained a latrine which could be used by 44 people simultaneously.

★ Gymnasium
A colonnade surrounded the rectangular palaestra *of the gymnasium, which was devoted to the training of athletes.*

Two pools with cold water were located beyond the east portico.

STAR SIGHTS
★ **Caldarium**
★ **Gymnasium**
★ **Roman Theatre**

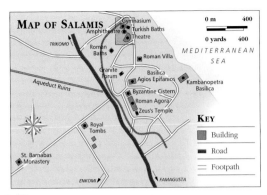

MAP OF SALAMIS

Gymnasium
Turkish Baths
Amphitheatre
Theatre
TRIKOMO
Roman
Baths
Roman Villa
Granite
Forum
Basilica
Agios Epifanios
Kambanopetra
Basilica
Byzantine Cistern
Roman Agora
Zeus's Temple
Royal
Tombs
St. Barnabas
Monastery
ENKOMI
FAMAGUSTA
MEDITERRANEAN SEA

0 m | 400
0 yards | 400

KEY

▨ Building
▬ Road
= Footpath

Aqueduct
To the east of the gymnasium are the stone cisterns and other remains of an aqueduct that used to supply the baths and the pools with water.

★ Roman Theatre
Built 2,000 years ago, during the reign of Emperor Augustus, this auditorium could hold 15,000 spectators. Today the restored theatre serves as a venue for summer performances.

Amphitheatre
Built by the Romans in the early years of the modern era, it was destroyed by an earthquake in the 6th century.

Backstage area,
with dressing rooms for the actors.

Famagusta (Gazimağusa) ●

Atatürk monument

ONCE THE WORLD'S wealthiest city, present-day Famagusta presents a somewhat depressing sight. Yet within the mighty Venetian fortifications that withstood the onslaught of the powerful Turkish army for nearly a year, and amid the many derelict buildings, are true gems of Gothic architecture. Former magnificent churches have been destroyed or turned into mosques. It was Famagusta – "a seaport in Cyprus" – that Shakespeare chose as the setting for *Othello*. South of the city lies the deserted district of Varosha, once Cyprus's biggest resort.

Namik Kemal Square, once the site of the Venetian Palace

Exploring Famagusta

Virtually all of Famagusta's major historic sites are found within the Old Town, surrounded by the Venetian fortifications. The best way to enter the city is through the Land Gate, leaving your car behind. The tourist information office is located by the gate. The city is not large; it is possible to explore it on foot.

⬛ Lala Mustafa Pasha Mosque

Namik Kemal Meydoni. 📷

This former cathedral was built in the Lusignan period between 1298 and 1312 to a Gothic design modelled on the French cathedral in Reims. It was here that Lusignan royalty, after the coronation in Nicosia, received the symbolic title of "King of Jerusalem".

Following the capture of the city in 1571, the

Gothic portal of Lala Mustafa Pasha Mosque

victorious Turks converted the cathedral into a mosque and named it after the commander of the besieging army - Lala Mustafa Pasha. They also added a minaret to the left tower. The building is still a functioning mosque; visitors are admitted only outside the hours of prayer with the purchase of a ticket.

The white interior has 12 columns to support the Gothic vaulting. There is a modest *minbar* (pulpit) in the right aisle. The façade with its unusual window and enormous rosette, basking in the light of the setting sun, is one of the most beautiful sights in Cyprus.

🏠 Agia Zoni & Agios Nikolaos

Hisar Yolou Sokagi.

This small, excellently preserved Byzantine-style church, decorated with wall paintings, dates from about the 15th century. It

stands in an empty square, surrounded by a handful of palm trees. Close by is the larger Church of St Nicholas, now partly demolished.

⬛ Fountain and Jafar Pasha Baths

Naim Effendi Sokagi.

Located northwest of Namik Kemal Square, the fountain and baths were built in 1601 in the Ottoman style by the Commander of the Sultan's Navy and the Turkish Governor of Cyprus.

Jafar Pasha ordered the building of the aqueduct in order to supply the city with water. Both the aqueduct and the original town fountain have been destroyed. The current fountain has been reconstructed using fragments salvaged from the original.

⬛ Sinan Pasha Mosque

Abdullah Paşa Sokagi.

The former church of Saints Peter and Paul was turned into a mosque after the capture of the city by the Turks. This beautiful Gothic edifice, built of yellow stone and maintained in excellent condition, now houses the municipal library collection.

A former church turned into the Sinan Pasha mosque

⬛ Venetian Palace

Namik Kemal Meydani.

Not much has survived of the former palace of the Lusignan kings and Venetian governors, constructed during Lusignan times. Nowadays the area marked by its jutting stone walls is a car park.

On the side of Namik Kemal Square stands a triple-arched façade supported by four granite columns from Salamis. Above the central arch is the coat of arms of Giovanni Renier – the Venetian military commander of Cyprus.

Remains of the Venetian Palace

VISITORS' CHECKLIST

Road map E3. 🏛 *30 000.*
ℹ️ *Land Gate, 366 2864.*
🚌 *Gazi Mustafa Kemak Boulv.*
🚏 *east of the Sea Gate (for tickets, call 366 4557).*
🎭 *Famagusta International Festival (Jun–Jul).*

Between 1873 and 1876, the left section of the building was used as a prison in which Turkish poet and playwright, Namik Kemal, was locked up on the Sultan's order. Now it houses his museum.

🏛 Nestorian Church

Somoundjouoglou Sokagi.

Francis Lakhas, a rich Syrian merchant, built this church in 1338 for Famagusta's Syrian community. The facade is adorned with a lovely rose window. Inscriptions inside the church are in Syrian – the language of the Nestorian liturgy.

Later, the church was taken over by Greek Cypriots and renamed Agios Georgios Exorinos. The word *exorinos* means "exiler". Greeks believe that dust taken from the church floor and sprinkled in the house of an enemy will make him die or leave the island within a year.

🏛 Churches of the Knights Templar and Knights Hospitaller

Kişla Sokagi.

These two adjacent medieval churches are known as the twins. On the north facade, above the entrance, you can still see the carved stone coats of arms of the Knights

Romantic ruins of the Gothic Church of St John (Latin)

Hospitaller. In the early 14th century, following the dissolution of the Knights Templar order, their monastery and the Chapel of St Anthony were handed over to the order of St John of Jerusalem (the Knights Hospitaller). The Hospitallers' chapel, featuring a lovely rose window in the facade, now houses a theatre and an art gallery.

🏛 Church of St John (Latin)

Cafer Paşa Sokagi.

Built in the late 13th century, during the reign of the French king Louis IX, the Church of St John was one of Famagusta's ealiest churches, and a splendid example of Gothic architecture. Now largely in ruins, the original north wall with the presbytery and tall Gothic windows remains standing. The capital of the surviving column is decorated with floral motifs and winged dragons.

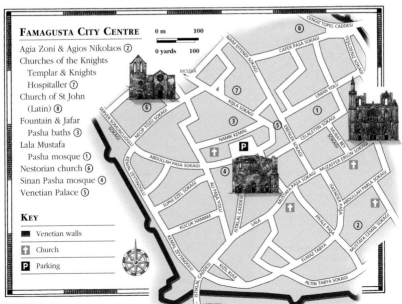

FAMAGUSTA CITY CENTRE

Agia Zoni & Agios Nikolaos ②
Churches of the Knights
  Templar & Knights
  Hospitaller ⑦
Church of St John
  (Latin) ⑧
Fountain & Jafar
  Pasha baths ③
Lala Mustafa
  Pasha mosque ①
Nestorian church ⑥
Sinan Pasha mosque ④
Venetian Palace ⑤

KEY

▬ Venetian walls
✝ Church
🅿 Parking

0 m   100
0 yards   100

🔒 Agios Ioannis

Varosha (Maraş). Polat Pasa Bulvari.
Icon Museum ☐ *summer: 9am–2pm; winter: 9am–1pm & 2–4:45pm.* 📷

The Neo-Byzantine Church of St John stands in the Varosha (Maras) district of Famagusta, where the Turkish army is currently stationed. The recently renovated church houses a museum of icons, mostly from the 18th century, that were gathered together from many destroyed Greek Orthodox churches.

The Varosha area, controlled by Turkish and UN forces, has been uninhabited for more than 30 years, ever since the expulsion of the Greek Cypriots. It is forbidden to photograph the crumbling houses or dozens of decaying beachfront

Iconostasis in Agios Ioannis Church

🏛 Canbulat Bastion

☐ *summer: 9am–5pm; winter: 9am–1pm & 2–4:45pm.* 📷

The bastion at the southeast corner of the Venetian defence walls was once called the Arsenal. Today it bears the name of the Turkish commander, Canbulat, who charged his horse at the Venetian war machine, which was studded with spinning knives, during the siege of Famagusta. Canbulat perished, cut to shreds, but his desperate attack put the machine out of action, and the Turks regard him as a hero. The bastion contains his tomb and a small museum with a collection of artifacts dating from antiquity and the Ottoman era.

🏛 Venetian City Walls

Famagusta's Old Town is encircled by huge defence walls erected by the Venetians, who felt threatened by the

Ruins of the Citadel (Othello's Tower)

Ottoman Empire's expansion into the eastern Mediterranean. The walls, 15 m (49 ft) high and up to 8 m (26 ft) thick, are reinforced with 15 bastions. The two gates leading to the town are the Land Gate and Sea Gate, which was constructed by the Venetian, Nicolo Prioli. His name, coat of arms, construction date (1496) and the Lion of St Mark have been carved in the marble brought from the ruins of Salamis.

To the right of the entrance are two marble statues of lions. Legend has it that one night the larger of the two will open its mouth, and the person who sticks his head in at that moment will win a fortune.

The entrance to the Old Town from the opposite side leads over a stone bridge that spans the moat. It is defended by the massive Rivettina (Ravelin) Bastion, which the Turks call Akkule ("White Tower"). It was here that the Venetians hoisted the white flag following the 10-month siege of

Famagusta in 1571 by the Turkish army. From the Old Town side you can see wall paintings and the coats of arms of the Venetian commanders.

The passageway features a small shrine. The restored rooms beyond the gate now house the tourist information bureau. Under the Rivettina Bastion are subterranean casemates. In 1619, a small mosque was built for the Muslim guards.

🏛 Citadel (Othello's Tower)

Cengiz Topel Caddesi (adjacent to the Sea Gate). ☐ *summer: 10am–5pm; winter: 9am–1pm & 2–4:45pm.* 📷

The Citadel was erected in the 12th century by the Lusignan Kings, to defend Famagusta Harbour from attack. Carved in marble above the gate are the Lions of St Mark (symbolizing Venice) and the name of Nicolo Foscari, who supervised the rebuilding of the fortress in 1492. This was a vast structure for its time, and it included a system of fortifications and subterranean casemates.

The Citadel is popularly known as Othello's Tower, after Shakespeare's play *Othello*, which was set largely in Famagusta. The empty interiors, Gothic rooms and gloomy casemates are now inhabited by pigeons, and the floors littered with discarded bullets and fragments of broken sculptures.

The Citadel walls afford a magnificent view over old Famagusta and the harbour.

The massive Venetian defence walls

🔒 St George of the Greeks Church

Mustafa Ersu Sokagi.
Erected in the 15th century, in Gothic-Byzantine style, just a shell remains of this church. The east apse still shows the fragments of wall paintings. The steps in the nave are typical of early Christian basilicas.

The roof was brought down by Turkish bombardment in the siege of Famagusta. To this day, the walls bear pockmarks of cannonballs. Legend says that a treasure belonging to St Epifanos (Archbishop of Salamis) lies under the floor.

Abutting the church to the south is the smaller church of Agios Symeon (St Simon's).

Biddulph Gate – a remnant of a Venetian merchant's home

🏛 Biddulph Gate

Naim Effendi Sokagi. ◯ 8am–5:30pm daily.
This Renaissance gate standing in a side street is a remnant of a medieval merchant's house. It was named in honour of Sir Robert Biddulph, British High Commissioner, who saved it from being pulled down in 1879. Departing from the usual custom of demolishing old structures, Biddulph pioneered the protection of Famagusta's historic sites.

Another interesting relic found along Naim Effendi Sokagi is an old, intact merchant's house, an excellent example of secular Renaissance architecture.

🔒 Churches in North Famagusta

The area at the north end of old Famagusta, around the Martinengo, San Luca and Pulacazara bastions, was, until recently, occupied by the Turkish army. Now some of its historic sites are open to visitors. Among them is the rectangular **church of St Mary**

Ruins of St George of the Greeks Church

of Carmel, built of a yellow stone. It may be viewed only from the outside. The adjacent **Armenian Church** was built in the 16th century, when the Armenians had their Bishops in Nicosia and Famagusta. The interior is covered with paintings and Armenian inscriptions. A short distance away, in the direction of the Moratto bastion and beyond the Tanner's mosque, stands the splendidly preserved medieval **church of St Anna**, featuring an unusual belfry rising above the facade; unfortunately it is closed to visitors.

🏛 Medresa

Liman Yolu Sokagi.
The single-storey domed building to the north of the Lala Mustafa Pasa mosque was once a college of Islamic studies, attached to an Ottoman mosque. Nowadays it would be difficult to discern any particular style in it, although it is often cited as an example of classic Ottoman architecture. The two granite columns brought from Salamis, and placed in front of the building, add to the overall impression of architectural chaos.

Coat of arms, St Mary of Carmel Church

The stone plinth opposite the entrance bears the bust of Namik Kemal, a 19th-century Turkish poet and playwright, who, on orders of the Sultan, was imprisoned in the Venetian Palace opposite. To the right are two domed Turkish tombs, one with an interesting wrought-iron gate.

After serving as a college, the former medresa was later used as offices, and then as bank premises. Today the building stands empty.

🏛 Tanner's Mosque

Somoundjouoglou Sokagi.
This small, yellow limestone building was erected in the late 16th century as a church. In 1571, following the capture of Famagusta by the Turks, it was converted into a mosque. Clay pots were built into its vaults, intended to improve the general acoustics of the building.

The mosque was later abandoned and left to decay. Since 1974 the building has been contained within a fenced-off compound used by the Turkish army; it now serves as a depot.

Ruins of St Mary of Carmel Church seen at sunset

Trikomo (İskele) ❽

Road map E2.

THIS SMALL TOWN lies close to the base of the Karpas peninsula. At its centre, right by the roundabout, stands the tiny Dominican **Church of St James** (Agios Iakovos). Intricately carved in stone, it resembles an encrusted jewellery box. At the western end of the town stands the two-aisled, single domed **church of Panagia Thetokos**, which was erected in the 12th century. The church was restored in 1804, when it was also given its marble-panelled belfry. Inside you can still see the original wall paintings dating from the 12th century.

The **Icon Museum**, opened here in 1991, houses a collection of icons removed from the local Greek churches. The images are modern and of little artistic merit, yet the museum is worth visiting for its lovely interior frescoes.

🏛 **Icon Museum**
Panagia Theotokos Church. ⬤ *summer: 9am–7pm; winter: 9am–1pm & 2–4:45pm.* 🖼

A mosque in Trikomo, a town at the base of the Karpas peninsula

Bogazi (Boğaz) ❾

Road map E2. On the road leading to the Karpas peninsula.

AT THIS LITTLE fishing port on Famagusta Bay you can watch the fishermen returning with their catch, and also buy fresh fish each morning. Fishing trips are available for visitors, as are lessons in scuba diving. There are good

The imposing walls of Kantara Castle, overlooking Famagusta Bay

long, sandy beaches in this area. A half-dozen local restaurants specialize in fish and seafood. European cuisine is on offer at Moon Over the Water, an English-run seaside restaurant 2 km (1.2 miles) south of Bogazi.

Kantara Castle ❿

Road map E2. ⬤ *summer: 10am–5pm; winter: 9am–1pm & 2–4:45pm.* 🖼

KANTARA CASTLE is the easternmost medieval fortress of North Cyprus. It lies 630 m (2,068 ft) above sea level, at the base of the Karpas peninsula, on a spot affording views of both Famagusta Bay and the shores of Asia Minor. This was already the site of a castle in Byzantine times. It was here that the English King Richard the Lionheart finally caught up with his adversary, Byzantine governor Isaac Komnenos, in 1191 and forced him to capitulate.

The castle rooms were mostly torn down by the Venetians, but the mighty walls survive in excellent condition. The route to the castle leads through a barbican with two towers; the vast southeastern tower has a water cistern at its base, also used as a dungeon. The two adjacent former army barracks are in good condition. The

southwestern wing of the castle features a secret passage that enabled the defenders to sneak out and launch a surprise attack on the besiegers. The north towers and the bastions afford magnificent views of the surrounding area.

ENVIRONS: A dozen or so kilometres (7.5 miles) west of the castle, close to the sea, is the lonely late-Byzantine **church of Panagia Pergaminiotissa**.

Karpas Peninsula ⓫

Road map E2, F1–2. ℹ️ *Yialoussa, 374 4984.*

THIS LONG, ROCKY SPIT is the least developed part of the island, with sandy beaches on its north and south coast, and a scattering of historic Christian churches, including the monastery of Apostolos Andreas, which is awaiting restoration, to be funded by the UN and the EU. Known as Kirpasa to the Turks, this depopulated

Picturesque Panagia Pergaminiotissa

peninsula has rolling hills, where wild donkeys roam, fringed by lovely empty beaches, which provide nesting grounds for sea turtles. The eastern part of the peninsula is a nature reserve, home to droves of birds and donkeys.

The best starting point for exploring the peninsula is the fishing village of **Bogazi**. A few kilometres to the left of the main road, near the village of **Komi** (Büyükkonuk), stands a small Byzantine church with beautiful 6th-century mosaics. The church is surrounded by the ruins of a Roman town. Only the apse remains of the 5th-century church of Panagia Kanakaria, on the edge of **Boltaşli** (Lythrangkomi), east of Ziyamet (Leonarisso); the mosaics that used to decorate it can be seen in the Makarios Museum, in Nicosia. The rest of the church dates from the 11th century, except the tamboured dome which was added in the 18th century. The church is now closed.

The last petrol station is in **Yialousa** (Yenierenköy). Further south is the village of **Sipahi** (Agia Trias) with a three-aisled early Christian basilica. Dating from the 5th century, it was discovered by archaeologists in 1957, and is noted for its handsome floor mosaics. The marble-encrusted, cruciform font in the baptistry is the biggest in the island.

Beyond the small village of **Agios Thyrsos** stands Hotel Theresa, with the best accommodation on the peninsula.

Dipkarpaz (Rizokarpaso) is the peninsula's biggest, if somewhat neglected, village. It has a population of 3,000, comprised mainly of immigrants from Anatolia. Some 3 km (1.8 miles) to the north are the ruins of the 5th-century church of **Agios Philon**, standing amid the ruins of the Phoenician town of Karpatia. The 10th-century basilica was subsequently replaced by a chapel; just the south wall and the apse remain.

North of Agios Philon stands an ancient stone breakwater. A narrow road running along the coast leads to **Aphendrika**, with the ruins of an ancient harbour, a Hellenic necropolis and a fortress erected on bare rock. It also has three ruined churches: the two-aisled, partly domed Agios Georgios dating from the Byzantine period; the 12th-century Romanesque Panagia Chrysiotissa; and the three-aisled Panagia Assomatos, the best preserved of the lot. On the opposite side of the peninsula is the beautiful Nangomi Beach.

Apostolos Andreas – the monastery of St Andrew

Apostolos Andreas ⑫

Road map F1.

ALMOST AT THE TIP of the Karpas peninsula stands the monastery of St Andrew (Apostolos Andreas), an irregular edifice built of yellow stone, with a white bell tower. According to legend, it was here that the Saint's invocation caused a miraculous spring to appear, whose water cures epilepsy and ailments of the eyes, and grants pilgrims their wishes. During the Byzantine period, a fortified monastery occupied the site; some historians believe that it was here, rather than in Kantara, that Richard the Lionheart caught up with Isaac Komnenos.

In the early 20th century the monastery gained a reputation for its miracles, and became the target of mass pilgrimages. After 1974, the site was taken over by the Turkish army. Today it is once again open to visitors.

The 19th-century church has been stripped of its icons, but on the Feast of the Assumption (15 August) and St Andrew's Day (30 November), services are held for the pilgrims arriving from southern Cyprus.

In the crypt beneath the church the holy well, famed for its healing properties, still gushes the "miraculous" water. The site is regarded as holy by Greeks and Turks alike.

ENVIRONS: Less than 5 km (3 miles) distance separates Apostolos Andreas monastery from **Zafer Burnu**, the furthest point of the Karpas peninsula. This cave-riddled rocky cape was a Neolithic settlement known as Kastros, one of the earliest places of known human habitation in Cyprus. In ancient times it became the site of a temple to the goddess Aphrodite.

The offshore **Klidhes islets** (the "Keys" islets) are a haven for a variety of sea birds.

Turtle Beach in the Karpas peninsula

Antifonitis Monastery ⑬

Road map D2. 29 km (18 miles) E of
Kyrenia via Esentepe (Agios Amvrosios).
◯ *summer: 9am–2pm Fri–Wed;*
winter: 9am–1pm & 2–4pm Fri–Wed. 🏛️

IN A PINE-COVERED VALLEY on
the northern slopes of the
Pentadaktylos mountains,
some 8 km (5 miles) south of
Esentepe, stands the disused
12th-century monastery church
of Antifonitis. This was once
the most important Byzantine
church in the mountains of
North Cyprus. Its Greek name,
meaning "He who responds",
is associated with a legend
about a pauper who met a
wealthy man and requested a
loan. When the rich man
asked who would vouchsafe
the loan, the pauper replied,
"God will". At this moment
they both heard a voice from
heaven. The monastery was
built on the site of this miracle.

The church was built in the
7th century; the narthex and
gallery date from the Lusignan
period and the loggia was
added by the Venetians. The
church was originally decorated with magnificent frescoes,
but since 1974 these have
been defaced and damaged.

Buffavento Castle ⑭

Road map D2. ◯ *summer: 9am–*
7pm; winter: 9am–1pm & 2–4:45pm.
🏛️

BUILT ON THE SITE of a
Byzantine watchtower
remodelled by the Lusignans,
this castle perches 950 m
(3,117 ft) above sea level. The

Buffavento, the highest castle in Cyprus

date of its construction is
unknown, but this mountain
stronghold was captured in
1191 by the Frankish king
Guy de Lusignan. The castle
was used for years as an
observation post and political
prison. Under Venetian rule
the castle lost its importance
and was abandoned.

Steep stairs lead from the
gate to the top of the tallest
tower, where a magnificent
view awaits. In fine weather
it is possible to see Kyrenia,
Nicosia and Famagusta, as
well as the Troodos moun-
tains and the coast of Turkey.

Cold winter wind blowing
from Anatolia explains the
name of the castle, meaning

the "wind blast". In old days
bonfires lit on top of the
tower served as means of
communication with the
garrisons stationed at St
Hilarion and Kantara castles.

A marble monument by the
car park commemorates the
passengers and crew of a
Turkish aircraft that crashed
in fog in February 1988 on its
approach to Ercan airport.

ENVIRONS: West of the castle,
on the southern slopes of the
juniper-covered mountains,
stands the 12th-century
Byzantine **Panagia
Apsinthiotissa monastery**. It
was restored in the 1960s, but
after 1974 the monks were
forced to abandon it. Its
church is crowned with a vast
dome; on its north side is a
lovely original refectory.

The site is reached by
turning off the Kyrenia-Nicosia
highway and passing through
Asagi Dikmen (Kato Dikomo)
and Tasken (Vouno) villages.

Along the way is a giant
stone flag erected by Turkish
Cypriot refugees from Tochni
where, in the 1960s, the Greek
EOKA organization murdered
all the Turkish men.

The breathtaking view from Buffavento castle

◁ **View of the impressive St Hilarion castle – a mountaintop fortress**

Bellapais ⓯

Road map C2. 7 km (4.3 miles) SE of Kyrenia. ⬛ *815 7540.* ⬜ *summer: 9am–7pm; winter: 9am–1pm & 2–4:45pm.* 🖉

ONE OF the most beautiful villages in Cyprus, Bellapais lies amid citrus groves on the northern slopes of the Pentadaktylos mountains. It features the splendidly preserved ruins of a Gothic abbey, to which the village owes its name. It is thought to be derived from the French *Abbaye de la Paix* (Peace Abbey).

The first monks to settle here were Augustinians from Jerusalem, forced to flee the city after its capture by Saladin. The first buildings were erected in the early 13th century, but the main section of the abbey was built during the reign of the Lusignan kings, Hugo III and Hugo IV. The abbey was destroyed by the Turks, following their conquest of the island.

Bellapais is one of the loveliest Gothic historic sites in the Middle East. The oldest part of the abbey is well-preserved church, built in the French Gothic style.

A spiral staircase in the western end of the garth (the garden close) leads to the roof, affording a magnificent view of the sea and the mountains. The remaining parts include the living quarters, the kitchen, and the old refectory illuminated by the light entering through the

Splendidly preserved ruins of Bellapais abbey

vast windows facing the steep crag. The garth cloisters once contained a carved marble sarcophagus and a lavatory, where the monks washed their hands before entering the refectory. Now they are used for concerts during music festivals.

The English writer Lawrence Durrell lived in Bellapais from 1953–6, and described the struggles of the EOKA fighters in his novel *Bitter Lemons*. The house in which he lived bears a commemorative plaque.

Sign from Durrell's house in Bellapais

saint from Palestine, who came to Cyprus in search of solitude, dying here in 372. The Byzantines built the church and monastery in his memory.

The outer defence wall was erected by the Lusignans. The castle played an important role in the 1228–31 struggle for the domination of Cyprus between German Emperor Frederick II of Hohenstaufen and Jean d'Ibelin; also during the 1373 Genoese invasion.

The lower section of the fortress held stables. A huge gate leads to the inner castle with a chapel and an imposing refectory, which in the Lusignan period was converted into a banqueting hall. From here you can pass to the belvedere and the adjoining kitchen. An arched gate leads to the upper castle.

The south part of the castle has the Gothic "queen's window", with a spectacular view over Karmi village.

St Hilarion Castle ⓰

⬜ *summer: 9am–5pm; winter: 9am–1pm & 2–4.45pm.* 🖉

THE BEST PRESERVED mountain-top stronghold in North Cyprus, this magnificent castle bristles with turrets from its walls built on sheer rock. It was named after the monastic

Ruins of St Hilarion castle, on top of a steep rock

Kyrenia (Girne) ⑰

ENJOYING A PICTURESQUE LOCATION flanked by a range of craggy hills and the sea, Kyrenia is built around a charming harbour – the most beautiful in Cyprus – guarded by a mighty medieval castle. Its compact Old Town is full of bars, tavernas and restaurants, yet remains a tranquil place. The nearby seashore is lined with the best hotels in North Cyprus. Home to a sizeable expatriate community until 1974, there is still a small number of expats living here today.

View of the Lusignan Tower in the castle (see pp148–9)

Exploring Kyrenia

Once you arrive in Kyrenia, it is best to leave the car at the large car park near the town hall, and then continue exploring on foot. Most of Kyrenia's historic sites are clustered around the old harbour. The tourist information office is housed in the former customs house. The town's main attractions – the harbour, castle and small museums – can be explored in a day.

⚏ Byzantine Tower

At the junction of Ziya Rizki Caddesi and Atilla Sokaki.
This massive stone defence structure, with walls several metres thick, once formed part of the town's defence walls. Nowadays it houses an art gallery selling local handicrafts, including rugs, paintings and other souvenirs. Strolling down Atilla Sokagi

you will come across a similar, but more derelict tower; also a number of Greek and Roman tombs.

🏛 Folk Art Museum

The old harbour. ◯ summer: 8am-2pm Mon–Fri; winter: 9am–1pm & 2–4:45pm Mon–Fri. 📷
Set in a centuries-old Venetian house midway along the harbour, this museum houses a modest collection of traditional village costumes, household implements, furniture and tools. Also on display is an interesting giant olive press made of olive wood.

⚏ Market

Canbulat Sokagi.
The covered town bazaar, where fish, meat, fruit, vegetables and spices are sold, stands along Canbulat street leading towards the shore. This fairly dilapidated building is currently being renovated with funding provided by the UN.

Art gallery inside the Byzantine Tower

Town hall building with the forecourt fountain

⚏ Town Hall

This modern single-storey building stands on a small square, just a stone's throw from the Old Town. Standing in the forecourt is a unique fountain with three huge birds carved in white stone.
The nearby Muslim cemetery is full of the distinctive tombs - *baldaken turbe*.

◖ Djafer Pasha Mosque (Cafer Paşa Camii)

In the Old Town, close to the castle and the harbour.
This small mosque with a stocky minaret was erected in 1589 by Djafer Pasha, commander of the Sultan's army and navy, and three times the Turkish governor of Cyprus. The founder's body rests in the small stone tomb to the right of the entrance. The simple prayer hall is lined with carpets.
About a dozen metres (40 ft) west of the mosque is the small, abandoned Chysospiliotissa church which was erected by the Lusignans in the early 14th century.

⛪ Archangelos Church & Icon Museum

Near the harbour. ◯ May–Sep: 9am–7pm daily; Oct–Apr: 9am–1pm & 2–4:45pm daily. 📷
The former church of the Archangel Michael, standing on top of a hill close to the old harbour, now houses the Icon Museum.
This white edifice with its slender belfry was built in 1860. Some of its original furnishings remain, including the exquisite carved wooden iconostasis and pulpit. The walls are now hung with over 50 icons, dating from the 18th-20th centuries, that were removed from local churches.

One of the oldest was painted in 1714. Other objects on display are sacral books and a carved crosier. Outside are marble sarcophagi, dating from the Byzantine period.

During summer, Catholic mass is celebrated in the late-Gothic **chapel of Terra Santa**, situated further west, in Ersin Aydin Sokagi. The only other Christian place of worship in Kyrenia is the Anglican **church of St Andrew**, which was built in 1913 close to the castle and the Muslim cemetery.

⚓ Harbour

Kyrenia's once important harbour was the safest haven along the north coast of Cyprus, so heavily fortified

The distinctive white silhouette and belfry of the Archangelos church

was it. In ancient times the Romans built a defence castle here; later on the Lusignans and the Venetians rebuilt it, creating a vast fortress. In the Middle Ages the harbour

VISITORS' CHECKLIST

Road map C2. 🏠 *8,000.*
🛈 *Kordon Boyou, by the entrance to the old harbour, 815 2145.*
🚌 *Fergün, 815 2344.*

entrance was protected by a strong iron chain. Evidence of its former importance are the medieval stone lugs that were used to fasten the mooring lines of large ships.

Now the old harbour is devoted exclusively to yachts and pleasure boats, ready to take visitors on cruises along the coast. It is lined with an array of dining spots, particularly fish restaurants, with tables set close to the water's edge. The harbour looks particularly enchanting at night, when the calm waters reflect myriad sparkling lights.

🏛 Fine Arts Museum

⏱ *summer: 9am–7pm; winter: 9am–1pm & 2–4:45pm.* 🔲
This museum is housed in a somewhat ostentatious villa built in 1938 in the western part of Kyrenia. Its collection comprises a variety of unrelated exhibits, from anonymous paintings (both oil and watercolour) to European porcelain, to Oriental jewellery.

Kyrenia's natural horseshoe harbour, the most beautiful in Cyprus

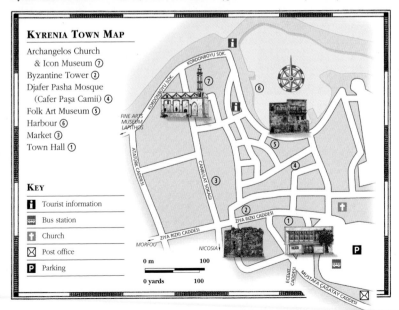

KYRENIA TOWN MAP

Archangelos Church
& Icon Museum ⑦
Byzantine Tower ②
Djafer Pasha Mosque
(Cafer Paşa Camii) ④
Folk Art Museum ⑤
Harbour ⑥
Market ③
Town Hall ①

KEY

🛈 Tourist information

🚌 Bus station

🕆 Church

☒ Post office

🅿 Parking

0 m   100

0 yards   100

Kyrenia Castle and Shipwreck Museum

Ancient amphora

KYRENIA CASTLE was built by the Byzantines on the site of a Roman fort and later extended by the Lusignans. The Venetians turned it into a vast fortress occupied by the Turks in 1570. The castle was never taken by force. Today it houses a Tomb-Finds Gallery and a Shipwreck Museum, with the wreck of an ancient vessel dating from the days of Alexander the Great. The magnificent view from the city walls encompasses the harbour and St Hilarion castle.

Amphorae
Nearly 400 clay amphorae for storing wine were found in the wreck of a sailing vessel, probably bound for Anatolia from the Greek islands.

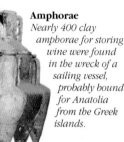

★ Shipwreck Museum
On display here is what remains of a merchant vessel that sank in a storm some 2,300 years ago.

★ The Lusignan Tower
Arranged in the vaulted rooms of the two-storey tower are figures of medieval soldiers standing by the guns.

The Tomb-Finds Gallery
comprises a reconstructed late Neolithic dwelling and tombs from both Kirini and Akdeniz (Agia Irini).

The Courtyard
Surrounded by stone walls, the large courtyard has a series of stone balls lying around and a quern (millstone) of volcanic rock.

VISITORS' CHECKLIST

Road map C2. **Kyrenia Castle
and Shipwreck Museum**
*summer: 9am–7pm, winter:
9am–1pm & 2–4:45pm.* *The
visitors' entrance is located in the
eastern part of the Old Harbour.*

The Venetian Tower
*The southeast section of Kyrenia Castle
includes the Venetian Tower. Arranged
in its gloomy casements are figures of
resting soldiers and Venetian
gunners in action.*

Defence Walls
*Once powerful castle fortifications
are now severely dilapidated.*

Square tower

Coat of Arms
*A medieval knight's
stone-carved coat of
arms is preserved in
the castle walls.*

West wall

Entrance
*The castle is reached
via a narrow bridge
spanning a moat, once
filled with sea water.*

STAR SIGHTS

★ **Shipwreck
   Museum**

★ **Lusignan Tower**

Lapithos (Lapta) – a popular destination for daytrips from Kyrenia

local Turks were forced to leave the village. After 1974 it was the Greeks' turn to leave.

Now, in addition to Turkish Cypriots, Lapithos' population includes settlers from Anatolia and a handful of foreigners.

Environs: Karman (Karmi) is one of the loveliest Cypriot villages, with whitewashed houses built on hillsides. The small church has a collection of icons removed from the abandoned Greek churches. Nearby is a necropolis dating from 2,300-1,625 BC. The village is now inhabited almost exclusively by British and German expatriates.

Lambousa (Lambusa) ⑱

Road map C2. Situated on the coast, 1.5 km (1 mile) from the village of Alsançak (Karavas).

O^N A SMALL, rocky peninsula near cape Acheiropitios, Lambousa was one of several ancient Cypriot kingdoms. This cosmopolitan city-state was inhabited by the Greeks, Phoenicians, Romans and Byzantines, as well as Hittites and Franks. The earliest inhabitants arrived in the 13th century BC. In the 8th century BC Lambousa was conquered by the Phoenicians, but its most glorious times were in the Roman and Byzantine periods.

In the course of excavation works carried out in the early

20th century, archaeologists discovered on this site a 6th-century Byzantine treasure consisting of gold and silver artifacts. Some of these are now on display in the Cyprus Museum in Nicosia (see p123), with the rest divided between the British Museum in London, the Metropolitan Museum in New York and the Dumbarton Oaks Collection in Washington, DC.

Only the eastern portion of ancient Lambousa is open to the public. It includes a dozen rock tombs and a series of vast tanks for keeping freshly caught fish alive.

Lapithos (Lapta) ⑲

Road map C2. 18 km (11 miles) west of Kyrenia.

T^HIS PICTURESQUE village, with its isolated dwellings scattered around mountain slopes, is a popular daytrip destination from Kyrenia.

The abundant water supply made this a natural supply base for ancient Lambousa, until the threat of Arab raids in the 7th century caused the inhabitants to move to a safer site inland. The settlement was once famous for its silks and exquisite ceramics.

Lapithos was formerly inhabited by both Cypriot communities living in concord; they left behind seven churches and two mosques. In 1963–4 the

Fragments of ruins from the ancient city-state of Lambousa

Larnaka tis Lapithou (Kozan) ⑳

Road map C2.

T^HIS VILLAGE ENJOYS a scenic location on the southern slopes of Selvii Dag (Kiparissovouno), the peak of the Kyrenian range at 1,024 m (3,360 ft). It makes an excellent base for hikes and bicycle trips around the neighbouring mountains. The local church was turned into a mosque, while the nearby monastery, Panagia ton Katharon, was sacked after 1974.

Kormakitis village, the capital of the Cypriot Maronites

Kormakitis (Koruçam) ㉑

Road map B2. 9 km (5.6 miles) west of Camlibel (Myrton). 🏠 140.

K^ORMAKITIS is the capital of the Cypriot Maronite Christian sect. As recently as the 1960s this was a bustling,

Views from the Kormakitis peninsula

prosperous small town with population of over 1,000. Now it has dwindled to about one tenth of that number. Although the Maronites tried to stay impartial in the Greek-Turkish conflict, after 1974 many were forced by Turkish persecution to leave their homes and emigrate. The current residents of the village are mostly elderly, and despite living through those difficult times, the people are unfailingly kind, cheerful and hospitable.

Daily mass is still celebrated in the local church, **Agios Gregorios**, which is now far too large for the needs of its current congregation. To visit the church you should contact the nearby convent or go to the next-door coffee-house to enquire about the church being opened. **Profitis Ilias**, standing close to the village, is the main Maronite monastery on the island.

ENVIRONS: Next to the village of Akdeniz (Agia Irini) that lies close to the Güzelyurt (Morfou) bay is an interesting archaeological site believed to date from the late Bronze era to the Archaic era. A reconstruction of a tomb that was discovered here can now be seen in the Kyrenia Castle museum.

Just off the road leading to Nicosia stands a Bronze Age shrine – the Pigadhes sanctuary. Its stone altar is decorated with geometric reliefs and crowned by a pair of bull horns, indicating the Minoan influence.

Cape Kormakitis (Koruçam Burnu) ㉒

Road map B2.

CAPE KORMAKITIS, called Koruçam Burnu by the Turks, is the northeasternmost part of Cyprus. In terms of landscape and wildlife it is similar to the Karpas and Akamas peninsulas; together they are the wildest and least accessible parts of the island. The few villages that existed in this areas have now been largely deserted. The North Cyprus authorities plan to turn this area into a nature reserve.

A rough track running among limestone hills covered with Mediterranean vegetation leads from the Maronite village of Kormakitis towards the small village of Sadrazamköy (Livera). From here, a 3.5-km (2.2-mile) unmade but serviceable road runs towards Cape Kormakitis.

Waves breaking off Cape Kormakitis

The cape lies in a desolate area of dreary rocks, a handful of deserted dwellings and an unmanned lighthouse at the very tip. The nearby rocky island of Nissi Kormakitis lies a mere 60 km (37 miles) from Cape Anamur on the Anatolian coast of Turkey.

For centuries, the cape has been inhabited by Maronites, a Christian sect that originated in Syria and Lebanon in the 7th century. This Eastern Christian sect, whose members proclaim themselves to be Catholic and to recognize the supremacy of the Pope, arose from a dispute between Monophysites (who postulated a single, divine nature of Jesus) and Christians (who believed Jesus to be both divine and human). The Maronites took their name from the 4th- or 5th-century Syrian hermit, St Maron. They arrived on Cyprus in the 12th century, together with the Crusaders, whom they served during their campaigns in the Holy Land.

ENDANGERED SEA TURTLES

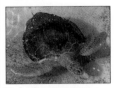

The legally protected green turtle (*Chylonia mydas*)

Both the loggerhead (*Caretta caretta*) and green (*Chylonia mydas*) species of sea turtle that nest on the beaches of Cyprus are endangered species subject to conservation programmes. Their nesting season lasts from mid-May to mid-October. The female digs a hole 30–60 cm (12–24 in) into the sand, in which she deposits her eggs. The hatchlings emerge after 55–60 days and head for the sea. Those that survive will return after 30 years to the same beach to breed. Only one in 40 turtles succeeds.

Morphou (Güzelyurt) ㉓

Road map B3.  *Orange Festival (May).*

THE TURKISH NAME Güzelyurt means "beautiful place". And, indeed, the local citrus groves and picturesque bay add to the lovely scenery here.

It was close to the town that archaeologists discovered the earliest traces of human habitation in Cyprus, dating from the Neolithic and Early Bronze eras when copper was produced and exported.

The best historic site in Güzelyurt is the **church and monastery of Agios Mamas**, built during the Byzantine period on the site of a former pagan temple. In the 15th century it acquired Gothic embellishments, and in the 18th century a dome.

The interior features the throne of St Mamas, a Gothic window carved in stone, an iconostasis and a marble sarcophagus of the saint.

Until 1974 swarms of pilgrims streamed to Agios Mamas from all over Cyprus, but after the Turkish invasion it was shut and used to store icons brought here from the nearby Orthodox churches. It is now an **Icon Museum**.

Other than Agios Mamas, the town has few tourist attractions. Next to the church is the **Archaeology and Natural History Museum**. Besides masses of stuffed animals and birds, and a

Monastery buildings of Agios Mamas in Morphou

Atatürk's statue in Lefke

collection of ancient ceramics, the museum also houses an exhibition of Late Bronze Age objects found in the course of excavations conducted in Töumba and Skourou.

🏛 **Icon Museum & Archaeology and Natural History Museum**
Agios Mamas. ◯ *summer: 9am– 7pm; winter: 9am–1pm and 2–4:45pm.* 📷

Léfka (Lefke) ㉔

Road map B3. 👥 *3,000.*

INHABITED FOR OVER 400 years by Turks, Lefke is a major centre of Islam on the island. The central square sports a huge equestrian statue of Atatürk. A few hundred metres further on stands the early 19th-century mosque of **Piri Osman Pasha**, built in the Cyprian style. The garden surrounding the mosque contains the tomb of Vizier Osman Pasha, who was supposedly killed by poison – a victim of a palace intrigue. His marble sarcophagus is one of the loveliest surviving works of its kind from the Ottoman period.

Lefke European University, one of five universities in North Cyprus, trains students from many countries of the Middle East and Central Asia. The pleasant **Lefke Garden Hotel** occupies a renovated 19th-century inn *(see p165)*. Lefke is also the seat of Kibrisli Syke Nazim, the *murshid* or

Logo of the university in Lefka

spiritual leader of the Naqshbandi order of Sufism, who decides on all spiritual aspects of life of the faithful.

ENVIRONS: In the nearby coastal town of Gemikonagi (Karavostasi) is the excellent **Mardinli** restaurant, standing on a small beach surrounded by a garden and orchard that provide its kitchen with fruit and vegetables. On the other side of the town, between the road and the sea, stands an imposing monument to a Turkish pilot killed during the 1974 invasion.

Soloi (Soli Harabeleri) ㉕

Road map B3. 20 km (12.5 miles) W of Güzelyurt. ◯ *summer: 9am–7pm; winter: 9am–1pm & 2–4:45pm.* 📷

SOLOI, A ONE TIME city-state of Cyprus, was supposedly founded at the suggestion of the Athenian law-giver Solon, who persuaded King Philocyprus of Aepea to build a new capital close to the river Ksero. In his honour, the town was named Soloi.

The reality, however, was probably quite different. As long ago as Assyrian times (c.700 BC) a town called Sillu stood on this site. It was a stronghold of Greek culture, and was the last town to fall to the Persians.

The town gave its name to the entire region of Solea, on the northern slopes of the Troodos mountains, where Cypriot copper was mined near the present-day town of Skouriotissa. The extraction and export of this metal spurred the growth of Soloi, particularly during Roman times. There was a good harbour, needed for the export of copper, and abundant water.

It was in Soloi that St Mark converted a Roman named Auxibius to Christianity; he later became bishop of Soloi.

Stones taken from the ruins of the ancient town were used by the British and the French in the building of the Suez Canal and the coastal town of Port Said. It was only in the late 1920s that Swedish archaeologists unearthed a theatre, and in 1964 a Canadian team uncovered the basilica and part of the agora (market place).

The Roman theatre was built for an audience of 4,000 people, and had a lovely view over the sea. It has been restored and during summer is often used as a venue for shows and concerts.

Above the theatre the archaeologists uncovered remains of palaces and a temple to Athena. The famous 1st-century marble statuette of Aphrodite, found nearby, can now be seen in the Cyprus Museum in Nicosia *(see p122)*. Lower down are the ruins of the 5th-century Byzantine basilica, which was destroyed in the course of the 632 Arab raid.

Displayed under a makeshift roof are some fairly well-preserved mosaics from the temple floor, featuring geometric and animal motifs. The most interesting mosaics depict water birds surrounded by dolphins. Another small medallion features a swan.

Unearthed to the north of the ruined basilica is a poorly preserved agora.

Soloi is surrounded by vast burial grounds, dating from various periods of antiquity.

Ruins of the ancient palace in Vouni

Vouni (Vuni Sarayi) ㉖

Road map B3. 27 km (17 miles) west of Güzelyurt. ☐ *summer: 10am–5pm; winter: 9am–1pm & 2–4:45 pm.* 📷

Mosaic from Soloi

This magnificent, somewhat mysterious palace stands atop a coastal hill, 250 m (820 ft) above sea level. The site is extraordinarily beautiful, with panoramic views over the North Cyprus coast and the Troodos mountains to the south. The palace was probably built by a pro-Persian king of Marion (a city near present-day Polis), as evidenced by its Oriental architectural details.

Occupying a strategic spot, the residence was probably intended to intimidate the nearby pro-Athenian town of Soloi. Following an anti-Persian insurrection, Vouni (which means "mountain" in Greek) was taken over by the supporters of Greece. Having occupied the palace, they rebuilt it, adding a temple to Athena, among other things. When the reversal of military fortunes resulted in the Persians returning to power, the palace was burned down in 380 BC.

Today the ruins are reached via a new, narrow and winding road. Above the car park are the scant remains of a temple to Athena, dating from the late 5th century BC. The stairs on the opposite side lead to the palace courtyard, which features a guitar-shape stone stele with a hole in it and an unfinished face of a woman, probably a goddess. The adjacent cistern was used to supply water to the luxurious baths in the northwestern portion of the palace, which reputedly had 137 rooms.

Environs: The small rocky island off the west coast, visible from Vouni palace, is **Petra tou Limniti**. This is the oldest inhabited part of Cyprus, colonized as early as the Neolithic era.

Remains of the ancient agora, in Soloi

TRAVELLERS'
NEEDS

WHERE TO STAY

Logo of the Grekosun
Hotels chain

CYPRUS HAS A CHOICE of places to stay that is every bit as wide as its portfolio of visitor attractions and holiday activities, with accommodation to suit all budgets. Its climate attracts holidaymakers throughout the year, and most of its hotels and guesthouses are also open year round. Accommodation ranges from simple, family-run guesthouses and small apartment complexes to large resort hotels with an array of facilities for families, luxury villas with private pools, and stylishly restored village houses. Hotels in the three- and four-star categories are generally more luxurious than similar hotels in other Mediterranean countries, and Cyprus has a well-deserved reputation for affordable comfort.

Grecian Bay Hotel in Agia Napa (see p159)

INFORMATION

MOST HOTELS in the popular resorts are block-booked by holiday companies, making it difficult for independent travellers to find good accommodation on arrival. Booking a holiday package (which includes flights and hotel) is the best and usually cheapest option. In low season, bargains may be found on the Internet. The **Cyprus Hotel Association** also has booking desks at Larnaka airport.

HOTELS

MOST HOTELS are clustered along the coast on either side of Larnaka and Limassol, and in the more recently developed resorts of Pafos, Agia Napa and Protaras. Few stretches of the island's coastline, however, are without a scattering of places to stay. In the Larnaka and Limassol areas most hotels are compact high-rise blocks, while many newer hotels in the Pafos and Agia Napa regions are low-rise resort complexes with a choice of swimming pools and play areas for children.

◁ A lovely sandy beach in Agia Napa

There are also small hotels and apartment complexes in these resorts, though most are reserved by tour operators. Visitors looking for a tranquil setting can head to some of the lesser-known places inland.

All major hotels are modern and well-equipped, with air-conditioning. The **Cyprus Tourism Organization (CTO)**, and the Turkish tourism ministry in the occupied North, grade hotels from one to five stars. Those rated one or two stars are likely to be slightly shabby, with few facilities. Upper-end hotels may offer a wide range of activities, from watersports, riding, tennis and golf to cabaret, traditional music and dancing, and discos.

RATES

RATES VARY depending on the season, with bargains available outside the peak spring and summer months. Rates are highest during Easter (both Greek Orthodox and non-Orthodox Easter), for the two weeks around Christmas, and from June to September.

Most larger hotels offer a choice of bed and breakfast, half-board or full-board pricing. Smaller hotels may not include breakfast in the quoted rate. Make sure the quoted rate includes local taxes.

Roman Hotel in Pafos, imitating an ancient Roman building (see p158)

PRIVATE ACCOMMODATION

IT IS NOT EASY to find accommodation in private homes, and when you do find it such accommodation does not usually offer a high standard of comfort or

Bellapais Gardens hotel, with its inviting swimming pool (see p164)

A camping site near the Baths of Aphrodite

facilities, or a competitive rate. However, the **CTO** can provide a list of small bed-and-breakfast establishments.

Lodgings in monasteries were once a popular option, but today are available only to Orthodox pilgrims.

AGROTOURISM

VISITORS WHO prefer the charm of a quiet, rural village to the hustle and bustle of a tourist resort can opt for agrotourism accommo-dation. You book your stay in a village, usually in a restored traditional house, and have the opportunity to participate in some of the traditions of this village. This is especially popular in the mountains, with Cypriots as well as visitors from abroad.

Village houses usually feature modern kitchens and bathrooms, but you must be prepared for the occasional cut in the water and power supplies. These houses almost always have a garden, where you can enjoy such delights as oranges fresh from the tree. Basic homemade foodstuffs, such as bread, fresh honey or jam, can be bought from neighbours; other supplies can be brought from the larger towns.

HOSTELS AND CAMPSITES

HOSTEL BEDS are in short supply, but there are some in Nicosia, Larnaka, Pafos and in the Troodos mountain resorts. None offer a high standard of comfort. The few youth hostels in South Cyprus that once belonged to the International Youth Hostel Association are no longer in operation. You can obtain

information about budget hotels and apartments on the Internet by keying in "Hostels in Cyprus".

There are five officially designated camping sites at Governor's Beach (Limassol district), Geroskipou, Pegeia and Polis (Pafos district), and at Troodos, run by the **CTO** and intended mainly for urban Cypriots seeking an inexpen-sive holiday. Governor's Beach and Pegeia are open all year round; the others are open March through October. Facilities are basic, but include shower and toilet facilities, and a simple bar-restaurant.

RESERVATIONS

ARRIVING IN CYPRUS without a hotel reservation is inad-visable, as most hotels have been built to meet demand from package holiday compa-nies and are block-booked by them. In resorts, including Pafos, Agia Napa and Protaras, few affordable and acceptably comfortable hotel rooms are available to independent travellers. However, the **CTO**

Tochni, the most popular agrotourism village in Cyprus

supplies a directory of hotels of all categories and independent travellers can book directly with hotels by phone, fax or e-mail, or with specialist hotel booking sites via the Internet. In the North, where good-quality hotels are far fewer, booking ahead is even more essential.

DISABLED TRAVELLERS

MOST NEWER, larger hotels in the South are wheel-chair-accessible (some even have ramps leading to the beach) and hotels here are working to meet European accessibility norms. Cheaper, smaller hotels, village houses and villas are unlikely to offer wheelchair access. In the North, hotels are far less likely to be wheelchair-accessible. Ask your hotel, travel agent or tour operator to confirm accessibility details in writing, by fax or e-mail.

DIRECTORY

INFORMATION

Cyprus Tourism Organization (CTO)
Leoforos Lemesou 19
1390 Nicosia.
☎ 226 91100.
FAX 223 34696.
W www.visitcyprus.org.cy

Cyprus Hotel Association
Andreas Araouzos 12
1303 Nicosia.
☎ 224 52820.
FAX 223 75460.
@ chaniccy@cylink.com.cy

AGROTOURISM

Cyprus Agrotourism Company
Leoforos Lemesou 19
PO Box 24535
1390 Nicosia.
☎ 223 40071.
FAX 223 39723.
W www.agrotourism.com.cy
@ helpdesk@agrotourism.com.cy

Choosing a Hotel

THE HOTELS LISTED BELOW have been selected across a range of price categories for their attractive location, value for money and standard of accommodation. They are listed by region, and within regions by town or village. Central Cyprus has been omitted from the list, since it has no tourism infrastructure. Colour-coded thumb tabs make it easy to find the right region.

	NUMBER OF ROOMS	RESTAURANT	GARDEN OR TERRACE	SWIMMING POOL	AIR CONDITIONING
WEST CYPRUS					
CHLORAKAS: *Azia Beach* €€€€€	183	●	■	●	■
CORAL BAY: *Crown Resorts Horizon* €€€€	210	●	■	●	■
GEROSKIPOU: *Ledra Beach* €€€€	261	●	■	●	■
LATSI: *Anassa* €€€€€	177	●	■	●	■
PAFOS: *Kissos Hotel* €	144	●	■	●	■
PAFOS: *New Olympus Hotel* €	22	●	■	●	■
PAFOS: *Roman Hotel* €€	87	●	■	●	■
PAFOS: *Alexander The Great* €€€€	202	●	■	●	■
PAFOS: *Elysium Mediterranean Beach Resort* €€€€€	250	●	■	●	■

CHLORAKAS: *Azia Beach*   €€€€€   183
Akamas Rd. **Road map** A4. 268 45100. FAX 268 45200. www.aziahotel.com info@aziahotel.com
The Azia Beach hotel stands 6 km (3.7 miles) north of Pafos. It has a private beach, a jetty and a swimming pool complex. It also has conference rooms.

CORAL BAY: *Crown Resorts Horizon*   €€€€   210
Coral Bay Ave. **Road map** A3. 268 13800. FAX 268 13888.
www.crownresortsgroup.com horizon@crownresortsgroup.com
Located on picturesque Coral Bay, this 4-star hotel provides comfortable, family-friendly accommodation. The facilities include indoor and outdoor pools, a sauna and tennis courts. Children will enjoy the playground and the children's club.

GEROSKIPOU: *Ledra Beach*   €€€€   261
Theas Aphrodites Ave. **Road map** A4. 269 64848. FAX 269 64611.
www.louishotels.com
All Ledra Beach rooms face the sea and the hotel's private marina. Facilities include laundry service and a hair salon.

LATSI: *Anassa*   €€€€€   177
Road map A3. 268 88000. FAX 263 22900. www.thanoshotels.com res.anassa@thanoshotels.com
Anassa is the most luxurious hotel in Cyprus. Situated on a beautiful site, this imposing hotel is equipped with every modern tourist facility. There are excellent tennis courts for adults and organized activities for children.

PAFOS: *Kissos Hotel*   €   144
Verenigis St. **Road map** A4. 269 36111. www.swaypage.com/kissos kissos@kissos.com.cy
A quiet, peaceful and clean hotel with a swimming pool, bowling alley, minigolf course, sauna, jacuzzi and a children's playground. It is situated 500 m (1,640 ft) from the sea.

PAFOS: *New Olympus Hotel*   €   22
Byron St. 12. **Road map** A4. 269 32020. FAX 269 32031. www.newolympus.com newolympus@cytanet.com
Built in the colonial style, the New Olympus is the oldest hotel in Pafos, and is visited mainly by the British. The terrace affords a magnificent view over the town.

PAFOS: *Roman Hotel*   €€   87
Tombs of the Kings Rd. **Road map** A4. 269 45411. FAX 269 46834.
www.romanhotel.com.cy romanhtl@cytanet.com.cy
This smart hotel is built in the style of an ancient Roman residence. The walls are hung with beautiful paintings.

PAFOS: *Alexander The Great*   €€€€   202
Poseidon Ave. **Road map** A4. 269 65000. FAX 269 65100.
www.kanikahotels.com alexander@kanikahotels.com
This hotel is surrounded by greenery, and its guest rooms overlook the sea. Cypriot and international cuisine.

PAFOS: *Elysium Mediterranean Beach Resort*   €€€€€   250
Queen Verenikis Ave. **Road map** A4. 268 44444. FAX 268 44333.
www.elysium.com.cy info@elysium.com.cy
The Elysium Mediterranean is a very pleasant and elegant seaside hotel with a private beach and yacht marina. The facilities include minigolf, tennis courts and indoor squash courts.

Price categories for a twin room with bath or shower, including service and tax, in Cypriot pounds:
- £ under CY£30
- ££ CY£30–CY£60
- £££ CY£60–CY£90
- ££££ CY£90–CY£120
- £££££ over CY£120

RESTAURANT
The restaurant is open also to non-residents.

GARDEN OR TERRACE
The hotel is set in a garden or has an outside terrace or courtyard with plants.

SWIMMING POOL
The hotel has a swimming pool.

AIR CONDITIONING
Most rooms are air-conditioned.

Hotel	Price	Number of Rooms	Restaurant	Garden or Terrace	Swimming Pool	Air Conditioning
PAFOS: *Paphos Amathus Beach* — Poseidon Ave. Road map A4. ☎ 268 83300. FAX 268 83333. W www.pamathus.com.cy @ pamathus@pamathus.com.cy — This luxury hotel is an excellent centre for water sports and other outdoor activities.	£££££	272	●	▪	●	▪
PEGEIA: *Leptos Coral Beach* — Road map A3. ☎ 266 21601. FAX 266 21742. W www.coral.com.cy @ info@coral.com.cy — Guest rooms overlook the sea at this Coral Bay hotel, 12 km (7.5 miles) north of Pafos. Guests can use a private beach.	£££££	421	●	▪	●	▪
POLIS: *Bougainvillea Apartments & Villas* — Road map A3. ☎ 268 12250. FAX 263 22203. W www.bougainvillea.com.cy @ reservations@bougainvillea.com.cy — This hotel is close to the beach as well as the town centre.	££	28		▪	●	▪
POLIS: *Natura Beach Hotel & Villas* — Road map A3. ☎ 263 23111. FAX 263 22822. W www.natura.com.cy @ natura@cytanet.com.cy — Natura Beach Hotel is a pleasant, family-run hotel (and 5 chalets) near the beach, with a lovely bay view. The fruit and vegetables served in the hotel restaurant come from the hotel's own garden.	££	60	●	▪	●	▪

SOUTHERN CYPRUS

Hotel	Price	Number of Rooms	Restaurant	Garden or Terrace	Swimming Pool	Air Conditioning
AGIA NAPA: *Grecian Bay Hotel* — PO Box 30006. Road map E3. ☎ 237 21301. FAX 237 21307. W www.grecianbay.com @ info@grecianbay.com — A 5-star luxury complex with private beach, Grecian Bay is known for its pleasant, quiet atmosphere. It is linked with the Grecian Park hotel, famous for beautiful gardens.	££	271	●	▪	●	▪
AGIA NAPA: *Limanaki Beach Hotel* — 1 October St 18. Road map E3. ☎ 237 21600. FAX 237 22345. W www.ayianapahotels.net @ limanaki@ayianapahotels.net — On a promenade leading to the old harbour, this hotel's main attraction is the terrace and restaurant overlooking the sea.	££	72	●	▪	●	▪
AGIA NAPA: *Nissi Beach* — Nissi Ave 5340. Road map E3. ☎ 237 21021. FAX 237 21623. W www.nissi-beach.com @ nissi@spidernet.com.cy — One of the most luxurious hotels in Agia Napia, this hotel is located on Nissi, the most famous beach in Cyprus. A tangle of footpaths winds through the exotic gardens that lead to the sea.	£££££	270	●	▪	●	▪
AMATHOUS: *Amathus Beach Hotel* — 9 km (5.6 miles) from Limassol. Road map C4. ☎ 258 32000. FAX 253 27494. W www.amathushotel.com @ amathusl@amathushotel.com — Beautifully situated hotel descending in a series of cascades towards the sea. There are also suites with private pools.	£££££	244	●	▪	●	▪
AMATHOUS: *Hawaii Grand Hotel & Resort* — Road map C4. ☎ 256 34333. FAX 256 34588. W www.hawaiihotel.com @ hawaii@hawaii.com.cy — This luxury hotel has a charming swimming pool fringed by palm trees, elegant restaurants, a fitness club and tennis courts.	£££££	255	●	▪	●	▪
EPISKOPI: *Episkopiana Hotel & Sports Resort* — Kremastis St. Road map B4. ☎ 259 35093. FAX 259 85094. W www.episkopiana.com @ info@episkopiana.com — Episkopiana is a good choice for families who wish to have a restful holiday. The facilities include a playground, children's pool, games area, football grounds and babysitting service upon request.	£££	100	●	▪	●	▪

For key to symbols see back flap

Price categories for a twin room with bath or shower, including service and tax, in Cypriot pounds: ⓔ under CY£30 ⓔⓔ CY£30–CY£60 ⓔⓔⓔ CY£60–CY£90 ⓔⓔⓔⓔ CY£90–CY£120 ⓔⓔⓔⓔⓔ over CY£120	**RESTAURANT** The restaurant is open also to non-residents. **GARDEN OR TERRACE** The hotel is set in a garden or has an outside terrace or courtyard with plants. **SWIMMING POOL** The hotel has a swimming pool. **AIR CONDITIONING** Most rooms are air-conditioned.	NUMBER OF ROOMS	RESTAURANT	GARDEN OR TERRACE	SWIMMING POOL	AIR CONDITIONING

LARNAKA: *Boronia Hotel Apartments* ⓔ
Larnaka-Dhekelia Rd. **Road map** D3. 246 46200. FAX 246 44120.
@ boronia@cytanet.com.cy
This small hotel located close to shops and restaurants, and 500 m (1,640 ft) from the sea, has a pleasant English-style restaurant.

21	●	■	●	■

LARNAKA: *Faros Village* ⓔⓔ
Road map D3. 244 22111. FAX 244 22114. W www.farosvillage.com
@ farosvillage@vavlitis.com
The rooms here are arranged in low buildings, which make the hotel look smaller than it is. The grounds include a minigolf course, tennis courts, private beach and swimming pool.

134	●	■	●	■

LARNAKA: *Larco* ⓔⓔ
Pontou. **Road map** D3. 246 57006. FAX 246 59168. W www.larco-hotel.com.cy
@ info@larco-hotel.com.cy
The Larco offers bed and breakfast accommodation. Guests are welcome to use the swimming pool and sauna.

55		■	●	■

LARNAKA: *Lenios Beach Hotel* ⓔⓔ
Larnaka-Dhekelia Rd. **Road map** D3. 246 46100. FAX 246 47104.
@ lenios@cytanet.com.cy
The facilities here include a swimming pool, sauna and gymnasium. The guest rooms are not large, but are comfortable.

27	●	■	●	■

LARNAKA: *Sandbeach Castle* ⓔⓔ
Piale Pasha. **Road map** D3. 246 55437. FAX 246 59804. W www.castlehotel.com.cy
@ castle.hotel@cytanet.com.cy
A rather small hotel with a large terrace, the Sandbeach Castle is situated right by the sea. Its design imitates the walls of a castle. The hotel is just a few minutes from the international airport.

26	●	■		■

LARNAKA: *Henipa* ⓔⓔⓔ
G. Afxentiou Ave. **Road map** D3. 246 46022. FAX 246 46212.
W www.crownresortsgroup.com.cy @ henipa@crownresortsgroup.com
The Henipa hotel is a pleasant place to stay, with good facilities for outdoor activities. A swimming pool and tennis courts await sporty visitors, while a sauna and jacuzzi guarantee relaxation for those in search of pampering.

131	●	■	●	■

LARNAKA: *Louis Princess Beach Hotel* ⓔⓔⓔ
Larnaka-Dhekelia Rd. **Road map** D3. 246 45500. FAX 246 45508.
W www.louishotels.com
This smart hotel is located on the outskirts of Larnaka. It is furnished in light colours.

138	●	■	●	■

LARNAKA: *Svetlos* ⓔⓔⓔ
Road map D3. 246 47100. FAX 246 45173. @ svetlos@cytanet.com.cy
The Svetlos is situated away from the town centre. The facilities here include a swimming pool and tennis courts. The guest rooms are small, but clean and comfortable.

46	●	■	●	■

LARNAKA: *Palm Beach Hotel* ⓔⓔⓔⓔⓔ
Larnaka-Dhekelia Rd. **Road map** D3. 248 46600. FAX 248 46601.
W www.palmbeachhotel.com @ palmotel@logos.cy.net
This large, conspicuous building, set amid greenery, is visible from afar.

228	●	■	●	■

LARNAKA: *The Golden Bay Beach Hotel* ⓔⓔⓔⓔⓔ
Larnaka-Dhekelia Rd. **Road map** D3. 246 45444. FAX 246 45451.
W www.lordos.com.cy @ reception@goldenbay.com.cy
The Golden Bay Beach Hotel is a vast luxury hotel complex that offers all the entertainment a holidaymaker might wish for, including evening concerts.

193	●	■	●	■

LIMASSOL: *Metropole* (£) 19
Iphigenia 6. **Road map** C4. (253 62686. FAX 253 62330.
One of the more modest and most inexpensive hotels in Limassol. The guest
rooms are tiny, but clean, and each has a telephone. P

LIMASSOL: *Aquarius Beach* (£)(£) 33
Amathus Ave 11. **Road map** C4. (253 66624. FAX 253 61562.
A small hotel standing right by the sea, with its own beach and swimming
pool surrounded by greenery. The hotel restaurant is open to non-residentss
and serves local and European cuisine. There is live music in the evenings.

LIMASSOL: *Avenida Beach Hotel* (£)(£) 68
Avenida Beach. **Road map** C4. (253 21122. FAX 253 21123.
The Avenida Beach Hotel stands right by the beach. The guest rooms
overlook Limassol Bay.

LIMASSOL: *Golden Arches* (£)(£) 110
Amathous Ave 166. **Road map** C4. (253 22433. FAX 253 25835.
W www.goldenarcheshotel.com @ goldenarches@cytanet.com.cy
The Golden Arches is a charming hotel with arch-vaulted balconies. The
swimming pool is surrounded by lovely hibiscus and bougainvillea shrubs.
You can enjoy a pleasant dinner served at the poolside.

LIMASSOL: *Pefkos Hotel* (£)(£) 110
Kavazoglou and Misiaouli 70. **Road map** C4. (256 60066. FAX 255 77083.
W www.cytop.net/pefkos
This 1970s-style hotel stands on the outskirts of town, away from the
promenade and tourist attractions. The hotel swimming pool is screened from
the busy road by a double row of trees.

LIMASSOL: *Arsinoe* (£)(£)(£) 179
Amathus Ave 62. **Road map** C4. (253 21444. FAX 253 29908.
W www.cyprus2000.com/arsinoe @ arsinoe@logos.cy.net
The Arsinoe hotel offers extensive sports facilities, including tennis and
squash, as well as a sauna and swimming pool. It is a favourite with those
who like active holidays.

LIMASSOL: *Marathon Beach* (£)(£)(£) 130
Amathus Ave 4046. **Road map** C4. (253 20122.
The hotel stands between the resort centre and the ruins of ancient Amathous.
It stands opposite a sandy beach, reached via an underground passage. The
grounds include tennis courts and a yacht marina. The comfortable guest
rooms afford lovely views of the sea.

LIMASSOL: *Pavemar Hotel* (£)(£)(£) 93
28 October Ave. **Road map** C4. (255 81166. FAX 255 91916.
A relatively small hotel compared to the vast complexes in Limassol's holiday
centre, the Pavemar is located on the main road, close to shops and
restaurants.

LIMASSOL: *Elias Beach* (£)(£)(£)(£) 175
Road map C4. (256 36000. FAX 256 35300. W www.eliasbeach.com
@ info@eliasbeach.com
The colour schemes of the rooms and furnishings at Elias Beach are inspired
by nature, and intended to reflect the warmth, sun and greenery of Cyprus.

LIMASSOL: *Four Seasons* (£)(£)(£)(£)(£) 323
Road map C4. (258 58000. FAX 253 10887. W www.fourseasons.com.cy
@ inquiries@fourseasons.com.cy
One of the finest and most expensive hotels in Cyprus, the Four Seasons has a
magnificent swimming and recreation complex and a private beach. The high-
vaulted hall is adorned with plants and a fountain. The guest rooms are large
and luxurious. There are organised activities, programmes for children, and
beach clubs to entertain guests.

LIMASSOL: *Mediterranean Beach* (£)(£)(£)(£)(£) 291
Amathus Ave 3105. **Road map** C4. (253 11777. FAX 253 24754.
W www.medbeach.com @ medbeach@spidernet.com.cy
The light hotel building surrounds the swimming pool complex. The hotel has
a private beach and yacht marina. There are special offers for couples who
want to get married on the island.

		Price categories for a twin room with bath or shower, including service and tax, in Cypriot pounds: £ under CY£30 ££ CY£30–CY£60 £££ CY£60–CY£90 ££££ CY£90–CY£120 £££££ over CY£120		

RESTAURANT
The restaurant is open also to non-residents.

GARDEN OR TERRACE
The hotel is set in a garden or has an outside terrace or courtyard with plants.

SWIMMING POOL
The hotel has a swimming pool.

AIR CONDITIONING
Most rooms are air-conditioned.

	NUMBER OF ROOMS	RESTAURANT	GARDEN OR TERRACE	SWIMMING POOL	AIR CONDITIONING
PANO LEFKARA: *Agora* ££ **Road map** C4. 243 42901. **FAX** 243 42905. @ hotelagora@hotmail.com.cy This hotel is situated in a village famous for its lace-making. Although not very large, it is clean and comfortable and provides a good base for mountain hikes.	19	●	■	●	■
PISSOURI: *Bunch of Grapes Inn*. £ **Road map** B4. 252 21275. **FAX** 252 22510. This small, delightful, family-run hotel occupies a specially adapted century-old building. The owners serve homemade food.	11	●			
PISSOURI: *Columbia Beach Hotel & Resort* ££££ **Road map** B4. 258 33333. **FAX** 252 21505. W www.columbia-hotels.com @ columbia@columbia-hotels.com The Columbia Beach is a large, comfortable hotel complex right by the sea. The restaurant offers excellent Cypriot cuisine. There are good opportunities here for sports and outdoor activities.	94	●	■	●	■
TOCHNI: *Cyprus Villages* £££££ **Road map** C4. 243 32998. W www.cyagrotourismo.com The centre of agrotourism stands on top of a hill, above the village of Tochni. Guests' chalets are in Tochni, Kalvassos, Psematismenos, Skarinou and Pentakomo. Agrotourism packages include angling, horseriding, and traditional workshops (such as cookery).	160	●	■	●	■
VAVATSINIA: *Maria's Inn* £ 7712 Vavatsinia Rd. **Road map** C4. 243 42640. Maria's Inn is a delightful, traditional family-run restaurant with guest rooms. The rooms are clean and heated, with windows overlooking the mountains. Honey and candied fruit are also sold here.	10	●	■		

TROODOS MOUNTAINS

	NUMBER OF ROOMS	RESTAURANT	GARDEN OR TERRACE	SWIMMING POOL	AIR CONDITIONING
AGROS: *Rodon* ££ Rodou 1. **Road map** C3. 255 21201. **FAX** 255 21235. W www.rodonhotel.com @ info@rodonhotel.com This is a large, pleasant mountain hotel. The facilities include a swimming pool and sauna, tennis courts and gymnasium.	155	●	■	●	■
KAKOPETRIA: *Makris* ££ Mammantos 48. **Road map** B3. 229 23366. **FAX** 229 23367. This hotel in the famous resort of Kakopetria is popular with visitors. It is surrounded by balmy pinewoods, with a swimming pool and tennis courts for guests' relaxation.	52	●	■	●	
KAKOPETRIA: *Mylos* £££ Mylou 8. **Road map** B3. 229 22536. **FAX** 228 13970. W www.cymillhotel.com A delightful hotel, with small but comfortable rooms. The restaurant serves tasty homemade cuisine.	14	●	■		■
PEDOULAS: *Health Habitat* ££ **Road map** B3. 229 52283. **FAX** 223 14017. A vast hotel complex, the Health Habitat offers all the entertainment that a holidaymaker could wish for. Live music concerts are held in the evening.	30	●	■		
PEDOULAS: *Pinewood Valley* £££ **Road map** B3. 229 52211. **FAX** 229 52439. W www.holiday-inn.com/limassolcyprus @ pinewood@churchill.com.cy Situated in a small side street, this traditional mountain-style hotel is popular with foreign visitors. The small-scale architecture of Pinewood Valley makes the hotel feel intimate, disguising the fact that there are nearly 50 rooms.	49	●	■	●	

PLATRES: *Edelweiss* £€ 22
Kalidonias St 53. **Road map** B3. 254 21335. FAX 254 22060.
www.edelweisshotel.com.cy edelweissl@cytanet.com.cy
The Edelweiss is a beautifully situated, delightful hotel. The restaurant serves homemade delicacies. There are fabulous mountain views from the windows.

PLATRES: *Minerva* £€ 12
Kalidonias St 36. **Road map** B3. 254 21731. FAX 254 21075.
minerva@globalsoftmail.com
A small hotel with plain furnishings, the Minerva is in the tourist district of the Troodos Mountains. Rooms are small but clean.

PLATRES: *Petit Palais Hotel* £€ 32
Road map B3. 254 22723. FAX 254 21065. www.petitpalaishotel.com
petitpalais@spidernet.com.cy
This small hotel on the road to Limassol, in the Troodos Mountains, serves tasty homemade food.

PLATRES: *New Helvetia* £€€ 32
Helvetia St 6. **Road map** B3. 254 21348. FAX 254 22148. www.minotel.com
helvetia@spidernet.com.cy
The hotel enjoys a beautiful location within the tourist district of the Troodos Mountains. The rooms are light and comfortable. There is a gymnasium for the use of guests.

PLATRES: *Forest Park* £€€€€ 149
Road map B3. 254 21751. FAX 254 21875. www.forestparkhotel.com.cy
forest@cytanet.com.cy
Forest Park is the largest and best hotel in the Troodos Mountains. Guests are offered the use of the swimming pools, fitness club and tennis courts. Luxuriously appointed, spacious rooms.

TROODOS: *Jubilee* £€ 37
Road map B3. 254 20107. FAX 226 73991. jubilee@cytanet.com.cy
The Jubilee is the only hotel in Troodos village, at the edge of the nature reserve. The rooms here are plain, but the atmosphere is splendid.

SOUTH NICOSIA

Averof £€ 25
Averof 19. **Road map** C3. 227 73447. FAX 227 73411.
A modest hotel, the Averof is inexpensive by Nicosia standards. Rooms have neither TV nor minibar, but guests are welcome to use the hotel bar and restaurant.

Excelsior £€ 36
Ph. Pitta 4. **Road map** C3. 226 76740. FAX 224 76740.
The Excelsior is a modest suite hotel. The guest accommodation is quite large and comfortable. The hotel also has a conference room.

Asty £€€ 52
Prince Charles 12. **Road map** C3. 227 73030. FAX 227 73311.
asty.hotel@cytanet.com.cy
This hotel is a member of the Cyprus Hoteliers' Association. The restaurant serves local and international cuisine, and the grounds feature a minigolf course.

Castelli £€€ 46
Ouzounian 38. **Road map** C3. 227 12812. FAX 226 80176.
hinnicres@cytanet.com.cy
The Castelli is one of the smaller hotels in Nicosia, and is comfortable for a visit while exploring the capital. The guest rooms and bathrooms are clean and tastefully furnished, and there is a hotel bar and large restaurant.

Europa £€€ 52
Alkaios 16. **Road map** C3. 226 92692. FAX 226 64417.
info@europahotel.com.cy
The Europa hotel is not very large, but the guest rooms, decorated in light colours, are clean and comfortable. The windows provide a magnificent panoramic view of the city.

					NUMBER OF ROOMS	RESTAURANT	GARDEN OR TERRACE	SWIMMING POOL	AIR CONDITIONING

Price categories for a twin room with bath or shower, including service and tax, in Cypriot pounds:
£ under CY£30
££ CY£30–CY£60
£££ CY£60–CY£90
££££ CY£90–CY£120
£££££ over CY£120

RESTAURANT
The restaurant is open also to non-residents.

GARDEN OR TERRACE
The hotel is set in a garden or has an outside terrace or courtyard with plants.

SWIMMING POOL
The hotel has a swimming pool.

AIR CONDITIONING
Most rooms are air-conditioned.

Best Western Classic Hotel   ££££   **60**
Rigenis St 94. **Road map C3.** 226 64006. FAX 226 70072.
www.classic.com.cy classichotel@gapgroup.com
The Best Western Classic is a smart hotel, located right in the city centre, close to the Cyprus Museum and about a quarter of an hour's walk from the Famagusta Gate. In the evenings the guests may retire to its elegant restaurant or to the Blue Bar.

Cleopatra   £££££   **89**
Florina St 8. **Road map C3.** 228 44000. FAX 228 44222. www.hotelworld.com
cleotel@cleopatra.com.cy
A luxurious hotel located in Nicosia's business and commercial centre, the Cleopatra was built in the 1950s, and renovated a few years ago. It is popular with business travellers and those who like to be in the centre of things.

Hilton Cyprus   £££££   **298**
Arch. Makarios Ave 1516. **Road map C3.** 223 77777. FAX 22377788.
www.hilton.com hilton.cyprus@hilton.com.cy
The Hilton Cyprus is, without question, one of the most luxurious hotels in Cyprus. It is also the only 5-star hotel in Nicosia. It is situated within walking distance of the historic Nicosia town centre. The luxuriously appointed guest rooms, with every possible amenity, provide a breathtaking view of the city.

Hilton Park Nicosia   £££££   **194**
G. Digenis 2413. **Road map C3.** 226 95111. FAX 223 51918. www.louishotels.com
forum@louishotels.com
The elegant, 4-star Hilton Park Nicosia is recommended as a good venue for business travellers. It is located close to the historic Nicosia town centre.

Holiday Inn Nicosia   £££££   **140**
Rigenis St 70. **Road map C3.** 227 12712. FAX 226 73337.
hinnicres@cytanet.com.cy
The Holiday Inn is the best hotel within the ramparts of old Nicosia. The rooms are comfortable, and there's an indoor pool and a rooftop bar. The hotel provides a smart venue for business and recreation. The banqueting rooms can accommodate up to 2,000 people, and the five restaurants serve European and international cuisine.

NORTH CYPRUS

BELLAPAIS: *Ambelia Village*   ££   **33**
Road map C2. 815 36 55. FAX 815 77 01.
ambelia@northcyprus.net
Ambelia Village features luxury bungalows with magnificent views of the impressive Bellapais Abbey. There are also smart villas surrounded by exotic greenery.

BELLAPAIS: *Bellapais Gardens*   £££   **17**
Crusader Rd. **Road map C2.** 815 60 66. FAX 815 76 67.
www.bellapaisgardens.com info@bellapaisgardens.com
The Bellapais Gardens hotel stands on a hillside, at the foot of the monastery. For safety reasons (there are steep banks at the hotel) children are not permitted. Accommodation is spread across a series of apartments and bungalows. The setting is ideal for a quiet, tranquil stay. The stylish restaurant serves local cuisine.

FAMAGUSTA (GAZIMAĞUSA): *Mimoza Beach Hotel*   ££   **52**
Road map E3. 378 8219. FAX 378 90 77.
An exceptionally pleasant small hotel located right by the sea, the Mimoza Beach Hotel has a private beach and a poolside/beach bar.

FAMAGUSTA (GAZIMAĞUSA): *Park Hotel* £€£ | 89
Salamis Rd. **Road map** E3. (378 82 13. FAX 378 91 11. @ parkhotel@ebim.net
The Park Hotel is a colonial-style hotel on the seashore. Car hire is available
on site.

KARAVAS (ALCANCAK): *Merit Crystal Cove Hotel & Casino* £€£€£ | 220
Karavas, Kyrenia. **Road map** C2. (821 23 45. FAX 821 87 74. W www.merithotels.com
@ meritcristal@superonline.com
This luxury hotel and casino has a private beach, water sports facilities and
sea views from every guest room.

KYRENIA (GIRNE): *Yalin Guest House* £ | 11
S. Ozdemir 5. **Road map** C2. (815 43 99. FAX 815 42 66. @ asaltur@kktc.net
The Yalin Guest House is a pleasant, family-run inn, located within a
15-minute walk of the centre of Kyrenia.

KYRENIA (GIRNE): *British Hotel* £ | 18
Yacht Harbour. **Road map** C2. (815 22 40. FAX 815 27 42.
W www.britishhotelcyprus.com @ info@britishhotelcyprus.com
A delightful, clean guesthouse set in a residential district, about a 10-minute
walk from the town centre.

KYRENIA (GIRNE): *Dome Hotel* £€£ | 160
Kordonboyu St, PO Box 6, Kyrenia. **Road map** C2. (815 24 53. FAX 815 24 52.
W www.domehotel.com @ thedome@kktc.net
The Dome Hotel is located in the old yacht harbour. Recently refurbished, the
hotel has a stylish interior. Friendly staff.

KYRENIA (GIRNE): *Pitoresk Holiday Village* £€£ | 64
Orhan Durusoy Ave, Kyrenia. **Road map** C2. (815 582 76. FAX 815 582 75.
W www.pitoresk-northcyprus.com @ info@pitoresk-northcyprus.com
This prestigious hotel is located in the town centre, close to the harbour. It
has private swimming pools and owns a stretch of the coast. The restaurant is
renowned for its excellent cuisine.

KYRENIA (GIRNE): *Acapulco Beach Club* £€£ | 430
Agios Epiktitos (Çatalcöy), Kyrenia. **Road map** C2. (824 41 10. FAX 824 44 55.
W www.acapulco.com.tr @ info@acapulco.com.tr
A holiday village perched on the mountain slope above Kyrenia, the Acapulco
Beach Club has a terrace overlooking Kyrenia and the Mediterranean.

KYRENIA (GIRNE): *The Colony* £€£€£ | 90
Ecevit Caddesi, Kyrenia. **Road map** C2. (815 15 18. FAX 815 59 88.
W www.parkheritage.com @ thecolony@parkheritage.com
The most luxurious hotel in Kyrenia, the Colony has all the amenities visiors
could wish for, including a rooftop swimming pool, fitness facilities, massage,
two restaurants and bars.

LAPITHOS (LAPTA): *LA Hotel & Resort* £ | 101
Road map C2. (282 189 81. FAX 282 189 92. W www.la-hotel_cyprus.com
@ info@la_hotel_cyprus.com
This hotel resort has a somewhat nostalgic feel to it. Guests can spend time
lounging by the lovely swimming pool surrounded by greenery, with a view
of the mountains.

LAPITHOS (LAPTA): *Manolya Hotel* £ | 48
Road map C2. (821 84 98. FAX 821 81 24.
W www.manolyahotel.com @ info@manolyahotel.com
A pleasant, family-run hotel set on a rocky seashore, the Manolya overlooks
the excavated ancient city ruins. Guests dining at the restaurant are cooled by
sea breezes.

LÉFKA (LEFKE): *Lefke Gardens Hotel* £ | 21
Road map C2. (728 82 23. FAX 728 82 22.
W www.lefkegardens.com @ lefkegardens@veezy.com
A delightful hotel with a charming stone courtyard, in the old part of Lefka. Its
main attractions include the stylish interior and rustic furniture.

NORTH NICOSIA (LEFKOŞA): *Saray Hotel* £€£ | 72
Road map C2. Atatürk Sq. (228 31 15. FAX 228 48 08. @ saray@northcyprus.net
The tallest building in North Nicosia, the Saray Hotel features the excitement of
its casino, as well as a restaurant and roof terrace with great views of Nicosia.
Lovely café on the square in front of the hotel.

For key to symbols see back flap

WHERE TO EAT

Signboard of a Cypriot tavern

The range of restaurants in Cyprus is wide enough to satisfy even the most discerning gastronome. The predominant type of eatery is the small, inexpensive bar; the most popular serving local cuisine. The true atmosphere of a Cypriot banquet can be experienced in a traditional *taverna*, while swanky restaurants tend more towards European style. Greek-style *tavernas* and Turkish-style restaurants *(meyhane)* guarantee an evening with a great Cypriot atmosphere, often featuring folk performances and music. In general, the further you go from the popular resorts, the more authentic the cuisine.

A traditional Cypriot *taverna* in Nicosia

There are hundreds of cafés and snack bars selling Cypriot specialities such as *souvlaki* and doner kebabs, as well as sandwiches, burgers and pizzas.

Dinner, the most celebrated meal of the day, is eaten between 8pm and late into the night. An evening around the table is a social event, and can last several hours, so it is worth selecting a table with a good view. The meal usually starts with a selection of *mezedhes* (appetisers), followed by a meat or fish main course accompanied by wine.

A popular waterfront bar on one of Kyrenia's beaches

CHOOSING A RESTAURANT

A VAST SELECTION of eating establishments exists in Cyprus. This is particularly evident in the popular resorts, where there are tavernas and restaurants on every street, serving a range of local and international cuisine. In addition to the traditional *tavernas*, serving Greek and Turkish-influenced dishes, there are French, Italian, Mexican, Chinese, Thai, Indian, Middle Eastern, Russian and even Japanese restaurants.

There are also hundreds of cafés and snack bars, as well as a growing number of international fast-food restaurants

Most restaurants are casual, without a dress code. In terms of value, restaurants in town are usually cheaper than hotel restaurants. Look out for establishments frequented by the locals – these tend to serve good-value, tasty food.

On the whole, eating out in Cyprus is reasonable. Do bear in mind, however, that imported wines are much more expensive than locally produced wines.

WHEN TO EAT

BREAKFAST IS usually eaten between 7:30 and 10am. Most budget and inexpensive hotels serve a Continental breakfast, consisting of tea or coffee, fruit juice, toast, white bread, jam, honey and butter. Upscale hotels usually provide guests with a self-service bar, stocked with light salads, a selection of cheeses, scrambled eggs and sausages. In North Cyprus it is customary to serve the traditional Turkish breakfast of bread, jam, white cheese and olives.

Lunch is usually eaten between noon and 2:30pm.

Menu boards outside a fish restaurant

WHAT TO EAT

THE EXQUISITE cuisine of Cyprus is famous for the simplicity of its ingredients and its ease of preparation. Traditional local recipes are influenced by modern European trends – British cuisine plays a major role here.

The most important items on a Cypriot menu are the starters – called *mezedhes* – a vital element of a meal in any Mediterranean country, accompanied by traditional Cypriot bread baked on a hotplate. A decent restaurant will always

Preparing pizza in one of Nicosia's pizzerias

include *halloumi* (grilled goat cheese), roast courgettes, and the real delicacy – *koupepia* – stuffed vine leaves. Other specialities include *hummus* (chick-pea dip), *tahini* (sesame sauce), and *kleftiko* (lamb roasted in a clay stove).

For main courses, the Cypriot menu is dominated by lamb and seafood, and an array of vegetables, usually served with rice or roast potatoes. Dishes of lamb are superbly complemented by strong Cypriot wines.

Fish is the most expensive item on the menu, although at coastal locales it is generally very fresh and tasty, so well worth the expense. Chicken is usually the cheapest meat dish available.

Happily for visitors, there should be no problem choosing from the menu, as the names of dishes are usually translated.

VEGETARIANS

CYPRIOT CUISINE is based on essentially healthy Mediterranean produce and includes many vegetarian dishes, traditionally eaten in Cypriot homes during the Lenten period and other Orthodox fasts, when meat is shunned. As well as huge "village salads" *(choriatiki)* of tomatoes, cucumber, onions, peppers, olives and feta cheese, there is plentiful fresh fruit and a good array of grilled and fried vegetable dishes, based on aubergines (eggplant), courgettes (zucchini), artichokes, peppers and tomatoes, and lots of tasty dips based on chick-peas,

fava beans and other pulses. Cypriot cheeses are also worth recommending, especially the traditional fried halloumi cheese.

However, there is little understanding in Cyprus of the pure vegetarian diet and it is not easy to find a restaurant that will prepare true vegetarian meals to order – even many so-called vegetable dishes may contain meat stock. In resorts vegetarians may find their choices limited to cheese, omelettes, fruit and salads.

ALCOHOL

A S FAR BACK as ancient times, Cyprus has produced good wines, helped by the fertile soil and warm, mild climate. The quality of local wine has been maintained to this day, thanks to the careful nurturing and traditional methods of wine production.

Wine-tasting sessions are held in wineries all over the island. Between them, these wineries produce nearly 40 varieties of wine, sherry and brandy. In the villages at the foot of the mountains you can try homemade liqueurs, which, in terms of quality and flavour, are often as good as branded products.

The best known product is the sweet dessert wine, Commandaria. Nicknamed the "Cypriot sun", this fortified wine with a raisin-like flavour makes an excellent digestive to round off a traditional Cypriot dinner, and a good

souvenir to take home. The strong, dry *zivania* aperitif is classified by the European Union as eau-de-vie.

The locally produced beers have a good flavour and are also inexpensive. In North Cyprus you should try cold Efes; in the south, try KEO or the island-bottled Carlsberg.

Tables set on the terrace of Kybele restaurant, in Bellapais

PRICES

T HE HIGHEST PRICES are charged by restaurants in fashionable resorts. Here the best-value meals are generally the chef's recommended dishes of the day. Set menus may be substantially cheaper than a selection of à la carte items. Seafood dishes are particularly expensive.

You can eat more reasonably at restaurants in town – especially those frequented by the locals.

The total bill always includes VAT (10%) and usually a service charge (around 10%). Most restaurants accept credit cards nowadays.

Bedrock – one of several themed restaurants in Agia Napa

What to Eat

Goat's cheese

WHILE STAYING IN CYPRUS it is worth switching over to the delights of the local cuisine. This draws on elements of the Mediterranean tradition, with fresh fruit and vegetables, olive oil, and delicious wines. The hearty local food is a mixture of Greek and Turkish cuisine, with British influences. Vegetables and meat (especially lamb, minced or in the form of *shashlik*) are prepared in a traditional way, and the delicious goat's cheese, *halloumi*, can be added to virtually any dish. Fresh seafood is abundant along the coast.

Cypriot Salad
The traditional fresh vegetable salad, popular on the island, is served with pita bread.

Pita bread

Fresh tomatoes

Aubergine slices

Green olives

Avgolemono (Düğün)
Lemon soup with egg, served with bread ,makes an ideal mid-morning light meal.

Meze
A popular tradition in Cyprus, meze is a selection of appetisers. It includes vegetables – usually olives, aubergine, capers, fried peppers and tomatoes – as well as loukanika (smoked sausage), tzatziki (a yoghurt and cucumber dip) and pita bread, served on small plates. This sumptuous dish can pass for an entire meal. Seaside restaurants specialize in seafood meze.

Laz böreği (North Cyprus)
are pancakes or pies filled with a tasty herb-seasoned meat or cheese mixture.

Kolokotes (Cyprus)
are dumplings filled with pasta with pumpkin, raisins and cracked wheat.

Börek (North Cyprus) *are pastries filled with chunks of meat or cheese - best when served hot.*

Moussaka *is a popular baked dish of ground lamb with aubergines and sweet potatoes, served with a bechamel sauce.*

Manti (North Cyprus)
is a Turkish meat-filled pasta, topped with garlic-spiced yoghurt and chilli. It is a very tasty dish.

Karniyarik (North Cyprus)
are baked aubergines stuffed with a meat mixture. They are delicious as hors-d'oeuvres, or a light snack on a hot day.

Sheftalia *are delicious grilled spicy pork sausages seasoned with herbs and served with pita bread and olives.*

Afélia (Cyprus) *is a pork dish simmered in a red wine and herb sauce, with ground coriander seeds.*

Souvlaki *is pork* shashlik *served with rice or wheat cakes, vegetables and various seasoned sauces.*

Kupepia (dolmades) *are the ubiquitous vine leaves stuffed with a mixture of minced lamb, rice and herbs.*

Fresh olives

Bay leaf

Baked onions

Lamb ribs

Kléftiko (küp kebap) *is a dish of lamb ribs roasted in a traditional clay oven. It is traditionally served with roasted stuffed peppers, rice and fresh olives.*

DESSERTS

The island of Aphrodite is famous for its grapes, and the best local desserts are fruit or almonds in grape juice, served with Cypriot-style coffee.

Bakláva (baklava) *is a very sweet dessert made of slices of pastry interlaid with grape syrup and honey.*

Loukoumia (lokum) *is the traditional Turkish delight – sugar-dusted fruit jelly, often with almonds and nuts.*

WHAT TO DRINK

Early in the day, a cup of strong Cypriot coffee, always served with a glass of cold water, will put you on your feet. Fresh fruit juices are delicious and relatively inexpensive. Local wines are of a high quality, and reasonably priced. There are nearly 40 varieties of locally produced wine (the sweet commandaria is particularly good), sherry and brandy. The local vodkas – *zivania* and *ouzo* – are also worth trying.

Cypriot brandy

Zivania vodka

Cypriot-style coffee, always served with water

Choosing a Restaurant

THE FOLLOWING RESTAURANTS have been selected across a wide range of price categories for their good value, exceptional food, and/or interesting location. The restaurants are listed by region. Central Cyprus has been omitted from this list, due to its non-existent tourist infrastructure. Colour-coded thumb tabs in the margin make it easy to find the right region.

	CREDIT CARDS ACCEPTED	OUTSIDE TABLES	VEGETARIAN DISHES	GOOD WINE LIST	OPEN LATE

WEST CYPRUS

LATCHI: *Yiangos & Peter Fish Tavern* €€€
Road map A3. 263 21411.
In the hands of the same fishing family since 1939, this is a restaurant with a strong tradition. Fresh fish and shellfish are brought in every day. Live shows are available on request. ⏰ 8:30am–midnight. 🅿 ♨ ♿ 🕴

LATCHI-POLIS: *Psaropolous Fish Tavern* €€€
Road map A3. 263 21089.
This seaside restaurant, with a spacious, modern interior, has access to the beach. The chef's specials include fish and seafood dishes. ⏰ 11am–11pm.
🅿 ♨ ♿ 🕴

PAFOS: *Petra Tou Romiou* €€
Road map A4. 269 99005.
The restaurant stands on the old coastal road to Limassol, 20 km (12.5 miles) from Pafos, overlooking the rocks of Aphrodite. It serves truly delicious souvla – grilled meat. ⏰ 8am–8:30pm (summer), 8am–5pm (winter). 🅿 🕴 ♿

PAFOS: *Roman Tavern* €€
Road map A4.
A charming stylized hotel restaurant, modelled on a Roman house with colourful frescos. In the evening, tables are set around the swimming pool. Specialties are grilled and barbecued food. ⏰ 7:45am–10pm. 📋 🅿 ♿ 🕴 ♨ 🎵 🈺

PAFOS: *Kastro Tavern* €€€
Apostolos Paulos Ave 110. Road map A4. 269 33088.
This popular harbour restaurant serves traditional and international dishes, and seafood. The Chef's special is the fish *meze*. ⏰ 10am–11pm. 📋

PAFOS: *O'Neills Irish Bar & Grill* €€€€
Tombs Of The Kings Rd. Road map A4. 269 35888.
O'Neill's is a restaurant with an Irish pub atmosphere, practically guaranteed to be noisy and packed. There is a large plasma screen to which everyone, including the staff, is glued during sports events. There are also live music concerts here. ⏰ 10am–2am. 📋 🅿 ♿ 🕴 🎵

PAFOS: *Phukhet Chinese* €€€
Tombs Of The King Rd. Road map A4. 269 36738.
🌐 www.3ds.com.cy/phukhet
Phuket Chinese is an oriental-style restaurant on the road to Polis, serving Chinese and Thai cuisine. Chinese dumplings and Peking duck are particularly recommended. ⏰ 6pm–midnight. 📋 🅿 ♨ ♿ 🕴 🎵

PAFOS: *Seven St. Georges Tavern* €€€€
Geroskipos. Road map A4. 996 55824. 🌐 www.7stgeorgestavern.com
@ 7st_geor@spidernet.net
This is one of the best restaurants in Cyprus, situated at the border of Pano Pafos, Kato Pafos and Geroskipou. It serves traditional *meze*, and delicious *kléftiko*. ⏰ 12:30–3pm & 7:30–11pm. ⬤ Jan. 🅿 ♿ 🕴 ♨

PAFOS: *The Pelican Restaurant* €€€€
Apostolos Paulos Ave 102. Road map A4. 262 52500.
This famous harbour restaurant is situated close to the historic fortifications in Pafos. Its main attraction is the trained pelican, Coco. The restaurant specializes in fish and other seafood. ⏰ 11am–midnight. 🅿 🕴 ♨ 📋

PAFOS: *Theo's Seafood Restaurant* €€€€
Apostolos Paulos Ave 100. Road map A4. 269 32829.
This harbour restaurant is popular, so it is worth booking a table in advance. Theo's is famous for its fish and shellfish. Its most eye-catching feature is the large aquarium. ⏰ 8:30am–midnight. 🅿 🕴 ♨

		CREDIT CARDS ACCEPTED	OUTSIDE TABLES	VEGETARIAN DISHES	GOOD WINE LIST	OPEN LATE

Price for a three-course meal for one, including half a bottle of wine, tax and service, in Cyprus pounds:
£ under £10
££ £10–15
£££ £15–20
££££ £20–30
£££££ over £30

CREDIT CARDS ACCEPTED
The restaurant accepts major credit cards.

OUTSIDE TABLES
The restaurant has tables outside on a terrace, in a garden or in a courtyard.

VEGETARIAN DISHES
The menu includes some vegetarian options.

GOOD WINE LIST
The menu includes a large selection of wines.

POLIS: *Archontariki Tavern*   **£££**
Makarios Ave. **Road map** A3. (263 21328. w www.archontariki.com.cy
This stylish old house, situated in the centre of this small town, serves delicious king prawns in white wine. ⃝ *9am–midnight.* 🍽 P 🥗 ⛹ 👥 🎵

POLIS: *Old Town*   **££££**
Kyproleontos 9. **Road map** A3. (263 22758.
This restaurant is renowned for its Mediterranean cuisine and famous guests, who include Albert, Prince of Monaco, and Jean-Paul Belmondo. ⃝ *5pm–midnight.* 🍽 P ⛹ 👥

SOUTH CYPRUS

AGIA NAPA: *La Casa di Napa*   **££**
D. Solomou 8. **Road map** E3. (237 22137. @ napacasa@cytanet.com.cy
An extremely pleasant Italian restaurant with a wood-fired pizza oven. Serves pizzas as well as other Italian dishes. ⃝ *5pm–midnight.* 🥗 ⛹ 👥

AGIA NAPA: *Liquid Café Bar*   **££**
Kryou Nerou 8. **Road map** E3.
Small, family-run restaurant with a giant TV screen. Spaghetti and sandwiches are particularly good. Large selection of soft drinks and alcoholic beverages. ⃝ *9am–2am.* P 🍽 ⛹ 👥

AGIA NAPA: *Garden's Restaurant*   **£££**
Asprovouniou 1. **Road map** E3. (237 22225.
A modern, smart restaurant on the main road with a large garden and live music. You can also watch live transmissions of sporting events on TV. Very good drinks. ⃝ *10am–11:30pm.* P ⛹ 👥 🥗 🎵 📺

AGIA NAPA: *Gui-Lin*   **£££**
Makariou 2. **Road map** E3. (237 21043. @ guilin@cytanet.com.cy
A smart Chinese restaurant in the town centre. The chef recommends the Peking duck. ⃝ *4–11pm.* 🍽 ⛹ 👥 🥗

AGIA NAPA: *Limanaki Fish and Grill Restaurant*   **£££**
1. Octavriou. **Road map** E3. (237 21600. w www.ayianapahotels.net
@ limanaki.beach@cytanet.com.cy
Limanaki is situated close to the town centre, by the old fishing harbour and near the largest sandy beach in Agia Napa. The restaurant specializes in fish *meze.* ⃝ *7am–11pm.* P 🍽 👥 ⛹ 🥗 🎵

AGIA NAPA: *Odyssos*   **£££**
Nissi Ave. **Road map** E3. (238 16231. @ info@tavernasportsbar.com
Opposite the famous Nissi beach, here at Odyssos palm trees grow on the terrace and cats sneak between tables. There is also a children's playground. The fresh fish dishes are well worth trying. ⃝ *9am–11:30pm.* P 👥 ⛹ 📺

AGIA NAPA: *Petinos Café Restaurant*   **£££**
1. Octavriou 3. **Road map** E3. (237 21645. @ ariskyn@yahoo.com
This restaurant is famous for its Cypriot specialities – particularly the extensive *meze* and very good local wines. ⃝ *3pm–midnight.* P ⛹ 👥 🥗

AGIA NAPA: *Vassos Fish Harbour Tavern*   **£££**
Makariou 51. **Road map** E3. (237 21884. w www.vassosfishrest.com
Resembling a small Cypriot town, this restaurant overlooks the ships and fishing vessels in the harbour. Try the seafood *meze.* ⃝ *8am–11pm.* P ⛹ 👥

AGIA NAPA: *Zorba's the Greek Restaurant*   **£££**
1. Octavriou 15. **Road map** E3. (237 23586.
Popular with tourists, this fish restaurant standing close to the harbour is always full. The traditional Cypriot *meze* is well worth recommending. ⃝ *8:30–midnight.* P ⛹ 👥

For key to symbols see back flap

Price for a three-course meal for one, including half a bottle of wine, tax and service, in Cyprus pounds:
£ under £10
££ £10–15
£££ £15–20
££££ £20–30
£££££ over £30

CREDIT CARDS ACCEPTED
The restaurant accepts major credit cards.

OUTSIDE TABLES
The restaurant has tables outside on a terrace, in a garden or in a courtyard.

VEGETARIAN DISHES
The menu includes some vegetarian options.

GOOD WINE LIST
The menu includes a large selection of wines.

	Credit Cards Accepted	Outside Tables	Vegetarian Dishes	Good Wine List	Open Late

AGIA NAPA: *Maistrali Beach Restaurant*   **££££**
Kriuy Nepoy 42. **Road map** E3. 237 23754.
Local and international cuisine, with an emphasis on fish. Maistrali has a beautiful view of the beach and the sea. ☐ *Mar–Oct: 6am–1pm.* **P** 🚻

AGIA NAPA: *Sage Restaurant and Vine Bar*   **££££**
Kryou Nerou 10. **Road map** E3. 238 16110. **W** www.sagerest.com
A smart restaurant, at the very heart of the resort, close to the famous monastery. ☐ *5–11pm.* **P** 🚻

LARNACA: *Paradise Restaurant*   **££**
Dheklia Rd. Galaxia St 2. **Road map** D3. 246 44321.
A pleasant restaurant plainly furnished but cosy, a short distance from the sea. The moussaka is delicious. ☐ *9am–11pm.* ● *Jan & Feb.* **P** 🍽

LARNACA: *Petalo Restaurant Taverna*   **££**
Larnaca-Dheklia Rd. **Road map** D3. 246 45127.
A family-run restaurant situated in a side street, surrounded by greenery. The tables are arranged on a large veranda under a thatched roof, with oleanders growing all around. ☐ *Apr–Oct: 9am–11pm.* **P**

LARNACA: *Faros*   **£££**
Okeanias 6. **Road map** D3. 248 15370. **W** www.farospub.com
This restaurant contains a lighthouse, and there are also tables in the pleasant garden. The menu features Cypriot dishes as well as pizzas, sandwiches and snacks. Reduced rates for children. ☐ *11am–3am.* **P**

LARNACA: *The Coral Inn*   **££££**
Dheklia Rd. **Road map** D3. 246 46200. @ boronia@cytanet.com.cy
A spacious hotel restaurant with a large veranda, furnished in native American style, with lots of wood and surrounded by exotic vegetation. The mussels in garlic sauce are particularly good. ☐ *7am until the last guest leaves.* **P**

LIMASSOL: *Mediterranean Pub-Taverna*   **££**
Promachon Eleftherias 1. **Road map** C4. 324 61109.
The restaurant, in the town centre, has a vine-covered arbour, citrus and palm trees, and attractive rockery. ● *Sun 4am–midnight.* **P**

LIMASSOL: *Pizza Plus*   **££**
Promachon Eleftherias 13. **Road map** C4. 233 11555.
Pizza is prepared in front of the guests, and baked in coal-fired oven, at this traditional-style Italian restaurant. The staff are extremely nice. The take-away pizza is much cheaper. ☐ *noon–midnight.* **P**

LIMASSOL: *Red Rum*   **££**
28. Octavriou 3322. **Road map** C4. 255 90946.
Red Rum is located on the main street in the town centre, facing the sea. The interior is modern, the staff are friendly, there is a large terrace, and most importantly the food is delicious. The chef's specials are moussaka and Cypriot *meze.* ☐ *9am–midnight.* **P**

LIMASSOL: *Feggaria*   **£££**
Limassol–Platres Rd. **Road map** C4. 259 91125.
W www.feggariarestaurant.com @ info@feggariarestaurant.com
A popular restaurant, decorated in wood. On Tuesday, Friday and Saturday evenings guests are treated to traditional music played by Cypriot groups.
☐ *10am until the last guest leaves.* **P**

LIMASSOL: *Kalymnos*   **£££**
Governor's Beach. **Road map** C4. FAX 256 32878.
Kalymnos lies on a picturesque bay, near the popular Governor's Beach. The vast terrace affords a lovely view of the bay. The staff are friendly and efficient. ☐ *9–11pm (summer), 9am–6pm (winter).* **P**

LIMASSOL: *Ladas Old Harbour* €€€
Road map C4. **[** 253 65760.
This marine-themed restaurant is located in a large building by the entrance to the harbour. Fish and other seafood feature strongly on the menu, and are definitely recommended. ☐ *noon–midnight.* ● *Sun.* **P** ▤

LIMASSOL: *O Mylos Café Lounge* €€€
Old Carob Mill Factory, adjacent to the medieval castle. **Road map** C4.
[258 20469. **W** www.carobmill-restaurants.com
Modern décor contrasts with old stone walls at this restaurant. House specials include sandwiches with prosciutto and mozzarella. ☐ *9am–2am.* **P** ▤ ⚡

LIMASSOL: *To Frourio Restaurant Tavern* €€€
Tsanakali 18. **Road map** C4. **[** 253 59332.
A delightful restaurant located by Limassol Castle, To Frourio occupies an old building with traditional interior. The *stifado* is particularly delicious. ☐ *10am–11pm (until 5pm in winter)* ● *Jan.*

LIMASSOL: *Artima Restaurant* €€€€
Vasilissis 3. **Road map** C4. **[** 258 20466. **W** www.e-restaurantsearch.com
@ dine@carobmill-restaurants.com
A luxurious restaurant with modern furnishings, based in an old building. The excellent bar and café nearby belong to the same owner. You can select your own live crab, which will arrive on your plate 20 minutes later. ☐ *noon–3pm & 7–11pm.* **P** 🏿 ▤ ⚡

LIMASSOL: *La Mer* €€€€
28. Octavriou 12. **Road map** C4. **[** 253 56095. **@** lamer@cytanet.com.cy
Elegant décor with plenty of wood, and local music. The speciality here at La Mer is freshly caught fish. ☐ *10am–midnight.* **P** ▤ 🏿 ⚡ ⚡

PROTARAS: *Paralimini Spartiatis* €€
Konnos 79. **Road map** E3. **[** 238 31386. **@** spartiatis@cy.net
Perched on high cliffs above the picturesque Konnos Bay, Paralimini Spartiatis is know for its fresh fish *meze.* ☐ *6–10:30pm (summer), noon–2pm (winter).* ● *Nov & Dec.* **P** 🏿 ⚡

PROTARAS: *Dragon Chinese Restaurant* €€€
Cavogreko-Protaras Ave. **Road map** E3. **[** 238 31414. **FAX** 237 21654.
The Dragon serves a range of Chinese food, as well as excellent hot wine. The spicy duck is highly recommended. ☐ *Apr–Nov: 6pm–midnight.* **P** ▤ 🏿 ⚡

PROTARAS: *Flintstones Inn* €€€
Cavogreko 357. **Road map** E3. **[** 238 33848.
This family-run restaurant that will particularly delight the children. It has a Flintstones' car, bingo, karaoke, and puts on magic shows. The staff all don costumes from the children's cartoon. ☐ *May–Oct: 4pm–2am.* **P** 🏿 ⚡ ⚡

PROTARAS: *La Cygne* €€€
Vizacia 15. **Road map** E3. **[** 238 31358. **W** www.lacygne.cy.com
La Cygne is a delightful restaurant on the outskirts of Protaras, with a lovely view of the sea. Its moussakas and *stifado* are definitely worth trying.
☐ *11:30am–midnight.* **P** ⚡

PROTARAS: *Sfinx* €€€
Cavogreko 381. **Road map** E3. **[** 238 11070. **W** www.sfinxbar.com
@ sfinxbar@yahoo.com
With an ancient Egyptian theme, Sfinx is a restaurant that caters to the whole family. The moussaka and sfinxburger are particularly good. There are also seven plasma screens that deliver live transmissions of various sport events.
☐ *10am until the last guest leaves.* **P** ▤ ⚡ 🏿 ⚡

PROTARAS: *Polixenia Isaak Restaurant* €€€
Road map E3. **[** 238 32929.
A relative newcomer to the Protaras restaurant scene, the Polixenia Isaak Restaurant is located by the beach, with a lovely sea view. The cuisine is predominantly traditional Cypriot, with an emphasis on fresh grilled fish.
☐ *Mar–Nov: 8am–midnight.* **P** ⚡ ♫

PROTARAS: *The Raj Indian Restaurant* €€€
Road map E3. **[** 238 32318. **@** chat@cytanet.com.cy
The island's most popular Indian restaurant, with live music and Indian dancing in the winter. ☐ *6pm–midnight.* ● *Dec.* **P** ⚡ 🏿 ⚡

Price for a three-course meal for one, including half a bottle of wine, tax and service, in Cyprus pounds: £ under £10 — ££ £10–15 — £££ £15–20 — ££££ £20–30 — £££££ over £30	**CREDIT CARDS ACCEPTED** The restaurant accepts major credit cards. **OUTSIDE TABLES** The restaurant has tables outside on a terrace, in a garden or in a courtyard. **VEGETARIAN DISHES** The menu includes some vegetarian options. **GOOD WINE LIST** The menu includes a large selection of wines.			

TROODOS MOUNTAINS

Restaurant	Credit Cards Accepted	Outside Tables	Vegetarian Dishes	Good Wine List	Open Late
KAKOPETRIA: *Pine Hill Lodge* ££ — On the Nicosia-Troodos road. **Road map** B3. 292 3142 — A hotel restaurant, close to the ski centre, Pine Hill Lodge has a spacious modern interior and a viewing terrace on the roof. Environment-friendly restaurant, with spring water flowing from the taps. ◯ 24 hours a day.	■	●	■	●	■
LANIA: *Platanos Tavern* ££ — **Road map** B3. 254 34273. — A delightful restaurant with traditional style décor. Particularly recommended are the delicious Cypriot dishes. ◯ 10–midnight.		●	■	●	
MONIATIS: *Andreas Makris Restaurant* ££ — **Road map** B3. 254 21275. — This restaurant, with a large wooden terrace, is located right by the road. Outdoor barbeques are held on Sundays and public holidays. ◯ 6am until the last guest leaves.		●	■	●	
MONIATIS: *Paraskeuas Restaurant* ££ — **Road map** B3. 254 33626. — This small but friendly restaurant has a charming vine-canopied garden. Guests are offered *kleftiko* roasted in a traditional outdoor oven, and the best kebab in the district. Paraskeuas also sells home-produced honey and preserves. ◯ Apr–Oct: 9am until the last guest leaves.		●	■		■
MONIATIS: *Ta Pefka* £££ — Limassol–Platres Rd. **Road map** B3. 254 34388. — Ta Pefka has a spacious wood-finished interior, with a fireplace and a dance floor. The house speciality is lamb's liver. There is also a well stocked bar. ◯ 9am–midnight.		●	■	●	■
PLATRES: *Psilo Dendro* ££ — **Road map** B3. 254 21350. — This restaurant set in the forest, close to the waterfalls, runs its own trout farm. The rustic character of its interior is emphasised by chickens running between the tables. ◯ 8am–6pm.	■	●	■	●	
PRODROMOS: *Louis Restaurant Kebab Cofee Bar* ££ — **Road map** B3. 254 62049. — This small family-run restaurant on the road to Kykkos serves kebabs and other Cypriot fare; it also sells home-made candied fruit. ◯ 8am–midnight.	■	●	■		■
PRODROMOS: *Overhill Restaurant Café* ££ — **Road map** B3. 254 62095. — Overlooking Mount Olympus, the Overhill Restaurant Café is located in the highest village in Cyprus. Guests can enjoy its spacious terrace, as well as the delicious food, including *stifado* and *kléftiko*. ◯ 8am–midnight.	■	●	■	●	■
PRODROMOS: *To Byzantio* ££ — **Road map** B3. 254 62047. — This restaurant along the road to Kykkos monastery is very popular with tourists. It has a view of Mount Olympus. ◯ noon–5pm.	■	●	■		
SAITTAS: *Okella Hotel Restaurant* £££ — **Road map** B4. 254 32521. @ efi@cytanet.com.cy — A hotel restaurant serving rustic cuisine, with a terrace overlooking the valley. The *souvla* and *kléftiko* are highly recommended. ◯ 6am–midnight.	■	●		●	■
TRIMIKLINI: *Green Valley Café Waterfalls Restaurant* £ — **Road map** B4. 996 28999. — This sandwich bar is set along a footpath leading to waterfalls. There are tables and stalls selling fruit from the owner's garden, as well as a souvenir shop. ◯ 8am–8pm.		●	■		

TRIMIKLINI: *J. R. Restaurant* ⓔ
Road map B4. 📞 254 32212.
Scenically perched on a mountain slope, J.R. features an arcaded terrace with view of the valley. Particularly recommended are the moussaka and *afélia* (pork cooked in red wine with coriander seeds).Postcards and souvenirs are sold here, too. ◐ *summer: 8am until the last guest leaves; winter 8am–6pm.* 🅿 ▤ ⅃ ⅃

TROODOS: *Dolfin* ⓔⓔ
Road map B3. 📞 254 20215.
The renovated 1940s building that houses Dolfin was once an army sports centre. Every Sunday there is a buffet of traditional Cypriot food. ◐ *9am–10pm.*
🅿 ▤ ⅃ ⅃

TROODOS: *Fereos Park Restaurant* ⓔⓔ
Road map B3. 📞 254 20114.
This small taverna, with a wood-finished interior, stands in the centre of the village, which is on the edge of the national park. There is also a wine shop here. ◐ *7am–midnight.* 🅿 ⅃

VASA: *Ariadne Restaurant* ⓔⓔ
On the road from Limassol to the Troodos mountains, near Omodos.
Road map B4. 📞 259 42185.
The speciality of this family-run restaurant is *kupepia* (stuffed vine leaves).
◐ *noon–4pm & 7–11pm.* 🅿 ⅃

SOUTH NICOSIA

Chilies Mexican Restaurant ⓔⓔ
Hippocrates 46/49. **Road map** C3. 📞 226 71647. W www.chilies.co.cy
Chilies Mexican Restaurant, with a pleasing décor of warm colours, serves supposedly the best Mexican food in the capital. Try the *fajitas* or spare ribs.
◐ *9am–midnight.* 🅿 ▤ ⅃ ⅃ ⅃

Finikas ⓔⓔ
Ledra St 51. **Road map** C3. 📞 226 60060.
A quiet restaurant with modern furnishings, Finikas stands close to the wall dividing Cyprus into Greek and Turkish zones, on a spot which, until recently, was just a pile of rubble. ◐ *11am–4pm & 7:30pm–midnight.* 🅿 ▤ ⅃ ⅃ ⅃

Kyklos Cafe ⓔⓔ
Hippocrates. **Road map** C3. 📞 226 69998.
A café in the city centre, housed in an 1850 building. It will serve you a sophisticated drink and *hookah.* ◐ *3pm–midnight.* ⅃

Xefoto Live Music Taverna ⓔⓔ
Aeschylou 6, Laïki Geitonia. **Road map** C3. 📞 226 66567.
A large restaurant with many rooms, traditional furnishings and a huge tree growing inside. Here you can listen to live folk music. Reservations are necessary at weekends. ◐ *morning–midnight.* 🅿 ▤ ⅃ ⅃ ⅃

To Steki Tis Loxandra ⓔⓔ
Phaneromeni 67/69. **Road map** C3. 📞 226 75757.
This restaurant is extremely popular with locals, as well as with tourists. Reservations are recommended. The traditional cuisine served here is particularly delicious. ◐ *6pm–midnight.* ● *Easter.* 🅿 ⅃ ⅃

N. Mike-Square-Alexandros ⓔⓔⓔ
C. Pantelides. **Road map** C3. 📞 226 71174.
This restaurant is situated by the entrance gate to the Old Town. The owner offers reduced rates to students, soldiers and groups. ◐ *8am–3pm.* ▤ ⅃ 📺

NORTH CYPRUS

ALSANCAK (KARAVAS): *Shanghai Chinese Restaurant* ⓔⓔⓔ
Karaoganoglu Cad. 28. **Road map** C2. 📞 0392 821 84 35.
@ eric_girne@hotmail.com
A lovely Chinese restaurant with a garden and a vine-covered roof. Small rooms decorated in Oriental style with Chinese lanterns and ornaments create an intimate atmosphere. ◐ *6:30pm–midnight.* 🅿 ▤ ⅃ ⅃ ⅃

BELLAPAIS: *The Abbey Bell Tower* ⓔⓔ
Opposite Bellapais Abbey. **Road map** C2. 📞 392 815 75 07.
This charming restaurant, surrounded by greenery, affords a magnificent view of the mountains and the sea. ◐ *9am–midnight.* 🅿 ⅃ ♫

<table>
<tr><td colspan="2">

Price for a three-course meal for one, including half a bottle of wine, tax and service, in Cyprus pounds:
(£) under £10
(£)(£) £10–15
(£)(£)(£) £15–20
(£)(£)(£)(£) £20–30
(£)(£)(£)(£)(£) over £30

</td><td colspan="2">

CREDIT CARDS ACCEPTED
The restaurant accepts major credit cards.

OUTSIDE TABLES
The restaurant has tables outside on a terrace, in a garden or in a courtyard.

VEGETARIAN DISHES
The menu includes some vegetarian options.

GOOD WINE LIST
The menu includes a large selection of wines.

</td></tr>
</table>

	CREDIT CARDS ACCEPTED	OUTSIDE TABLES	VEGETARIAN DISHES	GOOD WINE LIST	OPEN LATE
BOGAZI (BOĞAZ): *Moon Over The Water* **(£)(£)** Bogaz Rd 10. **Road map** E2. (392 371 32 57. W www.moonoverthewater98.TRIPOD.com @ moonoverthewater98@yahoo.com This wonderful European restaurant is the most delightful place on the east coast of North Cyprus. The restaurant overlooks the sea. ☐ *Tue–Sat: 6:30am–midnight; Sun: noon–midnight.* ● *Mon.* P & ♿	■	●	■	●	
BOGAZI (BOĞAZ): *Bogaz Terrace Restaurant* **(£)(£)(£)** Close to the harbour. **Road map** E2. (392 37 12 558. W www.bogazhotel.com @ bogazhotel@superonline.com Situated along the road leading to north Karpas, this restaurant has a timber-roofed dining room. Standing next to a sandy beach, it also has a bar and a disco. ☐ *9am–2am.* P ▤ & ♿ ✦ ♬	■	●	■	●	■
BOGAZI (BOĞAZ): *Neşe Fish Restaurant* **(£)(£)(£)** Karpoz Yolu. **Road map** E2. (392 371 26 41. This restaurant is situated 25 km (15.5 miles) from Famagusta, in the direction of Korpu. The menu features daily fish, freshly caught. Guests can sit right at the water's edge. The interior is decorated with fishing nets and exotic fish. ☐ *noon until the last guest leaves.* P & ♿ ✦	■	●	■	●	■
ÇATALKÖY (AGIOS EPIKTITOS): *Valley View Restaurant & Bar* **(£)(£)** Next door to the Acapulco Hotel. **Road map** C2. (533 86870. A delightful old-style restaurant with a sea view, shaded by palm trees. The house specials include meat, fish and *kleftiko* cooked in an earth oven. Dishes are prepared with own farm-grown produce. ☐ *10am–midnight.* P &	■	●	■		
FAMAGUSTA (GAZIMAĞUSA): *Hurma Restaurant* **(£)(£)** Nadir Yolu 8 – Maraş. **Road map** E3. (392 366 97 00. In a stylish building surrounded by palm trees and bougainvillea, Hurma Restaurant is by the seashore, on the edge of the Ghost Town. The house speciality is fresh fish with meze. ☐ *11am–11pm.* P ✦	■	●	■		
FAMAGUSTA (GAZIMAĞUSA): *La Veranda Café Restaurant* **(£)(£)** **Road map** E3. (357 0153. @ bugratansu@hotmail.com This pleasant restaurant with a garden standson the square close to the mosque. The chef's *piece de résistance* is roast chicken with wild mushrooms. La Veranda also serves fresh citrus fruit juices. ☐ *9am–10pm.* P	■	●	■		
FAMAGUSTA (GAZIMAĞUSA): *Petek Pattiserie* **(£)(£)** Yeàil Deniz 1, Stare Miasto. **Road map** E3. (392 366 71 04. W www.akpetek.com @ bar_demirci@yahoo.com A delightful patisserie housed in a stylish building in the main street of Old Famagusta. Whispering indoor fountains with swimming turtles; and a magnificent view from the terrace. ☐ *8am–1am.* P ▤ & ♿ ⊞	■	●	■		
FAMAGUSTA (GAZIMAĞUSA): *Sari Ismalin Yeri* **(£)(£)** Palm Beach Rd. **Road map** E3. (392 366 39 53. Right by the water's edge, with a view of the Old Famagusta towers, this unremarkable looking restaurant serves very tasty food, particularly the fish dishes. ☐ *11am–2am.* P & ♿	■	●	■		■
FAMAGUSTA (GAZIMAĞUSA): *DB Café* **(£)(£)(£)** Namik Kemal Meydani 14. **Road map** E3. (392 366 66 10. W www.db.com.tr DB Café is regarded as the queen of pizzerias. Its walls are adorned with photographs of movie stars. Besides pizza, there are steaks, Turkish dishes and salads. ☐ *10am–1am.*	■	●	■	●	■
GEMIKONAGI (KARAVOSTÁSI): *Mardin Restaurant* **(£)(£)(£)** **Road map** B3. (392 727 74 39, 727 81 50. A cosy little seafront restaurant, surrounded by plantations of citrus fruit, vegetables and figs. Tables are set outdoors, under the thatched roof. Specializes in fresh fish from daily catch. ☐ *11am–11pm.* P &	■	●	■	●	■

KYRENIA (GIRNE): *Körfez Beach Restaurant* €€
Çatalcöy Rd. **Road map** C2. (392 824 47 29.
This restaurant set on a craggy shore affords a magnificent view of the sea and the Pentadaktylos mountains. The grilled fish and *kléftiko* are particularly worth recommending. ○ May–mid-Nov: 8am–midnight. P &

KYRENIA (GIRNE): *Mirabelle Restaurant* €€
Ugur Mumen Rd 2. **Road map** C2. (392 815 73 90.
This roadside restaurant, set in a stylish building amid palms and olive trees, specializes in fresh fish and international cuisine. ○ 10am–3pm & 6pm until the last guest leaves. P 目 & ⚘ ⚮ ♬

KYRENIA (GIRNE): *Lemon Tree Fish Restaurant* €€€
On the Kyrenia–Çatalcöy road. **Road map** C2. (392 824 40 45.
This fish restaurant stands in a citrus tree orchard. A bubbling brook flows nearby. ○ 10am–midnight. P 目 &

KYRENIA (GIRNE): *Niazi's Restaurant* €€€
Kordonboyn Cad. **Road map** C2. (392 815 21 60.
This is a restaurant with a long tradition. It was established in 1949 in Limassol, and moved to Kyrenia following the island's partition. It is famous for its *kebabs* and *meze*, and a wide choice of alcoholic beverages. ○ 11am–midnight. P 目

KYRENIA (GIRNE): *Set Fish Restaurant* €€€
Yet Limani. **Road map** C2. (0392 815 23 36.
Set Fish Restaurant is housed in a building dating from the Venetian period, close to the yacht marina. Tables are set on a natural terrace. It specializes in fish, seafood, and fish *meze*. ○ 11am–midnight. ▦

NORTH NICOSIA (LEFKOŞA): *Sedirhan Café* €
Asmaalti 8. **Road map** C3. (392 228 77 60.
Set in the arcaded courtyard of a former caravanserai, the food at Sedirhan Café is prepared in front of the guests' eyes. There is also a wine and souvenir shop. ○ 8am–9pm (Tue & Fri 8am–midnight). P &

NORTH NICOSIA (LEFKOŞA): *Anibal Restaurant* €€
Karaoglanoglu. Caglajan. **Road map** C3. (392 227 48 35.
Near the moat encircling the defence walls, Anibal has a view of the Old Town. It is really a fast food bar that serves the best kebab in the whole of Cyprus. Also worth trying is the milk drink – *ayiran*. ○ 7:30am–10:30pm. ● Jun & Jul. 目

NORTH NICOSIA (LEFKOŞA): *Byer* €€
M. Akif St 61/1. Dereboyu. **Road map** C3. (392 228 01 43.
In a stone building resembling a country estate, Byer is located on the main street of North Nicosia. Its shady terrace makes a pleasant dining area. The fried meatballs with *halloumi* cheese are excellent. ○ for lunch and dinner.
P 目 ⚮ ♬ ▦

NORTH NICOSIA (LEFKOŞA): *Californian Bar Continental* €€
M. Akif 74. Dereboyu. **Road map** C3. (392 227 69 38.
ⓦ www.cyprusconstruction.com
A smart two-storey building houses this elegant restaurant and a fast food bar. Prices are affordable, much cheaper downstairs. ○ 7am–midnight. 目 ⚘

NORTH NICOSIA (LEFKOŞA): *Moyra Restaurant Bar* €€
Osman Pasa 32. Dereboyu. **Road map** C3.
An elegant restaurant in an older building with a garden. The walls are hung with maps and photographs of old Nicosia. The chef's special is the kebab with yoghurt and garlic sauce. ○ noon–midnight. 目 & ⚘ ♬ ▦

NORTH NICOSIA (LEFKOŞA): *Boghtalian Konak Restaurant* €€€
Salahi Sevket. **Road map** C3. (392 228 07 00.
ⓦ www.boghtalian.com.cy
The restaurant is based in an old house of an Armenian merchant, Boghtalian, with a stylish décor. The first floor features an air-conditioned dining room, and an Ottoman-style room; downstairs is a pleasant tree-shaded garden. This is one of the top 10 restaurants in Cyprus, where you can meet even members of the government. ○ noon–3:30pm & 6–11:30pm. P 目 & ▦

YEŞILIRMAK (LIMNITÍS): *Dillirga* €€
Road map B3. (392 726 20 05.
Dillirga, situated right on the beach, serves *meze* with a variety of meats. The restaurant has a lovely view, and lush ivy grows all around. ○ until the last guest leaves. P & ⚘ ♬

SHOPPING IN CYPRUS

CYPRUS IS FAMOUS for its handicrafts, especially the intricate laces and beautifully embroidered fabrics created by Cypriot women. Artisan food and drink, such as honey and jam as well as fruit- and herb-flavoured alcohol, are widely available. A variety of rose products, including oils, soap and perfume, are also gaining popularity.

Souvenir tray with a map of Cyprus

Other popular gifts are silver and copper jewellery, based on traditional designs, and inexpensive leather goods.

One of the pleasures of a trip to Cyprus is sampling the local food, whether in a market (where fresh fruit and spices abound) or bakery. *Halloumi* cheese, washed down with an inexpensive but enjoyable Cypriot wine, such as Othello, tastes delicious.

WHERE TO SHOP

SOUVENIRS CAN BE bought anywhere on the island. Shops, boutiques and street stalls are found in abundance in the larger towns and along the promenades of the famous resorts. In the mountain villages, small family-run shops sell basic commodities, while homemade foodstuffs, such as orange marmalade, jam and excellent honeys, can be bought directly from their producers at tree-shaded roadside stalls.

Near every major historic site you will find a stall that sells typical local souvenirs, postcards and handicrafts. The most common items for sale are clay amphorae and jugs, baskets and traditional lace and embroidery.

Supermarkets and small local shops, which are usually open late, have the best prices for foodstuffs, but you can also buy a variety of cold drinks and snacks at the beach. The larger hotels have their own shops.

A shop selling handicrafts in the centre of Larnaka

OPENING HOURS

THE PEAK HOLIDAY season is June to mid-September, when the shops have the longest hours. They open at 8am and close at 7:30pm (8:30pm on Fridays), with a 3-hour lunch break (1–4pm). On Wednesdays and Saturdays shops close at 2pm.

From April to May, and mid-September to October, the shops are open between 8am and 7pm (8pm on Fridays) .

Between November and March, shops are open from 8am to 6pm (7pm on Friday).

Markets are best seen early in the morning, when the choice of produce is largest and when both the fruit and the air are still fresh.

HOW TO PAY

IN SMALL BOUTIQUES, beach shops and markets it is customary to pay by cash. Credit cards are widely accepted in larger establishments, including supermarkets, souvenir and jewellery shops.

A stall with a variety of home-canned fruits and jams

MARKETS

AN INHERENT FEATURE of the Mediterranean scenery, markets can be found in all larger towns of Cyprus. The most picturesque of these are the fruit and vegetable markets in Nicosia and Larnaka. They are held mainly for the benefit of the local community, so even in high season few articles intended for visitors are available; nevertheless, their local colour and character make them a great tourist attraction. Haggling is a common practice.

A typical Cypriot market, brimming with fresh produce

Most markets sell fresh fruit, vegetables and spices. Those in seaside resorts may also have interesting costume jewellery, flip-flops and beach bags. Printed T-shirts are another popular tourist item.

Markets that specialize in fresh local produce are best visited early in the morning. At that time of day, the air is cool and you can take a leisurely stroll between the rows of stalls, savouring the flavours and scents. Here you will find readily available fresh produce, including exotic fruit and vegetable varieties little known in mainland Europe. You can also buy traditional cheeses, sausages, many types of fish, and a variety of nuts and sweets. Sacks full of fragrant, colourful spices stand next to the stalls.

Every now and then you can also find antiques offered at reasonable prices.

A well-stocked wine shop in Omodos, in the Troodos mountains

FOOD

O NE OF THE ISLAND'S specialist foods is *halloumi* – the traditional goat's cheese, which is excellent in salads and delicious when fried or grilled. Another tasty delicacy is *soujoukkos* – a sweet almond filling covered with thickened grape juice.

The best souvenir from Cyprus is the sweet "Cyprus sun" – the local full-bodied Commandaria wine with its rich, warm and truly sunny bouquet. Other noteworthy beverages include *ouzo*, also known in Greece and Turkey, and the very strong *zivania* (virtually pure grape alcohol) that will knock you off your feet, even in small quantities.

Other good food purchases include delicious dried fruit, and rose petal jam. The sweet fruit jellies – *loukoumia* – are the Cypriot version of Turkish delight. The highlanders pro-duce exquisite herb-scented honey. The most popular spices are small, hot peppers.

The owner of a jewellery studio at work on a new piece

SOUVENIRS

A WIDE RANGE of souvenirs is available in Cyprus, but the most popular are ceramics and wickerwork. The ceramic pitharia jugs and amphorae make lovely flower vases.

Traditional Cypriot lace is produced in the villages of Lefkara and Omodos, and make a beautiful gift and souvenir. In North Cyprus you can buy embroidery based on traditional Turkish patterns and designs.

Exquisite icons are sold in the mountain monasteries, sometimes painted by the monks themselves.

Traditional copper pots and bowls, and attractive and inexpensive leather goods, are available throughout Cyprus and make good gifts.

Beautifully embroidered, colourful shawls from Lefkara

What to Buy in Cyprus

THANKS TO THE centuries-long influence of a variety of cultures, Cyprus offers its visitors a wealth of souvenirs of every description, from beautiful icons in the south, to typical Turkish water pipes in the north. Some towns are famous for their unique lace designs, ceramics and exquisite jewellery. Leather goods are particularly attractive in the northern part of the island. The choice of souvenirs is truly astounding, and searching for that original item to take home with you is half the fun.

Icons

Icons, painted by Greek Orthodox monks, are very popular with tourists. They vary from simple to elaborate designs, some with robes depicted in silver or with golden floral motifs.

Madonna and Child icon

REPUBLIC OF CYPRUS

A beautifully embroidered tablecloth – a handsome gift

Textiles

Colourful stripes form the traditional pattern seen on tablecloths and rugs. The hand-woven fabric used in these articles is called lefkonika. *Its name comes from the town of Lefkonikon (now in North Cyprus) where the fabric was first produced.*

Woven rug with the distinctive striped pattern

Lace

The most famous Cypriot lace – lefkaritika – comes from Lefkara. The best-known motif is the Da Vinci pattern which, according to legend, was passed onto local lace-makers by the famous artist.

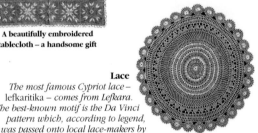

Exquisite lace

Tin and Copperware

Tin-plated kettles decorated with fine patterns are a practical, as well as a decorative present. Copper ornaments are also popular. The most beautiful of these include bracelets with traditional Greek designs.

An original tin kettle

A beautifully decorated silver trinket

Tray decorated with a map of Cyprus

Tourist Souvenirs

The most common souvenirs from Cyprus are plates, ashtrays, mugs and T-shirts decorated with the image of Aphrodite or a map of the island. But the inventiveness of the souvenir producers knows no bounds, and stalls are loaded with fancy knick-knacks.

Silver

In addition to lace, Lefkara prides itself on its silver creations. Here, you can find the finest jewellery made to unusual designs, and intricately decorated trinkets.

Statuette of Aphrodite – the patron goddess of Cyprus

Alcoholic Beverages

One of the best souvenirs from the island is "Cyprus sun" – sweet local Commandaria wine, full-bodied, with a rich bouquet reminiscent of the famous Madeira wine. Other noteworthy beverages include ouzo *and the strong* zivania *(grape spirit).*

"Cyprus sun" - the sweet Commandaria

Wicker basket

Bottle of white wine

Wickerwork

Inexpensive wicker baskets can be bought in the markets of Nicosia, Limassol and Larnaka, or directly from their makers in the villages of Liopetri or Sotira, near Agia Napa.

Cypriot Music

Traditional Cypriot music is based on Greek motifs. The famous "Zorba's Dance" is a favourite with tourists.

CD of traditional Cypriot music

Pottery

Cypriot markets are full of clay jugs, bowls and other vessels, of all shapes and sizes, often richly ornamented.

Local Delicacies

The outstanding local delicacy is halloumi *– a goat's cheese. People with a sweet tooth should try* soujoukkos *– made of almonds and grape juice, or* loukoumi *(Turkish Delight).*

Clay water jug

Cypriot sweets

NORTH CYPRUS

Ceramics

A wide variety of ceramic products is on offer. Available in all shapes and sizes, they are decorated in traditional patterns. The loveliest and most popular with tourists are the traditional bowls and jugs.

Hookah (or narghile)

The hookah is a typical souvenir from the north. Tourists buy these water pipes, tempted by the fruity aroma of tobacco. The full set also includes charcoal and tobacco.

A hookah – a typical souvenir from North Cyprus

A jug – a popular form of earthenware

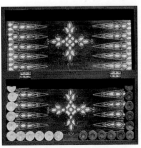

Tourist Souvenirs

The most popular souvenirs are hand-woven rugs and tablecloths, and plates decorated with pictures of popular historical sites, with commemorative inscriptions. The selection of souvenirs is not great, but prices are reasonable. Stalls selling souvenirs can be found at the main tourist sites.

A colourful souvenir plate

An encrusted wooden box with the popular game, backgammon

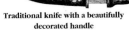

Traditional knife with a beautifully decorated handle

ENTERTAINMENT IN CYPRUS

EVERY VISITOR to Cyprus, whether young or old, will find plenty of entertainment to enjoy. Hotels stage folk evenings, with traditional music and dancing. Guests can dance to the tune from *Zorba the Greek*, watch an unusual display in which a

Having fun at one of the many water parks

dancer places a tower of glasses on his head, or join in games of skill based on traditional Greek entertainment.

In addition to this, every major resort has modern bars, pubs and clubs playing music mostly from the 1970s and 80s. Festivals, casinos and amusement parks provide even more diversions. In Cyprus, European-style fun and games combine with traditional local entertainment, which is very popular with the tourists.

CTO office in Pafos

INFORMATION

INFORMATION ON current cultural events can be obtained from tourist offices and hotel reception desks. Even before leaving for your trip, it's worth checking out Cyprus on the Internet, so that you can time your arrival to coincide with local festivals, such as the wonderful wine festivals, which are accompanied by free tastings. Leaflets handed out on the streets may contain interesting information on local events, as do posters displayed in public places.

CLUBS AND CAFÉS

THE ISLAND has a thriving nightlife. The major resorts, full of noisy clubs, modern bars and crowded pubs, are the most popular places to enjoy a lively night out. People looking for all-night parties and dancing should stay in Limassol - the centre of entertainment on the island. In the resort of Agia Napa it is customary to take a refreshing morning swim in the Mediterranean Sea after a night on the town. Tickets to the largest clubs can

be booked in advance over the telephone or via the Internet.

Cultural life in Cyprus is not limited to bars, cafés, nightclubs or folk shows staged on hotel terraces. Larger towns also have theatres performing a classical repertory as well as modern plays in historic settings.

It is worth dropping into one of the stylish cafés in the pedestrianised Laiki Geitonia area of Nicosia, to taste Cypriot coffee. Served in small glasses, this strong and sweet coffee will revive you in no time at all.

HOTEL ENTERTAINMENT

MANY HOTEL CONCIERGES and travel agents will arrange activities for visitors, including equipment hire for anything from tennis rackets or bicycles to a luxury yacht. They can also organize lessons for you. Their offers are displayed in hotels, where you can also book a boat cruise, an excursion or a diving course. Most hotels also sell tickets to

concerts, dance shows and other performances by local artists. In some venues, Cypriot orchestras entertain dinner guests nightly. Other traditional Cypriot evenings are popular and easy to book.

Children dressed up during the Flower Festival in Larnaka

FEASTS AND FESTIVALS

TRADITIONAL religious festivals in Cyprus coincide with those celebrated in Europe. On New Year's Day, Cypriots exchange presents and eat the traditional New Year cake – *vasilopitta*. Epiphany is

Café-patisserie in Famagusta

celebrated in the seaside towns with a swimming competition: the winner is the person who recovers the crucifix hurled out over the water. During Holy Week, an effigy of Judas is burned, and icons are covered with a pall. Anthestiria – the flower festival held in May, heralds the arrival of spring. In September the annual arts festival is held in Nicosia. The same month sees the Limassol wine festival.

The north celebrates mainly Muslim festivals. The most important widely celebrated of these is Eid-al-Fitr.

CASINOS

Gambling is not particularly popular in Cyprus, but there are some who enjoy casino games. Roulette and blackjack attract mainly tourists from Turkey. Casinos are found only in North Cyprus. Inhabitants of South Cyprus often cross the border to try their luck in one of the gambling dens. The best casinos are found in the larger, more upmarket hotels of Kyrenia and Famagusta.

A casino in the Colony hotel *(see p165)*, located in Kyrenia

EXCURSIONS

Information about organized excursions can be obtained from hotel reception desks or tourist information centres, which have lists of organizers recommended by the CTO. The most popular excursions are daytrips to major tourist attractions and historic sites, visits to traditional villages, and Cypriot evenings with traditional food, drink and dancing. Boat cruises are also available.

The colourful waterpark in Agia Napa

AMUSEMENT PARKS

Unlike most rival Mediterranean resorts, Cyprus has lots of purpose-built visitor attractions for younger visitors. A visit to an waterpark *(see p187)* or a mini-zoo is a must when on holiday with children. The vast waterparks, usually occupying several hectares, offer numerous amusements. In addition to swimming pool complexes, they have scenic routes that can be travelled by small boat, while admiring Greek ruins scattered along the shores. Large swimming pools have secret coves, artificial waves, thickets and diving sites. They vie with one another to provide the most unusual attractions, such as the Zenith Zeus slide with its 370 bends. The waterpark in Agia Napa, styled after ancient Greek designs, combines entertainment with a history lesson. Waterparks, being outdoor attractions, are open only during high season.

Educational parks and their collections of island fauna and flora are also sources of unforgettable delight and knowledge for youngsters.

In the summer the most popular parks are crowded. Every amusement park is virtually a small town in itself, with shops, restaurants and numerous attractions.

Those who fail to get their fill of fun during the daytime can stroll along the seaside promenades during the evening, and drop into a funfair for a ride on a carousel sparkling with flashing lights. Limassol and other large resorts have such funfairs.

DIRECTORY

EXCURSIONS

Airtour-Cyprus Sightseeing
Naxou 4, Nicosia.
224 52777. FAX 223 75220.
@ airtour@cytanet.com.cy

Amathus Tours
Plateia Syntagmatos 2, Limassol.
253 46464. FAX 253 71172.
@ main@tourism.amathus.com.cy

Louis Tours
Leoforos Evagorou 54-58, Nicosia.
777 78555. FAX 226 71894.
@ tourism@louisgroup.com

Salamis Tours Excursions
Salamis House, 28 Oktovriou, Limassol.
258 60000. FAX 253 67374.
@ info@salamis.tours.com.cy

WATERPARKS

Aphrodite Waterpark
Geroskipou-Pafos. Poseidonos Ave.
262 22722. Apr–Oct:
10am–6pm daily.

Ocean Aquarium
Protaras-Paralimni. 237 41111.
10am–5:30pm daily.

Octopus Aquapark
Catalköy. Beàparmark Caddesi.
853 9674. 8am–5pm daily.

Water World Waterpark
Agia Napa. 237 24444.
W www.waterworldwaterpark.com
Mar–mid Nov: 10am–6pm daily.

Wet'n Wild Waterpark
Limassol. 253 18000.
W www.wetnwild.com.cy
Apr–Oct: 10am–6pm daily.

OUTDOOR ACTIVITIES

CONTRARY TO popular belief, Cyprus offers much more in the way of recreation than splashing in the sea and sunbathing on the beaches. Certainly many visitors are drawn by the prospect of sunshine, peace and tranquillity. But the island's mild, warm climate, combined with its unique topography, attracts all types of outdoor enthusiasts. Visitors seeking an

Studying the map

active holiday will find numerous facilities for sport, as well as excellent and professional coaching and instruction. You can enjoy a wide array of water sports, including snorkelling, diving and windsurfing. On land there is excellent hiking, horse riding and cycling. In winter, you can even learn to ski or snowboard on the slopes of Mount Olympus.

Horse-lovers will appreciate a beautiful ride along the paths that wind their way gently through the pine-clad hills. An unhurried walk through a cypress grove, or a wild gallop over wooded hills, will be a memorable part of your holiday in Cyprus.

Virtually all you need to enjoy horse riding is a well-trained, docile animal. But for those who are nervous of horses, donkey rides are also widely available.

Hiking in the Troodos mountains

HIKING

THE ISLAND's best hiking areas are in the mountain regions. Clearly signposted walking trails and scenic nature trails, found mainly in the Troodos mountains and on the Akamas peninsula, help hikers to discover the most fascinating corners of Cyprus. The most enjoyable island hikes lead through nature reserves.

When hiking, you should always carry a detailed map of the region. And before setting off, it is important to pack appropriate warm clothing; even when it is hot on the coast, it can be quite chilly high up in the mountains. Also be sure to bring plenty of drinking water and sunblock.

CYCLING TRIPS

VIRTUALLY all tourist resorts on Cyprus have bicycles available for hire. The island's cycling routes are

magnificent, particularly in the mountains, and this is a great way to enjoy the scenery. Maps showing the routes are available from tourist information centres, in every resort and larger town.

It is a good idea to carry a pump with the correct tip, and self-adhesive patches for inner-tubes in case of punctures. For more complicated repairs, you can ask for help from a specialist bicycle shop.

HORSE RIDING

CYPRUS'S BEACHES and gentle hills provide the ideal terrain for horse riding.

A leisurely family cycling trip

Snowboarder on the slopes of Mount Olympus

SKIING AND SNOWBOARDING

DEPENDING on the weather, it is possible to ski and snowboard on the northeast slopes of Mount Olympus between December and mid-March. The island's highest mountain provides good snow conditions, with four ski lifts and an equipment hire centre for visitors. Individual and group tuition is available for both skiiers and snowboarders to help novices negotiate the complexities of a downhill run.

If you are planning to engage in snow sports during your holiday in Cyprus, you can keep an eye on the weather forecast and snow conditions by checking on the Internet or teletext information service, or asking your tour operator.

TENNIS

MOST TOP HOTELS have their own hard courts and tennis schools, and floodlit, all-weather public tennis courts can be found in most major towns. Aficionados will enjoy a game played at high altitude (above 1,500 m/ 4,921 ft), amid the pine and cedar woods. This is made possible by the location of one of the most scenic courts, near Troodos.

GOLF

CYPRUS HAS PERFECT golfing weather for much of the year, though some may find July and August uncomfortably hot. There are several 18-hole courses, all offering golf clubs for hire. Particularly note-worthy is the Tsada Golf Club, situated near Pafos on the picturesque grounds of a 12th-century monastery. There are many other high-quality, scenically-located golf courses of varying degrees of difficulty for golfers of every ability.

The north of the country has no public golf courses, but visitors may use the golf

Building sandcastles at the beach in Larnaka

course in Pentayia, which is located to the southwest of Morphou (Güzelyurt).

OTHER ACTIVITIES

INCREASINGLY popular excursions in four-wheel-drive vehicles give visitors the chance to discover the lesser-known parts of the island and to admire its beauty away from the tourist centres.

Rock-climbers may head for the crags of Troodos, Droushia or Cape Greco, around Agia Napa. Novice climbers should always be assisted by an experienced instructor.

Cyprus is full of ancient relics, and among its main attractions are the archaeo-logical sites. The ruins at Amathous, near Limassol, are partially flooded, so they can be viewed while swimming in the sea. Other important sights are Kato Pafos and Salamis, in the north.

CAR RALLIES

Drivers travelling around Cyprus will get enough excitement from driving the narrow streets of Nicosia or steep roads of the Troodos mountains. But if you want even more driving thrills, you can attend one of Cyprus' several car rallies, sprints or hill climbs. These are held at

Churning out clouds of dust at the popular International Rally of Cyprus

various locations including Limassol, Larnaca, Nicosia and Pafos. Further details, including the routes and the results of recent years, can be obtained from the website of the Cyprus Motor Sports Federa-tion (www.cmf.org.cy) or from any of the individual towns' automobile clubs.

Water Sports

THE BEACHES OF CYPRUS are fun places for the whole family. Sunbathing, volleyball and all kinds of water sports are available to keep you entertained. The numerous attractions include snorkelling, diving, windsurfing, waterskiing and sailing. Sea breezes moderate the high temperatures, and the clear water is ideal for swimming. There is no shortage of places to hire equipment, allowing you to practise even the most ambitious water sports or take a scuba-diving course.

Snorkelling in the clear blue waters near rock formations

DIVING

THE CLEAR, clean coastal waters of Cyprus simply beckon underwater exploration. Diving is extremely popular in Cyprus, and there are diving schools and centres in virtually every seaside resort in the island.

The greatest thrills can be experienced from underwater explorations in the regions of Larnaka and Agia Napa, famous for the island's loveliest beaches. Experienced divers may look for the local wrecks of cargo boats and naval vessels. This is quite a unique attraction since, unlike many countries, the Cyprus Tourism Organization does allow the exploration of vessels that have sunk off its coast.

Visitors will be flooded with offers from hundreds of diving clubs and schools. These organizations offer not only diving lessons for novices and children, but also sea cruises combined with diving. The initial lessons can often be taken in the hotel, since many of them run their own diving schools.

SNORKELLING

THERE IS PLENTY to see underwater, even within a few metres of the shore if you are a beginner at this sport. The shallows teem with tiny fish, sea anemones and urchins clinging to the rocks. If you're lucky, you may even see an octopus slither past.

It's well worth heading out to the more rocky shores where there is more to see than on the sandy bottom. One of the best places for snorkelling is the north coast of the Akamas peninsula, where rocky coves and tiny offshore islands abound in a variety of sealife.

Many hotels hire out snorkelling equipment. You can also buy masks with snorkels and flippers at local sports shops; these do not cost much.

It is prohibited to collect sponges or any archaeological items found on the seabed.

WINDSURFING AND KITEBOARDING

ALMOST ALL the beaches run courses for windsurfing. The gentle afternoon breezes may not meet the expectations of the more competitive windsurfers. The best winds blow around the capes, between Agia Napa and Protaras, and in the region of Pafos. Kiteboarding, which involves being towed at high speeds by a giant parachute-like kite, is starting to catch on in Agia Napa.

Dozens of yachts moored in Larnaka Marina

SAILING

SAILING IS VERY popular in Cyprus, and the island's marinas play host to vessels from practically every European country. Skippered yachts can be chartered from island marinas (Larnaka and Limassol are the main centres) by the day or for longer cruises, and smaller dinghies and catamarans are available by the day or half-day from beaches around Agia Napa, Protaras, Limassol and Latsi. The many boat charter companies have their offices in coastal resorts, where you will also find sailing schools.

The waters around Cyprus offer magnificent sailing conditions, and the island is often referred to as a "sailor's paradise". Southwesterly

A diver exploring the sights under water

The Cypriot coast - an ideal destination for an active holiday

winds prevail in the summer. The delicate westerly breeze blowing in the morning changes gently around noon to a westerly wind of 15-20 knots. In the winter, the temperatures are milder and the sun less scorching. In December and January the winds are mainly 10-20 knots from the southeast. There can be occasional rain at this time, but the prevailing clear weather makes sailing conditions close to ideal.

From Cyprus you can sail to nearby Israel, Lebanon, Egypt, the Greek islands and Turkey.

BEACH SPORTS

FOR THE MOST PART, beaches are found close to hotels, and are watched over by lifeguards in the summer, making them peaceful and comfortable recreation grounds. The beautiful sandy beaches in small sheltered coves are particularly welcoming to those who are lured by the charm and appeal of Aphrodite's island.

The delightful small rocky coves and beaches provide a quiet and charming spot for a refreshing dip. The best known of these scenic beaches is the rocky coast by Petra tou Romiou – the Rock of Aphrodite.

Private hotel beaches as well as public beaches become very crowded during peak season. One of the most famous beaches in Cyprus – Agia Napa's Nissi Beach – buzzes with activity from morning until night. Tourists remain in beach bars and

Colourful inflatable rings for children

nearby clubs until the small hours and, after a night of partying, head straight for the beach to enjoy a refreshing swim. Named after the nearby island (the word *nissi* means "island"), Nissi Beach has consequently been nick-named the "Cypriot Ibiza". The beach lures visitors with its clear water and sand, not seen in other parts of south Cyprus. According to legend, the sand was brought here from the Sahara.

Less famous but equally beautiful beaches can be found in the northern part of the island, in the region of Famagusta (Gazimagusa). Deckchairs, umbrellas and towels are available for hire, but watch out because in some places the owners charge exorbitant prices. Many beaches are set up with volleyball courts; you can also have a game of beach ball or frisbee. Numerous sport centres hire out diving or snorkelling equipment, as well as boats and canoes.

Since there is no shortage of daredevils, Cyprus's beaches also offer bungee jumping, water skiing, water scooters, paragliding and "banana" rides behind a motorboat.

The very popular water scooter

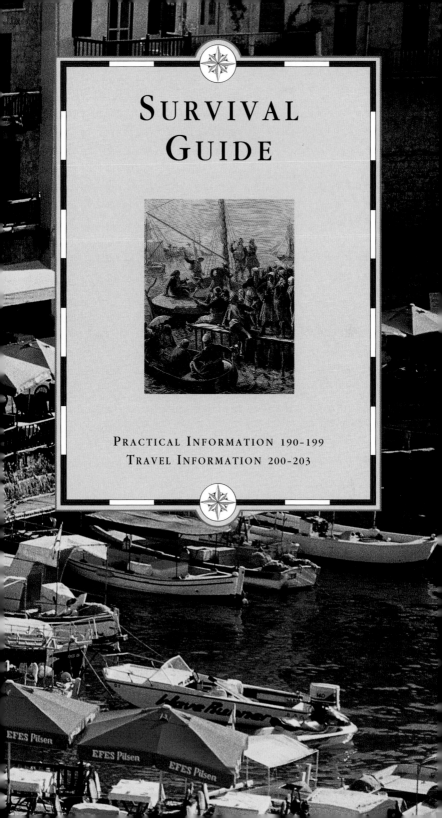

SURVIVAL
GUIDE

PRACTICAL INFORMATION

Stone road sign

Cyprus is a popular year-round destination, due to its Mediterranean climate. It is easily accessible from mainland Europe and the Middle East, yet being an island is a true getaway. The Cypriots are extremely friendly and well inclined towards tourists.

The Greek South and Turkish North have very different characters. Entry requirements are straightforward for visitors who travel solely to either the South or the North. But due to the island's partition, visitors wanting to see both parts of the island should follow the latest advice. The Cyprus Tourism Organization (CTO), representing Southern Cyprus, has offices overseas and throughout the South. The Turkish Republic of Northern Cyprus Ministry of Economy and Tourism represents the North.

WHEN TO GO

Cyprus is a year-round destination, so any time of year is suitable for a visit. The main tourist season runs from April until October, and peaks during July and August, when the air and water temperatures are at their highest. At this time the late-night bars, taverns and restaurants fill up to capacity, and the beaches are packed with sun worshippers. The hotel swimming pools, pubs and discos are equally crowded. During peak season you can hear an international mix of languages in the streets, dominated by English, German and Russian.

Those who enjoy the mild, warm climate but prefer to avoid the crowds should visit Cyprus outside the peak season. In April, May and October it is warm enough to swim in the sea, but the beaches are not crowded. In winter (December-February), it is cool for swimming, but good for beach walks, while in the Troodos mountains you can even ski. In spring, Cyprus is an ideal place for hiking, cycling and horse riding.

Viewpoint across the Green Line to the other side of Nicosia

PASSPORTS & VISAS (THE SOUTH)

MOST VISITORS, including citizens of the EU, the USA, Canada, Australia and New Zealand do not require a visa to visit the Republic of Cyprus, and can stay for up to 3 months. However, entry will be refused if visitors' passports show they have previously entered North Cyprus.

Tourists may be asked to show that they have adequate means to support themselves during their stay (approximately 15 Cyprus pounds per day). No vaccinations or health certificates are required.

PASSPORTS & VISAS (THE NORTH)

TO VISIT North Cyprus, most visitors (including citizens of the EU, USA, Canada, Australia and New Zealand) require only a valid passport. But to avoid being refused entry on later visits to the South, passports should be stamped on a separate loose sheet of paper.

There are no currency restrictions in the North, which has no currency of its own and uses the Turkish lira.

CROSSING THE BORDER

UNTIL RECENTLY the only entry route for travellers to North Cyprus was via plane or ferry from Turkey. Nowadays visitors can fly to the Republic of Cyprus and from there travel to the buffer zone. Most visitors do not require a visa to visit North Cyprus, but you will be issued a document free of charge when crossing the border between the two parts of the island.

A popular beach in a seaside resort

◁ **The picturesque Kyrenia harbour in North Cyprus**

There are four border crossings (one for pedestrians and one for cars in Nicosia; a further two for cars outside the capital).

Apart from the largest cities, such as North Nicosia, Kyrenia and Famagusta, North Cyprus is less crowded than the South. The climate is the same, so in spring it is pleasant to stroll among the orange groves, and in the summer to enjoy the beaches and the sea.

CUSTOMS

CUSTOMS REGULATIONS allow visitors to bring in, duty free, 200 cigarettes; one litre of spirits; two litres of wine; and 60 millilitres of perfume. The import of perishable food items is strictly prohibited. Visitors may import any amount of Cypriot or foreign banknotes, which should be declared to customs on arrival.

EMBASSIES & CONSULATES

MANY COUNTRIES have embassies or consulates in southern Nicosia, the capital of the Republic of Cyprus. There are no embassies or consulates north of the Green Line because North Cyprus is not recognized as an independent country.

WHAT TO TAKE

FOR THE MOST PART, Cyprus is a relaxed, casual holiday destination. Visitiors should pack beachwear, sunglasses, hats and smart casual wear for the resorts. If you're staying in an upmarket hotel, or dining in a fancy restaurant, you will fit in better if you dress up more, as the Cypriots themselves do.

In summer you'll seldom need a sweater, but in late autumn, winter and early spring temperatures are cooler and you will need to bring some warm clothing. If you plan to visit the mountains, at any time of year, it is advisable to bring warm clothes and rain gear.

Visitors taking medication should travel with an adequate supply. It's also a good idea to bring high-factor sun lotion and insect repellent.

Some hotels don't supply bath or sink plugs, so you may consider bringing a universal plug.

ETIQUETTE

WHEN VISITING religious buildings, modest attire is expected. For churches, monasteries and mosques this means long trousers or skirts, and a shirt that covers your back and shoulders. Shoes must be removed before entering a mosque.

A tourist information centre

TOURIST ORGANIZATIONS

TOURIST information bureaux can be found easily in all major tourist centres, such as Nicosia, Larnaka, Limassol, Pafos and Agia Napa. They distribute free information packs and maps, as well as providing useful advice on sightseeing. The **Cyprus Tourism Organization (CTO)**, with offices in many European cities, has a website with lots of information on the Republic of Cyprus. Visit their website at: www.visit cyprus.org.cy.

The **Turkish Republic of Northern Cyprus Ministry of Economy & Tourism** has

Automatic tourist information kiosk

overseas offices, too. You can learn more about the North at www.go-north cyprus.com.

Nowadays travel agents, hotels, car hire companies, and organizations that offer special activities have their own websites. These websites are often in several languages, with pictures to illustrate the services offered. It's a good idea to browse through their websites to look for good offers before travelling; many arrangements can be made before you leave home, allowing you to start enjoying your visit from the moment you arrive in Cyprus. Just be sure to check when the website was last updated, as some of the information, particularly for the North, may be out of date and quote the last season's prices.

A range of brochures and illustrated booklets covering individual tourist sights is usually available for sale at the sights themselves.

LANGUAGES

TWO LANGUAGES – Greek and Turkish – have co-existed in Cyprus in the centuries between the Turkish conquest of 1571 and the partition of the island in 1974. Due to the current political situation, however, the South uses only Greek and the North uses only Turkish. In the holiday resorts of the South, English (as well as German and Russian) is commonly understood. Restaurant menus and shop signs are in several languages.

In the North it is more difficult to communicate in English and other European languages, although there is usually no problem in hotels. Road signs throughout the island carry the names of towns written in the Latin alphabet. In the North, however, only the Turkish names are given, so check your map to ensure that you know where you are going.

RELIGION

THE CYPRIOT Orthodox Church, which is dominant in the south of the island, is independent from the Greek Orthodox Church. It is also the oldest national church in Christendom, its history tracing back to the times of St Paul.

In the towns you often encounter Orthodox priests dressed in long black robes. The main Orthodox services, lasting two to three hours, are held on Saturday evenings and Sunday mornings.

Monasteries have served as Cypriot pilgrimage sites for centuries. Today, they are visited by tourists in such vast numbers that access to some of them has been restricted.

In the North the dominant religion is Islam though, like Turkey, the North is a secular state. All larger towns and cities have mosques, from which the muezzin's voice calls the faithful to prayer five times a day. Services are held on Friday afternoons.

Men at prayer in a mosque in North Cyprus

TRAVELLING WITH CHILDREN

MAJOR BRANDS of baby food, medicines and toiletries, including nappies (diapers) are sold in all supermarkets and pharmacies. Both parts of the island are family-friendly, with children welcomed everywhere and plenty of kids' facilities. However, risks for smaller children include sunburn, occasional rough waters and pests such as jellyfish, sea urchins, and stinging insects.

Worshipper inside an Orthodox church in southern Cyprus

YOUNG VISITORS

CYPRUS IS an ideal holiday destination for young people. Its sunny beaches, clean waters, water-sports facilities, and rich and varied nightlife attract young people in their thousands. Hundreds of nightclubs, discos, pubs and bars await the revellers.

Holders of ISIC or Euro<26 cards qualify for discounts on public transport and reduced admission to museums and some other tourist sights.

WOMEN TRAVELLERS

WOMEN TRAVELLING alone or together should exercise normal caution. Cyprus is generally safe, but there has been a rise in sexual assaults against women travellers so avoid walking alone at night.

DISABLED VISITORS

IN RECENT YEARS, facilities for the disabled have improved somewhat. But even so, few public buildings, shops or visitor attractions have wheelchair ramps so access can be very difficult for wheelchair users. Many museums are in older buildings without lifts. Access to archaeological sites is also difficult. Pavements in towns and villages (if there are any) are often uneven. A

Sign prohibiting photography

leaflet with information on facilities for wheelchair users is available from the CTO.

Only a few museums and archaeological sites in the south (and none in the North) offer Braille or audio guides for visually impaired people or induction loop devices for those with hearing difficulties. The British charity RADAR (for people with hearing and visual impairment) can supply information on facilities in Cyprus (www.radar.org.uk)

GAY & LESBIAN VISITORS

HOMOSEXUALITY IS no longer illegal in southern Cyprus and gay visitors are generally tolerated; there are gay clubs and bars in Agia Napa, Larnaka, Limassol and Pafos.

In North Cyprus, homosexuality is still illegal.

SINGLE TRAVELLERS

MOST VISITORS to Cyprus come as couples, families, or groups of singles, and most hotels offer only double or twin rooms and charge a "single supplement" for those travelling alone. Individuals travelling independently may be able to negotiate a better deal out of season. Several companies specialize in tours for singles: lists are available from the CTO or the Association of Independent Tour Operators in the UK.

SENIOR CITIZENS

BOTH CYPRIOT communities are notably respectful to older people, but hazards include urban traffic (Cypriot drivers sometimes ignore pedestrian crossings) and noise – Agia Napa, especially, is geared to younger visitors.

PHOTOGRAPHY

PHOTOGRAPHY OF military bases or facilities, and the border between southern Cyprus and the North is strictly prohibited. UN soldiers guarding the "Green Line" are used to groups of tourists, but taking photos at any point other than at the checkpoint at the end of Ledra Street is strictly forbidden.

Archaeological sites can be photographed and filmed free of charge; the state museums charge an additional fee for taking photographs.

In places of worship, ask in advance whether photography is permitted. Most churches will not allow you to use flash photography.

ELECTRICAL EQUIPMENT

THE MAINS SUPPLY on the island is 220/240V, with standard British triple rectangular-pin plugs. Most hotel reception desks will provide you with a suitable adaptor. Some hotel rooms are equipped with hairdryers, and irons are usually available to borrow. Most hotels have adapted their supply sockets to suit European plugs, so in

theory there should be no problem using your own electrical equipment (but in practice this isn't always true).

TIME

CYPRUS LIES within the Eastern-European time zone. In the summer (end of March to the end of September) local time is three hours ahead of Greenwich Mean Time. In the winter, it is two hours ahead. "Morning" in Cyprus is *proí*; "afternoon" - *mesiméri*; "evening" - *vrádhi*; and "night" - *níchta*.

WEDDINGS

CYPRUS IS ONE of the world's most popular wedding destinations and some hotels have their own wedding chapel. The bride and groom are required to stay in Cyprus for 20 days.

DISCUSSING POLITICS

THE EVENTS of 1974, when the island was divided between the Turkish and the Greek Cypriots, are still remembered with bitterness. In both the south and the North, local people vehemently argue the justice of their cause. Politics and recent history are subjects that are best avoided.

MILITARY ZONES

BRITAIN'S SOVEREIGN bases in the south, at Akrotiri (Episkopi) and Dhekelia, are also used by US forces and are likely to be on heightened alert in these security-conscious times. Do not intrude on military installations. The same applies to Turkish Army personnel, equipment and installations in the occupied North.

DIRECTORY

EMBASSIES & CONSULATES

Australia
Annis Komninis 4,
Nicosia.
[227 53001.
@ auscomm@logos.cy.net

Canada
1 Odos Lampousas,
Nicosia.
[227 75508.

Ireland
Aianta 7,
1082 Nicosia.
[228 18183.

New Zealand
Kondalaki 6,
1090 Nicosia.
[228 18884.

Representation of the European Commission
2 Archiepiskopou Makariou III & Agapinoros,
Iris Tower,
Nicosia.
[228 17770.
@ ecdc@cytanet.com.cy

South Africa
101 Leoforos Archiepiskopou Makariou III,
Nicosia.
[223 74411.

UK
Alexandrou Palli 1,
Nicosia.
[228 61100.
@ infobhc@cylink.com.cy

USA
Ploutarchou,
Nicosia.
[227 764 00.
@ amembsys@spidernet.com.cy

TOURISM ORGANIZATIONS

Association of Independent Tour Operators
W www.aito.co.uk

Cyprus Tourism Organization (CTO)
Leoforos Lemesou 19,
Nicosia.
[226 91100.
W www.visitcyprus.org.cy

Cyprus Hotel Association
PO Box 24772,
CY 1303, Nicosia.
[224 52820.
@ chaniccy@cylink.com.cy

Association of Cyprus Travel Agents
[226 66435.
@ acta@ccci.org.cy

Cyprus Tourist Guides Association
[227 65755.
W www.cytourist-guides.com

Turkish Republic of Northern Cyprus Ministry of Economy & Tourism
[228 9629.
W www.holidayinnorthcyprus.com

DISABLED VISITORS

Cyprus Organization for the Deaf
[223 56767.

WEDDINGS

Union of Cyprus Municipalities
Nicosia.
[226 69150.
FAX 226 77230.
@ endeky@cytanet.com.cy
W www.ucm.org.cy

USEFUL WEBSITES IN THE REPUBLIC OF CYPRUS

W www.cypria.com
W www.cyprus-mail.com
W www.visitcyprus.org.cy
W www.kypros.org
W www.pio.gov.cy
W www.welcometocyprus.com
W www.windowoncyprus.com

USEFUL WEBSITES IN NORTH CYPRUS

W www.cypnet.com
W www.tourism.trnc.net
W www.northcyprus.net
W www.cyprustouristguide.com

Personal Security and Health

Policeman on a scooter

CYPRUS HAS a low crime rate, but even here crimes do occur; these can be minimized by taking simple precautions. The risk of mugging and theft is greatest in crowded places. Take extra care on crowded promenades or streets and in markets to protect your belongings. Keep documents, money and credit cards hidden from view, and leave what you don't need in the hotel safe. Never leave anything visible in your car when you park it. When in need, you can always ask a policeman for help. Basic medical advice is available at pharmacies. All medical treatment must be paid for; insurance is strongly advised.

military facilities, of which there is no shortage. In particular, resist the temptation to photograph any military installations, vehicles or soldiers. The latter are visible in great numbers, but if you follow the rules of normal behaviour, they will not interfere with your visit.

Roads in North Cyprus are comfortable, wide and of very high quality, including the mountain roads.

Entrance to a police station in the North

strap or inside the case. Your car should always be locked, with any valuables kept out of sight.

Any case of theft should be reported immediately to the police. Theft of a passport should also be reported to your embassy in Nicosia.

Manned lifeguard post at one of the beaches

PERSONAL BELONGINGS

BEFORE TRAVELLING abroad, it is wise to ensure that you have adequate insurance to protect yourself financially from the loss or theft of your property. Even so, it is advisable to take precautions against loss or theft in the first place. Be vigilant in crowded places, where risk of theft or mugging is greatest.

Make photocopies of your important documents and keep these with you, leaving the originals behind in the hotel safe (where you can also deposit money and jewellery).

Make a note of your credit card numbers and the phone number of the issuing bank, in the event of loss or theft.

Cameras and camcorders should be carried on a

CYPRUS POLICE

THE POLICE in Cyprus are friendly towards tourists, always ready to offer help and advice. The majority of them also speak English. But in the event that you are caught breaking the law, they are stern and unwilling to accept any excuses.

Heavy fines are levied for failing to wear a seat belt, and for using a mobile telephone when driving a vehicle.

PERSONAL SECURITY IN THE NORTH

IN TERMS of personal safety, North Cyprus is no different from the south, and the same common-sense precautions apply. Special care should be taken when visiting the buffer zone and when passing by

BEACHES

DURING THE HOLIDAY season, most beaches employ lifeguards. The areas allocated for swimming are marked with coloured buoys. While swimming outside the marked areas is not prohibited, it is inadvisable, particularly for weaker swimmers. Some beaches have first-aid stations, with lifeguards trained to help casualties.

Beach facilities, such as showers, are standard almost everywhere. Hotels with direct access to the sea have stretches of beach allocated to them. There are also a few private beaches, belonging to the owners of seaside properties; these are closed to the public.

Smaller beaches have no lifeguards; they are generally found in coves sheltered from the open sea, so their waters are calm and safe. The most beautiful beaches are found in the regions of Agia Napa in the south, and Famagusta in North Cyprus. The south coast beaches are generally rocky and pebbly.

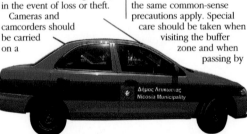

Typical southern Cyprus police car

In summer, Cyprus has some of the highest temperatures in Europe, and it's easy to get sunburnt anytime from early April to late October. Young children are especially vulnerable to the hot sun. Avoid being directly in the sun during the middle of the day, when the rays are strongest. Sunhats, sunglasses, a high factor sunscreen and sunblock are essential to protect your skin. During the day, carry bottled water with you, and drink plenty of it, to avoid dehydration.

MEDICAL CARE

Cyprus is free from most dangerous infectious diseases (although AIDS is present) and no immunizations are required. Drinking tap water is safe. However, all medical treatment must be paid for, and comprehensive insurance to cover hospital and medical charges, as well as emergency repatriation, is advisable. Before travelling to the North, double check that your insurance policy will cover you there.

Some medical procedures (such as dental treatment) are not covered by insurance.

Citizens of the European Union are entitled to use the national health service of the Republic of Cyprus. Accident and emergency patients are treated free of charge, and any subsequent treatment in national health establishments is reimbursed by the insurer.

Hotels can usually recommend a local doctor or dentist, many of whom speak

ΦΑΡΜΑΚΕΙΟ

ΠΑΝΑΓΙΩΤΑ ΚΑΛΑΙΤΖΗ

Pharmacy sign with the easily recognisable green cross

English. All bills must be settled at the time of treatment, but these practitioners will provide a receipt for you to claim a refund from your insurance company once you arrive back home.

Visitors to Cyprus on package holidays should check with their tour operator if medical insurance is included.

PHARMACIES

Most pharmacies keep normal shop opening hours *(see p178)*. They display the green cross sign and the word *farmakeio* or *eczane*. A list of pharmacies open at night and on holidays can be found in the English-language *Cyprus Mail*, or by dialling 192. In an emergency, an all-night pharmacy can offer medical help and advice.

In tourist resorts and large cities most pharmacists speak English. They can usually advise and provide remedies for minor ailments and injuries, but if you need specialist prescription drugs it is best to bring an adequate supply with you.

A uniformed fireman

FIRE SERVICE

Winters are dry and mild, and summers are hot, creating prime conditions for

fires, which can spread with alarming speed and present a particular danger to forests. Mountain fires, especially, are difficult to put out.

There are two types of fire brigade in Cyprus; one that responds to general emergency calls, the other specifically dedicated to forest fires.

During excursions to the island's dry interior, or when camping, you must take particular care not to start a fire. Be especially careful to extinguish cigarettes thoroughly, and dispose of them safely. When leaving a picnic area or campsite, ensure that bonfires are completely extinguished, and take all glass bottles with you to prevent accidental fires.

DIRECTORY

EMERGENCY SERVICES

Police
(112 (South), 155 (North).

Fire Brigade
(112 (South), 199 (North).

Forest Fire Teams
(1407 (South), 177 (North).

Ambulance (112.

HOSPITALS

General Enquiries
(1400.

General Hospitals
Agia Napa/Paralimni.
(238 21211.

Larnaka. (248 00500.

Limassol. (258 01100.

Nicosia. (228 01400.

Pafos. (268 03100.

PHARMACIES

Information in English
(192.

Agia Napa. (909 01403.

Larnaka. (909 01404.

Limassol. (909 01405.

Nicosia. (909 01402.

Pafos. (909 01406.

Standard fire engine of the Cyprus Fire Brigade

Communications

Post office logo in South Cyprus

THE QUALITY OF telecommunications services in Cyprus is very good, especially in the south. Public telephone booths are widespread. In larger towns and cities, you will have no trouble finding an Internet café, if your hotel doesn't have access. Postal services are decent. A good selection of newspapers is available, and there's no shortage of TV or radio stations.

A telephone card available in south Cyprus

USING THE TELEPHONE

CYPRUS HAS a well developed telephone network. Public phones accept 5, 10, 20 and 50 cent coins, as well as phonecards, which can be purchased from newsagent kiosks, post offices and banks in denominations of 3, 5 or 10 pounds. Instructions for using the phone are provided in both Greek and English. Calls to the police, fire brigade or ambulance service are free.

Hotel rooms are equipped with telephones, but calls made from them are very expensive; check the rates before using them.

The country code for Cyprus is 357. Local area codes in Cyprus include: Nicosia 22; Limassol 25; Larnaca 24; Pafos and Polis 26; Agia Napa and Protaras 23.

When making an international call from Cyprus, first dial 00, followed by the country code, and then the area code (omitting the zero that precedes some area codes). Useful country codes are: UK (44), USA and Canada (1), Ireland (353), Australia (61), New Zealand (64) and South Africa (27). All public telephones in the south can be used to make international calls. Calls are cheaper at night (after 6pm) and at weekends.

The mobile telephone (cellphone) network covers most of the island, although reception may be patchy in the mountain region. Mobile phone usage is widespread in Cyprus, and visitors who bring their own phone are likely to experience few problems. Although individual calls cost more than at home, the convenience usually more than compensates.

Making and receiving calls requires an active roaming facility. Bear in mind that, while abroad, mobile telephone users are charged for both outgoing and incoming calls, as well as text messages. Information on the cost of calls can be obtained from individual mobile network operators.

Every hotel and many public buildings have Yellow Pages directories where, in addition to local phone numbers, you can find information on hotels, restaurants, and many outfits offering outdoor activities or other types of entertainment.

Post office logo in North Cyprus

TELEPHONES IN NORTH CYPRUS

THERE ARE decidedly fewer public telephones in the North than in the south. The quality of connections also leaves much to be desired. In the North, phones don't accept coins; instead you insert a pre-paid *telekart* – a phone card that comes in denominations of 1, 1.5 and 2 Turkish lira. They are available from *Telekomünikasyon* offices, post offices and newsagents. There are also metred counter phones *(kontürlü telefon)* – where you speak first, and pay after completing your call. These calls are more

USING A CARDPHONE

1 Screen displaying the number and amount of credit.

2 Alpha-numerical keypad for dialling the number.

3 Phonecard slot; in some phones you need to press the card to make sure it doesn't pop out.

4 After lifting the receiver, insert the card into the slot and dial the number.

USEFUL NUMBERS

- Directory enquiries 192
- International directory enquiries 194
- International calls via the operator 80000198
- Speaking clock 1895
- Infoline 132
- International access code 00

REPUBLIC OF CYPRUS

Banknotes

Banknotes come in 4 denominations – 1, 5, 10 and 20 Cyprus pounds (£). The denominations differ slightly in terms of size and colour, but all bear images of figures who played an important role in the culture and history of Cyprus. The notes are inscribed in Greek and English and bear a serial number, written vertically and horizontally.

20 pounds

10 pounds

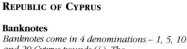

5 pounds

1 pound

50 cents

20 cents

10 cents

Coins

Coins come in denominations of 1, 2, 5, 10, 20 and 50 cents, in varying sizes and colour. The lower denominations are round, while the highest-value 50 cent coin is heptagonal.

5 cents   **2 cents**   **1 cent**

NORTH CYPRUS

Banknotes

North Cyprus does not have its own currency; it uses the New Turkish Lira (abbreviated to YTL), which was adopted in January 2005. The banknotes, in 6 denominations from 1 to 100 YTL, come in a range of colours, and bear Turkish national symbols and major historical figures. The Cyprus pound is also accepted in the North.

1 lira

5 lira

10 lira

20 lira

50 lira

100 lira

1 lira

50 kuruş

Coins

There are 6 new coins now in circulation, ranging in value from 1 kuruş, 5 kuruş, 10 kuruş, 25 kuruş and 50 kuruş to 1 YTL - New Turkish Lira (100 kuruş).

TRAVEL INFORMATION

MOST VISITORS travel to Cyprus on a package holiday which combines flights, accommodation, transport to and from the airport, and often car hire. This can be the most cost-effective option. International airports are located in Larnaka and Pafos; handling both scheduled flights and charters. Travel from mainland Europe to the island takes around 3-4 hours. Fares and

Cyprus Airways flight attendant

schedules can be obtained from travel agents, airline offices and on the Internet. You can also reach Cyprus by ferry, although this takes much longer. Boats sail from Greece to Limassol, and from Turkey to Kyrenia and Famagusta.

The road network is good, with clearly marked signs. Cars drive on the left side of the road. A decent bus service operates between main towns and big resorts.

AIR TRAVEL

THE INTERNATIONAL AIRPORTS in Pafos and Larnaka, both in the Republic of Cyprus, handle flights by the national carrier Cyprus Airways and other European airlines that serve many European capital cities and regional hubs. During summer, the airports become crowded due to the large number of charter flights. Scheduled flight tickets are generally more expensive than charters, but offer more flexibility and greater comfort.

Charter flights are at their busiest from April through October, with weekly departures. Most seats on charter flights are bought in blocks by tour operators, as part of their holiday packages, but "flight only" charters are also available. These can be affordable and convenient for holidaymakers who prefer independent arrangements. Information concerning ticket availability can be obtained from travel agents and airline representatives.

Terminal building at Larnaka airport

Airports have duty-free shops, cafés and restaurants, but the food and beverages on offer are over-priced.

Bus service from the airports to the main towns is infrequent, so it is worth checking the schedule to your destination in advance, to spare yourself a long wait with luggage. The tourist information centres should be able to help with this.

The best way of getting to town is by taxi or hired car. The taxi rank is situated immediately next to the exit from the arrivals hall. For short distances, taxis are a

comfortable and affordable mode of transport. Car hire companies have offices at the airports, as well as in towns.

Visitors travelling to Larnaka airport with a tour operator should turn left, towards the coach parking, after leaving the terminal building. Visitors hiring a car should turn towards the car park, situated some 400 m to the left, after leaving the terminal building.

At Larnaka as well as Pafos airport, services, amenities and transport links are clearly signposted at the terminal.

FERRIES

TRAVEL BY FERRY is often cheaper than flying, and all ferry operators quote roughly the same prices, but be prepared for a long journey. The ferry from Piraeus (Athens) to Cyprus takes about 40 hours, and from Crete to Limassol 24 hours. Ferry operators serving the south are Poseidon Lines and Salamis Lines. Information concerning prices and special offers can be obtained from travel agents or the Internet.

If you wish to travel to the island in your own car, or to ride the mountain roads on your own motorcycle, you would do best to use the services of a ferry operator. Ferries operate regularly between Limassol and the Greek ports of Piraeus, Patmos and Rhodes.

Check-in hall at Larnaka international airport

Passenger ships provide regular links between Cyprus and Haifa (Israel), Beirut (Lebanon) and Port Said (Egypt).

Regular service begins in spring, at the start of the tourist season. Between May and October, the ferries sailing to the Middle East are used mainly by people on holiday in Cyprus. From the south there are a number of popular trips, including the journeys to Israel, Egypt, Lebanon and the Greek islands. Regular services operate between North Cyprus and Turkey.

Some travel operators offer organized 3-day trips to Egypt and the Holy Land, which include visits to Jerusalem and Bethlehem. These excursion vessels depart from Limassol Port.

A number of luxury cruise-liners travel the Mediterranean and Middle East, with Cyprus a popular stopping-off point.

NORTH CYPRUS

THE QUICKEST way to reach North Cyprus is by plane. All flights to Ercan airport originate in Turkey – from Alanya, Dalaman, Istanbul and Izmir. It is not possible to fly direct to Northern Cyprus from any other country. Flights are operated by Cyprus Turkish Airlines and Turkish Airlines. In order to reach Ercan airport you have to travel to Turkey from one of the European airports and then change for the flight to North Cyprus.

Convenient package holidays offer the same combination of flights, accommodation, airport transfers and, generally, car hire as those to the south, making this the easiest way to visit.

Ferry harbour in Kyrenia, North Cyprus

You can also reach North Cyprus by ferry, which is a cheaper option, especially recommended for those who wish to bring their own car to the island. The ferry companies serving these routes include Turkish Maritime Lines and Fergun Lines. Ferry journeys take much longer than flying: the journey from Taşucu to Kyrenia lasts 6 hours and from Mersin to Famagusta 10 hours.

Travelling to North Cyprus can test your patience, as it usually involves long hours of waiting at Turkish airports for connecting flights – an important consideration when travelling with children or the elderly. These delays are due to the timetables not being very well coordinated.

Since the Republic of Cyprus joined the European Union in 2004, all citizens from the south are allowed to cross the border into North Cyprus without any hindrance, at least in theory, and stay as long as they wish. Visitors to the south who want to see North Cyprus can also cross the border to the North at the official checkpoints. Crossing anywhere other than an official checkpoint may result in arrest.

Airport terminal building at Ercan, North Cyprus

Travelling by Car

The logo of a Cypriot petrol station

Mᴏsᴛ ᴠɪsɪᴛᴏʀs to Cyprus explore the island by bus or hire car. Buses provide good links between the towns, while for shorter distances taxis are a good option – both comfortable and affordable. In Cyprus, vehicles are right-hand drive. The roads throughout the island are in good condition, and signposting is clear.

kmph (50 mph) on most other roads, and 50 kmph (30 mph) in built-up areas. There are on-the-spot fines for speeding and for failing to wear a seat belt. Driving under the influence of alcohol is a criminal offence with serious consequences, as is using a mobile phone while driving.

Roads

Tʜᴇ ᴄᴏɴᴅɪᴛɪᴏɴ of the roads in Cyprus is very good. In recent years many new stretches of road have been built, and others modernized. A number of new roundabouts (traffic islands) have also appeared at intersections; the right of way goes to drivers approaching from the right.

Finding your way to the major historic sites is not difficult, as brown road signs show the way. Difficulties may arise, however, in the narrow streets of small towns, where signs are usually absent.

Pedestrians, especially those who may not be used to left-hand traffic, should exercise caution when crossing the road, and warn children to be particularly careful when stepping into the road.

North Cyprus sign indicating cars should drive in the left lane

Car Hire

Iᴛ ɪs ᴇxᴘᴇɴsɪᴠᴇ to hire a car on the island, especially in the main tourist season from April through October. You may find more attractive prices during low season. The price usually includes full insurance, a certain mileage allowance and VAT (value-added tax). Drivers under the age of 25 require additional insurance. Cypriot authorities honour international diving licences, as well as foreign licences. Both manual and automatic cars are available for hire, as are motorcycles and scooters.

You really only need a four-wheel-drive vehicle if you are planning to tour the mountain regions in winter using some

of the rough tracks, or go off-road in the Akamas peninsula. Major international car hire companies – Hertz, Avis and Europcar – have offices at the airports and in large cities, including Nicosia, Larnaka, Limassol and Pafos. Driving a hire car across the border to North Cyprus is not prohibited, but you will have to take out extra insurance on the Turkish side.

Rules of the Road

Dʀɪᴠɪɴɢ is the easiest way to get around Cyprus. Roads are good, with motorways connecting Nicosia with Larnaka, Limassol, Pafos and Agia Napa. Distances are short – it is less than 160 km (100 miles) from Pafos to Nicosia.

Cypriots drive on the left side of the road, and drivers should give way to vehicles approaching from the right. Road signs are provided in both Greek and English in the south.

Distances and speed limits are in kilometres – 100 kmph (60 mph) on motorways, 80

Road sign in the south: sharp bend

Maps

Wʜᴇɴ ʜɪʀɪɴɢ a car, you will usually be given a very basic road map of the island. It is certainly worth purchasing a more detailed map of Cyprus or the part of the island you'll be exploring; these are available in many bookstores and petrol stations. It may be easier to purchase a map from home and bring it with you, so that you'll be prepared from the outset. Bear in mind that many mountain roads are accessible only by four-wheel drive vehicle or motorcycle (or scooter).

Remember, too, that place names in the North may be different from those on a map purchased in the South, so you may have to cross-reference maps.

A well-maintained road in the Troodos mountains

DRIVING IN NICOSIA

THE CAPITAL of Cyprus is the biggest and most congested city on the island. Traffic jams occur during rush hour and tourists may have difficulty negotiating the traffic here, and the narrow streets of parts of the city. The worst congestion can be expected on the trunk roads leading into and out of the city and – particularly in high season – on roads to the main historical sites. Outside the rush hour, driving in Nicosia is relatively easy and comfortable.

Street names throughout the city are clearly visible, and major tourist attractions are well signposted.

BUSES

BUS SERVICE between the large towns is efficient and comfortable, and tickets are inexpensive. There are at least 6 services daily between the four main southern towns. Transport links to major seaside resorts are also good.

Local buses also connect outlying communities with the nearest main town, but they are geared to the needs of schoolchildren and villagers, so departures are only early morning and mid-afternoon. Travellers will find it harder to get to and from the smaller towns and villages.

Before travelling, check the timetable to see when the last return bus departs, to ensure that you will be able to get back. At weekends, there are reduced services.

Traffic moving along one of Kyrenia's busy streets

TAXIS

METERED TAXIS operate in all the main towns in Cyprus. Unmetered rural taxis serve most larger villages, charging 15-25 cents per kilometre. There are also shared "service taxis" or mini-buses, which take passengers door to door so you can choose the most convenient point for getting on or off.

A taxi sign in North Cyprus

Service taxis operate between all the major towns half-hourly between 6am and 6pm (7pm summer) Monday to Friday, and 7am to 5pm at weekends.

Taxi fares are reasonable, particularly when you take a larger car and share the cost between several people, and provide a very convenient way of getting around.

HITCHHIKING

HITCHHIKING is not illegal in Cyprus, nor is it recommended. It is better avoided altogether in the larger towns, where a decent public transport system and affordable taxis provide safer alternatives. In remote areas, the locals readily give lifts to people standing by the road.

It can be difficult to hitch a lift during the peak holiday season, and temperatures soar, making the wait uncomfortable. Be sure to carry a bottle of water with you and wear a sunhat. Women who hitchhike should take special care.

DIRECTORY

BUS TIMETABLES

Plateia Solomou, Nicosia.
(226 65814.

Themistocleous 7, Limassol.
(253 70592.

King Evagorou 2/203, Larnaka.
(246 50477.

Karavella Bus Station, Pafos.
(269 34410.

Leoforos Makariou III 32A, Agia Napa. **(** 237 213 21.

TAXIS

Euro Taxi
Ifigenias 24, Nicosia.
(225 13000.

Orphanou Taxi & Minibus
Perikleous, Larnaka 3C.
(225 11511.

Acropolis Taxi
Gladstonos 25, Larnaka.
(246 52531.

Golden Taxi
Chr. Kranou 67, Limassol.
(258 79 787.

CAR HIRE

Avis
(227 13333.
W www.avis.com.cy

Hertz
(777 77411.
W www.hertz.com.cy

Europcar
(246 43085
W www.europcar-cyprus.com

Bus for carrying tourists on the island

Index

Acknowledgments

Dorling Kindersley and Wiedza i Życie would like to thank the following people and institutions, whose contributions and assistance have made the preparation of this guide possible.

PUBLISHING MANAGER
Kate Poole

MANAGING EDITORS
Vivien Antwi, Vicki Ingle

PUBLISHER
Douglas Amrine

SENIOR CARTOGRAPHIC EDITOR
Casper Morris

SENIOR DTP DESIGNER
Jason Little

EDITORIAL ASSISTANCE
Anna Freiberger, Dora Whitaker

PRODUCTION CO-ORDINATOR
Wendy Penn

JACKET DESIGN
Tessa Blindoss

CONSULTANT
Robin Gauldie

FACTCHECKER
John Vickers

PROOFREADER
Stewart Wild

INDEX
Hilary Bird

ADDITIONAL PHOTOGRAPHY
Wojciech Franus, Konrad Kalbarczyk, Grzegorz Micuła, Bernard Musyck, Ronald Sayegh, Andrzej Zygmuntowicz

SPECIAL ASSISTANCE
Dr. Fotos Fotiou, Aleksander Nikolaou, Irfan Kiliç, Suleyman Yalin, Latif Ince, Artur Mościcki, Joanna Egert-Romanowska, Maria Betlejewska, Małgorzata Merkel-Massé.
The publishers would also like to thank all the people and institutions who allowed us to use photographs from their archives:

Bernard Musyck, Ronald Sayegh
(www.CyprusDestinations.com, skiing and agrotourism site)

PICTURE CREDITS
t = top; tr = top right; tl = top left; cla = centre left above; ca = centre above; cra = centre right above; cl = centre left; c = centre; cr = centre right; clb = centre left below; cb = centre below; crb = centre right below; bl = bottom left; b = bottom; br = bottom right.

Every effort has been made to trace the copyright holders, and we apologize in advance for any unintentional omissions. We would be pleased to insert the appropriate acknowledgments in any subsequent edition of this publication.

Alamy Rawdon Wyatt 203t.
Corbis 10t; Nathan Benn 40; Bettmann 26, 34bl, 71br; Jonathan Blair 11t, 24c, 25c, 34t, 96–97; Tom Brakefield 151cr; James Davis/Eye Ubiquitous 16clb, 91crb, 148cla; Dave G. Houser 1; Jo Lillini 22b, 185bl; Chris Lisle 24b; Hans Georg Roth 8–9.
Grzegorz Micuła 12; 16t; 17ca, bl; 18t; 19br; 36–37; 52b; 57cb; 67cr; 92t; 186b; 187t; 190t; 196cla.
TAGO Konrad Kalbarczyk 13b, 182t; Wojciech Franus 15b.
Andrzej Zygmuntowicz 168–169 (except for the box).

Jacket
Front – DK IMAGES: K. Kur cb, bl, br; ©Zefa: Svenja-Foto main image
Bac – DK IMAGES: K. Kur tl, br.
Spine - ©Zefa: Svenja-Foto

All other images ©Dorling Kindersley
For further information see www.dkimages.com

English-Greek Phrase Book

There are no clear-cut rules for transliterating modern Greek into the Latin alphabet.

The system employed in this guide follows the rules generally applied in Greece, adjusted to fit in with English pronunciation. On the following pages, the English is given in the left-hand column, the right-hand column provides a literal system of pronounciation and indicates the stressed syllable in bold.

It is also worth remembering that both the Cypriot Greek and Cypriot Turkish alphabets differ slightly from those used on the mainland, and their accents are distinctive, too.

IN AN EMERGENCY

Help!	Voítheia	vo-ee-theea
Stop!	Stamatíste	sta-ma-tee-steh
Call a doctor!	Fonáxte éna yatro	fo-nak-steh e-na ya-tro
Call an ambulance!	Kaléste to asthenofóro	ka-le-steh to as-the-no-fo-ro
Call the police!	Kaléste tin astynomía	ka-le-steh teen a-sti-no mia
Call the fire brigade!	Kaléste tin pyrosvestikí	ka-le-steh teen pee-ro-zve-stee-kee
Where is the nearest telephone?	Poú eínai to plisiéstero tiléfono?	poo ee-ne to plee-see-e-ste-ro tee-le-pho-no?
Where is the nearest hospital?	Poú eínai to plisiéstero nosokomeío?	poo ee-ne to plee-see-e-ste-ro no-so-ko-mee-o?
Where is the nearest pharmacy?	Poú eínai to plisiéstero farmakeío?	poo ee-ne to plee-see-e-ste-ro far-ma-kee-o?

COMMUNICATION ESSENTIALS

Yes	Nai	neh
No	Ochi	o-chee
Please	Parakaló	pa-ra-ka-lo
Thank you	Efcharistó	ef-cha-ree-sto
Excuse me	Me synchoreíte	me seen cho-ree-teh
Goodbye	Antío	an-dee-o
Good morning	Kaliméra	ka-lee-me-ra
Good evening	Kalinychta	ka-lee-neech-ta
Morning	Proí	pro-ee
Afternoon	Apógevma	a-po-yev-ma
Evening	Vrádi	vrath-i
Yesterday	Chthés	chthes
Today	Símera	see-me-ra
Tomorrow	Avrio	av-ree-o
Here	Edó	ed-o
There	Ekeí	e-kee
What?	Tí?	tee?
Why?	Giatí?	ya-tee?
Where?	Poú?	poo?
How?	Pós?	pos?

USEFUL PHRASES

How are you?	Tí káneis?	tee ka-nees
Very well, thank you	Poly kalá, efcharistó	po-lee ka-la, ef-cha-ree-sto
Pleased to meet you	Cháiro polę	che-ro po-lee
What is your name?	Pós légeste?	pos le-ye-ste?
Where is/where are...?	Poú eínai?	poo ee-ne?
How far is it to...?	Póso apéchei...?	po-so a-pe-chee?
I understand	Katalavaíno	ka-ta-la-ve-no
I don't understand	Den katalavaíno	then ka-ta-la-ve-no
Can you speak more slowly?	Miláte lígo pio argá parakaló?	mee-la-te lee-go pyo ar-ga pa-ra-ka-lo?
I'm sorry	Me synchoreíte	me-seen-cho-ree teh

USEFUL WORDS

big	Megálo	me-ga-lo
small	Mikró	mi-kro
hot	Zestó	zes-to
cold	Kreyo	kree-o
good	Kaló	ka-lo
bad	Kakó	ka-ko
open	Anoichtá	a-neech-ta
closed	Kleistá	klee-sta
left	Aristerá	a-ree-ste-ra
right	Dexiá	dek-see-a
straight	Eftheía	ef-thee-a
between	Anámesa/ Metaxey	a-na-me-sa/ Metaxý
on the corner.....	Sti gonía tou...	stee go-nee-a too
near	Kontá	kon-da
far	Makriá	ma-kree-a
up	Epáno	e-pa-no
down	Káto	ka-to
early	Norís	no-rees
late	Argá	ar-ga
entrance	I eísodus	ee ee-so-thos
exit	I éxodos	ee e-kso-dos
toilets	Oi toualétes	ee e-kso-dos

SHOPPING

How much is it?	Póso kánei?	po-so ka-nee?
Do you have...?	Echete...?	e-che-teh
Do you accept credit cards?	Décheste pistotikés kártes	the-ches-teh pee-sto-tee-kes kar-tes
Do you accept ' travellers cheques?	Décheste pistotikés travellers' cheques?	the-ches-teh pee-sto-tee-kes ... travellers cheques
What time do you open?	Póte anoígete?	po-teh a-nee-ye-teh?
What time do you close?	Póte kleínete?	po-teh klee-ne-teh?
this one	Aftó edó	af-to e-do
that	Ekeíno	e-kee-no
expensive	Akrivó	e-kree-vo
cheap	Fthinó	fthee-no
size	To mégethos	to me-ge-thos
white	Lefkó	lef-ko
black	Mávro	mav-ro
red	Kókkino	ko-kee-no
yellow	Kítrino	kee-tree-no
green	Prásino	pra-see-no
blue	Mple	bleh
antique shop	Magazí me antíkes	ma-ga-zee me an-dee-kes
bakery	O foúrnos	o foor-nos
bank	I trápeza	I trápeza
bazaar	To pazári	to pa-za-ree
bookshop	To vivliopoleío	o vee-vlee-o-po-lee-o
pharmacy	To farmakeío	to far-ma-kee-o
post office	To tachy-dromeío	to ta-chee-thro-mee-o
supermarket	Supermarket	"Supermarket"

SIGHTSEEING

tourist information	CTO	CTO
beach	I paralía	ee pa-ra-lee-a
Byzantine	vyzantinós	vee-zan-dee-nos
castle	To kástro	to ka-stro
church	I ekklisía	ee e-klee-see-a
monastery	moní	mo-ni
museum	To mouseío	to moo-see-o
national	ethnikós	eth-nee-kos
river	To potámi	to po-ta-mee
road	O drómos	o thro-mos
saint	ágios	a-yee-os
theatre	To théatro	to the-a-tro

TRAVELLING

When does the ... leave?	Póte févgei to...?	po-teh fev-yee to..
Where is the bus stop?	Poú eínai i stási tou leoforeíou?	poo ce-neh ee sta-see too le-o-fo-ree-oo?
Is this bus going to..?	Ypárche I leoforeío gia...?	ee-par-chee le-o-fo-ree-o yia...?
bus ticket	Eisitírio leoforeíou	ee-see-tee-ree-o le-o-fo-ree-oo?
harbour	To limáni	to lee-ma-nee
bicycle	To podílato	to po-thee-la-to
taxi	To taxí	to tak-see
airport	To aero- drómio	to a-e-ro-thro- mee-o
ferry	To „ferry-boat"	to fe-ree-bot

IN A HOTEL

Do you have a vacant room?	Echete domátia?	e-che-teh tho- ma-tee-a?
double room	Díklino me dipló kreváti	thee-klee-no meh thee-plo kre-va-tee
single room	Monóklino	mo-no-klee-no
room with bathroom	Domátio me mpánio	tho-ma-tee-o meh ban-yo
shower	To douz	To dooz
key	To kleidí	to klee-dee
I have a reservation	Echo kánei krátisi	e-cho ka-nee kra-tee-see
room with sea view	Domátio me théasti thálassa	tho-ma-tee-o meh the-a stee tha-la-sa
room with a balcony	Domátio me théasti mpalkóni	tho-ma-tee-o meh the-a stee bal-ko-nee
Does the price include breakfast	To proïnó symperi- lamvánetai stin timí?	to pro-ce-no seem-be-ree-lam- va-ne-teh steen tee-mee?

EATING OUT

Have you got a free table?	Echete trapézi?	e-che-te tra-pe-zee?
I'd like to reserve a table	Thélo na kratíso éna trapézi	the-lo na kra-tee-so e-na tra-pe-zee
The bill, please	Ton logariazmó parakaló	ton lo-gar-yas-mo pa-ra-ka-lo
I'm a vegetarian	Eímai chortofágos	ee-meh chor-to- fa-gos
menu	O katálogos	o ka-ta-lo-gos
wine list	O katálogos me ta oin- opnevmatódi	o ka-ta-lo-gos meh ta ee-no- pnev-ma-to-thee
glass	To potíri	to po-tee-ree
bottle	To mpoukáli	to bou-ka-lee
knife	To machaíri	to ma-che-ree
fork	To piroúni	to pee-roo-nee
spoon	To koutáli	to koo-ta-lee
breakfast	To proïnó	to pro-ce-no
lunch	To mesimerianó	to me-see-mer-ya-no
dinner	To deípno	to theep-no
main course	To kyríos gévma	to kee-ree-os yev-ma
starter	Ta orektiká	ta o-rek-tee-ka
dessert	To glykó	to ylee-ko
dish of the day	To piáto tis iméras	to pya-to tees ee-me-ras
bar	To „bar"	To bar
tavern	I tavérna	ee ta-ver-na
café	To kafeneío	to ka-fe-nee-o
wine shop	To oinopoleío	to ee-no-po-lee-o
restaurant	To estiatório	to e-stee-a-to-ree-o
ouzeria	To ouzerí	To ouzerí
kebab take-away ko	To souvlatzidiko	To soo-vlat-zee dee-

MENU DECODER

coffee	O Kafés	o ka-fes
with milk	me gála	me ga-la
black coffee	skétos	ske-tos
without sugar	chorís záchari	cho-rees za-cha-ree
tea	tsái	tsa-ee
wine	krasí	kra-see
red	kókkino	ko-kee-no
white	lefkó	lef-ko
rosé	rozé	ro-ze
raki	To rakí	to ra-kee
ouzo	To oúzo	to oo-zo
retsina	I retsína	ee ret-see-na
water	To neró	to ne-ro
fish	To psári	to psa-ree
cheese	To tyrí	to tee-ree
halloumi cheese	To chaloúmi	
feta	I féta	ee fe-ta
bread	To psomí	to pso-mee
hummus	To houmous	to choo-moos
halva	O chalvás	o chal-vas
Turkish Delight	To loukoúmi	to loo-koo-mee loo-koo-mee
baklava	O mpaklavás	o bak-la-vas
kléftiko (lamb dish)	To kléftiko	to klef-tee-ko

NUMBERS

1	éna	e-na
2	dyo	thee-o
3	tría	tree-a
4	téssera	te-se-ra
5	pénte	pen-deh
6	éxi	ek-si
7	eptá	ep-ta
8	ochtó	och-to
9	ennéa	e-ne-a
10	déka	the-ka
100	ekató	e-ka-to
200	diakósia	thya-kos-ya
1,000	chília	cheel-ya
2,000	dychiliádes	thee-o cheel-ya-thes
1,000,000	éna ekat- -ommyrio	e-na e-ka-to-mee-ree-o

DAYS OF THE WEEK, MONTHS, TIME

one minute	éna leptó	e-na lep-to
one hour	mía óra	mee-a o-ra
half an hour	misí óra	mee-see o-ra
a day	mía méra	mee-a me-ra
week	mía evdomáda	mee-a ev-tho-ma-tha
month	énas mínas	e-nas mee-nas
year	énas chrónos	e-nas chro-nos
Monday	Deftéra	thef-te-ra
Tuesday	Tríti	tree-tee
Wednesday	Tetárti	te-tar-tee
Thursday	Pémpti	pemp-tee
Friday	Paraskeví	pa-ras-ke-vee
Saturday	Sávvato	sa-va-to
Sunday	Kyriakí	keer-ee-a-kee
January	Ianouários	ee-a-noo-a-ree-os
February	Fevrouários	fev-roo-a-ree-os
March	Mártios	mar-tee-os
April	Aprílios	a-pree-lee-os
May	Máios	ma-ee-os
June	Ioúnios	ee-oo-nee-os
July	Ioúlios	ee-oo-lee-os
August	Avgoustos	av-goo-stos
September	Septémvrios	sep-tem-vree-os
October	Októvrios	ok-to-vree-os
November	Noémvrios	no-em-vree-os
December	Dekémvrios	the-kem-vree-os

English-Turkish Phrase Book

PRONUNCIATION

Turkish uses a Roman alphabet. It has 29 letters: 8 vowels and 21 consonants. Letters that differ from the English alphabet are: c, pronounced "j" as in "jolly"; ç, pronounced "ch" as in "church"; ğ, which lengthens the preceding vowel and is not pronounced; ı, pronounced "uh"; ö, pronounced "ur" (like the sound in "further"); ş, pronounced "sh" as in "ship"; ü, pronounced "ew" as in "few".

IN AN EMERGENCY

Help!	İmdat!	eem-dat
Stop!	Dur!	door
Call a doctor!	Bir doktor çağrın!	beer dok-tor chah-ruhn
Call an ambulance!	Bir ambulans çağrın!	beer am-boo-lans chah-ruhn
Call the police!	Polis çağrın!	po-lees chah-ruhn
Fire!	Yangın!	yan-guhn
Where is the nearest telephone?	En yakın telefon nerede?	en ya-kuhn teh-leh-fon neh-reh-deh
Where is the nearest hospital?	En yakın hastane nerede?	en ya-kuhn has-ta-neh neh-reh-deh

COMMUNICATION ESSENTIALS

Yes	Evet	eh-vet
No	Hayır	h-'eye'-uhr
Thank you	Teşekkür ederim	teh-shek-kewr eh-deh-reem
Please	Lütfen	lewt-fen
Excuse me	Affedersiniz	af-feh-der-see-neez
Hello	Merhaba	mer-ha-ba
Goodbye	Hoşça kalın	bosh-cha ka-luhn
Good morning	Günaydın	gewn-'eye'-duhn
Good evening	İyi akşamlar	ee-yee ak-sham-lar
Morning	Sabah	sa-bah
Afternoon	Öğleden sonra	ur-leh-den son-ra
Evening	Akşam	ak-sham
Yesterday	Dün	dewn
Today	Bugün	boo-gewn
Tomorrow	Yarın	ya-ruhn
Here	Burada	boo-ra-da
There	Şurada	shoo-ra-da
Over there	Orada	o-ra-da
What?	Ne?	neh
When?	Ne zaman?	neh za-man
Why?	Neden?	neh-den
Where?	Nerede?	neh-reh-deh

USEFUL PHRASES

How are you?	Nasılsınız?	na-suhl-suh-nuhz
I'm fine	İyiyim	ee-yee-yeem
Pleased to meet you	Memnun oldum	mem-noon ol-doom
That's fine	Tamam	ta-mam
Where is/are ...?	... nerede?.	... neh-reh-deh
How far is it to ...?	... ne kadar uzakta?	... neh ka-dar oo-zak-ta
I want to go to ...	... a/e gitmek istiyorum	... a/eh geet-mek ees-tee-yo-room
Do you speak English?	İngilizce biliyor musunuz?	een-gee-leez-jeh bee-lee-yor moo-soo-nooz
I don't understand	Anlamıyorum	an-la-muh-yo-room
Can you help me?	Bana yardım edebilir misiniz?	ba-na yar-duhm eh-deh-bee-leer mee-see-neez?

USEFUL WORDS

big	büyük	bew-yewk
small	küçük	kew-chewk
hot	sıcak	suh-jak
cold	soğuk	soh-ook
good/well	iyi	ee-yee
bad	kötü	kur-tew
open	açık	a-chuhk
closed	kapalı	ka-pa-luh
left	sol	sol
right	sağ	saa
straight on	doğru	doh-roo
near	yakın	ya-kuhn
far	uzak	oo-zak
early	erken	er-ken
late	geç	gech
entrance	giriş	gee-reesh
exit	çıkış	chuh-kuhsh
toilets	tuvaletler	too-va-let-ler

SHOPPING

How much is this?	Bu kaç lira?	boo kach lee-ra
I would like ...	... istiyorum	... ees-tee-yo-room
Do you have ...?	... var mı?	... var muh?
Do you take credit cards?	Kredi kartı kabul ediyor musunuz?	kreh-dee kar-tuh ka-bool eh-dee-yor moo-soo-nooz?
What time do you open/close?	Saat kaçta açılıyor/kapanıyor?	Sa-at kach-ta a-chuh-luh-yor/ka-pa-nuh-yor
this one	bunu	boo-noo
that one	şunu	shoo-noo
expensive	pahalı	pa-ha-luh
cheap	ucuz	oo-jooz
size (clothes)	beden	beh-den
size (shoes)	numara	noo-ma-ra
white	beyaz	bay-yaz
black	siyah	see-yah
red	kırmızı	kuhr-muh-zuh
yellow	sarı	sa-ruh
green	yeşil	yeh-sheel
blue	mavi	ma-vee
bakery	fırın	fuh-ruhn
bank	banka	ban-ka
cake shop	pastane	pas-ta-neh
chemist's/pharmacy	eczane	ej-za-neh
hairdresser	kuaför	kwaf-fur
barber	berber	ber-ber
market/bazaar	çarşı/pazar	char-shuh/pa-zar
post office	postane	pos-ta-neh
travel agency	seyahat acentesi	say-ya-hat a-jen-teh-see

SIGHTSEEING

castle	hisar	bee-sar
church	kilise	kee-lee-seh
mosque	cami	ja-mee
museum	müze	mew-zeh
square	meydan	may-dan
theological college	medrese	med-reh-seh
tomb	türbe	tewr-beh
tourist information office	turizm danışma bürosu	too-reezm da-nuhsh-mah bew-ro-soo
town hall	belediye sarayı	beh-leh-dee-yeh sar-'eye'-uh
Turkish bath	hamam	ha-mam

TRAVELLING

airport	havalimanı	ha-va-lee-ma-nuh
bus/coach	otobüs	o-to-bewss
bus stop	otobüs durağı	o-to-bewss doo-ra-uh
ferry	vapur	va-poor
taxi	taksi	tak-see
ticket	bilet	bee-let
ticket office	bilet gişesi	bee-let gee-sheh-see
timetable	tarife	ta-ree-feh

STAYING IN A HOTEL

Do you have a vacant room?	Boş odanız var mı?	bosh o-da-nuhz var muh?
double room	iki kişilik bir oda	ee-kee kee-shee-leek beer o-da
twin room	çift yataklı bir oda	cheeft ya-tak-luh beer o-da
single room room	tek kişilik	tek kee-shee-leek
with a bathroom	banyolu bir oda	ban-yo-loo beer o-da

key	**anahtar**	*a-nah-tar*
room service	**oda servisi**	*o-da ser-vee-see*
I have a	**Rezervasyonum**	*reb-zer-vas-yo-noom*
reservation	**var**	*var*
Does the price	**Fiyata kahvaltı**	*fee-ya-ta kah-val-*
include breakfast?	**dahil mi?**	*tub da-beel mee?*

EATING OUT

Do you have a table	**... kişilik bir masa**	*... kee-shee-leek*
for ...people		
The bill please	**Hesap lütfen**	*heb-sap lewt-fen*
I am a vegetarian	**Et yemiyorum**	*et yeb-mee-yo-room*
restaurant	**lokanta**	*lo-kan-ta*
waiter	**garson**	*gar-son*
menu	**yemek listesi**	*ye-mek lees-teb-see*
wine list	**şarap listesi**	*sha-rap lees-teb-see*
breakfast	**kahvaltı**	*kab-val-tub*
lunch	**öğle yemeği**	*ur-leb yeb-meb-ee*
dinner	**akşam yemeği**	*ak-sham yeb-meb-ee*
starter	**meze**	*meb-zeb*
main course	**ana yemek**	*a-na yeb-mek*
dish of the day	**günün yemeği**	*gewn-ewn yeb-meb-ee*
dessert	**tatlı**	*tat-lub*
glass	**bardak**	*bar-dak*
bottle	**şişe**	*shee-sheb*
knife	**bıçak**	*bub-chak*
fork	**çatal**	*cha-tal*
spoon	**kaşık**	*ka-shubk*

MENU DECODER

bal	*bal*	honey
balık	*ba-lubk*	fish
bira	*bee-ra*	beer
bonfile	*bon-fee-leb*	fillet steak
buz	*booz*	ice
çay	*cb-'eye'*	tea
çilek	*chee-lek*	strawberry
çorba	*chor-ba*	soup
dondurma	*don-door-ma*	ice cream
ekmek	*ek-mek*	bread
elma	*el-ma*	apple
et	*et*	meat
fasulye	*fa-sool-yeb*	beans
fırında	*fub-rubn-da*	roast
gazoz	*ga-zoz*	fizzy drink
kkahve	*kab-veb*	coffee
karpuz	*kar-pooz*	water melon
kavun	*ka-voon*	melon
kayısı	*k-'eye'-ub-sub*	apricots
kıyma	*kuby-ma*	minced meat
kızartma	*kub-zart-ma*	fried
köfte	*kurf-teb*	meatballs
kuzu eti	*koo-zoo eb-tee*	lamb
lokum	*lo-koom*	Turkish delight
maden suyu	*ma-den soo-yoo*	mineral water

meyve suyu	*may-veb soo-yoo*	fruit juice
muz	*mooz*	banana
patlıcan	*pat-lub-jan*	aubergine (eggplant)
peynir	*pay-neer*	cheese
pilav	*pee-lav*	rice
piliç	*pee-leech*	roast chicken
şarap	*sha-rap*	wine
sebze	*seb-zeb*	vegetables
şeftali	*shef-ta-lee*	peach
şeker	*sheb-ker*	sugar
su	*soo*	water
süt	*sewt*	milk
sütlü	*sewt-lew*	with milk
tavuk	*ta-vook*	chicken
tereyağı	*teb-reb-yah-ub*	butter
tuz	*tooz*	salt
üzüm	*ew-zewm*	grapes
yoğurt	*yob-urt*	yoghurt
yumurta	*yoo-moor-ta*	egg
zeytin	*zay-teen*	olives
zeytinyağı	*zay-teen-yab-ub*	olive oil

NUMBERS

0	**sıfır**	*sub-fubr*
1	**bir**	*beer*
2	**iki**	*ee-kee*
3	**üç**	*ewch*
4	**dört**	*durt*
5	**beş**	*besh*
6	**altı**	*al-tub*
7	**yedi**	*yeb-dee*
8	**sekiz**	*seb-keez*
9	**dokuz**	*dob-kooz*
10	**on**	*on*
100	**yüz**	*yewz*
200	**iki yüz**	*ee-kee yewz*
1,000	**bin**	*been*
100,000	**yüz bin**	*yewz been*
1,000,000	**bir milyon**	*beer meel-yon*

TIME

one minute	**bir dakika**	*beer da-kee-ka*
one hour	**bir saat**	*beer sa-at*
half an hour	**yarım saat**	*ya-rubm sa-at*
day	**gün**	*gewn*
week	**hafta**	*baf-ta*
month	**ay**	*'eye'*
year	**yıl**	*yubl*
Sunday	**pazar**	*pa-zar*
Monday	**pazartesi**	*pa-zar-teb-see*
Tuesday	**salı**	*sa-lub*
Wednesday	**çarşamba**	*char-sham-ba*
Thursday	**perşembe**	*per-sbem-beb*
Friday	**cuma**	*joo-ma*
Saturday	**cumartesi**	*joo-mar-teb-see* 200

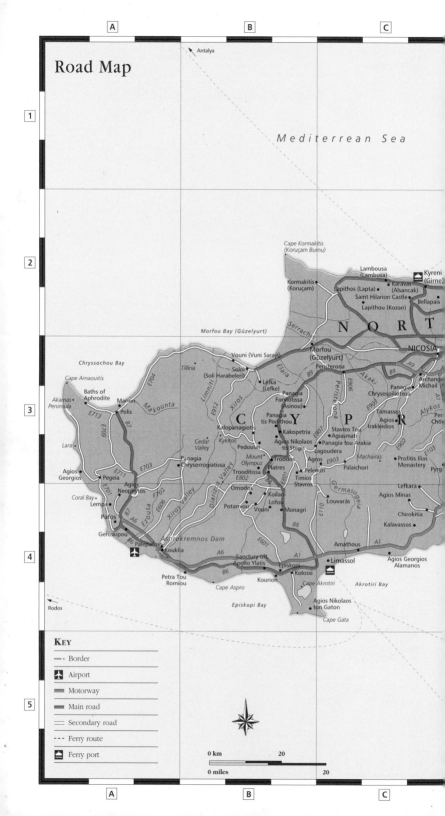